BREWER'S

DICTIONARY OF
PHRASE AND FABLE

fourteenth edition

by

IVOR H. EVANS

CASSELL

Cassell Publishers Ltd
Villiers House, 41/47 Strand, London WC2N 5JE

First published 1870
Fourteenth edition 1989
First published in paperback 1990
Reprinted 1990
Reprinted 1991
Reprinted 1992 (twice)

British Library Cataloguing in Publication Data
Evans, Ivor H. (Ivor Henry), *1913*
  Brewer's dictionary of phrase and fable. – 14th ed.
  1. English language. Idioms – Dictionaries
  I. Title II. Brewer, E. Cobham (Ebenezar Cobham), *1810–1897*. Brewer's dictionary of phrase and fable
  423.1

ISBN 0-304-34004-9 (paperback)
ISBN 0-304-31835-3 (hardback)

Typeset in Imprint by Belgrave Phototypesetters Limited, Scarborough, North Yorkshire.

Printed in Great Britain by The Bath Press, Avon

CONTENTS

PREFACE

Dr. Ebenezer Cobham Brewer's *Dictionary of Phrase and Fable* was first published by Cassell in 1870 and has long outlived most of his other forty or so miscellaneous publications, although at the time it was regarded as a dubious commercial venture. He completed his "New and Enlarged" edition in 1894, three years before his death in his eighty-seventh year. He expressed the hope in his preface "that this Treasury of Literary bric-à-brac will become a standard book of reference". This wish seems to have been fulfilled and, as I have said before, the book is very rarely seen on the shelves of second-hand bookshops. The Centenary Edition went through seven impressions, as has the second revised edition of 1981, the latter also having appeared as a paperback.

The core of the present edition is still substantially Dr. Brewer's and his close acquaintance with a very extensive range of subjects and authors becomes increasingly apparent the more one delves into the book. He seems to have been particularly familiar with the Bible, Lemprière's *Classical Dictionary*, the works of Chaucer, Shakespeare, Milton and Scott, as well as Percy's *Reliques of Ancient English Poetry*. Others of his favourite poets and authors were Dryden, Pope, Thomson, Byron, Thackeray, Dickens, Longfellow and Tennyson, but the total range of his gleanings extends over many fields, from the writings of ancient authors to those of the Victorian age.

The title page of the 1894 revision of Dr. Brewer's *Dictionary of Phrase and Fable* described it as "Giving the Derivation, Source or Origin of Common Phrases, Allusions and Words that have a Tale to Tell". Subsequent editors deleted some of the more obsolete and trifling entries and added new subject matter, including contemporary usages, as well as some material which was not really in keeping with a work of this character.

Since 1963, when I first became involved with this book, I have endeavoured to return to Dr. Brewer's terms of reference as outlined in his last edition. When preparing the Centenary Edition, which was then a complete revision, I discarded entries which seemed to have little claim to be in a dictionary of "Phrase and Fable" or were not really worth their space, as well as words and technical expressions which had no particular "tale to tell", although avoiding change for the sake of it. A good deal of repetition was excluded by introducing extensive cross-referencing and further space for new entries was obtained by making the existing text more concise wherever possible.

When preparing the 1981 edition I endeavoured, as before, to aim at clarity and conciseness to make the best possible use of space in order to prevent the book becoming unwieldy, but nevertheless it continued to grow with a substantial number of additional entries. In this present revised edition more than three hundred extra entries have been inserted, some on current usages (*e.g. Big Bang, Carpet bombing, Catch 22, Emmets and Grockles, Glasnost, Hobbit, Inner Cities, Mole, Murphy's Law, Switched on, etc.*), as well as many on those of former times (*e.g. Auld Lang Syne, Banshee, Bard of Erin, Br'er Fox, Darling Daisy, Falmouth for Orders, Gaudeamus Igitur, The Hermit of Warkworth, Jezebel, The Silk Road, Six-of-the-Best, Tin Tabernacle*). In addition many existing entries have been updated, expanded and, I hope, improved. Where space has permitted more quotations have been included to illustrate the use of a word or phrase, but they are not intended as examples of their earliest employment. I have not been pedantically consistent with my general plan but have continued to include items which may interest those who like to browse or use the book as a bedtime "lucky dip".

Letters concerning the last edition have been received from many readers in Great Britain, as well as from America, Canada, South Africa, Australia, New Zealand, Holland, Germany, Sweden, Japan and elsewhere. I must express my grateful thanks to those numerous correspondents for their constructive criticisms and helpful suggestions. I must also once more acknowledge the practical help given by my wife, especially in checking, criticizing and typing the script, and also thank Miss Jean Sharman, Plymouth Reference Librarian, for her friendly and productive co-operation. I hope this new edition will be as well received as its predecessors.

East Wheal Russell   I.H.E.
1989

INTRODUCTION

by John Buchanan-Brown

A reference book which has flourished for over a hundred years is clearly something exceptional. Its original compiler needs to hit upon not so much a new area of information of wide and permanent interest as a way of presenting that material and of providing access to it which satisfies and attracts generation after generation of readers. Equally such a compiler needs to place his book with publishers sensitive to changing tastes and aware of the need periodically to give the work that face-lift needed to attract fresh generations of readers to the mass of information within.

Both these conditions have been satisfied in the case of *Brewer's Dictionary of Phrase and Fable*. That this is a fresh revision of the Edition of 1981, entrusted once more to the sure hands of Ivor H. Evans, speaks loudly enough for the publishers' keeping their side of the bargain. Hence it is the purpose of this short Introduction to set the original edition in the context of 1870 and to show how skilfully the compiler was able to make available to a wider and predominantly self-educated working-class public some of the more specialized results of nineteenth-century scholarship.

But what of the compiler himself? What sort of man was Dr. E. Cobham Brewer? Some clue was given in the brief Memoir of Dr. Brewer with which his grandson, Captain P. M. C. Hayman, introduced the Centenary Edition, spicing the plain facts of biography with childhood memories of his grandfather. (After the death of his wife in 1878, Dr. Brewer had come to live with his eldest daughter, Captain Hayman's mother, and her husband, Canon H. T. Hayman, Vicar of Edwinstowe in Nottinghamshire.)

"Dr. Brewer," Captain Hayman wrote, "must have been nearly eighty years of age when I was old enough to remember him at the Vicarage. He had an upstairs room furnished as a bed-sitting-room, for he used to work far into the night, often until three or four in the morning. He always declared that he did his best work then—but he was always down to breakfast dead on time at nine o'clock.

"The walls of this room were papered with a plain white paper, upon which he used to write in pencil stray memoranda and the names of any particularly interesting visitors and the dates on which they came to see him. These names included that of the Duchess of Portland, then one of the most beautiful women in the country. She insisted on going upstairs to my grandfather's own room and carried on a long conversation with him, sitting on his bed, a highly informal proceeding in those days, which particularly pleased the old gentleman!

"He had a wonderful way with children and would put aside whatever he was doing to amuse the children of the house before they went to bed.

He was a great hand at cutting out, drawing, telling stories, showing his 'treasures' which he had collected in various countries and relating his experiences in France and at the Court of Napoleon III and his Empress. But it was his sense of humour, which he could adapt to the childish mind, which made Dr. Brewer in his old age such a very delightful companion to the youngest of his grandchildren.

"He was also quite fearless. On one occasion the Vicarage odd-job-man—not remarkable for either intelligence or courage—came up to the house to announce that a rough-looking man was asleep in the stable. Before my father, a county cricketer and a noted sportsman, could move, Dr. Brewer had seized a stick and, when the Vicar arrived at the stable, he found the old gentleman belabouring the trespasser, a hulking tramp, and exclaiming, 'Be off, you scoundrel!' This onslaught was too much for the tramp, who made off as hard as he could go."

However vivid and photographic a child's memories of a fascinating and much-loved figure, these memories, like the photograph, capture only a fleeting moment in a very long life. This is the patriarchal figure of the portrait by his younger daughter which was reproduced as a frontispiece to the Centenary Edition. But what of his youth and middle age? Here the information is tantalizingly scanty.

Ebenezer Cobham Brewer was born on 2 May 1810, the son of a Norwich schoolmaster. In 1832 he went up to Trinity Hall, Cambridge, to read for a degree in Law. At twenty-two, he was considerably older than most undergraduates: Thackeray, a year his junior, had departed from neighbouring Trinity College, prematurely, it is true, a couple of years earlier. Brewer's university career was, however, the antithesis of the novelist's. So far from leaving after a year and heavily in debt, Brewer, according to his grandson, worked his way through college and crowned his achievement by graduating with first-class honours in 1836. Undoubtedly he then hoped for a college fellowship for, such posts then being confined to clergy of the Church of England, he was ordained deacon in 1836 and priest two years later. Equally clearly he was disappointed in his ambition, for he next appears as assistant and then as successor to his father in their school, Mile End House, Norwich.

One is bound to wonder just how much of a living the school provided for Brewer and his father. It is, perhaps, indicative of financial stringency that Brewer went up to Cambridge so much later than the normal undergraduate, and that he had to support himself while at the University. Moreover, it is still more suggestive that we next find him in the early 1850s settled in Paris, for throughout the century the Continent was the refuge of English financial embarrassment. I am not hinting at anything dishonourable, but if Dr. Brewer had had to give up his school through financial pressure, the Continent was the ideal place in which to recuperate. Living was cheap and, above all, there was no need to keep up those middle class appearances so essential to one's native land.

How Brewer earned his living during those years it is impossible to say. The fact that in later life he was editor of *The Morning Chronicle* would point to journalism and his familiarity with French Imperial circles would seem to confirm this, since a foreign correspondent would have easy access to Napoleon III and his ministers. At the same time the list of his published books (all educational) shows that he continued in the vein he had first explored while still a Norwich schoolmaster. Around 1841 he had written his most successful *Guide to Science* for the Norwich printers and publishers, Jarrolds, who became his principal publishers thereafter. Turning, however, from speculation to known fact, we find that by 1856 Brewer had become well enough established to return to England, marry and settle at Lavant in West Sussex.

In the early 1860s he became associated with Messrs. Cassell, Petter and Galpin, to whom his facility as an educational writer and experience as a schoolmaster were particular recommendations. The publishing house which John Cassell had founded in 1848 and which George William Petter and Thomas Dixon Galpin had rescued in 1855 when success overstrained the founder's resources, was built upon those twin pillars of Victorian stability, religion and self-improvement, with a strong flavour of total abstinence, for John Cassell had started out as a temperance lecturer. His major contribution to the field of adult education was his *Popular Educator*, launched in 1850 as a penny weekly part-issue, and designed to enable the working man to educate himself to university entrance standards in a wide variety of subjects. This was followed by more specialized courses and it is interesting to note that what have become the mainstays of the Cassell list for so many years—the foreign-language dictionaries—started life as major elements in integrated language-teaching series. In 1853 French, German and Latin dictionaries began to be issued in threepenny numbers, along with the appropriate grammars, readers and exercises (for which keys were provided), all parts of complete "teach yourself" courses.

But if adult education had been the dominant strain in the first half of the century, by the 1850s the focus of concern had shifted to primary schooling. In 1858 a Royal Commission on popular education was appointed and although it was not until 1870 that the new school boards were empowered to make education compulsory in England and Wales if they so wished, the trend was apparent far earlier. Cassell's were therefore moving with this tide when they widened their horizons to include the children as well as their fathers in their *Child Educator* of 1855 and the later series, *My first book of* ... Of this, the first six titles were published in 1864 (the year before John Cassell died) and another six followed in 1868. All twelve were written by Dr. E. C. Brewer.

While the tradition in the family is that Dr. Brewer occupied a senior editorial post at Cassell's at this time, the evidence from the diary of another employee, Bonavia Hunt, which Simon Nowell-Smith quotes in *The House of Cassell* (1958), points to the conclusion that Brewer had simply been provided with an office at the firm's headquarters at La Belle Sauvage where he compiled his books for them. Very probably he was engaged in other projects, since the period of two years covered by the diary falls midway between the publication of the two batches of *My first book of* ... Nor, I fear, did the middle-aged Dr. Brewer make such a favourable impression upon his young colleague as he was to make upon his grandson in old age. "What a fussy old gentleman Dr. Brewer is!" Hunt wrote, "I find it very tedious to humour and be affable to him, he is so insufferably inquisitive and such an old gossip." However trying it may have been to the young editor, this inquisitiveness is surely the sustaining virtue of Dr. Brewer's enduring contribution to the fortunes of the house of Cassell, his *Dictionary of Phrase and Fable*.

From the compiler's own account it is not absolutely certain whether Cassell's were offered the finished manuscript of the *Dictionary of Phrase and Fable* for publication or whether they commissioned it from him on the basis of sample materials which he had already collected. The latter seems the more probable for, as he himself wrote:

> ... the popularity of this book [*A Guide to Science*] brought me in a large number of questions on all imaginary matters. I kept these questions and their answers till they grew into a large book, when I sorted them and made the nucleus of the *Dictionary of Phrase and Fable*. I consulted the Editor of *The Despatch*, to whom I was well known, but it was his opinion that the book would have no sale as it would be wholly impossible to exhaust the subject.

Fortunately Cassell's thought differently and despite their being "doubtful whether the book would pay the expense of printing"—a typical ploy when it comes to negotiating with an author—the *Dictionary* was an undoubted success. By 1886, that is, within sixteen years of its first publication, it had been reprinted eighteen times and with the first printing of the second edition of 1894–5 the publishers could claim that 100,000 copies of the book had been produced.

The *Dictionary* undoubtedly owed its popularity to the way in which its subject-matter, whether by intuition or by conscious design, responded to the needs of a reading public created by nineteenth-century conditions. From the rapidly growing towns and cities emerged a class of reader, literate if not educated in the academic sense, which looked beyond the pure entertainment of novels and poetry, the utility of self-education and the moral uplift of religious books to the satisfaction of simple intellectual curiosity. This is that spirit of enquiry which at one end of the scale leads to pure scholarship and at the other to the acquisition of what some would stigmatize as totally useless information. It was that lower end of the scale which turned to the compilations of John Timbs (1801–75), sometime editor of *The Mirror* and *The Illustrated London News*. Using Dr. Brewer's method of scissors, paste and pigeon-holes he abstracted the curiosities of science, history and human behaviour which came his way in the course of his editorial duties and rehashed them in such books as *Things not generally known, Curiosities of London*, and *Curiosities of History*, all of which enjoyed considerable popularity in the mid-1850s.

Certainly there is an element of Timbs in some of the subjects included in the *Dictionary*, but Brewer gives them a permanent rather than an ephemeral value because he presents them for information rather than entertainment. More important is that the mere quirks of history are subordinated to the popularization of a very important segment of nineteenth-century scholarship—the investigation of the language, customs and belief of the common people, all part and parcel of what may be loosely termed the Romantic Movement away from the Classicism which had dominated Europe since the Renaissance.

In England the trend had become apparent in the eighteenth century in the cult of the Gothic exemplified by Horace Walpole's villa at Strawberry Hill, in the interest in Norse and Celtic mythology evinced, for example, by Gray's poems and Macpherson's *Ossian*, in such collections of folk-custom and belief as the Newcastle antiquary, John Brand's *Observations of Popular Antiquities*, first published in 1777 and reprinted throughout the nineteenth century, and in Frederick Grose's *Classical Dictionary of the Vulgar Tongue* (1785). However, and as in so many other fields, German scholarship took the lead in the early years of the nineteenth century. *Grimm's Fairy Tales* have become one of the most popular of children's books, but they originated as a scholarly collection by those great philologists, the Brothers Grimm. Indeed philology and folklore go hand in hand and by 1839 we can find the specialist publisher, John

Russell Smith, including in his list not merely a new edition of Grose's *Glossary of Provincial and Local Words* but a whole series of similar vocabularies devoted to different parts of England and to stories and poems written in dialect. Again, while Joseph Jacobs's two classic collections of English fairy tales were not to appear until the last decade of the century, they are in some sense the culmination of the work of many others in the field. Thomas Crofton Croker, for example, had been collecting such material in the south of Ireland in the 1820s and the wider general interest in such lore is typified by the publication in 1850 of Thomas Keightley's wide-ranging *Fairy Mythology*.

Folk-customs and belief, Celtic and Norse mythology are all important elements in Dr. Brewer's compilation, but the philological is, perhaps, the most striking in the early editions. The century saw the publication of important etymological dictionaries by Wedgwood and Skeat, the whole brought together in the Philological Society's great work, *The New English Dictionary*. Better known by its current name of *The Oxford English Dictionary*, the first volume had been published in 1884 and it is very probably to this that Dr. Brewer referred in the Preface to the second edition of 1894–5 as principal among those researches into English philology in the twenty-five years previous which enabled him to make so many corrections and additions in this field. For the great feature of both the editions which Brewer himself prepared is the wealth of philological and etymological information with which they responded to the wide interest among the public at large in the meaning and derivation of English words.

Thus we can see how the *Dictionary of Phrase and Fable* was conceived in the mainstream of nineteenth-century philological and antiquarian research, but no consideration of the genesis of the book would be complete without mention of the work which, I would suggest, inspired Dr. Brewer to his masterpiece. This was *Noted Names of Fiction*, originally contributed as a supplement to the 1864 edition of *Webster's Dictionary* by William Adolphus Wheeler (1833–74) and subsequently enlarged and published as a separate book. Wheeler, who later helped to produce various abridgements of *Webster* and was employed in the Boston Public Library, also included in his work "familiar pseudonyms, surnames bestowed on eminent men, and analogous popular appellations often referred to in literature and conversation". Comparison between his book and Brewer's shows beyond any shadow of doubt that his was a source, and a very substantial source, of material for fields of common interest. Yet it was precisely what was *not* in *Noted Names* that very probably prompted Brewer's undertaking, for Wheeler wrote in his Preface that:

> The introduction of appellative or generic names, such as *abbot of unreason, lord of misrule, kobold*, etc., as well as the explanation of celebrated customs and phrases, such as *flap-dragon, nine-men's morrice, philosophy of the Porch, to send to Coventry, to carry coals to Newcastle*, etc., would open too vast a field of enquiry; and besides, there are copious special treatises on these subjects already before the public...

If Brewer really did take this hint, it is surely to his credit that he was undaunted by the vastness of the field and shrewd enough to realize that although there might be treatises before the public, his public, Cassell's working- and lower middle-class public, would either be unaware of or overawed by them. So when he came to compile his *Dictionary*, it was not only Wheeler's noted names which went into the mixing-bowl, but all those words and phrases which Wheeler had specifically declined—and many more like them—as well as generous helpings of philology, etymology, folklore, mythology and those curiosities which Timbs had collected before him. Thus, if its ingredients were drawn from common stock, the recipe was all Brewer's very own.

And what a successful recipe it has proved to be. Of course tastes have changed in the ensuing hundred years and more. Modern English dictionaries cater for the etymologies of words, we no longer feel the need to know the names of all the characters in Sir Walter Scott's novels or the *dramatis personae* of long-forgotten eighteenth-century comedies, but we still want to know the story of "words which have a tale to tell"—this is what makes *Brewer* such a splendid book for browsing.

In paying tribute to the compiler, let us not forget the publishers. Cassell's had created something new in dictionaries, but they seem to have realized that it needed to speak with a special accent to each succeeding generation of users. Accordingly they invited Dr. Brewer himself to revise, correct and expand a new edition in 1894–5, exactly twenty-five years from the date of the first *Brewer*. This edition ran up to and beyond World War I and in 1923 Lawrence H. Dawson edited the revised and up-dated version which was to carry *Brewer* through the years of slump and depression and the horrors of World War II. Once again it was time to bring *Brewer* up to date and a new edition of the *Dictionary of Phrase and Fable* was among the top priorities of the post-war publishing programme. The then Chairman of Cassell's, Dr. Desmond Flower, M.C., made it his especial concern and a new and revised edition duly appeared in 1952. Dr. Flower was again the moving spirit behind the Centenary Edition so ably prepared by Ivor H. Evans in 1970. In the intervening years Mr. Evans has kept a fatherly eye on his offspring and now incorporates the fruits of nineteen years' nurture in this new edition. Its users will find that the *Dictionary* of the 1990s will satisfy their needs as fully as those of their countless predecessors. For, if the publishers have always striven to make the name of Cassell synonymous with quality in the field of reference books, they have succeeded in making *Brewer* their hallmark and a household name.

CHRONOLOGICAL LIST OF BOOKS

Written or Edited by Dr. E. Cobham Brewer

c. 1841	A Guide to Science *The exact date of first publication is not known, although Brewer himself said 1840. A "Second Edition" was published in 1848 and by 1905 the book had gone through forty-seven editions and sold 319,000 copies in English alone*	**Jarrold**
1842	School Recitations	**Jarrold**
1842	Poetical Chronology *Second Edition 1853*	**Longmans** **Jarrold**
1844	A New Set of Arithmetical and Commercial Tables *At least twenty editions*	**Jarrold**
c. 1847	An Entire New System of Book-keeping by single-entry *At least thirteen editions*	**Jarrold**
1847	Allison's Guide to English History and Biography *Dr. Brewer revised this, the sixth edition, and his revision went through a further sixty editions*	**Jarrold**
c. 1850	A Guide to English Composition *A Second Edition was published in 1853*	**Longmans**
1853	A Guide to Roman History *Twenty-four editions*	**Jarrold**
1853	An Entire New System of Book-keeping by double-entry *At least six editions*	**Jarrold**
1854	Sound and Its Phenomena	**Longmans**
1858	A Guide to the Mythology, History and Literature of Ancient Greece *Fourteen editions*	**Jarrold**
1858/ 1860	A Guide to Scripture History (Two Parts, Old and New Testaments) *Twenty-four editions*	**Jarrold**

1859	Appendix to Dr. Brewer's Guide to Science, to which is added Poisons and Accidents, their antidotes and remedies *A third edition was published in this year.* *Date of first publication not known*	**Jarrold**
1860	Theology in Science *At least seven editions*	**Jarrold**
1863	The Political, Social and Literary History of France *At least ten editions*	**Jarrold**
1864	My First Book of Bible History	**Cassell**
	My First Book of Geography	**Cassell**
	My First Book of the History of England	**Cassell**
	My First Book of Reading and Spelling	**Cassell**
	My First Book of Science	**Cassell**
	My First Book of Common Things	**Cassell**
1864	The Young Tutor	**Cassell**
1868	My First Book of Astronomy	**Cassell**
	My First Book of Chemistry	**Cassell**
	My First Book of Facts and Discoveries	**Cassell**
	My First Book of French History	**Cassell**
	My First Book of Grecian History	**Cassell**
	My First Book of the History of Rome	**Cassell**
1870	**A Dictionary of Phrase and Fable**	**Cassell**
1870	Great Central Points of Medieval and Modern History selected from the Poetical Chronology	**Longmans**
1874	A Guide to Christian Evidences *At least three editions*	**Jarrold**
1874	The Pathway through the Bible and Gospel History *At least five editions*	**Jarrold**
1877	Errors of Speech and Spelling *(reissued 1882)*	**Jarrold**
1880	The Reader's Handbook *At least six editions*	**Chatto and Windus**
1880	Rules for English Spelling	**Jarrold**

KEY TO PRONUNCIATION

VOWELS

a	as in	far (far).	i	as in	bit (bit).	u	as in	bull (bul).
ă	"	fat (făt).	ī	"	bite (bīt).	ŭ	"	sun (sŭn).
ā	"	fate (fāt).				ū	"	muse (mūz).
aw	"	fall (fawl).	o	"	not (not).			
â	"	fair (fâr).	ō	"	no (nō).	ou	"	bout (bout).
			ô	"	north (nôrth).	oi	"	join (join).
e	"	bell (bel).	oo	"	food (food).			
ĕ	"	her (hĕr).						
ē	"	beef (bēf).						

A dot placed over a, e, o, or u (ȧ, ė, ȯ, u̇) signifies that the vowel has an obscure, indeterminate, or slurred sound, as in:—

advice (ȧd vīs′), current (kŭr′ ėnt), notion (nō′ shȯn).

y when used as a vowel is rendered by i as in Polycrates (pol i′ krȧ tēz), or by ī as in Gyges (gī′ jēz).

CONSONANTS

b, d, f, h (see the combinations below), k, l, m, n, p, r, t, v, w, x, z, and y when used as a consonant, have their usual values.

c (except in the combinations ch and *ch*) is not used, the hard c being rendered by k as in cachet (kăsh′ ā), and the soft c by s as in Circe (sĕr′ si).

q is not used and is rendered by k as in quey (kwā).

s is used only for the sibilant s, as in toast (tōst); the sonant is rendered by z, as in toes (tōz).

x is not used and is rendered by z or ks as in Xerxes (zĕrks′ ēz).

ch is rendered by k when thus pronounced, as in Acheron (ăk′ er on), and by sh in words of French origin as in panache (păn ăsh).

ph is rendered by f as in Pharaoh (fâr′ ō).

ch	as in	church (chĕrch).	hw	as in	white (hwīt).
ch	"	loch (lo*ch*).	sh	"	shawl (shawl).
g	"	get (get).	zh	"	measure (mezh′ u̇r).
j	"	join (join).	th	"	thin (thin).
			th	"	thine (*th* īn).

The soft g is rendered by j as in gin (jin) and in words of French origin by zh as in gendarme (zhon′ darm); j is also rendered by zh in words of French origin as in jeunesse (zhĕr nes′).

The accent (′) follows the syllable to be stressed.

ABBREVIATIONS

Arab.	Arabic		L. Lat.	Late Latin
Austr.	Australian		M.E.	Middle English
c.	*circa* (about)		Med. Lat.	Mediæval Latin
cp.	compare		Mod. Fr.	Modern French
Dan.	Danish		O.E.	Old English
Dut.	Dutch		O.Fr.	Old French
e.g.	*exempli gratia* (for example)		O.H.Ger.	Old High German
			O. Slav.	Old Slavonic
Fr.	French		O.W.	Old Welsh
Gael.	Gaelic		Pers.	Persian
Ger.	German		Port.	Portuguese
Gr.	Greek		*q.v.*	*quod vide* (which see)
Heb.	Hebrew		Russ.	Russian
Hind.	Hindustani		Sans.	Sanskrit
Icel.	Icelandic		Scot.	Scottish
i.e.	*id est* (that is)		Sp.	Spanish
Ital.	Italian		Swed.	Swedish
Jap.	Japanese		Turk.	Turkish
Lat.	Latin		*viz.*	*videlicet* (namely)

CROSS-REFERENCES

These are indicated in the text by the use of SMALL CAPITALS unless *q.v.* is used.

INDEX

Where the main a–z sequence does not include the word or phrase required, or where additional information is sought, the index may provide references to relevant entries. The index and a guide to its use may be found on page 1201.

NOTE

All biblical references are to the *Authorized Version* unless otherwise stated. Entries concerning liturgical customs of the Church of England refer to those associated with the *Book of Common Prayer*. Ecclesiastical usages are those of the Church of England except where otherwise indicated.

A

A. This letter is modified from the Egyptian hieroglyph representing the EAGLE. The Phœnician (Hebrew) symbol was k (*aleph* ✘ an ox), doubtfully assumed to represent an ox-head. The Greek A (*alpha*) was the symbol of a bad AUGURY in the sacrifices. *See also* SCARLET LETTER.

A in logic denotes a universal affirmative.

A1 means first-rate—the very best. In LLOYD'S *Register of British and Foreign Shipping* the state of a ship's hull is designated by *letters* and that of the anchors, cables, etc. by *figures*. Thus A1 is a mark of the first class.

A.E.I.O.U. The device adopted by Frederick V, Archduke of Austria, on becoming the Emperor Frederick III in 1440. The letters, used by his predecessor, Albert II, stood for:

> Albertus Electus Imperator Optimus Vivat.

Frederick gave them the meaning:

> Archidux Electus Imperator Optime Vivat.

Among other versions are:

> Austria Est Imperare Orbi Universo.
> Alles Erdreich Ist Oesterreich Unterthan.
> Austria's Empire is Overall Universal.

To which wags added after the war of 1866:

> Austria's Empire Is Ousted Utterly.

Frederick the Great of Prussia (1712–1786) is said to have translated the motto thus:

> Austria Erit In Orbe Ultima
> (*Austria will be lowest in the world*).

A.L.O.E. These initials represent A Lady of England, the pseudonym of Charlotte Maria Tucker (1821–1893), the author of popular tales and allegories for children.

A.M.D.G. An abbreviation for *ad majorem Dei gloriam* (Lat.) meaning "to the greater glory of God".

A.U.C. Abbreviations of the Lat. *ab urbe condita*, or *Anno urbis conditae*, "from the foundation of the city" (ROME) "in the year of the city's foundation". It is the starting point of the Roman system of dating, and corresponds with 753 B.C.

A from a windmill, Not to know. To be very obtuse or ignorant. Possibly suggested by the similarity between the shape of a capital A and that of a distant tower windmill. Current in popular speech until the late 19th century.

Aalu, or **Aaru.** In ancient Egyptian religion the fields of Aalu, where food was grown for the dead to supplement the votive offerings of their descendants, correspond roughly with the ELYSIAN FIELDS of Greek mythology.

Aaron (âr' on). The patriarch of the Jewish priesthood (*Exod.* xxviii), possibly connected with *haaron*, "the ark".

Aaron's Beard. The popular name of many wild plants, including Great St. John's Wort (Rose of Sharon), the Ivy-leaved Toadflax, Meadowsweet, *Saxifrage sarmentosa*, etc. The reference is to *Ps*. cxxxiii, 2.

Aaron's Rod. The name given (with reference to *Num*. xvii, 8) to various flowering plants including Golden Rod and Great Mullein. Also a name for the DIVINING ROD.

Aaron's serpent. Something so powerful as to swallow up minor powers (*Exod*. vii, 10–12). Thus Prussia was the Aaron's serpent that swallowed up the lesser German States between 1866 and 1870.

Aaru. *See* AALU.

Aarvak. *See* HORSE.

Aback, To be taken, to be astounded, taken by surprise. From the sailing-ship term *aback*, when the sails press against the mast (or the clew of a fore and aft sail is to windward) and progress is suddenly stayed.

Abacus (ăb' à kùs). The name given to a variety of counting devices first used by the ancient civilizations of the Mediterranean and China (where it is called *Suan-Pan* and is still in use), but most commonly to the familiar nursery frame with its horizontal wires, each carrying ten sliding balls. The word is derived from a tablet covered in dust or sand (Gr. *abax*). The multiplication table invented by PYTHAGORAS is called *Abacus Pythagoricus*. *See* NAPIER'S BONES.

In architecture the *abacus* is the topmost member of a capital.

Abaddon (à băd' òn). The angel of the bottomless pit (*Rev*. ix, 11), from Heb. *abad*, he perished. Milton used the name for the pit itself:

In all her gates Abaddon rues
Thy bold attempt.
Paradise Regained, IV, 624.

Abaris (ăb′ à ris). **The dart of Abaris.** A
mythical priest of APOLLO mentioned by
Herodotus, PINDAR, etc. and surnamed "the
Hyperborean". Apollo gave him a magic arrow which rendered him invisible and on
which he rode through the air. He cured diseases and spoke oracles. Abaris gave the dart
to PYTHAGORAS.

Abatement (O.Fr. *abatre*, to beat down). In
HERALDRY, a *difference* in coat armour for illegitimate birth, granted to a petitioner after
establishing paternity but indicating that the
possessor is outside the legitimate line of
succession.

Abaton (ăb′ à ton) (Gr. *a*, not; *baino*, I go).
As inaccessible as Abaton. Said of various
places of antiquity difficult of access.

Abbassides (ăb′ à sīdz). A dynasty of caliphs
who ruled the Arabian Empire from 750 to
1258, descended from Abbas, uncle of MO-
HAMMED. Haroun al-Raschid (b. 765,
reigned 786–808), of the ARABIAN NIGHTS,
was one of their number.

Abbot of Misrule. *See* KING OF MISRULE.

Abbot's Bromley Horn, or **Antler Dance.**
One of the rare European animal dances surviving from remote times. Originally danced
on Twelfth Day at Abbot's Bromley, Staffordshire, it now takes place on the first
Monday after 4 September. The six dancers, all male as in MORRIS DANCES, hold ant-
lers (three of which are painted blue or red
and three white) to their heads as they
dance. It may originally have been a form of
fertility rite since the dancers go the round of
neighbouring farms before the dance. *See*
SWEARING ON THE HORNS *under* HORN.

A B C. The alphabet. Hence "He doesn't know
his A B C" means he is very ignorant: "he
doesn't understand the A B C of the subject"
means that he has not grasped its rudiments.
An *Absey Book* or *A B C Book* was a child's
primer.

Abd in Arabic = slave or servant, as ABDIEL
and ABDALLAH (*servant of God*), Abd-el-
Kader (*servant of the Mighty One*), Abdul-
Latif (*servant of the Gracious One*), etc.

Abdallah (ăb dăl′ à). The father of MO-
HAMMED. He was so beautiful that when he
married Amina 200 virgins broke their
hearts from disappointed love. He died before his son was born. *See* Washington Irving's *Life of Mahomet*.

Abdals (ăb′ dàlz). The name given by MOS-
LEMS to certain mysterious persons whose
identity is known only to God and through
whom the world is able to continue in exis-

tence. When one dies another is secretly appointed by God to fill the vacant place.

Abdera (ăb dēr′ à). A maritime town of
Thrace, mythically founded by HERCULES in
memory of ABDERUS. The *Abderites* or *Ab-
deritans* were proverbial for stupidity, said
to be caused by the air, but among them
were DEMOCRITUS, the laughing philosopher
(hence *Abderitan laughter* = scoffing laughter, and *Abderite* = scoffer); Protagoras, the
sophist; Anaxarchos, the philosopher friend
of Alexander; and Hecatæus, the historian.

Abderus. A friend of HERCULES, who was devoured by the horses of DIOMEDES when
keeping guard over them.

Abdiel (ăb′ dēl). *See* ABD. In Milton's *Paradise Lost* (V, 805, 896, etc.) the faithful
seraph who withstood SATAN when he urged
the angels to revolt.

Abe, Old or **Honest Abe.** Abraham Lincoln,
President of the United States from 1861 to
1865.

Abecedarian (ă bè si dâr′ i àn). A teacher or
learner of the A B C or rudiments. Also an
ANABAPTIST sect, the ZWICKAU PROPHETS,
founded in 1520. Led by Nicholas Stork, a
weaver, they relied on direct inspiration
from God, rejecting all learning as a hindrance.

Abecedarian Hymns. Hymns the lines or
divisions of which begin with the letters of
the alphabet in regular succession. In Hebrew the 119th Psalm is abecedarian. *See*
ACROSTIC POETRY.

Abelard and Héloïse (ăb′ e lard, ā lō ēz). Peter Abelard (1079–1142), eminent scholar,
theologian and philosopher, studied under
William of Champeaux and Anselm, and
founded an internationally famous school of
theology in Paris. At the age of thirty-six he
became tutor to Héloïse, the beautiful and
accomplished seventeen-year-old niece of
Canon Fulbert of Notre Dame. They fell in
love, a son was born and they were secretly
married, but Héloïse soon disavowed the
marriage that she might not hinder Abelard's preferment. Fulbert, enraged at her
husband's seeming connivance, caused him
to be emasculated. Abelard entered the
monastery of St. Denis. Héloïse became a
nun. Abelard continued his highly controversial teaching and later founded another
school near Nogent-sur-Seine called PARA-
CLETE, which, after his departure to take
charge of the Abbey of St. Gildas in Brittany, was given to a sisterhood under
Héloïse. His stormy career ended in 1142
and Héloïse was laid by his side in 1164.
Their remains were transferred from Paraclete and re-buried in the PÈRE LACHAISE

cemetery (Paris) in 1817.

Abelites (ăb' e lītz), **Abelians,** or **Abelonians.** A Christian sect of the 4th century living in North Africa, mentioned by St. AUGUSTINE. They married but remained virgin, as they affirmed Abel did, since no children of his are mentioned in the SCRIPTURES. Children were adopted to maintain the sect.

Abenezra. *See* ADMIRABLE.

Abhidhamma (ăb id a' ma). The third pitaka of the three texts (TRIPITAKA) which together form the sacred canon of the Buddhists. In seven treatises it is essentially concerned with metaphysics.

Abhorrers. *See* PETITIONERS.

Abif. *See* HIRAM ABIF.

Abigail (ăb' i gāl). A lady's maid. Abigail (I *Sam.* xxv, 24–28) repeatedly called herself David's handmaid, hence the usage. Beaumont and Fletcher in *The Scornful Lady* called the "waiting gentlewoman" by this name, and it was used by Swift, Fielding and others. Probably the usage was popularized by the political notoriety of Abigail Hill (Mrs. Masham), waiting-woman to QUEEN ANNE and royal favourite.

Abingdon Law. *See* CUPAR JUSTICE.

Abiogenesis (Gr. *a*, without, *bios*, life + *genesis*), a term applied by T. H. Huxley in 1870 to the ancient theory that non-living matter could produce living. An example of such spontaneous generation is found in VIRGIL'S *Georgics* (Bk. IV), when the shepherd Aristæus, son of APOLLO and CYRENE, having lost his bees through disease and famine, slew four bulls at his mother's orders. On the ninth morning bees poured forth from the decomposing cattle.

Abo (ăb' ō). Shortened form of aborigine in general colloquial use in Australia.

Abolitionists. In Great Britain historically applied to supporters of the anti-slavery movement; in the U.S.A. specifically applied to those who agitated for the abolition of Negro slavery in the period 1830–1861; in Australia, to those, in the 19th century, who sought to end the transportation of British convicts.

Abominable Snowman. Name, popularized by Shipton's Everest Expedition of 1951, for the yeti, a rare, elusive, and supposedly bear-like animal of the Himalayas.

Abomination of Desolation. Probably refers to some statue set up in the TEMPLE by heathens or the Romans and is mentioned in *Dan.* ix, xi, xii, and *Matt.* xxiv, 15. The subject is very obscure.

Abou-Bekr (ă boo bekr), (*c.* 573–634), called Father of The Virgin (AYESHA). He was the immediate successor of MOHAMMED or first CALIPH (632–634) and was supported by the SUNNITES.

Abou Hassan (ă boo hăs' ăn). A rich merchant (in the ARABIAN NIGHTS, *The Sleeper Awakened*), transferred while asleep to the bed of the Caliph HAROUN AL-RASCHID. Next morning he was treated as the CALIPH and every effort was made to make him forget his identity. The same trick was played on Christopher SLY in the Induction of Shakespeare's *The Taming of the Shrew*; and according to Burton (*Anatomy of Melancholy*, 1621) by Philip the Good, duke of Burgundy, on a drunken rustic, the subject of *The Frolicsome Duke, or the Tinker's Good Fortune* found in PERCY'S RELIQUES. Calderón's play, *Life's a Dream* (*c.* 1633), contains another version.

Abou ibn Sina. *See* AVICENNA.

About the size of it. How matters stand, approximately the facts of the case.

Above-board. Honest and open. According to Johnson "borrowed from gamesters, who, when they put their hands under the table, are changing their cards."

Above oneself, To be. Temporarily more than ordinarily high-spirited, self-confident, or conceited.

Above par. *See* PAR.

Above your hook. *See* HOOK.

Ab ovo (Lat. from the egg). Laboriously from the very beginning. Stasinus in his *Cypria*, an introduction to the ILIAD, begins with the eggs of LEDA, from one of which HELEN was born. If Leda had not laid this egg Helen would never have been born, therefore PARIS could not have eloped with her, therefore there would have been no TROJAN WAR, etc. The English use of the phrase probably derives from the line in Horace's *De Arte Poetica*:

Nec gemino bellum Troianum orditur ab ovo.

Abracadabra. A cabbalistic charm, said to be made up from the initials of the Hebrew words Ab (Father), Ben (Son), and Ruach ACadsch (Holy Spirit), and formerly used against ague, flux, toothache etc. The word was written on parchment as shown and hung from the neck by a linen thread. *See* CABBALA.

```
A B R A C A D A B R A
 A B R A C A D A B R
  A B R A C A D A B
   A B R A C A D A
    A B R A C A D
     A B R A C A
      A B R A C
       A B R A
        A B R
         A B
          A
```

Abracax. *See* ABRAXAS.

Abraham. In addition to the BIBLE stories about the Hebrew patriarch, Mohammedan legend adds the following: His parents were Prince Azar and his wife Adna. As King Nimrod had been told that one shortly to be born would dethrone him, he proclaimed a "massacre of the innocents". Adna retired to a cave where Abraham was born and was nourished by sucking two of her fingers, one giving milk and the other honey. At fifteen months the boy was the size of a lad of fifteen, and so wise that Azar introduced him to Nimrod's court. Further, that Abraham and his son "Ismail" rebuilt for the fourth time the KAABA; that Abraham destroyed the idols made and worshipped by his father Terah; and that the mountain on which he offered up his son ("Mount Moriah" in the Bible) was "Arfaday".

The GHEBERS say that the infant Abraham was thrown into the fire by Nimrod's order but it turned into a bed of roses on which he went to sleep.

To sham Abraham. *See* ABRAM-MAN.

Abrahamic Covenant. The promise given by God to ABRAHAM because he left his father's house to live in a strange land as God told him, and interpreted to mean that the MESSIAH should spring from Abraham's seed (*Gen.* xii, 1–3 and xvii).

Abraham Newland, An. A bank-note: from Abraham Newland, chief cashier of the Bank of England (1782–1807), whose signature appeared on its notes.

Abraham's bosom. The repose of the happy in death:

> The sons of Edward sleep in Abraham's bosom.
> SHAKESPEARE: *Richard III*, IV, iii.

The allusion is to the ancient custom of allowing a dear friend to recline on one's bosom (*Luke* xvi, 22), as did John on the bosom of Jesus.

There is no leaping from Delilah's lap into Abraham's bosom—*i.e.* those who live and die in notorious sin must not expect to go to HEAVEN at death.

Abram-colour. "Abram" here is a corruption of *auburn*. In Shakespeare's *Coriolanus*, II, iii, the word is so printed in the first three folios.

> Our heads are some brown, some black, some Abram, some bald.

Abram-man, or **Abraham cove.** In Tudor and early Stuart times a pretended maniac who wandered about begging; a TOM O'BEDLAM; hence **to sham Abraham** meaning to sham illness in order to dodge work.

Inmates of BEDLAM who were not dangerous were kept in the "Abraham Ward" and occasionally allowed out in distinctive dress and permitted to beg. This gave an opportunity to many impostors. *The Canting Academy* (Richd. Head, 1674) says they used to beg alms but "for all their seeming madness, they had wit enough to steal as they went along."

They are also portrayed in *King Lear*, II, iii, and Beaumont and Fletcher's *Beggar's Bush*, II, i.

Abraham, Plains of, or **Heights of,** south-west of the city of Quebec, the scene of the decisive battle (13 September 1759) between the British under Wolfe and the French under Montcalm, as a result of which the conquest of Canada was effected. They were named after a pilot known as Maître Abraham (A. Martin). Both Montcalm and Wolfe died in the battle.

Abraxas (à bràks' às). A cabbalistic word used by the GNOSTICS to denote the Supreme Being, the source of 365 emanations, the sum of the numbers represented by the Greek letters of the word. It was often engraved on gems (*Abraxas stones*) used as TALISMANS. By some authorities the name is given as that of one of the horses of AURORA.

Absalom. The third son of DAVID, remarkable for his good looks, who rose in rebellion against his father, aided by AHITHOPHEL. In his flight after defeat, Absalom was trapped in the branches of a tree and slain by Joab, the King's general. David's great sorrow was thus expressed (II *Sam*. xviii, 33):

> O my son Absalom, my son, my son Absalom! would God I had died for thee, O Absalom my son, my son!

In Dryden and Tate's *Absalom and Achitophel*, Absalom stands for the Duke of Monmouth.

Absence. The Etonian term for "roll-call".

Absent. The proverb "Out of sight out of mind" appears as the title of one of Barnabe Googe's *Eglogs* in 1563. Fulke Greville, Lord Brooke (1554–1628) in his 56th *Sonnet* gives it as "Out of mind as soon as out of sight."

The absent are always wrong. From the French proverb, *les absents ont toujours tort*. It implies that it is always easy to blame those not present, who cannot defend themselves. Found in G. Herbert, *Outlandish Proverbs*, 1640.

Absence makes the heart grow fonder. A tag from the song, *the Isle of Beauty*, by T. Haynes Bayly (1797–1839).

Absinthe (ǎb' sinth). A green liqueur flavoured with wormwood (*Artemisia absinthium*) together with angelica root, etc. It appears frequently in accounts of the life of

French literary and artistic circles at the end of the 19th century and the early 20th century, and was first popularized by being prescribed as a febrifuge to French troops during the Algerian War (1830–1847). *L'Absinthe* is the title by which the painting "Au Café" by Degas (exhibited in London in 1893) is better known. Émile Zola vividly described the horrors of absinthe poisoning in *L'Assommoir*. Its sale and manufacture are now illegal in France.

Absolute, A Captain. A bold despotic man, determined to have his own way, so called from the character in Sheridan's *The Rivals*.

Abstinence. Ecclesiastically *Days of Abstinence* are those when the eating of meat is not permitted; on *Fasting Days* only one full meal is allowed in the twenty-four hours.

Abstract Numbers are numbers considered without reference to anything else, *i.e.* 1, 2, 3; if we say one year, two feet, three men, etc. the numbers are *concrete*.

Things are said to be **taken in the abstract** when considered absolutely without relation to other things.

An abstract of title is a legal phrase meaning a précis of the evidences of ownership of real property.

Abstraction. An empty abstraction, a mere ideality of no practical use and thus often eventually rejected as unsatisfying:

> Give us, for our abstractions, solid facts;
> For our disputes, plain pictures.
> WORDSWORTH: *Excursion*, V, 636.

Abudah (à bū' da). Thackeray's allusion:

> Like Abudah, he is always looking out for the Fury, and knows that the night will come with the inevitable hag with it,

is to a merchant of Baghdad, haunted every night by an old hag described in Ridley's *Tales of the Genii*.

Abundant Number, An. A number the sum of whose aliquot parts is greater than itself, *e.g.*, 12, because its divisors, 1, 2, 3, 4, 6, = 16, which is greater than 12. *Cp.* DEFICIENT NUMBER, PERFECT NUMBER.

Abyla. *See* CALPE.

Abyssinian Christians. A branch of the Coptic Church. *See* COPTS.

Academy. Originally a garden near Athens where PLATO taught (named after *Academos*). Hence the philosophical school or system of Plato, and later a place, society or institution where the arts and sciences are taught or fostered.

The teaching of Plato and his early followers came to be known as the Old Academy; the modified Platonic system founded by Arcesilaus (*c.* 224 B.C.), as the Middle; the half-sceptical school founded by Carneades (*c.* 160 B.C.), as the New. Plato's followers were known as *Academics*. In addition to its usage in reference to an academy or university the adjective academic has come to mean "theoretical, scholarly, abstract, unpractical". *See* PLATONISM.

Acadia (à kā' dià), **Acadie.** A former French settlement which now forms part of the provinces of Nova Scotia and New Brunswick. Ceded to Great Britain in 1713, the French inhabitants continued to intrigue against the British, and in 1755 were dispossessed and dispersed among the British colonies to the southward. This deportation provides the subject for Longfellow's *Evangeline*.

Acadine (ăk' à dīn). A Sicilian fountain mentioned by Diodorus Siculus as having magic properties. Writings were thrown into it to be tested; if genuine they floated, if spurious they sank to the bottom.

Acanthus (à kăn' thùs). The representation of the leaf of *Acanthus mollis* used to decorate the capitals of CORINTHIAN and composite columns. The story is that an acanthus sprang up around a basket of flowers that Callimachus had placed on his daughter's grave. This so struck the fancy of the architect that he introduced the design into his buildings.

Accessory after the fact is one who screens a felon or helps him in any way to profit from his crime. A receiver of stolen goods, knowing or even suspecting them to be stolen, is an accessory *ex post facto*.

Accessory before the fact is one who is aware that another intends to commit an offence, but is absent when the offence is committed.

Accident. A logical accident is some quality or property which a thing possesses but which is not essential to it, the removal or change of which would not necessarily affect it, as the height of our bodies, the whiteness of paper or the redness of a brick. *See* TRANSUBSTANTIATION.

Accidental colours. *See* COLOURS.

Accius Nævius (ăk' kiùs nē' vi ùs). A legendary Roman augur who forbade TARQUIN the Elder (616–579 B.C.) to increase the number of centuries (*i.e.* divisions of the army) instituted by ROMULUS, without consulting the augurs. Tarquin asked him if, according to the augurs, the thought then in his (Tarquin's) mind was feasible of accomplishment. "Undoubtedly", said Accius after consultation. "Then cut through this whet-stone with the razor in your hand". The priest gave a bold cut and the block fell in two (Livy, I, 36). *See* AUGURY.

Accommodation. In commercial use, a loan of money.

Accommodation note or **bill.** A BILL OF EXCHANGE for which value has not been received, used for the purpose of raising money on credit.

Account, To keep open. Merchants are said to keep open account when they agree to honour each other's BILLS OF EXCHANGE.

On the account. An old phrase for sailing on a piratical expedition.

The account on the STOCK EXCHANGE means the credit allowed on dealings for the fortnightly settlement, or the fortnightly settlement itself, which is also called *account-day* or *settling-day*.

To be called to one's last account. To die.

To be sent to one's account. To have final judgment passed on one. The ghost in *Hamlet* (I, v) uses the phrase as a synonym for death:

> Sent to my account
> With all my imperfections on my head.

To square accounts with someone means to get even with or retaliate upon. Derived from "square accounts" in which debit balances credit.

Accusative. Calvin was so called by his college companions. An "accusative age" is an obsolete expression denoting an age that is *searching*, one that eliminates error by accusing or censuring it.

> This hath been a very accusative age.
> SIR E. DERING (16th century).

Ace. The unit of cards or dice from *as*, the Latin unit of weight. In World War I the French word *as*, applied to an airman who had brought down ten enemy aeroplanes, was imported in its English equivalent *ace*, then extended to any especially expert flier, golfer, etc.

Within an ace. Within a hair's breadth of; he who wins with an ace wins within a single mark. *See* AMBS-AS.

To bate an ace. To make an abatement or to give a competitor some start or advantage making the combatants more equal. *See* BOLTON.

Aceldama (à sel' dà mà). The Aramaic for the "field of Blood" figuratively used for any place of great slaughter. It was the POTTER'S FIELD near Jerusalem bought to bury strangers in (*see Matt. xxvii*, 7, 8 and *Acts* i, 18, 19), and was used by Christians during the CRUSADES and as late as the 17th century.

Acephalites (à sef' à lītz) (Gr. *akephale*, without a head). A name given to various schismatical Christian bodies, principally to (i) those MONOPHYSITES who rejected the auth-ority of Peter Mongus, Bishop of Alexandria, in 482, and were later absorbed by the JACOBITES; (2) those NESTORIANS rejecting patriarchal condemnation of Nestorius in 431; (3) priests rejecting episcopal authority or bishops that of their metropolitans; (4) a group of English LEVELLERS in the reign of Henry I, who acknowledged no leader.

The name is also given to various legendary headless monsters.

Acestes (à ses' tēz). **The arrow of Acestes.** In a trial of skill Acestes, the Sicilian, shot his arrow with such force that it took fire (*Æneid*, V, 525).

Achates (à kā' tēz). **A fidus Achates** is a faithful companion, a bosom friend. Achates (in VIRGIL's *Æneid*) was the chosen comrade of ÆNEAS.

Achemon (à ke' mon). According to Greek legend, Achemon and his brother Basalas were two Cercopes (a people of Ephesus) for ever quarrelling. One day they saw HERCULES asleep under a tree and insulted him, so he tied them by their feet to his club and walked off with them, heads downwards. Everyone laughed at the sight, and it became a proverbial cry among the Greeks, when two men were seen quarrelling—"Look out for Melampygos!" (*i.e.* Hercules):

> Ne incidas in Melampygum.

Acheri. The ghost of a little girl, who, according to folk tradition of India, comes down at night from her mountain haunts to bring sickness to children in human habitations. A bright-red thread worn round the neck is believed to be a protection against such molestation.

Acheron (ăk' er on). The "woeful river" of the underworld into which flow the PHLEGETHON and COCYTUS. Also HADES itself. *See* CHARON; STYX.

> They pass the bitter waves of Acheron
> Where many souls sit wailing woefully.
> SPENSER: *Faerie Queene* I, v, 33.

See also VIRGIL's *Æneid*, Bk. VI.

Acherontian Books. *See* TAGES.

Acherusia (ăk er ooz' i à). A cavern on the borders of Pontus, through which HERCULES dragged CERBERUS from the infernal regions to earth.

Acheulean (à shĕr' li àn). The name given to stages of PALAEOLITHIC hand-axe culture typified by the tools found at St. Acheul, near Amiens.

Achillea (ăk il ē' à). A genus of plants of the aster family, including common yarrow (*Achillea millifolium*), so called from ACHILLES. The tale is that the Greeks, on the way to TROY, landed in Mysia and were opposed by Telephus, son of HERCULES. DIO-

NYSUS caused Telephus to stumble and he was wounded by Achilles with his spear. Told by the ORACLE that Achilles (the wounder) would be the healer (meaning milfoil or yarrow), Telephus sought out the Greek leader, promising to lead him to Troy in return for his help. Achilles agreed, scraped some rust from his spear from which sprang the plant milfoil, and this healed the wound. It is called carpenters' wort by the French (*herbe aux charpentiers*) because it is supposed to heal wounds made by carpenters' tools.

Achilles (à kil′ēz). Hero of the ILIAD, the son of Peleus, King of the MYRMIDONS in Thessaly, and grandson of Æacus. Brave and relentless, his quarrel with AGAMEMNON, the Greek commander-in-chief, caused him to withdraw from the struggle. The TROJANS prevailed and Achilles allowed PATROCLUS to lead the Myrmidons back. Patroclus was killed by HECTOR. Achilles then returned, routed the Trojans, and slew Hector. According to later poems Achilles was killed by PARIS at the Scæan gate. *See* ACHILLES TENDON.

Achilles and the tortoise. Alludes to a paradox by ZENO. In a race Achilles, who can run ten times as fast as a tortoise, gives the latter 100 yards start; but cannot win the race because while he is running the first 100 yards, the tortoise runs ten, while Achilles runs that ten the tortoise runs one, while Achilles is running one, the tortoise runs one-tenth of a yard, and so on *ad infinitum*.

Achilles of England. The Duke of Wellington (1769–1852).

Achilles of Germany. Albert, Elector of Brandenburg (1414–1486).

Achilles of Lombardy. In Tasso's JERUSALEM DELIVERED, the brother of Sforza and Palamedes in the allied army of Godfrey. He was slain by Corinna.

Achilles of Rome. Lucius Sicinius Dentatus, tribune of the Roman plebs, 454 B.C., also called the "*Second Achilles*".

Achilles of the West. ROLAND the PALADIN, also called "the Christian THESEUS".

Achilles tendon (*tendo Achillis*). A strong sinew connecting the heel and calf frequently strained by athletes. The tale is that THETIS took her son Achilles by the heel, and dipped him in the river STYX to make him invulnerable, but the heel in her hand remained dry. The hero was slain by an arrow wound in the heel—the one weak spot (a post-Homeric story).

Achilles's horses. Balios and XANTHUS. *See* HORSE.

Achilles's mistress in Troy. Hippodamia, surnamed BRISEIS.

Achilles's spear. *See* ACHILLEA. Shakespeare and Chaucer allude to its powers.

> Whose smile and frown, like to Achilles's spear,
> Is able with the change to kill and cure.
> SHAKESPEARE: *Henry VI, Part II*, V, i.
> And of Achilles with his queynte spere,
> For he coude with it both hele and dere [harm].
> CHAUCER: *Squire's Tale*, 238.

Achilles's tomb. In Sigeum, over which no bird ever flies. *Pliny*, X, 29.

Achilles's tutors. PHŒNIX, who taught him the arts of war and rhetoric, and CHIRON, the CENTAUR, the art of healing.

Achilles's wife. DEIDAMIA.

The English Achilles. John Talbot, first Earl of Shrewsbury (1388?–1453).

The heel of Achilles. The vulnerable spot in the character of a man or a nation. *See* ACHILLES TENDON.

Achitophel. *See* AHITHOPHEL.

Achor (ā kôr). Said by Pliny to be the deity prayed to by the Cyreneans for the averting of insect pests. *See* FLIES, GOD OF.

Acid. Acid Drop, The. Nickname by which Mr. Justice Avory (1851–1935) was known in legal circles, from his caustic wit in court.

Acid test. Gold is not attacked by most acids but reacts to AQUA FORTIS (and AQUA REGIA)—the acid test. Hence applied to a decisive or searching test.

To come the acid. To adopt an acid manner, to exaggerate one's authority, to be overbearing or offensive.

To put the acid on. Used originally in Australia and New Zealand meaning to ask for a loan. It has since come to mean to make excessive demands on. Possibly derived from ACID TEST.

Acis (ā′ sis). The son of FAUNUS, in love with GALATEA, crushed to death with a rock by his rival, POLYPHEMUS the CYCLOPS, and changed into the river Acis (Ovid, *Metam.* xiii, 750–968).

Ack Ack. Slang from World Wars I and II meaning Anti-Aircraft Guns. Field telephonese, *cp*. ACK EMMA.

Ack Emma. *See* PIP EMMA.

Acknowledge the corn. To admit the truth of the point at issue, an American expression. In a Congressional debate in 1828 one of the states which claimed to export corn admitted that the corn was actually used to feed hogs, and exported in that form.

> "I hope he will give up the argument, or to use a familiar phrase *acknowledge the corn*" (Mr Speight of Mississippi speaking in the U.S. Senate in 1846).

Acme (ăk′ mi) (Gr. a point). The highest pitch of perfection. Old medical writers divided the progress of a disease into the *arche*, or beginning; the *anabasis* or increase; the *acme*, or crisis; and the *paracme*, or decline.

Aconite (ăk ò nīt). The herb Monkshood or Wolfsbane. According to classic fable when HERCULES, at the command of Eurystheus, dragged CERBERUS from the infernal regions, the poisonous aconite grew from the foam which dropped from his mouths.

Acrasia (à krā' zi à). The personification of intemperance, the name signifying "lack of self control". In Spenser's *Faerie Queene* (II, xii) *Acrasia*, an enchantress, mistress of the "Bower of Bliss", transformed her lovers into monstrous shapes and kept them captive. Sir Guyon destroyed her bower, freed her victims, and sent her in chains of adamant to the Faerie Queene.

Acre. O.E. *œcer*, akin to Lat. *ager*, a field.

God's acre, a cemetery or churchyard. A modern borrowing from Germany, wrongly called by Longfellow an "ancient Saxon phrase".

Acre-Fight. *See under* FIGHT.

Acre-Shot. Obsolete name for a land-tax. "Shot" is *scot. See* SCOT AND LOT.

Acres, Bob. A coward is sometimes called "a regular Bob Acres" after a character in Sheridan's *The Rivals*, whose courage always "oozed out at his fingers' ends".

Acres of Diamonds. A lecture said to have been given 6,000 times by the American BAPTIST minister, R. H. Conwell (1843–1925), in which he urged the acquisition of riches as a social duty. His assertion that 3,900 of the 4,500 American millionaires were self-made men led to the growth of the popular "success story" in American magazines.

Across someone, To get. To quarrel with or annoy a person; *cp.* "cross" in the sense of obstruct or thwart.

Across, To put, or **get something**. Generally used of a speaker making his point and carrying his audience with him. Probably derived from the theatre where actors must reach their audience across the footlights, or possibly from the game of baseball.

Acrostic (Gr. *akros*, outermost; *stichos*, line of verse). Verse in which the initial letters of each line read downwards to form a word; if the final letters also form a word it is a double acrostic; if the middle letters also, it is a triple acrostic. The term was first applied to the obscure prophecies of the Erythræan SIBYL written on loose leaves, which made a word when sorted into order (*Dionys.* IV, 62).

Acrostic Poetry among the Hebrews consisted of twenty-two lines or stanzas beginning with the letters of the alphabet in succession (*cp.* ABECEDARIAN HYMNS).

Act and Opponency. An "act", at the universities of Oxford and Cambridge, consisted of a thesis publicly maintained by a candidate for a degree, with the "disputation" thereon. The person "disputing" with "the keeper of the Act" was called the "opponent" and his function was called an "opponency". In some degrees the student was required to keep his Act, and then to be the opponent of another disputant. This custom has long been given up, but at Cambridge the thesis and examination for the doctor's degree in Medicine is still called an "Act".

Act of God. A term applied by lawyers to happenings indisputably outside human control, for which there is no legal redress (*e.g.,* losses caused by flood, hurricane, earthquake, etc.).

Act of Parliament. A law or statute made by PARLIAMENT. Introduced as a BILL, it becomes an Act when passed, after it has received the royal assent. *See* REGNAL YEAR *under* YEAR.

Act of Truth. An event which, following a solemn oath, was held to prove or disprove its truth as in trial by ORDEAL.

Actæon (ăk tē' on). In Greek mythology a huntsman who, having surprised DIANA bathing (or according to Euripides boasted his superiority in the chase) was changed into a stag and torn to pieces by his own hounds. Thus (as a stag) he became representative of men whose wives are unfaithful. *See* TO WEAR THE HORNS *under* HORN.

Actian Games (ăk' ti àn). The games celebrated at Actium in honour of APOLLO, renewed by AUGUSTUS after his naval victory over Antony off Actium (31 B.C.).

Action Sermon. In the Scottish PRESBYTERIAN Church the sermon sometimes preached before administering the Communion.

Actresses. Thomas Coryate says "When I went to a theatre [in Venice] I observed certain things that I never saw before; for I saw women act... I have heard that it hath sometimes been used in London" (Coryate's *Crudities*, 1611). Female parts on the English stage were always taken by boys until the RESTORATION. The first actress to perform in public was Margaret Hughes (Prince Rupert's mistress) playing Desdemona in *Othello* at a theatre in Clare Market, London (8 December 1660). Edward Kynaston (d. 1706) seems to have been the last actor to take female parts in serious drama.

Whereas, women's parts in plays have hitherto been acted by men in the habits of women... we do permit and give leave for the time to come that all women's parts be acted by women.

Charles II's licence of 1662.

Ad inquirendum (ăd' in kwī ren' dum) (Lat.). A judicial writ commanding an inquiry to be made into some complaint.

Ad Kalendas Græcas (ăd ka len'dăs grē' kăs) (Lat.). (Deferred) to the Greek Calends—*i.e.* for ever. (It shall be done) on the Greek Calends—*i.e.* never—for the Greeks had no CALENDS. Suetonius says AUGUSTUS used this reply if asked when he was going to pay his creditors.

Ad libitum (ăd lib' i tum) (Lat.). To choice, at pleasure, without restraint.

Ad libbing. From *ad libitum*. In theatrical, broadcasting and musical parlance, to depart from the script or music and improvise.

Ad valorem (ăd văl ôr' em) (Lat.). According to the value. A term used in imposing customs and stamp duty, the duty increasing according to the value of the transaction or goods involved.

Ad vitam aut culpam (ăd vī' tam awt kŭl' pam) (Lat.). Literally "to lifetime or fault", used in Scottish law of the permanency of an appointment during good behaviour.

Adam. The Talmudists say that Adam lived in PARADISE only twelve hours before he was thrust out. Mohammedan legend says that:

God sent GABRIEL, MICHAEL, and ISRAFEL in turn to fetch seven handfuls of earth from different depths and of different colours for the creation of Adam (hence the varying colours of mankind), but they returned empty-handed because Earth foresaw that the creature to be made from her would rebel against God and draw down his curse on her. AZRAEL was then sent and he fulfilled the task, and so was appointed to separate the souls from the bodies, hence becoming the ANGEL of Death. The earth he fetched was taken to ARABIA to a place between MECCA and Tayef, kneaded by angels, fashioned into human form by God and left to dry for either 40 days or 40 years. The tradition holds that Adam was buried on Aboucais, a mountain in Arabia.

For the Bible story of Adam, see *Gen*. i-v.

Adam. The elegant neo-classical style of architecture and interior decoration created by the brothers Adam, especially Robert Adam (1728–1792). *See* ADELPHI.

As old as Adam. Means that something was well known long ago.

The curse of Adam. The necessity of working for a living. "In the sweat of thy face shalt thou eat bread, till thou return unto the ground" (*Gen*. ii, 19). In the story of the Creation, Adam and EVE were driven from the Garden of EDEN for disobedience, and

God cursed the earth, which had hitherto borne only plants "pleasant to the sight and good for food" (*Gen*. ii, 9) so that it now put forth "thorns also and thistles" (*Gen*. iii, 18).

Not to know someone from Adam. To regard someone as a complete stranger, to be completely unacquainted.

The old Adam. The offending Adam, etc.

> Consideration, like an angel, came
> And whipped the offending Adam out of him.
> SHAKESPEARE: *Henry V*, I, i.

Adam, as the head of unredeemed man, stands for "original sin", or "man without regenerating grace".

The Second Adam, the New Adam, etc. Jesus Christ is so called.

> The Tempter set
> Our second Adam in the wilderness,
> To show him all earth's Kingdoms and their glory.
> *Paradise Lost*, XI, 383.

In the same way Milton calls MARY our "second Eve" (*Paradise Lost*, V, 387 and X, 183).

When Adam delved:

> When Adam delved and Eve span,
> Who was then the gentleman?

This, according to the *Historia Anglicana* of Thos. Walsingham (d. 1422), was the text of John Ball's speech at Blackheath to the rebels in the PEASANTS' REVOLT (1381). Possibly adapted from lines by Richard Rolle of Hampole (d. *c*. 1349):

> When Adam dalfe and Eve spanne
> To spire of thou may spede,
> Where was then the pride of man,
> That now marres his meed?

Cp. JACK'S AS GOOD AS HIS MASTER—*under* JACK(1).

Adam Bell. *See* CLYM OF THE CLOUGH.

Adam Cupid, *i.e.* Archer CUPID, probably alluding to ADAM BELL. In all early editions the line in *Romeo and Juliet* (II, i, 13) "Young Adam Cupid, he that shot so trim", reads "Young Abraham Cupid". The emendation was suggested by George Stevens (1736–1800).

Adam's ale. Water; first man's only drink, sometimes called *Adam's wine* in Scotland.

Adam's apple. The protuberance in the forepart of the throat; so called from the supposition that a piece of the forbidden fruit stuck in Adam's throat.

Adam's bridge. *See* RAMA.

Adam's needle. A name given chiefly to the Yucca and to certain other plants with needle-like spines. *Gen*. iii, 7 tells us that Adam and EVE "sewed fig leaves together".

Adams, Parson. *See* PARSON.

Adam's Peak. A mountain in Ceylon where, according to Mohammedan legend, ADAM, after his expulsion from PARADISE, expiated his crime by standing on one foot for 200 years until GABRIEL took him to Mount Ararat, where he found EVE. In the granite there is a large impression resembling a human foot. Hindus assert that it was made by BUDDHA when he ascended into heaven.

Adam's profession. Gardening or agriculture. See *Gen*. ii, 15 and *Gen*. iii, 23.

> There is no ancient gentlemen but gardeners, ditchers, and grave-makers; they hold up Adam's profession.
>
> SHAKESPEARE: *Hamlet*, V, i.

Adamites (ăd' à mīts). The name given to various heretical sects, possibly of misguided ascetics, who practised nudity and rejected marriage. Such were the 2nd-century Adamites in North Africa, but similar ideas, leading to licentiousness, were revived in Europe by the *Brethren and Sisters of the Free Spirit* in the 13th century; the BEGHARDS in France, Germany and the Netherlands; and the PICARDS of Bohemia in the 14th and 15th centuries, etc. Adamites are mentioned in James Shirley's comedy *Hyde Park* (II, iv) (1632) and in the *Guardian*, No. 134 (1713).

Adamastor (ăd à măs' tôr). The spirit of the Cape of Storms (Good Hope), described by Camoëns (1524–1580) in the LUSIADS, who appeared to Vasco da Gama and foretold disaster to all attempting the voyage to India.

Add insult to injury. To wound by word or deed someone who has already suffered an act of violence or injustice. PHÆDRUS quotes the fable of ÆSOP about a bald man who, in attempting to kill a fly which had bitten his head, missed and dealt himself a sharp smack. Whereupon the fly said: "You wished to kill me for a mere touch. What will you do to yourself since you have added insult to injury?"

Add up, It does not. No sensible answer can be arrived at from the known facts, it does not make sense. A phrase derived from simple arithmetic.

Addison of the North. Henry Mackenzie (1745–1831), author of *The Man of Feeling*, literary leader in Edinburgh. So called by Sir Walter Scott.

Addisonian termination. The name given by Bishop Hurd (1720–1808) to the construction, frequently employed by Joseph Addison (1672–1719), which closes a sentence with a preposition, *e.g.*, "which the prophet took a distinct view of".

Addle is the Old English *adela*, mire or liquid filth, hence rotten, putrid, worthless. Thus *addled egg*, a rotten egg, and figuratively *addle-headed, addle-pate*, muddle-headed or lacking brains.

Addled Parliament (5 April–7 June 1614). So called for its sterility, being dissolved by James I without passing a single Act. It refused to grant supplies unless the king abandoned IMPOSITIONS.

Adelantado (ă de lăn ta' dō). Spanish for "his excellency". Hence a figure of importance.

> Open no door. If the adelantado of Spain were here he should not enter.
>
> BEN JONSON: *Every Man out of his Humour*, V, vi.

Middleton, in *Blurt, Master Constable* (IV, iii), used the abbreviation *lantedo*.

Adelphi, The. A small district between the STRAND and Thames designed by Robert ADAM and his brothers in 1768 (*Adelphoi* is the Greek word for brothers). Originally the site of the Bishop of Durham's palace, it is rich in literary and historical associations, having accommodated the Savage Club, Garrick, Rowlandson, Hardy, Barrie, etc. The arches upon which the streets were built, known as the SHADES or Darkies, became of ill repute. John Adam Street still accommodates the Royal Society of Arts but most of the Adelphi has been replaced by unneighbourly modern buildings.

Adept. One who has attained (Lat. *adeptus*). The alchemists applied the term *vere adeptus* to those who professed to have found out the ELIXIR OF LIFE or the PHILOSOPHER'S STONE.

Adiaphorists (ăd ĭ ăf' or ists) (Gr. indifferent). Moderate Lutherans, followers of Melanchthon, who accepted the Interim of Leipzig (1548) on ceremonies indifferent (*i.e.* neither sanctioned nor forbidden by the Scriptures), causing controversy among the Lutherans, which substantially ended in 1555. See AUGSBURG.

Adieu (a dū) (Fr. *à Dieu*, to God). An elliptical form for *I commend you to God*. *Cp.* GOOD-BYE.

Aditi. The great earth mother of Hindu mythology, sometimes an abstract concept of limitless space and time. Variously described as the mother, wife, and daughter of VISHNU.

Adityas. In the VEDAS they are the divine sons of ADITI, the chief being VARUNA, sustainer of the moral law, who is often called *Aditya*.

Adjective colours are those which require a mordant before they can be used as dyes.

Admass. Coined by J. B. Priestley in *Journey Down a Rainbow* (1955) to describe the vast mid-20th-century proliferation of commercial advertising and high-pressure salesmanship, especially in the U.S.A. The word has now come to mean the vast mass of the general public to which advertisers address their publicity.

Admirable, The. Abraham ben Meir ibn Ezra (1092–1167), a celebrated Spanish Jew was so called. He was a noted mathematician, philologist, poet, astronomer, and commentator on the BIBLE, and the Rabbi Ben Ezra of Robert Browning's poem of that name.

The Admirable Crichton. James Crichton (1560–1585), Scottish traveller, scholar and swordsman. So called and wonderfully portrayed by Sir Thomas Urquhart (1611–1660) in *The Exquisite Jewel*. Hence one distinguished by all-round talents. Harrison Ainsworth was much indebted to Urquhart for his novel, *The Admirable Crichton* (1837). Sir J. M. Barrie's play of this name appeared in 1902.

> And was in short (in their eyes at least) a very Admirable Crichton of the nineteenth century.
> CUTHBERT BEDE: *Adventures of Mr. Verdant Green*, ch. v.

Admirable Doctor (*Doctor Admirabilis*). Roger Bacon (*c.* 1214–1294), the great English philosopher.

Admiral, from the Arabic *amir* (lord or commander), with the article *al* as in *amir-al-bahr* (commander of the sea), *amir-al-Omra* (commander of the forces). Milton, speaking of SATAN, uses the old form for the ship itself:

> His spear—to equal which the tallest pine
> Hewn on Norwegian hills, to be the mast
> Of some great ammiral, were but a wand—
> He walked with.
> *Paradise Lost*, I, 292.

In the Royal Navy there are now four ranks of Admiral—Admiral of the Fleet, Admiral, Vice-Admiral, Rear-Admiral. Up to 1864 Flag-Officers were graded as Admirals, Vice-Admirals, and Rear-Admirals of the Red, White, and Blue, from the late 17th-century practice of dividing the fleets into squadrons—Red (centre), White (van), Blue (rear), the Admiral of the Red being Admiral of the Fleet until this eventually became a separate post. The junior appointment was that of Admiral of the Blue. Subsequently squadrons were sub-divided into centre, van and rear divisions each under a Flag Officer. As their numbers multiplied these posts became ranks.

Admiral of the Blue (*see above*), facetiously used for a butcher or a tapster from their blue aprons.

> As soon as customers begin to stir
> The Admiral of the Blue cries "Coming Sir!"
> *Poor Robin* (1731).

Admiral of the Red (*see above*), also applied to a wine-bibber whose nose and face are red.

Yellow Admiral, nickname for those promoted from Captain to Admiral but not employed actively (in allusion to the yellow QUARANTINE Flag). The Retired List proper dates from 1870.

Admonitionists, or **Admonitioners.** Those who in 1572 sent *admonitions* to PARLIAMENT condemning EPISCOPACY and advocating the doctrines and practices of Geneva.

Adonai (à dō nī) (Heb. pl. of *adon*, lord). A name for the Deity used by the Hebrews, instead of *Yahweh* (JEHOVAH), "the ineffable name", wherever it occurs. *See* TETRAGRAMMATON.

Adonists. Those Hebraists who maintain that the vowels of the word ADONAI are not those necessary to make the TETRAGRAMMATON J H V H into the name of the Deity. *See* JEHOVAH.

Adonais (àd ō nā' is). The name given by Shelley to Keats in his elegy (*Adonais*, 1821) lamenting the latter's death, probably in allusion to the mourning for ADONIS.

Adonia (àd ō' ni à). An eight-day feast of ADONIS, celebrated in Assyria, Alexandria, Egypt, Judæa, Persia, Cyprus, Greece and Rome. The women first lamented the death of ADONIS then wildly rejoiced at his resurrection—a custom referred to in the BIBLE (*Ezek*. viii, 14), where Adonis appears under his Phœnician name, Tammuz. *See* THAMMUZ.

Adonis (à dō' nis). In classical mythology, a beautiful youth, son of MYRRHA (or Smyrna), he was beloved by APHRODITE (Venus) and killed by a boar while hunting. Hence, usually ironical, any beautiful young man. Leigh Hunt was sent to prison for libelling the Prince Regent by calling him "a corpulent Adonis of fifty" (*Examiner*, 1813).

Adonis Flower, the rose, once white, but coloured red by the blood of APHRODITE when pricked by a thorn rushing to help the fallen ADONIS; the anemone which sprang from his blood or the tears of Aphrodite; and more commonly Pheasant's Eye (*Adonis autumnalis*), which arose from the hunter's blood.

Adonis garden. A worthless toy; very perishable goods.

> Thy promises are like Adonis' gardens.
> That one day bloomed and fruitful were the next.
> SHAKESPEARE: *Henry VI, Pt. I*, 1, vi.

Adonis River, the stream near Byblos

which ran red with the soil brought down from Lebanon.

> Thammuz came next behind,
> Whose annual wound in Lebanon allured
> The Syrian damsels to lament his fate
> In amorous ditties all a summer's day,
> While smooth Adonis from his native rock
> Ran purple to the sea, supposed with blood
> Of Thammuz yearly wounded.
> MILTON: *Paradise Lost*, I, 446.

Adoption. Adoption by arms. An ancient custom of giving arms to a person of merit, which put him under the obligation of being your champion and defender.

Adoption by baptism. Being godfather or godmother to a child.

Adoption by hair. Boso, King of Provence (879–889), is said to have cut off his hair and given it to Pope John VIII (872–882) as a sign that the latter had adopted him.

Adoption controversy. Elipand, Archbishop of Toledo, and Felix Bishop of Urgel (in the 8th century), maintained that Christ in his human nature was the son of God by adoption only (*Rom.* viii, 29), though in his pre-existing state he was the "begotten Son of God" in the ordinary Catholic acceptation. The **adoptionists** were condemned by the Council of Frankfurt in 794.

Adoptive Emperors. The five Emperors—Nerva, Trajan, Hadrian, Antoninus Pius, Marcus Aurelius—each of whom (except Nerva, who was elected by the Senate) was the adopted son of his predecessor. Their period (96–180) is said to have been the happiest in Roman history.

Adrammelech (à drăm' e lek). A Babylonian deity to whom infants were burnt in sacrifice (II *Kings* xvii, 31). Possibly the sun god worshipped at Sippar (Sepharvaim).

Adrastus (à drăs' tus). (i) A mythical Greek king of Argos, leader of the expedition of the SEVEN AGAINST THEBES. (ii) An Indian prince, slain by RINALDO (in Tasso's JERUSALEM DELIVERED, Bk, XX), who aided the king of Egypt against the crusaders.

Adriatic. *See* BRIDE OF THE SEA.

Adrift. At the mercy of wind and tide, something which has carried or broken away. In colloquial naval usage it means being late, overdue from leave or absent from place of duty.

All adrift, figuratively used, means an aimless and confused state of mind.

Adullamites (à dŭl' à mīts). A group of some thirty LIBERALS led by R. Lowe and E. Horsman, who led the opposition to Lord Russell's Reform Bill in 1866; likened by John Bright to the malcontents who joined David when he escaped to the cave of Adullam.

And every one that was in distress, and every one that was in debt, and every one that was discontented, gathered themselves unto him.
> I *Sam*. xxii, 1, 2

Adulterous Bible. *See* BIBLE, SOME SPECIALLY NAMED EDITIONS.

Advent (Lat. *adventus*, arrival). The four weeks before CHRISTMAS, beginning on St. ANDREW'S Day (30 November), or the Sunday nearest to it, commemorating the first and second coming of Christ; the first to redeem, and the second to judge the world.

Advent Sunday. The first Sunday in Advent, the beginning of the Church Year, except in the Greek Church where it begins on St. MARTIN'S Day (11 November).

Adventists. Those who expect a second coming of Christ on earth as imminent. They originated in the U.S.A. as MILLERITES. *See* MILLENARIANS; SEVENTH-DAY ADVENTISTS.

Adversary, The. SATAN or the DEVIL (from I *Pet*. v, 8).

Adversity Hume. Joseph Hume (1777–1855) was so called through his forebodings of national disaster in the mid-1820's. *Cp.* PROSPERITY ROBINSON.

Advocate. The Devil's Advocate. A carping or adverse critic, from *Advocatus Diaboli* (Devil's Advocate). In the ROMAN CATHOLIC CHURCH, the popular name given to the Promoter of the Faith whose duty it is to promote vigorously the arguments against a proposed BEATIFICATION or CANONIZATION. The supporter was (until 1983) called *Advocatus Dei* (God's Advocate).

Advocates' Library, was founded in Edinburgh (1682) by Sir George Mackenzie, Dean of the Faculty of Advocates (*i.e.* members of the Scottish bar). In 1925 it became the National Library of Scotland and has received a copy of all books published since the Copyright Act of 1709. *See* FAMOUS LIBRARIES *under* LIBRARY.

Advowson (Lat. *advocatio*, a summoning). The right of presentation to a church BENEFICE. Thus named because the patron was the advocate or defender of the living and of the claims of his candidate. The different advowsons are:

Advowson appendant. When the right of presentation belongs to and passes with the manor whose owner originally built, or endowed, the church.

Advowson collative. When the BISHOP himself is patron; presentation, admission, and institution are replaced by collation.

Advowson donative. When the patron (usually the Crown) donated the benefice without the bishop's playing any part in its disposal. These became presentative after 1898.

Advowson in gross. One which has been sold and become legally separated from the manor. *See* GROSS.

Advowson presentative. Where the patron presents the clerk to the BISHOP, who must institute the nominee unless there are legal or ecclesiastical grounds for refusal.

The transfer and sale of advowsons is now subject to restrictions.

Adytum (Gr. *aduton*, not to be entered). The HOLY OF HOLIES in Greek and Roman temples, into which the public was not admitted; hence a sanctum.

Ægeus (ē′ jūs). A mythical king of Attica, who sent his son THESEUS to Crete to deliver ATHENS from the yearly tribute of seven youths and seven maidens exacted by MINOS. If successful, Theseus was to hoist white sails (in place of black) on his return, as a signal of his safety. He omitted to do so. Ægeus, thinking his son was lost, threw himself into the sea. The story is repeated in the tale of TRISTRAM and Isolde.

Æginetan Sculptures consist of two groups of figures from the east and west pediments of the temple of ATHENE, on the island of Ægina, representing exploits of the Greek heroes at TROY. They date from *c.* 500 B.C., being found in 1811, and are preserved in the Glyptothek, in Munich.

Ægir (ē′ jir, ē′ gir). In Norse mythology the god of the ocean, husband of Ran. They had nine daughters (the billows), who wore white robes and veils.

Ægis (ē′ jis) (Gr. goat skin). The shield of ZEUS, made by HEPHÆSTOS and covered with the skin of the goat AMALTHEA, who had suckled the infant Zeus. With the GORGON'S head in the centre, it was also carried by his daughter ATHENE. By shaking his ægis Zeus produced storms and thunder. In relation to Athene it is usually represented as a cloak fringed with serpents and the Gorgon's head. It is symbolic of divine protection, hence *under my ægis*, under my protection.

Ægyptus (ē jip′ tus). In Greek legend a son of Belus and twin brother of Danaus who was king of that part of Africa named after him (Egypt).

Aemilian Law. The Roman prætor Aemilius Mamercus made a law (A.U.C. 391) empowering the eldest prætor to drive a nail in the Capitol on the IDES of September, with the supposition that it would stop pestilence or avert a calamity. It is mentioned in Livy VII, iii.

Æneas (ē nē′ as). In Greek mythology the son of Anchises, King of Dardanus, and APHRO-DITE. According to HOMER he fought in the TROJAN WAR, and after the sack of TROY withdrew to Mount IDA and reigned in the Troad. The post-Homeric legends are largely embodied in the ÆNEID.

Æneid (ē′ ne id or ē nē′ id). VIRGIL'S epic poem in twelve books, accounting for the settlement of ÆNEAS in Italy, thus claiming Trojan origins for the Roman state. The story tells how Æneas escaped from the flames of TROY carrying his father Anchises to Mount IDA. With his Trojan followers he sailed to Crete but learnt in a vision that he was destined for Italy, and eventually reached Sicily where his father died. Heading for the mainland, he was wrecked on the coast of Carthage. He left secretly, at JUPITER'S behest, whereupon the lovelorn queen DIDO of Carthage killed herself. Reaching Latium he was betrothed to LAVINIA, daughter of king LATINUS; but war arose with Turnus, king of the Rutuli, who also wished to marry Lavinia. Turnus was finally killed by Æneas.

Æolian Harp. A musical instrument rather like a zither consisting of a wooden resonating box with strings of different thickness tuned to the same note. Taking its name from ÆOLUS, when exposed to the wind the strings vibrate producing a series of chords depending on the speed of the wind. It developed to its present form at the end of the 16th century.

Æolian Mode, in music, the ninth of the "church modes" according to the classification established by Henricus Glareanus in 1547, the range being from A to A with dominant E.

Æolian Rocks. Those which have been deposited or eroded largely by the wind.

Æolus (ē′ ō lùs), in Homeric legend, was appointed ruler of the winds by ZEUS, and lived on his Æolian island.

Æon (ē′ on) (Gr. *aion*). An age of the universe, an infinite length of time. Also the personification of an age, a god, any being that is eternal. Basilides, in the early 2nd century, held that there had been 365 such Æons but Valentinus, the 2nd-century GNOSTIC, restricted the number to 30.

Æschylus (ēs′ ki lùs) (525–456 B.C.), the main father of Greek tragic drama. Only seven plays, of over seventy known titles, are extant. Fable says he was killed by a tortoise dropped by an eagle (to break the shell) on his bald head (mistaken for a stone).

Æschylus of France. Prosper Jolyot de Crébillon (1674–1762).

Æsculapius (ēs kū lā′ pi us). The Latin form of the Greek *Asklepios*, god of medicine and

of healing, son of APOLLO and father of HY-
GEIA. The usual offering to him was a cock,
hence "to sacrifice a cock to Æsculapius"—
to give thanks (or pay the doctor's bill) after
recovery from an illness.

When men a dangerous disease did scape,
Of old, they gave a cock to Æsculape.
BEN JONSON: *Epigram*.

Introduced to ROME (293 B.C.), in the form of
a snake, during a pestilence, the SERPENT entwined round a staff became his attribute.

Æsir (ē′zēr). The collective name of the
mythical gods of Scandinavia, who lived in
ASGARD. (1) ODIN the chief; (2) THOR; (3)
TIU; (4) BALDER; (5) BRAG, god of poetry;
(6) VIDAR, god of silence; (7) Hoder the
blind (slayer of Balder); (8) Hermoder,
Odin's son and messenger; (9) Hœnir, a
minor god; (10) Odnir, husband of FREYJA;
(11) LOKI; (12) Vali (Odin's youngest son).

Æson's Bath (ē′ son).

I perceive a man may be twice a child before the
days of dotage; and stands in need of Æson's Bath
before three score.
SIR THOMAS BROWNE: *Religio Medici, Section* xlii.

The reference is to MEDEA rejuvenating
Æson, father of JASON, with the juices of various magic herbs. After Æson had absorbed
these juices, Ovid says:

Barba comaeque,
Canitie posita, nigrum rapuere, colorem.
Metamorphoses, VII, 288.

Æsop's Fables (ē′ sop). These popular animal fables are traditionally the work of
Æsop, a deformed Phrygian slave (*c.*
620–560 B.C.), but many are far older, being
found on Egyptian papyri of 800–1,000
years earlier. SOCRATES, in prison, began
committing them to verse. A collection
made in CHOLIAMBIC by BABRIUS (early 3rd
century A.D.), was found in a monastery on
Mount Athos in 1844. *See* PHÆDRUS.

Æsop of England. John Gay (1685–1732).

Æsop of France. Jean de LA FONTAINE
(1621–1695).

Æsop of India. PILPAY has been so called.

Ætion (ē′ ti ōn) in Spenser's *Colin Clout's
Come Home Againe* (1595) typifies Michael
Drayton, the poet.

Aetites (ā ē tī′ tēz) (Gr. *aetos*, an eagle).
Eagle stones, also called *gagites*: according
to fable found in eagle's nests, possessing
magical and medical properties.

The stone in question is big with another inside it,
which rattles, as if in a jar when you shake it.
PLINY: *Natural History*, X, iv (*see also* XXX, xliv).

Lyly's *Euphues* (1578–1580) says:
The precious stone Aetites which is found in the
filthy nests of the eagle.

Affluent Society. A phrase, popular from the

later 1950s, denoting the overall growth in
material prosperity of British society as evidenced by the growingly widespread ownership of motor cars, television sets, washing
machines, refrigerators, etc.; a society
further cushioned by its "free" social services. J. K. Galbraith's *The Affluent Society*
was published in 1958.

Afreet, Afrit (ăf′ rēt). In Mohammedan
mythology the second most powerful of the
five classes of JINN or devils. They were of
gigantic stature, malicious and inspiring
great dread.

Africa. Teneo te, Africa. When CÆSAR
landed at Adrumetum, in Africa, he tripped
and fell—a bad omen; but with great presence of mind pretended that it was intentional. He kissed the soil, exclaiming, "Thus
do I take possession of thee, O Africa." The
story is told also of Scipio and again of Cæsar
on his landing in Britain.

Africa semper aliquid novi affert. "Africa is always producing some novelty." A
Greek proverb quoted by Pliny, in allusion
to the belief that Africa abounded in strange
monsters.

African Sisters, The. The HESPERIDES,
who dwelt in Africa.

Afrikander Bond. A party founded in Cape
Colony in 1874 to promote "a united South
Africa under its own Flag", essentially
under Boer domination.

After. After-cast. An obsolete expression for
something done too late; literally a throw of
the dice after the game is ended.

Ever he playeth an after-cast
Of all that he shall say or do.
GOWER.

After-clap. A catastrophe or misfortune
after an affair is supposedly over. In thun-
derstorms a "clap" is often heard after the
rain stops, and the clouds break.

What plaguy mischief and mishaps
Do dog him still with after-claps.
BUTLER: *Hudibras*, Pt. I, iii.

After-guard. The men who tended the gear
in the after part of a ship, also the officers,
who had their quarters aft.

After meat, mustard. *See under* MUS-
TARD.

After me the deluge. *See* APRÈS MOI LE
DÉLUGE.

Aft-meal. An extra meal; a meal taken after
and in addition to the ordinary meals.

At aft-meals who shall pay for the wine?
THYNNE: *Debate* (*c.* 1608).

Agamemnon (ăg à mem′ non). In Greek legend, the King of Mycenæ, son of Atreus,
grandson of PELOPS, brother of MENELAUS,
and leader of the Greeks at the siege of TROY.

He married CLYTEMNESTRA. ORESTES was their son. Their daughters were IPHIGENIA and/or Iphianassa, Laodice (in later legend ELECTRA), and Chrysothemis. He returned from Troy with CASSANDRA (daughter of King PRIAM) and both were murdered by his wife Clytemnestra and her paramour Ægisthus. The guilty pair were killed by Orestes, called Agamemnonides.
Vixere fortes ante Agamemnona, a quotation from HORACE (*Od.* IV, ix), paraphrased by BYRON in *Don Juan* (i, 5);

> Brave men were living before Agamemnon
> And since, exceeding valorous and sage,
> A good deal like him too, though quite the same none;
> But then they shone not on the poet's page,
> And so have been forgotten.

In general, we are not to suppose our own age or locality monopolizes all that is good.

Aganippe (ăg à nip' i). In Greek legend a fountain of BŒOTIA at the foot of Mount HELICON, dedicated to the MUSES because it imparted poetic inspiration. Hence the Muses are sometimes called *Aganippides*. Also the NYMPH of this fountain.

Agape (ăg' à pi). A love-feast (Gr. *agape*, love). The early Christians held a love-feast in conjunction with the Lord's Supper when the rich provided food for the poor. Eventually they became a scandal and were condemned by the Council of Carthage, 397. *Agape* was the mother of Priamond, Diamond, Triamond and Cambina in Spenser's *Faerie Queene* (IV, ii, 4188).

Agapemone (ăg à pem' ō ni). A sect of men and women, adherents of Henry James Prince (1811–1899), curate of Charlynch, Somerset, and his rector Samuel Starky (hence they were sometimes called *Starkyites*). These zealots founded an Agapemone or Abode of Love at Spaxton in 1849, living on a common fund, but their licentious conduct led to trouble with authority. After 1890 the movement revived as the "Children of the Resurrection" under Smyth-Pigott, who was unfrocked in 1909.

Agapetæ (ăg à pē' tē). (Gr. beloved). A group of 3rd-century ascetic women who, under vows of virginity, contracted spiritual marriage with monks and attended to their wants. The practice became widespread and the scandals arising led to their condemnation in the 4th century and suppression by the LATERAN COUNCIL of 1139.

Agate (ăg' àt). So called, says Pliny (XXXVII, 10), from Achates or Gagates, a river in Sicily, near which it is found in abundance. It was supposed to render a person invisible, and to turn the sword of foes against themselves.

A diminutive person has been called an *agate* from the custom of carving small figures on seals made from agate. Thus Shakespeare speaks of Queen MAB as no bigger than an agate-stone on the forefinger of an alderman.

Agatha, St. (ăg 'à thà), was tortured and murdered at Catania in Sicily, possibly during the Decian persecution of 250–253. She is sometimes represented holding a salver containing her severed breasts, and the shears or pincers with which she was mutilated. Her feast day is 5 February.

Agave (a gā' vi), named from Agave, daughter of CADMUS, a group of tropical American plants of the Amaryllis family including the gigantic "American Aloe" or Maguey of Mexico, mistakenly called the century plant, in the belief that it took 100 years to flower.

Agdistes (ăg dis' tēz). The god who kept the "Bower of Bliss" in Spenser's *Faerie Queene*.

Agdistis (ăg dis' tis). A Phrygian mother goddess sometimes identified with CYBELE the goddess of fertility. Originally hermaphrodite, she was made female by castration.

Age, a word used in mythology, geology, archaeology, history, etc. to denote a period of time marked by particular characteristics, *e.g.*, GOLDEN AGE, ICE AGE, STONE AGE, DARK AGES, MIDDLE AGES, Elizabethan Age, AUGUSTAN AGE, Machine Age, Atomic Age, etc.

Hesiod (? 8th century B.C.) names five ages: the Golden or patriarchal; the SILVER or voluptuous; the Brazen, warlike and violent; the Heroic or renaissant; the IRON or present, an age of misery and crime when justice and piety have vanished.

Lucretius (*c.* 94–55 B.C.) distinguishes three ages, stone, bronze, and iron, according to the material from which implements were made (V, 2128).

Varro (116–27 B.C.) recognizes three— from the beginning of mankind to the DELUGE; from the Deluge to the first OLYMPIAD, called the mythical period; from the first Olympiad to his own time, called the historic period (*Fragments*, p. 219 Scaliger's edition, 1623).

Ovid (B.C. 43–A.D. 18) describes four ages—Golden, Silver, Bronze and Iron (*Metamorphoses* I, 89–150).

Thomas Heywood (*c.* 1572–1650) has a series of plays based on classical mythology called *The Golden Age, The Silver Age, The Brazen Age*, and *The Iron Age*.

Shakespeare's seven ages of man are described in *As You Like It*, II, vii.

Age of Animals. According to an old

CELTIC rhyme:

Thrice the age of a dog is that of a horse;
Thrice the age of a horse is that of a man;
Thrice the age of a man is that of a deer;
Thrice the age of a deer is that of an eagle.

Age of Consent. The age at which a girl's consent to seduction is legal. In English and Scottish law the age is 16.

Age of Discretion. In English law, a child of 14 years is deemed to have sufficient discretion to be prosecuted for offences of commission.

Age of Reason, for Roman Catholics the end of the seventh year when they begin to assume moral responsibility, the obligation of confession, etc.

The 18th century is also called the *Age of Reason* as a period of ENLIGHTENMENT when philosophy was in vogue throughout Europe.

Canonical Age. Ages fixed by Canon Law when individuals may undertake various functions, duties, etc. In the CHURCH OF ENGLAND a man may become a deacon at 23, a priest at 24, and a BISHOP at 30. In the ROMAN CATHOLIC CHURCH a novice must be 16, a deacon 22, and a bishop 30. FASTING begins at the age of 21.

Age hoc (a' jē hok). "Attend to this." In sacrifice the Roman crier perpetually repeated these words to arouse attention. Somewhat similar is the frequent use of the exhortation "Let us pray" in the Church of England services.

Agelasta (ăj e lăs' tà), (Gr. joyless). The stone on which CERES (Demeter) rested when wearied in the search for her daughter, PERSEPHONE.

Agenor (ă jen' or). King of Tyre, son of POSEIDON (Neptune). His descendants Europa, CADMUS, PHŒNIX, Cilix, etc., are known as Agenorides.

Agent provocateur (Fr. provocative agent). A person used to incite or stir up others by posing as a partisan in order to induce them to commit treasonable or indictable actions.

Aggie Weston's, Aggies. The Royal Sailors' Rest Homes founded in Portsmouth, Chatham, and Devonport by Dame Agnes E. Weston (1840–1918).

Aglaia (à glī' à). One of the three GRACES.

Aglaonice (ăg lā ō nī' si), the Thessalian, being able to calculate eclipses, claimed power over the MOON and to be able to draw it from HEAVEN. Her vaunting became a laughing-stock and gave rise to the Greek proverb cast at braggarts, "Yes, as the Moon obeys Aglaonice."

Agnes. A sort of female "VERDANT GREEN", so unsophisticated that she does not even know what love means: from a character in Molière's *L'École des Femmes*.

Agnes, St., patron saint of young virgins, possibly martyred in the Diocletian persecution (*c.* 304) at the age of 13. There are various unreliable and conflicting accounts on the manner of her death; some say she was burnt at the stake and others that she was beheaded or stabbed. She vowed that her body was consecrated to Christ and rejected all her suitors. Her festival is on 21 January. Upon St. Agnes's night, says Aubrey in his *Miscellanies* (1696), you take a row of pins, and pull out every one, one after another. Saying a PATERNOSTER, stick a pin in your sleeve, and you will dream of him or her you shall marry. In Keats' *The Eve of St. Agnes*, we are told:

how upon St. Agnes' Eve,
Young virgins might have visions of delight,
And soft adorings from their loves receive
Upon the honey'd middle of the night,
If ceremonies due they did aright;
As, supperless to bed they must retire.

Tennyson has a poem called *St. Agnes' Eve*.

Agnoitæ (ăg' nō tē) (Gr. *a*, not; *gignoskein*, to know).—(1) Certain 4th-century Euomian heretics, who maintained that God was not completely omniscient.

(2) A group of 6th-century MONOPHYSITES, who maintained that Christ, by the limitations of his human nature, had incomplete knowledge of both present and future.

Agnostic (Gr. *a*, not; *gignoskein*, to know). A term coined by T. H. Huxley in 1869 (with allusion to St. PAUL'S mention of an altar "To the Unknown God" in *Acts* xvii, 23) to indicate the mental attitude of those who withhold their assent from whatever is incapable of proof, *e.g.* the existence of God, a First Cause, etc. An agnostic simply says 'I do not know". *See* THEIST.

Agnus Bell. *See* AGNUS DEI.

Agnus-castus. *See* VITEX.

Agnus Dei (ăg' nùs de' ī) (Lamb of God). (1) A title of Jesus; (2) the figure of a lamb bearing a cross or flag, the symbol of Christ; (3) the cake of wax or dough bearing this imprint, distributed by the POPE on the Sunday after EASTER—a relic of the ancient custom of distributing the wax of the Paschal candle, which was stamped with the lamb; (4) that part of the MASS introduced by the ringing of the *Agnus bell*, beginning with the words, *Agnus Dei, qui tollis peccata mundi* (O Lamb of God, that takest away the sins of the world); also part of the *Gloria* in the English Communion service.

Agonistes (ă gon is' tēz), (Gr. champion). The title of Milton's last poem, *Samson Agonistes* (1671), simply means "Samson the

Champion". Similarly *Sweeney Agonistes*, a poem by T. S. Eliot (1888–1965).

Agonistics (ă gon is' tiks). A group of roving DONATISTS in Africa in the early 4th century. The name means "Champions" (of Christ). They committed acts of violence and were called *Circumcellions* by the Catholics because they wandered among the dwellings of the peasants (*circum cellas*).

Agony aunt. A woman who conducts an advice column, page or pages in newspapers or magazines (especially women's) answering correspondents who seek help with their problems. Most of the letters are from girls and women and are mainly concerned with family relationships, marital problems, sex and boy friends. Nowadays agony aunts tend to adapt their advice to the circumstances of the PERMISSIVE SOCIETY.

Agony column. A column in a newspaper containing advertisements for missing relatives and friends. Now commonly applied to the columns in which the AGONY AUNT offers advice.

Aguecheek. Sir Andrew Aguecheek, a straight-haired country squire, stupid even to silliness, self-conceited, living to eat, and wholly unacquainted with the world of fashion. The character is in Shakespeare's *Twelfth Night*.

Agur's Wish (ā' gėrz) (*Prov.* xxx, 8). "Give me neither poverty nor riches."

Ahasuerus (à hăs ū ēr' ùs). Under this name the Emperor XERXES (485–465 B.C.), husband of Esther, appears in the Biblical books of *Ezra* and *Esther*. The Ahasuerus of *Daniel* has not been identified. It is also traditionally the name of the WANDERING JEW.

Ahithophel. A treacherous friend and adviser. Ahithophel was the traitorous counsellor of King DAVID, who deserted to ABSALOM but hanged himself when Absalom disregarded his advice (II *Sam.* xvii, 23). In Dryden and Tate's *Absalom and Achitophel*, Achitophel (Ahithophel) stands for Lord Shaftesbury.

Ahmed, Prince (a' med), in the ARABIAN NIGHTS, is noted for the tent given him by the fairy Paribanou, which would cover a whole army, but might be carried in one's pocket; and for the apple of Samarkand (*see* APPLE, PRINCE AHMED'S), which would cure all diseases. Similar qualities to those of the tent are common to many legends. *See* BAYARD; CARPET; SKIDBLADNIR.

Aholah and Aholibah (à hō' la, a hō lī' bà) (*Ezek.* xxiii). Personifications of prostitution. Used by the prophet to signify religious adultery or running after false faiths.

Ahriman (a' ri màn). In the dualism of later ZOROASTRIANISM, the spirit of evil, also called Angra Mainyu. He is in eternal conflict with Ahura Mazda or ORMUZD. The spirit of deceit and wickedness was earlier personified as Druj.

Ahura Mazda. *See* ORMUZD.

Aidan, St. A monk of Iona who was chosen in 635 in answer to King Oswald's request to spread and rekindle Christianity in Northumbria. He established a monastery on the island of Lindisfarne (HOLY ISLAND) and founded many churches and schools on the mainland. He died at Bamburgh in 651.

Aide-mémoire (Fr. *aider*, to help; *mémoire*, memory). A memorandum or reminder. In diplomatic parlance, a memorandum sent by one government through its ambassador to the Foreign Minister of another government summarizing the points he has been instructed to make by word of mouth.

Aide-toi, le Ciel t'aidera (ād twa lè sē el tà dė ra'). A line from LA FONTAINE (*Fables*, vi, 18). Literally "Help yourself, heaven will help you"; motto of a French liberal political society founded in 1824 to secure the advancement of the working classes. It helped in bringing about the Revolution in 1830 and was dissolved in 1832. Guizot was at one time its president and *Le Globe* and *Le National* its organs.

Aim. To give aim. To stand aloof. In archery, meaning to stand within a suitable distance from the butts, to inform the archers how near their arrows fall to the target.

> But, gentle people, give me aim awhile,
> For nature puts me to a heavy task;
> Stand all aloof.
> SHAKESPEARE: *Titus Andronicus*, V, iii.

Aim-crier. An abettor, one who encourages. In archery the one appointed to cry "aim".

> Thou smiling aim-crier at princess' fall.
> GERVAIS MARKHAM: *English Arcadia* (1638).

To cry aim. To applaud, encourage. In archery those chosen to cry "aim" to encourage the archer.

> All my neighbours shall cry aim.
> SHAKESPEARE: *Merry Wives of Windsor*, III, ii.

Air. Held by Anaxagoras (*c.* 500–*c.* 428 B.C.) to be the primary form of matter and one of the four elements according to Empedocles and ARISTOTLE. *See* ELEMENT.

Air-brained. A mis-spelling of HAREBRAINED.

Air-line. Often used in the U.S.A. comparably to the English BEE-LINE, as well as for railways which follow direct routes (*e.g.*, The Seaboard Air Line). Aeroplane companies flying on scheduled routes are also called *Air Lines*.

Hot Air. *See* HOT.

The air of the court, the air of gentility; hence **to give oneself airs**—to assume a manner, appearance, tone, superiority to which one has no real claim.

Aisle sitters. American theatre critics. Where in English *aisle* is usually restricted to the walks, or passages between the pews of a church, in the U.S.A. applied to any kind of gangway in public buildings and vehicles. In a theatre an *aisle sitter* could escape from a boring play before the end or leave to send copy to his newspaper without disturbing other theatregoers.

Aitch-bone. Corruption of "naitch-bone", *i.e.* the haunch-bone (Lat. *nates*). For other instances of the coalescence of the "n" of "an" with an initial vowel (or the coalescence of the "n" with the article), *see* APRON, NICKNAME.

Ajax (ā jăks). (1) *The Greater*. A famous hero of the TROJAN WAR. Son of Telamon and King of Salamis, a man of giant stature, daring and slow-witted. In the ODYSSEY, when the armour of ACHILLES was awarded to Odysseus (ULYSSES), as the champion, Ajax killed himself.

(2) *The Lesser*. In HOMER, son of Oileus, King of Locris, in Greece, and of small stature. In consequence of his attack on PRIAM'S daughter CASSANDRA he was drowned by POSEIDON after being shipwrecked.

Akbar (ăk' bar). An Arabic title, meaning "Very Great", especially applied to Jelaleddin-Mohammed, Akbar Khan, MOGUL emperor of India (1556–1605).

Alabama claims were made by the U.S.A. against Great Britain for losses caused during the CIVIL WAR (1861–5) by British-built Confederate raiders and notably the *Alabama*. In 1871 an international tribunal awarded the U.S.A. $15,500,000.

Aladdin (à lăd' in), in the ARABIAN NIGHTS, obtains a magic lamp and has a splendid palace built by the genie of the lamp. He marries the daughter of the SULTAN of China, who disposes of the lamp, and his palace is transported to Africa. He subsequently recovers the lamp and returns with both wife and palace to China to live happily for many years.

Aladdin's lamp. The source of wealth and good fortune. After his good luck and marriage Aladdin neglected his lamp and allowed it to rust.

To finish Aladdin's window—*i.e.* to attempt to complete something begun by a master hand or genius. The palace built by the genie of the lamp had a room with twenty-four windows, all but one being set in precious stones; the last being left for the SULTAN to finish but his resources proved unequal to the task.

Alamo (al' ămo). American cottonwood tree, hence the name *Alamo Mission* for the Franciscan mission at San Antonio, Texas, which stood in a grove of cottonwood trees. Founded in 1718, it was later used as a fort. During the Texas rebellion against Mexico in 1836 a garrison of 187 Texans, including David CROCKETT, was wiped out by 3,000 Mexicans under Santa Anna, after a thirteen-day siege. "Remember the Alamo" became the war cry with which Sam Houston led the Texans to victory. Alamo is sometimes called the "THERMOPYLÆ of America" and the buildings are now a national monument.

Alans. Large hunting dogs introduced to Britain from Spain, whither they are said to have been brought by the Alani, a barbarian tribe which entered Spain *c.* 410. Chaucer in *The Knight's Tale* describes Lycurgus on his throne guarded by "alaunts, twenty and mo, as grete as any steer". Scott mentions them in *The Talisman* (ch. vi). *Cp.* RACHE.

Al Araf (al' ă' răf) (Arab. the partition). In the KORAN, a region between PARADISE and Jahannam (HELL), for those who are neither morally good nor bad, such as infants, lunatics and idiots. Also where those whose good and evil deeds are equally balanced can await their ultimate admission to HEAVEN—a kind of LIMBO.

Alasnam (à lăs' năm). In the ARABIAN NIGHTS Alasnam had eight diamond statues, but was required to find a ninth more precious still, to fill the vacant pedestal. The prize was found in the woman who became his wife, at once the most beautiful and perfect of her race.

Alasnam's mirror. The "touchstone of virtue", given to him by one of the genii. If he looked into this mirror and it remained unsullied so would the maiden he had in mind; if it clouded she would prove faithless.

Alastor (à lăs' tor). The evil genius of a house; a NEMESIS, the Greek term for an avenging power who visits the sins of the fathers on their children. Shelley has a poem entitled *Alastor; or the Spirit of Solitude*.

Alauda. A Roman legion raised by Julius CÆSAR in GAUL, so called from the lark's tuft worn on top of their helmets.

Alban, St. (ôl' bàn). Britain's first martyr, beheaded *c.* 305 at Verulamium during the Diocletian persecution, for harbouring a Christian priest. The monastery of St. Albans was built by Offa in 795 on the spot where he died. His feast is on 22 June, although the CHURCH OF ENGLAND keeps 17 June. The story is given in the works of GILDAS. Like many other SAINTS he is sometimes represented carrying his head in his hands to signify death by beheading.

Albany, Albainn, or **Albin** (Celtic *alp* or *ailp*, rock or cliff). An ancient name applied to the northern part of Scotland, inhabited by PICTS, and called CALEDONIA by the Romans. The name Albany survives in Breadalbane, the hilly country of Albainn, *i.e.* western Perthshire.

In Spenser's *Fairie Queene* (II, x, 14, etc.) northern Britain is called Albania.

Also the name of a famous block of bachelors' chambers converted from the Duke of York's house in 1803 and adjoining Burlington House, PICCADILLY, where Macaulay wrote his *History of England*. BYRON and Lord Lytton also lived there. Albany is no longer exclusively restricted to bachelors.

Albatross. The largest of web-footed birds, called the Cape Sheep by sailors from its frequenting the CAPE of Good Hope. It was said to sleep in the air without any apparent motion of its wings, and sailors say that to shoot one is fatal. *See* ANCIENT MARINER.

Alberich. In Scandinavian mythology, the all-powerful King of the DWARFS. In Wagner's version of the NIBELUNGENLIED he appears as a hideous GNOME and steals the magic GOLD guarded by the Rhine Maidens but is later captured by the gods, and forced to give up all he has in return for freedom.

Albert, An. A watch-chain across the waistcoat from one pocket to another or to a buttonhole; so called from Albert, Prince Consort, who set the fashion. He was presented with such a chain by the jewellers of Birmingham, when visiting the town in 1849.

Albert the Bad (d. 1314). Landgrave of Thuringia and Margrave of Meissen.

Albert the Good. The Prince Consort (1819–1861).

> Beyond all titles, and a household name,
> Hereafter, thro' all times, Albert the Good.
> TENNYSON: Dedication to *Idylls of the King*.

Albert the Great. (1) Albertus Magnus (*c.* 1206–1280), Albert of Cologne, famous DOMINICAN scholastic philosopher, also called *doctor universalis*.

(2) A nickname, by analogy with Albert the Good, given to Albert Chevalier (1861–1923), the coster's LAUREATE and great favourite of the late Victorian and Edwardian MUSIC HALLS. Among the most famous of his songs are *Knock'd 'em in the Old Kent Road* and *My Old Dutch*. *See* DUTCH *and* KNOCK.

Albigenses (ăl bi jen' sēs). A common name for various 12th- and 13th-century MANICHEAN sects in southern France and northern Italy; so called from the city of Albi in LANGUEDOC, where their persecution began. Violent opponents of the CATHOLIC Church, they were subjected to a crusade by Innocent III in 1208 and they were finally exterminated by the end of the 14th century. They were also called Cathari and Bulgarians.

Albin. *See* ALBANY.

Albino (al bē' nō) (Lat. *albus*, white). This term denoting congenital absence of colouring pigment in human beings, animals, etc. is occasionally used figuratively. Thus Oliver Wendell Holmes, in THE AUTOCRAT OF THE BREAKFAST TABLE (ch. viii), speaks of Kirke White as one of the "sweet albino poets", whose "plaintive song" he admires; apparently implying some deficiency of virility and possibly playing upon the name.

Albion. An ancient and poetical name for Great Britain, probably from the white (Lat. *albus*) cliffs that face GAUL, but possibly from the CELTIC *alp*. Albion or ALBANY originally may have been the Celtic name of all Great Britain.

One legend is that a giant son of NEPTUNE, named Albion, discovered the country and ruled over it for forty-four years. Another such derivation is that the fifty daughters of the King of Syria (the eldest of whom was named Albia), were all married on the same day, and murdered their husbands on their wedding night. They were set adrift in a ship as punishment and eventually reached this western isle where they duly married natives.

In POLY-OLBION (1613) Michael Drayton says that Albion came from ROME and was the first Christian martyr in Britain.

Perfide Albion. Although the sentiment is often traced back to a mid-17th-century sermon by Bossuet, where the phrase "la perfide Angleterre" is used, he is referring to England's adoption of Protestantism, and there is no real connection with the subsequent expression which is first noticed in a poem of 1793 by the Marquis de Ximenez—"Attaquons dans ses eaux la perfide Albion". It attracted no particular attention and next appears in 1809 in both a poem by Henri Simon and a song. Its popular currency stems from its wide use in the Napoleonic recruiting drive of 1813 and it was well established by the end of the war in 1815.

New Albion. The name under which Sir Francis Drake annexed California in 1579, during his voyage of circumnavigation. He recorded this act by setting up a brass plate. Such a plate was found near San Francisco in 1937. *See* FORGERY.

Al Borak. *See* BORAK.

Alcaic Verse (ăl kā′ ik) or **Alcaics.** A Greek and Latin lyrical metre so called from Alcæus (7th century B.C.) who supposedly invented it.

Alcantara, Order of (ăl′kăn′ tà rà). A military and religious order, developing from the 12th-century order of St. Julian de Pereiro, founded to combat the MOORS in Spain, and following the CISTERCIAN rule. Charged with the defence of Alcantara since the early 13th century, it became a lay order in the mid-16th century and a civil and military decoration after 1875.

Alcestis. In Greek legend the daughter of Pelias and wife of Admetus, King of Pheræ in Sicily to whom the FATES agreed to grant deliverance from death if his mother, father, or wife would die for him instead. Alcestis thus sacrificed her life but was restored to her husband from the lower world by PERSEPHONE (another version says by HERCULES).

Alchemilla (ăl kè mil′à). A genus of plants of the rose family; so called because alchemists collected the dew of its leaves for their operations. Also called "Lady's Mantle", from the Virgin MARY, to whom the plant was dedicated.

Alchemy (ăl′kè mi). The derivation of this word is obscure; *al* is the Arabic article the, and *kimia* the Arabic form of the Greek *chemeia*, which seems to have meant "Egyptian art"; hence "the art of the Egyptians". Its main objects were the transmutation of base metals into gold, and the search for the PHILOSOPHER'S STONE, the universal solvent or ALKAHEST, the PANACEA, and the ELIXIR OF LIFE. It was the forerunner of the science of chemistry. Ben Jonson wrote a play called *The Alchemist* (1610).

Alcimedon (ăl sim′ è don). A generic name for a first-rate carver in wood.

> Pocula ponam
> Fagina, coelatum divini opus Alcimedontis.
> VIRGIL: *Eclogue* III, 36.

Alcina (ăl sē′ nà). In Ariosto's ORLANDO FURIOSO (1516) the personification of carnal pleasure; the CIRCE of fable and Labe of the Arabians. Handel's opera *Alcina* appeared in 1735.

Alcinoo poma dare (ăl′sin′ ō ō pō′ mà da′ re) (to give apples to Alcinous). "To carry COALS to Newcastle." The gardens of Alcinous, legendary king of the Phæacians, by whom ULYSSES was entertained, were famous for their fruits.

Alcmena (ălk mē′ nà). In Greek mythology, daughter of Electryon (King of Mycenæ), wife of AMPHITRYON, and mother (by ZEUS) of HERCULES. The legend is that at the conception of Hercules, Zeus (in the guise of Amphitryon), for additional pleasure with Alcmena, made the night the length of three ordinary nights.

Alcofribas Nasier (ăl ko′ fre băs nā′ syer). The anagrammatic pseudonym used by Rabelais under which the first two books of GARGANTUA and PANTAGRUEL appeared.

Aldebaran (al′deb′ à răn) (Arab. *al*, the; *davaran*, the follower, because its rising follows that of the PLEIADES). A red star of the first magnitude, a Tauri, it forms the bull's eye in the constellation of TAURUS.

Aldgate Pump, A draught on. A worthless cheque or bill. The pun is on the word "draught", which may mean either an order on a bank or a drink.

Aldine Editions. Internationally famous and reliable octavo editions of the Greek and Latin classics printed and published at Venice by the firm founded by Aldus Manutius in 1490. The type called *italics*, once called *Aldine*, was devised by his type-designer, Francesco Griffo. The founder's grandson (Aldus, the Younger) closed the business on taking charge of the VATICAN press in 1590.

Ale is the Old English *alu*, connected with the Scandinavian *ol*. Beer is the Old English *beor* connected with the German *bier*. A beverage made from barley is mentioned by Tacitus (*c.* 55–120?) and even Herodotus (5th century B.C.). Ale in Britain is of pre-Roman origin and was a malt brew without hops. Hopped or bitter beer was introduced by the Flemings in the 15th century. Fuggles hops are now used for most beers and goldings for pale ales—ale and beer now being largely synonymous terms, although the word ale is not used for the thick black beers (STOUT and porter) which became so popular in the 18th century. In some areas ale is used for the stronger malt liquors and beer for the weaker, in others the terms are reversed. *See also* AUDIT-ALE, CHURCH-ALE, ENTIRE.

Aleberry. A corruption of *ale-bree*. A drink made of hot ale, spice, sugar and toast. Burns speaks of the barley-bree (A.S. *briw*, broth).

Ale-dagger. A dagger used in self-defence in ale-house brawls.

> He that drinkes with cutters must not be without his ale-dagger.
> LYLY?: *Pappe with a Hatchet* (1589).

Ale-draper. The keeper of an ale-house. *Ale-drapery*, the selling of ale, etc.

No other occupation have I but to be an ale-draper.
CHETTLE: *Kind Harts Dreame* (1593).

Ale-knight. A tippler, a sot.

Ale-silver. Formerly, the annual fee paid to the Lord MAYOR of London for the privilege of selling ale within the city.

Ale-stake, or **ale-pole.** The pole set up before an ale-house by way of a sign, often surmounted by a bush or garland. Thus, Chaucer says of the Sompnour:

A garland hadde he sette upon his hede
As gret as it were for an ale-stake.
Canterbury Tales, Prologue, 666.

Ale-wife. The landlady of an ale-house. In America a fish of the herring family, possibly from supposed resemblance to a stout landlady; or from a corruption of aloofe, a North American Indian name; or from the French *alose*, a shad.

Alecto (à lek′ tō). In Greek mythology "she who rests not", one of the three ERINYES, goddesses of vengeance, the Latin FURIES.

Alectorian Stone (à lek tôr′ i àn) (Gr. *alector*, a COCK). A stone, fabled to be of talismanic power, found in the stomach of cocks. Those who possess one are strong, brave, and wealthy. MILO of Crotona owed his strength to one.

Alectryomancy (à lek′ tri ō măn si). DIVINATION by a COCK. Draw a circle, and write in succession round it the letters of the alphabet, on each of which lay a grain of corn. Then put a cock in the centre of the circle, and watch what grains he eats. The letters will prognosticate the answer. Libanus and Jamblicus thus discovered who was to succeed the emperor Valens. The cock ate the grains over the letters t, h, e, o, d = Theod (orus).

Alexander. So PARIS, son of PRIAM, was called by the shepherds who brought him up.

Alexander the Great. Alexander III of Macedon (356–323 B.C.).

Alexander and the Robber. The pirate Diomedes, having been captured, was asked by Alexander how he dared to molest the seas. "How darest thou molest the earth?" was the reply. "Because I am the master of a single galley I am termed a robber; but you who oppress the world with huge squadrons are called king." Alexander was so struck by this reasoning that he made Diomedes a rich prince, and a dispenser of justice. *See* GESTA ROMANORUM, *Tale* cxlvi.

Only two Alexanders. Alexander said, "There are but two Alexanders—the invincible son of Philip, and the inimitable painting of the hero by APELLES."

The continence of Alexander. Having won the battle of Issus (333 B.C.), the family of Darius III fell into his hand; but he treated the women with the greatest decorum. His CONTINENCE drew respect from Darius.

You are thinking of Parmenio and I of Alexander.—*i.e.* you are thinking of what you ought to receive, and I of what I ought to give; you are thinking of those castigated or rewarded, but I of my position, and what reward is consistent with my rank. The allusion is to the tale that Alexander said to Parmenio, "I consider not what Parmenio should receive, but what Alexander should give."

Alexander of the North. The war-loving Charles XII of Sweden (1682–1718), whose army was annihilated by Peter the Great at Pultawa (1709).

Alexander the Corrector. The self-assumed nickname of Alexander Cruden (1701–1770), bookseller and compiler of the *Complete Concordance to the Holy Scriptures* (1737). Several times confined to a lunatic asylum, his activities as a corrector of morals were many and varied. He carried a damped sponge to wipe out the obscene and profane scrawls found on walls and buildings. *See* GRAFFITI.

Alexander's beard. A beardless, smooth chin—an AMAZONIAN CHIN.

I like this trustie glass of Steele ...
Wherein I see a Sampson's grim regarde
Disgraced yet with Alexander's bearde.
GASCOIGNE: *The Steele Glas* (1576).

Alexandra Day. A day in June when rose emblems are sold for the hospital fund inaugurated in 1912 by Queen Alexandra (1844–1925), Danish consort of Edward VII, to celebrate the fiftieth year of her residence in England.

Alexandra limp. In the 1860s Queen Alexandra (then Princess of Wales), after a minor accident, developed a very slight limp, which was imitated in sycophantic fashion by many women about the court. Hence the description "Alexandra limp".

Alexandrian. Anything from the East was so called by the old writers because Alexandria was the depot from which Eastern goods reached Europe. Thus ARIOSTO says:

Reclined on Alexandrian carpets (*i.e.* Persian).
Orlando Furioso, X, 37.

Alexandrian Codex. A Greek MS. of the Scriptures, probably of the 5th century, written in UNCIALS on parchment, and supposed to have originated at Alexandria. It was presented to Charles I in 1628 by the PATRIARCH of Constantinople, and was placed in the BRITISH MUSEUM on its foundation.

Alexandrian Library. *See* LIBRARY.

Alexandrian School. An academy of learning founded about 310 B.C. at Alexandria by Ptolemy I (Soter) and Demetrius of Phaleron, especially noted for its literary scholars and mathematicians. Of the former the most noted were Aristarchus (*c.* 217–145 B.C.), Eratosthenes (*c.* 275–194 B.C.), and Harpocration (2nd century A.D.); and of its mathematicians EUCLID (fl. *c.* 300 B.C.), the author of the *Elements*, the celebrated treatise on geometry, and Claudius Ptolemæus (2nd century A.D.), the astronomer. Alexandria remained a centre of learning until 640 A.D. when the library was, supposedly, finally destroyed.

Alexandrine. In prosody, an IAMBIC or trochaic line of twelve syllables or six feet with, usually, a caesura (break) at the sixth syllable. So called either from the 12th-century French metrical romance, *Li Romans d'Alixandre* (commenced by Lambert-li-Cort and continued by Alexandre de Bernay), or from the old Castilian verse chronicle, *Poema de Alexandro Magno*, both of which are written in this metre. Pope sometimes used it but wrote:

> A needless Alexandrine ends the song
> That, like a wounded snake, drags its slow length along.
> *Essay on Criticism* (1709), ii, 356.

Alexandrine Age. When the Alexandrine school was the centre of literature, science and philosophy.

Alexandrine Philosophy. A school of philosophy which developed at Alexandria in the early centuries of the Christian era. It gave rise to Gnosticism and Neoplatonism and attempted to reconcile Christianity and Greek philosophy.

Alexis, St. Patron saint of hermits and beggars. According to the story in the GESTA ROMANORUM (*Tale* XV) he lived on his father's estate as a hermit until he died, but was never recognized.

Alfadir (al fa′ der) (father of all). In Scandinavian mythology, one of the epithets of ODIN.

Alfana. *See* HORSE.

Alfar. The elves of the northern mythology. In German legend the *döckalfar* frequent dark underground caverns and mines. The O.E. *Ælfric* means "ruler of the elves".

Alfonsin, Alfonsine Tables. *See* ALPHONSIN, etc.

Alfred the Great (849–899), King of WESSEX, especially noted for his resistance to the Danish invaders who in the winter of 877–8 occupied much of Wessex. Alfred withdrew to his base at Athelney and it is to this period that the story of Alfred and the cakes

belongs—the first known version probably dating from the 11th/12th century. The story is that the king, unrecognized, took refuge in a cowherd's hut. He was sitting by the fire seeing to his equipment and allowed the housewife's loaves to burn. For this he was vigorously scolded. The story is not found in Asser's *Life of Alfred* (written in 893). After the defeat of the Danes Alfred commanded the building of a monastery at Athelney.

The beautiful gold enamelled relic, known as *Alfred's Jewel*, and bearing his name, was dug up at Athelney in 1693. It is now in the ASHMOLEAN MUSEUM, Oxford.

Alfred's scholars. The name given to the group of learned men which Alfred the Great gathered around him in his devoted efforts to revive learning in WESSEX. Chief among them were the Mercian clerics Plegmund, afterwards Archbishop of Canterbury; Werferth, Bishop of Worcester; Werwulth and Athelstan; Grimbald of St. Omer; John, a continental Saxon; and Asser, priest of St. David's.

Algarsife (ăl′ gars īf). In Chaucer's unfinished *Squire's Tale*, son of CAMBUSCAN, and brother of Camballo, who "won Theodora to wife".

> This noble kyng, this Tartre Cambyuscan,
> Hadde two sones on Elpheta his wyf,
> Of which the eldest sone highte Algarsyf,
> That oother sone was cleped Camballo.
> A doghter hadde this worthy kyng also
> That yongest was and highte Canacee.

Hence the reference in Milton's *Il Penseroso*:

> Or call up him that left half told
> The story of Cambuscan bold
> Of Camball and of Algarsife,
> And who had Canace to wife.

Alhambra (ăl hăm′ brà) (Arab. *Kal'-at al hamra*, the red castle). The citadel and palace built at Granada by the Moorish kings in the 13th century. Also the name of a famous theatre and music hall in Leicester Square, built in Moorish style. *See* PANOPTICON.

Ali (a′ lē). MOHAMMED'S cousin and son-in-law, famed among Persians for the beauty of his eyes, hence *Ayn Hali* (eyes of Ali) as the highest expression for beauty.

Ali Baba (ă′ lē ba′ ba). The hero of a story in the ARABIAN NIGHTS ENTERTAINMENTS, who sees a band of robbers enter a cave by means of the magic password "Open SESAME". When they have gone away he enters the cave, loads his ass with treasure and returns home. The Forty Thieves discover that Ali Baba has learned their secret and resolve to kill him, but they are finally outwitted by the slave-girl MORGIANA.

Alias (ā' li ăs), "You have as many aliases as Robin of Bagshot," said to one who passes under many names. The phrase is from Gay's *Beggar's Opera*: Robin of Bagshot, one of Macheath's gang, was *alias* Gordon, *alias* Bluff Bob, *alias* Carbuncle, *alias* Bob Booty and intended for Sir Robert Walpole.

Alibi (ă' li bī) (Lat. elsewhere). A plea of having been elsewhere at a time that an offence is alleged to have been committed. A clock which strikes an hour, while the hands point to a different time, has been humorously called *an alibi clock*. A modern usage of the word is for an excuse or pretext.

Aliboron. The name of a jackass in LA FON-TAINE'S *Fables*; hence Maître Aliboron = Mr. Jackass.

Alice. The town of Alice Springs in Northern Territory, Australia, "the capital of the centre". Presumably named from Lady Alice Todd, wife of Sir Charles Todd, who supervised the building of the Overland Telegraph in the 1870s. It was formerly called Stuart after the explorer John McDouall Stuart. *See* GHAN.

> It's railhead of course, for trucking cattle down to Adelaide—that's one thing.—But it's a go-ahead place is Alice; all sorts of things go on there.
> NEVIL SHUTE: *A Town Like Alice*, Ch. vi.

Alice in Wonderland. *Alice's Adventures in Wonderland* (1865) and *Through the Looking Glass* (1871), widely read children's classics, originally illustrated by Sir John Tenniel, were written by C. L. Dodgson, an Oxford mathematician, under the pseudonym of Lewis Carroll. The original of Alice was Alice Liddell, daughter of Dean Liddell, famous as joint author of Liddell and Scott's Greek Lexicon. The Alice stories are noted for their whimsical humour and the "nonsense" verse included in them.

"Alice in Wonderland" schemes, projects, ideas etc., are those which are unreal, totally impractical, things which can only exist in the realm of fantasy. *Cp*. CLOUD-CUCKOO-LAND; LOOKING-GLASS.

Alien priory. A priory which was dependent upon a monastery in a foreign country.

Alifanfaron (ăl i fan' fà ron). Don QUIXOTE attacked a flock of sheep, and declared them to be the army of the giant Alifanfaron. Similarly AJAX, in a fit of madness, fell upon a flock of sheep, mistaking them for the sons of Atreus.

Al Kadr (ăl kădr) (the divine decree). A particular night in the month RAMADAN when Mohammedans say that angels descend to earth and GABRIEL reveals to man the decrees of God. — *Al Koran*, ch. xcvii.

Alkahest (ăl' kà hest). A sham-Arabic word

attributed to PARACELSUS. *See* ALCHEMY.

All. All abroad. To be confused in mind, or wide of the mark.

All adrift. *See* ADRIFT.

All and Some. An old expression meaning "one and all", confused sometimes with "all and sum", meaning the whole total.

> They that wolde nought Crystene become,
> Richard lect sleen hem alle and some.
> *Cœur de Lion*. 14th cent.

All Fools' Day (1 April). *See* APRIL FOOL.

All Fours. A game of cards; so called from the points at stake, *viz*. High, Low, Jack, and Game.

To go on all fours is to crawl about on all four limbs like a quadruped or an infant. The phrase used to be *all four*, as in *Lev*. xi, 42, "whatsoever goeth upon all four".

It does not go on all fours means it does not suit in every particular; it limps like a lame quadruped. Thus the Latin saying, *Omnis comparatio claudicat* (all similes limp) was translated by Macaulay as "No simile can go on all fours".

All-Hallows' Day. All Saints' Day (1 November), "hallows" being the Old English *halig*, a holy (man), a saint. Pope Boniface IV converted the PANTHEON at Rome into a Christian church, dedicated to all the martyrs, in 610. The festival of All Saints, originally held on 1 May, was changed to 1 November in 834.

All-Hallows' Eve or **Hallowe'en** (31 October), also called "NUTCRACK NIGHT" and "Holy Eve", is associated with many ancient customs including bobbing for apples (*see* BOB), cracking nuts (mentioned in *The Vicar of Wakefield*), finding one's lover by various rites, etc. Burns portrays the Scottish customs in his poem *Hallowe'en*, and Scottish tradition says that those born on HALLOW-E'EN have the gift of second sight. Thus Mary Avenel, in Scott's *The Monastery* (1820), is made to see the WHITE LADY.

All-Hallows Summer. Another name for St. Martin's SUMMER or an INDIAN SUMMER, so called because it set in about All-Hallows; similarly there is a St. Luke's Summer (from 18 October).

> Farewell, thou latter spring! farewell, All-hallown Summer!
> SHAKESPEARE: *Henry IV, Part I*, I, ii.

All hands and the cook (western U.S.A.). A state of total emergency when the herds were so restless that everyone, including the sacrosanct cook, had to ride to quieten them down.

All Heal. The common Valerian, formerly supposed to have many medicinal virtues, also called *Hercules Woundwort*, because

HERCULES is supposed to have learned its virtues from CHIRON. Spikenard, mentioned in the BIBLE (*Mark* xiv, 3), and extracted from a Himalayan member of the family, was used in perfumes by the ancient Egyptians, Greeks and Romans.

All in. Completely exhausted.

All my eye and Betty Martin. All nonsense, BOSH, rubbish. A curious phrase of uncertain origin. A common explanation was that it was a British soldiers' or sailors' rendering of "O mihi, beate Martine" an invocation to ST. MARTIN heard abroad. "All my eye" is the older saying:

> That's all my eye, the King only can pardon, as the law says.
> GOLDSMITH: *The Good Natur'd Man* (1767).

All of. Quite as much or possibly more than, for example: "It is all of fifty miles from London to Brighton".

All-overish. Not to be at one's best, beset with lassitude and indifference as before the onset of an illness.

All Saints. *See* ALL HALLOWS.

All serene (Sp. *sereno*). In Spain the word was used by night watchmen to indicate that the weather was fine and is equivalent to our "All's well". It was a popular CATCHPHRASE from the late 19th century.

All ship-shape and Bristol fashion. Everything stowed and the ship in every way ready for sea, thus "to be completely organized and ready". It derives from the port of Bristol's reputation for efficiency in the days of sail.

All Sir Garnet, meaning "everything is as it should be" began as an army phrase of the 1880s arising from Sir Garnet Wolseley's skilfully organized operations in Egypt.

All Souls College, Oxford, was founded in 1438 by Henry Chichele, Archbishop of Canterbury, with Henry VI a co-founder, as a CHANTRY, whose members were to study and pray for the souls of Henry V and Henry VI, and for those killed or who might be killed in their French wars. It has a Warden and fifty fellows (few of whom are in residence) and was unique, until the new foundations of the 1960s, in having no undergraduates.

All Souls' Day (2 November). The day which Roman Catholics devote to prayer and almsgiving on behalf of the faithful departed. According to tradition, a pilgrim returning from the HOLY LAND took refuge on a rocky island during a storm. There he met a hermit, who told him that among the cliffs was an opening to the infernal regions, through which flames ascended, and where the groans of the tormented were distinctly audible. The pilgrim told Odilo, abbot of Cluny, who appointed the day following (2 November 998) to be set apart for the benefit of those souls in PURGATORY.

All Souls' Parish Magazine. *The Times* was so nicknamed during the editorship (1923–1941) of G.G. Dawson, Fellow of All Souls. He and some of his associates, who were also fellows of the college, frequently met there for discussions.

All standing. A nautical expression meaning "fully equipped", "all sails set".

To be brought up all standing is to be suddenly checked when unprepared, or to be taken by surprise.

To turn in all standing is to go to one's hammock, bunk or bed fully dressed.

All Stuarts are not sib (O.E. *gesibb*, related), *i.e.* related to the Royal Family. An old Scottish proverb rebuking those who, sharing a surname with a famous person, advance false claims of kinship to inflate their self-esteem.

All the Talents. The unsuitable name given to Lord Grenville's ministry (1806–1807) formed on the death of the younger Pitt. It was an attempt at a broadly-based administration but largely consisted of the followers of Charles James Fox, who was Foreign Secretary. Its one great measure was the abolition of the slave trade in 1807.

All this for a song! *See* WHAT! ALL THIS FOR A SONG? *under* SONG.

All to break. "And a certain woman cast a piece of millstone upon Abimelech's head, and all to break his skull" (*Judges* ix, 53). This does not mean for the sake of breaking his skull but that she wholly smashed his skull. The *to*, signifying *in twain*, is used as an intensification, comparable to the inseparable verbal prefix *sehr* in German, and *all* being a natural addition. Compare Chaucer's

> Al is to-brosten [broken] thilke regioun.
> *Knight's Tale*, 1899.

Allah (äl′ ä). The Arabic name of the Supreme Being (*al*, the, *ilah*, god). The Mohammedan war-cry *Allah il Allah* is a form of *la illah illa allah* "there is no God but the God"—the first clause of their confession of faith. *Allah akbar* means "God is most mighty".

Allan-a-Dale. A minstrel in the ROBIN HOOD ballads who also appears in Scott's *Ivanhoe*. Robin Hood helped him to carry off his bride when she was on the point of being married against her will to a rich old knight.

Alleluiah. *See* HALLELUJAH.

Alley, or **Ally.** A choice, large playing-marble

made of stone or alabaster (from which it takes its name). The alley tor (taw) beloved of Master Bardell (*Pickwick Papers*, xxxiv) was a special alley that had won many taws or games. Also in Australia, a group of gamblers, or their den.

Alley, Right up one's. A variation of *right up one's street*, meaning some kind of activity in which one is specially skilled or particularly well informed. Current since the early 19th century.

Alley, The. An old name for Change Alley in the City of London, where dealings in the public funds, etc. used to take place.

Alley up. In Australia, to pay up one's debts.

Alliensis, Dies (ăl i en' sis, dī' ēz). The day when the Romans were cut to pieces by the Gauls (390 B.C.) near the banks of the river Allia. It was ever after held to be a DIES NEFASTUS, or unlucky day.

Alligator. When the Spaniards first saw this reptile in the New World, they called it *el lagarto* (the lizard). In American slang *alligator* has several figurative meanings, among them "a Mississippi River keel-boat sailor", derived from the real or supposed battles of early boatmen with alligators; hence it is a symbol of manliness.

Alligator Pear. The name given to the fruit of the West Indian tree, *Persea gratissima* (also called *avocado* or *aguacate*). It is a corruption of the Carib *aouacate*, called by the Spanish discoverers *avocado* or *avigato*, or the Aztec *abuacath*, which was transmitted through the Spanish *aguacate*.

Alliteration. The rhetorical device of commencing adjacent accented syllables with the same letter or sound, as ridiculed by Quince in *A Midsummer Night's Dream* (V, i):

> Whereat with blade, with bloody blameful blade,
> He bravely broach'd his boiling bloody breast.

Alliteration was a SINE QUA NON in Old and Middle English poetry, and is frequently used in modern poetry with great effect, as in Coleridge's *Ancient Mariner*:

> The fair breeze blew, the white foam flew,
> The furrow followed free.

Many fantastic examples of excessive alliteration are extant (*see* AMPHIGOURI). Henry Harder composed a poem of 100 lines in Latin hexameters on cats, each word beginning with c, called *Canum cum Catis certamen carmine compositum currente calamo C Catulli Caninii*.

Thomas Tusser (1524–1580) has a rhyming poem of twelve lines, every word of which begins with a *t*; and in the 1890s a Serenade of twenty-eight lines was published

"sung in M flat by Major Marmaduke Muttinhead to Mademoiselle Madeline Mendoza Marriott", which contained only one word not beginning with *M*—in the line "Meet me by moonlight, marry me". The alliterative alphabetic poem beginning:

> An Austrian army awfully arrayed
> Boldly by battery besieged Belgrade;
> Cossack commanders, cannonading come,
> Dealing destruction's devastating doom;

was published in *The Trifler* (7 May 1817), ascribed to the Rev. B. Poulter, later revised by Alaric A. Watts.

Ally Pally. A familiar and affectionate name for the Alexandra Palace in North London, first opened in 1863 but burnt down and rebuilt in 1873. A popular amusement centre like the CRYSTAL PALACE and partly used as a broadcasting and television centre, it was devastated by another disastrous fire in July 1980.

Ally Sloper's Cavalry. In the GREAT WAR, a nickname of the Army Service Corps which provided transport for men, rations and supplies generally. Ally Sloper was the jester in a pre-war comic paper of this name.

Alma (āl' mà) (Ital. soul, spirit, essence). In Matthew Prior's poem *Alma, or The Progress of the Mind*, the name typifies the mind or guiding principles of man. Alma is queen of "Body Castle", and is beset by a rabble rout of evil desires, foul imaginations and silly conceits for seven years. In Spenser's *Faerie Queene* (II, ix-xi) Alma typifies the soul. She is mistress of the House of Temperance, and there entertains Prince Arthur and Sir Guyon.

Alma Mater (Lat. bounteous mother). A collegian so calls his university. Also applied to one's school and other "fostering mothers".

> You might divert yourself, too, with Alma Mater, the Church.
> HORACE WALPOLE: *Letters* (1778).

Almack's (1) A gambling club opened in Pall Mall in 1764 by William Macall, a Scotsman, with the support of regular young gamesters from WHITE'S. In 1778 it was sold to one Brooks, a wine merchant and moneylender, and was subsequently known as BROOKS'S Club. (2) A suite of assembly rooms in King Street, St. James's (WESTMINSTER) opened in 1765. Success came early and weekly subscription balls, presided over by ladies of the highest rank, were held there during the London season for more than 75 years, and to be admitted was almost as great a distinction as being presented at Court. On Almack's death in 1781 the premises passed to his niece, Mrs Willis, hence the subsequent name Willis's Rooms. They were closed in 1890 and destroyed in an air raid in 1941.

Almagest (ăl' mà jest). The English form of the Arabic name (*al Majisti*) given to Ptolemy's *Mathematike syntaxis*, his classic astronomical treatise in thirteen books, of the mid-2nd century. An Arabic translation was made about 820. In the third book the length of the year was first fixed at 365¼ days. His geocentric astronomy lasted until the introduction of the COPERNICAN SYSTEM.

Almanac. A mediæval Latin word of obscure origin for a calendar of days and months with astronomical data, etc.

> A calendar, a calendar! look in the almanac; find out moonshine, find out moonshine.
> SHAKESPEARE: *A Midsummer Night's Dream*, III, i.

Some early almanacs before the invention of printing are:

By Solomon Jarchi	in and after 1150
Peter de Dacia	about 1307
Walter de Elvendene	1327
John Somers, Oxford	1380
Nicholas de Lynna	1386
Purbach	1457–1461

Examples after the invention of printing are:

By Regiomantanus at Nuremberg	1474
Zainer at Ulm	1478
Richard Pynson (Sheapeherd's Kalendar)	1497
Stoffler at Venice	1499
Poor Robin's Almanac (*q.v.*)	1652
Francis Moore's Almanack	1698–1713
Poor Richard's Almanack (U.S.A.)	1732–1757
Almanach de Gotha (Successively suppressed by Hitler, Stalin and Adenauer)	1764–1944
Whitaker's Almanack	from 1869

Almanzor (ăl măn' zor). The word, derived from the Arabic, means "the invincible" and was adopted as a title by several MOSLEM rulers, notably the second Abasside Caliph Abu Jafar Abdullah (712–775), who founded Baghdad.

> The kingdoms of Almanzor, Fez and Sus, Morocco, and Algiers, and Tremisen.
> MILTON: *Paradise Lost*, XI, 403.

One of the characters in Dryden's *Conquest of Granada* (1672) is an Almanzor; and it is also the name of one of the lackeys in Molière's *Précieuses Ridicules* (1659).

Almesbury. It was in a SANCTUARY at Almesbury that Queen GUINEVERE, according to Malory, took refuge after her adulterous passion for LANCELOT was revealed to King ARTHUR. Here she died; but her body was buried at GLASTONBURY.

Almighty Dollar. *See under* DOLLAR.

Almonry. The place where the almoner resides. In monasteries, one-tenth of the income was distributed to the poor by the almoner. *Almonry* is from the Latin *eleemosynarium*, a place for alms but the word became confused with AMBRY, thus "Ambry Close" in WESTMINSTER used to be called "Almonry Close".

> The place wherein this chapel or almshouse stands was called the "Elemosinary" or Almonry, now corrupted into Ambrey, for that the almis of the Abbey are there distributed to the poor.
> STOW: *Survey of London* (1598).

Alms (amz) (O.E. *ælmysse*, ultimately from Latin *eleemosina* from Greek *eleemosyne*, compassion), gifts to the poor. It is a singular word which, like riches (from Fr. *richesse*), has by usage become plural. In the BIBLE, we have "(he) asked an alms" (*Acts* iii, 3), but Dryden gives us "alms are but the vehicles of prayer" (*The Hind and the Panther*, iii, 106), 1687.

Alms Basket (in Shakespeare's *Love's Labour's Lost*, V, i). **To live on the alms basket.** To live on charity.

Alms-drink. Leavings; the liquor which a drinker finds too much, and therefore hands to another. *See* Shakespeare's *Antony and Cleopatra*, II, vii.

Almshouse. A house or group of dwellings built and endowed for the accommodation of the poor and aged.

Alms-man. One who lives on alms.

Alnaschar's Dream. Counting your chickens before they are hatched. In the ARABIAN NIGHTS, Alnaschar, the Talkative Barber's fifth (and deaf) brother, spent all his money on a basket of glassware, on which he was to make a profit which was to be invested to make more, and so on until he grew rich enough to marry the VIZIER's daughter. Being angry with his imaginary wife he gave a kick, overturned his basket and broke all his wares.

Aloe (Gr. *aloe*). A genus of very bitter plants of the family Liliaceæ; hence the line in Juvenal's sixth satire (181), *Plus aloes quam mellis habet*, "He has in him more bitters than sweets", said of a writer with a sarcastic pen. The French say, "*La côte d'Adam contient plus d'aloès que de miel*", where *côte d'Adam* means woman or one's wife.

Alombrados. *See* ALUMBRADO; ILLUMINATI.

Alonzo of Aguilar. When Fernando, King of Aragon, was laying siege to Granada in 1501, he asked who would undertake to plant his banner on the heights. Alonzo, "the lowmost of the dons", undertook the task but was cut down by the MOORS. His body was exposed in the wood of Oxijera and the Moorish damsels, struck with its beauty, buried it near the brook of Alpuxarra. The incident is the subject of a number of ballads.

À l'outrance (a loo' trons). To the uttermost, to the death. An incorrect English form of the French *à outrance*.

Alpha (ăl' fà). "I am Alpha and Omega, the first and the last" (*Rev*. i, II). *Alpha* (A) is the first and *Omega* (Ω) the last letter of the Greek alphabet. *See* TAU.

Alphabet. Compounded from *alpha* and *beta*, the first two letters of the Greek alphabet. *Ezra* vii, 21 contains all the letters of the English alphabet except j.

The number of letters in an alphabet varies in different languages. Although the English alphabet is capable of innumerable combinations and permutations, we have no means of differentiating our vowel sounds; take *a*, we have *fate, fat, Thames, war, orange, ware, abide, calm, swan*, etc. So with *e*, we have *era, the, there, prey, met, England, sew, herb, clerk*, etc. The other vowels are equally indefinite. *See* LETTER.

Alpheus and Arethusa (ăl fē' us, ăree-thū' za). Greek legend says that the river-god Alpheus fell in love with the nymph Arethusa, who fled from him in affright to Ortygia, an island near Syracuse, where ARTEMIS changed her into a fountain. Alpheus flowed under the sea from Peloponnesus to rise in Ortygia and so unite with his beloved. The myth seems to derive from the fact that the Alpheus, in places, does flow underground.

Alphonsin (ăl fon' sin). An old surgical instrument for extracting shot from wounds, named after Alphonso Ferri, a surgeon of Naples, who invented it in 1552.

Alphonsine Tables. Astronomical tables completed in 1252 by a group of Jewish, Arabian and Christian astronomers under the patronage of Alphonso X of Castile.

Alpine Race. Another name for the broad-headed CELTIC Race, because of its distribution in the mountainous regions from Armenia to the Pyrenees. They were a midway race between the Scandinavian Nordics and the dark Mediterranean folk. The LA TÈNE period (500 B.C.-? A.D.) witnessed the zenith of their culture.

Alruna-wife, An (ăl roo' nà). The Alrunes were the LARES or PENATES of the ancient Germans; and an Alruna-wife, the household goddess.

> She looked as fair as the sun, and talked like an Alruna-wife.
>
> KINGSLEY: *Hypatia* (1853), ch. xii.

Alsatia (ăl sā' shà). The Whitefriars district of London, which retained privileges derived from being a converted SANCTUARY un-

til 1697, and was the haunt of debtors and law-breakers. Bounded on the north and south by FLEET STREET and the THAMES, on the east and west by the Fleet river (now New Bridge Street) and the TEMPLE, it was probably named after Alsace (Lat. *Alsatia*), which was for centuries a disputed frontier and refuge of the disaffected. This rookery is described in Shadwell's *Squire of Alsatia* (1688), from which Scott borrowed freely when describing this precinct in *The Fortunes of Nigel* (1822), as did Leigh Hunt in *The Town* (1848).

Al-Sirat (Arab. the path). In Mohammedan mythology, the bridge leading to PARADISE; a bridge over a mid-HELL, no wider than the edge of a sword, across which all who enter HEAVEN must pass.

Also ran, An. In horse-racing this refers to a runner who fails to come in among the first three, hence, metaphorically, it denotes one who has failed to make his mark or to distinguish himself.

Altar (Lat. *altus*, high). The block or table used for religious sacrifice. In many Christian churches the term is applied to the Communion Table.

Led to the altar, *i.e.* married, said of a woman, who as a bride is led up to the altar-rail, where marriages are solemnized.

Alter ego (ăl'ter eg' ō) (Lat. other I, other self). One's double, one's intimate and thoroughly trusted friend; one who has full power to act for another. *Cp.* ONE'S SECOND SELF (*see* SECOND).

Alternative Services Book. *See* BOOK OF COMMON PRAYER.

Althæa's Brand (ăl' thē à), a fatal contingency. Althæa's son MELEAGER was to live just so long as a log of wood, then on the fire, remained unconsumed, so she snatched it from the fire. Years later, to avenge her brothers (slain by Meleager) she threw the brand into the fire, and her son died as it was consumed (Ovid: *Metamorphoses*, viii).

> As did the fatal brand Althæa burned.
>
> SHAKESPEARE: *Henry VI, Part II*, 1, i.

Althea. The divine Althea of Richard Lovelace (1618–1658) was Lucy Sacheverell, also called by the poet "Lucasta".

> When love with unconfinèd wings
> Hovers within my gates,
> And my divine Althea brings
> To whisper at my grates

Lovelace was imprisoned in the Gatehouse, Westminster, by the LONG PARLIAMENT for his royalist activities; hence the grates or railings referred to.

Altis. The sacred precinct of ZEUS at OLYMPIA combining the altar of Zeus, the temples of

Zeus and HERA, the Pelopion (grave of PE-LOPS), etc. It was connected by an arched passage with the STADIUM, where the games were held.

Altmark, The. In the Royal Navy an opprobrious synonym for a ship or an establishment with a reputation for very strict discipline. It derives from a famous naval exploit of February 1940 when Captain Vian, commanding the destroyer *H.M.S. Cossack*, entered Norwegian territorial waters to effect the release of 299 British prisoners of war from the German auxiliary-cum-prison ship *Altmark*, which had taken refuge in Josing Fiord.

Alto relievo. Italian for "high relief". A term used for sculptures so cut as to project more than one-half their thickness from the background. The ELGIN MARBLES are notable examples. *See* BAS-RELIEF.

Alumbrado (Sp. illuminated, enlightened). A perfectionist; so called from a Spanish sect claiming special "illumination", which arose in 1575. *See* ILLUMINATI.

Alvina weeps, or "Hark! Alvina weeps", *i.e.* the wind howls loudly, a Flemish saying. Alvina was the daughter of a king, who was cursed by her parents because she married unsuitably. From that day she roamed about the air invisible to the eye of man, but her moans are audible.

Alzire (ăl' zēr). A daughter of Montezuma, invented by VOLTAIRE and the central character of his play *Alzire* (1736), which is set in Peru instead of Mexico.

Amadis of Gaul (à ma' dis). The hero of the famous prose romance of the same title. The oldest extant edition (1508) is in Spanish by Montalvo but is probably an adaptation of a 14th-century Portuguese or Spanish original with his own additions. Many details are derived from ARTHURIAN legend, and subsequent writers increased the romance to fourteen books by adding other exploits. It long enjoyed popularity and exerted a wide influence on literature.

Amadis, called the "Lion-Knight", from the device on his shield, and "Beltenebros" (darkly beautiful), was a love-child of Perion, King of Gaula (Wales), and Elizena, Princess of Brittany. He was cast away at birth and became known as the Child of the Sun. After many adventures he secured the hand of ORIANA. He is represented as a poet and musician, a linguist and a gallant, a knight-errant and a king, the very model of CHIVALRY.

Other names by which Amadis was called were the *Lovely Obscure*, the *Knight of the Green Sword*, the *Knight of the Dwarf*, etc.

Amadis of Greece. A supplemental part of the romance *Amadis of Gaul* supposedly added by the Spaniard Feliciano de Silva in 1530.

Amaimon (à mī' i mon). A DEVIL, king of the eastern portion of HELL in mediæval demonology. He might be bound or restrained from doing hurt from the third hour till noon, and from the ninth hour till evening. ASMODEUS is his chief officer. *See* BARBASON; LUCIFER.

> Amaimon sounds well; Lucifer well; Barbason well; yet they are devils' additions, the names of fiends.
> SHAKESPEARE: *Merry Wives of Windsor*, II, ii.

Amalfitan Code (à măl' fi tàn). The oldest existing collection of maritime law, compiled in the 11th century at Amalfi, then an important trading centre.

Amalthea (ăm ăl thē' à). In Greek mythology a NYMPH, the nurse of ZEUS; (alternatively the she-goat which suckled him). In Roman legend a SIBYL of Cumæ who offered the SIBYLLINE Books to Tarquin II.

Amalthea's horn. The cornucopia or HORN OF PLENTY. The infant ZEUS was fed with goat's milk by Amalthea, daughter of Melisseus, King of Crete. Zeus, in gratitude, broke off one of the goat's horns, and gave it to Amalthea, promising that the possessor should always have in abundance everything desired. *See* ÆGIS.

> When Amalthea's horn
> O'er hill and dale the rose-crowned flora pours,
> And scatters corn and wine, and fruits and flowers.
> CAMOËNS: *Lusiad*, Bk. II.

Amaranth (ăm' à rănth) (Gr. *amarantos*, everlasting). In Pliny the name of some real or imaginary fadeless flower. Clement of Alexandria says:

> Amarantus flos, symbolum est immortalitatis.

It is so called because its flowers retain to the last much of their deep blood-red colour. The best-known species are "Love lies bleeding" (*Amarantus caudatus*), and "Prince's feather" (*amarantus hypochondriacus*). Wordsworth has a poem called *Love lies Bleeding*, and Milton refers to "Immortal amarant" in *Paradise Lost* (III, 353). Spenser has "sad Amaranthus" (*The Faerie Queene*, III, vi, 45), one of the flowers "to which sad lovers were transformed of yore", but there is no known legendary basis for this.

In 1653 Queen Christina of Sweden instituted an order of *Knights of the Amaranth* which lapsed on her death.

Amaryllis (ăm à ril' is). A rustic sweetheart, from a shepherdess in the pastorals of Theocritus and VIRGIL.

To sport with Amaryllis in the shade.
MILTON: *Lycidas*, 68.

In Spenser's *Colin Clout's Come Home Again*, Amaryllis is intended for Alice Spenser, Countess of Derby.

Amasis, Ring of (à mā′ sis). Herodotus tells us (III, iv) that Polycrates, tyrant of Samos, was so fortunate in everything that Amasis, King of Egypt, fearing such unprecedented luck boded ill, advised him to part with something which he highly prized. Polycrates accordingly threw into the sea an extremely valuable RING, but a few days afterwards a fish was presented to him, in which the ring was found. Amasis now renounced friendship with Polycrates, as a man doomed by the gods; and not long afterwards the latter was crucified by his host, the satrap Oroetes.

Amati (à ma′ ti). A first-rate violin; properly one made by the brothers Andrea and Nicolo Amati or their successors at CREMONA. *Cp.* STRAD.

Amaurote (ăm ô rō′ te) (Gr. the shadowy or unknown place). The chief city of Sir Thomas More's *Utopia*. Rabelais introduces Utopia and "the great city of the Amaurots" into his *Pantagruel* (Bk. II, ch. xxiii).

Amazement. Not afraid with any amazement (I *Pet*. iii, 6), introduced at the end of the marriage service in the BOOK OF COMMON PRAYER. The meaning is, you will be God's children so long as you do his bidding, and are not drawn aside by any distraction. Shakespeare uses the word in the same sense.

> Behold, destruction, frenzy, and amazement,
> Like witless antics, one another meet.
> *Troilus and Cressida*, V, iii.

Amazon (ăm′ à zon). A Greek word meaning *without breast*. In Greek mythology a race of female warriors living in Scythia, although some writers mention an older nation of Amazons in Africa. There were no men in the nation, but any sons born of their union with their neighbours were killed or sent to their fathers. The girls had their right breasts burnt off, that they might better draw the bow. The term is now applied to any strong brawny woman of masculine habits.

> She towered, fit person for a Queen
> To lead those ancient Amazonian files;
> Or ruling Bandit's wife among the Grecian isles.
> WORDSWORTH: *Beggars*.

Amazonia (ăm à zō′ ni à). An old name for the regions about the river Amazon in South America, which was so called by the early Spanish explorers under Orellana who claimed to have seen female warriors on its banks.

Amazonian chin. A beardless chin like that of a woman warrior.

> When with his Amazonian chin he drove
> The bristled lips before him.
> SHAKESPEARE: *Coriolanus*, II, ii.

Amber. A yellow, translucent, fossilized vegetable resin, the name of which originally belonged to ambergris. Legend says that amber is a concretion of the tears of birds who were the sisters of MELEAGER and who never ceased weeping for the death of their brother (Ovid: *Metamorphoses*, viii, 170).

Amber meaning a repository is an obsolete spelling of AMBRY.

Ambree, Mary. An English heroine whose valour in the siege of Ghent of 1584 is recorded in the ballad *Mary Ambree* in PERCY'S RELIQUES:

> When captaines couragious, whom death cold not daunte,
> Did march to the siege of the citty of Gaunt,
> They mustred their souldiers by two and by three,
> And the formost in battle was Mary Ambree.

Her name was proverbial for a woman of heroic spirit or a virago.

> My daughter will be valiant
> And prove a very Mary Ambry in the business.
> BEN JONSON: *Tale of a Tub*, I, ii.

Ambrose, St. (*c.* 340–397) became BISHOP of Milan in 374. He was noted for the penance he imposed on the Eastern Emperor Theodosius, for the massacre of the Thessalonians; also for his victory over the ARIANS at the synod of Aquileia (381), and for his organization of church music. The **Ambrosian Chant** was used until the GREGORIAN CHANT became the basis of church music two centuries later. His feast day is 7 December. His emblems are (1) a beehive, in allusion to the legend that a swarm of bees settled on his mouth when he was lying in his cradle—a favourable OMEN; (2) a scourge, by which he expelled the ARIANS from Italy.

Ambrosian Library, founded in Milan (1609) by Cardinal Borromeo, Archbishop of Milan, and named in honour of St. Ambrose. Its famous collection of manuscripts includes a 4th-century codex of HOMER, the earliest known.

Ambrosia (ăm brō′ zi à) (Gr. *a*, not, *brotos*, mortal). The food of the gods, so called because it made them immortal. Hence anything delicious to the taste. *See* NECTAR.

Ambrosian Nights. John Wilson ("Christopher North"), James Hogg and other literary figures forgathered at Ambrose's Tavern, Edinburgh, of an evening for convivial conversation, recorded largely by North (with embellishments) as a series of papers on literary and topical subjects in the form of dialogues. These famous *Noctes Ambrosianæ* (1822–1835) were published in *Blackwood's Magazine*. *Cp.* BANNATYNE CLUB.

Ambrosius Aurelianus. A shadowy 5th-century figure, according to GILDAS the last of the Roman nation in Britain, under whose leadership the Britons rallied to resist the SAXON invaders.

Ambry (am' bri) (Lat. *armarium*, cupboard, chest). A cupboard, wall-press, or locker. In church a closed recess for keeping books, vestments, sacramental plates, consecrated oil, etc. There are several variant forms such as *aumbry, awmry, almery*, etc., the latter leading to confusion with ALMONRY.

Ambs-as, or **ace,** or **Ames-ace** (ămz ās) (Lat. *ambo-asses*, both or two aces). Two aces, the lowest throw in dice; figuratively, bad luck.

> I had rather be in this choice than throw amesace for my life.
>
> SHAKESPEARE: *All's Well that Ends Well*, II, iii.

Also the name of a card game sometimes spelt **aumo-ace**.

Amelia. A model of conjugal affection in Fielding's last novel, *Amelia* (1751). It is said that the character was intended for his own wife. Amelia Sedley, "one of the best and dearest creatures", appears in Thackeray's *Vanity Fair* (1847–8).

Amen Corner, at the west end of PATERNOSTER ROW, London, was where the monks finished the PATER NOSTER, on CORPUS CHRISTI Day, as they went in procession to St. Paul's Cathedral. They began in *Paternoster* Row with the *Lord's Prayer* in Latin, which was continued to the end of the street; then said *Amen* at the corner of the Row; on turning down *Ave Maria* Lane, commenced chanting the *Hail Mary*! then, crossing LUDGATE entered *Creed* Lane chanting the CREDO. Paternoster Row, Amen Corner and much of Ave Maria Lane were destroyed in an air raid on 28 December 1940.

Amen-Ra, or **Amon-Ra.** The King of the gods during the ancient Egyptian Empire, a development from *Amon* ("the hidden one"), patron of Thebes. Usually figured as human-headed, with two long ostrich plumes rising above his head, sometimes with a ram's head. The ram was sacred to him and his ORACLE was at the oasis of Jupiter AMMON. The Greeks identified him with ZEUS.

Amende honorable. An anglicized French phrase for a full and public apology. In mediæval France the term was applied to the degrading punishment inflicted on traitors, parricides and the sacrilegious, who were brought into court with a rope round their necks, stripped to the shirt and made to beg pardon of God, the King and the court.

A mensa et thoro. *See* A VINCULO.

Amenthes (a men' thēz). The HADES of the ancient Egyptians, the abode of the spirits of the dead where judgment was passed by OSIRIS.

America. *See* UNITED STATES OF AMERICA.

Americans, Good—when they die go to Paris. Not an original witticism of Oscar Wilde, who used it in *A Woman of No Importance*, but attributed by Oliver Wendell Holmes to Thomas Appleton (1812–1884).

American Dream, The. A phrase epitomizing the democratic ideals and aspirations on which America had been founded, the American way of life at its best.

> It [the American dream] has been a dream of being able to grow to fullest development as man and woman, unhampered by the barriers which had slowly been erected in older civilizations, unrepressed by social orders which had developed for the benefit of classes rather than for the simple human being of any and every class.
>
> J.T. ADAMS: *The Epic of America, Epilogue* (1938).

American Workhouse, The. A name given to the Park Lane Hotel, London, by taxi-drivers because of its popularity with wealthy Americans, and hence in general a hotel offering luxurious accommodation.

Amerindian (ăm ėr in' di ản). A PORTMANTEAU WORD combining *American* and *Indian* applied to native peoples of the NEW WORLD as distinct from those of India and the East Indies.

Ames-ace. *See* AMBS-AS.

Amethea. *See* FAMOUS HORSES *under* HORSE.

Amethyst (ăm' e thist) (Gr. *a*, not; *methusko*, intoxicate). A violet-blue variety of quartz supposed by the ancients to prevent intoxication. Drinking-cups of amethyst were a charm against inebriety and it was especially cherished by Roman matrons from the belief that it would preserve inviolate the affection of their husbands.

Amiable, or **Amicable Numbers.** Any two numbers either of which is the sum of the aliquots of the other, *e.g.*, 220 and 284. The aliquots of 220 are 1, 2, 4, 5, 10, 11, 20, 22, 44, 55, 110, the sum of which is 284; and the aliquots of 284 are 1, 2, 4, 71, 142, the sum of which is 220.

Amiel (am' i el). In Dryden's *Absalom and Achitophel* (i, 899–913), this is meant for Sir Edward Seymour, Speaker of the House of Commons. The name is an anagram of *Eliam* (God is kinsman). *Eliam*, in II *Sam*. xxiii, 34, is the son of Ahithophel the Gilonite, and one of David's heroes; in II *Sam*. xi, 3 it appears as the name of BATHSHEBA'S father, which in I *Chron*. iii, 5 is given as *Ammiel*.

Aminadab (a min′ à dăb). A QUAKER. The Scripture name has a double *m*, but in old comedies, where the character represents a Quaker, the name has generally only one. Obadiah was also used to signify a Quaker and Rachel a Quakeress.

Amiral, or **Ammiral.** An early form of the word ADMIRAL.

Amis and Amile. *See* AMYS.

Amish, The. Followers of Jakob Ammann; a strictly conservative sect which separated from the MENNONITES in the late 17th century. They first appeared in Pennsylvania in *c*. 1714 and settlements in other parts of America followed. They are conspicuous for their colourful customs, industry, and frugality. They still use the German language, wear old-fashioned dress and beards without moustaches, use hooks and eyes instead of buttons, and employ horse-drawn vehicles.

Ammon, or **Hammon.** The Greek form of the name of the Libyan and Egyptian god Amun or Amon. *See* AMEN-RA.

Son of Ammon. ALEXANDER the Great was thus greeted by the priests of the Libyan temple of JUPITER Ammon.

> Ammon's great son one shoulder had too high.
> POPE: *Epistle to Dr. Arbuthnot*, 117.

Ammonites (ăm′ àn ītz). Fossil molluscs allied to the nautilus and cuttlefish. So called because they resemble the horn upon the ancient statues of Jupiter Ammon.

Also the children of Ammon; the descendants of Ben-ammi, the son of Lot by his younger daughter (*Gen*. xix, 38).

Amoret (ăm′ àr et), in Spenser's *Faerie Queene* (Bk. III), is the type of female loveliness—young, handsome, gay, witty, and good; soft as a rose, sweet as a violet, chaste as a lily, gentle as a dove, loving everybody and by all beloved.

Also a love-song, love-knot, love-affair, or love personified.

> He will be in his amorets, and his canzonets, his pastorals and his madrigals.
> THOMAS HEYWOOD: *Loves Maistresse* (1633).

Amorous, The. Philip I of France (1060–1108); he deserted his wife Bertha and carried off Bertrada, the wife of Fulk of Anjou.

Amour-propre (a′ moor propr) (Fr.). One's self-love, vanity, or opinion of what is due to oneself. *To wound his amour-propre* is to gall his good opinion of himself.

Ampersand. The character "&" for *and*. In the old HORNBOOKS, after giving the twenty-six letters, the character & was added (… x, y, z, &), and was called "Ampersand", a corruption of "and per se &" (and by itself, and). The symbol is an adaptation of *et* (Lat. *and*), as can be seen if we look at the italic ampersand—*&*—where the "e" and the cross of the "t" are clearly recognizable. *See* TIRONIAN.

Amphialus (ăm fī′ à lùs). In Sidney's *Arcadia* (1580–1590) the valiant and virtuous son of the wicked Cecropia, in love with Philoclea; he ultimately married Queen Helen of Corinth.

Amphictyonic Council (ăm fik ti on′ ik) (Gr. *amphiktyones*, dwellers round about). In Greek history, the council of the Amphictyonic League, consisting of the deputies of the twelve member tribes, who met twice a year, at DELPHI or THERMOPYLAE. With Delphi it administered the sanctuary of the Pythian APOLLO and it also conducted the PYTHIAN GAMES. It was named after its supposed founder Amphictyon, son of DEUCALION.

Amphigouri (ăm fi goor′ i). Verses which, while sounding well, contain no meaning. A good example is Swinburne's *Nephelidia*, a well-known parody of his own style, which begins:

> From the depth of the dreamy decline of the dawn through a notable nimbus of nebulous noonshine,
> Pallid and pink as the palm of the flag-flower that flickers with fear of the flies as they float,
> Are they looks of our lovers that lustrously lean from a marvel of mystic miraculous moonshine?
> *etc*.

Amphion (ăm fī′ on). The son of ZEUS and Antiope who, according to Greek legend, built Thebes by the music of his lute, which was so melodious that the stones danced into walls and houses of their own accord.

Amphisbæna (ăm fis bē′ nà), (Gr. *amphis*, both ways; *baino*, go). A fabulous venomous serpent with a head at each end and able to move in either direction. The name is applied to a genus of South American lizards.

Amphitrite (ăm fi trī′ ti). In classical mythology, the goddess of the sea, wife of POSEIDON, daughter of NEREUS and Doris (Gr. *amphi-trio* for *tribo*, rubbing or wearing away [the shore] on all sides).

Amphitryon (ăm fit′ ri on). Son of Alcæus and husband of ALCMENA.

> Le véritable Amphitryon
> Est l'Amphitryon où l'on dine.
> MOLIÈRE: *Amphitryon*.

That is, the person who provides the feast (whether master of the house or not) is the real host. The tale is that ZEUS assumed the likeness of Amphitryon, in order to visit Alcmena, and gave a banquet; but Amphitryon came home and claimed the honour of being master of the house. As far as the servants and guests were concerned "he who gave the feast was to them the host".

Amphrysian Prophetess (ăm fri′ zi ản). The Cumæan SIBYL; so called from Amphrysus, a river of Thessaly, on the banks of which APOLLO fed the herds of Admetus.

Ampoule, La Sainte (la sant am pool′). The vessel containing oil used in anointing the kings of France, and said to have been brought from heaven by a dove for the coronation service of St. LOUIS. It was preserved at Rheims till the French Revolution, when it was destroyed.

Amram's Son. Moses (*Exod.* vi, 20). Milton's reference in *Paradise Lost*, I, 338–40:

> As when the potent rod
> Of Amram's son, in Egypt's evil day,
> Waved round the coast,

is to *Exod.* x, 13.

Amrita (ăm rē′ tả). In Hindu mythology the ELIXIR of immortality, corresponding to the AMBROSIA of classical mythology.

Amulet (Lat. *amuletum*, a charm). Something worn, usually round the neck, as a preventive charm. The word was formerly connected with the Arabic *himalah*, the name given to the cord that secured the KORAN to the person.

The early Christians used to wear amulets called ICHTHUS. *See also* TALISMAN.

Amun, or **Amon.** *See* AMEN-RA.

Amyclæan Silence (ăm i klē′ ản). Amyclæ in the south of Sparta was so often alarmed by false rumour of the approach of the SPARTANS, that a decree was issued forbidding mention of the subject. When the Spartans actually came no one dared give warning and the town was taken. Hence the proverb, *more silent than Amyclæ*.

Ruled by the mythical Tyndareus, CASTOR AND POLLUX were born there and are hence sometimes called the **Amyclæan Brothers.**

Amyris plays the Fool (à mī′ ris). An expression used of one who assumes a false character with an ulterior object like JUNIUS BRUTUS. Amyris was a SYBARITE sent to DELPHI to consult the ORACLE, who informed him of the approaching destruction of his nation; he fled to Peloponnesus and his countrymen called him a fool; but like the madness of David, his "folly" was true wisdom, for thereby he saved his life.

Amys and Amylion, or **Amis et Amiles.** A late 12th-century French romance telling the story of the friendship of two knights in the reign of CHARLEMAGNE. At the end of the story Amylion slays his children to cure his friend of leprosy.

Anabaptists. At the time of the REFORMATION the name given to various sects which did not believe in infant baptism, and noted for their extremist views, especially at Zwickau and Munster in Germany. On coming to years of discretion they were re-baptized (Gr. *ana*, over again). In 17th-century England Baptists were often abusively called Anabaptists.

Anacharsis (ăn à kar′ sis). A Scythian PHILOSOPHER (*c.* 600 B.C.) and admirer of Greek civilization. He studied at Athens and became acquainted with SOLON.

In 1787 the Abbé Barthélemy published *Le Voyage du Jeune Anacharsis en Grèce*, giving an account of Greek customs and antiquities. It became a popular work, and was the imaginary narrative of a descendant of the Scythian philosopher.

Anacharsis Cloots. Anarchsis Jean Baptiste Du Val De Grâce, baron de Cloots (1755–1794), also known as "the Orator of the human race". A Prussian noble and apostle of revolution, who travelled Europe as a young man and became a member of the CONVENTION. He was guillotined by Robespierre in 1794.

Anachronism (Gr. *ana chronos*, out of time). Something wrongly dated, thus in the wrong chronological relationship with other things and events, and most commonly found in imaginative works which are in an historical setting. Thus in Shakespeare's *Henry IV, Pt. I*, II, i, the carrier complains "The turkeys in my pannier are quite starved", but turkeys were introduced from America, which was not discovered until nearly a century after Henry IV's time. In *Julius Cæsar*, II, i, the clock strikes and Cassius says "The clock has stricken three", yet striking clocks were not invented until 1400 years after the days of Cæsar. Mediæval romances abound with anachronisms.

Anaclethra. Another name for the AGELASTA.

Anacreon (ă năk′ ri on). A Greek lyric poet (born *c.* 570 B.C.) who wrote chiefly in praise of love and wine. Hence *Anacreontics* as a name for this kind of verse or the metrical form in which they were written.

Anacreon Moore. Thomas Moore (1779–1852), who not only translated Anacreon into English (1800), but also wrote original poems in the same style.

Anacreon of Painters. Francesco Albano (1578–1660), a painter of beautiful women.

Anacreon of the Guillotine. Bertrand Barère de Vieuzac (1755–1841), one of the Committee of Public Safety; so called from the flowery language and convivial jests directed towards his miserable victims.

Anacreon of the Temple. Abbé Guillaume Amfrye de Chaulieu (1639–1720), poet and wit and member of the LIBERTINE circle of the TEMPLE which influenced VOLTAIRE.

Anacreon of the Twelfth Century. Walter Map or Mapes, ecclesiastic (1140–1210), the "jovial archdeacon", was unsuitably so called. He is perhaps best known for the verse which became the famous drinking-song "Meum est propositum in taberna mori".

The French Anacreon. Pontus de Thiard or Tyard (1521–1605), one of the PLÉIADE poets; also Pierre Laujon (1727–1811).

The Persian Anacreon. Hafiz of Shiraz (c. 1320–1389) whose *Divan* of over 500 poems revealed him as the greatest Persian lyric poet.

The Scotch Anacreon. Alexander Scott, poet (c. 1520–1585).

The Sicilian Anacreon. Giovanni Meli (1740–1825).

Anadyomene (Gr. rising). In ancient Greece a name given to APHRODITE in allusion to her having risen from the sea as portrayed in the famous painting by APELLES.

Anagram (Gr. *ana graphein*, to write over again). A word or phrase formed by transposing letters of another word or phrase. Some famous examples are:

> Dame Eleanor Davies (prophetess in the reign of Charles I)=*Never so mad a ladie.*
> Gustavus=*Augustus.*
> Horatio Nelson=*Honor est a Nilo.*
> Florence Nightingale=*Flit on cheering angel.*
> Queen Victoria's Jubilee=*I require love in a subject.*
> Quid est Veritas (*John* xviii, 38)=*Vir est qui adest.*
> Marie Touchet (mistress of Charles IX of France)=*Je charme tout* (made by Henry IV).
> Voltaire is accepted as an anagram of *Arouet l(e) j(eune).*

These are *interchangeable words*: Alcuinus and Calvinus; Amor and Roma; Eros and Rose; Evil and Live.

Anagrams have been much employed since ancient times for serious, satirical or complimentary purposes and were very popular in Victorian days. They were often slightly strained by the omission, addition, or substitution of letters as will be noticed in some of the above examples. *See also* CABALIST.

Anastasia, St. (ăn a stā′ zi a), a Roman matron said to have been beheaded with St. Basilissa for having buried the bodies of St. PETER and St. PAUL.

Anathema (à năth′ i mà). A denunciation or curse. A Greek word meaning "a thing set up or hung up", an offering to the gods.

Thus Gordius (*see* GORDIAN KNOT) hung up his yoke and beam; the shipwrecked hung up their wet clothes; retired workmen hung up their tools, cripples their crutches, etc. Later it came to mean a thing devoted to evil since animals offered up were destined for death.

In the Catholic and Calvinistic churches it became a more extreme form of denunciation than EXCOMMUNICATION.

Anatomy. He was like an anatomy—*i.e.* a mere skeleton, very thin, like one whose flesh has been anatomized or cut off.

> They brought one Pinch; a hungry lean-faced villain,
> A mere anatomy, a mountebank.
> SHAKESPEARE: *The Comedy of Errors*, V, i.

Shakespeare also uses *atomy* as a synonym. Thus Quickly calls the Beadle "Thou atomy, thou!" in *Henry IV, Pt. II*, V, iv.

Ancæus (ăn sē′ ås). Helmsman of the ship ARGO, after the death of Tiphys. He was told by a hard-pressed slave that he would never live to taste the wine of his vineyards, and when wine, made from his own grapes, was set before him he sent for the slave to laugh at the latter's prognostications; but the slave made the answer "there's many a slip 'twixt the CUP and the lip". At this very instant a messenger informed Ancæus that the Calydonian BOAR was devastating his vineyard, whereupon he set down his cup, went out against the boar, and was slain in the encounter.

Anchises. In Greek mythology, ruler of DARDANUS. APHRODITE became enamoured of his beauty and bore him ÆNEAS, the Trojan hero. According to one legend Anchises was blinded or killed by lightning for naming his son's mother. Virgil gives a different legend.

Anchor. In Christian symbolism the anchor is the sign of hope, in allusion to *Heb.* vi, 19, "Hope we have as an anchor of the soul". It also symbolizes security. In art it is an attribute of Pope CLEMENT I who was said to have been tied to an anchor and cast into the sea (1st century); and St. Nicholas of Bari, the patron SAINT of sailors.

Anchor light. A white light visible all round the horizon, shown from the forepart of an anchored vessel. Vessels over 150 feet in length must carry two, one being aft.

Anchor watch. A watch kept when a vessel is anchored as a precaution against dragging, etc.

Swallowing the anchor. A sailor is said to do so when he retires from the sea.

The anchor is a-peak. In shortening cable, when the ship is drawn completely over the anchor.

The anchor comes home. When an anchor does not hold and drags out of the ground. Figuratively, the enterprise has failed, notwithstanding the precautions employed.

To weigh anchor. To haul in the anchor. When broken out of the ground it is *aweigh*. Figuratively to begin an enterprise which has hung on hand.

Ancien Régime (Fr.). The old order of things; a phrase used during the French Revolution for the system of government, with all its evils and shortcomings, which existed under the BOURBON monarchy.

Ancient. In the now obsolete sense of a flag or standard or bearer of same, is a corruption of *ensign*. Pistol was Falstaff's ancient and Iago Othello's.

> 'Tis one Iago, ancient to the general.
> SHAKESPEARE: *Othello*, II, i.
> My whole charge consists of Ancients, corporals, lieutenants, gentlemen of companies...
> SHAKESPEARE: *Henry IV, Pt. I*, IV, ii.

Ancient Lights on a notice board in England means that for at least 20 years uninterruptedly a certain building has enjoyed light, and no structure may be erected which substantially deprives it of such light.

Ancient Mariner. Having shot an albatross, he and his companions were subjected to fearful penalties. On repentance he was forgiven, and on reaching land told his story to a hermit. At times, however, distress of mind drove him from land to land, and wherever he abode told his tale of woe, to warn from cruelty and persuade men to love God's creatures. This story in Coleridge's *Rime of the Ancient Mariner*, which was first published in *Lyrical Ballads* (1798), is partly based on a dream told by his friend Cruickshank, and partly gathered from his reading. Wordsworth told him the story of the privateer George Shelvocke, who shot an albatross while rounding Cape Horn in 1720, and was dogged by bad weather. Other suggested sources are Thomas James's *Strange and Dangerous Voyage* (1683) and the *Letter of St. Paulinus to Macarius, in which he relates astounding wonders concerning the shipwreck of an old man* (1618). A full and definitive examination of the sources is to be found in *The Road to Xanadu* (1927) by J. L. Lowes.

Ancient of Days. A scriptural name given to God (*Dan.* vii, 9).

Ancile (ăn' sīl). The PALLADIUM of ROME; the sacred buckler said to have fallen from heaven in the reign of Numa. To prevent its being stolen, as the safety of the state depended on it, he caused eleven others, exactly similar, to be made, and entrusted them to twelve priests called SALII.

Ancren Riwle, or **Ancrene Wisse.** The rule of the Anchoresses; a mediæval treatise (? early 13th century) in rhythmical prose of great charm, written for the guidance of women who were trying to live the strict religious lives of anchoresses. Among the counsels given them is to work hard, avoid gossiping and to limit their pets to "but one cat" (unlike Chaucer's Prioress who possessed an unspecified number of small pet dogs). It is of uncertain authorship.

Andaman Marble. An exceptionally hard timber grown in the Andaman Islands, of the same family as ebony.

Andiron (ănd' ĭr ŏn). A firedog; that is, one of a pair of short horizontal iron bars, with legs or a supporting stand, for holding the ends of logs in an open fireplace. The word is from the Old French *andier*, after the Late Latin *andedus, andena*, or *anderius* and has nothing to do with *iron*. *End-iron* and *hand-iron* are variants.

Andrea Ferrara (ăn drā' á fĕ ra' rà). A sword, also called an *Andrew* and a *Ferrara* after the famous 16th-century sword maker of this name.

> Here's old tough Andrew.
> JOHN FLETCHER: *The Chances* (1618).

Andrew, a name used in old plays for a valet or man-servant. *Cp.* ABIGAIL. *See also* MERRY ANDREW.

St. Andrew was a fisherman and brother of St. PETER, depicted in Christian art as an old man with long white hair and beard, holding the Gospel in his right hand, and leaning on a St. Andrew's cross. His day is 30 November. It is said that he was crucified in Patræ (*c.* A.D. 70) on a *crux decussata* (*see* CROSS). He is also the patron saint of Russia and Scotland. *See* RULE, ST.; CONSTANTINE'S CROSS *under* CROSS.

The Andrew meaning "the Royal Navy" derives from the time of the French Revolutionary and Napoleonic Wars when one Andrew Miller acquired such a reputation in the Portsmouth area as a PRESSGANG operator that it came to be said that his victims had been snatched into "the Andrew". In the 19th century **Andrew Miller** was also used to mean "a warship" or "government authority".

Androcles and the Lion (ăn drō' klēz). Androcles was a runaway slave who took refuge in a cavern. A lion entered and, instead of tearing him to pieces, lifted up his forepaw that Androcles might extract from it a thorn. The slave, being subsequently captured, was doomed to fight with a lion in the Roman arena. It so happened that the same lion was led out against him, and recognizing his benefactor, showed towards him every demonstration of love and gratitude.

The tale is told by Aulus Gellius (*c*. 130–180) and similar stories are found in ÆSOP'S FABLES and the GESTA ROMANORUM. Bernard Shaw's *Androcles and the Lion* (1916) is based on the story.

Android. An old name for an AUTOMATON figure resembling a human being (Gr. *andros-eidos*, a man's likeness).

Andromache (ăn drom' à ki). In Greek legend she was the wife of HECTOR, on whose death she was given to Pyrrhus (Neoptolemus). The latter was killed by ORESTES and she became the wife of Helenus, Hector's brother. It is the title of a play by Euripides.

Andromeda (ăn drom' e dà). Daughter of CEPHEUS and CASSIOPEIA. Her mother boasted that her beauty surpassed that of the NEREIDS; so the Nereids induced NEPTUNE to send a sea-monster to the country, to which the oracle of Jupiter AMMON declared ANDROMEDA must be surrendered. She was accordingly chained to a rock but was delivered by PERSEUS, who married her and slew Phineus, her uncle, to whom she had been promised. After death she was placed among the stars.

Angel. In post-canonical and apocalyptic literature angels are grouped in varying orders. The commonly used hierarchy of nine orders is that popularized by the Pseudo-Areopagite or Pseudo-Dionysius (early 5th century) in his *De Hierarchia Celesti*, which arranges them in three triads:

(1) Seraphim, Cherubim, and Thrones in the first circle.

(2) Dominions, Virtues, and Powers in the second circle.

(3) Principalities, Archangels, and Angels in the third circle.

The names are taken from the *Old Testament* and *Eph*. i, 21 and *Col*. i, 16.

The seven holy angels are MICHAEL, GABRIEL, RAPHAEL, URIEL, Chamuel, Jophiel and ZADKIEL. Michael and Gabriel are mentioned in the BIBLE, Raphael in the APOCRYPHA and all appear in *Enoch* (viii, 2).

Milton in *Paradise Lost*, Bk. I, 392, gives a list of the fallen angels.

Mohammedans say that angels were created from pure bright gems; the genii from fire, and man from clay.

Angel. An English gold coin copied from the French *ange* and minted from 1465 to the reign of Charles I. It was to replace the NOBLE and was first called *angel noble*. Valued at 6*s*. 8*d*. and later at 10*s*., it bore the

figure of the archangel MICHAEL slaying the dragon, and was the coin presented to persons touched for the KING'S EVIL.

Angel. In modern theatrical parlance denotes the financial backer to a play.

Angel. *See* PUBLIC-HOUSE SIGNS.

Angel of the Schools. St. Thomas Aquinas. *See* ANGELIC DOCTOR.

A flying angel. A ride given to a youngster seated astride someone's shoulders, holding hands with arms held high at full stretch.

On the side of the angels. *See* SIDE.

To entertain an angel unawares. To meet and talk with someone famed for saintliness of life while unaware of their identity; nowadays more usually applied to the entertainment of persons of note rather than sanctity.

> Be not forgetful to entertain strangers: for thereby some have entertained angels unawares.
> *Hebrews*: xiii, 2. *Cp*. PHILEMON AND BAUCIS.

Angel-beast. A 17th-century card-game. The game was called *la bête* (beast), and an angel was a usual stake, hence *angel-beast*, much as we say "shilling-whist" or "half-penny nap".

> This gentleman offers to play at Angel-beast, though he scarce knows the cards.
> SEDLEY: *The Mulberry Garden* (1668).

Angels of Mons. The 3rd and 4th Divisions of the OLD CONTEMPTIBLES, under the command of General Dorrien-Smith, were sorely pressed in the retreat from Mons (26–27 August 1914). Their losses were heavy and that they survived at all was by some attributed to divine intervention. Arthur Machen, writing from FLEET STREET, described with great verisimilitude St. GEORGE and the angels, who, clad in white, with flaming swords held back the might of the German First Army. For some, the imaginary became a reality, and the *Angels of Mons* became a phrase and fable.

Angel visits. Delightful intercourse of short duration and rare occurrence.

> Like angel visits, few and far between.
> T. CAMPBELL: *Pleasures of Hope* (1799), II, 378.

Angel-water. An old Spanish cosmetic, made of roses, trefoil, and lavender; but originally mainly from ANGELICA, hence the name.

> Angel-water was the worst scent about her.
> SEDLEY: *Bellamira, or the Mistress* (1687).

Angelic. Angelic Brothers, or **Gichtelians.** A separatist sect founded in Holland in the latter part of the 17th century by the German mystic Johann Gichtel (1638–1710).

Angelic Doctor. Thomas Aquinas (*c*. 1225–1274) was so called, probably because of the purity and excellence of his teaching.

His exposition of the most recondite problems of theology and philosophy was judged to be the fruit of almost more than human intelligence and in 1879 Pope Leo XIII directed that the teachings of Aquinas should be the basis of theology. His *Summa Theologica* is the culmination of SCHOLASTICISM. *See* DUMB OX.

Angelic Hymn, The. The hymn beginning with *Glory to God in the highest* (*Luke* ii, 14), so called because the former part of it was sung by the angel host that appeared to the shepherds of Bethlehem.

Angelic Salutation, The. The AVE MARIA.

Angelica (ăn jel' i kà). This beautiful but fickle young woman was the heroine of Boiardo's ORLANDO INNAMORATO and Ariosto's ORLANDO FURIOSO. Orlando's unrequited love for her drove him mad. The name was used by Congreve for the principal character in *Love for Love* and by Farquhar in *The Constant Couple* and *Sir Harry Wildair*. Also the name of a plant (*Archangelica officinalis*) cultivated for its aromatic stalks which when candied are used in decorating cakes and confectionery. Called the **angelic herb** from a belief in its medicinal virtues, especially against plague and pestilence, it was also used as an ingredient of ABSINTHE, of gin and of "bitters".

Angelical Stone. The speculum of Dr. DEE. He asserted that it was given him by the angels RAPHAEL and GABRIEL. It passed into the possession of the Earl of Peterborough, thence to Lady Betty Germaine, by whom it was given to the Duke of Argyll, whose son presented it to Horace Walpole. It is now in the BRITISH MUSEUM.

Angelico, Fra. The name by which Giovanni da Fiesole (*c.* 1400–1455), who was famed for the spiritual quality of his paintings, is better known.

Angelus, The (ăn' je lùs). A Roman Catholic devotion in honour of the Annunciation. It begins with the words *Angelus Domini nuntiavit Mariae*. It is recited thrice daily, usually at 6 a.m., noon, and 6 p.m. at the sound of the *Angelus* bell.

Angevin Kings of England (ăn' je vin). The early PLANTAGENET kings from Henry II to John. Henry II (1154–1189) was the son of Matilda (daughter of Henry I) and Geoffrey "Plantagenet", Count of Anjou. John lost Anjou in 1204.

Angle, A Dead. A term applied in old books on fortification to the ground before an angle in a wall which can be neither seen nor defended from the parapet.

Angle with a silver hook. To buy fish at the market; said of an unsuccessful angler who buys fish to conceal his failure.

The Father of Angling. Izaak Walton (1593–1683). *See* THE GENTLE CRAFT.

Angles. Non Angli, sed angeli (Not Angles, but angels). The legend is that when Pope GREGORY THE GREAT (590–604) saw some fair-complexioned youths in the slave-market he asked whence they had come. He was told that they were Angles and also heathen. "Not Angles, but angels" was his comment and on becoming Pope he sent St. AUGUSTINE to effect their conversion.

Anglican. In America means "English" (sometimes with no ecclesiastical implications).

> ... suitable abodes for country gentlemen, in the strictly Anglican sense of the expression.
> C.E. CASON: *Culture in the South*.

In England it is used in connexion with the CHURCH OF ENGLAND.

Anglo-Saxon Chronicle. The first history in the English language to use the dating system ANNO DOMINI. It was probably begun in the reign of ALFRED THE GREAT (871–899). There are seven manuscript versions extant, which substantially deal with events from the time of Julius Cæsar to 1154, and four of these are usually distinct chronicles. It is the basic source for the history of Anglo-Saxon England.

Angra Mainyu. *See* AHRIMAN.

Angry Young Men. A name applied to certain living British dramatists, particularly John Osborne, from whose play *Look Back in Anger* (1956) the term was derived. They are characterized by dissatisfaction with established social, moral, political and intellectual values. By association it is also applied to some American writers of protest.

> In the absence of any really firm standards among those whom they sought to replace the temptation to exploit the gullibility of the public and those who were supposed to guide them was too strong for many of the 'Angry Young Men' to resist.
> BORIS FORD: *The Modern Age*, Pt. III, *The Novel Today*.

Angurvadel. FRITHIOF'S sword, inscribed with runic letters, which blazed in time of war, but gleamed with a dim light in time of peace. *See* SWORD.

Anima Mundi (ăn' i mà mŭn' dī) (Lat. the soul of the world), with the oldest of the ancient philosophers meant "the source of life"; with PLATO it meant "the animating principle of matter", inferior to pure spirit, with the STOICS it meant "the whole vital force of the universe".

G. E. Stahl (1660–1734) taught that the phenomena of animal life are due to an immortal *anima* or vital principle distinct from matter.

Animal Farm. A satirical "fairy story" by George Orwell (1903–1950) of totalitarianism of the Russian kind under Stalin. A modern fable in which the pigs, by cunning, treachery and ruthlessness, lord it over the more honest, gullible and hardworking farm animals. It was first published in 1945.

Animals in Christian Art. Some animals are appropriated to certain saints: as the calf or ox to St. LUKE; the cock to St. PETER; the eagle to St. JOHN the Divine; the lion to St. MARK and St. JEROME; the raven to St. Benedict, etc. *See* SYMBOLS OF SAINTS *under* SAINT.

Animals in Heaven. According to Mohammedan legend the following ten animals have been allowed to enter paradise: Jonah's whale; Solomon's ant; the ram caught by ABRAHAM and sacrificed instead of Isaac; the lapwing of BALKIS; the camel of the prophet Saleh; Balaam's ass; the ox of MOSES; the dog KRATIM of the SEVEN SLEEPERS; Al BORAK, MOHAMMED'S steed; and Noah's dove.

Animals in symbolism.

The lamb, the pelican, and the unicorn, are symbols of Christ.

The dragon, serpent, and swine, symbolize Satan and his crew. The ant symbolizes frugality and prevision; ape, uncleanness, malice, lust, and cunning; ass, stupidity; bantam cock, pluckiness, priggishness; bat, blindness; bear, ill-temper, uncouthness; bee, industry; beetle, blindness; bull, strength, straight-forwardness; bulldog, pertinacity; butterfly, sportiveness, living in pleasure; calf, lumpishness, cowardice; camel, submission; cat, deceit; cicada, poetry; cock, vigilance, overbearing insolence; crocodile, hypocrisy; crow, longevity; cuckoo, cuckoldom; dog, fidelity, dirty habits; dove, innocence, harmlessness; duck, deceit (French, *canard*, a hoax); eagle, majesty, inspiration; elephant, sagacity, ponderosity; fly, feebleness, insignificance; fox, cunning, artifice; frog and toad, inspiration; goat, lasciviousness; goose, conceit; folly; grasshopper, old age; gull, gullibility; hare, timidity; hawk, rapacity, penetration; hen, maternal care; hog, impurity; horse, speed, grace; jackdaw, vain assumption, empty conceit; jay, senseless chatter; kitten, playfulness; lamb, innocence, sacrifice; lark, cheerfulness; leopard, sin; lion, noble courage; lynx, suspicious vigilance; magpie, garrulity; mole, blindness, obtuseness; monkey, tricks; mule, obstinacy; nightingale, forlornness; ostrich, stupidity; owl, wisdom; ox, patience, strength, pride; parrot, mocking verbosity; peacock, pride; pig, obstinacy, dirtiness, gluttony; pigeon, cowardice (pigeon-livered); puppy, conceit; rabbit, fecundity; raven, ill-luck; robin redbreast, confiding trust; serpent, wisdom; sheep, silliness, timidity; sparrow, lasciviousness; spider, wiliness; stag, cuckoldom; swan, grace; tiger, ferocity; tortoise, chastity; turkey cock, official insolence; turtledove, conjugal fidelity; vulture, rapine; wolf, cruelty, ferocity; worm, cringing; etc.

Animals sacred to special deities:

To Æsculapius, the serpent; to Apollo, the wolf, the griffon, and the crow; to Bacchus, the dragon and the panther; to Diana, the stag; to Hercules, the deer; to Isis, the heifer; to Juno, the peacock and the lamb; to Jupiter, the eagle; to the Lares, the dog; to Mars, the horse and the vulture; to Mercury, the cock; to Minerva, the owl; to Neptune, the bull; to Tethys, the halcyon; to Venus, the dove, the swan, and the sparrow; to Vulcan, the lion, etc.

Animal, Cries of.

To the cry, call or voice of many animals a special name is given; to apply these names indiscriminately is always wrong and frequently ludicrous. Thus, we do not speak of the "croak" of a dog or the "bark" of a bee. Apes gibber; asses bray; bears growl; bees hum; beetles drone; bitterns boom; blackbirds and thrushes whistle; bulls bellow; calves bleat; cats mew, purr, swear and caterwaul; chaffinches chirp and pink; chickens peep; cocks crow; cows moo or low; crows caw; cuckoos cry cuckoo; deer bell; dogs bark, bay, howl and yelp; doves coo; ducks quack; eagles, vultures and peacocks scream; falcons chant; flies buzz; foxes bark and yelp; frogs croak; geese cackle and hiss; grasshoppers chirp and pitter; guineafowls cry "Come back"; guineapigs and hares squeak; hawks scream; hens cackle and cluck; horses neigh and whinny; hyenas laugh; jays and magpies chatter; kittens mew; linnets chuckle in their call; lions and tigers roar and growl; mice squeak and squeal; monkeys chatter and gibber; nightingales pipe and warble— we also speak of their "jug-jug"; owls hoot and screech; oxen low and bellow; parrots talk; peewits cry peewit; pigs grunt, squeak and squeal; pigeons coo; ravens croak; rooks caw; screech owls screech or shriek; sheep and lambs baa or bleat; snakes hiss; sparrows chirp; stags bellow and call; swallows twitter; swans cry and are said to sing just before death (*see* SWAN); turkey-cocks gobble; wolves howl. Most birds, besides many of those here mentioned, sing, but we speak of the chick-chick of the blackcap, the drumming of the grouse, and the chirr of the whitethroat.

Animosity meant originally animation, spirit, as the fire of a horse, called in Latin *equi animositas*. Its present exclusive use in a bad sense is an instance of the tendency by which words originally neutral have come to assume a bad meaning.

Animula, vagula, etc. (an im′ ū là, văg′ ū là). The opening of a poem to his soul, ascribed to the dying Emperor Hadrian (A.D. 76–138):

Animula, vagula, blandula,
Hospes, comesque, corporis;
Quae nunc abibis in loca,
Pallidula, rigida, nudula?

Sorry-lived, blithe little, flittering sprite,
Comrade and guest in this body of clay,
Whither, ah! whither, departing in flight,
Rigid, half-naked, pale minion, away?

E.C.B.

BYRON also has an English rendering.

Ann, Mother. Ann Lee (1736–1784), the founder and "spiritual mother" of the American sect of SHAKERS.

Annates (ăn′ ātz) (Lat. *annus*, a year), also called FIRST FRUITS. Payments to the POPE, on the appointment of a BISHOP or other ecclesiastic, of a year's income of the SEE or BENEFICE. In England these payments were finally stopped in 1534 and transferred to the Crown. *See* QUEEN ANNE'S BOUNTY.

Anne's Great Captain. The Duke of Marlborough (1650–1722).

Annie Laurie was the eldest of three daughters of Sir Robert Laurie of Maxwelton, born 16 December 1682. William Douglas of Fingland (Kirkcudbright) wrote the popular verses which were altered by Lady Scott (1810–1900), who composed the air. In 1709 Annie married Alexander Fergusson of Craigdarroch. She was the grandmother of Alexander Fergusson, the hero of Burns's song called *The Whistle*.

Annie Oakley. *See* OAKLEY.

Anno Domini (ăn′ ō dom′ i nī) (Lat.). In the Year of our Lord; *i.e.* in the year after the Nativity; or A.D. This system of dating was introduced by the monk Dionysius Exiguus who lived in the first half of the 6th century. *Anno Domini* is also used colloquially as a synonym for old age, *e.g.*, "Anno Domini is his complaint." *See* ANGLO-SAXON CHRONICLE.

Annunciation, The Feast of the. 25 March, also called LADY DAY, on which the angel GABRIEL announced to the Virgin MARY that she would be the mother of the MESSIAH (*Luke* i, 26–38).

Order of the Annunciation. An Italian order of military knights thus named from 1518, but founded by Amadeus VI, count of Savoy, in 1362 as the *Order of the Collar*, from its badge, a silver collar bearing devices in honour of the Virgin. *See* F.E.R.T.

Sisters of the Annunciation. *See* FRANCISCANS.

Annus Luctus (ăn′ ŭs lŭk′ tūs) (Lat. the year of mourning). The period during which a widow is supposed to remain unmarried. If she marries within about nine months from the death of her husband and a child is born, a doubt might arise as to its paternity. Such a marriage is not illegal.

Annus Mirabilis (ăn′ ŭs mir ăb′ i lis). The year of wonders. Such was 1666, memorable for the Great FIRE OF LONDON and the successes of English arms over the Dutch, commemorated in Dryden's poem entitled *Annus Mirabilis*.

Annwn (ăn′ oon), or **Annwyfn** (ăn oi′ vŭn). In Welsh legend, the land of the departed, the Celtic HADES.

Anodyne Necklace, An. An anodyne relieves pain: an anodyne necklace was an AMULET supposedly efficacious against suffering. Johnson's *Idler*, No. 40, says:

> The true pathos of advertisements must have sunk deep into the heart of every man that remembers the zeal shown by the seller of the *anodyne necklace*, for the ease and safety of poor soothing infants.

The term then came to be applied to a hangman's noose:

> May I die by an *anodyne necklace*, but I had rather be an under-turnkey than an usher in a boarding school.
>
> GOLDSMITH: *Vicar of Wakefield*, ch. x.

Anon. The O.E. *on ane*, in one mind (state, body, etc.), the present meaning *soon, in a little while*, is a misuse of the earlier meaning, *straightway, at once*. *Mark* i, 30 (AUTHORIZED VERSION) gives an instance of the old meaning:

> But Simon's wife's mother lay sick of a fever, and anon they tell him of her.

The REVISED VERSION gives *straightway*. Wordsworth in *The White Doe of Rylstone*, I, 31, exemplifies the later meaning:

> Fast the churchyard fills; — anon
> Look again, and they are all gone.

The word was also used by servants, tapsters, etc., as an interjectory reply meaning "Coming, sir!"

Anschluss, The. This German word meaning "junction" or "union" in a modern historical context refers to the seizure of Austria by Germany in March 1938.

Answer like a Norman, To, that is, evasively.

Answer more Scotico, To. Avoiding the direct question by starting another question or subject.

> "Hark you sirrah", said the doctor, "I trust you remember you are owing to the laird four stones of barleymeal and a bow of oats...". "I was thinking" replied the man *more Scotico* (in the Scottish fashion), that is returning no direct answer on the subject on which he was addressed "my best way would be to come to your honour, and take your advice yet, in case my trouble should come back".
>
> SIR WALTER SCOTT: *The Abbot*, ch. xxvi.

Answer to a Maiden's Prayer, The. A young good-looking and wealthy bachelor or generally anything which exactly meets requirements.

Ant. For many centuries the ant has been a symbol of thrift and industry. The *Bible* says "Go to the ant, thou sluggard; consider her ways and be wise" (*Proverbs* vi, 6). Æsop has a fable on the "Ant and the Grasshopper" in which the indolent grasshopper, in the winter, went to the busy little ants to beg food.

Antæus (ăn tē′ us), in Greek mythology, a gigantic wrestler, son of Earth and Sea (GÆA and POSEIDON), who became stronger whenever he touched the earth. HERRCULES lifted him from the ground and slew him.

Antediluvian. Before the DELUGE. Colloquially used for anything hopelessly outdated.

Anthology (Gr. garland of flowers). A collection of poems or prose extracts.

The Greek Anthology. A modern edition of sixteen books, largely of Greek epigrammatic poetry, based upon the 10th-century *Anthology* of Cephalas of Constantinople, which was rearranged by Maximus Planudes in 1301 and first published at Florence in 1494. The work of Cephalas incorporated the *Garland* of Meleager (1st century B.C.), the *Garland* of Philippus (1st century A.D.) and the *Circle* of Agathias (6th century). The text of Planudes was superseded by the Palatine MS., when the *Anthology* of Cephalas was discovered (1606) in the Count Palatine's Library at Heidelberg.

Anthony Eden. Popular name for the style of black felt homburg worn by Sir Anthony Eden (Lord Avon) when Foreign Secretary in the 1930s, and which was fashionable in WHITEHALL circles.

Anthony the Great, St. (*c.* 250–356), the patron saint of herdsmen and hermit of Upper Egypt; also the father of Christian monasticism. The story of his temptations by the devil was a popular subject in literature and art. His day is 17 January.

Anthony of Padua, St. (1195–1231), rigorous follower of St. FRANCIS of Assisi and famous preacher. He was canonized in 1232 by Pope Gregory IX. His day is 13 June.

St. Anthony's Cross. The TAU cross, T, called a lace.

St Anthony's fire. In mediæval times a pestilential disease, so called from the belief that those who sought the intercession of St. Anthony recovered from this epidemic or sacred fire. It was commonly supposed to be erysipelas (Gr. red skin) or the ROSE (from its colour) but in fact the disease was ergotism, a poisoning due to eating rye bread with fungal infection. *Cp.* ST. VITUS'S DANCE under VITUS.

St. Anthony's pig. A pet pig, the smallest of the litter, also called the TANTONY PIG.

Anthroposophus (ăn thrō pos' ō fùs). The nickname of Thomas Vaughan (1622–1666), cleric and alchemist and twin brother of Henry Vaughan the SILURIST. He was so called from his book *Anthroposophia Theomagica* (1650), which dealt with the condition of man after death.

Anthroposophy (ăn'thrō pos' ò fi). (Gr. *anthropos*, man; *sophia*, knowledge). The name given to the "spiritual science" developed by the Austrian philosopher Rudolf Steiner (1861–1925), a former theosophist. *See* THEOSOPHY.

Antic Hay. *See* HAY.

Antichrist, or the Man of Sin, due to appear at the end of time, is mentioned in the *Epistles of St. John* (I, ii, 18, 22) and is derived from Hebrew teachings. The belief that the arrival of Antichrist was to precede the second advent is chiefly founded on II *Thess*. ii, 1–12, and *Rev*. xiii. In the early Christian Church the ROMAN EMPIRE and its rulers were frequently referred to as Antichrist and later the title was bestowed upon the Emperor Frederick II and various Popes. With the REFORMATION the PROTESTANT conception of the papacy as Antichrist became widespread and its later use is largely as an abusive term and it has been applied even to NAPOLEON and William II of Germany. The Mohammedans have a legend that Christ will slay the Antichrist at the gate of the Church at Lydda, in Palestine. *See also* NUMBER OF THE BEAST.

Antigone (ăn tig' ò ni). The subject of a tragedy by Sophocles: she was the daughter of ŒDIPUS by his mother, Jocasta. She slew herself to avoid being buried alive for disobeying an edict of Creon. She was famed for her devotion to her brother Polynices, hence the Duchess of Angoulême (1778–1851) was called *the Modern Antigone* for her attachment to her brother Louis XVII.

Antimony (an' ti mon i). A word probably from the Arabic as it was introduced through ALCHEMY, but Johnson's *Dictionary* derives it erroneously from the Greek *antimonachos* (bad for monks). The explanation copied from earlier writers was that a prior gave some of this mineral to his convent pigs, who thrived upon it and became very fat. He next tried it on the monks, who died from its effects.

Antinomian (an ti no' mi an) (Gr. *antinomos*, exempt from the law). One who believes that Christians are not bound to observe the "law of God", but "may continue in sin that grace may abound". The term was first applied to John Agricola by Martin Luther, and was given to a sect that appeared in Germany about 1535. It was put forward as an excuse for immorality by extremist sects from early Christian times and appeared in England during the COMMONWEALTH period.

Antinous (ăn tin' ō ùs). A model of manly beauty. He was favourite and companion of Hadrian, the Roman Emperor.

Anti-pope. A usurping or rival pontiff set up in opposition to one canonically elected. Of the thirty-nine anti-popes, those residing at Avignon during the Great SCHISM (1378–1417) are perhaps best known. When John XXIII (a schismatic) summoned the Council of Constance (1414) to end the schism, there were three rival popes. John and Benedict XIII were deposed as schismatics, Gregory XIII resigned and a new POPE, Martin V, was elected in 1417.

Antisthenes (ăn tis' the nēz). Athenian philosopher (*c.* 455–*c.* 360 B.C.), founder of the CYNIC School. He wore a ragged cloak, and carried a wallet and staff like a beggar. SOCRATES, whose pupil he was, wittily said he could "see rank pride peering through the holes of Antisthenes' rags".

Antonine's Wall. A turf wall fronted by a deep ditch with forts at intervals stretching from Carriden on the Forth, to Old Kilpatrick on the Clyde (*c.* 36 miles). Built between 140 and 142 by Lollius Urbicus, governor of Britain under the Emperor Antoninus Pius, it was abandoned before the end of the 2nd century. *See* HADRIAN'S WALL.

Antrustions (ăn trŭs' ti ŏnz). Members of the military household of the Frankish kings (O.H. Ger. *Trost*, trust, fidelity). They survived as a bodyguard until the 8th century.

None but the king could have antrustions.
STUBBS: *Constitutional History*, I, ix.

Anu. Chief God of the Sumerians and Babylonians, king of heaven and ruler of destiny. The centre of his cult was at Erech, mentioned in *Genesis* (x, 10) as part of Nimrod's kingdom.

Anubis (à nū' bis). An Egyptian god similar to HERMES of Greece with whom he was sometimes identified. His office was to take the souls of the dead before the judge of the infernal regions. The son of OSIRIS, the judge, he was represented with a human body and a jackal's head.

Anvil. It is on the anvil, under deliberation, the project is in hand.

Anxious seat, To be on the. To be in a state of apprehension or suspense. A METAPHOR derived from American revivalist meetings where the penitents' bench was popularly known as the *anxious bench*.

Anzac. A word coined in 1915 from the initials of the Australian and New Zealand Army Corps. It was also applied to the cove and beach in Gallipoli where they landed.

Anzac Day. 25 April, commemorating the landing of the Anzacs in Gallipoli in 1915.

Anzac Pact. The agreement between Australia and New Zealand in 1944 to co-operate in their policies with regard to armistices with the AXIS powers, the post-war settlement, and in certain other matters.

Aonian (ā ō' ni an). Poetical, pertaining to the MUSES. The Muses, according to Greek mythology, dwelt in Aonia, that part of Bœotia which contains Mount HELICON and the MUSES' fountain. MILTON speaks of "the Aonian mount" (*Paradise Lost*, I, 15), and

Thomson calls the fraternity of poets:

The Aonian hive
Who praised are, and starve right merrily,
Castle of Indolence, ii, 2.

À outrance. *See* À L'OUTRANCE.

Apache (à păch' i). The name of a group of tribes of North American Indians, given to (or adopted by) the HOOLIGANS of Paris about the end of the 19th century (here pronounced à păsh'). This usage has a close parallel in the MOHOCKS of the 18th century.

Apache State. Arizona, the land of the Apache Indians.

Apartheid (Afrikaans, apart-hood). A policy adopted by the Afrikaner National Party in 1948 to ensure the dominance of the white minority. It divided South Africa into separate areas for whites and blacks causing its departure from the British Commonwealth in 1961 and leading to rioting, repression and isolation from other nations. Limited constitutional rights were granted to non-whites in 1985.

Ape. To copy, to imitate.

He keeps them, like an ape, in the corner of his jaw;
first mouthed, to be last swallowed.
SHAKESPEARE: *Hamlet*, IV, ii.

Most of the OLD WORLD monkeys have cheek pouches, used as receptacles for food.

The buffoon ape, in Dryden's *The Hind and the Panther*, means the Freethinkers.

Next her the buffoon ape, as atheists use,
Mimicked all sects, and had his own to chuse.
Part I, 39.

To lead apes in hell. It is an old saying (frequent in the Elizabethan dramatists) that it is the fate of old maids. Hence *apeleader*, an old maid. Thus Beatrice says:

I will even take sixpence in earnest of the bearward,
and lead his apes into hell.
SHAKESPEARE: *Much Ado About Nothing*, II, i.

To play the ape, to play practical jokes or silly tricks, to pull faces like an ape.

To put an ape into your hood or **cap,** *i.e.* to make a fool of you. Apes were formerly carried on the shoulders of fools and simpletons.

To say an ape's paternoster, is to chatter with fright or cold, like an ape. One of the books in Rabelais' *Library of St. Victor* is called "The Ape's Paternoster".

Apelles. *See* CHIAN PAINTER.

Apemantus (ăp e măn' tùs). A churlish philosopher in Shakespeare's *Timon of Athens*.

A-per-se (ā pĕr sē). An AI; a person or thing of unusual merit. "A" all alone with no one who can follow, *nemo proximus aut secundus*. Chaucer calls Cresseide "the floure A-per-se of Troi and Greek".

London, thou art of towns A-per-se.
DUNBAR: *In honour of the city of London* (1501).

Aphrodite (ăf′ rō dī ti) (Gr. *aphros*, foam). The Greek VENUS; so called because she sprang from the foam of the sea. In HOMER she is the daughter of ZEUS and DIONE.

Aphrodite's girdle. The CESTUS.

Apicius (a pis′ i ùs). A gourmand. The name of three famous Roman gourmands. Marcus Gavius Apicius, of the time of AUGUSTUS and Tiberius, whose income was reduced by luxurious living, put an end to his life to avoid the misery of a plain diet.

A-pigga-back. See PICK-A-BACK.

Apis (ā′pis). In Egyptian mythology, Hap, the bull of Memphis, sacred to Ptah (later associated and identified with OSIRIS) of whose soul it was supposed to be the image. SERAPIS was the dead Apis. The sacred bull had to be black with special markings. Sometimes it was not suffered to live more than twenty-five years, when it was sacrificed and embalmed with great ceremony. Cambyses, King of Persia (529–521 B.C.), and conqueror of Egypt, slew the bull of Memphis, and is said to have been punished with madness.

Apocalypse, Four Horsemen of. See under FOUR.

Apocalyptic Number. The mysterious number 666 (*Rev.* xiii, 15). See NUMBER OF THE BEAST.

Apocrypha (à pok′ ri fà) (Gr. *apokrupto*, hide away); hence the meaning "withheld from general circulation" (for various reasons), and therefore coming to be regarded as of doubtful origin, false or spurious. In the early 5th century JEROME was responsible for its inappropriate application to the non-canonical books of the Old Testament found in the SEPTUAGINT and VULGATE and not usually included in PROTESTANT Bibles. In the preface to the Apocrypha in the 1539 Bible the explanation that the books are so called "because they were wont to be read not openly" is untenable. The Apocrypha was included in the AUTHORIZED VERSION of 1611. The Apocrypha proper consists of:

> I and II Esdras, Tobit, Judith, additions to Esther, WISDOM OF SOLOMON, Ecclesiasticus, Baruch, part of the Epistle of Jeremiah, the SONG OF THE THREE HOLY CHILDREN, the History of Susanna, Bel and the Dragon, the Prayer of Manasses, I and II Maccabees.

Apart from other Old Testament Apocryphal books there are numerous New Testament Apocryphal Gospels, Acts and Teachings of the APOSTLES, Epistles and Apocalypses. See THE ACTS OF PILATE *under* PILATE; PROTEVANGELIUM; PSEUDEPIGRAPHA.

Apocryphal. Applied to a story or anecdote, especially one concerning a celebrity or well-known individual to indicate that it is in character but fictitious. See APOCRYPHA.

Apollinarians (à pol in âr′ i ànz). An heretical 4th-century sect, followers of Apollinaris, Bishop of Laodicea, a vigorous opponent of Arianism. They denied that Christ had a human soul and asserted that the *Logos* supplied its place. This heresy was condemned at the Council of Constantinople (381) and subsequently.

Apollo (à pol′ ō). In Greek mythology, son of ZEUS and Leto (LATONA), and sometimes identified with HELIOS the sun god. He was the brother of Artemis (*see* DIANA), half-brother of HERMES, and father of ÆSCULAPIUS. He was the god of music, poetry, archery, prophecy and the healing art. His plant was the LAUREL and he is represented as the perfection of youthful manhood.

> the fire rob'd god,
> Golden Apollo.
> SHAKESPEARE: *A Winter's Tale*, IV, iii.

A perfect Apollo is a model of manly beauty, referring to the APOLLO BELVEDERE.

Apollo Belvedere, so called from the Belvedere Gallery in the VATICAN, where it stands; an ancient statue of Apollo, supposedly a copy of a bronze votive statue of Delphi commemorating the repulse of an attack by the Gauls on his shrine in 279 B.C.. It was discovered at Antium (Anzio) in 1485.

Apollo of Portugal. Luis de Camoëns (1524–1580), author of the LUSIAD, so called for the beauty of his poetry.

Apollonius of Tyana. A Pythagorean philosopher (born shortly before the Christian era), accredited with exceptional powers of magic. It was he who discovered that the Phœnician woman whom Menippus Lycius intended to wed was in fact a serpent or LAMIA. This story was noted by Robert Burton in his *Anatomy of Melancholy*, and it forms the subject of Keats' *Lamia*.

Apollyon (à pol′ yòn). The Greek name of ABADDON, King of HELL. It is used by Bunyan in *The Pilgrim's Progress*.

Aposiopesis. See QUOS EGO.

Apostate, The. JULIAN, the Roman Emperor (c. 331–363). So called because he forsook the Christian faith for paganism, which he sought to promote after his accession (361).

A posteriori (ā pos tē′ ri ôr′ i) (Lat. from the latter). An *a posteriori* argument is proving the cause from the effect. Thus if we see a watch, we conclude there was a watchmaker. ROBINSON CRUSOE inferred there was another human being on the desert island, because he saw a human footprint in the wet sand. It is thus that the existence and character of God are inferred from his works. See A PRIORI.

41

Apostles. The word *apostle* (Gr. *apostolos*, envoy, messenger, one sent) was especially applied to the Twelve Disciples of Christ as those sent forth to preach the gospel. They are named in *Matthew* x, 1–4; *Mark* iii, 14–19; *Luke* vi, 13–16; and *Acts* i, 13. The original list comprises PETER, ANDREW, JAMES and JOHN (the sons of Zebedee), PHILIP, BARTHOLOMEW, THOMAS, MATTHEW, James (the son of Alphæus), Judas or JUDE, SIMON and JUDAS Iscariot. The Gospels of *St. Matthew* and *St. Mark* give Thaddæus in place of Jude, and the Gospel of *St. John* (xxi, 1–2) has Nathanael, who by some has been identified with Bartholomew. James the Less has also been identified, somewhat dubiously, with James, the son of Alphæus. MATTHIAS and PAUL were subsequent additions. The badges or symbols of the fourteen apostles (*i.e.* the original twelve with Matthias and Paul) are as follows:

Andrew, *an × -shaped cross* because he was crucified on one.

Bartholomew, *a knife*, because he was flayed with a knife.

James the Great, *a scallop shell, a pilgrim's staff*, or *a gourd bottle*, because he is the patron saint of pilgrims.

James the Less, *a fuller's pole*, because he was killed by a blow on the head with a pole, dealt him by Simeon the fuller.

John, *a cup with a winged serpent flying out of it*, in allusion to the tradition about Aristodemos, priest of Diana, who challenged John to drink a cup of poison. John made the sign of a cross on the cup, Satan like a dragon flew from it, and John then drank the cup which was quite innocuous.

Judas Iscariot, *a bag*, because he "had the bag and bare what was put therein" (*John* xii, 6).

Jude, *a club*, because he was martyred with a club.

Matthew, *a hatchet* or *halberd* because he was slain at Nadabar with a halberd.

Matthias, *a battleaxe*, because he was first stoned, and then beheaded with a battle axe.

Paul, *a sword*, because his head was cut off with a sword. The convent of La Lisla in Spain boasts of possessing the very instrument.

Peter, *a bunch of keys*, because Christ gave him "the keys of the kingdom of heaven". *A cock*, because he went out and wept bitterly when he heard the cock crow (*Matt.* xxvi, 75).

Philip, *a long staff surmounted with a cross*, because he suffered death by being suspended by the neck from a tall pillar.

Simon, *a saw*, because he was sawn to death, according to tradition.

Thomas, *a lance*, because he was pierced through the body, at Mylapore, with a lance.

According to tradition:

ANDREW lies buried at Amalfi (Naples).

BARTHOLOMEW, at Rome, in the church of Bartholomew, on the Tiber Island.

JAMES THE GREAT was buried at St. Jago de Compostella, in Spain.

JAMES THE LESS, at Rome, in the church of SS. Philip and James.

JOHN, at Ephesus.

JUDE, at Rome.

MATTHEW, at Salerno (Naples).

MATTHIAS, at Rome, in the church of St. Peter.

PAUL, at Rome, in the church of S. Paolo fuori le Mura.

PETER, at Rome, in the church of St. Peter.

PHILIP, at Rome.

SIMON or SIMEON, at Rome.

THOMAS, at Ortona (Naples). (?Madras).

The supposed remains of MARK THE EVANGELIST were buried at Venice, about 800.

LUKE THE EVANGELIST is said to have been buried at Padua.

See EVANGELISTS; SYMBOLS OF SAINTS *under* SAINT.

Apostles of

Abyssinians, St. Frumentius (*c.* 300–*c.* 360).

Alps, Felix Neff (1798–1829).

Andalusia, Juan de Avila (1500–1569).

Ardennes, St. Hubert (d. 727).

Armenians, Gregory the Illuminator (*c* 257–*c.* 337).

Brazil, José de Anchieta, Jesuit missionary (1533–1597).

English, St. Augustine (d. 604); St. George (d. *c.* 300).

Free Trade, Richard Cobden (1804–1865).

French, St. Denis (? 3rd century).

Frisians, St. Willibrod (*c.* 657–738).

Gauls, St. Irenæus (*c.* 130–*c.* 200); St. Martin of Tours (*c.* 316–400).

Gentiles, St. Paul (d. 67).

Germany, St. Boniface (680–754).

Highlanders, St. Columba (521–597).

Hungary, St. Stephen (975–1038), the Apostle King.

Indians (American), Bartolomé de Las Casas (1474–1566); John Eliot (1604–1690).

Indies (East), St. Francis Xavier (1506–1552).

Infidelity, Voltaire (1694–1778).

Ireland, St. Patrick (*c.* 389–461).

North, St. Ansgar or Anscarius (801–865), missionary to Scandinavia; Bernard Gilpin (1517–1583), Archdeacon of Durham, evangelist of the Scottish border.

Peru, Alonso de Barcena, Jesuit missionary (1528–1598).

Picts, St. Ninian (? 5th century).

Rome, St. Philip Neri (1515–1595) for his good works there. (*See* ORATORIANS).

Scottish Reformers, John Knox (1505–1572).

Slavs, St. Cyril (827–869).

Spain, St. James the Great (d. 44).

The Sword, Mohammed (*c.* 570–632).

Temperance, Father Mathew (1790–1856).

Yorkshire, Paulinus, Archbishop of York (d. 644).

Wales, St. David (*c.* 500–*c.* 600).

Prince of the Apostles. St. PETER (*Matt.* xvi, 18, 19).

The Apostles or **The Society.** *See* CAMBRIDGE APOSTLES.

Apostle spoons. Silver spoons having the figure of one of the APOSTLES at the top of the handle, formerly given at christenings. Sometimes twelve spoons, representing the twelve apostles; sometimes four, representing the four EVANGELISTS; and sometimes only one was presented. Occasionally a set occurs, containing in addition the "Master Spoon" and the "Lady Spoon". Silver spoons were given to children of the wealthier classes, hence the saying BORN WITH A SILVER SPOON IN ONE'S MOUTH. *See under* BORN.

Apostles' Creed. A Christian creed supposed to be an epitome of doctrine taught by the apostles. It was received into the Latin Church, in its present form, in the 11th century, but a formula somewhat like it existed in the 2nd century. Items were added in the 4th and 5th centuries, and verbal alterations much later. *See* ATHANASIAN CREED; NICENE CREED.

Apostolic Fathers. Christian writers born in the 1st century supposedly in contact with the original APOSTLES. Polycarp, the last of the Apostolic Fathers, born about 69, was believed to be the disciple of St. John the Apostle. Clement of Rome died *c*. 101, Ignatius *c*. 120, and Polycarp *c*. 155. Others are Barnabas, Hermas (author of *The Shepherd*) and Papias (a bishop of Hierapolis, mentioned by Eusebius).

Apostolic Majesty. A title borne by the Emperor of Austria, as King of Hungary, first conferred by Pope Sylvester II on King Stephen of Hungary in 1001.

Apostolic Succession. The doctrine that the mission given to the APOSTLES by Christ (*Matt*. xxviii, 19) must extend to their legitimate successors in an unbroken line. Thus the only valid ministry is that of clergy ordained by properly consecrated BISHOPS.

Apparel. One meaning of this word used to be "ornament" or "embellishment", especially applied to orphreys, the embroidered borders of ecclesiastical vestments, and in particular to the ornamental parts of the alb, at the lower edge and at the wrists.

> The albe should be made with apparels worked in silk or gold, embroidered with ornaments.
> PUGIN: *Glossary of Ecclesiastical Ornament* (1844).

Appeal to the Country, An. To ask the nation to express its opinion on some particular issue or issues by dissolving PARLIAMENT and holding a general election.

Appiades (ăp'i à dēz). Five divinities whose temple stood near the Appian aqueduct in ROME. Their names are VENUS, PALLAS, Concord, Peace, and VESTA. They were represented on horseback, like AMAZONS. Also a name for the courtesans of this locality.

Appian Way (ăp'i àn). The "queen of long-distance roads" leading from Rome to Brundusium (Brindisi). This most famous Roman road was begun by the censor Appius Claudius about 312 B.C. *See* DOMINE, QUO VADIS?

Apple. The apple appears more than once in Greek legend; *see* APPLE OF DISCORD; ATALANTA'S RACE; HESPERIDES.

There is no mention of an apple in the Bible story of Eve's temptation. She took "the fruit of the tree which is in the midst of the garden" (*Gen*. iii, 3).

For the story of William Tell and the apple, *see* TELL.

Apple, Newton and the. The well-known story of Newton and the apple originated with VOLTAIRE, who says that Mrs. Conduit, Newton's niece, told him that Newton was at Woolsthorpe (visiting his mother) in 1666 when, seeing an apple fall, he was led into the train of thought which resulted in his contribution to the laws of gravitation.

Apple, Prince Ahmed's, a cure for every disorder. In THE ARABIAN NIGHTS story of Prince Ahmed, the Prince purchased his apple at Samarkand.

Apple of Discord. A cause of dispute; something to contend about. At the marriage of THETIS and Peleus, where all the gods and goddesses assembled, Discord (Eris), who had not been invited, threw on the table a golden apple "for the most beautiful". Hera (JUNO), Pallas Athene (MINERVA), and Aphrodite (VENUS) put in their claims and PARIS, as referee, gave judgment in favour of Aphrodite. This brought upon him the vengeance of Hera and PALLAS, to whose spite the fall of TROY was attributed.

Apple of the eye. The pupil, because it was anciently supposed to be a round solid ball like an apple. Figuratively anything held extremely dear or much cherished.

> He kept him as the apple of his eye.
> *Deut*. xxxii, 10.

Apple Tree Gang. The name given to John Reid and his Scottish friends who introduced golf into the U.S.A. in 1888, at Yonkers, N.Y. The name was coined in 1892 when they moved to their third "course" at Yonkers—a 34-acre orchard which yielded six holes.

Apple-cart, To upset the. To ruin carefully laid plans. To have one's expectations blighted, as a farmer's might be when his load of apples was overturned. This phrase is recorded in use as early as 1796. Bernard Shaw has a play called *The Apple Cart*.

Apple-islanders. NICKNAME for the inhabitants of Tasmania, who are also known as Tassies and Mountain-devils.

Apple-jack. An apple-turnover is sometimes so called in East Anglia; in the U.S.A. the name of a drink distilled from fermented apple juice—like French Calvados.

Apple-john. An apple so called from its

being mature about St. JOHN THE BAPTIST'S Day, 24 June. The French call it *Pomme de Saint Jean*. We are told that apple-johns will keep for two years, and are best when shrivelled.

> I am withered like an old apple-john.
>
> SHAKESPEARE: *Henry IV, Part I*, III, iii.

Incorrectly called *Apples of King John*, other probable names are *Deus Ans, Dusand, Dewsum, Jewsum* and *Pomme de Fer*.

Apple-pie bed, or **pie bed.** A bed in which the sheets are so folded that a person cannot get his legs down. Perhaps a corruption of *nappe pliée* (French), a folded sheet or cloth.

Apple-pie order. Everything just so, in perfect order. The origin of the phrase is uncertain. Perhaps the suggestion *nappes pliées* (Fr. folded linen), neat as folded linen, is near the mark. *See* APPLE-PIE BED.

Apple-polishing. An attempt to win favour by gifts or flattery. From the practice of American schoolchildren bringing shiny apples to their teachers.

Apples, Isle of. *See* AVALON.

Apples of Iduna. *See* IDUNA.

Apples of Istakhar are "all sweetness on one side, and all bitterness on the other".

Apples of Paradise, according to tradition, had a bite on one side, to commemorate the bite given by Eve.

Apples of perpetual youth. *See* IDUNA.

Apples of Pyban, says Sir John MANDEVILLE, fed the pigmies with their odour only.

Apples of Sodom. Possibly the *madar* or *oschur* (*Caloptris procera*). The fruit of trees reputed to grow on the shores of the Dead Sea "which bear lovely fruit, but within are full of ashes". Josephus, Strabo and Tacitus refer to them.

Like an apple of Sodom, signifies disappointment and disillusion. "Dead Sea fruit" has a similar meaning.

> Like to the apples on the Dead Sea shore,
> All ashes to the taste.
>
> BYRON: *Childe Harold*, III, 34.

Après moi le déluge. After me the deluge—I care not what happens after I am dead. Madam de Pompadour (1721–1764), mistress of Louis XV, used the phrase, *Après nous le déluge*, when remonstrated with on account of the extravagances of the Court, possibly having heard her royal lover use it. Metternich (1773–1859), the Austrian statesman, used the expression, meaning that the existing order would collapse when his guiding hand was removed.

April. The opening month (probably derived from Lat. *aperire*, to open) when trees un-

fold and the earth opens with new life. The old Dutch name was *Gras-maand* (Grass month). In the French Republican CALENDAR it was called *Germinal*, the time of budding (21 March to 19 April).

April fool, called in France *un poisson d'avril*, and in Scotland a *gowk* (cuckoo), a person befooled or tricked on *All Fools' Day* (1 April). In India similar tricks are played at the Holi Festival (31 March), so that it cannot refer to the uncertainty of the weather, nor yet to a mockery of the trial of Christ, the two most popular explanations. A better solution is this: as 25 March used to be New Year's Day, 1 April was its octave, when its festivities culminated and ended.

It may be a relic of the Roman CEREALIA, held at the beginning of April. The tale is that PROSERPINA was sporting in the Elysian meadows, and had just filled her lap with daffodils, when PLUTO carried her off to the lower world. Her mother, CERES, heard the echo of her screams, and went in search of the voice; but her search was a fool's errand, it was "hunting the gowk", or looking for the "echo of a scream".

A priori (ā prī ôr′ i) (Lat. from an antecedent). An *a priori* argument is one in which a fact is deduced from something antecedent, as when we infer certain effects from given causes. Mathematical proofs are of this kind whereas judgments in the law courts are usually A POSTERIORI; we infer the animus from the act.

Apron (O. Fr. *napperon*). Originally *napron* in English, it is representative of many words that have either lost or gained an "n" through coalescence, or the reverse, with the article "a" or "an". *A napron* became *an apron*. Other examples are *adder* for *a nadder, auger* for *a nauger*, and *umpire* for *a numpire*. The opposite coalescence may be seen in *newt* for *an ewt*, NICKNAME for *an ekename*, and the obsolete *nuncle* for *mine uncle*. *See* NONCE.

Apron-string tenure. A tenure held in virtue of one's wife.

Tied to one's mother's apron strings. Completely under one's mother's thumb, particularly of a young man dominated by his mother.

Aqua Fortis (ăk′ wȧ for′ tis) (Lat. strong water). Nitric acid.

Aqua Regia (ăk′ wȧ rē′ jȧ) (Lat. royal water). A mixture usually of one part concentrated nitric acid with three parts concentrated hydrochloric acid; so called because it dissolves GOLD, *the king of metals*.

Aqua Tofana (ăk′ wȧ tof′ ā nȧ). A poisonous liquid containing arsenic, much used in Italy in the 18th century by young wives who wanted to get rid of their husbands. It was invented about 1690 by a Greek woman named Tofana, who called it the *Manna* of St. Nicholas of Bari, from a widespread notion that an oil of miraculous efficacy flowed from the tomb of that saint.

Aqua vitæ (ăk′ wà vī′ tē) (Lat. water of life). Brandy or distilled spirits. EAU DE VIE, *whisky*, and the Irish USQUEBAUGH have the same meaning. Also certain ardent spirits used by the alchemists. Ben Jonson calls a vendor of such an "acquavitæ man" (*Alchemist*, I, i). The ELIXIR OF LIFE was made from distilled spirits.

Aquarius (à kwâr′ i ùs) (Lat. the water-bearer). The eleventh sign of the ZODIAC (21 January to 18 February). Its symbol is a man pouring water from a vessel, its sign ≈ representing a stream of water.

Aquila non captat muscas (ăk′ wi là non kăp′ tăt mŭs′ kăs). A Latin phrase—"an eagle does not hawk at flies", a proverbial saying implying that little things are beneath a great man's contempt.

Aquiline. *See* FAMOUS HORSES *under* HORSE.

Aquinas, St. Thomas. *See under* THOMAS.

Aquinian Sage, The. Juvenal is so called because he was born at Aquinum, a town of the Volscians, in Latium.

Arabesque. A term now applied to forms of design derived from classical grotesque.

The original Moorish Arabesque (now usually called Moresque, Alhambresque or Saracenic) did not admit representation of natural objects.

Arabia. It was Ptolemy who was the author of the threefold division into **Arabia Petræa,** or Stony (Hejaz); **Arabia Felix,** or Fruitful (Hasa, Hadramaut, Oman and Yemen); **Arabia Deserta** or Desert (Nejd).

Arabian Bird, The. The PHŒNIX; hence, figuratively, a marvellous or unique person.

All of her that is out of door most rich!
If she be furnish'd with a mind so rare,
She is alone the Arabian bird.
SHAKESPEARE: *Cymbeline*, I, vi.

Arabian Nights Entertainments, The, or **The Thousand and One Nights.** These ancient Oriental tales were first introduced into western Europe in a French translation by Antoine Galland (12 vols., 1704–1717), derived from an Egyptian text probably of 14th- or 15th-century origin. English translations based on Galland were made by R. Heron (1792) and W. Beloe (1795). The later English translations by Henry Torrens (1838), E.W. Lane (1839–1841), John Payne (1882–1884), and Sir Richard Bur-

ton's unexpurgated edition published at Benares (16 vols., 1885–1888) are based on a late 18th-century Egyptian text. The standard French translation by J. C. Mardrus (1899–1904) has been severely criticized.

The framework of the tales is that they were told by SCHEHERAZADE, bride of Sultan Schahriah, to stave off her execution.

Arabians. An obscure Arabian Christian sect of the 3rd century who maintained that the soul dies with the body but rejoins the body on the last day. This heresy was overcome by Origen (*c*. 185–*c*. 254).

Arabic figures. The figures 0, 1, 2, 3, 4, etc., so called because they were introduced to Europe by the Arabs who brought them from India. They were familiar in Europe by the 12th century but did not generally supersede the Roman numerals (I, II, III, IV, V, VI, etc.) until the 16th century. The cipher or nought was an immensely valuable gain and the introduction of place value made possible a decimal system, the positional value of the numbers (*e.g.* 444) increasing tenfold to the left and decreasing correspondingly to the right. *See* NUMBERS.

Street Arabs. Children of the houseless poor; street urchins. So called from the nomadic habits of the Arabs who had no fixed abode.

He strode on just in time to avoid a flight of street-arabs, who had seen the scuffle from a distance and were bearing down eagerly upon him.
MRS. HUMPHRY WARD: *David Grieve*, Bk.II, ch.vii.

Arachne's Labours (à răk′ ni). Spinning and weaving. The story is that Arachne challenged ATHENE to a weaving contest and hanged herself when the goddess destroyed her web. Athene then changed her into a spider, hence Arachnida, the scientific name for spiders, scorpions and mites.

Aram, Eugene (âr′ àm) (1704–1759). A schoolmaster of considerable learning who, while at Knaresborough, was involved with one Daniel Clark in a series of frauds. He murdered Clark in 1745 but was not found out until 1758, when he was teaching at King's Lynn. He was executed on 6 August 1759. A competent scholar in Latin, Greek, Hebrew, Welsh, etc., his story is told in Hood's poem *The Dream of Eugene Aram* (1831), and Lytton's novel *Eugene Aram* (1832).

Arawn (à′ roun). King of ANNWN.

Arbor Day. A day set apart in Canada, the United States and New Zealand, for planting trees, first observed in Nebraska in 1872 where it became a legal holiday in 1885. The date varies according to locality.

Arbor Judæ. *See* JUDAS TREE.

Arcadia (ar' kā' di ā). A district of the Peloponnesus named after Arcas, son of JUPITER, chiefly inhabited by shepherds and the abode of PAN. According to VIRGIL it was the home of pastoral simplicity and happiness. The name was used by Sidney for the title of his romance (1590) and soon became a byword for rustic bliss.

Arcades ambo (ar' kȧ dēz ăm' bō) (Lat.). From VIRGIL'S seventh ECLOGUE: "*Ambo florentes ætatibus, Arcades ambo*" (Both in the flower of youth, Arcadians both), meaning "both poets or musicians", now extended to two persons having tastes or habits in common. BYRON gave the phrase a whimsical turn:

> Each pulled different ways with many an oath,
> "Arcades ambo"—*id est*, blackguards both.
> *Don Juan*, iv, 93.

Arcadian beasts. An old expression to be found in Plautus, Pliny, etc. *See* Persius, iii, 9:

> Arcadiae pecuaria rudere credas,

and Rabelais, V, vii. So called because the ancient Arcadians were renowned as simpletons. Juvenal (vii, 160) has *arcadicus juvenis*, meaning a stupid youth.

Arcas. *See* CALISTO.

Archangel. In Christian story the title is usually given to MICHAEL, the chief opponent of SATAN and his angels, and to GABRIEL, RAPHAEL, URIEL, Chamuel, Jophiel and ZADKIEL. *See* ANGEL.

According to the KORAN, there are four archangels; Gabriel, the angel of revelations, who writes down the divine decrees; Michael, the champion, who fights the battle of faith; AZRAEL, the angel of death; and ISRAFEL, who is commissioned to sound the trumpet of the resurrection.

Archbishop Parker's Table. *See under* TABLE.

Archers. The best archers in British legend are ROBIN HOOD, and his two companions LITTLE JOHN and Will Scarlet.

The famous archers of Henry II were Tepus, his bowman of the guards, Gilbert of the white hind, Hubert of Suffolk, and Clifton of Hampshire.

Nearly equal to these were Egbert of Kent and William of Southampton, and CLYM OF THE CLOUGH.

Domitian, the Roman emperor, we are told, could shoot four arrows between the spread of the fingers of a man's hand.

The story of TELL reproduces the Scandinavian tale of EGIL, who at the command of King Nidung performed a precisely similar feat.

Arches, Court of. The ecclesiastical court of appeal for the province of Canterbury, which was anciently held in the church of St. Mary-le-Bow (*Beata Maria de Arcubus*, St. Mary of the Arches), Cheapside, London.

Archeus (ar kē' us). According to PARACELSUS (*c*. 1490–1541), the immaterial principle which energizes all living substances. There were supposed to be numerous *archei*; the chief one was said to reside in the stomach.

Archies. In World War I anti-aircraft guns and batteries were thus nicknamed—probably from Archibald, the hero of one of George Robey's songs.

Archilochian Bitterness (ar ki lō' ki ȧn). Ill-natured SATIRE or bitter mockery, so named from Archilochus, a Greek satirical poet (fl. *c*. 650 B.C. and after).

Archimago (ar ki mā' gō). The enchanter in Spenser's *Faerie Queene* (Bks. I and II), typifying hypocrisy.

Archimedes' Principle (ar ki mē' dēz). The apparent loss in weight of a body immersed in liquid will equal the weight of the displaced liquid. This discovery was made by Archimedes of Syracuse (*c*. 287–212 B.C.). *See* EUREKA.

Archimedes Screw. A flexible tube twisted spirally round an axis; said to have been invented by Archimedes whilst in Egypt, as a method of irrigation. A carpenter's auger works on the same principle. Later it became a spiral screw contained in a close-fitting cylindrical case.

Architecture, Orders of. In classical architecture, DORIC, IONIC, CORINTHIAN, TUSCAN and Composite (a compound of Ionic and Corinthian).

Archontics. A 2nd-century GNOSTIC sect attributing the Creation to God's agents or *archons* (Greek *archon*, a chief magistrate or ruler).

Arcite (ar sī' ti, ar' sīt). A Theban knight made captive by Duke THESEUS, and imprisoned with Palamon at ATHENS. Both captives fell in love with Emily, the duke's sister (or daughter in some versions), and after gaining their liberty Emily was promised by the duke to the victor in a tournament. Arcite won but was thrown from his horse and killed when riding to receive his prize. Emily became the bride of Palamon. Chaucer, in his *Knight's Tale*, borrowed the story from Boccaccio's *Teseide* (1341), and it is told by Fletcher in his *Two Noble Kinsmen* (1634), and Dryden in his *Fables* (1699).

Arcos Barbs. War steeds of Arcos, in Andalusia, famous in Spanish ballads. *See* BARB.

Arctic Region means the region of the Bear stars, from *arktos*, bear (meaning both the animal and the constellation), hence northern. Arcturus (the bear-ward) or Alpha Boötes is the brightest star in the Northern Hemisphere and can be found by following the curve of the Great Bear's tail. In *Job* xxxviii, 32, Arcturus is used for the Great Bear itself. *See under* BEAR.

Arden, The Forest of. In north Warwickshire, once part of a large Midland forest, famous as the probable setting of Shakespeare's *As You Like It*.

Arden, Enoch. The story in Tennyson's poem of this name (1864), of a husband who mysteriously and unwillingly disappears, and returns years later to find that his wife (who still treasures his memory) is married to another, is not an uncommon theme. It is reminiscent of Crabbe's *The Parting Hour*, and a similar story appeared in Adelaide Anne Procter's *Homeward Bound* (in her *Legends and Lyrics*, 1858), and Mrs. Gaskell's *Manchester Marriage*.

Arden of Feversham. A play (printed in 1592) once attributed to Shakespeare and possibly written by Thomas Kyd (1558–1594), based on the murder of Thomas Arden, Mayor of Faversham, Kent (1548). Alice Arden plans the murder with the aid of two ruffians, who rush in on the signal "Now I take you", when her husband and her paramour, Mosbie, are playing draughts.

George Lillo's play of this name was completed after his death (1739) by Dr. John Hoadly and acted in 1759.

Areopagus (ăr e op′ à gus) (Gr. the hill of Mars or Ares). The seat of a famous tribunal in ATHENS; so called from the tradition that MARS was tried there for causing the death of NEPTUNE'S son Halirrothius.

Ares (âr′ ēz). The Greek god of war, son of ZEUS and HERA and identified with the Roman MARS.

Arethusa. *See* ALPHEUS AND ARETHUSA.

Aretinian Syllables. *Ut, re, mi, fa, sol, la,* used by Guido d'Arezzo or Aretino in the 11th century for his hexachord, or scale of six notes. These names were taken from the Latin hymn by Paulus Diaconus, addressed to St. JOHN, which Guido used in teaching singing:

Ut queant laxis, Re-sonare fibris,
Mi-ra gestorum Fa-muli tuorum,
Sol-ve pollutis La-biis reatum

Ut-tered be thy wondrous story,
Re-prehensive though I be,
Me make mindful of thy glory,
Fa-mous son of Zacharee;
Sol-ace to my spirit bring,
La-bouring thy praise to sing.

E.C.B.

Si was added in the 16th century and *do*

(doh), probably from *dominus*, took the place of *ut* in the 17th century. In England *te* replaced *si* in the 19th century (*ti* or *si* are used in the U.S.A.).

Argan (ar′ gàn). The principal character in Molière's *Malade Imaginaire*, a hypochondriac, uncertain whether to think more of his ailments or of his purse.

Argenis (ar′ jen is). A political allegory by John Barclay (1582–1621) written in Latin and published in 1621. It deals with the state of Europe, and France in particular, in the time of the CATHOLIC LEAGUE. "Sicily" is France, "Poliarchus" (with whom Argenis is in love) is Henry IV, "Hyanisbe" is Queen Elizabeth I, etc.

Argentine, Argentina (ar′ jen tīn, ar-jen tē′ nà). This South American republic, The Silver Republic, takes its name from the Rio de la Plata, or River of Silver, so called from the Indian silver work sent to Spain by Sebastian Cabot in 1526, assumed to indicate vast future wealth.

Argo (Gr. *argos*, swift). The galley of JASON in which he sailed in search of the GOLDEN FLEECE and finally succeeded with the help of MEDEA. Hence a sailing ship on any particularly adventurous voyage; also the name of a Southern constellation (the Ship).

Argonauts. The sailors of the ship Argo, who sailed from Iolcos to Colchis in quest of the GOLDEN FLEECE. Apollonius of Rhodes wrote an epic poem on the subject. The name is also given to a family of cephalopod molluscs (cuttlefish).

Argosy. A merchant ship. A corruption of *ragusea*. Large merchant ships were built and sailed from Ragusa (Dubrovnik) in Dalmatia.

> He hath an argosy bound to Tripolis, another to the Indies...a third at Mexico, a fourth for England.
> SHAKESPEARE: *The Merchant of Venice*, I, iii.

Argus-eyed. Jealously watchful. According to Grecian fable, Argus had 100 eyes, and JUNO set him to watch IO, of whom she was jealous. MERCURY, however, charmed him to sleep with his lyre, and slew him. Juno then set the eyes of Argus on the peacock's tail. *See* PEACOCK'S FEATHER.

> So praysen babes the Peacocks spotted traine,
> And wondren at bright Argus blazing eye.
> SPENSER: *The Shepheards Calendar*, October.

Argyle. God bless the Duke of Argyle, a phrase supposed to have been used by Scottish Highlanders when they scratched themselves. The story is that a Duke of Argyle (now Argyll) had posts erected on a treeless part of his estates so that his cattle might rub against them to ease themselves of the "torment of flies". The herdsmen saw the value of the practice, and as they rubbed their itching backs against the posts they thankfully uttered the above words.

Ariadne (ă ri ăd′ ni). In Greek mythology, daughter of the Cretan King, MINOS. She helped THESEUS to escape from the LABYRINTH, and later went with him to Naxos where he deserted her. Here DIONYSUS found her and married her.

Arians (âr′ i ănz). The followers of Arius, a presbyter of the Church of Alexandria in the 4th century. He maintained (1) that the Father and Son are distinct beings; (2) that the Son, though divine, is not equal to the Father; (3) that the Son had a state of existence prior to His appearance on earth, but not from eternity; (4) that the MESSIAH was not real man, but a divine being in a veil of flesh. The heresy was condemned by the Council of Nicæa (325), which upheld the orthodox view of Athanasius that the Son was "of the same substance" with the Father.

Ariel (âr′ iel). A Hebrew name signifying "lion of God". In *Isaiah* xxix, 1–7, it is applied to Jerusalem; in astronomy a satellite of URANUS; in demonology and literature, the name of a spirit. Thus Ariel is one of the seven angelic "princes" in Heywood's *Hierarchie of the Blessed Angels* (1635); one of the rebel angels in Milton's *Paradise Lost*, VI, 371 (1667); a SYLPH, the guardian of Belinda, in Pope's *Rape of the Lock* (1712); but best known as "an ayrie spirit" in Shakespeare's *Tempest*. According to the play Ariel was enslaved to the witch Sycorax (I, ii) who overtasked him, and in punishment for not doing what was beyond his power, shut him up in a pine-rift for twelve years. On the death of Sycorax, Ariel became the slave of CALIBAN, who tortured him most cruelly. PROSPERO liberated him and was gratefully served by the fairy until he set Ariel free.

Aries (âr′ ēz). The RAM. The first sign of the ZODIAC in which the sun is from 21 March to 20 April. The legend is that the ram with the GOLDEN FLEECE, which bore Phrixus and Helle on its back, was finally sacrificed to ZEUS, who set it in the heavens as a constellation.

Arimanes (a ri ma′ nēz). Another form of AHRIMAN. BYRON introduces him under this name in *Manfred*, seated "on a Globe of Fire, surrounded by the Spirits".

Arimaspians (ăr im ăs′ pi ănz). A one-eyed people of Scythia constantly at war with the GRIFFINS who guarded a hoard of gold. They are mentioned by Lucan (Pharsalia, iii, 280), Herodotus (iii, 116; iv, 13, 27), Pliny,

Strabo etc. Rabelais (IV, lvi, and V, xxix) so names the peoples of northern Europe who had accepted the REFORMATION, the suggestion being that they had lost one eye—that of faith.

> As when a gryphon, through the wilderness
> With winged course, o'er hill or moory dale
> Pursues the Arimaspian, who by stealth
> Had from his wakeful custody purloin'd
> The guarded gold.
>
> MILTON: *Paradise Lost*, II, 943–7.

Arioch (ăr′ i ok). The name means "a fierce lion" and was used for one of the fallen angels in *Paradise Lost* (VI, 371); Milton took it from *Dan*. ii, 14, where it is the name of the captain of the guard.

Arion (a rī′ on). A Greek poet and musician (7th century B.C.) reputed to have been cast into the sea by mariners but carried to Taenaros on a dolphin's back. *See* FAMOUS HORSES *under* HORSE.

Ariosto, Ludovico (ăr i os′ tō) (1474–1533). Italian poet, author of ORLANDO FURIOSO.

Ariosto of the North. So BYRON called Sir Walter Scott (*Childe Harold*, iv, 40).

Aristides (à ris′ ti dēz). Athenian statesman and general, surnamed "the Just" (*c.* 520–*c.* 468 B.C.), who took part in the battles of Marathon and Salamis, and was in command at Platæa.

The British Aristides. Andrew Marvell (1621–1678), poet and satirist.

The French Aristides. Jules Grévy (1807–1891), president of the Third Republic (1879–1887), a barrister by profession.

Aristophanes (ăr is tof′ à nēz) (*c.* 450–*c.* 385 B.C.). The great Athenian comic dramatist.

The English or **modern Aristophanes.** Samuel Foote (1722–1777), author of *The Mayor of Garret*.

The French Aristophanes. MOLIÈRE (Jean Baptiste Poquelin) (1622–1673).

Aristotle (ăr′ is totl) (384–322 B.C.). The great Greek philosopher, pupil of Plato, and founder of the PERIPATETIC SCHOOL.

Aristotelian philosophy (ăr is tot ē′ li àn). Aristotle maintained that four separate causes are necessary before anything exists: the material cause, the formal, the final, and the moving cause. The first is the antecedents from which the thing comes into existence; the second, that which gives it its individuality; the moving or efficient cause is that which causes matter to assume its individual forms; and the final cause is that for which the thing exists. According to Aristotle, matter is eternal.

Aristotelian Unities. *See* DRAMATIC UNITIES.

Arm, Arms. This word, with meaning of the

limb, has given rise to numerous common phrases, such as:

Arm of the sea. A narrow inlet.

Secular arm. Civil as opposed to ecclesiastical jurisdiction.

To chance your arm. *See* CHANCE.

To make a long arm. *See under* LONG.

At arm's length. At a good distance; hence with avoidance of familiarity.

Infant in arms. One too young to walk and so has to be carried.

With open arms. Cordially, as a dear friend is received, with arms open for an embrace.

Arm-shrines. In the MIDDLE AGES bodily relics of saints were often put in metal containers modelled on the shape of the contents. Arm-shrines were normally cylinders of silver ending in the shape of a hand. Head-shrines were called *Chefs*.

The word *arm* is almost always used in the plural nowadays when denoting implements or accoutrements for fighting, etc., and also in heraldic usage. Some common phrases are:

A nation in arms. One in which the people are armed for war.

A passage of arms. A literary controversy; a battle of words.

An assault at arms (or **of arms**). A hand-to-hand military exercise.

Coat of Arms. *See* ARMOUR.

Small arms. Those which do not, like artillery, require carriages.

To appeal to arms. To decide an issue by resorting to the test of war.

To arms. Make ready for battle.

To lay down arms. To cease from armed hostilities; to surrender.

Under arms. Prepared for battle; in battle array.

Up in arms. In open rebellion; figuratively, roused to anger.

King of Arms. *See* HERALDRY.

The right to bear arms. This is based on proven descent, through the male line, from an ancestor entitled to bear certain arms; or by a grant from the College of Arms (Heralds' College) in England and Wales; the NORROY and ULSTER King of Arms in Ulster; and the LYON King of Arms in Scotland. A person having such right is said to be *armigerous*. Actually there is little to prevent individuals from adopting arms without the consent of these authorities. *See* HERALDRY.

In the U.S.A. the right to bear arms means the right of a citizen to have a gun and is still zealously championed by many. It derives from Article II in the BILL OF RIGHTS which reads, "A well-regulated militia being necessary to the security of a free State, the right of the people to keep and bear arms shall not be infringed."

The Royal Arms of England. The systematic use of Royal Arms begins with Richard I, who introduced the three lions passant gardant. In 1340 Edward III styled himself "of Great Britain, France and Ireland, King", and quartered the arms of France with those of England. This title and practice was abandoned in 1801 when the Arms were re-marshalled consequent upon the Union with Ireland. During Mary Tudor's reign the arms of Philip II of Spain were impaled on the existing Arms. James I of England and VI of Scotland introduced the LION rampant of Scotland and the harp of Ireland (derived from the badge assigned to Ireland in the reign of Henry VIII). During the reign of William III and Mary II the arms of Nassau were added, and on the accession of George I the White Horse of Hanover was superimposed until the Hanoverian connection ended with the accession of Victoria in 1837. The lion supporter for England and the UNICORN for Scotland were introduced by James I. The lion statant gardant on the crest was first used by Edward III.

The corrct emblazoning of the arms of the United Kingdom of Great Britain and Northern Ireland is:

Quarterly, first and fourth gules, three lions passant gardant in pale, or, for England; second or, a lion rampant with a double tressure flory-counter-flory gules, for Scotland; third azure, a harp or, stringed argent, for Ireland; all surrounded by the Garter. *Crest.*—Upon the royal helm, the imperial crown proper, thereon a lion statant gardant or, imperial crown proper. *Supporters.*—A lion rampant gardant, or, crowned as the crest. Sinister, a unicorn argent, armed, crined, and unguled proper, gorged with a coronet composed of crosses patée and fleur de lis, a chain affixed thereto passing between the forelegs, and reflexed over the back, also or. *Motto.*—"Dieu et mon Droit" in the compartment below the shield, with the Union rose, shamrock, and thistle engrafted on the same stem.

Armageddon (ar mà ged' ón). The name given in the Apocalypse (*Rev.* xvi, 16) to the site of the last great "battle of that great day of God almighty" between the forces of good and evil. Hence any great battle or scene of slaughter.

Armchair general. A person who thinks he knows how to direct affairs in which he is not taking part. Somewhat similarly one talks of BACK SEAT DRIVER.

Arme Blanche (arm blonsh) (Fr. white arm). Steel weapons—the dagger, lance or spear, sabre, sword and bayonet—in contradistinction to firearms.

Armida (ar mē' da). In Tasso's JERUSALEM DELIVERED a beautiful sorceress, with whom

RINALDO fell in love and wasted his time in voluptuous pleasure. After his escape from her, Armida followed him, but being unable to lure him back, set fire to her palace, rushed into a combat, and was slain.

In 1806 Frederick William III of Prussia declared war on NAPOLEON, and his young queen rode about in military costume to arouse popular enthusiasm. When Napoleon was told of it, he said, "She is Armida, in her distraction setting fire to her own palace."

Arminians. Followers of Jacobus Hermansen or Arminius (1560–1609), anti-Calvinist theologian and professor at Leiden. They asserted that God bestows forgiveness and eternal life on all who repent and believe; that He wills all men to be saved and that His predestination is founded on His foreknowledge. His Dutch followers came to be called "Remonstrants" after their "remonstrance" of 1610 embodying their five points of difference from orthodox Calvinism. In England the name was applied to the supporters of William Laud, Archbishop of Canterbury (1633–1645).

Armistice Day. 11 November, the day set aside to commemorate the fallen in World War I, marked by a two-minute silence at 11 a.m. and religious ceremonies. The armistice ending the war was signed at 11 o'clock on 11 November 1918. In 1946 the name was changed to REMEMBRANCE DAY. In the U.S.A. and Canada 11 November is a legal holiday, its name being changed to *Veterans' Day* in 1954.

Armory. The old name for HERALDRY, the word originally used to describe arms, military equipment and their employment.

> Armory is an Art rightly prescribing the true knowledge and use of Armes.
> *Guillim's Display of Heraldrie* (1610).

Armory, Armoury. The place where armour and arms are kept. It may also mean armour collectively, as in *Paradise Lost*, IV, 553:

> but nigh at hand
> Celestial armoury, shields, helms, and spears,
> Hung high with diamond flaming and with gold.

Armour, Coat, or a **Coat of Arms,** was originally a coat of silk or linen used to cover the Knight's armour from the heat of the sun, or from rust and dirt, and it was colourfully embroidered with the distinguishing device of the wearer.

Arnauts (ar' nawts) (Turk. brave men). Albanian mountaineers.

> Stained with the best of Arnaut's blood.
> BYRON: *The Giaour*.

Arnold of Rugby. Dr. Thomas Arnold (1795–1842), father of the poet Matthew Arnold, and famous headmaster and reformer of Rugby School portrayed as "The Doctor" in *Tom Brown's Schooldays* by Thomas Hughes. His avowed aim in education was "if possible to form Christian men, for Christian boys I can scarcely hope to make."

Aroint thee. Get ye gone, be off. The phrase occurs in Shakespeare's *Macbeth* (I, iii, 6) and *King Lear* (III, iv, 129), on both occasions in connexion with witches. Its origin is unknown. The Brownings made a verb of it, Mrs. Browning in her *To Flush* ("Whiskered cats arointed flee") and Browning in *The Two Poets of Croisic*, and elsewhere.

Arondight (ar' on dīt). The sword of Sir LANCELOT OF THE LAKE.

Arras (ar' ás). Tapestry, so called from Arras in Artois, once famed for its manufacture. When rooms were hung with tapestry it was easy for persons to hide behind it; so Hubert hid the two villains who were to put out Arthur's eyes (Shakespeare, *King John*, IV, i, 2); Polonius was slain by Hamlet while concealed behind the arras (*Hamlet*, III, iv); Falstaff hid behind it in Ford's house (*Merry Wives of Windsor*, III, iii); etc.

Arrière-ban. *See* BAN.

Arrière-pensée. (Fr. behind-thought). A hidden or reserved motive, not apparent on the surface.

Arrow. *See* BROAD ARROW; JONATHAN'S ARROWS.

Art. Art Deco. The decorative style of the 1920s and 1930s in painting, glass, pottery, silverware, furniture, etc. It is distinguished by bold colours, ornateness, geometrical lines and lack of symmetry.

Art Nouveau (ăr noo vō') (Fr.). New art. A decorative art style of the 1890s and early 1900s freely ornamented with leaf-like and organic or natural forms. It is characterized by the use of curves and the absence of geometrical lines.

Art trouvé (ar troo vā') (Fr.). Found art. Not the direct creation of the artist but adapted from "found" or natural objects which have been primarily shaped by circumstances, nature, and the elements. Items found on the seashore are obvious examples of the raw material of *art trouvé*.

Art Union. Originally, in Europe and Great Britain, associations formed to promote art by purchasing paintings, etc., and dispersing them among the membership by lottery. In Australia, after a while, all kinds of prizes were offered and consequently *Art Union* came to be applied to a lottery with money prizes.

Artaxerxes (ár tàks ĕrks' ēz), younger son of XERXES and king of the Persians (465–425

B.C.). His Persian name was Artakhshatra and he was called the long-handed (*Longimanus*) because his right hand was longer than his left. He is mentioned in the BIBLE in connexion with his part in the restoration of Jerusalem after the Captivity (*Ezra* iv, vi, vii, and *Neh.* ii, v, and xiii).

Artegal, or **Arthegal, Sir** (ar' te gàl). The hero of Bk. V of Spenser's *Faerie Queene*, lover of BRITOMART, to whom he was made known by means of a magic mirror. He is emblematic of Justice, and in many of his deeds, such as the rescue of Irena (Ireland) from Grantorto, is mirrored on Arthur, 14th Lord Grey de Wilton, who became lord deputy of Ireland in 1580 with Spenser as his secretary. *See* ELIDURE.

Artemis. *See* DIANA.

Artemus Ward. The name of an imaginary YANKEE showman and writer, the guise adopted by the American humorist, Charles Farrer Browne (1834–1867), for a series of books which became popular in America and England.

Artesian State, The. South Dakota, better known as the *Coyote State*.

Artful Dodger. A young thief, a most perfect adept in villainy, up to every sort of wicked dodge. Such was the character of Jack Dawkins, pupil of Fagin, in Dickens's *Oliver Twist*.

Arthegal. *See* ARTEGAL.

Arthur. As a shadowy "historical" figure is first mentioned under the Latin name Artorius in the late 7th-century *Historia Britonum* (usually known by the name of Nennius, its 9th-century editor). Arthur, as *Dux Bellorum*, not king, is said to have led the Britons against the Saxons in twelve great battles culminating in the great victory of *Mons Badonicus* (fought between 493 and 516). He is mentioned again by William of Malmesbury (early 12th century), but ARTHURIAN ROMANCES owe most to Geoffrey of Monmouth. *See* CAMELOT.

Arthur's Seat. A hill overlooking Edinburgh from the East. The name is a corruption of the GAELIC *Ard-na-said*, the height of the arrows, a convenient shooting ground.

Arthurian Romances. The stories which have King Arthur as their central figure appear as early as 1136 in Geoffrey of Monmouth's mainly fabulous *Historia Regum Britanniæ*, which purported to be a translation (in Latin) of an ancient CELTIC history of Britain, lent to him by Walter Map, Archdeacon of Oxford. Geoffrey's *Historia* was dedicated to Robert, Earl of Gloucester, a natural son of Henry I. This was versified in French in Wace's *Roman de Brut* or *Brut d'Angleterre* (1155), which is the first to mention the ROUND TABLE. These were used by Layamon, the Worcestershire priest, whose BRUT (in English) was completed in about 1205, with additions such as the story of the fairies at Arthur's birth, who transported him to AVALON at his death. In France, in the late 12th century, Robert de Borron introduced the legend of the GRAIL and gave prominence to MERLIN; Chrestien de Troyes brought in the tale of ENID and GERAINT, the tragic loves of LANCELOT and GUINEVERE, the story of PERCEVAL and other material which was probably drawn from Welsh sources including the MABINOGION. Thus Walter Map and the Arthurian writers introduced the romantic spirit of CHIVALRY and courtly manners into European literature and King Arthur became the embodiment of the ideal Christian KNIGHT. Many other Welsh and Breton ballads, lays and romances popularized the legend and the whole corpus was collected and edited by Sir Thomas Malory (d. 1471), whose great prose romance *Le Morte d'Arthur* was produced by Caxton in 1485. Tennyson's *Morte d'Arthur* and *Idylls of the King* (1857–1885) were based upon it. *See* ALMESBURY, ARONDIGHT, ASTOLAT, BALIN, BAN, BEDIVERE, CAMELOT, CAMLAN, DAGONET, DIAMOND JOUSTS, ELAINE, EXCALIBUR, GLASTONBURY, LAUNFAL, LYONESSE, MODRED, MORGAN LE FAY, TRISTRAM, YSOLDE, etc.

Articles of Roup. The conditions of sale at a ROUP, as announced by a crier.

The Six Articles. *See under* SIX.

The Thirty-nine Articles. *See under* THIRTY.

Artists, the Prince of. Albrecht Dürer (1471–1528) of Nuremberg was so called by his countrymen.

Arts, Degrees in. In the mediæval universities the seven liberal arts consisted of the TRIVIUM (grammar, logic and rhetoric), and the QUADRIVIUM (arithmetic, geometry, music and astronomy).

In mediæval England the *Master of Arts* was the person qualified to teach or to be the master of the students in arts; as the *Doctor* was in theology, law, or medicine.

Arundel. *See* HORSE.

Arundelian Marbles. A collection of ancient sculptures made at great expense by Thomas Howard, 14th Earl of Arundel (1585–1646), and presented to Oxford University in 1667 by his grandson Henry, 6th Duke of Norfolk. They include the famous *Marmor Chronicon* or *Parian Chronicle* (said to have been executed in the island of Paros about 263 B.C.) which recorded events in Greek history from 1582 to 264 B.C., although now incomplete and ending at 354 B.C.

Arval Brothers (*Fratres Arvales*). An ancient Roman college of Priests, revived by AUGUSTUS. It consisted of twelve priests (including the Emperor), whose sole duty was to preside at the festival of *Dea Dia* in May. Ceremonies took place in Rome and in the grove of the goddess, who seems to be identical with *Acca Larentia*, goddess of cornfields.

Aryans. A name used for the parent stock of the Indo-European family of nations and popular with 19th-century philologists for the Indo-European languages (also sometimes called Indo-Germanic and JAPHETIC but more accurately Indo-Hittite). They include Sanskrit, Zend, Latin, Greek, Celtic, Persian, Hindu and all the European languages except Basque, Turkish, Hungarian, Finnish and Estonian. The name Aryan means "noble" and was used by early Hindus and Persians, to whose descendants it can be more properly applied. Anti-Semites prostituted the word and it was used by the German NAZIS to denote any people or thing that was not Semite, even the Japanese being classified as Aryans.

Asaph. In the Bible, a famous musician in David's time (I *Chron*, xvi, 5 and xxv, 1, 2). He is supposed to be the founder of the hereditary choir of *b'ne Asaph* in the Second Temple (*Ezra* iii, 10, 11 and *Neh*. vii, 44). *Psalms* 50 and 73–83 are ascribed to Asaph.

Tate lauds Dryden under this name in *Absalom and Achitophel*, Pt. II, 1063.

> While Judah's throne and Sion's rock stand fast,
> The song of Asaph and the fame shall last.

St. Asaph. A 6th-century Welsh saint, Abbot and first Welsh bishop of the see of Llanelwy which came to be called St. Asaph in the 12th century.

Ascalaphus. In Greek mythology, a son of ACHERON who said that PROSERPINE had partaken of a pomegranate when PLUTO had given her permission to return to the upper world if she had eaten nothing. In revenge Proserpine turned him into an owl by sprinkling him with the water of PHLEGETHON.

Ascendant. In casting a HOROSCOPE the point of the ECLIPTIC or degree of the ZODIAC which is nearest the eastern horizon at the time of birth is called the ascendant, and the easternmost star represents the house of life (*see* HOUSES, ASTROLOGICAL; STAR), because it is in the act of ascending. This is a man's strongest star, and when his outlook is bright, we say *his star is in the ascendant*.

The house of the Ascendant, includes five degrees of the ZODIAC above the point just rising, and twenty-five below it. Usually, the point of birth is referred to.

The lord of the ascendant, is any planet within the "house of the Ascendant". The house and lord of the ascendant at birth were said by astrologers to exercise great influence on the future life of the child. Deborah referred to the influence of the stars when she said "the stars in their courses fought against Sisera" (*Judges* v. 20).

Ascension Day, or **Holy Thursday** (*q.v.*). The day set apart by the Christian Churches to commemorate the ascent of Christ from earth to HEAVEN. It is the fortieth day after EASTER. *See* BOUNDS, BEATING THE.

Asclepiads, or **Asclepiadic Metre** (ăs klepī′ ădz). A Greek and Latin verseform, possibly invented by Asclepiades (3rd century B.C.) consisting of a spondee, two (or three) choriambi, and an iambus, usually with a central cæsura, thus:

$$— \; —|— \cup \cup —||— \cup \cup —|\cup —$$

The first ode of HORACE is Asclepiadic. Its first and last two lines have been translated in the same metre:

> Dear friend, patron of song, sprung from the race of kings;
> Thy name ever a grace and a protection brings...
> My name, if to the lyre haply you chance to wed,
> Pride would high as the stars lift my exalted head.
>
> E.C.B.

Ascot, Royal. A very fashionable race meeting held in June at Ascot Heath, Berkshire. Normally attended by the Royal Family, the meeting was instituted by Queen Anne in 1711. *Cp.* CLASSIC RACES.

Ascræan Poet, or **Sage** (ăs krē′ ăn). Hesiod, the Greek didactic poet, born at Ascra in Bœotia. VIRGIL (*Bucolics, Eclogues*, vi, 70) calls him "the Ascræan sage".

Asgard (ăs′ gard) (*As*, a god; *gard*, or *gardh*, an enclosure, garth or yard). The realm of the ÆSIR or the Northern gods, the OLYMPUS of Scandinavian mythology. It is said to be situated in the centre of the universe, and accessible only by the rainbow bridge, BIFROST. It contains many regions, and mansions such as Gladsheim and VALHALLA.

Ash Tree, or **Tree of the Universe.** *See* YGGDRASIL.

Ash Wednesday. The first day of LENT, so called from the Roman Catholic custom of sprinkling on the heads of penitents the consecrated ashes of palms remaining from the previous PALM SUNDAY. The custom is of uncertain date but is commonly held to have been introduced by GREGORY THE GREAT (Pope 590–604).

Ashes. Ashes to ashes, dust to dust. A

phrase from the English burial service, used sometimes to denote total finality. It is founded on scriptural texts such as "dust thou art, and unto dust thou shalt return" (*Gen.* iii, 19), and "I will bring thee to ashes upon the earth in the sight of all them that behold thee" (*Ezek.* xxvii, 18).

> Ashes to ashes and dust to dust,
> If God won't have him the Devil must.

According to Sir Walter Scott (see his edition of Swift's *Journal to Stella*, 25 March 1710–11) this was the form of burial service given by the sexton to the body of the French spy Guiscard, who, in 1711, had attempted the life of Robert Harley.

Dust and Ashes. *See under* DUST.

The Ashes. The mythical prize contended for in the test CRICKET matches between England and Australia. When England was beaten at the Oval in 1882 a humorous epitaph on English cricket appeared in the *Sporting Times*, winding up with the remark that "The body will be cremated and the ashes taken to Australia".

To wear sackcloth and ashes. *See under* SACK.

Ashmolean Museum (ăsh mō′ li ăn). The first public museum in England opened at the University of Oxford in 1683 from a collection presented by Elias Ashmole (1617–1692), the antiquarian, in 1677; also called the Tradescant from John Tradescant, whose coveted collection Ashmole had secured.

Ashtaroth, or **Ashtoreth.** The goddess of fertility and reproduction among the Canaanites and Phœnicians, called by the Babylonians ISHTAR (VENUS) and by the Greeks ASTARTE. She is referred to in I *Sam.* xxi, 10; I *Kings* xi, 5 and II *Kings* xxiii, 13; and she may be the "queen of heaven" mentioned by *Jeremiah* (vii, 18; xliv, 17, 25). Formerly she was supposed to be a moon-goddess, hence Milton's reference in his *Hymn on the Nativity*.

> And moonèd Ashtaroth,
> Heav'ns Queen and Mother both.

Ashur. *See* ASSHUR.

Asir. *See* ÆSIR.

Ask. The dialectal *ax* was common literary form until the late 16th century. The word is from the O.E. *ascian*, which by METATHESIS became *acsian*, and so *axian*.

> How sholde I axen mercy of Tisbe
> When I am he that have yow slain, allas!
> CHAUCER: *Legend of Good Women*, 835.

The Wyclif version of *Matt.* vii, 7–10 begins:

> Axe ye and it schal be gyven to you.

Askance at, To look. To regard obliquely, with suspicion or disapproval. Of uncertain origin but the expression of ill will sometimes used by gypsies "May the Lord look upon you sideways" probably stems from the same root idea.

Asleep at the switch. A failure in alertness of mind or lack of awareness of threatened danger. An American expression derived from the railroads. "To switch a train" is to transfer it to another set of rails by operating a switch. Failure to do this according to schedule might well lead to a catastrophe.

Also a derisive nickname for the American Defense Medal, given to those in the armed forces on Pearl Harbour Day (7 December 1941).

Asmodeus (ăs mō dē′ us, ăs mō′di ùs). The evil demon who appears in the Apocryphal book of TOBIT and is derived from the Persian *Aeshma*. In *Tobit* Asmodeus falls in love with Sara, daughter of Raguel, and causes the death of seven husbands in succession, each on his bridal night. He was finally driven into Egypt through a charm made by Tobias of the heart and liver of a fish burnt on perfumed ashes, as described by Milton in *Paradise Lost* (IV, 167–71). Hence Asmodeus often figures as the spirit of matrimonial jealousy or unhappiness. Le Sage gave the name to the companion of Don Cleofas in his *Le Diable Boiteux* (1707).

Asmodeus flight. Don Cleofas, catching hold of his companion's cloak, is perched on the steeple of St. Salvador. Here the foul fiend stretches out his hand, and the roofs of all the houses open in a moment, to show the Don what is going on privately in each respective dwelling.

> Could the reader take an Asmodeus-flight, and, waving open all roofs and privacies, look down from the roof of Notre Dame, what a Paris were it!
> CARLYLE: *French Revolution* II, vi.

Asoka (ăs′ ō kà). Emperor of India *c*. 274–232 B.C., who was converted to BUDDHISM by a miracle and became its "nursing father", as Constantine was of Christianity.

Aspasia (ă spā′ zi à). A courtesan. The most celebrated of the Greek Hetæræ. She lived at Athens as mistress of Pericles and after his death (429 B.C.) with Lysicles, the democratic leader.

Aspatia (ă spā′ shà), in the *Maid's Tragedy*, of Beaumont and Fletcher, is noted for her deep sorrows, her great resignation, and the pathos of her speeches. Amyntor deserts her, women point at her with scorn, she is the jest and byword of everyone, but she bears it all with patience.

Aspen, or trembling poplar. The aspen leaf is said to tremble, from shame and horror, because our Lord's cross was made of this wood. In fact, owing to the shape of the leaf and its long, flexible leafstalk, it is peculiarly liable to move with the least breath of air.

Asphaltic Lake. The DEAD SEA, where asphalt abounds both on the surface of the water and on the banks.

> There was an Asphaltick and Bituminous nature in that Lake before the fire of Gomorrah.
>
> SIR THOS. BROWNE: *Religio Medici*, i, 19.

Asphodel (ăs′ fō del). A plant genus of the lily family, particularly associated with death and the underworld in Greek legend. It was planted on graves, and the departed lived their phantom life in the *Plain of Asphodel*. The name DAFFODIL is a corruption of asphodel.

Aspidistra. A very hardy member of the lily family, with broad lance-shaped leaves and small inconspicuous flowers borne at soil level. It was a very popular house plant from late Victorian times until the 1920s owing to its ability to survive in heated gas-lit rooms. It has become a symbol of Victorian lower-middle-class philistinism, respectability and stuffiness. George ORWELL wrote a novel called *Keep the Aspidistra Flying*.

Ass. According to tradition the dark stripe running down the back of an ass, crossed by another at the shoulders, was the cross communicated to the creature when Christ rode on the back of an ass in His triumphant entry into Jerusalem.

Ass, deaf to music. This tradition arose from the hideous noise made by "Sir Balaam" in braying. *See* ASS-EARED.

An ass in a lion's skin. A coward who hectors, a fool that apes the wise man. The allusion is to the fable of an ass that put on a lion's skin, but was betrayed by his braying.

An ass with two panniers. A man out walking with a lady on each arm, called in Italy *a pitcher with two handles*, and formerly in London *walking bodkin* (*see* BODKIN). Our expression is from the French *faire le panier à deux anses*.

Ass-eared. MIDAS had the ears of an ass. The tale says APOLLO and PAN had a contest, and chose Midas to decide which was the better musician. Midas gave sentence in favour of Pan; and Apollo, in disgust, changed his ears into those of an ass.

> Avarice is as deaf to the voice of virtue, as the ass to the voice of Apollo.
>
> ARIOSTO: *Orlando Furioso*, xvii.

Golden Ass. *See* GOLDEN.

Sell your ass. Get rid of your foolish ways.

That which thou knowest not perchance thine ass can tell thee. An allusion to BALAAM's ass (*Num.* xxii, 21–33).

The ass waggeth his ears. A proverb applied to those who lack learning, and yet talk as if they were very wise; men wise in their own conceits. The ass, proverbial for having no "taste for music", will nevertheless wag its ears at a "concord of sweet sounds", just as if it could well appreciate it.

Till the ass ascends the ladder—*i.e.* NEVER. A rabbinical expression. The Romans had a similar one, *cum asinus in tegulis ascenderit* (when the ass climbs to the tiles).

Ass's bridge. *See* PONS ASINORUM.

Well, well! honey is not for the ass's mouth. Persuasion will not persuade fools. The gentlest words will not divert the anger of the unreasonable.

Wrangle for an ass's shadow. To contend about trifles. The tale told by Demosthenes is that a man hired an ass to take him to Megara; and at noon, the sun being very hot, the traveller dismounted, and set himself down in the shadow of the ass. Just then the owner came up and claimed the right of sitting in this shady spot, saying that he let out the ass for hire, but there was no bargain made about the ass's shade. The two men then fell to blows to settle the point in dispute. While they were wrangling the ass took to its heels and ran away, leaving them both in the glare of the sun.

Asses as well as pitchers have ears. Children and even the densest minds hear and understand many a word and hint which the speaker supposed would pass unheeded. *Cp.* WALLS HAVE EARS.

Feast of Asses. *See under* FOOL.

Asses that carry the mysteries (*asini portant mysteria*). A classical knock at the Roman clergy. The allusion is to the custom of employing asses to carry the *cista* which contained the sacred symbols, when processions were made through the streets (WARBURTON: *Divine Legation*, ii, 4).

Assassins (à săs′ inz). Killers by treachery and violence. Originally a sect of MOSLEM fanatics founded in Persia, about 1090, by Hassan ben Sabbah (better known as *the Old Man of the* MOUNTAIN), their terrorism was mainly directed against the SELJUK authority. From Persia and Iraq they extended their activities to Syria in the early 12th century. Their power was broken by 1273 through the attacks of the Mongols and the MAMELUKE Sultan Bibars. Their name *hashishin* is derived from their reputed habit of dosing themselves with *hashish* or *bhang* prior to their murderous assaults.

Assay (à sā), or **Essay** (through O.Fr. from Lat. *exagium*, weighing). To try or test metals, coin, etc.; and formerly to taste food or drink before it was offered to a monarch; hence, *to take the assay* is to taste wine to prove it is not poisoned.

The aphetic form of the word, "say", was common until the 17th century. Thus Edmund in *King Lear* (V, iii), says to Edgar, "thy tongue some say of breeding breathes"; *i.e.* thy speech gives indication of good breeding—it savours of it.

Assay as a noun means a test or trial.

> (He) makes vow before his uncle never more
> To give the assay of arms against your majesty.
> SHAKESPEARE: *Hamlet*, II, ii.

For the last 300 years the spelling *essay* (from French) has been used for the noun, except in connexion with the assaying of metals.

Assaye Regiment. *See* REGIMENTAL AND DIVISIONAL NICKNAMES.

Assemblage, Nouns of. Long custom and technical usage have ascribed certain words to assemblages of animals, things, or persons. Some of the principal are:

Animals, birds, etc.

antelopes: a herd.
asses: a pace or herd.
badgers: a cete.
bears: a sloth.
bees: a swarm, a grist.
birds: a flock, flight, congregation, volery.
bitterns: a sedge or siege.
boars: a singular.
bucks: a brace or leash.
cattle: a drove or herd.
chickens: a brood.
choughs: a chattering.
coots: a covert.
cranes: a herd, sedge, or siege.
crows: a murder.
cubs: a litter.
curlews: a herd.
deer: a herd.
doves: a flight.
ducks: (in flight) a team, (on water) a paddling.
elk: a gang.
ferrets: a fesnyng.
fishes: a shoal, draught, haul, run, or catch.
flies: a swarm.
foxes: a skulk.
geese: (in flight) a skein; (on the ground) a gaggle.
gnats: a swarm or cloud.
goats: a herd or tribe.
goldfinches: a charm.
grouse: (a single brood) a covey; (several broods) a pack.
hares: a down or husk.
hawks: a cast.
hens: a brood.
herons: a sedge or siege.
hounds: a pack or mute.
kangaroos: a troop.
kine: a drove.
kittens: a kindle.
larks: an exaltation.
leopards: a leap.
lions: a pride.
mares: a stud.
moles: a labour.

monkeys: a troop.
nightingales: a watch.
oxen: a yoke, drove, team or herd.
partridges: a covey.
peacocks: a muster.
pheasants: a nye or nide.
plovers: a wing or congregation.
porpoises: a school.
pups: a litter.
quails: a bevy.
rabbits: a nest.
rooks: a building or clamour.
seals: a herd or pod.
sheep: a flock.
starlings: a murmuration.
swans: a herd or bevy.
swifts: a flock.
swine: a sounder or drift.
teals: a spring.
whales: a school, gam or pod.
wolves: a pack, rout or herd.
woodcock: a fall.

Things.

aeroplanes: a flight, squadron.
arrows: a sheaf.
bells: a peal.
bowls: a set.
bread: a batch.
cars: a fleet.
cards: a pack, a deck (Am.).
eggs: a clutch.
flowers: a bunch, bouquet or nosegay.
golf-clubs: a set.
grapes: a cluster or bunch.
onions: a rope.
pearls: a rope or string.
rags: a bundle.
sails: a suit.
ships: a fleet, squadron or flotilla.
stars: a cluster or constellation.
steps: a flight.
trees: a clump.

Persons.

actors: a company, cast or troupe.
angels: a host.
baseball: team, a nine.
beaters: a squad.
bishops: a bench.
cricket team: an eleven.
dancers: a troupe.
football: (Association) an eleven or squad; (Rugby) a fifteen or squad.
girls: a bevy.
labourers: a gang.
magistrates: a bench.
minstrels: a troupe.
musicians: a band, an orchestra.
police: a posse.
rowing: an eight, a four, a pair.
runners: a field.
sailors: a crew.
savages: a horde.
servants: a staff.
worshippers: a congregation.

Asshur. Originally the local god of Asshur, the capital of Assyria, he became the chief god of the kingdom. His symbol was the winged sun disc enclosing a male figure wearing a horned cap, often with a bow in his hand. His name was frequently linked with the goddess ISHTAR of Nineveh. *See*

ASHTAROTH.

Assumption, Feast of the. 15 August, celebrated in the ROMAN CATHOLIC CHURCH to commemorate the death of the Virgin MARY and the assumption of her body into HEAVEN when it was reunited to her soul. It can be traced back to the 6th century and in 1950 Pope Pius XII declared that the Corporal Assumption was thenceforth a dogma of the Church.

Assurance. Audacity, self-confidence. "His assurance is quite unbearable". In insurance parlance *assurance* is applied to life policies only.

To make assurance doubly sure. To make security doubly sure or secure.

> But yet I'll make assurance double sure
> And take a bond of fate.
> SHAKESPEARE: *Macbeth*, IV, i.

Astarte (à star' ti). The Greek and Roman name for the supreme goddess of the Phoenicians, ASHTAROTH.

BYRON gave the name to the lady beloved by Manfred in his drama, *Manfred*. It has been suggested that Astarte was drawn from the poet's half-sister, Augusta (Mrs. Leigh).

Astley's. The popular name for an enterprising and much patronized place of entertainment from 1770 to 1862, opened and developed by Philip Astley (1742–1814). After service as a Sergeant-Major in the Dragoons under General Eliott during the SEVEN YEARS WAR, Astley, with his charger Gibraltar, opened a theatre with an unroofed circus at Lambeth in 1770 for equestrian displays. Eventually called the Royal Grove Theatre, it was burnt down in 1794 and rebuilt as the Royal Amphitheatre patronized by the Prince of Wales and the Duke of York, among other notabilities. It grew in repute as a centre for equestrian and circus entertainment under Astley's pioneering management—he was the best horse-tamer of his day. Astley's was destroyed again by fire in 1803 but was re-opened in 1804. Astley was eventually succeeded by his son who died seven years after his father, when the venture passed into other hands. *Cp.* SADLER'S WELLS.

> But many other "cunning tricks" ... have been performed by dogs some few years ago, at Sadler's Wells, and afterwards at Astley's, to the great amusement of the polite spectators.
> STRUTT: *Sports and Pastimes* (1801), Bk. III, Ch. vi, vii.

Astolat (ăs' tō lăt). This town, mentioned in the ARTHURIAN ROMANCES, is generally identified with Guildford, in Surrey.

The Lily Maid of Astolat. ELAINE.

Astoreth. *See* ASHTAROTH.

Astræa (ă s trē' à). Justice, innocence. During the GOLDEN AGE this goddess dwelt on earth, but when sin began to prevail, she reluctantly left it, and was metamorphosed into the constellation VIRGO.

Astral Body. In theosophical parlance, the phantasmal or spiritual appearance of the physical human form, that is existent both before and after the death of the material body, though during life it is not usually separated from it; also the "Kamarupa" or body of desires, which retains a finite life in the astral world after bodily death.

Astral spirits. The spirits animating the stars. According to occultists, each star had its special spirit; and PARACELSUS maintained that every man had his attendant star, which received him at death, and took charge of him until the great resurrection.

Astrea, Incomparable. Mrs. Aphra Behn (1640–1689), playwright and novelist, author of *Oroonoko*, the first English novel written by a woman.

> The stage how loosely does Astrea tread.
> POPE: *Satires*, V, 290.

Hymnes of Astrea in Acrosticke Verse, twenty-six poems written by Sir John Davies (1569–1626), in honour of Elizabeth I, the ACROSTICS being based on the name Elizabeth Regina.

Astrology. The pseudo-science of the ancient and mediæval world, concerned with DIVINATION, etc., based on the stars and heavenly bodies. *Natural Astrology* dealt with the movements and phenomena of the heavenly bodies, time, tides, eclipses, the fixing of EASTER, etc., and was the forerunner of the science of astronomy (*cp.* ALCHEMY); *Judicial Astrology* dealt with what is now known as astrology, the influence of the stars upon human affairs. *See* ASCENDANT; HOUSES, ASTROLOGICAL; HOROSCOPE; MICROCOSM; STAR.

Astronaut (Lat. *astrum*, star; *nauta*, sailor). One who voyages in interstellar space. This word, first used in 1929, gained popular acceptance after the first manned spacecraft flight by Major Yuri Gagarin of the U.S.S.R. in April 1961. He landed safely after orbiting the earth in 89 minutes at altitudes ranging from 110 to 188 miles. *See* COSMONAUT.

Astronomers Royal. (1) Rev. J. Flamsteed, 1675; (2) E. Halley, 1720; (3) Rev. J. Bradley, 1742; (4) Rev. N. Bliss, 1762; (5) Rev. N. Maskelyne, who originated the Nautical ALMANACK, 1765; (6) J. Pond, 1811; (7) Sir J. B. Airy, 1835; (8) Sir W. H. M. Christie, 1881; (9) Sir F. W. Dyson, 1910; (10) Sir H. S. Jones, 1933; (11) Sir Richard Wool-ley, 1955; (12) Sir Martin Ryle, 1972; (13) Professor Graham Smith, 1982.

Astrophel (ăs' trō fel). Sir Philip Sidney (1554–1586). "Phil. Sid." being a contraction of *Philos Sidus*, and the Latin *sidus* being changed to the Greek *astron*, we get *astron-philos* (star-lover), the "star" being Penelope Devereux, whom he called Stella in his collection of sonnets known as *Astrophel and Stella*. Spenser wrote a pastoral called *Astrophel* to the memory of his friend and patron, who fell at Zutphen.

Asur (ăs' ŭr). *See* ASSHUR.

Asurbanipal. *See* SARDANAPALUS.

Asynja (ăs in' yà). The goddesses of ASGARD; the feminine counterparts of the ÆSIR.

At Home. *See* HOME.

Atalanta's Race (ăt à lăn' tà). In Greek myth the daughter of Iasus or of Schoenus. She took part in the hunt of the Calydonian BOAR and, being very swift of foot, refused to marry unless the suitor should first defeat her in a race. Milanion (or HIPPOMENES) overcame her by dropping at intervals during the race three golden apples, the gift of VENUS. Atalanta stopped to pick them up, lost the race and became his wife.

Atargatis (ăt ar găt' is). The "Syrian Goddess", the "fish goddess". A fertility goddess represented at Ascalon as half woman, half fish.

Atatürk. Father of the Turks. A surname adopted in 1934 by Mustapha Kemal (1881–1938), the maker of modern Turkey, when all Turks were made to assume surnames. In World War I he held the Dardanelles and subsequently ruthlessly set out to westernize the republic he had established in 1923. European dress was imposed, polygamy abolished, women enfranchised, and the Latin script replaced the Arabic.

Ate (ā' tē). In Greek mythology, the goddess of vengeance and mischief; she was cast down to earth by ZEUS.

> With Ate by his side come hot from hell...
> Cry "Havoc" and let slip the dogs of war.
> SHAKESPEARE: *Julius Cæsar*, III, i.

In Spenser's *Faerie Queene* (IV, i, iv, ix, etc.), the name is given to a lying and slanderous hag, the companion of DUESSA.

Atellane, or **Atellan Farces** (ă tè la' nē). Coarse improvised interludes in the Roman theatres introduced from Atella, in Campania. The characters of Macchus and Bucco are the forerunners of our PUNCH and CLOWN.

Athanasian Creed (ăth à nā' shàn). One of the three creeds accepted by the Roman and Anglican churches; so called because it embodies the opinions of Athanasius (*c.*

298–373) respecting the TRINITY. It is of unknown authorship. *See* APOSTLES' CREED; NICENE CREED.

Atheists. During World War II Father W. T. Cummings, an American army chaplain in Bataan, in a sermon used the phrase "there are no atheists in foxholes", meaning that no one can deny the existence of God in the face of imminent death.

Atheling (O.E. *æthel*, noble). In Anglo-Saxon England a title of distinction to those of noble family but subsequently restricted to royal princes or the heirs apparent. The island of Athelney, a marsh near Taunton, means *royal* or *princes'* island and it is where King Alfred took refuge from the Danes (878–879) and is supposed to have burnt the cakes.

Athena. *See* ATHENE.

Athenæum (ăth è nē' ŭm). (1) A temple in Athens which became a meeting place of learned men. (2) A famous academy in Rome founded by Hadrian *c.* 135 A.D. The name is still used for literary and scientific institutions.

The Athenæum Club in PALL MALL was founded in 1824; the literary review called *The Athenæum* was founded by James Silk Buckingham in 1828 and was incorporated with *The Nation* in 1921, which merged with the *New Statesman* in 1931.

Athene, or **Pallas Athene** (à thē' nē). The patron goddess of ATHENS and patroness of arts and crafts; the goddess of wisdom and subsequently identified with MINERVA by the Romans.

Athens. When ATHENE and POSEIDON disputed for the honour of being the city's patron, the goddess of wisdom produced an olive branch, the symbol of peace and prosperity, and the sea-god created a horse, symbolic of war. The gods deemed the olive the better boon, and the city was called Athens.

Athens of Ireland. Belfast.

Athens of the New World. Boston.

Athens of the West. Cordoba, in Spain, was so called in the MIDDLE AGES.

The Modern Athens. Edinburgh.

Athenian Bee. PLATO (*c.* 429–347 B.C.), a native of ATHENS, was so called from the tradition that a swarm of bees alighted on his mouth when he was in his cradle, consequently his words flowed with the sweetness of honey. The same tale is told of St. AMBROSE, and others. *See* BEE. Xenophon (*c.* 430–*c.* 354 B.C.) was also called "the Athenian Bee" or "Bee of Athens". *See* ATTIC BEE.

Athole Brose (Scots). A compound of oatmeal, honey and whisky.

Charm'd with a drink which Highlanders compose,
A German traveller exclaim'd with glee,—
Potztausend! sare, if dis is Athol Brose,
How goot dere Athol Boetry must be!

THOMAS HOOD.

Atkins. *See* TOMMY ATKINS.

Atlantean Shoulders. Shoulders able to bear
a great weight, like those of ATLAS.

Sage he stood,
With Atlantean shoulders fit to bear
The weight of mightiest monarchies.

MILTON: *Paradise Lost*, II, 305–7.

Atlantes (ăt lăn' tēz). Figures of men, used in
architecture as pillars. So called from
ATLAS. Female figures are called CARYA-
TIDES. *See also* TELAMONES.

Atlantic Charter. During World War II, President Roosevelt and Winston Churchill met
at sea (14 August 1941) and made this
eight-point declaration of the principles on
which peace was to be based, consequent
upon Allied victory. It can be compared
with President Wilson's FOURTEEN POINTS.

Atlantic Ocean, is named after the Atlas
mountains or the mythical ATLANTIS.

Atlantic Wall. The name given by the Germans in World War II to their defences
along the Atlantic coast of Europe built to
resist invasion.

Atlantis. According to ancient myth, an extensive island in the Atlantic Ocean, mentioned by PLATO in the *Timaeus* and *Critias*.
It was said to have been a powerful kingdom
before it was overwhelmed by the sea. The
story was brought from Egypt by Solon. In
the 16th century it was suggested that America was Atlantis and there have been a number of other implausible identifications.
More recently, and more likely, the work of
archaeologists and scientists has placed it in
the Eastern Mediterranean. The centre of
the former island of Stronghyle (Santorin)
collapsed after catastrophic volcanic action
and was submerged (*c.* 1500 B.C.). The civilization of the island was Minoan and the
Minoan Empire suffered overwhelming disaster at this time. The general conclusion
equates Atlantis with Stronghyle-Santorin
and Minoan Crete. *Cp.* LEMURIA; LYONESSE.

The New Atlantis. An allegorical romance
by Francis Bacon (written in 1624) in which
he describes an imaginary island where was
established a philosophical commonwealth
bent on the cultivation of the natural sciences. *See* UTOPIA; CITY OF THE SUN.

Mrs. Manley, in 1709, published under
the same title a scandalous chronicle, in
which the names of contemporaries are so
thinly disguised as to be readily recognized.

Atlas. In Greek mythology, one of the TITANS,
condemned by ZEUS for his part in the war of
the Titans to uphold the heavens on his
shoulders. His abode became the Atlas
mountains in Africa, which accorded with
the legend that they supported the heavens.

A book of maps is so called because the
figure of Atlas with the world on his back
was put on the title page by Rumold Mercator when he published his father's maps in
1595. In the paper trade Atlas was a standard size of drawing paper, 26 × 34 in.

Atli. *See* ETZEL.

Atman. In Buddhist philosophy the noume-
non of one's own self. Not the EGO, but the
Ego divested of all that is objective; the
"spark of heavenly flame". In the UP-
ANISHADS the Atman is regarded as the sole
reality.

Atomic theory. From the 5th century B.C.
atomic theories were held by Greek philosophers, notably EMPEDOCLES, Leucippus,
DEMOCRITUS, and EPICURUS. Matter was
said to consist of minute, indivisible, and indestructible particles. Modern atomic theory largely begins with John Dalton
(1766–1844) who first wrote on the subject
in 1803. His hypotheses still remain of real
value in chemistry and to a lesser extent in
physics; but the indivisibility of the atom
was disproved and fresh concepts of the
structure of atoms resulted from the discovery of the electron and the nucleus. *See also*
CORPUSCULAR PHILOSOPHY.

Atomy. *See* ANATOMY.

Atonement (at-one-ment). Reconciliation,
expiation, making amends. In Christian
usage the *Atonement* denotes the reconciliation of God and man through the life, sufferings and crucifixion of Jesus Christ. It
presupposes man's alienation from God
through sin.

Day of Atonement or **Yom kippur** (Heb.
yom, day; *kippur*, atonement). The great
Jewish fast day held on the tenth day of *Tishri*, the seventh month (Sept.–Oct.). The
day is one of prayer, confession and repentance and the closing service of this most
sacred day ends with the sounding of the
SHOFAR. The ceremonies are described in
Leviticus, xvi.

And this shall be a statute for ever unto you: that in
the seventh month, on the tenth day of the month ye
shall afflict your souls, and do no work at all,
whether it be one of your own country, or a stranger
than sojourneth among you.

Leviticus, xvi, 29.

Atossa. Sarah, Duchess of Marlborough
(1660–1744), is said to be intended by Pope
(*Moral Essays*, ii). Her friend, Lady Mary
Wortley Montagu, is called SAPPHO. Somewhat convincingly the Duchess of Bucking-

58

ham has also been suggested for Atossa.

Atropos (ăt′ rō pos). In Greek mythology the eldest of the Three FATES, and the one who severs the thread of life.

Attaboy. An exclamation of enthusiastic approval or encouragement, originating in America and widely used in the 1930s by young people in the English-speaking countries of the British Commonwealth.

Attic. Of ATHENS or Attica.

The Attic Bee. Sophocles (*c.* 496–406 B.C.), the Athenian tragic poet, so called from the sweetness of his compositions. *See also* ATHENIAN BEE.

The Attic Bird. The NIGHTINGALE; so called because Philomel was the daughter of the King of Athens, or because of the abundance of nightingales in Attica.

> Where the Attic bird
> Trills her thick-warbled notes the summer long.
> MILTON: *Paradise Regained*, IV, 245.

The Attic Boy. Cephalos, beloved by AURORA or Morn; passionately fond of hunting.

> Till civil-suited Morn appeer,
> Not trickt and frounc't as she was wont,
> With the Attick Boy to hunt,
> But chercheft in a comly Cloud.
> MILTON: *Il Penseroso*.

Attic faith. Inviolable faith, the very opposite of PUNIC FAITH.

The Attic Muse. Xenophon (*c.* 430–*c.* 354 B.C.), the historian, a native of Athens; so called because the style of his composition is a model of elegance. *See* ATHENIAN BEE.

Attic salt. Elegant and delicate wit. Salt, both in Latin and Greek, was a common term for wit, or sparkling thought well expressed, thus CICERO says, *Scipio omnes sale superabat* (Scipio surpassed all in wit). The Athenians were noted for their wit and elegant turns of thought.

Atticus (ăt′ i kus). An elegant Roman scholar and master of Greek, publisher, and patron of the arts (109–32 B.C.). His taste and judgment were so highly thought of that even CICERO submitted several of his treatises to him.

The Christian Atticus. Reginald Heber (1783–1826), Bishop of Calcutta, a great hymn writer.

The English Atticus. Joseph Addison (1672–1719), so called by Pope (*Prologue to Satires*), on account of his refined taste and philosophical mind.

The Irish Atticus. George Faulkner (1700–1775), bookseller, publisher, and friend of Swift; so called by Lord Chesterfield when Lord Lieutenant of Ireland.

Attila. *See* ETZEL.

Attis. *See* ATYS.

Attorney (a tĕr′ ni) (Fr. *atourner*, to attorn or turn over to another). One who acts for another in business and especially legal matters. Solicitors practised in the courts of equity and attorneys in the courts of common law until the Judicature Act of 1873 declared "all persons admitted as solicitors, attorneys, or proctors … shall be called Solicitors of the Supreme Court". In the U.S.A. an attorney-at-law possesses the functions of both BARRISTER and solicitor.

Power of Attorney. Legal authority given to another to collect rents, pay wages, etc. or to act in matters stated in the legal instrument of **Warrant of Attorney,** according to his own judgment. In such cases *quod aliquis facit per aliquem, facit per se*.

The Attorney-General is the chief law officer of the Crown, chief legal adviser to the government and head of the BAR. Since the Revolution of 1688 the Attorney-General has sat in the HOUSE OF COMMONS.

In the U.S.A. the Attorney-General is the chief law officer of the Federal Government and his office dates from 1789. First giving legal advice to the government and conducting government cases in the Supreme Court, he became head of the new Department of Justice in 1870 with control over federal district attorneys and marshals. Many of his duties are now administrative. He is also a member of the CABINET. There is also a law officer in each state usually designated the attorney-general.

Atys (ā′ tis). A youth beloved by AGDISTIS (Cybele). Driven mad by her jealousy he castrated himself with a sharp stone. According to Ovid's *Metamorphoses* Cybele changed him into a pine tree as he was about to commit suicide.

Au courant (ō koo′ ron) (Fr.), "acquainted with" (literally, in the current of events). To keep one *au courant* of everything is to keep one informed of passing events.

Au fait (Fr.). Skilful, a thorough master of, conversant with.

Au pair (Fr.). An arrangement by which foreigners who wish to learn the language or study the way of life of another country offer their services as domestic help in return for board and lodging, and usually a small payment as well.

Au pied de la lettre (Fr.). *Litteratim et verbatim*; according to the strict letter of the text.

> Arthur is but a boy, and a wild and enthusiastic young fellow, whose opinions one must not take *au pied de la lettre*.
> THACKERAY: *Pendennis*, ch. xi.

Au revoir (Fr.). "Good-bye for the present". Literally, *till seeing you again*.

Aubaine. *See* DROIT D'AUBAINE.

Aubry's Dog. *See* DOG.

Auburn. The hamlet described by Goldsmith in *The Deserted Village*, said to be Lissoy, County Westmeath, Ireland.

Audit Ale. A strong ALE which was brewed at some of the Oxford and Cambridge colleges and originally broached on audit day when college accounts had to be paid up by the students. Whether this was intended as a consolation to the students or a mild form of celebration by the college authorities is uncertain.

Audley. We will John Audley it. A theatrical phrase meaning to abridge, or bring to a conclusion, a play in progress. It is said that an 18th-century travelling showman named Shuter used to lengthen out his performance until sufficient newcomers were waiting for the next house. An assistant would then call out, "Is John Audley here?" and the play was ended as soon as possible.

Audrey. In Shakespeare's *As You Like It*, an awkward country wench who jilted William for Touchstone. *See also* TAWDRY.

Auf Wiedersehen (ouf vē' der zān). The precise German equivalent of the French AU REVOIR.

Augean Stables (aw jē' àn). The stables of Augeas, the mythological King of Elis, in Greece, which housed his great herd of oxen. They were never cleaned and it was one of the labours of HERCULES to cleanse them, which he did by diverting the course of a river through them. Hence *to cleanse the Augean stables* means to clear away an accumulated mass of rubbish or corruption, physical, moral, religious or legal.

Augsburg Confession. The historical confession of faith compiled with MELANCHTHON in consultation with Luther and presented to Charles V at the Diet of Augsburg in 1530.

Augury (aw' gū ri) (etymology uncertain), means properly the function of an augur, a Roman religious official. The duty of members of the college of Augurs was to pronounce, by the observation of signs called AUSPICES, whether the gods favoured or disfavoured a proposed course of action, and they were consulted before any important public action. *See* DIVINATION; INAUGURATE; OMENS; SINISTER.

August. Formerly called *sextilis* in the Roman calendar, the sixth month from MARCH (when the year began). It was changed to *Augustus* in 8 B.C. in honour of AUGUSTUS (63 B.C.–A.D. 14), the first Roman Emperor, whose "lucky month" it was. *Cp.* JULY. It was the month in which he began his first consulship, celebrated three TRIUMPHS, received the allegiance of the legions on the Janiculum, reduced Egypt, and ended the civil wars.

The old Dutch name for August was *Oostmaand* (harvest month); the old Saxon *Weodmonath* (weed-month, weed meaning vegetation in general); the French Republicans called it THERMIDOR (hot month, 19 July to 17 August).

Augusta. A name given to many Roman provincial towns. London was called *Augusta Trinobantia*.

Augustan Age. The GOLDEN AGE of Latin literature, so called from the Emperor AUGUSTUS, in whose reign (27 B.C.–A.D. 14) HORACE, Ovid, VIRGIL, Livy, Propertius, Tibullus, etc., flourished.

Augustan Age of English Literature. The period of the classical writers of the time of Queen Anne and George I, or to interpret it more widely, from Dryden to Johnson.

Augustan Age of French Literature. The period of Corneille (1606–1684), MOLIÈRE (1622–1673), and Racine (1639–1699).

Augustan History. A series of biographies of the Roman Emperors from Hadrian to Carinus (A.D. 117–284), purporting to be the work of six authors, but possibly written as propaganda during the reign of JULIAN THE APOSTATE (361–363).

Augustine, St. (354–430). Bishop of Hippo, DOCTOR OF THE CHURCH, and the greatest of the Latin fathers. He was baptized in 387 after an earlier life of self-indulgence and in due course (396) became Bishop of Hippo in N. Africa. Distinguished by his zealous opposition to the heresies of his time and by his prolific writings, his best-known works are his *Confessions* and *De Civitate Dei* (The City of God).

Augustine of Canterbury, St. (d. 604). APOSTLE of the English and first Archbishop of Canterbury. He was sent from ROME by POPE Gregory the Great with a band of 40 monks to convert the English. They first landed on the Isle of Thanet, gained the support of King Aethelbert of Kent and established themselves at Canterbury in 597 when Aethelbert was baptized. Differences with the older British Church became apparent before Augustine's death.

Augustine, The Second. THOMAS AQUINAS, the ANGELIC DOCTOR.

Augustinian Canons. Regular CANONS who adopted the Rule of St. Augustine in the 11th century. Also called **Austin Canons,** their first house in England was established at Colchester between 1093 and 1099. They took religious vows like the monks but made clerical and parochial duties their predominant obligation.

Augustinian, or **Austin Friars,** also called **Augustinian Hermits** from whom they were formed (1243–1256). The fourth of the MENDICANT ORDERS, they first came to England in 1248.

Augustus. A title, meaning venerable, bestowed upon Gaius Julius Cæsar Octavianus, the first Roman Emperor, in 27 B.C., and borne by his successors. In the reign of Diocletian (284–305) the two emperors, of the East and the West, were called *Augustus*, each with his *Cæsar* or colleague.

Augustus was the name given to Philip II of France (1165–1223) and to Sigismund II of Poland (1520–1527), both of whom were born in August.

Auld Hornie. After the establishment of Christianity, the heathen deities were degraded by the Church into fallen angels; and PAN, with his horns, crooked nose, goat's beard, pointed ears, and goat's feet, was transformed to his Satanic majesty, and called Old Horny.

> O thou, whatever title suit thee,
> Auld Hornie, Satan, Nick, or Clootie.
> BURNS.

The Auld Kirk. The CHURCH OF SCOTLAND.
Auld Lang Syne. Old long since — the days of long ago. Words immortalized in the famous 18th-century Scottish ballad by Robert Burns, still frequently sung at the end of social gatherings and dances, particularly in the CHRISTMAS season.

> Should auld acquaintance be forgot,
> And never brought to min'?
> Should auld acquaintance be forgot,
> And days o' lang syne?

Auld Reekie. Edinburgh old town; so called because it generally appeared to be capped by cloud of "reek" or smoke.

Aulis (aw' lis). The port in BŒOTIA where the Greek fleet assembled before sailing against TROY. Becalmed by the intervention of ARTEMIS, because AGAMEMNON had killed a stag sacred to her, she was propitiated by the sacrifice of his daughter IPHIGENIA. This is the subject of Gluck's opera *Iphigénie en Aulide* (1774), based upon Racine's *Iphigénie* (1675).

Aums-ace. See AMBS-ACE.

Aunt Sally. A game in which sticks or cudgels are thrown at a wooden (woman's) head mounted on a pole, the object being to hit the nose of the figure, or break the pipe stuck in its mouth. The word *aunt* was anciently applied to any old woman. An Aunt Sally as a popular expression is applied to one who is an object of ridicule or a target of abuse.

Aureole (Fr. through Latin *aura*, air). A luminous radiance surrounding the whole figure in paintings of the Saviour and sometimes of the SAINTS. Du Cange (1610–1688) informs us that the aureole of nuns is white, of martyrs red, and of doctors green. *See* HALO; NIMBUS; VESICA PISCIS.

Auri sacra fames (aw' ri săk' rà fā' mēz). A Latin tag from the ÆNEID (III, 57), meaning "the cursed hunger for wealth", which almost amounts to monomania.

Aurignacian (aw rig nā' shàn). An upper PALÆOLITHIC culture characterized by the very extensive use of flint scrapers, blade flakes, and bone tools, probably originating in Palestine. It is the period of CRO-MAGNON man, notable for his cave paintings like those of Altamira in Spain.

Aurora (aw rôr' à). Early morning. According to Greek mythology, the dawn-goddess Eos (Lat. *Aurora*) called by HOMER "rosy-fingered", sets out before the sun to proclaim the coming of day.

Aurora's tears. The morning dew.

Aurora borealis. Bands of light usually seen in high latitudes, hence the name *Northern Lights*. (*See* MERRY DANCERS; DERWENTWATER.) The similar phenomenon in the southern hemisphere is called *Aurora Australis*. Both are forms of *Aurora Polaris* and the lights are probably due to electrically charged solar particles.

Ausone, Château (aw sōn'). A very fine claret, so called because the vineyard is reputed to be on the site of a villa at Lucaniacum (St. Émilion), built by the 4th-century Latin poet Ausonius.

Ausonia (aw sō' ni à). An ancient name of Italy; so called from Auson, son of ULYSSES, and father of the Ausones.

Auspices (aw' spi sēz) (Lat. *avis*, a bird; *specere*, to observe). In ancient ROME the name for the interpreters of signs from birds, animals, and other phenomena, who were later called augurs.

AUGURY depended on the observation and interpretation of signs which were known as auspices. Only the chief in command was allowed to take the auspices of war, thus if a subordinate gained a victory he won it "under the good auspices" of his superior. *Cp.* DIVINATION.

Aussie (aw' si, os' i). A familiar name given to Australian soldiers during and after World War I. Their own colloquial term was "DIGGER".

Auster (Gr. *austeros*, hot, dry). A wind pernicious to flowers and health. In Italy one of

61

the south winds was so called; its modern name is the *Sirocco*. In England it is a damp wind, generally bringing wet weather.

Australia. The States of Australia have their own familiar names:

South Australia, the Wheat State.
Queensland, Bananaland.
Victoria, the Cabbage Patch.
New South Wales, Ma State.
Northern Territory, The Top End, Land of the White Ant.
Western Australia, Westralia, Groperland.

Among the cities, Perth is called The Swan City; Adelaide, the City of the Churches; Melbourne, City of the Cabbage Garden.

Australia Day. 26 January, commemorating the first landing at Sydney Cove in 1788. The Monday following is a nationwide holiday since the establishment of the Commonwealth of Australia in 1901. It began in New South Wales in 1818 and was originally called *Foundation* or *Commemoration* Day.

Australian Capital Territory. The name given to an area in New South Wales, of just over 900 square miles, which is Federal territory, containing Canberra, the Federal capital and seat of government.

Austrian Lip. A characteristic of the royal family of HABSBURGS, one of the most famous cases of hereditary physical deformity, said to have been derived through marriage with a daughter of the Polish princely house of Jagellon. Motley (*The Rise of the Dutch Republic*) describing the Emperor Charles V, at the age of fifty-five, says, "the lower jaw protruding so far beyond the upper, that it was impossible for him to bring together the few fragments of teeth which still remained, or to speak a whole sentence in an intelligible voice." Of Philip II of Spain, he says "he had the same heavy, hanging lip, with a vast mouth, and monstrously protruding lower jaw." Macaulay (*History of England*) says of Charles II, the last of the Spanish Habsburgs, "the malformation of the jaw, characteristic of his family, was so serious that he could not masticate his food."

Aut Cæsar aut nullus (awt sē′ sàr-awt nŭl′ us) (Lat. either Cæsar or a nobody). Everything or nothing; all or not at all. CÆSAR used to say, "he would sooner be first in a village than second at Rome". The phrase was used as a motto by Pope Alexander VI's natural son, Cesare Borgia (1476–1507).

Authentic Doctor. A title bestowed on the scholastic philosopher, Gregory of Rimini (d. 1358).

Authorized Version, The. *See* BIBLE, THE ENGLISH.

Auto da fe (aw′ tō da fā) (Port. an act of faith). The ceremonial procedure of the Spanish INQUISITION when sentences against heretics were read. Persistent HERETICS were subsequently delivered to the secular ARM for punishment. The reason why their victims were *burnt* was because inquisitors were forbidden to "shed blood"; a tergiversation based on the axiom of the ROMAN CATHOLIC CHURCH, *Ecclesia non novit sanguinem* (The Church is untainted with blood).

Autocrat of the Breakfast Table. A name given to Oliver Wendell Holmes (1809–1894), who wrote a seres of essays under this title first published in the *Atlantic Monthly* in 1857.

Autolycus (aw tol′ i kùs). In Greek mythology, son of MERCURY, and the craftiest of thieves. He stole his neighbours' flocks and altered their marks; but SISYPHUS outwitted him by marking his sheep under their feet. Delighted with this device, Autolycus became friends with Sisyphus. Shakespeare uses his name for a rascally pedlar in *The Winter's Tale* (IV, ii).

My father named me Autolycus; who being, as I am, littered under Mercury, was likewise a snapper-up of unconsidered trifles.

Automedon (aw tom′ ė don). A coachman. He was the charioteer of ACHILLES.

Auto State, The. An alternative nickname to "the Wolverine State" for Michigan, in which Detroit is situated, and where Ford automobiles were originally made.

Autumn. The third season of the year, in the Northern Hemisphere AUGUST or SEPTEMBER, OCTOBER and NOVEMBER; astronomically 22/23 September to 21/22 DECEMBER. Figuratively a season of maturity or decay as in Shelley's *Alastor* (248):

And now his limbs were lean; his scattered hair, Sered by the autumn of strange suffering, Sung dirges in the wind.

Avalon (ăv′ á lon). Called *Avilion* in Tennyson's *Morte d'Arthur*, a CELTIC word meaning the "island of apples", and in Celtic mythology the *Island of Blessed Souls*. In the ARTHURIAN ROMANCES it is the abode and burial place of ARTHUR, who was carried thither by MORGAN LE FAY. Its identification with GLASTONBURY is due to etymological error. OGIER THE DANE and OBERON also held their courts at Avalon.

Avant-garde (ă′ von gard) (Fr.). The advanced guard of an army, usually nowadays shortened to *vanguard*. The term is also applied to ultra-modern and experimental young artists and writers.

Avars. *See* BANAT.

Avatar (Sans. *avatara*, descent; hence incarnation of a god). In Hindu mythology the advent to earth of a deity in a visible form. The ten avatars of VISHNU are the most celebrated. He appeared as (1) the fish (Matsya); (2) the tortoise (Kurma); (3) the boar (Varaha); (4) half-man, half-lion (Nrisinha); (5) the dwarf (Vamana); (6) RAMA with the Axe (Parasurama); (7) again as Rama (Ramachandra); (8) KRISHNA; (9) BUDDHA; the tenth advent is to occur at the end of the four ages and will be in the form of a white horse with wings (Kalki), to destroy the earth.

The word is used metaphorically to denote a manifestation or embodiment of some idea or phrase:

> I would take the last years of Queen Anne's reign as the zenith, or palmy state of Whiggism, in its divinist avatar of common sense.
>
> COLERIDGE: *Table-talk*.

Ave (ā′ vi, a′vā). Latin for "Hail!"

Ave atque vale. *See* VALE.

Ave Maria (Lat. Hail, Mary!). The first two words of the Latin prayer to the Virgin MARY used in the ROMAN CATHOLIC CHURCH. (*See Luke* i, 28.) The phrase is applied to the smaller beads of a ROSARY, the larger ones being termed PATERNOSTERS.

Avenger of Blood, The. The man who, in the Jewish polity, had the right of taking vengeance on him who had slain one of his kinsmen (*Josh.* xx, 5, etc.). The Avenger in Hebrew is called GOEL.

Cities of refuge were appointed for the protection of homicides, and of those who had caused another's death by accident (*Num.* xxxv, 12). The KORAN sanctions the Jewish custom.

Avernus (à věr′ nùs) (Gr. *a-ornis*, without a bird). A lake in CAMPANIA, so called from the belief that its sulphurous and mephitic vapours caused any bird that attempted to fly over it to fall into its waters. Latin mythology made it the entrance to Hell; hence VIRGIL'S lines:

> Facilis descensus Averno;
> Noctes atque dies patet atri janua Ditis;
> Sed revocare gradum, superas que evadere ad
> auras,
> Hoc opus, hic labor est.
>
> *Æneid*, vi, 126.

Rendered in Dryden's *Virgil* as:

> Smooth the descent and easy is the way
> (The Gates of Hell stand open night and day);
> But to return and view the cheerful skies,
> In this the task and mighty labour lies.

Avesta (à ves′ tà). The sacred writings of ZOROASTER, sometimes called ZENDAVESTA. The present fragment is from the Avesta compiled under the SASSANIDES, using earlier sources from the time of Zoroaster onwards and adding to them. It essentially comprises (1) the Yasna, the chief liturgical portion including the *Gathas*, or hymns; (2) the Vispered, another liturgical work; (3) the Vendidad, which like the Christian PENTATEUCH, contains the laws; (4) the Yashts, dealing with stories of the different gods, etc.; (5) the Khordah Avesta (Little Avesta), containing short prayers.

Avianus (ăv i ā′ nùs). A Roman fabulist whose work was a popular mediæval schoolbook. His material is largely based on BABRIUS.

Avicenna (Abu Ibn Sina) (980–1037). A great Moslem PHILOSOPHER, mathematician, astronomer and physician. About 100 treatises are attributed to him and his *Canon of Medicine* remained a standard text-book into the 17th century. He wrote mostly in Arabic although his native language was Persian.

Avignon Popes (ă vē′ nyon). In 1309 Pope Clement V (1305–1314), a Gascon, under pressure from Philip the Fair of France, transferred the papal court to Avignon, where it remained until 1377. This BABYLONIAN CAPTIVITY weakened the papacy and led to the GREAT SCHISM.

Other Avignon popes were:

John XXII	1316–34	Innocent VI	1352–62
Benedict XII	1334–42	Urban V	1362–70
Clement VI	1342–52	Gregory XI	1370–78

A vinculo matrimonii (ā vin′ kū lō măt ri-mō′ nĭī) (Lat.). A total divorce from the marriage bond. A divorce *a mensa et thoro* (*i.e.* from table and bed), equivalent to a modern decree of judicial separation, was formerly granted by the Church courts until the Matrimonial Causes Act of 1857 transferred this jurisdiction to the King's Court.

Avoid Extremes. A traditional wise saw of Pittacus of Mitylene (*c.* 650–570 B.C.).

Awar. One of the sons of EBLIS.

Awkward Squad. Military recruits not yet trained to take their place in the ranks. "Squad" is a contraction of "squadron". One who is unaccommodating and difficult is often said to be "one of the awkward squad".

Axe. *Cp.* ASK.

He has an axe to grind. Some selfish motive in the background; some personal interest to answer. Benjamin Franklin tells of a man who wanted to grind his axe, but had no time to turn the grindstone. Going to the yard where he saw young Franklin, he asked the boy to show him how the machine worked, kept praising him till his axe was ground, and then laughed at him for his pains.

To hang up one's axe. To retire from business, to give over a useless project. The allusion is to the battle-axe, formerly devoted to the gods and hung up when fighting was over.

To put the axe on the helve. To solve a problem, "hit the nail on the HEAD".

To send the axe after the helve. To spend more money in the hope of recovering bad debts.

Geddes axe. The drastic cuts in public expenditure, especially on the army, navy, and education, recommended by the Geddes Committee in 1922.

Axinomancy (ăks' in ō măn si). DIVINATION by the axe, practised by the ancient Greeks with a view to discovering crime. An agate or piece of jet was placed on a red-hot axe which indicated the guilty person by its motion.

Axis. The alliance of the FASCIST states of Germany and Italy (October 1936), described by Mussolini an "an axis round which all European states animated by the will to collaboration and peace can also assemble". It became the Rome–Berlin–Tokyo axis in 1937.

Axle grease. Money; an Australian colloquial expression. Money makes life run more smoothly, as axle grease helps the running of a wagon.

Ayesha, or **A'isha** (ī yesh' a). Favourite wife of MOHAMMED, daughter of ABOU BEKR. He married her when she was only a child, soon after the HEGIRA, and ultimately died in her arms. Sir Henry Rider Haggard (1856–1925) wrote a novel called *Ayesha*.

Aymon, The Four Sons of (ā' mon). The *geste* of *Doon de Mayence* (13th century) describes the struggle of certain feudal VASSALS against CHARLEMAGNE, including Doon of Mayence and Aymon of Dordone. The exploits of the four sons of Aymon—Renauld or RINALDO, Alard, Guichard, and Richard with their famous horse BAYARD is a central feature. They appear in many other poems and romances including Boiardo's ORLANDO INNAMORATO, Pulci's MORGANTE MAGGIORE, Ariosto's ORLANDO FURIOSO, Tasso's *Rinaldo* and JERUSALEM DELIVERED, etc.

Ayrshire poet. Robert Burns (1759–1796),

who was born at Alloway in Ayrshire.

Azazel (à zāz' el). In *Lev.* xvi, 7–8, we read that AARON, as an atonement, "shall cast lots" on two goats "one lot for the Lord, and the other lot for the scapegoat" (Azazel). Milton uses the name for the standard-bearer of the rebel angels (*Paradise Lost*, I, 534). In Mohammedan demonology Azazel is the counterpart of the DEVIL, cast out of HEAVEN for refusing to worship ADAM. His name was changed to EBLIS (Iblis), which means "despair".

Azaziel (à zāz' i el). In BYRON'S *Heaven and Earth*, a seraph who fell in love with Anah, a granddaughter of Cain. When the flood came he carried her under his wing to another planet.

Azilian (à zil' i àn). A MESOLITHIC culture of the transitional period between PALÆO-LITHIC and NEOLITHIC. Named from the bone and flint implements found in the cave at Mas d'Azil in the south of France.

Azoth (ăz'oth) (Arab.). The alchemists' name for mercury; also the PANACEA or universal remedy of PARACELSUS. In Browning's *Paracelsus* (Bk. V), it is the name of Paracelsus' sword:

> Last my good sword; ah, trusty Azoth, leapest
> Beneath thy master's grasp for the last time?

Azrael (ăz' rāl). The Mohammedan ANGEL of death. He will be the last to die, but will do so at the second trump of the ARCHANGEL. *See* ADAM.

> The bitter cold stole into the cottages, marking the old and feeble with the touch of Azrael.
> MRS. HUMPHRY WARD: *Marcella*, II, i.

The Wings of Azrael. The approach of death; the signs of death coming on the dying.

Azrafil. *See* ISRAFEL; ADAM.

Aztec State, The. One of the names by which Arizona, the *Apache State*, has been known. Also called the *Grand Canyon State* and the *Valentine State*, the latter because it was admitted as a state of the U.S.A. on St. VALENTINE'S DAY (14 February) 1912.

Azure (ăzh' ūr, ā' zūr). From the Arabic *lazura* (lapis-lazuli). Heraldic term for the colour blue. Represented in royal ARMS by the planet JUPITER, in noblemen's by the sapphire. The ground of the old shield of France was azure. Emblem of fidelity and truth. Represented in heraldic devices by horizontal lines. Also used as a synonym for the clear blue sky.

B

B. The form of the Roman capital "B" can be traced through early Greek to Phœnician and Egyptian hieratic; the small "b" is derived from the cursive form of the capital. In Hebrew the letter is called *beth* (a house); in Egyptian hieroglyphics it was represented by the crane.

B in Roman notation stands for 300; with a *line above*, it denotes 3,000.

Marked with a B. In the MIDDLE AGES, and as late as the 17th century (especially in America), this letter was branded on the forehead of convicted blasphemers. In France *être marqué au "b"* means to be one-eyed, hump-backed, or lame (*borgne, bossu, boiteux*); hence, an ill-favoured creature.

Not to know B from a battledore, or **from a bull's foot.** To be quite illiterate, not to know even one's letters. Conversely, *I know B from a bull's foot* means "I'm a sharp, knowing person; you can't catch me!" *Cp.* A FROM A WINDMILL; I KNOW A HAWK FROM A HANDSAW *under* HAWK. *See also* BATTLEDORE-BOOK.

B. and S. Brandy and soda.

B.C. In dating an abbreviation for "Before Christ", before the Christian era.

Marked with B.C. When a soldier disgraced himself by insubordination he was formerly marked with "B.C." (bad character) before he was finally drummed out of the regiment.

B Flats. Bugs; which obnoxious insects are characterized by their flatness.

B. of B.K. Mysterious initials applied to himself in Arthur Orton's diary (*see* TICHBORNE CASE). Supposed to denote "Baronet of British Kingdom", they were for some time popularly applied to anyone who put on airs.

Ba. The SOUL, which according to more primitive Egyptian belief roamed the burial places at night. Later belief held that it travelled to the realm of OSIRIS, after a harrowing journey, where its happiness was assured.

Baal. A Semitic word meaning proprietor or possessor, primarily the title of a god as lord of the place (*e.g. Baal-peor*, lord of Peor), or as possessor of some distinctive attribute (*e.g. Baal-zebub* or BEELZEBUB). The worship of local Baals was firmly established in Canaan when the Israelites arrived. The latter adopted many rites of the Canaanites and grafted them to their own worship of Jahweh (JEHOVAH), who thus tended to become merely the national Baal. It was this form of worship that Hosea and other prophets denounced as heathenism. BEL is the Assyrian form of the name. *See also* BELPHEGOR.

Baal, or **Bale Fires.** Fires lighted on the highest moorland hill-tops on Midsummer Eve, etc. The custom still survives in Cornwall. *See* BELTANE.

Baalbec. *See* CHILMINAR.

Baba Yaga. A cannibalistic ogress of Russian folk-lore who stole young children and cooked them. She lived in the remote forest, sailed through the air in an iron cauldron raising tempests on her way, and swept with a broom all traces of her passing. She bears a strong resemblance to BERCHTA of S. German folk-lore.

Babbitt (băb' it). The leading character in Sinclair Lewis's novel of this name (1922). He is a prosperous "realtor" or estate agent in the Western city of Zenith, a simple likeable fellow, with faint aspirations to culture that are forever smothered in the froth and futile hustle of American business life. Drive (which takes him nowhere), hustle (by which he saves no time) and efficiency (which does not enable him to do anything) are the keynotes of his life. Babbitt in present usage typifies the business man of orthodox outlook and virtues, with no interest in cultural values. *Cp.* MAIN STREET.

Babe the Blue Ox. A legendary and indeed remarkable beast that belonged to Paul BUNYAN.

Babel. A perfect Babel. A thorough confusion. "A Babel of sounds", a confused uproar and hubbub. The allusion is to the confusion of tongues at Babel (*Gen.* xi).

Babes in the Wood. *See* CHILDREN. The phrase has been humorously applied to (1) simple trustful folks, never suspicious and easily gulled; (2) Irish insurrectionaries who infested the mountains of Wicklow and the woods of Enniscorthy towards the close of the 18th century; and (3) men in the stocks or in the pillory.

Babes, Protecting deities of. According to Varro (116–27 B.C.), Roman infants were looked after by Vagitanus, the god who caused them to utter their first *cry*; FABULINUS, who presided over their *speech*; CUBA, the goddess who protected them in their cots; and Domiduca, who brought young children safe *home*, and guarded them when out of their parents' sight. In the Christian Church St. NICHOLAS is the patron SAINT of children.

Babies in the Eyes. Love in the expression of the eyes. Love is the little babe CUPID, hence the conceit, originating from the miniature image of a person in the pupil of another's eyes.

> She clung about his neck, gave him ten kisses.
> Toyed with his locks, looked babies in his eyes.
> HEYWOOD: *Love's Maistresse* (1633).

Babrius. Ancient fabulist, probably a Hellenized Roman of the early 3rd century, possibly dwelling in Syria. *See* ÆSOP'S FABLES.

Baby. To be left holding the baby. *See under* HOLD.

To throw out the baby with the bathwater. Over-zealous reform, reorganization or action, which in getting rid of unwanted elements casts away the essentials as well.

Babylon (băb' i lòn). **The Modern Babylon.** London is sometimes so called on account of its wealth, luxury and dissipation.

The hanging gardens of Babylon. *See* HANGING.

The whore of Babylon. A PURITAN epithet for the ROMAN CATHOLIC CHURCH. The allusion is to *Rev.* xvii-xix (*cp.* SCARLET WOMAN), where Babylon stands for Rome, the embodiment of luxury, vice, splendour, tyranny and all that the early Church held was against the spirit of Christ.

Babylonian Captivity. The period beginning from 597 B.C., when the Jews became captives in Babylon after the attacks by NEBUCHADNEZZAR, until their return (from 538 B.C.) after their release by Cyrus, consequent upon his conquest of Babylon.

Babylonian Captivity of the Papacy. *See* AVIGNON POPES.

Babylonian numbers. *Nec Babylonios temptaris numeros* (HORACE: *Odes*, Bk. 1, xi, 2). Do not make trial of Babylonian calculations, *i.e.* do not consult astrologers or fortune-tellers. The Babylonians or Chaldeans were the most noted of astrologers.

Baca, The Valley of (ba' ka). An unidentified place mentioned in *Ps.* lxxxiv, 6, meaning the "Valley of Weeping", and so translated in the Revised Version of the BIBLE.

Bacbuc (băk' bŭc). A Chaldean or Assyrian word for an earthenware pitcher, cruse, or bottle, taken by Rabelais as the ORACLE of the Holy Bottle (and of its priestess). PANURGE consulted the Holy Bottle on the question whether or not he ought to marry and it answered with a click, like the noise made by glass snapping. Bacbuc told Panurge the noise meant *trinc* (drink), and that was the response, the most direct and positive ever given by the oracle. Panurge might interpret it as he liked, the obscurity would always save the oracle.

Bacchus (băk' ŭs). In Roman mythology, the god of wine, the Dionysus of the Greeks, son of ZEUS and SEMELE. The name "Bacchus" is a corruption of the Gr. *Iacchus* (from *Iache*, a shout) and was originally merely an epithet of Dionysus as the noisy and rowdy god. First represented as a bearded man, he later appears as a beautiful youth with black eyes and flowing locks, crowned with vine and ivy. In peace his robe was purple, in war a panther's skin. According to some accounts he married ARIADNE after her desertion by THESEUS.

Bacchus, in the LUSIAD, is the evil demon or antagonist of JUPITER, the lord of destiny. As MARS is the guardian power of Christianity, Bacchus is the guardian power of Mohammedanism.

Bacchus sprang from the thigh of Zeus. The tale is that SEMELE, at the suggestion of JUNO, asked JUPITER to appear before her in all his glory, but the foolish request proved her death. Jupiter saved the child, which was prematurely born, by sewing it up in his thigh till it came to maturity.

What has that to do with Bacchus? *i.e.* What has that to do with the matter in hand? When Thespis introduced recitations in the vintage songs, the innovation was suffered to pass, so long as the subject of recitation bore on the exploits of BACCHUS; but when, for variety's sake, he wandered to other subjects, the Greeks pulled him up with the exclamation, "What has that to do with Bacchus?"

Bacchus a noyé plus d'hommes que Neptune (Fr.). The ale-house has overwhelmed more men than the ocean.

A priest, or **son of Bacchus.** A toper.

Bacchanalia. Roman festivals in honour of BACCHUS, the equivalent of the Greek Dionysia, characterized by drunkenness and licentiousness (although it must be noted that Greek drama had its origins in the Dionysia). Hence *Bacchanalian orgy* now denotes any wild and drunken revelry.

Bacchanals (băk′ à nálz), **Bacchants, Bacchantes.** Priests and priestesses, or male and female votaries of BACCHUS; hence drunken roysterers. *See also* BAG O'NAILS *under* PUBLIC HOUSE SIGNS.

Bach, or **Batch.** In Australia a hut or shanty, from the fact that a BACHELOR was the usual occupant of these simple dwellings.

Bachelor. A man who has not been married. The word is of uncertain etymology from the O.Fr. *bacheler*, derived from the late Latin word *baccalaris*. The word was applied to aspirants to knighthood, and KNIGHTS of the lowest rank were known as *knights bachelor*, those too young to display their own banners.

> With him ther was his sone, a young Squyer
> A lovyere, and a lusty bachelor.
> CHAUCER: *Prologue to the Canterbury Tales*, i, 80.

Bachelor of Arts, Science, Medicine, etc. In most British and American universities one who has taken his first degree in the appropriate faculty. Originally the degrees of "master" and "doctor" were for those further qualified to teach at the university.

Bachelor of Salamanca. The last novel of Le Sage (published in 1736); the hero, Don Cherubin de la Ronda, is a bachelor of arts.

Bachelor's buttons. Buttons, similar in principle to press-studs used in dressmaking, and affixed without the need of sewing, hence the name.

Also several button-shaped flowers are so called—red bachelor's buttons (double red campion), yellow (the upright crowfoot and buttercup), white (white ranunculus and white campion). Rustics were wont to put them in their pockets and their growth was an indication that they would find favour with their sweethearts. Maidens wore them under their aprons.

Bachelor's fare. Bread and cheese and kisses.

Bachelor's porch. An old name for the north door of a church. Menservants and old men used to sit on benches down the north aisle, and maidservants and poor women on the south side. After service the men formed one line and the women another, through which the clergy and gentry passed.

Bachelor's wife. A hypothetical ideal or perfect wife.

> Bachelors' wives and maids' children be well taught.
> JOHN HEYWOOD: *Proverbs*.

Back, To. To support with money, influence, or encouragement: to lay money on a horse or any other participant in a race or contest.

A commercial term meaning to endorse. When a merchant backs or endorses a bill he guarantees its value. Falstaff says to the Prince:

> You care not who sees your back: call you that backing of your friends?
> A plague upon such backing!
> SHAKESPEARE: *Henry IV, Pt. I*, II, iv.

Back and edge. Entirely, heartily, TOOTH AND NAIL, with might and main. The reference is, perhaps, to a wedge driven home to split wood.

> Old George Storefield and Mr Falkland … and one or two more people that had some say with the Government, was working back and edge for me.
> BOLDREWOOD: *Robbery Under Arms*, ch.lii.

Back-of-beyond. A phrase originating in Australia to describe the vast inland spaces, the *great Outback*. The term *back-block* is found in 1850, referring to those territories divided up by the government into blocks for settlement.

Back to Square One. Back to where one started from. Popularised from the early days of broadcast commentaries on football matches when, in order to make the course of the game easier to follow, a diagram of the pitch, divided into numbered squares, was printed in radio programmes. Possibly derived from earlier board games.

Laid on one's back. Laid up with ill health; helpless.

Thrown on his back. Completely beaten. A figure taken from wrestling.

To back and fill. A nautical phrase, denoting a mode of tacking when the tide is with the vessel and the wind against it. Metaphorically, to be irresolute.

To back down. To yield a point contrary to the stand one had previously made.

To back out. To withdraw from an engagement, commitment, etc.; to retreat from a difficult position.

To back the field. *See under* FIELD.

To back the oars, or **to back water,** is to row backwards to check way, or go astern.

To back the sails. In a fore and aft rigged vessel, to sheet the sails to windward to check its way; in a square-rigged ship, to brace the yards so that the wind will press on the front of the sail thereby retarding the ship's course.

To back up. To uphold, to support. As one who stands at your back to support you. In CRICKET an advance by the batsman not taking strike, in order to take a quick run if the striker makes an opportunity.

To be a back number. To be superseded, relegated, out of the SWIM, to be a person with outdated ideas. From old back numbers of newspapers which carry news that is no longer current.

To break the back of. To finish the hardest part of (one's work).

To get one's back up. To become annoyed or angry. The allusion is to a cat, which sets its back up when attacked by a dog or other animal.

To go back on one's word. To withdraw from what one has promised or said. **To go back on a person** is to betray him.

To have one's back to the wall. To act on the defensive against odds. One beset with foes tries to get his back against a wall to prevent attack from behind.

To take a back seat. To withdraw from a position one has occupied into relative obscurity; to submit to humiliation.

To turn one's back on. To have nothing more to do with.

Back-bencher. *See under* BENCH.

Back end, The. Autumn. Widely used in the North of England.

Back-friend. A secret enemy. SHAKESPEARE uses it in this sense.

> A back-friend, a shoulder clapper...
> One that, before the judgement, carries poor souls
> to hell.
>
> *The Comedy of Errors*, IV, ii.

Back-hander. A blow with the back of the hand. Also one who takes *back* the decanter to *hand* himself another glass before the decanter is passed on.

> I'll take a backhander, as Clive don't seem to drink.
> THACKERAY: *The Newcomes*, ch. xliii.

A back-handed compliment. One so phrased as to imply depreciation. Also shortened, *a backhander*.

Backroom boys. A name given to the unpublicized scientists and technicians in World War II who contributed so much to the development of scientific warfare and war production, and since applied generally to such anonymous laboratory workers. The phrase comes from a speech by Lord Beaverbrook on war production (24 March 1941): "To whom must praise be given ... to the boys in the backroom."

Back-seat driver. One who gives a motor-car driver advice and instructions from the back seat. Has the same meaning as ARM-CHAIR GENERAL.

Back-slang. A form of slang which consists in pronouncing the word as spelt backwards. Thus *police* becomes *ecilop* (hence the term *slop* for a policeman), *parsnips*, *spinsrap*, etc. It was formerly much used by "flash" cockneys (*see* COCKNEY), thieves, etc. The widely-used epithet *yob* may be aptly

defined as a "backward boy".

Backstairs influence. Private or unrecognized influence, especially at Court. Royal palaces have more than one staircase, and backstairs would be used by those who sought the sovereign upon private matters; it was, therefore, highly desirable to conciliate the servants or underlings in charge of the "backstairs".

Hence **backstairs gossip,** tittle-tattle obtained from servants; **backstairs plots,** or **politics,** underground or clandestine intrigue.

Backward. He is not backward in coming forward. He is by no means self-effacing, shy, or reluctant to make himself prominent, or to draw attention to himself.

Backwardation. A STOCK EXCHANGE term denoting the sum paid by a seller *i.e.* on a "BEAR ACCOUNT" (a speculation on a fall in the price of certain stock) in order to postpone the completion of the transaction till the next settling day. *Cp*. CONTANGO.

Backward blessing. A curse. To say the Lord's Prayer backwards was to invoke the DEVIL.

Backwater. Properly a pool or stretch of water fed by the backflow of a stream or river. Figuratively **to be in a backwater** is to be isolated from the active flow of life. *See above* TO BACK THE OARS.

Bacon. To baste your bacon. To strike or scourge one. Bacon is the outside portion of the sides of pork, and may be considered generally as the part which would receive a blow. Here *baste* means "to thrash".

Falstaff's remark to the travellers at Gadshill, "On, bacons, on!" (*Henry IV, Pt. I*, II, ii) is an allusion to the fact that formerly bacon was the normal meat of English rustics, hence such terms as *bacon-brains* and CHAW-BACON for a country yokel.

To bring home the bacon. To bring back the prize; to succeed. Possibly a reference to the DUNMOW flitch, or to the sport of catching a greased pig at country fairs.

To save one's bacon. To save oneself from injury; to escape loss. The allusion may be to the care taken by our forefathers to save from the dogs of the household the bacon which was stored for winter use.

> But here I say the Turks were much mistaken,
> Who, hating hogs, yet wished to save their bacon.
> BYRON: *Don Juan*, vii, 42.

He may fetch a flitch of bacon from Dunmow. He is so amiable and good-tempered he will never quarrel with his wife. *See* DUNMOW.

Baconian Philosophy. Inductive philosophy as formulated by Francis Bacon

(1561–1626) in the second book of the *Novum Organum*. He did not invent it but gave it a new importance.

Baconian Theory. *See* SHAKESPEARE.

Bacon's Brazen Head. *See* BRAZEN HEAD.

Bactrian Sage. ZOROASTER or Zarathustra, founder of the ancient Persian religion, who was probably either a Bactrian or a Mede.

Bad. Among rulers called "the Bad" are William I, King of Sicily from 1154 to 1166; Albert, Landgrave and Margrave of Meissen (d. 1314); Charles II, King of Navarre from 1349 to 1387.

Bad blood. Vindictiveness, ill-feeling; hence *to make bad blood* is to create or renew ill-feeling.

You are in my bad books. Under disgrace, in disfavour. Similarly "in my BLACK BOOKS".

Bad debts. Debts unlikely to be paid.

Bad egg. A disreputable character.

A bad excuse is better than none. An adage first appearing in Nicholas Udall's *Ralph Roister Doister*, the first English comedy, performed *c*. 1553.

Bad form. Not in good taste. "It's not done" is commonly used in the same sense.

Bad hat. A rascal or good-for-nothing. In America also applied to a bad actor.

Bad Lands, The. In particular the *Mauvaises Terres*, of the early French trappers in the west of South Dakota; extensive tracts of sterile, rocky and desolate hill-country.

A bad lot. One morally or commercially unsound. Also a commercial project or stock that is worthless. Perhaps from auctioneering meaning a lot for which no one will bid. Similarly an inefficient soldier is called one of the Queen's *bad bargains*.

A bad shot. A wrong guess. A sporting phrase for a shot that misses the mark.

He is gone to the bad. He is mixing with bad companions, has acquired bad habits, has become ruined or depraved.

To the bad. On the wrong side of the account; in arrears.

Badge-men. Licensed beggars, or alms-house men; so called from their special dress or badge, worn to indicate that they belonged to a particular foundation.

> He quits the gay and rich, the young and free,
> Among the badge-men with a badge to be.
> GEORGE CRABBE: *The Borough, Letter XIV* (1810).

Recipients of parish relief formerly wore a badge on the shoulder of the right sleeve, consisting of the letter P, with the initial of their parish, in red or blue cloth. *See* DYVOUR. In the Royal Navy a rating who holds Good Conduct Badges is called a "one", "two", or "three badgeman" according to the number of chevrons he wears on his left arm.

Badger, A. A hawker, huckster, or itinerant dealer, especially in corn, but also in butter, eggs, fish, etc. Its derivation is uncertain.

> This court taking notice of the great prices of corn and butter and cheese and all other commodities, it was ordered that from henceforth no badger whatsoever be licensed but in open sessions.
> *Somerset Quarter Sessions Records*, Vol. 24, p.120
> (1630).

In the U.S.A. *badger* is the slang name of an inhabitant of Wisconsin.

To badger. To tease, annoy, or persistently importune, in allusion to badger-baiting. The badger was kennelled in a tub and dogs were set upon him to "draw him out". When dragged from his tub the badger was allowed to retire to recover and then the process was repeated several times.

It is a vulgar error that the legs of a badger are shorter on one side than on the other.

> His [Titus Oates's] legs uneven as those of a badger.
> MACAULAY: *The History of England*, ch. iv.

Badinguet (ba' din gā). A nickname given to NAPOLEON III, reputedly the name of the workman whose clothes he wore when he escaped from the fortress of Ham in 1846. His adherents were known as *Badingueux*.

> If Badinguet and Bismarck have a row together let them settle it between them with their fists.
> ZOLA: *The Downfall*, ch. ii.

Badminton. The Gloucestershire seat of the Dukes of Beaufort which has given its name to a claret-cup and the game played with rackets and shuttlecocks. In pugilistic parlance blood, which is sometimes called CLARET, from the colour, is also called "badminton".

Badoura (ba doo' rà). "The most beautiful woman ever seen upon earth", heroine of the story of Camaralzaman and Badoura in the ARABIAN NIGHTS.

Baedeker (bā' dė kėr). Karl Baedeker (1801–1859) published the first of the famous series of guidebooks, modelled on John Murray's *Handbooks*, at Coblenz in 1839. Noted for reliability and thoroughness, they became widely used by tourists the world over. Baedeker inaugurated the practice of marking with one or more stars objects and places of interest according to their historic or aesthetic importance, hence **starred in Baedeker.**

Baedeker Raids. A phrase used in Britain, 29 April 1942, to describe German air attacks, in reprisal for British raids on Cologne and Lübeck, deliberately directed on historic monuments such as listed in Baedeker (*e.g.* Bath, Canterbury, Norwich).

Baffle. Originally a punishment or degradation of a recreant KNIGHT including hanging him or his effigy by the heels from a tree.

> He by his heeles him hung upon a tree
> And baffuld so, that all which passed by,
> The picture of his punishment might see.
>
> SPENSER: *The Faerie Queene*, VI, vii, xxvii.

Bag and Baggage. In entirety (*cp.* LOCK, STOCK AND BARREL). Originally a military phrase signifying the soldier with all his belongings or the whole of the equipment and stores of an army. (*See* BAGGAGE.) Hence Mr. Gladstone's **Bag and Baggage policy** with regard to the Near East, which implied that the Turks must be completely cleared out of the Balkans.

> Let the Turks now carry away their abuses in the only possible manner, namely by carrying away themselves,…one and all, bag and baggage, shall I hope, clear out from the province they have desolated and profaned.
>
> W.E. GLADSTONE: *The Bulgarian Horrors and the Question of the East*, 1876.

A bag of bones. Very emaciated.

Bag o'Nails. *See* PUBLIC HOUSE SIGNS.

A bag of tricks, or **the whole bag of tricks.** The whole lot, the entire collection. An allusion to the conjuror's bag, in which he carried his equipment for performing tricks.

An old bag. A slang term for an elderly and unattractive or slovenly woman; also a lady of easy virtue.

> Ah reckon you must have fired that old bag you had in the kitchen and got yourself a hundred per cent American cook.
>
> PAUL GALLICO: *Mrs Harris goes to New York*, ch. 16.

In the bag. As good as certain. In horseracing parlance in Australia it means that the horse referred to will not be running.

The bottom of the bag. The last expedient, after having emptied one's bag of all others. A trump card held in reserve.

To be left holding the bag. To be deserted by one's comrades and left with the entire onus of what was originally a group responsibility. Somewhat similar expressions are to be left HOLDING THE BABY, or left TO CARRY THE CAN.

To empty the bag. To tell everything and conceal nothing (Fr. *vider le sac*, to expose all to view).

To give the bag now means to give the sack, but it seems formerly to have meant the reverse. An employee who left without giving notice was said to have given his master "the bag".

To let the cat out of the bag. *See* CAT.

To bag. To secure for oneself, to purloin; probably from sporting or poaching use, to put into one's bag what one has shot or trapped. Hence, **a good bag,** a large catch of game, fish, etc.

To set one's bag. In America is used of someone setting out to secure political office or preferment.

Bag-man, A. A commercial traveller, from the bag of samples that he carries. Formerly the horses of commercial travellers often bore outsize saddle-bags.

The term *bagman* (or *Leadenhallers*) also denoted those who dealt in *bag-foxes*, which were regularly traded at Leadenhall Market. From the late-18th century until the mid-19th century, foxes were brought in (mainly from France) to overcome the scarcity created by the destruction of foxes by gamekeepers and farmers. The fox was released from the bag at the time of the hunt.

Bags. Slang for "trousers" which may be taken as the bags of the body. When the pattern was strong and "loud" they were once called *howling-bags*.

Bags I. Schoolboy slang assertion of a claim. *See* FAINS.

Oxford bags were wide-bottomed flannel trousers, popularized by Oxford undergraduates in the 1920s.

Bags of mystery. Slang for sausages and saveloys; the allusion is obvious.

Baga de Secretis. Records in the Public Record Office of treason and other State trials from 1477 to 1813. These records contain the proceedings in the trials of Anne Boleyn, Sir Walter Ralegh, Guy Fawkes, the regicides, and of the Jacobite risings of 1715 and 1745.

Baggage, as applied to a worthless or flirtatious woman, dates from the days when soldiers' wives, taken on foreign service with the regiment, travelled with the regimental stores and baggage.

Bail up! The Australian BUSHRANGER'S equivalent for the highwayman's "Stand and deliver!"

Bailey (probably ultimately from O.Fr. *bailler*, to enclose). The external wall of a mediæval castle, also the outer court, the space immediately within the outer wall. When there were two courts they were distinguished as the inner and outer bailey. Subsequently the word was attached to the buildings as the OLD BAILEY (London), the Bailey (Oxford). The paved surround at the back of a house is still called "the bailey" in South Wales.

Bailey bridge. In World War II a metal bridge of amazing strength made of easily portable sections and capable of speedy erection, invented by the British engineer D. C. Bailey. They were a major factor in the rapidity of Allied advances especially in N.W. Europe.

Bailiff. *See* BUM-BAILIFF.

Bailiff of Bedford. The overflowing of the River Ouse in former days was so called, possibly because it turned people out of their homes.

Bailiff of the Marshland. A feverish shivering fit to which newcomers to Fenland were supposed to be prone. It is mentioned in Fuller's *History of the Worthies of England*, published posthumously in 1662. The newcomer to the Fens was said to be arrested by the "Bailiff of the Marshland".

Bailiff's Daughter of Islington, The. A ballad given in PERCY'S RELIQUES on the popular theme of a pair of lovers separated by differences of social rank—a squire's son and a bailiff's daughter. Islington in Norfolk is the place meant. It has appeared in the U.S.A. as "Ireland Town" and "Hazelington Town".

Baily's Beads. *See* BEAD.

Bairam (bī răm). The name given to two Mohammedan feasts. The word in Turkish means "festival". The Lesser begins on the new moon of the month Shawwal, immediately after the feast of RAMADAN and lasts three days. The Greater (seventy days after the Lesser) lasts three days, beginning on the tenth day of the twelfth month, and forms the concluding ceremony of the pilgrimage to MECCA.

Bajadere. *See* BAYADERE.

Bajan, or **Bajanella.** *See* BEJAN.

Bajazet (băj' à zet), or **Bayezid I.** Ottoman SULTAN from 1389 to 1403, and a great warrior, noted for his victories especially against the Hungarians and their allies at Nicopolis in 1396. He was overwhelmed by TIMUR at Ankara in 1402 and held prisoner until his death. There is no evidence for the story, popularized by Christopher Marlowe (1564–1593) and Nicholas Rowe (1674–1718), that Timur carried him about in an iron cage.

Baked Meats, or **Bake meats.** Meat pies.

> The funeral bak'd meats
> Did coldly furnish forth the marriage tables.
>
> SHAKESPEARE: *Hamlet*, I, ii.

i.e. the hot meat pies, served at the funeral and not eaten, were served cold at the marriage banquet, so short was the interval between the death of Gertrude's husband (Hamlet's father) and her remarriage to Claudius.

Baker, The. Louis XVI was so called and his Queen "the baker's wife", and the DAUPHIN the "shop boy"; because they gave bread to the starving men and women who came to VERSAILLES on 6 October 1789.

The return of the baker, his wife, and the shop-boy to Paris had not the expected effect. Flour and bread were still scarce.

A. DUMAS: *The Countess de Charny*, ch. ix.

Baker's dozen. Thirteen for twelve. In earlier times when a heavy penalty was inflicted for short weight, bakers used to give a surplus number of loaves, called the *inbread*, to avoid all risk of incurring a fine. The 13th was the *vantage loaf*.

To give one a baker's dozen. To give one a sound drubbing, *i.e.* all he deserves and one stroke more.

Baker's knee. Knock-knee. Bakers were said to be particularly liable to this deformity owing to the constrained position in which they had to stand when kneading bread.

Bakha. The sacred bull of Hermonthis in Egypt, an incarnation of Menthu, a personification of the heat of the sun. He changed colour every hour of the day.

Baksheesh (băk' shēsh). A Persian word for a gratuity. These gifts are persistently demanded throughout the Near East by beggars, camel-men, servants, etc. more as a claim than a gratuity.

> I was to give the men, too, a "baksheish", that is a present of money, which is usually made upon the conclusion of any sort of treaty.
>
> KINGLAKE: *Eothen*.

Balaam (bā lăm). A misleading prophet or ally as Balaam was in *Numb.* xxii–xxiv. In Dryden's *Absalom and Achitophel* (l. 574), Balaam stands for the Earl of Huntingdon. The "citizen of sober fame" called Balaam in Pope's *Moral Essays*, Ep. iii, is partly drawn on DIAMOND PITT.

The word also denotes matter kept in type for filling up odd spaces in periodicals—the words of one who talks like Balaam's ASS (*Numb.* xxii, 30). Lockhart (*Life of Scott*, ch. lxx) tells us:

> Balaam is the cant name for asinine paragraphs about monstrous productions of nature and the like, kept standing in type to be used whenever the real news of the day leaves an awkward space that must be used up somehow.

Hence **Balaam basket,** or **box;** the printer's slang for the receptacle for such matter, and also (in America) for the place where stereotyped "fill-ups" are kept.

Balaamite. One who makes a profession of religion for profit or grain, as did Balaam.

Balaclava. *See* CARDIGAN.

Balafré, Le (băla' frā) (Fr. the gashed). Francis, second Duke of Guise (1519–1563). In the siege of Boulogne (1545) he received a sword-cut which left a frightful scar on his face. At Dormans (1575), his son Henri, third Duke of Guise

(1550–1588) earned the same title. It was given by Scott (in *Quentin Durward*) to Ludovic Lesly, an archer of the Scottish Guard.

Balan (bā' lăn). A strong and courageous giant in many old romances. In FIERABRAS the "Sowdan of Babylon", father of Fierabras, ultimately conquered by CHARLEMAGNE. In the Arthurian cycle, brother of BALIN.

Balance, The. LIBRA, an ancient zodiacal constellation between VIRGO and SCORPIO representing a pair of scales, the 7th sign of the ZODIAC, which the sun enters a few days before the autumnal equinox.

According to Persian mythology, at the LAST DAY there will be a huge balance as big as the vault of HEAVEN. The two scale pans will be called that of light and that of darkness. In the former all good will be placed, in the latter all evil; and everyone will be rewarded according to the verdict of the balance.

In commercial parlance one's *balance* is the money remaining after all assets are realized and liabilities discharged. Hence the phrases:

He has a good balance at his banker's. His credit side shows a large balance in his favour.

Balance of payments. The difference over a given period between a nation's gross receipts from other countries and its gross payments to them, the result being adverse or favourable.

Balance of power. Such an adjustment of power among sovereign states that no state has such a preponderance as to endanger the independence of the rest.

Balance of trade. The money-value difference between the exports and imports of a nation.

To strike a balance. To calculate the exact difference, if any, between the debit and credit sides of an account.

Balclutha (băl cloo' thà). A fortified town on the banks of the Clutha (*i.e.* the Clyde) mentioned in *Carthon*, one of the OSSIAN poems. It was captured and burnt by Comhal, father of FINGAL, in one of his forays against the Britons.

Bald. Charles le Chauve. Charles II of France (823, 840–877), son of Louis the Pious or le Débonnaire, was named "the Bald". Sometimes known as Charles I (when CHARLEMAGNE is omitted from the list).

Bald as a coot. Completely bald. The common coot, a water bird, has a white bill and frontal shield which give the impression of baldness.

Baldfaced Stag. Common among old PUBLIC-HOUSE SIGNS. *Baldfaced* was applied to horses and other animals with a white strip down the forehead. *Cp.* BLAZE.

Baldheaded. To go for someone baldheaded, that is, without constraint or compunction, probably dating from the days when men wore wigs, and any energetic action or fray required that the wig should be thrown aside. According to the *Army Quarterly* (July 1937) it commemorates a cavalry charge at Warburg (1760) led by the Marquis of Granby (*see* PUBLIC HOUSE SIGNS), whose WIG fell off in the battle.

Balder (bol' der). A Scandinavian god of light, son of ODIN and FRIGG who dwelt at Breidhablik, one of the mansions of ASGARD. One legend says that Frigg bound all things by oath not to harm him, but accidentally omitted MISTLETOE, with a twig of which he was slain. Another tells that he was slain by his rival Hodhr while fighting for the beautiful Nanna. His death was the final prelude to the overthrow of the gods.

Baldwin. (1) In the CHARLEMAGNE romances, nephew of ROLAND and the youngest and comeliest of Charlemagne's PALADINS.

(2) First King of Jerusalem (1100–1118), brother of Godfrey of Bouillon, the previous ruler, who declined the title of king. He figures in Tasso's JERUSALEM DELIVERED as the restless and ambitious Duke of Bologna, leader of 1,200 horse in the allied Christian army.

Bale. When bale is highest, boot is nighest. An old Icelandic proverb appearing in Heywood and other English writers. It means, when things have come to the worst they must needs mend. *Bale* means "evil", *boot* is the M.E. *bote*, relief, remedy, good.

Bale out. Literally to empty water out of a boat with pails, etc.; also an airman's phrase meaning to parachute from an aircraft in an emergency. In army usage it means hastily escaping from a tank when it is hit.

Balfour of Burley, John. Leader of the COVENANTERS in Sir Walter Scott's *Old Mortality* (1816).

Balfour's Poodle. The HOUSE OF LORDS. From 1906 the CONSERVATIVE leader A. J. Balfour exploited their majority in the House of Lords to block the legislation of the LIBERAL government which had an overwhelming majority in the Commons. When the Lords rejected the Licensing Bill of 1908, Mr. Henry Chaplin, M.P., claimed that the House of Lords was the "watchdog of the constitution", to which Mr. Lloyd George replied, "You mean it is Mr. Balfour's poodle! It fetches and carries for him. It barks for him. It bites anybody that he sets it on to!"

Bloody Balfour. See BLOODY BALFOUR.

Balin (bal' in). In the ARTHURIAN ROMANCES devoted brother of BALAN. They accidentally slew one another in ignorance of each other's identity and were buried in one grave by MERLIN. The story is told by Malory in Bk. II and an altered version appears in Tennyson's *Idylls of the King*.

Balios. See HORSE.

Balisarda. See SWORD.

Balk (bawlk, bawk). Originally a ridge (O.E. *balca*), then the ridge between two furrows left in ploughing (in the old OPEN FIELD SYSTEM of agriculture the cultivated strips were divided by unploughed turf balks). The word came to be applied to any obstacle, stumbling-block or check on one's actions. Thus in billiards, the balk is the part of the table behind the balk-line from which one has to play when in certain circumstances one's freedom is checked. So *to balk* is to place obstacles in one's way.

A balk of timber is a large roughly squared piece of timber.

To make a balk. To miss a part of the field in ploughing. Hence, to disappoint, to withhold deceitfully.

Balker. One who from an eminence on shore directs fishermen where shoals of herrings have gathered together (O.E. *baelcan*, to shout). See HUER.

Balkis (bol' kis). The Mohammedan name of the Queen of SHEBA, who visited SOLOMON.

Ball. "Ball", the spherical body, is a Middle English and old Teutonic word; "ball", the dancing assembly, is from O.Fr. *baler*, to dance, from Late Lat. *ballare*.

A ball of fortune. One tossed like a ball, from PILLAR to post; one who has experienced many vicissitudes of fortune.

The ball is with you, or **in your court.** It is your turn now.

To have the ball at your feet. To have an opportunity, a METAPHOR from football.

To keep the ball rolling. To continue without intermission. To keep the fun, conversation, or the matter going. A metaphor from ball games.

To open the ball. To lead off the first dance at a ball, hence to begin the matter by taking the lead.

To play ball. A colloquial phrase on both sides of the Atlantic, meaning to agree to a suggestion or to co-operate in some plan or action.

To strike the ball under the line. To fail in one's object. The allusion is to the earlier game of tennis in which a line was stretched across the middle of the court, and the players on each side had to strike and return the ball over the line. Strutt (*Sports and Pastimes*, ch. III, v) says:

> Hence the propriety of Heywoode's proverb (1566), "Thou hast stricken the ball under the line"; meaning he had failed in his purpose.

To take the ball before the bound. To anticipate an opportunity; to be over-hasty. A metaphor from CRICKET.

Ball's Bull. A person with no ear for music. According to an old tale this bull kicked a fiddler, whose music angered him, over a bridge.

The Three Golden Balls. The once familiar pawnbroker's sign was taken from the coat of arms of the MEDICI family and first introduced to London by the LOMBARD bankers and money-lenders. The positioning of the balls was popularly explained in that there were two chances to one that what was brought to UNCLE would be redeemed.

Also the emblem of St. NICHOLAS of Bari, who is said to have given three purses of gold to three virgin sisters to enable them to marry.

Ballad. Originally a song to dance-music (from Late Lat. *ballare*, to dance, through O.Fr. *balade*).

Let me make the ballads, and who will make the laws. Andrew Fletcher of Saltoun, in Scotland, wrote to the Marquis of Montrose, "I knew a very wise man of Sir Christopher Musgrave's sentiment. He believed, if a man were permitted to make all the ballads, he need not care who should make the laws" (1703).

Ballet. A theatrical representation combining PANTOMIME, music and dancing, introduced into France from Italy by Catherine de' MEDICI, whose valet, Baldas Baldassarino de Belgioso, produced the first ballet of importance in 1581, called *Le Ballet Comique de la Reyne*.

Balliol College, Oxford, founded in 1263, by Sir John de Baliol of Barnard Castle (father of Baliol, King of Scotland) as a penance, and augmented by his wife, Devorguilla. In the 19th century Balliol scholarships became a much coveted distinction. Benjamin Jowett, its most famous Master, was in office from 1870 to 1893.

> I know I'd rather win two schoolhouse matches running than get the Balliol scholarship any day.
> THOMAS HUGHES: *Tom Brown's Schooldays*, ch. vi.

Balloon, A pilot. Metaphorically, a feeler to ascertain opinion. *Cp.* TO FLY A KITE *under* KITE.

Ballot. This method of voting was common in

ancient Greece and Rome. (*See* BEANS.) The name comes from the use of small balls put secretly in a box (Fr. *ballotte*, a little ball). In more modern times secret voting at governmental elections was first used in South Australia in 1856, hence the term *Australian Ballot*. Although one of the six points of CHARTISM, voting by ballot was not adopted in Great Britain until the Ballot Act of 1872, and not until after 1884 in the U.S.A.

Ballplatz, The. The Foreign Office of Austria-Hungary was so called because it was situated in the square in Vienna named *Ballplatz* or *Ballhausplatz*.

Ballyhoo (băli hoo'). The word is said to come from Ballyhooly, a village in Co. Cork, but in its present sense of a noisy demonstration to attract attention, extravagant advertisement or publicity, originates from the U.S.A.

Balm (Fr. *baume*, a contraction of balsam). An aromatic, resinous gum exuded from certain trees and used in perfumery and medicine.

Is there no balm in Gilead? (*Jer.* viii, 22). Is there no remedy, no consolation? "Balm" here is the Geneva Bible's translation of the Heb. *sori*, which probably means "mastic", the resin yielded by the mastic tree, *Pistacia lentiscus*. In Wyclif's Bible the word is translated "gumme" and in Coverdale's "triacle". (*See* BIBLE, THE ENGLISH; TREACLE.)

The gold-coloured resin now known as "Balm of Gilead" is that from *Balamodendron gileadense*.

Balmerino (băl mer' i nō). The story was long current that when Lord Balmerino was executed for his part in the JACOBITE rebellion of 1745, the executioner bungled and only half cut off his head, whereupon his lordship turned round and grinned at him.

Balmy. I am going to the balmy—*i.e.* to "balmy sleep"; one of Dick Swiveller's pet phrases (Dickens: *Old Curiosity Shop*). *See also* BARMY.

Balnibarbi (băl ni bar' bi). A land occupied by projectors (Swift: *Gulliver's Travels*).

Balthazar (băl thăz' ar). One of the three kings of COLOGNE. *See* MAGI.

Baltic, The. In commercial parlance is the familiar name of the Baltic Mercantile and Shipping Exchange, which was founded in the 18th century. Originating from meetings, at the Baltic COFFEE House, of merchants concerned with the Baltic trade, it is now at St. Mary Axe as a centre for chartering ships for a world trade, also dealing in air freight, etc. Membership largely consists of shipowners, shipbrokers and merchants. *Cp.* LLOYD'S.

Bamberg Bible, The. *See* BIBLE, SOME SPECIALLY NAMED EDITIONS.

Bambocciades (băm boch' i ădz). Pictures of scenes in low life, such as country WAKES, PENNY WEDDINGS, and so on; so called from the Ital. *bamboccio*, a cripple, nickname given to Pieter van Laar (1592–*c.* 1675), a noted Dutch painter of such scenes.

Bamboo Curtain, The. Formed by analogy with IRON CURTAIN to denote the veil of secrecy and mistrust drawn between the Chinese Communist block and the non-Communist nations. *Cp.* GARLIC WALL, IRON CURTAIN.

Bampton Lectures. Founded by the Rev. John Bampton, minor CANON of Salisbury, who, in 1751, left £120 per annum to the University of Oxford, to pay for eight divinity lectures on given subjects to be preached yearly at Great St. Mary's and for their subsequent publication. Only M.A.s of Oxford and Cambridge are eligible as lecturers and the same person may not be chosen twice. First given in 1780, the lectures by Dr. Hampden in 1832 aroused great controversy in theological circles. *Cp.* HULSEAN LECTURES.

Ban (O.E. *bannan*, to summon, O.Teut. *bannan*, to proclaim). Originally meaning to summon, the verb came to mean to anathematize, to imprecate; and the noun was applied specifically to an ecclesiastical curse, a formal prohibition, a sentence of outlawry. *Banish* and BANNS are from the same root.

Lever le ban et l'arrière ban (Fr.). To levy the *ban* was to call the king's VASSALS to active service; to levy the *arrière ban* was to levy the vassals of a suzerain or under-lord.

Ban, King. In the ARTHURIAN ROMANCES, father of Sir LANCELOT DU LAC. He died of grief when his castle was taken and burnt through the treachery of his seneschal.

Banagher, That beats (băn' à her). Wonderfully inconsistent and absurd—exceedingly ridiculous. Banagher is a town in Ireland, on the Shannon, in Offaly. It formerly sent two members to PARLIAMENT and was a notorious POCKET BOROUGH. When a member spoke of a family borough where every voter was a man employed by the owner, it was not unusual to reply, "Well, that beats Banagher."

According to Francis Grose, however, Banagher (or Banaghan) was an Irish minstrel famous for telling wonderful stories of the MÜNCHAUSEN kind.

"Well," says he, "to gratify them I will. So just a morsel. But Jack, this beats Banagher."
W. B. YEATS: *Fairy Tales of the Irish Peasantry*.

Bananalanders. Nickname for the inhabitants of Queensland, Australia, who are also known as *Canecutters*.

Banana oil. Used colloquially in Australia and America for "nonsense" or "insincere talk".

Banat (băn′ ăt). A territory governed by a *ban* (Persian for lord, master) particularly certain districts of Hungary and Croatia. The word was imported by the Avars who settled in Dacia in the latter half of the 6th century.

Banbury. A town in Oxfordshire, proverbially known for its PURITANS, its "cheese-paring", its cakes and its cross. Hence a *Banbury man* is a Puritan or bigot. Zeal-of-the-land Busy, in Jonson's *Bartholomew Fair*, is described as a "Banbury Man".

> In my progress travelling Northward,
> Taking my farewell o'th Southward,
> To Banbery came I, O prophane one!
> Where I saw a Puritane one,
> Hanging of his cat on Monday,
> For killing of a Mouse on Sonday.
> RICHARD BRATHWAITE: *Barnabee's Journal* (1638).

As thin as Banbury cheese. In *Jack Drum's Entertainment* (1600) we read, "You are like a Banbury cheese, nothing but paring"; and Bardolph compares Slender to Banbury cheese (*Merry Wives*, I, i). The Banbury cheese is a rich milk cheese about an inch thick.

Banbury cake is a kind of spiced pastry turnover, once made exclusively at Banbury.

Banbury Cross of nursery rhyme fame was removed by the PURITANS as a heathenish memorial in 1646. Another CROSS was erected on the site in 1858.

Banbury Tinkers. People who try to put things right but only make them worse. The Banbury tinkers were said to make three holes in a pot while mending one.

Banco. A commercial term denoting bank money of account as distinguished from currency; used in exchange business when current money had depreciated from its former value.

In Banco, or **in Banc.** A Late Latin legal phrase, meaning "on the bench"; it is applied to sittings of a superior court of COMMON LAW in its own bench or court, and not on circuit or at NISI PRIUS. The work of the courts *in Banco* was transferred to Divisional Courts of the High Court of Justice by the Judicature Act of 1873.

Mark Banco. The mark of fixed value used as an invariable standard in the old Bank at Hamburg, and used by the HANSEATIC LEAGUE. Deposits in GOLD and SILVER were credited in *Mark Banco* in which all banking accounts were carried on so that they were unaffected by variations in exchange.

Bancus Communium Placitorum. The BENCH OF COMMON PLEAS.

Bancus Regius, or **Bancus Reginae.** The King's or Queen's Bench.

Bandbox. He looks as if he were just out of a. He is so neat and carefully got up in his dress and person, that he looks like some company dress, carefully kept in a bandbox, a cardboard box for millinery formerly used by parsons for keeping their BANDS in.

Neat as a bandbox. Neat as clothes folded and put by in a bandbox.

The Bandbox Plot. Paul de Rapin (1661–1725) in his *Histoire d'Angleterre* (Vol. IV) tells us that in Queen Anne's reign a bandbox was sent to the lord-treasurer containing three pistols charged and cocked, and triggers being tied to a pack-thread fastened to the lid. When the lid was lifted, the pistols would go off and shoot the person who opened the lid. Dean Swift happened to be by when the box arrived, and seeing the pack-thread, cut it, thus saving the life of the lord-treasurer.

Bandicoot. A small Australian marsupial (*Perameles*) which ravages garden and farm produce.

Bald as a bandicoot (Austr.). Quite bald. An alliterative variant of BALD AS A COOT. Meaning is sacrificed to euphony since the bandicoot is not bald. The expression *busy as a bandicoot* similarly means "extremely busy".

To bandicoot is an Australian phrase meaning to steal vegetables—often by removing the roots and leaving the tops standing so that the theft is not noticed.

Band of Hope. The name given (c. 1847) to children's temperance societies in the UNITED KINGDOM. The movement grew steadily and the Band of Hope Union was founded in 1855.

Bands. Clerical bands are a relic of the ancient *amice*, a square linen tippet tied about the neck of priests during the saying of MASS. Disused by ANGLICAN clergy in the late 19th century, they have partially come back into fashion of late and are also worn by PRESBYTERIAN ministers and continental clergy.

Legal bands are a relic of the wide falling collars which formed a part of the ordinary dress in the reign of Henry VIII, and which were especially conspicuous in Stuart times. In the showy days of Charles II the plain bands were changed for lace ends.

> The eighth Henry as I understand,
> Was the first prince that ever wore a band.
> JOHN TAYLOR (1580–1653).

Bandwagon. To climb on the bandwagon is to show support for a popular movement or trend with intent to profit or reap easy material benefit. It was customary in the U.S.A., particularly in southern States, for a band to play on a wagon through the streets to advertise a forthcoming meeting, political or otherwise. At election time local leaders would show their support of a candidate by climbing on the wagon and riding with the band.

Bandy. I am not going to bandy words with you, *i.e.*, to wrangle. The METAPHOR is from the Irish game bandy (the precursor of hockey), in which each player has a stick with a crook at the end. The ball is *bandied* from side to side, each party trying to beat it home to the opposite goal. It was earlier a term in tennis as is shown by the line in John Webster's *Victoria Corombona* (IV, iv):

> That while he had been bandying at tennis. (1612).

Bane really means ruin, death, or destruction (O.E. *bana*, a murderer); and "I will be his bane" means I will ruin or murder him. Bane is therefore a mortal injury.

Bangorian Controversy. A theological pamphlet-war occasioned by a sermon preached by Dr. Hoadly, Bishop of Bangor, before George I in 1717. Taking as his text "My kingdom is not of this world", he denied that Christ had delegated his authority to the Church. Convocations were prorogued to silence the opposition and the Convocation of Canterbury did not meet effectively until 1852 and that of York until 1861.

Bang-up. SWELL, fine, first-rate. Current as colloquial English by the end of the 18th century. A second meaning, now obsolete, was "overcoat".

> A green coat cut round in jockey fashion, and over it a white bang-up.
> C.J. LEVER: *Jack Hinton the Guardsman* (1843).

Banian, or **Banyan** (băn′ yȧn) (Sanskrit *vanij*, a merchant). A name applied to a caste of Hindu traders and moneylenders, who wore a particular dress, were strict in their observance of fasts, and abstained from eating any kind of flesh. It is from this circumstance that sailors speak of BANYAN DAY.

The word is also applied to a form of loose house-coat worn by Anglo-Indians.

Bank. Originally meaning "bench" or "shelf", in Italy the word BANCO was applied specially to a tradesman's counter, and hence to a money-changer's bench or table, from which the modern meaning of an establishment dealing with money, etc., is derived.

Banker. In Australia, a river in flood running as high as its banks. In North America, a cod fisherman of the Newfoundland Banks, or his ship.

Bank Holidays. Properly, when banks are legally closed. In 1830 Bank of England closures were limited from more than 40 to 18 and in 1834 to 4. By the Bank Holiday Act of 1871 days were again fixed for England, Wales and Ireland and with a slight variation for Scotland. These Bank Holidays soon became general public holidays. Alterations have taken place from 1967.

Bankrupt. In Italy, when a moneylender was unable to continue business, his bench or counter was broken up, and he was spoken of as a *bancorotto—i.e.* a bankrupt.

Bank of river. Stand with your back to the source, and face to the sea or outlet: the *left* bank is on your left, and *right* bank on your right hand.

Bankside. An historic part of the borough of SOUTHWARK on the right bank of the Thames between Blackfriars and London bridges. At one end stood the CLINK prison and the church of St. Mary OVERIE (now Southwark Cathedral). Also famous in Shakespeare's England for BULL-BAITING and the Globe theatre, and notorious for its brothels and evil-doers. Hence **Sisters of the Bank,** an old term for prostitutes.

> Come I will send for a whole coach or two of Bankside ladies, and we will be joyful.
> RANDOLPH: *The Muses' Looking Glass*, II, iv (*c.* 1632).

Banks's Horse. A horse called Marocco, belonging to one Banks about the end of Queen Elizabeth I's reign, and trained to do all manner of tricks. One of his exploits is said to have been the ascent of St. Paul's steeple. A favourite story of the time is of an apprentice who called his master to see the spectacle. "Away, you fool," said the shopkeeper, "what need I go to see a horse on the top when I can see so many horses at the bottom!" The horse is mentioned by Ralegh, Gayton, Kenelm Digby, Ben Jonson and others.

Bannatyne Club. The literary club founded by Sir Walter Scott, Archibald Constable and others in 1823 and named after George Bannatyne (1545?–1608), to whose manuscript (now in the ADVOCATES' LIBRARY) we owe the preservation of much 15th- and early 16th-century Scottish poetry. The club had convivial meetings and printed 116 rare works of Scottish history and literature. It was dissolved in 1861. *Cp.* MAITLAND CLUB; ROXBURGHE CLUB.

> Assist me ye friends of Old Books and Old Wine,
> To sing in the praises of sage Bannatyne,
> Who left such a treasure of old Scottish lore

As enables each age to print one volume more,
One volume more, my friends, one volume more
We'll ransack old Banny for one volume more.
                        SCOTT: *The Bannatyne Club*, I.

Banner of the Prophet, The. What purports to be the actual standard of MOHAMMED is present in the Eyab mosque of Istanbul. It is twelve feet in length and made of four layers of silk, the top-most being green, embroidered with GOLD. In times of peace it is kept in the hall of the "noble vestment" as the Prophet's garb is styled, along with his stirrup, sabre, bow and other relics.

Banner of France, The Sacred. The ORIFLAMME.

Banners in churches. These are suspended as thank offerings to God. Those in St. George's Chapel, Windsor, Henry VII's Chapel, WESTMINSTER, etc., are to indicate that the KNIGHT whose banner is hung up avows himself devoted to God's service.

Banner State. In the U.S.A. the State which, in a presidential election, gives the victor the biggest majority or vote. The adjective is used in other contexts to mean "leading" or "foremost".

Banneret. One who leads his vassals to battle under his own banner. Also an order of Knighthood conferred on the field of battle for deeds of valour by tearing off the points of the recipient's pennon. This mediæval order lapsed after the reign of Elizabeth I, and was last properly conferred by Charles I in 1642 on Colonel John Smith for his recovery of the Royal Standard at Edgehill.

Banns of Marriage. The publication in the parish church for three successive Sundays of an intended marriage. It is made after the second lesson of the Morning Service, or of Evening Service (if there be no Morning Service). The word is from the same root as BAN.

To forbid the banns. To object formally to the proposed marriage.

And a better fate did poor Maria deserve than to have a banns forbidden by the curate of the parish who published them.
                        STERNE: *Sentimental Journey* (1768).

Banquet in addition to its present meaning once also meant dessert. Thus in the *Pennyles Pilgrimage* (1618) John Taylor, the WATER POET, says: "Our first and second course being three-score dishes at one boord, and after that, always a banquet." The word is from the Italian *banco*, a bench or table (*see* BANK).

Banshee. In Irish folklore and that of the Western Highlands of Scotland, a female fairy who announces her presence by shrieking and wailing under the windows of a house when one of its occupants is awaiting death. The word is a phonetic spelling of the Irish *bean-sidhe*, a woman of the fairies.

Bantam. A little bantam cock. A plucky little fellow that will not be bullied by a person bigger than himself. The bantam cock will encounter a dunghill cock five times his own weight, and is therefore said to "have a great soul in a little body". The bantam originally came from Bantam in Java.

Banting. Reducing superfluous fat by living on an essentially protein diet, and abstaining from beer, port, etc., and farinaceous food, according to the method adopted by William Banting (1797–1878). This London undertaker explained in his pamphlet *Corpulence* (1864), how he reduced his weight from 202 lb. to 156 lb. between August 1862 and August 1863. The word was used by *The Times* on 12 August 1864.

A greater benefactor to mankind was Sir Frederick Grant Banting (1891–1941), the Canadian scientist who discovered insulin in 1922.

Bantling. A child, a brat; usually in a depreciatory sense, or meaning an illegitimate child. It is from Ger. *Bankling*, a bastard, from *Bank*, a bench; hence a child begotten casually, as on a bench or out of the marriage-bed. The word has been confused with *bandling*, taken to mean a little one in swaddling clothes.

Banyan Day. An English nautical phrase to describe a day on which no meat was issued in the rations. In Australia it is found in official documents of the late 18th century. On Australian out-stations Banyan Day for the hands was when meat supplies were exhausted, before the end of the ration period. *See* BANIAN.

I was not very much tempted with the appearance of this dish, of which, nevertheless, my messmates ate heartily, advising me to follow their example, as it was banyan day, and we could have no meat till next noon.
                        SMOLLETT: *Roderick Random* (1748), ch. xxv.

Baphomet (Fr. *Baphomet*; O.Sp. *Matomat*). A corruption of Mahomet, the imaginary idol which the TEMPLARS were said to worship with licentious rites.

Baptes. Priests of the goddess COTYTTO, the Thracian goddess of lewdness, whose midnight orgies were so obscene that they disgusted even the goddess herself. The name is derived from the Greek verb *bapto*, to wash, because of the so-called ceremonies of purification connected with her rites (*Juvenal*, ii, 91).

Baptism. This SACRAMENT of the Christian Church dates back in one form or another to pre-apostolic times.

Baptism for the dead was a kind of vicarious baptism of a living person for the sake of one dead. An heretical and superstitious custom referred to in I *Cor. xv*, 29.

Baptism of blood. Martyrdom for the sake of Christ which supplied the place of the sacrament if the martyr was unbaptized.

Baptism of desire is the grace or virtue of baptism acquired by one who earnestly desires baptism by water but dies before receiving it.

Baptism of fire is really martyrdom, but usually means experiencing the fire of battle for the first time. It was so used by NAPOLEON III.

Baptists. English Baptists are of 16th-century origin. Their first independent church, however, was founded from a group of separatists under John Smythe at Amsterdam in 1609, from whence an offshoot returned to London in 1612 to form the General Baptists. Their Arminianism (*see* ARMINIANS) led to the growth of the Strict, Particular, or Calvinistic Baptists in the 1630s. In the 18th century many General Baptists became UNITARIANS and the more orthodox formed the New Connection in 1770. The Baptist Union (1832) eventually led to closer co-operation and the Particular Baptists joined forces with the New Connection in 1891. Church government is congregational and baptism (by total immersion) is only for believers. *Cp*. BARROWISTS; BROWNISTS; CONGREGATIONALISTS; PRESBYTERIANS.

Bar. The whole body of barristers, *cp*. BENCH. The bar, in the INNS OF COURT, is the partition separating the benchers from the rest of the hall.

At the bar. The prisoner at the bar. The prisoner in the dock before the judge.

To be called to the bar. To be admitted a BARRISTER. Students having attained the necessary standing used to be called from the body of the hall to the bar. To *disbar* means to expel a barrister from his profession.

To be called within the bar. To be appointed QUEEN'S COUNSEL, *i.e.* to be admitted within the bar which separated the members of the court from the prisoners, junior counsel and public. Q.C.s are thus of the inner bar.

Trial at Bar. By full court of judges in the QUEEN'S BENCH division. These trials are for very difficult causes, before special juries, and occupy the attention of the four judges in the superior court, instead of at NISI PRIUS.

Bar. Excepting. In the language of the TURF, "two to one, bar one" means betting two to one against any horse in the field with one exception. The word means "barring out", "debarring", "excluding", as in Shakespeare's:

> Nay, but I bar to-night; you shall not gage me by what we do to-night.
> *Merchant of Venice*, II, ii.

Bar. In HERALDRY, a horizontal band across the shield taking up not more than one-fifth of the Field. A diminutive of the fesse.

> A barre ... is drawne overthwart the escochon ... it containeth the fifth part of the Field.
> JOHN GUILLIM: *The Display of Heraldry* (1610).

Bar sinister. An heraldic term popularly mistaken as an indication of bastardy, correctly denoted by a baton sinister. *See* BEND SINISTER.

Barring out. In bygone days, the practice of barricading the masters out of the classroom or the school. Maria Edgeworth (1767–1848) has a tale so called. In 1818 soldiers were called in to deal with a rebellious outbreak at Winchester College.

Bar Mitzvah (Heb. Son of duty). The ceremony celebrating the arrival of a Jewish boy at the age of responsibility, 13 years.

Barataria. SANCHO PANZA'S island-city, in Don QUIXOTE, over which he was appointed governor. The table was presided over by Doctor Pedro Rezio de Aguero, who caused every dish set upon the board to be removed without being tasted—some because they heated the blood, and others because they chilled it, some for one ill effect, and some for another; so that Sancho was allowed to eat nothing. The word is from Sp. *barato*, cheap.

Barataria is also the setting of Act II of *The Gondoliers*. *Cp*. BARMECIDE'S FEAST.

Barathron, or **Barathrum.** A deep ditch behind the Acropolis of ATHENS into which malefactors were thrown; somewhat in the same way as criminals at ROME were cast from the TARPEIAN ROCK. Sometimes used figuratively, as in Massinger's *New Way to Pay Old Debts*, where Sir Giles Overreach calls Greedy a "barathrum of the shambles" (III, ii), meaning that he was a sink into which any kind of food or offal could be thrown.

> *Carion*: Barathrum? What's Barathrum?
> *Mercury*: Why, Barathrum is Pluto's boggards [privy]: you must all be thrown into Barathrum.
> RANDOLPH: *Hey for Honesty*, V, i (*c*. 1630).

Barb (Lat. *barba*, a beard). Used in early times in England for the beard of a man and thus for the feathers under the beak of a HAWK (beard feathers). Its first English use was for a curved-back instrument such as a fish-hook. The barb of an arrow had two iron "feathers" or hooks near the point to hinder extraction.

Barb. A Barbary steed, noted for docility, speed, endurance and spirit; also called a *Barbary*. *See* BARBARY ROAN.

Barbara Allen. The heroine of an old ballad given in PERCY'S RELIQUES called *Barbara Allen's Cruelty*. She died of remorse after showing no pity for the young man who was dying of love for her.

> Farewell, she sayd, ye virgins all,
> And shun the fault I fell in:
> Henceforth take warning by the fall
> Of cruel Barbara Allen.

Barbara, St. Virgin and martyr (*c*. 4th century). Her father, a fanatical heathen, delivered her up to Martian, governor of Nicomedia, for being a Christian. After she had been subjected to the most cruel tortures, her unnatural father was about to strike off her head, when a lightning flash laid him dead at her feet. Hence she is invoked against lightning and is the patron saint of arsenals and artillery.

Barbari. Quod non fecerunt barbari, fecerunt Barberini. *i.e.* What the barbarians left standing, the Barberini contrived to destroy. A PASQUINADE current in ROME at the time when Pope Urban VIII (1623–1644) (Barberini) converted the bronze girders from the portico of the PANTHEON, which had remained in splendid condition since 27 B.C., into cannon and into pillars for the Baldacchino, or canopy of St. Peter's.

Barbarian. The Greeks and Romans called all foreigners *barbarians* (babblers; men who spoke a language not understood by them). The word was probably merely imitative of unintelligible speech. The extension of meaning to imply uncivilized, uncultured, is a natural consequence.

> Therefore if I know not the meaning of the voice, I shall be unto him that speaketh a barbarian, and he that speaketh shall be a barbarian unto me.
> I *Cor.* xiv. 11.

Barbarossa (Red-beard). The surname of Frederick I (*c*. 1123–1190), Holy Roman EMPEROR. He was drowned whilst on the Third CRUSADE. Also the name applied by the Christians to a family of Turkish sea rovers, especially well known being the famous corsair Khair ud-Din Barbarossa, who became Bey of Algiers in 1518 and High ADMIRAL of the Turkish fleet in 1537.

Barbary Coast. The western Mediterranean coast of Africa which was infested by MOSLEM sea rovers from the 16th century until the early 19th century. The native Berbers derive their name from the Roman habit of referring to indigenous peoples as *barbari*.

In Sydney, New South Wales it is a slang term for a part of one of that city's thoroughfares which runs from Taylor Square, through Oxford and Liverpool streets, to the Central Railway Station. In the U.S.A. the name was given, before the 1906 earthquake, to a rather disreputable district of San Francisco.

Barbary Roan, the favourite horse of Richard II.

> O, how it yearn'd my heart, when I beheld,
> In London streets, that coronation-day,
> When Bolingbroke rode on Roan Barbary,
> The horse that thou [Rich. II] so often hast bestrid,
> The horse that I so carefully have dress'd!
> SHAKESPEARE: *Richard II*, V, v.

Barbason (bar' bà son). A fiend mentioned by Shakespeare in *The Merry Wives of Windsor*, II, ii, and in *Henry V*, II, i.

> Amaimon sounds well; Lucifer, well; Barbason, well; yet they are devils' additions, the names of fiends.
> *Merry Wives*.

The name seems to have been obtained from Scot's *Discoverie of Witchcraft* (1584).

Barbecue (bar' be kū) (Sp. *barbacoa*, a wooden framework set up on posts). A West Indian term formerly used in America for a wooden bedstead, and also for a large gridiron upon which an animal could be roasted whole. Hence an animal, such as a hog, so cooked; also the feast at which it is roasted and eaten. Popularly applied in Britain to an outdoor party when the food is cooked on a fire in the open.

> Oldfield, with more than harpy throat subdued,
> Cries, "Send me, ye gods, a whole hog barbecued!"
> POPE: *Satires*, ii, 25.

Barbed Steed. A horse in armour. *Barbed* should properly be *barded*; it is from the Fr. *barde*, horse-armour. Horses' "bards" were the metal coverings for the breast and flanks.

> And now,—instead of mounting barbed steeds
> To fright the souls of fearful adversaries,—
> He capers nimbly in a lady's chamber
> To the lascivious pleasing of a lute.
> SHAKESPEARE: *Richard III*, I, i.

Barber. (Ultimately from Lat. *barba*, beard). One who cuts and trims beards, a hairdresser. Originally barbers also practised dentistry and surgery. The Company of Barber-Surgeons in London was first incorporated in 1461 and in 1540 it became the Company of Barbers and Surgeons limited (other than in its proper functions) to drawing teeth. In 1745 it was renamed the Barbers Company which is still one of the London LIVERY COMPANIES.

Every barber knows that.

> Omnibus notum tonsoribus.
> HORACE: *I Satires*, vii, 3

From ancient Roman times the barber's shop has been a centre for the dissemination of scandal, and the talk of the town.

Barber Poet. Jacques Jasmin (1798–1864), a Provençal poet, who was also known as "the last of the TROUBADOURS". He was a barber.

Barber's pole. This pole, painted spirally with two stripes of red and white, and displayed outside barber's shops as a sign, derives from the days when they also practised phlebotomy. The pole represents the staff gripped by persons in venesection, which was painted red since it was usually stained with blood. The white spiral represents the bandage twisted round the arm previous to blood-letting. The gilt knob at the end of the pole represents the brass basin which was sometimes actually suspended from it. The basin had a notch in it to fit the throat, and was used for lathering customers before shaving.

Barber of Seville. The comedy of this name (*Le Barbier de Séville*) was written by Beaumarchais and produced in Paris in 1775. In it appeared as the barber the famous character of FIGARO. Paisello's opera appeared in 1780 but was eclipsed by Rossini's *Barbiere di Siviglia*, with words by Sterbini. The latter was hissed on its first appearance in 1816 under the title of *Almaviva*.

Barber-shop. A term used to denote a style of close-harmony part singing by male quartets. Informal music-making existed in barber shops in the 16th and 17th centuries in Britain as well as Europe. It lapsed in the 18th century but continued in the U.S.A. where the barber-shop quartet came into being.

Barcelona. A fichu, piece of velvet for the neck, or small necktie, made at Barcelona, and common in England in the early 19th century. Also a neckcloth of some bright colour, as red with yellow spots.

> Now on this handkerchief so starch and white
> She pinned a Barcelona black and tight.
> > PETER PINDAR: *Portfolio (Dinah)*.
>
> A double Barcelona protected his neck.
> > SCOTT: *Peveril of the Peak (Prefatory Letter)*.

Barchester. An imaginary cathedral town (modelled on Winchester), in the county of Barsetshire; the setting of Anthony Trollope's "Barchester Novels". These are: *The Warden*, 1855; *Barchester Towers*, 1857; *Doctor Thorne*, 1858; *Framley Parsonage*, 1861; *The Small House at Allington*, 1864; and *The Last Chronicle of Barset*, 1867. Angela Thirkell (1890–1961) also used Barsetshire and Barchester as a setting for some of her stories.

Barcochebah, or **Barcochebas** (barkoch' e ba). In Hebrew means "Son of a star". One Simeon, a heroic Jewish leader against the Romans, who is reputed to have claimed to be the "Star out of Jacob" mentioned in *Num*. xxiv, 17, was so called. He took Jerusalem in 132 and was acclaimed by some as the MESSIAH. He was overwhelmed and slain by the forces of Julius Severus in 135.

Bard. The minstrel of the ancient Celtic peoples, the Gauls, British, Welsh, Irish and Scots. They celebrated the deeds of the gods and heroes, incited to battle, acted as heralds, and sang at festivities. The oldest extant bardic compositions are of the 5th century. *See* EISTEDDFOD.

Bard of Avon. William Shakespeare (1564–1616), who was born and buried at Stratford-upon-Avon.

Bard of Ayrshire. Robert Burns (1759–1796), a native of Ayrshire.

Bard of Erin. Thomas Moore (1779–1852). Born in Dublin, writer of *Irish Melodies*, *Lalla Rookh*, etc. He spent most of his life in England.

Bard of Hope. Thomas Campbell (1777–1844), author of *The Pleasures of Hope* (1799).

Bard of the Imagination. Mark Akenside (1721–1770), author of *The Pleasures of the Imagination* (1744, rewritten 1757).

Bard of Memory. Samuel Rogers (1763–1855), author of *The Pleasures of Memory* (1792).

Bard of Olney. William Cowper (1731–1800), who for many years lived at Olney, Buckinghamshire.

Bard of Prose. Boccaccio (1313–1375), author of the DECAMERON.

> The Bard of Prose, creative spirit! he
> Of the Hundred Tales of Love.
> > BYRON: *Childe Harold*, IV, lvi.

Bard of Rydal Mount. William Wordsworth (1770–1850); so called because Rydal Mount was his home.

Bard of Twickenham. Alexander Pope (1688–1744), who had a house at Twickenham. Also called the **Wasp of Twickenham** by some of his contemporaries.

Bardolph. One of FALSTAFF'S inferior officers. Falstaff calls him "the knight of the burning lamp", because his nose was so red, and his face "so full of meteors". He is a low-bred, drunken swaggerer, without principle, and "POOR AS A CHURCH MOUSE". (*Henry IV, Parts I and II, Henry V, Merry Wives*.)

Barebones Parliament (4 July–11 December 1653). The Nominated or Little PARLIA-MENT of 140 members approved by Cromwell and the officers and derisively named after one of its members, Praise-God Barebon.

Barefooted. Certain FRIARS and nuns (some of whom wear sandals instead of shoes), especially the reformed section of the CAR-MELITES (White Friars) founded by St. TER-ESA in the 16th century, known as the *Discalced Carmelites* (Lat. *calceus*, a shoe). The practice is defended by the command of our Lord to His disciples "Carry neither purse, nor scrip, nor shoes" (*Luke* x, 4). The Jews and Romans used to put off their shoes in mourning and public calamities, by way of humiliation.

Bare poles, Under. When a ship has no sails set due to bad weather and gale conditions. Figuratively applied to a man reduced to the last extremity.

Bargain. Into the bargain. In addition thereto; besides what was bargained for.

King's, or **Queen's bad bargain.** *See under* KING.

To make the best of a bad bargain. To make the best of a matter in which one has been worsted.

To stand to a bargain. To abide by it; the Lat. *stare conventis, conditionibus stare, pactis stare*, etc.

Barisal Guns. The name given to certain mysterious booming sounds which occur at Barisal (Eastern Bengal) and seem to come from the sea. Similar phenomena at Seneca Lake, New York, are called *Lake guns*; on the coast of Holland and Belgium *mistpoeffers*; and in Italy *bombiti, baturlio marina*, etc.

Bark. Dogs in their wild state never bark, but howl, whine, and growl. Barking is an acquired habit.

Bark and the tree, Put not thy hand between the. Do not interfere in disputes between the closely related. Thomas Tusser advises in 1573 "not to put thy hand betwixt bark and the tree, least through thy owne follie so pinched thou be."

Barker. A pistol, which barks or makes a loud report. Also the man who stands at the entrance of a sideshow of a circus, etc., or touts outside a shop, shouting to attract custom. In the U.S.A. it is also applied to a baseball coach.

Barking dogs seldom bite. Huffing, bouncing, hectoring fellows rarely possess cool courage. Similar proverbs are found in Latin, French, Italian and German.

His bark is worse than his bite. He scolds and abuses roundly, but does not bear malice or act harshly.

To bark at the moon. To rail uselessly, especially at those in high places, as a dog thinks to frighten the moon by baying at it. There is a superstition that when a dog does this it portends death or ill-luck.

> I had rather be a dog, and bay the moon,
> Than such a Roman.
>
> SHAKESPEARE: *Julius Caesar*, IV, iii.

To bark up the wrong tree. To waste energy, to be on the wrong scent. The phrase comes from raccoon hunting, which takes place in the dark. The dogs are used to mark the tree where the raccoon has taken refuge, but they can mistake the tree in the dark and bark up the wrong one.

Barkis is willin'. The message sent by Barkis to Peggotty through David Copperfield, expressing his desire to marry. It has become a proverbial expression indicating willingness.

Barlaam and Josaphat (bar′ lăm, jós à făt). An Indian romance telling how Barlaam, an ascetic of the desert of Sinai, converted Josaphat, a Hindu prince, to Christianity. Probably translated into Greek by the 6th century, and put into its final form by St. John of Damascus, a Syrian monk of the 8th century, in part it corresponds closely with the legendary story of BUDDHA'S youth. It became a widely popular mediæval romance. The Story of the Three Caskets was used by SHAKESPEARE in *The Merchant of Venice*.

Barley. To cry barley. An old country game akin to "Prisoners' Base", having a "home" which was called "hell". Herrick has a poem, *Barley-break, or Last in Hell*. Barley, a corruption of parley, was, in rough games, a cry for a truce.

Barley-bree. ALE: malt liquor brewed from barley, also called *barley-broth*.

> The cock may craw, the day may daw,
> And aye we'll taste the barley-bree.
>
> BURNS: *Willie Brew'd a Peck o' Maut*.

Barley-mow. A heap or stack of barley (O.E. *muga*; *cp*. Icel. *muge*, a swathe). *See* MOW.

John, or **Sir John Barleycorn.** A personification of malt liquor. The term was popularized by Burns.

> Inspiring bold John Barleycorn,
> What dangers thou canst make us scorn!
>
> *Tam o'Shanter*.

To wear the barley cap. To be top-heavy or tipsy with BARLEY-BREE.

Barmecide's Feast. An illusion, particularly one containing a great disappointment. In the ARABIAN NIGHTS, *The Barber's story of his sixth Brother*, a prince of the great Barmecide family in Baghdad, desirous of sport, asked Schacabac, a poor starving wretch, to dinner. Having set before him a series of empty plates, the merchant asked, "How do you like your soup?" "Excellently well," replied Schacabac. "Did you ever see whiter bread?" "Never, honourable sir," was the civil answer. Illusory wine was later offered, but Schacabac excused himself by pretending to be drunk already, and knocked the Barmecide down. The latter saw the humour of the situation, forgave Schacabac, and provided him with food to his heart's content.

Barmy. Mad, crazy, *i.e.* full of froth. Sometimes incorrectly spelled "balmy". Hence, in prison slang, **to put on the barmy stick** is to feign insanity. There is a popular misconception that the word comes from *Barming* (near Maidstone) because the county lunatic asylum was built at Barming Heath.

Barnabas. St. Barnabas's Day, 11 June. St. Barnabas was a fellow-labourer of St. PAUL. His symbol is a rake, because 11 June is the time of hay-harvest.

Barnabites. An order of regular clerks of St. PAUL, recognized by Clement VII in 1533. Probably so called from the Church of St. Barnabas in Milan which became their centre.

Barnaby Bright. An old provincial name for St. BARNABAS'S Day (11 June). Before the reform of the CALENDAR it was the longest day, hence the jingle in Ray's *Collection of Proverbs*—

Barnaby bright! Barnaby bright!
The longest day and the shortest night.

Barnaby Lecturers. In the University of Cambridge, four lecturers elected annually on St. BARNABAS'S Day, to lecture on mathematics, philosophy, rhetoric, and logic.

Barnaby Rudge. This novel by Charles Dickens, which first appeared in 1840, centres round the Gordon riots of 1780, and he drew upon the memories of survivors of these times. Barnaby was a half-witted lad whose companion was a raven.

Barnacle. A species of wild GOOSE allied to the Brent Goose, called in Germany the "duck-mussel". Also the popular name of the *Cirri-pedes*, especially those attached by a stalk to floating balks of timber and the bottoms of ships. In mediæval times it was held that the goose developed from it as a frog does from a tadpole.

The name is given figuratively to close and constant companions, hangers-on; and also to PLACEMEN who cling to office, like barnacles sticking to the bottoms of ships.

Barnacles. Spectacles, especially those of heavy make and clumsy appearance. A slang term from their supposed resemblance to the twitches or barnacles formerly used by farriers to restrain unruly horses while being shod, etc. This instrument, consisting of two branches joined at one end by a hinge, was used to grip the horse's nose. Probably a diminutive of the O.Fr. *bernac*, a kind of muzzle for horses.

Barnard's Inn. One of the old Inns of CHANCERY, formerly situated on the south side of HOLBORN and once known as "Mackworth's Inn", because Dean Mackworth of Lincoln (d. 1454) lived there.

Barn-burners. Destroyers, who, like the Dutchmen of story, would burn down their barns to rid themselves of the rats. In the U.S.A. the term was applied to the radical section of the Democratic party in New York State in the Presidential election of 1844 by their conservative opponents, who were called HUNKERS. The Barn-burners finally joined the Republican party in the 1850s to further the cause of anti-slavery.

Barney. A dispute, argument or rumpus. A contraction of BARNABAS, current in England and Australia. Barney was a fairly common name among Irish settlers in the 19th century, and the usage is probably an allusion to their reputed temperament and behaviour.

Barnstormer. A strolling player, and hence any second-rate actor, especially one whose style is an exaggerated declamatory kind. From the itinerant actors who performed in village barns.

In the U.S.A. the term has also been applied to a stunt pilot touring country districts or one giving trips for a fee; also to someone carrying out a speaking tour in rural areas, etc.

Barnwell, George. The subject of the 17th-century ballad in PERCY'S RELIQUES which formed the basis of George Lillo's prose tragedy *The London Merchant, or the History of George Barnwell*, produced in 1731. Barnwell was a London apprentice, who fell in with a wanton in SHOREDITCH, named Sarah Millwood, to whom he gave £200 of his master's money in return for her favours. He next robbed his uncle, a rich grazier at Ludlow, and beat out his brains. Having spent the money, Sarah turned him out; each informed against the other and both were hanged.

Baron is from Late Lat. *baro*, a man (especially opposed to something else, as a freeman to slave, etc.). After the Norman CONQUEST it denoted the man or VASSAL of a great noble, especially the king, and by the 13th century the distinction between greater and lesser barons was well established. The greater barons came to be summoned to the GREAT COUNCIL by individual writs and the term *baronage* became equated to peerage. It is now the lowest order of nobility.

In colloquial speech in the U.S.A. it is equivalent to "magnate" as in "beef baron" and "soap baron".

Baron and feme. An heraldic term for husband and wife, an example of the older use of the word BARON.

Baron Bung. Mine host, master of the beer bung.

Baron Münchausen. *See* MÜNCHAUSEN.

Baron of beef. A double SIRLOIN, left uncut at the backbone, and of great size, roasted at special festivities. Jocosely, but wrongly, said to be a pun upon *baron* and *sir* loin.

Barons of the Cinque Ports. The name given to the representatives of the CINQUE PORTS in the HOUSE OF COMMONS until the Reform Act of 1832.

Barons' War. The name applied to the civil war (1264–1267) between the baronial supporters of Simon de Montfort and the supporters of Henry III. Drayton's poem *The Barrons Wars* appeared in 1603.

Court Baron. A court dealing with matters concerning the duties and services relating to a MANOR, and with personal actions under 40 shillings. Freeholders were not subject to it but were under the COMMON LAW. *Cp.* COURT LEET *under* LEET; HUNDRED.

Tobacco Baron. *See* TOBACCO BARON.

Baronet. An hereditary title instituted by James I in 1611, the sale of which was to provide funds for the defence of the plantation of ULSTER. The Red Hand of Ulster became the badge of Baronets of England; of Great Britain; of the United Kingdom; and of Ireland (instituted in 1619). Baronets of Scotland and Nova Scotia were created from 1625. Nova Scotian patents ceased in 1638 after the colony had fallen to the French. Scottish creations ceased in 1707 and Irish from 1801, consequent upon the respective Acts of UNION.

Barrack. To barrack, is to jeer at, to receive with derisive applause, to interrupt with rude comments, particularly the players of games. In Australia, where the word came into use during the 1880s, it is nearly always used in the opposite sense meaning to cheer or support a team. It stems from the days when army supporters of the Victoria Barracks team entered the S. Melbourne cricket ground and were greeted with shouts of "here come the barrackers". *Barracking* was probably introduced into England by Australian cricketers and their supporters. That

it acquired an opposite meaning is understandable. *See* BORAK.

Barrack Hack. A lady who attends all barrack social events and hangs on the sleeves of the officers.

Barrack-room lawyer. A soldier with a real or professed knowledge of regulations who makes complaints against authority. A grouser. In American army parlance, a *latrine lawyer. Cp.* SEA LAWYER.

Barrack stanchion. In naval usage, a sailor who remains in barracks for a length of time instead of being sent to sea. The meaning is obvious.

Barrel House. A name applied in the U.S.A. in the late 19th century to a small squalid drinking saloon, where customers drew their own liquor from the cask. Also given to a rough uninhibited type of JAZZ.

Barrell's Blues. *See* REGIMENTAL AND DIVISIONAL NICKNAMES.

Barricade. To block up a street, building, etc., against attack. The term arose in France in 1588, when Henri of Guise returned to Paris in defiance of Henry III. The King called out the SWISS GUARDS, and the Parisians tore up the pavements, threw chains across the streets, and piled up barrels (Fr. *barriques*) filled with earth and stones, from behind which they shot down the Swiss.

The day of the Barricades—

(1) 12 May 1588, when the people forced Henry III to flee from Paris.

(2) 5 August 1648, the beginning of the FRONDE.

(3) 27 July 1830, the first day of *la grande semaine* which resulted in the abdication of Charles X.

(4) 24 February 1848, when Louis Philippe abdicated.

(5) 25 June 1848, when the Archbishop of Paris was shot in attempting to quell the insurrection consequent upon the closing of the national workshops.

(6) 2 December 1851, the day of Louis NAPOLEON III's *coup d'état*, when the RADICALS attempted resistance.

In spite of Napoleon III's street widening in Paris, partly to prevent the successful erection of barricades, the Communards made further use of them during the second siege of Paris in 1871.

Barrister. One who has been "called to the BAR", and is thereafter entitled to plead in any court, having received his brief from a solicitor. Formerly called "outer" or "UTTER" barristers, after ten years as junior counsel they may apply to "take SILK" to become QUEEN'S (King's) COUNSEL. Until 1877 there was a superior third group called SERGEANTS-AT-LAW. The Q.C. is a senior barrister and is entitled to wear a silk gown and full-bottomed wig. Other barristers wear a stiff gown and short wig.

A Revising Barrister. One appointed to

revise the list of electors for members of PARLIAMENT.

A Vacation Barrister. Formerly one newly called to the bar, who for three years had to attend in "Long Vacation". The practice is now obsolete.

Barrister's Bags. *See* LAWYER'S BAGS.

Barrister's gowns. "UTTER barristers wear a stiff or bombazine gown, and the puckered material between the shoulders of the gown is all that is now left of the purse into which, in early days, the successful litigant ... dropped his ... pecuniary tribute ... for services rendered" (*Notes and Queries*, 11 March 1893, p.124). Barristers' fees have always been treated as gratuities and even now are not recoverable at law.

Barrowists. In the reign of Elizabeth I, PURITAN followers of Henry Barrow, holding CONGREGATIONALIST views similar to the BROWNISTS.

Barry Cornwall. The NOM DE PLUME of Bryan Waller Procter (1787–1874). Writer of once popular songs.

Bartholomew, St. The symbol of this SAINT is a knife, in allusion to the knife with which he was flayed alive, reputedly in A.D. 44. His day is 24 August.

Bartholomew doll. A TAWDRY overdressed woman; like one of the flashy bespangled dolls offered for sale at Bartholomew Fair.

Bartholomew Fair. A FAIR opened annually at SMITHFIELD on St. Bartholomew's Day, from 1133 to 1752; after the reform of the CALENDAR it began on 3 September. It was removed to Islington in 1840 and was last held in 1855 (*see* CALEDONIAN MARKET). One of the great national fairs dealing in cloth, livestock, etc., accompanied by a variety of amusements and entertainments, it long held its place as a centre of London life. The PURITANS failed to suppress it. Ben Jonson's *Bartholomew Fair*, a comedy of manners, was first acted in 1614.

> Here's that will challenge all the fairs,
> Come buy my nuts and damsons and Burgamy pears!
> Here's the *Woman of Babylon, the Devil and the Pope*.
> And here's the little girl just going on the rope!
> Here's *Dives and Lazarus*, and the *World's Creation;*
> Here's the Tall Dutchwoman, the like's not in the nation.
> Here is the booths where the high Dutch maid is,
> Here are the bears that dance like any ladies;
> Tat, tat, tat, tat, says little penny trumpet;
> Here's Jacob Hall, that does so jump it, jump it;
> Sound trumpet, sound, for silver spoon and fork.
> Come, here's your dainty pig and pork!
> *Wit and Drollery* (1682).

Bartholomew, Massacre of St. The slaughter of the French HUGUENOTS begun on St. Bartholomew's Day, 24 August 1572, in Paris and the provinces, at the instigation of Catherine de' MEDICI, mother of Charles IX. Probably some 50,000 people perished.

Bartholomew pig. A very fat person. At BARTHOLOMEW FAIR one of the chief attractions used to be a pig, roasted whole and sold piping hot. Doll Tearsheet calls Falstaff—

> Thou whoreson little tidy Bartholomew boar-pig.
> *Henry IV, Pt. II*, II, iv.

Bartolist. One skilled in law, or specifically a student of Bartolus. Bartolus (1314–1357) was an eminent Italian lawyer who greatly enhanced the status of the law school of Perugia, particularly by his *Commentary on the Code of Justinian*.

Bas Bleu. *See* BLUE-STOCKING.

Base Tenure. Originally tenure not by military, but by base service, such as a serf or VILLEIN might give; later, villein tenure became COPYHOLD tenure.

Bashaw. An arrogant, domineering man; a corruption of the Turkish PASHA, a viceroy or provincial governor.

The Three Bashaws of Somerset House. A popular nickname for the three Poor Law Commissioners (T. Frankland Lewis, J. G. Shaw Lefevre, George Nicholls) appointed under the Poor Law Amendment Act of 1834. SOMERSET HOUSE was their headquarters.

A three-tailed bashaw. A *beglerbeg* or prince of princes among the Turks, who has a standard of three horse-tails borne before him. The next rank is the bashaw with two tails, and then the bey who has only one horse-tail.

Bashi-bazouk (băsh' i bă zook'). A savage and brutal ruffian (Turkish *bashi*, headdress; *bozuq*, unkempt). It was applied in Turkey to non-uniformed irregular soldiers who made up in plunder what they did not get in pay. The term came into prominence at the time of the Crimean War and again through the Bulgarian atrocities of 1876.

Basic English. A fundamental selection of 850 English words designed by C. K. Ogden as a common first step in the teaching of English and as an auxiliary language. The name comes from the initials of the words British, American, Scientific, International, Commercial. *Cp.* ESPERANTO; INTERLINGUA; VOLAPÜK.

Basilian Monks. A monastic order founded by St. Basil in *c.* 360 whose rule became the basis of monasticism in the Greek and Russian churches.

Basilica (bà zil' i kà) (Gr. *basilikos*, royal). Originally a royal palace, but afterwards (in

ROME) a large building with nave, aisles, and an apse at one end used as a court of justice and for public meetings. Some were adapted by the early Christians and many churches were modelled on them. Constantine built the great basilicas of St. PETER (rebuilt in the 16th century), St. PAUL, and St. John Lateran.

Basilisco. A braggart. Basilisco was a cowardly, bragging KNIGHT in Kyd's (?) tragedy *Solyman and Perseda* (?1588). SHAKESPEARE (*King John*, I, i) makes the BASTARD say to his mother, who asks him why he boasted of his ill-birth, "Knight, knight, good mother, Basilisco-like" *i.e.* my boasting has made me a knight.

Basilisk (baz' i lisk). The fabulous king of serpents (Gr. *basileus*, a king), also called a COCKATRICE and alleged to be hatched by a SERPENT from a cock's egg. It was reputed to be capable of "looking anyone dead on whom it fixed its eyes".

> The Basiliske…
> From powerful eyes close venim doth convay
> Into the lookers hart, and killeth farre away.
> SPENSER: *The Faerie Queene*, IV, vii, 37.

Also the name given to a genus of Central American lizard and to a large brass cannon of Tudor times.

Basin Street. A street in the RED-LIGHT DISTRICT of the French quarter of New Orleans which is possibly the original home of American JAZZ music. The well-known *Basin Street Blues* was composed by Spencer Williams in 1928.

Basket. To be left in the basket. Neglected or uncared for. Formerly foundling hospitals used to place baskets at their doors for the reception of abandoned infants. *Basket* is also a EUPHEMISM for BASTARD.

To give a basket. To refuse to marry. In Germany it was an old custom to fix a basket on the roof of one who had been jilted.

To go to the basket. Old slang for consignment to prison: referring to the dependence of the lowest grade of poor prisoners upon what passers-by put in the basket for their sustenance.

To put all your eggs in one basket. *See* EGG.

Basochians (bà sosh' yànz). An old French term for clerks of the PARLEMENTS, hence, lawyers. In Paris, their chief, called *le roi de la basoche*, had his court, coin and grand officers, and reviewed his subjects annually. Henry III (1574–1589) suppressed the office.

The *basoche* presented entertainments including farces, political satires, and moralities, thus contributing to the development of the theatre. There were also certain local *basoches*. All were abolished by 1790. *Cp.* Enfants SANS SOUCI.

Messager produced a comic opera called *La Basoche* in 1890.

Bast. *See* BUBASTIS.

Bastard. An illegitimate child, from the Old French *bast*, a pack-saddle, used by muleteers as a bed; hence, one begotten on a pack-saddle bed. *Cp.* BANTLING; BATMAN.

Also an old name for a sweetened Spanish wine made from the bastard muscadine grape.

> I will pledge you willingly in a cup of bastard.
> SIR WALTER SCOTT: *Kenilworth*, Ch. III.

Baste. I'll give you a thorough basting, *i.e.* beating. The word is of uncertain origin but may derive from the fact that lazy scullions and TURNSPITS were sometimes beaten by the enraged cook with the basting-stick, a long-handled wooden spoon ending in a funnel which was used for basting the joint of meat on the spit with hot fat from the dripping pan beneath.

Bastille (bàs tēl') (O.Fr. *Bastir*, now *bâtir*, to build). A fortress, but specifically the famous state prison in Paris built as a royal castle by Charles V between 1370 and 1383, seized and sacked by the mob in the French Revolution, 14 July 1789. Regarded as a symbol of tyranny, *bastille*, when used of a building or establishment, implies prison-like qualities. *Cp.* ALTMARK.

Bat. HARLEQUIN'S lath wand (Fr. *batte*, a wooden sword).

Off his own bat. By his own exertions; on his own account. A cricketer's phrase, meaning runs made by a single player.

Parliament of Bats. *See* CLUB PARLIAMENT.

To bat along, to get along at a great bat. Here the word means beat, pace, rate of speed.

To bat on a sticky wicket. To have to take action or carry on in difficult circumstances where things make success unlikely. In CRICKET the batsman playing on recently rained-on turf finds the movement of the ball very tricky.

To carry one's bat (in cricket). A batsman who goes in first and is "not out" at the end of the innings.

To have bats in the belfry, or **attic.** To be crazy in the head, bats here being the nocturnal variety.

On a bat, or **on the bat.**

> On a spree I went to a bat in S's rooms and we smoked till three.
> W. T. WASHFORD: *Fair Harvard* (1869).

Without batting an eyelid. Without betraying surprise. Here *batting* is derived from the now obsolete *bate* (from O.Fr. *batre*) meaning to beat the wings, to flutter.

Batman (Fr. *bat*, pack-saddle). Originally a soldier in charge of a **bat-horse** (pack-horse) and its load of officer's baggage. The name came to denote an army officer's servant in World War I through its inaccurate use by non-regular wartime officers. *Cp.* BASTARD.

It also now denotes the man on an aerodrome or an aircraft carrier who wields a pair of lightweight bats to assist aircraft to land or take off.

Bate me an Ace. *See* BOLTON.

Bath. Knights of the Bath. This order derives its name from the ceremony of bathing which was formerly practised at the inauguration of a KNIGHT as a symbol of purity. Established in the reign of Henry IV, the last knights were created in the ancient manner at the coronation of Charles II in 1661. G.C.B. stands for Grand Cross of the Bath (the first class); K.C.B., Knight Commander of the Bath (the second class); C.B., Companion of the Bath (the third class).

Bath brick. A scouring brick made at Bridgwater, Somerset, used for cleaning steel knives, metals, etc. made from sand and clay taken from the River Parret, which runs through the town.

Also a naval nickname for Malta, derived from the particular hue of its stone buildings.

Bath chair. An invalid chair mounted on wheels, first used at Bath, frequented by invalids on account of its hot springs.

Bath, King of. Richard Nash (1674–1762), commonly called BEAU NASH, for 56 years the celebrated master of ceremonies at Bath.

Bath King-of-Arms. *See* HERALDRY.

Bath metal. An alloy like PINCHBECK consisting of copper, zinc, lead and tin. Also called mosaic gold, DUTCH GOLD, etc.

Bath Oliver. A special kind of biscuit invented by Dr. William Oliver (1695–1764), founder of the Royal Mineral Water Hospital, Bath; an authority on GOUT, he left his biscuit recipe to his coachman, Atkins.

Bath post. A letter paper with a highly glazed surface, used by the ultra-fashionable visitors of Bath when that spa was in its prime. *See* POST PAPER.

Bath shillings. Silver tradesmen's tokens coined at Bath in 1811–1812 with face values of 4s., 2s., 1s.

Bath stone. An attractive, but not very durable building stone, quarried in the Lower Oolite, near Bath.

There, go to Bath with you! Don't talk

nonsense. Insane persons used to be sent to Bath for the benefit of its mineral waters. The implication of silliness is obvious.

Bathia (băth' i à). The name given in the TALMUD to the daughter of PHARAOH who found MOSES in the ark of bulrushes.

Bathos (bā' thos) (Gr. *bathos*, depth). First used by Pope (1727) in the sense of a ludicrous descent from grandiloquence to the commonplace.

> And, thou Dalhousie, the great god of war,
> Lieutenant-general to the Earl of Mar.
> *Bathos*, ix.

Bathyllus (băth' i lùs). A beautiful boy of Samos, greatly beloved by Polycrates the tyrant, and by the poet ANACREON (Horace: *Epistle* xiv, 9).

Bat-Kol (băt kol') (daughter of the voice). A heavenly or divine voice announcing the will of God. It existed in the time of the Jewish prophets but was also heard in post-prophetic times. The expression "daughter of a voice", meaning a small voice, differentiated it from the customary voice. Bat-Kol also denoted a kind of OMEN or AUGURY. After an appeal to Bat-Kol the first words heard were considered oracular.

Batrachomyomachia (bă' trak ō mi' ō mā kyà). A "STORM IN A TEACUP"; much ado about nothing. The word means *The Battle of the Frogs and Mice* and is the name of a mock heroic Greek epic once attributed to HOMER but probably by Pigres of Caria.

Batta (băt' à). An Anglo-Indian term for perquisites. Properly an extra allowance once paid to officers of the British army in India which varied according to where they were stationed, etc. Also spelt *batty*.

> He would rather live on half-pay in a garrison that could boast of a fives-court than vegetate on full batta where there was none.
> G. R. GLEIG: *Thomas Munro*, vol. I, ch. iv, p. 287.

Battels (băt' ĕlz). At Oxford University the accounts for board and provisions, etc., and more loosely for total college expenses for the term, including tuition fees, etc. The word, of uncertain origin, has also been used for the provisions or rations themselves.

Battersea. You must go to Battersea to get your simples cut. A reproof to a simpleton, or one who makes a very foolish observation. The market gardeners of Battersea used to grow simples (medicinal herbs), and the London apothecaries went there to cut or select such as they wanted.

Battle. A pitched battle. A battle which has been planned, and the ground pitched on or chosen beforehand.

A close battle. Originally a naval engagement **at close quarters** in which opposing ships engage each other alongside.

Half the battle. *See* THE FIRST BLOW IS HALF THE BATTLE *under* BLOW.

Line of battle. The formation of ships in line ahead or line abreast in a naval engagement. A *line of battle ship* was a CAPITAL SHIP built and equipped to take part in a main attack. Also a line or lines of troops drawn up for battle.

Order of battle. The arrangement and disposition of an army or fleet according to the situation prior to engagement.

Trial by battle or **by Combat; Wager of battle.** An ancient usage abolished by 59 Geo. III, c. 46 (1819), after a man accused of murder escaped conviction in 1818, by appealing to *wager of battel* by throwing down the glove, which his accuser did not take up. Originally one of the forms of ORDEAL, when the accuser and accused could settle a case by personal combat in the presence of the court under the assumption that God would give the victory to the innocent.

Battle above the clouds. *See* CLOUDS.

Battle bowler. A nickname given in World War I to the soldier's steel helmet or tin hat. In World War II it was also called a "tin topee".

Battle of Britain. The attempt of the German Luftwaffe by their prolonged attack on S.E. England (August–October 1940) to defeat the R.A.F., as a prelude to invasion. R.A.F. Fighter Command gained the victory and universal admiration. The name arose from Sir Winston Churchill's speech (18 June 1940)—"What General Weygand called the 'Battle of France' is over. I expect that the Battle of Britain is about to begin."

Battle of the Books. A satire by Swift (written 1697, published 1704) on the current literary dispute as to the relative merits of ancient and modern authors. In the battle, ancient and modern books assail each other in St. James's Library. *See* BOYLE CONTROVERSY.

Battle of the Frogs and Mice. *See* BATRACHOMYOMACHIA.

Battle of the Giants. *See* GIANTS.

Battle of the Herrings. *See* HERRINGS.

Battle of the Nations. *See* NATIONS.

Battle of the Poets, The. A satirical poem (1725) by John Sheffield, Duke of Buckingham, in which the versifiers of the time are brought into the field.

Battle of the Spurs. *See* SPURS.

Battle of the Standard. *See* STANDARD.

Battle of the Standards. The nickname given to the presidential election contest of 1896. The Republican candidate, William

McKinley, upheld the single GOLD STANDARD, and the Democratic candidate, William Jennings Bryan, fought for the free and unrestricted coinage of silver. The latter was defeated by a comparatively small margin. It was regarded as a victory for "big property".

Battle of the Three Emperors. *See* THREE EMPERORS.

Battle-painter, The. *See* MICHAEL ANGELO.

Battle Royal. In COCKFIGHTING, a certain number of birds are pitted together and left to fight until there is one survivor, the victor of the battle royal (*cp.* WELSH MAIN). Metaphorically the term is applied to any contest of wits, a general mêlée, etc.

Battledore-book. A name sometimes used for a HORN-BOOK, because of its shape like a shuttlecock bat or battledore. Hence, perhaps, the phrase "not to know B from a battledore". *See* CHRISSCROSS.

Batty. *See* BATTA. Also slang for crazy, to have "bats in the belfry" (*see* BAT).

Baturlio marina. *See* BARISAL GUNS.

Baubee. *See* BAWBEE.

Bauble. A fool should never hold a bauble in his hand. "'Tis a foolish bird that fouls its own nest", a fool should not advertise his folly. The bauble was a short stick, ornamented with ass's ears, carried by licensed fools (O.Fr. *bable*, or *baubel*, a child's toy; perhaps confused with M.E. *babyll* or *babulle*, a stick with a thong). Oliver Cromwell thus contemptuously alluded to the House of Commons MACE, when dismissing the RUMP. "What shall we do with this baubel?" he said, picking up the mace. "Take it away."

If every fool held a bauble, fuel would be dear. The proverb indicates that the world contains a vast number of fools.

To deserve the bauble. To be so foolish as to qualify for the fool's emblem.

Baucis. *See* PHILEMON.

Bauld Willie. *See* BELTED WILL.

Baulk. *See* BALK.

Baviad, The (băv′ i ăd). A merciless satire by William Gifford on the DELLA CRUSCAN poetry, published in 1794, and republished with *The Maeviad* in 1795. Bavius and Maevius were two minor poets pilloried by VIRGIL (*Eclogue* iii, 9).

> He may with foxes plough, and milk he-goats,
> Who praises Bavius or on Maevius dotes.

Their names are used for inferior poets.

> May some choice patron bless each grey goose quill,
> May every Bavius have his Bufo still.
> POPE: *Prologue to Satires*, 249–250.

Bavieca. *See* FAMOUS HORSES (under HORSE).

Bavius. *See* BAVIAD.

Bawbee. A Scottish small coin or half-penny first issued in 1541. The word is probably derived from a mint-master of that time, the laird of Sillebawby.

Jenny's bawbee. Her marriage portion.

Bawtry. Like the saddler of Bawtry, who was hanged for leaving his liquor (Yorkshire proverb). It was customary for criminals on their way to execution to stop at a certain tavern in York for a "parting draught". The saddler of Bawtry refused to accept the liquor and was hanged. If he had stopped a few minutes at the tavern, his reprieve, which was on the road, would have arrived in time to save his life.

Baxterians. Followers of Richard Baxter (1615–1691), eminent divine of PRESBYTERIAN sympathies, who took a prominent part in the SAVOY CONFERENCE, but was ejected by the Act of Uniformity (1662). His chief doctrines were—(1) That Christ died in a spiritual sense for the elect, and in a general sense for all; (2) that there is no such thing as reprobation; (3) that even saints may fall from grace.

Bay. A shrub of the LAUREL family, *Laurus nobilis*, used for flavouring, was the bay of the ancients. As the tree of APOLLO (*see* DAPHNE) it was held to be a safeguard against thunder and lightning. Hence, according to Pliny, Tiberius and other Roman emperors wore a wreath of bay as an AMULET.

> Reach the bays—
> I'll tie a garland here about his head;
> 'Twill keep my boy from lightning.
> WEBSTER: *Vittoria Corombona*, V, i.

The withering of a bay tree was supposed to be an OMEN of evil or death. Holinshed's reference to this superstition is used by SHAKESPEARE in *King Richard II* (II, iv).

> 'Tis thought the King is dead; we will not stay.
> The bay trees in our country all are wither'd.

In another sense *bay* is a reddish-brown colour, generally used of horses. The word is the Fr. *bai*, from Lat. *badius*, a term used by Varro in his list of colours appropriate to horses. Thus BAYARD means "bay-coloured".

Crowned with bays. A reward of victory: from the ancient Roman custom of so crowning a victorious general.

To bay at the moon. *See under* BARK.

To flourish like a green bay tree. To prosper exceedingly. The bay throws out many fresh green branches every year from both base and trunk. *Psalm* xxxvii has:

> I have seen the wicked in great power, and spreading himself like a green bay tree.

Bay Psalm Book, or **The Whole Booke of Psalmes.** A translation for colonial churches by Thomas Welde, Richard Mather and John Eliot and the first book published in NEW ENGLAND, printed by Stephen Daye and his family at Cambridge, Mass., in 1640, and of which only eleven copies are known to have survived. Now highly prized, a copy changed hands in 1947 for $151,000.

Bay salt. Coarse-grained salt, formerly obtained by slow evaporation of sea water and used for curing meat, etc. "Bay" here does not signify colour: perhaps the salt is so called because originally imported from the coast of the Bay of Biscay.

The Bay State. Massachusetts. Originally the Colony of Massachusetts Bay.

The Queen's Bays. *See* REGIMENTAL AND DIVISIONAL NICKNAMES.

Bay-window. An old nickname for a fat belly, which sticks out, as a bay-window does, from the house-front; the same as BOW-WINDOW.

Bayadere (bā ya′ dâr). A Hindu professional dancing girl or nautch-girl employed for religious dances and private amusements. The word is a French corruption of the Portuguese *bailadeira*, a female dancer.

Bayard (bā′ yard). A horse of incredible swiftness, given by CHARLEMAGNE to the four sons of AYMON. If only one of the sons mounted, the horse was of ordinary size; but if all four mounted, his body became elongated to the requisite length. He is introduced in Boiardo's ORLANDO INNAMORATO and Ariosto's ORLANDO FURIOSO, Tasso's RINALDO, etc. It is the name given to Fitz-James's horse in Scott's *The Lady of the Lake*. The name is used for any valuable or wonderful horse. *See* BAY.

Bold as a Blind Bayard. Foolhardy. If a blind horse leaps, the chance is that he will fall into a ditch. Francis Grose's *Dictionary of the Vulgar Tongue* (1823) has the following expression, **To ride Bayard of ten toes**—"Going by the MARROW-BONE STAGE"—*i.e.* walking.

Keep Bayard in the stable. Keep what is valuable under lock and key.

Bayard, Chevalier de. Pierre du Terrail (1475–1524), a celebrated French KNIGHT and national hero, distinguished in the Italian campaigns of Charles VIII, Louis XII and Francis I. *Le bon chevalier, le chevalier sans peur et sans reproche* were names bestowed upon him. *Cp.* ADMIRABLE CRICHTON.

Bayard of the Confederate Army. Robert E. Lee (1807–1870).

The Bayard of the East, or **of the Indian Army.** Sir James Outram (1803–1863).

The British Bayard. Sir Philip Sidney (1554–1586), the pride of Elizabeth I's court, who was mortally wounded at the battle of Zutphen (1586).

The Polish Bayard. Prince Joseph Poniatowski (1763–1813), who served with the greatest distinction under NAPOLEON.

Bayardo. The famous steed of RINALDO, which once belonged to AMADIS OF GAUL. *See* BAYARD.

Bayardo's Leap. Three stones, about thirty yards apart, near Sleaford. It is said that Rinaldo was riding on his favourite steed, when the demon of the place sprang up behind him; but Bayardo took three tremendous leaps and unhorsed the fiend.

Bayes (bāz). A character in the *Rehearsal* (1671), by the 2nd Duke of Buckingham, designed to satirize Dryden. The name is derived from the BAY Laurel of the laureateship.

Dead men may rise again, like Bayes's troops, or the savages in the Fantocini. In the *Rehearsal* a battle is fought between foot-soldiers and great HOBBY-HORSES. At last DRAWCANSIR kills all on both sides. Smith then asks how they are to go off, to which Bayes replies, "As they come on—upon their legs", upon which they all jump up alive again.

Bayonets. A synonym of "rank and FILE", that is, privates and corporals of infantry. As, "the number of bayonets was 25,000". In former times the strength of a cavalry force was indicated similarly by "Sabres".

Bayou State (bī' yoo). The State of Mississippi; so called from its numerous bayous. A bayou is a creek or sluggish and marshy offshoot of a river or lake. The word is probably a corruption of the Fr. *boyau*, gut.

Bazooka. (1) A comedian's trombone-type wind instrument. The name is perhaps modelled on *Kazoo*, a once popular submarine-shaped toy producing sounds of the "comb and paper" variety. (2) American infantry light rocket-firing tube used as an anti-tank weapon in World War II. It was then applied to the British P.I.A.T. (projectile, infantry anti-tank) and the German *Panzerfaust*.

To be bazookaed. To be in a tank struck by such a weapon and thus metaphorically to be "scuppered", put out of action, done for.

Beachcomber. One who subsists on what FLOTSAM AND JETSAM he can find on the seashore. The word originated in New Zealand, where it is found in print in 1844; an earlier form (1827) was beach ranger, analogous to BUSHRANGER.

Bead. From O.E. *-bed* (in *gebed*), a prayer. "Bead" thus originally meant "a prayer"; but as prayers were "told" (*i.e.* account was kept of them) on a PATERNOSTER, the word came to be transferred to the small globular object which, threaded on a string, made up the paternoster or ROSARY.

To count one's beads. To say one's prayers. *See* ROSARY.

To draw a bead on. *See* DRAW.

To pray without one's beads. To be out of one's reckoning.

Baily's beads. When the disc of the moon has (in an eclipse) reduced that of the sun to a thin crescent, the crescent assumes a resemblance to a string of beads. This phenomenon, caused by the sun shining through the depressions between the lunar mountains, was first accurately described by Francis Baily in 1836, hence the name.

St. Cuthbert's beads. *See under* CUTHBERT.

St. Martin's beads. *See under* MARTIN.

Bead-house. An almshouse for BEADSMEN.

Bead-roll. A list of persons to be prayed for; hence also any list.

Beadsman, or **Bedesman.** Properly, one who prays; hence an inmate of an ALMSHOUSE, since most of these charities, under the terms of their foundation, required the inmates to pray for the soul of the founder. *See* BEAD.

Beadle. One whose duty it is to bid or cite persons to appear in a court; also a church servant, whose duty it was to bid parishioners to attend the VESTRY and to execute its orders. The word is ultimately from the Old High Ger. *Bitel*, one who asks, but it came to us from the O.Fr. *badel*, a herald. *See* BEDEL.

Beak. Slang for a police magistrate, but formerly (16th and 17th cent.) for a constable. Of uncertain origin.

Beam. In nautical usage, that part of the ship's side between the bows and quarter; also the extreme breadth of a ship. Thus **on the port beam** means away on the left-hand side of the ship when facing the bows; **on the starboard beam** is similarly away on the right-hand side. **On the weather beam** is the side of the ship from which the wind is blowing.

To be on one's beam ends. To be driven to one's last shift, to be virtually destitute. The *beams* of a wooden ship are the transverse timbers which support the decks and retain the sides, and a vessel is said to be on her beam ends when heeling excessively, or laid on her side—an extremely dangerous situation.

To be on the beam is to be on the right course or track. A modern phrase coming from the directing of aircraft by means of a radio beam.

To kick the beam. *See* KICK.

Beam (of a stag). The main trunk of the horn, the part that bears the branches (O.E. *bēam*, a tree).

Bean. Every bean has its black. *Nemo sine vitis nascitur* (everyone has his faults). The bean has a black eye (*Ogni grano ha la sua semola*).

He has found the bean in the cake. He has got a prize in the lottery, has come to some unexpected good fortune. The allusion is to the custom of hiding a bean in TWELFTH-NIGHT cakes. When the cake is cut up, he who gets the bean is BEAN-KING.

Jack and the bean-stalk. *See* JACK.

Old bean. A colloquial expression of good-natured familiarity (*cp*. Old boy, Old chap, Old man, etc.). Very common early in the 20th century.

Bean-feast. Much the same as WAYZ-GOOSE. Properly an annual dinner given by an employer to his employees, possibly because beans or a BEAN-GOOSE were prominent in the meal. Now applied to various annual outings and jollifications or *beanos*.

Bean-goose. A grey goose (*Anser fabalis*) which arrives in England in the autumn; so named from a mark on its bill like a horse-bean. It is also reputed to be fond of newly sown beans.

Bean-king. *Rey de Habas*, the child appointed to play king on TWELFTH-NIGHT, the Bean-king's festival. The one who has found the bean in the Twelfth-night cake (*see above*).

Beans. Slang for property, money; also for a sovereign and a GUINEA, probably the O.Fr. cant, *biens*, meaning property. In such phrases as *not worth a bean*, the allusion is to the bean's small value. Similarly *without a bean* means penniless or "broke".

PYTHAGORAS forbade the use of beans to his disciples—not as a food, but the use of beans for political elections. Magistrates and other public officers were elected by beans cast by the voters into a helmet, and what Pythagoras advised was that his disciples should not interfere with politics or "love beans" (*i.e.* office). According to ARISTOTLE the word *bean* implied venery and that the prohibition "to abstain from beans" was equivalent to "keeping the body chaste".

Blue Beans. Lead shot. *Cp*. BLUEY.

Beans are in flower. A catch-phrase intended to account for a person's silliness. Our forefathers imagined that the perfume of bean flowers made people silly or light-headed.

He knows how many beans make five. He is no fool; he is "up to SNUFF"; he is not to be imposed upon. The reference is to an old catch. Everyone knows five beans make five, and on getting the correct answer the questioner says "But you don't know how many blue beans make five white ones." The correct answer to this is "Five—if peeled."

Full of beans. Said of a fresh and spirited horse; hence in good form; full of health and spirits.

I'll give him beans. I'll give him a thrashing. There is a similar French proverb, *S'il me donne des pois, je lui donnerai des fèves* (if he gives me peas I will give him beans), I will give him TIT FOR TAT, A ROLAND FOR AN OLIVER.

To spill the beans. To give away a secret, to let the cat out of the bag.

Bear. In STOCK EXCHANGE parlance, a speculator for a fall (*cp*. BULL). Thus **to operate for a bear,** or **to bear the market,** is to use every effort to depress prices so as to buy cheap and profit on the rise. Such a transaction is known as a **Bear account**. The term was current at least as early as the SOUTH SEA BUBBLE and probably derives from the proverb "Selling the SKIN before you have caught the bear". One who sold stocks in this way was formerly called a *bearskin jobber*. *See* BACKWARDATION.

The Bear. Albert (Albrecht), margrave of Brandenburg (*c.* 1100–1170).

The bloody bear, in Dryden's *The Hind and the Panther* (1687), means the INDEPENDENTS.

The Great Bear and Little Bear. These constellations were so named by the Greeks and their word, *arktos*, a bear, is still kept in the names, *Arcturus*, the bearward or guard, and *Arctic*. *See* ARCTIC REGION, CHARLES'S WAIN, NORTHERN WAGONER.

> The wind-shak'd surge, with high and monstrous mane,
> Seems to cast water on the burning bear
> And quench the guards of th'ever-fixed pole.
> SHAKESPEARE: *Othello*, II, i.

The "guards" referred to in this quotation are β and γ of URSA MINOR. One classical fable is that the nymph CALISTO had a son by ZEUS called Arcas. She was changed into a bear by the angry HERA. Calisto and her son were then set in the sky as constellations by Zeus.

> 'Twas here we saw Calisto's star retire
> Beneath the waves, unawed by Juno's ire.
> CAMOËNS: *Lusiad*, Bk. V.

The Northern Bear. An old nickname for Russia. In political cartoons the U.S.S.R. is still usually depicted as a bear.

A bridled bear. A young nobleman under the control of a travelling tutor. *See* BEAR-LEADER.

The bear and ragged staff. Crest of the Nevilles and later, Earls of Warwick, attracting particular note through the activities of WARWICK THE KINGMAKER and used as a PUBLIC HOUSE SIGN.

> Now by my father's badge, Old Nevil's crest,
> The rampant bear chain'd to the ragged staff.
> SHAKESPEARE: *Henry VI, Pt. II*, V, i.

Legend has it that the first earl was Arthgal of the ROUND TABLE, whose cognizance was a bear through having strangled one. Morvid, the second earl, slew a giant with a club made of a young tree stripped of its branches. To commemorate this victory he added the "ragged staff".

The bear and the tea-kettle. Said of a person who injures himself by foolish rage. The story is that one day the bear entered a hut in Kamchatka, when a kettle was on the fire. Master Bruin smelt at it and burnt his nose; greatly irritated he seized it and squeezed it against his breast, scalding himself terribly. He growled in agony till some neighbours killed him with their guns.

A bear sucking his paws. It was once held that when a bear was deprived of food it sustained life by sucking its paws. The same was said of the badger. The phrase is applied to industrious idleness.

As savage as a bear with a sore head. Unreasonably ill-tempered.

As a bear has no tail, for a lion he'll fail. The same as *Ne sutor supra crepidam* (let not the cobbler aspire above his last). Robert Dudley, Earl of Leicester, a descendant of the Warwick family, is said to have changed his own crest (a green lion with two tails) for the Warwick bear and ragged staff. Given command of the expedition to the Netherlands (1585), he was suspected of wider ambitions when the Netherlanders granted him "absolute authority" (1586). As the lion is monarch among beasts, some wit wrote under his crest set up in public, *Ursa caret cauda non queat esse leo, i.e.:*

> Your bear for lion needs must fail,
> Because your true bears have no tail.

If it were a bear it would bite you. An old expression applied to a person looking for something right in front of him, just under his nose.

To take the bear by the tooth. To "put your head into the LION's mouth"; needlessly to run into danger.

Bear garden, This place is a perfect. That is, full of confusion, noise, tumult and quarrels. In Tudor and Stuart times the gardens where bears were kept and baited for public amusement were notorious for noise and riotous disorder.

Bear-leader. In the 18th century denoted the tutor who conducted a young nobleman or youth of wealth and fashion on the GRAND TOUR. It is taken from the old custom of leading muzzled bears about the streets and making them show off to attract notice and money. (This practice was only made illegal in 1925.)

> Bear! (said Dr. Pangloss to his pupil). Under favour, young gentleman, I am the bear-leader, being appointed your tutor.
> G. COLMAN: *Heir-at-Law* (1797).

Bear. Come, bear a hand! Come and render help. Lend a hand, or bring your hand to bear on the work going on.

To bear arms. To do military service; to be entitled to heraldic coat of arms and crest.

To bear away (nautical). The same as TO BEAR UP but applied to the ship instead of the helm.

To bear one company. To be one's companion.

> His faithful dog shall bear him company.
> POPE: *Essay on Man, Epistle* i, 112.

To bear down. To overpower.

To bear down upon (nautical). To approach from the weather side.

To bear in mind. Not to forget; to remember for consideration.

To bear out. To corroborate, to confirm.

To bear up. To support; to keep the spirits up. In nautical language, to keep further away from the wind by putting the helm up. *Cp.* TO BEAR AWAY.

To bear with. To show forbearance.

To bear the bell. *See* BELL.

Beard. Among the Jews, Turks, Persians and many other peoples the beard has long been a sign of manly dignity and to cut it off wilfully is a deadly insult. MOSLEMS swore by the beard of the Prophet and to swear by one's beard was an assurance of good faith. To pluck or touch a man's beard was an extreme affront, hence the phrase *to beard one*, to defy or insult or contradict flatly.

To beard the lion in his den. To defy personally or have it out FACE TO FACE.

To make one's beard. To have one wholly at your mercy, as a barber when holding a man's beard to dress it, or shaving the chin of a customer. So, to be able to do what you like with one, to outwit or delude him.

> Though they preye Argus, with his hundred yën,
> To be my warde-cors, as he can best,
> In feith, he shal nat kepe me but me lest;
> Yet coude I make his berd, so moot I thee.
> CHAUCER: *Wife of Bath's Prologue*, 358.

I told him to his beard. I told him to his face, regardless of the consequences; openly and fearlessly.

Maugre his beard. In spite of him.

Old Man's Beard. *Clematis vitalba*, so called from its head of long-bearded fruits. Also known as Traveller's Joy.

"'Tis merry in hall when beards wag all"—*i.e.* when feasting goes on.

> With pleasure too did wag the minstrel's beard,
> For Plenty courted him to drink and bite.
> PETER PINDAR: *Elegy to Scotland*.

To laugh at a man's beard. To attempt to make a fool of him—to deceive by ridiculous exaggeration.

> "By the Prophet! but he laughs at our beards," exclaimed the Pacha angrily. "These are foolish lies."
> MARRYAT: *Pacha of many Tales*.

To laugh in one's beard. To laugh up one's SLEEVE, that is, surreptitiously.

To lie in one's beard. To accuse someone of doing so is to stress the severity of the accusation.

To run in one's beard. To offer opposition to a person; to do something obnoxious to a person before his face.

With the beard on the shoulder (Sp.). In the attitude of listening to overhear something; with circumspection, looking in all directions for surprises and ambuscades.

> They rode, as the Spanish proverb expresses it "with the beard on the shoulder", looking around, that is, from time to time, and using every precaution to have the speediest knowledge of any pursuit....
> SCOTT: *Peveril of the Peak*, ch. vii.

Tax upon beards. Peter the Great (1672–1725) encouraged shaving in Russia by imposing a tax upon beards. Clerks were stationed at the gate of every town to collect the tax. He personally cut off the beards of his chief boyars.

Bearded Master. So Persius styled SOCRATES, under the notion that the beard is a symbol of wisdom.

The bearded. A surname (*Pogonatus*) given to Constantine IV, Byzantine Emperor (668–685); also to Baldwin IV, Count of Flanders (988–1036); and St. Paula. Fidel Castro is known as *El Barbudo*.

Bearings. I'll bring him to his bearings. I'll bring him to his senses, put him on the right track. In navigation bearings are taken of the direction in which an object is seen. Thus to keep one's bearings is to keep on the right course, in the right direction.

To lose one's bearings. To be off course, to become lost, bewildered, to get perplexed.

To take the bearings. To ascertain the relative position of an object.

Béarnais, Le. Henry IV of France (1553–1610). So called from *Le Béarn*, his native province.

Beast. The number of the Beast. *See under* NUMBERS.

Beast of Belsen. In World War II the name given to Joseph Kramer, commandant of the infamous Belsen concentration camp.

Beasts of heraldry. In English HERALDRY all manner of creatures (many derived from BESTIARIES) have been borne as charges or as crests, notably the lion, leopard, bear, bull, boar, cat, eagle, swallow (called a martlet), pelican, unicorn, stag, griffin, wyvern. The attitude or position of the animal is thus described: *couchant*, lying down with head erect; *dormant*, sleeping, with head lowered; *passant*, walking; *passant gardant*, walking but looking at the beholder; RAMPANT, on its hind legs; *rampant combattant*, two beasts rampant facing one another; *rampant endorsed*, two beasts rampant back to back. A beast can be *proper*, that is, emblazoned in its natural colour; *naissant*, emerging out of a fesse or ordinary; *erased*, a head or limb torn from the body; etc.

Beauty and the Beast. *See under* BEAUTY.

Beat (O.E. *beatan*). The first sense of the word was that of striking; that of overcoming or defeating was a natural extension. Also a track, range or walk, trodden or beaten by the feet, as a **policeman's beat**.

Beat group. A type of "pop music" group of the 1950s and 1960s, characterized by a marked emphasis on rhythm or beat.

Dead beat. *See under* DEAD.

Dead beat escapement. *See under* DEAD.

Not in my beat. Not in my line; not in the range of my talents or inclination.

Off his beat. Not on duty; not in his appointed walk; not his speciality or line.

> Off his own beat his opinions were of no value.
> EMERSON: *English Traits*, ch. i.

On his beat. The reverse of the above.

Out of his beat. In his wrong walk; out of his proper sphere.

That beats Banagher. *See* BANAGHER; TERMAGANT.

To beat about. A nautical phrase meaning to TACK against the wind.

To beat about the bush. To approach a matter cautiously in a roundabout way, to SHILLY-SHALLY; perhaps because one goes carefully when beating a bush to find if any game is lurking within.

To beat an alarm. To give notice of danger by beat of a drum. *To beat to arms, to beat a charge*, are likewise military orders by drum beat.

To beat a retreat is to withdraw from or

abandon a position, undertaking, etc.

To beat retreat, in the military sense, was originally to summon men by drum beat to withdraw to camp or behind the lines when hostilities temporarily ceased at the approach of darkness; also to give warning to the guards to collect and be posted for the night.

The drums were later augmented by fifes and more recently, with the advent of military bands, *beat retreat* became an impressive ceremonial display.

To beat down. To make a seller abate his price.

To beat, or **drum a thing into someone.** To repeat as a drummer repeats his beats on the drum.

To beat hollow, or **to a mummy, a frazzle, to ribbons, a jelly,** etc. To beat wholly, utterly, completely.

To beat the air. To strike out at nothing as pugilists do before a fight; to toil without profit; to work to no purpose.

So fight I, not as one that beateth the air.
I *Cor*. ix, 26.

To beat the band. To excel, to exceed or surpass; from the idea of making more noise than the band.

To beat the booby. See BOOBY.

To beat the bounds. See BOUNDS.

To beat the bush. To allow another to profit by one's exertions; "one beat the bush and another caught the hare". The allusion is to beaters who start the game from the bushes for a shooting party.

To beat the devil's tattoo. See DEVIL.

To beat the Dutch. To "draw a very long BOW"; to say something very incredible.

To beat time. To indicate time in music by beating or moving the hands, feet or a baton.

To beat to Quarters. Formerly, in a man-of-war, to summon the crew to their respective stations by the beat of a drum.

To beat up someone. To make one the victim of vicious and brutal assault.

To beat up someone's quarters. To hunt out where he lives; to visit without ceremony. A military term signifying to make an unexpected attack on an enemy in camp.

To beat up the quarters of some of our less-known relations.
LAMB: *Essays of Elia*.

To beat up recruits, or **supporters.** To hunt them up or call them together, as soldiers are summoned by beat of drum.

To beat one with his own staff. To confute him with his own words. An *argumentum ad hominem*.

Can High Church bigotry go further than this? And how well have I since been beaten with mine own staff. — J. WESLEY (He refers to his excluding Bolzius from "the Lord's table", because he had not been canonically baptized.)

Beati Possidentes (bē a' tī pos i den' tēz). Blessed are those who have (for they shall receive). "Possession is nine points of the law." (*See under* NINE.)

Beatific Vision. The sight of God, or of the blessed in the realms of HEAVEN, especially that granted to the SOUL at the instant of death. See *Is*. vi, 1–3 and *Acts* vii, 55, 56.

Beatification (bē ăt i fi kā' shŭn). In the ROMAN CATHOLIC CHURCH this is a solemn act by which a deceased person is formally declared by the POPE to be one of the blessed departed and therefore a proper subject for a MASS and OFFICE in his honour, generally with some local restriction. Beatification is usually, though not necessarily, a step to CANONIZATION.

Beatitude (bē ăt' i tūd). Blessedness, perfect felicity.

The Beatitudes are the eight blessings pronounced by Our Lord at the opening of the Sermon on the Mount (*Matt*. v, 3–11).

Beatnik. A "beat" person, one who lives a beat life, akin to the American *hipster*. Socially, politically, intellectually and artistically the beatnik stands apart, and is an ANGRY YOUNG MAN or woman, ultra-BOHEMIAN, flouting all or most of the established conventions and values. The beatnik is distinguished by unconventional dress and slovenliness. The term may derive from the "beat generation" (meaning dissatisfied young people) and a Russian suffix (*nik*, as in SPUTNIK).

Beatrice. See DANTE.

Beau (bō) (Fr. fine or beautiful). In England and America used for a lover or admirer; formerly prefixed to the name of a fop or man of fashion, such as the following:

Beau Brummel. George Brummel (1778–1840), an intimate of the Prince Regent.

Beau Didapper, in Fielding's *Joseph Andrews*, a young fop with a passion for Fanny.

Beau D'Orsay. Count D'Orsay (1801–1852), called by BYRON *Jeune Cupidon*.

Beau Feilding. Robert Feilding (d. 1712), called "Handsome Feilding" by Charles II. He died in Scotland Yard, London, after having been convicted of bigamously marrying the Duchess of Cleveland, a former mistress of Charles II. He figures as Orlando in Steele's *Tatler* (Nos. 50 and 51).

Beau Hewitt. The model for Sir Fopling Flutter, hero of Etherege's *The Man of Mode* (1676).

Beau Nash. Richard Nash (1674–1762). Born at Swansea and educated at Jesus College, Oxford. As a noted gambler, he nevertheless achieved distinction as Master of Ceremonies at Bath, which he made the leading English spa.

Beau of Leadenhall Street. *See* DIRTY DICK'S.

Beau Tibbs, in Goldsmith's *Citizen of the World*, noted for his finery, vanity and poverty.

Beau ideal. "The ideal Beautiful" is the proper meaning of the original French, but often used in English to mean the beautiful ideal.

Beau monde. The fashionable world; people who make up the coterie of fashion.

Beau trap. An old name for a loose paving-stone under which water lodged and which squirted up filth when trodden on, to the discomfort of the smartly dressed.

Beauclerc (bō′ klĕrk) (good scholar). Applied to Henry I, King of England (1100–1135) for his scholarly accomplishments.

Beaumontague, Beaumontage, or **Beaumontique.** A filling compound used in joinery and metalwork said to be named after the French geologist Elie de Beaumont (1798–1874), who also gave his name to *beaumonlite*, a silicate of copper. As it can be used for disguising bad workmanship, it has the added meanings of bad joinery, literary padding and bad work generally.

Beautiful Parricide. Beatrice Cenci, daughter of Francesco Cenci, a dissolute Roman nobleman. Because of her father's cruelties to the family, she and two of her brothers contrived his murder. She was beheaded in 1599. Their story has been a favourite theme in literature and art; Shelley's tragedy, *The Cenci* (1819), is particularly noteworthy.

Beauty. Beauty is but skin deep.

> O formose puer, nimium ne crede colori.
>
> VIRGIL: *Bucolics, Eclogue* ii.

(O my pretty boy, trust not too much to your pretty looks.)

Beauty and the Beast. A handsome woman with an uncouth or uncomely male companion.

The heroine and hero of the well-known fairy tale in which Beauty saved the life of her father by consenting to live with the Beast; and the Beast, being disenchanted by Beauty's love, became a handsome prince, and married her. The story is found in Straparola's *Piacevoli Notti* (1550), and this is probably the source of Mme. deprince de Beaumont's popular French version (1757). It is the basis of Grétry's opera *Zémire et*

Azor (1771). The story is of great antiquity and takes various forms. *Cp.* LOATHLY LADY.

Beauty of Buttermere. *See* MAID OF BUTTERMERE.

Beauty sleep. Sleep taken before midnight. Those who habitually go to bed after midnight, especially during youth, are supposed to become pale and haggard.

Beaux Esprits (bō zā sprē′) (Fr.). Persons of wit or genius (singular, *Un bel esprit*, a wit, a genius).

Beaux yeux (bō zyĕr′) (Fr.). Beautiful eyes or attractive looks. "I will do it for your *beaux yeux*" (because you are so pretty, or because your eyes are so attractive).

Beaver. The lower and movable part of a helmet; so called from Fr. *bavière*, which meant a child's bib, to which it had some resemblance.

> Hamlet: Then you saw not his face?
> Horatio: O yes, my lord; he wore his beaver up.
>
> SHAKESPEARE: *Hamlet*, I, ii.

Beaver is also an old name for a man's hat because some hats used to be made of beaver fur. In the 1920s the word was popularly applied to anyone wearing a beard.

Beavers, or **Bevers.** Refreshments of bread and beer served in the afternoon, answering to the modern 5 o'clock tea. It is still a rural term for afternoon "ELEVENSES". *See* BEVER.

The Beaver. Name given in journalistic circles to Lord Beaverbrook (William Maxwell Aitken, 1879–1964), Canadian-born politician and newspaper magnate. He served in a number of capacities in World War I and as Minister of Aircraft Production in World War II, being responsible for stepping up the output of the Spitfire fighter and Whitley bomber. He became Minister of Supply in 1941.

Bed. The great bed of Ware. A fourposter bed eleven feet square and capable of holding twelve people. It dates from the late 16th century and was formerly at Rye House, Hertfordshire, but in 1931 it came into the possession of the Victoria and Albert Museum.

> Although the sheet were big enough for the bed of Ware in England.
>
> SHAKESPEARE: *Twelfth Night*, III, ii.

As you make your bed, so you must lie on it. Everyone must bear the consequences of his own acts.

To bed out. To transfer plants raised in pots or a greenhouse out into the open ground.

To make the bed. To arrange the bedding ready for use. In America, a room put ready is said to be made.

You got out of bed the wrong way, on the

wrong side, or **with the left leg foremost.** Said of a person who is moody or grumpy. It was held to be unlucky to set the left foot on the ground first when getting out of bed. The same superstition applies to putting on the left shoe first. AUGUSTUS Caesar was very superstitious in this respect.

Bed of Justice. *See* LIT.

A bed of roses. A situation of ease and pleasure.

A bed of thorns. A situation of great anxiety and apprehension.

In the twinkling of a bed-post, or **bed-staff.** As quickly as possible. A bed-staff was the loose slat across the bed-frame, also the staff sometimes used to beat the bed and clean it. Staves were also placed at the two sides of the bed to prevent the bedding slipping off. In the reign of Edward I, Sir John Chichester had a mock skirmish in which his servant was accidentally killed, Sir John wielding his rapier and the servant the bed-staff. Wright, in his *Domestic Manners*, shows us a chambermaid of the 17th century, using a bed-staff to beat up the bedding. "Twinkling" is from the O.E. *twinclian*, a twitch or flicker, an instant.

> I'll do it instantly, in the twinkling of a bed-staff.
> SHADWELL: *Virtuoso* I, i (1676).

Cp. In the twinkling of an EYE which has a similar and more self-evident meaning.

"In the twinkling of a *bed-post*" became the usual phrase when the *bed-staff* became obsolete.

Bedchamber Crisis, or **Question.** In May 1839, Lord Melbourne's insecure WHIG ministry resigned and when Sir Robert Peel accepted office he requested that some of the Whig ladies of the bedchamber be replaced by TORIES. Queen Victoria refused and Peel resigned, whereupon Melbourne was recalled to office. The question was resolved, with the intervention of the Prince Consort, before Melbourne's resignation in 1841.

Beddgelert (běth gĕl' ert). The name of a village in Caernarvonshire (the grave of Gelert). According to Welsh folklore, Prince Llewelyn returned to his castle to find his dog Gelert's jaws dripping with blood. His son had been left in Gelert's care but the baby was not to be found. In his distress, Llewelyn slew the faithful hound and found his son, close to the body of a wolf, which the hound had killed. This story has many variants in other ancient literatures.

Bede, The Venerable (*c.* 673–735). Also called the *English* DOCTOR. This most renowned of early English scholars became a monk at Jarrow and devoted his life to religion and learning. His industry, output and

range were remarkable, but he is probably best known for his *Ecclesiastical History of the English People*, a work of unusual merit and value, which has led him to be called the *Father of English History*. His book is a major source of information to the year 731. The title "venerable" is by one tradition assigned to an angelic hand; it is certainly not due to great age as is often thought.

Bedel, or **Bedell** (bē' del). Old forms of the word BEADLE, still used at Oxford and Cambridge universities for the officer who carries the mace before the Vice-Chancellor and performs certain other duties. At Oxford there are four *bedels*; at Cambridge two *bedells*, or *esquire-bedells*. London also has an *esquire-bedell* and a *Court bedell*.

Bedivere, or **Bedver**. In the ARTHURIAN ROMANCES, a knight of the ROUND TABLE, butler and staunch adherent of King ARTHUR. It was he who, at the request of the dying king, threw EXCALIBUR into the lake, and afterwards bore his body to the ladies in the barge which was to take him to AVALON.

Bedlam (A contraction of *Bethlehem*). A lunatic asylum, a madhouse; hence a place of hubbub and confusion. The priory of St. Mary of Bethlehem outside Bishopsgate was founded in 1247 and began to receive lunatics in 1377. It was given to the City of London as a hospital for lunatics by Henry VIII in 1547. In 1676 it was transferred to Moorfields and became one of the sights of London, where for twopence, anyone might gaze at the poor wretches and bait them. It was a place for assignations and one of the disgraces of 17th-century London.

> All that I can say of Bedlam is this; 'tis an almshouse for madmen, a showing room for harlots, a sure market for lechers, a dry walk for loiterers.
> NED WARD: *The London Spy* (1698).

In 1815 Bedlam was moved to St. George's Fields, Lambeth, the present site of the Imperial War Museum, when in 1931 the occupants were moved to West Wickham. Hannah SNELL died in Bedlam in 1792.

Bedlamite. A madman, a fool, an inmate of Bedlam. *See* ABRAM-MAN.

Bedlam, Tom o'. *See* TOM.

Bednall Green. *See* BEGGAR'S DAUGHTER.

Bedouin (bed' oo in). French (and thence English) form of an Arabic word meaning "a dweller in the desert", applied to the nomadic tribes of Arabia and Syria. Formerly also the homeless street poor. *Cp.* STREET ARABS.

Bedrock. American slang for one's last dollar. "I'm come down to bedrock", the end of one's resources. Bedrock is the miner's term for the hard basis rock which is reached when the mine is exhausted.

Bedroll (Western U.S.A.). A tarpaulin in which a COWBOY keeps his blanket and possessions. Once he has thrown it on the cook's chuck-wagon, he owes complete allegiance to the outfit.

Bee. Legend has it that JUPITER was nourished by bees, similarly PINDAR was nourished by bees with honey (instead of milk). The Greeks consecrated bees to the MOON. With the Romans a flight of bees was considered a bad OMEN. Appian (*Civil War*, Bk. II) says a swarm of bees lighted on the altar and prognosticated the fatal issue of the battle of Pharsalia. *See* AMBROSE; ATHENIAN BEE; ATTIC BEE.

The name *bee* is given, particularly in America, to a social gathering for some useful work (*see* ANIMALS IN SYMBOLISM), *e.g.* a *sewing bee*. A *spelling-bee* is a competition or gathering to compete in spelling.

Bee-line. The shortest distance between two given points such as a bee is supposed to take in making for its hive. *See* AIRLINE.

To have your head full of bees, or **to have a bee in your bonnet.** To be cranky; to have an idiosyncrasy; to be full of devices, crotchets, fancies, inventions and dreamy theories. The connexion between bees and the soul was once generally maintained; hence MOHAMMED admits bees to PARADISE. Porphyry says of fountains, "they are adapted to the NYMPHS or those souls which the ancients called bees." *Cp.* MAGGOT.

Beef. From the O.Fr. *boef*, an ox. Like mutton (O.Fr. *moton*) it is a reminder of the period after the Norman Conquest when the Saxon was the servant of the conquerors. The Saxon was the herdsman and used the word for the beast under his charge, the Normans had the cooked meat and used the appropriate French name for it.

Beefeaters. The popular name of the Yeomen of the Guard, first formed as a royal bodyguard at Henry VII's coronation in 1485; also of the Yeomen Extraordinary of the Guard, who were appointed as Warders of the TOWER of London by Edward VI, and wear the same Tudor-period costume. The name was probably first specifically applied to the Yeomen of the Guard about the middle of the 17th century.

That "eater" was formerly a synonym for "servant" is shown by the O.E. word *hláf-oeta* (loaf-eater), which meant "a menial servant" and by the passage in Ben Jonson's *Silent Woman*, III, ii (1609), where Morose, calling for his servants, shouts:

> Bar my doors! bar my doors! Where are all my eaters? My mouths, now? Bar up my doors you varlets!

The literal meaning "eaters of beef" is the probable origin of the word, rather than the Fr. word *buffetier*. It is found in a letter of Prince Rupert's (1645), quoted in Sir S. D. Scott's *The British Army* (I, 513). Also we have:

> Those goodly Juments of the guard would fight
> (As they eat beef) after six stone a day.
> WM. CARTWRIGHT: *The Ordinary*, II (c. 1635).

Beefsteak Club. The original club, frequented by the wits, where refreshment was limited to steaks and beer or wine, was established in LONDON in 1709, with a gridiron as its badge. In 1735 the Sublime Society of Steaks was inaugurated when Lord Peterborough supped with John Rich, manager of the COVENT GARDEN Theatre. His lordship was so delighted with the steak provided that he proposed to repeat the entertainment every Saturday. The Sublime Society continued to meet there until the fire of 1808, when it moved to other premises. The "Steaks" included many famous actors until its cessation in 1867. The modern Beefsteak Club was founded in 1876.

Beelzebub. Other forms are *Beelzebul*, *Baalzebub*. Baalzebub was the god of Ekron (II *Kings* i, 3), and the meaning is obscure although it has been popularly held to mean "lord of FLIES". In any event it was probably a derisory title. The most likely explanation so far is that Baalzebul means "lord of the lofty dwelling" and refers to the Syrian BAAL. This was altered to Baalzebub by the Jews, as the former title seemed only proper to JAHWEH. To the Jews he came to be the chief representative of the false gods. In *Matt.* xii, 24, he is referred to as "the prince of the devils" and similarly in *Mark* iii, 22, and *Luke* xi, 15. Hence Milton places him next in rank to SATAN.

> One next himself in power, and next in crime,
> Long after known in Palestine, and named
> Beelzebub.
> *Paradise Lost*, I, 79.

Beer. *See* ALE.

Beer-money. An allowance of one penny per day paid to British soldiers and N.C.O.s between 1800 and 1823 instead of an issue of beer. Now sometimes used to denote "spending money" for refreshment or pleasure.

Life is not all beer and skittles, *i.e.* not all eating, drinking, and play; not all pleasure.

Small beer. *See* SMALL.

Beeswing. Thus named from its appearance. A crust or film of tartar which forms in port and other wines after long keeping. It is not detrimental if it passes into the decanter.

Beetle, To. To overhang, to threaten, to jut

over. The word seems to have been first used by SHAKESPEARE:

> Or to the dreadful summit of the cliff
> That beetles o'er his base into the sea.
> *Hamlet*, I, iv.

It is formed from the adjective *beetle-browed*, having prominent or shaggy eyebrows. The derivation of *beetle* in this use is uncertain, but it probably refers to the tufted antennæ which, in some beetles, stand straight out from the head.

Beeton, Mrs. *The Book of Household Management*, a classic mid-Victorian work on "domestic economy", was written by Mrs. Isabella Beeton (1836–1865) and first published in 1861. The bulk of its contents consisted of some 4,000 recipes and it readily established itself as the most famous of all English cookery books. The name of Mrs. Beeton became synonymous with this book, although she compiled other lesser ones during her short life. In its revised editions it is still widely used. Mrs Beeton was doubtless familiar with the books written by the famous French cook, Alexis Soyer (1809–1858), who came to England after the French Revolution of July 1830.

Befana (be fa' na). The good fairy of Italian children, who is supposed to fill their stockings with toys when they go to bed on TWELFTH NIGHT. Someone enters the children's bedroom for the purpose and the wakeful youngsters cry out, "*Ecco la Befana.*" According to legend, Befana was too busy with house affairs to look after the MAGI when they went out to offer their gifts, and said she would wait to see them on their return; but they went another way, and Befana, every Twelfth Night, watches for them. The name is a corruption of *Epiphania*.

Before the Lights. *See* LIGHTS.

Before the Mast. *See* MAST.

Beg the Question, To. To assume a proposition which, in reality, involves the conclusion. Thus, to say that parallel lines will never meet because they are parallel, is simply to assume as a fact the very thing you profess to prove. The phrase is the common English equivalent of the Latin term, PETITIO PRINCIPII.

Beggar. A beggar may sing before a pickpocket. *Cantabit vacuus coram latrone viator* (*Juvenal*, x, 22). A beggar may sing in the presence of thieves because he has nothing in his pocket to lose.

Beggar's daughter of Bednall Green, Bessee the. An old ballad given in PERCY'S RELIQUES; the subject of a play by Chettle and Day (1600) and also one by Sheridan Knowles (1834). The beautiful Bessee had four suitors—a knight, a gentleman of fortune, a London merchant, and the son of the innkeeper at Romford. She told them that they must obtain the consent of her father, the poor blind beggar of Bethnal Green, whereupon they all slunk off except the knight, who went to ask the beggar's leave to wed the "pretty Bessee". The beggar gave her £3,000 for her dower, and £100 to buy her wedding gown. At the wedding feast he explained to the guests that he was Henry, son of Sir Simon de Montfort.

Beggars cannot be choosers. Beggars must take what is given to them and be thankful. They are not in a position to pick and choose or dictate terms to the giver.

Beggars' barm. The yeast-like scum which collects on the surface of ponds, brooks, etc. where the current is arrested. Unfit for use, it is only beggarly barm (froth) at best.

Beggars' bullets. Stones.

Beggars of the Sea. *See* GUEUX.

Beggar's Opera, The. Produced in 1728, its enormous success gave a new impetus to English comic opera. The hero is a highwayman, MacHeath, and it centres around NEWGATE. This topical satire by John Gay was produced by Rich (*see* BEEFSTEAK CLUB). It is said to have made Gay rich and Rich gay. The music was made up of traditional ballads and popular tunes of the day arranged by Pepusch.

Begging Friars. *See* MENDICANT ORDERS.

King of the Beggars. Bampfylde Moore Carew (1693–1770), a famous English vagrant who became King of the GIPSIES. Transported to Maryland, he escaped and is said to have joined the Young PRETENDER and followed him to Derby.

Set a beggar on horseback, and he'll ride to the de'il. There is no one so proud and arrogant as a beggar who has suddenly grown rich.

> Such is the sad effect of wealth—rank pride—
> Mount but a beggar, how the rogue will ride!
> PETER PINDAR: *Epistle to Lord Lonsdale*.

To go by beggar's bush, or **Go home by beggar's bush**—*i.e.* to go to ruin. Beggar's bush is the name of a tree which once stood on the left hand of the London road from Huntingdon to Caxton; so called because it was a noted rendezvous for beggars.

Beghards (be gardz). Monastic fraternities which first arose in the Low Countries in the late 12th century, named after Lambert le Bègue, a priest of Liège, who also founded the BÉGUINES. They took no vows and were free to leave the society at will. In the 17th century, those who survived Papal persecution joined the TERTIARIES of the FRANCIS-

CANS. The word *beggar* possibly derives from beghards. Le Bègue means "the stammerer". *Cp.* LOLLARDS; ORATORIANS.

Beglerbeg. *See* BASHAW.

Beguine (bĕ gēn'). A popular Martinique and South American dance, or music for this dance in bolero rhythm. It inspired Cole Porter's success of the 1930s, *Begin the Beguine*.

Béguines (bā gēn'). A sisterhood founded in the late 12th century by Lambert le Bègue (*see* BEGHARDS). They were free to quit the cloister and to marry, and formerly flourished in the Low Countries, Germany, France, Switzerland and Italy. There are still communities in Belgium. The cap called a *béguin* was named from this sisterhood.

Behemoth (be hē' moth). The animal described under this name in *Job* xl, 15–24, is probably the hippopotamus. The poet James Thomson apparently took it to be a rhinoceros.

> Behold! in plaited mail,
> Behemoth rears his head.
> > *The Seasons: Summer*, 709, 710.

The word is more often pronounced Be' hemoth; but Milton, like Thomson, places the accent on the second syllable.

> Scarce from his mould
> Behemoth, biggest born of earth, upheaved
> His vastness.
> > *Paradise Lost*, VII, 471.

Behistun, Rock of. A cliff-like mountain face in western Persia, east of Kermanshah, bearing CUNEIFORM inscriptions in Persian, Elamitic or Susian, and Babylonian, recounting the achievements of Darius I. By 1846 Henry Rawlinson had succeeded in translating the ancient Persian, thus providing the key for the subsequent translation of the Susian and Babylonian, and laying the foundations of scientific Assyriology. *Cp.* ROSETTA STONE.

Behmenists (bā' men ists). A sect of theosophical mystics, called after their founder Jacob Behman or Boehme (1575–1624). Jane Leade founded a Behmenist sect in England in 1697 called the Philadelphists.

Behram (bā' răm). The most holy kind of fire according to the PARSEES. *See also* GUEBRES.

Bejan (bē' jản). A freshman or greenhorn in the Scottish universities of St. Andrews and Aberdeen. A woman student is called a *bajanella* or *bejanella*. The word is a corruption of the Fr. *bec jaune*, yellow beak, with allusion to a nestling or unfledged bird, and was used in the University of Paris and elsewhere. In France *béjaune* is still the name for the repast that a freshman is supposed to

provide for his new companions. The word also means an "ignorant young man".

Bel. The name of the Assyrio-Babylonian gods En-lil and MARDUK. It has the same meaning as BAAL. The story of Bel and the Dragon, in which we are told how Daniel convinced the King that Bel was not an actual living deity but only an image, was formerly part of the book of *Daniel*, but is now relegated to the APOCRYPHA.

Bel Esprit (bel es prē') (Fr.). *See* BEAUX ESPRITS.

Belch, Sir Toby. A reckless, roistering jolly fellow; from the knight of that name in Shakespeare's *Twelfth Night*.

Belcher. A neckerchief of deep blue with large white spots, each containing a dark blue spot, darker than the ground. So called from Jim Belcher (1781–1811), the pugilist, who adopted it, as did many of his supporters. *Belcher* is also an old name for a beer drinker.

Belfast Regiment, The. *See* REGIMENTAL AND DIVISIONAL NICKNAMES.

Bel-fires. *See* BELTANE.

Belfry. Originally a movable tower used in sieges from which the attackers threw missiles. (O.Fr. *berfrei*. Mid. High Ger. *Bercfrit*, a place of safety. Thence a watch-tower, beacon or alarm bell-tower.) Thus a church bell tower is called a belfry not because bells are hung in it.

Belial (bē li ål) (Heb.). In Old Testament usage it has the meaning of worthlessness, wickedness, but later it is used as a proper noun in the sense of the wicked one.

> What concord hath Christ with Belial?
> > II *Cor.* vi, 15.

Milton thus uses it as a proper name:

> Belial came last—than whom a spirit more lewd
> Fell not from heaven, or more gross to love
> Vice for itself.
> > *Paradise Lost*, I, 490.

Sons of Belial. Lawless, worthless, rebellious people.

> Now the sons of Eli were sons of Belial; they knew not the Lord.
> > I *Sam.* ii, 12.

Belisarius (bel i sâr' i us). **Belisarius begging for an obolus.** Belisarius (d. 565), the greatest of Justinian's generals, was accused of conspiring against the emperor and imprisoned in 562, but restored to favour after six months. The later story that his eyes were put out and that he was reduced to asking passers-by to "Give an obolus to Belisarius" is without foundation.

Belisha Beacon. An amber-coloured globe mounted on a black and white banded pole, the sign of a pedestrian crossing. Named after Leslie Hore-Belisha, Minister of Transport (1934–1937), who introduced them.

Bell, Acton, Currer, and **Ellis.** These were the names under which Anne, Charlotte, and Emily Brontë wrote their novels.

Bell. As the bell clinks, so the fool thinks, or **As the fool thinks, so the bell clinks.** The tale says when Dick WHITTINGTON ran away from his master, and had got as far as Highgate Hill, he was hungry, tired, and wished to return. BOW BELLS began to ring, and Whittington fancied they said, "Turn again, Whittington, Lord Mayor of London." The bells clinked in response to the boy's thoughts.

At three bells, at five bells, etc. At sea a bell is rung at half-hourly intervals to mark the passing of time in the WATCH. Five of the seven watches last four hours. Thus "three bells" (three strokes on the bell) denotes the third half-hour of the watch, "five bells" the fifth, etc. "Eight bells" marks the ending of a watch. The two Dog watches are each of two hours duration (4 p.m. to 6 p.m. and 6 p.m. to 8 p.m.). The passing of the 1st DOG WATCH is marked by four bells and the 2nd or Last Dog by eight.

Bell, book, and candle. The popular phrase for ceremonial EXCOMMUNICATION in the ROMAN CATHOLIC CHURCH. After pronouncing sentence the officiating cleric closes his book, quenches the candle by throwing it to the ground and tolls the bell as for one who has died. The book symbolizes the book of life, the candle that the soul is removed from the sight of God as the candle from the sight of man.

Hence, **in spite of bell, book and candle** signifies in spite of all opposition the Christian hierarchy can offer.

Give her the bells and let her fly. Don't throw good money after bad; make the best of the matter but don't try to bolster it up. In falconry, when a HAWK was worthless it was allowed to escape, even at the expense of bells attached to it.

I'll not hang all my bells on one horse. I'll not leave all my property to one son. The allusion is manifest.

Like sweet bells jangled, out of tune and harsh (*Hamlet*, III, i). A metaphor for a deranged mind.

One bell in the Last Dog Watch. It is a common story in the Royal Navy that one bell has been struck at 6.30 p.m. instead of five since the mutinies of 1797, because in one port five bells in the dog watches was to be the signal for mutiny. This was prevented by the foreknowledge of officers, who caused one bell to be struck instead.

Passing bell. The hallowed bell which used to be rung when persons were *in extremis*, to scare away evil spirits which might be lurking ready to snatch the SOUL while *passing* from the body. A secondary object was to announce to the neighbourhood that all good Christians might pray for the safe passage of the soul into PARADISE. The bell rung at a funeral is sometimes improperly called the "passing bell".

Athenians used to beat on brazen kettles at the moment of decease to scare away the FURIES.

Ringing the bell backwards is ringing a muffled peal. *Backwards* is often used to denote "in a reverse manner", as, "I hear you are grown rich"—"Yes, backwards", meaning "quite the reverse". A muffled peal is one of sorrow, not of joy, and was formerly sometimes employed as a tocsin or notice of danger.

Ringing the hallowed bell. Consecrated bells were believed to be able to disperse storms and pestilence, drive away devils (*see* PASSING BELL) and extinguish fire. It is said that as late as 1852 the Bishop of Malta ordered the church bells to be rung for an hour to "lay a gale of wind".

Sound as a bell. Quite sound. A cracked bell is useless.

That rings a bell, that strikes a chord, that sounds familiar, that reminds me of something. It may have derived from the fairground, where a bell on top of a tall column could be struck by a contestant hammering a pivot at the base and sending a projectile upwards.

To bear, or **carry away the bell.** To be first fiddle; to carry off the palm; to be the best. The BELLWETHER bore the bell, hence the phrase; but it has been confused with an old custom of presenting to winners of horse-races, etc., a little GOLD or SILVER bell as a prize.

Tolling the bell for church. The "church-going bell" as Cowper called it (*Verses by Alexander Selkirk*) was in pre-Reformation days rung as an Ave Bell to invite worshippers to a preparatory prayer to the Virgin.

Warming the bell. A nautical phrase, doing something before the proper time, *e.g.* preparing to leave early, etc. Possibly from the idea that a bell, like a clock, if warmed moves faster.

Warwick shakes his bells. Beware of danger, for Warwick is in the field. "Trojans beware, ACHILLES has donned his armour." A METAPHOR from falconry, the bells being those of a HAWK.

> Neither the king, nor he that loves him best
> The proudest he that holds up Lancaster,
> Dares stir a wing, if Warwick shakes the bells.
> SHAKESPEARE: *Henry VI, Pt. III*, I, i.

Who is to bell the cat? Who will risk his own life to save his neighbour's? Anyone who encounters great personal hazard for the sake of others undertakes to "bell the cat". The allusion is to the fable of the cunning old mouse (given in *Piers Plowman* and elsewhere), who suggested that they should hang a bell on the cat's neck to give notice to all mice of her approach. "Excellent," said a wise young mouse, "but who is to undertake the job?"

Bell-the-Cat. Archibald Douglas, fifth Earl of Angus (d. 1514), was so called. James III made favourites of architects and masons, Cochrane, a mason, being created Earl of Mar. The Scottish nobles held a council in the church of Lauder for the purpose of putting down these upstarts, when Lord Gray asked "Who will bell the cat?" "That will I," said Douglas, and he fearlessly put to death, in the king's presence, the obnoxious minions.

Bell-man. *See* TOWN CRIER.

Bell-rope. A humorous name for a curl worn by a man—a "rope" for the "belles" to play with. *Cp.* BOW-CATCHER.

Bell Savage. *See* LA BELLE SAUVAGE.

Bell-wavering. Vacillating, swaying from side to side like a bell. A man whose mind jangles out of tune from delirium, drunkenness or temporary insanity, is said to have his wits gone bell-wavering.

> I doubt me his wits have gone a bell-wavering by the road.
> SIR WALTER SCOTT: *The Monastery*, ch. vii.

Bellwether of the flock. A jocose and rather deprecatory term applied to the leader of a party. The allusion is to the wether, or sheep, which leads the flock with a bell fastened to its neck.

Belladonna. The Deadly Nightshade. The name is Italian and means "beautiful lady". Its power of enlarging the pupils was put to use by would-be glamorous females. This is the usual explanation of the name but another is that it was used by an Italian poisoner named Leucota to poison beautiful women.

Bellarmine (bel′ ar mīn). A large Flemish GOTCH, or stone beer-jug, originally made in Flanders in ridicule of CARDINAL Bellarmine (1542–1621), a great defender of the ROMAN CATHOLIC CHURCH. It carried a rude likeness of the Cardinal. *Cp.* DEMIJOHN; GREYBEARD.

Belle (bel) (Fr.). A beauty.

The Belle of the ball. The most beautiful woman in the room.

Belles-lettres (bel letr). Polite literature; poetry and standard literary works: the study or pursuit of such.

Bellerophon (be ler′ ō fon). The JOSEPH of Greek mythology; Antæa, spouse of Prœtus, being the "POTIPHAR'S WIFE" who tempted him and afterwards falsely accused him. Prœtus sent Bellerophon with a letter to Iobates, King of Lycia, his wife's father, narrating the charge, and praying that the bearer might be put to death. Iobates, reluctant to slay Bellerophon himself, gave him many hazardous tasks, including the killing of the CHIMÆRA, but as he succeeded in all of them Iobates made him his heir. Later Bellerophon attempted to fly to heaven on PEGASUS, but ZEUS sent a gadfly to sting the horse, and the rider was thrown.

Bellerophon. The name of the former seventy-four-gun ship of the Royal Navy which took part in the Battle of the Nile and Trafalgar and to whose captain NAPOLEON finally surrendered himself after Waterloo. The name was corrupted by sailors to "Billy Ruffian", "Bully-ruffran", "Belly-ruffron", etc.

Letters of Bellerophon. Letters or documents either dangerous or prejudicial to the bearer. *See* BELLEROPHON.

Bellerus (bē lē′ rŭs). A Cornish giant invented by Milton to account for "Bellerium", the Roman name for the Land's End area.

> Sleep'st by the fable of Bellerus old.
> *Lycidas*, 160.

Bellona. The Roman goddess of war, wife (or sometimes sister) of MARS.

Belly. The belly and its members. The fable of Menenius Agrippa to the Roman people when they seceded to the Sacred Mount. "Once upon a time the members refused to work for the lazy belly; but, as the supply of food was thus stopped, they found there was a necessary and mutual dependence between them." The fable is given by ÆSOP and by Plutarch, whence Shakespeare introduced it in his *Coriolanus*, I, i.

The belly has no ears. A hungry man will not listen to advice or arguments. The Romans had the same proverb, *Venter non habet aures*; and in French, *Ventre affamé n'a point d'oreilles*.

Belly-timber. Food. An old expression used by the Elizabethans and given by Cotgrave (1611) as a translation of the French *Carrelure de ventre* (a resoling, or refurnishing of the stomach).

...through deserts vast
And regions desolate they pass'd
Where belly-timber above ground
Or under, was not to be found.
BUTLER: Hudibras.

Scott also uses it in *Peveril of the Peak*, ch. 48.

And now, Dame Peveril, to dinner, to dinner!—the
old fox must have his belly-timber, though the
hounds have been after him the whole day.

Belomancy (bel' ō măn si) (Gr.). DIVINA-
TION by arrows. Labels being attached to a
given number of arrows, the archers let
them fly, and the advice on the label of the
arrow which flies farthest is accepted. It was
anciently practised by the Babylonians,
Scythians, etc. Sir Thomas Browne describes it in *Pseudodoxia Epidemica*, v, 23,
and it is also mentioned in *Ezekiel* xxi, 21.

Beloved Disciple. St. JOHN (*John* xiii, 23).

Beloved Physician. St. LUKE (*Col.* iv, 14).

Belphegor (bel' fe gôr). The Assyrian form of
Baal-Peor (*see* BAAL), the Moabitish god to
whom the Israelites became attached in
Shittim (*Numb.* xxv, 3), which was associated with licentious orgies (*Hos.* ix, 10).

The name was given in mediæval Latin legend to a demon sent into the world by his
fellows to test rumours concerning the happiness of married life on earth. After a thorough trial, he fled to the happy regions
where female companionship was non-
existent. Hence the name is applied to a misanthrope and to a nasty, obscene, licentious
fellow. The story is found in MACHIAVELLI,
and occurs in English in Barnabe Rich's
Farewell to the Militarie Profession (1581)
and is used in *Grim, The Collier of Croyden*
(1600), Jonson's *The Divell is an Asse*
(1616), and John Wilson's *Belphegor, or the
Marriage of the Devil* (1691).

Belphoebe (bel fē' bi). The Huntress-
goddess in Spenser's *Faerie Queene*, daughter of Chrysogone and sister of AMORET,
typifies Queen Elizabeth I as a model of
chastity. She was of the DIANA and MINERVA
type; cold as an icicle, passionless, immovable and, like a moonbeam, light
without warmth.

Belt. To hit below the belt. To strike unfairly. It is prohibited in the QUEENSBERRY
RULES of prize-fighting to hit below the
waist-belt.

To hold the belt. To be the champion. In
pugilism, a belt usually forms part of the
prize in big fights.

To belt the grape. American slang meaning to drink heavily.

Belted earl, or knight. This refers to the
belt and spurs with which KNIGHTS, etc.,
were invested when raised to the dignity. In

American usage, *belted earl* is a person who
claims noble birth.

Belted Will. Lord William Howard
(1563–1640), third son of Thomas, fourth
Duke of Norfolk. Scott gives him this name
in *The Lay of the Last Minstrel* (IV, vi), and
also makes him warden of the western
marches, but he was known to contemporaries as Bauld (bold) Willie. He carried out
an enlightened policy in restoring order and
civilization to the border districts. His wife
was called "BESSIE WITH THE BRAID (broad)
APRON" from her ample dowry.

Beltane (bel' tān) (Gaelic, *bealtainn*). The
derivation is uncertain but it is not connected with *baal*. In Scotland, May Day
(O.S.); also an ancient Celtic festival when
bel-fires were kindled on the hill-tops and
cattle were driven between the flames, either
to protect them from disease, or as a preparatory to sacrifice.

Ben trovato. Well invented. A phrase from
the Italian rendered in French as *bien
trouvé*. The full Italian saying *Se non è vero,
è molto ben trovato* means "If it is not true, it
is very well invented".

Benares (ben âr' ēz). The holy city of the
Hindus, being to them what MECCA is to the
MOSLEMS. It contains many temples including the Golden Temple of SIVA and is much
frequented by pilgrims. It is of great antiquity and was for centuries a Buddhist
centre.

Bench. Originally the same word as BANK;
properly, a long wooden seat, hence the official seat of judges or magistrates in court,
BISHOPS in the HOUSE OF LORDS, aldermen in
the council chamber, etc.; hence by extension judges, bishops, etc., or the dignity of
holding such official status.

The front bench. In the HOUSE OF COM-
MONS the leading members of the government occupy the front bench to the right of
the SPEAKER. This is called the Treasury
Bench. The OPPOSITION leaders occupy the
opposite front bench; hence, by extension,
the leaders of the government, or of the opposition.

To be raised to the bench. To be made a
judge.

To be raised to the Episcopal bench. To
be made a BISHOP.

Bench and Bar. Judges and barristers. *See*
BAR; BARRISTER.

Benchers. Senior members who administer
the INNS OF COURT and call students to the
BAR. They also exercise powers of expulsion.

Back-benchers. Ordinary members of the
House of Commons who do not hold office
and occupy the back benches. *Cp.* THE

FRONT BENCH.

Bench-mark. A surveyor's mark cut in some lasting material such as rock, the wall of a building etc. as a located point of reference and to act as a starting point in a line of levels for determining the altitudes of an area. In Britain it consists of cuts in the shape of a broad arrow with a horizontal incision across its apex. When making the reading an angle-iron is inserted in the horizontal cut to form the *bench* on which the levelling-staff is rested. Hence the name.

Bend. In HERALDRY, an ORDINARY formed between the two parallel lines drawn across the shield from the DEXTER chief (*i.e.* the top left-hand corner when looking at the shield) to the SINISTER base (the opposite corner). It is said to represent the sword-belt.

Bend sinister. A bend running across the shield from the SINISTER chief, *i.e.* from right to left. It is occasionally an indication of bastardy (*cp.* BAR SINISTER) though more often a *baton sinister* is used. *He has a bend sinister* means he was not born in lawful wedlock.

Beyond my bend. *i.e.* beyond my means or power. It is probably a corruption of *beyond my bent*, but it may be in allusion to a bow or spring, which breaks if strained beyond its bending power.

To bend over backwards. To make exceptional or unnecessary efforts to please or appease.

To go round the bend, or **to be driven round the bend.** To go mad or to be driven crazy. Here *bend* is used in the sense of "taking a turn".

Bender. A sixpenny piece; perhaps because it could be bent fairly easily. In schoolboy slang a caning which was taken in a bent position. It is an old term for a hard drinker, also a drinking bout or spree.

Bendy, Old. The DEVIL; who is willing to bend to anyone's inclination.

Benedicite (ben e dīs' i ti) (Lat.). "Bless you", or "may you be blessed". In the first sense it is the opening word of many old graces; hence a grace or a blessing. The second sense accounts for its use as an expression of astonishment.

> The god of love, A benedicite,
> How myghty and how great a lord is he!
> CHAUCER: *Knight's Tale*, 927.

Benedick, or **Benedict.** A sworn bachelor caught in the snares of matrimony; from Benedick in SHAKESPEARE'S *Much Ado about Nothing*.

Benedictines. Monks who follow the rule of St. Benedict of Nursia (*c.* 480–*c.* 553), also known as the "Black Monks". Monte Cas-

sino became their chief centre and they were renowned for their learning. Apart from their religious exercises, the monks were to be employed in study, teaching and manual labour. The Benedictines were a great civilizing influence in western Europe. St. Benedict's sister Scholastica is regarded as the founder of the Benedictine nuns.

Benedictine. A liqueur still made on the site of the Benedictine abbey at Fécamp based on the original early 16th-century recipe of Brother Vincelli.

Benefice. Under the Romans certain grants of land made to veteran soldiers were called *beneficia*, and in early feudal times an estate held for life, in return for military service, was called a *benefice*. The term came to be applied to the possessions of the Church held by individuals as a recompense for their services. Hence a church "living".

Benefit of Clergy. Formerly, the privilege enjoyed by the English clergy of trial in an ecclesiastical court, where punishments were less harsh than in the secular courts, and where bishops could not impose the death penalty. A clerk came to be identified with one who could read the NECK VERSE. By an Act of Henry IV's reign, no woman was to suffer death for circumstances in which a man could "plead his clergy", and a blind man could avoid the rope if able to speak Latin "congruously". Benefit of clergy was steadily curtailed from the time of Henry VII and by the end of the 17th century most of the serious crimes were excluded, but it was not totally abolished until 1827.

Benefit Societies. *See* FRIENDLY SOCIETIES.

Benevolence. A royal expedient for raising money without consent of PARLIAMENT. First so called in 1473, when Edward IV raised such a forced loan as a mark of goodwill towards his reign. Last levied by James I in 1622, it was declared illegal by the BILL OF RIGHTS, 1689.

Bengal Tigers. *See* REGIMENTAL AND DIVISIONAL NICKNAMES.

Benghazi Cooker. An Australian name in World War II for a contrivance for heating water, made from a can containing petrol-soaked sand.

Bengodi (ben gō' di). A "land of COCKAIGNE" mentioned in Boccaccio's *Decameron* (viii, 3), where "they tie the vines with sausages, where you may buy a fat goose for a penny and have a gosling into the bargain; where there is also a mountain of grated Parmesan cheese, and people do nothing but make cheese-cakes and macaroons. There is also a river which runs MALMSEY wine of the very best quality," etc., etc.

Benjamin. The pet, the youngest; in allusion to Benjamin, the youngest son of Jacob (*Gen.* xxxv, 18). Also (in early and mid-19th century), an overcoat, so called from a tailor of this name, and rendered popular by its association with JOSEPH'S "coat of many colours".

Benjamin's mess. The largest share. The allusion is to the banquet given by Joseph, viceroy of Egypt, to his brethren. "Benjamin's mess was five times so much as any of theirs" (*Gen.* xliii, 34).

Benjamin tree. A tree of the Styrax family that yields benzoin, of which the name is a corruption. Friar's Balsam or Jesuit's Drops is compounded from its juice.

> Taste, smell; I assure you, sir, pure benjamin, the only spirited scent that ever awaked a Neapolitan nostril.
>
> BEN JONSON: *Cynthia's Revels*, V, ii.

Beowulf (bā' ō wulf). The hero of the Old English epic poem of the same name of unknown date and authorship, but certainly originally written before the Saxons came to England and modified subsequent to the introduction of Christianity. In its present form, it probably dates from the 8th century. It is the oldest epic in English and also in the whole Teutonic group of languages.

The scene is laid in Denmark or Sweden; the hall of King Hrothgar is raided nightly by GRENDEL, whom Beowulf mortally wounds after a fierce fight. Next night Grendel's mother comes to avenge his death. Beowulf pursues her to her lair under the water and slays her with a magic sword. He eventually becomes king and fifty years later is killed in combat with a DRAGON, which had ravished the land.

Berchta. A goddess of South German mythology akin to the HULDA of North Germany, but after the introduction of Christianity she was degraded into a BOGY to frighten children. She was sometimes represented with a long iron nose and one large foot. *See* BERTHA; WHITE LADY.

Berchtesgaden. A charmingly situated resort in Bavaria known for its salt mines, royal castle and abbey but subsequently for Adolf Hitler's strongly guarded and fortified retreat. His mountain villa could only be entered by an elevator and then a tunnel hewn through the rock.

Bereans. Followers of the Rev. John Barclay (1734–1798), who seceded from the Scottish kirk in 1773. They held that all we know of God is from the Bible alone; that all the *Psalms* refer to Christ; that assurance is the proof of faith; that unbelief is the unforgivable sin, etc. They took their name from the Bereans mentioned in *Acts* xvii, 10, 11, who "received the Word with all readiness of mind, and searched the Scriptures daily".

Berecynthian Hero. MIDAS, the mythological king of Phrygia; so called from Mount Berecynthus in Phrygia.

Berenice. The wife of Ptolemy III Euergetes (246–221 B.C.). She vowed to sacrifice her hair to the gods, if her husband returned home the vanquisher of Asia. She suspended her hair in the temple, but it was stolen the first night and Conon of Samos told the king that the winds had wafted it to heaven, where it still forms the seven stars near the tail of LEO, called *Coma Berenices*.

Bergomask (ber' gō mask). A rustic dance (*see Midsummer Night's Dream*, V, i); so called from Bergamo, a Venetian province, whose inhabitants were noted for their clownishness. Also a CLOWN.

Berlin. A four-wheeled carriage with a hooded seat behind. It was introduced into England by a German officer about 1670.

Bermoothes (bĕr mō ooth' ēz). The name of the island in *The Tempest*, feigned by SHAKESPEARE to be enchanted and inhabited by WITCHES and DEVILS. He almost certainly had the newly discovered Bermudas in mind.

Bermudas (bĕr mū' dàz). An old name for a district of WESTMINSTER, probably the narrow alleys in the neighbourhood of COVENT GARDEN, St. Martin's Lane, and the STRAND whose residents had certain privileges against arrest. Hence **to live in the Bermudas,** to skulk in some out-of-the-way place for cheapness or safety. *Cp.* ALSATIA.

Bermuda Triangle. The triangular sea area between Bermuda, Florida and Puerto Rico where the currents are very strong. It gained notoriety in the 1960s on account of the disappearance of numerous ships and aircraft without any trace of wreckage.

Bernard, St. (1090–1153). Abbot of Clairvaux. Renowned for his wisdom and abilities, he did much to promote the growth of the Cistercian Order, and exercised great influence in Church matters. He was nicknamed the "MELLIFLUOUS DOCTOR".

Bernardine. A monk of the Order of ST. BERNARD of Clairvaux; a CISTERCIAN.

Bonus Bernardus non videt omnia. The good Bernard does not see everything. We are all apt to forget sometimes; events do not always turn out according to plan. *Cp.* HOMER SOMETIMES NODS.

Lucullus Bernard. Samuel Bernard, famous French capitalist (1651–1739).

Petit Bernard. Bernard Salomon, engraver of Lyons (16th century).

Poor Bernard. Claude Bernard of Dijon, philanthropist (1588–1640).

St. Bernard dogs. *See* ST. BERNARD PASSES *under* PASSES.

St. Bernard Soup. *See* STONE SOUP.

Bernardo del Carpio. A semi-mythical Spanish hero of the 9th century and a favourite subject of minstrels. Lope de Vega wrote several plays around his exploits. He is credited with having defeated ROLAND at Roncesvalles.

Bernesque Poetry. Serio-comic poetry; so called from Francesco Berni (*c.* 1497–1536), the Italian cleric and poet who greatly excelled in it. BYRON'S *Beppo* is a good example of English bernesque, with reference to which he wrote to John Murray, his publisher:

> Whistlecraft is my immediate model, but Berni is the father of that kind of writing.

Berserk, Berserker. In Scandinavian mythology, the sons of Berserk, grandson of the eight-handed Starkadder and Alfhilde. The name probably means bear-sark, or bear-coat. Berserk always fought ferociously and recklessly, without armour. Hence *berserk* for a savage and reckless fighter, one with the fighting fever on him.

Berth. He has fallen into a good berth. A good situation or fortune. The place where a ship is anchored or tied up is called its berth. Nautically, a good berth is one that is safe and favourable. One's sleeping space in a ship is called a berth.

To give a wide berth. Not to come near a person; to keep at a safe distance from; literally to give a ship plenty of room to swing at anchor.

Bertha. A German impersonation of the EPIPHANY with some of the attributes of BERCHTA, and corresponding to the Italian BEFANA. She is a WHITE LADY, who steals softly into nurseries and rocks infants to sleep, but is the terror of all naughty children.

Berthe au Grand Pied (bert ō gron pē ā′). Mother of CHARLEMAGNE, and great-granddaughter of Charles Martel; she had a club-foot and died in 783. Many of her qualities, as described in the Charlemagne romances, appear to be derived from BERCHTA.

Bertram, Count of Roussillon, beloved by Helena, the hero of SHAKESPEARE'S *All's Well that Ends Well*.

> I cannot reconcile my heart to Bertram, a man noble without generosity, and young without truth; who married Helena as a coward, and leaves her as a profligate.
>
> DR. JOHNSON.

Besaile. A word once used in England for a great-grandfather; it is the French *bisaïeul*.

Besant. *See* BEZANT.

Beside the Cushion. An odd phrase first used by Judge Jeffreys in the sense of "beside the question", "not to the point".

Besom. Jumping the besom. Omitting the marriage service after the publication of BANNS, and living together as man and wife. In Lowland Scots, *besom* is a name applied to a prostitute or woman of low character.

To hang out the besom. To have a fling when your wife is gone on a visit. To be a quasi bachelor again. *Cp.* the French colloquialism, *rôtir le balai* (to roast the besom) which means "to live a fast life", "to go on the RAZZLE".

Bess, Good Queen. Queen Elizabeth I (1533–1603).

Bess o'Bedlam. A female lunatic vagrant. *See* BEDLAM.

Bess of Hardwick. Elizabeth Talbot, Countess of Shrewsbury (1518–1608), to whose husband's charge Mary Queen of Scots was committed in 1569. The countess treated the captive queen harshly, through real or feigned jealousy of her husband. Daughter of John Hardwick of Derbyshire, she married four times: Robert Barlow (when she was only fourteen); Sir William Cavendish; Sir William St. Loe, Captain of the Queen's Guard; and lastly George Talbot, 6th Earl of Shrewsbury. Known as "building Bess of Hardwick", she built Hardwick Hall, Oldcotes, Worksop, Bolsover, and completed Chatsworth.

Black Bess. Dick Turpin's mythical but celebrated mare, created by Harrison Ainsworth in his romance *Rookwood* (1834), particularly known for Dick's famous ride to York. *See* TURPIN.

Bessee of Bednall Green. *See* BEGGAR'S DAUGHTER.

Bessie Bell and Mary Gray. A ballad relating how two young women of Perth, to avoid the plague of 1666, retired to a rural retreat called the Burnbraes, near Lynedock, the residence of Mary Gray. A young man, in love with both, carried them provisions, and they all died of the plague and were buried at Dornock Hough.

Bessie with the braid apron. *See* BELTED WILL.

Best. At best, or **At the very best.** Looking at the matter in the most favourable light. Making every allowance.

> Man is a short-sighted creature at best.
>
> DEFOE: *Colonel Jack*.

At one's best. On top form in all respects.

For the best. With the best of motives; with the view of obtaining the best results.

I must make the best of my way home. It is getting late and I must use my utmost diligence to get home as soon as possible.

To best somebody. To get the better of him; to outwit him and so have the advantage.

To have the best of it, or **to have the best bargain.** To have the advantage or best of a transaction.

To make the best of the matter. To submit to ill-luck with the best grace in your power.

Best Man (at a wedding). The bridegroom's chosen friend who waits on him as the bridesmaids wait on the bride.

Bestiaries, or **Bestials.** Books which had a great vogue between the 11th and 14th centuries, describing the supposed habits and peculiarities of animals both real and fabled, with much legendary lore and moral symbolism. They were founded on the *Physiologi* of earlier centuries and those in English were mostly translations of continental originals. Among the most popular were those of Philippe de Thaun, Guillaume le Clerc, and Richard de Fournival's satirical *Bestiaire d'Amour* (c. 1250).

> The unicorn represents Jesus Christ, who took on him our nature in the virgin's womb, was betrayed to the Jews, and delivered into the hands of Pontius Pilate. Its one horn signifies the Gospel truth, that Christ is one with the Father, *etc*.
>
> GUILLAUME: *Le Bestiaire Divin*.

Bête Noire (bāt nwar) (Fr. black beast). The thorn in the side, the bitter in the cup, the SPOKE IN THE WHEEL, the BLACK SHEEP, one's pet aversion.

Beth Gelert. *See* BEDDGELERT.

Bethel (Heb. house of God). A hallowed place where God is worshipped (see *Gen*. xxviii, 18, 19). The name has frequently been given to Nonconformist chapels, especially in Wales, and also to religious meeting houses for seamen. They were sometimes referred to, somewhat disparagingly, by ANGLICANS as *little Bethels*.

> And God said unto Jacob, Arise, go up to Beth-el, and dwell there: and make there an altar unto God...
>
> *Gen*. xxxv, i.

Bethlehemites. (1) A monastic order existing at Cambridge in 1257. Members wore a red star on the breast in memory of the Star of Bethlehem. (2) A short-lived military order instituted by Pius II in 1459 against the Turks. (3) A religious society for tending the sick, founded in Guatemala, *c*. 1659, by Pierre de Bethencourt, a native of the Canaries. Innocent XI approved of the order in 1687. (4) Followers of John Hus, from the fact that he used to preach in the church of Bethlehem in Prague.

Better. Better off. In easier circumstances.

For better for worse. Forever. From the English marriage service, expressive of indissoluble union

My better half. My wife. As the twain are one, each is half. Horace calls his friend *animæ dimidium meæ* (*Odes* I, iii, 8).

No better than he or **she should be.** A phrase of disparagement implying immorality or an amoral character.

> ...and exprest some wonder at his having strayed so far out of his way, and at meeting him, as she said, 'in the company of that wench, who she feared was no better than she should be'.
>
> HENRY FIELDING: *Joseph Andrews*, Bk.II,ch.xiii.

To be better than his word. To do more than he promised.

To think better of the matter. To give it further consideration; to form a more correct opinion respecting it, and usually to revise one's intentions as a result.

Bettina. Elisabeth von Arnim (1785–1859), German writer and wife of the poet Ludwig Achim von Arnim. Her first book, *Letters to a Child* (1835), was based upon her letters to Goethe.

Betubium (be tū' bi um). The old poetic name for the Cape of St. Andrew, Scotland.

> The north-inflated tempest foams
> O'er Orka's and Betubium's highest peak.
> THOMSON: *Autumn*, 891, 2.

Between. Between hay and grass. Neither one thing nor yet another; a hobbledehoy, neither a man nor yet a boy.

Between cup and lip. *See* SLIP.

Between Scylla and Charybdis. Between equal dangers. *See* CHARYBDIS; SCYLLA. *Cp*. HOBSON'S CHOICE.

Between the devil and the deep (blue) sea. Similar in use to BETWEEN SCYLLA AND CHARYBDIS. *See under* DEVIL.

Between two fires. Between two dangers as soldiers caught between fire from opposite sides.

Between two stools, you fall to the ground. As when accidentally, or as the victim of a practical joke, you miss both stools and fall to the ground. To miss both chances through hesitance or indecision.

Between you and me. In confidence. Alternatively, **Between you and me and the gatepost,** or **bed-post;** between ourselves. Often an indication that some gossip or slander about a third person is to follow.

Betwixt and between. Neither one nor the other, but somewhere between the two. Thus, grey is neither white nor black, but *betwixt and between* the two.

Betwixt wind and water. In a most dangerous spot. The phrase refers to that part of a sailing ship's hull around the waterline, which is alternately wet and dry according to the motion of both ship and waves. A dangerous place for a ship to be holed.

Beulah. *See* LAND OF BEULAH.

Bever (bev' er). A snack (originally a drink) between meals; through O.Fr. *beivre* from Lat. *bibere*, to drink—*beverage* has the same origins. At Eton "Bever days" were when extra beer and bread were served during the afternoon in the College Hall to scholars and their friends. *See also* CRIB.

> He is none of these same ordinary eaters, that will devour three breakfasts and as many dinners without any prejudice to their bevers, drinkings, or suppers.
>
> BEAUMONT and FLETCHER: *Woman Hater*, I, iii.

Bevin Boys. Nickname for the young men directed to work in coal mines under the Emergency Powers (Defence) Act (1940). Ernest Bevin (1881–1951) was Minister of Labour and National Service at the time.

Bevis (bē' vis). In Scott's *Marmion*, Lord Marmion's red-roan charger.

Bevis of Hampton. Sir Bevis was the hero of this popular English mediæval romance slightly connected with the CHARLEMAGNE cycle. Bevis sought to avenge his father's death, which had been contrived by his mother. As a result he was sold to heathen merchants, and after many adventures he married Josian, daughter of King Ermyn, eventually returning to England to avenge his father. Hampton is usually interpreted as Southampton. The English version (14th century) is based on an earlier French version, but it is possible that the story had previous English origins. Drayton tells the story in his *Polyolbion*, Song ii, lines 260–384.

Bevoriskius (be vôr is' ki us), whose *Commentary on the Generations of Adam* is referred to by Sterne in the *Sentimental Journey*, was Johan van Beverwyck (1594–1647), a Dutch physician and author.

Bevy. A throng or company of ladies, roebucks, quails, or larks. The word is the Italian *beva*, a drink; possibly it acquired this meaning because timid, gregarious animals go down to the river to drink in company. Ladies in former times were regarded as timid creatures.

Bezant (be zănt') (from Byzantium, the old name of Constantinople, now Istanbul). A gold coin of varying value struck by the Byzantine Emperors and current in England until the time of Edward III. In HERALDRY the name is given to a plain gold ROUNDEL on the shield.

Bezoar (bē' zōr). A stone from the stomach or gall-bladder of an animal (usually goats and antelopes), set as a jewel and believed to be an antidote against poison. The word is of Persian origin (*pad-zahr*) and means "counter-poison".

Bezonian (be zō' ni an). A raw recruit; applied originally in derision to young, ill-equipped soldiers sent from Spain to the Italian Wars, who arrived in want of everything (Ital. *bisogni*, from *bisogno*, need; Fr. *besoin*). Hence a beggar, a knave, etc.

> Great men oft die by vile bezonians.
>
> SHAKESPEARE: *Henry VI, Pt. II*, IV, i.

Bhagavad Gita (The Song of the Blessed). One of the great religious and philosophical poems of India which occurs in the sixth book of the MAHABHARATA. In it, KRISHNA, in the form of a charioteer, instructs Arjuna, chief of the Pandus, in his duties and elaborates his ethical and pantheistic philosophy, finally revealing himself as the Supreme Being.

Bianchi (bē ăng' ki) (It. the Whites). In 1300 the GUELPH family in Florence split into two factions, "Whites" and "Blacks" (Neri). The Bianchi, among whom Dante was prominent, allied with their GHIBELLINE opponents. After the triumph of the Neri in 1301, Dante was exiled from Florence.

Bib. Best bib and tucker. *See* TUCKER.

Biberius Caldius Mero. The punning nickname of Tiberius Claudius Nero (Roman Emperor, A.D. 14–37). Biberius (Tiberius) drink-loving, Caldius Mero (Claudius Nero), by METATHESIS for *calidus mero*, hot with wine.

Bible. The word is derived from the Greek *Ta Biblia* through mediæval Latin and means *The Books*. *See* APOCRYPHA; DEAD SEA SCROLLS; NEW TESTAMENT; OLD TESTAMENT; PENTATEUCH; PSALMS; PSEUDEPIGRAPHA; "Q"; SEPTUAGINT; VULGATE.

Bible, The English. The principal versions in chronological order are:

Wyclif's Bible. The name given to two translations of the VULGATE. The earlier one completed *c.* 1384 is the first complete English Bible, although there were renderings of parts of the Scriptures from Anglo-Saxon times. Wyclif may have translated parts of it and one of his circle, Nicholas of Hereford, is known to have participated. The second and improved version, probably written between 1395 and 1397, is considered to owe much to John Purvey, a LOLLARD scholar. As a whole it remained unprinted until a monumental edition of both versions, prepared by Forshall and Madden, appeared in 1850.

Tyndale's Bible. This consists of the New Testament printed at Cologne in 1525 (Revisions 1534 and 1535); the PENTATEUCH, printed at Marburg, 1530; the Book of Jonah, 1531; Epistles of the Old Testament (after the Use of Salisbury), 1534; and a MS. translation of the Old Testament to the end of Chronicles, which was afterwards used in MATTHEW'S BIBLE. His work was chiefly based on Greek originals, while making use of the Greek and Latin versions of the New Testament by Erasmus, Luther's Bible, and the VULGATE. His work fixed the language and style of subsequent English versions which were more often revisions of his work rather than independent translations.

Coverdale's Bible. This first printed edition of a complete English Bible appeared in 1535, translated "out of Douche (German) and Latyn", by Miles Coverdale. It was based on Luther, the ZÜRICH BIBLE, the VULGATE, the Latin version of Pagninus, and Tyndale. The first edition was probably printed at Zürich, the second was printed by Nicolson at Southwark in 1537 (the first Bible printed in England). *See* BUG BIBLE.

Matthew's Bible. Printed in Antwerp in 1537 as the translation of Thomas Matthew, most probably an alias, for self-preservation, of John Rogers, an assistant of Tyndale. It is essentially made up from the work of Tyndale and Coverdale. Like Coverdale's third edition it appeared under the King's licence, but was soon superseded by the GREAT BIBLE. It is important as a basis of the approved editions which culminated in the AUTHORIZED VERSION. *See* BUG BIBLE.

Taverner's Bible. A revision of MATTHEW'S BIBLE by Richard Taverner printed in 1539. It had little influence on subsequent translations, but is notable for its idiomatic English.

The Great Bible. Published by Grafton and Whitchurch in 1539 as an authorized Bible sponsored by Cranmer and Cromwell, being a revision by Coverdale substantially based on MATTHEW'S BIBLE. It went through seven editions and it was made compulsory for all parish churches to possess a copy. *See* CRANMER'S BIBLE, CROMWELL'S BIBLE.

Cromwell's Bible. The GREAT BIBLE of 1539. The title-page includes a portrait of Thomas Cromwell, under whose direction the Bible was commissioned.

Cranmer's Bible. The name given to the 1540 edition of the GREAT BIBLE. It and later issues contained a prologue by Cranmer, and, on the woodcut title-page by Holbein, Henry VIII is shown seated handing copies to Cranmer and Cromwell. Its Psalter is still incorporated in the BOOK OF COMMON PRAYER.

The Geneva Bible. An important revision in the development of the English Bible, undertaken by English exiles in Geneva during the Marian persecutions, first published in 1560; largely the work of William Whittingham, assisted by Anthony Gilby and Thomas Sampson. Whittingham had previously (1557) published a translation of the New Testament. Based on the GREAT BIBLE, MATTHEW'S BIBLE, etc., it was the first English Bible to be printed in roman type instead of black letter, in QUARTO size, and the first in which the chapters were divided into verses (on the model of Robert Stephen's Greek-Latin Testament of 1537). It was immensely popular; from 1560 to 1616 no year passed without a new edition. *See* BREECHES BIBLE, GOOSE BIBLE, PLACEMAKER'S BIBLE.

The Bishops' Bible. A revision of the GREAT BIBLE to counter the growing popularity of the GENEVA BIBLE. Organized by Archbishop Matthew Parker, it appeared in 1568 and a number of the abler bishops took part in the work. It reached its 18th edition by 1602 and was the basis of the AUTHORIZED VERSION. *See* TREACLE BIBLE.

Matthew Parker's Bible. THE BISHOPS' BIBLE.

The Douai Bible (dou′ ā). A translation of the VULGATE by English Roman Catholics. The New Testament was published at the English College at Rheims in 1582, the Old Testament at Douai in 1609; hence called the **Rheims and Douai version.** *See* ROSIN BIBLE.

The Authorized Version. This version, still in general use in England, was produced by some 47 scholars, working at the command of King James I, and was a by-product of the HAMPTON COURT CONFERENCE. Begun in 1607 and published in 1611, it was based on the BISHOPS' BIBLE, but Tyndale's, Matthew's, Coverdale's and the Geneva Bibles were followed where they gave more accurate renderings. Since 1984 published as the *Authorized King James Version*.

King James's Bible. The AUTHORIZED VERSION.

The Revised Version. This revision of the AUTHORIZED VERSION resulted from a resolution passed by Houses of Convocation in 1870. It was the work of two companies of English scholars, with American co-operators. The New Testament appeared in 1881, the Old Testament in 1885, and the APOCRYPHA in 1895.

The American Standard Version (1901).

Essentially a modification of the Revised Version of 1881 to meet American preferences.

The New Testament in Modern Speech (1903). A new translation from the Greek by R. F. Weymouth.

Moffat's Translation. A revised edition of the Bible by James Moffat (N.T., 1913; O.T., 1924; complete edition, 1935).

Knox Version. A new Roman Catholic translation of the VULGATE by Monsignor R.A. Knox. The N.T. was authorized in 1945, the O.T. (for private use only) in 1949.

The Revised Standard Version. The work of American scholars issued between 1946 and 1952. It was to embody the results of modern scholarship "and to be in the diction of the simple classic English style of the King James version". The APOCRYPHA was published in 1957.

The New Testament in Modern English. A translation by J.B. Phillips aiming at clarity of expression, first published in 1958 with a revised version in 1973.

The New English Bible. A translation into contemporary English first proposed by the CHURCH OF SCOTLAND and directed by a joint committee of the PROTESTANT Churches of Great Britain and Ireland. The N.T. appeared in 1961 and the translations of the O.T. and the APOCRYPHA were finished in 1966. The complete bible was published in 1970. The 1989 edition was revised to eliminate "sexist language" such as *man*, *sons*, *brothers*, etc.

The Jerusalem Bible. A new translation of the Bible, prepared from the ancient originals by Roman Catholic scholars, largely in contemporary English. First published in 1966, it derives its notes and introduction from the French *La Bible de Jérusalem* produced under the editorship of Père Roland de Vaux in 1956. *Yahweh* replaces the traditional JEHOVAH.

The Revised Standard Version Common Bible. Published in 1973, based on both the Protestant and Roman Catholic (1966) editions of the REVISED STANDARD VERSION, and intended for interdenominational use. It has been accepted by the PROTESTANT churches generally as well as by the ROMAN CATHOLIC and EASTERN CHURCHES.

The Good News Bible: Today's English Version. An illustrated version, produced by the American Bible Society, designed to be easily understood, including by those whose first language is not English. The N.T. was published in 1966 and the complete Bible in 1976. It follows the traditional numbering of chapter and verse.

The New International Version. A new translation, the work of an Anglo-American team seeking to present a modernized version in good English. First published by the New York Bible Society in 1978 followed by a British edition in 1979.

Many other individually produced translations have appeared over the years.

BIBLE. SOME SPECIALLY NAMED EDITIONS.

The Adulterous Bible. The WICKED BIBLE.

The Affinity Bible, of 1923, which contains a table of affinity with the error, "A man may not marry his grandmother's wife."

The Bad Bible. A printing of 1653 with a deliberate perversion of *Acts* vi, 6, whereby the ordination of deacons was ascribed to the disciples and not to the apostles.

The Bear Bible. The Spanish Protestant version printed at Basle in 1569; so called because the woodcut device on the title-page is of a bear.

Bedell's Bible. An Irish translation of the Old Testament carried out under the direction of Bishop William Bedell (1571–1642). The Irish N.T. was published in 1601.

The Breeches Bible. The popular name for the GENEVA BIBLE because in it *Gen.* iii, 7, was rendered, "and they sowed figge-tree leaves together, and made themselves breeches." It is also given in the then unprinted Wyclif MS. (ya swiden ye levis of a fige tree and madin brechis), and also in the translation of the PENTATEUCH printed in Caxton's edition of Voragine's *Golden Legend* (1483).

The Brothers' Bible. The KRALITZ BIBLE.

The Bug Bible. COVERDALE'S BIBLE of 1535 is so called because *Ps.* xci, 5, is translated: "Thou shalt not nede to be afrayed for eny bugges by night." The same occurs in MATTHEW'S BIBLE and its reprints. Both the AUTHORIZED VERSION and REVISED VERSION read "terror".

Camel's Bible, of 1823. *Gen.* xxiv, 61, reads: "And Rebekah arose, and her camels (for *damsels*)."

Complutensian Polyglot. Published between 1514 and 1517 at Alcalá (the ancient Complutum), near Madrid, at the expense of Cardinal Ximenes. In six FOLIO volumes, it contains the Hebrew and Greek texts, the Septuagint, the VULGATE, and the Chaldee paraphrase of the PENTATEUCH with a Latin translation, together with Greek and Hebrew grammars and a Hebrew dictionary.

The Denial Bible. Printed at Oxford in 1792, in *Luke* xxii, 34, the name *Philip* is substituted for *Peter*, as the apostle who should deny Jesus.

The Discharge Bible. An edition of 1806 containing *discharge* for *charge* in I *Tim*. v, 21: "I dis-charge thee before God, ... that thou observe these things."

The Ears to Ear Bible. An edition of 1810, in which *Matt*. xiii, 43, reads: "Who hath ears to *ear*, let him hear."

The Ferrara Bible. The first Spanish edition of the Old Testament (1553) for the use of Spanish Jews. A second edition for Christians was published in the same year.

The Fool Bible. An edition of Charles I's reign in which *Psalm* xiv, 1, reads: "The fool hath said in his heart there is a God." (instead of *no god*). The printers were fined £3,000 and all copies were suppressed.

The Forgotten Sins Bible, of 1638. *Luke* vii, 47, reads: "Her sins which are many, are forgotten (instead of *forgiven*)."

The Forty-two-line Bible. The MAZARIN BIBLE.

The Goose Bible. The editions of the GENEVA BIBLE printed at Dort: the Dort press had a goose for its device.

The Gutenberg Bible. The MAZARIN BIBLE.

The He Bible. In the first of the two editions of the AUTHORIZED VERSION in 1611, known as "the He Bible", *Ruth* iii, 15, reads: "and he went into the city." The other, and nearly all modern editions (except the REVISED VERSION) have "she". "He" is the correct translation of the Hebrew.

The Idle Bible. An edition of 1809, in which "the idol shepherd" (*Zech*. xi, 17) is printed "the idle shepherd". In the REVISED VERSION the translation is "the worthless shepherd".

The Incunabula Bible. The date on the title page reads 1495 instead of 1594. The word INCUNABULA came to be applied to all books printed before 1500, the period when typography was in its "swaddling-clothes", or its beginnings.

The Indian Bible. The first complete Bible printed in America, translated into the dialect of the Indians of Massachusetts by the Rev. John Eliot and published by Samuel Green and Marmaduke Johnson in 1663.

Judas Bible, of 1611. *Matt*. xxvi, 36, reads "Judas" instead of "Jesus".

The Kralitz Bible, also called the *Brothers' Bible*, was published by the United Brethren of Moravia at Kralitz, 1579–1593.

The "Large Family" Bible. An Oxford edition of 1820 prints *Isaiah* lxvi, 9: "Shall I bring to the birth and not cease (for *cause*) to bring forth?"

The Leda Bible. The third edition (second folio) of the BISHOPS' BIBLE, published in 1572, and so called from the decoration of the initial at the Epistle to the Hebrews which is a startling and incongruous woodcut of JUPITER visiting LEDA in the guise of a swan. This and other decorations in the New Testament were from an edition of Ovid's *Metamorphoses*. Such was the protest that they were never used again.

The Leopolita Bible. A Polish translation of the VULGATE by John of Lemberg (Jan Nicz of Lwów) published at Cracow in 1561. So called from the Latin name, *Leopolis*, of his birthplace.

The Lions Bible. A Bible issued in 1804 containing many printers' errors such as: *Numbers* xxv, 18, "The murderer shall surely be put together (instead of *to death*)"; I *Kings* viii, 19, "but thy son that shall come forth out of thy lions (for *loins*)"; *Galatians* v, 17, "For the flesh lusteth after the Spirit (for *against the Spirit*)".

The Mazarin Bible. The first known book to be printed from movable type, probably by Fust and Schöffer at Mainz, who took over most of Gutenberg's presses in 1455. This edition of the VULGATE was on sale in 1456 and owes its name to the copy discovered in the Mazarin Library in Paris in 1760. A copy of Vol. I fetched a record price of £21,000 at a London auction in 1947. It was for long credited to Gutenberg and is frequently called the **Gutenberg Bible.** It is usually known to bibliographers as the **Forty-two-line Bible** (it having 42 lines to the column) to differentiate it from the THIRTY-SIX-LINE BIBLE.

More Sea Bible, of 1641. *Rev*. xxi, 1, reads: "and there was more sea", instead of "no more sea".

The Murderers' Bible. An edition of 1801 in which *Jude* 16 reads: "These are murderers (for *murmurers*), complainers", *etc*.

The Old Cracow Bible. The LEOPOLITA BIBLE.

The Ostrog Bible. The first complete Slavonic edition; printed at Ostrog, Volhynia, Russia, in 1581.

Pfister's Bible. The THIRTY-SIX-LINE BIBLE.

The Placemaker's Bible. The second edition of the GENEVA BIBLE, 1562. *Matt*. v, 9, reads: "Blessed are the placemakers (peacemakers): for they shall be called the children of God." It has also been called the WHIG BIBLE.

The Printers' Bible. An edition of about 1702 which makes David complain that "printers (princes) have persecuted me without a cause". (*Ps*. cxix, 161.)

The Proof Bible (Probe-Bibel). The revised version of the first impression of Luther's German Bible. A final revision appeared in 1892.

The Rosin Bible. The DOUAI BIBLE, 1609, is so called because it has in *Jer.* viii, 22: "Is there noe rosin in Galaad?" The AUTHORIZED VERSION translates the word by "balm", but gives "rosin" in the margin as an alternative. *Cp.* TREACLE BIBLE.

Sacy's Bible. A French translation by the JANSENIST, Louis Isaac le Maistre de Sacy, director of PORT ROYAL (1650–1679). He began his work when imprisoned in the BASTILLE.

Schelhorn's Bible. The THIRTY-SIX-LINE BIBLE.

The September Bible. Luther's German translation of the New Testament, published anonymously at Wittenberg in September 1522.

The She Bible. *See* HE BIBLE.

"Sin on" Bible. The first printed in Ireland was dated 1716. *John* v,14, reads: "sin on more", instead of "sin no more". The mistake was undiscovered until 8,000 copies had been printed and bound.

The Standing Fishes Bible. An edition of 1806 in which *Ezek.* xlvii, 10, reads: "And it shall come to pass that the fishes (fishers) shall stand upon it," *etc.*

The Sting Bible of 1746. *Mark* vii, 35, "the sting of his tongue", instead of "string".

The Thirty-six-line Bible. A Latin Bible of 36 lines to the column, probably printed by A. Pfister at Bamberg in 1460. It is also known as the Bamberg, and Pfister's, Bible and sometimes as Schelhorn's, as it was first described by the German bibliographer J. G. Schelhorn, in 1760.

The To-remain Bible. In a Bible printed at Cambridge in 1805 *Gal.* iv, 29, reads: "persecuted him that was born after the spirit to remain, even so it is now." The words "to remain" were added in error by the compositor, the editor having answered a proofreader's query as to the comma after "spirit", with the pencilled reply in the margin "to remain". The mistake was repeated in the Bible Society's first 8vo edition (1805) and their 12mo edition of 1819.

The Treacle Bible. A popular name for the BISHOPS' BIBLE, 1568, because *Jer.* viii, 22, reads: "is there no tryacle in Gilead, is there no phisition there?" "Tryacle" is also given for "balm" in *Jer.* xlvi, 11, and *Ezek.* xxvii, 17. *Cp.* ROSIN BIBLE. COVERDALE'S BIBLE also uses the word 'triacle'. *See* TREACLE.

The Unrighteous Bible. A Cambridge printing of 1653 contains: "know ye not that the unrighteous shall inherit the Kingdom

of God?", instead of "shall not inherit" (I *Cor.* vi, 9). Also in *Rom.* vi, 13, "neither yield ye your members as instruments of righteousness unto sin," in place of "unrighteousness". This edition is also sometimes known as the WICKED BIBLE.

The Vinegar Bible. An Oxford printing of 1717 in which part of the chapter heading to *Luke* xx reads: "The parable of the Vinegar" (for *Vineyard*).

The Whig Bible. Another name for the PLACEMAKERS' BIBLE. The jibe is obvious. *See* PLACEMEN.

The Wicked Bible. So called because the word "not" was omitted in the seventh commandment (*Exod.* xx, 14) making it, "Thou shalt commit adultery." It was printed by Barker and Lucas, the King's printers at Blackfriars in 1631. The fine of £300 helped to ruin the printer. It is also called the *Adulterous Bible. See* UNRIGHTEOUS BIBLE.

The Wife-hater Bible. An 1810 edition gives *Luke* xiv, 26: "If any man come to me, and hate not his father and mother ... yea, and his own wife," instead of "life".

Wujek's Bible. An authorized Polish translation by the Jesuit, Jacub Wujek, printed at Cracow in 1599.

The Zürich Bible. A German version of 1530 composed of Luther's translation of the New Testament and portions of the Old, with the remainder and the APOCRYPHA by other translators.

Bible, Statistics of. The following statistics are those given in the *Introduction to the Critical Study and Knowledge of the Bible*, by Thos. Hartwell Horne, D.D., first published in 1818. They apply to the English AUTHORIZED VERSION.

	O.T.	N.T.	Total
Books	39	27	66
Chapters	929	260	1,189
Verses	23,214	7,959	31,173
Words	593,493	181,253	774,746
Letters	2,728,100	838,380	3,566,480

APOCRYPHA. Books, 14; chapters, 183; verses, 6,031; words, 125,185; letters, 1,063,876.

	O.T.	N.T.
Middle book	*Proverbs*	*II Thess.*
Middle Chapter	*Job* xxix	*Rom.* xiii and xiv
Middle verse	*II Chron.* xx, 17 & 18	*Acts* xvii, 17
Shortest verse	I *Chron.* i, 25	*John* xi, 35
Shortest chapter	*Psalm* cxvii	
Longest chapter	*Psalm* cxix	

Ezra vii, 21, contains all the letters of the alphabet except j.

II *Kings* xix and *Isaiah* xxxvii are exactly alike.

The last two verses of II *Chron.* and the opening verses of *Ezra* are alike.

Ezra ii and *Nehemiah* vii are alike.

The word *and* occurs in the O.T. 35,543 times,

and in the N.T. 10,684 times.

The word *Jehovah* occurs 6,855 times, and *Lord* 1,855 times.

About thirty books are mentioned in the Bible, but not included in the canon.

In addition it is noteworthy that by the end of 1965 the United Bible Societies had circulated the Scriptures in 1,251 languages.
Bible-backed. Round-shouldered, like one who is always poring over a book.
Bible belt. In the U.S.A. the south central Mid-west, south of the MASON AND DIXON line reputedly associated with puritanism and religious fundamentalism.
Bible-carrier. A scornful term for an obtrusively pious person.

Some scoffe at such as carry the scriptures with them to church, terming them in reproach *Bible-carriers*.

GOUGE: *Whole Armour of God* (1616), p. 318.

Bible Christians. An evangelical sect founded in 1815 by William O'Bryan, a Cornish METHODIST; also called Bryanites. The movement grew steadily, beginning in the fishing and farming districts of Devon and Cornwall. They joined the United Methodist Church in 1907.
Bible-Clerk. A student at Oxford or Cambridge who formerly got pecuniary advantages for reading the Bible at chapel, etc.
Bible-puncher. A modern equivalent of BIBLE-CARRIER.
Biblia Pauperum (Lat., poor man's Bible). A MISNOMER coined long after the first appearance in the 1460s of these late mediæval BLOCK BOOKS. They contain a series of NEW TESTAMENT scenes from the life of Christ, each surrounded by their OLD TESTAMENT antetypes, and with a brief text engraved in the same block below the illustration. Despite their name, the *Biblia Pauperum* can hardly have been intended for the illiterate, their iconography and text being replete with allegory and symbol, and must rather have served itinerant preachers and the lower orders of clergy. *See* SPECULUM HUMANÆ SALVATIONIS.
Bibliomancy. DIVINATION by means of the Bible. *See* SORTES.
Bibliomania. A love of books pursued to the point of unreason or madness. One Don Vicente, a Spanish scholar, is reputed to have committed murder to obtain a supposedly unique book.
Bibliophilia. A devotion to books and book collecting within the limits of reason.

Sir Thomas Phillipps (1792–1872) is an especially notable example of a *bibliophile* whose manuscript collection surpassed all other private hoards. His obsession bordered on BIBLIOMANIA and kept him constantly on the edge of bankruptcy.
Bibulus. Colleague of Julius Caesar, a mere cipher in office; hence proverbial for one in office who is a mere *fainéant*.
Bickerstaff, Isaac. A name assumed by Dean Swift in a satirical pamphlet against Partridge, the ALMANAC-maker. So diverting was the ensuing paper war that Steele issued the *Tatler* under the editorial name of "Isaac Bickerstaff, Esq., Astrologer" (1709). An actual Isaac Bickerstaffe, playwright, was born in Ireland in 1735.
Bicorn (bī kôrn). A mythical beast, fabled by the early French romancers to grow very fat through living on good and enduring husbands. It was the antitype of CHICHEVACHE.
Bi-corn (two-horns) contains an allusion to the horned CUCKOLD.
Bid. The modern verb "to bid" may be from either of two Old English verbs, (1) *béodan*, to stretch out, offer, present, and hence to inform, proclaim, command, or (2) *biddan*, to importune, beg, pray, and hence also, command. The two words have now become very confused. The following four examples are from (1) *béodan*:
To bid fair. To seem likely; as "He bids fair to do well"; "It bids fair to be a fine day".
To bid for (votes). To promise to support certain measures in PARLIAMENT in order to obtain votes.
To bid against one. To offer a higher price for an article at auction.
I bid him defiance. I offer him defiance; I defy him.

The next examples are from (2) *biddan*:
I bid you good night. I wish you good night, or I pray that you may have a good night.

Neither bid him God speed.

II *John* 10.

To bid one's beads. To tell off one's prayers by beads. *See* BEAD; ROSARY.
To bid the (marriage) banns. To ask if anyone objects to the marriage of the persons named. *Cp.* SI QUIS.
To bid to the wedding. To ask to the wedding feast.
Bid-ale (or **Help-ale**). A gathering to drink ALE and to collect for the relief of some poor man or other charity. They frequently became an excuse for excessive conviviality.

There was an ancient custom called a Bidale or Bidder-ale... when any honest man decayed in his estate was set up again by the liberal benevolence and contributions of friends at a feast to which those friends were bid or invited. It was most used in the West of England, and in some counties called a Help-ale.

BRAND: *Popular Antiquities* (1777).

Bidding-prayer (O.E. *biddan*; *see* BID). In

the CHURCH OF ENGLAND this term is now commonly applied to a prayer for the souls of benefactors said before the sermon, in cathedrals, university churches, and on special occasions. It stems from the pre-REFORMATION vernacular prayer of the "bidding of the beads". "Bidding" was here used in the sense of "praying" and the priest told the people what to remember in their prayers. By the time of Elizabeth I the "bidding of prayers" came to mean the "directing" or "enjoining" of prayers, hence the modern meaning.

Biddy (*i.e.* Bridget). A generic name for an Irish servant-maid, as Mike is for an Irish labourer. Such names were once very common: for example Tom Tug, a waterman; Jack Pudding, a buffoon; JACK TAR, a sailor; TOMMY Atkins, a soldier; Colin Tampon, a Swiss; John Chinaman, etc. *See* NICKNAME.

Biddy also denotes a hen; sometimes *chick-a-biddy*, and also, in English dialect, a louse. In Australia it denotes a female teacher.

> The English hens had a contented cluck as if they never got nervous like Yankee biddies.
> L. M. ALCOTT: *Little Wives.*

Old Biddy. In the U.S.A. a term applied to an elderly woman who is somewhat of a busybody.

Red Biddy. A highly intoxicating concoction of red wine and methylated spirit.

Bideford Postman. Edward Capern (1819–1894), the DEVONSHIRE POET, so called from his former occupation and abode.

Bidpay. *See* PILPAY.

Bifrost (Icel. *bifa*, tremble; *rost*, path). In Scandinavian mythology, the bridge between HEAVEN and earth, ASGARD and MIDGARD. The rainbow may be considered to be this bridge, and its various colours are the reflections of its precious stones. HEIMDALL is its keeper.

Big. To look big. To assume a consequential air.

To look as big as bull beef. To look stout and hearty, as if fed on bull beef which was held to make men strong and muscular.

To talk big. To boast or brag.

Big Bang (in the City of LONDON). The deregulation of the STOCK EXCHANGE, the removal of fixed commissions charged by stockbrokers and the merging of the functions of STOCKJOBBER and STOCKBROKER operating with negotiated rates of commission. Foreign investment companies may now join the Stock Exchange and also own British brokers and jobbers. The intention was to maintain London's position as a leading international financial centre. It took place on 26 Oct. 1986 and its long term effects remain to be seen.

Big Bang (in cosmology). The theoretical origin of the universe. It presupposes that a very small fireball of an extraordinary high temperature was formed and when this exploded (the Big Bang) the result was the formation of the universe.

Big Ben. Properly, the famous hour bell in the Clock Tower (St. Stephen's Tower) of the Houses of PARLIAMENT, which came to be so called after Sir Benjamin Hall who was Chief Commissioner of Works at the time. The original casting of 1856, weighing some 15 tons, when being tested in Palace Yard developed serious cracks and was scrapped. The new bell weighing *c.* 13 tons was installed in October 1858. This also developed a crack, but of a less serious nature. There are also four Quarter bells whose weight varies between *c.* 4 tons and 1 ton. The clock as a whole is popularly and generally now called "Big Ben".

Big Bertha. The name given by the French to the large howitzers used by the Germans against Liége and Namur in 1914. In reality made at the Skoda works, they were mistakenly thought to be a product of the famous German armament firm, hence the allusion to Frau Bertha Krupp. In 1918 Paris was shelled from a range of 76 miles by the 142-ton "Paris" gun to which the name Big Bertha was again applied. In American slang "Big Bertha" means a fat woman.

Big bird, To get the (*i.e.* the goose). To be hissed; to receive one's *congé*; originally a theatrical expression. Today the usual phrase is "to get the bird".

Big Brother is watching you. Authority, totalitarian and bureaucratic, has you under its observation from which there is no escape. One of the telling phrases from George Orwell's *Nineteen Eighty-Four* (1949). The allusion is to the U.S.S.R. but its application is not without significance in other modern states.

> The posters that were plastered everywhere—BIG BROTHER IS WATCHING YOU the caption said, while the dark eyes looked into Winston's own.
> *Nineteen Eighty-Four*: Pt. I, i.

Big-endians. In Swift's *Gulliver's Travels*, a party in the empire of Lilliput who made it a matter of conscience to break their eggs at the *big end*; they were looked on as heretics by the orthodox party, who broke theirs at the *little end*. The *Big-endians* typify the CATHOLICS and the *Little-endians* the PROTESTANTS.

Big Gooseberry Season, The. The "SILLY

SEASON", the dead season, when newspapers are glad of any subject to fill their columns; monster gooseberries will do for such a purpose.

Big head. A conceited person.

Big House. American slang for a prison. Also the name given to the large structure formerly erected by the Delaware Indians for their twelve-night ceremony to propitiate the Great Spirit (*see* MANITOU).

Big nob. Big noise. *See* BIG-WIG.

Big Sea Day. An old-time custom in New Jersey, when, on the second Saturday in August, the farmers and their families drove to the sea-shore to picnic and to bathe in the clothes they were wearing. Also called "Farmers' Wash-Day".

Big shot. *See* BIG-WIG.

Big Smoke, The. One of the nicknames of London, more commonly "the SMOKE"; also of Sydney, N.S.W. *Cp.* AULD REEKIE.

Big stick diplomacy. Backing negotiations or policy with the threat of military force. The term was popularized by Theodore Roosevelt's declaration in 1900 that he had always been fond of the West African proverb "speak softly and carry a big stick". He used such tactics successfully (1902–4) in the Alaskan boundary dispute and the second Venezuelan crisis.

Big Triangle. A sailorman's term denoting the round trip frequently made by sailing ships from a British port to Australia, thence with New South Wales coal to South America, and back home with a cargo of nitrates.

Big-wig. A person in authority, an important person. The term arises from the custom of judges and BISHOPS, and so on, wearing large WIGS. Judges still wear them. *Big nob, Big noise, Big shot* are similarly used.

Bight (bit). **To hook the bight**—*i.e.* to get entangled. A nautical term; the bight is the loop or doubled part of a rope, and when the fluke of one anchor gets into the bight of another's cable it is "hooked".

Bikini. This atoll in the Marshall Islands, the scene of American nuclear weapon testing in 1946 (and 1954), has given its name to a scanty two-piece bathing outfit worn by women, apparently from the devastating effects of the atomic explosion and the overpowering effect of the costume.

Bilbo. A rapier or sword. So called from Bilbao, in Spain, once famous for its finely tempered blades. Falstaff says to Ford:

> I suffered the pangs of three several deaths; first an intolerable fright, to be detected... next, to be compassed like a good bilbo... hilt to point, heel to head.
> *Merry Wives*, III, v.

Cp. ANDREA FERRARA; TOLEDO.

Bilboes. A bar of iron with sliding fetters attached to it, by which mutinous sailors or prisoners were linked together. Possibly derived from Bilbao where they may have been first made. Some of the bilboes from the Spanish Armada are kept in the TOWER of London.

Bile. It rouses my bile. It makes me angry or indignant. In Latin, *biliosus* (a bilious man) meant a choleric one. According to ancient theory, bile is a HUMOUR of the body and black bile is indicative of melancholy. When excited abnormally, bile was supposed to produce choler or rage.

> It raised my bile
> To see him so reflect their grief aside.
> HOOD: *Plea of Midsummer Fairies*, stanza liv.

Bilge-water. Stale dregs; bad beer; any distasteful or nauseating drink. The bilge is the inside or curve of the ship immediately above the keel, where the rain or seawater collects and becomes foul. In slang *bilge* means worthless stuff or rubbish.

Bilk. Originally a term in cribbage meaning to spoil your adversary's score, to BALK him; perhaps the two words are mere variants.

It now usually means to cheat, to obtain goods and depart without paying.

> He cannot drink five bottles, bilk the score,
> Then kill a constable, and drink five more.
> COWPER: *Progress of Error*, l. 193.

Bill. The nose, also called the *beak*. Hence *billy* is slang for a pocket-handkerchief.

Bill, A. The draft of an ACT OF PARLIAMENT. When a Bill is passed and receives the royal assent it becomes an Act.

A Private Bill is the draft of an Act of Parliament affecting private persons, groups or corporations.

A Private Member's Bill is a public bill introduced by a private member as distinct from a member of the Government. Few reach the STATUTE Book.

A Public Bill is the draft of an Act of Parliament affecting the general public.

A True Bill. Under the old judicial system before a case went to the Criminal Assizes it was examined by the Grand Jury. If they decided that there was enough evidence to justify a trial they were said "to find a true bill"; if they decided to the contrary they were said to ignore the bill and it was endorsed *ignoramus*. Hence *to find a true bill* is a colloquial way of saying that something after examination can go forward as true.

Bill of Attainder. In mediæval England felons under sentence of death, outlaws, etc., were *attainted* and subject to forfeiture of goods, etc. Bills of Attainder were used for arbitrarily destroying political enemies of the government, for criminal offences against the State and public peace, PARLIAMENT acting as both judge and jury. First introduced in 1549, the last Bill of Attainder was passed against Lord Edward Fitzgerald, Irish rebel leader, in 1798.

Bill of Exchange. An order transferring a named sum of money at a given date from the debtor (drawee) to the creditor (drawer). The drawee having signed the bill becomes the "acceptor", and the document is then negotiable in commercial circles just as money itself.

Bill of Fare. A list of dishes provided in a restaurant, etc.; a menu.

Bill of Health. A document signed by the proper authorities to the master of a ship certifying that when the ship sailed no infectious disorder existed in the place. This is a *clean bill of health*, and the term is often used figuratively. *See* YELLOW JACK. **A foul bill of health,** or the absence of a clean bill, means that the place from which the vessel sailed was infected.

Bill of Lading. A document signed by the master of a ship in acknowledgment of goods laden in his vessel. In this document he binds himself to deliver the articles in good condition to the persons named, subject to certain circumstances. These bills are generally in triplicate—one for the sender, one for the receiver, and one for the master of the vessel.

Bill of Pains and Penalties. A Parliamentary proceeding like a BILL OF ATTAINDER imposing punishment less than capital. The last such bill against Queen Caroline, wife of George IV, was dropped in 1820.

Bill of Rights (Oct. 1689). A constitutional enactment of fundamental importance consolidating the GLORIOUS REVOLUTION of 1688. It asserted the liberties and rights of the nation, declared William and Mary King and Queen, and settled the succession.

A Bill of Rights, designed to guarantee civil liberties, was embodied in the American Constitution in 1791. It consists of the first ten amendments, proposed in 1789.

Bill of Sale. When a person borrows money and delivers goods as security, he gives the lender a "bill of sale", *i.e.* permission to sell the goods if the money is not returned on the stated day.

Bills of Mortality. In 1592, on the occasion of a great pestilence, the Company of Parish Clerks, representing 109 parishes in and around London, began to publish weekly returns of all deaths occurring; later they included births or baptisms. They were very inaccurate and were superseded by the Registrar-General's returns after 1836. **Within the Bills of Mortality** means within the districts covered by the Bills of Mortality, which grew with the growth of London.

Bills receivable. Promissory notes, bills of exchange, or other acceptances held by a person to whom the money stated is payable.

Billabong (Austr.). A backwater or a waterhole in a river-bed which only flows after a downpour; dead water. It is from the Aborigine *billa*, a creek or river (hence water) and *bong*, dead. *See* WALTZING MATILDA.

Billet. As a soldier's lodging place, from the official note or ticket requiring the addressee to provide accommodation for its bearer. *See* BULLET.

Billet-doux (Fr. a sweet note). A love letter, now usually given a humorous use.

Billingsgate. The site of an old passage through that part of the city wall that protected London on the river side, named from an early property-owner in the area; also the site of a fish-market for many centuries, where porters were famous for their foul and abusive language at least four centuries ago.

To talk Billingsgate. To slang; to use foul and abusive language; to scold in a vulgar fashion.

You are no better than a Billingsgate fish-fag. You are as rude and ill-mannered as the women of Billingsgate fish-market.

Billingsgate pheasant. A red herring; a bloater.

Billjim. A synonym for "Australian", supposedly on account of the frequency of the names William and James among the early settlers.

Billy. (1) A policeman's staff, which is a little bill or billet. (2) A pocket-handkerchief (*see* BILL). A *blue billy* is a handkerchief with blue ground and white spots (*cp.* BELCHER). (3) The can in which Australian stationhands originally made tea and did their cooking. Possibly from *billa*, a creek—hence water.

Billies and Charlies. *See under* FORGERY.

Billy Barlow. A street droll, A MERRY ANDREW; so called from a half-idiot of that name well known in the East End of London for witty and droll behaviour, in the early half of the 19th century. He died in a WHITECHAPEL workhouse.

Billy Blue. Admiral Sir William Cornwallis (1744–1819).

Billy boy. A bluff-bowed North Country coaster of river-barge build.

Billy goat. A male goat. From this came the

term once common for a tufted beard—a "billy" or goatee.

Billycock Hat. A round, low-crowned, hard felt hat with a wide brim. One account says the name is the same as "bully-cocked", that is, as worn by a bully or swell, a term used in Amhurst's *Terrae Filius* (1721). Another says that it was first used by Billy Coke (Mr. William Coke) at the great shooting parties at Holkham about 1850. Old established West End hatters used to call them "Coke hats". *See* BOWLER HAT; COKE'S CLIPPINGS.

Billy the Kid. William H. Bonney (1859–1881), baby-faced killer, who committed his first murder at the age of twelve. Prominent in the Lincoln County cattle war in New Mexico, he boasted that he had killed a man for every year of his life. He was finally shot (aged 21) by Sheriff Pat Garrett.

Billy Williams's Cabbage Patch. The English Rugby Football Union's ground at Twickenham, the headquarters of the game, also known as *Twickers*. Popularly so-called after W. (Billy) Williams (1860–1951), who discovered the site and through whose persistence the ground was acquired in 1907; also from the ground's former partial use as a market garden. The first match was played there on 2 October 1909. The nearby *Railway Tavern* changed its name to *The Cabbage Patch* in the early 1970s.

Bi-metallism. The employment for coinage of two metals, SILVER and GOLD which would be of fixed relative value; both being standard money or legal tender.

Bimini. A legendary island of the Bahamas where the fountain of youth gave everlasting life to all who drank from it.

Binary Arithmetic (bī′ nà ri). Arithmetic in which the base of the notation is 2 instead of 10, a method suggested for certain uses by Leibnitz. The unit followed by a cipher signifies two, by another unit signifies three, by two ciphers it signifies four, and so on. Thus 10 signifies 2; 100 signifies 4; while 11 signifies 3, etc. Most computers work on this system.

Bing Boys. The nickname of the Canadian troops in World War I from the name of their commanding officer, Lord Byng of Vimy. Also from the revue, *The Bing Boys Are Here*, which opened at the ALHAMBRA in 1915.

Bingham's Dandies. *See* REGIMENTAL AND DIVISIONAL NICKNAMES.

Birchin Lane. I must send you to Birchin Lane. *i.e.* whip you. The play is on *birch* (a rod), but the derivation of the name really means "the lane of barbers".

A suit in Birchin Lane. Birchin Lane was once famous for all sorts of apparel and was known for second-hand clothing in Shakespearean times.

> Passing through Birchin Lane amidst a camp-royal of hose and doublets, I took...occasion to slip into a captain's suit—a valiant buff doublet stuffed with points and pair of velvet slops scored thick with lace.
>
> MIDDLETON: *Black Book* (1604).

Bird. This is the Old English and Middle English *brid* (sometimes *byrde* in M.E.), which meant the *young* of feathered flying animals. *Foul, foule,* or *fowel* was the M.E. equivalent of the modern *bird*.

The now obsolete use as an endearing name for a girl is connected with BURD. In modern slang "bird" is often a somewhat disparaging term for a young female.

Bird is also a name for the shuttlecock used in Badminton.

A bird in the hand is worth two in the bush; a pound in the purse is worth two in the book. Possession is better than expectation.

It exists in several languages:

Italian: E meglio aver oggi un uovo, che domani una gallina.

French: Un tiens vaut, ce dit-on, mieux que deux tu l'auras.

German: Ein Vogel in der Hand ist besser als zehn über Land.

Besser ein Spatz in der Hand, als ein Storch auf dem Dache.

Latin: Certa amittimus dum incerta petimus (Plautus).

On the other side we have, "Qui ne s'aventure, n'a ni cheval ni mule." "Nothing venture, nothing win." "Use a sprat to catch a mackerel." "Chi non s'arrischia non guadagna."

A bird of ill omen. One who is regarded as unlucky or who is in the habit of bringing bad news. The phrase comes from the custom of AUGURY and even today OWLS, crows and RAVENS are often regarded as unlucky birds, SWALLOWS and STORKS as lucky ones. Ravens by their acute sense of smell can often locate dead and decaying bodies at a great distance, hence, perhaps, they indicate death. Owls screech when bad weather is at hand and, as foul weather often precedes sickness, so the owl is looked on as a funeral bird.

A bird of passage. A person who shifts from place to place, a temporary visitant, like a cuckoo, swallow, swift, etc.

A little bird told me so. From *Eccles.* x, 20:

> Curse not the King, no not in thy thought;...for a bird of the air shall carry the voice, and that which

hath wings shall tell the matter.

Birdcage Walk (St. James's Park, WEST-
MINSTER); named from the aviary kept there
by Charles II.

Birdie. A hole at golf which the player has
completed in one stroke less than par (the
official figure). Two strokes less is an *eagle*.

Bird's-eye view. A mode of perspective
drawing in which the artist is supposed to be
over the objects drawn, in which case he be-
holds them as a bird in the air would see
them; a general or overall view.

Birds of a feather flock together. Those
of similar character, taste or station associate
together. Hence, *of that feather*, of that
sort.

> I am not of that feather to shake off
> My friend, when he most need me.
> SHAKESPEARE: <i>Timon of Athens</i>, I, i.

Bird walking weather. A flying expression of American origin, indicating CEILING
ZERO, coined from the phrase, "the weather
is so bad, even the birds are walking."

Fine feathers make fine birds. *See*
FEATHER.

**Old birds are not to be caught with
chaff.** Experience teaches wisdom.

**One beats the bush, another takes the
bird.** The workman does the work, the master makes the money. *See* BEAT.

The Arabian bird. The PHŒNIX.

The bird of Juno. The peacock. MINERVA'S
bird is either the COCK or the owl; that of
VENUS is the DOVE.

The bird of Washington. The American
or bald-headed EAGLE.

**Thou hast kept well the bird in thy bo-
som.** Thou has remained faithful to thy allegiance or faith. The expression was used of
Sir Ralph Percy (slain in the battle of
Hedgeley Moor, 1464) to express his fidelity
to the House of Lancaster.

**'Tis the early bird that catches the
worm.** It is the early riser or one who acts
promptly who attains his objective.

To get the bird. To be hissed; to be given a
hostile reception. *See* BIG BIRD.

To kill two birds with one stone. To
achieve two ends with one effort or outlay.

Birds Protected by Superstitions:

The Chough was protected in CORNWALL
because the soul of King ARTHUR was fabled
to have migrated into one.

The arms of Cornwall contain "over the
crest on a wreath Argent and Azure a chough
proper resting the dexter claw upon a ducal
coronet Or".

The Falcon was held sacred by the Egyptians because it was the form assumed by RA
and HORUS; and the **Ibis** because the god

THOTH escaped from the pursuit of TYPHON
disguised as an Ibis.

Mother Carey's Chickens, or Stormy
Petrels, are protected by sailors from a
superstition that they are the living embodiment of the souls of dead mariners. *See also*
MOTHER.

The Robin is protected on account of
Christian tradition and nursery legend. *See*
ROBIN REDBREAST.

The Stork is held sacred in Sweden, from
the legend that it flew round the cross crying, "Styrka, Styrka!" when Jesus was crucified. *See* STORK.

Swans are protected in Ireland from the
legend of the FIONNUALA (daughter of LIR)
who was metamorphosed into a swan and
condemned to wander the waters until the
advent of Christianity. Moore wrote a poem
on the subject.

Birler. In Cumberland, a *birler* is the master
of revels at a bidden-wedding, who sees that
the guests are well furnished with drink. To
birl is to carouse or pour out liquor (O.E.
byrelian).

Birmingham by way of Beachy Head. Metaphorically, a roundabout approach. It is a
quotation from G. K. Chesterton's poem
The Rolling English Road.

> He (Mr. George Brown) grows impatient with a
> Civil Service that makes him travel to Birmingham
> by way of Beachy Head.
> <i>The Times</i>, London, 22 February 1965.

Birmingham Poet. John Freeth, who died
at the age of seventy-eight in 1808. He was a
wit, poet, and publican, who not only wrote
the words and tunes of songs, but sang them
also, and sang them well.

Birrellism. A good-humoured but penetra-
ting comment tinged with kindly irony.
Named after Augustine Birrell (1850–
1933), Professor of Law at University College, London, politician, and man of letters, who is probably best remembered for
his witty and urbane essays called *Obiter
Dicta*.

Birthday suit. He was in his birthday suit.
Quite nude, as when born.

Originally, the magnificent suit of clothes
specially ordered by courtiers to be worn on
the sovereign's birthday.

> The Sun himself, on this auspicious Day,
> Shines, like a Beau in a new Birth-day Suit.
> FIELDING: <i>Tom Thumb the Great</i>, I, i.

Bis (Lat. twice). French and Italians use this
as English audiences use *encore*.

Bis dat, qui cito dat. He gives twice who
gives promptly—*i.e.* quick relief will do as
much good as twice the sum later.

Bishop (O.E. *biscop*; from Lat. *episcopus*,

and Gr. *episcopos*, an overseer). One of the higher order of Christian priesthood who presides over a diocese and has powers of ordaining and confirming.

The name is given to one of the men in CHESS (formerly called the *archer*); to the LADYBIRD (*see* BISHOP BARNABEE); to a lady's bustle (sometimes called a "stern reality"); and to a drink made by pouring red wine, such as CLARET or burgundy, either hot or cold, on ripe bitter oranges, the liquor being sugared and spiced to taste. Similarly a *Cardinal* is made by using *white* wine instead of *red* and a *Pope* by using *tokay*. *See also* BOY BISHOP.

Bishop Barker. An Australian term used around Sydney for the largest glass of beer available, named from Frederick Barker (1808–1882), Bishop of Sydney, who was a very tall man.

Bishop Barnabee. The May-bug, ladybird, etc. There is an old Sussex rhyme:

Bishop, Bishop Barnabee,
Tell me when my wedding shall be;
If it be tomorrow day,
Ope your wings and fly away.

Bishop of Fleet Street. A nickname given to Hannen Swaffer (1879–1962) by his fellow journalists because of his pronouncements on public morality, and his sombre stylized mode of attire.

Bishop in Partibus. *See* IN PARTIBUS.

The bishop has put his foot in it. Said of milk or porridge that is burnt, or of meat over-roasted. Tyndale says, "If the porage be burned to, or the meate over rosted we saye the byshope hath put his fote in the potte"; and explains it thus, "because the bishopes burnt who they lust". Such food is also said to be *bishopped*.

The Bishops' Bible. *See* BIBLE, THE ENGLISH.

The Bishops' Wars. The name given to Charles I's two short wars (1639–1640) against the Scots when they renounced EPISCOPACY. The wars ended with his defeat and caused the summoning of the LONG PARLIAMENT.

To Bishop was formerly used in the sense of to confirm, to admit into the Church. There are two verbs *to bishop*, both from proper names. One is obsolete and meant to murder by drowning; from the name of a man who drowned a little boy in Bethnal Green and sold the body to the surgeons for dissection. The other means to conceal a horse's age by "faking" his teeth.

Bissextile (bi seks′ tīl). LEAP YEAR. We add a day to February in leap year, but the Romans counted 24 FEBRUARY twice, and called it *dies bissextus* (*sexto calendas Martias*), the sextile or sixth day before 1 MARCH. This day was reckoned twice (*bis*) in leap year, which was called *annus bissextus*.

Bistonians (bis tō′ ni ănz). The Thracians; after Biston, son of MARS, who allegedly built Bistonia on Lake Bistonis.

Bistro(t). A small, unpretentious café in France, where meals as well as drinks, can be obtained quickly. The suggestion that the word comes from the Russian, *bistro* (quick), and dates from the Allied Occupation of 1815, is open to doubt, since it is not found until 1884. It may possibly be derived from *bistouille*, rot-gut liquor, served in such a café.

Bit. A piece, a morsel. Really the same word as *bite* (O.E. *bitan*), meaning a piece bitten off. It is the substantive of *bite*, as morsel (Fr. *morceau*) is of *mordre*.

Also used for a piece of money as a "threepenny bit", a "two-shilling bit", etc. In the U.S.A. a *bit* was $12\frac{1}{2}$ cents; *two bits* are a QUARTER.

Bit is old thieves' slang for money and a coiner is called a "bit-maker".

In the 1920s *bit* was slang for a girl, short for a "bit of fluff", now a "bit of stuff". "Piece (or bit) of skirt" is similarly used.

Bit (of a horse). **To take the bit between, or in one's teeth.** To be obstinately self-willed; to make up one's mind not to yield. When a horse has a mind to run away, he catches the bit between his teeth and the driver no longer has control over him.

Bite. A cheat; one who bites us. "The biter bit" explains the origin. We say a man was "bitten" when "he burns his fingers", meddling with something that promised well but turned out a failure. "The biter bit" is the moral of ÆSOP's fable *The* VIPER AND THE FILE.

Bites and Bams. Hoaxes and quizzes; humbug.

(His) humble efforts at jocularity were chiefly confined to...bites and bams.
SCOTT: *Guy Mannering*, ch. iii.

Once bitten, twice shy. Having been caught, led up the garden path, or seen off once, to be wary or cautious in order not to be tricked a second time.

To bite off more than one can chew. To undertake more than one is capable of doing, or seeing through.

To bite on the bullet. To endure pain courageously, to face trouble or adversity with fortitude, to behave stoically.

To bite one's thumb at another. To insult or defy by putting the thumbnail into the mouth and clicking it against the teeth. Why this should be so provocative is not clear.

> *Gregory:* I will frown as I pass by; and let them take it as they list.
> *Sampson:* Nay, as they dare. I will bite my thumb at them: which is a disgrace to them, if they bear it.
>
> SHAKESPEARE: *Romeo and Juliet*, I, i.

To bite the dust or **the ground.** To fall, to be struck off one's horse, to be vanquished. The form "another Redskin bit the dust", derived from WILD WEST stories, was widely current in World War II, especially in the R.A.F.

To bite the lip, indicative of suppressed chagrin, passion, or annoyance.

To bite upon the bridle. To champ the bit, like an impatient or restless horse.

Bitt. To bitt the cable. To pass a bight of cable over the bitts, thus securing the cable. Bitts are now usually cast-iron bollards fitted on the foredeck, in small vessels often wooden posts.

Bitter end, The. *À outrance*, with relentless hostility; also applied to affliction, as "she bore it to the bitter end", meaning to the last stroke of adverse fortune. In nautical parlance the "bitter end" is that part of the cable abaft the bitts (*i.e.* the inboard end) when the vessel is riding at anchor.

> A Bitter is but the turne of a Cable about the bitts, and veare it out by little and little. And the Bitter's end is that part of the Cable doth stay within board.
>
> CAPT. SMITH: *Seaman's Grammar*, 1627.

In the Bible, *Proverbs* v, 4, reads: "But her end is bitter as wormwood." This may have some share in the present use of the phrase.

Bittock. A little bit: *-ock* as diminutive is preserved in bullock, hillock, buttock, etc. "A mile and a bittock" is a mile and a little bit.

Black. *See* COLOURS for its symbolism. Its use for mourning was a Roman custom (*Juvenal*, x, 245), borrowed from the Egyptians. At funerals mutes who wore black cloaks were sometimes known as the *blacks*, and sometimes as *Black Guards. See* BLACK-GUARDS.

> I do pray ye
> To give me leave to live a little longer.
> You stand about me like my Blacks.
>
> BEAUMONT and FLETCHER: *Monsieur Thomas*, III, i.

In several of the Oriental nations it is a badge of servitude, slavery and low birth. Our word *blackguard* seems to point to this meaning, and the Lat. *niger*, black, also meant bad, impropitious.

Beaten black and blue. A very severe beating when the skin is bruised black and blue.

Black as a crow, etc. Among the common similes used to denote "blackness" are black as a crow, a RAVEN, a raven's wing, ink, HELL, HADES, death, the grave, your hat, thunder or a thundercloud, Egypt's night, a NEWGATE KNOCKER, ebony, coal, pitch, soot, tar, etc. Most of these are self-explanatory.

Black in the face. Extremely angry. The face being discoloured with passion or distress.

> Mr Winkle pulled...till he was black in the face.
>
> DICKENS: *Pickwick Papers*.

He swore himself black in the face.

PETER PINDAR.

A black dog for a white monkey. A fair swop or exchange is no robbery.

I must have it in black and white, *i.e.* in writing; the paper being white and the ink black.

Not as black as he or **she is painted.** Not as bad or disreputable as he or she is said to be.

The pot calling the kettle black. *See under* POT.

To say black's his eye, *i.e.* to vituperate, to blame. **Black's the white of his eye** is a modern variant. To say the eye is black or evil is to accuse a person of an evil heart or great ignorance.

> I can say black's your eye though it be grey. I have connived at this.
>
> BEAUMONT and FLETCHER: *Love's Cure*, II, i.

To swear black is white. To swear to any falsehood no matter how glaring.

All Blacks, The. New Zealand's Rugby XV which first played in England in 1905.

Black and Tans. The name of a pack of hounds in County Limerick, applied to the irregulars enlisted by the British government in 1920 to supplement the Royal Irish Constabulary. This force (sometimes called the "Auxis") was so called from their dark blue uniforms with the black belts and dark-green caps of the R.I.C. Later the Irish used the name indiscriminately for all the armed constabulary.

Black Act. An Act of 1722 (9 Geo. I, c. 22) imposing the death penalty for certain offences against the Game Laws, and specially directed against the Waltham deer-stealers who blackened their faces and, under the name of *Blacks*, carried out their depredations in Epping Forest. Dick TURPIN was a member of such a gang at the outset of his career. This Act was repealed in 1827.

Blackamoor. Washing the blackamoor white—*i.e.* engaged upon a hopeless and useless task. The allusion is to one of ÆSOP'S FABLES of that name.

Black art, The. Magic, NECROMANCY. The name seems to have derived from Med. Lat.

nigromantia used erroneously for Gr. *nekromanteia*. The devil was also portrayed as black.

Black Assize. 6 July 1577, when a putrid pestilence broke out at Oxford and the SHERIFF and a large number of gentry died during the Assize.

Black-balled. Not admitted to, or rejected by a CLUB or suchlike. In the BALLOT those who accepted a candidate dropped a red or white ball into the box, those rejecting dropped a black one.

Blackbirds. Slang for negro slaves or indentured labourers. Hence **Blackbirding**, capturing or trafficking in slaves. *Cp.* BLACK CATTLE.

Blackboard Jungle, The. Downtown schools in which delinquency is rife and discipline is difficult to impose. The name is taken from the title of a novel by Evan Hunter published in 1954 and filmed in 1955, based on a New York school, which was a savage indictment of certain aspects of the American state educational system.

Black Book. Perhaps the most important bearing this title are: (1) *The Black Book of the Admiralty*, a 14th-century collection of maritime law; (2) *The Black Book of the Exchequer*, an official account of royal revenues, payments, perquisites, etc., in the reign of Henry II; (3) *The Black Book of the Household*, purporting to deal with court customs of the reign of Edward III; (4) The earliest records of LINCOLN'S INN (dating from 1422) are called *Black Books*; (5) The reports presented to Parliament in 1536 prior to the dissolution of the monasteries are collectively termed the *Black Book*; (6) *The Black Book* (1820) and the *Extraordinary Black Book* (1831), which set out to expose the abuses in Church and State of those times. There are also two notable Welsh MSS. of this name: (1) *The Black Book of Carmarthen*, a 12th-century collection of Welsh poetry containing references to King Arthur; (2) *The Black Book of Chirk*, a codex of Welsh law in the Welsh language (probably 12th century).

Black books. To be in my black books. Out of favour, in disgrace. A black book is one recording the names of those who are in disgrace or have merited punishment. Amhurst, in his *Terrae Filius, or the Secret History of the University of Oxford* (1726), speaks of the PROCTOR's black book, and tells us that no one can proceed to a degree whose name is found there.

Black Brunswickers. A corps of 700 volunteer hussars commanded by Frederick William, Duke of Brunswick, who had been deprived of his father's dukedom by NAPOLEON. They were called "Black" from their uniform.

Black Canons. The AUGUSTINIANS, from their black cloaks.

Black cap. A small square of black cloth. In Britain it was worn by a judge when passing the death sentence; it is part of a judge's full dress and is also worn on 9 November, when the new Lord Mayor of London takes the oath at the Law Courts. Covering the head was a sign of mourning among the Israelites, Greeks, Romans, and Anglo-Saxons. *Cp.* II *Sam.* xv, 30.

Black Cattle. Negro slaves. *Cp.* BLACKBIRDS, BLACK IVORY, and *see* BLACK OX.

Black coat. An old name for a parson.

Black-coated worker. A clerical worker as opposed to a manual worker, from their former convention of wearing a black jacket with pin-striped trousers. *Cp.* WHITE-COLLAR WORKER.

Black Country, The. The crowded manufacturing district in the Midlands comprising parts of South Staffordshire, Warwickshire and Worcestershire of which Dudley is the geographical centre. The collieries, blast furnaces, foundries and metal industries grimed and blackened the area with smoke, hence the name.

Black Death. The plague, both pneumonic and bubonic, which came from Asia and ravaged Europe between 1348 and 1351. It reached England in 1348 where it probably carried off one-eighth of the population, the clergy being particularly badly hit. The name does not appear before the 16th century and may be due to the devastating nature of the visitation but it is usually said that it comes from the dark skin haemorrhage (ecchymosis). Coughing and sneezing were doubtless accompanying symptoms, hence the somewhat improbable suggestion that the nursery rhyme:

Ring a ring o'roses,
A pocket full of posies,
A-tishoo! A-tishoo!
We all fall down.

was some form of folk memory of the Black Death. It reappeared in 1361–1362 and 1379, and there were periodic epidemics until the GREAT PLAGUE.

Black Diamonds. Coal. Coal and diamonds are both forms of carbon. Truffles are also called black DIAMONDS.

Black Dick. Richard, Earl Howe (1726–1799), British admiral and victor of the Battle of the First of June, 1794. So called from his swarthy complexion.

Black Dog. An early 18th-century name for

a counterfeit SHILLING or other "silver" coin made of pewter. Also another name for the BLUES. See also A BLACK DOG HAS WALKED OVER HIM *under* DOG.

Black Doll. The sign of a MARINE STORE. The doll was a dummy dressed to indicate that cast-off garments were bought. *See* DOLLY SHOP.

Black Douglas. *See* DOUGLAS.

Black Dwarf. *See under* DWARF.

Blackfellows. Australian aborigines are so called, although their complexion is but a dark coffee colour.

Black Flag. The pirate's flag; the JOLLY ROGER. A black flag was formerly hoisted over a prison immediately after an execution.

Chinese mercenaries who opposed the French in Tongkin in the 1880s were known as the *Black Flags*, as also were the troops of the CALIPH of Baghdad, because his banner, that of the ABASSIDES, was black. It is said that the black curtain which hung before the door of AYESHAH was taken for a national flag.

Blackfoot. A Scottish term for a matchmaker, or an intermediary in love affairs; if he chanced to play traitor he was called a *whitefoot*. Also the name of one of the Irish agrarian secret societies of the early 19th century.

> And the Blackfoot who courted each foeman's approach,
> Faith! 'tis hot-foot he'd fly from the stout Father Roach.
>
> LOVER.

Blackfeet. The popular name of two North American Indian tribes, one the Algonkin (Algonquin) calling themselves the *Silksika*, and the other, the *Sihasapa*.

Black Friars. The DOMINICAN Friars, from their black mantle. The London district of this name is on the site of the former Dominican monastery.

Black Friday. Notably (1) 6 December 1745, the day on which the news arrived in London that the Young PRETENDER had reached Derby; (2) 11 May 1866, when widespread financial panic was caused by Overend, Gurney and Co., the bankers, suspending payments; (3) 15 April 1921 was Black Friday for the British Labour Movement when the threatened General Strike was cancelled; (4) in the U.S.A., 24 September 1869, when many speculators were ruined by the Government's release of gold into the open market in order to bring down the price, which had been forced up by stock manipulators. *See also* RED FRIDAY.

Black Game. Heath-Fowl; in contradistinction to *red* game, as grouse. The male

bird is called a *black cock*.

Black Genevan. A black preaching gown formerly used in many Anglican churches and still used by NONCONFORMISTS. So called from Geneva, where Calvin preached in such a robe.

Blackguards. The origin of this term, long applied to rogues and scoundrels, is uncertain. In the 16th and 17th centuries it was applied to lowest menials in great houses, army hangers-on, scullions, camp-followers, etc. It was also given to the link-boys and torch-bearers at funerals. A proclamation of 1683 in the Lord Steward's office reads:

> Whereas... a sort of vicious, idle, and masterless boyes and rogues, commonly called the Black guard, with divers other lewd and loose fellows... do usually haunt and follow the court...

Black Hand. The popular name of the Slav secret society largely responsible for contriving the assassination of the Archduke Franz Ferdinand in Sarajevo, 28 June 1914. This was the event which precipitated World War I. Also a criminal society, once active in New York, largely made up of Italians.

Blackheath. A district of S.E. London once the haunt of footpads and highwaymen. The followers of Wat Tyler in 1381 and Jack CADE in 1450 assembled there. Here also the Londoners welcomed Henry V after Agincourt and Charles II met the army on his way to London in 1660.

Black Hole of Calcutta (20–21 June 1756). Surajah Dowlah, Nawab of Bengal, thoughtlessly confined 146 British prisoners, including one woman, in the small prison (eighteen feet by fourteen feet ten inches) of the East India Company's Fort William, after its capture. Only 22 men and the woman escaped suffocation in the Black Hole.

The punishment cell in barracks, etc., is often nicknamed the "Black Hole" and very dark stuffy places are often likened to the Black Hole of Calcutta.

Black Horse. *See* REGIMENTAL AND DIVISIONAL NICKNAMES.

Black Ivory. Negro slaves from Africa.

Black jack. A large leather GOTCH, or can for beer, so called from the outside being tarred.

> He hath not pledged one cup, but looked most wickedly
> Upon good Malaga; flies to the black-jack still,
> And sticks to small drink like a water-rat.
>
> MIDDLETON: *The Witch*, I, i.

Cornish miners called blende or sulphide of zinc "Black Jack", the occurrence of which was considered a favourable indication. Hence the saying *Black Jack rides a good horse*, the blende rides upon a lode of good ore.

A blackjack is a small club or cosh, usually leather covered; and the American scrub oak is called Black Jack.

The nickname Black Jack was given to the American General J. A. Logan (1826–1886) on account of his dark complexion and hair, and to General Pershing (1860–1948) who commanded the Americans in World War I.

Blacklead. *See* MISNOMERS.

Black-leg. An old name for a swindler, especially at cards or races; now almost solely used for a non-union member who works for less than trade-union rates, or especially one who works during a strike.

Black letter. Gothic or German type which in the early days of printing was the most commonly used. The term dates from *c.* 1600 because of its heavy black appearance in comparison with roman type.

Black letter day. An inauspicious or unlucky day. The allusion is to the old liturgical CALENDARS in which major saints' days and festivals were distinguished by being printed in red. Black was used for holy days of lesser importance. (*See* RED-LETTER DAY.) The Romans marked the unlucky days with a piece of charcoal and their lucky ones with white chalk.

Black list. A list of those in disgrace, or who have incurred censure or punishment; a list of bankrupts for the private guidance of the mercantile community. *Cp.* BLACK BOOKS.

Black looks. Looks of displeasure.

Blackmail. "Mail" here is the Old English and Scottish word meaning rent, tax, or tribute. In Scotland *mails* and *duties* are rents of an estate in money or otherwise. Blackmail was originally a tribute paid by the BORDER farmers to FREEBOOTERS in return for protection or immunity from molestation. Hence payment extorted by intimidation or threat, or extractions and exorbitant charges.

Black Maria. The police van used for the conveyance of prisoners. It is suggested that the name is derived from that of Maria Lee, a Boston negress who kept a lodging-house. She was of such great size that when the police required help they sent for Black Maria, who soon collared the refractory men and led them to the lock-up. The term was certainly in use at Boston in the 1840s.

Black market. A World War II phrase to describe illicit dealing in rationed goods. *See* UNDER THE COUNTER.

Black Mass. A sacrilegious MASS in which the DEVIL is invoked in place of God and var-

ious obscene rites performed in ridicule of the proper ceremony. *See* MEDMENHAM MONKS.

It is also a REQUIEM Mass from the custom of wearing black vestments.

Black Monday. Supposedly Easter Monday, 14 April 1360, when Edward III was besieging Paris. The day was so dark, windy and bitterly cold that many men and horses died. In fact 14 April 1360 fell on the Tuesday of the week after Easter. The Monday after Easter Monday is called "Black Monday" in allusion to this fatal day.

In Melbourne, 27 February 1865 was so called from a terrible wind from the N.N.W. which caused dreadful havoc between Sandhurst and Castlemaine.

Black money. *See* BLACK DOG.

Black Monks. The BENEDICTINES.

Black Nell. Wild Bill Hickok's famous mare. *See* DEAD MAN'S HAND.

Black-out. The term was first used in the theatre, certainly from the early 1920s, when the lighting was extinguished to darken the whole stage, but it is now largely associated with its wartime use. From the outbreak of war against Germany (3 September 1939) until 23 April 1945 (coastal areas, 11 May), it was obligatory throughout Great Britain to cover all windows, skylights, etc., before dark so that no gleam of light could be seen from outside. Moving vehicles were only allowed the dimmest of lights. This essential air raid precaution was called the *Black-out*.

Black-out also denotes a complete loss of consciousness.

Black ox. The black ox has trod on his foot, *i.e.* misfortune has come to him. Black oxen were sacrificed to PLUTO and other infernal deities.

Black Parliament. A name given to the REFORMATION Parliament (1529–1536) which effected the breach with ROME.

Black Pope. The General of the JESUITS.

Black Prince. Edward, Prince of Wales (1330–1376), eldest son of Edward III. He is popularly supposed to be named from wearing black armour, but there is no evidence for this. Froissart says he was "styled black by terror of his arms" (*c.* 169). The name does not appear to have been used before the latter part of the 16th century and first appeared in writing in 1569.

> Brave Gaunt, thy father and myself
> Rescued the Black Prince, that young Mars of men,
> From forth the ranks of many thousand French.
> SHAKESPEARE: *Richard II*, II, iii.

Black Rod. The short title of the "Gentleman Usher of the Black Rod", named from his staff of office—a black wand surmounted by a gold lion. He is responsible for maintaining order in the HOUSE OF LORDS and summoning the Commons to the Peers when the royal assent is given to bills, etc. He is also chief gentleman usher to the sovereign and usher to the order of the GARTER.

Black Rood of Scotland. The "piece of the true cross" or ROOD, set in an ebony crucifix, which St. MARGARET, wife of King Malcolm Canmore, left to the Scottish nation in 1093. It fell into English hands at the battle of Neville's Cross (1346) and was kept in Durham Cathedral until the REFORMATION when it was lost.

Black Russia. Central and southern Russia, from the black soil.

Blacks, The. *See* BLACK HORSE, *under* REGIMENTAL AND DIVISIONAL NICKNAMES; BIANCHI.

Black Saturday. In Scotland 4 August 1621, because a violent storm occurred at the very moment the PARLIAMENT was sitting to force EPISCOPACY upon the people.

Black Sea, The. Formerly called the EUXINE and probably given its present name by the Turks, possibly from its dangers and lack of shelter.

Black sheep. A disgrace to the family or community; a *mauvais sujet*. Black sheep are not as valuable as white and in times of superstition were looked on as bearing the devil's mark. A black sheep in a white flock is the ODD MAN OUT. *Cp.* BÊTE NOIRE.

Black Shirts. The distinguishing garment worn by Mussolini's Italian FASCISTS and adopted in England by their imitators. Also a name for the German S.S. or *Schutzstaffeln*, led by Himmler. *See* BROWN SHIRTS.

Blacksmith. A smith who works in black metal (such as iron). *See* HARMONIOUS; LEARNED. A mixture of Guinness and barley wine is called a *Blacksmith*.

Black Stone. The famous stone kissed by every pilgrim to the KAABA at MECCA. Moslems say that it was white when it fell from heaven but it turned black because of the sins of mankind. The stone was worshipped centuries before MOHAMMED. In Persian legend it was an emblem of SATURN.

Black strap. A sailor's term for any strong dark liquor, especially dark red wines. In North America, a mixture of rum or whisky with molasses, sometimes with vinegar added.

> The seething blackstrap was pronounced ready for use.
>
> PINKERTON: *Molly Maguires* (1882), ch. xvii.

Black Swan. *See* RARA AVIS.

Blackthorn winter. The cold weather, which frequently occurs when the blackthorn is in blossom. *See* ICE SAINTS; PEEWIT'S PINCH.

Black Thursday. In Australia 6 February 1851, from a terrible bush fire which occurred in Victoria.

Black Tom. The 10th Earl of Ormonde (1532–1614), Lord High Treasurer of Ireland, from his ungracious ways and "black looks".

Black Tom Tyrant. Thomas Wentworth (1593–1641), Earl of Strafford, Lord Lieutenant of Ireland, from his policies in support of Charles I.

Black velvet. A drink of champagne and Guinness in equal parts. It was the favourite drink of Bismarck, the IRON CHANCELLOR.

Black Watch. Originally companies, recruited from the WHIG clans, employed from 1729 by the English Government to watch the HIGHLANDS and to enforce the Disarming Act. Named Black Watch from their dark tartan, they were enrolled under the Earl of Crawford as the 42nd Regiment in 1739, later the Royal Highland Regiment. They are distinguished by the red hackle (small group of red feathers) on their bonnets.

Blade. A knowing blade, a sharp fellow; **a regular blade,** a BUCK or fop. Originally the word conveyed a sense of somewhat bullying bravado, and probably the name arose from the sword a swaggering buck would carry.

Bladud (blā' dŭd). A mythical English king, father of King LEAR. According to Geoffrey of Monmouth he built Bath and dedicated the medicinal springs to MINERVA, studied magic, and was dashed to pieces when he fell into the temple of APOLLO whilst trying to fly.

Blanch, To. A method of testing the quality of money paid in taxes to the King, used by Roger of Salisbury in the reign of Henry I. 44 shillings' worth of SILVER coin was taken from the amount being paid in, a pound's weight of it was melted down and the impurities were skimmed off. If then found to be light, the taxpayer had to throw in enough pennies to balance the scale.

Blanchefleur (blonsh' flĕr). The heroine of the Old French metrical romance, *Flore et Blanchefleur*, used by Boccaccio for his prose romance, *Il Filocolo*. It is substantially the same as that of Dianora and Ansaldo in the DECAMERON and that of DORIGEN and Aurelius by Chaucer. The tale is of a young Christian prince who is in love with the SARACEN slave-girl with whom he has been brought up. They are parted, but after many adventures he rescues her unharmed from the harem of the Emir of Babylon.

Blanco White. *See under* WHITE.

Blank. To draw blank. *See* DRAW.

Blank cartridge. Cartridge with powder only, without shot, bullet, or ball; used in drill and saluting. Thus figuratively, empty threats.

Blank cheque. A signed cheque, leaving the amount to be filled in by the payee. Thus **to give a blank cheque** is, figuratively, to give CARTE BLANCHE.

Blank verse. Rhymeless verse in continuous decasyllables with IAMBIC or trochaic rhythm, first used in English by the Earl of Surrey about 1540 in his version of Books II and IV of the ÆNEID. There is other unrhymed verse, but it is not usual to extend to such poems as Collins's *Ode to Evening*, Whitman's *Leaves of Grass*, or the *vers libre* of today, the name of blank verse.

Blanket. To be born on the wrong side of the blanket. To be illegitimate.

A wet blanket. A discouragement; a MARPLOT or spoilsport. A person who discourages a proposed scheme is a *wet blanket*. A wet blanket smothers fire and has a dampening effect.

Blanketeers. The starving handloom weavers and spinners who assembled in St. Peter's Field, Manchester, 10 March 1817, each equipped with a blanket for their march to London to present a petition to the Prince Regent. Only a few reached Macclesfield after intimidation from the authorities, and no organized marchers got farther than Derby.

Blarney. Soft wheedling speeches to gain some end; flattery or lying with unblushing effrontery. Legend has it that Cormac Macarthy in 1602 undertook to surrender Blarney Castle (near Cork) to the English, as part of an armistice. Daily the Lord President Carew looked for the fulfilment of the terms, but received nothing but soft speeches, till he became the laughing-stock of Elizabeth's ministers, and the dupe of the Lord of Blarney.

Among American criminals "to blarney" means to pick locks.

To kiss the Blarney Stone. In the wall of Blarney Castle about twenty feet from the top and difficult of access is a triangular stone inscribed, "Cormac Macarthy *fortis me fieri fecit*, A.D. 1446". Tradition says that whoever kisses it is endowed with wonderful powers of cajolery. As it is almost impossible to reach, a substitute has been provided, which is said to be as effective as the original. *Cp*. SHANNON.

Blasphemous Balfour. Sir James Balfour (d. 1583), Scottish judge, was so called for his apostasy. He "served with all parties, deserted all, and yet profited by all".

Blast. To strike by lightning; to cause to wither, *e.g.* the "blasted oak". This is the sense in which the word is used as an expletive.

In full blast. In full swing, all out. "The speakers at MARBLE ARCH on Sunday were in full blast." A METAPHOR from the blast furnace in full operation.

Blatant Beast. In Spenser's *Faerie Queene* (Bks. V, VI) "a dreadful fiend of gods and men, ydrad"; the type of calumny or slander. He was born of CERBERUS and CHIMÆRA, and had a hundred tongues and a sting; with his tongues he speaks things "most shameful, most unrighteous, most untrue"; and with his sting "steeps them in poison". Sir CALIDORE muzzled him and drew him with a chain to Fairyland but the beast escaped. The word *blatant* seems to have been coined by Spenser and is probably from the provincial word *blate*, to bellow.

Blayney's Bloodhounds. *See* REGIMENTAL AND DIVISIONAL NICKNAMES.

Blaze (Icel. *blesi*). A white spot on the forehead of a horse, also called a *star* (*cp*. CLOUD). Similarly, a white mark made on a tree by chipping off a piece of bark is called a *blaze*.

To blaze a trail. To notch trees as a guide. In America trees so marked are called *blazed trees*.

To blaze abroad (Icel. *blasa*, to blow), to noise abroad.

...and began to publish it much, and to blaze abroad the matter.
Mark i, 45.

Blazer. Originally a brightly coloured jacket used in boating, CRICKET, etc. These are now often called *sports blazers* to distinguish them from the more sober styles used as everyday wear by students, schoolchildren, etc.

A blazer is the red flannel boating jacket worn by the Lady Margaret, St. John's College, Cambridge Boat Club.
Daily News, 22 August 1889.

The name derives from H.M.S. Blazer, whose captain, in 1845, dressed his ship's company in somewhat striking blue and white jerseys, thus his men were nicknamed "Blazers". Much later the name was applied to the striped and coloured jackets.

Blazes. Go to blazes. Go to HELL. Here the word is from O.E. *blaese*, a torch.

Bleed. To bleed someone white is to extort the uttermost farthing from them. Money is the life-blood of commerce.

It makes my heart bleed. It makes me very sorrowful.

Bleeding of a dead body. It was once believed that at the approach of a murderer, the blood of the murdered body gushed out. If there was the slightest change observable in the eyes, mouth, feet, or hands of a corpse the murderer was supposed to be present.

Bleeding the monkey. The same as *Sucking the Monkey*. *See* MONKEY.

Blefuscu (ble fūs' kū). An island in Swift's *Gulliver's Travels*. In describing it he satirized France.

Blemmyes (blem' iz). An ancient Ethiopian tribe mentioned by Roman writers as inhabiting Nubia and Upper Egypt. They were fabled to have no head, their eyes and mouth being placed in the breast. *Cp.* ACE-PHALITES; CAORA.

Blenheim Palace (blen' im). This mansion, given to the Duke of Marlborough for his great victory over the French at Blenheim (1704), has given its name to the *Blenheim spaniel*, and to a golden-coloured apple, the *Blenheim Orange*.

Blenheim Steps. Going to Blenheim Steps meant going to be dissected, or unearthed from one's grave. Sir Astley Cooper (1768–1841), the great surgeon, presided over an anatomical school at Blenheim Steps, Bond Street. Here "RESURRECTION-ISTS" were sure to find a ready mart for their gruesome wares.

> The body-snatchers, they have come,
> And made a snatch at me;
> 'Tis very hard them kind of men
> Won't let a body be.
> The cock it crows—I must be gone—
> My William we must part;
> But I'll be yours in death although
> Sir Astley has my heart.
>
> HOOD: *Mary's Ghost*.

Bless. He has not a penny or **a sixpence to bless himself with,** *i.e.* in his possession; wherewith to make himself happy; he has no financial resources. Perhaps this expression goes back to the times when such coins were of silver and carried a cross on the reverse. Crossing the palm with silver is still practised by gipsies as a sign of good luck.

Blessing with three fingers in Christian churches is symbolical of the TRINITY.

Blest. I'll be blest if I do it. I will not do it. A EUPHEMISM for *damned*.

Blighty. Soldier's name for England or the homeland widely current in World War I, but was well known to soldiers who had served in India long before. It is the Hind. *bilayati*, foreign, from Arab. *wilayet* meaning "provincial", "removed at some distance"; hence adopted by the military for England. Its widespread use during the GREAT WAR is illustrated by three popular songs of the time — "There's a ship that's bound for Blighty", "We wish we were in Blighty", and "Take me back to dear old Blighty, put me on the train for London town".

Blimp. A word originally applied to an observation balloon in World War I. "Colonel Blimp" was created by David Low, the cartoonist, between the wars, to embody the elderly dyed-in-the-wool TORY, opposing all and any change. A *blimp* has come to mean an elderly, unprogressive, reactionary "gentleman" of somewhat limited intelligence.

Blind. A pretence; something ostensible to conceal a covert design. The METAPHOR is from window-blinds, which prevent outsiders from seeing in.

Blind Alley, A. A *cul-de-sac*. It is blind because it has no "eye" or passage through it. "A blind alley occupation" is one that leads nowhere; there are no prospects of promotion.

Blind as a bat, or **beetle,** or **mole,** or **owl.** Blind, with very poor sight. None of these creatures is actually blind. The phrase is often used sarcastically of one who is unable to see what is under his nose.

> Trust a woman for being as blind as a bat when she won't see.
>
> KIPLING: *The Story of the Gadsbys*
> (*The Tents of Kedar*).

Blind Department, The. In Post Office parlance, the Returned Letter Office (formerly Dead Letter Office), the department where efforts are made to trace the proper destination of inaccurately or illegibly addressed mail. The clerk in charge was called the "Blind Man". Dr. Brewer had one delivered from France addressed "A Mons. E. Cobham, brasseur, Angleterre".

Blind ditch. One which cannot be seen. Here *blind* means concealed, obscure.

Blind drunk. Very drunk, so drunk as to be unable to distinguish things clearly.

Blind Half-hundred, The. *See* REGIMENTAL AND DIVISIONAL NICKNAMES.

Blind Harper, The. John Parry, who died in 1782. He lived at Ruabon, and published collections of Welsh music.

Blind Harry. A Scottish minstrel who died *c.* 1492 and left in MS. an epic of 11,858 lines on Sir William Wallace.

Blind Hedge. A ha-ha. Milton used the word blind for *concealed*, as "In the blind mazes of this tangled wood" (*Comus*, line 181).

Blind leaders of the blind. Those who give advice to others or who take the lead but who are unfitted to do so, or incapable themselves. The allusion is to *Matt*. xv, 14.

Blind Magistrate, The. Sir John Fielding (1722–1780), Bow Street Magistrate, blinded in his youth, was reputed to know countless thieves by their voices.

Blind Man. *See* BLIND DEPARTMENT.

Blindman's buff. A very old-established children's game. "Buff" here is short for "buffet", and is an allusion to the three buffs or pats which the "blind man" gets when he has caught a player.

Blindman's holiday. The hour of dusk when it is too dark to work, and too soon to light candles. The phrase was in common use at least as early as the 16th century.

> What will not blind Cupid doe in the night, which is his blindman's holiday.
>
> T. NASHE: *Lenten Stuffe* (1599).

Blindmen's Dinner, The. A dinner unpaid for, the landlord being the victim. EULENSPIEGEL, being asked for alms by twelve blind men, said "Go to the inn; eat, drink and be merry, my men; and here are twenty florins to pay the bill." They thanked him, each supposing one of the others had received the money. After having provided them with food and drink at the inn, the landlord asked for payment, whereupon they all said, "let him who received the money pay for the dinner." But none had received a penny.

Blind spot. This is a small area not sensitive to light, situated on the retina where the optic nerve enters the eye. The term is used figuratively to denote some area in one's understanding where judgment and perception are always lacking.

To go it blind. To enter upon some project without sufficient forethought, inquiry, or preparation.

To turn a blind eye. To pretend tactfully not to see; to ignore, in order to avoid embarrassment to all concerned.

When the devil is blind. A circumlocution for NEVER.

You came on his blind side. His tender-hearted side. He yielded because he was not wide awake to his own interest. Said of persons who wheedle some favour out of another.

Blitzkrieg (Ger. *blitz*, lightning; *krieg*, war). A concentrated military offensive designed to produce a knock-out blow. The term was particularly applied to the attacks by Hitler's Germany on various European countries between 1939 and 1941. In 1940 in Western Europe the Germans captured Copenhagen on 9th April, Oslo on 10th April, The Hague on 14th May, Brussels on 17th May and Paris on 14th June resulting in the British withdrawal at DUNKIRK. *See* D DAY.

The Blitz. The name (an abbreviation of BLITZKRIEG) given to the intensive German air raids on London between July and December 1940 which resulted in the destruction of many buildings and the death of some 23,000 civilians. *See* BATTLE OF BRITAIN; BLACK-OUT.

To have a blitz or **thorough blitz**. To make a real attack on something, to go the whole HOG. An expression often used when a thorough clean-up or clear out is needed.

Block. To block a bill. In parliamentary language means to postpone or prevent the passage of a bill by giving notice of opposition, thus preventing its being taken after ten o'clock at night.

A chip of the old block. *See* CHIP.

A stumbling block. An obstacle in the path of progress, a snag or cause of difficulty.

> Let us not therefore judge one another any more: but judge this rather, that no man put a stumbling block or an occasion to fall in his brother's way.
>
> *Rom*. xiv, 13.

To cut blocks with a razor. *See* CUT.

Block books. Late mediæval books printed from wood-blocks in which both text and illustrations (if any) were carved in relief. The impression was taken by laying the paper on the block moistened with a brown or grey water-based ink and rubbing the verso by hand with a cloth, though some later block books were produced with black oil-based printer's ink in a press. As the water-based ink tended to soak through the paper, impressions were generally taken on one side of the leaf only. The most important block books were pictorial works of devotion, such as the BIBLIA PAUPERUM, *Ars Moriendi, Apocalypse, et al.*, but the same method was also used for printing various scientific works, Latin grammars, etc., with or without illustrations. Although there are references in earlier documents which might possibly imply that such books were current several decades before the invention of printing from movable type (*c*. 1450), the earliest of the surviving block books dates from the early 1450s, most of the remainder from the 1460s and 1470s, and a few from as late as the 1520s.

Blockhead. A stupid person; brainless. The allusion is to a wig-maker's dummy or *tête à perruque*.

> Nay, your wit will not so soon out as another man's will—'tis strongly wedged up in a blockhead.
>
> SHAKESPEARE: *Coriolanus*, II, iii.

Blockhousers. The oldest Negro Regiment in the U.S. Army, nicknamed from its gallant assault on a blockhouse in the Spanish-American War.

Blondin (blon' din). One of the most famous acrobats of all time. Born at St. Omer in 1824, his real name was Jean François Gravelet; he died at Ealing in 1897. His greatest feat was in 1859, when he crossed the Niagara Falls on a tightrope, embellishing the performance by repeating it blindfolded, wheeling a barrow, twirling an umbrella, and carrying a man on his back. He made a fortune by this feat and soon after settled in England, where he gave performances until old age forced him to retire.

Blood. In figurative use came to denote members of the same family or race, family descent generally, and thence one of noble or gentle birth, finally a BUCK or aristocratic rowdy.

> The gallants of those days pretty much resembled the bloods of ours.
>
> GOLDSMITH: *Reverie at the Boar's Head Tavern.*

It also denotes royalty, and the once popular "PENNY DREADFULS".

A blood horse. A thoroughbred; a horse of good parentage or stock.

A prince of the blood. One of a royal family.

Bad blood. Anger, etc., as, *It stirs up bad blood*. It provokes ill-feeling and resentment.

Blood and Guts. Nickname given by the soldiers in World War II to the American General George Smith Patton (1885–1945). Also a disrespectful term for the RED ENSIGN.

Blood and iron policy. A policy requiring war as its instrument. The phrase was coined by Bismarck in 1886.

Blood and thunder. Melodrama, sensational and blood-curdling stuff.

Bloodhound. Figuratively, one who follows up someone or something with real pertinacity.

Blood is thicker than water. Relationship has a claim which is generally acknowledged. It is better to seek kindness from a kinsman than from a stranger. The interest we take in a stranger is "thinner" and more evanescent than that which we take in a blood relation.

Bloodless Revolution. The revolution of 1688 when William of Orange, invited over by leading WHIGS and TORIES, landed at Torbay (5 November) and the army of James II deserted without firing a shot. James was captured but eventually escaped and fled to France.

Blood money. Money paid to a person for giving such evidence as shall lead to the conviction of another; or for the betrayal of another, as JUDAS was paid for his betrayal of Jesus. Also at one time money paid to the next of kin as compensation for the murder of his relative or to induce him to forgo his "right" of seeking for blood.

Blood-red wedding. *See under* WEDDING.

Blood relation. One in direct descent from the same father or mother; one of the same family stock.

Blood Royal. The royal family or royalty; also called "the blood".

Bloodstone. *See* HELIOTROPE.

Bloodsucker. A leech-like animal which, if allowed, will rob a person of all vitality. Hence a sponger, a parasite, an extortioner.

Blood, toil, tears and sweat. The words used by Sir Winston Churchill in his speech to the HOUSE OF COMMONS, on becoming Prime Minister, 13 May 1940. "I would say to the House, as I have said to those who have joined this Government. I have nothing to offer but blood, toil, tears and sweat." In his *Anatomie of the World*, John Donne, says, "Mollifie it with thy teares, or sweat, or blood", and Byron has,

> Year after year they voted cent per cent,
> Blood, sweat, and tear-wrung millions—why? for rent!
>
> *The Age of Bronze*, xiv, 621.

Gladstone's speech in Westminster Abbey (22 Feb. 1866) commemorating Lord Palmerston includes reference to "the unhappy African race, whose history is for the most part written in blood and tears".

Blue blood. *See* BLUE.

In cold blood. Deliberately; not in the excitement of passion or battle.

It makes one's blood boil. It provokes indignation and anger.

It runs in the blood. It is inherited or is characteristic of the family or race.

Laws written in blood. Demades said that the laws of Draco were written in blood, because every offence was punishable by death. *See* DRACONIAN CODE.

Man of Blood. Any man of violent temper. David was so called in II *Sam.* xvi, 7 (REVISED VERSION), and the PURITANS applied the term to Charles I.

My own flesh and blood. My own children, my own brothers and sisters, or other near kindred.

Nelson's blood. The Royal Navy's nickname for rum, issued to ratings since 1731 but tots were withdrawn on 31 July 1970. *See* GROG.

The Blood of the Grograms. TAFFETA gentility; make-believe aristocratic blood. *See* GROG; GROGRAM.

Our first tragedian was always boasting of his being "an old actor", and was full of the blood of the Grograms.

C. THOMSON: *Autobiography*, p. 200.

The Field of Blood. ACELDAMA, the piece of ground purchased with the blood-money of our Saviour.

The battlefield of CANNAE, where Hannibal defeated the Romans, 216 B.C., is also so called.

Young blood. Young members; as, "To bring young blood into the concern." The term with the article, "a young blood", signifies a young RIP, a young aristocrat of convivial habits.

Bloody. Several fanciful derivations are suggested for this expletive, that it is a corruption of "By our Lady", or associated with "bloods" or aristocratic rowdies; but the obvious meaning of the word with its unpleasant and lurid associations is a sufficient explanation of its origin and its use as an intensive.

It was bloody hot walking today.

SWIFT: *Journal to Stella*, letter xxii.

As a title the adjective has been bestowed on Otto II, Holy Roman Emperor (973–983) and Queen Mary Tudor (1553–1558) was called "Bloody MARY".

Bloody Angle. A section of the battlefield of Spottsylvania Court House, Virginia, where on 11 and 12 May 1864 the armies of Grant and Lee fought one of the bloodiest encounters of the CIVIL WAR.

Bloody Assizes. The Assizes conducted in the western circuit under Judge Jeffreys after MONMOUTH'S REBELLION, 1685. Named from the brutality, severity, and unfairness of the proceedings.

Bloody Balfour. In 1887, when A. J. Balfour became Chief Secretary for Ireland, the police fired on a riotous mass meeting at Mitchelstown, County Cork, occasioned by the prosecution of a nationalist leader, William O'Brien. Three people were killed. As a consequence of Balfour's resolute support of authority the nickname *Bloody Balfour* soon became current in Ireland. The meeting in Trafalgar Square on BLOODY SUNDAY was held to protest against O'Brien's imprisonment.

Bloody Bill, The. Better known as the Act of the SIX ARTICLES (31 Henry VIII, c. 14), it made the denial of TRANSUBSTANTIATION a heresy punishable by death.

Bloody-bones. A HOBGOBLIN; generally "RAW-HEAD and Bloody-bones".

Bloody Eleventh. *See* REGIMENTAL AND DIVISIONAL NICKNAMES.

Bloody Hand. A term in Old Forest Law denoting a man whose hand was bloody, and who was therefore presumed to be the one guilty of killing the deer. In HERALDRY it is the badge of a BARONET and the armorial device of ULSTER. *See* HAND.

Bloody Mary. *See under* MARY.

Bloody Pots, The. *See* KIRK OF SKULLS.

Bloody Sunday. (1) 13 November 1887. The dispersal of a socialist demonstration in Trafalgar Square which had been prohibited by the Commissioner of Police led to baton charges being made, Footguards and Life Guards being brought in, and the arrest of two M.P.s, R. Cunninghame-Graham and John Burns. Two of the crowd died of injuries. (2) 22 January 1905. A deputation of workers led by Father Gapon marched to St. Petersburg to present a petition to the Czar. They were attacked by troops and hundreds of unarmed peasants were killed. (3) 30 January 1972. The dispersal of anti-internment marchers in the Bogside, Londonderry by British troops when 13 civilians were killed.

Bloody Thursday. The Thursday in the first week of LENT, that is, the day after ASH WEDNESDAY, used to be so called.

Bloody Tower. *See under* TOWER.

Bloomer. An error, a mistake. An elliptical form of a "BLOOMING error", etc.

Bloomers. Originally a female costume consisting of jacket, skirt and Turkish trousers gathered closely round the ankles, introduced by Mrs. Amelia Bloomer of New York in 1849. Associated with the Woman's Rights Movement, the outfit met with little success. Nowadays "bloomers" is applied to the trouser portion of the outfit, or drawers.

Bombay bloomers. An old nickname for army shorts.

Blooming. A meaningless EUPHEMISM for BLOODY.

Bloomsbury Gang. In the 1760s the WHIG party faction adhering to the Duke of Bedford was so called. Bedford House was in Bloomsbury, the duke's London property.

Bloomsbury Group. The name given to a group of various callings — writer, artist, philosopher, economist, who, from about 1904 met at the Bloomsbury home of Clive and Vanessa Bell (née Stephen) in Gordon Square, that of Virginia and Adrian Stephen in Fitzroy Square and elsewhere. Virginia Stephen married Leonard Woolf; others prominent in the circle were Roger Fry, Duncan Grant, J.M. Keynes, David Garnett, Lytton Strachey and to a lesser extent E.M. Forster. They saw themselves as advocates of a new rational, civilized society and many of them had Cambridge links. The group had lost its cohesion by the end of the 1920s. They were considerably influenced by G.E. Moore's *Principia Ethica* (1903).

Bloomsbury Intellectuals. Since the 19th century, a popular designation of those many highbrows and intellectuals associated with the Bloomsbury area adjacent to the BRITISH MUSEUM. It is often used with critical implications.

Blot. To blot one's copybook. *See* COPYBOOK.

Blow. This represents three words of different origin: (1) To move as a current of air, to send a current of air from the mouth, etc., from the O.E. *blawan*, cognate with the Mod. Ger. *blähen* and Lat. *flare*.

A blow out. A "tuck in" or feast which swells out the paunch. Also the sudden collapse of a pneumatic tyre when the inner tube is punctured.

Blowing Stone. A roughly square block of red sarsen about $3\frac{1}{2}$ ft. high, perforated with two or three holes. If blown properly it produces a lingering moaning sound. It is situated at Kingston Lisle in the Vale of the WHITE HORSE.

> "Um do say, sir," says mine host, rising purple-faced, while the moan is still coming out of the Stwun, "as they used in old times to warn the countryside, by blowing the Stwun when the enemy was a comin' ".
>
> T. HUGHES: *Tom Brown's Schooldays*, ch. i.

Blow me down. An expletive of nautical origin, as in the sea shanty "Blow the man down" of sailing ship days.

Blow me tight. An expletive.

> If there's a soul, will give me food, or find me in employ,
> By day or night, then blow me tight! (he was a vulgar boy).
>
> R. H. BARHAM: *Ingoldsby Legends: Misadventures at Margate.*

Blown herrings. Herrings bloated, swollen or cured by smoking; another name for bloaters.

Blown upon. Blown upon by the breath of slander. *His reputation has been blown upon* means that he has been the subject of derogatory gossip. *Cp.* FLY-BLOWN.

Blow-point. A game similar to pea-shooting, only instead of peas small skewers of pointed wood were puffed through the tube. It is alluded to by Florio, Strutt and others.

Fly-blown. *See under* FLY.

It will soon blow over. It will soon cease to be talked about, as a gale blows over or ceases.

I will blow him (up) sky high. Give him a good scolding. The metaphor is from blasting by gunpowder.

To blow a cloud. To smoke a cigar, pipe,

etc. This term dates from Elizabeth I's reign.

To blow a trumpet. To sound a trumpet, but **to blow one's own trumpet** is to go in for self-advertisement, to boast.

To blow great guns. Said of a wind that blows so violently that its noise resembles the roar of artillery.

To blow hot and cold. To be inconsistent, to be irresolute, unable to make up one's mind. The allusion is to the fable of a traveller who was entertained by a SATYR. Being cold the traveller blew his fingers to warm them, and afterwards blew his hot broth to cool it. The satyr, in great indignation turned him out of doors, because he blew both hot and cold with the same breath.

To blow off steam. To get rid of superfluous temper. The allusion is to the forcible escape of superfluous steam no longer required. *See also under* LET.

To blow one's top. To lose one's temper.

To blow the gaff. To let out a secret; to inform against a companion; to "peach". Here *gaff* is a variant of GAB.

To blow up. To inflate, to explode, to burst into fragments; to censure severely. *See* I WILL BLOW HIM UP (*above*).

You be blowed. A mild imprecation or expletive.

> Don't link yourself with vulgar folks, who've got no fixed abode,
> Tell lies, use naughty words, and say "they wish they may be blow'd!"
>
> R. H. BARHAM: *Ingoldsby Legends: Misadventures at Margate.*

Blow it! is similarly used.

(2) To blossom, to flourish, from O.E. *blowan*, cognate with *bloom*, Ger. *blühen* and Lat. *florere*.

Full-blown. In full flower, hence fully developed or qualified. "He is a full-blown doctor now" means he is no longer a student but fully qualified to practise.

(3) A stroke with the fist, etc., probably from an old Dutch word *blau*, to strike.

A body-blow. *See under* BODY.

At one blow. By one stroke.

The first blow is half the battle. Well begun is half done, a good lather is half the shave. PYTHAGORAS used to say: "the beginning is half the whole". "*Incipe, Dimidium facti est cœpisse*" (Ausonius). "*Dimidium facti, qui cœpit, habet*" (Horace). "*Ce n'est que le premier pas qui coûte*" (*see under* PREMIER).

Without striking a blow. Without coming to a contest.

Blowzelinda (blou ze lin' dà). A common 18th-century name applied to a rustic girl.

Sweet is my toil when Blowzelind is near;
Of her bereft, 'tis winter all the year...
Come Blowzelinda, ease thy swain's desire,
My summer's shadow and my winter's fire.

GAY: *Shepherd's Week, Pastoral*, i.

A *blowse* was a ruddy fat-cheeked wench:

Sweet blowse you are a beauteous blossom, sure.

SHAKESPEARE: *Titus Andronicus*, IV, ii.

Bluchers (bloo′ kerz). Half-boots; named after the Prussian Field-Marshal von Blücher (1742–1819), of Waterloo fame. *See* WELLINGTON.

Bludger (Austr.). Originally (19th century) a pimp, but later any scrounger or one profiting without risk. In World War I *to bludge on the flag* meant to slack in the army.

Bludsoe, Jim. The hero of a poem by the American John M. Hay (1838–1905). Bludsoe was the engineer of a steamboat on the Mississippi who, when the vessel caught fire, sacrificed himself to save his passengers.

Blue, or AZURE. *See* COLOURS for its symbolisms.

The COVENANTERS wore blue as their badge in opposition to the scarlet of royalty. They based their choice on *Numb.* ix, 38. "Speak unto the children of Israel, and bid them that they make them fringes on the borders of their garments...and that they put upon the fringe...a ribband of blue." It was one of the traditional Whig colours, also blue and buff. The LIBERAL colours are now blue and yellow, and the CONSERVATIVES blue. It was also the colour of the Unionists in the American CIVIL WAR; the CONFEDERATE colour was grey.

A blue, or **a true blue,** politically speaking usually means a TORY. Also at Oxford and Cambridge *a blue* is a man who has been chosen to represent his 'VARSITY in rowing, CRICKET, etc. In the general sense "a true blue" is a person of unimpeachable integrity and staunch fidelity, probably from the idea of such qualities being characteristic of BLUE BLOOD.

A dark blue. An Oxford man or Harrow boy.

A light blue. A Cambridge man or Eton boy.

A priest of the blue bag. A CANT name for a BARRISTER. *See* LAWYER'S BAGS.

Bluebeard. A BOGEY, a murderous tyrant in Charles Perrault's *Contes du Temps* (1697). In this version Bluebeard goes on a journey leaving his new wife the keys of his castle, but forbidding her to enter one room. Curiosity overcomes her and she opens the door to find the bodies of all Bluebeard's former wives. On his return he finds a blood spot on the key which tells him of his wife's disobe-dience. He is about to cut off her head when her two brothers rush in and kill him. The tale is of an internationally widespread and ancient type and it is unprofitable to regard Gilles de Rais or Henry VIII as the historical Bluebeard.

Bluebeard's Key. When the bloodstain of this key was rubbed out on one side, it appeared on the other; so prodigality being overcome will appear in the form of meanness; and friends, over-fond, will often become enemies.

Blue beans. *See under* BEAN.

Blue Billy. *See under* BILLY.

Blue Bird of Happiness. This is an idea elaborated from Maeterlinck's play of that name, first produced in London in 1910. It tells the story of a boy and girl seeking "the blue bird" which typifies happiness.

Blue blood. High or noble birth or descent; it is of Spanish origin, from the fact that the veins of the pure-blooded Spanish aristocrat, whose race had suffered no Moorish admixture, were more blue than those of mixed ancestry.

Blue Boar. A cognizance of Richard, Duke of York, father of Edward IV. The cognizance of Richard III was a white boar—a popular inn sign. After his defeat at Bosworth, White Boars were changed into Blue Boars.

Blue Bonnets, or **Blue Caps.** The Highlanders of Scotland, or the Scots generally; from the blue woollen cap formerly in very general use in Scotland.

March, march Eskdale and Liddesdale,
All the Blue Bonnets are bound for the Border.

SCOTT: *Border Ballad*.

Blue Books. In Great Britain parliamentary reports and other official parliamentary publications. Each volume is in FOLIO with a blue cover. Short ACTS OF PARLIAMENT, etc., even without a wrapper, come under the same designation. *Cp.* WHITE PAPER.

Bluebottle. A constable, a policeman; also formerly an almsman, or anyone else whose distinctive dress was blue. Shakespeare makes Doll Tearsheet denounce the BEADLE as a "blue-bottle rogue". The large fly of this name has a blue abdomen.

I will have you as soundly swinged for this, you blue-bottle rogue.

Henry IV, Pt. II, V, iv.

Blue Caps. *See* BLUE BONNETS.

Blue-Coat School. Christ's Hospital is so called because the boys there wear a long blue coat girded at the loins with a leather belt. Formerly in the City of London, it moved to Horsham in 1902. There were other Charity schools so named; the building of the Westminster Blue-Coat School still remains although the funds were diverted in 1909 to Grey-Coat Hospital and the United Westminster Schools.

Blue Devils. *See* BLUES.

Blue-eyed Boy, The. The favourite, one highly thought of and shown preference or marks of favour.

Blue-eyed Maid. MINERVA, the goddess of wisdom, is so called by HOMER.

> Now Prudence gently pulled the poet's ear,
> And thus the daughter of the Blue-eyed Maid,
> In flattery's soothing sounds, divinely said,
> "O Peter, eldest-born of Phoebus, hear."
> PETER PINDAR: *A Falling Minister*.

Blue gown. A harlot. Formerly a blue gown was a dress of ignominy for a prostitute who had been put in the HOUSE OF CORRECTION.

The bedesmen to whom the Scottish kings distributed certain alms were known as *blue gowns* from their dress of coarse blue cloth. The number of these bedesmen was equal to the king's years and they were privileged to ask alms throughout Scotland. *See* GABERLUNZIE.

Blue Hen's Chickens. The inhabitants of the State of Delaware. It is said that in the Revolutionary War, one Captain Caldwell, commander of a very efficient Delaware regiment, used to say that no cock could be truly game whose mother was not a blue hen. Hence his regiment became known as "Blue Hen's Chickens", and the name was transferred to the inhabitants generally.

Blue jackets. Sailors in the naval service; from the colour of their jackets (worn 1857–1890 and subsequently replaced by jumpers). *Cp.* TARPAULIN.

Blue John. A blue fluorspar, found in the Blue John Mine near Castleton, Derbyshire; so called to distinguish it from BLACK JACK. Called John from John Kirk, a miner who first noticed it.

Blue laws. In the U.S.A. denotes laws such as SUMPTUARY LAWS and those regulating personal morals or interfering with personal freedom.

Blue-light Federalists. A name given to those Americans who were believed to have made friendly (blue-light) signals to British ships in the war of 1812.

Bluemantle. One of the four English PURSUIVANTS attached to the College of Arms or Heralds' College, so called from his official robe.

Blue Monday. The Monday before LENT, spent in dissipation, which is said to give everything a blue tinge. Hence "Blue" means tipsy.

Blue Monkey, The. The nickname given to the Marquis Luis Augusto Pinto de Soveral (d. 1922), from his swarthy complexion and blue-black hair. Portuguese ambassador at London almost continuously from 1884 to 1909, and intimate of King Edward VII, he was noted for his wit, discretion and ability as a raconteur. He held a unique position in Edwardian society and was pre-eminent as a philanderer among the upper CRUST. At the German embassy he was dubbed "Soveral-Uberall".

Blue moon. Once in a blue moon. Very rarely indeed.

Blue murder. To scream or **shout blue murder.** Indicative of terror and alarm rather than real danger. It appears to be a play on the French exclamation *morbleu*.

Blue-noses. The Nova Scotians.

> "Pray Sir," said one of my fellow-passengers, "can you tell me the reason why the Nova Scotians are called Blue-noses?"
> "It is the name of a potato," said I, "which they produce in the greatest perfection, and boast to be the best in the world. The Americans have, in consequence, given them the nickname of Blue Noses."
> HALIBURTON: *Sam Slick*.

Blue Peter. A blue flag with a white square in the centre, hoisted as a signal that a ship is about to sail. Here "Peter" is a corruption of "repeater", the flag having been originally used to mean that a signal had not been read and should be repeated. Also the letter "P" in the International Code of Signals.

Blue-pencil. The mark of editing or censorship.

Blue-pictures. Indecent cinema shows. The name derives from the custom of Chinese brothels being painted blue externally.

Blue-print. Properly the reproduction of a detailed architectural or engineering drawing, etc., in white lines on a blue ground. Now increasingly used for any project, scheme, or design.

Blue Riband of the Atlantic. The liner gaining the record for the fastest Atlantic crossing is said to hold the "Blue Riband of the Atlantic" and from 1907 to 1929 it was held by Cunard liner *Mauretania*. It then passed to the *Europa* (1930) and *Bremen* (1933) of Germany, to the *Rex* of Italy (1933), and to the French liner *Normandie* in 1935. It was next held by the *Queen Mary* of Britain from 1938 until its capture by the American-owned *United States* in 1952. A trophy offered in 1935 by H. K. Hales (1868–1942) was first accepted by the United States Lines in 1952. The average speed of the *Mauretania* was 27·4 knots, that of the *United States* 35·69 knots. *Cp.* BLUE RIBBON.

Blue Ribbon. The blue ribbon is the GAR-

TER, the most coveted Order of Knighthood in the gift of the British Crown; hence the term is used to denote the highest honour attainable in any profession or walk of life, etc. The Blue Ribbon of the Church is the Archbishopric of Canterbury, that of the Law, the office of Lord Chancellor. *See* CORDON BLEU.

A weal from a blow has had the term "blue ribbon" applied to it, because a bruise turns the skin blue.

> "Do you want a blue ribbon round those white sides of yours, you monkey?" answered Orestes: "because, if you do, the hippopotamus hide hangs ready outside."
>
> KINGSLEY: *Hypatia*, ch. iv.

Blue Ribbon of the Turf. The Derby. Lord George Bentinck sold his stud and found to his vexation that one of the horses sold won the Derby a few months later. Bewailing his ill-luck, he said to Disraeli, "Ah! You don't know what the Derby is." "Yes, I do," replied Disraeli, "it is the blue ribbon of the turf." *See* DERBY DAY.

Blue Ribbon Army. A TEETOTAL society founded in the U.S.A. and extending to Great Britain by 1878, whose members wore a piece of narrow blue ribbon as a badge. It became the Gospel Temperance Union in 1883. The phrase came in time to be applied to teetotallers generally.

Blue Shirts. An Irish FASCIST organization under General Eoin O'Duffy, former Commissioner of the Garda, which developed from the Army Comrades Association in the early 1930s. A Blue Shirt battalion led by O'Duffy fought for General Franco in the Spanish Civil War, 1936–1939.

Blue Sky Laws. In the U.S.A., laws passed to protect the inexperienced buyer of stocks and bonds against fraud. The name is said to have its origin in a phrase used by one of the supporters of the earliest of these laws, who said that certain business operators were trying to capitalize "the blue skies".

Blue Squadron. From 1625 until 1864 one of the three divisions of the British Fleet, and the third in order of precedence. *See* ADMIRAL OF THE BLUE.

Blue-stocking. A female pedant or learned woman who tends to neglect "feminine graces" and their accompaniments. In 1400 a society of men and women was formed in Venice, distinguished by the colour of their stockings and called *della calza*. A similar society appeared in Paris in 1590 and was the rage among lady *savants*. The name is derived directly from such a society, founded by Mrs. Montagu about 1750, from the fact that a prominent member, Mr. Benjamin

Stillingfleet, wore blue stockings. The last of the clique was Miss Monckton, afterwards Countess of Cork, who died in 1840. Mrs. Montagu is also said to have deliberately adopted the badge of the French *Bas-bleu* club.

Blues. A traditional form of American folk-song expressive of the unhappiness of the black man in the Deep South. The usual subject matter is love, the troubles that beset the singer, or a nostalgic longing for home but with an uncomplaining acceptance of life as it is. Blues usually consist of 12 bars made up of three 4-bar phrases in 4/4 time. They can be vocal or instrumental and have had more influence on JAZZ than RAGTIME.

Also low spirits, **to have a fit of the blues** is to be downcast or depressed. Here a contraction of **blue-devils**. *See also* REGIMENTAL AND DIVISIONAL NICKNAMES.

Bluey. A slang word for lead. Also an Australian name for blue-coloured blankets widely used in the 19th century, hence the SWAG which tramps carried in their blankets. In Tasmania a *bluey* was a blue shirt-like garment issued to convicts.

The Boys in blue. The police, from the colour of their uniforms.

The Oxford Blues. *See* REGIMENTAL AND DIVISIONAL NICKNAMES.

To be blue in the face. To have made a great effort; to be breathless and exhausted, either bodily or more usually with suppressed anger or emotion.

To look or **feel blue.** To be depressed.

True blue will never stain. A really noble heart will never disgrace itself. The reference is to blue aprons and blouses worn by butchers. They do not show bloodstains.

True as Coventry blue. The reference is to a blue cloth and blue thread made at Coventry, noted for its permanent dye.

'Twas Presbyterian true blue (*Hudibras*, I, i). The allusion is to the blue apron which some PRESBYTERIAN preachers used to throw over their preaching-tub before they began to address the people. In one of the RUMP songs we read of a person going to hear a lecture, and the song says:

> Where I a tub did view,
> Hung with an apron blue;
> 'Twas the preacher's I conjecture.

Bluff, To. In poker and other card-games, to stake on a bad hand. This is a ruse to lead an adversary to throw up his cards and forfeit his stake rather than risk them against the "bluffer".

So, by extension, to bluff is to deceive by pretence. **To call someone's bluff** is to unmask his deception.

Bluff Harry, or **Bluff King Hal.** Henry VIII (1509–1547), from his bluff hearty manner.

Blunderbore. A nursery-tale giant, brother of CORMORAN, who put JACK THE GIANT KILLER to bed and intended to kill him; but Jack thrust a billet of wood into the bed, and crept under the bedstead. Blunderbore came with his club and broke the billet to pieces and was amazed to see Jack next morning at breakfast. He asked Jack how he had slept. "Pretty well," said the Cornish hero, "but once or twice I fancied a mouse tickled me with its tail." This increased the giant's surprise. Hasty pudding being provided for breakfast, Jack stowed away such a bulk in a bag concealed within his dress that the giant could not keep pace. Jack cut the bag open to relieve the "gorge" and the giant, to effect the same relief, cut his throat and thus killed himself.

Blunt. Slang for ready money, origin unknown.

> To get a signora to warble a song,
> You must fork out the blunt with a haymaker's prong!
> HOOD : *A Tale of a Trumpet.*

Blurb. A publisher's note on the dustjacket or cover of a book purporting to tell what the book is about and usually of a laudatory nature. The word was coined by Gelett Burgess, the American novelist (1866–1951), about 1914, when he defined it as "self praise, to make a noise like a publisher".

Blush. At first blush. At first sight, on the first glance. The word is from the M.E. *blusche*, a gleam, a glimpse; a meaning now obsolete except in the above phrase.

> At the first blush we thought they had been shippes come from France.
> HAKLUYT : *Principal Navigations,* III.

To blush like a blue dog. Not to blush at all.

To put to the blush. To make someone blush with shame, annoyance, or confusion.

Bo. You cannot say Bo!, or **Boo! to a Goose.** A proverbial saying implying timidity.

Boa. Pliny (*Natural History,* VIII, xiv) says the word is from Lat. *bos* (a cow), and it arose from the belief that this snake sucked the milk of cows.

Boadicea (bō à dìsē′ à), or **Boudicca.** The famous British warrior queen, wife of Prasutagus, king of the Iceni. On her husband's death (A.D. 61) the Romans had seized the territory, scourged the widow for her opposition and violated her two daughters. Boudicca raised a revolt of the Iceni and Trinovantes, burned Camulodunum (Colchester), Londinium (London), and Veru-

lamium (St. Albans), but when finally routed by Suetonius Paulinus, she took poison. She is the subject of poems by Cowper and Tennyson.

Boanerges (bō à nĕr′ jēz). A name given to James and John, the sons of Zebedee, because they wanted to call down "fire from HEAVEN" to consume the Samaritans for not "receiving" the Lord Jesus. It is said in the Bible to signify "sons of thunder", but "sons of tumult" would be a better rendering. (*Luke* ix, 54; *Mark* iii, 17.)

Boar, The. Richard III. *See* BLUE BOAR.

> The wretched, bloody, and usurping boar,
> That spoiled your summer fields and fruitful vines,…this foul swine
> Lies now even in the centre of this isle,
> Near to the town of Leicester, as we learn.
> SHAKESPEARE : *Richard III,* v, ii.

Buddha and the boar. A Hindu legend relates that BUDDHA died from eating dried boar's flesh. The third AVATAR of VISHNU was in the form of a boar, and in the legend "dried boar's flesh" probably typifies ESOTERIC knowledge prepared for popular use. None but Buddha himself must take the responsibility of giving out occult secrets, and he died while preparing for the general esoteric knowledge.

The bristled Baptist boar. So Dryden denominates the ANABAPTISTS in his *Hind and Panther.*

> The bristled Baptist boar, impure as he [*the ape*],
> But whitened with the foam of sanctity,
> With fat pollutions filled the sacred place,
> And mountains levelled in his furious race.
> *Pt. I,* 43.

The Calydonian boar. In Greek legend, Œneus, King of Calydon in Ætolia, having neglected the sacrifices to ARTEMIS, was punished by the goddess sending a ferocious boar to ravage his lands. A band of princes collected to hunt the boar, which was wounded by Atalanta (*see* ATALANTA'S RACE), and killed by MELEAGER.

The wild boar of the Ardennes. Guillaume, Comte de la Marck, beheaded in 1485, was so called from his ferocity. He features in Scott's *Quentin Durward.*

Boar's Head. The old English custom of serving this as a Christmas dish is said to derive from Norse mythology. FREYR, the god of peace and plenty, used to ride on the boar Gullinbursti: his festival was held at YULETIDE, when a boar was sacrificed to his honour. The English custom is described in Washington Irving's *Sketch Book* (*The Christmas Dinner*). The Boar's Head was brought in ceremoniously to a flourish of trumpets and a carol was sung. The follow-

ing is the first verse of that sung before
Prince Henry at St. John's College, Oxford,
at Christmas, 1607:

> The Boar is dead
> So, here is his head;
> What man could have done more
> Than his head off to strike,
> Meleager like
> And bring it as I do before?

Irving gives the Boar's Head Carol of
Queen's College, Oxford.

The Boar's Head Tavern. Made immortal
by SHAKESPEARE and Prince Hal, this used to
stand in Eastcheap. Destroyed in the Great
Fire (*see* FIRE), it was rebuilt and annual
Shakespeare Dinners were held there until
1784. It was demolished in 1831. Washington Irving has an essay, "The Boar's Head
Tavern, Eastcheap", in his *Sketch Book*.

Board. In all its many senses it is the O.E.
bord, a board, plank, or table; the verb *to
board* meaning to enter a ship by force,
hence to embark in a ship, is from the Fr.
aborder, which is itself from the same word
bord, meaning the side of a ship, as in STAR-
BOARD, larboard, inboard, overboard, etc.

> For I will board her though she chide as loud
> As thunder, when the clouds in autumn crack.
> SHAKESPEARE: *The Taming of the Shrew*, I, ii.

A board. A council which sits at a board or
table: as Board of Directors, School Board,
Board of Trade, etc.

Board of Green Cloth. So called from the
green covered table at which the board originally sat under the Lord Steward. It examined all the accounts of the English Royal
Household and formerly dealt with all offenders within the verge of the palace, which
extended 200 yards from the palace gate. Its
powers were curtailed in 1782 and it is now
concerned with the royal domestic arrangements under the Master of the Household.

In modern slang *the board of green cloth* is
the card-table or the billiard-table.

Board School. *See* SCHOOL-BOARDS.

He is on the boards. He is an actor by profession.

To sweep the board. To win and carry off
all the stakes in a game of cards, or all the
prizes at some meeting.

To board. To feed and lodge. From the
custom of dining at table or board.

Boarding School. One where the pupils are
fed and lodged as well as being taught. The
term is sometimes applied euphemistically
to prison.

Board Wages. Wages paid to servants
which include the cost of food. Servants "on
board wages" provided their own victuals.
*Pretty little Polly Perkins of Paddington
Green*, the title and subject of Clifton's pop-

ular Victorian song, "lived on board wages".
Board in many nautical phrases is that part
of the sea which a ship passes over in tacking.

To go by the board. To go for good, to be
completely destroyed or finished with,
thrown overboard. When a ship's mast is
carried away it is said "to go by the board",
board here meaning the ship's side.

To make a long, good, or **short board.**
To make a long or short tack.

To make a stern board, *i.e.* to go backwards. To sail stern foremost.

To run aboard of. To run foul of another
ship.

Boast of England, The. A name given to TOM
THUMB or Tom-a-lin by Richard Johnson,
who in 1599 published a "history of this
ever-renowned soldier, the Red Rose
Knight, surnamed The Boast of England".

Boater. A flat-topped, shallow-crowned straw
hat, usually trimmed with a band of ribbon,
popular in late-Victorian and Edwardian
England and still seen until the early 1930s
for wear at CRICKET matches, picnics and
boating parties (hence the name). It is the
established headgear of Harrow School and
was formerly much favoured by butchers
and fishmongers and still worn by some.

Boaz. *See* JACHIN.

Bob. Slang for a SHILLING. This use, of unknown origin, dates from about 1800. Also a
term used in campanology denoting certain
CHANGES in the long peals. A *bob minor* is
rung on six bells, a *bob triple* on seven, a *bob
major* on eight, a *bob royal* on ten, and a *bob
maximus* on twelve.

Bob-a-Job-Week. An imaginative way of
raising funds by self-help, instituted by the
BOY SCOUTS in 1949. All kinds of jobs were
undertaken, some for their publicity value,
for the payment of one shilling. It became an
annual effort but with the declining value of
the "bob" and the advent of DECIMAL CUR-
RENCY, *Scout Job Week* took its place in 1972
thus encouraging patrons to give a fairer return for work done.

To bob for apples or cherries is to try and
catch them in the mouth while they swing
backwards and forwards. *Bob* here means to
move up and down buoyantly; hence the
word also means to "curtsy", as in the Scottish song **If it isn't weel bobbit we'll bob
it again,** signifying if it is not well done we'll
do it again.

To bob for eels is to fish for them with a *bob*,
which is a bunch of lobworms like a small
mop.

To bob also means to thump, and a *bob* is a
blow.

He that a fool doth very wisely hit,
Doth very foolishly, although he smart,
Not to seem senseless of the bob.

SHAKESPEARE: *As You Like It*, II, vii.

A bob wig. One in which the bottom locks are turned up into bobs or short curls.

Bear a bob. Be brisk. The allusion is to bobbing for apples which requires great agility and quickness.

Bobbed hair is hair that has been cut short; docked like a bobtailed horse.

Bobbing John. John Erskine, Earl of Mar (1675–1732), was so called from his frequent change of allegiance. He began as a WHIG but eventually led the JACOBITES in the rebellion of 1715.

Pretty bobbish. Pretty well (in spirits and health), from *bob* as in BEAR A BOB.

Bob's your uncle. That will be all right; you needn't bother any more, just leave it to me! The phrase was occasioned by A. J. Balfour's promotion by his uncle Robert (Lord Salisbury), the TORY Prime Minister, to the post of Chief Secretary for IRELAND. Balfour had previously been made President of the Local Government Board in 1886, then Secretary for SCOTLAND with a seat in the CABINET. The suggestion of nepotism was difficult to ignore.

Bobbery. Kicking up a bobbery. Making a squabble, kicking up a SHINDY. It was much used in India and probably comes from Hind. *bapre*, "Oh, father!" a common exclamation of surprise.

Bobby. A policeman, from Sir Robert Peel, Home Secretary, who established the Metropolitan Police in 1829. *Cp.* PEELER.

Bobby-sox. Long white cotton socks or ankle socks affected by teenage girls in the U.S.A. in the early 1940s. Hence the name *Bobby-soxers* for the young females who distinguished themselves for their intemperate and moronic behaviour at the public appearances of crooners and suchlike.

Bobadil. A military braggart of the first water, Captain Bobadil is a character in Ben Johnson's *Every Man in his Humour*. This name was probably derived from Bobadilla, the first governor of Cuba, who sent Columbus home in chains.

Bocland, or Bookland. Denotes land of inheritance granted from FOLKLAND in Anglo-Saxon England by the King and the Witan by written charter or book. It was at first given to the CHURCH, but also to lay subjects. The place-name *Buckland* is derived from this.

Bodkin. Originally signified a small dagger but in Elizabeth I's reign it was applied to the stiletto pin worn by ladies in their hair.

SHAKESPEARE probably used it in this sense.
When he himself might his quietus make
With a bare bodkin.

Hamlet, III, i.

To ride bodkin. To ride in a carriage between two others. Probably the allusion is to the bodkin, something so slender that it can be squeezed in anywhere.

There is barely room between Jos and Miss Sharp, who are on the front seat, Mr Osborne sitting bodkin opposite, between Captain Dobbin and Amelia.

THACKERAY: *Vanity Fair*, Ch. vi.

Bodle, or **Boddle.** A former Scottish COPPER coin of low value; said to be so-called from Bothwell, a mint-master.

To care not a boddle is equivalent to the English phrase "not to care a farthing".

Fair play, he car'd na deils a boddle.

BURNS: *Tam o'Shanter*, 110.

Bodleian Library (bod lē' an). The famous Oxford library, named from Sir Thomas Bodley who restored it in 1598. Rich in manuscript collections, in England it is second only to the BRITISH MUSEUM Library in importance, and receives copies of all publications under the Copyright Acts.

Body (O.E. *bodig*).

Body-blow. In boxing a punch between a breast-bone and the navel; figuratively, a shattering blow, a severe setback or shock.

Body colour. Paint containing body or density.

Body corporate. A group of individuals legally united into a corporation.

Body line. In CRICKET, fast bowling at the batsman rather than the wicket with the intention of forcing him to give a catch while defending his person. The accurate but dangerous bowling of Larwood and Voce won the ASHES for England 1932–1933, but roused a storm of indignation in Australia which caused a modification in the laws of cricket.

Body politic. A whole nation considered as a political corporation; the State.

Body-snatcher. One who stole newly buried corpses to sell them for dissection. *See* RESURRECTIONISTS; *Cp.* BURKE.

By a play on the words, a BUM-BAILIFF was so called, because his duty was to snatch or capture a delinquent.

A regular body, in geometry means one of the five regular solids called PLATONIC BODIES.

The heavenly bodies. The SUN, MOON, stars, etc.

The seven bodies (of alchemists). The seven metals supposed to correspond with the "seven planets".

	Planets	Metals
1.	Apollo, or the Sun	Gold
2.	Diana, or the Moon	Silver
3.	Mercury	Quicksilver
4.	Venus	Copper
5.	Mars	Iron
6.	Jupiter	Tin
7.	Saturn	Lead

To body forth. To give mental shape to an ideal form.

> And, as imagination bodies forth
> The forms of things unknown.
>
> SHAKESPEARE: *Midsummer Night's Dream*, V, i.

To keep body and soul together. To sustain life; from the notion that the SOUL gives life. The Lat. *anima*, and the Gr. *psyche*, mean both soul and life. According to Homeric mythology and the common theory of "ghosts", the departed soul retains the shape and semblance of the body. *See* ASTRAL BODY.

Bœotia (bē ō' shà). The ancient name for a district in central Greece, probably so called from its abundance of cattle. The fable is that CADMUS was conducted thence by an ox (Gr. *bous*) to the spot where he built THEBES.

Bœotian (bē ō' shàn). Rude and unlettered, a dullard. The ancient Bœotians were an agricultural and pastoral people, so the Athenians used to say that they were as dull and thick as their own atmosphere; yet Hesiod, Pindar, Corinna, Plutarch, Pelopidas, and Epaminondas were Bœotians.

Bœotian ears. Ears unable to appreciate music or rhetoric.

> Well, friend, I can assure thee thou has not got Bœotian ears (because you can appreciate the beauty of my sermons).
>
> LE SAGE: *Gil Blas*, vii, 3.

Boethius (bō ē' thi ùs). Roman philosopher and writer (c. 475–c. 525 A.D.). His manuals and translations from the Greek were widely used in the MIDDLE AGES. Both King Alfred and Chaucer translated his *De Consolatione Philosophiae*.

Boffin. A nickname used by the R.A.F. in World War II for research scientists or BACKROOM BOYS. It passed into general use in the 1940s and is said to be from the practice of a certain scientist giving his colleagues Dickensian nicknames, Mr Boffin being a character in *Our Mutual Friend*. There is a family of HOBBITS called Boffins.

Boggard or **Boggart**. A North of England name for a GOBLIN or spectre, especially one haunting a particular place. It is the same as a BROWNIE or KOBOLD and the Scottish *bogle*. When a horse took fright it was said to have seen a boggart. In the Isle of MAN a *buggane* was an evil creature with a great head and body, with long teeth and nails.

Bogey. *See* BOGY.

Bogomils. A long-lasting heretical sect which sprang up in Thrace and Bulgaria in the 10th century, named after the priest Bogomil. Their heresy was a compound of Manichæism and the errors of the Massalians, rejecting the TRINITY and the sacraments and holding that matter is evil. As a result *Bulgar* became an abusive term in the West, being identified with Bogomilism and evil practices generally. Hence the word *bugger* as a low term of abuse, etc. *See also* MANICHÆANS.

Bog-trotters. Irish tramps; from their skill in Irish bogs, trotting from tussock to tussock, either as guides or to escape pursuit.

Bogy. A HOBGOBLIN; a person or object of terror; a bugbear. The word first appeared in the 19th century and is perhaps connected with the Scottish *bogle* and so with the obsolete BUG. There was also an evil creature in Manx folklore called a *buggane* (*see* BOGGARD). A more recent suggestion is that *bogy* derives from the *Boogie* tribesmen's privateering and piratical activities in S.E. Asian waters.

Colonel Bogey. A name given in golf to an imaginary player whose score for each hole is settled by the committee of the particular club and is supposed to be the lowest that a good average player could do it in. It is usually one stroke above par at a hole.

Beating Bogey or *the Colonel*, is playing the hole in a lesser number of strokes.

Colonel Bogey is also the name of a well-known military march tune by K. J. Alford.

Bohemia, The Queen of. This old PUBLICHOUSE SIGN was in honour of Elizabeth, daughter of James I, and wife of Frederick, Elector of the Palatinate, whose election to the throne of Bohemia touched off the THIRTY YEARS WAR. George I, king of England, was their descendant. *See* WINTER.

Bohemian. A term applied to artists, writers and others of unconventional, loose or irregular habits. Originally the name was applied to a GIPSY from the belief that Bohemia was the home of the gipsies, or because the first to arrive in France (1427) came by way of Bohemia.

Bohemian Brethren. A religious sect formed from the HUSSITES which arose in Prague in the 15th century. They were the forerunners of the MORAVIANS.

Boiling point. He was at boiling point. Very angry indeed. Properly the point at which water under ordinary conditions boils (212° Fahrenheit, 100° Centigrade, 80° Réaumur).

Bold. Bold as Beauchamp. It is said that Thomas Beauchamp, Earl of Warwick, with one squire and six archers, overthrew 100 armed men at Hogges, in Normandy, in 1346. This exploit is not more incredible than that attributed to Captal-de-Buch, who, with forty followers, cleared Meaux of the JACQUERIE in 1358, slaying some 7,000!

Bold as brass. Downright impudent; without modesty. Similarly we say *brazenfaced*.

I make bold to say. I take the liberty of saying; I venture to say.

Boldon Book. A record of the possessions of the see of Durham in 1183. The DOMESDAY BOOK did not include the counties of Durham, Northumberland, Cumberland and Westmorland, probably because of their devastation by WILLIAM THE CONQUEROR. This survey, first republished in 1816 in one of the two supplementary volumes to the Domesday facsimile of 1783, partly covers the deficiency.

Boldrewood, Rolf. The pseudonym of Thomas Alexander Browne (1826–1915), author of novels on Australian life. Most notable are *Robbery under Arms*, *The Miner's Right*, and *The Squatter's Dream* dealing with BUSHRANGERS, the goldfields etc. He was born at London and taken to Melbourne by his father in 1830.

Bollandists. JESUIT WRITERS of the *Acta Sanctorum* or *Lives of the Saints*, the original editor being John Bolland, a Dutchman. The first two volumes giving the SAINTS commemorated in January were published in 1643. The disturbances of the French Revolution of 1789 led to cessation of the work in 1794 but the society was reconstituted in 1837. Sixty-seven volumes (from 1 Jan. to 10 Nov.) had been completed by 1967.

Bollen. Swollen. The past participle of the obsolete English verb, *bell*, to swell. The seed capsule of flax or cotton is called a *boll*.

> The barley was in the ear, and the flax was bolled.
> *Exod.* ix, 31.

Bolognese School. There were three periods to the Bolognese School in painting—the Early, the Roman, and the ECLECTIC. The first was founded by Marco Zoppo in the 15th century, and its best exponent was Francia. The second was founded in the 16th century by Bagnacavallo, and its chief exponents were Primaticcio, Tibaldi, and Niccolò dell'Abbate. The third was founded by Carracci at the close of the 16th century, and its best masters were Domenichino, Lanfranco, Guido, Schidone, Guercino, and Albani.

Boloney. It is all boloney. It is all nonsense, rubbish or pretence. Originally the name for a Bologna sausage. "Bunk" and "hooey" are similarly used.

Bolshevik (bol' she vik), or less correctly **Bolshevist**. Properly a member of the Russian revolutionary party under Lenin that seized power in 1917, aiming at the establishment of the supreme power of the proletariat and declaring war on capitalism. The Bolsheviks were so called from the fact that at the party conferences of 1902–1903 the Leninists were the majority group (*Bolsheviki* = majority). The defeated minority were called MENSHEVIKS.

Bolshie, or **Bolshy**. A contraction of "Bolshevik". Also used to denote a person with "red" or revolutionary tendencies, or sometimes a trouble-maker.

Bolt. Originally a short thick arrow with a blunt head as used in a cross-bow. It then came to be applied to the door fastening of similar shape, and these meanings have given rise to phrases of widely different implication. There is also an almost obsolete word *bolt* (O.Fr. *bulter*, connected with Lat. *burra*, a coarse cloth) meaning a sieve, or to sieve.

> The curious few
> Who care to sift a business to the bran
> Nor coarsely bolt it like the simpler sort.
> BROWNING: *The Ring and the Book*, i, 923.

Bolted arrow. A blunt arrow for shooting young rooks with a cross-bow; called "bolting rooks".

Bolt in tun. In HERALDRY, a bird-bolt, in pale, piercing through a tun, often used as a PUBLIC-HOUSE SIGN. The punning crest of Serjeant Bolton, who died in 1787, was "on a wreath a tun erect proper, transpierced by an arrow fesseways or". There is a Bolt-in-Tun Court off FLEET STREET, London. These punning signs or rebuses for such names as Luton, Hatton, Ashton, etc., were quite common. *See* REBUS.

Bolt upright. Straight as an arrow.

> Winsinge she was, as is a jolly colt,
> Long as a mast, and upright as a bolt.
> CHAUCER: *Miller's Tale*, 77.

A bolt from the blue. A sudden and wholly unexpected event or catastrophe, like a thunderbolt from the blue sky, or a flash of lightning without warning. Here "bolt" is used for lightning, although strictly a meteorite is a thunderbolt.

A fool's bolt is soon shot or **spent**. *See under* FOOL.

The horse bolted. The horse shot off like a bolt or arrow.

To bolt food. To swallow it quickly without

waiting to chew it; hence **to bolt a Bill,** a political phrase used of Bills passed without adequate time or opportunity for consideration.

To bolt out the truth. To blurt it out; also to bolt out, to exclude or shut out by bolting the door.

To have shot one's bolt. To have tried; to have done all that one can but with no avail. The bolt here is that of the archer.

Bolton. Bate me an ace, quoth Bolton. Give me some advantage. What you say must be qualified, as it is too strong. Ray says that a collection of proverbs was once presented to the VIRGIN QUEEN, with the assurance that it contained all the proverbs in the language; but the Queen rebuked the boaster with the proverb, "Bate me an ace, quoth Bolton", a proverb omitted in the compilation. John Bolton was one of the courtiers who used to play cards and dice with Henry VIII, and flattered the King by asking him to allow him an ACE or some advantage in the game.

Bomb. A metal shell filled with an explosive. From the Gr. *bombos*, any deep (especially humming) noise; ultimately the same word as *boom*.

Bombshell, To drop a. To suddenly deliver or release some shattering or surprising news. *Cp.* A BOLT FROM THE BLUE.

King Bomba. A nickname given to Ferdinand II, King of Naples, for his cruel and wanton bombardment of Messina in 1848. His son Francis II was called Bomba II, or *Bombalino* (Little Bomba), for his bombardment of Palermo in 1860.

Bombast literally means the produce of the bombyx, or silkworm (Gr. *bombux*); formerly applied to cotton-wool used for padding, and hence to inflated language.

> We have received your letters full of love...
> And, in our maiden council, rated them...
> As bombast and as lining to the time.
> SHAKESPEARE: *Love's Labour's Lost*, V, ii.

Bombastes Furioso (bom băs′ tēz fū ri ō′ zō). One who talks big or in an ultra bombastic way. From the hero of a burlesque opera so called, by William Barnes Rhodes, produced in 1813 in parody of ORLANDO FURIOSO.

Bombay Duck. A fish, the bummalo, which is dried and eaten with curries.

Bombiti. *See* BARISAL GUNS.

Bon Gaultier Ballads (bon gol′ tyèr). Parodies of contemporary poetry by W. E. Aytoun and Sir Theodore Martin. They first appeared in *Tait's*, *Fraser's* and *Blackwood's Magazine* in the 1840s, and in volume form in 1885.

Bon mot (bon mō) (Fr.). A good or witty saying; a pun; a clever repartee.

Bon ton (Fr.). Good manners or manners accredited by good society; also, the fashionable world.

Bon vivant (Fr.). A boon companion; one who indulges in the good things of the table.

Bon viveur (Fr.). One who enjoys high living, a fast man about town.

Bon voyage (Fr.). Have a good journey! Often used as a send-off to a departing traveller.

Bona Dea (Lat. the good goddess). A Roman goddess supposed to preside over the earth and all its blessings. She was worshipped by the VESTALS as the goddess of chastity and fertility. Her festival was 1 May and no men were allowed to be present at the celebration.

Bona Fide (bō′ na fī′ di) (Lat.). Without subterfuge or deception; really and truly. Literally, *in good faith*. **To produce bona fides** is to produce credentials, to give proof of identity or ability to perform what one professes.

Bona-roba (bō′ na rō′ ba) (Ital. *buona roba*, good stuff, fine gown, fine woman). A courtesan; so called from the smartness of her dress.

> We knew where the bona-robas were.
> SHAKESPEARE: *Henry IV, Pt. II*, III, ii.

Bonanza (Sp. a fair weather at sea, prosperity). The term was applied in the mining areas of the U.S.A. to the discovery of a rich vein or pocket when the mine was said to be *in bonanza*. Subsequently a *bonanza farm* was so called when it was very profitable and had all the latest machinery. Now in colloquial usage it implies an unexpected source of wealth or success, a run of good luck.

Bonduca (bon dū′ ka). Another form of BOADICEA, or Boudicca. Fletcher wrote a tragedy of this name in 1616.

Bone. Old thieves' slang for "good", "excellent". From the Fr. *bon*. The lozenge-shaped mark chalked by tramps on the walls of houses where they have been well received is known among the fraternity as a "bone".

Also slang for dice and counters used at cards; and the man who plays the clappers or bones in a Negro minstrel show is known as "Uncle Bones".

Bone, To. To filch, as, *I boned it*. SHAKESPEARE (*Henry VI, Pt. II*, I, iii) says, "By these ten bones, my lords," meaning the fingers and calls the ten fingers "pickers and stealers" (*Hamlet*, III, ii). So "to bone" may mean to finger, that is, "to pick and steal". Another explanation is that it is an allusion to the way a dog makes off with a bone.

You thought that I was buried deep
Quite decent-like and chary
But from her grave in Mary-bone,
They've come and boned your Mary!
                    HOOD: *Mary's Ghost*.

A bone in her mouth, or **teeth.** Said of a ship speeding along throwing up spray or foam under the bows. *Cp.* TO CUT A FEATHER *under* FEATHER.

See how she leaps, as the blasts o'ertake her,
And speeds away with a bone in her mouth.
            LONGFELLOW: *The Golden Legend*, V.

A bone of contention. A disputed point; a point not yet settled. The METAPHOR is taken from two dogs fighting for a bone.

Bone-lace. Lace made on a cushion with bobbins, which were originally made of bone.

Bone-shaker. An "antediluvian", dilapidated four-wheel cab; an old bicycle of the days before pneumatic tyres, spring saddles, etc.; any "old crock" of a vehicle.

Bred in the bone. A part of one's nature. "What's bred in the bone will come out in the flesh." A natural propensity cannot be repressed.

I have a bone in my leg. An excuse given to children for not moving from one's seat. Similarly "I have a bone in my arm", and must be excused using it for the present.

I have a bone in my throat. I cannot talk; I cannot answer your question.

Napier's bones. *See* NAPIER.

One end is sure to be bone. It won't come up to expectation. "All is not gold that glitters."

To give one a bone to pick. To throw a sop to CERBERUS; to give a lucrative appointment to a troublesome opponent to silence him, or to a colleague who is for any reason an embarrassment. It is used in political life, by removing members of the Commons to the Lords by gift of a peerage or by giving appointments in nationalized industries, etc.

To have a bone to pick with someone. To have an unpleasant matter to discuss and settle. This is another allusion from the kennel. Two dogs and one bone invariably form an excellent basis for a fight.

To make no bones about the matter. To do it, say it, etc., without hesitation or scruple; to offer no opposition, present no difficulty. Dice are called bones and the Fr. *flatter le dé* (to slide the dice, to soften a thing down) is the opposite of our expression. *To make no bones* of a thing is not to "make much of" or coax the dice in order to show favour. Hence *without more bones*, with- out further scruple or objection.

To make old bones. To live to a ripe old age.

To point a bone at (Austr.). To place a death curse on someone. In an Australian aboriginal ceremony a small sharp bone was pointed at the person to whom ill was wished while the curse was uttered.

Boney (bō′ ni). "If you aren't a good boy Boney will catch you," was an old threat from a children's nurse or harassed parent; Boney being NAPOLEON Bonaparte, whose threatened invasion of England was a real scare in the early years of the 19th century.

Bonfire. Originally a *bone-fire*, that is, a fire made of bones. The *Festyvall* of 1493, printed by Wynkyn de Worde in 1515, says, "in the worship of St. John the people ... made three manner of fires: one was of clean bones and no wood, and that is called a bone fire; another of clean wood and no bones, and that is called a wood-fire ... and the third is made of wood and bones, and is called St. John's fire." Also:

In some parts of Lincolnshire ... they make fires in the public streets ... with bones of oxen, sheep, etc, ... heaped together ... hence came the origin of bon-fires.
                              LELAND (1546).

Bonhomme. *See* JACQUES.

Boniface. A sleek, good-tempered, jolly landlord; from Farquhar's comedy of the *Beaux' Stratagem* (1707).

St. Boniface. The APOSTLE of Germany, a West Saxon whose English name was Wynfrith (680–754).

St. Boniface's cup. An extra cup of wine; an excuse for an extra glass. Pope Boniface, we are told in the *Ebrietatis Encomium*, instituted an indulgence to those who drank his good health after grace, or the health of the POPE of the day. This probably refers to Boniface VI, an abandoned profligate, who was elected Pope by the mob in 896 and died fifteen days later. The two Saints Boniface to be Pope were Boniface I (418–422) and Boniface IV (608–615).

Bonne Bouche (Fr.). A delicious morsel; a titbit.

Bonnet. In slang, a player at a gaming table or an accomplice at auctions, to lure others to play or bid, so called because he blinds the eyes of his dupes, just as if he had "bonneted them" or crashed their hats down over their eyes.

Balmoral bonnet. A flat Scottish cap.

Bonnet lairds. Local magnates or petty squires of SCOTLAND who wore the BRAID BONNET, like the common people.

Bonnet-piece. A gold coin of James V of SCOTLAND, on which the king's head wears a bonnet.

Bonnet Rouge. The red CAP OF LIBERTY worn by the leaders of the French Revolution in 1789.

Braid bonnet. The old Scottish cap, made of milled woollen, without seam or lining.

Glengarry bonnet. The highland bonnet, which rises to a point; named after the valley in Inverness.

He has a bee in his bonnet. *See* BEE.

He has a green bonnet. He has failed in trade. In France it used to be customary, even in the 17th century, for bankrupts to wear a green bonnet (cloth cap).

To cast one's bonnet over a windmill. To throw caution to the winds. To decide on a hazardous course of action.

Bonnie Dundee. John Graham of Claverhouse, Viscount Dundee (1649–1689). A noted supporter of the Stuart cause and a relative of Montrose. He was killed at the battle of Killiecrankie.

Bonny-clabber. Sour buttermilk used as a drink (Irish *bainne*, milk; *claba*, thick or thickened).

> It is against my freehold, my inheritance,
> My Magna Charta, *cor laetificat*,
> To drink such balderdash or bonny-clabber!
> Give me good wine!
> BEN JONSON: *The New Inn*, I, i.

Booby. A spiritless fool, who suffers himself to be imposed upon. The player who comes in last in whist-drives, etc.; the lowest boy in the class.

> Ye bread-and-butter rogues, do ye run from me?
> An my side would give me leave, I would so hunt ye,
> Ye porridge-gutted slaves, ye real-broth boobies!
> BEAUMONT and FLETCHER:
> *Humorous Lieutenant*, III, vii.

A species of gannet (*Sula piscator*) is called a booby, from its apparent stupidity.

A booby will never make a hawk. The booby, that allows itself to be fleeced by other birds, will never become a bird of prey itself.

Booby-prize. A prize, often of a humorous or worthless kind, given to the "booby" at whist-drives, parties, etc., *i.e.* to the player who has the lowest score, etc.

Booby trap. A trap set to discomfit an unsuspecting victim, such as placing an object on top of a door to fall on whoever opens it. More deadly "booby traps" are used in warfare.

To beat the booby. A sailor's term for warming the hands by striking them under the armpits.

Boogie-woogie. A style of piano playing. The left hand maintains a heavy repetitive pattern of eight beats to the bar over which the right hand improvises at will. Probably developed in the Middle West by JAZZ musicians early in the 20th century. It owes its name to Clarence "Pinetop" Smith's *Pinetop's Boogie-Woogie* (1928). *Boogie* in U.S. slang is a negro performer and *woogie* a rhyming additive. *Cp.* BLUES; RAGTIME; SWING.

Boojum. *See* SNARK.

Book (O.E. *boc*; Dan. *beuke*; Ger. *Buche*, a beech tree). Possibly derived from the use of beech bark for carving names before the days of printing.

In betting, the *book* is the record of people's bets on the various horses made by the *bookmaker*.

In WHIST, bridge, etc., the *book* is the first six tricks taken by either side. The whole pack of cards is sometimes called a "book"—short for "the DEVIL'S PICTURE-BOOK".

Bell, book and candle. *See under* BELL.

Beware of a man of one book. Never attempt to controvert the statement of anyone in his own special subject. A shepherd who cannot read will know more about sheep than the wisest bookworm. This caution is given by St. THOMAS AQUINAS.

Book-keeping is a system of keeping debtor and creditor accounts in books provided for the purpose, either by single or by double entry. In the former each debit or credit is entered only once in the ledger, either as a debit or credit item, under the customer's or salesman's name; in double entry, each item is entered twice in the ledger, once on the debit and once on the credit side. The daily debits and credits are entered in the **Day book** and these are ultimately "posted" in the ledger. In the **Waste book** each transaction is entered as it occurs.

Bookmaker, or **Bookie.** A professional betting man who makes his living by taking bets and recording his transactions.

Bookworm. One who is always poring over books, so called in allusion to the maggot that eats holes in books, and lives in and on their leaves.

He is in my books, or **in my good books.** The former is the older phrase; both mean to be in favour. The word book was at one time used more widely, a single sheet or even a list being called a book. *To be on my books* is to be on my list of friends.

He is in my black, or **bad books.** In disfavour. *See* BLACK BOOKS.

On the books. On the list of a club, on the list of candidates, or any official or members' list. At Cambridge University they say "on the boards".

Out of my books. Not in favour; no longer

on my list of friends.

That does not suit my book. Does not accord with my arrangements. The reference is to the betting-book of the BOOKMAKER in which bets are formally entered.

The Battle of the Books. *See under* BATTLE; BOYLE CONTROVERSY.

The Book of Books. The BIBLE; also called simply "the Book", or "the good Book".

The Book of Common Prayer. The official liturgy of the CHURCH OF ENGLAND first issued in 1549 under Cranmer. Modified in 1552, 1559, and 1604 it was revised after the RESTORATION and reissued in 1662. The amended Prayer Books of 1927 and 1928 were approved by Convocation but rejected by PARLIAMENT.

Since the 1960s *The Book of Common Prayer* has been increasingly displaced by alternative forms of service commonly known as Series 1, Series 2 and Series 3. The *Alternative Services Book* of 1980 contains three alternative forms of Communion Service, namely, revised versions of Series 1 and 2 (largely based on the *Book of Common Prayer*), and the more controversial Series 3 (Revised) in modern English. The other services are all in the Series 3 idiom, those for the Visitation and Communion of the Sick being dropped. None of the readings (formerly called *lessons*) is from the AUTHORIZED VERSION (*see* BIBLE) and perhaps more properly it should have been called "The Replacement Service Book", although this was not supposed to be the intention.

The Book of Kells. An exceptionally fine illustrated copy of the Gospels in Latin. It is kept in the Library of Trinity College, Dublin, and probably dates from the 8th century.

The Book of Life, or **of Fate.** In BIBLE language, a register of the names of those who are to inherit eternal life (*Phil*. iv, 3; *Rev*. xx, 12).

The Book of the Dead. A collection of ancient Egyptian texts, both religious and magical, concerned with guidance for the safe conduct of the soul through Amenti (the Egyptian HADES). The Egyptians called it *The Book of Going Forth by Day* and copies, or parts of it, were buried with the mummy. There is a variety of texts.

To be booked. Not to be available; to have a previous commitment in one's engagement book or diary. Also to have something booked or entered up against one, hence caught. Currently applied to being entered in a policeman's notebook for an offence and subsequently charged.

To book a ticket, or **seat.** Now means to purchase a ticket for a theatre, railway journey, etc. In coaching days and in the early days of railways, tickets sold at Booking Offices were written out and entered up in the books by clerks.

To book it. To take down an order; to enter it in a book; to make a memorandum.

To bring him to book. To call him to account; to make him prove his words. Make him show that what he says accords with the records, the written agreement, or the book which treats of the subject.

To kiss the book. *See* KISS.

To know one's book. To know one's own interest; to know on which side one's bread is buttered (*see under* BREAD). Also, to have made up one's mind.

To speak by the book. To speak with meticulous exactness. To speak *literatim*, according to what is in the book.

To speak like a book. To speak with great precision and accuracy; to be full of information. Often used of a pedant.

To speak without the book. To speak without authority; from memory only, without consulting or referring to the book.

To take one's name off the books. To withdraw from a club, from an organization or register, etc. In the passive voice it means to be excluded. *See* ON THE BOOKS, *above*.

To take a leaf out of someone else's book. To follow someone else's example; to copy.

Boom meaning the spar of a ship, etc., is the Dutch *boom* equivalent to our *beam*.

Booming along. Going along at a merry pace with a fair wind. A sailing ship under full sail with studding sails set (stun'sls), which were held at the foot by light booms extending from the yards, was said to *boom along*.

Boom passenger. A convict on board a transport ship, who was chained to a boom when made to take his daily exercise.

Boomer. Since the early 19th century an Australian name for the kangaroo, the national animal; possibly of Tasmanian aboriginal origin.

Boomerang. A remarkable wooden missile developed by the Australian aborigines, bent in a curve and varying from two feet to two feet nine inches long, which when thrown returns near to or behind the thrower.

Metaphorically a *boomerang* is a scheme or proposal that recoils upon its originator. A scheme can also be said *to boomerang* upon its author, *i.e.* to have repercussions to his disadvantage.

Boon Companion. A convivial or congenial

companion. (Fr. *bon*, good.)

Boon work, or **Bene work,** or **Precariæ.** Special work at request (*ad precem* or *at bene*), *i.e.*, extra work done by the mediæval VILLEIN from Saxon times for the lord at haytime and harvest, etc. *Boon days* were in addition to the normal WEEK WORK.

Boondoggling. An expression used in the early 1930s to denote useless spending, usually with reference to the U.S. government's expenditure in the effort to combat the depression. It apparently derives from the Scottish word *boondoggle*, meaning a marble you receive as a gift without having worked for it.

Boone, Daniel (1733–1820). American pioneer and frontiersman renowned for his prowess and exploits, who became a hunter when only twelve years old and at one time was captured and adopted by the Shawnees. He is now part of American folk-lore.

Boosening (M.E. *bousen*, to drink or tipple). An old method of treating insanity by immersing the patient in cold water. *See* BOOZE.

Boot. An instrument of torture made of four pieces of narrow board nailed together, of a length to fit the leg. Wedges were inserted till the victim confessed or fainted.

> All your empirics could never do the like cure upon the gout as the rack in England or your Scotch boots.
>
> JOHN MARSTON: *The Malcontent* (1604).

Boot and saddle. The order to cavalry to get packed and ready to go. It is a corruption of the Fr. *boute selle* (put on the saddle), and has nothing to do with boots.

Boot-hill (western U.S.A.). A frontier cemetery, thus called because so many of its occupants "died with their boots on".

Boot-jack. *See* JACK.

Bootless errand. An unprofitable or futile errand. *Cp.* I WILL GIVE YOU THAT TO BOOT, *below*.

> I sent him
> Bootless home and weather-beaten back.
> SHAKESPEARE: *Henry IV, Pt. I*, III, i.

Bootlegger. One who traffics illegally in alcoholic liquor, derived from the smuggling of flasks of liquor in boot legs.

Bootlegging became a major racket in the U.S.A. during the years of prohibition (1920–1934), MOONSHINERS and RUM-RUNNERS playing their part. Criminal elements took over and the profits of bootlegging fostered the growth of underworld bosses like CAPONE.

Bootlicker. A TOADY or creep. *See* TO LICK A MAN'S BOOTS *under* LICK.

Bootneck. A MARINE.

Boots. An inn or hotel servant whose duty it is to clean the boots. Dickens has a Christmas Tale (1855) called *The Boots of the Holly-tree Inn*.

The BISHOP with the shortest period of service in the HOUSE OF LORDS, whose duty it is to read prayers, is colloquially known as the "Boots"; the name is also applied to the youngest officer in a regimental mess.

I will give you that to boot, *i.e.* in addition. The O.E. *bot* means advantage, good, profit, as in Milton's "Alas! what boots it with incessant care" (*Lycidas*), Alas! what profit is it...?

It also meant compensation paid for injury; reparation. *Cp.* HOUSE-BOTE.

> As anyone shall be more powerful...or higher in degree, shall he the more deeply make boot for sin, and pay for every misdeed.
>
> *Laws of King Ethelred*.

Like old boots. Slang for vigorously; "like anything". "I was working like old boots," means "I was doing my very utmost."

Puss in Boots. *See under* PUSS.

Seven-leagued boots. The boots worn by the giant in the fairy tale called *The Seven-leagued Boots*. A pace taken in them measured seven leagues.

The boot is on the other foot. The CASE is altered; you and I have changed places; you have changed your tune now that the circumstances are different.

The order of the boot. "The sack"; notice of dismissal from one's employment or office.

To die with one's boots on. To die fighting.

To go to bed in one's boots. To be very tipsy.

To have one's heart in one's boots. To be utterly despondent.

When bale is highest boot is nighest. *See* BALE.

Boötes (bō oo′ tēz). Greek for "the ploughman"; the name of the constellation which contains the bright star, Arcturus (*see* ARCTIC REGION). According to ancient mythology Boötes invented the plough, to which he yoked two oxen, and at death was taken to HEAVEN with his plough and oxen and made a constellation. HOMER calls it "the wagoner", *i.e.* the wagoner of CHARLES'S WAIN, the Great Bear. *See* BEAR.

Booze. To drink steadily and continually. Though regarded as slang this is the M.E. *bousen*, to drink deeply, probably connected with Dut. *buizen*, and Ger. *bousen*, to drink to excess. Spenser uses the word in his description of Gluttony:

Still as he rode, he somewhat still did eat,
And in his hand did beare a bousing can,
Of which he supt so oft, that on his seat
His drunken corse he scarse upholden can.
Faerie Queene, I, iv, 22.

Bor. An East Anglian form of address to a lad or young man as, "Well, bor, I saw the mauther you spoke of"—*i.e.* "Well, boy, I saw the lass...". It is apparently O.E. *gebur*, neighbour, similar in use to Dut. *buur*, neighbour.

Borachio (bô ra' chō). Originally a wine bottle made of goat-skin; hence a drunkard, one who fills himself with wine. Sp. *borracha*; Ital. *borraccia*.

A follower of Don John, in SHAKESPEARE'S *Much Ado About Nothing*, is called Borachio; he thus plays upon his own name:

I will, like a true drunkard [borachio], utter all to thee.

III, iii.

Borak, or **Al Borak** (bôr' ak) (the lightning). The animal brought by GABRIEL to carry MOHAMMED to the seventh HEAVEN, and itself received into PARADISE. It had the face of a man but the cheeks of a HORSE; its eyes were like jacinths, but brilliant as the stars; it had the wings of an EAGLE, spoke with the voice of a man, and glittered all over with radiant light.

To poke Borak at. To make fun of or jeer at. From an Australian aboriginal word for "banter". It has been suggested as a possible source of BARRACK.

Bordar. In Anglo-Saxon England, a VILLEIN of the lowest rank who did menial service to his lord in return for his cottage; the *bordars* or *bordarii* were the labourers, and the word is from the Med. Lat. *bordarius*, a cottager. *See* COTTAR.

Border, The. The frontier of England and Scotland which from the 11th to the 15th century was a field of constant forays.

Border Minstrel. Sir Walter Scott (1771–1832), because he sang of the Border.

The Border States. The five "slave" states (Delaware, Maryland, Virginia, Kentucky, and Missouri) which lay next to the "free" states. So called in the American CIVIL WAR, 1861–1865.

Boreas (bôr' ë ăs). In Greek mythology, the god of the north wind, and the north wind itself. He was the son of Astræus, a TITAN, and Eos, the morning, and lived in a cave of Mount Hæmus, in Thrace.

Hence *boreal*, of or pertaining to the north.

In radiant streams,
Bright over Europe, bursts the Boreal morn.
THOMSON: *Autumn*, 98.

Borgias (bôr' jàz). **A glass of wine with the**

Borgias was a great and sometimes fatal honour, for Caesar and Lucretia Borgia, children of Pope Alexander VI, were reputed to be adept in ridding themselves of foes or unwanted friends by inducing them to pledges in poisoned wine.

Born. Born in the gutter. Of base origins; the child of beggars or vagrants.

Born in the purple. *See under* PURPLE; PORPHYROGENITUS.

Born with a silver spoon in one's mouth. Born to good luck; born with hereditary wealth. The reference is to the usual gift of a silver spoon by the godparents (*see* APOSTLE SPOONS). The lucky child does not need to wait for the gift for it inherits it at birth. A phrase with a similar meaning is **born under a lucky star;** here the allusion is to ASTROLOGY.

Born to be hanged. "He that is born to be hanged shall never be drowned." An old proverb quoted in different forms by SHAKESPEARE.

I have great comfort from this fellow: methinks he hath no drowning mark upon him; his complexion is perfect gallows.
The Tempest, I, i.

Go, go; begone to save your ship from wreck,
Which cannot perish, having thee aboard,
Being destined to a drier death on shore.
Two Gentlemen of Verona, I, i.

In all my born days. Ever since I was born; in all my experience.

Not born yesterday. Not inexperienced and gullible; not to be taken in.

Poets are born, not made. One can never be a poet by mere training if one has been born without the "divine afflatus". A translation of the Lat. phrase *Poeta nascitur non fit*, of which an extension is *Nascimur poetae fimus oratores*, we are born poets, we are made orators. The idea has, of course, been extended to other callings.

Borough or **Burgh.** Originally, a corporate town with privileges granted by royal charter. By the Local Government Act of 1888 many large towns became county boroughs with the same governing powers as a county, but they were abolished by an act of 1972. By the same act non-county boroughs lost their status except in the Greater London Council area set up by the London Government Act of 1963. Subsequently various District Councils have been granted the title of borough by royal charter, thus enabling their chairmen to become mayors. The word *borough* has lost its historical meaning since it has been bestowed upon rural districts.

A Parliamentary Borough was one that sent at least one "burgess" or member to PARLIAMENT.

A Rotten, or **Pocket Borough** was a borough of much diminished population with the parliamentary seat at the disposal of a patron (frequently the Crown). Fifty-six such boroughs were disfranchised by the Reform Act of 1832.

Borough English. A custom abolished in 1925 by which real estate passed to the youngest instead of the eldest son. It was of English origin and was so called to distinguish it from Norman custom. If there was no son, then the youngest daughter was sole heiress; failing a daughter, the youngest brother, then the youngest sister, etc. Land held by Borough English was sometimes termed *Cradle-Holding* or *Cradle-land*. It was found in Kent, Middlesex, Surrey, Sussex and Somerset. *See* GAVELKIND.

The Borough, used as a proper name denotes SOUTHWARK, a district rich in historical and literary associations. The TABARD INN, BANKSIDE, and the MARSHALSEA are but examples.

It is also the title of a collection of poetical tales by George Crabbe (1810) about the Suffolk borough of Aldeburgh, one of which forms the theme of Benjamin Britten's opera *Peter Grimes*.

Borrow. Originally a noun (O.E. *borg*) meaning a pledge or security; the modern sense of the verb depended originally on the actual pledging of something as security for the loan. Even today the idea that a loan is the property of the lender and must be returned some day is always present. The noun sense is seen in the old oath *St. George to borowe*, which is short for "I take St. George as pledge," or "as surety"; also in:

Ye may retain as borrows my two priests.
SCOTT: *Ivanhoe*, ch. xxxiii.

Borrowed, or **borrowing days.** The last three days of MARCH are said to be "borrowed from APRIL", as is shown by the proverb in Ray's Collection:

"March borrows three days of April, and they are ill." One old rhyme says:

March borrowed frae Aprile
Three days an' they were ill;
The first o' them was wind and weet,
The second o' them was snaw an' sleet,
The third o' them was sic a freeze,
That the birds' legs stack to the trees.

In Scotland, FEBRUARY also has its "borrowed days", the 12th, 13th, and 14th, which are said to be borrowed from JANUARY. If these prove stormy the year will be one of good weather; if fine, the year will be foul. They are called *Faoilteach*.

Borrowed time, To live on. To continue to live after every reasonable presumption is that one should be dead, *i.e.* living on time borrowed from Death.

Bosey (Austr.). In CRICKET, another name for a GOOGLY, so named from its inventor, the English bowler B. J. T. Bosanquet, who toured Australia in 1903–1904. The term was also applied in World War II to a single bomb dropped from a plane.

Bosh. A Turkish word meaning empty, worthless. It was popularized by James Morier in his novel *Ayesha* (1834), and other Eastern romances.

To talk bosh. To talk rubbish, to be quite on the wrong track.

Bosky. On the verge of drunkenness. A slang term possibly connected with the legitimate *bosky* meaning bushy, hence overshadowed, obscured.

And with each end of thy blue bow dost crown
My bosky acres and my unshrubb'd down.
SHAKESPEARE: *Tempest*, IV, i.

Bosom friend. A very dear friend. Nathan says it "lay in his bosom, and was unto him as a daughter" (II *Sam*. xii, 3). St. JOHN is represented in the New Testament as the "bosom friend" of Jesus.

Bosom sermons. Sermons committed to memory and learnt by heart; not extempore or delivered from notes.

The preaching from "bosom sermons", or from writing, being considered a lifeless practice before the Reformation.
BLUNT: *Reformation in England*, p. 179.

Bosporus (bos' pôr ùs), or less correctly **Bosphorus,** is a Greek compound meaning "ox-ford". The Thracian Bosporus unites the Sea of Marmora with the EUXINE or BLACK SEA. Greek legend says that ZEUS, enamoured of Io, changed her into a white heifer from fear of HERA, to flee from whom Io swam across the strait, which was thence called *bos porus*, the passage of the cow. Hera discovered the trick, and sent a gadfly to torment Io, who was made to wander, in a state of frenzy, from land to land, ultimately finding rest on the banks of the Nile. The wanderings of the Argive princess were a favourite theme among ancient writers.

Boss. (1) A master, is the Dut. *baas*, head of the household. Hence the great man, chief, overseer, and originally more widely used in the U.S.A. than England, for political leaders and financial magnates, etc. Thus **to boss someone about** is to try to take charge of them, to order them about, etc.

(2) *Boss* is also a protuberance like the shield or a raised ornament in architecture, etc. Hence **boss-backed,** a good old word for "hump-backed".

(3) **Boss-eyed.** Slang for having a bad squint or one eye injured, or only one eye.

Hence, **boss one's shot,** to miss one's aim, as a person with a defective eye might be expected to do; and **a boss,** a bad shot. In archery the *boss* is the straw-packed base to which the target proper is affixed. Thus to shoot clumsily, missing the target altogether and lodging one's arrow in the boss, would be a "boss shot", and the archer derisively dubbed "boss-eyed" by the more expert.

Boston. From colonial days until after the CIVIL WAR, it was the intellectual, social and literary capital of America, and was known as "the HUB".

> And this is good old Boston,
> The home of the bean and the cod,
> Where the Lowells talk only to Cabots,
> And the Cabots talk only to God.
>
> J. C. BOSSIDY: *On the Aristocracy of Harvard*.

Boston Tea-Party (1773). An incident serving to worsen the relations between Great Britain and her American colonies. By the Tea Act of 1773 the East India Company was enabled to ship its surplus stocks of tea direct to America to the disadvantage of American merchants. At Boston, patriots, disguised as Indians, boarded the tea ships and dumped all the tea into the harbour. As a consequence the British PARLIAMENT passed the INTOLERABLE ACTS.

Botanomancy (bot' ăn ō măn si). DIVINATION by leaves. One method was by writing sentences on leaves which were exposed to the wind, the answer being gathered from those which were left; another was through the crackling made by leaves of various plants when thrown on the fire or crushed in the hands.

Botany Bay. An inlet in the coast of New South Wales five miles south of Sydney discovered by Captain Cook in 1770, and so named by him on account of the great variety of new plants observed there. Although the first convicts landed there in 1788 the settlement was established at Sydney, Port Jackson. In contemporary parlance Botany Bay was an alternative name for New South Wales and **to be sent to Botany Bay** meant sentence of transportation to Australia.

> One of the great difficulties in Botany Bay is to find proper employment for the great mass of convicts who are sent out.
>
> SYDNEY SMITH: *Botany Bay* (*Edinburgh Review*, July 1819).

Botany wool is so called because Australian woollens were first made at Botany Bay by Simeon Lord in 1815.

Both ends against the middle, To play (western U.S.A.). A method of rigging a pack of cards in faro, from which the expression became common for any sharp practice

with a risk of being found out.

Bothie (perhaps from Gaelic *Bothag*). A humble cottage or hut. Particularly applied to the one-room farm servants' dwelling in the north-east of Scotland which was often part of the stabling. The *bothie system* was formerly widespread, and the unmarried men were crowded into these sparsely furnished habitations, often preparing their own food.

Botley Assizes. The joke is to ask a Botley man, "When are the Assizes coming on?" The reference is to the tradition that the men of Botley once hanged a man because he could not drink so deep as his neighbours.

Bo-tree. The pipal tree or *Ficus religiosa* of India, allied to the banyan and so called from Pali *Bodhi*, perfect knowledge, because it is under one of these trees that GAUTAMA attained enlightenment and so became the BUDDHA. At the ruined city of Anuradhapura in Ceylon is a bo-tree reputed to have grown from a cutting sent by King ASOKA in 288 B.C.

Bottle. The accepted commercial size of a wine bottle is one holding $26\frac{2}{3}$ fluid ounces per reputed quart. Large bottles are named as follows:

Magnum	holding	2	ordinary bottles.
Double-magnum or *Jeroboam*	,,	4	,, ,,
Rehoboam	,,	6	,, ,,
Methuselah	,,	8	,, ,,
Salmanazar	,,	12	,, ,,
Balthazar	,,	16	,, ,,
Nebuchadnezzar	,,	20	,, ,,

A *Nip* is $\frac{1}{4}$ of a bottle, a *Baby* is $\frac{1}{8}$.

A three-bottle man. A toper who can drink three bottles of port at a sitting.

Bottle-chart. A chart of ocean surface currents made from the track of sealed bottles thrown from ships into the sea.

Bottle-holder. One who gives moral but not material support. The allusion is to boxing or prize-fighting, where the attendant on each combatant, whose duty it is to wipe off blood, to refresh him with water, and to do other services to encourage his man to persevere and win, is called "the bottle-holder".

> Lord Palmerston considered himself the bottle-holder of oppressed States... He was the steadfast partisan of constitutional liberty in every part of the world.
>
> *The Times*.

Bottle-neck. Metaphorically, a narrowing of the main highway impeding the smooth flow of traffic; an impediment holding up production or trade.

Bottle-washer. Chief agent; the principal man employed by another; a factotum. The full phrase—which is usually applied more or less sarcastically—is "chief cook and bottle-washer".

Bottled moonshine. Unpractical social and benevolent schemes, as UTOPIA, Coleridge's PANTISOCRACY, the dreams of Owen, Fourier, St. Simon etc.

> Godwin! Hazlitt! Coleridge! Where now are their "novel philosophies and systems"? Bottled moonshine, which does not improve with keeping.
> BIRRELL: *Obiter Dicta*, p. 109 (1885).

Brought up on the bottle. Said of a baby which is artificially fed instead of being nursed at the breast.

Looking for a needle in a bottle of hay, or **in a haystack.** Looking for a very small article amidst a mass of other things. Bottle here is a diminutive of the Fr. *botte*, a bundle.

> Methinks I have a great desire to a bottle of hay.
> SHAKESPEARE: *Midsummer Night's Dream*, IV, i.

To be bottled. A colloquialism for being drunk.

To bottle up one's feelings, emotions, etc. To suppress them; to hold them well under control.

To put new wine into old bottles. A saying found in *Matt.* ix, 17; typical of incongruity. New wine expands as it matures. If put in a new skin (bottle), the skin expands with it; if in an old skin, when the wine expands, the skin bursts.

Bottom. Of a ship, the lower part of the hull, usually below the waterline; hence the hull itself or the whole ship as in such phrases as *goods imported in British bottoms* or *in foreign bottoms*.

A vessel is said to have a *full bottom* when the hull construction allows large stowage, and a *sharp bottom* when it is capable of speed.

At bottom. Radically, fundamentally; as, "the young prodigal lived a riotous life, but was good at bottom", or below the surface.

A horse of good bottom means of good stamina, good foundation.

From the bottom of my heart. Without reservation.

He was at the bottom of it. He really instigated it or prompted it.

Never venture all in one bottom. Do not put all your eggs in one basket. This has allusion to the marine use of the word.

> My ventures are not in one bottom trusted.
> SHAKESPEARE: *Merchant of Venice*, I, i.

To have no bottom. To be unfathomable; to be unstable.

To get to the bottom of the matter. To ascertain the entire truth; to "BOLT (sieve) a matter to its bran".

To knock the bottom out of anything. *See under* KNOCK.

To stand on one's own bottom. To be independent. "Every tub must stand on its own bottom."

To touch bottom. To reach the lowest depth.

Bottom drawer. *See under* DRAWER.

Bottom the Weaver. A man who fancies he can do everything, and do it better than anyone else. Shakespeare has drawn him as profoundly ignorant, brawny, mock heroic, and with an overflow of self-conceit. He is in one part of *Midsummer Night's Dream* represented with an ass's head, and Titania, queen of the fairies, under a spell caresses him as an ADONIS.

The name is very appropriate, as one meaning of *bottom* is a ball of thread used in weaving, etc. Thus in Clark's *Heraldry* we read, "The coat of Badland is argent, three bottoms in fess gules, the thread or."

Bottomless Pit, The. Hell is so called in *Revelation*, xx, 1. *See* ABADDON. William Pitt, the younger (1759–1806), was humorously called **the bottomless Pitt,** in allusion to his thinness.

Boudicca. Nowadays the preferred form of BOADICEA.

Bought and Sold, or **Bought, Sold, and Done For.** Ruined, done for, outwitted.

> It would make a man mad as a buck, to be so bought and sold.
> SHAKESPEARE: *Comedy of Errors*, III, i.

Bouillabaisse (boo′ ya bās). A soup, for which Marseilles is celebrated, made of fish boiled with herbs in water or white wine.

> This Bouillabaisse a noble dish is—
> A sort of soup, or broth, or brew
> Or hotchpotch of all sorts of fishes
> That Greenwich never could outdo:
> Green herbs, red peppers, mussels, saffron,
> Soles, onions, garlic, roach and dace;
> All these you eat at Terre's tavern,
> In that one dish of Bouillabaisse.
> W. M. THACKERAY: *The Ballad of Bouillabaisse*.

Boulangism (boo lonj′ izm). The name given to a wave of political hysteria that swept over France, especially in Paris, in 1886–1887, and to the movement in support of General Boulanger (1837–1891). As Minister of War (1886–1887), he achieved some popularity for army reforms, but more particularly for his handsome military figure and identification with the policy of revenge against Germany. Deprivation of command (1888) increased his popularity, but his plans for a COUP D'ÉTAT were never realized. His flight abroad, when sentenced to exile (1889) for crimes against the Republic, lost him his supporters, and he shot himself in Brussels in 1891.

Boule, or **Boulle** (bool). A kind of marquetry

in which brass, GOLD, or enamelled metal is inlaid into wood or tortoiseshell, named after André Charles Boulle (1642–1732), the celebrated cabinet-maker who worked for Louis XIV on the decorations and furniture at VERSAILLES. With English furniture dealers **buhl** (a Germanized form of the name) or **buhlwork** came to denote inlay work of this sort, however inferior or cheap.

Bounce. Brag, swagger; boastful and mendacious exaggeration.

> He speaks plain cannon, fire, and smoke, and bounce.
>
> SHAKESPEARE: *King John*, II, i.

On the bounce. Ostentatiously swaggering. Trying to achieve some object "on the bounce" is trying to attain one's end through making an impression that is unwarrantable.
That's a bouncer. A gross exaggeration, a braggart's lie. A *bouncing* lie is a *thumping* lie and a *bouncer* is a *thumper*. A *bouncer* is also a "chucker-out" at a dance-hall, etc.

Boundary Rider. An employee on an Australian pastoral station who looks for and repairs damaged fences, attends to water supplies and treats sick stock.

Bounds, Beating the. An old custom still kept up in a few English parishes, of going round the parish boundaries on Holy Thursday or ASCENSION DAY. The schoolchildren, accompanied by the clergymen and parish officers, walked round the boundaries, which the boys struck with peeled willow-wands. The boys were sometimes "whipped" at intervals and water was sometimes poured on them from house windows "to make them remember" the boundaries.

In Scotland beating the bounds was called *Riding the marches* (bounds), and in England the day is sometimes called *gang-day*.

Bounty. *See* QUEEN ANNE'S BOUNTY; ROYAL BOUNTY.

Bounty-jumpers. Men, often foreigners, who enlisted during the American CIVIL WAR and, having been paid their bounty, promptly deserted to re-enlist elsewhere.

Bounty, The Mutiny of the. This celebrated mutiny broke out on 28 April 1789, and was as much due to the mutineers' attachment to the damsels of Otaheite as to the exacting discipline of Captain William Bligh. The *Bounty* had been engaged in a bread-fruit collecting voyage in the South Seas and Bligh was unaware of the impending mutiny. The mutineers reached Tahiti and some of them, accompanied by native men and women, sailed to Pitcairn Island, where they were not discovered until 1808, John Adams being the only surviving mutineer. Bligh, with 18 loyal companions, was set adrift in an open boat and made the remarkable passage of 3,618 nautical miles to Timor near Java.

Bourbon (boor' bon). The family name of the kings of France from 1589 to 1793 (Henry IV, Louis XIII, XIV, XV, XVI), and from 1814 to 1830 (Louis XVIII, Charles X), derived from the seigniory of Bourbon, in the Bourbonnais in central France; the family is a branch of the house of CAPET. Bourbons also ruled in Spain, Naples and Sicily, and later in Lucca, Parma and Piacenza, as a result of the accession of Philip of Anjou (grandson of Louis XIV) to the Spanish throne in 1700.

It was said of the restored Bourbons that they had learned nothing and forgotten nothing. Hence in the U.S.A. the name *Bourbon* was applied to the Democratic Party leaders of the southern States, with the implication that they were guided by a pre-CIVIL WAR outlook.

In the U.S.A. the term *Bourbon* is also used for a whisky made from Indian corn, sometimes with rye or malt added. The first Kentucky whisky was made by a BAPTIST clergyman named Elijah Craig at Royal Spring, near Georgetown, in 1789. Georgetown (now County seat of Scott County) was then in Bourbon (*pron.* běr' bŭn) County.

Bourgeois (Fr.). Our *burgess*; a member of the class between the "upper" and "working" classes. It includes merchants, shopkeepers and professional people, the so-called "middle class".

In typography *bourgeois* (*pron.* burjois') is the name of a size of type between long PRIMER and brevier.

Bourgeoisie (Fr.). The merchants, manufacturers, master-tradesmen, etc., considered as a class; much maligned since the days of Karl Marx who portrayed it as the exploiting class.

> The bourgeoisie has stripped of its halo every occupation hitherto honoured and looked up to with reverent awe. It has converted the physician, the lawyer, the priest, the poet, the man of science, into its paid wage-labourers.
>
> MARX and ENGELS: *Communist Manifesto*, 1848.

More recently the word has also been used to denote the conventional, narrow-minded and philistine elements of the middle classes. *See* PHILISTINES.

Bouse. *See* BOOZE.

Boustrapa. A nickname of NAPOLEON III; in allusion to his unsuccessful attempts at a COUP D'ÉTAT at *Bou*logne (1840) and *Stra*sbourg (1836) and the successful one at *Pa*ris (1851).

Boustrophedon (boo strof' e dŏn). A method

of writing found in early Greek inscriptions in which the lines run alternately from right to left and left to right, like the path of oxen in ploughing. (Gr. *boustrophos*, ox-turning.)

Bouts-rimés (boo rē′ mā) (Fr. rhymed endings). A parlour game which had a considerable vogue in 18th-century literary circles as a test of skill. A list of words that rhyme with one another is drawn up; this is handed to the competitors, and they have to make a poem to the rhymes, each rhyme-word being kept in its place on the list.

Bow (bō) (O.E. *boga*; connected with the O.Teut. *beguan*, to bend).

Draw not your bow till your arrow is fixed. Have everything ready before you begin.

He has a famous bow up at the castle. Said of a braggart or pretender.

He has two strings to his bow. Two means of accomplishing his object; if one fails, he can try the other. The allusion is to the custom of bowmen carrying a reserve string for emergency.

To be too much of the bow-hand. To fail in a design; not to be sufficiently dexterous. The bow-hand is the left hand, the hand which holds the bow.

To draw a bow at a venture. To attack without proper aim; to make a random remark which may hit the truth.

> A certain man drew a bow at a venture, and smote the King of Israel.
> I *Kings* xxii, 34.

To draw the longbow. To exaggerate. It is said that a good archer could hit between the fingers of a man's hand at a considerable distance, and could propel his arrow a mile. The tales told about longbow exploits, especially in the ROBIN HOOD stories, fully justify the application of the phrase. *See* TELL.

To unstring the bow will not heal the wound (Ital.). René of Anjou (1409–1480), king of Sicily, on the death of his wife, Isabella of Lorraine, adopted the emblem of a bow with the string broken with the words given above for the motto, by which he meant, "Lamentation for the loss of one's wife is but poor satisfaction."

Bow (bou). The fore-part of a boat or ship. (O.E. *bog* or *boh*; connected with Dan. *boug*, Icel. *bogr*, a shoulder.)

On the bow. A bearing midway between ahead and abeam, *i.e.*, within 45° on either side of the stem.

Up in the bows, To be. To be enraged.

Bow Bells (bō). **Born within sound of Bow Bells.** Said of a true COCKNEY. St. Mary-le-Bow, Cheapside, long had one of the most celebrated bell-peals in London, until an air raid destroyed the bells and the interior of the church in 1941. John Dun, mercer, in 1472 gave two tenements to maintain the ringing of Bow Bell every night at nine o'clock, to direct travellers on the road to town. In 1520 William Copland gave a bigger bell for the purpose of "sounding a retreat from work". It is said that the sound of these bells, which seemed to say "Turn again, Whittington, Lord Mayor of London", encouraged the young Dick WHITTINGTON to return to THE CITY and try his luck again.

Bow Street Runners (bō). The first regular police and detective force in London, organized in the mid-18th century under the chief magistrate at Bow Street, near COVENT GARDEN. They were eventually superseded (1829–1839) by the Metropolitan Police.

Bow-catcher (bō). A corruption of "Beau catcher", a love-curl, termed by the French an *accroche-cœur*. A love-curl worn by a man is a *bell-rope*, *i.e.* a rope to pull the *belles* with.

Bow-window in Front. A big belly or corporation. The same as BAY-WINDOW.

> He was a very large man … with what is termed a considerable bow-window in front.
> CAPTAIN MARRYAT: *Poor Jack*, i.

Bow-wow (bou-wou). A word in imitation of the sound made, as hiss, cackle, murmur, cuckoo, etc. Hence *the bow-wow school* is derisively applied to those philologists who sought to derive speech and language from the sounds made by animals. The terms were first used by Max Müller. *See* ONOMATOPEIA.

Bowden (bou′den). **Not every man can be vicar of Bowden.** Not everyone can occupy the first place. Bowden was one of the best livings in Cheshire.

Bowdlerize (bou′ dler īz). To expurgate a book. Thomas Bowdler, in 1818, published a ten-volume edition of Shakespeare's works "in which nothing is added to the original text; but those words are omitted which cannot with propriety be read aloud in a family". He also expurgated Gibbon's *Decline and Fall*, hence the words bowdlerist, bowdlerizer, bowdlerism, etc.

Bowels of Mercy. Compassion, sympathy. The affections were once supposed to be the outcome of certain secretions or organs, as the bile, the kidneys, the heart, the liver, the bowels, the SPLEEN etc. Hence the word *melancholy* or "black bile"; the Psalmist says that his *reins*, or kidneys, instructed him (*Ps*. xvi, 7), meaning his inward conviction; the *head* is the seat of understanding, the *heart* of affection and memory (hence "learning by heart"); the *bowels* of mercy, the *spleen* of passion or anger, etc. *See* HUMOUR.

His bowels yearned over, upon, or **towards him.** He felt a secret affection for him.

> Joseph made haste; for his bowels did yearn upon his brother.
>
> *Gen.* xliii, 30; *see also* I *Kings* iii, 26.

Bower. A lady's private room (O.E. *bur*, a chamber).

> But come to my bower, my Glasgerion,
> When all men are att rest;
> As I am a ladie true of my promise,
> Thou shalt bee a welcome guest.
>
> PERCY: *Reliques* (*Glasgerion*).

Hence, *bower-woman*, a lady's maid and companion.

Bower, the term used in euchre, is from the Ger. *bauer*, a peasant or knave. The right *bower* is the knave of trumps, the left *bower* is the other knave of the same colour.

> But the hands that were played
> By that heathen Chinee,
> And the points that he made,
> Were quite frightful to see—
> Till at last he put down a right bower
> Which the same Nye had dealt unto me.
>
> BRET HARTE: *Plain Language from Truthful James*.

Bower anchor. The anchors normally in use carried at the bow of a ship. The larger vessels carry two, the *best bower* and the *small bower*.

> Starboard being the best bower, and port the small bower.
>
> SMYTH: *Sailor's Word-book*.

Bower of Bliss. In Spenser's *Faerie Queene* (Bk. II), the enchanted home of Acrasia. In Tasso's JERUSALEM DELIVERED, ARMIDA's garden.

Bowery, The (Dut. *bouwerij*, a farm). A densely populated cosmopolitan street in New York city which runs through the former farm or *bouwerij* of Governor Peter Stuyvesant (1592–1672). Noted for its many cheap lodging houses, saloons and shops, it was once the haunt of the notorious ruffians called the *Bowery Boys*.

Bowie Knife. James Bowie (*pron.* Boo-ee) was a Southerner who for some years from 1818 smuggled negro slaves with the great pirate Jean Laffitte. In 1827 he was present at a duel on a sandbar in Mississippi near Natchez which ended in a general mêlée. Six of the seconds and spectators were killed and fifteen wounded. Bowie killed one Major Norris Wright with a knife fashioned from a blacksmith's rasp some 10 to 15 inches long, with one sharp edge curving to the point. This knife attracted such attention that Bowie sent it to a cutler in Philadelphia who marketed copies as the *Bowie knife*. Bowie was with Davy CROCKETT at the fall of the ALAMO on 6 March 1836.

Bowing (bou' ing). We uncover the head when we wish to salute anyone with respect; but the Jews, Turks, Siamese, etc., uncover their feet. The reason is that with us the chief act of investiture is crowning or placing a cap on the head, but in the East it is the putting on of slippers.

Bowled. To be bowled out, or **to be clean bowled** are METAPHORS from CRICKET, meaning to be defeated in argument or detected in a falsehood.

Bowled over. To be knocked down; or figuratively to be overcome by a sudden assault on the emotions.

Bowler Hat. A hard felt hat, known in the U.S.A. as the DERBY hat. Like the BILLYCOCK HAT it is said to have been introduced by the Norfolk landowner, William Coke (*see* COKE'S CLIPPINGS). Because he found his tall riding hat frequently swept off by overhanging branches, he asked (1850) Locks, the famous hatters of St. James's to design him a lower-crowned hat. The first "Coke" or bowler was made from felt supplied by Thomas and William Bowler.

To be bowler-hatted. To be discharged from the forces with a gratuity before the normal termination of one's commission, a bowler hat being the emblem of CIVVIE STREET. *Cp.* GOLDEN HANDSHAKE.

Bowling, Tom (bō ling). The type of a model sailor; from the character of that name in Smollett's *Roderick Random*.

The Tom Bowling referred to in the long-famous sea-song was Captain Thomas Dibdin, brother of Charles Dibdin (1768–1833), who wrote the song, and father of Thomas Frognall Dibdin, the BIBLIOMANIAC.

Bowls. They who play bowls must expect to meet with rubbers. Those who touch PITCH must expect to defile their fingers. Those who enter upon affairs of chance, adventure, or dangerous hazard must make up their minds to encounter crosses, losses, or difficulties. *Rubbers*, in bowls, is the collision of two bowls.

Bowyer God. The "archer god", usually applied to CUPID.

Bowyang (Austr.). A string or strap used by labourers to hitch the trouser leg below the knee, hence a symbol of manual labour.

From bowyangs to bowyangs. The Australian equivalent of CLOGS TO CLOGS IS ONLY THREE GENERATIONS.

Box, The. An everyday name for a television

set.

"Box about, 'twill come to my father anon." During an argument with his son, Sir Walter Ralegh gave him a blow on the head. Not wishing to strike his father back, young Walter hit the man on his other side at table making the above remark, intending that the blow should go right round the table and get back to his father. According to Aubrey this became a common proverb in the 17th century.

Box and Cox has become a phrase which can only be explained by the story. Mrs Bouncer, a deceitful lodging-house landlady, let the same room to two men, Box and Cox, who unknown to each other occupied it alternately, one being out at work all day, the other all night. It is from the farce by J. M. Morton (1811–1891) called *Box and Cox* (adapted from the French).

Box-cars. In throwing dice, in the U.S.A., a double six is known as *box-cars* from its resemblance to freight cars or goods wagons.

Box Days. A custom established in the Scottish Court of Session in 1690, providing two days in spring and autumn, and one at CHRISTMAS (during vacation) on which pleadings could be filed. Informations were to be placed in a box for each judge and examined in private.

I've got into the wrong box. I am out of my element, or in the wrong place or in a false position.

To be in the same box. To be in the same predicament as somebody else; to be equally embarrassed. *To be in the same boat* is a similar phrase.

To box Harry. A commercial traveller's phrase; applied to one who avoids the TABLE D'HÔTE and has a substantial tea, in order to save expense, especially after a bout of extravagance. *To box a tree* is to cut the bark to procure the sap, and these travellers drain the landlady by having a cheap tea instead of an expensive dinner.

To box the compass. A nautical phrase meaning to name the thirty-two points of the compass in their correct order. Hence a wind is said to "box the compass" when it blows from every quarter in rapid succession; hence, figuratively, to go right round in political views, etc., and end at one's starting-place.

Boxing Day. *See* CHRISTMAS BOX.

Boxer Hat (Austr.). A BOWLER HAT.

Boxers. A branch of the White Lotus sect in China which took a prominent part in the rising against foreigners in 1900 and was suppressed by joint European action. The Chinese name was *I Ho Chuan* or "Right-

eous Harmony Fists", implying training for the purpose of developing righteousness and harmony.

Boy. In a number of connexions "boy" has no reference to age. It is a common term for a "native" servant or labourer of any age, and a ship's *boy* is the lowest category among mariners, being essentially a GREENHORN. An "old boy" can be a former member of a particular school or an elderly man, and "Hello, old boy," is quite a normal way in which to greet an acquaintance.

The Boy, meaning champagne, takes its origin from a shooting-party at which a boy with an iced bucket of wine was in attendance. When the Prince of Wales (Edward VII) needed a drink, he shouted "Where's the boy?", and thence the phrase found its way into would-be smart parlance.

> He will say that port and sherry his nice palate always cloy;
> He'll nothing drink but "B. and S." and big magnums of "the boy".
>
> *Punch* (1882).

Boy Bishop. St. NICHOLAS of Bari was called "the Boy Bishop" because from his cradle he manifested marvellous indications of piety.

The custom of choosing a boy from the cathedral or parish choir on his day (6 December), as a mock BISHOP, is very ancient. It was also the custom in schools and colleges such as St. Paul's, Eton, Winchester; King's College, Cambridge etc. The boy held office for three weeks and the rest of the choir were his prebendaries. If he died in office he was buried *in pontificalibus*. Probably the reference is to the boy Jesus sitting in the temple among the doctors. The custom was abolished by Henry VIII in 1541, revived in 1552, and finally abolished by Elizabeth I.

Boy Scouts. An outstandingly imaginative and successful youth movement started by General Sir Robert Baden-Powell (Lord Baden-Powell of Gilwell) in 1908. The aim was to train boys to be good citizens with high ideals of honour, service to others, cleanliness and self-reliance, based essentially on training in an outdoor setting. The movement became world-wide with a membership now of over eight million young people. A complete Scout Group now consists of Cub Scouts (formerly Wolf Cubs), age 8 to 11; Scouts 11 to 16; Venture Scouts (formerly Rover Scouts), 16 to 20. These new designations, as well as that of Scout Association, were introduced in 1967.

Naked boy. *See* NAKED.

The Boys in blue. *See under* BLUE.

The Gazelle Boy. *See* GAZELLE.

Boycott. To boycott is to coerce by preventing any social or commercial dealings with a person, group, or nation. The term dates from 1880, when such methods were used by the Irish Land League under Parnell, who advocated that anyone taking over a farm from an evicted tenant should be "isolated from his kind as if he were a leper of old". This treatment was first used against Captain Boycott, a land agent in County Mayo. *Cp.* TO SEND TO COVENTRY *under* COVENTRY.

Boyle Controversy. A book-battle between Charles Boyle, fourth Earl of Orrery (1676–1731), and Richard Bentley (1662–1742), respecting the *Epistles of Phalaris* which were edited by Boyle in 1695. In 1697 Bentley wrote an essay declaring the Epistles to be spurious, and finally routed his opponents in his famous *Dissertation* of 1699. SWIFT'S BATTLE OF THE BOOKS was one result of the controversy.

Boyle's Law that the volume of a gas is inversely proportional to the pressure if the temperature remains constant, was formulated by Robert Boyle (1627–1691) in the early 1660s.

Boyle Lectures. A course of eight sermons to be delivered annually, in defence of the Christian religion; endowed by the Hon. Robert Boyle, the natural philosopher, and first given in 1692.

Boz. Charles Dickens (1812–1870). "Boz, my signature in the *Morning Chronicle*," he tells us, "was the nickname of a pet child, a younger brother, whom I had dubbed Moses, in honour of the Vicar of Wakefield, which being pronounced Boses, got shortened into Boz."

Bozzy. James Boswell (1740–1795), the biographer of Dr. Johnson.

Brabançonne, La (bra ban son). The national anthem of Belgium, composed by Van Campenhout in the revolution of 1830, and so named from Brabant, of which Brussels is the chief city.

Braccata. *See* GENS BRACCATA; GALLIA.

Bradamante (brăd′ à mănt). The sister of RINALDO in ORLANDO FURIOSO and ORLANDO INNAMORATO. She is represented as a wonderful Christian AMAZON, possessed of an irresistible spear which unhorsed every KNIGHT it struck.

Bradbury. A £1 note, as issued by the Treasury 1914–1928, bearing the signature of J. S. Bradbury (first Baron Bradbury), who as Joint Permanent Secretary to the Treasury began the issue.

Bradman. A second Bradman. An outstanding batsman, likened to the great Australian cricketer, Sir Donald Bradman.

Bradshaw's Guide. This famous railway guide was started in 1839 by George Bradshaw (1801–1853), printer, in Manchester. The *Monthly Guide* was first issued in December 1841, and consisted of thirty-two pages, giving tables of forty-three lines of English railway. Publication ceased in 1961.

> "Just look up the trains in Bradshaw", said he, and turned back to his chemical studies.
>
> A. CONAN DOYLE: *Adventures of Sherlock Holmes* (*The Adventure of the Copper Beeches*).

Brag. A game at CARDS; so called because the players *brag* of their cards to induce the company to make bets. The principal sport of the game is occasioned by any player *bragging* that he holds a better hand than the rest of the party, which is declared by saying "I brag", and staking a sum of money on the issue.

Brag is a good dog, but Holdfast is a better. Talking is all very well, but doing is far better.

> Trust none;
> For oaths are straws, men's faiths are wafer-cakes,
> And holdfast is the only dog, my duck.
> SHAKESPEARE: *Henry V*, II, iii.

There is also the English proverb "Brag is a good dog but dare not bite", meaning braggarts fear to make good their pretensions.

Jack Brag. A vulgar, pretentious braggart, who gets into aristocratic society, where his vulgarity stands out in strong relief. The character is in Theodore Hook's novel (1837) of the same name.

Braggadocio (brăg à dō′ si ō). A braggart; one who is valiant with his tongue but a great coward at heart. *Cp.* ERYTHYNUS. The character is from Spenser's *Faerie Queene* and a type of the "Intemperance of the Tongue". After a time, like the jackdaw in borrowed plumes, Braggadocchio is stripped of all his glories; his shield is claimed by Sir Marinell; his lady is proved by the golden girdle to be the false Florimell; his horse is claimed by Sir Guyon; Talus shaves off his beard and scourges his squire; and the pretender sneaks off amidst the jeers of everyone. It is thought that the poet had the Duke of Alençon, a suitor of Queen Elizabeth I, in mind when he drew this character (*Faerie Queene*, II, iii; III, v, viii, x; IV, ii, iv; V, iii, etc.).

Bragi. In Norse mythology, the god of poetry and eloquence, son of ODIN and husband of IDUNA. He welcomes the slain heroes who arrive in VALHALLA.

Brahma (bra′ mà). In Hinduism Brahma, properly speaking, is the Absolute, or God conceived as entirely impersonal. This theological abstraction was later endowed with personality and became the Creator of the universe, the first in the divine Triad, of which the other partners were VISHNU the maintainer, and SIVA, the destroyer. As such the Brahmins claim Brahma as the founder of their religious system.

Brahma Somaj (Sans., the Society of Believers in the One God). A Hindu theistic religious movement founded in 1828 by Ram Mohan Roy (1772–1833), a wealthy and well-educated BRAHMIN who wished to purify his religion and found a national church which should be free from idolatry and superstition. It was further developed after 1841 by Debendra Nath Tagore, but schisms occurred before the end of the century.

Brahmin. A worshipper of BRAHMA, the highest CASTE in the system of Hinduism and of the priestly order.

Braille. A system of writing made up of varying combinations of raised dots enabling the blind to read by touch, invented by Louis Braille in 1829. It has been likened to a domino block as it consists of different groups of one to six raised points. Braille devised his system after becoming acquainted with a twelve dot system invented by Captain Charles Barbier for passing messages at night. Braille accidentally blinded himself in one eye as a child of three and soon lost his sight completely. In 1819, at the age of ten he was put in the *Institution Nationale des Aveugles* at Paris where he later became a teacher and organ player and modified his system for reading music. He devoted his life to his pupils and accepted his misfortune with religious fortitude. He died of consumption in 1852 and Braille was officially adopted by the Institution in 1854.

Brain-child. A project, scheme, invention, etc., the product of an individual's brain.

Brain Drain. A phrase used to denote the drift abroad (from the early 1960s), of British-trained scientists, technologists, doctors and university teachers (especially to the U.S.A.), attracted by higher salaries and often better facilities for their work.

Brain-washing. The subjection of a person to an intensive course of indoctrination in order to transform his opinions and transfer his political loyalties to those approved by the "washers".

Brain-wave. A sudden inspiration; "a happy thought".

Brains Trust. Originally the name "Brains Trust" was applied by James M. Kieran of the *New York Times* to the advisers of F. D. Roosevelt in his election campaign; later to the group of college professors who advised him in administering the NEW DEAL. In Britain it became the name of a popular B.B.C. programme in which well-known public figures aired their views on questions submitted by listeners. Now in general use for any such panel of experts or team which answers questions impromptu.

Bran. If not Bran, it is Bran's brother.

> "Mar e Bran, is e a brathair, if it be not Bran, it is Bran's brother", was the proverbial reply of Maccombich.
>
> SCOTT: *Waverley*, ch. xlv.

If not the real "SIMON PURE" it is just as good. A complimentary expression. Bran, the well-known dog of FINGAL, was a mighty favourite.

In Cornwall a crow is called *bran*, a word of Celtic origin.

Bran-new, or **Brand-new** (O.E. *brand*, a torch). Fire new, new from the forge. SHAKESPEARE, in *Love's Labour's Lost*, I, i, says, "A man of fire-new words"; again in *Twelfth Night*, III, ii, "Fire-new from the mint"; in *King Lear*, V, iii, "Fire-new fortune"; in *Richard III*, I, "Your fire-new stamp of honour is scarce current." Originally applied to metals and things manufactured in metal which shine. Subsequently applied generally to things quite new.

Brand. The merchant's or excise mark branded on a commodity or article.

He has the brand of villain in his looks. It was once customary to brand vagabonds and convicted offenders with a red-hot iron. In Tudor times vagabonds were branded with a V on the breast, and brawlers or "fray-makers in church" with an F, and so on. In the reign of William III it was enacted that branding for theft and larceny should be on the left cheek (1698). This was replaced in 1707 and in the 18th century "cold branding" was often passed as a normal sentence until branding was finally abolished in 1829. In the Army deserters were "branded" by tattooing below the left nipple until 1879. Deserters were branded with a D and incorrigibly bad characters with B.C. *Cp.* MAVERICK.

Brandan, St., or **Brendan.** A semi-legendary Irish saint, said to have been born at Tralee in 484. He founded the abbey of Clonfert and died in 577. The *Rule of St. Brendan* was dictated to him by an angel and he is said to have presided over 3,000 monks in the various houses of his foundation.

He is best known for the mediæval legend, widespread throughout Europe, of his seven-year voyage in search of the "Land of the Saints", the Isle of St. Brendan, reputed to be in mid-Atlantic. The very birds and beasts he encountered observed the Christian fasts and festivals. The earliest surviving version of the story is the *Navigatio Brendani* (11th century). *See* MAELDUNE.

> And we came to the isle of a saint who had
> sailed with St. Brendan of yore,
> He had lived ever since on the Isle and his
> winters were fifteen score.
> TENNYSON : Voyage of Maeldune.

Brandenburg Confession. A formulary of faith drawn up in the city of Brandenburg in 1610, by order of the elector, with the view of reconciling the tenets of Luther with those of Calvin, and to put an end to the disputes occasioned by the AUGSBURG CONFESSION.

Branding. *See* BRAND.

Brandon. An obsolete form of *brand*, a torch. *Dominica de brandonibus* (St. VALENTINE'S Day), when boys used to carry about *brandons* (CUPID's torches).

Brandy Nan. Queen Anne, who was very fond of brandy. On her statue in St. Paul's Churchyard a wit once wrote:

> Brandy Nan, Brandy Nan, left in the lurch,
> Her face to the gin-shop, her back to the church.

A "gin palace" used to stand at the southwest corner of St. Paul's Churchyard. *See* EST-IL POSSIBLE; QUEEN ANNE.

Brank (Scot.). A gag for scolds consisting of an iron framework fitting round the head with a piece projecting inward which went into the mouth and prevented the tongue wagging. There is one dated 1633 in the church vestry at Walton-on-Thames, inscribed:

> Chester presents Walton with a bridle
> To curb women's tongues that talk too idle.

Brasenose College (brāz′nōz) (Oxford). Over the gate is a brass nose, the arms of the college; but the word is a corruption of *brasenhuis*, a brasserie or brewhouse, the college having been built on the site of a brewery. For over 550 years the original nose was at Stamford, for in the reign of Edward III the students migrated thither in search of religious liberty, taking the nose with them. It was re-acquired by the college in 1890.

Brass. A slang term for money.

A church brass. A memorial brass plate engraved with details of the person commemorated. The earliest complete specimen is late 13th century in Stoke d'Abernon Church, Surrey.

Brassbounder. Formerly, a premium apprentice on a merchant ship, called by courtesy midshipman.

Brass Hat. A service term for an officer of high rank. It dates from the first Boer War (1880–1881), and refers to the gold oak leaves on the brim of senior officers' caps, sometimes nicknamed "scrambled egg". Officers of the highest rank are called **top brass**.

The Man of Brass. Talus, the work of Hephæstus (VULCAN). He was the guardian of Crete and threw rocks at the ARGONAUTS to prevent their landing; he used to make himself red-hot, and then hug intruders to death.

As bold as brass. With barefaced effrontery or impudence. Said to derive from Brass Crosby, Lord Mayor of LONDON in 1770, at which time publishing of reports of Parliamentary proceedings was still forbidden but Crosby, as chief magistrate, released the printer of the *London Evening Post* for so doing. Crosby was committed to the TOWER but public outcry soon secured his freedom.

To get down to brass tacks. To get down to the essentials. Probably from cockney RHYMING SLANG where *brass tacks* are *facts*.

Brave. A fighting man among the American Indians was so called.

Alphonso IV of Portugal (1290–1357) was called "the Brave".

Bravest of the Brave. Marshal Ney (1769–1815). So called by the troops of Friedland (1807), on account of his fearless bravery. NAPOLEON said of him, "That man is a lion."

Brawn. The test of the brawn's head (boar's head). In *The Boy and the Mantle* (PERCY'S RELIQUES), a little boy came to the court of King ARTHUR and brought in a boar's head saying "there never was a cuckold's knife that could carve it". No knight in the court except Sir Cradock was able to accomplish the feat.

> He brought in the boar's head,
> And was wondrous bold
> He said ther was never a cuckold's knife,
> Carve itt that cold.

Brazen Age. The age of war and violence. It followed the SILVER AGE. *See* AGE.

> To this next came in course the brazen age,
> A warlike offspring, prompt to bloody rage,
> Not impious yet. Hard steel succeeded them,
> And stubborn as the metal were the men.
> DRYDEN : Metamorphoses, i.

Brazen-faced. Bold (in a bad sense), without shame. *Cp.* BRASS.

> What a brazen-faced varlet art thou!
> SHAKESPEARE : King Lear, II, ii.

Brazen head. The legend of the wonderful head of brass that could speak and was omniscient, found in early romances, is of East-

ern origin. Ferragus in VALENTINE AND OR-
SON is an example but the most famous in
English legend is that fabled to have been
made by the great Roger Bacon. It was said
if Bacon heard it speak he would succeed in
his projects; if not, he would fail. His familiar, Miles, was set to watch, and while Bacon slept the Head spoke thrice: "Time is";
half an hour later it said, "Time was". In another half-hour it said, "Time's past", fell
down and was broken to atoms. Byron refers
to this legend.

> Like Friar Bacon's head, I've spoken,
> "Time is", "Time was", "Time's past."
> *Don Juan*, i, 217.

References to Bacon's brazen head are frequent in literature. Most notable is Robert
Greene's *Honourable History of Friar Bacon
and Friar Bungay*, 1594. Other allusions
are:

> Bacon for his brazen head.
> POPE: *Dunciad*, III, 104.

> Quoth he, "My head's not made of brass,
> As Friar Bacon's noddle was."
> BUTLER: *Hudibras*, II, i.

See also SPEAKING HEADS.

To brazen it out. To stick to an assertion
knowing it to be wrong; to outface in a
shameless manner; to disregard public
opinion.

Breach of Promise. A contract to marry was
as binding in English law as any other contract, and the man or woman who broke an
engagement was liable in law. The plaintiff
was entitled to recover any pecuniary loss
due to outlay in anticipation of marriage and
a woman might be awarded substantial damages in certain circumstances. If the man
was the injured party he was better advised
to seek consolation or compensation other
than in a court of law. "Breach of Promise"
was abolished for England and Wales as
from 1 January 1971.

Breaches, meaning *creeks* or *small bays*, is to
be found in *Judges* v, 17. Deborah, complaining of the tribes who refused to assist
her in her war with Sisera, says that Asher
"abode in his breaches", that is, creeks on
the seashore.

Spenser has the same usage:

> The headful boateman strongly forth did stretch
> His brawnie armes, and all his body straine,
> That the utmost sandy breach they shortly fetch.
> *Faerie Queene*, II, xii, 21.

Bread. Bread is the staff of life (17th-
century proverb).

Bread and cheese. The barest necessities
of life.

Bread and circuses. Free food and entertainment. *Panem et circenses* were, accord-

ing to Juvenal's *Satires*, the two things the
Roman populace desired.

Bread and point. *See* TO DINE ON POTATOES
AND POINT *under* POINT.

Bread-basket. The stomach.

**Bread never falls but on its buttered
side.** An old north country proverb.

> We express the completeness of ill-luck by saying
> "The bread never falls but on its buttered side".
> J. L. KIPLING: *Man and Beast in India* (1891).

Breaking of bread. The EUCHARIST. In
scriptural language *to break bread* is to partake of food.

> They continued... in breaking of bread, and in
> prayer.
> *Acts* ii, 42 (also 46).

**Cast thy bread upon the waters; for thou
shalt find it after many days** (*Eccles*. xi,
1). The interpretation of this well-known
passage is obscure. Perhaps the most likely
meaning is "do not be afraid to give generously without hope of immediate gain, sooner or later you will reap as you have sown."
Another common explanation is that seed
cast on flooded land will take root and profit
the sower when the waters recede, bread in
this context meaning "corn" or "seed".

**Don't quarrel with your bread and but-
ter.** Don't foolishly give up your job or take
action that will deprive you of your living.

He took bread and salt, *i.e.* he took his
oath. In Eastern lands bread and salt were
once eaten when an oath was taken.

**To know which side one's bread is but-
tered.** To be mindful of one's own interest.

**To take the bread out of someone's
mouth.** To forestall another; to take away
another's livelihood.

Break. A short solo improvisation in jazz music.

To break. To bankrupt.

To break a bond. To dishonour it.

To break a butterfly on a wheel. To employ superabundant effort in the accomplishment of a small matter.

> Satire or sense, alas! can Sporus feel?
> Who breaks a butterfly upon the wheel?
> POPE: *Epistle to Dr. Arbuthnot*, 307.

To break a journey. To stop before the
journey is accomplished, with the intention
of completing it later.

To break a matter to a person. To be the
first to impart it, and to do so cautiously and
piecemeal.

To break away. To escape, to go away
abruptly; to start too soon in a race.

To break bread. *See* BREAD.

To break cover. To start forth from a
hiding-place.

To break down. To lose all control of one's

feelings; to collapse, to become hysterical; also to demolish or to analyse. A *breakdown* is a temporary collapse in health; it is also the name given to a wild kind of Negro dance.

To break faith. To violate one's word or pledge; to act traitorously.

To break ground. To commence a new project, as a settler does.

To break in. To interpose a remark. To train a horse or animal to the saddle, harness, etc., or to train a person to a way of life. To enter as a burglar does.

To break off. To stop a conversation, etc. To end an engagement or friendship.

To break one's fast. To take food after long abstinence; to eat one's *breakfast* after the night's fast.

To break one's neck. To dislocate the bones of one's neck. To be in a violent hurry.

To break on the wheel. To torture on a "wheel" by breaking the long bones with an iron bar. *See* COUP DE GRÂCE.

To break out. To escape from prison. To throw off restraint.

To break out of bounds. To go beyond the prescribed limits.

To break the ice. To prepare the way; to get through the stiffness and reserve of a first meeting with a stranger; to impart distressing news to another delicately and tactfully.

To break through. To force a passage. To overcome major obstacles especially in the field of scientific or technical progress.

To break one's back. To make one bankrupt; to reduce one to a state of impotence. The METAPHOR is from carrying burdens on the back.

To break up. To break into pieces, to smash; to discontinue classes at the end of term and go home; to separate. A meeting is said to break up when it dissolves or disperses. Also to become rapidly decrepit and infirm.

To break with someone. To quarrel or discontinue relations.

To get a break. To have an unexpected chance; to have an opportunity of advancing oneself.

To make a break. To make a complete change; to commit a social error or make an unfortunate mistake.

To run up a score in billiards or snooker.

Breakers Ahead. Hidden danger at hand. Breakers in an open sea always announce sunken rocks, sandbanks, etc.

Breaking a Stick. Part of the marriage ceremony of certain North American Indians, as breaking a wineglass is part of the

marriage ceremony of the Jews.

One of Raphael's pictures shows an unsuccessful suitor of the Virgin Mary breaking his stick. This alludes to the legend that suitors were each to bring an almond stick to be laid up in the sanctuary overnight. The owner of the stick which budded was to be accounted the suitor approved by God. It was thus Joseph became the husband of Mary.

Breast. To make a clean breast of it. To make a full confession, concealing nothing.

Breath. All in a breath. Without taking breath (Lat. *continenti spiritu*).

It takes one's breath away. The news is so astounding it causes one to hold one's breath with surprise.

Out of breath. Panting from exertion; temporarily short of breath.

Save your breath to cool your porridge. Don't talk to me, it is only wasting your breath.

To catch one's breath. To check suddenly the free act of breathing.

To hold one's breath. Voluntarily to cease breathing for a time, as in fear, etc.

To take breath. To cease for a little time from some exertion in order to recover from exhaustion of breath.

Under one's breath. In a whisper or undertone.

To breathe fire and brimstone. To be manifestly wrathful.

To breathe one's last. To die.

Brèche de Roland. A deep defile in the crest of the Pyrenees, some three hundred feet wide. The legend is that ROLAND, the PALADIN, cleft the rocks in two with his sword DURANDAL, when he was set upon by the Gascons at RONCESVALLES.

Breeches. She wears the breeches or trousers. Said of a woman who usurps the prerogative of her husband. *Cp.* THE GREY MARE IS THE BETTER HORSE, *under* MARE.

Breeches Bible. *See* BIBLE.

Brehon Laws (brē' hon). The English name for the ancient laws of Ireland, which prevailed until the mid-17th century. They cover every phase of Irish life and provide an invaluable source of historical information.

Brendan, St. *See* BRANDAN, ST.

Bren-gun. A World War II light machine-gun, fired from the shoulder. Originally made in Brno, Czechoslovakia, then in Enfield, England. *Bren* is a blend of Brno and Enfield.

Brent (Scot.). Without a wrinkle. Burns says of Jo Anderson, in his prime of life, "his locks were like the raven", and his "bonnie brow was brent".

Brent-hill means the eyebrows. *Looking* or *gazing from under brent-hill*, in Devonshire means "frowning at one"; and in west Cornwall *to brend* means to wrinkle the brows.

Brentford. Like the two kings of Brentford smelling at one nosegay. Said of persons who were once rivals, but have become reconciled. The allusion is to *The Rehearsal* (1672), by the Duke of Buckingham. "The two kings of Brentford enter hand in hand", and the actors, to heighten the absurdity, used to make them enter "smelling at one nosegay". (Act. II, Sc. ii.)

Br'er Fox, he lay low. A hint that silence in speech or action is the wise course. The expression was in fairly common use in the early 1900s and was derived from the popular stories, largely concerning Br'er Fox and Br'er Rabbit, by the American writer Joel Chandler Harris (1848–1908). These animal stories in the Negro dialect, which began to appear in 1879, were supposedly told to a plantation owner's little boy by Uncle Remus, a kindly old Negro.

Bretwalda (bret wol' dà). The title given in the *Anglo-Saxon Chronicle* to Egbert of Wessex (802–839) and seven earlier English kings, who exercised a supremacy, often rather shadowy, over other English kings south of the Humber. The title probably means "overlord of the Brets (Britons)" and was sometimes assumed by later kings. *See* HEPTARCHY.

Breviary (brē' vi àr i). A book containing the ordinary and daily services of the ROMAN CATHOLIC CHURCH, which those in orders are bound to recite. It omits the EUCHARIST, which is contained in the MISSAL, and the special services (marriage, ordination, etc.), which are found in the *Ritual* or *Pontifical*. It is called a breviary because it is an abbreviation in the sense that it contains prayers, hymns, and lessons, etc., thus obviating the need to use a separate hymn book, and BIBLE.

Brew. Brew me a glass of grog, *i.e.* mix one for me. *Brew me a cup of tea, i.e.* make one for me. *The tea is set to brew, i.e.* to draw. The general meaning of the word is to boil or mix; the restricted meaning is to make malt liquor.

As you brew, so you will bake. As you will go on; you must take the consequences of your actions; "as you make your BED so you will lie on it."

To brew up. To burn. Said of tanks in World War II.

Brewer. The Brewer of Ghent. Jacob van Artevelde (d. 1345); a popular Flemish leader who allied with Edward III against France. Although by birth an aristocrat, he was a member of the Guild of Brewers.

Brian Boru, or **Boroma** (brī' àn bo roo', bo ro' ma) (926–1014). This great Irish chieftain became king of Munster in 978 and chief king of all Ireland in 1002. On Good Friday 1014, his forces defeated the Danes of Dublin at the battle of Clontarf, but Brian, too old to fight, was killed in his tent.

Briareus (brī âr' ē ùs), or **Ægeon**. A giant with fifty heads and a hundred hands. Homer says the gods called him Briareus, but men called him Aegeon (*Iliad*, I, 403). He was the offspring of HEAVEN and Earth and was one of the race of TITANS, against whom he fought in their war with ZEUS.

> He [Ajax] hath the joints of everything, but everything so out of joint that he is a gouty Briareus, many hands and no use, or purblind Argus, all eyes and no sight.
> SHAKESPEARE: *Troilus and Cressida*, I, ii.

Bold Briareus. Handel (1685–1759), so called by Pope:

> Strong in new arms, lo! giant Handel stands,
> Like bold Briareus, with a hundred hands;
> To stir, to rouse, to shake the soul he comes.
> And Jove's own thunders follow Mars's drums.
> *Dunciad*, IV, 65.

The Briareus of Languages. Cardinal Mezzofanti (1774–1849), who is said to have spoken fifty-eight different tongues. BYRON called him "a walking polyglot; a monster of languages; a Briareus of parts of speech".

Bric-à-brac. Odds and ends of curiosities. In French, a *marchand de bric-à-brac* is a seller of junk, old stores, etc., usually of small value; we employ the phrase for odds and ends of virtu. *Bricoler* in French means *faire toute espèce de métier*, to be Jack of all trades. *Brac* is the RICOCHET of *bric*, as FIDDLE-FADDLE and scores of other double words in English. Littré says that it is formed on the model of *de bric et de broc*, by hook or by crook.

Brick. A regular brick. A jolly good fellow; perhaps because a brick is solid, four-square, plain and reliable.

> A fellow like nobody else, and in fine, a brick.
> GEORGE ELIOT: *Daniel Deronda*, Bk. II, ch. xvi.

Brick and mortar franchise. A Chartist phrase for the £10 householder franchise.

Brickdusts. *See* REGIMENTAL AND DIVISIONAL NICKNAMES.

Brickfielder (Austr.). A southerly gale experienced at Sydney which used to blow dust into the city from the nearby brickfields.

Brick tea. The inferior leaves of the plant mixed with a glutinous substance (sometimes bullock's or sheep's blood), pressed into cubes and dried. In this form it was sent overland from China to Russia and these blocks were frequently used as a medium of exchange in central Asia.

To drop a brick. To make a highly tactless remark.

To make bricks without straw. To attempt to do something without having the necessary material supplied. The allusion is to the Israelites in Egypt, who were commanded by their taskmasters so to do (*Exod*. v, 7).

Bride. The bridal wreath is a relic of the *corona nuptialis* used by the Greeks and Romans to indicate triumph.

Bride, or **wedding favours** represent the TRUE-LOVER'S KNOT and symbolic union.

Bride-ale. *See* CHURCH-ALE. It is from this word that we get the adjective *bridal*.

Bride cake. A relic of the Roman *confarreatio*, a mode of marriage practised by the highest class in Rome. It was performed by the *Pontifex Maximus* before ten witnesses and the contracting parties mutually partook of a cake of salt, water, and flour (*far*). Only those born in such wedlock were eligible for the high sacred offices.

Bride of the Sea. Venice; so called from the ancient ceremony of the wedding of the sea by the Doge, who threw a ring into the Adriatic saying, "We wed thee, O sea, in token of perpetual domination." This took place annually on ASCENSION DAY, and was enjoined upon the Venetians in 1177 by Pope Alexander III, who gave the Doge a gold ring from his own finger in token of the Venetian fleet's victory over Frederick Barbarossa, in defence of the Pope's quarrel. At the same time his Holiness desired the event to be commemorated each year. *See* BUCENTAUR.

Bridegroom. In O.E. this word was *brydguma* (the latter element from the Old Teutonic *gumon*, man), becoming replaced by *bridegroom* in the 16th century. The last change appears to be due to the confusion of *gome* with M.E. *groom*, the word for a man-servant.

Bridegroom's men. In the Roman marriage by *confarreatio*, the bride was led to the *Pontifex Maximus* by bachelors, but was conducted home by married men. Polydore Virgil says that a married man preceded the bride on her return, bearing a vessel of GOLD and SILVER. *See* BRIDE CAKE.

Bridewell. A generic term for a HOUSE OF CORRECTION, or a prison, so called from the City Bridewell, BLACKFRIARS, formerly a royal palace built over the holy well of St. Bride (Bridget). After the REFORMATION, Edward

VI made it a penitentiary for unruly apprentices and vagrants. It was demolished in 1863 although much of the palace was destroyed in the GREAT FIRE OF LONDON. *See under* FIRE.

> At my first entrance it seemed to me rather a Prince's Palace than a House of Correction, till gazing round me, I saw in a large room a parcel of ill-looking mortals stripped to their shirts like hay-makers, pounding hemp ... From thence we turned to the women's apartment, who we found were shut up as close as nuns.
>
> NED WARD: *The London Spy* (1698).

Bridge of Gold. According to a German tradition, CHARLEMAGNE's spirit crosses the Rhine on a golden bridge at Bingen, in seasons of plenty, to bless the vineyards and cornfields.

> Thou standest, like imperial Charlemagne,
> Upon thy bridge of gold.
>
> LONGFELLOW: *Sonnets, Autumn*.

To make a bridge of gold for him is to enable a man to retreat from a false position without loss of dignity.

Bridge of Jehennam. Another name for AL SIRAT.

Bridge of Sighs. Over this bridge, which connects the Doge's palace with the state prisons of Venice, prisoners were conveyed from the judgment hall to the place of execution. The passageway which used to connect the Tombs prison in New York with the criminal court was so dubbed for similar reasons.

A bridge over the Cam at St. John's College, Cambridge, which resembles the Venetian original, is called by the same name.

Waterloo Bridge, London, was also called *The Bridge of Sighs* when suicides were frequent there. Hood gave the name to one of his poems:

> One more Unfortunate,
> Weary of breath,
> Rashly importunate,
> Gone to her death.

Bridget, St. (Bridig, Bride, Brigid) (453–523). The second patron saint of Ireland whose day is 1 February. She became a nun renowned for her piety and founded an abbey at Kildare — the first for women in Ireland. She is the protectress of dairy workers and became popular in England as St. Bride.

Bridgewater Treatises. Instituted by the Rev. Francis Howard Egerton, eighth Earl of Bridgewater. He left £8,000 to be given to the author or authors of the best treatise or treatises "On the Power, Wisdom, and Goodness of God, as manifested in the Creation". The money was divided between eight authors: Dr. Chalmers, Dr. John

Kidd, Dr. Whewell, Sir Charles Bell, Dr. Peter Roget, Dean Buckland, the Rev. W. Kirby, and Dr. William Prout. The award was made by the President of the Royal Society (Davies Gilbert) in consultation with the Archbishop of Canterbury (Dr. Howley) and the Bishop of London (Dr. Blomfield).

Bridle road, or **path.** A way for a riding-horse, but not for a HORSE and cart.

To bite on the bridle is to suffer great hardships. Horses bit on the bridle when trying, against odds, to get their own way.

To bridle up. In Fr. *se rengorger*, to draw in the chin and toss the head back in scorn or pride. The METAPHOR is from a HORSE pulled up suddenly and sharply.

A scold's bridle. A most uncomfortable metal bridle with an even more unpleasant tongue plate put upon shrewish women as a punishment. They were used from mediæval times until the 18th century. There was a ring over the nose aperture for a rope or chain by which the wearer was led through the streets. *See* SKIMMINGTON; STANG.

Bridport. Stabbed with a Bridport dagger, *i.e.* hanged. Bridport in Dorsetshire was famous for its hempen goods, supplying ropes and cables for the Royal Navy, and it is still a centre for net-making. The hangman's rope, being made at Bridport, gave rise to the phrase.

Brigade of Guards. *See* HOUSEHOLD TROOPS.

Brigand. A French word from the Ital. *brigante*, pres. part. of *brigare*, to quarrel. The 14th-century FREE COMPANIES of France, such as *The White Company* in Conan Doyle's story, were brigands, *i.e.* irregular troops addicted to marauding. In the course of time the Ital. *brigante* came to mean a robber or pirate; hence *brig, brigandine, brigantine* for a pirate ship, then a type of sailing vessel. *Brigade* and *Brigadier* are also derivatives.

Brigandine (brig' ản dīn). The armour of a BRIGAND, consisting of small plates of iron on quilted linen, and covered with leather, hemp, etc. The word occurs twice in *Jeremiah* (xlvi, 4; li, 3), and in both of these passages the REVISED VERSION reads "coats of mail".

Brighton. Doctor Brighton. The town of Brighton in Sussex, from its popularity as a health resort. Originally the fishing village of Brighthelmstone, it changed its name at the beginning of the 19th century. Dr. Richard Russell drew attention to its possibilities as a watering-place in the 1750s and it rapidly gained in favour after the PRINCE OF WALES first spent a holiday there in 1782.

Subsequently he built the Royal Pavilion, in which he resided on his annual visits, thereby making the town fashionable. This NICKNAME seems to have come into being about the end of the REGENCY.

> And then fell to talking about Brighton, and the sea-air and the gaieties of the place.
> THACKERAY: *Vanity Fair*, ch. xxv.

Brilliant. A form of cutting of precious stones introduced by Vincenzo Peruzzi at Venice in the late 17th century. Most diamonds are now brilliant cut and the word *brilliant* commonly means a DIAMOND cut in this way. In a perfect brilliant there are fifty-eight facets.

Brilliant Madman, The. Charles XII of Sweden (1682, 1697–1718).

> Macedonia's madman or the Swede.
> JOHNSON: *Vanity of Human Wishes*.

Bring. To bring about. To cause a thing to be done.

To bring down the house. To cause rapturous applause in a theatre.

To bring forth. To produce or give birth.

To bring in. To introduce, to pronounce a verdict.

To bring into play. To cause to act, to set in motion.

To bring off. To achieve successfully.

To bring on. To cause an event or speed it up.

To bring round. To restore to consciousness or health; to cause one to recover from a faint or fit, etc.

To bring to. To restore to consciousness, to resuscitate.

> "I'll bring her to!" said the driver, with a brutal grin. "I'll give her something better than camphire!" and, taking a pin from his coat-sleeve, he buried it to the head in her flesh.
> H. BEECHER STOWE: *Uncle Tom's Cabin*, ch. xxxiii.

Nautically, to luff, to heave to, to bend a sail to its yard; or used of a ship about to anchor, etc.

To bring to bear. To apply oneself to, to focus one's efforts or attention upon, as guns or searchlights are trained on a target.

To bring to book. To detect one in a mistake, to bring one to account.

To bring to pass. To cause to happen.

To bring to the hammer. To offer or sell by public auction.

To bring under. To bring into subjection.

To bring up. To rear from birth or an early age. To moor or anchor a ship. Also numerous other meanings.

Brinkmanship. A term coined by Adlai Stevenson in 1956 (though he disclaimed originality), with especial reference to the policy of J. Foster Dulles as leading to the brink of war. It is now generally used for policies leading to the verge, and possible outbreak, of war.

Brinvilliers, Marquise de (brin vē' yā) (*c.* 1630–1676), a notorious French poisoner. She married the Marquis in 1651 and became the mistress of the Seigneur de Sainte Croix in 1659. Her father secured the latter's consignment to the BASTILLE by *lettre de cachet*, where Sainte Croix learnt the use of poison (probably AQUA TOFANA). Together they plotted revenge and she poisoned her father in 1666 and two brothers in 1670. Her crimes were discovered when Sainte Croix died of accidental poisoning in 1672, and the Marquise was duly beheaded and burned. *See* CHAMBRE ARDENTE.

Briny. I'm on the briny. The sea, which is salt like brine.

Brioche (brē' osh). A kind of pâtisserie made with flour, butter and eggs. The French phrase *Qu'ils mangent de la brioche*, popularly translated as "Let them eat cake", has been commonly, but apocryphally, attributed to Queen Marie Antoinette. The remark was said to have been occasioned at the time of the bread riots at Paris (October 1789) when she was told that the starving populace could not afford bread. The saying in various forms has also been attributed to Yolande, duchesse de Polignac; the Princess Victoire; Queen Maria Theresa and others, but seems to have a considerably earlier ancestry. It is also said that Princess Charlotte (1796–1817), daughter of the then Prince Regent (later George IV), avowed that she would for her part "rather eat beef than starve" and wondered why the people should insist on bread when it was so scarce.

Briseis. The patronymic name of Hippodamia, daughter of Briseus. She was the cause of the quarrel between AGAMEMNON and ACHILLES, and when the former robbed Achilles of her, Achilles withdrew from battle and the Greeks lost ground daily. Ultimately, Achilles sent his friend PATROCLUS to supply his place; he was slain, and Achilles, towering with rage, rushed to battle, slew HECTOR, and TROY fell.

Brissotins. A name given to the republican group in the French Revolution led by Jaques Pierre Brissot (1754–1793), more commonly known as the GIRONDISTS.

Bristol Board. A stiff drawing paper or fine cardboard said to have been first made at Bristol.

Bristol Boy, The. Thomas Chatterton (1752–1770), who was born at Bristol and there composed his ROWLEY POEMS (*see under* FORGERIES).

> The marvellous boy,
> The sleepless soul that perished in his pride.
> WORDSWORTH: *Resolution and Independence*.

Bristol cream is a particularly fine rich brand of SHERRY. *See* BRISTOL MILK.

Bristol diamonds. Brilliant crystals of colourless quartz found in St. Vincent's Rock, Clifton, Bristol. Spenser refers to them as "adamants".

Bristol fashion. *See* ALL SHIP-SHAPE AND BRISTOL FASHION *under* ALL.

Bristol Milk. Sherry; the nickname arose in the 17th century when sherry SACK was a major import at Bristol.

> This metaphorical milk, whereby Xeres or Sherry-sack is intended.
> FULLER: *Worthies*.

Bristol waters. Mineral waters of Clifton, Bristol, formerly celebrated in cases of pulmonary consumption.

Britain (M.E. *Bretayne* through O.Fr. *Bretaigne* from Lat. *Britannia*). An anglicized form of the Latin name for what is now England, WALES and SCOTLAND, called *Britannia* by CAESAR and other Roman writers. In the 4th century B.C. the inhabitants were known as *Pritani* or *Priteni*, and under the Roman occupation they were known as *Britones*.

Great Britain consists of "Britannia prima" (England), "Britannia secunda" (Wales), and "North Britain" (Scotland), united under one sway. The term was first officially used in 1604 when James I was proclaimed "King of Great Britain" and was previously used by some writers to distinguish Britain from "Brittannia Minor", or Brittany, in France.

Britannia. The earliest figure of Britannia as a female figure reclining on a shield is on a Roman coin of Antoninus Pius, who died in A.D. 161. The figure reappeared on our copper coin in the reign of Charles II, 1665, and the model was Frances Stewart, afterwards Duchess of Richmond. The engraver was Philip Roetier.

> The king's new medall, where in little, there is Mrs. Stewart's face…and a pretty thing it is, that he should choose her face to represent Britannia by.
> PEPYS: *Diary*.

British. British disease. An uncomplimentary term used abroad with reference to the prevalence of strikes and INDUSTRIAL ACTION in Great Britain during the 1970s. *Cp.* TO WORK LIKE A BRITON *under* BRITON.

British Legion. *See under* LEGION.

British Lion, The. The pugnacity of the British nation, as opposed to the JOHN BULL, which symbolizes their substantiality, solidity and obstinacy.

To twist the tail of the British lion, or **to twist the lion's tail** used to be a favourite phrase particularly in America for attempting to annoy the British people or provoke them by abuse or to inflict a rebuff. This was a device used to gain the support of Irish Americans.

British Museum. This famous institution began in Montague House, Great Russell Street. It resulted from an Act of 1753 and its first collections were purchased from the proceeds of a public lottery.

Britomart (brit′ ō mart). In Spenser's *Faerie Queene*, a female knight, daughter of King Ryence of Wales. She is the personification of chastity and purity; encounters the "savage, fierce bandit mountaineer" without injury, and is assailed by "hag and unlaid ghost, goblin and swart fairy of the mine", but "dashes their brute violence into sudden adoration and blank awe". She finally marries ARTEGAL.

Spenser got the name, which means "sweet maiden", from Britomartis, a Cretan NYMPH of Greek mythology, who was very fond of the chase. King MINOS fell in love with her, and persisted in his advances for nine months, after which she threw herself into the sea.

Briton. To fight like a Briton is to fight with indomitable courage.

To work like a Briton is to work hard and perseveringly. A similar phrase is "To work like a Trojan". *Cp.* BRITISH DISEASE.

Brittany, The Damsel of. Eleanor, daughter of Geoffrey, second son of Henry II of England and Constance, daughter of Conan IV of Brittany. At the death of Prince Arthur (1203) she became heiress to the English throne, but King John confined her within Bristol castle, where she died in 1241.

Broach. To broach a subject. To open up a subject or start a topic in conversation. The allusion is to beer barrels which are tapped by means of a peg called a *broach*. So "to broach a subject" is to bring it to light, as beer is drawn from the cask after it has been broached.

> I did broach this business to your highness.
> SHAKESPEARE: *Henry VIII*, II, iv.

Broad Arrow. The symbol with which Government stores are marked as a precaution against theft, also once forming a pattern on convicts' uniforms. There are various explanations of its origin but in 1698 an Act was passed imposing heavy penalties on anyone found in possession of naval stores or other goods marked with the broad arrow. *See* ROGUE'S YARN.

Broad Bottom Ministry. A name particularly applied to Henry Pelham's administration (1743–1754) from 1744, which was reinforced by the admission of members of various opposition groups.

Broad Church. A group within the CHURCH OF ENGLAND favouring theological liberalism and tolerance, typified by the writers of *Essays and Reviews* (1860). The name dates from the mid-19th century and the party have certain affinities with the LATITUDINARIANS of former times. They were the forerunners of the MODERNISTS. *Cp.* HIGH CHURCH; LOW CHURCH.

Broadside. In naval language, the whole side of a ship, thus *to fire a broadside* is to discharge all the guns on one side simultaneously; figuratively, a telling verbal onslaught. It is also another name for a *broadsheet*, a large sheet of paper printed on one side, once a popular form of selling printed ballads, etc.

Brobdingnag. In Swift's *Gulliver's Travels*, the country of the giants, to whom Gulliver was a pigmy "not half so big as a round little worm plucked from the lazy finger of a maid". Hence the adjective, *Brobdingnagian*, colossal.

Brocken. *See* SPECTRE.

Brodie, Steve. He jumped off Brooklyn Bridge, 23 July 1886. Known as "the man who wouldn't take a dare" he made this leap to win a bet of $200.

Broken Music. In Tudor England this term meant: (1) Part, or concerted music, *i.e.* music performed on instruments of different classes such as the consorts given in Morley's *Consort Lessons* (1599), which are written for the treble lute, cithern, pandora, flute, treble viol, and bass viol; (2) Music played by a string orchestra, the term in this sense probably originating from harps, lutes, etc., played without a bow and unable to sustain a long note. Bacon uses it in this sense.

> Dancing to song is a thing of great state and pleasure. I understand it that the song be in quire, placed aloft and accompanied with some broken music.
> *Essays: Of Masques and Triumphs*.

SHAKESPEARE makes verbal play with the term:

> *Pand:* Fair prince, here is good broken music.
> *Paris:* You have broke it cousin: and by my life, you shall make it whole again.
> *Troilus and Cressida*, III, i.

Broker. This word originally meant a man who broached wine and then sold it; hence one who buys to sell again, a retailer, a second-hand dealer, a middleman. The word is formed in the same way as *tapster*, one who *taps* a cask. Thus bill-broker, cotton-broker, pawn-broker, ship-broker, STOCK-BROKER, etc.

Bromide. One given to trite remarks, then the remark itself. It was first used in this latter sense by Gelett Burgess (1866–1951) in his novel *Are You a Bromide?* (1906).

Brontes (bron' tēz). A blacksmith personified; in Greek mythology, one of the CYCLOPS. The name signifies *Thunder*.

Brontës, The. The three novelist sisters and their brother Branwell. *See* BELL.

Bronx cheer. The American term for a vulgar derisive sound made with the tongue between the lips, known in England as a "RASPBERRY".

Brooks's. This LIBERAL and social club was originally a gambling club, previously AL-MACK'S, which had acquired the former reputation of WHITE'S as the society centre for high play. In the late 18th century it led the fashion in hazard and faro and C. J. Fox was a notorious patron as was the Prince of Wales. The younger Pitt was a one-time member but subsequently withdrew to White's. It soon became associated with WHIG politics, a flavour which it retained.

Broom. The small wild shrub with yellow flowers (Lat. *planta genista*) from which the English royal dynasty unhistorically called PLANTAGENETS were named. The founder of the dynasty, Geoffrey of Anjou (father of Henry II), was nicknamed Plantagenet because he wore a sprig of broom in his hat, but it was not until about 1448 that the name was assumed by Richard, Duke of York (father of Edward IV) as a surname. It is more correct to refer to ANGEVIN, LANCASTRIAN, and YORKIST kings.

Broom. A broom hung at the masthead of a ship indicates that it is for sale or to be "swept away". The idea is popularly taken to be an allusion to Admiral Van Tromp (*see* PENDANT). It is more probably due to the custom of hanging up something special to attract notice, as a bush meant wine for sale; an old piece of carpet outside a window meant furniture for sale; a wisp of straw meant oysters for sale, etc.

New brooms sweep clean. Those new in office are generally very zealous at first, and sometimes ruthless in making changes.

Brosier my dame. A phrase used at Eton, meaning "to eat one out of house and home". When a dame kept an unusually bad table, the boys agreed on a day to eat, pocket, or waste everything eatable in the house. The hint was generally effective. (Gr. *broso*, to eat.)

Brother used attributively with another noun denotes a fellow-member of the same calling, order, corporation, etc. Apart from the more formal instances, we may note: *brother birch*, a fellow-schoolmaster; *brother blade*, a fellow-soldier or companion in arms; *brother brush*, a fellow-painter; *brother bung*, a fellow-innkeeper; *brother Crispin*, a fellow-shoemaker; *brother Mason*, a fellow-freemason; *brother string*, a fellow-violinist; etc.

Brother Jonathan. It is said that when Washington was in want of ammunition, he called a council of officers, but no practical suggestion was forthcoming. "We must consult brother Jonathan," said the general, meaning His Excellency Jonathan Trumbull, governor of the State of Connecticut. This was done and the difficulty was remedied. Hence the set phrase "To consult Brother Jonathan", and *Brother Jonathan* became the JOHN BULL of the United States until replaced by UNCLE SAM. (*See under* SAM.)

Brougham (brō' am, brum). A closed four-wheel carriage drawn by one horse, very similar to the old GROWLERS. It was named after Lord Brougham (1778–1868), a prominent WHIG politician and one-time Lord CHANCELLOR.

Brow-beat. To beat or put down with sternness, arrogance, in a bullying manner, etc.; from knitting the brows and frowning on one's opponent.

Brown. A copper coin; a penny; so called from its colour. *Cp.* YELLOW BOY.

Browned off. A slang phrase (derivation uncertain) widely current in World War II, signifying "fed up" or "bored stiff". *Cheesed off* is a similar expression. *See* COOKING.

To be done brown. To be deceived, taken in; seen off, to be "roasted". One of the many expressions connected with cooking. *See* ROAST; COOK.

Brown Bagger. A "swot" type of undergraduate, especially at the modern universities. The term is derived from the brown attaché case in which students (especially non-resident students) used to carry their books.

> A "Brown Bagger" I must explain, is a peculiar person; he is one who arrives at 10 a.m. (or earlier) and leaves at 5 p.m., takes no active part in the social life of the college, works at home or elsewhere on Boat Race and Athletic Days when the college is shut and perhaps knows only by hearsay where the Union is.
> *Westminster City School Magazine*, Dec. 1930.

In the U.S.A. a *brown bagger* is a workman who takes his lunch from a brown paper bag rather than use the cafeteria, etc.; or one who similarly takes his own liquor to a club or restaurant, usually where alcoholic drinks are not available.

Brown Bess. A familiar name for the old flint-lock musket formerly in use in the British Army. In 1808 a process of browning was introduced but the term was current long before this and probably referred to the colour of the stock. *Bess* is unexplained but may be a counterpart to *Bill* in BROWN BILL.

Brown Bill. A kind of halberd used by foot-soldiers before muskets took their place. The *brown* probably refers to their rusty condition though it may equally stand for *burnished* (Dut. *brun*, shining) as in the old phrases "my bonnie brown sword", "brown as glass", etc. Keeping the weapons *bright*, however, is a modern habit; our forefathers preferred the honour of bloodstains. In the following extract the term denotes the soldiers themselves:

> Lo, with a band of bowmen and of pikes
> Brown bills and targetiers.
> MARLOWE: *Edward II*, I, 1324.

Brown Bomber. Joe Louis (1914–1981), undefeated heavyweight champion of the world from 1937 until his retirement in 1949. On his return in 1950 he was defeated by Ezzard Charles. He began his career in 1934, winning 27 fights, all but four by knockouts. The phrase comes from his being a NEGRO and from the great power of his punches.

Brown George. A large earthenware vessel such as that mentioned by Thomas Hughes in *Tom Brown at Oxford* (1861).

Brown, Jones, and Robinson. The typification of middle-class Englishmen; from the adventures of three Continental tourists of these names which were told and illustrated by Richard Doyle in *Punch* in the 1870s. These sketches hold up to ridicule the gaucherie, insularity, vulgarity, extravagance, conceit, and snobbery of the middle class, and are in themselves an outstanding example of Victorian snobbery in their ill-mannered sneers at the uneducated.

Brown Shirts. Hitler's NAZI Party in Germany, so called from the colour of their shirts.

Brown study. Absence of mind; apparent thought but real vacuity. The corresponding French phrase explains it—*sombre rêverie*. *Sombre* and *brun* both mean sad, melancholy, gloomy, dull.

> Tom was in a brown study, brooding, like a young William Tell, upon the wrongs of fags in general, and his own in particular.
> T. HUGHES: *Tom Brown's Schooldays*, Pt. I, ch. viii.

Brownie. The home spirit in Scottish superstition. He is called in England ROBIN GOODFELLOW. At night he is supposed to busy himself on little jobs for the family over which he presides. Brownies are brown or tawny spirits and farms are their favourite abode. *See also* GIRL GUIDES.

Brownists. Followers of Robert Browne, who established a congregational society at Norwich in 1580. Both episcopal and presbyterian organization was rejected. Browne eventually left his own society and returned to the Church. *See* INDEPENDENTS.

> I had as lief be a Brownist as a politician.
> SHAKESPEARE: *Twelfth Night*, III, ii.

Browse his jib, To. A sailor's phrase meaning to drink till the face is flushed and swollen. The *jib* means the face and to *browse* here means "to fatten". Formed from "to browse the jib" which means to haul the jib taut, thus metaphorically signifying to be "TIGHT".

Bruderhof (Ger. Society of Brothers). A Christian sect founded in Germany in 1920 with beliefs similar to the MENNONITES. They came to Gloucestershire in 1937 when driven out by the NAZIS, but to avoid internment in World War II left for Paraguay in 1941. They re-established themselves in Sussex in 1971. The men wear beards and dark trousers with braces, the women are simply clad with long skirts and headscarves or caps. They support themselves by making quality wooden toys in community workshops and the children first go outside the community at the secondary school stage. There are four other groups in the Eastern U.S.A. and they are linked with the Hutterian Anabaptists in the Western U.S.A. and Canada. *Cp.* KIBBUTZ.

Bruin (bru' in). In Butler's *Hudibras*, one of the leaders arrayed against the hero. His prototype in real life was Talgol, a NEWGATE butcher who obtained a captaincy for valour at Naseby. He marched next to Orsin (Joshua Gosling, landlord of the bear-gardens at SOUTHWARK).

Sir Bruin. The bear in the famous mediæval beast-epic, REYNARD THE FOX.

Brumaire (brü' mâr). In the French Revolutionary CALENDAR, the month from 23 October to 21 November; named from *brume*, fog (Lat. *bruma*, winter). The celebrated COUP D'ÉTAT of 18 Brumaire (9 November 1799) was when NAPOLEON overthrew the DIRECTORY and established the Consulate, thus ending the sway of the revolutionary oligarchy.

Brumby. An Australian wild horse. The origin of the word is obscure.

Brummagem (brŭm' ä jem). Worthless or inferior metal articles made in imitation of better ones. The word is a local form of the name *Birmingham*, formerly noted for its output of cheap trinkets, toys, imitation jewellery, etc.

Brummel, George Bryan. *See* BEAU.

Brunhild (broon' hild). Daughter of the King of Islant, and of superhuman physique, beloved by GUNTHER, one of the two great chieftains in the NIBELUNGENLIED. She was to be won by strength, and SIEGFRIED contrived the matter but Brunhild never forgave him for his treachery.

Brunswicker. *See* BLACK BRUNSWICKERS.

Brunt. To bear the brunt. To bear the worst stress, the worst of the shock. The *brunt of the battle* is the hottest part of the fight. *Brunt* is possibly connected with the Icel. *bruna*, to advance like fire.

Brush. The tail of a fox or a squirrel, which is bushy and brush-like.

He brushed by me. He just touched me as he hurried by. Hence also *brush*, a slight skirmish.

Give it another brush. A little more attention; bestow a little more labour on it.

To brush aside. To sweep out of the way; to take no account of.

To brush up. To renovate or revive; to bring back into use that which has been neglected, as, "I must brush up my French."

To get the brush off (of American origin). To be given a curt rebuff; to be put aside, rejected or dismissed.

Brut. A rhyming chronicle of British history beginning with the mythical Brut, or BRUTE, and so named from him. Wace's *Le Roman de Brut*, or *Brut d'Angleterre* is a rhythmical translation of Geoffrey of Monmouth's *History*, with additional legends. Wace's work formed the basis of Layamon's *Brut* (early 13th century), a versified history of England from the fall of TROY to A.D. 698. (*See* ARTHURIAN ROMANCES.)

Brute (broot), or **Brutus.** In the mythological history of Britain the first king was Brute, the son of Sylvius (grandson of Ascanius and great-grandson of ÆNEAS). Having inadvertently killed his father, he first took refuge in Greece, and then in Britain. In remembrance of TROY he called the capital of his kingdom TROY NOVANT, now London.

Brutum fulmen (broo' tum fŭl' men) (Lat.). A noisy but harmless threatening; an innocuous thunderbolt. The phrase is from Pliny II, xliii, 113: "*Bruta fulmina et vana, ut quae nulla veniant ratione naturae*"— Thunderbolts that strike blindly and harmlessly, being traceable to no natural cause.

The actors do not value themselves upon the Clap, but regard it as a mere *Brutum fulmen*, or empty

Noise, when it has not the sound of the Oaken Plant in it.
ADDISON: *Spectator* (29 Nov. 1711).

Brutus, Junius (broo' tus, joo' ni ŭs). In legend, the first consul of ROME, fabled to have held office about 509 B.C. He condemned to death his own two sons for joining a conspiracy to restore the banished TARQUIN. *See* JUNIUS.

Brutus, Marcus (85–42 B.C.). Caesar's friend, who joined the conspiracy to murder him.

Et tu Brute. Thou, too, Brutus! Caesar's exclamation when he saw that his old friend was one of his assassins. "Does my old friend raise his hand against me?"

The Spanish Brutus. Alphonso Perez de Guzman (1258–1320). While he was governor, Castile was besieged by Don JUAN who had revolted against his brother Sancho IV. Juan threatened to cut the throat of Guzman's son, whom he held captive, unless Guzman surrendered the city. Guzman replied, "Sooner than be a traitor, I would myself lend you a sword to slay him," and he threw a sword over the city wall. With this the son was slain before his father's eyes.

Bryanites. *See* BIBLE CHRISTIANS.

Bub. Drink; particularly strong beer.

Drunk with Helicon's waters and double-brewed bub.
PRIOR: *To a Person who wrote ill*.

Bubastis. The ancient capital of Lower Egypt named after Bast, the local cat-headed goddess. The Greeks identified her with ARTEMIS and the CAT was sacred to her.

Bubble, or **Bubble Scheme.** A worthless, unstable, unsound project—an ephemeral scheme, frail as a bubble. *See* MISSISSIPPI; SOUTH-SEA.

The Bubble Act. An Act of 1719 which was designed to check the formation of "bubble" companies or schemes. It proved to be ineffectual and was repealed in 1825.

Bubble and Squeak. Cold boiled potatoes and greens fried up together (sometimes with meat). They first *bubbled* in water when boiled and afterwards hissed or *squeaked* in the frying pan.

Bubbles. The name given to the portrait of a curly-headed boy, clad in velvet, with pipe and bowl, blowing bubbles. It was painted by Sir John Millais in 1886 and it became widely familiar when used as an advertisement for Pears' Soap. The boy concerned came to be Admiral Sir William James (1881–1973), affectionately known in the Royal Navy as "Bubbles James".

Bubbly. Sparkling champagne. Until well into the 18th century champagne was fashionable as a still drink.

Bucca (bŭk′ ȧ). A GOBLIN of the wind, once supposed by Cornish people to foretell shipwrecks; also a sprite fabled to live in the tin mines.

Buccaneer (bŭc ȧ nēr′). This name is particularly applied to the PROTESTANT sea rovers and pirates of England, France and the Netherlands who haunted the Caribbean in the 17th century. It is derived through the Fr. *boucanier* from the Caribbean *boucan*, smoked dried meat, the preparation of which the adventurers learned from the natives of Hispaniola, where they carried on an illicit trade in *boucan*. This trade was inevitably combined with lawlessness and piracy and so the word came to signify a desperate piratical adventurer.

Bucentaur (bū sen′ tôr) (Gr. *bous*, ox; *centauros*, centaur). The name of the Venetian state galley used by the Doge on ASCENSION DAY when Venice was made BRIDE OF THE SEA. The original galley was probably ornamented with a manheaded ox. The third and last Bucentaur was destroyed by the French in 1798.

> The spouseless Adriatic mourns her lord
> And, annual marriage now no more renewed,
> The Bucentaur lies rotting unrestored,
> Neglected garment of her widowhood.
>
> BYRON: *Childe Harold*, iv. 9.

Bucephalus (bull-headed). A HORSE. The famous charger of ALEXANDER THE GREAT.

Buchan's Weather Periods (bŭ′ kȧn). Alexander Buchan (1829–1907) was secretary of the Scottish Meteorological Society which, under his influence, built an observatory on Ben Nevis. After many years' observation of weather and temperatures he worked out a curve of recurrent periods, six cold and two warm, in the year. The cold periods are 7–10 Feb.; 11–14 April; 9–14 May; 29 June–4 July; 6–11 Aug.; 6–12 Nov. The warm periods are 12–15 July; 12–15 Aug. It should be noted that these dates are the mean of many observations and do not predict the probable weather every year.

Buchanites. A deluded group of fanatics, appearing in the west of Scotland in the latter part of the 18th century, and named after their foundress Mrs., or Lucky, Buchan. She called herself the "Friend Mother" claiming to be the woman mentioned in *Rev*. xii and maintaining that the Rev. Hugh White, a convert, was the "man-child".

> I never heard of ale-wife that turned preacher, except Luckie Buchan in the west.
>
> SCOTT: *St. Ronan's Well*, ch. ii.

Buchmanism. *See* OXFORD GROUP.

Buck. A DANDY; a GAY and spirited fellow; a fast young man.

> A most tremendous buck he was, as he sat there serene, in state, driving his greys.
>
> THACKERAY: *Vanity Fair*, ch. vi.

The word is also American slang for a DOLLAR, derived from the time when skins were classified as "bucks" and "does", the former being the more valuable.

Buck-basket. A linen-basket. To *buck* is to wash clothes in lye. The word is probably connected with the Ger. *beuchen*, Fr. *buer*, to steep in lye, and perhaps with O.E. *bue*, a pitcher.

Buck board. An open four-wheeled horse-drawn vehicle formerly used in the U.S.A.; named from the "bucking" motion endured by the occupants due to the springy structure of the floor-boards.

Buckeye State. Ohio, from the abundance of *buckeyes* or horse-chestnut trees that grow there. A *buckeye* is a native of Ohio.

Buck horn. *See* STOCKFISH.

Buckhorse, A. A severe blow or slap on the face, from an 18th-century pugilist, John Smith, whose nickname was "Buckhorse". For a small sum he would allow anyone to strike him heavily on the side of the face.

Buck-tooth. A large projecting front-tooth, once called a butter-tooth.

To pass the buck. To evade a task or responsibility and shift it on to someone else. The term is from poker and was the equivalent of passing (*i.e.* not bidding) in a game of bridge.

Bucket, To. An obsolete slang term for *to cheat*, of American origin.

Bucket-shop. Probably derived from TO BUCKET, it denoted the office of an "outside" STOCKBROKER, *i.e.* a non-member of the STOCK EXCHANGE. As these offices are used for gambling in stocks rather than investing, the name usually implies a shady establishment.

To give the bucket, to get the bucket. To give (or receive) notice of dismissal from employment. Here *bucket* is synonymous with SACK.

To kick the bucket. To die. *Bucket* here is a beam or yoke (O.Fr. *buquet*, Fr. *trébuchet*, a balance), and in East Anglia the beam on which a pig is suspended by the heels for slaughter is called a bucket. Another theory is that the bucket was kicked away by a suicide, who stood on it the better to hang himself. A third explanation is that when a bucket was put out to collect for the widow of a workmate some who passed by kicked the bucket instead of throwing in a coin.

Buckle. I can't buckle to. I can't give my mind to work. The allusion is to buckling on one's armour or belt.

To cut the buckle. To caper about, to heel and toe it in dancing. In jigs the two feet buckle or twist into each other with great rapidity.

> Throth, it wouldn't lave a laugh in you to see the parson dancing down the road on his way home, and the ministher and methodist praicher cuttin' the buckle as they went along.
>
> W. B. YEATS: *Fairy tales of the Irish Peasantry*, p. 98.

To talk buckle. To talk about marriage.

Buckler. *See* SHIELD.

Bucklersbury (London) was at one time the noted street for druggists and herbalists; hence Falstaff says:

> I cannot cog, and say thou art this and that, like a many of these lisping hawthorn buds, that come like women in men's apparel, and smell like Bucklersbury in simple time.
>
> SHAKESPEARE: *Merry Wives of Windsor*, III, iii.

Buckley's Chance (Austr.). An extremely remote chance. One explanation of the phrase is that it comes from a convict named Buckley who escaped in 1803 and lived over thirty years with aborigines. The second explanation derives it from the Melbourne business house of Buckley and Nunn—hence the pun, "There are just two chances, Buckley's or None."

"To have two chances—mine and Buckley's" is a way of emphasizing that there is only one feasible course of action to take.

Buckmaster's Light Infantry. *See* REGIMENTAL AND DIVISIONAL NICKNAMES.

Buckram. A strong coarse kind of cloth.

Men in buckram. Imaginary men, as in Falstaff's vaunting tale to Prince Henry. Hence a "buckram army", one which exists only in the imagination.

> Four rogues in buckram let drive at me.
>
> SHAKESPEARE: *Henry IV, Pt. I*, II, iv.

Buckshee. Free, gratis. Military slang derived from BAKSHEESH.

Buckskin. A Virginian.

Buddha (bud′à) (Sans. the enlightened). The title given to Prince Siddhartha or GAUTAMA (*c.* 563–483 B.C.), the founder of BUDDHISM; also called Sakyamuni from the name of his tribe, the Sakyas.

Buddhism. A religion inaugurated by Buddha in India in the 6th century B.C. It holds that the way to *enlightenment* consists in knowledge of the *Four Truths*:

(1) That life is characterized by unsatisfactoriness.

(2) That this is due to desire or craving.

(3) That the state of unsatisfactoriness can be removed by eliminating desire.

(4) That NIRVANA, the state of non-, desire is attainable by means of the *Noble Eightfold Path*: right understanding, right thought, right speech, right action, right livelihood, right effort, right mindfulness and right concentration.

Esoteric Buddhism. *See* THEOSOPHY.

Bude, or **Gurney Light.** A very bright light obtained by supplying an argand gas jet with oxygen, invented by Sir Goldsworthy Gurney (1793–1875) about 1834 and first used in the lighthouse at Bude, Cornwall.

Budge. Lambskin with the wool dressed outwards, worn on the edges of capes, graduates' hoods, etc. Hence the word is used attributively to denote pedantry, stiff formality, etc. Budge Row, Cannon Street, is so called because it was chiefly occupied by budge-makers.

> O foolishness of men! that lend their ears
> To those budge-doctors of the stoic fur.
>
> MILTON: *Comus*, 706.

Budge Bachelors. A company of men clothed in long gowns lined with *budge* or lamb's wool, who used to accompany the Lord MAYOR at his inauguration.

Budget (O.Fr. *bougette*, a wallet). The present meaning of the (normally) annual estimate of revenue and expenditure and statement on financial policy, which the CHANCELLOR OF THE EXCHEQUER lays before the HOUSE OF COMMONS, arose from the custom of bringing the relevant papers to the House in a leather bag and laying them on the table. Hence to *budget*, to estimate, or to make proper provision for meeting one's expenses.

A budget of news. A bagful of news, a large stock of news.

Cry budget. A watchword or shibboleth; short for MUMBUDGET. Slender says to Shallow:

> We have a nay-word how to know one another. I come to her in white and cry *mum*: she cries *budget*; and by that time we know one another.
>
> SHAKESPEARE: *Merry Wives of Windsor*, V, ii.

Buff. Properly, soft stout leather prepared from the skin of a buffalo; hence any light-coloured leather; then figuratively, the bare skin. **To stand in buff** is to stand without clothing; **to strip to the buff** is to strip to the skin.

To stand buff. To stand firm; unflinching. Here buff means a blow or buffet. *Cp.* BLINDMAN'S BUFF.

The phrase also occurs as **to stand bluff.** Here the allusion is probably nautical; a "bluff shore" is one with a bold and upright front.

That he should have stood bluff to old bachelor so
long, and sink into a husband at last.
SHERIDAN: School for Scandal, II, iii.

Buffs. *See* REGIMENTAL AND DIVISIONAL
NICKNAMES.

Buffalo Bill. William Frederick Cody
(1847–1917) earned this name for his hunting the buffalo to provide meat for the
labourers constructing the Kansas Pacific
Railway in 1876–1878. He is held to have
killed 4,280 buffaloes in 18 months. He was
born in Iowa and, when little more than a
boy, was a rider of the PONY EXPRESS. In
1861 he became a scout for the U.S. army
and fought in the CIVIL WAR. Later on he was
fighting once more in the Indian wars and
single-handed killed Yellowhand, the Cheyenne chief. In 1883 he organized his Wild
West Show, which he brought to Europe for
the first time in 1887. He paid various subsequent visits and toured the Continent in
1910. His show, with its Indians, cowboys,
sharp-shooters and roughriders was outstanding.

Buffer. A chap, a silly old fellow. In M.E. it is
used for a stammerer or stutterer.

Buffer State. A small state between two larger neighbours acting as a shock-absorber
between the two.

Bug. An old word for GOBLIN, SPRITE, BOGY;
probably from the Welsh *bwg*, a ghost. The
word is used in the BUG BIBLE (*see* BIBLE, SPE-
CIALLY NAMED), and survives in *bogle, bogy*,
and in *bugaboo*, a monster or goblin, and
bugbear, a scarecrow, or sort of HOBGOBLIN
in the form of a bear.

Warwick was a bug that feared us all.
SHAKESPEARE: Henry VI, Pt. III, V, ii.

In common usage the word *bug* is applied to
almost any kind of insect or germ, especially
an insect of the creeping crawling sort, and
notably the *bed bug*. Also it is colloquially
used to refer to anyone "bitten" with a particular craze or obsession, from the *love-bug*
to the *money-bug*. *See* BUGHOUSE.

A big bug. A person of importance, especially in his own eyes, a SWELL, a conceited
man. There is an old adjective *bug*, meaning
pompous, proud.

Dainty sport toward, Dalyall! sit, come sit.
Sit and be quiet; here are kingly bug-words.
FORD: Perkin Warbeck, III, ii.

Bug-Eye. A flat-bottomed boat used by the
oyster fishermen of the coast of Maryland
and Virginia, especially in Chesapeake Bay.

Bug-eyed Monster. Generic for the creatures of the science-fiction writers' imaginations, inhabitants of, or visitors from, outer
space; from the American slang "bug" (*i.e.*
bulging) eyes. It is known as BEM to science-

fiction addicts.

Bughouse (U.S.A.). Crazy or demented.
Also used in England for the old-time cheap
cinema in the same way as *fleapit*.

Fire-bug. A person with a mania for incen-
diarism. A term of American origin.

Buggane. *See* BOGGARD.

Buhl. An incorrect form of BOULE.

Bull. (1) A blunder, or inadvertent contradiction of terms, for which the Irish are proverbial. *The British Apollo* (No. 22, 1708) says
the term is derived from one Obadiah Bull,
an Irish lawyer of London in the reign of
Henry VII, whose blundering in this way
was notorious, but there is no corroboration
of this story which must be put down as BEN
TROVATO. Another explanation is that it is
suggested by the contradiction in a PAPAL
BULL in which the POPE humbly styles himself "servant of servants" while asserting
complete authority. There was a M.E. verb
to bull, to befool, to cheat, and there is the
O.Fr. *boule* or *bole*, fraud, trickery; the
word may be connected with one of these.

(2) Slang for a five-shilling piece. *Half a
bull* is half a CROWN. Possibly from *bulla* (*see*
PAPAL BULL); but as BULL'S EYE was an older
slang term for the same thing, this is doubtful. Hood, in one of his comic sketches,
speaks of a crier who, being apprehended,
"swallowed three hogs (shillings) and a
bull".

(3) It is also short for BULL'S EYE.

(4) *Bull* (short for bull-shit), originally
army slang for excessive spit and polish and
unnecessary cleaning of equipment, etc.
Now used also for anything useless, unnecessary, or just rubbish and pretence.

(5) In STOCK EXCHANGE language, a *bull* is
a speculative purchase for a rise; also a buyer
who does this, the reverse of a BEAR. A *bull-
account* is a speculation made in the hope
that the stock purchased will rise before the
day of settlement. Since the early 18th century the terms *bull* and *bear* have been
broadly used on the Stock Exchange to describe an optimist or pessimist in share-
dealing.

(6) In astronomy, the English name of the
northern constellation (Lat. Taurus) which
contains ALDEBARAN and the PLEIADES; also
the sign of the ZODIAC that the sun enters
about 22 April.

(7) *Bull* is also the name given to a drink
from the swillings of empty spirit casks.

Bulling the barrel. Pouring water into a
nearly empty rum cask to prevent it leaking.
The water which gets impregnated with the
spirit is called *bull*. Hence the seaman's
phrase of *bulling the teapot* (making a sec-

ond brew).

A bull in a china shop. One who behaves clumsily or acts in a gauche manner, without finesse, or even with violence.

To roar like a bull of Bashan. To roar loudly and excessively. In OLD TESTAMENT times Bashan was a territory in northern Palestine noted for its breed of cattle.

> Many bulls have compassed me; strong bulls of Bashan have beset me round.
> They gaped upon me with their mouths, as a ravening and roaring lion.
> *Ps.* xxii, 12–13.

In the SCRIPTURES a bull of Bashan also denoted a loud-mouthed, tyrannical oppressor.

> Hear this word, ye kine of Bashan ... which oppress the poor, which crush the needy....
> *Amos* iv, 1.

To score a bull. *See* BULL'S EYE.

To take the bull by the horns. To attack or encounter a threatened danger fearlessly; to go forth boldly to meet a difficulty, just as a MATADOR will grasp the horns of a bull about to toss him.

A brazen bull. An instrument of torture. *See* INVENTORS.

Bull and Gate. Bull and Mouth. PUBLIC-HOUSE SIGNS. A corruption of Boulogne Gate or Mouth, adopted out of compliment to Henry VIII, who took Boulogne in 1544. Fielding's Tom Jones stayed at the "Bull and Gate" in HOLBORN, where there is still a public house of that name.

Bull sessions. In the U.S.A. this phrase is applied to long talks, among men only, about life in general or some particular problem.

Geneva Bull. *See under* GENEVA.

John Bull. *See* JOHN BULL.

Papal Bull. An edict issued by the POPE, named from the seal (Lat. *bulla*) appended to the document. *See* GOLDEN BULL.

Bull-baiting. Bull and bear-baiting were popular spectacles in Tudor and Stuart England. The beasts were usually tethered and set upon by dogs. It was made illegal in 1835.

Bull-ring. In Spain the arena where bullfights take place; in England, the place where bulls used to be baited. The name survives in many English towns, as in Birmingham. *See* MAYOR OF THE BULL-RING.

Bull-Roarer. A flat piece of wood, about eight inches long, attached to a cord and whirled above the head, producing a moaning or humming sound. It was used by the primitive peoples of Australia (called *tundun*) and North America in rain-making, initiation and fertility ceremonies.

Bull's eye. The inmost disc or centre of a target. Also a black and white streaked peppermint-flavoured sweet; a small cloud appearing seemingly in violent motion, and expanding till it covers the entire vault of heaven, producing a tumult of wind and rain (I *Kings* xviii, 44); and a thick disc or boss of glass. Hence a *bull's-eye lantern*, also called a *bull's-eye*.

To make a bull's-eye, or **to score a bull.** To gain some signal advantage; a successful coup. To hit the centre of the target.

Bulldog. A man of relentless, tenacious disposition is sometimes so called. A bulldog courage is one that flinches from no danger. The bulldog was formerly used for BULL-BAITING. At Oxford and Cambridge the *bulldogs* or *bullers* are the two MYRMIDONS of the proctor, who attend on his heels like dogs, ready to spring on any offending undergraduate.

Boys of the bulldog breed. Britons, especially with reference to their pugnacity. This phrase comes from Arthur Reece's music-hall song *Sons of the Sea, All British born* which had a tremendous vogue in late Victorian and Edwardian England. It came at the time of naval rivalry with the Kaiser's Germany and had the same kind of effect as the JINGO song.

Bullet. Every bullet has its billet. Nothing happens by chance and no act is altogether without effect.

To get the bullet. To be dismissed, TO GET THE SACK. (*See under* SACK.)

Bulletin. An official report of a public event or public news, or from medical attendants on the health of public personages. The word is borrowed from the Ital. *bullettino*, a theatre or lottery ticket, from *bulla* (*see* PAPAL BULL, *above*), because of their authentication by an official *bulla* or seal.

Bully. To overbear with words. A *bully* is a blustering menacer. The original meaning of the noun was "sweetheart" as in

> I kiss his dirty shoe, and from my heart-strings I love the lovely bully.
> SHAKESPEARE: *Henry V*, IV, i.

It is probably from the Dut. *boel*, a lover; and the later meaning may have been influenced by Dut. *bul*, a bull, also a clown, and *bulderen*, to bluster.

Bully-beef. Tinned corned beef. Probably from Fr. *boulli*, boiled meat.

Bully-rag. To intimidate; *bully-ragging* is abusive intimidation. A *rag* is a scold.

Bully-rook. SHAKESPEARE uses the term (*Merry Wives*, I, iii, 2) for a jolly companion, but later it came to mean a hired ruffian.

Bum. An old word for the buttocks or posterior. An American term for a vagrant, hence any worthless fellow.

Bum-bailiff. The Fr. *pousse-cul* seems to favour the view that *bum-bailiff* is no corruption. These officers, who made an arrest for debt by touching the debtor on the back, are frequently referred to as *bums*.

> Scout me for him at the corner of the orchard, like a bum-bailiff.
> SHAKESPEARE: *Twelfth Night*, III, iv.

Bum-boat. A small wide boat used to carry provisions to vessels lying off shore. Also called "dirt boats", being used for removing filth from ships lying in the Thames.

Bum-freezer. A short jacket, an Eton jacket, especially as formerly worn by schoolboys at Eton and elsewhere. *Cp.* MONKEY JACKET; SHELL JACKET.

Bumble. A BEADLE. So called from the officious, overbearing beadle in Dickens's *Oliver Twist*; hence **bumbledom**, fussy officialism, especially on the part of parish officers; also parochial officials collectively.

Bummaree. Middlemen or fishjobbers in BILLINGSGATE Market. It has been suggested that the word is a corruption of *bonne marée, good fresh fish, marée* being a French term for all kinds of fresh seafish.

Bump-off. To murder, a EUPHEMISM deriving from "to take for a ride" (*see* RIDE).

Bump Races. Rowing contests held annually at Oxford and Cambridge between the colleges, where the boats seek to bump each other, not to overtake.

Bump Suppers. Festivities which follow the BUMP RACES, often accompanied by hilarious behaviour from the undergraduates.

Bun. Hot cross buns on GOOD FRIDAY were supposed to be made of the dough kneaded for the HOST, and were marked with a cross accordingly. As they are said to keep for twelve months without turning mouldy, some persons still hang up one or more in their house as a "charm against evil".

The Greeks offered cakes with "horns" on them to APOLLO, DIANA, HECATE and the MOON. Such a cake was called a *bous*, and (it is said) never grew mouldy. The round bun represented the full moon, and the cross symbolized the four quarters.

> Good Friday comes this month: the old woman runs.
> With one a penny, two a penny "hot cross buns",
> Whose virtue is, if you believe what's said,
> They'll not grow mouldy like the common bread.
> *Poor Robin's Almanack*, 1733.

When women "put up" long hair, finished in a coil at the back of the neck, it is called a *bun*. The word is applied to a hare's tail and a rabbit. *See* BUNNY.

Bun fight. A tea party on a fairly large scale such as that of a SUNDAY SCHOOL, social club, parish organization, etc.

To put a bun in the oven. To make a woman pregnant.

Bunce. A slang term for money; particularly for something extra or unexpected in the way of profit. Also sometimes used in the sense of perquisites, which can be sold for money. Thought to be a corruption of *bonus* (in the sense of extra dividend).

Bunch, Mother. A noted London alewife of the late 16th century, on whose name have been fathered many jests and anecdotes, and who is mentioned more than once in the drama of the period.

> Now, now, Mother Bunch, how dost thou? What dost frowne, Queen Gwyniver, dost wrinkle?
> DEKKER: *Satiromastix*, III, i.

Pasquil's Jests, mixed with Mother Bunches Merriments was published in 1604 and she is humorously described in the "Epistle to the Merrie Reader":

> ... She spent most of her time in telling of tales, and when she laughed she was heard from Aldgate to the monuments at Westminster, and all Southwarke stood in amazement, the Lyons in the Tower, and the Bulls and Beares of Parish Garden roar'd louder than the great roaring Megge... She dwelt in Cornhill neere the exchange, and sold strong ale...and lived an hundred and seventy and five yeares, two days and a quarter, and halfe a minute.

Other books were named after her, such as *Mother Bunch's Closet newly Broke Open, containing rare secrets of art and nature, tried and experienced by learned philosophers, and recommended to all ingenious young men and maids, teaching them how to get good wives and husbands.*

Bunch of Fives. Slang for the hand or fist.

Bundle off. Get away. *To bundle a person off* is to send him away unceremoniously. Similar to *pack off*. The allusion is obvious.

Bundles for Britain. An organization founded in the U.S.A., January 1940, by Mrs. Wales Latham to send parcels of "comforts" to Britain during World War II.

Bundle of Sticks. ÆSOP, in one of his fables, shows that sticks one by one may be readily broken; not so when several are bound together in a bundle. The lesson taught is that "Union gives strength".

The bundle of rods with an axe or *Fasces*, the Roman symbol of absolute authority, was adopted by Mussolini's party. Hence the name FASCIST.

Bundling. The curious and now obsolete New England custom of engaged couples going to bed together fully dressed and thus spending the night. It was a recognized proceeding to which no suggestion of impropriety was attached.

> Stopping occasionally in the villages to eat pumpkin pie, dance at country frolics, and bundle with the Yankee lasses.
>
> WASHINGTON IRVING: *Knickerbocker*.

The same custom existed in Wales and the remoter parts of Scotland.

Bung. A CANT term for a publican; also for a toper. "Away, ... you filthy bung," says Doll to Pistol (SHAKESPEARE: *Henry IV, Pt. II*, II, iv).

Bung up. Close up, as a bung closes a cask.

Bungalow (Hind. *bangla*, of, or belonging to, Bengal). Originally, the house of a European in India, generally of one storey only with a verandah all round it, and the roof thatched to keep off the hot rays of the sun. A *dak-bungalow* is a caravansary or house built by the government for the use of travellers. Dr. Brewer says, in his 1894 edition of this dictionary, "There are English bungalows at Birchington and on the Norfolk coast near Cromer."

Bungay. *See* FRIAR BUNGAY.

Bungay play. Leading with the highest scoring cards in WHIST, instead of attempting any finesse. It may be a corruption of "bungling" or a reference to the supposed rustic slow-wittedness of the people of Bungay in Suffolk.

Castle of Bungay. *See* CASTLE.

Friar Bungay. *See under* FRIAR.

Go to Bungay with you!—*i.e.* get away and don't bother me; don't talk such stuff. Bungay in Suffolk was famous for the manufacture of leather breeches, once very fashionable. Persons who required new ones or old ones re-seated went or sent to Bungay for them. Hence rose the cant saying, "Go to Bungay, and get your breeches mended", shortened into "Go to Bungay with you!"

Bunkum. Claptrap. Now more commonly shortened to *bunk*. A representative at Washington being asked why he made such a flowery and angry speech, so wholly uncalled for, made answer, "I was not speaking to the House, but to Buncombe," which he represented (North Carolina).

Bunny. A rabbit. So called from the provincial word *bun*, a tail, especially of a hare, which is said to "cock her bun". *Bunny*, a diminutive applied to a rabbit, means the animal with the "little tail".

Bunny girl. A somewhat scantily dressed waitress or attendant in certain night clubs and Playboy clubs, equipped with a fluffy tail and a headdress with long ears to suggest a rabbit.

Bunting. In Somersetshire *bunting* means sifting flour. Sieves were once made of a strong gauzy woollen cloth, which was tough and capable of resisting wear. It has been suggested that this cloth was found suitable for making flags, hence its present meaning of a material for this purpose.

A "bunt-mill" is a machine for sifting corn.

Bunting-tosser, or sometimes shortened to *bunts*, a naval nickname for a signalman because he hoisted the bunting (flags and pennants), nowadays a Radio Operator (Tactical). *Cp.* SPARKER.

Bunyan, Paul. A legendary hero of the lumber camps of the north-western U.S.A. His feats—such as cutting the Grand Canyon of the Colorado by dragging his pick behind him—are told and retold with embellishments by the lumbermen; some of them were collected in a curious volume entitled, *Paul Bunyan Comes West*.

Bunyip. According to Australian aboriginal folk-lore, a man-eating bellowing monster who drags his victims down to the bottom of the lake or swamp that he inhabits. It is also used to mean an "impostor".

Burble (bĕr′bĕl). To mutter nonsense. In its modern use this is a word invented by Lewis Carroll (*Through the Looking Glass*) with the meaning to make a sound somewhere between a bubble and a gurgle.

> The Jabberwock, with eyes of flame,
> Came whiffling through the tulgy wood
> And burbled as it came.

Burd. A poetic word for a young lady (*cp.* BIRD). Obsolete except in ballads.

Burden of a song. A line repeated at intervals constituting a refrain or chorus. It is the Fr. *bourdon*, the big drone of a bagpipe, or double diapason of an organ, used in *forte* parts and choruses.

Burden of Isaiah. "The Burden of Babylon, which Isaiah the son of Amoz did see" (*Isaiah* iii, 1, etc.). Burden here is a literal translation of the Heb. *massa* (rendered in the Vulgate by *onus*), which means "lifting up", either a burden or the voice; hence utterance, hence a prophecy announcing a calamity, or a denunciation of hardships on those to whom the burden is uttered.

The burden of proof. The obligation to prove something.

Bureaucracy. A system of government in which business is carried on in *bureaux* or departments. The Fr. *bureau* means not only the office of a public functionary but the whole staff attached to it. Hence *bureaucrat*, the head of a department in a bureaucracy; now used to imply a short-sighted, bumptious, soulless RED-TAPE minded administrator, lacking vision and intelligent understanding.

Burglary in English law, used to mean breaking into a house by night with intent to commit a felony, and by the Larceny Act of 1861 "night" was limited to the hours between 9 p.m. and 6 a.m. At other times such an offence became *house-breaking*. The 1861 Act has been repealed and burglary, as defined by the Theft Act of 1968, is no longer restricted to particular hours and includes the damaging of premises entered and the infliction of "grievous bodily harm".

Burgoyne, Gentleman Johnny. General John Burgoyne (1722–1792), who surrendered to General Gates at Saratoga (1777). He later devoted his time to writing light literature and plays. He earned his nickname for his elegant manner and fondness of fashionable life.

Burgundian. A Burgundian blow, *i.e.* decapitation. The Duc de Biron, who was put to death for treason by Henry IV, was told in his youth by a fortune-teller, "to beware of a Burgundian blow". When going to execution, he asked who was to be his executioner, and was told he was a man from Burgundy.

Burial of an Ass. No burial at all, just thrown on a refuse heap.

> He shall be buried with the burial of an ass, drawn and cast forth beyond the gates of Jerusalem.
> *Jer.* xxii, 19.

Buridan's Ass. A man of indecision; like one on "double business bound, who stands in pause where he should first begin, and both neglects". Buridan was a French scholastic philosopher who died *c.* 1360, incorrectly reputed to be the father of the well-known SOPHISM:

> If a hungry ass were placed exactly between two haystacks in every respect equal, it would starve to death, because there would be no motive why it should go to one rather than to the other.

Burke. To murder by smothering. So called from William Burke, an Irish NAVVY, who with his accomplice William Hare, used to suffocate his victims and sell the bodies to Dr. Robert Knox, an Edinburgh surgeon. Aided by their wives they lured fifteen people to their deaths before discovery. Hare turned King's EVIDENCE and Burke was hanged in 1829. *Cp.* RESURRECTIONISTS.

To burke a question. To smother it at birth. *The publication was burked*, suppressed before it was circulated.

To be in Burke. To be of an aristocratic family. Burke's *Peerage, Baronetage and Knightage* has, since 1826, been a recognized authority on Britain's titled classes with their family pedigrees. *Cp.* DEBRETT.

Burlaw. *See* BYRLAW.

Burleigh. As significant as the shake of Lord Burleigh's head. In Sheridan's *Critic* is introduced a mock tragedy called *The Spanish Armada*. Lord Burleigh is supposed to be too full of state affairs to utter a word; he shakes his head, and Puff explains what the shake means.

Burler. *See* BIRLER.

Burlesque. Father of burlesque poetry. Hipponax of Ephesus (6th cent. B.C.).

Burlington Bertie. A would-be MASHER. Portrayed in Vesta Tilly's song of that name.

Burma Road. This great highway was made in 1937–1939 to open up the western interior of China by communication with the sea, and ran from Lashio to Kunming in Yunnan, a distance of 770 miles. It was the chief highway for supplies to China during World War II until the Japanese cut it in 1941. It was recaptured in 1945.

Burn. His ears must be burning. *See under* EAR.

His money burns a hole in his pocket. He cannot keep it in his pocket, he cannot refrain from spending it.

The burnt child dreads fire. Once caught twice shy. "What! wouldst thou have a serpent sting thee twice?"

To burn used adjectivally as in such phrases as *money to burn* or *time to burn* means to have much more than is needed and therefore it can be expended without causing any hardship or sense of deprivation.

To burn one's boats. To take an irrevocable step; to cut oneself off from all chance of retreat. When invading forces burned their boats they were impelled to conquer or die—there could be no going back. *Cp.* RUBICON.

To burn one's fingers. To suffer loss or mischance. The allusion is to taking chestnuts from the fire.

To burn the midnight oil. To work or study late into the night.

To burn the Thames. To set the Thames on fire. *See* HE'LL NEVER SET THE THAMES ON FIRE *under* THAMES.

To have a burn. A slang phrase meaning to have a "smoke".

The burning question. A question under hot discussion, the vital question.

You cannot burn the candle at both ends. You cannot do two opposite things at one and the same time, or more commonly, you cannot exhaust your energies in one direction and yet reserve them unimpaired for something else. If you overdo it your health will suffer. *To burn the candle at both ends* often implies a hectic and somewhat dissipated existence.

We burn daylight. We waste time in talk instead of action (SHAKESPEARE: *Merry Wives of Windsor*, II, i).

Burning Crown. A crown of red-hot iron set on the head of a regicide.

> He was adjudged
> To have his head seared with a burning crown.
> *Tragedy of Hoffman* (1631).

Burnt Candlemas. The name given by the Scots to the period around CANDLEMAS DAY, 1355–1356, when Edward III marched through the Lothians with fire and sword.

Burns' Night. The evening of 25th January, the birthday of the Scottish poet Robert Burns (1759–1796). In Scotland it is a celebration for many accompanied by feasting and drinking, the HAGGIS being a prominent dish on the bill of fare. *See* AULD LANG SYNE.

Bursa (Gr. a *hide*). So the citadel of Carthage was called. The tale is that when DIDO came to Africa she bought from the natives "as much land as could be encompassed by a bull's hide". The agreement was made, and Dido cut the hide into thongs so as to enclose a space sufficient for a citadel. *Cp.* DONCASTER.

The following is a similar story: The Yakuts granted to the Russian explorers as much land as they could encompass with a cow's hide; but the Russians, cutting the hide into strips, obtained land enough for the port and town of Yakutsk.

The Indians have a somewhat similar tradition. The fifth incarnation of VISHNU was in the form of a DWARF called Vamen who obtained permission to have as much land as he could measure in three paces to build a hut on. The request was laughed at but granted; whereupon the dwarf grew so prodigiously that with three paces he encircled the world.

Burst. To inform against an accomplice. The same as "split" (to turn King's EVIDENCE). The one who does this *splits* or breaks up the whole concern.

I'm bursting to tell you so-and-so. I'm all agog to tell you; I can't rest till I've told you.

On the burst. *See* BUST.

Burton. Gone for a Burton. Absent, missing or lost (referring to persons or things), dead or presumed dead. Widely used by the services in World War II it is of uncertain origin and date. Often claimed as an R.A.F. coinage derived from the training of Radio Telegraph operators in Burton's clothing premises at Blackpool. Those who failed their tests were said to have *gone for a Burton* and it was subsequently applied to those who

were killed. It may also possibly be connected with Burton beer meaning he has gone for a drink as an explanation of absence. Another interesting suggestion is that when George Cadbury was standing for Birmingham Council in 1878 and supporting the temperance interest his opponent, Dr. Burton, was openly backed by the licensed victuallers. The Birmingham Post (22 July) says "During the whole of the polling day men were seen coming from Dr. Burton's committee room, and, parading Steward St. with jugs of beer in their hands, on which were painted papers 'Vote for Burton'". This could have given rise to the expression "he's gone for a Burton" when inquiring of someone's whereabouts.

Bury the Hatchet. Let bygones be bygones. The "GREAT SPIRIT" commanded the North American Indians, when they smoked their calumet or peace-pipe, to bury their hatchets, scalping-knives, and war clubs, that all thought of hostility might be put out of sight.

> Buried was the bloody hatchet.
> Buried was the dreadful war club;
> Buried were all warlike weapons,
> And the war-cry was forgotten.
> There was peace among the nations.
> LONGFELLOW: *The Song of Hiawatha*, xiii.

Burying at the cross roads. *See* CROSS ROADS.

Bus. A contraction of *omnibus*. An affectionate term for a car, aeroplane, etc.

Busman's holiday. There is a story that in the old horse-bus days a driver spent his holiday travelling to and fro on a bus driven by one of his pals. From this has arisen the phrase, which means to occupy one's spare or free time on the same or similar work to one's everyday occupation, *i.e.* a holiday in name only.

To miss the bus. To miss a chance or opportunity.

Bush. One beats the bush but another has the hare. *See* BEAT THE BUSH.

Good wine needs no bush. That which has real worth, quality or merit does not need to be advertised. An ivy-bush (in the ancient world sacred to BACCHUS) was once the common sign of taverns and ale and wine vendors.

> Some ale-houses upon the road I saw,
> And some with bushes showing they wine did draw.
> *Poor Robin's Perambulations* (1678).

The proverb is a Latin one, and shows that the Romans introduced the custom into Europe. *Vino vendibili hedera non opus est* (Columella). It is also common to France (*Au vin qui se vend bien, il ne faut point de lierre*).

If it be true that good wine needs no bush, 'tis true that a good play needs no epilogue.
SHAKESPEARE: *As You Like It*, Epilogue.

Shakespeare does continue with words more encouraging to the modern advertiser: "Yet to good wine they do use good bushes; and good plays prove the better by the help of good epilogues."

Bush. An Australian term for wild wooded and sparsely populated country, derived from the Dut. *bosch* and imported from South Africa before 1820. It has given rise to a whole vocabulary.

Bush Baptist. A person of dubious religious convictions.

Bush Brotherhood. An association formed to take the Christian religion to the OUTBACK and remote cattle stations. Its members sacrifice their own personal and domestic comforts in so doing.

Bush carpenter. A clumsy, inept joiner.

Bush lawyer. One who argues glibly on a slight or inaccurate basis.

Bushed. An Australian word meaning "lost" or "confused". It has become so general that we find, "a small ship became bushed in the great Van Diemen's Gulf" (Barratt: *Coast of Adventure*, 1944).

Bushman. A Hyde Park Bushman. An ignoramus as regards bush life whose acquaintance with the outdoors is limited to city parks such as Sydney's Hyde Park.

Bushmen (Dut. *boschjesman*). The Cape of Good Hope aborigines; dwellers in the Australian bush; bush farmers.

Bushrangers. Originally escaped convicts in Australia who lived as robbers in the wilds to avoid recapture, in which sense it is found in the *Sydney Gazette* in 1805. The word has a modern sense of those who take advantage of their fellows by sharp practice or crime. *See* KELLY.

Bush-shanty. In Australia a hut selling illegal liquor, often in the gold-rush areas. Hence *to shanty* is to PUB-CRAWL.

Bush telegraph. In early Australian slang, one who informed the BUSHRANGERS of police movements. Now widespread to indicate any unofficial and undisclosed source of information.

Our 'bush telegraphs' were safe to let us know when the 'traps' were closing in on us, and then — why the coach would be 'stuck up' a hundred miles away, in a different direction, within twenty-four hours.
BOLDREWOOD: *Robbery Under Arms*, ch.i.

Bush-whacker (Dut. *bosch wachter*, forest-keeper). In Australia, one who lives in the bush, especially an axeman engaged in clearing scrub. In the U.S.A. a deserter in the CIVIL WAR, who looted behind the lines.

Pulling a boat along by means of bushes growing on the river banks was also known as *bushwhacking*.

It's Sydney or the bush (Austr.). To make a decisive choice between alternatives which might result in complete success or total disaster.

To take to the bush. To become a BUSH-RANGER and live by plunder like a runaway convict.

Bushel. To hide one's light under a bushel. To conceal one's talents; to be self-effacing and modest about one's abilities. The bushel was measured in a wooden or earthenware container, hence *under a bushel* is to hide something.

Neither do men light a candle and put it under a bushel, but on a candlestick.
Matt. v, 15.

To measure other people's corn by one's own bushel. To make oneself the standard of right and wrong; to appraise everything as it accords or disagrees with one's own habits of thought and opinions.

Bushido. The code of conduct of the SAMURAI of Japan. Courage, self-discipline, courtesy, gentleness, and keeping one's word are among the virtues enjoined. *Cp.* CHIVALRY.

Bushnell's Turtle. A Dutchman, Cornelius van Drebel, successfully demonstrated a submarine in the THAMES in the reign of James I; but the first to be used in naval warfare was David Bushnell's *Turtle* built at Saybrook, Conn., in 1775 and used to attack (unsuccessfully) the British 64-gun *Eagle* in New York harbour (1776). It was employed subsequently for laying mines in the Delaware River. It was made of oak, coated with tar and looked like two turtle shells joined together. A foot pedal operated a cock to let in water when it was desired to dive, and two other hand pumps expelled the water to make the vessel rise again.

Business. O.E. *bisignes* and *bisigian*, to occupy, to worry, to fatigue. In theatrical parlance "business" or "biz" means by-play, *e.g.* Hamlet trifling with Ophelia's fan. The "business" is usually the creation of the actor who plays the part and it is handed down by tradition.

Business tomorrow. When the SPARTANS seized upon Thebes they placed Archias over the garrison. Pelopidas with eleven others banded together to put Archias to the sword. A letter giving full details of the plot was given to Archias at the banquet table but he thrust the letter under his cushion, saying "Business tomorrow." But long ere the sun rose he was dead.

The business end. The end of the tool,

etc., with which the work is done. The *business end* of a chisel is the cutting edge, of a rifle the barrel.

Busiris (bū si′ ris). A mythical king of Egypt who, in order to avert a famine, used to sacrifice to the gods all strangers who set foot on his shores. HERCULES was seized by him; and would have fallen a victim, but he broke his chain and slew the inhospitable king.

Busker. There is an old verb *to busk*, meaning to improvise, and it is from this word that *busker* is derived, to describe a street or beach singer or performer.

Buskin. Tragedy. The Greek tragic actors used to wear a similar thick-soled boot or *cothurnus* to elevate their stature. *Cp.* SOCK.

> Or what (though rare) of later age
> Enobled hath the buskind stage.
> MILTON: *Il Penseroso.*

Buss. To kiss. An obsolete word, probably of onomatopœic origin, but *cp.* Lat. *basium*, Ital. *bacio*, Sp. *beso*, and Fr. *baiser*.

> Yon towers, whose wanton tops do buss the clouds
> Must kiss their own feet.
> SHAKESPEARE: *Troilus and Cressida*, IV, v.

Bust. A frolic; a drunken debauch. The word is a vulgarization of BURST.

Busted. Done for, exploded.

To be bust. To be spent up with no money left, to be "broke".

To go on the bust. To go on the SPREE; to PAINT THE TOWN RED.

Buster. Anything of large or unusual size or capacity; a "whacking great lie".

A southerly buster, in Australia, is a heavy gale from the south, striking the east coast of Australia and New Zealand.

To come a buster. To come a CROPPER; to meet with a serious set-back or fall.

Butcher. A title given to many soldiers and others noted for their bloodthirstiness. Achmed Pasha was called *djezzar* (the butcher), and is said to have whipped off the heads of seven wives. He was killed at the siege of Acre in 1804.

The Bloody Butcher. The Duke of Cumberland (1721–1765), second son of George II. So called for his ruthless suppression of the Highlanders after the rising under the Young PRETENDER. *See* JACOBITES.

The Royalist Butcher. Blaise de Montluc (1502–1577), a Marshal of France, distinguished for his cruelties to the PROTESTANTS in the reign of Charles IX.

Butter. Often used figuratively for flattery or "soft-soap", in order to appease or win somebody over. *To butter up* a person is to flatter them and smooth them down. *Punch* called it "the milk of human kindness churned into butter".

Butter-fingers. Said of a person who lets things fall out of his hands or slip through his fingers. Often used in the CRICKET field.

> I never was a butter-fingers, though a bad batter.
> H. KINGSLEY.

Buttered ale. A beverage made of ALE or beer mixed with butter, sugar and cinnamon.

He knows which side his bread is buttered. He knows his own interest.

He looks as if butter would not melt in his mouth. He seems suspiciously amiable. He looks quite harmless, but his innocence is probably misleading. He seems too good to be true.

Soft, or **fair words butter no parsnips.** Saying "Be thou fed" will not feed a hungry man. Mere words will not find salt for our porridge, or butter our parsnips.

To butter one's bread on both sides. To be wastefully extravagant and luxurious; also to run with the HARE and hunt with the hounds, to gain advantages from two sides at once.

Buttercups. So called because they were once supposed to increase the butter content of milk. Miller, in his *Gardener's Dictionary*, says that they were named "under the notion that the yellow colour of butter is owing to these plants".

Butterfly. A light, flippant, objectless young person who flutters from pleasure to pleasure. One who is bright when conditions are favourable but is "done for" when the clouds gather.

The name was once used in the cab trade for those drivers who took up the occupation at the best of the season, in summertime only.

> The feeling of the regular drivers against these "butterflies" is very strong.
> *Nineteenth Century* (March 1893, p.177).

Butterfly kiss. A kiss with the eyelashes, that is, stroking the cheek with one's eyelashes.

Button. A decoy in an auction room was known as a *button*, because he "buttoned" or tied the unwary to "bargains" offered for sale. The button fastens or fixes what otherwise would slip away.

Button's Coffee House was established by Daniel Button in 1712, a former servant of the Dowager Countess of Warwick whom Addison married in 1716. It stood on a site in Russell Street, COVENT GARDEN, which was later occupied by HUMMUMS. It was much frequented by Joseph Addison and his circle, which included Steele, Eustace Budgell, Ambrose Philips (*see* NAMBY-PAMBY), and Carey. It became as much a centre of the

WHIG literary fraternity as did WILL'S COFFEE-HOUSE that of the TORY. *Cp.* ALMACK'S; BROOKS'S; WHITE'S.

Buttons. A page whose jacket in front is remarkable for a display of small round buttons, as close as they can be fixed, from chin to waist. In the pantomime of CINDERELLA, Buttons, the page, is a stock character.

> So at last Mrs. Casey, her pangs to assuage,
> Having snapped off his buttonses, curried the page.
> WALTER DE LA MARE: *Buttons.*

Bachelor's buttons. *See* BACHELOR.

He has not all his buttons. He is half-silly; "not all there"; he is a "button short", a "screw loose".

The buttons come off the foils. Figuratively, the courtesies of controversy are neglected. The *button* of a foil is a ball of waxed thread about one third of an inch in diameter drawn round and over the tip of the blade to prevent injury in fencing.

The *button* of an épée is a three-pronged piece of metal bound on to the tip of the blade with waxed thread and, by catching in a fencer's clothing, simulates the drawing of blood in a duel. In competitive épée, the button is in two parts, fractionally divided; a hit closes the two parts together, thus completing an electric circuit which, via a thin wire in the blade itself and cables leading from each competitor to an apparatus in front of the judge, causes one of the two bulbs to light up and so automatically register a hit. A similar apparatus for foils is under development.

The button of the cap. The tip-top. Thus in *Hamlet* (II, ii), Guildenstern says, "On fortune's cap we are not the very button" *i.e.* the most highly favoured. The button on the cap was a mark of honour. In Imperial China the first grade of literary honour was the privilege of adding a gold button to the cap, and the several grades of MANDARINS are distinguished by a different coloured button on top of their caps. The idea has been used on schoolboys' caps. *See* PANJANDRUM.

'Tis in his buttons. He is destined to obtain the prize; he is the accepted lover. Boys used to count their buttons, as plum-stones, etc., are counted on one's dish, to see what trade they were to follow, whether to do a thing or not, and whether some favourite favoured them.

> 'Tis in his buttons; he will carry't.
> SHAKESPEARE: *Merry Wives of Windsor*, III, ii.

To have a soul above buttons. To be worthy, or rather, to consider oneself worthy, of better things; to believe that one has abilities too good for one's present employment. This is explained by George Col-

man in *Sylvester Daggerwood* (1795): "My father was an eminent button-maker ... but I had a soul above buttons ... and panted for a liberal profession."

To have something buttoned up. To have something organized; to have it under control, everything tied up.

To press the button. To set in motion, literally or figuratively; generally by simple means, as the pressing of a button will start electrically driven machinery.

To take by the button. TO BUTTONHOLE A PERSON.

Buttonhole. A flower or nosegay worn in the coat buttonhole.

To buttonhole a person. To detain him in conversation; to deliberately waylay someone to speak to them. The allusion is to a former habit of holding a person by the button or buttonhole while in conversation. The French have the same locution: *Serrer le bouton* (*à quelqu'un*).

To take one down a buttonhole. To take one down a PEG; to lower one's conceit.

> Better mind yerselves, or I'll take ye down a buttonhole lower.
> HARRIET BEECHER STOWE: *Uncle Tom's Cabin*, IV.

Buy. To buy in. To collect stock by purchase; to withhold the sale of something offered at auction because the bidding has not reached the reserve price. On the STOCK EXCHANGE *buying in* is the term used when, a seller having sold stock that he is unable to deliver, the buyer purchases the stock himself in the market and charges the extra cost, if any, to the original seller. *See* SELLING OUT.

Buying a pig in a poke. *See* PIG.

To buy off. To give a person money or some form of reward to drop a claim, put an end to contention, or throw up a partnership.

To buy out. To redeem or ransom.

> Not being able to buy out his life,
> Dies ere the weary sun set in the west.
> SHAKESPEARE: *Comedy of Errors*, I, ii.

To buy over. To induce one by a bribe to renounce a claim; to gain over by bribery.

To buy up. To purchase stock to such an amount as to obtain a virtual monopoly, and thus command the market; to make a CORNER, as to "buy up corn", etc.

Buzfuz (bŭz'fŭz). Sergeant Buzfuz was the windy, grandiloquent counsel for Mrs Bardell in the famous breach of promise trial described in *Pickwick Papers*. He represented a type of barrister of the early 19th century, seeking to gain his case by abuse of the other side and a distortion of the true facts.

Buzz. A rumour, a whispered report. An old usage. The word **buzzer** for a whisperer of rumours, a secret whisperer, etc., is now seldom used, instead we have **buzz-monger,** as a spreader of rumours, etc. *Cp.* BUSH TELEGRAPH.

To buzz. Either, to empty the bottle to the last drop, in which case the partially-filled glass is called a *buzz* and entitles the recipient to another full glass; or, when there is not enough liquor left to fill a glass for everyone, to share it out equally. Perhaps a corruption of *bouse. See* BOOZE.

> Get some more port, Bowls, old boy, whilst I buzz this bottle here.
> THACKERAY: *Vanity Fair*, ch. xxxiv.

Buzzard. In Dryden's *The Hind and the Panther* is meant for Dr. Burnet.

Between hawk and buzzard. Not quite the equal of master or mistress nor quite a servant. Applied to BEAR-LEADERS, governesses, and other adults who used to be allowed to come down to dessert, but not to the dinner table.

Buzzard called hawk by courtesy. It is a EUPHEMISM, a brevet rank, a complimentary title.

> The noble Buzzard ever pleased me best;
> Of small renown, 'tis true; for, not to lie
> We call him but a hawk by courtesy.
> DRYDEN: *The Hind and the Panther*, III, 1221.

By-and-by now means a little time hence, but at the time of the preparation of the AUTHORIZED VERSION of the Bible it meant *instantly*. "When tribulation or persecution ariseth ... by-and-by he is offended" (*Matt*. xiii, 21); rendered in *Mark* iv, 17, by the word "immediately". Our *presently* means in a little time, soon, but formerly it meant at present, at once; in this sense it is not an uncommon usage in the U.S.A.

By the street of by and by one arrives at the house of never. A Spanish proverb which is roughly the equivalent of "Procrastination is the thief of time." Things postponed never get done.

By and large. Taking one thing with another, generally speaking. This is really a nautical phrase. When a vessel is close-hauled, to sail by and large is to sail slightly off the wind, making it easier for the helmsman to steer and less likely for the vessel to be taken ABACK.

To sail "by" is to sail close to the wind, to sail large (*see under* LARGE) is to sail with the wind free or on the quarter. A ship's capability was evaluated from her performance sailing "by and large" *i.e.* from an overall or general view, hence the usage as an everyday expression.

> Taking it 'by and large', as the sailors say, we had a

pleasant ten days run from New York to the Azores islands....
> MARK TWAIN: *The Innocents Abroad*, ch.V.

By-blow. A bastard.

> I it is have been cheated all this while,
> Abominably and irreparably—my name
> Given to a cur-cast mongrel, a drab's brat,
> A beggar's bye-blow.
> BROWNING: *The Ring and the Book*, iv, 612.

By-laws. Local laws. From *by*, a town (*e.g.* Selby). Laws of local or restricted application introduced by local government authorities, joint-stock companies, etc. They must not conflict with the laws of the land. *See* BYRLAW.

By-line. A journalist's signature. When a newspaper reporter progresses from anonymous to signed contributions, he is said to have got a *by-line*.

By-the-by. *En passant*, laterally connected with the main subject. *By-play* is side or secondary play; *by-roads* and streets are those which branch out of the main thoroughfare. The first *by* means *passing from one to another*, as in the phrase "Day by day". Thus *By-the-by* is passing from the main subject to a *by* or secondary one.

By-the-way. An introduction to an incidental remark thrown in, and tending the same way as the discourse itself.

Bycorne. *See* BICORN.

Bye Plot, or Watson's Plot. So called from its presumed connection with Cobham's plot or the MAIN PLOT. In 1603, William Watson, a Roman Catholic priest, and others, plotted to capture James I and to secure toleration from him. Some PURITANS collaborated but the plans were revealed by a JESUIT and Watson was beheaded.

Byerly Turk. *See* DARLEY ARABIAN.

Byrlaw. A local law in the rural districts of Scotland. The inhabitants of a district used to make certain laws for their own observance, and appoint one of their neighbours, called the *Byrlaw-man*, to carry out the pains and penalties. *Byr* = *by*, common in such names as *Derby*, the town on the Derwent, Grimsby, Aswardby, Spilsby, etc., and is present in BY-LAWS.

Byron. Lord George Gordon Byron (1788–1824). The great English poet, much admired by his European contemporaries, who died at Missolonghi, serving the cause of Greek Independence.

The Polish Byron. Adam Mickiewicz (mĕs kā′ vĕtch) (1798–1855), orator and national poet, buried among the Polish kings in Wawel Cathedral.

The Russian Byron. Alexander Sergeivich Pushkin (1799–1837).

Byrsa. *See* BURSA.

Byzantine (bi zăn' tin). Another name for the BEZANT.

Byzantine Art (from Byzantium, the former name of Constantinople, now Istanbul). A blend of Roman and Eastern influence and Christian symbolism by the early Greek or Byzantine artists. Its chief features are the circle, dome and round arch; and its chief symbols the LILY, CROSS, VESICA and NIMBUS. St. Sophia at Istanbul and St. Mark at Venice are excellent examples of Byzantine architecture and decoration. Westminster Cathedral, the great Roman Catholic cathedral in Ashley Gardens, Westminster, first used in 1904, is a fine modern example of Early Byzantine style. It was designed by J. F. Bentley, who died in 1903. Cardinal Wiseman and Cardinal Manning are buried there.

Byzantine Empire. The Eastern or Greek Empire, which lasted from the separation of the eastern and western Roman Empires on the death of Theodosius in 395 until the capture of Constantinople by the Turks in 1453.

C

C. The form of the letter is a rounding of the Gr. *gamma*(G), which was a modification of the Phœnician sign for *gimel*, a camel. It originally corresponded with the Gr. *gamma*, as its place in the alphabet indicates.

C in Roman notation stands for *centum*, 100. Hence the Fr. *cent*, etc. When the French *c* has a mark called a cedilla under it, thus, ç, it is to be pronounced as an *s*. There are poems written in which every word begins with C. There is one by Hamconius called "*Certamen catholicum cum Calvinistis*" and another by Henry Harder in Latin on Cats. *See* ALLITERATION.

C3. Signifies a physical weakling or something of third-rate quality. The lowest category in the medical examination for service in the armed forces. *Cp.* A1.

Ca'canny. A Scots expression meaning "go easy", "don't exert yourself", much the same as "go slow". In trade-union parlance it means WORKING TO RULE, restricting output as a means of exerting pressure on employers. *Ca'* is *caw*, to drive, and *canny* here means "gently".

Ça ira (it will go). The name and refrain of a popular French patriotic song which became the *Carillon National* of the French Revolution. It went to the tune of the *Carillon National*, which Marie Antoinette was for ever strumming on her harpsichord.

As a rallying cry it was borrowed from Benjamin Franklin, who used to say, in reference to the American Revolution, "*Ah! ah! ça ira, ça ira!*" ('twill be sure to do). The refrain of the French revolutionary version was:

> Ah! ça ira, ça ira, ça ira,
> Les aristocrates à la lanterne.

Caaba. *See* KAABA.

Cab. A contraction of *cabriolet*, a small one-horse carriage, from the Ital. *capriola*, a caper, the leap of a kid, from the lightness of the carriage compared with its lumbering early predecessors. Cabs were introduced into London in the 19th century.

Cabal. A JUNTO, a council of intriguers. The famous Cabal (1667–1673) of Charles II's reign, the group of five ministers, the initial letters of whose names (Clifford, Ashley, Buckingham, Arlington, Lauderdale) by coincidence spelt this word, did not give rise to the usage. It was often applied in the 17th century to the king's inner group of advisers. *See* CABBALA.

Cabala, Cabalist. *See* CABBALA.

Cabbage. An old term for odd bits of cloth, etc., left over after making up suits and other garments, appropriated by working tailors as perquisites. Hence a tailor was sometimes nicknamed "cabbage", and *to cabbage* means to pilfer. It was formerly so used in schoolboy slang as well as for something "cribbed". *See* TO CRIB *under* CRIB.

Cabbage-garden, Battle of Widow McCormack's. The derisive name given to the scuffle in Ballingarry which terminated Smith O'Brien's pitiful insurrection of July 1848. The cabbages suffered most in the struggle.

Cabbage-garden patriots. Cowards. A reference to William Smith O'Brien's easily dispersed rebels.

Cabbage-patch, Billy Williams's. *See under* BILLY.

Cabbage-patchers. Nicknames for the inhabitants of Victoria, Australia, who are also known as YARRA-YABBIES.

Cabbage Tree Ned. Edward Devine, born in Tasmania, 1833, died at Ballarat, 1909. Australia's most famous coach driver who for many years drove the Geelong to Ballarat coach. In 1862 he drove the great twelve-horse coach which carried ninety passengers, among them the first visiting CRICKET team from England, whose driver he remained throughout their tour.

Cabbala. The word is the Heb. *qabbalah* or *kabbalah*, which means "accepted by tradition." It is particularly applied to a Jewish mystical system of theology and metaphysics, dating from the 11th and 12th centuries, but with much older antecedents in the teachings of the Neoplatonists and Neopythagoreans, etc. Its aim was to relate the finite and the infinite, which was brought about by emanations from the Absolute Being. Scriptural passages were treated as symbolic and interpretation was based on the significance of numbers. The most important Cabbalistic work is the *Zohar*, written in the 13th century, but based on earlier material. Our CABAL is from *Cabbala*.

Cabbalist. From the later MIDDLE AGES the cabbalists were chiefly occupied in concocting and deciphering charms, mystical anagrams, etc., by unintelligible combinations of letters, words and numbers; in searching for the PHILOSOPHER'S STONE; in prognostications, attempted or pretended relations with the dead, and suchlike fantasies.

Cabinet, The. In Britain, the inner committee of ministers, headed by the Prime Minister, who hold the highest executive offices and largely determine national policy. The Prime Minister chooses the many ministers and decides the composition of the Cabinet, which has varied in size, but latterly contained about twenty. Those included in 1979 were the Chancellor of the Exchequer; the Secretaries of State for Foreign and Commonwealth Affairs, Home Department, Scotland, Wales, Northern Ireland, Defence, Employment, Environment, Industry, Social Services, Trade, Energy, Education; the Minister of Agriculture, Fisheries and Food; the Chancellor of the Duchy of Lancaster; the Chief Secretary to the Treasury; the Paymaster General; the Lord High Chancellor; the Lord President of the Council; and the Lord Privy Seal. The Cabinet is collectively responsible to Parliament and its decisions are binding on all members of the government.

The word *cabinet* originally meant a small room and eventually came to apply to the group of politicians who met in the room. The Cabinet has its real origins in the reign of Charles II (1660–1685) and it developed steadily from Hanoverian times with the growth of the Prime Minister's influence, and by the latter part of the 18th century ministerial responsibility was fairly well established.

In the U.S.A. the Cabinet consists of the heads of the great departments of state (twelve in number), who are appointed by the President and serve as his advisers. Unlike their British counterparts they are not members of the legislature and cannot take part in debates. A new Cabinet post must be authorized by an Act of Congress. They hold office during the President's pleasure. If the President is elected for a second term they continue in office, except the Postmaster General, who has to be reappointed. The President is more independent of his cabinet's advice than is the British Prime Minister.

Shadow Cabinet. A potential cabinet formed from leaders of the OPPOSITION party in PARLIAMENT, who also take the lead as critics of particular features of government policy.

Cabiri (ka bī′ ri). Certain deities, probably of Phrygian origin, worshipped in Asia Minor, Greece and the islands. Samothrace was the centre of their worship, which involved scandalous obscenities. The traditional four deities are Axierus, Axiocersa, Axiocersus and Cadmilus who promoted fertility and safeguarded mariners.

Cable. In nautical usage commonly denotes the rope or chain to which the anchor is secured. Ship's cable is measured in *shackles*, a shackle being $12\frac{1}{2}$ fathoms.

A cable's length. Eight shackles or 100 fathoms, one-tenth of a nautical mile.

To range cable is to haul it out of the chain locker and lay it in lengths back and forth along the deck with the running part to the ship's side to ensure that the cable will run out freely.

To slip the cable. To release the cable from the inboard end letting it run out through the hawse, thus releasing the anchor.

> To preserve their close order the Armada's vessels were riding to two anchors each, and there was no time to weigh. The majority did not even slip, but cut their cables and drifted off in the darkness. ...
>
> J.A. WILLIAMSON: *The Age of Drake*, ch. xvi.

Figuratively, to slip one's cable is to die.

To veer cable is to pay or ease out cable.

Caboched (O.Fr. *caboche*, head). A term in HERALDRY when a beast's head is borne full face, without any part of the neck.

Caboodle (kȧ boodl′). **The whole caboodle.** The whole lot, the whole collection. Possibly from the Dut. *boedel*, possession, household goods, property. In this sense it has long been a common term among New England longshoremen. In America *kit and boodle* is another expression with the same meaning.

Caboshed, or **Cabossed.** See CABOCHED.

Cachecope Bell (kăsh′kōp). In some parts of England it was customary to ring a bell at a funeral when the PALL was thrown over the coffin. This was called the cachecope bell, from Fr. *cache corps*, conceal the body.

Cachet (kăsh′ā) (Fr.). A seal; hence a distinguishing mark, a stamp of individuality.

Lettres de cachet (letters sealed). Under the old régime in France, letters or orders issued by the king under the royal seal (*cachet*). The name is best known for those used to imprison or punish a subject without trial, there being no HABEAS CORPUS in France. In the 18th century they were often issued as blank warrants, leaving the name to be filled in subsequently by the authorities or parties concerned. They were used against lunatics and prostitutes, and obtained by heads of families against their relatives; thus Mirabeau was consigned to prison by his father. During the administration of Cardinal Fleury (1726–1734) 80,000 of these cachets are said to have been issued, mostly against the JANSENISTS. They were abolished by the CONSTITUENT ASSEMBLY (January 1790).

Cacodæmon (kăkō dē′mon) (Gr. *kakos daimon*). An evil spirit. Astrologers gave this name to the Twelfth House of HEAVEN, from which only evil prognostics proceed.

> Hie thee to hell for shame, and leave this world,
> Thou cacodemon.
> SHAKESPEARE: *Richard III*, I, iii.

Cacoethes (kăk ō ēth′ ēz) (Gr.) A bad habit.

> As soon as he came to town, the political Cacoethes began to break out upon him with greater violence because it had been suppressed.
> SWIFT: *Life of Steele*.

Cacoethes loquendi. A passion for making speeches or talking.

Cacoethes scribendi. The love of rushing into print; a mania for authorship.

> Tenet insanabile multos
> Scribendi cacoethes.
> JUVENAL: *Satires* vii, 51.
> The incurable itch for scribbling affects many.

Cactus, To be in the (Austr. and New Zealand). In an uncomfortable or awkward situation. The allusion is obvious.

Cacus (kā′kus). In classical mythology, a famous robber, son of VULCAN, represented as three-headed and vomiting flames. He lived in Italy and was strangled by HERCULES for stealing some of his cattle. The curate of La Mancha says of Lord Rinaldo and his friends, "They are greater thieves than Cacus" (*Don Quixote*).

Cad. A low, vulgar, nasty fellow; also, before the term fell into disrepute, an omnibus conductor. The word is like the Scots CADDIE, probably from CADET.

Caddice-garter, or **caddis.** A servant, a man of mean rank (*caddice*, worsted yarn or binding, crewel). When garters were worn in sight, the cheaper variety was worn by small tradesmen, servants, etc. Prince Henry calls Poins a "caddisgarter" (SHAKESPEARE: *Henry* IV, Pt. I, II, iv).

> Dost hear,
> My honest caddis-garter?
> CLAPTHORNE: *Wit in a Constable* (1639).

Caddie. This is now almost solely associated with the boy or man who carried a golfer's clubs on the links, and now and then gave the tyro advice, and the two-wheeled container which has largely replaced them. It is another form of CADET and was formerly commonly used in Scotland for errand boys, odd-job men, chairmen, etc.

> All Edinburgh men and boys know that when sedan-chairs were discontinued, the old caddies sank into ruinous poverty, and became synonymous with roughs. The word was brought to London by James Hannay, who frequently used it.
> M. PRINGLE.

Caddy. In some English dialects, a ghost, a bugbear; from *cad*, a word of uncertain origin which in the 17th century meant a FAMILIAR spirit. It is not connected with *caddis*, a grub, which is from *caddice*, the allusion being to the similarity of the caddis-worm to the larva of the silkworm.

Caddy in **tea-caddy** is a Malay word (*kati*), and properly denotes a weight of 1lb 5oz 2dr., that is used in China and the East Indies.

Cade. Jack Cade legislation. Pressure from without. An allusion to Jack Cade's Kentish insurrection of 1450. He marched on LONDON, encamped on BLACKHEATH and demanded redress of grievances from King Henry VI. He held London for two days, then his followers began to plunder and disperse. He was finally killed near Heathfield, Sussex. His popular name was JACK AMEND-ALL.

Cadency, Marks of. *See* DIFFERENCE.

Cader Idris (Kǎ′der id′ ris). *Cader* in Welsh means chair, and *Idris* is the name of one of the old Welsh giants. The legend is that anyone who passes the night in this "chair" will either be a poet or a madman.

Cadet (kà det). Younger branches of noble families are called cadets from Fr. *cadet*, a diminutive, ultimately from Lat. *caput*, head, hence little head, little chieftain. Their armorial shields bore the marks of cadency(Lat.*cadere*,to fall).*See*DIFFERENCE.

The word is now commonly used to denote certain categories of military trainees, etc.

Cadger. A SPONGER, one who sets out to obtain things from others without payment, a scrounger, etc. Originally an itinerant dealer in butter, eggs, etc. who visited remote farmhouses and probably made what extra he could by a little judicious wheedling or begging. The word is possibly connected with *catch*.

Cadmus. In Greek mythology, the son of AGENOR, King of Phœnicia and Telephassa, founder of THEBES (Bœotia) and the introducer of the alphabet into Greece. Legend says that, having slain the dragon which guarded the fountain of Dirce, in BŒOTIA, he sowed its teeth, and a number of armed men sprang up with intent to kill him. By the counsel of ATHENE, he threw a PRECIOUS STONE among them and they killed each other in the struggle to gain it, except five who helped to build the city. *See also* JASON.

Cadmean letters. The sixteen simple Greek letters, which CADMUS is supposed to have introduced from Phœnicia. *See also* PALAMEDES.

Cadmean victory. A victory purchased with great loss. The allusion is to the armed men who sprang from the dragon's teeth sown by CADMUS.

Cadogan (kȧ dŭg' an), or **Catogan.** A style of dressing the hair by securing it at the back with a ribbon, affected by men in the second half of the 18th century. Derived from a popular portrait of the first earl of Cadogan, it was imitated also by fashionable ladies and introduced at the court of Montbéliard by the Duchesse de Bourbon.

Caduceus. A white wand carried by Roman heralds when they went to treat for peace; the wand placed in the hands of MERCURY, the herald of the gods, with which, poets feign, he could give sleep to whomsoever he chose; wherefore Milton styles it his "opiate rod" (*Paradise Lost*, XI, 133). It is generally pictured with two SERPENTS twined about it (a symbol thought to have originated in Egypt), and—with reference to the serpents of ÆSCULAPIUS—it was adopted as the badge of the Royal Army Medical Corps.

Caedmon (kăd'mon) (d. 680). Anglo-Saxon poet famed for his *Hymn* preserved in Bede's Latin. All his other work is lost. BEDE says he was an ignorant man knowing nothing of poetry, but was commanded in a dream, by an ANGEL, to sing the Creation, which he straightway did. On waking he remembered his verses and composed more. He was received into the monastery at Whitby, where he spent his life praising God in poetry. He has been called the "father of English song".

Cærleon (kâr' lē on). The Isca Silurum of the Romans, about three miles N.E. of Newport in South Wales. It is the traditional residence of King ARTHUR, where he lived in splendid state, surrounded by hundreds of knights, twelve of whom he selected to be KNIGHTS OF THE ROUND TABLE. *See* CAMELOT.

Cæsar (sē' zȧr). The cognomen of Caius Julius Cæsar, assumed by his male successors, and by the heir-apparent to the imperial throne. The titles KAISER and *Czar* or *Tsar* are variants of the name.

Cæsarism. A term applied to rule by a quasi-popular dictatorship where power has been seized by a COUP D'ÉTAT as in the case of a NAPOLEON or Hitler.

Cæsar's wife must be above suspicion. The name of Pompeia having become involved with an accusation against P. Clodius, Cæsar divorced her, not because he believed her guilty, but because the wife of Cæsar must not be even suspected of crime (Suetonius, *Julius Cæsar*, 74).

Cæsarian operation. The extraction of a child from the womb by cutting the abdomen; supposedly so called because Julius Cæsar was thus brought into the world, but the obstetric use of the word *cæsarian* is most probably derived from Lat. *cæsus* (past participle of *cædere*, to cut).

Cage. To whistle, or **sing in the cage.** The *cage* is a jail, and to *whistle in a cage* is to turn King's EVIDENCE, or *peach* against a comrade. The lift in which miners descend the pit shaft is termed a *cage*.

Cagliostro (kă lyos' trō). Count Alessandro di Cagliostro was the assumed name of the notorious Italian adventurer and impostor Giuseppe Balsamo (1743–1795), of Palermo. He played a prominent part in the affair of the DIAMOND NECKLACE, and among his many frauds was the offer of everlasting youth to all who would pay him for his secret.

Cagmag (kăg' măg). Offal, bad meat; also a tough old goose; food which none can relish.

Cagots (ka' gō). In the MIDDLE AGES, a sort of GYPSY race, living in Gascony and Béarn, supposed to be descendants of the Visigoths and shunned as something loathsome, possibly because they may have been leprous. *Cp.* CAQUEUX; COLLIBERTS. In modern French, a hypocrite or ultra-devout person is called a *cagot*. From this came the word *cagoule*, meaning a penitent's hood or cowl, and from this the terrorist political organization of the latter 1930s, the *Cagoulards*, took their name.

Cahoot (Fr. *cahute*, cabin or small hut). In the U.S.A. **to go cahoots** is to share equally, to become partners.

In cahoots is to be in partnership or in league with someone.

Cain-coloured Beard. Yellowish, or sandy red, symbolic of treason. In the ancient tapestries Cain and JUDAS are represented with yellow beards. *See* YELLOW.

> He hath but a little wee face, with a little yellow beard, a Cain-coloured beard.
> SHAKESPEARE: *Merry Wives of Windsor*, I, iv.

Cainites (kā' nītz). An heretical sect of the 2nd century so named because they held that Cain was made by an almighty power and

Abel by a weak one. They renounced the NEW TESTAMENT in favour of *The Gospel of Judas* which justified the false disciple and the crucifixion of Jesus, and held that the way to salvation was to give way to every lust and make a trial of everything.

To raise Cain. To "raise the devil", to "play hell", to make an angry fuss or noisy disturbance. Cain is either used as an alternative to "the DEVIL", or is a direct allusion to Cain's violent anger which drove him to kill his brother. (*See Gen.* iv, 5.)

> Seven men from all the world back to Docks again
> Rolling down the Ratcliffe Road drunk and raising Cain.
>
> KIPLING: *Ballad of the 'Bolivar'* (1890).

Caius (kēz) **College,** or properly **Gonville and Caius.** Established by Edmund Gonville at Cambridge in 1348 as a hall, it was raised to the status of a college by Dr. John Caius (1510–1573), of Norwich, in 1558. He was first physician to Edward VI, Mary Tudor and Elizabeth I and wrote treatises on various subjects, including one on the antiquity of Cambridge University which, he asserted, was founded by *Cantaber* in 394 B.C.

Cake. Obsolete slang for a fool, a poor thing, *Cp.* HALF-BAKED.

Cakes and ale. A good time. *Life is not all cakes and ale.* Life is not all BEER AND SKITTLES—all pleasure. W. Somerset Maugham has a novel called *Cakes and Ale*.

It's a piece of cake. It's easy, it can be done with little trouble or effort—as easy as eating cake.

My cake is dough. All my swans are turned to geese. *Occisa est res mea*; my project has failed; *mon affaire est manquée*.

The land of cakes. Scotland, famous for its oatmeal cakes.

> Land o'cakes and brither Scots.
>
> BURNS.

To go like hot cakes. To be a great success, to sell well.

To take the cake, bun, or **biscuit.** To carry off the prize (ironically). That beats everything. The reference is to the negro *cake walk*, the prize for which was a cake. The competitors walk round the cake in pairs while the judges decide which couple walk the most gracefully. From this a dance developed which was popular in the early 20th century before the coming of JAZZ.

In ancient Greece, a cake was the award to the toper who held out longest, and in Ireland the best dancer in a dancing competition was rewarded, at one time, by a cake.

> A churn-dish stuck into the earth supported on its flat end a cake, which was to become the prize of the best dancer.
>
> BARTLETT and COYNE: *Scenery and Antiquities of Ireland*, vol. II, p. 64.

You cannot eat your cake and have it too. You cannot spend your money and yet keep it. You cannot serve God and MAMMON. You cannot have it both ways.

Calainos (kà lī' nos). The most ancient of Spanish ballads. Calainos the Moor asked a damsel to wife; she consented on condition that he should bring her the heads of the three PALADINS of CHARLEMAGNE— RINALDO, ROLAND, and OLIVER. Calainos went to Paris and challenged them. First Sir Baldwin, the youngest Knight, accepted the challenge and was overthrown; then his uncle Roland went against the Moor and smote him.

Calamity Howler, A. Colloquial American for a pessimist, particularly one given to voicing his misgivings widely and loudly.

Calas. The case of Jean Calas (căl' aš'). A celebrated case in French history. Jean Calas (1698–1762), a HUGUENOT cloth-merchant of Toulouse, was tortured, broken on the wheel and burnt in 1762, having been found guilty of the murder of his twenty-nine-year-old son Marc-Antoine. The motive was supposed to be that Jean was determined to prevent his son becoming a Roman Catholic. The evidence was circumstantial although suicide was perhaps the most obvious conclusion to draw. The widow's case was taken up by Voltaire in his book *Sur la Tolérance*, with the result that the family, who had also suffered the penalties of intolerance, were declared innocent and given 30,000 livres by Louis XV.

Calatrava, Order of (kăl á tra' va). A Spanish military order of knighthood, founded by Sancho III of Castile in 1158 from the many warriors who had concentrated there for the town's defence against the MOORS. They at first entered the order of Cîteaux and wore a white scapulary and hood; in 1397 they were permitted to wear secular dress, their badge being a red cross fleury. The knights took vows of poverty, obedience and conjugal chastity. It became an order of merit in 1808.

Calceolaria (kăl sē ō lár' i à). Little shoe-flowers; so called from their resemblance to fairy slippers (Lat. *calceolus*).

Calchas. The famous Greek soothsayer in the TROJAN WAR who told the Greeks that the aid of ACHILLES was essential for the taking of the city, that IPHIGENIA must be sacrificed before the fleet could sail from AULIS, and that the siege would take ten years. He died of disappointment when beaten in a trial of skill by the prophet Mopsus.

Calculate is from the Lat. *calculi* (pebbles), used by the Romans for counters. In the ABACUS the round balls were called *calculi*. The Greeks voted by pebbles dropped into an urn—a method adopted both in ancient Egypt and Syria; counting these pebbles was *calculating* the number of voters.

I calculate. An old Americanism for to think, guess or reckon. "I guess" is now the common expression.

> Your aunt sets two tables, I calculate, don't she?
> SUSAN WARNER: *Queechy*, Ch. xix.

The calculator. Among those of unusual mathematical prowess who have been awarded this title are:

Alfragan, the Arabian astronomer (d. 830).

Jedediah Buxton (1705–1772), of Elmton in Derbyshire; a farm labourer of no education, who exhibited in London in 1754.

George Bidder (1806–1878) of Moretonhampstead, Devon, and Zerah Colburn (1804–1840), of Vermont, U.S.A., who exhibited publicly.

Jacques Inaudi (1867–1950), an Italian who exhibited "his astounding powers of calculating" at Paris in 1880; his additions and subtractions, contrary to the usual procedure, were from left to right.

> Buxton, being asked "How many cubical eighths-of-an-inch there are in a body whose three sides are 23,145,786 yards, 5,642,732 yards and 54,965 yards?" replied correctly without setting down a figure.
> Colburn being asked the square root of 106,929 and the cube root of 268,336,125, replied before the audience had set the figures down.
> PRICE: *Parallel History*, vol. ii, p.570.

See TRACHTENBERG SYSTEM.

Caledonia. SCOTLAND; the ancient Roman name, now only used in poetry and in a few special connexions, such as the Caledonian Hotel, the Caledonian Canal, etc.

Caledonian Market. Until its closure at the outbreak of World War II, this Islington cattle and general market was especially noted for miscellaneous secondhand goods and was much frequented by bargain hunters. Dubbed the "thieves' market", it was partially a relic of the pedlar's part of London's BARTHOLOMEW FAIR, which ceased in 1855, the year in which the Caledonian Market opened.

Calembour (ka lom boor') (Fr.). A pun, a jest. From Wigan von Theben, a priest of Kahlenberg in Lower Austria, who was introduced in *Till* EULENSPIEGEL and other German tales. He was noted for his jests, puns, and witticisms. In the French translation he appeared as the Abbé de Calembourg or Calembour.

Calendar.
The Julian Calendar. *See* JULIAN.
The Gregorian Calendar. *See* GREGORIAN.
The Jewish Calendar. This dates from the Creation, fixed at 3761 B.C. and consists of 12 months of 29 and 30 days alternately, with an additional month of 30 days interposed in EMBOLISMIC years to prevent any great divergence from the months of the Solar year. The 3rd, 6th, 11th, 14th, 17th, and 19th years of the METONIC CYCLE are Embolismic Years.
The Mohammedan Calendar, used in Moslem countries, dates from 16 July 622, the day of the HEGIRA. It consists of 12 lunar months of 29 days 12 hours 44 minutes each; consequently the Mohammedan year consists of only 354 or 355 days. A cycle is 30 years.
The French Revolutionary Calendar. Adopted by the National CONVENTION on 5 October 1793, retrospectively as from 22 September 1792, and in force in France till 1 January 1806, when NAPOLEON restored the GREGORIAN CALENDAR. It consisted of 12 months of 30 days each, with 5 intercalary days, called SANSCULOTTIDES. Every fourth or Olympic Year was to have six such days. It was devised by Gilbert Romme (1750–1795), the months being named by the poet Fabre d'Eglantine (1755–1794).
The Newgate Calendar. *See* NEWGATE.

Calender. The Persian *galandar*, a member of a begging order of dervishes founded in the 13th century by Qalander Yusufal-Andalusi, a native of Spain. The took a vow of perpetual wandering and feature in the story of the *Three Calenders* in the ARABIAN NIGHTS.

Calends (from Lat. *calare*, to call). The first day of the Roman month. Varro says the term originated in the practice of calling the people together on the first day of the month, when the *pontifex* informed them of the time of the new moon, the day of the NONES, with the festivals and sacred days to be observed. The custom continued till A.U.C. 450, when the FASTI or *calendar* was posted in public places. *See* GREEK CALENDS.

Calepin, A (kăl' e pin). A dictionary. Ambrosio Calepino of Calepio in Italy was the author of a famous Latin dictionary (1502), so that *my Calepin* was used in earlier days as my EUCLID, my Liddell and Scott, my Lewis and Short, my Kennedy, etc., became common later.

> Whom do you prefer
> For the best linguist? And I sillily
> Said that I thought Calepine's Dictionary.
>
> DONNE: *Fourth Satire*.

Calf. Slang for a dolt, a "mutton-head", a raw, inexperienced, childish fellow. *See also* CALVES.

The golden calf. *See* GOLDEN.

There are many ways of dressing a calf's head. Many ways of saying or doing a foolish thing; a simpleton has many ways of showing his folly; or, generally, if one way won't do we must try another. The allusion is to the banquets of the CALVES' HEAD CLUB.

To eat the calf in the cow's belly. To be over-ready to anticipate; to count one's chickens before they are hatched. *See under* CHICKEN.

To kill the fatted calf. To celebrate, to welcome with the best of everything. The phrase is from the parable of the prodigal son (*Luke* xv, 30).

Calf-love. Youthful fancy, immature love as opposed to lasting attachment.

Calf-skin. Fools and jesters used to wear a calf-skin coat buttoned down the back. In SHAKESPEARE's *King John*, III, i. Constance says scathingly to the Archduke of Austria:

> Thou wear a lion's hide! Doff it for shame,
> And hang a calf's skin on those recreant limbs!

Caliban (kăl' i băn). Rude, uncouth, unknown. The allusion is to SHAKESPEARE's Caliban in *The Tempest*, the deformed half-human son of a DEVIL and a WITCH, slave to Prospero.

Caliburn (kăl' i bĕrn). Same as EXCALIBUR, King ARTHUR's well-known sword.

> And onward Arthur paced, with hand
> On Caliburn's resistless brand.
>
> SCOTT: *Bridal of Triermain*, xv.

Calidore, Sir (kăl' i dôr). In Spenser's *Faerie Queene* (Bk. VI) the type of courtesy, and the lover of "fair Pastorella". He is described as the most courteous of all knights, and is entitled the "all-beloved". He typifies Sir Philip Sidney or the Earl of Essex.

Caligula (kà lig' ū là). Roman Emperor (A.D. 37–41); so called because, when with the army as a boy, he wore a military sandal called a *caliga* which had no upper leather and was only used by the common soldiers.

Caligula was a voluptuary whose cruelties and excesses almost amounted to madness. Hence Horace Walpole coined the word *Caligulism*. Speaking of Frederick, Prince of Wales, he says:

> Alas! it would be endless to tell you all his Caligulisms.
>
> *Letter to France*. 29 Nov. 1745.

Calipash and Calipee (kăl i păsh, kăl i pē). These are apparently fancy terms (though the former may come from *carapace*, the upper shell of a tortoise and crustaceans), to describe choice portions of the turtle. Calipash is the fatty, dull-greenish substance of the upper shield; calipee is the light-yellow fatty stuff belonging to the lower. Only epicures and aldermen can tell the difference!

> Cut off the bottom shell, then cut off the meat that grows to it (which is the callepy or fowl).
>
> MRS. RAFFALD: *English Housekeeping* (1769).

Caliph (kā lif). A title given to the successors of MOHAMMED (Arab. *Khalifah*, a successor). The caliphate of Baghdad reached its highest splendour under Haroun al-Raschid (786–809). From the 13th century the titles of *Caliph*, *Sultan*, *Imam* came to be used indiscriminately, but in the 19th century Ottoman Sultans sought to revive their claim to the title, especially Abdul Hamid II (1876–1908). In 1924 the Turks declared the abolition of the Caliphate.

Calisto and Arcas. Calisto was an Arcadian NYMPH metamorphosed into a she-bear by JUPITER. Her son Arcas having met her in the chase, would have killed her, but Jupiter converted him into a he-bear, and placed them both in the heavens, where they are recognized as the Great and Little Bear. *See* ARCTIC REGION.

Calixtines (ka liks' tīnz). A Bohemian religious sect of the 15th century; so called from *calix* (the chalice), which they insisted should be given to the laity, *i.e.* communion of both kinds. They were also called UTRAQUISTS.

Call. A summons, or invitation felt to be divine, as a "call to the ministry".

A call bird. A bird trained as a decoy.

A call-boy. A boy employed in theatres to call or summon actors in time for them to appear on the stage.

A call-box. A public telephone booth.

A call-girl. A prostitute who uses her telephone for arranging to receive her customers.

A call of the House. An imperative summons sent to every Member of PARLIAMENT to attend. This is done when the opinion of the whole house is required.

A call on shareholders. A demand to pay the balance of money due for shares allotted in a company, or a part thereof.

A call to the pastorate. An invitation to a clergyman by the members of a PRESBYTERIAN or NONCONFORMIST congregation to serve as their minister.

A curtain call. *See under* CURTAIN.

Called to the Bar. *See under* BAR.

Payable at call. To be paid on demand.

The call of Abraham. The invitation or

command of God to ABRAHAM, to leave his idolatrous country, under the promise of becoming father of a great nation (*Gen*. xii, 1–2).

The call of God. An invitation, exhortation, or warning by the dispensations of Providence (*Isa*. xxii, 12); divine influence on the mind to do or avoid something (*Heb*. iii, 1).

To call a man out. To challenge him; to appeal to a man's honour to come forth and fight a duel.

To call God to witness. To declare solemnly that what one states is true.

To call in question. To doubt the truth of a statement; to challenge the truth of a statement. "*In dubium vocare*".

To call in. To summon a doctor or invite for consultation, etc. In banking, to take coins or notes out of circulation.

To call it a go, or **a day.** To give in, to give up, to stop work.

To call off. To cancel a forthcoming event, to withdraw from a deal.

To call over the coals. *See* COALS.

To call to account. To demand an explanation; to reprove.

To be called, or **sent to one's account.** To be removed by death, to be called to the judgement seat of God to give an account of one's deeds.

To call to arms. To summon, to prepare for battle. "*Ad arma vocare*."

To call to mind. To recollect, to remember.

To call up. To summon for military service.

Caller herrings. Fresh herrings. The adjective is also applied in SCOTLAND to fresh air, water, etc.

Calliope (kà lī̄ō pi) (Gr. beautiful voice). Chief of the nine MUSES; the muse of epic or heroic poetry, and of poetic inspiration and eloquence. Her emblems are a stylus and wax tablets.

The name is also applied to a steam organ, making raucous music on steam whistles.

Callippic Period (kà lip' ik). A correction of the METONIC CYCLE by Callippus, the Greek astronomer of the 4th century B.C. To remedy the defect in the Metonic Cycle, Callippus quadrupled the period of Meton, making his cycle one of seventy-six years, and deducted a day at the end of it, by which means he calculated that the new and full moons would be brought round to the same day and hour. His calculation, however, is not absolutely accurate, as there is one whole day lost every 553 years.

Calomel (kăl' ō mel). Hooper's *Medical Dictionary* says: This name, which means "beautiful black", was originally given to the Aethiop's mineral, or black sulphuret of mercury. It was afterwards applied in joke by Sir Theodore Mayerne to the chloride of mercury, in honour of a favourite negro servant whom he emloyed to prepare it. As calomel is a white powder, the name is merely a jocular misnomer. *See* MISNOMERS.

Calotte (kà lot'). **Régime de la calotte.** Administration of government by ecclesiastics. The *calotte* is the small skull-cap worn over the TONSURE.

Régiment de la calotte. A society of wits and satirists in the reign of Louis XIV. When any public character made himself ridiculous, a calotte was sent to him to "cover the bald or brainless part of his noddle"

Caloyers (kà lō' yěrz). Monks in the Greek church, who follow the rule of St. Basil. They are divided into *cenobites*, who recite the offices from midnight to sunrise; *anchorites*, who live in hermitages; and *recluses*, who shut themselves up in caverns and live on alms (Gr. *calos* and *geron*, beautiful old man).

Calpe (kăl' pi). Gibraltar, one of the PILLARS OF HERCULES; the other, the opposite promontory in Africa (Jebel Musa, or Apes' Hill), was anciently called Abyla. According to one account these two were originally one mountain which HERCULES tore asunder; but some say he piled up each mountain separately.

The pack of hounds introduced into the peninsula by Wellington's officers is the *Calpe Hunt*.

Caltrop, Caltrap, or **Chevaltrap**. A mediæval four-pronged iron device placed on the ground so that the horses of the attacking cavalry might be lamed. There is a similar modern one for puncturing pneumatic tyres.

Calumet (kăl' u met). The "pipe of peace" of the North American Indians. The word is of French Canadian origin, being the Norman form of the Fr. *chalumeau* (Lat. *calamus*, a reed); it was the name they gave to certain plants used by the natives as pipe stems, and hence, the pipe itself. The calumet is about two-and-a-half feet long, the stem is reed and the bowl is of highly polished red marble. To present the calumet to a stranger is a mark of hospitality and goodwill; to refuse the offer is an act of hostile defiance. *Cp*. MATÉ

Gitche Manito, the mighty
Smoked the calumet, the Peace-pipe
As a signal to the nations.
LONGFELLOW: *Hiawatha*, i.

Calvary. The Latin translation of the Gr. GOLGOTHA, which is a transliteration of the Hebrew word for a skull. It is the name given to the place of our Lord's crucifixion. Legend has it that the skull of ADAM was preserved here, but the name is probably due to a fancied resemblance of the configuration of the ground to the shape of a skull.

The actual site may be that occupied by the Church of the Holy Sepulchre, or possibly an eminence above the grotto of Jeremiah not far from the Damascus Gate.

A Calvary. A representation of the successive scenes of the PASSION of Christ in a series of pictures, etc., in a church; the shrine containing such representations. Wayside calvaries or crosses, representing the Crucifixion, are common in parts of Europe and some notable examples are to be found in Brittany.

A calvary cross. A Latin CROSS mounted on three steps (or grises).

Calvary clover. A common trefoil, *Medicago echinus*, said to have sprung up in the track made by PILATE when he went to the cross to see his "title affixed " (Jesus of Nazareth, King of the Jews). Each of the three leaves has a little carmine spot in the centre; in the daytime they form a sort of cross; and in the flowering season the plant bears a little yellow flower, like a "crown of thorns". Julian tells us that each of the three leaves had in his time a white cross in the centre, and that the centre cross remains visible longer than the others.

Calves. The inhabitants of the Isle of Wight were sometimes so called from a tradition that a CALF once got its head firmly wedged in a wooden pale, and instead of breaking up the pale, the farmhand cut off the calf's head.

His calves are gone to grass. Said of a spindle-legged man. And another mocking taunt is, "Veal will be dear, because there are no calves."

Calves' Head Club. Instituted in ridicule of Charles I, and apparently first mentioned in a tract (given in the *Harleian Miscellany*) of 1703 by Benjamin Bridgwater, stating that it first met in 1693. It lasted till about 1735. The annual banquet was held on 30 January, the anniversary of the King's execution, and according to the *Secret History of the Calves' Head Club, or the Republicans unmasked*, attributed to Ned Ward:

> Their bill of fare was a large dish of calves' heads, dressed several ways, by which they represented the king and his friends who had suffered in his cause; a large pike with a small one in its mouth, as an emblem of tyranny; a large cod's head by which they

intended to represent the person of the king singly; a boar's head with an apple in its mouth, to represent the king as bestial,...

We are also told that after the repast the EIKON BASILIKE was burnt and a calf's skull filled with wine was drunk to "those worthy patriots who had killed the tyrant". Furthermore "the company only consisted of INDEPENDENTS and ANABAPTISTS".

Calvinism. The doctrines of the Reformer Jean Calvin (1509–1564), particularly as expressed in his *Institutio Religionis Christianæ* (1536). Some chief points of his teaching are:

(1) the transcendence of God;
(2) the total depravity of natural man. He can achieve nothing without God;
(3) predestination of particular election. Before the world began God chose some men for salvation through Christ;
(4) the scriptures and the Holy Spirit are the sole authority;
(5) the community must enforce the Church's public discipline.

Calydon (kal' i don). In classical geography, a city in Ætolia, near the forest which was the scene of the legendary hunt of the CALYDONIAN BOAR (*see* BOAR). Also in Arthurian legend, the name given to a forest in northern England.

Calypso (kà lip' sō). In classical mythology, the queen of the island Ogygia on which ULYSSES was wrecked. She kept him there for seven years and promised him perpetual youth and immortality if he would remain with her for ever. She bore him two sons and was inconsolable when he left. Ogygia is generally identified with Gozo, near Malta.

A calypso is a type of popular song developed by the coloured folk of Trinidad, improvised on topical subjects.

Cam and Isis. The universities of Cambridge and Oxford; so called from the rivers on which they stand.

> May you, my Cam and Isis, preach it long,
> The right divine of kings to govern wrong.
> POPE: *Dunciad*, iv, 187.

Cama. The god of young love in Hindu mythology. His wife is Rati (voluptuousness), and he is represented as riding on a sparrow, holding in his hand a bow of flowers and five arrows. (*i.e.* the five senses).

> Over hills with peaky top engrail'd,
> And many a tract of palm and rice,
> The throne of Indian Cama slowly sail'd
> A summer fann'd with spice.
> TENNYSON: *The Palace of Art*.

Camacho (kàm a' chō). A rich but unfortunate man in one of the stories in *Don Quixote*, who is cheated of his bride just when he has prepared a great feast for the wedding; hence the phrase **Camacho's wedding** to describe useless show and expenditure.

Camarina. *Ne moveas Camarinam* (Don't meddle with Camarina). Camarina, a lake in Sicily, was a source of malaria to the inhabitants, who, when they consulted APOLLO about draining it, received the reply, "Do not disturb it." Nevertheless, they drained it, and ere long the enemy marched over the bed of the lake and plundered the city. The proverb is applied to those who remove one evil, but thus give place to a greater—"LEAVE WELL ALONE".

Cambalo's Ring. Cambalo was the second son of CAMBUSCAN in Chaucer's unfinished *Squire's Tale*. He is introduced as Cambel in the *Faerie Queene*. The ring, which was given him by his sister Canace, had the virtue of healing wounds.

Camber. In British legend, the second son of BRUTE. WALES fell to his portion; which is one way of accounting for its name of Cambria.

Cambria. The ancient name of WALES, the land of the Cymry.

Cambridge Apostles, The. An exclusive debating society founded at Cambridge in 1826 by John Sterling (1806–1844), which included dons and undergraduates, many of whom subsequently attained celebrity. Among them were Frederick Denison Maurice, Richard Chenevix-Trench, John Kemble, James Spedding, Monckton Milnes, A. H. Hallam and Tennyson; and somewhat more recently Henry Sidgwick, Roger Fry, Bertrand Russell, G. E. Moore, Desmond MacCarthy, Lytton Strachey, Leonard Woolf, J. M. Keynes, Lowes Dickinson. The Apostles have been greatly discredited by such members as the notorious traitors Anthony Blunt, Guy Burgess and Donald Maclean and associations with homosexuality.

Cambuscan. In Chaucer's unfinished *Squire's Tale*, the king of Sarra, in Tartary, model of all royal virtues. His wife was Elfeta; his two sons ALGARSIFE and Cambalo; and his daughter Canace.

Camden Society. An historical society founded in 1838 for the publication of early historical texts and documents, named after William Camden (1551–1623), schoolmaster, antiquary and author of *Britannia*, a survey of the British Isles. In 1897 it amalgamated with the Royal Historical Society, and its long series of publications were transferred to that body.

Camel. MOHAMMED's favourite camel was Al Kaswa. The mosque at Koba covers the spot where it knelt when he fled from MECCA. He considered the kneeling of the camel as a sign sent by God, and remained at Koba in safety for four days. The swiftest of his camels was Al Adha, who is fabled to have performed the whole journey from JERUSALEM to Mecca in four bounds, thereby gaining a place in heaven along with BORAK, Balaam's ass, Tobit's dog, and the DOG OF THE SEVEN SLEEPERS.

It is easier for a camel to go through the eye of a needle, than for a rich man to enter into the Kingdom of God (*Matt.* xix, 24 and *Mark* x, 25). In the KORAN we find a similar expression: "The impious shall find the gates of heaven shut; nor shall he enter till a camel shall pass through the eye of a needle." The meaning of the passage is reinforced by *Mark* x, 24, "How hard is it for them that trust in riches to enter into the Kingdom of God!" In the Rabbinical writings there is a variant of the expression, "Perhaps thou are one of the Pampedithians, who can make an elephant pass through the eye of a needle."

Camelot (kăm' e lot). In British fable, the legendary spot where King ARTHUR held his court. It has been tentatively located at CAERLEON, the hill-fort known as Cadbury castle in Somerset, and Camelford in Cornwall, where the Duke of Cornwall resided in his castle of TINTAGEL, etc. The Cadbury site is the most probable. It is mentioned in Shakespear's *King Lear*, II, ii, and Tennyson's *Idylls of the King*, etc. *See also* CAMELET.

> On either side the river lie
> Long fields of barley and rye,
> That clothe the wold and meet the sky;
> And through the field the road runs by
> To many-tower'd Camelot.
>
> TENNYSON: *The Lady of Shalott*.

Cameron Highlanders. The 79th Foot, raised by Allan Cameron of Errock in 1793. It became the Queen's Own Highlanders (Seaforth and Cameron).

Cameronians, or Reformed PRESBYTERIANS, were organized by the strict COVENANTER and field preacher, Richard Cameron, who was slain in battle at Aird's Moss in 1680. He objected to the alliance of Church and State under Charles II and seceded from the Kirk. His followers refused to take the Oath of Allegiance and thus deprived themselves of some of the privileges of citizenship. In 1876 the majority of Cameronians united with the Free Church.

Cameronian Regiment. The 26th Infantry, which had its origin in a body of CAMERONIANS in the Revolution of 1688, called the Cameronians (Scottish Rifles) from 1881.

Camford. A name, made up from Cambridge and Oxford, which has never acquired the same currency as OXBRIDGE. *Cp.* REDBRICK.

> He was a Camford man and very nearly got the English Prize Poem; it was said.
>
> THACKERAY: *Pendennis*, ch. iii.

Camilla (kà mil' à). In Roman legend a virgin queen of the Volscians. She helped Turnus against ÆNEAS. VIRGIL (*Aeneid* VII, 809) says she was so swift that she could run over a field of corn without bending a single blade, or make her way over the sea without even wetting her feet.

> Not so when swift Camilla scours the plain,
> Flies o'er the unbending corn and skims along the main.
>
> POPE: *Essay on Criticism*, 372.

Camisard, or **Camisardo** (kăm' i sard, kăm i sa' dō). A night attack; so called because the attacking party wore a *camise* or *camisard* over their armour, both to conceal it, and that they might better recognize each other in the dark.

Camisards. In French history the PROTESTANT insurgents of the Cévennes, who resisted the violence of the DRAGONNADES occasioned by the Revocation of the Edict of NANTES in 1685 and carried on a fierce war of reprisals with Louis XIV's forces until finally suppressed in 1705. Their leader was Jean Cavalier (1681–1740), afterwards governor of Jersey and later of the Isle of Wight. So called from the *camise* or blouse worn by the peasantry.

Camlan, Battle of. In Arthurian legend the battle which put an end to the KNIGHTS OF THE ROUND TABLE, and at which ARTHUR received his death wound from the hand of his nephew MODRED, who was also slain.

Camlet, camelot. A fabric. As far back as the 13th century camlet was a rich stuff made of silk and camel's hair. Later it was a durable cotton and woollen cloth mixture, etc.; also the name of a waterproof material before the introduction of indiarubber.

> After dinner I put on my new camelott suit, the best that I ever wore in my life, the suit costing me above £24.
>
> PEPYS: *Diary* (1 June 1664).

Cammock. As crooked as a cammock. A cammock is a staff or stick with a crook-end like a hockey stick or shinty club.

> Though the cammock, the more it is bowed the better it serveth; yet the bow, the more it is bent and occupied the weaker it waxeth.
>
> LYLY: *Euphues*.

Camorra (kà mor' à). A lawless secret society of the 19th century, run on gangster lines, which terrorized Naples. It began amongst prisoners in the gaols about 1820, and exacted tribute from traders and brothel-keepers alike. From 1848 it began to intervene in politics and continued to be a very real menace until 1911, when severe judicial action led to its extinction. The name is probably from the Sp. *Camorra*, a quarrel, and now has the same significance as THUG, APACHE, gangster, etc. *Cp.* MAFIA.

Camp. The origin of the use of this word in the following expressions is a matter of surmise.

High camp. Ostentatiously exaggerated movements and gestures akin to those of the ballet.

To camp it up is to use *camp* gestures in an affected and effeminate way.

> Look at that fellow who scored such a hit in the late-night show as Actaeon's mother, camping it up like mad.
>
> JUVENAL: *Satire VI* (*Peter Green's Translation*, 1967).

To make camp. To make affected gestures, to behave in an effeminate or homosexual fashion.

Camp-followers. The old-time armies which lived on the country, moved in a leisurely fashion and laid up in winter quarters, were accompanied by numerous civilian followers, such as washerwomen and sutlers who sold liquor and provisions, etc. These were called camp-followers.

> In the moment of failure (at Bannockburn) the sight of a body of camp-followers, whom they mistook for reinforcements to the enemy, spread panic through the English host.
>
> J. R. GREEN: *Short History of the English People*, ch. iv, 6.

Camp of the Tartars. The shopkeepers of part of the Palais Royal, Paris, in the early years of the 19th century, whose rapacity was said to equal that of the TARTAR hordes.

Campaign Wig. This style of WIG came from France in the early 18th century. It was very full, curled, and 18 inches in length at the front with deep locks. Sometimes the back part was put in a black silk bag. The name refers to Marlborough's campaign in the Netherlands.

Campania (kăm pā' ni à) (Lat. level country). The ancient geographical name for the fertile district south-east of the Tiber, containing the towns of Cumæ, Capua, Baiæ, Puteoli, Herculaneum, Pompeii, etc.

> Disdainful of Campania's gentle plains.
>
> THOMSON: *Summer*.

Campaspe (kăm păs' pe). A beautiful concubine, favourite of ALEXANDER THE GREAT, whom he handed over to APELLES, who it is said modelled his VENUS Anadyomene from her.

> Cupid and my Campaspe play'd
> At cards for kisses—Cupid paid.
>
> LYLY: Song from "*Campaspe*".

Campbellites. Followers of John McLeod Campbell (1800–1872), who taught the universality of the atonement, for which he was ejected from the CHURCH OF SCOTLAND in 1831.

In the U.S.A. the name is sometimes given to the *Disciples of Christ*, a body founded by Thomas and Alexander Campbell of Pennsylvania in 1809. They reject creeds and practise baptism by immersion and weekly communion, and uphold Christian union on the foundation of the Bible alone. They are also known simply as *Christians*.

Campbells are coming, The. This stirring song is supposed to have been composed in 1715 when John Campbell, Duke of Argyll, defeated the Earl of Mar and the JACOBITES. It became the regimental march of the Sutherland Highlanders (93rd Regiment) and after 1881 of the Argyll and Sutherland Highlanders when the two regiments merged.

At the second relief of Lucknow in November 1857 the beseiged in the Residency became aware of the approach of Sir Colin Campbell and the Sutherland Highlanders when they heard the distant sound of bagpipes playing "The Campbells are coming".

Campeador. The CID.

Canard (kăn′ ar) (Fr. a duck). A hoax, a ridiculously extravagant report. The French lexicographer Emile Littré (1801—1881) says that the term comes from an old expression, *vendre un canard à moitié*, to half-sell a duck. As this was no sale at all, it came to mean "to take in", "to make a fool of". Another explanation is that a certain Cornelissen, to try the gullibility of the public, reported in the papers that he had twenty ducks, one of which he cut up and threw to the nineteen, who devoured it greedily. He then cut up another, then a third, and so on till the nineteenth was gobbled up by the survivor—a wonderful proof of duck voracity.

Canary. Wine from these islands was very popular in the 16th and 17th centuries.

> Farewell, my hearts, I will to my honest knight Falstaff, and drink canary with him.
> SHAKESPEARE: *Merry Wives of Windsor*, III, ii.

It was also at one time slang for a GUINEA or SOVEREIGN, from its yellow colour.

Cancan. A fast and extremely dexterous dance, sometimes accompanied by extravagant and often indecent postures, originally performed in the casinos of Paris. The most famous example is in Offenbach's opera *Orpheus in the Underworld* (1858).

They were going through a quadrille with all those supplementary gestures introduced by the great Rigolboche, a notorious *danseuse*, to whom the notorious cancan owes its origin.
A. EGMONT HAKE: *Paris Originals* (1878).

Cancer (Lat. crab). One of the twelve signs of the ZODIAC, the Crab. It appears when the sun has reached its highest northern limit, and begins to go backward to the south; but like a crab the return is sideways (21 June to 23 July).

According to fable, JUNO sent Cancer against HERCULES when he combated the HYDRA of Lerna. It bit the hero's foot, but Hercules killed the creature, and Juno took it up to heaven.

Candaules (kăn daw′ lēz). King of Lydia about 710 to 668 B.C. Legend relates that he exposed the charms of his wife to GYGES, whereupon she compelled him to assassinate her husband, after which she married the murderer. Plato's version is that Gyges obtained possession of the queen by using the ring which made him invisible.

Candid Camera. An unseen camera which is used to photograph an unsuspecting subject. Candid camera shots, which are often ridiculous, are much used in pictorial journalism.

Candidate (Lat. *candidatus*, clothed in white). One who seeks or is proposed for some office, appointment, etc. Those who solicited the office of consul, quæstor, prætor, etc., among the Romans, arrayed themselves in a loose white robe. It was loose that they might show the people their scars, and white in sign of fidelity and humility.

Candide (kan′ dēd). The hero of VOLTAIRE'S philosophical novel, *Candide, ou l'Optimisme* (1759). All sorts of misfortunes are heaped upon him which he bears philosophically. It was written at the time of the Lisbon earthquake to satirise philosophical optimism.

Candle. Bell, book, and candle. *See* BELL.

Fine, or **Gay as the king's candle.** "*Bariolé comme la chandelle des rois*", in allusion to an ancient custom of presenting on 6 January a candle of various colours at the shrine of the three kings of COLOGNE. It is generally applied to an overdressed woman, especially one wearing gay ribbons and flowers. "FINE AS FIVEPENCE."

He is not fit to hold a candle to him. He is very inferior. The allusion is to link boys who held candles in theatres and other places of night amusement.

The game is not worth the candle. *Le jeu n'en vaut pas la chandelle*. The effort is not worth making; not worth even the cost of the candle that lights the players.

To burn the candle at both ends. *See* BURN.

To hold a candle to the Devil. To aid or countenance that which is wrong.

To sell by the candle. A form of sale by auction. A pin is thrust through a candle about an inch from the top, and bidding goes on till the candle is burnt down to the pin; when the pin drops into the candlestick the last bidder is declared the purchaser. Such an auction was held at Aldermaston and reported in the *Reading Mercury* (16 Dec.) in 1893.

> The Council thinks it meet to propose the way of selling by "inch" of candle, as being the most probable means to procure the true value of the goods.
> MILTON: *Letters*.

To vow a candle to the Devil. To seek to bribe or propitiate the DEVIL.

What is the Latin for candle? *See* TACE.

Candle-holder. An abettor. The reference is to the practice of holding a candle to assist a reader or worker where light is needed. In ordinary parlance it applies to one who assists in some slight degree but is not a real sharer in an action or undertaking.

> I'll be a candle-holder and look on.
> SHAKESPEARE: *Romeo and Juliet*, I, iv.

Candlemas Day. 2 February, formerly the Feast of the Purification of the Virgin Mary, now called the Presentation of Our Lord; one of the QUARTER DAYS in SCOTLAND. In ROMAN CATHOLIC churches all the candles which will be needed in the church throughout the year are consecrated on this day; they symbolize Jesus Christ, called "the light of the world", and "a light to lighten the Gentiles". The ancient Romans had a custom of burning candles to scare away evil spirits.

> If Candlemas Day be dry and fair,
> The half o'winter's come and mair;
> If Candlemas Day be wet and foul,
> The half o'winter was gone at Youl.
> *Scotch Proverb.*

> The badger peeps out of his hole on Candlemas Day, and, if he finds snow, walks abroad; but if he sees the sun shining he draws back into his hole.
> *German Proverb.*

Candlewick. The name given to a type of embroidery with tufts of soft cotton yarn, used mainly to decorate bedspreads. It is said that snippets of the thick yarn used for the wicks of candles were put to decorative use on the borders of the dust covers for beds by the thrifty wives of the early settlers in America.

Candour, Mrs. In *The School for Scandal* Sheridan drew the perfect type of female back-biter, concealing her venom under an affectation of frank amiability.

Canecutters. Nickname for the inhabitants of Queensland, Australia, who are also known as *Bananalanders*.

Canephorus (kà nef' ôr ùs). A sculptured figure of a youth or maiden bearing a basket on the head. In ancient ATHENS the *canephori* bore the sacred things necessary at the feasts of the gods.

Canicular Days (Lat. *canicula*, dim. of *canis*, a dog). The DOG-DAYS.

Canicular Period. The ancient Egyptian cycle of 1,461 years or 1,460 Julian years, also called a SOTHIC PERIOD, during which it was supposed that any given day had passed through all the seasons of the years.

Canicular Year. The ancient Egyptian year computed from one heliacal rising of the DOG STAR to the next.

Canker. The briar or dog-rose.

> To put down Richard, that sweet lovely rose,
> And plant this thorn, this canker, Bolingbroke.
> SHAKESPEARE: *Henry IV, Pt. 1*, I, iii.

Also a caterpillar that destroys leaves, buds, etc.

> As killing as the canker to the rose.
> MILTON: *Lycidas*.

Canmore. *See* GREAT HEAD.

Cannæ. The place where Hannibal defeated the Romans under Varro and Æmilius with great slaughter in 216 B.C. Any fatal battle that is the turning point of a great general's success may be called his *Cannæ*. Thus Moscow was the Cannæ of NAPOLEON.

Canned music. Music recorded and reproduced, as opposed to "live music", *i.e.* played by musicians present in person. Canned music, like canned foods, can be stored and used when required. *See* DISC JOCKEY.

Cannon. This term in billiards is a corruption of *carom*, which is short for Fr. *carambole*, the red ball (*caramboler*, to touch the red ball). A *cannon* is a stroke by which the player's ball touches one of the other balls in such a way as to glance off it and strike the remaining ball.

To cannon into, or **against someone.** An unexpected collision of persons or a chance encounter.

Canny. *See* CA'CANNY.

Canoe. A Haitian word brought to Europe by the Spaniards. It meant a boat hollowed out of a tree trunk.

Paddle your own canoe. Rely upon yourself. The caution was given by President Lincoln, but it is an older saying and was used by Captain Marryat (*Settlers in Canada*, ch. viii) in 1844. Sarah Bolton's poem in *Harper's Magazine* for May 1854 popularized it:

Voyage upon life's sea,
To yourself be true,
And, whatever your lot may be,
Paddle your own canoe.

Canon. From Lat. and Gr. *canon*, a carpenter's rule; a rule, hence a standard (as "the canons of criticism"), a model, an ordinance, as in SHAKESPEARE.

> Or that the everlasting had not fix'd
> His canon 'gainst self-slaughter.
> *Hamlet*, I, ii.

The canon. The body of books in the BIBLE which are accepted by the Christian Church generally as genuine and inspired; the whole Bible from *Genesis* to *Revelation*, excluding the APOCRYPHA. Called also the *sacred canon* and the *Canonical Books*.

The Church dignitary known as a *Canon* is a capitular member of a cathedral or COLLEGIATE CHURCH, usually living in the precincts, and observing the rule or *canon* of the body to which he is attached. The canons, with the DEAN or provost at their head, constitute the governing body, or CHAPTER, of the cathedral. These are the *canons-residentiary*; there are also *honorary canons* who have no share in the cathedral government, or emoluments. *Minor canons* are mainly concerned with the singing of the services and have no part in the decisions of the chapter.

The title once had a much wider application and was used to designate most of the diocesan clergy. When its use came to be limited to the secular clergy of a cathedral, they were called *secular canons* as distinct from the *canons regular* such as the Austin or AUGUSTINIAN CANONS.

Also in music, from the same derivation, a composition written strictly according to rule, for two or three voices which sang exactly the same melody, one a few beats after the other, either at the same or different pitch. Simple forms are the catch and the round such as *Three Blind Mice* and *London's Burning*. A London choral club was founded in 1843 called the "Round, Catch and Canon Club".

Canoness. The title was given to certain women living under rule, less strict than that of nuns, in the Frankish empire from the late 8th century. Like their male counterparts they came to be divided into canonesses *regular* and *secular*.

Canon law, or canons. A collection of ecclesiastical laws which serve as the rule of church government. The professors or students of canon law are called *canonists*.

> Doubt not, worthy senators! to vindicate the sacred honour and judgement of Moses your predecessor, from the shallow commenting of scholastics and canonists.
> MILTON: *Doctrine of Divorce*, Introd.

Book of Canons. A collection of 178 canons enacted by the councils of Nicæa, Ancyra, Neocesarea, Laodicea, Gangra, Antioch, Constantinople, Ephesus, and Chalcedon. It was first published in 1610 and is probably of late 4th or early 5th-century origin.

The CHURCH OF ENGLAND "Book of Canons" was adopted in 1604 as the basis of ecclesiastical law. A *Book of Canons* for the Scottish Church was drawn up under Charles I's command and issued in 1636. It mainly helped to precipitate religious strife in Scotland.

Canons of the Mass. The fixed form of consecratory prayer used in the GREEK and ROMAN CATHOLIC CHURCHES—from the *Sanctus* to the PATERNOSTER.

Canonical Age. *See under* AGE.

Canonical dress. The distinctive or appropriate costume worn by the clergy according to the direction of the canon; BISHOPS, DEANS and archdeacons, for instance, wear canonical hats. This distinctive dress is sometimes called simply "canonicals"; Macaulay speaks of "an ecclesiastic in full canonicals".

The same name is given also to the special parts of such robes, such as the pouch on the gown of an M.D., originally designed for carrying drugs; the lamb-skin on some B.A. hoods, in imitation of the *toga candida* of the Romans; the tippet on a BARRISTER'S gown, meant for a wallet to carry briefs in; and the PROCTORS' and proproctors' tippet for papers—a sort of sabre-tache.

Canonical Epistles. The seven CATHOLIC EPISTLES as distinct from those of Paul which were addressed to particular churches or individuals.

Canonical hours. The different parts of the Divine Office which follow, and are named after the hours of the day. They are seven—MATINS, PRIME, tierce, sext, NONES, VESPERS and COMPLINE. Prime, tierce, sext and nones are the first, third, sixth and ninth hours of the day, counting from six in the morning. (*See* BREVIARY.) The reason why there are seven canonical hours is that David says, "Seven times a day do I praise thee" (*Ps*. cxix, 164).

In England the phrase means more especially the time of the day within which persons can be legally married, *i.e.* from 8 in the morning to 6 p.m.

Canonical obedience. The obedience due by the inferior to the superior clergy. Thus bishops owe canonical obedience to the archbishop of the same province.

Canonization. The solemn act by which the Pope proclaims the sanctity of a person, subsequent to the lesser act of BEATIFICATION; whereupon he or she is worthy to be honoured as a SAINT and is put upon the *Canon* or Catalogue of Saints of the Church.

Canopus (kà nō′ pus). Alpha Argus or Canopus, in the constellation Argo Navis, is the brightest star in the heavens after SIRIUS.

Canopy properly means a gnat curtain. Herodotus tells us (II, 95) that the fishermen of the Nile used to lift their nets on a pole, and form thereby a rude sort of tent under which they slept securely, as gnats will not pass through the meshes of a net. Subsequently the hangings of a bed were so called, and lastly the canopy borne over kings (Gr. *konops*, a gnat).

Canossa (kà nos′ à). Canossa, in the duchy of Modena, is where the Holy Roman Emperor Henry IV humbled himself to Pope Gregory VII (Hildebrand) by standing for three days barefooted in the courtyard of the palace in the garb of a penitent (January 1077). This was during the INVESTITURE CONTROVERSY.

Hence, **to go to Canossa** is to undergo humiliation, to EAT HUMBLE PIE, to submit after having refused to do so. During Bismarck's quarrel with Pope Pius IX at the time of the KULTURKAMPF he said in the Reichstag (14 May 1872): "*Nach Canossa gehen wir nicht.*" (We shall not go to Canossa!)

Cant. Language peculiar to a social class; profession, sect, etc., jargon; technical language; insincere talk, hypocrisy. As its derivation (Lat. *cantus*, song) shows, the earlier application of the word was to music and thereby intonation. Soon the term came to be applied to the whining speech of beggars, who were known as the CANTING CREW. In Harman's *Caveat, or Warning for Common Cursetors, vulgarly called Vagabonds* (1567), we read:

As far as I can learne or understand by the examination of a number of them, their language—which they term pcddclars Frenche or Canting—began within these xxx yeeres.

One example of canting that he gives begins:

Bene Lightmans to they quarromes, in what tipken hast thou lypped in this darkemans, whether in a lybbege or in the strummel? (Good-morrow to thy body, in what house hast thou laid all night, whether in a bed or in the straw?)

The term was in use to denote professional slang by the 17th century.

The doctor here...
When he discourses of dissection...

Of vena cava and of vena porta...
What does he else but cant?

BEN JONSON: *The Staple of News*, IV, i (1625).

As insincerity or conventionality in speech or thought we have:

Rid your mind of cant.

DR. JOHNSON.

Canting crew. Beggars, gipsies, thieves and vagabonds, who use CANT. In 1696 E. B. Gent published the first English Slang Dictionary with the title *A New Dictionary of the terms, Ancient and Modern, of the Canting Crew in its several Tribes*.

Cantabrian Surge. The Bay of Biscay. So called from the Cantabri who dwelt about the Biscayan shore.

Cantate Sunday (kăn′ta′ te). ROGATION Sunday, the fifth Sunday after EASTER. So called from the first word of the introit of the MASS: "Sing to the Lord". Similarly "LÆTARE SUNDAY", the fourth in LENT, is so called from the first word of the introit of the mass. *Cp.* QUASIMODO SUNDAY.

Canter. An easy gallop; originally called a *Canterbury pace* or gallop, from the ambling gait adopted by mounted pilgrims to the shrine of St. Thomas à Becket at Canterbury.

A preliminary canter. Something which precedes the real business in hand, a trial run. The reference is to the trial trip of horses before racing.

To win in a canter. Easily; well ahead of all competitors.

Canterbury Tales. Chaucer represented that he was in company with a party of pilgrims going to Canterbury to pay their devotions to the shrine of St. Thomas à Becket. The party assembled at the TABARD INN, SOUTHWARK, and there agreed to tell one tale each, both in going and returning. He who told the best story was to be treated with a supper on the homeward journey. The work is incomplete and we have none of the tales told on the way home.

Canucks (ka nŭks′). The name given to Canadians generally, but in Canada to Canadians of French descent. Possibly a corruption of *Connaught*, a name originally applied by the French Canadians to Irish immigrants.

Canvas means cloth made of hemp (Lat. *cannabis*, hemp).

To be under canvas. To be in camp, in a tent.

To carry too much canvas means that a sailing ship has spread more sail than she can safely carry; figuratively that something far too big for one's resources is being attempted.

To canvas a subject is to strain it through a hemp strainer, to sift it.

To canvass a constituency is to solicit votes. In the U.S.A. it is also used to mean scrutinizing voting papers after the ballot.

Caora (ka ŏr´ à). A river described in Hakluyt's *Voyages*, on the banks of which dwelt a people whose heads grew beneath their shoulders. Their eyes were in their shoulders, and their mouths in the middle of their breasts. Ralegh, in his *Description of Guiana*, gives a similar account of a race of men. *Cp.* BLEMMYES.

Cap. The word is used figuratively by SHAKESPEARE for the top, the summit (of excellence, etc.); as in *They wear themselves in the cap of the time* (*All's Well*, II, i), *i.e.* "They are the ornaments of the age"; *a very riband in the cap of youth* (*Hamlet*, IV, vii); *Thou art the cap of all the fools alive* (*Timon*, IV, iii); *on fortune's cap we are not the very button* (*Hamlet*, II, ii); etc.

Black cap. *See* BLACK.

Cap acquaintance. A bowing acquaintance. One just sufficiently known to touch one's cap to.

Cap and bells. The insignia of a professional fool or jester.

Cap and feather days. The time of childhood.

> Here was I got into the scenes of my cap and feather days.
>
> COBBETT.

Cap and gown. The full academical costume of a university student, tutor or graduate, worn on formal occasions, etc.

> Is it cap and gown affair?
>
> "CUTHBERT BEDE": *Verdant Green.*

Cap and stocking. A public-house sign in Leicester commemorating the importance of these articles to the town's industry, especially the making of STATUTE CAPS (*see below*).

Cap in hand. Submissively. Like a servant.

Cap money. Money collected in a cap or hat; hence an improvised collection.

Cap of liberty. When a slave was manumitted by the Romans, a small Phrygian cap, usually of red felt, called a *pileus*, was placed on his head and he was termed *libertinus* (a freed-man). When Saturninus, in 100 B.C., possessed himself of the Capitol, he hoisted a similar cap to the top of his spear, to indicate that all slaves who joined his standard should be free. Marius employed the same symbol against Sulla, and when CÆSAR was murdered, the conspirators marched forth with a cap elevated on a spear in token of liberty.

In the French Revolution the cap of liberty (*bonnet rouge*) was adopted as an emblem of freedom from royal authority.

Cap of maintenance. A cap of dignity anciently belonging to the rank of duke; the fur cap of the Lord MAYOR of London, worn on days of state; a cap carried before the British sovereigns at their coronation. The significance of *maintenance* here is not known, but the cap was an emblem of very high honour, for it was conferred by the POPE three times on Henry VII and once on Henry VIII. By certain old families it is borne in the COAT OF ARMS, either as a charge or in place of the wreath.

Canterbury cap. A soft flat cloth cap sometimes worn by dignitaries of the CHURCH OF ENGLAND.

Cater cap. A square cap or MORTAR-BOARD (Fr. *quartier*).

College cap. A TRENCHER, like the caps worn at the English universities.

Dunce's cap. A conical cap worn by the class "dunce" as a symbol of disgrace and stupidity. *See* DUNCE.

Fool's cap. A conical cap with feather and bells, such as licensed fools used to wear.

Forked cap. A bishop's MITRE.

John Knox cap. An early form of the TRENCHER, MORTAR-BOARD, or COLLEGE CAP worn at the Scottish universities.

Monmouth cap. *see* MONMOUTH.

Phrygian cap. CAP OF LIBERTY.

Scotch cap. A cloth cap worn in Scotland as part of the national dress.

Square Cap. A TRENCHER or MORTAR-BOARD.

Statute cap. A "cap of wool knit", the wearing of which on holidays was enforced on all over six years of age (with certain exceptions for rank and sex) by a statute of Elizabeth I of 1571, for the benefit of the woollen trade. The fine for non-compliance was 3s. 4d. "for each day's transgression". The act was repealed in 1597. To a similar end, persons were at one time obliged to be buried in woollen shrouds. *See* CAP AND STOCKING.

> Well, better wits have worn plain statute caps.
>
> SHAKESPEARE: *Love's Labour's Lost*, V, ii.

Trencher cap, or MORTAR-BOARD. A cap with a square board on top, generally covered with black cloth, and with a tassel, worn with academical dress; a COLLEGE CAP.

A feather in one's cap. An achievement to be proud of; something creditable.

I must put on my thinking cap. I must consider before I give a final answer. The allusion is to the official cap of the judge, formerly donned when passing sentence, later reserved for passing the death sentence.

If the cap fits, wear it. If the remark applies to you, apply it to yourself. Hats and caps vary only slightly in size but everyone knows his own when he puts it on.

Setting her cap at him. Trying to catch for a sweetheart or husband. In the days when ladies habitually wore caps they would naturally put on the most becoming to attract the attention of the favoured gentleman.

To cap. To take off, or touch one's cap to, in token of respect; also to excel.

> Well, that caps the globe.
>
> C. BRONTE: *Jane Eyre*.

I cap to that. I assent to it. The allusion is to the custom among French judges. Those who assent to the opinion stated by any of the bench signify by lifting their toques from their heads.

To cap a story. To go one better; to follow a good story with a better one of the same kind.

To cap it all. To surpass what has gone before; to make things even worse.

To cap verses. Having the metre fixed and the last letter of the previous line given, to add a line beginning with that letter, thus:

> The way was long, the wind was cold (D).
> Dogs with their tongues their wounds do heal (L).
> Like words congealed in northern air (R).
> Regions Cæsar never knew (W).
> With all a poet's ecstasy (Y).
> You may decide my awkward pace, *etc., etc.*

There are parlour games of capping names, proverbs, etc., in the same way, as: Plato, Otway, Young, Goldsmith, etc., "Rome was not built in a day", "Ye are the salt of the earth", "Hunger is the best sauce", "Example is better than precept", "Time and tide wait for no man", etc.

To gain the cap. To obtain a bow from another out of respect.

> Such gains the cap of him that makes 'em fine,
> But keeps his book uncrossed.
>
> SHAKESPEARE: *Cymbeline*, III, iii.

To pull caps. To quarrel like two women who pull each other's caps. An obsolete phrase, used only of women. In a description of a rowdy party in 18th-century Bath we read:

> At length they fairly proceeded to pulling caps, and everything seemed to presage a general battle…they suddenly desisted, and gathered up their caps, ruffles and handkerchiefs.
>
> SMOLLET: *Humphry Clinker, Letter xix.*

To send the cap round. To make a collection. From the custom of street musicians, singers, etc., sending a cap round to collect pennies among the onlookers.

Wearing the cap and bells. Said of a person who is the butt of the company, or one who excites laughter at his own expense.

The reference is to licensed jesters, formerly attached to noblemen's establishments, who wore the CAP AND BELLS.

> One is bound to speak the truth—whether he mounts the cap and bells or a shovel hat [like a bishop].
>
> THACKERAY.

Your cap is all on one side. Many workmen, when they are perplexed or bothered, scratch their heads and in so doing push their cap on one side of the head, generally over the right ear, because the right hand is occupied.

Capful of wind. Olaus Magnus tells us that Eric, King of Sweden, was so familiar with evil spirits that whatsoever way he turned his cap the wind would blow, and for this he was called *Windy Cap*. The Laplanders drove a profitable trade in selling winds, and even so late as 1814, Bessie Millie of Pomona (Orkney), used to sell favourable winds to mariners for the small sum of sixpence.

To be capped. A player who has represented ENGLAND, SCOTLAND, IRELAND, or WALES in an international match at any of the major field sports may wear a cap bearing the national emblem. Hence the phrase, *he was capped for England*, etc.

Capability Brown. Lancelot Brown (1715–1783), landscape gardener and architect, patronized by most of the rich men of taste. He set their great country houses in a surround of parkland and informal pastoral charm. He was given this nickname because he habitually assured prospective employers that their land held "great capabilities".

Cap-à-pie (kăp á pē). From head to foot; usually with reference to arming or accoutring. From O.Fr. *cap-à-pie* (Mod. Fr. *de pied en cap*).

> Armed at all points exactly cap-a-pie.
>
> SHAKESPEARE: *Hamlet*, II, i.

Cape. The Cape. Cape of Good Hope (originally known as the Cape of STORMS), Cape Province.

Cape cart. A two-wheeled, hooded cart with a single shaft or pole, much used in Cape Colony and South Africa in colonial days.

Cape Gooseberry. *Physalis peruviana*, a plant much prized for its decorative bladder-like calyx, it takes its name from the Cape, but is of South American origin.

Cape Cod Turkey. Salt fish, a product of the Cape Cod fisheries, Massachusetts. *Cp.* BOMBAY DUCK. *See also* CAPON.

Cape Doctor. A bracing S.E. wind blowing at the Cape of Good Hope; so named from the time when the British in India used the Cape as a health resort, to recuperate from the more exacting climate of India, until hill stations came to be used for the same purpose.

Spirit of the Cape. See ADAMASTOR.

Capel Court. A lane adjacent to the London STOCK EXCHANGE where dealers congregate to do business; so called from Sir William Capel, Lord Mayor in 1504. Hence used sometimes for the Stock Exchange itself. Hence also *Capel Courtier*, a humorous term for a professional stock-dealer.

Caper. The weather is so foul not even a Caper would venture out Caper. A Manx proverb. A *Caper* is a fisherman of Cape Clear in Ireland, who will venture out in almost any weather.

Caper Merchant. A dancing master who "cuts capers".

Cut your capers! Be off with you!

I'll make him cut his capers, *i.e.* rue his conduct.

To cut capers. To spring upwards in dancing, and rapidly interlace one foot with the other; figuratively to act in a manner with the object of attracting notice. *Caper* here is from the Ital. *capra*, a she-goat, which will jump about in an erratic way.

Capet. Hugh Capet (938–996), the founder of the Capetian dynasty of France, is said to have been named from the *cappa*, or monk's hood, which he wore as a lay abbot of St. Martin de Tours. The Capetians of the direct line ruled from 987 till 1328 when they were succeeded by the collateral house of VALOIS and by that of BOURBON in 1589 (Henry of Navarre). Louis XVI was arraigned before the National CONVENTION under the name of Louis Capet.

Capital. Money or money's worth available for production.

> His capital is continually going from him (the merchant) in some shape and returning to him in another.
>
> ADAM SMITH: *Wealth of Nations*, Bk. II, ch. i.

Active capital. Ready money or property readily convertible into it.

Capital cross. See under CROSS.

Capital levy. A State exaction on capital. First proposed in the British HOUSE OF COMMONS in 1914. A Capital Gains tax was introduced in 1965.

Capital punishment. The imposition of the death penalty for crime (Lat. *caput*, head).

Capital ship. Warships of the largest class like the now obsolete battleship of which the DREADNOUGHT was the prototype.

Circulating capital. Wages or raw material. This sort of capital is not available a second time for the same propose.

Fixed, capital. Land, buildings, and machinery, which are only gradually consumed.

To make capital out of. To turn to account; thus, in politics, one party is always ready to make *political capital* out of the errors or misfortunes of the other.

Capitán, El Gran (el grăn kăp i ta′ n) (the Great Captain). The name given to the famous Spanish general Gonsalvo de Cordova (1453–1515), through whose efforts Granada and Castile were united.

Capitulary (kăp it′ ū lăr i). A collection of ordinances or laws, especially those of the Frankish kings. The laws were known as *capitulars*, from their being arranged in chapters (Med. Lat. *capitularius*). See CHAPTER.

Capon. (kā′ pon). Properly a castrated cock; but the name has been given to various fish, perhaps originally by humorous friars who wished to avoid the Friday fast and so eased their consciences by changing the name of the fish and calling a chicken a *fish out of the coop*. Thus we have:

A Crail's capon. A haddock dried and split, Crail being the borough in Fife, Scotland, which flourished from its fishing.

A Glasgow capon. A salt herring.

A Norfolk or **Yarmouth capon.** A red herring.

A Severn capon. A sole.

Capon is also an obsolete term for a love-letter, after the Fr. *poulet*, which means not only a chicken, but also a love-letter or a sheet of fancy notepaper. Thus Henry IV, consulting with Sully about his marriage, says: "My niece of Guise would please me best, though report says maliciously that she loves poulets in paper better than in fricassee."

> Boyet, you can break-up this capon (*i.e.* open this love-letter).
>
> SHAKESPEARE: *Love's Labour's Lost*, IV, i.

Capone, Alphonse (1899–1947). Al (Scarface) Capone, notorious Chicago gangster and racketeer of Sicilian origin. He rose to power in the heyday of BOOTLEGGING in the 1920s and made himself master of the rackets in the city by organizing the killing of most of the rival gunmen. After the St. Valentine's Day Massacre of 1929, when seven rival gangster leaders were machine-gunned, he was left in supreme control of the protection racket, speakeasies, brothels, etc. The suburb of Cicero was completely dominated by him. See also MAFIA.

Capricorn (kăp′ ri kôrn). Called by Thomson in his *Winter*, "the centaur archer". Anciently the winter SOLSTICE occurred on the entry of the sun into Capricorn, *i.e.* the

Goat; but the stars having advanced a whole sign to the east, the winter now falls at the sun's entrance into SAGITTARIUS (the Centaur Archer), so that the poet is strictly right, though we commonly retain the classical manner of speaking. Capricorn is the tenth, or strictly, eleventh sign of the ZODIAC (21 December–20 January).

In classical mythology Capricorn was PAN, who, from fear of the great TYPHON, changed himself into a goat, and was made by JUPITER one of the signs of the Zodiac.

Captain. The Great Captain. See CAPITÁN.
A led captain. An obsequious person, a hanger-on, who dances attendance on the master and mistress of a house, for which service he has a knife and fork at the dinner table.

Captain Armstrong. A name for a cheating jockey—one who pulls a horse with a strong arm, and so prevents him winning.

Captain Cauf's Tail. In Yorkshire, the chief MUMMER who led his following from house to house on PLOUGH MONDAY He was most fantastically dressed, with a cockade and many coloured ribbons; and he always had a genuine calf's (*cauf's*) tail affixed behind.

Captain Cooks, or **Cookers.** The popular name for the scrawny wild pig of New Zealand descended from those introduced by Captain Cook (1728–1779), the explorer.

Captain Moonlight. In Ireland a mythical person to whom was attributed the performance of atrocities by night especially in the latter part of the 19th century. Arson, murder, and the maiming of cattle were his specialities.

Captain of the Heads. In naval ships, the rating in charge of the *Heads* or lavatories. The name Heads arises from the original position of the ship's latrines, right forward in the beakhead or heads of the vessel.

Capua (kăp' ū à). **Capua corrupted Hannibal.** Luxury and self-indulgence will ruin anyone. Hannibal was everywhere victorious until he wintered at Capua, the most luxurious city of Italy, after which his star began to wane. Another form of the saying is **Capua was the Cannæ of Hannibal.** (*See* CANNÆ.)

Capuchin (kăp' ū chin). A friar of the strict group of FRANCISCANS that arose about 1520; so called from the *capuce* or pointed cowl. They became a separate order in 1619.

Capulet (kăp' ū let). A noble house in Verona, the rival of that of Montague; in Shakespeare's *Romeo and Juliet*, Juliet is of the former, and ROMEO of the latter. Lady Capulet is the BEAU IDEAL of a proud Italian ma-

tron of the 15th century.

> In as few years their few successors will go to the family vault of "all the Capulets."
> BURKE: *Reflections on the Revolution in France*.

Caput Mortuum (kăp' ut môr tū um) (Lat. dead head). An alchemist's term for the residuum left after exhaustive distillation or sublimation; hence, anything from which all that made it valuable has been removed. Thus a learned scholar paralysed is a mere *caput mortuum* of his former self. The French DIRECTORY, towards its close, was a mere *caput mortuum* of a government.

Caqueux (ka kė). A sort of gipsy race in Brittany, similar to the CAGOTS of Gascony and COLLIBERTS of Poitou.

Carabas (kăr' a ba). **He is a Marquis of Carabas.** An ultra-conservative nobleman of unbounded pretensions and vanity, who would restore the lavish foolery of the reign of Louis XIV; one with the purse of FORTUNATUS, which was never empty. The character is taken from Perrault's tale of PUSS IN BOOTS.

> Prêtres que nous vengeom
> Levez la dîme et partageons;
> Et toi, peuple animal,
> Porte encor le bat féodal...
> Chapeau bas! Chapeau bas!
> Gloire au marquis de Carabas!
> BÉRANGER (1816).

The Marquis of Carabas in Disraeli's *Vivian Grey* is intended for the Marquis of Clanricarde.

Carabinier. See CARBINEER.

Caracalla (kăr' a kăl' à). Aurelius Antonius, Roman Emperor (211–217), was so called because instead of the Roman TOGA he adopted the Gaulish *caracalla*. It was a large, close-fitting, hooded mantle, reaching to the heels, and slit up before and behind to the waist.

Caradoc (kà răd' ok). A Knight of the ROUND TABLE, noted for being the husband of the only lady in the queen's train who could wear "the mantle of matrimonial fidelity". He appears as Craddocke in the old ballad *The Boy and the Mantle* in PERCY'S RELIQUES. *See* BRAWN.

> Craddocke called forth his ladye,
> And bade her come in;
> Saith, Winne this mantle, ladye,
> With a little dinne.

Also in history, the British king whom the Romans called Caractacus, who was taken captive to Rome in A.D. 51.

Caran d'Ache (kă ràn dash'). The pseudonym of Emmanuel Poiré (1858–1909), a well-known French caricaturist, born and educated at Moscow. (Russ. *karandash*, pencil).

Carat. For precious stones, a measure of weight, about 1/142 of an ounce; for GOLD it is a ratio or proportional measure of 1/24th. Thus 22 carats of gold means 22 parts gold, 2 parts alloy. The name is perhaps from the Arab. *qirat*, meaning the seed of the locust tree, which was used for weighing gold and PRECIOUS STONES.

Caraway (kăr′ à wā). Once caraway "seeds" were very commonly used for flavouring cakes which were then called *caraways* or seed cakes. The liqueur kümmel is also distilled from caraway oil.

> Nay, you shall see my orchard, where in an arbour, we will eat a last year's pippin of my own graffing, with a dish of caraways.
> SHAKESPEARE: *Henry IV, Pt. II*, V, iii.

Carbineer, Carabineer, or **Carabinier.** In the 16th century light cavalry armed with *carabins*, later becoming troops armed with a short rifle called a *carbine*. The 9th Horse (subsequently the 6th Dragoon Guards) were named the *Carabiniers* by William III in 1692. Louis XIV's Royal Carabiniers were so named in 1693. In 1939 the 3rd and 6th Dragoon Guards amalgamated to form the 3rd Carabineers.

Carbonado (kar bon ā′ dō). Grilled meat or fish. Strictly speaking, a carbonado is a piece of meat cut crosswise for the grid-iron (Lat. *carbo*, a coal).

> If he do come in my way; so; if he do not—if I come in his willingly, let him make a carbonado of me.
> SHAKESPEARE: *Henry IV, Pt. I*, V, iii.

Carbonari (kar bo na′ rē). The name means *charcoal burners* and was assumed by a political secret society in Naples formed about 1808 with the aim of overthrowing despotic and foreign government. Their meeting-place was called a "hut", the inside "the place of selling charcoal", the outside "the forest", their opponents "wolves", etc. Much of their ritual was drawn from FREE-MASONRY and kindred societies grew up throughout Italy and also France. The Italian Carbonari were largely merged into YOUNG ITALY in the 1830s. BYRON and Mazzini were members, and NAPOLEON III was associated with the movement in his earlier days.

Card. Slang for a queer fellow, an eccentric, a "character". Arnold Bennett has a novel called *The Card* (1911).

> You're a shaky old card; and you can't be in love with this Lizzie.
> DICKENS: *Our Mutual Friend*, Bk. III, ch. i.

Perhaps suggested by the phrase A SURE CARD, we have such phrases as the following:

A cool card. A person who coolly asks for something preposterous or outrageous; "cool" here means "coolly impudent". *Cp.* A COOLING CARD.

A cooling card. An obsolete expression for something that cools one's ardour, probably derived from some old game of cards. It is quite common in Shakespeare's day. In *Euphues* (1579) Lyly calls the letter to Philantus "a cooling card for Philantus and all fond lovers", and says:

> The sick patient must keep a straight diet, the silly sheep a narrow fold, poor Philantus must believe Euphues, and all lovers (he only excepted) are cooled with a card of ten or rather fooled with a vain toy.

A card of ten was evidently an important card; SHAKESPEARE has:

> A vengeance on your crafty wither'd hide!
> Yet I have faced it with a card of ten.
> *Taming of the Shrew*, II, i.

which means either to put a bold face on it, or to meet an attack with craft and subtlety.

A great card. A BIG-WIG, a person of note.

A knowing card. A sharp fellow, next door to a sharper. The allusion is to card-sharpers and their tricks.

> ...whose great aim it was to be considered a "knowing card", a "fast-goer", and so forth,...
> DICKENS: *Sketches by Boz, Making a Night of It*.

A leading card. The strongest point in one's argument, etc.; a star actor. In card games a person leads from his strongest suit.

A loose card. A worthless fellow who lives on the loose.

> A loose card is a card of no value, and consequently the properest to throw away.
> HOYLE: *Games*, etc.

A queer card. An eccentric person, "indifferent honest"; one who may be "all right", but whose proceedings arouse mild suspicion and so not inspire confidence.

A sure card. A person one can fully depend on; one sure to command success. A project certainly to be depended on, as a winning card in one's hand.

> A clear conscience is a sure card.
> LYLY: *Euphues* (1579).

Court cards. *See* COURT.

He played his cards well. He acted judiciously and skilfully, like a WHIST-player who plays his hand with judgment.

On the cards. Likely to happen, projected, and talked about as likely to occur. Probably derived from fortune-telling by cards, but possibly an allusion to a racing programme or *card*.

That's the card. The right thing. It probably refers to card games—"that's the right card to play"—but it means the same as "that's the ticket" and may refer to a ticket, or a race-card, etc.

That was my trump card. My best chance, my last resort.

The cards are in my hands. I hold the disposal of events which will secure success; I have the upper hand, the whip-end of the stick.

The Devil's Four-poster. *See under* DEVIL.

To ask for one's cards. To resign one's job. The reference is to the National Insurance cards kept by a person's employer. Similarly **to be given one's cards** means to be dismissed or sacked.

To count on one's cards. To anticipate success under the circumstances; to rely on one's advantages.

To go in with good cards. To have good patronage; to have excellent grounds for expecting success.

To have a card up one's sleeve. To have resources unsuspected by one's opponents, to have a last stroke in reserve. From cheating at cards, but with no implication of dishonesty in the figurative use.

To play one's best card. To do that which one hopes is most likely to secure victory.

To speak by the card. Here the allusion is probably to the card of a mariner's compass. It means to be careful with one's words; to be deliberate and have as much claim to be right as a compass. It may, however, have reference to written agreements such as those made between a merchant and the master of a ship, *i.e.* to speak according to the written instructions.

> Law...is the card to guide the world by.
> HOOKER: *Ecclesiastical Policy*, Pt. II, sec. v.
> We must speak by the card, or equivocation will undo us.
> SHAKESPEARE: *Hamlet*, V, i.

When Osric tells Hamlet (V, ii) that Laertes is "the card and calendar of gentry" the compass card is implied with all its points.

Cardi. A native of Cardiganshire (now part of Dyfed), Wales. *Cardis* are popularly reputed to be clannish, parsimonious and excessively thrifty. Thus, among Welsh people "an old Cardi" denotes one reluctant to pay his turn of drinks, a stingy person.

Cardigan. A knitted woollen over-waistcoat with sleeves, named after the 7th Earl of Cardigan, who led the Light Brigade in the famous charge of Balaclava (1854). It appears to have been first worn by the British to protect themselves from the bitter cold of the Crimean winter. The Balaclava helmet or cap, a knitted woollen covering for the head and neck, has a similar origin. *See*

CHERRY; THE NOBLE YACHTSMAN *under* NOBLE.

Cardinal (Lat. *cardo*, a hinge). The adjective *cardinalis* meant originally "pertaining to a hinge" hence "that on which something turns or depends", thus "the principal or chief". In Rome, a cardinal church was a parish church as distinct from an oratory attached to it and the word was next applied to the senior priest of such a church. From the mid-8th century it denoted urban as distinct from rural clergy, and subsequently the clergy of a diocesan town and its cathedral but it was later restricted to the cardinals of the Roman see. In 1567 Pius V formally reserved the title for members of the Pope's Council, the COLLEGE OF CARDINALS.

The Cardinal's red hat was made part of the official vestments by Innocent IV in 1245. This 30-tasselled hat (not worn) was abolished in 1969. *See also* BISHOP.

College of Cardinals, or **Sacred College.** Originally formed from the clergy of the see of ROME, it now contains members from many nations who take their titles, as has always been customary, from a Roman parish. It consists of Cardinal-Bishops, Cardinal-Priests, and Cardinal-Deacons (the latter possibly deriving from the seven deacons appointed by St. PETER), but these terms are essentially of historical significance only, as all cardinals are now consecrated bishops. The number of cardinals was fixed at 70 by Sixtus V in 1586. John XXIII (1958–1963) raised it to 87, and in 1969 it reached 136. The POPE is elected by and from the College of Cardinals.

Cardinal humours. An obsolete medical term for the four principal humours of the body. *See* HUMOUR.

Cardinal numbers. The natural primitive numbers, which answer the question "how many?" such as 1, 2, 3, etc. 1st, 2nd, 3rd, etc., are *ordinal* numbers.

Cardinal points of the compass. Due north, south, east, and west, so called because they are the points on which the intermediate ones (NE., NW., NNE., etc.) hinge. The poles, being the points on which the earth turns, were called in Latin *cardines* (*See* CARDINAL.) The cardinal points are those which lie in the direction of the poles and of sunrise and sunset. Thus the winds which blow due north, east, west, and south, are called *cardinal winds*. It is probably from the fact that there are four cardinal points that there are four cardinal humours, virtues, etc.

Cardinal signs (of the ZODIAC). The two equinoctial and the two solstitial signs ARIES and LIBRA, CANCER and CAPRICORN.

Cardinal virtues. Justice, prudence, temperance, and fortitude, on which all other virtues hang or depend. A term of the SCHOOLMEN, to distinguish the "natural" virtues from the "theological" virtues (faith, hope and charity).

Care. Care killed the cat. It is said that "a cat has nine lives", yet care would wear them all out.

> Hang sorrow! care'll kill a cat.
> BEN JONSON: *Every Man in his Humour*, I, iii.

Care Sunday. The fifth Sunday in LENT. "Care" here means trouble, suffering; and Care Sunday means PASSION SUNDAY (as in O.H. Ger. *kar-fritag* is GOOD FRIDAY).

Care Sunday is also known as *Carle* or *Carling Sunday*. It was an old custom, especially in the north, to eat parched peas fried in butter on this day, and they were called *Carlings*.

Care-cloth. In the ROMAN CATHOLIC CHURCH, the fine silk or linen cloth formerly laid over the newly-married, or held over them as a canopy.

Carey Street, To be in. To be bankrupt. Carey Street is in the City of London, off Chancery Lane, and the bankruptcy court is situated there.

Carle Sunday; Carlings. *See* CARE SUNDAY.

Carlists. Don Carlos (1788–1855), second son of Charles IV of Spain, would have become king on the death of his brother Ferdinand VII, had not the SALIC LAW been set aside in favour of Ferdinand's daughter, Isabella. Don Carlos was supported by the Church, and the Carlist Wars ensued (1833–1840), but Isabella's supporters triumphed. Carlist intrigues continued until the death of Don Carlos II in 1909 and in 1937 the Carlists supported General Franco's FALANGE, maintaining Carlos Hugo de Borbón-Parma as claimant to the throne. On General Franco's death in 1975, Alphonso XIII's grandson became King of Spain as Juan Carlos I, his succession having been accepted by Franco in 1969.

Carlovingians (kar lo vin' jiànz). **Carolingians,** or **Karlings.** The dynasty named from *Carolus Magnus* or CHARLEMAGNE. They were descended from Arnulf, a 7th-century bishop of Metz, and ruled in France (751–987), Germany (752–911), and Italy (744–887).

Carmagnole (kar ma nyōl). Originally the name of a workman's jacket introduced into France from Carmagnola in Piedmont and adopted by French revolutionaries. Thus the name came to be applied to them, to the soldiers of the Republic, and to a widely popular song and dance which was almost invariably used at the executions of 1792 and 1793. The first verse of the song is:

> Madame Veto avait promis
> De faire égorger tout Paris,
> Madame Veto avait promis
> De faire égorger tout Paris,
> Mais son coup a manqué.
> Dansons la carmagnole, Vive le son, vive le son,
> Dansons la carmagnole, Vive le son du canon.

Madame VETO was their name for Marie Antoinette, as she was supposed to have instigated the king's unfortunate use of the veto. Carmagnole was subsequently applied to other revolutionary songs such as ÇA IRA, the MARSEILLAISE, the CHANT DU DÉPART, also to the speeches in favour of the execution of Louis XVI, called by Barère *des Carmagnoles*.

Carmelites (kar' me lītz). A mendicant order of friars of 12th-century origin, taking its name from Mount Carmel in Syria and with a mythical history associating them with the prophet Elijah. Also called WHITEFRIARS from their white mantle. *See* BAREFOOTED.

Carmen Sylva (kar' men sil' và). The penname of Queen Elizabeth of Roumania (1843–1916). She was a musician, painter, and writer of poems and stories.

Carnaby Street. In the 1960s the much publicized clothing centre for fashion-conscious young men, situated east of Regent Street. It became associated with trendy unisex costumes and was somewhat showily refurbished by Westminster City Council in 1973, but its popularity had declined by 1975 when boutiques in King's Road, Chelsea, began to attract this type of trade. *Cp.* MONMOUTH STREET.

Carnival. The season immediately preceding LENT, ending on SHROVE TUESDAY and a period in many Roman Catholic countries devoted to amusement; hence revelry, riotous amusement. From the Lat. *caro, carnis*, flesh; *levare*, to remove; signifying the abstinence from meat during Lent. The earlier word *carnilevamen* was altered in Italian to *carnevale* as though connected with *vale*, farewell—farewell to flesh.

Carol (O.Fr. *carole*, probably from Lat. *choraula*, a flute-player). The earliest use of the word in English was for a round dance, then later a light and joyous hymn particularly associated with the Nativity. The following verse is a translation from Old English of our earliest extant Christmas carol:

> Lordlings listen to our lay—
> We have come from far away
> To seek Christmas;
> In this mansion we are told
> He his yearly feast doth hold;
> 'Tis today!

May joy come from God above,
To all those who Christmas love.

The first printed collection came from the press of Wynkyn de Worde in 1521; it included the *Boar's Head Carol*, which is still sung at Queen's College, Oxford. *See* BOAR'S HEAD.

Carolingians. *See* CARLOVINGIANS.

Carolus (kà rō′ lus). A GOLD coin of the reign of Charles I. It was at first worth 20s., later 23s.

Carpathian Wizard. PROTEUS, who lived in the island of Carpathus (now Scarpanto), between Rhodes and Crete, and could transform himself into any shape he pleased. He is represented as carrying a sort of crook in his hand, because he was an ocean shepherd and had to manage a flock of sea-calves.

Carpe diem (kar′ pä dī′ em) (Lat.). Seize the present day. Enjoy yourself while you have the chance. *"Dum vivimus, vivamus"*.

> Carpe diem, quam minimum credula postero.
> HORACE: *Odes* I, xi, 8.
> Seize the present, trust tomorrow e'en as little as you may.
> CONNINGTON.

Carpet. The magic carpet. The apparently worthless carpet, which transported whoever sat upon it wheresoever they wished, is one of the stock properties of Eastern storytelling. It is sometimes *Prince Housain's carpet*, because of the popularity of the *Story of* PRINCE AHMED in the ARABIAN NIGHTS, when it supplies one of the main incidents; but the chief magic carpet is that of King SOLOMON which, according to the KORAN, was of green silk. His throne was placed on it when he travelled, and it was large enough for all his forces to stand upon, the men and women on his right hand, and the spirits on his left. When ready, Solomon told the wind where he wished to go, and the carpet rose in the air, and landed at the place required. The birds of the air, with outspread wings, protected the party from the sun.

To be on the carpet, or **to be carpeted**. To be reprimanded, to be "called over the COALS".

To bring a question on the carpet. To bring it up for consideration; a translation of the Fr. *sur le tapis* (on the tablecloth)—*i.e.* before the House, under debate.

To sweep under the carpet. To conceal or put something out of sight so that it will not be noticed; to try and forget unpleasant difficulties or realities.

Carpet-bagger. The name given in the U.S.A. to the northern political adventurers who sought a career in the southern states after the CIVIL WAR ended (1865). Their only "property qualification" was their "carpet bag" of personal belongings, and they were regarded by the southerners as parasites and exploiters. The southern state governments of this time are called *carpet-bagger* governments from the presence of these Republican office-holders from the north.

Hence a general term for one who comes to a place for political or particular ends, as a political candidate who has no real roots in the constituency he seeks to represent.

Carpet-biter. A person subject to violent fits of rage. Chewing and biting of this kind has always been a sign of uncontrolled temper, and there are many accounts of this type of behaviour among the notoriously violent-tempered from the ANGEVINS to Adolf Hitler.

Carpet bombing. Delivery by the postman of unsolicited (and mainly unwanted) advertising matter. Increasingly prevalent from the 1980s.

Carpet-knight. One dubbed at Court by favour, not having won his spurs by military service in the field. Perhaps because nonmilitary knighthoods were conferred "on the carpet", rather than "in the field", but more probably in allusion to the attachment shown to the carpeted drawing-room by non-martial knights.

> You are women
> Or, at the best, loose carpet-knights.
> MASSINGER: *Maid of Honour*, II, v.

Carriage. This used to mean things carried, luggage.

> And after those days we took up our carriages, and went up to Jerusalem.
> *Acts* xxi, 15.

Carriage company. People who kept their own carriage for visiting, etc.

> There is no phrase more elegant and to my taste than that in which people are described as "seeing a great deal of *carriage company*".
> THACKERAY: *The Newcomes*, ch. ix.

Carronade (kăr o nād). A short gun of large calibre like a mortar, having no trunnions and thus differing from howitzers. First made in 1779 at the Carron iron foundry in Scotland, carronades were fastened to their carriages by a loop underneath, and were chiefly used on ships to enable heavy shot to be thrown at close quarters.

Carry. Carry arms! Carry swords! Military commands directing that the rifle or drawn sword is to be held in a vertical position in the right hand and against the right shoulder.

To carry away. In nautical language, to break a spar, or rope or other part of a ship's gear.

To carry both ends of the log (Austr). To do all the work supposed to be shared by two.

To carry coals. *See* COAL.

To carry everything before one. To carry off all the prizes, to be highly successful in any form of sport, contest, or examination.

To carry fire in one hand and water in the other. To say one thing and mean another; to flatter, to deceive; to lull suspicion in order the better to work mischief.

> Altera manu fert aquam, altera ignem,
> Altera manu fert lapideum, altera panem ostentat.
> PLAUTUS.
> In one hand he carried water, in the other fire; in one hand he bears a stone, in the other he shows a piece of bread.

To carry on. (1) To continue an activity from the point already reached. (2) To make a scene, lose one's temper—"he carried on something dreadful".

To carry on with someone. To indulge in an amorous affair.

To carry one's bat. Said of a cricketer who goes in first and is "not out" at the innings close. Hence, figuratively, to outlast one's opponents, to succeed in one's undertaking.

To carry one's point. To succeed against opposition, to overrule, to win. Candidates in ROME were balloted for and the votes marked on a tablet by points. Hence, *omne punctum ferre* meant "to be carried *nem. con.*", or to gain every vote; and "to carry one's point" is to carry off the points at which one aimed.

To carry out, or **through.** To continue a project to its completion.

To carry the can. To receive the blame for the misdeeds or mistakes in which others have participated. Probably from the performance of menial tasks in the services, which benefit others.

To carry the day. To win the contest; to carry off the honours of the day.

To carry weight. To have influence. In horse-racing, to equalize the weight of two or more riders by adding to the lighter ones.

> He carries weight! he rides a race!
> 'Tis for a thousand pounds.
> COWPER: *John Gilpin.*

Cart. To put the cart before the horse is to reverse the right or natural order of things.

> This methinks is playnely to sett the carte before the horse.
> *The Babees Book* (Early English Tract Society, p. 23).

In other languages we have:

French:	Mettre la charrette avant les bœufs.
Latin:	Currus bovem trahit præpostere.
Greek:	HYSTERON PROTERON.
German:	Die Pferde hinter den Wagen spannen.
Italian:	Metter il carro innanzi ai buoi.

Carte. Carte blanche (Fr.). Literally a blank paper. A paper with only the signature written on it, so that the recipient may write his own terms upon it, knowing they will be accepted. Of military origin, referring to unconditional surrender, but now entirely used in a figurative sense meaning to confer absolute freedom of action on someone. *Cp.* BLANK CHEQUE.

Carte de visite (Fr.). A visiting card; a photographic likeness on a card, originally intended to be used as a visiting card; an idea which started in 1857 but never "caught on", although it made the small size of photograph very popular.

Cartesian Philosophy (kar tē' zhån). The philosophical system of René Descartes (1596–1650), often called the father of modern philosophy. The basis of his system is COGITO ERGO SUM. Thought must proceed from SOUL and therefore man is not wholly material; that soul must be from some Being not material, and that Being is God. As for physical phenomena, they must be the result of motion excited by God, and these motions he termed *vortices*, to explain the movement of heavenly bodies. This latter theory was replaced by Newton's theory of gravitation. *See* NEWTONIAN PHILOSOPHY.

Carthage of the North. This name was given to Lübeck when it was the head of the HANSEATIC LEAGUE.

Carthaginem esse delendam. *See* DELENDA EST CARTHAGO.

Carthaginian faith. Treachery. *See* PUNIC FAITH.

Carthusians. An order of monks founded about 1084 by St. Bruno of Cologne, who with six companions retired to the solitude of La Grande Chartreuse, thirteen miles north-east of Grenoble, and there built his famous monastery. It was here they made the famous liqueur called CHARTREUSE. In 1902 monks were evicted by order of the French government and they moved to the Certosa (Charterhouse) near Lucca.

The first English Charterhouse was founded by Sir Walter de Menny at London in 1371 and the Carthusians were among the staunchest opponents of Henry VIII at the time of the Dissolution of the Monasteries. In 1833 the Carthusians were re-established in the Charterhouse at Parkminster, Sussex.

Carucate (Med. Lat. *caruca*, a plough). The same as a HIDE.

Carvilia. *See* MORGAN LE FAY.

Caryatides, or **Caryatids** (kăr i ăt' idz). Figures of women in Greek costume, used in architecture to support entablatures. Caryæ, in Laconia, sided with the Persians at

THERMOPYLÆ, in consequence of which the Greeks destroyed the city, slew the men, and made the women slaves. Praxiteles, to perpetuate the disgrace, employed figures of these women instead of columns. *Cp*. AT-LANTES, CANEPHORUS, TELAMONES.

Casabianca (kăs á bi ăng' kà). At the Battle of the Nile (1798), Louis Casabianca, Captain of the French flagship *L'Orient* (120 guns), gallantly fought his ship to the end, although the Admiral had been killed. His thirteen-year-old son, Giacomo Jocante, refusing to leave him, perished with his father.

> The boy stood on the burning deck
> Whence all but he had fled;
> The flame that lit the battle's wreck
> Shone round him o'er the dead.
>
> MRS. HEMANS: *Casabianca*.

Casanova. To be regarded as a "regular Casanova" is to have a reputation for amorous escapades, in allusion to the notorious Giovanni Jacopo Casanova de Seingalt (1725-1798), who secured his own reputation as an insatiable amorist by the writing of his lengthy *Mémoires*. Expelled from a Venetian seminary for his immoral conduct, after a period in the household of Cardinal Acquaviva, he wandered the capitals of Europe mixing with aristocratic and wealthy society, posing as alchemist, preacher, gambler, diplomatist, etc., and generally leading a vicious life. He was also a knight of the papal order of the Golden Spur, and was acquainted with Stanislaus Poniatowski and Frederick the Great, but he soon exhausted the goodwill of those around him and found it necessary to move on.

Case. The case is altered. *See* PLOWDEN.

To case. To skin an animal; to deprive it of its "case". *See* FIRST CATCH YOUR HARE *under* CATCH.

To case a joint (Amer.). A criminal's expression for investigating, reconnoitring or inspecting a "joint" (the building or property concerned) preparatory to the intended robbery, etc.

Case-hardened. Impenetrable to all sense of honour or shame. The allusion is to steel hardened by carbonizing the surface.

Casket. A small chest or box.

Casket Homer. *See* HOMER.

Casket, Children of the. Between 1728 and 1751 the Mississippi Company sent regular shipments of respectable middle-class girls to New Orleans to provide wives for the French settlers in Louisiana; each was presented on her departure with a *casket* of suitable clothing. They were known as *filles à la cassette*, to distinguish them from the women of bad character shipped out from the Salpêtrière prison during the same period. Louisiana families like to claim descent from a casket girl as New Englanders do from a MAYFLOWER pilgrim.

Casket Letters, The. Letters supposed to have been written between Mary Queen of Scots and Bothwell, at least one of which was held to prove the complicity of the Queen in the murder of Darnley, her husband. They were kept in a *casket* which fell into the hands of the Earl of Morton in 1567; they were examined in England and used as evidence (though denounced as forgeries by the Queen, who was never allowed to see them), and they disappeared after the execution of the Earl of Gowrie (1584), into whose possession they had passed on Morton's execution in 1581. Their authenticity is still in dispute.

Cassandra (kà săn' drà). A prophetess. In Greek legend the daughter of PRIAM and HECUBA, gifted with the power of prophecy. She refused APOLLO's advances and he brought it to pass that no one believed in her predictions, although they were invariably correct. She appears in SHAKESPEARE's *Troilus and Cressida*. In the figurative sense the name is usually applied to a prophet of doom.

Cassation. The Court of Cassation, in France, is the highest Court of Appeal, the court which can *casser* (quash) the judgment of other courts.

Cassi. Inhabitants of the Cassio HUNDRED, Hertfordshire, referred to by CÆSAR in his *Commentaries*. The name survives in Cassiobury Park, Watford.

Cassibelan (kăs ib' el àn). Uncle to Cymbeline mentioned in Shakespeare's *Cymbeline*. He is the historical Cassivellaunus, a British king who ruled over the Catuvellauni (in Herts., Bucks., and Berks.), about 50 B.C., and was conquered by CÆSAR. *See* CUNOBELIN.

Cassiopeia (kaš i ō pē' à). In Greek mythology, the wife of CEPHEUS, King of Ethiopia, and mother of ANDROMEDA. In consequence of her boasting of her beauty, she was sent to the heavens as the constellation Cassiopeia, the chief stars of which form the outline of a woman sitting in a chair and holding up both arms in supplication.

Cassiterides (kăs i ter' i dēz). The tin islands, generally supposed to be the Scilly Islands and CORNWALL; but possibly the isles in Vigo Bay are meant. It is said that the Veneti procured tin from Cornwall and carried it to these islands, keeping its source a profound secret. The Phœnicians were the chief customers of the Veneti.

Cast. A cast of the eye. A squint. One meaning of the word cast is to twist or warp. Thus, a fabric is said to "cast" when it warps; seamen speak of "casting", or turning the head of a ship on the tack it is to sail. We also speak of a CASTING VOTE.

> My goode bowe clene cast (twisted) on one side.
> ASCHAM: *Toxophilus*.

Cast down. Dejected (Lat. *dejectus*).

Cast not a clout till May is out. *See under* MAY.

Casting vote. The vote of the presiding officer or chairman when the votes of the assembly are equal. The final vote casts, turns, or determines the issue.

To cast about. To deliberate, to consider, as, "I am casting about me how I am to meet the expenses." A sporting phrase. Dogs, when they have lost scent, "cast for it", *i.e.* spread out and search in different directions to recover it.

To cast accounts. To balance or keep accounts. **To cast up a line of figures** is to add them together and set down the sum they produce.

To cast anchor. To throw out the anchor in order to bring the vessel to a standstill (Lat. *anchoram jacere*).

To cast a sheep's eye at one. *See* SHEEP.

To cast beyond the moon. To form wild conjectures. One of Heywood's proverbs. At one time the MOON was supposed to influence the weather, to affect the ingathering of fruits, to rule the time of sowing, reaping and slaying cattle, etc.

> I talke of things impossible, and cast beyond the moon.
> HEYWOOD.

To cast in one's lot. To share the good or bad fortune of another.

To cast in one's teeth. To throw reproof at one. The allusion is to knocking one's teeth out by stones.

> All his faults observed,
> Set in a notebook, learn'd and conn'd by rote,
> To cast in my teeth.
> SHAKESPEARE: *Julius Cæsar*, IV, iii.

To cast pearls before swine. To offer what is precious to those who are unable to understand its value or appreciate it; a Biblical phrase (*Matt*. vii, 6). If pearls were cast to swine, the swine would trample them underfoot.

Castaly (kăs′ tà li). A fountain of PARNASSUS sacred to the MUSES. Its waters had the power of inspiring with the gift of poetry those who drank of them.

Caste (Port. *casta*, race). One of the hereditary classes of society among Hindus; hence any hereditary or exclusive class. The four Hindu castes are BRAHMINS (the priestly order), *Shatriya* (soldiers and rulers), *Vaisya* (husbandmen and merchants), *Sudra* (agricultural labourers and artisans). The first issued from the mouth of BRAHMA, the second from his arms, the third from his thighs, and the fourth from his feet. Below this come thirty-six inferior classes, to whom the VEDAS are sealed, and who are held cursed in this world and without hope in the next.

To lose caste. To lose position in society. To be degraded from one caste to an inferior one.

Castle. Castle in the air. A visionary project, day-dream, splendid imagining which has no real existence. In fairy tales we often have these castles built at a word and vanishing as soon, like that built for ALADDIN by the Genie of the Lamp. Also called *Castles in Spain*; the French call them *Châteaux en Espagne* or *Châteaux en Asie*.

Castle of Bungay. In Camden's *Britannia* (1607) the following lines are attributed to Lord Bigod of Bungay on the borders of Suffolk and Norfolk:

> Were I in my castle of Bungay
> Upon the river of Waveney,
> I would ne care for the king of Cockney.

The events referred to belong to the reign of Stephen or Henry II. The French have the proverb: *Je ne voudrais pas être roi, si j'étais prévôt de Bar-sur-Aube* (the most lucrative and honourable of all the provostships in France). A similar idea is expressed in the words:

> And often to our comfort, we shall find
> The sharded beetle in a safer hold
> Than is the full-winged eagle.
> SHAKESPEARE: *Cymbeline*, III, iii.

Similarly Pope says:

> And more true joy Marcellus exiled feels
> Than Cæsar with a senate at his heels.
> *Essay on Man*, iv, 257.

Castle of Indolence. In Thomson's poem of this name (1748) it is situated in the land of Drowsiness, where every sense is steeped in enervating delights. The owner was an enchanter, who deprived all who entered his domains of their energy and free will.

Castle Terabil, or **Terrible,** in ARTHURIAN legend stood in Launceston, Cornwall. It had a steep keep environed with a triple wall. Sometimes called Dunheved Castle.

Castor and Pollux (kăs′ tór, pol′ uks). In classical mythology, twin sons of JUPITER and LEDA, also known as the DIOSCURI. They had many adventures including sailing with JASON in quest of the GOLDEN FLEECE, were worshipped as gods, and finally placed among the constellations as the GEMINI.

Their names used to be given by sailors to the ST. ELMO'S FIRE, or CORPOSANT. If only one flame showed itself, the Romans called it HELEN, and said that the worst of the storm was yet to come; two or more luminous flames they called *Castor and Pollux*, and said that they boded the termination of the storm.

Casus belli (kā′ sŭs bel′ i) (Lat.). A ground for war; an occurrence warranting international hostilities.

Cat. Called a "FAMILIAR", from the mediæval superstition that SATAN's favourite form was a black cat. Hence witches were said to have a cat as their familiar. The superstition may have arisen from the classical legend of Galenthias who was turned into a cat and became a priestess of HECATE.

In ancient Rome the cat was a symbol of liberty and the goddess of Liberty was represented with a cat at her feet. No animal is so opposed to restraint as a cat.

In Ancient Egypt the cat was held sacred. The goddess Bast (*see* BUBASTIS), representative of the life-giving solar heat, was portrayed as having the head of a cat, probably because that animal likes to bask in the sun. Diodorus tells us that in Egypt whoever killed a cat, even by accident, was punished by death. According to tradition DIANA assumed the form of a cat, and thus excited the fury of the GIANTS.

The male, or Tom, cat in SCOTLAND is called a Gib cat; the female is a Doe cat. *Cat* is also a term for a spiteful woman, a spiteful remark is said to be "catty" and "cat" was once a slang term for a harlot.

A cat has nine lives. A cat is more tenacious of life than many animals, it is careful and hardy and after a fall generally lands upon its feet without injury, the foot and toes being well padded.

> *Tyb:* What wouldst thou have with me?
> *Mer:* Good king of cats, nothing but one of your nine lives.
> SHAKESPEARE: *Romeo and Juliet*, III, i
> A cat has nine lives, and a woman has nine cats' lives.
> FULLER: *Gnomologia*.

A cat may look at a king. An impertinent remark by an inferior, meaning, "I am as good as you." There was a political pamphlet published with this title in 1652.

All cats love fish but fear to wet their paws. An old adage said of one who is anxious to obtain something of value but does not care to incur the necessary trouble or risk. It is to this saying that SHAKESPEARE referred in *Macbeth*, I, vii:

> Letting "I dare not" wait upon "I would",
> Like the poor cat i' the adage.

Before the cat can lick her ear. Never; before the GREEK CALENDS. No cat can lick her ear. *See* NEVER.

Care killed the cat. *See* CARE.

Cat i' the adage. *See* ALL CATS LOVE FISH, ETC.

Dick Whittington and his cat. *See* WHITTINGTON.

Enough to make a cat laugh. Incongruously ridiculous.

Enough to make a cat speak. Said of something (usually good liquor) that will loosen one's tongue.

> Come on your ways; open your mouth; here is that which will give language to you, cat; open your mouth.
> SHAKESPEARE: *Tempest*, II, ii.

Hang me in a bottle like a cat. (*Much Ado about Nothing*, I, i). In olden times a cat was for sport enclosed in a bag or leather bottle, and hung to the branch of a tree, as a mark for bowmen to shoot at. Percy in his *Reliques of Ancient English Poetry* (1765) mentions a variant of the "sport":

> It is still a diversion in Scotland to hang up a cat in a small cask or firkin, half filled with soot; and then a parcel of clowns on horseback try to beat out the ends of it, in order to show their dexterity in escaping before the contents fall upon them.

It is raining cats and dogs. Very heavily. *See under* RAIN.

Like a cat on hot bricks. Very uneasy; not at all "at home" in the situation; very restless.

Like something the cat brought in. Said of a slovenly person or one of uncouth or unkempt appearance. Also used in fun.

Muffled cats catch no mice (Ital. *Gatta guantata non piglia sorce*). Said of those who work in gloves for fear of soiling their fingers.

Not room to swing a cat. Used to indicate that a space, room, house, etc., is very restricted and small. There are various suggested origins of the phrase. Swinging cats by their tails as a mark for sportsmen was once a popular amusement. There were several variants of the diversion; *see* HANG ME IN A BOTTLE, *above*; and TO FIGHT LIKE KILKENNY CATS, *below*. *Cat* was an abbreviation for CAT-O'-NINE-TAILS and in view of the restricted space in the old sailing ships where the cat was often administered, it is most likely derived from swinging this particular kind of cat. *Cat* is also an old Scottish word for rogue, and if the derivation is from this, the "swing" is that of the condemned rogue hanging from the gallows.

See how the cat jumps. See "which way the wind blows"; await the course of events, but see what is going to happen before you pass an opinion, support a course of action or commit yourself. The allusion is either to the game of "tip-cat", in which before you strike you must watch which way the "cat" has jumped up, or to the cruel pastimes mentioned under NOT ROOM TO SWING A CAT.

Sick as a cat. Cats are very prone to vomiting. Hence one is said *to cat* or *to shoot the cat* when vomiting.

The cat's pyjamas. Something superlatively good; first rate; attractive. An American colloquialism in use by 1900 and current in England in the 1920s and 1930s. **The cat's whiskers** is used in the same way and with the same meaning.

To bell the cat. *See* BELL.

To be made a cat's paw of. *See under* CAT'S PAW.

To cat the anchor. To secure the anchor on the **cathead,** a fitment on the ship's side near the hawse-pipe. It is used to hang the BOWER ANCHOR, when the hawse-pipe is needed for the cable in securing to a buoy.

To fight like Kilkenny cats. To fight till both sides have lost their all; to fight with the utmost determination and pertinacity. The story is that during the Irish rebellion of 1798 Kilkenny was garrisoned by a troop of Hessian soldiers, who amused themselves by tying two cats together by their tails and throwing them across a clothes-line to fight. When an officer approached to stop the "sport", a trooper cut the two tails with a sword and the two cats bolted. When an explanation of the two bleeding tails was asked for, he was told that two cats had been fighting and devoured each other all but the tails.

To grin like a Cheshire cat. An old simile popularized by Lewis Carroll:

> "please would you tell me," said Alice a little timidly,... "why your cat grins like that?" "It's a Cheshire cat," said the Duchess, "and that's why."
> *Alice in Wonderland* (1865), ch. vi.

The phrase has never been satisfactorily explained, but it has been said that Cheshire cheese was once sold moulded like a cat that appeared to be grinning. The waggish explanation is that the cats know that Cheshire is a COUNTY PALATINE and find the idea a source of perpetual amusement.

To lead a cat and dog life. To be always snapping and quarrelling, as a cat and a dog.

To let the cat out of the bag. To disclose a secret. *See* A PIG IN A POKE *under* PIG.

To live under the cat's foot. To be under PETTICOAT GOVERNMENT; to be HENPECKED. A mouse under the cat's paw lives but by sufferance and at the cat's pleasure.

To put the cat among the pigeons. To stir up trouble, to cause dissension. The allusion is obvious.

To turn cat-in-pan. To turn traitor, to be a TURNCOAT. The phrase seems to be the Fr. *tourner côté en peine* (to turn sides in trouble).

Touch not a cat but a glove. The punning motto of the Mackintosh clan, whose crest is a "cat-a-mountain salient guardant proper", with "two cats proper" for supporters. Their clan was the clan *Cattan* or *Chattan*, thus "touch not the clan Cattan". The meaning of "but" here is "without" or "except with".

What can you have of a cat but her skin? Said of something that is useless for any purpose but one. The cat's fur was used for trimming cloaks, etc., but the flesh was no good for anything.

When the cat's away the mice will play. Advantage will be taken of the absence of the person in authority. A proverb found in many languages. It is given in Ray's *Collection*.

Cat and Fiddle. There are several fanciful derivations for this inn sign but it most probably comes from the nursery rhyme:

> Heigh diddle diddle
> The cat and the fiddle, *etc.*

There is a possible reference to the once popular game of tip-cat or trap-ball and the fiddle for a dance that were provided as attractions for customers. The second highest English inn is the *Cat and Fiddle* near Buxton, Derbyshire.

Cat and Kittens. A PUBLIC-HOUSE SIGN alluding to the large and small pewter pots in which beer was served. Stealing these pots was called "cat and kitten sneaking".

Cat and Mouse Act. Popular name for the Prisoners (Temporary Discharge for Ill-Health) Act of 1913, passed during the SUFFRAGETTE disturbances to avoid the imprisoned law-breakers from achieving martyrdom through hunger strikes. They were released on licence when necessary, subject to re-arrest if need arose. **To play cat and mouse** is to do what you like with someone in your power.

Cat-call. A kind of whistling noise sometimes used by theatre audiences, etc., to express displeasure or impatience.

> I was very much surprised with the great consort of cat-calls...to see so many persons of quality of both sexes assembled together in a kind of caterwauling.
> ADDISON: *Spectator*, No. 361.

Cat-eyed. Able to see in the dark.

Cat-ice. Very thin, almost transparent ice, from under which the water has receded; unable to bear the weight of a cat.

Cat-lap. A contemptuous name for tea, or other "soft" drink such as a cat would drink; non-alcoholic liquor.

> A more accomplished old woman never drank cat-lap.
>
> SCOTT: *Redgauntlet*, ch. xiii.

Cat o'mountain. The wild-cat; also the leopard, or panther; hence a wild, savage sort of man.

Cat-o'-nine-tails. A whip with nine lashes used for punishing offenders, briefly known as the "cat". Once used for flogging in the Army and Navy and not formally abolished as a civil punishment for crimes of violence until 1948. Popular superstition says that the nine tails were because flogging by "a trinity of trinities" would be both more efficient and more efficacious. *See* NOT ROOM TO SWING A CAT *above*.

Cat Stane. Certain monoliths in Scotland (there is one near Kirkliston, Linlithgow), so called from the Celtic *cath*, a battle, because they mark the site of a battle. They are not Druidical stones.

Cat's-brains. This curious name is given to a geological formation of sandstone veined with chalk. It is frequently met with in old agricultural deeds and surveys.

Cats' concert. A noisy jangle, a discordant din; like the caterwauling of cats at night.

Cat's cradle. A game played with a piece of twine by two children. It has been suggested that the name is a corruption of *cratch-cradle*, or the manger cradle in which the infant Saviour was laid (*cratch* is the Fr. *crèche*, a rack or manger), but this is no more than surmise.

Cat's eye. A gem which possesses chatoyancy, or a changeable lustre. The true or precious cat's eye is a variety of chrysoberyl. The semi-precious kind is a form of quartz.

It is also the name of a reflector embedded in the road as a guide for motorists after lighting-up time or in fog.

Cat's paw. A light air, seen afar off, indicated by a ripple on a calm sea, and often heralding the end of the prevailing calm, is so called by sailors. It is also a nautical term for a loop formed in a rope for attaching a hook, etc.

To be made a cat's paw of, *i.e.* the tool of another, to do another's dirty work. The allusion is to the fable of the monkey who wanted to get some roasted chestnuts from the fire, and used the paw of his friend the cat for the purpose.

Cat's whisker. In the old fashioned "crystal" wireless sets, this was the name given to the very fine wire that made contact with the crystal. *See also* CAT'S PYJAMAS *above*.

Catacomb (kăt' á cōm). A subterranean gallery for the burial of the dead, especially those at ROME. The origin of the name is unknown but the cemetery of St. SEBASTIAN on the APPIAN WAY was called the *Catacumbas*, probably a place-name and in the course of time the name was applied to similar cemeteries. Their extensive development in Rome took place in the 3rd and 4th centuries and was due to the spread of Christianity. At times they were used by the Christians for their meetings. They suffered much destruction from the GOTHS and Lombards and eventually came to be forgotten until rediscovered in 1578 as the result of a landslip.

Cataian (kàt ā' yan) A native of CATHAY or China; hence a thief, liar or scoundrel, because the Chinese were supposed to have these characteristics.

> I will not believe such a Cataian, though the priest of the town commended him for a true man.
>
> SHAKESPEARE: *Merry Wives of Windsor*, II, i.

Catalogue raisonné (rā' zȯ nā) (Fr.). A catalogue of books, paintings, etc., classed according to their subjects and often with explanatory notes or comments.

Catamaran (kăt à mà răn'). A scraggy old woman, a vixen; so called from a play on the first syllable. It properly means a raft consisting of three logs lashed together with ropes; used on the coasts of Coromandel and Madras, etc. (Tamil *katta-maram*, tied-log).

> No, you old catamaran, though you pretend you never read novels.
>
> THACKERAY: *Lovel the Widower*, ch. i.

It is now largely used to denote a boat made of two hulls connected in parallel.

Catastrophe (kà tăs trò fi) (Gr. *kata* downwards; *strephein*, to turn). A turning upside down. Originally used of the change which produces the *dénouement* of a drama, which is usually a "turning upside down" of the beginning of the plot.

> All the actors must enter to complete and make up the catastrophe of this great piece.
>
> SIR THOMAS BROWNE: *Religio Medici*.
>
> Pat! he comes like the catastrophe of the old comedy.
>
> SHAKESPEARE: *King Lear*, I, ii.

Catch. Catch as catch can. Get by HOOK OR CROOK all you can; a phrase from the child's game of this name, or from the method of wrestling so called, in which the wrestlers are allowed to get a grip anyhow or anywhere.

Catch me at it. Most certainly I shall never do what you say, I will never do that.

Catch weights. A term in racing, wrestling or boxing, meaning without restrictions as to weight.

First catch your hare. This direction is generally attributed to Hannah Glasse, habit-maker to the Prince of Wales, and author of *The Art of Cookery made Plain and Easy* (1747). Her actual directions are, "Take your hare when it is cased, and make a pudding,... etc." To "case" means to take off the skin, as in Shakespeare's *All's Well that Ends Well*, iii, vi, "We'll make you some sport with the fox ere we case him." "First catch your hare," is a very old phrase and in the 13th century Bracton (Bk. IV, tit. i, ch. xxi, sec. 4) has these words:

> Vulgariter, quod primo oportet cervum capere, et postea, cum captus fuerit, illum excoriare. (It is commonly said that you must first catch your deer, when it is caught, skin it.)

To be caught bending. To be caught at a disadvantage. If you catch a small boy bending over it is easy to smack him on that portion of his anatomy provided by nature for the purpose. Some time about 1903 one of George Robey's songs declared:

> My word! If I catch you bending!

The expression also occurs, of course, in *Knees up, Mother Brown*.

To be caught napping. To suffer some disadvantage while off one's guard. Pheasants, hares, and other animals are sometimes surprised "napping".

To be caught out. To be unmasked in a lie or subterfuge, from CRICKET, etc., in which the striker is out when a catch is caught by a fieldsman.

To catch a crab. In rowing when the oarsman fails to strike the blade deeply enough into the water and falls backwards as a result, or too deeply and risks being thrown overboard.

To catch a tartar. To catch a troublesome prisoner; to have dealings with a person who is more than a match for one; to think one is going to manage a person, only to find it is no easy job.

To catch a Yankee. The equivalent of TO CATCH A TARTAR, before Yankee lost its derogatory implication.

To catch on. To make its way; something which becomes popular, such as a song, a phrase, a fashion, etc.

To catch someone with his pants down. An American METAPHOR meaning to take someone at a great disadvantage. Hardly a phrase of drawing-room origin but sufficiently vivid not to require explanation.

To catch the Speaker's eye. *See* SPEAKER.

To lie upon the catch. To lie in wait; to try to catch one tripping.

You'll catch it. You'll get severely punished. Here "it" stands for the undefined punishment, such as a whipping, a scolding, etc.

Catch crop. A quick-growing crop between the rows of a main crop or a substitute for one that has failed. A catch crop is often used by market gardeners to increase productivity.

Catch penny. A worthless article puffed up to catch the pennies of those who are foolish enough to buy it.

Catch -22. Whichever alternative you choose you can't win or you are in a different situation or tight spot — you lose either way. It is the title of Joseph Heller's book published in 1955. The story centres around Captain Yossarian of the 256th United States (Army) bombing squadron in World War II and his main aim is to avoid being killed. "There was only one catch and that was Catch -22 which specified that concern for one's own safety in the face of dangers that were real and immediate was the process of a rational mind. Orr was crazy and could be grounded. All he had to do was to ask and as soon as he did he would no longer be crazy and would have to fly more missions".

> How immediate is the response to a 999 call? The Catch 22 of the situation — as Chief Superintendant Eddie Gleeson of New Scotland Yard pointed out — is that the more violent and urgent the emergency, the less coherent the caller.
>
> *Sunday Telegraph*, 24 July, 1988.

Catchphrase. A phrase which has caught on and is repeated by all and sundry. Virtually the same as CATCHWORD.

Catchpole. A constable; a law officer whose business it was to apprehend criminals. This is nothing to do with a pole or staff, nor with *poll*, the head, but is the mediæval Latin *chassipullus*, one who hunts or chases fowls.

Catchpole, Margaret. (1773–1841). An almost legendary Suffolk character. She was the daughter of a farm labourer and eventually a servant of John Cobbold, the Ipswich brewer. According to the Revd. Richard Cobbold's *The History of Margaret Catchpole* (1845) she twice saved the lives of her employer's children but subsequently stole one of his horses and, dressed as a man, rode to London in ten hours. She intended to meet her lover, William Laud, a local sailor turned smuggler, but was captured and sentenced to death. Fortunately this was commuted to seven years imprisonment and she managed to escape to join Laud by scaling a twenty-two foot wall with the aid of a clothes line. Laud was shot dead in self defence by one of their pursuers, Margaret was caught and again sentenced to death but reprieved and transported to BOTANY BAY. There she duly established herself as a trusted and respectable character and by strange chance met up with John Barry, son of a Suffolk miller, now a very prosperous and influential settler, whose suit she had rejected formerly, thus causing him to emigrate. They married in 1812.

Catchword. A popular cry, a word or CATCHPHRASE, particularly adopted as a political slogan. "Three acres and a cow", "your food will cost you more", "CHINESE SLAVERY", "Scholarships not battleships", 'the NEW MORALITY", "the AFFLUENT SOCIETY", are examples.

In printing, the first word on a page which is printed at the foot of the preceding page is known as the catchword; the first printer to employ catchwords may be either Balthazar Azoguidus of Bologna (in his Italian and Latin editions of Antoninus' *Confessionale*, 1472) or Vindelinus de Spira of Venice (in his undated editions of Philelphus' *Epistolae*, and Tacitus' *Opera* printed before 1474).

Printers also use the name for the main words in a dictionary; *i.e.* those at the head of each article, printed in bold type so as to catch the eye.

In the theatre, the cue (the last word or so of an actor's lines) is called the *catchword*.

Catechumen (kăt e kū' men). One taught by word of mouth (Gr. *katecheein*, to din into the ears). Those about to be baptized in the Early Church were first taught by word of mouth, and then *catechized* on their religious faith and duties.

Caterans, or **Catherans** (kăt' e rănz). Highland Scottish FREEBOOTERS; the word occurs in Scottish romances and ballads.

Cater-cousin. An intimate friend, a remote kinsman. The word probably refers to persons being *catered* for together, "friends so familiar that they eat together".

Alternatively it may derive from *cater* or *quater* (Fr. *quatre*, four) meaning a fourth cousin or remote relation; or from the dialect word *cater* meaning "diagonally", hence an indirect relation.

> His master and he, saving your worship's reverence, are scarce cater-cousins.
> SHAKESPEARE: *Merchant of Venice*, II, ii.

Caterpillar Club. An unofficial club started by the Irvin Parachute Company during World War II and still in being; the caterpillar being that of the silkworm which supplied the material from which parachutes were formerly made. The Company presented a small gold caterpillar pin to any R.A.F. airman who had baled out in action,

on his supplying the number of the parachute which had saved his life. Similarly the *Goldfish Club* existed for those who had been forced to use their rubber dinghies. Since then, similar clubs have been formed to encourage the wearing of protective clothing by industrial workers.

Catgut. Cords of various thicknesses, made from the intestines of animals (usually sheep, but never cats) and used for the strings of musical instruments and racquets for ball-games. Why it is called catgut has never been satisfactorily explained, but it may be a corruption of *kitgut, kit* being an old word for a small fiddle.

> *Heresay:* Do you not hear her guts already squeak like kit-strings?
> *Slicer:* They must come to that within
> This two or three years: by that timeshe'llbe
> True perfect cat.
> CARTWRIGHT: *The Ordinary* (1634), I, ii.

> Here's a tune indeed! pish,
> I had rather hear one ballad sung i' the nose now
> Than all these simpering tunes played upon cat's guts
> And sung by little kitling.
> T. MIDDLETON: *Women Beware Women* (1657), III, ii.

SHAKESPEARE, however, gives catgut its true origin:

> Now divine air! Now is his soul ravished! Is it not strange that Sheep's guts should hale souls out of men's bodies? Well, a horn for my money when all's done.—*Much Ado*, II, iii.

Catgut scraper. A fiddler.

Catharine. *See* CATHERINE.

Cathay (kȧ thā'). The name used by Marco Polo for what roughly corresponds to northern China, and the name for that part of China which the 16th-century navigators sought to discover via a NORTH-EAST or NORTH-WEST PASSAGE. The word comes from *Khitai*, a Manchurian Tartar kingdom of the 10th century. It was also used less specifically for China in general. *See* MANGI.

> Paulus Venetus, who dwelt many yeres in Cataia, affirmed that he sayled 1500 miles upon the coastes of Mangia, and Anian, towards the Northeast: always finding the open seas before him...
> SIR HUMPHREY GILBERT: *Discourse to prove a passage by the Northwest to Cataya, etc.* (printed 1576).

An English Cathay Company was founded by Michael Lok in 1577 to develop Frobisher's discoveries. In more modern times the name remained as a poetic usage.

> Better fifty years of Europe than a cycle of Cathay.
> TENNYSON: *Locksley Hall*.

Cathedrals of the Old Foundation. The ancient cathedrals that existed in England before Henry VIII founded and endowed new cathedrals out of some of the revenues from the Dissolution of the Monasteries. These latter are known as **Cathedrals of**

the New Foundation; they are Chester, Gloucester, Peterborough, Bristol and Oxford.

Catherine, St. Virgin and martyr of noble birth in Alexandria. She adroitly defended the Christian faith at a public disputation (c. 310) with certain heathen philosophers at the command of the Emperor Maximinus, for which she was put on a wheel like that of a chaff-cutter. Legend says that as soon as the wheel turned, her bonds wre miraculously broken; so she was beheaded. Hence the name CATHERINE WHEEL. She is the patron saint of wheel-wrights.

Catherine of Siena, St. (1347–1380). A patron saint of Italy, she was canonised in 1461 and in 1970 the second woman to be made a DOCTOR OF THE CHURCH. As well as serving the poor she was instrumental in bringing about the return of the POPE from AVIGNON to ROME.

Catherine wheel. A kind of firework, in the form of a wheel, which is driven round by the recoil from the explosion of the various squibs of which it is composed.

Catherine-wheel window. A wheel window, sometimes called a *rose-window*, with radiating divisions.

The Order of St. Catherine. (1) An extinct military order established in 1063 to guard the remains of ST. CATHERINE and to protect pilgrims. It followed the rule of St. Basil.

(2) A Russian order founded by Peter the Great, confined to female members, and so named as a compliment to his second wife, who succeeded him as Catherine I in 1725.

To braid St. Catherine's tresses. To live a virgin.

> Thou art too fair to be left to braid St. Catherine's tresses.
> LONGFELLOW: *Evangeline*.

Catherine Théot (tā′ō). A French prophetess like the English Joanna Southcott, calling herself "The Mother of God" and changing her name to Theos (God). In the height of the Revolution she preached the worship of the Supreme Being and announced that Robespierre was the forerunner of The Word. She called him her well-beloved son and chief prophet. She died in prison in 1794.

> This Théot mystery they affect to regard as a Plot; but have evidently introduced a vein of satire, of irreverent banter, not against the Spinster alone but obliquely against her Regenerative Man!
> CARLYLE: *The French Revolution*, Pt. III, Bk. VI, ch. vi.

Catholic. The word (Gr. *katholikos*) means general, universal, comprehensive. It is used in this sense in the following extract:

> Creed and test
> Vanish before the unreserved embrace
> Of Catholic humanity.
> WORDSWORTH: *Ecclesiastical Sonnets*, III, xxxvi.

Hence from the Church viewpoint it distinguishes (1) the whole body of Christians as apart from "Jews, heretics and infidels", (2) a member of a church which claims the APOSTOLIC SUCCESSION and direct descent from the earliest body of Christians; (3) the ROMAN CATHOLIC CHURCH, *i.e.* the Western or Latin branch of the ancient Catholic or universal Church.

Alphonso I, King of the Asturias, 739–757, was surnamed *the Catholic* on account of his zeal in erecting and endowing monasteries and churches. *See* CATHOLIC KING.

A man of catholic tastes is one who is interested in a wide variety of subjects.

Catholic Church. The whole body of Christians as distinct from the Churches and sects into which they are divided. The Latin Church called itself Catholic after the separation from the Eastern or ORTHODOX CHURCH. At the REFORMATION the Reformers called the Western Church under papal jurisdiction the ROMAN CATHOLIC CHURCH as opposed to their own Reformed or PROTESTANT Churches. Members of the CHURCH OF ENGLAND hold themselves to be Catholics but in popular usage Catholic usually means Roman Catholic.

> I believe in the Holy Ghost; The holy Catholic Church; etc.
> Book of Common Prayer: Apostles' Creed.

Catholic and Apostolic Church. The name given to the followers of Edward Irving (1792–1824), and to the Church founded in 1835, after his death (also called IRVINGITES). He was a former member of the CHURCH OF SCOTLAND from which he was expelled for heresy in 1833.

Catholic Association (1823–1829). Founded in Ireland by Daniel O'Connell and supported by the Roman Catholic clergy to promote the political emancipation of Roman Catholics. It became a powerful organization, aided by the monthly subscriptions of the peasantry called "Catholic Rent", and achieved its objective with the passing of the Catholic Emancipation Act in 1829.

Catholic Epistles. Those Epistles in the NEW TESTAMENT not addressed to any particular church or individual; the epistles of James, Peter, and Jude and the first of John; II John is addressed to a "lady", and III John to Gaius, but they are often included. *See* CANONICAL.

Catholic King, or **His Most Catholic Majesty.** A title given by Pope Innocent VIII to Ferdinand of Aragon and Isabella of Castile, and confirmed by Pope Alexander VI on account of their conquest and subsequent expulsion of the MOORS in 1492. Those who remained and became nominal Christians were called Moriscos. The title was thereafter used as an appellation of the kings of Spain. *Cp.* RELIGIOUS.

Catholic League. (1) The party headed by the Guise faction in France (1584) in alliance with Philip II of Spain. Their object was to prevent the succession of Henry of Navarre to the French crown and place the Cardinal of BOURBON on the throne on the death of Henry III. (2) A Catholic confederacy formed in Germany in 1609 to counterbalance the Protestant Union of 1608. These rival groupings resulted in the THIRTY YEARS WAR (1618–1648).

Catholic Roll. A document which Roman Catholics were obliged to sign on taking their seats as Members of PARLIAMENT. It was abolished when a single oath was prescribed to all members by an Act of 1866.

Old Catholics. In the Netherlands, the Church of Utrecht which separated from ROME in 1724 after allegations of Jansenism. (*See* JANSENISTS). The term is more particularly associated with members of the German, Austrian and Swiss Churches who rejected the dogmas of papal INFALLIBILITY after the VATICAN COUNCIL of 1870 and were joined by others as a result of the KULTURKAMPF. Their episcopal succession is derived from the Church of Utrecht and they are in communion with the CHURCH OF ENGLAND. There are also others in the U.S.A. and small groups of Poles and Croats.

Catholicon (kȧ thol' i kȯn). A PANACEA, a universal remedy, from the Greek word meaning universal, all-embracing.

Also the name of a comprehensive work of the encyclopaedic dictionary type. A famous edition of the 13th century *Catholicon* (the first so called) of Johannes Balbus of Genoa was printed by Gutenberg at Mainz in 1460. An English—Latin dictionary compiled about 1483, called *Catholicon Anglicanum* was published by the Early English Text Society in 1881, and a Breton—Latin—French dictionary called the *Catholicon* was printed in 1499.

Catholicos (kȧ thol' ikȯs). The head of the Assyrian NESTORIANS. Since called the Patriarch of Armenia.

Catiline's Conspiracy (kăt' i līn). Lucius Sergius Catilina conspired with a number of dissolute young nobles (64 B.C.) to plunder the Roman treasury, destroy the senate, and fire the city as part of a political revolution. CICERO, who was consul, got full information of the plot and delivered his first Oration against Catiline (8 November 63 B.C.), whereupon Catiline left ROME. Next day Cicero delivered his second Oration, and several of the conspirators were arrested. His third Oration respecting the punishment to be accorded was made on 4 December and, after his fourth Oration the following day, sentence of death was passed. Catiline was slain with his supporters at Pistoria in Etruria (62 B.C.).

Cato (kā' tō). **He is a Cato.** A man of simple life, self-denying habits, strict justice, brusque manners, blunt of speech, like the Roman Censor Marcus Porcius Cato (234–149 B.C.).

Cato Street Conspiracy. A plot by Arthur Thistlewood (1770–1820) and his associates to murder the CABINET while the members were dining with the Earl of Harrowby in Grosvenor Square (23 February 1820). Hand grenades were to be used. The conspirators met in a loft in Cato Street, a small MEWS near the Edgware Road, where some were arrested. Thistlewood and others escaped, but he was caught the following morning. Five, including Thistlewood, were hanged and decapitated and five others were transported for life.

Caucasian (kaw kā' shȧn). The white or European race is so called. The term originated with J. F. Blumenbach (1752–1840) who, in 1775, selected a Georgian skull as the perfect type of Indo-European. His views are no longer held, but the word has been used with certain qualifications by later anthropologists.

Caucus (kaw' kús). An American word, first recorded as having been used in Boston about 1750 and popularized in England by Joseph Chamberlain about 1878 in Birmingham. In America it means a meeting of some division, large or small, of a political or legislative body for the purpose of agreeing upon a united course of action in the main assembly. In England it is applied opprobriously to an inner group which seeks to manipulate affairs behind the backs of its party. The origin of the word is unknown, but it may be connected with the Algonquin word *cau-cau-as-u*, one who advises.

> In all these places is a severall commander, which they call *Werowance*, except the *Chickhamanians*, who are governed by the priests and their Assistants, or their Elders, called *cawcawwassoughes*.
>
> CAPT. JOHN SMITH: *Travels in Virginia*, 6th voyage (1606).

Caudillo (kaw dil' yō). The title adopted by

General Franco, head of the FALANGIST government in Spain, in imitation of Mussolini's DUCE and Hitler's FÜHRER. Like them it means "Leader".

Caudine Forks. A narrow pass in the mountains near Capua, now called the Valley of Arpaia. It was here that the Roman army, under the consuls T. Veturius Calvinus and Sp. Postumius, fell into the hands of the Samnites (321 B.C.), and were made to pass "under the YOKE".

Caudle. Any sloppy mess, especially that sweet mixture of gruel and wine or spirits once given by nurses to recently confined women and their "gossips" who called to see the baby during the first month. The word means "something warm" (Lat. *calidus*).

Caudle lecture. A curtain lecture. The term is derived from a series of papers by Douglas Jerrold, *Mrs. Caudle's Curtain Lectures*, which were published in *Punch* (1846). These papers represent Job Caudle as a patient sufferer of the lectures of his nagging wife after they had gone to bed and the curtains were drawn.

> ...and General Jones, a hero in spite of costume, in his red *bonnet de nuit*, a more natural accompaniment to a Caudle lecture than to a siege.
> OUIDA: *Held in Bondage*, ch. xxx

Caught bending, napping, etc. *See under* CATCH.

Caul. The word was formerly used for a net in which women enclosed their hair, now called a SNOOD.

> Her head with ringlets of her hair is crowned,
> And in a golden caul the curls are bound.
> DRYDEN: *Æneid*, VII.

It was also used to describe any membrane enclosing the viscera, *e.g.* "The caul that is above the liver", *Exod*. xxix, 13.

The membrane on the head of some newborn infants is the *caul* and is held to be a charm, especially against death by drowning. They were once advertised for sale and frequently sought after by mariners. To be born with a caul was with the Romans tantamount to being BORN WITH A SILVER SPOON IN ONE'S MOUTH.

> You were born with a caul on your head.
> BEN JONSON: *Alchemist* I, i.

Cauld-lad, The, of Hilton Hall. A housespirit who moved about the furniture during the night. Being resolved to banish him, the inmates left for him a green cloak and hood, before the kitchen fire, which so delighted him that he never troubled the house any more; but sometimes he might be heard singing:

> Here's a cloak, and here's a hood,
> The cauld-lad of Hilton will do no more good.

Cauliflower ear. An ear permanently thickened and deformed by boxing injuries.

Caurus (kaw' rùs). The Latin name for the west-north-west wind, anglicized below as Chorus:

> ... the sonne is hid whan the sterres ben clustred by a swifte winde highte Chorus.
> CHAUCER: *Boethius*, Bk. I, Mett. iii.
> The ground by piercing Caurus seared.
> THOMSON: *Castle of Indolence*, ii, 78.

Causa causans (kaw' zà kaw' zănz). The initiating cause, the primary cause.

Causa causata. The cause which owes its existence to the CAUSA CAUSANS; the secondary cause.

Causa vera. (*a*) The immediate predecessor of an effect; (*b*) a cause verifiable by independent evidence (Mill).

In theology, God is the *causa causans*, and creation the *causa causata*. The presence of the sun above the horizon is the *causa vera* of daylight, and its withdrawal below the horizon is the *causa vera* of night.

Cause. Aristotelian causes.

(1) **The Efficient Cause.** That which immediately produces the effect.

(2) **The Material Cause.** The matter on which (1) works.

(3) **The Formal Cause.** The Essence or "Form" (or group of attributes) introduced into the matter by the *efficient cause*.

(4) **The Final,** or **Ultimate Cause.** The purpose or end for which the thing exists or the causal change takes place. But God is called the Ultimate Final Cause, since, according to ARISTOTLE, all things tend, so far as they can, to realize some Divine attribute.

God is also called the **First Cause,** or the **Cause Causeless,** beyond which even imagination cannot go.

Cause, The. A mission; the object or project.

The Cause, or **The Good Old Cause** in the 17th century is the PURITAN cause, and was commonly used by the supporters of the Puritan Revolution in Cromwellian times and afterwards.

> The army, resolute as it still remained for the maintenance of "the cause", was deceived by Monk's declarations of loyalty to it...
> J. R. GREEN: *A Short History of the English People*, ch. viii, sec. x.

To make common cause. To work for the same object. Here "cause" is the legal term meaning the cause or side of the question advocated.

Cause célèbre (Fr.). Any famous law case or trial, such as the TICHBORNE CASE or the case of Jean CALAS.

Caution. So-and-so's a caution, meaning

that he is odd in his ways, likely to do something unexpected, often with a quaint twist to it. The phrase is originally American and had a somewhat wider application:

> The way the icy blast would come down the bleak shore was a caution.
>
> C. F. HOFFMAN: *Winter West* (1835).
>
> His wife was what the Yankees call a Caution.
>
> MORTIMER COLLINS: *Vivien* (1870).

Caution money. A sum deposited with college authorities, at an INN OF COURT, etc., as a safeguard against misbehaviour. Some colleges retain a portion of the sum at the end of a student's course as a "gift" to augment their revenues.

Cavalier. A horseman; whence a knight, a gentleman (Span. *caballero, b* and *v* being pronounced alike in that language).
Personages styled The Cavalier.

Charles de Beaumont d'Eon (1728–1810), French diplomat and secret agent; *Chevalier d'Eon.* He stayed at the court of the Tsarina Elizabeth dressed as a woman.

Charles Breydel (1677–1744), Flemish landscape painter.

Francesco Cairo (*Cavaliere del Cairo*) (1598–1674), Italian historical and portrait painter.

Jean le Clerc, *le chevalier* (1587–1633), French painter.

Giovanni Battista Marini (1569–1625), Italian poet; *Il Cavaliere.*

Andrew Michael Ramsay (1686–1734), Scottish–French writer.

Cavalier, or **Chevalier of St. George.** James Francis Edward Stuart, called the PRETENDER, or the Old Pretender (1688–1766). *See* WARMING-PAN.
The Laughing Cavalier. The name given to the famous portrait of an unknown gallant, by the Dutch painter Frans Hals, now in the Wallace Collection, London.
The Young Cavalier, or **the Bonnie Chevalier.** Charles Edward Stuart, the Young Pretender (1720–1788). *See* PRETENDER.
Cavalier Parliament (1661–1679). The first PARLIAMENT of Charles II after the RESTORATION and thus named from its Royalist majority. It was also called the PENSIONARY PARLIAMENT or LONG PARLIAMENT of Charles II.
Cavaliers. The Royalists or adherents of Charles I at the time of the CIVIL WARS. Their opponents were called ROUNDHEADS.
Cavaliere servente (kăv a lyĕr'ĭsĕr ven' te) (Ital.). Much the same as a CICISBEO.

Cave of Adullam. *See* ADULLAMITES.
Caveat (kā' vē ăt) (Lat. let him beware). A notice directing the recipient to refrain from

some act pending the decision of the court. Hence, **to enter a caveat,** to give legal notice that the opponent is not to proceed with the suit in hand until the party giving notice has been heard; to give warning or admonition.

Caveat emptor (Lat. let the purchaser beware). The buyer must keep his eyes open, for the bargain he agrees to is binding. The full legal maxim is: *Caveat emptor, quia ignorare non debuit quod ius alienum emit.* (Let a purchaser beware, for he ought not to be ignorant of the nature of the property which he is buying from another party.)

Caviare (kăv' i ar). Sturgeon's roe, pickled, salted and used as a savoury or HORS D'ŒUVRE, etc. Caviare is usually only appreciated by those who have acquired a taste for it, hence Shakespeare's *caviare to the general* (*Hamlet*, II, ii), above the taste or comprehension of ordinary people.

> He (Cobbett) must, I think, be caviare to the Whigs.
>
> HAZLITT: *Table-talk.*

In the days of Tsarist Russia certain matter in imported periodicals was blacked out by over-stamping. Such matter came to be known as *caviare* because its appearance was reminiscent of black, salted caviare on a slice of bread.

Cavo-rilievo (ka' vō ril yā' vō). "Relief", cut below the original surface, the highest parts of the figure being on a level with the surface.

Caxon. A worn-out WIG; also a big cauliflower wig, worn out or not. It has been suggested that the word is from the personal name Caxon.

> People scarce could decide on its phiz,
> Which looked wisest—the caxon or jowl.
>
> PETER PINDAR: *The Portfolio.*

Caxton, William. Father of English printing, hence his name is widely applied to branded articles in the printing and paper trades. Born in the Weald of Kent, he learnt his printing in Cologne and Bruges. He set up shop at the sign of the Red Pole in the shadow of Westminster Abbey about 1476 and died in 1491, by which time he had printed about a hundred books. He was printer, publisher, retailer and translator.

Cayuse. An Indian pony. The Cayuses were a RED INDIAN tribe. Since about 1880 the word has meant "a horse of little value".

Cean (sē' an). **The Cean poet.** Simonides of Ceos, *c.* 556–468 B.C.

> The Cean and the Teian muse.
>
> BYRON: *Don Juan* (Song: *The Isles of Greece*).

Cecilia, St. (se sil' i à). Patron SAINT of the blind and patroness of music and especially of Church music. Born in Rome, she is usually supposed to have been martyred in A.D. 230, but the date is uncertain. She was blind, and according to tradition, was inventor of the organ. An ANGEL fell in love with her for her musical skill; her husband saw the heavenly visitant, who gave to both a crown of martyrdom which he brought from PARADISE. Her day is 22 November, on which the Worshipful Company of Musicians, a LIVERY COMPANY of the CITY of LONDON, meet and go in procession for divine service in St. Paul's Cathedral. Both Dryden and Pope wrote odes in her honour.

> At length divine Cecilia came,
> Inventress of the vocal frame.
> DRYDEN: *Alexander's Feast*, 7.

Cecil's Fast. A dinner of fish. William Cecil, Lord Burghley, for nearly forty years chief minister to Queen Elizabeth I, introduced a law to enjoin the eating of fish on certain days in order to promote the fishing industry.

Ceelict, St. An English name of St. Calixtus, who is commemorated on 14 October, the day of the Battle of Hastings. Browne Willis tells us there was once a tablet in Battle parish church with these words:

> This place of war is Battle called, because in battle here
> Quite conquered and o'erthrown the English nation were.
> This slaughter happened to them upon St. Ceelict's day.

Ceiling. The term is figuratively applied to the maximum height to which an aeroplane can rise, the highest price that can be reached for any article, etc. In aeronautical circles it denotes the height of the cloud base above ground level.

Ceiling zero means that the clouds or mist are down to ground level.

Celestial City. HEAVEN is so called by John Bunyan in his *Pilgrim's Progress*.

Celestial Empire. China; a translation of the Chinese *Tien Chao*, literally "heavenly dynasty", alluding to the belief that the old Emperors were in direct descent from the gods. Hence the Chinese are sometimes called *Celestials*.

Celestines. An order of reformed BENEDICTINES founded about 1260 by Pietro di Murrone, who became Pope Celestine V in 1294.

Celt (selt, kelt). A piece of stone, ground artificially into a wedge-like shape with a cutting edge, used for axes, chisels, etc. The term is also loosely applied to metal axe-heads, especially of bronze.

Celtic (sel′tik, kel′tik). Applied to the peoples and languages of that branch of the Aryan family which includes the Irish, Manx, Welsh, Cornish, Breton, and Scottish Gaels. Anciently the term was applied by the Greeks and Romans to the peoples of western Europe generally, but when CÆSAR wrote of the Celtæ he referred to the people of middle GAUL only. The word *Celt* probably means a warrior; fable accounts for it by the story of Celtina, daughter of Britannus, who had a son by HERCULES, named Celtus, who became the progenitor of the Celts.

Celtic Fringe. Those parts of Great Britain and Ireland whose population is predominantly of Celtic stock, namely WALES, CORNWALL, SCOTLAND and IRELAND.

Celtic Sea. Formally defined as "that part of the continental shelf lying between the 200 fathom contour, S. Ireland, the S.W. tip of Wales, Land's End and Ushant". The term derives from the neighbouring Celtic areas—Brittany, CORNWALL, WALES and IRELAND, and was first used by E. W. L. Holt in 1921.

Cemetery properly means a sleeping-place (Gr. *koimeterion*, a dormitory). The Persians call their cemeteries "the Cities of the Silent".

Cenci. *See* BEAUTIFUL PARRICIDE.

Cenomanni (sen ō ma′ ni). The name given to the inhabitants of Norfolk, Suffolk, and Cambridge by CÆSAR in his *Commentaries*.

Cenotaph (sen′ o tăf) (Gr. *kenos*, empty; *taphos*, tomb). A sepulchral monument raised to the memory of a person or persons buried elsewhere. By far the most noteworthy to all of British race is that in Whitehall, designed by Sir E. Lutyens, which was dedicated on 11 November 1920, to those who fell in World War I. It has since been adapted to commemorate the fallen of World War II.

Among the most noted cenotaphs of the ancients are those of:

ÆNEAS to Deiphobus (*Æneid*, I, 6; v, 505);

ANDROMACHE to Hector (*Æneid*, I, 3; v, 302);

ARISTOTLE to Hermias and Eubulus (*Diogenes Laertius*);

The Athenians to the poet Euripides;

Callimachus to Sopolis, son of Dioclides (*Epigram of Callimachus*, 22);

Catullus to his brother (*Epigram of Catullus*, 103);

DIDO to Sichæus (*Justin*, xviii, 6);

The Romans to Drusus in Germany, and to Alexander Severus, the emperor, in Gaul (Suetonius: *Life of Claudius*; and the *Anthologia*);

Statius to his father (*The Sylvae of Statius*, v, Epicedium 3);

Xenocrates to Lysidices (*Anthologia*).

Centaur. Mythological beast, half horse and

half man. Centaurs are said to have dwelt in ancient Thessaly; a myth the origin of which is probably to be found in the expert horsemanship of the inhabitants. (*See* IXION). The Thessalian centaurs were invited to a marriage feast and one of their number attempted to abduct the bride, whereupon conflict ensued and the centaurs were duly driven out of the country by the LAPITHAE.

Cent Nouvelles Nouvelles (son noo vel'). This collection of "a hundred new tales" first appeared in the MS. dated 1456. It is on much the same lines as the DECAMERON and tells in French some of the stories already made familiar by the Italian novelists. Saintsbury calls it the best of all the late mediæval prose works. Nicolas of Troyes produced his *Grand Parangon de Nouvelles Nouvelles* in 1535, containing tales of his own and drawing from the GESTA ROMANORUM and *Decameron*.

Cento (Lat. a patchwork). Poetry made up of lines borrowed from established authors, an art freely practised in the decadent days of Greece and Rome. Ausonius, who has a nuptial idyll composed from verses selected from VIRGIL, made rules for their composition. Well-known examples are the *Homerocentones*, the *Cento Virgilianus* by Proba Falconia (4th century), and the hymns made by Metellus out of the *Odes* of HORACE.

Centre Party. In politics, the party occupying a place between two extremes: the *left centre* is the most radical wing, and the *right centre* the more conservative. In the French Revolution *the Centre* of the Legislative Assembly included the friends of order.

Head Centre. The FENIAN Brotherhood (founded by Irishmen in the United States in 1858) was organized from *centres* and, at the time of the Fenian raid into Canada and the abortive rising in Ireland (1886), the leader or *Head Centre* was James Stephens.

The Centre, Dead Centre, Dead Heart, or **Red Centre.** The arid central areas of Australia were vegetation is sparse and short-lived and only briefly seen after one of the infrequent rainfalls.

Centurion (sen tū' ri on) (Lat. *centum*, a hundred). A Roman officer who had the command of 100 men. There were sixty centurions, of varying ranks, to a legion, the chief being the first centurion of the first maniple of the first cohort; his title was *Primus pilus prior* or *Primipilus*. The centurion's emblem of office was a vinestaff.

Century of the Common Man. The twentieth century, the age of democracy. *The Century of the Common Man* (1940) was the title of a book by Henry A. Wallace, New-Dealer

and Vice-President of the United States (1941–1945) under F. D. Roosevelt. The phrase speedily became popular on both sides of the Atlantic and was much favoured by Nancy, Viscountess Astor.

Cephalus and Procris (sel' a lùs, prok' ris). Cephalus was husband of PROCRIS, who deserted him through jealousy. He went in search of her and rested awhile under a tree. Procris crept through some bushes to ascertain if a rival was with him and Cephalus, hearing the noise and thinking it was made by some wild beast, hurled his javelin into the bushes and slew Procris. When he discovered what he had done he slew himself with the same javelin.

> *Pyramus:* Not Shafalus to Procrus was so true.
> *Thisbe:* As Shafalus to Procrus, I to you.
> SHAKESPEARE: *Midsummer Night's Dream*, V, i.

Cepheus (sē' fūs). A northern constellation; named from Cepheus, king of Ethiopia, husband of CASSIOPEIA and father of ANDROMEDA.

Cepola (sep' ō là). **Devices of Cepola.** Quips of law are so called from Bartholomew Cepola whose law-quirks, teaching how to elude the most express law, and to perpetuate lawsuits *ad infinitum*, have been frequently reprinted—once in 8vo, in BLACK LETTER, for John Petit of Paris, in 1503.

Cerberus (sĕr' bĕr ùs). A grim, watchful keeper, house-porter, guardian, etc. Cerberus according to classical mythology is the three-headed dog that keeps the entrance of the infernal regions. HERCULES dragged the monster to earth and let him go again. (*See* ACONITE.) ORPHEUS lulled Cerberus to sleep with his lyre and the SIBYL who conducted ÆNEAS through the INFERNO also threw the dog into a profound sleep with a cake seasoned with poppies and honey. (*See* SOP.)

The origin of the fable of Cerberus may be found in the custom of the ancient Egyptians of guarding graves with dogs.

Cerealia. Festivals in honour of CERES, celebrated by the Romans. First held in April, a second festival was introduced by CICERO in August.

Ceremonious, The. Pedro IV of Aragon (1336–1387) was so named.

Ceremony (Lat. *cærimonia*). By way of accounting for this word, which is probably connected with the Sans. *karman*, a religious action, a rite, Livy tells us that when the Romans fled before Brennus, one Albinus, who was carrying his wife and children in a cart to a place of safety, overtook at Janiculum the VESTALS bending under their load. He took them up and conveyed them to *Cære* in Etruria, where they remained and continued to perform their sacred rites, which were consequently called *Cære-monia*.

Master of the Ceremonies. A court official, first appointed by James I to superintend the reception of ambassadors and strangers of rank, and to prescribe the formalities to be observed in LEVEES and other public functions. The title is now given to one whose duty it is to superintend at a ball and similar social gatherings; usually now abbreviated to "M.C.".

Dont' stand on ceremony. Make yourself at home, be natural, don't be formal.

Ceres (sē' rēz). The Roman name of MOTHER EARTH, the protectress of agriculture, and of all the fruits of the earth. She is the Corn Goddess and she had a daughter by JUPITER, called PROSERPINE. She is identified with the Greek DEMETER.

Cess. A tax, contracted from assessment; as, a "church-cess". In Ireland the word is sometimes used as a contraction of success, meaning luck, as, "Bad cess to you!" It is also a common contraction of *cesspit* or *cesspool*.

Out of all cess. Beyond all estimation or valuation.

> The poor jade is wrung in the withers out of all cess.
> SHAKESPEARE: *Henry IV, Pt. I*, II, i.

To have a mind like a cesspool. To have a dirty mind that harbours unclean thoughts. A similar expression is **to have a mind like a sewer.**

C'est magnifique. C'est magnifique, mais ce n'est pas la guerre. "It is magnificent, but it is not war." The criticism on the charge of the Light Brigade at Balaclava (25 October 1854), made on the field at the time, by the French General Bosquet to A. H. Layard.

Cestui que vie. This and the two following are old Anglo-French legal terms (*cestui* = he, or him). The person for whose life any lands or hereditaments may be held.

Cestui que use, the person to whose use anyone is infeoffed of lands or tenements.

Cestui que trust, the person for whose benefit a trust has been created.

Cestus (ses' tus). The girdle of VENUS, made by her husband VULCAN; but when she wantoned with MARS it fell off, and was left on the "Acidalian Mount". It was of magical power to move to ardent love. By poetical fiction, all women of irresistible attraction are supposed to be wearers of Aphrodite's girdle, or the cestus. *Cp.* CHASTITY GIRDLE.

The word is also used for the Roman boxing-glove composed of leather thongs wound round the hand and wrist, and sometimes loaded with iron.

Ceteris paribus (set'ĕris pă' ribus) (Lat.). Other things being equal.

Chacun a son goût (shăk' ûn a son goo). "Everyone has his taste" is the correct French phrase. "Everyone to his taste" (*à*, to, instead of *a*, has) is English-French. The phrase is more common with us than it is in France, where we meet with the phrases, *Chacun a sa chacunerie* (everyone has his own idiosyncrasy), and *chacun a sa marotte* (everyone has his hobby). In Latin *sua cuique voluptas*, every man has his own pleasures.

Chad, St. (*Ceadda*). A Northumbrian by birth and a pupil of St. Aidan, he subsequently became BISHOP of MERCIA with Lichfield as his SEE. He died in 672 and was the patron SAINT of springs. The New River which was once London's main water supply has its source in Chad's Well Springs between Hertford and Ware. There was also a spa at King's Cross opened early in the reign of George III called St. Chad's Well.

Chadpennies. Lichfield Cathedral is dedicated to St. Mary and St. Chad; the WHITSUNTIDE offerings used to be devoted to the upkeep of the building and were called Chadpennies.

WOT NO CHAR?

Chad. A character whose bald head and large nose were depicted appearing over a wall and inquiring, "Wot, no [word filled in to suit the circumstances]?", as a comment or protest against a shortage or shortcoming. Widely current during World War II, especially among the forces, Chad provided scope for humorous relief in many a difficult situation. It was the happy creation (1938) of "Chat" the cartoonist (George Edward Chatterton). *Cp.* KILROY; *see also* GRAFFITI.

Chadband. This synonym for a religious hypocrite is taken from a character in Dickens's *Bleak House*—a gluttonous, unctuous, illiterate rogue, minister of some indeterminate sect.

Chaff. An old bird is not to be caught with chaff. An experienced man, or one with his wits about him, is not to be deluded by humbug. The reference is to throwing chaff instead of birdseed to allure birds. Hence perhaps:

You are chaffing me. Making fun of me. A singular custom used to exist in Nottinghamshire and Leicestershire. When a husband ill-treated his wife, the villagers emptied a sack of chaff at his door, to intimate that "thrashing was done within".

Chain letter. A letter, frequently anonymous, which the recipient is asked to copy and send to one or more friends, requesting that they should do the same, good luck being supposed by the superstitious to follow the faithful fulfilment of the conditions. It is sometimes used by the unscrupulous as a device for obtaining money from the credulous.

Chair, The. The seat of authority, or the office of same. The person in authority or the president of an assembly or meeting whose decisions, like those of the SPEAKER of the HOUSE OF COMMONS, are final in all points of doubt. When debaters call out "Chair", they mean that the Chairman is not being sufficiently heeded and properly supported. Similarly, "Pray support the chair", has the same significance.

A university professorship is also called a chair, as "the chair of poetry at Oxford".

Below the chair. Said of one who has not reached the presidential position, as of an alderman who has not yet served the mayoralty.

Passed the chair. One who has held the office.

To take the chair. To be the chairman of a meeting or assembly, committee, etc. Colloquially **to be in the chair** means to act as host or to be the one paying for the round of drinks.

Chair of St. Peter. The office of the POPE of Rome, founded by St. PETER, the apostle; but *St. Peter's Chair* means the Catholic festival held in commemoration of the two episcopates founded by the apostle, one at Rome, and the other at Antioch (18 January; 22 February). The reputed chair itself in St. Peter's at ROME is kept locked away and only exhibited once every century. It is of wood with ivory carvings, the wood being much decayed. It is probably 6th-century BYZANTINE work.

Chalk. Chalk it up. Put it on the SLATE, put it to his credit.

Chalk and talk. A common phrase in the scholastic profession to denote teaching essentially relying upon oral instruction and the use of the blackboard, a method not always popular with the professors of pedagogy, but likely to remain the basis of most good teaching.

I beat him by a long chalk. Thoroughly. A reference to the custom of making merit marks with chalk, before lead pencils were so common.

I'll chalk out your path for you, *i.e.* lay it down or plan it out, as a carpenter or shipwright plans out his work with a piece of chalk.

I can walk a chalk as well as you. I am no more drunk than you are. The allusion is to a test given to those suspected of drunkenness which consists of walking steadily along a line chalked on the floor.

I cannot make chalk of one and cheese of the other. I must treat both alike; I must show no favouritism.

I know the difference between chalk and cheese. Between what is worthless and what is valuable, between a counterfeit and a real article.

A popular phrase, no doubt helped by its alliteration.

> This Scotch scarecrow was no more to be compared to him than chalk was to cheese.
>
> SCOTT: *Woodstock*, xxiv.

They are no more alike than chalk and cheese is another common variant.

The tapster is undone by chalk, *i.e.* credit. The allusion is to the old custom of tavern-keepers scoring on a door or board the amounts owed by customers. This was a common practice early in the 19th century when milk and bread scores were also general.

Walk your chalk. Get you gone. Lodgings wanted for the royal retinue were once taken arbitrarily by the marshal and sergeant-chamberlain and the occupants of houses marked with the chalk were sent to the right-about. The phrase is "Walk, you're chalked", corrupted to *Walk your chalk*. When Marie de' MEDICI came to England in 1638, Sieur de Labat was employed to mark "all sorts of houses commodious for her retinue in Colchester".

At one time it was customary for a landlord to give the tenant notice to quit by chalking the door.

> The prisoner has cut his stick, and walked his chalk, and is off to London.
>
> C. KINGSLEY: *Two Years Ago*, i.

Challenge. This meant originally an accusation or charge, and secondly a claim, a defiance, etc. It comes through French from the Lat. *calumnia*, a false accusation, and is etymologically the same word as "calumny".

Challenging a jury. This may be to object to all the jurors from some informality in the way they have been "arrayed" or empanelled, or to one or more of the jurors, from some real or supposed disqualification or bias of judgment. In the first case it is **a challenge to the array,** and this must be based on some default of the sheriff or his officer.

Cham (kăm). The sovereign prince of Tartary, now written Khan.

Fetch you a hair off the great Cham's beard.
SHAKESPEARE: *Much Ado about Nothing*, II, i.

The great Cham of Literature. An epithet applied to Dr. Johnson (1709–1784) by Tobias Smollett.

Chamber of Horrors. *See* MADAME TUSSAUD'S.

Chambré (shom' brā). From Fr. *chambre*, a room. Used of wine which has been warmed to raise it from the cellar temperature to the temperature of the room in which it is to be served, which for red wine is ideal.

Chambre Ardente (shombr ar dont') (Fr.). In French history, the name given to certain courts of justice held under the ANCIEN RÉGIME, for trying exceptional cases such as charges of heresy, poisoning, etc. They were usually held at night, and both then and when held in daytime were lighted by torches. These courts were devised by the Cardinal of Lorraine and first used by Francis I in 1535. Louis XIV used a Chambre Ardente in 1679 to investigate suspected poisoners as a result of the scare caused by the trial of the Marquise de BRINVILLIERS. These courts were abolished in 1682.

Chambre Introuvable (shombr an'-troo vab là) (Fr. the chamber not to be found again). The French Chamber of Deputies, which met in 1815 after the second return of Louis XVIII, was so named by the king for its fervent royalist sympathies. It was afterwards used to denote any ultra-royalist assembly.

Chameleon. You are a chameleon, *i.e.* very changeable, like a VICAR OF BRAY, shifting according to the opinions of the others, as the chameleon (to a very limited extent) can change its hue to that of contiguous objects.

Would they ever change their hue
As the light camelions do,
Suiting it to every ray
Twenty times a day?
SHELLEY: *An Exhortation*.

Champ de Mars (shon dĕ mars). Clovis and the early Frankish kings held meetings in MARCH when feudal gifts and fees were paid and homage received. It was this ancient custom that was seized upon in the French Revolution when, in the summer of 1790, an enormous amphitheatre was dug by the Paris citizens, and the Federation of Freedom sworn at the altar of the Fatherland.

NAPOLEON gave the name of **Champ de Mai** to the assembly he called together on 1 May 1815, when he proclaimed the result of the plebiscite ratifying the liberal *Acte additionnel* on his return from Elba.

Champagne Charlie. The 4th Marquess of Hastings was the first so named (*see* PLUNGER) and another was Charles Philip Yorke, 5th Earl of Hardwicke (1836, 1873–1897), who was one time Comptroller of the Royal Household and prominent in the social circle around the Prince of Wales. He wasted his inheritance mostly by gambling and riotous living and finally went bankrupt in 1893.

Champak (chăm' păk). An Indian magnolia (*Michelia champaca*). The wood is sacred to BUDDHA, and the strongly scented golden flowers are worn in the black hair of Indian women.

The Champak odours fail.
SHELLEY: *Lines to an Indian Air*.

Champion of England, or **King's Champion.** A person whose office it was to ride up Westminster Hall on a Coronation Day, and challenge anyone who disputed the right of succession. The office was established by William the Conqueror and was given to Robert de Marmion and his male descendants with the manor of "broad Scrivelsby". De Ludlow received the office and manor through the female line, and at the coronation of Richard II Sir John Dymoke succeeded, also through the female line. Since then it has continued in the Dymoke family, but the custom of the challenge was last observed at the coronation of George IV. Instead the Champion bears the sovereign's standard at the coronation.

Chamuel. *See* ARCHANGEL.

Chance. *See* MAIN CHANCE.

To chance your arm, or **your luck.** To run a risk in the hope of "bringing it off' and obtaining a profit or advantage of some sort.

Chancel means a lattice screen. In the Roman law courts the lawyers were cut off from the public by such a screen (Lat. *cancellus*).

Chancel of a church. That part of the church (usually at the eastern end) containing the altar and choir, which is often separated from the nave by a screen of wood or iron lattice-work and often with a raised floor level.

Chancellery. "The chancelleries of Europe" is a favourite journalistic phrase and is the equivalent of saying the Foreign Offices or ministries of the European powers. *See* CHANCERY.

Chancellor. Originally an official (*cancellarius*) in the Roman law courts stationed at the CHANCEL as usher of the court and in the Eastern Empire a secretary or notary, subsequently invested with judicial functions. The name has been used in most European countries for an officer of state with varying powers and functions. In England, the office of Chancellor was introduced by Edward the Confessor and under the Normans the Chancellor became the chief secretary in charge of all important legal documents, head of CHANCERY, and keeper of the GREAT SEAL. In France, the Chancellor was the royal notary, president of the councils, and keeper of the Great Seal. Bismarck was made Chancellor of the newly created German Empire in 1871.

There are also diocesan chancellors who preside over the bishop's court, chancellors of cathedrals, academic chancellors who are usually the titular heads of universities, etc.

Chancellor, Dancing. *See* DANCING.

The Lord Chancellor, or the Lord High Chancellor. The highest judicial functionary of Great Britain, who ranks above all peers, except princes of the BLOOD and the Archbishop of Canterbury. He is keeper of the GREAT SEAL, is called "Keeper of His (or Her) Majesty's Conscience", and presides on the WOOLSACK in the House of Lords and in the CHANCERY Division of the Supreme Court of Judicature or High Court of Justice.

Chancellor of the Exchequer. The minister of finance in the British CABINET; the highest financial official of state in the kingdom.

Chancery. One of the three divisions of the High Court of Justice. It is mainly concerned with Equity and is presided over by the LORD CHANCELLOR. Not all its work is done in London; there is also a Chancery Court in Manchester, such jurisdiction having existed in the COUNTY PALATINE of Lancashire since the end of the 15th century. The word is shortened from Chancellery.

A Ward of Chancery is the term applied to a minor whose guardianship is vested in the Court of CHANCERY for various legal reasons. It is contempt of court to marry a ward of Chancery without the court's consent.

To get a man's head into Chancery is to get it under your arm, where you can pummel it as long as you like, and he cannot get it free without great difficulty. The allusion is to the long and exhausting suits for which the Court of Chancery was once notorious.

> Never can there come a fog too thick, never can there come mud and mire too deep, to assort with the groping and floundering condition which this High Court of Chancery, most pestilent of hoary sinners, holds, this day, in the sight of heaven and earth.
> DICKENS: *Bleak House*, ch. i.

If a man once got his head there, the lawyers could punish him to their heart's content.

> When I can perform my mile in eight minutes or a little less, then I feel as if I had old Time's head in chancery.
> HOLMES: *Autocrat of the Breakfast Table*, ch. vii.

Change. Ringing the changes. Repeating the same thing in differing ways. The allusion is to bell-ringing. For the sharper's meaning of the term, *see* RINGING.

To know how many changes can be rung on a peal, multiply the number of bells in the peal by the number of changes that can be rung on a peal consisting of one bell less, thus: 1 bell, no change; 2 bells, 1 by 2 = 2 changes; 3 bells, 2 by 3 = 6 changes; 4 bells, 6 by 4 = 24 changes; 5 bells, 24 by 5 = 120 changes; 6 bells, 120 by 6 = 720 changes, etc.

Changeling. A peevish, sickly child. The notion used to be that the fairies took a healthy child, and left in its place one of their starveling elves which never thrived.

Chansons de Geste (shon son dĕ zhest) (Fr.). Narrative poems dealing with the heroic families of French history and legend, and composed at various times between the 11th and 15th centuries. The famous *Chanson de Roland* is generally regarded as the finest. *See under* ROLAND.) *Gestes* (Lat. *gesta*) is used to mean the deeds of a hero and the account of his deeds.

Chant du départ (shon dū dā par). After the MARSEILLAISE, this was the most celebrated song of the French Revolution. It was written by M. J. Chénier for a public festival in 1794 to commemorate the taking of the BASTILLE. The music is by Méhul. A mother, an old man, a child, a wife, a girl, and three warriors sing a verse in turn, and the sentiment of each is, "We give up our claims on the men of France for the good of the Republic." *Cp.* CARMAGNOLE.

> La république nous appelle,
> Sachons vaincre ou sachons périr;
> Un Français doit vivre pour elle,
> Pour elle un Français doit mourir.

Chantage. BLACKMAIL; money accepted by low-class journals to prevent the publication of scandals, etc. *Chantage* is the common name in France for this form of subsidy; and the word has been used in the same way in England. *Cp.* CHEQUEBOOK JOURNALISM.

Chanticleer. The cock, in the tale of REYNARD THE FOX, and in Chaucer's *Nonnes Prestes Tale*; also in Rostand's play *Chantecleer*, produced in Paris in 1910 (Fr. *Chanter clair*, to sing clearly).

Chantrey Bequest. When Sir Francis Legatt Chantrey (1781–1841), the sculptor, died, he left a sum yielding £3,000 a year to the Royal Academy, of which the President was to receive £300, the secretary £50, and the remainder to be devoted to the purchase for the nation of works of art executed in Great Britain.

Chantry. A religious and often charitable endowment usually connected with a chapel (often part of the parish church) and mainly to provide for the chanting of masses for the founder. Their spoliation was begun by Henry VIII in 1545 and completed under Edward VI in 1547. Little of the proceeds was used for charitable or educational purposes.

Chaonian Bird (kā ō′ ni ȧn). This is the poetic name for a DOVE, and takes its origin from the legend that the dove bore the oracles of Chaonia.

Chaonian food. Acorns. So called from the acorns of Chaonia or DODONA. Some think beech-mast is meant, and tell us that the bells of the ORACLE were hung on beech-trees, not on oaks.

Chap. A man, properly a merchant. A **chapman** (O.E. *ceap-mann*) is a merchant or tradesman. "If you want to buy, I'm your chap." A good chap-man or chap became in time a good fellow. Hence, *a good sort of chap, a clever chap*, etc.

An awkward customer is an analogous phrase.

Chap-book. A cheap little book containing tales, ballads, lives, etc., sold by chapmen.

Chaps are wide leather leggings worn by American COWBOYS to protect their legs from injury, colloquially abbreviated from the S. American Sp. *chaparejos*, leather breeches. Also spelt *shaps* and so pronounced.

Chapeau bras (shăp ō bra) (Fr.). A soft three-cornered flat silk hat which could be folded and carried under the arm (Fr. *chapeau*, hat; *bras*, arm). It was worn in France with the court dress of the 18th century.

Chapel. Originally a chest containing relics or the shrine thereof, so called from the *capella* (little cloak or cope) of St. MARTIN, which was preserved by the Frankish kings as a sacred relic. The place in which it was kept when not in the field was called the *chapelle*, and the keeper thereof the *chapelain*. Hence the name came to be attached to a sanctuary, or a private place of worship other than a parish or cathedral church; and is also used for a place of worship belonging to the Free Churches, as a METHODIST Chapel, Baptist Chapel, etc., or a separately dedicated oratory within a church.

Among printers a *chapel* is an association of journeymen (compositors, machine-men, etc.), who meet periodically to discuss matters of common interest and take decisions affecting their conditions of employment, etc. The chairman is called the "father of the chapel". This use of the word possibly derives from the earliest days of English printing when presses were set up in chapels attached to abbeys. *See* CAXTON; FRIAR; MONK.

Chapel of ease. A place of worship for the use of parishioners residing at a distance from the parish church.

Lady chapel. A chapel dedicated to the Virgin within a larger church.

The Old Chapel. An unusual public house at the corner of Duke Street, Devonport, which still has some of its original features. It was opened as a Unitarian church in what was then Plymouth Dock, in 1791. This was the time of the French Revolution and UNITARIANS were suspect, as is evidenced by the burning down of Joseph Priestley's Unitarian church in Birmingham. Commissioner Fanshawe, Controller of the Dockyard, suspecting the Unitarians (many of whom were government employees), of revolutionary intrigues, closed their chapel and it was converted to a tavern in 1801.

Chapelle Ardente (shă pel′ ar dont′) (Fr.). The chapel or resting-place of kings or exalted personages when lying in state, so called from the many candles which were lit round the catafalque, a custom at least dating from the funeral rites of DAGOBERT, king of the FRANKS in 638. The term is now also applied to other mortuary chapels.

Chaperon (shăp′ e rōn). A married or mature woman who escorted a young unmarried girl in public places and acted as adviser and protector. So called from the Spanish hood worn by the duennas in former days. Also the hood or cap worn by Knights of the GARTER.

Chapter. From Lat. *caput*, a head. The chapter of a cathedral, composed of the canons (*see* CANON) and presided over by the DEAN or provost is so called from the ancient practice of the canons and monks reading at their meetings a *capitulum* (*cp.* CAPITULARY) or chapter of their Rule or of Scripture. *Ire ad capitulum* meant to go to the meeting for the reading of the chapter, hence to the meeting, hence to the body which made up the meeting.

Chapter of accidents. A series of unforeseen events. *To trust to a chapter of accidents* is to rely on something unforeseen turning up in your favour.

Chapter of possibilities. A maybe in the course of events.

To give chapter and verse. To give the exact authority for a statement, as the name of the author, the title of the book, the date, the chapter, etc., which may make verification readily possible.

To the end of the chapter. To the end of a proceeding. The allusion is obvious.

Char. This is a common abbreviation for "charwoman", or woman who chars or chares, *i.e.* works by the hour or day at house-cleaning. The word comes from O.E. *cerr, cerran*, meaning to turn. It has come back to England from the U.S.A. in the form of "chores", monotonous but necessary tasks.

The slang word "char" meaning tea appears to derive from the army in India from the Hind. *cha*, meaning tea.

Character. An oddity. One who has a distinctive peculiarity of manner. Sam Weller is a character, so is Pickwick.

In character. In harmony with personality and habitual behaviour.

Out of character. Not in harmony with a person's usual actions, writing, profession, age, status, etc.

Chare Thursday. Another form of *Shear* or *Shere* Thursday; the same as MAUNDY THURSDAY.

Charge, To. To make an attack or onset.

To be on charge. To be up before a magistrate.

To be on one's charge. To be responsible for the care or custody of something and answerable for it as members of the services are for government property.

To be put on a charge. In the Armed Forces to be entered up as a defaulter and brought before the appropriate officer for a hearing. If the charge is held proven, punishment is then awarded in accordance with Sevice regulations.

To charge a person. To accuse him formally of a crime or misdemeanour. It must be answered before the appropriate court or authority.

To charge like a bull at a gate. To go at something BALDHEADED, head first; to tackle something in a precipitate manner without due forethought.

To charge oneself with. To take upon oneself the onus of a given task.

To give charge over. To set in authority over.

> I gave my brother Hanani ... charge over Jerusalem.
>
> *Neh.* vii, 2.

To give in charge. To hand over a person to the charge of a policeman.

To have in charge. To have the care of something.

To return to the charge. To renew the attack.

To take in charge. To "take up" a person given in charge; to make an arrest; to take upon oneself the responsibility for something.

Charge-sheet. The form setting out in correct language and according to law the specific charges which an accused person has to answer.

Charing Cross. The original Charing Cross was erected in the centre of the ancient village of Charing, which stood midway between the cities of LONDON and WESTMINSTER, by Edward I to commemorate his Queen, Eleanor. It was the spot where her coffin was halted for the last time on it way from Harby, Notts., to Westminster.

The cross was sited where the statue of King Charles I now stands on the south side of Trafalgar Square, but it was destroyed by the PURITANS in 1647. The present Gothic cross in the courtyard of Charing Cross Station was designed by E. M. Barry and erected in 1865.

> Undone, undone, the lawyers are:
> They wander about the towne;
> Nor can they find the way to Westminster,
> Now Charing-cross is downe;
> At the end of the Strand they make a stand,
> Swearing they are at a loss,
> And chaffing say, that's not the way
> They must go by Charing-cross.
>
> PERCY: *Reliques* (*The Downfall of Charing-Cross*).

Chariot. According to Greek mythology, the chariot was invented by ERICHTHONIUS to conceal his feet, which were those of a dragon.

Chariot of the gods. So the Greeks appear to have called Sierra Leone, in Africa, a ridge of mountains of great height; but some suggest the title applies to Mount Cameroon.

> Her palmy forests, mingling with the skies,
> Leona's rugged steep behind us flies.
>
> CAMOËNS: *Lusiad*, Bk. V.

Chariots, or cars. That of:

> Admetus was drawn by lions and wild boars,
> BACCHUS by panthers,

CERES by winged dragons,
CYBELE by lions,
DIANA by stags,
JUNO by peacocks,
NEPTUNE by sea-horses,
PLUTO by black horses.
The SUN by seven horses (the seven days of the week),
VENUS by doves.

Charity. Charity begins at home. "Let them learn first to show piety at home" (I *Tim.* v, 4).

Charivari (shǎ ri va' ri). A French term for an uproar caused by banging pans and kettles and accompanied by hissing, shouting, etc., to express disapproval. As a verb (*charivariser*) it means to subject someone to disapproval. Originally a common practice at weddings in mediæval France, it was later only used as a derisive or satirical demonstration at unpopular weddings. The fracas resembled what we would call a CATS' CONCERT. The name *Charivari* was adopted for a satirical paper in Paris in 1832 and used in the sub-title for *Punch* which derided the shortcomings of society, the politicians, etc. *See* SHIVAREE; ROUGH MUSIC.

Charlatan (shar' lå tån). From the Ital. *ciarlare*, to prate, to chatter, to babble. One who pretends to knowledge or skill he does not possess; a MOUNTEBANK. It is usually applied to vendors of QUACK remedies who cover their ignorance in a spate of high-sounding and often meaningless words.

> Saltimbancoes, Quacksalvers, and Charlatans deceive the people in lower degrees.
> SIR T. BROWNE: *Pseudodoxia Epidemica*, I, iii.

It is difficult to make a choice among the charlatans of history. A striking example in modern times was Sequoa, a white man posing as RED INDIAN, who (about 1890) toured Britain in a coach with attendant Redskins and a brass band, drawing teeth "painlessly" (all squeals drowned by the band) and supplying an "Indian oil" to cure all manner of aches and pains. *Cp.* PSALMANAZAR.

Charlemagne (sharl' mān) (742–814). Charles the Great became sole king of the Franks in 771 and first Holy Roman EMPEROR in 800. He ruled over most of western Europe and was noted as a law-giver, administrator, protector of the Church and promoter of education. He was married nine times.

Charlemagne and his Paladins are the centre of a great series of chivalric romances. (*See* PALADIN). We are told that he was eight feet tall and of enormous strength and could bend three horseshoes at once in his hands. He was buried at Aix-la-Chapelle (Aachen), but according to legend he waits, crowned and armed, in Oldenburg, Hesse, for the day when ANTICHRIST shall appear; he will then go forth to battle and rescue Christendom. Another legend says that in years of plenty he crosses the Rhine on a BRIDGE OF GOLD, to bless the cornfields and vineyards.

Charles. Many rulers bearing this name have been afflicted with misfortune:
England:
    CHARLES I was beheaded by the Cromwellians (1649).
    Charles II lived long in exile. *See also* CHARLES AND THE OAK.
    Charles Edward, the Young PRETENDER, died in poverty in Rome in 1788.
France:
    Charles II, the Fat, reigned wretchedly, was deposed in 877, and died in poverty in 888.
    Charles III, the Simple, died a prisoner in the castle of Péronne in 929.
    Charles IV, the Fair, reigned six years (1322–1328), married thrice, buried all his children except one daughter, who was forbidden by THE SALIC LAW to succeed to the crown.
    Charles VI (reigned 1380–1422) went mad in 1392.
    Charles VII starved himself to death in 1461, partly through fear of being poisoned and partly because of a painful and incurable abscess in the mouth.
    Charles VIII accidentally smashed his head against the lintel of a doorway in the Château d'Amboise, and died in agony (1498), leaving no issue.
    Charles IX died at the age of twenty-four (1574), harrowed in conscience for the part he had taken in the Massacre of St. BARTHOLOMEW.
    Charles X spent a quarter of a century in exile, and after less than six years on the throne, fled for his life and died in exile (1836).
    Charles the Bold, of Burgundy, lost his life at Nancy in 1477, when he was utterly defeated by the Swiss.
Naples:
    Charles I (1266–1285) lost Sicily as a result of the SICILIAN VESPERS and experienced only disasters.
    Charles II, the Lame, was in captivity at the time of his father's death (died 1309).
    Charles III, his great-grandson, was killed (1386).

Charles I of England. When Bernini's bust of Charles I was brought home, the king was sitting in the garden of WHITEHALL Palace. He ordered the bust to be uncovered, and at that moment a hawk with a bird in its beak flew by, and a drop of blood fell on the throat of the bust. The bust was ultimately destroyed when the palace was burnt down.

The bronze statue of Charles I in Whitehall was modelled by Le Sueur and cast in 1633 for the Earl of Portland for his home in Roehampton. The earl died before the statue was finished and it was stored in the crypt of St. Paul's COVENT GARDEN, until it was sold for scrap by PARLIAMENT in 1650. John Revett, the purchaser, did a flourishing trade in knives, forks, etc., "made from the statue" which was in fact hidden away. It was recovered by the Earl of Portland's son at the RESTORATION and erected on the present site, roughly the old position of CHARING CROSS, in 1674. Wreaths are still laid on the statue, on the anniversary of the king's execution, by the JACOBITES of today. *See* REMEMBER.

Charles and the Oak. When Charles II fled from the Parliamentary army after the battle of Worcester (3 September 1651), he took refuge in Boscobel House; but it was unsafe to remain there, and he hid himself in an oak-tree. Dr. Stukeley says that this tree "stood just by a horse-track passing through the wood, and the king, with Colonel Carlos, climbed into it by means of the hen-roost ladder. The family reached them victuals with a nuthook" (*Itinerarium Curiosum*, ii, p. 57, 1724).

Charles's Wain. An old popular name for the seven bright stars of the Great Bear (*see under* BEAR). The constellation forms the rough outline of a wheelbarrow or rustic wagon and the name is held to be a corruption of "Churl's wain" (peasant's cart). Another version derives it from "CHARLEMAGNE'S wain". It is also called the *Wagon*, the *Plough*, and the *Dipper*, and by the Romans the *Septentriones* (the seven plough-oxen). *See* SEPTENTRIONAL SIGNS.

Charley Moore. An old navy term for anything honest and respectable, probably originating from a publican's advertisement in Malta, which read "Charley Moore—the Fair thing" (mid-19th century). Hence "that ain't no Charley Moore" means that isn't honest, that is underhand.

Charley Noble. The galley funnel. So called from a Merchant Service Captain who kept his copper galley funnel brightly polished.

Charleys, or **Charlies.** The old night watch, before the police force was organized in 1829. Possibly from Charles I, under whom London's WATCH system was reorganized in 1640.

Charlie, Bonnie Prince. *See* THE YOUNG PRETENDER *under* PRETENDER.

Charlie Dunn. To give a Charlie Dunn (Austr.). To expel for cheating. The origin is obscure.

Charleston. A FOX-TROT popular *c.* 1925–1927, originated as a dance among the American Negroes. Charleston is the name of a cotton-trading seaport in South Carolina, one-third of the population of which is Negro.

Charm. Deriving from the Lat. *carmen*, a song, a charm is an incantation that is alleged to work magic, although the word is usually applied to some object that averts bad luck or brings good.

Charon. In Greek mythology, the son of Erebus and Nox, the hideous old man who ferried the spirits of the dead over the rivers STYX and ACHERON for the fare of an *obolus*.

Charon's Toll. A coin placed in the mouth or hand of the dead by the ancient Greeks to pay Charon for ferrying the spirit across the rivers of the underworld to ELYSIUM.

Chartism. A working-class movement beginning in 1837 which embodied its agreed demands in the *People's Charter* of 1838. Its six points included: manhood suffrage, vote by ballot, annual parliaments, payment of M.P.s, equal constituencies and the abolition of the property qualification for M.P.s. It collapsed after the failure of their petition to Parliament in 1848.

Chartreuse. A greenish or yellowish liqueur made of brandy and various aromatic herbs. Made at La Grande Chartreuse by the CARTHUSIANS, but now commercially produced. Originally the money was spent on the maintenance of the Carthusian houses and mostly on charity.

Charybdis (kà rib' dis). A whirlpool on the coast of Sicily. SCYLLA and Charybdis are employed to signify two equal dangers. Thus HORACE says an author trying to avoid Scylla, drifts into Charybdis, *i.e.* seeking to avoid one fault, he falls into another.

The Homeric account says that Charybdis dwelt under an immense fig-tree on the rock, and that thrice every day he swallowed the waters of the sea and thrice threw them up again; but later writers have it that he stole the oxen of HERCULES, was killed by lightning, and changed into the gulf.

Chase (O.Fr. *chasier* from Lat. *captiare*, to chase). A small unenclosed deer forest held mainly by private individuals, and protected only by COMMON LAW. Forests were royal prerogatives and protected by the Forest Laws.

An iron frame used by printers for holding sufficient type for one side of a sheet, which is held tight by quoins, or small wedges of wood or metal, is also called a chase. Here the word is the Fr. *chasse* (Lat. *capsa*), a case.

Chasidim (chăs i dim). *See* HASIDEANS.

Chastity Girdle. A padded metal appliance in the shape of a belt that a man could fasten around his wife in such a way as to preclude possibility of unfaithfulness during his prolonged absence. It is said to have come into vogue at the time of the CRUSADES when such protracted absence was common. One or two examples exist in museums. *Cp.* CESTUS.

Chasuble (chăz' ū bl) (Fr. from Med. Lat. *casabula*, a little cottage). The principal vestment worn by the priests in celebrating MASS. It is a roughly rectangular sleeveless garment, with a hole for the head in the middle, thus hanging down both back and front. It is usually richly decorated with embroidery, and mediæval chasubles were finely ornamented with gold wire and gilded silver, this form of work being known throughout Europe as OPUS ANGLICANUM. The City of London was the home of some of the best work of the 12th and 13th centuries. The chasuble is said to represent the seamless coat of Christ.

> And ye, lonely ladyes, with youre longe fyngres,
> That ye han silke and sendal to sowe, what tyme is,
> Chesibles for chapelleynes cherches to honoure.
> PIERS PLOWMAN.

Château (shă tō). French for castle, mansion, or country seat.

The wines of various districts of France, especially Bordeaux, are named after the château or homestead of the estate from which they are produced. *Mise en bouteille au Château* or *Mise du Château* means that they were also bottled there.

Château en Espagne. A castle in the air. *See* CASTLE.

Chatelaine (shăt' e lān). Originally the mistress of a château, a chatelaine now usually signifies a brooch or clasp from which a variety of trinkets hang on short chains. They are the things which the mistress of a castle was likely to use, keys, scissors, knives, etc.

Chatelaine's (shăt' e lānz). This was a famous ORDINARY in COVENT GARDEN, established soon after the RESTORATION and a favourite resort of wits and men of fashion.

> *Sparkish:* Come, but where do we dine?
> *Horner:* Even where you will.
> *Sparkish:* At Chatelaine's.
> WYCHERLEY: *The Country Wife*.

Chatterbox. A talkative person. SHAKESPEARE speaks of the CLACK-DISH. "His use was to put a ducat in her clack-dish" (*Measure for*

Measure, III, ii), *i.e.* the beggars' alms-dish which was clattered or rattled to attract attention. We also find *chatter-basket* in old writers, referring to the child's rattle.

Chatterpie. The magpie, also used figuratively for a chatterbox.

Chautauqua (shȧ tawk' wȧ). In the U.S.A. the name given to an assembly for educational purposes with lectures, entertainments, etc., held largely out of doors, modelled on the Chautauqua Assembly. This was started in 1874 at the village and summer resort on Lake Chautauqua, New York State, which developed into the Chautauqua Literary and Scientific Circle in 1878 to promote home reading and study.

Chauvinism (shō' vin izm). Blind and exaggerated patriotism similar to jingoism (*see* JINGO). Nicholas Chauvin was a soldier of the French Republic and Empire well known by his contemporaries for his devoted enthusiasm for NAPOLEON. He was introduced as a type of exaggerated bellicose patriotism into a number of plays (*e.g.* Scribe's *Le Soldat laboureur*, Cogniard's *La Cocarde tricolore*, Bayard and Dumanoir's *Les Aides de camp*, and Charet's *Conscript Chauvin*), and his name was quickly adopted on both sides of the Channel.

Chawbacon. A contemptuous name for an uncouth rustic, whose only meat was bacon. (*Chaw*, chew.)

Che sarà, sarà (kā sa ra', sa ra'). What will be, will be. The motto of the Dukes of Bedford and the Russell family.

Cheap as a Sardinian. A Roman phrase referring to the great crowds of Sardinian prisoners brought to ROME by Tiberius Gracchus, and offered for sale at almost any price.

Cheap-jack. A travelling vendor of small wares who is usually ready to "cheapen" his goods, *i.e.* take less for them than the price he first named.

Cheapside bargain. A weak pun meaning that the article was bought cheap or under its market value. Cheapside; on the south side of the *Cheap* (or *Chepe*), was the principal market-place of old LONDON, so called from O.E. *ceaptan*, to buy; *cypan*, to sell; *ceap*, a price or sale.

Cheater. Originally an Escheator, or officer of the King's EXCHEQUER appointed to receive dues and taxes. The present meaning shows how these officers were wont to fleece the people. *Cp.* PUBLICANS.

A windcheater. A warm semi-weatherproof garment of the blouse or jacket type. The derivation is obvious.

Check. A sudden stop, hindrance or control.

From the game of CHESS in which a threat to the king is called a *check*. *Cp*. CHECKMATE.

Checkmate. A term in CHESS meaning to put your adversary's king into inescapable check. This wins the game. Figuratively "to checkmate" means to foil or outwit another. The term is from the Arabic *shāh māt*, the king is dead, and was introduced into Old Spanish and Portuguese as *xaque mate*.

In check. Under restraint.

To check in. To register on arrival at a hotel, conference, etc.

To check out. To settle one's account at a hotel on leaving, to register one's departure.

To check up on. To examine someone's personal record, etc.

Checks. To hand in one's checks. *See* HAND.

Cheek. Cheek by jowl. Side by side, close together.

> I'll go with thee, cheek by jowl.
> SHAKESPEARE: *Midsummer Night's Dream*, III, ii.

It is the same as "cheek by jaw".

> So cheek by cheek and jaw by jaw,
> We both sucked cider through a straw.
> *Popular song*.

None of your cheek. None of your insolence. A *cheeky* person is one who is saucy and presumptuous.

To cheek, or **to give cheek.** To be insolent, to be saucy.

To have the cheek. To have the face or assurance or presumption. "He hadn't the cheek to ask for more."

Cheese. Tusser in his *Five Hundred Points of Good Husbandry* (1573), says that a cheese to be perfect should be (1) not like Gehazi, *i.e.* dead white like a leper; (2) not like Lot's wife, all salt; (3) not like Argus, full of eyes; (4) not like Tom Piper, "hoven and puffed" like the cheeks of a piper; (5) not like CRISPIN, leathery; (6) not like LAZARUS, poor; (7) not like Esau, hairy; (8) not like MARY MAGDALENE, full of whey or maudlin; (9) not like the Gentiles, full of maggots or gentils; and (10) not like a bishop, made of burnt milk; this last is a reference to the old phrase, *the bishop has put his foot in it. See* BISHOP.

A green cheese. An unripe cheese; also a cheese that is eaten fresh (like a cream cheese) and is not kept to mature.

Big Cheese (slang). The boss, or someone in an important position.

Bread and cheese. Food generally, but of a frugal nature. CHARTISM has often been referred to as a "bread and cheese question", meaning it was largely caused by want and hunger, in this case lack of bread and cheese. "Come and take your bread and cheese with me this evening"—that is, come and have a light supper, anything that's going.

Cheese it! Stop it! Stow it! Also (in thieves' slang) clear off, make yourself scarce.

Cheesed off. Services' slang for disgusted, disgruntled.

Hard cheese. Hard lines; rotten luck.

He is quite the cheese, or **just the cheese**—*i.e.* quite the thing. Here "cheese" is the Persian and Urdu *chiz* (*cheez*), meaning "thing". The phrase is of Anglo-Indian origin; but it has been popularly treated as being connected with Eng. *cheese*, and thus we get the slang varieties, *That's prime Stilton, or double Gloster*—*i.e.* SLAP UP. Hence:

It is not the cheese. Not the right thing; said of something of rather dubious propriety or morals.

> Well, I've heard Nudity is not the cheese on public occasions!
> CHAS. READE: *Hard Cash*, ii, 186.

The moon made of green cheese. *See* MOON.

'Tis an old rat that won't eat cheese. It must be a very old man that is inaccessible to flattery or who can abandon his favourite indulgence; only a very cunning rat knows that cheese is a mere bait.

Cheesemongers. *See under* REGIMENTAL AND DIVISIONAL NICKNAMES.

Cheeseparer. A skinflint, one who would pare off the rind of his cheese so as to waste the minimum. The tale is told of a man who chose his wife out of three sisters by the way they ate their cheese. One pared it—she was mean (he said); one cut if off extravagantly thick—she was wasteful; The third sliced it off in a medium way, and there his choice fell.

Cheese-toaster. A sword; also called a "toasting-fork", etc.

> The sight of the blade, which glistened by moonlight in his face, checked in some sort, the ardour of his assailant, who desired he would lay aside his toaster, and take a bout with him at equal arms.
> SMOLLETT: *Peregrine Pickle*, ch. xxiv.

Cheesewring, The Devil's. A mass of eight stones towering to the height of thirty-two feet in the Valley of Rocks, Lynmouth, Devon, so called because it looks like a gigantic cheesepress.

Chefs. *See* ARM-SHRINES.

Chef d'œuvre (shā der vr) (Fr. a chief work). A masterpiece.

Chellean. (shell' ē ǎn). An early PALÆOLITHIC core-tool culture named by G. de Mortillet, French anthropologist, from the site at Chelles-sur-Marne where the remains were found.

Chelsea Pensioner. *See under* PENSIONER.

Chemosh (kē mosh). The national god of the

Moabites; very little is known of his cult, but human beings were sacrificed to him in times of crisis.

> Next Chemos, the obscene dread of Moab's sons,
> From Aroer to Nebo and the wild
> Of southmost Abarim.
>
> MILTON: *Paradise Lost*, I, 406–8.

Cheque. To give a blank cheque. *See under* BLANK.

Cheque-book journalism. A phrase introduced in the mid-1960s to describe the misuse of the wealth of the press to obtain copy by purchase, especially of exclusive rights, to the detriment of less wealthy competitors and possible corruption of the public. A particular abuse is the buying of stories from criminals, harlots, and notorious persons generally, thus financially rewarding the evildoer and tending to encourage others in vicious activities with the prospect of gain. Such conduct has been condemned by the Press Council.

Chequers (chek' ẽrz). A PUBLIC-HOUSE SIGN. The arms of Fitzwarren, the head of which house had the privilege of licensing alehouses in the reign of Edward IV, probably helped to popularize this sign, but it is of much older origin. It has been found on houses in Pompeii and probably referred to some game like draughts being played on the premises. One explanation is that in mediæval times some innkeepers were also money-changers and used an "exchequer board" as a sign of their calling. Also certain public houses were used by the parish authorities for the payment of doles, etc., and a chequer-board was provided for that purpose and also adopted as a sign.

Chequers, the country seat of the Prime Minister of Great Britain, in the Chiltern country near Princes Risborough, was presented to the nation for this purpose by Sir Arthur and Lady Lee (Lord and Lady Lee of Fareham) in 1917, and first officially used by Lloyd George in 1921.

Cheronean (kē rō nē' àn). **The Cheronean Sage.** Plutarch (A.D. 46–120), who was born at Cheronea in BŒOTIA.

Cherry. Cherry-breeches, Cherrybums, Cherry-Pickers. *See* CHERRY-PICKERS; CHERUBIMS *under* REGIMENTAL AND DIVISIONAL NICKNAMES.

Cherry fairs. Cherry orchards where sales of fruit were held, such gatherings frequently becoming boisterous. Their temporary character caused them to be used to typify the evanescence of life; thus Gower says of this world, "Alle is but a cheryefayre."

Cherry-trees and the cuckoo. The cherry-tree is strangely mixed up with the CUCKOO in many cuckoo stories, because of the tradition that the cuckoo must eat three good meals of cherries before he is allowed to cease singing.

> Cuckoo, cuckoo, cherry-tree,
> Good bird, prithee, tell to me
> How many years I am to see.

The answer is gathered from the number of times the cuckoo repeats its cry.

The whole tree or not a cherry on it. "AUT CÆSAR AUT NULLUS." All in all or none at all.

To make two bites of a cherry. To divide something too small to be worth dividing; to take two spells over a piece of work that should be done in one.

Cherubims. *See under* REGIMENTAL AND DIVISIONAL NICKNAMES.

Cheshire Cat. To grin like a Cheshire cat. *See under* CAT.

Chess. "The game of kings"; the word being the English equivalent of the Persian *shah* (*see* CHECKMATE), a king. In Arabic the word was pronounced *shag*, which gave rise to the late Lat. *scaccus*, whence the O.Fr. *eschec*, Mod. Fr. *échecs*, and E. *chess*. Derivatives in other languages are *scacco* (Ital.), *jaque* (Span.), *xaque* (Port.), *Schach* (Ger.).

Chestnut. A stale joke. The term is said to have been popularized in America by a Boston actor named Warren, who, on a certain apposite occasion, quoted from *The Broken Sword*, a forgotten melodrama by William Dimond, first produced at COVENT GARDEN in 1816, in which one of the characters, Captain Xavier, is forever telling the same jokes with variations, one of which concerned his exploits with a cork-tree. He is corrected by Pablo who says "A chestnut. I have heard you tell the joke twenty-seven times, and I am sure it was a chestnut."

Cheval (shẽ văl') (Fr. a horse).

Cheval de bataille (Fr. literally "horse of battle"). One's strong argument, one's favourite subject.

Cheval de frise. An apparatus consisting of a bar carrying rows of pointed stakes, set up so that the bar can revolve, and used in warfare as a defence against enemy cavalry. So called from its first use by the Frisians (who had few if any horses) in the siege of Groningen, Friesland, in 1594. A somewhat similar engine had been used before. In German it is "a Spanish horseman" (*ein spanischer Reiter*).

Cheval glass. A large, swinging mirror, long enough to reflect the whole of the figure; so called from the "horse" or framework which supports it.

Chevalier de St. George. *See* CAVALIER.

Chevalier d'industrie. A man who lives by his wits and calls himself a gentleman; an adventurer, a swindler.

> Be cautiously upon your guard against the infinite number of fine-dressed and fine-spoken *chevaliers d'industrie* and *aventuriers*, which swarm at Paris.
> CHESTERFIELD: *Letters to his son* (26 Apr. 1750).

Cheveril (chev' ĕr il). **He has a cheveril conscience.** An accommodating one; one that will easily stretch like kid leather.

> Oh, here's a wit of cheveril, that stretches from an inch narrow to an ell broad!
> SHAKESPEARE: *Romeo and Juliet*, II, iv.

Chevy Chase. There had long been a rivalry between the families of Percy and Douglas, which showed itself by incessant raids into each other's territory. Percy of Northumberland once vowed he would hunt for three days in the Scottish border, without condescending to ask leave of Earl Douglas. The Scots warden said in his anger, "Tell this vaunter he shall find one day more than sufficient." The ballad called *Chevy Chase* mixes up this hunt with the battle of Otterburn, which, Bishop Percy justly observes, was "a very different event". The ballad of *The Battle of Otterburn* is also given in PERCY'S RELIQUES.

Chew. To chew the fat or **rag.** An old colloquialism meaning to grumble or to "bellyache", to harp on an old sore; to argue the point. Also, less commonly, to hold familiar conversation. *Cp*. JAW.

Chian Painter, The. Appelles, famous Grecian painter and contemporary of ALEXANDER THE GREAT, born at Colophon on the coast of Asia Minor.

> The Chian painter, when he was required
> To portrait Venus in her perfect hue,
> To make his work more absolute, desired
> Of all the fairest maids to have the view.
> SPENSER: *Dedicatory Sonnets*, xvii.

Chicago piano. A World War II naval nickname for an eight-barrelled pom-pom anti-aircraft gun. The allusion is to the Chicago of the gangsters (*see* CAPONE). Similarly a four-barrelled pom-pom was called a **Chicago typewriter.**

Chicane (chi kān'). A term used in bridge for a hand containing no trumps. Its general meaning is the use of mean, petty subterfuge, especially legal dodges and quibbles. It is a French word which, before being used for sharp practice in lawsuits, meant a dispute in games, particularly mall, and originally the game of mall itself. (*See* PALL MALL). It seems to be ultimately from the Persian *chaugan*, the crooked stick used in polo, and

it is also applied to an obstacle on a racecourse, particularly to the artificial bends introduced on motor-racing tracks.

Chichevache (chich' e vash). A fabulous monster that lives only on good women, and was hence all skin and bone, because its food was so extremely scarce; the antitype to BICORN. Chaucer introduced and changed the word from the French *chichifache* (thin or ugly face) into *chichevache* (lean or meagre-looking cow).

> O noble wyves, ful of height prudence,
> Lat noon humylitee youre tonge naille,
> Ne lat no clerk have cause or diligence
> To write of yow a storie of swich mervaille
> As of Grisildis, pacient and kynde,
> Lest Chichivache yow swelwe in hire entraille.
> CHAUCER: *Lenvoy de Chaucer, Clerk's Tale*.

Lydgate wrote a poem called *Bycorne and Chichevache*.

Chicken. Chicken-feed, chick-feed, or **chicken-corn.** Trivial amounts of money, SMALL BEER, or comparatively trifling costs; from the fact that chicken corn usually consists of the smaller and cheaper grains.

Chicken-hearted, or **chicken-livered.** Cowardly. Young fowls are remarkably timid and run to the hen on the slightest alarm.

Children and chicken must always be pickin'. They are always hungry and ready to eat.

Curses, like chickens, come home to roost. *See* CURSE.

Don't count your chickens before they are hatched. Make sure that a thing is actually yours before you speak or act as if it were already yours. The saying in a slightly different form is first found in the writings of Erasmus. "Don't crow till you are out of the wood" has a similar meaning. *Cp*. ALNASCHAR'S DREAM; A BIRD IN THE HAND IS WORTH TWO IN THE BUSH (*See under* BIRD).

His chickens have come home to roost. His sins have found him out; he has got what he asked for; his actions have caught up on him.

Mother Carey's chickens. *See* MOTHER CAREY.

She's no chicken, or **she's no spring chicken.** She's no youngster, she is not young.

Where the chicken got the axe. *See* NECK. TO GET IT IN THE NECK.

Which came first, the chicken or the egg? A suitable reply to an unanswerable question.

Chicken of St. Nicholas. So the Piedmontese call our "LADYBIRD", the little red beetle with spots of black. The Russians call it "God's little cow".

Child. At one time this was a provincial term for a female infant, and was the correlative of *boy*.

> Mercy on's, a bairn; a very pretty bairn! A boy or a child, I wonder?
>
> SHAKESPEARE: *Winter's Tale*, III, iii.

Child of God. In the CHURCH OF ENGLAND and the ROMAN CATHOLIC CHURCH, one who has been baptized; others consider the phrase to mean one converted by special grace and adopted into the holy family of God's Church.

> In my baptism; wherein I was made a member of Christ, the child of God, and an inheritor of the kingdom of heaven.
>
> *Catechism, Book of Common Prayer.*

That's child's play. Said of something which can be done very easily or simply.

Childe. In *Childe Harold, Childe Roland, Childe Tristram*, etc., "childe" is a title of honour like the Sp. "infante". In the days of CHIVALRY, a noble youth who was a candidate for knighthood, during his time of probation, was called *infans, valet, damoysel, bachelier*, and *childe*.

Childe Harold. Byron's poem depicts a man sated of the world, who roams from place to place to escape from himself. The "Childe" was in fact BYRON himself, who was only twenty-one when he began the poem, and twenty-eight when he finished it. In Canto I (1809), he visited Portugal and Spain; in Canto II (1810), Turkey in Europe; in Canto III (1816), Belgium and Switzerland; and in Canto IV (1817), Venice, Rome and Florence.

Childermas. The Old English name for the festival, of MASS of the HOLY INNOCENTS (28 December).

Children. Three hundred and sixty-five at a birth. It is said that a countess of Henneberg accused a beggar of adultery because she carried twins, whereupon the beggar prayed that the countess might carry as many children as there are days in the year. According to the legend, this happened on Good Friday, 1276. All the males were named John, and all the females Elizabeth. The countess was forty-two at the time.

The Children, or Babes in the Wood. The story is that the master of Wayland Hall, Norfolk, left a little son and daughter to the care of his wife's brother; both were to have money, but if the children died first the uncle was to inherit. After twelve months the uncle hired two ruffians to murder the babes; one of them relented and killed his partner, leaving the children in a wood. They died during the night, and "ROBIN REDBREAST" covered them over with leaves. All things now went ill with the wicked uncle; his sons died, his barns were fired, his cattle died, and he finally perished in gaol. After seven years the ruffian was taken up for highway robbery, and confessed the whole affair.

The ballad *The Children in the Wood* appears in PERCYS' RELIQUES and also in a crude MELODRAMA, printed in 1601 and attributed on the title-page to Rob Yarington, called *Two Lamentable Tragedies; the one of the murder of Maister Beech, a chandler in Thames-streete, etc. The other of a young child murthered in a wood by two ruffians, with the consent of his unkle.* It is uncertain which is earlier, the play or the ballad.

Chiliasts (ki' li àsts) (Gr. *chilias*, a thousand). Also called MILLENARIANS. Those who believe that Christ will return to this earth and reign a thousand years in the midst of his SAINTS. Originally a Judaistic theory, it became a heresy in the early Christian Church, and though it was condemned by St. Damasus, who was POPE from 366 to 384, it was not extirpated. Article xli of the English Church further condemned Chiliasm in 1553; this Article was omitted in 1562.

Chillingham Cattle. A breed of cattle still preserved in the Northumberland park of the Earl of Tankerville, reputed to be the last remnant of the wild oxen of Britain.

Chillon (shē' yong). **Prisoner of Chillon.** François de Bonnivard (1493–1570), a Genevan prelate and politician. BYRON, in his poem, makes him one of six brothers, all of whom suffered for their opinions. The father and two sons died in battle, one was burnt at the stake; three were imprisoned in the dungeon of Chillon, on the edge of Lake Geneva—of these, two died, and François, who had been gaoled for republican principles by the Duke-Bishop of Savoy, was liberated, after four years, by the BÉARNAIS.

Chilminar and Baalbek (kil min ar', bāl' bek). According to legend, two cities built by the Genii, acting under the orders of Jinn bin Jann, who governed the world long before ADAM. Chilminar, or the "Forty Towers", is Persepolis. They were intended as lurking places for the Genii to hide in.

Chilo. One of the "Seven Sages of Greece". *See* WISE MEN.

Chiltern Hundreds. The HUNDREDS of Stoke, Desborough and Burnham, Buckinghamshire, over which a Steward was originally appointed to suppress the robbers who frequented the thickly wooded Chiltern Hills. The necessity has long since ceased, but the office remains. As a consequence of the Succession Act of 1701 and later Place

Acts, the holding of most non-political offices of profit under the Crown meant resignation from the HOUSE OF COMMONS, and after 1750 application for the stewardship of the Chiltern Hundreds was used as a means of relinquishing membership of Parliament (since members cannot resign directly). The Stewardships of Old Shoreham, East Hendred, Hempholme, Poynings, and Northstead were also used for this purpose, as were (till 1838) the Escheatorships of Munster and Ulster. By the House of Commons Disqualification Act (1957), the Stewardship of the Chiltern Hundreds and the Manor of Northstead (Yorks), were retained for this use and their gift remains with the CHANCELLOR OF THE EXCHEQUER.

Chimæra (ki mē' rà) (Gr. *chimaira*, a she-goat). A fabulous monster in Greek mythology. According to HOMER it has a lion's head, a goat's body, and a dragon's tail. It was born in Lycia and slain by BELLEROPHON. Hence the use of the name in English for an illusory fancy, a wild incongruous scheme.

Chime in. To join in a conversation already in progress, or to be in accord with or agree to suggestions made by others. The allusion is to the chiming of bells.

Chimney Money, or **Hearth Money.** A yearly tax of two shillings on every fire-place in all houses liable to church and poor rates, or above a minimum value of 20s. per year. First levied in 1663, it was abolished in 1689 and replaced by the WINDOW TAX in 1696.

Chimneypot hat. The same as a STOVEPIPE HAT; the ordinary cylindrical black silk hat or top-hat.

Chinaman. A cricketing term (not to be confused with GOOGLY) denoting an offbreak bowled from the back or side of the hand by a left-handed bowler. It is said that the name derives from the Chinese bowler Ellis Achong, who played for the West Indies, and who practised this kind of bowling, although he was not the first to do so.

Chinatown. That part of any city which forms the Chinese quarter, especially in the U.S.A.

Chindit. A corruption of *chinthe*, the lion-headed DRAGON gracing the outside of Burmese pagodas. It was adopted as the device of the troops under Major-General Orde Wingate operating in Burma behind the Japanese lines (1943–1945). Wingate himself was killed in an aircrash in March 1944.

Chinese Gordon. General Charles Gordon (1833–1885), who in 1863 was placed in command of the EVER-VICTORIOUS ARMY and after thirty-three engagements succeeded in suppressing the formidable TAI-PING rebel-

lion by 1864.

After the MAHDI'S revolt in the Sudan, he was sent out by Gladstone's government to effect the evacuation of the Egyptian garrisons, but allowed himself to be cut off in Khartoum and was killed (26 January) after a heroic defence lasting nearly a year. The relief force under Wolseley arrived two days too late, due to CABINET procrastination.

Chinese Slavery. Virtual slavery; excessively hard graft for negligible rewards. The phrase became widely used as a political slogan by the LIBERALS from 1903, when Balfour's CONSERVATIVE government (1902-1905) introduced indentured coolies from China to combat the shortage of Kaffir labour in the Rand gold mines after the dislocation caused by the South African War. They were kept in compounds and only allowed out under permit.

Chink. Money; so called because it *chinks* or jingles in the purse. It was formerly in good repute as a synonym for coin.

> Have chinks in thy purse.
> TUSSER: *Five Hundred Points* (1573).

Chinook. A warm, dry wind which blows down the east side of the Rockies in winter causing rapid rises in temperature and sudden thawing of snow. It is a cooling wind in the summer and takes its name from the Chinook Indians of the Columbia River area.

Chintz. A plural word that has erroneously become singular. The Hindi *chint* (from Sans. *chitra*, variegated) was the name given in the 17th century to the painted and stained calico imported from the East; but as the plural *chints* was more common in commercial use it came to be taken for the singular, and was written *chince* or *chinse* and finally *chintz*.

Chios (kī' os). **The man of Chios.** See SCIO'S BLIND OLD BARD.

Chip. A carpenter is known by his chips. A man is known to be a carpenter by the chips in his workshop, so the profession or taste of other men may be known by their manners or mode of speech.

A chip of the old block. A son or child of the same stuff as his father. The chip is the same wood as the block. Burke applied the words to William Pitt the younger.

Brother Chip. Properly a brother carpenter, but in its extended meaning applied to anyone of the same vocation as oneself. A ship's carpenter is commonly called "Chips" or "Chippy".

He's had his chips. He is finished or come to an end as far as this is concerned, he is out of it. Probably from the game of poker. See TO CHIP IN.

Such carpenters, such chips. As the workman, so his work will be.

The chips are down. The situation is urgent or desperate. Probably the same derivation as TO CHIP IN.

To chip in. It has two meanings; to make a contribution, and to interrupt. The former derives from the game of poker, in which the chips, representing money, are placed by the players in the "pot". The latter is obscure, but possibly from the same source.

To have a chip on one's shoulder. To be quarrelsome; to parade or have a grievance. Of 19th-century American origin, possibly as a man might carry a chip on his shoulder daring others to dislodge it.

Chippie. A knee-length frock worn in the RED-LIGHT DISTRICT of New Orleans; hence the U.S. term for a prostitute. It can be used as a back-handed term of affection, as with the Blues singer Bertha "Chippie" Hill.

Chiromancy. *See* PALMISTRY.

Chiron (kī'ron). The CENTAUR who taught ACHILLES, and many other heroes, music, medicine, and hunting. JUPITER placed him in heaven among the stars as SAGITTARIUS.

Dante, in his INFERNO, gives the name to the keeper of the lake of boiling blood, in the seventh circle of HELL.

Chirping Cup. A merry-making glass or cup of liquor. Wine that makes glad the heart of man, or makes him sing for joy.

> A chirping cup is my matin song,
> And my vesper bell is my bowl; Ding Dong!
> WILLIAM SHIELD: *A Friar of Orders Grey* (1784).

Chisel. I chiselled him means, I cheated him or cut him out of something. Hence a *chiseller*, a cheat or one who takes unfair advantage.

Chivalry (shiv' ál ri). A general term for all things pertaining to the romance of the old days of knighthood. The word is of similar origin to *cavalry*, coming from the Fr. *cheval*, a horse, and *chevalier*, a horseman. Chivalry embodied the mediæval conception of the ideal life, where valour, courtesy, generosity and dexterity in arms were the summit of any man's attainment.

> For him behoveth to be of soch chiualrie and so aventurouse that he com by hymselfe and enquere after the seint Graal that my feire doughter kepeth.
> *Merlin* (E.E.T.S., iii).

A great literature arose out of chivalry—the ROLAND epics, those of CHARLEMAGNE, and ARTHUR. It was, perhaps, prophetic of the fate of chivalry itself that in every case these great epics end in tragedy.

The PALADINS of CHARLEMAGNE were all scattered by the battle of RONCESVALLES.

The champions of Dietrich were all assassinated by the instigation of Chriemhild (KRIEMHILD), the bride of ETZEL, king of the Huns.

The KNIGHTS of the ROUND TABLE were all destroyed in the fatal battle of CAMLAN.

The flower of chivalry. *See* FLOWER.

Chivy. To chase or urge someone on; also a chase in the game of "Prisoner's Base". One boy "sets a chivy" by leaving his base, when one of the opposite side chases him, and if he succeeds in touching him before he reaches "home", the boy touched becomes a prisoner. The word is a variant of *chevy*, from CHEVY CHASE.

Chivy, or **chivvy.** The face. An example of RHYMING SLANG.

Chloe (klō' ē). The shepherdess beloved by DAPHNIS in the Greek pastoral romance of Longus called *Daphnis and Chloe*, and hence a generic name in literature for a rustic maiden—not always of the artless variety.

In Pope's *Moral Essays* (ii) Chloe is intended for Lady Suffolk, mistress of George II, "Content to dwell in decencies for ever"; and Prior uses the name for Mrs. Centlivre.

Chock-full. Chock-a-block. Full right up; no room for any more. When two blocks of a tackle meet preventing any more purchase being gained it is said to be *two blocks* or *chock-a-block*.

Chocolate. The produce of the cocoaberry was introduced into England from Central America in the early 16th century as a drink. It was sold in London coffee-houses from the middle of the 17th century. The *Cocoa Tree* was one of the famous coffee-houses of the early 18th century. *See* COFFEE.

Chocos (Austr.). A diminutive of *chocolate soldiers*, applied to militiamen and conscripts in World War II.

Choice spirit. A specially select or excellent person, a leader in some particular capacity. From Antony's speaking of Cæsar and Brutus as:

> The choice and master spirits of this age.
> SHAKESPEARE: *Julius Cæsar*, III, i.

Choice spirit of the age. Figuratively used for a gallant of the day; one who delights to exaggerate the whims of fashion.

Hobson's choice. *See* HOBSON'S CHOICE.

Of two evils choose the less. The proverb is given in John Heywood's collection (1546), but it is a good deal earlier and occurs in Chaucer's *Troilus and Criseyde* (ii, 470) as:

> Of harmes two, the lesse is for to chese.

Thomas a Kempis (*Imitatio Christi*, III, xii) has:

> De duobus malis minus est semper eligendum (Of two evils the lesser is always to be chosen.)

which is an echo of Cicero's:

> Ex malis eligere minima oportere. (Of evil one should select the least.)
>
> *De Officiis*, III, i.

Choke. May this piece of bread choke me, if what I say is not true. In ancient times, a person accused of robbery had a piece of barley bread given him over which MASS had been said. He put it in his mouth uttering the above words, and if he could swallow it without being choked he was pronounced innocent. Tradition ascribes the death of Earl Godwin to choking with a piece of bread after this solemn appeal. *See* CORSNED.

Choke-damp. The carbonic acid gas which accumulates in coal mines, and can cause suffocation. Also called *after-damp* or *foul-damp*.

Choke-pear. A kind of pear with a rough, astringent taste. From this the term was applied to anything that stopped speaking, such as an unanswerable argument or a biting sarcasm.

> He gave him a choake-peare to stoppe his breath.
> LYLY: *Euphues*.

Choke Weed. Hemp. An obsolete Americanism for the plant which provides the material for the hangmans' rope. The name is also applied to the parasitic plant broomrape (*Orobanche*).

Choker. Formerly a broad neck-cloth, worn in full dress by waiters, clergymen and others; then a high stiff collar or necklace or scarf worn tight round the neck.

Chop. (1) **to chop,** meaning to cut a piece off with a sudden blow, is a variant spelling of *chap*, a cleft in the skin, and *to chap*, to open in long slits or cracks. From this we get:

Chops of the Channel. The short, broken motion of the waves experienced in crossing the English Channel; also the place where such motion occurs. In this use, however, the word may be *chops*, the jaw (*see below*), because the *Chops of the Channel* is an old and well-understood term for the entrance to the Channel from the Atlantic.

Chop house. An eating-house where chops and steaks are served.

> I dine at the Chop-House three days a week, where the good company wonders they never see you of late.
> STEELE: *Spectator*, No. 308 (22 Feb. 1712).

(2) In the following phrases **chop** comes from the same root as *chap* in CHAPMAN and signifies to barter, exchange, or sell.

To chop an article means to dispose of it arbitrarily, even at a loss.

To chop and change. To barter by RULE OF THUMB; to fluctuate, to keep changing one's mind or vary continuously.

To chop logic. To bandy words; to altercate. Bacon says, "Let not the counsel chop with the judge."

> How now, how now, chop logic! What is this?
> "Proud", and "I thank you", and "I thank you not",
> And yet "not proud".
> SHAKESPEARE: *Romeo and Juliet*, III, v.

The wind chops about. Shifts from point to point suddenly. Hence *choppy*, said of a variable wind, and of the rough sea produced by such; and *to chop round*:

> How the House of Lords and House of Commons chopped round.
> THACKERAY: *The Four Georges* (*George I*).

(3) **Chop,** the face, and **chops,** the jaws or mouth, is a variant spelling of *chap* (as in *Bath chap*, the lower part of a pig's face, cured). From this come:

Chop-fallen, or **Chap-fallen.** CRESTFALLEN, down in the mouth.

Down in the chops. Down in the mouth; in a melancholy state; with the mouth drawn down.

To lick one's chops. To relish in anticipation.

(4) In the slang phrase **first chop**, meaning excellent, the word is the Hindi *chhāp*, a print or stamp, formerly used in India and China by English residents for an official seal, also for a passport or permit; and a Chinese custom-house is known as a *chop-house*.

Chop-chop. Hurry, hurry; get moving quickly. *See* PIDGIN ENGLISH.

Chopsticks. The two thin sticks of wood or ivory that the Chinese, Japanese and Koreans use to eat with. The word is a rendering of the Chin. *K'wai-tsze*, meaning "the quick ones".

Chopsticks is also the name of a quick traditional waltz tune played as a duet by schoolchildren. The French call it *Côtelettes* (Cutlets), and the Germans *Koteletten Walzer*.

Choragus (kor ā' gùs). The leader of the chorus in the ancient Athenian drama.

At Oxford, the title was given to the assistant of the Professor of Music, but formerly to the officer who superintended the practice of music. *See* CORYPHÆUS.

Choriambic Metre. HORACE gives us a great variety, but the main feature in all is the prevalence of the choriambus ($-\cup\cup-$). Specimen translations in two of these metres are subjoined:

(1) Horace, *Odes*, I, viii.

Lydia, why on Stanley,
By the great gods, tell me, I pray, ruinous love you
    centre?
Once he was strong and manly,
Never seen now, patient of toil Mars' sunny camp
    to enter.

E.C.B.

——|——⌣⌣—|⌣—
——|——⌣⌣—|⌣⌣—|⌣—

When you with an approving smile,
Praise those delicate arms, Lydy, of Telephus,
Ah me! how you stir up my bile!
Heart-sick that for a boy you should forsake me
    thus.

E.C.B.

Chouans (shoo′ ong). French peasant bands in Brittany, under the leadership of Jean Cottereau (1767–1794), who rose in revolt in 1793 and joined the royalists of La VEN- DÉE. *Chouan* (a corruption of *chat-huant*, a screech-owl) was the nickname given to Cot- tereau, who imitated the screech of the owl to warn his companions of danger, and the name was extended to his followers. Georges Cadoudal (executed 1804) was their leader after 1794. The movement reap- peared in 1814–1815 and again during the JULY REVOLUTION of 1830. *See also* COMPAN- IONS OF JEHU.

Choughs. *See under* BIRD.

Chouse (chouz). To cheat or swindle. It der- ives from the Turkish *cha′ ush*, an interpre- ter, messenger, etc. The interpreter of the Turkish embassy in England in 1609 de- frauded his government of £4,000, and the notoriety of the swindle gave rise to the term.

What do you think of me,
That I am a Chiause?

BEN JONSON: *Alchemist*, I, ii.
You shall chouse him out of horses, clothes, and
money, and I'll wink at it.

DRYDEN: *Wild Gallant*, II, i.

Chriem-hild. *See* KRIEMHILD.

Chrism, Chrisom (Gr. *chrisma*, anointing, unction). The mixture of oil and balm con- secrated for use in bap- tism, confirmation, etc. Originally *chrisom* was merely a variant of *chrism* resulting from a frequent form of pronunciation but later differentiated from the latter when it came to designate the white cloth or robe worn at baptism. This was used as a shroud if the child died within the ensuing month. In the BILLS OF MORTALITY, as late as 1726, such infants were called *chrisoms*.

'A made a finer end, and went away, an it had been
any chrisom child.

SHAKESPEARE: *Henry V*, II, iii.

Chriss-cross, or Christ-cross row. The alphabet in a HORNBOOK, which had a cross like the MALTESE CROSS (✝) at the beginning and end.

Sir Ralph. I wonder, wench, how I thy name might
know.

Mall. Why you may find it, sir, in th' Christcross
row.

PORTER: *Two Angry Women of Abington*, V, i (1599).

The word appears as *Christ-cross, criss- cross*, etc., and Shakespeare shortened it to *cross-row*:

He harkens after prophecies the dreams;
And from the cross-row plucks the letter G,
And says a wizard told him that by G
His issue disinherited should be.

Richard III, I, i.

As the Maltese cross was also sometimes used in place of XII to mark that hour on clocks, chriss-cross has occasionally been used for noon:

The feskewe of the Diall is upon the Chriss-cross of
Noone.

The Puritan Widow, IV, ii (ANON., 1607).

Christadelphians, or Brethren of Christ, sometimes called *Thomasites* after their founder Dr. John Thomas (1805–1871), who migrated from London to Brooklyn and established the sect in 1848. They believe in "conditional immortality" for the faithful and the full inspiration of the BIBLE, and look for the return of Christ to reign on this earth.

Christendom. All Christian countries gener- ally; formerly it also meant the state or con- dition of being a Christian.

By my christendom,
So I were out of prison, and kept sheep,
I should be as merry as the day is long.

SHAKESPEARE: *King John*, IV, i.

Christian. A follower of Christ. So called first at Antioch (*Acts* xi, 26). Also the hero of Bunyan's *Pilgrim's Progress* who fled from the CITY OF DESTRUCTION and journeyed to the CELESTIAL CITY. He started with a heavy burden on his back, which fell off when he stood at the foot of the cross.

Christian Brothers. A secret society formed in London in the early 16th century to distribute the NEW TESTAMENT in English. The name is now better known as that of the Roman Catholic teaching congregation of laymen, founded by the Abbé de la Salle in 1684. It still flourishes in France, Great Britain and elsewhere.

Christian Science. The religion founded at Boston by Mrs. Mary Baker Eddy in 1879, "the scientific system of divine healing". Her views were put forward in her book *Science and Health, with key to the Scriptures,* first published in 1875. Christian Science is founded on the BIBLE, but distinguishes be- tween what is taught in the NEW TESTAMENT and what is taught in the creeds and later dogma. It now has a considerable following and is not limited, as is popularly assumed, to the healing of those who are ill.

Most Christian Doctor. John Charlier de Gerson (1363–1429), French theologian.

Most Christian King. The style of the king of France since 1429, when it was conferred on Louis XI by POPE Paul II. Previously the title had been given in the 8th century to Pepin le Bref by Pope Stephen III (714–768), and again in the 9th century to Charles le Chauve. *See* RELIGIOUS.

Christiana (kris ti an' a). The wife of CHRISTIAN in Pt. II of Bunyan's *Pilgrim's Progress*, who journeyed with her children and Mercy from the CITY OF DESTRUCTION some time after her husband.

Christinos. Supporters of the Queen-Regent Christina during the CARLIST WARS in Spain, 1833–1840.

Christmas. 25 December is Christmas Day although almost certainly not the day on which Christ was born, as is popularly supposed. The date was eventually fixed by the Church in A.D. 440, the day of the winter SOLSTICE, which had anciently been a time of festival among heathen peoples. In Anglo-Saxon England, the year began on 25 December, but from the late 12th century until the adoption of the Gregorian Calendar in 1752 the year began on LADY DAY, 25 March. *See* GREGORIAN YEAR; OLD STYLE.

Christmas box. A gratuity given on Boxing Day (the day after Christmas Day), St. Stephen's Day. Boxes placed in churches for casual offerings used to be opened on Christmas Day, and the contents, called the "dole of the Christmas box", or the "box money", were distributed next day by priests. Apprentices also used to carry a box around to their masters' customers for small gratuities (*See* PIGGY-BANKS). Postmen received such gifts until after World War II, and some dustmen and errand-boys still call to collect them. *Cp.* HANDSEL.

Christmas cards. These boosters of post office and stationers' revenues are of comparatively recent origin. W. C. T. Dobson, R.A., is usually regarded as having sent the first such card in 1844. Sir Henry Cole and J. C. Horsley produced the first commercial Christmas card in 1846, although it was condemned by temperance enthusiasts because members of the family group in the centre piece were cheerfully drinking wine. After Tucks, the art printers, took to printing them in the 1870s, they really came into VOGUE.

Christmas Day in the Workhouse. The popular title of the much parodied long narrative poem (twenty-one verses) properly entitled *In the Workhouse: Christmas Day*, by George R. Sims (1847–1922). It was frequently burlesqued in the days of the MUSIC HALL and subsequently.

> It is Christmas Day in the Workhouse,
> And the cold bare walls are bright
> With garlands of green and holly,
> And the place is a pleasant sight:
> For with clean-washed hands and faces,
> In a long and hungry line
> The paupers sit at the tables
> For this is the hour they dine.

Christmas decorations. The Roman festival of SATURN was held in December and the temples were decorated with greenery; the DRUIDS are associated with MISTLETOE, and the Saxons used HOLLY and IVY. These customs have been transferred to the Christian festival. The holly or holy-tree is called Christ's thorn in Germany and Scandinavia, from its use in church decorations and its putting forth its berries about Christmas time. The early Christians gave an emblematic turn to the custom, referring to the "righteous branch", and justifying it from *Isaiah* lx, 13: "The glory of Lebanon shall come unto thee, the fir-tree, the pine-tree, and the box together, to beautify the place of my sanctuary."

The decorated Christmas tree was in use among the Romans and was introduced into England from Germany soon after Queen Victoria's marriage with Prince Albert of Saxe-Coburg-Gotha in 1840. SANTA CLAUS and his reindeer came to England at the same time.

Christopher, St. Legend relates that St. Christopher was a giant who one day carried a child over a brook, and said, "Chylde, thou hast put me in gret peryll. I might bere no greater burden." To which the child answered "Marvel thou nothing, for thou hast borne all the world upon thee, and its sins likewise." This is an allegory: Christopher means Christbearer; the child was Christ, and the river was the river of death.

Christy Minstrels. For many years the mid-Victorian publics of London and New York were entertained by the troupe of black-faced minstrels organized by the American Christy brothers (1815–1862). To an accompaniment of various stage-Negro antics they sang plantation songs and cracked innocent jokes with Bones, Sambo, and the rest. Stephen Collins Foster provided their best songs, of which *Beautiful Dreamer* is the most famous. They were succeeded by Moore and Burgess, and other troupes of the same genre.

> Why is it almost certain that Shakespeare was a broker?
> Because he furnished so many stock quotations.
> *The Merry Book of the Moore and Burgess Minstrels.*

Chronicle, Chronicon ex Chronicis. An early 12th-century chronicle from the creation to 1117 written by Florence, a monk of Worcester (d. 1118). It is largely based on Marianus Scotus, a lost version of the ANGLO-SAXON CHRONICLE, and Asser. His own contributions begin with 1106 and it was carried on to 1141 by John of Worcester.

To chronicle small beer. To note down events of no importance whatsoever. *See* SMALL BEER.

> She was a wight, if ever such wight were...
> To suckle fools and chronicle small beer.
>
> SHAKESPEARE: *Othello*, II, i.

Chronogram. A sentence or inscription in which certain letters stand for a date or epoch. In this double chronogram upon the year 1642 (one part in Latin and the other in the English of that Latin) the capitals in each produced the total of 1642.

TV DeVs IaM propItIVs sIs regI regnoq
Ve hVIC VnIVerso.
O goD noVV sheVV faVoVr to the kIng
anD thIs VVhoLe LanD.
VDVIMIIVIIVVICVIV   1642
DVVVVVVIDIVVLLD   1642

Chronon-hoton-thologos (krō' non hō' ton-thol' ō gos). A burlesque pomposo, king of Queerummania, in Henry Carey's farce of the same name—"the most tragical tragedy ever tragedized" (1734). The name is used for any bombastic person who delivers an inflated address.

Chrysippus. *Nisi Chrisippus fuisset, Porticus non est.* If Chrysippus had not been, there would be no Porticus (STOIC philosophy—the portico was the place where ZENO taught.). Chrysippus of Soli was a disciple of Zeno the Stoic and Cleanthes, his successor. He did for the Stoics what St. PAUL did for Christianity—that is, he explained the system, showed by plausible reasoning its truth, and how it was based on a solid foundation. Stoicism was founded by Zeno; but if Chrysippus had not been its advocate, it would never have taken root.

Chum. A crony, a familiar companion.

To chum up with. To become friendly with, to make a companion of.

Church. This is the O.E. *circe*, or *cirice*, which comes through W.Ger. *kirika*, from Gr. *kuriakon*, a church, the neuter of the adjective *kuriakos*, meaning of or belonging to the Lord. It denotes the whole body of Christians; the place of worship; a particular sect or group of Christians; the CLERGY.

Anglican Church The CHURCH OF ENGLAND.

Broad Church. *See* BROAD.

Catholic Church. *See* CATHOLIC.

Collegiate Churches. So called from having a college or chapter of CANONS or prebends under a DEAN. There were many such in mediæval England but they were mainly suppressed during the reign of Edward VI (1547–1553). St George's Chapel, Windsor and Westminster Abbey are surviving examples. Some of them eventually became cathedrals of new dioceses (*e.g.* at Manchester and Ripon).

Established Church. The church officially recognized and established by law and enjoying a privileged position. In England the established Church is Episcopalian, in Scotland it is PRESBYTERIAN. *See* EPISCOPACY.

Church of England. First severed its connexion with ROME under Henry VIII and subsequently under Elizabeth I (1559). Doctrinal changes were largely effected in the reign of Edward VI (1547–1553) and embodied in the BOOK OF COMMON PRAYER of 1549 and the more definitely PROTESTANT version of 1552.

Church of Ireland. This became PROTESTANT in the same way as the Church of England and, although most of the Irish remained Roman CATHOLIC, it was not disestablished and largely disendowed until 1869.

Church of North America (Episcopalian), was established in November 1784, when Bishop Seabury, chosen by the churches of Connecticut, was consecrated in Scotland. The first convention was held at Philadelphia in 1787.

Church of Scotland. It first became PRESBYTERIAN in 1560, but EPISCOPACY was cautiously restored by James VI and I from 1599, to be rejected finally in 1638. It is an ESTABLISHED CHURCH.

Church in Wales was separated from the province of Canterbury in 1920, after the long-standing agitation for disestablishment, which resulted in the Act of 1914 for this purpose.

Church Commissioners. *See* ECCLESIASTICAL COMMISSIONERS; QUEEN ANNE'S BOUNTY.

Church-ale. Also called *Easter-ale* and *Whitsun-ale* from their being sometimes held at EASTER and WHITSUNTIDE; a church festivity akin to the WAKES, when specially brewed ale was sold to the populace and money was collected in addition for church purposes. The word "ale" is used in such composite words as *bride-ale, church-ale, clerk-ale, lamb-ale, Midsummer-ale, Scot-*

ale etc., for revel or feast, ale being the chief liquor provided. Church-ales were unsuccessfully forbidden in 1603 but mostly came to an end during the INTERREGNUM.

> which mault being made into very strong ale, or beer, is set to sale, either in the church, or in some other place...If all be true which they say, they bestow the money which is got thereby for the repair of their churches and chappels; they buy bookes for the service, etc....
>
> PHILIP STUBBS: *Anatomie of Abuses* (1595).

Church scot. A tribute, earlier known as *food-rent*, paid on ST. MARTIN's Day (11 November) in corn and poultry, etc., to support the parish priests in Saxon times. It is named from the Early Saxon silver coin called a *sceat*.

High Church. *See* HIGH.

Low Church. *See* LOW.

Orthodox Church. *See* ORTHODOX.

The Church Army. A CHURCH OF ENGLAND evangelical body founded by the Rev. Wilson Carlile in 1882. It began its work among the poor of LONDON on somewhat similar lines to those of the SALVATION ARMY.

The Church Invisible. Those who are known to God alone as His sons and daughters by adoption and grace. *See* CHURCH VISIBLE.

> There is...a Church visible and a Church invisible; the latter consists of those spiritual persons who fulfil the notion of the Ideal Church—the former is the Church as it exists in any particular age, embracing within it all who profess Christianity.
>
> F. W. ROBERTSON: *Sermons* (series IV, ii).

The Church Militant. The Church or whole body of believers who are said to be "waging the war of faith" against "the world, the flesh and the DEVIL". It is therefore militant, or in warfare.

The Church Triumphant. Those who are dead and gone to their rest. Having fought the fight and triumphed, they belong to the Church Triumphant in HEAVEN.

The Church Visible. All ostensible Christians; all who profess to be Christians; all who have been baptized and admitted into the communion of the Church. *Cp.* CHURCH INVISIBLE.

The Seven Churches of Asia. *See* SEVEN.

To church a woman. To read the appointed service when a woman comes to church to give thanks after childbirth.

To go into the Church. To take HOLY ORDERS; to enter the ministry.

Uniat Churches. *See* UNIAT.

Churchwarden. A long clay pipe, such as churchwardens used to smoke a century or so ago when they met together in the parish tavern, after they had made up their accounts in the VESTRY, or been elected to office at the EASTER meeting.

Churchyard cough. A deep, chesty cough of an ominous kind. The allusion is obvious.

Churn Supper. *See* MELL SUPPER.

Churrigueresque (chu rig er esk'). Overornate as applied to architecture. The word, frequently used by Richard Ford (1796–1858) in his writings on Spain, derives from José Churriguera (1665–1725), a Spanish architect of the Baroque school.

Ci-devant (sē de vong) (Fr.). Former, of times gone by. As *Ci-devant governor*, once a governor but no longer so; *ci-devant philosophers*, philosophers of former days. In the time of the first French Republic the word was used as a noun meaning a nobleman of the ANCIEN RÉGIME.

Cicero (sis' er ō). Marcus Tullius, the great Roman orator, philosopher, and statesman (106–43 B.C.); said by Plutarch to have been called Cicero from Lat. *cicer* (a wart or vetch), because he had "a flat excrescence on the tip of his nose".

La Bouche de Cicéron. Philippe Pot, chief minister of Louis XI France (1428–1494).

The British Cicero. William Pitt, Earl of Chatham (1708–1778).

The Christian Cicero. Lucius Cœlius Lactantius or Lactantius Firmianus, a Christian Father (*c.* 260–*c.* 340).

The Cicero of France. Jean Baptiste Massillon (1663–1742), a noted pulpit orator.

The Cicero of Germany. John, Elector of Brandenburg (1486–1499).

The Cicero of the British Senate. George Canning (1770–1827).

The German Cicero, Johannes Sturm, printer and scholar (1507–1589).

Cicerone. A guide who points out objects of interest to strangers. So called from the great orator Cicero, in the same way as PAUL was called by the men of Lystra, "Mercurius, because he was the chief speaker."

Cicisbeo (chich is bā' ō). A dangler about women: the same as *cavaliere servente*; the professed gallant of a married woman. At one time in Italy it was unfashionable for a husband to associate with his wife in society or in public and she was accompanied by her cicisbeo. Also the knot of silk or ribbon which is attached to fans, walking sticks, umbrellas, etc.

Cid (sid). A corruption of *seyyid*, Arabic for lord. The title given to Roderigo or Ruy Diaz de Bivar (*c.* 1040–1099), also called El Campeador, the national hero of Spain and champion of Christianity against the MOORS. His exploits, real and legendary, form the basis of many Spanish romances and chronicles, as well as Corneille's tragedy *Le Cid* (1636).

Cid Hamet Benengeli. The supposititous author upon whom Cervantes fathered the *Adventures of Don Quixote*.

> If the two bad cassocks I am worth ... I would have given the latter of them freely as even as Cid Hamet offered his ... to have stood by.
>
> STERNE.

Cigars and Cigarettes. The word *cigar* comes from *cicada*, the Spanish name for the cigar-shaped insect. The natives of Cuba were already smoking tobacco in this form when Europeans first arrived. Cigars as we know them were introduced into the U.S.A. by General Putnam in 1762, on his return from the capture of Havana by the Earl of Albermarle.

Cheroots (from the Tamil *shuruttu*, a roll) are made from tobacco grown in Southern India, Burma or the Philippines, and are merely rolled with the ends cut square.

Cigarettes originated in Spain (Borrow calls them paper cigars, and the Spaniards *cigarrillos* or little cigars), first rolled by the smoker as he needed them. It was not until the late 19th century that they were sold in packets ready made.

Cimmerian Darkness (sĭ mēr' i àn). HOMER (possibly from some story as to the Arctic night) supposes the Cimmerians to dwell in a land "beyond the ocean stream", where the sun never shone (*Odys*. XI, 14). Spenser refers to "Cymerian shades" in *Virgil's Gnat* and Milton to "Cimmerian desert" in *L'Allegro*.

The Cimmerians were known in post-Homeric times as an historical people on the shores of the BLACK SEA, whence the name *Crimea*.

Cinch. It's a cinch. Dead easy, an absolute certainty. A phrase of American origin derived from the Mexican saddle girth which was strong, tight and safe (Sp. *cincha*, girth).

Cinchona (sin chō' na), or **Quinine.** So named from the wife of the Conte del Chinchon, viceroy of Peru, who was cured of a tertian fever by its use, and who brought it to Europe in 1640. Linnæus erroneously named it *Cin*chona for *Chin*chona. *See* PERUVIAN BARK.

Cincinnatus (sin si nā' tus). A legendary Roman hero of about 500 to 430 B.C., who, after having been consul years before, was taken from his plough to be Dictator. After he had conquered the Æquians and delivered his country from danger, he laid down his office and returned to his plough.

The Cincinnatus of the Americans. George Washington (1732–1799).

The Cincinnati were members of a society of officers of the American Army after the peace of 1783 "to perpetuate friendship, and to raise a fund for relieving the widows and orphans of those who have fallen during the war". On their badge was a figure of Cincinnatus.

The Ohio city of this name, formerly Losantiville, was renamed in 1790 in honour of General St. Clair, governor of the North West Territory, who was president of the Cincinnati.

Cinderella (sin der rel'à). Heroine of a fairy tale of very ancient, probably Eastern, origin, found in German literature in the 16th century and popularized by Perrault's *Contes de ma mère l'oye* (1697). Cinderella is drudge of the house, while her elder sisters go to fine balls. At length, a fairy enables her to go to the prince's ball; the prince falls in love with her, and she is found again by means of a glass slipper which she drops, and which will fit no foot but her own.

The glass slipper has been conjectured as a fur or sable slipper, supposedly from *pantoufle de vair* not *de verre*. Perrault's text of 1697 has "*de verre*", which is more in keeping with the story.

Cinquecento (ching' kwè chen' tō). The Italian name for the 16th century, applied as an epithet to art and literature with much the same significance as RENAISSANCE or Elizabethan. It was the revival of the classical or antique, but is also understood as a derogatory term, implying debased or inferior art.

Cinque Ports (sink). Originally the five Kent and Sussex seaports of Hastings, Sandwich, Dover, Romney, and Hythe, which were known by this name collectively from the 12th century and were granted special privileges in consideration of their providing ships and men for the defence of the Channel. Winchelsea and Rye were subsequently added and there were ultimately thirty-two lesser members. Their privileges were largely surrendered in 1685. The Duke of Wellington and Sir Winston Churchill are among those who have held the office of Lord Warden of the Cinque Ports. In 1965 Sir Robert Menzies, Prime Minister of Australia, was given this appointment. H.M. Queen Elizabeth, the Queen Mother, was made Lord Warden in 1978.

Barons of the Cinque Ports. *See under* BARON.

Circe (sĕr' si). A sorceress in Greek mythology, who lived in the island of Ææa. When ULYSSES landed there, Circe turned his companions into swine, but Ulysses resisted this metamorphosis by virtue of a herb called MOLY, given him by MERCURY.

Who knows not Circe,
The daughter of the sun, whose charmed cup
Whoever tasted, lost his upright shape,
And downward fell into a grovelling swine?

MILTON: *Comus*, 50–3.

Circle. Great circle. A line on the surface of a sphere which lies on a plane through its centre, or any circle which divides it into two equal parts. The great circle is of major importance in navigation by sea or in the air. The shortest distance between any two points on the earth's surface is on a great circle. The Equator and all lines of longitude are great circles.

Circle of Ulloa. A white rainbow or luminous ring sometimes seen in Alpine regions opposite the sun in foggy weather. Named from Antonio de Ulloa (1716–1795), a Spanish naval officer who founded the observatory at Cadiz and initiated many scientific enterprises.

Circuit, Judicial. The journey through the counties formerly made by the judges twice a year to administer justice at the Assizes, a system changed by the Courts Act of 1971. Circuit Judges are now appointed having criminal jurisdiction in the Crown Courts and civil jurisdiction in the County Courts. The circuits, each with their number of judicial centres, are now, the Western, the South-Eastern (including London), the Midland and Oxford, the Northern, the North-Eastern, and the Wales and Chester. Apart from Edinburgh, the Scottish circuits are the Western, the Northern and the Southern.

Circuit Rider. A METHODIST minister in America who rode on horseback round the outlying stations of his circuit to preach and perform other pastoral duties. Francis Asbury, a follower of John Wesley, began the practice in 1771.

Circumcellions. *See* AGONISTICS.

Circumlocution Office. A term applied in ridicule by Charles Dickens in *Little Dorrit* to our public offices, because each person tries to shuffle off every act to someone else; and before anything is done it has to pass through so many departments with such consequent delays that it is hardly worth having bothered about it.

Whatever was required to be done, the Circumlocution Office was beforehand with all the public departments in the art of perceiving—How not to do it.

DICKENS: *Little Dorrit*, ch. x.

Cist (kist) (Gr. *kiste*, Lat. *cista*). A chest or box, generally used as a coffer for the remains of the dead by prehistoric man, made from flat stones placed on edge with another stone as a lid, and usually covered by a round barrow. The Greek and Roman cist was a deep cylindrical basket made of wickerwork. The basket into which voters cast their tablets was called a *cist*; but the mystic cist used in the rites of CERES was latterly made of bronze. *Cp.* KIST OF WHISTLES.

Cistercians. A monastic order, founded at Cistercium or Cîteaux (near Dijon) in 1098, by Robert, abbot of Molesme, as strict BENEDICTINES. They are also known as Grey or White Monks from their habit and as *Bernadines* from St. Bernard of Clairvaux, who with thirty companions joined the abbey of Cîteaux in 1113. They were noted agriculturalists, and in the 13th-century England became a great producer of wool.

Citizen King, The. Louis Philippe of France. So called because he was elected King of the French (1830–1848), not King of France, after the downfall of Charles X. He was the son of PHILIPPE ÉGALITÉ

City. A town thus incorporated by charter; any large town is so called in ordinary speech. In England, the term is of historical and ceremonial rather than administrative significance. In the BIBLE, it means a town having walls and gates.

The City. The City of LONDON within its historic boundaries as distinct from other London boroughs; also a general term for the business and financial interests of the City of London.

The Big City. London.

The City College. An old irony for NEWGATE GAOL.

The City of a Hundred Towers. Pavia, in Italy; famous for its towers and steeples.

The City of Bells. Strasbourg.

The City of Brotherly Love. Philadelphia. A somewhat ironical but quite etymological nickname for this city (Gr. *philadelphia*, brotherly love).

The City of David. Jerusalem. So called in compliment to King David (II *Sam.* v, 7, 9).

The City of Destruction. In Bunyan's *Pilgrim's Progress*, the world of the unconverted.

The City of Dreaming Spires. Oxford. A name derived from Matthew Arnold's *Thyrsis*: "that sweet City with her dreaming spires".

The City of Dreadful Knights. Cardiff. After World War I, Lloyd George, Prime Minister in the Coalition government, made lavish grants of honours in a cynical and blatant fashion. In 1922 Lord Salisbury opened an attack and it was alleged that the government had fixed prices for the sale of titles, the money being put into party political funds. The CONSERVATIVE PARTY profited as did Lloyd George's private party chest. As a consequence, a Royal Commission was set up in 1922 to recommend future procedure. Three people connected with prominent South Wales newspapers were among the recipients of these honours, hence Cardiff was dubbed the "City of Dreadful Knights", a punning allusion to *The City of Dreadful Night*, a poem by James Thomson (1834–1882).

The City of Elms. New Haven, Connecticut.

The City of God. The Church, or whole body of believers; the Kingdom of Christ, in contradistinction to the CITY OF DESTRUCTION. The phrase is from St. Augustine's famous work, *De Civitate Dei*.

The City of Lanterns. A suppositious city in Lucian's *Verae Historiae*, situated somewhere beyond the ZODIAC. *Cp.* LANTERNLAND.

The City of Legions. Caerleon-on-Usk, where King ARTHUR held his court.

The City of Lilies. Florence.

The City of Magnificent Distances. Washington, D.C., famous for its wide avenues and splendid vistas.

The City of Palaces. Agrippa, in the reign of AUGUSTUS, converted ROME from "a city of brick huts to one of marble palaces".

> Marmoream se relinquere quam latericiam accepisset.
> SUETONIUS: *Aug.* xxix.

Calcutta is also called the "City of Palaces".

The City of St. Michael. Dumfries, of which St. MICHAEL is the patron SAINT.

The City of Saints. Montreal is so named because of its streets named after SAINTS. Salt Lake City, Utah, U.S.A., is also so called, from its MORMON inhabitants.

The City of the Golden Gate. San Francisco. *See* GOLDEN GATE.

The City of the Prophet. MEDINA. *See* CITIES OF REFUGE.

The City of the Seven Hills. ROME, built on seven hills (*Urbs Septacollis*). The hills are the Aventine, Cælian, Capitoline, Esquiline, Palatine, Quirinal, and Viminal.

> The Aventine Hill was given to the people. It was deemed unlucky because here Remus was slain. It was also called "Collis Dianæ", from the temple of DIANA which stood there.
> The Cælian Hill was given to Cælius Vibenna, the Tuscan, who came to the help of the Romans in the Sabine war.
> The Capitoline Hill of "Mons Tarpeius", also called "Mons Saturni", on which stood the great castle or citadel of Rome. It contained the Temple of Jupiter Capitolinus.
> The Esquiline Hill was given by AUGUSTUS to

MÆCENAS, who built thereon a magnificent mansion which he bequeathed to Augustus.
> The Palatine Hill was the largest of the seven. Here Romulus held his court, whence the word "palace" (*palatium*).
> The Quirinal Hill was where the Quirés or Curés settled. It was also called "Cabalinus", from two marble statues of a horse, one of which was the work of Phidias, the other of Praxiteles.
> The Viminal Hill was so called from the number of osiers (*vimines*) which grew there. It contained the Temple of Jupiter Viminalis.

The City of the Sun. Baalbec, Rhodes, and Heliopolis, which had the sun for tutelary deity, were so called. It is also the name of a treatise on the Ideal Republic by the Dominican Friar Campanella (1568–1639), similar to the REPUBLIC of Plato, UTOPIA of Sir Thomas More, and the NEW ATLANTIS of Bacon.

The City of the Three Kings. Cologne; the reputed burial place of the MAGI.

The City of the Tribes. Galway; because it was anciently the home of the thirteen "tribes" or chief families, who settled there in 1232 with Richard de Burgh.

The City of the Violated Treaty. Limerick; because of the way the Pacification of Limerick (1691) was broken by England.

The City of the Violet Crown. Athens is so called by Aristophanes (*Equites*, 1323 and 1329; and *Acharnians*, 637). Macaulay refers to Athens as the "violet-crowned city". Ion (a violet) was a legendary king of ATHENS, whose four sons gave names to the four Athenian tribes; and Greece in Asia Minor was called Ionia. Athens was the city of "Ion crowned its king" or "of the Violet crowned".

Cities of Refuge. Six walled cities (*Joshua*, xxxv, 6), three on each side of the Jordan, set aside under MOSAIC LAW as a refuge for those who committed accidental homicide. Such refuges were necessitated by the primitive law which exacted blood vengeance by next of kin. All seeking asylum were tried, and if found guilty of murder right of asylum was withdrawn. The cities were Ramoth, Kedesh, Bezer, Shechem, Hebron, and Golam (*Joshua* xx, 7, 8). In *Numbers* xxxv, and other references, the choice of cities is attributed to Moses, but in *Joshua* xx, to Joshua.

Among Mohammedans, MEDINA, in Arabia, where MOHAMMED took refuge when driven by conspirators from MECCA, is known as "the City of Refuge". He entered it, not as a fugitive, but in triumph (622 A.D.). Also called the *City of the Prophet*.

The Cities of the Plain. Sodom and Gomorrah.

> Abram dwelled in the land of Canaan, and Lot

dwelled in the cities of the plain, and pitched his tent towards Sodom.

Gen. xiii, 12.

Inner Cities. Properly speaking, the central areas of large towns but currently applied to those districts housing whites and non-whites where overcrowding, poverty and racial tension are prevalent although, geographically, they are often nearer the fringe than the centre. In numerous cases crime and violence have driven away established residents and businesses.

Civil List. The annual grant to the Crown and Royal Family, voted by PARLIAMENT for royal expenditure from the CONSOLIDATED FUND. It was so named in the early 18th century because the salaries of Civil Servants, Judges, etc., were paid from it (until 1831) and it has its origins in the reign of William III.

George III gave up most of the hereditary revenues in 1760 in return for an annual grant. In 1978 it was over £2,000,000. *See* ROYAL BOUNTY.

Civil Service. This name for all those employed in administering the civil business of the State was originally used by the English East India Company to distinguish its civilian employees from its soldiers.

Civil Service Estimates. The annual Parliamentary grant to cover the expenses of the diplomatic service, the Home Office, the prison service, education, the collection of the revenue, and various other expenses pertaining to neither the sovereign nor the armed services of the Crown.

Civil War. War between citizens (*civiles*) of the same state. In English history, the term is particularly applied to the war between Charles I and PARLIAMENT; but the BARONS' WAR and the Wars of the Roses (*see under* ROSE) were also civil wars. The U.S.A. was confronted with a costly civil war between 1861 and 1865, when the eleven CONFEDERATE STATES sought to secede from the Union.

Civis Romanus sum (siv' is rō mā'nus-sŭm). "I am a Roman citizen", a plea which sufficed to stop arbitrary condemnation, bonds, and scourging. No Roman citizen could be condemned unheard; by the Valerian Law he could not be bound; by the Sempronian Law it was forbidden to scourge him or beat him with rods. When the chief captain commanded PAUL "should be examined by scourging", he asked, "Is it lawful for you to scourge a man that is a Roman, and uncondemned?" (*Acts*, xxii, 24–25). *See also Acts* xvi, 37, etc.

The phrase gained an English fame from the peroration of Palmerston's great speech in the House of Commons (24 June, 1850) over the Don PACIFICO affair: "As the Roman, in days of old, held himself free from indignity, when he could say *Civis Romanus sum*, so also a British subject, in whatever land he may be, shall feel confident that the watchful eye and the strong arm of England will protect him against injustice and wrong."

Civvies. Civilians or civilian clothes as opposed to military uniform. *See* MUFTI.

Civvie Street (siv' i). The usual term by which members of the armed services refer to civilian life.

Clack Dish. A dish or basin with a movable lid. Some two or three centuries ago, beggars used to proclaim their want by clacking the lid of a wooden dish.

> Can you think, I get my living by a bell and clack-dish?—
> How's that?
> Why, begging, sir?
> THOMAS MIDDLETON: *Family of Love* (1608).

Clam. A bivalve mollusc like an oyster, which burrows in sand or mud. In America especially, clams are esteemed a delicacy and are gathered only when the tide is out. Hence the saying, "Happy as a clam at high tide." The word is also used as slang for the mouth, and for a close-mouthed person.

Close as a clam. Mean, close-fisted; from the difficulty with which a clam is made to open its shell.

Clameur de Haro *See* HARO.

Clan. This is from the mediæval Latin *planta*, a branch. The prevalent idea that the Scottish Highland clan consisted of the chief of a family and his followers, related by ties of kinship and bearing his name, is unsound. It comprised the chief and his followers irrespective of descent, and only in its narrowest sense applies to the chief, his family, and kindred. The legal power and hereditary jurisdiction of the head of a clan was abolished in 1747 after the '45 Rebellion. The phrase **a gathering of the clans** implies any assembly of like-minded persons, usually for convivial purposes.

Clan-na-Gael (Klăn'nà gāl'). An Irish FENIAN organization founded in Philadelphia in 1881, and known in secret as the "United Brotherhood". Its object was to secure "the complete and absolute independence of Ireland from Great Britain, and the complete severance of all political connexion between the two countries, to be effected by unceasing preparation for armed insurrection in Ireland".

Clancy of the Overflow. The hero of *Bush*

Ballads by A. B. (Banjo) Paterson (1864–1941), author of the words of WALTZ-ING MATILDA. Clancy may have been drawn in part from T. M. Macnamara, a first-class shot, horseman and bushman, who died in 1943 at the age of 94.

Clapham Sect. The name bestowed by Sydney Smith upon the group of EVANGELICALS with common social and political interests most of whom lived in Clapham at the end of the 18th and in the early 19th centuries. William Wilberforce (1759–1833) the ABOLITIONIST was their leader. Henry Thornton the banker, Zachary Macaulay, John Venn and James Stephen were among his close associates. Their opponents derisively called them "the Saints".

Clapperclaw. To jangle, to claw or scratch; to abuse, revile; originally meaning to claw with a clapper of some sort.

> Now they are clapper-clawing one another; I'll go look on.
>
> SHAKESPEARE: *Troilus and Cressida*. V, iv.

Clapper-dudgeon. An ABRAM-MAN, a beggar from birth. The clapper is the tongue of the bell, and in CANT language the tongue. Dudgeon is the hilt of a dagger; and perhaps the original meaning is one who knocks his *clap dish* or CLACK DISH with a dudgeon.

Clap-trap. Something introduced to win applause: something really worthless but sure to take with the groundlings. A *trap* to catch applause.

Claque (klăk). A body of hired applauders at a theatre, etc.; said to have been originated or first systematized by a M. Sauton, who, in 1820, established in Paris an office to secure the success of dramatic performances. The manager ordered the required number of *claqueurs*, who were divided into *commis-saires*, those who commit the piece to memory, and noisily point out its merits; *rieurs*, who laugh at the puns and jokes; *pleureurs*, chiefly women who hold their handkerchiefs to their eyes at the emotional parts; *chatouil-leurs*, who are to keep the audience in good humour; and *bisseurs*, who are to cry BIS (encore). *Claque* is also the French for an opera-hat. Thackeray thus uses it.

> A gentleman in black with ringlets and a tuft stood gazing fiercely about him, with one hand in the arm-hole of his waistcoat and the other holding his cla-que.
>
> *Pendennis*, ch. xxv.

Clare. County Clare Election. The famous election of 1828 which resulted in the return of the CATHOLIC candidate, Daniel O'Connell, and which brought about the Catholic Emancipation Act of 1829.

Clare, Order of St. A religious order of wo-men founded in 1212, the second that St. Francis instituted. The name derives from their first abbess, Clare of Assisi. The nuns are also called Clarisses, Poor Clares, Min-oresses, or Nuns of the Order of St. Francis. *See* FRANCISCANS.

Clarenceux King of Arms (klăr′ en sū). The second of the three English Kings of Arms, under the head of the College of Arms, having jurisdiction over the counties east, west and south of the Trent. The office was insti-tuted by the Duke of Clarence, third son of Edward III. *See* HERALDRY.

Clarendon Code. The famous four acts passed by the CAVALIER PARLIAMENT, named after the King's minister, the Earl of Claren-don, although he was not their originator. They comprise the Corporation Act (1661), the Act of Uniformity (1662), the Conven-ticle Act (1664), and the Five-Mile Act (1665). They were directed against the NON-CONFORMISTS.

Clarendon Press. The University of Ox-ford Press when housed in the Clarendon Building, and subsequently used as an im-print for many of its publications. Edward Hyde, Earl of Clarendon (1609–1674) be-queathed the copyright of his *History of the Rebellion* to the university, and the profits from its publication (1702–1704) were used to build a new printing-house named after him, the home of the press until 1830. Clar-endon was a former student of Magdalen Hall and Chancellor of the University from 1660 to 1667.

Clarendon type. A bold-faced condensed type, such as that used for a CATCHWORD or words.

The Constitutions of Clarendon. Laws made by Henry II at a council held at Clar-endon in Wiltshire in 1164, to check the power of the Church and to restrain the pre-rogatives of ecclesiastics. These sixteen or-dinances defined the limits of the patronage and jurisdiction of the POPE in England.

Claret. The English name for the red wines of Bordeaux, originally the yellowish or light red wines as distinguished from the white wines. The name (which is not used in France) is the O.Fr. *clairet*, diminutive of *clair*, from Lat. *clarus*, clear. The *colour* re-ceives its name from the wine.

Claret cup. A drink made of claret, brandy, lemon, borage, sugar, ice, and carbonated water. *See* BADMINTON.

To broach one's claret, or **to tap one's claret jug.** To give one a bloody nose, *See* BADMINTON.

Claribel. The pen-name of Mrs. Charlotte Alington-Barnard (1830–1869), writer of many one-time popular ballads, the best known being *Come back to Erin*.

Clark(e). Nobby Clark(e) is the popular name used by British army and navy personnel for every man of the name of Clark(e). It originated in the dressy or "NOBBY" turn-out affected by clerks and other blackcoated workers of the early 19th century.

Clary Water. A cordial of bygone days made from an infusion of the flowers of wild sage or clary in brandy, flavoured with cinnamon.

Classics. The best authors. The Romans were divided by Servius into five classes. Any citizen who belonged to the highest class was called *classicus*, all the rest were said to be *infra classem* (unclassed). From this the best authors were termed *classici auctores* (classic authors), *i.e.* authors of the best or first class. The high esteem in which Greek and Latin authors were held at the RENAISSANCE obtained for these authors the name of *classic*. When other first-rate works are intended some distinctive name is added, as the English, French, Spanish, etc., classics.

Classic Races. The five chief horse-races in England all for three-year-olds, namely: The One Thousand Guineas (fillies only), and the Two Thousand Guineas (fillies and colts), both run at Newmarket; the OAKS, the DERBY, and the ST. LEGER. *See* RACES.

Claude Lorraine (*i.e.* of Lorraine). This incorrect form is generally used in English for the name of Claude Gellée (1600–1682), the French landscape painter, born at Chamagne in Lorraine.

Clause Rolls. *See* CLOSE ROLLS.

Clavie. Burning of the Clavie on New Year's Eve (old style) in the village of Burghead, on the southern shore of the Moray Firth. The clavie is a sort of bonfire made of casks split up. One of the casks is split into two parts of different sizes, and an important item of the ceremony is to join these parts together with a huge nail made for the purpose. Whence the name, from *clavus* (Lat.), a nail. Chambers in his *Book of Days* (vol. II, p. 789) minutely describes the ceremony and suggests that it is a relic of DRUID worship. The two unequal divisions of the cask possibly symbolize the unequal parts of the old and new year.

Claw. Claw me I will claw thee. "Praise me, and I will praise you", or "scratch my back, and I'll scratch yours". To claw meaning to tear or scratch, formerly also meant to stroke or tickle; hence to please, flatter or praise.

> Laugh when I am merry, and claw no man in his humour.
> SHAKESPEARE: *Much Ado About Nothing*, I, iii.

Claw-backs. Flatterers. Bishop Jewel (1522–1571) speaks of "the Pope's claw-backs".

Clay, To have feet of. *See under* FOOT.

Clean. Free from blame or fault.

> Create in me a clean heart, O God, and renew a right spirit within me.
> *Psalm*, li, 10.

Used adverbially, it means entirely, wholly: as "you have grown clean out of knowledge", *i.e.* wholly beyond recognition.

> Contricioun hadde clene forgeten to crye and to wepe.
> *Piers Plowman*, xx.
> The people were passed clean over Jordan.
> *Joshua*, iii, 17.

A clean tongue. Not abusive, not profane, not addicted to swearing.

To clean down. To sweep down, to swill down.

To clean out. To purify, to make tidy. Also, to win another's money till his pocket is quite empty; to completely impoverish someone. De Quincey says that Richard Bentley, after his lawsuit with Dr. Colbatch, "must have been pretty well cleaned out".

To clean up. To wash up, to put in order; to wash oneself.

To have clean hands. To be quite clear of some stated evil. Hence *to keep the hands clean*, not to be involved in wrongdoing; and "clean handed".

> He that hath clean hands and pure heart.
> *Psalm* xxiv, 4.

To live a clean life. To live blameless and undefiled.

To make a clean breast of it. To make a full and unreserved confession.

To make a clean sweep. To dispose completely of anything; to get rid of materials, methods or staff regarded as obsolete or redundant. *See under* BROOM.

To show a clean bill of health. *See* BILL.

To show a clean pair of heels. To run away, to make one's escape by superior speed. Here *clean* means free from obstruction.

Clean and unclean animals. Among the Jews of the OLD TESTAMENT (*see Lev.* xi) those animals which chew the cud and part the hoof were clean and might be eaten. Hares and rabbits could not be eaten because (although they chew the cud) they do not part the hoof. Pigs and camels were unclean, because (although they part the hoof) they do not chew the cud. Birds of prey were accounted unclean. Fish with fins and scales were accounted fit food for man.

According to PYTHAGORAS, who taught

the doctrine of the TRANSMIGRATION OF THE SOUL, it was lawful for man to eat only those animals into which the human soul never entered, the others being held unclean. This notion existed long before the time of Pythagoras, who learnt it in Egypt.

Cleanliness is next to godliness. An old saying, quoted by John Wesley (*Sermon* xcii, *On Dress*), Matthew Henry, and others. The origin is said to be found in the writings of Phinehas ben Yair, an ancient rabbi.

Clear (verb). **To be quite cleared out.** To have spent all one's money; to have nothing left. *Cleared out* means, my purse or pocket is cleared out of money.

To clear an examination paper. To floor it, to answer every question.

To clear away. To remove, to melt away, to disappear.

To clear for action. To prepare for action, TO CLEAR THE DECKS.

To clear off. To make oneself scarce, to remove oneself or something.

To clear out. To eject; to empty out, to make tidy, to make off.

To clear out for Guam. An obsolete shipping phrase; used when a ship was bound for no specific port. In the height of the gold rushes ships carried passengers to Australia without making arrangements for return cargoes. They were, therefore, obliged to leave Melbourne in ballast, and to sail in search of homeward freights. The Customs regulations required that some port should be specified on clearing outwards, so it became the habit of captains to name Guam (a small island of the Ladrone group) as their hypothetical destination.

To clear the air. To get rid of sultriness, oppressiveness, etc.; figuratively, to remove misunderstandings or ambiguities of a situation, argument, etc.

To clear the court. To remove all strangers, or persons not officially concerned in the suit.

To clear the customs. To have been inspected and dealt with by the customs officers.

To clear the decks. To remove everything not required, especially when preparing for action; playfully used of eating everything available on the table at mealtimes.

To clear the dishes. To empty them of their contents, or TO CLEAR THE TABLE.

To clear the land. As a nautical phrase means to have good SEA ROOM, to escape from the land.

To clear the room. To remove from it everything or person not required.

To clear the table. To remove what has been placed upon it.

To clear up. To become fine after rain or cloudiness; to make manifest; to elucidate what was obscure; to tidy up.

Clear (adjective). Used adverbially, clear has much the same force as the adverb CLEAN—wholly, entirely: as, "He is gone clear away", "Clear out of sight".

A clear day. An entire, complete day. "The bonds must be left three clear days for examination", means that they must be left for three days not counting the first or last. It also means a cloudless day, or one free from engagements.

A clear head. A mind that is capable of understanding things clearly.

A clear statement. A straightforward and intelligible statement.

A clear style (of writing). A lucid method of expressing one's thoughts.

A clear voice. A voice of pure intonation, neither husky, mouthy, nor throaty.

Clear grit. The right spirit, real pluck; the genuine article, the real thing. A phrase of American origin.

In Canadian politics of the early 1880s the radicals were called *Clear-grits*.

Clearing House. The office or house where bankers do their "clearing", that is, the exchanging of bills and cheques and the payment of balances, etc. In LONDON, the bankers' clearing house has been in LOMBARD Street since 1775. Each bank sends to it daily all the bills and cheques not drawn on its own firm; these are sorted and distributed to their respective houses, and the balance is settled by transfer tickets. *A clearing banker* is a banker who has the ENTRÉE of the CLEARING HOUSE.

Similarly the railway companies formed a clearing house to organize through traffic on each others' lines and to adjust payment. Other examples are those existing for sorting out and passing on applications to the various teacher training colleges and universities.

Cleave. Two quite distinct words, the one meaning to *stick to*, and the other to *part asunder*. A man "shall cleave to his wife" (Matt. xix, 5), the former, is the O.E. *clifian*, to stick to; as one that "cleaveth wood" (*Ps*. cxli, 7), the latter, is *cleofan*, to split.

Cleft stick, To be caught in a. Figuratively to be caught in two awkward situations which combine to embarrass one. The form of torture inflicted on ARIEL by the witch Sycorax in SHAKESPEARE'S *The Tempest* (I, ii) was to confine him in the trunk of a cleft pine tree.

Clement, St. Patron SAINT of tanners, being

himself a tanner. His day is 23 November, and his symbol is an anchor, because he is said to have been martyred by being thrown into the sea tied to an anchor.

Clench, and **clinch.** The latter is a variant of the former, which is the M.E. *clenchen,* from O.E. *(be-) clencan,* to hold fast. In many uses the two words are practically synonymous, meaning to grasp firmly, to fasten firmly together, to make firm; but clench is used in such phrases as "he clenched his fists", "he clenched his fingers firmly to endure the pain", "to clench one's teeth"; while clinch is used in the more material senses, such as to turn the point of a nail in order to make it fast, and also in the phrase "to clinch an argument". In business "to clinch a deal" is to settle it, to make it certain.

That was a clincher. That argument was not to be gainsaid; that remark drove the matter home, and fixed it.

Cleopatra (klē ō pǎt′ rả). (69–30 B.C.). She was Queen of Egypt, being joint ruler with and wife of her brother Ptolemy Dionysius. In 48 B.C. she was driven from the throne, but was reinstated in 47 by Julius Cæsar, by whom she had a son. In 41 Mark Antony fell under her spell and repudiated his wife Octavia. When he was defeated at Actium by Octavian, he committed suicide, and Cleopatra is supposed to have killed herself by means of the bite of an asp.

Cleopatra and her pearl. It is said that Cleopatra gave a banquet for Antony at Alexandria, the costliness of which excited his astonishment. When Antony expressed his surprise she took a pearl eardrop and dissolved it in her drink, the further to impress him.

A similar story is told of Sir Thomas Gresham when Queen Elizabeth I visited the ROYAL EXCHANGE. He is said to have pledged her health in a cup of wine in which a precious stone worth £15,000 had been crushed to atoms.

Heywood refers to this in his play *If you know not me you know nobody* (1604):

Here fifteen thousand pounds at one clap goes
Instead of sugar; Gresham drinks the pearl
Unto his queen and mistress.

Cleopatra's Needle. The OBELISK so called, now on the Thames Embankment, was brought from Alexandria in 1877, whither it and its fellow (now in Central Park, New York) had been moved from Heliopolis by Augustus about 14 B.C. It has no connexion with Cleopatra other than having been in her capital, Alexandria, and was ori-

ginally set up by Thotmes III about 1500 B.C.

Cleopatra's nose. Blaise Pascal (1623-1662) wrote, "If the nose of Cleopatra had been shorter, the whole face of the earth would have been changed" (*Pensées* viii, 29). The allusion is to the momentous effects brought about by her conquest, through her charm and beauty, first of Julius Cæsar, then of Mark Antony.

Clergy. Ultimately from Gr. *kleros,* a lot or inheritance, with reference to *Deut.* xviii, 21 and *Acts* i, 17; thus, the men of God's lot or inheritance. In St. Peter's First Epistle (ch. v, 3) the Church is called "God's heritage" or lot. In the OLD TESTAMENT the tribe of Levi is called the "lot or heritage of the Lord".

Clergy, Benefit of. *See* BENEFIT.

Clerical Titles. *Clerk.* In remote times the clergyman was usually one of the few who could read and write, so the word *clerical,* as used in "clerical error", came to mean an orthographical error. As the respondent in church was able to read, he received the name of clerk, and the assistants in writing, etc., were so termed in business (Late Lat. *clericus,* a clergyman).

Curate. One who has the cure of souls in a parish. Properly a rector, vicar, or perpetual curate, but the word curate is now generally used to denote an "assistant" curate or unbeneficed clergyman.

Parson. The same word as *person.* As Blackstone says, a parson is *"persona ecclesiae,* one that hath full rights of the parochial church".

Though we write "parson" differently, yet 'tis but "person"; that is the individual person set apart for the service of such a church, and 'tis in Latin *persona,* and *personatus* is a parsonage. Indeed with the canon lawyers, *personatus* is any dignity or preferment in the church.

SELDEN: *Table-talk.*

Rector. One who received the great TITHES. From Lat. *rector,* a ruler—the man who rules and guides the parish.

Vicar. Originally one who does the "duty" of a parish for the owner or owners of the tithes (Lat. *vicarius,* a deputy). *Perpetual Curates* are now termed Vicars.

The French *curé* equals our vicar, and their *vicaire* our curate.

In the U.S.A. a vicar is the priest of a chapel, dependent on a church.

Clerical vestments. *White.* Emblem of purity, worn on all feasts, saints' days, and sacramental occasions.

Red. The colour of blood and of fire, worn on the days of martyrs, and on WHIT SUNDAY, when the HOLY GHOST came down like

tongues of fire. Now also used on GOOD FRI-
DAY.

Green. Worn on days which are neither
feasts nor fasts.

Purple. The colour of mourning, worn on
ADVENT Sundays, in LENT, and on EMBER
DAYS. Now used on Good Friday in some
churches.

Black. Formerly worn on Good Friday;
worn when masses are said for the dead.

Clerihew (kler´ i hū). The name given to a
particular kind of humorous verse invented
by E. Clerihew Bentley (1875–1956). It is
usually satirical and often biographical, consisting of four rhymed lines of uneven
length. For inclusion in this Dictionary Mr.
Bentley suggested the following:

> It was a weakness of Voltaire's
> To forget to say his prayers,
> And one which, to his shame,
> He never overcame.

He also wrote:

> Sir Christopher Wren
> Said "I'm going to dine with some men.
> If anyone calls,
> Say I'm designing St. Paul's."

Clerk-ale *See* CHURCH-ALE.

Clerk of the Weather. A humorous personification of whatever forces govern the
weather.

Clerkenwell (klark´ en wel). At the holy well
in this district the parish clerks of LONDON
used to assemble yearly to play some sacred
piece.

Clew up. To draw up the lower ends of square
sails to the upper yard ready for furling. Figuratively, to finish something completely, to tie it up leaving no loose ends.

Clicquot (klē kō). A nickname of Frederick
William IV of Prussia (1795–1861), so called
from his fondness for champagne, in allusion to the well-known brand Veuve Clicquot. *See* WIDOW.

Cliff-hanger. Figuratively, a state of affairs
producing anxiety. From the early serial adventure films where the hero was often left in
such a hazardous plight in order to whet the
cinema-goer's appetite for the next instalment.

Climacteric (klī măk´ tér ik). It was once believed by astrologers that the 7th and 9th
years, with their multiples, especially the
odd multiples (21, 27, 35, 45, 49, 63, and
81), were critical points in life; these were
called the *Climacteric Years* and were presided over by SATURN, the malevolent planet. 63, which is produced by multiplying 7
and 9 together, was termed the *Grand Climacteric*, which few persons succeeded in
outliving.

Climate of Opinion. The way people in general think and feel about matters, the state of
opinion. A hackneyed vogue phrase much
used in political speeches and writings of the
mid-20th century.

Climb down, To. To abandon as untenable
an attitude or opinion that one has hitherto
vigorously supported.

Climbing the ladder. To progress in one's
career or to move upwards, socially and
financially. **Why kick down the ladder by
which you have climbed?** is an allied expression, meaning — Why seek to destroy
the opportunities and facilities, educational
and otherwise, by means of which you have
risen?

Clinch, Clincher. *See* CLENCH.

Clink. Slang term for prison, derived from the
famous gaol, the Clink in SOUTHWARK, destroyed in the Gordon Riots of 1780.

Clio (klī´ ō). One of the nine MUSES, the inven-
tress of historical and heroic poetry, the
Muse of history. Hence the pun, "Can Clio
do more than amuse?"

Addison adopted the name as a pseudonym, and many of his papers in the *Spectator* are signed by one of the four letters in this
word, probably the initial letters of where
they were written—of Chelsea, LONDON, Islington, Office. *Cp.* NOTARIKON.

Clip-joint. A night club or place of entertainment where patrons are grossly overcharged
or cheated, *i.e.* clipped.

Clipper. A fast sailing-ship, first built at Baltimore about 1830; in Smyth's *Sailors Word
Book* (1867) described as "formerly applied
to the sharp-built raking schooners of America, and latterly to Australian passenger-
ships" (*see* CUTTY SARK). The name was applied in the mid-20th century to a transatlantic flying-boat.

She's a clipper. Said of a stylish or beautiful woman.

Clippie (klip´ i). A popular nickname for bus
conductresses during and since World War
II, since they clipped or punched the tickets.

Cliveden Set. The name given to the right-
wing politicians and journalists who gathered for week-end parties in the late 1930s at
Cliveden, the country home of Lord and
Lady Astor in Buckinghamshire. They were
alleged to favour the appeasement of NAZI
Germany. The name first appeared in *The
Week*, but the legend seems to be largely
supposititious.

Cloacina (klō a sī´ nà). (Lat. *cloaca*, a sewer). Goddess of sewers.

> Then Cloacina, goddess of the tide,
> Whose sable streams beneath the city glide,
> Indulged the modish flame: the town she roved,

A mortal scavenger she saw, she loved.

GAY: *Trivia, II.*

Cloak and Sword Plays. Swashbuckling plays, full of fighting and adventure. The name comes from the comedies of the 17th-century Spanish dramatists, Lope de Vega and Calderón—*Comedias de capa y espada*. With them it signified merely a drama of domestic intrigue and was named from the rank of the chief characters, but in France (and, through French influence, in England) it was applied as above. They are also called **Cloak and dagger plays.** The intrigues, undercover and often melodramatic activities of those involved in espionage, etc., are similarly called **cloak and dagger operations.**

Clock. So church bells were once called (Ger. *Glocke*: Fr. *cloche*: Med. Lat. *cloca*).

The tale about St. Paul's clock striking thirteen is given in Walcott's *Memorials of Westminster*, and refers to John Hatfield, a soldier of William III's reign who died in 1770, aged 102. Accused before a court martial of falling asleep on duty upon Windsor Terrace, he asserted in proof of his innocence that he heard St. Paul's strike thirteen. His statement was confirmed by several witnesses.

Another strange incident is related concerning BIG BEN. On the morning of Thursday, 14 March 1861, "the inhabitants of Westminster were roused by repeated strokes of the new great bell, and most persons supposed it was for the death of a member of the royal family. It proved, however, to be due to some derangement of the clock, for at four and five o'clock ten and twelve strokes were struck instead of the proper number." Within twenty-four hours of this the Duchess of Kent (Queen Victoria's mother) was declared to be dying and early on the 16th she was dead.

To put the clock back. To revert to an earlier practice or way of life; also to put back the hands of a clock especially at the end of DAYLIGHT SAVING.

To put the clock on. To put forward the hands of a clock, particularly at the commencement of a period of DAYLIGHT SAVING.

Clockwork. Like clockwork. Used of any enterprise that runs as planned, without any hitch.

Clog Almanac. A primitive almanac or calendar, originally made of a foursquare "clog" or log of wood. The sharp edges were divided by notches into three months each, every week being marked by a bigger notch. The faces contained the saints' days, the festivals, the phases of the moon, and so on, sometimes in Runic characters (*see* RUNE), whence the clog was also called a "Runic Staff". They are not uncommon and specimens may be seen in the BRITISH MUSEUM, the BODLEIAN, the ASHMOLEAN, and elsewhere.

Clogs to clogs is only three generations is an old Lancashire saying, implying that however a man may prosper and raise himself from poverty, his grandson will be wearing clogs, and back to the condition the family started from.

He'll clog again. An old saying in Lancashire and Yorkshire mill towns meaning that the person would recover from an illness or accident. It derives from the mending of repairable clogs.

Cloister. He retired into a cloister, he entered a monastery. Most monasteries had a cloister or covered walk, which generally occupied three sides of a quadrangle. Hence *cloistered*, confined, withdrawn from the world in the manner of a recluse.

> I cannot praise a fugitive, and cloistered virtue, unexercised and unbreathed, that never sallies out and sees her adversary, but slinks out of the race where that immortal garland is to be run for, not without dust and heat.
>
> MILTON: *Areopagitica*.

Clootie. Auld Clootie. OLD NICK (*see* NICK). The Scots call a cloven hoof a *cloot*, so that Auld Clootie is Old Clovenfoot.

> And maybe Tam, for a' my cants,
> My wicked rhymes an' drucken rants
> I'll gie auld Cloven Clootie's haunts
> An unco slip yet,
> An' snugly sit amang the saunts
> At Davie's hip yet!
>
> BURNS: *Reply to a Trimming Epistle.*

Close Rolls. CHANCERY enrolments of royal letters closed with the GREAT SEAL. Close writs date from 1204 but in the 16th century the Close Rolls came to consist only of private deeds, enclosure awards, etc. They ceased in 1903. *Cp.* PATENT ROLLS.

Close Shave. A narrow escape; a figure based on the extremely small margin between a smooth, closely shaven skin and a painful gash.

Close-time for Game. *See* SPORTING SEASONS.

Closed Shop. *See* SHOP.

Closure. The ending of a HOUSE OF COMMONS debate by a member moving "that the question be now put". The chair is not bound to accept the motion. The procedure was derived from the French *clôture* and first asked by Speaker Brand in 1881 against Parnell and his Irish obstructionists, consequent upon the famous sitting of February 1881 which lasted from 4 p.m. Monday until 9.30 a.m. on the following Wednesday. *See* FILI-

BUSTER; GUILLOTINE; KANGAROO.

Cloth, The. Once applied to the customary garb of any calling and similar in usage to the word LIVERY. In the 17th century it became restricted to the CLERGY and clerical office. Thus we say "having respect for the cloth".

Cloth of Gold, Field of. *See* FIELD.

Cloth-yard. A measure for cloth, slightly differing from the yard of today.

Cloth-yard shaft. An arrow a cloth-yard in length.

Clotho (Gr. *klotho*, to draw thread from a distaff). One of the three FATES in classic mythology. She presided over birth and drew from her distaff the thread of life. *See* ATROPOS; LACHESIS.

Cloud. A dark spot on the forehead of a horse between the eyes. *Cp*. BLAZE.

> *Agrippa:*   He [Antony] has a cloud in's face.
> *Enobarbus:*   He were the worse for that, were he
>   a horse:
>   SHAKESPEARE: *Antony and Cleopatra*, III, ii.

A clouded cane. A malacca cane clouded or mottled from age and use. These canes were very popular in the first quarter of the 18th century and earlier.

> Sir Plume of amber snuff-box justly vain,
> And the nice conduct of a clouded cane.
>   POPE: *Rape of the Lock*, iv, 123.

Cloud-Cuckoo-Land. The *Nephelococcygia* of *The Birds*, by Aristophanes; an imaginary city built in the air by the birds. Hence any impractical Utopian scheme.

Every cloud has a silver lining. There is some redeeming brightness in the darkest prospect; while there is life there is hope.

He is in the clouds. In dreamland; entertaining visionary notions and so having no distinct idea about the matter in question.

He is under a cloud. Under suspicion, in disrepute.

The Battle above the Clouds. A name given to the battle of Lookout Mountain, part of the battle of Chattanooga, fought during the American CIVIL WAR, on 24 November 1863. The Union forces defeated the Confederates and part of the fighting took place in a heavy mist on the mountains, hence the name.

To blow a cloud. *See* BLOW.

Cloven Foot. To show the cloven foot, or **hoof.** *i.e.* to show a knavish intention; a base motive. The allusion is to SATAN, represented with the legs and feet of a goat. However disguised he could never conceal his cloven feet. *See* CLOOTIE.

Clover. He's in clover. In luck, in prosperous circumstances, in a good situation. The allusion is to cattle feeding in fields of clover.

Clown. The clown of circus and PANTOMIME,

in his baggy costume, whitened face, grotesque red lips, and odd little tuft of black hair is probably a relic of the DEVIL as he appeared in mediæval miracle plays. He is the descendant of many court fools and jesters. Of all the clowns, Joseph GRIMALDI (1779–1837), and the Swiss "Grock", Adrien Wettach (1880–1959), were outstanding. *See* HARLEQUIN.

Club. In England the club has played an important part in social life. John Aubrey (1626–1697) says "we now used the word clubbe for a sodality in a taverne". Some were political, such as the ROTA, the OCTOBER, the GREEN RIBBON and the somewhat eccentric CALVES' HEAD CLUB; others more riotous like the MOHOCKS and the HELL FIRE CLUB. Clubs came into vogue in the reign of Queen Anne as is evidenced by the *Tatler* and *Spectator*. Dr. Johnson's Ivy Lane Club (1749) and the Literary Club (1764), which he founded with Sir Joshua Reynolds, set a new standard in social clubs where like-minded men of culture could meet and converse. The latter included Burke, Garrick, Goldsmith, and Boswell among its members. For many years clubs met in taverns and COFFEE houses and did not begin to occupy their own premises until the REGENCY. Many more sprang up in the early 19th century, some such as Watiers' (1806–1819) and CROCKFORD'S (1828–1844), being solely gaming clubs. The first exclusive modern ladies' club was the Alexandra (1883), to which no man was allowed admittance. Among the principal London clubs (with the dates of their foundation) are the following:

Army and Navy, 1838	Guards, 1813
ATHENÆUM, 1824	Junior Carlton, 1864
Bath, 1894	Lansdowne, 1935
BEEFSTEAK, 1876	National Liberal, 1822
Boodle's, 1762	Reform, 1832
BROOKS'S, 1764	Savage, 1857
Carlton, 1832	Savile, 1868
Cavalry, 1890	Thatched House, 1865
Conservative, 1840	Travellers, 1819
Constitutional, 1883	United Services, 1815
Devonshire, 1875	WHITE'S, 1693
Garrick, 1831	

In 1976 the Guards Club moved to the home of the Cavalry Club to form the Cavalry and Guards Club. The United Services' Club and the Royal Aero Club merged with the IN AND OUT in 1976.

Among the famous clubs associated with sport are:

M.C.C., 1787	Royal Automobile, 1897
Royal Aero, 1901	Turf, 1868

Clubs of many kinds have long been a common feature of national and provincial life among all classes and range from the serenity of the Athenæum to the less austere atmosphere of the STRIP-TEASE Club. *See also* CORDELIER; JACOBINS; OTHER CLUB; THE RAG *under* RAG.

Club-bearer, The. In Greek mythology, Periphetes, the robber of Argolis, is so called because he murdered his victims with an iron club.

Club car. A railway carriage furnished as a lounge, often with a refreshment bar. Club cars, reserved for subscribing season ticket holders, were formerly provided on the Lancashire and Yorkshire Railway's business expresses between Blackpool and Manchester and by the London and North Western Railway between Llandudno and Manchester.

Club-land. That part of the West End of London centred around PALL MALL where the principal clubs are situated; also the members of such clubs.

Club-law. The law of might or compulsion through fear of chastisement; "might is right"; "do it or get a hiding".

Club men. The bands of rustics, formed in the southern and western counties in 1645 to resist the exactions of both CAVALIERS and ROUNDHEADS, were so called from their cudgels.

Club Parliament, or **the Parliament of Bats,** was held at Northampton in 1426, during the quarrel between the Duke of Gloucester and Cardinal Beaufort. Forbidden to bear arms by the Regent Bedford, the members came armed with clubs or "bats".

Club sandwich. An American term for a "three decker" sandwich, usually with different fillings between the layers.

Clue. I have not yet got the clue; to give a clue, *i.e.* a hint. A clue is a ball of thread (O.E. *cleowen*). The only way of finding the way out of the Cretan LABYRINTH was by a skein of thread, which, being followed, led the right way.

I haven't a clue. A colloquial usage meaning "I haven't an inkling", "I haven't the vaguest idea" (of what you are asking or talking about, etc.).

Cluniacs. In 10th century France discipline in the Benedictine abbeys had declined almost completely and wealth and luxury predominated. At Cluny, N.W. of Mâcon a reformed abbey was established in 910 and in due course many old abbeys adopted the rigid rule of the Cluniacs. By the end of the 12th century there were over 300 European monasteries linked with Cluny and some 30 or so Cluniac houses in England, including those of Bermondsey, Reading and Faversham. As with the BENEDICTINES wealth and laxity took over and the next major revival was that of the CISTERCIANS.

Cluricaune. An ELF in Irish folklore. He is of evil disposition and usually appears as a wrinkled old man. He has a knowledge of hidden treasure and is the fairies' shoemaker. Another name for him is LEPRECHAUN.

Clydesdale Horses. *See* SHIRE HORSES.

Clydesiders, The. A loosely attached group of left-wing M.P.s representing Glasgow and Clydeside constituencies, who enlivened British politics and Parliament from 1922 until they were much diminished in numbers by the 1931 election. Notable among them were John Wheatley, of Housing Act fame, Campbell Stephen, Emanuel Shinwell, and best known of all James Maxton who became chairman of the Independent LABOUR Party. They acted as a GINGER GROUP on the Labour Party and were notable champions of the poor and unemployed.

Clym of the Clough. A noted archer and outlaw, who, with Adam Bell and WILLIAM OF CLOUDESLEY, forms the subject of a ballad in PERCY'S RELIQUES. The three became as famous in the north of England as ROBIN HOOD and LITTLE JOHN in the midland counties. They were presumed to have lived before Robin Hood and abode in Englewood Forest, near Carlisle. Clym of the Clough means Clement of the Cliff. He is mentioned in Ben Jonson's *Alchemist* (I, ii, 46).

Clytemnestra. In Greek legend, the faithless wife of AGAMEMNON. She was a daughter of Tyndarus and LEDA. *See also* ELECTRA.

Clytie. In classical mythology an ocean NYMPH, in love with APOLLO. She was deserted by him and changed into the heliotrope or sunflower, which, traditionally, still turns to the sun, following him through his daily course.

Cnidian Venus, The. The exquisite statue of VENUS by Praxiteles, formerly in her temple at Cnidus. It is known through the antique reproduction now in the VATICAN.

Coach. When railways replaced horsedrawn road transport in the 1830s and 1840s they took over the old coaching terms as the steamship did from the days of sail. Carriage, coach, driver, guard, "Right away"! are all reminiscent of former coaching days.

To get on fast you took a *coach*. It is from this association that a private tutor or a sports trainer is called a coach, for it is his job to get his pupils trained as fast as possible.

A slow coach. A dullard, an unprogressive person.

To dine in the coach. In the captain's private apartment. The *coach* or *couch* of one of the old wooden battleships was the small compartment built on the aftmost part of the QUARTERDECK and under the poop. In small yachts the raised cabin-top, which increases the headroom in the cabin, is called a *coach roof*.

To drive a coach and four through an Act of Parliament. To find a way of flagrantly ignoring or evading its provisions wholesale, thereby reducing it to an absurdity. In effect, to make it useless.

Coade Stone. An artificial stone of great durability and firmness of outline, much used from the 1770s until the 1830s for statues and ornamentations for buildings (CARYATIDS, keystone masks, friezes, vases, etc.). Made from a kind of frost-resistant terracotta, and presumably invented by the sculptor John Bacon (1740–1799), it was produced in Mrs. Eleanor Coade's factory at Lambeth (later the firm of Coade and Sealy). The huge red lion which was long a familiar figure on the SOUTH BANK from 1837 is an excellent example. The secret of its manufacture has been lost.

Coal. To blow the coals. To fan dissensions, to excite smouldering animosity into open hostility, as dull coals are blown into a blaze with a pair of bellows.

To call, or **haul over the coals.** To bring to task for shortcomings; to scold. At one time the Jews were "bled" whenever the kings or barons wanted money. One very common tortue, if they resisted, was to haul them over the coals of a slow fire, to give them a "roasting". In Scott's *Ivanhoe*, Front-de-Bœuf threatens to haul Isaac over the coals. *See* ROAST.

To carry coals. To be put upon. "Gregory, o'my word, we'll not carry coals"—*i.e.* submit to be "put upon" (*Romeo and Juliet*, I, i). So in *Every Man out of his Humour*, "Here comes one that will carry coals, ergo, will hold my dog." The allusion is to the dirty, laborious occupation of charcoal carriers.

To carry coals to Newcastle. To do what is superfluous; to take something where it is already plentiful. The French say, *"Porter de l'eau à la rivière"* (to carry water to the river). ALCINOO POMA DARE is a Latin equivalent.

To heap coals of fire on one's head. To melt down one's animosity by deeds of kindness: to repay bad treatment with good.

> If thine enemy be hungry, give him bread to eat; and if he be thirsty, give him water to drink; for thou shalt heap coals of fire upon his head, and the Lord shall reward thee.
>
> *Prov. XXV*, 21, 22.

To post the coal, or **cole.** *See* COLE.

Coal brandy. Burnt brandy. The old way to set brandy on fire was to drop in it a live or red-hot piece of charcoal.

Coaling, in theatrical slang, means telling phrases and speeches, as, "My part is full of *coaling lines*." Possibly from COLE (money), such a part being profitable.

Coalition Government. One formed of rival parties, usually in times of crisis, when party differences are set aside. Examples are those of Fox and North in 1783; of WHIGS and PEELITES under Aberdeen, 1852–1855; of CONSERVATIVES and LIBERAL-UNIONISTS under Salisbury 1895–1902; of LIBERALS, UNIONISTS, and LABOUR under Asquith 1915–1916 (reformed under Lloyd George 1916–1922); Macdonald's NATIONAL GOVERNMENT, 1931–1935; and Winston Churchill's Coalition Government, 1940–1945.

Coast. The coast is clear. There is no likelihood of interference. It was originally a smuggling term, implying that no coastguards were about.

Coastal Eastern. The form of American English which has much the same relation to other variants of that language as Standard Received English has to variants in England. Both developed in those districts where academic and cultural influences were strongest.

Coasters. Vessels engaged in the coasting trade. Also travelling containers, often on castors or wheels, for passing food and drink (such as cheese, wine and beer) along large tables. They were commonly used in England in the 18th and early 19th centuries and some were elaborate representations of carts and other wheeled vehicles.

Coasting lead. A sounding lead used in shallow water.

Coasting waiter. An officer of Customs in the Port of London, whose duty it was to visit and make a return of coasting vessels which (from the nature of their cargo) were not required to report or make entry at the Custom House, but which were liable to payment of certain small dues. The coasting waiter collected these, and searched the cargo for contraband. Like TIDE WAITERS, they were abolished in the latter part of the 19th century and their duties taken over by the examining officer.

Coat. Coat Card. *See* COURT CARDS.

Cut your coat according to your cloth. Curtail your expenses to the amount of your income; live within your means. *Si non possis quod velis, velis id quod possis.*

To baste someone's coat. To DUST his jacket; to beat him.

To trail one's coat. To try deliberately to pick a quarrel. From an old Irish custom of trailing one's coat along the ground as a sign that the owner was prepared to fight anyone daring to tread on his coat-tails.

To wear the King's coat. To be a soldier.

Turning one's coat for luck. It was an ancient superstition that this was a charm against evil spirits. See TURNCOAT.

> William found
> A means for our deliverance: "Turn your cloaks".
> Quoth hee, "for Pucke is busy in these oakes".
> RICHARD CORBETT (1582–1635): *Iter* Boreale.

Coat of Arms. Originally a linen or silken surcoat worn by KNIGHTS to protect their armour from the sun's heat, dirt, etc., with their arms embroidered upon it. The use of coats of arms probably began in the 12th century. In HERALDRY the coat of arms comprises shield, helmet, crest, mantling and supporters. The shield is the central part.

Cob. A short-legged, stout variety of horse, rather larger than a pony, from thirteen to nearly fifteen hands high. (*See* HAND.) The word means big, stout. It also meant a tuft or head (from *cop*), hence eminent, large, powerful. The *cob of the county* is the great boss thereof. A *rich cob* is a plutocrat. Hence also a male is a *cobswan*.

Cobalt. From the Ger. *kobold*, a GNOME, the demon of the mines. This metal, from which a deep blue pigment is made, was so called by miners partly because it was thought to be useless and partly because the arsenic and sulphur, with which it was found in combination, had bad effects on their health and on the silver ores. Its presence was therefore attributed to the mine demon.

Cobb and Co. The mail and passenger coach company whose fame is legendary in Australia. Founded by Freeman Cobb and three other Americans in 1854, during the Ballarat gold rush, they provided reliable and comfortable transport between Melbourne and Bendigo in American-built coaches. Later, under the ownership of James Rutherford, another American, the company absorbed or eclipsed rival firms and secured a monopoly throughout Victoria, New South Wales and Queensland. At the height of its prosperity the company covered 28,000 miles per week, but the growth of railway and motor transport brought inevitable decline, although the last run was made as late as 1924. Tales of the exploits of Cobb and Co.'s crack drivers are as exciting as any told of WELLS FARGO.

> Behind six foaming horses, and lit by flashing lamps,

Old Cobb and Co., in royal state, went dashing past the camps.

> HENRY LAWSON (1867–1922): *The Roaring Days*.

Cobber (Austr.). A friend or companion; possibly from the old Suffolk *to cob*, to form a friendship.

Cobber Kain. Flying Officer E. J. Kain, D.F.C., the first New Zealand air ace, who was killed on active service in June 1940.

Cobbler. A drink made of sherry, sugar, lemon and ice. *See* COBBLER'S PUNCH.

> This wonderful invention, sir, ... is called a cobbler: Sherry cobbler, when you name it long, cobbler when you name it short.
> DICKENS: *Martin Chuzzlewit*, xvii.

Also the name of a deep fruit pie with no bottom crust and a top crust resembling scone or plain cake dough. The name is possibly suggested by the resemblance of the uneven surface of the top crust to cobble stones.

A cobbler should stick to his last. Let no one presume to interfere in matters of which he is ignorant.

> Ne supra crepidam sutor judicaret
> PLINY, XXV, x, 85.

There is the story of a cobbler who detected a fault in a shoe-latchet in a painting by APELLES. The artist rectified the fault. The cobbler then ventured to criticize the legs but Apelles answered, "Keep to your trade—you understand about shoes, but not about anatomy."

The Cobbler Poet. Hans Sachs of Nuremberg (1494–1576), prince of the MEISTER-SINGER of Germany. He was trained as a cobbler.

Cobbler's punch. Gin and water, with a little treacle and vinegar.

Cobbler's toast. Schoolboy's bread and butter, toasted on the dry side and eaten hot.

Cobham's Plot. *See* MAIN PLOT.

Coburg. A corded or ribbed cotton-cloth made in Coburg (Saxony), or an imitation thereof. Chiefly used for ladies' dresses.

Also a type of round loaf, said to have been named in honour of the Prince Consort, who was of the House of Saxe-Coburg-Gotha.

Cobweb. To blow away the cobwebs. To clear one's mind by taking fresh air; to freshen oneself up.

Cock (noun). In classical mythology the cock was dedicated to APOLLO because it gives notice of the rising sun. It was also dedicated to MERCURY, because it summons men to business by its crowing; and to ÆSCULAPIUS, because "early to bed and early to rise makes a man healthy".

Mohammedan legend says that the Prophet found in the first HEAVEN a cock of such enormous size that its crest touched the second heaven. The crowing of this celestial bird arouses every living creature except man. When this cock ceases to crow, the Day of JUDGMENT will be at hand.

Peter Le Neve (1661–1729), English antiquary, affirms that a cock was the warlike ensign of the GOTHS and therefore used in GOTHIC churches for ornament.

The weathercock is a very old symbol of vigilance. As the cock heralds the coming of day, so does the weathercock tell the wise man what the weather will likely be.

A cock and bull story. A long highly coloured or incredible story, a CANARD. It possibly derives from old fables in which cocks and bulls and other animals conversed. In Bentley's *Boyle Lecture* (1692) we find:

> That cocks and bulls might discourse, and hinds and panthers hold conferences about religion.

The "hind and panther" allusion is an obvious reference to Dryden's poem of 1687 and "cocks and bulls" probably had a well-known meaning at the time. The last words in Sterne's *Tristram Shandy* are:

> Lord! said my mother, what is all this story about?
> A Cock and a Bull, said Yorick—And one of the best of its kind, I ever heard.

The *Cock and Bull* inn sign is found in the 17th century and both *Cock* and *Bull* as separate signs were always popular. There is a story at Stony Stratford, Buckinghamshire that in the coaching days the London coach changed horses at the Bull Inn and the Birmingham coach at the Cock. From the exchange of jests and stories between the waiting passengers of both coaches the "Cock and Bull" story is said to have originated.

The French equivalents are *faire un coq à l'âne* and *un conte de ma mère l'oie* (a mother goose tale). In Scotland a satire or rambling story was a *cockalayne* from the Fr. *coq à l'âne*.

A cock of hay, or **haycock.** A small heap of hay thrown up temporarily (Ger. dialect *kocke*, a heap of hay; Norw. *kok*, a heap).

By cock and pie. We meet with *cock's bones, cock's wounds, cock's mother, cock's body, cock's passion,* etc., where there is no doubt that the word is a minced oath, and stands for God. The *pie* is the table or rule in the old Catholic office, showing how to find out the service for each day (from Med. Lat. *pica*).

> By cock and pie, sir, you shall not away to-night.
> SHAKESPEARE: *Henry IV, Pt. II*, V, i.

Cock and Bottle, Cock and Pie. Both are PUBLIC HOUSE SIGNS. The latter is probably "The Cock and Magpie" and the former probably means that draught and bottled beer are sold on the premises (here *cock* would mean the tap).

Cock of the North. George, fifth Duke of Gordon (1770–1836), who raised the Gordon Highlanders in 1795, is so called on a monument erected to his honour at Fochabers in Morayshire.

The brambling, or mountain finch, is also known by this name.

Cock of the walk. The dominant bully or master spirit. The place where barn-door fowls are fed is the *walk*, and if there is more than one cock, they will fight for the supremacy of this domain.

Every cock crows on its own dunghill, or **Ilka cock crows on its ain midden.** It is easy to brag of your deeds in your own castle when safe from danger and not likely to be put to proof.

Nourish a cock, but offer it not in a sacrifice. This is the eighteenth Symbolic Saying in the *Protreptics* of Iamblichus. The cock was sacred to MINERVA, and also to the SUN and MOON, and it would be impious to offer a sacrilegious offering to the gods. What is already consecrated to God cannot be employed in sacrifice.

That cock won't fight. That dodge won't answer; that tale won't wash. The allusion is to COCK-FIGHTING.

The red cock will crow in his house. His house will be set on fire.

> "We'll see if the red cock craw not in his bonnie barnyard ae morning." ... "What does she mean?" said Mannering ... "Fire-raising", answered the ... dominie
> SCOTT: *Guy Mannering*, ch. iii.

To cry cock. To claim the victory; to assert oneself to be the superior. To assert oneself as COCK OF THE WALK.

Cock-boat. A small ship's boat; a very light or frail craft.

> That now no more we can the maine-land see,
> Have care, I pray, to guide the cock-bote well.
> SPENSER: *Faerie Queene*, III, viii, 24.

This "cock-bote" is previously (III, vii, 27) called a "little bote" and a "shallop". *Cokke* or *cocke* is an obsolete word for a small boat, and is probably connected with *cog*, a mediæval cargo-ship, from Scan. *kog, kogge*, originally a wicker frame covered with leather, akin to the Welsh coracle.

Cock-crow. The Hebrews divided the night into four watches: (1) The "beginning of the watches" or "even" (*Lam*. ii, 10); (2) the "middle WATCH" or "midnight" (*Judges* vii, 19); (3) the "cock-crowing"; (4) The "morning watch" or "dawning" (*Exod.* xiv, 24).

> Ye know not when the master of the house cometh, at even, or at midnight, or at the cock-crowing, or in the morning.
>
> *Mark* xiii, 35.

The Romans divided the day into sixteen parts, each one hour and a half, beginning at midnight. The third of these divisions (3 a.m.) they called *gallicinium*, the time when cocks begin to crow; the next was *conticinium*, when they ceased to crow; and the fifth was *diluculum*, dawn.

If the Romans sounded the hour on a trumpet three times it would explain the diversity of the Gospels: "Before the cock crow" (*John* xiii, 38; *Luke* xxii, 34; *Matt.* xxvi, 34) and "Before the cock crow twice" (*Mark* xiv, 30)—that is, before the trumpet has finished sounding.

Apparitions vanish at cock-crow. This is a Christian superstition, the cock being the watch-bird placed on church spires, and therefore sacred.

> The morning cock crew loud,
> And at the sound it [the Ghost] shrunk in haste away,
> And vanish'd from our sight.
>
> SHAKESPEARE: *Hamlet*, I, ii.

Cock-eye. A squint. **Cock-eyed,** having a squint; cross-eyed. It may mean that such an eye has to be *cocked*, as the trigger of a gun is cocked, before it can do its work effectively; or it may be from the verb *to cock* in the sense of "turning up" as in *to cock the nose*. *Cock-eyed* also means not straight, out of true, out of line, as well as nonsensical.

Cockfighting was a favourite sport with both Greeks and Romans and was introduced into Britain by the Romans.

From the 12th to the 19th century cockfighting and throwing at cocks was the sport of schoolboys on SHROVE TUESDAY and the triumphant boy, holding the winning bird in his hands, was sometimes carried aloft by some of his companions. This may be the origin of the old schoolboy phrase "cock of the school". The COCKPIT at WHITEHALL was added by Henry VIII and the "royal diversion" was very popular with James I and Charles II. Cockfighting was made illegal in Britain in 1849. *See also* BATTLE ROYAL; WELSH MAIN.

That beats cockfighting. That is most improbable and extraordinary. The allusion is to the extravagant tales told of fighting cocks.

To live like fighting cocks. To live in luxury. Fighting cocks were highly fed to increase their mettle and powers of endurance.

Cock-horse. To ride a cock-horse. A cock-horse is really a HOBBY-HORSE, but the phrase means to sit astride a person's foot or knee while he jigs it up and down.

A horse kept ready at the bottom of a steep hill to help a coach and its team to the top, was called a *cock-horse*. It was hitched to the front of the team.

Cock Lane Ghost. A tale of terror without truth; an imaginary tale of horrors. In Cock Lane, Smithfield (1762), certain knockings were heard, which Mr. Parsons, the owner, declared proceeded from the ghost of Fanny Kent, who died suddenly. Parsons, with the hope of blackmail, wished people to suppose that she had been murdered by her husband. All London was agog with the story. Royalty and the nobility made up parties to go to Cock Lane to hear the ghost. Dr. Johnson and others of learning and repute investigated the alleged phenomena. Eventually it was found that the knockings were made by Parson's eleven-year-old daughter rapping on a board which she took into her bed. Parsons was condemned to the pillory. *Cp.* STOCKWELL GHOST.

Cock Lorell's Bote. An imitation of Alexander Barclay's *Ship of Fools* (1509) published by Wynkyn de Worde about 1510. It satirized low-class life. Cock Lorell, a tinker, was the captain of a motley crew of rogues and vagabonds.

Cockpit. The arena in which game-cocks were set to fight; also the name of a theatre built about 1618 on the site of a cockpit in DRURY LANE. The after part of the orlop deck of an old man-of-war (formerly used as quarters for junior officers and as a sick-bay in battle), and the well of a small yacht where the helmsman sits, are also so called.

> Captain Hardy, some fifty minutes after he had left the cock-pit, returned; and, again taking the hand of his dying commander, congratulated him on having gained a complete victory.
>
> SOUTHEY: *Life of Nelson*, ch. ix.

In aeroplanes the space where the pilot sits is called the cockpit.

The judicial committee of the PRIVY COUNCIL was called the cockpit of Whitehall Palace.

> Great consultations at the cockpit about battles, duels, victories, and what not.
>
> *Poor Robin's Almanack*, 1730.

Cockpit of Europe. Belgium is so called because it has so frequently been the battleground of Europe, as is evidenced by Ramillies (1706); Oudenarde (1708); Fontenoy (1745); Fleurus (1794); Jemmapes (1792); Ligny, Quatre Bras and Waterloo (1815); Mons, Ypres and the continuous battles of

World War I; the German invasion of 1940.

Cockshut, or **Cockshut time.** Twilight; the time when the *cockshut* (a large net to catch woodcocks) was spread. The net was so named from being used in a glade through which the woodcocks might *shoot* or dart.

> Let me never draw a sword again,
> Nor prosper in the twilight, cockshut light
> When I would fleece the wealthy passenger...
> If I, the next time that I meet the slave,
> Cut not the nose from off the coward's face.
> *Arden of Feversham* (1592), III, ii.

See also SHAKESPEARE'S *Richard III*, V, iii.

Cockshy. A free fling or "shy" at something. The allusion is to the once popular SHROVE TUESDAY sport of shying or casting stones or sticks at cocks.

The phrase was popular in military circles in World War II, implying an ill-considered, ill-prepared attempt at something.

Cock sure. As sure as a cock, brazenly self-confident; meaning either "with all the assurance of a game-cock", or "as sure as the cock is to crow in the morning". Shakespeare uses it in the sense of "sure as the cock of a fire-lock".

> We steal as in a castle, cock-sure,
> *Henry IV, Pt. I*, II, i.

The phrase "sure as a gun" seems to favour the latter explanation.

Cock (verb). In the following phrases, all of which connote assertiveness, obtrusiveness, or aggressiveness in some degree, the allusion is to game-cocks, whose strutting about, swaggering, and ostentatious pugnacity is proverbial.

To cock the ears. To prick up the ears, or turn them as a horse does when he listens to a strange sound.

To cock the nose, or **cock up the nose.** To turn up the nose in contempt. *See* TO COCK YOUR EYE.

To cock up your head, foot, etc. To lift up or turn up your head or foot.

To cock your eye. To shut one eye and look with the other in a somewhat cheeky fashion; to glance at questioningly. *Cp.* COCK-EYE.

To cock your hat. To set your hat on one side of the head; to look knowing and pert.

To cock a snook. To make a long nose; to put the thumb to the nose and spread wide the fingers. A gesture of contempt; also known as Anne's fan or Queen Anne's fan.

Cock-a-hoop. Jubilant; exultant; as a cock crowing boastfully; but the saying may come from the fact that when the spigot or *cock* is removed from the beer barrel and laid on a hoop of the barrel, the beer flows for jollity and high spirits.

Cocked hat. A hat with an upturned brim like that of a BISHOP, DEAN, etc.: also applied to the CHAPEAU BRAS. It now denotes the brimless triangular hat, pointed at the back and front, worn as part of full-dress by diplomats and naval and army officers, the *chapeau à cornes*. *Cocked* here means turned up.

Knocked into a cocked hat. To beat someone in a contest of skill, etc., by a wide margin. In the game of ninepins, three pins were set up in the form of a triangle and when all the pins except these three were knocked down, the set was said to be "knocked into a cocked hat". From the idea of a hat being knocked out of shape.

Cockade (Fr. *cocarde*, a plume, rosette, or bunch of ribbons). A badge worn on the head-dress of menservants of Royalty, naval and military officers, diplomatists, lord-lieutenants, high sheriffs, etc. The English cockade is black and circular in shape with a projecting fan at the top, except for naval officers, for whom the shape is oval without the fan. This form was introduced from Hanover by George I; under Charles I the cockade was scarlet but Charles II changed it to white. Thus the white cockade became the badge of the House of Stuart; William III (as Prince of Orange) adopted an orange cockade. *See* DOG-VANE.

To mount the cockade. To become a soldier.

Cockaigne, Land of (kok ān'). An imaginary land of idleness and luxury, famous in mediæval story. Ellis in his *Specimens of Early English Poets* gives an early translation of a 13th-century French poem called *The Land of Cockaign* in which "the houses were made of barley sugar cakes, the streets were paved with pastry, and the shops supplied goods for nothing".

LONDON has been so called, with punning reference to COCKNEY. Boileau applies the name to Paris.

The name may well mean the "land of cakes", ultimately from Lat. *coquere*, to cook. Scotland is called the "land of cakes" (*see under* CAKE).

Cockatoo. Old Australian slang for a convict serving his sentence on Cockatoo Island, Sydney, which was first used for convicts in 1839. Also used for small farmers in Australia who were "just picking up the grains of a livelihood like cockatoos do maize".

Cockatrice. A fabulous and heraldic monster with the wings of a fowl, tail of a DRAGON, and head of a cock; the same as BASILISK. Isaiah says, "The weaned child shall put his hand on the cockatrice' den" (xi, 8), to signify that the most obnoxious animal shall not hurt the most feeble of God's creatures.

Figuratively, it means an insidious, treacherous person bent on mischief.

> They will kill one another by the look, like cockatrices.
>
> SHAKESPEARE: *Twelfth Night*, III, iv.

Cocker. According to Cocker. All right according to Cocker. According to established rules, according to what is correct. Edward Cocker (1631–1675) published his *Arithmetick* which ran through over a hundred editions. The phrase was popularized by Murphy in his farce, *The Apprentice* (1756). *Cp.* GUNTER.

Cockle. Cockle-boat. *See* COCK-BOAT.

Cockle hat. A pilgrim's hat. Pilgrims used to wear cockle (scallop) shells on their hats, the symbol of St. JAMES of COMPOSTELA in Spain. This supposed shrine of James, the son of Zebedee, was especially favoured by English pilgrims. The polished side of the shell was scratched with some crude drawing of the Virgin, the Crucifixion, or some other object related to the pilgrimage. Being blessed by the priest, the shells were considered as amulets against spiritual foes, and might be used as drinking vessels.

> How should I your true love know
> From another one?
> By his cockle hat and staff,
> And by his sandal shoon.
>
> SHAKESPEARE: *Hamlet*, IV, v.

Cockle shell. A small boat or frail craft. *See also* COCKLE HAT.

Hot cockles. *See* HOT.

To try cockles. To be hanged; from the gurgling noises made in strangulation.

To warm the cockles of one's heart. Said of good wine and anything which particularly warms and gratifies one's feelings (Lat. *cochleæ cordis*, the ventricles of the heart).

Cockney. This is the M.E. *cokeney*, meaning "a cock's egg" (-ey = O.E. *æg*, an egg), applied to the small malformed egg occasionally laid by young hens; hence applied to a foolish or spoilt child, or a simpleton.

> I made thee a wanton and thou hast made me a fool. I brought thee up like a cockney and thou hast handled me like a cock's-comb, I made more of thee than became a father and thou less of me than beseemed a child.
>
> LYLY: *Euphues* (1578).

The word then came to be applied by country folk, the majority of the population, to townsfolk generally for their reputed ignorance of country life, customs and habits. Its restriction to Londoners, particularly those born within the sound of the bells of St. Mary-le-Bow, dates from the 17th century. It is also used to denote London peculiarities of speech. *See* BOW BELLS: RHYMING SLANG.

> As Frenchmen love to be bold, Flemings to be drunk, Welchmen to be called Britons, and Irish to be costermongers; so cockneys, especially she cockneys, love not aqua-vitae when 'tis good for them.
>
> DEKKER and WEBSTER: *Westward Hoe*, II, ii (1607).

SHAKESPEARE uses the word for a squeamish woman.

> Cry to it, nuncle, as the cockney did to the eels, when she put them i' the paste alive.
>
> *King Lear*, II, iv.

The Cockney School. A nickname given by Lockhart to a group of writers including Leigh Hunt, Hazlitt, Shelley, and Keats. It was used derogatorily on account of the kind of rhymes they used in their verse, which smacked too much of everyday life instead of the classic purity preferred by the critics.

> If I may be permitted to have the honour of christening it, it may be henceforth referred to by the designation of the "Cockney School".
>
> LOCKHART: *Blackwood's Magazine* (Oct., 1817).

The King of Cockneys. A master of the revels chosen by the students of LINCOLN'S INN on CHILDERMAS Day.

Cocktail. An aperitif, or short drink taken before a meal, usually concocted of spirits, bitters, fruit-juice or other flavourings, etc. There are many varieties of the American appetizer. The origin of the name is uncertain but suggestions vary from "a tail that cocks up" and "the tail of a cock" to the name of an Aztec princess Xochitl, who is supposed to have given a drink to the king with romantic results. *Coquetel*, a mixed drink from the wine-growing district of the Gironde, has also been suggested as a possible source. Dickens says of Major Pawkins (of Pennsylvanian origin):

> He could ... chew more tobacco, smoke more tobacco, drink more rum-toddy, mint-julep, gin-sling and cock-tail, than any private gentleman of his acquaintance.
>
> *Martin Chuzzlewit*, ch. xvi (1844).

The name also applies to a horse with a docked tail which "cocks up"; and to a halfbred horse, from the custom of docking stage-coach horses and hunters.

Coconut. Milk in the coconut. *See* MILK.

Cocqcigrues. At the coming of the Cocqcigrues. (kok′ sē groo). (More correctly *coquecigrues*.) Imaginary animals that have become labels for an idle story. The phrase *à la venue des cocquecigrues* used by Rabelais (*Gargantua*, Ch. V) means "NEVER".

> "That is one of the seven things", said the fairy Bedonebyasyoudid, "I am forbidden to tell till the coming of the Cocqcigrues."
>
> C. KINGSLEY: *The Water Babies*, ch. vi.

Cocytus (ko si' tŭs). One of the five rivers of HELL, which flows into the ACHERON. The word means the "river of lamentation". The unburied were doomed to wander about its banks for 100 years. *See* CHARON; STYX.

Cod. You can't cod me. You can't take me in, or deceive me.

Codille (kòdil'). Triumph. In the game of OMBRE, when one of the two opponents of ombre has more tricks than ombre, he is said to have won *codille* and takes all the stakes for which ombre played. Thus, Belinda is said, in the *Rape of the Lock*, to have been "between the jaws of ruin and Codille". She wins with the "King of hearts", and *she wins codille*.

Codswallop. A lot, or **a load of codswallop.** Simply nonsense or rubbish; said of something silly, far-fetched or fanciful when advanced as serious information or explanation. In 1875 Hiram Codd patented a mineral water bottle with a marble stopper. *Wallop* here is a slang term for beer. Thus *Codd's wallop* is said to have become a disparaging term among beer drinkers for mineral waters and weak drinks and in due course the term acquired a more general application.

Coehorn, or **Coehoorn.** A small mortar named after Baron von Coehoorn of Holland (1641–1704), who was called the Dutch Vauban, after Louis XIV's famous siege engineer and fortifications expert, Sebastien Le Prestre de Vauban (1633–1707).

Coelacanth (see'. lĕkanth). *See* FOURLEGS, OLD.

Cœnobites, or **Cenobites** (sen' ō bīts) (Gr. *koinos bios*). Monks who live in common, in contradistinction to hermits or anchorites.

Cœur de Lion (kĕr de lē' on). Richard I of England (1157, 1189–1199); called the lion-hearted for his valour in the Third CRUSADE.

Coffee. From the Turkish form *kahveh* of the Arabic *qahwah*, the drink. The first coffee-house in England opened at Oxford in 1650 and the first in London about 1652. They soon became centres for social and political gossip and meeting places for the wits and literary men of the day. *See also* BALTIC; BUTTON'S COFFEE-HOUSE; CHOCOLATE; CLUB; GARRAWAY'S; GRECIAN; GREAT PIAZZA COFFEE-HOUSE *under* PIAZZA; JONATHAN'S; LLOYD'S; TOM'S; WILL'S; WHITE'S.

> I date all gallantry from White's; all poetry from Will's; all foreign and domestic news from St. James's, and all learned articles from the Grecian.
> SIR RICHARD STEELE: *The Tatler*, 12 April 1709.

Coffee housing. Talking and gossiping, especially when waiting for something to happen or when there is work to be done. The expression was used in the hunting field certainly from the 1860s when riders were waiting for the hounds to draw a fox from a covert and gossiping at the same time.

Pousse café. Liqueur served after coffee. Also a drink of various liqueurs in layers in a glass.

Coffin. A raised pie crust, like the lid of a basket (Gr. *kophinos*, a basket). Hence Shakespeare speaks of a "custard-coffin" (*Taming of the Shrew*, IV, iii) meaning a custard under a crust. Also,

> And of the paste a coffin I will rear.
> *Titus Andronicus*, V, ii.

Coffin nail. A cigarette. An expression in use long before the association between cigarette smoking and lung cancer but probably connected with the risk to health.

To drive a nail into one's coffin. To do anything that would tend to hasten one's death, or finish one off, usually by annoyance and frustration.

> Care to our coffin adds a nail, no doubt;
> But every grin so merry draws one out.
> PETER PINDAR: *Expostulatory Odes*, xv.

Cog. A boat. *See* COCK-BOAT.

Coggeshall (kog' shăl). **A Coggeshall job.** Something foolish. It is said that the Coggeshall (Essex) folk wanted to divert the current of a stream, and so fixed hurdles in its bed. Another tale is that a mad dog bit a wheelbarrow, and the people, fearing the wheelbarrow's madness, chained it up in a shed. *Cp.* GOTHAM.

Cogito, ergo sum. The axiom formulated by Descartes (1596–1650) as the starting point of his philosophic system: it means, "I think, therefore I am." He provisionally doubted everything until he concluded that "I think" presupposed the existence of "I". *See* PETITIO PRINCIPII.

> He [Descartes] stopped at the famous formula, "I think, therefore I am." Yet a little consideration will show this formula to be full of snares and verbal entanglements. In the first place, the "therefore" has no business there. The "I am" is assumed in the "I think", which is simply another way of saying "I am thinking". And, in the second place, "I think" is not one simple proposition, but three distinct assertions rolled into one. The first of these is "something called I exists"; the second is "something called thought exists"; and the third is "the thought is the result of the action of the I".
> Now it will be obvious to you, that the only one of these three propositions which can stand the Cartesian test of certainty is the second.
> T. H. HUXLEY: *Descartes' Discourse on Method*.

Cognoscente (Latinized form of It. *conoscente* from *cognoscere*, to know). One with a critical, expert and thorough knowledge of a subject, especially in literature, music, works of art, etc. The plural form *cognos-*

centi is the more widely used.

Coif. Serjeants of the Coif. SERJEANTS-AT-LAW were so called from the close-fitting white lawn or silk cap once worn as a symbol of their rank (O.Fr. *coife*, a cap).

Coin. *See* ANGEL, BAWBEE, CAROLUS, CROSS AND PILE, CROWN, DECIMAL CURRENCY, DOLLAR, FARTHING, FLORIN, GROAT, GUINEA, MANCUS, PENNY, PIECES OF EIGHT, SHILLING, SOVEREIGN, etc.

Coinage (Fr. *coin*, corner). Derived from the practice in the STANNARY towns of Devon and Cornwall of collecting a "coinage" duty. In the towns appointed for the purpose the blocks of tin were weighed by the assay-master, then a piece called a *coign* was struck from the corner of each block. This was assayed for quality to fix the dues before stamping the block.

Paid in his own coin. TIT FOR TAT.

To coin a phrase. To invent a phrase. If it is a telling phrase it may *gain currency, i.e.* become popular and widespread.

To coin money. To make money with rapidity and ease.

Coke. Slang for cocaine.

Coke's Clippings. The colloquial name for the famous sheep-shearing gatherings held at Holkham, Norfolk, from 1778, by Thomas William Coke, Earl of Leicester (1752–1842), renowned for his pioneering work in agriculture. That of 1818 lasted a week, during which time he kept open house for some 600 people from all ranks of society, including foreign visitors. As many as 7,000 people attended annually. Mornings were spent inspecting the land and stock, and after a three o'clock dinner the remainder of the day was taken up with discussions, toasts and speeches on farming topics. Similar gatherings were instituted by the Duke of Bedford at Woburn, Lord Egremont at Petworth etc.

Coke upon Littleton. Eighteenth-century slang for a mixture of tent (a deep-red Spanish wine) and brandy. *Coke upon Littleton* is the lawyers' name for the reprint and translation of Littleton's *Tenures* (first printed *c.* 1481), published in 1628 with a commentary by Sir Edward Coke (1552–1634).

Colbronde, or **Colbrand.** The Danish giant slain by Guy of Warwick. By his death the land was delivered from Danish tribute.

I am not Samson, nor Sir Guy, nor Colbrand,
To mow 'em down before me.
SHAKESPEARE: *Henry VIII*, V, iii.

Colcannon (kŏl kăn' ŏn). Potatoes and cabbage pounded together and then fried in butter (Irish). "Col" is cole or cale, *i.e.* cabbage. *Cp.* BUBBLE AND SQUEAK.

About 1774 Isaac Sparks, the Irish comedian, founded in Long Acre a Colcannon Club.
The Athenæum, 20 January 1875.

Colcannon Night. HALLOWEEN in parts of N.E. Canada, when it is traditional to eat this dish.

Cold. Cold as Charity. *See* CHARITY.

Cold blood. Done in cold blood (Fr. *sang froid*). Not in the heat of temper; deliberately, and with forethought. The allusion is to the old notion that the temperature of the blood ruled the temper.

Cold-blooded animals. As a rule, all invertebrates, and all fishes and reptiles, the temperature of their blood being about equal to the medium in which they live.

Cold-blooded people. Those not easily excited. Those with little feeling.

Cold chisel. A steel chisel made in one piece and so tempered that it will cut cold metal when struck with a hammer.

Cold comfort. Comfort that is found chilling by the receiver, discouraging, little or no consolation.

Cold feet, To have or **to get.** To be really discouraged, to be afraid, or in a state of fear.

Cold fish, He is a. He has no warm feelings, he is unemotional and impassive.

Cold shoulder. To show, or **to give one the cold shoulder.** To assume a distant manner, to indicate that you wish to CUT someone.

Cold steel. The persuasion of cold steel. Persuasion enforced at the point of the sword or bayonet.

Cold war. The term applied to the state of tension between states which behave with marked distrust and hostility towards each other without recourse to actual fighting.

Cold-water ordeal. An ancient method of testing guilt or innocence. The accused, being tied under the arms, was thrown into a river. If he sank, he was held guiltless and drawn up by the cord; if he floated, the water rejected him because of his guilt.

Cold water. To pour cold water on. To discourage. To damp the fires of enthusiasm.

Cold without. An elliptical expression, meaning spirits mixed with cold water without sugar, the alternative being "hot with".

Cold Bath Fields. A district of CLERKENWELL, London, so called from the cold baths established there in 1697, for the cure of rheumatism, convulsions, and other nervous disorders. The Fields were famous for the prison which was established there in 1794 and closed in 1877. Leigh Hunt's brother, John, was an inmate from 1813 to

1815, for his part in an article ridiculing the Prince Regent. *See* ADONIS.

Cold Comfort Farm. As a phrase, it is used to imply that a particular domicile is untidy and comfortless. It is from a humorous book of this title by Stella Gibbons (1932).

> If she intended to tidy up life at Cold Comfort she would find herself opposed at every turn by the influence of Aunt Ada. Persons of Aunt Ada's temperament were not fond of a tidy life.
>
> STELLA GIBBONS : *Cold Comfort Farm*, Ch. v.

Coldbrand. *See* COLBRONDE.

Coldstream Guards. One of the five regiments of Foot Guards. General Monk's Regiment which crossed the border at Coldstream in Berwickshire to effect the RESTORATION of Charles II in 1660. It became the 2nd Regiment of Footguards in 1661 and in 1670 was officially called the Coldstream Guards.

Cole. An old canting term for money. *Cp.* COALING.

> My lusty rustic, learn and be instructed. Cole is, in the language of the witty, money: the ready, the rhino.
>
> SHADWELL : *Squire of Alsatia*, IV, xvi (1688).

To post, or **tip the cole.** To pay or put down the cash.

> If he don't tip the cole without more ado, give him a taste of the pump, that's all.
>
> HARRISON AINSWORTH : *Jack Sheppard*.

Cole, King. A legendary British king, described in the nursery rhyme as "a merry old soul" fond of his pipe, fond of his glass, and fond of his fiddlers three. Robert of Gloucester says he was father of St. HELENA (and consequently grandfather of the Emperor Constantine). Colchester was said to have been named after him.

Colettines. *See* FRANCISCANS.

Colin Clout. A name which Spenser assumes as a shepherd's boy in *The Shepheardes Calender* (1579), and in the pastoral *Colin Clout's Come Home Again* (1595), which represents his return from a visit to Sir Walter Ralegh, "the Shepherd of the Ocean". Skelton had previously (*c.* 1520) used the name as a title of a satire directed against the abuses of the Church.

Colin Tampon. The old NICKNAME of a Swiss, as JOHN BULL is of an Englishman. *Cp.* BROTHER JONATHAN ; CRAPAUD.

Coliseum. *See* COLOSSEUM.

Collar. Against the collar. Somewhat fatiguing. When a horse travels uphill the collar distresses his neck, so foot travellers often find the last mile or so "against the collar", or distressing.

Out of collar. Out of work, out of a place.

Collar-day. A day on which KNIGHTS of the different orders when present at LEVEES or other Court functions wear all their insignia and decorations, including the collar.

In the late 18th century it was a slang term for execution day.

Collar of S's. A decoration restricted to the Lord Chief Justice, the Lord Mayor of London, the Kings of Arms, the HERALDS, the SERJEANTS-AT-ARMS, and the Serjeant Trumpeter. It is composed of a series of golden S's joined together, and was originally the badge of the adherents of the House of Lancaster.

To collar. To seize (a person) by the collar ; to steal ; to appropriate without leave ; to acquire (of possessions).

To collar the bowling. In CRICKET, to hit the bowling all over the field so that it becomes easier to score, through the bowlers losing their length.

To collar the cole. To steal the money. *See* COLE.

To get hot under the collar. To become indignant, angry or irritated.

To slip the collar. To escape from restraint ; to draw back from a task begun.

To work up to the collar. To work TOOTH AND NAIL ; not to shirk the work in hand. A horse that lets his collar lie loose on his neck without bearing on it does not draw the vehicle at all, but leaves another to do the real work.

Dog-collar. *See under* DOG.

Spit and rub collar. A jocular term for the "celluloid" collar worn by clerics, which does not need laundering but can be cleaned by rubbing with a damp cloth.

White collar workers. *See* WHITE.

College. From Lat. *collegium*, a colleague ; hence a body of colleagues with common duties and privileges, etc. In English the word has a wide range, as College of Surgeons, Heralds' College, College of Justice, College of Preceptors. It is most commonly used for a separate foundation of teachers and scholars within a university and for a wide range of educational institutions, including many schools.

In old slang a prison was known as a college, and the prisoners as *collegiates*. NEWGATE was "New College" and *to take one's final degree at New College* was to be hanged. The King's Bench Prison was "King's College" and so on.

College port. The vintage port laid down in university college cellars for the special use of the senior Common Room. The excellence of this is a source of college pride.

College pudding. A small, sweet, individual-sized pudding. The name may be an abbreviation of New College Pudding.

Colliberts. A sort of GYPSY race similar to the CAQOTS and CAQUEUX, living in boats, chiefly on the rivers of Poitou. In feudal times a collibert was a partly free serf but still bound to certain services (Lat. *collibertus*, a fellow freedman).

Collins. A word sometimes applied to the "thank you letter" one writes after staying at another person's house. In *Pride and Prejudice* Mr. Collins appears as a bore and a snob of the first water; after a protracted and unwanted visit at the Bennets' his parting words are: "Depend upon it, you will speedily receive from me a letter of thanks for this, as for every mark of your regard during my stay in Hertfordshire" (ch. xxi).

Tom Collins. *See* TOM.

Colly. An old popular name for a blackbird. *Colly* is the black grime of coal (A.S. *Col*, coal). The traditional song, "The Twelve Days of Christmas", has:

> The Fourth day of Christmas my true love sent to me,
> Four colly birds, Three French hens, Two turtle doves,
> And a partridge in a pear tree.

Colly, my Cow. Colly, an old term of endearment for a cow, properly refers only to a polled cow (one deprived of its horns). It is from Scan. *kolla*, a beast without horns (Icel. *kollr*, a shaven crown).

Cologne (ko lōn′). **The Three Kings of Cologne.** The three Wise Men of the East, the MAGI, whose bones, according to mediæval legend, were deposited in Cologne Cathedral.

Eau de Cologne. *See* EAU DE COLOGNE.

Colonel. When an officer in the British Army is promoted to the rank of colonel he loses his regimental identity and becomes a member of the Staff Corps. The titular head of a regiment is also called the colonel and is usually a distinguished serving or retired General. The titular head of a Territorial Army regiment is called the Honorary Colonel.

Colonial Goose. A roast leg of mutton which has been boned and the cavity filled with a stuffing of onions, breadcrumbs and savoury herbs. A recipe intended to vary the monotony of too frequently recurring mutton on Australian sheep stations. *Cp*. BOMBAY DUCK; CAPE COD TURKEY.

Colophon. Originally, as the name implies, the *tail-piece* at the end of a book giving the printer's name, the date and place of printing, etc., sometimes with laudatory remarks designed to promote sales. It survives in the brief information usually given on the front or back of the title-page. The term is now loosely applied to a printer's or publisher's house device, such as LA BELLE SAUVAGE formerly used on the title-pages of books from the House of Cassell

Colophon, an Ionian city, was famed for its horsemen who were always reputed to turn the tide of battle by their last charge, hence this name for the final part of the book. **To add a colophon** means "to supply the finishing stroke".

Coloquintida, St. (col ō kwin′ ti dà). Charles I was so called by the LEVELLERS, to whom he was as bitter as gall or coloquintida (colocynth), the bitter-apple.

Colorado (U.S.A.). The river (and hence the State) was so named by the Spanish explorers from its *coloured* (*i.e.* reddish) appearance.

Colosseum (kol o sē′ ùm). The great Flavian amphitheatre of ancient ROME, said to be named from the colossal statue of NERO that stood close by in the Via Sacra. It was begun by Vespasian in A.D. 72, and for 400 years was the scene of gladiatorial contests. The name has since been applied to other amphitheatres and places of amusement. *Cp*. PALLADIUM.

Colossus, or Colossos (ko los′ ùs) (Lat. and Gr. for a giant statue). The bronze colossus of Rhodes, completed by Chares about 280 B.C., was a representation of the sun-god HELIOS, and commemorated the successful defence of Rhodes (305–304 B.C.) against Demetrius Poliorcetes. It was one of the Seven WONDERS of the World and probably stood some 100 ft. high. It was destroyed by an earthquake in 224 B.C. The story that it was built striding across the harbour and that ships could pass between its legs is of 16th-century origin and is not found in Strabo or Pliny's descriptions,

> He doth bestride the narrow world
> Like a Colossus.
> SHAKESPEARE: *Julius Cæsar*, I, ii.

Colour. A man of colour, or **a coloured man,** a Negro or one with Negro blood.

His coward lips did from their colour fly. (Shakespeare: *Julius Cæsar*, I, ii). He was unable to speak. As cowards run away from their regimental colour, so Cæsar's lips, when he was ill, ran away from their colour and turned pale.

I should like to see the colour of your money. I should like proof that you have any; I should like to be paid.

Off colour. Not up to the mark; run down; seedy. In the U.S.A. a risqué joke is called *off colour*.

To change colour. To blush; especially to look awkward and perplexed when found out in some deceit or meanness.

To colour up. To turn red in the face; to blush.

To give colour, or **some plausible colour to the matter.** To render it more plausible; to give it a more specious appearance.

To put a false colour on a matter. To misinterpret it, or put a false construction on it.

Under colour of. Under pretence of; under the alleged authority of.

Colours. Accidental colours. Those colours seen on a white ground after looking for some time at a bright object such as the sun. The accidental colour of red is bluish green, of orange dark blue, of violet yellow, and the converse.

Complementary colours. Colours which in combination, produce white light.

Fast colours. Colours which do not run or wash out in water.

Fundamental colours. The seven colours of the spectrum: violet, indigo, blue, green, yellow, orange, and red.

Primary, or **simple colours.** Colours which cannot be made by mixing other colours. Usually red, yellow, and blue (violet is sometimes substituted for blue).

Secondary colours. Those which result from the mixture of two or more PRIMARY COLOURS, such as orange, green, and purple.

Regimental colours. The flags peculiar to regiments, carried into battle until 1881, on which they are entitled to embroider their battle honours, by permission of the sovereign. The Royal Regiment of Artillery has no colours, regarding the capture of its guns as the same disgrace as having one's colours captured. The regimental colours of NAPOLEON's Army were the famous eagle standards, copied from the eagles of the Roman legions. The capture of a Napoleonic eagle was such an unusual feat that regiments which did so (such as the Scots Greys) usually incorporated the eagle into their regimental device. *See* QUEEN'S COLOUR.

Colours.

To come off with flying colours. To be completely triumphant, to win "hands down". The allusion is to a victorious fleet sailing into port with their flags still flying at the mastheads.

To come out in one's true colours. To reveal one's proper character, divested of all that is meretricious.

To describe (a matter) in very black colours. To see it with a jaundiced eye, and describe it accordingly; to describe it under the bias of strong prejudice.

To desert one's colours. To become a TURNCOAT; to turn tail. The allusion is to the military flag.

To get one's colours. To be rewarded for prowess in sport by the privilege of wearing school, college, or university colours on the appropriate garment, blazer, etc. *See* TO BE CAPPED, *under* CAP; FLANNELS.

To paint in bright, or **lovely colours.** To see or describe things in COULEUR DE ROSE.

To sail under false colours. To try to attain your object by appearing to be other than you are, to act hypocritically. The allusion is to the practice of pirate ships approaching their unsuspecting victim with false colours at the mast.

To see things in their true colours. To see them as they really are.

University colours. Cambridge, light blue; Oxford, dark blue; London, purple; etc. Used as distinguishing dress in all sport. Oxford and Cambridge teams are commonly referred to as the Dark Blues and the Light Blues. *See* TO GET ONE'S COLOURS *above*.

Wearing his colours. Taking his part; being strongly attached to him. The idea is from livery.

With colours nailed to the mast. Holding out to the bitter end. Colours so fixed cannot be lowered in sign of defeat or submission.

> If they catch you at disadvantage, the mines for your life is the word,—and so we fight them with our colours nailed to the mast.
> SIR W. SCOTT: *The Pirate*, ch. xxi.

With the colours. Said of a soldier who is on the active strength of a regiment, as opposed to the reserve.

Colours IN SYMBOLISM, ECCLESIASTICAL USE, etc.

Black:

> *In blazonry*, sable, signifying prudence, wisdom and constancy; it is engraved by perpendicular and horizontal lines crossing each other at right angles.
> *In art*, signifying evil, falsehood, and error.
> *In Church decoration* it was used for GOOD FRIDAY.
> *As a mortuary colour*, signifying grief, despair, death. (In the Catholic Church violet may be substituted for black.)
> *In metals* it is represented by lead.
> *In precious stones* it is represented by the DIAMOND.
> *In planets* it stands for SATURN.

Blue:

> Hope, love of divine works; (in dresses) divine contemplation, piety, sincerity.
> *In blazonry*, azure, signifying chastity, loyalty, fidelity, it is engraved by horizontal lines.
> *In art* (as an angel's robe) it signifies fidelity and faith; (as the robe of the Virgin Mary) modesty and (in the Catholic Church) humility and expiation.

In Church decoration, blue and green were used indifferently for ordinary Sundays in the pre-Reformation Church.

As a mortuary colour it signifies eternity (applied to Deity), immortality (applied to man).

In metals it is represented by tin.

In precious stones it is represented by sapphire.

In planets it stands for JUPITER.

Pale Blue:

Peace, Christian prudence, love of good works, a serene conscience.

Green:

Faith, gladness, immortality, the resurrection of the just; (in dresses) the gladness of the faithful.

In blazonry, vert, signifying love, joy, abundance; it is engraved by diagonal lines from left to right.

In art, signifying hope, joy, youth, spirit (among the Greeks and Moors it signifies victory).

In Church decoration it signifies God's bounty, mirth, gladness, the resurrection; used for week-days and Sundays after TRINITY.

In metals it is represented by COPPER.

In precious stones it is represented by the emerald.

In planets it stands for VENUS.

Pale Green:

Baptism.

Purple:

Justice, royalty.

In blazonry, purpure, signifying temperance; it is engraved by diagonal lines from right to left.

In art signifying royalty.

In Church decoration it is used for ASH WEDNESDAY and HOLY SATURDAY.

In metals it is represented by quicksilver.

In precious stones it is represented by amethyst.

In planets it stands for MERCURY.

Red:

Martyrdom for faith, charity; (in dresses) divine love.

In blazonry, gules; blood-red is called sanguine. The former signifies magnanimity, and the latter fortitude; it is engraved by perpendicular lines.

In Church decoration it is used for martyrs and for WHIT SUNDAY.

In metals it is represented by iron (the metal of war).

In precious stones it is represented by the ruby.

In planets it stands for MARS.

White:

In blazonry, argent; signifying purity, truth, innocence; in engravings argent is left blank.

In art, priests, MAGI, and DRUIDS are arrayed in white. Jesus after the resurrection should be draped in white.

In Church decoration it is used for festivals of Our Lord, for MAUNDY THURSDAY, and for all Saints except Martyrs.

As a mortuary colour it indicates hope.

In metals it is represented by SILVER.

In precious stones it is represented by the pearl.

In planets it stands for DIANA or the MOON.

Yellow:

In blazonry, or; signifying faith, constancy, wisdom, glory; in engravings it is shown by dots.

In modern art, signifying jealousy, inconstancy, incontinence. In France the doors of traitors used to be daubed with yellow, and in some countries Jews were obliged to dress in yellow. In Spain the executioner is dressed in red and yellow.

In Christian art JUDAS is arrayed in yellow; but St. PETER is also arrayed in golden yellow.

In metals it is represented by GOLD.

In precious stones it is represented by the topaz.

In planets it stands for APOLLO or the SUN.

Violet, Brown or Grey:

are used in Church decoration for ADVENT and LENT; and in other symbolism violet usually stands for penitence, and grey for tribulation.

Colour-blindness. A term introduced by Sir David Brewster (1781–1868), the inventor of the kaleidoscope, to denote the various forms of defective colour vision or perception. Also known as *Daltonism* after John Dalton (1766–1844) the scientist, who first described it in 1794, and who also suffered from it. Inability to perceive any colours as such is called *total* colour-blindness. *Complete partial* colour blindness is where some bright colours are confused, as opposed to *incomplete partial* colour-blindness where composite and neutral shades are not recognized.

Colour sergeant. From 1813 to 1915 the senior non-commissioned officer of an infantry company who had charge of the regimental colours. It is now a staff-sergeant's appointment whose badge is a sergeant's chevrons surmounted by a crown. The original badge was of crossed colours above the chevrons.

Colporteur. A hawker or PEDLAR; so called because he carried his basket or pack round his neck (Fr. *col.* neck; *porter*, to carry). The name is especially given to hawkers of religious books.

Colt. A person new to office; an awkward young fellow who needs "breaking in"; specifically in legal use, a BARRISTER who attended a SERJEANT-AT-LAW at his induction.

> I accompanied the newly made Chief Baron as his colt.
>
> POLLOCK.

In CRICKET and football a Colt team consists of a club's most promising young players.

Colt is also an abbreviation for "Colt's revolver," patented by the American Col. Sam Colt in 1835, as well as an old nautical term for an 18-inch length of knotted rope for use on the ship's boys; a CAT-O'-NINE-TAILS.

To colt. Obsolete slang for to befool, gull, cheat.

Harebrain: We are fools, tame fools!
Bellamore: Come, let's go seek him.
                He shall be hanged before he colt us so basely.

BEAUMONT and FLETCHER: *With Without Money*, III, ii.

The verb is still used in some provincial dialects for making a newcomer pay his footing.

Colt-pixy. A PIXY, PUCK, or mischievous fairy. To *colt-pixy* is to take what belongs to the pixies, and is specially applied to the gleaning of apples after the crop has been gathered in.

Colt's-tooth. The love of youthful pleasure. Chaucer uses the word "coltish" for skittish.

> He was, I trowe, a twenty winter old,
> And I was fourty, if I shall seye sooth;
> But I hadde alwey a coltes tooth.
> *Wife of Bath's Tale, Prologue,* 602.

Horses have colt's teeth at three years old, a period of life when their passions are strongest.

> Your colt's-tooth is not cat yet.
> SHAKESPEARE: *Henry VIII,* I, iii.

Columbine. A stock character in old Italian comedy from about 1560 and transferred to English PANTOMIME. She was the daughter of PANTALOON and the sweetheart of HARLE-QUIN, and, like him, was supposed to be invisible to mortal eyes. Columbina in Italian is a pet name for a lady-love, and means dove-like.

Columbus of the Skies, The. Sir William Herschel (1738–1822), German born discoverer of URANUS, was so called. The name has also been applied to others—Galileo (1564–1642), Tycho Brahe (1546–1601), and Sir Isaac Newton (1642–1727).

Columbus's Egg. An easy task once one knows the trick. The story is that Columbus, in reply to a suggestion that other pioneers might have discovered America had he not done so, is said to have challenged the guests at a banquet in his honour to make an egg stand on end. All having failed, he flattened one end of the egg by tapping it against the table and so standing it up, thus indicating that others might follow but he had discovered the way.

Column. The Column of Marcus Aurelius, or **Antonine Column.** Erected at Rome in honour of the Emperor Marcus Aurelius Antoninus (A.D. 121–180), covered like that of TRAJAN with spiral bas-reliefs representing the emperor's wars. It is a Roman DORIC column of marble 95 ft. in height on a square pedestal.

Sixtus V caused the original statue on this column to be replaced by a figure of St. PAUL in 1589.

The Column at Boulogne, or **The Column of the Grand Army,** a marble DORIC column 176 ft. high carrying a bronze statue of NAPOLEON I, to commemorate the camp at Boulogne 1804–1805, formed there for the invasion of England.

The Duke of York's Column, in London, at the top of Waterloo Steps leading from Waterloo Place into the MALL. Completed in 1833 in memory of Frederick, Duke of York, George III's second son, who died in 1827. It is of the TUSCAN ORDER, designed by R. Wyatt, and is made of Aberdeen granite, surmounted by a statue of the Duke by R. Westmacott. It contains a winding staircase to the platform and is 124 ft. high. *See* NOBLE DUKE OF YORK.

Columns, or **Pillars, of Hercules.** *See* PILLAR.

The Column of July. Erected in Paris in 1840 on the site of the BASTILLE to commemorate the July revolution of 1830 when Charles X abdicated. It is a bronze column 154 ft. high surmounted by a gilded statue of LIBERTY.

London's Column. *See* MONUMENT.

Nelson's Column. A CORINTHIAN column of Devonshire granite on a square base in Trafalgar Square, London, completed in 1843. The four lions, by Landseer, were added in 1867. It stands 185 ft. high overall; the column is a copy of one in the temple of MARS Ultor (the Avenger) at ROME. The statue, by E. H. Bailey, R.A., is 17 ft. high. The following bronze reliefs are on the sides of the pedestal; (north) the battle of the Nile, 1798, (south) Nelson's death at Trafalgar, 1805; (east) the battle of Copenhagen (1801); (west) the battle of Cape St. Vincent (1797). *See* NELSON'S PILLAR *under* PILLAR.

Column of the Place Vendôme. Erected in Paris (1806–1810) in honour of Napoleon I. Made of marble encased with bronze, the spiral outside in bas-relief represents his battles ending with Austerlitz (1805). This imitation of TRAJAN'S COLUMN is 142 ft. high and the statue of NAPOLEON at the top was hurled down by the COMMUNARDS in 1871 and replaced in 1874.

Trajan's Column. At ROME. Built of marble (A.D. 114) by Apollodorus of Damascus, it is a Roman DORIC column $127\frac{1}{2}$ ft. high, on a square pedestal with a spiral staircase inside lighted by 40 windows. It was surmounted by a statue of the Emperor Trajan but Sixtus V substituted one of St. PETER. The outside spiral represents in bas-relief the emperor's battles.

Flying Column. A column of soldiers trained and equipped for rapid movement.

To dodge the column. To avoid one's duties or allotted tasks.

Coma Berenices. *See* BERENICE.

Comazant (kom' à zănt). *See* CORPOSANT.

Comb. A crabtree comb. Slang for a cudgel. To *smooth your hair with a crabtree comb* is to give the head a knock with a stick.

Reynard's wonderful comb. This comb existed only in the brain of Master Fox. He said it was made of the Panthera's bone (*see* PANTHER), the perfume of which was so fragrant that no one could resist following it; and the wearer of the comb was always cheerful and merry.—*Reynard the Fox* (*q.v.*).

To comb out. To disentangle the hair or remove foreign bodies from it with a comb. A thorough clearing out from offices, works, etc., of men of military age, into the Army, in accordance with the Military Service Acts of World War I, was called a *comb-out*.

To comb the cat. An old military and naval phrase for untangling the cords of a CAT-O'-NINE-TAILS by drawing it through the fingers.

To comb your noddle with a three-legged stool (SHAKESPEARE: *Taming of the Shrew*, I, i) is to beat you about the head with a stool. The three-legged milking stool is the weapon in question.

To cut someone's comb. To take down a person's conceit. In allusion to the practice of cutting the combs of capons.

To set one's combs. To be cocky and vainglorious.

Come. A come down. Loss of prestige or position.

Can you come that? Can you equal it? Here "come" means to arrive at, to accomplish.

Come February, Michaelmas, etc. A colloquialism for "next February", etc.

> Come Lammas-eve at night shall she be fourteen.
> SHAKESPEARE: *Romeo and Juliet*, I, iii.

Come hell or high water. No matter what happens.

Come home. Return to your house; to touch one's feelings or interest.

> I doe now publish my Essayes: which, of all my other workes, have been most currant: for that, as it seems, they come home to men's businesse and bosomes.
> BACON: *Epistle Dedicatory to the Essays*, 1625.

Come out. Formerly said of a young woman after she had been presented at Court, and more generally, when she comes out into society as a "grown up" person.

Come-ye-all. A type of ballad consisting of a strong simple narrative with little dialogue and usually ending with a moral reflection. Double ballad metre is the traditional form, and a typical first line is "Come all ye young maidens". Hence the name.

Don't try to come it over me. Don't try to boss me or order me about; don't set yourself in a position above me.

Has he come it? Has he lent the money? Has he hearkened to your request? Has he come over to your side?

If the worst comes to the worst. *See* WORST.

Marry come up. *See* MARRY.

To come a cropper. *See* CROPPER.

To come by. To acquire, with a hint of premeditation in the transaction.

To come clean. To tell the whole truth, to make a full and frank admission, to reveal completely.

> The President of the Board of Trade will not "come clean".
> *Hansard* (1950), Vol. 473, p. 627.

To come down. To leave the university finally or to commence vacation.

To come down handsome. To pay a good price, reward, subscription, etc.

To come down upon one. To reproach, to punish severely, to make a peremptory demand.

To come it strong. To LAY IT ON THICK; to exaggerate or overdo. *See* DRAW IT MILD.

To come of good stock. To be descended from a good family.

To come off. To occur, as "my holiday didn't come off after all". Also to be accomplished successfully.

To come over one. To wheedle one to do or given something; to cheat or overreach one; to conquer or get one's own way.

To come round. To recover consciousness; to recover from a fit of the sulks; return to friendship; "he is coming round to my way of thinking", he is beginning to think as I do.

To come short. Not to be sufficient. "To come short of" means to miss or fail to attain.

To come the old soldier over one. To attempt to intimidate or bully one by an assumption of authority.

To come through the side door. To be born as an illegitimate child.

To come to. To amount to, as in "It will not come to much"; to obtain possession; to regain consciousness after fainting; etc.

To come to blows. To start fighting.

To come to grief. To meet with disaster; to be ruined.

To come to hand. *See under* HAND.

To come to pass. To happen, to befall, to come about.

> It came to pass in those days, that there went out a decree.
> *Luke* ii, I.

To come to stay. To come as a guest, also used of something which will be permanent or long-lasting.

To come to the point. *See* POINT.

To come under. To be classified under.

To come under the hammer. *See* HAMMER.

To come up against. To encounter opposition; to come across; to encounter by chance.

To come up smiling. To laugh at discomfiture or punishment; to emerge from disaster unruffled.

To come upon the parish. To enter the workhouse, to be supported by the parish.

To come up to. To equal, to amount to the same quantity.

To come up to scratch. *See* SCRATCH.

To come Yorkshire over one. To bamboozle one, to overreach one. Yorkshire has been proverbial for shrewdness and sharp practice. "I's Yorkshire too" means I am as sharp as you and am not to be taken in.

To stage a come-back. To return successfully to former standing in political or professional life, etc., after withdrawing from it.

What's to come of it? What's to come of him? A contracted form of *become*.

Comedy (Gr. *komē-ōdē*). Originally a village song, referring to the village merrymakings, in which songs still take a conspicuous place. Greek comedy appears to have originated from such village revels and certain elements of the festivities connected with the worship of DIONYSUS. The chorus probably derives from the practice of Attic revellers masquerading as birds, frogs, fishes, etc. *Cp.* TRAGEDY.

The Father of Comedy. Aristophanes (*c.* 450–385 B.C.), the Athenian dramatist.

Comet Wine. A term denoting wine of a superior quality from the notion that grapes of "comet years" (*i.e.* years in which remarkable comets appear) are are better in flavour than those of other years.

Commandment, The Ten Commandments. *See* DECALOGUE; *also under* TEN.

The ten commandments. A common expression in Elizabethan days for the ten fingers and nails, especially when used by an angry woman for scratching her opponent's face.

> Could I come near your beauty with my nails
> I'd set my ten commandments in your face.
> SHAKESPEARE: *Henry VI, Pt II*, I, iii.

The eleventh commandment. An ironical expression, signifying "Thou shalt not be found out".

Commando (Port. *commandar*, command). Originally armed units of Boer horsemen on military service. They achieved notable successes for their daring and nobility during the South African War (1899–1902).

> Lord Kitchener's relentless policy of attrition was

slowly breaking the hearts of the commandos.
> DENEYS REITZ: *Commando*, ch. xxvi.

In World War II it was adopted as the name of the especially trained British assault troops formed from volunteers to undertake particularly hazardous tasks, and also used for a member of these units.

Comme il faut (kom ēl fō) (Fr.). As it should be; quite proper; quite according to etiquette or rule.

Commemoration. *See* ENCÆNIA.

Commendam. A living in commendam is one temporarily held by someone (often a BISHOP) until an incumbent is appointed, and the practice arose of commending several livings to the bishops of poorer sees. The custom was abolished in 1836.

Commendation Ninepence. This was a bent ninepenny silver piece, commonly used in the 17th century as a love-token, giver and receiver saying. "To my love, from my love." Sometimes the coin was broken, each keeping a part.

> Like commendation ninepence, crooked,
> With "To and from my love" it looked,
> SAMUEL BUTLER: *Hudibras*, Pt. I, i.

Committee. A Committee of the whole House, in parliamentary language is when the SPEAKER leaves the chair, the mace is placed under the table, and the chair is taken by the Chairman of WAYS AND MEANS. Any member may speak more than once.

A Joint Committee is a committee nominated by the HOUSE OR LORDS and the HOUSE OF COMMONS, in practice a Select Committee of the Commons which meets a Select Committee of the Lords.

A Select Committee is fact-finding body of members selected from the whole House.

A Standing Committee in the Commons is formed so as to represent the different parties according to their relative strength in the House. They are appointed for the Session to deal with bills in the Committee stage.

Commodore. A corruption of "commander" (Fr. *commandeur*; Dut. *kommandeur*). A naval officer ranking above a captain and below a rear-admiral, of equivalent rank to a brigadier in the army. By courtesy, the title is given to the senior captain when two or more ships are in company; also to the president of a yacht club.

In the United States Navy the title was abolished in 1899, except as a retiring rank for captains.

Common. Short for common land which cannot be enclosed without an ACT OF PARLIAMENT. The enclosure of common land was a source of friction and discontent over the centuries and was not halted until the Commons Preservation Act of 1876. *See* MANOR; OPEN FIELD SYSTEM.

Rights of Common are (1) Pasture, the right of feeding stock; (2) Piscary, the right of fishing; (3) Estovers, the right of cutting wood, furze, etc.; (4) Turbary, the right of cutting turves.

Common Law. Originally the unwritten law of custom of the King's courts (except of Equity). From the late 15th century precedent began to be accepted and gradually superseded local customs until the 19th century when precedent and case-made law predominated. *Cp.* STATUTE.

Common Law Wife. A common term applied to a woman cohabiting with a man as in a marriage relationship but based on mutual agreement and not on any civil or religious rite. Her partner has to maintain their children but she has no legal status under COMMON LAW. *Cp.* TO LIVE TALLY *under* TALLY.

A judge objected to the use of the phrase "Common Law Wife" by a barrister at a trial at Southend Crown Court yesterday ...." Nowadays there is no stigma about unmarried people living together".
DAILY TELEGRAPH, 4 Dec. 1974.

Common Market. The popular name for the European Economic Community set up in 1957, consisting of Belgium, France, West Germany, Italy, Luxembourg and the Netherlands, to promote economic co-operation and common development with the ultimate aim of economic and a degree of political unity. It was joined by Great Britain, Denmark and the Irish Republic in 1974, by Greece in 1981 and by Spain and Portugal in 1985. Free Trade between members was established in 1984. A commission implements policies decided by a Council of Ministers which is subject to a European Parliament.

Common Pleas. Actions between subject and subject at Common Law. The Court of Common Pleas was for the trial of civil actions and was transferred to the High Court of Justice by the Judicature Act of 1873 and then merged in the Queen's Bench Division (1881).

Common Prayer. The Book of Common Prayer. *See under* BOOK.

Common sense. Good, sound, practical sense; general sagacity. Formerly it denoted a supposed internal sense held to be common to all the senses, or one that acted as a link between them. *See* SEVEN SENSES *under* SENSE.

Commoneer. One of the common people, one below the rank of peer, a member of the British HOUSE OF COMMONS; also one with RIGHTS OF COMMON and, at Oxford colleges,

a student not on the foundation.

The Great Commoner. William Pitt the elder (1708–1778), Earl of Chatham, famous statesman, and, like Sir Winston Churchill, a great House of Commons man.

Commons. Doctors' Commons. *See under* DOCTOR.

To come into commons. To enter a society in which the members have a common or general dinner table. To be removed from the society is to be *discommonsed*:

He [Dryden] was in trouble [at Cambridge] on 19 July 1652, when he was discommonsed and gated for a fortnight for disobedience and contumacy.
SAINTSBURY: *Dryden*, ch. i.

To put someone on short commons. To stint him, to give him scanty meals. At the universities of Oxford and Cambridge the food provided for each student (at a common table) at breakfast was called his *commons*; hence food in general or meals.

Commonwealth, The. A term specifically applied to England in 1649 by the RUMP, after it had abolished the HOUSE OF LORDS and the monarchy and established the Council of State. Oliver Cromwell was styled Lord PROTECTOR of the Commonwealth in 1653, and the period of his rule is usually called the Protectorate.

In current usage the term is applied to the British Commonwealth, the free association of most nations of the former British Empire.

Ideal Commonwealths. The best known ideal or imaginary Commonwealths are those sketched by Plato in the *Republic* (from which later examples derive), by CICERO in his *De Republica*, by St. Augustine in his *De Civitate Dei*, by Dante in his *De Monarchia*, by Sir Thomas More in UTOPIA, by Bacon in the *New Atlantis* (*see under* ATLANTIS), by Campanella in his *Civitas Solis*, and by Samuel Butler in EREWHON.

Others are Johnson's *Rasselas*, Lytton's *Coming Race*, Bellamy's *Looking Backward*, Wm. Morris's *News from Nowhere*, H. G. Wells's *In the Days of the Comet*, and *The World Set Free*.

Communards (From *commune*, in France, a unit of local government). After the Franco-Prussian War and the fall of Napoleon III, bitter political divisions arose between the people of Paris and the government at Versailles under Adolphe Thiers. Radicals, revolutionaries, socialists and workmen of the Paris Commune, adopting the name *Communards*, took control of the city in March 1871. They were ruthlessly suppressed by 29 May, with heavy loss of life, especially at the PÈRE LACHAISE cemetery.

Communism, in the general sense of a society or community based on common ownership of property and common labour with all sharing the common product, has been practised in many primitive societies and particular groups (*See* DIGGERS). Since the time of Plato's *Republic* various forms of communism have been elaborated, but in current usage it derives from the theories of Karl Marx (1818–1883) and Friedrich Engels (1820–1895) as set out in their *Communist Manifesto* (1848) and in the former's *Capital* (1867–1894). *See* MARXISM; MATERIALISM.

> The distinguishing feature of Communism is not the abolition of property generally, but the abolition of bourgeois property.
> *Communist Manifesto, II.*

Companions of Jehu. The CHOUANS were so called, from a fanciful analogy between their self-imposed task, and that given to Jehu when anointed king over Israel. Jehu was to cut off Ahab and Jezebel, with all their house (II *Kings* ix, 6–8). The Chouans were to cut off all who murdered Louis XVI, and to place his brother Louis XVIII (Jehu) on the throne.

Comparisons are odorous. So says Dogberry (SHAKESPEARE: *Much Ado About Nothing*, III, v) (a blunder for *odious*).

> We own your verses are melodious,
> But then comparisons are odious.
> SWIFT: *Answer to Sheridan's "Simile".*

Complementary Colours. *See* COLOURS.

Complex. A combination of memories and wishes which exercise an influence on the personality. *See also under* ŒDIPUS.

Inferiority complex. A feeling of inferiority in persons who appear over-conscious of their own shortcomings.

To have a complex about something. To have a strong feeling either for or against something; to be over concerned about it.

Compline (kom' plin). The last of the CANONICAL HOURS, said about 8 or 9 p.m., and so called because it completes the series of the daily prayers or hours. From M.E. and O.Fr. *complie*, Lat. *completa* (*hora*).

In ecclesiastical Lat. *vesperinus*, from *vesper*, means evening service, and *completinus* appears to be formed on this model.

Complutensian Polyglot. *See* BIBLE, SOME SPECIALLY NAMED EDITIONS.

Compos Mentis. *See* NON COMPOS MENTIS.

Compostela, or Compostella (kom postel' à). Santiago de Compostela, the city in Spain where the relics of St. JAMES the Great are supposed to be preserved; a corruption of *Giacomopostolo* (James the Apostle). *See* COCKLE HAT.

Comstockery. The vigorous suppression of books, plays, and other literature deemed to be salacious or corrupting, as advocated by the New York Society for the Suppression of Vice, whose moving spirit was Anthony Comstock (1844–1915). The word was coined by G. B. Shaw. *Cp.* BOWDLERIZE.

Comus. (kō' mus) (Gr. *komos*, carousal). In Milton's masque of this name, the god of sensual pleasure, the son of BACCHUS and CIRCE.

In the masque, the elder brother is meant for Viscount Brackley, the younger brother is Thomas Egerton, and the lady is Lady Alice Egerton, children of the Earl of Bridgewater, at whose castle in Ludlow it was first presented in 1634. *See* SABRINA.

Con amore (kon a môr' i) (Ital.). With heart and soul; as, "he did it *con amore*"—*i.e.* lovingly, with delight, and therefore in good earnest.

Con brio (Ital.). In music, forcefully and with spirit.

Con spirito (Ital.). With quickness and vivacity. A musical term.

Conan (kō' nan). In the literature of OSSIAN "a kind of Thersites, but brave even to rashness".

Blow for blow or claw for claw, as Conan said. Conan made a vow never to take a blow without returning it. When he descended into the infernal regions, the arch fiend gave him a cuff, which Conan instantly returned, saying, "Claw for claw."

Conceptionists. *See* FRANCISCANS.

Concert of Europe. In the 19th century, the name given to the general policy of the major European powers to maintain peace after the Vienna Settlement, and to regulate international relations by consultation and agreement, and to act in concert when the need arose. *See* CONGRESS SYSTEM.

> Mr Disraeli's refusal [to be party to the Berlin Memorandum of 1876] created, as was inevitable, profound perturbation abroad, and evoked a storm of criticism at home. There can be no question that the European Concert, whatever it was worth, was broken by the policy of Great Britain.
> J.A.R. MARRIOTT: *History of Europe, 1815–1939*, ch. xvii.

Concert Pitch is the pitch, internationally agreed in 1939, to which musical instruments are usually tuned.

Hence figuratively **to screw oneself up to concert pitch** is to make oneself absolutely ready, prepared for any emergency or anything one may have to do.

Conchobar (kon ko' bar). In ancient Irish romance, son of Nessa, and king of ULSTER at the opening of the Christian era. He was uncle and guardian of CUCHULAIN and also responsible for the upbringing of DEIRDRE. He is said to have died of anger on the day of Christ's crucifixion.

Conchy. *See* CONSCIENTIOUS OBJECTOR.

Conclamatio. Amongst the ancient Romans, the loud cry raised by those standing round a death-bed at the moment of death. It probably had its origin in the idea of recalling the departed spirit and was similar to the Irish howl over the dead. "One not howled over" (*corpus nondum clamatum*) meant one at the point of death; and "one howled for" was one given up for dead or actually deceased. Hence the phrase *conclamatum est*, he is dead past all hope, he has been called and gives no sign. VIRGIL makes the palace ring with howls when DIDO burnt herself to death.

> Lamentis, gemituque, et fœmineo ululato,
> Texta fremunt.
> *Æneid*, iv, 667.

Conclave. Literally, a room or set of rooms, all of which can be opened by one key (Lat. *cum clavis*). The word is applied to small cells erected for the CARDINALS who meet, after the death of a POPE, to elect a successor; hence the assembly of cardinals for this purpose; hence any private assembly for discussion. The conclave of cardinals dates from 1274 and was limited to 120 cardinals in 1973. Those assembled in the VATICAN are secluded in the conclave apartments and votes are taken morning and evening until one candidate has secured a two-thirds majority of votes. He is then acclaimed Pope.

> And once more in my arms I bid him [Cardinal Campeius] welcome,
> And thank the holy conclave for their loves.
> SHAKESPEARE: *Henry VIII*, II, ii.

To meet in solemn conclave is to meet together to decide matters of importance.

Concordat (kon kôr′ dăt). An agreement, especially between a secular ruler and the POPE; as the Germanic Concordat of 1448 between the Emperor Frederick III and Nicholas V; the Concordat of 1516 between Francis I of France and Leo X to abolish the PRAGMATIC SANCTION; and the Concordat of 1801 between NAPOLEON and Pius VII. In 1929 a concordat between the Papacy and the Italian Government established the VATICAN City State.

Concrete Numbers. *See* ABSTRACT NUMBERS.

Condottieri (It. *condotto*, hired). A name applied to the leaders of bands of FREEBOOTERS, mercenaries, or military adventurers of the 14th and 15th centuries. Notable among them were Sir John Hawkwood at Florence, Francesco of Carmagnola, and Francesco Sforza. Italy was particularly pla-

gued by them. The singular is *condottiere*.

Confederate States. The eleven states which seceded from the Union in the American Civil War (1861–1865)—*viz*. Alabama, Arkansas, North and South Carolina, Georgia, Florida, Louisiana, Mississippi, Tennessee, Texas, Virginia.

Confederation of the Rhine. The sixteen German states which allied themselves with France in 1806. The confederation was dissolved in 1813.

The North German Confederation was formed in 1867 under the presidency of the King of Prussia, consequent upon the defeat of Austria in 1866. It consisted of all 22 states north of the river Main.

Confession, Seal of. The obligation which binds a priest not to divulge outside the confessional anything he may hear therein. He cannot be forced to reveal in the witness-box of a court of law any information he may have thus obtained.

Confetti. The practice of throwing confetti over the bridal pair after their wedding is a substitute for the old custom of throwing corn and later, rice. It derives from an ancient fertility rite the intent of which was to ensure prosperity and fruitfulness.

Confidence trick. Usually the work of a professional swindler, who creates a false impression to secure a person's trust with the direct purpose of cheating him. Often the victim is induced to hand over money, valuables, etc., as a mark of confidence but such trickery takes many forms. From this the current slang expression **all a con** is derived to imply *a take in*, *a see off*, or *a swindle*.

Confusion worse confounded. Disorder made worse than before.

Congé (kon zhā′) (Fr. leave). "To give a person his congé" is to dismiss him from your service. "To take one's congé" is to give notice to friends of your departure by leaving a card at the friend's house inscribed P.P.C. (*pour prendre congé* to take leave) on the left-hand corner.

Congé d'élire (Fr. leave to elect). A royal writ given to a CHAPTER to elect a named priest to a vacant SEE. Its use dates from 1533.

Congleton Bears. Men of Congleton, or Beartowners. Congleton in Cheshire was a noted north of England bear-baiting centre in the 16th and 17th centuries. Tradition has it that at some time in the 16th century the town bear died just before the annual wakes (*see* WAKE). Money intended to purchase a Bible was diverted to purchase a bear, hence Congleton came to be called *Bear Town* and its inhabitants *Congleton Bears*. In the

words of the jingle—
> Congleton rare, Congleton rare,
> Sold the Bible to buy a bear.

Congregationalists. Those PROTESTANT Dissenters maintaining that each congregation was independent with a right to govern its own affairs and choose its own minister. They derived from the BROWNISTS and BARROWISTS of Elizabeth I's reign. The Congregational Union was formed in 1832. *See* UNITED REFORMED CHURCH.

Congress System. Refers to the attempts made after the Vienna Settlement of 1815 to settle problems affecting the peace of Europe by congresses or conferences between the major powers. The experiment ended with the Congress of St. Petersburg (1825). *See* CONCERT OF EUROPE.

Congreve Rocket. A rocket invented in 1808 for use in war by Sir William Congreve (1772–1828). It was not very successfully used at Leipzig in 1813. He was Comptroller of the Royal Laboratory at Woolwich.

> But vaccination certainly has been
> A kind antithesis to Congreve's rockets.
> > BYRON: *Don Juan*, I, cxxix.

Congreves. Predecessors of the LUCIFERMATCH, invented by Sir William Congreve. The splints were dipped in sulphur then tipped with chlorate of potash paste, in which gum was substituted for sugar, then a small quantity of sulphide of antimony was added. The match was ignited by being drawn through a fold of sand-paper. *Cp.* PROMETHEAN.

Conjuring Cap. I must put on my conjuring cap—*i.e.* your question requires deliberate thought, and I must reflect upon it. Tradition says that Eric XIV, King of Sweden (1560–1568), who became insane, was a great believer in magic and had an "enchanted cap" by means of which he pretended to exercise power over the elements. When a storm arose, his subjects used to say, "The King has got on his conjuring cap." *Cp.* I MUST PUT ON MY THINKING CAP *under* CAP.

Conker (kon' kĕr). A children's name for a horse-chestnut; possibly derived from the Fr. *conque*, a shell. Schoolboys thread a chestnut on a string knotted at one end, and then play conkers by each taking a turn at striking his opponent's conker until one or other is broken from the string. Perhaps **conk**, slang for nose, is similarly derived; hence, *conky*, a big- or beak-nosed person. **Old Conky.** The Duke of Wellington (1769–1852) was so nicknamed from the shape of his nose or CONK.

To conk out, used of an engine or motor, means to break down or stop running. This usage is probably onomatopoeic. It also means to die.

Connecticut (kȯ net' i kŭt) is the Mohegan dialect word *Quonaughicut*, meaning "long tidal river". *See* NUTMEG STATE.

Conqueror. The title was applied to the following:
> ALEXANDER THE GREAT. *The conqueror of the world* (356–323 B.C.).
> Alfonso I of Portugal (*c.* 1114–1185).
> Aurungzebe, Mogul Emperor of India (1659–1707).
> James I of Aragon (1213–1276).
> Mohammed II, Sultan of Turkey (1451–1481).
> Othman or Osman I, founder of the Ottoman dynasty in Turkey (1300–1326).
> Francisco Pizarro. *Conquistador*, conqueror of Peru (*c.* 1470–1541).
> William, Duke of Normandy, conqueror of England (1066–1087).

Conqueror's nose. A prominent straight nose, rising at the bridge. CHARLEMAGNE had such a nose, so had Henry the Fowler of Germany, Rudolf I of Germany; Frederick I of Hohenzollern; Bismarck, the IRON CHANCELLOR of Germany, etc. *See* OLD CONKY *under* CONKER.

Conquest, The. William of Normandy's conquest of England (1066).

Conscience. Conscience clause. A clause in an ACT OF PARLIAMENT to relieve persons with conscientious scruples from certain requirements in it (usually of a religious character). It acquired a wider significance in connexion with the Compulsory Vaccination Act of 1898.

Conscience money. Usually refers to money paid anonymously to the government by persons who have defrauded the revenue, most frequently by understating their income-tax liabilities. The sum is advertised in the *London Gazette*. It also has a more general connotation.

Court of Conscience. Courts of the recovery of small debts, established at LONDON and various other commercial centres, eventually superseded by County Courts.

> Why should not Conscience have vacation,
> As well as other courts o' th' nation.
> > BUTLER: *Hudibras*, II, ii.

Have you the conscience to [demand such a price]? Can your conscience allow you to [demand such a price]?

In all conscience. As, "And enough too, in all conscience", *i.e.* the demand made is as much as conscience would tolerate; verging on the border of sharp practice or of that fine line which divides honesty from dishonesty.

My conscience! An oath. I swear by my conscience.

To have a Nonconformist Conscience. To have opinions as to right or wrong like those commonly held by NONCONFORMISTS; to have a puritan conscience especially with regard to drinking and gambling.

To make a matter of conscience of it. To deal with it according to the dictates of conscience, to treat it conscientiously.

To speak one's conscience. To speak one's own mind, give one's own candid thoughts and opinions.

> By my troth I will speak my conscience of the king.
> SHAKESPEARE: *Henry V*, IV, i.

Conscientious objector. One who takes advantage of a conscience clause, and so evades some particular requirement of the law in question. Once specially applied to those who had a conscientious objection to vaccination, but since World War I it has come to mean one who obtains exemption from military service on grounds of conscience. Such people are also called. *C.O.*s or *Conchies*.

Conscript Fathers. Lat *Patres Conscripti*, the Roman Senate. One explanation is that ROMULUS is supposed to have instituted a senate of a hundred elders called *Patres* (Fathers). After the SABINES joined the State, another hundred were added. Tarquinius Priscus, the fifth king, added a third hundred, called *Patres Minorum Gentium*. When Tarquinius Superbus, the seventh and last king of Rome, was banished, several of the senate followed him, and the vacancies were filled up by Junius Brutus, the first consul. The new members were enrolled in the senatorial register and so called *conscripti*; the entire body was then addressed as *Patres [et] Conscripti* or *Patres, Conscripti*. See TARQUIN.

Consentes Dii. The twelve chief Roman deities, six male and six female, the same as the Athenian Twelve Gods:

> JUPITER, APOLLO, NEPTUNE, MARS,
> MERCURY, VULCAN, JUNO, DIANA,
> MINERVA, VENUS, CERES, VESTA.

Ennius puts them into two hexameter verses:

> Juno, Vesta, Minerva, Ceres, Diana, Venus, Mars,
> Mercurius, Jovi', Neptunus, Vulcanus, Apollo.

Called *consentes*, says Varro.

> Quia in consilium Jovis adhibebantur.
> *De Lingua Latina*, vii, 28.

Consenting Stars. Stars forming configurations for good or evil. In *Judges* v, 20, we read that "the stars in their courses fought against Sisera", *i.e.* formed unlucky or malignant configurations.

> ... Scourge the bad revolting stars
> That have consented unto Henry's death.
> SHAKESPEARE: *Henry VI, Pt. I*, I, i.

Conservative. One who essentially believes in amending existing institutions cautiously and who opposes doctrinaire changes. The name came to be applied to the TORY party from the 1830s after its use by J. W. Croker in the *Quarterly Review* of January 1830. "We have always been conscientiously attached to what is called Tory, and which might with more propriety be called the Conservative Party" (P. 276). Canning somewhat similarly used the word in a speech at Liverpool in March 1820.

Conservator of the Peace. The predecessor of the JUSTICE OF THE PEACE and usually a function of the KNIGHT OF THE SHIRE.

Consistory (Lat. *consistorium*, a place of assembly). As an ecclesiastical court in the Church of ROME it is the assembly in council of the POPE and CARDINALS; in England it is a diocesan court presided over by the CHANCELLOR of the diocese.

Consolidated Fund. The national revenue from all sources is paid into this fund and held in the EXCHEQUER account at the Bank of England. The fund, which dates from 1787, is pledged for meeting the interest and management costs of the National Debt, CIVIL LIST, etc.

Consols. A contraction of *Consolidated Annuities*, part of the public debt.

Constable (Lat. *comes stabuli*) means Court of the Stable or Master of the Horse. In the BYZANTINE EMPIRE the Constable was master of the imperial stables and a great officer of state, hence the use of the name for an official of a royal household or a military commander. It was adopted by the Frankish kings and the office grew steadily more important under their successors. (*See* CONSTABLE OF FRANCE.) Constable is also the term for a governor of a fortress, as the Constable of the TOWER of London. From Tudor times it became the designation of a parish officer, and later a policeman, as officers appointed to keep the peace. In England a *Special Constable* is one enrolled to help the regular constabulary in time of pressure or emergency.

The Constable of England, or **Lord High Constable** is first identifiable in Henry I's reign (1100–1135), but since 1521 has been appointed for coronation days only.

The Constable of France was once a great household official, judge of all matters pertaining to CHIVALRY, etc., and from the 14th century commander-in-chief of the army. The office was suppressed by Louis XIII in

1627, but temporarily revived by NAPOLEON.

The Lord High Constable of Scotland. An office similar to those of England and France instituted by David I about 1147. It was conferred by Robert Bruce in 1315 on Sir Gilbert Hay, created Earl of Erroll, in which family it was made hereditary and is still held.

Drink the constable. *See* MOROCCO.

To overrun, or **outrun the constable.** To fall into debt; to overspend one's income; to talk about what you do not understand.

> Quoth Hudibras, Friend Ralph, thou hast
> Outrun the constable at last:
> For thou art fallen on a new
> Dispute, as senseless as untrue.
> BUTLER: *Hudibras*, I, iii.

Who's to pay the constable? Who is to pay the score?

Constantine, Donation of. *See* DECRETALS.

Constantine's Cross. *See* CROSS.

Constituent Assembly. The first of the National Assemblies of the French Revolution which sat from July 1789 until 1791; so called from its main objective of drawing up a new constitution.

After World War II a National Constituent Assembly of 522 deputies was elected in France, according to the constitution promulgated in October 1945.

Constitution. The fundamental law or body of custom by which a state is organized and governed, *i.e.* constituted.

To give a nation a constitution usually means to establish a system of government limiting the arbitrary power of the head of the state thus preventing a despotism or autocracy.

Apostolic Constitutions. A comprehensive rule in eight books concerning church doctrines and customs. Of unknown authorship, they are probably of Syrian origin and probably date from the 4th century. They are certainly post-Apostolic.

Constitutions of Clarendon. *See* CLARENDON.

Consummatum est. (kon sŭm ā′ tum est) (Lat.). It is finished; the last words of our Lord on the CROSS (*John* xix, 30).

> Meph.: O, what will I not do to obtain his soul?
> Faust.: Consummatum est: this bill is ended.
> And Faustus hath bequeathed his soul to Lucifer.
> MARLOWE: *Doctor Faustus*, V, 74.

Contango. In STOCK EXCHANGE parlance, the sum paid by the purchaser of stock to the seller, for the privilege of deferring the completion of the bargain till the next, or some future settling day. *Cp.* BACKWARDATION.

Contemplate. To meditate or reflect upon: to consider attentively. The word takes us back

to the ancient Roman augurs (*see* AUGURY), for the *templum* (whence our *temple*) was that part of the heavens which he wished to consult. Having mentally divided it into two parts from top to bottom, he watched to see what would occur; and this watching of the *templum* was called *contemplating*.

Contempt of Court. A term of wide coverage which briefly defined consists of refusal to obey the rules, orders, and processes of the courts of law, or interference with the course of justice. Offenders can be jurors, parties, witnesses, solicitors, etc.

Contempt of Parliament. Any disobedience or disrespect or obstruction to the due course of proceedings or gross reflection on the character of a member is a breach of PRIVILEGE.

Contemptibles, The Old. Members of the British Expeditionary Force of 160,000 men that left Britain in 1914 to join the French and Belgians against Germany. The soldiers gave themselves this name from an army order (almost certainly apocryphal) said to have been given at Aix on 19 August by the Kaiser.

> It is my royal and imperial command that you exterminate the treacherous English, and walk over General French's contemptible little army.

It is said by some that actually he called the B.E.F. "a contemptibly little army", which is not nearly so disparaging.

The surviving veterans held their last parade at the garrison church of All Saints, Aldershot on Sunday 4 August 1974, in the presence of Queen Elizabeth II, who took tea with them before their final dispersal.

Contest of Wartburg. Sometimes called the *Battle of the Minstrels*, the famous poetical contest of MINNESINGER held in 1207 at the Wartburg, a castle in Saxe-Weimar. The best of the contestants was Walther von der Vogelweide and the contest is commemorated in Wagner's TANNHÄUSER.

Continence of a Scipio. It is said that a beautiful princess fell into the hands of Scipio Africanus, and he refused to see her, "lest he should be tempted to forget his principles". Similar stories are told of many historical characters including Cyrus and ALEXANDER.

Continental. Not worth a continental. Worthless like the paper money issued by the American Continental Congress during the War of Independence, which became valueless by the end of 1780.

Continental System. The name given to NAPOLEON'S plan to cripple Britain by economic warfare when the invasion plan had failed. The Berlin Decrees of 21 NOVEMBER 1806 excluded all British goods from the ports of France and her allies, and declared the British Isles in a state of blockade.

Continuity Man, or **Girl.** The technique of cinematography allows of a play, etc., being photographed in scenes and incidents not necessarily in sequence and each scene, etc., may be "shot" many times. It is essential that every detail of costume, scenery, etc., is correctly repeated each time a scene is "shot". It is the task of the continuity man or girl to ensure this.

Contra (Lat.). Against: generally in the phrase *pro and contra* or *pro and con*. In bookkeeping a *contra* is an entry on the right-hand or credit side of the ledger. *See* PER CONTRA.

A contra-account is one kept by a firm which both buys from and sells to the same client, so that the transactions cancel out as paper entries.

Contra bonos mores (Lat.). Not in accordance with good manners; not COMME IL FAUT.

Contra jus gentium (Lat.). Against the law of nations; specially applied to usages in war which are contrary to the laws or customs of civilized peoples.

Contra mundum (Lat.). Against the world at large. Used of an innovator or reformer who sets his opinion against that of everyone else, and specially connected with Athanasius in his vehement opposition to the ARIANS.

Contretemps (Fr.). A mischance, something inopportune, a "hitch". Literally "out of time".

Conventicle. The word was applied by the early Christians to their meeting places and inevitably acquired the derogatory sense of a clandestine meeting. With the advent of Protestantism in England it came to be applied to the meetings and meeting-places of DISSENTERS.

Conventicle Act. In 1593 such an Act was passed containing severe penalties against those attending religious conventicles. The better-known Act of 1664 forbade religious conventicles of more than five persons except in accordance with the BOOK OF COMMON PRAYER. It was repealed in 1812.

Convention Parliaments. Two parliaments were so called: one in 1660, because it was not summoned by the king, but was convened by General Monk to effect the RESTORATION of Charles II; and that authorized by William of Orange in January 1689 which offered the throne to William and Mary as joint sovereigns.

In 1787 the Constitution of the U.S.A. was drawn up by a convention at Philadel-phia. In the U.S.A. National Party Conventions elect the official candidates for the Presidency and Vice-Presidency.

In the French Revolution, the National Convention succeeded the Legislative Assembly (21 September 1792), proclaimed the Republic (22 September) and governed France until October 1795, when it was succeeded by the DIRECTORY.

Convey (Lat. *conveho*, to carry away). A polite term for *steal*. Thieves, by a similar euphemism are called *conveyers*.

> Convey, the wise it call: Steal! foh! a fico for the phrase!
>
> SHAKESPEARE: *Merry Wives of Windsor*, I, iii.

Convict. In circus parlance a zebra, because of the resemblance of its stripes to a convict's one-time striped shirt.

Cooing and Billing, like Philip and Mary on a shilling. The reference is to coins struck in 1555, in which Mary and her consort are placed face to face, and not cheek by jowl, the usual way.

> Still amorous, and fond, and billing,
> Like Philip and Mary on a shilling.
>
> BUTLER: *Hudibras*, Pt. III, i.

Cook, Cooking. Terms belonging to cuisine applied to man under different circumstances: Sometimes he is well *basted*; he *boils* with rage, is *baked* with heat, and *burns* with love or jealousy. Sometimes he is *buttered* and *well buttered;* he is often *cut up, devoured* with a flame and *done brown*. We *dress his jacket* for him; sometimes he is *eaten up* with care, sometimes he is *fried*. We *cook his goose* for him, and sometimes he makes a goose of himself. We make a *hash* of him, and at times he makes a hash of something else. He gets into *hot water*, and sometimes into a *mess*. Is made into *mincemeat*, makes mincemeat of his money, and is often in a *pickle*. We are often asked to *toast* him, sometimes he gets well *roasted*, is sometimes *set on fire*, put into a *stew*, or is in a *stew*.

A "softie" is *half-baked*, one severely handled is well *peppered*. To falsify accounts is to *cook* or *salt* them, wit is *Attic salt*, and an exaggerated statement must be taken *cum grano salis*.

A pert young person is a *sauce* box, a shy lover is a *spoon*, a rich father has to *fork out*, and is sometimes *dished* of his money.

A conceited man does not think small *beer* (or small *potatoes*) of himself, and one's mouth is called a *potato-trap*. A simpleton is a *cake*, a *gudgeon*, and a *pigeon*. Some are *cool as a cucumber*, others *hot as a quail*. A chubby child is a little *dumpling*. A woman may be a *duck*; a courtesan was called *mut-*

ton or *laced mutton*, and a large coarse hand is a *mutton fist*. Side whiskers are called *mutton chops*. A greedy person is a *pig*, a fat one is a *sausage*, and a shy one, if not a sheep, is certainly *sheepish*; while a Lubin casts *sheep's eyes* at his lady-love. A coward is *chicken-hearted*, a fat person is *crummy*, and a cross one is *crusty*, while an aristocrat belongs to the *upper crust* of society. Yeomen of the Guard are BEEFEATERS, a soldier is a *red herring*, or a *lobster*, and a stingy, ill-tempered old man is a *crab*. A walking advertiser between two boards is a *sandwich-man*. An alderman in his chain is a *turkey hung with sausages*. Two persons resembling each other are like as *two peas*. A chit is a mere *sprat*, a delicate maiden is a *titbit*, and a colourless countenenace is called a *wheyface*. Anything unexpectedly easy is a *piece of cake*.

Cooked. The books have been cooked. The accounts have been falsified.

Cook your goose. *See* GOOSE.

What's cooking? What's in hand? What's doing?

Cookie-pusher (U.S.A.). A young and junior diplomat whose most onerous duties appear to consist in handing round plates and food at official receptions.

Cool. Cool card; cooling card. *See* CARD.

Cool as a cucumber. Perfectly composed; not in the least angry or agitated.

Cool hundred, thousand (or any other sum). The whole of the sum named, cool being emphatic; it may have originally had reference to the calm deliberation with which the sum was counted out.

> He had lost a cool hundred, and would play no longer.
>
> FIELDING: *Tom Jones*, VIII, xii.

Cool tankard, or **cool cup.** A drink made of wine and water, with lemon, sugar, and borage; sometimes also slices of cucumber.

Cooler. A slang term, of American origin, for a prison or prison cell.

Coon. Short for raccoon, a small North American arboreal animal, about the size of a fox, valued for its fur. The animal was adopted as a badge by the old WHIG party in the United States about 1840. In the 19th century the word became slang for a Negro.

A coon's age. Quite a long time; a "month of Sundays" (U.S.A.).

A gone coon. A person in a terrible fix; one on the verge of ruin. The coon being hunted for its fur is a "gone coon" when it is treed and so has no escape from its pursuers.

To go the whole coon. An American equivalent of the English "to go the whole hog". *See* HOG.

Coop. U.S. slang for prison.

To fly the coop is to escape from prison.

Cooper. Half STOUT and half porter. The term arose from the old practice at breweries of allowing the coopers a daily portion of stout and porter. As they did not like to drink porter after stout, they mixed the two together. *See also* ALE; ENTIRE.

Coot. A silly coot, Stupid as a coot. The coot is a small waterfowl.

Bald as a Coot. *See under* BALD.

Cop. To catch, lay hold of, capture. To "get copped" is to get caught, especially by the police, whence *cop* and COPPER for a policeman. Perhaps connected with Lat. *capere*, to take, etc. The word is used for catching almost anything, as punishment at school, or even an illness.

> They thought I was sleepin', ye know,
> And they sed as I'd copped it o' Jim;
> Well, it come like a bit of a blow,
> For I watched by the deathbed of him.
>
> SIMS: *Dagonet Ballads (The Last Letter).*

A fair cop is applied to one caught *in flagrante delicto*.

Cope, Johnnie. *See* JOHNNIE COPE.

Copenhagen (kō pėn hā'gėn). The famous chestnut horse ridden by the Duke of Wellington at Waterloo. The name commemorates the Duke's part in the Copenhagen expedition of 1807. Copenhagen was pensioned off at Stratfield Saye and lived to the age of twenty-seven.

Copernican System, Copernicanism. The heliocentric or sun-centred theory of the universe postulated by Nicolaus Copernicus (1473–1543) in his book *De Revolutionibus Orbium*. This superseded the PTOLEMAIC SYSTEM in which the sun is supposed to move round the earth. The idea was not entirely new and was vaguely held by the School of PYTHAGORAS. Pope Gregory XIII used *De Revolutionibus* when constructing his CALENDAR but the book was placed on the INDEX in 1616. *See* ALMAGEST.

Cophetua (ko fet' ū à). An imaginary king of Africa who fell in love with Penelophon (SHAKESPEARE'S Zenelophon in *Love's Labour's Lost*, IV, i) and married her. They lived happily and were widely lamented at death. The story is given in the ballad *King Cophetua and the Beggar-Maid* in PERCY'S RELIQUES and is referred to in Shakespeare's *Romeo and Juliet* (II, i) and *Richard II* (V, iii).

Copper. Among the old alchemists copper was the symbol of VENUS.

The name is also given to the large boiler used for laundry purposes, cooking, etc., which was originally made of copper but later of iron; also to pence, half-pence, farthings, etc., once minted of copper but from 1860 of bronze.

In slang a **copper** is a policeman, *i.e.* one who "cops" or catches offenders.

Copper captain. A "BRUMMAGEM", or sham captain; a man who "swanks about" with the title but has no right to it. Michael Perez is so called in Beaumont and Fletcher's *Rule a Wife and have a Wife*.

> To this copper-captain was confided the command of the troops.—W. IRVING: *Knickerbocker*.

Copper Nose. Oliver Cromwell; also called "Ruby Nose", "Nosey", and "Nose Almighty", no doubt from *acne rosacea* which showed itself in a big red nose.

Copper-nose Harry. Henry VIII was notorious for his debasement of the coinage (from 1526). The copper content in the "silver" coins soon showed itself on the more prominent parts, especially the nose. Hence the king came to be called "Old Copper Nose" or "Copper-nose Harry".

Copperheads. Secret foes. Copperheads are North American poisonous snakes which attack without warning. The name was applied by the early colonists to the Indians, then to the Dutch (see Washington Irving's *History of New York*). In the American CIVIL WAR it was given to those Northerners who were against the coercion of the CONFEDERATE STATES of the South. Copperhead badges were devised from one cent copper pieces and some Copperheads engaged in subversive activities joining secret societies such as the KNIGHTS OF THE GOLDEN CIRCLE.

Copts. Christian descendants of the Ancient Egyptians who became MONOPHYSITES and JACOBITES and who have retained the patriarchal chair of Alexandria since the Council of Chalcedon in 451, which still has nominal jurisdiction over the Ethiopian Church. Coptic ceased to be a living language in the 16th or early 17th century but is still used in their liturgy. The word is derived from the Gr. *Agyiptos* which became *Qibt* after the 7th-century Arab invasion.

Copus (kō'pùs). Old university slang for a drink made of beer, wine, and spice heated together and served in a LOVING CUP. Variously accounted for as being DOG-LATIN for *cupellon Hippocratis* (a cup of Hippocras), or short for *episcopus*, in which case it would be the same as the drink BISHOP. Another suggestion is that it is from Lat. *copulo* (couple, unite).

Copy. That's a mere copy of your countenance. Not your real wish or meaning, but merely one you choose to present to me.

Copy-book. A book in which specimen entries of handwriting, letters, and figures are printed with blank spaces for the learner to imitate or copy them. Such exercise books were used in schools until the present century.

> Fair as a text B in a copy-book.
> SHAKESPEARE: *Love's Labour's Lost*, V, ii.

Copy-book maxims. Commonplace moral precepts, etc., of the sort found in copy-books. Actual examples are:

> All good subjects love their country.
> Your aim in life should be a noble one.
> Britannia must ever rule the waves.

To blot one's copy-book. To make a serious blunder, to mar one's reputation, to do something disgraceful. The derivation is obvious.

Copyhold estate. Land held by possession of a copy made by the steward of a manor from the court-roll of the manor. Copyhold was enfranchised in 1925.

Coq à l'âne. *See* A COCK AND BULL STORY *under* COCK.

Corah (kôr' à). In Dryden's *Absalom and Achitophel*, is meant for Titus Oates, notorious inventor of the POPISH PLOT. *See Numb*, xvi.

Coral. The Romans used to hang beads of red coral on the cradles and round the necks of infants as a charm against sickness, etc., and soothsayers held that it was a charm against lightning, whirlwind, shipwreck and fire. PARACELSUS similarly advocated its use "against fits, sorcery, charms and poison". The bells on an infant's coral were a Roman Catholic addition to frighten away evil spirits.

> Coral is good to be hanged about the neck of children...to preserve them from the falling sickness. It has also some special sympathy with nature, for the best coral...will turn pale and wan if the party that wears it be sick, and it comes to its former colour again as they recover.
> SIR HUGH PLATT: *Jewel House of Art and Nature* (1594).

Sir Thomas Browne, *Pseudoxica Epidemica*, V, xxiii, says:

> Though Coral doth properly preserve and fasten the Teeth in men, yet it is used in Children to make an easier passage for them; and for that intent is worn about their necks.

Coram judice (kôr' am joo' di si) (Lat.). Under consideration; still before the judge.

Cordelia (kôr dē' li à). The youngest of King LEAR's three daughters, and the only one that loved him. *Cp.* GONERIL.

Cordelia's gift. "Her voice was ever soft, gentle, and low—an excellent thing in woman". SHAKESPEARE: *King Lear*, V, iii.

Cordelier (kôr dē' lyà, kôr de lēr'), *i.e.* cord-wearer. Franciscan Observantists or "brethren of more strict observance" are called Cordeliers in France on account of their girdles of knotted cord (*see* FRANCISCANS). The story is that when these Minorites repulsed an army of infidels. St. LOUIS of France (Louis IX, 1226–1270) is reputed to have asked who those *gens de cordeliés* (corded people) were. From this they received their name.

Cordeliers' Club. A French Revolutionary political club of the extreme left founded in 1790 by Danton, Marat, and Camille Desmoulins, which met originally in the old convent of the Cordeliers; also called the "Society of the Friends of the Rights of Man and of the Citizen" and nicknamed the "PANDEMONIUM". In advance of their rivals, the JACOBINS, in demanding the abolition of the monarchy, the club rapidly declined after the execution of its leaders in March and April 1794.

Il ne faut pas parler latin devant les Cordeliers. Don't talk Latin before the Cordeliers, *i.e.* FRANCISCANS. A common French proverb, meaning that one should be careful what one says before those who are masters of the subject.

Cordon (Fr.). A ribbon or cord; especially the ribbon of an order of chivalry; also a line of sentries or military posts encircling some position, hence an encircling line.

Cordon bleu. Originally in France a knight of the Order of the *St. Esprit* (HOLY GHOST) from the fact that their insignia was suspended on a blue ribbon. Hence **un repas de cordon bleu** is a well-cooked and well-appointed dinner. The Commandeur de Souvé, Comte d'Olonne, and other *cordons bleus* (*i.e.* knights of St. Esprit), met together as a sort of club, and were noted for their excellent dinners. Hence when anyone has dined well he says, *"Bien, c'est un vrai repas de cordon blue."* Thus the title was playfully bestowed on good cooks.

Cordon noir. A knight of the Order of St. MICHAEL, distinguished by a black ribbon.

Cordon rouge. A chevalier of the Order of St. LOUIS, distinguished by a red ribbon.

Cordon sanitaire. A sanitary cordon, a barrier line enclosing an infected area patrolled by watchers.

Un grand cordon. The highest grade in the French *Légion d'Honneur*. The cross is attached to a *grand* (broad) ribbon.

Corduroy. A corded fabric, originally made of silk, and worn by the kings of France in the chase (Fr. *corde du roy*). It is also a coarse, thick, ribbed cotton stuff, capable of standing hard wear. Hence corduroys as a name for trousers made of such material.

Corduroy road. Roads formed of tree trunks sawn in two longitudinally and laid transversely, thus presenting a ribbed appearance like corduroy.

> Even slow walking on the Corduroy, demoralised by the heavy traffic, was exasperating. Many logs were missing altogether.
> BOLDREWOOD: *The Ghost-Camp*, ch. vii.

Corineus. A mythical hero in the suite of BRUTE, who conquered the giant GOEMAGOT, for which achievement the whole western horn of England was allotted to him. He called it Corinea, and the people Corineans from his own name. This is the legendary explanation of the name of the county of CORNWALL. *See also* BELLARUS.

> In meed of these great conquests by them got,
> Corineus had that province utmost west
> To him assyned for his worthy lot,
> Which of his name and memorable gest,
> He called Cornwall.
> SPENSER: *Faerie Queene*, II, x.

Corinth. Non cuivis homini contingit adire Corinthum. A tag from HORACE (*Ep.*, I, xvii), quoted of some difficult attainment that can be achieved only by good fortune or great wealth. Professor Conington translates it:

> You know the proverb "Corinth town is fair,
> But 'tis not every man that can get there".

Gellius in his *Noctes Atticæ*, I, viii, says that Horace refers to LAIS who sold her favours at so high a price that not everyone could afford to buy them; but Horace says (I *Odes*, vii), "To please princes is no little praise, for it falls not to every man's lot to go to Corinth." That is, it is as hard to please princes, as it is to get to Corinth, either because of the expense, or because it is situated between two seas, and hence called *Bimaris Corinthus*.

Corinthian. A licentious libertine. The loose living of Corinth was proverbial both in Greece and ROME.

In the REGENCY the term was applied to a hard-living group of sportsmen devoted to pugilism and horse-racing. The sporting rake in Pierce Egan's *Life in London* (1821) was known as "Corinthian Tom"; in SHAKESPEARE's day a "Corinthian" was the "fast man" of the period. *Cp.* EPHESIAN.

> I am no proud Jack, like Falstaff; but a Corinthian, a lad of mettle, a good boy.
> *Henry IV, Pt. I*, II, iv.

The term survives in the Royal Corinthian Yacht Club and the Corinthian Amateur Football Club.

Corinthian brass. An alloy made of a variety of metals (said to be gold, silver and copper) melted at the conflagration of Corinth in 146 B.C., when the city was burnt to the ground by the consul Mummius. Vases and other ornaments, made of this metal by the Romans, were more highly prized than if they had been of SILVER and GOLD.

> I think it may be of Corinthian brass,
> Which was a mixture of all metals, but
> The brazen uppermost.
>
> BYRON: *Don Juan*, vi, 56.

Corinthian Order. The most richly decorated of the five orders of Greek architecture. The shaft is fluted, and the capital is bell-shaped and adorned with ACANTHUS leaves. *See* DORIC; IONIC; TUSCAN.

Corked. This wine is corked, *i.e.* it tastes of the cork.

Corker. That's a corker. That's a tremendous example of whatever is in question—something very difficult to answer or deal with—said of a story, a problem, a ball in CRICKET, etc.

Corking-pins. Pins of the largest size, at one time used by ladies to keep curls on the forehead fixed and in trim.

Cormoran. The Cornish giant, who in the nursery tale fell into a pit dug by JACK THE GIANT-KILLER. For this doughty achievement Jack received a belt from King ARTHUR, with this inscription—

> This is the valiant Cornish man
> That slew the giant Cormoran.
>
> *Jack the Giant-killer*

Corn. Acknowledge the corn. *See* ACKNOWLEDGE.

There's corn in Egypt. There is abundance; there is a plentiful supply. The reference is to the BIBLE story of Joseph in Egypt (*Gen*. xliii, 2).

To tread on his corns. To irritate his prejudices; to annoy another by disregarding his pet opinions or habits or to offend his susceptibilities.

Up corn, down horn. An old saying suggesting that when corn is up or dear, beef is down or cheap, because people had less money to spend on meat.

Corn Dolly. Customarily, when the last load of the corn harvest was carried home, a Corn Dolly (called in some areas a Kern Baby or Mel Doll) was made from the last sheaf and carried by one of those riding on top of the load. This female symbol of the Corn Spirit was hung in the farm kitchen until the next harvest. *See* CRYING THE NECK; HARVEST HOME; HARVEST THANKSGIVING; HOCKEY; MELL SUPPER.

Corn Laws. Enactments beginning in 1360 which were designed to regulate the export, and subsequently the import of grain. Particularly noteworthy and unpopular was the Corn Law of 1815 which forbade the import of foreign wheat until the home price reached 80s. per quarter. This kept the price of bread unduly high in times of bad harvests, thus increasing the hardships of the poor. A sliding scale was introduced in 1828 which was further modified in 1842. In 1839 the Anti-Corn Law League was founded in Manchester, and in 1846 Sir Robert Peel secured the virtual repeal of the duties. A nominal duty of 1s per quarter remained until 1869.

The Corn-Law Rhymer. Ebenezer Elliott (1781–1849) denounced the Corn Laws by portraying the sufferings and miseries of the poor in terms which gave them a wide appeal. His *Corn-Law Rhymes* appeared in 1831.

> Ye coop us up and tax our bread,
> And wonder why we pine;
> But ye are fat, and round and red,
> And filled with tax-bought wine.
>
> *Caged Rats.*

Cornage. A feudal rent for pasture paid by free men and fixed with relation to the number of horned cattle in their possession. It was most common in the north of England. In Littleton's *Tenures* (*c*. 1481) (*see* COKE) it was mistakenly said to be "a kind of tenure in grand serjeanty", the service being to blow a horn when an invasion of the Scots was imminent.

Cornelia, Mother of the Gracchi. The model of Roman matronly virtue. She was the second daughter of Scipio Africanus. On the death of her husband, T. Sempronius Gracchus, in 154 B.C. she refused to remarry and devoted herself to the education of her three surviving children, Tiberius, Gaius, and Sempronia. When asked to show her jewels, Cornelia produced her two sons, saying, "These are the only jewels of which I can boast."

Corner, To. To buy up the whole of any stock in the market, to buy up the available stocks of a commodity to secure a virtual monopoly in order to raise the price. The idea is that the goods are piled and hidden in a corner out of sight.

> The price of bread rose like a rocket, and speculators wished to corner what little wheat there was.
>
> *New York Weekly Times* (13 June 1894).

To be driven into a corner. Placed where there is no escape; driven from all subterfuges and excuses.

To make a corner. To combine in order to control the price of a given article, and thus secure greater profits.

To turn the corner. To have got over the worst; after an illness, to be on the mend. In nautical parlance "turning the corner" implied sailing on, either to port or starboard, after reaching either the CAPE of Good Hope or CAPE HORN (*See under* HORN).

Corner-stone. A large stone laid at the base of a building to strengthen the two walls forming a right-angle. In figurative use, Christ is called (*Eph*. ii, 20) the chief corner-stone because He united the Jews and Gentiles into one family; and daughters are called corner-stones (*Ps*. cxliv, 12) because, as wives and mothers, they unite together two families.

Cornet. The Terrible Cornet of Horse. A nickname of William Pitt the Elder (1708–1778). He obtained a cornetcy in Cobham's Horse in 1731.

Cornish. The Cornish hug. A hug to overthrow you. Cornish men were noted wrestlers and tried to throttle their antagonist with a particular grip or embrace called the Cornish hug.

> The Cornish are Masters of the Art of Wrestling...
> Their Hugg is a cunning close with their fellow
> combatant; the fruits whereof is his fair fall, or foil
> at the least. It is figuratively appliable to the deceit-
> ful dealing of such who secretly design their over-
> throw, whom they openly embrace.
> FULLER: *Worthies* (1662).

Cornish language. A Brythonic branch of the CELTIC language now only used as an acquired speech by a few. It is supposed that Dolly Pentreath (Dorothy Jeffery, 1685–1778) was the last to speak Cornish as a native language.

Cornish names.

> By Tre, Pol, and Pen
> You shall know the Cornishmen.

Thus *Tre* (a hamlet) gives Trebilcock, Tredinnick, Tregaskis, Tregenza, Trelawny, Treloar, Tremayne, Trenowth, Treseder, etc.

Pol (a pool) gives Polglase, Polkinghorne, Polmear, Polwhele, etc.

Pen (a top) gives Penberthy, Pengelly, Penhale, Penprase, Penrose, Penruddock, etc.

There are countless similarly formed place-names.

The Cornish Wonder. John Opie (1761–1807), the Cornish painter. It was "Peter Pindar" (John Wolcot) who gave him this name.

Cornstalks. In Australia, especially in New South Wales, from colonial times a name for youths, perhaps from their being taller and more slender than their parents.

Cornubian Shore. Cornwall, formerly famous for its tin mines.

> ... from the bleak Cornubian shore
> Dispense the mineral treasure, which of old

Sidonian pilots sought.
> AKENSIDE: *Hymn to the Naiads*.

Cornucopia. *See* AMALTHEA'S HORN.

Cornwall (Cornish, *Kernow*). Probably from the tribal name *Cornovii*. The O.E. *Cornwealas* means "the Welsh in Cornwall". *See also* CORINEUS.

Barry Cornwall. The pseudonym of Bryan Waller Proctor (1787–1874), based on an inaccurate anagram of his name. Trained as a lawyer, he published poems, songs, memoirs of Edmund Kean and Charles Lamb, etc. He was very popular with the eminent poets and other writers of his time including Scott, Tennyson, Macaulay, Dickens and Thackeray.

Coronation Chair. *See* SCONE.

Coronet. A crown inferior to the royal crown. The coronet of the Prince of Wales has one arch less than the royal crown; those of other princes are without arches; a duke's coronet is adorned with strawberry leaves above the band; that of a marquis with strawberry leaves alternating with pearls; that of an earl has pearls elevated on stalks, alternating with strawberry leaves above the band; that of a viscount has a string of pearls above the band, but no leaves; that of a baron has only six pearls.

Coronis. (kôr ō′ nis). Mother of ÆSCULAPIUS by APOLLO, who slew her for her infidelity; also the daughter of Coronæus, King of Phocis, changed by ATHENE into a crow to enable her to escape from NEPTUNE.

Corporal Violet. *See* VIOLET.

Corporation. A body or succession of persons having legal existence, rights and duties, as distinct from the individuals from whom it is formed. In Britain its usual application is to the body of individuals elected for the local government of a city or town. In America it commonly applies to a company. The word *corporation* is also facetiously given to a fat paunch, from the tendency of civic bodies to indulge in well-provided feasts, thus acquiring generous figures.

Corposant. The ball of fire which is sometimes seen playing around the masts of ships in a storm. So called from the Ital. *corpo santo*, holy body. To the Romans the phenomenon was known as CASTOR AND POLLUX, and it is also known as ST. ELMO'S FIRE, HELEN'S FIRE, and Comazant.

> Upon the maintopgallant mast-head, was a ball of
> light, which the sailors call a corposant (*corpus
> sancti*), and which the mate had called out to us to
> look at ... for sailors have a notion that if the corpo-
> sant rises in the rigging ti is sign of fair weather, but
> if it comes lower down there will be a storm.
> R. H. DANA: *Two Years Before the Mast*, ch. XXIV.

Corps Diplomatique (Fr.). The diplomatic

body in a capital made up of the diplomatic representatives of the various foreign states.

Corps législatif (Fr.). At various times in modern French history this name has been used for the lower house of the legislature. In 1799 NAPOLEON substituted a *Corps législatif* and a tribunal for the two councils of the DIRECTORY. In 1807 there was a *c.l.* and a *conseil d'état* (council of state); in 1849 a *c.l.* was formed with 750 deputies; and under NAPOLEON III the legislative power was vested in the Emperor, the Senate, and the *c.l.*

Corpse Candle. The IGNIS FATUUS is so called by the Welsh because it was supposed to forbode death, and to show the road the corpse would take. The large candle used at LICH WAKES was similarly named.

> When any Christian is drowned in the river Dee, there will appear over the water where the corpse is, a light, by which means they do find the body: and it is therefore called the Holy Dee.
>
> AUBREY: *Miscellanies* (1721), p. 179

Corpse coins. An old name for the pennies placed on the eyelids of dead persons to prevent them from opening. In the New England states a half-dollar was the traditional coin.

Corpus (Lat. a body). The whole body or substance; especially the complete collection of writings on one subject or by one person, as the *Corpus poetarum Latinorum*, the *Corpus historicum medii œvi*, etc. Also short for CORPUS CHRISTI COLLEGE.

Corpus Christi. A church festival kept on the Thursday after TRINITY SUNDAY, in honour of the Blessed Sacrament. It was instituted by Pope Urban IV in 1264. It was the regular time for the performance of religious dramas by the trade guilds and in England, many of the Corpus Christi plays of York, Coventry, and Chester are extant.

Corpus Christi College at Cambridge was founded in 1352, and the college of the same name at Oxford in 1516.

Corpus delicti (Lat. the body of the crime or offence). The material thing in respect to which a crime has been committed; thus a murdered body or some of the stolen property would be a *"corpus delicti"*.

Corpuscular Philosophy. The theory promulgated by Robert Boyle which sought to account for all natural phenomena by the position and motion of corpuscles. *Cp.* ATOMIC THEORY.

Corrector. *See* ALEXANDER THE CORRECTOR.

Corridors of Power. Collectively the ministries in WHITEHALL with their top-ranking civil servants. The phrase was first used by C. P. (Lord) Snow in his novel *Homecom-*

ings (1956) and gained speedy acceptance. It was used in the title of a later novel *Corridors of Power* (1964).

> Boffins at Daggers Drawn in Corridors of Power.
>
> *The Times* (Headline 8 April 1965).

Corroboree. A dance practised by Australian aborigines on festal or warlike occasions; hence any hilarious or slightly riotous assembly.

> He roared, stamped, and danced corrobory, like any blackfellow.
>
> KINGSLEY: *The Water-Babies*, ch. viii.

Corruption of Blood. Loss of title and entailed estates in consequence of treason, by which a man's *blood was attainted* and his issue suffered.

Corsican. An epithet applied to NAPOLEON who was born in Corsica, which became a French possession in 1768. He was often referred to as "the Corsican upstart".

Corsned (kôrs' ned) (O.E. *cor*, choice, trial; *snaed*, piece). The piece of bread "consecrated for exorcism", formerly given to a person to swallow as a test of his guilt, a form of trial by ORDEAL. The words of "consecration" were: "May this morsel cause convulsions and find no passage if the accused is guilty, but turn to wholesome nourishment if he is innocent." *See* CHOKE.

Cortina (kôr' tĭ nà) (Lat. cauldron). The tripod of APOLLO, which was in the form of a cauldron; hence any tripod used for religious purposes by the ancient Romans.

Corvinus (kôr vī' nus). Matthias I, King of Hungary (1458–90), younger son of John (Janos) Hunyadi, was so called from the raven (Lat. *corvus*) on his shield. He was one of the greatest of all book collectors and some of the earliest European gilt-tooled bindings were executed for his library. They may be recognized by the raven stamped in the centre of the covers.

Corvus, Marcus Valerius (*c.* 370–270 B.C.) was so called because while in combat with a gigantic Gaul during the Gallic War he was helped by a raven (*corvus*) which flew at the Gaul's face.

Corybantes (kor i băn' tēz). The Phrygian priests of CYBELE, whose worship was celebrated with orgiastic dances and loud, wild music. Hence a wild, unrestrained dancer is sometimes called a *corybant*. In 1890 Prof. T. H. Huxley referred to the members of the SALVATION ARMY as being "militant missionaries of a somewhat corybantic Christianity".

Corycian Cave (kor is' i àn). A cave on Mount PARNASSUS named after the NYMPH Corycia. The MUSES are sometimes in poetry called Corycides or the Corycian Nymphs.

> The immortal Muse
> To your calm habitations, to the cave
> Corycian...will guide his footsteps.
> AKENSIDE: *Hymn to the Naiads*.

Corydon (kor′ i don). A conventional name for a rustic, a shepherd; a brainless lovesick fellow; from the shepherd in Virgil's *Eclogue* vii, and in Theocritus.

Coryphæus (kôr i fē′ us). The leader and speaker of the chorus in Greek dramas; hence figuratively, the leader generally, the most active member of a board, company, expedition, etc. At Oxford University the assistant of the CHORAGUS was so called. The offices of Choragus and Coryphæus have long since disappeared.

> In the year 1626, William Heather,\ desirous to ensure the study and practice of music at Oxford in future ages, established the offices of Professor, Choragus, and Coryphaeus, and endowed them with modest stipends.
>
> *Grove's Dictionary of Music*.

The Coryphæus of German Literature. Goethe, "prince of German poets" (1749–1832).

The Coryphæus of Grammarians. Aristarches of Samothrace (2nd century B.C.), an outstanding grammarian and critic.

The Coryphæus of Learning. Richard Porson (1759–1801), renowned for his knowledge of Greek.

Coryphée. A ballet-dancer; strictly speaking, the leader of the ballet.

Cosmonaut. An inflated form of ASTRONAUT, similarly coined when the Russians and Americans began their adventures into space.

Coss, Rule of. An old name for algebra (also called the *Cossic Art*), from the Ital. *regola de cosa, cosa* being an unknown quantity, or a "thing". *See* WHETSTONE OF WITTE.

Costard. A large ribbed apple, and metaphorically, a man's head. *Cp.* COSTERMONGER.

> Take him on the costard with the hilts of they sword.
>
> SHAKESPEARE: *Richard III*, I, iv.

SHAKESPEARE gives the name to a clown in *Love's Labour's Lost*, who apes the court wit of the period, but miscalls like Mrs. MALAPROP or Dogberry.

Costermonger. A street vendor of fruit, vegetables, fish, etc., properly an apple-seller; from COSTARD and *monger*, a dealer or trader (O.E. *mangian*, to trade), as in ironmonger, fishmonger, etc. Often abbreviated to *coster*, the word is generally applied in London to "barrow boys" and COCKNEY dealers. *See* PEARLIES.

Cotillion, Cotillon (ko til′ yon) (Fr. petticoat). Originally a brisk dance by four or eight persons, in which the ladies held up their gowns and showed their under petticoats. It later became a form of quick waltz. The French phrase for PETTICOAT GOVERNMENT is *régime du cotillon*.

Cotset. A word found in DOMESDAY BOOK denoting one of the lowliest types of feudal bondsmen from O.E. *cot-saeta*, a cottage-dweller.

Cotswold. You are as long a-coming as Cotswold barley. The Cotswold Hills in Gloucestershire are bleak and cold, and wind-exposed. Backward in vegetation, they yield a good supply of late barley.

Cotswold lion. An ironical name for a sheep, for which the Cotswold hills are famous.

> Then will he look as fierce as a Cotssold lion.
>
> UDALL: *Ralph Roister Doister*, IV, vi (*c*. 1553).

Cottage Countess, The. Sarah Hoggins of Shropshire, daughter of a small farmer, who in 1791 married Henry Cecil, nephew and heir-presumptive of the 9th Earl of Exeter, Lord of Burleigh. He was living under the name of John Jones at the time, and separated from his wife (Emma Vernon), who eloped with a clergyman. He subsequently obtained a divorce to legitimize the children of his second wife. Sarah was seventeen at the time of her marriage at Bolas Magna, Salop, and "John Jones" was thirty. They lived there for two years until his succession to the peerage made her a countess. She died in 1797. Tennyson has a poem on the subject, called *The Lord of Burleigh*.

Cottage loaf. A loaf of bread in two round lumps, the smaller being on top, and baked with a good crust.

Cottage Orné (Fr. *orné*, adorned). A picturesque country cottage or small house designed for the well-to-do.

Cottage piano. A small upright pianoforte.

Cottar. In England a class of VILLEIN, a cottager, virtually the same as a BORDAR; one who usually held a few acres in the village fields and who had to give one or two days each week to working for his lord.

In the Highlands of Scotland and in the Orkney and Shetland Isles the name applied to certain tenants with small patches of land owing no services.

Cotton. A cotton king. A rich Lancashire or Manchester cotton manufacturer, a king in wealth, style of living, equipage, etc. Sir Robert Peel, the statesman, could be so designated.

Cotton kingdom. In the U.S.A., the agricultural states of the South, where cotton production expanded rapidly from the close of the 18th century, and stimulated the support for slavery.

Cottonopolis. Manchester, the headquarters of cotton manufacture; Great Britain's largest single export during the 19th century.

Cotton snobs. In the U.S.A., a name applied in the 19th century to the slave-owning cotton magnates of the South, reputed to be pompous and overbearing, without the merits of an older aristocracy.

To cotton on. To catch on, to grasp a line of thought.

To cotton on to a person. To cling to or take a fancy to someone. To stick to a person as cotton sticks to our clothes.

Cottonian Library. The remarkable library founded by Sir Robert Cotton (1571–1631), the antiquary. Rich in early MSS., and augmented by his son and grandson, it was secured for the nation in 1700 and transferred first to Essex House and then to Ashburnham House, Westminster, in 1730. A disastrous fire in 1731 destroyed over 100 volumes of irreplaceable MSS., and the remainder (some 800 volumes) were moved to Westminster School and finally lodged in the BRITISH MUSEUM in 1753.

Cottus (kot' ūs). One of the hundred-handed giants, son of URANUS (HEAVEN) and GÆA (Earth). His two brothers were BRIAREUS and Gyes.

Cotytto (ko tī tō). The Thracian goddess of immodesty and debauchery, worshipped at Athens with licentious rites. *See* BAPTES.

> Hail! goddess of nocturnal sport,
> Dark-veiled Cotytto.
>
> MILTON: *Comus*, 128, 129.

Couéism. A form of psychotherapy dependent, upon auto-suggestion, propagated by Emile Coué (1857–1926), a French pharmacist. The key phrase of his system was, "Every day, and in every way, I am becoming better and better."

Couleur de rose (koo lĕr de rōz). (Fr. rose-coloured). Highly coloured; too favourably viewed; overdrawn with romantic embellishments, like objects viewed through rose-tinted spectacles.

Council. Privy, Œcumenical, etc. *See these words.*

Count (Lat. *comitem*, accusative of *comes*, a companion). The continental equivalent of the English EARL (O.E. *eorl*, a warrior), of which COUNTESS is still the feminine.

Count of the Saxon Shore. *Comes Litoris Saxonici*, the Roman general in charge of the coastline of Britain from the Wash to the Solent, whose task it was to combat Saxon and Frankish raiders. In the later 4th century his jurisdiction was extended to the Yorkshire coast.

Count, To. From O.Fr. *conter*; Lat. *computare*, to compute, to reckon.

Don't count your chickens before they are hatched. *See under* CHICKEN.

To count kin with someone. A Scots expression meaning to compare one's pedigree with that of another.

To count out the house. When the SPEAKER adjourns a sitting of the HOUSE OF COMMONS because there are not forty members present, after his attention has been called to the fact.

To be counted out is said of a boxer who, after being knocked down, fails to rise during the ten seconds counted out loud by the referee. **Count me out.** Do not reckon me in this.

To count upon. To rely with confidence on someone or something; to reckon on.

To count without one's host. *See* TO RECKON WITHOUT YOUR HOST, *under* HOST.

Countenance, To. To sanction, to support. Approval or disapproval is shown by the countenance. The Scriptures speak of "the light of God's countenance", *i.e.* the smile of approbation; and to "hide His face" (or countenance) is to manifest displeasure.

Out of countenance. Ashamed, confounded. With countenance fallen or cast down.

To keep in countenance. To encourage, or prevent someone losing his countenance or feeling dismayed.

To keep one's countenance. To refrain from smiling or appearing downcast, to avoid revealing one's thoughts by the face.

To put one out of countenance is to make one ashamed or disconcerted. To *discountenance* is to set your face against something done or propounded.

Counter. Under the counter. A phrase that became current in World War II, to denote a common practice of dishonest tradesmen. Articles in short supply were kept out of sight, or under the counter, for sale to favoured customers, often at enhanced prices. *Cp.* BLACK MARKET.

Counter-caster. One who keeps accounts or casts up accounts by counters. Thus Iago (*Othello*, I, i) contemptuously calls Cassio "a great arithmetician", and "this counter-caster"; and the Clown in *The Winter's Tale* (IV, ii) says: "Fifteen hundred shorn: what comes the wool to? I cannot do't without counters."

Countercheck Quarrelsome. Sir, how dare you utter such a falsehood? Sir, you know that it is not true. This, in Touchstone's classification (SHAKESPEARE's *As You Like It*, V, iv), is the third remove from the lie direct; or rather, the lie direct in the third degree.

The REPROOF VALIANT, the Countercheck Quarrelsome, the Lie Circumstantial and the Lie Direct, are not clearly defined by Touchstone. That is not true; how dare you utter such a falsehood; if you say so you are a liar; you lie or are a liar, seem to fit the four degrees.

Counter-jumper. A contemptuous epithet applied to a shop assistant who may be supposed to have to jump over the counter to go from one part of the shop to another.

Counter-Reformation. *See under* REFORMATION.

Countess. *See* COUNT; COTTAGE COUNTESS.

Country. Black Country. *See* BLACK.

Country dance. A corruption of the Fr. *contre danse; i.e.* a dance where the partners face each other, as in the Sir Roger de Coverley. *See* COVERLEY.

Father of his country. *See* FATHER.

To appeal, or **go to the country.** To dissolve PARLIAMENT in order to ascertain the wishes of the country by a general election.

County (Fr. *comté*). A SHIRE. After the Local Government Act of 1888 until 1972, certain of the larger towns had county status as county BOROUGHS. *See also* HUNDRED.

County family. A family belonging to the nobility or gentry with an ancestral seat in the county.

County Palatine, or **Palatinate** (Lat. *palatinus*, of the palace). Properly the dominion of an earl palatine over which he had quasi-royal jurisdiction. Cheshire, Shropshire, Durham and Kent became Counties Palatine after the Norman Conquest as frontier districts, and Lancaster in 1351. At one time Pembroke, Hexhamshire and the Isle of Ely were so designated but only Cheshire, Durham and Lancaster still retain the title, and the Chancellor of the Duchy of Lancaster is a member of the Government. Their jurisdictions are now vested in the Crown. *See* PALATINATE.

Coup (koo) (Fr.). A blow or stroke. Now used in English for a successful move or stroke in certain games (chess, billiards), a stroke of policy or a sudden and successful act, an illegal attempt to overthrow an established government. *See* COUP D'ÉTAT.

A good coup. A good hit or haul.

Coup d'essai. A trial-piece; a piece of work serving for practice.

Coup d'état. A state stroke, one of those bold measures taken by a government to forestall a supposed or actual danger to the régime; more commonly a violent or illegal seizure of power from above.

The famous *coup d'état* by which Louis Napoleon seized power occurred on 2 December 1851. *See* MAN OF DECEMBER *under* DECEMBER.

Coupa de grâce. The finishing stroke; the stroke of mercy. When a prisoner was being tortured, the executioner finished him off with a *coup de grâce* to put him out of his misery.

Coup de main. A sudden stroke, a stratagem whereby something is effected suddenly; a *coup*.

> It appears more like a line of march than a body intended for a *coup de main*, as there are with it bullocks and baggage of different kinds.
>
> WELLINGTON: *Dispatches*, vol. I, p. 25.

Coup d'œil. A view, glance, prospect; the effect of things at the first glance; literally "a stroke of the eye".

Coup de pied de l'âne. A kick from the ass's hoof; figuratively, a blow given to a vanquished or fallen man; a cowardly blow; an insult offered to one who has not the power of returning or avenging it. The allusion is to the fable of the sick lion kicked by the ass.

Coup de soleil. A sunstroke or any malady produced by exposure to the sun.

Coup de théâtre. An unforeseen or unexpected turn in a drama producing a sensational effect; something planned for effect, such as Burke's throwing down of the dagger in the HOUSE OF COMMONS. *See* DAGGER SCENE.

Coup manqué. A false stroke, a miss, a failure.

> Shoot dead, or don't aim at all; but never make a coup manqué.
>
> OUIDA: *Under Two Flags*, ch. xx.

Coupon (Fr. a remnant, a piece cut off). In commercial usage a detachable ticket cut off a bond entitling the owner to payment of interest. Also used for a variety of slips and tickets which can be detached or cut out for special uses such as food coupons from ration books, coupons from advertisements, etc.

Coupon Election. The General Election of 1918, when PRIME MINISTER Lloyd George and Mr. Bonar Law sent a certificate of coupon to all candidates supporting the Coalition. The coupon was not accepted by the Asquith LIBERALS nor by the LABOUR Party. A *couponeer* was a politician who accepted the coupon.

Course. Another course would have done it. A little more would have effected our purpose. It is said that the peasants of a Yorkshire village tried to wall in a cuckoo in order to enjoy an eternal spring. They built a wall round the bird, and the cuckoo just skimmed over it. "Ah!" said one of the peasants, "another carse would 'a' done it".

In the course of nature. In the due of proper time or order, etc.; in the ordinary procedure of nature.

Of course. Naturally; as would be expected. **A matter of course** is something that belongs to ordinary procedure, or that is customary.

To hold, or **keep on the course.** To go straight; to do one's duty in that course [path] of life in which we are placed. The allusion is to navigation.

Court. From Lat. *cohors, cohortis*, originally an enclosure for sheep or cattle; subsequently as many soldiers as could be cooped together in such an enclosure was called a *cohort*. The cattle-yard, being the nucleus of the farm, became the centre of a group of farm buildings and cottages, then of a hamlet, town, fortified place, and lastly of a royal residence.

Court Baron. *See* BARON.

Court cards. A corruption of *coat card*, becauase they bore the representation of a clothed or *coated* figure, and not because the king, queen, and knave belonged to a court.

The King of Clubs may originally have represented the arms of the Pope; of Spades, the king of France; of Diamonds, the king of Spain; and of Hearts, the king of England. The French kings of cards are called David (Spades), Alexander (Clubs), Cæsar (Diamonds), and Charles (Hearts)—representing the Jewish, Greek, Roman and Frankish empires. The queens or dames are Argine, *i.e.* Juno (Hearts), Judith (Clubs), Rachel (Diamonds), and Pallas (Spades)—representing royalty, fortitude, piety and wisdom. They were likenesses of Maria d'Anjou, the queen of Charles VII; Isabeau, the queen-mother; Agnès Sorel, the royal mistress; and Jeanne d'Arc, the dame of Spades or war.

Court Circular. Daily information concerning the official engagements of royalty for publication in the newspapers. George III introduced the custom in 1803 to prevent misstatements.

Court cupboard. A movable buffet to hold flagons, cans, cups, and beakers.

Court fools. *See* FOOLS.

Court-hand. A cursive form of handwriting which developed in England by the late 12th century as the legal script employed in the writing of the king's business, the law courts, etc. It was abolished in the reign of George II.

Court holy water. An obsolete term of Eli-

zabeth I's reign for fair speeches, which look like promises of favour, but end in nothing.

> On nuncle, court holy-water in a dry house is better than this rain-water out o'door.
> SHAKESPEARE: *King Lear*, III, ii.

In Florio's Italian Dictionary (1598) *Mantellizzare* is translated by "to flutter or fawne upon, to court one with faire words or give court holywater".

Court-leet. *See* LEET.

Court martial. A court convened to try a person subject to military law. In Great Britain, such courts resulted from the Mutiny Act of 1689.

Court plaster. Sticking-plaster, so called from the fashion of court ladies patching their faces with fanciful shapes cut out from such plaster. This fashion was in vogue in the reign of Charles I and in Queen Anne's time was employed as a political badge.

> Your black patches you wear variously,
> Some cut like stars, some in half-moons, some lozenges.
> FLETCHER and MASSINGER: *The Elder Brother*, III, ii.

Court of Arches. *See* ARCHES.

Court of Love. A judicial court for deciding affairs of the heart, established in Provence during the days of the TROUBADOURS. The following is a case submitted to their judgment: A lady listened to one admirer, squeezed the hand of another, and touched with her toe the foot of a third. Query: Which of these three was the favoured suitor?

Court of Piepowder. *See* PIEPOWDER.

Court of Session. The supreme court of civil jurisdiction in SCOTLAND, first established in 1532, and originally modelled on the PARLEMENT of Paris.

Out of court. Not admissible evidence within the terms of reference of the trial being conducted; ruled as being out of consideration.

They are but in the Court of the Gentiles. They are not wholly God's people; they are not the elect, but have only a smattering of the truth. The "Court of the Israelites" in the Jewish Temple was for Jewish men; the "Court of Women" for Jewish women; the "Court of the Gentiles" was for those who were not Jews.

To pay court to someone is to pay attention to or cultivate someone whose favour or interest is wanted.

To settle out of court. A case, almost always involving damages, which is settled by the respective litigants' solicitors, before it is called to court, agreeing on a sum to be paid by the litigant who admits himself to be in the wrong.

Courtesy (kĕr′ tĕ si). Civility, politeness. It was at court that those in attendance practised the refinements of the age. The word originally meant the manners of the court.

Courtesy titles. Titles assumed or granted by social custom, without legal status. The courtesy title of the eldest son of a peer is normally one of his father's inferior titles, usually his second, but sometimes lower ones are used. Younger sons of DUKES and MARQUISES have the courtesy title LORD. The daughters of Dukes, Marquises, and EARLS are styled LADY. Sons of Earls, VISCOUNTS and BARONS are entitled *Honourable* as are daughters of barons. Courtesy titles are allowed to the eldest son of courtesy marquises and earls. None of these titles carry the right to sit in the HOUSE OF LORDS.

Cousin. Sir William Blackstone (1723–1780) says that Henry IV, being related or allied to every EARL in the kingdom, artfully and constantly acknowledged the connexion in all public acts. The usage has descended to his successors, and in royal writs and commissions an *earl* is addressed "Our right trusty and well-beloved cousin", a MARQUIS "Our right trusty and entirely-beloved cousin", and a DUKE "Our right trusty and right-entirely-beloved cousin".

The word is also used by sovereigns in addressing one another formally.

Cousin Betsy, or **Betty.** A half-witted person, a BESS OF BEDLAM.

> Nobody can say Fosters wronged him of a penny or gave short measure to a child or a cousin Betty.
> MRS. GASKELL: *Sylvia's Lovers*, ch. xiv.

Cousin-german. The children of brothers and sisters, first cousins or full cousins; kinsfolk (Lat. *germanus*, a brother, one of the same stock).

> There is three cousin-germans that has cozened all the hosts of Reading, of Maidenhead, of Colebrook, of horses and money.
> SHAKESPEARE: *Merry Wives of Windsor*, IV, v.

Cousin Jack. So Cornishmen are called in the western counties, and in places where they are working as miners.

> Mr Tregonwell was a thoroughbred Cornishman ... His coal-black close-curled hair, with dark, deep-set eyes, short upright forehead, and square jaw proclaimed him a "Cousin Jack" ....
> BOLDREWOOD: *The Ghost Camp*. ch.vi.

Cousin Michael. The Germans were so called. *Michel*, in Old German, means "gross"; *Cousin Michael* is meant to indicate a slow, heavy, unrefined, coarse-feeding people.

I wouldn't call the king my cousin. I am perfectly satisfied with things as they are; they couldn't be bettered even if I were cousin to the king.

To call cousins. This formerly meant to claim relationship.

> He is half-brother to this Witwoud by a former wife, who was sister to my Lady Wishfort, my wife's mother; if you marry Millamant you must call cousins too.
> CONGREVE: *Way of the World*, I, v.

Cove. An individual; as a *flash cover* (a swell), a *rum cove* (a man whose position and character are not quite obvious, a queer fish), a *gentry cove* (a gentleman), a *downy cove* (a very knowing individual), etc. The word is old thieves' CANT.

> A ben cove, a brave cove, a gentry coffin.
> MIDDLETON and DEKKER: *The Roaring Girle*, V, i (1611).

Covenanters. A term applied to those Scottish PRESBYTERIANS subscribing to various bonds or covenants for the security and advancement of their cause. The first was entered into by the Lords of the Congregation in 1557 and another by ordinance of King James VI in 1581. In 1638 the National Covenant was directed against the Laudian prayer-book imposed by Charles I. In 1643 a Solemn League and Covenant pledged the Scots and their English Parlimentarian allies to preserve Presbyterianism in SCOTLAND and to establish it in ENGLAND and IRELAND.

The name Covenanter is particularly applied to those who adhered to the Covenants after they were declared unlawful in 1662. Between the RESTORATION and the Revolution of 1688 they were harried and proscribed but exhibited a brave and often fanatical resistance. *See* CAMERONIANS.

> The envoy of the Covenanters, to judge by his mein and manners, seemed fully imbued with that spiritual pride, which distinguished his sect.
> SCOTT: *Old Mortality*, ch. xxv.

Covent Garden. A corruption of *Convent* Garden; the garden and burial ground attached to the convent or Abbey of WESTMINSTER, granted at the dissolution of the monasteries to the Duke of Somerset and on his attainder in 1552 it passed to the Earl of Bedford, in whose family it remained until 1910. The original church of St. Paul's Convent Garden was built by Inigo Jones between 1631 and 1638, separated from St. Martin's parish in 1645, and rebuilt after a disastrous fire in 1795. Its peculiar feature is that the portico that appears to be the front is really the back.

The fruit, flower, and vegetable market developed from the 17th century, when the square became popular with stallholders. The nucleus of the existing market buildings dates from 1850 but the market itself moved to Nine Elms, Battersea in 1974. In the 17th and 18th centuries the area was the stamping ground of the MOHOCKS and other semi-fashionable ruffians, and its COFFEE-houses, bagnios and taverns the favourite resorts of poets, actors and artists.

Covent Garden Theatre was opened by John Rich the HARLEQUIN in 1732 but was burnt down in 1808 and again in 1856. It became the Royal Italian Opera House in 1847 and the new opera house was opened in 1858. Since 1949 it has been State-owned. *See* BOW STREET RUNNERS; BUTTON'S COFFEE-HOUSE; EVANS'S SUPPER ROOMS; HUMMUMS; WILL'S COFFEE-HOUSE.

Coventry. As true as Coventry blue. A proverbial saying, derived from Coventry's connexion with the wool trade, and its reputation for the quality of its dyeing.

Coventry Mysteries. Miracle plays supposed to have been acted at CORPUS CHRISTI at Coventry until 1591. Called *Ludus Coventriæ* by Sir Robert Bruce, Cotton's librarian in the time of James I, their special connexion with Coventry or Corpus Christi is doubtful, although there are two such plays extant, the play of the Shearman and Tailors, and the play of the Weavers. *See also* MYSTERY.

Peeping Tom of Coventry. *See* GODIVA.

To send one to Coventry. To take no notice of him; to make him feel that he is in disgrace by ignoring him. *Cp.* BOYCOTT. It is said that the citizens of Coventry once had so great a dislike of soldiers that a woman seen speaking to one was instantly tabooed; hence when a soldier was sent to Coventry he was cut off from all social intercourse. Clarendon, in his *History of the Great Rebellion*, says that Royalist prisoners captured in Birmingham were sent to Coventry, which was a Parliamentary stronghold.

Cover. To break cover. To start from the covert or temporary lair. The usual earthholes of a fox being blocked the night before a hunt, the fox seeks some other cover, and as soon as it quits it the hunt begins.

Coverley. Sir Roger de Coverley. A member of an imaginary club in the *Spectator*, "who lived in SOHO Square when he was in town". Sir Roger is the type of an English squire in the reign of Queen Anne.

The country dance of this name (or rather the *Roger of Coverly*) was well known before Addison's time.

Cow. The cow that nourished YMIR with four streams of milk was called Audhumla.

Always behind, like a cow's tail. A proverbial saying of ancient date. *Cp. Tanquam coda vituli* (Petronius).

Cow Cockie. A New Zealand or Australian dairy farmer. *See* COCKATOO.

Curst cows have curt horns. Angry men cannot do all the mischief they wish. Curst means "angry" or "fierce", and curt is "short", as curt-mantle, CURT-HOSE. The Latin proverb is, *Dat Deus immiti cornua curta bovi*.

Not until the cows come home. Not for a very long time, if at all.

The cow knows not the worth of her tail till she loses it, and is troubled with flies, which her tail brushed off.

The tune the old cow died of. *See* TUNE.

The whiter the cow, the surer it is to go to the altar. The richer the prey, the more likely it is to be seized. Pagan sacrifices demanded white cattle.

Cowboy. The term used for the cattlemen of the American West, much romanticized in popular ballad and story. Their "ten-gallon" hats, leather CHAPS, and high-heeled boots, were characteristic dress in the great days of the Cattle Kingdom. The name was also applied during the Revolutionary Wars to TORY partisans of New York State, notorious for their harsh treatment of their opponents. In current colloquial usage the term *cowboy* is applied to clumsy and unskilled lorry drivers and workers in many occupations.

Cow-lick. A tuft of hair on the forehead that cannot be made to lie in the same direction as the rest of the hair.

> This term must have been adopted from a comparison with that part of a...cow's hide where the hairs, having different directions, meet and form a projecting ridge, supposed to be occasioned by the animals licking themselves.
> BROCHETT: *Glossary of North Country Words*.

Cowpuncher. A COWBOY, derived from the metal-tipped pole with which cattle are driven when being loaded on rail.

Cow with the iron tail, The. A pump, from its use in dishonestly watering-down milk.

Dun Cow, The Book of the Dun Cow, The Old Dun Cow. *See under* DUN.

Sacred Cow. *See under* SACRED.

Coward. Ultimately from Lat. *cauda*, a tail, either from an animal "turning tail" when frightened, or from cowering with its tail between its legs.

A beast *cowarded*, in HERALDRY, is one drawn with its tail between its legs.

Cowper Justice. *See* CUPAR JUSTICE.

Cowper-Temple Clause. A famous amendment to the Education Act of 1870 secured by W. Cowper-Temple (1811–1888) which enacted that, "in any school provided by a SCHOOL BOARD, no religious catechism or religious formulary which is distinctive of any particular denomination, shall be taught."

Coxcomb. An empty-headed vain person. The ancient licensed JESTERS were so called because they wore a cock's comb in their caps.

> Let me hire him too; here's my coxcomb.
> SHAKESPEARE: *King Lear*, I, iv.

Coxswain (cok' sọn). The helmsman; originally the *swain* or man in charge of the COCK-BOAT, formerly spelt *cockswain*.

Coyne and livery. An old Irish term for food and entertainment for soldiers and forage for their horses, formerly exacted by Irish chiefs when on the march. *Coyne* is Irish *coinnemh*, billeting, or one billeted.

Coystril. A term of reproach, meaning a low fellow, a knave, a varlet.

> He's a coward and a coystril that will not drink to my niece.
> SHAKESPEARE: *Twelfth Night*, I, iii.

It is a variant of the obsolete *custrel*, an attendant on a KNIGHT, seemingly from O.Fr. *coustillier*, a soldier armed with a *coustille* (a two-edged dagger). Every soldier in the life-guards of Henry VIII was attended by a man called a *coystrel* or *coystril*.

Cozen. To cheat. This is the same word as *cousin*; the Fr. *cousiner* means "to sponge on" as well as "to call cousin" (*see under* COUSIN). In England one who *cozened* another was one who lived on another just as though they were "cousins". *See* SHAKESPEARE'S *Merry Wives*, IV, ii, and V, v.

Crab. A walking-stick made of crab-apple wood; a *crabstick*.

> Out bolts her husband upon me with a fine taper crab in his hand.
> GARRICK: *Lying Valet*, I, ii.

To catch a crab. *See* CATCH.

Crack. First-rate, excellent, quite at the top of its class; as a crack regiment, a crack shot, a crack hand of cards, etc. (*See* TO CRACK UP.) Formerly the word was used substantively for a lively young fellow, a WAG.

> Indeed, La! 'tis a noble child; a crack, madam.
> SHAKESPEARE: *Coriolanus*, I, iii.

Nowadays **a crack** or **a wisecrack** is a sharp, witty, or humorous saying, or just "a dig" at someone. Both derive from O.E. *cracian*, to make a sudden sharp noise.

A gude crack. In Scottish dialect, a good chat or conversation, also a good talker.

> Wi' merry sangs an' friendly cracks,
> I wat they did na weary;
> And unco tales, an' funnie jokes—
> Their sports were cheap an' cheery.
> BURNS: *Halloween*.

To be a gude crack, that is, to possess talents for conversation, was essential to the trade of a "puir body" of the more esteemed class.
SCOTT: *The Antiquary (Advertisement)*.

Crack-brained. Eccentric; slightly mad.

Cracked pipkins are discovered by their sound. Ignorance is betrayed by speech.

> They bid you talk—my honest song
> Bids you forever hold your tongue;
> Silence with some is wisdom most profound—
> Cracked pipkins are discovered by the sound.
> PETER PINDAR: *Lord B. and his Motions*.

Cracked pots last longest. An old proverb. Long-sufferers from ill health or some disability often outlive the seemingly fit and healthy.

Cracks and slams (U.S.A.). Jokes and jibes directed against institutions or individuals (*See* CRACK.) Slam is to hit or put in place with force.

In a crack. Instantly. In a snap of the fingers, in the time taken by a crack or shot.

> Do pray undo the bolt a little faster—
> They're on the stair just now, and in a crack
> Will all be here.
> BYRON: *Don Juan*, I, cxxxvii.

To be given a fair crack of the whip. To be fairly treated; to receive just treatment; to be given a fair share of something.

To crack a bottle. In this phrase the word implies to open and drink.

> You'll crack a quart together, ha! will you not, Master Bardolph.
> SHAKESPEARE: *Henry IV, Pt. II*, V, iii.
> Dear Tom, this brown jug that now foams with mild ale,
> From which I now drink to sweet Nan of the Vale,
> Was once Toby Filpot's, a thirsty old soul
> As e'er cracked a bottle, or fathomed a bowl.
> O'KEEFE: *Poor Soldier*.

To crack a crib. To break into a house and steal. (*See* CRIB.) Hence, *cracksman*, a burglar.

To crack up. To praise highly, to eulogize.

> We find them cracking up the country they belong to, no matter how absurd may be the boast.
> JAMES PAYN: *By Proxy*, ch. i.

It also means to break down in health or mind.

Cracker-barrel philosophy (U.S.A.) is roughly the same as homespun philosophy. The barrels in which crackers, or biscuits, used to be kept, were often used as seats in the country stores by local folk who met there and exchanged views on topics of the day, etc. *See* CROSS-ROADS.

Crackers. In colloquial usage means CRACK-BRAINED.

Cradle Crown. In mediæval England a fine paid by a priest (in lieu of penance) for fathering a child in his house and keeping a concubine. *Cp.* SIN RENT.

Cradle-holding. Land held by BOROUGH ENGLISH.

Cradle-snatching. Said of a grown man who consorts with a young girl well below his own age.

Craft. The Craft. A name given to FREE-MASONRY by its members.

The Gentle Craft. *See under* GENTLE.

Crambo. A game which consists in someone setting a line which another is to rhyme to, but no word of the first line must occur in the second. The word is of uncertain origin.

> Get the maids to crambo of an evening and learn the knack of rhyming.
>
> CONGREVE: *Love for Love*, I, i.

Dumb crambo is a somewhat similar game where rhymes of the given word are pantomimed or acted in dumb show until guessed.

Cramp-rings. Rings blessed by English sovereigns and distributed on GOOD FRIDAY, supposed to cure cramp and "falling sickness" (epilepsy). The custom grew up after the time of Edward the Confessor, who was said to have been given such a ring by a pilgrim, and was continued until the reign of Queen Mary Tudor. *Cp.* KING'S EVIL.

> Because Coshawk goes in a shag-ruff band, with a face sticking up in't which shows like an agate set in a cramp-ring, he thinks I'm in love with him.
>
> MIDDLETON: *The Roaring Girle*, IV, ii (1611).
>
> The superstitious|use of cramp-rings, as a preservative against fits, is not entirely abandoned; instances occur where nine young men of a parish each subscribe a crooked sixpence, to be moulded into a ring for a young woman afflicted with this malady.
>
> ROKEWODE: *The Hundred of Thingoe* (Suffolk), *Introd*. (1838).

Shackles or fetters, in colloquial usage, came to be called *cramp-rings*.

Cranmer's Bible. *See* BIBLE, THE ENGLISH.

Crannock. An Irish measure which, in the time of Edward II, contained either eight or sixteen pecks. *Curnock* is another form of the word: this was a dry measure of varying capacity, but usually 3 bushels for wheat, 4 bushels for corn, and from 10 to 15 bushels for coal, lime, etc.

Crapaud, or **Johnny Crapaud.** A Frenchman. *See* FLEUR-DE-LIS.

Les anciens crapauds prendront Sara. One of the cryptic prophecies of NOSTRADAMUS (1503–1566). Sara is *Aras* reversed, and when the French under Louis XIV took Arras from the Spaniards, this verse was remembered.

Crape. A saint in crape is twice a saint in lawn. (Pope: *Ep. to Cobham*, 136.) Crape (a sort of bombazine or alpaca) is the stuff of which cheap clerical gowns used to be made, lawn refers to the sleeves of a BISHOP. A saintly parson is all very well but the same goodness in a bishop is exalted into something much more noteworthy.

Craps. The American term for dice, a most popular form of gambling in the U.S.A. About 1800, when New Orleans was a French city, Bernard Marigny introduced dice-playing from France. He was a CREOLE and known as Johnny CRAPAUD, thus dice-playing, or Johnny Crapaud's game, became shortened into "craps". Burgundy Street in the Vieux Carré of New Orleans was, until 1860, known as Craps Street, after Marigny.

Cravat. This neckcloth was introduced into France in the 17th century. Croatian soldiers or Cravates (O.Slav. *khruvat*) guarded the Turkish frontier of HABSBURG territories and when France organized a regiment on the model of the Croats, their linen neckcloth was imitated, and the regiment was called "The Royal Cravat".

To wear a hempen cravat. To be hanged.

Craven. The word is derived from O.Fr. *cravant*, pres. part. of *craver* or *crever*, to burst or break, hence to be overcome.

When controversies were decided by an appeal to battle, the combatants fought with batons, and if the accused could either kill his adversary or maintain the fight till sundown he was acquitted. If he wished to call off, he cried out "Craven!" and was held infamous.

Crawler (Austr.). A convict who escaped with the connivance of the overseer, allowing himself to be recaptured in order that the overseer might collect the reward. In this sense it is found in *The Adventures of Philip Rashleigh* (1825), and thus considerably antedates the modern use as a sycophant or "creep".

Crawley. Crooked as Crawley, or **Crawley brook.** This brook rising near Woburn in Bedfordshire and running into the Ouse was noted for its meanderings. The proverb is given in Fuller's *Worthies*.

Creaking doors hang the longest. Delicate persons often outlive the more robust. *Cp.* CRACKED POTS.

Creatura Christi, or **Creature.** At one time newly-born children, in danger of dying before the arrival of a priest, were often baptized by a midwife. In the flurry of the moment mistakes could occur over the sex of the child, and to avoid the possibility of boys being baptized with girls' names, or the reverse, midwives often named them *Creature* or *Creatura Christi*—Christ's Creature being suitable in either case.

Creature. That which is created, animate or inanimate. Thus we speak of a man or animals as "God's creatures" and in the Communion Service (BOOK OF COMMON PRAYER), "these thy creatures of bread and wine".

Creature in the sense of whisky or other liquors is a facetious adaptation of the passage "Every creature of God is good" (I *Tim*. iv, 4), used in the defence of the drinking of alcoholic beverages.

> I find my master took too much of the creature last night, and is now angling for a quarrel.
> DRYDEN: *Amphitryon*, III, i.

Sergeant-Major Cruse writing to his wife (3 January 1855) during the Crimean winter said "It is only a drop of the creature that keeps us in any sort of spirit now-a-days".

Creature also has the meaning of a dependent or hanger-on.

Creature-comforts. Food and other things necessary for the comfort of the body. Man being supposed to consist of body and soul, the body is the creature, but the soul is the "vital spark of the heavenly flame".

> A very strong smell of brandy and water forewarned the visito that Mr. Squeers had been seeking in creature comforts a temporary forgetfulness of his unpleasant situation.
> DICKENS: *Nicholas Nickleby*, ch. lx.

Credat Judæus, or **Credat Judæus Apella** (Lat.). Let the Jew Apella believe it (HORACE, I *Satires*, v, 100); tell that to the Marines. (*See* HORSE MARINES.) Who this Apella was is not known.

Credence Table (kré' dèns). The table near the altar on which the bread and wine are placed before they are consecrated. In former times food was placed on a credence table to be tasted prior to being set before the guests, to assure them that the meat was not poisoned (Ital. *credenza*, a shelf or buffet).

Credit Squeeze. A comprehensive term to cover governmental attempts to check internal consumption and spending in order to curb inflationary tendencies, and often with the further aim of improving the BALANCE OF PAYMENTS. Tight control over borrowing and lending is exercised by raising the bank rate, resulting in dearer money, the restriction of bank lending, hire purchase, etc.

Credo (Lat.). A statement of belief. Literally "I believe".

Credo quia impossibile (Lat.). I believe it because it is impossible. A paradox ascribed to St. Augustine, but founded on a passage in Tertullian's *De Carne Christi, IV*:

> Credibile est, quia ineptum est... certum est quia impossibile.

Crème de la Crème (krām de la krām) (Fr.). Literally "cream of the cream"; used figuratively for the very choicest part of something which itself is very choice; the very best.

Cremona (kre mō' nà). A town in Lombardy famous for its violin makers (1550–1750). The most famous makers were Nicolo AMATI (1596–1684), teacher of Andreas GUARNIERI (*c.* 1626 – 1698) and Antonio Stradivari (1644–1737). The term is loosely applied to any good instrument. *See also* STRAD.

The organ-stop known as the cremona is a corruption of the German *krummhorn*, crooked horn.It is a|reed|stop|of 8-foot tone.

Cremorne Gardens. Famous Victorian pleasure gardens opened in 1845 as a rival to VAUXHALL GARDENS on the land of Chelsea Farm, the former property of Thomas Dawson, Viscount Cremorne. A popular venue for fêtes and entertainments, their clientèle degenerated and they were closed in 1877 after many local complaints. Lots Road Power Station, on the left bank of the Thames near Battersea Bridge, largely occupies their site. Their memory is preserved in Whistler's *Nocturnes*. *Cp.* ROSHERVILLE GARDENS.

Creole (krē ōl) (Fr. from Sp. *criollo*; W. Indian corruption of *criadillo* from *criado*, bred, brought up). Originally a person of Spanish parentage born in the West Indies as against those of mixed blood, Negroes, new immigrants, and aboriginals. It is often wrongly used to denote those of mixed blood but its usage varies in different places. In the West Indies it implies European descent; in Louisiana the French-speaking whites; in Mexico, whites of Spanish blood. Non-whites are called Negro creoles, but in Mauritius, Réunion, etc., creole is usually applied to Negroes. The Empress Josephine was a creole from Martinique and the liberated slaves of Liberia called themselves creoles.

Crescent. Tradition says that, "Philip, the father of Alexander, meeting with great difficulties in the siege of Byzantium, set the workmen to undermine the walls, but a crescent moon discovered the design, which miscarried; consequently the Byzantines erected a statue to DIANA, and the crescent became the symbol of the state."

Another legend is that Othman, the SULTAN, saw in a vision a crescent moon, which kept increasing till its horns extended from east to west, and he adopted the crescent of his dream for his standard, adding the motto, "*Donec repleat orbem*".

The crescent as a symbol was used by the Seljuk Sultan Ala-ud-din in the mid-13th century, and it was reputedly adopted from this source by Osman, who founded the Ottoman dynasty in *c.* 1281. It is also said that the crescent was placed on the Turkish flag by Mohammed II, after the capture of Constantinople in 1453.

Crescent City. The descriptive name in the

U.S.A. for New Orleans.

Cresset. A beacon light. The original cresset was an open metal cup at the top of a pole, the cup being filled with burning grease or oil. Hence the name; from O.Fr. *craisse* (Mod. Fr. *graisse*), grease.

> At my nativity
> The front of heaven was full of fiery shapes,
> Of burning cressets.
>
> SHAKESPEARE: *King Henry IV, Pt. I*, III, i.

Cressida, or **Cressid.** Daughter of Calchas, a priest, beloved by TROILUS. They vowed eternal fidelity and as pledges Troilus gave the maiden a sleeve, and Cressid gave the Trojan prince a glove. Scarce had the vow been made when an exchange of prisoners was agreed to. Diomed gave up three Trojan princes, and was to receive Cressid in lieu thereof. Cressid vowed to remain constant, and Troilus swore to rescue her. She was led off to the Grecian's tent and soon gave all her affections to Diomed—nay, even bade him wear the sleeve that Troilus had given her in token of his love.

> As false
> As air, as water, wind, or sandy earth,
> As fox to lambs, as wolf to heifer's calf,
> Pard to the hind, or step-dame to her son;
> "Yea," let them say, to stick the heart of falsehood,
> "As false as Cressid".
>
> SHAKESPEARE: *Troilus and Cressida*, III, i.

Cresswell, Madam. A notorious bawd and procuress who flourished in London between *c.* 1670 and 1684 and was much patronized by RESTORATION courtiers and politicians. She wintered in CLERKENWELL and kept house in Camberwell in the summer. "Old Mother Cresswell" was not married, although Sir Thomas Player went by the nickname of Sir Thomas Cresswell. In her old age she became religiously inclined and bequeathed £10 for a funeral sermon, in which nothing ill should be said of her. Scott attributes the sermon to the Duke of Buckingham.

> "Why," said the Duke, "I had caused the little Quodling to go through his oration thus—'That whatever evil reports had passed current during the lifetime of the worthy matron whom they had restored to dust that day, malice itself could not deny that she was born well, married well, lived well, and died well; since she was born in Shadwell, married to Cresswell, lived in Camberwell, and died in Bridewell."
>
> *Peveril of the Peak*, ch. xliv.

Crestfallen. Dispirited. The allusion is to fighting cocks, whose crest falls in defeat, and rises rigid and of a deep-red colour in victory.

> Shall I seem crest-fallen in my father's sight?
>
> SHAKESPEARE: *Richard II*, I, i.

Cretan Labyrinth. *See* LABYRINTH.

Crete. Hound of Crete. A bloodhound.

> *Coupe la gorge*, that's the word. I thee defy again, O hound of Crete.
>
> SHAKESPEARE: *Henry V*, II, i.

The infamy of Crete. The MINOTAUR.

> At the point of the disparted ridge lay stretch'd
> The infamy of Crete, detested brood
> Of the feigned heifer.
>
> DANTE: *Hell*, xii (*Cary's Translation*).

Cretinism (kret' in izm). Mental imbecility accompanied by goitre, so called from the Crétins of the Alps. The word is a corruption of Christian (*Chrétien*), because being baptized, and only idiots, they were "washed from original sin", and incapable of actual sin. Similarly, idiots are called *innocents*.

Crew Cut. A form of hair-cut popularized by U.S. athletes, particularly college rowing teams, in the decade following World War II. The hair is cut very short all over and brushed upright on top, reminiscent of a hedgehog.

Crewel Garters. Garters made of worsted or yarn. The resemblance in sound between *crewel* (the derivation of which is unknown) and *cruel* gave rise to many puns.

> Ha, ha! he wears cruel garters.
>
> SHAKESPEARE: *King Lear*, II, iv.

Crewian Oration. A Latin oration delivered in alternate years by the Public Orator and Professor of Poetry at the ENCÆNIA of Oxford University, essentially to commemorate the benefactions of Nathaniel, third Baron Crew (1633–1721), Bishop of Oxford and later of Durham. He was a notorious sycophant and a favourite of the Duke of York, afterwards James II. From 1688 he was in disgrace and his benefactions may be regarded as belated attempts to restore his name.

Crib. Thieves' slang for a house or dwelling as "Stocking Crib" (a hosier's shop), "Thimble Crib" (a silversmith's); also slang for a petty theft; and for a literal translation of a Greek or Latin text used as an aid in translating, either openly or surreptitiously.

The word originally denoted a fodder rack with bars in a stable or shippen; hence its application to a child's cot.

In the West Country a working man still has his mid-morning *crib* or refreshment during his *crib-break*. *See* BEVER.

To crack a crib. *See* CRACK.

To crib is to pilfer, purloin, or to copy someone else's work (especially applied to cheating or "copying" among school children), also to plagiarize.

Crichton. *See under* ADMIRABLE.

Cricket. Probably from O.E. *cric*, *cryec*, a staff or stick, and thus connected with *crutch*. Strutt in his *Sports and Pastimes of the People of England* (1801) suggests that cricket originated from the mediæval game of club-ball. John Derrick of Guildford in 1598 (being then aged *c*. 59) states that as a boy at school "hee and several of his fellowes did runne and play there at Crickett and other plaies". An earlier reference to *criquet* has been traced to 15th-century Flanders. The game was certainly played at Winchester school before the Civil Wars. It began to come into its own in the 18th century and owed much to the Hambledon Club matches on Broad Halfpenny Down, which came to an end in 1793. The Marylebone Cricket Club (M.C.C.), which is regarded as the governing body of the game, was founded in 1787, and the present LORD'S CRICKET GROUND was opened in 1814.

Single and double wicket was played from early on, and sizes of wicket, etc., varied considerably. At the beginning of the 18th century two stumps, 12 inches high and 24 inches apart, were used. In the rules made in 1774 the stumps were to be 22 inches high with a bail of 6 inches. The third stump was added by the Hambledon Club in 1775 and the height of the stump raised from 27 to 28 inches in 1929. *See also* CHINAMAN; GOOGLY.

> Who would think that a little bit of leather and two pieces of wood, has such a delightful and delighting power!
>
> MISS MITFORD: *Our Village* (*A Country Cricket-Match*).

It's not cricket. It's not done in a fair and sportsmanlike way.

Merry as a cricket. *See* GRIG.

Crillon (krē′ yon). **Where wert thou, Crillon?** Louis Balbis de Berton de Crillon (1543–1615) was one of the greatest warrior captains of the 16th century. Henry IV entitled him "*le brave des braves*". Crillon, in his old age, was in church listening intently to the story of the Crucifixion. In the middle of the narrative he grew excited, and, unable to contain himself, cried out, '*Où étais-tu, Crillon?*". Henry IV, after the battle of Arques (1589) wrote to Crillon: "*Pends-toi, brave Crillon, nous avons combattu à Arques, et tu n'y étais pas*". This letter has become proverbial.

Crimen Læsæ Majestatis (krī′ men lē′ ze-mǎj es tā′ tis) (Lat.). *See* LESE-MAJESTÉ

Cripplegate. The origin of the name for this district in the City of London is uncertain. St. GILES is the patron SAINT of cripples, but the name is not derived from the former parish church of St. Giles, Cripplegate, which was spelt *Crupelgate* in the early 13th century. It is possibly from O.E. *crepel* (a burrow) or *crypele* (a den). The gate was demolished in 1760.

Crisis (Gr. *krinein*, to decide or to determine), properly means the "ability to judge". HIPPOCRATES said that all diseases had their periods, when the humours of the body (*see* HUMOUR) ebbed and flowed like the tide of the sea. These tidal days he called *critical days*, and the tide itself a *crisis*, because it was on these days the physician could determine whether the disorder was taking a good or bad turn. The seventh and all its multiples were critical days of a favourable character.

Crispin and Crispianus. Shoemakers who became patron saints of their craft. It is said that the two brothers born at Rome, went to Soissons in France to propagate the Christian religion, and they maintained themselves wholly by making and mending shoes. They were martyred in *c*.286.

St. Crispin's Day. 25 October, the day of the battle of Agincourt. SHAKESPEARE makes Crispin Crispian one person, and not two brothers. Hence Henry V says to his soldiers:

> And Crispin Crispian shall ne'er go by—
> But we in it shall be remembered.
>
> *Henry V*, IV, iii.

St. Crispin's holiday. Every Monday, with those who begin the working week on Tuesday, still a common practice with some butchers, fishmongers, etc.; a no-work day with shoemakers.

St. Crispin's lance. A shoemaker's awl.

Criss-cross Row. *See* CHRISS-CROSS.

Critic. A judge, an arbiter. (*See* CRISIS.) A captious, malignant critic is called a ZOILUS.

Prince of Critics. Aristarchus of Byzantium (2nd century B.C.), who compiled a critical edition of the Homeric poems, commentaries, etc.

Stop-watch critics.

> "And how did Garrick speak the soliloquy last night?" "Oh, against all rule, my lord, most ungrammatically. Betwixt the substantive and the adjective, which should agree together in number, case, and gender, he made a breach, thus—stopping as if the point wanted settling; and betwixt the nominative case, which, your lordship knows, should govern the verb, he suspended his voice in the epilogue a dozen times, three seconds and three-fifths by a stop-watch, my lord, each time." "Admirable grammarian! But in suspending his voice was the sense suspended likewise? Did no expression of attitude or countenance fill up the chasm? Was the eye silent? Did you narrowly look?" "I looked only at the stop-watch my lord." "Excellent observer!"
>
> STERNE: *Tristram Shandy*, vol. III, ch. xii.

Croak, To. In slang this means to die, the

term probably coming from the hoarse death rattle or croak of the expiring breath. A HEDGE doctor or wandering QUACK is known as a *Crocus*, or one who makes his patients croak.

Croaker. A raven, so called from its croak; one who takes a despondent view of things. Goldsmith, in his *Good-natured Man*, has a character so named.

Croakumshire. A name given to the county of Northumberland because the natives were alleged to speak with a peculiar croak. It was supposed to be especially observable in Newcastle and Morpeth, where the people were said to be born with a burr in their throats preventing their giving effect to the letter *r*.

Crockett, Davy (1786–1836). American folk hero famed as a marksman, bear hunter, and fighter. He served under Andrew Jackson in the Creek War (1813–1814). His popularity led him to Congress where his natural wit and homespun stories made him a noted character. He was killed at the ALAMO in 1836.

Crockford. The popular name for *Crockford's Clerical Directory*, published since 1838 and first compiled by John Crockford. It is a reference book of all the clergy of the CHURCH OF ENGLAND and of the other churches in communion with the SEE of Canterbury.

Crockford's was established as an exclusive gambling club at 50 St. James's Street in 1827 by William Crockford (1775–1844), the son of a fishmonger. It became the favourite haunt of the world of fashion, and fortunes were staked there. Crockford made more than £1,000,000 before he retired in 1840.

Crockford's closed down (*c.* 1848), consequent upon a change in the Gaming Laws. A new "Crockford's" opened in 1928, essentially as a bridge club at 21 Hertford Street, subsequently moving to sumptuous premises at Carlton House Terrace. The new Betting and Gaming Act of 1960 permitting the revival of games of chance enabled it to acquire a leading position, with *chemin de fer* as its main game.

Crocodile. A symbol of deity among the Egyptians, because, says Plutarch, it is the only aquatic animal which has its eyes covered with a thin transparent membrane, by reason of which it sees and is not seen, as God sees all, Himself not being seen. To this he adds: "The Egyptians worship God symbolically in the crocodile, that being the only animal without a tongue, like the Divine Logos, which standeth not in need of speech." (*De Iside et Osiride*, vol. II, p. 381).

Achilles Tatius says, "The number of its teeth equals the number of days in a year." Another tradition is that, during the seven days held sacred to APIS, the crocodile will harm no one. At Crocodilopolis in the Faiyum, he was worshipped under the name of Sobek.

Crocodile tears. Hypocritical tears. The tale is that crocodiles moan and sigh like a person in deep distress, to allure travellers to the spot, and even shed tears over their prey while devouring it.

> As the mournful crocodile
> With sorrow snares relenting passengers.
> SHAKESPEARE: *Henry VI, Pt. II*, III, i.

Crœsus (krē' sùs). **Rich as Crœsus.** Crœsus, the last king of Lydia (560–546 B.C.), was so rich and powerful that his name became proverbial for wealth. Many of the wise men of Greece were drawn to his court, including Æsop (*see under* ÆSOP'S FABLES) and SOLON. He was overthrown by Cyrus of Persia. *See* ORACLE.

Crofters. Smallholders in the Highlands of Scotland and the Western Isles, holding their land by a variety of ancient tenures; a COTTAR is somewhat similar to a crofter.

Cro-Magnon Man. A prehistoric race-type named after the Cro-Magnon cave near Les Eyzies in the Dordogne, France, where four of their skeletons were discovered in 1868. Cro-Magnon man is associated with the AURIGNACIAN culture. His skull was long and narrow and larger than that of the average European of today.

Cromlech (krom' lek). A name formerly used by British archæologists for a NEOLITHIC AGE monument consisting of a large flat stone resting on top of two or more others, like a table (Welsh *crom*, bent; *llech*, a flat stone). They appear to be the uncovered remains of burial chambers or cairns, and the French name DOLMEN is now more commonly used.

WAYLAND SMITH's Cave (Berkshire), Trethevy Quoit (Cornwall), Kit's Coty House (Kent), and the "killing-stone" at Louth (Ireland), are examples among many.

Cromwell's Bible. *See* BIBLE, THE ENGLISH.

Cronian Sea. The north polar sea; so called from Cronos (*see* KRONOS). Pliny says, "*A Thule unius diei navigatione mare concretum, a nonnullis cronium appellatur.*" (*Nat. Hist.*, iv, 16.)

> As when two polar winds blowing adverse
> Upon the Cronian sea.
> MILTON: *Paradise Lost*, x, 290.

Cronos, or **Cronus.** *See* KRONOS.

Crook. By hook or crook. *See* HOOK.

Crooked as Crawley. *See* CRAWLEY.

There is a crook in the lot of every one. There is trial or vexation in every person's life. When LOTS were drawn by bits of stick it was desirable to get sticks which were smooth and straight; but one without a crook or some other defect is rare. Thomas Boston (1676–1732), a Scottish pastor, published a popular book entitled *The Crook in the Lot*.

To crook the elbow, or **finger.** This occurs in England before the mid-1780s. It is the American equivalent to ELBOW-LIFTING. More recently in England *to crook the finger* means to drink from a tea or coffee cup with the little finger noticeably crooked. This is often regarded as a somewhat ostentatious mark of gentility.

Crooning as a sentimental type of singing began in the U.S.A. about 1929 and rapidly became popular. The singing is very soft "somewhere near the written notes, but preferably never actually on those notes" (Eric Blom), and its effects depend largely on electrical amplification.

Crop Up, or **Out.** To rise out of, to appear at the surface; hence to occur or arise. A mining term. Strata which appear near the surface are said to crop out. We say a subject *crops up* from time to time and such and such a thing *crops out* of what you were saying.

Cropper. To come a cropper. To get a bad fall, literally or metaphorically. "Neck and crop" means altogether, and "to come a cropper" is to come to the ground neck and crop.

Croquemitaine. A HOBGOBLIN, an evil sprite or ugly monster, used by French nurses and parents to frighten children into good behaviour. In 1863 M. L'Epine published a romance with this title, telling the story of a god-daughter of CHARLEMAGNE whom he called "Mitaine". It was translated by Tom Hood (the younger).

Croquet (krō'ki). The garden game takes its name from the Fr. *croc*, a hook, as the early croquet mallets were shaped like hockey-sticks. It is probably descended from the earlier game of pell mell or PALL MALL. It became popular in England from the 1850s.

Crosier, or **Crozier** (from L. Lat. *crocia*; connected with our *crook*; confused with Fr. *croisier* from *crois*, a cross). The pastoral staff of an abbot or BISHOP, and sometimes applied to an archbishop's staff, which terminates in a cross and not in a crook as does the bishop's crosier.

A bishop turns his staff outwards to denote his wider authority; an abbot turns it inwards to show that his authority is limited to his own convent. The abbot covers his staff with a veil when walking in the presence of a bishop, his superior.

Cross. The cross is not solely a Christian symbol originating with the crucifixion of the Redeemer. In Carthage it was used for ornamental purposes; runic crosses were set up by the Scandinavians as boundary marks, and were erected over the graves of kings and heroes. CICERO tells us (*De Divinatione*, ii, 27, and 80, 81) that the augur's staff with which they marked out the heaven was a cross; the Egyptians employed it as a sacred symbol, and two buns marked with a cross were discovered at Herculaneum. It was also a sacred symbol among the Aztecs; in Cozumel it was an object of worship; at Tabasco it symbolized the god of rain. It was one of the emblems of QUETZALCOATL, as lord of the four cardinal points, and the four winds that blow therefrom.

The cross of the crucifixion is said to have been made of palm, cedar, olive, and cypress, to signify the four quarters of the globe.

In his *Monasteries of the Levant* (1848) Curzon gives the legend that SOLOMON cut down a cedar and buried it on the spot where the pool of Bethesda stood later. A few days before the crucifixion the cedar floated to the surface of the pool, and was used as the upright of the Saviour's cross.

Constantine's Cross. It is said that Constantine on his march to ROME saw a luminous cross in the sky with the motto *In hoc vinces*, by this [sign] conquer. In the night before the battle of Saxa Rubra (312) he was commanded in a vision to inscribe the cross and motto on the shields of his soldiers. He obeyed the voice and prevailed. The LABARUM of Constantine was not really in the form of a cross but a monogram ☧ (XPI) formed of the first three letters of the word *Christ* in Greek. The legend of the DANNEBROG is similar and there are others. The Scots are said to have adopted St. ANDREW'S cross because it appeared in the heavens the night before Achaius, King of the Scots, and Hungus, King of the Picts, defeated Athelstan.

The Cross in heraldry. As many as 285 varieties of cross have been recognized, but the twelve in ordinary use, from which the others are derived, are: (1) the ordinary cross; (2) the cross humetté, or couped; (3) the cross urdé, or pointed; (4) the cross potent; (5) the cross crosslet; (6) the cross botoneé, or treflé; (7) the cross moline; (8) the cross potence; (9) the cross fleury; (10) the cross patté; (11) the Maltese cross (or eight-pointed cross); (12) the cross cleché and fitché.

The cross as a mystic emblem may be reduced to the four following:

1. **The Greek cross,** found on Assyrian tablets, Egyptian and Persian monuments, and on Etruscan pottery.

2. **The crux decussata,** generally called St. ANDREW'S cross, an x-shaped cross. Quite common in ancient sculpture.

3. **The Latin cross,** or **crux immissa.** This symbol is found on coins, monuments, and medals long before the Christian era.

4. **The tau cross** or **crux commissa.** Very ancient indeed. It is also the cross of St. ANTHONY.

The tau cross with a handle, or **crux ansata,** is common to several Egyptian deities as ISIS, OSIRIS, etc.; and is the emblem of immortality and life generally. The circle on the top signifies the eternal preserver of the world, and the T is the monogram of THOTH, the Egyptian MERCURY, meaning wisdom.

Capital Cross. In HERALDRY, a Greek cross with terminations similar to the architectural capital of the TUSCAN ORDER. Also called *brick-axed* because the ends resembled a mason's brick-axe.

The Cross of Lorraine, with two bars, was adopted as the emblem of the Free French during World War II. It is the patriarchal cross.

Long Cross. *See* DAGGER.

The Red Cross on a white ground, sometimes called the *Cross of Geneva*, is the Swiss flag reversed, and indicates the neutrality of hospitals and ambulances. *See* GENEVA CONVENTION *under* GENEVA; *Cp.* THE RED CRESCENT *under* RED. The Red Cross is also the cross of St. GEORGE.

True Cross. *See* THE INVENTION OF THE CROSS.

Creeping to the Cross. The GOOD FRIDAY ceremony of the *Veneration of the Cross* was commonly so called in England, when priest and people kneel and kiss the cross on the sanctuary steps. The custom derives from the veneration of the True Cross at Jerusalem. *See* THE INVENTION OF THE CROSS.

> On Good Friday above all in holy Church men creep to the church and worship the cross.
> *Dives and Pauper* (printed by Wynkyn de Worde in 1496).

Everyone must bear his own cross. Everyone must carry his own burden or troubles. The allusion is to the practice of the person condemned to crucifixion being made to carry his cross to the place of execution.

Exaltation of the Cross. *See under* EXALTATION.

Hot cross buns. *See* BUN.

The Invention of the Cross. Until its abolition by Pope John XXIII in 1960, a church festival held on 3 May, in commemoration of the finding (Lat. *invenire*, to find) of the "true cross of Christ" by St. HELENA. At her direction, after a long and difficult search in the neighbourhood of the HOLY SEPULCHRE (which had been over-built with heathen temples), the remains of the three buried crosses were found. These were applied to a sick woman, and that which affected her cure was declared the True Cross. The Empress had this enclosed in a silver shring (after having taken a large piece to ROME) and placed in a church built on the spot for the purpose. *See* IRON CROWN OF LOMBARDY *under* CROWN.

The Judgment of the Cross. An ordeal instituted in the reign of CHARLEMAGNE. The plaintiff and defendant were required to cross their arms upon their breast; and he who could hold out the longest gained the suit.

The Stations of the Cross. *See under* STATION.

To take the Cross. In mediaeval times to take the pledge to become a crusader. *See* CRUSADES.

Veneration of the Cross. *See* CREEPING TO THE CROSS.

Cut on the cross. *See under* CUT.

On the cross. Not "on the square", not straightforward. To get anything "on the cross" is to get it unfairly or dishonestly.

To cross it off, or **out.** To cancel it by running your pen across it.

To cross swords. To fight a duel; metaphorically to encounter someone in argument or debate.

To cross the hand, or **palm.** Gipsy fortune-tellers always bid their dupe to "cross their hand with a bit of silver". This, they say, is for luck. The coin remains with the owner of the crossed hand. The sign of the cross warded off witches and all other evil spirits, and as fortune-telling belongs to the black arts, the palm is signed with a cross to keep off the wiles of the DEVIL.

Crossing the palm is also used colloquially to mean giving a tip or small "bribe".

To cross the line is to cross or pass the Equator. *See* CROSSING THE LINE *under* LINE.

Cross and Ball. The orb of royalty is a sphere or ball surmounted by a cross, an emblem of empire introduced in represen-

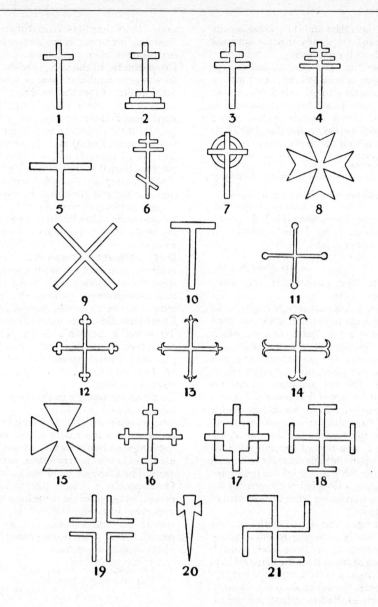

CROSSES.—1. Latin. 2. Calvary. 3. Patriarchal, Archiepiscopal, Lorraine.
4. Papal. 5. Greek. 6. Russian. 7. Celtic. 8. Maltese. 9. St. Andrew's.
10. Tau. 11. Pommé. 12. Botonné. 13. Fleury. 14. Moline. 15. Patté.
16. Crosslet. 17. Quadrate. 18. Potent. 19. Voided and couped. 20 Patté fiché.
21. Fylfot, Swastika.

tations of our Saviour. The cross stands above the ball, to signify that the spiritual power is above the temporal.

Cross and Pile. The obverse and reverse sides of a coin or head and tail; hence money generally and the game of PITCH AND TOSS in particular, to which Edward II was said to be partial. Coins were in former times stamped with a cross on one side. *Pile* (Lat. *pila*) is French for the reverse of a coin.

> A man may now justifiably throw up cross and pile for his opinions.
>
> LOCKE: *Essay Concerning Human Understanding* (1690).

> Marriage is worse than cross I win, pile you lose.
>
> SHADWELL: *Epsom Wells* (1672).

I have neither cross nor pile. Not a penny in the world. The French phrase is, "*N'avoir ni croix ni pile*."

> Whachum had neither cross nor pile.
>
> BUTLER: *Hudibras*, II, iii.

Crossbelts. *See* REGIMENTAL AND DIVISIONAL NICKNAMES.

Cross-bench. Seats set at right angles to the rest of the seats in the HOUSE OF COMMONS and the HOUSE OF LORDS, and on which members independent of party usually sit. Hence *cross-bencher*, an independent, and the *cross-bench mind*, open or unbiased.

Crossbill. The red plumage and curious crossing of the upper and lower bill-halves are accounted for by a mediæval fable which says that these distinctive marks were bestowed on the bird by the Saviour at the Crucifixion, as a reward for its having attempted to pull the nails from the cross with its beak. The fable is best known to English readers through Longfellow's *Legend of the Crossbill*, a translation from the German of Julius Mosen.

Cross-biting. Cheating; properly cheating one who has been trying to cheat you—biting in return. Hence *cross-biter*, a swindler. *Laurence Crossbiter* is the name given to one of the rogues in COCK LORELL'S BOTE.

Cross-bones. *See* SKULL AND CROSS-BONES.

Cross-grained. Bad-tempered, self-willed. Wood only works smoothly with the grain; when the grain crosses we get a knot or curling which is hard to work.

Cross-legged Knights. Crusaders were generally represented on their tombs with crossed legs.

> From him descended cross-legg'd knights,
> Fam'd for their faith and warlike fights.
>
> BUTLER: *Hudibras*, I, i, 471.

To dine with cross-legged knights. *See* DINE.

Cross questions and crooked answers. A parlour game which consists in giving ludicrous or irrelevant answers to simple questions. Hence the phrase is used of one who is "hedging" or trying by his answers to conceal the truth when questioned.

Cross-roads. In the U.S.A. when used as an adjective implies a rural or unsophisticated quality. From the building of general stores at cross-roads which in thinly populated areas became meeting places for gossip. *Cp.* CRACKER-BARREL PHILOSOPHY.

Cross-roads, Burial at. All excluded from holy rites (criminals and suicides) were at one time buried at cross-roads. The ancient Teutonic peoples used such places for holding sacrifice and they thus by association came to be places of execution.

Cross-roads of the Pacific. A nickname of Honolulu, from its position on shipping and air routes.

Dirty work at the cross-roads. Foul play; nefarious activity. Probably the phrase arose from the association with burial at crossroads (*see above*), or from the fact that cross-roads were often the scene of foul play.

Cross-row. Short for CHRISS-CROSS ROW.

To cross a person's bows. To cause annoyance to another and incur his displeasure. A naval phrase. It is a breach of good manners for a junior ship to cross the bows of a senior.

To cross someone's path. To meet or to thwart a person.

Cross, meaning irritable, bad-tempered.

As cross as a bear with a sore head, as the tongs, as two sticks. Common phrases used of one who is very vexed, peevish, or cross. The allusions are obvious.

Cross-patch. A disagreeable, ill-tempered person. PATCH is an old name for a fool, and with the meaning "fellow" is common enough in SHAKESPEARE, as a "scurvy patch", "What patch is our porter?" etc.

> Cross-patch, draw the latch,
> Sit by the fire and spin;
> Take a cup, and drink it up,
> Then call your neighbours in.
>
> *Old Nursery Rhyme*.

Crotona's Sage (Kro tō′ nà). PYTHAGORAS. So called because he established his chief school of philosophy at Crotona in Italy (*c.* 530 B.C.). Such success followed his teaching that the whole aspect of the town became more moral and decorous in a very short time.

Crouchmas. An old name for the festival of the INVENTION OF THE CROSS, also for ROGATION Sunday and Rogation week. "Crouch", here from Lat. *crux*, means cross.

> From bull-cow fast,
> Till Crouchmas be past.
>
> TUSSER: *May Remembrances*.

Croud. See CROWD.

Crow. A crow symbolizes contention, discord, strife.

As the crow flies. The shortest distance between two places. The crow flies straight to its destination. *Cp.* AIR-LINE; BEE-LINE.

I must pluck a crow with you; I have a crow to pick with you. I am displeased with you, and must call you to account. I have a small complaint to make against you. In Howell's proverbs (1659) we find the following used in the same sense, "I have a goose to pluck with you." *Cp.* TO HAVE A BONE TO PICK WITH SOMEONE *under* BONE.

> If a crow help us, sirrah, we'll pluck a crow together.
> SHAKESPEARE: *Comedy of Errors*, III, i.

Jim Crow. See JIM.

To crow over one. To exult over a vanquished or abased person. The allusion is to cocks who habitually crow when victorious.

To eat crow. To be forced to do something extremely distasteful. The expression derives from an incident during an armistice of the Anglo-American War of 1812–1814. A New Englander unwittingly crossed the British lines while hunting and brought down a crow. An unarmed British officer heard the shot and determined to punish the offender. He gained hold of the American's gun by praising his marksmanship and asking to see his weapon. The Britisher then told the American he was guilty of trespass and forced him at the point of the gun to take a bite out of the crow. When the officer returned the gun the American in his turn covered the soldier and compelled him to eat the remainder of the crow.

Crow-eaters. Nickname for the inhabitants of South Australia.

Crow's nest. A barrel or cylindrical box fitted to the crosstrees of the maintop mast of a sailing ship for the lookout man.

Crowd, Croud, or **Cruth** (*Crwth*). A mediæval rectangular shaped instrument, with from three to six strings, played with a bow. Hence *crowder*, a player of the *crowd*. It lingered on in WALES much longer than elsewhere. John Morgan who died in 1720 was a noted player, and the Welsh *crwth* survived until the end of the 18th century.

> Harke! how the Minstrils gin to shrill aloud
> Their merry musick that resounds from far,
> The pipe, the tabor, and the trembling croud.
> SPENSER: *Epithalamion*.
> I never heard the old song of *Percy and Duglas*, that
> I found not my heart mooved more than with a
> trumpet: and yet it is sung by some blinde Crouder,
> with no rougher voyce, then rude stile.
> SIDNEY: *Apology for Poetrie*.

Crown. In HERALDRY, nine crowns are recognized: the oriental, the triumphal or imperial, the DIADEM, the obsidional crown, the civic, the crown vallary, the mural crown, the naval, and the crown celestial.

Among the Romans of the Republic and Empire, crowns of various patterns formed marks of distinction for different services; the principal ones were:

1. *The blockade crown* (*corona obsidionalis*), given to the general who liberated a beleaguered army. This was made of grass and wild flowers gathered from the spot.

2. *A camp crown* (*corona castrensis*) was given to the first to force his way into the enemy's camp. It was made of GOLD, and decorated with palisades.

3. *A civic Crown* to one who saved a *civis* (Roman citizen) in battle. It was of oak leaves, and bore the inscription H.O.C.S.—*i.e., hostem occidit, civem servavit*, a foe he slew, a citizen saved).

4. *A mural crown* was given to the first to scale the wall of a besieged town. It was made of gold and decorated with battlements.

5. *A naval crown*, of gold, decorated with the beaks of ships, was given to him who won a naval victory.

6. *An olive crown* was given to those who distinguished themselves in battle in some way not specially provided for.

7. *An ovation crown* (*corona ovatio*), made of myrtle, was given to the general who won a lesser victory.

8. *A triumphal crown* was given to the general granted a triumph. It was made of LAUREL or bay leaves. Sometimes a massive gold crown was given to the victorious general.

The Iron Crown of Lombardy is the crown of the ancient Longobardic kings, said to have been bestowed by Pope GREGORY THE GREAT. CHARLEMAGNE was crowned (774) with it as King of Italy, as was Charles V in 1530. In 1805 NAPOLEON put it on his head with his own hands. It was restored to the King of Italy by the Emperor of Austria in 1866 and replaced in the cathedral at Monza. It is so called from the inner fillet of iron which is said to have been beaten out of a nail from the True Cross which was given to Constantine by his mother, St. HELENA (*See* INVENTION OF THE CROSS.) The outer circlet is of beaten GOLD, and set with PRECIOUS STONES.

The crown in English coinage when first minted (1526) was valued at 4s. 6d. and called the *crown of the rose*, but in the same year it was replaced by one worth 5 s. It was a GOLD coin and did not disappear as such until the reign of Charles II. Silver crowns were struck from 1551. The name derives from the French gold coin (*couronne*) first issued by Philip of Valois in 1339, which bore a crown on the obverse.

In the paper trade **crown** was a standard size of printing paper measuring 15 by 20 inches (before metrification); so called from an ancient watermark.

Crowns of Egypt. *See under* EGYPT.

Crown of the East. Antioch, ancient capital of Syria, which consisted of four walled cities, encompassed by a common rampart that "enrounded them like a coronet".

The Crown of St. Stephen. *See under* STEPHEN, ST.

Crown of Thorns. The crown of Christ upon the Cross.

Crown of Wild Olive. The satisfaction of having performed a worthwhile task for its own sake rather than for gain. This crown was the only prize awarded to victors in the ancient OLYMPIC GAMES, the wild olive being held sacred from its having been first planted by HERCULES. John Ruskin has a book of this title, first published in 1866, which is a series of four essays or lectures on work, traffic, war, and the future of ENGLAND.

Crowquill, Alfred. This was the name used by Alfred Henry Forrester (1805–1872), the black-and-white artist of *Punch* and the *Illustrated London News*. He was famous in his day as the illustrator of DR. SYNTAX, the BON GAULTIER BALLADS, Baron MÜNCHAUSEN and other popular works.

Crozier. *See* CROSIER.

Crucial (kroo' shàl). **A crucial test.** A very severe and undeniable test. The allusion is to a fancy of Francis Bacon, who said that two different diseases or sciences might run parallel for a time but would ultimately cross each other; thus, the plague might for a time resemble other diseases, but when the *bubo* or boil appeared, the plague would assume its special character. Hence the phrases *instantiacrucis* (a crucial or unmistakable symptom), a crucial experiment, example, question, etc. *Cp.* CRUX.

Cruel, The. Pedro, King of Castile (1333, 1350–1369), so called for the murders he perpetrated. He was finally overthrown and slain in Du Guesclin's tent by his brother Henry.

Cruel Garters. *See* CREWEL.

Cruft's. The usual name for the internationally famous Cruft's Dog Show, now held at Olympia and founded by Charles Cruft in 1891. Some years after his death in 1938, the show was taken over by the Kennel Club. Cruft's interest in dogs largely arose from his

apprenticeship to James Spratt in 1876. Spratt had recently started a "dog cake" business in HOLBORN, having got the idea from America.

Crummy. In obsolete slang, expressive of something desirable, as *that's crummy*, that's good; also meaning plump, well developed, as *she's a crummy woman*, a fine, handsome woman. No doubt from *crumb*, being the soft or fleshy part of the bread. Among soldiers the word has usually meant lousy, infested with lice, and this is its present meaning. Here it is probably from the likeness in appearance between breadcrumbs and the eggs of a louse. *Cp.* CRUSTY.

Crumpet. *See* MUFFINS.

Crusades. Wars undertaken by Christians in the late MIDDLE AGES to secure the right of Christian pilgrims to visit the Holy Sepulchre and to recover the HOLY LAND from its Mohammedan conquerors. The name is derived from the CROSS which the Crusaders wore on their dress. Ideas of CHIVALRY as well as hopes of material gain were prominent. According to Matthew Paris, each nation had its special colour, which was *red* for France; *white* for ENGLAND; *green* for Flanders; *blue* or *azure* for Italy; *gules* for Spain; for SCOTLAND, a *St. Andrew's cross*; for the Knights TEMPLAR, *red on white. See* TO TAKE THE CROSS *under* CROSS; PALMER. There were eight principal crusades:

1. Proclaimed by Urban II in 1095. The futile expeditions under PETER THE HERMIT and Walter the Penniless were destroyed by the Turks, but the main expedition (1096–1099) under Raymond of Toulouse, Robert of Normandy, and Godfrey of Bouillon, ended with the capture of Jerusalem. The Latin Kingdom of Jerusalem was set up in 1100 under Baldwin I.

2. After the loss of Edessa an unsuccessful expedition (1147–1149) was promoted by St. BERNARD under the leadership of the Emperor Conrad III and Louis VII of France.

3. Inspired by the fall of Jerusalem in 1187, and led by Frederick Barbarossa, Philip Augustus of France and Richard I of England. Begun in 1188, it reached a stalemate in 1192.

4. Promoted by Innocent III in 1202 and led by Thibaut of Champagne and Baldwin of Flanders it was diverted, in spite of the Pope's prohibitions, into an attack on Constantinople. Baldwin became the first Latin Emperor of Constantinople in 1204.

5. Proclaimed by Innocent III for 1217 to recover Jerusalem. The main force was directed against Egypt. Damietta was taken but given up in 1221.

6. The Emperor Frederick II obtained Nazareth, Bethlehem and Jerusalem by negotiation (1222–1229), although he was under excommunication at the time, but was absolved on his return.

7. Followed the loss of Jerusalem in 1244. It was organized and led by St. LOUIS (Louis IX) of France in 1248. The main expedition against Egypt led to his capture in 1250. After release he made fruitless efforts to recover the Holy Land and returned home in 1254.

8. The Last Crusade. Undertaken by St. Louis, Charles of Anjou, and Prince Edward of England. St. Louis died in 1270 at Tunis and the project finally petered out in 1272.

The Children's Crusade of 1212 was due to misguided zeal. There were two main expeditions. Some 40,000 German children under one Nicholas, set off over the Alps for Italy. Only a few reached Genoa and ROME, where Innocent III ordered them home. Some hundreds possibly sailed from Brindisi to disappear from history. Another 30,000 French children, under Stephen of Cloyes, set out for Marseilles and about 5,000 were eventually offered passage by scoundrelly ship masters only to be wrecked or sold as slaves to the MOSLEMS. *See* PIED PIPER OF HAMELIN.

Crush. To crush a bottle—*i.e.* to drink one. Milton has *crush't the sweet poison* (*Comus*, 47). The idea is that of crushing grapes. SHAKESPEARE also has *burst* a glass in the same sense (Induction of *The Taming of the Shrew*), *Cp.* TO CRACK A BOTTLE *under* CRACK.

> Come and crush a cup of wine.
> SHAKESPEARE: *Romeo and Juliet*, I, ii.

To crush a fly on a wheel. Another form of "to break a butterfly on a wheel". *See under* BREAK.

To have a crush on someone is to have an infatuation for someone—a schoolgirl's phrase.

Crush-room. An old term for a room in a theatre or opera-house, etc., where the audience can collect and talk during intervals, wait for their carriages, and so on.

Crust. The upper crust (of society). The aristorcracy; the UPPER TEN thousand. The phrase was first used in Haliburton's *Sayings and Doings of Sam Slick*. The upper crust was at one time the part of the loaf placed before the most honoured guests.

Crusted port. When port is first bottled its fermentation is not complete; in time it precipitates argol on the sides of the bottle, where it forms a crust. Crusted port, there-

fore, is port which has completed its fermentation.

Crusting. An American hunting term for taking big game in winter when the ice of ponds, rivers and lakes will bear the weight of a man but not that of a moose or deer.

Crusty. Ill-tempered, apt to take offence, cross, irritable, peevish. (*Cp.* CRUMMY) ACHILLES addresses the bitter THERSITES with:

> Thou crusty batch of nature, what's the news?
> SHAKESPEARE: *Troilus and Cressida*, V, i.

Crutched Friars. Crutched is the Lat. *cruciati*, crossed, from the cross at the top of their staves, later embroidered on their dress. They were a mendicant order established in Italy by 1169 and followed an Augustinian rule. They arrived in England in 1244 and the order was suppressed by the POPE in 1656.

Crux. A knotty point, an essential point, that on which a decision depends. It does not refer to the CROSS as an instrument of punishment, but to the crossing of two lines, called a *node* or knot; hence trouble or difficulty. *Quæ te mala crux agitat?* (Plautus); What evil cross distresses you?—*i.e.* what difficulty, what trouble are you under? *See* CRUCIAL.

Crux Ansata. *See* TAU CROSS *under* CROSS.

Crux Decussata. *See* CROSS.

Crux petoralis (Lat. *pectus*, breast). A cross suspended over the breast usually worn by BISHOPS, abbots and CARDINALS.

Cry. For the distinctive cries of animals, *see* ANIMALS.

A far cry. A long way; a very considerable distance; used both of space and time, as, "it is a far cry from David to Disraeli, but they were both Jews"; "it's a far cry from Clapham to Kamchatka".

> One of the Campbells replied, "It is a far cry to Lochow"; a proverbial expression of the tribe, meaning that their ancient hereditary domains lay beyond the reach of an invading enemy.
> SCOTT: *Legend of Montrose*, ch. xii.

Crying the Mare. *See* CRYING THE NECK.

Crying the Neck. Formerly, at the end of the harvest, especially in the north and west of England, the last sheaf of corn, the *Neck* (or the *Mare*) was held aloft by the leader or Harvest Lord, who shouted "I have it! I have it! I have it!" The harvesters around him cried "What have 'ee? What have 'ee? What have 'ee?". The leader shouted back, "A Neck! A Neck! A Neck!" The noise made it plain that the harvest on that particular farm was complete. There were numerous regional variants of these proceedings. *See* CORN DOLLY; HARVEST HOME; HARVEST

THANKSGIVING; HOCKEY: MELL SUPPER.

For crying out loud. A colloquial exclamation of astonishment or annoyance current since the 1920s, probably a subconscious EUPHEMISM for a blasphemous utterance.

Great cry and little wool. A proverbial equivalent expressive of contempt for one who promises great things but never fulfils the promises—*i.e.* "all talk and no do". Originally the proverb ran, "Great cry and little wool, as the Devil said when he sheared the hogs." It appears in this form in the ancient MYSTERY of *David and Abigail*, in which Nabal is represented as shearing his sheep and the DEVIL imitates him by shearing a hog.

> Thou wilt at best but suck a bull,
> Or shear swine, all cry and no wool.
> BUTLER: *Hudibras*, I, i, 851.

Hue and cry. *See* HUE.

In full cry. In full pursuit. A hunting phrase, with allusion to a yelping pack of hounds in full chase.

It's no good crying over spilt milk. It's useless lamenting what has happened, it is done and cannot be undone.

To cry aim. *See* AIM.

To cry cave (kā' vi). To give warning (Lat. *cave*, beware); a traditional schoolboy's warning given to his fellows on the approach of a master.

To cry down. To condemn, to belittle.

To cry havoc. *See* HAVOCK.

To cry off. To go back on a bargain or arrangement. In the U.S.A. it means to sell at auction.

To cry quits. *See under* QUIT.

To cry stinking fish. To belittle one's own endeavours, offerings, etc. "To cry" here is to offer for sale by shouting one's wares in the street.

To cry up. To praise loudly and publicly.

To cry wolf. *See under* WOLF.

Crystal Gazing, or, as it is sometimes called, **Scrying,** is a very ancient form of DIVINATION. By gazing fixedly and deeply into a polished crystal ball, was held that those possessing the gift could see what is about to happen or what was actually happening at some distant place, etc. *To gaze into the crystal ball* it is to see into the future, to seek inspiration to answer questions. *See* CRYSTALLOMANCY.

Crystal Palace. One of the glories of the Victorian era. It was designed entirely of glass and iron by Joseph Paxton, a former head gardener at Chatsworth, to house the Great Exhibition of 1851, or to give it its full name, the *Great Exhibition of the Works of Industry of All Nations*. It was originally erected in Hyde Park but moved to Sydenham in 1854 with some alterations, including the addition of two towers, and used as an exhibition, entertainment, and recreational centre. It became national property in 1911 and was destroyed by fire in 1936.

The Crystalline Sphere. According to Ptolemy, the ninth orb, identified by some with "the waters which were above the firmament" (*Gen.* i, 7); it was placed between the "PRIMUM MOBILE" and the firmament, or sphere, of the fixed stars, and was held to have a shivering movement that interfered with the regular motion of the stars.

> They pass the planets seven, and pass the fixed,
> And that crystalline sphere, whose balance weighs
> The trepidation talked.
> MILTON: *Paradise Lost*, III, 481.

Crystallomancy. DIVINATION by means of transparent bodies such as a crystal globe, polished quartz, and precious stones, especially a beryl. *See* CRYSTAL GAZING.

Cub. Properly the young of fox, wolf, bear, etc., figuratively a raw or unpolished young fellow. *See* TO LICK INTO SHAPE *under* LICK.

Cubbing, or **Cub-hunting.** Preliminary training for young foxhounds. Fox cubs have not the cunning nor the staying power of the grown fox, and thus offer better sport for young hounds and young riders.

Wolf Cub. *See* BOY SCOUT.

Cuba. The Roman deity who guarded infants in their cribs and sent them to sleep (Lat. *cubo*, I lie down in bed). *See* BABES, PROTECTING DEITIES OF.

Cubism. The style of an early 20th-century school of painters who depict surfaces, figures, tints, light and shade, etc., by means of a multiplicity of shapes of a cubical and geometrical character. The name was given somewhat disparagingly by Henri Matisse in 1908. It was essentially abstract and divorced from realism. It rejected any attempt to depict actual appearances and turned its back on all accepted canons of art. Its chief exponents were Braque, Derain, Léger, and notably Picasso. *Cp.* DADAISM; FAUVISM, FUTURISM; IMPRESSIONISM; ORPHISM; SURREALISM; SYNCHRONISM; VORTICISM.

Cubit. (Lat. *cubitum*, elbow). An ancient measurement of length from the elbow to the tip of the longest finger. The Roman cubit was *c*. 17½ in., the Egyptian *c*. 21 in. (which was divided into seven palms), and that of the Hebrews *c*. 22 in. The English cubit was 18 in.

> Which of you by taking thought can add one cubit unto his stature?
> *Matt.* vi, 27.

Cuchulain, or **Cú Chulainn** (koo kŭ lin, koo koo lin). A legendary Irish hero, called the "Hound of Culann" because, having accidentally slain the watchdog of the smith, Culann, in penance he had to take the animal's place. He was brought up in the court of King CONCHOBAR of Ulster, whose kingdom he defended single-handed against the Queen of Connaught. He is called Cuthullin by OSSIAN.

Cucking-stool. A kind of stool once used for ducking scolds, disorderly women, dishonest apprentices, etc., in a pond. "Cucking" is from the old verb *cuck*, to void excrement, and the stool used was often a close-stool.

> Now, if one cucking-stool was for each scold,
> Some towns, I fear, would not their numbers hold.
> *Poor Robin* (1746).

Cuckold. The husband of an adulterous wife; so called from the CUCKOO, whose chief characteristic is to deposit its eggs in other birds' nests. Johnson says, "it was usual to alarm a husband at the approach of an adulterer by calling out 'Cuckoo', which by mistake was applied in time to the person warned." Greene calls the cuckoo "the cuckold's quirister" (*Quip for an Upstart Courtier*, 1592), and the Romans used to call an adulterer a "cuckoo", as "*Te cuculum uxor ex lustris rapit*" (Plautus: *Asinaria*, V, iii). *Cp.* ACTÆON; HORN.

> The cuckoo then, on every tree,
> Mocks married men, for thus sings he—Cuckoo;
> Cuckoo, cuckoo, —O word of fear
> Unpleasing to a married ear!
> SHAKESPEARE: *Love's Labour's Lost*, V, ii.

Cuckold's Point. A spot on the Thamesside near Deptford so called from a tradition that King John there made love successfully to a labourer's wife.

Cuckoo. Cuckoo folklore and superstitions abound and are often tokens of the bird's popularity as a herald of spring. There are many old rhymes and proverbs about this bird; one says:

> In April the cuckoo shows his bill;
> In May he sings all day;
> In June he alters his tune;
> In July away he'll fly;
> In August go he must.

Also:

> Turn your money when you hear the cuckoo, and you'll have money in your purse till he come again.

And:

> The cuckoo sings from St. Tiburtius' Day (14 April) to St. John's Day (24 June).

Cuckoo oats and woodcock hay make a farmer run away. If the spring is so backward that oats cannot be sown till the cuckoo is heard (*i.e.* April), or if the autumn is so wet that the aftermath of hay cannot be got in till woodcock shooting (middle of November), then the farmer is in a bad way.

Cuckoo flowers, etc. There are many flower and plant names associated with the cuckoo. As a representative selection may be mentioned cuckoo-flower or lady's smock; cuckoo's joy, marsh marigold; cuckoo's sorrow, sheep sorrel; cuckoo-pint, LORDS AND LADIES or priest in the pulpit; cuckoo-grass, woodrush; cuckoo's potatoes, pignut; cuckoo's sorrel, wood sorrel.

Cuckoo-spit, or **Frog-spit.** A frothy exudation deposited on plants by certain insects, especially the froghopper (*Aphrophora spumaria*), for the purpose of protecting the larvæ. So called from an erroneous popular notion that the froth was spat out by cuckoos.

> Cicades are bred out of cuccow spittle or Woodsear; that is, that spumous, frothy dew or exudation or both, found upon Plants, especially about the joints of Lavender and Rosemary, observable with us about the latter end of May.
> SIR THOMAS BROWNE: *Pseudodoxia Epidemica*, v, 3. (1646).

Cloud-cuckoo-land. *See under* CLOUD.

Don't be a cuckoo. Dont' be a silly ass; don't go and make a fool of yourself.

To wall in the cuckoo. *See* COURSE.

Cucullus non facit monachum (ku kul′ lus non făk′ it mo na′ kum) (Lat. The cowl does not make the monk). Do not judge a person by external appearances. An old proverb quoted by SHAKESPEARE in *Twelfth Night*, I, v.

Cuddy, an abbreviation of Cuthbert, and the North Country and Scottish familiar name for a donkey, elsewhere called NEDDY or Jack. As an ass it also means a fool or dolt.

Cudgel. To cudgel one's brains. To make a painful effort to remember or understand something. The idea is from taking a stick to beat a dull boy under the notion that dullness is the result of temper or inattention.

> Cudgel thy brains no more about it; for your dull ass will not mend his pace with beating.
> SHAKESPEARE: *Hamlet*, V. i.

To take up the cudgels. To maintain an argument or position. To fight, as with a cudgel, for one's own way or point of view.

Cue. Besides the usual dictionary meaning of a catchword for an actor or a hint, as SHAKESPEARE's "When my cue comes, call me, and I will answer" (*Midsummer Night's Dream*, IV, i), it also meant a humour or frame of mind.

> The lassies were pretty and agreeable; the baillie's wife one of the best creatures that ever lived; and my uncle in thoroughly good cue.
> DICKENS: *Pickwick Papers*. ch. xlix.

Cuff. Speaking off the Cuff. Without previous preparation. Probably from the habit of some after-dinner speakers of making jottings on their stiff shirt cuffs as ideas occurred to them during the meal.

Cuffy, or **Cuffee.** A Negro. Both a generic word and a proper name; probably from the Gold Coast name *Kofi. Cp.* SAMBO; JIM CROW.

> Boots blacked—pass in pocket—all grand as Cuffee.
>
> H. BEECHER STOWE, *Uncle Tom's Cabin*, ch. vi.

Cufuffle, Curfuffle, or **Carfuffle.** A fuss or excitement. An old and expressive word of uncertain origin, but possibly from a verb used in Northern Ireland meaning to shake up and toss hay or straw. *Cufuffled* is also to be ruffled or rumpled.

> And wha suld come whirling there in a post-chaise but Monkbarns in an unco carfuffle—now it's no little thing that will make his honour take a chaise and post-horse twa days rinnin'.
>
> SCOTT: *The Antiquary*, ch. xx (1816).

Cui bono? (kwī bō′ nō). Who is benefited thereby? To whom is it a gain? A common but wrong meaning attached to the phrase is, "What good will it do?" "For what good purpose?" It was the question of the Roman judge L. Cassius Pedanius (*see* Cicero, *Rosc. Am.*, xxv, 84).

> Cato, that great and grave philosopher, did commonly demand, when any new project was propounded unto him, *cui bono*, what good will ensue in case the same is effected?
>
> FULLER: *Worthies* (*The Design*, i).

Culdees (kŭl dēz′). A religious order in IRELAND and SCOTLAND from about the 8th century to the 13th, although they continued in Ireland until the REFORMATION. So called from the Old Irish *céle dé* servants of God. They seem to have originated as independent communities of hermits or anchorites and latterly were essentially secular CANONS.

Cullinan Diamond. The largest known DIAMOND, named after the chairman of the Premier Mine, Johannesburg, where it was found in 1905. Its uncut weight was 3,025¾ carats (about 1 lb. 6 oz.). It was presented to King Edward VII by the South African Government and was cut into a number of stones (the largest weighing some 516 carats), which now form part of the Crown Jewels.

Cullion. *See* CULLY.

Cully. A fop, a fool, a dupe, a strumpet. Possibly a contraction of *cullion*, a despicable creature, a sponger (Ital. *coglione*, Lat. *coleus*, a leather bag or sheath). SHAKESPEARE says "Away, base cullions!" (*Henry VI, Pt. II*, I, iii), and in *The Taming of the Shrew*,

IV, ii—"And makes a god of such a cullion".
Cp. GULL.

> You base cullion, you.
>
> JONSON: *Every Man in his Humour*, III, ii.

Culross Girdles. The thin plate of iron on which oaten cakes, scones, etc., are cooked is called a "girdle" in Scotland and is similar in use to the Welsh bakestone. Thus we speak of girdle cakes and bakestone cakes. Culross was formerly celebrated for its iron girdles.

> Locks and bars, plough-graith and harrow-teeth! and why not grates and fireprongs, and Culross girdles?
>
> SCOTT: *Fair Maid of Perth*, ch. ii.

Cultures, The Two. The existence in England, and to a great extent in Western Europe, of two separate cultures with few points of contact between them; one based on the humanities and the other on the sciences. The phrase gained immediate popularity after C. P. (Lord) Snow's Rede Lecture, subsequently published as *The Two Cultures and the Scientific Revolution* (1959). A useful comparison may be made with the ideas expressed in Matthew Arnold's *Culture and Anarchy* (1869) and his Rede Lecture entitled *Literature and Science* (1882).

Culver (kŭl′ vêr). A dove or pigeon; from O.E. *culfre*, hence culver-house, a dove-cote or pigeonhouse. The word is not connected with Lat. *columba*, dove.

Pigeons formed a very useful addition to the table in former times and the culver-houses were maintained by manorial lords, monasteries, and parish clergy. There were some thousands still in use in 17th-century England.

Culverkeys. An old popular name for such plants as the bluebell, columbine, squill, etc., the flowers of which have some resemblance to a bunch of keys (O.E. *culfre*, a dove).

Cumberland Poets. *See* LAKE SCHOOL.

Cumberland Presbyterians. A separatist group formed in Cumberland, Kentucky, in 1810, following a dispute with the Kentucky Synod of the American PRESBYTERIAN Church over the formal requirements for the ministry. Those of the Cumberland presbytery unsuccessfully urged the need to dispense with the usual high educational standards in a frontier environment.

Cum grano salis (kŭm grā′ nō sā′ lis) (Lat. with a grain of salt). There is some truth in the statement but we must use great caution in accepting it. Similarly we "take something with a pinch of salt", *i.e.* it is not wholly palatable as it is, therefore it is accepted or believed with some reserve or allowance.

Cummer. A gude wife, old woman, mid-wife, gossip, neighbour (Fr. *commère*). Frequently used in Scott's novels. *Cp.* GAFFER; GAMMER.

Cunctator (kŭngk tā tôr) (Lat. the delayer). Used of one given to delay and especially of Quintus Fabius Maximus. He gained the epithet as an abusive title for his delaying tactics against Hannibal and avoidance of pitched battles, but subsequent events, such as Hannibal's great victory at CANNÆ (216 B.C.), seemed to justify his policy, and what started as a slur became an honour. Du Guesclin used similar tactics successfully against the English during the HUNDRED YEARS WAR. *See* FABIUS.

Cuneiform Letters. Wedge-shaped letters, also called arrow-headed (Lat. *cuneus*, a wedge). A name for the writing of ancient Babylonia, Assyria, Persia, and the Hittites, which was made up of wedge-shaped impressions made on soft clay. The name cuneiform is said to have been first used by the Orientalist Thomas Hyde, Regius Professor of Hebrew at Oxford (1636–1703). Cuneiform script was used from *c.* 3800 B.C. until the early years of the Christian era. The first to decipher the letters was Grotefend of Hanover in 1802.

Cunning. A word with several meanings which comes from the O.E. *cunnan*, as does "ken", to know, and was applied to someone who knew things. As WYCLIF'S BIBLE translates *Genesis* ii, 9:

> A tree of kunnynge of good and euil.

By extension of this came the meaning of skill:

> If I forget thee, O Jerusalem, let my right hand forget her cunning.
>
> *Psalm* cxxxvii.

The word had already begun to imply a knowledge of occult and evil matters:

> We take cunning for a sinister, or crooked wisdom.
> BACON: *Of Cunning* (1612).

and a Cunning Man or Woman was merely another name for a WIZARD, or WITCH. Hence the usual present meaning of sly and crafty.

The originally American usage meaning charming, pretty, engaging or clever was customary there by the mid-19th century.

Cunobelin (kū' nō bel' in). Cunobelinus, King of the Catuvellauni (A.D. 5–40), and the father of Caractacus (*see* CARADOC). His name is preserved in modified form in Cymbeline, and in "Cunobelin's goldmines", the local name for the den-eholes in the chalk beds of Little Thurrock, Essex, traditionally said to have been used by Cunobelin (and also by the Danes) for refuge.

Cup. A mixture of strong ale with sugar, spice, and a lemon, properly served up hot in a silver cup. Sometimes a roasted orange takes the place of a lemon. *Cp.* BISHOP.

Cider cup, claret cup, etc., are drinks made of these beverages, with sugar, fruit, and herbs.

Cup Final. The final round of a football contest, etc., on the result of which a championship cup is awarded. In England the most popular is for the Football Association Cup. An engraved cup, usually of silver, is a common form of trophy for many sporting events.

Divination by cup. An ancient method of DIVINATION by floating certain articles on a cup of water and reading the signs. The practice survives in fortune-telling with a cup of tea. After the last of the liquid is disposed of, the arrangement of the sediment is examined for signs.

Grace Cup. *See* LOVING or GRACE CUP *under* LOVE.

He was in his cups. Drunk. *Inter pocula, inter vina* (Horace: *Odes* III, vi, 20).

Let this cup pass from me. Let this trouble or affliction be taken away, that I may not be compelled to undergo it. The reference is to Christ's agony in the Garden of GETHSEMANE (*Matt.* xxvi, 39).

Loving, or **Grace Cup.** *See under* LOVE.

My cup runs over. My blessings overflow. Here cup signifies portion or blessing.

> My cup runneth over. Surely goodness and mercy shall follow me all the days of my life.
> *Ps.* xxiii, 5, 6.

Not my cup of tea. This does not suit me, this is not my line, this is not the sort of thing I want.

Stirrup cup. *See under* STIRRUP.

The cup of vows. In Scandinavia it was anciently customary at feasts to drink from cups of mead, and vow to perform some great deed worthy of the song of the skald. There were four cups: one to ODIN, for victory; one to FREYJA, for a good year; one to NIORD, for peace, and one to BRAGI, for celebration of the dead in poetry.

The Cups that cheer but not inebriate. Tea. A quotation from Cowper's *Task*, iv, 36, 40.

There's many a slip 'twixt the cup and the lip. Success is not always certain, things can go wrong at the last moment. *See* ANCÆUS.

We must drink the cup. We must bear our allotted burden, the sorrow which falls to our lot.

Cupar (koo' par). **He that will to Cupar maun to Cupar.** A wilful man must have his way, even to his own injury. A Scottish proverbial saying. Caleb Balderston uses it in Scott's *Bride of Lammermoor*, ch. xviii. The reference is to the fact that the Fife Courts of Justice were formerly at Cupar.

Cupar justice, The same as "Jedburgh justice", hang first and try afterwards. It is sometimes called "Cowper law" and it owed its rise to a baron-baile in Coupar-Angus before heritable jurisdictions were abolished. *Abingdon Law* is a similar phrase. It is said that during the COMMONWEALTH Major-General Browne of Abingdon first hanged his prisoners, then tried them. *Cp.* JEDDART JUSTICE; LYDFORD LAW.

Cupboard Love. Love from self-interest or hope of gain. The allusion is to the love of children for some indulgent person who gives them something nice from the cupboard.

Cupid (Lat. *cupido*, desire, love). The Roman god of love, identified with the Greek EROS. He is usually represented as a beautiful winged boy, blindfolded, and carrying a bow and arrows. There are varying legends of his parentage.

Cupid and Psyche (sī′ ki). The story is told in the GOLDEN ASS of Apuleius. *See* PSYCHE.

Cupid's golden arrow. Virtuous love.
Cupid's leaden arrow. Sensual passion.

> Deque sagittifera promisit duo tela pharetra
> Diversorum operum; fugat hoc, facit illud amorem.
> Quod facit auratum est, et cuspide fulget acuta.—
> Quod fugat obtusum est, et habet sub arundine plumbum.
> OVID: *Apollo and Daphne*.

> I swear to thee by Cupid's strongest bow;
> By his best arrow with the golden head...
> By that which knitteth souls and prospers love.
> SHAKESPEARE: *Midsummer Night's Dream*, I, i.

Cupid's torches. *See* BRANDON.

Cupidon, Le Jeune (lė zhėrn kū′ pe dong) (Fr. young Cupid). Count D'Orsay (1801–1852), famous dandy and wit and extremely good looking, was so styled by Lord Byron. The Count's father was styled *Le beau d'Orsay*.

Curate. *See* CLERICAL TITLES.

Curate's Egg. Among the catch-phrases that Punch (*see* MR. PUNCH *under* PUNCH) has introduced into the language, "Good in parts, like the curate's egg" is proverbial. The illustration shows a nervous young curate at his bishop's breakfast table. Asked by his lordship whether the egg is to his liking, he is terrified to say that it is bad and stammers out that, "Parts of it are excellent!"

Curé de Meudon (kū′ r ā de mė don) *i.e.* Rabelais (*c.* 1495–1553), who was first a monk, then a physician, then a CANON of St. Maur,

and lastly (1550) non-resident curé of Meudon.

Curfew (kĕr′ fū). The custom of ringing a bell every evening as a signal to put out fires and go to bed; also the hour for this and the bell itself. The word is from O.Fr. *couvrefeu*, cover-fire, which reveals its Norman origin. WILLIAM THE CONQUEROR instituted the curfew in England in 1068, at the hour of 8 p.m. The word is now extended to mean the period commonly ordered by occupying armies or government authorities in time of war or civil commotion when civilians must stay within doors.

> The curfew tolls the knell of parting day.
> GRAY: *Elegy written in a Country Churchyard*.

Curlies (Austr.). GOOGLIES. Used figuratively of awkward and embarrassing situations as "the question was a curly one".

Curmudgeon (kĕr mŭj′ ón). A grasping, miserly fellow. A word of unknown origin, but of it Johnson's *Dictionary* says: "It is a vitious manner of pronouncing *cœur méchant*, Fr., an unknown correspondent", meaning that this suggestion was supplied by some corespondent unknown. By a ridiculous blunder, Ash (1775) copied it into his dictionary as "from Fr. *cœur*, unknown, *méchant*, correspondent"!

Curnock. *See* CRANNOCK.

Currant. A corruption of Corinth, whence currants were imported. Originally called "raisins of Corauntz", *Corauntz* being Anglo-French for Corinth.

Currency. A word applied in early colonial Australia to the wide variety of coins then in circulation, as distinct from English gold coins, which were called STERLING. Female convicts sent to Australia became known as the "currency" and the majority of first generation Australian-born whites were descended from them.

Currency lad, or **lass.** In the early 19th century this meant one of European descent born in Australia, as opposed to *sterling, i.e.* English-born settlers.

Current. The drift of the current is the rate per hour at which the current runs.

The setting of the current is the direction or point of the compass towards which the current flows.

Curry Favour. A corruption of the M.E. *to curry favel*, to rub down Favel: *Favel* (or *Fauvel*) being the name of the CENTAUR in the early 14th-century French satirical romance *Fauvel*. This fallow-coloured creature symbolizes cunning and bestial degradation; hence to curry, or smooth down, Favel, was to enlist the services of duplicity, and so to seek to obtain by insincere flattery, to ingratiate oneself by sycophantic officiousness, etc.

Curse. Curses, like chickens, come home to roost. Curses rebound on the head of the curser, as chickens which stray during the day return to their roost at night.

Cursing by bell, book, and candle. *See under* BELL.

Curst cows have curt horns. *See under* COW.

Not worth a curse. I don't care (or **give**) **a** (**tinker's**) curse (or **cuss**), *i.e.* not worth anything, I care not at all. Similar expressions are "not a STRAW", "not a PIN", "not a bit", "not a RAP", "not a jot", "not a pin's point", "not a button".

The curse of Cain. One who is always on the move and has no abiding place is said to be "cursed with the curse of Cain". The allusion is to God's judgment on Cain after he had slain his brother Abel.

> And now art thou cursed from the earth…a fugitive and a vagabond shalt thou be in the earth.
> *Gen*, iv, 11–12.

The curse of Scotland. The nine of diamonds. The phrase seems to be first recorded in the early 18th century, for in Houston's *Memoirs* (1715–1747) we are told that Lord Justice Clerk Ormistone became universally hated in SCOTLAND and was called the Curse of Scotland; and when the ladies encountered the Nine of Diamonds at cards they called it Justice Clerk. Among the suggested origins of the phrase are:

(1) It may refer to the arms of Dalrymple, Earl of Stair—*viz*. or, on a saltire azure, nine lozenges of the first. The earl was justly held in abhorrence for his share in the massacre of GLENCOE.

(2) The nine of diamonds in the game of POPE JOAN is called the Pope, the ANTICHRIST of the Scottish reformers.

(3) In the game of *comette*, introduced by Queen Mary, it was the great winning card, and the game was the curse of Scotland because it was the ruin of many.

(4) The word "curse" is a corruption of cross, and the nine of diamonds is so arranged as to form a St. Andrew's Cross; but so are the other nines.

(5) Some say it was the card on which BUTCHER Cumberland wrote his cruel order after the battle of Culloden (1746); but the term was apparently already in vogue.

(6) Grose says somewhat inaccurately in his *Tour Thro' Scotland* (1789): "Diamonds …imply royalty…and every ninth king of Scotland has been observed for many ages to be a tyrant and a curse to the country."

The curse of Tutankhamun. A legend arising from the death of the 5th Earl of Carnarvon during the excavations at Tutankhamun's tomb. He died from pneumonia after an infection from a mosquito bite but Sir Arthur Conan Doyle, a convinced spiritualist, suggested that it might be attributed to elementals created by the priests of Tutankhamun. Coincidentally there was a power failure at Cairo when Carnarvon died and his dog in England expired at the same time. Howard Carter survived until 1939. *See also* THE VALLEY OF THE KINGS *under* VALLEY.

Cursitors. The 24 junior clerks who wrote out in COURT HAND the formal common-form (*de cursu*) CHANCERY writs in their office in Chancery Lane, London, adjoining Cursitor Street. The growth of printed forms led to their abolition in 1835.

Cursor Mundi (Lat. *cursor*, runner, *mundus*, world). An early 14th-century English poem of some 24,000 lines in northern dialect. It describes the "Course of the World" from the Creation until Doomsday. It is essentially scriptural and designed to edify and supplant chivalric romance. The author wrote in English so those who had not the more fashionable French might understand. It is a valuable source of legend.

Curtain. Curtain Call. An invitation to an actor or actress to appear in front of the curtain and receive the applause of the audience.

Curtain Lecture. The nagging by a wife after she and her husband are in bed. *See* CAUDLE LECTURE.

> If one must be your choice, which d'ye approve,
> The Curtain -Lecture or the Curtain-Love?
> DRYDEN: *Epilogue to Henry II*.

Curtain Raiser. *See* LEVER DE RIDEAU.

To ring down the curtain. To bring a matter to an end. A theatrical term. *See* RABELAIS *under* DYING SAYINGS.

Curtal Friar (kẽr tål). A curtal was a horse with its tail docked, whence its application to other things that were cut down or shortened. A curtal friar was one who wore a short cloak. In later use, especially by Scott, it acquired a vaguely derisory or belittling significance.

Curtana (kẽr tā' nà). The sword of mercy borne before kings of ENGLAND at their coronation; it has no point and is therefore shortened (O.Fr. *curt*; Lat. *curtus*). It is also called the sword of Edward the Confessor, which, having no point, was the emblem of mercy.

> But when Curtana will not do the deed
> You lay the pointless clergy-weapon by,
> And to the laws, your sword of justice, fly.
> DRYDEN: *The Hind and the Panther*, Pt. II, 419.

Curthose (kĕrt' hoz). Robert II, Duke of Normandy (1087–1134), eldest son of WILLIAM THE CONQUEROR, was so named from his short stature. He was also called "Shortthigh", as in Drayton's *The Tragicall Legend of Robert, Duke of Normandy, surnamed Short-thigh* (1596).

Curtmantle (kĕrt' măn tàl). Henry II (1133, 1154–1189), who introduced the Anjou mantle, which was shorter than the robe worn by his predecessors. *Cp.* CARACALLA.

Curule Chair. (kū' rùl). A folding stool inlaid with ivory, and with curved legs, from Lat. *currus*, a chariot, because it was originally a chariot chair. It was the ancient Roman chair of office of the higher magistrates (*e.g.* dictators, consuls, prætors, censors, and the chief ædiles), termed *curules* or *curule* magistrates, and emperors.

> Those mounted in a chair-curule,
> Which Moderns call a Cucking-stool.
>   BUTLER: *Hudibras*, II, ii.

Cushcow Lady. A Yorkshire name for a LADYBIRD.

Cushion Dance. A lively dance, popular in early Stuart times, in which kissing while kneeling on a cushion was a major feature.

> In our court in Queen Elizabeth's time, gravity and state was kept up; in King James's time things were pretty well; but in King Charles's time there has been nothing but Trench-more and the cushion dance, omnium gatherum, tolly polly, hoyte cum toyte.
>   SELDEN: *Table Talk (King of England)*.

It survived quite late in rural districts. John Clare (1793–1864), the peasant poet of Northamptonshire, mentions it in his *May-Day Ballad*:

> And then comes the cushion, the girls they all shriek,
> And fly to the door from the old fiddler's squeak:
> But the doors they are fastened, so all must kneel down,
> And take the rude kiss from th' unmannerly clown.

To miss the cushion. To make a mistake, to miss the mark.

Custard Coffin. *See* COFFIN.

Custer's Last Stand. In America in the late 19th century as favourite a subject for paintings and engravings as the "Relief of Ladysmith" became in England. Lt.-Col. George A. Custer was a dashing cavalry man with a popular reputation. The annihilation of his force of over 200 men by some 2,000 Indian warriors under Sitting Bull at the Battle of Little Big Horn, Montana (25 June 1876) made a tremendous impact, and the episode became part of the national epic. Custer's body was spared mutilation unlike most or all of the others.

Custom clothes, or **custom tailoring.** The American equivalent of "made to measure",

or "bespoke tailoring". These terms were appearing in English fashion magazines by the 1960s.

Customer. A rum customer. A queer or strange fellow, one not to meddle with. Here *rum* is the old CANT term meaning "fine", "gallant", or "spirited".

A slim customer. A sly or crafty character, a "wily bird".

An ugly customer. One better left alone as he is likely to prove vicious if interfered with.

Custos Rotulorum (Lat. keeper of the rolls). Those officers charged with keeping the records of the courts in a county. The Lord-Lieutenant is now the Custos Rotulorum and the work is done by the Clerk of the Peace in his capacity of deputy.

Cut. Cut and come again. Take a cut from the joint, and come for another if you like it, *i.e.* "there's plenty of it, have as much as you like." It is used by Swift in his *Polite Conversation*, ii.

Cut and dried. All ready, fixed or arranged beforehand. "He had a speech all cut and dried." The allusion is to timber, cut, dried and ready for use.

> Sets of phrases, cut and dry,
> Evermore thy tongùe supply.
>   SWIFT: *Betty the Grisette*.

Cut neither nails nor hair at sea. Petronius says:

> Non licere cuiquam mortalium in nave neque ungues neque capillos deponere nisi cum pelago ventus irascitur.

The cuttings of the nails and hair were votive offerings to PROSERPINE, and it would excite the jealousy of NEPTUNE to make offerings to another in his own special kingdom.

Cut of his jib. The contour or expression of his face. "I don't like the cut of his jib" means, "I don't like the look of him." The phrase is of nautical origin. The cut of the jib or headsail betokened the quality or character of the vessel.

Cut-off. The American equivalent of the English "short cut".

Cut off with a shilling. Disinherited. To be left a shilling showed that the testator had not forgotten, but had intentionally disinherited a person by bequeathing a trifling sum.

Cut on the cross. A dressmaking and tailoring term. The material is folded so that the weft is parallel to the warp and the cut is then made along the fold.

Cut out. Left in the lurch; superseded. When there are too many for a game of cards (say whist or bridge), it is customary for the players to cut out after a rubber, in order that another may have a turn. The players cut the cards on the table the lowest turn-up gives place to a newcomer.

Cut your coat according to your cloth. *See* COAT.

Diamond cut diamond. *See under* DIAMOND.

He has cut his eye teeth. *See under* TOOTH.

He is cut, he is half cut. Drunk or nearly so.

He'll cut up well. He is rich and on his death his property will cut into good slices among his heirs.

His life was cut short. He died prematurely. The allusion is to ATROPOS, one of the three FATES, cutting the thread of life spun by her sister CLOTHO.

I must cut my stick, *i.e.* depart. The Irish usually cut a SHILLELAGH before starting on an expedition. *Punch* gives the following derivation: "Pilgrims on leaving the Holy Land used to cut a palmstick, to prove that they had really been to the Holy Sepulchre. So brother Francis would say to brother Paul, 'Where is brother Benedict?' 'Oh (says Paul), he has cut his stick!'—*i.e.* he is on his way home."

To be cut out for. To be naturally suited for, as, "He is cut out for a sailor." The allusion is to cutting out cloth for specific purposes.

To cut. To renounce or ignore acquaintance. There are four sorts of cut—

1. The *cut direct* is to stare an acquaintance in the face and pretend not to know him.

2. The *cut indirect*, to look another way, and pretend not to see him.

3. The *cut sublime*, to admire the top of some tall edifice or the clouds of heaven till the acquaintance has passed by.

4. The *cut infernal*, to stoop and adjust your boots till he has gone past.

To cut blocks with a razor. To do something remarkable by insignificant means; to do something more eccentric than expedient; to "make pin-cushions of sunbeams" (Swift). It is an allusion to the story of ACCIUS NÆVIUS, which is used in the BON GAULTIER BALLADS and is also referred to by Goldsmith in his *Retaliation*.

> In short, 'twas his [Burke's] fate, unemployed or in place, sir,
> To eat mutton cold, and cut blocks with a razor.

To cut capers. *See under* CAPER.

To cut one's comb. *See under* COMB.

To cut a dash. To make a show; to get oneself looked at and talked about for a showy or striking appearance. "Dashing" means showy or striking, as a "dashing fellow", a "dashing equipage".

To cut the ground from under one, or **from under his feet.** To leave an adversary no ground to stand upon, by disproving or forestalling all his arguments or undermining his case.

To cut no ice. Be of no account, make no impression, possibly borrowed from figure skating.

To cut the knot. To break through an obstacle. The reference is to the GORDIAN KNOT.

To cut the painter. *See under* PAINTER.

To cut up rough. To be disagreeable or quarrelsome about anything.

To cut and run. To escape in a hurry, to quit. In the days when a ship's anchor cable was made of hemp, the cable was cut, if the occasion demanded it, and the vessel allowed to run before the wind. A classical example of this was when the Spanish Armada was anchored off Calais. Most of the captains cut their cables on the approach of Howard's fireships.

Sails were also set in a hurry by cutting their gaskets.

To cut it short means to bring to an end. *Cp.* AUDLEY.

To cut short is to shorten, to silence by interruption.

To cut a swath. To make an impression. An American expression usually used in the negative. A swath is the amount cut by one sweep of a scythe.

To cut your wisdom teeth. *See under* WISDOM.

Cuthbert. A name coined by "Poy", the cartoonist of the *Evening News*, during World War I for the fit men of military age, especially in Government offices, who were not called for military service, or who positively avoided it. These civilians were depicted as frightened-looking rabbits. *See* TO COMB OUT *under* COMB.

Cuthbert Bede. The pen-name of the Rev. Edward Bradley (1827–1889), author of *The Adventures of Mr.* VERDANT GREEN and other humorous works.

St. Cuthbert's Beads. Single joints of the articulated stems of encrinites (fossil crinoids), also called *stone lilies*. They are perforated in the centre and bear a fanciful resemblance to a CROSS; hence they were once used for ROSARIES. Legend relates that the 7th-century St. Cuthbert sits at night on a rock in HOLY ISLAND and uses the opposite rock as an anvil while he forges the beads.

St. Cuthbert's Duck. The eider duck, so called because it breeds in the Farne Islands, the headquarters of St. Cuthbert.

Cutler's poetry. Mere jingles or rhymes. At one time knives had a distich inscribed on the blade by means of AQUA FORTIS.

> Whose posy was
> For all the world like cutler's poetry
> Upon a knife.
>
> SHAKESPEARE: *Merchant of Venice*, V, i.

Cutpurse. A pickpocket nowadays. When purses were worn suspended from a girdle, thieves cut the strings by which the purse was attached. When purses, etc., came to be kept in pockets the cut-purse became a pickpocket.

> To have an open ear, a quick eye, and a nimble hand, is necessary for a cutpurse.
>
> SHAKESPEARE: *Winter's Tale*, IV, ii.

Moll Cutpurse. The familiar name of Mary Frith (*c.* 1585–1660), a woman of masculine vigour, and who often dressed as one. In 1611 she was sentenced to do public penance by the Court of ARCHES for parading about FLEET STREET and the STRAND in male costume. She was a notorious thief and once attacked General Fairfax on Hounslow Heath, for which she was sent to NEWGATE. She escaped by bribery and finally died of dropsy. Middleton and Dekker's *The Roaring Girle* is founded on her exploits.

Cutter's law. Not to see a fellow want while we have cash in our purse. Cutter's law means the law of CUTPURSES, robbers, brigands, and highwaymen.

> I must put you in cash with some of your old uncle's broad pieces. This is cutter's law; we must not see a pretty fellow want, if we have cash ourselves.
>
> SCOTT: *Old Mortality*, ch. ix.

Cuttle. Captain Cuttle. An eccentric, kind-hearted sailor in Dickens's *Dombey and Son*, simple as a child, credulous of every tale, and generous as the sun. He is immortalized by his saying "When found, make a note of" (*see* ch. xv.) This phrase was adopted by *Notes and Queries*.

Cutty. Scots for short, as *cutty pipe*, a short clay pipe; *cutty spoons*; *a cutty gun*, a pop-gun; a *cutty*, a dumpy girl or a woman of dubious character. *See* CUTTY SARK.

> Not a gleed of fire, then, except the bit kindling peat, and maybe a spunk in Mysie's cutty-pie.
>
> SCOTT: *Bride of Lammermoor*, ch. xxvi.

Cutty Sark (Scot.). A short petticoat or short-tailed shirt. The name of the famous clipper built at Dumbarton in 1869 for Captain John Willis, shipowner and master mariner. After a long career, mainly in the China tea trade and in shipping wool from Australia, she became a Portuguese trader in 1895 and was renamed the *Ferreira*. Purchased by Captain Dowman in 1922, and restored at Falmouth as a boys' training ship, she was towed round to the Thames in 1938 and taken over by the Cutty Sark Preservation Society in 1952—the last survivor of the clippers. The name is taken from Burns' poem "Tam O'Shanter" which was illustrated on the carvings round the ship's bows, but the figurehead was of a woman in flowing garments with outstretched arm. The accompanying "witches" round the bows were naked. At one stage in the ship's career a short shirt emblem was flown at the main truck.

> Whene'er to drink you are inclined
> Or Cutty Sarks run in your mind
> Think: you may buy the joys ower dear,
> Remember Tam O'Shanter's mare.

Cutty stool. A short-legged wooden stool; in Scotland the familiar name for the STOOL OF REPENTANCE.

Cwt. is C. *centum*, wt. *weight*, meaning hundred-weight. *Cp.* DWT.

Cyanean Rocks, The (sī ān' i ăn). Two rocky islands at the entrance of the EUXINE SEA, where the breakers make the passage very hazardous. It was anciently supposed that they floated and closed together to crush a vessel when it attempted to sail between them.

Cybele. Mother goddess of Phrygia, also goddess of fertility and of the mountains. Commonly identified with AGDISTIS her favourite was ATYS and her priests were called CORYBANTES. She is also associated with DEMETER.

Cycle. A period or series of events or numbers which recur everlastingly in the same order.

Cycle of the moon. The METONIC CYCLE, from its discoverer Meton of ATHENS (5th century B.C.). It is a period of nineteen years, at the expiration of which the phases of the MOON repeat themselves on the same days as they did nineteen years previously. *See* CALLIPPIC PERIOD.

Cycle of the sun. A period of twenty-eight years, at the expiration of which the days of the month fall on the same days of the week as they did twenty-eight years previously.

The Platonic Cycle, or **Great Year.** That space of time which, according to ancient astronomers, elapses before all the stars and constellations return to their former positions in respect to the equinoxes. Tycho Brahe calculated this period at 25,816 years, and Riccioli at 25,920 years.

> Cut out more work than can be done
> In Plato's year, but finish none.
>
> BUTLER: *Hudibras*, III, ii

Cyclic Poets (sī' klik). Post-Homeric epic poets who wrote continuations, illustrations or additions to Homer's poems. These poets wrote between 800 and 550 B.C., and were called *cyclic* because they confined themselves to the cycle of the TROJAN WAR. The chief were Agias, Arctinus, Eugammon, Lesches, and Stasinus.

Cyclops (sī klops) (Gr. circular-eye). One of a group or race of GIANTS. They had only one eye each and that in the centre of the forehead, and their work was to forge iron for VULCAN. Hesiod limits their number to three: Arges, Steropes, and Brontes. *Cp.* ARIMASPIANS.

Cyclopean Masonry (sī klō′ piȧn). The old Pelasgic ruins of Greece, Asia Minor, and Italy, such as the Gallery of Tiryns, the Gate of Lions at Mycenæ, the Treasury of ATHENS, and the tombs of Phoroneus and Danaos. They are made of huge blocks fitted together without mortar and are fabled to be the work of the CYCLOPS. The term is applied to similar huge structures elsewhere.

Cygnus. *See* PHAETON'S BIRD.

Cylleneius (sī lē′ ni ȕs). MERCURY. So called from Mount Cyllene, in Peloponnesus, where he was born.

Cymbeline. *See* CUNOBELIN; CASSIBELAN.

Cymodoce (sī mod′ ō si). One of the NEREIDS, a companion of VENUS in Virgil's *Georgics* (IV, 338) and ÆNEID (V, 826). In Spenser's *Faerie Queene* (III, iv, and IV, xii), she is a daughter of Nereus and mother of Marinell by Dumarin. She frees Florimel from the power of PROTEUS. The word means "wave-receiving".

The Garden of Cymodoce. Sark, one of the Channel Islands. It is the title of a poem by Swinburne in his *Songs of the Springtides*.

Cynic. The ancient school of Greek philosophers known as the *Cynics* was founded by ANTISTHENES and made famous by his pupil DIOGENES. They were ostentatiously contemptuous of ease, luxury or wealth, and convention. The name is either derived from their dog-like, slovenly, and uncouth habits or from the fact that Antisthenes held his school in the Gymnasium called *Cynosarges* (white dog), from the incident when a white dog carried away part of a victim which was then being offered to HERCULES. The effigy over the pillar of Diogenes was a dog with the inscription, (as rendered by Dr. Brewer):

"Say, dog, I pray, what guard you in that tomb?"
"A dog."—"His name?"—"Diogenes."—"From far?"
"Sinope."—"What! who made a tub his home?"
"The same; now dead, amongst the stars a star."

Cynic Tub. The tub from which Diogenes

lectured. Similarly we speak of the PORCH, meaning STOIC philosophy; the GARDEN, Epicurean philosophy; the ACADEMY, Platonic philosophy; and the *Colonnade*, meaning Aristotelian philosophy. *See* PERIPATETIC SCHOOL.

And fetch their precepts from the Cynic tub.
MILTON: *Comus*, line 708.

Cynosure (sin′ ō shur). The Pole star; hence the observed of all observers. Greek for *dog's tail*, and applied to the constellation called URSA MINOR. As mariners guide their ships by the north star, and observe it as well, the word "cynosure" is used for whatever attracts attention, as "The cynosure of neighbouring eyes" (Milton, *L'Allegro*), especially for guidance in some doubtful matter.

Cynthia. The MOON; a surname of Artemis or DIANA, who represented the moon, and was called Cynthia from Mount Cynthius in Delos, where she was born.

The name was one of many applied to Elizabeth I by contemporary poets.

Cypress. A funeral tree; dedicated by the Romans to PLUTO, because when once cut it never grows again. It is said that its wood was once used for making coffins; hence SHAKESPEARE'S "In sad cypress let me be laid" (*Twelfth Night*, II, iv). The Greeks and Romans put cypress twigs in the coffins of the dead and it is much associated with cemeteries. It was also traditionally the wood from which CUPID'S arrows were made.

Cyprian (sip′ ri ȧn). Cyprus was formerly famous for the worship of VENUS; hence the application of the adjective to lewd and profligate persons and prostitutes.

A Night Charge at Bow Street Office; with other matters worth knowing, respecting the unfortunate Cyprian, the feeling Coachman, and the generous Magistrate.
PIERCE EGAN: *Life in London*, Bk. II, ii.

Cyprian brass, or *æs Cyprium*, copper. Pliny (Bk. XXXIV, c, ii) says, "*in Cypro enim prima æris inventio fuit*".

Cyrene. A Thessalian nymph, daughter or granddaughter of the river god Peneus. She was carried off by APOLLO to the country which came to be called Cyrenaica, where she bore him a son named Aristæus. *See* ABIOGENESIS.

Cyrillic Alphabet. The form of letters traditionally used by the Slavonic peoples, a form of the Greek alphabet invented by two brothers, the apostles of the Slavs, Constantine (827–869) and Methodius (*c.* 825–885) of Thessalonica. Constantine was more popularly known by his religious name of Cyril.

D

D. This letter is the outline of a rude archway or door. It is called in Phœnician and Hebrew *daleth* (a door) and Gr. *delta*. In Egyptian hieroglyphics it is a man's hand.

D., or **d.** indicating a penny or pence is the initial of the Lat. *denarius*. As a Roman numeral **D** stands for 500, and represents the second half of **CIƆ**, the ancient Tuscan sign for one thousand. **D** stands for 5,000.

D.C. *See* DA CAPO.

D Day. In World War II, the day appointed for the Allied invasion of Europe and the opening of the long-awaited second front. It was eventually fixed for 5 June 1944, but owing to impossible weather conditions, it was postponed at the last moment until 6 June. *See* OVERLORD.

D.O. Demi-official. A British War Office term for a letter on official business but addressed personally from one officer to another.

D.O.M. An abbreviation of the Lat., *Deo Optimo Maximo* (to God the best the greatest) or *Datur omnibus mori* (it is alloted to all to die). In the former sense it is inscribed on bottles of BENEDICTINE.

D.T.s. A contraction of *delirium tremens*.

D.V. *See* DEO VOLENTE.

Da Capo (D.C.) (Ital.). A musical term meaning from the beginning—that is, finish with a repetition from the beginning to the point indicated.

Dab. Clever, skilled; as "dab-hand at it". Possibly a contraction of the Lat. *adeptus*, an adept. *Dabster* is another form.

> An Eton stripling training for the law,
> A dunce at learning, but a dab at taw [marbles].
> ANON: *Logic; or, The Biter Bit*.

Dab, Din, etc.

> Hab Dab and David Din
> Ding the deil o'er Dabson's Linn.

"Hab Dab" (Halbert Dobson) and "David Din" (David Dun) were CAMERONIANS who lived in a cave near "Dabson's Linn", a waterfall near the head of Moffat Water. Here, legend relates, they saw the DEVIL in the form of a pack of dried hides, and after fighting him for some time, they "dinged" him into the waterfall.

Dabbat (Arab. *Dabbatu'l-ard)*. In Mohammedan mythology the monster, reptile of the earth, that shall arise at the last day and cry that mankind has not believed in the Divine revelations.

By some it is identified with the Beast of the Apocalypse (*Rev*. xix, 19; xx, 10).

Dactyls. Mythical beings connected with the worship of CYBELE in Crete, supposed to be the discoverers of iron and copper; also called *Idæan Dactyls* (the fingers of IDA), after their mountain home. Their number is given as ten or more but was originally three—the Smelter, the Hammer, and the Anvil.

In prosody a dactyl is a foot of three syllables, the first long and the others short (— ∪∪), again from the similarity to the joints of a finger.

Dad, or **Daddy.** A child's word for "father" common to many languages, Gaelic, *daidein*; Welsh, *tad*; Cornish, *tat*; Latin, *tata, tatula* (papa); Greek, *tata, tetta*, used by youths to an elder; Sanskrit, *tata*; Lap, *dadda*; are examples.

Dad and Dave. Two figures becoming traditional in Australian humour, invented by A. H. Davis (Steele Rudd), 1868–1935. They first appeared in his humorous sketches, *On Our Selection*, 1899, which deals with the hard lives of the small farmers of the period. Dad and Dave have since been widely used in Australian broadcasting serials.

Daddy Long-legs. A crane-fly, applied also to the long-legged spiders called "harvestmen".

Dadaism (da′ da izm). An anarchic and iconoclastic art movement which began at Zürich in 1916, arising from indignation and despair at the catastrophe of World War I. Its supporters, writers and painters, sought to free themselves from all artistic conventions, and what they considered cultural shams. Dadaism was influenced by CUBISM and FUTURISM and after about 1922 it was succeeded by SURREALISM. The name Dadaism was derived from *dada*, the French word for a hobby-horse, and was named by Tristan Tzara after opening a dictionary at random. Arp, Ernst and Janco were among their number. There was a similar outbreak at New York at the same time associated with Duchamp, Picabia and Man Ray. A plaque, showing a human navel, was unveiled at Zürich in February 1966, to commemorate the fiftieth anniversary of the movement. *Cp.* FAUVISM; IMPRESSIONISM; ORPHISM; SYNCHRONISM; VORTICISM.

Dædalus (dē' dà lùs). A legendary Athenian, father of ICARUS, who formed the Cretan LABYRINTH and made wings, by means of which he flew from Crete across the archipelago. He is said to have invented the saw, the axe, the gimlet, etc., and his name is perpetuated in our *dædal*, skilful, fertile of invention; *dædalian*, labyrinthine or ingenious.

Daffodil. Legend says that the daffodil, or LENT LILY was once white; but Persephone (PROSERPINA), who had wreathed her head with them and fallen asleep in the meadow, was captured by PLUTO and carried off in his chariot. She let fall some of the lilies and they turned to a golden yellow. Theophilus and Pliny tell us that they grow on the banks of ACHERON and that the spirits of the dead delight in the flower, called by them the ASPHODEL. In England it used to be called the Affodil (Fr. *asphodile*: Lat. *asphodelus*; Gr. *asphodelos*).

In the present century it has become an alternative to the LEEK as a Welsh emblem, because the leek was considered vulgar by some.

> O Proserpina,
> For the flowers now, that, frighted, thou lett'st fall
> From Dis's waggon!—daffodils,
> That come before the swallow dares, and take
> The winds of March with beauty.
> SHAKESPEARE: *Winter's Tale*, IV, iii.

Dagger, or **Long Cross** (†), used for reference to a note after the asterisk (*), was originally used in church books, prayers of EXORCISM, at benedictions, and so on, to remind the priest where to make the sign of the cross. It is sometimes called an obelisk (Gr. *obelos*, a spit).

In the arms of the City of LONDON, the dagger supposedly commemorates Sir William Walworth's dagger, with which he slew Wat Tyler in 1381. Before this time the cognizance of the City was the sword of St. PAUL. The inscription below Sir William's statue in Fishmonger's Hall announced:

> Brave Walworth Knyght Lord Mayor that slew
> Rebellious Tyler in his alarmes—
> The king therefore did give in lieu
> The Dagger to the Cytyes armes.

Dagger ale. The ale of the *Dagger*, a low class gambling-house in HOLBORN, famous in the time of Elizabeth I for its strong drink, furmety, and meat-pies. There was another tavern of the same name in Cheapside.

> My lawyer's clerk I lighted on last night
> In Holborn at the Dagger.
> BEN JONSON: *The Alchemist*, I, i.

Dagger Money. The sum once paid to judges on the Northern Circuit for the purchase of weapons as a protection against thieves and robbers.

Dagger-scene in the House of Commons. Edmund Burke, during the French Revolution, threw down a dagger on the floor of the House, exclaiming as he did so: "There's French fraternity for you! Such is the weapon which French Jacobins would plunge into the heart of our beloved king." Sheridan spoilt the dramatic effect, and set the House in a roar by his remark: "The gentleman, I see, has brought his knife with him, but where is his fork?" *See* COUP DE THÉÂTRE.

To be at daggers drawn. To be fiercely opposed, at great enmity.

> Boffins at Daggers Drawn in Corridors of Power.
> *The Times* (Headline of 8 April 1965).

To speak, or **look daggers.** To speak or look so as to wound, to convey open hostility.

> I will speak daggers to her, but use none.
> SHAKESPEARE: *Hamlet*, III, ii.

Daggle-tail, or **Draggle-tail.** A slovenly woman, the bottom of whose dress trails in the dirt. *Dag* (of uncertain origin) means loose ends, mire, dirt; whence *dag-locks*, the soiled locks of a sheep's fleece, and *dag-wool*, refuse wool.

Dagobert (dăg' ō bert). **King Dagobert and St. Eloi.** There is a traditional French song in which the king's minister St. Eloi tells Dagobert that his coat has a hole in it, and the king replies, *"C'est vrai, le tien est bon; prête-le moi."* After many such complaints and answers St. Eloi says, "My lord, death is at hand!" "Why can't you die instead of me?" says the king.

In the time of the Revolution, and subsequently, the song has been adapted to suit the political events of the day. In 1814, for example, it was banned by the authorities on account of verses against NAPOLEON and the Russian campaign of 1812.

Dagon. A semitic god worshipped by the PHILISTINES after their arrival in Canaan, supposed to have been symbolized as half man and half fish. Samson's vengeance on the Philistines occurred after their riotous celebrations to Dagon (*Judges* xvi, 23–30).

Dagon his name, sea-monster, upward man
And downward fish: yet had his temple high
Rear'd in Azotus, dreaded through the coast
Of Palestine, in Gath and Ascalon,
And Accaron and Gaza's frontier bounds.
MILTON: Paradise Lost, I, 462.

Dagonet, Sir. In ARTHURIAN ROMANCES, the fool of King Arthur, knighted by the king himself.

Dagonet was the name under which G. R. Sims (1847–1922) wrote his popular articles in *The Referee*.

Daikoku (da ē′ kō ku). One of the seven Japanese gods of luck. He is god of wealth and good fortune and is represented sitting on bags of rice.

Daisy. An emblem of deceit. Greene (*Quip for an Upstart Courtier*) speaks of the "dissembling daisie". "Light of love wenches" are warned by it "not to trust every fair promise that such amorous bachelors make them". Ophelia in SHAKESPEARE'S *Hamlet* gives the queen a daisy to signify, "that her light and fickle love ought not to expect constancy in her husband".

The word is *Day's eye* (O.E. *dæges eage*), and the flower is so called because it closes its pinky lashes and goes to sleep when the sun sets, but in the morning expands its petals to the light. *See* VIOLET.

That well by reason men call it maie,
The daisie, or else the eie of daie.
CHAUCER: Legend of Good Women (Prol.).

Darling Daisy. Frances, Countess of Warwick, adulterous wife of the 5th Earl of Warwick and for nine years mistress of King Edward VII, whom he often addressed as "My Darling Daisy wife" when writing to her. In 1914 she sought to bring in money by threatening to publish her memoirs, which would include the late King's letters. This was prevented by three prominent courtiers acting on behalf of King George V.

Daisy-cutter. In CRICKET a ball that fails to rise when delivered, and in tennis a service which behaves similarly. In the 19th century a horse that lifted its feet very little above the ground was so described, and more recently it was applied colloquially by the R.A.F. to a perfect landing.

Daisy-roots. Legend says that these, like the berries of dwarf elder, stunt the growth, a superstition which probably arose from the notion that everything had the property of bestowing its own speciality on others. *Cp.* FERN SEED.

She robbed dwarf-elders of their fragrant fruit
And fed him early with the daisy root,
Whence through his veins the powerful juices ran,
And formed the beauteous miniature of man.
TICKELL: Kensington Gardens.

Pushing up the daisies. To be dead and buried.

Dak-bungalow. *See* BUNGALOW.

Dalai-Lama. *See* LAMAISM.

Dalkey, King of. A burlesque officer, like the Mayor of GARRATT. Dalkey is a small island near Dun Laoghaire, to the south of Dublin Bay.

Daltonism. *See* COLOUR-BLINDNESS.

Damiens' Bed of Steel (Dăm′ i enz). Robert François Damiens, in 1757, attempted to stab Louis XV. As a punishment he was chained to an iron bed that was heated, his right hand was burned in a slow fire, his flesh was torn with pincers and the wounds dressed with molten lead, boiling wax, oil and resin. He was finally torn to pieces by wild horses.

The uplifted axe, the agonising wheel,
Luke's iron crown, and Damien's bed of steel.
GOLDSMITH: The Traveller (1768).

Damn. Not worth a damn. Worthless; not even worth a curse. Goldsmith in his *Citizen of the World*, uses the expression "Not that I care three damns" and a common expression of the Duke of Wellington was "Not a twopenny damn". The derivation of these phrases from the coin, a dam, is without foundation.

To damn with faint praise. To praise in such restrained terms as to deprive the praise of any value.

Damn with faint praise, assent with civil leer,
And, without sneering teach the rest to sneer.
POPE: Epistle to Dr. Arbuthnot.

Damocles. The Sword of Damocles. Impending evil or danger. Damocles, a sycophant of Dionysius the Elder, of Syracuse, was invited by the TYRANT to try the felicity he so much envied. Accepting, he was set down to a sumptuous banquet, but overhead was a sword suspended by a hair. Damocles was afraid to stir, and the banquet was a tantalizing torment to him.

Damon (dā′ mon). The name of a goatherd in VIRGIL's *Eclogues*, and hence used by pastoral poets for rustic swains. *Cp.* CORYDON.

Damon and Pythias. Models of devoted friendship. In the 4th century B.C. Pythias (correctly Phintias) was condemned to death by Dionysius, the TYRANT of Syracuse, but obtained leave to go home too arrange his affairs after his friend Damon had agreed to take his place and be executed should Pythias not return. Pythias returned in time to save Damon, and Dionysius was so struck with this honourable friendship that he released both of them.

Damper. An Australian name for a simple type of unleavened bread made with water and wheat flour into a flat cake and baked in the ashes of a fire. Made by the settlers travelling in the bush, the name may derive from the fact that it damps down the ashes when placed upon them. Small dampers are called "beggars-on-the-coals".

A damp squib. *See under* SQUIB.

Damsel. A maiden or young woman, a waiting-maid or attendant. The word is the O.Fr. *damoisele*, the feminine of *damoisel*, a squire; this is from Med. Lat. *domicellus*, a contracted form of *dominicellus*, the dimunutive of *dominus*, lord (*cp.* DONZEL). In mediæval France the *domicellus* or *damoiseau* was the son of a king, prince, KNIGHT, or lord before he entered the order of knighthood; the king's bodyguards were called his *damoiseaux* or *damsels*. Froissart styles Richard II *le jeune damoisel Richart*, and Louis VII (Le Jeune) was called the *royal damsel*.

Dan. A title meaning *Sir* or *Master* (Lat. *dominus*; *cp.* Span. *Don*) common with the old poets, as Dan Phœbus, Dan Cupid, Dan Chaucer, etc. *Cp.* DOM.

> Dan Chaucer, well of English undefiled,
> On Fame's eternal beadroll worthy to be filed.
> SPENSER: *Faerie Queene*, IV, ii, 32.

From Dan to Beersheba. From one end of the kingdom to the other; everywhere. The phrase is scriptural, Dan being the most northern and Beersheba the most southern cities of the HOLY LAND. We have the similar expression, "From Land's End to John o'Groats".

Danace (Dăn′ ās). An ancient Persian coin, worth rather more than the Greek OBOLUS, and sometimes placed by the Greeks in the mouth of the dead to pay CHARON'S TOLL.

Danaë (Dăn′ à ē). Daughter of Acrisius, King of Argos. He was told that his daughter's son would put him to death, and so resolved that Danaë should never marry. She was accordingly locked up in an inaccessible tower. ZEUS foiled the King by changing himself into a shower of gold, under which guise he readily found access to the fair prisoner, and she thus became the mother of PERSEUS.

Danaides (dăn ā′ i dēz). The fifty daughters of Danaus, King of Argos. They married fifty sons of ÆGYPTUS, and all but HYPERMNESTRA, wife of LYNCEUS, at the command of their father murdered their husbands on their wedding night. They were punished in HADES by having to draw water everlastingly in sieves from a deep well.

Dance. I'll lead you a pretty dance. I'll bother or put you to trouble. The French say *Donner le bal à quelqu'un*. The reference is to the complicated dances of former times, when all followed the leader.

St. Vitus's Dance. *See* VITUS.

To dance and pay the piper. To work hard to amuse and have to take all the trouble and bear the expense as well. The allusion is to *Matt*. xi, 17: "We have piped unto you, and ye have not danced."

To dance attendance. To wait obsequiously, to be at the beck and call of another. It was an ancient custom at weddings for the bride, not matter how tired she was, to dance with every guest.

> I had thought
> They had parted so much honesty among 'em
> (At least good manners) as not thus to suffer
> A man of his place, and so near our favour,
> To dance attendance on their lordship's pleasures
> SHAKESPEARE: *Henry VIII*, v, ii.

To dance the Tyburn jig. To be hanged. *See* TYBURN.

To dance upon nothing. To be hanged.

Dance of Death, or Danse Macabre. An allegorical representation of Death (usually a dancing skeleton or corpse) leading all sorts and conditions of men to the grave. It is first found in the 14th century, and there is a famous series of woodcuts on the subject by Hans Holbein the Younger (1497–1543). In the cloister of Old St. Paul's a "Dance of Death" called the "Dance of St. Paul's" was painted at the cost of John Carpenter, town clerk of London (15th century), with translations of French verses by John Lydgate. There is a copy in the LAMBETH PALACE library. W. H. Auden's poem *The Dance of Death* was published in 1933.

Floral Dance, or Furry Dance. *See* FURRY DANCE.

Horn Dance. *See* ABBOT'S BROMLEY.

Morris Dance. *See* MORRIS.

Dances of the Ancient World.

> *Astronomical dances*, invented by the Egyptians, designed to represent the movements of the heavenly bodies.
> *Bacchic dances* were of three sorts: grave (like the minuet), gay (like the gavotte), and a mixture of grave and gay.
> The *Danse champêtre*, invented by PAN, quick and lively. The dancers (in the open air) wore wreaths of oak and garlands of flowers.
> *Children's dances*, in Lacedæmonia, in honour of DIANA. The children were nude; and their movements were grave, modest, and graceful.
> *Corybantic dances*, in honour of BACCHUS, accompanied with timbrels, fifes, flutes, and a tumultuous noise produced by the clashing of swords and spears against brazen bucklers.
> *Funeral dances*, in Athens, slow, solemn dances in which the priests took part. The performers wore long white robes, and carried cypress slips in their hands.
> *Hymeneal dances* were lively and joyous. The dancers were crowned with flowers.
> *Jewish dances*. David danced in certain religious

processions (II *Sam.* vi, 14). The people sang and danced before the GOLDEN CALF (*Exod.* xxxii, 19). And in the book of *Psalms* (cl, 4) we read, "Praise him with the timbrel and dance". Miriam, the sister of Moses, after the passage of the Red Sea, was followed by all the women with timbrels and dances (*Exod.* xv, 20).

Of the Lapithæ, invented by Pirithous. These were performed after some famous victory, designed to imitate the combats of the CENTAURS and LAPITHÆ, and were both difficult and dangerous.

May-day dances at Rome. At daybreak lads and lasses went out to gather "May" and other flowers for themselves and their elders; and the day was spent in dances and festivities.

Military dances. The oldest of all dances, executed with swords, javelins and bucklers. Said to be invented by Minerva to celebrate the victory of the gods over the TITANS.

Nuptial dances. A Roman pantomimic performance representing the dances of our HARLE-QUIN and COLUMBINE.

Pyrrhic dance. See PYRRHIC.

Salic dances, instituted by Numa Pompilius in honour of MARS. They were executed by twelve priests selected from the highest of the nobility, and were performed in the temple while sacrifices were being made and hymns sung to the god.

Dances, National. When Handel was asked to point out the peculiar taste of the different nations of Europe in dancing, he ascribed the *minuet* to the French, the *saraband* to the Spaniard, the *arietta* to the Italian, and the HORNPIPE and the MORRIS DANCE to the English. To these might be added the *reel* to the Scots, and the JIG to the Irish.

Dancing Chancellor, The. Sir Christopher Hatton (1540–1591) was so called, because he first attracted Queen Elizabeth I's notice by his graceful dancing in a masque at Court. He was Lord Chancellor from 1587 till his death.

> His bushy beard and shoestrings green,
> His high-crowned hat and satin doublet,
> Moved the stout heart of England's queen,
> Though Pope and Spaniard could not trouble it.
> GRAY: *A Long Story.*

Dancing Dervishes. The Mawlawis, one of the many MOSLEM religious fraternities of dervishes for whom their dirge or *zikr* is a devotional rite. The chant is accompanied by a slow whirling movement with their eyes shut and arms stretched out. It lasts until a state of catalepsy is attained.

Dancing round the Maypole *See* MAY-POLE.

Dancing-water. A magic elixir, common to many fairy tales, which beautifies ladies, makes them young again and enriches them. In the Countess d'Aulnoy's *Contes des Fées* it fell in a cascade in the Burning Forest, and could only be reached by an underground passage. Prince Chery fetched a bottle of it for his beloved Fairstar, but was aided by a dove.

Dander. Is your dander up, or **riz?** Is your anger excited? Are you in a range? This is generally considered to be an Americanism but as a synonym for *anger* has been a common dialect word in several English counties. It is more likely that it was imported into America by the early Dutch colonists and is from their *donder*, thunder; the Dutch *op donderen* is to burst into a sudden rage.

> He was as spunky as thunder, and when a Quaker gets his dander up, it's like a Northwester.
> SEBA SMITH: *Letters of Major Jack Downing* (1830).

Dandiprat. A small coin issued in the reign of Henry VII, value three halfpence. The term is also applied to a DWARF and a page and to a conceited little fellow, much as we speak of a "little twopenny-ha'penny fellow". Stanyhurst calls CUPID a "dandiprat" in his translation of VIRGIL's *Æneid*, Bk I (1582).

Dando. One who frequents hotels, restaurants, and such places, satisfies his appetite, and decamps without payment. From Dando, hero of many popular songs in the early 19th century, who was famous for this.

Dandy. A COXCOMB, a fop. Of late 18th-century Scottish origin; possibly one who has been spoilt by overmuch dandying, or from the name *Andrew*, or corruption of DANDIPRAT or the earlier JACK-A-DANDY.

In paper-making the *dandy*, or *dandy-roller*, is the cylinder of wire gauze which comes into contact with paper while on the machine in a wet and elementary stage. It impresses the watermark, and also the ribs in "laid" papers.

Dandy King, The. Joachim Murat (1767–1815), NAPOLEON's dashing cavalry leader, made King of Naples in 1808, was so nicknamed from his fondness for personal adornment. Napoleon is reputed to have called him "*un roi de théâtre*" (a player king).

Dandy traps. The same as BEAU TRAPS.

Danegeld. The geld or tax on land originally raised to buy peace from the Danes in the time of Ethelred II (978-1016) and continued as a tax long after it was needed for its original purpose.

> And that is called paying the Dane-geld;
> But we've proved it again and again,
> That if once you paid him the Dane-geld
> You never get rid of the Dane.
> KIPLING: *Dane-Geld.*

Danelaw, or **Danelagh** (O.E. *Dena lagu*, law of the Danes). That part of north and east England, roughly bounded by a line from LONDON to Chester, to which ALFRED THE GREAT (871–899) succeeded in containing the Danes and where Danish law was thus in force. The term was not used until the reign of King Cnut (1017–1035).

Danesblood, or **Danewort.** Dwarf elder (*Sambucus ebulus*), called Danesblood from a belief that it was supposed to flourish in places where there had been battles against the Danes; called Danewort because it is believed to have been introduced by the Danes.

Dane's skin. A freckled skin. Red hair and a freckled skin were regarded as the traditional characteristics of Danish blood.

Dannebrog, or **Danebrog.** (dăn' e brog). The national flag of Denmark (*brog* is Old Danish for cloth). The tradition is that Waldemar II of Denmark saw a fiery cross in the heavens which betokened his victory over the Estonians (1219). For similar legends of St. ANDREW and Constantine *see* CONSTANTINE'S CROSS *under* CROSS.

The Order of Danebrog. The second of the Danish orders of Knighthood; traditionally instituted in 1219 by Waldemar II, but the present order derives from that founded by Christian V in 1671.

Daniel. A Daniel come to judgment. One who displays wisdom beyond his years.

In SHAKESPEARE's *Merchant of Venice*, IV, i, Shylock says:

A Daniel come to judgement! yea, a Daniel!
O wise young judge, how I do honour thee!

The History of Susanna in the APOCRYPHA tells how Susanna rejected the advances of two elders, who falsely accused her and condemned to death. They claimed to have seen her lying under a tree with a young man. Her innocence was established by the youthful Daniel, who asked both accusers separately under what kind of tree the adultery took place. They each named a different tree.

Dannocks. Hedging-gloves. The word is said to be a corruption of *Doornick*, the Flemish name of Tournai, where they may have been originally manufactured. *Cp.* DORNICK.

Dansker. A Dane. Denmark used to be called Danskë. Hence Polonius says to Reynaldo, "Inquire me first what Danskers are in Paris." (SHAKESPEARE: *Hamlet*, II, i).

Dante and Beatrice. Beatrice Portinari was only eight years old when Dante first saw her. The poet's love for her was pure as it was tender. Beatrice married a nobleman, Simone de Bardi, in 1287 and she died in 1290 (under the age of twenty-four). Dante, a few years later, married Gemma Donati. Beatrice is celebrated and idealized in Dante's *Vita Nuova* and *Divina Commedia*. In the latter work the poet is conducted first by VIRGIL (who represents human reason)

through HELL and PURGATORY; then by the spirit of Beatrice (who represents the wisdom of faith); and finally by St. BERNARD (who represents the wisdom from on high).

Again mine eyes were fix'd on Beatrice;
And, with mine eyes, my soul that in her looks
Found all contentment.
DANTE: *Divine Comedy*, Canto XXI.

Dantesque (Dăn tesk). Dante-like—that is, a minute lifelike representation of horrors, whether by words, as in the poet, or in visual form, as in Doré's illustrations of the *Inferno*.

Daphne (dăf' ni). Daughter of the river-god Peneus in Thessaly, beloved by APOLLO. She had resolved to spend her life in perpetual virginity and fled from him, seeking the protection of the gods, who changed her into a LAUREL or BAY-tree. Apollo declared that henceforth he would wear bay-leaves instead of the oak, and that all who sought his favour should follow his example.

Daphnis (dăf' nis). In Greek mythology, a Sicilian shepherd who invented pastoral poetry. He was a son of MERCURY and a Sicilian nymph and was protected by DIANA. He was taught by PAN and the MUSES.

Also the lover of CHLOE. Daphnis was the model of Allan Ramsay's *Gentle Shepherd* (1725), and the tale is the basis of Bernardin de St-Pierre's *Paul et Virginie* (1787).

Dapple. The name given in Smollett's translation of *Don Quixote* to SANCHO PANZA's donkey (in the original it has no name). The word is probably connected with Icel. *depill*, a spot, and means blotched, speckled in patches. A *dapple-grey* horse is one of a light grey shaded with a deeper hue; a *dapple-bay* is of a light bay spotted with a bay of deeper colour.

Darbies. Handcuffs. Probably derived from a personal name; the phrase "father Derbies bands" for handcuffs is found in George Gascoigne's *Steel Glas* (1576).

An hark ye! Jem Clink will fetch you the darbies.
SCOTT: *Peveril of the Peak*, ch xxxiii.

Johnny Darbies, policeman, is a perversion of the Fr. *gendarmes*, in conjunction with the above.

Darby and Joan. The type of loving, old-fashioned, virtuous couples. The names belong to a ballad written by Henry Woodfall, first published in the *Gentleman's Magazine* in 1735. The characters are said to be John Darby, of Bartholomew Close, who died in 1730, and his wife "As chaste as a picture cut in alabaster. You might sooner move a Scythian rock than shoot fire into her bosom." Woodfall served his apprenticeship to John Darby; but another account localizes the couple in the West Riding of Yorkshire.

The French equivalent *C'est St. Roch et son chien* (*see* ROCH).

Darbyites (dar' bi iitz). A name sometimes given to the PLYMOUTH BRETHREN, from John Nelson Darby (1800–1882), their founder.

Dardanus. A son of ZEUS and ELECTRA and legendary founder of the royal house of TROY. He eventually married Batea, daughter of King Teucer, who gave him land near Abydos where he established the town of Dardania or Dardanus. Hence the name *Dardanelles* for what was once called the HELLESPONT.

Daric. An ancient Persian gold coin, probably so called from *dara*, a king (*see* DARIUS), much in the same way as our SOVEREIGN. There was also a silver daric, worth one-twentieth of the gold.

Darius (dà rī' ùs). A Greek form of Persian *dara*, a king, or of Sanskrit *darj*, the mountaineer. Darius the Great, son of Hystaspes (Vishtaspa), governor of Persia, assumed the name when he became king in 521 B.C.

Legend relates that he conspired with six other Persian nobles to overthrow Smerdis, the usurper, and that they agreed that he should be king whose horse neighed first; and the horse of Darius was the first to neigh. His exploits are recorded on the rock of BEHISTUN.

It is said that Darius III (Codomannus), the last king of the Persian empire, who was conquered by ALEXANDER the Great (331 B.C.), sent for the tribute of golden eggs on Alexander's accession. The Macedonian replied: "The bird which laid them is flown to the other world, where Darius must seek them." The Persian king then sent him a bat and ball, in ridicule of his youth; but Alexander told the messengers, with the bat he would beat the ball of power from their master's hand. Lastly, Darius sent him a bitter melon as emblem of the grief in store for him; but the Macedonian declared that he would make the Persian eat his own fruit.

Dark. A dark Horse. A racing term for a horse of possible promise, but of which nothing is positively known by the general public. The epithet is applied to a person whose abilities or probable course of action are unknown.

A leap in the dark. A step the consequences of which cannot be foreseen. *See* HOBBES *under* DYING SAYINGS. Lord Derby applied the words to the 1867 Reform Act.

Dark Ages, The. A term applied to the MIDDLE AGES, but more particularly to the early centuries; so called because of the intellectual darkness, held to be characteristic of the period, consequent upon the collapse of classical civilization. Hallam considered this term to apply to the period from the 5th to the 12th century, but it is now applied to a much more limited period "darkened" by the lack of contemporary written sources.

Dark and bloody ground. Kentucky. So called by the Indians because of the fierce wars waged in the forests, and later so known by the whites for the same reason in their struggle against the redman.

Dark Continent, The. Africa; concerning which the world was so long "in the dark", and much of which was an unknown land of mystery. It is also the land of dark races. H.M. Stanley's *Through the Dark Continent* appeared in 1878, *In Darkest Africa* in 1890, and *My Dark Companions and their Strange Stories* in 1893.

Dark Lady of the Sonnets. *See* LADY.

Darkie. A colloquial name for an American Negro, found as early as 1775.

Darkies, The. A popular name for the former ADELPHI arches.

The darkest hour is that before the dawn. When things come to their worst, they must mend. In Lat., *Post nubila Phœbus.*

To darken counsel. To confuse an issue by introducing irrelevant or ill-founded considerations.

Who is this that darkeneth counsel by words without knowledge?

Job xxxviii, 2.

To keep dark. To lie perdu; to lurk in concealment.

To keep it dark. To keep it a dead secret; not to *enlighten* anyone about the matter.

To darken one's door. To cross one's threshold. Usually used in a threatening way as "Don't you dare to darken my door again!" The door is darkened by one's shadow.

Darley Arabian. In 1704 Thomas Darley sent from Aleppo to his father Richard Darley, of Aldby Park, Yorks, an Arab horse of the best Maneghi breed. From this thoroughbred stallion came a famous breed of race-horses, including ECLIPSE.

All thoroughbred racehorses throughout the world are descended from three Arabs, of which Darley Arabian was one. The others were Byerly Turk, the charger of Colonel Byerly at the battle of the Boyne (1690), and Godolphin Arabian, brought to England in 1730 by Edward Coke, from whom it passed into the possession of the Earl of Godolphin.

Darling, Daisy. *See under* DAISY.

Grace Darling (1815–1842). An English heroine of almost legendary fame, the daughter of William Darling, keeper of the Longstone Lighthouse, Farne Islands, Northumberland. She and her father attempted the rescue of survivors of the wrecked *Forfarshire* in 1838. They launched their small boat in perilous seas and brought back five survivors to the lighthouse. Darling made a second trip with two of the *Forfarshire's* crew and saved four more, 43 being drowned. Grace died of consumption in 1842.

England's Darling. *See under* ENGLAND.

Darnex. *See* DORNICK.

Dart. *See* ABARIS.

Dartmoor. The extensive moorland in Devon, some 400 square miles in area, noted for its tors, hut circles, stone rows, barrows, pounds and stannaries and synonymous with the prison at Princetown. This was founded in 1809 to house prisoners during the Napoleonic Wars.

Darwinian Theory. The theory of evolution as put forward by Charles Darwin (1809–1882), notably in his famous book of 1859 *The Origin of Species by Natural Selection*, summed up by Herbert Spencer as "the survival of the fittest". Evolution was not a new idea to science but the shock to established science and orthodox Christian belief was profound.

Dash. Cut a dash. *See* CUT.

Dash it all, dash my wig, buttons, etc. In these expressions dash is a EUPHEMISM for "damn". *Wig, buttons*, etc., are relics of a fashion adopted by "MASHERS" of "swearing" without using profane or obscene language.

Date. Not up to date. Behind the times, not in the latest fashion, behindhand.

To date. As yet, up to the present time.

To have a date. To have an appointment, especially with one of the opposite sex.

Datum Line (Dā' tùm). A term used in surveying and engineering to describe a line from which all heights and depths are measured. The datum line upon which the Ordnance Survey maps of Great Britain were based until 1921 was the mean sea-level at Liverpool. Since 1921 it has been the mean sea-level at Newlyn, Cornwall.

Daughter. The daughter of Peneus. The bay-tree was so called because it grew in greatest perfection on the banks of the river Peneus. *See* BAY; DAPHNE.

The daughter of the horseleech. One very exigent; one for ever sponging on another, *Prov.* xxx, 15.

The horseleech hath two daughters crying, Give, give.

The scavenger's daughter. *See* SCAVENGER.

Dauphin (daw' fin). The heir of the French crown under the VALOIS and BOURBON Dynasties. Guy IX, Count of Vienne, was the first so styled, and he wore a *dolphin* as his cognizance. The title descended in the family till 1349, when Humbert III sold his seigneurie, the Dauphiné, to Philippe VI (de Valois), one condition being that the heir of France assumed the title of *le Dauphin*. The first French prince so called was Jean, who succeeded Philippe; and the last was the Duc d'Angoulême, son of Charles X, and he renounced the title in 1830.

The dauphinate of Auvergne appeared as a title in the 13th century, was joined to the French royal family by marriage in 1428, and was annexed to the crown in 1693. The heir to the French monarchy was called the "King Dauphin" and the Dauphin of Auvergne the "Prince Dauphin".

Grand Dauphin. Louis (1661–1711), eldest son of Louis XIV, for whose use the DELPHIN CLASSICS were prepared.

Second, or **Little Dauphin.** Louis (1682–1712), son of the Grand Dauphin.

Davenport. Two different articles of furniture bear this name, which is probably that of some forgotten craftsman. One is a small desk with drawers each side, the other is a large upholstered sofa or settee.

Davenport-trick. A trick by which a person can release himself when bound round and tied with rope. The term derives from the Davenport brothers, two American impostors who professed that spirits would untie them when bound with cords. Their imposition was exposed in 1865. *Cp.* HOUDINI.

David. The youngest son of Jesse and slayer of GOLIATH. He temporarily rose in favour through comforting Saul by his skill as a harpist. Saul's eventual jealousy led to David's flight, effected with the aid of his wife Michal and her brother Jonathan, both children of Saul. After many vicissitudes David eventually became King of Israel (I *Sam.* xvi–xxxi, II *Sam.*; I *Kings* i–ii). The Davidic authorship of the *Psalms* has largely been discounted. In Dryden and Tate's *Absalom and Achitophel*, David represents Charles II. *See* ABSALOM; ADULLAMITES.

St. David, or **Dewi Sant.** Patron SAINT of WALES, whose day is 1 March. Historical information is scanty. He lived in the 6th century and died *c.* 600, and as the chief bishop of South Wales moved the ecclesiastical centre from CAERLEON to MENEVIA (St. David's). Legend is far more prolific and says that he was the son of Xantus, prince of Cereticu (Cardiganshire), and became an ascetic in the Isle of Wight; that he visited Jerusalem, confuted Pelagius, and was preferred to the see of Caerleon. Geoffrey of Monmouth makes him the uncle of King ARTHUR.

David and Chad, sow peas good and bad. An old proverb meaning that one should sow peas by the saints' days on the first and second of March regardless of weather conditions. St David's day is 1 March, St. CHAD'S 2 March.

David and Jonathan. A type of inseparable friends. *Cp.* DAMON AND PYTHIAS; PYLADES AND ORESTES.

> I am distressed for thee, my brother Jonathan; very pleasant hast thou been unto me. Thy love to me was wonderful, passing the love of women.
> II *Sam.* i, 26.

The Shield of David. *See under* SHIELD.
Davidians, Davists. *See* FAMILISTS.
Davus sum, non Œdipus. I am Davus, not ŒDIPUS; I am a plain simple fellow, and no solver of riddles like Œdipus. The words are from Terence's *Andria*, I, ii, 23, and the reference is to the riddle of the SPHINX.
Davy Crockett *See* CROCKETT.

Davy Jones. An 18th-century sailor's term for the evil spirit of the sea. Of the many conjectures as to its derivation the most plausible are that Davy is a corruption of the West Indian *duppy* (devil) and that Jones is a corruption of Jonah, or that Davy Jones was a pirate.

Davy Jones's Locker. The sea, especially as the grave of drowned sailors.

Davy's sow. Drunk as Davy's sow. According to Grose (*Classical Dictionary of the Vulgar Tongue*), one David Lloyd, a Welshman who kept an ale-house at Hereford, had a sow with six legs, which was an object of great curiosity. One day David's wife, having indulged too freely, lay down in the sty to sleep, and a company came to see the sow. David led them to the sty saying as usual, "There is a sow for you! Did you ever see the like?" One of the visitors replied, "Well it is the drunkenest sow I ever beheld." Whence the woman was ever after called "Davy's sow".

Dawson, Bully. A noted London sharper, who swaggered and led a most abandoned life about Blackfriars in the reign of Charles II.

Jemmy Dawson. The hero of Shenstone's ballad of this name given in PERCY'S RELIQUES. James Dawson joined the Young CHEVALIER and was one of the Manchester rebels who were hanged, drawn, and quartered on Kennington Common in 1746. A lady of gentle blood was in love with the gallant young rebel, and died of a broken heart after witnessing his execution.

> The dismal scene was o'er and past,
> The lover's mournful hearse retir'd;
> The maid drew back her languid head,
> And sighing forth his name expir'd.

Day. When it begins. (1) At *sunset*: for the Jews in their "sacred year", and the Christian Church, hence the eve of feastdays; Tacitus tells us that the ancient Britons "*non dierum numerum, ut nos, sed noctium computant*," hence "se'n-night" and "fort'night"; the ancient Greeks, Chinese, Mohammedans, etc.; (2) At *sunrise*: for the Babylonians, Syrians, Persians, and modern Greeks; (3) At *noon*: for the ancient Egyptians and modern astronomers; (4) At *midnight*: for the Romans, English, French, Dutch, Germans, Spaniards, Portuguese, Americans, etc.

A day after the fair. Too late; the fair you came to see is over.

Day in, day out. All day long and every day.

Day of Atonement, or **Day of Coverings.** *See under* ATONEMENT.

Day of the Barricades. *See under* BARRICADE.

Day of Dupes. *See* DUPES.

Days of Grace. *See* GRACE DAYS.

Every dog has its day. *See* DOG.

I have had my day. My prime of life is over. I am no longer in the SWIM and am of little account now.

> "Old Joe, Sir," said the Major, "was a bit of a favourite ... once. But Joe has had his day."
> DICKENS: *Dombey and Son*, ch. xx.

I have lost a day. The exclamation (*Perdidi diem*) of the Roman emperor Titus, when on occasion he could recall nothing done during the past day for the benefit of his subjects. *See* DELIGHT.

Today a man, tomorrow a mouse. Fortune is so fickle that one day we may be at the top of the WHEEL, and the next day at the bottom. The French equivalent is, "*Aujourd'hui roi, demain rien*."

To lose the day. To lose the battle, to be defeated.

To win, or **gain the day** is to be victorious or successful.

Daylight. In drinking bumpers, means the light seen between the wine and the rim of the glass when the wine-glass is not full. Toastmasters used to cry out "Gentlemen, no daylights nor heeltaps." *See* HEEL-TAP *under* HEEL.

Daylight robbery. Flagrant over-charging or swindling.

Daylight Saving. The idea of making fuller use of the hours of daylight by advancing the clock originated with Benjamin Franklin, but its introduction was due to its advocacy from 1907 by William Willett (1856–1915), a Chelsea builder. It was adopted in 1916 in Germany, then England, as a wartime measure, when clocks were advanced one hour. In Britain it became permanent by an Act of 1925. *Summer Time*, as it was called, until 1939, and again in 1946 and from 1948 till 1959, began on the day following the third Saturday in April (unless that was Easter Day, in which case it was the day following the second Saturday in April). It ended on the day following the first Saturday in October. In 1961 Summer Time was extended by six weeks, beginning in March and ending in October, and similar extensions were made in 1962 and subsequent years. During World War II it extended from 25 February in 1940 and 1 January 1941–1944, until 31 December. In 1945 it ended in October. *Double Summer Time* (*i.e.* two hours in advance of G.M.T. instead of one hour) was in force during 1941–1945 and 1947 to save fuel. *See also* GREENWICH TIME.

In the U.S.A. Summer Time (March to October) was in force in 1917 and 1918 and again from 1942 to 1945 (all the year round and known as War Time). In 1966 the Uniform Time Act re-introduced Summer Time (from the last Sunday in April until the last Sunday in October) whilst allowing individual states the right of option. In the years following World War II a number of other countries have adopted some form of Summer Time.

Daylights. Pugilists' slang for eyes.

To beat the living daylights out of him, to chastise heavily.

To let daylight into him. To pierce a man with sword or bullet.

Daysman. An umpire, judge, or intercessor. The obsolete verb *to day* meant to appoint a day for the hearing of a suit, hence to judge between; the man who *dayed* was the *daysman*.

> Neither is there any daysman betwixt us, that might lay his hand upon us both.
>
> *Job* ix, 33.

Dayspring. The dawn.

> The dayspring from on high hath visited us.
>
> *Luke* i, 78.

Daystar. The morning star; hence the emblem of hope and better prospects.

> Again o'er the vine-covered regions of France,
> See the day-star of Liberty rise.
>
> WILSON: *Noctes Ambrosianæ* (Jan. 1831).

De die in diem (dē dī' ē in dī' em) (Lat.). From day to day continuously, till the business is completed.

De facto (Lat.). Actually, in reality; as opposed to **de jure,** lawfully or rightfully. Thus John was *de facto* king, but Arthur was so *de jure*. A legal axiom says: "*De jure Judices, de facto Juratores, respondent*"; Judges look to the law, juries to the facts.

De gustibus non est disputandum (Lat.). There is no accounting for tastes; a somewhat similar English proverb is, "One man's meat is another man's poison". *Cp.* CHACUN A SON GOÛT.

De Jure. *See* DE FACTO.

De mortuis nil nisi bonum (dē môr' tū is nil nī'sī bō' num) (Lat.). Of the dead speak kindly or not at all. "Speak not evil of the dead" was one of the maxims of Chilo (*see* WISE MEN).

De novo (dē nō'vō) (Lat.). Afresh; over again from the beginning.

De profundis (dē prō fǔn' dis) (Lat.). Out of the deep; hence a bitter cry of wretchedness. *Ps* cxxx is so called from the first two words in the Latin version. It forms part of the Roman Catholic burial service.

These words were chosen as the title of Oscar Wilde's apologia, published posthumously in 1905.

De rigueur (dĕ rigēr') (Fr.). According to strict etiquette; quite COMME IL FAUT, in the height of fashion.

De trop (dĕ trō) (Fr.). One too many; when a person's presence is not wished for, that person is *de trop*.

Deacon. To deacon apples, etc. An American phrase arising out of the thrifty habits ascribed to the rural NEW ENGLAND deacons who are said to have put the best of the fruit, etc., on the top of the baskets in which they were being sold, concealing the inferior goods beneath.

Dead. Dead as a door-nail. The door-nail is either one of the heavy-headed nails with which large outer doors used to be studded, or the knob on which the knocker strikes. As this is frequently knocked on the head, it cannot be supposed to have much life left in it. The expression is found in PIERS PLOWMAN.

> Old Marley was as dead as a door-nail.
>
> DICKENS: *Christmas Carol*, Stave i.

Other well-known similes are "Dead as a shotten herring", "as the nail in a coffin", "as mutton", and Chaucer's "as stoon [stone]", and "as the Dodo" (*see below*).

Dead as the Dodo. *See* DODO.

Let the dead bury their dead (*Matt,* viii, 22). Let bygones be bygones. Don't rake up old scores and dead grievances.

Gladstone, speaking on the second Home Rule Bill for Ireland (13 Feb. 1893), explains the phrase:

"Let me entreat you to let the dead bury the dead, to cast behind you every recollection of bygone evils."

Dead beat. Completely exhausted, absolutely "whacked", like a dead man with no fight left in him. A *dead beat* is a down and out. In the U.S.A. it denotes a sponger, one who deliberately avoids settling his debts.

Dead beat escapement (of a clock or a watch). One in which there is no reverse motion of the escape-wheel.

Dead. Book of the Dead. *See under* BOOK.

Dead certainty. An absolute certainty.

Dead drunk. So drunk as to be totally incapable or senseless.

Dead duck. *See under* DUCK.

Dead end kids. Children from poverty-stricken back streets for whom the future seems to hold little promise.

Dead-eye. A wooden block with three holes but without sheaves used for the setting up of shrouds in sailing ships. The holes are the eyes.

Dead fire. CORPOSANT, believed at one time by the credulous to presage death.

Dead hand. A "dead hand" at anything can do it every time without fail. *Cp.* DAB.

First-rate work it was too; he was always a dead hand at splitting.

BOLDREWOOD:*Robbery Under Arms,* xv.

Dead-heads. Those admitted to theatres, etc., without payment; they are "dead" so far as box office receipts are concerned.

As a nautical usage, logs or obstructions floating low in the water, only a small part being visible.

Dead heat. A race in which two or more competitors tie for first place.

Dead horse. To flog a dead horse is to attempt to revive a question already settled or worn thin, thereby wasting time and energy.

To work a dead horse is to perform work already paid for, or to pay off a debt.

Dead knock. A knocking at the door caused by no visible agent, supposed to presage the death of an occupant of the house or someone closely connected with it.

Dead languages. Languages no longer spoken, such as Latin and Sanskrit.

Dead letter. A law or regulation no longer acted upon. A letter which the post office has been unable to deliver either because of an incorrect address or because the person addressed is untraceable.

Dead-letter office. *See* BLIND DEPART-MENT; DEAD LETTER.

Dead lift. I am at a dead lift. In a strait or difficulty where I greatly need help; a hopeless exigency. A dead lift is the lifting of a dead or inactive mass which depends on sheer strength.

Deadlights. Formerly strong wooden shutters to darken or protect the cabin windows of a ship. In a modern vessel they are steel plates fitted over the scuttles of portholes to strengthen the ship's side and to prevent the internal lighting showing outboard. *To ship the deadlights* was to shut or fasten them in position, they are now usually *closed*.

Deadline. The final date or time when a task or assignment must be completed, etc. This sense of strict demarcation derives from the "deadline" round a military prison camp. The phrase was coined in the notorious Confederate prisoner of war camp, Andersonville, during the American CIVIL WAR. Some distance from the peripheral wire fence a line was marked out and any prisoner crossing this line was shot at sight.

Deadlock. A lock which has no spring catch. Metaphorically a state of things so entangled that there seems to be no solution; to reach a complete standstill.

Dead Man's Hand. In the western states of U.S.A., a combination of aces and eights in poker, so called because when Sheriff Wild Bill Hickok was shot in the back at Deadwood, S. Dakota, he held such cards in his hand.

It is said that carrying a dead man's hand will provide a dead sleep. Another superstition is that a lighted candle placed in the hand of a dead man gives no light to anyone but him who carries the hand. *See* HAND OF GLORY *under* GLORY; *Cp.* DEAD HAND.

Dead man's handle. A handle on the controller of an electric train, etc., so designed that it cut off the current and applied the brakes if the driver released his pressure from illness or some other cause. It was formerly applied to electric, diesel-electric, diesel-mechanical, and diesel-hydraulic trains but is now called *Driver's Safety Device*, a term with less distressing associations.

Dead Marines. Empty bottles. Of this it is said: "an empty bottle is no good to anyone", and "an empty bottle has done good service and is ready to do it again".

Dead men. Empty bottles. When the "spirit" is out of the bottle it is dead. In the U.S.A. *dead soldiers* has the same meaning.

Down among the dead men let me lie. Let me get so drunk as to slip from my chair, and lie under the table with the empty bottles.

Dead men's fingers. (1) The common British *Alcyonium digitatum*, a form of marine animal found attached to rocks and seaweed, so called from its appearance when out of the water. (2) The early purple orchis (*Orchis mascula*) which has tuberous roots somewhat resembling distorted hands.

> long purples
> That liberal shepherds give a grosser name,
> But our cold maids do dead men's fingers call them.
>
> SHAKESPEARE: *Hamlet*, IV, vii.

Dead men's shoes. *See under* SHOE.

Dead pays. In the 15th and 16th centuries the pay of English officers on land and sea was augmented by permitting a fictitious increase in the numbers borne on the muster-roll. These "dead pays" were divided among the officers.

Dead Reckoning. Calculating a ship's position by plotting on from the last fix, or trustworthy observed position, the speed made good through the water along the compass course steered.

Dead right. Entirely right.

Dead ropes. Those which are fixed or do not run on blocks.

Dead Sea. The Palestinian Salt Sea or Sea of the Plain of the OLD TESTAMENT, in the ancient Vale of Siddim; called by the Romans *Mare Mortuum* and *Lacus Asphaltites*. It is about 46 miles long and 5 to 9 miles wide and is fed by the Jordan from the north, but has seemingly no outlet. The water is of bluish-green colour and its surface is about 1,300 ft. below the level of the Mediterranean. The northern end is some 1,300 ft. deep and its salt content is 25 per cent while that of sea-water is usually between 3 and 4 per cent. It supports no life other than microbes and a few very low organisms.

Dead Sea Fruit. *See* APPLES OF SODOM.

Dead Sea Scrolls. In 1947 a Bedouin goatherd, Muhammed the Wolf, made the first scroll discoveries in a cave at the N.W. end of the DEAD SEA, since when some hundreds more have been found and more discoveries are probable. Most scholars accept them as originating from the monastery of the Jewish sect of the ESSENES at Qumran. There is still much controversy over their interpretation but it is expected that these manuscripts (from the period 150 B.C. to A.D. 70) will add very considerably to the understanding of Old Testament textual criticism and the background of the NEW TESTAMENT.

Dead Set. To be at a dead set. To be set fast, so as not be able to move. The allusion is to machinery.

To make a dead set upon someone. To concentrate steadfastly upon gaining someone's attention or notice; to concentrate on gaining someone's affection, particularly of the opposite sex; to make a prolonged and resolute onslaught. The allusion is to dogs, etc., set on each other to fight.

Dead soldiers. *See* DEAD MEN.

Dead to the world. In a deep sleep, or state of exhaustion or intoxication, so that a person is totally unconscious of his surroundings.

Dead water. The eddy-water which closes in round a ship's stern as it passes through the water.

Dead weight. The weight of something without life; a burden that does nothing towards easing its own weight; a person who encumbers us and renders no assistance. *Cp.* DEAD LIFT.

Deaf. Deaf as an adder. "Even like the adder that stoppeth her ears; which refuseth to hear the voice of the charmer: charm he never so wisely" (*Ps.* lviii, 4, 5). In the East, if a viper entered the house, the charmer was sent for, who enticed the serpent and put it into a bag. According to tradition, the viper tried to stop its ears when the charmer uttered his incantation, by applying one ear to the ground and twisting its tail into the other.

In the United States deaf adders are sometimes called COPPERHEADS.

Deaf as a beetle. This does not refer to the insect but to the heavy wooden mallet used to level paving-stones or drive in stakes.

Deaf as a post. Quite deaf; or so inattentive as not to hear what is said. One might as well speak to a gatepost or log of wood.

Deaf as a white cat. It is said that white cats are deaf and stupid.

None so deaf as those who won't hear. The French have the same saying: *Il n'y a de pire sourd que celui qui ne veut pas entendre*.

Dean (Lat. *decanus*, one set over ten). The ecclesiastical dignitary who presides over the CHAPTER of a cathedral or COLLEGIATE CHURCH, this having formerly consisted of ten canons. In the more recent foundations decanal functions are carried out by a PROVOST. The Bishop of London is an *ex officio* Dean of the Province of Canterbury and Dean of the Chapels Royal. The Dean of the Chapel Royal of Scotland (Holyrood), is also Dean of the Order of the THISTLE. The Dean of Christchurch, Oxford, is head of the college and also Dean of the cathedral. The Dean of King's College, London, controls the Theological Department.

In the colleges of Oxford and Cambridge, the resident don responsible for under-graduate discipline, or in charge of the chapel, is called a dean.

In Scottish and most modern English universities the title is given to the head of a faculty, as in America, where it is applied to certain other college and administrative officers. *Cp.* DOYEN.

Dean of the Arches. The judge presiding over the Court of ARCHES, formerly at Bow Church, once a PECULIAR.

Dean of Faculty. In Scotland the barrister who presides over the Faculty of Advocates.

Dean of Guild. One who formerly decided mercantile and maritime causes in a Scottish burgh, but more recently largely concerned with regulations affecting buildings.

Deans of Peculiars. Once numerous, and including those of Collegiate Churches such as Westminster and Windsor, surviving examples are those of Battle, Bocking, Jersey and Guernsey. *See* COLLEGIATE CHURCH; PECULIARS.

Dean of the Sacred College, is the senior cardinal-bishop who is given the title of Bishop of Ostia and Velletri. He ranks next to the POPE in the hierarchy. *See* CARDINAL.

Rural Dean. An incumbent who assists in adminstering part of an archdeaconry. An ancient office effectively revived from the mid-19th century.

Dear. Dear bought and far brought, or **felt.** A gentle reproof for some extravagant purchase or luxury.

My dearest foe. As "my dearest friend" is my greatest friend, so "my dearest foe" is my greatest enemy.

> Would I had met my dearest foe in heaven,
> Or ever I had seen that day, Horatio!
>
> SHAKESPEARE: *Hamlet*, I, ii.

Oh, dear me! A very common exclamation, most likely a EUPHEMISM for "Oh, damn me!"

Death. Angel of Death. *See* AZRAEL.

Black Death. *See* BLACK.

At death's door. On the point of death; very dangerously ill.

In at the death. Present when the fox was caught and killed; hence, present at the climax or final act of an exciting event.

Till death us do part. *See* DEPART.

To feel like death warmed up. To be utterly exhausted, to be quite done up, to feel ghastly.

> "If I had scored the try I would have jumped for joy. I hadn't the heart to tell him I felt like death warmed up".
>
> W. REYBURN: *Twickenham*, ch. 17.

Death from Strange Causes.

Æschylus was killed by a tortoise, dropped on his bald head by an eagle (Valerius Maximus, IX, xii, and Pliny, *History*, VII, vii).

Anacreon was choked by a grape-stone (Pliny, *History*, VII, vii).

Bacon died of a cold contracted when stuffing a fowl with snow as an experiment in refrigeration.

Burton, author of the *Anatomy of Melancholy*, died on the very day that he had himself astrologically predicted.

Chalchas, the soothsayer, died of laughter at the thought of having outlived the predicted hour of his death.

Charles VIII, of France, conducting his queen into a tennis-court, struck his head against the lintel, which caused his death.

Fabius, the Roman prætor, was choked by the presence of a single goat-hair in the milk which he was drinking (Pliny, *History*, VII, vii).

Frederick Lewis, Prince of Wales, son of George II, died from the blow of a cricket-ball.

George, Duke of Clarence, brother of Edward IV, was drowned in a butt of MALMSEY.

King John, traditionally said to have died from a surfeit of lampreys but more probably from dysentery resulting from excessive fatigue and indulgence in food and drink.

Lepidus (*Quintus Æmilius*), going out of his house, struck his big toe against the threshold and died.

Lully (*Jean Baptiste*), the composer, when beating time by tapping the floor with his staff while directing a performance of the *Te Deum*, struck his foot and subsequently died from the abscess which set in.

Otway, the poet, in a starving condition, had a guinea given him, with which he bought a loaf of bread and died while swallowing the first mouthful.

Philomenes died of laughter at seeing an ass eating the figs provided for his own dessert (Valerius Maximus).

Prince Philip, eldest son of Louis VI of France, met his death when a pig ran between his horse's legs causing him to be thrown.

William III died from a fall from his horse which stumbled over a mole-hill.

Death in the pot. During a dearth in Gilgal, there was made for the sons of the prophets a potage of wild herbs, some of which were poisonous. When they tasted the potage, they cried out "there is death in the pot". Then Elisha put into it some meal and the poisonous qualities were counteracted (II *Kings* iv, 40).

Death or Glory Boys. *See* REGIMENTAL AND DIVISIONAL NICKNAMES.

Death under shield. Death in battle.

> Her imagination has been familiarized with wild and bloody events ... and had been trained up to consider an honourable "death under shield" (as that in a field of battle was termed) a desirable termination to the life of a warrior.
>
> SCOTT: *The Betrothed*, ch. vi.

Death-bell. A tinkling in the ears, supposed by the Scottish peasantry to announce the death of a friend.

> O lay, 'tis dark, an' I heard the death-bell,
> An' I darena gae yonder for gowd nor fee.
>
> JAMES HOGG: *Mountain Bard*.

Death coach. A ghostly carriage, whose coachman is sometimes headless, which, in Irish and Breton superstition, is reputed to stop in front of a house where a death is about to occur.

Death-watch. Any species of *Anobium*, a genus of wood-boring beetles, that make a clicking sound, once supposed to presage death.

Death's head. A skull. Bawds and procuresses used to wear a ring bearing the impression of a death's head in the time of Queen Elizabeth I.

> Sell some of thy cloaths to buy thee a death's head, and put upon thy middle finger: your least considering bawd does so much.
>
> MASSINGER: *The Old Law*, IV, i.

Death's-head Moth. *Acheronitia atropos* is so called from the markings on the back of the thorax which closely resemble a skull. It is the largest British Hawkmoth.

Death's-man. An executioner; a person who kills another brutally but lawfully.

> He's dead, I'm only sorry
> He had not other death's-man.
>
> SHAKESPEARE: *King Lear*, IV, vi.

Debatable Land. A tract of land between the Esk and Sark claimed by both ENGLAND and SCOTLAND and for long in dispute. It was the haunt of thieves and vagabonds.

Debon. *See* DEVONSHIRE.

Debonair (de bon âr') (*Le Débonnaire*). Louis I of France (778, 814–840), son and successor of CHARLEMAGNE as Holy Roman Emperor; also called the PIOUS.

Debrett. To be in Debrett is to be included in *Debrett's Peerage, Baronetage, Knightage, and Companionage, i.e.* to be of an aristrocatic or titled family. *Debrett's Peerage* was originally composed by John Debrett and first published in 1802, and followed by *Debrett's Baronetage* in 1808. *Cp.* TO BE IN BURKE *under* BURKE.

Debt of Nature. To pay the debt of Nature. To die. Life is a loan and the debt is paid off by the death.

> The slender debt to Nature's quickly paid.
>
> QUARLES: *Emblems*.

Decabrists, Dekabrists. *See* DECEMBRISTS.

Decalogue (Gr. *deka logos*, ten words or sentences). The name given by the Greek Fathers to the TEN COMMANDMENTS referred to in *Exodus* xxxiv, 28 and elsewhere. They have sometimes been divided into those which define our duty to God and those which state our duty to others. The 'classic' version occurs in *Exodus* xx, 2–17; another is found in *Deuteronomy* v, 6–21. The form adopted by the CHURCH OF ENGLAND and most Protestant churches is that which Josephus says was used by his Jewish contemporaries.

Decameron (de kăm' ėrȯn). The collection of 100 tales by Boccaccio, completed *c.* 1353, represented as having been told in ten days (Gr. *deka*, ten, *hemera*, day) during the plague at Florence in 1348, seven ladies and three gentlemen each telling a tale daily. *Cp.* HEPTAMERON; CANTERBURY TALES.

Decathlon. An athletic contest in the modern OLYMPIC GAMES consisting of ten events: 100 metres race, long jump, putting the shot, high jump, 400 metres race, 110 metres hurdles, discus, pole vault, throwing the javelin, and 1,500 metres race.

December (Lat. the tenth month). So it was when the year began in MARCH with the vernal equinox; but, since JANUARY and FEBRUARY have been inserted before it, the name is somewhat misplaced. The old Dutch name was *Winter-maand* and the old Saxon *Winter-monath* (winter month), also called YULE month. After the Saxons became Christians it was known as *Helighmonath* (holy month). In Germany it is known as *Christmonat*. In the French Republican Calendar it was *Frimaire* (hoar-frost month, from 22 November to 20 December).

The Man of December. NAPOLEON III (1808–1873). He was elected President of the Second French Republic 10 December 1848; made his COUP D'ÉTAT 2 December 1851; and became Emperor 2 December 1852.

Decembrists. Conspirators in the Russian army who tried to overthrow the Czar Nicholas I in December 1825.

Decimal Currency was introduced in Great Britain on 15 February 1971, the new POUND consisting of 100 pence. The new coins were the seven-sided 50p piece, the 10p piece (the same size as the former FLORIN), the 5p piece (the same size as the former SHILLING), the 2p piece, the 1p piece and the ½p piece. The first three coins are silver in colour and the remainder copper-coloured. The introduction of a decimal currency was first mooted by the Tory M.P., John Croker, 1816. The idea was again put forward in Parliament in 1824, 1847, 1853 and 1855.

> During the last two years he had devoted himself to decimal coinage with a zeal only second to that displayed by Plantagenet Palliser....
>
> ANTHONY TROLLOPE: *Phineas Redux* (1874), Vol i, ch. xxxii.

Decimo-sexto. An obsolete expression for a small, insignificant person. The term comes from the book trade: *sexto-decimo* (16mo) is a book in which each sheet is folded to a sixteenth of its size, giving 32 pages; hence it is a small book. *Cp.* DUODECIMO.

> How now! my dancing braggart in decimosexto! Charm your skipping tongue.
>
> BEN JONSON: *Cynthia's Revels*, I, i.

Deck. A pack of cards, or that part of the pack left after the hands have been dealt. The term was current in England until the 19th century, it is now mostly used in the U.S.A.

> But, while he thought to steal the single ten, The king was slyly finger'd from the deck.
>
> SHAKESPEARE: *Henry VI, Pt. III*, V, i.

To sweep the deck. To clear off all the stakes.

Clear the decks. Get everything out of the way that is not essential, also to clear the decks of personnel. A nautical expression.

To clear lower deck is to assemble the ship's company from below.

Decoration Day. *See* MEMORIAL DAY.

Decree nisi. *See* NISI.

Decretals. The name given to papal decrees or letters which embody decisions in ecclesiastical law.

The False, or **Forged Decretals** aimed at enhancing the position of BISHOPS and papacy and strengthening the Church against inroads by the temporal power. The collection contains many spurious letters and documents, ranging from the 1st to the 7th century, including the pretended DONATION OF CONSTANTINE, intermingled with, and thus supported by, genuine decretals. They appeared in the mid-9th century and were issued under the name of Isidore Mercator. They were first seriously challenged in the 15th century and finally discredited by the PROTESTANT minister David Blondel in 1620. They are also known as the ISIDORIAN DECRETALS.

The Isidorian Decretals. The False Decretals wrongly assigned to Isidore, Archbishop of Seville, a noted 7th-century scholar and codifier of canon law. They were probably compiled in France and accepted by Pope Nicholas I. Since their forgery became manifest they commonly came to be called the *Pseudo-Isidorian Decretals*.

Decuman Gate. The principal entrance to a Roman military camp, situated on the farthest side from the enemy, and so called because it was guarded by the 10th cohort of each legion (*decimus*, tenth).

Dedalian. *See* DÆDALUS.

Dee, Dr. John Dee (1527–1608), famous mathematician, alchemist and astrologer, was patronized by Queen Elizabeth I, but eventually died a pauper at Mortlake, where he was buried. he wrote 79 treatises on a variety of subjects. Dee's *Speculum* or Mirror, of solid pink-tinted glass, about the size of an orange, once in Horace Walpole's collection at Strawberry Hill, is now in the BRITISH MUSEUM.

Deed Poll. A deed made by one party, and so called because it was written on parchment with a *polled* or straight edge as opposed to an INDENTURE, one with an indented or wavy edge.

Deemster, Dempster, or **Doomster.** The two judges of the Isle of Man are called Deemsters and they take an oath to execute the laws "as indifferently as the herring backbone doth lie in the midst of the fish." (*See* DOOM.) Hall Caine's once popular romance *The Deemster* appeared in 1887.

In SCOTLAND, a Dempster or Doomster was formerly appointed to recite the sentence after it had been pronounced by the court. He combined this office with that of executioner.

> "And this," said the Doomster, aggravating his harsh voice, "I pronounce for doom".
>
> SCOTT: *Heart of Midlothian*, ch. xxiv.

Deer. Supposed by poets to shed tears. The drops, however, which fall from their eyes are not tears but an oily secretion from the so-called tear-pits.

> A poor sequester'd stag...
> Did come to languish... and the big round tears
> Cours'd one another down his innocent nose
> In piteous chase.
>
> SHAKESPEARE: *As You Like It*, II, ii.

Small deer. Any small animal; and used metaphorically for trifling matters or any collection of trifles. *Cp.* SMALL BEER.

> But mice and rats, and such small deer
> Have been Tom's food for seven long year.
>
> SHAKESPEARE: *King Lear*, III, iv.

Default. Judgment by default is when the defendant does not appear in court on the day appointed. The judge gives sentence in favour of the plaintiff, not because the plaintiff is right, but from the default of the defendent. Hence used of a judgement made in a person's absence.

Defender of the Faith (Lat. *fidei defensor*).

A title given to Henry VIII by Pope Leo X (11 October 1521) for his treatise *Assertio Septem Sacramentorum* attacking Luther's teachings. The initials 'F.D.' continuously appeared on the British coinage from the reign of George I.

Defenders. An association of Irish Catholics (1784–1798), formed in Northern IRELAND in opposition to the PEEP-OF-DAY BOYS. In 1795 a pitched battle was fought between the two and the Defenders suffered severe losses.

Defenestration of Prague. An incident in Bohemia prior to the outbreak of the THIRTY YEARS WAR when the two leading Roman Catholic members of the Bohemian National Council were thrown out of a window of the castle of Prague by the PROTESTANT members. They landed in the moat and sustained only minor injuries.

Deficient. A deficient number is one of which the sum of all its divisors is less than itself, as 10, the divisors of which are 1, 2, 5=8, which is less than 10.

Déficit, Madame. Marie Antoinette, because she was always in need of money. She was noted for her extravagance and popularly regarded as being responsible for the nation's bankruptcy. According to the Revolutionary song:

La Boulangère a des écus,
Qui ne lui comptent guère.

See BAKER.

Degrees, Songs of. Another name for the GRADUAL PSALMS.

Dei Gratia (dē ī grā' shà) (Lat.). By the grace of God. As early as *c*. 690 we find "I, Ine, by God's grace King of the West Saxons", and in an ordinance of William I, *"Willelmus gratia Dei Rex Anglorum"*. It was first used on the GREAT SEAL by William II and all Great Seals from the reign of Edward I. It still appears on British coins, where it was originally introduced on the gold coins of Edward III in 1344. *See* GRACELESS FLORIN.

The style was also sometimes used by the Archbishops of Canterbury and York, until as late as the 17th century, and is still so used by BISHOPS of the ROMAN CATHOLIC CHURCH.

Dei Judicium (dē ī yoo dis' i um) (Lat.). The judgment of God; so the judgment by ORDEAL was called, because it was taken as certain that God would deal rightly with appellants.

Deianira (dē ī ăn ira). Wife of HERCULES and the unwitting cause of his death. NESSUS, the CENTAUR, having carried her across a river, attempted to assault her and was shot by Hercules with a poisoned arrow. The expiring centaur gave Deianira his tunic, steeped in blood, telling her that it would reclaim her husband from illicit loves. When she had occasion to give it to Hercules, the poisoned blood brought about his death.

Deidamia (dē ī dā' mia). Daughter of Lycomedes, King of Scyros. ACHILLES, when sojourning there disguised as a woman, became the father of her son Pyrrhus, or Neoptolemus.

Deiphobus (dē ī fō' bus). Third husband of HELEN of Troy whom she married after the death of his brother PARIS. Helen betrayed Deiphobus to her first husband, MENELAUS who killed his rival.

Deirdre (dir' drē). In Irish romance the daughter of the king of ULSTER's storyteller. At her birth it was prophesied that she would bring ruin to IRELAND. King CONCHOBAR brought her up and planned to marry her, but she fell in love with Naoise, the eldest of the three sons of USNECH. She escaped to Scotland, with the three brothers but they were lured back by Conchobar with false promises. The jealous king killed the three young men. One version of the story says that Deirdre killed herself, another that she died the following year after living unhappily with Conchobar. Deirdre is the subject and title of a play by W.B. Yeats, and J.M. Synge also dramatized the legend in his *Deirdre of the Sorrows*.

Deist. *See* THEIST.

Deities. The more important classical, Teutonic, and Scandinavian deities appear under their own names; the present list is only intended to include certain collective names and some better-known gods, sprites, etc., of special localities, functions, etc.

Air: ARIEL; *Elves. See* ELF.
Caves or *Caverns*: HILL-FOLK or Hill-people, Pixies (*see* PIXIE).
Corn: CERES (Gr. DEMETER).
Domestic Life: VESTA.
Eloquence: MERCURY (Gr. HERMES).
Evening: Vesper.
Fairies. See FAIRY.
Fates: (*q.v.*); NORNS.
Fire: VULCAN (Gr. Hephaistos), VESTA, MULCIBER.
Furies: (*q.v.*), (Gr. EUMENIDES, ERINYES).
Gardens: PRIAPUS; VERTUMNUS; POMONA.
Graces: See under GRACE (Gr. Charites).
Hades (*q.v.*): PLUTO with his wife PROSERPINA (Gr. Aidēs and Persephóne).
Hills: Pixies (*see* PIXIE), TROLLS; also Wood Trolls and Water Trolls.
Home Spirits: LARES AND PENATES.
Hunting: DIANA (Gr. Artemis).
Justice: THEMIS, ASTRÆA, NEMESIS.
Love: VENUS (Gr. APHRODITE), CUPID (Gr. EROS).
Marriage: HYMEN.
Medicine: ÆSCULAPIUS.
Morning: AURORA (Gr. EOS).
Mountains: OREADS, TROLLS.

Ocean: OCEANIDES. *See* SEA *below*.
Poetry and Music: APOLLO, the nine MUSES.
Rainbow: IRIS.
Riches: PLUTUS.
Rivers and Streams: Fluviales (Gr. Potamēides, NAIADS, Nymphs).
Sea: NEPTUNE (Gr. POSEIDON), TRITON, Nixies, MERMAIDS, NEREIDS.
Shepherds and their flocks: PAN, the SATYRS.
Springs, Lakes, Brooks, etc.: NEREIDS, NAIADS. See RIVERS, *above*.
Time: SATURN (Gr. CHRONOS).
Trees: See WOODS, *below*.
War: MARS (Gr. ARES), BELLONA, THOR.
Water-nymphs: NAIADS, UNDINE.
Winds: ÆŌLUS.
Wine: BACCHUS (Gr. DIONYSUS).
Wisdom: MINERVA (Gr. PALLAS, ATHENE, or PALLAS-ATHENE).
Woods: DRYADS (a Hamadryad presides over some particular tree), Wood Trolls.
Youth: HEBE.

Déjeuner à la fourchette (dējĕnā' ǎ lǎ foorshet') (Fr.). A fork lunch; a cold collation with meat and wine.

Dekko, To take a. To glance at, to have a look at. This is one of the many phrases brought back from India by the British Army. In Hindustani *dekho* means "look". *Cp.* CHAR.

Delectable Mountains. In Bunyan's *Pilgrim's Progress*, a range of mountains from which the "CELESTIAL CITY" may be seen.

Delenda est Carthago (dė len'då est kar tha' gō) (Lat.). Carthage must be destroyed; the words with which Cato the Elder concluded every speech in the Senate after his visit to Carthage in 157 B.C. where he saw in her revived prosperity a standing threat to ROME. The phrase is now proverbial and means "that which stands in the way of our greatness must be removed at all costs".

Delight. The delight of mankind. So Titus the Roman emperor (40, 79–81) was called on account of his benevolence and munificence. *See* I HAVE LOST A DAY *under* DAY.

Delilah, A. A beautiful but treacherous woman, from the story of Samson and Delilah (*Judges* xvi).

Delinquents. During the English civil wars (1642–1645) a term applied to the royalists by their opponents. Charles I was called the "chief delinquent".

Delirium. From the Lat. *lira* (the ridge left by the plough), hence the verb *de-lilare*, to make an irregular ridge in ploughing. Thus *delirus* for one who could not plough straight, and hence a crazy, dotty person, one whose mind wandered from the subject in hand. *Delirium* is that state of such a person. *Cp.* PREVARICATION.

Della Cruscans (del' a krŭs' kånz), or **Della Cruscan School.** A school of poetry started by some young Englishmen in Florence in the latter part of the 18th century. Their silly, sentimental affectations, which appeared in *The World* and *The Oracle*, created a temporary stir but were mercilessly pilloried in *The* BAVIAD and *The Mœviad*. The clique took its name from the famous Accademia della Crusca (Academy of Chaff) which was founded in Florence in 1582 with the object of purifying the Italian language by sifting away its "chaff", and which in 1611 published an important dictionary.

Delos. The smallest island of the Cyclades, sacred to APOLLO. It comes from the Greek word for a ring, as the rest of the islands encircle Delos. It was fabled to have been called out of the deep by POSEIDON, and remained a floating island until ZEUS chained it to the bottom of the sea. It was the legendary birthplace of Apollo and Artemis (DIANA).

Delphi, or **Delphos** (now Kastri). A town of Phocis at the foot of Mount PARNASSUS famous for a temple of APOLLO and for its celebrated oracle which was silenced only in the 4th century by the Emperor Theodosius. Delphi was regarded by the ancients as the "navel of the earth", and in the temple there was a white stone bound with a red ribbon to represent the navel and umbilical cord.

In the *Winter's Tale* (the same play in which he gives Bohemia a sea-coast) SHAKESPEARE makes Delphos an island.

A Delphic utterance is one which has the ambiguity associated with the words of the ORACLE.

> The president's broad wishes, as expressed in his periodic but carefully Delphic press conferences.
> *The Times*, 3 Jan. 1966.

Delphin Classics. A set of Latin classics prepared under the superintendence of Pierre Daniel Huet and Anne Lefebvre (Madame Dacier) for the use of the Grand DAUPHIN (*ad usum Delphini*). They were published between 1674 and 1730 and were subsequently reprinted in various parts of Europe.

Deluge. The Biblical story of the flood (*Gen.* vi, vii, viii) has its counterpart in a variety of mythologies. In Babylonia it appears in the 11th tablet of the GILGAMESH EPIC, but on a higher level of civilization, for UTNAPISHTIM takes both craftsmen and treasure into his ark.

Apollodorus tells the story of DEUCALION AND PYRRHA in some versions of which Deucalion is replaced by Ogyges. (*See* OGYGIAN DELUGE.) The story is also found in Ovid's *Metamorphoses*, Bk. I, 253–415.

In India one legend tells how MANU was

warned by a fish of the approaching flood and the fish subsequently towed his vessel to safety.

Kindred stories are found in China, Burma, New Guinea, etc., and in both the American continents.

Delusion. A snare and a delusion. Something that raises hopes only to dash them. Lord Denman's judgment in O'Connell *v.* the Crown (September 1844) has, "Trial by jury … will be a delusion, a mockery and a snare."

Demesne. *See* MANOR.

Demeter (de mē' ter). The corn goddess of Greek legend, identified with the Roman CERES. She was the mother of Persephone (PROSERPINE) and the goddess of fruit, crops, and vegetation.

Demijohn (dem' i jon). A glass or stoneware vessel with a large body and a small neck enclosed in wickerwork and containing more than a bottle. A common capacity is five gallons. The word is probably from the Fr. *dame-jeanne*, Dame Jane. *Cp.* BELLARMINE.

Demi-monde (dem' i mond) (Fr. d*emi*, half; *monde*, world, society). As *le beau monde* is society, *le demi-monde* denotes that class of women whose social standing is only half acknowledged or who are of uncertain reputation. The term was first used by Dumas *fils* for the title of a play (*Le Demi-Monde*, 1855), and sometimes incorrectly applied to fashionable courtesans.

> [Dumas'] *demi-monde* is the link between good and bad society … the world of compromised women, a social limbo, the inmates of which … are perpetually struggling to emerge into the paradise of honourable and respectable ladies.
>
> *Fraser's Magazine*, 1885.

Demi-rep (dem' i rep). A woman whose character has been blown upon, one "whom everybody knows to be what nobody calls her" (Fielding). A contraction of *demireputable*.

Demiurge (demi' i ĕrj) (Gr. *demiourgos*, artisan, handicraftsman, etc.). In the language of the Platonists, that mysterious agent which made the world and all that it contains. The Logos, or Word, spoken of by St. JOHN in the first chapter of his gospel, is the *Demiurgus* of Platonizing Christians. Among the GNOSTICS JEHOVAH (as an eon or emanation of the Supreme Being) is the Demiurge. *See* MARCIONITES.

Certain officials in some of the ancient Greek states were called *Demiurgoi*.

Democritus (de mok' ri tus) (*c.* 460–370 B.C.). Called "Wisdom" during his life and later the "laughing philosopher". He was a follower of Leucippus and head of the school of ABDERA in Thrace. He should rather be termed the *deriding* philosopher, because he derided or laughed at people's folly or vanity. It is said that he put out his eyes that he might think the more deeply. He was no mere scoffer, and in many ways is to be ranked with PLATO and ARISTOTLE.

> Democritus, dear droll, revisit earth,
> And with our follies glut thy heightened mirth.
> PRIOR: *Democritus and Heraclitus.*

Democritus Junior. The name under which Robert Burton's (1577–1640) *The Anatomy of Melancholy* first appeared in 1621.

Demogorgon (dem ō gor' gon). A terrible deity, whose very name was capable of producing the most horrible effects. He is first mentioned by the 4th-century Christian writer, Lactantius, who in doing so broke with the superstition that the very reference to Demogorgon by name brought death and disaster.

> Must I call your master to my aid,
> At whose dread name the trembling furies quake,
> Hell stands abashed, and earth's foundations shake?
> ROWE: *Lucan's Pharsalia,* vi.

Milton speaks of "the dreaded name of Demogorgon" (*Paradise Lost*, II, 966). According to Ariosto, Demogorgon was king of the elves and fays who lived on the Himalayas, and once in five years summoned all his subjects before him to give an account of their stewardship. Spenser (*Faerie Queene*, IV, ii, 47) says that he dwells "down in the bottom of the deep abyss" with the three fatal sisters. In Dryden's *The Flower and the Leaf* (493) he appears as "cruel Demogorgon" and in Shelley's *Prometheus Unbound* he is the eternal principle that ousts false gods.

Demon (Austra.). A convict serving his sentence of transportation in Van Diemen's Land (Tasmania) was so called.

Demons, Prince of. ASMODEUS, also called "the Demon of Matrimonial Unhappiness".

Demos, King (dē' mos). The electorate, the proletariat; those who choose the rulers of the nation and are therefore ultimately sovereign. A facetious or derisive term (Gr. *demos*, people).

Demy (Fr. *demi*, half). A demy of Magdalen College, Oxford, is a foundation scholar, whose allowance or "commons" was originally half that of a Fellow.

Den. God ye good den! An abbreviated form of the old salutation "God give you good even(ing)".

> Nurse: God ye morrow, gentlemen.
> Mer: God ye good den, fair gentlewoman.
> SHAKESPEARE: *Romeo and Juliet*, II, iv.

Denarius (den âr' i ùs). A Roman silver coin

originally equal to ten ases (*deniases*). The word was used in France and England for the inferior coins whether of silver or copper, and for ready money generally. The initial "d" for PENNY (£ *s. d.*) is from *denarius*.

Denarius Dei (Lat. God's penny). An earnest of a bargain, which was given to the Church or poor.

Denarii St. Petri. Peter's pence. (*See under* PETER).

Denims. Coloured twilled cotton material used for overalls and especially jeans. A contraction of *serge de Nimes*. Originally made at Nimes in the south of France.

Denis, St. *See* DENYS.

Denmark. According to the *Roman de la Rose*, Denmark means the country of Danaos, who settled there after the siege of TROY, as BRUTUS is said by the same sort of legend to have settled in BRITAIN. SAXO-GRAMMATICUS (*c.* 1150–*c.* 1206) in his *Gesta Danorum*, with equal fancifulness, explains the name by making Dan, the son of Humble, the first king. His work is largely a collection of myths and oral tradition dealing with kings, heroes and national gods.

Something is rotten in the state of Denmark. A hidden cause of uneasiness which is felt but cannot be precisely defined; there is a scent of corruption or something dubious going on. Often used facetiously. From SHAKESPEARE's *Hamlet*, IV, i.

Denys, St. (dė nē´) or **St. Dionysius.** The apostle to the Gauls and a traditional patron saint of France, said to have been beheaded at Paris in 272. Legendarily, after martyrdom he carried his head in his hands for two miles and laid it on the spot where stands the cathedral bearing his name. The tale may have arisen from an ancient painting of his martyrdom in which the artist placed the head between the hands so that the martyr might be identified. *See* CE N'EST QUE LE PREMIER PAS QUI COÛTE *under* PREMIER.

Montjoie Saint Denys! *See* MONTJOIE.

Deo gratias (dē´ ō grā shǎs) (Lat.). Thanks to God. *Cp.* DEI GRATIA.

Deo juvante, or **adjuvante** (dē´ ō yoo-vǎn´ te) (Lat.). With God's help.

Deo volente (dē´ ō vō len´ te) (Lat.). God be willing; by God's will; usually contracted into D.V.

Deoch-an-dorius. *See* DOCH-AN-DORIS.

Deodand (dē´ ō dǎnd). Literally, something which should be given to God (Lat. *deodandum*). In English law a personal chattel responsible for the death of an individual was forfeited to the crown for some pious use. For example, if a man met his death from the fall of a ladder, the kick of a horse, etc., the cause of death was sold and the proceeds given to the Church. It originated from the idea that as the sufferer was sent to his account without the sacrament of extreme unction, the money could serve to pay for masses for his repose. Deodands were abolished in 1846.

Depart. Literally, to part thoroughly; to separate effectually. The marriage service in the old prayer-books had "till death us depart", which has been corrupted into "till death us do part".

> "Depart" is sound English for "part asunder", which was altered to "do part" in 1661, at the pressing request of the Puritans, who knew as little of the history of their national language as they did of that of their national Church.
> J.H. BLUNT: *Annotated Book of Common Prayer*.

Derby (dĕr´ bi). The American name for the hat known as the BOWLER in England. The *Brown Derby* is a well-known Hollywood restaurant, shaped like a hat, and frequented by the film colony.

The Derby is the DERBY STAKES.

Derby Day (dar´ bi) is the day when the DERBY STAKES are run for, during the great Epsom Summer Meeting.

Derby Dog. The stray dog that so often wanders on to the race-course on Epsom Downs as soon as it has been cleared for the main race. Something that inevitably "turns up".

Derby Stakes (dar´ bi). One of the CLASSIC RACES, also called the BLUE RIBAND OF THE TURF, was instituted by the Twelfth Earl of Derby in 1780, one year after he established the OAKS. The Derby is for three-year-old colts and fillies only, therefore no horse can win it twice. *See* EPSOM RACES; HERMIT'S DERBY.

Kiplingcotes Derby. *See* KIPLINGCOTES.

Derbyite. In World War I, a soldier enlisted under the Derby Scheme of 1915. The Earl of Derby was Director of Recruiting and sought to promote a scheme of voluntary enlistment by age groups. The response was quite inadequate and conscription was instituted in May 1916.

Derbyshire neck. Goitre, from its occurrence in that county more commonly than in other parts of Britain.

Derrick. A contrivance or form of crane used for hoisting heavy objects; so called from Derrick, the TYBURN hangman of the early 17th century. The name was first applied to the gibbet and, from its similarity, to the crane.

> He rides circuit with the devil, and Derrick must be his host, and Tyborne the inn at which he will light.
> DEKKER: *Bellman of London* (1608).

Derwentwater. Lord Derwentwater's Lights. A local name of the AURORA BOREALIS; James, Earl of Derwentwater, was beheaded 24 February 1716 for his part in the 1715 rebellion in support of the Old Pretender. (*See* PRETENDER). It is said that the northern lights were unusually bright that night.

Deseret. Deseret was the MORMON name for a honey bee and their original name for the State of Utah.

Desert Fathers. *See under* FATHER.

Desert Rats. *See* REGIMENTAL AND DIVISIONAL NICKNAMES.

Desmas. *See* DYSMAS.

Despair. Giant Despair, in Bunyan's *Pilgrim's Progress*, dwelt in DOUBTING CASTLE.

Destruction. Prince of Destruction. TAMERLANE, or Timur, the Tartar (1336–1405), the famous oriental conqueror of Persia and a great part of India. He was threatening China when he died.

Desultory. Roman circus-riders who used to leap from one horse to another were called *desultores*; hence used figuratively in Latin to mean an inconstant person, or one who went from one thing to another; and desultory thus means after the manner of a *desultor* (Lat. *desilio*, leap down, alight).

Deucalion and Pyrrha. Deucalion (the Greek counterpart of Noah) was a son of PROMETHEUS and married Pyrrha, daughter of Epimetheus. He was king of part of Thessaly. When ZEUS, angered at the evils of the Bronze Age (*See* AGE), caused the DELUGE, Deucalion built an ark to save himself and his wife, which came to rest on Mount PARNASSUS. Told by the ORACLE of THEMIS that to restore the human race they must cast the bones of their mother behind them (which they interpreted as the stones of Mother Earth), he and his wife obeyed the direction. The stones thrown by Deucalion became men and those thrown by Pyrrha became women.

> And men themselves, the which at first were framed
> Of earthly mould, and form'd of flesh and bone,
> Are now transformed into hardest stone;
> Such as behind their backs (so backward bred)
> Were thrown by Pyrrha and Decucalione.
>
> SPENSER: *Faerie Queene*, V, *Introd.*, ii.

Deuce. The two, in games with cards, dice, etc. (fr. *deux*). The three is called "tray" (Fr. *trois*).

Deuce-ace. A throw of two dice, one showing one spot and the other showing two; hence, exceptionally bad luck.

Among the origins ascribed to the word *deuce* used as a EUPHEMISM for DEVIL is that it may come from the two at dice being an unlucky throw. Other suggestions are that it is from the Latin expletive *Deus*! My God!; from the Celtic *dus, teuz*, phantom, spectre; or from the Old German *Durce, Turse*, giant.

Deuce take you. Get away! you annoy me.

Go to the deuce. Go to the devil!

It played the deuce with me. It made me very ill; it disagreed with me. It gave me the devil of a time.

The deuce is in you. You are a very demon.

What the deuce is the matter? What the devil is up? What in the world is amiss?

Deus. Deux ex machina (Lat.). The intervention of some unlikely or providential event just in time to extricate one from difficulties or to save a situation; especially as contrived in a novel or a play. Literally it means "a god let down upon the stage from the machine", the "machine" being part of the stage equipment in an ancient Greek theatre.

Deus vult (Lat. God wills it). The warcry of the First CRUSADE, enjoined by Pope Urban II because these words were spontaneously used by the crowd in response to his address at Clermont in 1095.

Deva. The Roman legionary fortress on the site of the present Chester; the river Dee.

> Nor yet where Deva spreads her wizard stream.
> MILTON: *Lycidas*.

Devil, The. Represented with a cloven foot, because by the Rabbinical writers he is called *seirizzim* (a goat). As the goat is a type of uncleanness, the prince of unclean spirits is aptly represented under this emblem. As the Prince of Evil he is also called SATAN.

In legal parlance a counsel who prepares a brief for another is called a *devil* and the process is called *devilling*. It is also applied where one counsel transfers his brief to another to represent him in court.

The Attorney-General's Devils are the Counsel of the Treasury, who not infrequently get promoted to the BENCH.

A printer's devil. A printer's errand boy; formerly the boy who took the printed sheets from the tympan of the press. Moxon says (1683): "They do commonly so black and bedaub themselves that the workmen do jocosely call them devils".

DEVIL PHRASES.

As the Devil loves holy water. That is, not at all. HOLY WATER drives away the devil. The Latin proverb is, "*Sicut sus amaricinum amat*" (as swine love marjoram), which similarly means not at all, since Lucretius, VI, 974, says, "*amaricinum fugitat sus*."

Beating the Devil's tattoo. Drumming on the table with one's fingers a wearisome number of times, or on the floor with one's foot; repeating any rhythmical mechanical sound with annoying persistence.

Between the Devil and the deep (blue) sea. Between SCYLLA and CHARYBDIS; between two evils or alternatives, to be in a hazardous or precarious position. It is seemingly of nautical origin and means between the devil and the waterline of a ship. *See* THE DEVIL TO PAY AND NO PITCH HOT, *below*.

Cheating the Devil. Mincing an oath; doing evil for gain, and giving part of the profits to the Church, etc. It is not unusual in monkish traditions. Thus the "DEVIL'S BRIDGE", over the Fall of Reuss in Switzerland, is a single arch over a cataract. It is said that Satan knocked down several bridges but promised the abbot, Giraldus of Einsiedeln, to let this one stand, provided he would give him the first living thing that crossed it:

> The Abbot, standing at its head,
> Threw across it a loaf of bread,
> Which a hungry dog sprang after,
> And the rocks re-echoed with peals of laughter
> To see the Devil thus defeated!
>
> LONGFELLOW: *Golden Legend*, V.

Rabelais (*Pantagruel*, Bk. IV, ch. xlvi), says that a farmer once bargained with the Devil for each to have on alternate years what grew under and over the soil. The canny farmer sowed carrots and turnips when it was his turn to have the under-soil share, and wheat and barley the year following.

Devil dodger. A sly hypocrite; a ranting preacher, a parson.

Devil-may-care. Wildly reckless; also a reckless individual.

Give the Devil his due. Give even a bad person, or one hated like the devil, such credit as he deserves.

Go to the Devil. Go to ruin. In the 17th century wits used to make a play on the applicability of the phrase to the Devil Tavern, TEMPLE BAR, a favoured rendezvous among lawyers and writers. The sign was St. DUNSTAN pulling the Devil's nose.

> *Bloodhound:* As you come by Temple Bar make a step to the Devil.
> *Tim:* To the Devil, father?
> *Sim:* My master means the sign of the devil, and he cannot hurt you, fool; there's a saint holds him by the nose.
>
> W. ROWLEY: *A Match at Midnight*, 1633

He needs a long spoon who sups with the Devil. *See* SPOON.

Here's the very Devil to pay. Here's a pretty KETTLE OF FISH. I'm in a pretty mess. *Cp.* **The devil to pay and no pitch hot,** *below*.

Needs must when the Devil drives. If I must, I must; there is no option. The French say: "*Il faut marcher quand le diable*

est aux trousses." The Italian version is: "*Bisogna andare, quando il diavolo è nella coda.*"

> He must needs go that the Devil drives.
>
> SHAKESPEARE: *All's Well that Ends Well*, I, iii.

Pull Devil, pull baker. Lie, cheat and wrangle away, "have a go at each other". Sometimes "parson" is substituted for "baker".

> Then my mither and her quarrelled, and pu'ed me twa ways at anes, as if ilk ane had an end o' me, like Punch and the Deevil rugging about the Baker at the fair.
>
> SCOTT: *Old Mortality*, ch. xxxviii.

Talk of the Devil and he's sure to appear. Said of a person who has been the subject of conversation and who unexpectedly makes his appearance. An older proverb still is: "Talk of the Dule and he'll put out his horns"; and a more modern version is "Talk of an angel and you'll hear the fluttering of its wings."

> Forthwith the devil did appear,
> For name him, and he's always near.
>
> PRIOR: *Hans Carvel*.

Tell the truth and shame the Devil. A very old saying, of obvious meaning.

The Devil among the tailors. Said when a god slanging match is in progress; it is also the name of a game in which a top (the "devil") is spun among a number of wooden men (the "tailors") to knock down as many as possible.

The phrase is said to have originated from a fracas made at a benefit performance about 1830 for the actor William Dowton (1764–1851). The piece was a burlesque called *The Tailors: a Tragedy for Warm Weather*, and the row was made outside the Haymarket Theatre by a large crowd of tailors, who considered the play a slur on their trade.

The Devil and all. Everything, especially everything bad.

The Devil and his dam. The Devil and something worse. Dam here may mean *mother* or *wife* and numerous quotations may be adduced in support of either interpretation. Rabbinical tradition relates that LILITH was the wife of ADAM, but was such a vixen that Adam could not live with her, and she became the Devil's dam. We also read that BELPHEGOR "came to earth to seek him out a dam". In many mythologies the Devil is typified by an animal, and in such cases *dam* for mother is not inappropriate.

The Devil catch the hindmost. A phrase from late mediæval magic. The Devil was supposed to have had a school at Toledo, or at Salamanca, where the students, after making certain progress in their mystic studies, were obliged to run through a subterranean hall, and the last man was seized by the Devil and became his imp. *See also under* SHADOW.

The Devil dances in an empty pocket. An old proverb. Poverty or an empty pocket leads to temptation or crime. Many coins bore a cross on the obverse and so the Devil could not gain entrance to the pocket if they were present.

The Devil in Dublin City. The Scandinavian form of Dublin was *Divelin [a]*, and the Latin *Dublinia*. Dublin is the Gael. *dhu linn*, the black pool. Devlin, in Co. Mayo, is the same word and preserves the Scandinavian form.

> Is just as true's the devil's in hell
> Or Dublin City.
>
> BURNS: *Death and Dr. Hornbrook*.

The Devil is not so black as he is painted. Said in extenuation or mitigation, especially when it seems that exaggerated censure has been given.

The Devil looking over Lincoln. Said of a vitriolic critic or a backbiter. Fuller in his *Worthies* (under *Oxford*), says the phrase may allude either to the "stone picture of the Devil which doth [1661] or lately did, overlook Lincoln College", or to a grotesque sculpture at Lincoln Cathedral. *See* LINCOLN IMP.

> Than wolde ye looke ouer me with stomoke swolne
> Like as the divell lookt ourer Lincolne.
>
> JOHN HEYWOOD: *Proverbs* (1562).

The Devil rides on a fiddlestick. Much ado about nothing. Beaumont and Fletcher, SHAKESPEARE and others, use the phrase "Fiddlesticks!" as an exclamation meaning rubbish! nonsense! When the prince and his merry companions are at the *Boar's Head*, first Bardolph rushes in to warn them that the sheriff's officers are at hand, then the hostess enters to warn her guests. But the prince says:

> Heigh, heigh! the devil rides upon a fiddlestick:
> what's the matter?
>
> *Henry IV, Pt. I*, II, iv.

The Devil's advocate. *See* ADVOCATE.

The Devil's dancing-hour. Midnight.

The Devil's daughter's portion. The saying:

> Deal, Dover, and Harwich,
> The Devil gave with his daughter in marriage.

occasioned by the scandalous impositions once practised in these ports on sailors and casual visitors.

The Devil's door. A small door in the north wall of some old churches, which used to be opened at baptisms and communions to "let the Devil out". The north used to be known as "the Devil's side", where SATAN and his legion lurked to catch the unwary.

The Devil sick would be a monk.

> When the Devil was sick, the Devil a monk would be;
> When the Devil got well, the devil a monk was he.

Said of those persons who in times of sickness or danger make pious resolutions, but forget them when danger is past and health recovered.

The Devil to pay and no pitch hot. There will be serious trouble arising from this. The "devil" was the seam between the outboard plank and the waterways of a ship and very awkward of access. It also needed more pitch when caulking and paying, hence "the devil". *See* PAY.

To hold a candle to the Devil. *See* CANDLE.

To kindle a fire for the Devil. To offer sacrifice, to do what is really sinful, under the delusion that you are doing God's service.

To lead one the Devil's own dance. To give one endless trouble.

To play the very Devil with something. To thoroughly mar or spoil.

To pull the Devil by the tail. To struggle constantly against adversity.

To say the Devil's paternoster. To grumble; to rail at providence.

To vow a candle to the Devil. *See* CANDLE.

To ship the Devil round the stump. An American phrase meaning to enjoy the fruits of evil-doing without having to suffer the penalty; to dodge a difficulty dishonestly but successfully.

When the Devil is blind. Never.

Why should the Devil have all the good tunes? A saying originating with Charles Wesley about 1740, when he adapted the music of current popular songs to promote the use of his hymns.

DEVIL. SOME TOPOGRAPHICAL USAGES.

Devil's Arrows. Three remarkable "Druid" stones near Boroughbridge, Yorkshire.

Devil's Bridge. A popular name in mountainous areas for bridges built over ravines and chasms. There is a notable one over the Reuss in the Swiss canton of Uri. (*See* CHEATING THE DEVIL.) The Cardiganshire hamlet of this name is so called from the bridge across the gorge of the Mynach. The lower or Monk's Bridge was built by the monks of Strata Florida in the 12th century and the upper tiers in the 18th and 20th.

Devil's Cheesewring. *See* CHEESEWRING.

Devil's Coits. *See* HACKELL'S COIT.

Devil's Current. Part of the current of the BOSPORUS is so called, from its great rapidity.

Devil's Den. A CROMLECH near Marlborough.

Devil's Dyke. (1) An ancient earthwork in Cambridgeshire stretching from Reach to Wood Ditton. On the eastern side it is 18 ft. high. (2) A ravine in the South Downs to the N.W. of Brighton. The legend is that St. Cuthman, priding himself on having christianized the area and having built a nunnery where the dyke-house was later built, was confronted by the Devil and told that all his labour was vain for he would swamp the whole country before morning. St. Cuthman went to the nunnery and told the abbess to keep the sisters in prayer till after midnight and then illuminate the windows. The Devil came at sunset with mattock and spade, and began cutting a dyke into the sea, but was seized with rheumatic pains all over his body. He flung down his tools, and the cocks, mistaking the illuminated windows for sunrise, began to crow; whereupon the Devil fled in alarm, leaving his work not half done. (3) *See* GRIM'S DYKE *under* GRIM.

Devil's Frying-pan. A curious rock basin filled by the sea at high tide, situated near the village of Cadgwith, east of Lizard Point, CORNWALL.

Devil's Hole. A name of the Peak Cavern in Derbyshire.

Devil's Island. A small island off the coast of French Guiana, formerly used as a convict settlement. Captain Alfred Dreyfus was confined there (*see* DREYFUSARD).

Devil's Lake. A lake in North Dakota, U.S.A.; also the name of a city on its shore.

Devil's Nostrils. Two vast caverns separated by a huge pillar of natural rock on the Mainland of Zetland.

Devil's Punch Bowl. A deep combe on the S.W. side of Hindhead Hills, in Surrey, scene of the murder of an unknown sailor in 1786. His assassins, Lonagan, Casey and Marshall, were hanged in chains on nearby Hindhead Common. A similar dell in Mangerton Mountain, near Killarney, has the same name.

Devil's Throat. Cromer Bay, so called from the danger to navigation.

Devil's Tower. A natural tower of volcanic rock some 600 ft. high on the Belle Fourche River, Wyoming, U.S.A.

DEVIL. IN PERSONAL NOMENCLATURE.

Devil Dick. A nickname of Richard Porson (1759–1808), Regius Professor of Greek in the University of Cambridge and an outstanding Greek scholar.

The Devil's Missionary. A nickname given to VOLTAIRE (1694–1778).

The French Devil. Jean Bart (1651–1702), French admiral and a native of Dunkirk. He was a terror to English shipping during the wars between William III and Louis XIV.

Robert the Devil. *See under* ROBERT.

Son of the Devil. Ezzelino da Romano (1194–1259), the noted GHIBELLINE leader and Governor of Vicenza; so called for his infamous cruelty.

White Devil. Vittoria Corombona, an Italian murderess whose story was dramatized (1608) by John Webster under this name. "White devils" was 16th- and 17th-century slang for prostitutes.

The White Devil of Wallachia. SCANDERBEG or George Castriota (1403–1468), the Albanian leader, was so called by the Turks.

DEVIL. IN MISCELLANEOUS TERMS AND NAMES.

Devil and bag o'nails. *See* BAG O'NAILS *under* PUBLIC-HOUSE SIGNS.

Devil on two sticks. *See* DIABOLO. It is also the English name of Le Sage's novel *Le Diable Boiteux* (1707) in which ASMODEUS features.

Devil's apple. The MANDRAKE; also the thorn apple.

Devil's bedpost. In card games, the four of clubs. *Cp.* DEVIL'S FOUR-POSTER *below*.

Devil's Bible. *See* DEVIL'S BOOKS *below*.

Devil's bird. A Scots name for the yellow bunting; from its note, *deil*.

Devil's-bit. A species of scabious, *Scabiosa succisa*, the root of which ends abruptly and is supposed to have been bitten off by the devil to destroy its usefulness to mankind.

Devil's bones. Dice, which were made of bones and led to ruin.

Devil's books, or **Devil's picture-book.** Playing cards. A PRESBYTERIAN phrase, used in reproof of the name *King's Books*, applied to a pack of cards, from the Fr. *livre des quatre rois* (the book of the four kings). Also called the **Devil's Bible.**

Devil's candle. So the Arabs call the MANDRAKE from its shining appearance at night.

Devil's candlestick. The common stinkhorn fungus. *Phallus impudicus*; also called the **devil's horn** and the **devil's stinkpot.**

Devil's coach-horse. The cock-tail beetle, *Ocypus olens*. Also called **devil's cow.**

Devil's coach-wheel. The corn crowfoot.

Devil's daughter. A shrew. *Cp.* DEVIL'S DAUGHTER'S PORTION *in* PHRASES *above*.

Devil's dozen. Thirteen; twelve and one for the Devil. *Cp.* BAKER'S DOZEN.

Devil's dung. An old pharmaceutical nickname for the *asafœtida*, an evil-smelling resinous gum.

Devil's dust. Flock and shoddy made from old rags torn up by a machine called a "devil".

> Does it beseem thee to weave cloth of devil's dust instead of true wool?
>
> CARLYLE: *Miscellanies, IV: Dr Francis* (1843).

Devil's fingers. The starfish; also belemnites.

Devil's four-poster. A hand of cards containing four clubs. It is said that there never was a good hand at WHIST containing four clubs. *Cp.* DEVIL'S BEDPOST, *above.*

Devil's guts. The long, thin, red stems of the leafless, parasitic dodder plant; also the creeping buttercup.

Devil's horn. *See* DEVIL'S CANDLESTICK, *above.*

Devil's livery. Black and yellow. Black for death, yellow for quarantine.

Devil's luck. Astounding good luck. Such lucky people were thought at one time to have compounded with the Devil.

Devil's Mass. Swearing at everybody and everything.

Devil's milk. The sun-spurge, from its poisonous milky juice.

Devil's Own, The. *See* REGIMENTAL AND DIVISIONAL NICKNAMES.

Devil's Parliament. The parliament which met at Coventry in 1459 and passed Acts of Attainder against the YORKIST leaders.

Devil's Paternoster. *See* TO SAY THE DEVIL'S PATERNOSTER *in* PHRASES *above.*

Devil's shoestrings. Goats-rue *Tephrosia virginiana*, from its tough thin roots.

Devil's snuff-box. A puff-ball of the genus *Lycoperdon*; a fungus full of dust.

Devil's stinkpot. *See* DEVIL'S CANDLESTICK *above.*

Devil's stones. The field gromwell, probably from its hard twin fruits. This plant is reputed to have contraceptive qualities.

Devonshire. The name is derived from the early CELTIC inhabitants, the Defnas. According to legend it is from Debon, one of the heroes who came with BRUTUS from TROY, and who was allotted this part of ALBION which was thus Debon's share.

> In meed of these great conquests by them gott,
> Corineus had that province utmost west ...
> And Debon's shayre was that is Devonshyre.
>
> SPENSER: *Faerie Queene*, II, x, 12.

The Devonshire Poet. O. Jones, a journeyman wool-comber who lived at the close of the 18th century. Other Devonshire poets are John Gay (1685–1732) of Barnstaple and Edward Capern (1819–1894), the postman poet of Bideford. The bell which Capern carried on his rounds still hangs in a niche on his tombstone at Heanton Punchardon.

Dew-beater. One who is out early and treads through the dew.

Dew-beaters. The feet; shoes to resist the wet.

> Hold put your dew-beaters till I take off the darbies.
>
> SCOTT: *Peveril of the Peak*, ch xxxvi.

Dew-cup, or **dew-drink.** An early morning allowance of beer formerly given to harvest-workers.

Dew Ponds. Artificial ponds or pools on the heights of the chalk downs of southern ENGLAND and elsewhere, which very rarely dry out even in the most severe drought. Formerly providing water for sheep, and known locally as "sheep ponds", their water supply depends upon rain and mist. Some date from the NEOLITHIC AGE. The pits were first lined with flints and stones, followed by a layer of straw, and finally a thick coating of puddled clay.

> Only the dewpond on the height,
> Unfed, that never fails.
>
> RUDYARD KIPLING: *Sussex.*

Dexter. A Latin word meaning "to the right-hand side", hence *dextrous* originally meant "right-handed". In HERALDRY the term *dexter* is applied to that side of the shield to the right of the person holding it, hence it is the left side of the shield as seen by the viewer.

Diable, Le. Olivier Le Dain, the tool of Louis XI, and once the king's barber. Much feared and even more disliked, he was hanged in 1484, after the king's death.

> Olivier le Dain, called sometimes Oliver le Mauvais, and sometimes Oliver le Diable, epithets derived from the unscrupulous cunning with which he assisted in the execution of the schemes of his master's tortuous policy.
>
> SCOTT: *Quentin Durward*, ch. viii.

Diabolo. A modern name for an old toy formerly called the "devil on two sticks". The "devil" is a hollow turned piece of wood, roughly the shape of two cones joined at the points. The player places the "devil" on a cord, held loosely between two sticks, and it is then made to spin by manipulating the sticks.

Diadem (Gr. *dia*, round; *deo*, bind). In ancient times the headband or fillet worn by kings as a badge of royalty was so called; it was made of silk, linen, or wool, and was tied at the back with the ends falling on the neck. The diadem of BACCHUS was a broad band which might be unfolded to make a veil. The diadem eventually became a flexible band of gold and its development and decoration became largely inseparable from that of the CROWN.

All hail the power of Jesu's Name;
Let Angels prostrate fall;
Bring forth the royal diadem
To crown him Lord of all.

EDWARD PERRONET: *Hymn*.

Dial of Ahaz. The only time-measuring device mentioned in the BIBLE. It was probably a form of sun-clock and its introduction by Ahaz may have been due to his contacts with the Assyrians. It is referred to in II *Kings* xx, 9–11 and *Is*. xxxviii, 8.

And he brought the shadow ten degrees backward, by which it had gone down in the dial of Ahaz.
II *Kings* xx, ii.

Dialectic, or **Dialectics** (Gr. *dialektikos*, belonging to discussion or disputation). Commonly used to mean abstract discussion, logic in general, or the investigation of truth by analysis, but the word has various technical implications in the language of philosophy. Under SOCRATES dialectic became a search for definition by the systematic use of question and answer, and for PLATO the method of the highest kind of speculation. For ARISTOTLE a dialective proof was a probable deduction as opposed to a scientific or demonstrative proof. From the time of the STOICS until the end of the mediæval period dialectic was synonymous with logic.

Hegel (1770–1831) gave dialectic a new meaning—the action and reaction between opposites (thesis and antithesis), out of which the new or higher synthesis emerges. *See also* MATERIALISM.

Dialectical Materialism. *See under* MATERIALISM.

Diamond (Gr *adamas*, unconquerable.) A corruption of adamant. So called because the diamond, which cuts other substances, can only be cut or polished by one of its kind. *See* CULLINAN; FLORENTINE; FRENCH PASTE; GLAUCUS; HOPE DIAMOND; KOH-I-NOOR; PITT DIAMOND; SANCY; STAR OF SOUTH AFRICA.

In Spenser's *Faerie Queene* (Bk. IV), Diamond is one of the three sons of AGAPE. He was slain by Cambell.

Diamond. In baseball the four-sided space enclosed within the four bases. In cards the suit marked with red diamond-shapes.

A diamond of the first water. A specially fine diamond, one of the greatest value for its size (the colour or lustre of a diamond is called its "water"). Thus we speak of a "genius of the first water" meaning a very great genius; "a rogue of the first water" meaning one who excels in roguery; "a blunder of the first water" meaning an outstanding blunder, etc.

A rough diamond. An uncultivated person but intrinsically of great merit; a person of excellent parts, but lacking social polish.

Black diamonds. *See under* BLACK.

Diamond cut diamond. Cunning outwitting cunning; a hard bargain over-reached; an encounter of two acute minds. A diamond is so hard that it can only be ground by diamond dust or by rubbing one against another.

He had been conducting a difficult negotiation all day of the diamond-cut-diamond order, and was tired out and disgusted by the amount of knowledge of books which even a gentleman may possess.
MRS. HUMPHRY WARD: *David Grieve*, Bk. II, ch, ii.

Diamond Jim. Jim Brady, or more correctly James Buchanan Brady (1856–1917), American speculator and philanthropist, who started life as a bell-boy in a New York hotel. A well-known character in the night life of Broadway, he attracted attention and gained this nickname from the valuable and varied diamond ornaments with which he adorned his person.

Diamond Jousts, The. Jousts instituted by King ARTHUR "who by that name had named them, since a diamond was the prize". The story as embroidered by Tennyson in his *Lancelot and Elaine* (from Malory, Bk. XVIII) is that Arthur once picked nine diamonds from the crown of a slain KNIGHT and when he became king he offered them as a prize for nine successive annual jousts, all of which were won by Sir LANCELOT. The knight attempted to present them to Queen GUINEVERE but she flung them out of the casement into the river below, through jealousy of ELAINE.

Diamond Jubilee. *See under* WEDDING ANNIVERSARIES.

Diamond Necklace, The Affair of the. A notorious scandal in French history (1784–1786) centering round Queen Marie Antoinette, Cardinal de Rohan, an ambitious profligate, and an adventuress, Jeanne, Countess de la Motte, who cleverly tricked Rohan by pretending to conduct for him a correspondence with the queen. Thus Rohan was induced to purchase for the queen (for 1,600,000 livres) the diamond necklace, originally intended for Madame du Barry, giving it to Jeanne de la Motte to pass to her. It was never delivered. When the jewellers, Boehmer and Bassenge of Paris, claimed payment, the queen denied all knowledge of the matter. The arrest of Rohan and Jeanne de la Motte followed. After a sensational trial, the Cardinal was acquitted and exiled to the abbey of *La Chaise-Dieu*, and the Countess was branded as a thief and consigned to the Salpêtrière, but subsequently escaped.

That extraordinary 'Procès du Collier Necklace Trial", spinning itself through Nine other ever-memorable Months, to the astonishment of the hundred and eighty-seven assembled *parlementiers*.

CARLYLE: *The Diamond Necklace* (1837).

Diamond Pitt. Thomas Pitt (1653–1726), East India merchant and owner of the famous PITT DIAMOND, and grandfather of the first Earl of Chatham.

Diamond Sculls, The. An annual race for amateur single scullers at the Henley Royal Regatta, first rowed in 1844. The prize is a pair of crossed silver sculls nearly a foot in length, surmounted by an imitation wreath of LAUREL, and having a pendant of diamonds. The trophy passes from winner to winner but each winner retains a silver cup.

Diana. An ancient Italian goddess identified with Artemis. Commonly regarded as a moon-goddess, on somewhat slender evidence, she was also the goddess of hunting and the woodlands. Associated with fertility, she was largely worshipped by women, and was invoked by the Romans under her three aspects. *Cp.* SELENE.

> Queen and huntress, chaste and fair,
> Now the sun is laid to sleep,
> Seated in thy silver chair,
> State in wonted manner keep.
>
> BEN JONSON: *Hymn to Diana*.

Diana of Ephesus. This statue, we are told, fell from heaven. She is represented with many breasts and with trunk and legs enclosed in an ornamental sheath. The temple of Diana of Ephesus was one of the Seven Wonders of the World (*see under* WONDER), with a roof supported by 127 columns. It was set on fire by Eratostratus for the sake of perpetuating his name.

Diana's Worshippers. Midnight revellers. So called because they return home by moonlight, and so, figuratively, put themselves under the protection of DIANA.

Great is Diana of the Ephesians. A phrase sometimes used to signify that self-interest blinds the eyes, from the story of Demetrius, the Ephesian silversmith in *Acts* xix, 24–28, who made shrines for the temple of DIANA. Demetrius stirred the people to riot, claiming that, "this Paul hath persuaded and turned away much people, saying that they be no gods, which are made with hands: so that not only this our craft is in danger to be set at naught; but also that the great goddess Diana should be despised ..." Hence their cry "Great is Diana of the Ephesians".

The Tree of Diana. *See* PHILOSOPHER'S TREE.

Diapason (dī á pā′ zon). A Greek word (short for *dia pason chordon*, through all the strings) which means an harmonious combination of notes, hence harmony itself. According to the Pythagorean system (*see* PYTHAGORAS) the world is a piece of harmony and man the full chord.

> From harmony, from heavenly harmony
> This universal frame began;
> From harmony to harmony
> Through all the compass of the notes it ran,
> The diapason closing full in man.
>
> DRYDEN: *Song for St. Cecilia's Day*.

Diavolo. Another form of DIABOLO.

Diavolo, Fra. Michele Pozza (1771–1806), an Italian brigand and enemy of the French occupation, renowned for his atrocities. He features in Auber's light opera of this name.

Dibs. Money. *Cp.* TIP. The knuckle-bones of sheep used for gambling games were called *dibbs* and stones used for the same purpose were called *dibstones*.

Dicers' oaths. False as dicers' oaths. Worthless or untrustworthy, as when a gambler swears never to touch dice again (*see* *Hamlet*, III, iv).

Dick. Slang for detective.

A clever dick. A know-all, a SMART ALEC.

Dick Turpin. *See* TURPIN.

Dick Whittington. *See* WHITTINGTON.

Dirty Dick's. *See under* DIRT.

King Dick. A scornful term for Richard Cromwell (1626–1712), who succeeded his father Oliver as Lord protector in September 1658 and showed no capacity to govern. *See also* TUMBLEDOWN DICK.

Dick's hatband. A popular reference to Richard Cromwell's "crown" as in:

> *Dick's hatband was made of sand*. His regal honours were a "rope of sand".
> *As queer as Dick's hatband*. Few things have been more ridiculous than the exaltation and abdication of Oliver's son.
> *As tight as Dick's hatband*. The crown was too tight for him to wear with safety.

Queen Dick, That happened in the reign of Queen Dick *i.e.* NEVER; there never was a Queen Richard.

Tumbledown Dick. Anything that will not stand firmly. "Dick" is KING DICK (*see above*), who was but a tottering wall at best.

Dickens. To play the dickens. To play the devil. *Dickens* here is probably a EUPHEMISM for the DEVIL or OLD NICK, and is nothing to do with Charles Dickens.

What the dickens. What the devil. *See* TO PLAY THE DICKENS *above*.

> I cannot tell what the dickens his name is.
> SHAKESPEARE: *Merry Wives of Windsor*, III, ii.

Dickey, or Dicky. In George III's time, a flannel petticoat.

> A hundred instances I soon could pick ye—
> Without a cap we view the fair,

The bosom heaving also bare,
The hips ashamed, forsooth to wear a dicky.
PETER PINDAR: *Lord Auckland's Triumph*.

It was afterwards applied to what were called false shirts—*i.e.* a starched shirt front worn over another; also to leather aprons and children's bibs. It was also applied to the driver's seat in a carriage and the servant's seat behind. In the earlier "two-seater" motor-cars the dickey was the additional seating at the rear, where the occupants were exposed to the weather in the space corresponding to the *boot* of later models.

Dickey. A donkey; especially in East Anglia, where it was anciently called Dickass or dicky-ass. It is a term of endearment, as we call a little bird a *dicky-bird*. The ass is also called Dicky (little Richard), CUDDY, NEDDY, Jack-ass, MOKE or MIKE.

Dicky Sam. A native born inhabitant of Liverpool. *Cp.* TIM BOBBIN.

Dictys Cretensis (Dictys of Crete). A companion of Idomeneus at TROY and reputed author of an eyewitness account of the siege of Troy. The manuscript was probably written in the 2nd or 3rd century A.D. and translated into Latin in the 4th century. It is important as the chief source used by mediæval writers on the Trojan legend.

Didache (Gr. teaching). An early Christian treatise, also known as *The Teaching of the Twelve Apostles*, probably belonging to the late 1st or early 2nd century. It was discovered in the Patriarchal Library at Constantinople in 1875 and falls into two parts. The first is concerned with moral teachings and is based on an earlier document, seemingly of Jewish origin, called *The Two Ways*, with additions from the Sermon on the Mount, etc. The second part is concerned with church ordinances.

Diderick. *See* DIETRICH.

Dido, also called Elissa, was the legendary daughter of Belus of Tyre and founder Queen of Carthage, after the murder of her husband Sichæus by PYGMALION. According to VIRGIL's *Æneid* she fell in love with Æneas, who was driven by a storm to her shores, and committed herself to the flames through grief at his departure. Older legend says that she did it to avoid marriage with the king of Libya.

Porson (*see* DEVIL DICK) said he could rhyme on any subject; and being asked to rhyme upon the three Latin gerunds, which appeared in the old Eton Latin grammar as *-di, -do, -dum*, gave this couplet:

When Dido found Æneas would not come,
She mourned in silence and was Di-do-dum(b).

Cutting a dido, or **dancing dido.** The American equivalent of cutting a CAPER. The phrase appears as early as 1807 in the autobiographical work *A Narrative of the Life and Travels of John Robert Shaw, the Well-Digger*. Its origin is unknown but it has been fancifully suggested that Dido, Queen of Carthage, by a smart piece of work, managed to secure more land than she had agreed to buy, on which she built the city of Carthage.

Didymus (did′ i mŭs). This Greek word for a twin was applied to St. THOMAS, as the name Thomas in Aramaic means a twin.

Die. The die is cast. The step is taken and there is no drawing back. So said Julius CÆSAR when he crossed the RUBICON—*jacta alea est! Die* here is ultimately from Lat. *datum*, given.

I have set my life upon a cast,
And I will stand the hazard of the die.
SHAKESPEARE: *Richard III*, V, iv.

Die. Never say die. Never despair; never give up. *Die* here is "to cease to live".

To die in harness. To die working, while still in active employment or before retirement; like the draught horse which drops dead between the shafts of a cart, or the soldier who dies fighting in harness [armour].

Blow, wind! come wrack!
At least we'll die with harness on our back.
SHAKESPEARE: *Macbeth*, V, v.

To die in the last ditch. To fight to the death or last gasp.

"There is one certain means," replied the Prince William of Orange, "by which I can be sure never to see my country's ruin—I will die in the last ditch."
HUME: *History of England*.

What did your last servant die of? Said to someone who is expecting you to help and work like a galley slave doing one thing after another — asking a bit too much. An expression from the days when household servants were often grossly overworked from morning till night.

Whom the gods love die young. This is from Menander—*Hon hoi theoi philousin apothneskei neos*. Demosthenes has a similar apophthegm. Plautus has the line, *Quem di diligunt adolescens moritur* (*Bacch.* IV, vii, 18).

Die-hards. In political phraseology those members of a party who refuse to abandon long-held theories and attitudes regardless of the changes that time and situation may bring. They would rather "DIE IN THE LAST DITCH" than give way.

Die-hards, The. *See* REGIMENTAL AND DIVISIONAL NICKNAMES.

Dies (dī′ ēz). **Dies Alliensis.** *See* ALLIENSIS.

Dies Iræ (Lat. Day of Wrath). A famous mediæval hymn on the Last JUDGMENT, probably the composition of Thomas of Celano (in the Abruzzi), who died *c.* 1255. It is derived from the VULGATE version of *Zeph* i, 15, and is used by Roman Catholics in the MASS for the Dead and on ALL SOULS' DAY. Scott has introduced the opening into his *Lay of the Last Minstrel* (Canto vi, xxx).

> Dies iræ, dies illa
> Solvet sæclum in favilla.

Dies nefastus (Lat. *dies*, day, *nefas*, that which is contrary to divine law, sinful), An unlucky or inauspicious day. For the Romans *Dies nefasti* were days on which no judgment could be pronounced nor any public business transacted. *See* ALLIENSIS.

Dies non (Lat. a "not" day). A non-business day, a contracted form of *Dies non juridicus*, a non-judicial day, when the courts do not sit and legal business is not transacted, as SUNDAYS; the PURIFICATION in HILARY TERM; the ASCENSION, in EASTER term; and ALL SAINTS' Day, with ALL SOULS' in MICHAELMAS term.

Dietrich of Bern (dē' trik). The name given by the German MINNESINGER to THEODORIC the Great (*c.* 454–526), King of the Ostrogoths (Bern=Verona). He appears as a liegeman of King ETZEL in the NIBELUNGENLIED and other Middle High German poems.

Dieu. et mon droit (dyĕ ā mō drwa') (Fr. God and my right). The parole of Richard I at the battle of Gisors (1198), meaning that he was no vassal of France, but owed his royalty to God alone. The French were signally beaten, but the battle-word does not seem to have been adopted as the royal motto of ENGLAND till the time of Henry VI.

Difference. When Ophelia is distributing flowers (*Hamlet*, IV, v) and says: "You must wear your rue with a difference", she is using the word in the heraldic sense, probably implying that she and the queen were *to rue*; herself as the affianced of Hamlet, eldest son of the late king; the queen with a *difference* as the wife of Claudius, the late king's brother, and therefore the cadet branch.

In HERALDRY *differences* or *marks of cadency* indicate the various branches of a family. The eldest son, during the lifetime of his father, bears a *label, i.e.* a bar or fillet having three pendants often now shaped like a dovetail. The second son bears a *crescent*. The third, a *mullet* (*i.e.* a star with five points). The fourth, a *martlet*. The fifth, an *annulet*. The sixth, a *fleur-de-lis*. The seventh, a *rose*. The eighth, a *cross-moline*. The ninth, a *double quatrefoil*.

To difference is to make different by the superimposition of a further symbol.

Digest. A compendium, synopsis, or summary, especially the *Digest* of Roman Law, or PANDECTS, compiled by Tribonian and his sixteen assistants (530–533) by order of Justinian.

Digger. An Australian. The name was in use before 1850, consequent upon the discovery of GOLD, and was applied to ANZAC troops fighting in Flanders in World War I and again in World War II.

Diggers. A small group of extreme RADICALS and social revolutionaries under Winstanley who began to dig the common at St. George's Hill, Surrey in 1649. Their aim was to give back the land to the common people, but they were soon suppressed by the Cromwellian army leaders. *Cp.* LEVELLERS.

In the U.S.A. the name has been adopted by those HIPPIES given to helping others, especially fellow hippies.

Diggings, or digs. Lodgings, rooms. A word imported from California and its gold diggings.

> My friend here wants to take diggings; and as you were complaining that you would get someone to go halves with you, I thought I had better bring you together.
> SIR ARTHUR CONAN DOYLE: *A Study in Scarlet*, ch. 1.

Digits (Lat *digitus*, a finger). The first nine numerals are so called from the habit of counting as far as ten on the fingers.

Dii Penates (dī' i pe nā' tēz) (Lat.). Household gods; now colloquially used for specially prized household possessions. *See* LARES AND PENATES.

Dilemma. The horns of a dilemma. A difficult choice in which the alternatives appear equally distasteful or undesirable. "Lemma" means an assumption, a thing taken for granted (Gr. *lambanein*, to take). "Dilemma" is a double lemma, a two-edged sword, called by the SCHOOLMEN *argumentum cornutum*, or a bull which will toss you whichever horn you lay hold upon. Thus:

> A young rhetorician said to an old sophist, "Teach me to plead, and I will pay you when I gain a cause." When his old tutor sued for payment, he argued, "If I gain the cause I shall not pay you, because the judge will say I am not to pay; and if I lose my case I shall not be required to pay, according to the terms of our agreement." To this the master replied: "Not so; if you gain your cause you must pay me according to the terms of our agreement; and if you lose your cause the judge will condemn you to pay me."

Diligence. A four wheeled stage-coach common in France before the days of the railway. The word meant speed, dispatch, promptitude, as in Shakespeare's "If your diligence be not speedy I shall be there before you" (*King Lear*, I, v).

Dilly. A stage-coach, as in the Derby Dilly. The word is an abbreviation of *diligence*.

Dime (U.S.A.). A ten-cent piece. From French *dîme* (tithe).

Dime novel (U.S.A.). A cheap and lurid publication, formerly obtainable for a dime. *Cp.* PENNY-DREADFUL.

Dimensions. *See* FOURTH DIMENSION.

Dimissory. A letter dimissory is a letter from the bishop of one diocese to some other bishop, giving leave for the bearer to be ordained by him (Lat. *dimittere*, to send away).

Dimity. Stout cotton cloth woven with raised patterns. It has been said to be so called from Damietta, in Egypt, but is really from Gr. *dimitos*, double-thread. *Cp.* SAMITE.

Dine. To dine with Democritus. To be cheated out of one's dinner. DEMOCRITUS was the derider, or philosopher who laughed at men's folly.

To dine with Duke Humphrey; to dine with Sir Thomas Gresham. To go dinnerless. *See* HUMPHREY.

To dine with Mohammed. To die, and dine in paradise.

To dine with the cross-legged knights. To have no dinner at all. The knights referred to are the stone effigies of the TEMPLE Church where lawyers once met their clients and where vagabonds loitered in the hope of being hired as witnesses. *See* CROSSLEGGED KNIGHTS. *Cp.* TO DINE WITH DUKE HUMPHREY.

Dingbats. An Australian colloquial term for *delirium tremens*.

Ding-dong. A ding-dong battle. A fight in good earnest. Ding-dong is an onomatopœic word reproducing the sound of a bell; the idea is that the blows fall regularly and steadily, like the hammer-strokes of a bell.

Dinkum (Austr.). Genuine, sincere, honest. The word probably derives from English country dialect. Also applied especially to the second shipment of ANZACS sent abroad in World War I. The third shipment were called "Superdinkums". A "dinkum-Aussie" denotes a native-born Australian.

Dinkum oil (Austr.). Genuine information.

Hard dinkum meaning hard work was first used in Australia by Rolf Boldrewood in *Robbery Under Arms* (1881).

Dinmont. *See* SHEEP.

Dinnyhayser (Austr.). A knock-out blow, as delivered by the fighter Dinny Hayes.

Dinos. *See* FAMOUS HORSES *under* HORSES.

Dint. By dint of war; by dint of argument; by dint of hard work. Dint means a blow or striking (O.E. *dynt*); whence perseverance, power exerted, force; it also means the indentation made by a blow, now *dent*.

> Strong were our sires, and as they fought they writ,
> Conquering with force of arms and dint of wit.
> DRYDEN: *To Mr. Congreve, On The Double Dealer.*

Diogenes (dī oj' ė nēz). Founder of the CYNIC sect at Athens (*c.* 400–*c.* 325 B.C.), who, according to Seneca, lived in a tub. ALEXANDER THE GREAT so admired him that he said, "If I were not Alexander I would wish to be Diogenes."

> The whole world was not half so wide
> To Alexander, when he cry'd
> Because he had but one to subdue
> As was a paltry narrow tub to
> Diogenes.
> BUTLER: *Hudibras*, I, iii.

Diogenes Crab. A West Indian hermit crab which lives in another creature's shell as Diogenes in his tub.

Diogenes Cup. The cup-like hollow formed by the palm of the hand with closed fingers bent upward. An allusion to the philosopher's simple mode of life.

Diomedes (dī ō mē' dėz), or **Diomed.** In Greek legend, a hero of the siege of TROY, second only to ACHILLES in bravery. With ULYSSES he removed the PALLADIUM from TROY. He appears as the lover of CRESSIDA in Boccaccio's *Filostrato* and in later works.

Also the name of a king in Thrace, son of ARES, who fed his horses on human flesh. One of the labours of HERCULES was to destroy Diomedes and his body was thrown to his own horses to be devoured.

Diomedean exchange. One in which all the benefit is on one side. The expression is founded on an incident related in the ILIAD. GLAUCUS recognizes Diomed on the battlefield, and the friends change armour:

> For Diomed's brass arms, of mean device,
> For which nine oxen paid (a vulgar price),
> He gave his own, of gold divinely wrought,
> An hundred beeves the shining purchase bought.
> POPE: Iliad, VI.

Dione (dī ō' ni). Daughter of OCEANUS and TETHYS and mother by JUPITER of VENUS. Also applied to Venus herself; Julius CÆSAR, who claimed descent from her, was sometimes called *Dionœus Cæsar*.

> So young Dione, nursed beneath the waves,
> And rocked by Nereids in their coral caves ...
> Lisped her sweet tones, and tried her tender smiles.
> ERASMUS DARWIN: *Economy of Vegetation*, ii.

Dionysia. *See* BACCHANALIA.

Dionysius, St. *See* DENYS.

Dionysius's Ear. *See under* EAR.

Dionysus (Dī ō nī' sùs). *See* BACCHUS.

Dioscuri. CASTOR AND POLLUX (Gr. *Dios Kouroi*, sons of ZEUS).

The horses of the Dioscuri. Cyllaros and Harpagus. *See* HORSE.

Dip, or **angle of dip.** The angle between a freely suspended needle and the horizontal. It is zero at the magnetic equator, where the needle rests horizontal, and 90 degrees at the magnetic poles. In geology it is the angle between the horizontal and the line of greatest slope of a stratum.

Dip. A candle made by dipping the cotton wick into melted tallow.

A farthing dip. A synonym for something almost valueless. *Cp.* NOT WORTH A RUSH *under* RUSH.

A lucky dip. A bran tub or other receptacle into which the hand is dipped to withdraw a prize or present at random.

The dip of the horizon is the apparent slope of the horizon as seen by an observer standing above sea-level. This slope is due to the convexity of the earth.

To dip snuff (U.S.A.). A once prevalent habit in the southern states of dipping a stick into snuff and smearing it on the teeth and gums.

To dip a flag. *See under* FLAG.

To dip the headlights of a car is to lower them, usually when meeting oncoming traffic.

To go for a dip. To go bathing.

Diphthera (dif' thē rà) (Gr.). A piece of prepared hide or leather; specifically the skin of the goat AMALTHEA on which JOVE wrote the destiny of man.

Diphtheria. An infectious disease of the throat; is so called from its tendency to form a false membrane.

Diplomat. One provided with a diploma or letter authorizing him to represent his government abroad.

A diplomatic cold, illness, etc. When indisposition is pleaded as a tactful excuse for avoiding a meeting or engagement which might prove awkward or embarrassing.

Diplomatic. The scientific study of the official sources of history, namely characters, treaties, statutes, registers, etc., as opposed to literary and other sources. The name comes from an extended use of the Latin word *diploma* for an historical document. As a modern study it was largely established by one of the BOLLANDISTS, Jean Mabillon, with his famous text-book *De re diplomatica* which appeared in 1681. His work was further advanced by Dom Toustain and Dom Tassin in their six-volume *Nouveau Traité de Diplomatique* (1750–1765).

Diplomatic Revolution. A phrase specifically applied to the reversal of alliances in 1756 under which Austria, France, Prussia and Great Britain had fought the War of the Austrian succession, with the result that, in the ensuing SEVEN YEARS WAR, France and her former enemy Austria fought against Great Britain and her former enemy Prussia.

Dipper. An old name for the seven principal stars of the constellation URSA MAJOR (Great Bear); also known as the Plough or CHARLES'S WAIN. The name is derived from the supposed resemblance to the kitchen utensil of this name—a pan with a long handle.

Dircæan Swan. Pindar (518–438 B.C.), so called from the fountain of Dirce near Thebes, the poet's birthplace. Dirce was changed into a fountain by the gods, out of pity for the sufferings inflicted upon her by the sons of Antiope, who were avenging torments she had imposed upon their mother.

Direct action. To seek to attain industrial or political ends by coercive action such as strikes, etc., as opposed to industrial or political negotiation and agitation.

Direct tax. Taxation such as income tax or land tax collected directly from the individual liable for such tax. *Indirect taxes* are those levied on marketable commodities, etc., which are thus paid by the citizen indirectly.

Directory, The. The French constitution of 1795 which vested the executive authority in five Directors. The "Five Majesties" were Barras, Ruebell, Sieyès, Letourneur, and La Revellière. Sieyès retired at the outset and was replaced by Carnot. Its rule was ended by NAPOLEON's *coup d'état* of 18 BRUMAIRE (9 November) 1799 and the Consulate was established in its place.

Dirleton. Doubting with Dirleton, and resolving those doubts with Stewart. Doubting and answering those doubts, but doubting still. It is a Scottish phrase and the allusion is to the *Doubts and Questions in Law* (1698), by Sir John Nisbet of Dirleton, the Lord President, and Sir James Stewart's *Dirleton's Doubts and Questions ... Resolved and Answered* (1715). Of the former work Lord Chancellor Hardwicke remarked, "His *Doubts* are better than most people's *certainties*."

Dirt (M.E. *drit* probably from Icel. *drit*, excrement). It has been extended to include filth generally, soil, dust, etc., and obscenity of any kind, especially language.

Pay dirt. Soil containing gold or diamonds, whichever is being sought.

Dirt cheap. Very low-priced, as cheap as dirt.

Throw plenty of dirt and some will be

sure to stick. Scandal always leaves a trail behind; some of it will be believed. In Lat., *Fortiter calumniari, aliquid adhœrebit*.

To eat dirt. To put up with insults and mortification.

Dirt-track racing. Motor-cycle racing on a track of cinders or similar material; introduced into England from Australia in 1928.

Dirty Dick's. A tavern in Bishopsgate, London, the interior of which is festooned with cobwebs and grimed with dirt. The name was taken from the once famous *Dirty Warehouse* in Leadenhall Street, owned by Nathaniel Bentley (*c*. 1735–1809). Brought up in easy circumstances and a frequent visitor to Paris, he was known as the Beau of Leadenhall Street, but suddenly his mode of life altered completely to one of miserly squalor and he came to be called "Dirty Dick". His hardware store became famous for its dirt and decay which increased with the years and after his death some of its contents were bought by the tavern keeper to attract custom. Bentley's change from a man of fashion to excessive slovenliness was reputedly the consequence of a broken engagement.

Dirty Half-Hundred, The. *See* REGIMENTAL AND DIVISIONAL NICKNAMES.

Dirty money. Money acquired by dishonest or disreputable means.

Dirty Shirts, The. *See* REGIMENTAL AND DIVISIONAL NICKNAMES.

Dirty Warehouse. *See* DIRTY DICK'S.

Dirty word. An obscene word; also currently used of something which has become socially or politically unpopular or suspect, often through unmerited criticism and denigration or from being out of line with current trends.

Disastrous Peace, The (*La Paix Malheureuse*). The Treaty of Cateau-Cambrésis (1559), essentially between France and Spain. It recognized Spanish supremacy in Italy and involved renunciation of the VALOIS claims there.

Disc. Disc Jockey. The established name for those who present broadcast programmes of gramophone records or discs, interspersed with commentary. Christopher Stone (1882—1965) was the pioneer of such performances in England.

Discalced. *See* BAREFOOTED.

Discharge Bible, The. *See* BIBLE, SOME SPECIALLY NAMED EDITIONS.

Disciples of Christ. *See* CAMPBELLITES.

Discipline, A. A scourge used for penitential purposes.

> Before the cross and altar, ... a lamp was still burning, ... and on the floor lay a discipline, or peniten-

tial scourge of small cord and wire, the lashes of which were stained with recent blood.
> SCOTT: *The Talisman*, ch. iv.

This is a transferred sense of one of the ecclesiastical uses of the word—the mortification of the flesh by penance.

Discipline, Books of. The books which formed the basis of the constitution and procedure of the CHURCH OF SCOTLAND after the REFORMATION. The first was drawn up under John Knox in 1566, and the second, which amplified the first, between 1575 and 1578.

Discord. Literally, severance of hearts (Lat. *discorda*). It is the opposite of *concord*, the coming together of hearts. In music it means disagreement of sounds, as when a note is followed by, or played with another which is disagreeable to a musical ear.

Apple of Discord. *See* APPLE.

Discount. At a discount. Not in demand; little valued; less esteemed than formerly; below PAR (Med. Lat. *dis-computare*, to deduct, to discount).

Dished. I was dished out of it. Cheated out of it; or rather, someone else contrived to obtain it. When one is *dished* or *dished up* he is completely done for, and the allusion is to food which, when it is quite *done*, is *dished*. Thus Disraeli "dished the Whigs" with his Reform Bill of 1867.

> Where's Brummel? Dished!
> BYRON: *Don Juan*.

Disjecta membra (dis yek' tà mem' brà) (Lat.). Scattered limbs, remains, fragments. The phrase occurs in Ovid (*Met*., III, 724) and HORACE has "*Etiam disjecti membra poetæ*" (*Sat*., I, iv. 62).

Dismal Science. *See* SCIENCE.

Dismas, St. *See* DYSMAS.

Dispensation (Lat. *dispensatio*, from *dis-* and *pendere*, to dispense, distribute, arrange). The system which God chooses to dispense or establish between himself and man. The dispensation of ADAM was between Adam and God; the dispensation of ABRAHAM, and that of MOSES, were those imparted to these holy men; the GOSPEL dispensation is that explained in the Gospels.

A Papal dispensation. Permission from the POPE to dispense with something enjoined; a licence to do what is forbidden, or to omit what is commanded by the law of the ROMAN CATHOLIC CHURCH.

> A Papal dispensation enabled Catherine to wed the brother of her late husband, the younger sovereign himself.
> J.R. GREEN: *History of the English People*, ch. vi.

Displaced Persons. A phrase applied to the

millions of homeless and uprooted people in Europe, India and Asia whose misfortunes were due to the havoc produced by World War II and subsequent events.

Dissenters. In England another name for the NONCONFORMISTS and commonly used from the RESTORATION until the 19th century, when it gradually fell into disuse.

Distaff. The staff from which the flax was drawn in spinning; hence, figuratively, woman's work, and a woman herself, in allusion to what was women's common daily task. *Cp.* SPINSTER.

> I blush that we should owe our lives to such
> A king of distaffs!
>
> BYRON: *Sardanapalus*, II, i.

St. Distaff's Day. 7 JANUARY. So called because the CHRISTMAS festival terminated on Twelfth Day, and on the day following the women returned to their distaffs or daily occupations. *Cp.* PLOUGH MONDAY.

> Give St. Distaff all the right,
> Then give Christmas sport good night,
> And next morrow every one
> To his own vocation.—(1657).

It is also called ROCK DAY, "rock" being an old name for the distaff.

> What! shall a woman with a rock drive thee away?
> Fye on thee, traitor!
>
> *Digby Mysteries.*

The distaff side. The female side of a family; a branch descended from the female side. *See also* SPINDLE-SIDE.

To have tow on the distaff. To have work, or serious business on hand.

> He hadde more tow on his distaff
> Than Gerveys knew.
>
> CHAUCER: *Miller's Tale*, 558.

Distrain. To seize goods for non-payment, to coerce by exacting fines, etc. (Lat. *distringere*, to pull asunder, to draw tight.).

Distraint of Knighthood. The compelling of persons with lands of certain value and tenants of KNIGHTS fees to become knights and assume the obligations and liabilities of such rank (relief, wardship, SCUTAGE, etc.). It was introduced in the reign of Henry III (1216–1272). The fines levied by Charles I on those who neglected this obligation angered many of the gentry. It was abolished by the LONG PARLIAMENT in 1641.

Dithyramb (dith i răm') (Gr. *dithyrambos*, a choric hymn). *Dithyrambic poetry* was originally a wild impetuous kind of Dorian lyric in honours of BACCHUS, traditionally ascribed to the invention of ARION of Lesbos who gave it a more definite form (*c*. 600 B.C.) and who has hence been called the father of dithyrambic poetry.

Dittany (dit' à ni). This plant (*Origanum dic-*

tamnus), so named from Dicte in Crete, where it grew in profusion, was anciently credited with many medicinal virtues, especially in enabling arrows to be drawn from wounds and curing such wounds. In Tasso's JERUSALEM DELIVERED (Bk. IX) Godfrey is healed in this way.

> Stags and hinds, when deeply wounded with darts, arrows, and bolts, if they do but meet the herb called dittany, which is common in Candia, and eat a little of it, presently the shafts come out, and all is well again; even as kind Venus cured her beloved by-blow Æneas.
>
> RABELAIS (URQUHART and MOTTEUX), Bk. IV, ch. lxii.

Ditto (dit' ō) (Ital. *detto*, said; from Lat. *dictum*). That which has been said before; the same or a similar thing. In writing the word is often contracted to *do*.

Dittoes, or **a suit of dittoes.** Coat, waistcoat, and trousers to match, all alike.

To say ditto. To endorse or agree with somebody else's expressed opinion.

Divan (Turk. and Pers.). A countinghouse, a tribunal; hence the account book or register; the office or room where they are kept; a collection of poems; a long seat or bench covered with cushions; a court of justice and custom-house (whence, Fr. *douane*). The order of derivation is not certain but the word in its ramifications and extensions is rather like our BOARD. In England its chief meanings are a sofa without back or sides, a low bed, and formerly a coffee-house used for smoking.

Divan of the Sublime Porte. The former council of the Turkish Empire presided over by the Grand VIZIER.

Dives (Dī' vēz). The name popularly given to the rich man (Lat. *dives*) in the parable of the Rich Man and LAZARUS (*Luke* xvi, 19).

> Lazar and Dives liveden diversely
> And diverse guerdon haddon they ther-by.
>
> CHAUCER: *Somnour's Tale*, 169.

Divide. When the members in the British HOUSE OF COMMONS interrupt a speaker by crying out *Divide*, they mean, bring the debate to an end and put the motion to the vote—*i.e.* let the ayes divide from the noes, one group going into one LOBBY, and the others into another.

Divide and rule, or **govern** (Lat. *divide et impera*). Divide a nation into parties or set people at loggerheads and you can have your own way or exercise control.

> Every city or house divided against itself shall not stand.
>
> *Matt.* xii, 25.

Divination. There are numerous forms of divination. The following appear in the BIBLE: ASTROLOGY (Judicial) (*Dan*. ii, 2).

CASTING LOTS (*See* LOTS) (*Josh*, xviii, 6).
HEPATOSCOPY (*Ezek*. xxi, 21–26).
ONEIROMANCY (*Gen*. xxxvii, 10).
NECROMANCY (I *Sam*. xxviii, 12–20).
RHABDOMANCY (*Hos*. iv, 12).
TERAPHIM (*Gen*. xxxi, *Zech*. x, 2).
WITCHCRAFT (I *Sam*. xxviii).

There are numerous other references including divination by fire, air, and water; thunder, lightning, meteors, etc. Consult: *Gen*. xxxvii, 5–11; xl, xli; I *Sam*. xxviii; II Kings xvii, 17; II *Chron*. xxxiii, 6; *Prov*. xvi, 33; *Ezek*. xxi, iii, 4, etc. *See also* ALECTRYOMANCY; AUGURY; AXINOMANCY; BELOMANCY; BIBLIOMANCY; BOTANOMANCY; CHIROMANCY; CRYSTALLOMANCY; DIVINATION BY CUP *under* CUP; EMPYROMANCY; EXTISPICY; GEOMANCY; GYROMANCY; HARUSPEX; OMENS; PALMISTRY; PYROMANCY; RUNE; SIEVE AND SHEARS; SINISTER; SORTES; URIM AND THUMMIN; XYLOMANCY; WITCH OF ENDOR. *See also* ORACLE.

Divine, The. Theophrastus (*c*. 372–*c*. 287 B.C.), the philosopher pupil of PLATO and whose name means *the Divine Speaker*, is said to have changed his name from Tyrtamus when this epithet was bestowed upon him by ARISTOTLE.

Hypatia (*c*. 370–415), daughter of Theon, who presided over the Neoplatonic School at Alexandria, was known as *the Divine* Pagan.

Jean de Ruysbroeck (1293–1381), the ECSTATIC DOCTOR, was also called the *Divine Doctor*.

Michelangelo (1475–1564) was called the *Divine Madman*.

Ariosto (1474–1533), the Italian poet; Raphael (1483–1520), the painter; Luis de Morales (*c*. 1509–1586), Spanish religious painter; and Fernando de Herrera (1534–1597), Spanish lyric poet, were all known as *the Divine. See also* ST. JOHN THE DIVINE *under* JOHN.

The Divine Plant. Vervain. *See* HERBA SACRA.

The Divine Right of Kings. A theory, of mediæval origin, that kings reign by divine ordination, was first formulated in a rudimentary way during the struggle between the Papacy and the Empire. It was developed more fully to strengthen the European monarchies when they were later threatened by the activities of PROTESTANT and CATHOLIC extremists and others. Monarchy based on primogeniture was held to be divinely anointed and therefore unquestioning obedience could be demanded from subjects. Monarchs were responsible to God alone and their model was the patriarchal rule portrayed in the OLD TESTAMENT. The theory was expounded fully by James I in his *True Law of Free Monarchies* (1598) and in Sir Robert Filmer's *Patriarcha* (1642—published 1680). Divine Right was destroyed in Great Britain by the GLORIOUS REVOLUTION of 1688.

The Right Divine of Kings to govern wrong.
POPE: *Dunciad*, IV, 188.

Divining Rod, or **virgula divina,** also called AARON'S ROD or the *Wand of Mercury*. It is usually a forked branch of hazel or willow which when manipulated by the diviner or *dowser* inclines towards the place where a concealed spring or a metallic lode is to be found. The Romans used the *virgular divina* in AUGURY and the forked twig, or *virgula furcata*, was introduced into the Cornish mines from Germany in the reign of Elizabeth I. With the decline of mining in the West Country dowsing is now confined to waterfinding.

"Pray, Mr. Dousterswivel ... will you assist us with your triangular vial of May-dew, or with your divining-rod of witch's hazel?"
SCOTT: *The Antiquary*, ch. xxiii.

Divison. The sign $\div$ for division was introduced by John Pell (1611–1685), the noted Cambridge mathematician who became professor of Mathematics at Amsterdam in 1643.

In the military sense a *division* (originated by Napoleon) is the largest formation in an army, so designed as to be self-contained and capable of operating independently. It normally contains infantry, mechanized units, engineers, signals, etc. There are also specialized armoured divisions.

Division of labour. The division of an employment or manufacture into particular parts so that each individual is concerned with one part or process of the whole. Adam Smith in his *Wealth of Nations* (1776) argued strongly in its favour.

Divisions. In the Royal Navy the formal morning parade of officers and ship's company is so called, the custom being introduced by Kempenfelt in 1780. The name derives from the fact that the ship's complement is customarily divided or organized into parts of ship or divisions, usually Quarterdeck, Maintop, Foretop, and Forecastle. Divisions are subdivided into watches. *See* WATCH.

Divisionist technique. *See* POINTILLISME.

Divorcement. A Bill of Divorcement is a phrase from former days of divorce procedure. Before the Matrimonial Causes Act, 1857, "divorce", or in effect judicial separation, could be granted only by the ecclesiastical courts, but remarriage was prohibited except when a special bill was promoted and passed in PARLIAMENT for either of the parties. Few could afford such an expensive process. *See* A VINCULO MATRIMONII.

Divus (dī' vŭs) (Lat. a god; godlike). After the Augustan period this was conferred as an epithet on deceased Roman Emperors proclaiming them "of blessed memory" rather than enrolling them among the gods.

Dix. One-time American slang for a ten-dollar bill, apparently derived from the fact that a bank in New Orleans used to issue ten-dollar bills with the French word *dix* (ten) printed on the back.

Dixie or **Dixieland** is a popular name for the southern states of the U.S.A., south of the MASON-DIXON LINE. One suggestion is that the name originated from *Dix*. Another is that it derives from *Dixieland*, the estate of a kind slave-owner, Dixie, on Manhattan Island, whose slaves lamented Dixie when transferred South. *Dixieland* also denotes the type of JAZZ played in New Orleans about 1910.

Dixiecrat, or **Dixiegop.** In the U.S.A. those BOURBON members of the Democratic Party in the southern states who stand for the retention of white supremacy over the Negroes.

Dixie, the oval-shaped army cooking kettle is from the Hindi *degshi*, a pot or vessel. Its naval counterpart is called a FANNY.

Dizzy. A nickname of Benjamin Disraeli, Earl of Beaconsfield (1804–1881), Queen Victoria's favourite Prime Minster. *See* PRIMROSE DAY.

Djinn. *See* JINN.

Djinnestan. The realms of the jinns or genii of Oriental mythology.

Do. *See* DITTO, DOH.

Do. A verb and auxiliary that forms part of countless phrases and has equally numerous uses. Some chief modern significations are:

1. Transitive: To put, as in *To do to death*; to bestow, cause to render, give, etc., as, *It did him no harm, To do a good turn*; to perform, perpetrate, effect, etc., as *To do one's work, Thou shalt do no murder, All is done and finished.*

2. Intransitive: To exert actively, act, make an end, fare, suffice, etc., as *Let us do or die, I have done with you, How do you do? I'm doing very well, That will do.*

3. Casual and Auxiliary: Used instead of a preceding verb, as *He plays as well as you do.* Periphrastically as an auxiliary of the Present and Past Indicative and the Imperative, used for the sake of emphasis, euphony, or clarity, also in negative and interrogative sentences: *I do wish you would let me alone, Not a word did he say, Billiards and drinking do make the money fly, Do you like jazz? I do not care for it, Do tell me where you have been! don't stop!*

A do. A regular swindle, a fraud; a party.

Do as you would be done by. Behave to others as you would have them behave to you.

Do-it-yourself. A post-World War II phrase applied primarily to the efforts of the amateur house-repairer, improver, and decorator, etc., but also more widely applied to many forms of self-help. A "do-it-yourself" shop is one which caters for the growing needs of the amateur decorator, furniture repairer, etc.

To do away with. To abolish, put an end to, destroy entirely.

To do for. To act for or manage for. *A man ought to do well for his children*; a landlady *does for* her lodgers. Also to ruin, destroy, wear out. *I'll do for him*, I'll ruin him utterly, or even, I'll kill him; *taken in and done for*, cheated and fleeced; *this watch is about done for*, it's nearly worn out.

To do it on one's head. Said of doing something with consummate ease; "I bet you couldn't walk a mile in seven minutes"; "Nonsense! I could do it on my head."

To do on. *See* DON.

To do one, to do one down, or **brown, to do one out of something.** To cheat or trick one out of something; to get the better of one.

To do one proud. To make much of one; to treat one in an exceptionally lavish and hospitable way.

To do oneself proud, or **well.** To give oneself a treat.

To do someone in. A common expression for killing a person.

To do the grand, amiable, etc. To act (usually with some ostentation) in the matter indicated by the adjective.

To do to death. To murder savagely, or to overcook excessively; to wear out or render stale by frequent repetition.

To do up. To repair, put in order, renovate. *This room wants doing up, i.e.* needs redecorating. Also to fasten a shoe-lace, a parcel, a button, etc., and to wear out or tire. *He has quite done himself up*, he is thoroughly worn out or exhausted.

To do up brown (U.S.A.). To do thoroughly in a good or bad sense—as beating someone up badly.

To do without so-and-so. To deny oneself something, to manage without it.

To have to do with. To have dealings with,

to have relation to. "That has nothing to do with the case."

Well-to-do. In good circumstances, well off.

Dobbin. A steady old horse, a child's horse.

Dobby, a silly old man, also a GOBLIN or house-elf. Like DOBBIN, it is an adaptation of Robin, diminutive of Robert.

> The Dobby's walk was within the inhibited domains of the Hall.
>
> SCOTT: *Peveril of the Peak*, ch. x.

Docetes. An early GNOSTIC sect, which maintained that Jesus Christ was divine only, and that his visible form, the crucifixion, resurrection, etc., were merely illusions. Christ had no real body on earth, but only a phantom body. The word is Greek and means phantomists.

Doch-an-doris (Gael. *deoch*, drink, *an*, the, *doruis*, of the door). A Scottish term for a STIRRUP CUP or a final drink before departing, made familiar in England by one of Sir Harry Lauder's songs. Variants are *doch-an-doroch, deuch-an-doris*, etc.

> After the lord keeper, the Master, and the domestics, had drunk doch-an-dorroch, or the stirrup-cup ... the cavalcade resumed its progress.
>
> SCOTT: *Bride of Lammermoor*, ch. xviii.

Dock Brief. When a prisoner in the dock pleads inability to employ counsel, the presiding judge can instruct a BARRISTER present in court to undertake the defence, a fee for this being paid by the court.

Dock defence. The instruction of counsel by a prisoner in the dock without the aid of a solicitor.

Dockers' K.C. A nickname gained by Ernest Bevin (1881–1951) for his successful championing of the dockers' case before the Commission of Inquiry of 1920. Many of his union's demands were met.

Doctor. (Lat. *doctor*, a teacher, instructor). One who has obtained the highest university degree (a doctorate) in any Faculty (i.e. arts, science, law, medicine, etc.), but the word has acquired a special meaning by constant use in a particular context. In common parlance a doctor is a medical practitioner whether or not in possession of a doctorate. Because the doctor of medicine was most widely known the title came to be applied generally to members of the medical profession.

> "Now, if you are dying and call in some Dr. So-and-so, you may find him a young fellow of three or four and twenty. As likely as not only an M.B. in reality, who has arrogated to himself the title of Doctor. For I hear some of them do it."
>
> MRS HENRY WOOD: *Johnny Ludlow* (4th Series) *Roger Bevere* ii.

The name *Doctor* is also given to various adulterated or falsified articles because they are "doctored" *i.e.* treated in some way that strengthens them or otherwise makes them appear better than they actually are. Thus a mixture of milk, water, nutmeg, and rum is called *Doctor*; the two former ingredients being "doctored" by the two latter. Brown sherry is also called *Doctor* because it is concocted from thin wine with the addition of unfermented juice and some spirituous liquor.

In nautical parlance, the ship's cook is known as "the doctor" because he is supposed to doctor the food; and a seventh son used to be so dubbed from the popular belief that he was endowed with power to cure agues, the KING'S EVIL and other diseases.

Doctored dice, or **Doctors.** Loaded dice; dice which are so "doctored" as to make them turn up winning numbers.

> "The whole antechamber is full, my lord—knights and squires, doctors and dicers."
> "The dicers, with their doctors in their pockets, I presume!"
>
> SCOTT: *Peveril of the Peak*, ch. xxviii.

The three best doctors are Dr. Quiet, Dr. Diet, and Dr. Merryman.

> Si tibi deficiant medici, medici tibi fiant
> Hæc tria: Mens-læta, Requies, Moderata-Diæta.

To doctor the accounts. To falsify them, to COOK them; the allusion is to drugging wine, beer, etc., and adulteration generally.

To doctor the wine. To drug it, or strengthen it with brandy; to make wine stronger, and "sick" wine more palatable. The fermentation of cheap wines is increased by fermentable sugar. As such wines fail in aroma, connoisseurs smell at their wine.

To have a cat doctored. To have a TOM-cat "cut", or castrated.

To put the doctor on a man. To cheat him. The allusion is to DOCTORED DICE.

Who shall decide when doctors disagree? When authorities differ, the question SUB JUDICE must be left undecided. (POPE: *Moral Essays*, Ep. ii. line 1.)

Doctors of the Church. Certain early Christian Fathers, and other saints whose doctrinal writings gained special acceptance and authority.

(a) *Eastern Church*. St. Athanasius, who defended the divinity of Christ against the ARIANS; St. Basil the Great; St. Gregory of Nazianzus; ST. JOHN CHRYSOSTOM.

(b) *Western Church*. St. Alphonsus Liguore; St. AMBROSE; St. Anselm of Canterbury; St. AUGUSTINE of Hippo; St. BERNARD of Clairvaux; St. Bonaventura; St. Francis de Sales; St. GREGORY THE GREAT; St. Hilary; St. JEROME; St. THOMAS AQUINAS.

Doctors of Learning, Piety, etc.

ADMIRABLE DOCTOR (*Doctor Admirabilis*) Roger Bacon (*c.* 1214—1294).

ANGELIC DOCTOR: St. Thomas Aquinas (*c.* 1225–1274).

DIVINE *Doctor* } *Jan van Ruysbroeck*
ECSTATIC DOCTOR } (1293–1381)

ELOQUENT DOCTOR: Peter Aureolus (14th Century).

EVANGELIC DOCTOR: John Wyclif (*c.* 1320–1384).

Illuminated Doctor: Raymond Lully (1235–1315); Johann Tauler (*c.* 1300–1361).

Illustrious Doctor: Adam de Marisco (*d.* 1257).

INVINCIBLE DOCTOR: William of Occam (*c.* 1280–1349).

IRREFRAGABLE DOCTOR: Alexander of Hales (*c.* 1175–1245).

MELLIFLUOUS DOCTOR: St. Bernard of Clairvaux (1090–1153).

Perspicuous Doctor: Walter Burley (1275–1345).

Profound Doctor: Thomas Bradwardine (*c.* 1290–1349).

Resolute Doctor: John Baconthorpe (*d.* 1346).

SERAPHIC DOCTOR: St. Bonaventura (John of Fidanza) (1221–1274).

SINGULAR DOCTOR: William of Occam (*c.* 1280–1349).

Solid Doctor (*i.e.* sound); Richard Middleton (*fl.* 1280).

SUBTLE DOCTOR: Duns Scotus (*c.* 1265–1308).

UNIVERSAL DOCTOR: Albert of Cologne or Albertus Magnus (*c.* 1206–1280); Alain de Lille (*c.* 1128–1202).

Wonderful Doctor: Roger Bacon (*c.* 1214–1294).

See SCHOLASTICISM; SCHOOLMEN.

Dr. Brighton. *See* BRIGHTON.

Dr. Dee. *See* DEE.

Dr. Faustus. *See* FAUST.

Dr. Fell. *See* FELL.

Dr. Sangrado. *See* SANGRADO.

Dr. Slop. *See* SLOP.

Dr. Syntax. *See* SYNTAX.

Doctors' Commons. The association and buildings established on St. Bennet's Hill, St. Paul's Churchyard, for practitioners of canon and civil law, under the presidency of the DEAN OF ARCHES. This self-governing body was established in the 16th century and dissolved after the passing of the Court of Probate Act and the Matrimonial Causes Act of 1857. The buildings were demolished in 1867. The name arises from the fact that the doctors had to dine there four days in each term. *See* TO COME INTO COMMONS *under* COMMONS.

Documentary film. A film devised and produced for the sole purpose of giving a realistic and accurate picture of some aspect of everyday life or work.

Doddypoll. A blockhead, a silly ass. *Poll* is head and *doddy* is the modern dotty, silly, from the verb to dote, to be foolish or silly. There is a comedy called *The Wisdom of Doctor Doddypoll* (*c.* 1595), attributed by some to George Peele.

As wise as Dr. Doddypoll. Not wise at all; a DUNCE.

Dodger. The Artful Dodger. The sobriquet of John Dawkins, a young thief in Dicken's *Oliver Twist*.

Dodman. A snail; a word still used in Norfolk. Fairfax, in his *Bulk and Selvedge* (1674), speaks of "a snayl or Dodman". The eastern point of Veryan Bay, CORNWALL, is called the Dodman. *See* DUDMAN.

Doddiman, doddiman, put our your horn,
Here comes a thief to steal your corn.
Norfolk rhyme.

Hodmandod, a variant of DODMAN.

Dodo (Port. *doudo*, silly). *Didus ineptus*, a large bird about the size of a turkey last known to exist in Mauritius in the 1680s.

As dead as the dodo. Long since dead and forgotten and finished with; very much a thing of the past, completely extinct.

Dodona (do dō' nà). The site of a most ancient ORACLE of Epirus dedicated to ZEUS. The oracles were delivered from the tops of oak-trees, the rustling of the leaves being interpreted by the priests. The cooing of the sacred pigeons, and the clanging of brass plates suspended in the trees when the wind blew, gave further signs to the priests and priestesses. The Greek phrase *khalkos Dodones* (brass of Dodona), meaning a babbler, probably stems from this.

The black pigeons of Dodona. Two black pigeons, we are told, took their flight from Thebes, in Egypt; one flew to Libya, and the other to Dodona. On the spot where the former alighted, the temple of Jupiter AMMON was erected; in the place where the other settled the ORACLE of JUPITER was established, and there responses were made by the black pigeons that inhabited the surrounding groves. The fable is possibly based on a pun upon the word *peleiai* which usually meant "old women", but in the dialect of the Epirots signified pigeons or doves.

Doe. John Doe and Richard Roe. Any plaintiff and defendant in an action of ejectment. They were sham names formerly used to save certain "niceties of law". This legal fiction was abolished by the Common Law Procedure Act, 1852. The names "John o'Noakes" and "Tom Styles" were similarly used.

Doff is do-off, as "Doff your hat". So DON is do-on, as "Don your clothes". *Cp.* DUP, DOUT.

Dog. "Dog" entries are arranged as follows:
1. Dogs in Phrases and Colloquialisms.
2. Dogs of note in the Classics and in Legend.
3. Dogs of noted people and in Literature, etc.
4. Dogs in Symbolism and Metaphor.
5. Combinations of Dog or Dog's.

(1) IN PHRASES AND COLLOQUIALISMS.

A black dog has walked over him. Said of a sullen person. HORACE tells us that the sight of a black dog with its pups was an unlucky omen, and the DEVIL has been frequently symbolized by a black dog.

A dead dog. Something utterly worthless.
> After whom is the king of Israel come out? ... after a dead dog, after a flea (I *Sam*. xxiv, 14).
> *Cp.* IS THY SERVANT A DOG, etc., *below*.

A dirty dog. One morally filthy, a CAD, a rotter, etc. In the East the dog is still the scavenger of the streets. "Him that dieth of Jeroboam in the city shall the dogs eat" (I *Kings* xiv, 11).

A dog in a doublet. A bold resolute fellow. In Germany and Flanders, the strong dogs used in hunting the wild boar wore a kind of buff doublet round their bodies. **A dog in one's doublet.** A false friend.

A dog in the manger. A mean-spirited individual who will not use what is wanted by another, nor yet let the other have it to use; one who prevents another enjoying something without any benefit to himself. The allusion is to the fable of the dog that fixed his place in a manger and would not allow the ox to come near the hay but would not eat it himself.

A dog's age. A long time.

A dog's chance. Virtually no chance at all.

A gay dog. Said of one who gets around and enjoys himself, especially with the ladies.

A living dog is better than a dead lion (*Eccles*. ix, 4). The meanest thing with life in it is better than the noblest without. The Italians say, "A live ass is worth more than a dead doctor."

A surly dog. A surly tempered fellow. Dog is often used for "chap" or "fellow" as in a *a dull dog*, A GAY DOG, etc.

A well-bred dog hunts by nature. Breeding "tells". The French proverb is *"Bon chien chasse de race."*

Barking dogs seldom bite. *See under* BARK.

Brag's a good dog, etc. *See under* BRAG.

Dog eat dog. The equivalent of, "No quarter given."

Dog don't eat dog. The equivalent of, "There's honour among thieves."

Dogs howl at death. A widespread superstition.
> In the rabbinical book, it saith
> The dogs howl, when, with icy breath
> Great Sammael, the Angel of Death,
> Takes through the town his flight!
> LONGFELLOW: *Golden Legend*, III, vii.

Every dog has his day. You may crow over me today, but my turn will come by and by. In Latin, *Hodie mihi, cras tibi,* "Today to me, tomorrow to thee." *Nunc mihi, nunc tibi, benigna fortuna*, FORTUNE visits every man once; she favours me now, but she will favour you in your turn.
> Thus, every dog at last will have his day—
> He who this morning smiled, at night may sorrow;
> The grub today's a butterfly tomorrow.
> PETER PINDAR: *Oldes of Condolence*.

Give a dog a bad name and hang him. If you besmirch a person's reputation he will be as good as condemned. Give a person a bad reputation and he might as well be hanged as try to recover his good name. *Cp.* THROW PLENTY OF DIRT, etc., *under* DIRT.

He who has a mind to beat his dog will easily find a stick. If you want to abuse a person, you will easily find something to blame. Dean Swift, says, "If you want to throw a stone, every lane will furnish one."

Hungry dogs will eat dirty pudding. Those really hungry are not particular about what they eat, and are by no means dainty. "To the hungry soul every bitter thing is sweet" (Heywod, *Prov.* xxvii, 7).

I am his Highness' dog at Kew; Pray tell me sir, whose dog are you? Frederick, Prince of Wales, had a dog given him by Alexander Pope, and these words are said to have been engraved on his collar. They are sometimes quoted with reference to an overbearing, bumptious person.

I don't keep dogs and bark myself. I don't keep servants to do their work for them, or to do the work myself.

In the doghouse. To be *in the doghouse* is to be in disgrace, as a dog confined to his kennel. Usually applied to a husband who has been misbehaving or has thoroughly displeased his wife, and is consequently treated with marked disfavour. In J.M. Barrie's PETER PAN, Mr. Darling lived in the dog kennel until his children returned, as a penance for his treatment of NANA.

Is thy servant a dog, that he should do this thing? Said in contempt when asked to do something derogatory or beneath one.

The phrase (slightly modified) is from II *Kings* viii, 13.

When Landseer, the celebrated painter of dogs and animals, asked Lockhart if he would like to sit for his portrait, Lockhart's answer was: "Is thy servant a dog that he should do this thing?" The phrase was adopted and much used by Sydney Smith.

It was the story of the dog and the shadow. A case of one who gives up the substance for its shadow. The allusion is to the fable of the dog who dropped his bone into the stream because he opened his mouth to seize the reflection of it.

Lazy as Lawrence's, or **Ludlam's dog.** *See* LAZY.

Let sleeping dogs lie; don't wake a sleeping dog. Let well alone. Don't stir up trouble by seeking to make changes. If your course of action is likely to cause trouble, let things be. *Cp.* QUIETA NON MOVERE.

> It is nought good a sleping hound to wake,
> Nor yeve a wight a cause to devyne.
> CHAUCER: *Troilus and Criseyde*, iii, 764.

Love me love my dog. *See under* LOVE.

Not to have a word to throw at a dog. Said of one who is sullen or sulky.

> *Cel:* Why, cousin; why Rosalind;—Cupid have mercy!—Not a word?
> *Ros:* Not one to throw at a dog.
> SHAKESPEARE: *As You Like It*, I, iii.

St. Roch and his dog. Emblematic of inseparable companions. *See* ROCH, ST.

Sick as a dog. Very sick. We also say, "Sick as a cat." (*See* CAT.) The Bible speaks of dogs returning to their vomit (*Prov.* xxvi, 11; II *Pet.* ii, 22).

The dogs of war. The horrors of war, especially fire, sword and famine.

> Cry *Havoc* and let slip the dogs of war.
> SHAKESPEARE: *Julius Cæsar*, III, i.

The hair of the dog that bit you. *See under* HAIR.

The more I see of men the more I love dogs. A misanthropic saying of obvious meaning, attributed to Mme. de Sévigné (1626–1696). *Plus je vois les hommes, plus j'admire les chiens*; also to Mme Roland (1754–1793) and Frederick the Great of Prussia (1712–1786).

There are more ways of killing a dog than by hanging. There is more than one way of achieving your object. The proverb is found in Ray's *Collection* (1742).

Throw it to the dogs. Throw it away, it is useless and worthless.

> Throw physic to the dogs, I'll none of it.
> SHAKESPEARE: *Macbeth*, V, iii.

To blush like a dog, or **like a blue,** or **black dog.** Not to blush at all.

To call off the dogs. To desist from some pursuit or inquiry; to break up a disagreeable conversation. In the chase the huntsman calls off the dogs if they are on the wrong track.

To die like a dog. To have a shameful or miserable end.

To go to the dogs. To go to ruin, morally or materially.

To help a lame dog over a stile. To give assistance to one in distress; to hold out a helping hand; to encourage.

> Do the work that's nearest,
> Though it's dull at whiles,
> Helping, when we meet them,
> Lame dogs over stiles.
> CHARLES KINGSLEY: *The Invitation*.

To lead a cat and dog life. *See under* CAT.

To lead a dog's life. To be harried from PILLAR to post, to be nagged constantly, never to be left in peace.

To put on the dog. To behave in a conceited or bumptious manner.

To rain cats and dogs. To rain very heavily. *See under* RAIN.

To wake a sleeping dog. To take action which stirs up or leads to trouble. *See* LET SLEEPING DOGS LIE, *above*.

Try it on the dog! A jocular phrase used of medicine that is expected to be unpalatable or of food that is suspect or dubious.

You can never scare a dog away from a greasy hide. It is difficult to free oneself from bad habits. The line is from HORACE'S *Satires* (II, v, 83): *Canis a corio nunquam absterrebitur uncto*.

You cannot teach old dogs new tricks. Elderly people are not adaptable. They do not readily take to new ways.

(2) DOGS OF NOTE IN THE CLASSICS AND IN LEGEND.

Aubry's Dog, or **the Dog of Montargis.** Aubry of Montdidier was murdered in 1371 in the forest of Bondy. His dog Dragon excited suspicion of Richard of Macaire by always snarling and flying at his throat whenever he appeared. Richard, condemned to a judicial combat with the dog, was killed, and, in his dying moments, confessed the crime.

Cuchulain's Hound. Luath.

Fingal's Dog. BRAN.

Geryon's Dogs. Gargittios and the two-headed Orthos. Both were slain by HERCULES.

Icarius's Dog. Mœra (the glistener). *See* ICARIUS.

King Arthur's Favourite Hound. Cavall.

Llewelyn's Greyhound. Gelert. *See* BEDDGELERT.

Mauthe Dog. *See* MAUTHE.

Montargis, Dog of. AUBRY'S DOG.

Orion's Dogs. Arctophonos (bear-killer), and Ptoophagos (the glutton of Ptoon, in Bœtia).

Procris's Dog. Lælaps. *See* PROCRIS.

Roderick the Goth's Dog. Theron.

Seven Sleepers, Dog of the. Katmir who, according to Mohammedan tradition, was admitted to HEAVEN. He accompanied the seven noble youths (*see* SEVEN SLEEPERS) to the cavern in which they were walled up. He remained standing for the whole time, neither moving, eating, drinking nor sleeping.

Tristran's Dog. Hodain, or Leon.

Ulysses's Dog. Argos; he recognized his master after his return from TROY, and died of joy.

(3) DOGS OF NOTED PEOPLE AND IN LITERATURE, etc.

Boatswain. Byron's favourite dog; buried at Newstead Abbey. His master wrote the epitaph.

Bounce. Alexander Pope's dog.

Boy. Prince Rupert's dog, killed at the battle of Marston Moor.

Brutus. Landseer's greyhound; jocularly called "The Invader of the Larder".

Dash. Charles Lamb's dog, also the much-loved spaniel of the young Queen Victoria.

Diamond. Sir Isaac Newton's little dog which one winter's morning upset a candle on his master's desk causing the destruction of the records of many years' experiments. On perceiving this disaster Newton exclaimed: "Oh, Diamond, Diamond, thou little knowest the mischief thou hast done!" And at once set to work to repair the loss.

Flush. Elizabeth Barrett Browning's dog.

Geist. One of Matthew Arnold's dachshunds. He wrote the poem *Geist's Grave* in memory of him.

Giallo. Walter Savage Landor's dog.

Greyfriars Bobby. A terrier who watched over the grave of his master (John Gray) in Greyfriars Kirkyard, Edinburgh, from 1852 to 1872. A drinking fountain surmounted by a statue of Bobby stands in nearby Candlemaker Row.

Hamlet. Sir Walter Scott's black greyhound.

Kaiser. Another of Matthew Arnold's dachshunds commemorated in his *Kaiser Dead*. *See* GEIST *above*.

Luath. The favourite of Robert Burns.

Lufra. The hound of Douglas, in Scott's *Lady of the Lake*.

Maida. Sir Walter Scott's favourite deerhound.

Mathe. Richard II's greyhound which left him in favour of Bolingbroke.

Nana. Mr. and Mrs. Darling's dog in J.M. Barrie's PETER PAN.

Rufus. Sir Winston Churchill's poodle.

St. Bernard Dogs. *See* PASSES, ST. BERNARD.

Toby. PUNCH's famous dog; named after the dog that followed TOBIT in his journeys, a favourite in mediæval Biblical stories and plays.

(4) DOGS IN SYMBOLISM AND METAPHOR.

Dogs in mediæval art, symbolize fidelity. A dog is represented as lying at the feet of St. BERNARD, St. Benignus, and St. Wendelon; as licking the wounds of St. ROCH; as carrying a lighted torch in representations of St. DOMINIC.

Dogs in effigy. In funeral monuments a dog in effigy is usually a memento of the dead person's pet with no symbolical significance.

Lovell the Dog. *See* RAT, CAT AND DOG *under* RAT.

The Derby Dog. *See under* DERBY

The Dog. DIOGENES (412–323 B.C.). When ALEXANDER of Macedon went to see him he introduced himself with these words: "I am Alexander, surnamed the Great." To which the philosopher replied: "And I am Diogenes, surnamed the Dog." The Athenians raised to his memory a pillar of Parian marble, surmounted by a dog. *See* CYNIC.

The Dog of God. So the Laplanders call the bear, which "has the strength of ten men and the wit of twelve".

The Thracian Dog. ZOILUS, the carping critic of ancient Greece.

> Like curs, our critics haunt the poet's feast,
> And feed on scraps refused by every guest;
> From the old Thracian dog they learned the way
> To snarl in want, and grumble o'er their prey.
> PITT: *To Mr. Spence.*

(5) COMBINATIONS OF DOG OR DOG'S.

Dog—or dog's—in combination, is used, besides in its literal sense (as in dog-biscuit) for

(*a*) denoting the male of certain animals, as dog-ape, dog-fox, dog-otter.

(*b*) denoting inferior plants, or those which are worthless as food for man, as dog-briar, dog-cabbage, dog-leek, dog-lichen, dog's mercury, dog-parsley, dog-violets (scentless), dog-wheat. *See below* DOG-GRASS, DOG-ROSE.

(*c*) expressing spuriousness or some mongrel quality, as dog's-logic, DOG-LATIN.

Dog-cart. A light one-horse trap popular for informal country use in Victorian and Edwardian times, originally designed for carrying sportsmen's dogs. Also the name carrying sportsmen's dogs. Also the name of a small cart drawn by dogs.

Dog-cheap. Extremely cheap; "dirt-cheap".

Dog-collar. As well as its literal meaning, it is the popular name for a clergyman's "back to front" collar. Also the ornamental band or collar worn close to the throat by women.

Dog-days. Days of great heat. The Romans called the hottest weeks of the summer *caniculares dies*. Their theory was that the DOG-STAR, rising with the SUN, added to its heat, and the dog-days (about 3 July to 11 August) bore the combined heat of both.

Dog-ears. The corners of pages crumpled and folded down; *dog-eared* pages are so crumpled, like the turned-down ears of many dogs.

Dog-fall. A fall in wrestling when the two combatants touch the ground together.

Dog-grass. Couch-grass (*Triticum repens*), which is eaten by dogs when they have lost their appetite; it acts as an emetic and purgative.

Dog-head. In a flintlock, the part of the gun which bites or holds the flint.

Dog-Latin. Pretended or mongrel Latin. An excellent example is Stevens's definition of a kitchen:

> As the law classically expresses it, a kitchen is "camera necessaria pro usus cookare; cum saucepannis, stewpannis, scullero, dressero, coalholo, stovis, smoak-jacko; pro roastandum boilandum fryandum et plum-pudding-mixandum ...".
>
> *A Law Report* (Daniel *v.* Dishclout).

Dog-leech. A dog-doctor; formerly applied contemptuously to a medical practitioner.

Dog-rose. The common wild rose (*Rosa canina*, Pliny's *cynorrodon*), so called because it was supposed by the ancient Greeks to cure the bite of mad dogs.

Dogs, Isle of. See ISLE.

Dog's-nose. Gin and beer, etc.

> "Dog's-nose, which your committee find upon inquiry, to be compounded of warm porter, moist sugar, gin and nutmeg."
>
> DICKENS: *Pickwick Papers*, ch. xxxiii.

Dogsbody. A drudge, one who is generally exploited and used as a menial.

Dog-sleep. A pretended sleep; also a light, easily broken sleep. Dogs seem to sleep with "one eye open".

Dog-star. Sirius, the brightest star in the firmament in the constellation of the Big Dog, *Alpha Canis Majoris*. See DOG-DAYS *above*.

Dog-tags Identity discs of members of the U.S. armed forces (World War II).

Dog-tired. Exhausted, usually after exercise or hard manual labour; and wanting only to curl up like a dog and go to sleep.

Dog-vane. A nautical term for a small vane placed on the weather gunwale to show the direction of the wind. Sailors also apply it to a COCKADE.

Dog-watch. Two-hour watches (4–6 p.m. and 6–8 p.m.) instead of the usual four-hour watches introduced to enable seamen to vary their daily watch-keeping rota. Among various suggested origins are that it is a "docked" or shortened watch or a corruption of "dodge" watch. *See* WATCH.

Dog-whipper. A minor church officer of the days when sheepdogs, TURNSPITS and others accompanied their owners to church. His job was to keep order among the canine congregation, to eject the badly behaved and to exclude troublsome dogs generally. Whips and dog-tongs were used. The office became redundant in the 19th century. Even as late as 1856 Mr John Pickard was appointed dog-whipper in Exeter Cathedral.

Dog-whipping Day. 18 October (St. LUKE's Day). It is said that a dog once swallowed a consecrated wafer on this day.

Doggo. To lie doggo. To get into hiding and remain there; to keep quiet and out of sight.

Dog-goned. An American EUPHEMISM for "God-damned."

> But when that choir got up to sing.
> I couldn't catch a word;
> They sang the most doggonest thing
> A body ever heard!
>
> WILL CARLETON: *Farm Ballad.*

Dogaressa. The wife of a DOGE.

Dogberry. An officious and ignorant JACK IN OFFICE. The allusion is to the ignorant, self-satisfied, overbearing, but good-natured night-constable of this name in SHAKESPEARE's *Much Ado About Nothing*.

Doge (dōj) (Lat. *dux*, a leader or duke). The chief magistrate of the Venetian Republic. The first doge was Paolo Anafesto (Paoluccio), 697, and the last Luigi Manin, 1789. *See* BRIDE OF THE SEA.

> For six hundred years ... her [Venice's] government was an elective monarchy, her ... doge possessing, in early times at least, as much independent authority as any other European sovereign.
>
> RUSKIN: *Stones of Venice*, vol. I, ch. i.

The chief magistrate of Genoa was also called a doge from 1339 until 1796 when the French established the Ligurian Republic.

Dogget's Coat and Badge. The prize given in an annual rowing match for Thames watermen held under the auspices of the Fishmongers' Company on or near 1 August. So called from Thomas Dogget, an actor of DRURY LANE, who signalized the accession of George I by instituting the race in

1715. It is from the Swan Steps at London Bridge to the "Swan" at Chelsea, the average time taken being 30 mins. The coat is an orange-coloured livery jacket.

Dogie, or dogy (dō′gi). In the western U.S.A. the term for an undersized calf. At round-up time all motherless calves were called "dough-guts", which became contracted into *dogie*. Being prematurely weaned, their stomachs could not digest and swelled accordingly.

Doh, or Do (dō). The first or tonic note of the solfeggio system of music. *See* ARETINIAN SYLLABLES.

Doily, or Doyley. A small ornamental mat or napkin used on cake dishes, etc., or on which to stand glasses, bottles, etc. In the 17th century it denoted a kind of woollen material; thus Dryden speaks of "doyley petticoats", and Steele in No. 102 of the *Tatler* speaks of his "doiley suit". The Doyleys, from which the stuff was named, were linen drapers in the STRAND from the time of Queen Anne until 1850.

Doit. An old Dutch coin of low value; hence any coin of little worth, a trifle.

> When they will not give a doit to relieve a lame beggar, they will lay out ten to see a dead Indian.
> SHAKESPEARE: *The Tempest*, II, ii.

Dolce far niente (dol′chi far ni en′ti) (Ital. sweet doing nothing). Delightful idleness. Pliny has *"Jucundum tamen nihil agere"* (*Ep.* viii, 9).

Doldrums, The. A condition of depression, slackness, or inactivity; hence applied by sailors to regions where ships were likely to be becalmed, especially those parts of the ocean near the Equator noted for calms, light winds, etc.

> But from the bluff-head, where I watched today,
> I saw her in the doldrums.
> BYRON: *The Island*, II, xxi

Dole (Lat. *dolor* grief, sorrow). Lamentation.
To make dole. To lament, mourn.

> Yonder they lie; the poor old man, their father, making such pitiful dole over them that all the beholders take his part with weeping.
> SHAKESPEARE: *As You Like It*, I, ii.

Dole (O.E. *dale*, a portion; *dael*, deal). A portion allotted, a charitable gift, alms. From Saxon times the strips of land, especially of common meadow, distributed annually were called *doles*. Since the National Insurance Act of 1911, it is the everyday name for "unemployment benefit".

Happy man be his dole. May his share or lot be that of a happy or fortunate man.

> Your father and my uncle have made motions: if it be my luck, so: if not, happy man be his dole!
> SHAKESPEARE: *Merry Wives of Windsor*, III, iv.

Dollar. The sign $ is possibly a modification of the figure 8 as it appeared on the old Spanish "pieces of eight" which were of the same value as the dollar. There are various other derivations put forward, most notably that it is the U of the United States superimposed on the S.

In pre-metric colloquial English a dollar was a CROWN or five shilling piece and half a dollar was a half crown and sometimes a two shilling piece.

The word is a variant of *thaler* (Low. Ger. *Dahler*; Dan. *daler*), and means valley (our *dale*). The Counts of Schlick, at the close of the 15th century, coined ounce-pieces from the silver extracted from the mines at *Joachim's Tal* (Joachim's valley). These pieces called *Joachim's Talers* or *Schlickenthalers* gained such repute that they became standard coin. Other coins made like them came to be called *thalers*.

Bank of England dollars were struck as bank tokens in 1797 and subsequently. Dollars were first coined in the U.S.A. in 1794.

The Almighty Dollar. An expressive term emphasizing the power of money. Washington Irving seems to have first used this expression:

> The almighty dollar, that great object of universal devotion throughout our land....
> *Wolfert's Roost, Creole Village*, p.40 (1837).

Ben Jonson (1573–1637) in his *Epistle to Elizabeth, Countess of Rutland*, speaks of "almighty gold".

Dollar Diplomacy. A term applied to governmental support and furtherance of commercial interest abroad for both political and economic ends. The phrase, popular with critics of American policy, stems from the Taft administration (1909–1913), which fostered such policies in the Far East and Latin America. Their intention was to control as well as to promote enterprise abroad by substituting dollars for bullets and lending "all proper support to every legitimate and beneficial American enterprise abroad".

Dolly bird. A current colloquialism for an attractive and well dressed young woman.

Dolly shop. A MARINE STORE where rags and old clothes are bought; so called from the BLACK DOLL hung up as a sign. It is suggested that the name was originally a corruption of *tally shop*.

Dolly-tub. A wash-tub, the predecessor of the electric washing machine, with a *dolly* or revolving wooden disc with projecting dowels which stirred up its contents and was manually operated. The name was earlier applied to the keeve or tub which was part of the dollying-machine used in the Cornish tin-mining industry.

Dolmen (dol' men). A word of CELTIC origin, the equivalent of the Welsh CROMLECH. The name is particularly used in Brittany. They are often called devils' tables, fairies' tables, etc.

The Constantine Dolmen, CORNWALL, is 33 ft. long, 14½ ft. deep, and 18½ ft. across and estimated to weigh 750 tons. It is poised on the points of two natural rocks.

Dolphin. *See* DAUPHIN. The dolphin in mediæval art symbolizes social love.

Dom (Lat. *dominus*). A title applied in the MIDDLE AGES to the POPE, and later to other Church dignitaries. It is now largely restricted to monks of the BENEDICTINE and CARTHUSIAN Orders. The Sp. *don*, Port. *dom*, and M.E. *dan* are the same word. *See* DAN; DON.

Domboc. *See* DOOM.

Domdaniel. A fabled abode of evil spirits, GNOMES, and enchanters "under the roots of the ocean" off Tunis, or elsewhere. It first appears in Chaves and Gazotte's *Continuation of the Arabian Nights* (1788–1793), was introduced by Southey into his *Thalaba*, and used by Carlyle as synonymous with a den of iniquity. The word is made up from Lat. *domus*, a house, and *Danielis*, of Daniel, the latter being taken as a magician.

Domesday Book consists of one folio volume of 382 pp. and one quarto of 450 pp., written in Latin, now housed in the Public Record Office, but formerly kept in the EXCHEQUER. They contain the records of a survey of England begun in 1085 by order of WILLIAM THE CONQUEROR. Certain remote areas (Northumberland, Cumberland, Westmorland, and Durham) were omitted (*See* BOLDON BOOK).

Details of the ownership, extent, value, population, stock, etc., of all holdings are given for the time of Edward the Confessor and also at the time of the survey. The value is also given for the time of the Conquest. It was long used for taxation purposes and as a general governmental reference book. It is also called *The King's Book* and *The Winchester Roll* because it was once kept there. It was reproduced in typographical facsimile in 1783. The name is from O.E. *dom*, judgment. *Cp.* EXON DOMESDAY.

Dominations. *See* DOMINIONS.

Domine, quo vadis? (Lat. Master, whither goest thou?). According to tradition, when St. PETER was fleeing from NERO's persecution in ROME, he met Christ on the APPIAN WAY and greeted Our Lord with these words. The reply "*Veno Roman, iterum crucifigi*" (I am coming to Rome to be crucified again) so shamed the apostle that he returned to martyrdom in Rome. The meeting is commemorated by a church on the Appian Way. He is said to have requested to be crucified head downwards and to have given this account when nailed upon the cross. The story is found in the Gnostic *Acts* and other texts and is featured in an historical novel by H. Sienkiewicz, *Quo Vadis?* (1896).

Dominic, St., de Guzman (1170–1221), the founder of the Dominican Order, or Preaching Friars, noted for his vehemence against the ALBIGENSES and called by the POPE "Inquisitor-General". He was canonized by Gregory IX. He is represented with a sparrow at his side and a dog carrying in its mouth a burning torch. It is said that the DEVIL appeared to him in the form of a sparrow, and the dog refers to his mother's dream, during her pregnancy, that she had given birth to a dog which lighted the world with a burning torch.

Dominical Letters, or **Sunday Letters.** The first seven letters of the alphabet used in calendars, almanacs, etc., to mark the Sundays throughout the year (Lat. *Dominica Dies*, the Lord's Day, Sunday). If 1 January is a Sunday the Dominical Letter for the year will be A and if 2 January is a Sunday the Letter will be B, and so on. Dominical Letters are used for finding on what day of the week any day of the month falls in any particular year, also in determining EASTER. Tables and instructions are to be found in Prayer Books, Breviaries, etc.

Dominicans. The order of preaching friars founded by St. DOMINIC de Guzman in 1215, their rule being based on that of St. AUGUSTINE. Their first home in England was at Oxford (1221). They gained the name of BLACK FRIARS and in France they were called JACOBINS. They were also called *Domini canes* or Hounds of the Lord. Albertus Magnus, St. Thomas Aquinas and Savonarola were representatives of an order notable for its intellectual distinction.

Dominions. The sixth of the nine orders in the mediæval hierarchy of angels, also known as *Dominations* and symbolized in art by an ensign. *See* ANGEL.

From the formation of the Dominion of Canada (1867) the word also came to be applied to the self-governing units of the British Empire as they were formed, and their relations with the mother country were handled by the Dominions Office. As the word *Empire* came to be replaced by that of COMMONWEALTH, the Dominions Office became the Commonwealth Relations Office in 1947 and Commonwealth Office in 1966, which was combined with the Foreign Office in 1968.

The Old Dominion. The State of Virginia, formerly an English colony.

Domino (Ital.). Originally a hooded clerical cloak; hence such a hooded garment worn at masquerades, then a hood only, and finally the half mask covering an inch or two above and below the eyes, worn as a disguise. The black ebony pieces used in the game of dominoes may have derived their name from some allusion to the black domino cloak or the black mask with the eyes showing through as the white pips.

Don is do-on, as "Don your bonnet". *See* DOFF; DOUT; DUP.

> Then up he rose, and donn'd his clothes,
> And dupp'd the chamber-door.
> SHAKESPEARE: *Hamlet*, IV, v.

Don (Lat. *dominus* lord). A Spanish gentleman, any Spaniard, an aristocrat, a man of mark, a university tutor, fellow, etc.

Don Juan. *See under* JUAN.

Don Pacifico. *See under* PACIFICO.

Don Quixote. *See under* QUIXOTE.

Donation of Constantine. The presumed grant by the Emperor Constantine (306–337) to Pope Silvester and his successors in perpetuity, consequent upon his baptism of Constantine in 326, of the temporal jurisdiction over ROME and Italy, etc. The document is now accepted as an 8th-century forgery. *See* DECRETALS.

Donation of Pepin, or **Pippin.** When Pippin III (the Short) conquered Aistulf the Lombard king, the exarchate of Ravenna fell into his hands (756). Pippin gave it with the surrounding country and the Republic of Rome to Pope Stephen II, thus founding the Papal States and the temporal power of the papacy.

With the exception of the city of ROME, the Papal States were incorporated in the Kingdom of Italy in 1860 and when Rome was made the Italian capital in 1870 the Pope declared himself a "prisoner" in the VATICAN. This seclusion was ended by the CONCORDAT with Mussolini's government in 1929.

Donatists. Schismatic followers of Donatus, a Numidian bishop of the 4th century who, on puritanical grounds, opposed the election of Cæcilianus to the bishopric of Carthage (311).

Their chief dogma was that the Church was a society of holy people and that mortal sinners were to be excluded. St. AUGUSTINE of Hippo vigorously combated their heresies.

Doncaster. The "City on the river Don" (Celt. *don*, that which spreads). Sigebert, monk of Gemblours, in 1100, derived the name from *Thong-ceaster*, "the castle of the thong", and says that HENGIST AND HORSA purchased from the British king as much as they could encompass with a leather thong, which they cut into strips and so encompassed the land occupied by the city. *Cp.* CUTTING A DIDO *under* DIDO.

Done. The done thing. That which is recognized as socially acceptable and proper. *Cp.* U AND NON-U.

Donkey. An ass. The word is first found in the later 18th century and is a diminutive probably derived from *dun* with reference to its colour. For the story concerning the cross on the donkey's back, *see* ASS.

A donkey's breakfast. A merchant navy term for a straw-filled mattress.

Not for donkey's ears. Not for a very long time. Probably from the mispronunciation of *years* with *ears* and an allusion to the length of a donkey's ears.

The donkey means one thing and the driver another. Different people see things from different standpoints, according to their interests. The allusion is to a fable in PHÆDRUS, where a donkey-driver exhorts his donkey to flee, as the enemy is at hand. The donkey asks if the enemy will load him with double pack-saddles. "No," says the man. "Then," replies the donkey, "what care I whether you are my master or some other?"

To ride the black donkey. To be pig-headed, obstinate like a donkey. Black is added in the sense of bad, as in BLACK BOOKS, BLACK LOOKS, etc.

To talk the hind leg off a donkey. To talk non-stop, to talk incessantly, and, less commonly, to wheedle. *Jackass, horse, cow*, etc. sometimes take the place of the donkey in this phrase.

Two more, and up goes the donkey. An old cry at fairs, the showman having promised his credulous hearers that as soon as enough pennies are collected his donkey will balance himself on the top of a pole or ladder. Always a matter of "two more pennies", the trick is never performed.

Who stole the donkey? An old gibe against policemen. The story is that in the early days of the force a donkey was stolen, but the police failed to discover the thief, and this gave rise to the laugh against them. The correct answer is "The man with the white hat", because white hats were made from the skins of donkeys, many of which were stolen and sold to hatters.

Donkey engine, pump, etc. Small auxiliary engines or pumps used for subsidiary work, just as the horse does more important work than the donkey.

Donkey-work. Uninteresting work; less responsible work, drudgery.

Donnybrook Fair. This FAIR, held in August from the time of King John till 1855, was noted for its bacchanalian routs and light-hearted rioting. Hence it is proverbial for a disorderly gathering or regular rumpus. The village is now one of the south-eastern suburbs of Dublin.

Donzel. A SQUIRE or young man of good birth not yet knighted (Ital. *doncello*, from Late Lat. *domicellus*). *See* DAMSEL.

> He is esquire to a knight-errant, donzel to the damsels.
> S. BUTLER: *Characters.*

Doolalli (Doolally) or **Doolalli tap.** An army expression for an unbalanced state of mind or mental derangement. Formerly, time-expired soldiers in India were sent to *Deolali*, a town near Bombay to await passage home. There were often long, frustrating delays, when boredom and the climate may have led to some odd behaviour, which caused some of them to become "doolalli". *Tap* when used in conjunction is the E. Indian word for fever.

Doom (O.E. *dom*). The original meaning was law, or judgment, and a *doomsman* was a judge. (*See* DEEMSTER.) The book of laws compiled by King Alfred was called the *Domboc*.

Crack of doom. The last trump, the signal for the final judgment.

To false a doom. A Scottish term meaning to protest against a sentence.

Doomsday Book. *See* DOMESDAY.

Doomsday Sedgwick (*c*. 1610–1669), a Puritan zealot during the COMMONWEALTH. He claimed to have had it revealed to him in a vision that doomsday was at hand; and going to the house of Sir Francis Russell, in Cambridgeshire, he called upon a party of gentlemen playing at bowls to leave off and prepare for the approaching dissolution.

Doones, The. Outlaws and desperadoes who supposedly settled in the Badgworthy area of Exmoor, Devon about 1620. They lived by highway robbery and plundering of farmsteads. They also abducted women. Numerous murders were attributed to them. When in *c*. 1699 they killed a child and seized the mother, the people of the district stormed their stronghold and those who were not destroyed fled. Some stories claim them to be of Scottish origin but the legends vary and they were adapted and romanticised by R. D. Blackmore in *Lorna Doone* (1869).

Door. The O.E. *dor (fem. duru)*. The word is similar in many other languages, thus, Dan. *dor*, Icel. *dyrr*; Gr. *thura*; Lat. *fores*; Ger. *Tür*.

Dead as a door-nail. *See* DEAD.

Door-money. Payment taken at the doors for admission to an entertainment, dance, etc.

Doors of Perception. The senses; the greatly increased sensitivity achieved by the taking of certain drugs, as described by Aldous Huxley in his book of that title.

He laid the charge at my door. He accused me of doing it.

Indoors. Inside the house; also attributively, as, *an indoor servant, indoor clothes*.

Next door to it. Within an ace of it (*see* ACE); very like it; next-door neighbour to it.

Outdoor, or **Out of doors.** Outside the house; in the open air.

Sin lieth at the door. (*Gen.* iv. 7). The blame of sin attaches to the wrongdoer, and he must take the consequences.

The door must be either shut or open. It must be one way or the other. This is from de Brueys and Palaprat's comedy, *le Grondeur*, (produced 1691): the master scolds his servant for leaving the door open. The servant says that he was scolded the last time for shutting it, and adds: "Do you wish it shut?"—"No."—"Do you wish it open?"—"No."—"Why," says the man, "it must be either shut or open."

To darken one's door. *See under* DARK.

To make the door. To make it fast by shutting and bolting it.

> Make the door upon a woman's wit, and it will out at the casement.
> SHAKESPEARE: *As You Like It*, IV, i.

To meet behind closed doors. In secret; without the press or public present.

To show someone the door. Peremptorily to ask a person to leave one's house; to get rid of someone whose presence is unwelcome.

To shut the door in someone's face. To shut the door deliberately and to refuse to have any dealings with the caller.

Dora. The popular name of the Defence of the Realm Acts (D.O.R.A.) which imposed many temporary restrictions. Their application to munitions factories and the drink trade caused particular irritation. It passed into common speech after being used in the Law courts by Mr Justice Scrutton. In numerous newspaper cartoons *Dora* was portrayed as a long-nosed elderly female, the personification of restriction (*Cp*. GRUNDY). There have been countless similar coinages since World War II and their derivation is usually, but not always, obvious. "Ernie" (Electronic Random Number Indicating

Equipment), the selector of prizewinning numbers for holders of Government Premium Bonds; "Unesco" (United Nations Educational, Scientific and Cultural Organization); and "Sweb" (South Western Electricity Board) are typical examples. *Cp.* ENSA.

Dorado, El. *See* EL DORADO.

Dorcas Society. A woman's circle making clothing for charitable purposes. So called from Dorcas in *Acts* ix, 39, who made "coats and garments" for widows.

Dorian, Doric. Pertaining to Doris, a district of ancient Greece; or to the Doric or Dorian race, one of the four main divisions of the ancient Greeks, the others being the Aeolians, the Ionians, and the Achaeans. The Dorians maintained some of the characteristics of a simple-living, pastoral people and were dominant in the southern and western Peloponnesus, including Sparta, Megara, Corinth, Argos, Halicarnassus, Rhodes, Syracuse, Crete etc.

Dorian Mode. The scale represented by the white keys on a pianoforte, beginning with D. A simple, solemn form of music, the first of the authentic Church modes.

Doric Dialect The broad, hard dialect spoken by the natives of Doris, in Greece. Hence any broad rustic dialect, and especially that of Scotland, of which Robert Burns's verses are a notable example.

Doric Order. The oldest, strongest, and simplest of the Grecian orders of architecture. The Greek Doric is simpler than the Roman imitation. A characteristic of the Grecian is that the column stands directly on the pavement, whereas the Roman is placed on a plinth. *See* CORINTHIAN; IONIC; TUSCAN.

The Doric Land. Greece, of which Doris forms a part.

The Doric Reed. Pastoral poetry. Everything Doric was very plain, but cheerful, chaste and solid.

> The Doric reed once more
> Well pleased, I tune.
>
> THOMSON: *The Seasons, Autumn*, line 3.

Doris. *See* NEREIDS.

Dornick. Stout figured linen for tableclothes, etc.; so called from Doornick, the Flemish name of Tournai, where it was originally made. The word is also spelt Dornock, Darnex, etc. *See* DANNOCKS.

> I have got ... a fair Darnex carpet of my own
> Laid cross for the more state.
>
> FLETCHER: *The Noble Gentleman*, V, i.

Dorothea, St. (dor ō thē' à). A martyr under Diocletian about 300. She is represented with a rose-branch in her hand, a wreath of roses on her head, and roses with fruit by her side. The legend is that Theophilus, the judge's secretary, scoffingly said to her as she was going to execution, "Send me some fruit and roses, Dorothea, when you get to Paradise." Immediately after her execution, a young angel brought him a basket of apples and roses, saying "From Dorothea in Paradise", and vanished. Theophilus was a convert from that moment. The story forms the basis of Massinger and Dekker's tragedy, *The Virgin Martir* (1622). Her day is 6 February.

Dorset. Once the seat of a British tribe, calling themselves *Dwr-trigs* (dwellers by the water). The Romans latinized *Dwrtrigs* into *Duro-triges*. Lastly came the Saxons, who translated the original words into their own tongue, *dor-saetta*, *saetta* being a seat or settlement.

The Dorsetshire Poet. William Barnes (1800–1886), a clergyman who was born and lived in Dorset, and who wrote much poetry in the local dialect.

The Dorsetshire Novelist. Thomas Hardy (1840–1928), of Dorset stock on both sides, who made the Dorset rustic and countryside a central feature of his novels.

Dot. Dot and carry one. An infant just beginning to toddle; one who limps in walking; a person who has one leg longer than the other.

On the dot. Precisely on time. A probable reference to the minute-hand of the clock being exactly over the dot marking the given minute on the dial.

To dot the i's and cross the t's. To be meticulous; to give most careful attention to detail; to finalize the details of an agreement. From the liability to confuse these letters if carelessly written without cross or dot.

Dotheboys Hall (doo' the boiz). A private boarding school in Dickens's *Nicholas Nickleby* where boys were taken in and done for by Mr. Wackford Squeers, a brutish, ignorant, overbearing knave, who starved them and taught them nothing. The ruthless exposure of this kind of school led to the closing or reformation of many.

Dotterel. A doting old fool; an old man easily cajoled. So called from the bird, a species of plover, which is easily approached and caught.

To dor the dotterel. *Dor* is an obsolete word meaning to trick or cheat, whence the phrase means to cheat the simpleton.

Douai Bible. *See* BIBLE, THE ENGLISH.

Double (Lat. *duplus*, twofold). One's double is one's *alter ego*. The word is applied to such pairs as the Corsican brothers in the play *Les frères corses*, the DROMIO brothers, and the brothers Antipholus.

Double-barrelled. A double-barrelled gun is one with two barrels; to have *a double-barrelled name* is to have a hyphenated surname; a *double-barrelled compliment* is an ambiguous or two-edged compliment. *Cp.* BACK-HANDED COMPLIMENT.

Double dealing. Deceit or duplicity; professing one thing and practising another.

Double Dutch. Gibberish or jargon, as of infants or of a foreign tongue not understood by the hearer. Dutch is a synonym for foreign in this context; and double implies to an excessive degree.

Double-edged. Able to cut either way; used metaphorically of an argument which makes for and against the person employing it or of a compliment or statement with a double meaning.

> "Your Delphic sword," the panther then replied,
> "Is double-edged and cuts on either side."
> DRYDEN: *The Hind and the Panther, Pt. III, 191.*

Double entendre (doo' blŏn tŏn dra). An incorrect English version of the French *double entente*. Used of a word or phrase with a double meaning, one of which is usually coarse or indelicate.

A double first. Formerly in the first class both of the classical and mathematical triposes at Cambridge. Now, a first class in any two final examinations.

Double-headed Eagle. *See* THE TWO-HEADED EAGLE *under* EAGLE.

Double or quits. The winner stakes his stake, and the loser promises to pay twice the stake if he loses again; but if he wins the second throw, etc., his loss is cancelled and no money passes.

Double-quick. In military usage, means to proceed at double-quickstep or double-time, the quickest step next to a run. *See* TO DOUBLE-UP.

Double Summer Time. *See* DAYLIGHT SAVING.

Double take. An actor's trick. It is to look away from the person who has addressed a remark to you, and then to look back at him quickly when the purport of the remark sinks in. A second look occasioned by surprise or admiration.

Double-talk. An expression of American origin. Talk that sounds promising but in reality means nothing, or can be made to mean what the speaker wishes.

Double-think. A term used by George Orwell in his *Nineteen Eighty-four* (1949) to describe what unscrupulous propagandists achieved by "NEWSPEAK", a kind of DOUBLE-TALK. It denoted the mental ability to hold and accept simultaneously two entirely conflicting views or beliefs.

Double-time. As a military expression, the same as DOUBLE-QUICK.

Double-tongued. Making contrary declarations on the same subject at different times; deceitful; insincere.

> Be grave, not double-tongued.
> I *Tim*. iii, 8.

Double X. *See* X.

To double a cape. Said of a ship that sails round a cape to the other side; hence its course proceeds along both sides.

To double a part. Said of an actor playing two parts in the same piece.

To double and twist. To prevaricate, act evasively or to try to extract oneself from a difficulty by tortuous means. The phrase is taken from coursing—a hare "doubles and twists" in seeking to escape the hounds. In weaving, "to double and twist" is to add one thread to another and twist them together.

To double back. To turn back on one's course.

To double-cross. Properly to cheat or cross each of two parties, to betray both sides; but now commonly used to mean the betrayal or deception of an associate.

To double up. To fold together. "To double up the fist" is to clench the fist. "To double a person up" is to strike him in the wind and make him fold double with pain. In military language, "Double up" is an order to hurry or run.

To word double tides. To work extra hard, with all one's might. It implies doing three days work in two, or a minimum of two tides work in 24 hours. When a ship is left aground between tides for repairs below the waterline, a tide's work is that period of labour possible during the ebb and slack water.

> We...were working double tides, doing our very best to make up a pile worth while leaving the country with.
> BOLDREWOOD: *Robbery Under Arms*, Ch. xxix.

Doubting Castle. In Bunyans's *Pilgrim's Progress*, the castle of the giant Despair and his wife Diffidence, in which CHRISTIAN and Hopeful were incarcerated, but from which they escaped by means of the key called Promise.

Doubting Thomas. *See* THOMAS.

Doughboy. Originally a dough cake baked for sailors, but from the late 1840s the name came to be given to American soldiers until World War II when "G.I." generally took its place. The common explanation is that the large brass buttons of the soldier's uniform resembled the dough cake.

Doughface (U.S.A.). An inhabitant of the northern states who was in favour of maintaining slavery in the South.

Douglas. The Scottish family name is from the river Douglas in Lanarkshire, which is the Celt. *dhu glaise*, black stream, a name in use also in IRELAND, the Isle of Man, etc., and in Lancashire corrupted to *Diggles*. Legend explains it by the story that in 770 an unknown chief came to the assistance of a Scottish king. After the battle the king asked who was the "Duglass" chieftain, his deliverer, and received for answer *Sholto Duglas* which means "Behold the dark grey man".

> The complexion of the day is congenial with the original derivation of the name of the country, and the description of the chiefs to whom it belonged—Sholto Dhu Glass—(See yon dark grey man).
> SCOTT: *Castle Dangerous*, ch. iii.

Black Douglas. Sir James Douglas (1286–1330), or "Good Sir James", champion of Robert Bruce, was called "Black Douglas" by the English of the Border to whom he became a figure of dread. He twice took Douglas Castle from its English occupants by stratagem. The story is told in Scott's *Castle Dangerous*.

The Douglas Larder. On PALM SUNDAY 1307. Sir James Douglas regained his castle by a ruse and, knowing that he could not hold it, caused all the provisions to be heaped together in the cellar along with the bodies of the slain prisoners and dead horses. Drink was then poured over all and salt cast upon it. The castle was then fired. This cellar is known as the "Douglas Larder".

Douse, or **dowse.** To strike, to *douse a sail* is to lower it hastily; to extinguish; to drench. The origin of the word is uncertain but possibly from Old Dut. *doesen*, to beat, to strike. *See also* DOWSE.

A douse in the chops. A heavy blow in the face.

Douse the Glim. Put out the candle, put out the light, also to knock out a man's eye.

> "What though he has his humours, and made my eye dowse the glim in his fancies and frolics."
> SCOTT: *The Pirate*, ch. xxiv.

Dout. A contraction of *do out*. In some southern counties we find *dout the candle* and *dout the fire*, and extinguishers are called *douters*. *Cp*. DOFF; DON; DUP.

Dove. The name means "the diver-bird"; perhaps from its habit of ducking its head. So also Lat. *columba* is the Gr. *kolumbis*, a diver.

In Christian art the dove symbolizes the HOLY GHOST, and the seven rays proceeding from it the seven gifts of the Holy Ghost. It also symbolizes the SOUL and as such is sometimes represented coming out of the mouth of saints at death. A dove bearing a ring is an attribute of St. AGNES; St. DAVID is shown with a dove on his shoulder; St. DUNSTAN and St. Gregory the Great with one at the ear; St. Enurchus with one on his head; and St. REMIGIUS with the dove bringing him holy chrism.

The clergy of the CHURCH OF ENGLAND are allegorized as doves in Dryden's *The Hind and the Panther*, Pt. III, 947.

The dove is also the symbol of peace, tenderness, innocence, and gentleness.

To cause a flutter in the dovecot. To alarm, disturb, or cause confusion among those conventionally minded or settled in their ways, as would a bird of prey in a dovecot.

Dover. In the professional slang of English cooks a *resurrection pie* or any *réchauffé* is called a dover (do over again).

A Jack of Dover. *See* JACK.

When Dover and Calais meet. *See* NEVER.

Dovercourt. A confused gabble, a babel. According to legend, Dovercourt church in Essex once possessed a cross that spoke; and Foxe says that the crowd in the church was so great "that no man could shut the door". Dovercourt also seems to have been noted for its scolds and chattering women.

> And now the rood of Dovercourt did speak.
> Confirming his opinions to be true.
> *Grim, the Collier of Croydon* (1600).
> When bells ring round and in their order be,
> They do denote how neighbours should agree;
> But when they clam, the harsh sound spoils the sport
> And 'tis like women keeping Dovercourt.
> *Lines in the Belfry of St. Peter's, Shaftesbury.*

Dowelling Money. Dwelling-house money. In mediæval England the equivalent of a church rate *i.e.*, a parochial levy in each household. *See* PENTECOSTAL; SMOKE-FARTHINGS *under* SMOKE.

Dowlas, Mr. A generic name for a linen-draper, who sold dowlas, a coarse linen cloth (so called from Daoulas, in Brittany, where it was made).

> *Mrs. Quickly:* I bought you a dozen of shirts to your back.
> *Falstaff:* Dowlas, filthy dowlas: I have given them away to bakers' wives, and they have made bolsters of them.
> *Mrs. Quickly:* Now, as I am a true woman, holland of eight shillings an ell.
> SHAKESPEARE: *Henry IV, Pt. I*, III, iii.

Down. Down and out. At the end of one's resources with no apparent chance of recovery. Homeless vagrants are termed down-and-outs. The allusion is to boxing.

Down at heel. In decayed circumstances, of which worn-down heels are a sign.

> A good man's fortune may grow out at heels
> SHAKESPEARE: *King Lear*, II, ii.

Down in the dumps. *See* DUMPS.

Down in the jib. The nautical equivalent of DOWN IN THE MOUTH.

Down in the mouth. Out of spirits; disheartened. When persons are very sad and low-spirited, the corners of the mouth are drawn down.

Down on his luck. In ill luck; short of cash and credit.

Down with! Away with! A cry of rage and exasperation, like the Fr. *à bas*.

He is run down. Out of condition. In need of a thorough rest. Like a clock that has *run down* and needs rewinding.

I was down on him in a minute. I pounced on him directly. I detected his trick immediately. The allusion is to birds of prey.

That suits me down to the ground. Wholly and entirely, like a well-tailored garment.

The down train. The train away from London or the local centre, in contradistinction to the *up train*, which goes to it. We also have the *down platform*, etc.

To be sent down. To be sent from a university as a punishment.

To down tools. To lay one's tools aside and stop work; to come out on strike.

To go down. In university parlance, to commence vacation or to leave the university finally.

To have a down on. To have a grudge or spite against.

To run a man down. To denigrate or discredit someone to a third party.

Ups and downs. The twists and turns of fortune; one's successes and reverses.

> Fraudulent transactions have their downs as well as their ups.
> DICKENS: *Martin Chuzzlewit*, ch. xvi.

Down-easter. An American from New England.

Down-town. The business district of an American city, so called from New York, where financial houses are concentrated on the southern tip of Manhattan Island; the lower part of a town.

Down under. At the Antipodes; in Australia.

Downing Street. A street leading off WHITE-HALL and a synonym for the British Government.

No. 10 was given in 1725 by George II to Sir Robert Walpole as the official residence of the PRIME MINISTER, and it is there that CABINET meetings are usually held. No. 11 is the official residence of the CHANCELLOR OF THE EXCHEQUER; No. 12 is the Government WHIP's Office. The street was named after Sir George Downing (*c.* 1623–1684), a noted parliamentarian and ambassador, who served under both Cromwell and Charles II, and owned property there.

Downright. Downright Dunstable. *See* DUNSTABLE.

Downy. A downy cove. A knowing or cunning fellow *up to* or, as formerly, *down to* every dodge. In Vaux's *Flash Dictionary* (1812) *down* is given as a synonym for "awake".

> When the party you are about to rob sees or suspects your intention, it is then said that *the cove is down*.

Dowsabell. A common name in 16th-century poetry for a sweetheart, especially an unsophisticated country girl. It is the Fr. *douce et belle*, sweet and beautiful.

> He had, as antique stories tell,
> A daughter cleaped Dowsabel,
> A mayden fayre and free.
> DRAYTON: *The Ballad of Dowsabell*.

Dowse (*see also* DOUSE). To search for water etc., with a DIVINING-ROD or *dowsing-rod*.

Doxology (Gr. *Doxologia*). The word means a hymn of praise to God. The Greater Doxology is the hymn *Gloria in Excelsis Deo* at the EUCHARIST. The Lesser Doxology is the *Gloria Patri* (Glory be to the Father, etc.) sung or said at the end of each psalm in the liturgy. The hymn "Praise God from whom all blessings flow" is also known as the Doxology.

Doyen. Fr. for DEAN (Lat. *decanus*). Denotes the senior accredited ambassador in a capital, but if there is a Papal Nuncio he is *ipso facto* the doyen. It is also applied to the senior member of a profession, etc.

> Professor John Orr, F.B.A., Emeritus Professor in the University of Edinburgh, and the doyen and outstanding representative of Romance philology in Britain, and in the English speaking world, died on Wednesday at Edinburgh.
> *The Times*, 15 Aug. 1966.

Dozen. Twelve. The word is derived from the Lat. *duodecim*.

A long dozen is thirteen. *See* BAKER'S DOZEN.

To talk nineteen to the dozen. To talk at a tremendous speed or with excessive vehemence.

Drachenfels (Ger. Dragon's Rock). The German mountain on the right bank of the Rhine, south-east of Bonn. The legendary haunt of the DRAGON which SIEGFRIED slew. He bathed in its blood and so became invulnerable except in one spot on which a linden leaf had fallen. *See* NIBELUNGENLIED.

> The castled crag of Drachenfels
> Frowns o'er the wide and winding Rhine,
> Whose breast of waters broadly swells
> Between the banks which bear the vine.
> BYRON: Childe Harold, iii, 55.

Draconian Code (drȧ kō′ ni ȧn). A very severe code. Draco was an Athenian of the 7th century B.C. who drew up a code of laws noted for their severity. As nearly every violation of his laws was a capital offence, Demades, the orator, said that Draco's code was written in blood.

Dracula. *See* VAMPIRE.

Draft. Draft on Aldgate pump. *See* ALDGATE.

Drag. In slang, feminine dress worn by men; transvestite clothing.

To go on the drag. To wear women's clothes with immoral intentions.

Draggle-tail. *See* DAGGLE-TAIL.

Dragon. The Greek word *drakon* comes from a verb meaning "to see", to "look at", and more remotely "to watch" and "to flash".

In classical legend the idea of *watching* is retained in the story of the dragon who guards the golden apples in the Garden of the HESPERIDES, and in the story of CADMUS. In mediæval romance captive ladies were often guarded by dragons.

A dragon is a fabulous winged crocodile, usually represented as of large size, with a serpent's tail; whence the words dragon and SERPENT are sometimes interchangeable. In the Middle Ages the word was the symbol of sin in general and paganism in particular, the METAPHOR being derived from *Rev.* xii, 9, where SATAN is termed "the great dragon" and *Ps.* xci, 13, where it is said "the dragon shalt thou trample under feet". Hence, in Christian art it has the same significance.

Among the many SAINTS usually pictured as dragon-slayers are St. MICHAEL, St. GEORGE, St. MARGARET, St. Samson (Archbishop of Dol), St. Clement of Metz; St. Romain of Rouen, who destroyed the huge dragon La GARGOUILLE, which ravaged the Seine; St. PHILIP the Apostle; St. MARTHA, slayer of the terrible dragon Tarasque, at Aix-la-Chapelle; St. Florent, who killed a dragon which haunted the Loire; St. Cado, St. Maudet, and St. Pol, who performed similar feats in Brittany; and St. KEYNE of CORNWALL.

Among the ancient Britons and the Welsh the dragon was the national symbol on the war standard; hence the term PENDRAGON for the *dux bellorum*, or leader in war. *See* RED DRAGON.

Dragon's Blood. An old name in pharmacy for the resin from certain plants, formerly used in certain preparations, etc. The East Indian palm (*Calamus draco*) is used as a colouring matter for artists' varnishes, etc.

In German legend, when SIEGFRIED was told to bathe in the blood of a dragon in order to make him immune from injury, a linden leaf fell on him and the place it covered remained vulnerable. There is a possible connexion between this story and the term "dragon's blood" applied to a powder used in printing which, applied to a block for processing, prevents the etching of that portion covered.

A flying dragon. A meteor.

The Chinese dragon. In China, a five-clawed dragon is introduced into pictures and embroidered on dresses as an AMULET.

The Dragon of Wantley. *See* WANTLEY.

To sow dragon's teeth. To foment contentions; to stir up strife or war; especially to do something which is intended to put an end to strife but which brings it about. The Philistines "sowed dragons' teeth" when they took SAMSON, bound him, and put out his eyes; Ethelred II did the same when he ordered the massacre of the Danes on St. Brice's Day (1002), as did the Germans when they took Alsace-Lorraine from France in 1871.

The reference is to the classical story of CADMUS.

Dragon's Hill. A site in Berkshire where one legend has it that St. GEORGE killed the dragon. A bare place is shown on the hill, where nothing will grow, for there the dragon's blood was spilled.

In Saxon annals we are told that Cerdic, founder of the West Saxon kingdom, there slew Naud or Natanleod, the PENDRAGON, and five thousand men.

Dragon Mountains. The Drakensberg Mountains in South Africa.

Dragonnades. The name given to Louis XIV's persecutions of the HUGUENOTS from 1681, until after the Revocation of the Edict of NANTES in 1685. The name arises from the billeting of DRAGOONS on those PROTESTANTS who refused to renounced their "heresy". The soldiery were given a free hand with the obvious results.

Dragoon. The name of certain cavalry regiments; originally a mounted infantryman. The name is taken from the carbine called a *dragon* which spouted fire like the fabulous beast of this name.

To dragoon is to persecute; to coerce. The derivation is obvious from the above. "He was dragooned into" means that he was coerced into it.

Drake. Drake Brass Plate. *See under* FOR-
GERY.

Drake's Drum. *See under* DRUM.

Drama. Closet Drama. An American expression denoting plays which are better
suited for reading rather than acting.

Father of Danish Drama. Ludwig von
Holberg (1684–1754).

Father of French Drama. Étienne Jodelle
(1532–1573).

Father of Greek Drama. Thespis (6th
century B.C.).

Father of Modern German Drama. Andreas Gryphius (1616–1664).

Father of Spanish Drama. Lope de Vega
(1562–1635).

Dramatic Unities. The three dramatic
unities, the rules governing the so-called
"classical' dramas, are founded on RENAIS-
SANCE misconceptions of passages in AR-
ISTOTLE's *Poetics*, and are hence often,
though very incorrectly, styled the *Aristotelian Unities*. They are, that in dramas there
should be (1) Unity of Action, (2) Unity of
Time, (3) Unity of Place. Aristotle lays
stress on the first, the second was deduced
by Castelvetro (1505–1571), the Italian
scholar and critic, from an incidental reference to it by Aristotle, and the third followed
almost perforce.

The convention of the three unities was
adopted in France, especially after the triumph of Corneille's *Le Cid* (1636), but met
with little success in ENGLAND. SHAKE-
SPEARE, like Aristotle, was only concerned
with the Unity of Action but the three unities were purposely adhered to in Ben Jonson's *Alchemist* (1610).

Dramatis personæ (drăm' ȧ tis pĕr-
sō' nē). The characters of a drama, novel
or, by extension, of an actual transaction.

Drapier's Letters (drā' pēr). A series of letters written by Dean Swift to the people of
Ireland, appearing in 1724 under the signature of M.B. Drapier, rousing them against
the copper coinage called WOOD'S HALF-
PENCE.

Drat. A variant of *Od rot!* "Od" being a minced
form of "God", and the vowel showing the
same modifications as in "Gad!" or "Gadzooks!" *See* OD'S.

Draupnir (drawp' nēr). ODIN's magic ring,
from which every ninth night dropped eight
rings equal in size and beauty to itself. It was
made by the DWARFS.

Draw. A drawn game, battle, etc. One in
which neither side can claim a victory; perhaps so called from a battle in which the
troops are drawn off on both sides when no
decision seems possible.

A good draw. A first-rate attraction. "Performing elephants are always a good draw at
circuses."

Draw it mild! Don't exaggerate! Don't
make your remarks (or actions) stronger
than necessary. The allusion is to the drawing of ALE.

Hanged, drawn, and quartered. Strictly,
the phrase should read *Drawn, hanged, and
quartered*; for the allusion is to the sentence
usually passed on those guilty of high treason, which was that they should be drawn to
the place of execution on a hurdle or at a
horse's tail. Later, drawing (or disembowelling) was added to the punishment after the
hanging and before the quartering. Thus the
sentence (August 1305) on Sir William WAL-
LACE was that he should be drawn (*detraha-
tur*) from the Palace of WESTMINSTER to the
TOWER, then hanged (*suspendatur*), then
disembowelled or drawn (*devaletur*), then
beheaded and quartered (*decapitetur et de-
colletur*). His quarters were gibbeted at
Newcastle, Berwick, Stirling and Perth.

Lord Chief Justice Ellenborough
(1750–1818) used to say to those condemned:

> "You are drawn on hurdles to the place of exec-
> ution, where you are to be hanged, but not till you
> are dead; for, while still living, your body is to be ta-
> ken down, your bowels torn out and burnt before
> your face; your head is then cut off, and your body is
> divided into four quarters."
>
> *Gentleman's Magazine*, 1803.

To draw a badger. *See* BADGER.

To draw a bead on somebody. To take
aim at him with a rifle or revolver. The *bead*
referred to is the foresight.

**To draw a bow at a venture; to draw the
long bow.** *See* BOW.

To draw a furrow. To plough or to make a
furrow.

To draw a person out. To entice a
person to speak on any subject, to encourage
one too shy to talk, to obtain information.

To draw amiss. To take the wrong direction. A hunting term, *to draw* meaning to
follow a scent.

To draw a veil over. To say no more about
a matter; to conceal something from the
knowledge of others as a veil conceals a
woman's face.

To draw blank. To meet with failure in
one's pursuit. The allusion is to sportsmen
"drawing" a covert and finding no game. **To
draw a blank** means having no luck in a lottery, etc., to fail in a search.

To draw in one's horns. *See under* HORN.

To draw the cork. To give one a bloody
nose. *Cp.* CLARET.

To draw the King's, or **Queen's picture.**

To coin false money.

To draw the line. To set a definite limit beyond which one refuses to go; to impose a restriction on one's behaviour for fear of going too far. "He was utterly unprincipled, but he drew the line at blackmail," *i.e.* he would not stoop to blackmail, he would stop short of that.

To draw the nail. To release oneself from a vow. It was a Cheshire custom to register a vow by driving a nail into a tree, swearing to keep your vow as long as it remained there. If you withdrew the nail, the vow was cancelled.

To draw rations, stores, etc. A military phrase; to go to the place of issue and collect same.

To draw rein. To pull up short, to check one's course.

To draw stumps. At the end of a game of CRICKET the wickets are dismantled, the stumps being drawn out of the ground.

Drawcansir. A bustling braggart, from the burlesque tyrant in Buckingham's *Rehearsal* (1671). He was a caricature of Dryden's ALMANZOR. Drawcansir's opening speech (he has only three) is:

> He that dares drink, and for that drink dares die,
> And knowing this, dare yet drink on, am I.
> *Rehearsal*, IV, i.

which parodies Almanzor's:

> He who dares love, and for that love must die,
> And, knowing this, dare yet love on, am I.
> *Almanzor*, IV, iii.

Cp. BAYES; BOBADIL.

Drawer. Bottom Drawer. The most capacious drawer in a chest is usually at the bottom, and when a young woman who is engaged starts collecting articles for setting up her future home, she is said to be putting them in her bottom drawer.

> As soon as a girl passed her fifteenth birthday she began to sew for the "bottom drawer".
> ARNOLD BENNETT: *Anna of the Five Towns*, Ch.13.

Out of the top drawer. Upper class, to be of good family, to be of top grade socially. The expression probably derives from the fact that the top drawers of a chest often contain the more valued of one's personal effects.

Drawing-room. Originally the *withdrawing room* to which the ladies retired after dinner leaving the men to continue their drinking, etc.

Drawing-room of Europe. So NAPOLEON called St. Mark's Square in Venice.

Drawlatch. An old name for a robber, a house-breaker; *i.e.* one who entered by drawing up the latch with the string provided for the purpose.

Dreadnought. The name given to the 17,900-ton turbine-engined big-gun battleship completed in 1906, the first of a famous class, which greatly influenced subsequent naval construction. The first ship of this name was in use in the reign of Queen Elizabeth I.

The Seamen's Hospital at Greenwich, known as the Dreadnought Hospital, takes its name from the seventh *Dreadnought*, which was first in action in 1809, and from 1857 was anchored off Greenwich as a seamen's hospital. It was broken up in 1875.

Dreams, The Gates of. There are two, that of ivory and that of horn. Dreams which delude pass through the Ivory gate, those which come true pass through the Gate of Horn. This fancy depends upon two puns: ivory in Greek is *elephas*, and the verb *elephairo* means "to cheat with empty hopes"; the Greek for horn is *keras*, and the verb *karanoo* means to accomplish.

> That children dream not the first half-year; that men dream not in some countries, with many more, are unto me sick men's dreams; dreams out of the ivory gate, and visions before midnight.
> SIR THOMAS BROWNE: *On Dreams*.

The Immortal Dreamer. John Bunyan (1628–1688), whose allegory, *The Pilgrim's Progress*, is in the form of a dream.

Pipe dream. *See under* PIPE.

Drengage. An ancient form of tenure, connected with hunting services. Such service existed on the manors of the Bishop of Durham before the CONQUEST. The word is from Dan. *dreng*, a boy, a servant.

> Thus there are persons holding in "drengage", who have had to feed a horse and a dog and "to go in the great hunt (*magna caza*) with two harriers and 15 cordons", etc.
> F. SEEBOHM: *The English Village Community*, ch. II, 10.

Dresden China. This fine hard porcelain, which attained such high repute in the 18th century and afterwards, was made at Meissen (some 12 miles from Dresden) from about 1709. Among the many figurines produced there, the Dresden Shepherdess has remained a favourite for daintiness and grace. The factory was established by Augustus II, King of Poland and Elector of Saxony, and its success was the result of the discovery of kaolin at Aue. Every effort was made to retain the process of manufacture, the kaolin was dispatched from Aue in casks sealed by dumb persons and the workmen at Meissen sworn to secrecy, but by 1718 the secret was known in Vienna. In the 1750s beautifully ornamented "table services" were selling at prices between 100 and 1,000 guineas.

Dressed. Dressed to kill. Dress in the height of fashion. Very smartly dressed. The idea is from that of so dressing to make a conquest or "kill" of one of the opposite sex. **To dress to death** has a similar meaning. We also say **dressed up to the nines** which is perhaps a corruption of **to then eyne** (to the eyes).

Dreyfusard. An advocate of the innocence of Capt. Alfred Dreyfus (1859–1935), a French artillery officer of Jewish descent who was convicted in 1894 on a charge of betraying military secrets to Germany and sent to DEVIL'S ISLAND. In 1898 Clemenceau and Zola took up his case and Zola wrote his famous open letter *J'accuse*. In 1899 Dreyfus was retried, again condemned, but shortly afterwards pardoned. In 1906 the proceedings were finally quashed. The whole affair reflected the greatest discredit on the French military hierarchy of the time.

Drink. Drink-money. A "tip"; a small gratuity to be spent on drinking the health of the giver; a *pourboire* (Fr. for drink); also money allocated for drink.

Drinking of healths. *See* GABBARA; HEALTH.

In the drink. In the sea, in the water; long-established nautical slang.

It is meat and drink to me. Something that is almost essential to my well-being; something very much to my liking; just what I appreciate.

> It is meat and drink to me to see a clown.
> SHAKESPEARE: *As You Like It*, V, i.

One must drink as one brews. One must take the consequences of one's actions; "as one makes one's bed so must one lie on it".

> I am grieved it should be said he is my brother, and take these courses; well, as he brews, so shall he drink.
> JONSON: *Every Man in His Humour*, II, i.

The big drink. An American expression for any large stretch of water, such as the Atlantic (*cp.* HERRING-POND) or Lake Superior.

Those who drink beer will think beer. A saying attributed to Warburton, Bishop of Gloucester (1698–1779). Some non-teetotaller capped it with, "And those that drink water will think water."

To drink at Freeman's Quay. To get one's drink at someone else's expense. It is said, somewhat improbably, that at one time all porters and carmen calling at Freeman's Quay, near London Bridge, had a pot of beer given them gratis.

To drink deep. To take a deep draught; to drink heavily.

> A little learning is a dangerous thing;
> Drink deep, or taste not the Pierian spring.
> POPE: *Essay on Criticism*, I, 216.

SHAKESPEARE uses the expression metaphorically as in Henry V, I, i.

> *Cant:* If it pass against us,
> We lose the better half of our possession;
> ...And to the coffers of the king, beside,
> A thousand pounds by the year: thus runs the bill.
> *Ely:* This would drink deep.
> *Cant:* 'Twould drink the cup and all.

To drink like a fish. To drink abundantly or excessively. Many fish swim open-mouthed, thus appearing to be continually drinking. The expression is found in Beaumont and Fletcher.

To drink the cup of sorrow. To undergo affliction, to suffer one's share of sorrow. "To drink the cup" is used in the sense of "being allotted one's portion".

To drink the waters. To take medicinal waters, especially at a spa.

Drive. He is driving pigs, or **driving pigs to market.** Said of one who is snoring, because the grunt of a pig resembles the snore of a sleeper.

To drive a coach and four through an Act of Parliament. *See under* COACH.

To drive a good, or **hard bargain.** To exact more than is quite equitable.

> Heaven would no bargain for its blessings drive.
> DRYDEN: *Astræa Redux*, line 137.

To drive a nail into one's coffin. *See under* COFFIN.

To drive a point home. To stress a point with the utmost persistence; to ensure the acceptance of one's point and to make sure that it is understood; like driving a nail to its full extent.

To drive a roaring trade. To do a brisk business.

To drive a ship is to press on with full sail.

To drive someone up the wall. To drive a person to desperation; metaphorically, to drive one crazy.

To drive the swine through the hanks of yarn. To spoil what has been painfully done; to squander thrift. In Scotland, the yarn wrought in the winter (called *the gudewife's thrift*) was laide down by the burnside to bleach, and was thus exposed to damage from passing animals, such as a herd of pigs.

To drive to the wall. To push to extremity; to break or crush.

To let drive. To attack.

> Thou knowest my old ward; here I Falstaff lay, and thus I bore my point. Four rogues in buckram let drive at me.
> SHAKESPEARE: *Henry IV, Pt. I*, II, iv.

What are you driving at? What do you want to prove? What do you want to infer?

Who drives fat oxen shall himself be fat.
Henry Brooke in his *Gustavus Vasa* (1739)
says: "Who rules o'er free-men should himself be free". Dr. Johnson parodied the
line—and the sentiment, with which he did
not agree.

Droit. Droit d'Aubaine (drwa′ dō bān)
(Fr.). *Aubain* means an "alien", a non-naturalized foreigner", and *droit d'aubaine*
the "right over an alien's property". In
France the king was entitled, at the death of
foreign residents (except Swiss and Scots),
to all their movable estates, a right that was
not finally abolished until 1819.

> Had I died that night of an indigestion, the whole
> world could not have suspended the *droit
> d'aubaine*. My shirts and black pair of breeches,
> portmanteau, and all must have gone to the King of
> France.
>
> STERNE: *Sentimental Journey* (Intro.).

Droit de fauteuil (drwa′ dĕ fotēē′). *See*
TABOURET.

Droit du seigneur (drwa′ doo sen yĕr′)
(Fr.). *See* JUS PRIMÆ NOCTIS.

Droit de Tabouret (drwa′ dĕ tăb′ oo rā′).
See TABOURET.

Dromio (drō′ mi ō). **The brothers Dromio.**
Two brothers who were exactly alike, who
served two brothers who were exactly alike.
The mistakes of masters and men form the
fun of SHAKESPEARE's *Comedy of Errors*,
based on the *Menæchmi* of Plautus.

Drone. The male of the honey bee which does
no work but lives on the labour of the worker
bees; hence a sluggard, an idler, a parasite.

The three lower pipes of a bagpipe are
called the drones because they produce a
monotonous bass humming like that of a
bee.

> I am as melancholy as a gib-cat ... or the drone of a
> Lincolnshire bagpipe.
>
> SHAKESPEARE: *Henry IV, Pt. I,* I, ii.

Drop. Acid drop, The. *See* ACID.

A drop in one's eye. Not exactly intoxicated, but having had quite enough.

> We are no fou, we're nae that fou,
> But just a drappie in our e'e!
>
> BURNS: *Willie Brew'd a Peck o' Maut.*

A drop in the ocean, or **bucket.** A negligible or tiny quantity; something that makes
little difference.

A drop of the cratur. *See* CREATURE.

A dropping fire. An irregular fusillade from
small-arms, machine-guns, etc.

Drop-outs. An American name for those
who fail to complete their college courses or
those who drift into hoodlum gangs on leaving school.

Drope serene (Lat. *gutta serena*). An old
name for *amaurosis*, a disease of the optic
nerve, causing blindness without affecting
the appearance of the eye. It was at one time
thought that it was caused by a transparent,
watery humour, distilling on the nerve.

> So thick a drop serene hath quenched their orbs.
>
> MILTON: *Paradise Lost*, III, 25.

Prince Rupert's Drops. *See* RUPERT.

To drop across. To encounter accidentally
or casually.

To drop an acquaintance. To allow
acquaintanceship to lapse.

To drop in. To make a casual call or informal visit.

To drop off. To fall asleep (especially from
weariness). When "friends drop off" they
fall away gradually.

To drop someone a line. To write to
them.

To drop the pilot. To dismiss a well-tried
and trusted leader. The phrase was popularized by Tenniel's famous *Punch* cartoon (29
March 1890) showing Count von Bismarck,
wearing pilot's uniform, being dismissed by
Kaiser Wilhelm II.

To get the drop on someone. To have him
in your power; a phrase taken from pistol
shooting, where it means being ready to
shoot before your opponent.

To take a drop. A EUPHEMISM for taking
anything from a sip to a DUTCHMAN's
DRAUGHT.

To take one's drops. To drink spirits in
private.

Drown. Drowning men catch, or **clutch at
straws.** People in acute danger or desperate
circumstances cling in hope to trifles wholly
inadequate to be of use.

To drown the miller. *See* MILLER.

Drows. *See* TROWS.

Drug. A drug in the market. Something
which no one wants, something for which
there is little or no demand, especially from
there being a surfeit of the particular product in question.

Druids. The ancient order of priestly officials
in pre-Roman Gaul, pre-Roman Britain,
and IRELAND. They seem to have combined
priestly, judicial, and political functions.
The Druidic cult presents many obscurities
and our main literacy sources are Pliny and
the *Commentaries* of CÆSAR. We are told
that their rites were conducted in oak-groves, that human sacrifices were offered
up, and that they regarded the OAK and
MISTLETOE with particular veneration. It is
now suggested that the name Druid is derived from some "oak" word. They practised
DIVINATION and ASTROLOGY and taught that
the soul at death was transferred to another
body. Their distinguishing badge was a serpent's egg. (*See* DRUID'S EGG).

In the 18th and 19th centuries there was a revival of interest in Druidism and a new romantic and unhistorical cult grew up associated with the Welsh Eisteddfodau. This is usually termed Neo-Druidism. *See* EISTEDDFOD.

Druid's Circles. A popular name for circles of standing stones, of which STONEHENGE is the most famous example.

The Druid's Egg. According to Pliny, who claimed to possess one, this wonderful egg was hatched by the joint labour of several serpents and was buoyed in the air by their hissing. The person who caught it had to escape at full speed to avoid being stung to death; but the possessor was sure to prevail in every contest, and to be courted by those in power.

United Ancient Order of Druids. A secret benefit society, akin to FREEMASONRY, founded in London in 1781 and introduced into the U.S.A. in 1833. It now has lodges, or "groves", in many parts of the world.

Druj. *See* AHRIMAN.

Drum. A popular name in the 18th century and later for a crowded evening party, so called from its resemblance in noise to the drumming up of recruits. The more riotous of these parties were called *drum-majors*. *Cp.* HURRICANE; ROUT.

> This is a riotous assembly of fashionable people of both sexes, at a private house, consisting of some hundred, not unaptly stiled a drum, from the noise and emptiness.
> SMOLLETT: *Advice, a Satire* (1746).

A kettle drum. An afternoon tea. An obvious derivative of *drum* and a pun upon the tea kettle. A tea party was also called a *drum*.

Drake's Drum. Sir Francis Drake's (*c.* 1541–1596) drum of legendary fame.

> Take my drum to England, hang et by the shore.
> Strike et when your powder's runnin' low;
> If the Dons sight Devon, I'll quit the port o'heaven.
> An'drum them up the Channel as we drummed them long ago.
> SIR HENRY NEWBOLT: *Drake's Drum.*

John, or **Jack Drum's entertainment.** Turning an unwelcome guest out of doors.

> O! for the love of laughter, let him fetch off his drum; he says he has a stratagem for't. When your lordship sees the bottom of his success in't, and to what metal this counterfeit lump of ore will be melted if you give him not John Drum's entertainment, your inclining cannot be removed.
> SHAKESPEARE: *All's Well that Ends Well*, III, vi.

John Marston wrote a comedy with the title *Jack Drum's Entertainment* (1600), in which he is supposed to have satirized Ben Jonson.

Drum ecclesiastic. The pulpit cushion or pulpit, often vigorously thumped by "rousing preachers".

> When Gospel-trumpeter, surrounded
> With long-ear'd rout, to battle sounded;
> And pulpit, drum ecclesiastic,
> Was beat with fist instead of a stick.
> BUTLER: *Hudibras*, I, i.

Drum-head court martial. One held in haste in the field to punish on the spot; from the one-time custom of holding it round the big drum.

To be drummed out. To be expelled ignominiously, as a soldier in disgrace was dismissed the regiment to the accompaniment of drum beats.

To drum up. To get together unexpectedly or in an emergency, as "to drum up a meal".

Drumsticks. Legs, especially thin ones. Also the legs of dress or cooked poultry.

Drummer. An old name for a BAGMAN. In former days pedlars often drew attention to their arrival by beating a drum. The word was also current in the U.S.A. until the early 20th century.

Drummond Light. *See* LIME-LIGHT.

Drunk. Drunk as a fiddler, or **fiddler's bitch.** The fiddler at WAKES, FAIRS, and aboard ship, used to be paid in liquor for playing to the dancers.

Drunk as a lord. Obviously the nobility of bygone days could afford to indulge in excessive drinking if they were so inclined. In the 18th and 19th centuries gross intoxication was common and many men of fashion prided themselves on the number of bottles of wine they could consume at a sitting.

Drunk as blazes. Very drunk. Blazes here means the DEVIL, or HELL, etc., or, as has been suggested, it is a corruption of "blaiziers", *i.e.* those gildsmen who took part in the feastings and revelry in honour of St. Blaize, the patron of woolcombers.

Drunk as Chloe. Chloe was the cobbler's wife of Linden Grove to whom the poet Prior was attached. She was notorious for her drinking habits.

Drunk as David's sow. *See* DAVY'S SOW. There are many other common similes, such as *drunk as a coot, drunk as a newt, drunk as an owl*; Chaucer has *drunk as a mouse*, Massinger *drunk as a beggar*.

Drunkard's cloak. A tub with holes for the arms to pass through, used in the 17th century for drunkards and scolds by way of punishment.

Drunken Parliament, The. The Parliament assembled at Edinburgh, January 1661, of which Burnet says the members "were almost perpetually drunk".

Drury Lane. This famous London thoroughfare and its theatre takes its name from Drury House, built by Sir William Drury in the time of Henry VIII.

The parent of the present Drury Lane Theatre was opened in 1663 but was burned down nine years later. Its successor was designed by Wren but replaced by a new structure in 1794. This was destroyed by fire in 1809. The present theatre, designed by Wyatt, was opened in 1812. Many famous actors have appeared at Drury Lane, including Garrick, Kemble, and Kean.

Sweet Nell of Old Drury. Nell GWYN.

Druses. A people and sect of Syria of 11th-century origin, living about the mountains of Lebanon and Anti-Libanus. Their faith is a mixture of the PENTATEUCH, the GOSPEL, the KORAN and Sufism. They worship in both mosques and churches, but have their own SCRIPTURES. Their name is derived from their first apostle Ismail Ad-darazi.

Dry. I am dry with talking, *i.e.* I am thirsty after talking so long. Thus *to dry up* is to cease speaking. *Cp.* WET. **To go dry** is to adopt prohibition.

Not dry behind the ears. As innocent as a new-born child. When young animals are born, the last place to become dry after birth is the small depression behind each ear.

Dry-bob. A boy at Eton College who plays CRICKET and football instead of rowing. *See* WET-BOB.

Dry lodgings. An old expression for sleeping accommodation without board. Gentlemen who took their meals at clubs lived in "dry lodgings".

Dry shave. A shave without lathering the face; to scratch the face and bruise it. *To give someone a dry shave* is also to rub their cheeks with one's own bristly face.

> I'll shave her, like a punished soldier, dry.
> PETER PINDAR: *The Lousiad*, canto ii.

Dry wine. Opposed to sweet. In sweet wine some of the sugar is not yet decomposed; in dry wine all the sugar has been converted into alcohol.

Dryad. In classical mythology, a tree nymph (Gr. *drus*, an oak-tree), who was supposed to die when the tree died. Also called Hamadryads (Gr. *hama*, with). EURYDICE, the wife of ORPHEUS, was a dryad.

Dryasdust. The name given by Scott to the fictitious "reverend doctor", a learned pundit to whom he addressed some of his prefaces, hence a heavy, plodding author, very prosy, very dull, and very learned; and antiquary without imagination.

Dual (Lat. *dualis*, twofold, divided in two).

Dual personality. Used of someone who, on different occasions, reveals two quite different characters.

Dual Monarchy. When two states share

the same monarchy but remain politically separate, as in the case of England and Scotland from 1603. The Stuart kings reigned in both countries which, however, remained politically independent of each other until the Act of Union of 1707.

Historically the phrase is specifically applied to Austria-Hungary from the time of the *Ausgleich*, or Compromise, of 1867, until the collapse of 1918. During this period Francis Joseph was Emperor of Austria and King of Hungary.

Dualism. A system of philosophy which refers all things that exist to two ultimate principles, such as Descartes's Thought (*res cogitans*) and Extension (*res extensa*), or—in the theological sense—good and evil. In modern philosophy it is opposed to MONISM and insists that creator and creation, mind and body, are distinct entities. *See* MANICHÆANS.

Dub. The original meaning (from O.E. *dubban*, to equip with arms) was to confer knighthood by a stroke of a sword; whence it acquired figurative meanings, such as to nickname some thing or person, *e.g.* "he was dubbed a ladies' man".

Dub up. Pay down the money; "fork out". *Dub* another form of DUP.

Dubglas. *See* DUGLAS.

Ducat (dŭk' ăt). A coin first minted in 1140 by Roger II of Sicily as Duke of the Duchy (*ducato*) of Apulia. In 1284 the Venetians struck a GOLD coin bearing the legend *Sit tibi, Christe, datus, quem tu regis, iste ducatus* (may this duchy which you rule be devoted to you, O Christ), and through this the name ducat gained wider use.

Duce (doo' chā) (Ital. leader). The title adopted by Benito Mussolini (1883–1945), the FASCIST dictator of Italy from 1922 to 1943.

Duck. *See* DUCK'S EGG.

A dead duck. Figuratively, something of no further interest. *To feel like a dead duck* is to be exhausted.

> At the last election Britains' relationship with Europe was a dead duck.
> *The Times*, 17 June 1966.

A lame duck. A STOCK-JOBBER or dealer who will not, or cannot, pay his losses, he has to "waddle out the alley like a lame duck". Also a defaulter or one who is disabled.

> "I don't like the looks of Mr. Sedley's affairs ... He's been dabbling on his own account I fear ... unless I see Amelia's ten thousand down you don't marry. I'll have no lame duck's daughter in my family."
> THACKERAY: *Vanity Fairy*, ch. xiii.

Duck Lane. Duck Lane (now Duke Street,

leading from LITTLE BRITAIN to Long Lane, in the City of LONDON) in Queen Anne's time was famous for its secondhand bookstalls.

> Scotists and Thomists now in peace remain
> Amidst their kindred cobwebs in Duck Lane.
> POPE: *Essay on Criticism*, Pt. II.

Duck's egg. Now always used in the shortened form of "a duck", meaning in CRICKET no score at all. It arose from the resemblance of o to a duck's egg. In American usage *goose-egg* is used for no score at all in a game. *See* SPECTACLES.

Ducks and Drakes. The ricocheting or rebounding of a stone thrown to skim along the surface of a pond, etc. **To play ducks and drakes with one's money** is to throw it away carelessly, just for the sake of amusement and watching it make a splash.

> What figured slates are best to make
> On watery surface duck and drake.
> BUTLER: *Hudibras*, II, iii.

Like a dying duck in a thunderstorm. Quite CHOP-FALLEN (*see under* CHOP (3)), very woebegone. Young ducks die speedily of chill if caught by a sudden downpour away from warmth and shelter.

To get one's ducks in a row. An American expression meaning to have one's arrangements completed, to have things organized or lined up; or, literally, to have one's skittles set up. In an American bowling alley the smaller sets of skittles, or pins, are called ducks.

Ducking stool, or **Scold's chair.** A specially made chair in which the culprit was bound and publicly "ducked" or immersed in the water. It was commonly used until the early 18th century, but its last recorded use in England was at Leominster, Herefordshire, in 1809, when Jenny Pipes was ducked.

Dude. A fop or dandy, a MASHER.

Dude Ranch. In the western states of the U.S.A., one especially organized as a holiday camp for inexperienced riders.

Dudman and Ramhead. When Dudman and Ramhead meet, *i.e.* NEVER. The DODMAN and Ramehead (as they are now spelt) are two forelands on the south coast of CORNWALL about 23 sea miles apart.

Duds. A very old word of unknown origin once applied to coarse cloaks but now used for clothes of any kind, as "He was dressed in his best duds", or "He was wearing his oldest duds". A *dudder* or *dudsman* or *dudman* is a scarecrow, or a pedlar who sells dress materials, etc.

Duglas. According to the *Historia Brittonum* by Nennius, King ARTHUR fought twelve great battles against the Saxons. "The second, third, fourth, and fifth, were on another river, by the Britons called Duglas in the region Linius." The topography is vague and the whereabouts of the river Duglas (or Dubglas) is open to conjecture.

Duke (Lat. *dux*, leader). The title of the highest rank of nobility in Great Britain. The first English dukedom to be created was that bestowed by Edward III on his eldest son the BLACK PRINCE in 1338, when he was raised from Earl of CORNWALL to Duke of Cornwall. The title is very rarely conferred except for royal dukes; and since 1874 (when Hugh Lupus Grosvenor, 3rd Marquis of Westminster, was made Duke of Westminster), it has been conferred only on the Earl of Fife, who was created Duke of Fife on his marriage with Princess Louise in 1889. On his death in 1912, his daughter, Princess Arthur of Connaught, became Duchess of Fife in her own right, by special remainder. Prince Philip was created Duke of Edinburgh in 1947. Other than royal dukes there are twenty-six noble dukedoms.

Duke Combe. William Combe (1741–1823), also called *Count Combe*, author of *The Tour of Dr. Syntax*, etc., was so called from the splendour of his dress, the profusion of his table, and the magnificence of his deportment, in the days of his prosperity. Having spent all his money he turned author, but passed much of his life in the King's Bench Prison. He died at Lambeth. *See* SYNTAX.

Duke Humphrey. *See* HUMPHREY.

Duke or Darling. Heads or tails. When the scandals about the Duke of York (1763–1827) and his mistress, Mrs. Mary Anne Clarke, were the talk of the town, boys in the street used to cry *Duke or Darling*, instead of *Heads or Tails*.

Iron Duke. *See* THE GREAT DUKE.

The Duke of Exeter's daughter. The rack. It was introduced into England in 1447, when the Duke of Exeter was Constable of the TOWER, hence the name.

The Great Duke. The Duke of Wellington (1769–1852), the victor at the battle of Waterloo, who was also called the IRON DUKE.

To meet one in the Duke's Walk. To fight a duel. Duke's Walk, near Holyrood Palace, was the favourite promenade of the Duke of York (afterwards James II), during his residence in SCOTLAND and it became the common rendezvous for settling "affairs of honour", as did the fields behind the site of the BRITISH MUSEUM in ENGLAND.

Dukeries. That part of Nottinghamshire so called from the number of ducal residences established in the area from the 1680s, including Welbeck Abbey (Duke of Portland), Clumber (Duke of Newcastle), Thoresby (Duke of Kingston till 1773), Worksop Manor (formerly Duke of Norfolk). The land was formerly part of the Royal Forest of Sherwood.

Dulcarnon (dŭl kar′ non). The horns of a DI-LEMMA (or *syllogismum cornutum*); at my wit's end; a puzzling question. From an Arabic word meaning "the possessor of two horns". The 47th proposition of the First Book of EUCLID is called the Dulcarnon (the theorem of PYTHAGORAS), because the two squares which contain the right angle roughly represent horns.

To be at Dulcarnon. To be in a quandary, or on the horns of a dilemna.

> "I am, til god me bettere mynde sende,
> At dulcarnon, right at my wittes end."
> CHAUCER: *Troilus and Criseyde*, Bk. III, 931.

To send me to Dulcarnon. To daze with puzzles.

Dulce Domum (Dŭl′ si dō′ mŭm). A school holiday song originating at Winchester College. The words mean "the sweet (sound of the word) home" not as often interpreted "sweet home". It is said to have been written by a boy detained, during the WHITSUN holidays, for misconduct "as report says, tied to a pillar". According to tradition he pined away and died. On the evening preceding the Whitsun holidays, the masters, scholars and choristers still walk in procession round the pillar, chanting the six stanzas of the song. The music is by John Reading (d. 1692), organist of Winchester Cathedral and of the college.

> Dulce domum resonemus.
> Let us make the sweet sound of home to resound.

Dulce est desipere in loco (dŭll′ si est dȯ sip′ ė ri in lō′ kō). It is delightful to play the fool occasionally; it is nice to throw aside one's dignity and relax at the proper time (HORACE: *Odes* IV, xii, 28).

Dulce et decorum est pro patria mori (dŭl si et de kôr′ um est prō pắt′ ri ȧ môr′ ĭ). It is sweet and becoming to die on one's country's behalf, or to die for one's country (HORACE: III *Odes*, ii, 13).

Dulcinea (dŭl sin′ ē ȧ). A lady-love. Taken from the name of the lady to whom Don QUIXOTE paid his knightly homage. Her real name was Aldonza Lorenzo, but the knight dubbed her Dulcinea del Toboso.

Dulcinists (dŭl′ si nists). Heretical followers of Dulcinus (in northern Italy) who rejected papal authority and church rites and ceremonies. Dulcinus was burnt (1307) by order of Clement IV.

Dulia. *See* LATRIA.

Dullness. King of Dullness. So Pope called Colley Cibber (1671–1757), appointed Poet Laureate in 1730.

> "God save King Cibber!" mounts in every note ....
> So when Jove's block descended from on high ...
> Loud thunder to its bottom shook the bog,
> And the hoarse nation croaked, "God save King Log!"
> POPE: *Dunciad*, Bk. I.

As dull as ditchwater. Applied to those who are boring and uninteresting, likewise to such tasks and employments. An allusion to the dull and muddy water in ditches.

Dum sola (Lat.). While single or unmarried.

Dum vivimus vivamus (dûm vi vī′ mùs vi vā′ mùs) (Lat.) While we live, let us enjoy life. This was the motto of the Epicureans. (*See* EPICURUS.) Catullus has a similar theme: *Vivamus, mea Lesbia, atque amemus* (Lesbia mine, let us live and love). The motto was adopted on Dr. Doddridge's coat of arms and converted into the following epigram:

> "Live, while you live," the epicure would say,
> "And seize the pleasures of the present day."
> "Live, while you live," the sacred preacher cries,
> "And give to God each moment as it flies."
> Lord, in my views, let each united be;
> I live in pleasure, when I live to thee.

Dumb. Dumb crambo. *See* CRAMBO.

Dumb Ox, The. St. Thomas Aquinas (1224–1274), known afterwards as "the ANGELIC DOCTOR", or "Angel of the Schools". Albertus Magnus, his tutor, said of him: "The dumb ox will one day fill the world with his lowing." So called from his great bulk and taciturnity.

Dumb-waiter. An 18th-century English contribution to the amenities of the DRAWING-ROOM. The mahogany dumb-waiter introduced in the 1730s consisted of two or three circular trays of graduated sizes pivoted on a central stem, the legs of which were on castors. The trays usually contained wine and glasses, etc., thus obviating the need for keeping servants hovering around the guests on social occasions. In the days when servants were noted for making improper use of overheard confidences, the dumb-waiter was a notable asset.

Dumdum. A half-covered steel-cased bullet which expands on impact and causes a very terrible wound. So called from the arsenal at Dumdum, near Calcutta, where they were first made in the 1890s. Their use was proscribed by the Second Hague Conference in 1899. At the time of the INDIAN MUTINY (1857), Dumdum was the scene of the first protests against the "greased cartridges".

Dumps. To be in, or **down in the dumps.** Out of spirits; Gay's Third Pastoral is *Wednesday, or the Dumps*.

Why, how now, daughter Katherine? In your dumps?
SHAKESPEARE: *The Taming of the Shrew*, II, i.

In the 16th century the name was given to any plaintive tune, and also to a slow and mournful sort of dance.

They would have handled me a new way;
The devil's dump had been danced then.
BEAUMONT and FLETCHER: *The Pilgrim*, V, iv.

Dun. One who importunes for payment of a bill. The tradition is that it refers to Joe Dun, a bailiff of Lincoln in the reign of Henry VII. The *British Apollo* (1708) said he was so active and dexterous in collecting bad debts that when anyone became "slow to pay" the neighbours used to say to the creditors. "Dun him" (send Dun after him).

An Universitie dunne ... is an inferior creditor of some ten shillings or downewards, contracted for horse hire, or perchance drinke, to weake to be put in suite.
EARLE: *Micro-cosmographie* (1628).

Squire Dun. The hangman between Richard Brandon (executioner of Strafford, Laud, and Charles) and JACK KETCH (executioner of Russell and Monmouth).

And presently a halter got,
Made of the best strong hempen teer;
And, ere a cat could lick his ear,
Had tied him up with as much art
As Dunn himself could do for's heart
CHARLES COTTON: *Virgil Travestied*, Bk. IV.

Dun Cow. The savage beast slain by GUY OF WARWICK. A huge tusk, probably that of an elephant, is still shown at Warwick Castle as one of the horns of the dun cow. The fable is that it belonged to a giant, and was kept on Mitchell Fold, Shropshire. Its milk was inexhaustible; but one day an old woman who had filled her pail wanted to fill her sieve also. This so enraged the cow that she broke loose from the fold and wandered to Dunsmore Heath, where she was slain.

On Dunsmore heath I alsoe slewe
A monstrous wyld and cruell beast,
Calld the Dun-cow of Dunsmore heath;
Which many people had opprest.
Some of her bones in Warwicke yett
Still for a monument doe lye.
PERCY: *Reliques (The Legend of Sir Guy)*.

The Book of the Dun Cow. An early 12th-century manuscript account of earlier Irish romance. It derives its name from the story that it is a copy of those written down on the hide of a cow by St. Kieran of Clonmacnoise in the 6th century.

The Old Dun Cow. A derisive nickname given by the troops to the steamer *River Clyde* beached at Gallipoli in 1915 during World War I. It was probably a reference to the popular song containing the words "The Old Dun Cow she's done for now", the *Old Dun Cow* in question being a public house that had run dry.

To draw Dun out of the mire. To lend a helping hand to one in distress; to assist when things are at a standstill. The allusion is to an old English game, in which a log of wood, called Dun (a name formerly given to a cart-horse), is supposed to have fallen into the mire, and the players are to pull it out. Each does all he can to obstruct the other, and as often as possible the log is made to fall on someone's toes.

Sires, what? Dun is in the mire.
CHAUCER: *Prologue to the Maunciples Tale*.
If thou art dun, we'll draw thee from the mire.
SHAKESPEARE: *Romeo and Juliet*, I, iv.

Dunce. A dolt; a stupid person. The word is taken from Duns Scotus (*c.* 1265–1308), the famous SCHOOLMAN so called from his birthplace, Dunse, in Scotland. His followers were called Dunsers or SCOTISTS. Tyndal says, when they saw that their hair-splitting divinity was giving way to modern theology, "the old barking curs raged in every pulpit" against the CLASSICS and new notions, so that the name indicated an opponent to progress, to learning, and hence a dunce.

Duns Scotus was buried at Cologne; his epitaph reads:
Scotia me genuit, Anglia me suscepit, Gallia me docuit, Colonia me tenet.

The Parliament of Dunces. Convened by Henry IV at Coventry in 1404, and so called because all lawyers were excluded from it. Also known as the Lawless, and Unlearned Parliament.

Dunciad. The dunce-epic, a satire by Alexander Pope, first published in 1728 with Theobald featuring as the Poet Laureate of the realm of Dullness, but republished with an added fourth part in 1741 with Colley Cibber in that role. Many contemporary writers who were pilloried in this poem would have otherwise been unnoticed by posterity.

Dundreary Whiskers. Lord Dundreary was the chief character in Tom Taylor's *Our American Cousin* (1858), the personification of a good-natured, indolent, blundering, empty-headed SWELL. E.A. Sothern created the character by the brilliance of his acting and the liberties he took with the original text. The theatrical make-up for the part included long side-whiskers which set a fashion among the young men about town.

Dunedin. *See* EDINBURGH.

Dunghill! Coward! Villain! This is a cockpit expression; all cocks, except gamecocks, being called dunghills.

Out, dunghill! dar'st thou brave a nobleman?
SHAKESPEARE: *King John*, IV, iii.

Every cock crows on its own dunghill.
See under COCK.

Dunheved Castle. *See* CASTLE TERABIL.

Dunkers. *See* TUNKERS.

Dunkirk. This once notorious haunt of pirates and privateers has acquired fresh associations since World War II. The name is now used figuratively to denote a forced military evacuation by sea to avoid disaster, a speedy and complete withdrawal, an entire abandonment of a position. The allusion is to the heroic evacuation of the main British expeditionary force (26 May–4 June 1940), in the face of imminent disaster, by Vice-Admiral Ramsay's motley force of destroyers, yachts, etc., with essential air cover from R.A.F. Fighter Command.

Dunmow (dŭn' mō). **To eat Dunmow bacon.** To live in conjugal amity, without even wishing the marriage knot to be less firmly tied. The allusion is to a custom said to have been instituted by Juga, a noble lady, in 1111, and restored by Robert de Fitzwalter in 1244. It was that any person going to Dunmow, in Essex, and humbly kneeling on two sharp stones at the church door, might claim a gammon of bacon if he could swear that for twelve months and a day he had never had a household brawl or wished himself unmarried.

Between 1244 and 1772 eight claimants were awarded the flitch. Their names merit immortality:

1445 Richard Wright, labourer, Bawburgh, near Norwich.
1467 Steven Samuel, Little Ayston, Essex.
1510 Thomas Ley, fuller, Coggeshall, Essex.
1710 William (and Jane) Parsley, butcher, Much-Easton, Essex.
     Also John (and Ann) Reynolds of Hatfield Regis
1751 Thomas Shakeshaft, woolcomber, Weathersfield, Essex.
1763 Names not recorded.
1773 John and Susan Gilder, Tarling, Essex.

Allusions to the custom are frequent in 17th- and 18th-century literature and the custom was revived again in the second half of the 19th century.

"Ah madam! cease to be mistaken;
Few married folk peck Dunmow bacon".
PRIOR: *Turtle and Sparrow*, 233.

W. Harrison Ainsworth's *The Flitch of Bacon or The Custom of Dunmow* (1854) is dedicated to Baron and Baroness TAUCHNITZ "As a record of rare conjugal attachment, this Tale may be appropriately inscribed to you, my good friends: than whom I have never known a more fondly-united couple".

Dunscore. The saut lairds o'Dunscore.
Gentlefolk who have a name but no money. The tale is that the "puir wee lairds of Dunscore" (a parish near Dumfries) clubbed together to buy a stone of salt, which was doled out to the subscribers in spoonfuls, that no one should get more than his due quota.

Duns Scotus. *See* DOCTORS OF LEARNING; DUNCE.

Dunstable. Nathan Bailey (d. 1742), lexicographer, gives the etymology of the name of this Bedfordshire town as *Duns' stable*; adding "Duns or Dunus was a robber in the reign of Henry I, who made it dangerous for travellers to pass that way". The actual derivation is *Dunn's* (or *Duma's*) *stapol* (O.E. for pillar or post).

Downright Dunstable. Very blunt, plain speaking, straightforward; like the Dunstable to London road (a part of Watling Street) which has many long straight stretches. Hence also **Plain as the road to Dunstable,** *i.e.* quite clear and straightforward.

Dunstable larks. Once a highly prized dish, in the same way as Whitstable oysters. Famed from the 17th century, they were served as a speciality in the local inns, which were much patronized by the visiting gentry.

Dunstan, St. (*d*. 925–988). Archbishop of Canterbury (961), and patron saint of goldsmiths, being himself a noted worker in GOLD. He is represented in pontifical robes, and carrying a pair of pincers in his right hand, the latter referring to the legend that on one occasion he seized the DEVIL by the nose with a pair of red-hot tongs and refused to release him till he promised never to tempt Dunstan again. *See also* HORSESHOE.

Dunsterforce. The name given to the men sent to Baku in 1918 under the command of Maj.-Gen. L.C. Dunsterville (1865–1946), who had been a schoolfellow of Rudyard Kipling and was the hero of *Stalky and Co.* The purpose of this expedition was to prevent the Turks and Germans seizing the oil-wells and Dunsterforce adequately accomplished its object.

Duodecimo (dū ō des' i mō). A book whose sheets are folded into twelve leaves each (Lat. *duodecim*, twelve), often called "twelvemo", from the contraction 12mo. The book is naturally a small one, hence the expression is sometimes applied to other things or persons of small size. *Cp.* DECIMO-SEXTO.

Dup is do up. Thus Ophelia says, "he ... dupp'd the chamber door", *i.e.* he did up or pushed up the latch, in order to open the door, that he might "let in the maid"

(*Hamlet*, IV, v). *Cp.* DOFF, DON.

> Iche weene the porters are drunk. Will they not dup the gate today.
>
> RICHARD EDWARDS: *Damon and Pithias* (*c.* 1564).

Dupes, Day of the. In French history, 11 November 1630 when Marie de' MEDICI, the queen mother, and others sought the overthrow of Louis XIII's minister, Cardinal Richelieu. The cardinal's friends interviewed Louis at Versailles later in the day and by the evening Richelieu was reassured of the royal favour. This was the "day of dupes" for those who counted upon the minister's fall.

Durandal, or **Duranda,** or **Durenda,** etc. *See* ROLAND'S SWORDS *under* ROLAND.

Durden, Dame. A generic name for a good old-fashioned housewife. In the old song she kept five serving girls to carry the milking pails, and five serving men to use the flail and spade; and of course, the five men love the five maids.

> 'Twas Moll and Bet, Doll and Kate, and Dorothy Draggletail;
> And John and Dick, and Joe and Jack, and Humphrey with his flail.
>
> ANON.

Dust. Slang for money; probably in allusion to the moralist's contention that money is worthless.

Ashes to ashes, dust to dust. *See* ASHES.

Down with the dust! Out with the money; DUB UP! The expression is at least three hundred years old, and it is said that Swift once took for the text of a charity sermon, "He who giveth to the poor, lendeth to the Lord". Having thrice repeated his text, he added: "Now brethren, if you like the security, down with your dust." That ended his sermon.

Dust and ashes. In Old Testament times, a person sprinkled earth, dust and ashes over the head as a sign of mourning. *Dust and ashes* was expressive of one's deep humiliation, insignificance and worthlessness. *Cp.* TO WEAR SACKCLOTH AND ASHES *under* SACK.

> And Abraham answered and said, Behold now, I have taken upon me to speak unto the Lord, which am but dust and ashes.
>
> *Gen.* xviii, 27.

I'll dust your jacket for you. Give you a good beating; also used with *doublet, trousers, pants*, etc., in place of *jacket*.

To bite the dust. *See under* BITE.

To kiss, or **lick the dust.** *See under* KISS.

To raise a dust, to kick up a dust. To make a commotion or disturbance.

To shake the dust from one's feet. To show extreme dislike of a place, and to leave it with the intention of never returning. The allusion is to the Eastern custom.

> And whosoever shall not receive you, nor hear your words, when ye depart out of that house or city, shake off the dust of your feet.
>
> *Matt.* x, 14.

> But the Jews ... raised persecution against Paul and Barnabas, expelled them out of their coasts. But they shook off the dust of their feet against them, and came into Iconium....
>
> *Acts.* xiii, 50, 51.

To throw dust in his eyes. To mislead, to dupe or trick. The allusion is to "the swiftest runner in a sandy race, who to make his fellows aloofe, casteth dust with his heeles into their envious eyes" (*Cotgrave*, 1611).

The Mohammedans had a practice of casting dust into the air for the sake of confounding the enemies of the Faith. This was done by the Prophet on two or three occasions, as in the battle of Honein; and the KORAN refers to it when it says: "Neither didst thou, O Mahomet, cast dust into their eyes; but it was God who confounded them."

The dustman has arrived, or more usually nowadays "The sandman is about", the "dustman" having lost popularity in nursery talk since the association with refuse collecting. The phrase means that it is bedtime, for the children rub their eyes, as if sand or dust was in them.

A dusty answer. To get a dusty answer is to receive an unsatisfactory reply akin to a BRUSH off; substantially the same as to be sent off with a flea in the ear (*see under* FLEA).

Well, it is not so dusty, or **Not so dusty.** I don't call it bad; rather smart in fact, just as "not bad" is often used too mean "very good". Here *dusty* means soiled, bad, worthless.

A dust-up. A row, a bit of a SHEMOZZLE or a SHINDY.

Dustyfoot. *See* PIEPOWDER COURT.

Dusty Miller. A common nickname, particularly in the Royal Navy, for all those with the surname Miller, just as all Clarks are called "NOBBY", and Bells "Daisy" or "Dinger". Its origin is obvious and appropriate. The auricula is also known as *Dusty Miller* from the white mealiness of its leaves.

Dutch. This word, properly meaning "Hollandish", is the M.Dut. *Dutsch* or Ger. *Deutsch*, and formerly denoted the people of Germany or of Teutonic stock, not merely the Low Dutch or Netherlanders. (*See* PENNSYLVANIA DUTCH.) The derogatory implications of some of the undermentioned phrases derive from the Anglo-Dutch wars of the 17th century.

Dutch auction. An auction in which the auctioneer offers the goods at gradually decreasing prices, the first bidder to accept becoming the purchaser; to reverse the process of a normal auction.

Dutch bargain, or **wet bargain.** A bargain settled over drinks, the Dutch being formerly reputed to be steady drinkers.

Dutch collar. A horse collar.

Dutch comfort. Cold comfort, *i.e.* things might have been worse.

Dutch concert. A great noise and uproar, like that made by a party of drunken Dutchmen, some singing, others quarrelling, speechifying, etc.

Dutch courage. The courage exerted by drink; POT VALOUR. The Dutch were considered heavy drinkers. *Cp.* DUTCH BARGAIN.

Dutch cousins. Close friends, a play upon COUSINS GERMAN.

Dutch defence. A sham defence.

> To confess the truth, I am afraid Mr. Jones maintained a kind of Dutch defence, and treacherously delivered up the garrison, without duly weighing his allegiance to the fair Sophia.
>
> FIELDING: *Tom Jones*, IX, v.

Dutch gleek. Tippling. GLEEK is a game and the name implies that the game loved by Dutchmen is drinking.

> Nor could be partaker of any of the good cheer except it were the liquid part of it, which they call "Dutch Gleek".
>
> GAYTON: *Pleasant Notes upon Don Quixote* (1654).

Dutch gold. "German" gold, an alloy of copper and zinc, yellow in colour, which easily tarnishes unless lacquered. Imitation gold leaf is made from it, hence the name *Dutch leaf*. It is also called *Dutch metal*.

Dutch nightingales. Frogs. Similarly we have *Cambridgeshire nightingales; Liège nightingales*, etc.

Dutch talent. That which is not done in true nautical and shipshape fashion, more the result of brawn than brain.

Dutch treat. A meal, amusement, etc., at which each person pays for himself. *To go Dutch* has the same meaning.

Dutch wife. An open frame constructed of cane, originally used in the Dutch East Indies and other hot countries to rest the limbs in bed; also a bolster used for the same purpose.

Double Dutch. *See under* DOUBLE.

His Dutch is up. His DANDER is riz.

In Dutch. In trouble, out of favour, under suspicion.

My old Dutch. Here the word is a contraction of *duchess* and has nothing to do with Holland or Germany. It is a colloquial term for one's wife, especially the wife of a coster,

as in the song *My Old Dutch. See* ALBERT THE GREAT.

The Dutch have taken Holland. A quiz when anyone tells what is well known as a piece of wonderful news. Similar to *Queen Bess* (or *Queen Anne*) *is dead*.

To talk like a Dutch uncle. To reprove firmly but kindly. The Dutch were noted for their discipline.

Dutchman. I'm a Dutchman if I do. A strong refusal. During the Anglo-Dutch rivalry of the 17th century the name was synonymous with all that was despicable and when a man said, "I would rather be a Dutchman than do what you ask me," he used the strongest possible terms of refusal.

If not, I'm a Dutchman. Used to strengthen an affirmation or assertion—if I am found to be wrong, then I am a Dutchman which I manifestly am not.

The Flying Dutchman. *See under* FLY.

Well, I'm a Dutchman! An exclamation of strong incredulity.

Dutchman's breeches, or **sailor's trousers.** Two patches of blue appearing in a stormy sky giving the promise of better weather, *i.e.* enough blue sky to make a Dutchman (or sailor) a pair of breeches.

The plant *dicentra cucullaria* is also called Dutchman's Breeches from its two-spurred flowers.

Dutchman's draught. A "big swig", a copious draught; an allusion to the Dutchman's reputed fondness for heavy drinking. *Cp.* DUTCH COURAGE; DUTCH GLEEK.

Dutchman's log. A rough method for finding a ship's speed by throwing a piece of wood, etc., into the sea well forward and timing its passage between two marks on the vessel of known distance apart.

Dwarf. Dwarfs have figured in the legends and mythology of nearly every people, and the success of Walt Disney's children's classic *Snow White and the Seven Dwarfs* (1938) is evidence of their enduring appeal. Pliny gives particulars of whole races of them, possibly following travellers' tales of African pygmies. They are prominent in Teutonic and Scandinavian legend and generally dwelt in rocks and caves, and recesses of the earth. They were guardians of mineral wealth and precious stones and very skilful at their work. They were not unfriendly to man, but could on occasions be intensely vindictive and mischievous.

In England, dwarfs or midgets were popular down to the 18th century as court favourites or household pets. In later times they were often exhibited as curiosities at circuses, etc.

Among those recorded in legend or history (with their reputed heights) the following are, perhaps, the most famous:

ALBERICH, the dwarf of the NIBELUNGEN-LIED.

ANDROMEDA and CONOPAS, each 2 ft. 4 in. Dwarfs of Julia, niece of Augustus.

BEBE, or NICHOLAS FERRY, 2 ft. 9 in. A native of France (1714–1737). He had a brother and sister, both dwarfs.

BORUWLASKI (*Count Joseph*), 3 ft. 3 in. (d. 1837).

CHE-MAH (a Chinaman), 2 ft. 1 in., weight 52 lb. Exhibited in London in 1880.

COLOBRI (*Prince*) of Sleswig. 2 ft. 1 in., weight 25 lb. at the age of twenty-five (1851).

CONOPAS. *See* ANDROMEDA, *above*.

COPPERNIN, the dwarf of the Princess of Wales, mother of George III. The last court dwarf in England.

CRACHAMI (*Caroline*). Born at Palermo; 1 ft. 8 in. (1814–1824). Exhibited in Bond Street, London, 1824.

DECKER or DUCKER (*John*), 2 ft. 6 in. An Englishman (1610).

FAIRY QUEEN (*The*), 1 ft. 4 in., weight 4 lb. Exhibited in Regent Street, London, 1850. Her feet were less than two inches.

GIBSON (*Richard*), a good portrait painter (1615–1690). His wife's maiden name was Anne Shepherd. Each measured 3 ft. 10 in. Waller sang their praises:

> Design or chance makes others wive,
> But Nature did this match contrive.

HOPKINS (*Harry*). Born at Llantrisant, Glamorgan: 2 ft. 7 in. (1737–1754).

HUDSON (*Sir Jeffrey*). Born at Oakham, Rutland; 3 ft. 9 in. at the age of thirty (1619–1682); he figures in Scott's *Peveril of the Peak*.

JACKSON (*William E.*). Born at Dunedin, New Zealand; 2 ft. 3 in. and commonly known as *Major Mite* (1864–1900).

JARVIS (*John*), 2 ft. Page of honour to Queen Mary (1508–1556).

KELLY (*Mrs. Catherine, The Irish Fairy*), 2 ft. 10 in. (1756–1785).

LOLKES (*Wybrand*), 2 ft. 3 in., weight 57 lb. Exhibited at ASTLEY's in 1790.

LUCIUS, 2 ft., weight 17 lb. The dwarf of the Emperor Augustus.

MAGRI (*Count Primo*), *see* WARREN, *below*.

MARINE (*Lizzie*), 2 ft. 9 in., weight 45 lb.

MIDGETS (*The*). Lucia Zarate, the elder sister, 1 ft. 8 in., weight 4¾ lb., at the age of eighteen. Her sister was a little taller. Exhibited in London, 1881.

NUTT, COMMODORE. *See* TOM THUMB, *below*.

PAAP (*Simon*). A Dutch dwarf, 2 ft. 4 in., weight 27 lb.

SAWYER (*A.L.*), 2 ft. 6½ in., weight 39 lb. Editor in 1833 of the *Democrat* a paper of considerable repute in Florida.

STOBERIN (*C.H.*), of Nuremberg, 2 ft. 11 in. at the age of twenty.

STOCKER (*Nannette*), 2 ft. 9 in. Exhibited in London in 1815.

STRASSE DAVIT Family. Man 1 ft. 8 in.; woman, 1 ft. 6 in.; child at seventeen only 6 in.

TERESIA (*Madame*). A Corsican, 2 ft. 10 in., weight 27 lb. Exhibited in London, 1773.

TOM THUMB (*General*), whose name was Charles S. Stratton, born at Bridgeport in Connecticut, U.S.A. (1838–1883). Exhibited first in London in 1844. In 1863 he married Lavinia WARREN,

and was then 31 in. in height, she being 32 in. and 21 years old. They visited England in the following year with their dwarf son, Commodore NUTT.

WANMER (*Lucy*), 2 ft. 6 in., weight 45 lb. Exhibited in London 1801, at the age of forty-five.

WARREN (*Lavinia*). *See* TOM THUMB *above*. In 1884 she married another dwarf, Count Primo Magri, who was 2 ft. 8 in.

WORMBERG (*John*), 2 ft. 7 in. at the age of thirty-eight (Hanoverian period).

XIT was the dwarf of Edward VI.

ZARATE. *See* MIDGETS, *above*.

Cp. GIANTS; HEAVIEST MEN.

The Black Dwarf. A GNOME of the most malignant character, once held by the dalesmen of the BORDER as the author of all the mischief that befell their flocks and herds. In Scott's novel of this title (1816), the name is given to Sir Edward Mauley, *alias* Elshander, the recluse, Cannie Elshie, and the Wise Wight of Mucklestane Moor.

Dwt. *D-wt.*, *i.e. denarius-weight* (pennyweight). *Cp.* CWT.

Dye. A villain of the deepest dye. One steeped in villainy, a villain of the worst kind.

Dyed in the wool. Thorough-going 100 per cent (16th-century origin).

Dying Sayings. Many are either APOCRYPHAL or have survived in inaccurate versions.

ADAMS (*President*): "Independence for ever."

ADAMS (*John Q.*): "It is the last of earth. I am content."

ADDISON: "See in what peace a Christian can die."

ALBERT (*Prince Consort*): "I have such sweet thoughts." *Or*, "I have had wealth, rank, and power; but, if these were all I had, how wretched I should be!"

ALEXANDER I (of Russia; to his wife Elizabeth): "Que voux devez être fatiguée."

ALEXANDER II (of Russia): "I am sweeping through the gates, washed in the blood of the Lamb."

ALFIERI: "Clasp my hand, dear friend, I am dying."

ANAXAGORAS (the philosopher, who kept a school; being asked if he wished for anything, replied): "Give the boys a holiday."

ANTONY (of Padua): "I see my God. He calls me to Him."

ARCHIMEDES (being ordered by a Roman soldier to follow him, replied): "Wait till I have finished my problem."

AUGUSTUS (to his friends): "Do you think I have played my part pretty well through the farce of life?"

BACON (*Francis*): "My name and memory I leave to men's charitable speeches, to foreign nations and to the next age."

BECKETT (*Archbishop*; before he was struck dead by Sir William de Tracy): "I am prepared to die for Christ and His Church."

BEDE (*The Venerable*; having dictated the last sentence of his translation of St. John's Gospel, and being told by the Scribe that the sentence was now written): "It is well; you have said the truth: it is in deed."

BEECHER (*Henry Ward*): "Now comes the mystery."

BEETHOVEN (who was deaf): "I shall hear in heaven."

BLOOD (*Colonel*): "I do not fear death."

BOILEAU: "It is a great consolation to a poet on the point of death that he has never written a line injurious to good morals."

BOLEYN (*Anne*): "The executioner is, I believe, very expert; and my neck is very slender."

BURKE: "God bless you."

BURNS: "Don't let the awkward squad fire over my grave."

BYRON: "I must sleep now."

CÆSAR (to Brutus, his most intimate friend when he stabbed him): "Et tu, Brute?"

CASTLEREAGH (said to his doctor): "Bankhead, let me fall into your arms. It is all over."

CATESBY (a conspirator in the Gunpowder Plot): "Stand by me, Tom, and we will die together."

CATO THE YOUNGER (on seeing that the sword's point was sharp and before thrusting it into his body): "Now I am master of myself."

CAVELL (*Nurse*; before facing the German firing party in 1915): "Patriotism is not enough. I must have no hatred or bitterness towards anyone."

CHARLEMAGNE: "Lord, into Thy hands I commend my spirit." *Cp.* COLUMBUS, LADY JANE GREY, and TASSO.

CHARLES I: "From a corruptible to an incorruptible crown where no disturbance can be, no disturbance in the world". *See* REMEMBER.

CHARLES II: "I have been a most unconscionable time a-dying; but I hope you will excuse it." (To his brother, James II): "Do not, do not let poor Nelly starve."

CHARLES VIII (of France): "I hope never again to commit a mortal sin, nor even a venial one, if I can help it."

CHARLES IX (of France, in whose reign occurred the Massacre of St. BARTHOLOMEW): "Nurse, nurse, what murder! what blood! O! I have done wrong: God pardon me."

CHESTERFIELD (*Lord*): "Give Dayrolles a chair."

CHRYSOSTOM: "Glory to God for all things. Amen."

CICERO (to his assassins): "Strike."

COKE (*Sir Edward*): "Thy kingdom come; Thy willbe done."

COLIGNY (to the German who assassinated him): "Honour these grey hairs, young man."

COLUMBUS: "Lord, into Thy hands I commend my spirit." *Cp.* CHARLEMAGNE and TASSO.

COPERNICUS: "Now, O Lord, set Thy servant free." (*See Luke* ii, 29.)

CRANMER (as he held in the flames his right hand which had signed his apostasy): "That unworthy hand! That unworthy hand!"

CROMWELL: "My design is to make what haste I can to be gone."

CUVIER (to the nurse who was applying leeches): "Nurse, it was I who discovered that leeches have red blood."

DANTON (to the executioner): "Be sure you show the mob my head. It will be a long time ere they see its like."

DARWIN: "I am not in the least afraid to die."

DEMONAX (the philosopher): "You may go home, the show is over" (*Lucian*). *Cp.* RABELAIS.

DIDEROT: "The first step towards philosophy is incredulity."

DOUGLAS "Fight on, my merry men."

EDWARD I: "Carry my bones before you on your march, for the rebels will not be able to endure the sight of me, alive or dead."

EDWARDS (*Jonathan*): "Trust in God, and you need not fear."

ELDON (*Lord*): "It matters not where I am going whether the weather be cold or hot."

ELIZABETH I: "All my possessions for a moment of time."

ELLIOTT (*Ebenezer*); "A strange sight, sir, an old man unwilling to die."

ENGHIEN (*Duc d'*; shot by order of Napoleon I in (1804): "I die for my king and for France."

EPAMINONDAS (wounded; on being told that the Thebans were victorious): "Then I die happy." *Cp.*WOLFE.

ETTY: "Wonderful! Wonderful this death!"

FONTENELLE: "I suffer nothing, but I feel a sort of difficulty in living longer."

FOX (*C.J.*; to his wife): "It don't signify, my dearest, dearest Liz."

FOX (*George*, the Quaker): "Never heed! the Lord's power is over all weakness and death."

FREDERICK V (of Denmark): "There is not a drop of blood on my hands." *Cp.* PERICLES.

GAINSBOROUGH: "We are all going to heaven and Van Dyck is of the company."

GARTH (*Sir Samuel*; to his physicians—Garth was a doctor himself!): "Dear gentlemen, let me die a natural death."

GASTON DE FOIX: "I am a dead man! Lord, have mercy upon me!"

GEORGE IV (said to his page, Sir Walthen Waller): "Wally, what is this? It is death, my boy. They have deceived me."

GOETHE: "Light, more light!"

GRANT (*General*): "I want nobody distressed on my account."

GRATTAN: "I am perfectly resigned. I am surrounded by my family. I have served my country. I have reliance upon God and I am not afraid of the Devil."

GREELEY (*Horace*): "It is done."

GREGORY VII (he had retired to Salerno after his disputes with the Emperor, Henry IV): "I have loved justice and hated iniquity, therefore I die in exile."

GREY (*Lady Jane*): "Lord, into Thy hands I commend my spirit." *Cp.* CHARLEMAGNE.

GUSTAVUS ADOLPHUS: "I am sped, brother. Save thyself."

HALE (*Capt. Nathan*; hanged by the British Army in America for espionage): "I regret that I have but one life to give for my country."

HANNIBAL: "Let us now relieve the Romans of their fears by the death of a feeble old man."

HAVELOCK (*Sir Henry*): "Come, my son, and see how a Christian can die."

HAYDN died singing "God preserve the Emperor!"

HAZLITT: "Well, I've had a good life."

HENRY II (when told that his favourite son John was one of those who were conspiring against him): "Now let the world go as it will; I care for nothing more."

HENRY VIII: "All is lost! Monks, Monks, Monks!"

HERBERT (*George*): "Now, Lord, receive my soul."

HOBBES: "I am taking a fearful leap in the dark."

HOLLAND (*Lord*): "If Mr. Selwyn calls, let him in; if I am alive I shall be very glad to see him, and if I am dead he will be very glad to see me." [Selwyn was noted for his interest in viewing corpses and in attending executions.]

HUMBOLDT: "How grand these rays! They seem to beckon earth to heaven."

HUNTER (*Dr. William*): "If I had strength to hold a pen, I would write down how easy and pleasant a thing it is to die."

HUS (*John*; to an old woman thrusting another

faggot on the pile to burn him): "Sancta simplicitas!"

JACKSON ("*Stonewall*"): "Let us pass over the river, and rest under the shade of the trees."

JAMES V (of Scotland; this he said when told that the Queen had given birth to a daughter—the future Mary Queen of Scots): "It [the crown of Scotland] came [to the Stewarts] with a lass and it will go with a lass."

JEFFERSON (of America): "I resign my spirit to God, my daughter to my country."

JEROME (of Prague): "Thou knowest, Lord, that I have loved the truth!"

JOAN OF ARC "Jesus! Jesus! Jesus! Blessed be God."

JOHNSON (*Dr.*; to Miss Morris): "God bless you, my dear."

JULIAN (called the "Apostate"): "Vicisti, O Galilæe." (Thou hast conquered, O Galilean.)

KEATS: "Severn—I—lift me up—I am dying—I shall die easy; don't be frightened—be firm, and thank God it has come."

KEN (*Bishop Thomas*): "God's will be done."

KNOX (*John*): "Now it is come."

LAMB (*Charles*): "My bed-fellows are cramp and cough—we three all in one bed."

LAMBERT (the Martyr; as he was pitched into the flames): "None but Christ! None but Christ!"

LATIMER (to Ridley at the stake): "Be of good comfort, Mr. Ridley, and play the man, we shall this day light a candle by God's grace in England, as I trust never shall be put out."

LAUD (*Archbishop*): "No one can be more willing to send me out of life than I am desirous to go."

LAWRENCE (*Sir Henry*): "Let there be no fuss about me, let me be buried with the men."

LEICESTER (*Earl of*): "By the arm of St. James, it is time to die."

LEOPOLD I (*Kaiser*): "Let me die to the sound of sweet music." *Cp.* MIRABEAU.

LOCKE (*John*; to Lady Masham, who was reading to him some of the Psalms): "Oh! the depth of the riches of the goodness and knowledge of God. Cease now."

LOUIS IX (he died in 1270 while on a crusade): "Jerusalem, Jerusalem."

LOUIS XIV: "Why weep you! Did you think I should live for ever? I thought dying had been harder."

LOUIS XVI (on the scaffold): "Frenchmen, I die guiltless of the crimes imputed to me. Pray God my blood fall not on France!"

MACAULAY: "I shall retire early; I am very tired."

MACHIAVELLI: "I love my country more than my soul."

MALESHERBES (to the priest): "Hold your tongue! your wretched chatter disgusts me."

MARIE ANTOINETTE: "Farewell, my children, for ever. I am going to your father."

MARTINEAU (*Harriet*): "I see no reason why the existence of Harriet Martineau should be perpetuated."

MARY I (*Queen of England*): "You will find the word Calais written on my heart."

MARY II (to Archbishop Tillotson, who had paused in reading a prayer): "My Lord, why do you not go on? I am not afraid to die."

MELANCHTHON (in reply to the question, "Do you want anything?"): "Nothing but heaven."

MICHELANGELO: "My soul I resign to God, my body to the earth, my worldly goods to my next of kin."

MIRABEAU: "Let me fall asleep to the sound of delicious music." *Cp.* LEOPOLD.

MOHAMMED: "O Allah! Pardon my sins. Yes, I come."

MONICA (*St.*): "In peace I will sleep with Him and take my rest". (St. Augustine: *Confessions*.)

MONMOUTH (*Duke of*; to his executioner): "There are six guineas for you and do not hack me as you did my Lord Russell."

MONTAGU (*Lady Mary Wortley*): "It has all been very interesting."

MOODY (the evangelist): "I see earth receding: Heaven is opening; God is calling me."

MOORE (*Sir John*): "I hope my country will do me justice."

MORE (*Sir Thomas*): "See me safe up [*i.e.* on ascending the scaffold]; for my coming down, let me shift for myself."

MOZART: "You spoke of a refreshment, Emile; take my last notes, and let me hear once more my solace and delight."

MURAT (*King of Naples*; said to the men detailed to shoot him): "Soldiers, save my face; aim at my heart. Farewell."

NAPOLEON I: "Mon Dieu! La Nation Française. Tête d'armée."

NAPOLEON III (to Dr. Conneau): "Were you at Sedan?"

NELSON: "I thank God I have done my duty. Kiss me, Hardy."

NERO: "Qualis artifex pereo." ("What an artist the world is losing in me!")

NEWTON: "I don't know what I may seem to the world. But as to myself I seem to have been only like a boy playing on the seashore and diverting myself in now and then finding a smoother pebble or prettier shell than ordinary, whilst the great ocean of truth lay all undiscovered before me."

PALMER (*John*, the actor): "There is another and a better world." (Said on the stage. It is a line in the part he was playing—*The Stranger*)

PALMERSTON: "Die, my dear doctor! that's the last thing I shall do."

PASCAL: "My God, forsake me not."

PERICLES: "I have never caused any citizen to put on mourning on my account." *Cp.* FREDERICK V.

PETERS (*Hugh*, the regicide; to his executioner): "Friend, you do not well to trample on a dying man."

PITT (*William, the Younger*): "My country! How I leave my country!"

PLATO: "I thank the guiding providence and fortune of my life, first, that I was born a man and a Greek, not a barbarian nor a brute; and next, that I happened to live in the age of Socrates."

POE (*Edgar Allan*): "Lord, help my soul!"

POMPADOUR (*Madame de*): "Stay a little longer, M. le Curé, and we will go together."

POPE: "Friendship itself is but a part of virtue."

QUIN (the actor): "I could wish this tragic scene were over, but I hope to go through it with becoming dignity."

RABELAIS: "Let down the curtain, the farce is over." *Cp.* DEMONAX. Also, "I am going to seek the great perhaps."

RALEGH (said on the scaffold where he was beheaded): "It matters little how the head lies, so the heart be right."

RENAN: "We perish, we disappear, but the march of time goes on for ever."

REYNOLDS (*Sir Joshua*): "I know that all things on earth must have an end, and now I am come to mine."

RHODES (*C.J.*): "So little done, so much to do."

RICHARD I: "Youth, I forgive thee!" (Said to Bertrand de Gourdon, who shot him with an arrow at

Chalus. Then, to his attendants, he added): "Take off his chains, give him 100 shillings, and let him go."

RICHARD III (at Bosworth, where his best men deserted him): "Treason! treason!"

ROLAND (*Madame*; on her way to the guillotine): "O Liberty! What crimes are committed in thy name!"

ROSCOMMON (*Earl of*):
"My God, my Father, and my Friend,
Do not forsake me at my end."
(Quoting from his own translation of *Dies Iræ*.)

RUSSELL (*Lord*; executed 1683): "The bitterness of death is now past."

SALADIN: "When I am buried, carry my winding-sheet on the point of a spear, and say these words: Behold the spoils which Saladin carries with him! Of all his victories, realms and riches, nothing remains to him but this." *Cp.* SEVERUS.

SCARRON: "Ah, my children, you cannot cry for me so much as I have made you laugh."

SCHILLER: "Many things are growing plain and clear to my understanding."

SCOTT (*Sir Walter*; to his family): "God bless you all, I feel myself again."

SERVETUS (at the stake): "Christ, Son of the eternal God, Have mercy upon me." (Calvin insisted on his saying, "the eternal Son of God" but he would not, and was burnt to death.)

SEVERUS: "I have been everything, and everything is nothing. A little urn will contain all that remains of one for whom the whole world was too little." *Cp.* SALADIN.

SHERIDAN: "I am absolutely undone."

SIDNEY (*Sir Philip*; to his brother Robert): "Govern your will and affections by the will and word of your creator: in me beholding the end of this world with all her vanities."

SIWARD (the Dane): "Lift me up that I may die standing, not lying down like a cow." *Cp.* VESPASIAN.

SOCRATES: "Crito, I owe a cock to ÆSCULAPIUS."

STAËL (*Madame de*): "I have loved God, my father, and liberty."

STEPHEN (the first Christian martyr): "Lord, lay not this sin to their charge."

STRAFFORD (before his execution in 1641): "Put not your trust in princes."

TASSO: "Lord, into Thy hands I commend my spirit." Also recorded of Charlemagne, Lady Jane Grey, Columbus, and others.

TAYLOR (*General Zachary*): "I have tried to do my duty, and am not afraid to die. I am ready."

TAYLOR (the "Water-Poet"): "How sweet it is to rest!"

TENTERDEN (*Lord Chief Justice*): "Gentlemen of the jury, you may retire."

THERAMENES (the Athenian condemned by Critias to drink hemlock, said as he drank the poison): "To the health of the fair Critias."

THISTLEWOOD (executed for high treason, 1820): "I shall soon know the grand secret."

THOREAU: "I leave this world without a regret."

THURLOW (*Lord*): "I'll be shot if I don't believe I'm dying."

TYNDALE: "Lord, open the eyes of the King of England [*i.e.* Henry VIII]."

VANE (*Sir Harry*): "It is a bad cause which cannot bear the words of a dying man."

VESPASIAN: "A king should die standing" (*see* SIWARD); but his last words were "Ut puto, deus fio," *i.e.* "I suppose I am now becoming a god," referring to the apotheosization of Cæsars after death.

VICTORIA (*Queen*; referring to the war in South Africa then in progress): "Oh, that peace may come."

VOLTAIRE: "Do let me die in peace."

WASHINGTON: "It is well, I die hard, but am not afraid to go."

WEBSTER (*Daniel*): "Life, life! Death, death! How curious it is!"

WESLEY (*Charles*): "I shall be satisfied with Thy likeness—satisfied."

WESLEY (*John*): "The best of all is, God is with us."

WILLIAM (*the Silent*): "O my God have mercy upon my soul! O my God, have mercy upon this poor people!"

WILSON (the ornithologist): "Bury me where the birds will sing over my grave."

WISHART (at the stake): "I fear not this fire."

WOLCOTT ("*Peter Pindar*"): "Give me back my youth!"

WOLFE (*General*): "What! do they run already? Then I die happy." *Cp.* EPAMINONDAS.

WOLSEY (*Cardinal*): "Had I but served God as diligently as I have served the King, He would not have given me over in my grey hairs."

WORDSWORTH: "God bless you! Is that you, Dora?"

ZISKA (*John*): "Make my skin into drum-heads for the Bohemian cause."

See CONSUMMATUM EST.

Dymoke. The name of the family which has held the office of CHAMPION OF ENGLAND since the coronation of Richard II (1377).

Dymphna (dimf' nà). The patron SAINT of the insane. She is said to have been the daughter of a 6th-century Irish chieftain, who fled to Gheel in Belgium to escape her father's incestuous attentions, and devoted herself to charitable works. She was eventually murdered by her father. In art she is shown dragging away a DEVIL. Gheel has long been a centre for the treatment of the mentally afflicted.

Dysmas (diz' măs). The traditional name of the Penitent Thief, who suffered with Christ at the Crucifixion. His relics are claimed by Bologna, and in some calendars he is commemorated on 25 March. In the apocryphal GOSPEL OF NICODEMUS he is called *Dimas* (and elsewhere *Titus*), and the Impenitent Thief *Gestas*.

In Longfellow's *The Golden Legend* (*The Miracle Play*, V), *Dumachus* (Dysmus) and *Titus* both belonged to a band of robbers who molested the HOLY FAMILY on their flight into Egypt.

Dyvour (dī' vôr). The old name in Scotland for a bankrupt (Fr. *devoir*, to owe). From the 17th century *dyvours* were by law compelled to wear an upper garment half yellow and half brown, with part-coloured cap and hose. This requirement was not formally abolished until 1836.

Dyzemas Day (diz' măs). Tithe day (Port. *dizimas*, tithes; Lat. *decima*, a tenth, a tithe).

E

E. This letter is derived from the Egyptian hieroglyph ⌓, and the Phœnician and Hebrew sign called *he*.

The following legend is sometimes found in churches under the two tables of the Ten Commandments:

> PRSVR Y PRFCT MN
> VR KP THS PRCPTS TN
> The vowel E
> Supplies the key.

E.G., e.g. (Lat. *exempli gratia*). By way of example; for instance.

E pluribus unum (ē ploo′ ri bus ū′ nùm) (Lat.) One out of many. It is taken from *Moretum* (l. 103), a Latin poem attributed to VIRGIL, and is the motto on the Great Seal of the United States of America.

Eager beaver. An American expression in World War II for an over-zealous recruit whose keenness was marked by volunteering on every possible occasion, and subsequently applied in civilian life to similar enthusiasts.

Eagle. In mythology, the eagle commonly represents the SUN, but in Scandinavian myth is usually associated with storm and gloom. It is also emblematic of courage, immortality, etc. In Christian art, it is the symbol of St. JOHN THE EVANGELIST (hence its use on church lecterns), St. Augustine, St. GREGORY THE GREAT, and St. PRISCA. Emblematically, or in HERALDRY, the eagle is a charge of great honour. It was called the Bird of JOVE by the Romans and was borne on their military standards; they used to let an eagle fly from the funeral pile of a deceased emperor, symbolizing the reception of his soul among the Gods. Dryden alludes to this custom in the opening stanza of his poem on the death of Oliver Cromwell:

> Like eager Romans ere all rites were past,
> Did let too soon the sacred eagle fly.

An *eagle* is also an American gold ten-dollar piece, first coined in 1795.

The Golden Eagle and **the Spread Eagle** are commemorative of the CRUSADES and were the devices of the Eastern Roman Empire. France (under the Empires), Germany, Austria, Prussia and Russia also adopted the eagle as a royal or imperial emblem. *See* THE TWO-HEADED EAGLE.

The white-headed American eagle, *Haliœtus leucocephalus* (sometimes wrongly termed the Bald Eagle), with outspread wings or spread-eagle (the "eagle displayed" of HERALDRY) is specifically the emblem of the U.S.A.

The term **Spread-eaglism** denotes bombastic display and ostentation of speech or action, especially of vulgar patriotism, and in the United States was the counterpart of JINGOISM in Britain. In the navy a man was said to be **spread-eagled** when he was lashed to the rigging for flogging, with outstretched arms and legs.

The Two-headed Eagle. The German eagle has its head turned to our left hand and the Roman eagle to our right hand. CHARLEMAGNE, as successor to the Roman EMPERORS, is said to have adopted the eagle as a badge, but the two-headed eagle, reputedly symbolizing the eastern and western divisions of the empire, did not appear on the arms of the HOLY ROMAN EMPIRE until the early 15th century. It was retained by the Austrian Emperors as successors to the Holy Roman Emperors. In 1472 Ivan III of Russia assumed the two-headed eagle after his marriage to Sophia, daughter of Thomas Palæologus, and niece of Constantine XIV.

An eagle eye. One with keen and piercing sight; figuratively used of acute intellectual vision.

Eagle stones. *See* ÆTITES.

Grand eagle. Before metrification, paper 28¾ in. by 42 in.; so called from a watermark first met with in 1314.

The Eagle. Gaudenzio Ferrari (*c.* 1480–1549), the Milanese painter.

The Eagle of Brittany. Bertrand Du Guesclin (1320–1380), CONSTABLE of France.

The Eagle of the Divines. St. THOMAS AQUINAS (*c.* 1225–1274).

The Eagle of the Doctors of France. Pierre d'Ailly (1350–1420), French cardinal and SCHOOLMAN, who helped to end the Papal schism.

The Eagle of Meaux. Jacques Bénigne Bossuet (1627–1704), Bishop of Meaux, the great pulpit orator, theologian, and historian.

The Eagle of the North. Count Axel Oxenstierna (1583–1654), the Swedish statesman.

The Eagle and Child. The crest of the Stanley family and Earls of Derby, and a well-known PUBLIC-HOUSE SIGN. The legend is that Sir Thomas Latham, an ancestor of the house, caused his illegitimate son to be placed under the foot of a tree in which an eagle had built its nest. When out walking with his wife, they "accidentally" found the child, which he persuaded her to adopt as their heir. Later he changed his mind and left most of his wealth to his daughter, and the family altered the eagle crest of Sir Thomas to that of an eagle preying upon a child.

The eagle does not hawk at flies. *See* AQUILA NON CAPTAT MUSCAS.

Land of the White Eagle. *See under* LAND.

Thy youth is renewed like the eagle's (*Ps*. ciii, 5). This refers to the ancient superstition that every ten years the eagle soars into the "fiery region", and plunges into the sea, where, moulting its feathers, it acquires new life. *Cp*. PHOENIX.

> At last she saw where he upstarted brave
> Out of the well, wherein he drenched lay:
> As eagle fresh out of the ocean wave,
> Where he hath lefte his plumes all hory gray,
> And deckt himself with fethers youthly gay.
> SPENSER: *Faerie Queene*, I, xi, 34.

Ear (O.E. *eare*). If your ears burn, someone is talking about you. This is a very old superstition; Pliny says, "When our ears do glow and tingle, some do talk of us in our absence." In SHAKESPEARE's *Much Ado About Nothing* (III, i), Beatrice says when Ursula and Hero had been talking of her, "What fire is in mine ears?" Sir Thomas Browne ascribes the conceit to guardian angels, who touch the right ear if the talk is favourable and the left if otherwise. This is done to cheer or warn.

> One ear tingles; some there be
> That are snarling now at me.
> HERRICK: *Hesperides*.

About one's ears. Causing trouble. The allusion is to a hornet's nest buzzing about one's head; thus "to bring the house about one's ears" is to set the whole family against one.

Ass-eared. *See under* ASS.

Asses as well as pitchers have ears. *See under* ASS.

Bow down thine ear. Condescend to hear or listen (*Ps*. xxxi, 2).

By ear. To sing or play by ear is to sing or play without reading the music, depending on the ear alone.

Dionysius's Ear. A large ear-shaped underground cave cut in a rock and so connected that Dionysius, TYRANT of Syracuse, could overhear the conversation of his prisoners from another chamber. A similar whispering gallery exists beneath Hastings Castle. It is cut from the solid rock and the listening post is shaped like an ear.

Give ear to. Listen to; give attention to.

His ears must be burning. Said of someone being talked about in his absence.

I am all ear. All attention.

> I was all ear,
> And took in strains that might create a soul
> Under the ribs of death.
> MILTON: *Comus*, 560.

In one ear and out of the other. Forgotten as soon as heard.

> the sermon ... of Dame Resoun ...
> It toke no sojour in myn hede.
> For alle yede out at oon er
> That in at that other she did leve.
> *Romaunt of the Rose*, 5148 (*c*. 1400).

Jew's ear. *See* ELDER TREE.

Lend me your ears. Pay attention to what I am about to say.

> Friends, Romans, countrymen, lend me your ears;
> I come to bury Cæsar, not to praise him.
> SHAKESPEARE: *Julius Cæsar*, III, ii.

Little pitchers have long ears. *See* PITCHER.

Mine ears hast thou bored. Thou hast accepted me as thy bond-slave for life. If a Hebrew servant declined to go free after six years' service, the master was to bore his ear with an awl, in token of his voluntary servitude for life (*Exod*. xxi, 6).

No ear. A bad ear for music, the opposite of a good ear.

Over head and ears, or **up to the ears.** Wholly, desperately; said of being in love, debt, etc.

To be sent off with a flea in your ear. *See under* FLEA.

To be willing to give one's ears. To be prepared to make a considerable sacrifice. The allusion is to the old practice of cutting off the ears for various offences.

To come to the ears of. To come to someone's knowledge, especially by hearsay.

To fall together by the ears. To fight and scuffle together; to contend in strife. *See* TO SET PEOPLE TOGETHER BY THE EARS *below*.

To get the wrong sow by the ear. *See under* SOW.

To have itching ears. To enjoy scandal-mongering, hearing news or current gossip (II *Tim*. iv, 3).

To have one's ear to the ground. To be alert and well informed of what is taking place, to be alive to the probable trend of events. A figure derived from woodcraft.

To prick up one's ears. To listen attentively to something not expected, as horses prick up their ears at a sudden sound.

> Like unbacked colts, they pricked their ears.
> SHAKESPEARE: *Tempest*, IV, i.

To set people together by the ears. To create ill will among them; to set them quarrelling and, metaphorically, pulling each other's ears as dogs do when fighting.

> When civil dudgeon first grew high,
> And men fell out, they knew not why;
> When hard words, jealousies, and fears
> Set folks together by the ears.
> BUTLER: *Hudibras* (opening lines).

To tickle the ears. To gratify the ear either by pleasing sounds or gratifying words.

To turn a deaf ear. To refuse to listen; to refuse to accede to a request.

Walls have ears. *See under* WALL.

Within earshot. Within hearing.

You cannot make a silk purse out of a sow's ear. *See under* SILK.

Ear-finger. The little finger, which, because of its convenient size, is thrust into the ear when it tickles.

Ear-marked. Marked so as to be recognized; figuratively, something allocated or set aside for a special purpose. The allusion is to owner's marks on the ears of cattle and sheep.

Ears to Ear Bible, The. *See* BIBLE, SOME SPECIALLY NAMED EDITIONS.

Earing. Ploughing (O.E. *erian*, to plough; cp. Lat. *aro*).

> And yet there are five years, in which there shall neither be earing nor harvest.
> *Gen*. xiv, 6.

Earl (O.E. *eorl*, a man of position in opposition to a *ceorl* or churl; *cp*. Dan. *jarl*). The third in dignity in the British peerage, ranking next below MARQUESS. In later Anglo-Saxon England, earls became important administrative officers commanding the MILITIA of their areas, and their growing political power is exemplified by that of Earl Godwin. William the Conqueror tried to introduce the name COUNT unsuccessfully, but the wife of an earl is still called a *countess*. An earl's coronet has eight silver balls mounted on gold rays which reach to the top of the cap, with small strawberry leaves alternating between them. *Cp*. VISCOUNT.

> The sheriff is called in Latin vice-comes, as being the deputy of an earl or comes, to whom the custody

of a shire is said to have been committed.
> BLACKSTONE: *Commentaries*, I, ix.

Earl Marshal. The officer of State who presides over the College of Arms, grants armorial bearings and is responsible for the arrangements of State ceremonials, processions, etc. Since 1483 the office has been hereditary in the line of the Dukes of Norfolk. *See* MARSHAL.

> 'Tis the list
> Of those that claim their offices this day,
> By custom of the coronation ...
> ... next, the Duke of Norfolk,
> He to be earl marshal.
> SHAKESPEARE: *Henry VIII*, IV, i.

Earl of Mar's Grey-Breeks. *See* REGIMENTAL AND DIVISIONAL NICKNAMES.

Earth. Down to earth. Forthright and plain spoken.

Gone to earth. Gone into hiding. A figure derived from fox-hunting.

> They crouched and shuddered like beaten dogs as the terrible cry once more roused the shivering echoes!
> "Gone to earth! Gone to earth!"
> MARY WEBB: *Gone to Earth*, ch. xxxvi.

The ends of the earth. *See under* END.

To come back to earth. To abandon fantasy for reality.

To run something to earth. To trace something to its source, as a fox is chased or traced to its earth.

Earthquakes. According to Indian mythology the world rests on the head of a great elephant, "Muhu-pudma", and when, for the sake of rest, the huge monster refreshes itself by moving its head, an earthquake is produced.

The lamas say that the earth is placed on the back of a gigantic frog and when it moves its limbs or head it shakes the earth. Other Eastern myths place the earth on the back of a tortoise.

Greek and Roman mythologists ascribe earthquakes to the restlessness of the giants whom JUPITER buried under high mountains. Thus VIRGIL (*Aeneid*, III, 578) ascribes the eruption of Etna to the giant ENCELADUS.

Earwig. (O.E. *ear-wicga*, ear-beetle). So called from the erroneous notion that these insects are apt to enter the ears and penetrate the brain.

Metaphorically, one who whispers scandal, etc., in order to CURRY FAVOUR.

Ease. From O.Fr. *eise*, Mod. Fr. *aise*.

At ease. Resting; without pain or anxiety.

Chapel of Ease. *See* CHAPEL.

Ill at ease. Uneasy, anxious, uncomfortable.

Stand at ease! A military command for a

position less rigid than attention, with the feet apart and the hands joined behind the back (unless arms are being carried).

Stand easy. In a military drill a position in which relaxation is permitted, short of moving away. In the Royal Navy a short break during working hours is called a *stand easy*.

To ease one of his money, or **purse**. To steal it.

East. In the Christian Church the custom of turning to the east when the creed is repeated is to express the belief that Christ is the Dayspring and Sun of Righteousness. The altar is placed at the east end of the church to remind us of Christ, the DAY-SPRING and Resurrection; and persons are buried with their feet to the East to signify they died in the hope of the Resurrection.

The ancient Greeks always buried their dead with the face upwards, looking towards HEAVEN; and the feet turned to the east, or the rising SUN, indicating that the deceased was on his way to ELYSIUM, and not to the region of night (Diogenes Laertius: *Life of Solon*).

East End. Specifically the inner London boroughs east of the CITY itself, essentially working-class areas, the inhabitants of which are known as *East Enders*. *Cp*. COCK-NEY; WEST END.

East is East and West is West. A phrase from Rudyard Kipling, emphasizing the divergence of views on ethics and life in general between the Oriental and Western peoples.

> Oh, East is East, and West is West and never the twain shall meet,
> Till Earth and Sky stand presently at God's great Judgement Seat.
> *The Ballad of East and West*.

Far East. South-East Asia, China, Japan, etc.

Middle East and **Near East.** The precise meaning of these terms has become blurred by recent usage, which has either treated them as interchangeable or used Middle East for what was formerly called the Near East. Iran, Iraq, Afghanistan, India, and Burma used to be called Middle East, and the Near East comprised Libya, Egypt, Arabia, Palestine, Syria and Turkey.

The Eastern Question, as an historical term, essentially refers to the problem created by the decay and disintegration of the Turkish Empire in south-eastern Europe and the NEAR EAST from the time of the Greek revolt in 1821, until the establishment of the Turkish Republic in 1922, which began a new chapter.

He came safe from the East Indies, and was drowned in the Thames. He survived many great dangers, but was at last killed when he thought himself secure.

To send to the East Indies for Kentish pippins. To go round about to accomplish a very simple thing. To BREAK A BUTTERFLY ON A WHEEL. *See under* BREAK.

Eastern Association, The. Formed in December 1642 from the counties of Norfolk, Suffolk, Essex, Cambridge and Hertford to defend their territory against the ROYALISTS in the CIVIL WAR. Oliver Cromwell as the Puritan leader in East Anglia organized a disciplined army. His cavalry consisted of the pick of the yeomen of the area, voluntarily enlisted. *See* IRONSIDES; NEW MODEL.

Eastern Church. The Orthodox Church. *Cp.* GREEK CHURCH.

Eastern Empire. The East Roman or BYZANTINE EMPIRE.

Easter. The name was adopted for the Christian Paschal festival from O.E. *eastre*, a heathen festival held at the vernal equinox in honour of the Teutonic goddess of dawn, called *Eostre* by Bede, which fell about the same time.

Easter Day is the first Sunday after the Paschal full MOON, *i.e.* the full moon that occurs on the day of the vernal equinox (21 March) or on any of the next 28 days. Thus Easter Sunday cannot be earlier than 22 March, or later than 25 April, as laid down by the COUNCIL OF NICÆA in 325. The Eastern Church still celebrates Easter independently and in 1963 the VATICAN Council declared itself in favour of fixing the date of Easter when agreement with other churches could be reached.

It was formerly a common belief that the sun danced on Easter Day.

> But oh, she dances such a way,
> No sun upon an Easter day
> Is half so fine a sight.
> SIR JOHN SUCKLING: *Ballad upon a Wedding*.

Sir Thomas Browne combats the superstition:

> We shall not, I hope, disparage the Resurrection of our Redeemer, if we say the Sun doth not dance on Easter day. And though we would willingly assent unto any sympathetical exultation, yet cannot conceive therein any more than a Tropical expression.
> *Pseudodoxia Epidemica*, V, xxii.

Easter-ale. *See* CHURCH-ALE.

Easter Eggs, or **Pasch Eggs.** The egg as a symbol of fertility and renewal of life derives from the ancient world, as did the practice of colouring and eating eggs at the spring festival. The custom of eating eggs on Easter Sunday and of making gifts of Easter Eggs to children probably derives from the Easter payment of eggs by the VILLEIN to his overlord. The idea of the egg as a symbol of new life was adopted to symbolize the Resurrection. *Pasch Eggs* or *pace eggs*, hard-boiled and coloured, were rolled down slopes as one of the Easter games, a practice surviving in the yearly egg rolling held on the lawn of the WHITE HOUSE in Washington.

Eat. To eat together was, in the East, a sure pledge of protection. There is a story of a Persian grandee who gave the remainder of a peach which he was eating to a man who implored his protection, only to find that his own son had been slain by this man. The nobleman would not allow the murderer to be punished, but said, "We have eaten together; go in peace." *Cp*. CALUMET; TO EAT A MAN'S SALT *under* SALT.

Go and eat coke! Go away and don't bother me; GO TO HALIFAX. An expression of annoyance and impatience.

Let us eat and drink, for tomorrow we shall die. *Is*. xxii, 13. A traditional saying of the Egyptians who, at their banquets, exhibited a skeleton to the guests to remind them of the brevity of life.

To eat a man's salt. *See under* SALT.

To eat dirt. *See under* DIRT.

To eat dog. An American Indian custom at councils of importance. Later, when white men took exception, they were allowed to avoid offence by placing a silver dollar on the dish; the next man ate dog and took the dollar. Hence the expression in American politics *to eat dog for another*.

To eat humble pie. To come down from a position you have assumed and to be obliged to defer to others, to submit to humiliation. Here "humble" is a pun on *umble*, the umbles being the heart, liver, and entrails of the deer, the huntsmen's perquisites. When the lord and his household dined off the venison on the dais, the huntsman and his fellows took lower seats and partook of the umbles made into a pie.

To eat its head off. Said of an animal (usually a horse) that eats more than it is worth, or whose work does not cover the cost of its keep.

To eat one out of house and home. Literally, to eat so much that the householder or host is ruined. A favourite complaint of the mother of a growing family. Mistress Quickly in SHAKESPEARE's *Henry IV, Pt. II* (II, i), when the Lord Chief Justice asks her "for what sum" she had caused Sir John Falstaff to be arrested, answers, "He hath eaten me out of house and home; he hath put all my substance into that fat belly of his."

To eat one's heart out. To fret or worry excessively; to allow grief or vexation to pre-dominate and tincture all one's ideas, and absorb all other emotions.

To eat one's terms. To be studying for the BAR. Students are required to dine in the hall of an INN OF COURT at least thrice in each of the twelve terms before they are "called" to the bar.

To eat one's words. To retract in a humiliating manner; to unsay what you have said.

To eat out of someone's hand. To be submissive and compliant to someone, as a tame animal will eat from its master's hand.

To eat the leek. *See under* LEEK.

To eat up into the wind. A sailing-ship expression meaning to make good progress to windward.

To eat well. To have a good appetite. *It eats well* means that what is eaten is agreeable. **To eat badly** is to eat without appetite or too little.

Eau de Cologne (Fr. water of Cologne). A perfumed spirit invented by an Italian chemist, Johann Maria Farina, who settled in Cologne in 1709. The usual recipe prescribes twelve drops of each of the essential oils, bergamot, citron, neroli, orange, and rosemary, with one dram of Malabar cardamoms and a gallon of rectified spirits, which are distilled together.

Eau de vie (Fr. water of life). Brandy. A translation of the Lat. *aqua vitæ*. This is a curious perversion of the Ital. *acqua di vite* (water, or juice of the vine), rendered by the monks into *aqua vitæ* instead of *aqua vitis*, and confounding the juice of the grape with the alchemists' ELIXIR OF LIFE. *Cp*. USQUEBAUGH.

Eavesdropper. One who listens stealthily to other people's conversation. The *eavesdrop* or *eavesdrip* was the space of ground around the house which received the water dripping from the eaves. An eavesdropper was one who stationed himself in the eaves-drip to overhear what was said in the house.

> Under our tents I'll play the eavesdropper,
> To hear if any mean to shrink from me.
> SHAKESPEARE: *Richard III*, V, iii.

Ebenezer. A name often adopted by NONCONFORMIST chapels from the Heb. word meaning "stone of help" (I *Sam*. vii, 12) and thus sometimes used as a symbol of Nonconformity. *See* EXETER HALL.

> Lest there should be any well-intentioned persons who do not perceive the difference ... between religion and the cant of religion ... let them understand that it is always the latter and never the former which is satirized here ... whether it establish its headquarters, for the time being, in Exeter Hall or Ebenezer Chapel, or both.
> CHARLES DICKENS: *Posthumous Papers of the Pickwick Club (Preface)*.

Ebionites (Heb. *ebion*, poor). In the early Church the name was given to the ultra-Jewish Christians, many of whom rejected the Virgin Birth and who kept the Jewish Sabbath as well as the Lord's Day. As a separate heretical sect from the 2nd century, they called themselves the Poor Men, and remained isolated from the Church, developing a mixture of creeds.

Eblis. A jinn of Arabian mythology, the ruler of the evil genii, or fallen angels. Before his fall he was called AZAZEL. When ADAM was created, God commanded all the angels to worship him; but Eblis replied, "Me thou hast created of smokeless fire, and shall I reverence a creature made of dust?" God turned the disobedient ANGEL into a Sheytan (DEVIL), and he became the father of devils.

> When he said unto the angels, "Worship Adam", all worshipped him except Eblis.
> *Al Koran*, ii.

E-boat. In World War II an abbreviation for "Enemy War Motorboat", the British name for the German motor torpedo boat.

E-boat alley. In World War II, the name given to the coastal convoy route approximately off the Norfolk and Suffolk coast which was the scene of much successful E-boat activity in the early years of the war.

Ebony. God's image done in ebony, Negroes. An expression coined by Thomas Fuller. *Cp.* BLACK IVORY.

Ebrew Jew, *i.e.* Hebrew Jew meaning a Jew of the purest stock, completely a Jew. "You ebrew Jew" is an old expression of abuse meaning "you utter Jew" and therefore one not to be believed, trusted, or one who is excessively mean. It derives from the days when Jews were subjected to recurrent persecution and were also unpopular from their association with usury.

> You rogue, they were bound, every man of them; or I am a Jew else, an Ebrew Jew.
> SHAKESPEARE: *Henry IV, Pt. I*, II, iv.

Ecce homo (ek' ki hō' mō) (Lat. Behold the man). The name given to many paintings of Our Lord crowned with thorns and bound with ropes, as He was shown to the people by PILATE, who said to them, "Ecce homo!" (*John* xix, 5). Especially notable are those by Correggio, Titian, Guido Reni, Van Dyck, Rembrandt, Poussin, and Albrecht Dürer. In 1865 Sir John Seeley published a study of Christ under this title.

Ecce signum (ek' ki sig' nùm). See it, in proof. Behold the proof.

> I am eight times thrust through the doublet, four through the hose; my buckler cut through and through; my sword hacked like a handsaw—ecce signum!
> SHAKESPEARE: *Henry IV, Pt. I*, II, iv.

Ecclesiastes. This book of the OLD TESTAMENT was formerly ascribed to SOLOMON, because it says (i, I), "The words of the Preacher, the son of David, King in Jerusalem." It is now generally assigned to an unknown author of about the 3rd century B.C.

Ecclesiastical. Ecclesiastical Commissioners, The, of the CHURCH OF ENGLAND were established in 1836 consisting of the archbishops, bishops and deans of Canterbury, St. Paul's and Westminster with certain judges and ministers of State together with eleven eminent laymen. Essentially they administered surplus episcopal and cathedral endowments for relief of the poorer clergy and parochial ministries. In 1948 they merged with QUEEN ANNE'S BOUNTY as the Church Commissioners, basically to manage the ancient endowments of the Church for the support of the ministry.

The Father of Ecclesiastical History. Eusebius of Cæsarea (*c.* 264–340).

Ecclesiasticus. The Latin name, probably meaning "church book" (from its frequent use in the church), for the Book of Sirach, traditionally ascribed to Jesus the son of Sira. It is perhaps the most important book of the OLD TESTAMENT APOCRYPHA and both the German hymn *Nun danket alle Gott* (Now thank we all our God) and the *Jubilee Rhythm* of St. BERNARD of Clairvaux are taken from it. It has been much used by the Lutheran Church.

Echidna (e kid' nà). In classical mythology, a celebrated monster, half woman, half SERPENT and mother of the CHIMÆRA, the many-headed dog ORTHOS, the hundred-headed DRAGON of the HESPERIDES, the Colchian dragon, the SPHINX, CERBERUS, SCYLLA, the GORGONS, the Lernæan HYDRA, the vulture that gnawed away the liver of PROMETHEUS, and the NEMEAN LION.

Spenser makes her the mother of the BLATANT BEAST in the *Faerie Queene*, VI, vi, 10.

In zoology an echidna is a porcupine ant-eater found in Australia, Tasmania, and New Guinea, allied to the platypus.

Echo (ek' ō). The Romans say that Echo was a NYMPH in love with NARCISSUS, but her love not being returned, she pined away until only her voice remained.

> Sweet Echo, sweetest nymph, that liv'st unseen
> Within thy airy shell,
> By slow Meander's margent green—
> Canst thou not tell me of a gentle pair
> That likest thy Narcissus are?
> MILTON: *Comus*, 230.

To applaud to the echo. To applaud vigorously — so loudly as to produce an echo.

Eckhardt (ek' hart). **A faithful Eckhardt, who warneth everyone.** Eckhardt, in German legends, appears on the evening of MAUNDY THURSDAY to warn all persons to go home, that they may not be injured by the headless bodies and two-legged horses which traverse the streets on that night. He also warned those who followed Frau Holle or Holda (VENUS) of evils to come; sometimes he appears as the companion of TANN-HÄUSER.

Eclectics (ek lek' tiks). The name given to those who do not attach themselves to any special school (especially philosophers and painters), but pick and choose from many (Gr. *eklegein*, to choose, select). The name was first given to such a group of Greek philosophers of the 2nd and 1st centuries B.C. The 17th-century Italian painters who followed the great masters are known as the *Eclectic School*.

Eclipse, one of the most famous of English race-horses, the great-grandson of DARLEY ARABIAN, foaled 1 April 1764. He ran his first race 3 May 1769, and from then until October 1770 ran in eighteen races, never being beaten. His skeleton is preserved in the Royal Veterinary College, London. His fame gave rise to a saying applied to a person of outstanding ability who outstrips all rivals, "Eclipse first and the rest nowhere."

The Eclipse Stakes is a race inaugurated in 1884 for horses of three years and upwards, run at Sandown Park.

Eclipses were considered by the Greeks and Romans as bad OMENS and the latter would never hold a public assembly during an eclipse. Some of their poets feign that an eclipse of the MOON is because she is on a visit to ENDYMION.

A general notion among some races was that the SUN or moon was devoured by some monster, hence the beating of drums and kettles to scare it away. The Chinese, Lapps and Persians call the evil beast a DRAGON. The East Indians say it is a black GRIFFIN.

The ancient Mexicans thought that eclipses were caused by quarrels between sun and moon.

Ecliptic. The track in the heavens along which the sun appears to perform its annual march. It lies in the middle of the ZODIAC and is an imaginary line produced by the earth's motion about the sun.

Eclogue (Gr. a selection). The word was originally used for VIRGIL's *Bucolics*, because they were selected poems; as they were all pastoral dialogues it came to denote such poems, and hence an *Eclogue* is now a pastoral or rustic dialogue in verse.

Economy. Literally, household management (Lat. *œconomia*, from Gr. *oikos*, house; *nemein*, to deal out).

> I was going, to-day, by the side of a plat of ground where there was a very fine flock of turkey. I stopped to admire them, and observed to the owner how fine they were, when he answered, "We owe them entirely to you, sir, for we never raised one till we read your *Cottage Economy*."
> WM. COBBETT: *Rural Rides (From Kensington across Surrey).*

Sound economy includes the avoidance of waste, hence the sense of frugality which is illustrated by numerous proverbs: "Ever save, ever have"; "TAKE CARE OF THE PENCE (*under* PENNY) and the pounds will take care of themselves"; "MANY A MICKLE MAKES A MUCKLE"; "A PENNY SAVED IS A PENNY GAINED"; "Little and often fills the purse"; etc.

The Christian Economy. The religious system based on the teachings of Jesus Christ as recorded in the NEW TESTAMENT.

The Economy of Nature. The laws and provisions of nature whereby the greatest amount of good is obtained, and by which the animal and vegetable kingdoms are regulated.

> If we forget, for an instant, that each species tends to increase inordinately, and that some check is always in action, yet seldom perceived by us, the whole economy of Nature will be utterly obscured.
> CHARLES DARWIN: *Origin of Species*, ch. xi.

The Mosaic Economy. The religious system revealed by God to Moses and set forth in the OLD TESTAMENT.

Political Economy. The science of the production and distribution of wealth, etc., which in the 20th century came to be called *economics*.

Ecstasy (Gr. *ek*, out; *stasis*, a standing). Literally, a condition in which one stands out of one's mind, or is "beside oneself". St. PAUL refers to this when he says he was caught up to the third HEAVEN and heard unutterable words, "whether in the body, or out of the body, I cannot tell" (II *Cor.* xii, 2–4). St. JOHN also says he was "in the spirit"—*i.e.* in an ecstasy—when he saw the apocalyptic vision (*Rev.* i, 10). The belief that the soul left the body at times was common in former ages, and there was a class of diviners among the ancient Greeks called **Ecstatici,** who used to lie in trances, and when they came to themselves gave strange accounts of what they had seen while they were "out of the body".

The Ecstatic Doctor. Jan van Ruysbroeck (1293–1381), the Dutch mystic.

Ector, Sir. In ARTHURIAN ROMANCES the foster-father of King ARTHUR.

Edda. This name, which may be from Icel. *edda*, great-grandmother, or from Old Norse *odhr*, poetry, is given to two works or collections, *The Elder*, or *Poetic Edda*, and *The Younger Edda*, or *Prose Edda of Snorri*. The first-named was found in 1643 by an Icelandic bishop and consists of mythological and heroic poetry dating from about the 9th century. Erroneously attributed to Sæmund Sigfusson (d. 1133), it is sometimes called *Sæmund's Edda*. The *Younger Edda* by Snorri Sturluson (d. 1242) is in prose and verse and forms a guide to poets and poetry. Found in 1628, it consists of the *Gylfaginning* (an epitome of Scandinavian mythology), the *Skaldskaparmal* (a glossary of poetical expressions, etc.), the *Hattatal* (a list of metres with examples, lists of poets, etc.).

Eden. PARADISE, the country and garden in which ADAM was placed by God (*Gen.* ii, 15). The word means delight, pleasure.

Eden Hall. The Luck of Eden Hall. An enamelled drinking-glass (probably made in Venice in the 10th century) in the possession of the Musgrave family at Eden Hall, Cumberland, and supposed to be endowed with fortune-bringing properties. The tale is told that it was taken from St. Cuthbert's Well in the garden where it was left by the fairies while they danced. The superstition is:

> If that glass should break or fall,
> Farewell the luck of Eden Hall.

The estate was broken up in 1920 and the glass is now in the Victoria and Albert Museum, London.

Edge (O.E. *ecg*). **Back and edge.** *See* BACK.
It is dangerous to play with edged tools. It is dangerous to tamper with mischief or that which may bring you into trouble.
Not to put too fine an edge on it. Not to mince the matter; to speak plainly.
To be on edge. To be very eager or nervously impatient.
To edge away. To move away very gradually, as a ship moves away from the edge of the shore.
To edge on. *See* EGG ON.
To fall by the edge of the sword. By a cut from the sword; to be slain in battle.
To have the edge on someone. To have an advantage.
To set one's teeth on edge. To induce a tingling or grating sensation in one's teeth as from acids or harsh noises; to jar one's nerves or to feel aversion.

> In those days they shall say no more, the fathers have eaten a sour grape, and the children's teeth are set on edge.
> *Jer.* xxxi, 29.

> I had rather hear a brazen canstick turn'd,
> Or a dry wheel grate on the axle-tree;
> And that would set my teeth nothing on edge,
> Nothing so much as mincing poetry.
> SHAKESPEARE: *Henry IV, Pt. I*, III, i.

Edge-bone. *See* AITCH-BONE.

Edinburgh. Edwin's burgh; the fort built by Edwin, king of Northumbria (616–632). Dunedin (Gael. *dun*, a fortress) and Edina are poetical forms. Also called the Modern ATHENS, or Athens of the North. *See* AULD REEKIE.

Edinburgh Review. An outstanding quarterly magazine founded at Edinburgh in 1802 by Francis Jeffrey, Sydney Smith, and Henry Brougham, and originally published in the buff and blue colours of the WHIG party by Constable. The first three numbers were edited by Smith, who then handed over to Jeffrey. Its brilliance and wit gave it great literary and political influence, especially in the earlier decades, but the unfairness and savageness of some of its reviews were particularly marked in the case of Wordsworth and Southey, and it drew forth Byron's satire *English Bards and Scotch Reviewers* (1809). Its contributors included Hazlitt, Macaulay and Carlyle. It ceased publication in 1929.

Edward the Confessor. The last Anglo-Saxon king (1042–1066) of the old royal house, so called for his piety and monk-like virtues although conspicuously deficient as a ruler. He was canonized in 1161 by Pope Alexander III.

Edwardian. Belonging to the reign of King Edward VII (1901–1910). Edwardian style of dress was affected by many young men and youths in the 1950s, who soon came to be called *Teddy Boys*. They were as much distinguished for anti-social behaviour as for their peculiarities of costume. *Cp.* BEATNIK; MODS AND ROCKERS; MOHOCKS.

Eel. A salt eel. A rope's end used for scourging. At one time eelskins were used for whips.

> With my salt eele, went down in the parler, and there got my boy and did beat him.
> PEPYS: *Diary.*

Eel-skins. Old slang for very tight trousers or tightly fitting frocks.
Holding the eel of science by the tail. To have a smattering of the subject, the kind which slips from the memory as an eel would wriggle out of one's fingers if held by the tail.
To get used to it, as a skinned eel. It may be unpleasant at first, but habit will get the better of such annoyance; arising from the curious old notion that eels feel little more than a slight discomfort when skinned alive.

To skin an eel by the tail. To do things the wrong way.

Effigy. To burn, or **hang one in effigy.** To burn or hang the dummy or representation of someone in order to show dislike or contempt. From earliest times it has been believed that magic was worked by treating an effigy as one would fain treat the original. In France the public executioner used to hang the criminal in effigy when the criminal himself could not be found.

Égalité (ā găl′ itā). Philippe, Duc d'Orléans (1747–1793) (father of Louis-Philippe, King of the French) assumed this name when he renounced his title and voted for the death of Louis XVI. It is taken from the revolutionary motto "Liberty, Equality (*égalité*), and Fraternity". He was guillotined in 1793.

Egeria (e jēr′ i à). The NYMPH who instructed Numa Pompilius, second king of ROME (753–673 B.C.), in his wise legislation; hence a counsellor, adviser.

> It is in these moments that we gaze upon the moon. It is in these moments that Nature becomes our Egeria.
> LORD BEACONSFIELD: *Vivian Grey*, III, vi.

Egg. *See also* SHELL.
A bad egg. *See under* BAD.
A duck's egg. *See under* DUCK.
Curate's egg. *See under* CURATE.
Druid's egg. *See under* DRUIDS.
Easter eggs. *See under* EASTER; EGG FEAST.
Golden eggs. Great profits. *See under* GOOSE.
Scrambled egg. *See* BRASS HAT.
The mundane egg. The Phœnicians, Egyptians, Hindus, Japanese and others maintained that the world was egg-shaped and was hatched from an egg made by the Creator. In some mythologies a bird is represented as laying the mundane egg on the primordial waters. Anciently this idea was attributed to ORPHEUS, hence the "mundane egg" is also called the *Orphic egg*.

> The opinion of the oval figure of the earth is ascrib'd to Orpheus and his disciples; and the doctrine of the mundane egg is so peculiarly his that 'tis called by Proclus the Orphick egg.
> BURNET: *The Sacred Theory of the Earth* (1684).

As sure as eggs is eggs. Very sure, certain in fact. It has been suggested that this is a corruption of the logician's formula "*x* is *x*".
Don't put all your eggs in one basket. Don't venture all you have in one speculation or enterprise. The allusion is obvious.
I have eggs on the spit. I am very busy, and cannot attend to anything else. The reference is to roasting eggs on a spit. They were first boiled, then the yolk was taken out, braided up with spices, and put back again; the eggs were then drawn on a spit and roasted. The process needed constant attention.

Like as two eggs. Exactly alike.
> They say we are almost as like as eggs.
> SHAKESPEARE: *Winter's Tale*, I, ii.

Show him an egg and instantly the whole air is full of feathers. Said of a very sanguine man, because he is "counting his chickens before they are hatched".

Teach, or **tell your grandmother to suck eggs.** Said derisively to someone who tries to teach his elders or those more experienced than himself.

There is reason in roasting egg. Even the most trivial thing has a reason for being done in one way rather than some other. When wood fires were usual, it was more common to roast eggs than to boil them, and some care was required to prevent their being "ill-roasted", "all on one side", as Touchstone says in SHAKESPEARE'S *As You Like It*, III, ii.

> One likes the pheasant's wing, and one the leg;
> The vulgar boil, the learned roast an egg.
> POPE: *Second Epistle of the Second Book of Horace*.

To crush in the egg. TO NIP IN THE BUD; to ruin some scheme before it has been fairly started.

To egg on. To incite, to urge on. Here *egg* is another form of edge, thus it means to encourage one to move little by little in the direction of the edge.

To take eggs for money. To allow yourself to be imposed upon. The saying derives from the days when eggs were plentiful and exceedingly cheap.

> *Leon*: Mine honest friend
> Will you take eggs for money?
> *Mam*: No, my lord, I'll fight.
> SHAKESPEARE: *Winter's Tale*, I, ii.

To tread upon eggs. To walk gingerly, as if walking over eggs, which are easily broken.

Egg Feast, or **Egg Saturday.** The Saturday before SHROVE TUESDAY used to be so called, particularly in Oxfordshire, as the eating of eggs was forbidden during LENT.

Egg-head. A bald person or an intellectual person. The latter derives from the former on the supposition that intellectuals are often bald. *See also* HIGHBROW; SQUARE.

Egg-trot, or **Egg-wife's trot.** A cautious jog-trot pace, like that of a housewife riding to market with eggs in her panniers.

Egil. Brother of Weland (*see* WAYLAND), the VULCAN of Northern mythology. He was a great archer and in the Saga of Thidrik there is a tale told of him exactly similar to that about William TELL and the apple.

Eglington Tournament. *See under* TOURNA-MENT.

Ego (Lat. "I"). In various philosophical systems, *ego* is used of the conscious thinking subject and *non-ego* of the object. The term *ego* was introduced into philosophy by Descartes, who employed it to denote the whole man, body and mind. Fichte later used the term the *absolute ego*, meaning thereby

the non-individual being, neither subject nor object, which posits the world of individual egos and non-egos.

In psychoanalysis the ego is that part of the mind that perceives and takes cognizance of external reality and adjusts responses to it. *See* ID; QUIS.

Egypt. Crown of Egypt. In ancient Egypt there were many worn by kings and gods. As rulers of Upper Egypt, or the South Land, and Lower Egypt, or the Northern Land, the kings wore the double crown (*pschent*) made up of the Red Crown, the head-dress of the Delta, to which was added the White Mitre of the South. The Khepresh, called the war-helmet of the PHARAOHS, was blue with round dots. Each of the many crowns had its particular significance and symbolism and the gods wore crowns which indicated their attributes.

Egyptian Days. Unlucky days, days on which no business should be undertaken. The Egyptian astrologers named two in each month, but the last Monday in APRIL, the second Monday of AUGUST, and the third Monday of DECEMBER seem to have been specially baneful. *Cp.* DIES NEFASTUS.

Eight. Behind the eight ball. In a dangerous position from which it is impossible to escape. The phrase comes from the game of Kelly pool, in one variety of which all the balls must be pocketed in a certain order, except the black ball, numbered eight. If another ball touches the eight ball, the player is penalized. Therefore, if the eight ball is in front of the one which he intends to pocket, he is in a hazardous position.

One over the eight. Slightly drunk.

Eikon Basilike (ī′ kon bǎz il′ i ki) (Gr. royal likeness). *Eikon Basilike: The Pourtraicture of His Sacred Majestie in His Solitudes and Sufferings* appeared in 1649 very soon after the execution of Charles I. It purported to be his own account of his reflections and feelings during, and before, his imprisonment. It greatly strengthened royalist sentiment and led to Milton's less influential *Eikonoklastes*. Dr. John Gauden (1605–1662) afterwards claimed authorship at the time of his election to the bishopric of Worcester. It appears that he had edited the king's papers

and his version received the royal approval.

Eisel (ī′ sel). An old name for vinegar; through Old Fr. from Late Lat. *acetillum*, diminutive of *acetum* (vinegar). Hamlet asks Laertes, *Would'st drink up eisell*—to show his love for the dead Ophelia (V, i).

Whilst, like a willing patient, I will drink
Potions of eysell, 'gainst my strong infection.
SHAKESPEARE: *Sonnet* cxi.

Eisenhower Platz. Nickname of Grosvenor Square, London, during World War II, when all the buildings surrounding the square were occupied by American Military Headquarters.

Eisteddfod (ī steth′ vod) (Welsh, a session; from *eistedd*, to sit). Eisteddfodau were held in mediæval Wales and later, largely to regulate the admission of aspirants seeking to qualify as bards or minstrels. Thus in 1568, the Council for the Marches of Wales commissioned the holding of an Eisteddfod at Caerwys because "vagraunt and idle persons, naming theim selfes mynstrelles Rithmrs, and Barthes, are lately growen into such an intollerable multitude ... that not only gentlemen and other by theire shameles disorders are oftentymes disquieted in their habitacions. But also thexpert mynstrelles and musicions in tonge and Conyng therby much discouraged ..." All such minstrels and bards were to appear before the experts and those found not worthy of their professions were "to returne to some honest Labor and due Exercise, such as they be most apt unto maytenaunce of their lyvinges, upon paine to be taken as sturdy and idle vacaboundes ..." Revival of the Eisteddfodau was largely due to the romantic movement and their modern development grew from the Corwen Eisteddfod of 1789, the druidic rites being introduced by Iolo Morgannwg in the early 19th century. They have been held annually since 1880, primarily for the encouragement of Welsh literature and music. *See* DRUIDS.

Elagabalus, or **Heliogabalus.** A Syro-Phœnician sun-god. Two temples were built at Rome for this god, who was represented by a huge conical stone. Varius Avitus Bassanius (205–222), who became Roman emperor as Marcus Aurelius Antonius (218–222), was called Elagabalus because he had been a high priest of the sun-god at Emesa. His brief reign was marked by unparalleled debaucheries, cruelties, and loathsome practices. He and his mother were slain by the PRÆTORIAN GUARD.

Elaine. The Lily Maid of ASTOLAT, whose unrequited love for Sir LANCELOT caused her death. The story is told in Tennyson's *Lan-*

celot and Elaine (*Idylls of the King*) based upon Malory (Bk. XVIII, ch. ix-xx). She loved him "with that love which was her doom". Sir Lancelot wore her favour at the ninth of the DIAMOND JOUSTS, thus arousing the jealousy of Queen GUINEVERE.

Elbow. *See* ELL.

A knight of the elbow. A gambler. *Cp.* ELBOW-SHAKER.

At one's elbow. Close at hand.

Elbow grease, use plenty of elbow grease, etc. The pressure and physical effort applied when rubbing, polishing, scrubbing, etc. A jocular expression in use for more than three centuries. A time-hallowed joke was to send the GREENHORN to the shop to buy "elbow-grease".

Elbow-lifting. Drinking. *To lift the elbow* is to drink and both expressions are used to indicate fondness of alcohol.

Elbow-room. Sufficient space for the work in hand; room to extend the elbows.

Elbow-shaker. A dicer, a sharper or gambler.

More power to your elbow. A jocular toast of encouragement and support implying that a stronger elbow will lift more glasses to the mouth.

Out at elbow. Shabbily dressed, like one who wears a coat worn out at the elbows. "Down at heel" has a similar meaning. *See under* HEEL.

To elbow one's way in. To push one's way through a crowd; to get a place by HOOK OR CROOK. *See under* HOOK.

To elbow out; to be elbowed out. To supersede; to be ousted by a rival. A thruster or pusher who selfishly pursues his own interest is said to *use his elbows*.

Up to one's elbows. Very busy, with work piled up to one's elbows. *Cp.* UP TO THE EYES *under* EYE.

Elden Hole. Elden Hole needs filling. A reproof given to great braggarts. Elden Hole is a deep chasm in the Derbyshire Peak, long reputed to be bottomless. It is mentioned in Scott's *Peveril of the Peak*, ch. iii.

Elder. The importance of elders as people of authority in ancient communities was a natural development. In the OLD TESTAMENT they appear as official authorities of a locality; and as the elders of the SYNAGOGUE they exercised religious discipline. The members of the SANHEDRIN were called elders. The name was also applied to officers of the early Christian Church and is still used in this sense by the PRESBYTERIAN CHURCH.

Elder Brethren. *See* TRINITY HOUSE.

Elder tree. There are many popular tradi-

tions and superstitions associated with this tree. The CROSS is supposed to have been made from its wood and, according to legend, JUDAS hanged himself on an elder, cup-shaped fungal excrescences on the bark still being known as Judas's (or Jew's) ears. *The Travels* of Sir John MANDEVILLE and SHAKESPEARE in *Love's Labour's Lost*, V, ii, say that Judas was hanged on an elder.

> Judas he japed
> With Jewen silver
> And sithen on an eller
> Hanged hymselve.
> *Vision of Piers Plowman: Passus* I.

Warts are cured by being rubbed with elder and it is a protection against witchcraft. *See also* FIG-TREE; JUDAS TREE.

El Dorado (el dôr a' dō) (Sp. the gilded). Originally the name given to the supposed king of the fabulous city of MANOA believed to be on the Amazon. The king was said to be covered with oil and then periodically powdered with gold-dust so that he was permanently, and literally, gilded. Expeditions from Spain and England (two of which were led by Sir Walter Ralegh) tried to discover this territory. El Dorado and Manoa were used by the explorers as interchangeable names for the "golden city". Metaphorically it is applied to any place which offers opportunities of getting rich quickly or acquiring wealth easily.

Eleanor Crosses. The crosses erected by Edward I to commemorate his first wife Eleanor of Castile, who died at Hadby in Nottinghamshire in 1290. She was buried in Westminster Abbey and crosses were set up at each of the twelve places where her body rested on its journey—Lincoln, Grantham, Stamford, Geddington, Northampton, Stony Stratford, Woburn, Dunstable, St. Albans, Waltham, West Cheap (Cheapside) and CHARING CROSS. Only those at Geddington, Northampton and Waltham survive.

Eleatic Philosophy. A school of philosophy founded at Elea in Italy in the latter part of the 6th century B.C. Parmenides and ZENO were its chief exponents, although Xenophanes of COLOPHON is usually regarded as the founder. He had attacked the current polytheism and anthropomorphism and the *Eleatics* maintained a conception of the universal unity of being. Their thought considerably influenced PLATO.

Elecampane (*Inula helenium*), one of the Compositae, allied to the aster. Its candied roots are used as a sweetmeat and were formerly held to confer immortality and to cure wounds. Pliny tells us that the plant sprang from HELEN's tears. It was much used in old medicines and herb remedies.

Elector. In the HOLY ROMAN EMPIRE those rulers who formed an Electoral College to appoint the Emperor were called Electors. Their number was eventually regularized by the GOLDEN BULL of 1356 and the seven Electors were to be the archbishops of Mainz, Trier, and Cologne, with the rulers of the Rhine Palatinate, Saxony, Brandenburg and Bohemia. The ruler of Bavaria gained admission during the THIRTY YEARS WAR and Hanover became an Electorate in 1708. The office disappeared with the abolition of the Holy Roman Empire in 1806.

The Great Elector. Frederick William of Brandenburg (1620–1688), who left for his successors a position in Germany next in importance to that of Austria.

Electra (1) One of the PLEIADES, mother of Dardanus, the mythical ancestor of the Trojans. She is known as "the Lost Pleiad", for she is said to have disappeared a little before the TROJAN WAR to avoid seeing the ruin of her beloved city. She showed herself occasionally to mortal eye, but always in the guise of a comet. *See Odyssey*, V, and *Iliad*, XVIII.

(2) A sister of ORESTES who features in the *Oresteia* of Aeschylus and the two other dramas entitled *Electra* by Sophocles and Euripides. The daughter of AGAMEMNON and CLYTEMNESTRA, she incited Orestes to kill their mother in revenge for the latter's murder of Agamemnon. In modern psychology, an *Electra Complex* is a girl's attraction towards her father accompanied by hostility towards her mother.

Electricity (Gr. *elektron*, amber). Thales of Miletus (600 B.C.) observed that amber when rubbed attracted small particles. From such observations of electrical phenomena the modern science of electricity has developed.

Electronic Brain. A popular name for a computer.

Electuary. Coming from a Greek word meaning to lick up, this term is applied in pharmacy to medicines sweetened with honey or syrup, and originally meant to be licked off the spoon by the patient.

Elegant Extracts. At Cambridge, in former days, men too good to be PLUCKED and not good enough for the POLL, but nevertheless luckily allowed to pass, were nicknamed the *Elegant Extracts*, from the usual name for the popular anthology compiled by Vicesimus Knox and frequently reprinted in the 19th century. (It was published in 1791 as *Extracts, Elegant, Instructive, and Entertaining in Poetry; from the most approved authors*.) There was a similar LIMBO in the

honours list called the GULF. *See also* REGIMENTAL AND DIVISIONAL NICKNAMES.

Elegiacs. Verse consisting of alternate hexameters and pentameters, so called because it was the usual metre in which Greek and Roman elegies were written. In Latin it was commonly used by Ovid, Catullus, Propertius, Tibullus, and others; the following is a good specimen of English elegiacs:

> Man with inviolate caverns, impregnable holds in his nature,
> Depths no storm can pierce, pierced with a shaft of the sun:
> Man that is galled with his confines, and burdened yet more with his vastness,
> Born too great for his ends, never at peace with his goal.
>
> SIR WILLIAM WATSON: *Hymn to the Sea* (1899).

Element (Lat. *elementum*, first principle). In ancient and mediæval philosophy, earth, air, fire and water were the four elements from which all other substances were composed. This conception was introduced by EMPEDOCLES in the 5th century B.C. Later a fifth immaterial element was added, called the QUINTESSENCE, or *quinta essentia*, supposed by ARISTOTLE to permeate everything.

The use of the word in chemistry to denote substances which resist analysis into simpler substances begins with Robert Boyle.

In one's element. One's natural surroundings, within one's ordinary range of activity, enjoying oneself thoroughly. The allusion is to the natural abode of any animals, as the air to birds, water to fish.

> God who created me
> Nimble and light of limb,
> In three elements free
> To run, to ride, to swim.
>
> H. C. BEECHING: *A Hymn*.

To brave the elements. To venture out into the weather, to defy adverse weather conditions. The elements here are the atmospheric powers; the winds, storms, etc.

> I tax not you, you elements, with unkindness;
> I never gave you kingdom, call'd you children;
> You owe me no subscription; then, let fall
> Your horrible pleasure.
>
> SHAKESPEARE: *King Lear*, III, ii.

Elephant. The Order of the Elephant. A Danish order of knighthood said to have been instituted by Christian I in 1462, but reputedly of earlier origin. It was reconstituted by Christian V in 1693 and, besides the SOVEREIGN and his sons, consists of 30 KNIGHTS. The collar is of gold elephants and towers.

A white elephant. Some possession the expense or responsibility of which is not worth while; a burdensome possession. The allusion is to the story of a king of Siam who used to make a present of a white elephant to courtiers he wished to ruin.

King of the White Elephant. The proudest title borne by former kings of Ava and Siam. In Ava the white elephant bore the title of "lord", and had a minister of high rank to superintend his household.

Only an elephant can bear an elephant's load. An Indian proverb: Only a great man can do the work of a great man; also, the burden is more than I can bear; it is a load fit for an elephant.

Elephant paper. Before metrification a large-sized drawing paper measuring 23 inches by 28 inches; *Double Elephant*; a standard size of printing paper 27 inches by 40 inches. The name is probably from an ancient watermark.

To see the elephant (U.S.A.). To see all there is to see.

Elephant and Castle. The sign of a public house at Newington Butts that has given its name to a railway station and to a district in South London. The Elephant and Castle is the crest of the Cutlers' Company, into whose trade the use of ivory entered largely.

In ancient times, war-elephants bore "castles" on their backs containing bowmen and armed knights.

A legendary explanation is that it is a corruption of *Infanta de Castile*, Eleanor of Castile, who was the wife of Edward I.

Eleusinian Mysteries. The religious rites in honour of DEMETER or CERES, originally an agrarian cult, performed at Eleusis in Attica and later taken over by the Athenian state and partly celebrated at ATHENS. The rites included sea bathing, processions, religious dramas, etc., and the initiated obtained thereby a happy life beyond the grave. Little is known about the chief rites, hence the figurative use of the phrase to mean something deeply mysterious. The Eleusinian Mysteries were abolished by the Emperor Theodosius about the end of the 4th century A.D.

Elevation of the Host. In the MASS, after the consecration, the raising of the Host and the Chalice by the celebrant for the adoration of the faithful.

Eleven. At the eleventh hour. Just in time; from the parable in *Matt.* xx, 1–16.

Eleven Days. Give us back our eleven days. When ENGLAND adopted the Gregorian CALENDAR (by Chesterfield's Act of 1751) in place of the JULIAN CALENDAR, eleven days were dropped, 2 September 1752 being followed by 14 September. Many people thought that they were being cheated out of eleven days and also eleven days' pay. Hence the popular cry from the populace, "Give us back our eleven days!"

The Eleven Plus. The name given to the much-abused selection tests set to schoolchildren at the age of eleven, or just over that age, and used as a means of judging their suitability for the various types of secondary education provided by the Education Act of 1944 (secondary modern, secondary technical, secondary grammar, etc.). It soon became the WHIPPING BOY for all those who, for reasons political and social rather than essentially educational, were seeking to demolish the existing pattern of education in England in favour of comprehensive schools. Most of the attacks made on the efficiency or fairness of the "eleven plus", although tendentious and often unsubstantiated, nevertheless succeeded in creating a popular bogy.

The Eleven Thousand Virgins. *See* URSULA.

The Eleven Years' Tyranny. Denotes the period from 1629 to 1640 when Charles I, with the support of Strafford and Laud, governed without summoning a PARLIAMENT.

Elevenses. A popular name for a mid-morning refreshment snack with tea or coffee. *See also* CRIB.

Elf. Originally a dwarfish being of Teutonic mythology, possessed of magical powers which it used for the good or ill of mankind. Later the name was used for a malignant imp, and then for FAIRY creatures that dance on the grass in the full MOON, etc.

> Every elf and fairy sprite
> Hop as light as bird from brier.
> SHAKESPEARE: *A Midsummer Night's Dream*, V, ii.

The derivation of elf and GOBLIN from GUELF AND GHIBELLINE is mentioned in Johnson (with disapproval); the word is O.E. *ælf*, from Icel, *alfr*, and Teut. *alp*, a nightmare.

Elf-arrows. Arrow-heads of the NEOLITHIC AGE. At one time they were supposed to be shot by elves at people and cattle out of malice or revenge.

Elf-fire. The IGNIS FATUUS.

Elf-locks. Tangled hair. It used to be said that one of the favourite amusements of Queen MAB was to tie people's hair in knots. When Edgar impersonates a madman in SHAKESPEARE's *King Lear*, II, iii, he says, "I'll ... elf all my hair in knots."

> That is that very Mab
> That plats the manes of horses in the night;
> And bakes the elf-locks in foul sluttish hairs.
> SHAKESPEARE: *Romeo and Juliet*, I, iv.

Elf-marked. Those born with a natural defect, according to ancient Scottish superstition, are marked by the elves for mischief. SHAKESPEARE makes Queen Margaret call Richard III:

> Thou elvish-mark'd, abortive, rooting hog!
> *Richard III*, i, iii.

Elf-shot. Afflicted with some unknown disease which was supposed to have been caused by an ELF-ARROW.

Elgin Marbles. The 7th Earl of Elgin (1766–1841) was envoy to the Sublime PORTE from 1799 to 1803 and noticed that many of the classical sculptures at ATHENS were suffering from neglect and depredations. At his own expense, he made a collection of statuary and sculpture, including the frieze from the PARTHENON and works of Phidias, and brought them to England. He sold the "Elgin Marbles" to the BRITISH MUSEUM in 1816 for £36,000, a good deal less than they had cost him.

Elia. A *nom de plume* used by Charles Lamb (1775–1834), under which a series of essays appeared. The first of these (in the *London Magazine*, 1820) was a description of the Old South-Sea House, with which he associated the name of Elia, an Italian clerk, a "gay light-hearted foreigner", who was a fellow employee.

Elidure. A legendary king of Britain, who in some accounts was advanced to the throne in place of his brother, Arthgallo (or ARTEGAL), supposed by him to be dead. Arthgallo, after a long exile, returned to his country, and Elidure resigned the throne. Wordsworth has a poem on the subject called *Artegal and Elidure*.

Eligius, St. *See* ELOI, ST.

Elijah's Mantle. Metaphorically the assumption of powers previously enjoyed by another, as Elisha took up the mantle of Elijah (II *Kings* ii, 13).

Elijah's Melons. Certain stones on Mount Carmel are so called from the legend that the owner of the land refused to supply food for the prophet, and for punishment his melons were turned into stones.

Eliot, George. The pseudonym of Mary Ann, or Marian, Evans (1819–1880). Her first novel appearing under this name was *Scenes of Clerical Life*, 1858.

Eliott's Tailors. *See* REGIMENTAL AND DIVISIONAL NICKNAMES.

Elissa. DIDO, Queen of Carthage, was sometimes called Elissa.

Elixir of Life. The supposed potion of the alchemists that would prolong life indefinitely. It was sometimes imagined as a powder, sometimes as a fluid (Arab. a powder for sprinkling on wounds). It also meant the PHILOSOPHER'S STONE, use for transmuting base metals into GOLD. The name is now given to any sovereign remedy—especially of the "QUACK" variety.

Elizabeth. St. Elizabeth of Hungary (1207–1231). Patron SAINT of the Third Order of St. FRANCIS of which she was a member. Her day is 19 November and she was noted for her good works and love of the poor. She is commemorated in Kingsley's poem *The Saint's Tragedy*. The story is told that her husband Louis at first forbade her abounding gifts to the poor. One day he saw her carrying away a bundle of bread and told her to open it asking what it contained. "Only flowers, my lord," said Elizabeth and, to save the lie, God converted the loaves into flowers and the king was confronted with a mass of red roses. This miracle converted him.

Ell. An old measure of length, which, like FOOT, was taken from a part of the body, *viz.* the forearm and was originally 18 inches. The word (O.E. *eln*) from a Teutonic word *alina*, the forearm to the tip of the middle finger, is cognate with Lat. *ulna*. The measure varied at different times and the English ell of 45 inches seems to have been introduced from France in the 16th century and was chiefly used as a measurement for cloth. The Scotch ell was 37 inches, the Flemish ell *c.* 27 inches and the French ell *c.* 47 inches.

Give him an inch and he'll take an ell. Give him a little licence, and he will take great liberties or make great encroachments.

The King's Ell-wand. The group of stars called "ORION's Belt".

Elmo's Fire, St. *Elmo* through *Ermo*, is an Italian corruption of St. *Erasmus*, a 4th century Syrian bishop who came to be regarded as the patron SAINT of seamen, and St. Elmo's Fire was attributed to him. Through some confusion the name St. Elmo was also applied by Spanish sailors to the 13th century DOMINICAN, Blessed Peter Gonzalez, who revered him as their particular guardian for his labours among them. *See* CORPOSANT.

Elohim. The plural form of the Heb. *eloah*, God. It expresses the general notion of Deity in the same way as the more widely used *El*, which is found in Babylonian, Aramæan, Phœnician, Hebrew, and Arabic. JEHOVAH (*Jahweh* or *Yahve*), however, is used with the special meaning of the God of Israel.

Elohistic and Yahwistic Sources. The Mosaic authorship of the PENTATEUCH is no longer held by Biblical scholars and the first six books of the BIBLE (the Hexateuch) are usually regarded as a literary entity compounded of a variety of sources. Among the evidence used to support this view, is the use of the names ELOHIM and YAHWEH. In some sections of the Hexateuch Elohim is used, in others Yahweh, and in some the names are used indifferently, the general conclusion being that the various sources, written at different periods, were subsequently blended. *See also* JEHOVAH, ADONAI.

Eloi, St., or **St. Eligius** (el′ oi, el ij′ i us) (588–659). Patron SAINT of goldsmiths and metal-workers, and apostle of Flanders. Trained as a goldsmith, he was treasurer to DAGOBERT I (King of the Franks) and Bishop of Noyon.

Eloquent. The old man eloquent. Isocrates (436–338 B.C.), the Greek orator. He wrote a letter to Philip of Macedon congratulating him on his victory at Chæronea and died soon after. He was a Greek patriot in the wider sense and possibly thought Philip's triumph would promote peace and unity. The old view was that he died of grief at the Macedonian victory.

> That dishonest victory
> At Chæronea, fatal to liberty,
> Killed with report that old man eloquent.
> MILTON: *Sonnets* (*To Lady Margaret Ley*).

The Eloquent Doctor. The SCHOOLMAN, Peter Aureolus (Pierre d'Auriol, 14th century), Archbishop of Aix.

Elysium (e liz′ i ûm). In Greek mythology, the abode of the blessed; hence the **Elysian Fields**, the PARADISE or Happy Land in Greek poetry. *Elysian* means happy, delightful.

> Would take the prison'd soul,
> And lap it in Elysium.
> MILTON: *Comus*, 256, 7.

Elzevir. An edition of a classic author from the house of Elzevir, booksellers, printers and publishers, who made such works their chief concern. The firm was founded in 1580 by Louis, a Calvinist of Louvain, who settled at Leiden to escape persecution, and it continued in business until 1712. Members of the family established branches at The Hague, Utrecht, and Amsterdam, and Isaak (1596–1651) was appointed printer to the University of Leiden in 1620. The firm was at its best in the first half of the 17th century and their DUODECIMO classics sold all over Europe. The Amsterdam branch closed in 1680, having published works of Bacon, Comenius, Descartes, Milton, Hobbes, Molière, and Pascal. Elzevirs were cheap, soundly produced, and recognized for the quality of their scholarship. The cult of collecting them reached its height during the 19th century.

Em. The unit of measure in printing. The square of the body of any size of type. For standard purposes the pica em is taken, measuring 12 points or one-sixth of an inch. The depth and width of a printed page is measured in ems. An *en* is half an *em*, and is the average width of the letters in a fount; it is thus used as a basis for casting-off or estimating a quantity of typed matter.

Embargo. To lay an embargo on. To prohibit, to forbid. The word comes from the Sp. *embargar*, to detain, and is especially applied to the prohibition of foreign ships to enter or leave a port, or to undertake any commercial transaction; also to the seizure of a ship, goods, etc., for the use of the State.

Embarras de richesse (om ba ra′ de rē shes′) (Fr.). A perplexing amount of wealth, or too great an abundance of anything; more matter than can be conveniently employed. The phrase was used as the title of a play by the Abbé d'Allainval (1753).

Ember Days. The Wednesday, Friday, and Saturday of the four EMBER WEEKS once observed as days of fasting and abstinence, the following Sundays being the days of Ordination. The name is the M.E. *ymber*, from O.E. *ymbren*, a period, course or circuit (as the rotation of the seasons).

Ember Weeks. The weeks next after the first Sunday in LENT, WHIT SUNDAY, HOLY CROSS DAY (14 September), and St. Lucia's Day (13 December). Uniformity of observance was fixed by the Council of Placentia in 1095, but they were introduced into Britain by AUGUSTINE.

Ember goose. The northern diver or loon; called in Norway *imbre*, because it appears on the coast about the time of Ember days in ADVENT. In Germany it is called *Adventsvogel*.

Emblem. A symbolic figure or representation; a pictorial design with an allusive meaning which is inserted or "cast into" the visible device (Gr. *em*, in; *balein*, to cast). Thus a *balance* is an emblem of justice, *white* of purity, a *sceptre* of sovereignty.
Some of the most common and simple emblems of the Christian Church are:
A chalice. The eucharist.
The circle inscribed in an equilateral triangle, or *the triangle in a circle*. To denote the co-equality and co-eternity of the TRINITY.
A cross. The Christian's life and conflict; the death of Christ for man's redemption.
A crown. The reward of the perseverance of the SAINTS.
A dove. The HOLY GHOST.

A hand from the clouds. To denote God the Father.

A lamb, fish, pelican etc. The Lord Jesus Christ.

A phœnix. The resurrection.

Emblematical poems. Poems consisting of lines of different lengths so that the outline of the poem on the written page can be made to represent the object of the verse. Thus, George Herbert in the *Temple* wrote a poem on the *Altar* that is shaped like an altar, and one on *Easter Wings* like wings. George Puttenham in his *Arte of English Poesie* (1589) gives a chapter on this form of word-torture (which he calls "Proportion in Figure"), giving examples of eggs, crosses, pillars, pyramids, etc., and it was gibbeted by Ben Jonson, Dryden, Addison, and others.

> As for altars and pyramids in poetry, he has outdone all men that way; for he has made a gridiron and a frying-pan in verse, that besides the likeness in shape, the very tone and sound of the words did perfectly represent the noise that is made by these utensils.
>
> SAMUEL BUTLER: *Character of a Small Poet*.

Embolismic (Late Lat. *embolismus*, intercalation). Pertaining to intercalation, that which is inserted; thus in the Jewish CALENDAR an embolismic year consists of thirteen lunar months, an ordinary year of twelve.

Emerald. According to legend, an emerald protected the chastity of the wearer. It also warded off evil spirits, and epilepsy, cured dysentery, and was anciently supposed to aid weak eyesight.

The Emerald Isle. Ireland, from its bright-green vegetation. The term was first used by Dr. Drennan (1754–1820) in his poem called *Erin*.

> Nor one feeling of vengeance presume to defile
> The cause or the men of the Emerald Isle.
>
> WILLIAM DRENNAN: *Erin*.

Émigré (ā' mē grā) (Fr.). An emigrant or refugee. The word is particularly applied to those royalists and members of the privileged classes who left France during the Revolution. Their co-operation with foreign powers led to severe laws against them. NAPOLEON, as First Consul, proclaimed a general amnesty, when many returned to France. After the fall of the Empire they were rewarded with political favours by Louis XVIII, but did not recover their estates and former privileges.

Emilie. The "divine Emilie" to whom VOLTAIRE wrote verses, was the Marquise du Châtelet, with whom he lived at Cirey for some ten years, between 1735 and 1749.

Eminence Grise (ā mē nos' grēz) (Fr.). *See* GREY EMINENCE.

Emmanuel, or **Immanuel** (Heb. God with us). The name of the child whose birth was foretold by Isaiah, and who was to be a sign from God to Ahaz (*Is*. vii, 14). The name was later applied in the NEW TESTAMENT to the Messiah.

> Behold, a virgin shall be with child, and shall bring forth a son, and they shall call his name Emmanuel, which being interpreted is, God with us.
>
> *Matt*. i, 23.

Emmets and Grockles. A current Westcountry expression applied to tourists and holiday-makers.

Emmet is an archaic word for an ant and such insects swarm everywhere. The word *Grockle* apparently derives from *Grock*, the famous CLOWN, implying someone to be laughed at. It arose in 1963 from comments made on holiday-makers at the Globe Inn, Brixham, and was used by Peter Draper in his film *The System* (1963), made at Brixham, Torquay and other parts of Devon.

Empedocles (em ped' ō klēz). Greek philosopher, statesman, and poet (*c*. 493–*c*. 433 B.C.). According to Lucian, he cast himself into the crater of ETNA, that people might believe he was returned to the gods; but Etna threw out his sandal and destroyed the illusion (HORACE, *Ars Poetica*, 404).

> He who to be deemed
> A god, leaped fondly into Etna flames,
> Empedocles.
>
> MILTON: *Paradise Lost*, III, 469.

Matthew Arnold published (1853) a classical drama with the title *Empedocles on Etna*.

Emperor (Lat. *Imperator*). This title, borne by certain monarchs as a mark of the highest regal dignity, derives from its use by the rulers of the Roman Empire. In the days of the Roman Republic, the title *imperator* was given to magistrates vested with *imperium*, the supreme administrative power, which included military command. It came to be applied as a title of honour to military commanders after a victory until the celebration of their triumph. Julius Cæsar was the first to use the title permanently and it was adopted by Octavian as a *prænomen* (*i.e. imperator Cæsar*, not *Cæsar imperator*). In due course it became the monarchical title of the head of the Empire. Constantine Palæologus, the last of the emperors, fell in the siege of Constantinople in 1453.

CHARLEMAGNE was crowned Roman emperor in 800 but the first known use of the title HOLY ROMAN EMPIRE occurs in 1254. The so-called Holy Roman Emperors, whose office was abandoned by Francis II in 1806, were at best rulers of Germany, Burgundy and northern Italy, and from 1556 the HABSBURG emperors were but virtual presidents of a loose Germanic federation.

In 1804 the Holy Roman Emperor Francis II assumed the hereditary title of Emperor of Austria (as Francis I), a title last borne by Charles I (1916–1918).

In 1804 NAPOLEON crowned himself Emperor of the French. The First Empire lasted until 1815. NAPOLEON III ruled the Second Empire from 1852 until 1870.

Peter the Great was proclaimed "Emperor of All Russia" in 1721. The Russian Empire lasted until 1917.

In 1871 King William I of Prussia was proclaimed Emperor of Germany at Versailles. William II, the last German Emperor, abdicated in 1918.

King Victor Emmanuel III of Italy was declared Emperor of Abyssinia in 1936, when Italian forces invaded the country and the rightful Emperor, Haile Selassie I, went into exile until his return to his capital in 1941. Italy became a Republic in 1946.

Queen Victoria assumed the title of Empress of India in 1876. The title was relinquished by British sovereigns in 1947.

Emperors ruled Brazil from 1822 to 1889; Mexico from 1822 to 1823 and from 1864 to 1867 (the ill-fated Maximilian of Austria); Haiti from 1804 to 1806. The title has also been given to the Mogul of India, and to the sovereigns of China, Japan, Ethiopia, etc.

Emperor. Before metrification, a standard size of drawing paper measuring 48 inches by 72 inches, the largest sheet made by hand.

Emperor, not for myself, but for my people. The maxim of the Roman Emperor Hadrian (117–138).

The Emperor of Believers. Omar I (581–644), father-in-law of MOHAMMED, and second of the Mohammedan caliphs.

The Emperor's Chambermaids. *See* REGIMENTAL AND DIVISIONAL NICKNAMES.

Empire City, The. New York, the great commercial city of the United States, from its situation in the **Empire State**, the name given to New York State on account of its wealth and importance. Hence the name of the famous and tallest New York skyscraper.

Empire Day. Instituted by the Earl of Meath in 1902, after the end of the South African War, as a way to encourage schoolchildren to be aware of their duties and responsibilities as citizens of the British Empire. The day set aside was 24 May, Queen Victoria's birthday. In 1916 it was given official recognition in the United Kingdom, and was renamed Commonwealth Day in December 1958.

Empire Loyalist. *See* UNITED EMPIRE LOYALISTS.

Empire Promenade, The. A once famous feature of the former Empire Theatre, Leicester Square. This open space behind the dress circle was a regular parade of the "ladies of the town". In 1894, Mrs. Ormiston Chant of the London County Council directed a purity campaign against the MUSIC-HALLS and sought to effect the closure of the Empire Promenade and its adjoining bars. This led to the erection of canvas screens between them, but these were soon demolished by a riotous crowd, a prominent member being the young Winston Churchill. Brick partitions were subsequently built.

> Thus the temples of Venus and Bacchus, though adjacent, would be separated, and their attack on human frailties could only be delivered in a successive or alternating and not in a concentrated form.
> W. S. CHURCHILL: *My Early Life*, ch. iv.

Empire Style. The style of furniture, decoration, costume, etc., that came into vogue in Napoleonic France lasting from about 1800 until 1820. The Empire style followed the pseudo-classical fervour of the Revolution, but was much influenced by NAPOLEON's wish to emulate the splendour of Imperial Rome, hence the imitation of Roman architecture. The Egyptian campaign led to the introduction of Egyptian embellishments, notably the SPHINX. There was much use of bronze appliqué ornament, mirrors, and brocade, and court costume was rich and ornate. Women's fashions changed frequently, but the high-waisted Grecian style remained a constant motif.

Empirics. A school of medicine founded by Serapion of Alexandria (*c.* 200–150 B.C.) who made observation and experiment the first guide to treatment (Gr. *empeiros*, experienced). The statements of established authorities were placed second. Hence any medical QUACK or pretender is called an empiric.

> We must not
> So stain our judgement, or corrupt our hope,
> To prostitute our past-cure malady
> To empirics.
> SHAKESPEARE: *All's Well That Ends Well*, II,i.

Empyrean (em pi rē′ ản). According to Ptolemy, there are five heavens, the last of which is pure elemental fire and the seat of deity; this fifth heaven is called the empyrean (Gr. *empuros*, fiery); hence in Christian angelology, the abode of God and the angels. *See* HEAVEN.

> Now had the Almighty Father from above,
> From the pure Empyrean where he sits
> High thron'd above all height, bent down his eye.
> MILTON: *Paradise Lost*, III, 56.

Empyromancy. An ancient method of DIVI-NATION by observing the behaviour of certain objects when placed on a sacrificial fire. Eggs, flour and incense were used for this purpose as well as a shoulderblade.

En avant (on ă von) (Fr.). Forward.

En bloc (on blok) (Fr.). The whole lot together. *Cp.* EN MASSE.

En famille (on fa mē) (Fr.). In the privacy of one's own home.

En garçon (on gar' son) (Fr.). As a bachelor. "To take me *en garçon*", without ceremony, as a bachelor fares in ordinary life.

En grande toilette; en grande tenue (on grond twa let; on grond tĕ nū) (Fr.). In full dress; dressed for a great occasion.

En masse (on mǎs) (Fr.). The whole lot, just as it stands; the whole.

En papillotes (on papē yot) (Fr.). in a state of undress; literally, in curl-papers. Cutlets with frills on them are *en papillote*.

En passant (on pǎs' on) (Fr.). By the way. A remark made *en passant* is one dropped in, almost an aside.

En pension (on pon' si on) (Fr.). Pension is payment for board and lodging; hence, a boarding-house. "To live *en pension*" is to live at a boarding-house or hotel, etc., for a charge that includes board and lodging.

En rapport (on ra pôr) (Fr.). In harmony with; in agreement.

En route (on root) (Fr.). On the way; on the road or journey.

Encænia (en sē' ni ȧ) (Lat. from Gr., commemoration). The annual commemoration in June, which concludes the academic year at Oxford, held in the SHELDONIAN THEATRE. Benefactors are commemorated, honorary degrees conferred, prize compositions recited, etc.

Enceladus (en sel' ȧ dus). The most powerful of the hundred-armed giants, sons of URANUS and GE, who conspired against ZEUS. The king of gods and men cast him down at Phlegra, in Macedonia, and threw Mount ETNA over him. The poets say that the flames of the volcano arise from the breath of this giant.

Encomium (en kō' mi um) (Gr. *komos*, revel). In ancient Greece, a eulogy or panegyric in honour of a victor in the games; hence, praise, eulogy, especially of a formal nature. The encomium was sung in the procession which escorted the victor home.

Encore (on kôr). A good example of "ENGLISH FRENCH". Our use of this word is not as in France, where they say *bis* (twice) if they wish a thing to be repeated. *Encore une tasse* is "another cup", *encore une fois*, "once again".

Encratites (en krăt' i tēz). In the early Church, and especially among the GNOSTICS, those ascetics who condemned marriage, forbade eating flesh or drinking wine, and rejected all the luxuries and comforts of life. The name is Greek, and signifies "the self-disciplined" or "continent".

Encyclopedia (en sî klō pē' di ȧ) or **Encyclopædia.** A book or books giving information on all branches of knowledge or on a particular subject, usually arranged alphabetically. The Greek word was used to denote a complete system of learning. The earliest encyclopedia extant is Pliny's *Naturalis historia* in 37 books (1st century A.D.). In *c.* 1360 Bartholomew de Glanville, an English Franciscan friar, wrote *De proprietatibus rerum*, in 19 books, starting with an article on God and ending with a list of birds' eggs, but the first encyclopedia in English was that of John Harris (*c.* 1667–1719) who in 1704 produced a *Lexicon technicum or an Universal English Dictionary of Arts and Sciences*. This was soon overshadowed by the work of Ephraim Chambers (d. 1740), who, in 1728, brought out his *Cyclopædia, or an Universal Dictionary of Art and Sciences*, *etc.*, in two volumes, the forerunner of *Chambers's Encyclopædia* which is still the leading British production in this field. The *Encyclopædia Britannica*, edited by C. Macfarquhar, was first published at Edinburgh in three volumes (1768–1771). It was later taken over by Constable, then by A. and C. Black, and in 1920 it passed into American hands. The 11th edition (1908) in 29 volumes was issued by the Cambridge University Press, by arrangement. It is now published "with the editorial advice of the faculties of the University of Chicago and a committee of members of Oxford, Cambridge, and London Universities".

The French *Encyclopédie* developed from a translation of Chambers's *Cyclopædia*. The new work appeared at Paris between 1751 and 1772 in 28 volumes (including 11 volumes of plates) under the editorship of Diderot, assisted by d'Alembert, and many of the leading men of letters contributed to it. The **Encyclopedists** were exponents of sceptical, deistic and heretical opinions and their attacks on the Church and despotic government served the cause of revolution. Thus the name Encyclopedist designated a certain form of philosophy and gave their work conspicuous political importance resulting in censorship and attempts at suppression.

The above are but examples of the growth

of a multitude of such reference books now too numerous to mention.

End. A rope's end. A short length of rope used for beating someone, a once convenient and common disciplinary weapon in a ship. **A shoemaker's end.** A length of thread pointed with a bristle, and used by shoemakers.

At a loose end. *See* LOOSE.

At my wits' end. In a quandary how to proceed further; not knowing what further to do; nonplussed.

East End. *See under* EAST.

End for end. In reverse position, as to turn a rope or plank so that each end occupies the opposite to its former position.

End it or mend it. Said when an *impasse* or a crisis is reached, when things are intolerable and something simply must be done.

> The Labour Party declared for the total abolition of the Second Chamber, but the Government preferred "mending" to "ending".
> J. A. R. MARRIOTT: *Modern England*, ch. xvii.

He is no end of a fellow. A capital chap; a most agreeable companion.

Odds and ends. Fragments, remnants; bits and pieces of trifling value.

On end. Erect; also, in succession, without a break, as, "He'll go on talking for days on end."

One's latter end. The close of one's life.

> So the Lord blessed the latter end of Job more than his beginning.
> *Job* xlii, 12.

The end justifies the means. A false doctrine, frequently condemned by various Popes, which teaches that evil means may be employed to produce a good result.

> The End must justifie the means;
> He only sins who Ill intends;
> Since therefore 'tis to combat Evil;
> 'Tis lawful to employ the Devil.
> PRIOR: *Hans Carvel*.

The End of the World. According to rabbinical legend, the world was to last six thousand years. The reasons assigned are (1) because the name *Yahweh* contains six letters; (2) because the Hebrew letter *m* occurs six times in the book of *Genesis*; (3) because the patriarch Enoch, who was taken to heaven without dying, was the sixth generation from ADAM (Seth, Enos, Cainan, Mahalaleel, Jared, Enoch); (4) because God created the world in six days; (5) because six contains three binaries—the first 2,000 years were for the law of nature, the next 2,000 the written law, and the last 2,000 the law of grace. *See* LAST TRUMP *under* TRUMP.

The ends of the earth. The remotest parts of the earth, the regions farthest from civilization.

> All the ends of the earth have seen the salvation of our God.
> *Ps.* xcviii, 3.

To begin at the wrong end. To take things in the wrong order; to attempt to do something without any method.

To be one's end. The cause or agent of his death.

> This apoplexy will certain be his end.
> SHAKESPEARE: *Henry IV, Pt. II*, IV, iv.

To burn the candle at both ends. *See under* BURN.

To come to the end of one's tether. *See* TETHER.

To go off the deep end. To get unnecessarily excited or angry.

To have something at one's fingers' ends. *See under* FINGER.

To make ends, or **both ends meet.** To make one's income cover expenses; to manage to live without getting into debt.

To put an end to. To terminate, or cause to terminate.

To the bitter end. *See* BITTER.

West End. *See under* WEST.

End-irons. Two movable iron cheeks or plates, formerly used in cooking-stoves to enlarge or contract the grate at pleasure. The term explains itself but must not be mistaken for "dogs". *See* ANDIRON.

End papers. The two leaves at the front and back of a book, one of which is pasted down on to the inside of the cover and the other is a fly-leaf. They were formerly usually coloured or marbled. Sometimes maps, plans, etc., are printed on them.

End-stopped. A term in prosody denoting that the sense of the line to which it is applied is completed with that line and does not run over to the next; the opposite of *enjambement*. In the following lines the first is an example of enjambement, and the second is end-stopped.

> Awake, my St. John, leave all meaner things
> To low ambition, and the pride of Kings.
> POPE: *Essay on Man*, I, i.

Endor, Witch of. *See under* WITCH.

Endymion (en dim' i on). In Greek mythology, the shepherd son of Aethlius, loved by SELENE, the Moon goddess who bore him fifty daughters. Another story is that ZEUS gave him eternal life and youth by allowing him to sleep perpetually on Mount Latmus and Selene came down nightly to embrace him. The story is used by Keats in his *Endymion* (1818) and it forms the basis of Lyly's comedy, *Endimion, the Man in the Moone* (1585).

The moon sleeps with Endymion,
And would not be awaked.
SHAKESPEARE: *Merchant of Venice*, V, i.

Disraeli's novel *Endymion*, was published in 1880.

Enemy. How goes the enemy? or **What says the enemy?** What o'clock is it? Time is the enemy of man, especially of those who are behindhand.

Enfant terrible (on fon te rēbl) (Fr.). Literally, a terrible child. An embarrassing person, one who says or does awkward things at embarrassing times; one who stirs up trouble for his cause or party by his impetuousness.

England. In O.E. it is *Engla land*, meaning the land of the Angles, a Germanic people who began to invade Britain in the late 5th century from the Baltic coastlands, Angeln at the south of the Danish peninsula being their chief centre. Their kingdoms were those of the East and Middle Angles, Mercia, and Northumbria.

England's Darling. A name given to Hereward the Wake (*fl.* 1070), the patriot who held the Isle of Ely against WILLIAM THE CONQUEROR and eventually escaped with a few followers when the isle was beset by William's forces.

England expects that every man will do his duty. Nelson's famous signal to his fleet before the battle of Trafalgar. The intended signal was "England confides, etc.", but the signal officer obtained permission to substitute "expects" in order to save seven hoists, as the word "confides" was not in the signal book.

Little Englander. A name applied to those RADICAL and LIBERAL politicians and propagandists of Victorian England who, influenced by the doctrines of LAISSER-FAIRE and the MANCHESTER SCHOOL, or from more positive and idealistic reasons, opposed IMPERIALISM and advocated retrenchment in the colonial field. Gladstone, Granville, Cobden, and Bright are examples.

> That is why I distrust ... the late Government, because in their ranks were men who notoriously were "Little England" men, who took every opportunity of carping at and criticizing those brave Englishmen who have made for us homes across the sea, men who are opposed to any extension of the responsibilities and obligations of Empire, men who are unworthy sons of the ancestors who have made this country what it is.
> JOSEPH CHAMBERLAIN: *Speech at Walsall* (15 July 1895).

English. The language of the people of ENGLAND. It is derived from the West Germanic branch of the Germanic or Teutonic division of the Indo-European or Aryan family of languages. Historically it is divided into three main stages of development—*Old English*, or *Anglo-Saxon*, from the invasion to *c.* 1100; *Middle English* from *c.* 1100 to *c.* 1500; *Modern*, or *New English*, from *c.* 1500. It is the most widely used language in the world.

In typography *English* was the name given to a large size of type, two points (*i.e.* one-thirty-sixth of an inch) larger than pica and four points smaller than great primer.

Basic English. *See* BASIC.

Borough English. *See under* BOROUGH.

King's or **Queen's English.** English as it should be spoken. The term occurs in SHAKESPEARE's *Merry Wives of Windsor* (I, iv), but it is older and was evidently common. *Queene's English* is found in Nashe's *Strange Newes of the Intercepting Certaine Letters* (1593), and "thou clipst the Kinge's English" in Dekker's *Satiro-Mastix* (1602).

> These fine English clerkes will saih thei speake in their mother tongue, if a manne should charge them for counterfeiting the kinges Englishe.
> THOMAS WILSON: *Arte of Rhetorique* (1553).

Plain English. Plain, unmistakable speech or writing. To tell a person *in plain English* what you think of him is to give your very candid opinion without any beating about the bush.

To put on English (U.S.A.). In billiards and in baseball, to apply spin to the ball.

English French. A kind of perversity seems to pervade many of the words which we have borrowed from the French. Thus our *curate* is the Fr. *vicaire*, and our *vicar* the Fr. *curé*. Also note *epergne* (Fr. *surtout*); *surtout* (Fr. *pardessus*). *Screw* (Fr. *vis*), whereas the Fr. *écrou* we call a *nut*; and our vice is the Fr. *étau*. Some still say *à l'outrance* (Fr. *à outrance*). We say *double entendre*, the French *à double entente*. *See* ENCORE.

Englishman. The national nickname of an Englishman is JOHN BULL. The old nickname for him in France was GODDAM.

An Englishman's home, or **house is his castle.** Because so long as a man shuts himself up in his own house, no bailiff can break through the door to arrest him or seize his goods. It is generally used to mean that an Englishman is inviolable in his own home. In the third of his *Institutes* Sir Edward Coke (1552–1634) says:

> A man's house is his castle, *et domus sua cuique tutissimum refugium*.

And, again, in his report on Semayne's case:

> The house of everyone is to him as his castle and fortress, as well for his defence against injury and violence as for his repose.

Nowadays, it is less of a "castle" than it

was, various public authorities having right of entry under certain conditions; the premises may even be taken over and destroyed, consequent upon a compulsory purchase order.

> Lord Wilberforce said that the integrity and privacy of a man's home and of his place of business, an important human right, had since the Second World War, been eroded by a number of Acts passed by Parliament … Many people, as well as the present respondents, thought that the process had gone too far; that was an issue to be debated in Parliament and the press.
> *The Times* (*Law Report*, 13 December 1979).

Englishry. The differentiation between English and Normans or Anglo-Normans and Welsh. WILLIAM THE CONQUEROR introduced the *murdrum*, or fine for murder, to protect his fellow Normans. The fine was payable by the HUNDRED if the murderer could not be found. If it could be proved Englishry, *ie*, that the corpse was English, the Hundred was exempt.

Enid. The daughter and only child of Yniol, and wife of Prince GERAINT, one of the Knights of the ROUND TABLE. Ladies called her "Enid the Fair", but the people named her "Enid the Good". Her story is told in Tennyson's *Geraint and Enid* (*Idylls of the King*).

Enjambement. *See* END-STOPPED.

Enlightened Despot. A term applied to those sovereigns in 18th-century Europe whose rule reflected in various ways some of the ideas of the philosophers of the ENLIGHTENMENT. As despots their rule reflected the dictum attributed to Louis XIV of France—"*L'État, c'est moi*". Generally, they sought to break the power of the nobles and to govern through a centralized middle class bureaucracy, to advance the material and commercial strength of their states, and to improve the condition of their peoples. Frederick the Great of Prussia (1712, 1740–1786), Joseph II of Austria (1741, 1765–1790), and Catherine II of Russia (1729, 1762–1796) are notable examples.

Enlightened Doctor, The. Raymond Lully of Palma (*c*. 1235–1315), a Spaniard, and one of the most distinguished of the 13th-century SCHOOLMEN.

Enlightenment, The. The name given to the general intellectual and literary trend in Europe between *c*. 1690 and *c*. 1790. In England it is more commonly known as the AGE OF REASON. It was characterized by steadily increasing philosophical and radical criticisms of the existing order. In the political sphere the writings of Locke, Montesquieu, Voltaire, Diderot and Rousseau are typical. It led to the growth of Deism (*see*

THEIST), MATERIALISM and humanitarianism, as well as ideas of popular sovereignty and somewhat facile ideas of progress. The better ENLIGHTENED DESPOT was influenced by these tendencies.

Enniskillens. *See* INNISKILLINGS.

Ennius. "The father of Roman poetry" (239–169 B.C.). Noted for his dramas and epic poetry.

The English Ennius. Layamon (*fl. c.* 1200), who made a late Old English paraphrase of Wace's *Brut d'Angleterre*. Chaucer is also called the English Ennius.

The French Ennius. Guillaume de Loris (*fl.* 1230), author of the *Roman de la Rose*; also Jean de Meung (*c*. 1240–*c*. 1305) who wrote a continuation of the romance, is sometimes so called.

The Spanish Ennius. Juan de Mena (1411–1456), Spanish poet and author of *El Laborinto de Fortuna*.

Ensa Concerts. In World War II, concerts provided for the British fighting forces on active service by the Entertainments National Service Association (E.N.S.A.). Many famous figures in the entertainment and musical world took part, greatly helping to boost morale.

Entail. An estate in which the rights of the owner are *cut down* (Fr. *tailler*, to cut) by his being deprived of the right of the power of alienating them at pleasure and so depriving the rights of his issue; also the settlement of an estate in such a manner. *Tail males* or *tail females* were entails where the property passed exclusively to the males or females respectively.

To cut off the entail. To put an end to the limitation of an inheritance to a particular line or class of heirs.

Entente Cordiale (on tont' kôr di al') (Fr.) A cordial understanding between nations; not amounting to an alliance but something more than a *rapprochement*. The term is particularly applied to the Anglo-French Entente of 1904, for which King Edward VII's visit to Paris in 1903 was a valuable preliminary. The phrase was used in the time of Louis-Philippe when Guizot was in power. He achieved a "cordial understanding" with Lord Aberdeen in 1844.

> If Guizot remains in office Normanby must be recalled, as the only chance of a renewal of the entente cordiale.
> GREVILLE: *Diary*, p. 189 (1847).

Enter. To enter the lists. Figuratively, to enter any field of rivalry or controversy; an allusion to the arrival of a challenger in the tilting-ground in mediæval TOURNAMENTS.

Entertain. To entertain an angel un-

awares. *See under* ANGEL.

Enthusiast (Gr. *en theos*). Literally, one who is possessed or inspired by a god. "Inspired" is very similar, being the Lat. *in spirare*, to breathe in (the god-like essence). In the 17th and 18th centuries the word *enthusiasm* was applied disparagingly to emotional religion.

Entire. As the name of a beer, the term is now rarely used, but is still occasionally seen on public-house signs and advertisements. In the early 18th century the chief malt liquors were ALE, beer, and twopenny (a superior kind of ale sold at 2d. a pint). The constant demand for mixtures induced the brewers to combine the qualities of the three in a liquor called *entire* (from its being drawn from one cask). Being much drunk by porters it also came to be called *porter*.

> The Fokers had been at the Cistercian school from father to son; at which place, our friend, whose name could be seen over the playground wall, on a public-house sign, under which "Foker's Entire" was painted, had been dreadfully bullied on account of his trade.
>
> THACKERAY: *Pendennis*, ch. v.

Entrée (on' trā) (Fr.). **To have entrée.** To have the right or privilege of entry or admission.

Entre nous (on trè noo') (Fr.). Between you and me; in confidence.

Eolithic Age, The. The name given to the earliest part of the STONE AGE (Gr. *eos*, dawn; *lithos*, a stone). It is characterized by the rudest stone implements.

Eolus. *See* ÆOLUS.

Eon. *See* ÆON.

Epact (Gr. *epagein*, to intercalate). The excess of the solar over the lunar year, the former consisting of 365 days, and the latter of 354, or eleven days less. The epact of any year is the number of days from the last new moon of the old year to the first of the following January, and used in determining the date of EASTER. (See *Table of Movable Feasts* at the beginning of the BOOK OF COMMON PRAYER).

Epaulette (ep' aw let). A shoulder ornament worn by officers of the Royal Navy above the rank of sub-lieutenant, when in full dress. Epaulettes ceased to be worn in the army in 1855. Officers of the U.S. Navy above the rank of ensign wear epaulettes, but since 1872, in the army, they are worn by generals only.

Ephebi (e fē' bi) (Gr.). Youths who had reached the age of puberty. At Athens it denoted a youth who had reached the age of eighteen, and who had to spend a year in military training and a second year on garrison duty. When fully trained, he was given his shield and spear. He also attended public functions and was immune from taxation.

The system was adopted throughout the Greek world and, during the Roman period, athletic, cultural and religious studies took the place of military training, and admission for ephebi was by selection.

Ephesian. A jolly companion; a roysterer. The origin of the term is unknown. SHAKESPEARE also uses CORINTHIAN in much the same way.

> It is thine host, thine Ephesian calls.
>
> *Merry Wives of Windsor*, IV, v.

Diana of the Ephesians. *See under* DIANA.

The Ephesian Poet. Hipponax, born at Ephesus in the 6th century B.C.

Ephialtes. A giant, son of POSEIDON and brother of Otus. When nine years old, they were nine fathoms tall and nine cubits broad. They were slain by APOLLO.

Ephors. In Sparta, the five magistrates annually elected from the ruling caste. They exercised control over the king, the *Gerousia* (Council of Elders) and the *Apella* (Assembly).

Epic Poetry. Narrative poetry of an elevated and dignified style dealing with heroic and historical events, real or fictitious and mythical. The ILIAD and ODYSSEY, Virgil's ÆNEID and Milton's *Paradise Lost* are outstanding examples.

Father of Epic Poetry. HOMER.

Epicurus (ep i kū' rus). The Greek philosopher (*c.* 341–*c.* 270 B.C.) who founded the *Epicurean School* and taught that "pleasure" was the natural aim and highest good, but a pleasure which consisted of right living which led to tranquillity of mind and body. The idea that "good living" and luxury were the pleasures to be sought was a corruption of his teaching.

Hence, *epicure*, one devoted to the pleasures of the table, but fastidious in his choice; *epicurean*, pertaining to good eating and drinking.

> Epicurean cooks
> Sharpen with cloyless sauce his appetite.
>
> SHAKESPEARE: *Antony and Cleopatra*, II, i.

See DUM VIVIMUS VIVAMUS.

Epigoni. *See* THE SEVEN AGAINST THEBES *under* THEBES.

Epigram. A short piece of verse ending in a witty or ingenious thought, or WITH A STING IN ITS TAIL (*under* TAIL); or any short, pointed or witty saying. The original Greek verse epigrams were graceful lines for inscription on tombstones, etc.

> Treason doth never prosper; what's the reason?
> For if it prosper, none dare call it treason.
>
> SIR JOHN HARINGTON.
>
> You beat your pate, and fancy wit will come:
> Knock as you please, there's nobody at home.
>
> ALEXANDER POPE.

The Devil having nothing else to do
Went off to tempt My Lady Poltargrue.
My Lady, tempted by a private whim,
To his extreme annoyance, tempted him.
                                        HILAIRE BELLOC.

Sir, I admit your general rule,
That every poet is a fool:
But you yourself may serve to show it,
That every fool is not a poet.
        Attributed to, COLERIDGE, POPE, PRIOR and SWIFT.

Epimenides (e pi men′ i dēz). A religious
teacher and wonder worker of Crete (6th or
7th century B.C.). According to Pliny (*Natural History*), he fell asleep in a cave when a
boy, and did not wake for 57 years. He is
supposed to have lived for 299 years. *Cp*. RIP
VAN WINKLE *under* WINKLE.

Epiphany (e pif′ à ni) (Gr. *epiphaneia*, an
appearance, manifestation). The manifestation of Christ to the Gentiles, *i.e.* to the Wise
Men from East. 6 January is the feast of the
Epiphany in commemoration of this. The
vigil of the Epiphany (5 January) was the
time for choosing the BEAN-KING. *See*
TWELFTH NIGHT *under* TWELVE.

Episcopacy (Gr. *episkopos*, overseer, Late
Lat. *episcopus*, bishop). Church government by BISHOPS. Hence an *episcopalian
church* is a church governed by bishops and
its supporters are designated *episcopalians*.
Episcopacy in the CHURCH OF ENGLAND was
contested early on by Calvinists, who advocated a PRESBYTERIAN system, and was abolished by PARLIAMENT in 1643, but restored
with the return of the Stuarts. *See* ROOT AND
BRANCH.

Episcopal Signatures. It is the custom of
BISHOPS of the CHURCH OF ENGLAND to sign
themselves with their Christian name and
name of their SEE. In some of the older dioceses the Latin form is used, sometimes abbreviated:

Cantuar:	Canterbury.	*Gloucestr:*	Gloucester
Ebor:	York.	*Norvic:*	Norwich
Carliol:	Carlisle.	*Oxon:*	Oxford
Cestr:	Chester.	*Petriburg:*	Peterborough
Cicestr:	Chichester.	*Roffen:*	Rochester
Dunelm:	Durham.	*Sarum:*	Salisbury
Exon:	Exeter.	*Winton:*	Winchester

Episode (Gr. coming in besides, adventitious). Originally the parts in dialogue
which were interpolated between the choric
songs in Greek tragedy; hence an adventitious tale introduced into the main story; an
incident or happening standing by itself, but
part of a wider series of events as, "an episode in the Egyptian campaign".

In music, an intermediate or connective
passage in certain forms of composition,
especially a fugue.

Epistle (e pis′ èl). This word, related in origin
to APOSTLE, comes from a Greek verb meaning "to send to". The word is particularly applied to the NEW TESTAMENT letters, from
which extracts are read at the Communion
service. There are thirteen from St. PAUL,
one from St. JAMES, two from St. PETER,
three from St. JOHN, and one from St. JUDE,
and the *Epistle to the Hebrews*, of unknown
authorship, written to the various churches
with which they were concerned.

The epistle side of the altar. That side
from which the Epistle has been customarily
read at the Communion service according to
the BOOK OF COMMON PRAYER. It is to the
right of the celebrant as he faces the altar.

Epitaph (ep′ i taf). Strictly, an inscription on
a tomb, but usually it refers to any brief
verses or apt commemoration of the departed.

Here a pretty baby lies
Sung asleep with lullabies;
Pray be silent, and not stir
Th' easy earth that covers her.
                    ROBERT HERRICK, *Upon a child*.
Fuller's Earth.
                    Thomas Fuller's epitaph on himself, 1661.
His foe was folly and his weapon wit.
                    Epitaph on W. S. Gilbert
                    by "*Anthony Hope*" *Hawkins*.
Life is a jest, and all things show it;
I thought so once, and now I know it.
                    John Gay's epitaph on himself, 1732.
Si monumentum requiris circumspice.
                    Sir Christopher Wren's epitaph in St. Paul's.

Epithalamium (e pi thà lā′ mi um). In ancient Greece, a song sung by youths and
maidens outside the bridal chamber. The
poets developed it as a special literary form,
notably SAPPHO, ANACREON, Stesichorus and
Pindar. Spenser's *Epithalamion* (1595) is
the most celebrated English poem of this
kind. *Cp*. PROTHALAMION.

Epoch (ē′ pok) (Gr. a stop or pause). A definite point in time. The succession of events
in the period following, and reckoned from
an epoch, is called an ERA. In general usage
epoch and *era* are treated as interchangeable
terms.

Epode (Gr. *epodos*; an aftersong). A Greek
ode, the part after the strophe and antistrophe; in the epode the chorus returned to
their places and remained stationary. Also a
form of lyric poetry invented by Archilochus
in which a longer verse is followed by a
shorter one. The *Epodes* of HORACE are the
best known examples.

Father of Choral Epode. Stesichorus of
Sicily (*c*. 632–*c*. 553 B.C.).

Eppur si muove (e poor sē mwô′ vē) (Ital.
and yet it [the earth] does move). The
phrase said to have been uttered by Galileo
immediately after his recantation of belief in
the COPERNICAN SYSTEM. He appeared be-

fore the INQUISITION at ROME in 1633, and record of the saying (certainly APOCRYPHAL), first occurs in 1761.

Epsom Races. Horse races instituted in the reign of James I and held on Epsom Downs (continuously from 1730, except during World Wars I and II). The main meeting is held in May or June. The second day (Wednesday) is DERBY DAY, and on the fourth the OAKS is run.

Epsom Salts. Magnesium sulphate; used as a purgative, etc., and so called because it was originally obtained by the evaporation of the water of a mineral spring at Epsom in Surrey. According to Fuller's *Worthies*, the spring was discovered by a farmer in 1618, who noticed that, in spite of the drought, his cows refused to drink water from the spring. On analysis, it was found to contain the bitter purgative, sulphate of magnesia. Epsom Wells developed, like Tunbridge Wells, as a favourite LONDON spa. Aubrey, Pepys, Nell GWYN, and Queen Anne's consort were among its visitors. Shadwell's comedy *Epsom Wells* (1672) portrays the loose life of the spa in those times.

Equality. The sign of equality in mathematics, two parallel lines (=), was invented by Robert Recorde, who died in 1558. As he said, nothing is more equal than parallel lines.

Equation of Time. The difference between mean time (as on a perfect clock) and apparent time (as indicated by a sundial). The greatest difference is at the beginning of November, when the sun is somewhat more than sixteen minutes slow. There are days in December, April, June, and September when the sun and the clocks agree.

Era. A series of years beginning from some EPOCH or starting-point as:

		B.C.
The Era of	the Chinese	2697
,,	Abraham (1 Oct.)	2016
,,	the Greek Olympiads	776
,,	the Foundation of Rome	753
,,	Nabonassar (Babylon)	747
,,	Alexander the Great	324
,,	the Selucidæ	312
,,	the Maccabees	166
,,	Tyre (19 Oct.)	125
,,	Julian	45
,,	Actium (1 Jan.)	30
,,	Augustus (27 June)	27
		A.D.
,,	Diocletian (29 Aug.)	284
,,	Armenia (9 July)	552
,,	the Hegira (16 July)	622
,,	Yezdegird (Persian) (16 June)	632
,,	American Independence (4 July)	1776
,,	the French Republic (22 Sept.)	1792

The Christian Era begins theoretically from the birth of Christ, though the actual date of the Nativity is uncertain and was probably B.C. 6 or 7. The EPOCH of the Christian Era was fixed by the calculations of Dionysius Exiguus in 527 A.D. and was inexact.

Erastianism. A term derived from Thomas Erastus (1524–1583), denoting the supremacy of the State in ecclesiastical affairs. *Erastus* (Gr. lovely, or beloved) was the name adopted by Thomas Lieber (Liebler, or Luber), professor of medicine at Heidelberg and at Basel, where he later held the chair of ethics. He was a follower of Zwingli, noted for his opposition to Calvinistic claims, and held that punishment for sin was the prerogative of the civil authority.

The term was popularized in England after its use in the WESTMINSTER ASSEMBLY, and the CHURCH OF ENGLAND is sometimes called Erastian because in certain matters it is subject to State control. *See* BANGORIAN CONTROVERSY; CONGÉ D'ÉLIRE.

Erato. One of the nine MUSES; the Muse of erotic poetry, usually represented with a lyre.

Erebus. In Greek mythology, the son of Chaos and brother of Night; hence darkness personified. His name was given to the gloomy underground cavern through which the Shades had to walk in their passage to HADES.

> Not Erebus itself were dim enough
> To hide thee from prevention.
> SHAKESPEARE: *Julius Cæsar*, II, i.

Eretrian. The Eretrian Bull. Menedemus of Eretria (*c.* 319–*c.* 265 B.C.) was so called from his gravity. He was a follower of the MEGARIAN SCHOOL of philosophy and founder of the Eretrian School.

Erewhon (ēr' won, âr' e won). An ANAGRAM of "Nowhere", the name of the ideal commonwealth in Samuel Butler's philosophical novel of the same name (1872). *Cp.* IDEAL COMMONWEALTHS *under* COMMONWEALTH.

Erichthonius. Fathered by VULCAN and very deformed. ATHENE put him in a box and gave its charge to the daughters of Cecrops with strict orders not to open it but they did so and out of fright at what they saw jumped off the Acropolis to their death. He became King of ATHENS and established the worship of ATHENE. He was set up as the constellation *Auriga* (Lat. charioteer). *See* CHARIOT.

Erigena. Johannes Scotus, or John the Scot (*c.* 815–*c.* 877), philosopher and theologian. The name *Erigena* is taken to mean "born in Erin" (Ireland) but nothing is known of his early life.

Erigone. *See* ICARIUS.

Erin. An ancient name for Ireland.

Erin go bragh. Ireland for ever. *See* MAVOURNIN.

Erinyes (e rin' yēz). In Greek mythology, avengers of wrong, the Latin FURIES. *See* EUMENIDES.

Erk. Originally "airk", an R.A.F. nickname of World War I given to aircraftmen and mechanics. It later became "erk" and is applied to beginners, juniors, and underlings generally.

Erlking. In German legend, a malevolent GOBLIN who haunts forests and lures people, especially children, to destruction. Goethe has a poem on him, set to music by Schubert.

Ermine (ĕr' min). Another name for the stoat (*Putorius erminea*), but more usually used for its fur which is brown in summer and white in winter. It is one of the furs used in HERALDRY and is represented by a white field flecked with black ermine tails. Black tails on a white field is now called *ermines*. Other variants are *erminois*, a gold field with black tails; *erminites*, the same as *ermine* but with a red hair on either side of each black tail.

Ermine Street. The name of this essentially Roman road from LONDON to Lincoln, through Braughing and Huntingdon, is of later origin. It derives from *Earningastrœt* (the road to Earn's people), a group of Anglo-Saxons who settled near part of its route through Cambridgeshire.

Eros. The Greek god of love, usually personified as a young boy with bow and arrows; the equivalent of the Roman CUPID. It is also the popular name for the winged archer surmounting the memorial fountain to the 7th Earl of Shaftesbury, in the centre of Piccadilly Circus, London, which is actually a symbol of Christian charity. It is the work of Sir Alfred Gilbert (1854–1934) and was unveiled in 1893.

Erra-Pater. The supposititious author of an ALMANAC published about 1535 as *The Pronostycacion for ever of Erra Pater: a Jewe born in Jewery, a Doctour in Astronomye and Physycke*. It is a collection of astrological tables, rules of health, etc., and is arranged for use in any year. He is alluded to in Beaumont and Fletcher's *Scornful Lady* and *Elder Brother*, and by John Taylor, the WATER POET.

> He had got him a suit of durance, that would last longer than one of Erra Pater's almanacks, or a cunstable's browne bill.
>
> NASHE: *Nashe's Lenten Stuffe* (1599).

The almanacs were frequently reprinted and nearly a hundred years later Butler (*Hudibras*, I, i) says of William Lilly, the almanac-maker and astrologer:

> In mathematics he was greater
> Than Tycho Brahe or Erra Pater.

Erse. The native language of the HIGHLANDS and Western Isles of SCOTLAND. The word is a variant of Irish, the Scots coming originally from IRELAND. It was formerly applied by the Lowlanders to the CELTIC tongue of the Highlanders. It is now usually called GAELIC and the term Erse is more usually applied to the native language of Ireland.

> Of the Earse language as I understand nothing, I cannot say more than I have been told. It is the rude speech of a barbarous people, who had few thoughts to express, and were content, as they conceived grossly, to be grossly understood.
>
> JOHNSON: *A Journey to the Western Islands* (*Ostig in Sky*) (1775).

Erudite. Most erudite of the Romans. Marcus Terentius Varro (116–27 B.C.), a man of vast and varied erudition in almost every department of literature, the greatest of Roman scholars.

Erythynus (e rith' i nůs). **Have no doings with the Erythynus,** *i.e.* "don't trust a braggart". The Erythynus is mentioned by Pliny (ix, 77) as a red fish with a white belly, and PYTHAGORAS used it as a symbol of a BRAGGADOCIO, who fable says is whitelivered.

Escorial, or **Escurial.** The royal palace, MAUSOLEUM, and monastery built by Philip II of Spain some 27 miles northwest of Madrid. It was erected between 1563 and 1584 on a rocky altitude to commemorate his victory of St. Lawrence's Day over the French at St. Quentin (1557). It is generally believed that the shape of its plan represents the gridiron on which St. LAWRENCE was martyred. It takes its name from the adjacent hamlet, which is itself apparently so called from the waste of local iron mines (Lat. *scoria*, slag or dross).

Escuage. *See* SCUTAGE.

Esculapius. *See* ÆSCULAPIUS.

Escutcheon. In HERALDRY, the shield on which armorial bearings are depicted. The word is from O.Fr. *escuchon* from Lat. *scutum* (Late Lat. *scutionem*), a shield.

Escutcheon of Pretence. In heraldry, the small shield of a wife, either heiress or coheiress, placed in the centre of her husband's shield.

To blot one's escutcheon. To incur disgrace or mar one's reputation. *Cp.* TO BLOT ONE'S COPYBOOK *under* COPYBOOK.

> ... he shrank ... from the abrupt question which told him that his connexion with the woman who dishonoured his name, who cursed his career, who blotted his escutcheon, and had now sunk so low that any honest day-labourer might have shrunk from acknowledging her as his wife ...
>
> OUIDA: *Held in Bondage*, ch. xxxiii.

Esoteric (Gr.) Secret, only for the initiated. Those within, as opposed to *exoteric*, those

without. The term originated with PYTHAG-
ORAS, who stood behind a curtain when he
gave his lectures. Those who were allowed
to attend lectures, but not to see his face, he
called his *exoteric disciples*; but those who
were allowed to enter the veil, his *esoteric*.

ARISTOTLE adopted the same terms; those
who attended his evening lectures, which
were of a popular character, he called his *ex-
oterics*; and those who attended his more ab-
struse morning lectures, his *esoterics*.

Esoteric Buddhism. *See* THEOSOPHY.

Esperanto. A constructed international language first published in 1887 by L. L. Za-
menhof which soon superseded VOLAPÜK. It
means "the hopeful one", the pseudonym of
its inventor.

Esprit (es' prē) (Fr. spirit, mind, wit).

Esprit de corps (es' prē de kôr) (Fr.). The
spirit of pride in the organization with which
you are associated, and regard for its traditions and associations, as a naval man speaks
of "pride of ship".

Esprit d'escalier (es' prē des kăl yā) (Fr.,
staircase wit). The effective rejoinder which
comes too late, the witty retort which comes
to one after the moment has passed. The
correct French is *l'esprit de l'escalier*, the
afterthought which occurs when going
downstairs from the salon to the street door.

Beaux Esprits. *See* BEAUX.

Bel Esprit. *See* BEL.

Esquire. (O.Fr. *esquier* from Lat. *scutarius*,
shield-bearer). One who carried the shield
of a KNIGHT and who ranked immediately
below him. William Camden (1551–1623),
the antiquary and one-time CLARENCEUX
KING OF ARMS, defined four classes of esquire:

(1) The eldest sons of knights, and their
eldest sons in perpetual succession.

(2) The eldest sons of the younger sons of
peers, and their eldest sons in perpetual succession.

(3) Those created by the King's LETTERS
PATENT or other investiture, and their eldest
sons.

(4) Esquires by virtue of their offices, as
Justices of the Peace and others who bear
any office of trust under the crown.

Sir William Blackstone (1723–1780)
added to the list but the title was loosely used
before this time and the various attempts to
legally define its use have met with little success. Esquires still feature in the "Scale of
General or Social Precedence", immediately
before Gentlemen, the last on the list. In
practice, it is mainly used in correspondence
(abbreviated to "Esq."), as an alternative to
"Mr."

I am Robert Shallow, sir; a poor esquire of this
county, and one of the King's justices of the peace.
SHAKESPEARE: *Henry IV, Pt. II*, III, ii.

Essays. Bacon's essays were the first in English to bear this name.

Certain brief notes ... which I have called essays.
The word is late but the thing is ancient.
Suppressed Dedication to Prince Henry.

Essenes. A Jewish fraternity originating about
the 2nd century B.C. who lived a monastic
kind of life and who rejected animal sacrifices. They were distinguished for their
piety and virtue and were strict observers of
the SABBATH. They were given to acts of
charity and maintained themselves by manual labour (chiefly agriculture), lived in fellowship, and held their goods in common.
Their way of life was akin to that of Jesus
and His disciples. *See* DEAD SEA SCROLLS;
HASIDEANS.

Essex Lions. Calves, for which the county is
famous.

Valiant as an Essex lion. Said ironically of
a timid person. *Cp.* COTSWOLD LION.

Establishment, The (O.Fr. *establissement*).
A term long used to denote in particular the
established CHURCH OF ENGLAND, but now a
popular designation for the influential hierarchy or inner circle in any particular sphere
of the community, or of the community in
general. It has a somewhat derogatory significance associated with reaction, privilege,
and lack of imagination.

They were in fact appointed, of course, because
they had been trained to think in the way that what
is now called "the establishment" thinks and it was
clear that they did not dissent from this manner of
thinking.
S. G. EVANS: *The Social Hope of the Christian Church*,
ch. vi (1965).

Estate (O.Fr. *estat*; Lat. *status* from *stare*, to
stand).

Estates General (*États généraux*. Fr.).
The French assembly first summoned in
1302 as a consultative body consisting of
clergy, nobility and THE THIRD ESTATE. It
did not meet again after 1614 until 1789
when the Revolution began.

Estates of the Realm. Those classes, or orders, which have a recognized share or part
in the body politic. In Britain the three estates are the Lords Spiritual, the Lords
Temporal, and the Commons, although the
term is now anachronistic.

The King and the three estates of the realm assembled in parliament.
Collect for 5 Nov.

The Third Estate. The Commons. Historically the term usually refers to the third
chamber (*Tiers État*) of the French ESTATES

GENERAL at the time of the Revolution.

The Fourth Estate. The Press. Burke, referring to the Reporters' Gallery in the HOUSE OF COMMONS, is reputed to have said, "Yonder sits the Fourth Estate, more important than them all", but it does not appear in his published works. In former days the phrase has also been applied to the working classes. It occurs in Hazlitt's *Table Talk* (vi, 115) of 1821 referring to the influence of William Cobbett.

> The gallery [in the Commons] where the reporters sit has become a fourth estate of the realm.
> MACAULAY: *Hallam* (1828).

The Fifth Estate. The British Broadcasting Corporation has jocularly been so called.

Est-il possible (ā tēl pos ēbl). A nickname of Prince George of Denmark (1653–1708), the consort of Queen Anne. The story goes that when he was told of the abdication of his father-in-law, James II, all he did was to exclaim, "Est-il possible?" and when told further of the various noblemen who had deserted him, could only add, "Est-il possible?" *See also* BRANDY NAN.

Estotiland. An imaginary tract of land near the Arctic Circle in North America, said to have been discovered by John Scalve, a Pole. It is mentioned and shown in Peter Heylin's *Microcosmos* (1622).

> The snow
> From cold Estotiland.
> MILTON: *Paradise Lost*, x, 685.

Estrich. The old name for ostrich.

Eternal, The. God.

The Eternal City. ROME. The epithet occurs in Ovid, Tibullus, etc., and in many official documents of the Empire. It has also been applied to the "City of God".

The eternal fitness of things. The congruity between an action and the agent.

> Can any man have a higher notion of the rule of right, and the eternal fitness of things?
> FIELDING: *Tom Jones*, Bk. IV, ch. iv.

The Eternal Tables. In Mohammedan legend, a white PEARL extending from east to west, and from HEAVEN to earth, on which God has recorded every event, past, present, and to come.

The Eternal Triangle. The oft-recurring comic or tragic situation of the amorous involvement of one of a married couple with another member of the opposite sex.

Etesian Wind (e tē' zhȧn). A Mediterranean wind which rises annually (Gr. *etos*, a year) about the DOG-DAYS, and blows mainly from the north for about 40 days. It is gentle and mild.

> And he who rules the raging wind,
> To thee, O sacred ship, be kind;

> And gentle breezes fill thy sails,
> Supplying soft Etesian gales.
> DRYDEN: *Tr. of Horace's Odes*, I, 3.

Ethon. The EAGLE or vulture that gnawed the liver of PROMETHEUS.

Etna, or Ætna (et' nȧ). The highest active volcano in Europe. It stands over the Straits of Messina, *c.* 10,700 ft. high, covering an area of 460 sq. miles. In Sicily, Etna is known as Monte Gibello and many towns and villages live under its continual threat. The last serious eruption was in 1928. VIRGIL (*Æneid* III, 578, etc.) ascribes its eruption to the restlessness of ENCELADUS, the most powerful of all the giants who plotted against JUPITER and who lies buried under the mountain. According to the Greek and Latin poets it is the site of the smithy of CYCLOPS and the forges of VULCAN.

Eton Crop. A short boyish hairstyle, fairly popular among English women in the 1920s, called after the famous school for boys at Eton.

Etrenne. *See* STRENIA.

Etruria is a district of Hanley, Stoke-upon-Trent, where Josiah Wedgwood established his famous Etruria pottery works in 1769, named after the ancient Etruria in Italy, the home of the celebrated Etruscan ware.

Ettrick Shepherd. The name given to James Hogg (1770–1835), the Scottish poet who was born at Ettrick, Selkirkshire, the son of a shepherd, and, for a time, a shepherd himself.

Etzel. In German heroic legend, Attila, King of the Huns *(d.* 453).

Eucharist (ū' kȧ rist) (Gr. *eucharistos*, grateful). An ancient name for the *Lord's Supper*, *Holy Communion*, or MASS; also the consecrated *Elements* in the Communion. Literally, a thank-offering. Our Lord gave thanks before giving the bread and wine to His disciples at the LAST SUPPER. The Church offers the Eucharist as a service of praise and thanksgiving. *See* IMPANATION.

Euchre (ū' kėr). A word of doubtful etymology and the name of the most popular card game in the United States before it was replaced by auction bridge.

To be euchred is when the side that makes the trumps fails to win three tricks. Hence, figuratively, to be beaten, to be at a disadvantage. *Cp.* TO TURN THE TABLES *under* TABLE.

> "See here, men" said Bradfield, a tall powerful native chiel wi' a black beard, a grand bushman, too: "this here battle's over, your euchred ..."
> BOLDREWOOD: *The Ghost Camp*, ch. iii.

Euclid (ū' klid). Many generations of schoolboys knew geometry only as "Euclid", because the teaching of that branch of mathematics was based on the *Elements* of Eucleides, a Greek mathematician, who taught at Alexandria about 300 B.C. Although many rival text-books have been produced to supplant Euclid, none yet commands the same respect.

Eucrates (ū krā′ tēz). **More shifts than Eucrates.** Eucrates, the miller, was one of the archons of Athens, noted for his shifts and excuses for neglecting the duties of his office.

Eudoxians (ū doks′ i ȧnz). Followers of Eudoxius, a 4th-century patriarch of Constantinople, who maintained the heresies of the ARIANS.

Euhemerus (ū hē′ mě rŭs). A Greek philosopher of the 4th century B.C., who lived at the court of Cassander, King of Macedonia. In his *Sacred History*, he maintained the theory that the gods were formerly kings and heroes of exceptional ability, reverenced after death and finally deified. Hence the term *euhemerism* for such explanations of primitive myth and the derivation of mythology from an historical basis.

Eulalia, St. (ū′ lȧ lia). Eulalon (*i.e.* the sweetly spoken) is one of the names of APOLLO, and there are two 4th-century virgin martyrs called Eulalia both presumed to have been put to death under Diocletian in 304—St. Eulalia of Barcelona and St. Eulalia of Merida, whose ashes were scattered over a field upon which a pall of snow is said to have descended.

Eulenspiegel, Till (oi len shpē′ gěl). The name (owl-glass) of a 14th-century villager of Brunswick round whom gathered a large number of popular tales of mischievous pranks and often crude jests, first printed in 1515. The work was translated into many languages and rapidly achieved wide popularity. Till Eulenspiegel is the subject of the picaresque novel *Ulenspiegel* by Charles de Coster (1867), of various operas and a symphonic poem by Richard Strauss, *Till Eulenspiegel's Merry Pranks* (1895).

Eumæus (ū mē′ ŭs). The slave and swineherd of ULYSSES; hence a swineherd.

Eumenides (ū men′ i dēz) (Gr. the good-tempered ones). The name given by the Greeks to the FURIES, as it would have been bad policy to call them ERINYES, their right name.

Euphemism (ū′ fěmizm) (Gr. *euphemimos*, speaking fair). A word or phrase substituted to soften an offensive expression. Thus— His Satanic Majesty (the DEVIL); light-fingered gentry (pickpockets or thieves); an obliquity of vision (a squint); a lady of the town (a prostitute), are common examples. *Cp.* EUMENIDES; EUXINE SEA; FOUR-LETTER MAN.

Euphuism (ū′ fū izm). An affected and artificial literary style, characterized by alliteration, ornate language, lengthy similes taken from myth and fable, etc., after the manner of John Lyly (1554–1606), author of *Euphues: the Anatomy of Wit* (1578) and *Euphues and his England* (1580). Euphues, the hero of Lyly's romance, is taken from the Greek, implying a man "well-endowed by nature". Euphuism was much imitated by Lyly's contemporaries, including Queen Elizabeth I, Robert Greene and Thomas Lodge.

Eureka (ū rē′kȧ) (Gr. *Heureka*, I have found it). An exclamation of delight at having made a discovery; originally that of Archimedes, the Syracusan philosopher, when he discovered how to test the purity of Hiero's crown. The tale is, that Hiero gave some GOLD to a smith to be made into a votive crown, but suspecting that the gold had been alloyed with an inferior metal, asked Archimedes to test it. The philosopher did not know how to proceed, but in getting into his bath, which was full, observed that some of the water ran over and immediately concluded that a body must displace its own bulk of water when immersed; silver is lighter than gold, therefore a pound weight of silver is bulkier than a pound weight of gold and would consequently displace more water. Thus he found that the crown was deficient in gold. Vitruvius says:

> When the idea flashed across his mind, the philosopher jumped out of the bath exclaiming, "Heureka! heureka!" and, without waiting to dress himself, ran home to try the experiment.

"Eureka!" is the motto of California, in allusion to the gold discovered there.

The Eureka stockade. A fortified stockade erected by the diggers at the Ballarat goldfield in 1854, after the arrest of three of their fellows. It was the climax to their protests against ill treatment by the police, lack of political representation, and the licence system. Troops carried the stockade, twenty miners and two police being killed. Some improvements resulted as a consequence.

Eurus (ū′ rŭs). The east wind; connected with Gr. *eos* and Lat. *aurora*, the dawn.

> While southern gales or western oceans roll,
> And Eurus steals his ice-winds from the pole.
> DARWIN: *Economy of Vegetation*, canto vi.

Euryalus. *See* NISUS.

Eurydice (ū rid′ i si). In Greek mythology the wife of ORPHEUS, killed by a serpent

when fleeing from the attentions of Aristæus. Orpheus sought her in HADES,
charmed PLUTO by his music, and was promised her return on condition that he did
not look back until Eurydice had reached the
upper world. Nearing the end of his journey
he turned his head to see if Eurydice was following and she was instantly caught back
into Hades.

Euterpe (ū tĕr′ pi). One of the nine MUSES,
daughter of JUPITER and MNEMOSYNE, inven-
tress of the double flute, muse of Dionysiac
music, patroness of joy and pleasure, and of
flute-players.

Eutychians (ū tik′ i ănz). Followers of Eu-
tyches (c. 380–c. 456), archimandrite of
Constantinople, and author of the Eutychian controversy. He fiercely opposed
the NESTORIANS and held that Christ, after
the incarnation, had only one nature, the divine. He was excommunicated, reinstated,
and later exiled. They were the forerunners
of the MONOPHYSITES.

Euxine Sea (ūks′ in). The ancient Greek
name for the BLACK SEA, meaning the "hospitable". It was originally called *Axeinos*, inhospitable, on account of its stormy character and rocky shores but the name was probably changed euphemistically to propitiate
the powers supposedly controlling the elements. *Cp.* ERINYES; EUMENIDES.

Evangelic Doctor, The. John Wyclif
(c.1320–1384), "the morning star of the
Reformation".

Evangelical. From the time of the REFORMA-
TION, Protestant Churches were often called
Evangelical Churches from their insistence
that their teachings were based on the *evan-
gel*, or Gospel (*i.e.* the BIBLE). Those known
as *Evangelicals* in the CHURCH OF ENGLAND
emerged at the same time as the METHODISTS
and they notably emphasized the importance of scriptural authority and salvation by
faith in Christ, etc. *Cp.* CLAPHAM SECT; LOW
CHURCH.

Evangelists. The four Evangelists, MAT-
THEW, MARK, LUKE and JOHN, are usually
represented in art as follows:
Matthew. With pen in hand and scroll before him, looking over his left shoulder at an
ANGEL.
Mark. Seated writing, and by his side a
couchant winged LION.
Luke. With a pen, in deep thought, looking over a scroll, with a cow or ox nearby
chewing the cud. Also shown painting a picture, from the tradition that he painted a
portrait of the Virgin.
John. As a young man of great delicacy,
with an EAGLE in the background to denote

sublimity.
The more ancient symbols were: for Matthew, a man's face; for Mark, a lion; for
Luke, an ox; and for John, a flying eagle, in
allusion to the four living creatures before
the throne of God, described by St. John the
Divine.

> And the first beast was like a lion, and the second
> beast was like a calf, and the third beast had a face as
> a man, and the fourth beast was like a flying eagle.
> *Rev.* iv, 7.

Another explanation is that Matthew is
symbolized by a man because he begins his
gospel with the humanity of Jesus, as a descendant of David; Mark by a lion, because
he begins with the scenes of JOHN THE BAP-
TIST and Jesus in the Wilderness; Luke by a
calf, because he begins with the priest sacrificing in the temple; and John by an eagle,
because he soars high, and begins with the
divinity of the Logos. The four symbols are
those of Ezekiel's cherubim (*Ezek.* i, 10).

Irenæus says: "The lion signifies the royalty of Christ; the calf His sacerdotal office;
the man's face His incarnation; and the eagle
the grace of the Holy Ghost."

The name evangelist was applied in the
early Church to preachers of the Gospel and
is often used today to denote a revivalist
preacher.

Evans's Supper Room. In the 19th century,
one of the best-known resorts of London
night life; situated at the corner of King
Street, COVENT GARDEN. The premises, used
by the National Sporting Club, were opened
as a family hotel (1773) and in the 1830s occupied by the Star Dinner and Coffee Room
which was much frequented by the nobility.
The name *Evans's Supper Room*, by which
the premises were known until their closure
in 1880, derives from W. C. Evans, a member of the chorus of the Covent Garden
Theatre, who was one-time owner. He made
it the most famous song and supper room in
London giving entertainment of the "blue"
variety and allowing his patrons to outdo
each other in singing dirty songs. John
Greenmore (Paddy Green) took over in
1844 and added a splendid new hall with a
platform at one end. All the performers were
male, and women were only admitted on
giving their names and addresses, and even
then only enjoyed the privilege of watching
from behind a screen. The standard of entertainment under Green was outstanding
and Evans's more than any other song and
supper room can be regarded as the precursor of the MUSIC HALL. The Prince of Wales
(afterwards Edward VII) was a frequent visitor in the 1860s.

Eve (Heb. *havvah*, life, lifegiving, or possibly, snake). The first woman, formed from one of the ribs of ADAM.

> And Adam called his wife's name Eve; because she was the mother of all living.
>
> *Gen.* iii, 20.

Daughter of Eve. Woman. Often used with reference to feminine curiosity.

Even-Christian. An old term for a fellow-Christian, a neighbour in the Gospel sense.

> He that hath desdayn of his neighebore, that is to seyn, of his evene Cristene.
>
> CHAUCER: *Parson's Tale* (*De Superbia*).
>
> The more pity that great folk should have countenance in this world to drown and hang themselves more than their even Christian.
>
> SHAKESPEARE: *Hamlet*, V, i.

Events. At all events. In any case; be the issue what it may; *utcumque ceciderit*.

In the event. "In the event of his being elected", means in case, or provided he is elected; if the result is that he is elected.

To be wise after the event. To give advice on what should have been done to prevent some happening after it has occurred.

Ever and anon. From time to time, every now and then. *See* ANON.

Ever-Sworded. *See* REGIMENTAL AND DIVISIONAL NICKNAMES.

Ever-Victorious Army, The. A force of Chinese, officered by Europeans and Americans at Shanghai in 1861, and placed under the command of CHINESE GORDON in 1863. It stamped out the TAIPING REBELLION.

Everlasting staircase. The treadmill.

Everyman. The central character in the most famous English MORALITY PLAY (*c.* 1529) drawn from a late 15th-century Dutch original. Everyman is summoned by Death and invites all his acquaintances (such as Kindred, Good Deeds, Goods, Knowledge, Beauty, Strength, etc.) to accompany him on his journey, but only Good Deeds will go with him.

Every man Jack. Everyone, without exception.

> Sir Pitt had numbered every "Man Jack" of them.
>
> THACKERAY: *Vanity Fair*, ch. viii.

Evidence (Lat. *evidentia*, clearness). Evidence, meaning testimony in proof of something, has a wide variety of classifications, such as:

> *Circumstantial evidence.* That based on relevant fact and circumstances to the fact in issue.
>
> *Conclusive evidence.* That which establishes proof beyond doubt.
>
> *Demonstrative evidence.* That which can be proved without leaving a doubt.
>
> *Direct evidence.* Evidence of a fact in issue; that of an eyewitness.
>
> *Documentary evidence.* Evidence supplied in written documents.
>
> *External evidence.* That derived from history or tradition.
>
> *Hearsay evidence.* That which is heard from another but not known to be true.
>
> *Internal evidence.* That derived from conformity with what is known.
>
> *King's* or *Queen's evidence.* That of an accessory against his accomplices.
>
> *Material evidence.* That which|is|essential in order to carry proof.
>
> *Moral evidence.* That which accords with general experience.
>
> *Presumptive evidence.* That which is highly probable.
>
> *Prima facie evidence.* That which seems likely unless it can be explained away.
>
> *Self evidence.* That derived from the senses: manifest and indubitable.

In evidence. Before the eyes of the people; to the front; actually present.

Evil. Evil communications corrupt good manners. The words used by St. PAUL (I *Cor.* xv, 33); but he was evidently quoting Menander (*Thais*). Similar proverbs are, "he that toucheth pitch shall be defiled therewith" (*Ecclesiasticus*, xiii, 1); "one scabbed sheep infests a whole flock"; "the rotten apple injures its neighbours".

Evil Eye. An ancient and widespread belief that certain individuals had the power to harm or even kill with a glance. Various charms and gestures, many of an obscene kind, were employed to counteract it. Virgil speaks of an evil eye bewitching lambs.

> Nescio quis teneros oculus mihi fascinat agnos.
>
> *Bucolics, Ecl.* iii, 103.

Evil May Day. The name given to the serious rioting of 1 May 1517, when the London apprentices attacked the foreign merchants and artisans. It forms the basis of an anonymous play of SHAKESPEARE'S day, *Sir Thomas More*.

The Evil One. The DEVIL.

Evil Principle. AHRIMAN.

King's Evil. *See under* KING.

Of two evils, choose the less. *See* CHOICE.

Ewe-lamb. A single possession greatly prized; in allusion to the story told in II *Sam.* xii, 1–14.

Ex (Lat. from, out of, after, or by reason of). It forms part of many adverbial phrases, of which those in common use in English are given below. As a prefix to the name of an office or dignity it denotes a former holder of that office (e.g. *an ex-president*), or the present holder's immediate predecessor (e.g. *the ex-president*).

Ex cathedra. With authority. The POPE speaking *ex cathedra* (from the chair, or Papal throne) is said to speak with an infallible voice—as the successor and representative of St. PETER. The phrase is applied to dicta uttered by authority and ironically to self-sufficient, dogmatic assertions.

Ex hypothesi. According to what is supposed or assumed; in consequence of assumption made.

Ex libris. Literally, "from the (collection of) books". It is written in books or on bookplates followed by the name of the owner (properly in the genitive). Hence, a bookplate is often called an *ex-libris*.

Ex luce lucellum. A gain or small profit out of light. It was originally said of the old window tax, and when, in 1871, Robert Lowe, CHANCELLOR OF THE EXCHEQUER, proposed a tax on matches he intended this Latin pun to be printed on the revenue stamps on the matchboxes. The tax had to be withdrawn after protests.

Ex officio. By virtue of office. As, "the Vicar shall be *ex officio* one of the trustees."

Ex parte. Proceeding only from one of the parties; hence likely to be prejudiced. An *ex-parte* statement is a one-sided or partial statement, made by one side without modification from the other.

Ex pede Herculem. From the foot (we judge) a HERCULES; from this sample we can judge the whole. PYTHAGORAS calculated the height of Hercules by comparing the length of various stadia in Greece. A stadium was 600 feet in length but Hercules' stadium at OLYMPIA was much longer; therefore, said the philosopher, the foot of Hercules was proportionally longer than an ordinary foot; and as the foot bears a certain ratio to the height, so the height of Hercules can be easily ascertained. **Ex ungue leonem,** a lion (may be drawn) from its claw, is a similar phrase.

Ex post facto. From what is done afterwards; retrospective. An *ex post facto* law is one made to operate retrospectively.

Ex professo. Avowedly, expressly.

Ex proprio motu. Of his (or its) own accord; voluntarily.

Ex uno (disce) omnes. From one instance you may infer the rest. A general inference from a particular example; if one OAK bears acorns, all oaks will.

Exaltation. In ASTROLOGY, a planet was said to be in its "exaltation" when it was in that sign of the ZODIAC in which it was supposed to exercise its strongest influence. Thus the exaltation of VENUS is in Pisces, and her "dejection" in Virgo.

> And thus, god wot, Mercurie is desolat
> In Pisces, wher Venus is exaltat.
> CHAUCER: *Wife of Bath's Prologue*.

Exaltation of the Cross. A feast held in the ROMAN CATHOLIC CHURCH on 14 September (HOLY CROSS DAY), in commemoration of the restoration of the true cross to CAVALRY in

629, after the victory of Heraclius over the Persians. The CROSS had been taken by Chosroes in 614.

Excalibur (ekskăl' i běr). The name of King Arthur's sword (O.Fr. *Escalibor*), called by Geoffrey Monmouth *Caliburn*, and in the MABINOGION, *Caledvvlch*. There was also a legendary Irish sword called *Caladbolg* (hard-belly), *i.e.* capable of consuming anything.

According to Sir Thomas Malory's *Le Morte d'Arthur* (1470), Arthur, being the only one who could pull the sword from a great stone in which it had been magically fixed, was acclaimed king. The name *Excalibur* does not appear until later in the book. Later still, Chapter XXV is headed "How Arthur by the mean of MERLIN got Excalibur his sword of the LADY OF THE LAKE." After his last battle, when he lay sore wounded, it was returned at his command, by Sir Bedivere to the water. (See Malory, *Le Morte d'Arthur*, Bk. XXI, ch. v, and Tennyson's *Passing of Arthur*, *Idylls of the King*. There are some obvious inconsistencies in the story.

Excelsior (Lat. higher). Aim at higher things still. It is the motto of New York State and has been popularized by Longfellow's poem of this name:

> And from the sky, serene and far,
> A voice fell, like a falling star,
> Excelsior!

Exception. The exception proves the rule. The very fact of an exception proves or tests the rule.

To take exception. To feel offended; to find fault with or to object.

Exchequer. The name derives from the chequered cloth used for calculations. It dealt with the Crown's income and expenditure and was in being by Henry I's reign (1100–1135). It was presided over by the Treasurer until 1714 (when the Treasury board took over) and was abolished in 1833. **Chancellor of the Exchequer.** See under CHANCELLOR.

Excommunication. An ecclesiastical censure which excludes a person from the communion of the Church and sometimes accompanied by other deprivations. If clerics, they are forbidden to administer the sacraments. As a form of discipline, it no doubt derives from the Jewish practice at the time of Christ, which entailed exclusion from religious and social intercourse. It was a common punishment in mediæval times and was on occasions applied to whole nations. Pope Adrian IV used it against ROME in 1155, and Pope Innocent III employed it against ENG-

LAND in 1208. (*See* I *Cor.* v, 5.) The practice was also adopted by PROTESTANT Churches at the REFORMATION. The thirty-third of the *Articles of Religion* in the *Book of Common Prayer* is headed "Of Excommunicate Persons, how they are to be avoided". *Cp.* INTERDICT; BELL, BOOK AND CANDLE.

Exempli gratia (Lat.). For the sake of example: abbreviated to "e.g." when used as the introduction to an example.

Exequatur (Lat. he may perform or exercise). The letter PATENT issued to a diplomat by the government to which he is accredited authorizing him to exercise his power; a temporal sovereign's recognition of a BISHOP under papal authority, or of a PAPAL BULL, thus implying the right of rejection.

Exeter. An episcopal SEE and county town of Devonshire; called *Isca Dumnoniorum* by the Romans. *See also* EXTER.

The Duke of Exeter's daughter. *See* DUKE.

The Exeter Book. A MS. collection of Old English poetry presented (*c.* 1060) by Bishop Leofric to Exeter Cathedral, and still preserved in the cathedral library. It includes riddles, proverbs, poems, and legal documents. Among them are Cynewulf's *Christ*, *Juliana*, *Guthlac*; Widsith, *Deor's Lament*, and *The Wanderer*. Widsith is the earliest English poet known by name. The Exeter or EXON DOMESDAY is also sometimes called the "Exeter Book".

Exeter Hall. A public hall opened in the STRAND, London, in 1831 and largely used for the MAY MEETINGS of religious and philanthropic organizations. Their influence on colonial policy and in humanitarian causes was considerable, especially in the 1830s, and is generally known as "the Exeter Hall influence". It was acquired by the Y.M.C.A. in 1880 and demolished in 1907, the site being used for the Strand Palace Hotel.

> The spiritual successors of the Clapham Sect were the large body of people who in the mid-nineteenth century were grouped under the generic title of the Exeter Hall party, from the use of that building for their public demonstrations ...
> Exeter Hall was a dominant force until 1870, and powerful to a later date.
>
> J. A. WILLIAMSON: *Short History of British Expansion*, vol. II, ch. I.

> Mr. David has since had a "serious call",
> He never drinks ale, wine, or spirits, at all,
> And they say he is going to Exeter Hall
> To make a grand speech, and to preach and to teach
> People that "they can't brew their malt liquor too small".
>
> BARHAM: *Ingoldsby Legends* (*Look at the Clock*), 1840.

Exhibition. The Great Exhibition. The Exhibition of 1851, largely inspired by the Prince Consort and housed in the CYSTAL PALACE, Hyde Park, LONDON.

There were over 13,000 exhibitors in the four classes—raw materials, machinery, manufacturers, and fine arts. It was a conspicuous success and the profits were mainly used for educational foundations at South Kensington. Its centenary was celebrated by another Exhibition on the SOUTH BANK in 1951.

Existentialism. A philosophical attitude owing much to the writings of Søren Kierkegaard (1813–1855) which developed in Germany after World War I and somewhat later in France and Italy. Atheistic existentialism was popularized in France by Jean-Paul Sartre (1905–1980) during World War II. Existentialists emphasize the freedom and importance of individual "existence" and personality, and show a distrust of philosophical idealism. Much of their writing is characterized by disillusionment. The term is the translation of the German *Existenz-philosophie*.

Exon. One of the four officers in command of the YEOMEN OF THE GUARD, who are exempt from regimental duties. The word is an Anglicized pronunciation of the Fr. *exempt*, for former title of a junior officer who commanded in the absence of his superiors and was exempt from ordinary duty.

Exon (short for Lat. *Exoniensis*, of *Exonia*, i.e. Exeter. *See* EPISCOPAL SIGNATURES).

Exon Domesday. A magnificent MS. transcript of the Great, or Exchequer Domesday for the counties of Wiltshire, Dorset, Somerset, Devon, and Cornwall, preserved in the muniments of Exeter Cathedral. It was published in 1816. *See* DOMESDAY BOOK.

Exorcism. The expelling of evil spirits by prayers and incantations. An ancient practice taken over by the Christian Church, after the example of Jesus Christ and the APOSTLES who healed those possessed of evil spirits. The use of this rite in the ROMAN CATHOLIC CHURCH is now carefully regulated.

> And when he had called unto him his twelve disciples, he gave them power against unclean spirits, to cast them out.
>
> *Matt.* x, 1.

Exoteric. *See* ESOTERIC.

Expectation Week. Between ASCENSION and WHIT SUNDAY, when the APOSTLES continued praying "in earnest expectation of the Comforter".

Experimental Philosophy. Science founded on experiments or data, in contradistinction to moral and mathematical sciences; also called *natural philosophy*.

Experto crede (Lat.). Believe one who has had experience in the matter. The phrase is used to add significance or weight to a warning.

Exter. That's Exter, as the old woman said when she saw Kerton. A Devonshire saying, meaning, I thought my work was done, but I find much still remains before it is completed. The story is that the woman in question was going to Exeter for the first time, and seeing the fine old church of Kerton (Crediton) supposed it to be Exeter Cathedral. "That's Exter" (a local pronunciation of Exeter), she said, "and my journey is over"; but alas! she had still eight miles to walk.

Extispicy. The ancient practice of Roman soothsayers of divination by the inspection of the entrails of sacrificed animals—the same as HARUSPEX.

Extreme Unction. The last sacramental unction, the anointing with oil when a person is *in extremis*, now usually called "The Anointing of the Sick". One of the seven SACRAMENTS of the ROMAN CATHOLIC CHURCH founded on *James* v, 14, "Is there any sick among you? let him call for the elders of the church; and let them pray over him, anointing him with oil in the name of the Lord."

Eye. Apple of the Eye. *See under* APPLE.

Bull's eye. *See under* BULL.

Cat's eye. *See under* CAT.

Eagle eye. *See under* EAGLE.

Evil eye. *see under* EVIL.

Eye of the Baltic. Gotland.

Eye of Greece. ATHENS.

> Athens, the eye of Greece, mother of arts.
> MILTON: *Paradise Regained*, IV, 240.

Eye of a needle, It is easier for a camel to go through the. *See under* CAMEL.

Eye of the storm. An opening between the storm clouds. *Cp.* BULL'S EYE.

Eyes and no eyes. Unobservant. "Eyes have they, but they see not". *Ps.* cxv, 5.

Eyes to the blind. A staff; perhaps in allusion to that given to TIRESIAS.

A green eye. A jealous or envious eye; jealousy is figuratively described as "a green-eyed monster".

An eye for an eye and a tooth for a tooth. Let the punishment be equal to the crime or offence. A phrase derived from the OLD TESTAMENT.

> Eye for eye, tooth for tooth, hand for hand, foot for foot.
> *Exod.* xxi, 24.

Do you see any green in my eye? Do I look credulous and easily bamboozled? Do I look a GREENHORN?

My eye! or **Oh, my eye!** An exclamation of astonishment.

All my eye and Betty Martin. *See* ALL.

One-eyed. An expression of contempt, as, "I've never seen such a one-eyed town," *i.e.* such a hopeless and lifeless place.

One-eyed peoples. *See* ARIMASPIANS; CYCLOPS.

In my mind's eye. In my perceptive thought.

In the twinkling of an eye. Immediately, in a very short time.

> In a moment, in the twinkling of an eye, at the last trump; for the trumpet shall sound, and the dead shall be raised incorruptible.
> I *Cor.* xv, 52.

In the wind's eye. Directly opposed to the wind.

A sheet in the winds eye. An early stage of intoxication. An expression of nautical origin. *See* THREE SHEETS IN THE WIND, *under* SHEET.

A sight for sore eyes. A proverbial expression used of something that is very welcome, pleasant, and unexpected.

Mind your eye. Look out, be careful; keep your eyes open to guard against mischief.

There's more in that than meets the eye. There is more to it than appears at first sight or on the surface.

To cry one's eyes out. To cry immoderately or excessively.

To get one'e eye in. To adjust one's sight at CRICKET, billiards, golf, bowls, etc.

To give the glad eye to. To cast inviting or amorous glances at.

To have, or **keep an eye on.** To keep watch over someone or something.

To have an eye for. To have due sense of appreciation and judgment for.

To have an eye to. To keep constantly in view; to act from motives of policy.

To have an eye to the future. To bear future circumstances in mind when acting or making a decision.

To have an eye to the main chance. To keep self-advantage or profit constantly in view.

To have bags under one's eyes. Bulges under the eyes, often a sign of dissipation.

To keep one's eyes skinned. To be particularly watchful.

To look babies in one's eyes. *See* BABIES.

To make eyes at. To look amorously or lovingly at. *Cp.* TO MAKE SHEEP'S EYES.

To make sheep's eyes. *See under* SHEEP.

To make someone open his eyes. To surprise him very much, and make him stare with wonder or admiration; to bring someone to realize what is happening, to enlighten him.

To meet the eye. To arrest the sight, to come into notice.

To pipe your eye. *See under* PIPE.

To see eye to eye. To be precisely of the opinion; to agree completely or think alike.

To see with half an eye. Easily, at a mere glance.

To set, or **lay eyes on.** To have sight of.

To throw dust in his eyes. *See* DUST.

Up to the eyes. Wholly, completely; as, *up to the eyes in work*, very fully occupied; *up to the eyes in debt*, very heavily in debt.

Eyebrow. To raise an eyebrow. A natural sign of surprise.

Eyelid. Without batting an eyelid. Without the involuntary lowering or flicker of the eyelids that betrays surprise. "Batting" is from the O.Fr. *batre*, to beat or flap.

Eye-opener. Something that provides enlightenment; also, a strong mixed drink, especially a morning pick-me-up.

Eye-picking. An Australian expression in the days of the settlers for the practice of buying up the choice lots of land, leaving the waste parts in between to settlers of smaller

means; it was called "picking the eyes out of the country". Those who adopted this practice were called *peacockers*. *Cp.* GRIDIRONER.

Eye-service. Unwilling service, of the sort only done when one's master is looking.

> Servants, be obedient to them that are your masters, ... not with eyeservice, as menpleasers; but as the servants of Christ.
>
> *Eph.* vi, 5, 6.

Eye-teeth. The canine teeth; so called because they are located (in the upper and lower jaw) just under the eyes.

He has cut his eye-teeth. *See under* TOOTH.

To draw one's eye-teeth. *See under* TOOTH.

Eye-wash. In colloquial usage means "BUNKUM", "humbug"; something to blind one to the real state of affairs.

Eyre (âr) (Lat. *iter*; O.Fr. *eire*, a journey).

Justices in Eyre. From the time of Henry II (1154–1189), itinerant judges travelled the country on circuit to hear pleas, etc., usually sitting in the SHIRE court. They lapsed in the mid-14th century, being made redundant by the Justices of Assize.

F

F. The first letter in the Runic FUTHORC, but the sixth in the Phœnician and Latin alphabets and their derivatives. The Egyptian hieroglyph represented a horned asp and the Phœnician character a peg. *Ph* represents the same sound.

Double F(Ff, or ff) as an initial in a few personal names, as *Ffoukes, ffrench*, etc., is a mistaken use in print of the mediæval or Old English capital F (*ﬀ*) as it appears written in engrossed leases, etc. In script the old capital F looked very much like two small F's entwined. Its modern use is an affectation.

F is written on his face. The letter F (for fraymaker) used to be branded on the cheek of brawlers in church or churchyard. The practice was begun in the reign of Edward VI (1547–1553) to check the violent outbursts occasioned by changes in ritual. It was abolished in 1822.

F.E.R.T. The Order of the Annunciation (*see under* ANNUNCIATION) has these letters on its collar. *Fert* (Lat. he bears) is an ancient motto of the House of Savoy. But the letters have also been held to be the initials of *Fortitudo Ejus Rhodum Tenuit* (His courage held Rhodes), in allusion to the succour rendered to Rhodes by Savoy in 1310; *Fœdere et Religione Tenemur* (We are bound by our word and oath), on the gold doubloon of Victor Amadeus I (1630–1637); or, *Fortitudo Ejus Rempublicam Tenet* (His courage holds the State).

F.F.I. *Forces françaises de l'intérieur* (French Forces of the Interior). The grouping together in February 1944 of the various forces fighting for liberation after the fall of France in 1940. It included partisans, francs-tireurs, MAQUIS and others, and was subsequently merged with the army (Nov. 1944).

F.F.L. *Forces françaises libres.* After the German occupation of France, the Free French Forces organized, from June 1940, by General de Gaulle to continue the struggle in co-operation with the Allies. Later called "The FIGHTING FRENCH".

F.F.V. First Families of Virginia, a snobbish term used in the 19th century by those claiming descent from the first settlers.

Fabius (fā′ bi ús). Quintus Fabius Maximus (*d.* 203 B.C.), surnamed CUNCTATOR. According to Ennius (*Annals*, XII):

Unus homo nobis cunctando restituit rem.

i.e. one man by delaying saved the State for us.

The American Fabius. George Washington (1732–1799), whose tactics as commander-in-chief in the American War of Independence were somewhat similar to those of FABIUS.

Fabian Society. A society founded in January 1884 by a small group of middle-class intellectuals to propagate evolutionary socialism by transforming the State to an organization to promote social welfare through increasing state intervention in the economy. They took their name from Quintus FABIUS Maximus, believing that "long taking of counsel" was necessary before they could achieve their objective. George Bernard Shaw (1856–1950), Sidney Webb (1859–1947), Beatrice Webb (1858–1943), Graham Wallas (1858–1932), and Annie Besant (1847–1933) were prominent among them.

It envisaged socialism as a heap of reforms to be built by the droppings of a host of successive swallows who would in the end make a Socialist summer.

COLE and POSTGATE: *The Common People*, ch. xxiv.

Fabian tactics. Delaying tactics, masterly inactivity, winning by delay; after the manner of FABIUS called CUNCTATOR.

Fables (Lat. *fabula*, a narrative story or fable). Although this name is applied in a general sense to fictitious tales, legends and myths, it is more particularly applied to didactic stories of which a moral forms an integral part. In this more restricted class, human thoughts and attributes are usually portrayed by members of the animal and insect world. *See* ÆSOP; BABRIUS; LA FONTAINE; PHÆDRUS; PILPAY.

Fabliaux (fab′ lē ō). Mediæval French metrical tales, mostly comical and satirical, and intended primarily for recitation by the

TROUVÈRES, or early poets north of the Loire, and essentially of the latter part of the 12th century to the latter half of the 14th. They have little connexion with the fable proper, beyond the name, and were usually in octosyllabic couplets. They were essentially to entertain the common people and were characterized by coarseness and satirical treatment of the weaknesses of the clergy and feminine frailty, and the familiar incidents of ordinary life.

Fabricius (fà brish' ùs), Gaius Lusinus. A Roman consul (d. *c*. 270 B.C.) and hero of the war against Pyrrhus, representative of incorruptibility and honesty. Roman writers tell of the frugal way in which he lived on his farm; how he refused the rich bribes offered him by the Samnite ambassadors, and how at death he was too poor to leave a portion for his daughters, for whom the Senate provided.

Fabulinus (*fabulari*, to speak). The god, mentioned by Varro, who taught Roman children to utter their first word. *See* BABES, PROTECTING DEITIES OF.

Face. A colloquialism for cheek, impudence, self-confidence, etc., as "He has face enough for anything", *i.e.* cheek or assurance enough. The use is quite an old one. *Cp*. NECK.

A brazen face. *See* BRAZEN-FACED. *Cp*. BRASS.

A pasty face. Pale faced, like paste; unhealthy looking.

A wry face. The features drawn awry, expressive of distaste.

Face to face. In the immediate presence of each other; two or more persons facing each other.

On the face of it. To all appearances; in the literal sense of the words.

That puts a new face on the matter. Said when fresh evidence has been produced, or something has happened which puts things in a new or different light.

The face that launched a thousand ships. That of HELEN, the ships being the Greek fleet which sailed for Troy to avenge Menelaus. The phrase is from Marlowe's *Faustus* (*l*. 1354).

To be doubled-faced, or **two-faced.** To be hypocritical. To say one thing and act differently.

To draw, or **wear a long face.** To look dissatisfied or sorrowful, as when the mouth is drawn down at the corners, and the eyes are dejected, giving the face an elongated appearance.

To face about. To turn round on one's ground.

To face down. To withstand with boldness and effrontery. To abash by fixity of look.

To face it out. To persist in an assertion which is not true. To maintain a bold front.

To face the music. To brave the consequences of one's actions or to put on a bold front in an unpleasant situation. Possibly derived from the stage.

To face up to something. To meet one's difficulties without weakening.

To fly in the face of. To set at defiance rashly; to oppose violently and unreasonably.

To have two faces, or **to keep two faces under one hood.** To pretend to be very religious, and yet live an evil life; TO BE DOUBLE-FACED.

To laugh on the wrong side of one's face. *See under* LAUGH.

To look a person in the face, or **full in the face.** To meet with a steady gaze, implying lack of fear, or, sometimes, a spirit of defiance.

To lose face. To be lowered in the esteem of others through an affront to one's dignity—a matter of especial concern in the Far East.

To make faces. To grimace or "pull faces".

To put a bold, or **a good face on the matter.** To make the best of a bad matter; to bear up under something disagreeable.

To save one's face. To avoid disgrace or discomfiture.

To set one's face against something. To oppose it firmly; to resist its being done.

To shut the door in someone's face. To put an end to negotiations; to refuse to have dealings with.

To take things at their face value. To judge matters on their apparent worth.

Face-lifting. A method of enhancing looks or concealing the marks of age by treatment which tightens the skin of the face and removes the wrinkles.

To give something a face-lift. To renovate and give it a new look.

Faced. With a facing; covering the surface of one material with another; dressing the surface of a material. *See* FACINGS.

Bare-faced. The present meaning, audacious, shameless, impudent, is a depreciation of its earlier sense of open or unconcealed. A "bare-face" is a beardless face, where the features are in no way hidden. The French equivalent is *à visage découvert*, with uncovered face.

Shame-faced. Having shame expressed in the face.

Face-card, or **Faced-card.** A COURT CARD, a card with a face on it; also a card which has been dealt face up.

Facings. Lapels and cuffs on uniforms, etc., which differ in colour from the body of the coat. *Cp.* BUFFS *under* REGIMENTAL AND DIVISIONAL NICKNAMES.

To put someone through his facings. To examine or test; to ascertain if what appears on the surface is superficial only.

Facile princeps (făk' i lā prin keps) (Lat.). Easily first.

Facilis descensus Averno. *See* AVERNUS.

Façon de parler (fă son dė par lā) (Fr.). Idiomatic or unusual form of speech.

Fact. The Facts of life. The realities of a situation, knowledge of the details of reproduction, particularly of human reproductive functions.

Faction. In Roman and Byzantine history the *factiones* were originally the companies into which the charioteers were divided, each group having its special colour. The original two factions at ROME were the white (*albata*) and red (*russata*), to which the green (*prasina*) and blue (*veneta*) were added when the number of competing chariots was increased from two to four. From this the "factions" of the circus and hippodrome arose as political partisans.

Factory King. The name given to Richard Oastler (1789–1861) for his strenuous and lifelong efforts to improve the lot of the factory workers, especially children. He initially aroused attention by writing to the Leeds press on "Yorkshire Slavery" and was the constant advocate of a ten-hour day.

Factotum (Lat. *facere totum*, to do everything required). One who does all kinds of services for his employer; sometimes called a *Johannes Factotum*. Formerly the term meant a "JACK-OF-ALL-TRADES", and it was in this sense that Greene used it in his famous reference to SHAKESPEARE:

There is an upstart Crow, beautified with our feathers, that with his Tygers heart wrapt in a Players hide, supposes he is as well able to bumbast out a blanke verse as the best of you; but being an absolute *Johannes fac totum*, is in his owne conceit the onely Shake-scene in a countrie.

GREENE: *Groatsworth of Wit* (1591).

Fadge. Probably a Scandinavian word, connected with *faga*, to suit. To suit or fit together, as, *It won't fadge; we cannot fadge together; he does not fadge with me*.

How will this fadge?

SHAKESPEARE: *Twelfth Night*, II, ii.

Fadge is also old slang for a FARTHING.

Faerie (fā' ėr i). The land of the fays or fairies, the dominions of OBERON. *See* AVALON.

The land of faery,
Where nobody gets old and godly and grave,
Where nobody gets old and crafty and wise,
Where nobody gets old and bitter of tongue.

W.B. YEATS: *The Land of Heart's Desire*.

Faerie Queene, The. An allegorical romance of CHIVALRY by Edmund Spenser (*c.* 1552–1599), originally intended to have been in twelve books, each of which was to have portrayed one of the twelve moral virtues, but only six books were completed. It details the adventures of various knights, who personify different virtues (*e.g.* ARTEGAL, justice; Sir CALIDORE, courtesy), and who belong to the court of GLORIANA, who sometimes typifies Queen Elizabeth I.

Fag. A schoolboy drudge who performs menial tasks for his seniors in certain boarding schools. Perhaps from *flag* in the sense of "drooping", *to fag* is to work until weary.

From supper until nine o'clock three fags taken in order stood in the passages, and answered any praeposter who called "Fag", racing to the door, the last comer having to do the work ... And besides this night-work, each praeposter had three or four fags specially allotted to him, of whom he was supposed to be the guide, philosopher, and friend.

T. HUGHES: *Tom Brown's Schooldays*, Pt. I, ch. vii.

Fag is also slang for a cigarette, possibly connected with "vag", a Devonshire term for a turf for burning. *Cp.* COFFIN-NAIL.

It's too much fag. Too much trouble, too much needless exertion.

Quite fagged out. Tired out, wearied with hard work.

Fag-end. Originally the coarse end of a piece of cloth; hence the remaining part of anything; as "the fag-end of a leg of mutton", "the fag-end of a conversation". It is also slang for a cigarette stub (*see* FAG *above*).

The Kitchen and Gutters and other Offices of noise and drudgery are at the fag-end.

Howell's Familiar Letters (20 May 1619).

Faggot. A bundle of sticks. In the days when heretics were burnt at the stake, an embroidered representation of a faggot was worn on the arm by those who recanted, thus showing what they merited but had narrowly escaped. *Faggot* was also applied to a hireling who took the place of another at the muster of a regiment. An *old faggot* is a dreary old woman.

Faggot votes. Votes obtained by the nominal transfer of property to individuals in the days when this was a necessary qualification for voting rights, the minimum necessary being the forty-shilling freehold. The "faggot" was in this context a bundle of property divided into small lots.

Fainéant. Les Rois Fainéants. "Do-nothing" or puppet kings (Fr. *faire*, do; *néant*, nothing). An epithet particularly applied to the later MEROVINGIAN kings of France, whose powers were increasingly wielded by the MAYOR OF THE PALACE. The first of these largely nominal monarchs was Thierry III (d. 690), followed by Clovis III, Childebert III, Dagobert III, Chilperic II, Thierry IV, and lastly Childeric III who was deposed by Pepin the SHORT, Mayor of the Palace, who assumed the title of king in 751. Louis V (d. 987), last of the CARLOVINGIANS, was likewise so called.

> "My signet you shall command with all my heart, madam," said Earl Philip.... "I am, you know, a most complete Roi Fainéant, and never once interfered with my Maire de palais in her proceedings."
> SIR WALTER SCOTT: *Peveril of the Peak*, ch. xv.

Fains. A schoolchildren's term of unknown origin exempting the first to call: "fains I goal-keeping". The opposite of "Bags I", by means of which a positive claim is asserted.

Faint. Faint heart never won fair lady. An old proverb with obvious meaning.

Fair (O.E. *fæger*, beautiful, pleasing; also light in colouring, clear, clean, satisfactory, just, etc.). The following have been given this epithet:

Edwy, or Eadwig, King of Wessex (938–958).

Philip the Fair, King of France, *le Bel* (1268, 1285–1314).

Charles IV, King of France, *le Bel* (1294, 1322–1328), youngest son of Philip the Fair.

The Fair. The FAIR SEX.

The Fair-haired. Harold I, King of Norway (872–930).

Fair Isle. One of the Shetland islands, where a special pattern of knitting is done, which is believed to be of Moorish origin and to have been derived from contacts with shipwrecked sailors from the Spanish Armada of 1588. The Duke of Medina Sidonia, admiral of the Armada, was wrecked on Fair Isle.

Fair Maid of Anjou. Lady Edith Plantagenet, a kinswoman of Richard I and an attendant on Queen Berengaria, who married David, Earl of Huntingdon, Prince Royal of Scotland. She is a central character in Scott's *Talisman*.

Fair Maid of Brittany. Eleanor (*d.* 1241), granddaughter of Henry II and, after the death of her brother Arthur, the rightful sovereign of ENGLAND. Her uncle, the usurper King John, imprisoned her in Bristol Castle, which she eventually left to enter a nunnery at Amesbury. Her father, Geoffrey, John's elder brother, was Count of Brittany.

Fair Maid of February. A once popular name for a snowdrop.

Fair Maid of Kent. Joan (1328–1385), Countess of Kent, wife of the BLACK PRINCE, and only daughter of Edmund Plantagenet, Earl of Kent. The Prince was her second husband.

Fair Maid of Norway. Margaret (1283–1290), daughter of Eric II of Norway, and granddaughter of Alexander III of SCOTLAND. Acknowledged as heir to the throne of Scotland and affianced to Prince Edward, son of Edward I of England, she died in the Orkney islands on her way to Britain.

Fair Maid of Perth. Katie Glover, heroine of Scott's novel of this name, is supposed to have lived in the early 15th century, but is not a definite historical character, though her house is still shown at Perth. Bizet's opera, *La Jolie Fille de Perth* (1867), is based on the novel.

Fair Maid of Ross. *See under* ROSS.

Fair Rosamond. *See* ROSAMOND.

A fair field and no favour. Every opportunity being given.

By fair means. Straightforwardly; without deception or compulsion.

Fair and soft goes far in a day. Courtesy and moderation will help one to effect a good deal of one's purpose.

Fair and square. Honestly, justly, with straightforwardness.

Fair fall you. Good befall you; good luck to you.

Fair game. A worthy subject of banter; legitimately to be pursued or attacked.

Fair play. Honest or straight dealing. Fair or impartial treatment.

Fair to middling. Moderately good; reasonably well.

Fair trade. An old EUPHEMISM for smuggling. It also signifies reciprocal trading privileges with another country as a condition of free trade or tariff concessions.

Fair weather friends. *See under* WEATHER.

Fair words butter no parsnips. *See under* BUTTER.

The fair sex. Women; a phrase modelled on the French *le beau sexe*.

Pretty fair. Fairly well; reasonably satisfactory; "not bad".

To bid fair. To give good promise; to indicate future success as, 'He bids fair to be a good preacher."

To speak fair. To speak civilly or courteously.

Fairs (O.Fr. *feire*; Lat. *feria*, a holiday). These great periodical markets of former days were often held at the time of Church festivals and came to be associated with side-shows, amusements and merry-making. Although trade fairs or exhibitions are a link with the commercial aspect of the fairs of the past, the name is now largely associated with the travelling amusement fair. *See* BARTHOLOMEW FAIR; DONNYBROOK FAIR; GOOSE FAIR; PIE-POWDER COURT. *Cp.* PADDINGTON FAIR.

A day after the fair. *See under* DAY.

Hiring Fair. A STATUTE FAIR, virtually the same as a MOP FAIR; once an annual event in most market towns in England and Wales on MARTINMAS Day (11 Nov.), when men and maids stood in rows to be inspected by those seeking servants, farm workers, etc.

Mop Fair. A HIRING FAIR, probably taking its name from the tufts or badges worn by those seeking employment. Carters fastened a piece of whipcord to their hats; shepherds, a lock of wool; grooms, a piece of sponge. Others carried a pail, a broom, a mop, etc.

Statute Fair. A fair legalized by statute as opposed to custom or usage; a HIRING FAIR.

Fairlop Oak. A huge tree in Hainault Forest, Essex, blown down in 1820. Prior to that, a FAIR was held annually in July beneath its spreading branches.

Fairy, or **Fay**. In folk-lore and legend, a diminutive supernatural being of human shape, with magical powers. The names of the principal fairies and sprites, etc., known in fable and legend appear in this dictionary as individual entries. *See also* BROWNIE, DEITIES, DWARF, ELF, FAUNI, GNOME, GOBLIN, LEPRECHAUN, PIXIE.

Fairy darts. Flint arrow-heads. *Cp.* ELF ARROWS.

Fairy loaves, or **stones.** Fossil sea-urchins, said to be made by the fairies.

Fairy money. Found money, said to be placed by some good fairy at the spot where it is picked up. Also in legend, money given by the fairies which soon turned into "leaves" or other worthless forms.

Fairy of the Mine. A malevolent GNOME supposed to live in mines who busied himself cutting ore, turning the windlass, etc.

> No goblin or swart fairy of the mine
> Hath hurtful power o'er true virginity.
> MILTON: *Comus*, 436.

Fairy rings. Circles of dark green grass often found in lawns and meadows and popularly supposed to be produced by fairies dancing on the spot. They are due to the growth of certain fungi below the surface. The spawn radiates from the centre at a similar rate annually and darker colour is due to the increased nitrogen produced by the action of the fungus.

> You demi-puppets that
> By moonshine do the green sour ringlets make,
> Whereof the ewe not bites.
> SHAKESPEARE: *Tempest*, V, i.

Fairy sparks. The phosphoric light from decaying wood, fish, and other substances. Thought at one time to be lights prepared for the fairies at their revels.

Fait accompli (fā tà kom′ plē) (Fr.). An accomplished fact, something already done; often used in the sense of some act carried out in order to steal a march on some other party.

> I pointed out to Herr von Jagow that this fait accompli of the violation of the Belgian frontier rendered, as he would readily understand, the situation exceedingly grave.
> *Sir Edward Goschen, Ambassador in Berlin, to Sir Edward Grey*, 8 Aug. 1914.

Faith. Act of faith. *See* AUTO DA FE.

Defender of the Faith. *See* DEFENDER.

In good faith. "*Bona fide*", "*de bonne foi*"; with no ulterior motive, with complete sincerity.

Punic Faith. *See* PUNIC.

To pin one's faith on. *See under* PIN.

Faithful. The active supporters of any cult are called *the faithful* and in former times a PURITAN was sometimes *Brother Faithful*.

Commander of the Faithful. The CALIPH was so called by Mohammedans.

Father of the Faithful. ABRAHAM (*Rom.* iv, 16; *Gal.* iii, 6–9).

The Most Faithful King. The epithet by which the kings of Portugal used to be addressed by the VATICAN. *Cp.* RELIGIOUS.

Falange (Sp. *Phalanx*). At first a right-wing party in Spain formed in 1932 by José Antonio Primo de Rivera to uphold his father's memory against republican criticism, and later adopted by General Franco as the one official party in the State. Essentially representing a combination of European fascism and Spanish nationalism, it was used to counterbalance royalist, army, and Church influence and in 1937 forced the CARLISTS to join with it. Since 1957 the latter group has re-emerged. The Falange (latterly known as the National Movement) lost its unique position after the CAUDILLO's death in 1975, and was formally disbanded in 1977.

Falernian. A choice Italian wine esteemed by the ancient Romans and celebrated by VIRGIL and HORACE; so called because it was made of grapes from Falernus.

Falkiner. In New South Wales, a once popular name for a former Australian SHILLING. It derives from the association of a ram's head, which it bore, with the name of the Falkiner family, noted sheep breeders.

Fall. In music, a sinking of tone, a cadence.

> That strain again; it had a dying fall.
> SHAKESPEARE: *Twelfth Night*, I, i.

In the fall. In the autumn, at the fall of the leaf. Though now commonly classed as an

Americanism, the term is found in the works of Drayton, Middleton, Ralegh, and others.

> What crowds of patients the town doctor kills,
> Or how, last fall, he raised the weekly bills.
>
> DRYDEN: *Juvenal*.

Did she fall or was she pushed? Seldom used for its obvious and literal meaning concerning one who has fallen down but almost exclusively applied to a young woman who has lost her virginity.

It fell off the back of a lorry. Said of something picked up or acquired fortuitously or by somewhat questionable means. The origin is obvious.

The Fall of Man. The degeneracy of the human race in consequence of the disobedience of ADAM.

The fall of the drop. In theatrical parlance, means the fall of the drop-curtain at the end of the act or play.

To fall away. To lose flesh; to degenerate; to quit a party, as, "His adherents fell away one by one."

To fall back upon. To have recourse to.

To fall between two stools. To fail, through hesitating between two choices. The French say, *Être assis entre deux chaises*.

To fall flat. To fall prostrate; to fail to interest as "The last act fell flat."

To fall for. To be captivated by; to be taken in by; to become enamoured of.

To fall foul of one. To quarrel with; to make an assault on someone. A nautical term. A rope is said to be *foul* when it is entangled; one ship *falls foul* of another when they run against each other.

To fall from. To tumble or slip off; to violate, as "to fall from one's word"; to abandon or depart from, as "to fall from grace", to lapse into error or sin, to lose favour.

To fall in. To take one's place in the ranks; to take one's place with others. *Cp.* TO FALL OUT.

To fall in love with. To become enamoured of.

To fall in with. To meet accidentally; to come across; to agree with, as, "He fell in with my views."

To fall into a snare. To stumble accidentally into a snare. This is a Latin phrase, *insidias incidere*. Similarly, to fall into disgrace is the Latin *in offensionem cadere*.

To fall on deaf ears. To go unheeded or to be deliberately ignored.

To fall on evil days. To go unheeded or to be deliberately ignored.

To fall on evil days. To sink into poverty or suffer similar misfortune.

To fall on stony ground. Said of ideas, etc., which meet with no response and fail to take root. The allusion is to the parable of the sower (*Matt*. xiii, 5, 6).

To fall out. To quarrel; to happen.

> See that ye fall not out by the way.
>
> *Gen.* xlv, 24.

Also, in military language, to be dismissed or to disperse from the ranks. *Cp.* TO FALL IN.

To fall short of. To be deficient of a supply; not to come up to standard. To *fall short of the mark* is a figure taken from archery, quoits, etc., where the missile falls to the ground before reaching the mark.

To fall sick. To be unwell. A Latin phrase, *in morbum incidere*. *Cp.* FALLING SICKNESS.

To fall through. To come to nothing; not to be carried out.

To fall to. To begin (eating, fighting, etc.).

> Come, sir, fall to then; you see my little supper is always ready when I come home, and I'll make no stranger of you.
>
> WALTON and COTTON: *The Compleat Angler*, Pt. II, ch. ii.

To fall to the ground. To fail; to come to nothing, as, "His hopes fell to the ground."

To fall together by the ears. *See under* EAR.

To fall under. To incur, as, "to fall under the reproach of carelessness"; to become subject to, as, "He fell under the influence of bad companions."

To fall upon. To attack, as, "to fall upon the enemy"; to throw oneself on, as, "he fell on his sword"; to happen on, as, "On what day does Easter fall?"

To fall upon one's feet. To be unexpectedly lucky; to find oneself unexpectedly in a very favourable situation. Evidently from the old theory that the CAT always falls upon its feet unharmed.

To ride for a fall. *See under* RIDE.

To try a fall. To wrestle, when each tries to "fall", or throw the other.

> I am given, sir, secretly to understand that your younger brother, Orlando, hath a disposition to come in disguis'd against me to try a fall.
>
> SHAKESPEARE: *As You Like It*, I, i.

Fall-back chaise. A chaise with an adjustable hood.

Fall Guy (U.S.A.). A loser, dupe or victim. Towards the end of the nineteenth century professional wrestling became widely popular in America and many of the bouts were "rigged". One wrestler would promise to "take a fall" if the other agreed to deal with him gently, but the winner often broke his word and handled his opponent roughly. In such circumstances the loser came to be known as a "fall guy".

Fall Line. The line formed by the edge of a plateau where rivers and streams make a sudden fall to the coastal plain; in particular, the boundary in the U.S.A. between the older Appalachian uplands and the Atlantic coastal plain, where its influence in determining the location of cities emphasizes its economic importance. Those living in this belt are sometimes referred to as *Fall Liners*.

Fall-out. A name given to radioactive dust resulting from atomic and nuclear explosions. Figuratively, the effect of an action which extends beyond the intended range.

Fallen angels. Those cast out of HEAVEN; colloquially, women who have slipped from the paths of virtue.

Falling-bands. Neck bands or broad collars of cambric, lace or linen, made to lie upon the shoulders. Also called *falls* as distinct from the stiff ruff. They were common in the 17th century.

> Under that fayre ruffe so sprucely set
> Appears a fall, a falling-band forsooth!
> MARSTON: *Scourge of Villainie*, iii (1599).

Falling sickness. Epilepsy, in which the patient falls suddenly to the ground. SHAKESPEARE plays upon the term:

> Brutus: He hath the falling-sickness.
> Cassius: No, Cæsar hath it not; but you, and I,
> And honest Casca, we have the falling-sickness.
> *Julius Caesar*, I, ii.

Falling stars. Meteors. A wish made as a star falls is supposed to come true. Mohammedans believe them to be firebrands flung by good ANGELS against evil spirits when they approach too near the gates of HEAVEN.

Falmouth for Orders. In the 19th century with the advent of the electric telegraph, Falmouth, accessible to big sailing ships, became the port of arrival for vessels from Southern Asia, Australia and the west coast of America. Instructions from home might be many months old when they reached the English Channel and it was often necessary to alter the destination of their cargoes. They therefore called in at "Falmouth for orders" to receive the latest instructions by telegraph and then sailed on to British or North European ports.

False. False quantity. A term used in prosody to denote the incorrect use of a long for a short vowel or syllable, or vice versa.

To play false. To act treacherously, to be faithless.

To sail under false colours. *See under* COLOUR.

Falstaff. A fat, sensual, boastful, and menda-

cious KNIGHT; full of wit and humour; the boon companion of Henry, Prince of Wales (the future King Henry V); as portrayed by SHAKESPEARE in *Henry IV, Pts. I and II*, and *Merry Wives of Windsor*. Hence, **Falstaffian,** possessing the qualities and characteristics of Falstaff.

Falutin. *See* HIGH FALUTIN'.

Fame. Temple of Fame. A PANTHEON where monuments to the famous dead of a nation are erected and their memories honoured. Hence, *he will have a niche in the Temple of Fame* means his achievements will cause his people to honour him and keep his memory green.

Familiar, or **familiar spirit** (Lat. *famulus*, a servant). A spirit slave, sometimes in human shape, sometimes appearing as a cat, dog, raven, etc., attendant upon a WITCH, WIZARD, or magician, and supposed to be a demon in disguise.

> Away with him! he has a familiar under his tongue.
> SHAKESPEARE: *Henry VI, Pt. II*, IV, vii.

Familiarity. Familiarity breeds contempt. The proverb appears in English at least as early as the mid-16th century and was well known in Latin. The same idea is conveyed in the saying that a prophet is not appreciated in his own country.

Familists. Members of the "Family of Love", an extremist sect founded by Hendrik Niclaes at Emden, about 1540. He derived his mysticism from David George, or Jorizoon, an ANABAPTIST of Delft, whose followers are sometimes called Davidists or Davists. He implanted his ideas in England in the reign of Edward VI and the sect gained a hold in the eastern counties in spite of persecution. It revived under the COMMONWEALTH, and lingered on until the 18th century. They maintained that all people were of one family and that religion consisted essentially of love.

Family Compact. (1) The name given to the three agreements (1733, 1743, and 1761) between the BOURBON Kings of France and Spain to assert their interests. They were essentially directed against Austrian ascendancy in Italy and British mercantile and maritime supremacy. (2) The social coterie in early 19th-century Connecticut under the Dwight brothers which dominated Connecticut. So called from their inter-relationship. (3) The clique, of UNITED EMPIRE LOYALIST origins, which dominated political and social life in Upper Canada prior to the rebellion of 1837, and which was of an anti-democratic character.

Family of Love. *See* FAMILISTS.

Fan. I could brain him with his lady's fan.

Hotspur's words in SHAKESPEARE'S *Henry IV, Pt. I*, II, iii. Fans were made of feathers, and were the lightest of weapons; a contemptuous phrase.

Queen Anne's Fan. *See under* QUEEN.

Fan. Used from about 1900 for an ardent admirer or devotee. It is an abbreviation of FANATIC. Admiring letters written to the object of such admiration are known as **fan mail.**

Fanatic (Lat. *fanum*, temple). Literally, one who is possessed of the enthusiasm or madness of the temple engendered by over-indulgence in religious rites.

> Earth's fanatics make
> Too frequently heaven's saints.
> MRS. BROWNING: *Aurora Leigh*, ii, 448.

Fancy. Love—*i.e.* the passion of the fantasy or imagination.

> Tell me, where is fancy bred,
> Or in the heart or in the head?
> SHAKESPEARE: *Merchant of Venice*, III, ii.

The Fancy. In early 19th-century slang parlance a collective name for prize-fighters and devotees of the prize-ring. It is now sometimes applied to supporters of other pastimes.

> Du Loo was a heavy good-humoured stupid fellow in the Blues, who prided himself on ... his boxing, and who was going, at half-past twelve, to have a little play with Fighting Chatney, one of the Fancy ...
> OUIDA: *Held in Bondage*, ch. vi.

Fancy-free. Not in love.

> And the imperial votaress passed on,
> In maiden meditation, fancy-free.
> SHAKESPEARE: *Midsummer Night's Dream*, II, ii.

Fancy-man. Originally a CAVALIERE SER-VENTE or CICISBEO; one selected by a married woman to escort her to theatres, etc., to ride about with her, and to amuse her. It is now more usually applied to a sweetheart, and a harlot's *souteneur*.

Fancy-sick. Love-sick.

> All fancy-sick she is, and pale of cheer.
> SHAKESPEARE: *Midsummer Night's Dream*, III, ii.

To fancy oneself. To be conceited.

To tickle one's fancy. To tickle one's imagination, thus exciting amusement.

Fanfaron (Fr. *fanfare*, a flourish of trumpets). A swaggering bully, a cowardly boaster who blows his own trumpet. Scott uses the word for finery, especially for the gold lace worn by military men.

Hence **fanfaronade,** swaggering; vain boasting; ostentatious display.

Fanny. A naval mess kettle, somewhat similar in size and use to an army DIXIE. The name is said to have been applied to the tins in which preserved mutton or FANNY ADAMS was first issued. The sailors found them useful as mess traps and the name was transferred to the official kettle subsequently provided from naval stores.

Fanny, Lord. A nickname given by Pope to Lord Hervey (1696–1743) for his effeminate and foppish manners. He painted his face, and was as pretty in his ways as a boarding-school miss.

> The lines are weak, another's pleased to say,
> Lord Fanny spins a thousand such a day.
> POPE: *Satires of Horace*, I.

Fanny Adams, or **Sweet Fanny Adams,** or **Sweet F.A.** means "nothing at all" or "sweet nothing" though (especially by its initials) it has a somewhat ambiguous connotation. It is a phrase of tragic origin. In 1867 Fanny Adams, a child of eight, was murdered in a hop-garden at Alton, Hants, and her body horribly dismembered. The Royal Navy, with gruesome humour, adopted her name as a synonym for tinned mutton, which was first issued at this time. Sweet Fanny Adams became, as a consequence, a phrase for anything worthless, and then for "nothing at all". *Cp.* HARRIET LANE.

Fantom. An old spelling of PHANTOM.

Far. A far cry. *See* CRY.

Far and away. Beyond comparison; as "far and away the best", incomparably the best.

Far and wide. To a good distance in every direction. "To spread the news far and wide", to blazon it everywhere.

Far-fetched. Brought from afar; remotely connected, strained, as "a far-fetched simile", "a far-fetched conceit".

Far from it. Not in the least; by no means; quite the contrary. If the answer to, "Was he sober at the time?" is, "Far from it", the implication is that he was more than a little drunk.

Far gone. Deeply affected, as, "far gone in love".

Fare (O.E. *faran*, to go, to travel, etc., ultimately connected with Lat. *portare*, to carry). The noun formerly denoted a journey for which a sum was paid; then the sum itself, and by extension, the person who pays it. In certain English dialects, *e.g.* Suffolk, the verb *fare* is used in its original sense, "to go". The noun also means food and drink, the provisions of the table.

He cannot fare well but he must cry out roast meat. Said of one who blazons his good fortune from the house-top.

Farmer George. George III (1738, 1760–1820). A keen and progressive farmer who transformed his agricultural holdings. Under the name of *Ralph Robinson* he contributed the Robinson Letters to Arthur Young's *Annals of Agriculture*. His nickname of farmer was used by his political critics to arouse ridicule but:

A better farmer ne'er brushed dew from lawn.
BYRON: *Vision of Judgement*.

Farmers General. *See* FERMIERS GÉNÉRAUX.

Farnese (far nā' zē). A noted Italian family who ruled Parma and Piacenza from 1545 to 1731. Alessandro Farnese, as Pope Paul III (1534–1549), set up his son Pierluigi in the duchy and established the family politically.

The Farnese Bull. A marble group executed by Apollonius of Tralles and his brother Tauriscus in the 2nd century B.C. The group represents Dirce bound to the horns of a bull by Zethus and AMPHION for ill-using their mother. It was discovered in the Baths of Caracalla in 1546, and placed in the Farnese Palace at ROME. It is now in the Museo Nazionale at Naples.

The Farnese Hercules. Glykon's copy of the famous statue by Lysippus, the Greek sculptor of the time of ALEXANDER THE GREAT. It represents the hero leaning on his club, with one hand on his back, as if he had just got possession of the apple of the HESPERIDES. It was removed from the Farnese Palace at Rome, with other famous sculptures, to the Museo Nazionale at Naples.

Farrago (fá ra' gō). **A farrago of nonsense.** A confused heap of nonsense. *Farrago* (Lat.) is properly a mixture of *far* (meal) with other ingredients for the use of cattle, *i.e.* mixed fodder.

Farthing (O.E. *feorthing*, a fourthling or fourth part). The early silver penny was divided into two or four parts on the reverse thus ⊕ on the lines of the cross. Each of these quarters was a farthing. Farthings were demonetized on 31 December 1960.

Not worth a brass farthing. Virtually worthless. Erasmus, when Professor of Greek at Cambridge, described his profits as "not worth a brass farthing" and the phrase is possibly an allusion to the Nuremberg Monastic token; the expression probably gained further use from the 17th-century farthing tokens or HARRINGTONS, and Gunmoney. (*See under* GUN.)

Farthingale. The hooped understructure of the large protruding skirt fashionable in the reigns of Elizabeth I and James I. The word is the O.Fr. *verdugale*, a corruption of Span. *verdugado*, green rods, which were used for the framework before WHALEBONE took their place.

Fasces (Lat.). A bundle of rods tied round with a red thong from which an axe projected. In ancient ROME *fasces* were assigned to the higher magistrates as symbols of authority, representing power over life and limb. In modern times the fasces became the emblem of the Italian FASCISTS.

Fascines (fǎs' ēnz). Bundles of faggots used to build up military defences or to fill ditches for impeding attack. They were much used in World War I for road foundations and for horse standings and also used to impede attack in World War II. The name derives from the Roman FASCES.

Fascist. Originally an Italian political movement taking its name from the old Roman FASCES. It was founded in 1919 by Benito Mussolini (1883–1945) who took advantage of the discontent in Italy after World War I to form a totalitarian nationalist party against left-wing radicalism and socialism. In 1922 the Fascists marched on ROME and demanded power, and King Victor Emmanuel III made Mussolini Prime Minister. He styled himself DUCE (leader) and made himself Dictator in 1925, suppressing all other political parties the following year. The Fascists controlled Italy until 1943.

The term Fascism soon came to be applied to similar totalitarian movements in other countries. Ruthlessness, inhumanity, and dishonest and disreputable practices were notable characteristics of its adherents. *See* HITLERISM; NAZI.

Benito Mussolini provided Italy with a new theme of government which, while it claimed to save the Italian people from Communism, raised himself to dictatorial power. As Fascism sprang from Communism, so Nazism developed from Fascism.
WINSTON CHURCHILL: *The Gathering Storm*, ch. i.

Fash. Dinna fash yoursel'! Don't get excited; don't get into a flurry about it. The word is not of Scottish origin, it is the O.Fr. *fascher* (Mod. Fr. *fâcher*), to anger.

Fashion. In a fashion, or **after a fashion.** "In a sort of way", as "He spoke French after a fashion."

In the fashion. Dressed in the latest style, modish; in accordance with current trends.

Fast. The adjective is used figuratively of someone of either sex who is addicted to pleasure and dissipation; of a young man or woman who "goes the pace", which amounts to the same thing.

To play fast and loose. To run with the HARE and hunt with the hounds; to blow both hot and cold; to say one thing and do another. The allusion is probably to an old cheating game once practised at FAIRS. A belt or strap was doubled and rolled up with the loop in the centre and placed on edge on a table. The player then had to catch the loop with a skewer while the belt was unrolled, but this was done in such a way by the trickster as to make the feat impossible.

> Like a right gipsy, hath, at fast and loose,
> Beguiled me to the very heart of loss.
>
> SHAKESPEARE: *Antony and Cleopatra*, IV, xii.

To pull a fast one. *See under* PULL..

Fasti. In ancient ROME, working days when the law courts were open. Holy days (DIES NON) when the law courts, etc., were not open were called *nefasti*.

The *Fasti* were listed in calendars, and the list of events occurring during the year of office of a pair of consuls was called *fasti consulares*; hence, any chronological list of events of office-holders became known as *fasti*. The surviving six books of Ovid's *Fasti* are a poetical account of the Roman festivals of the first six months of the year. *Cp.* CALENDS.

Fasting. Strictly a complete abstention from food and drink, but the word is more usually applied to an extreme or fairly strict limitation of diet, and is of proved value in treating certain complaints. It is ancient and widespread as a form of penance, or purification, and was so used by the Jews. It was practised by Christ and adopted by the early Church. As currently practised in the Church, it is marked by abstinence from flesh meat and observance of a light diet. Throughout the ROMAN CATHOLIC CHURCH fasting is obligatory on ASH WEDNESDAY and GOOD FRIDAY. The main fast of the Mohammedans is during the month of RAMADAN.

Mahatma Gandhi (1869–1948) practised fasting, an ancient Hindu observance, as a form of asceticism and as a political protest. *See* HUNGER-STRIKE; CAT AND MOUSE ACT *under* CAT.

> Moreover when ye fast, be not, as the hypocrites, of a sad countenance; for they disfigure their faces, that they may appear unto men to fast.
>
> *Matt.* vi, 16.

Fat. In printer's slang, composition that does not entail a lot of setting, and hence can be done quickly.

A bit of fat. An unexpected stroke of luck; also, the best part of anything, especially among actors, a good part in a play.

The fat is in the fire. Something has been let out inadvertently which will cause a "regular flare up"; it's all over, all's up with it, the damage is done. If, in cooking, the grease spills into the fire, it blazes up and smokes, there is a risk of trouble and the food is spoilt.

The Fat. Alphonso II of Portugal (1185, 1211–1223); Charles III of France, *le Gros* (839, 884–888), also known as Charles II when CHARLEMAGNE is excluded from the list of French kings; Louis VI of France, *le*

Gros (1081, 1108–1137), were so called.

Fat-head. A silly fool, a dolt.

Fata (fa´ ta) (Ital. a fairy). Female supernatural beings introduced in Italian mediæval romance, usually under the sway of DEMOGORGON.

Fata Morgana. The fay, or fairy Morgana, sister of King ARTHUR; also a mirage often visible in the Straits of Messina, so named from MORGAN LE FAY who was fabled by the Norman settlers in England to dwell in Calabria.

Fatal Gifts. *See* CADMUS; GOLD OF TOLOSA *under* GOLD; HARMONIA; FATAL NECKLACE *under* NECKLACE; NESSUS; NIBELUNGENLIED; OPAL; SEIAN HORSE.

Fates. The Cruel Fates. The Greeks and Romans supposed there were three Parcæ or Fates, who arbitrarily controlled the birth, life and death of everyone. They were CLOTHO, LACHESIS and ATROPOS; called cruel because they paid no regard to the wishes of anyone.

Father. In the HOLY TRINITY, God. The name is given as a title to Roman Catholic priests, and sometimes to CHURCH OF ENGLAND clergy of the HIGH CHURCH persuasion; also to the senior member of a body or profession, as the *Father of the House of Commons*; and to the originator or first leader of some movement or school, etc., as the *Father of Comedy*, the *Father of History*. In ancient Rome the title was given to the senators (*cp.* PATRICIAN; CONSCRIPT FATHERS), and in ecclesiastical history to the early Church writers and doctors.

Father Mathew, Neptune, etc. *See these names.*

Father Thoughtful. Nicholas de Catinat (1637–1712), a marshal of France; so called by his soldiers for his cautious and thoughtful policy.

Father of Angling. Izaak Walton (1593–1683).

Father of the Chapel. *See* CHAPEL.

Father of Chemistry. Robert Boyle (1627–1691).

Father of Christian Monasticism. St. Anthony (*c.* 250–350). *See* FATHERS OF THE DESERT.

Father of Comedy. Aristophanes (*c.* 450-*c.* 385 B.C.).

Father of Courtesy. Richard de Beauchamp, Earl of Warwick (1382–1439).

Father of Ecclesiastical History. Eusebius of Cæsarea (*c.* 260-*c.* 340).

Father of English Botany. William Turner (*c.* 1520–1568), Dean of Wells, who wrote his *New Herball* (1551–1562), which is held to begin the scientific study of botany in

ENGLAND.

Father of English History. The Venerable Bede (673–735), author of the famous *Ecclesiastical History of the English People* (written in Latin).

Father of the English Novel. Both Samuel Richardson (1689–1761) and Henry Fielding (1707–1754) have been given the title.

Father of English Poetry. Chaucer (*c.* 1340–1400).

Father of English Song. Caedmon (*fl.* 670).

Father of Epic Poetry. HOMER.

Father of the Faithful. ABRAHAM.

Father of Greek Tragedy. Æschylus (*c.* 525–456 B.C.).

Father of his Country. CICERO (106–43 B.C.) was so entitled by the Roman senate; also Julius CÆSAR (100–44 B.C.) and Augustus (63 B.C.–A.D. 14) were among the several Cæsars given the title.

Andronicus Palæologus II (*c.* 1260–1332), who assumed the title.

Cosimo de' MEDICI of Florence (1389–1464).

Andrea Doria (1466–1560) of Genoa.

George Washington (1732–1799), first President of the United States.

Victor Emmanuel II (1820–1878), first King of Italy, was popularly so designated in allusion to his unnumbered progeny of bastard children.

Father of History. Herodotus (*c.* 485–*c.* 424 B.C.).

Father of Letters. Francis I (1494–1547), King of France.

Lorenzo de' MEDICI (1449–1492), the Magnificent.

Father of Lies. SATAN.

Father of Medicine. Hippocrates (469–399 B.C.).

Father of Moral Philosophy. St. THOMAS AQUINAS (*c.* 1225–1274).

Father of the People. Louis XII, King of France (1462–1515). Henry IV (1553–1610) was also termed "the Father and Friend of the people".

Christian III (1552–1559), King of Denmark and Norway.

Father of Ridicule. Rabelais (*c.* 1495–1553). *See* RABELAISIAN.

Father of the Waters. The Irrawaddy in Burma and the Mississippi in North America. The Nile is so called by Dr. Johnson in his *Rasselas*.

The epithet *Father* is not uncommonly applied to rivers, especially those on which cities are built.

> Say, Father Thames, for thou hast seen
> Full many a sprightly race

> Disporting on thy margent green,
> The paths of pleasure trace.
> GRAY: *Distant Prospect of Eton College*.
> O Tiber, Father Tiber,
> To whom the Romans pray.
> MACAULAY: *Lay of Horatius*.

Fathers of the Church. All those church writers of the first twelve centuries whose works on Christian doctrine are considered of weight and worthy of respect. But the term is more strictly applied to those teachers of the first twelve, and especially of the first six, centuries who added notable holiness and complete orthodoxy to their learning. Representative among them are: 1st cent., Clement of Rome; 2nd cent., Ignatius of Antioch, Justin, Irenæus, Polycarp; 3rd cent., Cyprian, Dionysius, Origen, Tertullian, Clement of Alexandria, Gregory Thaumaturgus; 4th cent., Hilary, Cyril of Jerusalem, Gregory Nyssen, John Chrysostom, Eusebius, Jerome, Epiphanius, Athanasius, Basil, Ambrose; 5th cent., Rufinus, Augustine, Pope Leo the Great, Cyril of Alexandria, Vincent of Lerins; 6th cent., Cæsarius of Arles; 7th cent., Isidore, Pope Gregory the Great; 8th cent., John of Damascus, Venerable Bede; 11th cent., Peter Damian; 12th cent., Anselm, Bernard.

Cp. APOSTOLIC FATHERS.

Fathers of the Constitution. The framers of the constitution of the United States who took part in the Constitutional Convention at Philadelphia in 1787. In particular, James Madison (1751–1836) is known as *the Father of the Constitution* for the part he played in its formation.

Fathers of the Desert, or **Desert Fathers.** The monks and hermits of the Egyptian deserts in the 4th century from whom Christian monasticism derives. The most famous were St. ANTHONY, who founded his first monastery in 305; St. Pachomius, the hermit and founder of monasteries; and St. Hilarion. There is a good description of their mode of life in Kingsley's *Hypatia*.

Pilgrim Fathers. *See* PILGRIM.

Fatima. The last wife of BLUEBEARD. MOHAMMED's daughter was also called Fatima.

Fatimids, or **Fatimites.** An Arab dynasty ruling in Egypt and North Africa (909–1171), descended from Fatima and her husband ALI.

Fatted Calf. *See* TO KILL THE FATTED CALF *under* CALF.

Fault. In geology, the break or displacement of a stratum of rock.

At fault. Not on the right track. Hounds are *at fault* when the fox has jumped upon a wall, crossed a river, cut through a flock of sheep, or doubled like a hare, because the scent, *i.e.*, the track, is broken.

For fault of a better. For want of a better; no one (or nothing) better being available.

SHAKESPEARE uses the expression in the *Merry Wives of Windsor* (I, iv).

In fault, at fault. To blame.

Is Antony or we in fault for this?
SHAKESPEARE: *Antony and Cleopatra*, iii, xiii.

No one is without his faults. No one is perfect.

To a fault. In excess; as, "kind to a fault". Excess of every kind is almost a defect; there is a similar idea expressed in the phrase *to kill by kindness* (*see* KILL).

To find fault. To blame; to express disapprobation.

Fauna (faw' nà). The animals of a country at any given period. The term was first used by Linnæus in the title of his *Fauna Suecica* (1746), a companion volume to his *Flora Suecica* (1745), and is the name of a rural goddess, of like attributes to FAUNUS (*see* PAN).

Nor less the place of curious plant he knows;
He both his Flora and his Fauna shows.
CRABBE: *The Borough*, Letter viii.

Fauni or **Fauns.** Minor Roman deities of the countryside, merry and mischievous, small counterparts of FAUNUS. *Cp.* SATYR.

Faunus. A good spirit of forest and field, and a god of prophecy. He had the form of a SATYR and is identified with the Greek PAN. FAUNA is sometimes given as his wife, sometimes as his daughter. At his festivals, called FAUNALIA, peasants brought rustic offerings and made merry. He was also fabled to have been a king of Latium subsequently deified for his devotion to agriculture.

Fauntleroy. Little Lord. *See under* LITTLE.

Faust (foust). The hero of Marlowe's *Tragical History of Dr. Faustus* (*c.* 1592) and Goethe's *Faust* (1772–1831) is founded on Dr. Johann Faust, or Faustus, a magician and astrologer, who was born in Württemberg and died about 1538, and about whom many stories soon began to circulate crediting him with supernatural gifts and evil living. The suggestion that Johann Fust, or Faust, the printer and one-time partner of Gutenberg, was the original upon whom the Faust stories were built, is now completely rejected. In 1587 *The History of Dr. Faustus, the Notorious Magician and Master of the Black Art* was published by Johann Spies at Frankfurt. It immediately became popular and was soon translated into English, French, and other languages. Many other accounts followed and the Faust, theme was developed by writers, artists and musicians over the years. It was Goethe who was responsible, however, for transforming the necromancer into a personification of the struggle between the higher and lower na-

tures in man. Notable among musical compositions on the story are Spohr's opera *Faust,* 1813, Wagner's overture *Faust,* 1840; Berlioz's *Damnation de Faust,* 1846; Gounod's opera *Faust,* 1859; Boito's *Mefistofele,* 1868; and Busoni's *Doktor Faust,* 1925.

The idea of making a pact with a DEVIL for worldly reasons is of Jewish origin. The basis of the Faust story is that he sold his soul to the Devil in return for twenty-four years of further life during which he is to have every pleasure and all knowledge at his command. The climax comes when the Devil claims him for his own.

O lente, lente currite noctis equi!
The stars move still, time runs, the clock will strike,
The Devil will come, and Faustus must be damned.
O' I'll leap up to my God! Who pulls me down?
See, see where Christ's blood streams in the firmament!
MARLOWE: *Doctor Faustus*, V, iii.

Faute de mieux (fōt'dė mē ĕr) (Fr.). For want of something better. *Cp.* FOR FAULT OF A BETTER *under* FAULT.

Fauvism (fō' vizm). The name given to the work of a group of young French artists of the first decade of the 20th century, whose leader was Henri Matisse, and which included Derain, Braque, Vlaminck, Dufy, Marquet, Friez, and Rouault. There was a corresponding German movement known as *Die Brücke* (The Bridge). The French school derives from the influence of Van Gogh and their work was characterized by the imaginative use of brilliant colour, decorative simplicity, vitality and gaiety. The name *Fauves* (wild beasts) arose from a remark of the critic Vauxcelles at an exhibition of their work in 1905, *Donatello au milieu des fauves*, occasioned by the sight of their spectacularly coloured pictures. *Cp.* CUBISM; DADAISM; FUTURISM; IMPRESSIONISM; ORPHISM; SURREALISM; SYNCHRONISM; VORTICISM.

Faux pas (fō pa) (Fr. a false step). A breach of manners or good conduct.

The fact is his Lordship, who hadn't, it seems,
Form'd the slightest idea, not ev'n in his dreams,
That the pair had been wedded according to law,
Conceived that his daughter had made a faux pas.
BARHAM: *Ingoldsby Legends* (*Some account of a New Play*).

Favonius. The Latin name for the ZEPHYR or west wind. It means the wind favourable to vegetation.

If to the torrid zone her way she bend,
Her the cool breathing of Favonius lend,
Thither command the birds to sing their quires,
That zone is temp'rate.
HABINGTON: *Castara: To the Spring* (1634).

Favour. Ribbons made into a bow are called

favours from being bestowed by ladies on the successful champions of tournaments. *Cp*. TRUE-LOVERS' KNOT.

> Here, Fluellen; wear thou this favour for me, and stick it in thy cap.
>
> SHAKESPEARE: *Henry V*, IV, vii.

To curry favour. *See* CURRY.

Favourites. False curls on the temples; a curl of hair on the temples plastered with some cosmetic; whiskers made to meet the mouth.

> You tell me, sire, don't you as nice appear
> With your false calves, bardash, and fav'rites here?
>
> MRS. CENTLIVRE: *The Platonic Lady: Epilogue* (1721).

Fay. *See* FAIRY.

Morgan le Fay. *See* FATA MORGANA *and* MORGAN.

Feal and Divot. In SCOTLAND, the right to cut turf or peat, from which, by jocular derivation, comes the *divot* of golf, a piece of turf removed by a player's club. Both words mean "turf".

Fearless (Fr. *sans peur*). Jean, Duke of Burgundy (1371–1419) was so called. *Cp*. BAYARD.

Feast, or **Festival.** A day or days specially set apart for religious observances which is an ancient practice common to all religions. The number of Feasts in the ROMAN CATHO-LIC and GREEK CHURCHes is extensive; the CHURCH OF ENGLAND after the REFORMATION only retained a certain number. The Feasts in the Christian CALENDAR have been divided in various ways, one of which is to group them as **movable** or **immovable.** All SUNDAYS are Feast Days.

The chief immovable feasts are the four quarter-days—*viz*. the ANNUNCIATION, or LADY DAY (25 March); The Nativity of ST. JOHN THE BAPTIST (24 June); MICHAELMAS DAY (29 September); CHRISTMAS DAY (25 December). Others are the Circumcision (1 January), EPIPHANY (6 January), ALL SAINTS (1 November), the several Apostles' days and the anniversaries of martyrs and saints.

The movable feasts depend upon EAST-ER Day and also among them are the Sundays after the EPIPHANY, SEPTUAGESIMA SUNDAY, the Sundays of LENT, Rogation Sunday, ASCENSION DAY, PENTECOST or WHIT SUNDAY, TRINITY SUNDAY, and the Sundays after Trinity.

Feast of Reason. Conversation on and discussion of learned and congenial subjects.

> There St. John mingles with my friendly bowl
> The feast of reason and the flow of soul.
>
> POPE: *Imitations of Horace*, II, i.

Feasts of Reason. *See* REASON, THE GODDESS OF.

Feather. A broken feather in one's wing. A scandal connected with someone.

A feather in your cap. An honour to you. The allusion is to the very general custom in Asia and among the American Indians of adding a feather to the headgear for every enemy slain. The ancient Lycians and many others had a similar custom, just as the sportsman who kills the first woodcock puts a feather in his cap. In Hungary, at one time, none might wear a feather but he who had slain a Turk. When CHINESE GORDON quelled the TAI-PING rebellion he was honoured by the Chinese Government with the "yellow jacket and peacock's feather".

Birds of a feather flock together. *See under* BIRD.

Fine feathers make fine birds. Said of an overdressed person who does not really match up to his or her clothes.

In full feather. Well supplied with money. In allusion to birds not on the moult.

In grand feather. Dressed "up to the nines" (*see under* NINE). Also, in perfect health, thoroughly fit.

In high feather. In exuberant spirits, joyous.

Of that feather. *See* BIRDS OF A FEATHER.

Prince of Wales's feathers. *See* WALES, PRINCE OF.

Tarred and feathered. *See* TAR.

Tickled with a feather. Easily moved to laughter. Pope in his *Essay on Man* (II, 276) has, "Pleased with a rattle, tickled with a straw."

To cut a feather. A ship moving at speed is said *to cut a feather* in allusion to the foam set up by her bows. Metaphorically "to cut a dash" (*see under* DASH). *Cp*. A BONE IN HER MOUTH *under* BONE.

To feather an oar. To turn the blade parallel with and move it along the surface of the water as the hands are moved forward for a fresh stroke. The oar throws off the water in a feathery spray.

To feather one's nest well. To provide for one's own interests, especially financial. The phrase is commonly used with implications of disapproval.

To feather one's propeller. In flying to rotate the aeroplane's propeller blades, when the engine is stopped, to an angle at which they produce minimum drag. In boats to perform a similar operation to lessen water resistance on the screw.

To make the feathers fly. To make a noisy scene when angered, to make the "fur fly": an allusion to the fighting of cock birds.

To show the white feather. *See* WHITE.

To smooth one's ruffled feathers. To recover one's equanimity after an insult, etc.

To featherbed. To pamper, to cushion; the allusion is obvious.

Featherweight. Something of extreme lightness in comparison with others of its kind. The term is applied to a jockey weighing not more than 4 st. 7 lb. or to a boxer weighing not more than 9 st. In the paper trade, the name is given to very light antique, laid, or wove book papers, which are loosely woven and made mainly from esparto.

February. The month of purification amongst the ancient Romans (Lat. *februo*, I purify by sacrifice).

2 February, CANDLEMAS DAY, is the feast of the Purification of the Blessed Virgin Mary. It is said that if the weather is fine and frosty at the close of JANUARY and the beginning of February, there is more winter ahead than behind.

Si sol splendescat Maria Purificante,
Major erit glacies post festum quam fuit ante.
SIR T. BROWNE: *Vulgar Errors*.

The Dutch used to call the month *Spokkel-maand* (vegetation-month); the Anglo-Saxons *Sprote-cal* (Sprout-Kale) from the sprouting of cabbage or kale and subsequently *sol-monath* (from the returning of the sun). In the French Republican Calendar it was called *Pluviôse* (rain-month, 20 January to 20 February). *See also* FILL-DYKE.

Fecit (fā' kit) (Lat. he made it). A word often inscribed after the name of an artist, sculptor, etc., as David *fecit*, Goujon *fecit*; *i.e.*, David painted it, Goujon sculptured it, etc.

Federalists. Those Americans who supported the proposed new constitution of 1787, led by Alexander Hamilton, James Madison, John Adams, John Jay, and others. Hamilton, Madison and Jay published 85 essays under the name *Publius*, in support of Federalism, known in their collected form as *The Federalist* (1788). The party controlled the government until 1801 and came to an end in 1816. *Cp.* CONFEDERATE STATES.

Fee. An Anglo-French word, from Old High Ger. *Fehu*, wages, money, property, and it is connected with the O.E. *feoh*, cattle, goods, money. So in Lat. *pecunia*, money, from *pecus*, cattle. Capital is *capita*, heads (of cattle), and chattels is a mere variant.

At a pin's fee. *See* PIN.

Fee-farm. A tenure by which land is held in FEE SIMPLE without any services from the tenant other than a perpetual fixed rent.

Fee-penny. A fine for money overdue; an earnest or pledge for a bargain.

Fee simple. A property held by a person in his own right, free from condition or limitation. A conditional fee simple is one granted subject to conditions which if unfulfilled give the grantor the right to re-enter and is not a legal estate.

Fee-tail. An estate limited to a person and his lawful heirs; an entailed estate (*see* ENTAIL). Fee-tail as such was abolished by the Law of Property Act, 1925.

Retaining fee. To secure the right to call on the services of someone, especially a lawyer, by a fee paid.

To hold in fee. To hold as one's lawful, absolute possession.

Once did she hold the gorgeous east in fee;
And was the safeguard of the west.
WORDSWORTH: *The Venetian Republic*.

Feeble. Most forcible Feeble. Said of one whose language is pretentious but whose ideas are very jejune. Feeble is a woman's tailor brought to Sir John Falstaff as a recruit (SHAKESPEARE, *Henry IV, Pt. II*, III, ii). He tells Sir John he will do his good will, and the knight replies. "Well said, courageous Feeble! Thou wilt be as valiant as the wrathful or magnanimous mouse ... most forcible Feeble."

Fehmgerichte. *See* VEHMGERICHTE.

Felix, the Cat. Hero of early animated film cartoons which appeared in 1921 in a production by Pat Sullivan. Throughout his many adventures **Felix kept on walking** and thus originated the once-familiar catchphrase.

Fell. Doctor Fell.

I do not like thee, Dr. Fell,
The reason why I cannot tell;
But this I know, I know full well,
I do not like thee, Dr. Fell.

These well-known lines are by the "facetious" Tom Brown (1663–1704) and the person referred to was Dr. John Fell, Dean of Christ Church and Bishop of Oxford (1625–1686), who expelled him, but said he would remit the sentence if Brown translated the thirty-third Epigram of Martial:

Non amo te, Sabidi, nec possum dicere quare;
Hoc tantum possum dicere, non amo te.

The foregoing translation is said to have been given impromptu.

It was this Dr. Fell who in 1667 presented to the University of Oxford a complete typefoundry containing punches and matrices of a large number of founts—Arabic, Syriac, Coptic and other learned alphabets, as well as the celebrated "Fell" Roman.

Fellow. At the colleges of Oxford and Cambridge, and at Trinity College, Dublin, a Fellow is a member of the foundation sharing in its government and drawing a stipend from the college revenues. There are also Honorary Fellowships, etc. At University College and King's College, London, election as a Fellow is a mark of honour to a distinguished member. At other universities there are Research or Postgraduate Fellowships for further study.

Fellow-Commoner. An undergraduate at Cambridge who was formerly privileged to "common" (*i.e.* dine) at the fellows' table for extra payment, the corresponding Oxford term being **Gentleman Commoner.**

In 'varsity slang these names were given to empty bottles, from the implication that such students were empty-headed.

Fellow-traveller. A person in sympathy with a political party but not a member of that party; usually restricted to Communist sympathizers. The term (Rus. *poputchik*) was coined by Leon Trotsky.

> "He is but one of a reputed short list of seven fellow-travellers under threat of expulsion."— Comment in *Time and Tide*, 1 May 1948, on the Labour Party's expulsion of one of its members.

Felo de se (fē′ lō dē sē). Self-destruction, the act of suicide; also the self-murderer himself. Murder is felony, and a man who murders himself commits this felony on himself. An Anglo-Latin expression.

Feme-covert (fem kŭv′ ėrt). A married woman, one under the cover, authority, or protection of her husband. The expression is derived from Old French.

Feme sole (fem sōl). A single woman.

Feme sole merchant. A woman, married or single, who carries on a trade on her own account.

Feminine ending. An extra unaccented syllable at the end of a line of verse, *e.g.* in lines 1 and 3 of the following:

> With rue my heart is laden
> For golden friends I had,
> For many a rose-lipt maiden
> And many a light-foot lad.
>
> A. E. HOUSMAN.

Femynye (fem′ i ni). A mediæval name for the kingdom of the AMAZONS. John Gower (*c.* 1313–1408) terms PENTHESILEA "queen of Feminee".

> He [Theseus] conquered al the regne of Femynye
> That whylom was y-claped Scithia;
> And weddede the quene Ipolita.
>
> CHAUCER: *Knight's Tale*, 8.

Fen Nightingale. A frog, which sings at night in the fens, as nightingales sing in the groves.

Fence. A slang term for a receiver of stolen goods.

Fence month, or **season.** The fawning

time of deer, therefore the close time, *i.e.* from about fifteen days before midsummer until fifteen days after it. Also a close time for fishing, etc.

To sit on the fence. To take care not to commit oneself; to hedge. The characteristic attitude of "Mr. Facing-Both-Ways".

Fencibles. Companies of regular troops of horse and foot, raised for home service in 1759, again in 1778–1779, and 1794 for special emergencies. The word is short for *defensibles*.

Fenians. An anti-British secret society of Irishmen founded in New York in 1858 by John O'Mahony and in IRELAND by James Stephens, with the object of making Ireland a republic and bringing English domination to an end. The word is from the Old Irish *Fene*, a name of the ancient Irish, confused with *Fianna*, the legendary warriors who defended Ireland in the time of Finn.

The Fenian Brotherhood, or Irish Republican Brotherhood, attempted invasions of Canada in 1866 and 1870–1871. In 1867 there were insurrectionary attempts in Ireland, attacks on Chester Castle, Clerkenwell Gaol, and an attack on a policeman in Manchester, etc. The movement petered out in the late 1870s. *Cp.* CLAN-NA-GAEL; PHŒNIX PARK MURDERS; SINN FEIN.

Fennel. This herb was anciently supposed to be an aphrodisiac, thus "to eat conger and fennel" was provocative of sexual licence. Hence Falstaff's remark to Poins:

> He plays at quoits well, and eats conger and fennel, and drinks off candles' ends for flap-dragons, and rides the wild mare with the boys.
>
> SHAKESPEARE: *Henry IV, Pt. II*, II, iv.

It was also emblematical of flattery, and may have been included among the herbs distributed by Ophelia (*Hamlet*, IV, v) for this reason.

> Upon a banke, bordring by, grew women's weedes, Fenell I meane for flatterers, fit generally for that sexe.
>
> GREENE: *A Quip for an Upstart Courtier* (1592).

Culpeper also says:

> A decoction of the leaves and root is good for serpent bites, and to neutralise vegetable poison, as mushrooms, etc.
>
> *The New English Physician Enlarged* (1653).

Fenrir or **Fenris** (fen′ rėr). In Scandinavian mythology, the wolf of LOKI. He was the brother of HEL and when he gaped one jaw touched earth and the other HEAVEN. At the RAGNAROK he broke his fetters and swallowed ODIN, who was avenged by VIDAR thrusting his sword into the yawning gullet and piercing the beast's heart.

Feræ Naturæ (fer′ ī nȧ tū′ rī) (Lat. of savage

nature). The legal term for animals living in a wild state, as distinguished from those which are domesticated.

> Women are not comprised in our Laws of Friendship: they are *Feræ Naturæ*.
> DRYDEN: *The Mock Astrologer*, IV.

Ferdiad. A hero of Irish legend who was persuaded to fight for Queen MAEVE against CUCHULAIN, his dearest friend. After a struggle lasting three days he was killed, to Cuchulain's bitter grief.

Fergus mac Roich. The heroic tutor of CUCHULAIN, who left CONCHOBAR'S court after the treacherous murder of the sons of USNECH.

Ferguson, You can't lodge here, Mr Ferguson; you mustn't go there, Mr. Ferguson, etc. A popular catch phrase of the mid-19th century, the equivalent of the 20th-century "you can't do that there 'ere". The general explanation is that the phrase was originated and generally popularized by young men out ON THE SPREE. As to the Ferguson in question, one assertion is that he was a young Scotsman who got very drunk at EPSOM RACES and was refused a lodging by the local landlords. He was driven to town by his fellow roisterers who kept up the cry "You can't lodge here, Mr. Ferguson". Another account names a Captain Ferguson, a companion of the Marquis of Waterford. When out on the town they got separated and the Marquis went home to bed at his uncle's house. Awakened by a thunderous knocking and guessing who it was, he called from the window "It is all very fine, Ferguson, but you don't lodge here".

Fern Seed. We have the receipt of fern seed, we walk invisible (SHAKESPEARE *Henry IV, Pt. I*, II, i). Fern seed was popularly supposed only to be visible on St. JOHN's Eve, and as it was thus so seldom seen it was believed to confer invisibility on those who carried it. Plants were often supposed to convey their own particular quality on their wearer. Thus the yellow celandine was said to cure jaundice; wood-sorrel, which has a heart-shaped leaf, to cheer the heart; liverwort to be good for the liver, etc.

> I had
> No medicine, sir, to go invisible
> No fern-seed in any pocket.
> BEN JONSON: *New Inn*, I, i.

Ferney. The Patriarch, or **Philosopher of Ferney.** VOLTAIRE (1694–1778); so called because for the last twenty years of his life he lived at Ferney, a village near Geneva.

Ferragus. The giant of Portugal in VALENTINE AND ORSON. The great BRAZEN HEAD, that told those who consulted it whatever they required to know, was kept in this giant's castle.

Ferrara. *See* ANDREA FERRARA.

Ferrara Bible, The. *See* BIBLE, SOME SPECIALLY NAMED EDITIONS.

Ferrex and Porrex. Two sons of Gorboduc, a mythical British king, who divided his kingdom between them. Porrex drove his brother from Britain, and when Ferrex returned with an army he was slain, but Porrex was shortly after torn to pieces by his mother with the assistance of her women. The story is told in Geoffrey of Monmouth's *Historia Britonum* (ch. xvi), and it forms the basis of the first regular English tragedy, *Gorboduc, or Ferrex and Porrex*, written by Thomas Norton and Thomas Sackville, Lord Buckhurst, and acted in 1562.

Ferry Pilot. A World War II term for a pilot flying new aircraft from the factory to the air station.

Fescennine Verses. LAMPOONS; so called from Fescennium in Tuscany, where performers at merry-makings used to extemporize scurrilous jests of a personal nature to amuse the audience.

Fesse. *See* HERALDRY.

Festina Lente. (fes tēn′ a len tā) (Lat.). Make haste slowly. It is the punning motto of the Onslow family.

Festschrift (fest′shrift) (Ger. *fest*, festival; *schrift*, writings). This term is commonly used for the volume of essays, papers, etc., prepared by colleagues and friends as a tribute to a scholar on some special occasion (usually on retirement or a particular anniversary).

> The "Festschrift", the present *English Miscellany*, speaks for itself, and will remain a permanent record of the esteem in which Dr. Furnivall is held wherever English literature is read, or the English language studied.
> *An English Miscellany (Presented to Dr. Furnivall in Honour of his Seventy-fifth Birthday)*.

Fetch. A WRAITH—the disembodied ghost of a living person; hence *fetch-light*, or *fetch candle*, a light appearing at night supposed to foretell someone's death. *Fetches* most commonly appear to distant friends and relations at the very moment before the death of those they represent. The word is of uncertain origin.

> The very fetch and ghost of Mrs. Gamp, bonnet and all, might be seen hanging up, any hour in the day, in at least a dozen secondhand clothes-shops about Holborn.
> DICKENS: *Martin Chuzzlewit*, xix.

It is also used in the sense of a stratagem, artifice, or trick.

> Deny to speak with me? They are sick? they are weary?

They have travelled all night? Mere fetches.
SHAKESPEARE: *King Lear*, II, iv.

Fetish (fet' ish) (Port. *fetico*, sorcery, charm; Lat. *facticius*, artificial). The name given by early Portuguese voyagers to AMULETS and other objects supposed by the natives of the Guinea Coast to possess magic powers: hence an idol, an object of devotion. Fetishism is found in all primitive nations in which the services of a spirit may be appropriated by the possession of its material emblem. In psycho-pathology the word is used to denote a condition or perversion in which sexual gratification is obtained from some object, etc., that has become emotionally charged.

Fettle, as a verb, means to bind, repair, put in order, etc.; as a noun it means condition, state of health, as, *in good fettle*. It is probably from O.E. *fetel*, bond or girdle, with allusion to girding oneself up.

Fettle ale. ALE warmed and spiced.

Feu de joie (fĕr dĕ zhwa) (Fr. fire of joy). A ceremonial discharge of musketry into the air by a line of soldiers on an occasion of rejoicing.

Feudalism, or **Feudal system** (Med. Lat. *feodum*, fee). The name given to an institutional growth in Europe from the time of the decay of the Roman Empire. It arose from the need of the individual and society to gain protection from attack, occasioned by internal disorder and external threat. In return for protection from some powerful individual, the dependant offered services or surrendered to an overlord his land which was then held subject to conditions. English feudalism is commonly held to begin with WILLIAM THE CONQUEROR who acted on the principle that all land belonged to him. It was granted to the tenant-in-chief in return for homage and military service, etc., who passed on land to sub-tenants in return for other services. Thus a pyramidal social structure developed in which every man was bound to an overlord and ultimately to the King.

Feuillant (fĕr' yon). A reformed CISTERCIAN order instituted in 1577 by Jean de la Barrière, Abbot of the Cistercian monastery of Feuillants in Languedoc.

The Club of the Feuillants in the French Revolution was formed by moderate JACOBINS in 1791. Among its members were Sieyès, Barère, Lafayette, Lameth and Barnave. The club's proper title, indicative of its attitude, was the *Société des Amis de la Constitution* and the popular name was derived from its premises in the Rue St. Honoré, formerly a convent of the Feuillants. In June 1792 all its members were disfranchised.

Few. The Few. The R.A.F. pilots of the BATTLE OF BRITAIN, so called from Prime Minister Winston Churchill's memorable tribute in the HOUSE OF COMMONS (20 August 1940), "Never in the field of human conflict was so much owed by so many to so few."

Fiacre (fē akr'). A French cab or HACKNEY coach, so called from the hotel of St. Fiacre, Paris, where the first station of these coaches was established by M. Sauvage, about 1650.

Legend has it that **St. Fiacre** was a 7th-century hermit of Irish origin. He settled in France and built a monastery at Breuil. His day is 30 August and he is the patron saint of gardeners.

Fiars (fē' àrs). **Striking the fiars.** Fixing the prices of the different varieties of grain in the various counties of Scotland. The decision was made by the sheriff on the advice of a jury. The system was originally used for determining crown rents, clerical stipends, etc., and applied to all contracts where the prices were not fixed by the parties concerned. The word is from M.E. and O.Fr. *feor*, Lat. *forum*, a market.

Fiasco (Ital. a flask). A complete failure. In Italy an unpopular singer is sometimes greeted with the cry *Olà olà fiasco!* The word was used by the glassblowers of Venice to describe bad workmanship and it may have some allusion to the bursting of a bottle. Various incidents in the Italian theatre have been put forward as the origin of this usage.

Fiat (fī' at) (Lat. let it be done). **I give my fiat to that proposal.** I consent to it. A fiat in law is a certificate of the ATTORNEY-GENERAL giving leave to take certain proceedings for which Crown permission is required.

Fiat justitia ruat coelum (Lat.). Let justice be done though the heavens should fall. *See* PISO'S JUSTICE.

Fico (Ital. a fig, from Lat. *ficus*). A popular term in Shakespeare's England for a gesture of contempt such as made by thrusting the thumb between the first and second fingers; much as we say, "I don't care that for you", snapping the fingers at the same time. *Figo* is another form.

Convey, the wise it call, Steal! foh! a fico for the phrase.
SHAKESPEARE: *Merry Wives of Windsor*, I, iii.
Pist: And fico for thy friendship.
Flu: It is well.
Pist: The fig of Spain!
SHAKESPEARE: *Henry V*, III, v.

See also I DON'T CARE A FIG FOR YOU *under* FIG.

Fiddle (M.E. *fithele*; possibly connected with

Med.Lat. *vitula*, viol). The word *fithele* occurs in Layamon's *Brut* (line 7002) and Chaucer refers to the *fidel* in the *Canterbury Tales* (*Prol*. line 298). A stringed instrument of the violin type.

> For him was lever have at his beddes hed
> A twenty bokes, clothed in black or red,
> Of Aristotle and his Philosophie,
> Than robes riche or fidel or sautrie.

In Stock Exchange slang *a fiddle* was one-sixteenth of a pound—1s. 3d.

To fiddle. To manipulate accounts, etc., in a dishonest way in order to gain some advantage or to cover up a deficiency. **To work a fiddle** is substantially the same and usually implies some dishonest or "smart work".

To fiddle about. To trifle, fritter away one's time, mess about. **To fiddle with one's fingers** is to move them about as a fiddler does on the strings of a violin.

To fiddle while Rome burns. *See under* ROME.

Fit as a fiddle. In fine condition.

He was first fiddle. The leading or most distinguished of the company. The allusion is to the first violin, who leads the orchestra.

To play second fiddle. To take a subordinate part, but next after the leader.

Fiddle-de-dee! An exclamation signifying what you say is nonsense.

> All the return he ever had ... was a word, too common, I regret to say, in female lips, *viz.* fiddle-de-dee.
>
> DE QUINCEY: *Secret Societies*.

Fiddle-faddle. To busy oneself with nothing; to dawdle; to talk nonsense.

> Ye may as easily
> Outrun a cloud, driven by a northern blast,
> As fiddle-faddle so.
>
> JOHN FORD: *The Broken Heart*, I, iii (1633).

Fiddler. Slang for sixpence; also for a FARTHING.

Drunk as a fiddler. *See under* DRUNK.

Fiddler's fare, or **pay.** Meat, drink, and money.

Fiddler's Green. The happy land imagined by sailors where there is perpetual mirth, a fiddle that never stops playing for dancers who never tire, plenty of GROG, and unlimited tobacco.

Fiddler's money. A silver penny. The fee given to a fiddler at a WAKE by each dancer.

Fiddler's news. Stale or late news, because fiddlers were long reputed to be purveyors of out-of-date news.

Fiddlesticks! Much the same as FIDDLE-DE-DEE, *i.e.* you are talking nonsense.

The devil rides on a fiddlestick. *See* DEVIL PHRASES *under* DEVIL.

Fidei Defensor. *See* DEFENDER OF THE FAITH.

Fiduciary. Fiduciary Issue. That part of a note issue which is not backed by coin or bullion although it may be backed by government securities, etc. If there is no such backing for the paper currency as a whole, then the whole issue is fiduciary. Fiduciary means that which is held or given in trust (Lat. *fiduciarius*).

Field. In huntsman's language *the field* means all the riders; in horse-racing it means all the horses in any one race. In military parlance it is the place of battle, the battle itself or the place of campaign. In HERALDRY it means the entire surface of the shield.

Field of Blood. *See* ACELDAMA.

Field of Cloth of Gold. The plain in Picardy between Guines and Ardres where Henry VIII met Francis I of France in June 1520. Francis hoped for English support against the Emperor, Charles V. A temporary palace was erected, lavish and spectacular arrangements were made for jousting, dancing, and banqueting, and Henry was accompanied by a magnificent retinue. Henry, however, later met the Emperor with whom he effected a treaty.

Field of fire. That part of the terrain before infantry or machine-guns which their weapons can cover, uninterrupted by contours, woods or other obstructions.

Field of force. A term used in physics to denote the range within which a force, such as magnetism, is effective.

Field of the Forty Footsteps, or **The Brothers' Steps.** The land at the back of the BRITISH MUSEUM, once called Southampton Fields, near the extreme north-east of the present Montague Street. The tradition is that at the time of the Duke of MONMOUTH'S REBELLION (1685) two brothers fought each other here until both were killed, and for many years forty impressions of their feet remained on the field. No grass would grow there, nor upon the bank where the young woman sat who was the object of their contest. The site was built upon about 1800.

Field of vision, or **view.** The space over which things can be seen; the space or range within which objects are visible when looking through an instrument such as a telescope or microscope, etc.

In the field. A competitor for a prize, a term from horse-racing. In military usage it denotes being on active campaign.

Master of the field. The winner; the conqueror in battle.

To back the field means to bet on all the horses except one, the favourite.

To keep back the field is to keep back the riders.

To take to the field. To make the opening moves in a military campaign.

To win the field. To win the battle.

Field allowance. An extra allowance paid to officers in the field or on campaign.

Field-day. A military term for a day when troops have manœuvres or exercises. Generally, a day of unusual activity and success; to have a thorough turn-out and clean-up. In the U.S. Navy a day devoted to cleaning-ship and preparing for inspection.

Field-Marshal. In the British army this title, the highest rank, is conferred on generals who have rendered conspicuous services, and on royalty. The title was first used in ENGLAND in 1736. A Field Marshal remains on the active list (on half pay) for life, as does an ADMIRAL of the Fleet and an Air Marshal.

Field Officer. In the British army an officer above the rank of captain and below that of general.

Field piece. A piece of field artillery, a field gun.

Field works. Defensive or protective works, or temporary fortifications, made by an army to strengthen its positions.

Open-field System. *See under* OPEN.

Three-field System. *See under* THREE.

Fierabras, Sir (fī ёr à brăs). The son of BALAN, King of Spain. For height of stature, breadth of shoulder, and hardness of muscle, he knew no equal, but his pride was laid low by OLIVER. He became a Christian, was accepted by CHARLEMAGNE as a PALADIN and ended his days in an odour of sanctity.

Fieri facias (fī' er i făk'i ås) (Lat. cause it to be done). A writ of execution to a sheriff to levy from the goods of a debtor the sum according to the judgment given. The phrase is often abbreviated to *fi fa*. The term was also punningly used in the 16th century in connection with red noses and "fiery faces" through drink.

Fiery Cross, The. An ancient signal in the Scottish Highlands when a chieftain wished to summon his clan in an emergency. It was symbolical of fire and sword and consisted of a light wooden cross the ends of which were dipped in the blood of a goat slain for the purpose. It was carried from settlement to settlement by swift runners. Disobedience to the summons implied infamy, hence the alternative name of *Cross of Shame.*

Scott's *Lady of the Lake* (canto iii) contains a graphic account of the custom.

When the KU KLUX KLAN arose after the American CIVIL WAR, it adopted this symbol.

Fifteen, The. The Jacobite rebellion of 1715 when James Edward Stewart, the Old PRETENDER, made an unsuccessful attempt to gain the throne. The Earl of Mar's Scottish forces were defeated at Sheriffmuir and the English JACOBITES under Squire Foster were beaten at Preston. *Cp.* BOBBING JOHN.

Fifth. Fifth-Amendment Communist. In the United States, one who refused to answer the charge of Communist activities by invoking the Fifth Amendment to the Constitution (1791), which states that no person "shall be compelled in any criminal case to be a witness against himself".

Fifth Column. Traitors; those within a country who are working for the enemy, often by infiltrating into key positions, and seeking to undermine the body politic from within. The origin of the phrase is attributed to General Mola, who, in the Spanish Civil War (1936–1939), said that he had four columns encircling Madrid, and a fifth column working for him in the city.

Fifth-Monarchy Men. Religious extremists of Cromwellian times who maintained that the time had come for the rule of Christ and His Saints—the Fifth Monarchy, succeeding those of Assyria, Persia, Macedonia, and Rome; as the four monarchies described in the *Book of Daniel* (ch. ii) give way to that set up by the "God of Heaven". VENNER'S RISING of 1661 marked the end of their attempts to establish the Fifth Monarchy.

Fifty-four Forty or Fight. The slogan of the Democratic party in the U.S. presidential election campaign of 1844 which won the day for President Polk. It arose from the long-standing Oregon boundary dispute between Great Britain and the U.S.A. A convention of 1818 had provided for a ten-year joint occupation of the disputed area and this was renewed in 1827 for an indefinite period. The question came to the forefront again in the 1840s with the growing popularity of the OREGON TRAIL, hence the appeal of the slogan. Nevertheless Polk and the Senate agreed to the British proposal that the boundary between Canada and the U.S.A. be continued along the 49th parallel to the Pacific. Such a boundary had been proposed by the Americans as early as 1826 but it was then rejected by the British.

Fig. Most phrases that include the word fig have reference to the fruit as being an object of trifling value; but in the phrases **in full fig**, meaning "in full dress", **figged out**, etc., "dressed up", the word is a variant of *feague*.

I don't care a fig for you; not worth a fig. Nothing at all. Here fig is either an example of something of little value, or alternatively the *fig of Spain* or FICO.

> A fig for Peter.
>
> SHAKESPEARE: *Henry VI, Pt. II*, II, iii.

I shan't buy my Attic figs in future, but grow them. Said by way of warning to one who is building CASTLES IN THE AIR—"don't count your chickens before they are hatched". XERXES boasted that he was going to conquer Attica, where the figs grew, and add it to his own empire; but he met defeat at Salamis, and "never loosed his sandal till he reached Abdera".

In the name of the Prophet, Figs! A burlesque of the solemn language in the common business of life associated with eastern countries. The line occurs in imitation of Dr. Johnson's pompous style, in *Rejected Addresses* (1812), by James and Horace Smith.

To fig up a horse. To make it lively and spirited by artificial means.

Fig leaf. The leaf of the fig-tree was used by ADAM and EVE to cover their nakedness after the Fall (*Gen.* iii, 7). Hence its use in statuary and paintings in times when "modesty" was in fashion, notably in the Victorian period.

Fig Sunday. An old provincial name for PALM SUNDAY. Figs were eaten on that day in commemoration of the blasting of the barren fig-tree by Our Lord (*Mark* xi). Many festivals still have their special dishes, as, the goose for MICHAELMAS, pancakes for SHROVE TUESDAY, hot cross BUNS for GOOD FRIDAY, etc.

Fig-tree. It is said that Judas hanged himself on a fig-tree. *See* ELDER-TREE; JUDAS TREE.

Mercury fig. *See under* MERCURY.

Figaro. A type of daring, cunning and witty roguery and intrigue. The character is in *Le Barbier de Séville* (1775), and *Le Mariage de Figaro* (1784) by Beaumarchais. There are several operas based on these dramas, as Mozart's *Nozze di Figaro*, and Paisiello's and Rossini's *Il Barbiere di Siviglia*.

Hence the name of the famous Parisian periodical which appeared from 1826 to 1833 and its successor which began life in 1854. *Le Figaro* is one of the foremost French dailies to survive World War II.

Fight. Acre-fight. A good example of a GHOST-WORD. It was wrongly explained by Cowell as a duel in the open field, fought with sword and lance by single combatants, on the Anglo-Scottish border. It is actually a transliteration of Med. Lat. *acram committere* where *acram* (for *pugnam*) is a poor translation of "camp combat" which was confused with Lat. *campus* (field), Fr. *champ* and so with the English *acre*. It is found only in Cowell and some modern dictionaries which have perpetuated the error.

He that fights and runs away may live to fight another day. An old saw found in many languages. Demosthenes, being reproached for fleeing from Philip of Macedon at Chæronea, replied, "A man that runs away may fight again." The same sentiment is expressed in Butler's *Hudibras*, III, iii.

> For those that fly may fight again
> Which he can never do that's slain.

The Fighting Fifth. *See* REGIMENTAL AND DIVISIONAL NICKNAMES.

Fighting French, or **La France Combattante.** All those Frenchmen at home and abroad who combined with the Allied nations in their war against the AXIS powers after the fall of France (in June 1940). General de Gaulle and others escaped to England and he formed them into "The Free French" with the CROSS OF LORRAINE for their emblem. The name was later changed to "The Fighting French" (14 July 1942). One of their most noted feats was the march of General Leclerc's column across the Sahara, from Lake Chad, to join the British 8th Army in Libya. These men were honoured by being the first formation to enter Paris on 23 August 1944. The Fighting French supported the Allies in Africa, Italy and elsewhere and made a valuable contribution to the liberation of France, in conjunction with the F.F.I.

The Fighting Prelate. Henry Spenser, or Despenser, Bishop of Norwich (1370–1406), who put down the insurgents of Norfolk and Suffolk during the PEASANTS' REVOLT of 1381. At North Walsham he burnt down the church in which they took refuge. He later fought in Flanders and France for Pope Urban VI against the antipope's followers, and was denounced by Wyclif as a fighting bishop.

To fight for one's own hand. To uphold one's own cause, to struggle for one's own interest.

To fight like Kilkenny cats. *See under* CAT.

To fight shy of. To avoid; to resist being brought into contest or conflict.

To fight the tiger. To play against the bank at faro.

To fight with the gloves off. To dispute mercilessly "WITH NO HOLDS BARRED" (*see under* HOLD); without any regard to the courtesies of debate, not "PULLING ANY PUNCHES" (*see under* PULL).

To fight with the gloves on. Figuratively,

to spar or dispute without open animosity, to observe the courtesies and to show some consideration for one's opponent.

To live like fighting cocks. *See under* COCK.

Figo. *See* FICO.

Figure. From Lat. *fingere*, to shape or fashion; not etymologically connected with Eng. *finger*, though fingers were used as a primitive method of calculating.

A figure of fun. Of droll appearance, whether from untidiness, quaintness or other peculiarity; one to be scoffed at.

A figure of speech. An established form of abnormal expression designed to produce a special effect, such as hyperbole, METAPHOR, METATHESIS, etc.

A figure of speech only, or **only a figure of speech** is another name for a piece of exaggeration.

To cut a figure. To make an imposing appearance through dress, bearing, etc. *Cp.* CUT A DASH *under* CUT.

To cut a pretty, or **a sorry figure.** To give a poor impression, little to one's credit.

To make a figure. To make a name or reputation, to be a notability.

What's the figure? How much am I to pay? What do I owe?

Figure-head. A carved figure on the head or bows of a sailing ship, which has ornamental value but is of no practical use (*see* CUTTY SARK). Hence, a nominal leader who plays no real part, but often one whose social or other position inspires confidence.

Figures, Roman. *See* NUMERALS.

Filch. To steal or purloin. A piece of 16th-century thieves' slang of uncertain origin (*cp.* FILE).

> With cunning hast thou filched my daughter's heart.
> SHAKESPEARE: *Midsummer Night's Dream*, I, ii.

A **filch,** or **filchman** was a staff with a hook at the end, for plucking clothes from hedges, articles from shop windows, etc.

File. Old slang for a rapscallion or worthless person; also a pickpocket. It comes from the same original as the word *vile*.

In single file. Single line; one behind another (Fr. *file*, a row). *Cp.* INDIAN FILE.

Rank and file. Soldiers and non-commissioned officers as apart from commissioned officers; hence the followers in a movement as distinct from its leaders. *Rank* refers to men in line abreast or side by side, *file* to men standing one behind another.

Filibuster (Dut. *vrijbuiter*, a freebooter). The earlier form of the word *flibuster* (Fr. *flibustier*) was applied to the pirates plundering in West Indian waters in the 17th century. *Filibuster* was later used of certain 19th-century bands organized from the United States, in defiance of international law, to invade and revolutionize certain Spanish-American territories. The most notable of these filibusters were those led by Narcisco Lopez against Cuba (1850–1851) and William Walker against Sonora (1853–1854). *See also* FREEBOOTER.

> After an abortive filibuster in Lower California he appeared in 1855 in Nicaragua with a few hundred hard-boiled Californians.
> L. D. BALDWIN: *Stream of American History*, I, xxiii, 2.

To filibuster. As a term meaning the use of obstructive tactics in a legislature, by excessive use of technicalities, lengthy speeches, etc., first came into use in the U.S.A. in 1841. Such tactics were notably employed by the Irish Nationalists under Parnell. In July 1877 the HOUSE OF COMMONS sat for 26 hours. *See* CLOSURE.

Filioque Controversy (fil i ō' kwė). An argument concerning the "Procession of the Holy Spirit" that long disturbed the Eastern and Western Churches, and the difference of opinion concerning which still forms one of the principal barriers between them. The point was: Did the HOLY GHOST proceed from the Father *and the Son* (*Filio-que*), or from the Father only? The argument basically is this: If the Son is one with the Father, whatever proceeds from the Father must proceed from the Son also. The *filioque* was first introduced by the Western Church at the Council of Toledo in 589 and was added to the NICENE CREED in the 11th century.

Fill-dyke. The month of FEBRUARY, when the rain and melted snow fills the ditches to overflowing.

> February fill dyke, be it black or be it white;
> But if it be white it's the better to like.
> *Old Proverb.*

Fille de joie (fē dė zhwa) (Fr. daughter of joy). A prostitute.

Fimbul-Winter. In Norse legend, such a severe winter of horrors as never before known which lasted three years without any summer to lessen its onslaught; trees, plants and men died of hunger. It was the forerunner of RAGNAROK.

Fin de siècle (făn dė sē ekl) (Fr. end of century). It has come to imply decadent, with particular reference to the end of the 19th century.

Finality Jack. Lord John Russell (1792–1878), 1st Earl Russell, who originally maintained that the Reform Act of 1832 was a finality, yet made further attempts to extend Parliamentary reform in 1854, 1860, and 1866.

Financial Year. *See* YEAR.

Find. Findings, keepings! An exclamation made when one has accidentally found something, implying that it is now the finder's property. This old saying is very faulty law.

Findabair. In Irish legend, the wondrously beautiful daughter of Queen MAEVE of Connacht. She was promised in marriage to the man who would challenge CUCHULAIN in the WAR OF THE BROWN BULL and died after her lover, Fraech, was slain in battle by Cuchulain.

Fine. Fine as fivepence. An old alliterative saying meaning splendidly dressed or turned out.

Fine feathers make fine birds. *See under* FEATHER.

In fine. In short; to sum up; to come to a conclusion.

One of these fine days. Some time or other; when the opportunity occurs; at some indefinite time in the future.

The Fine Arts. Those arts which depend upon creative imagination and the quest for the expression of beauty, as music, painting, poetry, sculpture and architecture, as opposed to the useful arts, *i.e.*, those which are practised primarily for their utility, as the arts of weaving, metal-working, etc.

He's got it down to a fine art. He has got it to a fine degree of proficiency. He's got the complete knack, he has got it completely "wrapped up".

Fingal. The great Gaelic legendary hero, father of OSSIAN, who was purported by Macpherson to have been the original author of the long epic poem *Fingal* (1762), which narrates the hero's adventures.

Fingal's Cave. The basaltic cavern on Staffa, said to have been a home of FINGAL. It is the name given to Mendelssohn's *Hebridean Overture* (1830).

Finger (O.E. *finger*). The old names for the fingers are:

Thuma (O.E.), the thumb.

Towcher (M.E. the finger that touches), *foreman*, or pointer. This was called the *scite-finger* (shooting finger) by the Anglo-Saxons, now usually known as the first or fore-finger and *index finger* because it is used for pointing.

Long-man, or *long-finger*.

Lech-man, or *ring-finger*. The former means the "medical finger" and the latter is the roman *digitus annularis*, called by the Anglo-Saxons the *gold-finger*. This finger was used as the ring finger (also *annular finger*) in the belief that a nerve ran through it to the heart. Hence the Greeks and Ro-

mans called it the *medical finger*, and used it for stirring mixtures under the notion that it would give instant warning to the heart if in contact with anything noxious. It is still a popular superstition that it is bad to rub salve or scratch the skin with any other finger.

> At last he put on her medical finger a pretty, handsome gold ring, whereinto was enchased a precious toadstone of Beausse.
> RABELAIS: *Pantagruel*, III, xviii.

Little man, or *little finger*. Called by the Anglo-Saxons the EAR-FINGER. It is also known as the *auricular finger*.

The fingers each had their special significance in ALCHEMY, and Ben Jonson says:

> The thumb, in chiromancy, we give to Venus,
> The fore-finger to Jove; the midst to Saturn;
> The ring to Sol; the least to Mercury.
> *Alchemist*, I, ii.

Blessing with the fingers. *See* BLESSING.

Cry, baby, cry; put your fingers in your eye, etc. This nursery rhyme seems to be referred to in SHAKESPEARE's *Comedy of Errors*, II, ii:

> Come, Come, no longer will I be a fool,
> To put the finger in the eye and weep.

Fingers and toes. A popular name for anbury, or ambury, a soft tumour on horses and oxen, and club-root, which affects cabbages, turnips, etc.

Fingers were made before forks. A saying used especially at mealtimes to imply that ceremony is unnecessary. Forks were not introduced into England until about 1620, before which period fingers were used.

Finished to the finger-nail. Complete and perfect in every detail, to all the extremities. The allusion is obvious.

His fingers are all thumbs. Said of a person who is clumsy with his hands.

Lifting the little finger. Tippling. Many people in holding a tankard or glass stick out or lift up the little finger. *Cp.* TO CROOK THE ELBOW, or FINGER *under* CROOK; ELBOW-LIFTING.

Lightfingered gentry. Pickpockets, thieves.

My little finger told me that. The same as "A little bird told me that" (*see under* BIRD), meaning, I know it, although you did not expect it. The popular belief was that an itching or tingling foretold that something was about to happen.

> By the pricking of my thumbs,
> Something wicked this way comes.
> SHAKESPEARE: *Macbeth*, IV, i.

Not to lift a finger. Not to make the slightest effort; not to give any assistance.

To be finger and glove with another. To be in close collusion with, to be in the closest co-operation. The more common expression is TO BE HAND IN GLOVE WITH. (*See under* HAND).

To burn one's fingers. *See under* BURN.

To have a finger in. To be concerned in.

To have a finger in the pie. To have a share in doing something, usually with the implication of officious interference or meddling.

> The devil speed him! no man's pie is freed
> From his ambitious finger.
> SHAKESPEARE: *Henry VIII*, I, i.

To have it at one's fingers' ends. To be completely familiar with it and able to do it adequately and readily. The Latin proverb is, *Scire tanquam ungues digitosque suos*, to know it as well as one's fingers and nails. The allusion is self-evident. The Latin tag is referred to by Shakespeare in *Love's Labour's Lost*, V, i:

> *Costard:* Go to; thou has it ad dunghill, at the fingers' ends, as they say.
> *Holofernes:* I smell false Latin; dunghill for unguem.

To keep one's fingers crossed. To hope for success, to try to ensure against disaster. From the superstition that making the sign of the CROSS will avert bad luck.

To lay, or **put one's finger upon.** To point out precisely the meaning, cause, etc.; to detect with complete accuracy.

To slip through one's fingers. To miss an opportunity, to let something elude one, just as a fielder in CRICKET fumbles a catch.

To twist someone round one's little finger. To do just what one likes with him.

With a wet finger. Easily, directly. The allusion is to spinning, in which the spinner constantly wetted the fore-finger with the mouth.

> *Flores:* Canst thou bring me thither?
> *Peasant:* With a wet finger.
> *Wisdom of Doctor Dodipoll (c.* 1596).

Sailors find the wind by holding up a wet finger for the breeze to cool it, thus finding that side whence it comes.

Finger-print. An impression taken in ink of the whorls of lines on the finger. In no two persons are they alike, and they never change throughout life, hence their great value as a means of indentifying criminals. From ancient times they were used for certifying documents by the Chinese and Japanese. Sir Francis Galton's *Finger Prints* (1892) and *Finger Print Directories* (1895) drew attention to their usefulness. Sir Edward Henry, Commissioner of the Metropolitan Police (1903–1918), devised a system for classifying impressions which was widely adopted. The American Federal Bureau of Investigation uses his method.

Fingle-fangle. A RICOCHET word from *fangle* meaning a fanciful trifle. It was fairly common in the 17th century and was evolved from *new fangle* (new-*fangled*).

Fionnuala. In Irish legend, the daughter of LIR, who was transformed into a swan and condemned to wander over the lakes and rivers until Christianity came to IRELAND. Moore has a poem on the subject in his *Irish Melodies*.

Firbolgs. *See* MILESIANS.

Fire (O.E. *fyr*; Gr. *pur*).

St. Anthony's Fire. *See under* ANTHONY.

St. Elmo's Fire; St. Helen's Fire. *See* CORPOSANT.

The Great Fire of London (Sept. 1666) broke out at Master Farryner's bakehouse in Pudding Lane, Thames Street, in the early hours of Sunday (2 Sept.) and aided by high winds spread from the TOWER to the TEMPLE and from the THAMES to SMITHFIELD. St. Pauls' Cathedral and eighty-nine other churches were destroyed and 13,200 houses. In five days it covered 387 acres within the walls and 73 without. It was not the reason for the disappearance of the Plague, as is commonly held, since most of the slum quarters escaped. The fire was halted by blowing up houses at Pie Corner, Smithfield.

Greek Fire. *See under* GREEK.

Kentish Fire. *See under* KENT.

Between two fires. Subjected to attack, criticism, etc., from both sides at once.

The burnt child dreads the fire. *See under* BURN.

The fat is in the fire. *See under* FAT.

Fire away! Say on; say what you have to say. The allusion to the firing of a gun is obvious. You are loaded up to the muzzle with something to say; fire away and discharge your thoughts.

Fire in the fern. Trouble brewing; smouldering discontent. A New Zealand expression.

I have myself passed through the fire; I have smelt the smell of fire. I have had experience in trouble, and am all the better for it. The allusion is to the refining of GOLD, which is passed through fire and so purged of all its dross.

I will go through fire and water to serve you, *i.e.* through any hardships or any test. It may derive from the ORDEAL OF FIRE (*see under* ORDEAL).

If you would enjoy the fire you must put up with the smoke. You must take the rough with the smooth. Every convenience has its inconvenience.

Letter of fire and sword. In SCOTLAND, before the Union with ENGLAND (1707), an order issued by the Scottish Privy Council authorizing a sheriff to dispossess a tenant, or to proceed against a delinquent by all the means of force at his disposal.

Men stand with their backs to the fire. An old explanation is that when the dog's nose proved too small to stop a leak in the Ark, Noah sat on the hole to keep the water out. Ever since men have felt the need to warm their backs, and the dogs have had cold noses.

More fire in the bedstraw. More mischief brewing. A relic of the time when straw was used for beds.

No smoke without fire. To every scandal there is some foundation. Every effect is the result of some cause.

Out of the frying-pan into the fire. *See* FRYING-PAN.

To fire, or **to fire out.** To discharge from employment suddenly and unexpectedly. An expression originating in the U.S.A.

To fire up. To become indignantly angry; to flare up; to get unduly and suddenly excited.

To hang fire. To delay; to be irresolute; to be slow in taking action. An expression derived from gunnery, when the gun is slow in firing the charge.

To heap coals of fire on one's head. *See under* COAL.

To play with fire. To meddle with that which is perpetually dangerous or harmful.

To set the Thames on fire. *See* HE'LL NEVER SET THE THAMES ON FIRE *under* THAMES.

We do not fire first, gentlemen. According to tradition this very chivalrous reply was made to Lord Charles Hay (commanding the Guards) at the opening of the battle of Fontenoy (1745) by the French Comte d'Auteroche after Hay had invited the French commander to order his men to fire. The story is told by the historian Espagnac and by VOLTAIRE, but it is not borne out by the description of the battle written shortly after the conflict by Lord Charles to his father, the Marquis of Tweeddale.

> Lord Charles Hay ... stepped to the front of his battalion and saluted with his hat. Then he took out a pocket-flask and ironically drank to their health, shouting, "We are the English Guards, and hope you will stand till we come up to you, and not swim the Scheldt as you did the Main at Dettingen!"
> F.H.SKRINE: *Fontenoy* (1906).

Fire-brand. An incendiary; one who incites to rebellion; like a blazing brand which sets on fire all it touches.

> Our fire-brand brother, Paris, burns us all
> SHAKESPEARE: *Troilus and Cressida*, II, ii.

Fire-bug. An habitual perpetrator of arson; a FIRE-RAISER. The term is also applied to a glow-worm.

Fire-cross. *See* FIERY CROSS.

Fire dog. *See* ANDIRON.

Fire-drake, or **fire-dragon.** A fiery serpent, an IGNIS FATUUS of large proportions, superstitiously believed to be a flying DRAGON keeping guard over hidden treasures.

> There is a fellow somewhat near the door, he should be a brazier by his face, for, o' my conscience, twenty of the dog-days now reign in 's nose ... that fire-drake did I hit three times on the head.
> SHAKESPEARE: *King Henry VIII*, V, iii.

Fire-eaters. Those ready to quarrel with anyone; those looking for trouble; eager fighters. The allusion is to the jugglers who swallow flaming tow, etc.

Fire-hunting. An American term for hunting at night with the aid of fire-pans or links.

Fire-new. SPICK AND SPAN NEW.

> You should then have accosted her; and with some excellent jests, fire-new from the mint...
> SHAKESPEARE: *Twelfth Night*, III, ii.

Fire-raiser. One guilty of arson, often to collect the insurance money.

Fire-ship. A ship filled with combustibles sent against enemy vessels to set them on fire. English fire-ships scattered the Spanish Armada in confusion when anchored off Calais in 1588. Also a venereally infected strumpet.

> At that instant a sea-lieutenant came in ... when this wit advised him to keep clear of me, for I was a fire-ship.
> T.SMOLLETT: *Roderick Random*, ch. xxiii.

Fire-spaniel. Applied to one who hugs the fire and is loathe to stir from it.

Fire-watcher. The name given to those volunteers in Britain who kept watch for fires started by enemy air raids during World War II.

Fire-worship is said to have been introduced into Persia by Phœdima, widow of Smerdis, and wife of Hystaspes. It is not the SUN that is worshipped, but the god who is supposed to reside in it; at the same time the fire worshippers reverence the sun as the throne of the deity. *Cp.* PARSEES.

Fireside Chats. The name adopted by President F. D. Roosevelt for his broadcasts to the American people on topics of national interest and importance. They began in 1933 and became customary during his administration.

First. A diamond of the first water. *See under* DIAMOND.

At first hand. From one's own knowledge or personal observation.

First catch your hare. *See under* CATCH.

First cause. A cause that does not depend on any other. The Creator.

First chop. *See* CHOP.

First come first served. Promptness reaps its own reward. Chaucer in *The Wife of Bath's Tale* (*Prologue*) says:

> Whoso first cometh to the mill, first grint.

The first stroke is half the battle. *See* THE FIRST BLOW IS HALF THE BATTLE *under* BLOW.

First Fleet. The first expedition of eleven ships under Captain Arthur Phillip, R.N. bringing convicts to Australia in 1788. The second fleet arrived in 1790. To have been a *first fleeter* became a matter of pride.

First floor. In ENGLAND the first floor is that immediately above the ground floor; in America it is the ground floor.

First foot, or **first footer.** The first visitor at a house after midnight on New Year's Eve. In SCOTLAND and the North of ENGLAND the custom of *first footing* is still popular.

First-fruits. The first profitable results of labour. In husbandry, the first corn that is cut at harvest, which by the ancient Hebrews was offered to JEHOVAH. Such offerings became customary in the early Christian Church. ANNATES were also called Firstfruits. The word is used figuratively as well in such expressions as "the first fruits of sin", "the first fruits of repentance".

First light. In the armed forces "first light" denotes the earliest time (roughly dawn) at which light is sufficient for movement of ships, or for military operations to begin. Similarly *last light* is the latest time when such movements can take place. The expression was current in World War II.

First nighter. One who makes a practice of attending opening performances of plays.

The First Gentleman of Europe. A nickname given to George IV, but Thackeray says in *The Four Georges*, "We can tell of better gentlemen."

The First Grenadier of the Republic. A title given by NAPOLEON to La Tour d'Auvergne (1743–1800) a man of extraordinary courage and self-effacement. He refused all promotion beyond that of captain, as well as this title.

Fish. The fish was used as a symbol of Christ by the early Christians because the letters of its Greek name *ichthus* (*see* ICHTHYS) formed an acronym of the initial letters of the words Jesus Christ, Son of God, Saviour.

Ivory and mother-of-pearl counters used in card games, some of which are more or less fish-shaped, are so called, not from this shape, but from Fr. *fiche*, a peg, a card counter. *La fiche de consolation* (a little piece of comfort or consolation) is the name given in some games to the points allowed for the rubber.

A fish out of water. Said of a person out of his usual environment and who thus feels awkward; also of one who is without his usual occupation and is restless in consequence.

A loose fish. A man of loose or dissolute habits. Fish as applied to a human being is mildly derogatory.

A pretty kettle of fish. *See under* KETTLE.

A queer fish. An eccentric person.

All is fish that comes to my net. I turn everything to some use; I am willing to deal in anything out of which I can make a profit.

He eats no fish. In the time of Elizabeth I, a way of saying he is an honest man and one to be trusted, because he is not a Papist. Roman Catholics were naturally suspect at this time, and PROTESTANTS refused to adopt their custom of eating fish on Fridays (*see* FISH DAY).

> I do profess to be no less than I seem; to serve him truly that will put me in trust ... to fight when I cannot choose, and to eat no fish.
> SHAKESPEARE: *King Lear*, I, iv.

The government, however, sought to enforce the observance of fish days in order to help the fishing ports and the seafaring population; and to check the consumption of meat which encouraged the conversion of arable into pasture.

> It shall not be lawfull ... to eat any flesh upon any days now usually observed as fish dayes, or upon any Wednesday now newly limited to observed as fish day.
> *Act 5 Eliz.* c. 5, 1564.

I have other fish to fry. I have other things to do. I am busy and cannot attend to anything else now.

Neither fish, flesh, nor fowl, or **neither fish, flesh nor good red herring.** Suitable to no class of people; neither one thing nor another. Not fish (food for the monk), nor flesh (food for the people generally), nor yet red herring (food for the poor).

> Damned neuters in their middle way of steering,
> Are neither fish nor flesh nor good red-herring.
> DRYDEN: *Epilogue to "The Duke of Guise"*.

The best fish swim near the bottom. What is most valuable is not to be found near the surface, nor is anything really worth having to be obtained without effort and trouble.

There's as good fish in the sea as ever came out of it. Don't be disheartened if you've lost the chance of something good, you'll get another. Those who get preferment are not the only capable people.

To cry stinking fish. *See under* CRY.

To drink like a fish. *See under* DRINK.

To feed the fishes. To be sea-sick; to be drowned.

To fish for compliments. To try to obtain praise, usually by putting leading questions.

To fish in troubled waters. To scramble for personal advantage in times of stress, political unrest, etc.; to try to make a calamity a means to personal gain.

To fish the anchor. To hoist the flukes of an anchor to the bulwarks after the anchor has been "catted" (*see* CAT THE ANCHOR *under* CAT).

You must not make fish of one and flesh of the other. You must treat both alike. You must not discriminate.

Fish day. In France known as *jour maigre* (a lean day), a day when Roman Catholics and others used to abstain from meat and customarily eat fish. In the ROMAN CATHOLIC CHURCH there was a general law of abstinence on all Fridays (unless FEASTS), but BISHOPS now urge the faithful voluntarily to practise this or some other form of self-denial.

Fish Royal. Sturgeon and whale (although the latter is not a fish). If caught near the coast they are the property of the Crown.

Fish-wife. A woman who sells fish in a fish market or who hawks fish. Fishwives are renowned for their flow of invective, hence the term is sometimes applied to a vulgar, scolding female.

Fisher King. In the legends of the Holy GRAIL, the uncle of PERCEVAL.

Fisherman's Ring. A seal-ring with which the POPE is invested at his election, bearing the device of St. PETER fishing from a boat. It is used for sealing papal briefs, and is officially broken up at the Pope's death by the Chamberlain of the Roman Church.

Fitz. The Norman form of the modern French *fils*, son of; as Fitz-Herbert, Fitz-William, Fitz-Peter, etc. It is sometimes assumed by the illegitimate or morganatic children of royalty, as Fitz-Clarence, Fitz-roy, etc.

Fitzroy Cocktail (Austr.). One of the many concoctions drunk by strong men "OUT BACK". The recipe is methylated spirits, ginger beer, and one teaspoonful of boot polish.

Fitzwilliam Museum (Cambridge). So called from the 7th and last Viscount Fitz-william (1745–1816), who in 1816 left £100,000, with books, paintings, etc., to form the nucleus of a museum for the benefit of the university. The present building was begun in 1837 and was considerably extended in 1930–1931.

Five. The pentad, one of the mystic numbers, being the sum of 2 and 3, the first *even* and first *odd* compound. Unity is God alone, *i.e.*, without creation. Two is diversity, and three (being 1 and 2) is the compound of unity and diversity, or the two principles in operation since creation, and representing all the powers of nature.

Bunch of fives. Pugilistic slang for the fist.

The Five Alls. *See* PUBLIC-HOUSE SIGNS.

The Five Boroughs. In English history, the Danish confederation of Derby, Leicester, Lincoln, Nottingham, and Stamford in the 9th and 10th centuries.

Five fingers. A fisherman's name for the starfish.

The Five Members. Pym, Hampden, Haselrig, Holles, and Strode; the five members of the LONG PARLIAMENT whom Charles I attempted to arrest in 1642.

The Five-Mile Act. An Act passed in 1665 (repealed in 1812), the last act of the CLARENDON CODE prohibiting NONCONFORMIST clergy from coming within five miles of any corporate town or within that distance of the place where they had formerly ministered.

The Five Nations. A description applied by Kipling to the British Empire—the Old Country, with Canada, Australia, South Africa, and India.

In American history the term refers to the five confederated Indian tribes inhabiting the present State of New York, *viz.* the Mohawks, Oneidas, Onondagas, Cayugas, and Senecas; also known as the IROQUOIS Confederacy. HIAWATHA is traditionally regarded as the founder of this league, to which the Tuscarora were admitted as a Sixth Nation about 1715.

The Five Points of Calvinism. *See* CALVINISM.

The Five Senses. These are hearing, sight, smell, taste and touch.

The Five Towns. Towns in the Potteries which Arnold Bennett (1867–1931) used as the scene of the best known of his novels and stories. They are Tunstall, Burslem, Hanley, Stoke-upon-Trent, Longton, and Fenton—actually six—but for artistic purpose Bennett called them five. All are now part of Stoke-on-Trent. *Cp.* ETRURIA.

The Five Wits. Common sense, imagination, fantasy, estimation and memory; in general, the faculties of the mind; also an alternative expression for the five senses.

> If thy wits run the wild-goose chase, I have done; for thou hast more of the wild-goose in one of thy wits than, I am sure, I have in my whole five.
> SHAKESPEARE: *Romeo and Juliet*, II, i, v.

> These are the five witts removvying inwardly:
> First, "Common witte", and then "Ymagination",
> "Fantasy", and "Estimation" truely,
> And "Memory".
> STEPHEN HAWES: *The Passetyme of Pleasure* (1507).

Five-Year Plans. In the U.S.S.R., plans for developing the whole of the nation's economy in a co-ordinated effort by a five-year programme. The first Five-Year Plan was launched by Stalin in 1928 with the aims of making the Soviet Union self-supporting, mechanizing agriculture, promoting literacy, etc. Further Five-Year Plans followed and the example was copied by other countries.

Fiver. A five-pound note.

Fix, A. In modern slang and of American origin, a shot of heroin or other narcotic drug.

In a fix. In an awkward predicament.

To fix on, or **upon.** To determine upon; to settle upon; to choose.

To fix up. To mend or repair; to arrange.

To obtain a fix. In navigation to fix one's exact position by the intersection at a suitable angle of two or more position lines obtained at the same time.

Fixed Air. An old name of carbonic acid gas (carbon dioxide), given to it by Dr. Joseph Black (1728–1799), because it is "fixed" in solid carbonates until driven out by heat.

Fixed Oils. The true oils; *i.e.,* those which do not volatilize by heating without decomposition, and which harden on exposure to the air, thus differing from *essential oils*. The glycerides, such as linseed and walnut oils, are examples. Such oils make a permanent greasy stain on paper.

Fixed Stars. Stars whose relative position to other stars is always the same, as distinguished from planets, which shift their relative positions.

Flaccus (flăk' ùs). HORACE (65–8 B.C.), the Roman poet, whose full name was Quintus Horatius Flaccus.

Flag. A word of uncertain origin. National flags are flown as the symbols of a state and are particularly important as a means of recognition of ships at sea. Merchant ships usually wear their flag or ensign at the stern, warships wear their flag or jack at the bows and their ensign at the stern. Flags are also used as personal banners or standards, especially by royalty and high-ranking naval and military officers, by regiments, as house flags by companies, for signalling purposes,

etc. That part of a flag which is nearest the mast is called the *hoist* and the disc at the top of the flagstaff is the *truck*. The *fly* is the end of the flag furthest from the staff. *See* TRICOLOUR.

Flags on Church flagstaffs. In the CHURCH OF ENGLAND the proper flag to be flown is that of St. GEORGE, with the arms of the SEE in the first quarter.

A black flag is the emblem of piracy or of no QUARTER (*see under* BLACK); also the anarchists' flag. In World War II, submarines, on returning to base, sometimes hoisted a black flag to indicate a "kill".

A green flag is used on railways, roads, etc. for signalling "Go ahead".

A red flag is generally used to indicate danger or as a stop signal. It is also the symbol of international socialism and *The Red Flag* is a socialist anthem still used, somewhat incongruously, by the British LABOUR PARTY.

> Then raise the scarlet standard high,
> Beneath its shade we'll live and die
> Though cowards flinch and traitors sneer
> We'll keep the Red Flag flying here.
> JAMES CONNELL: *The Red Flag*.

A white flag is the flag of truce or surrender, hence **to hang out the white flag** is to sue for QUARTER, to give in.

A yellow flag is one of the three "quarantine flags". *See* YELLOW JACK; YELLOW ADMIRAL *under* ADMIRAL.

A flag of convenience is a foreign flag under which a vessel is registered, usually to lessen taxation and manning costs. Liberia, Honduras and Panama are the most widely used flags of convenience and Liberia has the largest merchant fleet in the world.

The flag of distress. When a ship's ensign is flown upside down it is a signal of distress.

The flag's down. Indicative of distress; also the start of a race. When the face is pale the "flag is down"; alluding to the old custom of taking down the flag of theatres when they were closed during LENT.

> 'Tis Lent in your cheeks, the flag's down.
> *Dodsley's Old Plays*, vol. V (*Mad World*).

To break a flag is to hoist it rolled up and to "break" it by pulling the halyard to release the hitch which holds it together.

To dip a flag is to haul it down to a half-mast position and then rehoist it. This is the usual salute between ships at sea. It is also flown **at the dip** as a sign of mourning.

To flag down. To stop someone, nowadays usually a motor-driver; from the practice of stopping a train or other vehicle by waving or displaying a flag. Formerly, trains which did not usually stop at little-used wayside stations did so if the appropriate flag was displayed. Such stations were known as *flag-stations* or *flag-stops*.

To fly the flag at half-mast is a sign of mourning.

To get one's flag. To become an admiral. *See* FLAG OFFICER.

> I do not believe that the bullet is cast that is to deprive you of life, Jack; you'll get your flag, as I hope to get mine.
>
> KINGSTON: *The Three Admirals*, xiii.

To lower one's flag. TO EAT HUMBLE PIE; *see under* HUMBLE), to yield or confess oneself in the wrong; to eat one's own words.

To strike the flag. To lower it completely. It is also a token of surrender; and when an ADMIRAL relinquishes his command he *strikes his flag*.

Trade follows the flag. *See under* TRADE.

Flag Captain. The captain commanding the vessel in which the ADMIRAL is flying his flag.

Flag Day. In the U.S.A., 14 June, the anniversary of the adoption of the STARS AND STRIPES in 1777. In Britain **a flag day** is any day on which small paper flags or emblems for wearing on the apparel are sold for the support of charities, etc.

Flag Lieutenant. An ADMIRAL'S aide-de-camp, colloquially known as "Flags".

Flag Officer. An ADMIRAL, vice-admiral or rear-admiral who flies the flag appropriate to his rank. An Admiral of the Fleet flies a UNION JACK; an admiral a ST. GEORGE's Cross on a white ground, a vice-admiral the same, with on red ball in the upper canton next the staff, and a rear admiral a second red ball in the canton immediately below.

Flag-ship. A ship carrying the FLAG OFFICER.

Flagellants (flă jel′ ănts). The Latin *flagellum* means a scourge, and this name is given to those extremists who scourged themselves in public processions in mediæval times, and subsequently, as penance for the sins of the world. There was a particular outbreak in Italy in 1260 and again in 1348–1349, at the time of the BLACK DEATH, when the movement spread over Europe. The Church has never encouraged such practices.

Flagellum Dei (Lat. the scourge of God). *See* SCOURGE OF GOD.

Flamboyant Architecture. The last phase of French GOTHIC architecture, named from O.Fr. *flambe* (flame). Characterized by the flame-like tracery and elaboration of detail, it flourished from about 1460 until the 16th century.

Flame. A sweetheart. **An old flame**, a quondam sweetheart.

Flaming swords. Swords with a wavy or flamboyant edge, used now only for state ceremonies. The Dukes of Burgundy carried such swords, and they were worn in Britain until the time of William III (1689–1702).

Flaminian Way. The great northern road, the *Via Flaminia*, of ancient Italy, constructed by G. Flaminius in 220 B.C. It led from the Flaminian gate of Rome to Ariminum (Rimini).

Flanders Babies. Cheap wooden jointed dolls common in the early 19th century.

Flanders Mare. So Henry VIII called Anne of Cleves, his fourth wife whom he married in January 1540, and divorced the following July. She died at Chelsea in 1557.

Flanders Poppies. The name given to the red artificial poppies sold for REMEMBRANCE DAY to benefit ex-service men. The connexion with poppies comes from a poem by John McCrae, which appeared in *Punch*, 8 December 1915:

> If ye break faith with us who die
> We shall not sleep, though poppies grow
> In Flanders fields.

Flannel. That's all flannel. That's all soft soap. What you say does not really impress me. *Flannel* may have acquired this kind of connotation in the same way as BOMBAST and FUSTIAN.

To be awarded one's flannels. Formerly, at Eton "to get one's flannels" was to row in the eight at Henley, or to get into the Cricket XI (1st), where white flannels were part of the outfit; all others wearing grey flannels. Similarly, in the Field Game "to be given one's shorts" was to represent the House; the others wearing knickerbockers.

Flannelled fools. Cricketers. This term, used either derisively or humorously, is taken from Kipling's poem *The Islanders*.

> Then ye returned to your trinkets; then ye contented your souls.
> With the flannelled fools at the wicket or the muddied oafs at the goals.

Flap. To be in a flap. A colloquial expression meaning to be in a state of anxious excitement, as birds flap and flutter when disturbed.

Flap-dragons. An old name for SNAPDRAGON, *i.e.* raisins soaked in spirit, lighted and floating in a bowl of spirituous liquor. GALLANTS used to drink flap-dragons to the health of their mistresses, and would frequently have lighted candle-ends floating in the liquor to heighten the effect. Hence:

> And drinks off candles' ends for flap-dragons.
> SHAKESPEARE: *Henry IV, Pt. II*, II, iv.

Flapjack. A flat cake of batter baked on a griddle or in a shallow pan, and so called from turning it by tossing it into the air.

> We'll have flesh for holidays, fish for fasting-days, and moreo'er puddings and flapjacks.
>
> SHAKESPEARE: *Pericles*, II, i.

In the 20th century the word has been applied to a woman's flat powder compact.

Flapper. In the early years of the 20th century a term applied to a girl in her teens, now called a teenager, from her plaited pigtail tied at the end with a large bow. When stepping along the pigtail flapped her back. Subsequently her hair was "put up" in a "bun" or other hairstyle. By the 1920s the name was commonly applied to a young woman, or "bright young thing". *See also* LAPUTA.

The Flapper Vote. An irreverent name for the vote granted to women of 21 by the Equal Franchise Act of 1928, sponsored by Baldwin's Conservative government. *See* FLAPPER.

Flash. Showy, smart, "swagger"; as a *flash wedding*, a *flash hotel*. In Australia the term *flash* or *flashy* is applied to

> anyone who is proud and has nothing to be proud of.
>
> J. KIRBY: *Old Times in the Bush of Australia*, 1895.

Also counterfeit, sham, fraudulent.

Flash notes are forged notes, a **flash man** is a thief or an associate of one; and a **flash-house** is one frequented by thieves and prostitutes.

> The excesses of that age [the Restoration] remind us of the humours of a gang of footpads, revelling with their favourite beauties at a flash-house.
>
> MACAULAY: *Essays (Hallam's Constitutional History)*.

A mere flash in the pan. A failure after a showy beginning; like the attempt to discharge an old flint-lock gun that ends with a flash in the lock-pan, the gun itself "hanging-fire" (*see* TO HANG FIRE *under* FIRE).

Flat. Flat as a flounder. I knocked him down "flat as a flounder". A flounder is one of the flatfish.

Flat as a pancake. Quite flat.

Flat out. At full speed, all out, fully extended.

He is a regular flatfish. A dull, stupid fellow. The play is upon *flat* (not sharp, *i.e.* dull), and such fish as plaice, dabs, etc.

To lie like a flatfish. To lie blatantly. The punning derivation is obvious.

To be caught flat-footed. To be caught unprepared, as a football player who is tackled by an opponent before he has been able to advance.

To be in a flat spin. To be very flurried, to be in a panic. In flying, a flat spin is when the longitudinal axis of an aircraft inclines downwards at an angle of less than 45°. In the early days this inevitably involved loss of control. It is now an aerial manœuvre performed at low level in air combat as an evasive action.

To come out flat-footed. To state one's beliefs positively, as though firmly planted on one's feet.

Flat-foot. A policeman. Sometimes called a **flattie**.

Flat race. A race on the "flat" or level ground without obstacles, as opposed to hurdling, STEEPLECHASING, etc.

Flat top. A World War II name for an aircraft-carrier.

Flatterer. Lucius Vitellius, father of Aulus Vitellius, Roman Emperor for most of A.D. 69. He obtained his honours through flattery of the emperors and especially Messalina, a wife of the Emperor Claudius. His name became a Roman synonym for a flatterer (Tacitus, *Ann.*, vi, 32).

When flatterers meet, the devil goes to dinner. Flattery is so pernicious, so fills the heart with pride and conceit, so perverts the judgment and disturbs the balance of mind, that SATAN himself could do no greater mischief, so he may go to dinner and leave the leaven of wickedness to work its own mischief.

Flea. A flea's jump. It has been estimated that if a man, in proportion to his weight, could jump as high as a flea, he could clear St. Paul's Cathedral with ease (365 ft. high).

Aristophanes, in the *Clouds*, says that SOCRATES and Chærephon tried to measure how many times its own length a flea jumped. They took in wax the size of a flea's foot; then on the principle of EX PEDE HERCULEM, calculated the length of its body. They then measured the distance of a flea's jump from the hand of Socrates to Chærephon and the problem was resolved by simple multiplication.

A mere flea-bite. A thing of no moment, a very small portion or contribution.

Great fleas have lesser fleas. No matter what our station in life, we all have some hangers-on.

> Hobbes clearly proves that every creature
> Lives in a state of war by nature.
> So naturalists observe, a flea
> Has smaller fleas that on him prey;
> And these have smaller still to bite 'em,
> And so proceed *ad infinitum*.
>
> SWIFT: *Poetry; a Rhapsody*.

To be sent off with a flea in the ear. Sent away discomfited by a reproof or repulse. A dog which has a flea in the ear is very restless, and runs off in terror and distress.

An old phrase dating at least from the 15th

century in English, and earlier in French. It
is found in Scogan's *Jests*, Heywood's *Proverbs*, Nashe's *Pierce Penilesse*, etc.

> Ferardo ... whispering Philautus in his eare (who
> stoode as though he had a leaf in his eare), desired
> him to kepe silence.
>
> LYLY: *Euphues, the Anatomy of Wit* (1579).

Here the phrase implies that vexatious
news has been heard; and in Deloney's *Gentle Craft* (1597) there is a similar instance,
where a servant goes away shaking his head
"like one that hath a flea in his eare".

Flecknoe, Richard. A Roman Catholic
priest, and author of poems, plays and other
works. He died about 1678. He is now only
remembered through Dryden's satire *Mac
Flecknoe*, where it is said he reigned

> without dispute
> Through all the realms of Nonsense, absolute.

Fleet, The. A famous London prison of mediæval origin which stood on the east side of
Farringdon Street, until its demolition
(1845–1846), on the site now partly occupied by the Memorial Hall. It took its name
from the river Fleet which (now piped) enters the THAMES at Blackfriars Bridge. As a
royal prison it housed some distinguished
prisoners in Tudor and Stuart times, including those committed by STAR CHAMBER, but
mainly owes its notoriety to its subsequent
use as a debtor's prison. It was destroyed in
the GREAT FIRE OF LONDON (*see under* FIRE),
rebuilt, and again burned during the Gordon Riots. The Warden farmed out the prison to the highest bidder which encouraged
the shameful treatment of its occupants. *Cp.*
FLEET MARRIAGES.

> Most of our readers will remember that, until with-
> in a very few years past, there was a kind of iron cage
> in the wall of the Fleet Prison, within which was
> posted some man of hungry looks, who, from time
> to time, rattled a money-box, and explained, in a
> mournful voice "Pray, remember the poor debtors;
> pray, remember the poor debtors".
>
> DICKENS: *Pickwick Papers*, ch. xlii.

Fleet Book Evidence. No evidence at all.
The books of the Old Fleet prison are not ad-
missible as evidence of a marriage. *See*
FLEET MARRIAGES *below*.

Fleet Marriages. Clandestine marriages,
especially of minors, at one time performed
without BANNS or licence in the chapel of the
FLEET, but from the latter part of Queen
Anne's reign performed by the Fleet clergy
in rooms of nearby taverns and houses.

> Before the door of the Fleet prison, men plied in be-
> half of a clergyman, literally insisting people to walk
> in and be married. They performed the ceremony
> inside the prison, to sailors and others for what they
> could get.
>
> LEIGH HUNT: *The Town*, ch. ii.

James Malcolm, the topographer, tells us
that as many as "thirty couple were joined in
one day" and that 2,954 marriages were
registered in the four months ending 12
February 1705. The practice was destroyed by Lord Hardwicke's Marriage
Act of 1753 which declared such marriages void. *Cp.* GRETNA GREEN MARRIAGES;
MAY-FAIR MARRIAGES.

Fleet Street. The famous thoroughfare
which runs from LUDGATE Circus to the
STRAND taking its name from the Fleet river,
once navigable for coal barges as far as HOL-
BORN. Formerly noted for its bookshops, it is
now synonymous with journalism and the
newspaper world.

The Liberties of the Fleet. The district
immediately surrounding the FLEET, in
which prisoners were sometimes allowed to
reside, and beyond which they were not permitted to go. They included the north side
of LUDGATE Hill and the OLD BAILEY to Fleet
Lane, down the lane to the market, and on
the east side along by the prison wall to the
foot of Ludgate Hill.

Flemish Account. A sum less than expected.
When accounts in Amsterdam were kept in
livres, *sols*, and *pence*, the *livre* or pound
consisted of 12*s.*; hence an account of 100
livres Flemish was worth only £60 to an English creditor.

Flemish School. A school of painting
founded by the brothers van Eyck, in the
15th century. The chief early masters were
Memling, Weyden, Matsys, and Mabuse; of
the second period, Rubens and Van Dyck,
Snyders, and the younger Teniers. As well
as the invention of oil painting by Jan van
Eyck the school was notable for the perfection and unsurpassed representation of reality.

Flesh. A thorn in the flesh. *See* THORN.

To be one flesh. To be closely united, as in
marriage.

He fleshed his sword, *i.e.* used it for the
first time.

Men fleshed in cruelty. Those initiated or
used to it when being trained. Young sporting dogs and hawks are rewarded with the
first game they catch. This first introduction
to flesh encourages the taste for blood.

> The wild dog
> Shall flesh his tooth in every innocent.
>
> SHAKESPEARE: *Henry IV, Pt. II*, IV, iv.

The Fleshly School. In the *Contemporary
Review* for October 1871, Robert Buchanan
published a violent attack on the poetry and
literary methods of Swinburne, Rossetti,
Morris, O'Shaughnessy, John Payne, and
one or two others under the heading *The

Fleshly School of Poetry, over the signature "Thomas Maitland". The incident created a literary sensation; Buchanan first denied the authorship but was soon obliged to admit it, and was reconciled to Rossetti, his chief victim, some years later. Swinburne's very trenchant reply is to be found in his *Under the Microscope* (1872).

Fleur-de-lis, -lys, or **-luce** (flĕr de lē, lēs, loos) (Fr. lily-flower). The name of several varieties of iris or flags, and also of the heraldic LILY here shown and which was borne as a charge on the old French royal COAT OF ARMS. In the reign of Louis VII (1137–1180) the national STANDARD was thickly charged with lilies but in 1376 the number was reduced to three by Charles V in honour of the TRINITY. Guillim's *Display of Heraldrie* (1610) says the device is "Three TOADS erect, saltant"; in allusion to which NOSTRADAMUS in the 16th century called Frenchmen CRAPAUDS. The *fleur-de-lis* was used to decorate the north point on the mariner's card before the end of the 15th century and in the 20th century it was adopted as the badge of the BOY SCOUTS. *See also* FLORIN.

Flibbertigibbet. One of the five fiends that possessed "poor Tom" in *King Lear* (IV, i). SHAKESPEARE got the name from Harsnet's *Declaration of Egregious Popish Impostures* (1603), where we are told of forty fiends which the JESUITS cast out, and among the number was "Fliberdigibet", a name which had been previously used by Latimer and others for a mischievous GOSSIP. Elsewhere the name is apparently a synonym for PUCK.

Flicks. To go to the flicks. To go to a film show, an expression derived from the early days of such shows when the pictures "flickered" on the screen.

Flimsy. A journalist's term for newspaper copy, arising from the thin paper (often used with a sheet of carbon paper to take a copy) on which reporters and others wrote up their matter for the press. The white £5 Bank of England note, which ceased to be legal tender in March 1961, was kown as a *flimsy*. In the Royal Navy the name is also given to the brief certificate of conduct issued to an officer by his Captain on the termination of his appointment to a ship or establishment; the name again derives from the thin quality paper.

Fling. I must have a fling at. Metaphorically, throw a stone at, *i.e.* attack with words, especially sarcasm; to make a haphazard venture.

To have his fling. To have full freedom of action; to indulge in pleasure to the fullest extent; to sow his wild OATS. The Scots have a proverb:

> Let him tak' his fling and find oot his ain wecht [weight]

meaning, give him a free hand and he'll soon find his level.

Flint. To skin a flint. *See under* SKIN.

Floating Academy. A convict ship, one of the HULKS.

Flogging a dead horse. *See under* HORSE.

Flogging round, or **through the fleet.** In the Royal Navy, according to the ancient practice of the sea, this barbarous punishment consisted of a number of lashes from the CAT-O'-NINE-TAILS administered alongside each ship present, usually to the accompaniment of the ROGUE'S MARCH. Death was a common result. It ceased before the end of the 18th century but flogging at the gangway was not finally "suspended" until 1879. After the mutiny at the Nore in 1797 one seaman of the *Monmouth* was sentenced to 380 lashes.

Flood, The. *See* DELUGE.

Floor. I floored him. Knocked him down on the floor; hence figuratively, to overcome or beat.

To cross the floor. In Parliamentary usage, means to change parties; from the fact that government and OPPOSITION benches are on opposite sides of the floor of the HOUSE OF COMMONS.

To get in on the ground floor. *See under* GROUND.

To take the floor. To speak in a debate; to begin to dance.

Floor traders, or **Room traders.** A name particularly used in New York for those members of a stock exchange who buy and sell stock on their own account, unlike commission brokers who act exclusively on behalf of clients.

Flora. The Roman goddess of flowers especially associated with Spring. Her festivals, the *Floralia*, were from 28 April to 3 May. The term *Flora* also denotes the native or indigenous plants of a country or region. *Cp.* FAUNA.

Flora's Dial. A fanciful dial formed of flowers which open or close at the various hours.

Flora Macdonald (1722–1790). The Scottish heroine who aided the escape of Prince Charles Edward after the failure of the FORTY-FIVE Rebellion. She conducted the YOUNG PRETENDER (*see* PRETENDER), disguised as Betty Bourke, an Irish woman, from Benbecula to Monkstadt in Skye and thence via Kingsburgh to Portree, often in imminent danger from the military search parties. She was subsequently imprisoned in the TOWER OF LONDON but released in 1747 under the Act of Indemnity. She married Allan Macdonald in 1750, emigrated to North Carolina, 1774, but returned to Scotland in 1779.

> After dinner, Flora Macdonald on horseback, and her supposed maid and Kingsburgh, with a servant carrying some linen, all on foot, proceeded towards that gentleman's house. Upon the road was a small rivulet which they were obliged to cross. The Wanderer [the Prince], forgetting his assumed sex, that his clothes might not be wet, held them up a great deal too high. Kingsburgh mentioned this to him, observing, it might make a discovery.
> BOSWELL: *Journal of a Tour to the Hebrides* (13 September).

Florentine Diamond. A large and famous DIAMOND weighing 133 carats. It formed part of the Austrian crown jewels and previously belonged to Charles, Duke of Burgundy.

Florida. In 1512 Ponce de León sailed to the west in search of "the Fountain of Youth". He first saw land on Easter Day which was then popularly called in Spain *Pascua florida*, flowery EASTER, and on that account called the land "Florida". It is also called the "Peninsula State". Its city of St. AUGUSTINE is the oldest European settlement in the original UNITED STATES.

Florin (Ital. *fiorino*, a little flower). As a gold coin it was first minted in 13th-century Florence and named after the lily on the reverse. The FLEUR-DE-LIS was the badge of Florence. Edward III coined an English gold florin in 1344 valued at 6s. The English silver florin representing 2s. was first issued in 1849 as a tentative introduction of a DECIMAL CURRENCY.

Graceless, or Godless florin. The first English silver florin struck in 1849, called "graceless" because the usual "*Dei Gratia*" (by God's grace) was omitted; and "Godless" because of the omission of F.D. (DEFENDER OF THE FAITH).

Some attributed the cholera outbreak of that year to the new florin. The coins were called in and the Master of the Mint, Richard Lalor Sheil (1791–1851), a Roman Catholic, left the MINT the following year.

Florizel. George IV, when Prince of Wales, corresponded under this name with Mrs. Robinson, the actress, generally known as PERDITA, in which character she first attracted his attention. The name comes from SHAKESPEARE's *Winter's Tale*.

In Lord Beaconsfield's *Endymion* (1880), *Prince Florizel* is meant for NAPOLEON III.

Flotsam and Jetsam. Properly wreckage and other goods found in the sea. "Flotsam", goods found floating on the sea (O.Fr. *floter*, to float); "jetsam", things thrown overboard (Fr. *jeter*, to throw out). The term is now also applied to wreckage found on the shore. *Lagan*, a word of uncertain origin, applies to goods thrown overboard but tied to a float for later recovery.

> The house bore sufficient witness to the ravages of the ocean, and to the exercise of those rights which the lawyers term Flotsome and Jetsome.
> SCOTT: *The Pirate*: ch. xii.

Flotsam and Jetsam were also the names adopted by two popular entertainers of variety stage and broadcasting fame. B.C. Hilliam (1890–1968), English composer and pianist, took the name *Flotsam* and his partner, the Australian bass singer, Malcolm McEachern (1884–1945), that of *Jetsam*.

Flowers and Trees, etc.

(1) Dedicated to heathen gods:

The Cornel cherry-tree	to	APOLLO
,, CYPRESS	,,	PLUTO
,, DITTANY	,,	DIANA
,, LAUREL	,,	APOLLO
,, LILY	,,	JUNO
,, Maidenhair	,,	PLUTO
,, MYRTLE	,,	VENUS
,, Narcissus	,,	CERES
,, OAK	,,	JUPITER
,, OLIVE	,,	MINERVA
,, POPPY	,,	CERES
,, VINE	,,	BACCHUS

(2) Dedicated to saints:

Canterbury Bells	to	St. AUGUSTINE of CANTERBURY
Crocus	,,	St. VALENTINE
Crown Imperial	,,	Edward the Confessor
DAISY	,,	St. MARGARET
Herb Christopher	,,	St. CHRISTOPHER
LADY'S-SMOCK	,,	the Virgin MARY
ROSE	,,	MARY MAGDALENE
St. John's-wort	,,	St. JOHN
St. Barnaby's Thistle	,,	St. BARNABAS

(3) National emblems:

LEEK, Daffodil	emblem of	Wales
LILY (FLEUR-DE-LYS)	,,	BOURBON France
,, (Giglio bianco)	,,	Florence
Lily, White	,,	GHIBELLINES
,, red	,,	the GUELPHS
LINDEN	,,	Prussia
Mignonette	,,	Saxony
Pomegranate	,,	Spain
Rose	,,	ENGLAND
,, red, LANCASTRIANS:	white, YORKISTS	
SHAMROCK	emblem of	IRELAND
THISTLE	,,	SCOTLAND
VIOLET	,,	ATHENS
Sugar Maple	,,	Canada

(4) In Christian Symbolism:

Box	a symbol of	the Resurrection
Cedars	,,	the faithful
Corn-ears	,,	the Holy Communion
Dates	,,	the faithful
Grapes	,,	this is my blood
HOLLY	,,	the Resurrection

IVY	,,	the Resurrection
Lily	,,	purity
OLIVE	,,	peace
ORANGE-BLOSSOM	,,	virginity
PALM	,,	victory
Rose	,,	incorruption
Vine	,,	Christ our Life
YEW	,,	death

N.B.—The laurel, oak, olive, myrtle, rosemary, cypress, and amaranth are all funereal plants.

Flowers in Christian Tradition. Many plants and flowers play a part in Christian tradition. The ASPEN is said to tremble because the cross was made of its wood and there are other traditions connected with the ELDER-TREE, FIG-TREE, PASSION FLOWER, THISTLE, etc. *See also* FIG LEAF; GLASTONBURY.

The following are said to owe their stained blossoms to the blood which trickled from the CROSS: the red anemone; the arum; the purple orchis; the crimson-spotted leaves of the roodselken (vervain, or the "herb of the cross"); the spotted persicaria or snakeweed.

The Language of Flowers. The traditional symbolic meanings attached to numerous flowers and plants. Some examples are:

Asphodel	my regret follows you to the grave
Bay leaf	I change but in death
Bluebell	constancy
Foxglove	insincerity
Honeysuckle	generous and devoted affection
Jasmine	amiability
Nasturtium	patriotism
Oak leaves	bravery
Peony	shame, bashfulness
Quince	temptation
Snowdrop	hope
Veronica	fidelity

There's rosemary, that's for remembrance; pray love, remember; and there is pansies, that's for thoughts.
SHAKESPEARE: *Hamlet*, IV, v.

The Flower of Chivalry. A name given to several knights of spotless reputation, *e.g.*:
Sir William Douglas, Knight of Liddesdale (*c.* 1300–1353).
Chevalier de Bayard. *See under* BAYARD.
Sir Philip Sidney (1554–1586).

The Flower of Kings (Lat. *Flos regum*). King ARTHUR was so called by John of Exeter, Bishop of Winchester (d. 1268).

Flower people. Supporters of a brightly clad cult of the mid-1960s who advocated "universal love" as a substitute for materialism.

The Flowery Kingdom. China; a translation of the Chinese *Hwa-Kwo*.

Fluff. A little bit of fluff. A girl or woman, especially one of the fluffy variety. A colloquial expression of Edwardian origin, fluff being the light, downy, soft stuff.

Flush. In cards, a whole hand of one suit.

Flush of, or **with money.** Very well supplied with money. Similarly *a flush of water* means a sudden and full flow of water (Lat. *fluxus*, flowing).

To flush game. A gun-dog is said to *flush game* when he disturbs them and they take to the air.

Flute. The Magic Flute. In Mozart's opera of this name (*Die Zauberflöte*, 1791) the magic flute was bestowed by the powers of darkness, and had the power of inspiring love. By it Tamino and Pamina are guided through all worldly dangers to knowledge of Divine Truth.

Flutter. A colloquial term for a small gamble.

To flutter, or **cause a flutter in the dovecotes.** To disturb the equanimity of a group of people. In Shakespeare's *Coriolanus* (V, vi) we have:

That, like an eagle in a dove-cote, I
Flutter'd your Volscians in Corioli.

Fly (*plural* flys). A one-horse hackney-carriage. A contraction of *Fly-by-night*, as sedan chairs on wheels used to be called in the REGENCY. These "Fly-by-nights", much patronized by the Regent and his boon companions at Brighton, were invented in 1809 by John Butcher, a carpenter.

Fly. An insect (*plural* flies). For the theatrical use, *see* FLYMAN.

It is said that no fly was ever seen in Solomon's temple, and according to Mohammedan legend, all flies shall perish except one, the bee-fly.

The God, or **Lord of Flies.** Every year, in the temple of Actium, the Greeks used to sacrifice an ox to ZEUS, who in this capacity was surnamed Apomyios, the averter of flies. Pliny tells us that at ROME sacrifice was offered to flies in the temple of HERCULES Victor, and the Syrians also offered sacrifice to these insects. *See* ACHOR; BEELZEBUB.

An eagle does not hawk at flies. *See* AQUILA.

The fly in the ointment. The trifling cause that spoils everything; a Biblical phrase.

Dead flies cause the ointment of the apothecary to send forth a stinking savour; so doth a little folly him that is in reputation for wisdom and honour.
Eccles. x, 1.

The fly on the coach-wheel. One who fancies himself of great importance, one who is in reality of none at all. The allusion is to ÆSOP's fable of a fly sitting on a chariot-wheel and saying, "See what dust I make."

There are no flies on him. He's very shrewd and wide awake; he won't be CAUGHT NAPPING (*see under* CATCH).

To crush a fly on a wheel. An allusion to

the absurdity of taking a wheel used for torturing criminals and heretics for killing a fly. *Cp.* TO USE A SLEDGEHAMMER TO CRUSH A NUT *under* NUT; TO BREAK A BUTTERFLY ON A WHEEL *under* BREAK.

To rise to the fly. To rise to the bait, to fall for a hoax or trap, as a fish rises to the angler's fly and is caught.

Fly-blown. Fouled by flyblows; hence tainted, spoiled. At one time naturalists thought that maggots were actually blown on to the meat by blow-flies.

Fly, To fly. To move through the air by means of wings, to move swiftly, to depart rapidly, etc.

A flying angel. *See under* ANGEL.

As the crow flies. *See under* CROW.

Fly bird. A knowing one, a WIDE BOY.

To fly a kite. *See under* KITE.

To fly blind. To pilot an aircraft solely by means of instruments; the opposite of visual navigation.

To fly in one's face. To get into a passion with someone; to insult; as a HAWK, when irritated, flies in the face of its master.

To fly in the face of danger. To defy danger in a foolhardy manner, as a hen flies in the face of a dog.

To fly in the face of providence. To act rashly, and throw away good opportunities; to court danger.

To fly off the handle. To burst out into angry and violent speech without control, as a hammer loses its head when loose after a blow has been struck.

To fly out at. To burst or break into a passion.

To let fly. To make a violent attack upon, either literally or by a torrent of abuse, etc.

To make the feathers, or **fur fly.** To create a violent disturbance or to attack vigorously, either physically or by speech or writing, as when birds or animals are attacked.

No flying without wings. Nothing can be done without the proper means.

To come off with flying colours. *See under* COLOUR.

Fly-boy. The boy in a printing-office who lifts the printed sheets off the press; so called because he catches the sheets as they fly from the tympan immediately the frisket is opened.

Fly-by-night. One who defrauds his creditors by decamping in the night; a dubious character. *See also* FLY (a cab).

Fly-flat. A racing man's term for a punter who thinks he knows all the ins and outs of the turf, but doesn't. *Cp.* FLAT.

Flying bedstead. Nickname of the experimental wingless and rotorless vertical take-off jet aircraft demonstrated in Britain in 1954. Built by Rolls-Royce, the name was inspired by its appearance.

Flying Column. *See under* COLUMN.

Flying-the-garter. *See under* GARTER.

The Flying Duchess. Mary du Caurroy Russell, Duchess of Bedford (1865–1937). After making record-breaking return flights to India (1929) and South Africa (1930) with Captain Barnard, she obtained an "A" pilot's licence in 1933 and disappeared on a solo flight over the North Sea in March 1937.

The Flying Dutchman. In maritime legend, a spectral ship that is supposed to haunt the seas around the Cape of Good Hope and to lure other vessels to their destruction or to cause other misfortune. According to Jal's *Scènes de la Vie Maritime*, he is said to be a Dutch captain, who persisted in trying to round the Cape, in spite of the violence of the storm, and the protests of passengers and crew. Eventually a form, said to be the Almighty, appeared on the deck, but the Captain did not even touch his cap but fired upon the form and cursed and blasphemed. For punishment, the Dutchman was condemned to sail and to be a torment to sailors until the Day of JUDGMENT. A skeleton ship appears in Coleridge's *Ancient Mariner*, and Washington Irving tells of "the Flying Dutchman of the Tappan Sea" in his *Chronicles of Woolfert's Roost*. Wagner has an opera *Der Fliegende Holländer* (1843) and Captain Marryat's novel *The Phantom Ship* (1839) tells of Philip Vanderdecken's successful but disastrous search for his father, the captain of the Flying Dutchman. Similar legends are found in many other countries.

> The Demon Frigate braves the gale;
> And well the doom'd spectators know
> The harbinger of wreck and woe.
> SCOTT: *Rokeby*, canto II, xi.

Flying Tigers. The nickname of a volunteer group of American airmen who supported China against Japanese aggression. Formed in August 1941, under Major-General C. L. Chennault, some months before America's entry into the war, they fought with distinction until merged with the 23rd Fighter Squadron of the U.S.A.A.F. in July 1942.

Flyman. In the theatre, the sceneshifter, or man in the "flies", *i.e.* the gallery over the proscenium where the curtains, scenery, etc., are controlled.

The flyman's plot. The list of all the articles required by the flyman in the play concerned.

Fob. You are trying to fob, or fub me off. You are trying to put me off (with something inferior or by deception). *Fob* is connected with Ger. *foppen*, to hoax.

Fo'c's'le. *See* FORECASTLE.

Foil. That which sets off something to advantage. The allusion is to the metallic leaf used by jewellers to set off PRECIOUS STONES (Fr. *feuille*; Lat. *folium*; Gr. *phullon*, a leaf).

> I'll be your foil, Laertes; in mine ignorance
> Your skill shall, like a star in the darkest night,
> Stick fiery off indeed.
> SHAKESPEARE: *Hamlet*, V, ii.

The buttons come off the foil. *See under* BUTTON.

To run a foil. To puzzle; to lead astray. The track of game is called its foil; and a hunted animal will sometimes run back over its foil to mislead its pursuers. The word also means "to baffle, frustrate, parry". It comes from the O.Fr. *fouler*, to trample upon (it is the same word in the phrase "to full cloth").

Folio. The word is the ablative of the Lat. *folium*, a leaf.

In bibliography and printing it has distinct applications. (1) A sheet of paper (for printing) in its standard size. (2) A book *in folio*, in [one] sheet, is a book, the sheets of which have been folded once only, so that each sheet makes two leaves; hence a book of large size. (3) It is also applied to the leaf of a book of any size. Until the mid-16th century, when printed pagination became common, books were *foliated, i.e.* numbered on the recto or front of the leaf only and not on the verso. (4) Printers call a page of MS. or printed matter a *folio* regardless of size.

In BOOK-KEEPING *Folio so-and-so* means page so-and-so, and also two pages which lie exposed at the same time, one containing the credit and the other the debit of one and the same account. So called because ledgers, etc., are made *in folio*.

In conveyances, MSS., type-written documents etc., 72 words, and in Parliamentary proceedings 90 words, make a *folio*, where it is used for assessing the length of a document. In the U.S.A. it is 100 words.

Folkland. An uncommon Anglo-Saxon term formerly explained as land which was the common property of the "folk" from which the king could grant land to his followers. The more accepted theory, initiated by Vinogradoff in 1893, is that folkland is land held by *folkright*. Folkland was subject to FOOD-RENT and other duties to the king, from which BOCLAND was exempt.

Folk-lore. The traditional beliefs, customs, popular superstitions and legends of a people. The word was coined in 1846 by W.

J. Thomas (1803–1885), editor of the *Athenæum* (*see under* ATHENÆUM CLUB), and founder of *Notes and Queries*.

Folk-mote. The meeting of the free men in the shire MOOT.

Follow. Follow-my-leader. A parlour game in which each player must exactly imitate the actions of the leader, or pay a forfeit.

Follow your nose. Go straight on.

He who follows truth too closely will have dirt kicked in his face. Be not too strict to pry into abuse.

To follow suit. To do as the person before you has done. A phrase from card-playing.

Follower. In addition to its usual meaning of one who follows a leader, the word was used in Victorian days to designate a maidservant's young man.

> Mrs Marker ... offers eighteen guineas ...
> Five servants kept ... No followers.
> DICKENS: *Nicholas Nickleby*, ch. xvi.

Folly. A fantastic or foolishly extravagant country seat or costly structure, built for amusement or vainglory. Fisher's Folly, a large and beautiful house in Bishopsgate, with pleasure-gardens, bowling green and hothouses, built by Jasper Fisher, one of the six clerks of CHANCERY, is an historical example. Queen Elizabeth I lodged there; in 1625 it was acquired by the Earl of Devonshire and its site is now occupied by Devonshire Square.

> Kirkby's castle, and Fisher's folly,
> Spinola's pleasure, and Megse's glory.
> STOWE: *Survey* (1603).

A classic example was that of Fonthill, Wiltshire, built by William Beckford (1760–1844), author of *Vathek*, at a cost of some £273,000. It took 18 years to complete and was sold in 1822 for £330,000. Three years later the tower, 260 ft. high, collapsed, destroying part of the house. With the growth of landscaping in the 18th century follies multiplied rapidly taking many forms. Towers, obelisks, mock ruins of castles and abbeys, chapels, temples, hermitages and grottoes became the pride of their owners. The style varied from "gothick" to classical and Chinese pagodas were not uncommon.

Palmerston's Follies. The nickname given to the line of forts surrounding Portsmouth and Plymouth, the building of which was supported by the Prime Minister, Lord Palmerston, in 1859 when he thought attack from NAPOLEON III's France was a possibility. They were called follies because they were never used for their original purposes. Fort Southwick, near Portsmouth, was used as the headquarters of the Commander-in-

Chief, Portsmouth, during World War II.

Fond. A foolish, fond parent. Here fond does not mean affectionate, but silly, from the obsolete *fon*, to act the fool, to become foolish (connected with our fun). Chaucer uses the word *fonne* for a simpleton (Reeve's Tale, 169); SHAKESPEARE has "fond desire", "fond wretch", "fond madwoman", etc.

Font, or **Fount.** A complete set of type of the same body and face with all the points, accents, figures, fractions, signs, etc., that ordinarily occur in printed books and papers. A complete fount (which includes italics) comprises over 200 separate pieces of type, without the special characters needed in AL-MANACS, astronomical and medical works, etc. The word is French, *fonte*, from *fondre* (to melt or cast). *See also* LETTER.

Fontange (fôn tonzh). A head-dress introduced in France about 1680, and named after Louis XIV's mistress, the Duchesse de Fontanges (1661–1681). It became progressively more extravagant in height and similar to the English *Tower* or *Commode* of the same period.

Fontarabia (font à rā′ bi à). Now called Fuenterrabia (Lat. *Fons rapidus*), near the Gulf of Gascony. Here, according to legend, CHARLEMAGNE and all his chivalry fell by the swords of the SARACENS. The French romancers say that, the rear of the king's army being cut to pieces, Charlemagne returned to life and avenged them by a complete victory.

> When Charlemain with all his peerage fell
> By Fontarabia.
> MILTON: *Paradise Lost*, I, 587.

Food. Food for powder. Soldiers; especially raw recruits levied in time of war; cannon fodder.

> *Prince:* I did never see such pitiful rascals.
> *Fal.:* Tut, tut; good enough to toss; food for powder; they'll fill a pit as well as better: tush, man, mortal men, mortal men.
> SHAKESPEARE: *Henry IV, Pt. I*, IV, ii.

Food for thought. Something to cogitate upon.

The food of the gods. *See* AMBROSIA; NECTAR.

To become food for worms, or **for the fishes.** To be dead and buried, or to be drowned.

Food-rent. In Anglo-Saxon England the victuals payable by a group of vills (townships) on the royal estates sufficient to provide for the king and his household for 24 hours. A food-rent used for the endowment of parish churches came to be called CHURCH SCOT.

Fool. A fool and his money are soon parted; Fortune favours fools; There's no fool like an old fool, etc., are among the "fool phrases" which need no explanation. Others are:

A fool's bolt is soon shot (SHAKESPEARE, *Henry V*, III, vii). Simpletons cannot wait for the fit and proper time, but waste their resources in random endeavours. The allusion is to bowmen, *bolt* being the arrow of a crossbow; the good soldier shot with a purpose, the foolish soldier at random. *Cp. Prov.* xxix, 11.

A fool's errand. A fruitless errand which is a waste of time.

A fool's paradise. A state of contentment or happiness founded on unreal, fanciful, or insecure foundations.

As the fool thinks, so the bell clinks. A foolish person believes what he desires. *See under* BELL.

At forty every man is a fool or his own physician. Said by Plutarch (*Treatise on the Preservation of Health*) to have been a saying of Tiberius. A man at the age of forty ought to have learnt enough about his own constitution to be able to keep himself healthy.

Every man hath a fool in his sleeve. No one is always wise; there is something of the fool in everyone.

Fools rush in where angels fear to tread. The unintelligent and thoughtless get involved where those with superior wisdom and understanding think twice.

> ... there they'll talk you dead:
> For fools rush in where angels fear to tread.
> Distrustful sense with modest caution speaks.
> POPE: *Essay on Criticism*, 624–626.

To be a fool for one's pains. To have worked ineffectively; to have had no reward for one's labours.

To be a fool to. Not to come up to; to be very inferior to; as, "Bagatelle is a fool to billiards."

To make a fool of someone. To mislead him; to trick him; to make him appear foolish.

Young men think old men fools, old men know young men are. An old saying quoted by Camden in his *Remains* (1605), as by a certain Dr. Metcalfe. It also occurs in Chapman's *All Fools*, V, ii (acted 1599).

To fool about, or **around.** To play the fool; to play around in an aimless fashion.

To fool away one's time, money, etc. To squander it; to fritter it away.

All Fools' Day. The first day of April. *See* APRIL FOOL.

April Fool. *See* APRIL.

Court Fools. From mediæval times until

the 17th century licensed fools or jesters were commonly kept at court; and frequently in the retinue of wealthy nobles. Holbein painted Sir Thomas More's jester, Patison, in his picture of the chancellor; the Earl of Morton, Scottish Regent (executed 1581), had a fool called Patrick Bonny; and as late as 1728 Swift wrote an epitaph on Dickie Pierce, the Earl of Suffolk's fool, who is buried in Berkeley Churchyard, Gloucestershire. *See also* DAGONET.

Among the most celebrated court fools are:

Rahère (founder of St. Bartholomew's Hospital), of Henry I (according to a tradition); John Scogan (*see* SCOGAN'S JESTS), of Edward IV; PATCH, of Elizabeth, wife of Henry VII; Will Somers, of Henry VIII; Jenny Colquhoun and James Geddes, of Mary Queen of Scots; Robert Grene, of Queen Elizabeth I; Archie Armstrong and Thomas Derrie, of James I; Muckle John, of CHARLES I, who was probably also the last court fool in England.

In France, Miton and Thévenin de St. Léger were fools of Charles V; Haincelin Coq belonged to Charles VI, and Guillaume Louel to Charles VII, Triboulet was the jester of Louis XII and Francis I; Brusquet, of Henri II; Sibilot and Chicot, of Henri III and IV; and l'Angély, of Louis XIII and Louis XIV.

In chess the French name for the "bishop" is *fou* (a fool) and they used to represent it in a fool's dress. *See* GONNELLA'S HORSE.

Gooseberry Fool. *See* GOOSEBERRY.

Tom Fool. *See under* TOM.

The Feast of Fools. A kind of clerical SATURNALIA, popular in the MIDDLE AGES and not successfully suppressed until the REFORMATION, and even later in France. The feast was usually centred on a cathedral and most commonly held on the Feasts of St. STEPHEN (26 December), St. JOHN (27 December), HOLY INNOCENTS (28 December). The mass was burlesqued and braying often took the place of the customary responses. Obscene jests and dances were common as well as the singing of indecent songs. The ass was a central feature and the **Feast of Asses** was sometimes a separate festival. *Cp.* BOY BISHOP.

The wisest fool in Christendom. James I was so called by Henri IV of France, who learnt the phrase from Sully.

Foolscap. Properly the jester's cap and bells or the conical paper hat of a DUNCE. The standard size of printing paper measuring $13\frac{1}{2} \times 17$ in. and of writing paper measuring $13\frac{1}{4} \times 16\frac{1}{2}$ in. took their name from an ancient watermark showing a fool's head and cap.

Fool's gold. *See under* GOLD.

Foot. The foot as a measure of length (12 in., $\frac{1}{3}$ of a yard, or 0.3047075 of a metre) is common to most peoples, and has never varied much more than does the length of men's feet, from which the name is taken.

In prosody, the term denotes a division in verse which consists of a certain number of syllables (or pauses), one of which is stressed. Here the term, which comes from Greece, refers to beating time with the foot.

Enter a house right foot foremost (*Petronius*). It is unlucky to enter a house or to leave one's room left foot foremost. Augustus was very superstitious on this point. PYTHAGORAS taught that it is necessary to put the shoe on the right foot first.

First foot. *See under* FIRST.

How are your poor feet? A cry said to have originated at the Great Exhibition of 1851 (*see* CRYSTAL PALACE), from the excessive amount of tramping about involved in visiting its galleries.

I have not yet got my foot in. I am not yet familiar and at home with the work. The allusion is to the preliminary exercises in Roman foot-races. While the starting signal was awaited the contestants made essays at jumping, running, etc., to limber up. This was "getting one's foot in" for the race. *Cp.* TO GET ONE'S HAND IN *under* HAND.

To be carried out feet foremost. To be dead.

To cast oneself at someone's feet. To be entirely submissive to him, to throw oneself on his mercy.

To fall, or **land on one's feet.** To secure a good position; to be fortunately placed. As a cat luckily lands on its feet.

To find one's feet. To get on one's feet; to settle down and develop a grip on one's work.

To have feet of clay. Said of someone hitherto held in high regard or in an important position who shows disappointing weaknesses of character. The allusion is to *Dan.* ii, 31–45. The image in Nebuchadnezzar's dream had a head of gold, breast and arms of silver, belly and thighs of brass, legs of iron and feet of iron and clay.

To have one's foot on another's neck. To have him at one's mercy; to tyrannize over, or domineer over him completely. *See Josh.* x, 24.

To measure another's foot by one's own last. To apply one's personal standards to the conduct or actions of another; to judge people by oneself.

To put one's best foot foremost. To walk as fast as possible, with all dispatch; to try to make a good impression.

To put one's foot down. To take a firm stand, to refuse or insist upon something firmly and finally. In driving, to depress the accelerator and drive fast.

To put one's foot in it. To perpetrate a blunder, to make a FAUX PAS, to get into trouble. The allusion is obvious. There is a famous Irish BULL. "Every time I open my mouth I put my foot in it".

To set a man on his feet. To start him off in business, etc., especially after he has "come a CROPPER".

To set on foot. To set going.

To show the cloven foot, or **hoof.** To betray an evil intention. An allusion to the DEVIL who is represented with a cloven hoof.

To trample under foot. To oppress, or outrage; to treat with the greatest contempt and discourtesy.

With one foot in the grave. In a dying state.

To foot it. To walk the distance instead of riding; also to dance.

> Lo! how finely the Graces can it foote.
> To the instrument:
> They dancen deffly, and singen soote,
> In their meriment.
>
> SPENSER: *Shepheard's Calendar: April.*

To foot the bill. To pay it; to promise to pay the account by signing one's name at the foot of the bill.

Washing the feet. *See* MAUNDY THURSDAY; MAUNDS.

He is on good footing with the world. He stands well with the world. *Cp.* TO BE ON A GOOD FOOTING.

To be on a good footing (with someone). To be on friendly terms with a person; to be in good standing.

To pay your footing. To give money for drink when you first enter a trade, etc. Entry money for being allowed to put your foot in the premises occupied by fellow craftsmen. *Cp.* GARNISH.

Footloose and fancy free. Unfettered, unattached to a member of the opposite sex.

Footmen. *See* RUNNING FOOTMEN.

Footlights. To appear before the footlights. To appear on the stage. The footlights are placed near the front edge of the stage.

Fop's Alley. An old name for a promenade in a theatre, especially the central passage between the stalls (right and left in the opera-house).

Forbidden. Forbidden City. Lhasa (the seat of the gods), the ancient religious and political capital of Tibet, some 12,000 ft. above sea level. The palace of the Dalai-Lama or Grand Lama stands on the neighbouring Potala hill. This sacred city of Lamaist BUDDHISM containing fifteen monasteries fell under Chinese control (*c.* 1720) and when, in 1959, the Tibetans unsuccessfully tried to cast off the Chinese yoke, the Dalai-Lama fled to India. Its first European mention was by Friar Odoric, the famous traveller (*c.* 1330). Long closed to Europeans, hence the epithet, it is still largely a forbidden city.

Forbidden Fruit. Forbidden or unlawful pleasure of any kind, especially illicit love. The reference is to *Gen*. ii, 17, "But of the tree of knowledge of good and evil, thou shalt not eat of it." According to Mohammedan tradition the forbidden fruit partaken of by ADAM and EVE was the banyan or Indian fig.

Forcible Feeble. *See* FEEBLE.

Fore! A cry of warning used by golfers before driving.

To come to the fore. To stand forth; to stand out prominently; to distinguish oneself.

To the fore. In the front rank; eminent.

Fore-and-aft. The whole length of the ship from stem to stern; lengthwise. Fore here is the *fore* or front part and *aft* the after or rear part. Sailing vessels are classed as square-rigged or fore-and-aft rigged, the latter having their sails extending from the fore-and-aft line to the lee side. Such vessels carry no square sails and can sail closer to the wind. In the Royal Navy a seaman's uniform of cap, jumper, and bell-bottomed trousers is termed *square-rig*, while the peaked cap, jacket, and trousers of petty officers and above is called *fore-and-aft rig*.

Forecastle, or **fo'c's'le** (fōk' sŭl). So called because anciently the fore part of a ship was raised and protected like a castle, so that it could command the enemy's deck. Similarly the after part (now termed the QUARTER DECK) was called the *after castle*. Soldiers were stationed in these castles to carry on the fighting. It has always been customary to place the crew's quarters in the fo'c's'le and the officers' quarters aft.

Forestick. The front log laid across the ANDIRONS on a wood fire, which holds the others in. Its opposite number at the back is the *backlog*.

Forest City. Cleveland, Ohio, from its many well-shaded, tree-lined streets.

Forest Courts. The ancient courts established for the conduct of forest business and the administration of the forest laws, the main aim of which was to preserve the wild animals for the royal chase. Such laws existed in Saxon England and were reinforced by the Norman kings. William I created the New Forest in the sense that he placed the area under Forest Law, and the forests reached their greatest extent under Henry II (1154–1189). The young Henry III was forced to concede a Forest Charter in 1217 modifying the laws and disafforesting lands afforested by Henry II. *See* REGARD; ROBIN HOOD; SWANIMOTE; WOODMOTE.

Forgery (O.F. *forgier*, Lat. *fabricare*, to fabricate or make). Generally speaking a forgery is an attempt to pass off as genuine some piece of spurious work or writing with the intent to deceive or defraud. It is not always easy to distinguish a forgery and an *imposture*. Among the notable examples given here, the ROWLEY POEMS (*see below*) are perhaps impostures rather than forgeries. *See also* OSSIAN.

Billies and Charlies. Bogus mediæval metal objects, chiefly plaques, cast in lead or an alloy of lead and copper known as cock metal, and artificially pitted with acid. Between 1847 and 1848 William Smith and Charles Eaton (Billy and Charley) produced these objects by the thousand and planted them on sites being excavated in and around London. Many simple folk and the more naïve collectors were taken in, though the crudity of the work was obvious. The business was exposed at a meeting of the British Archæological Association in 1858.

The Drake Brass Plate. Sir Francis Drake during his voyage of circumnavigation (1577–1580), anchored off the Californian coast in 1579 and set up a brass plate naming the territory New Albion and claiming it in the name of Queen Elizabeth. In 1936 the plate was said to have been found near San Francisco and the inscription seemed to be reasonably authentic although some authorities expressed doubt. A replica was, in due course, presented to Queen Elizabeth II which is kept in Buckland Abbey, Drake's Devonshire property, now a museum. In 1977 a reported analysis of the composition of the brass by the Lawrence Berkeley Institute of the University of California and the Research Laboratory for Archaeology at Oxford found that it was of late 19th- or early 20th-century manufacture.

Hitler Diaries. In April 1983 *The Sunday Times* reported the discovery of 60 volumes of Hitler's diaries which had been acquired by the Hamburg colour magazine *Stern* for £2,460,000 and delivered to them by their reporter Gert Heidemann. They were said to have been salvaged from an aircraft wrecked in 1945 and found in a hayloft. Professor Hugh Trevor-Roper (Lord Dacre) had vouched for their authenticity and *The Sunday Times* (after paying *Stern* for publication rights) obtained two volumes (1932 and 1935) for testing. Dr. Julius Grant, a chemical expert, proved that the paper in the diaries was not in use until after World War II. Two weeks after their alleged discovery the Bonn government also declared them to be forgeries. Heidemann revealed that he had obtained them from a Stuttgart dealer in military relics, Konrad Fischer, whose real name was Kujau and the latter confessed to forgery. Both were imprisoned in May 1983, brought to trial in August 1984 and sentenced in July 1985. Kujau was jailed for 4 years 6 months for forgery and Heidemann 4 years 8 months for fraud.

The Ireland Forgeries. One of the most famous literary forgers was William Henry Ireland (1777–1835), the son of a bookseller and amateur antiquarian. When only 19, young Ireland produced a number of seemingly ancient leases and other documents purporting to be in SHAKESPEARE's handwriting, including a love poem to "Anna Hatherrawaye". Emboldened by their acceptance he next came out with two "lost" Shakespeare plays—*Vortigern* and *Henry II*. Ignoring the suspicions of Kemble, Sheridan produced *Vortigern* at DRURY LANE in 1796. During the rehearsals Mrs. Siddons and Mrs. Palmer resigned their roles and Kemble helped to ensure the play was laughed off the stage. When he spoke the line "When this solemn mockery is o'er", the house yelled and hissed until the curtain fell. Meanwhile Malone and Steevens had studied the *Miscellaneous Papers*, said to be Shakespeare's, and had declared them forgeries. Ireland confessed later in the same year. His motive appears to have been a craving to secure the regard and admiration of his father, whose antiquarian interests amounted to an obsession.

The Macaroni parson. The Revd. Dr. William Dodd (1729–1777) was so nicknamed from his expensive habits which resulted in a famous forgery. He graduated in mathematics at Cambridge in 1750 and was soon ordained, becoming chaplain of the recently opened Magdalen hospital in London for unfortunate and fallen women, and his sermons soon attracted a fashionable following. He was editor of *The Christian Magazine* (1760–1767) and published numerous books during his lifetime. He became a royal

439

chaplain in 1763 but his attempt to secure the rich living of St. George's Hanover Square by improperly offering money through the Lord Chancellor's wife cost him his chaplaincy. He held various other preferments during his career but became deeply in debt and signed a cheque for £4,200 in the name of his former pupil, the 5th Lord Chesterfield. When the forgery was discovered he repaid much of the money but was imprisoned in NEWGATE and sentenced to death. He received support from Dr. Johnson and many others but George III refused clemency to his one-time chaplain who was hanged in July 1777. *See* MACARONI.

The Pictures of Tom Keating. Keating (1918–1984), beginning as a picture restorer, produced about 2,000 drawings and paintings and sold them as originals by Constable, Gainsborough, Turner, Rembrandt and others. He admitted they were fakes in 1976.

The Pigott Forgeries. In April 1887, *The Times* published in facsimile a letter attributed to Charles Stewart Parnell, the Irish leader, condoning the PHOENIX PARK MURDERS. Parnell denounced this as a forgery, but *The Times* continued to publish its damaging articles on "Parnellism and Crime" which deeply influenced English opinion. In 1888 O'Donnell, one of those besmirched, sued *The Times* for libel. From the judicial inquiry which resulted, the letters were found to be forged by Richard Pigott, who sold them to *The Times* for a large sum, money being his only motive. *The Times* had to pay £250,000 in costs. Pigott fled to Madrid and shot himself when arrest was impending.

The Piltdown Skull, or **Piltdown Man.** In 1908 and 1911 Charles Dawson of Lewes "found" two pieces of a highly mineralized human skull in a gravel bed near Piltdown Common, Sussex. By 1912 he and Sir Arthur Smith Woodward had discovered the whole skull. This was thought to be that of a new genus of man and was called *Eoanthropus Dawsoni*. It came to be accepted as such by most prehistorians, archaeologists, etc., although a few were sceptical. In 1953 J. S. Weiner, K. P. Oakley and W. E. Le Gros Clark issued a report (*Bulletin of the British Museum* (Natural History), Vol. II, No. 3) announcing that the Piltdown mandible was a fake, in reality the jaw of a modern ape, the rest of the skull being that of *Homo sapiens*. The hoax, which took in most of the experts, was apparently planned by William Sollas, Professor of Geology at Oxford (1897–1937), through his dislike of

Sir Arthur Smith Woodward.

The Poems of Ossian. *See* OSSIAN.

The Protocols of the Elders of Zion. *See under* PROTOCOL.

Psalmanazar, George. *See* PSALMANAZAR.

The Rowley Poems. Certain poems written by Thomas Chatterton (1752–1770), and said by him to have been the work of a 15th-century priest of Bristol called Thomas Rowley (a fictitious character). Chatterton began to write them before he was 15 and, after having been refused by Dodsley, they were published in 1769. Many prominent connoisseurs and litterateurs, including Horace Walpole (until he consulted friends), were hoaxed.

The Turin Shroud. The shroud of twill linen kept in Turin Cathedral and claimed to be that which wrapped the body of Christ after His crucifixion. The POPE agreed to RADIOCARBON DATING in 1987 and in 1988 the Archbishop of Turin appointed the Oxford Research Laboratory for Archaeology, the Department of Physics of Arizona University and the Swiss Federal Institute of Technology at Zurich, to date the shroud, pieces of which were given to these institutes in April 1988. The results were announced on 13 October and the cloth was dated between 1260 and 1390. There is no historical evidence that it was known before the 14th century. Although not accepted by all the general conclusion is that the shroud is a mediæval forgery.

The Vermeer Forgeries. Hans (Henri) van Meegeren (1889–1947) began his series of brilliant fakes of Dutch masters in 1937 with *The Supper at Emmaus* which was sold as a "Vermeer" for 550,000 gulden. It was, of course, vetted by the experts! His intention seems to have been to indulge his contempt and hatred of the art critics by a superlative hoax, but the financial success of his first fake led to others, mostly "Vermeers". Discovery only came in 1945 when Allied commissioners were seeking to restore to their former owners the art treasures which had found their way to Germany during the war. Among Goering's collection was an unknown Vermeer—*The Woman taken in Adultery*—and its original vendor was found to be van Meegeren. Sale of such a work of national importance involved a charge of collaboration with the enemy. To escape the heavy penalty, van Meegeren confessed to the faking of 14 Dutch masterpieces, 9 of which had been sold for a total of 7,167,000 gulden, and to prove his story agreed to paint another "old masterpiece" in prison in the presence of the experts. He was sentenced to one year's imprisonment in October 1947 but died on 30 December.

The Vinland Map. Norse exploration from the end of the 10th century led to the discovery of part of North America. According to the Norse Saga, *Flateyjarbók*, "When spring came they made ready and left, and Leif named the land after its fruits, and called it *Vinland*". In 1957 the discovery of a map of the N.E. American coast was announced and said to be the most exciting cartographic find of the century. Supposedly drawn about 1440, it substantially preceded the voyages of Columbus (1492) and of John Cabot (1497), thus conclusively establishing the extent of the Viking explorations. It was presented to Yale University by an anonymous giver in 1965. In 1974 Yale announced that it was a fake. The pigment of the ink with which it was drawn was found to contain titanium dioxide, first used in the 1920s.

The Zinoviev Letter, or **Red Letter Scare.** A letter, which purported to be signed by Zinoviev, president of the Presidium of the Third Communist International, summoning the British Communist Party to intensify its revolutionary activities and to subvert the armed forces of the crown, was published (25 October 1924), four days before a General Election. It helped to promote a "red scare" and possibly increased an almost certain CONSERVATIVE majority. Many Labour leaders held it to be a forgery and its authenticity was denied by the Russians. In December 1966 *The Sunday Times* published an article establishing that the letter was a forgery perpetrated by a group of WHITE RUSSIAN *émigrés*, at the same time suggesting that certain leaders at the Conservative Central Office knew that it was a fake, although the Conservative party as a whole assumed it to be genuine. The "informant" was paid for his services.

Forget-me-not. According to German legend this flower takes its name from the last words of a knight, who was drowned while trying to pick some from the riverside for his lady. The botanical name *myosotis* (mouse-ear) refers to the shape of the leaves.

Forgotten Man, The. A phrase derived from W. G. Summer (1840–1910), the American sociologist, to describe the decent, hardworking, ordinary citizen. It was later popularized by F. D. Roosevelt in 1932 during the Presidential election campaign, although he actually used the expression before his nomination. He advocated a NEW DEAL and appealed to the "forgotten man at the bottom of the economic pyramid".

Fork. To fork out. Fork is old thieves' slang for a finger, hence "to fork out" is to produce and hand over, to pay up.

Fingers were made before forks. See FINGERS.

Forked cap. A bishop's MITRE; so called by John Skelton (*c.* 1460–1529). It is cleft or forked.

The forks. The gallows (Lat. *furca*). Among the Romans the word also meant a kind of yoke, with two arms stretching over the shoulders, to which the criminal's hands were tied. The punishment was of three degrees of severity; (1) the *furca ignominiosa*; (2) the *furca pœnalis*; and (3) the *furca capitalis*. The first, for slight offences, consisted of carrying the *furca* (usually weighted) on the shoulders; the second involved scourging as well; and the third being scourged to death.

The Caudine Forks. See CAUDINE.

Forlorn Hope. This is the Dutch *verloren hoop*, the lost squad or troop. The French equivalent is *enfants perdus*, lost children. The *forlorn hope* was a picked body of men sent in front to begin an attack, particularly the body of volunteers who first entered the breach in the storming of defensive fortifications. The phrase is now usually applied to a body of men selected for some desperate enterprise.

Hoop means a troop or company, and word play or mistaken etymology have resulted in the phrase being used to mean a "faint hope" or an enterprise offering little chance of success.

Form (O.Fr. *forme*, Lat. *forma*). Shape, figure, manner, etc. *Good* or *bad form* is behaving in accordance—or otherwise—with the established conventions of good manners and behaviour.

> We'll eat the dinner and have a dance together, or we shall transgress all form.
> STEELE: *Tender Husband*, V, ii.

Forma pauperis (fôr′ ma pou′ per is) (Lat. in the character of a pauper, *i.e.*, as a poor man). To sue or defend an action *in forma pauperis* was when a person was unable to bring or defend a High Court action because of inability to pay the legal expenses, and arrangements were made for such to receive legal services gratuitously. The Legal Aid and Advice Act, 1949, replaced these proceedings although appeals *in forma pauperis* may still be taken to the HOUSE OF LORDS.

Fortiter in re (fôr′ ti tĕr in rē) (Lat.). Firmness in doing what is to be done; an unflinching resolution to persevere to the end. See SUAVITER.

Fortunatus. A hero of mediæval legend (derived from Eastern sources) who possessed an inexhaustible purse, a wishing cap, etc. He appears in a German *Volksbuch* of 1509. Hans Sachs dramatized the story in 1553, and Dekker's *Pleasant Comedy of Old Fortunatus* was first performed in December 1599.

You have found Fortunatus's purse. You are in luck's way.

Fortune. Fortune favours the brave. The expression is found in Terence—"Fortis fortuna adjuvat" (*Phormio*, I, iv); also in VIRGIL—"Audentis fortuna adjuvat" (*Æn*. X. 284), and many other classic writers.

Fortunate Islands. An ancient name for the Canary Islands; also, for any imaginary lands set in distant seas, like the "Islands of the Blest".

> Their place of birth alone is mute
> To sounds that echo farther west
> Than your sire's Islands of the Blest.
> BYRON: *Don Juan*, canto III, lxxxvi, 2.

Forty. A number of frequent occurrence in the SCRIPTURES and hence formerly treated as, in a manner, sacrosanct. Moses was "in the mount forty days and forty nights"; Elijah was fed by ravens for forty days; the rain of the FLOOD fell forty days; and another forty days expired before NOAH opened the window of the ark; forty days was the period of embalming; Nineveh had forty days to repent; Our Lord fasted forty days; He was seen forty days after His Resurrection, etc.

St. SWITHIN betokens forty days' rain or dry weather; a QUARANTINE extended to forty days; in Old English law forty days was the limit for the payment of the fine for manslaughter; a stranger, at the end of forty days, was compelled to be enrolled in the TITHING; the privilege of SANCTUARY was for forty days; the widow was allowed to remain in her husband's house for forty days after his decease; a KNIGHT enjoined forty days' service of his tenant; a new-made burgess had to forfeit forty pence unless he built a house within forty days, etc., etc.

Field of the Forty Footsteps. *See under* FIELD.

Fool or physician at forty. *See* FOOL.

Forty stripes save one. The Jews were forbidden by MOSAIC LAW to inflict more than forty stripes on an offender, and for fear of breaking the law, they stopped short of the number. If the scourge contained three lashes, thirteen strokes would equal "forty save one".

The THIRTY-NINE ARTICLES of the CHURCH OF ENGLAND used sometimes to be called "the forty stripes save one" by theological students.

Forty winks. A short nap.

The Forty Immortals, or simply **The Forty.** The members of the French Academy, who number forty.

The Hungry Forties. *See* HUNGRY.

The Roaring Forties. A sailor's term for the stormy regions between 40° and 50° south latitude, where heavy westerly winds (known as Brave West Winds) prevail. In the days of sail, owing to these winds, mariners used often to return to Europe via Cape Horn instead of the Cape of Good Hope. The term has also been applied to the North Atlantic crossing between Europe and America between 40° and 50° north latitude.

> Twice I have entered the Roaring Forties and been driven out by gales and squalls. The last one was on Tuesday when I handled the boat badly and it was damaged.
> SIR FRANCIS CHICHESTER: *Article in The Sunday Times* (30 October 1966).

The Forty-Five. The name given to the rebellion of 1745 led by Charles Edward Stuart, the Young PRETENDER. He landed on Eriskay Island (23 July) and raised his standard at Glenfinnan (19 August). Joined by many Scottish clansmen, he proclaimed the Old Pretender King, as James III, and defeated Sir John Cope at Prestonpans (21 September), and marched south reaching Derby (4 December). His plan to proceed to London was frustrated by the advice of his supporters and lack of support from English JACOBITES. He retreated to SCOTLAND and was decisively defeated by the Duke of Cumberland at Culloden Moor (16 April 1746). The Young Pretender escaped to France (20 September) with the help of FLORA MACDONALD and others. Cumberland earned the nickname "Butcher" for the subsequent reprisals taken against the Highlanders.

"Number 45" is the celebrated number of John Wilkes's *North Briton* (23 April 1763), in which the KING'S SPEECH referring to the Treaty of Paris of that year as "honourable to my Crown and beneficial to my people" was held to be a lie. *See* GENERAL WARRANTS.

Forty-niners. Those who took part in the Californian gold rush, after the discovery of gold there in 1848. Most of the adventurers arrived in 1849, coming from many parts of the world, including Australia and China.

> In a cavern, in a canyon,
> Excavated for a mine,
> Dwelt a miner, forty-niner,
> And his daughter Clementine.
> PERCY MONTROSE: *Clementine*.

Forty-two Line Bible, The. *See* BIBLE, SOME SPECIALLY NAMED EDITIONS.

Forty Years On. This oft quoted phrase

forms the opening of the famous Harrow Football Song, the first four lines of which are given below. It is also the school song. The words by Edward Bowen were set to music by his colleague John Farmer, who directed the music at Harrow from 1862 to 1885.

> Forty years on, when afar and asunder
> Parted are those who are singing today,
> When you look back and forgetfully wonder
> What you were like in your work and your play ...

Forwards, Marshal. Blücher (1742–1819) was called *Marschall Vorwärts*, from his constant exhortation to his soldiers in the campaigns preceding Waterloo. *Vorwärts!* always *Vorwärts!*

Fosse, or **Foss Way.** One of the principal Roman roads in Britain. It runs on the line Axmouth — Ilchester — Bath — Cirencester — Leicester — Lincoln. Its name derives from the ditch (Lat. *fossa*) on each side of the road. *Cp.* ERMINE STREET.

Fou. A Scottish expression for drunk. It is a variant of full.

> The clachan yill had made me canty
> I was na fou, but just had plenty.
>   BURNS: *Death and Dr. Hornbook.*

Foul anchor. When the ship's cable has taken a turn round the anchor. It was used as an official seal by Charles Howard, Earl of Nottingham (1536–1624), when Lord High Admiral, and later as a badge on naval uniform buttons, cap badges and the Admiralty crest.

Foul-weather Jack. Admiral John Byron (1723–1786), grandfather of the poet, said to have been as notorious for foul weather as Queen Victoria was for fine (*see* QUEEN'S WEATHER). Admiral Sir John Norris (*c.* 1660–1749) was also so called.

Fountain of Arethusa. *See* ALPHEUS AND ARETHUSA.

Fountain of Youth. In popular legend, a fountain with the power of restoring youth. Much sought after, at one time it was supposed to be in one of the Bahama Islands. Ponce de León, discoverer of FLORIDA, set out in search of BIMINI.

Four. Four-ale. Small ALE or cheap ale, originally sold at fourpence per quart. Hence *four-ale bar* as a name in a public house or inn for the public bar, where prices are lowest.

Four-eyes. An old and somewhat derisive nickname often used by children when teasing a bespectacled acquaintance.

The Four Corners of the Earth. Generally speaking, the uttermost ends of the earth, the remotest parts of the world.

In 1965 members of the Johns Hopkins Applied Physics Laboratory named the four corners of the earth as being in Ireland, south-east of the Cape of Good Hope, west of the Peruvian coast, and between New Guinea and Japan. Each of these "corners" (of several thousand square miles in area) is some 120 ft. above the geodetic mean and the gravitational pull is measurably greater at these locations.

The Four Freedoms. These were defined by President Franklin D. Roosevelt in his message to Congress, 6 January 1941, as the freedom of speech, and expression, the freedom of worship, and the freedom from fear and want. They were to be the aims of the U.S.A. and ultimately of the world. The occasion was his proposal to make the U.S.A. "the arsenal of democracy" and to extend Lease-Lend to Britain.

Four Horsemen of the Apocalypse. In *The Revelation of St. John the Divine* (ch. vi), four agents of destruction, two being agents of war and two of famine and pestilence. The first appeared on a white horse, the second on a red horse, the third on a black horse, and the fourth on a pale horse.

Vicente Blasco Ibáñez (1867–1928), the Spanish writer, published a novel of this title in 1916 which appeared in English in 1918.

The Four Hundred. A late 19th-century term for New York's most exclusive social set, which came into general use as a designation of social exclusiveness. In 1892, Mrs. William Astor finding the need to limit her guests to the capacity of her ballroom, which was asserted to be suitable for 400 guests, asked Ward McAllister, the self-appointed organizer of New York society, to prune her invitations. McAllister is also reported to have claimed that there were only 400 people in New York city who could claim to be "society". *Cp.* UPPER TEN *under* TEN.

The History of the Four Kings (Livre des Quatre Rois). A pack of cards. In a French pack the four kings are CHARLEMAGNE, David, ALEXANDER THE GREAT and CÆSAR. *See* COURT CARDS *under* COURT.

Four Letters, The. *See* TETRAGRAMMATON.

Four-letter man. A EUPHEMISM for one who is sufficiently obnoxious to be designated by certain of the FOUR-LETTER WORDS.

Four-letter words. The long established term for the blunt O.E. words for certain parts and functions of the body. Such words, not used in polite society, gained a much wider currency during the two World Wars and have since attained a degree of literary usage, especially after the *Lady Chatterley's Lover* case in 1960, when Penguin Books were acquitted of issuing an obscene publication. The most widely used of these words has since found its way into the *Oxford History of England* (vol. XV), if only in a footnote. The attempt to restore such words to normal usage is somewhat curious in a society which has converted "W.C.s" and "lavatories" into "toilets", and "urinals" into "Gentlemen".

The Annals of the Four Masters is the name usually given to a collection of old Irish chronicles published (1632–1636) as *Annals of the Kingdom of Ireland*. The Four Masters (authors or compilers) were Michael O'Clery (1575–1643), Conaire his brother, his cousin Cucoigriche O'Clery (d. 1664), and Fearfeasa O'Mulconry.

Four-minute men. In the U.S.A. during World War I, the name given to the members of a volunteer organization some 75,000 strong who, in 1917–1918, set out to promote the sale of Liberty Loan Bonds and stir up support for the war in Europe. They gave talks of four minutes duration to church congregations, cinema audiences, lodges, etc.

Four-minute mile. The running of a mile in four minutes was for many years the hoped-for achievement of first-class athletes. The rigorous training and timed pacing of P. J. Nurmi (Finland) achieved a time of 4 mins. 10·4 secs. in 1924 but R. G. Bannister (b. 1929) was the first man to reach the goal in 1954. He achieved a *sub-four-minute mile* at Oxford in 1954 (3 mins. 59·4 secs.) after constant and carefully planned efforts. In July 1979 Sebastian Coe achieved a new world record of 3 mins. 49 secs. only to be beaten almost immediately by Steve Ovett, who reduced this time by one-fifth of a second. In 1981 Coe ran the mile in 3 mins. 47·33 secs.

> The four-minute mile had become rather like an Everest—a challenge to the human spirit.
>
> R. BANNISTER: *First Four Minutes*, ch. xiii.

Four Sons of Aymon. *See* AYMON.

Fourlegs, Old. Nickname for the coelacanth, a species of fish held to be extinct for millions of years until a specimen was caught in 1938 off East London, South Africa. Another was caught off the Comoro Islands, north of Madagascar, in 1952 and subsequently numerous others. The lobate fins, which could be used more or less as limbs, give rise to the name.

Fourth dimension. As a mathematical concept, a hypothetical dimension, whose relation to the recognized three of length, breadth and thickness, is analogous to their relation with each other. Albert Einstein in 1921 introduced time as the fourth dimension in his THEORY OF RELATIVITY. The expression is also sometimes used to describe something beyond the limits of normal experience.

Fourth Estate. *See under* ESTATE.

Fourth of July. *See* INDEPENDENCE DAY.

The Fourth of June. King George III's birthday and SPEECH DAY at Eton. The day is celebrated with a procession of boats, cricket matches, and fireworks. George III was a particular patron of the school.

Fourth Party. The nickname of a group of four members of the CONSERVATIVE opposition, who harassed Gladstone's second administration (1880–1885). It consisted of Sir Henry Drummond Wolff, Sir John Gorst, A. J. Balfour and their leader, Lord Randolph Churchill. They seized their first opening during the disputes over Bradlaugh's admission to Parliament, when as an atheist he refused to take the Parliamentary oath of allegiance. They made every use of their political opportunities against the government, and strongly criticized their own front bench under the somewhat ineffective leadership of Sir Stafford Northcote. The name "Fourth Party" arose when a member of the Commons referred to two parties (LIBERAL and Conservative) and Parnell, the Irish leader, called out "three"; Randolph Churchill then interjected to make it "four".

Fourth Republic. The French Republic established in 1946 which replaced the provisional governments that followed the collapse of the VICHY régime after D-DAY. Essentially a continuation of the THIRD REPUBLIC, it gave way to the *Fifth Republic* in 1958.

Fourierism. A utopian socialist system advocated by François Marie Charles Fourier (1772–1837) of Besançon. Society was to be organized into "phalanges" each consisting of about 1,600 people sharing common buildings (the *phalanstère*) and working about 5,000 acres of land, with suitable facilities for the development of handicrafts and sources of amusement and a harmonious social life. The most menial tasks were to be the best rewarded out of the common gain and pleasant labour the least. The "phalanges" were to be linked together in suitable groups and finally into one great federation with the capital Constantinople. A number of short-lived Fourierist phalanges were established in the U.S.A. in the middle years of the 19th century but all had disappeared by 1860.

Fourteen. In its connection with Henri IV

and Louis XIV of France are the following curious coincidences:

HENRI IV:

There are 14 letters in the name Henri de Bourbon. He was the 14th King of France and Navarre on the extinction of the family of Navarre. He was born on 14 December, 1553, the sum of which year amounts to 14. His first wife, Marguerite de Valois, was born on 14 May 1553; on 14 March 1590 he won his decisive victory at Ivry and on 14 May 1590 a great ecclesiastical and military demonstration was organized in Paris against him. Gregory XIV placed Henri under the papal ban, and on 14 May 1610 Henri was assassinated by Ravaillac.

LOUIS XIV:

The fourteenth king of this name. He ascended the throne in 1643, the sum of which figures equals 14. He died in 1715, the sum of which figures equals 14. He reigned 77 years, the sum of which figures equals 14. He was born in 1638 and died in 1715, which added together equals 3353, the sum of which figures equals 14.

Fourteen Hundred. The cry raised on the Stock Exchange to give notice that a stranger has entered the "HOUSE". The term is said to have been in use in Defoe's time, and to have originated when, for a considerable period, the number of members had remained stationary at 1,399.

Fourteen Points. The 14 conditions laid down by President Woodrow Wilson (1856–1924) as those on which the Allies were prepared to make peace with Germany on the conclusion of World War I. He outlined them in a speech to Congress on 8 January 1918 and they were eventually accepted as the basis for the peace. They included the evacuation by Germany of all allied territory, the restoration of an independent Poland, freedom of the seas, reduction of armaments, and OPEN DIPLOMACY.

Fowler, The. Henry I (876–936), son of Otto, Duke of Saxony and King of Germany from 919 to 936. According to 11th-century tradition, when the deputies announced to him his election to the throne, they found him fowling with a HAWK on his fist.

Fox. As a name for the old English broadsword, *fox* probably refers to a maker's mark of a dog, wolf, or fox. Such swords were manufactured by Julian del Rei of Toledo, whose trade mark was a little dog, mistaken for a fox.

> O signieur Dew, thou diest on a point of fox,
> Except, O signieur, thou do give to me
> Egregious ransom.
>
> SHAKESPEARE: *Henry V*, IV, iv.

The Old Fox. Marshal Soult (1769–1851) was so nicknamed from his strategic talents and fertility of resource.

Reynard the Fox. *See* REYNARD.

A case of the fox and the grapes. Said of one who wants something badly, but cannot obtain it, and so tries to pretend that he does not really want it at all. *See* GRAPES.

A fox's sleep. A sleep with one eye open. Assumed indifference to what is going on. *Cp.* TO FOX.

A wise fox will never rob his neighbour's henroost. It would soon be found out, so he goes farther afield where he is less likely to be discovered.

Every fox must pay his skin to the furrier. The crafty will be taken in by their own wiliness.

I gave him a flap with a fox-tail. I cajoled him; I made a fool of him. The fox-tail was one of the badges of the MOTLEY, and *to flap with a fox-tail* is to treat one like a fool.

To set a fox to keep the geese (Lat. *ovem lupo committere*). Said of one who entrusts his money to sharpers.

To fox. To steal or cheat; to keep an eye on somebody without seeming to do so; to baffle. A dog, a fox, and a weasel sleep, as they say, "with one eye open".

Foxed. A print or page of a book stained with reddish-brown marks is said to be "foxed" because of its colour. *Foxed* is also used to imply "baffled" or "bewildered", and fuddled or the worse for liquor.

Fox-fire. The phosphoric light, without heat, which occurs on decaying matter. It is the Fr. *faux* or false.

Foxglove (*Digitalis purpurea*). The flower is named from the animal and the glove. It is not known how the fox came to be associated with it, but one suggestion is that it is a corruption of "folk's glove", folks being the fairies or little people. In Welsh it is called *menygellyllon* (elves' gloves) or *menyg y llwynog* (fox's gloves) and in Ireland it is called a *fairy thimble*.

Fox-hole. A small slit trench for one or more men.

There are no atheists in foxholes. *See* ATHEISTS.

Fox-trot. The short quick walking pace, as of a fox. "Only a fox's step away" means a very small distance away. It is also the name of a ballroom dance originating in America, popular from the 1920s until the 1950s.

Fra Diavolo. *See* DIAVOLO.

Frame-up. A cooked-up criminal charge against an innocent victim, a trumped-up affair. A term of American origin (from the early 1900s), derived from the framed photographs of criminals kept by law-enforcement agencies.

France. *See* FRANKS.

Francesca da Rimini (frăn ches′ kà da rim′ i ni). Daughter of Guido da Polenta, Lord of Ravenna. Her story is told in DANTE's *Inferno* (canto v). She was married to Giovanni Malatesta, Lord of Rimini, but her guilty love for his younger brother, Paolo, was discovered and both were put to death about 1289. Leigh Hunt wrote a poem of this name (1816) and there are tragedies on the subject by Silvio Pellico (1818), Stephen Phillips (1900), Gabriele d'Annunzio (1902), and F. M. Crawford (1902).

Francis of Assisi, St. The founder of the FRANCISCANS. Born in 1182, son of a wealthy merchant, he was rejected by his father for his generous gifts to the poor folk of Assisi and his little chapel, called the *Portiuncula*, was soon thronged with disciples. His love of nature was a characteristic as was his purity and gentleness of spirit and his preaching to the birds became a favourite subject for artists. His begging friars lived in extreme poverty and he was canonized two years after his death (1226).

Franciscans (frăn sis′ kànz). The Friars Minor, founded by St. FRANCIS OF ASSISI in 1209 and now divided into three distinct and independent branches, the Friars Minor, the Friars Minor Conventual and the Friars Minor CAPUCHIN. These constitute the First Order. The Franciscans first appeared in England in 1224 and were called *Grey Friars* from the indeterminate colour of their habit, which is now brown. They had 65 religious houses in England at the time of the REFORMATION. Especially notable for its preaching among the poor, the distinguishing feature of the order at the outset was insistence on poverty, which later produced dissension. Many of the stricter members called *Spirituals* or *Zealots*, the less strict FRATICELLI, and in 1517 the *Observants*, separated from the *Conventuals*, and in the 1520s the Capuchins became another Order. Later groups were the *Reformati*, the *Recollects*, and the *Discalced* (*see* BAREFOOTED). The whole Order was reorganized into its present branches by Pope Leo XIII in 1897. *See* CORDELIER; TERTIARIES. For the Second Order (or Nuns) *see* CLARE, ORDER OF ST.

Those nuns following a milder rule instituted by Urban IV in 1263 were called *Urbanists*, and a reformed order of *Colettines* founded by St. Colette arose in the 15th century, other offshoots being the *Grey Sisters*, *Capuchin Nuns*, *Sisters of the Annunciation*, and *Conceptionists*.

St. Francis's Distemper. Impecuniosity; being moneyless. Those of the Order of St. Francis were not allowed to carry any money about them.

Francs-tireurs (frong tē rĕr) (Fr. free-shooters). Sharp-shooters, skirmishers, or irregular troops. Originally unofficial military units or rifle clubs formed in France during the Luxembourg crisis of 1867, they gave notable service in the Franco-German War of 1870–1871. At first wearing no uniform, until brought under proper French military control, they were shot if captured by the Germans.

Frankalmoin, or **frankalmoigne tenure** (frăngk′ ăl moin) (free alms). A form of feudal tenure whereby the Church held land granted by pious benefactors in return for some form of praying service, usually praying for the soul of the donor. The Church also held some of its lands by KNIGHT SERVICE. *See* CHANTRY; MORTMAIN.

Frankenstein. The young student in Mary Wollstonecraft Shelley's romance of that name (1818), a classic horror story. Frankenstein made a soulless monster out of corpses from churchyards and dissecting-rooms and endued it with life by galvanism. The tale shows the creature longed for sympathy, but was shunned by everyone and became the instrument of dreadful retribution on the student who usurped the prerogative of the Creator. *Cp*. VAMPIRE.

Frankincense. The literal meaning of this is pure or true incense. It is a fragrant gum exuded from several trees of the genus *Boswellia*, abundant on the Somali coast and in South Arabia. It was ceremonially used by the Egyptians, Persians, Babylonians, Hebrews, Greeks, and Romans and is an ingredient of the modern incense used in certain churches.

> They presented unto him gifts; gold, and frankincense, and myrrh.
>
> *Matt*. ii, 11.

Frankpledge. A system originating in Anglo-Saxon times by which all men were to be grouped in a TITHING or frankpledge with the responsibility for each other's actions. If one of their number committed an offence the others would compel him to answer for it or see that reparation was made. Men of position were excused as were freeholders and the system came only to apply to the unfree, when over 12 years of age.

Franks. Free letters for government officials and Members of PARLIAMENT. The privilege of franking a letter was held by numerous court officials in Tudor times. By writing their name and title on the corner of the letter they secured free delivery. This concession was abused from the outset and after the RESTORATION was increasingly exploited by members of both Houses of Parliament signing the letters of friends and others. By an act of 1764 each member of either house of Parliament was permitted to send 10 free letters daily and to receive 15. The abuse still continued and the right was abolished in 1840 on the introduction of the penny post although it still exists in the U.S.A. for Members of Congress and others.

Franks. The Germanic tribe which conquered GAUL after the fall of the Roman Empire, whence the name France.

Frater (frā'tèr). The refectory or dining-room of a monastery, where the brothers (Lat. *fratres*) met together for meals. Also called the *fratry*.

In old vagabond's slang a *frater* was much the same as an ABRAM-MAN, a usage derived from the friar's begging habits.

> A Frater goeth wyth a Lisence to beg for some Spittelhouse or Hospital. Their pray is commonly upon poore women as they go and come to the markets.
> AWDELEY: *Fraternitye of Vacabondes* (1575).

Fraternity, The. A term highwaymen used to apply to themselves as a body but the "Gentlemen of the road" were by no means always on friendly terms with one another.

Fraticelli (frăt i chel'ē) (Ital. Little Brethren). A name given to several groups of monks and friars in Italy in the 13th, 14th, and 15th centuries, many of whom were originally FRANCISCANS. They were mostly fanatical ascetics and came to be branded as HERETICS.

Frazzle. Beaten, or **licked to a frazzle.** Completely beaten and reduced to a state of exhaustion; an expression of American origin, *frazzle* being a "frayed edge".

Worn to a frazzle. Reduced to a state of nervous exhaustion.

Fred Karno's army. *See* KARNO.

Free. A free and easy. An informal social gathering where people chat and smoke together. A public-house social and sing-song. Thus **in a free and easy way** is with entire absence of ceremony.

A free fight. A fight in which all engage, rules being disregarded. **A free-for-all** is much the same whether applied to a scuffle or an argument.

Free on board, or **F.O.B.** Used of goods delivered on board ship or into a conveyance at the seller's expense.

I'm free to confess. There's nothing to prevent my admitting.

To have a free hand. *See under* HAND.

To make free with. To take liberties with; to treat whatever it is as one's own.

Free Bench (*francus bancus*) (Lat.). A legal term denoting a widow's free right to the interest in a COPYHOLD estate. Called *bench* because, on acceding, she became a tenant of the MANOR, and entitled to sit on the bench at manorial courts. It was abolished by Acts of 1922 and 1925.

Free Churches. The NONCONFORMIST churches, so called because they are free from any kind of official connexion with the State.

Free Church of Scotland or **Free Church.** Formed by those who left the established CHURCH OF SCOTLAND after the disruption of 1843.

Free companies. A name given to groups of disbanded soldiery who in the mid-14th century roamed France, plundering and pillaging. Sir Arthur Conan Doyle's story, *The White Company*, is based upon the exploits of one of them, which had the white cross for its emblem. *Cp.* CONDOTTIERI.

Free coup (in SCOTLAND) means a piece of waste land where rubbish may be dumped free of charge; also the right of doing so.

Free French. *See* FIGHTING FRENCH.

Free House. A public house or inn which is not tied to a brewery; its landlord is thus free to sell any kind of beer he chooses.

Free lance. *See under* LANCE.

Free Soilers. In the U.S.A. members of the Free Soil Party which arose in 1847–1848 to oppose the extension of slavery into further territories. It was made of ABOLITIONISTS and BARNBURNERS and ended its separate existence in 1856, being absorbed by the newly formed Republican Party.

Free Trade. The opposite of PROTECTION; when a government does not impose duties on imports to favour the home producer. Such a policy in Britain aroused increasing advocacy from the time of Adam Smith's *Wealth of Nations* (1776) when he attacked the existing protectionist policies which he called the *Mercantile System*. Largely as a result of Peel's Budgets of 1842 and 1845, the activities of the Anti-Corn Law League and the repeal of the CORN LAWS in 1846, and Gladstone's Budgets of 1853 and 1860, Great Britain became a Free Trade country. In spite of changed economic circumstances Free Trade long remained a SACRED COW but the country reverted to Protection in 1932. *Free Trade* is also an old slang term for smuggling.

The Apostle of Free Trade. Richard Cobden (1804–1865), the principal founder of the Anti-Corn Law League in 1838.

Free Verse. A breakaway from the regular classical metres, which dominated European and English poetry from the later mediæval period, and the substitution of ordinary speech rhythms and little or loose rhyme-patterns, in place of regular stanza forms. Milton experimented with irregular forms and much of Browning's poetry breaks away from the older tradition. From the early 20th century, free verse came into its own through the influence of Ezra Pound, T. S. Eliot, and others. There was a similar trend in France towards *vers libre*.

Wee Frees. A minority of the FREE CHURCH which refused to join the United Free Church in 1900. It had some 16,000 members in 1988.

Freebooter. A pirate, an adventurer who makes his living by plundering; literally one who obtains his booty free (Dut. *vrij*, free; *buit*, booty). *See also* FILIBUSTER.

Freehold. An estate held in FEE SIMPLE. *Cp.* COPYHOLD.

Freeman, Mrs. The name assumed by Sarah, Duchess of Marlborough (1660–1744), in her correspondence with Queen Anne. The Queen called herself Mrs. Morley.

Freeman of Bucks. A CUCKOLD. The allusion is to the buck's horn. *See* HORNS.

Freemasonry. As a secret society it has existed for many centuries and professes to trace its origins to the building of SOLOMON'S TEMPLE. In mediæval times stonemasons banded together with their secret signs, passwords and tests. Freemasonry in its modern form, as a body with no trade connexions, began to flourish in the 17th century and it is likely that Sir Christopher Wren was a member. Ashmole (*see* ASHMOLEAN MUSEUM) was initiated in 1646. The mother Grand Lodge of England was founded in London in 1717 and took under its aegis the many small lodges in the provinces. Even the ancient York Lodge, which has given its name to the rites of the Continent and the U.S.A., acknowledged its authority. From this Grand Lodge of England derive all Masonic lodges throughout the world.

In Britain, Masonry has three degrees, the first is called Entered Apprentice; the second Fellow Craft, the third, Master Mason. Royal Arch Masonry is an adjunct to these, and is peculiar to Britain. In the U.S.A. the first regular lodge was founded at Boston in 1733, though there are minutes extant of a lodge in Philadelphia in 1730. The ritual side of Freemasonry has appealed to American more than it has to British Masons, and many degrees are worked in the U.S.A. with elaborate ritual and mysteries. In addition to the three degrees of British Masonry there are the Cryptic Degrees of Royal and Select Masters; the Chivalric Rite, with three degrees of Knights Red Cross, Temple and of Malta; and the 33 degrees of the Ancient and Accepted Scottish Rite. The various Grand Orients of the Continent (all disowned by the Grand Lodge of England on account of their political activities) were founded at different times and work modifications of the Scottish Rite. The part played by Masonic lodges in the French Revolution is still obscure; Philippe ÉGALITÉ was head of the Grand Orient, but repudiated it during the TERROR. NAPOLEON was reported to have been initiated at Malta in 1798; he certainly favoured Masonry and during the Empire Cambacérès, Murat, and Joseph Bonaparte were successive Grand Masters. Freemasonry has been condemned by the HOLY SEE, not only for being a secret society, but for its alleged subversive aims which, if supported by Continental Masons, were quite unknown to their British and American brethren. Charity and "brotherly love" are characteristics of the fraternity and much is done to help members and their dependants with the provision of hospitals, schools etc., and relief for widows and orphans. It is, however, commonly held that Masonry is responsible for a good deal of favouritism in appointments and promotions.

The Lady Freemason. Women were not admitted into FREEMASONRY, but the story goes that a lady was initiated in the early 18th century. She was the Hon. Elizabeth St. Leger, daughter of Lord Doneraile, who hid herself in an empty clock-case when the lodge was held in her father's house, and witnessed the proceedings. She was discovered, and compelled to submit to initiation as a member of the craft.

Freeze Bank. A term of American origin for a refrigerated stock of perishable organic substances, such as human blood and bone, kept in large modern hospitals for surgical use.

Freezing-point. The temperature at which liquid becomes solid; if mentioned without qualification, the freezing-point of water is meant (32° Fahrenheit, 0° Centigrade, and Réaumur). The zero of Fahrenheit's thermometer is 32° below freezing-point, being the lowest temperature recorded by him in the winter of 1709.

Freischütz (frī' shutz) (the freeshooter). A legendary German marksman in league with the DEVIL, who gave him seven balls, six of which were to hit infallibly whatever the marksman aimed at, and the seventh was to be directed as the devil wished. Weber's opera, *Der Freischütz*, based on the legend (libretto by F. Kind) was first produced in Berlin in 1821.

Fremd. Better kinde fremd than fremd kyne. The motto of the Waterton family. It means "better kind strangers than estranged kindred" (cp. *Prov.* xxvii, 10, "Better is a neighbour that is near than a brother far off"). *Fremd* is an O.E. word meaning foreign, strange, unfriendly, estranged; *Kyne* is kin.

> What says our old Scottish proverb? "Better kind fremit, than fremit kindred."
> SCOTT: *Quentin Durward*, ch. vi.

French. French of Stratford atte Bow. This has often been taken to mean French as spoken by an Englishman, and a COCKNEY at that, but it had no such connotation in Chaucer's day. Stratford and Bromley were then fashionable suburbs, and at Bromley was the convent of ST. LEONARDS' where the daughters of well-to-do citizens and others were taught French by the nuns. French was a common acquirement of the time and freely used at Court and in society; but it was somewhat archaic French, descending from Norman times, and not such as was current in Paris.

> And Frensh she [the nun] spake ful faire and fetisly,
> After the scole of Stratford atte Bowe,
> For Frensh of Paris was to hir unknowe.
> CHAUCER: *Canterbury Tales, Prologue*, 124–6.

To take French leave. To take without asking; also to leave without asking or announcing one's departure. This kind of backhander to the French was once common (*cp.* "French gout" for venereal disease).

The French returned the compliment similarly. The French equivalent of "to take French leave" is *s'en aller* (or *filer*) *à l'anglaise*. In the 16th century a creditor used to be called *un Anglais*.

French cream. Brandy: from the custom originating in France of taking a cup of coffee after dinner with brandy in it instead of cream.

French paste. A kind of glass into which a certain quantity of oxide of lead is introduced. It gives a very good imitation of a DIAMOND. *See* GLAUCUS.

French Prophets. The name bestowed upon a group of CAMISARDS who arrived in England in 1706 claiming prophetic and wonder-working gifts and the speedy arrival of the second ADVENT.

French Shore. Parts of the western and northern coasts of Newfoundland, where the French were given the monopoly to catch and dry fish by the Treaty of Utrecht (1713). France gave up her monopoly in 1904 but retained the right to fish.

Frenchman. *See* NATIONAL NICKNAMES *under* NICKNAME.

Done like a Frenchman, turn and turn again (*Henry VI, Pt. I*, III, iii). The French were frequently ridiculed as a fickle, wavering nation. Dr. Johnson says he once read a treatise, the object of which was to show that a weathercock is a satire on the word *Gallus* (a Gaul or cock).

Freyja (frā' yà). In Scandinavian mythology the sister of FREYR, goddess of love, marriage and of the dead. She was the wife of ODIN and always wore the shining necklace called *Brisingamen* and was consequently called "ornament loving". Her husband is also given in some legends as *Odhr*, and she shed golden tears when he left her. The counterpart of VENUS, she is also commonly identified with Frigg, wife of Odin, who in Scandinavian myth ranked highest among the goddesses. *See* FRIDAY.

Freyr. In Norse mythology, god of fruitfulness and crops, and of the sun and rain. His horse was called Bloodyhoof and his ship SKIDBLADNIR.

Friar (Lat. *frater*, a brother). A member of one of the mendicant orders, notably the AUGUSTINIANS, CARMELITES, DOMINICANS, and FRANCISCANS. *See also* CRUTCHED FRIARS.

In printer's slang a *friar* is a part of the sheet which has failed to receive the ink properly, and is therefore paler than the rest. As CAXTON set up his press in Westminster Abbey, it is but natural that monks and friars should give rise to some of the printer's slang. *Cp.* MONK.

Crutched Friars. *See* CRUTCHED.

Curtal Friar. *See* BRAZEN HEAD.

Friar Bungay. Thomas de Bungay of Suffolk, a FRANCISCAN who lectured at Oxford and Cambridge in the 13th century, whose story is much overlaid with legend. He came to be portrayed as a magician and necromancer. In the old prose romance, *The Famous History of Friar Bacon*, and in Greene's *Honourable History of Friar Bacon and Friar Bungay* (1587), he appears as the assistant to Roger Bacon (d. 1292). He also features anachronistically in Lytton's *Last of the Barons*.

Friar Rush. A legendary house-spirit who originated as a kind of ultramischievous ROBIN GOODFELLOW in German folk-lore. He later acquired more devilish attributes and appeared in the habit of a Friar to lead astray those under religious vows. Dekker's play, *If it be not Good, the Divel is in it* (printed 1612), was based upon *The Pleasant History of Friar Rush* (1567).

Friar Tuck. Chaplain and steward of ROBIN HOOD.

> In this our spacious isle I think there is not one
> But he hath heard some talk of Hood and Little John;
> Of Tuck the merry friar, which many a sermon made
> In praise of Robin Hood, his outlaws, and their trade.
>
> DRAYTON: *Polyolbion*, xxvi, 311–16.

Friar's Lanthorn. One of the many names given to the Will o' the Wisp. *See* IGNIS FATUUS.

Friars Major (*Fratres majores*). Sometimes applied to the DOMINICANS in contrast to the FRIARS MINOR.

Friars Minor (*Fratres minores*). The FRANCISCANS.

Friars of the Sack. *See under* SACK.

Friday. The sixth day of the week (until 1971 when it became the fifth (*see* SUNDAY); in ancient ROME called *dies Veneris*, the day dedicated to VENUS, hence the French *vendredi*. The northern nations adopted the same nomenclature and the nearest equivalent to Venus was Frigg or FREYJA, hence Friday (O.E. *frige dæg*).

Friday was regarded by the Norsemen as the luckiest day of the week, the day of weddings, etc., but among Christians it has been regarded as the unluckiest, because it was the day of the Crucifixion. While no longer a day of compulsory abstinence for Roman Catholics, they are urged to set Friday apart for some voluntary act of self-denial.

Friday is the SABBATH for Mohammedans and they say that ADAM was created on a Friday and it was on Friday that Adam and EVE ate the forbidden fruit, and on a Friday they died. It is also held unlucky among Buddhists and BRAHMINS.

In England the proverb is that "a Friday moon brings foul weather"; but it is not unlucky to be born on this day, since "Friday's child is loving and giving". It is held to be a bad day for ships to put to sea, but in 1492 Columbus set sail on a Friday and sighted land on a Friday. It was also sometimes called *Hanging day* as it was a common day for executing condemned criminals.

Black Friday. *See under* BLACK.

Good Friday. *See under* GOOD.

Friday the Thirteenth. A particularly unlucky Friday. *See* THIRTEEN.

Long Friday. GOOD FRIDAY was so called by the SAXONS, probably because of the long fasts and offices associated with that day.

Man Friday. The young savage found by ROBINSON CRUSOE on a Friday and kept as his servant and companion on the desert island. Hence a faithful and willing attendant, ready to turn his hand to anything.

Red Friday. *See under* RED.

He who laughs on Friday will weep on Sunday. Sorrow follows in the wake of joy. The line is taken from Racine's comedy, *Les Plaideurs*.

Friend. A QUAKER, *i.e.* a member of the Society of Friends; also one's second in a duel. In the law courts counsel refer to each other as "my learned friend", though they may be entire strangers, just as in the HOUSE OF COMMONS one member speaks of another as "my honourable friend".

A friend at court. A friend who is in a position to help by influencing those in power or authority.

A friend of the court (*amicus curiæ*). A legal term to denote anyone not concerned in a case who brings to the attention of the court some point or decision of law which seems to have been overlooked.

A friend in need is a friend indeed. The Latin saying (from Ennius) is, *Amicus certus in re incerta cernitur*, a sure friend is made known when (one is) in difficulty.

Friends of the Earth. An organization founded in Great Britain in 1971, with some 250 local groups, to campaign for the protection of the environment. It now has branches in a number of other countries. Protests and propaganda are furthered by public meetings, demonstrations, etc. They are active against all forms of pollution (especially nuclear power), developments which ruin the countryside and the destruction of wildlife. *Cp.* GREENPEACE *under* GREEN.

The Friend of Man. The name given to the Marquis de Mirabeau (1715–1789), father of Mirabeau, of French revolutionary fame. His great work was *L'Ami des Hommes*, hence the nickname.

The Prisoner's friend. At a naval court martial, the person (usually an officer) who acts on behalf of, or assists, the accused, unless the person charged conducts his own case.

The Society of Friends. The QUAKERS.

The Society of Friends of the People. A society founded at London (1792) largely of young aristocrats, and which included Lauderdale, Charles Grey, and Sheridan. They advocated reform of PARLIAMENT and estimated that 51 English and Welsh boroughs, with a total voting strength of under 1,500, returned 100 members to Parliament. It dissolved itself in 1795 after one of its members, Thomas Muir, was sentenced to 14 years transportation, it being held by Lord Braxfield that "to agitate for equal representation of the people in the House of the People was in the circumstances of itself sedition".

The soldier's friend. An official appointed to assist soldiers in making out and presenting their claims to the various pension boards.

A friendly suit, or **action.** An action at law between parties by mutual arrangement with the object of obtaining a legal decision upon some point which concerns them both.

Friendly Societies. Voluntary self-help organizations providing insurance against sickness, infirmity, death, etc., payable from central funds. Preceded by the old village Benefit Clubs, they developed from the late 17th century and became widespread in the 19th and early 20th centuries.

Friendship. The classical examples of lasting friendship between man and man are ACHILLES and PATROCLUS, PYLADES and ORESTES, NISUS and EURYALUS, DAMON and PYTHIAS. To these should be added DAVID and JONATHAN.

Frigg. See FREYJA.

Frills. To put on frills. To give oneself airs, frill being an affectation of dress or manner, similarly we say "to put on airs and graces".

Fringe. The fringe, or more correctly twisted cords or tassels worn on the four corners of the Jewish outer garment (*tzitzith*) in OLD TESTAMENT times and later, were anciently supposed to have a special virtue. Hence the desire of the woman who had the issue of blood to touch the fringe of Our Lord's garment (*Matt.* ix, 20–22). From the 13th century an undergarment with tassels attached, the *arba kanfoth* (four corners) worn at all times by orthodox Jews, replaced the *tzitzith*.

> Thou shalt make thee fringes upon the four quarters of thy vesture, wherewith thou coverest thyself.
> *Deut.* xxii, 12.

Fringe benefits. Concessions and benefits given to employees, or extra "perks" that go with a job or appointment such as free coal, use of a motor car, pensions, insurances, medical benefits etc.

> The main "fringe benefit" is a Government chauffeur-driven car. [Referring to the Leader of H.M. Opposition.]
> *Daily Telegraph,* 11 Feb. 1795.

The lunatic fringe. The small section of the community who follow and originate extremist ideas, and whose behaviour is often markedly eccentric by conventional standards, but whose influence on the majority is of little account.

Frippery. Rubbish of a tawdry character, worthless finery; foolish levity. A *friperer* or *fripperer* was one who dealt in old clothes (*cp.* Fr. *friperie*, old clothes, cast-off furniture, etc.).

> Old clothes, cast dresses, tattered rags,
> Whose works are e'en the frippery of wit.
> BEN JONSON: *Epig.* I, lvi.

Also a shop where odds and ends, old clothes, and so on are dealt in.

Frith. By frith and fell. By wold and wild, wood and COMMON. *Frith* here means ground covered with scrub or underwood; *fell* is a common.

Frithiof (frit' yof). A hero of Icelandic myth who married Ingeborg, daughter of a minor king of Norway, and widow of Sigurd Ring, to whose dominions he succeeded. His name signifies "the peacemaker" and his adventures are recorded in the saga which bears his name. It was paraphrased by Esaias Tegner in his famous poem (1825) of the same name.

Fritz. Frederick the Great of Prussia (1712, 1740–1786) was known as *Old Fritz.* In World War I the men in the trenches commonly called any German in the enemy lines *Fritz.* See NATIONAL NICKNAMES *under* NICKNAME.

Froebel System. The name given to a system of KINDERGARTEN teaching where children's abilities are developed by means of clay-modelling, mat-plaiting, and other forms of self-activity, developed by Friedrich Froebel (1782–1852), a German schoolmaster.

Frog. A frog and a mouse agreed to settle by a single combat their claims to a marsh; but, while they fought, a kite carried them both off (ÆSOP: *Fables*, clxviii).

> Old Æsop's fable, where he told
> What fate unto the mouse and frog befel.
> CARY: *Dante*, xxiii.

In Ovid's *Metamorphoses* (vi, 4) we are told that the Lycian shepherds were changed into frogs for mocking LATONA.

> As when those hinds that were transformed to frogs
> Railed at Latona's twin-born progeny.
> MILTON: *Sonnets*, xi.

Frenchmen, properly *Parisians*, have been nicknamed Frogs or Froggies, from their ancient heraldic device which was three frogs or toads. (*See* FLEUR-DE-LIS.) *Qu'en disent les grenouilles?* What do the frogs (people of Paris) say?—was in 1791 a common court phrase at VERSAILLES. There was point in the pleasantry, Paris having once been a quagmire, called *Lutetia* (mud-land). Further point is given to the nickname by the fact that the back legs of the edible frog (*Rana esculenta*) form a delicacy in French cuisine that aroused much disparaging humour from the English. *See* NATIONAL NICKNAMES *under* NICKNAME.

Nic Frog. The Dutchman in Arbuthnot's *History of John Bull* (1712). Frogs are called "Dutch Nightingales". *See* NATIONAL NICKNAMES *under* NICKNAME.

Frog, or **frog's march.** Carrying an obstreperous prisoner face downwards by his four limbs.

A frog in the throat. A temporary loss of voice, hoarseness.

It may be fun to you, but it is death to the frogs. A caution, meaning that one's sport should not be at the expense of other people's happiness. The allusion is to ÆSOP's fable of a boy stoning frogs for amusement.

Frogmen. In World War II, strong swimmers dressed in rubber suits with paddles on their feet resembling the feet of frogs, who operated in enemy harbours by night attaching explosives to shipping, etc. They are now used in salvage operations, etc.

Fronde (frond). The name given to a civil contest in France (1648–1653) during the minority of Louis XIV. It began as a struggle against the Court party for the redress of grievances, but soon became a faction fight among the nobles to undo the work of Cardinal Richelieu and to overthrow Cardinal MAZARIN. *Fronde* means sling and the name arose from the occasion when the Paris mob pelted Cardinal Mazarin's windows with stones.

The Spanish Fronde. The war between France and Spain (1653–1659), which was a sequel of the FRONDE and in which the *frondeur* Condé fought for Spain.

Frost Saints. *See* ICE SAINTS.

Frozen Words. A conceit used by the ancient Greeks. Antiphanes applies it to the discourses of PLATO: "As the cold of certain cities is so intense that it freezes the very words we utter, which remain congealed till the heat of summer thaws them, so the mind of youth is so thoughtless that the wisdom of Plato lies there frozen, as it were, till it is thawed by the ripened judgment of mature age." MÜNCHAUSEN relates an incident of the "frozen horn" and Rabelais (Bk. IV, ch. lvi) tells how PANTAGRUEL and his friends, on the confines of the Frozen Sea, heard the uproar of a battle, which had been frozen the preceding winter, released by a thaw.

> Where truth in person doth appear.
> Like words congeal'd in northern air.
> BUTLER: *Hudibras*, canto I, 147–8.

Frying-pan. Out of the frying-pan into the fire. In trying to extricate yourself from one evil you fall into a greater. The Greeks used to say, "Out of the smoke into the flame"; and the French say, "*Tomber de la poêle dans la braise*".

Frying-pan brand. An Australian term of the mid-19th century to describe the large brand superimposed by cattle thieves to blot out the rightful owner's brand.

Fub. *See* FOB.

Fuchsia (fū′ shà). A genus of highly ornamental flowering shrubs coming from Mexico and the Andes, though two species are found in New Zealand. They were so named in 1703 in honour of the German botanist Leonhard Fuchs (1501–1566).

Fudge. A word of contempt meaning "nonsense!", "absurd!" Its derivation is uncertain. It is also a kind of soft candy.

Fudge-box. An attachment on newspaper printing machines to allow of late news being added to the machine while it is running. This news appears in the "Stop-press" column, which is consequently called the *fudge-box*. In this sense the word is another form of FADGE.

Fuel. Adding fuel to the fire, or **flames.** Saying or doing something to increase the anger of a person already incensed.

Fugger. A famous family of German merchant bankers, particularly influential in the 15th and 16th centuries, and proverbial for their great wealth, their newsletter and fine library. **Rich as a fugger** is common in Elizabethan dramatists. Charles V introduced some of the family into Spain, where they superintended the mines.

Fugit irreparabile tempus (Lat.). Time, which cannot be retrieved, is flying. A classic reminder derived from VIRGIL's *Georgics* (III, 284).

Führer (fü′ rėr) (Ger. leader). The title assumed by Adolf Hitler (1889–1945) when he acceded to supreme power in Germany on the death of Hindenburg in 1934.

Fulhams, or **Fullams.** An Elizabethan name for loaded dice. Dice made with a cavity were called *gourds*; those made to throw the high numbers were *high fullams* or *gourds*, and those made to throw low numbers were *low fullams* or *gourds*.

> For gourd and fullam holds
> And "high" and "low" beguile the rich and poor.
> SHAKESPEARE: *Merry Wives of Windsor*, I, iii.

The name was probably from Fulham, which was then a notorious resort of crooks and rogues.

Full. Full dress. Ceremonial dress; court dress, full uniform, academicals, evening dress, etc.

A full dress debate is one for which proper preparations and arrangements have been made, as opposed to one arising casually.

Full house. A term in the game of poker for a hand holding three of one kind and two of another, *e.g.* 3 tens and 2 sixes.

Full of beans. *See under* BEAN.

In full cry. Said of hounds that have caught the scent, and give tongue in chorus; hence hurrying in full pursuit.

In full fig. *See* FIG.

In full swing. *See under* SWING.

Fum, or **Fung-hwang.** The PHŒNIX of Chinese legend, one of the four symbolical creatures presiding over the destinies of China. It originated from fire, was born in the Hill of the Sun's HALO, and has its body inscribed with the five CARDINAL virtues. It is this curious creature that was embroidered on the dresses of certain MANDARINS.

Fum. *See* GEORGE IV.

Fumage. Another name for Hearth-money or CHIMNEY-MONEY (Lat. *fumus*, smoke).

Fume. In a fume. In a bad temper, especially from impatience.

Fun. To make fun of. To make a butt of; to ridicule.

A figure of fun. *See under* FIGURE.

Like fun. Thoroughly, energetically, with delight.

> On'y look at the dimmercrats, see what they've done,
> Jest simply by stickin' together like fun.
> LOWELL: *Biglow Papers* (First series, iv, st. v).
> Then that the sound stopped all of a sudden, and the bolts went to like fun.
> T. HUGHES: *Tom Brown's Schooldays*, II, iii.

Fund. The Funds, or **The Public Funds.** Money lent at interest to Government or Government security.

The Sinking Fund. Money set aside by the Government for paying off the principal of the NATIONAL DEBT. According to Blackstone, it was intended "to sink and lower the National Debt". The first such fund was established at the end of the reign of Queen Anne.

> The Sinking Fund's unfathomable sea,
> That most unliquidating liquid, leaves
> The debt unsunk, yet sinks all it receives.
> BYRON: *Don Juan*, canto XVI, xcix.

To be out of funds. To be out of money.

Fundamentalism. The maintenance of traditional PROTESTANT Christian beliefs based upon a literal acceptance of the SCRIPTURES as fundamentals. Fundamentalism as a religious movement arose in the U.S.A. about 1919 among various denominations. What was new was not so much its ideas and attitudes, but its widespread extent and the zeal

of its supporters. It opposed all theories of evolution and anthropology, holding that God transcends all laws of nature and that He manifests Himself by exceptional and extraordinary activities, belief in the literal meaning of the Scriptures being an essential tenet. In 1925, John T. Scopes, a science teacher of Rhea High School, Dayton, Tennessee, was convicted of violating the State laws by teaching evolution, an incident arousing interest and controversy far beyond the religious circles of the U.S.A. Their leader was William Jennings Bryan (1860–1925), the politician and orator. *Cp.* MODERNISM.

Funeral (Late Lat. *funeralis*, adj. from *funus*, a burial). *Funus* is connected with *fumus*, smoke, and the word seems to refer to the ancient practice of disposing of the dead by cremation. Roman funerals were conducted by torchlight at night, that magistrates and priests might not be made ceremonially unclean by seeing the corpse.

Most of our funeral customs derive from the Romans; as dressing in BLACK, walking in procession, carrying insignia on the bier, raising a mound on the grave (called *tumulus*, whence *tomb*), etc. The Greeks crowned the dead body with flowers, and also placed flowers on the tomb; the Romans had similar customs. In England the PASSING BELL or the *Soul Bell* used to be tolled from the church when a parishioner was dying and the funeral bell would be tolled as many times as the dead person's years of age.

Public games were held in Greece and Rome in honour of departed heroes; as the games instituted by HERCULES at the death of Pelops, those held by ACHILLES in honour of PATROCLUS (*Iliad*, Bk. xxiii), those held by ÆNEAS in honour of his father Anchises (Æneid, Bk. V), etc. The custom of giving a feast at funerals came to us from the Romans, who not only feasted the friends of the deceased, but also distributed meat to the persons employed. *See* ISTHMIAN GAMES; NEMEAN GAMES.

Fung-hwang. *See* FUM.

Funk. To be in a funk or **a blue funk,** may be the Walloon "*In de fonk zun*", literally to "be in the smoke". Colloquially, to be in a state of apprehensive fear or abject fear. The phrase first appears at Oxford in the first half of the 18th century.

> Pryce, usually brimful of valour when drunk,
> Now experienced what schoolboys denominate funk.
> BARHAM: *Ingoldsby Legends*, I.

Funny Bone. A pun on the word *humerus*, the

Latin name for the arm bone. It is the inner condyle or knob at the end of the bone where the ulnar nerve is exposed at the elbow. A knock on this part is naturally painful and produces a tingling sensation.

Furcam et Flagellum (fĕr′ kăm et flà jel′ ùm) (Lat. gallows and whip). In the early MIDDLE AGES, the lowest form of tenure, that of the slave, whose life and limbs were at his lord's disposal. *Cp.* FORKS.

Furies, The. The Roman name (*Furiæ*) for the Greek ERINYES, said by Hesiod to have been the daughters of GÆA (the Earth) and to have sprung from the blood of URANUS, and by other accounts to be daughters of Night or of Earth and Darkness. They were three in number, Tisiphone (the Avenger of blood), ALECTO (the Implacable), and Megæra (the Jealous one).

They were merciless goddesses of vengeance and punished all transgressors, especially those who neglected filial duty or claims of kinship, etc. Their punishments continued after death. *See* EUMENIDES.

The Furies of the Guillotine. *See* TRICOTEUSES.

Furphy. In World War I containers for sanitary purposes were supplied to Australian military camps by the firm of Furphy and Co., whose name appeared on all their products. Hence a "furphy" was a latrine rumour or a report of doubtful reliability. *Cp.* BARRACK-ROOM LAWYER.

Furry Dance. Part of the spring festival held at Helston, Cornwall, on 8 May (now the nearest Saturday). Furry Day, which is derived from the Lat. *Feriæ* (festivals, holidays), was incorrectly changed to *Flora* in the 18th century and in the 19th century the dance was called the *Floral Dance*, as in the well-known song. It is derived from a pre-Christian festivity and is copied in some other towns. In its present form prominent townsfolk dance through the town. There is a similar spring festival at Padstow beginning at midnight on 30 April. *See under* HOBBY.

Fustian. A coarse twilled cotton cloth with a velvety pile, probably so called from Fustat, a suburb of Cairo. It is chiefly used now in a figurative sense meaning inflated or pompous talk, CLAPTRAP, BOMBAST, pretentious words. *Cp.* FLANNEL.

> Discourse fustian with one's own shadow.
> SHAKESPEARE: *Othello*, II, iii.
> Some scurvy quaint collection of fustian phrases and uplandish words.
> HEYWOOD: *Faire Maide of the Exchange*, II, ii.

Futhorc (foo′ thôrk). The ancient Runic alphabet of the Anglo-Saxons and other Teutons; so called (on the same principle as the A B C) from its first six letters, *viz., f, u, th, o, r, k*.

Futurism. An art movement which originated at Turin in 1909 under the influence of E.F.T. Marinetti. Its adherents sought to introduce into paintings a "poetry of motion" whereby, for example, the painted gesture should become actually "a dynamic condition". The Futurists tried to indicate not only the state of mind of the painter but also that of the figures in the picture. It was another movement to shake off the influence of the past. The original Futurists included Marinetti, Boccioni, Carra, Russolo, and Severini, and they first exhibited at Paris in 1912. *Cp.* CUBISM; DADAISM; FAUVISM; IMPRESSIONISM; ORPHISM; SURREALISM; SYNCHRONISM; VORTICISM.

Fylfot. A mystic sign or emblem known also as the SWASTIKA and GAMMADION, and in HERALDRY as the *cross cramponnée*, used (especially in Byzantine architecture and among the North American Indians) as an ornament of religious import. It has been found at Hissarlik, on ancient Etruscan tombs, CELTIC monuments, Buddhist inscriptions, Greek coins, etc. It has been thought to have represented the power of the SUN, of the four winds, of lightning, and so on. It is used nowadays in jewellery as an emblem of luck and was also adopted as the NAZI badge. (*See* diagram 21, p. 287.)

The name *fylfot* was adopted by antiquaries from a MS. of the 15th century, and is possibly *fill foot*, signifying a device to fill the foot of a stained-glass window.

G

G. This letter is a modification of the Latin C (which was a rounding of the Greek *gamma*, Γ); until the 3rd century B.C. the *g* and *k* sounds were both represented by the letter C. In the Hebrew and old Phœnician alphabets G is the outline of a camel's head and neck. Heb. *gimel*, a camel.

G.C.B. *See* BATH.

G.I. In World War II, American enlisted men called themselves G.I.s, from an abbreviation of Government Issue. After becoming accustomed to G.I. shirts, G.I. blankets, etc., the soldiers began to apply the term to themselves.

G-man, short for Government Man, an agent of the U.S. Federal Bureau of Investigation (F.B.I.)

G.O.M. The initial letters of "Grand Old Man", a nickname of honour given to W. E. Gladstone (1809–1898), in his later years. Lord Rosebery first used the expression in 1882.

G.P.U. *See* OGPU.

Gab. The gift of the gab, or **gob.** Fluency of speech, also the gift of boasting. The word *gab* may be onomatopœic or derive from the identical Gaelic word for mouth.

Gabbara. The giant who, according to Rabelais, was "the first inventor of the drinking of HEALTHS".

Gabble Ratchet. *See* GABRIEL'S HOUNDS.

Gabelle (gȧ bel'). The French tax on salt, first levied in 1286 and abolished in 1790. The word was originally applied to any indirect tax. All the salt made in France had to be brought to the royal warehouses and was there sold at a price fixed by the government. The iniquity was that some provinces had to pay twice as much as others and everyone above the age of eight had to purchase a minimum quantity weekly.

Gaberlunzie. A Scottish term of uncertain origin for a mendicant; or one of the king's BEADSMEN. The name has also been given to the wallet carried by the gaberlunzie-man. *See* BLUE GOWN.

> Though I should die at the back of a dike, they'll find as muckle quilted in this auld blue gown as will bury me like a Christian, and gie the lads and lasses a blithe lykewake too; sae there's the gaberlunzie's burial provided for, and I need nae mair.
> SCOTT: *The Antiquary*, ch. xii.

Gabriel (*i.e.* man of God). One of the ARCHANGELS, sometimes regarded as the ANGEL of death, the prince of fire and thunder, but more frequently as one of God's chief messengers, and traditionally said to be the only angel that can speak Syriac and Chaldee. The Mohammedans call him the chief of the four favoured angels and the spirit of truth. Milton makes him chief of the angelic guards placed over PARADISE (*Paradise Lost*, IV, 549).

In the TALMUD Gabriel appears as the destroyer of the hosts of Sennacherib, as the man who showed Joseph the way, and as one of the angels who buried MOSES.

According to the KORAN it was Gabriel who took MOHAMMED to heaven on Al BORAK and revealed to him his "prophetic love". In the OLD TESTAMENT Gabriel is said to have explained to DANIEL certain visions (*Dan.* viii. 16–26); in the NEW TESTAMENT he announced to Zacharias the future birth of JOHN THE BAPTIST (*Luke* i, 13, etc.) and appeared to Mary the mother of Jesus (*Luke* i, 26, etc.).

Gabriel Bell. In mediæval England, another name for the ANGELUS or AVE Bell, in remembrance of the archangel's salutation of the Virgin Mary.

Gabriel's horse. Haizum.

Gabriel's hounds, called also *Gabble Ratchet.* Wild geese. The noise of geese in flight is like that of a pack of hounds in full cry. The legend is that they are the souls of unbaptized children wandering through the air till the Day of JUDGMENT.

Gabrielle. La Belle Gabrielle (1573–1599). Daughter of Antoine d'Estrées, grandmaster of artillery, and governor of the Ile de France. Towards the close of 1590, Henri IV happened to sojourn for a night at the Château de Cœuvres, and fell in love with her. She married Liancourt-Damerval, but in 1592 went to live at court as the king's mistress. She was made Duchess of Beaufort in 1597.

Gad. By Gad. A minced form of God, occurring also in *Gadzooks*, *Begad*, *Egad*.

> How he still cries "Gad!" and talks of popery coming in, as all fanatiques do.
>
> PEPYS: *Diary*, 24 Nov. 1662.

Gad-steel. Flemish steel. So called from its being wrought in *gads*, or small bars (O.E. *gad*, a small bar or spike).

Gæa (jē′ à) or **Ge.** The Greek goddess of the Earth who gave birth to sky, mountains, and sea. By URANUS she brought forth the TITANS, the CYCLOPS and other GIANTS and according to some legends she was the mother of the EUMENIDES.

Gaelic (gā′ lik). The language of the Gaelic branch of the CELTIC race. The name is now usually restricted to the Celtic language of the Scottish Highlands, but also includes that of Irish and Manx Celts. *See* ERSE.

Gaff. Slang for humbug; also for a cheap public entertainment or a low-class MUSIC HALL, often called *penny gaffs* from the price of admission. Such theatres were once common on the Surrey side of the Thames.

It is also the spar to which the upper edge of a fore-and-aft sail is bent such as the mainsail of a sloop.

Crooked as a gaff. Here a *gaff* is an iron hook at the end of a short pole, used for landing salmon, etc., or the metal spur of fighting-cocks (Span. and Port. *gafa*, a boat-hook).

To blow the gaff. *See under* BLOW.

To stand the gaff. To beat punishment or raillery with calmness.

Gaffer. An old country fellow; the boss, overseer, or foreman; a corruption of "grandfather". *Cp.* GAMMER.

Gag. In theatrical parlance, an interpolation. When SHAKESPEARE makes Hamlet direct the players to say no more "than is set down" (III, ii) he cautions them against gagging; also a joke.

Gag-man. One who is employed to supply jokes for films, radio programmes, etc.

That's just a gag. A mere trick or deception. Something to "take one in".

To apply the gag. Said of applying the CLOSURE in the HOUSE OF COMMONS. Here *gag* is something forced into the mouth to prevent speech.

Gaiety. The Gaiety of Nations. This phrase, now often used ironically, such as "that won't add much to the gaiety of nations", derives from Dr. Johnson's words alluding to the death of David Garrick—"I am disappointed by that stroke of death which has eclipsed the gaiety of nations and impoverished the public stock of harmless pleasure."

Gaiety Girl. One of the beauty chorus for which the Old Gaiety Theatre in the STRAND was famous in the '90s and Edwardian days. Several of them married into the peerage. *Cp.* GIBSON GIRL.

Gala Day. A festive day; a day when people put on their best attire (Ital. *gala*, festivity).

Galahad, Sir (găl′a hăd). In Arthurian legend the purest and noblest knight of the ROUND TABLE. He is a late addition and was invented by Walter Map in his *Quest of the San Graal*. He was the son of LANCELOT and ELAINE. At the institution of the Round Table one seat (the Siege Perilous) was left unoccupied for the knight who could succeed in the Quest. When Sir Galahad sat there it was discovered that it had been left for him. The story is found in Malory's *Morte d'Arthur*, Tennyson's *The Holy Grail*, etc.

Galatea (găl à tē′ a). A sea NYMPH, beloved by the monster POLYPHEMUS, but herself in love with the beautiful ACIS, who was killed by the jealous CYCLOPS. Galatea threw herself into the sea where she joined her sister nymphs. Handel has an opera entitled *Acis and Galatea* (1720). The Galatea beloved by PYGMALION was a different person.

Galaxy, The (Gr. *gala*, *galaktos*, milk). The "Milky Way". A long white luminous track of stars which seems to encompass the heavens like a girdle. It is composed of a vast collection of stars so distant that they are indistinguishable as separate stars, and they appear as a combined light. According to classic fable, it is the path to the palace of ZEUS.

Galen (gā′ len). A Greek physician and philosopher of the 2nd century A.D. For centuries he was the supreme authority in medicine. Hence *Galenist*, a follower of Galen's medical theories; *Galenical*, a simple, vegetable medicine.

Galen says "Nay" and Hippocrates "Yea". The doctors disagree, and who is to decide? HIPPOCRATES, born at Cos (460 B.C.), was the most celebrated physician of antiquity.

Galère. Que diable allait-il faire dans cette galère? What the devil was he doing in that galley? This is from MOLIÈRE's comedy of *Les Fourberies de Scapin*. Scapin wants to bamboozle Géronte out of his money, and tells him that his master (Géronte's son) is detained prisoner on a Turkish galley, where he went out of curiosity. The above was Géronte's reply. The phrase is applied to one who finds himself in difficulties through being where he ought not to be, or to express astonishment that he should be found in such least expected company, situation, etc.

> "One of the St. Wilfrid's priests, I suppose," Flaxman said to himself. "What on earth is he doing *dans cette galère*? Are we to have a disputation? That would be dramatic."
> MRS. HUMPHRY WARD: *Robert Elsmere*, ch. xl.

Vogue la galère. *See under* VOGUE.

Galilee. A chapel or porch at the west end of some mediæval churches where penitents waited before admission to the body of the church and where clergy received women who had business with them. Examples remain at Durham, Ely and Lincoln cathedrals. The name derives from *Matt.* iv, 15.

Galilean. An inhabitant of Galilee, and specifically Jesus Christ, who was called "the Galilean". The term was also applied to Christians as his followers. The dying words attributed to the Roman Emperor Julian the Apostate were "*Vicisti, Galilæe*".

> Thou hast conquered, O pale Galilean; the world has grown grey from thy breath.
> SWINBURNE: *Hymn to Proserpine*.

Galimatias (gǎl i mā′ shiǎs). Nonsense, unmeaning gibberish. The word first appeared in France in the 16th century, but its origin is unknown; perhaps it is connected with GALLIMAUFRY. In his translation of Rabelais, Urquart heads ch. ii of Bk. I a "Galimatias of Extravagant Conceits found in an Ancient Monument".

Gall (gawl). Bile; the very bitter fluid secreted by the liver; hence used figuratively as a symbol for anything of extreme bitterness.

Gall and wormwood. Extremely bitter and mortifying.

> And I said, My strength and my hope is perished from the Lord: Remembering mine affliction and my misery, the wormwood and the gall.
> *Lam.* iii, 18, 19.

The gall of bitterness. The bitterest grief; extreme affliction. The ancients taught that grief and joy were subject to the gall as affection was to the heart, and knowledge to the kidneys. The "gall of bitterness" means the bitter centre of bitterness, as the "heart of hearts" means the innermost recesses of the heart or affections. In the *Acts* it is used to signify "the sinfulness of sin", which leads to the bitterest grief.

> For I perceive that thou art in the gall of bitterness, and in the bond of iniquity.
> *Acts* viii, 23.

Gall of Pigeons. The story goes that pigeons have no gall, because the dove sent from the ark by Noah burst its gall out of grief, and none of the pigeon family has had a gall ever since.

> For sin' the Flood of Noah
> The dow she has nae ga'.
> JAMIESON: *Pop_lar Ballads*
> (*Lord of Rorlin's Daughter*).

Gallant. The meaning of this word varies with its pronunciation. As Gǎl′ ǎnt, it is an adjective meaning brave, grand, fine, chivalrous; as gǎl′ ǎnt′, it means the cavalier or admirer of women, a flirt, or the adjective and verb implying this.

> That gallant spirit hath aspir'd the clouds,
> Which too untimely here did scorn the earth.
> SHAKESPEARE: *Romeo and Juliet*, III, i.
> These two gallants passed Peveril more than once, linked arm in arm ... staring broadly at Peveril and his female companions.
> SCOTT: *Peveril of the Peak*, ch. xxxii.

Gallery. A gallery hit. In CRICKET is an exceptionally stylish stroke which arouses the crowd's enthusiasm.

To play to the gallery. An appeal to the lower elements of one's audience, to court popularity by such methods as an actor seeking popular applause from the patrons of the cheapest seats in the theatre, these being in the gallery.

> The instant we begin to think about success and the effect of our work—to play with one eye on the gallery—we lose power and touch and everything else.
> KIPLING: *The Light that Failed*, ch. VII.

Gallery Halfpence. Small silver coin, chiefly from Genoa, brought over by Italian wine merchants ("galley men") in the 15th century. Stowe says they used Galley Quay in Thames Street. The use of such coins was forbidden in England.

> Galleymen ... had certain coin of silver amongst themselves, which were halfpence of Genoe, and were called Galley Halfpence; these halfpence were forbidden in the 13th of Henry IV, and again by Parliament in the 4th of Henry V.
> STOWE: *Survey of London*.

Gallia. France, as in Thomson's

> Impending hangs o'er Gallia's humbled coast.
> *The Seasons: Summer*.

More properly the Latin name for Gaul, the much more extensive areas then populated by CELTIC peoples.

Gallia Bracata, or **Braccata** (trousered Gaul). South-western Gaul from the Pyrenees to the Alps, or *Gallia Narbonensis* (from the Gaulish town of Narbo, the modern Narbonne), part of GALLIA TRANSALPINA. *See* GENS BRACCATA *under* GENS.

Gallia Cisalpina, or **Citerior.** Gaul this side of the Alps, *i.e.* Northern Italy; also called *Gallia Togata* from the Roman form of dress worn.

Gallia Comata. That part of Gaul which belonged to the Roman Emperor was so called from the hair (*coma*) of the inhabitants, which flowed over their shoulders. Also called *Tres Provinciæ*, it included the three provinces *Aquitania*, *Lugdununensis*, and *Belgica*, with a common capital at *Lugdunum* (Lyon).

Gallia Togata. *See* GALLIA CISALPINA; TOGA.

Gallia Transalpina, or **Ulterior**. Often called simply GALLIA, it included the modern France, Belgium, and parts of Holland, Germany, and Switzerland.

Gallicism. A phrase or sentence constructed after the French idiom; as, "When you shall have returned home you will find a letter on your table." In *Matt.* xv, 32, "I have compassion on the multitude, because they continue with me now three days, and have nothing to eat", is a Gallicism. *Cp. Mark* viii, 2. Also the use of a word in a sense peculiar to the French language, as "assist" in the sense of to "be present", using a word common to both languages in a French sense, etc.

Galligaskins. A loose wide kind of breeches worn by men in the 16th and 17th centuries.

> My galligaskins, that have long withstood
> The winter's fury and encroaching frosts ...
> A horrid chasm disclos'd, with orifice
> Wide, discontinuous.
>
> J. PHILIPS: *The Splendid Shilling* (1701).

The word is a corruption of Fr. *garguesque*, which is the Ital. *grechesca*, Greekish, referring to a Greek article of clothing.

Gallimaufry. A medley; any confused jumble of things; but strictly speaking, a HOTCH-POTCH made of all the scraps of the larder (Fr. *galimafrée*, the origin of which is unknown, though it is probably related to GALIMATIAS).

> They have a kind of dance which the wenches say is a gallimaufry of gambols, because they are not in't.
>
> SHAKESPEARE: *Winter's Tale*, IV, iii.

Gallio. A name applied to a person, particularly an official whose chief characteristic is one of indifference, especially to things outside his province.

> And Gallio cared for none of those things.
>
> *Acts* xviii, 17.

Gallo-Belgicus (găl ō bel′ ji kús). An annual register in Latin for European circulation, first published in 1598.

> It is believed,
> And told for news with as much diligence
> As if 'twere writ in Gallo-Belgicus.
>
> THOMAS MAY: *The Heir*, 1615.

Galloglass, or **Gallowglass**. An armed servitor or foot-soldier in ancient IRELAND (O.Ir. and Gael. *gall*, a stranger; *oglach*, a warrior). SHAKESPEARE speaks of *kerns and gallowglasses* as coming from the Western Isles of SCOTLAND. *See* KERN.

> The merciless Macdonwald ... from the Western Isles
> Of kerns and gallowglasses is supplied.
>
> *Macbeth*, I, ii.

Gallup Poll. The best known of the public opinion surveys, instituted by Dr. George Gallup of the American Institute of Public Opinion in 1935. Trained interviewers interrogate a carefully selected but small cross-section of the population. For the British Parliamentary election of 1945, out of 25 million voters, 1,809 were interviewed, but the Gallup Poll forecast was within 1 per cent; but the forecast was wrong for the American Presidential Election of 1948. The LABOUR PARTY victory was forecast for the British Parliamentary Elections in 1964 and 1966. It is held that such polls in themselves influence the result. STRAW POLLS and market research surveys were the forerunners of the Gallup Poll. *Cp.* MASS OBSERVATION.

Galosh. The word comes from the Span. *galocha* (wooden shoes); Ger. *Galosche*; Fr. *galoche*, which is probably from Gr. *Kalopous*, a shoemaker's last.

It was originally applied to a kind of clog or patten worn as a protection against wet in the days when silk or cloth shoes were worn. It is used in this sense by Langland.

> ... the kynde of Knyght that cometh to be doubed,
> To geten hus gilte spores and galoches y-couped.
>
> *Piers Plowman*, xxi, 12.

Galway Jury. An enlightened, independent jury. The expression has its origin when Thomas Wentworth, Lord Deputy of IRELAND, revived the king's claim to all the lands of Connaught. The juries of Mayo, Sligo, and Roscommon found verdicts in favour of the Crown, but that of Galway stood out against the plan; whereupon the SHERIFF was sentenced to a fine of £1,000 and each of the jurors £4,000.

Gambrel. Also known as cambrel, chambrel, chambren, gambril (O.Fr. *gambe*, the leg); the hock of a horse or other animal, also a crooked stick somewhat similarly shaped once used by butchers, from which they suspended carcases. *See* MANSARD ROOF.

> "Gambrel?—Gambrel?"—Let me beg
> You'll look at a horse's hinder leg—
> First great angle above the hoof,—
> That's the gambrel; hence gambrel-roof.
>
> O. W. HOLMES: *Autocrat of the Breakfast-Table*, xii.

Game (O.E. *gamen*, joy, sport). This word is variously used to mean play, sport, contest, trick, jest, etc.; it is also applied collectively to certain wild animals and birds legally protected and pursued for sport. *See* SPORTING SEASONS.

The game's afoot. The hare has started; the enterprise has begun.

> I see you stand like greyhounds in the slips,
> Straining upon the start. The game's afoot!
> Follow your spirit!
>
> SHAKESPEARE: *Henry V*, III, i.

The game is not worth the candle. *See under* CANDLE.

The game is up. The scheme, endeavour, plot, etc., has come to grief; all is at an end. In hunting it has the same significance as THE GAME'S AFOOT.

He's a game 'un. He's got some pluck, he's "a plucked 'un". Another allusion to gamecocks.

He's at his little games again, or **at the same old game.** He's at his old tricks; he's gone back to his old habits or practices.

To die game. To maintain a courageous attitude to the end. A phrase from COCK-FIGHTING.

To have the game in one's hands. To have such an advantage that success is assured; to hold the winning cards.

To play a waiting game. To bide one's time, knowing that that is the best way of winning; to adopt FABIAN TACTICS (*see under* FABIUS).

To play the game. To act in a straightforward, honourable manner; to keep to the rules of fair play.

> This they all with a joyful mind
> Bear through life like a torch in flame,
> And falling, fling to the host behind—
> "Play up! Play up! and play the game!"
>
> SIR HENRY NEWBOLT: *Vitaï Lampada*.

You are making game of me. You are bamboozling me, holding me up to ridicule. *Cp.* TO PULL SOMEONE'S LEG *under* PULL.

Game Chicken. The sobriquet of the pugilist Hen Pearce. Beginning as a pupil of James Belcher, he eventually defeated his teacher in a terrible battle on Barnby Moor near Doncaster, 6 December, 1805.

Game Laws. A series of enactments akin to the old FOREST LAW, designed to protect game for the landowner and to prevent poaching, and formerly noted for their harshness. In 1671 a Game Law was passed which prevented all freeholders killing game except those with lands worth £100 a year. *The Extraordinary Black Book* of 1831 pointed out that 50 times more property was required to kill a partridge than to vote for a KNIGHT OF THE SHIRE. In the reign of George III, 32 Game Laws were passed. The modern game licence for the killing of game stems from the Game Act of 1831, which also demarcated the seasons during which certain game might be taken. From 1671 to 1831 the sale of game was totally prohibited, thus providing a lucrative market for poachers.

> A labourer in Christian England,
> Where they cant of a Saviour's name,
> And yet waste men's lives like the vermin's
> For a few more brace of game.
>
> CHARLES KINGSLEY: *Yeast*, ch. xi.

Game leg. A lame leg. In this instance game is a dialect form of the CELTIC *cam*, meaning crooked. It is of comparatively modern usage. **Gammy** is also in this sense.

Gamecock State. An old nickname for South Carolina, from the supposedly warlike nature of its inhabitants. *See* PALMETTO STATE.

Gamesmanship. A term popularized by Stephen Potter, whose book *The Theory and Practice of Gamesmanship* (1947) defines the meaning in its sub-title. "The Art of Winning Games without actually Cheating".

Gamelyn, The Tale of (găm' lin). A Middle English metrical romance, found among the Chaucer MSS. and supposed to have been intended by him to form the basis of one of the unwritten *Canterbury Tales*, although the authorship is still in doubt. Gamelyn is a younger son to whom a large share of property has been bequeathed by his father. He is kept in servitude and tyrannically used by his elder brother until he is old enough to rebel. After many adventures during which he becomes a leader of outlaws in the woods, he comes to his own again with the help of the king, and justice is meted out to the elder brother. Thomas Lodge uses the story in his book, *Rosalynde, or Euphues' Golden Legacie* (1590), from which SHAKESPEARE drew a large part of *As You Like It*.

Gammadion (ga mā' di ón). The FYLFOT or SWASTIKA, so called because it resembles four Greek capital Gammas (G) set at right angles.

Gammer. A former rustic term for an old woman; a corruption of *grandmother*, with an intermediate form of *granmer*. *Cp.* GAFFER.

Gammer Gurton's Needle. The second earliest extant English comedy, which was probably written by William Stevenson of Christ's College, Cambridge, in the early 1550s but not published until 1575. The comedy is vigorous and it closes with the discovery of Gammer Gurton's missing needle in the seat of Hodge's breeches.

Gammon. This word derives from the same original as *game* and *gamble*, but in Victorian and later slang it means to impose upon, delude, cheat, or play a game upon. As an exclamation it means, "Nonsense, you're pulling my leg".

> A landsman said, "I twig the chap—he's been upon the Mill,
> And 'cause he gammons so the flats, ve calls him Veeping Bill."
>
> BARHAM: *Ingoldsby Legends (Misadventures at Margate)*.

Gamp. Sarah Gamp is a disreputable monthly nurse in Dickens's *Martin Chuzzlewit*, famous for her bulky umbrella and perpetual reference to an imaginary Mrs. Harris, whose opinions always confirmed her own. Hence a *gamp* as a common term for an umbrella.

Gamut (găm' ŭt). Originally, the first or lowest note in Guido d'Arezzo's scale, corresponding to G on the lowest line of the modern bass stave; later the whole series of notes recognized by musicians; hence, the whole range or compass.

It is *gamma ut*; *gamma* (the third letter of the Greek alphabet) was used by Guido to mark the first or lowest note in the mediæval scale; and *ut* is the first word in the mnemonic stanza. *Ut queant laxis resonare fibris*, etc., containing the names of the hexachord. *See* ARETINIAN SYLLABLES.

Gandermonth. An old term for the month following a wife's confinement, when the husband was at a loose end, and sometimes went *gandermooning* or playing the GALLANT. The term possibly derives from the aimless meanderings of the gander when the goose is sitting.

Ganelon. A type of black-hearted treachery, figuring in Dante's *Inferno* and grouped by Chaucer (*Nun's Priest's Tale*, 407) with JUDAS Iscariot and—

> Greek Sinon,
> That broghtest Troye al outrely to sorwe.

He was Count of Mayence, and PALADIN of CHARLEMAGNE. Jealousy of ROLAND made him a traitor; and in order to destroy his rival, he planned with Marsillus, the Moorish king, the attack of RONCESVALLES.

Ganesha (găn' esh à). In Hindu mythology, the god of wisdom and good luck, lord of the Ganas, or lesser deities. He was the son of SIVA and is invoked at the beginning of a journey, or when commencing important work, and on the first pages of books, especially ledgers.

Gang. A gang of saws. A number of power-driven circular saws mounted together so that they can reduce a tree trunk to planks at one operation. *Gang* is similarly applied to various collections of tools, machines, etc., working in combination.

Apple Tree Gang. *See under* APPLE.

Gang of Four (1). Leaders of a Chinese radical group who unsuccessfully attempted to seize control after the death of Mao Tse-tung in 1976. The gang consisted of Jiang Qing (Mao's widow and third wife), Zang Chunjao, Wang Hungwen and Yao Wenyuan.

(2) In Great Britain the name was given to the four M.P.s who left the LABOUR PARTY in 1981 to form the Social Democratic Party (S.D.P.), namely Roy Jenkins (leader until 1983), David Owen, Shirley Williams and William Rodgers. Owen became leader in 1983 and was succeeded by Robert Maclennan in 1987. *See* LIBERAL.

Gang agley, To (Scot.). To go wrong. The verb *to glee*, or *gley*, means to look asquint, sideways.

> The best-laid schemes of mice and men
> Gang aft agley.
>
> BURNS: *To a Mouse*.

Gang-day. *See* ROGATION DAYS.

To gang-up. To form a closely-knit group, usually in a spirit of antagonism.

Ganges, The (găn' jēz). So named from *ganga* or *gunga*, a river; as in *Kishenganga* (the black river), *Neelganga* (the blue river), *Naraingunga* (the river of Naranyana or VISHNU). The Ganges is the *Borra Ganga*, or great river. This sacred river of the Hindus is said to flow from the toe of Vishnu.

> Those who through the curse, have fallen from heaven, having performed ablution in this stream, become free from sin; cleansed from sin by this water and restored to happiness, they shall enter heaven and return again to the gods.
>
> *The Ramayana* (section xxxv).

Gangway. Originally the boarded way (sometimes called the *gang-board*) in the old galleys made for the rowers to pass from stem to stern, and where the mast was laid when it was unshipped (*gang*, an alley). Now the footboards with protecting railings by which passengers enter or leave a ship. When used as an exclamation it means "make way".

Below the gangway. In the HOUSE OF COMMONS, on the farther side of the passageway between the seats which separate the Ministry from the rest of the Members. Thus "to sit below the gangway" is to sit among the members in general, and not among the Ministers or ex-Ministers and leaders of the OPPOSITION.

Gauntlet. *See* GAUNTLET.

Ganymede, or **Ganymedes.** In Greek mythology, the cup-bearer of ZEUS, successor to HEBE, and the type of youthful male beauty. This Trojan youth was taken up to OLYMPUS and made immortal. Hence a cup-bearer generally.

Nature waits upon thee still,
And thy verdant cup does fill;
'Tis fill'd wherever thou dost tread,
Nature's self's thy Ganimede.
COWLEY: *The Grasshopper (Anacreontics)*.

Gaora (gā ôr′ a). According to Hakluyt this was a tract of land inhabited by people without heads, with eyes in their shoulders and their mouths in their breasts. *Cp.* BLEMMYES.

Gape. Looking for gape-seed. Gaping about and doing nothing. A corruption of "Looking agapesing"; *gapesing* (still used in Norfolk) is staring about with one's mouth open.

Seeking a gape's nest (Devon). A gape's nest is a sight which one stares at with wide-open mouth. *Cp.* MARE'S NEST.

Garcia (gar′ si à). **To take a message to Garcia** is to be resourceful and courageous, to be able to accept responsibility and carry one's task through to the end. The phrase originated in the exploit of Lieut. Andrew Rowan who, in the Spanish-American War of 1898, made his way through the Spanish blockade into Cuba, made contact with General Calixto Garcia, chief of the Cuban insurgent forces, and carried news from him back to Washington.

Garcias. The soul of Pedro Garcias. Money. The story is that two scholars of Salamanca discovered a tombstone with the inscription "Here lies the soul of the licentiate Pedro Garcias". On searching they found a purse containing a hundred golden ducats (Lesage: *Gil Blas*, Preface).

Garden, or Garden Sect, The. The disciples of EPICURUS, who taught them in his own garden.

The Garden of Eden. *See* EDEN. Traditionally supposed to be sited in Mesopotamia.

Garden of the Hesperides. *See* HESPERIDES.

Garden City. A name given to both Norwich and Chicago; also, as a general name, to model townships specially planned to provide attractive layouts for housing and industry with a surrounding rural belt and adequate open spaces. The term was first used by an American, A. T. Stewart, in 1869, and applied to an estate development on Long Island. The "garden city" movement in England was due to the social ideas of Sir Ebenezer Howard (1850–1928) set out in his book *To-morrow* (1898). His first garden city was founded at Letchworth, Hertfordshire, in 1903 and his second at Welwyn (1919–1920).

Garden Suburb. A name applied to certain model suburbs (*e.g.* Hampstead Garden Suburb) with certain characteristics of a GARDEN CITY.

The Garden Suburb. The nickname applied to Lloyd George's personal secretariat, of which he made increasing use after he became head of the War Cabinet (December 1916), to help him in effecting his policies. The name derives from the fact that they were accommodated in huts in St. James's Park. The "Garden Suburb" was dispersed when Bonar Law assumed the premiership in 1922.

Garden. A term commonly applied to the more fertile areas as:

Garden of England. Kent and Worcester are both so called.

Garden of Europe. Italy.

Garden of France. Amboise, in the department of Indre-et-Loire; also Touraine.

Garden of the Gods. In the U.S.A., an area west of COLORADO Springs at the foot of Pikes Peak, consisting of massive beds of red and pink sandstone rocks taking their colour from red oxide deposits. There are many fanciful shapes resembling cathedral spires, animals and carved faces.

Garden of India. Oudh.

Garden of Ireland. Carlow.

Garden of Italy. The island of Sicily.

Garden of Spain. Andalusia.

Garden of Switzerland. Thurgau.

Garden of the Sun. The East Indian (or Malayan) Archipelago.

Garden of the West. Illinois; also applied to Kansas ("the Garden State").

Garden of the World. The region of the Mississippi.

To lead up the garden, or **garden path.** To deceive, to trick, to entice with false promises of fair prospects, etc.

Gardy loo. The cry of warning formerly given by Edinburgh housewives and servants when about to empty the contents of the slop-pail out of the window into the street below. It is a corruption of the Fr. *gare de l'eau*, beware of the water.

At ten o'clock at night the whole cargo of the chamber utensils is flung out of a back window that looks into some street or lane, and the maid calls "Gardy loo" to the passengers.
SMOLLETT: *Humphry Clinker*.

Gargantua. A giant of mediæval or possibly CELTIC legend famous for his enormous appetite (Sp. *garganta*, gullet), adopted by Rabelais in his great satire (1535), and made the father of PANTAGRUEL. One of his exploits was to swallow five pilgrims, complete with their staves, in a salad. He is the subject of a number of CHAP-BOOKS, and became proverbial as a voracious and insatiable guzzler.

> You must borrow me Gargantua's mouth first before I can utter so long a word; 'tis a word too great for any mouth of this age's size.
>
> SHAKESPEARE: *As You Like It*, III, ii.

Gargouille (gar goo ēl'). The great DRAGON that lived in the Seine, ravaged Rouen, and was slain by St. Romanus, Archbishop of Rouen, in the 7th century.

Garibaldi's red shirt. The famous red shirt worn by Garibaldi and his followers during the liberation of Italy was of accidental origin. When Garibaldi was raising an Italian legion at Montevideo in 1843 a number of red woollen shirts came on the market owing to the difficulties in trade due to the war with Argentina. The government of Uruguay bought them up cheaply and gave them to Garibaldi for his men. When the Italian Legion came over to Italy in 1848 they brought their red shirts with them.

The Garibaldi biscuit, in which currants are mixed in the pastry, was a form of food much favoured by the General on his farm in Caprera.

The name *Garibaldi* was also given to a loose-fitting blouse for women, fashionable in the late 19th century.

Garland. Primarily a wreath of flowers either worn or festooned around something. Its use has also been extended to apply to an anthology of prose or verse.

> What I now offer to your lordships is a collection of Poetry, a kind of Garland of Good Will.
>
> PRIOR'S dedication to his *Poems*.

Garlic. The old superstition that garlic can destroy the magnetic power of the LODESTONE has the sanction of Pliny, Solinus, Ptolemy, Plutarch, Albertus, Mathiolus, Rueus, Rulandus, Renodæus, Langius, and others. Sir Thomas Browne places it among *Vulgar Errors* (Bk. II, ch. iii).

> Martin Rulandus saith that Onions and Garlick ... hinder the attractive power of the magnet and rob it of its virtue of drawing iron, to which Renodæus agrees; but this is all lies.
>
> W. SALMON: *The Complete English Physician*, ch. xxv (1693).

Garlic Wall. The satirical name applied by Gibraltarians to the Spanish barrier which closed the frontier to La Línea in 1969 as a consequence of Spain's claim to the Rock. GIBRALTAR was ceded to Great Britain by the Treaty of Utrecht, 1713. Spain reopened the frontier at La Linea in 1985. *See* ROCK SCORPION.

Garnish. In old prison slang, the entrance money, to be spent on drink, demanded by gaol-birds from new arrivals. *Garnish* means embellishment, extra decoration to dress, etc.; hence it was applied by prisoners to fetters, and the *garnish-money* was money given for the "honour" of wearing them; the bigger the "garnish", the lighter the fetters.

In its original meaning, to *garnish* was to warn (Fr. *garnir*), and it is in this sense still used in the legal term *garnishee*, one warned not to pay money he owes to another, because the latter is in debt to the *garnisher* who issues the warning.

Garratt. The Mayor of Garratt. The "mayor" of Garratt, Wandsworth, was really the chairman of an association of villagers formed to resist encroachments on the common in the latter part of the 18th century. It became the practice to choose a new "mayor" at the same time as the occurrence of a General Election. These events became popular public occasions and at one such there were more than 80,000 people present—the candidates usually being lively characters. During one election a dead cat was thrown at the hustings and a bystander remarked that it stank "worse than a fox." "That's no wonder", replied Sir John Harper (one of the mayors), "For you see, it's a poll-cat."

The election addresses were written by Garrick, Wilkes, and others, and were satires on electoral corruption and contemporary political life. The first recorded mayor was "Squire Blowmedown"; the last (1796) was "Sir" Harry Dimsdale, a muffin-seller and dealer in tinware.

Foote has a farce called *The Mayor of Garratt* (1764). The place-name still survives in Garratt Lane.

Garraway's. A famous coffee-house in Change Alley, Cornhill, opened about 1670 by Thomas Garraway (or Garway, etc.) although he was probably trading in the late 1650s in Sweetings Rents. He also sold tea "in leaf and drink" and claimed to be the first vendor (1657) of that commodity to the general public (this claim probably refers to his former premises). Garraway's came to be much frequented by merchants, bankers, the South Sea Company Directors and other City men and was long used by such as a business address. In 1719 and 1720 various "bubble companies" advertised from Garraway's and a wide variety of merchandise was auctioned there, including ships, beaver coats for the Hudson's Bay Company, and house property. Garraway's closed in 1866 and the building was demolished about 1873. *See* SOUTH SEA BUBBLE.

> There is an old monastery-crypt under Garraway's (I have been in it among the port wine), and perhaps Garraway taking pity on the mouldy men who

wait in its public room all their lives, gives them cool house-room down there over Sundays.

DICKENS: *The Uncommercial Traveller*, ch. xxii.

Garter. The Most Noble Order of the Garter. The highest order of Knighthood in Great Britain, traditionally instituted by King Edward III about 1348, and reconstituted in 1805 and 1831. The popular legend is that the Countess of Salisbury accidentally slipped her garter at a court ball. It was picked up by the king who, noticing the significant looks of the spectators, rebuked them by binding the blue band round his own knee, saying as he did so, HONI SOIT QUI MAL Y PENSE. The lady has also been named as Joan the FAIR MAID OF KENT, her cousin, Alice Montague and Queen Philippa. The order is limited to the Sovereign, and other members of the Royal Family, with 25 knights, and such foreign royalties as may be admitted by statute. The only Ladies of the Garter are the Sovereign's Queen and his eldest daughter when she is heir presumptive to the throne. Until Viscount Grey (then Sir Edward Grey) was admitted to the order in 1912, no commoner for centuries had been able to put "K.G." after his name. Sir Winston Churchill received the Order of the Garter from Queen Elizabeth II in 1953.

St. GEORGE was from the outset the special patron of the Order; it is sometimes called the Order of St. George, and each Knight is allotted a stall in St. George's Chapel, Windsor. The habits and insignia are the garter, mantle, surcoat, hood, star, collar, and GEORGE.

Garters. Wearing the garters of a pretty girl either on the hat or knee was a common custom with our forefathers. Brides usually wore on their legs a host of gay ribbons, to be distributed after the marriage ceremony amongst the bridegroom's friends; and the piper at the wedding dance never failed to tie a piece of the bride's garter round his pipe.

Magic garters. In the old romances, etc., garters made of the strips of a young hare's skin saturated with motherwort. Those who wore them excelled in speed.

Flying-the-garter. Springing or jumping lightly over something. Flying-the-garter was a one-time children's game, in which the players jumped over the *garter* or line (usually of stones), and the back of another player. In circuses, the tapes held up for performers to jump over were called *garters*.

> "Who do you suppose will ever employ a professional man, when they see his boy playing at marbles, or flying the garter in the horse road?"
> DICKENS: *The Pickwick Papers*, ch. xxxviii.

Prick the garter. An old swindling game, better known as "Fast and Loose". *See under* FAST.

Garvies. Sprats; perhaps so called from Inch-garvie, the island in the Firth of Forth.

Gasconade. Absurd boasting, vainglorious BRAGGADOCIO. It is said that a Gascon, being asked what he thought of the Louvre in Paris, replied "Pretty well; it reminds me of the back part of my father's stables"; an especially boastful answer when the Gascons were proverbial for their poverty. Another Gascon, in proof of his ancient nobility, asserted that they used no other fuel in his father's house than the batons of the family MARSHALS.

Gat. An American slang term for an automatic pistol. It is a contraction of *Gatling*, from the machine-gun invented (1861–1862) by Richard Jordan Gatling (1818–1903), of North Carolina.

Gat-tooth. Chaucer's "Wife of Bath" was *gat-toothed* (*see Prol.* to *Canterbury Tales*, 468, and *Wife of Bath's Prol.*, 603); this probably means that her teeth were set wide apart, with *gats*, *i.e.* openings or gaps between them. Some editors suggest it is *goat-toothed* (O.E. *gat*), *i.e.* lascivious, like a GOAT.

Gate. Gate of Italy. A narrow gorge between two mountain ridges in the valley of the Adige, in the vicinity of Trent and Rovereto.

Gate of Tears. The passage into the Red Sea so called by the Arabs (*Bab-el-Mandeb*) from the number of shipwrecks that took place there.

Golden Gate. *See under* GOLD.

Tom Gate. *See under* TOM.

Traitors' Gate. *See* TRAITORS'.

Gate crasher. One who gains entrance to a social function without invitation or ticket of admission. The origin is obvious.

Gate money. Money paid at the door or gate for admission to an enclosure where some entertainment or contest, etc., is to take place.

Gate-posts. The post on which a gate hangs is called the hanging-post; that against which it shuts is called the banging-post.

Gate-post bargain. A "cash down" deal. An old country custom of placing the purchase money on the gate-post before the stock being sold left the field. *Cp.* LUCK MONEY; TO PAY ON THE NAIL *under* NAIL.

Between you and me and the gate-post. Strictly confidentially.

Gath. Tell it not in Gath. Don't let your enemies hear it. Gath was famed as the birthplace of the giant GOLIATH.

> Tell it not in Gath, publish it not in the streets of Askelon: lest the daughters of the Philistines

rejoice, lest the daughters of the uncircumcised triumph.

II *Sam*. i, 20.

Gatling Gun. *See* GAT.

Gaudeamus igitur (Lat). The opening words of the famous students' song of mediæval origin, the first line being — *Gaudeamus igitur juvenes dum sumus* (Let us therefore rejoice while we are young). It has seven verses and was formerly often sung at student celebrations.

Gaudy, or **Gaudy-day** (gaw′ di) (Lat. *gaudium*, joy). A holiday, a feast-day; especially an annual celebration of some event, such as the foundation of a college.

Gaudy is also one of the beads in the ROSARY marking the five joys or JOYFUL MYSTERIES of the Virgin, and the name given to one of the tapers burnt at the commemoration of the same.

Gaul. The country inhabited by the Gauls. *See* GALLIA.

Gaunt. John of Gaunt (1340–1399), fourth son of Edward III; so called from his birthplace, Ghent in Flanders.

Gauntlet. To run the gauntlet. To be attacked on all sides, to be severely criticized. The word came into English at the time of the THIRTY YEARS WAR (1618–1648) as *gantlope*, meaning the passage between two files of soldiers. It is the Swedish *gata*, a way, passage (*cp.* GAT-TOOTH) and *lopp* (connected with our *leap*, a course). The reference is to the former punishment among soldiers and sailors; the company or crew, provided with rope ends, were drawn up in two rows facing each other, and the delinquent had to run between them, while every man dealt him as severe a punishment as he could. The spelling *gauntlet* (*gantlet*) here is a due to confused etymology with *gauntlet*, a glove (O.Fr. *gantelet*, a diminutive of *gant*, a glove).

To take up the gauntlet. To accept a challenge. *See* GLOVE.

To throw down the gauntlet. To challenge. In mediæval times, when one KNIGHT challenged another, the custom was for the challenger to throw his gauntlet on the ground, and if the challenge was accepted the person to whom it was thrown picked it up. Such a challenge was used by the CHAMPION OF ENGLAND.

Gautama (gaw ta′ ma). The family name of BUDDHA. His personal name was Siddhartha, his father's name Suddhodana, and his mother's name Maya. He assumed the title Buddha at about the age of 36, when, after seven years of seclusion and spiritual struggle, he believed himself to have attained to perfect truth.

Gauvaine. GAWAIN.

Gavelkind. A system of tenure, especially in Kent and Wales and also in other parts of England. It was based on the freemen who gave rent or *gafol* to their lord instead of services. Some of its principal features were that if a person died intestate his property was divided equally among his sons or his daughters in the absence of sons. The dower was half instead of a third of a husband's land; a widower's courtesy one half of the land while remaining unmarried. After the Norman conquest it was replaced in England by the custom of primogeniture, except in Kent. It was abolished in Wales during the reign of Henry VIII and completely by Acts of Parliament of 1922 and 1925.

Gawain (gà wān′). One of the most famous of the Arthurian knights, nephew of King ARTHUR and probably the original hero of the GRAIL·quest. He appears in the Welsh Triads and in the MABINOGION as Gwalchmei, and in the Arthurian cycle is the centre of many episodes and poems. The Middle English poem *Sir Gawain and the Green Knight* (*c.* 1360) is a romance telling how Gawain beheads the Green Knight in single combat.

Gay (O.Fr. *gai*). Light-hearted, merry, in high good spirits; also bright looking, as "she wore a gay-coloured dress".

Belinda smiled and all the world was gay.

POPE: *The Rape of the Lock*, II, 52.

Gay also acquired the sense of "given to pleasure" and hence dissipated; thus we say "he's a bit of a gay dog" and a *gay house* was a once common term for a brothel. In current slang, even less happily, the word is applied to homosexuals, who are now the "gay people".

A gay deceiver. A LOTHARIO, a LIBERTINE; also in modern slang a brassière lined with sponge-like plastic padding.

The Gay Science. A translation of *gai saber*, the old Provençal name for the art of poetry. A guild formed at Toulouse in 1323 with the object of keeping in existence the dying Provençal language and culture was called the *Gai Saber*. Its full title was "The Very Gay Company of the Seven Troubadours of Toulouse".

Gaze. To stand at gaze. To stand in doubt as to what to do. When a stag first hears the hounds it stands dazed, looking all round, and in doubt as to what to do. Heralds call a stag represented full-faced, "a stag at gaze".

As the poor frightened deer, that stands at gaze,
Wildly determining which way to fly.

SHAKESPEARE: *Rape of Lucrece*, 1149.

Gaze-hound. *See* LYME-HOUND.

Gazelle boy, The. In 1961, Jean-Claude Armen, travelling by camel through the Spanish Sahara in W. Africa, was told by nomad tribesmen of the whereabouts of a young boy living with a herd of gazelles. In due time he sighted the boy and eventually attracted him to close quarters by playing a Berber flute. The boy fed on the same plants as the animals, sometimes eating worms and lizards. On a subsequent expedition in 1963, this time in a jeep, the speed of the boy when galloping with the herd was established at over 30 m.p.h. *Cp.* PETER THE WILD BOY.

Gazette. A newspaper. A word of Italian origin derived from the government newspaper issued in Venice from about 1536. It may be a diminutive of *gazza*, a magpie, in the sense of gossip, tittle-tattle, chatter (*cp.* the English *Tatler, Chatterbox, Town Talk*), or from *gazetta*, a small coin charged as a fee for reading the Venetian newspaper.

The London Gazette, an official government organ, appeared first as the *Oxford Gazette* in 1665, when the Court was at Oxford. It was transferred to LONDON in 1666 and has appeared on Tuesdays and Fridays ever since. It contains announcements of pensions, promotions, bankruptcies, dissolutions of partnerships, etc. *Cp.* NEWS; YELLOW PRESS.

Similar journals are published at Edinburgh and Belfast, the latter being transferred from Dublin after the establishment of the Irish Free State.

Gazetted. Posted in the LONDON GAZETTE as having received some official appointment, service promotion, etc., or on being declared bankrupt, etc.

Gazetteer. A geographical and topographical index or dictionary; so called because the name of one of the earliest such works in English was Laurence Echard's *The Gazetteer's or Newsman's Interpreter* (1703), *i.e.* it was intended for the use of journalists, *gazetteer* being a word applied to writers of news.

Gazumping. A colloquial usage (derivation uncertain) from the early 1970s particularly with relation to the property market. It denotes the somewhat dubious practice of raising a selling price after agreement has been reached with an intending purchaser. After having fixed a price with the vendor the purchaser finds that he is *gazumped* by the vendor accepting an increased offer from another buyer before contracts have been signed and exchanged.

Ge. *See* GÆA.

Gear. Clothing, equipment, etc., as, for ex-ample, *sports gear* (O.E. *gearwe*, dress). Also the combination of toothed wheels and levers which connect a motor with its work, etc. *High gear* is the arrangement whereby the driving part moves slowly in relation to the driven part; *low gear* is when the driving part moves relatively more quickly than the driven.

In good gear. To be in good working order.

Out of gear. Not in working condition; out of health.

Gee-up! and **Gee-whoa!** Interjections addressed to horses meaning respectively "Go ahead!" and "Stop!" From them came the children's term "gee-gee", a horse, which was adopted by sporting men and others, as in "Backing the gee-gees".

Geese. *See* GOOSE.

Gehenna (ge hen' à) (Heb.). The place of eternal torment. Strictly speaking, it means the "Valley of Hinnom" (Ge-Hinnom), where sacrifices to BAAL and MOLOCH were offered (*Jer.* xix, 6, etc.). It came to be regarded as a place of unquenchable fire, possibly from the fires of Moloch.

> And made his grove
> The pleasant valley of Hinnom, Tophet thence
> And black Gehenna called, the type of hell.
> MILTON: *Paradise Lost*, I, 403.

Go to Gehenna. The same as saying "Go to Hell".

Gelert (gel' ĕrt). Llewelyn's dog. *See* BEDD-GELERT.

Gemara (ge ma' rà) (Aramaic, completion). The second part of the TALMUD, consisting of annotations, discussions and amplifications of the MISHNA, which is the first part. The *Mishna* is the codification of the oral law, the *Gemara* is supplementary and commentary on the *Mishna*.

The Palestinian or Jerusalem *Gemara* was completed by the Palestinian academics in the 5th century A.D. and the much fuller Babylonian *Gemara* by the academics of Babylon during the 4th and 5th centuries A.D.

Gemini. Lat. the Twins, a constellation and one of the signs of the ZODIAC (21 May to 21 June); representing CASTOR AND POLLUX, the "great twin brethren" of classical mythology.

Gen (jen). **Give us the gen.** Tell us the news, give us the detailed information; hence **to gen up** means to inform oneself fully or to "swot up" a subject. A phrase from Service slang, especially in the R.A.F.; it comes from either "General information" or "Genuine".

Gendarmes (zhon' darm) (Fr. *gens d'armes*, men-at-arms), the armed police of France. The term was first applied to an armed

KNIGHT or CAVALIER, then to the cavalry. In the time of Louis XIV it was applied to a body of horse charged with the preservation of order, and after the Revolution to a military police chosen from old soldiers of good character; and now to the ordinary police.

Gender Words. These are words which, prefixed to the noun, indicate an animal's sex, e.g.:

Bull, cow: elephant, rhinoceros, seal and whale.

Dog, bitch: ape, fox (the bitch is usually called a vixen), otter, wolf.

Buck, doe: hare, rabbit, deer.

He, she: general gender words for quadrupeds.

Cock, hen: gender words for most birds.

In many cases a different word is used for each of the sexes, e.g.: Boar, sow; cockerel, pullet; colt, filly; drake, duck; gander, goose; hart, roe; ram, ewe; stag, hind; stallion, mare; steer (in the U.S.A. used of beef cattle of any age), heifer.

General. General Average. In marine insurance, the apportionment of the contribution to be made by the owners or insurers, of a ship and cargo for "intentional damage", *i.e.* the jettisoning of cargo, masts etc., in an emergency, acceptance of towage and so on.

General Issue. An old legal term for a plea of "not guilty"; the issue formed by a general denial of the plaintiff's charge.

General Warrants. Warrants issued for the arrest of unspecified persons, first by the Court of STAR CHAMBER and subsequently authorized by the Licensing Act of 1662, and continued after its lapse in 1695, when they were used against the authors and publishers of allegedly seditious or libellous writings. They were declared illegal as a result of actions brought against the Crown (1763–1765) by John Wilkes, who was arrested with others after the publication of NUMBER 45 (*see under* FORTY) of the *North Briton*. The Incitement to Disaffection Act passed in 1934 to prevent Communist propaganda in the armed forces permitted the issue of a general warrant by a High Court Judge.

Generalissimo. The supreme commander, especially of a force drawn from two or more nations, or of a combined military and naval force; the equivalent of *Tagus* among the ancient Thessalians, *Brennus* among the ancient Gauls, and PENDRAGON among the ancient Welsh or Celts. The title is said to have been coined by Cardinal Richelieu on taking supreme command of the French armies in Italy, in 1629.

In modern times the title has been applied to Marshal Foch (1851–1929), who commanded the Allied forces in France in 1918; to Joseph Stalin (1879–1953), who was made generalissimo of the Soviet forces in 1943; to General Franco (1892–1975) who proclaimed himself generalissimo of the Spanish army in 1939; and to Marshal Chiang Kai-shek (1888–1975), leader of the KUOMINTANG, who was in power in China from 1927 to 1949.

Generic Names. *See* BIDDY.

Generous. Generous as Hatim. An Arabian expression. Hatim was a Bedouin chief famous for his warlike deeds and boundless generosity. His son was a contemporary of MOHAMMED.

> Let Zal and Rustum bluster as they will,
> Or Hatim call to supper—heed not you.
> FITZGERALD: *Rubáiyát of Omar Khayyám*, x.

Geneva (je nē' và). *See* GIN.

Geneva Bible. *See* BIBLE, THE ENGLISH.

Geneva Bull. A nickname given to Stephen Marshal (c. 1594–1655), a PRESBYTERIAN divine and one of the authors of SMECTYMNUUS, because he was a disciple of John Calvin of Geneva, and when preaching "roared like a BULL of Bashan". His influence on political and religious affairs was considerable.

Geneva Convention. In 1862, Jean Henri Dunant, a Swiss, published an account of the sufferings of the wounded at the battle of Solferino in 1859. From this sprang the RED CROSS movement and an international conference at Geneva in 1864. The resulting Geneva Convention provided for the care of the wounded and the protection of the military medical services, under the international emblem of the RED CROSS (*see under* CROSS).

Geneva courage. POT VALOUR; the BRAGGADOCIO resulting from having drunk too much GIN or *geneva*. *Cp.* DUTCH COURAGE.

Geneva Cross. *See* THE RED CROSS *under* CROSS.

Geneva doctrines. CALVINISM.

Geneviève, St. (je nà vēv) (422–512). Patroness of PARIS. Her day is 3 January, and she is represented in art with the keys of Paris at her girdle, a DEVIL blowing out her candle, and an ANGEL relighting it; or as restoring sight to her blind mother; or guarding her father's sheep. She was born at Nanterre and was influential in saving Paris from the FRANKS and the threatened attack of ATTILA the Hun. Her church has since become the PANTHEON.

Genius (pl. *Genii*). In Roman mythology the tutelary spirit that attended a man from cradle to grave, governed his fortunes, determined his character. The *Genius* wished a man to enjoy pleasure in life, thus to *indulge one's Genius* was to enjoy pleasure. The *Genius* only existed for man, the woman had her JUNO. Another belief was that a man had two *genii*, one good and one evil, and bad luck was due to his *evil genius*. The Roman *genii* were somewhat similar to the guardian angels spoken of in *Matt*. xviii, 10. The word is from the Lat. *gignere*, to beget (Gr. *gignesthai*, to be born), from the notion that birth and life were due to these *dii genitales*. Thus it is used for birth-wit or innate talent; hence propensity, nature, inner man.

The Eastern *genii* (sing. *genie*) were JINNS, who were not attendant spirits but fallen angels under the dominion of EBLIS.

Genius loci. The tutelary deity of a place.

> In the midst of this wreck of ancient books and utensils, with a gravity equal to Marius among the ruins of Carthage, sat a large black cat, which to a superstitious eye, might have presented the *genius loci*, the tutelar demon of the apartment.
> SCOTT: *The Antiquary*, ch. iii.

Genocide (jen′ ō sīd). A word invented by Professor Raphael Lemkin, of Duke University, U.S.A., and used in the drafting of the official indictment of war criminals in 1945. It is a combination of Gr. *genos*, race; and Lat. *cædere*, to kill. It is defined as acts intended to destroy, in whole or in part, national, ethnical, racial, or religious groups, and in 1948 was declared by the United Nations General Assembly to be a crime in international law.

Genre Painter (zhon′ rė) (Fr. mode, style). A term applied to those who paint scenes of everyday life in the home, the village, the countryside, etc. The Dutch artists of Rembrandt's time were particularly characteristic of this style. The term is sometimes used of drama in the same sense.

Gens (jenz) (Lat. pl. *gentes*). A CLAN or SEPT in ancient ROME; a number of families deriving from a common ancestor, having the same name, religion, etc.

Gens bracata, or **braccata** (Lat.). Trousered people. Unlike the Gauls, Scythians, and Persians, the Romans wore no trousers or breeches. *Cp*. GALLIA BRACCATA.

Gens togata. *See* TOGA.

Gentle. Belonging to a family of position; well-born; having the manners of genteel persons. The word is from Lat. *gentilis*, of the same family or *gens*, through O.Fr. *gentil*, high-born.

> We must be gentle, now we are gentlemen.
> SHAKESPEARE: *The Winter's Tale*, V, ii.

The gentle craft. Shoe-making. CRISPIN and Crispianus, the patron saints of shoe-making, were said to be brothers of noble birth.

> As I am a true shoemaker, and a gentleman of the Gentle Craft, buy spurs yourselfes, and I'll find ye bootes these seven yeeres.
> DEKKER: *The Shoemaker's Holiday, or the Gentle Craft*, I, i (1599).

Angling is also known as "the gentle craft". It is a pun on *gentle*, the maggot of the flesh-fly or blue-bottle, used as a bait.

> Every little pitiful coarse fish in the Avon was on the alert for flies ... and every lover of the gentle craft was out to avenge the poor may-flies.
> T. HUGHES: *Tom Brown's Schooldays*, ch. ix.

The gentle sex. Women.

The Gentle Shepherd. A nickname given by the elder Pitt to George Grenville (1712–1770). In the course of a speech on the cider tax (1763) Grenville addressed the HOUSE somewhat plaintively: "Tell me where? Tell me where?" Pitt mimicked him with the words of the song "Gentle shepherd, tell me where?" The House burst into laughter and the name stuck to Grenville. The line is from a song by Samuel Howard (1710–1782).

Gentleman (from O.Fr. *gentilz hom*). Historically a man entitled to bear arms but not of the nobility; hence one of gentle birth, of some position in society, and with manners, bearing and behaviour appropriate to one in such a position.

> Be it spoken (with all reverent reservation of duty) the king who hath power to make Esquires, Knights, Baronets, Barons, Viscounts, Earls, Marquesses, and Dukes, *cannot make a gentleman*, for Gentilitie is a matter of race, and of blood, and of descent, from Gentle and noble parents and ancestors, which no kings can give to any, but to such as they beget.
> EDMUND HOWES (*fl*. 1607–1631).

In the *York Mysteries* (*c*. 1440) we read, "Ther schall a gentilman, Jesu, unjustly be judged."

A gentleman at large. A man of means, who does not have to earn a living, and is free to come and go as he pleases. Formerly the term denoted a gentleman attached to the court but having no special duties.

A gentleman of fortune. A pirate, an adventurer, etc.

A gentleman of the four outs. A vulgar upstart, with-out manners, with-out wit, with-out money, and with-out credit. There are variants of the phrase, and sometimes the outs are increased to five:

> Out of money, and out of clothes,
> Out at the heels, and out at the toes,
> Out of credit—but don't forget,
> Never *out of* but aye *in* debt!

A gentleman of the road. A highwayman.

A gentleman's agreement. An agreement or understanding as between gentlemen in which the one guarantee is the honour of the parties concerned.

A gentleman's gentleman. A manservant, especially a valet.

> *Fag:* My master shall know this—and if he don't call him out I will
> *Lucy:* Ha! ha! ha! You gentlemen's gentlemen are so hasty!
>
> SHERIDAN: *The Rivals*, II, ii.

A nation of gentlemen. So George IV called the Scots when, in 1822, he visited their country and was received with great expressions of loyalty.

Gentleman Commoner. *See* FELLOW COMMONER.

Gentleman Pensioner. *See* GENTLEMEN AT ARMS, *below*.

Gentleman-ranker. In the days of the small regular army before World War I, this term was applied to a well-born or educated man who enlisted as a private solider. It was considered as a last resort of one who had made a mess of things.

> We're poor little lambs who've lost our way,
>   Baa! Baa! Baa!
> We're little black sheep who've gone astray,
>   Baa-aa-aa!
> Gentleman-rankers out on the spree,
> Damned from here to eternity,
> God ha' mercy on such as we.
>   Baa! Yah! Bah!
>
> KIPLING: *Gentlemen Rankers*.

Gentlemen Ushers. Court attendants in the Royal Household. They comprise Gentlemen Ushers, Extra Gentlemen Ushers, the Gentleman Usher to the Sword of State, and the Gentleman Usher of the BLACK ROD.

Gentlemen at Arms, The Honourable Corps of. The Bodyguard of the sovereign (formerly called *Gentlemen Pensioners*), acting in conjunction with the *Yeomen of the Guard* (*see* BEEFEATERS). It has a Captain, Lieutenant, Standard Bearer, Clerk of the Cheque, Sub-officer, and 39 Gentlemen at Arms, chosen from retired officers of ranks from General to Major of the Regular Army and Royal Marines.

The gentleman in black velvet. It was in these words that the JACOBITES used to drink to the mole that made the molehill that caused William III's horse to stumble and so brought about his death.

> He urged his horse to strike into a gallop just at a spot where a mole had been at work. Sorrel stumbled on the mole-hill, and went down on his knees. The king fell off and broke his collar bone.
>
> MACAULAY: *History of England*, ch. xxv.

The Old Gentleman. The DEVIL; Old Nick (*see under* NICK). Also a special card in a prepared pack, used for tricks or cheating.

To put a churl upon a gentleman. To

drink beer just after drinking wine.

Geomancy (jē' ō măn si) (Gr. *ge*, the earth; *manteia*, prophecy). DIVINATION by means of the observation of points on the earth or by the patterns made by throwing some earth into the air and allowing it to fall on a flat surface.

Geopolitics. The name given to the German theories of applied political geography developed by Karl Haushofer in the 1920s and earlier by F. Ratzel, whose pupil Kjellen coined the term. Sir Halford Mackinder (1861–1947) and others formulated similar theories. These teachings were used by the NAZIS to support their demand for LEBENSRAUM.

George, St. George. The patron SAINT of ENGLAND since his "adoption" by Edward III (*see* GARTER). His day is 23 April. The popularity of St. George in England stems from the time of the early CRUSADES, for he was said to have come to the assistance of the Crusaders at Antioch in 1098. Many of the Normans under Robert CURTHOSE, son of WILLIAM THE CONQUEROR, took him as their patron.

Gibbon and others argued that George of Cappadocia, the Arian bishop of Alexandria, became the English patron saint but it is more generally accepted that he was a Roman officer martyred (*c.* 300) near Lydda during the Diocletian persecution. He is also the patron saint of Aragon and Portugal.

The legend of St. George and the DRAGON is simply an allegorical expression of the triumph of the Christian hero over evil, which St. JOHN THE DIVINE beheld under the image of a dragon. Similarly, St. MICHAEL, St. MARGARET, St. SYLVESTER, and St. MARTHA are all depicted as slaying dragons; the Saviour and the Virgin as treading them under their feet; St. John the Evangelist as charming a winged dragon from a poisoned chalice given him to drink; and Bunyan avails himself of the same figure when he makes CHRISTIAN prevail upon APOLLYON.

The legend forms the subject of the ballad *St. George for England* in PERCY'S RELIQUES. **St. George he was for England, St. Denis was for France.** This refers to the battle-cries of the two nations—that of England was "St. George!" that of France, "MONTJOIE ST. DENIS!"

> St. George he was for England; St. Denis was for France;
> Sing, Honi soit qui mal y pense.
>
> PERCY: *Reliques: St. George for England*.

St. George's Cross. A red cross on a white background.

When St. George goes on horseback St.

Yves goes on foot. In times of war it was supposed that lawyers have nothing to do. St. GEORGE is the patron of soldiers and St. YVES or Yvo patron of lawyers.

George. A jewelled pendant representing St. GEORGE and the DRAGON, part of the insignia of the GARTER.

> Meanwhile Monmouth ... was flying from the field of battle. At Chedzoy he stopped a moment to mount a fresh horse and to hide his blue riband and his George.
>
> MACAULAY: *History of England*, ch. v.

George IV (1760, 1820–1830) was given many nicknames. As Prince Regent he was known as "Prinny", "Prince FLORIZEL" (the name under which he corresponded with Mrs. Robinson), "The First Gentleman of Europe", "The Adonis of Fifty". As King he was called, among less offensive titles, "Fum the Fourth", as by Byron in *Don Juan*, xi, 78.

George Eliot. The pseudonym of the author of *The Mill on the Floss*, *Silas Marner*, *Romola*, etc.—Mary Ann Evans (1819–1880). She lived with George Henry Lewes from 1854 until his death in 1878, and married her "second" husband John Walter Cross as Mary Ann Evans Lewes.

George Sand. The pen-name of the famous French novelist Amandine Lucile Aurore Dupin, baronne Dudevant (1804–1876). It was adopted during her liaison with Jules Sandeau.

George Cross and Medal. The George Cross is second only to the VICTORIA CROSS. It consists of a plain silver cross with a medallion showing St. GEORGE and the DRAGON in the centre. The words "For Gallantry" appear round the medallion, and in the angle of each limb of the cross is the royal cipher. It hangs from a dark blue ribbon. The George Cross was founded in 1940 for acts of conspicuous heroism, primarily by civilians. It is only awarded to service personnel for acts of heroism not covered by existing military honours.

The George Medal (red ribbon with five narrow blue stripes) is awarded for similar somewhat less outstanding acts of bravery.

George Cross Island. Malta is so called from the award of the George Cross to the island by King George VI in April 1942, in recognition of the steadfastness and fortitude of its people while under siege in World War II. It had suffered constant aerial attacks from Italian and German bombers.

As good as George-a-Green. Resolute-minded; one who will do his duty come what may. George-a-Green was the mythical *Pinder* (*Pinner* or *Pindar*) or pound-keeper of Wakefield, who resisted ROBIN HOOD, Will Scarlet, and LITTLE JOHN single-handed when they attempted to commit a trespass in Wakefield.

Robert Greene wrote a comedy (published 1599) called *George-a-Greene*, or *the Pinner of Wakefield*.

By George. An oath or exclamation. "St. George" was the battle-cry of English soldiers, and from this arose such expressions as "before George", "fore George". In American usage it is "George", which has additional meanings, one of which, applied to any person or thing, has the same significance as the CAT'S PYJAMAS (*see under* CAT).

Let George do it. Let someone else do it. Derived from Louis XII of France who, when an unpleasant task arose, was apt to say "Let Georges do it", referring to his minister, Cardinal Georges.

Geraint (ge rīnt'). In Arthurian legend, a tributory prince of Devon, and one of the Knights of the ROUND TABLE. In the MABINOGION, he is the son of Erbin, as he is in the French original *Erec et Enide*, from which Tennyson drew his *Geraint and Enid* in the *Idylls of the King*.

Geranium. The Turks say this was a common mallow changed by the touch of MOHAMMED's garment.

The word is Gr. *geranos*, a crane; and the wild plant is called "Crane's Bill", from the resemblance of the fruit to the bill of a crane.

Gerda, or **Gerdhr** (gĕr' dà). In Scandinavian mythology (the *Skirnismal*) daughter of the Frost-giant Gymir and wife of Frey. She was so beautiful that the brightness of her naked arms illumined both air and sea.

Germain. St. Germain-en-Laye. The favourite summer residence of the Kings of France until Louis XIV moved the court to VERSAILLES. Situated some 13 miles S.W. of Paris, the chateau was the childhood home of Mary Queen of Scots and sheltered the exiled James II after the Revolution of 1688.

German, or **Germane.** Pertaining to, nearly related to, as *cousins-german* (first cousins), *germane to the subject* (bearing on or pertinent to the subject). The word is Lat. *germanus*, of the same germ or stock, and has no connection with the German nation.

> Those that are germane to him, though removed fifty times, shall all come under the hangman.
>
> SHAKESPEARE: *The Winter's Tale*, IV, iii.

Germany. The English name for *Deutschland* (Fr. *Allemagne*) is the Lat. *Germania*, the source of which is uncertain, but possibly a Roman form of a CELTIC or Gaulish name for the TEUTONS; in which case it may be connected with Celt. *gair*, neighbour, *gavin*, war-cry, or with *ger*, spear.

Geoffrey of Monmouth says that Ebrancus, a mythological descendant of BRUTE, and founder of York (*Eboracum*), had twenty sons and thirty daughters by twenty wives. The twenty sons departed to Germany and obtained possession of it. Thus Spenser, speaking of Ebranck, tells us:

> An happy man in his first dayes he was,
> And happy father of faire progeny:
> For all so many weekes as the yeare has,
> So many children he did multiply:
> Of which were twentie sonnes, which did apply
> Their minds to prayse and chevalrous desyre:
> Those germans did subdew all Germany,
> Of whom it hight.
>
> *The Faerie Queene*, II, x, 22.

German comb. The four fingers and thumb. The Germans were late in adopting periwigs; and while the French were never seen without a comb in one hand, the Germans tidied their hair by running their fingers through it.

> He apparalled himself according to the season, and afterwards combed his head with an Alman comb.
>
> RABELAIS: *Gargantua and Pantagruel*, Bk. I, xxi.

German silver. A silvery-looking cheap alloy of copper, zinc and nickel. It was first made in Europe at Hildburghausen, in Germany, in the early 19th century but had long been used by the Chinese.

Gerrymander (jer i măn´ dĕr). So to redraw the boundaries of electoral districts as to give one political party undue advantage over others. The word is derived from Elbridge Gerry (1744–1814), governor of Massachusetts, who did this in 1812 in order to preserve control for his party. Gilbert Stuart, the artist, looking at a map of the new distribution, with a little invention converted the outline of one district in Essex County to a salamander and showed it to Benjamin Russell, editor of the Boston *Sentinel*. "Better say a gerrymander," said Russell, and the name caught on. The practice was not new.

Gertrude of Nivelles, St. The daughter of Pepin of Landen, aunt of Charles Martel's father, Pepin of Heristal. As abbess of Nivelles she was noted for her care of the poor and was reputed to have known most of the BIBLE by heart. In art she is usually represented as so rapt in contemplation that a mouse climbs her pastoral staff unnoticed. She died about 664 and her day is 17 March.

Geryon (gēr´ i on). In Greek mythology, a monster with three bodies and three heads, whose oxen ate human flesh, and were guarded by Orthrus, a two-headed dog. HERCULES slew both Geryon and the dog.

Gessler, Hermann. The tyrannical Austrian governor of the three Forest Cantons of Switzerland who figures in the TELL legend.

Gesta Danorum or **Historica Danica.** *See* SAXO GRAMMATICUS.

Gesta Romanorum. A collection of popular tales in Latin, each with a moral attached, compiled at the end of the 13th century or beginning of the 14th. The name, meaning "Deeds of the Romans", is merely fanciful and some of the episodes are of Oriental origin. It was first printed at Utrecht and the earliest English edition is that of Wynkyn de Worde about 1510. It is the source of many stories used in later literature. Chaucer, Shakespeare, Rossetti, Longfellow and many others use tales and plots which are found in it. It seems to have been compiled for the use of preachers.

Gestapo (ge sta´ pō). Shortened from the Ger. *Geheime Staatspolizei*, secret state police, which acquired such sinister fame in NAZI Germany after 1933. It was formed by Goering and later controlled by Himmler and was responsible for terrorizing both the Germans and the peoples of occupied territories. It was declared a criminal organization by the Nuremberg Tribunal in 1946.

Gestas (ges´ tăs). The traditional name of the impenitent thief. *See* DYSMAS.

Get. With its past and past participle *got*, one of the hardest-worked words in the English language, as the following example from a mid-Victorian writer (Dr. Withers) shows:

> I got on horseback within ten minutes after I got your letter. When I got to Canterbury I got a chaise for town; but I got wet through, and have got such a cold that I shall not get rid of it in a hurry. I got to the Treasury about noon, but first of all got shaved and dressed. I soon got into the secret of getting a memorial before the Board, but I could not get an answer then; however, I got intelligence from a messenger that I should get one next morning. As soon as I got back to my inn, I got my supper, and then got to bed. When I got up next morning, I got my breakfast, and, having got dressed, I got out in time to get an answer to my memorial. As soon as I got it, I got into a chaise, and got back to Canterbury by three, and got home for tea. I have got nothing for you, and so adieu.

How are you getting on? How do things fare with you? How are you prospering?

To get about. To travel about, to attend many social events. Also used to denote the spreading of news or rumour. **To get around,** an expression of American origin, has the same meanings.

To get at. To reach; to tamper with, bribe, influence to a wrong end; to attack, tease, to make a butt of, etc.

To get away with it. To do something dangerous, unlawful, wrong, etc., and escape the usual penalty.

To get by. To get along all right, to manage just satisfactorily, to pass MUSTER.

To get cracking. A popular expression with the same meaning as TO GET WEAVING.

To get down to it. To set about a task in downright earnest.

To get it in the neck. To receive a thorough dressing-down, beating, punishment, etc.

To get off. To escape, not to be punished; also (of a girl) to become engaged or to catch a man.

To get over it. To recover from illness, shock, or sorrow.

To get round someone. To persuade by coaxing or flattery.

To get there. To succeed, to "arrive", attain one's object.

To get up. To rise from one's bed. To learn, as, "I must get up my history". To organize and arrange, as "We will get up a bazaar".

To get weaving. To set about a task briskly. A colloquial Services expression in World War II. Weaving implies dexterous movement, as when aircraft make rapid directional changes to escape enemy fire.

To get well on, or **well oiled.** To become intoxicated.

Your get-up was excellent. Your style of dress was entirely suitable for the part you professed to enact. In the same way, "She was got up regardless". Her dress was splendid—regardless of expense.

For phrases such as **You got out of bed the wrong way, To get the mitten, To get the wind up,** etc., see the main word in the phrase.

Gethsemane (geth sem' à ni). The word means "oil-press" and the traditional site of the Garden of Gethsemane, the scene of Our Lord's agony, is on the Mount of Olives, east of the ravine of the Kidron. There was presumably an oil-press on this plot of ground.

The *Orchis maculata* is called "gethsemane" from the legend that is was spotted by the blood of Christ.

Ghan, The. In Australia, a weekly train from Adelaide to ALICE. The construction of a railway line from Adelaide to the northern coast was begun in 1877 but got no further than Oodnadatta (472 km. from Alice Springs). For about 40 years camel trains conducted by Afghans carried goods and passengers from Oodnadatta to Alice. When the railway reached Alice in 1929 the train came to be known as "The Ghan".

Ghebers. See GUEBRES.

Ghibelline. See GUELPH.

Ghost. The Holy Ghost. See under HOLY.

The ghost of a chance. The least likelihood. "He has not the ghost of a chance of being elected", not the shadow of a probability.

The ghost walks. Theatrical slang for "salaries are about to be paid"; when there is no money available actors say "the ghost won't walk this time". The allusion is to SHAKESPEARE's *Hamlet*, I, i, where Horatio asks the ghost if it "walks" because—

> Thou hast uphoarded in thy life
> Extorted treasure in the womb of earth.

To give up the ghost. To die. The idea is that life is independent of the body, and is due to the habitation of the ghost or spirit in the material body.

> Man dieth, and wasteth away: yea, man giveth up the ghost, and where is he?
> *Job* vix, 10.

To look like a ghost. To look deathly pale, pale as a ghost.

Ghost-word. A term invented by W. W. Skeat (*Philol. Soc. Transactions*, 1886) to denote words that had no real existence but are due to the errors of scribes, printers, or editors, etc. Like ghosts we may seem to see them, or may fancy that they exist; but they have no real being. ACRE-FIGHT (*see under* FIGHT) and SLUG-HORN are examples.

Intrusive letters that have no etymological right in a word but have been inserted through false analogy with words similarly pronounced (like the *gh* in *sprightly*, the *h* in *aghast* or the *h* in *ghost*) are sometimes called **ghost-letters**.

Ghost writer. The anonymous author who writes speeches, articles or books—especially autobiographies—for which another and better-known person gets the credit.

Giants, *i.e.* persons well above normal height and size, are found as "sports" or "freaks of nature"; but the widespread belief in pre-existing races of giants among primitive peoples is due partly to the ingrained idea that mankind has degenerated—"There were giants in the earth in those days" (*Gen.* vi, 4)—and partly to the existence from remote antiquity of cyclopæan buildings, gigantic SARCOPHAGI etc., and to the discovery from time to time in pre-scientific days of the bones of extinct monsters which were taken to be those of men. Among instances of the latter may be mentioned:

A 19 ft. skeleton was discovered at Lucerne in 1577. Dr. Plater is our authority for this measurement.

"Teutobochus", whose remains were discovered near the Rhône in 1613. They occupied a tomb 30 ft. long. The bones of another gigantic skeleton were exposed by the action of the Rhône in 1456. If this was a human skeleton, the height of living man must have been 30 ft.

Pliny records that an earthquake in Crete exposed the bones of a giant 46 cubits (*i.e.* roughly 75 ft.) in height; he called this the skeleton of ORION, others held it to be that of Otus.

Antæus is said by Plutarch to have been 60 cubits (about 90 ft.) in height. He furthermore adds that the grave of the giant was opened by Serbonius.

The "monster Polypheme". It is said that his skeleton was discovered at Trapani, in Sicily, in the 14th century. If this skeleton was that of a man, he must have been 300 ft. in height.

Giants of the Bible.

Anak. The eponymous progenitor of the Anakim (*see below*). The Hebrew spies said they were mere grasshoppers in comparison with these giants (*Josh*. xv, 14; *Judges* i, 20; and *Numb*, xiii, 33).

GOLIATH of Gath (I *Sam*. xvii, etc.). His height is given as 6 cubits and a span: the cubit varied and might be anything from about 18 in. to 22 in., and a span was about 9 in.; this would give Goliath a height of between 9 ft. 9 in. and 11 ft. 3 in.

OG, King of Bashan (*Josh*. xii, 4; *Deut*. iii, 10, iv, 47, etc.), was "of the remnant of the Rephaim". According to tradition, he lived 3,000 years and walked beside the Ark during the Flood. One of his bones formed a bridge over a river. His bed (*Deut*. iii, 11) was 9 cubits by 4 cubits.

The Anakim and Rephaim were tribes of reputed giants inhabiting the territory on both sides of the Jordan before the coming of the Israelites. The Nephilim, the offspring of the sons of God and the daughters of men (*Gen*. vi, 4), a mythological race of semi-divine heroes, were also giants.

Giants of Legend and Literature.

The giants of Greek mythology were, for the most part, sons of URANUS and GÆA. When they attempted to storm heaven, they were hurled to earth by the aid of HERCULES, and buried under Mount ETNA (*see* TITANS). Those of Scandinavian mythology dwelt in JOTUNHEIM and these "voracious ones" personified the unbridled forces of nature with superhuman powers against which man strove with the help of the gods. Giants feature prominently in nursery tales such as JACK THE GIANT-KILLER and Swift peopled BROBDINGNAG with giants. *See* ALIFANFARON; ANTÆUS; ATLAS; BALAN; BELLERUS; BLUNDERBORE; BRIAREUS; BRONTES; CACUS; COLBRONDE; CORMORAN; COTTUS; CYCLOPS; DESPAIR; ENCELADUS; EPHIALTES; FERRAGUS; FIERABRAS; GARGANTUA; GOG AND MAGOG; IRUS; MORGANTE MAGGIORE; ORGOGLIO; ORION; PALLAS; PANTAGRUEL; POLYPHEMUS; TYPHŒUS; YMIR.

Giants of Other Note.

Anak. *See* BRICE *below*.

Andronicus II, grandson of Alexius Comnenus, was 10 ft. in height. Nicetas asserts that he had seen him.

Bamford (Edward) was 7 ft. 4 in. He died in 1768 and was buried in St. Dunstan's churchyard, London.

Bates (Captain) was 7 ft. 11½ in. A native of Kentucky, he was exhibited in London in 1871. His wife, Anne Hannen Swan, a native of Nova Scotia, was the same height.

Blacker (Henry) was 7ft. 4 in. and most symmetrical. A native of Cuckfield, Sussex, he was called "the British Giant".

Bradley (William) was 7 ft. 9 in. Born in 1787 at Market Weight, Yorkshire, he died in 1820. His right hand is preserved in the museum of the Royal College of Surgeons.

Brice (M. J.), exhibited under the name of Anak, was 7 ft. 8 in. at the age of 26. He was born in 1840 at Ramonchamp in the Vosges and visited England 1862–1865. His arms had a stretch of 95½ in.

Brusted (Von) of Norway was 8 ft. He was exhibited at London in 1880.

Byrne. *See* O'BRIEN *below*.

Chang, the Chinese giant, was 8 ft. 2 in. He was exhibited in London in 1865–1866 and in 1880.

CHARLEMAGNE, according to tradition, was nearly 8 ft. and was so strong that he could squeeze together three horseshoes with his hands.

Cotter (Patrick), an Irish bricklayer, who exhibited as O'Brien, was 8 ft. 1 in. Born in 1761, he died at Clifton, Bristol, in 1806. A cast of his hand is preserved in the museum of the Royal College of Surgeons.

Daniel, the porter of Oliver Cromwell, was a man of gigantic stature.

Eleazer was 7 cubits (nearly 11 ft.). Vitellius sent this giant to Rome. He is mentioned by Josephus who also speaks of a Jew of 10 ft. 2 in.

Eleizegue (Joachim) was 7 ft. 10 in. A Spaniard, he was exhibited in the Cosmorama, Regent Street, London, in the mid-19th century.

Evans (William) was 8 ft. He was a porter of Charles I, and died in 1632.

Frank (Big) was 7 ft. 8 in. He was Francis Sheridan, an Irishman, and died in 1870.

Gabara, the Arabian giant, was 9 ft. 9 in. Pliny says he was the tallest man seen in the days of Claudius.

Gilly was 8 ft. This Swedish giant was exhibited at London in the early part of the 19th century.

Gordon (Alice) was 7 ft. She was a native of Essex, and died in 1737, at the age of 19.

Hale (Robert) was 7 ft. 6 in. and was born at Somerton, Norfolk in 1802. He died in 1862 and was called "the Norfolk Giant".

Hardrada (Harald) was nearly 7 ft. and was called "the Norway Giant". He was slain at Stamford Bridge in 1066.

Holmes (Benjamin) of Northumberland was 7 ft. 7 in. He became sword-bearer to the Corporation of Worcester and died in 1892.

McDonald (James) of Cork, Ireland, was 7 ft. 6 in. He died in 1760.

McDonald (Samuel) was 6 ft. 10 in. This Scot was usually called "Big Sam". He was the Prince of Wales's footman, and died in 1802.

Macgrath (Cornelius) was 7 ft. 10 in. at the age of 16. He was an orphan reared by Bishop Berkeley and died in 1760 at the age of 20.

Maximus I, Roman Emperor (235–238) was 8 ft. 6 in.

Middleton (John) was 9 ft. 3 in. He was born at Hale, Lancashire, in the reign of James I. "His hand was 17 in. long and 8½ in. broad" (Dr. Plot: *Natural History of Staffordshire*).

Miller (Maximilian Christopher) was 8 ft. His hand measured 12 in., and his forefinger 9 in. He died at London in 1734 at the age of 60.

Murphy, an Irish giant of the late 18th century, was 8 ft. 10 in. He died at Marseilles.

O'Brien, or Charles Byrne (1761–1783), was 8 ft. 4 in. He died in Cockspur Street, London and the skeleton of this Irish giant is preserved in the Royal College of Surgeons.

O'Brien (Patrick). *See* COTTER *above*.

Porus was 5 cubits in height (about 7½ ft.). He was an Indian king who fought against ALEXANDER the Great near the Hydaspes. (Quintus Curtius: *De rebus gestis Alexandri Magni*.)

Sam (Big). *See* MACDONALD *above*.

Sheridan. *See* FRANK *above*.

Swan (Anne Hannen). *See* BATES *above*.

Toller (James) was 8 ft. at the age of 24. He died in 1819.

Wadlow (Robert P.) of Illinois, U.S.A., was 8 ft. 11.1 in. (1918–1940), the tallest man of whose measurements there is complete certainty.

Winkelmaier (Josef), an Austrian, was 8 ft. 9 in. (1865–1887).

In addition to the above:

Del Rio tells us that he saw a Piedmontese in 1572 more than 9 ft. high.

M. Thevet published (1575) an account of a South American giant, the skeleton of which he measured. It was 11 ft. 5 in.

Gaspard Bauhin (1560–1624), the anatomist and botanist, speaks of a Swiss 8 ft. high.

A Mr. Warren (in *Notes and Queries*, 14 August 1875) said that his father knew a woman 9 ft. in height, and adds "her head touched the ceiling of a good-sized room".

There is a human skeleton 8 ft. 6 in. in height in the museum of Trinity College, Dublin.

There were over 100 applicants in response to an advertisement in *The Times* (25 July 1966) for "giants" of minimum height 6 ft. 7 in. for the premiere of *Cast a Giant Shadow* at the London Pavilion. The tallest was 7 ft. 3 in. *Cp*. DWARF; HEAVIEST MEN.

Giants, Battle of the. A name given to the battle of Marignano, or Melegnano (10 miles south-east of Milan), where in 1515 Francis I, after a fierce contest, defeated the Swiss mercenaries defending Milan.

Giants' Cauldrons. *See* GIANTS' KETTLES.

Giant's Causeway. A formation of some 40,000 basaltic columns, projecting into the sea about 8 miles ENE of Portrush, Co. Antrim, on the north coast of IRELAND. It is fabled to be the beginning of a road to be constructed by the giants across the channel from Ireland to SCOTLAND. Here are to be found the *Giants' Loom*, the *Giants' Well* and the *Giants' Chair*. Other formations in the district are called the *Giants' Organ*, the *Giants' Peep-hole*, and the *Giants' Granny*, also reefs called the *Giants' Eye-glass*.

Giants' Dance, The. STONEHENGE, which Geoffrey of Monmouth says was removed from Killaurus, a mountain in IRELAND, by Uther PENDRAGON and his men under the direction of MERLIN.

Giants' Kettles, or **Giants' Cauldrons.** A name given to glacial pot-shaped cylindrical holes worn in rocks by the rotary currents of sub-glacial streams, often containing water-worn stones, boulders, etc. They are found in Norway, GERMANY, the U.S.A., etc.

Giants' Leap, The. A popular name in many mountainous districts given to two prominent rocks separated from each other by a wide chasm or stretch of open country across which some giant is fabled to have leapt and so baffled his pursuers.

Giants' Ring. A prehistoric circular mound near Milltown, Co. Down, IRELAND. It is 580 ft. in diameter and has a CROMLECH in the centre.

Giants' Staircase. The staircase which rises from the courtyard of the Doge's Palace, Venice. So named from the figures of two giants at its head.

Giants' War with Zeus. The War of the Giants and the War of the TITANS should be kept distinct. The latter was before ZEUS became god of HEAVEN and earth, the former was after that time. The Giants' War was a revolt by the giants against Zeus, which was readily put down by the help of the other gods and the aid of HERCULES.

Giaour (jour). A word used by the Turks for one who was not a Mohammedan, especially a CHRISTIAN. The word was popularized by Byron who wrote a poem called *The Giaour*.

The city won for Allah from the Giaour,
The Giaour from Othman's race again may wrest.
BYRON: *Childe Harold's Pilgrimage*,
canto II, stanza 77.

Gib Cat (jib kăt). A tomcat. The male cat used to be called *Gilbert*. Tibert, or TYBALT, is the French form of Gilbert, and hence Chaucer, or whoever it was that translated that part of the *Romaunt of the Rose*, renders "Thibert le cas" by "Gibbe, our Cat" (line 6204). It is generally used of a castrated cat.

I am as melancholy as a gib cat or a lugged bear.
SHAKESPEARE: *Henry IV, Pt. I*, I, ii.

Gibeonite (gib' i on īt). A slave's slave, a workman's labourer, a farmer's understrapper, or Jack-of-all-work. The Gibeonites were made "hewers of wood and drawers of water" to the Israelites (*Josh*. ix, 27).

Gibraltar (jib rawl tàr). The "CALPE" of the ancients and one of the PILLARS OF HERCULES. The name is a corruption of *Gebel-al-Tarik*, the hill of Tarik, Tarik being the SARACEN leader, who utterly defeated RODERICK, the Gothic king of Spain in 711, and built a castle on the Rock. The Spaniards finally took it from the Moors in 1462. It was captured by a combined English and Dutch force under Sir George Rooke in 1704 and unsuccessfully besieged by the Spaniards and French in 1704, 1705 and subsequently, most memorably from 1779 to 1783, when it was heroically defended by General Eliott (later Lord Heathfield). *See also* GARLIC WALL; ROCK SCORPION.

Gibson Girl. A type of elegant female beauty characteristic of its period depicted by

Charles Dana Gibson (1867–1944) in several series of black-and-white drawings dating from 1896. His delineations of the American girl enjoyed an enormous vogue and the series entitled *The Adventures of Mr. Pipp*, which appeared in *Collier's Weekly* (1899), formed the basis of a successful play. The Gibson Girl was portrayed in various poses and occupations, her individuality accentuated by the sweeping skirts and large hats of the period.

Her type was based on his wife Irene (neé Langhorne) and her sisters, among whom was the late Nancy, Viscountess Astor.

Gibus (ji'bùs). An opera-hat named after its inventor, a Parisian hat-maker of the early 19th century. It is a cloth top-hat with a collapsible crown that enables the wearer to fold it up when not in use.

Gichtelians. *See* ANGELIC BROTHERS.

Gideons. An international association of Christian business and professional men founded in 1899 and now functioning in over 65 countries. They seek to lead others to Christianity, particularly by the distribution of Bibles and New Testaments on a large scale. Bibles are provided in hotel bedrooms and hospitals and New Testaments are presented to pupils in schools. They are named after Gideon's men who overthrew the Midianites (*Judges* vii).

Giff Gaff. Give and take; good turn for good turn. A variant repetition from *give*.

Gifford Lectureships. Lectureships in Natural Theology without reference to creed or sect founded in the universities of Edinburgh, Glasgow, Aberdeen, and St. Andrews in 1887 by a bequest of Adam, Lord Gifford.

Gift-Horse. Don't look a gift-horse in the mouth. When given a present do not inquire too minutely into its intrinsic value. The normal way of assessing the age of a horse is to inspect its front teeth. The proverb has its counterpart in many languages.

Giggle. Have you found a giggle's nest? A question asked in Norfolk when anyone laughs immoderately and senselessly. The meaning is obvious—have you found the place where giggles abound—a nest of giggling girls? *Cp.* GAPE'S NEST; TO FIND A MARE'S NEST *under* MARE.

Gig-lamps. Once popular for spectacles, especially large round ones—an allusion to the lanterns attached to a gig. It is also a local nickname for a fire-fly.

Giglet, or **giglot.** A light, wanton woman.

> If this be
> The recompense of striving to preserve
> A wanton gigglet honest, very shortly

'Twill make all mankind panders.
>
> MASSINGER: *The Fatal Dowry*, III, i (1619).

Gigman. Used derisively or comtemptuously for a quite respectable person; hence *gigmanity*, smug respectability, a word invented by Carlyle. A witness in the trial for murder of John Thurtell (1824) said, "I always thought him [Thurtell] a respectable man." Being asked by the judge why he thought so, the witness replied, "He kept a gig."

> A Princess of the Blood, yet whose father had sold his inexpressibles ... in a word, *Gigmanity disgigged*.
>
> CARLYLE: *The Diamond Necklace*, ch. V.

Gilbertian. A term applied to anything humorously topsy-turvy, any situation such as those W. S. Gilbert (1836–1911) depicted in the Gilbert and Sullivan operas. Of these perhaps the *Mikado* furnishes the best examples.

Gilbertines. The only mediæval religious order of English origin, founded at Sempringham in Lincolnshire *c.* 1135 by Gilbert of Sempringham (*c.* 1083–1189). The monks observed the rule of the AUGUSTINIANS and the nuns that of the BENEDICTINES. There were some 25 houses at the Dissolution.

Gild. To gild the lily. To add superfluous ornament to that which is already beautiful.

To gild the pill. It was the custom of old-time doctors—QUACKS and genuine—to make their nauseous pills more attractive, at least to the sight, by gilding them with a thin coating of sugar. Hence to make an unattractive thing at least appear desirable.

Gilded Chamber, The. A familiar name for the HOUSE OF LORDS.

Gilded Youth. Wealthy and fashionable young men, principally engaged in the pursuit of pleasure. A parallel expression to the Fr. JEUNESSE DORÉE.

Gildas (*c.* 516–*c.* 570). The earliest British "historian", also called *Sapiens* and *Badonicus*. Very little is known about him, but he was most probably an ecclesiastic and much of his writing consists of a tirade against his countrymen. His works contain much scriptural matter, and the history covers the period from the Roman invasion to his own times. Although vague and inaccurate, his sketch is important. Written *c.* 547, his treatise was first published in modified form by Polydore Virgil in 1525.

> Britain has kings, but they are tyrants; she has judges but unrighteous ones ... they have an abundance of wives, yet they are addicted to fornication and adultery.
>
> *The Works of Gildas*: III, *The Epistle*.

Gilderoy. A noted robber and cattle-stealer of Perthshire who was hanged with five of his gang in July 1638, at Gallowlee near Edinburgh. He was noted for his handsome person and his real name was said to be Patrick Macgregor. He is credited with having picked the pocket of Cardinal Richelieu, robbed Oliver Cromwell, and hanged a judge. There are ballads on him in PERCY'S RELIQUES, Ritson's *Collection*, etc., and a modern one by Campbell.

> Oh! sike twa charming een he had,
> A breath as sweet as rose,
> He never ware a Highland plaid,
> But costly silken clothes.
> PERCY: Reliques: Gilderoy.

To be hung higher than Gilderoy's kite is to be punished more severely than the very worst criminal. The greater the crime, the higher the gallows, was at one time a legal axiom. The gallows of Montrose was 30 ft. high. The ballad in Percy's *Reliques* says:

> Of Gilderoy sae fraid they were,
> They bound him mickle strong,
> Tull Edenburrow they led him thair,
> And on a gallows hung;
> They hung him high aboon the rest,
> He was sae trim a boy ...

Giles. A mildly humorous generic name for a farmer; the subject of Bloomfield's poem *The Farmer's Boy* (1800) was so named.

Giles, St. Patron SAINT of cripples. The tradition is that Childeric, king of France, accidentally wounded the hermit in the knee when hunting; and he remained a cripple for life, refusing to be cured that he might the better mortify the flesh.

His symbol is a hind, in allusion to the "heaven-directed hind", which went daily to his cave near the mouth of the Rhône to give him milk. He is sometimes represented as an old man with an arrow in his hand and a hind by his side.

Churches dedicated to St. Giles were usually situated in the outskirts of a city, and originally outside the walls, cripples and beggars not being permitted to pass the gates. *Cp.* CRIPPLEGATE.

Giles of Antwerp. Gilles Coignet, the Flemish painter (1538–1599).

Gilgamesh Epic. A collection of ancient Babylonian stories and myths, older than HOMER, seemingly brought together around Gilgamesh, king of Erech, as the central hero. He was two-thirds a god, one-third a man. It appears to have covered 12 tablets (*c.* 3,000 lines), portions of which were found among the relics of the library of Assur-bani-pal, King of Assyria (668–626 B.C.). Some of the tablets date back to *c.* 2000 B.C. *See* DELUGE.

Gillie. A Gaelic word for a boy or lad, manservant or attendant, especially one who waits on a sportsman fishing or hunting.

Gillies' Hill. In the battle of Bannockburn (1314), King Robert Bruce ordered all the gillies, drivers of carts, and camp followers to go behind a hill. Those, when the battle seemed to favour the Scots, desirous of sharing in the plunder, rushed from their concealment with such arms as they could lay hands on. The English, thinking them to be a new army, fled in panic. The height was ever after called the Gillies' Hill.

Gillie-wet-foot. A barefooted Highland lad; a running footman who had to carry his master over brooks and watery places when travelling.

> These gillie-wet-foots, as they were called, were destined to beat the bushes.
> SCOTT: Waverley, ch. xiii.

Gills. Humorous slang for the mouth.

Blue about the gills. Down in the mouth; depressed looking.

Pale about the gills. *See* WHITE *below*.

Rosy, or **red about the gills.** Flushed with liquor.

White about the gills. Showing unmistakable signs of fear or terror or sickness.

Gilpin, John, of Cowper's famous ballad (1782), is a caricature of a Mr. Beyer, a noted linendraper at the end of PATERNOSTER ROW, where it joins CHEAPSIDE. He died in 1791 at the age of 98. It was Lady Austin who told Cowper the story to divert him from his melancholy. The marriage adventure of Commodore Trunnion in Smollett's *Peregrine Pickle* is very similar to that of Gilpin's wedding anniversary.

Gilt. To take the gilt off the gingerbread. *See under* GINGERBREAD.

Gilt-edged Investments. A phrase introduced in the last quarter of the 19th century to denote securities of the most reliable character, such as CONSOLS and other Government and Colonial Stock, first mortgages, debentures, and shares in first-rate companies, etc.

Gimlet-eyed. Keen-eyed, very sharpsighted, given to watching or peering into things; eyes which bore through one. A squint is sometimes called a *gimlet-eye*.

Gimmick. The first use of this word in U.S.A. slang was to describe some device by which a conjurer or fairground showman worked his trick. In later usage it applied to some distinctive quirk or trick associated with a film or radio star, then to any such.

Gin. A contraction of *geneva*, the older name of the spirit, from Fr. *genièvre* (O.Fr. *genèvre*), juniper, the berries of which are used to flavour the spirit. *See* HOLLANDS.

> This calls the Church to deprecate our sin,
> And hurls the thunder of the laws on gin.
> POPE: *Epilogue to the Satires*, I, 130.

Gin and It. A mixture of gin and Italian vermouth.

Gin-palace. A garishly ornate gin-shop, especially of Victorian and Edwardian times.

Gin-Sling. A long drink composed mainly of gin and lemon. It has been attributed to JOHN COLLINS, famous bartender of Limmer's Hotel in London, but it dates from before his time and was found in the U.S.A. by 1800.

Ginger. A hot spicy root used in cooking and in medicine, hence as a nickname applied to someone with red hair.

Ginger group. A small group of people whose object is to stir the more passive majority into activity, especially in politics. The allusion to the spice is obvious. The FOURTH PARTY is a notable example of a political ginger group.

A stone ginger. A certainty, from the New Zealand racehorse of this name which (*c.* 1910) won every race for which it entered.

Gingerbread. A cake mixed with treacle and flavoured with ginger made up into toy shapes such as gingerbread men, etc., and with gilded decorations of DUTCH GOLD or gold leaf, it was commonly sold at FAIRS up to the middle of the 19th century. Hence TAWDRY wares, showy but worthless.

Gingerbread-work. A contemptuous term for fanciful shapes, ornate carvings, etc., used to decorate furniture, buildings, etc.

To take the gilt off the gingerbread. To destroy the illusion; to appropriate all the fun or profit and leave the dull base behind; to rob something of its attraction.

Gingerly. Cautiously, with hesitating, mincing, or faltering steps. The word is over 400 years old in English and has nothing to do with ginger. It is probably from O.Fr. *gensour*, comparative of *gent*, delicate, dainty.

> They spend their goods ... upon their dansing minions, that mins it fel gingerlie, God wot, tripping like gotes, that an egge would not brek under their feet.
> STUBBES: *Anatomie of Abuses*, II, i (1583).

Ginnunga gap. In Scandinavian mythology, the great abyss between NIFLHEIM, the region of fogs and MUSPELHEIM, the region of intense heat. It was without beginning and without end, there was neither day or night, and it existed before either land or sea, HEAVEN or earth.

Gioconda smile. An enigmatic smile, as that of Mona Lisa. Leonardo da Vinci's famous painting, also known as *La Gioconda* or *La Joconde*, is a portrait of the wife of Francesco del Giocondo.

Giotto's O. The old story goes that the POPE, wishing to employ artists from all over Italy, sent a messenger to collect specimens of their work. When the man visited Giotto (*c.* 1267–1337) the artist paused for a moment from the picture he was working on and with his brush drew a perfect circle on a piece of paper. In some surprise the man returned to the Pope, who, appreciating the perfection of Giotto's artistry and skill by his unerring circle, employed Giotto forthwith.

> I saw ... that the practical teaching of the masters of Art was summed up by the O of Giotto.
> RUSKIN: *Queen of the Air*, iii.

Giovanni, Don. *See* DON JUAN.

Gipsy. *See* GYPSY.

Giralda (Sp. a weather-vane). The name given to the great square tower of the cathedral at Seville (formerly a Moorish minaret) which is surmounted by a statue of Faith, so pivoted as to turn with the wind.

Gird. To gird up the loins. To prepare for hard work or for a journey. The Jews wore a girdle only when at work or on a journey.

To gird with a sword. To raise to a peerage. It was the SAXON method of investiture to an earldom, continued after the CONQUEST. Thus Richard I "girded with the sword" Hugh de Pudsey, the aged Bishop of Durham, making (as he said) "a young earl of an old prelate".

Girdle. A good name is better than a good girdle. A good reputation is better than money. It used to be customary to carry money in the belt or in a purse suspended from it, and a girdle of gold meant a "purse of gold".

Children under the girdle. Not yet born.

He has a large mouth but small girdle. Great expenses but small means.

He has undone her girdle. Taken her for his wife. The Roman bride wore a chaplet of flowers on her head, and a girdle of sheep's wool about her waist. A part of the marriage ceremony was for the bridegroom to loose this.

If he be angry, he knows how to turn his girdle. A quotation from Shakespeare's *Much Ado About Nothing*, V, i. He knows how to prepare himself to fight. Before wrestlers engaged in combat, they turned the buckle of the girth behind them. Thus, Sir Ralph Winwood writes to Mr. Secretary Cecil:

> I said, "What I spake was not to make him angry." He replied, "If I were angry, I might turn the buckle of my girdle behind me."
> 17 December 1602.

The Girdle of Venus. *See* CESTUS.

To put a girdle round the earth. To travel round it. PUCK says:

I'll put a girdle round about the earth
In forty minutes.

SHAKESPEARE: *Midsummer Night's Dream*, II, i.

Girdle-cake. A cake cooked over the fire on a girdle or griddle, a circular iron plate, also called a bakestone.

Girl. The word first appears in Middle English and its etymology has given rise to many guesses. It was formerly applicable to a child of either sex (a boy was sometimes distinguished as a "knave-girl"), and is now applied particularly to a young female or young woman. When they become "old girls" is somewhat elastic. It is probably a diminutive of some lost word cognate with Pomeranian *goer* and Old Low German *gor*, a child. It appears nearly 70 times in SHAKESPEARE, but only twice in the Authorized Version (*Joel* iii, 3; *Zech*. viii, 5).

Girl Guides. The feminine counterpart to the BOY SCOUTS, organized in 1910 by General Baden-Powell, and his sister Miss Agnes Baden-Powell. Their training and organization is essentially the same as the Scouts and is based on similar promises and laws. The three sections of the movement were called Brownies, Guides, and Rangers, but the names and groupings have now been modified to Brownie Guides (7–11 years); Guides (10–16 years); Ranger Guides (14–19 years).

In the U.S.A., where they were formed in 1921, they are called Girl Scouts, with different age groupings and names, other than that of Brownie.

Girondists, or **The Gironde.** The moderate republicans in the French Revolution (1791–1793). So called from the department of the Gironde which elected for the Legislative Assembly men such as Vergniaud and Gensonné who championed its point of view. Condorcet, Madame Roland, and Pétion were among them. Brissot became their chief spokesman, hence they were sometimes called *Brissotins*. They were the dominant party in 1792 but were overthrown in the Convention by the MOUNTAIN in 1793 and many of their leaders were guillotined.

Gis. A corruption of Jesus or J. H. S. Ophelia says "By Gis and by St. Charity" (*Hamlet*, IV, v).

Give. For such phrases as **Give the devil his due, Give a dog a bad name and hang him, I'll give him beans,** etc., see the principal noun.

A given name. In American usage, a given name is a first or Christian name.

A give-away is a revealing or betraying circumstance.

To give and take. To be fair; to practise forbearance and consideration. In horse-racing *a give and take plate* is a prize for a race in which the runners which exceed a standard height carry more, and those who come short of it less, than the standard weight.

To give away. To hand the bride in marriage to the bridegroom, to act the part of the bride's father. Also, to let out a secret, inadvertently or on purpose; to betray an accomplice.

To give in. To confess oneself beaten, to yield.

To give it anyone, to give it him hot. To scold or thrash a person. As "I gave it him right and left", "I'll give it you when I catch you".

To give oneself away. To betray oneself by some thoughtless action or remark; to damage one's own cause by carelessly letting something out.

To give out. To make public. Also, to come to an end, to become exhausted; as, "My money has quite given out."

To give way. To break down; to yield.

To give what for. To administer a sound thrashing, to castigate thoroughly.

Gizzard. The strong, muscular second stomach of birds, where the food is ground, attributed humorously to man in some phrases.

That stuck in his gizzard. Annoyed him, was more than he could stomach, or digest.

Glad. To give the glad eye. *See* EYE.

Glad rags. A slang term for evening dress.

Gladiators (Lat. *gladius*, a sword). These combatants who fought to the death in Roman arenas were first drawn from condemned criminals and originally appeared at FUNERAL ceremonies in 164 B.C. Slaves and prisoners of war came to be employed as the taste for these revolting spectacles grew, and their employment as hired bodyguards by wealthy patrons became a threat to law and order. They were trained in special schools (*ludi*) and gladiatorial games spread throughout the provinces. Such combats were suppressed in the Eastern Empire by Constantine in A.D. 325 and in the West by Theodoric in A.D. 500. *See* THUMB.

Gladstone. A name given to cheap claret after W. E. Gladstone (1809–1898) when CHANCELLOR OF THE EXCHEQUER reduced the duty on French wines in his famous budget of 1860.

Gladstone bag. A kind of leather portmanteau made in various sizes and named after the great Victorian statesman, W. E. Gladstone.

Glamorgan. The southernmost county of Wales. Geoffrey of Monmouth says that Margan and Cunedagius, the sons of Gonorilla and Regan, divided the Kingdom of Britain between them after the death of their aunt Cordeilla. Margan, resolving to take the whole, attacked Cunedagius but was put to flight and killed "in a town of Kambria, which since his death has been by the country people called Margan to this day". Spenser says:

> But fierce Cundah gan shortly to envy
> His Brother Morgan ...
> Whence as he to those woody hilles did fly,
> Which hight of him Glamorgan, there him slew.
> *The Faerie Queene*, II, x, 33.

The name actually appears to be a corruption of *Gwlad Morgan*, the land or territory of Morgan, alternatively called *Morganwg* (or *Morgannwg*), the suffix *wg* after the name indicating the ruler's domain, Morgan probably being a native prince of the 10th century. Geoffrey of Monmouth wrote in the 12th century.

Glasgow, Arms of. *See* KENTIGERN, ST.

Glasgow magistrate. A salt herring. The phrase is said to have originated when some wag placed a salt herring on the iron guard of the carriage of a well-known magistrate who made up part of a deputation attending on King George IV.

Glasnost (Russ. openness). Mikhail Gorbachev became General Secretary of the Soviet Communist party in 1985 and in 1986 he introduced a policy of *glasnost* (in conjunction with PERESTROIKA) relaxing repression on human rights, but within the framework of socialism. The intention is to give more freedom in social and cultural affairs.

> Mr Gorbachev has said Moscow no longer claims a monopoly on the right path to Communism but he has been at pains to stress the international benefits of a bit of *glasnost*.
> *Sunday Telegraph*, 17 July, 1988.

Glass. Glass breaker. A wine bibber. In the early part of the 19th century topers often threw the empty glass under the table or broke off the stand so that they might not be able to set it down and were compelled to drink it clean off, without HEEL-TAPS.

> We never were glass-breakers in this house, Mr. Lovel.
> SCOTT: *The Antiquary*, ch. ix.

Glass House. Army slang for a military prison. It was originally applied to the prison at North Camp, Aldershot, which had a glass roof.

To live in a glass house. To be in a vulnerable position morally, to be open to attack. An expression arising from the old proverb **those who live in glass houses should not throw stones.** It is found in varying forms from the time of Chaucer. *Cp. also Matt*. vii, 1–4.

> And forthy, who that hath a head of verre,
> From cast of stones wave him in the werre.
> CHAUCER: *Troylus and Cresseide*, Bk. II.

Glass slipper (of Cinderella). *See* CINDERELLA.

Glasse, Mrs. Hannah. A name immortalized by the reputed saying in her cookery book, FIRST CATCH YOUR HARE (*see under* CATCH).

Glasites or **Glassites.** *See* SANDEMANIANS.

Glastonbury. An ancient town in Somerset, almost twelve miles from Cadbury Castle, "the many-towered CAMELOT". It is fabled to be the place where Joseph of Arimathea brought the Christian faith to Britain, and the Holy GRAIL in the year 63. It was here Joseph's staff took root and budded—the famous Glastonbury Thorn, which flowers every Christmas in honour of Christ's birth. The name is now given to a variety of *Cratægus* or hawthorn, which flowers about old Christmas Day. It is the isle of AVALON, the burial place of King ARTHUR.

Glauber Salts (glou′bèr). A strong purgative, so called from Johann Rudolph Glauber (1604–1668), a German chemist who discovered it in 1658 in his search for the PHILOSOPHER'S STONE. It is sodium sulphate, crystallized below 34°C.

Glaucus (glaw′kùs). The name of a number of heroes in classical legend, including:

(1) A fisherman of Bœotia, who became a sea-god endowed with the gift of prophecy by APOLLO. Milton alludes to him in *Comus* (1. 895), and Spenser mentions him in *The Faerie Queene* (IV, xi, 13):

> And Glaucus, that wise soothsayer understood,

and Keats gives his name to the old magician whom ENDYMION met in NEPTUNE'S hall beneath the sea (*Endymion*, Bk. III). *See also* SCYLLA.

(2) A son of SISYPHUS who would not allow his horses to breed; VENUS so infuriated them that they tore him to pieces. Hence the name is given to one who is so overfond of horses that he is ruined by them.

(3) A commander of the Lycians in the TROJAN WAR (*Iliad*, Bk. VI) who was connected by ties of ancient family friendship with his enemy, DIOMED. When they met in battle they not only refrained from fighting but exchanged arms in token of amity. As the armour of the Lycian was of GOLD, and that of the Greek of bronze, it was like bar-

tering precious stones for FRENCH PASTE. Hence the phrase **A Glaucus swap**.

Gleek (Ger. *gleich*, like). An old card-game popular from the 16th to the 18th century, the object being to get three cards alike, as three aces, three kings, etc. Four cards all alike, as four aces, four kings, etc., is known as *mournival*.

Gleek is played by three persons. The twos and threes are thrown out of the pack; twelve cards are then dealt to each player, and eight are left for stock, which is offered in rotation to the players for purchase. The trumps are called Tiddy, Tumbler, Tib, Tom, and Towser. *Cp.* DUTCH GLEEK.

Gleipnir (glīp' nėr) (Old Norse, the fetter). In Scandinavian legend the fetter by which the dwarfs bound the wolf FENRIR. It was extremely light and made of the miaul of a cat, the roots of a mountain, the sinews of a bear, the breath of a fish, the beard of a woman, and the spittle of a bird.

Glim. *See* DOUSE THE GLIM.

Gloria. A cup of coffee with brandy in it instead of milk.

Gloria in Excelsis (glôr i a in ek sel' sis, ek shel' sis). The opening words of the ANGELIC HYMN, also called the Greater DOXOLOGY. The Latin *Gloria in Excelsis Deo*, etc., is part of the ORDINARY OF THE MASS and the English translation "Glory be to God on high" forms part of the CHURCH OF ENGLAND service for Holy Communion.

Gloria Patri. *See* DOXOLOGY.

Gloria Tibi (glôr i a ti bē). The brief DOXOLOGY, *Gloria tibi Domine*, Glory be to thee, O Lord. In the Roman Catholic Mass the Latin words are used after the announcement of the Gospel. In the CHURCH OF ENGLAND service for Holy Communion the English version is used similarly.

Gloria mundi, Sic transit (Lat.). So passes away the glory of the world. A quotation from *De Imitatione Christi* (Bk. I, ch. iii) by Thomas à Kempis (*c.* 1380–1471)—a classic statement on the transitory nature of human vanities. At the coronation ceremony of the POPE, a reed surmounted with flax is burnt, and as it flickers and dies the chaplain intones—*Pater sancte, sic transit gloria mundi*.

Gloriana. Spenser's name in *The Faerie Queene* for the typification of Queen Elizabeth I. Gloriana held an annual feast for twelve days, during which time adventurers appeared before her to undertake whatever task she chose to impose upon them. On one occasion twelve knights presented themselves before her, and their exploits form the scheme of Spenser's allegory of which only six and a half books remain.

Glory. Hand of Glory. In folk-lore, a dead man's hand, preferably one cut from the body of a man who has been hanged, soaked in oil, and used as a magic torch by thieves. Robert Graves points out that the *Hand of Glory* is a translation of the French *main de gloire*, a corruption of *mandragore*, the plant *mandragora* (mandrake), whose roots had a similar magic value to thieves. *Cp.* DEAD MAN'S HAND.

Glory-hole. A small room, cupboard, etc., where all sorts of odds and ends and junk are dumped.

Glorious. The Glorious First of June. 1 June 1794, when the Channel Fleet under Lord Howe gained a decisive victory over the French under Admiral Villaret Joyeuse. Off Ushant, six French ships were captured and one sunk but the convoy of corn ships, which they were escorting, got through to Brest.

Glorious Fourth, The. *See* INDEPENDENCE DAY.

Glorious John. John Dryden, the poet (1631–1700). George Borrow also gave this name to the publisher John Murray (1778–1843).

Glorious Revolution, The. The revolution of 1688 which established parliamentary sovereignty, when James II, deserted by his followers, fled to France in December 1688 and William of Orange and his wife Mary (daughter of James II) were declared joint sovereigns.

Glorious Twelfth, The. 12 August, "St. Grouse's Day"; the day grouse-shooting begins, unless it be on a Sunday, when it is postponed until the Monday in accordance with the Game Act of 1831. Shooting ends on 10 December. *See* PARTRIDGE; SPORTING SEASONS.

Glorious Uncertainty of the Law. The toast at a dinner given to the judges and counsel in Serjeant's Hall. The occasion was the elevation of Lord Mansfield to the peerage and to the office of Lord Chief Justice (1756).

Gloucestershire. As sure as God's in Gloucestershire. A strong asseveration. "As sure as God made little apples" is similarly used.

Glove. In the days of CHIVALRY it was customary for knights to wear a lady's glove in their helmets, and to defend it with their life.

One ware on his headpiece his ladies sleve, and another bare on hys helme the glove of his dearlynge.
HALL: *Chronicle, Henry IV*.

On ceremonial occasions gloves are not worn in the presence of royalty, because one is to stand unarmed, with helmet and gauntlets off to show there is no hostile intention.

In mediæval times a folded glove was used as a gage or pledge to fulfil a judgment of a court of law. A glove was also thrown down as a challenge. (*See* HERE I THROW DOWN MY GLOVE *below*). VASSALS were often enfeoffed by investing them with a glove, and fiefs were held by presenting a glove to the sovereign. Gloves used to be worn by the clergy to indicate that their hands were clean and not open for bribes. BISHOPS were sometimes given gloves as a symbol of accession to their SEE. Anciently, judges were not allowed to wear gloves on the BENCH; so to give a judge a pair of gloves symbolized that he need not take his seat, and in a MAIDEN ASSIZE the SHERIFF presented the judge with a pair of white gloves.

The ancient Glovers Company of London was refounded in 1556.

Glove money. A bribe, a perquisite: so called from the ancient custom of a client presenting a pair of gloves to a counsel who undertook a cause. Mrs. Croaker presented Sir Thomas More, the Lord Chancellor, with a pair of gloves lined with forty pounds in "angels" as a "token". Sir Thomas kept the gloves but returned the "lining".

A round with gloves. A friendly contest; a fight with gloves.

Hand in glove. Sworn friends; on most intimate terms, like glove and hand.

He bit his glove. He resolved on mortal revenge. On the BORDER, to bite the glove was considered a pledge of deadly vengeance.

> Stern Rutherford right little said,
> But bit his glove and shook his head.
>   SCOTT: *Lay of the Last Minstrel*, VI, vii.

Here I throw down my glove. I challenge you. *See* TO THROW DOWN THE GAUNTLET *under* GAUNTLET.

> I will throw my glove to Death himself,
> That there's no maculation in thy heart.
>   SHAKESPEARE: *Troilus and Cressida*, IV, iv.

With the gloves off. Figuratively, to oppose without restraint. An allusion to the old pugilists who fought with bare fists.

Glubbdubdrib. The land of sorcerers and magicians visited by Gulliver in Swift's *Gulliver's Travels*.

Gluckists. C. W. von Gluck (1714–1787), the German operatic composer and a notable innovator, came to Paris in 1773 and his controversial *Iphigénie en Aulide* was produced the following year with the support of the dauphiness, Marie Antoinette. The Italian composer Piccinni (1728–1800) arrived in 1776 at the invitation of Madame du Barry as champion of the Italian school, and in Parisian musical circles a foolish rivalry developed between the adherents of Gluck (Gluckists) and the supporters of Piccinni (Piccinnists). Gluck remained in Paris until 1779 when his *Iphigénie en Tauride* marked the triumph of the Gluckists.

Glumdalclitch. A girl, nine years old, and forty feet high, who, in Swift's *Gulliver's Travels*, had charge of Gulliver in BROBDINGNAG.

Glutton, The. Vitellius, the Roman Emperor, who reigned from 2 January to 22 December, A.D. 69. *Cp.* APICIUS.

Glyndebourne. The country estate, near Lewes in Sussex, where Mr. John Christie (1882–1962) opened the Glyndebourne Festival Theatre in 1934 for operatic and musical performancs which became an annual event.

Gnome (nōm). According to the ROSICRUCIAN system, a misshapen elemental spirit, dwelling in the bowels of the earth, and guarding the mines and quarries. Gnomes of various sorts appear in many FAIRY tales and legends. The word seems to have been first used (and perhaps invented) by PARACELSUS and is probably the Gr. *ge-nomos*, earth-dweller. *Cp.* SALAMANDER.

Gnomes of Zürich. An uncomplimentary name given to those financiers of Zürich controlling international monetary funds. The phrase became popular after its use in November 1964 by Mr. George Brown (then the Socialist Minister of Economic Affairs) at the time of a sterling crisis.

> What most infuriated George Brown, and Labour M.P.s such as John Mendelson and Ian Mikardo ... was that the men they disparaged as the "gnomes of Zürich" were really giants.
>   T. R. FEHRENBACH: *The Gnomes of Zurich*.

Gnomic Verse. Verse characterized by pithy expression of sententious or weighty maxims. The Gr. word *gnome*, (thought, judgment), acquired specialized meanings such as EPIGRAM, proverb, maxim; hence *gnomic verse*. A group of gnomic poets existed in Greece in the 6th century B.C. An English exemplar is Francis Quarles (1592–1644).

Gnostics (nos' tiks). Various sects, mainly of Christian inspiration, which arose and flourished in the 2nd century with offshoots which survived into the 5th century. The name derives from the Gr. word *gnosis*, knowledge, but it was usually used by the Gnostics in the sense of "revelation" which gave them certain mystic knowledge for salvation which others did not possess. It was essentially based on oriental DUALISM, the existence of two worlds, good and evil, the divine and the material. The body was regarded as the enemy of spiritual life. In most Gnostic systems there were seven world-creating powers, in a few their place was taken by one DEMIURGE. Christ was the final and perfect ÆON. The Gnostic movement caused the Christian Church to develop its organization and doctrinal discipline. In 1945 fifty-two Gnostic texts were found in Upper Egypt which underline its intellectual challenge to the early Church. *See also* MANICHÆANS; MARCIONITES.

Go (O.E. *gan*, start, depart, move, etc.). Both the verb and the noun are used in a wide range of expressions, some of which are recorded below. For others such as **to go by the board,** etc., *See under* the principal word.

A go. A fix, a scrape; as in **here's a go** or **here's a fine go**—here's a mess or awkward state of affairs. Also a share, a portion, or tot, as **a go of gin**; and an attempt, as **have a go at something.**

A go-between. One who acts as an intermediary; one who interposes between two parties.

A regular goer. One with plenty of dash, a man of mettle.

All the go. All the fashion, all the rage, quite in VOGUE.

> Her *carte* is hung in the West-end shops,
> With her name in full on the white below;
> And all day long there's a big crowd stops
> To look at the lady who's "all the go".
> SIMS: *Ballads of Babylon (Beauty and the Beast).*

Go along with you. A jocular expression of disbelief in what someone is saying, stop fooling, etc., used in the sense of "run off with you". Also, when someone agrees to participate in a course of action suggested by you, he is said to "go along with you".

Go as you please. Not bound by any rules; do as you like; unceremonious.

Go it! An exclamation of encouragement, sometimes ironical.

Go it alone. To play a lone hand; to carry on or do something without help; to assume sole responsibility.

Go to! An exclamation, often of impatience or reproof, or as an exhortation like "come".

> *Cassius:* I am a soldier, I,
> Older in practice, abler than yourself
> To make conditions.
> *Brutus:* Go to; you are not, Cassius.
> SHAKESPEARE: *Julius Cæsar*, IV, iii.

Go to Halifax. A EUPHEMISM for "Go to hell". The coinage probably derives from association with the saying "From Hull, Hell and Halifax, Good Lord, deliver us". *See* HULL.

Go-to-meeting clothes, behaviour, etc. One's best.

I've been on the go all day. I have been very busy and active with no time to rest.

I've gone and done it! or **I've been and gone and done it!** There! I've done the very thing I ought not to have done! I've made a pretty mess of it.

I will go through fire and water to serve you. *See under* FIRE.

It is no go. It is not workable.

That goes for nothing. It doesn't count; it doesn't matter one way or the other.

That goes without saying. That is self-evident, that is well understood or indisputable. The French say *Cela va sans dire*.

To give one the go-by. To pass by and ignore someone, to disregard.

To go ahead. To make progress, to prosper, to start.

To give the go ahead. To give permission to proceed in an undertaking.

To go back on one's word. To fail to keep one's promise.

To go down. *See under* DOWN.

To go farther and fare worse. To take more pains and trouble and find oneself in a worse position.

To go for a man. To attack him, either physically or in an argument, etc.

To go hard with one. To prove a troublesome matter. "It will go hard with me before I give up the attempt", *i.e.* I won't give up until I have tried every means to success, however difficult, dangerous, or painful it may prove.

To go in for. To follow as a pursuit or occupation, as in "to go in for medicine".

To go into a matter. To explore or investigate it thoroughly.

To go it. To be fast, extravagant, headstrong in one's behaviour and habits.

To go it blind. To act without stopping to consider. In poker, if a player chooses to "go it blind", he doubles the *ante* before looking at his cards.

To go off one's head, nut, onion, rocker, etc. Completely to lose control of oneself; to go mad, either temporarily or for good; to go out of one's mind.

To go off the rails. To behave abnormally, to go crazy.

To go on all fours. *See under* ALL FOURS.

To go round the bend. *See under* BEND.

To go the pace. *See* FAST.

To go through the motions. To make a pretence of doing something; to carry out an obligation or duty in a very half-hearted manner.

To go to Birmingham by way of Beachy

Head. *See* BIRMINGHAM.

To go under. To become ruined; to fail utterly, to lose caste.

Also to pass as, to be known as; as, "She goes under the name of 'Mrs. Harlow', but we all know she is really 'Miss Smith'."

Go-backs. Would-be settlers in the Far West of the U.S.A. who returned East discouraged and spread gloomy rumours about the difficulties met with.

Go-cart. A device for training toddlers to walk which at the same time combined some of the features of a playpen. They were in use from the later MIDDLE AGES and were introduced into England in the early 17th century. They consisted of a small framework on wheels or rollers splayed out at the base so that they could not be overturned. The top was usually in the form of a tray for containing toys with a circular opening in which the child could stand upright, and be held secure at waist height.

The name was also applied to a kind of two-wheeled cabriolet and to light children's cart, etc. The name *Go kart* now denotes a small one-man racing vehicle propelled by a light engine.

Godown (gō′ down). In India, China, etc., a warehouse. It is a corruption of the Malay word *gadong* or *godong*. The English form of the name may have been influenced by the fact that these storehouses were often partly below ground level.

Go-getter. An enterprising, ambitious, person.

Go slow. The deliberate slowing down of work or production by employees engaged in an industrial dispute. In Canada and the U.S.A. the term is *Slowdown*.

Goat. From early times the goat has been associated with the idea of sin (*see* SCAPEGOAT) and associated with devil-lore. The legend that the DEVIL created the goat may well be due to its destructiveness, and the Devil was frequently depicted as a goat. It is also a type of lust and lechery.

Don't play the giddy goat. Don't make a ridiculous fool of yourself; keep yourself within bounds. The derivation is obvious.

To get one's goat. An old Americanism for annoying one, making one wild.

To separate the sheep from the goats. To divide the worthy from the unworthy, the good from the evil, the favoured from the disfavoured. The allusion is to *Matt.* xxv, 32:

> And before him shall be gathered all nations; and he shall separate them one from another, as a shepherd divideth his sheep from the goats.

The Goat and Compasses. The origin of this PUBLIC-HOUSE SIGN is uncertain. A once popular suggestion was that it is a corruption of "God encompasseth us". Other suggestions are that it was derived from the arms of the Wine Cooper's Company of Cologne, or merely the addition of the masonic emblem of the compasses to an original sign of a goat.

Goatsucker, or **goat-owl.** A name popularly given to the nightjar, from the ancient and very widespread belief that this bird sucks the udders of goats. In Greek, Latin, French, German, Spanish, and some other languages its name has the same signification.

Gobbledygook. A word invented by Henry Maverick of Texas to describe the convoluted, pretentious and often meaningless language of bureaucracy. It was an allusion to the gobble-gobble sound of a turkey.

Gobelin Tapestry (go′ be lin). So called from a French family of dyers founded by Jehan Gobelin (d. 1476); their tapestry works in the Faubourg St. Marcel, Paris, were taken over by Colbert as a royal establishment in 1662.

Goblin. A familiar demon, dwelling, according to popular legend, in private houses, chinks of trees, etc. In many parts miners attributed to them the strange noises they heard in the mine. The word is Fr. *gobelin*, probably a diminutive of the surname *Gobel*, but perhaps connected with Gr. *kobalos*, an impudent rogue, a mischievous sprite, or with the Ger. *Kobold*. *Cp.* GNOME.

God. A word common, in slightly varying forms, to all Teutonic languages, probably from an Aryan root, *gheu*—to invoke; it is in no way connected with *good*.

It was VOLTAIRE who said, "*Si Dieu n'existait pas, il faudrait l'inventer.*" For the various gods listed in this Dictionary see under their individual names.

Greek and Roman gods were divided into *Dii Majores* and *Dii Minores*, the greater and the lesser. The *Dii Majores* were twelve in number:

Greek	Latin
ZEUS	JUPITER (King)
Apollon	APOLLO (the sun)
ARES	MARS (war)
HERMES	MERCURY (messenger)
POSEIDON	NEPTUNE (ocean)
Hephaistos	VULCAN (smith)
HERA	JUNO (Queen)
DEMETER	CERES (tillage)
Artemis	DIANA (moon, hunting)
ATHENE	MINERVA (wisdom)
APHRODITE	VENUS (love and beauty)
Hestia	VESTA (home-life)

Their blood was ICHOR, their food was AMBROSIA, their drink NECTAR.

Four other deities are often referred to:

Dionysos	BACCHUS (wine)
EROS	CUPID (love)
Pluton	PLUTO (the underworld)
KRONOS	SATURN (time).

Persephone (Greek) or PROSERPINE (Latin), was the wife of Pluto, CYBELE was the wife of Saturn, and RHEA of Kronos.

Hesiod says (i, 250):

Some thirty thousand gods on earth we find
Subjects of Zeus, and guardians of mankind.

The Greeks observed a *Feast of the Unknown Gods* that none might be neglected.

A god from the machine. *See* DEUS EX MACHINA.

Among the gods, or **up in the gods.** In the uppermost gallery of a theatre, just below the ceiling, which was frequently embellished with a representation of a mythological heaven. The French call this the *paradis*.

God bless the Duke of Argyle. *See* ARGYLE.

God helps those who help themselves. To this a wag has added "but God help those who are caught helping themselves". The French say AIDE-TOI, LE CIEL T'AIDERA. Among the *Fragments* of Euripides (No. 435) is:

Bestir yourself, and then call on the gods,
For heaven assists the man that laboureth.

God-intoxicated man. The name given to Spinoza by Novalis (Friedrich Leopold von Hardenberg).

God made the country and man made the town. So said Cowper in *The Task* (*The Sofa*, 749). *Cp.* Bacon's "God Almighty first planted a garden" (*Of Gardens*) and Cowley's "God the first garden made, and the first city Cain" (*On Gardens*). Varro says in *De Re Rustica*: "*Divina Natura dedit agros: ars humana aedificavit urbes.*" Marx and Engels say that the bourgeoisie "has created enormous cities ... and has thus rescued a considerable part of the population from the idiocy of rural life" (*Communist Manifesto*, I).

God save the King, or **Queen.** *See* NATIONAL ANTHEM.

God sides with the strongest. Fortune favours the strong. NAPOLEON said, "*Le bon Dieu est toujours du côté des gros bataillons*" (God is always on the side of the big battalions), but the phrase is of much earlier origin. Tacitus (*Hist*. IV, 17) has *Deos fortioribus adesse* (the gods are on the side of the strongest); the Comte de Bussy, writing to the Comte de Limoges, used it in 1677, as did VOLTAIRE in his *Epître à M. le Riche*, 6 February 1770.

God tempers the wind to the shorn lamb. The phrase comes from Sterne's *Sentimental Journey* (1768) but it was not original, for "*Dieu mesure le froid à la brebis tondue*" appears in Henri Estienne's *Les Prémices* (1594) and Herbert's *Jacula Prudentum* (1651) has "To a close-shorn sheep God gives wind by measure." Although Sterne's version is more poetical he did not improve the sense by substituting lamb for sheep—lambs are never shorn!

Man proposes, God disposes. An old proverb found in Hebrew, Greek, Latin, etc. In *Prov*. xvi, 9, it is rendered:

A man's heart deviseth his way; but the Lord directeth his steps;

and Publius Syrus (No. 216) has:

Homo semper aliud, Fortuna aliud cogitat.
(Man has one thing in view, Fate has another).

Whom God would destroy He first makes mad. A translation of the Latin version (*Quos Deus vult perdere, prius dementat*) of one of the *Fragments of* Euripides. *Cp.* also *Stultum facit fortuna quem vult perdere* (Publius Syrus, No 612), He whom Fortune would ruin she robs of his wits.

Whom the gods love die young. A translation of the Latin *Quem Di diligunt adolescens moritur* (Plautus, *Bacchides*, IV, vii, 18). For the popular saying "Only the good die young" *see under* GOOD.

God's Acre. *See under* ACRE.

Goddam, or **Godon** (gò dăm', gò don'). A name given by the French to the English at least as early as the 15th century, on account of the favourite oath of the English soldiers. JOAN OF ARC is reported to have used the word on a number of occasions in contemptuous reference to her enemies.

Godfather. To stand godfather. To pay the reckoning, godfathers being sometimes chosen for the sake of the present they are expected to make to the child at christening or in their wills.

Godless Florin. *See* GRACELESS FLORIN.

Godlike Daniel, The. A nickname given by his followers to Daniel Webster (1782–1852), the famous statesman, lawyer, and orator. In his youth he was known as *Black Dan* from his raven hair and dark skin.

Godiva, Lady (gò dī' và). Patroness of Coventry. In 1040 Leofric, Earl of Mercia and Lord of Coventry, imposed certain exactions on his tenants, which his lady besought him to remove. He said he would do so if she would ride naked through the town. Lady Godiva did so and the Earl faithfully kept his promise.

The legend is recorded by Roger of Wendover (d. 1236), in his *Flores Historiarum*, and this was adapted by Rapin in his *History of England* (1723–1727) into the story commonly known. An addition of the time of Charles II asserts that everyone kept indoors at the time, but a certain tailor peeped through his window to see the lady pass and was struck blind as a consequence. He has ever since been called "Peeping Tom of Coventry". Since 1768 the ride has been annually commemorated at Coventry by a procession in which "Lady Godiva" features centrally.

Godolphin Barb. *See* DARLEY ARABIAN.

Goel (gō′ el) (Heb. claimant). Among the ancient Hebrews the *goel* was the next of kin whose duty it was to redeem the property of a kinsman who had been forced to sell under stress of circumstances; he was also the AVENGER OF BLOOD.

Goemagot, or **Goemot** (gō em′ à got or gō′mot). The names given in Geoffrey of Monmouth's *Historia Britonum* (I, xvi), and Spenser's *The Faerie Queene* (II, x, 10), etc. to the giant who dominated the western horn of England (CORNWALL or *Cornubia*). He was slain by CORINEUS. *See* GOG AND MAGOG.

Gog and Magog. In British legend, the sole survivors of a monstrous brood, the offspring of demons and the thirty-three infamous daughters of the Emperor Diocletian, who murdered their husbands. Gog and Magog were taken as prisoners to LONDON after their fellow giants had been killed by BRUTE and his companions, where they were made to do duty as porters at the royal palace, on the site of the Guildhall, where their effigies have stood at least from the reign of Henry V. The old giants were destroyed in the GREAT FIRE, and were replaced by figures 14 ft. high, carved in 1708 by Richard Saunders. These were subsequently demolished in an air raid in 1940 and new figures were set up in 1953. Formerly wickerwork models were carried in the LORD MAYOR'S SHOWS.

In the BIBLE Magog is spoken of as a son of Japhet (*Gen*. x, 2), in the *Revelation* Gog and Magog symbolize all future enemies of the Kingdom of God, and in *Ezekiel* Gog is prince of Magog, a ruler of hordes to the north of Israel.

Gogmagog Hill. The higher of two hills some 3 miles south-east of Cambridge. The legend is that Gogmagog fell in love with the nymph Granta, but she would have nothing to say to the giant, and he was metamorphosed into the hill (Drayton, *Polyolbion*, xxi).

Golconda (gol kon′ dà). An ancient kingdom and city in India, west of Hyderabad, which was conquered by Aurangzeb in 1687. The name is emblematic of great wealth and pro-

verbially famous for its DIAMONDS, but the gems were only cut and polished there.

Gold. According to the ancient alchemists, gold represented the SUN, and SILVER the MOON. In HERALDRY gold (called "or") is depicted by dots. The gold CARAT is the unit used by goldsmiths, assayers, etc., for expressing the proportion of gold in any article in gold. Gold coins were struck in England as regular currency from the reign of Edward III until 1917.

The gold of Nibelungen. *See* NIBELUNGENLIED.

Dutch gold. *See under* DUTCH.

Fool's Gold. A name given to iron pyrites or pyrite, which being of a brassy yellow colour was sometimes mistaken for gold. It is often found in coal-seams. Martin Frobisher returned with supposed "gold minerall" from his voyage of 1576 in search of the NORTH-WEST PASSAGE. Two further voyages were made in 1577 and 1578 for cargoes of the supposed ore which proved to be nothing but fool's gold.

Healing gold. Gold given to a monarch for "healing" the KING'S EVIL.

Mannheim gold. A sort of PINCHBECK, made of copper, zinc, and tin, used for cheap jewellery and invented at Mannheim, Germany. *Cp*. DUTCH GOLD.

The Gold Standard. A currency system based upon keeping the monetary unit at the value of a fixed weight of gold. Great Britain adopted the Gold Standard from 1821 but suspended gold payments in 1914, returned to the Gold Standard in 1925 and abandoned it in 1931 during the slump. Most countries of the world were on the Gold Standard from 1894 to 1914. Gold became the monetary standard of the U.S.A. by the Coinage Act of 1873 but the Gold Standard was abandoned in 1933.

Gold Stick. The gilt rod carried before the Sovereign on State occasions by the Colonel of the Life Guards or the Captain of the Gentlemen-at-arms; also the bearer of the Stick.

A gold brick. An American phrase descriptive of any form of swindling. It originated in the gold-rush days when a cheat would sell his dupe an alleged (or even a real) gold brick, in the latter case substituting a sham one before making his get-away. In World War II **gold-bricking** was synonymous with idling, shirking, or getting a comrade to do one's job.

All he touches turns to gold. All his ventures succeed; he is invariably lucky. The allusion is to MIDAS.

All that glistens is not gold. (Shakespeare: *Merchant of Venice*, II, vii.) Do not be deceived by appearances.

> But al thing which that shyneth as the gold
> Nit nat gold, as that I have herd it told.
> CHAUCER: *Canon's Yeoman's Tale*, 243.

He has got gold of Tolosa. His ill-gotten gains will never prosper. Cæpio, the Roman consul, in his march, to *Gallia Narbonensis*, desecrated the temple of the Celtic APOLLO at Tolosa (Toulouse) and stole from it all the gold and silver vessels and treasure belonging to the Cimbrian DRUIDS. This, in turn, was stolen from him while it was being taken to Massilia (Marseilles). When he encountered the Cimbrians both he and his fellow-consul Maximus were defeated, and 112,000 of their men were left upon the field (106 B.C.).

To be worth its, or **his** (etc.), **weight in gold.** To be of great value or use. The phrase is applied both literally and metaphorically to persons and things.

The Gold Purse of Spain. Andalusia, because it is the most fertile area of Spain.

Golden Age. An age in the history of peoples when life was idyllic, or when the nation was at its summit of power, glory, and reputation; the best age, as the *golden age of innocence*, the *golden age of literature*. *See* AGE.

The "Golden Ages" of the various nations are often given as follows:

ASSYRIA. From the reign of Esarhaddon, third son of Sennacherib, to the fall of Nineveh (*c.* 700 to 600 B.C.).

ATHENS. During the supremacy of Pericles (443 to 429 B.C.).

CHALDAEO-BABYLONIAN EMPIRE. From the reign of Nabopolassar to that of Belshazzar (*c.* 625–538 B.C.).

CHINA. The era of the T'ang dynasty (618–906).

EGYPT. The reign of Seti I and Rameses II (*c.* 1312–1235 B.C.).

MEDIA. The reign of Cyaxares (*c.* 634–594 B.C.).

PERSIA. From the reign of Khosru, or Chosroes I, to that of Khosru II (*c.* A.D. 531–628).

ENGLAND. The reign of Elizabeth I (1558–1603).

FRANCE. The century including the reign of Louis XIV (1640–1740).

GERMANY. The reign of Charles V (1519–1558).

PORTUGAL. From John I to the close of Sebastian's reign (1385–1578).

PRUSSIA. The reign of Frederick the Great (1740–1786).

ROMAN EMPIRE. Gibbon (*Decline and Fall*, ch. iii), considered it to be from the death of Domitian to the accession of Commodus (A.D. 96–180).

RUSSIA. The reign of Peter the Great (1672–1725).

SPAIN. The reign of Ferdinand and Isabella when the crowns of Castile and Aragon were united (1474–1516).

SWEDEN. From Gustavus Vasa to the close of the reign of Gustavus Adolphus (1523–1632).

Golden Apples. *See* APPLE OF DISCORD; ATALANTA'S RACE; HESPERIDES.

The Golden Ass, properly, *Metamorphoses*, a 2nd-century satirical romance by Apuleius, and seemingly called the *Golden Ass* because of its excellency. It tells the adventures of Lucian, a young man who, being accidentally metamorphosed into an ass while sojourning in Thessaly, fell into the hands of robbers, eunuchs, magistrates, and so on, by whom he was ill-treated; but ultimately he recovered his human form. It contains the story of CUPID AND PSYCHE.

Golden Ball. Edward Hughes Ball, a REGENCY dandy.

The Golden Bull. In particular, an edict the Emperor Charles IV issued at the Diet of Nuremberg in 1356 for the purpose of regularizing the election to the throne of the Empire. It was sealed with a golden *bulla* or seal. *Cp.* PAPAL BULL *under* BULL.

Golden calf, To worship the. To bow down to money, to abandon one's principles for the sake of gain. The reference is to the golden calf made by AARON when Moses was absent on Mount Sinai. For their sin in worshipping the calf the Israelites paid dearly (*Exod.* xxxii).

The Golden Fleece. The old Greek story is that Ino persuaded her husband Athamus that his son Phryxus was the cause of a famine which desolated the land. Phryxus was thereupon ordered to be sacrificed but, being apprised of this, he made his escape over the sea on the winged ram, Chrysomallus, which had a golden fleece (*see* HELLESPONT). When he arrived at Colchis, he sacrificed the ram to ZEUS, and gave the fleece to king Æetes, who hung it on a sacred OAK. JASON subsequently set out to recover it.

Australia has been called "The Land of the Golden Fleece" from its abundant wool production.

Golden Fleece, The Order of the (Fr. *l'ordre de la toison d'or*). An historic order of knighthood once common to Spain and Austria, instituted in 1429, for the protection of the Church by Philip the Good, Duke of Burgundy, on his marriage with the Infanta

Isabella of Portugal. It became two separate orders in 1713. Its badge is a golden sheepskin with head and feet attached, adopted in allusion to Greek legend. It has been suggested that it may also have been influenced by the fact that the manufacture of woollens had long been the staple industry of the Netherlands.

> ... cette Toison rapporte la fable de la conqueste faicte par Iason Prince Grec, ... & par cette fable est representee l'acquisition de vertu qui ne peut estre sinon avec peine & travail. Autres dient que c'estoit par representation d'une devise amoureuse, comme en ce temps l'ordinaire estoit que les Chevaliers, a l'exemple des Chevaliers errans, prenoient les faveurs des Dames pour leurs emprises au faict d'armes.
>
> GUY COQUILLE : *Histoire du pays ... de Nivernois* (1612).

The Golden Gate. The strait forming the entrance to San Francisco Bay. San Francisco is hence called "The City of the Golden Gate". The name was given by John C. Frémont in 1846.

The state entrance to the city of Constantinople built of three arches to commemorate the victory of Theodosius I over Maximus (388), and incorporated in the walls built by Theodosius II, was called the Golden Gate. The 11th-century fortifications of Kiev also incorporated a Golden Gate.

Golden Handshake. A phrase applied to the often considerable terminal payments made to individuals, especially business executives, whose services are prematurely dispensed with. It has also been applied to the final grants made to colonial dependencies on attaining their independence. The phrase was coined by Frederick Ellis (d. 1979), City Editor of the *Daily Express*. *Cp.* TO BE BOWLER-HATTED *under* BOWLER HAT.

> This year promises to be an expensive one for the British taxpayer in "golden handshakes".
>
> *The Times*, 4 June 1964.

The Golden Hind. The famous ship in which Drake made his voyage of circumnavigation (1577–1580). Originally called the *Pelican*, it was renamed the *Golden Hind* at Port St. Julian, near the entrance to the Straits of Magellan, in 1578. Drake was knighted on board the *Golden Hind* in the presence of Queen Elizabeth I on 4 April 1581. *See* THE DRAKE BRASS PLATE *under* FORGERY.

Golden Horde. The Mongolian TARTARS who in the 13th century established an empire in S.E. Russia under Batu, grandson of Genghis Khan. They over-ran eastern Europe and parts of western Asia, being eventually defeated by TIMUR in 1395. The name golden derives from Batu's magnificent tent.

The Golden Horn. The inlet of the BOS-PORUS around which Istanbul (formerly Constantinople) is situated. Some five miles long, it may have derived its name both from its shape and its abundance of fish which made it a real CORNUCOPIA.

The Golden Legend (*Aurea Legenda*). A collection of so-called lives of the SAINTS made by the Dominican, Jacobus de Voragine, in the 13th century; valuable for the picture it gives of mediæval manners, customs, and thought. It was translated from the Latin into most of the languages of western Europe and an English edition was published by CAXTON in 1483.

Longfellow's *The Golden Legend* is based on a story by Hartmann von Aue, a German MINNESINGER of the 12th century.

The Golden-mouthed. St. JOHN CHRYSOSTOM (d. 407), a FATHER of the GREEK CHURCH, was so called for his great eloquence.

Golden Number. The number of the year in the METONIC CYCLE which may therefore consist of any number from 1 to 19. In the ancient Roman and Alexandrian CALENDARS this number was marked in gold, hence the name. The rule for finding the golden number is:

> Add one to the Year of our Lord, and then divide by 19; the Remainder, if any, is the Golden Number; but if nothing remaineth, then 19 is the Golden Number.
>
> *Book of Common Prayer* (*Table to find Easter Day*).

It is used in determining the EPACT and the date of EASTER.

Golden ointment. Eye ointment, in allusion to the ancient practice of rubbing a sty on the eye with a gold ring, which was supposed to cure it.

> "I have a sty here, Chilax."
> "I have no gold to cure it."
>
> BEAUMONT and FLETCHER: *Mad Lover*, V, iv.

Present-day "golden eye ointment" is made from yellow mercuric oxide.

Golden Rivet. A practice of LEG-PULLING among old hands in certain callings, especially in ships and shipyards, where young newcomers or GREENHORNS are sent to look for the *golden rivet*, which is, of course, non-existent. *Cp.* SKYHOOK.

Golden Rose. An ornament made of gold in imitation of a spray of roses, one rose containing a receptacle into which is poured balsam and musk. The rose is solemnly blessed by the POPE on LÆTARE SUNDAY, and is conferred from time to time on sovereigns and others, as well as churches and cities distinguished for their services to the ROMAN CATHOLIC CHURCH. The last to receive it was Princess Charlotte of Nassau, Grand Duchess of Luxembourg in 1956. That presented by Pius IX to the Empress Eugénie in 1856 is preserved in Farnborough Abbey.

The Golden Rule. "Do as you would be done by."

> Whatsoever ye would that men should do to you, do ye even so to them: for this is the law and the prophets.
>
> *Matt.* vii, 12.

Golden Shower, or **Shower of Gold.** A bribe, money. The allusion is to the classical tale of ZEUS and DANAË

The Golden State. California. So called from the gold discoveries of 1848. (*See* FORTY-NINERS *under* FORTY.)

The Golden Stream. St. JOHN DAMASCENE (d. *c.* 752), author of the first systematic treatise on dogmatic theology, was so called (*Chrysorrhoes*) for his flowing eloquence.

The Golden-tongued (Gr. *Chrysologos*). St. Peter, Archbishop of Ravenna (d. *c.* 450).

The Golden Town. Mainz or Mayence was so called in CARLOVINGIAN times.

Golden Vale or **Valley.** The rich plain of Munster in Ireland, of which Tipperary is the central town, is so called. The appellation is also given to the valley from Pontrilas to Dorestone in Herefordshire but it arose from mistaken etymology. The valley of the river Dore (O.W. Istratour) is not the "valley of gold". Dore derives from *dwfr*, water (O.W. *dovr*; O.E. *dor*).

Golden Verses. Greek verses containing the moral rules of PYTHAGORAS, usually thought to have been composed by some of his scholars. He enjoins, among other things, obedience to God and one's rulers, deliberation before action, fortitude, and temperance in exercise and diet. He also suggests making a critical review each night of the actions of that day.

Golden Wedding. The fiftieth anniversary of marriage, husband and wife being both alive.

A good name is better than a golden girdle. *See* GIRDLE.

The golden bowl is broken. Death. A Biblical allusion:

> Or ever the silver cord be loosed, or the golden bowl be broken, or the pitcher be broken at the fountain, or the wheel broken at the cistern; then shall the dust return to the earth as it was; and the spirit shall return unto God who gave it.
>
> *Eccles.* xii, 6, 7.

The golden section of a line. Its division into two such parts that the area of the rectangle contained by the smaller segment and the whole line equals that of the square on the larger segment (*Euclid*, ii, 11).

The Three Golden Balls. *See* BALLS.

To keep the golden mean. To practise moderation in all things. The wise saw of Cleobulus (*see* WISE MAN OF GREECE) and a virtue admired by the Romans, the *aurea mediocritas* of HORACE (*Odes* II, x, 5).

Goldfish Club. *See* CATERPILLAR CLUB.

Golgotha (gol' goth à). The place outside Jerusalem where Christ was crucified. The word is Aramaic and means a "skull". It may have been a place of execution where bodies were picked clean by animals or named from the round and skull-like contour of the site. There is no Biblical evidence for supposing that it was a hillock. The traditional site is that recovered by Constantine. *Calvaria* is the Greek and Latin equivalent of Golgotha. *See* CALVARY.

Golgotha, at the University church, Cambridge, was the gallery in which the "heads of the houses" sat; so called because it was the place of skulls or heads. It has been more wittily than truly said that Golgotha was the place of empty skulls.

Goliards. Educated jesters and buffoons who wrote ribald Latin verse, and who were noted for riotous behaviour. They flourished mainly in the 12th and 13th centuries. The word comes from the Old Fr. *goliard* (glutton) which derived from the Lat. *gula* (gluttony).

Goliath (go lī' áth). The Philistine GIANT, slain by the stripling David with a small stone hurled from a sling (I *Sam.* xvii, 49–51). See GIANTS OF THE BIBLE.

Golosh. *See* GALOSH.

Gombeen Man. A village usurer, a money-lender. A word of Irish origin.

> They suppose that the tenants can have no other supply of capital than from the gombeen man.
>
> EGMONT HAKE: *Free Trade in Capital.*

Gone. Gone with the Wind. Said of events or persons that have left no trace by which to be remembered. It is also the title of what probably remains America's most widely read novel, a story of the CIVIL WAR as seen through Southern eyes. It was written by Margaret Mitchell and published in 1936.

Goneril. One of LEAR's three daughters. Having received her moiety of Lear's Kingdom, the unnatural daughter first curtailed the old man's retinue, then gave him to understand that his company was troublesome. In Holinshed she appears as "Gonerilla". *Cp.* CORDELIA; REGAN.

> After two years' stay with his son-in-law, his daughter Gonerilla grudged the number of his men.
>
> GEOFFREY OF MONMOUTH: *Historia Britonum*, ch. XII.

Gong. A service nickname for a medal.

To be gonged. To be signalled to stop by motorized police for some breach of the traffic laws. A colloquial usage from the loud electric bell used to attract the offender's attention.

Gonnella's Horse. Gonnella, the domestic jester of the Duke of Ferrara, rode on a horse all skin and bone. The *Jests of Gonella* were printed in 1506. *See* COURT FOOLS *under* FOOL.

> His horse, whose bones stuck out like the corners of a Spanish real, being a worse jade than Gonela's *qui tantum pellis et ossa fuit.*
> CERVANTES: *Don Quixote*, ch. I.

Gonville and Caius. *See* CAIUS.

Good. The Good. Among the many who earned, or were given, this appellation are:

Alfonso VIII (or IX) of León, "The Noble and Good" (1158–1214).

Haco I, King of Norway (*c.* 920–961).

John II of France, *le Bon* (1319, 1350–1364).

John III, Duke of Brittany (1286, 1312–1341).

Philip the Good, Duke of Burgundy (1396, 1419–1467).

René called *The Good King René*, Duke of Anjou, Count of Provence, Duke of Lorraine, and King of Sicily (1409–1480).

The Prince Consort, ALBERT THE GOOD (1819–1861), husband of Queen Victoria.

Good Duke Humphrey. Humphrey, Duke of Gloucester (1391–1447), youngest son of Henry IV, said to have been murdered by Suffolk and Cardinal Beaufort (Shakespeare, *Henry VI*, *Pt. II*, III, ii); so called because of his devotion to the Church.

To Dine with Duke Humphrey. *See* HUMPHREY.

Good Friday. The Friday preceding EASTER Day, held as the anniversary of the Crucifixion. "Good" here means *holy*; CHRISTMAS, as well as SHROVE TUESDAY, used to be called "the Good Tide".

Born on Good Friday. According to old superstition, those born on CHRISTMAS Day or GOOD FRIDAY have the power of seeing and commanding spirits.

The Good Parliament. Edward III's Parliament of 1376; so called because of the severity with which it pursued the unpopular party of the Duke of Lancaster.

The Good Regent. James Stewart, Earl of Moray (d. 1570), a natural son of James V and half-brother of Mary Queen of Scots. He was appointed Regent of Scotland after the abdication of Queen Mary in 1567.

Good Samaritan. *See* SAMARITAN.

For good and all. Permanently, finally, conclusively.

> The good woman never died after this, till she came to die for good and all.
> L'ESTRANGE: *Fables.*

Never had it so good. *See under* NEVER.

Only the good die young. A popular saying derived ultimately from one of the Greek Gnomic poets (*see* GNOMIC VERSE), and echoed by several writers. Plautus says *Quem Di deligunt, adolescens moritur* (he whom the gods love dies young). Byron says "Heaven gives its favourites early death" (*Childe Harold*, iv, 102) and "Whom the gods love die young" (*Don Juan*, iv, 12), Defoe, in *Character of the late Dr. S. Annesley*, has "The good die early and the bad late", and Wordsworth "The good die first" (*The Excursion*, Bk. I).

There is a good time coming. A long established familiar saying in Scotland. Charles Mackay wrote his once-popular song of this title in 1846.

> "I could have wished it had been ... when I could have better paid the compliments I owe your Grace; but there's a gude time coming."
> SCOTT: *Rob Roy*, ch. xxxii.

Good-bye. A contraction of *God be with you*. Similar to the French *adieu*.

Good-den. *See* DEN.

Goodfellow. *See* ROBIN GOODFELLOW.

Goodman. A husband or master. In *Matt*. xxiv, 43, "If the goodman of the house had known in what watch the thief would come, he would have watched."

> It's like we maun wait then till the gudeman comes hame.
> SCOTT: *The Antiquary*, ch. xv.

Goodman of Ballengeich. The assumed name of James V of Scotland when he made his disguised visits through the country districts around Edinburgh and Stirling, after the fashion of HAROUN-AL-RASCHID, Louis XI, etc.

Goodman's Croft. The name given in SCOTLAND to a strip of ground or corner of a field left untilled in the belief that unless such a place were left, the DEVIL (called *Goodman* as a propitiatory gesture) would spoil the crop.

Goodwife is the feminine counterpart of GOODMAN.

Goods. I carry all my goods with me (*omnia mea mecum porto*). Said by Bias, one of the Seven Sages (*see* WISE MEN OF GREECE), when Priene was besieged and the inhabitants were preparing for flight.

"He's got the goods on you!" He's got evidence against you.

That fellow's the goods. He's first class, just the man for the job.

To deliver the goods. To perform adequately; to carry out one's promise effectively; to deliver the "real thing".

Goodwin Sands. It is said that these danger-ous sandbanks, stretching about 10 miles N.E. and S.W. some $5\frac{1}{2}$ miles off the East Kent coast, consisted at one time of about 4,000 acres of low land called Lomea (the *In-fera Insula* of the Romans) fenced from the sea by a wall, and belonging to Earl Godwin. WILLIAM THE CONQUEROR gave them to the abbey of St. Augustine, Canterbury, but the abbot allowed the sea wall to decay and in 1099 the sea inundated the whole. *See* TEN-TERDEN.

Goodwood Races. So called from the park in which they are held in Sussex, the property of the Duke of Richmond. Racing at "Glori-ous Goodwood" dates from 1801 and the course was laid out under the direction of Lord George Bentinck. The Gold Cup, "Cup Day" was instituted in 1812; the Goodwood Stakes in 1823; the Stewards' Cup in 1840. In 1814 the meeting was moved from April to July and in 1965 was extended from 4 to 5 days with fixtures, totalling an additional 6 days, in April, August, and September. *See* RACES.

Goody. A depreciative, meaning primly or sentimentally virtuous but with no strength of character or independence of spirit; NAMBY-PAMBY. It also denotes a sweet, jam tart, etc. The word is also a rustic variant of *goodwife* (*see* GOODMAN) and is sometimes used as a title, like GAMMER, as "Goody Blake", "Goody Dobson".

Goody-goody. A reduplication of GOODY, obtrusively virtuous.

Goody Two-shoes. This nursery tale first appeared in 1765. It was written for John Newbery (1713–1767), a notable publisher of children's books, probably by Oliver Goldsmith. She owned but one shoe and when given a pair she was so pleased that she showed them to everyone, saying "Two shoes!".

Googly. In CRICKET, a deceptive delivery de-pending on hand action by the bowler in which an off-break is bowled to a right-handed batsman with what appears to be a leg-break action. *Cp.* CHINAMAN.

It was invented and developed by B. J. T. Bosanquet from 1890 and he used it against the Australians in 1903. In Australia it is called a "BOSEY".

Goose. A foolish or ignorant person is called a goose beause of the alleged stupidity of this bird; a tailor's smoothing-iron is so called because its handle resembles the neck of a goose. The plural of the iron is *gooses* not geese. *Cp.* BOOBY.

Come in, tailor; here you may roast your goose.
SHAKESPEARE: *Macbeth*, II, i.

Geese save the Capitol. When the Gauls attacked ROME in 390 B.C. it is said that a de-tachment advanced up the Capitoline Hill so silently that the foremost man reached the top unchallenged, but when climbing over the rampart disturbed some sacred geese whose cackle awoke the garrison. Marcus Manlius rushed to the wall and hurled the fellow over the precipice. To commemorate this event, the Romans carried a golden goose in procession to the Capitol every year. Manlius was given the name *Capitoli-nus*.

Those consecrated geese in orders,
That to the capitol were warders;
And being then upon patrol,
With noise alone beat off the Gaul.
BUTLER: *Hudibras*, II, iii.

The Goose Bible. *See* BIBLE, SOME SPECI-ALLY NAMED EDITIONS.

Goose and Gridiron, The. A PUBLIC-HOUSE SIGN, probably in ridicule of the Swan and Harp, a popular sign for the early music-houses (*see* MUSIC HALL), but pro-perly the coat-of-arms of the Company of Musicians—*viz.* azure, a *swan* with wings expanded argent, within *double tressure* [the gridiron] flory counterflory.

In the United States the name is humor-ously applied to the national coat-of-arms—the American EAGLE with a gridiron-like shield on its breast.

Goose-egg. *See* DUCK'S EGG under DUCK: in the U.S.A. a zero.

Goose Fair. A fair formerly held in many English towns about the time of MICHAEL-MAS, when geese were plentiful. That still held at Nottingham was the most important. Tavistock Goosey Fair is still held, though geese are seldom sold, but goose lunches, etc., are available.

Tes jist a month cum Vriday nex'
Bill Champernown an' me
Us druv a-crost ole Dartymoor
Th' Goozey Vair to zee.
Tavistock Goozey Vair Song.

Goose flesh. A rough, pimply condition of the skin especially on the arms and legs like that of a plucked goose or fowl. It is usually occasioned by cold or shock.

Goose-month. The lying-in month for women. *Cp.* GANDERMONTH.

Goose-step. A military step in which the legs are moved from the hips, the knees being kept rigid, each leg being swung as high as possible. (It was introduced as a form of recruit drill in the British army but never became popular; it exists in a modified form in the slow march). The goose-step (*Stechschritt*) has been a full dress and processional march in the German army since the time of Frederick the Great. When the AXIS flourished it was adopted by the Italian army (*il passo romano*) but was soon ridiculed into desuetude.

Goose-trap. A late-18th-century American colloquialism for a swindle.

Michaelmas Goose. *See* MICHAELMAS DAY.

Mother Goose. Famous as giving the name to *Mother Goose's Nursery Rhymes*, which first seems to have been used in *Songs for the Nursery*: or, *Mother Goose's Melodies for Children*, published by T. Fleet in Boston, Mass., in 1719. The rhymes were free adaptations of Perrault's *Contes de ma mère l'oye* (Tales of My Mother Goose) which appeared in 1697.

Tuning Goose. The entertainment given in Yorkshire when the corn at harvest was all safely stacked.

Wayzgoose. *See* WAYZGOOSE.

All his geese are swans. He overestimates, he sees things in too rosy a light, he paints too rosy a picture.

He's cooked his goose. He's done for himself, he's made a fatal mistake, ruined his chances, "DISHED" himself. "To cook someone's goose" is to spoil his plans, to "fix" him, to "SETTLE HIS HASH" (*see* HASH). It is apparently of 19th-century origin.

At the time of the "Papal Aggression" when Cardinal Wiseman was designated Archbishop of Westminster and Administrator Apostolic of the Diocese of SOUTHWARK a street ballad of 1851 says:

> If they come here we'll cook their goose,
> The Pope and Cardinal Wiseman.

He can't say Bo! to a goose. *See* BO.

He killed the goose that laid the golden eggs. He grasped at what was more than his due and lost what was a regular source of supply; he has sacrificed future reward for present gain. The Greek fable says a countryman had a goose that laid golden eggs; thinking to make himself rich, he killed the goose to get the whole stock of eggs at once, thus ending the supply.

He steals a goose, and gives the giblets in alms. He amasses wealth by overreaching, and salves his conscience by giving small sums for charity.

The old woman is plucking her goose. A children's way of saying "it is snowing".

The royal game of goose. The game referred to by Goldsmith (*Deserted Village* 232) as being present in the alehouse—

> The pictures placed for ornament and use,
> The twelve good rules, the royal game of goose—

was a game of counters in which the player progressed through compartments according to the cast of the dice. At certain divisions a goose was depicted, and if the player fell into one of these he doubled the number of his last throw and moved forward accordingly. *See* TWELVE GOOD RULES *under* RULE.

To beat the goose. The same as to beat the BOOBY.

To shoe the goose. To fritter away one's times on unnecessary work; to play about, to trifle.

What's sauce for the goose is sauce for the gander. What's good for one is good for the other; what the husband can do so can the wife.

Gooseberry. Gooseberry Fool. A dish essentially made of gooseberries, cream or custard, and sugar, the fruit being crushed through a sieve. Here the word *fool* comes from the Fr. *fouler*, to crush.

The big gooseberry season. *See under* BIG.

He played old gooseberry with me. He took great liberties with my property, and greatly abused it; in fact, he played the very deuce with me and my belongings.

To play, or **be gooseberry.** To act as chaperon; to be an unwanted third when lovers are together. The origin of the phrase is obscure but it may derive from the tact of the chaperon occupying the time in picking gooseberries while the others were more romantically engaged.

Goosebridge. Go to Goosebridge. "Rule a wife and have a wife." Boccaccio (ix, 9) tells us that a man who had married a shrew asked Solomon what he would do to make her more submissive; and the wise king answered, "Go to Goosebridge." Returning home, deeply perplexed, he came to a bridge which a muleteer was trying to induce a mule to cross. The beast resisted, but the stronger will of his master at length prevailed. The man asked the name of the bridge, and was told it was "Goosebridge".

Gopher (gō' fẻr). A native of Minnesota, U.S.A. The word probably comes from the prairie rodent of that name.

Gopher wood. The wood of which Noah made his ark (*Gen*. vi, 14). It was probably some kind of cedar.

Gorboduc. *See* FERREX AND PORREX.

Gordian Knot. A great difficulty. Gordius, a peasant, being chosen king of Phrygia, dedicated his wagon to JUPITER, and fastened the yoke to a beam with a rope of bark so ingeniously that no one could untie it. ALEXANDER was told that "whoever undid the knot would reign over the whole East". "Well then," said the conqueror, "it is thus I perform the task," and, so saying, he cut the knot in twain with his sword; thus **To cut the Gordian Knot** is to get out of a difficult position by one decisive step; to resolve a situation by force or by evasive action.

> If then such praise the Macedonian got
> For having rudely cut the Gordian Knot.
> WALLER: *To the King*.

> Turn him to any cause of policy,
> The Gordian Knot of it he will unloose,
> Familiar as his garter.
> SHAKESPEARE: *Henry V*, I, i.

Gore. A triangular or wedge-shaped piece of cloth in dressmaking; also a similarly shaped piece of land, as in the name Kensington Gore. It is the O.E. *gara* cognate with *gar*, a spear.

> Corners of the fields which, from their shape, could not be cut up into the usual acre or half-acre strips, were sometimes divided into tapering strips pointed at one end, and called "gores", or "gored acres".
> SEEBOHM: *The English Village Community*, ch. I.

Gorgon. Anything unusually hideous, especially such a woman. In classical mythology there were three Gorgons, with serpents on their heads instead of hair. MEDUSA was their chief, the others, Stheno and Euryale, were immortal. They also had brazen claws and monstrous teeth. Their glance turned their victims to stone. *Cp.* PERSEUS.

Gorham Controversy (gôr' am). This arose out of the refusal (1848) of the Bishop of Exeter to institute the Rev. G. C. Gorham to the living of Bramford Speke, "because he held unsound views on the doctrine of baptism". After two years' controversy, the PRIVY COUNCIL decided in favour of Mr. Gorham, whose views were opposed by the HIGH CHURCH party. The PUSEYITES contested the decision of a lay court on a doctrinal matter, the Privy Council having reversed the judgment of the ARCHES Court of Canterbury made in 1849.

> The judgment in the Gorham case has enabled Evangelical clergymen to remain with a quiet conscience ministers of the Church of England.
> DICEY: *Law and Public Opinion in England*, Lecture X.

Gospel. From O.E. *godspel* (good tidings), a translation of the Med. Lat. *bonus nuntius*. It is used to describe collectively the lives of Christ as told by the EVANGELISTS in the NEW TESTAMENT; it signifies the message of redemption set forth in those books; it is used to denote the entire Christian message; and it is also applied to any doctrine or teaching set forth for some specific purpose.

The first four books of the New Testament, known as **The Gospels,** are ascribed to MATTHEW, MARK, LUKE and JOHN, although their exact authorship is uncertain. The first three of these are called the **Synop-**

tic Gospels as they follow the same lines and may be readily brought under one general view or *synopsis*. The fourth Gospel stands apart as the work of one mind. There are many **Apocryphal Gospels,** examples of which are given below. *See* APOCRYPHA.

The Gospel of Nicodemus, or "The Acts of Pilate", is an apocryphal book of uncertain date between the 2nd and 5th centuries. It gives an elaborate and fanciful description of the trial, death, and resurrection of Our Lord; names the two thieves (DYSMAS and GESTAS); PILATE'S wife (Procla); the centurion (Longinus), etc., and ends with an account of the *descensus ad inferos* of Jesus, by Charinus and Leucius, two men risen from the dead. The title first appears in the 13th century and the Gospel was much used by the writers of Miracle and MYSTERY plays.

The Gospel of Peter is an apocryphal book in fragmentary form, first mentioned by Serapion, bishop of Antioch in the last decade of the 2nd century, and part of which was found in 1892.

The Gospel of Thomas is a GNOSTIC work, probably of the 2nd century, containing much that is fanciful.

Gospel according to ... The chief teaching of [so-and-so]. *The Gospel according to* MAMMON is the amassing of wealth or money.

The Gospel side of the altar is to the left of the celebrant facing the altar.

The Gospel of wealth. Wealth is the great end and aim of man, the one thing needful, the Gospel according to MAMMON.

Gospeller. The priest who reads the Gospel in the Communion Service; also a follower of Wyclif, called the "Gospel Doctor".

Hot Gospellers was an old nickname for PURITANS and is now frequently applied to the more energetic and colourful EVANGELISTS and revivalists.

Gossamer. According to legend, this delicate thread is the ravelling of the Virgin Mary's winding-sheet, which fell to earth on her ascension to HEAVEN. It is said to be *God's seam*, *i.e.* God's thread. Probably the name is from M.E. *gossomer*, goose-summer or ST. MARTIN'S SUMMER (early November), when geese are plentiful. Other suggestions are *God's summer* and *gaze à Marie* (gauze of Mary).

Gossip. A tattler; formerly a sponsor at baptism, a corruption of *God-sibb*, a kinsman in the Lord. (O.E. *sibb*, relationship, whence *sibman*, kinsman). *Cp.* ALL STUARTS ARE NOT SIB.

> 'Tis not a maid, for she hath had gossips sponsors for her child; yet 'tis a maid, for she is her master's

servant, and serves for wages.
> SHAKESPEARE: *Two Gentlemen of Verona*, III, i.

Also (archaic) a boon companion, a familiar friend.

> Steenie, in spite of the begging and sobbing of his dear dad and gossip, carried off baby Charles in triumph to Madrid.
> MACAULAY: *Lord Nugent's Memorials of Hampden.*

Gotch. In East Anglian dialect, a large earthenware jug or pitcher. *Fetch the gotch, mor—i.e.* fetch the water-jug, my girl.

Gotham. Wise men of Gotham—fools, wiseacres. The village of Gotham in Nottinghamshire was proverbial for the folly of its inhabitants and many tales have been fathered on them, one of which is their joining hands round a thorn-bush to shut in a cuckoo. *Cp.* COGGESHALL.

It is said that King John intended to make a progress through the town with the view of establishing a hunting lodge but the townsmen had no wish to be saddled with the cost of supporting the court. Wherever the royal messengers went they saw the people engaged in some idiotic pursuit and the king, when told, abandoned his intention and the "wise men" cunningly remarked, "We ween there are more fools pass through Gotham than remain in it." The nursery rhyme says:

> Three wise men of Gotham
> Went to sea in a bowl,
> If the bowl had been stronger,
> My story would have been longer.

A collection of popular tales of stupidity was published in the reign of Henry VIII as *Merie tales of the Mad Men of Gotam*, gathered together by *A. B. Phisike, Doctour*. This "A. B." is assumed to be Andrew Boorde (*c.* 1490–1549), physician and traveller, but the use of his initials was probably to promote sales.

Most nations have some locality renowned for fools; thus we have Phrygia as the fools' home of Asia Minor, ABDERA of the Thracians, BŒOTIA of the Greeks, Nazareth of the ancient Jews, Swabia of the Germans, etc.

Gothamites. Inhabitants of New York. The term was in use in 1800. The name of Gotham was given to New York by Washington Irving in his *Salmagundi*, 1807.

Goths. A Germanic barbarian tribe which invaded and devastated Europe in the 3rd to 5th centuries, establishing kingdoms in Italy, France, and Spain. Hence the use of the name to imply uncultured, uncivilized, destructive. *Cp.* VANDALS.

Gothic Architecture. The name for the style prevalent in Western Europe from the 12th to the 16th centuries. The name was given contemptuously to imply "barbaric" by the architects of the RENAISSANCE period who revived classical styles. A revival of Gothic architecture was started by wealthy dilettanti such as Horace Walpole in the 18th century and was further popularized by Sir Walter Scott and Ruskin. The works of A. W. Pugin (1812–1852) and Sir G. Gilbert Scott (1811–1878) are notable examples of 19th-century Gothic.

The last of the Goths. *See* RODERICK.

Gouk. *See* GOWK.

Gourd. *See* FULHAMS.

Jonah's gourd. This plant (*see Jonah* iv, 6–10) was most probably the bottle-gourd. *Cucurbita lagenaria*, the *Karah* of the Arabs. This was often planted near such booths as the one in which JONAH sat. It is a very rapid grower and its broad leaves give plenty of shade. That it was such a vine is much more likely than the suggestion that it was the castor-oil plant, called in Hebrew *Kikayon*.

Gourmand and **gourmet** (goor' mond, goor' mā) (Fr.). The *gourmand* is one whose chief pleasure is eating; but a *gourmet* is a connoisseur of food and wines. The *gourmand* regards quantity more than quality, the *gourmet*, the reverse. *See* APICIUS.

The gourmand's prayer. "O Philoxenos, philoxenos, why were you not Prometheus?" PROMETHEUS was the mythological creator of man, and Philoxenos was a great epicure, whose constant wish was to have the neck of a crane, that he might enjoy the taste of his food longer before it passed into his stomach (Aristotle, *Ethics*, III, x, 10).

Gout (Fr. *goutte*, Lat. *gutta*, a drop). This disease is so called from the belief that it was due to a "drop of acrid matter in the joints".

Goven. St. Goven's Bell. *See* INCHCAPE ROCK.

Government men. In Australia an early and customary name for convicts.

Government Stroke. A well-established Australian expression for taking a long time over very little work. It is probably derived from the way GOVERNMENT MEN worked.

> You may see him do the Gov'ment stroke
> At eight bob every day.
> C. R. THATCHER: *The Bond Street Swell.*

Gowk. The cuckoo (from Icel. *gaukr*); hence a fool, a simpleton.

Hunting the gowk is making one an APRIL FOOL.

A gowk storm is one consisting of several days of tempestuous weather; believed by country-folk to take place periodically in early April, at the time that the gowk arrives in this country; it is also, curiously enough, a storm that is short and sharp, a "STORM IN A TEA-CUP".

Gown. Gown and town row. In university towns scrimmages between the students and citizens were once common. In the reign of King John, 3,000 students left Oxford for Reading owing to a quarrel with the townsmen.

Gownsman. A university student; so called from his academical robe.

Graal. *See* GRAIL.

Grace. A courtesy title used in addressing or speaking of dukes, duchesses, and archbishops. "His Grace the Duke of Devonshire", "My Lord Archbishop, may it please Your Grace", etc.

Act of Grace. A pardon; a general pardon granted by Act of Parliament, especially that of 1690, when William III pardoned political offenders; and that of 1784, when the estates forfeited for high treason in connexion with the FORTY-FIVE were restored.

Grace before, or **after meat.** A short prayer asking a blessing on, or giving thanks for, one's food; as the old college grace *Benedictus benedicat* before the meal followed by *Benedicto benedicatur* at the end. Here the word (which used to be plural) is a relic of the old phrase to *do graces* or to *give graces*, meaning to render thanks (Fr. *rendre grâces*; Lat. *gratias agere*), as in Chaucer's "yeldinge graces and thankinges to hir lord Melibee" (*Tale of Melibeus*, 71).

The Grace of God. The free and unmerited love and favour of God.

It is also an old Cornish term for a shipwreck because, to the poor fishermen and their families, the goods salvaged by them from the beaches seemed a gift of Providence.

There but for the grace of God go I. A phrase used by the self-critical when others are faced with disaster, disgrace etc., through their actions or misdoings. It implies that most of us have committed the same follies, sins etc., or had similar temptations, but have been fortunate enough to escape the consequences.

Grace and Favour Residence. A residence belonging to the Crown bestowed upon a notable person as free accommodation.

Grace card, or **Grace's card.** The six of hearts is so called in Kilkenny. One of the family of Grace, of Courtstown in IRELAND, equipped at his own expense a regiment of foot and a troop of horse in the service of James II. William III promised him high honours for his support, but the indignant nobleman wrote on a card, "Tell your master I despise his offer." The card was a six of hearts.

Grace Cup, or **Loving Cup.** *See* LOVING CUP.

Grace Days, or **Days of Grace.** The three days over and above the time stated in a commercial bill. Thus, if a bill is drawn on 20 June, and is payable in one month, it is due on 20 July, but three "days of grace" are added, bringing the date to 23 July.

Grace Darling. *See* DARLING.

Grace, Herb of. *See* HERB OF GRACE.

Grace Notes are musical embellishments not essential to the harmony or melody of a piece; more common in 16th-century music than in music of the present day.

Time of Grace. *See* SPORTING SEASONS.

To fall from grace. Apart from a theological implication, this means to relapse from a moral position attained or to fall from favour.

To get into ones' good graces. To insinuate oneself into the favour of.

To take heart of grace. To take courage because of favour or indulgence shown.

With a good, or **bad grace.** Gracefully or ungracefully, willingly or unwillingly. *With a good grace* has an air of rather forced acquiescence.

Year of Grace. The year of Our Lord, *Anno Domini*. Also the favour of benefiting from a year's delay in resigning an appointment, etc. *Cp.* GRACE DAYS.

The Three Graces. In classical mythology, the goddesses who bestowed beauty and charm and were themselves the embodiment of both. They were the sisters AGLAIA, THALIA, and Euphrosyne. *Cp.* MUSES.

> They were the daughters of sky-ruling Jove,
> By him begot of faire Eurynome, ...
> The first of them hight mylde Euphrosyne,
> Next faire Aglaia, last Thalia merry;
> Sweete Goddesses all three, which me in mirth do cherry.
>
> SPENSER: *Faerie Queene*, VI, x, 22.

Andrea Appiani (1754–1817), the Italian fresco artist, was known as *the Painter of the Graces*.

Graceless, or **Godless Florin.** *See under* FLORIN.

Grade. This word is commonly used to denote a pupil's mark of attainment in schools and colleges. In American usage it also replaces the English *gradient*.

At grade. On the same level.

Grade crossing. The American equivalent of the British level crossing. From Lat. *gradus*, a step.

Grade separation. Where one road is an overpass or underpass.

To make the grade. To rise to the occasion, to reach the required standard or level, to overcome obstacles. From the analogy of climbing a hill or gradient.

Gradual. An antiphon sung between the Epistle and the GOSPEL as the deacon ascends the steps (Late Lat. *graduales*) of the altar or pulpit. Also the book containing the musical portions of the service at mass—the *graduals*, *introits*, *kyries*, GLORIA IN EXCELSIS, *credo*, etc.

The Gradual Psalms. Ps. cxx to cxxxiv inclusive; probably because they were sung when the priests made the ascent to the inner court of the temple at JERUSALEM. In the Authorized Version of the BIBLE they are called *Songs of Degrees*, and in the Revised Version *Songs of Ascents*. *Cp.* HALLEL.

Graffiti (gră fē′ tē) (Ital. *graffito*, a scratching). A name applied originally to the "wall scribblings" found at Pompeii and other Italian cities, the work of schoolboys, idlers, etc., many of them obscene and accompanied by rough drawings. A collection of graffiti of Pompeii was published by Bishop Wordsworth in 1837 and it provides a useful insight into the life of the ancient Romans. Modern graffiti are found on walls, especially in lavatories, on posters, etc. They are usually crude and mostly erotic, but political graffiti are quite common and were much in evidence in the 1930s. *See* ALEXANDER THE CORRECTOR; CHAD; KILROY.

Grahame's, Graham's, Grime's, or **Grim's Dyke.** A popular name for the remains of Antonine's wall between the Firth of Forth and Firth of Clyde. GRIM is an old name for the DEVIL. Scott in his *Tales of a Grandfather* (ch. i) says that when the Picts and Scots attacked, after the Romans left, Grahame was the first to climb over it.

Grail, The Holy. The cup or chalice traditionally used by Christ at the LAST SUPPER, the subject of a great amount of mediæval legend, romance, and allegory.

According to one account, JOSEPH OF ARIMATHÆA preserved the Grail and received into it some of the blood of the Saviour at the Crucifixion. He brought it to England, but it disappeared. According to others it was brought by angels from HEAVEN and entrusted to a body of knights who guarded it on top of a mountain. When approached by anyone not of perfect purity it vanished, and its quest became the source of most of the adventures of the knights of the ROUND TABLE. *See also* PERCEFOREST.

There is a great mass of literature concerning the Grail Cycle, and it appears to be a fusion of Christian legend and pre-Christian ritual origins. Part of the subject matter appears in the MABINOGION in the story of *Peredur son of Efrawg*. The first Christian Grail romance was that of the French TROUVÈRE Robert de Borron who wrote his *Joseph d'Arimathie* at the end of the 12th century, and it next became attached to the Arthurian legend. In Robert de Borron's work the Grail took the form of a dish on which the Last Supper was served.

Malory's *Le Morte d'Arthur* (printed by CAXTON in 1485) is an abridgement from French sources. The framework of Tennyson's *Holy Grail* (*Idylls of the King*) in which the poet expressed his "strong feeling as to the Reality of the Unseen" is based upon Malory.

Grain. A knave in grain. A knave through and through, a complete knave. A phrase from dyeing. The dried bodies of kermes and cochineal insects, from which a brilliant red dye is obtained, have the appearance of grains. The dye being of a very durable and lasting nature, it dyed an article through and through. Hence also the word *ingrained* as, "an ingrained, ineradicable habit".

> How the red roses flush up in her cheekes,
> And the pure snow with goodly vermill stayne
> Like crimsin dyde in grayne!
> SPENSER: *Epithalamion*, 226.

> 'Tis in grain, sir; 'twill endure wind and weather.
> SHAKESPEARE: *Twelfth Night*, I, v.

To go against the grain. Against one's inclination. The allusion is to wood which cannot be properly planed the wrong way of the grain.

> Your minds,
> Pre-occupied with what you rather must do
> Than what you should, made you against the grain
> To voice him consul.
> SHAKESPEARE: *Coriolanus*, II, iii.

With a grain of salt. *See under* SALT.

Grammar. Cæsar is not above the grammarians. Suetonius tells us (*De Grammaticis*, 22) that Tiberius was rebuked by a grammarian for some verbal slip, and upon a courtier remarking that if the word was not good Latin it would be in future, now that it had received imperial recognition, he was rebuked with the words, *Tu enim Cæsar civitatem dare potes hominibus, verbis non potes* (Cæsar, you can grant citizenship to men, but not to words). Hence the saying, *Cæsar non supra grammaticos*.

When, however, the German Emperor Sigismund I stumbled into a wrong gender at the Council of Constance (1414), no such limitation would be admitted; he replied *Ego sum Imperator Romanorum, et supra grammaticam* (I am the Roman Emperor and am above grammar!).

Prince of Grammarians. Apollonius the

SOPHIST of Alexandria (1st century A.D.), so called by Priscian.

The Scourge of Grammar. So Pope in the *Dunciad* (iii, 149), called Giles Jacob (1686–1744), a very minor poet, who, in his *Register of the Poets*, made an unprovoked attack on Pope's friend, Gay.

Grammont. The Count de Grammont's short memory is a phrase arising from a story told of the Count's marriage to Elizabeth Hamilton—La Belle Hamilton—of the RESTORATION court. When leaving England in 1663, after a visit in which this young lady's name had been compromised by him, he was followed by her brothers with drawn swords, who asked him if he had not forgotten something. "True, true," said the Count pleasantly; "I promised to marry your sister." With which he returned to London and married Elizabeth.

Granby, The Marquis of. At one time this was a popular PUBLIC-HOUSE SIGN, and such signs are still numerous. John Manners, Marquis of Granby (1721–1770), commanded the Leicester Blues against the PRETENDER in the FORTY-FIVE; was a Lieutenant-General at Minden (1759), and commander-in-chief of the British army in 1766. He was a very bald man and this was exaggerated on most of the inn-signs. *See* BALDHEADED.

Grand, Le. (Fr. the Great).
Le Grand Bâtard. Antoine de Bourgogne (d. 1504), a bastard son of Philip the Good, famous for his deeds and prowess.
Le Grand Condé. Louis II of Bourbon, Prince de Condé, one of France's greatest military commanders (1621–1686). The funeral oration pronounced at his death was Bossuet's finest composition.
Le Grand Corneille. Pierre Corneille (1606–1684), the French dramatist.
Le Grand Dauphin. *See* DAUPHIN.
La Grande Mademoiselle. The Duchesse de Montpensier (1627–1693), daughter of Gaston, Duc d'Orleans, and cousin of Louis XIV.
Le Grand Monarque. Louis XIV, King of France (1638, 1643–1715).
Le Grand Pan. VOLTAIRE (1694–1778).
Monsieur le Grand. The Grand Equerry of France. The ill-fated Marquis de Cinq-Mars (1620–1642) held this office in the reign of Louis XIII.
Grand. Grand Alliance. The coalition against Louis XIV consisting of the Empire, Holland, Spain, Great Britain, etc., which fought the War of the Grand Alliance or War of the League of Augsburg (1689–1697) to check French aggression.

Grand Guignol. *See* GUIGNOL.
Grand Lama. *See* LAMA.
Grand National. The principal event in English steeplechasing, instituted at Liverpool in 1839, and now run at Aintree on a 4½-mile course of 30 jumps, including the famous Beecher's Brook. *See* RACES.
Grand Seignior. A term applied to the former Sultans of Turkey.
Grand Old Duke of York, The, of nursery rhyme fame was Frederick Augustus, Duke of York and Albany (1763–1827), second son of George III, who commanded the English Army in Flanders (1794–1795), co-operating with the Austrians against revolutionary France. His part in the campaign of 1794 was derisively summarized in the rhyme:

> The grand old Duke of York
> He had ten thousand men
> He marched 'em up to the top of the hill
> And he marched 'em down again.

In fact, there was no hill, he was young, and he commanded some 30,000 men. In variants of the rhyme he is the "brave" or "rare old Duke". He was made commander-in-chief in 1798. *See* THE DUKE OF YORK'S COLUMN *under* COLUMN.

Grandfather. Grandfather clock. The well-established name for the once commonly used weight and pendulum tall-case clock, or long-case clock. It derives from the popular song *My Grandfather's Clock* (1878) by Henry Clay Work (1832–1884) of Connecticut, author of the temperance song *Come Home Father* (1864) and *Marching through Georgia* (1865).

Grandison, Sir Charles, the hero of Samuel Richardson's *History of Sir Charles Grandison*, published in 1753. Sir Charles is the perfect hero and English Christian gentleman, aptly described by Sir Walter Scott as "a faultless monster that the world never saw". Richardson's model for Sir Charles may have been the worthy Robert Nelson (1656–1715), a religious writer and eminent non-juror, whose life was devoted to good works.

Grandison Cromwell. Mirabeau's nickname for Lafayette (1757–1834), implying that he had all the ambition of a Cromwell, but wanted to appear before men as a Sir Charles Grandison.

Grandmontines. An order of BENEDICTINE hermits, founded by St. Stephen of Thiers in Auvergne about 1100, with its mother house at Grandmont. They came to England soon after the foundation and established a few small houses in remote places as that at Craswall, Herefordshire.

Grange. Properly the *granum* (granary) or farm of a monastery, where the corn was stored. Houses attached to monasteries where rent was paid in grain were also called granges, and in Lincolnshire and the northern counties the name is given to any lone farm.

> Till thou return, the Court I will exchange
> For some poor cottage, or some country grange.
> DRAYTON: *Lady Geraldine to Earl of Surrey.*

"The Grange" became a popular name for country houses built for the more prosperous Victorians.

In the U.S.A. **The Grange** of *Patrons of Husbandry* is a secret organization of farmers and their families. Founded at Washington, D.C., in 1867 by O. H. Kelley, a clerk in the Department of Agriculture, as a social fraternity, it stressed cultural and educational objectives and became politically involved in the agrarian discontent of the 1870s. The name derives from the local lodges called granges.

Granger States. Wisconsin, Illinois, Minnesota, Iowa.

Grangerize. To "extra-illustrate" a book; to supplement it by the addition of illustrations, portraits, autograph letters, caricatures, prints, broadsheets, biographical sketches, anecdotes, scandals, press notices, parallel passages, and any other matter directly or indirectly bearing on the subject. So called from James Granger (1723–1776), vicar of Shiplake, Oxon, who published his *Biographical History of England from Egbert the Great to the Revolution* ... "with a preface showing the utility of a collection of engraved portraits". The book went through several editions with added material and it was continued by Mark Noble in 1806. Collectors made this book a core around which to assemble great collections of portraits, etc., and in 1856 two copies were sold in London, one in 27 vols, with 1,300 portraits, the other in 19 vols. with 3,000 portraits. *Grangerizing* books became a fashion with the result that many excellent editions of biographies, etc., were ruined by having the plates removed for pasting in some dilettante's collection.

Granite. The Granite City. Aberdeen.

Granite Redoubt. The grenadiers of the Consular Guard were so called at the battle of Marengo in 1800, because when the French had given way they formed into a square, stood like a stone against the Austrians, and stopped all further advance.

The Granite State. New Hampshire, because the mountainous parts are chiefly granite.

Granny. The affectionate and mildly derisive nickname of the *Sydney Morning Herald*, from the signature to its front-page column of news snippets and gossip.

Granny-knot. A knot that slips, a fumbled attempt at a reef-knot.

Granny Smith. A green-skinned, crisp-fleshed dessert apple, the best known Australian APPLE. Named after its first cultivator, Maria Ann Smith of Eastwood, New South Wales.

Grantchester. This village, of ancient origin, two miles south of Cambridge, has a fine old church with many interesting features but it owes its present celebrity to its associations with Rupert Brooke (1887-1915). He lived at the Old Vicarage, and saw active service in the Great War, his reputation being much enhanced by his last poems.

> But Grantchester! ah, Grantchester,
> There's peace and holy quiet there.
> RUPERT BROOKE: *The Old Vicarage, Grantchester.*

Grape. Sour grapes. Something disparaged because it is beyond one's reach. The allusion is to ÆSOP's well-known fable of the FOX who tried in vain to get at some grapes, but when he found they were beyond his reach went away saying, "I see they are sour."

Grape shot. A form of projectile, once much used with smooth-bore guns, consisting of cast-iron balls packed between iron plates which were arranged in layers or tiers and held together by a central iron pin. Also called *tier-shot*. When fired there was a wide spread of shot. The well-known phrase **A whiff of grape shot** occurs in Carlyle's *French Revolution* (III, vii, 7) and refers to the ease with which Bonaparte and his artillery dispersed the Paris insurrection of VENDÉMIAIRE, 1795.

Grapevine, or **Grapevine telegraph.** Somewhat the same as the BUSH TELEGRAPH, the mysterious means and covert whisperings by which information, rumours, etc., are spread around.

Grass. An old usage for spring or early summer, the time when the grass grows.

> ... she is five years old this grass ...
> MISS MITFORD: *Our Village, The Copse* 1819).

It is also the name given to the dried leaves and flowers of the cannabis plant or hemp (*cp.* HASH), also called marijuana and bhang. In criminal slang *to grass* is to inform, which may derive from rhyming slang "grasshopper" for COPPER. A *supergrass* is one who informs on a number of his associates. *See also* GRASS HAND.

Not to let the grass grow under one's feet. To act with all dispatch, not to delay in taking steps to deal with a matter.

To go to grass, or **to be put out to grass.** Primarily to turn out an animal to pasture, especially an old horse too old to work. Hence, to be retired, to rusticate, to be sent on holiday, or even to go to the grave.

A grass hand is a compositor who fills a temporary vacancy; hence *to grass*, to take only temporary jobs as a compositor.

Grass roots. Used to denote that which is rooted in the earth, *i.e.* that which has its origins among the peasantry or common folk.

Grass widow. Formerly, an unmarried woman who has had a child. The origin of the term is uncertain but "grass" here may be the equivalent of "bed". It now implies a wife temporarily parted from her husband and in this sense it became current again in the days of British rule in India. By extension it also denotes a divorced woman or one deserted by her husband. Its counterpart is grass widower. *Cp.* TO GIVE A GIRL A GREEN GOWN *under* GREEN.

Grasshopper. The grasshoppers used on London signboards of goldsmiths, bankers, etc., commemorated the crest of Sir Thomas Gresham (1519–1579), founder of the ROYAL EXCHANGE, the original building being decorated with stone grasshoppers. The grasshopper still forms part of the crest of Martin's Bank.

Grattan's Parliament. The free Irish Parliament at Dublin between 1782 and 1800, so named after Henry Grattan (1746–1820), who obtained the repeal of Poynings' Law and the Declaratory Act of 1719, thereby theoretically abolishing English control. It came to an end with the Act of UNION (1800), which was a result of English bribery and influence.

Grave. Solemn, sedate, and serious in look and manner. This is Lat. *gravis*, heavy, grave; but "grave", a place of interment, is O.E. *graef*, a pit or trench.

Close as the grave. Very secret indeed.

It's enough to make him turn in his grave. Said when something happens to which the deceased person would have strongly objected.

Someone is walking over my grave. An exclamation when one is seized with an involuntary convulsive shuddering.

To carry away the meat from graves. *See under* MEAT.

With one foot in the grave. At the verge of death. The parallel Greek phrase is, "With one foot in the ferry-boat", meaning that of Charon. *See* CHARON'S TOLL.

Graveyard Shift. In World War II the name given by shift workers in munitions factories, etc., to the shift covering the midnight hours.

Gravelled. I'm regularly gravelled. Nonplussed, like a ship run aground and unable to move.

> When you were gravelled for lack of matter.
> SHAKESPEARE: *As You Like It*, IV, i.

Gray. *See* GREY.

Gray-back. A Confederate soldier in the American CIVIL WAR. So called from the colour of the Confederate army uniform.

Gray's Inn. One of the four INNS OF COURT and formerly the residence of the de Greys, a family which, in the 13th century, had high-ranking legal associations. After the death of the first Lord Grey de Wilton (1308) the property was vacated and at some time in the 14th century it was occupied by the Society of Gray's Inn. In 1594 SHAKESPEARE's *Comedy of Errors* was first acted in the hall of Gray's Inn and the walks and gardens were laid out by Sir Francis Bacon, Lord Verulam. The library containing some 30,000 vols. and MSS. and the original hall were destroyed in the air raids of 1940–1941.

Grease. Slang for money, especially that given as a bribe; "PALM-OIL".

Like greased lightning. Very quick indeed.

To grease one's palm, or **fist**. To give a bribe.

> Grease my fist with a tester or two, and ye shall find it in your pennyworth.
> QUARLES: *The Virgin Widow*, IV, i.

To grease the wheels. To make things run smoothly, usually by the application of a little money.

Grease-boy. A LICKSPITTLE or time-server.

Great, The. The term is usually applied to the following:

Abbas I, Shah of Persia (1571, 1587–1629)
Albertus Magnus, the SCHOOLMAN (1206–1280)
Alexander, of Macedon (356, 336–323 B.C.)
Alfonso III, King of Asturias and León (838, 866–910)
ALFRED, of England (849, 871–899)
St. Basil, Bishop of Cæsarea (4th century)
Canute, of England and Denmark (995, 1016–1035)
Casimir III, of Poland (1310, 1333–1370)
Catherine II, Empress of Russia (1729, 1762–1796)
Charles, King of the Franks and Emperor of the Romans, called CHARLEMAGNE (742, 768–814)
Charles III, Duke of Lorraine (1543, 1545–1608)
Charles Emmanuel I, Duke of Savoy (1562, 1580–1630)
Clovis, King of the Franks (465, 481–511)
Condé, *see* Louis II *below*
Constantine I, Emperor of Rome (*c.* 288, 306–337)
Cyrus, founder of the Persian Empire (559–529 B.C.)
Darius, King of Persia (548, 521–486 B.C.)
Douglas, Archibald, the great Earl of Angus, also called BELL-THE-CAT (*c.* 1449–1514)
Ferdinand I, of Castile and León (reigned 1028–1065)

Frederick William, Elector of Brandenburg, surnamed the Great Elector (1620, 1640–1688)
Frederick II, of Prussia (1712, 1740–1786)
GREGORY I, Pope (540, 590–604)
Gustavus Adolphus of Sweden (1594, 1611–1632)
Henri IV, of France (1553, 1589–1610)
Herod, King of Judea (c. 73, 40–4 B.C.)
John I, of Portugal (1357, 1385–1433)
Justinian I, Emperor of the East (483, 527–565)
Leo I, Pope (440–461)
Leo I, Emperor of the East (400, 457–474)
Leopold I, of Germany (1640, 1658–1705)
Lewis I, of Hungary (1326, 1342–1382)
Louis II, de Bourbon, Duc d'Enghien, Prince of Condé (1621, 1646–1686), always known as The Great Condé
Louis XIV, called LE GRAND MONARQUE (1638, 1643–1715)
Maximilian, Duke of Bavaria, victor of Prague (1573, 1597–1651)
Cosmo de' Medici, first Grand Duke of Tuscany (1519, 1537–1574)
Gonzales Pedro de Mendoza, great Cardinal of Spain, statesman and scholar (1428, 1473–1495)
Mohammed II, Sultan of the Turks (1430, 1451–1481)
NAPOLEON I, Emperor of the French (1769–1821, 1804–1815)
Nicholas I, Pope (858–867)
Otho I, Emperor of the Romans (912, 936–973)
Peter I, Tsar of Russia (1672, 1689–1725)
Pierre III, of Aragon (1239, 1276–1285)
Sancho III, King of Navarre (c. 970, 1001–1035)
Shapur I, King of Persia from birth (310–379)
Sigismund II, King of Poland (1467, 1506–1548)
Theodoric, King of the Ostrogoths (c. 454, 474–526)
Theodosius I, Emperor (346, 378–395)
Matteo Visconti, Lord of Milan (1255, 1295–1322)
Vladimir, Grand Duke of Russia (c. 956, 973–1015)
Waldemar I, of Denmark (1131, 1157–1182)

Great Bear, The. *See under* BEAR.

Great Bible, The. *See* BIBLE, THE ENGLISH.

Great Bullet-head, Georges Cadoudal (1771–1804), a leader of the CHOUANS.

Great Captain. *See* CAPITANO, EL GRAN.

Great Cham of Literature. So Smollett called Dr. Johnson (1709–1784).

Great Commoner. William Pitt, 1st Earl of Chatham (1708–1778).

Great Council. The *Magnum Concilium* of the Norman kings and their successors, the assembly of tenants-in-chief meeting at regular intervals with the king and his principal officers for consultation. It was the *curia regis* from which governmental, legal, and political institutions derived.

Great Dauphin. *See* DAUPHIN.

Great Divide. The Rocky Mountains.

To cross the Great Divide, figuratively speaking, is to die.

Great Elector, The. Frederick William, Elector of Brandenburg (1620–1688).

Great Exhibition. The CRYSTAL PALACE exhibition of 1851.

Great Fire. *See under* FIRE.

Great Go. At Cambridge a traditional term for the B.A. final examinations. At Oxford called *Greats*, especially in *Literæ Humaniores*. *Cp.* LITTLE GO.

Great Harry. The name popularly given to the famous warship *Henry Grâce à Dieu* built at Erith and launched in 1514. Of about 1,000 tons, the vessel had five masts and 21 guns as well as a multitude of small pieces.

Great Head. Malcolm III of Scotland (reigned 1057–1093); also called *Canmore* (Gael. *Ceann-mor*, Great Head).

Great Lakes. Lakes Erie, Huron, Michigan, Ontario, and Superior.

Great Mogul. The ruler of the former MOGUL Empire.

Great Plague (1665–1666). The last occurrence of the bubonic plague, which had frequently erupted in various localities since the Black Death but less disastrously. Outbreaks were particularly bad in London in 1603, 1625 and 1636, doubtless due to growing congestion. That of 1625 was known as the Great Plague until it was overshadowed by that of 1665. Deaths in London are estimated at *c.* 100,000, but the Lord Mayor remained at his post. *See* THE GREAT FIRE OF LONDON *under* FIRE.

Great Plains. The area east of the Rocky Mountains from the border of Canada to the mouth of the Arkansas river.

Great Rebellion. In English history the period of the CIVIL WARS, the time of the rebellion against Charles I; also called the PURITAN Revolution.

Great Schism. *See* SCHISM.

Great Scott, or **Scot!** An exclamation of surprise, wonder, admiration, indignation, etc. It seems to have originated in America in the late 1860s, perhaps evocative of General Winfield-Scott (1786–1866), a popular figure after his victorious Mexican campaign of 1847.

Great Seal. The chief seal of the Sovereign used to authenticate important state documents. It is always round in shape and one side shows the sovereign crowned and enthroned (*i.e.* in majesty) and the other the sovereign mounted. The seal is kept by the LORD CHANCELLOR (*see under* CHANCELLOR). *See also* E PLURIBUS UNUM.

Great Spirit. *See* MANITOU.

Great Trek. The exodus of some fifth part of the Dutch-speaking South Africans from Cape Colony from 1835 and into the 1840s, leading to the establishment of Boer Republics across the Orange and Vaal rivers and to British control of Natal.

The Great Unknown. Sir Walter Scott, who published *Waverley* (1814) and the subsequent novels as "by the author of

Waverley". First so called by his publisher, James Ballantyne. It was not until 1827 that he admitted the authorship, though it was then well known.

The Great War. The war of 1914–18 was so called until that of 1939–1945, when the term World War I largely replaced it, the latter becoming World War II.

The Great White Way. A once popular name for Broadway, the theatrical district of New York City.

The Greatest Show on Earth. The name of the gigantic travelling combination of circus, menagerie and collection of human freaks in the U.S.A., displayed by the American showman Phineas T. Barnum (1810–1891) and his partners in 1871. In 1842 Barnum had exhibited General TOM THUMB and in 1850 had toured America with the SWEDISH NIGHTINGALE. He had a varied career of success and failure but the *Greatest Show* again made his fortune and that of his partner Bailey. In 1889 the show was presented at the LONDON OLYMPIA.

Grecian. A senior boy of Christ's Hospital, the BLUE-COAT SCHOOL.

Grecian bend. An affectation in walking with the body stooped slightly forward, assumed by English women in 1868. *Cp.* ALEXANDRA LIMP.

Grecian Coffee-House in Devereux Court, Essex Street, was possibly named after one Constantine, a Greek who opened one in Essex Buildings in 1681, but there is no written record of the Grecian until the reign of Anne (1709), and they were not necessarily connected. It is mentioned by Steele in the *Tatler* and by Addison in the *Spectator*. There was also a Grecian COFFEE-House in King Street, COVENT GARDEN in 1673, and it was possibly older than that in Devereux Court, which closed in 1843.

A Grecian nose, or **profile,** is one where the line of the nose continues that of the forehead without a dip.

Greco, El (grek' ō), or **The Greek.** Domenico Theotocopuli, a Cretan, who studied under Titian and MICHELANGELO, and moved to Spain about 1570. He was the foremost 16th-century painter of the Castilian school.

Greegrees. The name given in Africa to AMULETS, CHARMS, FETISHES, etc.

A greegree man. One who sells these.

Greek. A merry Greek. In *Troilus and Cressida* (I, ii) SHAKESPEARE makes Pandarus, bantering Helen for her love to Troilus, say, "I think Helen loves him better than Paris", to which Cressida, whose wit is to parry and

pervert, replies, "Then she's a merry Greek indeed", insinuating that she was a "woman of pleasure". *See* GRIG.

All Greek to me. Quite unintelligible; quite a foreign language. SHAKESPEARE'S Casca says, "For mine own part, it was Greek to me" (*Julius Cæsar*, I, ii).

Last of the Greeks. Philopœmen, of Megalopolis (252–182 B.C.), whose great object was to infuse into the Achæans a military spirit, and establish their independence.

To play the Greek. To indulge in one's cups. The Greeks have always been considered to have been addicted to CREATURE COMFORTS. The rule in Greek banquets was *E pithi e apithi* (Quaff, or be off!).

When Greek meets Greek, then is the tug of war. When two men or armies of undoubted courage fight, the contest will be very severe. The line is slightly altered from a 17th-century play, and the reference is to the obstinate resistance of the Greek cities to Philip and Alexander, the Macedonian kings.

> When Greeks joined Greeks, then was the tug of war.
> NATHANIEL LEE: *The Rival Queens*, IV, ii.

Greek Anthology. *See* ANTHOLOGY.

Greek Calends. Never. To defer anything to the Greek CALENDS is to defer it *sine die*. There were no Calends in the Greek months. *See* NEVER.

Greek Church. A name often given to the Eastern or ORTHODOX Church of which the Greek Church proper is an autocephalous unit, recognized as independent by the Patriarch of Constantinople in 1850.

Greek Cross. *See* CROSS.

Greek fire. A combination of nitre, sulphur, and naphtha used for setting fire to ships, fortifications, etc. Tow steeped in the mixture was hurled in a blazing state through tubes or tied to arrows. The invention is ascribed to Callinicus of Heliopolis, A.D. 668.

Greek gift. A treacherous gift. The reference is to the WOODEN HORSE OF TROY, or to VIRGIL'S *Timeo Danaos et dona ferentes* (*Æneid* II, 49), "I fear the Greeks, even when they offer gifts".

Greek trust. No trust at all. *Græca fides* with the Romans was much the same as PUNIC FAITH.

Green. Young, fresh, as *green cheese*, cream cheese which is eaten fresh; *a green old age*, an old age in which the faculties are not impaired and the spirits are still youthful; *green goose*, a young or midsummer goose.

Hence, immature in age or judgment, inexperienced (*see* SALAD DAYS).

Simple, raw, easily imposed upon; the characteristic GREENHORN.

> "He is so jolly green," said Charley.
>> DICKENS: *Oliver Twist*, ch. ix.

For its symbolism, etc., *see* COLOURS.

Do you see any green in my eye? *see under* EYE.

The green-eyed monster. So SHAKESPEARE called jealousy:

> *Iago:* O! beware my lord, of jealousy;
> It is the green-ey'd monster which doth mock
> The meat it feeds on.
>> *Othello*, III, iii.

A greenish complexion was formerly held to be indicative of jealousy, and as all the green-eyed cat family "mock the meat they feed on", so jealousy mocks its victim by loving and loathing it at the same time.

If they do these things in a green tree, what shall be done in the dry? (*Luke* xxiii, 31). If they start like this, how will they finish? Or as Pope says (*Moral Essays*, Ep. i), "Just as the twig is bent, the tree's inclined."

Rub of the Green. An expression used in golf, and which has spread thence into ordinary life, meaning a piece of good or ill fortune which is outside the competence of the player (or individual). By way of example, *A* hits a shot to the green which glances off a stone into the woods; *B* hits the same stone at a different angle and his ball runs on to the green and into the hole. Since neither was aiming at, or aware of, the stone, the resulting disparity of fortune is "the rub of the green".

To be green with envy. To be extremely envious of someone's achievements, attainments, wealth, etc. Literally, to have one's face acquire a pale greenish hue as a result of envy.

To get the green light. To get permission to proceed with an undertaking, green being the "Go" sign on road and rail signals.

To give a girl a green gown. A 16th-century descriptive phrase for romping with a girl in the fields and rolling her on the grass so that her dress is stained green.

> There's not a budding Boy or Girle this day,
> But is got up, and gone to bring in May ...
> Many a green gown has been given;
> Many a kiss, both odde and even.
>> HERRICK: *Corinna'a Going a-Maying*.

To look through green glasses. To feel jealous of one: to be envious of another's success. *Cp.* GREEN-EYED MONSTER.

You would have me believe that the moon is made of green cheese. *See under* MOON.

The Board of Green Cloth. *See under* BOARD.

Gentlemen of the Green Baize Road. WHIST players. Dickens uses the phrase in *Bleak House*, ch. xxvi. **Gentlemen of the Green Cloth Road.** Billiard players. Probably the idea of sharpers is implied. *Cp.* GENTLEMEN OF THE ROAD.

The wearing of the green. An Irish patriotic and revolutionary song dating from 1798. Green (*cp.* EMERALD ISLE) was the emblematic colour of Irish patriots.

> For they're hangin' men an' women there for wearin'
> o' the Green.

Green Belt. A stretch of country around a large urban area that has been scheduled for comparative preservation and where building development is restricted.

Green Dragoons. *See* REGIMENTAL AND DIVISIONAL NICKNAMES.

Green fingers. Said of a successful gardener.

Green hands. Inexperienced sailors. *Cp.* GREENHORN.

The Green Howards. Since 1920, the official name of the Yorkshire Regiment, the 19th of the line. Sir Charles Howard was their colonel from 1738 to 1748 and green is the colour of the regimental facings. The name was originally given to distinguish them from the 3rd BUFFS who were also commanded by a Colonel Howard.

The Green Isle. Ireland. *Cp.* EMERALD ISLE.

Green Linnets. *See* REGIMENTAL AND DIVISIONAL NICKNAMES.

Green Man. This common PUBLIC-HOUSE SIGN probably represents either a JACK-IN-THE-GREEN or a forester, who, like ROBIN HOOD, was once clad in green.

> But the "Green Man" shall I pass by unsung,
> Which mine own James upon his sign-post hung?
> His sign, his image—for he once was seen
> A squire's attendant, clad in keeper's green.
>> CRABBE: *The Borough*.

The public-house sign, *The Green Man and Still*, is probably a modification of the arms of the Distiller's Company, the supporters of which were two Indians, for which the sign painters usually substituted foresters or green men drinking out of a glass barrel.

On a golf course the **green-man** is the club employee responsible for the putting greens.

Green Mountain Boys. Vermont (*Vert Mont*) is called the *Green Mountain State* from the evergreen forests on its mountains. The Green Mountain Boys were organized on a military basis under Ethan Allen when the settlers of the area found their titles to land in dispute between New York and New

Hampshire. From 1775 they fought successfully in the American Revolution and Vermont declared itself an independent state in 1777.

Green Ribbon. A short-lived political club formed *c.* 1675 as the King's Head Club, after the tavern in Chancery Lane where it met. The name was changed to the Green Ribbon Club about 1679 from the bow of green ribbon which its members wore in their hats. Shaftesbury, Buckingham, Mulgrave, Shadwell, Dangerfield and Oates and others of the WHIG party were among its members. The failure of the Exclusion Bill, the flight of Shaftesbury, and the RYE HOUSE PLOT made membership a risk and by 1688 the club petered out.

Green Ribbon Day in IRELAND is 17 March, ST. PATRICK's Day, when the SHAMROCK and green ribbon are worn as the national badge.

Green room. In a theatre the common waiting-room for the performers near the stage. Originally such rooms were painted green to relieve the eyes from the glare of the stage.

Green sickness. The old name for chlorosis, a form of anaemia once common in adolescent girls. It was characterized by a greenish pallor.

Green wax. In the old Court of EXCHEQUER practice, an estreat (certified extract from an official record) formerly delivered to the SHERIFF for levy. It was under the seal of the court, which was impressed upon green wax.

Greenbacks. Legal tender notes first issued in the United States in 1862, during the CIVIL WAR, as a war-revenue expedient. So called because the back is printed in green. The name is now applied to paper currency issued by any national American bank.

Greengage. A variety of plum introduced into England from France by Sir William Gage of Hengrave, Suffolk, about 1725, and named in his honour. Called by the French "reine-claude" out of compliment to the daughter of Anne of Brittany and Louis XII, first wife of Francis I.

Greenhorn. A novice at any trade, profession, sport, etc. In allusion to the "green horns" of a young horned animal. *Cp.* GREEN; GREEN HANDS.

Greenpeace. A movement originating in Canada in 1971, aiming to persuade governments to change industrial activities which threaten natural resources and the environment. It supports direct non-violent action and has gained wide attention by its efforts to protect whales and to prevent the killing of young seals. When acting against French nuclear tests in the South Pacific in 1985 their ship, *Rainbow Warrior* was sunk by a French saboteur. *Cp.* FRIENDS OF THE EARTH.

Greenshirt. A supporter of the Social Credit Movement established in England by Major Douglas in the 1920s, and so named from the green uniform shirt adopted.

Greensleeves. A very popular ballad in the time of Elizabeth I, published in 1581, given in Clement Robinson's *Handefull of Pleasant Delites* (1584) and mentioned by SHAKESPEARE (*Merry Wives*, II, i, and V, v). The air is of the same period and was used for many ballads. During the CIVIL WAR it was used by the CAVALIERS as a tune for political ballads, and Pepys (23 April 1660) mentions it under the title of *The Blacksmith*.

Greenlander. A native of Greenland, discovered by Eric the Red in 985 and called Grœnland "for he said it would make men's minds long to go there if it had a fine name". *Greenlander* is facetiously applied to a GREENHORN.

Greenwich. Greenwich barbers. Retailers of sand; so called because the inhabitants of Greenwich used to "shave the pits" in the neighbourhood to supply London.

Greenwich Stars. The stars used by astronomers for the lunar computations in the nautical ephemeris.

Greenwich Time. Mean time for the meridian of Greenwich, *i.e.* the system of time in which noon occurs at the moment of passage of the mean sun over the meridian of Greenwich. It is the standard time adopted by astronomers and was used throughout the British Isles until 18 February, 1968, when clocks were advanced one hour and Summer Time became "permanent". The new system was designated British Standard Time (as from 27 October 1968), but the arguments against it duly prevailed and the country reverted to Greenwich Mean Time on 31 October 1971. *See* DAYLIGHT SAVING; STANDARD TIME.

Gregorian. Gregorian Calendar. A modification of the JULIAN CALENDAR, introduced in 1582 by Pope Gregory XIII. This is called "the New Style". *See* GREGORIAN YEAR.

Gregorian chant. Plainsong; the traditional ritual melody of the Christian Church of the West, so called because it was reformed and elaborated by GREGORY THE GREAT at the end of the 6th century.

Gregorian Epoch. The epoch or day on which the Gregorian CALENDAR commenced in October 1582. *See* GREGORIAN YEAR.

Gregorian telescope. The first form of the reflecting telescope, invented in 1663 by James Gregory (1638–1675), professor of mathematics at St. Andrews.

Gregorian tree. The gallows; so named from Gregory Brandon and his son Richard ("Young Gregory"), HANGMEN from the time of James I to 1649. Gregory was granted a coat of arms.

Gregorian Year. The civil year according to the correction introduced by Pope Greg - ory XIII in 1582. The equinox which occurred on 25 March in the time of Julius Cæsar fell on 11 March in the year 1582. This was because the Julian calculation of $365\frac{1}{4}$ days to a year was 11 min. 14 sec. too long. Gregory suppressed 10 days by altering 5 October to 15 October, thus making the equinox fall on 21 March 1583. Further simple arrangements prevented the recurrence of a similar error in the future. The change was soon adopted by most CATHOLIC countries, but the PROTESTANT countries did not accept it until much later. The *New Style* was not adopted by ENGLAND and SCOTLAND until 1752. At the same time the beginning of the civil or legal year was altered from LADY DAY (25 March) to 1 January, a change adopted in Scotland in 1600. *See* ELEVEN DAYS.

Gregories. HANGMEN. *See* GREGORIAN TREE.

Gregory. A feast held on St. GREGORY's Day (12 March), especially in IRELAND.

Gregory the Great, or **St. Gregory** (540–604), the first Pope of this name, and DOCTOR OF THE CHURCH. The outstanding figure of his age, notable for church and monastic reform, for dealing with heresies, for wise administration, and kindness to the poor. He also re-fashioned the liturgy of the Church and made a lasting contribution to Church music (*see* GREGORIAN CHANT). He sent St. AUGUSTINE on his mission to the Anglo-Saxons, thus earning the title of *Apostle of England*.

Gremlin. One of a tribe of imaginary GNOMES or GOBLINS humorously blamed by the R.A.F. in World War II for everything that went wrong in an aircraft or an operation. The name was probably coined at the end of World War I or in the 1920s and was apparently in use on R.A.F. stations in India and the Middle East in the 1930s. The name is first traced in print in *The Aeroplane* (10 April 1929). A common explanation is that a gremlin was the goblin which came out of Fremlin's beer bottles (Fremlin being a brewer in Kent), although there are numerous other stories.

Grenadier. Originally a soldier, picked for his stature, whose duty in battle was to throw *grenades*. In time each regiment had a special company of them, and when in the 18th century the use of grenades was discontinued (not to be revived until World War I) the name was retained for the company composed of the tallest and finest men. In the British Army it now survives only in the Grenadier Guards, the First Regiment of Foot Guards, noted for their height, physique, traditions, and discipline.

Grendel. The mythical half-human monster killed by BEOWULF. Grendel nightly raided the king's hall and slew the sleepers.

Gresham, Sir Thomas. *See* CLEOPATRA AND HER PEARL; GRASSHOPPER.

Gresham's Law can be briefly summarized as stating that bad money drives out good, and was promulgated by Gresham to Elizabeth I in 1558, though the same law had been explained earlier by COPERNICUS.

To dine with Sir Thomas Gresham. *See* HUMPHREY.

Greta Hall. The poet of Greta Hall. Robert Southey (1774–1843), who lived at Greta Hall, Keswick, Cumberland.

Gretna Green Marriages. Runaway marriages. Elopers from England reaching Gretna, near Springfield, Dumfriesshire, 8 miles N.W. of Carlisle, could (up to 1856) get legally married without licence, banns, or priest. All that was required was a declaration before witnesses of the couple's willingness to marry. This declaration was generally made to a blacksmith, landlord, toll-keeper, etc. By an Act of 1856, the residence in Scotland for at least 21 days of one of the parties became essential before a marriage was possible. Gretna Green's prominence arose from the abolition of FLEET MARRIAGES. Although marriage by declaration ceased to be legal in July 1940, Gretna Green and other places in Scotland continue to attract young couples because minors may still marry there without parental consent. *Cp.* MAY-FAIR MARRIAGES.

Grève (Grev). **Place de Grève.** The TYBURN of old PARIS, where for centuries public executions took place, now called the *Place de l'Hôtel de Ville*. It is on the bank of the Seine, the word *grève* here meaning the strand of a river.

Who has e'er been at Paris must needs know the
    Grève,
The fatal retreat of th' unfortunate brave,
Where honour and justice most oddly contribute
To ease heroes' pains by a halter or gibbet.
    PRIOR: *The Thief and the Cordelier.*

Grey. Grey as a badger. Said of one with

dark hair thickly sprinkled with grey and white, from the resemblance to the grey brindled fur of the badger.

The Greys. *See* REGIMENTAL AND DIVISIONAL NICKNAMES.

The Earl of Mar's Grey Breeks. *See* REGIMENTAL AND DIVISIONAL NICKNAMES.

Grey Cloak. A City of London alderman who has passed the chair; so called because his official robe is furred with grey amis.

Grey Eminence. The name given to François Le Clerc du Tremblay (1577–1638), or Père Joseph, as he was called, the CAPUCHIN agent and trusty counsellor of Cardinal Richelieu. It was inspired by his influence over Cardinal Richelieu's policies; he was, as it were, a shadowy CARDINAL in the background. Hence a close adviser who exercises power behind the scenes.

Grey Friars. FRANCISCANS.

Grey goose feather, or **wing.** The arrow, which is winged with grey goose feathers.

Grey Mare. *See under* MARE.

Grey Market. In World War II a transaction regarded as a lesser breach of the rationing regulations than the BLACK MARKET.

Grey matter. A pseudo-scientific name for the brain, for common sense. The active part of the brain is composed of a greyish tissue which contains the nerve-endings.

Grey Sisters. *See* FRANCISCANS.

Greybeard. An old man—generally a doddering old fellow; also an earthen pot for holding spirits; a large stone jar. *Cp.* BELLARMINE.

The Old Grey Whistle test. In TIN-PAN ALLEY song writers used to play their compositions to the "old greys", the elderly doorkeepers and suchlike workers in the offices of the music publishers. If the "old greys" were still whistling the tunes after a week or so, then they were likely to be worth publishing.

Gridiron. The emblem of St. LAWRENCE of ROME. One legend says that he was roasted on a gridiron; another that he was bound to an iron chair and thus roasted alive. He was martyred in 258, under Valerian. *See* ESCORIAL.

It is also the American term for a football playing field, from the fact that the field was marked with squares or grids. *See also* GOOSE AND GRIDIRON.

Gridironer. An Australian settler who bought land in strips like the bars of a gridiron, so that the land lying between was of little use and could be acquired later at a bargain price.

Griffin. A mythical monster; also called *Griffon, Gryphon*, etc., fabled to be the offspring of the LION and the EAGLE. Its legs and all from the shoulders to the head are like an eagle, the rest of the body is that of a lion. This creature was sacred to the sun and kept guard over hidden treasures. *See* ARIMASPIANS.

> [The Griffin is] an Emblem of valour and magnanimity, as being compounded of the Eagle and the Lion, the noblest Animals in their kinds; and so is it appliable unto Princes, Presidents, Generals, and all heroik Commanders; and so is it also born in the Coat-arms of many noble Families of Europe.
> SIR THOMAS BROWNE: *Pseudodoxia Epidemica*, III, xi.

The Londoner's familiar name for the figure on the site of TEMPLE BAR is *The Griffin*.

Among Anglo-Indians a newcomer, a GREENHORN, was called a *griffin*; and the residue of a contract feast, taken away by the contractor, half the buyer's and half the seller's, is known in the trade as *griffins*.

A griffon is a small rough-haired terrier used in France for hunting.

Grig. Merry as a grig. A grig is a small eel, a cricket or grasshopper; but grig here may be a corruption of Greek, "merry as a Greek". Both phrases were in use in the 16th century. *See* A MERRY GREEK *under* GREEK. Among the Romans *græcari* signified "to play the reveller".

Grim as an element in the naming of ancient earthworks and prehistoric sites derives from Old Norse *grimr*, a nickname of ODIN, supposedly from their size which made people attribute them to superhuman hands. From the 16th century they were often regarded as works of the DEVIL, with whom Grim was equated. *Cp.* GRAHAME'S DYKE. *See* HAVELOCK THE DANE.

Grim's Ditch, or **Grim's Dyke.** There are ancient earthworks of this name in Wiltshire, Buckinghamshire, Oxfordshire, Hertfordshire, Berkshire, etc. *See also* GRAHAME'S DYKE; WANSDYKE.

Grimes' Graves. NEOLITHIC flint quarries at Weeting, Norfolk.

Grimspound. The largest prehistoric work on Dartmoor, consisting of 24 hut circles in an oval enclosure some 150 yards long.

Grimaldi, Joseph (1779–1837). The most celebrated and irresistible clown of English PANTOMIME was born at LONDON, the son of an Italian actor. He appeared at Drury Lane theatre before he was two years old and at SADLER'S WELLS at the age of three. He was forced to retire in 1828, worn out by continuous overwork. He dressed in what became the traditional clown costume and the name "Joey the clown" attests his popularity and importance.

Grimalkin. An old she-cat, especially a wicked or eerie-looking one; from *grey* and

MALKIN. In Shakespeare's *Macbeth* (I, i) a Witch says "I come, Graymalkin". The cat was supposed to be a witch.

Grimm's Law. The law of permutation of consonants in the Indo-Germanic, Low and High German languages. It was first comprehensively formulated by Jakob L. Grimm, the German philologist, in 1822. Thus what is *p* in Greek, Latin, or Sanskrit, becomes *f* in Gothic and *b* or *f* in the Old High German; what is *t* in Greek, Latin or Sanskrit, *th* in Gothic and *d* in Old High German, etc. Thus changing *p* into *f*, and *t* into *th*, "pater" becomes "father". Grimm's Law is of the greatest importance in philological studies.

Grin. To Grin like a Cheshire cat. *See under* CAT.

You must grin and bear it. Resistance is hopeless; you may make a face if you like, but you must put up with things.

Grind. To work up for an examination.

He has an axe to grind. *See under* AXE.

To grind one down. To reduce the price asked; to oppress.

To grind to a halt. To gradually come to a standstill. From the clogging up of a piece of machinery until it can no longer function. In the days of the windmill, when the wind fell away, the grinding action of the millstones on the grain stopped the mill—it ground to a halt.

To take a grind. To walk for exercise.

Grinder. To take a grinder. An obsolete gesture of contempt defined by Dickens in *Pickwick Papers* (ch. xxxi):

> Here Mr. Jackson smiled once more upon the company, and, applying his left thumb to the tip of the nose, worked a visionary coffee-mill with his right hand ... which was familiarly denominated "taking a grinder".

Grindstone. To keep one's nose to the grindstone. *See* NOSE.

Griselda, or **Grisilda,** also called Patient Grisel, Grazel, etc. The model of enduring patience and wifely obedience. She was the heroine of the last tale in Boccaccio's *Decameron*. It was translated into Latin by Petrarch under the title *De Obidentia ac Fide uxoria Mythologia* and thence used by Chaucer for his *Clerkes Tale* and by Dekker, Chettle and Haughton for their *Patient Grissil* (1603). The story is of the Marquis of Saluzzo, who marries a poor girl of great beauty. He subjects her to almost unendurable trials, including the pretence that he has married another. At last convinced of her patience and devotion, Chaucer tells us:

> Ful many a yeer in heigh prosperitee
> Lyven thise two in concord and in reste.

Grist. All's grist that comes to my mill. All is appropriated that comes to me; I can make advantage out of anything or use all that comes my way. Grist is that quantity of corn which is to be ground at one time.

To bring grist to the mill. To bring profitable business or gain; to furnish supplies.

Groaning Chair. An old rustic name for a chair in which a woman sat after her confinement to receive congratulations. Similarly "groaning cake" and "groaning cheese" (called in some dialects KENNO) are the cake and cheese which were provided in GOOSE MONTH, and "groaning malt" was a strong ale brewed for the occasion.

> For a nurse, the child to dandle,
> Sugar, soap, spiced pots and candle,
> A groaning chair and eke a cradle.
> *Poor Robin's Almanack*, 1676.

Groat. The name given in mediæval times to all thick silver coins; derived from *denarii grossi*, large denarii. In ENGLAND the name was given specifically to the fourpenny piece first made in the reign of Edward I. Later it became a very small silver coin, the issue of which ceased in 1662 although they were still struck as MAUNDY MONEY. In 1836 the small fourpenny piece reappeared as the *Britannia Groat* (*see* JOEY).

You half-faced groat. A 16th-century colloquialism for "You worthless fellow". The debased groats issued in the reign of Henry VIII had the king's head in profile, but those in the reign of Henry VII had the king's head with full face.

> With that half-face would he have all my land;
> A half-fac'd groat five hundred pounds a-year!
> SHAKESPEARE: *King John*, I, i.

Groats. Husked oat or wheat fragments rather larger than grits (O.E. *grut*, coarse meal).

Blood without groats is nothing. Family without fortune is worthless. The allusion is perhaps to black pudding which consists chiefly of blood and groats formed into a sausage.

Grog. Spirits. Properly rum diluted with water. In 1740 Admiral Vernon, when Commander-in-Chief West Indies, substituted watered-down rum for the neat spirit then issued to both officers and men. The Admiral was nicknamed *Old Grog* from his GROGRAM coat and the name was transferred to the new beverage.

> But Jack with smiles each danger meets,
> Casts anchor, heaves the log,
> Trims all the sails, belays the sheets,
> And drinks his can of grog.
> DIBDIN: *The Friendly Tars*.

Originally issued twice daily (a quarter of a pint of rum with a pint of water), the ration was cut to one issue in 1824 and reduced to a half-gill in 1850. The issue to officers was stopped in 1881 and to Warrant Officers in 1918. Grog ration to all ratings ended on 31 July 1970.

Grog-blossoms. Blotches or pimples on the face produced by heavy drinking.

Grogram. A coarse fabric made of silk and mohair or silk and wool, stiffened with gum. It is the Fr. *grosgrain*.

> Gossips in grief and grograms clad.
>
> PRAED: *The Troubadour*, c. i, st. v.

The Blood of the Grograms. *See under* BLOOD.

Grommet. Once a common word for a young serving-man or a ship's boy (O.Fr. *gromet*). It is also the name of a ring formed from a single strand of rope by crossing the two ends to make a loop of the requisite size and passing the ends round and round in their original lay, the ends being finished off as in a long splice. In this sense the word is from 15th-century Fr. *gromette*, a curb.

Groom of the Stole. *See* STOLE.

Groove. To get into a groove. To get into a rut, a narrow undeviating course of life or habit, to become restricted in outlook and ways.

To be in the groove or **groovy.** To be in the right mood, to be doing something successfully, to be up to the current style or "with it"; from the accurate reproduction of music by a needle set in the groove of a gramophone record or disc.

Gross. The French word *gros*, big, bulky, corpulent, coarse, in English has developed many additional meanings. Thus a *gross* is twelve dozen; a *great gross*, twelve gross; *gross weight* is the entire weight without deductions; *gross average* is the GENERAL AVERAGE. A VILLEIN *in gross* was the property of his master, and not part of the property of the manor; a *common in gross* is one which is entirely personal property. *Cp.* AD-VOWSON IN GROSS.

Grotesque. Literally, in "Grotto style". The chambers of ancient buildings revealed in mediæval times in ROME were called *grottoes*, and as their walls were frequently decorated with fanciful ornaments and *outré* designs, the word grotesque (*grotesco*) came to be applied to similar ornamentations.

Grotto. Pray remember the grotto. This cry was raised in the streets (as late as the 1920s in the poorer parts of London) by small children, who collected old shells, bits of coloured stone or pottery, with leaves, flowers, etc., built a little "grotto" and knelt beside it with their caps ready for pennies. The custom should be restricted to 25 July (St.

JAMES's Day), for it is a relic of the old shell grottoes which were erected with an image of the saint for the use of those who could not afford the pilgrimage necessary to pay a visit on that day to the shrine of St. James of COM-POSTELA. *See* COCKLE HAT.

Ground. Ground floor. The storey level with the ground, or, in a basement-house, the floor above the basement. In the U.S.A. known as the first floor.

To get in on the ground floor. To secure an advantageous position in an enterprise through participation at the outset, especially in securing investments before they are available to the general public.

Ground and lofty tumbling. An 18th-century phrase for an acrobatic performance on the ground and upon a tightrope, or swing.

Ground hog. The wood-chuck or North American marmot.

Ground-hog Day. CANDLEMAS (2 February), from the saying that the ground-hog first appears from hibernation on that day. If he sees his shadow, he goes back for another six weeks—indicating six more weeks of bad weather.

Ground swell. A long, deep rolling or swell of the sea, caused by a recent or distant storm, or by an earthquake.

That suits me down to the ground. *See under* DOWN.

To break ground. To be the first to commence a project, etc.; to take the first step in an enterprise, as the first stage in siege operations was to break ground to dig trenches.

To gain ground. To make headway; to be improving one's position.

To have the ground cut from under one's feet. To see what one has relied on for support suddenly removed.

To hold one's ground. To maintain one's position, authority, etc. Not to budge or give way.

To lose ground. To become less successful or popular; to drift away from the object aimed at.

To shift one's ground. To try a different plan of attack; to change one's argument or the basis of one's reasoning.

To stand one's ground. Not to yield or give way; to stick to one's COLOURS; to have the courage of one's opinion.

Groundlings. Those who occupied the cheapest part of an Elizabethan theatre, *i.e.* the pit, which was the bare ground in front of the stage. The actor, who today "plays to the gallery", in Elizabethan times

Split the ears of groundlings.
SHAKESPEARE: *Hamlet*, III, ii.

Groundnut Scheme. Figuratively, an expensive failure or ill-considered enterprise; from a hastily organized and badly planned British government scheme (1947) to clear large areas of hitherto unprofitable land in Africa to grow groundnuts. The venture was abandoned three years later at considerable cost to the Taxpayer.

Growlers. The old four-wheeled horse-drawn cabs were called "growlers" from the surly attitude of their drivers, and "crawlers" from their slow pace.

Grub. To grub stake. A miner's term for equipping a gold prospector with his requirements in exchange for a share of his finds.

Grub Street. The former name of a London street in the ward of CRIPPLEGATE Without, changed to Milton Street in 1830 after the carpenter and builder who was the ground landlord. It leads north out of Fore Street, Moorfields, to Chiswell Street.

> Not with less glory mighty Dulness crowned
> Shall take through Grub Street her triumphant round;
> And her Parnassus glancing o'er at once,
> Behold an hundred sons, and each a dunce
> POPE: *The Dunciad*, III, 135 (1727).

Dr. Johnson says it was

> Much inhabited by writers of small histories, dictionaries, and temporary poems; whence any mean production is called *grubstreet*.

The name is used allusively for needy authors, literary hacks, and their work. *Cp.* HACK.

Hermit of Grub Street. *See under* HERMIT.

Gruel. A gruelling time, gruelling heat, etc. Exhausting, overpowering.

He had a gruelling. He was given a pasting, he was punished severely (in boxing, etc.).

To take one's gruel. To accept one's punishment, to take what is coming to one.

Grummet. *See* GROMMET.

Grundy. What will Mrs. Grundy say? What will our strait-laced neighbours say? The phrase is from Tom Morton's *Speed the Plough* (1798). In the first scene Mrs. Ashfield shows herself very jealous of neighbour Grundy, and farmer Ashfield says to her: "Be quiet, wool ye? Always ding dinging Dame Grundy into my ears—What will Mrs. Grundy zay? What will Mrs. Grundy think?"

Gryll. Let Gryll be Gryll and have his hoggish mind (Spenser: *The Faerie Queene*, II, xii, 87). Don't attempt to wash a blackamoor white; the leopard will never change his spots. Gryll is the Gr. *grullos*, a hog.

When Sir Guyon disenchanted the forms in the BOWER OF BLISS some were exceedingly angry, and Gryll, who had been metamorphosed by ACRASIA into a hog, abused him most roundly.

Gryphon. *See* GRIFFIN.

Guardiana. According to the old legend the Spanish river was so called from Durandarte's Squire of this name. Mourning the fall of his master at RONCESVALLES, he was turned into a river (*see Don Quixote*, ii, 23). Actually, it is Arab. *wadi*, a river, and *Anas*, its classical name.

Guard. To be off one's guard. To be careless, to be caught unawares.

To be put on his guard. To "give him the tip", to show him where the danger lies.

Guards, The. *See* HOUSEHOLD TROOPS.

Guards of the Pole. *See* GREAT BEAR *under* BEAR.

Guarneri, or **Guarnerius.** The name of one of the famous violin-makers of CREMONA of the 17th and 18th centuries. Andreas (*c.* 1626–1698) was a pupil of Nicolo AMATI. Giuseppe (1687–1745), known as Giuseppe del Gesù, from his habit of inscribing the sacred initials I.H.S. inside his violins, was held to be the greatest. *Cp.* STRAD.

Gubbins. The wild and savage inhabitants of the neighbourhood of Brentor, Devon, who according to Fuller in his *Worthies* (1661)—

> lived in cots (rather holes than houses) ..., having all in common, multiplying without marriage into many hundreds ... Their language is the dross of the dregs of the vulgar Devonian ... They held together like burrs.

As explanation of the name he says, "We call the shavings of fish (which are of little worth) *gubbins*".

William Browne in a poem on LYDFORD LAW (1644) says:

> And near hereto's the Gubbins Cave;
> A people that no knowledge have
> Of law, of God, or men;
> Whom Cæsar never yet subdued;
> Who've lawless lived; of manners rude
> All savage in their den.

Gudgeon. Gaping for gudgeons. Looking out for things extremely improbable. As a gudgeon is a small fish used as bait, it means here a snare, a lie, a deception.

To swallow a gudgeon. To be bamboozled with a most palpable lie, as silly fish are caught by gudgeons (Fr. *goujon*; whence the phrase *avaler le goujon*, to swallow the bait, to die).

> Make fools believe in their foreseeing
> Of things before they are in being;
> To swallow gudgeons ere they're catched,
> And count their chickens ere they're hatched.
> BUTLER: *Hudibras*, II, iii.

Gudrun, or **Kudrun.** The heroine of the great

13th-century German epic poem of this name founded on a passage in the *Prose* EDDA. The third part describes how Gudrun, daughter of King Hettel, was carried off by Hochmut of Normandy and made to work like a menial in his mother's house, because she would not break her troth to Herwig, King of Zealand. She was eventually rescued by her brother. This poem is sometimes known as the German ODYSSEY.

Gudule, Gudula, or **Gudila, St.** Patron saint of Brussels, daughter of Count Witger, died 712. She is represented with a lantern, from a tradition that she was one day going to the church of St. Morzelle with a lantern which went out, but the Holy Virgin lighted it again with her prayers. Her feast day is 8 January.

Guebres, or **Ghebers** (gā' bĕrz). Followers of the ancient Persian religion, reformed by ZOROASTER; fire-worshippers, PARSEES. The name, which was given them by their Mohammedan conquerors, is now applied to fire-worshippers generally.

Guelphs and Ghibellines (gwelfs, gib' e lēnz). In mediæval Italy two rival factions whose quarrels occupy much of the political history of the period. The Guelphs were the papal and popular party, the Ghibellines, the imperial and aristocratic party. Both names are derived from two rival German factions of the 12th century. *Ghibelline* is an Italian form of *Waiblingen*, a small town in Württemberg and a possession of the Hohenstaufen Emperor Conrad III, the name of which is said to have been used as a war-cry by his followers at the battle of Weinsberg (1140). Their opponents similarly used the war-cry *Welf*, the personal name of their leader, Welf VI of Bavaria. *Guelph* is the Italian form of *Welf*.

The Guelph dynasty ruled in Hanover until 1866 and the reigning dynasty of Great Britain is descended from it. Guelphs ruled in Brunswick from its erection into a Duchy in 1235 until 1918.

Guenever. *See* GUINEVERE.

Guerinists (ger' i nists). An early 17th-century sect of French ILLUMINATI, founded by Peter Guérin.

Guernsey Lily. *See* MISNOMERS.

Guerrilla War (ge ril' à). Irregular warfare carried on by small groups acting independently; especially by patriots when their country is being invaded. From Span. *guerrilla*, diminutive of *guerra*, war. *See* F.F.I.

Gueux, Les (lā ger), or **The Beggars.** The name adopted by the confederates who rose against Spanish rule in the Netherlands in the 16th century. In 1556 Baron Berlaymont

is said to have exclaimed to the Regent, Margaret of Parma: "Is it possible that your highness can entertain fear of these beggars?" (Motley, *Rise of the Dutch Republic*, II, vi). The name then became an honoured title. **The Beggars of the Sea** were the Dutch and HUGUENOT privateers who harassed Spanish shipping in the same struggle. **The Wild Beggars** were the bands of marauders and robbers who took advantage of the times to plunder and commit outrage, especially against monasteries and clergy.

Guides. *See* GIRL GUIDES.

Guignol (gē' nyol). The principal character in a popular 18th-century French puppet-show, similar to PUNCH. As the performance involved macabre and gruesome incidents the name came to be attached to short plays of this nature; hence **Grand Guignol,** a series of such plays, or the theatre in which they were performed.

Guilds, or **Gilds.** *See* LIVERY COMPANIES.

Guillotine (gil' ō tēn). An instrument for inflicting capital punishment by decapitation, so named from Joseph Ignace Guillotin (1738–1814), a French physician, who proposed its adoption to prevent unnecessary pain. It was first used in the Place de GRÈVE, 25 April, 1792. For a time it was known as a *Louisette* after Antoine Louis (1723–1792), the French surgeon who devised it. Similar instruments had been used in some countries from the 13th century. *Cp.* MAIDEN.

It is also the name of a paper-cutting machine and a surgical instrument.

In British Parliamentary procedure, a development of the CLOSURE to arbitrarily cut delay by passing a *guillotine motion*, when, at the committee stage or report stage, a BILL is divided into compartments, each of which has to be dealt with in the specified time. It is also known as *closure by compartments*.

Guinea. A gold coin current in England from 1663 to 1817 (last struck 1813), originally made of gold from Guinea in West Africa. The early issues bore a small elephant below the head of the king. Its original LEGAL TENDER value was 20s. but from 1717 it was fixed at 21s. The actual value varied; in 1694 it was as high as 30s. Before the advent of DECIMAL CURRENCY, it was still customary for professional fees, subscriptions, the price of racehorses, pictures and other luxuries to be paid in guineas as money of account. *See also* SPADE GUINEA.

Guinea-dropper. A cheat. It alludes to an old cheating dodge of dropping counterfeit guineas which is of comparable significance to THIMBLE-RIGGING.

Who now the guinea-dropper's bait regards,
Tricked by the sharper's dice or juggler's cards?
GAY: *Trivia*, II, 249.

Guinea fowl. So called because it was introduced from Guinea, where it is common.

Guinea Grains, or **Grains of Paradise.** The seeds of *Amomum melugueta* and *Amomum Granum-Paradisi*, two West African plants. Aromatic and pungent, they were formerly used in making HIPPOCRAS and are a constituent in some cattle-powders.

Guinea-hen. An Elizabethan synonym for a prostitute, who is won by gold.

Ere ... I would drown myself for the love of a Guinea-hen, I would change my humanity with a baboon.
SHAKESPEARE: *Othello*, I, iii.

Guinea-pig. Properly the cavy, a small South American rodent. A former Stock Exchange name for a person of standing who allowed his name to be put on a company director's list for a fee in guineas, but who was inactive. Guinea-pig is also an old name for a midshipman or a clergyman without a cure. The former because he was neither a fully-fledged officer nor a rating, as guinea-pigs are not pigs, nor do they come from Guinea; the latter because he did occasional duty for a guinea a sermon. Guinea-pigs are often used in scientific and medical experiments and the name is now applied to anyone used in this way or upon whom something is tried out.

Guinevere, Guinever, or **Guenever** (gwin′ e vēr). The wife of King ARTHUR. The name is a corruption of *Guanhumara* (from Welsh *Gwenhwyfar*) as she appears in Geoffrey of Monmouth's *Historia Britonum*, a principal source of ARTHURIAN ROMANCES.

Gule. The Gule of August. 1 August, LAMMAS DAY. The word is probably the Welsh *gwyl* (Lat. *vigilia*), a festival.

Gules. The heraldic term for red. In engraving it is shown by perpendicular parallel lines. From the plural of O.E. *gole*, *goule*, the mouth, the jaws; the reference is probably to the colour of the open jaws.

With man's blood paint the ground, gules, gules.
SHAKESPEARE: *Timon of Athens*, IV, iii.

Gulf. At the universities of Oxford and Cambridge, an old name for the position of a candidate who goes in for honours and is not good enough to be classed but has shown sufficient merit to pass. When the list is made out a line is drawn after the classes, and the few names put below are in the "gulf", those so listed being "gulfed". *See also* ELEGANT EXTRACTS.

A great gulf fixed. An impassable separation. The allusion is to the parable of DIVES and LAZARUS (*Luke* xvi, 26).

Gulf Stream. The great warm ocean current which flows out of the Gulf of Mexico (whence its name) and, passing by the eastern coast of the United States, is, near the banks of Newfoundland, deflected across the Atlantic to modify the climate of Western Europe as far north as Spitzbergen and Novaya Zemlya. It washes the shores of the British Isles.

Gulistan (Pers. the garden of roses). The famous moral miscellany renowned for the quality of its prose and wit, written by Sadi (1194–1282 or 1292), the name adopted by Sheikh Muslih Uddin, the most celebrated Persian poet and writer after OMAR KHAYYÁM. It contains sections on kings, dervishes, contentment, love, youth, old age, etc. with numerous stories and philosophical sayings.

Gull. An Elizabethan synonym for one who is easily duped, especially a high-born gentleman (*cp.* BEJAN). Dekker wrote his *Gull's Hornbook* (1609) as a kind of guide to the behaviour of contemporary GALLANTS.

The most notorious geek and gull
That e'er invention played on.
SHAKESPEARE: *Twelfth Night*, V, i.

Gully-raker. In early Australian slang, one who combs wild country and appropriates any unbranded cattle he finds there.

Gum. To gum up the works. To clog up the proceedings, to throw an enterprise into confusion.

Up a gum tree. To be in real difficulty, unable to get any further with a project or task; to be virtually stuck. Possibly an allusion to the gum tree being a refuge for the opossum. (*See* POSSUM.)

Gummed. He frets like gummed velvet, or **gummed taffety.** Velvet and taffeta were sometimes stiffened with gum to make them "sit better" but, being very stiff, they fretted out quickly.

Gun. This word was formerly used for a large stone-throwing military device of the catapult or mangonel type. In the *Legend of Good Women* (*Cleopatra*, 58) Chaucer seems to refer to the ballista:

With grisley soun out goth the grete gonne,
And hertely they hurtlen al at ones,
And fro the top doun cometh the grete stones.

But in the *House of Fame* (iii, 553) he says:
As swift as pelet out of gonne
Whan fyr is in the poudre ronne.

The word is perhaps a shortened form of the old Scandinavian female name Gunnildr (*gunnr* is Icel. for war, and *hildr* for battle). The bestowing of female names on arms is not uncommon; there are the famous MONS

MEG, Queen Elizabeth's pocket pistol (*see under* POCKET), as well as BIG BERTHA of World War I—the long-range gun that bombarded Paris, named after Bertha Krupp, wife of the head of the great armament factory at Essen.

Barisal guns, or **Lake guns.** *See* BARISAL.

Evening, or **sunset gun.** A gun fired at sunset, or about 9 p.m.

Minute gun. The firing of a gun at minute intervals, generally as a salute at a royal or state funeral.

He's a great gun. A man of note or consequence.

Son of a gun. This familiar designation implying contempt but now used with jocular familiarity derives from the days when women were allowed to live in naval ships. The "son of a gun" was one born in the ship, often near the midship gun, behind a canvas screen. If paternity was uncertain the child was entered in the log as "Son of a gun".

Sure as a gun. Quite certain. It is as certain to happen as a gun is to fire when the trigger is pressed.

To blow great guns. To be very boisterous, rough and windy, as the noise of great guns.

To give it the gun. In R.F.C. parlance in World War I and that of the R.A.F. in World War II, to open the throttle of an aeroplane suddenly and hard.

To jump the gun. To anticipate, to get started before the proper time, usually with a view to gaining an advantage; as when a competitor in a race starts just before the gun is fired.

To lay a gun. To aim it, to direct it on the target (not used of small-arms).

To run away from one's own guns. To eat one's words; to desert what is laid down as a principle.

To stick to one's guns. To maintain one's position, argument, etc., in spite of opposition.

To gun for someone. To set out deliberately to get a person and do him a mischief or get even with him.

Gunboat. Gunboat Diplomacy. In the days of the Victorian colonial empire, gunboats and other naval vessels were often called upon to coerce local rulers in the interests of British traders, etc., usually in response to local clamour. Hence "gunboat diplomacy", to imply the settling of issues with weaker powers by the use or threat of force. *Cp.* PACIFICO.

Gun-cotton. A highly explosive compound, prepared by saturating cotton or other cellulose material with nitric and sulphuric acids. *Cp.* GREEK FIRE.

Gunman. An armed criminal prepared to use his gun recklessly. A term of American origin.

Gun money. Money issued in IRELAND by James II between 1689 and 1690 made from old brass cannon, bells, copper utensils, etc.

Gun room. In a large warship a room for the accommodation of junior officers, originally under the charge of the gunner. *Cp.* WARD ROOM.

> The subordinate officers in a big ship mess together in the gun-room, and the King of the gun room is the Sub-Lieutenant.
> GIEVES LTD. *How to Become a Naval Officer,* ch. iv (1933).

Gun-runner. One who unlawfully smuggles guns into a country for belligerent purposes.

Gunnar. The Norse form of GUNTHER.

Gunner. Kissing the gunner's daughter. Being flogged on board ship. At one time sailors in the Royal Navy who were to be flogged were tied to the breech of a cannon.

Gunpowder Plot. A plan to destroy James I, with Lords and Commons at the opening of PARLIAMENT, 5 November 1605, as a prelude to a CATHOLIC rising. Barrels of powder were stored in a vault under the HOUSE OF LORDS and Guy Fawkes was to fire the train. Tresham, one of the plotters, warned his Catholic relative, Lord Monteagle, who revealed the plot to the authorities. The cellars were searched and Guy Fawkes was taken. The ceremony of searching the vaults of Parliament prior to the annual opening is a result of this plot. *See* GUY.

Gunter. According to Gunter. Carefully and correctly done; with no possibility of a mistake. It is the American counterpart of our "according to COCKER".

Gunter's Chain, for land surveying, is so named from Edward Gunter (1581–1626), the great mathematician and professor of astronomy at Gresham College. It is 66 ft. long, and divided into 100 links. As 10 square chains make an acre, it follows that an acre contains 100,000 square links.

Gunter's scale is a 2-ft. rule having scales of chords, tangents, logarithmic lines, etc., marked on it, used for the mechanical solving of problems in surveying, navigation, etc.

Gunther (gun' ter), or **Gunnar.** In the Nibelungen saga, a Burgundian king, brother of KRIEMHILD, the wife of SIEGFRIED. He resolved to wed the martial BRUNHILD (or Brynhild) who had made a vow to marry only the man who could ride through the flames that encircled her castle. Gunther failed, but Siegfried did so in the shape of Gunther, and remained with her three nights, his sword between them all the time. Gunther then married Brunhild, but later Kriemhild told Brunhild that it was Siegfried who had ridden through the fire, thus arousing her jealousy. Siegfried was slain at Brunhild's instigation, and she then killed herself, her dying wish being to be burnt at Siegfried's side. Gunther was slain by ATLI because he refused to reveal where he had hidden the hoard of the Nibelungs. Gundaharius, a Burgundian king, who, with his men, perished by the sword of the Huns in 436, is supposed to be the historical character around which these legends collected. *See also* NIBELUNGENLIED.

Gurney Light. *See* BUDE.

Guru (goo′ roo). A Sanskrit word meaning venerable; it is now applied to a Hindu spiritual teacher and leader.

Guthlac, St., of Crowland, Lincolnshire, is represented in Christian art as a hermit punishing demons with a scourge, or consoled by ANGELS while demons torment him. He was a Mercian prince who died as a hermit in 714.

Guthrum. Silver of Guthrum's Lane. Fine silver was once so called because the chief GOLD and SILVER smiths of London lived there in the 13th and 14th centuries. The street, which is now called *Gutter Lane*, running from Cheapside into Gresham Street, was originally *Godrun Lane*. The hall of the Goldsmiths' Company is still in this locality.

Gutter press. A term applied contemptuously to those widely circulating low-brow newspapers, which indulge in sensationalism and scandal-mongering.

Guy. An effigy of a man stuffed with combustibles in mockery of Guy Fawkes, carried round and burnt on a BONFIRE on 5 November, in memory of the GUNPOWDER PLOT. Hence, any dowdy or fantastic figure. From American usage, the word as applied to a person is the equivalent of "CHAP".

Fall Guy. *See under* FALL.

To do a guy. To decamp.

To guy a person. To chaff him, to make fun of him.

Guy of Warwick. An English hero of legend and romance, whose exploits were first written down by an Anglo-Norman poet of the 12th century and were accepted as history by the 14th century.

To obtain the hand of the fair Félice or Phelis, daughter of the Earl of Warwick, he performed many doughty deeds abroad. Returning to England he married Phelis, but after forty days set off on pilgrimage to the HOLY LAND again performing deeds of prowess. Back in England he slew COLBRONDE, and then the DUN COW. After these achievements he became a hermit near Warwick and daily begged bread of his wife at his own castle gate. On his death-bed he sent her a ring, by which she recognized her lord, and she went to close his dying eyes. The story is told in the *Legend of Sir Guy* in PERCY'S RELIQUES.

Guy's Hospital. Founded in 1721 by Thomas Guy (*c.* 1645–1724), bookseller and philanthropist. He amassed an immense fortune in 1720 by speculations in South Sea Stock (*see* SOUTH SEA BUBBLE) and gave £238,295 to found and endow the hospital which is situated in SOUTHWARK.

Gwyn, Eleanor, or **Nell** (1651–1687). Popular actress and mistress of Charles II. She first became known when selling oranges at the Theatre Royal, DRURY LANE, and in 1665 appeared as Clydaria in Dryden's *Indian Emperor*. An illiterate child of the back streets, she was lively and infectious company. She had two sons by the king, the elder becoming Duke of St. Albans, and the younger James, Lord Beauclerk. She finally left the stage in 1682, and on his death-bed Charles said to his brother James, "Let not poor Nelly starve." James II fulfilled the request. She was buried in St. Martin-in-the-Fields and the funeral sermon was given by Thomas Tenison, later Archbishop of Canterbury.

Nell Gwyn is said to have suggested to her royal lover the building of Chelsea Hospital, and to have made him a present of the ground for it.
LEIGH HUNT: *The Town*, ch. vii.

Gyges (gī′ jēz). A king of Lydia of the 7th century B.C., who founded a new dynasty, warred against Asurbanipal of Assyria, and is memorable in legend for his ring and for his prodigious wealth.

According to PLATO, Gyges went down into a chasm in the earth, where he found a brazen horse; opening the sides of the animal, he found the carcass of a man, from whose finger he drew a brazen ring which rendered him invisible.

Why, did you think that you had Gyges ring
Or the herb that gives invisibility [FERN-SEED]?
BEAUMONT and FLETCHER:
Fair Maid of the Inn, I, i.

It was by the aid of the ring that Gyges obtained possession of the wife of CANDAULES and through her, of his kingdom.

Gymnosophists (jim nos′ o fists). A sect of ancient Hindu philosophers who went about with naked feet and almost without clothing. They lived in woods, subsisted on roots, and never married. They believed in the TRANS-MIGRATION OF SOULS. (Gr. *gumnos*, naked; *sophistes*, sage.)

Gyp (jip). At Cambridge (and at Durham) the name for a college servant, who acted as the valet to two or more undergraduates, the counterpart of the Oxford SCOUT. He ran errands, waited at table, woke men for morning chapel, brushed their clothes, etc. The word is probably from *gippo*, a 17th-century term for a scullion. Also in American, slang for the verb or noun *cheat*.

To give a person gyp. To give him a rough time, to make him suffer, as, "I'll give him gyp", "This tooth is giving me gyp", etc. An expression of unknown origin.

Gyp joint. In the U.S.A. an inordinately overpriced business establishment, as for example a restaurant or store.

Gypped. Many of the rivers and creeks in the cattle country of the U.S.A. contain so much gypsum, or alkali salts, that anyone drinking immoderately therefrom suffers a stomach attack, and is referred to as "gypped".

Gypsy, or **Gipsy.** A dark-skinned nomadic people which first appeared in England in the 16th century, called *Romanies* by George Borrow from their native name Rom (Fem. *Romni*). Their language is called *Romani*. Originally of low-caste Indian origin, they migrated to Persia and thence to Eur-ope, reaching Germany and France in the 15th century. As they were first thought to have come from Egypt they were called *Egyptians*, which became corrupted to *Gypians*, and so to the present form. The largest group of European Gypsies is *Atzigan*. In Turkey and Greece this became *Tshingian*, in the Balkans and Rumania *Tsigan*, in Hungary *Czigany*, in Germany *Zigeuner*, in Italy *Zingaro*, in Portugal *Cigano*, and in Spain *Zincalo*. The original name is said to mean "dark man". *See also* BOHEMIAN; ZINGARI.

Under the NAZIS they suffered the same fate as the Jews and large numbers were exterminated. Gypsies have an old reputation as smiths, tinkers, horse-dealers, fortune-tellers, and musicians. They practise a wide variety of crafts in many countries.

> That the Egyptians and Chaldean strangers,
> Known by the name of Gipsies, shall henceforth
> Be banished from the realm, as vagabonds.
> LONGFELLOW: *The Spanish Student*, III, ii.

Gyromancy. A kind of DIVINATION performed by walking round in a circle or ring until one fell from dizziness, the direction of the fall being of significance. (Gr. *guros*, ring; *manteia*, divination.)

Gytrash. A north of England spirit, which in the form of horse, mule, or large dog, haunts solitary ways, and sometimes comes upon belated travellers.

> I remember certain of Bessie's tales, wherein figured a ... spirit called a Gytrash.
> CHARLOTTE BRONTË: *Jane Eyre*, ch, xii.

H

H. The form of our capital **H** is through the Roman and Greek directly from the Phœnician (Semitic) letter *Heth* or *Cheth*, which, having two crossbars instead of one, represented a fence. The corresponding Egyptian HIEROGLYPH was a sieve, and the Anglo-Saxon RUNE is called hægl, hail.

Habeas Corpus (hā′ bē às kôr′ pùs) (Lat. have the body). The name given to a prerogative writ (from the opening words) to one who detains a person in custody ordering him to produce or "have the body" of the accused before the Court. Various forms of this writ developed from the 13th century, and by Charles I's reign such writs were the established means of testing illegal imprisonment. The freedom of the subject from wrongful imprisonment was formally established by the *Habeas Corpus Act* of 1679 and the *Habeas Corpus Act* of 1816 provided for the issue of such writs in vacation as well as in term. By an Act of 1862 the writ of *Habeas Corpus* runs in all dominions of the Crown excepting such dominions where there is a court having authority to issue such a writ. An Irish *Habeas Corpus Act* was passed in 1782. In Scotland its place is taken by the *Wrongous Imprisonment Act* of 1701.

The *Habeas Corpus Act* has been suspended in times of political and social disturbance and its importance is that it prevents people being imprisoned on mere suspicion or left in prison an indefinite time without trial.

Haberdasher. A dealer in small articles of dress, etc. The word is of uncertain etymology. The Haberdashers' Company was one of the "twelve great" LIVERY COMPANIES and was noted for its benefactions, especially in the field of education.

> An Haberdasher and a Carpenter,
> A Webbe, a Dyer, and a Tapiser,
> Were with us eke, cloth'd in one livery,
> Of a solemn and great fraternity.
> CHAUCER: *Prologue.*

Habit is Second Nature. The wise saw of DIOGENES.

French: *L'habitude est une seconde nature.*

Latin: *Usus est optimus magister.*

SHAKESPEARE (*Hamlet*, III, iv) says: "Use almost can change the stamp of nature."

Habsburg, or **Hapsburg.** The name of the famous dynasty which ruled in Austria, Hungary, Bohemia, Spain, etc., is a contraction of *Habichts-burg* (Hawk's Castle). So called from the castle built in the 11th century near the junction of the Aar and the Rhine, in present-day Switzerland, by Werner, Bishop of Strassburg, whose nephew, Werner, was the first to assume the title of "Count of Hapsburg." *See* EMPEROR.

Habsburg Lip. *See* AUSTRIAN LIP.

Hack. Short for HACKNEY, a horse let out for hire; hence, one whose services are for hire, especially a literary drudge, compiler, furbisher-up of other men's work. *Cp.* GRUB STREET. Goldsmith, who well knew from experience what the life was, wrote this epitaph on Edward Purdon:

> Here lies poor Ned Purdon, from misery freed,
> Who long was a bookseller's hack:
> He led such a damnable life in this world,
> I don't think he'll wish to come back.

Hackell's Coit. A huge stone said to weigh about 30 tons, near Stanton Drew, Somerset; so called from a tradition that it was a quoit or coit thrown by Sir John Hautville (13th century). In Wiltshire three huge stones near Kennet are called the *Devil's Coits* and there is a DOLMEN at St. Breock, Wadebridge, Cornwall, called the *Giant's Quoit.*

Hackney (O. Fr. *Haquenée*, ambling horse). Originally (14th century) the name given to a class of medium-sized horses, distinguishing them from war-horses. They were used for riding, and later the name was applied to a horse let out for hire, whence *hackney carriage. Cp.* HACK.

The name of the London borough of Hackney has no etymological connexion with the foregoing.

A hackneyed expression. One that is well-worn or over used.

Had it, To have. A colloquial expression widely popularized during World War II and possibly of Australian origin. It is applied to that which "finished with" or "done for". Thus a man seriously wounded was said to "have had it". At Roman gladiatorial combats the spectators cried *hoc habet* or *habet* (he has it, he is hit) when a gladiator was wounded or received his death-wound. It is also applied to one who has missed his chance or opportunity.

Never had it so good. *See under* NEVER.

Haddock. Traditionally it was in a haddock's mouth that St. PETER found the piece of money, the *stater* or *shekel* (*Matt.* xvii, 27), and the two marks on the fish's neck are said to be impressions of the finger and thumb of the apostle. Haddocks, however, cannot live in the fresh water of the Lake of Gennesaret. *Cp.* JOHN DORY.

Hades (hā' dēz). In HOMER, the name of the god (PLUTO) who reigns over the dead; but in later classical mythology the abode of the departed spirits, a place of gloom but not necessarily a place of punishment and torture. As the state or abode of the dead it corresponds to the Heb. *Sheol*, a word which, in the Authorized Version of the BIBLE, has frequently been translated by the misleading HELL. Hence *Hades* is often used as a EUPHEMISM for Hell. *Cp.* INFERNO.

Hadith (hā'dith) (Arab., a saying or tradition). A 10th-century compilation by the Moslem jurists Moshin and Bokhari of the traditional sayings and doings of MOHAMMED. It forms a supplement to the KORAN, as the TALMUD does to the Jewish Scriptures. Originally the Hadith was not allowed to be committed to writing, but this became necessary later for its preservation.

Hadj (haj). The pilgrimage to the KAABA which every Mohammedan feels bound to make once at least before death. Those who neglect to do so "might as well die Jews or Christians". These pilgrimages take place in the twelfth month of each year, Dhu'l-Hijja, roughly corresponding to our AUGUST.

Until comparatively recent times none but a MOSLEM could make this pilgrimage except at risk of life, and the Hadj was only performed by Burckhardt, Burton, and a few other travellers in the guise of Moslems.

Hadji (ha' jē). A MOSLEM who has made the HADJ and who is therefore entitled to wear a green turban.

Hadrian's Wall. The Roman wall that runs for $73\frac{1}{2}$ miles between Wallsend-on-Tyne and Bowness on the Solway Firth. It was built between A.D. 122 and 127, after the Emperor Hadrian had inspected the site, to keep back the PICTS. It was 16 ft. high with mile-castles and turrets between the castles.

There were 17 forts on the south side and a parallel vallum or ditch (*c.* 10 ft. deep and 30 ft. wide) on the north. It was attacked and overrun in the 2nd and 3rd centuries and ceased to be an effective barrier by the latter part of the 4th century. *Cp.* ANTONINE'S WALL.

Hafiz. Shams-ud-din Mohammed, a 14th-century Persian poet, "the Persian ANACREON". His *ghazels* (*i.e.* songs, odes) tell of love and wine, nightingales, flowers, the instability of all things human, of ALLAH and the PROPHET, etc. He was a professed dervish and his tomb at Shiraz is still the resort of pilgrims. Hafiz is Arabic for one who knows the KORAN and HADITH by heart.

Hag. A witch or sorceress, an ugly old woman.

How now, you secret, black, and midnight hags?
SHAKESPEARE: *Macbeth*, IV, i.

Hag-knots. Tangles in the manes of horses and ponies, supposed to be used by witches for stirrups.

Hag's teeth. A seaman's term to express those parts of a matting, etc., which spoil its general uniformity.

Hagarenes (hăg a rēnz). An old name for the Saracens, Arabs, or Moors, who were supposed to be descendants of Hagar, ABRAHAM's bondswoman. *See* ISHMAEL.

Haganah. A clandestine Jewish militia organized in Palestine, when under British mandate, in preparation for the coming struggle for Zionist independence at the end of World War II. It formed the nucleus of the army of Israel which was established as an independent state in 1948.

Haggadah (Heb., narrative). The variety of MIDRASH which contains rabbinical interpretations of the historical and legendary, ethical, parabolic, and speculative parts of the Hebrew Scriptures. The variety devoted to law, practice, and doctrine is called *Halakhah* (rule by which to walk).

Haggis. A traditional Scottish dish (popular on BURNS' NIGHT) made from the heart, lungs, and liver of a sheep or calf chopped up with suet, oatmeal, onions and seasonings, and boiled like a big sausage in a sheep's stomach bag.

It was also an English dish until the 18th century. Gervase Markham (1568?–1637) says in his *English Housewife*:

"... and this small oatmeal mixed blood and the Liver of either Calfe, Sheep or Swine maketh that pudding which is called haggas, or haggus, of whose goodness it is in vain to boast because there is hardly to be found a man that does not affect them".

Hail. An exclamation of welcome like the Lat. *salve*. It is from the Icel. *heill*, hale, healthy, and represents the O.E. greeting *wes hal* (may you) be in whole (or good) health. Hail (the frozen rain) is O.E. *hagol*. *Cp*. WASSAIL.

> All hail, Macbeth! Hail to thee, than of Glamis!
> SHAKESPEARE: *Macbeth*, I, iii.

Hail fellow well met. One on easy, familiar terms; an intimate acquaintance.

Hail Mary. *See* AVE MARIA.

To hail a ship. To call to those on board.

To hail an omnibus, or **a cab,** etc. To attract the driver's attention in order to board or hire the vehicle.

To hail from. To come from or belong to a place by birth or residence. An expression of nautical origin from the custom of hailing passing ships to ascertain their port of departure.

Within hail. Within calling distance.

Hair. One single tuft is left on the shaven crown of a Moslem for MOHAMMED to grasp hold of when drawing the deceased to PARADISE.

The scalp-lock on the otherwise bald head of North American Indians is for a conquering enemy to seize when he tears off the scalp.

The ancients believed that till a lock of hair was devoted to PROSERPINE, she refused to release the SOUL from the dying body. When DIDO mounted the funeral pile, she lingered in suffering till JUNO sent IRIS to cut off a lock of her hair; THANATOS did the same for Alcestis when she gave her life for her husband; and in all sacrifices a forelock was first cut off from the head of the victim as an offering to the black queen.

It was an old idea that a person with red hair could not be trusted, from the tradition that JUDAS had red hair. Shakespeare says:

> *Rosalind:* His very hair is of the dissembling colour.
> *Celia:* Something browner than Judas's.
> *As You Like It*, III, iv.

See also RED-HAIRED PERSONS.

A man with black hair but a red beard was the worst of all. The old rhyme says:

> A red beard and a black head,
> Catch him with a good trick and take him dead.

BYRON says in *The Prisoner of Chillon:*

> My hair is grey, but not with years,
> Nor grew it white
> In a single night,
> As men's have grown from sudden fears.

It is a well-authenticated fact that this can happen, and has happened. It is said that Ludovico Sforza became grey in a single night; Charles I, also, while he was undergoing trial, and Marie Antoinette grew grey from grief during her imprisonment.

Adoption by Hair. *See under* ADOPTION.

Against the hair. Against the grain, contrary to its nature.

> If you should fight, you go against the hair of your professions.
> SHAKESPEARE: *Merry Wives of Windsor*, II, iii.

Both of a hair. As like as two peas or hairs; also, similar in disposition, taste, or trade, etc.

Hair-breadth escape. A very narrow escape from some danger or evil. In measurement, the forth-eighth part of an inch is called a "hair-breadth."

> Wherein I spake of most disastrous chances
> Of moving accidents by flood and field,
> Of hair-breadth 'scapes i' th' imminent deadly breach.
> SHAKESPEARE: *Othello*, I, iii.

Hair by hair you will pull out the horse's tail. Slow and sure wins the race. Plutarch says that Sertorius, in order to teach his soldiers that "perserverance is irresistible", had two horses brought before them, one old and feeble, the other large and strong. Two men were set to pull at their tails. One of the men, robust and strong, pulled the tail of the weak HORSE with no effect; the other, a contemptible little fellow, plucked out the hairs from the great horse's tail one by one and soon stripped it bare.

The hair of the dog that bit you. The idea that the thing which causes the malady is the best cure or means of relief, as another drink in the morning is considered by some the best answer to a HANGOVER. The allusion is to the old notion that the burnt hair of a DOG is an antidote to its bite. *Simila similibus curantur.*

Keep your hair on! Don't lose your temper, don't get excited. *Keep your wool on* is an alternative form.

To a hair, or **To the turn of a hair.** To a nicety.

To comb his hair the wrong way. To cross him or vex him by running counter to his prejudices, opinions, or habits.

To let one's hair down. To behave in a free informal manner; to give free vent to private opinions, etc., among friends. The allusion is to the days when women wore long hair pinned up in various ways over their head for their public appearances, but occasionally "let it down" and let it flow freely in the privacy of their homes.

To make one's hair stand on end. To terrify. Dr. Andrews, once of Beresford Chapel, Walworth, who attended an execution said: "When the executioner put the cords on the criminal's wrists, his hair, though long and lanky, of a weak iron-grey, rose gradually and stood perfectly upright, and so remained for some time, and then fell gradually down again."

Fear came upon me and trembling ... and the hair of my flesh stood up.

Job iv, 14, 15.

To split hairs. To argue over petty points, make fine, cavilling distinctions, quibble over trifles. The French equivalent is *couper les cheveux en quatre*.

To tear one's hair. To show signs of extreme vexation, anxiety, anguish, or grief. Tearing the hair was anciently a sign of mourning.

Without turning a hair. Without indicating any sign of distress or agitation, to be quite unruffled.

Hair-brained. *See* HARE-BRAINED.

Hair shirt. A garment of coarse hair-cloth (made from horsehair and wool or cotton) worn next to the skin by ascetics and penitents.

Hair-spring. The fine spiral spring in a clock or a watch for regulating the movement of the balance.

Hair Stane. *See* HOARSTONE.

Hair trigger. A trigger that allows the firing mechanism of a rifle or pistol to be operated by a very slight pressure. Invented in the 16th century.

Hake. We lose in hake, but gain in herring. Lose one way, but gain in another. herring are persecuted by the hake, which are therefore driven away from a herring fishery.

Halakhah. *See* HAGGADAH.

Hal-an-tow. The song and procession at Helston which preceded the FURRY DANCE on Furry Day. Men and maids went into the country in early morning, returning with green boughs and flowers, with twigs in their hats and caps. Led by an elderly person riding a donkey they entered the decorated streets singing the *Morning Song,* the chorus being:

Hal-an-Tow, jolly rumble-O
And for to fetch the Summer home, the Summer and the May-O,
For Summer is acome-O and Winter is agone-O.

Of considerable antiquity, the Hal-an-Tow eventually lapsed but was revived in 1930. The name is possibly from Cornish *hayl* and *tyow,* which freely rendered would mean "in the moorland and in the town".

Halcyon Days (hăl′ si on). Times of happiness and prosperity. *Halcyon* is the Greek for a kingfisher, compounded of *hals* (the sea) and *kuo* (to brood on). The ancient Sicilians believed that the kingfisher laid its eggs, and incubated them for fourteen days on the surface of the sea, during which period, before the winter SOLSTICE, the waves were always unruffled.

And wars have that respect for his repose
As winds for halcyons when they breed at sea.
DRYDEN: *Stanzas on Oliver Cromwell*, xxxvi.

Half. Half and half. A mixture of two liquors in equal quantities, such as PORTER and ALE, old and mild, mild and bitter, etc.

Half an eye. *See under* EYE.

Half a mind. To have half a mind. To be disposed to, to have an inclination towards doing something.

Half cock. To go off at half cock. To act or start unexpectedly, before one is ready; as a gun goes off when the hammer is set at half cock and supposedly secure.

Half done, as Elgin was burnt. In the wars between James II of SCOTLAND and the Douglases in 1452, the Earl of Huntly burnt one half of the town of Elgin, being the side which belonged to the Douglases, but left the other side standing because it belonged to his own family. (Scott: *Tales of a Grandfather*, xxii).

Half is more than the whole. This is what Hesiod said to his brother Perseus, when he wished him to settle a dispute without going to law. He meant, "Half of the estate without the expense of law will be better than the whole estate after the lawyers have had their pickings." The remark, however, has a wide signification. Thus a large estate, to one who cannot keep it up, is impoverishing.

Unhappy they to whom God has not revealed,
By a strong light which must their sense control,
That half a great estate's more than the whole.
COWLEY: *Essays in Verse and Prose*, iv.

Half-seas over. Well on the way, pretty far gone. Usually applied to a person half drunk.

Our Friend the Alderman was half Seas over.
Spectator, No. 616 (5 Nov. 1714).

Half the Battle. *See under* BATTLE.

He is only half-baked. He is raw or soft, *i.e.* of weak mind, a noodle.

My better half. *See under* BETTER.

Not half. Very much; "Rather! I should think so." **Not half bad** means "not at all bad"; pretty good, in fact.

To do a thing by halves. To do it in a SLAPDASH manner, very imperfectly.

To go halves. To share something equally with another.

Half-deck. In old sailing ships the quarters of the second mate, carpenters, coopers, boatswain, and all secondary officers. The afterpart of the deck below the spar-deck, extending to the cabin bulkheads. *Cp.* QUARTERDECK.

Half Joe. Portuguese coin (worth about $4) current on the Atlantic coast of the U.S.A. in the 18th century. A *Johannes* was an eight-escudo piece first struck in the reign of John V, and popularly called a *Joe* in America.

Half-life. As a scientific term, the time taken for half the atoms of a given amount of radioactive substance to decay. This time may vary from a fraction of a second to millions of years according to the given substance. A knowledge of this process has enabled archaeologists and geologists, etc., to date materials with considerable accuracy.

Half-mast high. *See* TO FLY THE FLAG AT HALF-MAST *under* FLAG.

Half-timer. One engaged in some occupation for only half the usual time; the term formerly applied to a child attending school for half time and working the rest of the day. This practice was terminated by the Education Act of 1918.

Half-tone block. A typographic printing-block for illustrations, produced by photographing on to a prepared plate through a screen or grating which breaks up the picture to be reproduced into small dots of varying intensity, thus giving the lights and shades, or tones.

Half-way House. A fairly common name for an inn situated midway between two towns or villages. It is figuratively used for a compromise or moderate policy.

Half-world. *See* DEMI-MONDE.

Halgaver. Summoned before the mayor of Halgaver. The mayor of Halgaver is an imaginary worthy, and the threat for those whose offence is slovenliness and untidiness. Halgaver or Goat's Moor near Bodmin, CORNWALL, was famous for an annual carnival held there in the middle of July. Charles II was so pleased with the diversions when he passed through on his way to Scilly that he became a member of the "self-constituted" corporation. *Cp.* MAYOR OF GARRATT *under* GARRATT.

Halifax. Halifax Gibbet Law. By this local law, whoever committed theft above the value of 13½d. in the liberty of Halifax, Yorkshire, was to be executed on the Halifax gibbet, a kind of GUILLOTINE. Originally enacted against those who stole cloth from the tenters or drying frames, it ceased to operate after 1650. The site of the gibbet, at the end of Gibbet Lane, has been preserved and restored.

> At Hallifax the law so sharpe doth deale,
> That whoso more than thirteen pence doth steale,
> They have a jyn that wondrous quick and well
> Sends thieves all headless into heaven or hell.
>
> JOHN TAYLOR: *Works*, II (1630).

Go to Halifax. *See under* GO.
Hull, Hell, and Halifax. *See* HULL.

Hall Mark. The official mark stamped on gold and silver articles after they have been assayed, so called because the assaying or testing and stamping was done at the Goldsmiths' Hall. The hall mark includes (1) the standard mark, (2) the assay office, or "hall" mark, (3) the date letter, and sometimes (4) the duty mark. With it is found (5) the maker's mark.

(1) The standard mark. For GOLD, a *crown* in ENGLAND and a *thistle* in SCOTLAND; for 22 and 18 CARAT gold, followed by the number of carats in figures. In IRELAND a *crowned harp* for 22 carat, *three feathers* for 20 carat, and a *unicorn's head* for 18 carat. Lower standards of gold have the number of carats in figures, without the device.

For SILVER, a *lion passant* in England, a *thistle* in Edinburgh, a *thistle* and a *lion rampant* in Glasgow, and a *crowned harp* in Dublin. In 1697 Britannia Standard was introduced enforcing a higher proportion of silver to prevent the melting down of coins. *Britannia* and a *Lion's head erased* replaced the *lion passant* and *leopard*. Britannia Standard or New Sterling was abolished in 1729 because the alloy was too soft.

(2) The Assay Office mark.

> London—a leopard's head (*see* LEOPARD).
>
> Sheffield—A York Rose for gold, a crown for silver.
>
> Edinburgh—a castle.
>
> Glasgow—the city arms: a tree, a bird, a bell, and a salmon with a ring in its mouth.
>
> Dublin—Hibernia.

Marks of Assay Offices now closed and dates of closing:

> Chester—three sheaves and sword (1962).
>
> Exeter—a castle (1883).
>
> Newcastle—castle over lion (1697).
>
> York—five lions on a cross (1856).

(3) The date letter. A letter of the alphabet indicates the date of an article. The London Assay Office used 20 letters of the alphabet, Glasgow 26 and most of the others 25. The letter is changed annually and a new type-face is adopted and the shape of the letter's frame is changed. Given the date letter and the Assay Office mark, the date of manufacture may be easily discovered on referring to a table.

(4) The duty mark was introduced in 1784 when a duty was imposed on silver plate. This was abolished in 1890. The mark was that of the head of the reigning sovereign (George III, George IV, William IV, Victoria).

(5) The maker's mark, originally a device, but since 1739 the maker's initials.

(6) Other marks.

(a) A voluntary silver jubilee mark in 1935 consisting of the crowned heads of George V and Queen Mary.

(b) A voluntary mark in 1952–1953 and 1953–1954 consisting of the crowned head of Queen Elizabeth II, to commemorate her coronation.

Hall Sunday. The Sunday before SHROVE TUESDAY; the next day is called *Hall Monday* or *Hall Night. Hall* is a contraction of *hallow* meaning holy. *Hall Monday* is also known as *Collop Monday* from the custom of celebrating with a dish of collops.

Hallel (hăl′ el). A Jewish hymn of praise recited at certain festivals, consisting of *Ps.* cxiii to cxviii inclusive, also called the *Egyptian* or *Common Hallel.* The name *Great Hallel* is given to *Ps.* cxxvi and sometimes to *Ps.* cxx–cxxxvi, thus including the GRADUAL PSALMS.

Hallelujah is the Heb. *halelu-Jah*, "Praise ye Jehovah". *Alleluia* is one of the several variant spellings.

Hallelujah Lass. In the early days of the SALVATION ARMY, a name given to female members. Defined somewhat censoriously by Dr. Brewer as: "A young woman who wanders about with what is called 'The Salvation Army'."

Hallelujah Victory. A victory by the Britons in *c.* 429 over the combined Picts and Saxons probably somewhere in the North Midlands. The Britons, many newly baptized, were led by Germanus, Bishop of Auxerre, and when they raised the war-cry "Hallelujah", the Picts and Saxons, seeing themselves surrounded, fled without fighting.

Halloween (hăl ō ēn′). 31 October, which in the old CELTIC calendar was the last day of the year, its night being the time when all the witches and warlocks were abroad. On the introduction of Christianity it was taken over as the Eve of ALL HALLOWS or All Saints.

Hallstatt. The name given to a culture marking the transition between the Bronze and Iron Ages in central and western Europe and the Balkans. It takes its name from Hallstatt in Upper Austria, where between 1846 and 1899 over 2,000 graves were found, the earliest dating from *c.* 900 B.C.. They contained many objects typical of the earliest IRON AGE.

Halo. In Christian art, the same as a NIMBUS. The luminous circle round the SUN or MOON caused by the refraction of light through a mist is called a halo. Figuratively it implies the ideal or saintly glory surrounding a person and is often used derisively, as "you ought to be wearing a halo". It is the Gr. *halo*, originally a circular threshing-floor, then the sun or moon's disc. *Cp.* AUREOLE.

Ham Actor. A ranting, inferior actor. Among the suggested contributory origins of the terms are (1) that in the 19th century, theatrical make-up was removed with ham fat; (2) that one Hamish McCullough (1835–1885), who toured with his troupe in Illinois, was known as "Ham" and his company as "Ham's actors";(3) there was also a popular American minstrel song "The Hamfat Man", about an inept actor; (4) an allusion to the word "amateur"; (5) the tradition that down-at-heel actors had performed *Hamlet* in better days.

Shakespeare's *Hamlet* may well be the original source, since Hamlet in his speech to the players (III, ii) describes the essence of ham acting: to "saw the air too much with your hand", to "tear a passion to tatters" and to "strut and bellow".

Hamadryads. *See* DRYAD.

Haman. To hang as high as Haman. To be well and truly hanged, to be hoist with one's own PETARD. Haman, having gained favour with King Ahasuerus (XERXES) of Persia, was provoked by the Jew Mordecai's refusal to bow before him, and obtained permission to exterminate all Jews in the kingdom. He prepared a gallows fifty cubits high on which to hang Mordecai. Queen Esther, aware of the threat to her former guardian, secured the downfall of Haman, who was hanged on his own gallows. (*Esther*, vii, 9). *Cp.* HARM SET, HARM GET.

Hambletonian. The name given to a superior strain of horse bred in the U.S.A. for trotting and descended from the stallion Hambletonian (1849–1876).

Hamburgers, or **Hamburg Steaks.** This popular American dish of fried minced beef, onion, egg, etc. made into a flat cake, takes its name from Hamburg in Germany. It appears to have originated in the Baltic region some centuries ago and was introduced into America in the 19th century by sailors from Hamburg and subsequently "naturalized". The infelicitous beefburger is an attempt by caterers to avoid confusion by association with the name of ham.

Hamet. *See* CID HAMET.

Hamiltonian System. A method of teaching foreign languages by interlinear translations suggested by James Hamilton (1769–1829).

Hamlet. It's Hamlet without the Prince.

Said when the person who was to have taken the principal place at some function is absent. SHAKESPEARE's *Hamlet* would lose all its meaning if the part of the Prince were omitted.

Hammer. In personal appellatives:

Pierre d'Ailly (1350–1420), *Le Mareau* (hammer) *des Hérétiques*, president of the council that condemned John Hus.

John Faber (1478–1541), the German controversialist, was surnamed *Malleus Hereticorum*, from the title of one of his works.

St. Hilary, Bishop of Poitiers (*d.* 368), was known as "The Hammer of the ADRIANS".

Charles the Hammer. *See* MARTEL.

Edward I (1239–1307), nicknamed "Longshanks" and called "The Hammer of the Scots." The inscription on his tomb in Westminster Abbey reads "*Edwardus Primus Malleus Scotorum hic est*".

Thomas Cromwell (*c.* 1485–1540) called the "Hammer of the monks" (*Malleus Monachorum*). He carried out the dissolution of the monasteries (1536–1540) as Henry VIII's right hand man.

The second name of Judas MACCABÆUS the son of Mattathias the Hasmonean, is thought by some to denote that he was a "Hammer" or "Hammerer" and to be derived from Heb. *makkabah*, hammer.

Hammer and Sickle. Since 1923, the emblem of the U.S.S.R., symbolic of productive work in the factory and on the land.

Knight of the Hammer. A blacksmith.

Throwing the hammer. An athletic contest involving the throwing of a 16 lb. hammer. The original hammer used was a blacksmith's sledge.

To be hammered. A Stock Exchange term, used of a broking firm which is in the "HOUSE" and cannot meet its commitments. This is done by the "Head Waiter", who goes into the rostrum and attracts the attention of the members present by striking the desk with a hammer before making the announcement.

To come, or **sell under the hammer,** or **Gone to the hammer.** Said of goods and property sent for sale by auction; from the rap of the auctioneer's hammer to denote that a lot is sold.

To go at it hammer and tongs. To go at it with might and main, to fight or quarrel vigorously.

To hammer away at anything. To go at it doggedly; to persevere.

To hammer out. To arrive at the final form of a plan or scheme by effort, careful thought, and discussion. A METAPHOR from the blacksmith's shop.

To live hammer and tongs. To be always quarrelling.

Hampden Clubs. A series of clubs centred on the Hampden Club set up in London in 1811 by the veteran agitator Major Cartwright (1740–1824). Their aim was to agitate for reform of PARLIAMENT and the extension of the franchise to all payers of direct taxes, although some years later they became more democratic, extending membership to all willing to pay a penny per week subscription. Each club was technically a separate organization in order to evade the existing law which forbade societies with affiliated branches. The name is derived from the famous 17th-century parliamentarian, John Hampden, of SHIP MONEY fame.

Hampton Court Conference. Discussions held at Hampton Court in 1604 between James I, the BISHOPS, and four PURITAN clergy in the presence of the Council. The bishops would make no concessions of importance and their most valuable decision was to effect a new translation of the BIBLE, which became the Authorized Version of 1611.

Hanaper. *Hanap* was the mediæval name for a goblet or wine-cup, and the *hanaper* (connected with *hamper*) was the wicker-work case that surrounded it. Hence the name was given to any round wicker basket and especially to one kept in the Court of CHANCERY containing documents that had passed the GREAT SEAL. The office was under the charge of the Clerk of the Hanaper until its abolition in 1842.

Hancock. *See* JOHN HANCOCK.

Hand. A symbol of fortitude in Egypt, of fidelity in ROME. Two hands symbolize concord; by a closed hand ZENO represented dialectics and by an open hand eloquence.

In early art, the Deity was frequently represented by a hand extended from the clouds, with rays issuing from the fingers, but generally it was in the act of benediction, *i.e.* two fingers raised.

In card-games the word is used for the game itself, for an individual player (as "a good *hand* at WHIST") or the cards held.

> A saint in heaven would grieve to see such hand
> Cut up by one who will not understand.
> CRABBE: *The Borough.*

Also for style of workmanship, handwriting, etc. ("he is a good *hand* at carpentry", "he writes a good *hand*"). Workmen and sailors are also called *hands*.

As a measure of length *a hand* equals 4 inches. Horses are measured up the foreleg to the withers, and their height is expressed in *hands*.

Dead Hand. *See under* DEAD.

Dead Man's hand. *See under* DEAD.

Hand of Glory. *See* GLORY.

The Red Hand, or **Bloody Hand,** in coat armour is the device of ULSTER and is carried as a charge on the coats of arms of English and Irish BARONETS (not on those of SCOTLAND or Nova Scotia). The "bloody hand" is also borne privately by a few families when its presence is generally connected with some traditional tale of blood. *Cp.* BLOODY HAND.

Hand gallop. A slow and easy gallop, in which the horse is kept well IN HAND.

Hand paper. A particular kind of paper well known in the Record Office, and so called from its watermark, which goes back to the early 16th century.

Also a hand-made paper.

A bird in the hand. *See under* BIRD.

A dab hand. One who is adept.

An empty hand is no lure for a hawk. You must not expect to receive anything without giving a return.

A note of hand. A promise to pay made in writing and duly signed.

An old hand at it. One who is experienced at it.

A poor hand. An unskilful one.

All hands. The nautical term for the whole crew.

It is believed on all hands. It is generally or universally believed.

At first, or **second, hand.** As the original (first) purchaser, owner, hearer, or (second) as one deriving, learning, etc., through another party.

At hand. Conveniently near. "Near *at hand*", quite close by.

By hand. Without the aid of machinery or an intermediate agent. A letter "sent by hand" is one deliverted by a personal messenger, not sent through the post. But a child "brought up by hand" is one reared on the bottle instead of being breast-fed.

Cap in hand. *See under* CAP.

From hand to hand. From one person to another.

Hand and thigh. An ancient Irish form of inheritance of land by daughters in default of sons was known as *inheritance of hand and thigh*.

Hand in hand. In a friendly fashion; unitedly.

Hand-out. Primarily something handed out or given away, as oranges or buns at a children's party or gifts of food or clothing, etc., to tramps. It is now more commonly used to designate (1) free advertising material, brochures, etc., given to potential customers, (2) a press release by a news service, and (3) a prepared statement to the Press by a government, official body, publicity agent, etc.

Hand over hand. To put one hand above the other, as when climbing a rope or ladder; also to overtake or overhaul rapidly. Sailors when hauling a rope put one hand before the other alternately and rapidly. The French say *main sur main*.

Hands up! The order given by captors when taking prisoners, etc. The hands are to be held high above the head to preclude possibility of resistance, the use of firearms, etc.

He is my right hand. My principal assistant, my best and most trustworthy man.

In hand. Under control, in possession, in progress.

In one's own hands. In one's sole control, ownership, management, responsibility, etc.

Kings have long hands. *See under* KING.

Laying on of hands. In church usage, the imposition of hands is the laying on or touch of a BISHOP's hands in confirmation and ordination.

Among the Romans, a hand laid on the head of a person indicated the right of property, as when someone laid claim to a slave in the presence of the prætor. *Cp.* TO LAY HANDS ON, *below*.

Many hands make light work. An old proverb (given in Ray's *Collection*, 1670) enshrining the wisdom of the division of labour.

The Romans had a similar saying, *Multorum manibus magnum levatur onus*, by the hands of many a great load is lightened.

My hands are full. I am fully occupied; I have as much work as I can manage.

My hands are tied. I am not free to act.

Offhand. In a casual, unceremonious fashion, curt, rude; extempore, without premeditation.

Off one's hands. No longer one's responsibility. If something or somebody is **left on one's hands,** one has to take full responsibility.

On the one hand ... on the other hand. Expressions used to introduce contrasting viewpoints, etc., with the meaning of, "from this point of view ... from that point of view".

Out of hand. At once; done with, over:

We will proclaim you out of hand.
SHAKESPEARE: *Henry VI, Pt. III*, IV, vii.

And were these inward wars once out of hand,
We would, dear lords, unto the Holy Land.
SHAKESPEARE: *Henry IV, Pt. II*, III, i.

Also meaning "beyond control", as in "These children are quite out of hand."

The hand that rocks the cradle rules the world. The line is from *The Hand that Rules the World* by the American poet, William Ross Wallace (1819–1881):

They say that man is mighty,
He governs land and sea,
He wields a mighty sceptre
O'er lesser powers that be;
But a mightier power and stronger
Man from his throne has hurled,
And the hand that rocks the cradle
Is the hand that rules the world.

To be hand in glove with. To be inseparable companions, of like tastes and affections; thick as thieves; to fit each other like hand and glove.

To ask, or **give the hand of so-and-so.** To ask or give her hand in marriage.

To bear a hand. To come and help.

To bite the hand that feeds you. To wound or upset one on whom you depend; to treat a benefactor cavalierly, as a surly dog snaps at the hand of a person offering food.

To change hands. To pass from one possessor to another.

To come to hand. To be received, to come within reach.

To come to one's hand. To do or perform with ease.

To force one's hand. To make a person reveal his intentions, plans, etc., earlier than intended, as in card-playing.

To get one's hand in. To familiarize oneself with the task; to begin to take over a task or duty.

To get the upper hand. To obtain mastery.

To give one's hands upon something. To take one's oath on it; to pledge one's honour to keep the promise.

To hand down to posterity. To leave for future generations.

To hand in one's checks or **chips.** To die. A phrase of American origin derived from poker, etc. Checks (counters) were handed in when one had finished or was "cleaned out". Variants are, *to pass in* or *cash one's checks*.

To hand or **hand in** sail. To take in sail, to furl it.

To hand it to someone. To give well-merited credit to someone. A colloquial usage.

To hand round. To pass from one person to another, to distribute.

To have a free hand. To have freedom of action without the need of referring to others for agreement or approval.

To have a hand in the matter. To be associated with; to have a finger in the pie (*see under* FINGER).

To have clean hands. *See under* CLEAN.

To keep one's hand in. To maintain one's skill by practice.

To lay hands on. To apprehend; to lay hold of. *Cp.* LAYING ON OF HANDS, *above*.

To lend a hand. To help, to give assistance.

To live from hand to mouth. Improvidently, without thought for the morrow. The phrase implies the ready consumption of whatever one gets.

To play into someone's hands. To act unwittingly or carelessly, thus giving the advantage to the other party; to do just what will help him and not advance your own cause.

To play one's own hand. To look after NUMBER ONE; to act entirely for self-advantage.

To serve someone hand and foot. To be at someone's beck and call; to be someone's slave.

To shake hands. To greet by giving the hand clasped into your own a shake; to bid farewell.

Fortune and Antony part here; even here
Do we shake hands,
SHAKESPEARE: *Antony and Cleopatra*, IV, xii.

It is customary to shake hands after settling a quarrel, also to confirm an agreement or a business deal, and before the commencement of a boxing context.

To show one's hand. To reveal one's intentions or resources, as when exposing a hand of cards to an opponent.

To strike hands. To make a contract, to become surety for another. *See Prov.* xvii, 18, and xxii, 26.

To take a hand. To play a part, especially in a game of cards.

To take in hand. To undertake to do something; to take charge of.

To take something off someone's hands. To relieve someone of something troublesome.

To wash one's hands of a thing. To have nothing to do with it after having been concerned in the matter; to abandon it entirely. The allusion is to PILATE's washing his hands at the trial of Jesus.

When Pilate saw that he could prevail nothing, but that rather a tumult was made, he took water, and washed his hands before the multitude, saying, I am innocent of the blood of this just person: see ye to it.
Matt. xxvii, 24.

To win hands down. To win easily. A

jockey rides with hands down when he is winning comfortably and easily.

With a heavy hand. Oppressively; without sparing.

> It is a damned and a bloody work;
> The graceless action of a heavy hand
> If that it be the work of any hand.
> SHAKESPEARE: *King John*, IV, iii.

With a high hand. Arrogantly.

Handcuff King. The nickname of Harry HOUDINI (1874–1926), American entertainer and expert escapist, especially from handcuffs. *Cp.* DAVENPORT-TRICK.

Handfasting. A marriage "on approval", was formerly in vogue on the BORDER. A fair was at one time held in Dumfries-shire, at which a young man was allowed to pick a female companion to live with. If they both liked the arrangement after 12 months they became man and wife. This was called *handfasting* or *handfastening*. *Cp.* BUNDLING.

This sort of contract was common among the Romans and Jews.

Handiron. *See* ANDIRON.

Handkerchief. With handkerchief in one hand and sword in the other. Pretending to be sorry at a calamity, but prepared to make capital out of it.

> Maria Theresa stands, with the handkerchief in one hand, weeping the woes of Poland; but with the sword in the other hand, ready to cut Poland in sections, and take her share.
> CARLYLE: *The Diamond Necklace*, ch. iv.

Handle. A handle to one's name. Some title, as "lord", "sir", "doctor", etc.

To fly off the handle. *See under* FLY.

To give a handle to. To give grounds for suspicion, as "He certainly gave a handle to the rumour."

To go off the handle. To die, a 19th-century colloquial Americanism.

> My old gentleman means to be Mayor or Governor or President or something or other before he goes off the handle.
> O.W. HOLMES: *The Poet at the Breakfast Table*, ch. x.

Dead Man's Handle. *See under* DEAD.

Handsel (O.E. *handselen*, delivery into the hand). A gift for luck; earnest-money; the first money received in a day. Hence *Handsel Monday*, the first MONDAY of the year, when small gifts were given, before *Boxing Day* (*see* CHRISTMAS BOX) took its place. To "handsel a sword" is to use it for the first time; to "handsel a coat", to wear it for the first time, etc.

Handsome. Handsome is as handsome does. It is one's actions that count, not merely one's appearances or promises. The proverb is in Ray's *Collection*, and is also found in Goldsmith's *The Vicar of Wakefield* (ch. i).

Handwriting on the wall. The sign of impending calamity or disaster. The allusion is to the handwriting on Belshazzar's palace wall announcing the loss of his kingdom (*Dan.* v).

Hang. Hang it all!, I'll be hanged! Exclamations of astonishment or annoyance; mild imprecations. A mincing form of 'damned'.

Hanged, drawn and quartered. *See under* DRAW.

Hanging and wiving go by destiny. This comforting proverb is given in Heywood's *Collection* (1546) as "Wedding's destiny and hanging likewise."

> The ancient saying is no heresy,
> Hanging and wiving goes by destiny.
> SHAKESPEARE: *Merchant of Venice*, II, ix.

Hanging Day. *See* FRIDAY.

To get the hang of a thing. To understand the drift or connexion; to acquire the knack.

As well be hanged for a sheep as a lamb. *See under* SHEEP.

To hang a jury. To reduce them to disagreement so that they fail to bring in a verdict.

To hang about, or **around.** To loiter, loaf, wait about.

To hang back. To hesitate to proceed.

To hang by a thread. To be in a very precarious situation. The allusion is to the sword of DAMOCLES.

To hang fire. *See under* FIRE.

To hang in the balance. A state of doubt or suspense with regard to the outcome of a situation; not knowing on which side the scales of fate may descend.

To hang in the bell ropes. To have one's marriage postponed after the BANNS have been published in church.

To hang on. To cling to; to persevere; to be dependent on.

To hang on by the eyelids. To maintain one's position only with the greatest difficulty or by the slightest holds.

To hang on like grim death. To cling tenaciously, literally or metaphorically; not to be shaken off, as death persists having once marked down its victim.

Where do you hang out? Where are you living or lodging? The phrase may arise from the old custom of innkeepers, shopkeepers, tradesmen, etc., hanging a sign outside their premises.

> "I say old boy, where do you hang out?" Mr. Pickwick replied that he was at present suspended at the George and Vulture.
> DICKENS: *Pickwick Papers*, ch. xxx.

In the U.S.A. it implies, "Where do you pass your spare time?"

Hangdog look. A guilty, shame-faced look.

Hanging Gardens of Babylon. A square garden (according to Diodorus Siculus), 400 ft. each way, rising in a series of terraces, and provided with earth to a sufficient depth to accommodate trees of a great size. Water was lifted from the Euphrates by a screw and the gardens were irrigated from a reservoir at the top.

These famous gardens were one of the SEVEN WONDERS OF THE WORLD (*see under* WONDERS) and were said to have been built by Queen SEMIRAMIS and by NEBUCHADNEZZAR, to gratify his wife Amyitis, who felt weary of the flat plains of Babylon, and longed for something to remind her of her native Median Hills. They may have been associated with the great ziggurat of Babylon.

Hangmen and Executioners. Some practitioners have achieved a particular notice, *e.g.*:

BULL (*c.* 1593), the earliest hangman whose name survives.

DERRICK (*q.v.*), who cut off the head of Essex in 1601.

GREGORY BRANDON and his son RICHARD (1640), who executed Charles I, known as "the two Gregories". *See* GREGORIAN TREE.

SQUIRE DUN, mentioned in *Hudibras* (Pt. III, ii).

JACK KETCH (1663) executed Lord Russell and the Duke of Monmouth. His name later became a generic word for a hangman.

ROSE, the butcher (1686).

EDWARD DENNIS (1780), introduced in Dicken's *Barnaby Rudge*.

THOMAS CHESHIRE, nicknamed "Old Cheese".

WILLIAM CALCRAFT (1800–1879) was appointed hangman in 1829 and was pensioned off in 1874.

WILLIAM MARWOOD (1820–1883), who invented the "long drop".

Of French executioners, the most celebrated are Capeluche, headsman of Paris during the days of the Burgundians and Armagnacs; and the two brothers Sanson who worked the GUILLOTINE during the French Revolution.

The fee given to the hangman at TYBURN used to be 13½d., with 1½d., for the rope.

> For half of thirteen-pence ha'penny wages
> I would have cleared all the town cages,
> And you should have been rid of all the stages
> I and my gallows groan.
> *The Hangman's Last Will and Testament*
> *(Rump Songe).*

Noblemen who were to be beheaded were expected to give the executioner from £7 to £10 for cutting off their head; any peer who came to the halter could claim the privilege of being suspended by a silken rope.

Hangover. Something remaining from a previous occasion; especially the headache and nausea experienced the "morning after the night before", *i.e.* the morning after an evening of alcoholic overindulgence.

Hanky-panky. Jugglery, underhand dealing. *Cp.* HOCUS POCUS.

Hannah. In World War II, a nickname given to a Wren serving with the Royal Marines, after Hannah Snell, the female MARINE.

Hansard. The printed official report of the proceeding and debates in the British Houses of PARLIAMENT and its standing committees and also those of some of the COMMONWEALTH parliaments.

The name is derived from T.C. Hansard (1776–1833), printer, then publisher, of the unofficial *Parliamentary Debates* begun by William Cobbett in 1803. After 1855 the firm was helped by government grants, until 1890, when the work was undertaken by several successive printers working at a loss. The name "Hansard" was omitted from the title page in 1891 and restored in 1943. Luke Hansard, the father of T.C. Hansard, was the printer of the HOUSE OF COMMONS Journals from 1774 until his death in 1828.

Hanse, or **Hanseatic League.** Originating in the 13th century as an organization of German merchants trading in northern Europe, it became a loose federation of nearly 100 towns by the mid-14th century, headed by Lübeck. It acquired a monopoly of the Baltic trade and dominated the North Sea routes until challenged by English, Dutch, and Scandinavian competitors in the 15th century. The last Diet of the Hanse met in 1669 and only Lübeck, Bremen and Hamburg remained in the League. Its London STEELYARD was sold in 1853 and its Antwerp premises in 1863.

Hanse Towns. Member towns of the HANSEATIC LEAGUE.

Hansel. *See* HANDSEL.

Hänsel and Gretel. The inseparables of the famous fairy story found among the tales of the brothers Grimm. Hänsel was a woodcutter's son and the little girl Gretel was found in the forest. When starvation threatened the household the woodcutter, at his wife's behest, abandoned the children in the forest. Hänsel laid a trail by which they found their way home, but they were subsequently again cast adrift. After several escapes from the machinations of a wicked fairy, Hänsel was at last transformed into a fawn and taken with Gretel to the king's castle, where Hänsel was restored to human form and enabled to marry Gretel. The story forms the basis of Humperdinck's opera (1893) of this name.

Hansom. A light two-wheeled cab, very popular in London before the introduction of taxicabs early in the 20th century. It was invented in 1834 by J. Aloysius Hansom (1803–1882), the architect of Birmingham Town Hall. The original vehicle had two very large wheels with sunk axle trees and a seat for the driver beside the passenger. The size of the wheels was subsequently reduced and the driver placed in a DICKEY at the rear.

Happy. Bomb Happy. A World War II expression to describe one in a state of near hysteria induced by bombing, which often took the form of wild elation of the spirits.

Call no man happy. Properly, "Call no man happy till he dies, he is at best fortunate". It implies that no man can be called happy until his life has ended happily. The saying is attributed by Herodotus (*Histories*, I, 32, to Solon) and is also used by Sophocles (*Œdipus Tyrannus*, 1195) and Aristotle.

Happy as a clam. *See* CLAM.

Happy as Larry. Very happy. An Australian expression. It is suggested that the original Larry may have been Larry Foley (1847–1917), the noted boxer.

Happy (jolly or **merry) as a sand-boy.** Very happy or merry. An old-established expression from the days when sand-boys (or men) drove their donkeys through the streets hawking bags of sand, usually obtained from beaches. The sand was used by people for their gardens, by builders and by publicans for sanding their floors. The happiness of sand-boys was due to their habit of indulging in liquor with their takings.

Happy dispatch. *See* HARA-KIRI.

A happy expression. A well-turned phrase; one especially apt.

Happy Family. In travelling menageries, etc., the name given to an assortment of animals living together peaceably. The phrase is now more usually associated with the children's card game.

Happy-go-lucky. Thoughtless, indifferent, carefree.

Happy hunting ground. The North American Indians' HEAVEN. Figuratively, where one finds happy leisure occupation.

Happy is the country that has no history. The old proverb implies that such a nation avoids the wars, rebellions, etc., that forms so much of human history. Gibbon in *The Decline and Fall of the Roman Empire* (ch. iii) says:

> History, which is, indeed, little more than the register of the crimes, follies and misfortunes of mankind.

Hapsburg *See* HABSBURG.

Hara-Kiri (Jap. *Hara*, the belly; *kiri*, to cut). A method of suicide by disembowelling practised by Japanese military and governmental officials, daimios, etc., when in serious disgrace, or when their honour was positively impugned. *Hara-kiri* or *Happy dispatch* was practised from mediæval times but ceased to be obligatory in 1868. The act was performed with due ceremony. A law of 1870 granted the privilege of Hara-Kiri to the SAMURAI, in lieu of the death penalty. It was abolished as an official practice in 1873.

Hard. Hard and fast. Strict, unalterable, fixed. A "hard and fast rule" is one that must be rigidly kept. Originally a nautical phrase, used of a ship run aground.

Hard-bitten. Tough, doggedly stubborn, unyielding, Probably derived from *hard-bitten*, a term used of horses, hard-mouthed and difficult to control.

Hard-boiled. One who is toughened by experience, a person with no illusions or sentimentalities.

Hard by. In close proximity to. *Hard* here means close, pressed close together.

Hard cash. Money; especially actual currency as opposed to cheques or promises— "down on the nail" (*see* ON THE NAIL *under* NAIL); formerly coin as distinguished from banknotes.

Hard currency. Now usually refers to currency of a country which is hard to obtain by another country having an adverse balance of payments with it. The term has also been used to mean metallic money (*see* HARDS AND SOFTS) and to mean currency which is stable and unlikely to depreciate suddenly or change its value.

Hard-headed. Shrewd, intelligent, and businesslike. Not easily bamboozled.

Hard-hearted. Unfeeling, callous, pitiless.

Hard hit. Badly affected, especially by monetary losses.

Hard labour. A punishment of enforced labour additional to that of imprisonment, introduced by statute in 1706. For a long time it consisted of working the treadmill, stone-breaking, oakum picking, etc. Hard labour was abolished by the Criminal Justice Act of 1948.

Hard lines. A hard lot, hard luck. *Lines* here means one's lot or portion marked off as if by a line, "one's lot in life", as, "The lines are fallen unto me in pleasant places: yea, I have a goodly heritage." *Ps.* xvi, 6.

Hard of hearing. Somewhat deaf.

Hard-shell Baptists. Extreme Calvinistic Baptists in the Southern U.S.A. who opposed all missionary activities and benevolent schemes. Also known as *Anti-Mission Baptists*. *Hard-shell* here is the colloquial American term meaning rigid, uncompromising, narrowly orthodox.

Hard tack. Ship's biscuit; coarse bread.

Hard up. Short of money. Originally a nautical phrase; when a vessel was forced by stress of weather to turn away from the wind the helm was put *hard up* to windward to alter course. So, when a man is "hard up" he has to weather the storm as best he may.

To go hard with. To fare ill with; to result in danger, hardship, etc.

Hards and Softs. In the U.S.A. in the 19th century the advocates of "Hard" and "Soft" money policies; the former meaning metallic currency with emphasis on gold and silver and the latter, paper money.

Hardware. A long established term for ironmongery—kettles, pots and pans, cutlery, tools, etc. which were sold in *Hardware Stores*. Currently the word usually denotes the equipment used in a computer system. *See* SOFTWARE.

Hardy. Brave or daring, hence the phrase *hardi comme un lion*. Among those surnamed "The Hardy" are:

William Douglas, defender of Berwick (d. 1298).

Philip III of France (1245, 1270–85).

Philip II, Duke of Burgundy (1342, 1363–1404).

Kiss me, Hardy. These famous words, often used facetiously, if somewhat irreverently, were uttered by the dying Lord Nelson when taking leave of his Flag-Captain, Thomas Masterman Hardy, in the moment of victory. Hardy knelt down and kissed his cheek. They were preceded by the request, "Take care of poor Lady Hamilton."

> "You revolt me," said Lypiatt.
> "Not mortually, I 'ope?" Coleman turned with solicitude to his neighbour; then shook his head. "Mortually I fear. Kiss me 'Ardy, and I die happy." He blew a kiss into the air.
> ALDOUS HUXLEY: *Antic Hay*, ch. iv.

Hare. *See* BURKE.

Hare. It is unlucky for a hare to cross your path, because witches were said to transform themselves into hares.

> *Geo.:* A witch is a kind of hare.
> *Scath.:* And marks the weather
> As the hare doth.
> BEN JONSON: *Sad Shepherd*, II, iii.

> The superstitious is fond in observation, servile in feare...This man does not stirre forth till his breat be crossed, and his face sprinkled: if but an hare crosse him the way, he returnes.
> BP. HALL: *Characters of Virtues and Vices* (1608).

According to mediæval "science", the hare was a melancholy animal, and ate wild succory in the hope of curing itself; its flesh was supposed to generate melancholy in any who partook of it.

> *Fal.:* 'Sblood, I am so melancholy as a gib cat, or a lugged bear.
> *Prince:* Or an old lion, or a lover's lute.
> *Fal.:* Yea, or the drone of a Lincolnshire bagpipe.
> *Prince:* What sayest thou to a hare, or the melancholy of Moor-ditch?
> SHAKESPEARE: *Henry IV, Pt. I*, I, ii.

Another superstition was that hares are sexless, or that they change their sex annually.

> Snakes that cast your coats for new,
> Camelions, that alter hue,
> Hares that yearly sexes change.
> FLETCHER: *Faithful Shepherdess*, III, i.

Among the Hindus the hare is sacred to the MOON, because, as they affirm, the hare is distinctly visible in the full disc.

First catch your hare. *See under* CATCH.

Hare and Hounds. The name given to a form of cross-country running when one or two runners act as hares and set off in advance scattering a trail of paper; the remainder, the hounds, duly set off in pursuit. It is also a fairly common PUBLIC-HOUSE SIGN.

> Well, my little fellows," began the Doctor ... "what makes you so late?"
> "Please sir, we've been out Big-side Hare-and-hounds, and lost our way."
> THOMAS HUGHES: *Tom Brown's Schooldays*, I, vii.

The Hare and the Tortoise. An allusion to the well-known fable of the race between them, which was won by the tortoise; the moral being, "Slow and steady wins the race."

Mad as a March Hare. Hares are unusually shy and wild in March, which is their rutting season.

> The March Hare will be much the more interesting, and perhaps, as this is May, it won't be raving mad—at least not so mad as it was in March.
> LEWIS CARROLL: *Alice in Wonderland*, ch. vi.

Erasmus in his *Aphorisms* says "Mad as a marsh hare", and adds, "Hares are wilder in marshes from the absence of hedges and cover."

To hold with the hare and run with the hounds, or **To run with the hare and hunt with the hounds.** To play a double game, to try to keep in with both sides.

To kiss the hare's foot. To be late for anything, to be a DAY AFTER THE FAIR. The hare has gone by and left its footprint for you to salute. A similar phrase is *to kiss the post*.

To start a hare. To introduce or raise an irrelevant issue in an argument or discussion. To start a hare in the literal sense is to rouse a hare from its form.

Hare-brained. Giddy, foolhardy, MAD AS A

MARCH HARE (*see above*).

> Let's leave this town for they are hair-brained slaves.
> SHAKESPEARE: *Henry VI, Pt. 1*, I, ii.

Harefoot. The surname given to Harold son of Canute and Ælfgifu of Northampton, King of England, 1035–1040.

Hare-lip. A cleft lip; so called from its resemblance to the upper lip of a hare. It was fabled to be caused at birth by an ELF or malicious FAIRY.

> This is the foul fiend Flibbertigibbit. He begins at curfew, and walks till the first cock. He ... squints the eye and makes the hare-lip.
> SHAKESPEARE: *King Lear*, III, iv.

Hare-stone. Another form of HOARSTONE.

Harikiri. See HARA-KIRI.

Hark back, To. To return to the subject. A call to hounds in fox-hunting, when they have overrun the scent, "Hark, hounds, come back"; so "Hark forrard!", "Hark away!", etc.

Harleian (har le' àn). Robert Harley, Earl of Oxford (1661–1724), and his son Edward, the second earl (1689–1741), were great collectors of manuscripts, scarce tracts, etc. The widow of the second earl sold his prints and printed books to Thomas Osborne, the Gray's Inn bookseller, for £13,000 (considerably less than the cost of their binding alone) in 1742, and in 1753 the manuscript books, charters and rolls were purchased at the bargain price of £10,000 for the BRITISH MUSEUM, where the *Harleian MSS.* are among its most valuable literary and historical possessions. The *Harleian Miscellany* (10 vols.; first published 1744–1746 in 8 vols.) contains reprints of nearly 700 tracts, etc., mostly of the 16th and 17th centuries. Since 1870, the Harleian society has published numerous volumes of Registers, Herald's Visitations, and Pedigrees.

Harlem. The main Negro district of New York City, so named by the original Dutch settlers after the town of Haarlem in the Netherlands.

Harlequin (har' le kwin). In British PANTO-MIME, a mischievous fellow supposed to be invisible to all eyes but those of his faithful COLUMBINE. His function is to dance through the world and frustrate all the knavish tricks of the CLOWN, who is supposed to be in love with Columbine. He wears a tight-fitting spangled or parti-coloured dress and is usually masked. He derives from Arlecchino, a stock character of Italian comedy (like PANTALOON and SCARAMOUCH), whose name was in origin probably that of a sprite or HOBGOBLIN. One of the demons in Dante is named "Alichino", and another DEVIL of

mediæval demonology was "Hennequin".

> What Momus was of old to Jove
> The same a Harlequin is now.
> The former was buffoon above,
> The latter is a Punch below.
> SWIFT: *The Puppet Show*.

The prince of Harlequins was John Rich (1682–1761).

Harlequin. So the Emperor Charles V or Charles Quint (1550–1558) was called by Francis I of France.

Harley Street. A street in Marylebone, London, which is generally regarded as the necessary address for leading and fashionable medical specialists. By extension the name includes a surrounding area, including Wimpole Street, which houses many consultants and dental specialists. Its growth as a medical centre dates from late Victorian days.

Harm. Harm set, harm get. Those who lay traps for others get caught themselves. HAMAN (*see Esther*, vii, 10) was hanged on his own gallows. Our Lord says, "They that take the sword shall perish with the sword." (*Matt.* xxvi, 52).

Harmonia. Harmonia's Necklace. An unlucky possession, something that brings evil to all who possess it. Harmonia was the daughter of MARS and VENUS and she received such a necklace on her marriage to King CADMUS. VULCAN, to avenge the infidelity of her mother, also made the bride a present of a robe dyed in all sorts of crimes which infused wickedness and impiety into all her offspring. *Cp.* NESSUS. Both Harmonia and Cadmus, having suffered many misfortunes, were changed into serpents.

MEDEA, in a fit of jealousy, likewise sent Creusa a wedding robe, which burnt her to death. *Cp.* FATAL GIFTS.

Harmonious Blacksmith, The. The name given, after his death, to a well-known air by Handel. An ingenious but completely baseless fabrication ascribed its origin to the hammering at his forge of a blacksmith, William Powell (d. 1780), said to have set Handel to work on this air.

Harmonists. A sect founded in Württemberg by George and Frederick Rapp. They emigrated to western Pennsylvania in 1803 and moved to Indiana, founding New Harmony in 1815. This was sold to Robert Owen in 1824 and they returned to Pennsylvania. They looked forward to the second ADVENT, practised strict economy and self-denial, amassed wealth, and favoured celibacy.

Harness. Out of harness. Not in practice, retired. A horse out of harness is one not at work.

To die in harness. To continue in one's work or occupation till death. The allusion is to a horse working and dying in harness, or to soldiers in armour or harness.

At least we'll die with harness on our back.
SHAKESPEARE: *Macbeth*, V, v.

Haro (hă′ rō). **Clameur de haro.** To cry out haro to anyone (*haro* being in O.Fr. an exclamation or call for help). This cry is an ancient practice in the Channel Islands, usually as a form of protest against trespass, which must then cease until the matter is settled in court. It dates from the time of the first Duke of Normandy. The cry, *Haro, to my aid, my prince, wrong is being done to me*, was raised in the Guernsey PARLIAMENT in January 1966 by a government employee seeking redress.

Haroun al Raschid (hà roon′ ăl răsh′ id). CALIPH of Baghdad. *See* ABBASSIDES.

Harp. The cognizance of IRELAND. Traditionally, one of the early Irish kings was named David, and this king took the harp of the Psalmist as his badge. King John, to distinguish his Irish coins from the English, had them marked with a triangle, either in allusion to St. PATRICK'S explanation of the TRINITY, or to signify that he was king of England, Ireland, and France. The harp may have originated from this. Henry VIII was the first to adopt it as the Irish device, and James I placed it in the third quarter of the royal achievement of Great Britain.

To harp forever on the same string. To reiterate, to return continually to one point of argument.

Harpocrates (har pok′ rà tēz). The Greek form of the Egyptian Harpa-Khruti (HORUS the child). Represented as a naked boy sucking his finger, the Greeks made him the god of silence and secrecy.

I assured my mistress she might make herself perfectly easy on that score for I was the Harpocrates of trusty valets.
A.R. LESAGE: *Gil Blas*, IV, ii.

Harpy. In classical mythology, a winged monster with the head and breasts of a woman, very fierce, starved-looking and loathsome, living in an atmosphere of filth and stench and contaminating everything it came near. HOMER mentions but one harpy, Hesiod gives two, and later writers three. Their names, *Aello* (storm), *Celeno* (blackness), and *Ocypete* (rapid), indicate their early association with whirlwinds and storms.

A regular harpy. A merciless sponger; one who wants to appropriate everything.

I will ... do you any embassage ... rather than hold three words conference with this harpy.
SHAKESPEARE: *Much Ado about Nothing*, II, i.

Harriet Lane. A merchant navy term for canned meat, especially Australian, because of its chopped-up character. One Harriet Lane was purported to have been thus disposed of. It is the merchant service counterpart of FANNY ADAMS.

Harringtons. FARTHINGS. More correctly, *Haringtons*, so called from John, 1st Baron Harington (d. 1613), to whom James I granted a patent (1613) for making these coins of brass. The patent was stopped in 1643, having finally passed to Lord Maltravers.

I will not bate a Harrington of the sume.
BEN JONSON: *The Devil is an Ass*, II, i.

Harry. Harry Tate's Navy. A good-humoured sobriquet applied to the Royal Naval Volunteer Reserve from about the time of World War I or a little earlier. The allusion is to the famous music hall artiste Harry Tate (Ronald Macdonald Hutchinson, d. 1940), perhaps best known of all for his motoring sketch. The term "Harry Tate" came to signify anything that was disorganized or chaotic. *Cp.* FRED KARNO' ARMY; WAVY NAVY.

Bell Harry. The splendid late-15th century central tower of Canterbury Cathedral is so called after the one bell "Harry" contained therein. It replaced the square Norman tower of Lanfranc's day known as the Angel Tower.

Great Harry. *See under* GREAT.

Old Harry. A familiar name for the DEVIL; probably from the personal name (*cp.* OLD NICK *under* NICK), but perhaps with some allusion to the word *harry*, meaning to plunder, harass, lay waste, from which comes the old *harrow*, as in the title of the 13th-century MIRACLE PLAY, *The Harrowing of Hell*.

Pitch Greek to Old Harry, and stick to conundrums!!
R.H. BARHAM: *Ingoldsby Legends*, II (*The Merchant of Venice*).

By the Lord Harry. A mild imprecation, *Lord Harry* here being the equivalent of the DEVIL.

By the Lord Harry, he says true.
CONGREVE: *Old Bachelor*, II, ii.

To play Old Harry. To play the DEVIL; to ruin, or seriously damage.

Hart. In Christian art, the emblem of solitude and purity of life. It was the attribute of St. HUBERT, St. JULIAN, and St. Eustace. It was also the type of piety and religious aspiration (*Ps.* xlii, 1). *Cp.* HIND.

Hart of grease. A hunter's phrase for a fat venison; a stag full of the pasture, called by Jaques in SHAKESPEARE's *As You Like It* (II, i) "a fat and greasy citizen".

Hart Royal. A male red deer, when the crown of the antler has made its appearance, and the creature has been hunted by a king.

The White Hart, or **Hind,** with a golden chain in PUBLIC-HOUSE SIGNS, is the badge of Richard II, which was worn by his adherents. It was adopted by his mother, Joan of Kent, whose cognizance it was.

Harum Scarum. Giddy, HARE-BRAINED; or a person so constituted. From the old *hare*, to harass, and scare; perhaps with the additional allusion to the madness of a March hare (*see under* HARE).

Haruspex (pl. *haruspices*). A Roman official of Etruscan origins who interpreted the will of the gods by inspecting the entrails of animals offered in sacrifice (O. Lat. *haruga*, a victim; *specio*, I inspect). Cato said, "I wonder how one haruspex can keep from laughing when he sees another." *Cp.* AUSPICES. *See* DIVINATION.

Harvard University. The senior university in the U.S.A. situated at Cambridge, Massachusetts. A college was founded in 1636 by the general court of the colony and in 1639 was named after John Harvard (1607–1638) who left to it his library and half his estate. In due course it developed into a complete university, especially after 1869, but the college remained its core.

Harvest Home. In former days the bringing in of the last load of the corn of the harvest with the harvesters singing the Harvest Home song; or the supper provided by the farmer followed by a general jollification. It is also a common PUBLIC-HOUSE SIGN. *See* CORN DOLLY; CRYING THE NECK; HARVEST THANKSGIVING; HOCKEY; MELL SUPPER.

Harvest Moon. The full moon nearest the autumnal equinox, which rises for several days at about the same time (nearly sunset) giving a longer proportion of moonlit evenings than usual.

Harvest Thanksgiving. On 1 October 1843, the Rev. R.S. Hawker, Vicar of Morwenstow in Cornwall, set aside that Sunday in order to thank God for the harvest. The popular CHURCH OF ENGLAND festival largely derives from this; the practice became widespread and nowadays churches are decorated with corn, fruit, vegetables and produce of all kinds, especially in country parishes. Hawker also reverted to the offering of the LAMMAS DAY bread at the EUCHARIST. *See* HARVEST HOME.

> Come, ye thankful people, come,
> Raise the song of harvest-home!
> All is safely gathered in,
> Ere the winter storms begin.
> H. ALFORD: *Harvest Hymn.*

The modern harvest-festival, as a parochial thanksgiving for the bounties of Providence, is an excellent institution, in addition to the old harvest-feast, but it should not be considered as a substitute for it.
R. CHAMBERS: *The Book of Days*, Sept. 25.

Hash. A mess, a muddle; as "a pretty hash he made of it". An allusion to the dish of recooked mixed-up meat and potatoes, etc. It is also the name given to the compacted resin of the cannabis plant, often mixed with molasses: an abbreviation of hashish. *Cp.* GRASS.

I'll soon settle his hash for him. I will soon deal with him; ruin his schemes; "cook his goose"; "put my finger in his pie" (*see* FINGER); "make mincemeat of him" (*see* MINCE). Our slang is full of such phrases. *See* COOKING.

> About earls as goes mad in their castles
> And females what settles their hash.
> G.R. SIMS: *The Dagonet Ballads.*

Hasideans (Heb. *Chasidim*, the pious). The forerunners of the PHARISEES. A religious party in Palestine, who, in the 2nd century B.C., sought to maintain strick adherence to the Hebrew law and Mosaism against Greek influences.

Hasmonæn. The family afterwards known as the MACCABEES.

Hassan-ben-Sabah, or **Hassan-ibn-Sabah.** The OLD MAN OF THE MOUNTAIN (*see under* MOUNTAIN), founder of the sect of the ASSASSINS.

Hat. According to the story, Lord Kingsale is supposed to have acquired the right of wearing his hat in the royal presence when King John and Philip II of France agreed to settle a dispute respecting the duchy of Normandy by single combat. John de Courcy, conqueror of ULSTER and founder of the Kingsale family, was the English champion and no sooner appeared than the French champion put spurs to his horse and fled. The King asked the EARL what reward he would like, and he replied, "Titles and lands I want not, of these I have enough; but in remembrance of this day I beg the boon, for myself and successors, to remain covered in the presence of your highness and all future sovereigns of the realm." The 18th Lord Kingsale wore his hat three times in the presence chamber of William III.

Motley informs us that all the Spanish grandees had the privilege of being covered in the presence of the reigning monarch; and to this day, in England, any peer of the realm has the right to sit in a court of justice with his hat on.

In the HOUSE OF COMMONS, whilst a division is proceeding, a member may speak on a point of order arising out of or during a division, but if he does so he must speak sitting and with his head covered.

It was a point of principle with the early QUAKERS not to remove the hat, the usual mark of respect, even in the presence of royalty. The story goes that William Penn once entered the presence of Charles II and kept his hat on; whereupon Charles removed his own hat. "Friend Charles," said Penn, "Why dost thou uncover thy head?" "Friend Penn," answered Charles with a smile, "it is the custom here that only one person wears his hat in the King's presence."

A cockle hat. *See* COCKLE.

A white hat. A white hat used to be emblematical of RADICAL proclivities because the radical, Orator Hunt (1773–1835), wore one at the time of the Wellington administration.

Hats and Caps. In the 18th century two political factions in the Swedish Rikstag. The Hats (*Hattar*) favoured war with Russia to regain the provinces (Livonia, Esthonia, Ingria, and part of Karelia) surrendered by the Peace of Nystad (1721). The Caps (*Mussorna*) were the peace party, who were nicknamed the "Nightcaps" by their opponents because they were averse to action and war. The Hats were so named from their three-cornered officer's hats and controlled Sweden until the 1760s.

As black as your hat. Quite black, black being a common colour for hats.

At the drop of a hat. On a signal, immediately, without delay; from the American frontier practice of dropping a hat as a signal for a fight to begin, usually the only formality observed. Races are sometimes started by the downward sweep of a hat.

> The man's [Lord Radcliffe's] personal charm, clarity of mind, and unrufflable equanimity certainly did an enormous amount to save the public from being put into blinkers during the Second World War, when D notices were invoke at the drop of a brass hat.
> *The Times*, 15 June 1967.

Hat in hand. *See* CAP IN HAND.

Knocked into a cocked hat. *See* COCKED.

Never wear a brown hat in Friesland. WHEN AT ROME DO AS ROME DOES (*see under* ROME). In Friesland the inhabitants used to cover the head with a knitted cap, a high silk skull-cap, then a metal turban, and over all a huge flaunting bonnet. A traveller once passed through the province with a common brown WIDE-AWAKE, and was hustled, jeered at, and pelted by the boys, because of his unusual attire.

Old hat. Outworn or obsolete. The expression probably arises from the fact that hats tend to date long before they are worn out.

To eat one's hat. Indicative of strong emphasis. "I'd eat my hat first". "I'd be hanged first".

To hang up one's hat in a house. To make oneself at home; to become one of the family.

To keep something under one's hat. To keep something to oneself, not to divulge it; to keep it under cover.

To pass round the hat. To gather subscriptions into a hat.

To take off one's hat to someone. Figuratively, to express admiration for a person's achievements, etc. From the custom of removing the hat as a mark of deference.

To throw one's hat into the ring. To enter a contest or to become a candidate for office. From the custom of throwing one's hat into the ring as the sign of accepting a pugilist's challenge.

Where did you get that hat? A catchphrase of the early 1890s originating from J. Rolmaz's comic song of 1888, with the refrain:

> Where did you get that hat?
> Where did you get that tile?
> Isn't it a nobby one
> And just the proper style?

You are only fit to wear a steeple-crowned hat. To be burnt as a heretic. The victims of the INQUISITION were always decorated with such headgear.

You are talking through your hat. You are talking nonsense; what you say is rubbish; you don't know what you are talking about.

Hat-trick. In CRICKET, the taking of three wickets with three successive balls. A bowler who did this used to be entitled to a new hat at the expense of the club. The phrase is now also applied to a variety of thrice repeated successes or achievements.

Hatches. Batten down the hatches. Figuratively, to make oneself secure, to shut out the weather, etc., as the *hatches* of a ship are secured for sea by battens and wedges.

Hatches, Matches and Dispatches. A long established colloquialism for births, marriages and deaths.

Put on the hatches. Figuratively, shut the door (O.E. *haec*, a gate).

Under hatches. Down in the world, depressed; under arrest; dead. The hatches of a ship are the coverings over the hatchways and to be *under hatches* is to be below deck—with various implications.

> For, though his body's under hatches,
> His soul is gone aloft.
> DIBDIN: *Tom Bowling.*

These lines were inscribed on Dibdin's tombstone at St. Martin-in-the Fields.

Hatchet. To bury the hatchet. *See* BURY.

To throw the hatchet. To exaggerate heavily, to tell falsehoods. In allusion to an ancient game where hatchets were thrown at a mark. *Cp.* TO DRAW THE LONGBOW *under* BOW.

Hatter. In Australia, a lone dweller in the OUTBACK. Possibly from association with the phrase MAD AS A HATTER (*see under* MAD).

Hatto. A 10th-century archbishop of Mainz, a noted statesman and counsellor of Otto the Great, who, according to some, was noted for his oppression of the poor. In time of famine, that there might be more for the rich, he was supposed to have assembled the poor in a barn and burnt them to death, saying: "They are like mice, only good to devour the corn." Presently an army of mice came against the archbishop, who removed to a tower on the Rhine to escape the plague, but the mice followed in their thousands and devoured him. The tower is still called the MOUSE TOWER. Southey has a ballad on Bishop Hatto.

Many similar legends, or versions of the same legend, are told of the mediæval Rhineland:

Count Graaf raised a tower in the midst of the Rhine, and if any boat attempted to avoid payment of toll, the warders shot the crew with crossbows. In a famine year the count profiteered greatly by cornering wheat, but the tower was invaded by hungry rats who worried the old baron to death and then devoured him.

Widerolf, bishop of Strassburg (in 997), was devoured by mice because he suppressed the convent of Seltzen, on the Rhine.

Bishop Adolf of Cologne was devoured by mice or rats in 1112.

Freiherr von Güttingen collected the poor in a great barn and burnt them to death. He was pursued to his castle of Güttingen by rats and mice who ate him clean to the bones. His castle then sank to the bottom of the lake "where it may still be seen". *Cp.* PIED PIPER OF HAMELIN.

Haussmannization. The demolition of buildings, whole districts, etc., and the construction on the site of new streets and cities; after Baron Haussman (1809–1891) who remodelled PARIS between 1835 and 1870. By 1868 he had saddled Paris with a debt of £34 million and was dismissed from his office of Prefect of the Seine in 1870.

Hautville Coit. *See* HACKELL'S COIT.

Havelock (hăv′ lok). A white cloth covering for a soldier's cap with a flap hanging down, worn in hot climates to protect the back of the neck from the sun. So called after General Sir Henry Havelock (1795–1857), who effected the first relief of Lucknow (1857) during the INDIAN MUTINY.

Havelock the Dane. A hero of mediæval romance, the orphan son of Birkabegn, King of Denmark. He was cast adrift on the sea through the treachery of his guardians and the raft bore him to the Lincolnshire coast. He was rescued by a fisherman called GRIM and brought up as his son. He eventually became King of Denmark and of part of England; Grim was suitably rewarded and with the money built Grim's town or Grimsby.

Haver-cakes. Oaten cakes (Icel. *hafr*; Ger. *hafer*, oat).

Haversack (Ger. *hafersack*, oat sack). Originally a bag to carry oats to feed a horse. Hence any small bag for rations, etc., slung over the shoulder.

Havock. An old military command to massacre without quarter. This cry was forbidden in the ninth year of Richard II's reign on pain of death. In a 14th-century tract entitled *The Office of the Constable and Mareschall in the Tyme of Werre* (contained in the *Black Book of the Admiralty*), one of the chapters is, "The peyne of hym that crieth havock, and of them that followeth him"— *Item si quis inventus fuerit qui clamorem inceperit qui vocatur havok.*

> Cry Havoc, and let slip the dogs of war.
> SHAKESPEARE: *Julius Cæsar*, III, i.

Hawcubites. Street bullies in the reign of Queen Anne who molested and ill-treated the old watermen, women, and children who chanced to be in the streets after sunset. The succession of these London pests after the RESTORATION was: The Muns, the TITYRE TUS, the Hectors, the SCOWERERS, the Nickers, then the Hawcubites (1711–1714), and worst of all the MOHOCKS. The name is probably a combination of Mohawk and JACOBITE. *Cp.* MODS AND ROCKERS.

> From Mohock and from Hawcubite,
> Good Lord deliver me,
> Who wander through the streets at nighte,
> Committing cruelty.
> They slash our sons with bloody knives,
> And on our daughters fall:
> And, if they murder not our wives,
> We have good luck withal.

Haw-haw, Lord. In World War II, the name given (originally by a FLEET STREET journalist, Jonah Barrington of the *Daily Express*, in allusion to his accent) to William Joyce, who broadcast anti-British propaganda in

English from Germany. He was hanged for treason in 1946.

Hawk. Falconry, as a sport for kings and gentry, had a tremendous vogue and it retained its popularity until the advent of the shotgun. The various hawks used in England mostly came from Norway and the chief market was the fair of St. Botolph, Boston, Lincs. Their maintenance was very expensive. In recent times there has been a serious revival of the sport.

(1) Different parts of a hawk:

Arms. The legs from the thigh to the foot.
Beak. The upper and crooked part of the bill.
Beams. The long feathers of the wings.
Clap. The nether part of the bill.
Feathers summed and *unsummed.* Feathers full *or* not full grown.
Flags. The feathers next to the principals.
Glut. The slimy substance in the pannel.
Gorge. The crow or crop.
Haglurs. The spots on the feathers.
Mails. The breast feathers.
Nares. The two little holes on the top of the beak.
Pannel. The pipe next to the fundament.
Pendant feathers. Those behind the toes.
Petty singles. The toes.
Pounces. The claws.
Principal feathers. The two longest feathers.
Sails. The wings.
Sear or *sere.* The yellow part under the eyes.
Train. The tail.

(2) Different sorts of hawk:

Gerfalcon. A Gerfalcon (esp. the Tercel, or male) is for a king.
Falcon or *Tercel gentle.* For a prince.
Falcon of the rock. For a duke.
Falcon peregrine. For an earl.
Bastard hawk. For a baron.
Sacre and *sacret.* For a knight.
Lanner and *Lanneret.* For a squire.
Merlin. For a lady.
Hobby. For a young man.
Goshawk. For a yeoman.
Tercel. For a poor man.
Sparrow-hawk. For a priest.
Musket. For a holy-water clerk.
Kestrel. For a knave or servant.

This somewhat fanciful list of hawks proper to the various individual is taken from the *Boke of St. Albans* (1486) by "Dame Juliana Berners".

The "Sore-hawk" is a hawk of the first year; so called from the French, *sor* or *saure,* brownish-yellow.

(3) The dress of a hawk:

Bewits. The leathers with the hawk-bells, buttoned to the bird's legs.
Creanse. A packthread or thin twine fastened to the leash in disciplining a hawk.
Hood. A cover for the head, to keep the hawk in the dark. A *rufter hood* is a wide one, open behind. *To unstrike the hood* is to draw the strings so that the hood may be in readiness to be pulled off.
Jesses. The little straps by which the leash is fastened to the legs.
Leash. The leather thong for holding the hawk.

(4) Terms used in falconry:

Casting. Something given to a hawk to cleanse their

gorge.
Cawking. Treading.
Cowering. When young hawks, in obedience to their elders, quiver and shake their wings.
Crabbing. Fighting with each other when they stand too near.
Hack. The place where a hawk's meat is laid.
Imping. Repairing a hawk's wing by engrafting a new feather.
Inke or *ink.* The breast and neck of a bird that a hawk preys on.
Intermewing. The time of changing the coat.
Lure. A figure of a fowl made of leather and feathers.
Make. An old staunch hawk that sets an example to/young ones.
Mantling. Stretching first one wing then the other over the legs.
Mew. The place where hawks sit when moulting.
Muting. The dung of hawks.
Pelf or *pill.* What a hawk leaves of her prey.
Pelt. The dead body of a fowl killed by a hawk.
Perch. The resting-place of a hawk when off the falconer's wrist.
Plumage. Small feathers given to a hawk to make her cast.
Quarry. The fowl or game that a hawk flies at.
Rangle. Gravel given to a hawk to bring down her stomach.
Sharp set. Hungry.
Tiring. Giving a hawk a leg or wing of a fowl to pull at.

The peregrine when full grown is called a *blue-hawk.*

Hawks and Doves. Politically, and generally, the Hawks are those who favour war and resolute military action, the Doves those who support peace or compromise and negotiation. In the U.S.A., the term *Warhawk* came into particular prominence for those agitating for war with Great Britain in 1811–1812.

I know a hawk from a handsaw (*Hamlet,* II, ii). Handsaw is probably a corruption of *hernshaw* (a young heron). I know a hawk from a heron, the bird of prey from the game flown at; I know one thing from another.

Neither hawk nor buzzard. Of doubtful social position—too good for the kitchen, and not good enough for the family; not hawks to be fondled and petted as the "tasselled gentlemen" of the days of falconry, nor yet buzzrds—a dull kind of falcon synonymous with dunce or plebeian. *Cp.* NEITHER FISH, FLESH, NOR GOOD RED HERRING *under* HERRING.

Hawker's News. "PIPER'S NEWS", news known to all the world. *Un secret de polichinelle.*

Hawkeye. An inhabitant of the state of Iowa. *See also* LEATHERSTOCKING NOVELS.

Hawse-hole. He has a crept through the hawse-hole, or hawse-pipe, or He has come in at the hawse-hole, or hawse-pipe. A naval phrase meaning entered the service in the lowest grade; he has risen from the ranks. The hawse-hole of a ship is the hole in the bows through which the anchor cable runs.

Hawthorn. The symbol of "Good Hope" in the language of FLOWERS because it shows winter is over and spring is at hand. The Athenian girls used to crown themselves with hawthorn flowers at weddings, and the marriage-torch was made of hawthorn. The Romans considered it a charm against sorcery, and placed leaves of it on the cradles of new-born infants.

The hawthorn was chosen by Henry VII, as his device, because Richard III's crown was recovered from a hawthorn bush at Bosworth. *Haw* here is the O.E. *haga*, hedge. *Cp.* HAYWARD.

Hay. Antic Hay. The hay was an old English country dance (O.E. *haga*, hedge, bush), somewhat of the nature of a reel, with winding movements around other dancers or bushes, etc., when danced in the open.

> My men, like satyrs grazing on the lawns,
> Shall with their goat-feet dance an antic hay.
> MARLOWE: *Edward II*, I, i.

Aldous Huxley wrote a novel of this title.

Hay, Hagh, or **Haugh** (all pron. ha). An enclosed estate; rich pasture-land, especially a royal park; as Bilhagh (*Billahaugh*), Beskwood- or Bestwood-hay, Lindeby-hay, Welley-hay or Wel-hay.

Hay. In the following phrases hay (O.E. *hieg*) is the cut, dried grass used as fodder.

Between hay and grass. Too late for one and too soon for the other.

Neither hay nor grass. That awkward stage when a youth is neither boy nor man.

To look for a needle in a bottle of hay, or **in a haystack.** *See under* BOTTLE.

To make hay of something. To disorganize and throw things into confusion and disorder. Before the days of the hay-baler, hay was tossed around with a pitchfork before being gathered in.

To make hay while the sun shines. To strike while the iron is hot; to take advantage of the opportunity. *Cp.* TAKE TIME BY THE FORELOCK *under* TIME.

Haybote. The right of a tenant of an estate to take wood for repairing hedges and fences. Other estovers are HOUSEBOTE and PLOUGHBOTE.

Hayseed. An American term for a rustic, a countryman.

Haysugge. *See* ISAAC.

Hayward (O.E. *haege, haga*, hedge; *weard*, keeper). A manorial and village officer whose duty it was to look after the hedges and boundaries and to impound straying livestock. He sometimes regulated the use of the common. *Cp.* HAWTHORN.

> Other haue an horne and be hawarde and liggen
> oute a nyghtes
> And kepe my corn in my croft fro pykers and
> theeues.
> *Piers Plowman* (*Text C*), vi, 16.

Haywire. To go haywire is to run riot, to behave in an uncontrolled manner. This American phrase probably arises from the difficulty of handling the coils of wire used for binding bundles of hay, which easily became entangled and unmanageable if handled unskilfully.

Hazazel. The scapegoat. *See* AZAZEL.

Haze. To bully, to punish by hard work. A nautical expression.

> Every shifting of the studding-sails was only to "haze" the crew.
> R.H. DANA: *Two Years Before the Mast* (1840), ch. viii.

In the U.S.A., to subject to horseplay or punishment in school or fraternity initiations.

He Bible. *See* BIBLE, SOME SPECIALLY NAMED EDITIONS.

Head. Cattle are counted by the *head*; labourers by *hands*, as "How many hands do you employ?"; soldiers once by their *arms*, as "so many rifles, bayonets, etc."; guests at dinner by the *cover*, "covers for ten", etc.

People are sometimes counted by *heads* as when a caterer undertakes to provide for a party at so much *a head*. *See also* SPEAKING HEADS *under* SPEAKING.

Better be the head of an ass than the tail of a horse. Better the foremost amongst commoners than the lowest of the aristocracy; "better to reign in hell than serve in Heav'n" (Milton: *Paradise Lost*, I, 263).

Get you head shaved. You are a dotard. Go and get your head shaved like other lunatics. *See* BATH.

> Thou thinkst that monarchs never can act ill,
> Get thy head shaved, poor fool, or think so still.
> PETER PINDAR: *Ode upon Ode*.

Head and shoulders. A phrase of sundry shades of meaning. Thus "head and shoulders taller" means considerably taller; "to turn one out head and shoulders" means to drive one out forcibly.

Heads I win, tails you lose. Descriptive of a one-sided arrangement. *See* HEADS OR TAILS *below*.

Heads or tails. Guess whether the coin spun will come down with head-side uppermost or not. The word *tail* includes all the various devices appearing on the reverse of a coin. The Romans said "Heads or ships".

He has a head on his shoulders. He is a clever fellow, he has got brains.

He has quite lost his head. He is so excited and confused that he does not know the right thing to do.

He has quite turned her head. She is so infatuated with him that she is unable to take a reasonable view of the situation.

I can make neither head nor tail or it. I cannot understand it at all. I can make nothing of it.

Off one's head. Deranged; delirious; extremely excited.

Over head and ears. *See under* EAR.

To bite a person's head off. A scathing or irritable answer to a mild remark or request.

To bury one's head in the sand. To shirk facing realities. Ostriches were popularly reputed to hide their head in the sand when pursued, and by thus not seeing their enemy believe that they themselves were not seen.

To come to a head. To reach a crisis. The allusion is to the ripening, or coming to a head, of a boil, ulcer, etc.

To eat its head off. *See under* EAT.

To give someone his head. To allow him complete freedom, let him go just as he pleases. A phrase from horse management.

To head off. To intercept; get ahead of and force to turn back.

To hit the nail on the head. To guess aright; to arrive at the exact conclusion. The allusion is obvious. The French say, *Voux avez frappé au but* (You have hit the mark); the Italians, *Avete dato in brocca* (You have hit the pitcher), alluding to a game where a pitcher took the place of AUNT SALLY. The Lat. *rem acu tetigisti* (You have touched the thing with a needle), refers to the custom of probing sores.

To keep one's head. To remain calm in an emergency; to keep one's wits about one. *Not to lose one's head* is another way of saying the same thing.

To keep one's head above water. To avoid insolvency; to avoid being overwhelmed by one's tasks or commitments. The derivation is obvious.

To go to one's head. To be unduly influenced; to become conceited, etc., as a result of success, praise, etc. A figure based on the heady effect of intoxicating drinks.

To make head, or **headway.** To get on, to struggle effectually against something, as a ship makes headway against a tide or current.

To run one's head against a brick, or **stone wall.** To make fruitless attempts against insuperable difficulties.

To take it into one's head. To conceive a notion.

To talk a person's head off. To weary a person with so much talking that he is mentally benumbed; to talk incessantly.

Heal. To heal the breach. To effect a reconciliation.

Health. Drinking Healths. This custom, of immemorial antiquity, William of Malmesbury says, took its rise from the death of young Edward the Martyr (978), who was traitorously stabbed in the back while drinking a horn of wine presented by his mother Ælfthryth. (*See also* GABBARA.)

The Greeks handed the cup to the person toasted and said, "This to thee." Our holding out the wineglass is a relic of this Greek custom.

The Romans in drinking the health of a mistress used to drink a bumper to each letter of her name. Samuel Butler (*Hudibras*, II, i) satirizes this custom in the line, "And spell names over beer-glasses." In Plautus (*Stich*. V, iv) we read of a man drinking to his mistress with these words: *Bene vos, bene nos, bene te, bene me, bene nostram etiam Stephanium* (Here's to you, here's to us all, here's to thee, here's to me, here's to our dear—) Martial, Ovid, HORACE, etc. refer to the same custom.

The Saxons were great health-drinkers, and Geoffrey of Monmouth (*Historia Britonum*, Bk. VI, xii) says that Hengist invited King Vortigern to a banquet to see his new levies. After the banquet, Rowena, Hengist's beautiful daughter, entered with a gold cup full of wine, and curtseying said to him "*Lauerd king wacht heil!*" (Lord King, your health). The king then drank and replied, "Drinc heil" (Here's to you). *See* WASSAIL.

Heap. Struck all of a heap. Struck with astonishment.

Hear, hear! An exclamation approving what a speaker says. Originally disapproval was marked by humming; those supporting the speaker protested by saying "Hear him", which eventually became "Hear, hear!"

Heart. In Christian art the heart is an attribute of St. TERESA of Avila.

The flaming heart is a symbol of charity, and an attribute of St. AUGUSTINE, denoting the fervency of his devotion. The heart of the Saviour is sometimes so represented.

Heart of Midlothian. The old TOLBOOTH of Edinburgh. This old prison was demolished in 1817.

> "Then the tolbooth of Edinburgh is called the Heart of Midlothian?" said I. "So termed and reputed. I assure you."
>
> SCOTT: *Heart of Midlothian*, ch. i.

Heart of Oak. This famous sea song and naval march is from Garrick's pantomime,

Harlequin's Invasion, with music by Dr. Boyce. It was written in 1759, "the year of victories" (Quiberon Bay, Quecbec, Minden), hence the allusion to "this wonderful year" in the opening lines. "Heart of Oak" refers, of course, to the timber from which the ships were built.

> Come, cheer up my lads! 'tis to glory we steer,
> To add something more to this wonderful year.

The Immaculate Heart of Mary. In the ROMAN CATHOLIC CHURCH, devotion to the heart of Mary is a special form of devotion to Our Lady which developed from the 17th century. In 1947 Pius XII recognized 22 August as the Feast of the Immaculate Heart of Mary.

The Sacred Heart. In the ROMAN CATHOLIC CHURCH, devotion to the Sacred Heart of Jesus, essentially directed at the Saviour himself. It originated from a vision experienced by a French nun, Marguerite Marie Alacoque (1647–1690). This devotion in France was approved by Clement XIII in 1758 and extended to the whole church in 1856 by Pius IX. The festival is celebrated on the Friday after the Octave of CORPUS CHRISTI. There are various Congregations of the Sacred Heart. *Cp.* IMMACULATE HEART.

A heart to heart talk. A confidential talk in private; generally one in which good advice is offered, or a warning or reprimand given.

After my own heart. Just what I like; in accordance with my wish.

At heart. At bottom; substantially; in real character.

Be of good heart. Cheer up.

From the bottom of one's heart. Fervently; with absolute sincerity.

His heart is in the right place. He is kind and sympathetic, in spite, perhaps, of appearances.

His heart sank into his boots. In Latin, *Cor illi in genua decidet.* In French *Avoir la peur au ventre.* The last two phrases are very expressive: fear makes the knees shake, and it gives one a stomach-ache; but the English phrase suggests that his heart or spirits sank as low as possible short of absolutely deserting him.

His heart was in his mouth. That choky feeling in throat which arises from fear, conscious guilt, shyness, etc.

In one's heart of heart. In the innermost, most secure recesses of one's heart.

> Give me that man
> That is not passion's slave, and I will wear him
> In my heart's core, ay in my heart of heart.
>
> SHAKESPEARE: *Hamlet*, III, ii.

The phrase is often heard of as "heart of hearts", but this is incorrect, as will be seen from SHAKESPEARE's clear reference to the "heart's core". *Cp.* also:

> Even the very middle of my heart
> Is warmed.
>
> *Cymbeline*, I, vi.

Out of heart. Despondent; without sanguine hope.

Set your heart at rest. Be quite easy about the matter.

Take heart. Be of good courage. At one time moral courage was supposed to reside in the heart, physical courage in the stomach, wisdom in the head, affection in the REINS, melancholy in the BILE, spirit in the blood, etc.

To break one's heart. To waste away or die of disappointment. "Brokenhearted", hopelessly distressed. It is not impossible to die "of a broken heart".

To eat one's heart out. To brood over some trouble to such an extent that one wears oneself out with the worry of it; to suffer from hopeless disappointment in expectations.

To have at heart. To cherish as a great hope or desire; to be earnestly set on.

To learn by heart. By rote, to memorize.

To lose one's heart to. To fall in love with somebody.

To set one's heart upon something. To earnestly desire it.

To take heart of grace. To pluck up courage; not to be disheartened or downhearted when all seems to go against one. This expression may be based on the promise, "My grace is sufficient for thee" (II *Cor.* xii, 9); by this grace St. PAUL says, "When I am weak then am I strong." Take grace into your heart, rely on God's grace for strength.

To take to heart. To feel deeply pained at something which has occurred; to appreciate fully the implications of.

To warm the cockles of one's heart. *See under* COCKLE.

To wear one's heart upon one's sleeve. To expose one's secret thoughts or intentions to general notice.; to show plainly one's feelings. The reference is to the custom of tying one's lady's favour to one's sleeve, and thus exposing the secret of the heart.

> For I come from Castlepatrick and me heart is on
> me sleeve,
> But a lady stole it from me on St. Gallowglass's Eve.
>
> G.K. CHESTERTON: *Me Heart*.

With all my heart, or **With my whole heart and soul.** With all the energy and enthusiasm of which I am capable.

With heart and hand. With enthusiastic energy.

Heart-breaker. A flirt. Also a particular kind of curl. A loose ringlet worn over the shoulders, or a curl over the temples.

Heartsease. The *Viola tricolor*. It has a host of fancy names; as the "Butterfly flower", "Kiss me quick", a "Kiss behind the garden gate", "LOVE-IN-IDLENESS", "Pansy", "Three faces under one hood", the "Variegated Violet", "Herba Trinitatis", etc.

Hearth money. *See* CHIMNEY MONEY.

Hearth-penny. An old name for PETER'S PENCE, a tax of one penny on every household.

Heat. One course of a race; that part of a race when the competitors are too numerous to run at the same time.

> Feign'd Zeal, you saw, set out the speedier pace,
> But, the last Heat, Plain Dealing won the Race.
> DRYDEN: *Albion and Albanius, Epilogue.*

A dead heat. When two or more competitors in a race cross the line together.

Its all for heat and pilchards. An old Cornish expression said of a warm foggy day in summer implying that hot weather is on the way and the pilchards will be gathering in shoals ready for the fisherman.

The heat of the day. The hottest part of the day; that part of the day when the heat is oppressive.

To turn the heat on. To subject to a severe cross-examination, to grill.

Heath Robinson, or **Heath Robinsonian,** is a phrase commonly applied to complicated, ingenious, and fantastic contraptions of machinery, etc., after W. Heath Robinson (1872–1944). His amusing drawings of such absurdities in *Punch* and elsewhere were distinctive of their kind.

Heaven (O.E. *heofon*). The word properly denotes the abode of the Deity and His ANGELS—"heaven is my throne" (*Is.* lxvi, 1, and *Matt.* v, 34)—but it is also used in the BIBLE and elsewhere for the air, the upper heights, as "the fowls of heaven", "the dew of heaven", "the clouds of heaven"; "the cities are walled up to heaven" (*Deut.* i, 28); and a tower whose top should "reach unto heaven" (*Gen.* xi, 4); the starry firmament, as "Let there be lights in the firmament of the heaven" (*Gen.* i, 14).

In the PTOLEMAIC SYSTEM, the heavens were the successive spheres surrounding the central earth. *See also* EMPYREAN; PARADISE.

The Seven Heavens (of the Mohammedans).

The first heaven is of pure SILVER, and here the stars, each with its ANGEL warder, are hung out like lamps on golden chains. It is the abode of ADAM and EVE.

The second heaven is of pure GOLD and is the domain of JOHN THE BAPTIST and Jesus.

The third heaven is of PEARL, and is allotted to JOSEPH. Here AZRAEL is stationed, and is forever writing in a large book (the names of the new-born) or blotting names out (those of the newly dead).

The fourth heaven is of white gold, and is Enoch's. Here dwells the angel of Tears, whose height is "500 days' journey", and who sheds ceaseless tears for the sins of man.

The fifth heaven is of silver and is AARON's. Here dwells the Avenging Angel, who presides over elemental fire.

The sixth heaven is composed of ruby and garnet, and is presided over by MOSES. Here dwells the Guardian Angel of heaven and earth, half-snow and half-fire.

The seventh heaven is formed of divine light beyond the power of tongue to describe, and is ruled by ABRAHAM. Each inhabitant is bigger than the whole earth, and has 70,000 heads, each head 70,000 faces and each face 70,000 mouths, each mouth 70,000 tongues and each tongue speaks 70,000 languages, all for ever employed in chanting the praises of the Most High.

To be in the seventh heaven. Supremely happy. The CABBALISTS maintained that there are seven heavens, each rising above the other, the seventh being the abode of God and the highest class of ANGELS.

Heavy. Heavy man. In theatrical parlance, an actor who plays foil to the hero, such as the King in SHAKESPEARE'S *Hamlet*, or Iago to Othello.

The Heavies. *See* REGIMENTAL AND DIVISIONAL NICKNAMES.

Heaviest Men.

Robert Earl Hughes (1926–1958) of Illinois, U.S.A., was the heaviest recorded man. His greatest weight was 74 st. 5 lb.

William Campbell (1856–1878), born at Glasgow, was the heaviest man recorded in Great Britain. He attained 53 st. 8 lb.

Daniel Lambert (1770–1809) of Leicester was the previous record-holder at 52 st. 11 lb. He was a keeper at Leicester gaol.

There are others said to have been heavier, but their weights are not verified. *Cp.* DWARF; GIANTS.

Hebe (hē' bi). In Greek mythology, daughter of ZEUS and HERA, goddess of youth, and cup-bearer to the gods. She had the power of restoring youth and vigour to gods and men.

Hecate (hek' à ti). In Greek mythology, daughter of the TITAN Perses and of Asteria, and high in favour with ZEUS. Her powers extended over HEAVEN and HELL, the earth and the sea. She came to combine the attributes of SELENE, ARTEMIS, and PERSEPHONE and to be identified with them. She was represented as a triple goddess sometimes with three heads, one of a horse, one of a dog, and one of a boar; sometimes with three bodies standing back to back. As goddess of the lower world she became the goddess of magic, ghosts and WITCHCRAFT. Her offerings consisted of dogs, honey and black lambs, which were sacrificed to her at crossroads. SHAKESPEARE refers to the triple character of this goddess:

> And we fairies that do run
> By the triple Hecate's team.
> *Midsummer Night's Dream*, V, ii.

Hecatomb (hek′ à tom, *or* toom). In ancient Greece, originally the sacrifice of a hundred head of oxen (Gr. *hekatombe*; *hekaton*, a hundred, *bous*, an ox); hence any large sacrifice or large number. Keats speaks of "hecatombs of vows", and Shelley of "hecatombs of broken hearts".

It is said that PYTHAGORAS, who, we know, would never take life, offered up 100 oxen when he discovered that the square of the hypotenuse of a right-angled triangle equals the sum of the squares of the other two sides. *See* DULCARNON.

Hector. Eldest son of PRIAM, the noblest and most magnanimous of all the Trojan chieftains in Homer's ILIAD. After holding out for ten years, he was slain by ACHILLES, who lashed him to his chariot, and dragged the dead body in triumph thrice round the walls of TROY.

Somewhat curiously his name has come to be applied to a swaggering bully, and "to hector" means to browbeat, bully, bluster.

The Hector of Germany. Joachim II, Elector of Brandenburg (1505, 1535–1571).

You wear Hector's cloak. You are paid in your own coin for trying to deceive another. When Thomas Percy, Earl of Northumberland, was routed in 1569, he hid in the house of Hector Graham of Harlaw, who betrayed him for the reward offered. Fortune never favoured this traitor thereafter, and he eventually died a beggar on the roadside.

Hecuba (hek′ ū bà). Second wife of PRIAM and mother of nineteen children, including HECTOR. When TROY was taken she fell to the lot of ULYSSES. She was afterwards metamorphosed into a bitch and finding she could only bark, threw herself into the sea. Her sorrows and misfortunes are featured in numerous Greek tragedies.

Hedge. To hedge, in betting, is to protect oneself against loss by cross bets. It is also to prevaricate.

> He [Godolphin] began to think ... that he had betted too deep on the Revolution and that it was time to hedge.
> MACAULAY: *History of England*, ch. xvii.

The word is used attributively for persons of low origin, vagabonds who plied their trade in the open, under or between the hedges, etc.; hence *hedge-priest*, a poor or vagabond parson; *hedge-writer*, a GRUB-STREET author; *hedge-marriage*, a clandestine union, one performed by a hedge-priest; *hedge-born swain*, a person of mean or illegitimate birth (as in Shakespeare's *Henry VI, PT. I*, IV, i); *hedge-school*, a school conducted in the open air, as in IRELAND in former days.

To hedge-hop. An airman's term for flying so low as almost to skim the hedgetops.

Hedgers and Ditchers. In 1911, during the struggle against the PARLIAMENT Bill proposing to curtail the powers of the HOUSE OF LORDS, the Conservative majority in the Lords was split. The "Hedgers" under Lord Landsdowne were prepared to acquiesce rather than risk the creation of enough Liberal peers to ensure the bill's passage. The "Ditchers" led by Lord Halsbury were prepared to to die in the last ditch rather than yield. The Hedgers ("the JUDAS group") prevailed and the bill passed thus formally ending the power of the Lords over Money Bills and limiting that over other legislation to two years. *See* BALFOUR'S POODLE.

Hedonism. The doctrine of Aristippus, that pleasure or happiness is the chief good and end of man (Gr. *hedone*, pleasure). *Cp.* EPICURUS.

Heebie-jeebies. An American slang term descriptive of intense nervousness or JITTERS.

Heel. In American slang a *heel* is a CAD, a despicable fellow with no sense of decency or honour.

The heel of Achilles. *See under* ACHILLES.

Down, or **out at heels.** *See under* DOWN.

To cool, or **kick one's heels.** To be kept waiting a long time, especially after an appointment has been given one.

To lay by the heels. To render powerless. The allusion is to the stocks, in which vagrants and other petty offenders were confined by the ankles.

To lift up the heel against. To spurn, physically or figuratively; to treat with contumely or contempt; to oppose, to become an enemy.

> Yea, mine own family friend, in whom I trusted which did eat of my bread, hath lifted up his heel against me.
> *Ps.* xli, 9.

To show a clean, or **fair pair of heels.** To abscond, run away and get clear.

To take to one's heels. To run off.

Heeled in Western U.S.A. means supplied with all necessities, particularly money and firearms. It derives from metal spurs or "heels" fitted to the spurs of fighting cocks.

A heeler is the hanger-on of a political boss.

Heel-taps. Bumpers all round and no heel-taps. The bumpers are to be drained to the bottom of the glass. A *heel-tap* is the small amount left in the glass after the bulk has been drunk.

Heep, Uriah. An abject toady and a malignant hypocrite, making a great play of being "'umble", but in the end falling a victim of his own malice (Dickens: *David Copperfield*).

Hegira (hej' i ra, he ji' ra) (Arab. *hejira*, the departure). The flight of MOHAMMED from MECCA to Yathrib, 16 July 622, which soon came to be called MEDINA, the City of the Prophet. The Mohammedan CALENDAR starts from this event.

Heidelberg Man. A type of Prehistoric man found near Heidelberg in 1907, possibly of the genus *Pithecanthropus*. A chinless jaw was found along with other extinct mammal fossils of the Pleistocene period.

Heimdall (hīm' dal). In Scandinavian mythology, a god of light who guards the rainbow bridge, BIFROST. He was the son of the nine daughters of ÆGIR, and in many attributes identical with TIW.

Heimskringla (hīm skring' là) (Orb of the world). An important collection of sixteen sagas on the lives of the early kings of Norway to 1184, the work of Snorri Sturluson (1179–1241). *See* EDDA.

Heir-apparent. The actual heir who will succeed if he outlives the present holder of the crown, title, etc., as distinguished from the *heir-presumptive*, whose succession may be broken by the birth of someone nearer akin, or of a son (who takes priority over daughters) to the holder. Thus the Princess Royal was heir-presumptive to Queen Victoria until the Prince of Wales (the future Edward VII), was born and became heir-apparent. At the death of his predecessor the heir-apparent becomes *heir-at-law*.

Hel. In early Scandinavian mythology the name of the abode of the dead and of its goddess; later, the home of those not slain in battle; slain warriors entered VALHALLA. Hel and her realm eventually acquired more sinister attributes after the advent of Christianity.

Heldenbuch (hel' den buk) (Ger., Book of Heroes). The name given to a collection of 13th-century German epic poetry. The stories are based upon national sagas, DIETRICH OF BERN being a central figure.

Helen. The type of female beauty. In Greek legend, she was the daughter of ZEUS and LEDA, and wife of MENELAUS, King of Sparta. She eloped with PARIS and thus brought about the siege and destruction of TROY.

> For which men all the life they here enjoy
> Still fight, as for the Helens of their Troy.
> FULKE GREVILLE, LORD BROOKE:
> *Treatise of Humane Learning.*

Helen's fire. *See* CORPOSANT.

St. Helena. Mother of Constantine the Great (*c.* 250–*c.* 330). She is represented in royal robes, wearing an imperial crown as an empress, sometimes carrying a model of the HOLY SEPULCHRE, sometimes carrying a large cross (*see* INVENTION OF THE CROSS *under* CROSS). Sometimes she also bears the three nails by which the Saviour was affixed to the cross. Her day is 18 August.

The island of St. Helena in the South Atlantic was discovered by the Portuguese on 21 May 1502 (St. Helena's Day as observed in the Eastern Church). It was the place of NAPOLEON's exile from 1815 until his death in 1821.

Helicon. The home of the MUSES, a part of PARNASSUS. It contained the fountains of AGANIPPE and HIPPOCRENE, connected by "Helicon's harmonious stream". The name is used allusively of poetic inspiration.

> From Helicon's harmonious springs
> A thousand rills their mazy progress take.
> The laughing flowers, that round them blow,
> Drink life and fragrance as they flow.
> GRAY: *The Progress of Poesy.*

Heliogabalus. *See* ELAGABALUS.

Heliopolis. The City of the Sun, a Greek form of (1) Baalbek, in Syria, and (2) On, in ancient Egypt (to the north-east of Cairo), where the sun was worshipped in the name of Re or RA or Aton.

Helios (Hē' li os). The Greek sun-god, who climbed the vault of HEAVEN in a chariot drawn by snow-white horses to give light, and in the evening descended into the Ocean. He is called HYPERION by HOMER, and in later times, APOLLO.

Heliotrope (Gr., "turn-to-sun"). for the story of the flower *see* CLYTIE.

The bloodstone, a greenish quartz with veins and spots of red, used to be called "heliotrope", the story being that if thrown into water it turned the rays of the sun to blood-colours. This stone also had the power of rendering its bearer invisible.

> Nor hope had they of crevice where to hide,
> Or heliotrope to charm them out of view.
> DANTE: *Vision, Hell*, xxiv (*Cary's Translation*).

Hell. The abode of the dead, then traditionally the place of torment or punishment after death (O.E. *hel*, hell, from root *hel-*, hide).

According to the KORAN, Hell has seven portals leading into seven divisions (*Surah* XV, 44).

True Buddhism admits of no Hell properly so called (*cp.* NIRVANA), but certain of the more superstitious Buddhists acknowledge as many as 136 places of punishment after death, where the dead are sent according to their deserts.

Classic authors tell us that the INFERNO is encompassed by five rivers: ACHERON, COCYTUS, STYX, PHLEGETHON, and LETHE. *See also* AVERNUS, GEHENNA, HADES, HEAVEN, PURGATORY, TARTARUS.

Hell and Chancery are always open. There's not much to choose between lawyers and the DEVIL. An old saying.

Hell, Hull and Halifax. *See* HULL.

Hell is paved with good intentions. This occurs as a saying of Dr. Johnson (Boswell's *Life*, entry for 16 April 1775), but it is a good deal older. It is given by George Herbert (*Jacula Prudentum*, 1633) as "Hell is full of good meanings and wishings." The usual form today is, "The road to hell is paved with good intentions."

It was all hell broken loose. Said of a state of riot or disorder.

The road to hell is easy. *Facilis descensus Averno. See* AVERNUS.

The Vicar of Hell. *See* VICAR.

To give someone hell. To make things very unpleasant for someone.

To Hell or Connaught. This phrase arose after the Act for the Settlement of IRELAND, 1652, following the Cromwellian defeat of the Irish insurrection. After September 1653, every Irish CATHOLIC owning property over the annual value of £10, and not guiltless of involvement in the revolt, was to be dispossessed and transplanted to the poorer parts of Connaught. Those remaining had to speak English and rear their children as PROTESTANTS.

To lead apes in hell. *See under* APE.

To ride hell for leather. To ride with the utmost speed, "all out".

To work, play, etc., **like hell.** To do it with all the power at one's disposal, with the utmost vigour.

Hell broth. A magical mixture prepared for evil purposes (SHAKESPEARE: *Macbeth*, IV, i).

Hell's Angels. Members of a group of unruly and trouble-making motor-cyclists originating in California in the 1950s. Usually wearing leather jackets, their symbol is a winged DEATH'S HEAD.

In due course Hell's Angels appeared in Britain and Europe among devotees of the motor-cycle. Often tatooed and badge-bestrewn, they still have a somewhat dubious image.

Hell's Corner. The triangle of Kent about Dover was so called in World War II from its being both under fire from German cross-channel gunnery and the scene of so much of the fiercest air combat during the BATTLE OF BRITAIN, 1940.

Hell-fire Club. A notorious 18th-century coterie founded about 1755 by Sir Francis Dashwood, afterwards Baron Le Despencer. Its thirteen members conducted their profanities and revelries at Medmenham Abbey, Buckinghamshire, which formed part of the Dashwood property. Among the "Monks of Medmenham" were John Wilkes, Paul Whitehead, the satirist, who was secretary and steward, Charles Churchill and the Earl of Sandwich.

The motto of the fraternity was: "*Fay ce que voudras.*"

Hell Gate. A dangerous passage in the East River between Long Island and New York City. The Dutch settlers called it *Hoellgat* (whirling-gut), which was corrupted into Hell Gate. Flood Island, its most dangerous reef, was removed by mining and blasting in 1885.

Hellenes (hel′ ēnz). "This word had in Palestine three different meanings: sometimes it designated the pagans; sometimes the Jews, speaking Greek and dwelling among the pagans; and sometimes proselytes of the gate, that is, men of pagan origin converted to Judaism, but not circumcised (*John* vii, 35, xii, 20; *Acts* xiv, 1, xvii, 4, xviii, 4, xxi, 28)" (Renan: *Life of Jesus*, xiv).

The Greeks were called *Hellenes*, from Hellen, son of DEUCALION AND PYRRHA, their legendary ancestors; the name has descended to the modern Greeks, and their sovereign was not "King of Greece", but "King of the Hellenes". After the abolition of the monarchy in 1973 a "Hellenic Republic" was instituted. The ancient Greeks called their country "Hellas"; it was the Romans who called it "Græcia", which, among the inhabitants themselves, referred only to Epirus.

Hellenic. The common dialect of the Greek writers after the age of ALEXANDER THE GREAT. It was based on the ATTIC.

Hellenistic. The dialect of the Greek language used by the Jews. It was full of Oriental idioms and METAPHORS. The term likewise particularly denotes Greek culture and art modified by foreign and oriental influences after the conquests of ALEXANDER THE GREAT.

Hellenists. Those Jews who used the Greek or Hellenic language; also a Greek scholar.

Hellespont (hel' es pont). The "sea of Helle"; so called because Helle, the sister of Phryxus, was drowned there. She was fleeing with her brother through the air to Colchis on the golden ram to escape from INO, her mother-in-law, who most cruelly oppressed her, but, turning giddy, she fell into the sea. It is the ancient name of the Dardanelles and is celebrated in the legend of HERO AND LEANDER. *See also* GOLDEN FLEECE.

Helmet. The helmets of Saragossa were in most repute in the days of CHIVALRY.

Bever, or *drinking-piece*. One of the movable parts, which was lifted up when the wearer ate or drank. It comes from the old Italian verb *bevere*, to drink.

Close helmet. The complete headpiece, having in front two movable parts, which could be lifted up or down at pleasure.

Morion. A low iron cap, worn only by infantry.

Visor. One of the movable parts; it was to look through.

The helmet in Heraldry, resting on the chief of the shield, and bearing the crest, indicates rank.

> *Gold, with six bars*, or *with the visor raised* (in full face), for royalty.
> *Silver, with five bars* (in full face), for a duke or marquis.
> *Silver, with four bars, with visor raised* (in profile), for an earl, viscount, or baron.
> *Steel, without bars*, and *with visor open* (in full face), for a knight or a baronet.
> *Steel, with visor closed* (in profile), for a squire or a gentleman.

A helmet is never put over the arms of a woman, other than the sovereign.

The helmet of Mohammed. MOHAMMED wore a double helmet; the exterior one was called *al-mawashah* (the wreathed garland).

The helmet of Perseus rendered the wearer invisible. This was the "helmet of HADES", which, with winged sandals and magic wallet, he took from certain NYMPHS; but after he had slain MEDUSA he restored them again, and presented the GORGON's head to ATHENE, who placed it in the middle of her ÆGIS.

Heloïse. *See* ABELARD.

Helot. A drunken helot. The Spartans used to make a helot (slave) drunk as an object-lesson to the youths of the evils of intemperance. Dr. Johnson said of one of his old acquaintances:

> He is a man of good principles; and there would be no danger that a young gentleman should catch his manner; for it is so very bad, that it must be avoided. In that respect he would be like the drunken Helot.
> BOSWELL'S *Life:* 2 April 1779.

Help-ale. *See* BID ALE.

Hemlock (*conium maculatum*). A poisonous biennial plant with umbels of small white flowers found in Britain, Europe and parts of Asia and W. Africa, also naturalized in North and South America. The roots and fruit are especially dangerous. Poisoning by hemlock was used in ancient Greece to kill condemned criminals and evil-doers. *See* SOCRATES.

Helve. To throw the helve after the hatchet. To be reckless, to throw away what remains because your losses have been so great. The allusions is to the fable of the wood-cutter who lost the head of his axe in a river and threw the handle in after it.

Hempe. When hempe is spun England is done. Bacon says he heard the prophecy when he was a child, and he interpreted it thus: Hempe is composed of the initial letters of Henry, Edward, Mary, Philip, and Elizabeth. At the close of the last reign "England was done", for the sovereign no longer styled himself "King of England", but, "King of Great Britain and Ireland". *See* NOTARIKON.

Hempen caudle, collar, etc. A hangman's rope.

> Ye shall have a hempen caudle then, and the help of hatchet.
> SHAKESPEARE: *Henry VI, Pt. II*, IV, vii.

Hempen fever. Death on the gallows, the rope being of hemp.

Hempen widow. The widow of a man that has been hanged.

Hen. A grey hen. A stone bottle for holding liquor. Large and small pewter pots mixed together are called "hens and chickens".

> A dirty leather wallet lay near the sleeper ... also a grey-hen which had contained some sort of strong liquor.
> EMMA ROBINSON: *Whitefriars*, ch. viii.

A hen on a hot griddle. A Scottish phrase descriptive of a restless person.

A whistling maid and a crowing hen is fit for neither God nor men. A whistling maid is a WITCH, who whistles to call up the winds and was supposed to be in league with the DEVIL. The crowning of a hen was supposed to forbode a death. The usual interpretation is that masculine qualities in women are undesirable.

As fussy as a hen with one chick. Over-anxious about small matters; over-particular and fussy. A hen with one chick is for ever clucking it and never leaves it alone.

Hen and chickens. In Christian art this device is emblematical of God's providence. *See also* GREY HEN, *above*.

Hen-pecked. A man who submits to the lectures and nagging of his wife and is domineered by her. *See* CAUDLE LECTURE.

Tappit-hen. *See* TAPPIT.

Hengist and Horsa. The semi-legendary leaders who led the first Saxon war-band to settle in England. They are said to have arrived in KENT in 449 at the invitation of Vortigern, who offered them land on the understanding that they would help against the PICTS. Horsa is said to have been slain at the battle of Aylesford (*c.* 455), and Hengist to have ruled in Kent till his death in 488. The name Horsa is connected with our word *horse* and Hengist is the Ger. *hengst*, a stallion. The traditional badge of Kent is a white horse.

Henry Grâce à Dieu. *See* GREAT HARRY.

Henry the Navigator (1394–1460). The fourth son of King John I of Portugal. In 1415 he took part in the capture of Ceuta from the Moors and then settled at Sagres, Cape St. Vincent, where he built an observatory and training school for navigation. As a result the Madeiras were discovered in 1418 and systematic exploration of the Guinea coast began in 1430. Cape Verde was rounded in 1446 and the Azores reached in 1448, by which time Prince Henry had aroused a national interest in further exploration.

Hep, or **Hip.** American slang meaning "alive to, aware of, wise to". It is probably from the West African Wolof word *hipi*, meaning "to open one's eyes". *See* HIPPIE.

Hep-cat. One who is fond of and moved by fast and noisy music. The American use of *cat* here denotes "person". In Wolof, *hipi-kat* denotes "one who has opened his eyes".

Hepatoscopy. A very ancient form of DIVINATION based upon inspection of the liver from the animal sacrificed (Gr. *hepar, hepatos*, liver). It rested on the belief that the liver was the seat of vitality and of the soul.

> For the king of Babylon stood at the parting of the way ... to use divination: he made his arrows bright, he consulted with images, he looked in the liver.
> *Ezek.* xxi, 21.

Hephæstus (hē fes' tus). The Greek VULCAN.

Heptameron, The. A collection of Italian and other mediæval stories written by, or ascribed to, Marguerite of Angoulême, Queen of Navarre (1492–1549), and published posthumously in 1558. They were supposed to have been related in seven days (Gr. *hepta*, seven; *hemera*, day). *Cp.* DECAMERON, HEXAMERON.

Heptarchy (Gr., seven governments). The term is used of the seven English kingdoms of Kent, Sussex, Wessex, Essex, East Anglia, Mercia, and Northumbria during the period of their co-existence, *i.e.* from the 6th to the 8th centuries. This is the period when overlordship was exercised by a BRETWALDA.

Heptateuch. (Gr. *hepta*, seven; *teuchos*, a tool, book). A name given to the first seven books of the BIBLE, the PENTATEUCH plus *Joshua* and *Judges*.

Hera (hē' rà) (Gr. *haireo*, chosen one). The Greek JUNO, the wife of ZEUS.

Herald (O.Fr. *heralt, heraut*). The herald was an officer whose duty it was to proclaim war or peace, carry challenges to battle, and messages between sovereigns, etc. Heralds had their attendants called PURSUIVANTS. Nowadays war or peace is still proclaimed by the heralds, but their chief duty as court functionaries is to superintend state ceremonies such as coronations, installations, etc., and also to grant arms, trace genealogies, attend to matters of precedence, honours, etc.

Edward III appointed two heraldic kings-at-arms for south and north—Surroy and Norroy. The English College of Heralds was incorporated by Richard II in 1483–1484. It consists of three Kings of Arms, six heralds and four Pursuivants, under the EARL MARSHAL, an hereditary office in the line of the Dukes of Norfolk.

The three Kings of Arms are Garter (blue), CLARENCEUX, and Norroy and Ulster (purple).

The six heralds are styled Somerset, Richmond, Lancaster, Windsor, Chester, and York.

The four Pursuivants are Rouge Dragon, Blue Mantle, Portcullis, and Rouge Croix.

Garter King of Arms is so called from his special duty to attend at the solemnities of election, investiture, and installation of Knights of the GARTER; he is Principal King of Arms for all England.

CLARENCEUX *King of Arms*. So called from the Duke of Clarence, brother of Edward IV. His jurisdiction extends over England south of the Trent.

Norroy and Ulster King of Arms has jurisdiction over England on the north side of the Trent and over Northern Ireland.

The "Bath King of Arms" is not a member of the Herald's College, and is concerned only with the Order of the BATH.

In Scotland heraldry is the function of the Lyon office and it consists of the *Lord Lyon King of Arms*, three Heralds (*Albany, Marchmont,* and *Rothesay*), three ordinary

Pursuivants (*Unicorn, Carrick, Dingwell* or *Kintyre*) and two Pursuivants Extraordinary (*Linlithgow* and *Falkland*).

Heraldry. Originally a term applied to the science and functions of a HERALD but now more usually restricted to the knowledge or science of armorial bearings, formerly known as ARMORY.

A COAT OF ARMS consists of the *shield*, the HELMET, *crest, mantling* and *supporters*. The motto is not strictly part of the coat of arms or *armorial achievement*.

The *shield* is the main part of the *achievement* and the colours used upon it are *azure* (blue); *gules* (red); *purpure* (purple); *sable* (black); *vert* (green). *Argent* (silver) and *or* (gold) are known as *metals* and the other tinctures are called *furs* (*ermine, ermines, erminois, pean, potent,* and *vair*). The items put on the ground of the shield are called *charges* (*e.g. bends, chevrons, piles, fesses, bars, crosses,* animals, birds, reptiles, and inanimate objects, etc.).

Differencing is the alteration of a coat to distinguish between the various members and branches of a family.

Marshalling is the science of bringing together the arms of several families in one escutcheon.

In heraldry, punning on names and words is called *canting*.

The following are some of the principal terms used in heraldry:

Bars, horizontal bands (more than one) across the middle of the shield.

Bend, a diagonal stripe.

Bordure, an edge of a different colour round the whole shield.

Chevron, a bent stripe, as worn by non-commissioned officers in the army, but the point upwards.

Chief, the upper one-third of the shield divided horizontally.

Cinquefoil, a five-petalled formalized flower.

Couchant, lying down.

Counter-passant, moving in opposite directions.

Couped, cut straight at the stem or neck.

Coward, coué, with tail hanging between the legs.

Displayed (of birds), with wings and talons outspread.

Dormant, sleeping.

Endorse, a very narrow vertical stripe; *see* PALE.

Erased, with nothing below the stem or neck, which ends roughly as opposed to the sharp edge of *couped*.

Fesse, a broad horizontal stripe across the middle of the shield.

File, a horizontal bar from which normally depend one or more smaller bars called *labels*.

Gardant, full-faced.

Hauriant, standing on its tail (of fishes).

Issuant, rising from the stop or bottom of an *ordinary*.

Lodged, reposing (of stags, etc.).

Martlet, a swallow with no feet.

Mullet, a star of a stated number of points.

Naiant, swimming (of fishes).

Nascent, rising out of the middle of an ORDINARY.

Ordinary. A primary charge (*e.g. bend, pale, fesse, chevron, pile, cross, lozenge, roundel,* etc.).

Pale, a wide vertical stripe down the centre of the shield.

Pallet, a narrow vertical stripe.

Passant, walking, the face in profile (emblematic of resolution).

Passant gardant, walking, with full face (emblematic of resolution and prudence).

Passant regardant, walking and looking behind.

Pile, a narrow triangle.

Rampant, rearing, with face in profile (emblematic of magnanimity).

Rampant gardant, erect on the hind legs, full face (emblematic of prudence).

Rampant regardant, erect on the hind legs, side face looking behind (emblematic of circumspection).

Regardant, looking back (emblematic of circumspection).

Salient, springing (emblematic of valour).

Sejant, seated (emblematic of counsel).

Statant, standing still.

Trippant, running (of stags, etc.).

Volant, flying.

Herb. Herb of Grace. Rue is so called probably because (owing to its extreme bitterness) it is the symbol of repentance.

> Here did she fall a tear; here in this place,
> I'll set a bank of rue, sour herb of grace;
> Rue, even for ruth, here shortly shall be seen,
> In the remembrance of a weeping queen.
> SHAKESPEARE: *Richard II*, III, iv.

Jeremy Taylor, in *A Dissuasive from Popery*, I, ii, 9 (1664), says:

> First, they are to try the devil by holy water, incense, sulphur, rue, which from thence, as we suppose, came to be called "herb of grace",— and especially St. John's wort, which therefore they call "devils' flight", with which if they cannot cast the devil out, yet they may do good to the patient.

Herba sacra. The "divine weed", vervain, said by the Romans to cure the bites of all rabid animals, to arrest the progress of venom, to cure the plague, to avert sorcery and WITCHCRAFT, to reconcile enemies, etc. So highly esteemed was it that feasts called *Verbenalia* were annually held in its honour. HERALDS wore a wreath of vervain when they declared war; and the DRUIDS are supposed to have held it in veneration.

> Lift your boughs of vervain blue.
> Dipt in cold September dew;
> And dash the moisture, chaste and clear,
> O'er the ground, and through the air.
> Now the place is purged and pure.
>
> W. MASON: *Caractacus* (1759).

Herb Trinity. A popular name for the pansy, *Viola tricolor. See* HEARTSEASE.

Hercules (hĕr′ kū lēz). In Greek mythology, a hero of superhuman physical strength, son of ZEUS and ALCMENA. He is represented as brawny, muscular, short-necked, often holding a club and a lion's skin. In a fit of madness inflicted on him by JUNO, he slew his wife and children, and as penance was ordered by APOLLO to serve for 12 years the Argive king, Eurystheus, who imposed upon him twelve tasks of great difficulty and danger:

(1) To slay the NEMEAN LION.
(2) To kill the Lernean HYDRA.
(3) To catch and retain the Arcadian stag.
(4) To destroy the Erymanthian boar.
(5) To cleanse the AUGEAN STABLES.
(6) To destroy the cannibal birds of the Lake Stymphalis.
(7) To take captive the Cretan bull.
(8) To catch the horses of the Thracian Diomedes.
(9) To get possession of the girdle of HIPPOLYTA, Queen of the Amazons.
(10) To capture the oxen of the monster GERYON.
(11) To obtain the apples of the HESPERIDES.
(12) To bring CERBERUS from the infernal regions.

After these labours and many other adventures he was rewarded with immortality.
The Attic Hercules. THESEUS, who went about like Hercules, destroying robbers and achieving wondrous exploits.
The Farnese Hercules. *See under* FARNESE.
Hercules and his load. The sign of the Globe Theatre showing Hercules carrying the globe upon his shoulders. SHAKESPEARE alludes to it in *Hamlet*, II, ii:

> *Ham.:* Do the boys carry it away?
> *Ros.:* Ay, that they do, my lord; Hercules and his load too.

Hercules' choice. Immortality, the reward of toil in preference to pleasure. Xenophon tells us that when Hercules was a youth he was accosted by Virtue and Pleasure, and asked to choose between them. Pleasure promised him all carnal delights, but Virtue promised immortality. Hercules gave his hand to the latter, and, after a life of toil, was received amongst the gods.
Hercules' horse. *See* FAMOUS HORSES *under* HORSE.
Hercules' Pillars. *See under* PILLAR.
Hercules Secundus. Commodus, the Roman Emperor (A.D. 161, 180–192), gave himself this title. Dissipated and inordinately cruel, he claimed divine honours and caused himself to be worshipped as Hercules. It is said that he killed 100 lions in the amphitheatre, and that he slew over 1,000 defenceless gladiators.
Herculean knot (hĕr kū lē′ ăn). A snaky complication on the rod or CADUCEUS of MERCURY, adopted by Grecian brides as the fastening of their woollen girdles, which only the bridegroom was allowed to untie. As he did so he invoked JUNO to render his marriage as those of Hercules, whose numerous wives all had families, among them being the 50 daughters of Thestius, all of whom conceived in one night. *See* TRUE LOVER'S KNOT *under* KNOT.
Ex pede Herculem. *See under* EX.
Herefordshire kindness. A good turn rendered for a good turn received. Thomas Fuller says the people of Herefordshire "drink back to him who drinks to them".
Heretic. From a Greek word meaning "one who chooses". A heretic is one who holds unorthodox opinions in matters of religion, *i.e.* he chooses his own creed.

The principal heretical sects of the first six centuries were:

FIRST CENTURY: The *Simonians* (from Simon Magus), *Cerinthians* (Cerinthus), EBIONITES (Ebion), and *Nicolaitans* (Nicholas, deacon of Antioch).

SECOND CENTURY: The *Basilidians* (Basilides), *Carpocratians* (Carpocrates), *Valentinians* (Valentinus), GNOSTICS (Knowing Ones), NAZARENES, MILLENARIANS, CAINITES (Cain), *Sethians* (Seth), *Quartodecimans* (who kept EASTER on the 14th day of *Nisan*, our April), *Cerdonians* (Cerdon), MARCIONITES (Marcion), MONTANISTS (Montanus), *Alogians* (who denied the "Word"), *Angelics* (who worshipped angels), *Tatianists* (Tatian), QUINTILIANS.

THIRD CENTURY: The *Patri-passians, Arabici, Aquarians,* NOVATIANS, *Origenists* (followers of Origen), *Melchisedechians* (who believed Melchisedec was the Messiah), SABELLIANS (from Sabellius), and

MANICHEANS (followers of Mani).

FOURTH CENTURY: The ARIANS (from Arius), *Colluthians* (Colluthus), MACEDONIANS, AGNOETÆ (they denied that God knew the past and the future), APOLLINARIANS (Apollinaris), *Collyridians* (who offered cakes to the Virgin Mary), *Seleucians* (Seleucus), *Priscillians* (Priscillian), *Anthropomorphites* (who ascribed to God a human form), *Jovinianists* (Jovinian), *Messalians*, and *Bonosians* (Bonosus).

FIFTH CENTURY: The PELAGIANS (Pelagius), NESTORIANS (Nestorius), EUTYCHIANS (Eutychus), MONOPHYSITES (who held that Christ had but a single, and that a Divine, nature), *Predestinarians, Timotheans* (Timothy, Monophysite Patriarch of Alexandria).

SIXTH CENTURY: *Theopaschites* (Monophysites who held that God was crucified in Christ's Passion), the new *Agnoetæ* (Monophysite followers of Themistus). *See also* ALBIGENSES; BOGOMILS; WALDENSIANS.

Heriot. A feudal kind of death duty. The lord of the manor's right to the best beast or chattel of a deceased VILLEIN. Freemen also owed heriots to their overlords of horses and armour. The word is from the O.E. *here geatu*, military apparel, which was originally on loan to the tenant.

Hermæ. *See* HERMES.

Hermaphrodite (hĕr măf′ rō dīt). A person or animal with indeterminate sexual organs, or those of both sexes; a flower containing both male and female reproductive organs. The word is derived from Hermaphroditus, son of HERMES and APHRODITE. The nymph Salmacis became enamoured of him, and prayed that she might be so closely united that "the twain might become one flesh". Her prayer being heard, the NYMPH and boy became one body (Ovid: *Metamorphoses*, IV, 347–88).

According to fable, all persons who bathed in the fountain Salmacis, in Caria, became hermaphrodites.

Hermas. One of the APOSTOLIC FATHERS (2nd century), author of *The Shepherd* which consists of Visions, Commandments, and Similitudes or Parables.

Hermes. The Greek MERCURY, whose busts, known as *Hermæ*, were affixed to pillars and set up as boundary marks at street corners, etc. The Romans also used them for garden ornaments.

Among alchemists, Hermes was the usual name for quicksilver or mercury (*see* Milton: *Paradise Lost*, III, 603).

Hermetic Art, or **Philosophy.** The art or science of ALCHEMY; so called from Hermes Trismegistus (the Thrice Greatest Hermes) the name given by the Neoplatonists to the Egyptian god THOTH, its hypothetical founder.

Hermetic books. Forty-two books fabled to have been written from the dictation of Hermes Trismegistus, dealing with the life and thought of ancient Egypt. They state that the world was made out of fluid; that the SOUL is the union of light and life; that nothing is destructible; that the soul transmigrates, and that suffering is the result of motion.

Hermetic powder. A sympathetic powder, supposed to possess a healing influence from a distance; so called by mediæval philosophers out of compliment to Hermes Trismegistus (Sir Kenelm Digby: *Discourse Touching the Cure of Wounds by the Powder of Sympathy*, 1658).

> For by his side a pouch he wore
> Replete with strange hermetic powder,
> That wounds nine miles point-black would solder.
> BUTLER: *Hudibras*, I, ii.

Hermetically sealed. Closed securely; from sealing a vessel hermetically, *i.e.* as a chemist, a disciple of Hermes Trismegistus, would, by heating the neck of the vessel till it is soft, and then twisting it till the aperture is closed up.

Hermit. The Hermit of Grub Street. Henry Welby of Lincolnshire who became a recluse in GRUB STREET at the age of 40, having resolved to live alone after suffering a pistol attack from his younger brother. He was never seen outside his house and died in 1636 at the age of 84. He lived abstemiously and was attended by an elderly servant maid, spending his means on the sick and the poor. He had been a student at St. John's College, Cambridge and seems to have spent his time reading.

The Hermit of Warkworth. The subject of a poem of this name by Bishop Percy, one-time chaplain to the Duke of Northumberland. His ballad, which appeared in 1771, gives a realistic picture of the early hermitage on the north bank of the river Cocquet about a quarter of a mile upstream of Warkworth Castle. It is hollowed out of the freestone cliff on the river bank and has an arched chapel with an altar and two other cells as well as steps cut in the rock leading to the hermit's small garden. The chapel is still used for occasional services. *See* PERCY'S RELIQUES.

> Then, scooped within the solid rock,
> Three sacred vaults he shows;
> The chief, a chapel, neatly arch'd,
> On branching columns rose.

Peter the Hermit. *See under* PETER.

Hermit's Derby. One of the famous RACES in the history of the TURF, when Hermit, belonging to Henry Chaplin (1840–1923), later Viscount Chaplin, won the DERBY STAKES of 1867 against all expectations, and the notorious Marquess of Hastings lost £120,000 in bets.

Herne the Hunter. *See* WILD HUNTSMAN.

Hero. No man is a hero to his valet. An old saying. The idea is found in Plutarch and Montaigne (*Essays*, Bk. III, ii), but Bacon in his essay *Of Honour and Reputation* says, "Discreet followers and servants help much to reputation: '*Omnis fama a domesticis emanat*'." (All fame comes from one's own household.) *Cp. Matt.* xiii, 57, "A prophet is not without honour save in … his own house."

Hero and Leander. The old Greek tale is that Hero, a priestess of VENUS, fell in love with Leander, who swam across the HELLE-SPONT every night to visit her. One night he was drowned, and heart-broken Hero drowned herself in the same sea. The story is told in one of the poems of Musæus, and in Marlowe and Chapman's *Hero and Leander*.

Lord Byron and Lieutenant Ekenhead repeated the experiment of Leander in 1810 and accomplished it in 1 hour 10 minutes. The distance, allowing for drifting, would be about four miles. In *Don Juan* (Canto II, cv), BYRON says of his hero:

A better swimmer you could scarce see ever,
He could, perhaps, have pass'd the Hellespont,
As once (a feat on which ourselves we prided)
Leander, Mr. Ekenhead, and I did.

Heroic age. That age of a nation which comes between the purely mythical period and the historic. This is the age when the sons of the gods were said to take unto themselves the daughters of men, and the offspring partake of the twofold character.

Heroic size in sculpture denotes a stature superior to ordinary life, but not colossal.

Heroic verse. That verse in which epic poetry is generally written. In Greek and Latin it is HEXAMETER verse; in English it is ten-syllable IAMBIC verse, either in rhymes or not; in Italian it is the ottava rima. So called because it is employed to celebrate heroic exploits.

Herod. To out-herod Herod. To outdo in wickedness, violence, or rant, the worst of tyrants. Herod, who destroyed the babes of Bethlehem (*Matt.* ii., 16), was made (in the old mediæval MYSTERIES) a ranting, roaring tyrant.

Herrenvolk. A German word meaning broadly "master race". In NAZI usage it implied the superiority of the German peoples.

Herring. A shotten herring. One that has shot off or ejected its spawn, and hence is worthless.

Go thy ways, old jack; die when thou wilt. If manhood, good manhood, be not forget upon the face of the earth, then am I a shotten herring. There live not three good men unhanged in England, and one of them is fat and grows old.
SHAKESPEARE: *Henry IV, Pt. I*, II, iv.

Drawing a red herring across the path. Trying to divert attention from the main question by some side issue. A red herring (*i.e.* one dried, smoked, and salted) drawn across a fox's path destroys the scent and sets the hounds at fault.

Neither barrel the better herring. Much of a muchness; not a pin to choose between them; SIX OF ONE AND HALF A DOZEN OF THE OTHER. The herrings of both barrels are so much alike that there is no choice whatever.

Neither fish, flesh, nor good red herring. *See under* FISH.

The Battle of the Herrings (12 February 1429). During the HUNDRED YEARS WAR Sir John Fastolf was conveying provisions to the English besiegers of Orleans and was unsuccessfully attacked by superior French forces seeking to intercept the supplies. The English used the barrels of herrings with which their wagons were loaded, as a defence; hence the name.

The King of the Herrings. The *Chimæra*, or sea-ape, a cartilaginous fish which accompanies a shoal of herrings in their migrations.

Herring-bone (in building). Courses of stone or brick laid angularly, thus: ❮ ❮ ❮ ❮. Also applied to strutting placed between thin joists to increase their strength.

In needlework, an embroidery stitch, or alternatively a kind of cross-stich used to fasten down heavy material.

The Herring-pond. The ocean or dividing seas, especially the Atlantic which separates America from the British Isles. Also called the "fishpond".

I'le send an account of the wonders I meet on the Great Herring Pond.
JOHN DUNTON: *Letters from New England*, 1686.

Herriot, James. The pen name of James Alfred Wright (1916–) who was born, and trained as a veterinary surgeon, at Glasgow and began practising in North Yorkshire in 1940. The first of his many entertaining stories, based on his professional experiences in the Yorkshire Dales, appeared in 1970.

'Now then, young man,' he cried in the nasal twang of the West Riding, 'I'm Mr Dinsdale's brother. I farm over in Listondale'.

I put down my equipment and nodded. 'How do you do? My name is Herriot'.

JAMES HERRIOT: *If Only They Could Talk*, ch. i.

Hershey Bar. In the U.S.A. a Hershey Bar is a famous trade-marked chocolate bar which was only available to the troops in World War II. General L.B. Hershey was Director of the Selective Service System, 1941–1946. Hence in U.S. army slang the term was applied to the narrow gold bar worn by troops on the left sleeve to indicate that they had done six months' overseas service.

Hertha. *See* NERTHUS.

Hesperia (hes pēr' i à) (Gr. western). Italy was so called by the Greeks, because it was to them the "Western Land"; and afterwards the Romans, for a similar reason, transferred the name to Spain.

Hesperides (hes per' i dēz). Three sisters who guarded the golden apples which HERA received as a marriage gift. They were assisted by the dragon LADON. HERCULES, as the eleventh of his "twelve labours", slew the DRAGON and carried some of the apples to Eurystheus.

Many poets call the place where these golden apples grew the "Garden of the Hesperides". SHAKESPEARE (*Love's Labour's Lost*, IV, iii) speaks of "climbing trees in the Hesperides". (*Cp.* Milton's *Comus*, lines 393–7.)

Hesperus (hes' per ùs). The name given by the Greeks to the planet VENUS as an evening star. As a morning star it was called LUCIFER or *Phosphorus*. *See* HESPERIA.

Ere twice in murk and occidental damp
Moist Hesperus hath quenched his sleepy lamp.

SHAKESPEARE: *All's Well that Ends Well*, II, i.

The Wreck of the Hesperus. An episode made famous by Longfellow's ballad of 1840, formerly widely learnt by schoolchildren. The *Hesperus* was wrecked on Norman's Woe, near Gloucester, Massachusetts, in 1839.

It was the schooner Hesperus,
That sailed the wintry sea;
And the skipper had taken his little daughter,
To bear him company.

Hessian. A coarse, strong cloth made from jute or hemp, originally made in Hesse in Germany.

Hessian boots were first worn by troops in Germany and became fashionable in England in the 19th century.

While a lover's professions,
When uttered in Hessian,
Are eloquent ev'rywhere.

W.S. GILBERT: *Patience*.

Hesychasts. In the Eastern Church, supporters of the ascetic mysticism propagated by the monks of Mount Athos in the 14th century. Also called *Palamists* after Gregory Palamas (*c.* 1296–1350), who became the chief exponent of Hesychasm. The object of their exercises was to attain a vision of the "Divine Light" which they held to be God's "energy". Hesychasm lasted until the 17th century; the name is from the Gr. *hesychos*, quiet.

Hexameron (Gr). A period of six days, especially the six days of the Creation.

Hexameter. The metre in which Greek and Latin epics were written, and which has been imitated in English in such poems as Longfellow's *Evangeline*, Clough's *Bothie*, Kingsley's *Andromeda* (probably the best), etc.

The line consists of six feet, dactyls or spondees for the first four, the fifth is almost always a dactyl (but sometimes a spondee), and the sixth a spondee or trochee.

Verse consisting of alternate hexameters and pentameters is known as ELEGIAC. Coleridge illustrates this in his:

In the hexameter rises the fountain's silvery column;
In the pentameter aye falling in melody back.

The Ovidian Elegiac Metre.

Hexateuch. *See* ELOHISTIC; *cp.* HEPTATEUCH, PENTATEUCH.

Hiawatha. The Iroquois name of a hero of miraculous birth who came (under a variety of names) among the North American Indian tribes to bring peace and goodwill to man.

In Longfellow's poem (1855) he is an Ojibway, son of Mudjekeewis (the west wind) and Wenonah, and married Minnehaha, "Laughing Water". He represents the progress of civilization among his people. When the white man landed and taught the Indians the faith of Jesus, Hiawatha exhorted them to receive the words of wisdom, to reverence the missionaries who had come so far to see them.

Hibernia. The Latin name for IRELAND, a variant of the old CELTIC *Erin*, common in poetic usage.

Hic Jacets. Tombstones, so called from the first two words of the Latin inscription: *Hic Jacet* (Here lies ...)

And by the cold Hic Jacets of the dead.

TENNYSON: *Idylls of the King (Merlin and Vivien)*.

Hickathrift, Tom. A hero of nursery rhyme and mythical strong man, fabled to have been a labourer at the time of the CONQUEST. Armed with an axle-tree and cartwheel he killed a GIANT who dwelt in a marsh at Tilney, Norfolk. He was knighted and made a governor of Thanet. *Cp.* JACK THE GIANT-KILLER.

Hickory. Hickory cloth. Cloth dyed with hickory juice.

Hickory Mormons. MORMONS of half-hearted persuasions

Old Hickory. General Andrew Jackson (1767–1845), President of the United States (1829–1837). He was first called "Tough", from his great powers of endurance, then "Tough as hickory", and lastly, "Old Hickory". *Cp.* STONEWALL JACKSON.

Hicksites. QUAKERS in the U.S.A. who seceded from the main body in 1827 under the leadership of Elias Hicks.

Hide of land. In feudal England the term denoted the amount of land that was sufficient to support a family; usually varying between 60 and 120 acres according to the locality or quality of the land. A hide of good land was smaller than one of poorer quality. It was long used as the basis for assessing taxes. The name may derive from the possibility that the original tribute was payable in hides.

To hide one's light under a bushel. *See* BUSHEL.

Hieroglyphs (hī′ ér ō glifs). The name applied to the picture characters of ancient Egyptian writing (Gr. *hieros*, sacred; *glyph*, what is carved). For many years these inscribed symbols of beasts and birds, men and women, etc. were indecipherable. Dr. Thomas Young (1773–1829) was the first to decipher part of the demotic text of the RO-SETTA STONE in 1819, and prove the alphabetic nature of the signs. This provided a basis for the construction of a complete alphabet (1821–1822) by J.F. Champollion (1790–1832). Since then, our knowledge of ancient Egypt and its customs has been transformed.

High. An all-time high. A record achievement, an expression of American origin.

High and dry. Stranded, left out of the current of events. A nautical metaphor.

High and low. People of all estates and conditions.

High and mighty. Powerful, or more usually, arrogant and overbearing.

High days and holidays. Special occasions, a high day being a festival or great occasion. *See* HOLIDAY.

High falutin'. Oratorical bombast, affected pomposity.

To be on one's high horse. *See under* HORSE.

With a high hand. Arrogantly.

High Church. That section of the CHURCH OF ENGLAND distinguished by its "high" conception of Church authority, upholding sacerdotal claims and asserting the efficacy of the SACRAMENTS. It also stresses the historical links with CATHOLIC Christianity. It has its origins in the reign of Elizabeth I, although the name is of the late 17th century. Archbishop Laud was of this persuasion and High Church opinions were again strengthened and re-established by the OXFORD MOVEMENT. *Cp.* LOW CHURCH *under* LOW.

High German. Official and literary German, derived from the language of *High* or South Germany. Low German is the name applied to all other German dialects, or the language of *Low* or North Germany. *Cp.* LANGUE D'OC; LANGUE D'OÏL.

High Heels and Low Heels. The names of two factions in Swift's tale of Lilliput (*Gulliver's Travels*), satirizing the HIGH and LOW CHURCH parties.

High places. In the Authorized Version of the BIBLE this is a literal translation of the Heb. *bamah* and applied to the local places of sacrifice where JEHOVAH was worshipped. Such sites were often on a hilltop or mound, which may account for the origin of the name. Because of their association with forms of idolatry, and sometimes immoral rites, they were denounced by Hosea. Hezekiah removed the high places. (II *Kings* xviii, 4), so did Asa (II *Chron.* xiv, 3) and others. *Cp.* HILLS.

High seas. As defined in international law, all the area of sea not under the sovereignty of any state. *Cp.* TERRITORIAL WATERS.

High table. In a college dining-hall, the table at which the dons sit.

High tea. A meal of a substantial character about the usual tea-time which can include fish, meats, pastry, etc. It is common in Scotland and the North of England and in agricultural areas.

High words. Angry words.

High-ball, the American term for whisky, diluted with water, soda-water or ginger ale and served in a tall glass with ice.

High-brow. A learned person, an intellectual. The term originated in the U.S.A. about 1911 and is also used to denote cultural, artistic, and intellectual matters above one's head. Derivatives are *low-brow* and *middle-brow*.

Highbinders. The name given to those rowdies, ruffians, and members of malevolent gangs who troubled New York and other American cities from the early 19th century.

Higher Criticism. Critical inquiry into the literary composition and sources, especially of the BIBLE, also called *historical criticism*.

The term is used in contradistinction to textual or verbal criticism which is to establish the correctness of the text.

Highgate. Sworn at Highgate. In public houses at Highgate it was once customary to administer an oath to travellers who called. They were sworn on a pair of horns fastened to a stick—(1) Never to kiss a maid when the mistress could be kissed. (2) Never to eat brown bread when white could be got. (3) Never to drink small beer when strong could be got (unless preferred). *See* SWEARING ON THE HORNS *under* HORN.

> And many to the steep of Highgate hie,
> Ask ye Bœotian shades! the reason why,
> 'Tis to the worship of the solemn horn,
> Grasp'd in the holy hand of mystery,
> In whose dread name both men and maids are sworn,
> And consecrate the oath with draught and dance till morn.
>
> BYRON: *Childe Harold*, canto I, lxx.

Highlands, The. That part of SCOTLAND lying north of the line approximately Dumbarton to Stonehaven. Stirling is known as the "gateway to the Highlands"; in the wars between ENGLAND and Scotland, possession of this strong point gave great advantage.

Highland bail. Fists and cuffs; to escape the constable by knocking him down with the aid of a companion.

Highland Mary. The most shadowy of Robert Burns's sweethearts, but the one to whom he addressed some of his finest poetry, including "The Highland Lassie, O", "Highland Mary", "'To Mary in Heaven", and perhaps "Will ye go to the Indies, my Mary?"

She is said to have been a daughter of Archibald Campbell, a Clyde sailor, and to have died young about 1784 or 1786.

Highness. Royal Highness. In Great Britain this title is now confined (since 1917) to the sovereign and his or her Consort, to the children of the sovereign, to grandchildren in the male line, and the eldest son of the eldest son of the PRINCE OF WALES. It was formerly granted to a somewhat wider group of relations.

Hijacker (hī' jăk ẻr). A term of American origin denoting a bandit who preys on BOOTLEGGERS, and other criminals; now applied more generally to one who steals goods in transit, particularly lorries loaded with valuable merchandise. The name may derive from the gunman's command to his victim, "Stick 'em up high, Jack," meaning that the arms were to be raised well above the head. *Cp.* SKYJACKER.

Hilary Term. The former legal term, and the university term at Oxford and Trinity College Dublin corresponding to the LENT term elsewhere. It is named in honour of St. Hilary whose day is 13 January (14 January in the R.C. Church), near which day these terms begin.

The Hilary Law Sittings usually begin on 11 January, and end on the Wednesday before EASTER.

Hildebrand (hil' de brand). A celebrated character of German romance whose story is told in *Das Hildebrandslied*, an old German alliterative poem (written *c.* 800), and he also appears in the NIBELUNGENLIED, DIETRICH VON BERN, etc. He is an old man, who returns home after many years among the Huns through following his master Theodoric, only to be challenged to single combat by his own son Hadubrand.

The name is better known as that of the great reforming pope St. Gregory VII (*c.* 1020, 1073–1085) whose attempts to prohibit lay investiture brought Henry IV to CANOSSA and made him many enemies. He did much to remove abuses and to regenerate the Church.

Hildesheim (hil' des hīm). Legend relates that a monk of Hildesheim, an old city of Hanover, doubting how with God a thousand years could be as one day, listened to the singing of a bird in a wood, as he thought for three minutes, but found the time had been three hundred years. Longfellow makes use of the story in his *Golden Legend* (II), calling the monk Felix.

Hill. Hill-billy. An American rustic or countryman of the hilly regions; also applied to the characteristic traditional songs of the hill regions of the southeastern parts of the U.S.A.

Hill folk. So Scott calls the CAMERONIAN Scottish COVENANTERS, who met clandestinely among the hills. Sometimes the Covenanters generally are so called.

In Scandinavian tradition they are a type of being between elves and human beings. The "hill people" were supposed to dwell in caves and small hills.

Hills. Prayers were offered on the tops of high hills, and temples built on "HIGH PLACES", from the notion that the gods could better hear prayer on such places, as they were nearer HEAVEN. It will be remembered that Balak (*Num.* xxiii, xxiv) took BALAAM to the top of Peor and other high places when Balaam wished to consult God. We often read of "idols on every high hill' (*Ezek.* vi, 13).

Old as the hills. Very old indeed.

Hinc illæ lachrimæ (hink il ē lăk' ri mē) (Lat., "hence those tears", Terence: *An-*

dria, I, i, 99). This was the real offence; this was the true secret of the annoyance; the real source of the vexation.

> *Lady Loadstone:* He keeps off all her suitors, keeps the portion
> Still in his hands; and will not part withal,
> On any terms.
> *Palate: Hinc illæ lachrymæ,*
> *Thence flows the cause of the main grievance.*
> BEN JONSON: *Magnetic Lady*, I, i.

Hind. Emblematic of St. Giles. *See under* GILES. *Cp.* HART.

The Hind of Sertorius. Sertorius (*c.* 122–72 B.C.), Marian governor of Hispania Citerior was proscribed by Sulla and forced to flee. Later he was invited to return by the Lusitani and held Spain against the Senatorial party until his death through treachery. He had a tame white hind, which he taught to follow him, and from which he pretended to receive the instructions of DIANA. By this artifice, says Plutarch, he imposed on the superstition of the people.

The milk-white hind, in Dryden's *Hind and the Panther*, means the ROMAN CATHOLIC CHURCH, milk-white because "infallible". The panther, full of the spots of error, is the CHURCH OF ENGLAND.

> Without unspotted, innocent within,
> She fear'd no danger, for she knew no sin.
> Part I, 3, 4.

Hindustan. Hindustan Regiment. *See* REGIMENTAL AND DIVISIONAL NICKNAMES.

Hinny. *See* MULE.

Hip. *See* HEP.

Hip. To have one on the hip. To have the mastery over him in a struggle, a term derived from a throw in wrestling.

> Now, infidel, I have thee on the hip.
> SHAKESPEARE: *Merchant of Venice*, IV, i.

To smite hip and thigh. To slay with great carnage. A Biblical phrase.

> An he smote them hip and thigh with a great slaughter.
> *Judges* xv, 8.

Hip! Hip! Hurrah! The old fanciful explanation of the origin of this cry is that hip is a NOTARIKON, composed of the initials *Hierosolyma est perdita*, and that when German knights headed a Jew-hunt in the MIDDLE AGES, they ran shouting "Hip! Hip!" as much as to say "Jerusalem is destroyed."

Hurrah was similarly derived from Slavonic *hu-raj* (to Paradise), so that Hip! Hip! Hurrah! would mean "Jerusalem is lost to the infidel, and we are on the road to Paradise."

Hipped. Melancholy, low-spirited, suffering from a "fit of the blues". *The hip* was formerly a common expression for morbid depression (now superseded by *the*

pip); it is an abbreviation of *hypochondria*.

Hipper-switches. A dialect name for coarse willow withies. A *hipper* is a coarse osier used in basket-making, and an osier field is a *hipperholm*. A suburb of Halifax, Yorks., is called Hipperholme-cum-Brighouse.

Hippie. A name derived from HEP. Hippies originated in San Francisco in the late 1960s among young people who were anarchists but with regard for the environment. The movement spread to Britain where they have adopted fantastic styles of dress, travel around in ramshackle vehicles, and are often given to drink and drugs. They live largely by begging, scrounging, and the help of the Department of Social Security, and are particularly known for their attempts to occupy STONEHENGE at the time of the Summer Solstice (21 June), where they have become a public nuisance. *See* BEATNIK; DROP-OUTS; HELL'S ANGELS, etc.

Hippocampus (hip' ō kăm' pŭs) (Gr. *hippos*, horse; *kampos*, sea monster). A sea-horse, having the head and forequarters resembling those of a horse, with the tail and hindquarters of a fish or dolphin. It was the steed of NEPTUNE.

Hippocras (hip' ō krăs). A cordial of the late MIDDLE AGES and down to Stuart times, made of Lisbon and Canary wines, bruised spices, and sugar; so called from being passed through HIPPOCRATES' SLEEVE.

> When these [*i.e.* other wines] have had their course which nature yeeldeth, sundrie sorts of artificial stuffe as ypocras and wormewood wine, must in like maner succeed in their turnes.
> HARRISON: *Description of England*, II, vi (1577).

Hippocrates (hip ok' rà tēz). A Greek physician (*c.* 460–*c.* 375 B.C.), known as the FATHER of Medicine. He was a member of the famous family of priest-physicians, the Asclepidae, and was an acute and indefatigable observer, practising as both physician and surgeon. More than seventy treatises known as the *Hippocratic Collection* are extant, but their authorship is uncertain. In the MIDDLE AGES he was called "Ypocras" or "Hippocras". Thus:

> Well knew he th'olde Esculapius,
> And Deiscorides, and eek Rufus,
> Old Ypocras, Haly, and Galien.
> CHAUCER: *Canterbury Tales* (*Prologue*, 431).

Hippocratean School. The "Dogmatic" school of medicine, founded by HIPPOCRATES. *See* EMPIRICS.

Hippocrates' sleeve. A woollen bag of a square piece of flannel, having the opposite corners joined, so as to make it triangular. Used by apothecaries for straining syrups, decoctions, etc., and anciently by vintners, whence the name of HIPPOCRAS.

Hippocratic Oath. An outstanding code of medical ethics contained in the *Hippocratic Collection* (*see* HIPPOCRATES). The oath related particularly to the inviolability of secrecy concerning any communication made by a patient during consultation, and demanded absolute integrity concerning the patient's welfare. It also enjoined members of the profession not to aid a woman to procure an abortion.

Hippocrene (hip' ō krēn) (Gr. *hippos*, horse; *krene*, fountain). The fountain of the MUSES on Mount HELICON, produced by a stroke of the hoof of PEGASUS; hence, poetic inspiration.

> O for a beaker full of the warm South,
> Full of the true, the blushful Hippocrene.
> KEATS: *Ode to a Nightingale.*

Hippodamia. *See* BRISEIS.

Hippogriff (Gr. *hippos*, a horse; *gryphos*, a griffin). The winged horse, whose father was a GRIFFIN and mother a filly. A symbol of love (Ariosto: *Orlando Furioso*, iv, 18, 19).

> So saying, he caught him up, and without wing
> Of hippogriff, bore through the air sublime,
> Over the wilderness and o'er the plain.
> MILTON: *Paradise Regained*, IV, 541–3.

Hippolyta (hip ol'i tà). Queen of the AMAZONS, and daughter of MARS. SHAKESPEARE introduced the character in his *A Midsummer Night's Dream*, where he betroths her to THESEUS, Duke of Athens. In classic fable it is her sister Antiope who married Theseus, although some writers justify Shakespeare's account. Hippolyta was famous for a girdle given by her father, and it was one of the "twelve labours" of HERCULES to possess himself of this prize.

Hippolytus (hip ol' it ùs). Son of THESEUS, King of Athens; when he repulsed his stepmother PHÆDRA's advances she accused him of attempting her seduction. In anger his father sought NEPTUNE's aid, who sent a sea monster which so terrified Hippolytus' horses that they dragged him to death. He was restored to life by ÆSCULAPIUS.

Hippomenes (hip om' en ēz). In Bœotian legend, the Greek prince who won the race with Atalanta. *See* ATALANTA'S RACE.

Hipster. A skirt or trousers hanging from the hips instead of the waist; also one of the terms denoting young people of the BEATNIK type. *Cp.* HIPPIE.

Hiram Abif (hī ràm a bif') is a central figure in the legend and ritual of FREEMASONRY, the craftsman builder of King Solomon's TEMPLE who died rather than yield up the secrets of masonry. He appears as Huram, the alternative form of the name, in II *Chron*. ii and iv. He must not be confused with Hiram or Huram, King of Tyre, who supplied much of the material.

Hiren. A strumpet. She was a character in Greene's lost play (*c.* 1594), *The Turkish Mahomet and Hyren the Fair Greek*, and is frequently referred to by Elizabethan dramatists. *See Henry IV, PT. II*, II, iv, Dekker's *Satironmastix*, IV, iii, Massinger's *Old Law*, IV, i, Chapman's *Eastwood Hoe*, II, i, etc. The name is a corruption of the Greek "Irene".

Hiring Fair. *See under* FAIR.

Hiroshima (hi rō shē' mà). A Japanese city and military base, the target of the first atomic bomb dropped in warfare (6 August 1945). Over 160,000 people were killed or injured and far more rendered homeless. The flash of the explosion was seen 170 miles away and a column of black smoke rose over the city to a height of 40,000 feet. Hiroshima remains a solemn portent of the fate overshadowing mankind in the event of major world conflict.

Historia Augusta. *See* AUGUSTAN HISTORY.

History. The Father of History, Ecclesiastical History, English History, *see under* FATHER.

Father of French History. André Duchesne (1584–1640).

Father of Historic Painting. Polygnotus of Thaos (*c.* 500–440 B.C.).

The Muse of History. CLIO.

To make history. To take part in events and actions that will shape the future, or which will be of such significance as to become part of the historical record.

Happy is the country that has no history. *See under* HAPPY.

Historical Materialism. *See under* MATERIALISM.

Hit. A capital, or **great hit.** A great success, a piece of good luck. From the game *hit and miss* or the game of backgammon, where "two *hits* equal a gammon".

Hit hard, or **hard hit.** Hurt or distressed by adversities of fortune.

Hitting on all six. Doing well, giving a fine performance. A motor-car engine when running well is described as having the pistons in all six cylinders *hitting* perfectly (*cp.* FIRING ON ALL FOUR).

Hit or miss. *See* HOB-NOB.

To hit below the belt. To hurt another unfairly, to ignore the rules of fair play; an allusion to the boxing ring.

To hit it off. To describe a thing tersely and epigrammatically; to make a sketch truthfully and quickly.

To hit it off together. To agree or get on well with each other.

To hit the high spots. To excel or to go to excesses in "gay living". In American parlance, to do something superficially.

To hit the nail on the head. *See under* HEAD.

To make a hit. To meet with great approval, to meet with unexpected success.

Hitch. Hitch your wagon to a star. Aim high; don't be content with low aspirations. The phrase is from Emerson's essay, *Civilization* (*Society and Solitude*). Young expressed much the same idea in his *Night Thoughts* (viii).

> Too low they build who build beneath the stars.

There is some hitch. Some impediment. A horse is said to have a hitch in his gait where he is lame.

To get hitched. To get married.

To go without a hitch. Entirely sucessfully or smoothly; without any obstruction or impediment.

To hitch. To get on smoothly; to fit in consistently; also on harness: as, "You and I hitch on well together"; "These two accounts do not hitch in with each other."

To hitch-hike. To travel from place to place by getting lifts from passing vehicles.

Hitched land. Part of the common field in which common rights were withdrawn or suspended to allow the cultivation of special crops such as turnips, clover, or potatoes. In Wiltshire, such land was said to be "hooked".

Hitlerism. A generic term for the whole doctrine and practice of Fascism as exemplified by the NAZI régime of Adolf Hitler (1889–1945), who became German Chancellor in 1933 and ruled until his death. His régime was marked by tyranny, aggression, and mass persecution of Communists and Jews.

Heil Hitler (Hail Hitler). The familiar salutation to the FÜHRER, often used derisively of one adopting dictatorial methods or attempting dictatorial policies.

Hoarstone. A stone marking out the boundary of an extate, properly an old, grey, lichen-covered stone. They are also called "Hour-stones", and in Scotland, "Harestanes". They have been wrongly taken for Druidical remains.

Hob. An abbreviated form of Robin.

Hob and nob. *See* HOB-NOB.

Hob's Pound. Difficulties, great embarrassment. **To be in Hob's pound** is to be in the pound of a *hob* or *hoberd*—*i.e.* a fool or ne'er-do-well—paying for one's folly.

Hobbema (hob′ e mȧ). Meindert Hobbema (1638–1709), the Dutch landscape painter.

The English Hobbema, John Crome (1768–1821), "Old Crome", of Norwich, whose last words were, "O Hobbema, my dear Hobbema, how I have loved you!"

The Scottish Hobbema. Patrick Nasmyth (b. at Edinburgh, 1787, d. 1831), the landscape painter, was so called.

Hobbism. The principles of Thomas Hobbes (1588–1679), author of *Leviathan* (1651). He was a sceptic noted for his MATERIALISM and ERASTIANISM. He emphasized the doctrine of state sovereignty based on the theory of a social contract which he used as a support for absolutism. Man, according to Hobbes, is motivated by self-interest and the urge for self-preservation. Many regarded *Hobbism* as subversive free-thinking.

Hobbit. A benevolent hospitable burrow people, two to four feet high, and fond of bright colours, the creation of Professor J.R.R. Tolkien. They are featured in his two works, *The Hobbit* (1937) and *The Lord of the Rings* (1954–1955).

Hobble Skirts. This women's fashion of skirts so tight around the ankles that the wearer was impeded in walking (much as a horse is hobbled) was at its height in 1912 and was gone by 1914.

Hobblers. A light-cavalry soldier, probably from his mount, a HOBBY or small horse. It was a feudal obligation for tenants of a certain class to provide hobblers for military service. They were often used to carry intelligence, to act as sentinels, and to reconnoitre.

Hobby. A favourite pursuit; a personal pastime that interests or amuses one. There are two words *hobby*. The earlier, meaning a smaller or medium-sized horse, is the M.E. *hoby* (*cp*. DOBBIN); the later, a small species of falcon, is the O.Fr. *hobé*, from Lat. *hobetus*, a falcon. It is from the first that our "hobby", a pursuit, comes. It is through *hobby-horse,* a light wickerwork frame, appropriately draped, in which someone gambolled in the old MORRIS DANCES. Padstow in Cornwall has its ancient Hobby Horse parade on May Day. The horse is preceded by men clad in white known as "teazers". The name is also applied to the child's plaything, consisting of a stick, across which he straddles, with a horse's head at one end.

To ride a hobby-horse was to play an infantile game of which one soon tired. It now implies to dwell to excess on a pet theory; the transition is shown in a sentence in one of John Wesley's sermons (No. lxxxiii):

> Every one has (to use the cant term of the day) his hobby-horse!

Hobgoblin. An impish, ugly, and mischievous sprite, particularly PUCK or ROBIN GOODFELLOW. The word is a variant of Rob-goblin—*i.e.* the goblin Robin (*cp.* HODGE).

> Those that Hobgoblin call you, and sweet Puck,
> You do their work, and they shall have good luck.
> SHAKESPEARE: *A Midsummer Night's Dream*, II, i.

Hob-nob. A corruption of *Hab-nab*, meaning "have or not have". Hence, hit or miss, at random; and, give or take, whence also an open defiance.

> The citizens in their rage shot habbe or nabbe [hit or miss] at random.
> HOLINSHED: *History of Ireland*.
> He is a devil in private brawl ... hob, nob, is his word give't or take't.
> SHAKESPEARE: *Twelfth Night* III, iv.
> Not of Jack Straw with his rebellious crew,
> That set King, realm and laws at hab or nab [defiance].
> SIR J. HARINGTON: *Epigrams*, IV.

To hobnob, or **hob and nob together.** To be on intimate terms of good fellowship, hold close and friendly conversation with, etc.; especially to drink together as cronies—probably with the meaning of "give and take".

> "Have another glass!" "With you hob and nob," returned the sergeant. "The top of mine to the foot of yours—the foot of yours to the top of mine—Ring once, ring twice—the best tune on the Musical Glasses! Your health."
> DICKENS: *Great Expectations*, ch. v.

Hobo. In American usage, a migratory worker who likes to travel, in contrast to a tramp, who travels without working, and a BUM, who neither travels nor works. It derives probably from *hoe-boy*, which meant a migratory farm worker.

Hobson's Choice means no choice at all. The saying derives eponymously from Thomas Hobson (1544?–1631), a Cambridge carrier well known in his day (he is celebrated in Fuller's *Worthies* and in two epitaphs by Milton), who refused to let out any horse except in its proper turn.

Hobson-Jobson. An expression used by British soldiers in India in the 19th century for the Muharram festival. It was their corruption of the Shi'ites' cry *Ya Hasan! Ya Hosain!* Hasan and Hosain were the sons of Ali, the fourth Mohammedan CALIPH and his wife Fatima (MOHAMMED's daughter).

Hoccamore. An old name for hock or hochheimer (the wine of Hochheim on the River Main), at one time called *Rhenish*.

> Restor'd the fainting high and mighty
> With brandy-wine, and aqua-vitæ:
> And made 'em stoutly overcome
> With Bacrack, Hoccamore, and Mum.
> BUTLER: *Hudibras*, III, iii, 297.

Hock cart. The last cartload of harvest. The word, like HOCKEY, is of unknown origin.

> The Harvest Swaines, and Wenches bound
> For joy, to see the Hock-cart crown'd.
> HERRICK: *Hesperides* (*The Hock-cart, or Harvest home*).

Hock-day, or **Hock Tuesday.** The second Tuesday after EASTER Day, long held as a festival in England and observed until the 16th century. According to custom, on Hock Monday, the women of the village seized and bound men, demanding a small payment for their release. On the Tuesday of Hocktide the men similarly waylaid the women. The takings were paid to the churchwardens for parish work. This was later modified, as shown below:

> Hock Monday was for the men and Hock Tuesday for the women. On both days the men and women, alternately, with great merriment, intercepted the public roads with ropes, and pullsed passengers to them, from whom they exacted money, to be laid out in pious uses.
> BRAND: *Antiquities*, vol. I.

Hock-shop. A pawnshop. In America *to hock* is to pawn. It derives from the earlier English Hocktide when small ransoms were demanded from those caught and bound.

Hockey, or **Horkey** is the old name in the eastern counties for the HARVEST-HOME feast.

Hockey cake. The cake given out to the harvesters when the HOCK CART reached home.

Hockley-in-the-Hole. A well-known resort in former days for bear-baiting, bull-baiting, and prize-fighting in what was then a squalid locality near Clerkenwell Green. It was closed about 1730. Mrs. Peachum, in Gay's *Beggar's Opera*, says, "you should go to Hockley-in-the-Hole to learn valour."

Hocus Pocus (hō' kŭs pō' kŭs). Words formerly uttered by conjurers when performing a trick: hence the trick or deception itself, also the juggler himself.

The phrase dates from the early 17th century, and is the opening of a ridiculous string of mock Latin used by the performer (*Hocus pocus, toutous talontus, vade celerita jubes*), the first two words possibly being a parody of the words of consecration in the Mass (*Hoc est Corpus*), while the remainder was reeled off to occupy the attention of the audience.

Our word *hoax* is probably a contraction of hocus pocus, which also supplies the verb **to hocus,** to bamboozle, to cheat, etc.

Hodge. A familiar and condescending name for a farm labourer or peasant, a country clown or rustic; an abbreviated form of *Roger*. It was in use in the 16th century.

Hodge-podge. A medley, a mixed dish of

"bits and pieces" all cooked together. The word is a corruption of HOTCH-POT.

Hodmandod. *See* DODMAN.

Hoe-cake (U.S.A.). Flat cake of coarse bread, originally baked on the blade of a cotton-field hoe.

Hog. A swine, properly a male swine castrated, and, as it is raised solely for slaughter, killed young. The origin of the word is uncertain. The name is also applied to a gelded boar, a sheep in its first year unshorn, and yearling, colts and bullocks are also termed *hogs* or *hoggetts*. A *hog-steer* is a three-year-old boar.

In slang use, a *hog* is a gluttonous, greedy or unmannered person, thus a selfish, reckless, thrusting motorist is termed a *road-hog*.

Hog was also slang for a SHILLING or sixpence, or (in the U.S.A.) a ten-cent piece.

Hampshire hog. An old established nickname for a native of Hampshire, from its famous breed of pigs.

As independent as a hog on ice. Supremely confident, cocky, self-assured. A phrase used in America, of unknown origin, though it may be Scottish, having connexion with the hog used in curling. The phrase is discussed in detail by Charles Earle Funk in his book *A Hog on Ice* (1950).

To drive one's hog to market. To snore very loudly.

To eat high off the hog. To be greedy, to have more than one's fair share.

To go the whole hog. To do the thing completely and thoroughly; without compromise or reservation; to go the whole way. William Cowper says (*The Love of the World; or Hypocrisy Detected*, 1779) that the Moslem divines sought to ascertain which part of the hog was forbidden as food by the PROPHET.

> But for one piece they thought it hard
> From the whole hog to be debarred.

Unable to reach a decision, each thought to be excepted the portion of the meat he most preferred. As the tastes of the worthy IMAMS differed:

> Thus conscience freed from every clog,
> Mahometans eat up the hog.

A more probable origin of the phrase is that "to go the whole hog" was to spend the whole *hog* or SHILLING at one go.

In the U.S.A. the phrase became popular during Andrew Jackson's campaign for the presidency in 1828. Hence the expression *whole-hogger*, one who will see the thing through to the bitter end, and "damn the consequences". During Joseph Chamberlain's controversial Protectionist campaign (1903, *et seq.*) the advocates of complete protection were called *whole-hoggers*.

To hear as a hog in harvest. In at one ear and out at the other; to hear without registering or paying attention. Giles Firmin says, "If you call hogs out of the harvest stubble, they will just lift up their heads to listen, and fall to their shack again." (*Real Christian*, 1670).

To hog. To cut the hair short, especially a horse's mane. Also to scrub a ship's bottom under water with a stiff scrubbing broom called a *hog*. *Cp.* TO ROACH *under* ROACH.

To hog it, or **to pig it.** In colloquial usage means to live in a rough, uncouth fashion or to eat unceremoniously and greedily in a piggish fashion; also to act selfishly and greedily, to grasp everything for oneself.

To live high off the hog. To be in affluent circumstances, to live very sumptuously.

You have brought your hogs to a fine market. You have made a pretty KETTLE OF FISH; said in derision when one's project turns out badly.

Hog and hominy (U.S.A.). Pork and maize, the latter being coarsely ground and boiled and considered poor food. In the Southern States it is often known as "Hog jowls and grits" or "Hog jowls and black-eyed peas". It is eaten on New Year's Day for good luck.

Hog in armour. A person of awkward manner dressed so finely that he cannot move easily; perhaps a corruption of "Hodge in armour". *See* HODGE.

Hog-shearing. Much ado about nothing. "Great cry and little wool." (*See under* CRY.)

Hog-wallows. American prairie which has become a series of mounds and depressions through the alternate action of rain and drought.

Hog wild. In American parlance to go berserk (*see* BERSERKER).

Hog's Back. The western end of the North Downs, the chalk ridge from Guildford to Farnham in Surrey; so called from its outline.

Hogs-Norton. A village in Oxfordshire, now called Hook Norton. The name owes its more recent fame to Gillie Potter, the English comedian and broadcaster, who described in mock erudite fashion a long series of unlikely events taking place in this village.

I think you were born at Hogs-Norton. A reproof to an ill-mannered person.

> I think thou wast born at Hoggs-Norton where piggs play upon the organs.
> HOWELL: *English Proverbs.*

Hogen Mogen. Holland or the Netherlands; so called from *Hooge en Mogende* (high and mighty), the Dutch style of addressing the STATES-GENERAL.

> But I have sent him for a token
> To your low country Hogen-Mogen
> BUTLER: *Hudibras*, III, i.

It has a secondary meaning, "Dutch".

> Well, in short, I was drunk; damnably drunk with Ale;
> Great Hogen Mogen bloody Ale.
> DRYDEN: *The Wild Gallant*, I, i.

Hogmanay. In SCOTLAND, the last day of the year, the day when children demanded gifts or *hogmanay* of oat-cake or oaten bread, etc.

> Hogmanay, Trollolay,
> Give us your white bread and none of your gray.

In olden times it was a kind of annual SATURNALIA. The word is of uncertain origin and of the numerous suggestions made, the most likely is that it is from the North French dialect word *hoginane*, O.Fr. *aguillaneuf* (to the mistletoe go this New Year).

Hoi Polloi (Gr., the many). The masses, usually used in a slighting sense. At Cambridge, a name given to poll men. *See* POLL.

> If by the people you understand the multitude, the *hoi polloi*, 'tis no matter what they think; They are sometimes in the right, sometimes in the wrong; their judgement is a mere lottery.
> DRYDEN: *Essay of Dramatic Poesy* (1668).

Hoity-toity. A reduplicated word (like *harum-scarum, mingle-mangle, hugger-mugger*, etc.), probably formed from the obsolete verb *hoit*, to romp about noisily. It is used as an adjective, meaning "stuck up", haughty, or petulant; as a noun, meaning a good romp or frolic; and as an interjection expressing disapproval or contempt of someone's airs, assumptions, etc.

See the quotation from Selden given *under* CUSHION DANCE, where *hoyte-cum-toyte* is used of rowdy behaviour.

Hokey cokey. A light-hearted dance popular during the 1940s dependent on the song and tune of this name.

Hokey-pokey. An early form of cheap ice-cream sold by street-vendors until the 1920s with the cry "Hokey-pokey penny a lump". The name is derived from HOCUS POCUS although mistakenly said by some to be from the Ital. *Ecco un poco* (Here is a little). *Hokey-pokey* is also used to mean nonsense.

Holborn. A thoroughfare and district of London taking its name from the *Holebourne* (the stream in the hollow), which was the name of the upper part of the Fleet River.

To ride backwards up Holborn Hill. To go to be hanged. The way to TYBURN from NEWGATE was up Holborn Hill which led steeply from Farringdon Street to what is now Holborn Circus, and criminals used to sit or stand with their backs to the horse when drawn to the place of execution.

The spanning of the valley by Holborn Viaduct (1867–1869) did away with the old hill.

Hold. He is not fit to hold a candle to him. *See under* CANDLE.

Hold hard! Stop; go easy; keep a firm hold, seat, or footing, or else there is danger of being overthrown.

Hold off! Keep at a distance.

Hold the fort! Maintain your position at all costs. Immortalized as a phrase by General Sherman (During the American CIVIL WAR), who signalled it to General Corse from the top of Kennesaw in 1864.

To hold the fort. To be left to keep things running during the absence of others.

Hold your horses. *See under* HORSE.

To be left holding the baby, or **bag.** To be left in the LURCH, to carry the responsibility for faults committed by others, to carry the can (*see under* CARRY).

To cry hold. To give the order to stop; in the old TOURNAMENTS, when the umpires wished to stop the contest they cried out, "Hold!"

> Lay on, Macduff
> And damn'd be him that first cries, "Hold, enough!"
> SHAKESPEARE: *Macbeth*, V, viii.

To have, or **hold under one's girdle.** To have in subjection.

To hold the candle to someone, a candle to the devil. *See under* CANDLE.

To hold forth. To speak in public, to harangue, to declaim. An author also *holds forth* certain opinions or ideas in his book, *i.e.* exhibits, or holds them out to view.

To hold good. To be valid, or applicable.

To hold in. To restrain. The allusion is to horses reined in tightly.

To hold in esteem. To regard with esteem.

To hold on one's way. To proceed steadily; to go on without heeding interruptions.

To hold someone guilty. To adjudge or regard as guilty.

To hold someone in hand, or **in play.** To keep control of; keep in expectation; to amuse in order to get some advantage.

To hold one's own. To maintain one's own position, opinion, advantage; to stand one's ground.

To hold one's tongue. To keep silence. In Coverdale's BIBLE, where the Authorized Version has, "But Jesus held his peace" (*Matt.* xxvi, 63), the reading is, "Jesus helde his tonge."

To hold out. To endure, persist, not to succumb.

To hold over. To keep back, retain in reserve, defer.

To hold the purse-strings. To be the one who controls the money and its expenditure. *See* CUTPURSE.

To hold up. To stop, as a highwayman did, with the intention of robbing. In this connexion the order "Hold 'em up!" or "Hold up your hands!" means that the victim must hold them above his head to ensure that he is not reaching for a weapon. *Cp.* HIJACKER. *A hold-up* is therefore an outdoor robbery where people or vehicles are held up. It also means a delay or obstacle.

To hold water. To bear close inspection; to be thoroughly sound and consistent, as a vessel that holds water is sound. In this sense it is usually used negatively, as "That statement will not hold water," *i.e.*, on examination it will be proved faulty. The expression also means to stay the progress of a boat by stemming the current with the oars.

Holdfast. That which is used to secure something in place, a cramp, a hook, etc.; a support.

Brag is a good dog, but Holdfast is better. *See* BRAG.

Hole. A better 'ole. Any situation that is better than the present one. It originated in World War I from a drawing by Bruce Bairnsfather, depicting "Old Bill" taking cover in a wet and muddy shellhole and rebutting the complaints of his companion with the remark, "If you know better 'ole, go to it."

A hold and corner business. Something clandestine and underhand.

In a hole. In an awkward predicament; in a mess.

To hole out. In golf, to drive the ball into the appropriate hole of the course.

To make a hole in something. To consume a considerable portion of it.

To pick holes in. To find fault with. The older phrase was to *pick a hole in one's coat*, thus a hole in one's coat is a blot on one's reputation.

> And shall such mob as thou, not worth a groat,
> Dare pick a hold in such a great man's coat.
>
> PETER PINDAR: *Epistle to John Nichols.*

Foxhole. An American name for a small slit-trench to hold one man.

There are no atheists in foxholes. *See* ATHEISTS.

Holger Danske. The national hero of Denmark. *See* OGIER THE DANE.

Holiday. Give the boys a holiday. A phrase attributed to Anaxagoras (*see* DYING SAYINGS). The old custom of so marking a noteworthy event has always been popular with pupils, but the unexpected holiday is less readily given now that most schools are subject to closer bureaucratic regulation.

Holiday speeches. Fine or well-turned speeches or phrases; complimentary speeches. We have also "holiday manners", "holiday clothes", meaning the best we have.

> With many holiday and lady terms
> He question'd me.
>
> SHAKESPEARE: *Henry, IV, Pt. I*, I, iii.

Holidays, or **Holy days of Obligation.** Days on which Roman Catholics are bound to hear MASS and to abstain "from servile work". These *Feasts of Obligation* vary slightly in different countries. In ENGLAND and WALES they are: all SUNDAYS, CHRISTMAS DAY, the EPIPHANY (6 January), ASCENSION DAY (40th day after EASTER Sunday), CORPUS CHRISTI (Thursday after Trinity Sunday), SS. PETER and PAUL (29 June), the ASSUMPTION of B.V.M. (15 August), ALL SAINTS (1 November). St. JOSEPH (19 March) and St. PATRICK (17 March) are observed in IRELAND and SCOTLAND. The former and the feasts of the Octave Day of Christmas (1 January) and the IMMACULATE CONCEPTION (8 December) are not observed in England and Wales. Epiphany, Corpus Christi, SS. Peter and Paul, and St. Joseph are not kept in the U.S.A.

Holland, The cloth, so called because it was originally made in Holland; its full name was *holland cloth.*

Hollands, or properly Hollands gin, is the Dut. *Hollandsch genever.*

Hollow. I beat him hollow. Completely, thoroughly. *Hollow* here is perhaps a corruption of *Wholly.*

Holly. The custom of decorating churches and houses with holly at CHRISTMAS-time is of great antiquity and may derive from its earlier use by the Romans in the festival of the SATURNALIA, which occurred at the same season, or from the old Teutonic custom. It is held to be unlucky by some to bring it into the house before Christmas Eve. *See also* IVY; MISTLETOE.

Holmes. *See* SHERLOCK HOLMES.

Holy. Holy Alliance. A treaty signed originally by the rulers of Austria, Prussia, and Russia in 1815 (after the fall of NAPOLEON) and joined by all the kings of Europe, except Great Britain and the President of the Swiss Republic. Sponsored by the Tsar Alexander, the rulers undertook to base their relations "upon the sublime truths which the Holy religion of Our Savious teaches". In effect it became a reactionary influence seeking to maintain autocratic rule.

Holy Boys, The. *See* REGIMENTAL AND DIVISIONAL NICKNAMES.

Holy City. The city which the religious consider most expecially connected with their faith. Thus:

Benares is the Holy City of the Hindus.
Cuzco of the ancient Incas.
Fez of the Western Arabs.
Jerusalem of the Jews and Christians.
Mecca and *Medina* as the places of the birth and burial of MOHAMMED.

Figuratively, the Holy City is HEAVEN.

Holy Club. The nickname given to the group of earnest Christians formed at Oxford in 1729 by Charles and John Wesley and joined by George Whitefield. They held meetings to study the Scriptures, fasted, and carried out pastoral worlk. *See* METHODISTS.

Holy Coat. Both the cathedral at Trèves (Trier) and the parish church of Argenteuil claim the ownership of Christ's seamless coat, which the soldiers would not rend and therefore cast lots for it (*John* xix, 23, 25). The traditions date from about the 12th century and the coat was supposed to have been found and preserved by the Empress HELENA in the 4th century. There are other places claiming this relic.

Holy Cross, or **Holy Rood Day.** 14 September, the day of the Feast of the EXALTATION OF THE CROSS, called by the Anglo-Saxons "Roodmass-day".

It was on this day that Jews in ROME used to be compelled to go to church and listen to a sermon—a custom abolished about 1840 by Pope Gregory XVI. It is the subject of Browning's *Holy-Cross Day* (1845).

Holy Door. The specially walled-up door of each of the four great basilicas at ROME (St. Peter's, St. John Lateran, St. Paul's-Outside-the-Walls, St. Mary's Major). That of St. Peter's is ceremoniously opened by the Pope on Christmas Eve, to inaugurate the Holy Year (*see* JUBILEE); the others are opened by Cardinals-Legate. They are similarly closed the following Christmas Eve. Many Pilgrims pass through these doors during the year to perform their devotions and receive INDULGENCES.

Holy Family. Properly, the infant Jesus, MARY, and JOSEPH; in art, the infant Saviour and His attendants, usually Joseph, Mary, Elisabeth, Anne the mother of Mary, and JOHN THE BAPTIST.

Holy Ghost. The third person of the TRINITY, the Divine Spirit, also called the Holy Spirit; represented in art as a dove.

The seven gifts of the Holy Ghost are: (1) Counsel, (2) the fear of the Lord, (3) fortitude, (4) piety, (5) understanding, (6) wisdom, and (7) knowledge.

The Procession of the Holy Ghost. *See* FILIOQUE CONTROVERSY.

The Sin against the Holy Ghost. Much has been written about this sin, the definition of which has been based upon several passages in the GOSPELS such as *Matt*. xii, 31, 32 and *Mark* iii, 29, and it has been interpreted as the wilful denouncing as evil that which is manifestly good, thus revealing a state of heart beyond the divine influence. Borrow in his *Lavengro* draws a graphic picture inspired by fear of this sin and its consequences, the danger of "eternal damnation".

The Order of the Holy Ghost. A French order of knighthood (*Ordre du Saint-Esprit*), instituted by Henry III in 1578 to replace the Order of St. MICHAEL. It was limited to 100 KNIGHTS and was not revived after the revolution of 1830. *Cp.* CORDON BLEU.

Holy Grail. *See* GRAIL.

Holy Innocents, or **Childermas.** This Feast is celebrated on 28 December, to commemorate Herod's MASSACRE OF THE INNOCENTS. It used to be the custom on *Childermas* to whip the children (and even adults) "that the memory of Herod's murder of the Innocents might stick the closer". This practice forms the plot of several tales in the DECAMERON.

Holy Island, or Lindisfarne. In the North Sea, some 9 miles south-east from Berwick-on-Tweed, it became the SEE of St. Aidan in 635 and a missionary centre. St. CHAD, St. Oswy, St. Egbert, and St. WILFRID were among those educated there. It was the see of St. CUTHBERT (685—687) and is now in the diocese of Newcastle. At low-water it can be reached across the sands by a causeway.

IRELAND was called the Holy Island on account of its numerous saints.

Guernsey was so called in the 10th century in consequence of the great number of monks residing there.

The Holy Land (1) Christians call Palestine the Holy Land, because it was the scene of Christ's birth, ministry, and death.

(2) Mohammedans call MECCA the Holy Land, because MOHAMMED was born there.

(3) The Chinese Buddhists call India the Holy Land, because it was the native land of Sakya-muni, the BUDDHA.

(4) The Greeks considered Elis as Holy Land, from the temple of Olympian ZEUS and the sacred festival held there. *See* OLYMPIC GAMES.

The Holy League. A combination formed by Pope Julius II in 1511 with Venice, Ferdinand of Aragon and the Emperor Maximilian of Germany to drive the French out of Italy. ENGLAND joined subsequently.

Among other leagues of the same name, that formed by Henry II of France in 1576, with the support of Henry of Guise and the JESUITS is noteworthy. It was formed to defend the Holy Catholic Church against the encoachments of the reformers, *i.e.* to destroy the HUGUENOTS.

The Holy Maid of Kent. Elizabeth Barton (*c.* 1506–1534) who incited the Roman Catholics to resist the REFORMATION, and imagined that she acted under inspiration. Having announced the doom and speedy death of Henry VIII for his marriage with Anne Boleyn, she was hanged at TYBURN in 1534.

Holy of Holies. The innermost apartment of the Jewish temple, in which the Ark of the Covenant was kept, and into which only the High Priest was allowed to enter, and that but once a year on the Day of Atonement (*see* YOM KIPPUR). Hence, a private apartment, a *sanctum sanctorum. Cp.* ADYTUM.

The Holy Office. *See* INQUISITION.

Holy Orders. *See* ORDERS.

Holy Places. A name particularly applied to those places in Palestine and especially Jerusalem, associated with some of the chief events in the life of Christ, his death, and Resurrection. Jerusalem is also a HOLY CITY for Jews and MOSLEMS and in the course of history this has produced bitter quarrels. Christian pilgrimages to the Holy Places were a familiar feature of mediæval life and the CRUSADES began when Moslems interfered with pilgrims visiting the HOLY SEPULCHRE.

The Crimean War (1854–1856) had its origins in a dispute between orthodox and Roman Catholic rights over the Holy Places, which included the churches of the Holy Sepulchre and the Virgin in Jerusalem, GOLGOTHA, and the church of the Nativity at Bethlehem.

Holy Roman Empire. The mediæval Western Empire, said to be neither Holy, nor Roman, nor an Empire. *See* EMPEROR.

Holy Rood Day. *See* HOLY CROSS DAY.

Holy Saturday. *See* HOLY WEEK.

Holy See. The SEE of Rome. Often used to denote the Papacy and papal jurisdiction, authority, etc.

Holy Sepulchre. The cave in Jerusalem, where according to tradition Christ was entombed, said to have been found by St. HELENA. Successive churches have been built on the site which includes that of CALVARY.

The Holy Spirit. *See* HOLY GHOST.

Holy Thursday. In England an old name for ASCENSION DAY, the Thursday next but one before WHITSUN; by Roman Catholics and others MAUNDY THURSDAY, *i.e.* the Thursday before GOOD FRIDAY, is meant. *See also* IN CŒNA DOMINI.

Holy Trinity. *See* TRINITY.

Holy War. A war in which religious motivation plays, or is purported to play, a prominent part. The CRUSADES, the THIRTY YEARS WAR, the wars against the ALBIGENSES, etc., were so called.

The *Jehad*, or Holy War of the Moslems, is a call to the whole Islamic world to take arms against the Unbelievers.

John Bunyans's *Holy War*, published in 1682, tells of the capture of Mansoul by SATAN and its recapture by the forces of Shaddai (EMMANUEL).

Holy Water. Water blessed by a priest for religious purposes. It is particularly used in the ROMAN CATHOLIC CHURCH at the *Asperges*, the sprinkling of the altar and congregation before High MASS, and generally in the Church at blessings, dedications, etc., and kept in Holy Water stoups near church doors for the use of those entering.

As the Devil loves Holy Water. *See* DEVIL PHRASES *under* DEVIL.

Holy water sprinkler. A military club of mediæval times, set with spikes. So called facetiously because it makes the blood to flow as water sprinkled by an aspergillum.

Holy Week. The last week in LENT. It begins on PALM SUNDAY; the fourth day is called SPY WEDNESDAY; the fifth is MAUNDY THURSDAY; the sixth is GOOD FRIDAY; and the last "Holy Saturday", or the "Great Sabbath".

Holy Week has been called *Hebdomada Muta; Hebdomada Inofficiosa; Hebdomada Penitentialis; Hebdomada Indulgentiæ; Hebdomada Luctuosa; Hebdomada Nigra;* and *Hebdomada Ultima.*

Holy Writ. The BIBLE.

Holy Year. *See* JUBILEE.

Homburg. A soft felt hat popularized by Edward VII. It was originally made at Homburg in Prussia where the king "took the waters" (*see under* WATER).

Home. At home. At one's own home and prepared to receive visitors. An *at home* is a more or less informal reception for which arrangements have been made. *To be at home to somebody* is to be ready and willing to receive him; *to be at home with a subject* is to be quite conversant with it.

Not at home. A familiar locution for "not

prepared to receive visitors", it does not necessarily mean "away from home". "Say I am not at home", is an instruction often given to the person sent to fob off a caller.

> There is an old story that Scipio Nasica called on the poet Ennius and was told by a slave "Ennius is not at home", although Nasica espied him in the house. When Ennius returned the visit later, Nasica called out, "Not at home." Ennius recognised the voice and remonstrated. Nasica replied, "You are a nice fellow, why, I believed your slave, and you won't believe me."

Home James, and don't spare the horses. An expression from the days when the well-to-do commanded their coachmen to drive them home as fast as possible. It is still used jocularly to imply "let us get home as fast as we can", or to tell the car-driver to proceed home without delay.

Home, sweet home. This popular English song first appeared in the opera *Clari, the Maid of Milan* (COVENT GARDEN, 1823). The words were by John Howard Payne (an American), and the music by Sir Henry Bishop, who professed to have founded it on a Sicilian air.

One's long home. The grave.

> Man goeth to his long home, and the mourners go about the streets.
>
> *Eccles.* xii, 5.

To come home to one. To reach one's heart; to become thoroughly understood or realized.

> I doe now publish my Essayes; which, of all my other workes have beene most Currant: For that, as it seemes they come home to Mens Businesse, and Bosomes.
>
> BACON: *Epistle Dedicatorie to the "Essays"* (1625).

To come home to roost. Usually said of a lie, fault, misdeed, etc., which eventually rebounds or "catches up" on its perpetrator. "His chickens have come home to roost" is a common form of the expression, "his chickens" being his misdeeds, mistakes, etc.

To do one's homework. To make adequate preparation for the task facing one; especially to acquaint oneself thoroughly with the relevant material for a discussion, debate or speech, as a day-school pupil is expected to do preparation at home.

To make oneself at home. To dispense with ceremony in another person's house, to act as though one were at home.

Who goes home? When the HOUSE OF COMMONS adjourns at night the doorkeeper asks this question of the members. In bygone days, when danger lurked in the unlit streets from cut-throats and thieves, the cry was raised to enable them to depart in groups, and to escort the SPEAKER to his residence.

Home Counties. The counties nearest London; formerly Kent, Surrey, Essex, Middlesex; now Buckinghamshire, Berkshire, Hertfordshire and Sussex are usually included in the term, but Middlesex was swallowed up by the Greater London Council in 1965.

Home Guard. In Britain, the force of volunteers raised early in World War II and trained for defence against the threat of invasion. Originally known as the L.D.V. (Local Defence Volunteers), it was renamed the "Home Guard" at Winston Churchill's suggestion.

Home Rule. The name given by Isaac Butt, its first leader, to the movement for securing governmental independence for IRELAND under the British crown, after failures of earlier movements to secure the repeal of the Act of Union of 1800. *The Home Government Association* was founded in 1870 (renamed the *Home Rule Association* in 1873) and when C.S. Parnell became leader in 1879 its policy of obstruction in PARLIAMENT became a growing bugbear to English governments. A *Home Rule Bill* was eventually passed in 1914 but its implementation postponed by the advent of World War I. The Easter Rising in 1916, the activities of SINN FÉIN, and resistance in ULSTER led to the establishment of the Irish Free State in 1921, but Northern Ireland continues to be represented in the British Parliament.

Home truth. An unwelcome or uncomplimentary truth delivered by another person about oneself, which "goes home".

Homer. The traditional author of the ILIAD and the ODYSSEY. Estimates of his birth date vary between 685 B.C. and 1159 B.C.. In antiquity seven cities claimed the honour of being Homer's birthplace (Argos, ATHENS, Chios, COLPHON, Rhodes, Salamis in Cyprus, and Smyrna). *See also* MÆONIDES; SCIO'S BLIND OLD BARD.

> PLATO has been called the Homer of philosophers, Milton the English Homer, and OSSIAN the Gaelic Homer. BYRON called Fielding the prose Homer of human nature, and Dryden said that "SHAKESPEARE was the Homer, or father, of our dramatic poets."

The Casket Homer. An edition corrected by ARISTOTLE, which ALEXANDER THE GREAT always carried about with him, and laid under his pillow at night with his sword. After the battle of Arbela, a golden casket richly studded with gems was found in the tent of DARIUS; and Alexander, being asked to what purpose it should be assigned, replied, "There is but one thing in the world worthy of so costly a depository," saying which he placed therein his edition of Homer.

Homer, a cure for the ague. Among the old cures it was held that if the fourth book of the ILIAD was laid under the head of a patient, it would provide instant remedy. This book contains the cure of MENELAUS (when wounded by Pandarus) by Machaon, "a son of ÆSCULAPIUS".

Homer sometimes nods. Even the best of us is liable to make mistakes. The line is from HORACE'S *De Arte Poetica* (359):

> Indignor quandoque bonus dormitat Homerus,
> Verum operi longo fas est obrepere somnum.
> (I think it shame when the worthy Homer nods; but in so long a work it is allowable if drowsiness comes on.)

Honeysuckle. *See* MISNOMERS.

Hong Merchants. Those Chinese merchants who, under licence from the Imperial Government of China, held the monopoly of trade with Europeans, and under the Hong system, were restricted to Canton. The restriction was abolished in 1842 after the OPIUM WAR. *Hong* or *hang* means row, range; hence a warehouse, particularly one for foreign merchants.

Honi soit qui mal y pense (on' ē swa kē-măl ē pons). The motto of the Most Noble Order of the GARTER, usually rendered as "Evil be to him who evil thinks," although "shame to him" would be more accurate.

Honky-tonk. A disreputable night club or low roadhouse. A place of cheap entertainment. *A honky-tonk piano* is one from which the felts of the hammers have been removed, thus making the instrument more percussive and giving it a noticeably different tone quality. Such pianos are often used for playing ragtime and popular melodies in public houses.

Honor. A feudal term for a number of KNIGHT'S fees administered as a unit, an aggregation of manors. It gave "honour" to its holder, hence the name.

Honorificabilitudinitatibus. A made-up word on the Lat. *honorificabilitudo*, honourableness, found in SHAKESPEARE and elsewhere. *See* LONG WORDS.

> Thou are not so long by the head as honorificabilitudinitatibus.
> *Love's Labour's Lost*, V, i.

Honour. An affair of honour. A dispute to be settled by a duel.

Duels were generally provoked by offences against the arbitrary rules of courtesy and etiquette, not recognized at law and thus to be settled by private combat. *See* LAWS OF HONOUR, *below*.

Debts of honour. Debts contracted by betting or gambling, so called because these debts cannot be enforced as such by law.

Laws of honour. Certain conventional rules which the fashionable world tacitly holds with regard to honourable conduct; the accepted conventions for the conducting of duels.

Legion of Honour. *See under* LEGION.

Point of honour. An obligation which is binding because its violation would offend some scruple or notion of self-respect.

Word of honour. A pledge which cannot be broken without disgrace.

Honours. Titles, distinctions, civilities, etc. At bridge, the *honours* are the five highest trump cards—ace, king, queen, knave (or jack), and ten.

Crushed by one's honours. The allusion is to the legend of the Roman damsel, Tarpeia, who agreed to open the gates of Rome to King Tatius, provided his soldiers would give her the ornaments which they wore on their arms (meaning their bracelets). As they entered, they threw their shields on her and crushed her, saying as they did so, "These are the ornaments worn by SABINES on their arms." *See also* TARPEIAN ROCK.

Draco, the Athenian legislator (*see* DRACONIAN CODE), was crushed to death in the theatre of Ægina, by the number of caps and cloaks showered on him by the audience, as a mark of their high appreciation of his merits. A similar story is told of the mad Emperor, ELAGABALUS, who smothered the leading citizens of Rome with roses.

Honours of war. The privilege, allowed to an enemy on capitulation, of being allowed to retain his weapons. This is the highest honour a victor can pay a vanquished foe. Sometimes the troops so treated are allowed to march with all their arms, drums beating, and colours flying.

Last honours. Funeral rites; last tributes of respect to the dead.

Military honours. Ceremonial marks of respect rendered by troops to royalty and high-ranking military and civil officials and also at military funerals.

To do the honours. To render necessary civilities, courtesies, hospitalities, etc., as at a reception or entertainment.

Honourable. As applied to the nobility, *see* COURTESY TITLES. This title of honour is also given to the children of life peers, to MAIDS OF HONOUR, and to Justices of the High Court, except Lord Justices and Justices of Appeal. In the HOUSE OF COMMONS one member speaks of another as "the honourable member for—". In the U.S.A. "honourable" is a courtesy title applied to persons of distinction in legal or civic life. The title was also borne by the East India

Company (*see* JOHN COMPANY).

Most Honourable. The form of address for a MARQUESS.

Right Honourable. A prefix to the title of EARLS, VISCOUNTS, BARONS, and the younger sons of DUKES and MARQUESSES, Lord Justices and Justices of Appeal, all privy councillors, some lord mayors and lord provosts, and certain other civic dignitaries, and some COMMONWEALTH ministers.

Honourable Artillery Company. The oldest surviving unit in the British Army, having been founded by Henry VIII, in 1537, as the Guild of St. George. In Tudor and Stuart days, the officers for the TRAIN-BANDS of London were supplied by the H.A.C., in whose ranks Milton, Wren, and Samuel Pepys served at one time or another. It has the privilege of marching through the CITY with fixed bayonets.

In 1638 Robert Keayne, a member of the London company, founded the Ancient and Honourable Artillery Company of Boston, Mass., the oldest military unit in the U.S.A.

Hooch. An American slang term for whisky or crude raw spirits, often made surreptitiously or obtained illegally. The word comes from the Alaskan Indian *hoochinoo*, a crude distilled liquor. *Cp.* MOONSHINE.

Hood. The hood, or **cowl does not make the monk.** It is a man's way of life, not what he professes to be, that really matters; from the Lat. *Cucullus non facit monachum*. The expression is probably derived from the lines in St. Anselm's *Carmen de Contemptu Mundi* (11th century):

> Non tonsura facit monachum, non horrida vestis;
> Sed virtus animi, perpetuusque rigor.

Hood, Robin. *See* ROBIN HOOD.

Hoodman Blind. A game now called BLINDMAN'S BUFF.

> What devil was't
> That thus hath cozen'd you at hoodman-blind?
> SHAKESPEARE: *Hamlet*, III, iv.

Hook. Above your hook. Beyond your comprehension; beyond your mark. Perhaps an allusion to hat-pegs fixed in rows, the higher ones being beyond the reach of small people.

By hook or by crook. Either rightfully or wrongfully; by some means or other; one way or another. It possibly derives from an old manorial custom which authorized tenants to take as much firewood as could be reached down by a shepherd's crook and cut down with a bill-hook.

> Dynmure wood was ever open and common to the ... inhabitants of Bodmin ... to bear away upon their backs a burden of lop, crop, hook, crook, and bag wood.
> *Bodmin Register* (1525).

> In hope her to attaine by hooke or crooke
> SPENSER: *Faerie Queene*, III, i, 17

He is off the hooks. Unhinged, out of spirits, put out, annoyed; also LAID ON THE SHELF, superseded, dead; the hooks being the pieces of iron on which gates hinges rest.

Hook it! Take your hook! Sling your hook! Be off! Buzz off! Go away! *Take your hook* refers to the practice in some Victorian MUSIC HALLS of the manager waiting in the wings with a long hooked pole ready to pull off a performer outrunning his time or welcome.

Hook, line and sinker. To swallow a tale *hook, line and sinker* is to be extremely gullible, like the hungry fish that swallows not only the baited hook, but the lead weight, and some of the line as well.

Let off the hook. To get out of a difficult situation. Also, of a married man, let out on his own, usually for a night with convivial male companions.

On one's own hook. On one's own responsibility or account. An angler's phrase.

To be hooked. To be caught, usually of a man "hooked" by a woman, *i.e.*, secured for marriage. More recently it also means to become addicted to the use of a drug.

With a hook at the end. Assent given with a mental reservation. It was a custom in some parts for a witness, when he swore the oath falsely, to crook his finger into a sort of hook with the idea of annulling the perjury. It is a crooked oath, an oath *with a hook at the end*.

A hook-up is a radio term for an arrangement of wiring for extended transmission or reception; it is applied to a network of radio stations connected for the transmission of the same programme.

Hookey Walker. *See* WALKER.

Hookey, or **hooky. To play hookey.** To play truant, from the idea that "to hook" something is to make off with it.

Hooligan. A violent young rough; of late 19th-century origin from the name of a family of such people. Hence the word *hooliganism*.

> The original Hooligans were a spirited Irish family of that name whose proceedings enlivened the drab monotony of life in Southwark about fourteen years ago. The word is younger than the Australian *larrikin*, of doubtful origin, but older than Fr. *apache*.
> ERNEST WEEKLEY: *Romance of Words* (1912).

Hooped Pots. Drinking pots at one time were marked with bands or hoops, set at equal distances, so that when two or more drank from the same tankard no one should take more than his share. Jack Cade promises his followers that "there shall be in England seven halfpenny loaves sold for a penny; the

three-hooped pot shall have ten hoops; and I will make it a felony to drink small beer."
(SHAKESPEARE: *Henry VI, Pt. II*, IV, ii.)

> I beleeve hoopers in quart pots were invented to that ende, that every man should take his hoope, and no more.
>
> NASH: *Pierce Pennilesse* (1592).

Hooray. Normally used as an exclamation of joy, approbation, etc., but in Australia and New Zealand it is used as a farewell. Why this has come about is obscure, but it may have the implication of encouragement as a joyful send-off.

Hoosier. An inhabitant of the state of Indiana, the *Hoosier State*. Probably from *hoosier*, a mountainer, an extension of *hoojee, hoojin*, a dirty person or tramp. The south of Indiana was mainly settled by Kentucky mountaineers.

Hoover. The trade name of a firm of vacuum-cleaner makers which has come to be used as a noun and a verb relating to vacuum-cleaners and vacuum-cleaning in general.

Hop Hop it. Be off with you, buzz off, go away.

To hop the twig. Usually to die; but sometimes to run away from one's creditors, as a bird eludes a fowler.

There are numerous phrases to express the cessation of life; for example, "to kick the bucket" (*see under* BUCKET); "to lay down one's knife and fork"; "to peg out" (from cribbage); "to snuff it" (*see under* SNUFF); "to fall asleep"; "to enter Charon's boat"; "to give up the ghost" (*see under* GHOST); etc.

Hopping mad. Very angry, jumping mad. So mad as to jump or hop about.

Hop-o'-my-thumb. A pygmy or dwarf. *Cp.* TOM THUMB.

> Plaine friend, Hop-o'-my-Thumb, know you who we are?
>
> *Taming of a Shrew* (Anon., 1594).

Hope. *See* PANDORA'S BOX.

Band of Hope. *See* BAND OF HOPE *under* BAND.

Bard of Hope. Thomas Campbell (1777–1844) was so called on account of his poem *The Pleasures of Hope* (1799).

Hope Diamond. A rare sapphire-blue Indian stone weighing $44\frac{3}{8}$ carats (now in America), which appeared on the market in 1830 and became the one-time property of Henry Thomas Hope. It is believed to be part of the large blue DIAMOND cut to 68 carats and sold to Louis XIV by Tavernier. Like the SANCY DIAMOND, it disappeared (1792) during the French Revolution.

Hopkinsians. A sect of Independent Calvinists (*see* CALVINISM) who followed the teach-

ings of Samuel Hopkins (1721–1803) a minister of Newport, Rhode Island. He was one of the first NEW ENGLAND Congregational ministers to oppose slavery. His theological teachings are to be found in his *System of Doctrines contained in Divine Revelation* (1793).

Horace. Quintus Horatius Flaccus (65 B.C.–8 B.C.), the Roman lyric poet.

Horace of England. George, Duke of Buckingham, preposterously declared Cowley to be the PINDAR, Horace, and VIRGIL of England. Ben Jonson was nicknamed Horace by Dekker in the so-called "War of the Theatres".

Horace of France. Jean Macrinus, or Salmon (1490–1557); and Pierre Jean de Béranger (1780–1857), also called the French Burns.

Horace of Spain. The brothers Lupercio (1559–1613) and Bartolomé de Argensola (1562–1631).

Horae (hôr' ī) (Lat. hours, seasons). In classical mythology, the three sisters Eunomia (Good order), Dice (Justice), and Irene (Peace), who presided over spring, summer, and winter. According to Hesiod they were the daughters of JUPITER and THEMIS.

Horn. The horn was a symbol of power and dominion and as such is found in classical writers and similarly in the OLD TESTAMENT. The original Hebrew SHOFAR or trumpet was made of a ram's horn.

Astolpho's horn. Logistilla gave Astolpho at parting a horn that had the virtue of being able to appal and put to flight the boldest KNIGHT or most savage beast (ARIOSTO: *Orlando Furioso*, Bk. VIII).

The Horn Gate. See DREAMS, THE GATES OF.

Horn of Fidelity. MORGAN LE FAY sent a horn to King ARTHUR, which had the following "virtue": No lady could drink out of it who was not "to her husband true"; all others who attempted to drink were sure to spill what it contained. This horn was carried to King MARK, and "his queene with a hundred ladies more" tried the experiment, but only four managed to "drink cleane". ARISTO'S *enchanted cup* possessed a similar spell.

Horn of Plenty or **Cornucopia.** AMALTHEA'S horn, an emblem of plenty. CERES is drawn with a ram's horn in her left arm, filled with fruits and flowers; sometimes they are being poured on the earth, and sometimes they are piled high in the horn as in a basket.

The horns of a dilemma. *See* DILEMMA.

The horns of Moses' face. *See* MOSES.

Horn with horn, or **horn under horn.** The promiscuous feeding of bulls and cows, or, in fact, all horned beasts that are allowed to run together on the same common.

Horne and Thorne shall make England forlorne. An old saying popularly held to have been fulfilled by the enclosures of the 16th century, when sheep and quickthorn hedges seemed to be devouring the open fields at an ever-increasing rate.

My horn hath He exalted (I *Sam.* ii, 10; *Ps.* lxxxix, 24, etc). He has given me the victory, increased my sway. Thus, *Lift not up your horn on high* (*Ps.* lxxv, 5) means, do not behave scornfully, maliciously, or arrogantly. In these passages "horn" symbolizes power, and its exaltation signifies victory or deliverance. In DANIEL's vision (*Dan.* vii, 7) the "fourth beast, dreadful and terrible, and strong exceedingly," had ten horns, symbolic of its great might.

Swearing on the Horns. Drovers and cattle dealers formerly practised this custom among their fraternity and a drover would have to show his skill by holding a bullock by the horns. The custom developed into a ceremony attracting travellers who were "sworn" and made to kiss the horns and beguiled into standing drinks. Nearly every inn at HIGHGATE, where drovers and graziers congregated en route to SMITHFIELD, kept a pair of horns for this purpose, the most frequented being the Gatehouse Inn.

To come, or **be squeezed out at the little end of the horn.** To come off badly in some affair; get the worst of it; fail conspicuously.

To draw in one's horns. To retrench, to curtail one's expenditure; to retract or mitigate an expressed opinion; to restrain pride. The allusion is to the snail.

To make horns at. To thrust out the fist with the first and fourth fingers extended, the others doubled in. An ancient gesture of insult to a person implying that he is a CUCKOLD.

> He would have laine withe the Countess of Nottinghame, making horns in derision at her husband the Lord High Admiral.
>
> SIR E. PEYTON: *The Divine Catastrophe of the ... House of Stuarts* (1652).

To put to the horn. To denounce as a rebel or pronounce as an outlaw, for not answering to a summons. In SCOTLAND the messenger-at-arms used to go the Cross at Edinburgh and give three blasts with his horn when proclaiming judgment of outlawry.

To show one's horns. To let one's evil intentions appear. The allusion, like that in "to show the cloven hoof", is to the DEVIL—

"Old Hornie" (*see under* AULD).

To take the bull by the horns. See under BULL.

To the horns of the altar. *Usque ad aras amicus,* Your friend even to the horns of the altar, *i.e.* through thick and thin. In swearing the ancient Romans held the horns of the altar, and one who did so in testimony of friendship could not break his oath without incurring the vengeance of the gods.

On heathen altars the horn was probably ornamental. In the TEMPLE OF SOLOMON the altar had a projection or horn at each of the four corners and they were regarded as especially sacred. Animals awaiting slaughter may have been bound to them and the horns were smeared with the blood of sacrifices (*Exod.* xxix, 12). Criminals were safe from vengeance if they grasped these horns.

> And Adonijah feared because of Solomon, and arose, and went, and caught hold on the horns of the altar.
>
> I *Kings* i, 50.

To wear the horns. To be a CUCKOLD. This old term is connected with the chase. In the rutting season, one stag selects several females for his consorts. If challenged and beaten by another stag he is without associates unless he defeats another stag in turn. As stags are horned, and have their mates taken from them by their fellows, the application is palpable. *See also* ACTÆON.

Another explanation is that it is due to the former practice of engrafting the spurs of a castrated cock on the root of the excised comb, where they grew and became "horns." In support of this it is noteworthy that *Hahnrei,* the German equivalent for *cuckold,* originally signified a capon.

Auld Hornie. *See* AULD.

Cape Horn. So named by Schouten, a Dutch mariner, who first doubled it (1616). He was a native of Hoorn, in north Holland, and named the cape after his native town. To seamen it was simply known as "the Horn". *Cp.* CAPE.

Horn Childe. An early 14th-century metrical romance with a story closely related to that of KING HORN.

Horn Dance. *See* ABBOT'S BROMLEY.

Hornbook. A thin board about nine inches long and five or six wide (with a handle) serving as backing to a leaf of vellum or sheet of paper on which was usually written (later printed) the alphabet, an exorcism, the Lord's Prayer, and the Roman numerals; the whole being covered by a thin piece of transparent horn. The handle had a hole in it so that it could be tied to a schoolchild's girdle. Hornbooks continued to be used in

England until well into the 18th century. *See* CHRISS-CROSS.

> He teaches boys the hornbook.
> SHAKESPEARE: *Love's Labour's Lost*, V, i.

Hornpipe. An obsolete wooden pipe with a reed mouthpiece at one end and horn at the other. The dance of this name, once particularly associated with mariners, was originally accompanied by this instrument.

Horner, Little Jack. *See under* JACK.

Horoscope (Gr. *horoskopos, hora,* an hour; *skopos,* observer). The observation of the heavens at the hour of a person's birth, used by astrologers for predicting the future events of his life. Also the figure or diagram of the twelve houses of HEAVEN, showing the positions of the planets at a given time as used by astrologers for calculating nativities and working out answers to horary questions. *See* HOUSES, ASTROLOGICAL.

Hors de combat (ô di kom′ ba) (Fr. out of battle). Incapable of taking any further part in the fight; disabled.

> He [Cobbett] levels his antagonists, he lays his friends low, and puts his own party *hors de combat.*
> HAZLITT: *Table Talk, Essay VI.*

Hors d'œuvre (ôr dĕrvr) (Fr., outside the work). Something served as a relish at the beginning of a dinner to whet the appetite, such as anchovies, caviar, continental sausages, ham, soused herrings, etc. In French, the expression also means an outbuilding and a literary digression.

Horsa. *See* HENGIST.

Horse. According to classical mythology, PO-SEIDON created the horse; and according to VIRGIL, the first person that drove a four-in-hand was ERICHTHONIUS. In Christian art, the horse is held to represent courage and generosity. It is an attribute of St. MARTIN, St. Maurice, St. GEORGE, and St. Victor, all of whom are represented on horseback.

It is a not uncommon emblem in the CATACOMBS and probably typifies the swiftness of life.

The use of *horse* attributively usually denotes something that is coarse, inferior, unrefined, as in *horse-parsley, horse-radish, horse mushroom. See* COB; HAND.

The fifteen points of a good horse:

> A good horse sholde have three propyrtees of a man, three of a woman, three of a foxe, three of a hare, and three of an asse.
> *Of a man.* Bolde, prowde, and hardye.
> *Of a woman.* Fayre-breasted, fair of haire, and easy to move.
> *Of a foxe.* A fair taylle, short eers, with a good trotte.
> *Of a hare.* A grate eye, a dry head, and well rennynge.
> *Of an asse.* A bygge chynn, a flat legge, and a good hoof.
> *Wynkyn de Worde* (1946).

The brazen horse. A magic horse given to CAMBUSCAN by the king of Arabia and India. By giving it instructions and turning a pin in its ear it would carry its rider anywhere.

> Or, if you list to bid him thennes gon,
> Trill this pin, and he will vanish anon.
> CHAUCER: *The Squire's Tale* (Pars Prima).

Flesh-eating horses. The horses of Diomedes, tyrant of Thrace, who fed his horses on the strangers who visited his kingdom. HERCULES vanquished the tyrant and gave the carcass to the horses to eat.

Hobby Horse. *See* HOBBY.

Iron horse. A steam locomotive.

The Pale Horse. Death. "I looked and behold a pale horse; and his name that sat on him was Death" (*Rev.* vi, 8). *See also* FOUR HORSEMEN OF THE APOCALYPSE *under* FOUR.

The White Horse. The standard of the ancient Saxons; hence the emblem of Kent.

The name is also given to the hillside figures formed by removing the turf, thus revealing the underlying chalk. The most famous of these is at Uffington, Berkshire, traditionally said to commemorate ALFRED THE GREAT's victory over the Danes in 871. It measures some 350 feet from nose to tail and gives its name to the *Vale of White Horse*, west of Abingdon. The scouring of the White Horse was once a local ceremony.

> And then what a hill is the White Horse Hill! There it stands right up above all the rest, nine hundred feet above the sea, and the boldest bravest shape for a chalk hill that you ever saw.
> T. HUGHES: *Tom Brown's Schooldays*, ch. i.

There are other white horses, that at Westbury, Wiltshire, being the best known.

A galloping white horse is the device of the House of Hanover and, during the reign of the first two Georges, the *White Horse* replaced the *Royal Oak* of Stuart fame on many PUBLIC-HOUSE SIGNS.

White horses. A poetic phrase for the white-capped breakers as they roll in from the sea.

O'Donohue's white horses. Waves which come on a windy day, crested with foam. The hero reappears every seventh year on MAY-DAY, and is seen gliding, to sweet but unearthly music, over the lakes of Killarney, on his favourite white horse. He is preceded by fairies who strew spring flowers in his path. Moore has a poem on the subject in his *Irish Melodies*.

Winged horse. *See* PEGASUS.

The Wooden Horse, called *Clavileno el Aligero,* in DON QUIXOTE, is governed by a peg in its forehead and has the same magical qualities as the BRAZEN HORSE given to CAMBUSCAN. The similar *Magic Horse* in the ARABIAN NIGHTS was of ivory and ebony.

A former instrument of military punishment was called a *wooden horse*. The victim was seated on the horse's back, a beam of ridged oak, with a firelock tied to both feet to keep him in this painful position. This was known as **riding the wooden horse.**

Before the days of iron and steel construction, a ship was sometimes called a *wooden horse*.

The Wooden Horse of Troy. VIRGIL tells us that, after the death of HECTOR, ULYSSES had a monster wooden horse made by Epios and gave out that it was an offering to the gods to secure a prosperous voyage back to Greece. The Trojans dragged the horse within their city, but it was full of Grecian soldiers, including MENELAUS, who stole out at night, slew the guards, opened the city gates, and set fire to TROY.

Famous Horses of Myth and History.

In classical mythology the names given to the horses of HELIOS, the Sun, are:

> *Actæon* (effulgence); *Æthon* (fiery red); *Amethes* (no loiterer); *Bronte* (thunderer); *Erythreos* (red producer); *Lampos* (shining like a lamp); *Phlegon* (the burning one); and *Purocis* (fiery hot).

AURORA'S horses were:

> *Abraxa, Eoos* (dawn) and *Phæthon* (the shining one).

PLUTO'S horses were:

> *Abaster* (away from the stars); *Abatos* (inaccessible); *Æton* (swift as an eagle); and *Nonios*.

The ensuing list is arranged alphabetically:

> *Aarvak*, or *Arvak* ("early-waker"). In Norse mythology, the horse that draws the sun's chariot driven by the maiden Sol.
> *Alborak. See* BORAK.
> *Alfana* ("mare"). Gradasso's horse, in ORLANDO FURIOSO.
> *Alsvid*, or *Alswider* ("All-swift"). The horse that draws the chariot of the moon (Norse mythology).
> *Aquiline* ("like an eagle"). Raymond's steed, bred on the banks of the Tagus (Tasso: *Jerusalem Delivered*).
> *Arion* ("martial"). HERCULES' horse, given to ADRASTUS. Formerly the horse of NEPTUNE, brought out of the earth by striking it with his trident; its right feet were those of a man, it spoke with a human voice and ran with incredible swiftness.
> *Arundel*. The horse of BEVIS OF HAMPTON. The word means "swift as a swallow" (Fr. *hirondelle*).
> *Balios* (Gr., "swift"). One of the horses given by NEPTUNE to Peleus. It afterwards belonged to ACHILLES. Like Xanthos (*see below*), its sire was the west wind, and its dam Swift-foot the HARPY.
> *Barbary. See* BARBARY ROAN.
> *Bavieca*. The CID's horse. He survived his master two years and a half, during which time no one was allowed to mount him; he was buried before the gates of the monastery at Valencia and two elms were planted to mark the grave.
> *Bayard. See* BAYARD.
> *Bayardo. See* BAYARDO.
> *Black Agnes*. A palfrey of Mary Queen of Scots

given by her brother Moray, and named after Agnes of Dunbar.
> *Black Bess*. The mythical mare, created for Dick TURPIN by Harrison Ainsworth in his *Rookwood*, which carried Dick from London to York.
> *Black Saladin*. Warwick's famous coal-black horse. Its sire was Malech, and according to tradition, when the race of Malech failed, the race of Warwick would fail also. And thus it was.
> *Brigadore*, or *Brigliadore* ("Golden bridle"). Sir Guyon's horse in Spenser's *Faerie Queene* (V, iii, etc.). It had a distinguishing black spot on its mouth, like a horseshoe.
> ORLANDO'S famous charger, second only to BAYARDO in swiftness and wonderful powers, was called *Brigiliadoro*.
> *Bucephalus* ("ox-head"). The famous charger of ALEXANDER THE GREAT, who was the only person who could mount him, and he always knelt down to take up his master. He was 30 years old at death and Alexander built the city of Bucephala for a mausoleum.
> *Carman*. The Chevalier BAYARD's horse, given to him by the Duke of Lorraine. It was a Persian horse from Kerman or Carmen (Laristan).
> *Celer* ("swift"). The horse of the Roman Emperor Lucius Versus. It was fed on almonds and raisins, covered with royal purple, and stalled in the imperial palace.
> *Cerus* ("fit"). The horse of ADRASTUS, swifter than the wind.
> *Clavileno. See* WOODEN HORSE *under* HORSE.
> *Copenhagen. See* COPENHAGEN.
> *Cyllaros*. Named from Cylla in Troas, a celebrated horse of CASTOR AND POLLUX.
> *Dapple. See* DAPPLE.
> *Dinos* ("the marvel"). DIOMEDES' horse.
> *Ethon* ("fiery"). One of the horses of HECTOR.
> *Fadda*. MOHAMMED's white mule.
> *Ferrant d'Espagne* ("The Spanish traveller"). The horse of OLIVER.
> *Galathe* ("cream-coloured"). One of the horses of HECTOR.
> *Grani* ("grey-coloured"). SIEGFRIED's horse, of marvellous swiftness.
> *Grizzle*. All skin and bone, the horse of Dr. SYNTAX.
> *Haizum*. The horse of the archangel GABRIEL (KORAN).
> *Harpagus* ("one that carried off rapidly"). One of the horses of CASTOR AND POLLUX.
> *Hippocampus*. One of NEPTUNE's horses. It had only two legs, the hind quarter being that of a dragon or fish.
> *Hrimfaxi* ("frost-mane"). The horse of Night, from whose bit fall the "rime-drops" which nightly bedew the earth (Scandinavian legend).
> *Incitatus* ("spurred-on"). The Roman Emperor CALIGULA's horse, made priest and consul. It had an ivory manger and drank wine from a golden pail.
> *Kantaka*. The white horse of Prince GAUTAMA, the BUDDHA.
> *Lampon* ("the bright one"). One of DIOMEDES' horses.
> *Lamri* ("the curvetter"). King ARTHUR's mare.
> *Malech. See* BLACK SALADIN, *above*.
> *Marengo*. The white stallion which NAPOLEON rode at Waterloo. It is represented in Vernet's picture of *Napoleon Crossing the Alps*.
> *Marocco. See* BANKS'S HORSE.
> *Pegasus. See* PEGASUS.
> *Phallus* ("stallion"). The horse of Heraclius.
> *Phrenicos* ("intelligent"). The horse of Hiero of Syracuse, that won the prize for single horses in the 73rd OLYMPIAD.

Podarge ("swift-foot"). One of the horses of HEC-TOR.

Roan Barbary. See BARBARY ROAN.

Rosabelle. The favourite palfrey of Mary Queen of Scots.

Rosinante ("formerly a hack"). DON QUIXOTE's horse, all skin and bone. *Cp.* GRIZZLE, above.

Savoy. The favourite black horse of Charles VIII of France; so called from its donor, the Duke of Savoy. It had but one eye, and "was mean in stature".

Shibdiz. The Persian BUCEPHALUS, fleeter than the wind; charger of Chosroes II.

Skinfaxi ("shining-mane"). The horse of day (Norse legend). *Cp.* HRIMFAXI, *above.*

Sleipnir. ODIN's eight-footed grey horse which could traverse both land and sea. The horse typifies the wind which blows from the eight principal points.

Sorrel. The horse of William III was blind in one eye and "mean of stature" (*cp.* SAVOY, *above*). It stumbled over a mole-hill and the king's fall led to his death. *See* GENTLEMAN IN BLACK VELVET.

Strymon. The horse immolated by XERXES before he invaded Greece. It came from the vicinity of the river Strymon in Thrace.

Tachebrune. The horse of OGIER THE DANE.

Trebizond. The grey horse of Guarinos, one of the French Knights taken at RONCESVALLES.

Vegliantino ("the little vigilant one"). ORLANDO's famous steed, called in Fr. romance *Veillantif*, Orlando there appearing as ROLAND.

White Surrey. Richard III's favourite horse.

> Saddle White Surrey for the field to-morrow.
> SHAKESPEARE: *Richard III*, V, iii.

Xanthos. See XANTHUS.

A dark horse. One whose capabilities are not known to the general public; hence a person whose abilities are undisclosed or who conceals them till he can reveal them to the best advantage.

A horse of another colour. A different affair altogether.

A horse wins a kingdom. It is said that on the death of Smerdis (522 B.C.) the several competitors for the throne of Persia agreed that he should be king whose horse neighed first when they met on the following day. The groom of Darius showed his horse a mare on the place appointed, and as soon as it arrived at the spot the following day, the horse began to neigh and won the crown for DARIUS.

A nod is as good as wink to a blind horse. However obvious a hint or suggestion may be, it is useless if the other person cannot see it or will not take the hint. Nowadays it is more generally used in the contrary sense and usually abbreviated to "a nod is as good as a wink",—the hint is sufficient, I understand, and MUM'S THE WORD. *Cp.* VERB SAP.

> But you're a dutiful son, so I'll say no more about it—a nod's as good as a wink to a blind horse.
> CAPTAIN MARRYAT: *Peter Simple*, ch. li.

As strong as a horse. Very strong. *Horse* is often used with intensive effect; as *to work,* or *to eat like a horse.*

A Trojan horse. A deception, a concealed danger. *See* WOODEN HORSE OF TROY, *above.*

Don't look a gift horse in the mouth. *See* GIFT-HORSE.

Flogging a dead horse. Trying to revive interest in a worn-out topic, matter, etc.

Hold your horses! Be patient, wait a moment; don't be too precipitate; hold up for a while on whatever you are doing.

Horse and foot. The cavalry and infantry; hence all one's forces; with all one's might.

I will win the horse or loose the saddle. NECK OR NOTHING; DOUBLE OR QUITS. The story is that a man made the bet of a horse that another could not say the Lord's Prayer without a wandering thought. The bet was accepted, but before being half-way through the reciter looked up and said, "By the by, do you mean the saddle also?"

One man may steal a horse, while another may not look over the hedge. Some people are specially privileged, and can take liberties, or commit offences, etc., with impunity, while others get punished for trivialities. An old proverb given by Heywood (1546).

Straight from the horse's mouth. Direct from the highest source, which cannot be questioned. The only certain way of discovering the age of a horse is by examining its front teeth, the incisors.

The grey mare is the better horse. *See under* MARE.

They cannot draw, or **set horses together.** They cannot agree together.

'Tis a good horse that never stumbles. Everyone makes mistakes sometimes; HOMER SOMETIMES NODS.

To back the wrong horse. To make an error in judgment. A phrase from THE TURF.

To be on one's high horse, to ride the high horse. To be overbearing and arrogant; to give oneself airs. Formerly people of rank rode on tall horses or chargers.

To lock the stable after the horse is stolen or **has bolted.** To take precautions after the mischief has happened.

To put the cart before the horse. *See* CART.

To ride on the horse with ten toes. To walk; to ride on SHANKS'S MARE.

Working with a dead horse. Doing work which has already been paid for. Such work is a *dead horse*, because you can get no more out of it.

You can take a horse to the water but you cannot make him drink. There is always some point at which it is impossible to get an obstinate or determined man to proceed farther in the desired direction. The proverb is found in Heywood (1546).

Horsebridge. Another name for a *pack-horse bridge*, sometimes called a riding bridge or bridle bridge. The hamlet of Horsebridge on the Tamar above Gunnislake takes its name from such a bridge.

Horse-chestnut. Gerard tells us in his *Herball* (1597) that the tree is so called —

> For that the people of the East countries do with the fruit thereof cure their horses of the cough ... and such like diseases.

Another explanation is that when a leaf-stalk is pulled off, it presents a miniature of a horse's hock and foot with shoe and nail marks.

Horse latitudes. A region of calms about 30° North and South; perhaps from the fact that sailing ships carrying horses to America and the West Indies were sometimes obliged to jettison their cargoes when becalmed in these latitudes through shortage of water for the animals.

Horse-laugh. A coarse, vulgar laugh.

Horse-leech. A type of insatiable voracity; founded on the blood-sucking habits of the worm and the passage in the BIBLE; "The horseleach hath two daughters, crying, Give, give" (*Prov.* xxx, 15).

Marbeck, commentating in 1581, explains the "two daughters"—

> That is, two forks in her tongue, which she heere calleth her two daughters, whereby she sucketh the bloud, and is never saciate.

Horse Marines. Go and tell that to the horse marines! Said in derision to the teller of some "tall" yarn or unbelievable story, the horse marine being an apparent absurdity (*but see under* REGIMENTAL AND DIVISIONAL NICKNAMES). The more common phrase is "tell that to the marines" (*see under* MARINES). To belong to the "Horse Marines" is the virtual equivalent of belonging to the "AWKWARD SQUAD". *Cp.* CREDAT JUDÆUS.

Horsemen. Four Horsemen of the Apocalypse. *See under* FOUR.

Horse-milliner. One who makes and supplies decorations for horses; hence a horse-soldier more fit for the dressing room than the battlefield. The expression was used by Chatterton in his *Excelente Balade of Charitie* (ROWLEY POEMS), and Scott revived it.

Horse-power. A common unit of power measurement as applied to machines, engines, motors, etc., equal to the raising of 33,000 lb. one foot high in one minute. It was first fixed by Watt when seeking a suitable way of indicating the power exerted by his steam engine. He estimated that a strong dray horse working at a gin for eight hours a day averaged 22,000 foot-pounds per minute. He increased this by 50 per cent, and this became the recognized unit.

Horseshoes. The belief that it is lucky to pick up a horse shoe is from the idea that it was a protection against WITCHES and evil generally. According to Aubrey, the reason is "since MARS (iron) is the enemy of SATURN (God of the Witches)". Consequently they were nailed to the house door with two ends uppermost, so that the luck did not "run out". Nelson had one nailed to the mast of the *Victory*.

One legend is that the DEVIL one day asked St. DUNSTAN, who was noted for his skill as a farrier, to shoe his "single hoof". Dunstan, knowing who his customer was, tied him tightly to the wall, and proceeded with the job, but purposely put the devil to such pain that he roared for mercy. Dunstan at last agreed to release his captive on condition that he would never again enter a place where he saw a horseshoe displayed.

Horse-trading. Hard, shrewd, bargaining.

Horse-wrangler. A western American term for a breaker-in and herder of horses.

Hortus Siccus (Lat., a dry garden). A collection of plants dried and arranged in a book.

Horus. One of the major gods of the ancient Egyptians, originally a great sky-god and sun-god, who became merged with Horus the son of OSIRIS and ISIS, and Horus the Child (*see* HARPOCRATES). He was also identified with the King himself and the Horus-name was the first of the five names of the Egyptian King. He was the most famous of the Falcon-gods and was represented in hieroglyphics by the winged sun-disc.

Hospital (Lat. *hospitale*, *hospitium*, from *hospes*, a guest). Originally a hospice or hostel for the reception of pilgrims; later applied to a charitable institution for the aged and infirm (as in Greenwich Hospital, Chelsea Hospital), to charitable institutions for the education of children (as in Christ's Hospital, Emmanuel Hospital, Greycoat Hospital), and finally to the present institutions for treatment of the sick and injured. *Hotel* and *spital* are related forms. *See also* LOCK HOSPITAL; MAGDALENE.

Hospital Sunday. The SUNDAY nearest St. LUKE's day (18th OCTOBER), when churches have special collections for hospitals. The practice began in London in 1873.

Hospitallers. First applied to those whose duty it was too provide *hospitium* (lodging and entertainment) for pilgrims. The most noted institution of the kind was founded at

Jerusalem (*c.* 1048), which gave its name to an order call the Knights Hospitallers or the Knights of St. John of Jerusalem; later they were styled the Knights of Rhodes; and then the Knights of MALTA; the islands of Rhodes (1310) and Malta (1529) being, in turn, their headquarters. The order became predominantly military in the 12th century but in late 18th century reverted to its earlier purposes of tending the sick and poor, moving to ROME in 1834.

. The order came to an end in England after the REFORMATION but a branch was revived in 1831 which declared itself an independent order in 1858, now styled the Order of the Hospital of St. John of Jerusalem. It founded the St. John Ambulance Association in 1877.

Host (Lat. *hostia*, a sacrifice). The consecrated bread of the EUCHARIST regarded as the sacrifice of the Body of Christ.

The Elevation of the Host. At the EUCHARIST, the raising by the celebrant of the sacred elements immediately after consecration to symbolize the offering to God and to show them for adoration.

Host, as an army or multitude, is from the Lat. *hostis*, enemy. In Med. Lat. *hostem facere* came to mean "to perform military service". *Hostis* (military service) then came to mean the army that went against the foe, whence our word *host*.

The heavenly host. The ANGELS and ARCHANGELS.

The Lord God of Hosts, Lord of Hosts JEHOVAH, the hosts being the ANGELS and celestial spheres.

Host as one who entertains guests is from the Lat. *hospes*, a guest.

To reckon without your host. To reckon from your own standpoint only; not to allow for what the other man may do or think or decide.

> Found in few minutes to his cost,
> He did but count without his host.
>
> BUTLER: *Hudibras*, I, iii, 21.

Hostler, or **Ostler** (os' lĕr). The name given to the man who looked after the horses of travellers at an inn was originally applied to the innkeeper (*hosteller*) himself. It has been jokingly said to be derived from *oat-stealer* for obvious reasons.

Hot. Hot air. Empty talk, boasting, threats, etc.; bombast. Hence *hot-air merchant*, one whose utterances are "full of sound and fury, signifying nothing"; a declamatory WIND-BAG.

Hot and hot. Food cooked and served in hot dishes straight from the stove.

Hot cockles. A CHRISTMAS game. One player kneels down with his eyes covered and lays his head in another's lap and on being struck has to guess who gave the blow.

> As at Hot cockles once I laid me down,
> And felt the weighty hand of many a clown,
> Buxoma gave a gentle tap, and I
> Quick rose, and read soft mischief in her eye.
>
> GAY: *Shepherd's Week* (Monday).

Hot cross buns. *See* BUN.

Hot-foot. With speed; rapidly.

Hot jazz. The term used for JAZZ music when the tone is less pure than in "cool" jazz, and when vibrato is prominently employed.

Hot-pot. A dish of mutton or beef with sliced potatoes cooked in a tight-lidded pot in an oven. A popular dish in the North of England.

Hot rod. An old car stripped and tuned for speed, and, by transference, the owner of such a vehicle or other unruly youth.

Hot stuff. Formerly said of a girl or woman of amorous inclination and flirtatious habits.

Hot under the collar. Agitated, angry.

I'll give it him hot and strong. I'll rate him most soundly and severely. *To get it hot* is to get severe punishment.

I'll make this place too hot to hold him. I'll "show him up", or otherwise make things so unpleasant that he will not be able to endure it.

Like hot cakes. Very rapidly; as in "to sell like hot cakes".

Not so hot. Not so good, not very satisfactory.

Hotch-pot, Hotchpotch (Fr. *hochepot*; *hocher*, to shake, and *pot*). A thick broth containing meat and vegetables and other mixed ingredients; a confused mixture or jumble. *Hodge-podge* is another alternative form and *hotchpot* is also a legal term. When a fund or estate has to be divided among certain beneficiaries and one of the number has already received a share, that person may be required to bring his special share into *hotchpot*, *i.e.* to add it to the total before the individual shares are computed. *A hotch-pot provision* is a clause in a settlement requiring the carrying out of the above procedure.

Hotspur. A fiery person of uncontrolled temper. Harry Percy (1364–1403), son of the first Earl of Nothumberland (*see* SHAKESPEARE's *Henry IV, Pt. I*), was so called. The 14th Earl of Derby, the CONSERVATIVE Prime Minister, was sometimes called the "Hotspur of Debate". *See also* RUPERT OF DEBATE.

Houdini, Harry. The stage name of Erik Weiz (1874–1926), the most celebrated illusionist and escapologist to date. Born at

Budapest of Jewish parents, who emigrated to New York, he began his career as a magician in 1890 but world fame began with his appearance at London in 1900. No lock could hold him, even that of the condemned cell at Washington gaol. He escaped from handcuffs, ropes, safes, etc., etc., and was deservedly called "the Great Houdini". He died from a punch in the stomach, delivered before he had tensed his muscles. *Cp.* DAVENPORT-TRICK.

Hound. To hound a person is to harass and persecute him as hounds worry a fox or stag.

Hour. Book of Hours. A book of devotions for private use, especially during the CANONICAL HOURS (*see under* CANON). Such books in the later MIDDLE AGES were often beautifully and lavishly illuminated and have a particular importance in the history of the book arts.

Canonical Hours. *See under* CANON.

A bad quarter of an hour. A short disagreeable experience.

At the eleventh hour. Just in time; only just in time to obtain some benefit. The allusion is to the parable of the labourers hired for the vineyard (*Matt.* xx).

In an evil hour. Acting under an unfortunate impulse. In ASTROLOGY there are lucky and unlucky hours.

In the small hours (of the morning). One, two, and three, after midnight.

My hour is not yet come. The time for action has not yet arrived; properly, the hour of my death is not yet fully come; from the idea that the hour of one's death is preordained.

> When Jesus knew that his hour was come.
> *John* xiii, 1.

Their finest hour. The famous phrase from Winston Churchill's speech (18 June 1940) given at the time when the collapse of France was imminent and the BATTLE OF BRITAIN about to begin.

> Let us therefore brace ourselves to our duties, and so bear ourselves that, if the British Empire and its Commonwealth last for a thousand years, men will say: "This was their finest hour."

To keep good hours. To go home early every night; to go to bed betimes; to be punctual at one's work.

Houri (hoo' ri). One of the black-eyed damsels of the Mohammedan PARADISE, possessed of perpetual youth and beauty, whose virginity is renewable at pleasure, and who are the reward of every believer; hence, in English use, any dark-eyed attractive beauty.

House. The House. A familiar name for Christ Church, Oxford, the London Stock Exchange, the HOUSE OF LORD, HOUSE OF COMMONS, etc.

The House of ... denotes a royal or noble family with its ancestors and branches, as the *House of Windsor* (the British Royal Family), the *House of Hanover*, etc.; also a commercial establishment such as the *House of Rothschild*, the bankers, the *House of Cassell*, the publishers, etc.

House of Assembly. The lower legislative chamber in the Republic of South Africa.

A house of call. Some house, frequently a public house, that one visits or uses regularly; a house where journeymen and workmen assembled for hire when out of work.

House of Commons. The elected house of the British PARLIAMENT. It is also the lower house in the Canadian Parliament.

A house of correction. A jail. Originally a place where vagrants were made to work and offenders were kept in ward for the correction of small offences.

A or **The House of God.** A church or place of worship; also any place sanctified by God's presence. Thus JACOB in the wilderness, where he saw the ladder leading from earth to HEAVEN, said, "This is none other but the House of God, and this is the gate of heaven" (*Gen.* xxvii, 17).

House of ill fame, or **repute.** An brothel.

House of Issue. An investment banking house which advertises, underwrites, and sells stocks or bonds on behalf of a corporation.

House of Keys. *See* TYNWALD.

House of Lords. The upper house of the British PARLIAMENT, consisting of the lords spiritual and temporal, namely: hereditary peers, life peers (Lords of Appeal and those created under the Life Peerages Act of 1958), Scottish Representative Peers, the archbishops and certain BISHOPS of the CHURCH OF ENGLAND.

House of Office. A 17th-century term for a privy.

House of Representatives. The lower legislative chamber in the U.S.A., Australia, and New Zealand.

The House that Jack built.

> This is the man, all tattered and torn,
> That kissed the maiden all forlorn,
> That milked the cow with the crumpled horn
> That tossed the dog
> That worried the cat ...
> That lay in the house that Jack built.

There are numerous similar constructions. For example the Hebrew parable of *The Two Zuzim*, the summation of which runs thus:

> 10. Then came the Most Holy, blessed be He, and slew

Philippe de Mornay (1549–1623) called Duplessis-Mornay, their great supporter, was nicknamed "the Huguenot Pope".

Huitzilopochtli. *See* MEXITL.

Hulda. The old German goddess of marriage and fecundity. The name means "the Benignant".

Hulda is making her bed. It snows.

Hulks, The. Old dismasted men-of-war anchored in the Thames and off Portsmouth and used as prison ships, first established as a "temporary expedient" in 1778 and remaining until 1857. An impression of the Hulks is given by Dickens in the opening chapters of *Great Expectations*.

Hull, Hell and Halifax. An old beggars' and vagabonds' "prayer" quoted by Taylor the WATER POET (1580–1653) as

From Hull, Hell and Halifax
Good Lord, deliver us.

It is said that *Hull* was to be avoided because the beggars had little chance of getting anything there without doing hard labour for it, and *Halifax* (*q.v.*) because anyone caught stealing cloth there was beheaded without further ado. A probable suggestion is that "Hell" is a corruption of Elland, another clothmaking town near Halifax.

Hulled (U.S.A.). Made a prisoner after capitulating; from the surrender of General Hull to the British at Detroit, 16 August 1812. The term is now archaic.

Hulsean Lectures. Since 1777, a course of lectures on Christian evidence, etc., delivered annually at Cambridge, instituted and endowed by the Rev. John Hulse (1708–1790) of Cheshire.

Hum, or **Hem and Haw, To.** To hesitate in giving a positive answer; to speak with frequent pauses and interjections of such sounds.

Huma (hū′mȧ). A fabulous oriental bird which never alights, but is always on the wing. It is said that every head which it overshadows will wear a CROWN. The bird suspended over the throne of Tippoo Sahib at Seringapatam represented this poetical fancy.

Humanitarians. A name given to certain ARIANS who held that Christ was only man. The name was also used of the UNITARIANS and of the followers of Saint-Simon (1760–1825), an early exponent of socialism.

Nowadays the term is usually applied to philanthropists in general.

Humanities. Grammar, rhetoric, and poetry, with Greek and Latin (*literæ humaniores*); in contradistinction to divinity (*literæ divinæ*). Also of more general application to polite scholarship in general.

The use of 'humanities' ... to designate those studies which are esteemed the fittest for training the true humanity in man.
TRENCH: *Study of Words*, Lect. iii.

Humanity Martin. Richard Martin (1754–1834), one of the founders of the Royal Society for the Prevention of Cruelty to Animals. He secured the passage of several laws for the suppression of cruelty to animals.

Humber. The legendary king of the HUNS, fabled by Geoffrey of Monmouth to have invaded Britain about 1000 B.C. He was defeated in a great battle by LOCRIN near the river which bears his name. "Humber made towards the river in his flight, and was drowned in it, on account of which it has since borne his name."

Humble. A man of humble birth is one of low estate, born of the common people. Here "humble" is from the Lat. *humilis*, lowly.

A humble bee, a bumble bee, or dumble-dor. Here "humble" is probably a derivative of *hum* in imitation of the droning noise of the bee. *Cp.* Ger. *Hummel*.

A humble cow is a polled cow, a cow without horns. Here "humble" is a variant of *hamble*, to mutilate.

To eat humble pie. *See under* EAT.

Humming Ale. Strong liquor that froths well and causes a humming in the head of the drinker.

Let us fortify our stomacks with a slice or two of hung beef, and a horn or so of humming stingo.
PIERCE EGAN: *Tom and Jerry*, ch. vii.

Hummums. The old hotel and COFFEE-house of this name on the south-west corner of Russell Street, COVENT GARDEN was on the site of the Turkish bath-house founded about 1631 and a fashionable resort after the RESTORATION. The name is from Arab. *hamam*, a hot bath or a Turkish bath. The hotel lasted until 1865.

"Now," says my friend, "we are so near, I'll carry you to see the Hummums ... and if you will pay your club towards eight shillings, we'll go in and sweat."
NED WARD: *The London Spy*, 1703.

Humour, Good humour, ill, or **bad humour,** etc. According to the ancients there are four principal humours in the body: phlegm, blood, choler and black BILE. As any one of these predominates it determines the temper of the mind and body; hence the expressions sanguine, choleric, phlegmatic, melancholic humours. A just balance made a "good humour" and a preponderance of any one of the four an "ill" or "evil humour". See Ben Jonson's *Every Man Out of His Humour* (*Prologue*).

Humpback, The. Geronimo Amelunghi, *Il Gobbo di Pisa*, an Italian burlesque poet of the mid-16th century.

Cristoforo Solario (or Solari), Italian sculptor and architect, *Il gobbo* (1460–1527).

Humphrey. To dine with Duke Humphrey. To have no dinner to go to. The Good Duke Humphrey (*see under* GOOD) was renowned for his hospitality. At death it was reported that a monument would be erected to him in St. Paul's, but he was buried at St. Alban's. The tomb of Sir John Beauchamp (d. 1358), on the south side of the nave of old St. Paul's was popularly supposed to be that of the Duke, and when the promenaders left for dinner, the poor stay-behinds who had no dinner to go to, or who feared arrest for debt if they left the precincts, used to say, when asked by the gay sparks if they were going, that they would "dine with Duke Humphrey" that day.

The expression was once very common, as was the similar one *To sup with Sir Thomas Gresham*, the Exchange built by Sir Thomas being a common lounge.

> Though little coin thy purseless pocket line,
> Yet with great company thou art taken up;
> For often with Duke Humphrey thou dost dine,
> And often with Sir Thomas Gresham sup.
> HAYMAN: *Quodlibets* (*Epigram on a Loafer*), 1628.

Humpty Dumpty. Short and broad, like the egg-shaped figure of the nursery rhyme; also a gypsy drink made of ale boiled with brandy.

Hun. An uncivilized brute; from the barbarian tribe of Huns who invaded the East Roman Empire in the 4th and 5th centuries. In World War I a slang name applied to the Germans.

Hundred. From pre-CONQUEST times, a division of the English shire, corresponding to the WAPENTAKE of Danish areas. Originally the Hundred probably consisted of 100 hides, hence the name (*see* HIDE). The Hundred Court or MOOT, which survived until late in the 19th century, met regularly in mediæval times to deal with private pleas, criminals, matters of taxation, etc.

The equivalent unit in Northumberland, Cumberland, Westmorland and Durham was called a WARD.

Yorkshire, Lincolnshire, Nottinghamshire, Derbyshire, Leicestershire and Rutland were divided into WAPENTAKES. Yorkshire had also three larger divisions called RIDINGS. Similarly Kent was divided into five LATHES and Sussex into six RAPES each with subordinate hundreds.

Chiltern Hundreds. *See* CHILTERN.

Great, or **Long hundreds.** Six score, a hundred and twenty.

The Hundred Days. The days between 20 March 1815, when NAPOLEON reached the TUILERIES (after his escape from Elba) and 28 June, the date of the second restoration of Louis XVIII. Napoleon left Elba, 26 February; landed near Cannes, 1 March; and finally abdicated 22 June.

The address of the prefect of PARIS to Louis XVIII on his second restoration begins: "A hundred days, sire, have elapsed since the fatal moment when your majesty was forced to quit your capital in the midst of tears." This is the origin of the phrase.

Hundred Years War. The long series of wars between England and France, beginning in the reign of Edward III, 1337, and ending in that of Henry VI, 1453.

The first battle was the naval victory of Sluys, 1340, and the last a defeat at Castillon, 1453. It originated in English claims to the French crown and results in the English losing all their possessions except Calais, which was held until 1558.

Old Hundred, or **Old Hundredth.** A famous and dignified Psalm tune that owes its name to its being so designated in the Tate and Brady *Psalter* of 1696 to indicate the retention of the setting of Kethe's version of the 100th Psalm in the *Psalter* of 1563 (by Sternhold and Hopkins). The tune is of older origin and is found as a setting to the 134th psalm in Marot and Beza's *Genevan Psalter* of 1551.

Hero of the hundred fights. Conn, a semi-legendary Irish king, of the 2nd century.

Hundred and thousands. A name given by confectioners to very tiny comfits.

It will all be the same a hundred years hence. An exclamation of resignation—it doesn't much matter what happens. It is an old saying and occurs in Ray's *Collection*.

Not a hundred miles off. An indirect way of saying "in this very neighbourhood" or "very spot". The phrase is used when it would be indiscreet or dangerous to refer more directly to the person or place hinted at.

The hundred-eyed. ARGUS in Greek and Latin fable. JUNO appointed him guardian of IO (the cow), but JUPITER caused him to be put to death; whereupon Juno transplanted his eyes into the tail of her peacock.

The Hundred-handed. Three of the sons of URANUS, namely, Ægæon or BRIAREUS, Cottys or COTTUS, and Gyges or Gyes. After the TITANS were overcome during the war with ZEUS and hurled into TARTARUS, the

Hundred-handed ones were set to keep watch and ward over them.

CERBERUS is sometimes so called because from its three necks sprang writhing snakes instead of hair.

Hungary Water. Made of ROSEMARY flowers and spirit, said to be so called because a hermit gave the recipe to a Queen of Hungary.

Hunger. Hunger march. A march of the unemployed to call attention to their grievances, as that of 1932, the year in which Wal Hannington, the leader of the National Union of Unemployed Workers, led a march on London. The biggest of the marches organized by the N.U.W.M. was that against the MEANS TEST in 1936.

The march of the Blanketeers (*see under* BLANKET) was in effect the first such march.

Hunger Strike. The refusal of prisoners to take food in order to embarrass the authorities or to secure release; a notable SUFFRA-GETTE tactic. *See* CAT AND MOUSE ACT.

Hungry. There are many common similes expressive of hunger, including—hungry as a hawk, a hunter, a church mouse, a dog. James Thomson (*The Seasons: Winter*) has "Hungry as the grave" and Oliver Wendell Holmes, "Hungry as the chap that said a turkey was too much for one, not enough for two."

Hungry dogs will eat dirty puddings. *See under* DOG.

The Hungry Forties. The 1840s in Great Britain, from the widespread distress among the poor, especially before 1843. Characterized by bad harvests, dear bread, and unemployment, it was the period of CHARTISM. 1847 and 1848 were also bad years; but the 1820s were probably worse than the 1840s. The situation was helped by the railway boom and Peel's financial measures.

Hunkers. In the 1840s, the conservative faction of the Democratic Party in New York, so named because they "hunkered" for the spoils of office (Dut. *hunkeren*, hanker). *See* BARNBURNERS.

Hunks. An old hunks. An OLD SCREW, a hard, selfish, mean fellow. In the late 16th century it was a name commonly given to performing bears (*cp.* CROSS AS A BEAR *under* CROSS) and may have its origin in some unknown person of cross or miserly character.

Hunky. Hunky dory (Amer.). An expression of approval, all's right or satisfactory. It is an elaborated form of 'hunky", derived from Dut. *honk*, goal, station, or "home" as in TAG and other games; hence, adjectivally, to be in a good or satisfactory position.

Hunt. Like Hunt's dog, he would neither go to church nor stay at home. A Shropshire saying. The story is that one Hunt, a labouring man, kept a mastiff, which, on being shut up while his master went to church, howled and barked so as to disturb the whole congregation. Hunt thought he would take him to church the next Sunday, but the dog positively refused to enter. The proverb is applied to a self-willed person, who will neither be led nor driven.

He who hunts two hares leaves one and loses the other. No one can do well or properly two things at once, he "falls between two stools". "No man can serve two masters."

> Like a man to double business bound,
> I stand in pause where I shall first begin
> And both neglect.
> SHAKESPEARE: *Hamlet*, III, iii.

To hunt with the hounds and run with the hare. *See under* HARE.

Hunters and Runners of classic renown:
ACASTUS who took part in the famous Calydonian hunt (*see under* BOAR).
ACTÆON, the famous huntsman who was transformed by DIANA into a stag, because he chanced to see her bathing.
ADONIS, beloved by VENUS, slain by a wild boar whil hunting.
ADRASTUS, who was saved at the siege of Thebes by the speed of his horse Arion, given him by HERCULES.
ATALANTA, who promised to marry the man who could outstrip her in running.
CAMILLA, the swiftest-footed of all the companions of DIANA.
LADAS, the swiftest-footed of all the runners of ALEXANDER THE GREAT.
MELEAGER, who took part in the great Calydonian boar-hunt (*see under* BOAR).
ORION, the great and famous hunter, changed into the constellation so conspicuous in November.
PHEIDIPPIDES, who ran 150 miles in two days.

The mighty hunter. NIMROD was so called (*Gen.* x, 9). The meaning seems to be a conqueror. Jeremiah says, "I [the Lord] will send for many hunters [warriors], and they shall hunt [chase] them [the Jews] from every mountain ... and out of the holes of the rocks." (xvi, 16).

> Proud Nimrod first the bloody chase began—
> A mighty hunter, and his prey was man.
> POPE: *Windsor Forest*.

Hunting the gowk, snark, etc. *See* these words.

Huntingdonians. Members of "the Countess of Huntingdon's Connexion", a sect of Calvinistic METHODISTS founded in 1748 by Selina, widow of the ninth Earl of Huntingdon, and George Whitefield, who had become her chaplain. The churches founded by the countess, numbering some 36, were mostly affiliated with the Congregational

Union. *See* UNITED REFORMED CHURCH.

Hurdy-gurdy. A stringed musical instrument, the music of which is produced by the friction of a rosined wheel on the strings, which are stopped by means of keys. It had nothing to do with the barrel-organ or piano-organ of the streets which is sometimes so called, probably from its being played by a handle. *Cp.* SQUEEZE BOX.

Hurlo-thrumbo. A ridiculous burlesque, which in 1729–1730 had an extraordinary run at the Haymarket Theatre. So great was its popularity that a club called "The Hurlo-Thrumbo Society" was formed. The author was Samuel Johnson (1691–1773), a half-mad dancing master, who put this motto on the title-page when the burlesque was printed:

> Ye sons of fire, read my *Hurlo-Thrumbo*,
> Turn it betwixt your finger and your thumbo,
> And being quite undone, be quite struck dumbo.

Hurricane. A very violent storm of wind, a West Indian word introduced through Spanish. In the 18th century the word was used for a large private party or ROUT; so called from its hurry, bustle, and noise. *Cp.* DRUM.

Hurry. Don't hurry, Hopkins. A satirical reproof to those who are not prompt in their payments. It is said that one Hopkins of Kentucky gave a creditor a promissory note on which was written, "The said Hopkins is not to be hurried in paying the above."

Husband. The word is from O.E. *hus*, house, and Old Norse *bondi*, a freeholder or yeoman, from *bua*, to dwell; hence literally *husband* is a house-owner in his capacity as head of the household, and so it came to be applied to a married man, who was the natural head of the household. When Sir John Paston, writing to his mother in 1475, said:

> I purpose to leeffe alle heer, and come to you, and be your hosbonde and balyff,

he was proposing to come and manage her household for her. We still use the word in this sense in such phrases as **To husband one's resources.**

Ship's husband. A man who has the care of a ship in port or one who oversees the general interests of a vessel in clearing and entering, berthing and provisioning, etc.

Husbandry is merely the occupation of the *husband* (in the original sense), the management of the household; later restricted to farm management, and the *husband* became the *husbandman*.

> I commit into your hands
> The husbandry and manage of my house.
> SHAKESPEARE: *Merchant of Venice*, III, iv.

Hush. Hush-hush. A term that came into use in World War I to describe very secret operations, designs, or inventions; from the exclamation "hush" enjoining silence. *Cp.* TOP SECRET.

Hush-money. Money given as a bribe for silence or "hushing" a matter up.

Husking. Husking-bee, Husking frolic, Corn husking. In North America in the 18th century this was a gathering for husking Indian corn, usually with feasting and merrymaking.

Hussites. Followers of John Hus, the Bohemian religious reformer (1369–1415), sometimes called WYCLIFFITES from the fact that many of the teachings of John Hus were derived from those of Wyclif.

Hussy. Nowadays a word implying an ill-balanced girl, a "jade" or "minx", it is none other than the honourable appellation *housewife* from the pronounciation "hussif". The portable sewing outfit is still pronounced "hussif".

Hustings. A Norse word *hus-thing* (*Hus*, house; *thing*, assembly); hence the assembly of a KING, EARL or chief. Hence its application to open-air meetings connected with Parliamentary elections. In many towns the *hustings court* transacted some legal business, particularly that of the City of London, which still exists and is presided over by the Lord Mayor and sheriffs, although shorn of most of its former powers. The use of the word for the platform on which nominations, etc., of Parliamentary candidates were made (until the passing of the Ballot Act of 1872) derives from its first application to the platform in the Guildhall on which the London court was held. A realistic impression of the old hustings at a Parliamentary election is given by Dickens in *Pickwick Papers* (ch. xiii).

To be beaten at the hustings. To lose an election.

Hutber's Law. "Improvement means deterioration". A telling phrase coined by Patrick Hutber (1928–1980), City Editor of the *Sunday Telegraph* from 1966 to 1979. It pin-pointed the growing tendency of officialdom to palm off reduced services of poorer quality as "new and improved". *Cp.* PARKINSON'S LAW.

Hutin (ū' tan). **Louis le Hutin.** Louis X of France (1289, 1314–16) was so called. It means "the quarreller", "the stubborn or headstrong one". He gained the epithet after his quarrel with the Archbishop of Lyon, who was arrested. His father's Treasurer, Enguerrand de Marigny was hanged and his first wife, Margaret of Burgundy, was executed for alleged adultery.

Hyacinth (hī′à sinth). According to Greek fable, the son of Amyclas, a Spartan king. The lad was beloved by APOLLO and ZEPHYR and as he preferred the sun-god, Zephyr drove Apollo's quoit at his head, and killed him. The blood became a flower, and the petals are inscribed with the signature AI, meaning woe (VIRGIL; *Eclogues*, iii, 106).

> The hyacinth bewrays the doleful "A I",
> And culls the tribute of Apollo's sigh.
> Still on its bloom the mournful flower retains
> The lovely blue that dyed the stripling's veins.
> CAMŌENS: *Lusiad*, ix.

Hyades (hī′ à dēz) (Gr. *huein*, to rain). Seven NYMPHS, daughters of ATLAS and Pleione, placed among the stars, in the constellation TAURUS, which threaten rain when they rise with the sun. The fable is that they wept at the death of their brother Hyas so bitterly that ZEUS out of compassion took them to HEAVEN. *Cp.* PLEIADES.

> The seaman sees the Hyades
> Gather an army of Cimmerian clouds ...
> All-fearful folds his sails, and sounds the main,
> Lifting his prayers to the heavens for aid
> Against the terror of the winds and waves
> MARLOWE: *Tamburlaine*, Pt, I, III, ii.

Hybla. A city and mountain in Sicily famous for its honey. *Cp.* HYMETTUS.

Hydra. A many-headed water-snake of the Lernaean marshes in Argolis. It was the off-spring of TYPHON and ECHIDNA and was variously reputed to have one hundred heads, or fifty, or nine. It was one of the "twelve labours" of HERCULES to kill it, and, as soon as he struck off one of its heads, two shot up in its place. Hence **Hydra-headed** applied to a difficulty which goes on increasing as it is combated. The monster was eventually destroyed by Hercules with the assistance of his charioteer, who applied burning brands to its wounds as soon as each head was severed by his master.

Hyena (hī ē′ nà). Held in veneration by the ancient Egyptians, because it is fabled that a certain stone, called the "hyænia", is found in the eye of the creature, and Pliny asserts (*Nat. Hist.*, xxxvii, 60), that when placed under the tongue it imparts the gift of prophecy.

> The skilful Lapidarists of Germany affirm that this beast hath a stone in his eye (or rather his head) called Hyæna or Hyænius.
> TOPSELL: *Historie of foure-footed Beasts* (1607).

Hygeia (hī jē′ à). Goddess of health in Greek mythology, and the daughter of ÆSCULA-PIUS. Her symbol was a serpent drinking from a cup in her hand.

Hyksos. The so-called "Shepherd Kings" who ruled Egypt from the end of the 18th century B.C. to the beginning of the 16th, the period between the Middle and New King-doms. They were Asiatic invaders, and the name derives from a mistranslation of the Egyptian word, which more correctly means "foreign princes".

Hylas (hī làs). A boy beloved by HERCULES, carried off by the NYMPHS while drawing water from a fountain in Mysia.

Hymen (hī′ men). Properly, a marriage song of the ancient Greeks; later personified as the god of marriage, represented as a youth carrying a torch and veil—a more mature EROS, or CUPID.

Hymettus (hī met′ ùs). A mountain in Attica, famous for its honey. *Cp.* HYBLA.

> There, flowery hill, Hymettus, with the sound
> Of bees' industrious murmur, oft invites
> To studious musing.
> MILTON: *Paradise Regained*, IV, 247.

Hype. A slang abbreviation of *hypodermic* meaning a hypodermic needle or an injection from same. *Hyped up* is to be self-injected with a drug or to be artificially excited or stimulated. *Hype* used in the sense of a deception, racket or for misleading, inflated, or highly exaggerated advertising publicity, may be derived from the prefix *hyper*—meaning more than normal, excessive, or possibly from *hypodermic*.

Hyperboreans. In Greek legend, a happy people dwelling beyond the North Wind, BOREAS from which their name was supposedly derived. They were said to live for a thousand years under a cloudless sky, knowing no strife or violence. The word is applied in general to those living in the extreme north.

Hyperion. In Greek mythology, one of the TITANS, son of URANUS and GÆA, and father of HELIOS, SELENE, and Eos (the Sun, Moon, and Dawn). The name is sometimes given by poets to the sun itself, but not by Keats in his "Fragment" of this name.

Hypermnestra. Wife of LYNCEUS and the only one of the fifty daughters of Danaus who did not murder her husband on their bridal night. *See* DANAIDES.

Hypnotism. The art of producing trance-sleep, or the state of being hypnotized. Dr. James Braid of Manchester gave it this name (1843), after first calling it *neuro-hypnotism* (Gr., an inducing to sleep of the nerves).

Hypocrite. Prince of Hypocrites. Tiberius Cæsar (42 B.C., A.D. 14–37) was so called because he affected a great regard for decency, but indulged in the most detestable lust and cruelty.

Abdullah Ibn Obba and his partisans were called *The Hypocrites* by MOHAMMED, because they feigned to be friends, but were in reality foes.

Hypostatic Union. The union of three Persons in the TRINITY; also the union of the Divine and Human in Christ, in which the two elements, although inseparably united, each retain their distinctness. The *hypostasis* (Gr. *hypo*, under; *stasis*, standing; hence foundation, essence) is the personal existence as distinguished from both *nature* and *substance*.

Hyssop. David says (*Ps.* li, 7): "Purge me with hyssop, and I shall be clean." The reference is to the custom of ceremonially sprinkling the unclean with a bunch of hyssop (marjoram or the thorny caper) dipped in water in which had been mixed the ashes of a red heifer. This was done as they left the Court of the Gentiles to enter the Court of the Women (*Numb.* xix, 17, 18).

Hysteron proteron (his' tèr on prō' tèr on) from the Greek meaning "hinder foremost". A term used in rhetoric to describe a figure of speech in which the word that should come last is placed first or the second of two consecutive propositions is stated first, *e.g.* "*Moriamur, et in media arma ruamus*"— Let us die, and rush into the midst of the fray (VIRGIL, *Æneid*, ii, 353).

In logic, the offering of what is essentially an axiom as a proof of some theorem the proof of which depends upon the axiom. *Cp.* PETITIO PRINCIPII.

I

I. The ninth letter of the alphabet, also the FUTHORC, representing the Greek *iota* and Semitic *yod*. The written and printed *i* and *j* were for long interchangeable; it was only in the 19th century that in dictionaries, etc., they were treated as separate letters (in Johnson's Dictionary, *iambic* comes between *jamb* and *jangle*), and hence in many series—such as the signatures of sheets in a book, hallmarks on plate, etc.—either I or J is omitted. *Cp.* U. I is number one in Roman notation.

The dot on the small *i* was introduced about the 11th century as a diacritic in cases where two i's came together (e.g. *filii*), to distinguish between these and *u*.

I in logic denotes a particular affirmative.

To dot the i's and cross the t's. *See* DOT.

I.H.S. The Greek I H S, meaning IHΣoyQ (Jesus), the long h (H) being mistaken for capital *H*, the abbreviation 'ihs' was often expanded as 'Ihsesus'. St. Bernadine of Siena in 1424 applied them to *Jesus Hominum Salvator* (Jesus, the Saviour of men). Other explanations were *In Hac Salus* (safety in this, *i.e.* the Cross) and *In Hoc Signo* [*vinces*] (in this sign [ye shall conquer]). *See* CONSTANTINE'S CROSS *under* CROSS.

I.N.R.I. The initial letters of the inscription affixed to the CROSS of Christ by order of Pontius Pilate—*Iesus Nazarenus, Rex Iudæorum*, Jesus of Nazareth, King of the Jews (*John* xix, 19). It was written in Greek, Latin, and Hebrew (*Luke* xxiii, 38).

I.O.U., *i.e.* "I owe you". The acknowledgement of a debt given by the borrower to the lender. As such it requires no stamp. *See* HURRY.

I.R.A. The Irish Republican Army, a guerrilla force largely reorganized by Michael Collins from the former Irish Volunteers, which confronted the Royal Irish Constabulary and the BLACK AND TANS from 1919 to 1923. After the CIVIL WAR, extremists kept it in being as a secret organization and although proscribed in 1936, it continued to make occasional raids into ULSTER, its aim now being to establish a united Irish Republic. After a period of quiescence, violence steadily increased from the mid-1950s. Since 1969 its senseless acts of terrorism in Ulster, England and elsewhere have made a settlement of the Ulster problem increasingly difficult.

I.R.B. The Irish Republican Brotherhood, another name for the Irish branch of the FENIANS, which continued in use after the latter had ceased to operate.

Iambic. An *iamb*, or *iambus*, is a metrical foot consisting of a short syllable followed by a long one, as *away*, *deduce*, or an unaccented followed by an accented, as *be gone!* Iambic verse is verse based on iambs, as for instance, the ALEXANDRINE measure, which consists of six iambuses:

> I think the thoughts you think; and if I have the knack
> Of fitting thoughts to words, you peradventure lack,
> Envy me not the chance, yourselves more fortunate!
>
> BROWNING: *Fifine at the Fair*, lxxvi.

Father of Iambic verse. Archilochos of Paros (*fl. c.* 700 B.C.).

Ianthe. A Cretan girl who, as told in Ovid's METAMORPHOSES, ix, 714–797, married Iphis, who had been transformed for the purpose from a girl into a young man. The Ianthe to whom Lord BYRON dedicated his *Childe Harold* was Lady Charlotte Harley, born 1801, and only eleven years old at the time. Shelley gave the name to his eldest daughter.

Iapetus (ī ăp′ ė tŭs). Son of URANUS and GÆA, father of ATLAS, PROMETHEUS, Epimetheus, and Menœtius, and, for the Greeks, father of the human race, hence called *genus Iapeti*, the progeny of Iapetus.

Iberia (ī bēr′ i à). Spain, the country of the *Iberus*, the ancient name of the river Ebro.

Iberia's Pilot. Christopher Columbus (*c.* 1446–1506), a Genoese by birth but a servant of Spain from 1492.

Ibis (ī′ bis). A sacred bird of the ancient Egyptians, with white body and black head and tail. It was the incarnation of THOTH. It is still found in the Nile marshes of the upper Sudan. The sacred ibis was often mummified after death.

Iblis. *See* EBLIS.

Ibn Sina. *See* AVICENNA.

Ibraham. The ABRAHAM of the Koran.

Ibsenism. A concern in drama with social problems, realistically rather than romantically treated, as in the works of the Norwegian dramatist Henrik Ibsen (1828–1906), whose plays, translated by William Archer and championed by G. B. Shaw (1856–1950), infused new vigour into English drama.

Icarius. In Greek legend an Athenian who was taught the cultivation of the vine by DIONYSUS. He was slain by some peasants who had become intoxicated with wine he had given them, and who thought they had been poisoned. They buried him under a tree; his daughter Erigone, searching for her father, was directed to the spot by the howling of his dog Mœra, and when she discovered the body she hanged herself for grief. Icarius, according to this legend, became the constellation BOÖTES, Erigone the constellation VIRGO, and Mœra the star PROCYON, which rises in July, a little before the dog-star.

Icarus. Son of DÆDALUS. He flew with his father from Crete; but the sun melted the wax with which his wings were fastened on, and he fell into the sea. Those waters of the Ægean were thenceforward called the Icarian Sea.

Ice. Ice Age. This term is usually applied to the earlier part of the existing geological period, the Pleistocene, when a considerable portion of the northern hemisphere was overwhelmed by ice caps. PALÆOLITHIC man was contemporary with at least the latter periods of the Ice Age, his remains having been found, together with the mammoth and reindeer, in glacial deposits.

The Antarctic continent was also more completely ice-covered and glaciers existed on the heights of Hawaii, New Guinea, and Japan. The Ice Age is also called the *glacial epoch*.

Ice Saints, or **Frost Saints.** Those saints whose days fall in what is called "the blackthorn winter"—that is, the second week in May (between 11 and 14). Some give only three days, but whether 11, 12, 13, or 12, 13, 14, it is not agreed. 11 May is the day of St. Mamertus, 12 May of St. PANCRAS, 13 May of St. Servatius, and 14 May of St. BONIFACE.

Iceberg. The tip of an iceberg. That which is merely on the surface, a small or superficial manifestation of something with the implication that there is much more, or worse to follow of which the present is only a beginning.

The ice-blink. The mariner's name for a luminous appearance of the sky, caused by the reflection of light from ice. If the sky is dark or brown, the navigator may be sure there is water; if it is white, rosy, or orange-coloured he may be certain there is ice. The former is called a "water-sky", the latter an "ice-sky".

The Danish name for the great ice-cliffs of Greenland is "The Ice-blink".

Ice-brook. A sword of ice-brook temper. Of the very best quality. The Spaniards used to plunge their swords and other weapons, while hot from the forge, into the brook Salo (Xalon), near Bibilis, in Celtiberia, to harden them. The water of the brook is very cold.

> It is sword of Spain, the ice-brook's temper.
> SHAKESPEARE: *Othello*, V, ii.

Ice-house. In the days before the domestic refrigerator, large private houses often had their own stores of ice kept in a specially constructed chamber, usually below ground level, which was known as an ice-house.

To break the ice. *See under* BREAK.

To cut no ice. To make no impression on others or have no influence or effect.

To skate over thin ice. To take unnecessary risks, especially in conversation or argument; to touch on a dangerous subject very lightly.

Iceni. *See* BOADICEA.

Ich Dien (ish dēn) (Ger., I serve). The motto of the PRINCE OF WALES since the time of Edward, the BLACK PRINCE (1330–1376); said, without foundation, to have been adopted, together with the three white ostrich feathers, from John, King of Bohemia, who fell at the battle of Crécy in 1346.

According to Welsh tradition Edward I promised to provide WALES with a prince "who could speak no word of English", and when his second son Edward (later Edward II) was born at Caernarvon he presented him to the assembly, saying in Welsh *Eich dyn* (Your Man).

Ichabod (ik′ à bod). A son of Phinehas, born just after the death of his father and grandfather (I *Sam.* iv, 19). The name ("no glory") is translated "The glory has departed", hence the use of Ichabod as an exclamation.

Ichneumon. A species of mongoose venerated by the ancient Egyptians and called "Pharaoh's rat" because it fed on vermin, crocodiles' eggs, etc. The word is Gr. and means "the tracker".

Ichor (ī′ kôr). In classical mythology, the colourless blood of the gods (Gr. juice).

> [St. Peter] patter'd with his keys at a great rate,
> And sweated through his apostolic skin:
> Of course his perspiration was but ichor,

Or some such other spiritual liquor.
BYRON: *Vision of Judgment*, xxv.

Ichthys (ik' this) (Gr. *ichthus*, fish). From the 2nd century the fish was used as a symbol of Christ and the word is also an acronym formed from the initial letters of *Jesous CHristos, THeou Uios, Soter* (Jesus Christ, Son of God, Saviour). It is found on many seals, rings, urns and tombstones of the early Christian period and was believed to be a charm of mystical efficacy.

Icknield Way. An ancient trackway from the Wash to the source of the river Kennet in Wiltshire, running through Cambridgeshire, Letchworth, Tring, and the Berkshire Downs (crossing the Thames near Goring). Part of it in East Anglia became a Roman road. The origin of the name is unknown.

Icon, or **Ikon** (Gr. *eikon*, an image or likeness). A representation in the form of painting, low-relief sculpture or mosaic of Our Lord, The Blessed Virgin, or a SAINT, and held as objects of veneration in the EASTERN CHURCH. Excepting the face and hands, the whole is often covered with an embossed metal plaque representing the figure and drapery.

Icon Basilike. *See* EIKON BASILIKE.

Iconoclasts (Gr., image-breakers). In the 8th century reformers, essentially in the EASTERN CHURCH, opposed to the use of sacred pictures, statues, emblems, etc. The movement against the use of images was begun by the Emperor Leo III, the Isaurian, who was strongly opposed by the monks and also by Pope Gregory II and Pope Gregory III. The controversy continued under successive *Iconoclast Emperors*, notably Constantine V, called insultingly "Copronymus" by his opponents (he is said to have fouled the font at baptism). It was finally ended by the Empress Theodora in 843 in favour of the image-lovers, and Iconoclasm was proscribed.

Id, in Freudian psychology, is the whole reservoir of impulsive reactions that forms the mind, of which the EGO is a superficial layer. It is the totality of impulses or instincts comprising the true unconscious mind.

Id est. (Lat., that is). Normally abbreviated to *i.e.*

Ida. Mount Ida. A mountain or ridge of mountains in the vicinity of TROY; the scene of the Judgment of PARIS. *See* APPLE OF DISCORD.

Idæan Dactyls. *See* DACTYLS.

Ideal Commonwealths. *See* COMMONWEALTHS.

Idealism, as a philosophical theory, takes a variety of forms, all of which agree that the mind is more fundamental than matter and that mind does not originate in matter; also that the material world is less real than that of the mind or spirit. Modern idealism has its roots in the philosophy of Bishop Berkeley (1685–1753), sometimes called *theistic idealism*. The more important theories of idealism are:

Transcendental Idealism taught by I. Kant (1724–1804); *Subjective Idealism* taught by J. G. Fichte (1762–1814); *Absolute Idealism*, taught by G. W. F. Hegel (1770–1831); and *Objective Idealism* taught by F. W. J. von Schelling (1775–1854).

Idealism in the general sense is applied to ethical and aesthetic concepts, etc., which adopt "ideal" or perfectionist standards. *Cp.* MATERIALISM.

Identikit. A method of identifying criminals from composite photographs based on an assemblage of individual features selected by witnesses from a wide variety of drawings. The method was developed by Hugh C. McDonald and first used at Los Angeles in 1959.

Ides. In the ancient Roman CALENDAR the 15th of March, May, July, and October, and the 13th of all the other months; always eight days after the NONES.

Beware the Ides of March. Said as a warning of impending and certain danger. The allusion is to the warning received by Julius CÆSAR before his assassination:

> What is still more extraordinary, many report that a certain soothsayer forewarned him of a great danger which threatened him on the ides of March, and that when the day was come, as he was going to the senate-house, he called to the soothsayer, and said, laughing, "The ides of March are come"; to which he answered, softly, "Yes; but they are not gone."
> PLUTARCH: *Julius Cæsar (Langhorne trans.)*.

Idiot. A mentally deficient or stupid person, originally (in Greece), a private person, one not engaged in any public office hence an uneducated, ignorant individual. The Greeks have the expressions, "a priest or an idiot" (layman), "a poet or an idiot" (prose-writer). In I *Cor.* xiv, 16, where the AUTHORIZED VERSION reads, "how shall he that occupieth the room of the unlearned say Amen...?" Wyclif's version reads, "who fillith the place of an idyot, how schal he seie amen...?"

Idiot cards. In the U.S.A., the name given to large cards held up in the wings of a theatre to give a comedian on stage the cue for his next joke.

Idle Bible, The. *See* BIBLE, SOME SPECIALLY NAMED EDITIONS.

Idomeneus. King of Crete and ally of the Greeks at TROY. After the city was burnt he made a vow to sacrifice whatever he first encountered if the gods granted him a safe return to his kingdom. He met his own son and duly sacrificed him, but a plague followed, and the king was banished from Crete as a murderer. *Cp.* IPHIGENIA.

Idris. Traditionally a Welsh giant, prince and astronomer. His rock hewn seat is on the summit of *Cader Idris* (the chair of Idris) in Gwynedd. According to legend, any person passing a night upon this will be either dead in the morning, in a state of frenzy, or endowed with the highest poetical inspiration.

> And, as from the grave, I awoke to inherit
> A flame all immortal, a voice, and a power!
> Day burst on that rock with the purple cloud crested,
> And high Cader Idris rejoiced in the sun;
> MRS HEMANS: *The Rock of Cader Idris*, iv.

Iduna. In Scandinavian mythology, daughter of the dwarf Svald and wife of BRAGI. She was guardian of the golden apples which the gods tasted whenever they wished to renew their youth. Iduna was lured away from AS-GARD by LOKI, but eventually restored, and the gods were once more able to grow youthful again and Spring came back to the earth.

Ifreet. *See* AFREET.

If. If youth but knew and age could do. This probably derives from Louis VI of France (1081–1137), also called Louis the Fat. Abbot Suger, his friend and counsellor, said that it was the King's frequent regret never to be able to have knowledge and strength together: "In my youth had knowledge, and in my old age had strength been mine, I might have conquered many Kingdoms".

Ifs and Ans.

> If ifs and ans
> Were pots and pans
> Where would be the tinker?

An old-fashioned jingle to describe wishful thinking; "if wishes were horses beggars could ride". The "ans", often erroneously written "ands", are merely the old use of "an" for "if".

Igerna. *See* IGRAINE.

Ignatius, St. According to tradition St. Ignatius was the little child whom our Saviour set in the midst of his disciples for their example. He was a convert of St. JOHN THE EVANGELIST, was consecrated Bishop of Antioch by St. PETER, and is said to have been thrown to the beasts in the amphitheatre by TRAJAN about 107. His day is 17 October and he is represented in art with lions, or chained and exposed to them.

Ignatius Loyola, St. *See* LOYOLA.

Father Ignatius. The Rev. Joseph Leycester Lyne (1837–1908), a deacon of the CHURCH OF ENGLAND, who founded a pseudo-BENEDICTINE monastery at Capel-y-ffin, near Llanthony, Monmouthshire, in 1870. He was an eloquent preacher, but his ritualistic practices brought him into conflict with his ecclesiastical superiors who would not admit him to priest's orders. In 1898 he was ordained by Joseph Villatte, a wandering BISHOP who had been consecrated by a schismatic "JACOBITE" prelate in Ceylon.

The Rev. and Hon. Geo. Spencer (1799–1864), a clergyman of the Church of England, who joined the ROMAN CATHOLIC CHURCH and became Superior of the English province of the Congregation of Passionists, was also known as "Father Ignatius".

Ignis Fatuus. The "Will o' the wisp" or "Friar's lanthorn", a flame-like phosphorescence flitting over marshy ground (due to the spontaneous combustion of gases from decaying vegetable matter), and deluding people who attempt to follow it; hence any delusive aim or object, or some Utopian scheme that is utterly impracticable. The name means "a foolish fire" and is also called "Elf-fire", "Jack o'lantern", "Peg-a-lantern", "Kit o' the canstick", "Spunkie", "Walking Fire", "Fair Maid of Ireland", "John in the Wad".

> When thou rannest up Gadshill in the night to catch my horse, if I did not think thou hadst been an *ignis fatuus* or a ball of wildfire, there's no purchase in money.
> SHAKESPEARE: *Henry IV, Pt. I*, III, iii.

According to Russian folklore, these wandering fires are the spirits of stillborn children which flit between HEAVEN and the IN-FERNO.

Ignoramus (Lat., we take no notice of it. The grand jury used to write *ignoramus* on the back of indictments "not found" or not to be sent to court. This was often construed as an indication of the stupidity of the jury, hence its present meaning.

Ignorantines. A name given to the Brothers of the Christian Schools, A Roman Catholic religious fraternity founded at Reims by the Abbé de la Salle in 1680 for giving free education to the children of the poor. They now carry out teaching work in many countries. A clause in their constitution prohibited the admission of priests with theological training, hence the name, which was also given to a body of Augustinian mendicants, the Brothers of Charity, or Brethren of Saint Jean-de-Dieu, founded in Portugal in 1495.

Igraine, Igerna. In ARTHURIAN ROMANCE, the wife of Gerlois (Gorlois), Duke of Tintagel, in CORNWALL, and mother of King ARTHUR.

His father, UTHER Pendragon, married Igraine the day after her husband was slain.

Ihram (i răm). The ceremonial garb of Mohammedan pilgrims to MECCA; also the ceremony of assuming it.

> We prepared to perform the ceremony of *Al-Ihram* (assuming the pilgrim garb) ... we donned the attire, which is nothing but two new cotton cloths, each six feet long by three and a half broad, white with narrow red stripes and fringes.... One of these sheets, technically termed the *Rida*, is thrown over the back, and, exposing the arm and shoulder, is knotted at the right side in the style *Wishah*. The *Izar* is wrapped round the loins from waist to knee, and knotted or tucked in at the middle, supports itself.
>
> BURTON: *Pilgrimage to Al-Madinah* and Mecca, xxvi.

Il Milione. *See* MILIONE.

Iliad (Gr. *Iliados*, of Ilium or Troy). The epic poem of twenty-four books attributed to HOMER, recounting the siege of TROY, PARIS, son of King PRIAM of Troy, when guest of MENELAUS, King of Sparta, ran away with his host's wife, HELEN. Menelaus induced the Greeks to lay siege to Troy to avenge the perfidy, and the siege lasted ten years. The poem begins in the tenth year with a quarrel between AGAMEMNON, King of Mycenae and commander-in-chief of the allied Greeks, and ACHILLES, the hero who had retired from the army in ill temper. The Trojans now prevail and Achilles sends his friend PATROCLUS to oppose them, but Patroclus is slain. Achilles in a desperate rage rushes into the battle and slays HECTOR, the commander of the Trojan army. The poem ends with the funeral rites of Hector.

An Iliad of woes. A number of evils falling one after another; virtually the whole catalogue of human ills finds mention in the *Iliad*.

Demosthenes used the phrase (*Ilias kakon*) and it was adopted by CICERO (*Ilias malorum*) in his *Ad Atticum*, viii, II,

> It opens another Iliad of woes to Europe.
> BURKE: *On a Regicide Peace*, ii.

The "Iliad" in a nutshell. *See* NUTSHELL.

The French Iliad. The *Romance of the Rose* (*see under* ROSE) has been so called. Similarly the NIBELUNGENLIED has been called **the German Iliad,** and the *Lusiad*, the **Portuguese Iliad**.

Ilk, Of that (O.E. *ilca*, the same). This phrase is often misused to mean "of the same kind", but is only correctly used when the surname of the person spoken of is the same as the name of his estate; *Bethune of that ilk* means "Bethune of Bethune". Used adjectively it means "every", "each"; as in "Ilka lassie has her laddie."

Ill May-Day. *See* EVIL MAY-DAY.

Ill-starred. Unlucky; fated to be unfortunate. In SHAKESPEARE's *Othello* (v, ii), Othello says of Desdemona, 'O ill-starr'd wench!" The allusion is to the astrological dogma that the stars influence the fortunes of mankind.

Illegitimates. An old Australian slang name for free settlers who came voluntarily, and not for "legal" reasons—*i.e.* as convicts.

Illuminated Doctor. *See* DOCTORS OF LEARNING.

Illuminati. The baptized were at one time so called, because a lighted candle was given them to hold as a symbol that they were illuminated by the HOLY GHOST.

The name has been given to, or adopted by, several sects and secret societies professing to have superior enlightenment, especially to a republican society of deists founded by Adam Weishaupt (1748–1830), at Ingolstadt in Bavaria in 1776, to establish a religion consistent with "sound reasons". They were also called *Perfectibilists*.

Among others to whom the name has been applied are the HESYCHASTS; the Alombrados of 16th-century Spain; the French GUERINISTS; the ROSICRUCIANS; the French and Russian MARTINISTS; and in the U.S.A. to the Jeffersonians, etc.

The Illuminator. The surname given to St. Gregory of Armenia (*c.* 240–322), the apostle of Christianity among the Armenians.

Illustrious, The. Albert V, Duke of Austria, and Emperor Albert II (1397, 1438–1439). Ptolemy V, Epiphanes (Illustrious), King of Egypt (*c.* 210, 205–180 B.C.).

JAMSHID (Jam the Illustrious), fourth king of the mythical Pishdadian dynasty of Persia.

Ch'ien-lug, fourth of the Manchu dynasty of China (1711, 1736–1796).

Image-breakers, The. ICONOCLASTS.

Imagism. A school of poetry founded by Ezra Pound (1885–1972), derived from the ideas of the philosopher T. E. Hulme (1883–1917). The imagist poets were in revolt against excessive romanticism, and proclaimed that poetry should use the language of common speech, create new rhythms, be uninhibited in choice of subject, and present an image.

Imam. An Arabic word meaning "leader", *i.e.* one whose example is to be followed. The title is given to the head of the MOSLEM community but is more familiar through its application to those leading the prayers in the Mosques, the *lesser Imams*. The name is also given as an honorary title and to the ruler of the Yemen.

Hidden Imam. *See* MAHDI.

Imbroccata, or **imbrocata** (Ital.). An old fencing term for a thrust over the arm.

> The special rules, as your punto, your reverso, your staccato, your imbroccato, your passado, your montanto.
>
> JONSON: *Every Man in His Humour*, iv, 5.

Immaculate Conception. This dogma, that the Blessed Virgin Mary was "preserved immaculate from all stain of original sin" from "the first moment of her conception" was not declared by the ROMAN CATHOLIC CHURCH to be an article of faith until 1854 when Pius IX issued the Bull *Ineffabilis Deus*. It has a long history as a belief and was debated by the SCHOOLMEN. It was denied by St. THOMAS AQUINAS (*see* THOMISTS), but upheld by Duns Scotus. (*See* DUNCE).

The Feast of the Immaculate Conception is on 8 December; it is a HOLIDAY OF OBLIGATION in some countries.

Immolate. To sacrifice (Lat. *immolare*, to sprinkle with meal). The reference is to the ancient Roman custom of sprinkling wine and fragments of the sacred cake (*mola salsa*) on the head of a victim to be offered in sacrifice.

Immortal. The Immortal. Yung-Cheng, 3rd Manchu Emperor of China (1723–1733), assumed this title.

The Immortal Tinker. John Bunyan (1628–1688), a tinker by trade.

The Immortals. The bodyguard of the kings of ancient Persia. *See also* REGIMENTAL AND DIVISIONAL NICKNAMES.

The Forty Immortals. The forty members of the French Academy are so nicknamed.

Imp. Lincoln Imp. *See* LINCOLN.

Impanation. The dogma that the body and blood of Christ are locally present in the consecrated bread and wine of the EUCHARIST, just as God was present in the body and soul of Christ. The word means "putting into the bread" and is found as early as the 11th century. *Cp.* TRANSUBSTANTIATION.

Imperial. From the Lat. *imperialis* (from *imperium*), meaning pertaining to an emperor or empire. The following are some of its special and particular applications:

A standard size of printing and writing paper measuring 22 × 30 in. (before metrification).

A Russian gold coin of the 18th century, 10 roubles in value.

A trunk for luggage of former days adapted for the roof of a coach or diligence. Also the carriage-top itself.

A tuft of hair on the chin, all the rest being clean-shaven. So called from the fashion set by the Emperor NAPOLEON III (1808–1873).

Imperial Conference. The name given to the conferences held in London between the prime ministers of the various dominions of the British Empire between 1907 and 1946 inclusive. These conferences had their origin in the first Colonial Conference which met in 1887 on the occasion of Queen Victoria's JUBILEE. Since 1948 the COMMONWEALTH Prime Ministers' Conference has replaced the Imperial Conference.

Imposition. Imposition of hands. *See* LAYING ON OF HANDS *under* HAND.

Impositions, as duties levied on imports under royal prerogative, were a point of dispute between James I and the Commons. CHARLES I continued to levy them until the fall of Strafford in 1642, when he consented to an ACT OF PARLIAMENT rendering them illegal. Extra written work, lines, etc., given to schoolchildren as punishments are also called *impositions*.

Impossibilities. Examples of the many familiar expressions denoting the impossible are:

> Gathering grapes from thistles.
> Fetching water in a sieve.
> Washing a blackamoor white.
> Catching wind in cabbage nets.
> Flaying eels by the tail.
> Making cheese of chalk.
> Squaring the circle.
> Turning base metal into gold.
> Making a silk purse of a sow's ear.

Impressionism. The first of the modern art movements, taking its name from a condemnatory criticism of Claude Monet's painting *Impression: Sunrise*, shown in 1874, Edouard Manet, Auguste Renoir, Camille Pissaro and Edgar Degas were the leading impressionist painters who upheld the new approach. As the name implies, they rejected the established conventions and sought to capture the impression of colour of transitory and volatile nature rather than its form. It broke down the distinction between a sketch and a finished painting. *See* SALON DES REFUSÉS. *Cp.* CUBISM; DADAISM; FAUVISM; FUTURISM; ORPHISM; POINTILLISM; POST-IMPRESSIONISM; SURREALISM; SYNCHRONISM; VORTICISM.

Imprimatur (Lat., let it be printed). An official licence to print a book. Such a licence or *royal imprimatur* was required under the Licensing Act of 1662 to secure ecclesiastical conformity. The act was initially for two years, was not renewed after 1695, and was in abeyance from 1679 to 1685.

In the ROMAN CATHOLIC CHURCH, if a priest writes on theological and moral subjects the book has to receive an *imprimatur* and NIHIL OBSTAT. The former is granted by the BISHOP or his delegate. *Cp.* INDEX.

Impropriation (Lat. *impropriare*, to take as one's own). Profits of an ecclesiastical BENE-FICE in the hands of a layman, who is called the *impropriator*. When the benefice is in the hands of a spiritual corporation it is called *appropriation*. At the REFORMATION, many appropriated monastic benefices passed into the hands of lay rectors, who usually paid only a small part of the TITHE to incumbents, hence the need for QUEEN ANNE'S BOUNTY.

In. In-and-in. A game for three, played with four dice, once very common. "In" is a throw of doubles, "in-and-in" a throw of double doubles, which sweeps the board.

> He is a merchant still, adventurer,
> At in-and-in.
> JONSON: *New Inn*, iii, 1.

The In and Out. The nickname of the Naval and Military Club (94, PICCADILLY) since HANSOM cab days. To avoid confusion between the various service clubs of that time, the cabbies bestowed nicknames upon them and the *In* and *Out* directions on the posts of the respective gateways suggested the name "In and Out". *See* CLUB.

Ins and outs. All the details of a subject, event, etc.

To be in for it. To be due for something unpleasant; to be due for a telling off; punishment is to be expected.

To have it in for a person is to be planning to work off a grudge against him; to be waiting the opportunity to get one's own back.

In Camera (Lat. vault or chamber). In judicial proceedings, the hearing of a case, either in the Judge's private room, or in Court, the public being excluded. Criminal cases may not be heard *in camera*.

In Cœna Domini (in chā' na dom' i ni) (Lat., on the Lord's Supper). A papal BULL issued from the 13th century until its suspension in 1773 owing to the opposition of the civil authorities. It contained excommunications and censures against heresies, schism, sacrilege, and the infringement of papal and ecclesiastical privileges by temporal powers, etc. Its publication came to be restricted to MAUNDY THURSDAY and many of its ecclesiastical censures were incorporated in Pius IX's bull *Apostolicæ Sedis* (1869).

In commendam (in kom en' dâm) (Lat., in trust). The holding of church preferment for a time, during a vacancy; and later restricted to livings held by a BISHOP in conjunction with his SEE. There were many abuses, and the practice was ended in England in 1836.

In esse (in es' i) (Lat. *esse*, to be). In actual existence, as opposed to *in posse*, in poten-tiality. Thus a living child is "in esse", but before birth is only "in posse".

In extenso (Lat.). At full length, word for word, without abridgement.

In extremis (in eks trē' mis). At the very point of death; *in articulo mortis*.

In flagrante delicto (Lat., while the offence is flagrant). RED-HANDED; in the very act.

In forma pauperis. *See* FORMA PAUPERIS.

In gremio legis (in grē' mi ō lē' jis) (Lat., in the bosom of the law). Under the protection of the law.

In loco parentis (in lō' kō pa ren' tis) (Lat., in place of a parent). Usually applied to those having temporary charge of minors in some capacity and therefore taking over parental functions.

In medias res (in mē' di ăs rāz) (Lat., in the middle of things). In novels and epic poetry, the author generally begins *in medias res*. *Cp.* AB OVO.

In memoriam (Lat.). In memory of.

In partibus (infidelium) (Lat., in the regions of the faithless.) A "bishop *in partibus*" was a Roman Catholic BISHOP in any country, Christian or otherwise and usually without a diocese, whose title was from some old SEE fallen away from the Catholic faith. Pope Leo XIII abolished the designation in 1882 and substituted that of "titular bishop".

In pectore. *See* IN PETTO.

In petto (Ital.). Held in reserve, kept back, something done privately and not announced to the general public. (Lat. *in pectore*, in the breast.)

Cardinals in petto. CARDINALS chosen by the POPE, but not yet proclaimed publicly. Their names are in *pectore* [of the Pope].

In posse. *See* IN ESSE.

In propria persona (Lat.). Personally, and not by deputy or agents.

In re (in rē) (Lat.). In the matter of; on the subject of; as *In re* Jones *v.* Robinson.

In rem. against the property or thing referred to.

In situ (Lat.). In its original place.

> I at first mistook it for a rock *in situ*, and took my compass to observe the direction of its cleavage.
> CHARLES DARWIN: *The Voyage of the "Beagle"*, ch. ix.

In statu quo (in stăt' ū kwō) or, **In statu quo ante** (Lat.). In the state in which things were before the change took place.

To maintain the status quo is to keep things as they are.

In statu pupillari (L. Lat.). Under guardianship.

In toto (in tō' tō) (Lat.). Entirely, altogether.

In vacuo (in văk′ ū ō) (Lat.). In a vacuum.

In vino veritas (Lat.). *See* VINO.

Inaugurate. To install into some office with appropriate ceremonies; to open formally. From Lat. *inaugurare*, which meant first to take OMENS by AUGURY, and then to consecrate or install after taking such omens.

Inbread. *See* BAKER'S DOZEN.

Inca. A king or royal prince of the dynasty governing Peru before the Spanish conquest; a member of the tribe in Peru at that time. The capital of their extensive empire was at Cuzco, and the dynasty was mythologically descended from Manco Capac, who was high priest of the Sun. His brothers were Cachi (Salt), Uchu (Pepper), and Auca (Pleasure). It was prophesied that Manco's golden rod would sink into the ground on reaching their destined home. This happened at Cuzco—

> Here the children of the Sun ... soon entered upon their beneficent mission among the rude inhabitants of the country; Manco Capac teaching the men the art of agriculture and Mama Oello initiating her own sex in the mysteries of weaving and spinning.
>
> H. M. PRESCOTT: *The Conquest of Peru*, I, i.

The last of the Inca dynasty Atahuallpa was murdered by the Spaniards in 1533.

Incarnation. The Christian doctrine that the Son of God took human flesh and that Jesus Christ is truly God and truly man (L.Lat. *incarnari*, to be made flesh).

Inchcape Rock. A dangerous rocky reef (also called the Bell Rock) about 12 miles from Arbroath in the North Sea (Inch or Innis means *island*). The abbot of Arbroath or "Aberbrothok" fixed a bell on a timber float as a warning to mariners. Southey's ballad of this name tells how the pirate Ralph the Rover cut the bell adrift and was himself wrecked on the very rock as a consequence.

A similar tale is told of St. Govan's bell in Pembrokeshire. In the chapel was a silver bell, which was stolen one summer evening by pirates, but no sooner had their boat put to sea than it was wrecked.

Incog.—*i.e.* **Incognito** (Ital. from Lat. *incognitus*, unknown). Under an assumed name or title. When a royal person, public figure, or a celebrity travels and does not wish to be treated ceremoniously or desires to avoid the public gaze he temporarily adopts another name and travels *incog*.

Incorruptible, The. Robespierre. *See* SEA-GREEN.

Incubus. A nightmare, anything that weighs heavily on the mind. In mediæval times it denoted an evil demon who was supposed to have sexual intercourse with women during their sleep (L.Lat. *incubus*, a nightmare). *Cp.* SUCCUBUS.

> Wommen may now go saufly up and doun;
> In every bussh or under every tree,
> Ther is noon oother incubus but he,
> And he ne wol doon hem but dishonour.
>
> CHAUCER: *Wife of Bath's Tale*, 1.24.

Incunabula (Lat., swaddling clothes; from *cunae*, a cradle). The cradle, birthplace, origins, or early stages of anything. The word is particularly and arbitrarily applied to early days of printing and book production up to 1500, although this date does not mark any significant change in these crafts. The middle of the 16th century is a much more satisfactory termination of the early period of printing and book production.

> The word incunabula was first used in connexion with printing by Bernard von Mallinckrodt ... in a tract, *De ortu et progressu artis typographicæ* (Cologne, 1639), which he contributed to the second centenary of Gutenberg's invention. Here he describes the period from Gutenberg to 1500 as '*prima typographiæ incunabula*', the time when typography was in its swaddling-clothes.
>
> S. H. STEINBERG: *Five Hundred Years of Printing*, ch. I.

Indenture. A document or agreement devised to prevent forgery; especially one between an apprentice and his master. So called because they were duplicated on a single sheet and separated or indented by a zigzag cut so that each party held identical documents. Their authenticity could be proved by joining the cuts. *Cp.* TALLY.

Independence Day. 4 July, which is kept as a national holiday in the United States of America, because the Declaration of Independence asserting the sovereign independence of the former British colonies was adopted on 4 July 1776.

Independents. A collective name for the various PROTESTANT separatist sects, especially prominent in 17th-century England, who rejected both Presbyterianism and EPISCOPACY, holding that each congregation should be autonomous or independent. The earliest were the BARROWISTS and BROWNISTS of Elizabeth I's reign, and the BAPTISTS and CONGREGATIONALISTS became the two main groups, but there were others more eccentric such as the FIFTH-MONARCHY MEN. They were notably strong in the Cromwellian army.

Index, The (Index Librorum Prohibitorum). The "List of Prohibited Books" of the ROMAN CATHOLIC CHURCH which members were forbidden to read except in special circumstances. The first Index was made by the INQUISITION in 1557, although Pope Gelasius issued a list of prohibited writings in 494 and there had been earlier condemnations and prohibitions. In 1571 Pius V set up a *Congregation of the Index* to supervise the list, and in 1917 its duties were transferred to the Holy Office. The Index was abolished 14 June 1966. In addition to the Index there was the *Codex Expurgatorius* of writings from which offensive doctrinal or moral passages were removed. Since 1897 diocesan bishops were given greater responsibility in the control of literature and the Index became less prominent.

All books likely to be contrary to faith and morals, including translations of the BIBLE not authorized by the Church, were formerly placed on the Index. Among authors wholly or partly prohibited were Chaucer, Bacon, Milton, Addison, Goldsmith, Locke, Gibbon; Montaigne, Descartes, VOLTAIRE, Hugo, Renan; Savonarola, Croce, D'Annunzio; and for a long time Galen, Copernicus, and Dante. *Cp.* IMPRIMATUR.

India is so named from *Indus*, in Sanskrit *Sindhu* (the river), in O.Persian *Hindu*. *Hindustan* is the *stan* or "country" of the river *Hindus*.

India paper. A creamy-coloured printing-paper originally made in China and Japan from vegetable fibre, and used for taking off the finest proofs of engraved plates; hence **India proof**, the proof of an engraving on India paper, before lettering.

The *India paper* (or *Oxford India paper*) used for printing Bibles and high-class "thin paper" and "pocket" editions is a very thin, tough, and opaque imitation. The name "India" given to these papers arises from their original importation through the "India trade" which brought in the products of the Far East.

Indian. American Indians. When Columbus left Spain in 1492 he set out to reach India and China, etc., by sailing west. When he reached the Bahamas the natives were called Indians in the belief that he had reached the fringes of the East. Hence the later name *West Indies*. *See* AMERINDIANS.

The Indian drug, or weed. Tobacco. Here the reference is to the West Indies.

> His breath compounded of strong English beere,
> And th' Indian drug, would suffer none come neere.
> JOHN TAYLOR: *The Water Poet*, 1630.

Indian file. Singly, one after another. From the American Indian practice of progressing in single file, each one of the column stepping in his predecessor's footprints, and the last man obliterating them. Thus neither the track nor the number of warriors could be traced.

Indian giver. An expression of U.S. origin, one who gives a present and later asks for its return, as American Indians did, if they got nothing in exchange for their gifts.

Indian Mutiny. The name given to the revolt in parts of British India (1857–1859) which was primarily a mutiny of sepoys in the East India Company's Bengal army rather than a national revolt against British rule.

Indian ringworm. Dhobie itch.

Indian summer. A term of American origin now generally applied to a period of fine sunny weather in late autumn. In America it is applied to such a period of mild dry weather usually accompanied by a haze. The name arose from the fact that such weather was more pronounced in the lands formerly occupied by the Indians than in the eastern regions inhabited by the white population. *Cp.* St. MARTIN'S SUMMER.

Indirect taxation. Tax levied on consumer commodities as opposed to *direct taxation* on land, incomes and capital.

Indo-European. A term invented by Thomas Young, the Egyptologist, in 1813, and later adopted by scientists, anthropologists, and philologists to describe the racial and linguistic origins of the main Indian and European peoples. Philologists have classified the Indo-European languages in groups such as Indo-Iranian, Greek, Italic, CELTIC, Germanic, etc.

Indra. An ancient Hindu god of the sky, originally the greatest, who was the hurler of thunderbolts and giver of rain, a god of warriors and of nature. He is represented as four-armed and his steed is an elephant. He is the son of HEAVEN and Earth and lives on the fabulous Mount MERU, the centre of the earth, north of the Himalayas.

Induction (Lat., the act of leading in). When a clergyman is inducted to a living he is led to the church door, and his hand is laid on the key by the archdeacon. The new incumbent then tolls the bell.

Indulgence. In the ROMAN CATHOLIC CHURCH, the remission before God of the earthly punishment due for sins of which the guilt has been forgiven in the sacrament of Penance. Such indulgences are granted out of the TREASURY OF THE CHURCH; they are either plenary or partial. In the later MIDDLE AGES the sale of indulgences by PARDONERS became a grave abuse and it was the hawking of indulgences by Tetzel and the DOMINICANS in Germany that roused Luther and precipitated the REFORMATION.

Declarations of Indulgence. Declarations issued by Charles II (1662 and 1672) and James II (1687 and 1688) suspending the penal laws against DISSENTERS and Roman

Catholics. Except for that of 1662, they were issued under royal prerogative; that of 1688 led to the trial of the SEVEN BISHOPS.

Industrial action. A term covering a variety of practices resorted to by dissatisfied employees collectively with the intent to disrupt industry, or to embarrass the general public, or even the government of the day. Such action includes bans on overtime, GO-SLOW tactics, WORKING TO RULE, strikes and picketing.

Industrial Revolution. A term popularized by Arnold Toynbee whose *Lectures on The Industrial Revolution of the 18th century in England* were published in 1884, although used half a century earlier by French observers. It generally denotes the whole range of technological and economic changes which transformed Great Britain from an essentially rural society into an urban industrialized state. The limiting dates usually assigned to this period of change vary somewhat, between 1750 to 1780 as the beginning and 1830 to 1850 as the end. The Industrial Revolution in this country occurred earlier than elsewhere.

Inexpressibles. A 19th-century EUPHEMISM for trousers, also called *unmentionables*. This absurdity is attributed to PETER PINDAR (*see* PINDAR) who used it in a biting LAMPOON on the DANDY Prince Regent.

Infallibility. In the ROMAN CATHOLIC CHURCH, the POPE, when speaking EX CATHEDRA on a question of faith and morals is held to be free from error. This dogma was adopted by the VATICAN COUNCIL of 1870 (many members dissenting or abstaining from voting) and was publicly announced by Pius IX at St. Peter's.

Infant (Lat. *infans*; ultimately from *in*, negative, and *fari*, to speak). Literally, one who is unable to speak; a child. It was used as a synonym of CHILDE, as "The Infant hearkened wisely to her tale" (Spenser, *The Faerie Queene*, VI, viii, 25). Hence **Infanta,** any princess of the royal blood in Spain and Portugal except an heiress of the crown; and **Infante,** any son of the sovereigns of Spain and Portugal except the crown prince who, in Spain, is called the Prince of the Asturias.

Infantry. Foot-soldiers. This is the same word as INFANT; it is the Ital. *infanteria*, from *infante*, a youth; hence one young and inexperienced who acted as a page to a KNIGHT, hence a foot-soldier.

Inferiority complex. A psycho-analytical term for a complex resulting from a sense of inferiority dating from childhood. It is supposed to cause an exaggerated desire for success and power, and frequently a conceited and pushing manner.

Infernal Column. So the corps of La Tour d'Auvergne (1743–1800)—"THE FIRST GRENADIER OF THE REPUBLIC"—was called by the Spaniards, from its terrible charges with the bayonet.

The same name—*Colonnes infernales*—was given, because of their brutality, to the twelve bodies of republican troops which "pacified" La Vendée in 1793, under General Turreau.

Inferno. We have DANTE'S notion of the infernal regions in his *Inferno*: HOMER'S in the ODYSSEY, Bk. XI; VIRGIL'S in the ÆNEID, Bk. VI; Spenser's in THE FAERIE QUEENE, Bk. II, canto vii; Ariosto's in ORLANDO FURIOSO, Bk. XVII; Tasso's in JERUSALEM DELIVERED, Bk. IV; Milton's in PARADISE LOST; Fénelon's in *Télémaque*, Bk. XVIII; and Beckford's in his romance of VATHEK. *See* HELL; HADES.

Infra dig. Not befitting one's position and public character. Short for Lat. *infra dignitatem*, beneath (one's) dignity.

Infralapsarian. The same as SUBLAPSARIAN.

Ingoldsby, Thomas. The pseudonym of the Rev. Richard Harris Barham (1788–1845) as author of the *Ingoldsby Legends*, which appeared in Bentley's *Miscellany* and the *New Monthly Magazine*, and in 1840 in book form.

Ingrained. *See* KNAVE IN GRAIN *under* GRAIN.

Ink. From Lat. *encaustus*, burnt in, encaustic.

Inkhorn terms. A common 16th-century term for pedantic expressions which smell of the lamp (*see under* LAMP). The inkhorn was the receptacle of horn, wood or metal which pedants and pedagogues carried with them.

> I know them that thinke Rhetorique to stande wholie upon darke wordes; and hee that can catch an ynke horne terme by the taile him they coumpt to be a fine Englishman.
> WILSON: *Arte of Rhetorique* (1533).

SHAKESPEARE used the phrase, an "inkhorn mate" (*Henry VI, Pt. I*, III, i).

Ink-slinger (U.S.A., ink-jerker). A contemptuous term for a writer, especially a newspaper journalist.

Inn. The word is Old English and originally meant a private dwelling-house or lodging. Hence Clifford's Inn, once the mansion of De Clifford; Lincoln's Inn, the abode of the Earls of Lincoln; GRAY'S INN. The word then came to be applied to a public house giving lodging and entertainment, or a tavern.

> Now when as Phœbus with his fiery waine
> Unto his Inne began to draw apace.
> SPENSER: *The Faerie Queene*, VI, iii, 29.

Inns of Court. The four voluntary societies in London which have the exclusive right of calling to the English BAR. They are the Inner Temple, The Middle Temple, Lincoln's Inn and GRAY'S INN. Each is governed by a board of BENCHERS.

Innings. He has had a long, or **a good innings.** A good long run of luck, a long time in office, etc. An innings in cricket is the time that the eleven or an individual has in batting at the wicket.

Inniskillings. In 1689, one cavalry and one infantry regiment were raised in Enniskillen to defend the town in the cause of William III, the former becoming the 6th (Inniskilling) Dragoons in 1751. These latter were amalgamated with the 5th Dragoon Guards in 1922 to form the 5th/6th Dragoons and were renamed the 5th Inniskilling Dragoon Guards in 1927. The title "Royal" was granted on the occasion of George V's JUBILEE (1935).

In 1751, the infantry regiment became the 27th (Inniskilling) Regiment of Foot. In 1881, they were renamed the Royal Inniskilling Fusiliers, with the 108th Foot as their 2nd battalion, becoming in 1968 the 1st Battalion Royal Irish Rangers.

Innocent, An. An idiot or born fool was formerly so called.

> Although he be in body deformed, in minde foolish, an innocent borne, a beggar by misfortune, yet doth he deserve a better then thy selfe.
> LYLY: *Euphues* (1579).

The Feast of the Holy Innocents. *See under* HOLY.

The massacre of the Innocents. *See* MASSACRE.

Ino. *See* LEUCOTHEA.

Inquisition, The (Lat. *inquisitio*, an enquiry). The name given to the ecclesiastical jurisdiction in the CATHOLIC Church dealing with the prosecution of heresy. In the earlier days of the Church excommunication was the normal punishment, but in the later 12th and early 13th centuries, disturbed by the growth of the Cathari (*see* ALBIGENSES), the Church began to favour seeking the aid of the State. The Inquisition as such was instituted by Pope Gregory IX in 1231, influenced by the activities of the Emperor Frederick II against HERETICS. Inquisitors were appointed, chiefly from the DOMINICAN and FRANCISCAN Orders to uphold the authority of the Church in these matters. They held court in the local monastery of their order. Proceedings were in secret, and torture, as a means of breaking the will of the accused, was authorized by Pope Innocent IV in 1252. Obstinate heretics were handed over to the secular authorities for punishment which usually meant death at the stake (*see* AUTO DA FÉ). In 1542 the *Congregation of the Inquisition* was set up as the final court of appeal in trials of heresy, and its title was changed to *The Congregation of the Holy Office* in 1908 and it was renamed *The Sacred Congregation for the Doctrine of the Faith* in 1965, concerned with the maintenance of ecclesiastical discipline.

The famous Spanish Inquisition was established in 1479, closely bound up with the State, and at first directed against "converts" from Judaism and ISLAM. Its famous first Grand Inquisitor was Torquemada (1420–1498), and during his term of office some 2,000 heretics were burned. The Spanish Inquisition was abolished by Joseph Bonaparte in 1808, reintroduced in 1814 and finally terminated in 1834.

Insane Root, The. A plant, probably henbane or hemlock, supposed to deprive of his senses anyone who partook of it. Banquo says of the witches:

> Were such things here as we do speak about?
> Or have we eaten of the insane root
> That takes the reason prisoner?
> SHAKESPEARE: *Macbeth*, I, iii.

Similar properties were attributed to MANDRAKE, BELLADONNA, poppy, etc. *Cp.* MOLY.

Inscription (on coins). *See* LEGEND.

Inspired Idiot, The. Oliver Goldsmith (1728–1774) was so called by Horace Walpole.

Installation. The correct term for the induction of a CANON or prebendary to his *stall* in a cathedral or collegiate church. Members of certain orders of CHIVALRY are also *installed*.

Institutes (Lat. *instituere*, to set up). A digest of the elements of a subject, especially law, as Coke's *Institutes of the Laws of England* and Erskine's *Institutes of the Laws of Scotland*. The most celebrated is the *Institutes of Justinian* completed in 533. It was intended as an introduction to the PANDECTS and was closely based on the earlier *Institutes of Gaius* and also on those of Callistratus, Paulus, Ulpian, and Marcian. Calvin's doctrines were summarily expressed in his famous *Institutio Religionis Christianæ*, or *Institutes*.

Insult. Literally, to leap on (the prostrate body of a foe); hence, to treat with contumely (Lat. *insultare*, to leap upon). Terence says, *Insultare fores calcibus* (*Eunuchus*, II, ii, 54). The priests of BAAL, to show their indignation against their gods, "leaped upon the altar which they had made" (I *Kings* xviii, 26). *Cp.* DESULTORY.

Intelligence Quotient, or **I.Q.,** is the ratio,

expressed as a percentage, of a person's mental age to his actual age, the former being the level of test performance which is median for that age tested by the Binet type scale or some similar system. Thus if a 10-year-old has a mental age of 9, his I.Q. is 90. 100 indicates average intelligence. The term was introduced by William Stern and popularized by L. M. Terman.

Inter alia (Lat.) Among other things or matters.

Intercalary (Lat. *inter*, between; *calare*, to proclaim solemnly). An *intercalary day* is a day inserted between two others, as 29 February in a LEAP YEAR; so called because, among the Romans, this was a subject of solemn proclamation. *Cp.* CALENDS.

Interdict. In the ROMAN CATHOLIC CHURCH, an ecclesiastical punishment placed upon individuals, particular places, or a district, restrictions being placed upon participation in, or performance of, certain SACRAMENTS, solemn services and public worship. *Cp.* EXCOMMUNICATION. Notable instances are:

1081. Poland was put under an interdict by Pope Gregory VII because Boleslaw II, the Bold, slew Stanislaus, Bishop of Cracow, on the altar steps of his church.

1180. SCOTLAND was similarly treated by Pope Alexander III for the expulsion of the Bishop of St. Andrews.

1200. France was interdicted by Pope Innocent III because Philip Augustus had his marriage with Ingelburge annulled.

1208. ENGLAND was put under an interdict lasting until 1213 by Innocent III for King John's refusal to admit Stephen Langton as archbishop of Canterbury.

Interest (Lat. *interesse*, to be a concern to). The interest on money is the sum which a borrower agrees to pay a lender for its use. *Simple interest* is interest on the principal, or money lent, only; *compound interest* is interest on the principal plus the interest as it accrues.

In an interesting condition. Said of an expectant mother. The phrase came into use in the 18th century.

Interlard (O.Fr. *entrelarder*). Originally to "lard" meat, *i.e.* to put strips of fat between layers of lean meat; hence, metaphorically, to mix irrelevant matter with the solid part of a discourse. Thus we say, "To interlard with oaths", "to interlard with compliments", etc.

> They interlard their native drinks with choice
> Of strongest brandy.
> JOHN PHILIPS: *Cyder* II.

Interlingua. An international language consisting of the living Latin roots in all European languages. It dates from about 1908 and was the product of the former VOLAPÜK academy. *Cp.* ESPERANTO.

International, or **Internationale.** The recognized international socialist and communist anthem. The words were written in 1871 by Eugène Pottier, a woodworker of Lille, and set to music by P. Degeyter.

Internationals. The name usually applied to the international federations of Socialist and Communist parties (*see under* COMMUNISM), the first of which was set up under the auspices of Karl Marx in 1864 as the International Working Men's Association, lasting till 1872. The INTERNATIONALE was adopted as its anthem. The Second, or Social-Democratic International, was formed in 1889 and the Third or Communist International was set up by Lenin in 1919 and lasted until 1941. The abortive Trotskyite Fourth International dates from 1936.

Interregnum, The. In British history usually implies the period of the COMMONWEALTH and Protectorate from the execution of Charles I (30 Jan. 1649) until the RESTORATION (18 May 1660). The period between the flight of James II (22 Dec. 1688) and the accession of William and Mary (23 Feb. 1689; 20 April 1689 in Scotland) was also an Interregnum.

Intolerable Acts. The American name for a group of British measures directed against Massachusetts in 1774, after the BOSTON TEA PARTY. They consisted of the Boston Port Act, closing the port of Boston; the Massachusetts Government Act, increasing British control; the Transportation Act, permitting British officials accused of capital offences to be tried outside Massachusetts; and the Quartering Act, which stationed royal troops in the barracks of Boston.

Invalides (an' và lēd). *Hôtel des Invalides*. The great institution founded by Louis XIV at Paris in 1670 for infirm soldiers. It contains a museum of military objects and notably the parish church of Saint-Louis containing the tomb of NAPOLEON, whose body was brought thither from St. Helena in 1840. Close by are the tombs of his son, The Duc de Reichstadt (L'Aiglon), and Marshal Foch (1851–1929). Others buried there are Joseph Bonaparte (1768–1844), King of Naples and Spain; Jerome Bonaparte (1784–1860), King of Westphalia; Marshal Turenne (1611–1675); General Bertrand (1773–1844); Marshals Duroc (1772–1813) and Grouchy (1766–1847); General Kleber (1753–1800).

Invention of the Cross. *See under* CROSS.

Inventors. Among the inventors and innovators "hoist with their own petard" (*see* PE-TARD), the following examples are of interest, although some no doubt belong to the realm of fable.

Bastille. Hugues Aubriot, Provost of Paris, who built the BASTILLE (*c*. 1369), was the first person confined therein. The charge against him was heresy.

Brazen Bull. Perillus of Athens made a brazen bull for PHALARIS, Tyrant of Agrigentum, intended for the execution of criminals, who were shut up in the bull, fires being lighted under the belly. Phalaris admired the invention and tested it on Perillus, who was the first person baked to death in the horrible monster.

Eddystone Lighthouse. Henry Winstanley erected the first Eddystone lighthouse. It was a wooden polygon, 100 feet high, on a stone base. The architect perished in his own edifice when it was washed away by a storm in 1703.

Gallows and gibbet. We are told in the *Book of Esther* (vii, 9) that HAMAN devised a gallows 50 cubits high on which to hang Mordecai, by way of commencing the extirpation of the Jews; but the favourite of Ahasuerus was himself hanged thereon. Similarly Enguerrand de Marigny, Minister of Finance to Philip the Fair (1284–1314), was hanged on the gibbet which he had caused to be erected at Montfaucon for the execution of certain felons; four of his successors in office suffered the same fate.

Guillotine. Dr. J. B. V. Guillotin of Lyons was guillotined, but he was not the man after whom the GUILLOTINE was named.

Iron Cage. The Bishop of Verdun, who invented the Iron Cage, too small to allow the person confined in it to stand upright or lie at full length, was the first to be shut up in one. Cardinal La Balue, who recommended them to Louis XI, was himself confined in one for ten years.

Ostracism. Cleisthenes of Athens introduced the practice of OSTRACISM and was the first to be banished thereby.

Sanctuary. Eutropius induced the Emperor Arcadius to abolish the benefit of SANCTUARY; but a few days afterwards he committed some offence and fled for safety to the nearest church. St. Chrysostom told him that he had fallen into his own net, and he was put to death.

Turret-ship. Cowper Coles, inventor of the Turret-ship, perished in the *Captain* off Finisterre, 7 September 1870.

Witch-finding. Matthew Hopkins, the witch-finder, was himself tried by his own

tests, and put to death as a WIZARD in 1647. *Cp*. DEATH FROM STRANGE CAUSES.

Investiture (Med.Lat. *investitura*, investing; from *vestire*, to clothe). The ceremonial clothing or investing of an official, dignitary, etc., with the special robes or insignia of his office.

Investiture Controversy. The name given to disputes between the Church and the Emperor and other princes over the right to invest abbots and BISHOPS with the ring and staff and to receive homage. The political and religious issues were strongly contested in the 11th and 12th centuries, especially between HILDEBRAND and the Emperor Henry IV (*see* CANOSSA). A compromise was reached in 1122, when the Emperor gave up his claim to invest with the ring and the staff but continued to grant the temporalities. In England the controversy between Anselm and Henry I over lay investiture was settled in a similar fashion in 1107.

Invincible Doctor. William of Occam (*c*. 1280–1349) or Ockham (a village in Surrey), FRANCISCAN friar and scholastic philosopher. He was also called *Doctor Singularis*, and *Princeps Nominalium*, for he was the reviver of NOMINALISM.

Invincibles. An Irish secret society of FENIANS founded in Dublin in 1881 with the object of doing away with the English "tyranny" and killing the "tyrants". They were responsible for the PHŒNIX PARK MURDERS.

Invisibility, according to fable, was obtainable in many ways. For example:

Alberich's cap, "Tarnkappe", which SIEGFRIED obtained, rendered him invisible (NIBELUNGENLIED).

The helmet of PERSEUS, loaned by PLUTO and made by the CYCLOPS for the god of the underworld, rendered its wearer invisible.

JACK THE GIANT-KILLER had a cloak of invisibility as well as a cap of knowledge.

Otnit's ring. The ring of Otnit, King of Lombardy, according to the HELDENBUCH, rendered its wearer invisible.

Reynard's wonderful ring, according to REYNARD THE FOX, had three colours, one of which (green), made the wearer invisible.

See also FERN SEED; GYGES; HELIOTROPE; DEAD MAN'S HAND.

Invulnerability. There are many fabulous instances of this having been acquired. According to Greek legend, a dip in the river STYX rendered ACHILLES invulnerable, and MEDEA rendered JASON, with whom she had fallen in love, proof against wounds and fire by anointing him with the PROMETHEAN UNGUENT.

SIEGFRIED was rendered invulnerable by

anointing his body with dragon's blood.

Io. The priestess of JUNO of whom JUPITER became enamoured. When Juno discovered his liaison, Jupiter transformed Io into a heifer and she wandered over the earth, finally settling in Egypt, when she was restored to human form.

Ionic Order. One of the three Greek orders of architecture, so called from Ionia, where it took its rise. The capitals are decorated with volutes, which are the characteristic feature of this order. *Cp*. CORINTHIAN ORDER; DORIC ORDER; TUSCAN ORDER.

Ionic School. A school of philosophy that arose in the 6th century B.C. in Ionia, notable as the nursery of Greek philosophy. It included Thales, Anaximander, Anaximenes, Heraclitus, Anaxagoras, and Archelaus. They sought a primal substance from which the infinite diversity of phenomena have evolved. Thales said it was water, Anaximenes thought it was air. Heraclitus maintained that it was fire. Anaxagoras developed a theory of fragments or particles from which all things emerged by process of aggregation and segregation.

Iota. *See* I; JOT.

Iphigenia. In classical legend, the daughter of AGAMEMNON and CLYTEMNESTRA. One account says that her father, having offended ARTEMIS by killing her favourite stag, vowed to sacrifice the most beautiful thing the year brought forth; this was his infant daughter. He deferred the sacrifice till the Greek fleet that was proceeding to TROY reached AULIS and Iphigenia had grown to womanhood. Then CALCHAS told him that the fleet would be wind-bound till he had fulfilled his vow; accordingly the king prepared to sacrifice his daughter, but Artemis at the last moment snatched her from the altar and carried her to HEAVEN, substituting a hind in her place. Euripides wrote a tragedy *Iphigenia in Tauris* and Gluck has an opera *Iphigénie en Tauride* (1779); the former's *Iphigenia in Aulis* was incomplete at his death. *Cp*. IDOMENEUS.

Ipse dixit (Lat., he himself said so). A mere assertion, wholly unsupported. "It is his *ipse dixit*" implies that there is no guarantee that what he says is so.

Ipso facto (Lat., by the very fact). Irrespective of all external circumstances of right or wrong; absolutely. It sometimes means the act itself carries the consequences. Thus by burning the PAPAL BULL (*see under* BULL), Luther *ipso facto* denied the POPE's supremacy.

Ireland. *Iar-en-land*, the land of the west. Called by the natives Erin, *i.e. Erinnis* or *Iar-innis*, west island; by the Welsh *Iwerddon*, west valley; by Apuleius Hibernia, which is *Iernia*, a corruption of *Iar-inni-a*; by Juvenal (ii, 160) Iuverna, the same as *Ierna* or *Iernia*; and by Claudian *Ouernia*.

The fair maid of Ireland. Another name for the IGNIS FATUUS.

The three great saints of Ireland. St. PATRICK, St. Columba, and St. Bridget.

Ireland forgeries. *See under* FORGERY.

Irene (I rē' nē). The Greek goddess of peace and wealth (Gr. *Eirene*). She is represented as a young woman carrying PLUTUS in her arms. Among her attributes are the OLIVE branch and CORNUCOPIA.

Iris. Goddess of the rainbow, or the rainbow itself. In classical mythology she was the messenger of the gods, and of JUNO in particular, and the RAINBOW is the bridge or road let down from heaven for her accommodation.

Besides being poetically applied to the rainbow, the name, in English, is given to the coloured membrane surrounding the pupil of the eye, and to a family of plants (Iridaceæ) having large, bright-coloured flowers and tuberous roots.

Iron. The Iron Age. An archæological term denoting the cultural phase conditioned by the introduction of the use of iron for edged-tools, implements, weapons, etc. In the Near East the preceding Bronze Age ended about 1200 B.C. and by 1000 B.C. the Iron Age was established. North of the Alps the first Iron Age, known as the HALLSTATT period, began about 750 B.C., in England about 500 B.C. and in Scotland the Bronze Age lasted till about 250 B.C. *See* LA TÈNE.

The era between the death of CHARLEMAGNE and the close of the Carlovingian dynasty (814–987) is sometimes so called from its ceaseless wars. It is sometimes called the *leaden age* for its worthlessness. *Cp*. DARK AGES. *See also* AGE.

Iron Chancellor. The name given to Prince Bismarck (1815–1898), the creator of the German Empire. *See* BLOOD AND IRON POLICY *under* BLOOD.

The Iron Cross. A Prussian military decoration (an iron Maltese CROSS, edged with silver), instituted by Frederick William III in 1813 during the struggle against NAPOLEON. Remodelled by William I in 1870 with three grades, in civil and military divisions, some 3,000,000 Iron Crosses were awarded in World War I.

The Iron Crown of Lombardy. *See under* CROWN.

Iron Curtain. The phrase denoting the barrier of secrecy created by the U.S.S.R. and her satellites along the Stettin-Trieste line, the Communist countries east of this line having cut themselves off from Western Europe after World War II. The phrase was popularized by Sir Winston Churchill in his Fulton Speech (5 March 1946) but it was used previously in Germany by Count Schwerin von Krosigk on 2 May 1945; and by Lord Conesford in February of that year. It has an earlier antecedent; Ethel Snowden used it in 1920 with reference to BOLSHEVIK Russia, Lord D'Abernon used it in 1925 with regard to the proposed Locarno Treaties, and the Queen of the Belgians, in 1914, spoke of a "bloody iron curtain", between her and the Germans. The phrase occurs in the Earl of Munster's journal as far back as 1817.

From Stettin on the Baltic to Trieste on the Adriatic, an iron curtain has descended across Europe.
SIR WINSTON CHURCHILL: *Fulton Speech*.

The Iron Duke. The Duke of Wellington (1769–1852) was so called from his iron will.

Iron Gates. The narrowing of the Danube below Orsova in south-west Rumania is so called. It is about 1½ miles long, with great rapids and an island in midstream. More popularly the term refers to the rocky bed of the river in this stretch which was dangerous to navigation until a ship canal was opened in 1898.

Iron Guard. The title adopted by the Rumanian FASCIST party of the 1930s.

The Iron Horse. The railway locomotive.

The Iron Lady. The name bestowed upon Mrs Margaret Thatcher, when leader of the Opposition in the HOUSE OF COMMONS, by the Soviet Defence Ministry newspaper *Red Star* (24 January 1976). After having warned the Commons of the increasing Russian threat to the West, the Red Star accused the "Iron Lady" of trying to revive the cold war referring to her "viciously anti-Soviet speech", and to "the peace-loving policy of the Soviet Union".

The Iron Maiden of Nuremberg. A mediæval instrument of torture used in Germany for traitors, heretics, parricides, etc. It was a box big enough to admit a man with folding doors, the whole studded with sharp iron spikes. When the doors were closed on him these spikes were forced into the body of the victim, and he was left to die.

Iron Mask, The Man in the. In the reign of Louis XIV, a mysterious state prisoner held for over forty years in various gaols until he finally died in the BASTILLE on 19 November 1703. When travelling from prison to prison he always wore a mask of black velvet, not iron. His name was never revealed but he was buried under the name of "M. de Marchiel". Many conjectures have been made about his identity, one of them being that he was the Duc de Vermandois, an illegitimate son of Louis XIV. Dumas, in his romantic novel on the subject, adopted VOLTAIRE's suggestion that he was an illegitimate elder brother of Louis XIV with Cardinal Mazarin for his father. The most plausible suggestion is that of the historians Lord Acton and Funck-Brentano, who suggested a minister of the Duke of Mantua (Count Mattiolo, b. 1640), who, in his negotiations with Louis XIV, was found to be treacherous, and imprisoned at Pignerol.

Iron rations. Emergency rations, especially as provided in the army; usually tinned food, particularly BULLY BEEF and biscuit. Also, in World War I a popular name for hot shell-fire.

Iron-arm. François de la Noue (1531–1591), *Bras de fer*, the HUGUENOT soldier, was so called. FIERABRAS is another form of the name.

Ironclads. The name originally applied to wooden warships when their hulls were first clad with iron armour plating. The idea originated with Napoleon III and the French floating batteries used in the Crimean war (1853–1856) were plated with iron. The first British warship of this type was the *Warrior* (1860), which was covered in plating to the water-line. The name persisted when warships were built of iron faced with steel.

Iron-hand, or The iron-handed. Götz von Berlichingen (1480–1562), a German knight who lost his right hand at the siege of Landshut (1505) and contrived one of steel to replace it. He was brave and chivalrous but something of a brigand. His autobiography was used by Goethe for his drama *Götz von Berlichingen* (1773).

Iron-man. U.S. colloquialism for a DOLLAR.

Ironside. Edmund II (*c.* 998–1016), King of England from April to November, 1016, was so called from his iron armour.

Ironsides. Cromwell's soldiers were so called after 1644. Their resolution at Marston Moor caused Prince Rupert to nickname Cromwell "Old Ironsides", and the name was thereafter applied to his men.

"Old Ironsides" was also the nickname of the famous U.S. frigate *Constitution*, said to have been so called by American sailors when the British shot failed to penetrate her oaken sides during her victory over the *Guerrière* in 1812. She was saved from the breakers by Oliver Wendell Holmes' poem *Old Ironsides* (1828).

Iron-tooth. Frederick II, Elector of Brandenburg (1440–1470).

Shooting-iron. Slang for a small firearm, especially a pistol or revolver.

The iron entered his soul. This expression, used of one experiencing the pangs of anguish and embitterment, is found in the Prayer Book Version of *Ps*. cv (verse 18). It is a mistranslation of the Hebrew which appeared in the VULGATE. It was corrected in the Authorized Version of the BIBLE which says "whose feet they hurt with fetters: he was laid in iron", *i.e.* he was put in irons or fetters. Coverdale, following the Vulgate, says—"They hurte his feet in the stocks, the yron pearsed his herte."

The iron fist, or **hand in the velvet glove.** Ruthlessness, extreme severity, or tyranny covered by a polite and courteous manner.

In irons. In fetters. A sailing vessel is said to be *in irons* when head to wind without way and will not pay off on either tack. The vessel is temporarily unmanageable.

Strike while the iron is hot. Don't miss a good opportunity; take action while the situation lends chance of success. An allusion to the blacksmith's shop.

Too many irons in the fire. More affairs in hand than you can properly attend to. The allusion is to the smithy.

To rule with a rod of iron. To rule tyrannically.

Irony (ī' ron i) (Gr. *eironeia*, simulated ignorance). The use of expressions having a meaning different from the ostensible one; a subtle form of sarcasm understood correctly by the initiated.

Socratic irony. The assumption of ignorance as a means of leading on and eventually confuting an opponent.

The irony of fate. That which brings about quite the opposite of what might have been expected. Thus by an irony of fate Joseph became the saviour of his brethren who had cast him into the pit.

Iroquois (ir' ō kwa). The French form of the Indian name of the FIVE NATIONS.

Irredentism. The name given to national minority movements seeking to break away from alien rule and to join up with neighbours of their own nationality and language. It derives from *Italia Irredenta* (unredeemed Italy), the name given by the Italians, between 1861 and 1920, to those Italian-speaking areas still under foreign rule. When the kingdom of Italy was formed in 1861 Venetia, ROME, Trieste, the Trentino, Nice, etc., were not included.

Irrefragable Doctor. Alexander of Hales (d. 1245), an English FRANCISCAN, author of *Summa Universæ Theologiæ. See* DOCTORS OF LEARNING.

Irresistible. ALEXANDER THE GREAT, before starting on his expedition against Persia, went to consult the Delphic ORACLE on a day when no responses were made. Nothing daunted he sought out PYTHIA and when she refused to attend took her to the temple by force. "Son," said the priestess, "thou art irresistible." "Enough," cried Alexander, "I accept your words as an answer."

Irus. The gigantic beggar who carried out the commissions of the suitors of PENELOPE. When he sought to hinder the returning ULYSSES, he was felled to the ground by a single blow. "Poorer than Irus" was a classical proverb.

Irvingites. Members of the CATHOLIC AND APOSTOLIC CHURCH. Edward Irving, a friend of the Carlyles, claimed to revive the college of the APOSTLES, and established a complex hierarchy, with such symbolical titles as "ANGEL", "Prophet", etc. In their early days they claimed to have manifested the gift of tongues.

Isaac. A hedge-sparrow; a dialect form of *haysuck* (in Chaucer *heisuagge*). The name meant a *sucker* (small thing) that lived in a *hay* (hedge).

Isabel. *See* SHE-WOLF OF FRANCE *under* WOLF.

Isabel, or **Isabelle.** The colour so called is the yellow of soiled calico. A yellow-dun horse is, in France, *un cheval isabelle*. According to Isaac D'Israeli (*Curiosities of Literature*) Isabel of Austria, daughter of Philip II, at the siege of Ostend vowed not to change her linen till the place was taken. The siege lasted three years!

Another story, equally unlikely, attaches to Isabella of Castile, who, we are told, made a vow to the Virgin not to change her linen till Granada fell into her hands.

There is no reason for accepting these fanciful derivations. The word appears in an extant list of Queen Elizabeth's clothes of July, 1600 ("one rounde gowne of Isabelle-colour satten").

Isenbras, or **Isumbras, Sir.** A hero of mediæval romance who made visits to the HOLY LAND and slaughtered thousands of SARACENS. At first proud and presumptuous, when he was visited by all sorts of punishments; afterwards penitent and humble when his afflictions were turned into blessings. It was in this latter stage that he one day carried on his horse two children of a poor woodman across a ford.

Iseult. *See* YSOLDE.

Ishbosheth, in Dryden and Tate's *Absalom*

and Achitophel, is meant for Richard Cromwell. His father Oliver is Saul.

The biblical Ishbosheth (man of shame) was the son of Saul, who was proclaimed King of Israel at his father's death (*see* II *Sam*. iv), and was almost immediately superseded by David.

Ishmael. An outcast. From the son of ABRAHAM and his concubine Hagar, handmaid of his wife Sarah. Hagar was driven into the wilderness by Sarah's harshness before her son was born. The Arabs regard Ishmael as their ancestor. *See* HAGARENES.

> And he will be a wild man; his hand will be against every man, and every man's hand against him.
> *Genesis* xvi, 12.

Ishtar. The Babylonian goddess of love and war (Gr. *Astarte*), corresponding to the Phœnician ASHTORETH, except that, while the latter was identified with the moon, Ishtar was more frequently identified with the planet VENUS.

Isidorian Decretals. *See* DECRETALS.

Isis (ī′ sis). The principal goddess of ancient Egypt, sister and wife of OSIRIS, and mother of HORUS, she typified the faithful wife and devoted mother. The cow was sacred to her, and she is represented as a queen, her head being surmounted by horns and the solar disc or by the double crown (*see* EGYPT). Her chief shrines were at Abydos and Busiris; later a splendid temple was built at Philæ. Proclus mentions a statue of her which bore the inscription "I am that which is, has been, and shall be. My veil no one has lifted. The fruit I bore was the Sun", hence **to lift the veil of Isis** is to pierce the heart of a great mystery.

She was worshipped as a nature goddess throughout the Roman world and was identified with JUNO, IO, APHRODITE, ASTARTE and a others, and in due course she became an embodiment of the universal goddess. Milton, in *Paradise Lost* (I, 478), places her among the fallen ANGELS.

Isis, River. *See* THAMES.

Islam. The Mohammedan religion, the whole body of the Mohammedans. The word means resignation or submission to the will of God.

Islam involves five duties:
(1) Recital of the creed (There is but one God and MOHAMMED is his Prophet).
(2) Reciting daily prayers.
(3) Fasting in the month of RAMADAN.
(4) Giving the appointed legal alms.
(5) Making a pilgrimage to MECCA at least once in a lifetime.

Islands of the blest. *See* FORTUNATE ISLANDS.

Isle of Dogs. A peninsula on the left bank of the THAMES between LIMEHOUSE and Blackwall reaches, opposite Greenwich. Traditionally said to be named from the fact that Edward III kept hounds here for hunting in Waltham Forest. Another explanation is that it is a corruption of *Isle of Ducks*, from the number of wild fowl inhabiting the marshes. It has long been part of dockland.

> The working men of the Isle of Dogs number some 15,000, engaged in the numerous factories and shipyards; for whose recreation has been formed a Free Library, to provide them with amusement for evenings too often spent in dissipation.
> JOHN TIMBS: *Curiosities of London*, 1867.

Ismene. In Greek legend, daughter of ŒDIPUS and Jocasta. ANTIGONE was to be buried alive by order of King Creon for burying her brother Polynices (slain in combat with his brother Eteocles) against the tyrant's express command. Ismene declared that she had aided her sister and asked to share the same fate.

Isocrates (ī sok′ rȧ tēz). One of the great orators of ATHENS, distinguished as a teacher of eloquence. He died 338 B.C.

The French Isocrates. Esprit Fléchier (1632–1710), Bishop of Nîmes, specially famous for his funeral orations.

Israfel. The angel of music for the Mohammedans. He possesses the most melodious voice of all God's creatures, and is to sound the Resurrection Trump which will ravish the ears of the saints in PARADISE. Israfel, GABRIEL, and MICHAEL were the three ANGELS that, according to legend, warned ABRAHAM of Sodom's destruction.

> In Heaven a spirit doth dwell
> Whose heart-strings are a lute;
> None sing so wildly well
> As the angel Israfel,
> And the giddy stars (so legends tell),
> Ceasing their hymns, attend the spell
> Of his voice, all mute.
> E. A. POE: *Israfel*.

Issachar, in Dryden and Tate's *Absalom and Achitophel*, means Thomas Thynne (1648–1682), of Longleat, known as "Tom of Ten Thousand".

Issachar's ears. Ass's ears. The allusion is to *Gen*. xlix, 14: "Issachar is a strong ass couching down between two burdens."

> Is't possible that you, whose ears
> Are of the tribe of Issachar's ...
> Should be deaf against a noise
> So roaring as the public voice?
> SAMUEL BUTLER: *Hudibras to Sidrophel*.

Issue. The point in debate or in question, especially in law.

At issue. Under dispute.

Side issues. Subsidiary issues; those of secondary importance to the main issue.

To join, or **take issue.** To dispute or take opposite views of a question, or opposite sides in a suit.

To join issues. In law is to leave a suit to the decision of the court because the parties interested cannot agree.

Istar. ISHTAR.

Isthmian Games. One of the four national festivals of the ancient Greeks, held every alternate spring, the second and fourth of each OLYMPIAD. They took place on the isthmus of Corinth, hence the name. According to one legend they were instituted as FUNERAL games in honour of MELICERTES. They included gymnastics, horse racing, and contests in music.

Isumbras. *See* ISENBRAS.

It. A humorous synonym for sex appeal, popularized by the novelist Elinor Glyn in *It* (1927), though Kipling had used the word earlier in the same sense in his story *Mrs. Bathurst (Traffics and Discoveries* 1904).

It. I'm it! I'm a person of some importance; also an expression used in children's games such as TAG by the one claiming the right to chase and touch the others, etc. It is also used as the name of the game.

In for it. About "to catch it" or be in trouble. In this phrase, and others, as to **come it strong, to rough it,** etc., *it* is the definite object of the verb.

To be with it. A much-used mid-20th century phrase meaning to be completely in with current trends, fashions, music etc., especially of the kind popular with certain sections of the young.

Its. One of the words by the use of which Chatterton betrayed his forgeries (*see* ROWLEY POEMS *under* FORGERY). In a poem, purporting to be the work of a 15th-century priest, he wrote, "Life and *its* goods I scorn," but the word was not in use till more than two centuries later, *it* (*hit*) and *his* being the possessive case.

> For love and devocioun towards god also hath *it* infancie and it hath *it* comyng forewarde in groweth of age.
> *Udal's Erasmus: Luke*, vii (1542).
> Learning hath *his* infancy, when it is but beginning and almost childish; then *his* youth ... then *his* strength of years ... and, lastly, *his* old age.
> BACON: *Essays; Of Vicissitudes of Things* (1625).

Its does not occur in any play of SHAKESPEARE published in his lifetime, but there is one instance in the First Folio of 1623 (*Measure for Measure*, I, ii), as well as nine instances of *it's*. Nor does it occur in the Authorized Version of the BIBLE (1611), the one instance of it in modern editions (*Lev.* xxv, 5) having been substituted for *it* in the Bible printed for Hills and Field in 1660.

Italia Irredenta. *See* IRREDENTISM.

Italian hand. I see his fine Italian hand in this may be said of a picture in which certain characteristics reveal the particular artist, or it may be remarked of an intriguer in which the characteristics of a particular plotter are apparent. The Italian hand was the *cancelleresca* type of handwriting used by the Apostolic Secretaries, and distinguishable by its grace and fineness from the Gothic styles of Northern Europe.

Italic. Pertaining to Italy, especially ancient Italy and the parts other than ROME.

Italic School of Philosophy. The Pythagorean, because PYTHAGORAS taught in Italy.

Italic type, or **italics.** The type in which the letters, instead of being erect, as in roman, slope from the left to right, *thus*. It was first used by Aldus Manutius in 1501, being the work of his type-designer, Francesco Griffo of Bologna, and based on the *cancelleresca corsiva* of the papal chancery. *Cp.* ITALIAN HAND.

Italic version. An old Latin version of the BIBLE, prepared from the SEPTUAGINT. It preceded the VULGATE.

The words italicized in the Bible have no corresponding words in the originals but were supplied by the translators to make the sense of the passage clearer.

Itch, To. Properly, to have an irritation of the skin which gives one a desire to scratch the part affected; hence, figuratively, to feel a constant teasing desire for something. The figure of speech enters into many phrases; as, *to itch* or *to have an itch for gold*, to have a longing desire for money; *an itching palm* means the same thing.

> Let me tell you, Cassius, you yourself
> Are much condemned to have an itching palm.
> SHAKESPEARE: *Julius Cæsar*, IV, iii.

To have itching ears. To be very desirous for news or novelty.

> For the time will come when they will not endure the sound doctrine; but, having itching ears, will heap to themselves teachers after their own lusts.
> II *Tim*. iv, 3 (R.V.).

My fingers itch to be at him. I am longing to give him a sound thrashing.

In popular belief, itching of various parts foretold certain occurrences; for instance, if your right palm itched you were going to receive money, the itching of the left eye betokened grief, and of the right pleasure. Itching of the lips foretold kissing; of the nose, that strangers were at hand, and the thumb, that evil approaches;

> By the pricking of my thumbs,
> Something wicked this way comes.
> SHAKESPEARE: *Macbeth*, IV, i.

ITMA (initials of "It's That Man Again"). The famous and once most popular of British radio features, and one which did much to brighten up the dreariness of the BLACK-OUT years of World War II. It was devised and maintained by the comedian Tommy Handley (1896–1949), the script being written by Ted Kavanagh. It ran from 1939 until Handley's death in 1949. Mrs. Mopp and Funf were among the characters in this hilarious weekly skit on English life.

Ivan Ivanovitch. Used of a Russian, as Johnny CRAPAUD was of a Frenchman.

Ivan the Terrible. Ivan IV of Russia (1530, 1533–1584), infamous for his cruelties, but a man of great energy. He first adopted the title of Tsar (1547).

Ivanhoe. Sir Walter Scott took the name and hero from the village of Ivinghoe in Bucks.; he recalled an old rhyme but misspelt the place-name.

> Tring, Wing and Ivinghoe
> For striking of a blow
> Hampden did forego
> And glad he could escape so.

The Hampden of this tradition, ancestor of the squire of SHIP-MONEY fame, is said to have quarrelled with the BLACK PRINCE at tennis and struck him with his racket.

Ivory, Ivory Gate. *See* DREAMS, GATES OF.

Ivory shoulder. *See under* PELOPS.

Ivory tower (Fr. *tour d'ivoire*). To live in an ivory tower is to live in seclusion, divorced from everyday life, excluding the harsh realities of the outside world. Contemporaries of the French poet, Alfred de Vigny (1797–1863), often said that he shut himself up in an ivory tower (a common phrase in the literary circles of his time).

Ivories. Teeth; also dice, keys of the piano, billiard balls, dominoes, etc.

Ivy (O.E. *ifig*). Dedicated to BACCHUS from the notion that it is a preventive of drunkenness. In Christian symbolism ivy typifies the everlasting life, from its remaining continually green.

Like an owl in an ivy-bush. *See* OWL.

Ixion. In Greek legend, a treacherous king of the LAPITHÆ who was bound to a revolving wheel of fire in the Infernal regions for boasting of having won the favours of HERA, ZEUS having sent a cloud to him in the form of Hera, and the cloud having become by him the mother of the CENTAURS.

J

J. The tenth letter of the alphabet, a modern introduction, only differentiated from I in the 17th century, and not completely separated till the 19th. It was a mediæval practice to lengthen the *I* when it was the initial letter, usually with the consonantal function now assumed by *J*. There is no roman *J* or *j* in the Authorized Version of the BIBLE. In the Roman system of numeration it was (and in medical prescriptions still is) used in place of *i* as the final figure in a series—iij, vij, etc., for iii, vii.

Jabberwocky. The eponymous central figure of a strange, almost gibberish poem in Lewis Carroll's *Through the Looking-glass*. It contains many significant PORTMANTEAU WORDS, as subsequently explained to Alice by HUMPTY DUMPTY.

Jachin and Boaz (jā′kin, bō′ăz). The two great bronze pillars set up at the entrance of the TEMPLE OF SOLOMON—*Jachin* being the right-hand (southern) pillar, the name probably expressing permanence, immovability, and *Boaz* being the left-hand (northern) pillar, typifying the Lord of all strength. *See* I *Kings* vii, 21; *Ezek*. xl, 49.

Jack. (1) A favourite name for JOHN, derived from *Jan* and *Jankin* which developed from *Johannes*; a generic name for a boy, man, husband, etc., and a familiar term of address among sailors, workmen and others.

In Australia, *Jack* has several connotations. It is slang for a policeman and in schoolboy parlance denotes an expert, as "a jack at games" (one who excels at games). *See* JACK SYSTEM *below*.

Cheap Jack. *See* CHEAP.

Cousin Jack. *See under* COUSIN.

Finality Jack. *See* FINALITY.

Jack Adams. A fool.

Jack Amend-All. One of the nicknames given to Jack Cade, leader of the Kentish rebellion of 1450. He promised to remedy all abuses.

Jack-a-dandy. A smart, foppish, bright little fellow.

> Tom did not understand French, but...despised it as a jack-a-dandy acquirement.
>
> SAMUEL LOVER: *Handy Andy*, xix.

Jack-a-dandy is also rhyming slang for brandy.

Jack-a-dreams. *See* JOHN-A-DREAMS.

Jack-a-Lent. A kind of AUNT SALLY which was thrown at in LENT; hence a puppet, a sheepish booby. SHAKESPEARE says: "You little Jack-a-Lent, have you been true to us?" (*Merry Wives of Windsor*, III, iii).

Jack among the maids. A favourite with the ladies; a ladies' man.

Jack-a-Napes. The nickname of William de la Pole, Duke of Suffolk, who was beheaded at sea (off Dover) in 1450, possibly at the instigation of the Duke of York. The name arose from his badge, the clog and chain of an ape, which also gave rise to his name "Ape-clogge". *See* JACKANAPES.

Jack and the Beanstalk. A nursery tale found among many peoples in varying forms. In the English version Jack exchanges his poor mother's cow for a handful of beans which miraculously produce stalks reaching the sky. Jack climbs up them and steals treasures from the ogre's castle—a bag of gold, a wonderful lamp, and the hen that lays the golden eggs, thus redeeming their poverty.

Jack and Jill. In the familiar nursery rhyme Jack and Jill who went up the hill "to fetch a pail of water" are probably generic names for lad and lass. Somewhat unconvincingly, attempts have been made to link them with Norse legend.

Jack-at-a-pinch. One who lends a hand in an emergency (pinch).

Jack-boot. A large boot extending over the knee, acting as protective armour for the leg, worn by troopers in the 17th and 18th centuries and later. It is still the type of boot worn by the Household Cavalry and was adopted by fishermen and others before the advent of gum boots. Figuratively, *to be under the jack-boot* is to be controlled by a brutal military regime. *Cp.* MAILED FIST; PRUSSIANISM.

Jack Brag. *See under* BRAG.

Jack Drum's Entertainment. *See under* DRUM.

Jack Dusty. A stores rating in the Royal Navy, formerly called a Supply Assistant, is so named. Handling naval stores, especially flour, is sometimes a dusty job.

Jack Frost. The personification of frost or frosty weather.

Jack the Giant-killer. The hero of the old nursery tale owed much of his success to his four marvellous possessions. When he put on his coat no eye could see him; when he had his shoes on no one could overtake him; when he put on his cap he knew everything he required to know and his sword cut through everything. The story is given by Walter Map (d. c. 1209), who obtained it from a French source.

Jack Horner. A very fanciful explanation of the old nursery rhyme "Little Jack Horner" is that Jack was steward to the Abbot of Glastonbury at the time of the Dissolution of the Monasteries, and that by a subterfuge he gained the deeds of the Manor of Mells. It is said that these deeds, with others, were sent to Henry VIII concealed, for safety, in a pasty; that "Jack Horner" was the bearer and that on the way, he lifted the crust and extracted this "plum".

Jack-in-the-basket. The basket or kindred device on the top of a pole which serves as a leading mark to shipping.

> To approach the entrance to Lymington river in the deepest water, bring Jack-in-the-basket beacon in line with the Lymington church.
> *Channel Pilot*, Pt. I (H.M.S.O.).

Jack-in-the-box. A toy consisting of a box out of which "Jack" springs, when the lid is raised.

Jack in the cellar. Old slang for an unborn child: a translation of the Dutch expression for the same, *Hans in Kelder*.

Jack-in-the-green. A youth or boy who moves about concealed in a wooden framework covered with leaves and boughs as part of the chimney-sweeps' revels on MAY DAY. An obsolete English custom.

Jack in office. A pompous overbearing official, usually with a RED-TAPE MIND, who uses his powers unimaginatively.

Jack Ketch. A notorious hangman and executioner, who was appointed about 1663 and died in 1686. He was the executioner of William, Lord Russell, for his share in the RYE HOUSE PLOT (1683), and of Monmouth (1685). In 1686 he was removed from office for insulting a SHERIFF and succeeded by a butcher named Rose, who was himself hanged within four months, when Ketch was reinstated. As early as 1678 his name had appeared in a ballad, and by 1702 was associated with the PUNCH AND JUDY

puppet-play, which had recently been introduced from Italy.

Jack-knife. Phrases from the similitude of a jack-knife in which the big blade doubles up into the handle.

(1) In logging, where two logs join end to end and hold up the rest;

(2) In swimming, a form of fancy dive;

(3) In road transport, when the main chassis of an articulated lorry swings towards the cab; a common cause of accidents.

Jack o' the bowl. The BROWNIE or house spirit of Switzerland; so called from the nightly custom of placing for him a bowl of fresh cream on the cowhouse roof. The contents are sure to disappear before morning.

Jack-o'-the clock, or **clock-house.** The figure which, in some old public clocks, comes out to strike the hours on the bell.

> Must I strike like Jack o'th'clock-house, never but in season.
> WM. STRODE: *Floating Island* I, ii (1655)

Jack-o'-lantern. The IGNIS FATUUS; in the U.S.A., the hollowed pumpkin of HALLOWEEN games.

Jack of both sides. One who tries to favour two antagonistic parties, either from fear or for profit.

Jack of cards. The knave or servant of the king and queen of the same suit.

Jack of Dover. Some unidentified eatable mentioned by Chaucer in the *Cook's Prologue*. "Our host," addressing the cook, says:

> For many a pastee hastow laten blood,
> And many a Jakke of Dover hastow sold
> That hath been twyes hoot and twyes cold.

Skeat says that it is "probably a pie that has been cooked more than once", another suggestion is that is is some seafish (*cp.* JOHN DORY).

Jack of Newbury. John Winchcombe alias Smallwood (d. 1520), a wealthy clothier in the reign of Henry VIII. He was the hero of many CHAP-BOOKS, and is said to have kept 100 looms in his own house at Newbury, and equipped at his own expense 100–200 of his men to aid the king against the Scots at Flodden Field.

Jack out of Office. One no longer in office; one dismissed from his employment.

> I am left out; for me nothing remains,
> But long I will not be Jack-out-of office.
> SHAKESPEARE: *Henry VI, Pt. I*, I, i.

Jack or John the Painter, James Aitken, alias James Hill, alias James Hinde, alias James Actzen was born at Edinburgh in 1752, the son of a whitesmith. He showed skill as an artist but abandoned his apprenticeship for the lure of London, where he lived by theft until capture seemed imminent. He joined the army but soon deserted. Early in the American war he apparently offered his services to the Americans, promising to burn British ships and dockyards. His first, but unsuccessful attempts, were at Portsmouth Dock and Plymouth and in January 1777 he set out for Bristol where he destroyed ships and warehouses and created panic. Rewards for his arrest were offered by the corporation, Edmund Burke, M.P. for Bristol and King George III. He was eventually arrested at Andover and in due course made his confession. He was hanged at the yardarm of the Arethusa at Portsmouth on 10 March 1777.

Jack-pot. In poker, a pot which cannot be opened until a player has a pair of jacks, or better. Generally applied to the "pool" disgorged by ONE-ARMED BANDITS, etc.

Jack Pudding. A buffoon, a MOUNTEBANK.

Jack Rice. An Australian race-horse once noted for his performance over the hurdles; hence **to have a roll Jack Rice couldn't jump over** is to have a lot of money.

Jack the Ripper. The name adopted by an unknown killer who murdered at least five prostitutes in Whitechapel in 1888 and mutilated their bodies.

> I'm not a butcher,
> I'm not a Yid,
> Nor yet a 'oreign skipper,
> But I'm your own light-hearted friend,
> Yours truly, Jack the Ripper.

Among suspects at the time were Michael Ostrog, a Russian doctor; Kosminski, a Polish Jew; and M.J. Druitt, unsuccessful son of a Dorsetshire surgeon. One recent fanciful theory was that the murders were planned by a group of high-ranking FREEMASONS, among them being Sir William Gull, the royal physician, their motive being to suppress scandals involving Prince Albert Victor, Duke of Clarence (1846–1892), elder son of the then Prince of Wales (later King Edward VII). Another theory was that it was the Duke of Clarence himself but a more likely candidate is J.K. Stephen, the Duke's lover.

Jack Russell. A white-coloured sporting terrier first bred by the Devonshire cleric John Russell (1759–1883). Much addicted to foxhunting and otter hunting, Jack Russell at one time kept his own pack of hounds and came to be known as "The Sporting Parson". See SQUARSON.

Jack-sauce. An insolent sauce-box, "the worst Jack of the pack".

Jack-snip. A botching tailor.

Jack Sprat. A DWARF; as if sprats were dwarf herrings. Children, by a similar META-PHOR, are called SMALL FRY.

> Jack Sprat could eat no fat,
> His wife could eat no lean,
> And so, betwixt them both you see,
> They licked the platter clean.
> *Nursery Rhyme.*

Jack Straw. One of the leaders in the PEASANTS' REVOLT of 1381, mentioned in Chaucer's *Nonnes Preestes Tale* (line 628). The name came to signify a man of STRAW, a worthless sort of person.

> It shall be but the weight of a strawe, or the weight of Jack Straw more.
> T. NASHE: *Nashe's Lenten Stuffe* (1599).

Jack Tar. A sailor. *See* TARPAULIN.

Radical Jack. *See under* RADICAL.

Yellow Jack. *See under* YELLOW.

A good Jack makes a good Jill. A good husband makes a good wife, a good master makes a good servant. Jill is a generic name for a woman. *See* JACK; *cp.* JACKEROO.

Before you can say Jack Robinson. Immediately, instantly. Grose says that the saying had its birth from a very volatile gentleman of that name who used to pay flying visits to his neighbours, and was no sooner announced than he was off again. Halliwell says (*Archaic Dictionary*, 1846):

> The following lines from "an old play" are elsewhere given as the original phrase—

> A warke it ys as easie to be done,
> As tys to saye Jacke! robys on.

But the "old play" has never been identified and both these accounts are palpably BEN TROVATO. The phrase was in use in the 18th century, and is to be found in Fanny Burney's *Evelina* (1778):

> "Done!" cried Lord Merton; "I take your odds!"
> "Will you?" returned he: "why then 'fore George, I'd do it as soon as say Jack Robinson".
> Letter Lxxxiii.

Sheridan, who became an M.P. in 1780, when attacking government bribery, retorted in response to shouts of "Name, Name", looking directly at John Robinson, Secretary of the Treasury; "Yes, I could name him as soon as I could say Jack Robinson". Thomas Hudson's ditty *Jack Robinson* was immensely popular in the early 19th century. It tells how the sailor Jack Robinson returned to find his lady married to another:

> says she, "I couldn't wait,
> For no tidings could I gain of you Jack Robinson."
> "But to fret and to stew about it's all in vain,
> I'll get a ship and go to Holland, France or Spain,
> No matter where; to Portsmouth I'll ne'er come again,"
> And he was off afore you could say Jack Robinson.

Every Jack shall have his Jill. Every man shall have a wife of his own.

> Jack shall have Jill
> Nought shall go ill;
> The man shall have his mare again, and all shall be well.
> SHAKESPEARE: *Midsummer Night's Dream*, III, ii.

Every man Jack of them. All without exception.

> Sir Pitt had numbered every "Man Jack" of them., and it would be as much his place was worth to give any away.
> THACKERAY: *Vanity Fair*, viii.

I'm all right, Jack. *See* PULL UP THE LADDER, JACK, *below.*

Jack of all trades and master of none. One who turns his hand to everything is not usually expert in any one field. *Jack of all trades* is a contemptuous expression—more grandiloquently he is a *sciolist*.

Jack policy, A. Virtually the same as a JACK SYSTEM.

Jack's as good as his master. An old proverb indicating the equality of man. *Cp.* WHEN ADAM DELVED *under* ADAM. It was the wise Agur (*see Proverbs*, xxx, 22) who placed "a servant when he reigneth" as the first of the four things that the earth cannot bear.

Jack system. An Australian phrase denoting the pursuit of one's own interests and welfare at the expense of others. *Cp.* PULL UP THE LADDER, JACK, *below.*

President of the Jack Club. In Australia this nickname is given to one who excels in the selfish pursuit of his own interests. *See* JACK SYSTEM.

Pull up the ladder, Jack, I'm inboard. The nautical equivalent of *I'm all right, Jack* denoting the pursuit of self-interest and the complete disregard of the interest of others. The allusion is obvious. *Cp.* JACK SYSTEM.

To play the Jack. To play the rogue, the knave. To deceive or lead astray like Jack-o'-lantern, or IGNIS FATUUS.

> Your fairy which you say, is a harmless fairy, has done little better than played the Jack with us.
> SHAKESPEARE: *The Tempest*, IV, i.

Jack (2), applied to animals, usually denotes the male sex or smallness of size; hence, **Jackass; Jack-baker** (a kind of owl); **Jack,** or **dog fox; Jack hare; Jack rat; Jack shark; Jack snipe; Jack curlew,** the whimbrel, a small species of curlew. A young pike is called a *Jack*, so also were the male birds used in falconry.

Jack-in-a-bottle. The long-tailed titmouse, or bottle-tit; so called from the shape of its nest.

Jack-rabbit. A large prairie-hare of North America; shortened from **Jackass-rabbit,** a name given to it on account of its very long ears and legs.

Jack (3) also forms part of the name of certain common wild plants, as in: **Jack-at-the-hedge** or cleavers; **Jack-by-the-hedge** or garlic mustard; **Jack-go-to-bed-at-noon** or goat's beard; etc. **Jack-in-the-pulpit** is a North American woodland plant, *Arisaema triphyllum*, so called from its upright spadix over-arched by the spathe.

Jack (4) when applied to certain articles usually implies smallness or inferiority of some kind. The *Jack* is the flag smaller than the ensign, worn on the jackstaff in the bows of a warship, although the Union flag is usually called the UNION JACK. The small waxed leather vessel for liquor was called a *jack* (*cp.* BLACK JACK). *Jack* was also the inferior kind of armour consisting of a leather surcoat worn by foot soldiers, formed by overlapping pieces of metal fastened between two layers of canvas, leather or quilted material. The *jack* at bowls is so called because it is small in comparison with the bowls themselves. A *jack* is an obsolete term for a FARTHING and a *jack* and *half-jack* were names given to counters, used in gambling, resembling a SOVEREIGN and half-sovereign.

To be upon their jacks. To have the advantage over one. The reference is to the *jack*, or jerkin worn by soldiers of olden times.

Jack rafter. A rafter in a hipped roof, shorter than a full-sized one.

Jack rib. An inferior rib in an arch, being shorter than the rest.

Jack timbers. Timbers in a building shorter than the rest.

Jack (5). Numerous appliances and contrivances which obviate the use of an assistant, etc., are called *Jacks*. A *jack* is used for lifting heavy weights and is also applied to the rough stool or horse used for sawing timber on; a **bottle-jack,** or **roasting-jack** was used for turning the meat when roasting before an open fire. Some others are:

Boot-jack. An appliance for pulling off boots by inserting the heel in a V-shaped opening.

Jack-block. A block attached to the masthead of a sailing shop for sending the topgallant yards up and down.

Jack-roll. The cylinder round which the rope of a well coils; a windlass.

Jack-screw. A large screw rotating in a threaded socket, used for lifting heavy weights.

Smoke-jack. An apparatus in a chimneyflue for turning a spit, made to revolve by the upward drought.

Jackal. A toady. One who does the dirty work for another. It was once thought that the jackal hunted in troops to provide the lion with prey. *See* LION'S PROVIDER.

Jackanapes. A pert, vulgar, apish little fellow; a prig. It is uncertain whether the *-napes* is connected originally with the ape or with *Naples*, *Jackanapes* being a *Jack* (monkey) of (imported from) *Naples*, just as *fustian-a-napes* was fustian from Naples. By the 16th century *Jackanapes* was in use as a proper name for a tame ape. *See* JACK-A-NAPES *above*.

> I will teach a scurvy jackanape priest to meddle or make
>
> SHAKESPEARE: *Merry Wives of Windsor*, I, iv.

Jackass. An unmitigated fool

Jackdaw. A prating nuisance.

The Jackdaw of Rheims. One of the best known of the INGOLDSBY *Legends* in which the cardinal's ring mysteriously vanished and he solemnly cursed the thief by BELL, BOOK, AND CANDLE. The jackdaw's bedraggled appearance brought on by the curse revealed him as the culprit.

Jackeroo. A name used in Australia in the first half of the 19th century to describe a young Englishman newly arrived to learn farming, derived, according to some, from the Queensland *tchareroo*, the shrike, noted for its garrulity. Others derive it from *Jack Carew*; *Jack* and *Kangaroo*; etc. Later the name was applied simply to a station hand. **Jilleroo,** its feminine counterpart, was applied to the Australian land girls of World War II.

Jacket. Diminutive of *jack*, a surcoat. Potatoes when cooked unpeeled are said to be "cooked in their jackets".

To dust one's jacket, or **to give one a good jacketing.** *See* I'LL DUST YOUR JACKET FOR YOU *under* DUST.

Jackey. A monkey. *Cp.* JACKANAPES.

Jackie Howe (Austr.) A sleeveless shirt worn by sheep shearers in Queensland, after Jack Howe (1855–1922), a champion shearer. His unbeaten record (1892) of hand shearing 321 merinos in one working day was not beaten by a machine shearer until 58 years later.

Jackstones. A children's game played with a set of small stones and a small ball or marble. They are thrown up and caught on the back of the hand in various ways, etc.

Jackstraws. In the U.S.A., a children's game similar to Spillikanes or Pik-a-Stik, but played with straws.

Jacob. Jacob's ladder. The ladder seen by Jacob leading up to HEAVEN (*Gen.* xxviii,

12); hence its application to steep ladders and steps, especially the rope ladder with wooden rungs slung from a ship's boom to the water. There is also a garden plant of this name so called from the ladder-like arrangement of its leaflets.

Jacob's staff. A pilgrim's staff; from the Apostle JAMES (Lat. *Jacobus*), who is usually represented with a staff and SCALLOP SHELL.

> As he had traveild many a sommers day
> Through boyling sands of Arabie and Ynde;
> And in his hand a Jacobs staffe, to stay
> His wearie limbes upon.
>
> SPENSER: *The Faerie Queene*, I, vi, 35.

Also a surveyor's rod, used instead of a tripod, and an obsolete instrument for taking heights and distances.

> Reach then a soaring quill, that I may write
> As with a Jacob's staff to take a height.
>
> CLEVELAND: *The Hecatomb to his Mistress*.

Jacob's stone. The Coronation stone of SCONE is sometimes called, from the legend that Jacob's head had rested on this stone when he had the vision of the ANGELS ascending and descending the ladder (*Gen.* xxviii, 11).

Jacobins. The DOMINICANS were so called in France from the "Rue St. Jacques", the location of their first house in PARIS. The famous French Revolutionary *Jacobin Club*, founded at Versailles in 1789 as the *Breton Club*, removed to Paris and met in a former Jacobin convent, hence the name. Among its famous members were Mirabeau, Robespierre, St. Just, Marat, and Couthon. It controlled the country at one stage through its hundreds of daughter societies in the provinces. The club was suppressed in November 1794, after the fall of Robespierre. Their badge was the Phrygian CAP OF LIBERTY.

Jacobites. A sect of Syrian MONOPHYSITES, so called from Jacobus Baradaeus, BISHOP of Edessa in the 6th century. The present head of their church is called the PATRIARCH of Antioch. The term is also applied to the Monophysite Christians in Egypt.

Jacobites. The name given to the supporters of James II (Lat. *Jacobus*) and of his descendants who claimed the throne of Great Britain and IRELAND. They came into existence after the flight of James II in 1688 and were strong in SCOTLAND and the north of ENGLAND. They were responsible for the risings of 1715 and 1745, the latter rising marking their virtual end as a political force. The last male representative of the Stuarts was Henry (IX), a cardinal and a pensioner of George III, who died in 1807.

Jacobus. The unofficial name of a hammered

gold coin struck in the reign of James I, originally worth 20s. It was properly called a UNITE. (Lat. *Jacobus*, James.)

Jacquard Loom (jăk′ ard). So called from Joseph Marie Jacquard (1752–1834), of Lyons, its inventor. Its particular importance was in facilitating the weaving of patterns, especially in silks.

Jacques (zhak) (Fr., James, Jim). A generic name for the French peasant, the equivalent of HODGE. *Jacques Bonhomme* is similarly used.

Jacquerie (zhăk′ e rē). An insurrection of the French peasantry in 1358, provoked by the hardships caused by the HUNDRED YEARS WAR, the oppressions of the privileged classes and Charles the BAD of Navarre. The Jacquerie committed many atrocities and savage reprisals followed. The name derives from JACQUES.

Jactitation of Marriage. A false assertion by a person of being married to another. This is actionable. *Jactitation* means literally "a throwing out", and here means "to utter", *i.e.* "to throw out publicly". The term comes from the old CANON LAW.

Jade. The fact that in mediaeval times this ornamental stone was supposed, if applied to the side, to act as a preservative against colic is enshrined in its name, for jade is from the Spanish *piedra de ijada*, stone of the side; and its other name, *nephrite*, is from Gr. *nephros*, kidney. Among the North American Indians it is still worn as an AMULET against the bite of venomous snakes, and to cure the gravel, epilepsy, etc.

Jade. A word of unknown etymology applied to a worthless horse, an old woman (contemptuously), and a young woman (often in the sense of "HUSSY" but not necessarily contemptuously).

Jagganath. *See* JUGGERNAUT.

Jahveh, or **Jahweh.** *See* JEHOVAH.

Jains. A sect of dissenters from Hinduism, of as early an origin as BUDDHISM. Jains, being largely traders, are usually wealthy, and therefore influential for their numbers.

Jakes. An old word for a privy.

Jakes-farmer. A contractor for cleaning out privies, a scavenger.

Jam. Used colloquially for something really nice or which comes very easily, especially if unexpected.

Money for jam. Money (or money's worth) for nothing or very little; an unexpected bit of luck.

Jam session. A meeting of JAZZ musicians improvising spontaneously without rehearsal.

To be in a jam. To be in a predicament;

from the verb *jam*, to compress, to squeeze or press down, to block, etc., akin to *champ*.

James. *See* JACOBUS.

St. James. The APOSTLE **St. James the Great** is the patron saint of Spain. One legend states that after his death in Palestine his body was placed in a boat with sails set, and that next day it reached the Spanish coast. At Padron, near COMPOSTELA, they used to show a huge stone as the veritable boat. Another legend says that it was the relics of St. James that were miraculously conveyed from Jerusalem, where he was BISHOP, to Spain, in a marble ship. A KNIGHT saw the ship entering port and his horse took fright and plunged into the sea but the knight saved himself by boarding the vessel and found his clothes entirely covered with SCALLOP SHELLS.

The saint's body was discovered in 840 by Bishop Theudemirus of Iria through divine revelation, and a church was built at Compostela for its shrine.

St. James is commemorated on 25 July and is represented in art sometimes with the sword by which he was beheaded, and sometimes attired as a pilgrim, with his cloak covered with shells. *Cp.* GROTTO.

St. James the Less, or **James the Little.** He has been identified both with the APOSTLE James, the son of Alphaeus, and with James the brother of the Lord. He is commemorated with St. PHILIP on 1 May. (3 May by Roman Catholics).

The Court of St. James. The British court to which foreign ambassadors are officially credited. St. James's Palace, PALL MALL, stands on the site of an ancient leper hospital dedicated to St. JAMES THE LESS. The palace was begun by Henry VIII in 1532 and was used as a residence by various monarchs and their children. After the burning of WHITEHALL in 1697, it came to be used for state ceremonies, hence the Court of St. James. It ceased to be a monarchical residence in 1837, but was used for LEVEES and other official functions. The office of the BOARD OF GREEN CLOTH was at St. James's.

Jesse James (1837–1882). A notorious American bandit. In 1867 he organized a band of bank and train robbers who perpetrated a number of infamous murders and daring crimes. A reward of $10,000 was put on his head. He retired to St. Joseph, Missouri, under the name of Howard and was shot by a reward-seeker while hanging a picture in his house. He undeservedly passed into legend as another ROBIN HOOD.

Poor Jesse left a wife to mourn all her life,
His children three were brave

But the dirty little coward that shot Mr. Howard,
He laid Jesse James in his grave.

Jameson Raid. A foolhardy attempt by Dr. L. S. Jameson to overthrow the Transvaal government of Paul Kruger. On 29 December 1875, Jameson crossed the border with 470 men in the expectation of a simultaneous UITLANDER rising in the Transvaal. He was surrounded at Doornkop (2 January 1896) and subsequently handed over to the British authorities. Rhodes, the Cape Prime Minister, was involved and the Colonial Secretary, Joseph Chamberlain, almost certainly implicated. *See* KRUGER TELEGRAM.

Jamshid. In Persian legend, the fourth king of the Pishdadian, or earliest, dynasty who reigned for 700 years and had Devs or demons as his slaves. He was credited with 300 years of beneficent rule, but when he forgot God, was driven out and remained hidden for 100 years. He was eventually sawn apart. Among his magical possessions was a cup containing the ELIXIR OF LIFE which is mentioned in Fitzgerald's *Omar Khayyám* and Moore's *Lalla Rookh*.

Jane. A small Genoese silver coin; so called from Fr. *Gênes*, Genoa.

Because I could not give her many a jane.
SPENSER: *The Faerie Queene*, III, vii, 58.

A *jane* is a slang term for a woman, derived from the name.

Jane-of-apes. The female equivalent of JACKANAPES.

Janissaries, or **Janizaries** (Turk, *yenitscheri*, new corps). Celebrated troops of the OTTOMAN EMPIRE, raised by Orchan in 1330; originally, and for some centuries, compulsorily recruited from Christian subjects of the Sultan. It was blessed by Hadji Becktash, a saint, who cut off the sleeve of his fur mantle and gave it to the captain, who put in on his head. Hence the fur cap worn by these footguards. In 1826 the Janissaries, long a tyrannical military caste, rebelled when their privileges were threatened, and they were abolished by total massacre.

Janissary music. Military music of the Turkish kind. Also called Turkish music.

Jannes, and **Jambres** (Jăn′ ēz, jăm′ brēz). The names under which St. PAUL (II *Tim.* iii, 8) referred to the two magicians of PHARAOH who imitated some of the miracles of MOSES (*Exod.* vii). The names are not mentioned in the OLD TESTAMENT, but they appear in the TARGUMS and other rabbinical writings, where tradition has it that they were sons of BALAAM, and that they perished either in the crossing of the Red Sea, or in the tumult after the worship of the GOLDEN CALF.

Jansenists. A sect of Christians, who held the doctrines of Cornelius Jansen (1585–1638), Bishop of Ypres. Jansen professed to have formulated the teaching of AUGUSTINE, which resembled CALVINISM in many respects. He taught the doctrines of "irresistible grace", "original sin" (*see under* SIN), and "the utter helplessness of the natural man to turn to God". Louis XIV took part against them and they were put down by Pope Clement XI, in 1713, in the famous Bull UNIGENITUS.

Januarius, St. The patron saint of Naples, a bishop of Benevento who was martyred during the Diocletian persecution, 304. He is commemorated on 19 September and his head and two vials of his blood are preserved in the cathedral at Naples. This congealed blood is said to liquefy several times a year.

January. The month dedicated by the Romans to JANUS, who presided over the entrance to the year and, having two faces, could look back to the year past and forward on the current year.

The Dutch used to call this month *Lauwmaand* (frosty-month); the Saxons *Wulfmonath*, because wolves were very troublesome then from the great scarcity of food. After the introduction of Christianity, the name was changed to *Se æfterageola* (the after-yule); it was also called *Forma monath* (first month). In the French Revolutionary CALENDAR of the first French Republic it was called *Nivôse* (snow-month, 21, 22 or 23 December to 20, 21 or 22 January).

It's a case of January and May. Said when an old man marries a young girl. The allusion is to the *Merchant's Tale* in Chaucer's *Canterbury Tales*, in which May, a lovely girl, married January, a Lombard baron sixty years of age.

Janus (jā′ nŭs). The ancient Roman deity who kept the gate of HEAVEN; hence the guardian of gates and doors. He was represented with two faces, one in front and one behind, and the doors of this temple in ROME were thrown open in times of war and closed in times of peace. The name is used allusively both with reference to the double-facedness and to war. Thus Milton says of the Cherubim:

Four faces each
Had, like a double-Janus.
Paradise Lost, XI, 129.

And Tennyson:

State-policy and church-policy are conjoint,
But Janus-faces looking diverse ways.
Queen Mary, III, ii.

While Dante says of the Roman eagle that it:

composed the world to such a peace,
That of his temple Janus barr'd the door.
Paradiso, vi, 83 (*Cary's tr.*).

Japhetic. An adjective sometimes applied to the ARYANS, from their supposed descent from *Japheth*, one of the sons of Noah. *Cp.* JAVAN.

Jarkman. Sixteenth-century slang for an ABRAM-MAN, especially an educated beggar able to forge passes, licences, etc. *Jark* was rogues' CANT for a seal, whence also a licence of the Bethlehem Hospital to beg.

Jarnac. Coup de Jarnac. A treacherous and unexpected attack; so called from Guy Chabot, Sieur de Jarnac, who, in a duel with La Châteigneraie, on 1 July 1547, in the presence of Henry II, first "hamstrung" his opponent, and then, when he was helpless, slew him.

Jarndyce *v.* **Jarndyce.** An interminable CHANCERY suit in *Bleak House*. Dickens probably founded his story on the long-drawn-out Chancery suit of Jennens *v.* Jennens, which related to property in Nacton, Suffolk, belonging to an intestate miser who died in 1798. The case was only finally concluded more than eighty years after its start.

Jarvey. Old slang for a HACKNEY-coach driver; from the personal name *Jarvis*, with a possible allusion to St. Gervaise, whose symbol in art is a whip.

I pity them 'ere jarvies sitting on their boxes all the night and waiting for the nobs what is dancing.
DISRAELI: *Sybil*, V, vii (1845).

Jason. The hero of Greek legend who led the ARGONAUTS in the quest of the GOLDEN FLEECE, the son of Æson, King of Iolcus, brought up by the centaur CHIRON. When he demanded his kingdom from his uncle Pelias who had deprived him of it, and was told he could have it in return for the Golden Fleece, Jason gathered around him the chief heroes of Greece and set sail in the ARGO. After many tests and trials, including sowing the remaining dragon's teeth left unsown by CADMUS, he was successful through the help of MEDEA, whom he married. He later deserted her and subsequently killed himself through melancholy. Another account says he was crushed to death by the stern of his old ship Argo, while resting beneath it. *See* ÆSON'S BATH.

Jaundice. A jaundiced eye. A prejudiced eye which only sees faults. It was a popular belief that to the eye of a person who had jaundice (Fr. *jaune*, yellow), everything looked yellow.

All seems infected that the infected spy.
As all looks yellow to the jaundiced eye.
POPE: *Essay on Criticism*, ii, 358–359.

Jaunty. In the Royal Navy the usual nickname for a Chief Petty Officer of the Regulating Branch, officially called a MASTER-AT-ARMS. It is a corruption of the Fr. *gendarme*.

Java man. *See* PITHECANTHROPUS.

Javan. In the BIBLE, the collective name of the Greeks (*Is.* lxvi, 19, and elsewhere), who were supposed to be descended from *Javan*, the son of Japheth (*Gen.* x, 2).

Jaw. To jaw, to annoy with words, to jabber, wrangle, cackle, etc.

Like a sheep's head, all jaw. Said of one who never stops talking but does little.

A break-jaw word; a jaw-breaker. A very long word, or one hard to pronounce.

Jaw-box, or **Jaw-hole** (Scotch). A sewer or sink.

Before the door of Saunders Jaup...yawned that odoriferous gulf, ycleped, in Scottish phrase, the jawhole, in other words an uncovered common sewer.
SCOTT: *St. Roman's Well*, ch. xxviii.

Pi jaw. A contemptuous term for pious talk, or for an ostentatious GOODY-GOODY.

Jay. Old slang for a frivolous person, a wanton.

Some jay of Italy...hath betrayed him.
SHAKESPEARE: *Cymbeline*, III, iv.

Jay hawker. In old Australian slang, a bandit.

Jaywalker. One who crosses a thoroughfare throughtlessly, regardless of passing traffic. A jay hops in an undulating fashion.

Jazey. A WIG; a corruption of *Jersey*, so called because wigs were once made of Jersey flax and fine wool.

Jazz. A type of dance music originating in the folk-music of the American Negro of the cotton fields. It first developed in New Orleans and reached Chicago by 1914 where it gained its name. It was slightly influenced by RAGTIME and is characterised by syncopation and the noisy use of percussion instruments, together with the trombone, trumpet and saxophone. Its impact grew steadily and it has had many notable exponents. The name has been somewhat loosely appropriated by popular dance orchestras playing their own conception of the jazz idiom. *Cp.* BLUES; BOOGIE-WOOGIE; SWING.

A load of jazz. A load of nonsense, a lot of CODSWALLOP.

Je ne sais quoi (zhe ne sā kwa) (Fr., I know not what). An indescribable something; as, "There was a *je ne sais quoi* about him which made us dislike him from the first."

Jeames. A flunkey. A former colloquial form of James. Thackeray's *Diary of C. Jeames de la Pluche, Esq.* first appeared in *Punch*.

O Evns! it vas the best of sights,

Behind his Master's coach and pair,
To see our Jeames in red plush tights,
A driving hoff from Buckley Square.
THACKERAY: *Jeames's Diary*

The old *Morning Post* used sometimes to be called *Jeames* because of its concern for the "flunkey-employing" classes and for its supposed subservience towards them.

Jean Crapaud. *See* CRAPAUD.

Jeddart, Jedburgh, or **Jedwood Justice.** Putting a person to death and trying him afterwards. From Jedburgh, the Scottish border town where MOSSTROOPERS were given this kind of treatment. The same as CUPAR JUSTICE and Abingdon law.

We will have Jedwood justice,—hang in haste, and try at leisure.
SCOTT: *The Fair Maid of Perth*, xxxii.

Jeep. A small all-purpose car first developed by the U.S.A. during World War II and known as G.P., *i.e.* General Purpose Vehicle, hence the name. Its four-wheel drive and high and low gearboxes gave it astonishing cross-country performance. The experimental models were also called Beeps, Peeps, and Blitz Buggies, but the name Jeep came to stay in 1941.

Jehad. *See* HOLY WAR.

Jehovah. The name *Jehovah* is an instance of the extreme sanctity with which the name of God was invested, for this is a disguised form of JHVH, the TETRAGRAMMATON which was too sacred to use, so the scribes added the vowels of ADONAI, thereby indicating that the reader was to say Adonai instead of JHVH. At the time of the RENAISSANCE these vowels and consonants were taken for the sacred name itself and hence *Jehovah* or *Yahweh*.

Jehovah's Witnesses. A religious movement founded in 1872 by Charles Taze Russel in Philadelphia, and known as International Bible Students until 1931. It does not ascribe divinity to Jesus Christ, regarding him as the perfect man and agent of God. Recognition of JEHOVAH as their sole authority involves the Witnesses in refusal to salute a national flag or to do military service. *The Watch Tower* is their official organ.

Jehovistic. *See* ELOHISTIC.

Jehu. A coachman, especially one who drives at a rattling pace.

The watchman told, saying...the driving is like the driving of Jehu the son of Nimshi; for he driveth furiously.
II *Kings*, ix, 20.

Jekyll (jek' il). **Dr. Jekyll and Mr. Hyde.** Two aspects of one man. Jekyll is the "would do good," Hyde is "the evil that is present". The phrase comes from R. L. Stevenson's *The Strange Case of Dr. Jekyll and Mr. Hyde*, first published in 1886.

Jellyby, Mrs. The type of enthusiastic, unthinking philanthropist who forgets that charity should begin at home (Dickens: *Bleak House*).

Jemmy (a diminutive of *James*). Slang for a number of things, as a burglar's crowbar (*see* JIMMY); a sheep's head, boiled or baked, said to be so called from the tradition that James IV of Scotland breakfasted on one just before the battle of Flodden (1513); also, a greatcoat; and, as an adjective, spruce, dandified. *See* JEMMY JESSAMY.

Jemmy Dawson. *See* DAWSON.

Jemmy Jessamy. A JACK-A-DANDY; a lady's fondling, "sweet as sugar-candy".

This was very different language to that she had been in the habit of hearing from her Jemmy Jessamy adorers.
THACKERAY: *Barry Lyndon*, ch. xiii.

Jemmy O'Goblin. Slang for a sovereign.

Jemmy Twitcher. *See* TWITCHER.

Jenkins's Ear. The name given to an incident that largely helped to provoke war between England and Spain in 1739, which became merged into the War of the Austrian Succession (1740–1748) since Spain and Britain took opposite sides. Captain Robert Jenkins, of the brig *Rebecca*, claimed to have been attacked by a Spanish *guarda costa* off Havana in 1731, when homeward bound from the West Indies; and that his ship was plundered and his ear severed. He carried his complaint to the king on reaching London. The case was revived in 1738 and Walpole was forced to yield to the general clamour for war backed by the trading interests. The main incidents of this maritime war, basically caused by Spanish interference with British shipping, occasioned by large-scale illicit trading, were Vernon's capture of Portobello (1739) and Anson's voyage round the world (1740–1744).

Jeofail. An old legal term for an error, omission, or oversight in proceedings at law. The word is the Anglo-French, *jeo fail*, O.Fr. *je faille*, I am at fault. There were several statutes of Jeofail for the remedy of irregularities and mistakes.

Jeremiah. A doleful prophet; from allusion to the *Lamentations of Jeremiah*, the OLD TESTAMENT prophet.

The British Jeremiah. Gildas (*fl.* 6th cent.), author of *Lamentations over the Destruction of Britain*, was so called by Gibbon.

Jeremiad. A pitiful tale, a tale of woe to produce compassion; so called from the *Lamentations of Jeremiah*.

Jerez. Jerez-de-la-Frontera, in southern Spain, once a frontier fortress between Moors and Christians, was the centre which produced the best SACK, which in the early 17th century came to be called "sherry", from *Scheris*, the Moorish rendering of Jerez. Drake brought home some 3,000 butts of Jerez wine when returning from the sack of Cadiz in 1587. *See* SINGEING THE KING OF SPAIN'S BEARD.

Jericho (Jer' i kō). Used in various phrases to give verbal location to some altogether indefinite place, possibly in allusion to II *Sam*. x, 5, and I *Chron*. xix, 5.

Go to Jericho. The equivalent of "GO TO HALIFAX," "Go and hang yourself," "Go to hell," etc.

Gone to Jericho. No one knows where.

I wish you were at Jericho. Anywhere out of my way.

Jerked Beef. "Jerked" is here a corruption of Chilian *charqui*, meat cut into strips and dried in the sun.

Jerkwater. An early American term for a small train on a branch railway; also a small township of little consequence, something of trifling importance. In such out of the way situations water was "jerked" by the bucketful into steam trains in need of replenishing their supply. *Cp*. ONE-HORSE TOWN.

Jeroboam. A very large wine bottle, flagon or goblet, so called in allusion to the "mighty man of valour" of this name who "made Israel to sin" (I *Kings* xi, 28, and xiv, 16). Its capacity is not very definite but it usually contains the equivalent of four bottles. An English wine bottle contains approximately one-sixth of a gallon or 26⅔ fluid ounces, also called a *reputed quart*. *Cp*. JORUM; MAGNUM; REHOBOAM; TAPPIT-HEN.

Jerome, St. A father of the Western Church, and compiler of the VULGATE (*c*. 340–420). He died at Bethlehem and is usually represented as an aged man in a cardinal's dress, writing or studying, with a lion seated beside him. His day is 30 September.

Jerrican. A 4½-gallon petrol or water container which would stand rough handling and stack easily, developed by the Germans for the Afrika Korps in World War II. Borrowed by the British in Libya, it became the standard unit of fuel replenishment throughout the Allied armies. The name is an allusion to its origin. *See* JERRY.

Jerry. Since World War I a nickname for a German, or Germans collectively. Also an old colloquialism for a chamber-pot.

Jerry-built. Unsubstantial. A "jerry-builder" is a builder of cheap unsubstantial properties. Possibly the name may be connected with Jericho, the walls of which collapsed at the sound of a trumpet. The phrase, however, may have originated at Liverpool about 1830 and a possible suggestion is that it is a corruption of "jury" as used in "jury mast" and "jury rigging", the temporary or makeshift replacements in an emergency. This could be a natural usage in a major seaport such as Liverpool where the housing shortage was acute in the post-Waterloo years and much accentuated by the influx of Irish labourers. Rapid and cheap construction by small builders with inadequate resources was the inevitable consequence.

Jerry, or **Jeremy Diddler.** In Kenny's farce *Raising the Wind* (1803), one who frequently borrowed small sums of money which he failed to return. The word *diddle* in the sense of to swindle is probably based on this name.

Jerry-shop, or **Tom and Jerry shop.** A low-class beerhouse.

Jerrymander. *See* GERRYMANDER.

Jersey Lily, The. Emily Charlotte Langtry (1852–1929), or Lillie Langtry, was so called after her debut on the professional stage in 1881. A famous Edwardian beauty and one-time intimate of the Prince of Wales (later Edward VII), she was the wife of Edward Langtry and daughter of W. C. Le Breton, Dean of Jersey. After Langtry's death she married Sir Hugo Gerald de Bathe in 1899.

Jerusalem. JULIAN THE APOSTATE, the Roman Emperor (d.363), to please the Jews and humble the Christians, said that he would rebuild the temple and city, but was mortally wounded before the foundations were laid, and his work set at nought by "an earthquake, a whirlwind, and a fiery eruption" (*see* Gibbon's *Decline and Fall*, ch. dxiii).

Much has been made of this by early Christian writers, who dwell on the prohibition and curse pronounced against those who should attempt to rebuild the city. The fate of Julian is cited as an example of Divine wrath.

The New Jerusalem. The paradise of Christians, in allusion to *Rev*. xxi.

Jerusalem artichoke. Jerusalem is here a corruption of Ital. *girasole*. Girasole is the sunflower, which this vegetable resembles in leaf and stem. *Cp*. HELIOTROPE.

Jerusalem Chamber. This chamber adjoins the south tower of the west front of Westminster Abbey and probably owes its name to the tapestries hung on its walls depicting scenes of Jerusalem. Henry IV died there, 20 March 1413.

It hath been prophesied to me many years,
I should not die but in Jerusalem.
SHAKESPEARE: *Henry IV, Pt. II*, IV, iv.

The WESTMINSTER ASSEMBLY (1643–1649) which drew up the Calvinistic WESTMINSTER CONFESSION met in the Jerusalem Chamber, as did the compilers of the Revised Version of the BIBLE. It is now the chapter-room.

Jerusalem Cross. A CROSS potent.

Jerusalem Delivered. An Italian epic poem in twenty books by Torquato Tasso (1544–1595). Published in 1581, it was translated into English by Edward Fairfax in 1600. It tells the story of the First CRUSADE and the capture of Jerusalem by Godfrey of Bouillon in 1099.

Jerusalem pony. A donkey.

Jess (through Fr. from Lat. *jactus*, a throw). A short strap of leather tied about the legs of a HAWK to hold it on the fist. Hence, metaphorically, a bond of affection, etc.

If I do prove her haggard,
Though that her jesses were my dear heart-strings,
I'd whistle her off.
SHAKESPEARE: *Othello*, III, iii.

Jessamy Bride. The fancy name given by Goldsmith to Mary Horneck when he fell in love with her in 1769. *Cp.* JEMMY JESSAMY.

Jesse, or **Jesse Tree.** A genealogical tree, usually represented as a large vine or as a large brass candlestick with many branches, tracing the ancestry of Christ, called a "rod out of the stem of Jesse" (*Is.* xi, 1). Jesse is himself sometimes represented in a recumbent position with the vine rising out of his loins; hence a stained glass window representing him thus with a tree shooting from him containing the pedigree of Jesus is called a *Jesse window*.

Jesse James. *See under* JAMES.

Jessie. More hide than Jessie at the zoo (Austr.). Insensitive. Jessie being an elephant, the phrase is similar to the English "having a hide like a rhinoceros".

Jesters. *See* COURT FOOLS *under* FOOLS.

Jesuit. The name given to members of the Society of Jesus, begun by Ignatius LOYOLA in 1534, and formally approved by Pope Paul III in 1540. It was founded to combat the REFORMATION and to propagate the faith among the heathen. Through its discipline, organization, and methods of secrecy it acquired such power that it came into conflict with both the civil and religious authorities. It was driven from France in 1594, from Portugal in 1759, and from Spain in 1767, was suppressed by Pope Clement XIV in 1773, but formally reconstituted by Pius VII in 1814.

Owing to the casuistical principles maintained by many of its leaders, the name Jesuit acquired an opprobrious signification and a *Jesuit* or *Jesuitical person* means (secondarily) a deceiver, a prevaricator, etc. Such associations have often obscured the extent of their achievements.

Jesuit's bark. *See* PERUVIAN BARK.

Jesus Paper. Before metrification, paper of large size (about 28½ in. × 21½ in.) chiefly used for engravings. Originally it was stamped with the initials I.H.S.

Jet. The Jet Set. A phrase applied to those affluent socialites who can afford to travel by jet aircraft to the various fashionable resorts around the world.

The Royal Family can hardly be said to belong to the Jet Set–all the aircraft in the Queen's Flight are prop-driven (and 15 years old).
Sunday Telegraph (3 February 1980).

Jetsam, or **Jetson.** Goods cast into the sea to lighten a ship. *See* FLOTSAM.

Jettatura (Ital.). The evil eye, a superstition that certain persons have the power, by looking at one, of casting a malevolent spell.

Jeu d'esprit (zhĕr des prē) (Fr.) A witticism.

Jeu de mots (zhĕr dȧ mō) (Fr.). A pun; a play on some words or phrase.

Jeune Cupidon. *See* BEAU D'ORSAY.

Jeunesse Dorée (zhĕr nes' dôr' ā) (Fr.). The "gilded youth" of a nation; the rich, fashionable young bachelors.

Jew. A Hebrew. Used opprobriously to denote a mean or hard-fisted person.

Ebrew Jew. *See* EBREW.

Wandering Jew. *See* WANDERING.

Jews born with tails. *See* TAILED MEN.

Jew's ear. A fungus that grows on the JUDAS-TREE; its name is due to a mistranslation of its Latin name, *Auricula Judæ i.e.* Judas's ear.

Jew's harp. A simple musical instrument held between the teeth and twanged with the hand. The origin of the name is a matter of surmise, hence *Jaw's harp* as a popular supposition. It has also been called **Jew's trump**. Hakluyt uses the former term and the latter is used by Fletcher (*Humerous Lieutenant*, V, ii). It is also applied to a shackle from its similarity of shape.

Jew's myrtle. Butcher's Broom is so called, from the popular notion that it formed the crown of thorns placed by the Jews on the head of the Saviour.

Worth a Jew's eye. Something precious or highly prized. An allusion to the torture by which money was extracted from Jews in the days of King John. There is a story of a Bristol Jew who resisted the tallage of 10,000 marks demanded of him. He was condemned to have one tooth tugged out every day until he paid up. He gave up after the seventh had been extracted. John is supposed to have jestingly remarked. "A Jew's eye may be a quick ransom, but a Jew's teeth give the richer harvest."

> There will come a Christian by,
> Will be worth a Jewess' eye.
> SHAKESPEARE: *Merchant of Venice*, II, v.

Jewels. *See* PRECIOUS STONES.

These are my jewels! *See* CORNELIA; *cp.* TREASURE.

Jezebel. The infamous wife of Ahab, King of Israel, who was denounced by Elijah for bringing in the worship of BAAL. Her name came to be used for an objectionable or abandoned woman, known to have used cosmetics. It is used for such a woman who paints her face, frequently referred to as a **painted Jezebel**.

> And when Jehu was come to Jezreel, Jezebel heard of it; and she painted her face, and tired her head, and looked out at a window.
> II *Kings*, ix, 30.

Jezreelites. A small sect founded in 1875 by James White (1849–1885), a one-time army private, who took the name James Jershom Jezreel. They were also called the "New and Latter House of Israel" and believed that Christ redeemed only souls, and that the body is saved by belief in the Law. Their object was to be numbered among the 144,000 (see *Rev.* vii, 4) who, at the Last JUDGEMENT, will be endowed with immortal bodies. Their headquarters were at Gillingham, Kent, where their Tower of Jezreel was formerly a familiar landmark.

Jib. The cut of his jib. The expression of a person's face. "Jib" here is the triangular foresail. Sailors used to recognize vessels at sea by the "cut of their jibs".

Jib is also applied to the lower lip. Thus **to hang the jib,** or **to make,** or **pull a jib** is to protrude the lower lip in an ill-tempered or discontented fashion.

To jib. To start aside, to back out; a "jibbing horse" is one that is easily startled. It is probably from the nautical *gybe*, which, with a fore-and-aft rig, is to bring a vessel so much by the lee (*i.e.* when the wind begins to blow on the same side as she is carrying her mainsail) that the mainsail swings to the other side. Accidental gybing can be dangerous.

Jiffy. In a jiffy. In a moment; in a brace of shakes; before you can say "Jack Robinson". (*See under* JACK). The origin of the word is unknown.

Jig (Fr. *gigue*). A lively tune or dance in six-eight time.

> You jig, you amble, and you lisp.
> SHAKESPEARE: *Hamlet*, III, i.

The jig is up. Your trickery is discovered. "Jig" was old slang for a joke or trick.

Jiggery. An American slang term for a dance-hall.

Jiggery-pokery. Fraud, "wangling", "fiddling", etc.

Jigot (jig′ ot). A Scots term for a leg of mutton or lamb. It is the Fr. *gigot*, and is one of the Scottish words arising from the close connexion between the two countries in the 16th and 17th centuries.

Jill. A generic name for a lass, a sweetheart. *See* JACK AND JILL *under* JACK.

Jilleroo. *See* JACKEROO.

Jim Crow. A popular "nigger minstrel" song first introduced in Louisville by Thomas D. Rice (Daddy Rice) in 1828. It was brought to the Surrey Theatre, London, in 1836. A renegade or TURNCOAT was called "Jim Crow", from the burden of the song:

> Wheel about and turn about
> And do jis so,
> Ebry time I wheel about
> I jump Jim Crow.

The song was so popular that it was translated into French;

> Je tourne, re-tourne, je caracole,
> Je fais des sauts;
> Chaque fois je fais le tour,
> Je saute 'Jim Crow'.

Jim Crow cars. Railway coaches set apart for the segregation of Negroes.

Jim Crow Regulations. Any regulations which prohibit Negroes from associating with or enjoying the same privileges as white people.

Jimmy. In the U.S.A., the burglar's JEMMY is called a "jimmy" and to *jimmy* is to force an entry.

Jimmy Woodser (Austr.). A solitary drinker; possibly based on the name of a bibulous "Jimmy Woods" or his drink. In Victoria a solitary drinker *goes Ballarat*.

Jingo. A word from the patter and jargon of 17th-century conjurers (*cp.* HOCUS-POCUS) probably substituted for *God*, in the same way as *Gosh*, *Golly*, etc. See JINGOISM, below.

Jingoism. Aggressive "patriotism", the equivalent of the Fr. *chauvinisme*. The term derives from the popular music-hall song by G. W. Hunt which appeared at the time of the Russo-Turkish War (1877–1878) when anti-Russian feeling ran high and Disraeli ordered the Mediterranean fleet to Constantinople.

> We don't want to fight, but by Jingo if we do,
> We've got the ships, we've got the men, and got the money too.

We've fought the Bear before, and while we're Britons true,
The Russians shall not have Constantinople.

The Russophobes became known as
Jingoes, and a noisy war-mongering policy
has been labelled jingoism ever since. *See*
CHAUVINISM.

Jinks. High Jinks. Nowadays the phrase expresses the idea of pranks, fun, and jollity.

The frolicsome company had begun to practise the
ancient and now forgotten pastime of *high jinks*.
This game was played in several different ways.
Most frequently the dice were thrown by the company, and those upon whom the lot fell were obliged
to assume and maintain for a time, a certain fictitious character, or to repeat a certain number of fescennine verses in a particular order. If they departed from the characters assigned...they incurred
forfeits, which were...compounded for by swallowing an additional bumper...

SCOTT: *Guy Mannering*, xxxvi.

Jinn. Demons of Arabian mythology fabled to
dwell in the mountains of Kâf, which encompass the earth; they were created two
thousand years before ADAM and assume the
forms of serpents, dogs, cats, monsters and
even human shape. The evil *jinn* are hid-
eously ugly, but the good are singularly
beautiful. The word is plural; its singular is
jinnee; *genii* is a variant form.

Jitters. To have the jitters. A phrase of
American origin meaning to be nervously
apprehensive; in a state of nerves. *Jittery* is
nervous or jumpy.

Jive. A canting name for the livelier and debased forms of JAZZ music, largely accomplished by the uninspired improvisations of
short phrases. *Jive-talk* is the specialized
vocabulary of its adepts. In Black
American-English *jive* originally signified
"misleading talk".

Jix. The nickname of Sir William Joynson-
Hicks, first Viscount Brentford
(1865–1932), noted puritan and tactless
speaker. He was Home Secretary
(1924–1929), and was prominent in defeating the adoption of the Revised Prayer Book
of 1928.

We mean to tread the Primrose Path,
In spite of Mr. Joynson-Hicks.
We're People of the Aftermath
We're girls of 1926

JACQUES REVAL: *Mother's advice on Father's fears*
(*The Woman of 1926*).

Joachim, St. (jō' á kim). The father of the
Virgin Mary. Generally represented as an
old man carrying in a basket two turtle-
doves, an allusion to the offering made for
the purification of his daughter. His wife
was St. Anne.

Joan of Arc. St. (1412–1431), the Maid of Orleans (*La Pucelle d'Orléans*). Born at Dom-
rémy in Lorraine, the daughter of a peasant,
she was directed by heavenly voices to undertake her mission to deliver France, then
undergoing the ravages of the HUNDRED
YEARS WAR. She convinced the DAUPHIN of
her sincerity, donned male dress, and inspired the French army in the relief of Orléans (1429) and then the advance to
Rheims. She was captured by the Burgundians at Compiègne (May 1430) and sold to
the English by the Count of Luxembourg
for 10,000 livres. She was condemned to
death by the Bishop of Beauvais for WITCH-
CRAFT and heresy and burned at the stake at
Rouen (30 May 1431). Her last words were
the name of Jesus repeated thrice. She was
canonized in 1920 as the second patron of
France but as such is not recognised by the
State. There has been no official patron saint
of France since the separation of Church and
State in 1905. *See* TERESA, ST. (2).

Pope Joan. *See under* POPE.

Joanna Southcott. *See* SOUTHCOTTIANS.

Job (jōb). The personification of poverty and
patience, in allusion to the PATRIARCH whose
history is given in the BIBLE.

I am as poor as Job, my lord, but not so patient.
SHAKESPEARE: *Henry IV, Pt. II*, I, ii.

Job's comforter. One who means to sym-
pathize with you in your grief, but says that
you brought it on yourself, thus adding to
your sorrow. An allusion to the rebukes Job
received from his "comforters".

Job's post. A bringer of bad news.

Job's Pound. BRIDEWELL; prison.

As poor as Job's turkey. An expression invented by "Sam Slick" (Thomas Chandler
Haliburton, 1796–1865), Canadian judge
and humorous writer, to denote someone
even poorer than JOB.

Jobation. A scolding; so called from the patriarch JOB.

Job (job). Employment, work, something
managed for undue private gain, etc.

A bad job. An unfortunate happening, a
bad speculation.

A job lot. A collection of miscellaneous
goods sold as one lot and usually bought as a
speculation at a low price.

A ministerial job. According to Sheridan:
"Whenever any emolument, profit, salary or
honour is conferred on any person not de-
serving it—that is a job; if from private
friendship, personal attachment, or any
view except the interest of the public, anyone is appointed to any public office...that is
a job."

Jobs for the boys. A form of favouritism
giving jobs and appointments to friends and
acquaintances or through the OLD BOY
NETWORK—not by fair and open competition. *Cp.* NEPOTISM.

Just the job. Exactly what is needed or required.

To do a job. Colloquially, to commit a robbery.

A jobber. One who does small jobs; a jobmaster hiring out horses or carriages by the week or by the month; one who buys from merchants to sell to retailers, a middle-man.

> Nobody in fact was paid. Not the blacksmith who opened the lock; nor the glazier who mended the pane; nor the jobber who let the carriage.
>
> THACKERAY: *Vanity Fair*, ch. xxxvii.

Stock-jobber. *See* STOCK-BROKER *under* STOCK.

Jocasta. *See* ŒDIPUS.

Jock. A popular nickname for a Scotsman.

Jockey. Properly "a little Jack". So the Scots say, "'Ilka Jeanie has her Jockie."

All fellows, Jockey and the laird. All fellows, man and master (Scots proverb).

To jockey. To deceive in trade; to cheat; to indulge in sharp practice.

To jockey for position. To manoeuvre for position, literally or figuratively, as in a horse race.

Jockey Club. The select body which controls the English TURF. Its headquarters are at Newmarket. It arose from a group of "noblemen and gentlemen" who first met in 1750 at the Star and Garter COFFEE-house in PALL MALL to remedy the abuses at Newmarket. It also controls the *General Stud Book* and, since 1902, the *Racing Calendar*. Its French counterpart was formed in 1833 and the American Jockey Club in 1880.

Jockey of Norfolk. Sir John Howard (*c*. 1430–1485), the first Howard to be Duke of Norfolk, and a firm adherent of Richard III. On the night before the battle of Bosworth where he was slain, he found in his tent the warning couplet:

> Jockey of Norfolk, be not too bold,
> For Dickon thy master is bought and sold.

Jodhpurs. In the 1860s the Maharajah of the Rajputanian State of Jodhpur was an extreme devotee of polo which he played in breeches that were tight-fitting from near to the ankle and loose-fitting above. British army officers imported the game and the breeches.

Joe. American slang for the man in the street, and as a form of address for some-one whose name is unknown (*cp*. JACK). G.I. Joe was applied to an American soldier but G.I. is more general.

In Australian usage it was once an insult and a digger's name for a policeman, after Charles Joseph La Trobe, Lieutenant-Governor of Victoria in 1851, whose unpopularity was occasioned by setting the police to check up on every digger's licence. Hence "Joe!" was a warning cry at the approach of the law. It is also suggested that the cry was formed on "Yo ho!"

Joe Miller. *see* MILLER.

Joe Muggins. A simpleton, a dupe. *See* MUG.

Joe Soap. One who is imposed upon, substantially a Joe Muggins.

Joey. The small silver GROAT struck between 1836 and 1855 at the suggestion of Joseph Hume, M.P. (1777–1855), who advocated their usefulness for paying short cab fares, etc. The name was sometimes later colloquially applied to the silver threepenny piece.

In Australia a young kangaroo is called a *joey*.

Jog. Jog away; jog off; jog on. Get away; be off; keep moving. SHAKESPEARE uses the word *shog* in the same sense, as, "Will you shog off?" (*Henry V*, II, i); and again in the same play "Shall we shog?" (II, iii). The word is connected with *shock and shake*.

Give his memory a jog. Remind him about it.

Jog-trot. A slow but regular pace.

Joggis, or **Jogges.** *See* JOUGS.

John. The English form of Lat. and Gr. *Johannes*, from Heb. *Jochanan*, meaning "God is gracious". The feminine form, *Johanna* or *Joanna*, is nearer the original. The French equivalent of "John" is *Jean* (formerly *Jehan*), the Italian *Giovanni*, Russian *Ivan*, Gaelic *Ian*, Irish *Sean* or *Shaun*, Welsh *Evan*, German *Johann* or *Johannes*, which is contracted to *Jan*, *Jahn*, and *Hans*. "John" is also American slang for water-closet.

For many centuries *John* has been one of the most popular of masculine names in England—probably because it is that of St. JOHN THE EVANGELIST, St. JOHN THE BAPTIST and many other saints.

The name *John* has been used by Popes more than any other, its last holder being John XXIII. The most famous "Johns" of history are probably King John of England (*c*. 1167, 1199–1216); John of Gaunt (1340–1399), the fourth son of Edward III; and Don John of Austria (1547–1578), illegitimate son of the Emperor Charles V, celebrated as a military leader, for his naval victory over the Turks at Lepanto (1571), and as Governor of the Netherlands.

Among the SAINTS of this name are:

St. John the Evangelist, or **the Divine.** The "beloved disciple". Tradition says that he took the Virgin Mary to Ephesus after the

Crucifixion and that in the persecution of Domitian (A.D. 93–96) he was plunged into a cauldron of boiling oil but was delivered unharmed, and afterwards banished to the Isle of Patmos where he wrote the *Book of Revelation*. He died at Ephesus. His day is 27 December, and he is usually represented bearing a chalice from which a serpent issues, in allusion to his driving the poison from a cup presented to him to drink.

St. John the Baptist. The forerunner of Jesus, who was sent "to prepare the way of the Lord". His day is 24 June, and he is represented in a coat of sheepskin (in allusion to his life in the desert), either holding a rude wooden CROSS with a pennon bearing the words, *Ecce Agnus Dei*; or with a book on which a lamb is seated; or holding in his right hand a lamb surrounded by a HALO, and bearing a cross on the right foot.

St. John of Beverley (*c*. 640–721). Bishop of Hexham and subsequently Archbishop of York. The Venerable BEDE was one of his pupils. His healing gifts are recorded by his biographers and his shrine at Beverley Minster (which he founded) became a favourite resort of pilgrims. His day is 7 May.

St. John Chrysostom (*c*. 347–407) (Golden tongued), Bishop of Constantinople and DOCTOR OF THE CHURCH, he did much to purify the life of his SEE. He was banished by his enemies in 403 and died in exile. He was noted for his holiness and liturgical reforms. His day is 13 September (formerly 27 January).

St. John of the Cross (1542–1591). Founder of the Discalced CARMELITES under the influence of St. TERESA. He is noted for his mystical writings, *The Ascent of Mount Carmel*, *The Dark Night*, *The Spiritual Canticle*, etc. He was canonized in 1726, his day being 14 December.

St. John Damascene (*c*. 675–*c*. 749). DOCTOR OF THE CHURCH and a defender of images during the Iconoclastic controversy. (*See* ICONOCLAST.) His day is 4 December (formerly 27 March).

St. John of God (1495–1550). Patron of hospitals, nurses and the sick, and a native of Portugal. In IRELAND he is also held popularly to be the patron of alcoholics, through association with the Dublin clinic devoted to their cure and bearing his name. He founded the Order of Charity for the Service of the Sick, or Brothers Hospitallers. His day is 8 March.

St. John of Nepomuk (*c*. 1340–1393). Patron saint of Bohemia, he was drowned by order of the dissolute King Wenceslaus IV, allegedly because he refused to reveal to the king the confessions of the queen. His day is 16 May.

General John. A nickname of John Churchill (1650–1722), first Duke of Marlborough.

John Anderson, my Jo. Burns's well-known poem is founded on an 18th-century version given in PERCY'S RELIQUES and is said to have been sung in derision of a Catholic Latin hymn. The first verse is:

> John Anderson my jo, cum in as ze gae bye,
> And ze zall get a sheip's heid weel baken in a pye;
> Weel baken in a pye, and the haggis in a pat;
> John Anderson my jo, cum in, and ze's get that.

Jo is an old Scottish word for a sweetheart.

John Audley. *See* AUDLEY.

John Barleycorn. *See under* BARLEY.

John Brown (1800–1859). An American abolitionist who led a body of men to free Negro slaves at Harper's Ferry, Virginia, 16 October 1859, and who was subsequently executed for treason. The famous Union song of the CIVIL WAR, *John Brown's Body*, made him a legend. It arose among the soldiers at Fort Warren, Boston, in 1861, around Sergeant John Brown of their regiment, who was jokingly connected with the "martyr" of Harper's Ferry.

John Bull. The nickname for an Englishman or Englishmen collectively. The name was used in Dr. John Arbuthnot's satire, *Law is a bottomless Pit* (1712), republished as *The History of John Bull*. Arbuthnot did not invent the name but established it.

John Chinaman. A Chinaman or the Chinese as a people.

John Collins. A long drink of gin, lemon or lime, and soda-water, sugar and a lump of ice. Curaçao is sometimes added. Possibly the name of the bar-tender who originally dispensed it. In the U.S.A. it is called a *Tom Collins*.

John Doe. *See* DOE.

John Drum's Entertainment. *See* DRUM.

John Hancock. American slang for one's own signature, derived from the fact that John Hancock (1737–1793), the first of the signatories to the Declaration of Independence (1776), had an especially large and clear signature.

John o' Groats. The site of a legendary house $1\frac{3}{4}$ miles west of Duncansby Head, Caithness, SCOTLAND. The story is that Malcolm, Gavin, and John o'Groat (or Jan de Groot), three Dutch brothers, came to this part of Scotland in the reign of James IV. There came to be eight families of the name and they met annually to celebrate. On one occasion a question of precedence arose, consequently John o'Groat built an eight-sided room with a door to each side and placed an octagonal table therein so that all were "head of the table". This building went ever after with the name of *John o'Groat's House*.

From Land's End to John o'Groats. From one end of Great Britain to the other; from DAN TO BEERSHEBA.

John Roberts. Obsolete slang for a very large tankard, supposed to hold enough for any ordinary drinker to last through Saturday and Sunday. It was introduced in Wales in 1886 to compensate topers for Sunday closing of public houses, and derived its name from John Roberts, M.P., author of the Sunday Closing Act.

John with the leaden Sword. John of Lancaster, Duke of Bedford (1389–1435), third son of Henry IV, who acted as regent of France from 1422 to 1429, was so called by Earl Douglas.

John-a-Dreams. A stupid, dreamy fellow, always in a BROWN STUDY and half asleep.

Yet I,
A dull and muddy-mettled rascal, peak,
Like John-a-dreams, unpregnant of my cause,
And can say nothing.
SHAKESPEARE: *Hamlet*, II, ii.

John-a-Droynes. A 16th-century term for a country bumpkin. There is such a character in Whetstone's *Promos and Cassandra* (1578), who, being seized by informers, stands dazed, and suffers to be quietly cheated out of his money.

John-a-Nokes and John-a-Stiles. Names formerly given, instead of the very impersonal "A and B", to fictitious persons in an imaginary action at law; hence either may stand for "just anybody". *Cp.* DOE.

And doth the Lawyer lye then, when under the names of John a stile and John a noaks, hee puts his case?
SIDNEY: *An Apologie for Poetrie* (1595).

John Company. The old Honourable East India Company. It is said that "John" is a pervision of "Hon"; but it is possible that "John Company" is allied to the familiar JOHN BULL. The Company was founded in 1600 and finally abolished in 1858.

John Dory. A golden yellow fish, the *Zeus faber*, common in the Mediterranean and round the south-western coasts of England. Its name was dory (Fr. *doré*, golden) long before the John was added.

There is a tradition that it was from this fish that ST. PETER took the stater or SHEKEL and it has an oval black spot on each side, said to be his finger-marks when he held the fish to extract the coin. It is called in France

le poisson de St. Pierre, and in Gascon the *golden* or *sacred cock*, meaning St. Peter's cock. *Cp.* HADDOCK.

John in the Wad. The IGNIS FATUUS.

John Tamson's man. A henpecked husband; one ordered about here, there and everywhere. Tamson is a *Tame-son*, a spiritless character.

John Scotus. *See* ERIGENA.

Little John. *See* ROBIN HOOD.

Prester John. In mediaeval legend a fabulous Christian emperor of Asia who occurs in documents from the 12th century onwards. In Marco Polo's *Travels* he is lord of the TARTARS. From the 14th century he becomes the Emperor of Ethiopia or Abyssinia where he was apparently still reigning in the time of Vasco da Gama.

To wait for John Long, the carrier. To wait a long time.

Johnnie Cope, or Hey, Johnnie Cope. This famous Scottish song celebrates the Young PRETENDER'S victory at Prestonpans (20 September 1745). Sir John Cope, who led the Government troops, was surprised by the Highlanders at day-break and routed. He escaped and brought the news of his own defeat to Berwick.

Hey, Johnnie Cope, are ye wauking yet?
Or are ye sleeping, I would wit?
Oh, haste ye, get up, for the drums do beat!
O fye, Cope, rise in the morning.

The Scots attacked before the English were awake.

Johnny. A superfine, dandified youth was known as a *Johnny*, in the latter part of the 19th century. Vesta Tilley in the days of the MUSIC HALL, used to sing about "Algy, or the Piccadilly Johnny with the little glass eye." The name is also used generally in the sense of "fellow".

Johnny-cake. An American name for a cake made of maize-meal, once much esteemed as a delicacy. It is said to be a corruption of *journey-cake*.

Johnny Crapaud. A Frenchman. *See* FLEUR-DE-LIS.

Johnny Raw. A nervous novice, a raw recruit.

Johnny Reb. In the American CIVIL WAR a Federal name for a CONFEDERATE soldier, a *rebel* from the Northern standpoint.

Johnstone. St. Johnstone's Tippet. A halter; so called from Johnstone the HANGMAN.

Joint. In U.S.A. slang, originally a sordid place where illicit spirits were drunk, etc.; hence, disparagingly, any cheap restaurant, dive, etc.

To case a joint. *See under* CASE.

Out of joint. Figuratively, a disrupted or

confused state of affairs, as a broken joint is out of order.

> The time is out of joint.
>
> SHAKESPEARE: *Hamlet*, I, v.

To put one's nose out of joint. *See under* NOSE.

Jolly. A sailor's nickname for a MARINE. A militiaman was called a *tame jolly*.

> To stand and be still to the Birken'ead drill is a damn tough bullet to chew,
> An' they done it, the Jollies, – 'Er Majesty's Jollies – soldier and sailor too!
>
> KIPLING: *Soldier an' Sailor Too*.

The noun is also slang for a man who bids at an auction with no intention of buying, but merely to force up the price.

In American usage **to jolly** is to chaff or banter and "to jolly someone along" is to wheedle him, to keep him in a good humour in order to coax something out of him.

A jolly dog. A *bon vivant*, a jovial fellow.

The jolly god. BACCHUS. The BIBLE speaks of wine "that maketh glad the heart of man" (*Ps*. civ, 15).

A jolly good fellow. A very social, popular, or thoroughly commendable person. When toasts are drunk "with musical honours" the chorus usually is –

> For he's a jolly good fellow [thrice],
> And so say all of us [thrice],
> For he's a jolly good fellow [thrice],
> And so say all of us!

The Jolly Roger. *See under* ROGER.

Jolly-boat. A small clinker-built ship's boat. *Jolly* is probably the Dan. *jolle* or Dut. *jol*, our yawl.

Jonah. A person whose presence brings misfortune upon his companions as did Jonah to the mariners when he took ship to Tarshish to "flee from the presence of the Lord". (*Jon*.i.) *Jonas* is also similarly used, being an alternative name of the prophet Jonah.

Jonathan. *See* BROTHER JONATHAN.

Jonathan's. A noted COFFEE house in Change Alley described in the *Tatler* as the general mart of stock-jobbers. In 1773 those brokers who used Jonathan's moved to premises in Sweating's Alley which came to be known as the STOCK EXCHANGE coffee house. In 1801 they raised capital to build the Stock Exchange in CAPEL COURT.

Jonathan's arrows. They were shot to give warning, and not to hurt (I *Sam*. xx, 36).

Jones, Davy. *See* DAVY JONES.

Jones, Paul. *See* PAUL JONES.

Joneses, Keeping up with the. *See under* KEEP.

Jongleur (zhong' glĕr). A mediaeval minstrel who recited verses to his own musical accompaniment. They wandered from castle to castle performing the CHANSONS DE GESTE and are linked with the TROUBADOURS. The word is O. Fr. *jiglere*, Lat. *joculator*, our juggler.

Jophiel. *See* ARCHANGEL.

Jordan. A name anciently given to the pot used by alchemists and doctors, then transferred to a chamber-pot. It was perhaps originally *Jordan-bottle*, *i.e.* a bottle in which pilgrims and crusaders brought back water from the River Jordan.

> Why, they will allow us ne'er a jordan, and then we leak in your chimney; and your chamber-lie breeds fleas like a loach.
>
> SHAKESPEARE: *Henry IV, Pt. I*, II, i.

Jordan almond. Here Jordan has nothing to do with the river (*cp*. JERUSALEM ARTICHOKE), but is a corruption of Fr. *jardin*, garden. The Jordan almond is a fine variety which comes chiefly from Malaga.

Jordan passed. Death over. The Jordan separated the wilderness of the world from the PROMISED LAND, and thus came to be regarded as the Christian STYX.

Jorum. A large drinking-bowl, intended especially for PUNCH. The name is thought to be connected with King Joram (*cp*. JEROBOAM), who "brought with him vessels of silver, and vessels of gold, and vessels of brass" (II *Sam*. viii, 10).

Josaphat. *See* BARLAAM AND JOSAPHAT.

Joseph. One not to be seduced from his continency by the severest temptation is sometimes so called. The reference is to Joseph in Potiphar's house (*Gen*. xxxix). *Cp*. BELLEROPHON.

A form of great-coat used to be known by the same name, in allusion to Joseph's coat of many colours (*Gen*. xxxvii, 3).

Joseph, St. Husband of the Virgin Mary and the lawful father of Jesus. He is patron saint of carpenters, because he was of that craft.

In art Joseph is represented as an aged man with a budding staff in his hand. His day is 19 March, and in 1955 Pope Pius XII instituted the feast of St. Joseph the Workman on 1 May.

Joseph of Arimathea, St. The rich JEW, probably a member of the SANHEDRIN, who believed in Christ, but feared to confess it, and, after the Crucifixion, begged the body of the Saviour and deposited it in his own tomb (*see Matt*. xxvii, 57–60; *Mark* xv, 43–46). His day is 17 March.

Legend relates that he was imprisoned for 12 years and was kept alive miraculously by the holy GRAIL, and that on his release by Vespasian, about the year 63, he brought the Grail and the spear with which Longinus wounded the crucified Saviour to Britain, and founded the abbey of GLASTONBURY whence he commenced the conversion of Britain.

The origin of these legends is to be found in a group of APOCRYPHAL writings of which the *Evangelium Nicodemi* is the chief; these were worked upon at Glastonbury and further established by Robert de Borron in the 13th century, the latter version (by way of Walter Map) being woven by Malory into his *Morte d'Arthur*.

Josephus (*c*. A.D. 37–95). Flavius Josephus, the celebrated Jewish historian, and PHARISEE, took a prominent part in the last Jewish revolt against the Romans (A.D. 66–70) and later wrote his *History of the Jewish War*. According to his own account, his prophecy that Vespasian, the captor of Jerusalem, would become emperor of ROME, saved his life. The most important of his other writings was his *Jewish Antiquities*, dealing with the history of the Jews down to the end of Nero's reign.

Joss. A Chinese god or idol. The word is probably a PIDGIN-ENGLISH corruption of Port. *deos*, Lat. *deus*, god. A temple is called a *joss-house*, and a *joss-stick* is a stick made from clay mixed with the powder of various scented woods burnt as incense.

Jot. A very little, the least possible. The iota i (*see* I) is the smallest letter of the Greek alphabet, called the *Lacedaemonian letter*.

This bond doth give thee here no jot of blood.
SHAKESPEARE: *Merchant of Venice*, IV, i.

Jot or tittle. A tiny amount. The jot is i or iota, and the tittle, from Lat. *titulus*, is the mark or dot over the *i*.

Jotunheim (jŏ' tŭn'hīm). The land of the Scandinavian *Jotuns* or GIANTS.

Jougs (joogz). The Scottish PILLORY, or more properly an iron ring or collar fastened to a wall by a short chain, and used as a pillory (O. Fr. *joug*, a yoke).

Jourdain, Monsieur. The type of bourgeois placed by wealth in the ranks of gentlemen, who makes himself ridiculous by his endeavours to acquire their accomplishments. The character is from MOLIERE'S *Le Bourgeois Gentilhomme* (1670). He is chiefly remembered for his delight in discovering that, whereas some men write poetry, he had been speaking prose all his life.

Journal (O. Fr. from Lat. *diurnalis*, diurnal; *dies*, a day). Applied to newspapers, the word strictly means a daily paper; but it has come to be applied to weekly and other periodicals.

Journey-weight (Fr. *journée*, a day). Originally the quantity of coins that could be minted in a day. A *journey-weight* of gold is fifteen pounds troy, which was coined into 701 SOVEREIGNS or double that number of half-sovereigns. A *journey* of silver is sixty pounds troy, which, before the alteration in the silver coinage of 1920, was coined into 3,960 shillings. The trial of the Pyx (*see under* PYX) depends on these journey-weights.

Jove. Another name for JUPITER, being *Jovis pater*, father Jove. Milton, in *Paradise Lost*, makes Jove one of the fallen angels (I, 512).

Jovial. Merry and sociable, like those born under the planet JUPITER, which astrologers considered the happiest of the natal stars. *Cp.* SATURNINE.

Our Jovial star reign'd at his birth.
SHAKESPEARE: *Cymbeline*, V, iv.

Joy. To get no joy. Not to meet with any success.

The five Joyful Mysteries. The first chaplet of the ROSARY, made up of the ANNUNCIATION, the Visitation, the Nativity of Christ, the Presentation of Christ in the TEMPLE, and the finding of the Child Jesus in the Temple.

The seven joys of the Virgin. *See* MARY.

Joy-ride. A pleasure-ride or stolen ride in a motor-car or other vehicle, especially when driven fast.

Joy-stick. The control column of an aeroplane or glider, which is linked to the elevators and ailerons to control them.

Joyeuse (zhwa yĕrz). A name given to more than one famous sword in romance, especially to CHARLEMAGNE'S, which bore the inscription *Decem praeceptorum custos Carolus*, and was buried with him.

Joyeuse Entrée (Fr., joyous entry; Dut. *blyde inkomst*). The name given to the constitution granted to Brabant by Duke John III in 1354. It checked the power of the Church and the appointment of foreigners to offices of state. The dukes were obliged to swear to uphold these privileges before entering the ducal residence. Should the prince violate these privileges, "the inhabitants of Brabant, after regular protest entered, are discharged of their oaths of allegiance, and...may conduct themselves exactly as seems to them best." Motley tells us (*The Rise of the Dutch Republic*, Pt. II, ch. II) "that mothers came to the province in order to give birth to their children, who might thus enjoy, as birthright, the privileges of Brabant."

Joyeuse Garde, or **Garde-Joyeuse.** The estate given by King ARTHUR to Sir LANCELOT of the Lake for defending the Queen's honour against Sir Mador. It is supposed to have been at Berwick-on-Tweed.

Juan, Don. Don Juan Tenorio, the legendary hero of many plays, poems, stories and operas, was the son of a notable family in 14th-century Seville. The story is that he killed the commandant of Ulloa after seducing his daughter. He then invited the statue of the murdered man (erected in the FRANCISCAN convent) to a feast, at the end of which the sculptured figure delivered him over to HELL. He is presented as the complete profligate.

His name is synonymous with rake, roué and aristocratic libertine, and in Mozart's opera *Don Giovanni* (1787) the valet says that his master had "in Italy 700 mistresses, in Germany 800, in Turkey and France 91, in Spain 1,003". Don Juan's dissolute life was dramatized by the monk Gabriel Tellez in the 17th century, followed by MOLIÈRE, Corneille, Shadwell and others. BYRON, the elder Dumas, Balzac, de Musset, and Shaw (*Man and Superman*) all utilized the story and helped to maintain its popularity.

Juan Fernandez. *See* ROBINSON CRUSOE.

Jubilate (joo bi la′ ti) (Lat., Cry aloud) is the name given to two psalms which begin with this word in the VULGATE (lxv and xcix). In the English psalter they are *Psalms* lxvi and c.

Jubilate Sunday is the third Sunday after EASTER, when the introit at the MASS begins with two verses of the first of the Jubilate Psalms.

Jubilee. In Jewish history the year of *jubilee* was every fiftieth year, which was held sacred in commemoration of the deliverance from Egypt. In this year the fields were allowed to lie fallow, land that had passed out of the possession of those to whom it originally belonged was restored to them, and all who had been obliged to let themselves out for hire were released from bondage. The jubilee was proclaimed with trumpets of ram's horn (*see Lev.* xxv, 11–34, 39–54, and xxvii 17–24).

Hence any fiftieth anniversary, especially one kept with great rejoicings, is called a *Jubilee*, and the name has been applied to other outbursts of joy or celebrations, such as the *Shakespeare Jubilee*, held at Stratford-upon-Avon in 1769, and the *Protestant Jubilee*, celebrated in Germany in 1617, the centenary of Luther's protest.

King George III's *Jubilee* was on 25 October 1809, the day before the commencement of the fiftieth year of his reign, Queen Victoria celebrated hers on 21 June 1887, and kept her *Diamond Jubilee* ten years later. George V celebrated the twenty-fifth year of his accession by a *Silver Jubilee* on 6 May 1935, and Queen Elizabeth II's Silver Jubilee was celebrated on 7 June 1977.

In the ROMAN CATHOLIC CHURCH Pope Boniface VIII instituted a *jubilee* in 1300 and INDULGENCES were granted to pilgrims visiting ROME. It was to be held at intervals of 100 years but in 1343 Clement VI altered it to 50 years and in 1389 Urban IV to 33. In 1470 Paul II reduced the interval to 25 years. The jubilee is the only occasion when the *Porta Santa* (HOLY DOOR) of St. Peter's Rome is opened. PILGRIMAGE to Rome ceased to be obligatory in 1500. A jubilee is also known as a *Holy Year*, and extends from Christmas to Christmas.

Jubilee Juggins. A nickname given to Ernest Benzon, a foolish and wealthy young man about town who squandered a fortune on horse-racing about the time of Queen Victoria's JUBILEE (1887). The name *Juggins* is generally applied to any simpleton.

Judas. Judas Iscariot, who betrayed Christ, his Master; hence a traitor.

Judas Kiss. A deceitful act of courtesy or simulated affection. JUDAS betrayed his Master with a kiss (*Matt.* xxvi, 49).

> So Judas kiss'd his Master,
> And cried, all hail! when as he meant all harm.
> SHAKESPEARE: *Henry VI, Pt. III*, V, vii.

Judas slits, or **holes.** The peep-holes in a prison door which the guard uncovers to check up on the prisoners.

Judas tree. A leguminous tree of southern Europe (*Cercis siliquastrum*) which flowers before the leaves appear, so called from a Greek tradition that Judas hanged himself on such a tree. *Cp.* ELDER-TREE, which is sometimes also so named. The American Judas tree is the *Cercis canadensis* or redbud.

Judas-coloured hair. Fiery red. In the MIDDLE AGES Judas Iscariot was represented with red hair and beard. *Cp.* CAIN-COLOURED BEARD

> *Ros:* His very hair is of the dissembling colour.
> *Cel:* Something browner than Judas's: marry, his kisses are Judas's own children.
> SHAKESPEARE: *As You Like It*, III, iv.

Judas's Ear. *See* JEW'S EAR.

Jude, St. One of the twelve apostles, brother of James (*i.e.* the Lord's brother), also identified as brother of JAMES THE LESS. He is represented in art with a club or staff, and a carpenter's square in allusion to his trade. His day, 28 October, coincides with that of St. SIMON, with whom he suffered martyrdom in Persia. He is the author of the *Epistle of Jude* and nowadays is regarded as the patron of hopeless cases.

Judge. Judge Lynch. *See* LYNCH LAW.

Judge's black cap. *See* BLACK CAP.

Judge's robes. In the English criminal courts, where the judges represent the sovereign, they appear in full court dress, and wear a scarlet robe; but in NISI PRIUS courts the judge sits merely to balance the law between citizens, and therefore appears in his judicial undress, or violet gown.

Judges' Rules. Rules concerning the questioning of suspects by the police, and the taking of statements. First formulated in 1912 and revised in 1918, they were reformulated in 1964 by a committee of judges and approved by a meeting of all judges of the QUEEN'S BENCH.

Judgement, The Last, or **General Judgement,** is God's final sentence on mankind on the LAST DAY. The **Particular Judgement** is the judgement on each individual soul after death.

Judgement of Paris. See PARIS.

Judica Sunday (joo' di kà). The fifth Sunday in LENT (formerly also known as Passion Sunday) is so called from the first word of the Introit at the MASS, *Judica me, Deus*, Give sentence with me, O God (*Ps.* xliii).

Judicial Astrology. See ASTROLOGY.

Judicium Crucis (jū dis' i um kroo' sis). Trial of the CROSS. A form of ORDEAL which consisted in stretching out the arms before a cross, till one party could hold out no longer, and lost his cause.

Judy. See PUNCH, MR.

Jug, or **Stone Jug.** A prison. *Cp.* JOUGS.

To be jugged, or **to be in the jug.** To be imprisoned.

Bottle and jug. A once common name for a public-house bar where beer was sold in bottles and draught beer could be collected in jugs for consumption off the premises.

Jugged hare. Hare stewed with wine and seasoning, properly in a jug or jar.

Juggernaut, or **Jagganath.** A Hindu god, "Lord of the World", having his temple at Puri in Orissa. It is a cult-title of VISHNU, and the pyramidal temple was erected in the 12th century and held the Golden Tooth of BUDDHA. The chief festival is the car festival when Jagganath is dragged in his car (35 feet square and 45 feet high) over the sand to another temple. The car has sixteen wheels, each seven feet in diameter. The belief that fanatical pilgrims cast themselves under the wheels of the car to be crushed to death on the last day of the festival is largely without foundation. However, it has led to the phrase the **car of the juggernaut,** used to denote customs institutions, etc., beneath which people are ruthlessly and unnecessarily crushed. The word *juggernaut* is also applied humorously to any wheeled "mon-

ster". More recently, juggernaut is the name given to the giant articulated lorries increasingly prevalent since Britain's entry into the Common Market, which pose another threat to the environment.

Juggins. See JUBILEE JUGGINS.

Juggler (Lat. *joculator*, a jester, joker). In the MIDDLE AGES, jugglers accompanied the MINSTRELS and TROUBADOURS and added to their musical talents sleight of hand, antics and feats of prowess to amuse their audience. In time the music was omitted and tricks became their staple. *Cp.* JONGLEUR.

Juke Box. An American term for an automatic musical box or record-player that churns out selected pieces when coins are inserted.

Julian. Pertaining to Julius CAESAR (100–44 B.C.).

Julian the Apostate (332, 361–363). Flavius Claudius Julianus, Roman EMPEROR, and nephew of Constantine the GREAT. So called from his attempts to restore paganism, having abandoned Christianity at about the age of 20. He set an example by the austerity of his life and zeal for the public welfare and was notable for his literary and philosophical interests. Christians were not actively persecuted but there was discrimination against them. *See* GALILEAN.

Julian Calendar. The calendar instituted by Julius CÆSAR in 46 B.C., which was in general use in Western Europe until the introduction of the GREGORIAN CALENDAR in 1582, and still used in England until 1752 and until 1918 in Russia. To allow for the odd quarter of a day, Cæsar ordained that every fourth year should contain 366 days, the additional day being introduced after the 6th before the CALENDS of March, *i.e.* 24 February. Cæsar also divided the months into the number of days they at present contain. It is now called "the Old Style". *See* JULY.

Julian Year. The average year of 365¼ days, according to the Julian Calendar.

Julian, St. A patron SAINT of travellers and of hospitality, looked upon in the MIDDLE AGES as the epicure of saints. Thus Chaucer says that the Franklin was "Epicurus owne sone", and:

An house holdere, and that a greet was he;
Seint Julian in his contree.
Canterbury Tales: Prologue, 339.

He seems to be essentially a mythical saint. He is supposed to have unwittingly slain his parents and devoted his life to helping strangers by way of atonement.

Juliana (or **Mother Julian**) **of Norwich** (c. 1342–c. 1413). A religious recluse and mystic who recorded her visions in

XVI *Revelations of Divine Love*.

Juliet. *See* ROMEO.

Julium Sidus. The comet which appeared at the death of Julius CÆSAR, and which in court flattery was called the apotheosis of the murdered man.

Jullien's Concerts were features of the London season in the 1840s and 1850s. Louis Antoine Jullien came to London in 1838 from PARIS and began a series of summer concerts at DRURY LANE, and later winter concerts, at which the best artists were engaged. He raised the level of musical appreciation and introduced the PROMENADE CONCERT. He went bankrupt in 1857, returned to Paris and died in a lunatic asylum in 1860.

July. The seventh month, named by Mark Anthony in honour of Julius CÆSAR. It was formerly called *Quintilis*, as it was the fifth month of the Roman year. The old Dutch name for it was *Hooy-maand* (hay-month); the old Saxon, *Mœdd-Monath* (because the cattle were turned into the meadows to feed) and *Lida œftevr* (the second mild or genial month). In the French Revolutionary CALENDAR it was called *Messidor* (harvest-month, 19 June to 18 July).

Until the 18th century, *July* was accented on the first syllable. Even as late as 1798 Wordsworth wrote:

In March, December, and in July,
'Tis all the same with Harry Gill;
The neighbours tell, and tell you truly,
His teeth they chatter, chatter still.
Goody Blake and Harry Gill.

The July Monarchy. That of Louis Philippe, also called the Orleanist monarchy. *See* JULY REVOLUTION.

The July Revolution. The French revolution of 1830 (17–29 July) which overthrew Charles X and gave the throne to Louis Philippe, Duke of Orleans, the CITIZEN KING.

Jumbo. The name of an exceptionally large African elephant, which, after giving rides to thousands of children in the London Zoo, was sold to Barnum's "Greatest Show on Earth" in 1882. He weighed 6½ tons and was accidentally killed by a railway engine in 1885. His name is now synonymous with *elephant* in children's minds.

Jumbuck (Austr.) A sheep, formerly applied to a shaggy kangaroo. Possibly from the native word *jïmbuc*.

Jump. As well as meaning "to leap" or "move quickly" or "jerk suddenly with shock", it also means "to go along", "agree with", "coincide", "tally".

In some sort it jumps with my humour.
SHAKESPEARE: *Henry IV*, *Pt. I*, I, ii.

To jump a claim. An expression from the miners' camps meaning to seize someone else's claim or diggings in his absence; hence to seize that which properly belongs to another by stealing a march on the owner.

To jump at an offer. To accept eagerly.

To jump at, or **to conclusions.** To draw inferences too hastily from insufficient evidence.

To jump bail. To forfeit bail by absconding before trial.

To jump down a person's throat. *See under* THROAT.

To jump from the frying-pan into the fire. *See* FRYING-PAN.

To jump over the broomstick. To live together without the proper ceremony of marriage. To "jump the besom" is an alternative form. The derivation is uncertain.

To jump the gun. *See under* GUN.

To jump upon someone. To come down upon them heavily with a crushing remark, etc.

Counter-jumper. *See* COUNTER.

Jumping-off place. The edge of the earth, the end of civilization from which one leaped into nothingness. Thus used by settlers of any remote, desolate spot. Also a starting point from which to begin an enterprise, etc.

Jumpers. A nickname applied to the SHAKERS, and also to Welsh METHODISTS who were supposed to "jump for joy" during divine service.

June. The sixth month, named from the Roman *Junius*, a gens or clan name akin to *juvenis*, young. Ovid says *Junius a juvenum nomine dictus* (*Fasti*, v, 79). Alternatively, it may derive from JUNO.

The old Dutch name was *Zomermaand* (summer-month); the old Saxon, *Seremonath* (dry-month) and *Lida œrra* (joy time). In the French Revolutionary CALENDAR the month was called *Prairial* (meadow month, 20 May to 18 June).

June marriages lucky. "Good to the man and happy to the maid." This is an old Roman superstition. The festival of Juno Moneta was held on the CALENDS of JUNE, and JUNO was the great guardian of women from birth to death.

Junius. Junius Brutus. Son of M. Junius and Tarquinia and nephew of Tarquin. When his father and elder brother were murdered by Tarquin the Proud, he feigned insanity, thereby saving his life, and was called *Brutus* for his apparent stupidity. He later inspired the Romans to get rid of the Tarquins and became a consul. *Cp.* AMYRIS PLAYS THE FOOL.

The Letters of Junius. A series of anonymous letters, the authorship of which has never been finally settled, which appeared in the London *Public Advertiser* from 21 November 1768 to 21 January 1772. They were directed against Sir William Draper, the Duke of Grafton, and the Ministers generally. The author said in his Dedication, "I am the sole depository of my own secret, and it shall perish with me." Among the many suggested authors are Edmund Burke, John Wilkes, George Grenville, Lord Temple, Chatham, Henry Grattan, Edward Gibbon, Alexander Wedderburn, Lord George Sackville, Horne Tooke, Philip Francis, and Lord Shelburne. The two latter find most favour at present. The vitriolic quality of the writer is evidenced by the following extract from *Letter* lxvii, addressed to the Duke of Grafton:

> The unhappy baronet [Sir James Lowther] has no friends even among those who resemble him. You, my Lord, are not yet reduced to so deplorable a state of dereliction. Every villain in the kingdom is your friend: and, in compliment to such amity, I think you should suffer your dismal countenance to clear up. Besides, my Lord, I am a little anxious for the consistency of your character. You violate your own rules of decorum, when you do not insult the man whom you have betrayed.

Junk. Nautically speaking is old, discarded or condemned cordage; **salt junk,** the salt meat supplied to ships for long voyages, from its toughness and likeness to old rope-ends. The term probably derives from Lat. *juncus*, a rush, once used in the making of cordage (*cp.* JUNKET). The word is now applied generally to a miscellany of cast-off or unwanted articles. It is now also the slang term for narcotic drugs such as heroin and cocaine and an addict of such is called a *junker* or *junkie*.

Junker (yung'ker). A German landowning aristocrat or squire, who formerly provided most of the officer class. Bismarck, the German chancellor, came frm the Prussian junker class. *See also* JUNK.

Junket. Curdled cream with spice, etc.; any dainty. So called because it was originally made in a rush basket (Ital. *giuncata*; from Lat. *juncus*, a rush).

> You know there wants no junkets at the feast.
> SHAKESPEARE: *Taming of the Shrew*, II, ii.

Juno. In Roman mythology "the venerable ox-eyed" wife and sister of JUPITER, and queen of HEAVEN. She is identified with the Greek HERA, was the special protectress of marriage and of women, and was represented as a war goddess. *Cp.* GENIUS.

Junonian Bird. The peacock, dedicated to the goddess-queen.

Junta (Sp. *juntar*, to join, congregate). In Spain a committee or council, especially a consultative or legislative assembly for the whole part of the country, the best known being the Junta of Regency set up under Murat's presidency after NAPOLEON had secured King Ferdinand's abdication, and the local Juntas, backed by a central Junta at Seville, formed to resist the French. A group of army officers who seize political power is called a "military junta".

The name was also applied by Sidney and Beatrice Webb to a group of TRADE UNION general secretaries in London who were influential in trade union affairs in the 1860s. Their contemporaries called them the "Clique".

Junto. A corruption of JUNTA, denoting a clique or faction. It is particularly used of the WHIG leaders of the reigns of William III and Anne. The lords of the Whig Junto were Wharton, Somers, Sunderland, Orford, and Halifax. *Cp.* CABAL.

Jupiter. Also called JOVE, the supreme god of Roman mythology, corresponding to the Greek ZEUS, son of SATURN or Kronos (whom he dethroned) and Ops or Rhea. He was the special protector of ROME, and as Jupiter Capitolinus (his temple being on the Capitoline Hill) presided over the Roman games. He determined the course of human affairs and made known the future through signs in the heavens, the flight of birds, etc. *See* AUGURY.

As Jupiter was lord of HEAVEN and bringer of light, white was the colour sacred to him; hence among the alchemists Jupiter designated tin. In HERALDRY Jupiter stands for AZURE, the blue of the heavens. *See* COLOURS.

His statue by Phidias at OLYMPIA was one of the Seven Wonders of the World (*see under* WONDER). It was removed to Constantinople by Theodosius I and destroyed by fire in 475. *See* THEMIS.

Jupiter is also the name of the largest of the planets.

Jupiter Ammon. A name under which JUPITER was worshipped in Libya where his temple was famous for its ORACLE which was consulted by HERCULES. *Cp.* AMMON.

Jupiter Scapin. A nickname of NAPOLEON, given him by the Abbé de Pradt. Scapin is a valet famous for his knavish tricks, in MOLIÈRE'S comedy *Les Fourberies de Scapin*.

Jupiter tonans (the thundering Jupiter). A complimentary nickname given to *The Times* in the mid-19th century. *Cp.* PRINTING HOUSE SQUARE.

Jupiter's beard. HOUSE LEEK.

Jury mast. A temporary mast erected to replace one that has been carried away. Similarly *jury rudder*, *jury rig*, etc., and humorously *jury leg* for a wooden leg. The etymology of "jury" here is a matter of surmise.

Jus. Latin for law.

Jus civile (Lat.). Civil law; Roman law.

Jus divinum (Lat.). Divine law.

Jus gentium (Lat.). The law of nations or law common to all nations; used by moderns as an expression for international law for which the Roman term was *jus feciale*.

Jus mariti (Lat.). The right of the husband to the wife's property.

Jus naturae, or **naturale** (Lat.). Natural law, originally virtually the same as *Jus gentium*. The law of reason common to nature and man.

Jus primae noctis (Lat. right of the first night). The same as *droit du seigneur* (lord's right), the right of the lord to share the bed of the bride of any one of his vassals on the wedding night. The custom seems to have existed in early mediaeval Europe to a limited extent but was more often the excuse for levying dues in lieu.

Just, The. Among rulers and others who have been given this surname are:

Aristides, the Athenian (d.*c.* 468 B.C.).

Bahram II (276–293), fifth of the Sassanidæ.

Casimir II, King of Poland (1177–1194).

Chosroes I, or Khosru of Persia (531–579), called by the Arabs *Malk-aladel* (the Just King).

Ferdinand I, King of Aragon (1412–1416).

Haroun al-Raschid (Aaron the Just).

The most renowned of the Abbassid caliphs (786–809) (*see under* ABBASSIDES). He appears in the ARABIAN NIGHTS stories.

James II, King of Aragon (1291–1327).

Peter I, King of Portugal (1356–1367).

Juste-milieu (zhoost mil yĕr) (Fr.) The golden mean.

Le mot juste (lĕ mó zhoost) (Fr.). The word or phrase which exactly conveys the meaning desired.

Justice. *See* JEDDART.

Justices in Eyre. *See* EYRE.

Justices of the peace. Local lords and gentry were initially given judicial authority as Conservators of the Peace in 1361. As unpaid Justices of the Peace they acted firstly through the courts or QUARTER SESSIONS. Summary jurisdiction developed in the 16th century and they also carried out much administrative work until the Local Government Acts of 1888 and 1894. Today, as lay magistrates appointed by the Lord Chancellor, they largely deal summarily with the lesser offences, the licensing of premises, affiliation orders, etc.

Poetic justice. The ideal justice which poets exercise in making the good happy and the bad unsuccessful.

Juvenal (Lat. *juvenis*). A youth; common in SHAKESPEARE, as "The juvenal, the prince your master, whose chin is not yet fledged" (*Henry IV, Pt. II*, I, ii).

Juveniles. In theatrical parlance, actors playing young men's parts; in the journalistic and book-trade, periodicals or books intended for the young.

K

K. The eleventh letter of the alphabet, representing the Greek *kappa* and the Hebrew *kaph*. The Egyptian hieroglyphic for K was a bowl. The Romans, after the C was given the K sound, only used the latter for abbreviated forms of a few words from Greek; thus, false accusers were branded on the forehead with a K (*Kalumnia*), and the Carians, Cretans, and Cilicians were known as *the three bad K's*. K is the recognized abbreviation of *Knight* in British Orders but the abbreviation of KNIGHT *per se* is *Kt*.

K.B. or **Kt.Bach.** Knight Bachelor.

Ka me, ka thee. You scratch my back and I'll scratch yours; one good turn deserves another; do me a service, and I will give you a helping hand when you require one. It is an old proverb, and appears in Heywood's collection (1546).

Kaaba (ka' bà) (Arab. *kabah*, a cube). The ancient stone building said to have been first built by ISHMAEL and ABRAHAM and incorporated in the centre of the Great Mosque at MECCA. It forms a rough square and is about 40 feet high, containing the BLACK STONE in the east corner. The present Kaaba was built in 1626 and is covered with a cloth of black brocade that is replaced with annual ceremony.

Kabbalah. *See* CABBALA.

Kaf, Mount. *See* JINN.

Kaffir (kăf' úr) (Arab. *kafir*, an infidel). A name given to all Africans who were not MOSLEMS. The British and other Europeans restricted the term to the Bantu races.

Kaffir King. A nickname given to Barney Barnato (1852–1897) the South African diamond magnate and speculator, who became an associate of Cecil Rhodes. *See* KAFFIRS.

Kaffirs, Kaffir market. The STOCK EXCHANGE term for South African mining shares, etc., and for the market dealing with them.

Kailyard School. A school of writers flourishing in the 1890s, who took their subjects from Scottish humble life. It included Ian Maclaren, J. J. Bell, S. R. Crockett, and J. M. Barrie. The name is from the motto—

"There grows a bonnie brier bush in our Kailyard"—used by Maclaren for his *Beside the Bonnie Brier Bush* (1894).

Kaiser (kī' zer). The German form of CÆSAR; the title formerly used by the head of the HOLY ROMAN EMPIRE, and by the Emperors of Austria and Germany. It was Diocletian (*c*. 284) who ordained that *Cæsar* should be the title of the EMPEROR of the West.

Kalevala. The national epic of the Finns, compiled from popular songs and oral tradition by the Finnish philologist, Elias Lönnroth (1802–1884), who published his first edition of 12,000 verses in 1835, and a second, of some 22,900 verses, in 1849. Its name is taken from the three sons of Kalewa (Finland), who are the heroes of the poem—Väinämöinen, Ilmarinen, and Lemminkäinen. Prominent in the action is the magical mill, the Sampo, an object that grants all one's wishes. The epic is influenced by Teutonic and Scandinavian mythology, and to a lesser extent by Christianity. It is written in unrhymed alliterative trochaic verse, and is the prototype both in form and content of Longfellow's *Hiawatha*.

Kali (ka' lē). The cult name of the Hindu goddess Durga, wife of SIVA goddess of death and destruction. Calcutta receives its name from her, Kali-ghat, the steps of Kali, by which her worshippers descended from the bank to the waters of the Ganges. It was to her that the THUGS sacrificed their victims. Her idol is black, besmeared with blood; she has red eyes, four arms, matted hair, huge fang-like teeth, and a protruding tongue that drips with blood. She wears a necklace of skulls, ear-rings of corpses, and is girdled with serpents.

Kalki. *See* AVATAR.

Kalyb (kă' lib). The "Lady of the Woods", who stole St. GEORGE from his nurse, and endowed him with gifts. St. George enclosed her in a rock where she was torn to pieces by spirits. The story occurs in the *Famous History of the Seven Champions of Christendom*, Pt. I. *See* SEVEN CHAMPIONS.

Kam. Crooked; a CELTIC word. *Clean kam*, perverted into *kim kam*, means wholly awry, clean from the purpose.

> *fic:* This is clean kam.
> *Brut:* Merely awry.
> SHAKESPEARE: <i>Coriolanus</i>, III, i.

Kamerad (Ger., comrade, mate). A word used by the Germans in World War I as an appeal for quarter. It is now used in English with the meaning, "I surrender."

Kami (ka' mē). A god or divinity in SHINTO-ISM, the native religion of Japan; also the title given to daimios and governors, comparable to our "lord". Their respective ideographs are different.

Kamikaze (ka mi ka zi). A Japanese word meaning "divine wind", in reference to the providential typhoon which once balked a Mongol invasion. In World War II it was applied to the "suicide" aircraft attacks organized under Vice-Admiral Onishi in the Philippines between October 1944 and January 1945. Some 5,000 young pilots gave their lives when their bomb-loaded fighters crashed into their objectives.

Kamsa. *See* KRISHNA.

Kangaroo, or **Kangaroo Closure.** In British Parliamentary procedure, the process by which the SPEAKER (on the Report stage of a bill), or the Chairman of the Committee of the Whole House (or standing committee) selects the amendments to be debated. So named because the debate leaps from clause to clause. *Cp.* CLOSURE; GUILLOTINE.

Kangaroo Court. An irregular court or tribunal conducted in disregard of proper legal procedure, as a mock court held among prisoners in a gaol. "To kangaroo" means to convict a person on false evidence. The term, which probably arose from some likening of the "jumps" of the kangaroo to the progress of "justice" in such courts, was common in the U.S.A. during the 19th century. It obtained wide currency in England in 1966 when applied to the irregular punitive measures taken by certain TRADE UNIONS against their members.

Karaites. *See* SCRIPTURISTS.

Karma (Sans., action, fate). In Buddhist philosophy, the name given to the results of action, especially the cumulative results of a person's deeds in one stage of his existence as controlling his destiny in the next.

Among Theosophists the word has a rather wider meaning, *viz.* the unbroken sequence of cause and effect; each effect being, in its turn, the cause of a subsequent effect.

Karmathians. A 9th-century Mohammedan sect in Iraq founded by Karmut, a labourer who professed to be a prophet. They were socialistic pantheists and rejected the forms and ceremonies of the KORAN, which they regarded as a purely allegorical work.

Karno. Fred Karno's army. A humorous nickname applied to the new British army raised during the war of 1914–1918 in allusion to the famous comedian and producer of stage burlesques, properly, Fred John Westcott (d. 1941). Fred Karno's company was a household name at the time from its merry and eccentric performances. The well-known army chorus, sung to the tune of "The Church's one foundation", runs:

> We are Fred Karno's army,
> Fred Karno's infantry;
> We cannot fight, we cannot shoot,
> So what damn good are we?
> But when we get to Berlin
> The Kaiser he will say
> Hoch, hoch, mein Gott
> Vot a bloody fine lot,
> Fred Karno's infantry.

There are, of course, variants and in World War II "Old Hitler" was substituted for "The Kaiser". The name is also applied derisively to other nondescript bodies. *Cp.* HARRY TATE'S NAVY; MEREDITH.

Karttikeya. The Hindu god of war. He is shown riding on a peacock, with a bow in one hand and an arrow in the other, and is known also as *Skanda* and *Kumara*.

Kaswa, Al. MOHAMMED'S favourite camel, which fell on its knees when the prophet delivered the last clause of the KORAN to the assembled multitude at MECCA.

Katerfelto. A generic name for a QUACK or CHARLATAN. Gustavus Katerfelto was a celebrated quack who became famous during the influenza epidemic of 1782, when he exhibited his solar microscope at London and created immense excitement by showing the infusoria of muddy water. He was a tall man, dressed in a long black gown and square cap, and accompanied by a black cat. He died in 1799.

> And Katerfelto, with his hair on end,
> At his own wonders, wondering for his bread.
> COWPER: <i>The Task; The Winter Evening</i> (1785).

Kathay. *See* CATHAY.

Kay, Sir. In ARTHURIAN ROMANCE, son of Sir Ector and foster-brother of King ARTHUR who made him his seneschal.

Keblah. *See* KIBLAH.

Kedar's Tents (kē dà). This world. Kedar was a son of ISHMAEL (*Gen.* xxv, 13), and was the ancestor of an important tribe of nomadic Arabs. The phrase means "houses in the wilderness of this world", and comes from *Ps.* cxx, 5: "Woe is me, that I sojourn in Mesech, that I dwell in the tents of Kedar!"

Keel. Keel-hauling. An old naval punishment consisting of dragging the offender under the keel of the ship from one side to the other by means of ropes and tackles attached to the yards. The result was often fatal. Figuratively it is "to haul over the coals" (*see under* COAL), to castigate harshly.

On an even keel. Figuratively, a state of stability or balance.

Keening. A weird lamentation for the dead, once common in Ireland, practised at funerals. It is from the Irish word *caoine*, pronounced *keen*, and was a similar musical dirge to the Scottish *coronach*.

Keep. One's *keep* is the amount that it takes to maintain one; heard in such phrases as **You're not worth your keep.** The *keep* of a mediæval castle was the main tower or stronghold of the donjon.

Keep, or **save your breath to cool your porridge.** Look after your own business, and do not put your SPOKE into another person's wheel.

Keep your hair on. *See under* HAIR.

Keep your powder dry. Keep prepared for action; keep your courage up. The phrase comes from a story told of Oliver Cromwell. During his campaign in IRELAND, he concluded an address to his troops, who were about to cross a river before attacking, with the words: "Put your trust in God; but be sure to keep your powder dry."

To keep, or **set a good table.** To provide a good and generous standard of fare at one's table.

To keep a stiff upper lip. To preserve a resolute appearance; not to give way to grief.

To keep at arm's length. To keep at a distance from one; to prevent another from being too familiar.

To keep at it. To continue hard at work; to persist.

To keep body and soul together. *See under* BODY.

To keep company with. A friendship preliminary to courtship.

To keep down. To prevent another from rising to an independent position; to keep in subjection; also to keep expenses low.

To keep good hours. *See under* HOUR.

To keep house, open house, etc. *See under* HOUSE.

To keep in. To repress, to restrain; also to confine pupils in the classroom as a punishment after school hours.

To keep in countenance, etc. *See under* COUNTENANCE.

To keep it dark, etc. *See under* DARK.

To keep oneself to oneself. To avoid the society of others; to keep aloof.

To keep one's hand in. *See under* HAND.

To keep one's terms. To reside in college, attend the INNS OF COURT, etc., during the recognized term times.

To keep tab, to keep tabs on. To keep a record; to keep a check on.

To keep the pot a-boiling. *See under* POT.

To keep up. To continue, as "to keep up a discussion"; to maintain, as, "to keep up one's courage", "to keep up appearances"; to continue PARI PASSU, as, "to keep up with the rest".

Keeper of the King's conscience. The LORD CHANCELLOR. (*See under* CHANCELLOR.)

Keeping up with the Joneses. Trying to keep up the social level or to keep up appearances with your neighbours. The phrase was invented by Arthur R. ("Pop") Momand, the comic-strip artist, for a series which began in the New York *Globe* in 1913, and ran in that and other papers for 28 years. It was originally based on the artist's own attempts to keep up with his neighbours.

Keeping-room. The common sitting-room of a family.

Kells, The Book of. Kells is an ancient Irish town in County Meath, and was the SEE of a BISHOP until the 13th century. Among its antiquities, but now preserved in Trinity College, Dublin, is the 8th-century *Book of Kells*, one of the finest extant illuminated manuscripts of the Gospels in Latin.

Kelly. As game as Ned Kelly. The phrase refers to the noted Australian desperado and BUSHRANGER, Ned Kelly (1855–1880) who, after a legendary career of crime, was captured in a suit of armour of his own making, and hanged at Melbourne. He died bravely, his last words being, "Such is life."

Kelmscott Press. A private printing press founded in 1890 by William Morris (1834–1896) in a cottage adjoining his residence, Kelmscott House, Hammersmith. Assisted by Emery Walker, who initially gave Morris the inspiration, and Sidney Cockerell, the aim was to revive good printing as an art, and their publications made a serious impact on printing and book production.

Kelpie, or **kelpy.** A spirit of the waters in the form of a horse, in Scottish fairy-lore. It was supposed to delight in the drowning of travellers, but also occasionally helped millers by keeping the mill-wheel going at night.

Every lake has its Kelpie or Water-horse, often seen by the shepherd sitting upon the brow of a rock, dashing along the surface of the deep, or browsing upon the pasture on its verge.

GRAHAM: *Sketches of Perthshire*.

Kelter or **Kilter**. Good condition, health, order or spirits. Of unknown origin, it occurs in various local dialects in such expressions as *out of kelter, in good kelter, to get into kelter*.

Kendal Green. Green cloth for foresters; so called from Kendal, Westmorland, formerly famous for its manufacture. LINCOLN was also famous for its green cloth.

Kenelm, St. An English SAINT, son of Kenwulf, King of Mercia in the early 9th century. He was only seven years old when, by his sister's order, he was murdered at Clent, Worcestershire. The murder, says Roger of Wendover, was miraculously notified at ROME by a white dove, which alighted on the altar at St. Peter's, bearing in its beak a scroll with

> In Clent cow pasture, under a thorn,
> Of head bereft, lies Kenelm, King-born.

His day is 17 July.

Kenne. A stone, fabled by mediæval naturalists to be formed in the eye of a stag. It was used as an antidote to poison. *Cp.* HYENA.

Kenno. A dialect name for a large rich cheese made by the women of the family for the refreshment of the GOSSIPS who were in the house at the birth of a child, any remnant being divided among them and taken home. Said to be derived from *ken*, to know, and so called because its making was kept secret. *Cp.* GROANING CHAIR.

Kensal Green. Churchyard burials in London had presented problems long before suburban cemeteries were established by joint-stock companies. Kensal Green, off the Harrow Road, was the first such cemetery and was opened in 1832. It contains the tombs of many notable 19th-century figures, including the Duke of Sussex (sixth son of George III) and his sister, the Princess Sophia, Thomas Hood, Sydney Smith, Brunel, Leigh Hunt, Buckle, Thackeray, Trollope, Wilkie Collins and Blondin.

> For there is good news yet to hear and fine things to be seen,
> Before we go to Paradise by way of Kensal Green.
> G. K. CHESTERTON: *The Rolling English Road*.

Kent. A man of Kent. One born east of the Medway. These men went out with green boughs to meet the CONQUEROR, and obtained in consequence a confirmation of their ancient privileges from the new King. *See* HENGIST AND HORSA.

A Kentish man. A native of West Kent.
The Fair Maid of Kent. *See under* FAIR.
The Holy Maid of Kent. *See under* HOLY.

Kent cap. Before metrification, a standard size of brown paper measuring 21 in. × 18 in.

Kentish Fire. Rapturous applause, or three times three and one more. The expression probably originated with the protracted cheers given in Kent to the No-Popery orators in 1828–1829. Lord Winchelsea, proposing the health of the Earl of Roden on 15 August 1834, said: "Let it be given with the Kentish Fire."

Kentish Rag. A dark-coloured tough limestone used for building, found in parts of Kent.

Kentishman's Tails. *See* TAILED MEN.

Kent's Cavern. A limestone cave at Torquay, Devon, a mile eastward from the harbour, once known as *Kent's Hole*. Apart from the fascination of its natural features, including the beauty of its stalagmite grotto, it is of major importance to students of prehistory. Many relics, human and animal, have been found, including those of the mammoth and sabre-toothed tiger. The origin of the cave's name is a matter for surmise.

Kentigern, St. (kent' i jĕrn). The patron SAINT of Glasgow (*c.* 510–*c.* 600); apostle of north-west ENGLAND and south-east SCOTLAND, and traditional founder of Glasgow Cathedral. He is represented with his episcopal cross in one hand, and in the other a salmon and a ring in allusion to the popular legend:

> Queen Langoureth had been false to her husband, King Roderich, and had given her lover a ring. The king, aware of the fact, stole upon the knight in sleep, abstracted the ring, threw it into the Clyde, and then asked the queen for it. The queen, in alarm, applied to St. Kentigern, who after praying, went to the Clyde, caught a salmon with the ring in its mouth, handed it to the queen and was thus the means of restoring peace to the royal couple.

The Glasgow arms include the salmon with the ring in its mouth, an oak-tree with a bell hanging on one of the branches, and a bird at the top of the tree:

> The tree that never grew,
> The bird that never flew,
> The fish that never swam,
> The bell that never rang.

The oak and the bell are in allusion to the story that St. Kentigern hung a bell upon an oak to summon the wild natives to worship.

St. Kentigern is also known as "St. Mungo", for *Mungho* (dearest) was the name by which St. Servan, his first preceptor, called him.

His day is 13 January.

Kentucky Derby. One of the classic races in the U.S.A., run since 1875 at Churchill Downs, Louisville, Ky. It is a mile and a half, for three-year-olds.

Kentucky Pill. A bullet.

Kepler's Laws. Astronomical laws first enunciated by Johann Kepler (1571–1630). They formed the basis of Newton's work, and are the starting-point of modern astronomy. They are:

(1) That the orbit of a planet is an ellipse, the sun being in one of the foci.

(2) That every planet so moves that the line drawn from it to the sun describes equal areas in equal times.

(3) That the squares of the times of the planetary revolutions are as the cubes of their mean distances from the sun.

Kerb-crawling. A motorist driving very slowly alongside the stone edging of the pavement seeking to entice someone into the car; especially a male motorist approaching and picking up a prostitute.

Kermesse, Kermis, or **Kirmess.** Originally the *Kirkmass* or church mass held in most towns of the Low Countries on the anniversary of the dedication of the parish church. It was accompanied by processions, and by feasting, and sports and games often of a somewhat riotous nature. It still survives, essentially as a FAIR.

Kern (M.E. *kerne* from Ir. *ceithern*). In mediæval Ireland, a light-armed foot soldier, one of the lowest grade. *Cp.* GALLOGLASS.

Kern Baby. *See* CORN DOLLY.

Kernel. The kernel of the matter. Its gist, true import; the core or central part of it. The word is O.E. *cyrnel*, diminutive of *corn*.

Kersey. A coarse cloth, usually ribbed, and woven from long wool; said to be originally made at Kersey in Suffolk. Hence, figuratively, "homely", "homespun".

> Henceforth my wooing mind shall be express'd
> In russet, yeas, and honest kersey noes.
> SHAKESPEARE: *Love's Labour's Lost*, V, ii.

Kerton. *See* EXTER.

Kestrel. A common European falcon, or small hawk, once regarded as of a mean or base variety; hence contemptuously, a worthless fellow.

> Ne thought of honour ever did assay
> His baser breast; but in his kestrell kynd
> A pleasing vaine of glory he did fynd.
> SPENSER: *The Faerie Queene*, II, iii, 4.

Ketch. *See* JACK KETCH *under* JACK.

Kettle. As well as meaning the vessel used for boiling water and cooking, it is old thieves' slang for a watch; a *tin kettle* is a silver watch and a *red kettle* a gold one.

A kettle of fish. An old Border name for a kind of *fête champêtre* or riverside picnic where a newly caught salmon is boiled and eaten. The discomfort of this sort of party may have led to the phrase, "A pretty kettle of fish", meaning an awkward state of affairs, a mess, a muddle.

> As the whole company go to the water-side today to eat a kettle of fish, there will be no risk of interruption.
> SCOTT: *St. Roman's Well*, ch. XII.

Kettledrum. A drum made of a thin hemispherical shell of brass or copper with a parchment top. Also an obsolete name for an afternoon tea party, on a somewhat smaller scale than the regular DRUM, and also in playful allusion to the presence of the tea kettle.

Kevin, St. An Irish saint of the 6th century, of whom legend relates that he retired to a cave on the steep shore of a lake where he vowed no woman should ever land. A girl named Kathleen followed him, but the saint flogged her with a bunch of nettles or, according to the more romantic story, hurled her from a rock and her ghost never left the place where he lived. A cave at Glendalough, Wicklow, is shown as the bed of St. Kevin. Moore has a poem on this tradition (*Irish Melodies*, IV).

Key. Metaphorically, that which explains or solves some difficulty, problem, etc., as *the key to a problem*, the means of solving it, *Keys to the Classics*, a well-known title for a series of CRIBS or literal translations. Also a place which commands a large area of land or sea, as Gibraltar is the **Key to the Mediterranean,** and, in the Peninsular War, Ciudad Rodrigo was known as the **Key to Spain.**

In music the lowest note of a scale is the **keynote,** and gives its name to the scale or key itself: hence the figurative phrases **in key, out of key,** in or out of harmony with.

St. Peter's Keys. The cross-keys, the insignia of the Papacy borne, saltire-wise, one of gold and the other of silver, symbolizing the POWER OF THE KEYS.

The Cross Keys. The emblem of St. PETER and also St. Servatius, St. Hippolytus, St. GENEVIÈVE, St. Petronilla, St. Osyth, St. MARTHA, and St. Germanus of Paris. They also form the arms of the Archbishop of York. The Bishop of Winchester bears two keys and a sword in saltire and the bishops of St. Asaph, Gloucester, Exeter, and Peterborough bear two keys in saltire. The Cross Keys are also used as a PUBLIC-HOUSE SIGN.

The Ceremony of the Keys. When the gates of the TOWER OF LONDON are locked at 10 p.m. each night by the Chief Yeoman Warder and his escort the party is challenged on its return by the sentry with the words "Halt, who comes there?" The Chief

Warder answers, "The Keys." The sentry asks, "Whose keys?" "Queen Elizabeth's keys", is the reply. The guard presents arms and the Chief Warder calls "God preserve Queen Elizabeth," to which the guard says "Amen," and the keys are deposited in the Queen's House. *See* BEEFEATERS.

The Gold Key. The office of GROOM OF THE STOLE (*see under* STOLE), the holder of which had a golden key as his emblem.

The House of Keys. *See* TYNWALD.

The Power of the Keys. The supreme ecclesiastical authority claimed by the POPE as the successor of St. PETER. The phrase is derived from *Matt*. xvi, 19:

> And I will give unto thee the keys of the kingdom of heaven: and whatsoever thou shalt bind on earth shall be bound in heaven: and whatsoever thou shalt loose on earth shall be loosed in heaven.

The queen's keys. An old legal phrase for the crowbars, hammers, etc., used to force an entrance so that a warrant could be executed.

To have the key of the door. A symbol of independence; much favoured on 21st and 18th birthday cards.

To have the key of the street. To be locked out of doors; to be turned out of one's home.

The key shall be on his shoulder. He shall have the dominion, shall be in authority, have the keeping of something. It is said of Eliakim that God would lay upon his shoulder the key of the house of David (*Is*. xxii, 22). The cumbersome wooden or iron keys of Biblical times were often carried across the shoulder.

Key-cold. Deadly cold, lifeless. A key, on account of its metallic coldness, is still sometimes used to stop bleeding at the nose.

> Poor key-cold figure of a holy king!
> Pale ashes of the house of Lancaster!
> Thou bloodless remnant of that royal blood!
> SHAKESPEARE: *Richard III*, I, ii.

The Keystone State. Pennsylvania; so called from its position and importance.

Keystone Comedies. Mack Sennett's notable early film comedies made by the Keystone Comedy Company at Hollywood. The first of their slapstick burlesques appeared in 1913. Charlie Chaplin worked with this company between 1916 and 1918.

Keyne, St. A CELTIC saint of the 5th century, daughter of Brychan, King of Brecknock. St. Keyne's Well, near Liskeard, Cornwall, is reputed to give the upper hand to the first of the marriage partners to drink from it.

Khaki (ka'ki). A Hindu word, meaning dusty, or dust-coloured, from *khak*, dust. Khaki uniform was first used by an irregular corps of Guides raised by the British at Meerut during the INDIAN MUTINY known as the *Khaki Risala* (khaki squadron), nicknamed "the Mudlarks". It was adopted as an active service uniform by several regiments and in the Omdurman campaign, etc., but was not generally introduced until the South African War of 1899–1902.

Khaki Election. The name given to the General Election of 1900 (28 September–24 October) by which the CONSERVATIVES sought to profit from the recent military victories in the South African War. It was promoted by Joseph Chamberlain and the Conservatives won, although the gain in seats was very slight. *See* KHAKI.

Khalifa (ka lē'fà). An Arabic word meaning "successor", and the title adopted by Abdullah el Taashi, the successor of the MAHDI, in 1885. His power was broken by Kitchener at the battle of Omdurman in 1898.

Khedive (ke dēv'). The title, meaning "prince" or "sovereign", by which the ruler of Egypt as viceroy of the Turkish Sultan was known from 1867 to 1914. In 1914, when Turkey joined the Central Powers, Khedive Abbas II was deposed by the British and Hussein Kamil set up as SULTAN. The title of King was adopted by Fuad in 1922 when the British terminated their Protectorate.

Kibbutz (Heb. a gathering). A Jewish communal settlement in Israel organised on socialist lines where land and property are shared. Work and meals are arranged collectively. Adults have private quarters but children are housed together. Originally agricultural only but later various factories and industries developed. The first Kibbutz was set up in the Jordan Valley in 1909 by Jewish immigrants from Europe. There are now c.280 *Kibbutzim* and they have played a considerable part in defending Jewish territory.

Kiblah. The point towards which Mohammedans turn when they worship, *i.e.* the KAABA at MECCA; also the niche or slab (called the *mihrab*) on the interior wall of a mosque indicating this direction.

Kibosh (kī' bosh). **To put the kibosh on.** To put an end to; to dispose of. It has been suggested that it is derived from the Irish *cie bais* (the last word being pronounced "bosh"), cap of death.

Kick. Former slang for a sixpence, but only in compounds, as, "Two-and-a-kick", two shillings and sixpence.

He's not got a kick left in him. He's done for, DOWN AND OUT. The phrase is from pugilism.

More kicks than ha'pence. More abuse than ha'pence. Called "monkey's allowance" in allusion to the monkeys once led about to collect ha'pence by performing tricks. The monkeys got kicks if they performed unsatisfactorily, but their owners collected the ha'pence.

Quite the kick. Quite dandy. The Italians called a dandy a *chic*. The French *chic* means knack, as *avoir le chic*, to have the knack of doing a thing smartly.

> I cocked my hat and twirled my stick,
> And the girls they called me quite the kick.
> GEORGE COLMAN THE YOUNGER.

To get a kick out of something. To derive pleasurable excitement from it. Young people today do things "for kicks".

To get the kick, or **kick out.** To be summarily dismissed; TO GET THE SACK (*see under* SACK) or the "order of the boot".

To kick against the pricks. To struggle against fate; to protest when the odds are against one. See *Acts* ix, 5, and xxvi, 14, where the reference is to an ox kicking when goaded, or a horse when pricked with the rowels of a spur. *Cp.* also I *Sam*. ii, 29— "Wherefore kick ye at my sacrifice and at mine offering?"

To kick one's heels. *See under* HEEL.

To kick over the traces. To break away from control; to throw off restraint; as a horse refusing to run in harness kicks over the traces.

To kick the beam. To be of light weight; to be of inferior consequence. When one scalepan is weighted less than the other, it flies upwards and "kicks the beam" of the scales.

To kick the bucket. *See* BUCKET.

To kick up a dust, row, etc. To create a disturbance.

Kick-off. In football, the start or resumption of a game by kicking the ball from the centre of the field.

Kickshaws. Made dishes, odds and ends, dainty trifles of small value. Formerly written "kickshose" (Fr. *quelque chose*).

> Some pigeons, Davy, a couple of short-legged hens, a joint of mutton, and any pretty little tiny kickshaws.
> SHAKESPEARE: *Henry IV, Pt. II*, V, i.

Kicksy-wicksy. Full of whims and fancies, uncertain; hence, figuratively, a wife. Taylor, the WATER POET, calls it *kicksie-winsie*, but Shakespeare spells it *kicky-wicky*.

Kid. A faggot or bundle of firewood. **To kid** is to bind up faggots. In the parish register of Kneesal church there is the following item: "Leading kids to church, 2*s*. 6*d*.", that is, carting faggots to church.

Kid. A young child; in allusion to kid, the young of the goat, a very playful and frisky little animal.

The verb **to kid** means to make a fool of, to hoax, and in the U.S.A. to tease or banter.

Kiddies, The. *See* REGIMENTAL AND DIVISIONAL NICKNAMES.

Kidnapping. A slang word of 17th-century origin. "Nabbing" a "kid" or a child was the popular term for the stealing of young children and selling them to sea captains and others who transported them to the colonial plantations. Usually, nowadays, people are kidnapped to be held to ransom, the kidnappers often being politically motivated. *Cp.* HIJACKER; SKYJACKER.

Kidd, Captain William Kidd (*c.* 1645–1701), famous privateer and pirate, about whom many stories and legends have arisen. Commissioned with LETTERS OF MARQUE in 1696 to attack the French and seize pirates, he turned the expedition into one of piracy. He was eventually arrested at Boston and subsequently hanged at Execution Dock, Wapping.

Kiddleywinks. A name given to the Cornish ale-houses which opened up as a consequence of the Beer Act of 1830, designed to encourage the consumption of beer as a means of decreasing the evils of gin-drinking. Any householder could obtain a licence for two guineas and some of them sold stronger beverages supplied by the smugglers.

Kidney. Temperament, disposition, stamp, as **men of another kidney,** or **of the same kidney.** The REINS or kidneys were formerly supposed to be the seat of the affections.

Kildare's Holy Fane. Famous for the "Fire of St. Bridget" which the nuns never allowed to go out. Every twentieth night St. Bridget was fabled to return to tend the fire. St. Bridget founded a nunnery at Kildare in the 5th century. Part of the chapel still remains and is called "The Firehouse".

Kill. To kill by kindness. To overwhelm with benevolence, etc. It is said that Draco, the Athenian legislator, was killed by his popularity, being smothered in the theatre of Ægina by the number of caps and cloaks showered on him by the spectators (590 B.C.). Thomas Heywood wrote a play called *A Woman Killed by Kindness* (1607).

Killing. Irresistible, overpowering, fascinating, or bewitching; so as to compel admiration and notice.

A killing pace. Too strong or hot to last; exhausting.

Killing no murder. A pamphlet published

in Holland and sent over to England in 1657 advising the assassination of Oliver Cromwell. It purported to be by one William Allen, a JESUIT, and has frequently been attributed to Silas Titus (later made a colonel and Groom of the Bedchamber by Charles II), but it was actually by Col. Edward Sexby, a LEVELLER, who had gone over to the Royalists, and who, in 1657, narrowly failed in an attempt to murder Cromwell.

To kill time. To while away spare time with amusements or occupations of various kinds in order to avoid or relieve boredom.

Kilroy. During World War II, the phrase "Kilroy was here" was found written up wherever the Americans (particularly Air Transport Command) had been. Its origin is a matter of conjecture. One suggestion is that a certain shipyard inspector at Quincy, Mass., chalked up the words on material he had inspected. *Cp.* CHAD; *see* GRAFFITI.

Kilter. *See* KELTER.

Kin. *See* KITH; FREMD.

Kindergarten, meaning in German "garden of children", is a name applied to schools for training young children where the child is led rather than taught through play materials, handwork, songs, etc. The system was initiated by Friedrich Froebel (1782–1852) when he opened his first kindergarten at Blankenburg in 1837.

Milner's Kindergarten. The nickname given to the notable group of young men gathered together by Sir Alfred (Viscount) Milner, High Commissioner for South Africa, for the work of reconstruction after the South African War (1899–1902). They were Robert Brand, Lionel Curtis, John Dove, Patrick Duncan, Richard Feetham, Lionel Hitchens, Philip Kerr, Douglas Malcolm, J. F. Perry, Geoffrey Robinson, and Hugh Wyndham. Among those associated with them were L. S. Amery, Basil Blackwood, John Buchan and Basil Williams. They duly became advocates of closer imperial ties, both political and economic, and remained an important propagandist group for the imperial idea in the years before World War I. The name was probably invented by the lawyer, Sir William Marriott.

Kindhart. A jocular name for a toothdrawer in the time of Elizabeth I. Kindhart, the dentist, is mentioned by Rowland in his *Letting of Humours—Blood in the Bead-vaine* (1600); and in Rowley's *New Wonder* (Act I, i).

> Mistake me not, Kindhart...
> He calls you tooth-drawer.

The dedication in Chettle's *Kindheartes Dreame* (1592) begins:

> Gentleman and good-fellowes (whose kindnes having christened mee with the name of kindheart, ... let it not seeme strange (I beseech ye) that he that all dayes of his life hath beene famous for drawing teeth, should now in drooping age hazard contemptible infamie by drawing himselfe into print.

King. The O.E. *cyning,* from *cyn,* a nation or people, and the suffix *-ing,* meaning "of" in the sense of "belonging to". In the game of chess a *king* is the chief piece; in draughts a crowned man is called a King, and in cards it is a card carrying a picture of a king.

The Factory King. *See* FACTORY.

King Alfred, H.M.S. The name given to the shore establishment at Brighton where R.N.V.R. officers were trained during World War II.

King Charles's head. A phrase applied to an obsession, a fixed fancy. It comes from Mr. Dick, the harmless half-wit in Dickens' *David Copperfield,* who, whatever he wrote or said, always got round to the subject of King Charles's head, about which he was composing a memorial—he could not keep it out of his thoughts.

King Charles's Spaniel. A small black and tan spaniel with a rounded head, short muzzle, and full eyes, silky coat and long, soft, drooping ears. The variety came into favour at the RESTORATION, but the colour of the dogs at that time was liver and white.

King Cole. *See* COLE.

King Cotton. Cotton, the staple of the American South, called at one time the Cotton Kingdom. The expression was first used by James H. Hammond in the United States Senate in 1858. *See* COTTON.

King Dick. *See under* DICK. Richard John Seddon, Liberal Prime Minister of New Zealand (1893–1906), was also so called because his leadership appeared to some to partake of the nature of benevolent despotism.

King Franconi. Joachim Murat (1767–1815), NAPOLEON's great cavalry leader who became king of Naples in 1808, was so named after the gold-laced circus-master.

King Horn. The hero of a late 13th-century English metrical romance. His father, King of Sudenne, was killed by SARACEN pirates who set young Horn adrift in a boat with twelve other children. After many adventures he reconquers his father's kingdom and marries Rymenhild, daughter of King Aylmer of Westernesse. *Cp.* HORN CHILDE *under* HORN.

King James's Bible. *See* BIBLE, THE ENGLISH.

King Kong. A towering ape-like monster. From the gigantic character of this kind which played the title role in Cooper and

Schoedsack's horror film of this name (1933).

King Log and King Stork. *See under* LOG.

King Pétaud. *See* PÉTAUD.

King of Arms. *See* HERALD.

The King of Bath. *See under* BATH.

King of the Bean. *See* BEAN-KING *under* BEAN.

King of the Beasts. The lion.

King of the Beggars. *See under* BEGGARS.

The King of the Border. A nickname of Adam Scott of Tushielaw (executed 1529), a famous border outlaw and chief.

The King of the Dunces. In his first version of the *Dunciad* (1712), Pope gave this place of honour to Lewis Theobald (1688–1744); but in the edition of 1742 Colley Cibber (1671–1757) was put in his stead.

The King of the Forest. The OAK.

King of Kings. The Deity. The title has also been assumed by various Eastern rulers, especially the sovereigns of Ethiopia.

King of the King. Cardinal Richelieu (1585–1642) was so called, because of his influence over Louis XIII of France.

The King of Men. A title given to both ZEUS and AGAMEMNON.

The King of Metals. GOLD.

King of Misrule. In mediæval and Tudor times the director of the Christmas-time horseplay and festivities, called also the Abbot, or Lord, of Misrule, and in SCOTLAND the Abbot of Unreason. A King of Misrule was appointed at the royal court, and at Oxford and Cambridge one of the Masters of Arts superintended the revelries. Stow tells us that the Lord Mayor of London, the sheriffs, and the noblemen each had their Lord of Misrule. Philip Stubbs (*Anatomie of Abuses*, 1595) says that these mock dignitaries had from twenty to a hundred officers under them, furnished with HOBBY-HORSES, dragons, and musicians. They first paraded in church with such a babble of noise that no one could hear his own voice. Polydore Vergil says that the Feast of Misrule was derived from the Roman SATURNALIA. According to Stow, "this pageant potentate began his rule at ALL-HALLOWS' EVE, and continued the same till the morrow after the Feast of the Purification."

The King of Painters. A title assumed by Parrhasius, the painter, a contemporary of Zeuxis (*c*. 400 B.C.). Plutarch says he wore a purple robe and a golden crown.

The King of Rome. A title conferred by NAPOLEON on his son Francis Charles Joseph Napoleon, Duke of Reichstadt (1811–1832), on the day of his birth. His mother was the Empress Marie Louise. He was called *L'Aiglon* (the young eagle) by Edmond Rostand in his play. His ashes were transferred to the INVALIDES in 1940.

The King of Spain's Trumpeter. A donkey. A pun on the word *don*, a Spanish magnate.

The King of Terrors. Death.

The King of Waters. The river Amazon, in South America. Although not as long as the Mississippi—Missouri (the longest river in the world), it discharges a greater volume of water.

The King of the World. The title (in Hindi *Shah Jehan*) assumed by Khorrum Shah, third son of Selim Jehangir, and fifth of the MOGUL Emperors of Delhi (reigned 1627–1658).

King of Yvetot. *See* YVETOT.

The King over the Water. The name given by JACOBITES to James II after his flight to France; to his son the Old PRETENDER (James III), and to his grandsons Charles Edward the Young Pretender (Charles III), and Henry, Cardinal of York (Henry IX).

> My father ... so far compromised his loyalty as to announce merely "The King," as his first toast after dinner, instead of the emphatic "King George".... Our guest made a motion with his glass, so as to pass it over the water-decanter which stood beside him, and added, "Over the water."
>
> SCOTT: *Redgauntlet*, Letter V.

The Three Kings of Cologne. THE MAGI.

King's, or **Queen's Bench.** *See under* QUEEN.

The King's Book. The usual name given to Henry VIII's *Necessary Doctrine and Evolution for any Christian Man* (1543) issued after presentation to Convocation. It was based on the *Bishops' Book* of 1537 and the royal supremacy was more strongly emphasized. Its doctrinal tone was more CATHOLIC than that of its predecessor. It was probably the work of Cranmer, although Henry VIII seems to have contributed the preface.

The King's Cave. On the west coast of the Isle of Arran; so called because it was here that King Robert Bruce and his retinue are said to have lodged before they landed in Carrick (1307).

King's Champion. *See* CHAMPION OF ENGLAND.

King's, or **Queen's Colour.** *See under* QUEEN.

King's, or **Queen's Counsel.** *See under* QUEEN.

King's County in the province of Leinster in Eire was so called in 1556 when planted by English settlers, but is now called Offaly, its former name. Similarly *Queen's County* is once more called Leix.

King's Crag. Fife in SCOTLAND, so called

because Alexander III of Scotland was killed there in 1286.

> As he was riding in the dusk of the evening along the sea-coast of Fife, betwixt Burnt-island and King-horn, he approached too near the brink of the precipice, and his horse starting or stumbling, he was thrown over the rock and killed on the spot.... The people of the country still point out the very spot where it happened, and which is called "the King's Crag".
>
> SCOTT: *Tales of a Grandfather*, vi.

The King's or **Queen's English.** *See under* ENGLISH.

King's, or **Queen's Evidence.** *See* EVIDENCE.

King's Evil. Scrofula; supposedly cured by the royal touch, hence the name. The custom existed in France long before its introduction into England by Edward the Confessor. Ceremonial touching was introduced by Henry VII and the sufferers were presented with gold coins, although CHARLES I sometimes gave silver touch pieces instead of gold. The practice reached its height under Charles II, who, according to Macaulay (*History of England*, ch. xiv) touched nearly 100,000 people and in 1682 alone some 8,500. "In 1684, the throng was such that six or seven of the sick were trampled to death." William III called it "a silly superstition" and it was last practised by Queen Anne who touched Dr. Johnson without effecting a cure in 1712. Between the reign of Charles I and 1719 the *Book of Common Prayer* contained an office for the touching. The PRETENDERS also claimed this power.

King's Friends. In the early years of George III the name given to those politicians, mainly Tories, who for various reasons supported the crown and its ministries. The term was used with derogatory implications by the WHIGS. Their subservience to the king has been over-estimated as well as their importance as a coherent political group.

King's, or **Queen's Messenger.** *See under* QUEEN.

The King's Oak. The OAK under which Henry VIII sat in Epping Forest, while Queen Anne (Boleyn) was being executed.

The King's, or **Queen's picture.** Money; so called because it bears the portrait of the reigning sovereign.

King's or **Queen's Proctor.** A law official entitled to intervene in probate, divorce, or nullity cases where collusion or fraud is suspected.

King's, or **Queen's Regulations.** Regulations governing the organization and discipline of the Royal Navy, the Army and the Royal Air Force.

King's, or **Queen's Remembrancer.** *See under* QUEEN.

King's Scholar. One who holds a school or college scholarship in a royal foundation.

The King's, or **Queen's Shilling.** *See under* SHILLING.

The King's, or **Queen's Speech.** *See under* QUEEN.

The books of the four kings. A pack of cards.

A cat may look at a king. *See under* CAT.

Days fatal to kings. Certain days were superstitiously held to be fatal to the sovereigns of Great Britain, but with little resemblance to the facts. Of those who have died since 1066 *Sunday* has been the last day of the reign of seven, *Monday, Tuesday*, and *Thursday* that of six each, *Friday* and *Wednesday* of five, and *Saturday* of four.

> *Sunday:* Henry I, Edward III, Henry VI, James I, William III, Anne, George I.
> *Monday:* Stephen, Richard II, Henry IV, Henry V, Richard III, George V.
> *Tuesday:* Richard I, Edward II, Charles I, James II, William IV, Victoria.
> *Wednesday:* John, Henry III, Edward IV, Edward V, George VI.
> *Thursday:* William I, William II, Henry II, Edward VI, Mary I, Elizabeth I.
> *Friday:* Edward I, Henry VIII, Charles II, Mary II, Edward VII.
> *Saturday:* Henry VII, George II, George III, George IV.

A king of shreds and patches. In the old MYSTERIES, Vice used to be dressed in the motley of a clown or buffoon, as a mimic king in a parti-coloured suit. Thus SHAKESPEARE says (*Hamlet*, III, iv)—

> A vice of kings;
> A cutpurse of the empire and the rule...
> A king of shreds and patches.

Gilbert and Sullivan's *Mikado* has—

> A wandering minstrel I—
> A thing of shreds and patches.

The phrase has also been applied to HACKS who compile books for publishers but supply no originality of thought or matter. *Cp.* GRUB STREET.

A king should die standing. The reputed DYING SAYING of Louis XVIII.

A King's, or **Queen's bad,** or **hard bargain.** Said of a soldier who turns out to be a malingerer or to be of no use; in allusion to the SHILLING formerly given to the serviceman on enlistment.

The king's cheese goes half in paring. A king's income is half consumed by the numerous calls on his purse.

Kings are above grammar. *See* GRAMMAR.

Kings have long hands. Do not quarrel with the king, as his power and authority reach to the end of his dominions. The Latin proverb is, *An nescis longas regibus esse manus* (Ovid, *Heroides*, XVII, 166).

Like a king. When Porus, the Indian prince, was taken prisoner, ALEXANDER THE GREAT asked him how he expected to be treated. "Like a king," he replied; and Alexander made him his friend, restoring Porus to his kingdom.

King-maker, The. Richard Neville, Earl of Warwick (1428–1471); so called because when he supported Henry VI, Henry was King, but when he sided with Edward IV, Henry was deposed and Edward crowned. He was killed at the battle of Barnet after seeking to re-establish Henry VI. He was apparently first called "the king-maker" by John Major in his *History of Greater Britain, both England and Scotland*, 1521.

King-pin. In skittles, etc., the pin in the centre when all the pins are in place, or the pin at the front apex, because if struck successfully it knocks down the others. Figuratively the word is applied to the principal person in a company, enterprise, etc.

Kingdom come. The next world.

> And forty pounds be theirs, a pretty sum,
> For sending such a rogue to kingdom come.
> PETER PINDAR: *Subjects for Painters*.

Kingsale. *See* HAT.

Kingston Bridge. A card bent so that when the pack is cut, it is cut at this card.

Kinless Loons. The judges whom Cromwell sent into SCOTLAND were so termed, because they had no relations in that country and so were free from temptations to nepotism.

Kiplingcotes Derby. The oldest flat race in Great Britain run in March, near Market Weighton, North Yorkshire. The four-mile course of narrow roads and tracks dates from 1519. The second prize is often worth more than the first.

> Miss Cole-Walton's three-length lead cost her £24 (the first prize was £16, the second £40). "But I don't really mind; it's much better to win".
> *The Times* (17 March 1972).

Kirk of Skulls. Gamrie Church in Banffshire; so called because the skulls and other bones of the Norsemen who fell in the neighbouring field, the *Bloody Pots*, were built into its walls.

Kirke's Lambs. *See* REGIMENTAL AND DIVISIONAL NICKNAMES.

Kismet. Fate, destiny; or the fulfilment of destiny; from Turk. *qismet*, portion, lot.

Kiss (O.E. *cyssan*). An ancient and widespread mode of salutation frequently mentioned in the BIBLE as an expression of reverence and adoration, and as a greeting or farewell among friends. Esau embraced Jacob,

"fell on his neck, and kissed him" (*Gen.* xxxiii, 4), the repentant woman kissed the feet of Christ (*Luke*, vii, 45), and the disciples of Ephesus "fell on Paul's neck, and kissed him" (*Acts* xx, 37). In the NEW TESTAMENT the kiss becomes a token of Christian brotherhood, "Salute one another with an holy kiss" (*Rom.* xvi, 16). Kissing between the sexes occurs in *Prov.* vii, 13, "So she caught him, and kissed him, and with an impudent face said unto him…"

The old custom of "kissing the bride" comes from the Salisbury rubric concerning the PAX.

In billiards (and bowls) a *kiss* is a very slight touch of one moving ball on another, especially a second touch; and the name also used to be given to a drop of sealing-wax accidentally let fall beside the seal.

Kiss-behind-the-garden-gate. A country name for a pansy.

Kiss it better, or **kiss the place and make it well.** Said to be a relic of the custom of sucking poison from wounds. St. MARTIN of Tours observed at the city gates of Paris a leper covered with sores; he went up to him and kissed the sores and the leper instantly became whole (Sulpicius Severus: *Dialogues*). There are many such stories.

> Who ran to help me when I fell,
> And would some pretty story tell,
> Or kiss the place to make it well.
> ANN TAYLOR: *My Mother*.

Kiss of Life. The name applied to the mouth-to-mouth method of artificial respiration. SLEEPING-BEAUTY was awakened from her death-like sleep by the Prince's kiss.

Kissing the Pope's toe. Matthew of Westminster (15th century) says it was customary formerly to kiss the hand of his Holiness; but that a certain woman in the 8th century not only kissed the POPE'S hand but "squeezed it". Seeing the danger to which he was exposed, the Pope cut off his hand, and was compelled in future to offer his foot. In reality the Pope's foot (*i.e.* the cross embroidered on his right shoe) may be kissed by the visitor; BISHOPS kiss the knee as well. This is an old sign of respect and does not imply servility. It is customary to bend the knee and kiss the ring of a CARDINAL, bishop, or abbot.

To kiss the book. To kiss the BIBLE, or the NEW TESTAMENT, after taking an oath; the kiss of confirmation or promise to act in accordance with the words of the oath and a public acknowledgment of its sanctity.

In the English courts, the Houses of PARLIAMENT, etc., non-Christians are permitted to affirm without kissing the book, as a result of the struggle waged by the atheist Charles Bradlaugh to take his seat in the HOUSE OF COMMONS. First elected in 1880 he was finally admitted to the House in 1886. Previously, in 1858, Baron Lionel de Rothschild, the first Jew to be admitted to Parliament, as a Jew, had been allowed to swear on the OLD TESTAMENT. He had been elected as WHIG M.P. for the City of London in 1847. The position was legalized by the Oaths Act of 1888.

In Roman Catholic churches it is customary for the priest to kiss the Bible after reading the Gospel.

To kiss, or **lick the dust.** To be completely overwhelmed and humiliated; to be slain.

His enemies shall lick the dust.

Ps. lxxii, 9.

To kiss the gunner's daughter. *See* GUNNER.

To kiss hands. To kiss the hand of the sovereign either on accepting or retiring from office.

Kissing the hand of, or one's own hand to, an idol, etc., was a usual form of adoration. God said he had in Israel seven thousand persons who had not bowed unto Baal, "every mouth which hath not kissed him" (I *Kings* xix, 18).

To kiss the hare's foot. *See under* HARE.

To kiss the rod. *See under* ROD.

Kissing-comfit. The candied root of the Sea Holly (*Eryngium maritimum*) prepared as a lozenge, to perfume the breath.

Kissing-crust. The crust where the lower lump of a cottage loaf kisses the upper. In French, *baisure de pain*.

Kist of Whistles. A church-organ (Scots). *Kist* is the same word as *cist* (a chest).

Kit and boodle. *See* CABOODLE.

Kit-Cat Club. A club formed about 1700 by the aristocratic WHIGS of the day who dined in the house of Christopher Cat, a pastry-cook of Shire Lane. His famous mutton pies, called *kit-kats*, always formed part of their repasts. Among the distinguished noblemen and gentlemen were Steele, Addison, Congreve, Garth, Vanbrugh, Manwaring, Stepney, Walpole, Pulteney and the Duke of Somerset. Jacob Tonson, the publisher, was the secretary.

Sir Godfrey Kneller painted forty-two portraits (now in the National Portrait Gallery) of the club members for Tonson, in whose villa at Barn Elms the meetings were latterly held. The paintings were made three-quarter length (36 in. × 28 in.) in order to accommodate them to the size of the club-room. Hence a three-quarter length

portrait came to be called a *kit-cat*. The club ceased about 1720.

Kit's Coty House. A great CROMLECH, $3\frac{1}{2}$ m. north-west of Maidstone on the Rochester road, consisting of a 12-feet long block of sandstone resting on three standing blocks. The name may be British for "the tomb in the wood" (Wel. *coed*, a wood). It is near the ancient battlefield where Vortigern is supposed to have fought HENGIST AND HORSA.

Kitchen. An old Scottish term for a cooked relish, as toasted cheese, eggs, sausages, bacon, etc.

Kitchen cabinet. An American term for an informal group of advisers used by a president and given more weight than the proper cabinet. The term was first used of such an unofficial group advising President Andrew Jackson (OLD HICKORY) in 1829.

Kitchen-middens. Prehistoric mounds (referred to the NEOLITHIC AGE) composed of sea-shells, bones, kitchen refuse, stone implements, and other relics of ancient man. They were first noticed on the coast of Denmark, but have since been found in the British Isles, North America, etc.

All but the kitchen sink. A comment on someone's excessive amount of luggage, particularly applicable to those travelling in motor cars crammed with bags, suitcases, etc.

Kite. In lawyer's slang, a junior counsel who was allotted at an assize court to advocate the cause of a prisoner who was without other defence.

In R.A.F. slang, any aircraft.

In STOCK EXCHANGE slang, an accommodation bill.

Go fly a kite. The American equivalent to "buzz off".

To fly a kite. In commercial slang, to raise money by means of accommodation bills, etc. The phrase is more commonly used nowadays to denote an experiment to test public opinion.

Kith and Kin (O.E. *cyth*, relationship; *cynn*, kind, family). One's own people and kindred; friends and relations.

Kiwanis. An organization founded in the U.S.A. in 1915 aiming to improve business ethics and provide leadership for raising the level of business and professional ideals. There are many Kiwanis clubs in the U.S.A. and Canada.

Kiwi. A New Zealand bird incapable of flight. In flying circles the word is applied to a man of the ground staff of an aerodrome. It also denotes a New Zealander.

Klephts, or **Klepts** (Gr., robbers). The name given to those Greeks who maintained their independence in the mountains after the Turkish conquest in the 15th century. After the War of Independence (1821–1828) they relapsed into brigandage.

Klondike. A river and district of the Yukon, Canada. The rich gold-bearing gravel found at Bonanza Creek in 1896 resulted in a wild rush of prospectors. GOLD production reached its peak in 1900.

Knave (O.E. *cnafa*; Ger. *Knabe*). Originally a boy or male child, then a male servant, or one in low condition, and subsequently a dishonourable rascal.

> The tyme is come, a knave-child she ber;
> Mauricius at the font-stoon they him calle.
> > CHAUCER: *Man of Lawe's Tale*, 722.
> Three misbegotten knaves in Kendal green came at my back.
> > SHAKESPEARE: *Henry IV, Pt. I*, II, iv.

In cards the *knave* (or *Jack*), the lowest court card of each suit, is the common soldier or servant of the royalties.

He lived like a knave and died like a fool. Said by Warburton of Henry Rich, first Earl of Holland (1590–1649), the TURN-COAT. He went to the scaffold dressed in white satin, trimmed with silver.

Knave of hearts. A flirt.

Knee. Housemaid's knee. *See under* HOUSE.

Knee tribute. Adoration or reverence by bending the knee; an act of homage. *Cp.* LIP-SERVICE.

> Coming to receive from us
> Knee-tribute yet unpaid, prostration vile.
> > MILTON: *Paradise Lost*, V, 778–9.

Weak-kneed. Irresolute, infirm of purpose or conviction, as a *weak-kneed Christian*, a LAODICEAN, neither hot nor cold.

Knickerbockers, or **knickers.** Loose-fitting breeches, gathered in below the knees, once worn by boys, cyclists, sportsmen, etc., and by women as an undergarment. So named from George Cruickshank's illustrations of *Knickerbocker's History of New York* (1809) by Washington Irving, where the Dutch worthies wore such knee-breeches. The name probably signified a baker of *knickers*, *i.e.* clay marbles. *Cp.* BLOOMERS.

Knife. The emblem of St. AGATHA, St. Albert, and St. Christina.

The **flaying knife** is the emblem of St. BARTHOLOMEW, because he was flayed.

The custom of demanding a small coin when making a present of a knife or a pair of scissors comes from Sheffield, the home of the Cutler's Company. The "gift" having been "bought" makes the purchaser responsible for any injury that may be sustained when using the knife or scissors.

He is a capital knife-and-fork. He has a good appetite.

To live on a knife's edge. Metaphorically, to occupy such a precarious position that the slightest false move may result in disaster.

> His [Mr. Wilson's] tactical appreciation of the problems of living on a knife-edge through the next few months in Parliament could not be cooler.
> > *The Times* (24 May 1965).

War to the knife. Deadly strife.

Knifeboard. The long, back-to-back seats that used to run longitudinally along the top of the old horse omnibuses. In the 1890s transverse "garden seats" gradually took their place. The allusion is to the old board used for cleaning steel table-knives.

Knight (O.E. *cniht*). Originally a boy or servant, the word came to denote a man of gentle birth who, after serving at court or in the retinue of some lord as a page and ESQUIRE, was admitted with appropriate ceremonies to an honourable degree of military rank and given the right to bear arms. *See* BACHELOR; BANNERET; BARONET.

Since the disappearance of KNIGHT-SERVICE, knights, as men of standing in England, continued to give service as KNIGHTS OF THE SHIRE, SHERIFFS, etc. Titles have long been bestowed on administrative officials, professional men, politicians, scholars, artists, etc., as well as those serving in the armed forces, and trade union officials and professional sportsmen have joined the throng in the present century.

There are nine existing British *Orders of Knighthood*, the oldest being that of the GARTER, which takes precedence. The others are (in order of precedence): the THISTLE (1687); St. PATRICK (1788); the BATH (1399, but revived in 1715 and subsequently reorganized); the STAR OF INDIA (1861); St. MICHAEL AND St. GEORGE (1818); the Indian Empire (1877); the Royal Victorian Order (1896); the British Empire (1917–1918).

The modern *Knights Bachelor* do not constitute an order and rank lowest in precedence. The wife of a Knight is designated "Dame", or more usually "Lady".

The word *knight* is used jocularly to denote a member of some trade, calling, etc. Thus we have *Knight of the blade*, a roystering bully; *Knight of the cleaver*, a butcher; *Knight of the cue*, a billiard player; *Knight of the needle*, a tailor; *Knight of the pestle*, a druggist; *Knight of the road*, a footpad or highwayman; *Knight of the spigot*, a tapster; *Knight of the wheel*, a cyclist; etc., etc.

Carpet-knight. *See under* CARPET.

Cross-legged Knights. *See* CROSS-LEGGED.

Knight Bachelor. *See* KNIGHT *above*; BACHELOR.

Knight Banneret. *See* BANNERET.

Knight Baronet. The original title of a BARONET.

Knight errant. A mediæval knight, especially a hero of those long romances satirized by Cervantes in *Don* QUIXOTE, who wandered about the world in quest of adventure and in search of opportunities of rescuing damsels in distress and performing other chivalrous deeds.

Knights Hospitallers. *See* HOSPITALLERS.

Knight Marshal. *See* MARSHALSEA.

Knights of Columbus. A Roman Catholic fraternal and philanthropic society in the U.S.A., founded in 1882 with the aim of uniting laymen of that Church in corporate religious and civic usefulness.

Knights of the Golden Circle. In the U.S.A. a COPPERHEAD secret society in the Middle West which opposed the war policy of the Republicans and sought to end the CIVIL WAR.

Knight of Grace. A member of the lower order of the Knights of MALTA.

Knight of Industry. Slang for a sharper; one who lives on his wits.

Knights of Labor. An organization of working men (at first secret), founded at Philadelphia in 1869, which subsequently played an important part in the early development of the American TRADE UNION movement. It secured the recognition of LABOR DAY (*see under* LABOUR) and sought to organize all workers, but it was eclipsed by the American Federation of Labor (founded 1886) and rapidly declined.

Knight of the post. A man who had stood in the pillory or had been flogged at the whipping-post was so called; hence one who haunted the purlieus of the courts, ready to give false witness, go bail for a debtor for pay, etc.

> "A knight of the post," quoth he, "for so I am termed; a fellow that will sweare you anything for twelve pence."
>
> NASHE: *Pierce Penilesse* (1592).

Knights of the Round Table. *See* ROUND TABLE.

The Knight of the Rueful Countenance. Don QUIXOTE.

Knight of the Shire. The original name for the two men of the rank of knight who formerly represented a shire or county in PARLIAMENT. The boroughs were represented by burgesses.

Knight of the square flag. A knight BANNERET in allusion to cutting off the points of his pennon when he was raised to this rank on the battlefield.

The Knight of the Swan. LOHENGRIN.

Knights Templar. *See* TEMPLARS.

Knights of the White Camelia. *See* KU KLUX KLAN.

Knights of Windsor. Originally a small order of knights founded by Edward III in 1349 as the "Poor Knights of the Order of the Garter". It was formed of 26 veterans, but since the time of Charles I the numbers have been fixed at 13 for the Royal Foundation and 5 for the Lower (since abolished) with a Governor. The members are meritorious military officers who are granted apartments in Windsor Castle with small pensions. They have to be in residence for nine months of the year, attend St. George's Chapel on saints' days, and occasionally act as guards of honour. Every Knight of the GARTER on appointment has to give a sum of money for distribution among them. Their present uniform was designed by William IV, who made their title "Military Knights of Windsor". *See* POOR MAN.

Knight Service. The tenure of land in feudal times, on the condition of rendering military service to the Crown for 40 days, etc. By the reign of Edward III knights were paid for their military service.

Knight's fee (Lat. *feodum*). The amount of land for which, under the FEUDAL SYSTEM, the services of a knight were due to the Crown. It was probably determined by valuation rather than area, in any case the number of HIDES in a Knight's Fee varied.

Knightenguild. The guild of thirteen "cnihts" (probably youthful scions of noble houses attached to the court) to which King Edgar, or, according to other accounts, Canute, gave that portion of the City of London now called PORTSOKEN WARD on the following conditions: (1) Each knight was to be victorious in three combats—one on the earth, and one under, and one in the water; and (2) each was, on a given day, to run with spears against all comers in East Smithfield. WILLIAM THE CONQUEROR, confirmed the same unto the heirs of these knights, whose descendants, in 1125, gave all the property and their rights to the newly founded Priory of the Holy Trinity.

Knipperdollings. ANABAPTIST followers of Bernard Knipperdolling (*c.* 1490–1536), who was one of the leaders of the Munster theocracy (1532–1535). After the city was taken by the BISHOP and his supporters, Knipperdolling was tortured to death with red-hot pincers.

Knobstick. A **knobstick wedding.** The name given to an 18th-century practice whereby the churchwardens of a parish used their authority virtually to enforce the marriage of a pregnant woman, which they attended officially. The term "knobstick" was in allusion to the churchwarden's staff, his symbol of office. *Cp.* SHOTGUN WEDDING.

Knock, To. In slang of former days, to create a great impression, to be irresistible; as in Albert Chevalier's song "Knocked 'em in the Old Kent Road" (1892), *i.e.* astonished the inhabitants, filled them with admiration. *See* ALBERT THE GREAT.

In current colloquial usage it means to criticize adversely, to look for faults in someone or something, to disparage.

To be knocked into a cocked hat, or **into the middle of next week.** To be thoroughly beaten. *See under* COCK.

To get a knock, or **a nasty knock.** To receive a blow, literally or figuratively, that finishes one off.

To knock about, or **around.** To wander about the town "seeing life" and enjoying oneself; to be in the vicinity or in the neighbourhood.

To knock the bottom, or **the stuffing out of anything.** To confound, bring to naught; especially to show that some argument or theory is invalid and "won't hold water". (*See under* WATER.)

To knock down. To dispose of an article to the highest bidder at an auction when a sale is indicated by a knock of the auctioneer's gavel.

To knock for six. To completely demolish an argument or to completely defeat an opponent figuratively or literally. In CRICKET the ball is "knocked for six" when the batsman, by hitting it over the boundary of the cricket field, scores six runs, and shows, in that instance, an easy mastery of the bowling.

To knock off. To cease work; to purloin.

To knock out of the box. In baseball, to score so highly against a pitcher that he is replaced by another in the box. Figuratively, to achieve an easy and decisive victory over an opponent.

To knock out of time. To settle one's HASH, to double him up. A phrase from pugilism referring to disabling an opponent so that he is unable to resume when the referee calls, "Time".

To knock spots off someone, or **something.** To beat him soundly, to get the better of it. The allusion is probably to pistol-shooting at a playing-card, when a good shot will knock out the pips or spots.

To knock under. Virtually the same as to KNUCKLE UNDER.

You could have knocked me down with a feather. I was overcome with surprise.

A knock-about turn. A MUSIC HALL term for a noisy boisterous act usually involving horseplay and SLAPSTICK.

Knock-kneed. With the knees turned inwards so that they virtually knock or rub together in walking.

Knock-out. A disabling blow, especially in boxing, on the point of the chin, or under the ear, etc., which puts the receiver to sleep, thus finishing the fight. Hence a complete surprise is "a fair knock-out".

In the auction room a *knock-out* is a sale at which a ring of dealers combine to keep prices artificially low to obtain the goods for subsequent profit divided among themselves.

Knockers. GOBLINS or KOBOLDS who dwell in mines and indicate rich veins of ore by their presence. In Cardiganshire and elsewhere miners attributed the strange noises so frequently heard in mines to these spirits.

Knot (Lat. *nodus*, Fr. *nœud*, Dan. *Knude*, Dut. *knot*, O.E. *cnotta*, allied to *knit*).

Gordian knot. *See* GORDIAN.

Knots of May. *See* HERE WE GO GATHERING NUTS IN MAY *under* NUT.

True lovers' knots. Sir Thomas Browne thinks the knot owes its origin to the *nodus Herculanus*, a snaky complication in the CADUCEUS or rod of MERCURY in which form the woollen girdle of the Greek brides was fastened (*Pseudodoxia Epidemica*, V, xxii). This interlacing knot is a symbol of interwoven affection.

He has tied a knot with his tongue he cannot untie with his teeth. He has got married. He has tied the marriage knot by saying "I take thee to my wedded wife", etc., but it is not to be untied so easily.

She was making 15 knots. The vessel was travelling 15 nautical miles per hour. The nautical MILE varies in different latitudes owing to the irregular shape of the earth but in practice it is 6,080 ft., its value in latitude 48°. The knot, as a speed, is that of one nautical mile per hour and is from the knots tied on the LOG line formerly used in conjunction with the sand glass, the speed being the number of such knots run out during the sand glass interval.

To seek for a knot in an rush. Seeking for something that does not exist.

Knotgrass. This plant, *Polygonum aviculare*, was formerly supposed, if taken in an infusion, to stop growth.

> Get you gone, you dwarf;
> You minimus of hindering knotgrass made.
> SHAKESPEARE: *Midsummer Night's Dream*, III, ii.

Know Nothings. An anti-Catholic, anti-immigrant movement which developed in the U.S.A. after 1852 but which faded out after 1856. Properly known as the Native American party, their nickname came from their stock reply to any awkward question on what they stood for, *i.e.* "I know nothing".

Know Thyself. The admonition of the oracle of APOLLO at DELPHI; also attributed (Diogenes Laertius, I, xl) to Thales; also to SOLON the Athenian lawgiver, SOCRATES, PYTHAGORAS, and others.

Do you know the Bishop of Norwich? A reminder to those who forget to pass the port wine to their neighbour because they are too busy conversing. The hint stems from a certain Bishop of Norwich who was said to be such a persistent talker that he often forgot to pass the port.

To know all the answers. To be well informed, resourceful, and intelligent. One who thinks he knows all the answers is one who conceitedly assumes a knowledge he does not really possess, a "CLEVER DICK".

To know the ropes. *See under* ROPE.

Knuckle. Near the knuckle. Said of a remark, story, joke, performance etc. that is bordering on the improper or indecent.

To knuckle down to. To submit to.

To knuckle down to it. To work away at it; to get on with it.

To knuckle under. To acknowledge defeat, to give in, to submit; in allusion to the old custom of striking the under side of a table with the knuckles when defeated in an argument. *Cp.* TO KNOCK UNDER.

Knuckle-duster. A loop of heavy, shaped brass, gripped in the hand and fitting over the knuckles, used as an offensive weapon. Its origin goes back to the days of Roman pugilism.

Knurr and Spell. An old English game resembling trap ball and played with a *knurr* or wooden ball which is released from a little brass cup at the end of a tongue of steel called a *spell* or *spill*. After the player has touched the spring the ball flies into the air and is struck with the bat.

Knut. *See* NUT.

Kobold. A house-spirit in German folklore; similar to our ROBIN GOODFELLOW and the Scots BROWNIE. Also a GNOME who works in mines and forests. *Cp.* KNOCKERS.

Kochlani (kok la' ni). Arabian horses of royal stock, of which the genealogies have been preserved for more than 2,000 years. It is said that they are the offspring of SOLOMON's stud.

Koh-i-Noor (kó i nôr) (Pers., mountain of light). A famous DIAMOND, so called by Nadir Shah, and now kept in the TOWER OF LONDON. Its early history is uncertain, but

when Aurangzeb (*d.* 1707), MOGUL Emperor of India, possessed the stone it was used for the eye of a peacock in his famous peacock throne at Delhi. In 1739 it was acquired by Nadir Shah of Persia and later passed to Afghanistan, but when Shah Shuja was deposed he gave it to Ranjit Singh of the Punjab for promised assistance towards his recovery of the Afghan throne. Ten years after Ranjit's death (1839) the Punjab was annexed to the British Crown and in 1849, by stipulation, it was presented to Queen Victoria. At this time it weighed $186\frac{1}{16}$ carats, but was subsequently cut down to $106\frac{1}{16}$ carats. There is a tradition that it always brings ill luck to its possessor.

Kon-Tiki Expedition. The unique voyage made by the Norwegian Thor Heyerdahl with five companions in 1947, who sailed a balsa raft from Callao in Peru to Tuamotu Island in the South Pacific. Their object was to support the theory that the Polynesian race reached the Pacific islands in this fashion and were descendants of the Incas of Peru. Their raft was called *Kon-Tiki* after the INCA sun-god.

Koppa. An ancient Greek letter, disused as a letter in classical Greek, but retained as the sign for the numeral 90.

Koran, or **Al Koran** (Arab. *qurān*, recitation). The sacred book of the Mohammedans, containing the religious teaching of the prophet with instructions on morality and Islamic institutions. The Koran, which contains 114 chapters or *Suras*, is said to have been communicated to the prophet at MECCA and MEDINA by an angel, to the sound of bells. It is written in Arabic and was compiled from MOHAMMED's own lips. The present text is of the 7th century, the chapters being arranged, except the first, in descending order of length.

Kosher (kō'sher). A Hebrew word denoting that which is "right", "fit" or "proper". It is applied usually to food—especially meat which has been slaughtered and prepared in the prescribed manner. Food must not be obtained from the animals, birds, and fish prohibited in *Lev*. xi and *Deut*. xiv and animals must be killed by cutting the windpipe.

Kowtow (Chin. knocking the head). A Chinese custom of kneeling down and knocking the head on the ground as a sign of reverence, homage, respect, etc. Hence in popular usage to behave obsequiously to someone, to fawn or grovel.

Kraken. A fabulous sea-monster supposed to have been seen off the coast of Norway and probably founded on an observation of a gigantic cuttle-fish. It was first described by

Pontoppidan in his *History of Norway* (1752). It was supposed to be capable of dragging down the largest ships and when submerging could suck down a vessel by the whirlpool it created. *Cp.* LOCH NESS MONSTER.

Kralitz Bible. *See* BIBLE, SOME SPECIALLY NAMED EDITIONS.

Kratim. The dog of the SEVEN SLEEPERS, more correctly called Katmir or Ketmir, which according to MOHAMMED sleeps with them and is one of the ten animals to be admitted into his PARADISE.

Kremlin (Russ. *kreml*, a citadel). The Moscow Kremlin is on a scale of its own, comprising buildings of many architectural styles (Arabesque, Gothic, Greek, Italian, Chinese, etc.) enclosed by battlemented and many-towered walls $1\frac{1}{2}$ miles in circuit. The Tsars and the PATRIARCH lived in the Kremlin until Peter the Great's reign when the court moved to St. Petersburg (Leningrad). Much of it was damaged in the revolution of 1917 but considerable repairs have been made. Its bells now ring out the INTERNATIONAL at 12 o'clock daily. The Imperial Palace was built in 1849.

As the seat of government of the U.S.S.R. the word is used symbolically of that government, just as the VATICAN is of the Papacy.

Kreutzer, or **Kreuzer.** An old German copper or silver coin marked with a cross (Ger. *Kreuz*, cross). There is a modern Austrian copper coin of this name.

Kriegspiel. *See* WAR GAME.

Kriemhild (krēm' hild). The legendary heroine of the NIBELUNGENLIED, a woman of unrivalled beauty, daughter of King Dankrat, and sister of GUNTHER, Gernot, and Giselher. She first married SIEGFRIED and next Etzel (Attila), King of the Huns.

Krishna (the black one). A popular Hindu deity and an avatar of VISHNU. One myth says he was the son of Vasudeva and Devaki and was born at Mathura between Delhi and Agra. His uncle King Kamsa, who had been warned that one of his nephews would kill him, murdered Devaki's children on birth; accordingly Krishna was smuggled away and brought up among cow-herds and lived to kill his uncle. He was the APOLLO of India and the idol of women. He features in the MAHABHARATA, the BHAGAVAD-GITA and the *Bhagavata-Purana*. Another story is that Vishnu plucked out two of his own hairs, one white and one black, and the black one became Krishna.

Kronos, or **Cronos.** One of the TITANS of Greek mythology, son of URANUS and GE,

father (by RHEA) of Hestia, DEMETER, HERA, HADES, POSEIDON, and ZEUS. He dethroned his father as ruler of the world, and was in turn dethroned by his son Zeus. By the Romans he was identified with SATURN.

Kruger Telegram. The famous congratulatory message sent by Kaiser William II to President Kruger (3 January 1896) after the defeat of the JAMESON RAID. It embittered Anglo-German relations and encouraged Kruger in his policies.

Ku Klux Klan. An American secret society founded at Pulaski, Tennessee, in 1866 at the close of the CIVIL WAR as a social club with a fanciful ritual and hooded white robes. The name is a corruption of the Gr. *kuklos*, a circle. It soon developed into a society to overawe the newly emancipated Negroes, and similar societies such as the Knights of the White Camelia, the White League, the Pale Faces and the Invisible Circle sprang up in 1867–1868. Its terroristic activities led to laws against it in 1870 and 1871. Although it had been disbanded by the Grand Wizard in 1869 local activities continued for some time.

In 1915 a new organization, The Invisible Empire, Knights of the Ku Klux Klan, was founded by the Rev. William Simmonds, preacher, near Atlanta, Georgia. He adopted much of the ritual of the original, adding further puerile ceremonies, titles, nomenclature, etc., of his own. *Klansmen* held *Klonvocations* and their local *Klaverns* were ruled by an *Exalted Cyclops*, a *Klaliff*, etc., etc. As well as anti-Negro it was anti-Catholic, anti-Jewish, and xenophobic. Advocating Protestant supremacy for the native-born whites, it grew rapidly from 1920 and gained considerable political control in the Southern States by unsavoury methods. By 1930 it had shrunk again to small proportions but a revival began before World War II and the Klan became noted for its FASCIST sympathies. In 1944 it was again disbanded but continued locally and in 1965 a Congressional Committee was set up to investigate Klan activities.

Kufic. Ancient Arabic letters, so called from Kufa, on the Hindiya branch of the Euphrates and capital of the CALIPHS before the building of Baghdad. It was noted for its skilled copyists. The KORAN was originally written in Kufic.

Kufic coins. Early Mohammedan coins inscribed in Kufic, which was superseded by Nashki characters in the 13th century A.D. Their inscriptions carry much useful information for the historian.

Kultur (Ger., civilization). When used in

English it implies civilization as conceived by the Germans. The English word "culture" is translated by *Bildung*.

Kulturkampf (Ger. *Kampf*, struggle). The Kulturkampf, or so-called struggle for civilization, was the name used for Chancellor Bismarck's struggle with the Roman Catholic hierarchy in the 1870s to assert the supreme authority of the State over the individual and the Church, at a time when the latter, under Pope Pius IX, was asserting CATHOLIC claims. The conflict began over the control of education and developed into a wider attack on the Church, but Bismarck eventually (1879) effected a reconciliation with the Catholic Centre Party in order to avoid control by the National Liberal Party.

Kuomintang (kwō min tăng). The National People's Party, a Chinese political party formed by Sun Yat-sen in 1905 which, after his death in 1925, passed under the control of General Chiang Kai-shek. From 1927 to 1949 the Kuomintang was in power in China when it was driven out by the Communist Party under Mao Tse-tung. The Nationalists still maintain themselves in Formosa (Taiwan).

Kurma. *See* AVATAR.

Kyle. The central district of Ayrshire.

Kyle for a man, Carrick for a coo [cow],
Cunningham for butter, Galloway for woo' [wool].

Kyle, a strong corn-growing soil; Carrick, a wild hilly portion, only fit for feeding cattle; Cunningham, a rich dairy land, and Galloway, long famous as pastoral country.

Kyrie Eleison (ki ri ā e lī' son) (Gr., "Lord have mercy"). The short petition used in the liturgies of the Eastern and Western Churches, as a response at the beginning of the MASS and in the Anglican Communion Service. Also, the musical setting for this.

Kyrle Society, The (kĕrl). Founded 1877 for decorating the walls of hospitals, schoolrooms, mission-rooms, cottages, etc.; for the cultivation of small open spaces, window gardening, the love of flowers, etc.; and improving the artistic taste of the poorer classes. *See* MAN OF ROSS *under* ROSS.

L

L. The twelfth letter of the alphabet. In Phœnician and Hebrew it represents an ox-goad, *lamedh*, and in the Egyptian hieroglyhic a lioness.

L. For a pound sterling it is from the Lat. *libra*, a pound. In the Roman notation it stands for 50, and with a line drawn above the letter, for 50,000.

LL.D. Doctor of Laws—*i.e.* both civil and canon. The double L is the plural, as in MSS., the plural of MS., pp., pages, etc.

L.S. Lat. *locus sigilli*, that is, the place for the seal.

L.S.D. Lat. *libra*, a pound; *solidus*, a shilling; and *denarius*, a penny; introduced by the Lombard merchants, from whom we also have *Cr.*, creditor; *Dr.*, debtor, BANKRUPT, *do.* or DITTO, etc.

   L.S.D. also stands for Dextro-lysergic acid diethylamide 25, a powerful drug inducing hallucinations, used by certain drug addicts of today. Those who take this drug are said to "take a trip" and to have PSYCHEDELIC EXPERIENCES.

LXX. A common abbreviation for the SEPTUAGINT.

La Belle Sauvage (la bel sō vazh'). The site on the north side of LUDGATE Hill occupied by the House of Cassell from 1852 until 11 May 1941, when the whole area was demolished in an air raid. The name is a corruption of "Savage's Bell Inn" and the French form appears to have been first used by Addison in *The Spectator* (No. 82). There seems to have been an inn on the site from about the 14th century, originally called "The Bell on the Hope", the *Hope* or *hoop* being the garlanded ivy-bush (*see* IVY). From its position just outside LUDGATE its yard became a rendezvous for bear-baiting, play-acting, etc., and, from the 17th century until the mid-19th, it was a starting place for coach traffic. The inn licence was not renewed after 1857. *See* COLOPHON; POCAHONTAS.

   Tom had never been in London, and would have liked to have stopped at the Belle Savage. Where they had been put down by the Star, just at dusk,

that he might have gone roving about those endless, mysterious gas-lit streets....
   T. HUGHES: *Tom Brown's Schooldays*, ch, iv.

La Fontaine Jean de la Fontaine (1621–1695) essentially depends for his fame on his *Contes* (1664–1671) and his *Fables* (1668–1693), the first six books of the latter being dedicated to the DAUPHIN. The complete collection comprises twelve books.

   Je chante les héros dont Ésope est le père;
   Troupe de qui l'histoire, encore que mensongère,
   Contient des véritiés qui servent de leçons.
   À Monseigneur le Dauphin.

La Mancha, The Knight of (la man' chà). Don QUIXOTE de la Mancha, the hero of Cervantes' romance *Don Quixote*. La Mancha was a province of Spain now the main part of Ciudad Real, an arid land with much heath and waste, and the most thinly populated part of Spain.

La Tène (la tän), or the Shallows. A site at the eastern end of the Lake of Neuchâtel, Switzerland, where extensive remains of the late IRON AGE have been found. The term covers a period of CELTIC culture from the 5th century B.C. to about the beginning of the Christian era.

La-di-da. A yea-nay sort of fellow, with no backbone; an affected fop with a drawl in his voice. Also used adjectively, as "in a la-di-da sort of way".
   The phrase was popularized by a song sung by the once famous Arthur Lloyd, the refrain of which was:

   La-di-da, la-di-do, I'm the pet of all the ladies,
   The darlings like to flirt with Captain
   La-di-da-di-do.

Labarum. The standard of the later Roman emperors. It consisted of a gilded spear with an eagle on the top, while from a cross-staff hung a splendid purple streamer, with a gold fringe, adorned with precious stones. *See also* CONSTANTINE'S CROSS *under* CROSS.

Labour. Independent Labour Party. A small socialist party formed by Keir Hardie in 1893 to establish independent labour candidates in PARLIAMENT. It played a prominent part in the early days of the LABOUR PAR-

TY and continued to advocate more radical policies. In 1923 it had 46 members in the Commons. When James Maxton, then its Leader, died in 1946, it petered out as a parliamentary party. *See* CLYDESIDERS.

Labor Day. A legal holiday in the U.S.A. and some provinces of Canada, held on the first Monday in September (*see* KNIGHTS OF LABOR). Labour rallies in Great Britain and elsewhere are held on MAY DAY.

Labour Party. One of the major political parties of Great Britain and aiming to promote socialism; so called from 1906 but first formed as the Labour Representation Committee in 1900 from such elements as the INDEPENDENT LABOUR PARTY (*see above*), the TRADE UNIONS, and the FABIAN SOCIETY (*see under* FABIUS). The first Labour Government was that of Ramsay MacDonald in 1924, the second lasted from 1929 to 1931, when the party split over the cuts in unemployment benefit (*see* NATIONAL GOVERNMENT). It was not returned to power again until 1945 and was replaced by the CONSERVATIVES in October 1951. It was again in office from 1964 to 1970 and from 1974 to 1979.

A labour of love. *See under* LOVE.

The labourer is worthy of his hire (*Luke* x, 7). In Latin: *Digna canis pabulo*. "The dog must be bad indeed that is not worth a bone." Hence the Mosaic law, "Thou shalt not muzzle the ox that treadeth out the corn."

The Statute of Labourers. An attempt made in 1351 to fix the rates of wages consequent upon the demand for labour after the BLACK DEATH. It attempted to hold them at their pre-plague levels. The ensuing discontent helped to bring about the PEASANTS' REVOLT.

Labyrinth (lăb′i rinth). A Greek word of unknown (but probably Egyptian) origin, denoting a structure with complicated passages through which it is baffling to find one's way. The maze at Hampton Court, formed of high hedges, is a labyrinth on a small scale. The chief labyrinths of antiquity were:

(1) The Egyptian, by Petesuchis or Tithoes, near the Lake Mœris. It had 3,000 apartments, half of which were underground (1800 B.C.).—*Pliny*, xxxvi, 13; and *Pomponius Mela*, I, ix.

(2) The Cretan, by DÆDALUS, for imprisoning the MINOTAUR. The only means of finding a way out was by help of a skein of thread. (*see* Virgil:*Æneid*, V.)

(3) The Cretan conduit, which had 1,000 branches or turnings.

(4) The Lemnian, by the architects Smilis, Rholus, and Theodorus. It had 150 columns, so nicely adjusted that a child could turn them. Vestiges of this labyrinth were still in existence in the time of Pliny.

(5) The labyrinth of Clusium, made by Lars Porsena, King of Etruria, for his tomb.

(6) The Samian, by Theodorus (540 B.C.). Referred to by Pliny; by Herodotus, II, 145; by Strabo, X; and by Diodorus Siculus, I.

(7) The labyrinth at Woodstock, built by Henry II to protect Fair ROSAMOND.

Lace. I'll lace your jacket for you, beat you, flog you severely. Perhaps a play on the word *lash*.

Laced mutton. *See* MUTTON.

Tea, or **coffee laced with spirits.** Tea or coffee fortified with brandy or whisky.

> Deacon Bearcliff ... had his pipe, and his teacup, the latter being laced with a little spirits.
> SCOTT: *Guy Mannering*, ch. xi.

Lacedæmonians. *See* REGIMENTAL AND DIVISIONAL NICKNAMES.

Lacedæmonian Letter. The Greek ι (*iota*), the smallest of the letters. *See* JOT.

Laches (lăch′ iz). A legal term for negligence and delay in enforcing a right, from the O.Fr. *laschesse*, negligence.

Lachesis (lăk′ e sis). The Fate who spins life's thread and determines its length. *See* FATES.

Lack-learning, or **Unlearned Parliament.** The PARLIAMENT held at Coventry (October 1404) by Henry IV; so called because SHERIFFS were directed not to return any lawyers as members, in the hope that it would be more tractable.

Laconic. Pertaining to Laconia or Sparta; hence very concise and pithy, for the Spartans were noted for their brusque and aphoristic speech. When Philip of Macedon wrote to the SPARTAN magistrates, "If I enter Laconia, I will level Lacedæmon to the ground," the ephors sent back the single word, "If." CÆSAR's words "VENI, VIDI, VICI" and Sir Charles Napier's "PECCAVI" are well-known laconicisms.

Ladon. The name of the DRAGON which guarded the apples of the HESPERIDES, also one of the dogs of ACTÆON.

Ladrones (la′ drōnz) (Thieves' Islands). The name given to the Marianas by Magellan's sailors in 1521, owing to the thievish habits of the natives.

Lady. Literally "the bread-maker", from O.E. *hlœfdige* (*hlaf*, loaf; and supposed root *dige*, to knead). The original meaning was simply the female head of the family, the mistress of the household. *Cp.* LORD. *See* COURTESY TITLES; COUSIN.

Dark Lady of the Sonnets. The woman about whom SHAKESPEARE wrote the sonnets numbered cxxvii-clii. Among the candidates favoured by the critics for this claim to fame are Mary Fitton, Penelope Rich and Mrs. Davenant, wife of an Oxford innkeeper. Dr. Leslie Hotson arrives at Black Lucy or Luce, alias Lucy Negro, *née* Morgan, married to one Parker; she was a former gentlewoman to Queen Elizabeth I and had become a notorious bawd and brothel keeper at CLERKENWELL. More convincingly Dr. A.L. Rowse, with considerable supporting evidence, has identified her with Emilia Lanier (*née* Bassano), illegitimate daughter of a Venetian court musician. She was married to Alfonso Lanier, another court musician, in 1592, at the end of which year the affair with Shakespeare probably began. She had previously been a mistress of Lord Hunsdon, the Lord Chamberlain.

A lady of easy virtue. A "lady of the town", one who readily gives way to amorous advances, an unchaste woman.

Naked Lady. *See* NAKED BOY.

Ladybird, Ladyfly, or **Ladycow.** The small red coleopterous insect with black spots, *coccinella septempunctata*, called also *Ladybug* and BISHOP BARNABEE, and in Yorkshire, the *Cushcow Lady*. The name means bird or beetle of Our Lady because of the wonderful service it performs by feeding exclusively on greenfly, one of the worst plant pests.

Lady Bountiful. The original character comes from Farquhar's *Beaux' Stratagem* (1706), and about a century later the term acquired the generic application of a village benefactress now in use.

Lady Chapel. *See under* CHAPEL.

Lady Day. 25 March, to commemorate the ANNUNCIATION of Our Lady, the Virgin Mary; formerly called "St. Mary's Day in Lent", to distinguish it from other festivals in honour of the Virgin which were also, properly speaking, "Lady Days". Until 1752, Lady Day was the legal beginning of the year and dates between 1 January and that day are shown with the two years, *e.g.* 29 January 1648/9, on present reckoning 29 January 1649. *See* GREGORIAN YEAR.

Our Lady of Mercy. A Spanish order of knighthood instituted in 1218 by James I of Aragon, for the deliverance of Christian captives among the Moors.

Our Lady of the Snows. A fanciful name given by Kipling in *The Five Nations* (1903) to Canada. Wordsworth has a poem *Our Lady of the Snow* (1820).

The Lady of England and Normandy.
The Empress Maud, or Matilda (1102–1167), daughter of Henry I of England and wife of the Emperor Henry V of Germany, who died in 1125. She then married Geoffrey of Anjou and long contested Stephen's possession of the English crown on her father's death. She was acknowledged as "Lady of England and Normandy" by a council at Winchester in 1141, but finally withdrew to Normandy in 1145. Her son by Geoffrey of Anjou became king, as Henry II, in 1154. *See also* A.L.O.E.

The Lady of the Lake. In Arthurian legend, Vivien, the mistress of MERLIN. She lived in the midst of a lake surrounded by knights and damsels. *See* LANCELOT OF THE LAKE.

In Scott's poem of this name (1810), the lady is Ellen Douglas, who lived with her father near Loch Katrine.

The Lady of the Lamp. A name given to Florence Nightingale (1820–1910), from her nightly rounds of the hospital wards at Scutari during the Crimean War, carrying a lighted lamp.

The Lady of Shalott. *See* SHALOTT.

Lady's Man. One who is fond of the company of women and very attentive to them; usually without the more amorous implications of LADY-KILLER.

Lady's Mantle. *See* ALCHEMILLA.

Lady's Slipper. The largest of British wild orchids of the genus *Cypripedium*, now rare. The flower has yellow petals, akin to a slipper in shape, and is found in Yorkshire on limestone soil. It also occurs in Europe and the U.S.A.

Lady's Smock. A common name for the Cuckoo-Flower or Bittercress (*Cardamine pratensis*), so called because the flowers are supposed to resemble linen exposed to bleach on the grass. There are many other such names of plants, *e.g.*: Lady's bedstraw, Lady's cushion, Lady's delight, Lady's glove, Lady's eardrops, Lady's hair, Lady's tresses, Lady's seal, etc., etc.

The Ladies' Mile. A stretch of the road on the north side of the Serpentine, Hyde Park, much favoured in Victorian days by "equestriennes". The Coaching and Four-in-Hand Clubs held their meets there in spring.

Lady-Killer. A male flirt; a great favourite with the ladies, or one who devotes himself to their conquest.

Læstrygones. *See* LESTRIGONS.

Lætare Sunday (Lat., rejoice). The fourth Sunday in LENT, so called from the first word of the Introit, which is from *Is.* lxvi, 10: "Rejoice ye with Jerusalem, and be glad with her, all ye that love her."

It is also known as MOTHERING SUNDAY.

Lagado. In Swift's *Gulliver's Travels*, the capital of Balnibarbi, celebrated for its grand academy of projectors, where the scholars spend their time in such projects as making pincushions from softened rocks, extracting sunbeams from cucumbers, and converting ice into gunpowder.

Lagan, or **Ligan.** *See* FLOTSAM AND JETSAM.

Lager louts. A term in use from 1988 and applied to young hooligans who create disturbances, damage property and commit violent assaults after drinking too much lager beer—their favourite tipple.

Laid. Laid paper. Paper having a ribbed appearance due to manufacture on a mould or by a DANDY on which the wires are laid side by side, instead of being woven transversely.

Lais (lā' is). The name of three celebrated Greek courtesans. One flourished in Corinth in the 5th century B.C. and was visited by Aristippus the philosopher, but the best known was the daughter of Timandra, the mistress of Alcibiades. She was born *c*. 420 B.C. and came to Corinth as a child. She was patronized by princes, philosophers, and plebeians alike. Her charges were sufficiently exorbitant to deter Demosthenes. Her later success in Thessaly so enraged the women that they pricked her to death with their bodkins. There was a third Lais, contemporary with ALEXANDER THE GREAT, who sat for Apelles.

Laissez faire (lā sā fâr) (Fr., let alone). The principle of allowing things to look after themselves, especially the non-interference by government in economic affairs. The originator of the phrase may have been Legendre, a contemporary of Colbert, or possibly D'Argenson, a one-time minister of Louis XV. It became the accepted maxim of the French PHYSIOCRATS in the 18th century as a reaction against Colbertism and MERCANTILISM. Adam Smith was its advocate in Britain, as the prophet of FREE TRADE. The principle was extended to politics by Jeremy Bentham, the leader of the individualist school and philosopher of UTILITARIANISM. Since the 1870s the doctrine has steadily been eroded by collectivist policies which ever increasingly limit the freedoms and activities of the individual in the name of public good. *Laissez passer, laissez aller* are similar phrases.

Lake. Lake District. The picturesque and mountainous district of Cumbria and part of Lancashire (Furness) which contains the principal English lakes, including Windermere, Grasmere, Derwentwater and Ullswater. Noted as the home of the Lake Poets, Lowell called it Wordsworthshire, and it has many literary associations.

Lake Poets. *See* LAKE SCHOOL.

Lake School. The name applied derisively by the *Edinburgh Review* to Wordsworth, Coleridge, and Southey, who lived in the LAKE DISTRICT and sought inspiration in nature, and to the writers who followed them. Charles Lamb, Charles Lloyd and Christopher North (John Wilson) are sometimes placed among the "Lake Poets" or "Lakers".

Lady of the Lake. *See* LADY.

Lancelot of the Lake. *See* LANCELOT.

Lakin. By'r lakin. An oath, meaning "By our Ladykin" or Little Lady, where *little* does not refer to size, but is equivalent to *dear*.

> By'r lakin, a parlous fear.
> SHAKESPEARE: *A Midsummer Night's Dream*, III, i.

Laksmi, or **Lakshmi.** One of the consorts of VISHNU, and mother of Kama. She is the goddess of beauty, wealth and pleasure, and the RAMAYANA describes her as springing from the foam of the sea. *Cp.* APHRODITE.

Lamaism (Tibetan, *blama*, spiritual teacher, lord). A modified form of BUDDHISM, the religion of Tibet and Mongolia. The name is from the title given to monks in the higher ranks. The Grand Lama or Dalai Lama (the Sacred Lama) was the ruler of Tibet, although it came under Chinese control (1720) during the time of the 7th Dalai Lama. This control declined to nominal suzerainty, but the Chinese again invaded in 1950, and in 1959 the 14th Dalai Lama fled to India. There is another Grand Lama, the Tashi Lama or Panchen Lama, whose authority was confined to one province but who was supported by the Chinese as rival to the Dalai Lama. The priests are housed in *lamaseries*.

Lamb. In Christian art, the emblem of the Redeemer, in allusion to *John* i, 29, "Behold the Lamb of God, which taketh away the sins of the world."

It is also the attribute of St. AGNES, St. CATHERINE, St. GENEVIÈVE, and St. Regina. JOHN THE BAPTIST either carries a lamb or is accompanied by one.

Paschal Lamb. *See under* PASCH.

Lamb-ale. The "ale" or merry-making given by the farmer when his lambing was over. *Cp.* CHURCH-ALE.

Lamb's wool. An old beverage consisting of the juice of apples roasted with ale, sugar, and nutmeg. Probably in allusion to its "softness".

The Vegetable, Tartarian, or **Scythian Lamb.** The woolly rootstalk of a fern (*Cibotium barometz*), found in Asia, and supposed in mediæval times to be a kind of hybrid animal and vegetable. The down is used in India for staunching wounds.

Lambert's Day, St. 17 September. St. Lambert, a native of Maestricht, lived in the 7th century. He supported the missionary work of St. Willibrord and was energetic in suppressing vice.

> Be ready, as your lives shall answer it,
> At Coventry, upon St. Lambert's day.
> SHAKESPEARE: *Richard II*, I, i.

Lambeth. A LONDON borough on the south side of the THAMES, once part of Surrey. The name is commonly derived from *lam*, mud, and *hythe*, haven. It includes the districts of VAUXHALL, Kennington, and Brixton.

Lambeth Palace. The London residence of the archbishops of Canterbury since the 12th century. The oldest part is the chapel built by Archbishop Boniface in 1245 and the buildings have been steadily added to and modified through the centuries. Originally called Lambeth House, it came to be called Lambeth Palace about 1658 owing to the decay of the palace at Canterbury. It is the archbishop's principal residence, but he now has another palace at Canterbury. The library and chapel were badly damaged in an air raid in 1940.

Lambeth Degrees in divinity, arts, law, medicine, music, etc., are conferred by the Archbishop of Canterbury, who was empowered to do so by a statute of 1533.

Lambeth walk, a thoroughfare in Lambeth leading from Black Prince Road to the Lambeth Road. It gave its name to an immensely popular "COCKNEY" dance featured by Lupino Lane (from 1937) in the musical show *Me And My Gal* at the Victoria Palace.

Lamia. Among the Greeks and Romans a female demon who devoured children and whose name was used to frighten them. She was a Libyan queen beloved by JUPITER, but, robbed of her offspring by the jealous JUNO, she became insane and vowed vengeance on all children, whom she delighted to entice and devour. The race of *Lamiæ*, in Africa, were said to have the head and breasts of a woman and the body of a serpent and they enticed strangers into their embraces to devour them.

Witches in the MIDDLE AGES were called *Lamiæ*, and Keats' poem *Lamia* (1820) relates the story of how a bride, when recognized by APOLLONIUS as a serpent or lamia, vanished in an instant. Keats took the substance of his poem from Burton's *Anatomy of Melancholy* (Pt. III, sect. ii, memb. i, subsect. i) whose source was Philostratus (*De Vita Apollonii*, Bk. IV). *Cp.* LILITH.

Lammas Day. 1 August, one of the regular QUARTER-DAYS in SCOTLAND and a half-quarter or cross-quarter-day in ENGLAND, the day on which, in Anglo-Saxon times, the FIRST-FRUITS were offered. Formerly, bread for the Lammas Day EUCHARIST was made from the new corn of the harvest. So called from O.E. *hlaf-mæsse*, the loaf-mass. It is also the feast of St. PETER ad Vincula. *See* HARVEST THANKSGIVING.

At latter Lammas. Another way of saying "Never".

Lamourette's Kiss (la moo ret'). A French term (*baiser Lamourette*) to denote an insincere or ephemeral reconciliation. On 7 July 1792, the Abbé Lamourette induced the different factions of the Legislative Assembly to lay aside their differences and give the kiss of peace; but the reconciliation was unsound and very short-lived.

> The Assembly dispersed in tears. And within the space of a few short hours they were all "tearing each other's eyes again".
> LOUIS MADELIN: *The French Revolution*, ch. xix.

Lamp. The Lamp of Heaven. The MOON. MILTON calls the stars "lamps":

> Why shouldst thou...
> In thy dark lantern thus close up the stars,
> That Nature hung in heaven and filled their lamps
> With everlasting oil, to give due light
> To the misled and lonely traveller?
> *Comus*, 196–200.

The Lady of the Lamp. *See under* LADY.

The Lamp of the Law. Irnerius, the Italian jurist, was so called. He was the first to lecture on the PANDECTS OF JUSTINIAN after their discovery at Amalfi in 1137.

The Lamp of Phœbus. The sun. PHŒBUS is the mythological personification of the sun.

It smells of the lamp. Said of a literary composition that bears manifest signs of midnight study; one that is over-laboured. In Lat., *olet lucernam*.

Lampadion. The received name of a lively, petulant courtesan, in the later Greek comedy.

Lampoon. A sarcastic or scurrilous personal satire, so called from Fr. *lampons*, let us drink, which formed part of the refrain of a 17th-century French drinking song. According to Scott:

> These personal and scandalous libels, carried to excess in the reign of Charles II, acquired the name of lampoons from the burden sung to them: "Lampone, lampone, camerada lampone"—"Guzzler, guzzler, my fellow guzzler".

Lampos. One of the steeds of AURORA, also the name of one of the horses of DIOMEDES, and of HECTOR.

Lancasterian. Of or pertaining to Joseph Lancaster (1778–1838), the QUAKER educational reformer, who claimed to have invented the MONITORIAL SYSTEM. His supporters founded the Royal Lancasterian Society in 1808, which later became The British and Foreign School Society. *See* MADRAS SYSTEM; VOLUNTARY SCHOOLS.

Lancastrian. An adherent of the Lancastrian line of kings, or one of those kings (*Henry IV, V, VI*), who were descendants of Edward III. *See* RED ROSE, WARS OF THE ROSES *under* ROSE; YORKIST.

Lance. An attribute in Christian art of St. MATTHEW and St. THOMAS, the apostles; also of St. Longinus, St. GEORGE, St. Adalbert, St. BARBARA, St. MICHAEL, and others.

A free lance. One who acts on his own judgment and is not bound to party; a journalist, musician, writer, etc., who is not definitely attached to, or on the salaried staff of, any one organization. The reference is to the FREE COMPANIES of the MIDDLE AGES which were free to sell themselves to any cause or master.

Lance-corporal. The lowest grade of N.C.O. in the army; a **lance-sergeant** is a corporal performing (on probation) the duties of a sergeant. Presumably formed on Ital. *lancia spezzata*, broken lance; *i.e.* an experienced soldier, one who has had his lance shivered in battle.

Lance-knight. An old term for a foot-soldier; a corruption of *Landsknecht*, a German mercenary foot-soldier of the 16th century, the French equivalent being *lansquenet*.

Lancers. The dance so called, an amplified kind of QUADRILLE, was introduced by Laborde in Paris in 1836 and brought over to England in 1850.

Lancelot du lac , or of the Lake. One of the Knights of the ROUND TABLE, son of King BAN of Brittany, and stolen in infancy by the LADY OF THE LAKE. She plunged with the baby into the lake (whence the cognomen *du Lac*), and when her protégé was grown to manhood, presented him to King ARTHUR. Sir Lancelot went in search of the GRAIL and twice caught sight of it. Though always represented in ARTHURIAN ROMANCE as the model of CHIVALRY, bravery, and fidelity, Sir Lancelot was the adulterous lover of Queen GUINEVERE, and it was through this liaison that war resulted which led to the disruption of the Round Table and the death of King Arthur.

Land. The Land of Beulah (*Is*. lxii, 4). In Bunyan's *Pilgrim's Progress* it is that land of heavenly joy where the pilgrims tarry till they are summoned to enter the CELESTIAL CITY.

The Land of Cakes. *See under* CAKE.

Land of Enchantment. A name given to Mexico.

Land of Hope and Glory. Great Britain was so protrayed in the heyday of imperialism in Elgar's famous melody with words by A. C. Benson. Sung by Dame Clara Butt in 1902, and widely used at EMPIRE DAY celebrations and other occasions. The tune was taken from the first of the *Pomp and Circumstance* marches (1901). The words were originally used in Benson's *Coronation Ode* of 1902.

> Land of Hope and Glory, Mother of the Free,
> How shall we extol thee, who are born of thee?
> Wider still and wider shall thy bounds be set;
> God, who made thee mighty, make thee mightier yet.

Land of My Fathers. In particular Wales, from the song *Hen Wlad fy Nhadau*, Land of My Fathers, which is the national anthem of Wales. The Welsh words are by Evan James and the tune by James James, first published in 1860.

Land of Nod. This was the land to which Cain was exiled after he had slain Abel (*Gen.* iv, 16). Swift, in *A Complete Collection of Genteel and Ingenious Conversation*, said that he was "going into the land of Nod", meaning that he was going to sleep, which meaning it has retained ever since.

The Land of Promise, or **the Promised Land.** Canaan, which God promised to give to Abraham for his obedience. *See Ex.* xii, 25, *Deut.* ix, 28, etc.

The Land o' the Leal. The land of the faithful or blessed; a Scotticism for a Happy Land or HEAVEN, as in Lady Nairn's song of this title:

> I'm wearin' awa'
> To the land o' the leal.

Land of the Midnight Sun. Norway. In the Arctic and Antarctic during summer the sun shines at midnight, a phenomenon observable from several lands within the high latitudes of the Arctic Circle. The name has been applied only to Norway where this phenomenon has been observed most by visitors.

Land of the Rising Sun. Japan.

Land of the White Eagle. Poland. The White Eagle, with a crown on its head, formed part of the Polish coat-of-arms. An old legend tells us that Prince Lech, when out hunting, came to a great oak-tree, where he saw a pair of huge white eagles over their nest. The prince regarded this as a prophetic sign and decided to establish his capital there. He called it *Gniezno* ("Nest-town"), saying, "Here shall be our nest."

Land League. An Irish association formed in 1879 under the leadership of Michael Davitt, with Parnell as president and two FE-NIANS as secretaries. It stimulated agrarian revolt and aimed to secure peasant proprietorship by forceful methods. It was declared illegal in 1881, but renewed as the National League in 1882.

Land Office business. The U.S. government land office of the 19th century was overburdened with work allotting land to a multitude of land-seekers. Hence the use of the phrase to mean a tremendous amount of business, a rush of business.

See how the land lies. See whether things are propitious or otherwise; see in what state the land is that we have to travel over.

Land-girl. Girls or women recruited for farm-work during the two World Wars. In World War II they were organized as a "Women's Land Army".

Land-grabber. One who grabs or seizes land rapaciously. Particularly used in late 19th-century Ireland of one who took over the land of an evicted tenant, in the 18th century usually called a *land pirate*.

Land-hunger. Desire to acquire land or to extend territory.

Land-loupers. Vagrants. *Louper* is from the Dut. *loopen*, to run. Persons who abscond for crime or debt and rove the country, vagabonds. Loafer, and luffer are variants of the Ger. *Läufer*, a vagrant, a runner.

Land-lubber. An awkward or inept sailor is so called, a mere landsman. A *lubber* is a heavy, clumsy fellow, a looby.

Land-slide. Used metaphorically of a crushing defeat at the polls, or a complete reversal of votes or support.

Landau (lăn dō). A four-wheeled carriage with a divided top or hood, the two halves of which can be raised or lowered separately. Said to have been first made in the 18th century at Landau in Bavaria.

Landaulet. A coupé with a LANDAU top; also an early style of motor-car body with a folding hood.

Landscape. A country scene or a picture representing this. The word is from the Dut. *schap*, connected with our *shape*. The old word in English was *land-skip*.

Father of landscape gardening. André Lenôtre (1631–1700), who landscaped VERSAILLES.

Landsknecht. *See* LANCE-KNIGHT.

Landsturm (lant' shtoorm). German forces of the militia type not used as first-line troops but usually employed on garrison duties or as labour forces, etc. Usually formed from those unfit for full military service or from the older age-groups.

Landtag (lant' tak). The legislative assembly of a German state.

Landwehr (lant' vār). In Germany, reserve forces used only in time of war.

Lane. 'Tis a long lane that has no turning. Every calamity has an ending, things will eventually improve.

Lang syne (Scot., long since). In the olden time, in days gone by.

Auld Lang Syne. This song, commonly sung at the conclusion of dances and revelries and usually attributed to Robert Burns, is really a new version by him of a very much older song. In Watson's Collection (1711), it is attributed to Francis Sempill (d. 1682), but is probably older. Burns says in a letter to Thomson "It is the old song of the olden times, which has never been in print.... I took it down from an old man's singing." And in another letter, "Light be on the turf of the heaven-inspired poet who composed this glorious fragment."

Langtry, Lillie. *See* JERSEY LILY.

Language. Language was given to men to conceal their thoughts. *See* SPEECH.

The three primitive languages. The Persians say that Arabic, Persian, and Turkish are three primitive languages. Legend has it that the serpent that seduced EVE spoke Arabic, the most suasive language in the world; that ADAM and Eve spoke Persian, the most poetic of all languages; and that the angel GABRIEL spoke Turkish, the most menacing.

Langue d'oc; langue d'oïl (lang dok; lang doil) (Fr. *langue*, tongue). The former is the old Provençal language, spoken south of the River Loire; the latter, Northern French, spoken in the MIDDLE AGES to the north of that river, the original of modern French. So called because our "yes" was in Provençal *oc*, and in the northern speech *oïl*, which later became *oui* (from Lat. *hoc illud*). *Cp.* HIGH GERMAN.

Lansbury's Lido. *See* LIDO.

Lansquenet. *See* LANCE-KNIGHT.

Lantern. In Christian art, the attribute of St. GUDULE and St. Hugh.

À la lanterne! (Fr., to the lamp-post). Hang him from the lamp-post! A cry and practice at Paris during the French Revolution. Many of the street lamp brackets were suitable for this purpose.

The Feast of Lanterns. A popular Chinese festival, celebrated annually at the first full moon. Tradition says that the daughter of a famous mandarin one evening fell into a lake. Her father and his neighbour took lanterns to look for her, and happily she was rescued. A festival was ordained to commemorate the rescue, which in time developed into the "Feast of Lanterns".

Lantern jaws. Cheeks so thin and hollow that one may almost see daylight through them, as light shone through the horn of the lantern.

Lantern Land. The land of literary charlatans, pedantic graduates in arts, doctors, professors, prelates, etc., ridiculed as "Lanterns" by Rabelais (with a side alusion to the divines assembled in conference at the Council of Trent) in his *Pantagruel*, v, 33. *Cp.* CITY OF LANTERNS.

Laocoön. A son of PRIAM and priest of APOLLO, famous for the tragic fate of himself and his two sons, who were squeezed to death by serpents while he was sacrificing to POSEIDON. Their death was said to be in consequence of his having offended Apollo, or for having sought to prevent the entry of the WOODEN HORSE into TROY. The group representing these three in their death agony, now in the VATICAN, was discovered in 1506 at ROME. It is a single block of marble, and is attributed to Agesandrus, Athenodorus, and Polydorus of the School of Rhodes in the 2nd century B.C.

Lessing called his treatise on the limits of poetry and the plastic arts (1766) *Laocoön*, because he uses the famous group as the peg on which to hang his dissertation.

Since I have, as it were, set out from the Laocoön, and several times return to it, I have wished to give it a share also in the title.
Preface.

Laodamia. The wife of Protesilaus, who was slain before TROY by HECTOR. According to one account, she begged to be allowed to converse with her dead husband for only three hours, and her request was granted; she afterwards voluntarily accompanied the dead hero to the shades. Wordsworth had a poem on the subject (1814).

Laodicean. One indifferent to religion, caring little or nothing about the matter, like the Christians of that church mentioned in the *Book of Revelation* (iii, 14–18).

Lao-tse. *See* TAOISM.

Lap. In the lap of the gods. The unknown chances of the future, whatever may fall from the lap of the gods. **The lap of fortune** expresses the same idea.

To live in the lap of luxury is to have every material comfort and need supplied; "lap" here is a place for repose "in luxury".

Lapithæ. A people of Thessaly, noted in Greek legend for their defeat of the CENTAURS at the marriage-feast of HIPPODAMIA, when the latter were driven out of PELION.

The contest was represented on the PARTHENON, the Theseum at ATHENS, the Temple of APOLLO at Bassæ, and on numberless vases.

Lapsus Linguæ (Lat.). A slip of the tongue, a mistake in uttering a word, an imprudent word inadvertently spoken. Similar adoptions from Latin are *lapsus calami*, a slip of the pen; and *lapsus memoriæ*, a slip of the memory.

Laputa. The flying island inhabited by scientific quacks, and visited by Gulliver on his "travels". These dreamy philosophers were so absorbed in their speculations that they employed attendants called "flappers", to flap them on the mouth and ears with a blown bladder when their attention was to be called off from "high things" to vulgar mundane matters.

Lapwing. SHAKESPEARE refers to two peculiarities of this bird; (1) to allure persons from its nest, it flies away and cries loudest when farthest from its nest; and (2) the young birds fly from their shells with part thereof still sticking to their heads.

Far from her nest the lapwing cries away.
Comedy of Errors, IV, ii.

This lapwing runs away with the shell on his head.
Hamlet, V, ii.

The first peculiarity made the lapwing a symbol of insincerity, and the second that of a forward person, one who is scarcely hatched.

Lar. *See* LARES.

Larboard. *See* STARBOARD AND LARBOARD.

Larder. A place for keeping bacon (Lat. *laridum*), from O.Fr. *lardier* or *lardoir*, a storeroom for bacon. This shows that swine were the chief animals salted and preserved in olden times.

The Douglas Larder. *See under* DOUGLAS.

Robin Hood's Larder. *See* SOME FAMOUS OAKS *under* OAK.

Wallace's Larder. Similar to the DOUGLAS LARDER. It consisted of the dead bodies of the garrison of Ardrossan, in Ayrshire, cast into the dungeon keep. The castle was surprised by Wallace in the reign of Edward I.

Lares and Penates. Used as a collective expression for home, and for those personal belongings that make it homely and individual. In ancient ROME the *lares* (sing. *lar*) were the household gods, usually deified ancestors or heroes, and the *lar familiaris* was the spirit of the founder of the house which never left it. The *penates* were the gods of the storeroom and guardian deities of the household and the state, whose duty was to protect and ward off dangers. Their images stood in a special shrine in each house and offerings were made to them of wine, incense, cakes and honey on special family occasions.

Large. A vulgarism for excess, as **That's all very fine and large,** that's a trifle steep, "coming it a bit thick", etc.; **to talk large,** to brag or swank in conversation, to talk big; **a large order,** an exaggerated claim or statement, a difficult undertaking.

By and large. *See under* BY.

Set at large. At liberty. It is a French phrase; *prendre le large* is to stand out to sea so as to free to move.

To sail large. To stand before the wind with the wind free or on the quarter.

> We continued running large before the north-east trade-winds for several days.
> R.H. DANA: *Two Years before the Mast*, ch. iv.

Lark. A spree or frolic. The word is a modern adaptation (*c.* 1800) of the dialectical *lake*, sport, from M.E. *laik*, play, and O.E. *lac*, contest. *Skylark*, as in *skylarking about*, etc., is a more recent extension.

If the sky falls we shall catch larks. *See under* SKY.

Larrikin. An Australian term dating from the 19th century denoting a young ruffian or rowdy given to acts of hooliganism. They flourished particularly in the 1880s and were known by their own style of dress, recognizable by its excessive neatness and severe colours. Possibly derived from the name *Larry* or from an Irishman's pronounciation of "larking".

Larvæ. Among the ancient Romans, a name for malignant spirits and ghosts. The larva or ghost of Caligula was often seen (according to Suetonius) in his palace.

> [Fear] sometimes representeth strange apparitions, as their fathers and grandfathers ghosts, risen out of their graves, and in their winding sheets: and to others it sometimes sheweth Larves, Hobgoblins, Robbin-good-fellows, and such other Bug-beares and Chimeraes.
> *Florio's Montaigne*, I, xvii.

Last. Last Day. The final day of the present dispensation when Christ is to return to earth for the last judgment; the day of judgment. *Cp.* BALANCE.

The Last Judgment. *See* JUDGMENT.

Last Light. *See* FIRST LIGHT.

The Last Man. CHARLES I was so called by the Parliamentarians, meaning that he would be the last king of Great Britain. His son, Charles II, was called *The Son of the Last Man.*

The Last Supper. The last meal Christ partook with his disciples on the night before the Crucifixion and the institution of the EUCHARIST.

Leonardo da Vinci's famous picture of this was painted on a wall of the refectory of the Convent of Santa Maria delle Grazie, Milan, in 1494–1497. Although the refectory was reduced to ruins by Allied bombs in August 1943, the wall on which the Last Supper is painted was practically undamaged and the picture left quite intact. It has worn badly with time and is now protected against further deterioration.

The Last Trump. *See* TRUMP.

The Last Word. That which is conclusive or definite; also, like the Fr. *le dernier cri* it has the meaning of the latest, most fashionable, and up-to-date style in anything.

To have the last word. To have the final say or decision; to make the last rejoinder in an argument.

Last Words. *See* DYING SAYINGS.

The Last of the Barons. Warwick the KING-MAKER. Lord Lytton has a novel of this title (1843).

The Last of the Dandies. A title given to Count Alfred D'Orsay (1801–1852).

The Last of the English. Hereward the Wake (*fl.* 1070–1071) who led the rising of the English at Ely against William the Conqueror.

The Last of the Fathers. St. BERNARD (1090–1153), Abbot of Clairvaux.

The Last of the Goths. Roderick (d. 711), last king of the Visigoths in Spain. Southey has a poem on him.

The Last of the Greeks. The general, Philopœmen of Arcadia (253–183 B.C.).

The Last of the Knights. The Emperor Maximilan I (1459, 1493–1519).

The Last of the Mohicans. The Indian chief Uncas is so called by Fenimore Cooper in his novel of this title (1826).

The Last of the Romans. A title given to a number of historical characters, including:

Marcus Junius Brutus (*c.* 85–42 B.C.), one of the murderers of Julius Cæsar.

Caius Cassius Longinus (d. 42 B.C.), so called by Brutus.

Stilicho (*c.* 359–408), VANDAL, and Roman general under Theodosius.

Ætius, the general who defended the Gauls against the FRANKS and other barbarians and defeated Attila near Châlons in 451. So called by Procopius.

François Joseph Terrasse Desbillons (1711–1789), a French Jesuit; so called from the elegance and purity of his Latin.

Pope called Congreve *Ultimus Romanorum*, and the same title was conferred on Dr. Johnson, Horace Walpole and C. J. Fox. *See also* ROMAN.

The Last of the Saxons. King Harold

(1022–1066), who was defeated and slain at the Battle of Hastings. Lord Lytton has this as a sub-title for his novel *Harold* (1848).

The Last of the Tribunes. Cola di Rienzi (*c.* 1313–1354), who led the Roman people against the barons.

The Last of the Troubadours. Jacques Boé called Jasmin (1798–1864), the Gascon poet who wrote in patois.

Lateran. The ancient palace of the Laterani family which was appropriated by NERO (A.D. 66) and later given to Pope (St.) Sylvester by the Emperor Constantine. It remained the official residence of the Popes until the departure to AVIGNON in 1309. The present palace is now a museum. Fable derives the name from *lateo*, to hide, and *rana*, a frog, and accounts for it by saying that Nero once vomited a frog covered with blood, which he believed to be his own progeny, and had it hidden in a vault. The palace built on its site was called the "Lateran", or the palace of the hidden frog.

Lateran Council. The name given to each of five ŒCUMENICAL COUNCILS held in the Lateran church at ROME. They are (1) 1123, held under Calixtus II; it confirmed the Concordat of Worms which ended the INVESTITURE CONTROVERSY; (2) 1139, when Innocent II condemned Anacletus II and Arnold of Brescia; (3) 1179, convoked by Alexander III to regularize papal elections; (4) 1215, when Innocent III condemned the ALBIGENSES and further defined CATHOLIC doctrine; and (5) 1512–1517, under Julius II and Leo X, to invalidate the work of the antipapal Council of Pisa.

Lateran Treaty. A treaty concluded between the Holy SEE and the Kingdom of Italy in 1929, establishing the VATICAN CITY as a sovereign state, thus ending the "Roman Question" begun in 1870 when the temporal power of the papacy was finally abrogated and ROME became the capital of the Italian Kingdom. *See* PRISONER OF THE VATICAN *under* VATICAN.

St. John Lateran is called the *Mother and Head of all Churches* and is the cathedral church of ROME. It occupies part of the site of the old Lateran palace.

Lathe (O.E. *laeth*, estate, district). An ancient unit of local government in Kent, which was ultimately divided into five lathes. These still exist and the divisions for petty sessions are based on them. *Cp.* RAPE.

Spenser in his *View of the Present State of Ireland* (1596), uses *lathe* or *lath* for the division of a HUNDRED.

If all that tything failed, then all that lath was charged for that tything; and if the lath failed, then all that hundred was demanded for them, and if the hundred, then the shire.

Latin. The language of the ancient inhabitants of Latium in Italy and spoken by the ancient Romans (Alba Longa was head of the Latin League and ROME was a colony of Alba Longa). According to one story Latium is from *lateo*, I lie hid, and was so called because SATURN lay hid there, when he was driven out of HEAVEN by the gods. According to Roman tradition the Latini were the aborigines. *See* LATINUS.

The earliest specimen of the Latin language is an inscription on the Præneste fibula (a gold brooch) found in 1886; it dates from the 6th century B.C.

Classical Latin. The Latin of the best authors centred around the Golden or AUGUSTAN AGE, as Livy, CICERO, etc. (prose); HORACE, VIRGIL, Ovid, etc. (poets).

Dog-Latin. *See under* DOG.

Late Latin. The period which followed the AUGUSTAN AGE to about A.D. 600; it includes the works of the Church FATHERS.

Law Latin. The debased Latin used in legal documents. *Cp.* DOG-LATIN.

Low Latin. MEDIÆVAL LATIN.

Mediæval, or **Middle Latin.** Latin from the 6th to the 16th century, both inclusive. In this Latin prepositions frequently supply the cases of nouns.

New Latin. Latin written since *c.* 1500, especially that used in scientific classifications, and in theological and philosophical works.

Thieves' Latin. Cant or jargon employed as a secret language by rogues and vagabonds.

The Latin Church. The Western Church, in contradistinction to the Greek or Eastern Church.

The Latin Cross. *See under* CROSS.

Latin Quarter. *See* QUARTERS.

The Latin Races. The peoples whose language is based on Latin; *i.e.* the Italians, Spanish, Portuguese, French, Rumanians, etc.

Latinus. Legendary king of the Latini, the ancient inhabitants of Latium (*see* LATIN). According to Virgil, he opposed ÆNEAS on his first landing, but later formed an alliance with him, and gave him his daughter, Lavinia, in marriage. Turnus, King of the Rutuli, declared that Lavinia had been betrothed to him and the issue was decided by single combat. Æneas, being the victor, became the husband of Lavinia and ancestor of ROMULUS and Remus (Virgil, *Æneid*, VII).

Latitudinarians. In the CHURCH OF ENGLAND a name applied, at first opprobriously, from the mid-17th century to those clergy attaching little importance to dogma and practice in religion, which in the 18th century encouraged laxity and indifference. The Cambridge Platonists were prominent among them. Latitudinarianism was checked by the advent of the EVANGELICALS and the OXFORD MOVEMENT. The term is widely applied to those attaching little importance to dogma and orthodoxy.

Latium. *See* LATIN.

Latona. The Roman name of the Gr. Leto, mother by JUPITER of APOLLO and DIANA. Milton (*Sonnet XII*) refers to the legend that when she knelt with her infants in arms by a fountain at Delos to quench her thirst, some Lycian clowns insulted her and were turned into frogs.

> As when those hinds that were transformed to frogs
> Railed at Latona's twin-born progeny,
> Which after held the sun and moon in fee.

Latria and **Dulia.** Greek words adopted by the Roman Catholics; the former to express that supreme reverence and adoration which is offered to God alone; and the latter, that secondary reverence which is offered to saints. *Latria* is from the Greek suffix *-latreia*, worship, as in ido*latry*; *dulia* is the reverence of a *doulos* or slave. **Hyperdulia** is the special reverence paid to the Virgin Mary.

Latrine lawyer. *See* BARRACK-ROOM LAWYER.

Latter-day Saints. *See* MORMONS.

Lattice. *see* RED-LATTICE PHRASES.

Lauds. In the Western Church, the traditional morning prayer, so called from the repeated occurrence of the word *laudate* (praise ye) in *Pss.* cxlvii-cl which form part of the office. It is said in the early morning by religious orders who rise for the Night Office, otherwise it is nowadays coupled with MATINS and said overnight. It forms part of the BREVIARY of the ROMAN CATHOLIC CHURCH, and the service of Morning Prayer, in the BOOK OF COMMON PRAYER, is essentially composed of parts of Lauds and Matins.

Laugh. He laughs best that laughs last. Don't crow too soon, a game's not finished till it's won; to have the last laugh. In Ray's *Collection* (1742) is, "Better the last smile than the first laughter," and the French have the proverb *Rira bien qui rira le dernier*.

Laugh and grow fat. An old saw, expressive of the wisdom of keeping a cheerful mind. Taylor, the WATER POET, has a poem *Laugh and be Fat* (c. 1625), and in Trapps' *Commentaries* (1647), on II *Thess.* iii, 11, he says, "Whose life is to eat and drink ... and laugh themselves fat."

To have the laugh on one. To be able to make merry at another's expense, generally to that other's surprise and confusion.

To laugh in one's sleeve. *See under* SLEEVE.

To laugh like a drain. To gurgle or laugh noisily, as water gurgles down a drain.

To laugh off. To dismiss a matter lightly; to shake off embarrassment with a jest.

To laugh on the wrong side, or **on the other side of one's face** or **mouth.** To be made to feel vexation and annoyance after mirth or satisfaction; to be bitterly disappointed; to cry.

To laugh out of court. To cover with ridicule, and so treat as not worth considering.

To laugh to scorn. To treat with the utmost contempt.

> All they that see me laugh me to scorn; they shoot out the lip; they shake the head.
> *Ps.* xxii, 7.

Laughing gas. Nitrous oxide (N_2O), discovered by Joseph Priestley in 1772 and suggested as an anaesthetic by Sir Humphry Davy in 1802. Formerly much used in dentistry and for minor operations. After inhalation it produces a feeling of exhilaration followed by unconsciousness, hence the name.

Laughing Murderer of Verdun. Friedrich Wilhelm, Crown Prince of Germany, who commanded the armies that tried to capture Verdun in World War I. He is said to have taken lightly the enormous casualties sustained on both sides, hence the nickname. British troops also called him "Little Willie".

Laughing Philosopher. Democrítus of ABDERA (5th century B.C.), who viewed with supreme contempt the feeble powers of man. *Cp.* WEEPING PHILOSOPHER.

Laughing stock. A butt for jokes.

No laughing matter. Something to be treated seriously. The expression is an example of LITOTES.

Launcelot. *See* LANCELOT.

Launching-pad. Figuratively, the place which gives an impetus to, or sees the start of, an important enterprise. From the technical term in rocketry.

Launfal, Sir. One of the Knights of the ROUND TABLE. His story is told in a metrical romance written by Thomas Chestre in the reigh of Henry VI. James Russell Lowell has a poem entitled *The Vision of Sir Launfal* (1845).

Laura (la belle Laure). Laure de Noves (1308–1348) was immortalized by Petrarch (1304–1374) in his poems. He first saw her in the church of St. Clara, Avignon, on 6 April 1327, and it was this event which, he said, made him a poet.

Laura. (Gr. *laura*, an alley). In early monachism, a collection of separate cells under a superior, their occupants meeting in chapel and for a common meal in the refectory. Monastic life proper was a much more communal affair.

Laureate. *See* POET LAUREATE.

Laurel. The Greeks gave a wreath of laurels to the victor in the PYTHIAN GAMES, but the victor in the OLYMPIC GAMES had a wreath of wild olives, in the NEMEAN GAMES, a wreath of green parsley, and in the ISTHMIAN GAMES, a wreath of dry parsley or green pine leaves.

The ancients held that laurel communicated the spirit of prophecy and poetry, hence the custom of crowning the Pythoness (the PYTHIA) and poets, and of putting laurel leaves under one's pillow to acquire inspiration. Another superstition was that the bay laurel (*see* DAPHNE) was antagonistic to the stroke of lightning; but Sir Thomas Browne, in his *Vulgar Errors*, tells us that Vicomereatus proves from personal knowledge that this is untrue.

The Laurel in modern times is a symbol of victory and peace, and of excellence in literature and the arts. St. GUDULE (patron saint of Brussels), in Christian art, carries a laurel crown. *See also* APOLLO.

To look to one's laurels. To have to try to maintain the lead in any field in which one has already excelled.

To rest on one's laurels. To be satisfied with the degree of success one has already achieved and to refrain from further effort.

Laurence, St. *See* LAWRENCE.

Laurentian Library. A library opened by Cosimo de' MEDICI in 1571, noted for its collection of Greek and Latin MSS., and named after Laurentius or Lorenzo de' Medici. It was designed by MICHELANGELO and formed from the collections of Cosimo the Elder, Pietro de' Medici, and Lorenzo the Magnificent.

Laurin. The dwarf-king in the German folk-legend *Laurin*, or *Der Kleine Rosengarten*. He possesses a magic ring, girdle, and cap, and is attacked by DIETRICH OF BERN in his rose-garden, which no one may enter on pain of death. The poem belongs to the late 13th century and is attributed to Heinrich von Ofterdingen.

Lavender. The earliest form of the word is Med. Lat. *livendula*, and is probably, like our livid, from *livere*, to make bluish; as, however, the plant has been used by laundresses for scenting linen, and in connection with the bath, later forms of the word are associated with *lavare*, to wash. The modern botanical name is *Lavendula*. It is a token of affection.

> He from his lass him lavender hath sent,
> Showing her love and doth requital crave.
> DRAYTON: *Ninth Eclogue*, 17.

Laid up in lavender. Taken great care of, laid away.

> The poore gentleman paies so deere for the lavender it is laid up in, that if it lies long at the broker's house he seems to buy his apparel twice.
> GREENE: *A Quip for an Upstart Courtier* (1592).

Lavinia. *See* LATINUS.

Lavolta (Ital., the turn). A lively dance, in which was a good deal of jumping or capering, whence its name. Troilus says: "I cannot sing, nor heel the high lavolt" (SHAKESPEARE, *Troilus and Cressida*, IV, iv). It originated in 16th-century Provence or Italy, and is thus described:

> A lofty jumping or a leaping round,
> Where arm in arm two dancers are entwined,
> And whirl themselves with strict embracements bound.
> And still their feet an anapest do sound.
> SIR JOHN DAVIES: *The Orchestra* (1594).

Law. In-Laws. A way of referring to one's relations by marriage—mother-in-law, sisters-in-law, etc. *In-law* is short for in CANON LAW, the reference being to the degrees of a affinity within which marriage is allowed or prohibited.

Law-calf. A bookseller's term for a special kind of binding in plain sheep or calf used largely for law books.

> Other gentlemen who had no briefs to show carried under their arms goodly octavos, with a red label behind, and that under-done-pie-crust-coloured cover, which is technically known as "law-calf".
> DICKENS: *Pickwick Papers*, ch.xxxiv.

Law Latin. *See under* LATIN.

Law Lords. The Lords of Appeal in Ordinary; also, additionally, those members of the HOUSE OF LORDS who are qualified to deal with the judicial business of the House, *i.e.* the Lord CHANCELLOR, the Lord Chief Justice, the Master of the ROLLS, and any peer who has held high judicial office. The Lords of Appeal in Ordinary were instituted in 1877 as life BARONS, being now seven to nine in number. Until 1873 the appellate jurisdiction of the Lords was open to the whole House.

Law Merchant. Formerly, the practice of merchants as established by judicial decisions and administered in the Courts of markets and FAIRS such as a PIE-POWDER COURT. From the time of Lord Mansfield (Lord Chief Justice, 1756–1788), Law Merchant became assimilated to the COMMON LAW.

The Law of Moses, or **Mosaic Law.** *See under* MOSES.

Law's Bubble. *See* MISSISSIPPI BUBBLE.

The law of the Medes and Persians. That which is unalterable.

> Now O King, establish the decree, and sign the writing, that it be not changed, according to the law of the Medes and Persians, which altereth not.
> *Dan.* vi, 8.

Possession is nine points of the law. *See under* NINE.

Quips of the law. *See* CEPOLA.

To give one law. A sporting term, "law" meaning the chance of saving oneself. Thus a hare or a stag is allowed "law"—*i.e.* a certain start before any hound is permitted to attack it; and a tradesman allowed "law" is one to whom time is given to "find his legs".

To go to law, to have the law on someone. To take legal proceedings.

To take the law into one's own hands. To try to secure satisfaction by force or personal action; to punish, reward, etc., entirely on one's own resonsibility.

Lawless Parliament. *See* PARLIAMENT OF DUNCES *under* DUNCE.

Lawn. Fine, thin cambric, used for the rochets of Anglican BISHOPS, ladies' handkerchiefs, etc. So called from *Laon* (O.Fr. *Lan*), a town in the Aisne department of France, once noted for its linen manufacture.

Man of lawn. A BISHOP.

Lawn-market. The higher end of High Street, Edinburgh, once a place for executions; hence, **to go up the lawn-market** is to go to be hanged.

> They [the stolen clothes] may serve him to gang up the Lawn-market in, the scoundrel.
> SCOTT: *Guy Mannering*, ch. xxxii.

Lawrence, St. (of Rome). The patron saint of curriers, who was roasted on a GRID-IRON. He was archdecaon to Pope (St.) Sixtus II and was charged with the care of the poor, the orphans, and the widows. When summoned by the prætor to deliver up the treasures of the church, he produced the poor, etc., under his charge, and said, "These are the church's treasures." His day is 10 August. (*Cp* CORNELIA). Fragments of his relics were taken to the ESCORIAL.

The phrase **Lazy as Lawrence** is said to originate from the story that when being roasted over a slow fire he asked to be turned. "For", said he, "that side is quite done." This expression of Christian fortitude was interpreted by his torturers as evidence of the height of laziness, the martyr being too indolent to wriggle.

> "Flo and I have got a new name for you; it's 'Lazy Laurence.' How do you like it?"
> LOUISA M. ALCOTT: *Good Wives*, ch. xxxix.

St. Laurence's tears or **The fiery tears of St. Laurence.** *See* SHOOTING STARS.

Lawyer's Bags, or more properly **Barrister's Bags,** since they are not used by solicitors. Counsel traditionally use bags made of cotton damask to carry their robes from home or Chambers to Court. The ordinary bag of a junior Counsel is blue but it is customary for a Q.C. to present a junior who has given him outstanding assistance in a particular case with a red bag, which that junior thereafter always uses, during the remainder of a career both as a junior and as a Q.C. Bags are normally carried from Chambers to Court by Counsel's Clerk. The bag is closed by pulling the ends of a cord which is threaded round the mouth. It is carried over the shoulder, the ends of the cord being held in one hand.

Lay. Pertaining to the people of laity (Lat. *laicus*) as distinguished from the clergy. Thus, a lay brother is one who, though not in HOLY ORDERS (*see under* ORDERS), is received into a monastery and is bound by its vows.

A layman is, properly speaking, anyone not in HOLY ORDERS; (*see under* ORDERS); it is also used by professional men, especially doctors and lawyers, to denote one not of their particular calling or specialized learning.

Lay Days. Days allowed under the terms of a charter party (the contract for hiring the whole or part if a ship for the delivery of cargo) for loading and unloading a ship; possibly from *delay* and *day*.

Lay figures. Wooden figures with free joints, used by artists chiefly for the study of how drapery falls. The word was earlier *layman* from Dut. *leeman*, a contraction of *ledenman* (*led*, a joint). Horace Walpole uses *layman* (1762), but *lay figure* had taken its place by the end of the 18th century. Hence, figuratively, a character who is a mere foil or puppet.

Lay investiture. *See* INVESTITURE CONTROVERSY.

Lay (the verb). **To lay about one.** To strike out lustily on all sides.

> He'll lay about him today.
> SHAKESPEARE: *Troilus and Cressida*, I, ii.

To lay into. To attack vigorously, either physically or verbally.

To lay it on thick. To flatter or over-praise.

To lay it on with a trowel. To flatter excessively.

> Well said; that was laid on with a trowel.
> SHAKESPEAR: *As You Like It*, I, ii.

To lay off. To dismiss workmen, usually temporarily; to cease to annoy, attack, tease, etc.

To lay on the table. *See under* TABLE.

To lay, or **put yourself out.** To go to a great deal of trouble; to go to especial pains.

To lay out. To disburse; to display goods, to arrange, etc.; to prepare a corpse for the coffin; to disable or render unconscious.

To lay to one's charge. To attribute an offence to a person; a Biblical phrase, see *Deut*. xxi, 8; *Rom*. viii, 33, etc.

> And he [Stephen] kneeled down, and cried with a loud voice, Lord, lay not this sin to their charge.
> *Acts* vii, 60.

To lay up. The store away; to dismantle and berth a vessel for a period of disuse. A person temporarily incapacitated through injury or illness is said to be "laid up", especially if confined to bed.

Laylock. Ancient rustic name for lilac.

Lazar House, or **Lazaretto.** *See under* LAZARUS.

Lazarillo de Tormes. A Spanish PICARESQUE novel something in the *Gil Blas* style, published in 1554, and of uncertain authorship, although formerly attributed to Diego Hurtado de Mendoza. Its full title is *Vida de Lazarillo de Tormes y de sus fortunas y adversidades*. Lazarillo, a light, jovial, audacious manservant, sees his masters in their undress and exposes their foibles.

Lazarus. Any poor beggar; so called from the Lazarus of the parable, who was laid daily at the rich man's gate. *See* DIVES.

Lazar house, or **Lazaretto.** A house for lazars or poor persons affected with contagious diseases; so called from LAZARUS.

Lazy. Lazy as Ludlam's dog, which leaned his head against the wall to bark. Ludlam was reputed to be a sorceress who lived in a cave near Farnham, Surrey. Her dog was so lazy that when the rustics came to consult her it would hardly condescend to announce their approach, even with the ghost of a bark (Ray: *Proverbs*).

Lazy as Lawrence's dog is a similar saying to the above. *See* LAWRENCE.

Lazy man's load. One too heavy to be carried; so called because lazy people are apt to overload themselves to save a second journey.

Lazzarone (lăts à rō ni) (Ital.). Originally applied to Neapolitan vagrants who lived in the streets and idled about begging, etc. So called from the hospital of St. LAZARUS which served as a refuge for the destitute of Naples. Every year they elected a chief, called the *Capo Lazzaro*. In 1674 Masaniello effected a revolution with the support of these vagabonds, and in 1798 Michele Sforza, at the head of the Lazzaroni, successfully resisted Championnet, the French general.

L'état, c'est moi (lā ta sā mwa) (Fr., I am the State). The reply traditionally ascribed to Louis XIV when the President of the PARLEMENT of Paris objected "in the interests of the State" to the King's fiscal demands. This was in 1655, when Louis was only 17 years old. He acted on this principle with fair consistency throughout his long reign (1643–1715).

Le roy, or **La reyne le veult** (O.Fr., The King, or Queen, wills it). The form of royal assent to Parliamentary Bills. The dissent is expressed by *Le roy* (*La reyne*) *s'avisera*, the King (Queen) will give it consideration, but this has not been used since 1707. The formula for money bills is *Le roy* (*la reyne*) *remercie ses bons sujets, accepte leur benevolence, et ainsi, le veult*, and for personal bills, *Soit fait comme il est désiré*.

Lead (led) was, by the ancient alchemists, called SATURN.

The *lead*, or *blacklead*, of a *lead* pencil contains no lead at all, but is composed of plumbago or graphite, an almost pure carbon with a touch of iron. It was so named in the 16th century when it was thought to be of or to contain the metal.

Swinging the lead. Malingering, usually by concocting some plausible yarn, or by feigning an indisposition. An allusion to the lazy leadsman idly swinging the line and protracting the job of taking soundings.

To strike lead. To make a good hit.

The Leads. The famous prison in Venice in which CASANOVA was incarcerated and from which he escaped.

Lead (lēd) (the verb) (O.E. *lædan*).

To lead apes in hell. *See under* APE.

To lead by the nose. *See* LED BY THE NOSE *under* NOSE.

To lead one a pretty dance. *See* DANCE.

Leader. The first violin of an orchestra, the first cornet of a military band, etc., is called the *leader*.

Bear-leader. *See under* BEAR.

Leading article, or **Leader.** A newspaper article by the editor or a special writer. It takes the lead or chief place as commentary on current issues, and expresses the policy of the paper.

Leading case. A lawsuit that forms a precedent in deciding others of a similar kind.

Leading counsel in a case, the senior counsel on a circuit.

Leading Lady, or **man.** The actress or actor who takes the chief role in a play.

Leading note (music). The seventh note of the diatonic scale, which leads to the octave, only half a tone higher.

Leading question. A question so worded

as to suggest an answer. "Was he not dressed in a black coat?" leads to the answer "Yes." In cross-examining a witness, leading questions are permitted, because the chief object of a cross-examination is to obtain contradictions.

To be in leading-strings is to be under the control of another. Infants just learning to walk are held up by "leading-strings".

Leaf. Before the invention of paper, leaves of certain plants were among the materials used for writing upon. The reverse and obverse pages are still called leaves; and the double page of a ledger is termed a "FOLIO", from Lat. *folium*, a leaf. *Cp.* the derivation of *paper* itself, from *papyrus*; and *book* from *boc*, a beech-tree.

To take a leaf out of my book. To imitate me; to do as I do. The allusion is to literary plagiarisms.

To turn over a new leaf. To amend one's ways, to start afresh.

League. The Holy League. Several leagues are so called. The best-known are: (1) 1511, between Pope Julius II, Ferdinand of Aragon, Henry VIII and Venice to drive the French out of Italy, and joined by the Emperor Maximilian and the Swiss; (2) 1526, the Holy League of Cognac between Clement VII and Francis I of France against the Emperor Charles V; (3) 1576, formed by Henry, Duke of Guise, and the JESUITS and joined by Henry III against the HUGUENOTS and for the defence of the CATHOLIC Church.

The League of Nations. A league, having at one time about 60 member nations with headquarters at Geneva, with the essential aim of preventing war as well as promoting other forms of international co-operation. It was formed on 10 January 1920, after the close of World War I, but was weakened from the outset by the refusal of the U.S.A. to participate (although President Woodrow Wilson had played a major part in its foundation), and the exclusion of Russia. Its achievements were considerable in many fields, but it failed in its primary purpose. It last met on 18 April 1946, being replaced by the UNITED NATIONS Organization which had been established on 24 October 1945.

Leak. To leak out. To come surreptitiously to public knowledge. As a liquid leaks out of an unsound vessel, so the secret filters through.

To spring a leak. Said of ships, etc., that open at the seams, etc., to admit water.

Leal. Anglo-French and O.Fr. *leel*, our *loyal*; trusty, law-abiding; now practically confined to SCOTLAND.

Land o' the leal. *See* LAND.

Leander. *See* HERO AND LEANDER.

Leaning Tower. While there are a number of leaning campanili, or bell-towers, in Italy, the most celebrated is that of the cathedral of Pisa which stands apart from the main building. It is 179 ft. high, 57½ ft. in diameter at the base, and leans about 17 ft. from the perpendicular. It was begun in 1174 and the sinking commenced during construction, but it still stands because the centre of gravity is within its walls. Galileo availed himself of the overhanging tower to make his experiments in gravitation. Caerphilly Castle, Glamorganshire, has a tower which leans 10° from the perpendicular, due to attempts to dismantle the castle with gunpowder after the CIVIL WARS. The church spires at Chesterfield, Derby, and Ermington, Devonshire, also lean.

Leap. The Leap in the Dark. The famous phrase used by Lord Derby, the Prime Minister, of his government's policy in promoting the Parliamentary Reform Act of 1867, He adopted the expression from Lord Cranborne who first "taunted the government with taking a leap in the dark" (Justin McCarthy, *Short History of Our Own Times*, ch. xxi). Thomas Hobbes is also supposed to have used it (*see* DYING SAYINGS).

Leap Year. A year of 366 days, a BISSEXTILE year: *i.e.*, in the Julian and Gregorian calendars (*see* CALENDAR), any year whose date is exactly divisible by 4 except those which are divisible by 100 but not by 400. Thus 1900 (though divisible by 4) was not a leap year, but 2000 will be.

In ordinary years, the day of the month which falls in Monday this year will fall on Tuesday next year, and Wednesday the year after; but the fourth year will *leap* over Thursday to Friday. This is because a day is added to February, the reason being that the astronomical year (*i.e.* the time that it takes the earth to go round the sun) is approximately 365¼ days (365·2422), the difference between ·25 and ·2422 being righted by the loss of the three days in 400 years.

It is an old saying that during leap year the ladies may propose, and, if not accepted, claim a silk gown. A Scottish law of 1288 says that "during the rein of hir maist blissit Megeste, for ilke yeare knowne as lepe yeare, ilk mayden ladye ... shal hae liberte, to bespeke ye man she like, albeit he refuses to taik hir to be his lawful wyfe, he shall be mulcted in ye sum of ane pundis...." There was a similar law passed in France and it became legal custom in Genoa and Florence in the 15th century.

Lear, King. A legendary king of Britain

whose story is told by SHAKESPEARE. His immediate source was Holinshed, who in turn derived it from Geoffrey of Monmouth's *Historia Britonum*. It is also given in the GESTA ROMANORUM and in PERCE-FOREST. Spenser uses it in his *Faerie Queene* (ii, x) and Camden tells a similar story of Ina, King of the West Saxons. According to Shakespeare's version, King Lear in his old age divided his kingdom between his daughters GONERIL and REGAN, who professed great love for him but then harassed him into madness. CORDELIA, left portionless, succoured him and came with an army to dethrone her sisters, but was captured and slain. King Lear died over her body. *See* LIR.

Learn. To learn a person a thing, or **to do something** is now a provincialism or regarded as illiterate speech, but was formerly quite good English. In the Prayer Book version of the *Psalms* we have "Lead me forth in thy truth and learn me," and "such as are gentle, them shall he learn his way" (xxv, 4, 8). Other examples of this use of learn as an active verb will be found in *Ps*. cxic, 66, and cxxxii, 13.

> The new plague rid you
> For learning me your language.
> SHAKESPEARE: *Tempest*, I, ii.

"I'll learn you" or "I'll larn you" is still frequently used as a threat, especially by indignant housewives to troublesome children.

The Learned. Kalman, or Koloman, King of Hungary (1095–1116), was so called. *Cp.* BEAUCLERC.

The learned Blacksmith. Elihu Burritt (1810–1879), the American philanthropist, a one-time blacksmith, who by the age of 30 could read nearly 50 languages.

The learned Painter. Charles Lebrun (1619–1690), so called from the great accuracy of his costumes.

The learned Tailor. Henry Wild of Norwich (1684–1734), who mastered, while he worked at his trade, Greek, Latin, Hebrew, Chaldaic, Syriac, Persian and Arabic.

Leash. To strain at the leash. To be eager to be off; to be impatient of restraint or delay. From the lead used to restrain hounds in coursing.

Leather. Nothing like leather. The story is that a town in danger of a siege called together a council of the chief inhabitants to know what defence they recommended. A mason suggested a strong wall, a shipbuilder advised "WOODEN WALLS", and when others had spoken, a currier arose and said, "There's nothing like leather."

Another version is, "Nothing like leather to administer a thrashing."

It's all leather or prunella. Nothing of any moment, all rubbish; through a misunderstanding of the lines by Pope, who was drawing a distinction between the work of a cobbler and that of a parson.

> Worth makes the man, and want of it the fellow;
> The rest is all but leather or prunella.
> POPE: *Essay on Man*, iv, 203.

Prunella is a worsted stuff, formerly used for clergymen's gowns, etc., and for the uppers of ladies' boots, and is probably so called because it was the colour of a prune.

Leather medal. An American colloquial term for a BOOBY PRIZE.

To give one a leathering. To flog him with a leather strap; to give him a drubbing.

Leatherneck. A soldier or a MARINE.

Leatherstocking Novels. The novels by Fenimore Cooper (1789–1851) in which Natty Bumppo, nicknamed *Leatherstocking* and *Hawkeye*, is a leading character. They are *The Pioneers* (1823), THE LAST OF THE MOHICANS (1826), *The Prairie* (1827), *The Pathfinder* (1840), and *The Deerslayer* (1841). "Leatherstocking" was a hardy backwoodsman, a type of North American pioneer, ignorant of books but a philosopher of the woods.

Leave in the lurch. *See* LURCH.

Leave well alone. Do not try to alter a state of affairs which is reasonably satisfactory lest you make things worse. "Why not let it alone" was a maxim of Lord Melbourne, the WHIG Prime Minister (1835–1841); and the motto of his 18th-century predecessor, Sir Robert Walpole, was virtually the same— *Quieta non movere*, the equivalent of "let sleeping dogs lie".

To take French leave. *See under* FRENCH.

Lebensraum (lā bènz roum'). A German phrase (room for living), somewhat akin to LAND HUNGER. It is applied especially to the territory required by a nation for overseas expansion, both for settlement and trade, to meet the population pressures in the mother country.

Leda. In Greek mythology, the wife of Tyndarus. JUPITER came to her in the guise of a swan when she was bathing, and in due time she brought forth two eggs, from one of which came CASTOR and CLYTEMNESTRA, and from the other POLLUX and HELEN. The two former are usually held to be the children of Tyndarus.

Leda Bible, The. *See* BIBLE, SOME SPECIALLY NAMED EDITIONS.

Lee (O.E. *helo, hleow*, a covering or shelter). Nautically, the side or quarter opposite to that against which the wind blows; the side away from the windward or weather side; the sheltered side.

Lee board. A wooden board fixed on the side of a vessel and lowered on the lee side when on a wind, to prevent making too much leeway. The once familiar THAMES sailing barge was equipped with lee boards.

Lee shore. The shore under the lee of a ship, or that towards which the wind blows. It is very dangerous for a vessel to come close to a lee shore.

Lee side. *See* LEEWARD.

Lee tide. A tide running in the same direction as the wind blows; if in the opposite direction is called a *tide under the lee*.

To lay a ship by the lee. An obsolete phrase for heaving-to, *i.e.* to bring a vessel up into the wind by suitably trimming sail so that she lies nearly head to wind. The vessel is then practically motionless, comparable to marking time in marching.

Under the lee of the land. Under the shelter of the land.

Under the lee of a ship. On the side away from the wind, so that the ship provides shelter and breaks the force of the wind.

Leeward (loo′ àrd). Towards the LEE, or that part towards which the wind blows; *windward* is the opposite direction, the WEATHER side.

Leech. One skilled in medicine or "leech-craft", a doctor; the word, now obsolete, is the O.E. *læce*, one who relieves pain, from *lacnian*, to heal. The blood-sucking worm, the *leech*, gets its name, *the healer*, probably from the same word.

> And straightway sent, with careful diligence,
> To fetch a leach the which had great insight
> In that disease.
>
> SPENSER: *The Faerie Queene*, I, x, 23.

Leech-finger. *See* MEDICINAL FINGER.

Leek. The national emblem of WALES. (*Cp.* DAFFODIL). The story is that St. DAVID, on one occasion, caused his countrymen under King Cadwaladr to distinguish themselves from their Saxon foes by wearing a leek in their caps.

SHAKESPEARE makes out that the Welsh wore leeks at the battle of Poitiers, for Fluellen says:

> If your majesties is remembered of it, the Welshmen did goot service in a garden where leeks did grow, wearing leeks in their Monmouth caps; which, your majesty knows, to this hour is an honourable padge of the service; and I do believe your majesty takes no scorn to wear the leek upon Saint Tavy's Day.
>
> *Henry V*, IV, vii.

To eat the leek. To be forced to eat your own words, or retract what you have said. Fluellen (in Shakespeare's *Henry V*, V, i) is taunted by Pistol for wearing a leek in his hat. "Hence," says Pistol, "I am qualmish at the smell of leek." Fluellen replies "I peseech you...at my desires...to eat...this leek." The ancient answers, "Not for Cadwallader and all his goats." Then the peppery Welshman beats him, nor desists till Pistol has swallowed the entire abhorrence.

Lees. There are lees to every wine. Everything has its dregs; the best things have some defect. A French proverb.

Settling on the lees. Making the best of a bad job; settling down on what is left, after having squandered the main part of one's fortune.

Leet. In East Anglia, a division of the HUNDRED formed of a group of vills for local government and taxation. The word occurs in DOMESDAY and is probably from the Dan. *lægd*, a division of the country for purposes of military service.

Court-leet. A court of record granted by the crown to a HUNDRED, lordship, MANOR, BOROUGH, etc. It took view of FRANKPLEDGE and dealt with minor criminal offences and a variety of administrative work. In its early days it was substantially the same as the COURT BARON.

> Who has a breast so pure,
> But some uncleanly apprehensions
> Keep leets and law-days, and in sessions sit
> With meditations lawful?
>
> SHAKESPEARE: *Othello*, III, iii.

Left. The *left* side of anything is frequently considered to be unlucky, of bad omen (*cp.* AUGURY; SINISTER), the *right* the reverse.

In politics the *left* denotes the more RADICAL political group, and today is usually applied to Socialists and Communists (*see* COMMUNISM). Within a particular party the *left wing* is made up of the "progressives" or "radicals". Communists are often known as the "extreme left". In many legislatures the radicals sit on the left-hand side (as seen from the chair) and in most of the British Commonwealth assemblies the opposition sits on the left.

In the French National Assembly of 1789, the reactionaries sat on the right, moderates in the centre, and democrats and extremists on the left, and this established the custom.

A left-handed compliment. A compliment which insinuates a reproach.

A left-handed marriage. A MORGANATIC MARRIAGE.

A left-handed oath. One not intended to be binding.

Over the left. In early Victorian days, a way of expressing disbelief, incredulity, or a negative.

Each gentleman pointed with his right thumb over his left shoulder. This action, imperfectly described in words by the very feeble term "over the left", when performed by any number of ladies or gentleman who are accustomed to act in unison, has a very graceful and airy effect; its expression is one of light and playful sarcasm.

DICKENS: *Pickwick Papers*, ch. xlii.

Leg. In many phrases, *e.g.* "To find one's legs", "to put one's best leg foremost", leg is interchangeable with FOOT.

Leg and leg. Equal, or nearly so, in a race, game, etc. *Cp.* NECK AND NECK.

On its last legs. Moribund; obsolete; about to collapse or break up; practically worn out.

Shake a leg! Hurry up! Also, *to shake a leg* is to dance.

Show a leg. Jump out of bed and be sharp about it. A naval phrase, from the monologue used to call the hands from their hammocks, "Wakey Wakey, rise and shine, the morning's fine ... show a leg, show a leg, a show leg, etc." It comes from the days when women were allowed to sleep on board; they were allowed to "lie in" and had to "show a leg" to ensure that no rating was still turned in.

To give a leg up. To render timely assistance, "to help a lame dog over a stile". Originally from horsemanship—to help one into the saddle.

To have good sea-legs. To be a good sailor, to be able to stand up to the ship's motion without getting seasick.

To make a leg. To make a bow, especially an old-fashioned obeisance by advancing the right leg.

The pursuivant smiled at their simplicitye,
And making many leggs, tooke their reward.

PERCY: *Reliques (The King and the Miller of Mansfield*, Pt, II).

To set on his legs. To be independent, to be earning one's own living. The allusion is to being nursed, and standing "alone".

To stretch one's legs. To take a walk for exercise, particularly after long sitting.

Without a leg to stand on. Having no excuse; no hope of getting away with it.

Leg-bail. A runaway. **To give leg-bail,** to abscond, make a "get-away".

Leg-break. In CRICKET, a ball which, after striking the ground from the batsman's leg side, turns towards the wicket.

Leg bye. In CRICKET, a run scored from a ball which has glanced off any part of the batsman's person except his hand.

Leg-pulling means teasing, chaffing, or befooling.

Legal tender. Money which, by the law of a particular country, constitutes payment which a creditor is bound to accept; formerly in England the tender of gold, Bank of England notes, silver up to 40s., and bronze up to one shilling. Since decimalization amounts of legal tender are (1) all English banknotes in England and Wales, but only £1 notes in Scotland and Northern Ireland; (2) all gold coins; (3) "silver" or cupronickel of more than 10p face value up to £10; (4) "silver" up to 10p face value totalling £5; (5) bronze up to 10p.

Legem Pone (lē′ jem pō ne). Old slang for money paid down on the NAIL, ready money; from the opening words of the first of the PSALMS appointed to be read on the twenty-fifth morning of the month—*Legem pone mihi, Domine, viam justificationum tuarum* (Teach me, O Lord, the way of thy statutes, *Ps*. cxix, 33). 25 March is the first QUARTER-DAY and Settlement Day of the year, and thus the phrase became associated with cash down.

Use *Legem pone* to pay at thy day,
But use not *oremus* for often delay.

TUSSER: *Good Husbandry* (1557).

Oremus (let us pray) occurs frequently in the Roman Catholic liturgy. Its application to a debtor who is suing for further time is obvious.

Legend (Lat. *legenda*; from *legere*, to read). Literally and originally "something to be read"; hence the narratives of saints and martyrs were so termed from their being read, especially at MATINS, and after dinner in monastic refectories. Exaggeration and a love for the wonderful so predominated in these readings, that the word came to signify a traditional story, a fable, a myth.

In numismatics the legend is the inscription impressed in letters on the edge or rim of a coin or medal and often used synonymously with *inscription*, which is strictly the words in the *field* of a coin. The *field* is the whole part of a coin not occupied by the device. Legend is also applied to the title on a map or under a picture.

Legenda Aurea. See GOLDEN LEGEND.

Leger. St. Leger Sweepstakes. One of the CLASSIC RACES, run at Doncaster early in September. It was instituted in 1776 by Colonel Anthony St. Leger, of Park Hill near Doncaster, and called the "St. Leger" two years later.

Legion. My name is Legion: for we are many (*Mark* v, 9). A proverbial expression somewhat similar to hydra-headed (*see* HYDRA). Thus we say of a plague of rats, "Their name is legion."

British Legion. An organisation for

promoting the welfare of ex-service personnel, especially for the aged, sick and disabled. It was founded in 1921 largely through the exertions of Field Marshal Earl Haig (1861–1928) and it became the *Royal British Legion* in 1971. There are many local branches and much of the funds are raised by the sale of Flanders poppies. *See* ARMISTICE DAY; REMEMBRANCE DAY.

Foreign Legion. A body of volunteer sympathizers fighting to aid a foreign cause. The name is now particularly associated with the French Foreign Legion, a regular force composed of volunteers of many nationalities.

The Thundering Legion. *See* THUNDERING.

Legion of Honour. An order of distinction and reward instituted by NAPOLEON in 1802, for either military or civil merit.

It was originally limited to 15 *cohortes*, each composed of 7 *grands officiers*, 20 *commandants*, 30 *officiers*, and 350 *légionnaires*, making in all 6,105 members; it was reorganized by Louis XVIII in 1814, and again by Napoleon III in 1852, and now comprises 80 *grand-croix*, 200 *grands officiers*, 1,000 *commandeurs*, 4,000 *officiers*, with *chevaliers* to whose creation there is no fixed limit.

The badge is a five-branched cross with a medallion bearing a symbolical figure of the republic and round it the legend, "République Française". This is crowned by a LAUREL wreath, and the ribbon is of red watered silk.

Leglen-girth. To cast a leglen-girth. To have made a *faux pas*, particularly by having an illegitimate child; to have one's reputation blown upon. *Leglen* is Scottish for a milk pail, and a *leglen-girth* is the girth of a milk pail.

> Did you ever hear of the umquhile Lady Huntinglen, the departed Countess of this noble earl, ganging a wee bit gleed in her walk through the world; I mean in the way of slipping a foot, casting a leglengirth, ye understand me?
> SCOTT: *The Fortunes of Nigel*, ch. xxxii.

Leitmotiv (līt' mō tēf'). A German word meaning the "leading motive", and it is applied in music to a theme associated with a personality in an opera or similar work, repeatedly recurring to emphasize the dramatic situation. The term first came into use with Wagner. In general usage it describes any phrase or turn of thought that continually recurs with a certain association.

Lemnos. The island were VULCAN fell, when JUPITER flung him out of HEAVEN. Lemnos was mythically celebrated for two massacres. The men were said to have killed all the children of their abducted Athenian consorts, and the Lemnian women to have murdered their husbands; hence **Lemnian actions** signifies barbarous and inhuman actions. The ARGONAUTS were received with great favour by the women of Lemnos and as a result of their short stay the island was repopulated; the queen Hypsipyle became the mother of twins by JASON.

Lemnian earth. A kind of bole or clayey earth of reddish colour found in the island of Lemnos, said to cure festering wounds and snake bites. This medical earth was made into blocks and anciently stamped with the head of DIANA and hence called *terra sigillata* ("sealed earth"). It is still used locally, and a ceremonial digging of this earth took place on a particular day under the supervision of a priestess. The ceremony eventually became fixed on 6 August, the feast of Christ the Saviour in the GREEK CHURCH.

Lemon. Salts of Lemon. *See* MISNOMERS.

Lemon sole. The name of the flatfish has nothing to do with the lemon but is from Fr. *limande*, a flat board, though it may also be from Lat. *limus*, mud, the fish being essentially a bottom fish.

The answer's a lemon. Nothing doing; a suitable answer to an unreasonable or ridiculous request or question.

Lemures (lem' ū rēz). The name given by the Romans to evil spirits of the dead, especially spectres which wandered about at nighttime to terrify the living. *Cp.* LARVÆ.

> The lars and lemures moan with midnight plaint.
> MILTON: *On the Morning of the Christ's Nativity*
> (*The Hymn* xxi).

Lemuria. The lost land that is supposed to have connected Madagascar with India and Sumatra in prehistoric times. The German biologist E. H. Haeckel (1834–1919) thought that it was the original habitat of the lemur. *See* W. Scott Elliott's *The Lost Lemuria* (1904). *Cp.* ATLANTIS; LYONESSE.

Lend-Lease. Reciprocal agreements made by the U.S.A. with Great Britain and the Allied Forces in World War II to foster the pooling of resources. The policy began with the destroyers (*see* RUM-RUNNERS) sent to Great Britain in return for naval and air bases in parts of the British Commonwealth, and was formalized by the Lend-Lease Act of March 1941. When Lend-Lease ended in 1945 the United States had received somewhat less than one-sixth, in monetary terms, of what she had expended in aid to her allies, over 60 per cent of which went to the British COMMONWEALTH.

Leningrad. The name given in 1924 to Petrograd which, until 1914, was known as St. Petersburg, the former capital of Tsarist Russia founded by Peter the Great in 1703.

Lens (Lat., a lentil or bean). Glasses used in optical instruments are so called because the double convex one, which may be termed the perfect lens, is of a bean shape.

Lent (O.E. *lencten*, the spring). The Saxons called MARCH *lencten monath* because in this month the days noticeably lengthen. As the chief part of the great fast, from ASH WEDNESDAY to EATER, falls in March, it received the name *Lencten-faesten* or Lent.

The fast of 36 days was introduced in the 4th century, but it did not become fixed at 40 days until the early 7th century, thus corresponding with Our Lord's fast in the wilderness.

Lent lily. The daffodil, which blooms in LENT.

Lenten. Frugal, stinted, as food in LENT. SHAKESPEARE has "lenten entertainment" (*Hamlet*, II, ii); "a lenten answer" (*Twelfth Night*, I, v); "a lenten pye" (*Romeo and Juliet*, II, iv).

Lenten curtain, or **Lenten veil.** In the mediæval Western Church, a white curtain hung down in parish churches between the altar and the nave, and parted on feast days kept during LENT. It was taken down in the last three days of HOLY WEEK and said to betoken "the prophecy of Christ's Passion, which was hidden and unknown till these days" (*Liber Festivalis*). Similarly, all crucifixes and images were covered, a practice still followed in some Anglican churches.

Leo. A constellation, and fifth sign of the ZODIAC.

Leonard, St. A Frank at the court of Clovis in the 6th century, founder of the monastery of Noblac and patron SAINT of prisoners, Clovis having given him permission to release all whom he visited. He is usually represented as a deacon holding chains or broken fetters in his hand. His day is 6 November.

Leonidas. King of Sparta, who defended the pass of THERMOPYLAE against the Persians in 480 B.C. Only one of the 300 SPARTANS survived.

The Leonidas of Modern Greece. Marco Bozzaris, who with 1,200 men put to rout 4,000 Turco-Albanians at Kerpenisi, but was killed in the attack (1823). He was buried at Missolonghi.

Leonine (lē' ō nīn). Lion-like; also relating to one of the popes named Leo (especially Leo I); as **the Leonine City** the part of ROME surrounding the VATICAN, which was fortified by Leo IV in the 9th century.

Leonine contract. A one-sided agreement; so called in allusion to the fable of *The Lion and His Fellow Hunters*. *Cp.* GLAUCUS SWAP.

Leonine verses. Latin HEXAMETERS, or alternate hexameters and PENTAMETERS rhyming at the middle and end of each respective line. These fancies were common in the 12th century, and are said to have been popularized by and so called from Leoninus, a canon of the church of St. Victor, in Paris; but there are many such lines in the classic poets, particularly Ovid. In English verse, any metre which rhymes middle and end may be called Leonine verse.

Leopard. So called because it was thought in mediæval times to be a cross between the lion (*leo*) and the *pard*, which was the name given to a panther that had no white specks on it.

In Christian art, the leopard represents that beast spoken of in *Revelation* xiii, 1–8, with seven heads and ten horns; six of the heads bear a NIMBUS, but the seventh, being "wounded to death", lost its power, and consequently is bare.

> And the beast which I saw was like unto a leopard, and his feet were as the feet of a bear, and his mouth as the mouth of a lion.
>
> *Rev.* xiii, 2.

The leopard's head, or King's Mark, on silver is really a lion's head. It is called a leopard, because the O.Fr. heraldic term *leopard* means a lion passant gardant. *See also* THE LION IN HERALDRY *under* LION.

The leopard can never change its spots. A person's character never changes fundamentally; what's "bred in the BONE" remains. The allusion is to *Jeremiah* xiii, 23.

> *K. Richard:* Lions make leopards tame.
> *Norfolk:* Yea, but not change his spots.
>
> SHAKESPEARE: *Richard II*, I, i.

Leopolita Bible. *See* BIBLE, SOME SPECIALLY NAMED EDITIONS.

Leprechaun (lep' rà kawn). The fairy shoemaker of Ireland, so called because he is always seen working at a single shoe (*leith*, half; *brog*, a shoe or brogue). Another of his peculiarities is that he has a purse that never contains more than a single shilling.

> Do you not catch the tiny clamour,
> Busy click of an elfin hammer,
> Voice of the Leprecaun singing shrill,
> As he merrily plies his trade.
>
> WM. ALLINGHAM: *The Leprecaun;*
> *or Fairy Shoemaker*.

He is also called lubrican, CLURICAUNE, etc. In Dekker and Middleton's *Honest Whore* (Pt. II, III, i), Hippolito speaks of Bryan, the Irish footman, as "your Irish footman, as "your Irish lubrican".

Lernæan Hydra. *See* HYDRA.

Lesbian. Pertaining to Lesbos, one of the islands of the Greek Archipelago, or to SAP-

PHO, the famous poetess of Lesbos, and the homosexual practices attributed to her.

The Lesbian Poets. Terpander, Alcæus, Arion, and SAPPHO, all of whom came from Lesbos.

The Lesbian rule. A flexible rule used by ancient Greek masons for measuring curved mouldings, etc.; hence, figuratively, a pliant and accommodating principle or rule of conduct.

Lèse-majesté (lez mazh′ estā) (Fr. from Lat. *læsa majestas*, injured or violated majesty). A phrase commonly applied to presumptuous conduct on the part of the inferiors who do not show sufficient respect for their "betters". The legal phrase **Lese-majesty** (lēz) denotes TREASON, a crime against the sovereign.

Lestrigons, or **Læstrygones.** A fabulous race of cannibal giants who lived in Sicily. ULYSSES (*Odyss.*, X) sent two sailors and a messenger to request that he might land, but the king of the place ate one for dinner and the other fled. The Lestrigons gathered on the coast and threw stones at Ulysses and his crew; they departed with all speed, but many men were lost. *Cp.* POLYPHEMUS.

Let. Let her go, Gallagher! (Austr.). Let's get going, let's start without delay. Tom Gallagher was a well-known driver in Queensland for COBB AND CO.

Letter-gae. A jocular Scottish name (after Allan Ramsay, 1686–1758) for the precentor of a kirk, he who leads off the singing, and lets go.

> There were no sae money hairs on the warlock's face as there's on Letter-gae's ain at this moment.
>
> SCOTT: *Guy Mannering*, ch. xi.

To let down. To disappoint; not to keep faith or trust; to fail in an obligation.

To let off steam. To give vent to pent up feelings in words, or to work off superabundant energy and high spirits in vigorous physical activity. From the noisy escape of steam from the safety valve of a steam locomotive.

To let up. To relax; to cease to act vigorously; to ease up.

Lethe (lē′ thi). In Greek mythology, one of the rivers of HADES, which the souls of all the dead are obliged to taste, that they may forget everything said and done when alive. The word means "forgetfulness".

> Here, in a dusky vale where Lethe rolls
> Old Bavius sits, to dip poetic souls,
> And blunt the sense.
>
> POPE: *Dunciad*, III, 23.

Letter. The name of a character used to represent a sound, and of a missive or written message. Through O.Fr. *lettre*, from Lat.

littera, a letter of the alphabet, the plural of which (*litteræ*) denoted an epistle. The plural, with the meaning literature, learning, erudition (as in *man of letters, republic of letters*, etc.), dates in English at least from the time of King Alfred, and is seen in CICERO'S *otium literatum*, lettered ease.

There are 26 letters in the English alphabet, but in a fount of type over 200 characters are required; these being made up of small letters (LOWER CASE, capitals, and small capitals; included also are the dipthongs (Æ, æ etc.) and ligatures (ff, fi, fl, ffi, ffl), accented letters, figures, fractions, points (, ; : ! ?, etc.), brackets, reference marks, and the common commercial and mathematical signs (£, %, +, ÷ etc.). *See* FONT.

Letter of Bellerophon. *See* BELLEROPHON.

Letter of Credit. A letter written by a merchant or banker to another, requesting him to credit the bearer with certain sums of money. *Circular notes* are letters of credit carried by travellers.

Letter of the law. To keep to the letter of the law is to observe it strictly; to follow out the regulations thoroughly and to avoid breaking them.

Letter of Licence. An instrument in writing made by a creditor, allowing a debtor longer time for payment of his debt.

Letter of Marque. A commission from the crown making a merchantman a PRIVATEER or legalized ship of war able to take reprisals on a hostile nation. Without such authorization the vessel would be a pirate. Marque is from Provençal *marcar*, Med. Lat. *marcare*, to seize as a pledge.

Letter of safe conduct. A writ under the GREAT SEAL, guaranteeing safety to and from to the person named in the passport.

Letter of Slains. In old Scottish law, a petition to the crown from the relatives of a murdered person, declaring that they have received satisfaction (*assythment*), and asking pardon for the murderer.

Letter of Uriah. *See* URIAH.

Letter-lock. A lock that cannot be opened unless letters on exterior movable rings are arranged in a certain order.

> A strange lock that opens with A M E N.
>
> BEAUMONT and FLETCHER: *The Noble Gentleman*.

Letters Missive. An official letter from the Lord CHANCELLOR to a peer requesting him to put in an appearance to a bill filed in CHANCERY and sent in lieu of a summons; also a letter from the sovereign to a DEAN and CHAPTER nominating the person to be elected BISHOP.

Letters Patent, or **Overt.** *See* PATENT.

Letters of Administration. The legal instrument granted by the Probate Court to a person appointed administrator to one who has died intestate.

Letters of Credence, or **Letters Credential.** Formal documents with which a diplomatic agent is furnished accrediting him on his appointment to a post at the seat of a foreign government. They are signed by the sovereign or head of the state and he is not officially recognized until his letters have been presented.

Letters of Horning. In Scottish law, a process issued under the signet instructing a messenger to charge a debtor to pay under penalty of caption if he fails to do so. *Cp.* TO PUT TO THE HORN *under* HORN.

Letters of Junius. *See* JUNIUS.

Lettres de Cachet. *See* CACHET.

Leucothea (The White Goddess). So Ino, the mortal daughter of CADMUS and wife of Athamas, was called after she became a sea goddess. Athamas in a fit of madness slew one of her sons; she threw herself into the sea with the other, imploring assistance of the gods, who deified both of them. Her son, then renamed PALÆMON, was called by the Romans Portunus or Portumnus, and became the protecting genius of harbours.

Levant (le vănt'). **He has levanted,** *i.e.* made off, decamped. a *levanter* is an absconder, especially one who makes a bet and runs away without paying if he loses. From Span. *levantar el campo*, or *la casa*, to break up the camp or house.

Levant and Couchant (lev' ănt, kou' chănt) (Fr. rising up and lying down). In legal parlance, cattle which have strayed into another's field, and have been there long enough to lie down and sleep. The owner of the field can demand compensation for such intrusion.

Levant and Ponent Winds. The east wind is the Levant, and the west wind the Ponent. The former is from Lat. *levare*, to raise (sunrise), and the latter from *ponere*, to set (sunset).

Forth rush the Levant and the Ponent winds.
MILTON: *Paradise Lost*, X, 704.

Levant, the region, strictly applies to the eastern shore of the Mediterranean, but is often used to denote the lands from Greece to Egypt. In the 16th and 17th centuries the Far East was sometimes known as the High Levant.

Levee (le' vi) (Fr. *lever*, to rise). A morning assembly or reception. In Britain the word is particularly associated with the royal levees formerly held at St. James's Palace, official occasions when the sovereign received men only, most usually in the afternoon. Before the French Revolution, it was customary for the French monarch to receive visitors (court physicians, nobles, messengers, etc.) at the time of this *levée—i.e.* while making his morning toilet on rising from bed.

The word *levee* is also applied to an embankment.

Levée en masse (Fr.). A levy of all the able-bodied men of a country for its defence or other military service.

On the twenty-third of August, Committee of Public Salvation, as usual through Barrère, had promulgated in words ... their Report, which is soon made into a Law, of Levy in Mass.
CARLYLE: *The French Revolution*, Pt. III, Bk. iv, ch. vi.

Level. On the level. Honest and sincere in whatever one is doing or saying. A term from FREEMASONRY.

To do one's level best. To do one's utmost. An expression originating in the Californian gold-diggings.

To find one's own level. To arrive at that position in society, or in an occupation, etc., best suited to one's gifts and attainments.

To level up, or **down.** To raise or lower to another level, status, or condition.

Your levellers wish to level down as far as themselves; but they cannot bear levelling up to themselves.
DR. JOHNSON: *Remark to Boswell*, 1763.

Level-headed. Shrewd, business-like, full of common sense; said of one who "has his head screwed on the right way".

Level pegging. To have even scores in a contest or an equality of achievements with another person. The expression is from those games (e.g. cribbage) in which a peg-board is used for scoring.

Levellers. In Cromwellian times, a group of RADICAL republicans who wanted the franchise for "freeborn Englishmen" (this did not necessarily include servants and labourers) and who were prominent at London and in the ranks of the Army until their power was broken by Cromwell, after the mutinies of 1647 and 1649. Their influence waned steadily, especially after the suppression (1652–1653) of their leader, John LILBURNE.

In Irish history, the WHITEBOYS were also called *Levellers. Cp.* ACEPHALITES.

Lever de Rideau (lev' ă de rē' dō) (Fr. curtain-raiser). A short sketch, etc., performed on the stage before the main play begins.

Leviathan (le vī' ǎ thǎn). The Hebrew name for a monster of the waters. In *Job* xli, 1, and *Ps.* lxxiv, 14, it appears to refer to the crocodile; in *Ps.* civ, 26, it is probably the whale;

and in *Is*. xxvii, 1, it is a sea-serpent.

> This great and wide sea, wherein are things creeping innumerable, both small and great beasts. There go the ships: there is that leviathan, whom thou hast made to play therein.
>
> *Ps*. civ, 26.

Hence the name is applied to any huge sea-animal or ship of great size.

> Like leviathans afloat,
> Lay their bulwarks on the brine.
> T. CAMPBELL: *The Battle of the Baltic*.

Hobbes took the name as the title for his famous treatise on "the Matter, Forme, and Power of a Commonwealth Ecclesiastical and Civil" (1651) from the Scriptures as he also did for his BEHEMOTH. His *Leviathan* is the absolute state.

> I have set forth the nature of man (whose Pride and other Passions have compelled him to submit himselfe to Government;) together with the great power of his Governour, whom I compared to Leviathan, taking that comparison out of the two last verses of the one and fortieth of Job; where God having set forth the great power of Leviathan, called him King of the Proud.
>
> *Leviathan*: Pt. II, ch. xxviii.

The Leviathan of Literature. Dr. Johnson (1709–1784). *Cp*. CHAM.

Levitation is a term applied to the phenomenon of heavy bodies rising and floating in the air. It is frequently mentioned in Hindu and other writings, and is a not uncommon attribute of Roman Catholic saints. Joseph of Cupertino (1603–1663) was the subject of such frequent levitation that he was forbidden by his superiors to attend choir, and performed his devotions privately where he would not distract others. D. D. Home was alleged by Sir W. Crookes to have this power. Science has not yet found an explanation.

Lex (Lat., law).
Lex non scripta (Lat., unwritten law). The COMMON LAW as distinct from STATUTE or written law. It does not derive its force from being recorded, such compilations being simply remembrancers.
Lex talionis (Lat.). The law of retaliation; TIT FOR TAT.

Lia-fail. The Irish name for the Coronation Stone, or Stone of Destiny, of the ancient Irish Kings. *See* SCONE; TANIST STONE.

Liars. Liars should have good memories. An old proverb in many languages, quoted by St. JEROME in the 4th century and traced to Quintilian's *Mendacem memorem esse oportet*, "It is fitting that a liar should be a man of good memory" (*Institutes*, IV, ii, 91). It also occurs in Erasmus's *Proverbs* (1539) and Montaigne's *Essays* (I, ix).

Libel. Originally the word denoted a little book (Lat. *libellus*), as in *The Libel of English Policy* (*c*. 1436), the title of a poetical essay advocating a strong navy. Also a plaintiff's statement of his case, which often "defames" the defendant, was called a libel, for it made a "little book". Today it usually applies to a written defamation and is actionable.

In 1637 the three PURITANS, Prynne, Burton and Bastwick, among other punishments, were branded on the cheeks and forehead with the letters "S.L." for "seditious libeller". Prynne later interpreted them as representing *Stigmata Laudi*.

The greater the truth, the greater the libel, a dictum of Lord Ellenborough (1750–1818), who amplified it by the explanation—"if the language used were true, the person would suffer more than if it were false."

Burns, in *The Reproof*, attributes the saying to Lord Mansfield:

> Dost not know that old Mansfield, who writes like the Bible,
> Says: "The more 'tis a truth, sir, the more 'tis a libel"?

Liber (Lat., a book).
Liber Albus (Lat., the white book). A compilation of the laws and customs of the City of LONDON, made in 1419 by John Carpenter, town clerk.
Liber Niger. *See* BLACK BOOK.

Liberal. as a political term, came to be applied to the more "advanced" Whigs in the early 19th century and acquired respectability after the Reform Act of 1832, when the name gradually supplanted that of WHIG. The first administration generally called Liberal was that of Gladstone (1868–1874), the last, that of Asquith (1908–1915). In March 1988 the Liberals merged with Social Democratic Party members to form the Social and Liberal Democrats. A minority of the S.D.P. continued under the leadership of David Owen.

Liberal Nationals, or **National Liberals.** Those Liberals who supported the NATIONAL GOVERNMENTS formed after the financial crisis of 1931 and who remained in close co-operation with the CONSERVATIVE party.

Liberal Unionists. Those Liberals who supported the maintenance of the parliamentary union with IRELAND and who opposed Gladstone's HOME RULE measures. From 1886, under Lord Hartington and Joseph Chamberlain, they supported the CONSERVATIVES.

Liberator, The. Simon Bolivar (1783–1830), who established the independence of Bolivia, Columbia, Ecuador, Panama, Peru and

Venezuela from Spain in 1825.

Daniel O'Connell (1755–1847), who secured emancipation for Roman Catholics in 1829, was also thus styled. The title derived from the "Order of Liberators" which he founded in 1826 and which was open to anyone who had done an act of service to Ireland. He was also known as "The Counsellor".

Liberator of the World. A name given to Benjamin Franklin (1706–1790).

Libertine. A free-thinker in religion and morals, hence (more commonly) a debauchee, a profligate; one who puts no restraint on his personal indulgence. The application of the word to 16th-century ANABAPTIST sects in the Low Countries and certain of Calvin's opponents at Geneva had derogatory implications. In the NEW TESTAMENT (*Acts* vi, 9) it is probably used to mean a freedman (Lat. *libertinus*):

> Then there arose certain of the synagogue, which is called the synagogue of the Libertines, ... disputing with Stephen.

Liberty. Freedom from restraint or control (Lat. *liber*, free).

Cap of Liberty. *See under* CAP.

Civil liberty. Freedom from arbitrary restraint in the citizen's conduct of his own affairs; limited only by the laws established on behalf of the community.

Natural liberty. Unrestricted liberty limited only by the laws of nature.

Political liberty. The freedom of a nation from any unjust abridgement of its rights and independence; also the right of the citizen to participate in political government and public office.

Press, Liberty of the. The right to publish without censorshop or restraint, subject to the laws of LIBEL and proper judicial processes.

Religious liberty. The freedom to adopt whatever religious beliefs or opinions one chooses and to practise them, provided such freedom in no way interferes with the equal liberty of others.

Liberty Enlightening the World. The colossal statue standing on Bedloe's (or Liberty) Island at the entrance of New York Harbour, presented to the American people by the Republic of France in commemoration of the centenary of the American Declaration of INDEPENDENCE. It was unveiled in 1886 and is the work of the Alsatian sculptor Frédéric-Auguste Bartholdi (1834–1904). The bronze, 151 ft. high (standing on a pedestal 154 ft. high) is of a woman, draped, and holding a lighted torch in her upraised hand.

The statue of Liberty, placed over the entrance of the Palais Royal, Paris, was modelled from Mme Tallien, "Notre-Dame-de-Thermidor".

The price of liberty is eternal vigilance. This oft-quoted maxim is found in a speech made in 1790 by the Irish judge John Philpot Curran (1750–1817), in which he said that "The condition upon which God hath given liberty to man is eternal vigilance." The phrase "eternal vigilance is the price of Liberty" was apparently first used by Wendell Phillips (1811–1884), the American reformer, in 1852.

Liberty boat. The boat taking seamen from a ship for shore leave, such passengers being designated **liberty men.**

Liberty Hall. The numerous applications of this descriptive phrase may be gathered from Goldsmith's definition—

> This is Liberty-hall, gentlemen. You may do just as you please here.
> *She Stoops to Conquer*, II, i

Dibdin has an opera *Liberty Hall*, which was first performed in 1785.

Liberty horses. Circus horses that perform evolutions without riders.

Liberty Ships. Standardized prefabricated cargo ships of about 10,000 tons much used by the U.S.A. during World War II.

Liberty Tree, or Pole. In America, the first so called was an elm on Boston Common. A pole inscribed "To his Gracious Majesty George III, Mr. Pitt, and Liberty" was set up in New York in 1766. It was cut down by the British four times, but the fifth remained for ten years.

Liberties. In mediæval England, areas of varying extent free from royal jurisdictions in whole or in part, such as the Marcher lordships (*see* MARCHES) and Palatine earldoms (*see* PALATINATE). The areas belonging to the City of London immediately without the City walls were called *liberties* and in course of time were attached to the nearest ward within the walls. *Cp.* TOWER LIBERTY.

The Liberties of the Fleet. *See under* FLEET.

To take liberties. To be unduly familiar, to over-presume; not to be overscrupulous in handling facts or observing rules.

Libitina. In ancient Italy, the goddess who presided over funerals, her name often being a synonym for death itself. The Romans identified her with PROSERPINA.

Libra (Lat., the balance). The seventh sign of the ZODIAC and the name of one of the ancient constellations, which the SUN enters about 22 September and leaves about 22 October. At this time the day and night being "weighed" would be found equal.

Library. Before the invention of paper the thin inner bark of certain trees was used for writing on; this was in Lat. called *liber*, which came in time to signify also a "book". Hence our *library*, the place for books; and *librarian*, the keeper of books.

A circulating library. A library from which books may be borrowed and taken by members to their homes.

Famous libraries. Strabo says that ARISTOTLE was the first to own a private library. From an uncertain date, there were public libraries in ATHENS, and these were known to Demetrius of Phalerum (4th century B.C.) who suggested to Ptolemy I the founding of a library at Alexandria. This was begun but greatly increased by Ptolemy II and Alexandria became the great library centre of the Greek world. It continued to flourish under the Romans but decline and destruction set in from the end of the 4th century A.D.

Among the numerous great libraries of modern Europe, the VATICAN Library is especially notable for its antiquity and manuscript wealth. The present building was erected by Sixtus V in 1588 and it contains some 905,000 vols. and 60,000 MSS. The Biblioteca Mediceo-Laurenziana, Florence (opened to the public in 1571), has a particularly fine collection of precious classical MSS. Others are the great national libraries, such as the Biblioteca Nazionale Centrale at ROME, founded in 1875; the Biblioteca Nacional, Madrid (founded 1716, formerly the Royal Library); the Bibliothèque Nationale, PARIS (originating under Charles V and re-created under Louis XI); the Lenin State Library, Moscow (formerly the Rumyantzov Museum Collection), among the largest in the world with some 10,000,000 vols. The library of the Academy of Sciences in Leningrad is a noteworthy example of the specialized library.

The British Library, founded as the BRITISH MUSEUM library in 1753, is world-famous, with about 6,500,000 vols. and 75,000 MSS. The BODLEIAN LIBRARY, Oxford (1598), includes the original University Library based on the collection of Humphrey, Duke of Gloucester, and has c. 2,250,000 vols. and a large MSS. collection. Cambridge University Library (15th century) has 2,000,000 vols., 225,000 maps, and some 17,000 MSS. John Rylands Library, Manchester, founded 1888, has a notable collection of MSS. The oldest library in Scotland is that of St. Andrews University, founded in 1456. The National Library of

Scotland was founded as the ADVOCATES LIBRARY. The National Library of Wales was founded at Aberystwyth in 1907. The Library of Trinity College, Dublin, possesses many valuable MSS. as well as the BOOK OF KELLS. All thse libraries (except John Rylands and St. Andrews) possess the copyright privilege.

The oldest library in the U.S.A. is that of Harvard University (1638) which has over 7,245,000 vols. The Library of Congress, founded in 1800, has some 14,000,000 books and pamphlets and over 18,000,000 MSS., plus maps (over 2,000,000) and music (over 3,000,000 volumes and pieces) and is probably the largest library in the world. New York Public Library has c. 7,000,000 vols. and 9,000,000 manuscript letters and documents. The Henry E. Huntington Library and Art Gallery, San Marino, California, is noted for rare books, and the Pierpont Morgan Library, New York, for INCUNABULA and MSS. Folger Shakespeare Library, Wahington, D.C., with 250,000 vols., has the largest collection of Shakespeareana in the world. It must, however, be stressed that figures for holdings of larger libraries can only be approximate and comparison is difficult due to different methods of computation.

Lich. A body (O.E. *lik*).

Lich fowls. Birds that feed on carrion, as night-ravens, etc.

Lich-gate. The covered entrance to churchyards intended to afford shelter to the coffin and mourners while awaiting the clergyman who is to conduct the cortège into church.

Lich-owl. The screech-owl, superstitiously supposed to foretell death.

Lich-wake, or **Lyke-wake.** The funeral feast or the *waking* of a corpse, *i.e.* watching it all night.

In a pastoral written by Ælfric in 998 for Wilfsige, Bishop of Sherborne, the attendance of the clergy at lyke-wakes is forbidden.

Lich-way. The path by which a funeral is conveyed to church, which not infrequently deviates from the ordinary road. It was long supposed that wherever a dead body passed became a public thoroughfare.

Lick. A lick and a promise. A superficial wash or clean up, as a cat might give a quick lick to its face.

I licked him. I flogged or beat him. A licking is a thrashing, or, in games, a defeat.

To go at a great lick, To run, ride, etc., at a great speed.

To lick a man's boots, shoes, etc. To CUR-

RY FAVOUR, to be abjectly servile, to be a LICKSPITTLE or BOOTLICKER.

To lick into shape. To make presentable; to bring children up well, etc. Derived from the widespread mediæval belief that bear cubs are born shapeless and have to be licked into shape by their mothers. The story gained currency apparently from the Arab physician AVICENNA (979–1037) who tells it in his encyclopædia.

To lick one's lips. To give evident signs of the enjoyment of anticipation.

To lick the dust, or **the ground.** *See* TO KISS THE DUST *under* KISS.

Lickpenny. Something or someone that makes the money go—that "licks up" the pennies. Lydgate (*c.* 1370–*c.* 1451) wrote a humorous poem called *London Lyckpenny* in which he shows that life in London makes the money fly.

Lickspittle. A toady; the meanest of sycophants.

Lictors. Binders (Lat. *ligo*, I bind or tie). These Roman officers were so called because they bound the hands and feet of criminals before they executed the sentence of the law.

Lido (lē′ dō). An outdoor bathing-place, usually with sunbathing facilities and often providing entertainments, etc. The name is taken from the sandy island called the Lido, facing the Adriatic outside Venice, and a fashionable bathing resort.

Lansbury's Lido. The bathing-place on the bank of the Serpentine in Hyde Park, London, sponsored by George Lansbury when First Commissioner of Works in the second Labour government (1929–1931).

Lie. A falsehood (O.E. *lyge*; from *leogan*, to lie).

The greatest lie. In Heywood's *Four P's*, an interlude (*c.* 1544), a Palmer, a Pardoner, a Poticary, and a Pedlar disputed as to which could tell the greatest lie. The Palmer said he had never seen a woman out of patience; whereupon the other three threw up the SPONGE, saying such falsehood could not possibly be outdone.

The lie circumstantial, direct, etc. *See* COUNTERCHECK QUARRELSOME.

A lie hath no feet. Because it cannot stand alone. In fact, a lie wants twenty others to support it, and even then is in constant danger of tripping. *Cp.* LIARS SHOULD HAVE GOOD MEMORIES.

A white lie. A conventional lie, such as telling a caller that Mrs. X is not at home (*see under* HOME).

To give one the lie. To accuse him to his face of telling a falsehood.

To give the lie to. To show that such a statement is false; to belie.

The Father of Lies. SATAN (*John* viii, 44).

Lie detector. An American invention which records the heart beats of a man under questioning. It is based on the supposedly proven assumption that a human being cannot tell a lie without the pulse of his heart increasing, and this increase of pulsation is recorded. In some States of the Union, the findings of this device are accepted as legal evidence.

Lie (O.E. *licgan*, to bide or rest).

To lie at the catch. In Bunyan's *Pilgrim's Progress* (ch. xii), Talkative says to Faithful, "You lie at the catch, I perceive." To which Faithful replies, "No, not I; I am only for setting things right." To lie at or on the catch is to lie in wait or to lay a trap to catch one.

To lie in. To be confined in childbirth; to stay in bed beyond one's usual time of rising.

To lie in state. Said of a corpse of a royal or distinguished person that is displayed to the general public.

To lie low. To conceal oneself or one's intentions; to avoid notice.

All this while Brer Rabbit lay low.
JOEL CHANDLER HARRIS: *Uncle Remus*.

To lie over. To be deferred; as, "This question must lie over till next session."

To lie to. To stop the progress of a vessel at sea by reducing the sails and counterbracing the yards (in a power-driven vessel, to slow down the engines) and to keep head to wind; hence to cease from doing something.

To lie to one's work. To work energetically.

To lie up. To refrain from work, especially through ill health; to rest.

To lie with one's fathers. To be buried in one's native place or with one's ancestors.

I will lie with my fathers, and thou shalt carry me out of Egypt.
Gen. xlvii, 30.

Lieutenant (in the British Army, lef ten′ ånt; in the U.S.A., loo ten′ ånt; in the Royal Navy, lå ten′ ånt). It is from the Lat. *locum-tenens* through the Fr. In combination with other ranks and offices it has the general implication of deputy or subordinate as, *Lord Lieutenant*, *Lieutenant Governor*, *Lieutenant-General*.

Lord Lieutenant. *See under* LORD.

Life (O.E. *lif*). **Drawn from life.** Drawn or described from some real person or object.

For life. As long as life continues.

For the life of me. True as I am alive. Even if my life depended on it.

Nor could I for my life see how the creation of the world had anything to do with what I was talking about.
GOLDSMITH: *Vicar of Wakefield*, ch. xiv.

High life. The life of high society.

Large as life. Of the same size as the object represented, life size; in person, in the flesh, "Here she is, large as life."

Low life. The life of the poor and lower grades of society.

On my life. I will answer for it by my life.

To bear a charmed life. To escape accidents or danger with amazing good luck.

To see life. To "KNOCK ABOUT" town, where life may be seen at its fullest; to move in smart or fast society.

To the life. In exact imitation. "Done to the life."

Life Guards. The senior cavalry regiment of the HOUSEHOLD TROOPS, the members of which are not less than six feet tall; hence a fine, tall, manly fellow was called "a regular Life Guardsman".

Life preserver. A loaded short stick for self-defence; also a buoyant jacket, belt, etc., to support the human body in water.

Still life. In artistic representation, inanimate objects such as books, furniture, fruit, etc.

Lift. To have one at a lift is to have one in one's power. When a wrestler has his antagonist in his hands and lifts him from the ground, he has him "at a lift", or in his power.

"Sirra," says he, "I have you at a lift.
Now you are come unto your latest shift."
PERCY: *Reliques (Guy and Amarant)*.

Air-lift. An organized manœuvre to transport troops or stores to a destination by air. The Berlin air-lift, to victual the British and American zones of the city after the Russian embargo on all land transport, began 26 June 1948, and ended 12 May 1949, having made 195,530 flights and carried 1,414,000 tons of food, coal and other stores.

Lifter. A thief, one who lifts to purloin. We still speak of a "shop-lifter" and *lifter* is a Scottish term for a cattle-stealer.

Is he so young a man, and so old a lifter?
SHAKESPEARE: *Troilus and Cressida*, I, ii.

In 18th-century English "a lifter" denoted a heavy drinker. *Cp.* ELBOW-LIFTING.

Lifting the little finger. *See* FINGER.

Ligan, or **Lagan** *See* FLOTSAM AND JETSAM.

Light. (O.E. *leoht*). The O.E. is the same for both senses of this word, *i.e.* illumination and smallness of weight, but in the former sense it is the O.H.Ger. *lioht* and in the latter O.H.Ger. *liht*.

Ancient lights. *See under* ANCIENT.

Inner Light. Inward or spiritual light; knowledge divinely imparted; as used by QUAKERS, the light of Christ in the soul.

Quakers (that, like to lanthorns, bear

Their light within 'em) will not swear.
BUTLER: *Hudibras*, II, ii.

The Light of the Age. Maimonides or Rabbi Moses ben Maimon of Cordova (1135–1204).

The Light of Asia. Gautama BUDDHA. *The Light of Asia, or the Great Renunciation* was the name given by Sir Edwin Arnold to his famous narrative poem dealing with the life and teachings of Buddha (1879).

The Light of the World (Lat. *Lux Mundi*). Jesus Christ; allegoricaly portrayed by Holman Hunt in his famous picture (1854) showing Christ carrying a lantern knocking at the door of the soul. Sir Arthur Sullivan has an oratorio of this title (1873); and Sir Edwin Arnold a poem (1891) in which Christ is the central figure as the founder of Christianity. *Cp.* LIGHT OF ASIA.

Then spake Jesus unto them, saying, I am the light of the world: he that followeth me shall not walk in darkness, but shall have the light of life.
John viii, 12.

The light of thy countenance. God's smile of approbation and love.

Lift thou up the light of thy countenance upon us.
Ps. iv, 6.

According to his lights. According to his information or knowledge of the matter; according to his way of looking at things.

Before the lights. In theatrical parlance, on the stage, *i.e.* before the foot-lights.

Light o' love. An inconstant capricious or loose woman; a harlot.

Men of light and leading. Men capable of illuminating the way and guiding the steps of others. The phrase is Burke's:

The men of England, the men, I mean, of light and leading in England ... would be ashamed ... to profess any religion in name, which by their proceedings, they appear to contemn.
Reflections on the Revolution in France.

He seems to have derived it from Milton, who, in his *Addresses to the Parliament*, prefixed to his notes on the *Judgment of Martin Bucer Concerning Divorce*, says:

I owe no light, or leading received from any man in the discovery of this truth, what time I first undertook it in "the Doctrine and Discipline of Divorce".

Light gains make a heavy purse. Small profits and a quick return is the best way of gaining wealth.

The light of one's eye. A much loved one.

To bring to light. To discover and expose; to reveal.

The duke yet would have dark deeds darkly answered; he would never bring them to light.
SHAKESPEARE: *Measure for Measure*, III, ii.

To light upon. To come across by chance; to discover by accident. Thus, Dr. Johnson wrote to Mrs. Thrale: "How did you light upon your specifick for the tooth-ach?"

To make light of. To treat as of no importance; to take little notice of.

> Behold, I have prepared my dinner: my oxen and my fatlings are killed, and all things are ready: come unto the marriage.
> But they made light of it, and went their ways, one to his farm, another to his merchandise.
> *Matt*. xxii, 4, 5.

To put out one's light. To kill him, "send him into the outer darkness". SHAKESPEARE'S Othello says, "Put out the light and then put put out the light" (V, ii), meaning first the light in the room and then Desdemona's light (life).

To see the light. To be born; to be converted; to come to a full understanding or realization of something.

To stand in one's own light. To act in such a way as to hinder one's own advancement.

To throw, or **shed light upon.** To elucidate, to explain.

Light comedian. One who takes humorous, but not low parts.

Light-fingered. *See under* FINGER.

Light Horse Harry. Nickname of Henry Lee (1756–1818), American cavalry officer and father of the Confederate Commander-in-Chief, Robert E. Lee. He defeated the British at Paulus Hook in the War of Independence.

Light Infantry. In the British Army, infantry carrying less equipment than normal and trained to manœuvre at high speed. they were introduced into the British Army by Sir John Moore (1761–1809).

Light troops. A term formerly applied to light cavalry, *i.e.* lancers and hussars, who were neither such large men as the "Heavies" or DRAGOONS, nor so heavily equipped: it also applies to lightly equipped forces generally.

Light Year. A scientific unit for measuring stellar distances. Light travels at the rate of 186,000 miles per second; a light year, or the distance travelled by light in a year, is about 6 million million miles.

Lighthouse. *See* PHAROS.

Lighthouse of the Mediterranean. The name given to the volcano Stromboli, one of the Lipari Islands in the Tyrrhenian Sea.

Lightning. Hamilcar (d. 228 B.C.), the Carthaginian general, was called "Barca", the Phœnician for "lightning" (Heb. *Barak*), both on account of the rapidity of his march and for the severity of his attacks.

Chain lightning. Two or more flashes of lightning repeated without intermission.

Forked lightning. Zigzag lightning.

Globular lightning. A ball of fire which sometimes falls on the earth and flies off with an explosion.

Sheet lightning. A diffuse discharge, caused by a flash of lightning in a cloud, or cloud to cloud discharge.

Lightning conductor. A metal rod raised above a building in metallic contact with the earth, to carry off the lightning and prevent its injuring the building. Benjamin Franklin (1706–1790) was the inventor.

Lightning preservers. The EAGLE, the sea-calf, and the LAUREL were the most approved classical preservatives against lightning. JUPITER chose the first, Augustus CÆSAR the second, and Tiberius the third (Columella, x; Suetonius in *Vit. Aug.*, xc; ditto in *Vit. Tib.*, lxix). *Cp.* HOUSE-LEEK.

Liguria. The ancient name of a part of Cisalpine GAUL, and now a modern territorial division of Italy including the provinces of Genoa, Imperia, Savona, and Spezia. NAPOLEON founded a "Ligurian Republic" with Genoa as its capital, and embracing also Venetia and a part of Sardinia. It was annexed to France in 1805.

The Ligurian Sage. Aulus Persius Flaccus (A.D. 34–63), born at Volaterræ, in Etruria, and famous for his *Satires*.

Like Billyo, or **Billio** With great gusto or enthusiasm. Among the suggested origins of the slang term are (1) that Joseph Billio, rector of Wickham Bishops, ejected for nonconformity and first NONCONFORMIST minister of Maldon (1696), was noted for his energy and enthusiasm; (2) one of Garibaldi's Lieutenants, a SWASHBUCKLER, Nino Biglio, used to dash enthusiastically into action shouting "I am Biglio! Follow me, you rascals, and fight like Biglio!" (3) that it has arisen from George Stephenson's locomotive "Puffing Billy" and "Puffing like Billy-o" and "running like Billy-o" were common phrases.

Lilburne. If no one else were alive, John would quarrel with Lilburne. John Lilburne was a leader of the LEVELLERS and much given to quarrelling with authority in many forms.

> Is John departed? and is Lilburne gone?
> Farewell to both—to Lilburne and to John.
> Yet, being gone, take this advice from me.
> Let them not both in one grave buried be.
> Here lay ye John, lay Lilburne thereabout;
> For if they both should meet, they would fall out.
> *Epigrammatic Epitaph.*

Lilith. A night monster and VAMPIRE, probably of Babylonian origin, supposed to haunt wildernesses in stormy weather, and to be especially dangerous to children. The name is from a Semitic root meaning "night" which was the special time of this demon's activities. In Rabbinical writings, she is supposed to have been the first wife of ADAM. *See* THE DEVIL AND HIS DAM *under* DEVIL. She is referred to in *Is*. xxxiv, 14, as the "screech-owl" in the Authorized Version; in the Revised Version as the "night-monster", and in the VULGATE as LAMIA. A superstitious cult of Lilith persisted among certain Jews until the 7th century. Goethe introduced her in his *Faust*, and Rossetti in his *Eden Bower* made the serpent the instrument of Lilith's vengeance—

> "Help, sweet snake, sweet lover of Lilith!
> (Alas the hour!)
> And let God learn how I loved and hated
> Men in the image of God created."

Lilliburlero (lil′ i bĕr lēr′ ō). The refrain of a piece of political doggerel written by Lord Thomas Wharton (1648–1716) which influenced popular sentiment at the time of the GLORIOUS REVOLUTION of 1688. Burnet says, "It made an impression on the [King's] army that cannot be imagined.... The whole army, and at last the people, both in city and country, were singing it perpetually ... never had so slight a thing so great an effect". The Orange Lily was the symbol of the Irish supporters of William of Orange and the words *Lilliburlero Bullenala* are apparently a corruption of the Erse *An lile ba léir é ba linn an lá* (the lily was triumphant and we won the day).

The song is referred to in *Tristram Shandy*, and is given in PERCY'S RELIQUES. The air is attributed to Purcell but it has been traced back to a book of psalm-tunes published at Antwerp in 1540.

> Wharton afterwards boasted that he had sung a king out of three kingdoms. But in truth, the success of Lilliburlero was the effect, and not the cause, of that excited state of public feeling which produced the Revolution.
> MACAULAY: *History of England*, ch. ix.

Lili Marlene. A German song of World War II (based on a poem written by a German soldier, Hans Leip, in 1917) composed by Norbert Schultze in 1938 and sung by the German singer Lale Andersen. It became increasingly popular during the 1940s, especially with the Afrika Korps, and the recorded version was played nightly by Radio Belgrade from the late summer of 1941 virtually until the end of hostilities. Other German stations plugged it and it was picked up and adopted by the British 8th Army, the English version of the lyric being by T. Connor. There were French, Italian and numerous other renderings of what became the classic song of the war.

> Underneath the lantern
> By the barrack gate,
> Darling I remember
> The way you used to wait
> ....
> My Lili of the lamplight,
> My own Lili Marlene.

Lilliput. The land of pigmies or Lilliputians (Swift: *Gulliver's Travels*).

Lily, The. There is a tradition that the lily sprang from the repentant tears of EVE as she went forth from PARADISE.

In Christian art the lily is an emblem of chastity, innocence, and purity, In pictures of the ANNUNCIATION, GABRIEL is sometimes represented as carrying a lily-branch, while a vase containing a lily stands before the Virgin who is kneeling in prayer. St. JOSEPH holds a lily-branch in his hand, indicating that his wife Mary was a virgin.

The lily in the field in *Matt*. vi, 29, "that even Solomon in all his glory was not arrayed like one of these", is the wild lily, probably a species of iris. Our "lily of the valley", with which this is sometimes confused, is a different plant, one of the genus *Convallaria*.

Lily of France. The device of Clovis was three black toads, but the story goes that an aged hermit of Joye-en-valle saw a miraculous light stream into his cell one night and an ANGEL appeared to him holding an azure shield of wonderful beauty, emblazoned with three gold lilies that shone like stars. This he was commanded to give to Queen Clothilde, who gave it to her husband, and his arms were everywhere victorious. The device thereupon became the emblem of France (*see Les Petits Bollandistes*, Vol. VI). *Cp*. FLEUR-DE-LIS.

The Jersey Lily. *See under* JERSEY.

The City of Lilies. Florence is so called from its coat-of-arms.

Lily-livered. *See* LIVER.

To paint, or **gild the lily.** *See* PAINT.

Limb. Slang for a mischievous rascal, a young imp; it is short for the older *Limb of the Devil*, where the word implies "agent" or "scion". Dryden called Fletcher "a limb of Shakespeare".

Limb of law. A clerk articled to a lawyer, or SHERIFF'S officer, a police officer, or other agent of the law; they obey the head of their office or department.

Limbo (Lat. *limbus*, border, fringe, edge). The borders of HELL; that portion assigned by the SCHOOLMEN to those departed spirits to whom the benefits of redemption did not apply through no fault of their own.

The Limbo of Children (Lat. *limbus infantium*). The limbo for children who die before baptism or before they are responsible for their actions.

Limbo of the Fathers (Lat. *limbus patrum*). The half-way house between earth and HEAVEN, where the PATRIARCHS and prophets who died before Christ's crucifixion await the last day, when they will be received into HEAVEN. Some hold that this is the "HELL" into which Christ descended after He gave up the ghost on the cross.

SHAKESPEARE (*Henry VIII*, V, iv) uses *limbo patrum* for "QUOD", jail, confinement.

> I have some of 'em in Limbo Patrum, and there they are like to dance these three days.

The Limbus of Fools, or **Limbus Fatuorum,** or **Paradise of Fools.** As fools or idiots are not responsible for their works, the SCHOOLMEN held that they were not punished in PURGATORY and could not be received into HEAVEN, so they were destined to go to a special "Paradise of Fools" (*cp.* FOOL'S PARADISE *under* FOOL).

> Then might you see
> Cowls, hoods, habits, with their wearers tossed
> And fluttered into rags; then relics, beads,
> Indulgences, dispenses, pardons, bulls,
> The sport of winds. All these, upwhirled aloft,
> Fly o'er the backside of the world far-off,
> Into a Limbo large and broad, since called
> The Paradise of Fools
> MILTON: *Paradise Lost*, III, 498.

Limbus of the Moon. *See* MOON.

Limehouse, or **Limehousing.** Once common for violent abuse of one's political opponents: so called from a speech by Lloyd George at Limehouse, London, on 30 July 1909, when he poured forth scorn and abuse on dukes, landlords, financial magnates, etc.

Lime-light. A vivid light, giving off little heat, produced by the combustion of oxygen and hydrogen on a surface of lime. Also called *Drummond Light*, after Thomas Drummond (1797–1840) who invented it in 1826. It was tried at the South Foreland lighthouse in 1861, but its main use developed in the theatre, where it was used to throw a powerful beam upon one player on the stage to the exclusion of others. Hence the phrase **to be in the lime-light,** to be in the full glare of public attention.

Limerick. A nonsense verse in the metre popularized by Edward Lear in his *Book of Nonsense* (1846), of which the following is an example:

> There was a young lady of Wilts,
> Who walked up to Scotland on stilts;
> When they said it was shocking
> To show so much stocking,
> She answered, "Then what about kilts?"

The name has been said to come from the chorus "Will you come up to Limerick" which was supposed to follow each verse as it was improvised by a member of a convivial party, but there is no real evidence for this.

Limey. In American and Australian slang, a British sailor or ship, or just a Briton. It derives from the practice of issuing lime juice to a ship's crew to combat scurvy.

Limp. This word, formed from the initials Louis (XIV), James (II), his wife Mary (of Modena), and the Prince (of Wales) was used as a JACOBITE toast in the time of William III. *Cp.* NOTARIKON.

Alexandra limp. *See* ALEXANDRA.

Lincoln. The devil looking over Lincoln. *See under* DEVIL.

Lincoln Green. Lincoln was noted formerly for its light green, as was Coventry for its blue, and Yorkshire for its grey cloth. *Cp.* KENDAL GREEN.

Lincoln Imp. A grotesque carving having weird and prominent ears and nursing the right leg crossed over the left, in the ANGEL choir of Lincoln Cathedral. He is said to have been turned to stone by the angels for misbehaving in the Angel Choir. The Imp is now the county emblem.

Lincoln's Inn. One of the four INNS OF COURT in London. The inn takes its name from its landlord Thomas de Lincoln, king's serjeant, and is probably of late 14th-century origin. The Old Hall dates from the reign of Henry VII. The chapel was completed by Inigo Jones in 1643.

Lindabrides (lin dà brī′ dez). A heroine in *The Mirror Knighthood*, whose name at one time was a synonym for a kept mistress or courtesan.

> "Well—I have my Master Tressilian's head under my belt by this lucky discovery, that is one thing certain; and I will try to get a sight of this Lindabrides of his, that is another."
> SCOTT: *Kenilworth*, ch. xxviii.

Linden. The German name (widely used in England) for lime-trees. *Unter den Linden* (under the limes) is the name of the principal street in Berlin.

Baucis (*see* PHILEMON) was converted into a linden tree.

Lindor. One of the conventional names given by the classical poets to a rustic swain, a lover *en bergère*.

Line. The Line. The Equator; also in the British Army all regular infantry regiments except the Foot Guards, and the Rifle Brigade, are called line regiments. The term sometimes includes cavalry regiments.

All along the line. In every particular, as, "The accuracy of the statement is contested all along the line by persons on the spot."

Crossing the line. Sailing across the Equator; advantage is usually taken of this for ceremonial practical joking aboard ship. Those who have not previously crossed the line are summoned to the court of NEPTUNE for trial, and are usually ducked by "bears", sometimes lathered and roughtly shaved, given "soap pills" to swallow, etc. As at present practised the whole affair constitutes a good-humoured and amusing interlude, but in former days some of the buffoonery and horse-play was decidedly rough. Such performances have a long history and may have begun as propitiatory rites to the deities of the ocean. At one time similar ceremonies were performed when a ship crossed the thirty-ninth parallel (about the latitude of Lisbon) and also when passing through the Straits of GIBRALTAR and rounding the CAPE of Good Hope.

Hard lines. Hard luck, a hard lot. Here *lines* means an allotment measured out.

Line of battle. *See under* BATTLE.

To break the enemy's line is to create a gap in his ORDER OF BATTLE (as Nelson did at Trafalgar and Wellington at Salamanca), and so put him to confusion.

Line of beauty. In art, a line of undulating curvature, usually in the form of a slender elongated letter S.

Line of country. One's business or occupation or specialization.

Line of direction. In mechanics, the line in which a body moves, a force acts, or motion is communicated; or the line drawn from the centre of gravity of a body perpendicular to the horizon.

Line of life. In palmistry, the crease in the left hand beginning above the web of the thumb, and running towards or up to the wrist. The nearer it approaches the wrist, the longer will be the life, according to palmists. If long and deeply marked, it indicates long life with very little trouble; if crossed or cut with other marks, it indicates sickness.

Line upon line. Admonition or instruction repeated little by little (a line at a time).

> Line upon line, line upon line, here a little and there a little.
>
> *Is*. xxviii, 10.

No day without its line. A saying attributed to the Greek artist Apelles (*nulla dies sine linea*), who said he never passed a day without doing at least one line, and to this steady industry owed his great success. The words were adopted by Anthony Trollope as his motto.

On the line. Said of a picture that, at the Royal Academy, is hung in a position that places its centre about the level of the spectator's eye.

The lines are fallen unto me in pleasant places (*Ps*. xvi, 6). The part allotted to me and measured off by a measuring line. The allusion is to drawing a line to mark out the lot of each tribe, hence line became the synonym of lot, and lot means position or destiny.

The thin red line. British infantrymen in action. The old 93rd Highlanders were so described at the battle of Balaclava (1854) by W. H. Russell, because they did not take the trouble to form into a square. Their regimental magazine was later called *The Thin Red Line*.

To fall into line with. To agree with; to act in conformity with. Derived from the falling-in of soldiers into straight lines. *See also* TO FALL IN *under* FALL.

To lay it on the line. In American usage means "to give money"; "to give the information required", "to speak openly, or frankly about something".

To line one's pockets. *See under* POCKET.

To read between the lines. To discern the hidden meaning; to draw certain conclusions which are not apparent on the surface. One method of cryptography is to write so that the hidden message is revealed only when alternate lines are read.

To shoot a line. To exaggerate; to tell a tall story; to boast.

To toe the line. To obey orders; to conform with. Athletes awaiting the starting signal of a race line up with their toes just touching the starting line.

What line are you in? What is your trade or profession? Commercial travellers are said to be in the "grocery line", "the hardware line", etc. *Cp*. LINE OF COUNTRY *above*.

Line engraving. The incising of lines on a metal plate for subsequent printing. It differs from etching in that no chemicals are used. The process dates from the first half of the 15th century. *See* LITTLE MASTER.

Line-up. A phrase with various meanings; a parade of persons, especially criminals, for inspection or recognition; an arrangment of players at the start of a game; the deploying of opposing forces before a battle.

Lingua Franca. A species of Italian mixed with French, Greek, Arabic, etc., spoken on the coasts of the Mediterranean; also any mixture of languages serving as a means of communication between different peoples. *Cp*. PIDGIN ENGLISH.

Lining. Lining of the Pocket. Money. When the court tailor wished to obtain the patronage of BEAU BRUMMEL, he made him a present of a dress-coat lined with bank-notes. Brummel wrote a letter of thanks stating that he quite approved of the coat, and especially admired the lining.

To be well-lined. Is to be rich, *i.e.* to have one's pockets well-lined with money.

Linnæan System. The system of classification adopted by the great Swedish botanist Linnæus (1707–1778), who arranged his three kingdoms of animals, vegetables, and minerals into classes, orders, genera, species, and varieties, according to certain characteristics.

Linne, The Heir of. The hero of an old ballad given in PERCY'S RELIQUES, which tells how he wasted his substance in riotous living, and, having spent all, sold his estates to his steward, keeping only a poor lodge. When no one would lend him more money he tried to hang himself but fell to the ground instead. When he came to he espied two chests full of beaten gold, and a third full of white money, over which was written:

Once more, my sonne, I sette thee clere;
Amend they life and follies past;
For but thou amend thee of thy life,
That rope must be thy end at last.

He now returned to his old hall, where he was refused the loan of forty pence by his quondam steward; one of the guests remarked to the steward that he ought to have lent it, as he had bought the estate cheap enough. "Cheap call you it?" said the steward, "why, he shall have it back for 100 marks less." "Done," said the heir of Linne, and recovered his estates.

Lion. An honourable nickname. Among its recipients are:

Ali, son of Abu Taleb, and son-in-law of MOHAMMED, called *The Lion of God* (*c.* 597–661). His mother called him at birth *Al Haidara*, "the Rugged Lion".

Ali Pasha, called *The Lion of Janina* (1741, 1788–1822).

Damelowicz, Prince of Halicz, who founded Lemburg (*Lion City*) in 1259.

Gustavus Adolphus, called *The Lion of the North* (1594, 1611–1632).

Henry, Duke of Bavaria and Saxony, was called *The Lion* for his courage and daring (1129, 1142–1195).

John Nicholson, Brigadier-General of Indian Mutiny fame, was called *The Lion of the Punjab* from his services in the Punjab and from his outstanding valour (1821–1857).

Louis VIII of France was called *The Lion* because he was born under the sign LEO (1187, 1223–1226).

Mohammed ibn Daud, nephew of Togrul Beg, the Perso-Turkish monarch (*c.* 1029, 1063–1072), was surnamed Alp Arslan, *The Valiant Lion*.

Richard I Cœur de Lion (*Lion's Heart*), so called for his bravery (1157, 1189–1199).

William of Scotland, *The Lion*, so called because he chose a *red lion rampant* for his cognizance (1143, 1165–1214).

St. MARK the EVANGELIST is symbolized by a lion because he begins his gospel with the scenes of St. JOHN THE BAPTIST and Christ in the wilderness.

A lion is the emblem of the tribe of Judah; Christ is called "the Lion of the tribe of Judah".

Judah is a lion's whelp:...he couched as a lion, and as an old lion; who shall rouse him up?
Gen. xlix, 9.

Among the titles of the Emperor of Ethiopia were *Conquering Lion of the tribe of Judah, Elect of God, King of Kings of Ethiopia*.

A lion is a symbol of Britain.

The Lion in Story and Legend.

CYBELE is represented as riding in a chariot drawn by two lions.

Hippomenes and ATALANTA (fond lovers) were metamorphosed into lions by Cybele.

HERCULES is sometimes represented clad in the skin of the NEMEAN LION.

The story of ANDROCLES and the lion has many parallels, the most famous of which are those related of St. JEROME and St. Gerasimus:

While St. Jerome was lecturing one day, a lion entered the schoolroom, and lifted up one of its paws. All his disciples fled; but Jerome, seeing that the paw was wounded, drew a thorn out of it and dressed the wound. The lion, out of gratitude, showed a wish to stay with its benefactor, hence the SAINT is represented as accompanied by a lion.

St. Gerasimus, says the story, saw on the banks of the Jordan a lion coming to him limping on three feet. When it reached the saint it held up to him the right paw, from which St. Gerasimus extracted a large thorn. The grateful beast attached itself to the saint, and followed him about as a dog.

Similar tales are told by the BOLLANDISTS in the *Acta Sanctorum*; and in more recent times a story was told of Sir George Davis, an English consul at Florence at the beginning of the 19th century, when he went to see the Duke of Tuscany's lions. There was one that the keepers could not tame; but no sooner did Sir George appear than it showed every symptom of joy. He entered its cage, and the lion licked his face and wagged his tail. Sir George told the duke that he had brought up the creature, but had sold it when it became older and more dangerous.

Sir Iwain de Galles, a hero of romance, was attended by a lion which he had delivered from the attacks of a serpent.

Sir Geoffrey de Latour was aided by a lion against the SARACENS, but it was drowned on attempting to board the vessel which was carrying Sir Geoffrey away from the HOLY LAND.

George Adamson, a game warden of Kenya, and his wife brought up the lioness Elsa. After returning to the jungle and rearing cubs she frequently visited the Adamsons. She died in 1961.

The Lion in Heraldry.

Ever since 1164, when it was adopted as a device by Philip I, Duke of Flanders, the lion has figured prominently as an emblem in HERALDRY and consequently in PUBLIC-HOUSE SIGNS. The earliest and most important attitude of the heraldic lion is *rampant* (the device of SCOTLAND), but it is also shown as *passant, passant gardant* (as in the shield of ENGLAND), *salient, sejant*, etc., and even *dormant*. A lion *statant gardant* is the device of the Duke of Norfolk; a lion *rampant*, with the tail between the legs and turned over its back, the badge of Edward IV as Earl of March; a sleeping lion, the device of Richard I; and a crowned lion the badge of Henry VIII.

The lions in the arms of England. Three lions *passant gardant, i.e.* walking and showing full face. The first was that of Rollo, Duke of Normandy, and the second that of Maine, which was added to Normandy. These were the two lions borne by WILLIAM THE CONQUEROR and his descendants. Henry II added a third to represent the Duchy of Aquitaine, which came to him through his wife Eleanor. Any lion not *rampant* is called a *lion leopardé*, and the French call the *lion passant* a *léopard; accordingly* NAPOLEON said to his soldiers "Let us drive these leopards (the English) into the sea."

Since 1603 the royal ARMS have been supported by (DEXTER) the English lion and (SINISTER) the Scottish UNICORN, but prior to the accession of James I the sinister supporter was a family badge. Edward III, with whom supporters began, had a lion and an EAGLE; Henry IV, an antelope and SWAN; Henry V, a lion and antelope; Edward IV, a lion and bull; Richard III, a lion and boar; Henry VII, a lion and DRAGON; Henry VIII, Mary I, and Elizabeth I, a lion and greyhound.

The lion in the arms of Scotland is derived from the earls of Northumberland and Huntingdon, from whom some of the Scottish monarchs were descended. *See* LYON KING OF ARMS.

The Lion as an emblem of the Resurrec-tion. According to tradition, the lion's whelp is born dead, and remains so for three days, when the father breathes on it and it receives life.

A lion at the feet of crusaders, or **martyrs,** in effigy, signifies that they died for their cause.

The Lion of St. Mark, or of Venice. A winged lion *sejant*, holding an open book with the inscription *Pax tibi, Marce, Evangelista Meus*. A sword-point rises above the book on the DEXTER side, and the whole is encircled by an AUREOLE.

Lions in Public-house Signs. *See* PUBLIC-HOUSE SIGNS.

The Lion will not touch the true prince (Shakespeare, *Henry IV, Pt. I*, II, iv). This is an old superstition, and has been given a Christian significance, the "true prince" being the MESSIAH. It is applied to any prince of blood royal, supposed at one time to be hedged around with a sort of divinity.

> Fetch the Numidian lion I brought over;
> If she be sprung from royal blood, the lion
> He'll do her reverence, else...
> He'll tear her all to pieces.
> JOHN FLETCHER: *The Mad Lover*, IV, v.

To lionize a person is either to show him the LIONS, or to make a lion of him by fêting him and treating him as a celebrity.

To meet a lion in one's path. To encounter a daunting obstacle.

To place oneself in the lion's mouth. To expose oneself to danger needlessly and recklessly.

To twist the Lion's tail. To insult or impose humiliating treatment on Great Britain when she is unable to retaliate; the lion being a British national emblem.

Lion-hunter. One who hunts up a celebrity, especially to adorn or give prestige to a party. Mrs. Leo Hunter in Dickens's *Pickwick Papers* is a good satire on the name and character of a lion-hunter.

The Lion Sermon. Preached annually on 16 October at St. Katharine Cree Church, Leadenhall Street, LONDON, to commemorate "the wonderful escape" of Sir John Gayer from a lion which he met in the desert whilst travelling in Turkish dominions. Sir John was Lord Mayor of London in 1646.

Lion's Head. In fountains the water is often made to issue from the mouth of a lion, an ancient custom. The Egyptians thus symbolized the inundation of the Nile, which happens when the SUN is in LEO (23 July to 22 August), and the Greeks and Romans adopted the device for their fountains.

Lion's Provider. A JACKAL; a foil to another man's wit, a humble friend who plays into your hand to show you to the best advantage. The jackal feeds on the lion's leavings, and is said to yell to advise the lion that it has roused up his prey, serving the lion in much the same way as a dog serves a sportsman.

> ... the poor jackals are less foul,
> As being the brave lion's keen providers
> Than human insects catering for spiders.
> BYRON: *Don Juan*, ix, 27.

Lion's share. The larger part: all or nearly all. In *Æsop's Fables*, several beasts joined the lion in a hunt; but, when the spoil was divided, the lion claimed one quarter in right of his prerogative, one for his superior courage, one for his dam and cubs, "and as for the fourth, let who will dispute it with me". Awed by his frown, the other beasts silently withdrew.

Lions. The *lions* of a place are the sights worth seeing, or the celebrities; so called from the ancient custom of showing visitors the lions at the TOWER, as chief of LONDON sights. The Tower menagerie was abolished in 1834.

Lip. Austrian lip. *See* AUSTRIAN LIP.

Lip homage, or **service.** Verbal devotion; insincere regard; honouring with the lips while the heart takes no part or lot in the matter. See *Matt.* xv, 8; *Is.* xxix, 13.

To bite one's lip. To express vexation and annoyance, or to suppress some emotion as anger or laughter.

To curl the lip. To express contempt or disgust with the mouth.

To keep a stiff upper lip. To be self-reliant; to bear difficulties and danger with fortitude.

To give someone lip. To be cheeky or abusive.

To hang the lip. To drop the under lip in sullenness or contempt.

> A foolish hanging of thy nether lip.
> SHAKESPEARE: *Henry IV, Pt. I*, II, iv.

To shoot out the lip. To show scorn.

> All they that see me laugh me to scorn: they shoot out the lip, they shake the head.
> *Ps.* xxii, 7.

Lir, King. The earliest known original of the king in SHAKESPEARE's *King Lear*, an ocean god of early Irish and British legend. He figures in the romance *The Fate of the Children of Lir* as the father of FIONNUALA. On the death of Fingula, the mother of his daughter, he married the wicked Aoife, who, through spite, transformed the children of Lir into swans.

Lir appears in the MABINOGION as *Llyr* and Geoffrey of Monmouth's *Historia Britonum*

as *Leir*, the founder of Leicester, from which later source Shakespeare derived his plot. *See* LEAR, KING.

Lisbon. Camoëns, in the LUSIADS, derives the name from *Ulyssippo* (Ulysses' *polis*, or city), and says that it was founded by ULYSSES; it is in fact the Phœnician *Olisippo*, the walled town.

Lit de justice (lē dĕ zhus tēs) (Fr., bed of justice). Properly the bed on which the French king reclined when he attended the deliberations of a *parlement* (a judicial body, which also registered royal edicts, etc.); hence the session itself. When the king was present he was the fount of authority. The first *lit de justice* is supposed to have been held by Louis XI and the last was that of Louis XVI in 1787.

Litotes (lī tō' tēz). Understatement, especially emphasizing an affirmative by a negative of its contrary, as, "a citizen of no mean city", *i.e.* of a great or illustrious city.

Little. Little by little. Gradually; a little at a time.

Many a little makes a mickle. The real Scottish proverb is: "A wheen o'mickles mak's a muckle", where mickle means *little* and muckel *much*; but the O.E. *micel* or *mycel* means "much", so that if the Scots proverb is accepted we must give a forced meaning to the word "mickle".

Little Britain. The name given in the old romances to Armorica, now Brittany; also called Benwic.

Also a street in the City of LONDON, originally Bretton-Strete, becoming eventually Lyttell Bretton in late Elizabethan times. It is said to be named from a Duke of Brittany who had a residence there. It was once noted for its booksellers.

> Little Britain may truly be called the heart's core of the city, the stronghold of true John Bullism.
> WASHINGTON IRVING: *The Sketch Book*
> (*Little Britain*).

Little Corporal. NAPOLEON Bonaparte. So called after the battle of Lodi in 1796, from his low stature, youthful age, and great courage. He was barely 5 ft. 2 in. in height.

Little-endians. *See* BIG-ENDIANS *under* BIG.

Little Englanders. An uncomplimentary term first applied in Victorian times to critics and opponents of imperialism and overseas expansion.

> That is why I distrust ... the late Government, because in their ranks were men who notoriously were "Little England" men, who took every opportunity of carping at and criticizing those brave Englishmen who have made for us homes across the sea, men who are opposed to any extension of the responsibilities and obligations of Empire, men who are un-

worthy sons of the ancestors who have made this country what it is.
>
> JOSEPH CHAMBERLAIN: *Speech at Walsall* (15 July 1895).

Little Entente. The name given to the political alliance formed between Czechoslovakia, Yugoslavia, and Rumania (1920–1922). Originally to prevent the restoration of HABSBURG power, it became broader in scope. It was brought to an end by the destruction of Czechoslovakia after the Munich Agreement (1938).

Little Gentleman in Velvet. A favourite JACOBITE toast in the reign of Queen Anne. The reference was to the mole that raised the molehill against which William III's horse Sorrel stumbled (21 February 1702). The king broke his collar-bone and died at Kensington (8 March).

Little go. A nickname for the former Previous (Entrance) Examination for undergraduates at Cambridge, unless excused on account of successes at other examinations. It ceased to operate after 1961, owing to new regulations. *Cp.* SMALLS.

Little Jack Horner. *See* JACK HORNER *under* JACK.

Little John. A character in the ROBIN HOOD cycle, a big stalwart man whose surname was also said to be Nailor. On his first encounter with Robin Hood he "tumbl'd him into the brook" and the outlaws changed the victor's name from John Little to "Little John".

> He was, I must tell you, but seven foot high,
> And, maybe, an ell in the waste;
> A sweet pretty lad; much feasting they had;
> Bold Robin the christ'ning grac'd.
>
> *Robin Hood and Little John*
> (given in RITSON'S *Robin Hood*).

Little Lord Fauntleroy. The title of an amazingly successful children's book by Frances E. Hodgson Burnett (1849–1924) which became a household name in late-Victorian and Edwardian days. First published in book form by Scribners in 1886, it was adapted as a play, *The Real Lord Fauntleroy*, in 1888. As a consequence many small boys, often to their embarrassment, were made to pattern themseles on the Fauntleroy image of polished manners, curly hair, and black velvet suits with lace collars. The garb was in vogue for at least a generation.

Little Magician. The nickname of Martin van Buren, President of the U.S.A. (1837–1841).

Little Mary. *See under* MARY.

Little Master. A name applied to certain German designers who worked for engravers, etc., in the 16th century, because their designs were on a small scale, fit for copper or wood. They were Hans Sebald and Barthel Beham, George Pencz, Jacob Binck, Heinrich Aldegraver, and Albrecht Altdorfer. They continued in the tradition begun by Albrecht Dürer of Nuremberg (1471–1528). *See* LINE ENGRAVING.

Little Parliament. BAREBONES PARLIAMENT.

Little People. Fairies (*see* FAIRY).

Little Red Ridinghood. This nursery story is also common to Sweden, Germany, and France. It comes from the French *Le Petit Chaperon Rouge*, in Charles Perrault's *Contes des Temps*, and was probably derived from Italy. The finale, which tells of the arrival of a huntsman who slits open the wolf and restores Little Red Ridinghood and her grandmother to life, is a German addition.

Little Rhody. The State of Rhode Island, U.S.A.

Little Willie. *See* LAUGHING MURDERER.

Liver. In the AUSPICES taken by the Greeks and Romans before battle, if the liver of the animals sacrificed was healthy and blood-red, the OMEN was favourable; but if pale it augured defeat.

The liver was anciently supposed to be the seat of love; hence in SHAKESPEARE'S *Love's Labour's Lost* (IV, iii), when Longaville reads the verses, Biron says in an aside. "This is the liver-vein, which makes flesh a deity." In the *Merry Wives of Windsor* (II, i) Pistol speaks of Falstaff as loving Ford's wife "with liver burning hot".

Another superstition was that the liver of a coward contained no blood; hence such expressions as **white-livered, lily-livered,** PIGEON-LIVERED, and Sir Toby's remark in Shakespeare's *Twelfth Night* (III, ii):

> For Andrew, if he were opened, and you find so much blood in his liver as will clog the foot of a flea, I'll eat the rest of the anatomy.

Liverpool. A native of Liverpool is called a *Liverpudlian*, a *Dicky Sam*, or SCOUSE.

Livery. What is delivered. The clothes of a manservant delivered to him by his master. The stables to which a horse is delivered for keep. Splendid uniforms were formerly given to members of royal households. BARONS and KNIGHTS gave them to their retainers, but in the reign of Edward IV a statute of 1468 forbade the latter practice and Henry VII prosecuted those giving or receiving liveries.

The colours of the livery of manservants were those of the field and principal charge of the armorial shield; hence the royal livery is scarlet trimmed with gold.

> What liverye is we by common use in England knowe well enough, namelye, that it is allowaunce of horse-meate, as they commonly use the woord in stabling, as to keepe horses at livereye; the which

woord, as I gess, is derived of livering or delivering
foorth theyr nightlye foode.

SPENCER: *A view of the Present State of Ireland*.

Livery Companies. The modern representatives of the City of LONDON of the old
City Craft Gilds, which were originally associations for religious and social purposes and
later trade organizations for fixing wages,
standards of craftsmanship, etc. They also
acted as Friendly Societies. Their members
wore distinctive *livery* on special occasions,
hence the name livery company.

The twelve "great" companies in order of
precedence are:

Mercers (1393)	Merchant Taylors (1326)
Grocers (1345)	Haberdashers (1448)
Drapers (1364)	Salters (1558)
Fishmongers (1364)	Ironmongers (1454)
Goldsmiths (1327)	Vintners (1436)
Skinners (1327)	Clothworkers (1528)

The Pepperers and Spicers amalgamated
in 1345 to become later known as the Gro-
cers, and the Haberdashers were originally
known as the Hurrers. Samuel Pepys was
Master (1677) of the Clothworkers, which
was a 16th-century incorporation of the
Shearman and Fullers.

Among the seventy-odd lesser livery companies are:

Apothecaries (1606)	Farmers (1952)
Armourers and	Furniture Makers (1963)
Brasiers (1453)	Glovers (1639)
Blacksmiths (1571)	Leathersellers (1444)
Butchers (1606)	Plasterers (1501)
Cordwainers (1438)	Stationers and Newspaper
Dyers (1471)	Makers (1556)

The Weavers (1184) claim to be the oldest
company. Many still have their halls in the
City and contribute largely from their funds
to charities, especially to almshouses and
education. Merchant Taylors' School, the
Haberdashers' schools, St. Paul's School,
Goldsmith's College and numerous such institutions, owe much to their benevolence.
See AT SIXES AND SEVENS *under* SIX.

Liverymen. The freemen of the London
LIVERY COMPANIES are so called because they
were entitled to wear the livery of their respective companies.

Livy. The Livy of Spain. Juan de Mariana
(1536–1624), author of *Historiæ de Rebus
Hispaniæ* in 35 books.

The Livy of Portugal. João de Barros
(1496–1570), the great Portuguese historian.

Lizard. Supposed, at one time, to be venomous, hence a "lizard's leg" was an ingredient of the witches' cauldron in Shakespeare's *Macbeth*.

Poison be their drink!...
Their chiefest prospect murd'ring basilisks!
Their softest touch as smart as lizard's stings!

SHAKESPEARE: *Henry VI, Pt. II*, III, ii

Lounge lizard. A popular phrase in the
1920s to describe a young man who spent his
time, or often made his living, by dancing
and waiting upon elderly women.

Lliannan-She. In the Isle of MAN, a spirit
friend, a female FAIRY who waited to encounter men. If one spoke to her she followed him always, but remained invisible to
everyone else.

Lloyd's. An international insurance market in
the City of LONDON and the world centre of
shipping intelligence that began in the
17th-century COFFEE house of Edward
Lloyd in LOMBARD Street. Originally a market for marine insurance only, it now deals
with nearly all forms of insurance. Lloyd's
was incorporated by Act of PARLIAMENT in
1871. *Cp.* BALTIC.

Insurance is accepted at Lloyd's by individual underwriters, not by Lloyd's, which
provides the premises, intelligence, and
other facilities. Lloyd's Agents throughout
the world send shipping information which
is published in *Lloyd's List* and *Lloyd's Shipping Index*.

Load Line. Another name for the PLIMSOLL
LINE.

Loaf. In sacred art, a loaf held in the hand is an
attribute of St. PHILIP the Apostle, St.
Osyth, St. Joanna, St. NICHOLAS, St. Godfrey, and other saints noted for their charity
to the poor.

Half a loaf is better than no bread. If you
can't get all you want, try to be content with
what you do get; something is better than
nothing.

Heywood (1546) says:

Throw no gift at the giver's head;
Better is half a loaf than no bread.

**Never turn a loaf in the presence of a
Menteith.** An old Scottish saying. It was Sir
John Menteith who betrayed WALLACE to the
English. When he turned a loaf set on the table, his guests were to rush upon the patriot
and secure him (Scott: *Tales of a Grandfather*, vii).

Use your loaf. A slang expression meaning
"use your brains", use "your head". *loaf* (of
bread) here means one's head.

With an eye to the loaves and fishes.
With a view to the material benefits to be
derived. The allusion is to the GOSPEL story
of the crowd following Christ, not for His
spiritual teachings but for the food He distributed among them.

Jesus answered them and said, Verily, verily, I say
unto you, Ye seek me, not because ye saw the miracles, but because ye did eat of the loaves and were
filled.

John vi, 26

Loamshire. An imaginary county of southern England used as a setting by writers of fiction to avoid identification with actual towns and villages. Hence the *Loamshires* as an equally fictitious regiment of the LINE.

Loamshire dialect. Said of a rustic dialogue used by a writer with no real knowledge of the forms of speech peculiar to a given district.

Loathly Lady. A stock character of old romance who is so hideous that everyone is deterred from marrying her. When, however, she at last finds a husand her ugliness, the effect of enchantment, disappears, and she becomes a model of beauty. Her story is the feminine countepart of BEAUTY AND THE BEAST.

Lob. Old thieves' slang for a till. Hence *lobsneak*, one who robs the till; *lobcrawling*, on the prowl to rob tills.

Lob's Pound. Old slang for prison, the stocks, or any other place of confinement.

Lobby. A vestibule or corridor, from Med. Lat. *lobia*, lodge, a covered way. In the HOUSE OF COMMONS, the large hall to which the public are admitted, especially for interiews with members. Division Lobbies are the corridors to which members retire to vote and **to lobby** is to solicit the vote of a member or to seek to influence members; a **lobbyist** is one who does this.

The Bill will cross the lobbies. Be sent from the HOUSE OF COMMONS to the HOUSE OF LORDS.

Loblolly. A sailor's term for spoon-victuals, pap, gruel, etc.

Loblolly boy. A surgeon's mate of former days, a lad not yet out of his spoon-meat. Also a ship's steward.

> I not only suffered from the rude insults of the sailors and petty officers, among whom I was known by the name of Loblolly Boy.
> SMOLLETT: *Roderick Random*, xxvii.

Lobsters. Soldiers were popularly so called because they were "turned red" when they enlisted (*i.e.* they wore red coats). The name is also applied to Royal MARINES. The term was originally given to a troop of Parliamentary horse in the GREAT REBELLION.

> Sir William Waller, having received from London (in 1643) a fresh regiment of 500 horse...which were so prodigiously armed that they were called by the king's party "the regiment of lobsters", because of their bright iron shells with which they were covered, being perfect cuirassiers, and were the first seen so armed on either side.
> CLARENDON: *History of the Great Rebellion*, III, 91.

Died for want of lobster sauce. Sometimes said of one who dies or suffers severely because of some trifling disappointment, pique, or wounded vanity. At a grand feast given by the great Condé to Louis XIV at Chantilly, Vatel, the chef, was told that the lobsters intended for sauce had not arrived, where upon he retired to his room and ran his sword through his body, unable to survive the disgrace thus brought upon him.

Local, The. In colloquial parlance, the local hostelry; also the local paper.

Local Defence Volunteers. *See* HOME GUARD.

Local option is the choice allowed to a local authority to decide what course it shall take on a given question, specifically the sale of liquor. In 1913 Scotland was given local option. Parishes, small towns, and wards of large towns were allowed to vote on liquor licensing—for no licence, reduction of licences, or no change. Very few places went "dry".

Loch Ness Monster. In April 1933, a motorist driving along the shore of Loch Ness, Scotland, saw a strange object at some distance out, subsequently described as being 30 ft. long with two humps, a snake-like head at the end of a long neck, and two flippers about the middle of the body. It was "seen" by others and much featured by the newspapers. Investigations showed no substantial evidence of the existence of the supposed prehistoric monster but more recent observations have increased the belief in its presence.

Lochiel (lo*ch* ēl). The title of the head of the CLAN Cameron, so called from his domain.

The hero of Thomas Campbell's poem, *Lochiel's Warning* (1802), is Donald Cameron, known as *The Gentle Lochiel*. He was one of the Young PRETENDER'S staunchest, adherents, and escaped to France with him after Culloden (1746). He took service with the French army, but died two years later.

Lock hospital. A hospital for the treatment of venereal diseases. Such a hospital was established in the Harrow Road, London, in 1746, and that at Kingsland had a sundial which bore the inscription "*Post voluptatem misericordia*". The name was originally used in mediæval times for a leper hospital and probably comes from the word *lock* meaning to shut in or seclude, a necessary precaution with lepers.

Lock, Stock, and Barrel. The whole of anything; in entirety. The lock, stock, and barrel of a gun is the complete firearm.

Lockhart. Legend has it that the good Lord James, on his way to the HOLY LAND with the heart of the King Robert Bruce, was killed in Spain fighting against the MOORS. Sir Simon Locard of Lee was commissioned to carry the heart back to SCOTLAND and it was interred in Melrose Abbey. In consequence he changed his name to *Lock-heart*, and adopted the device of *a heart within a fetter-lock*, with the motto *Corda serrata pando* (Locked hearts I open).

Locksmith's Daughter. A key.

Locofoco. An American name for a self-igniting cigar patented in New York in 1834 and soon applied to a friction or LUCIFER MATCH. The name is seemingly based on *locomotive*, taken to mean "self-moving"; thus *loco-foco* was intended to mean "self-lighting". The name was then applied to the RADICAL wing of the Democratic Party and then to the Democratic Party generally. It arose from an incident which occurred at a party meeting in TAMMANY HALL (1835) when the gas lights were turned out by the opponents of the radicals to break up the assembly, but the radicals produced candles which they lit with *loco-focos*.

> Here's full particulars of the patriotic loco-foco movement yesterday in which the Whigs was so chawed up.
>
> DICKENS: *Martin Chuzzlewit*, ch. xvi (1843).

Locrin. Father of SABRINA, and eldest son of the mythical BRUTUS, King of Britain. On the death of his father he became King of LOEGRIA (Geoffrey of Monmouth: *Historia Britonum*, ch. I-V).

An anonymous tragedy, based on Holinshed and Geoffrey of Monmouth, called *Locrine* was published in 1595 bearing Shakespeare's initials (W.S.). This tragedy contains borrowings from Spenser, and Marlowe has also been suggested as its author. It is almost certainly not by SHAKESPEARE.

Locum tenens, or **locum** (Med. Lat., one holding place). One acting temporarily for another, especially a doctor or a clergyman. *See* LIEUTENANT.

Locus Lat., a place).

Locus classicus (Lat.). The most cited or most authoritative passage on a subject.

Locus delicti. The place where a crime was committed (Lat. *delictum*, crime).

Locus in quo (Lat., the place in which). The place in question, the spot mentioned.

Locus pœnitentiæ (Lat., a place or opportunity of repentance). The interval when it is possible to withdraw from a bargain or course before being committed to it. In the interview between Esau and his father Isaac, St. PAUL says that the former "found no place of repentance, though he sought it carefully with tears" (*Heb.* xii, 17)—*i.e.* no means whereby Isaac could break his bargain with Jacob.

Locus sigilli (Lat., the place of the seal). The place where the seal is to be set; usually abbreviated in documents to "L.S.", or designated by a small circle.

Locus standi (Lat., a place of standing). Recognized position, acknowledged right or claim. In law, the right to be heard in court. We say of a person that he has no *locus standi* in society.

Locusta. A woman who murders those she professes to nurse, or those whom it is her duty to take care of. Locusta lived in the early days of the Roman Empire, poisoned Claudius and Britannicus, and attempted to destroy NERO. Being found out, she was put to death.

Lode. Originally a ditch that guides or leads water into a river or sewer, from O.E. *lad*, way, course (connected with *to lead*); hence in mines the vein that leads or guides to ore.

Lodestar. The North Star or Pole Star; the *leading-star* by which mariners are guided (*see* LODE). *Cp.* CYNOSURE.

> Your eyes are lodestars.
>
> SHAKESPEARE: *A Midsummer Night's Dream*, I, i.

Lodestone, Loadstone. The MAGNET or stone that guides, the magnetic oxide of iron. In the MIDDLE AGES pilots were called *lodesmen*.

> Among the ancients the lodestone was believed to have many strange virtues. Placed on the pillow of a guilty wife, it would make her confess her iniquities while she slept. It could be used for the treatment of many ailments and also as a contraceptive. There was a curious belief that its effect could be countered by garlic or onion. It was said that sailors ought to be forbidden to eat these vegetables in case their breath should demagnetize the compass needles.
>
> HITCHINS and MAY:
> *From Lodestone to Gyro-Compass*, ch. i.

Lodona. The Loddon, an affluent entering the Thames at Shiplake. Pope, in *Windsor Forest*, says it was a NYMPH, fond of the chase, like DIANA. It chanced one day that PAN saw her, and tried to catch her; but Lodona fled from him, imploring CYNTHIA to save her. No sooner had she spoken that she became "a silver stream" which "virgin coldness keeps".

Leogria, or **Logres** (lo eg'ri à, lō' gres). ENGLAND is so called by Geoffrey of Monmouth, from LOCRIN.

> Thus Cambria to her right, what would herself restore,
> And rather than to lose Loegria, looks for more.
>
> DRAYTON: *Polyolbion*, iv.

Log. An instrument for measuring the speed of a ship. In its simplest form it is a flat piece of wood, some 6 in. in radius, in the shape of a quadrant, and made so that it will float perpendicularly. To this is fastened the log-line, knotted at intervals. *See* KNOT.

A King Log. A king who rules in peace and

quietness, but never makes his power felt. In allusion to the FABLE of *The Frogs desiring a King*: JUPITER first threw them down a log of wood, but they grumbled at so spiritless a King. He then sent them a stork, which devoured them eagerly. *See* KING STORK *under* STORK.

Log-book. In a ship, the journal in which the "logs" are entered (*see* LOG). It also contains the general record of proceedings on board, especially the navigational and meteorological records.

To be logged. To have one's name recorded in the ship's log for some misdemeanour or offence.

Log-cabin and Hard Cider Campaign (U.S.A.). The name given to the Presidential campaign of 1840. The WHIGS adopted General W. H. Harrison of Ohio and the Democrats, ridiculed him as a "log-cabin candidate". The Whigs turned the situation against them by making a popular parade of portable log cabins and barrels of cider and succeeded in popularizing the old general.

Log-rolling. Applied in politics to the "give and take" principle, by which one party will further certain interests of another in return for help given in passing its own measures.

In literary circles it means mutual admiration, the mutual admirers being called "log-rollers". The allusion, originally American, is to neighbours who assist a new settler to roll away the logs of his clearing.

Logs. An early Australian name for prison, changed with time and circumstances to *The Bricks*.

Logan Stones. Rocking stones; large masses of stone so delicately poised by nature that they will rock to and fro at a touch. There are many such, especially in Cornwall, Derbyshire, Yorkshire and Wales; also in Scotland and Ireland.

The famous Logan Rock (about 70 tons) at Land's End was displaced by Lieutenant Goldsmith, R.N. (nephew of the poet Oliver Goldsmith) and his boat's crew in 1824. It cost him over £2,000 to get it replaced.

Pliny tells of a rock near Harpasa which might be moved with a finger.

Ptolemy says the Gygonian rock might be stirred with a stalk of ASPHODEL.

Half a mile from St. David's is a Logan stone, mounted on divers other stones, which may be shaken with one finger.

Loggerheads. Fall to loggerheads, to squabbling and fisticuffs, perhaps with the idea of establishing which "blockhead" was the harder. The word is used by SHAKESPEARE (*Taming of the Shrew*, IV, i.) *Logger* was the name given to the heavy wooden block fastened to the legs of grazing horses to prevent their straying, thus suggesting a block head, a thick head, a dolt.

To be at loggerheads with someone is to be in a state of disagreement or dispute.

Logres, Logria. *See* LOEGRIA.

Logris. Same as LOCRIN.

Lohengrin. A son of PERCIVAL in the German legend of the Knight of the Swan and attached to the GRAIL cycle. In France it was used to enhance the family of Godfrey of Bouillon. He appears at the close of Wolfram von Eschenbach's *Parzival* (*c*. 1210), and in other German romances, where he is the deliverer of Elsa, Princess of Brabant, who has been dispossessed by Tetramund and Ortrud. He arrives at Antwerp in a skiff drawn by a swan, champions Elsa, and becomes her husband on the sole condition that she shall not ask him his name or lineage. She is prevailed upon to do so on the marriage night, and he, by his vows to the Grail, is obliged to disclose his identity, but at the same time disappears. The swan returns for him, and he goes; but not before retransforming the swan into Elsa's brother Gottfried, who, by the wiles of the sorceress Ortrud, had been obliged to assume that form. Wagner's opera of this name was first produced in 1850.

Loins. Gird up our loins. Brace yourself for vigorous action, or energetic endurance. The Jews wore loose garments, which they girded about their loins when travelling or working.

Gird up the loins of your mind.
I Pet. i, 13.

My little finger shall be thicker than my father's loins (I *Kings* xii, 10). My lightest tax shall be heavier than the most oppressive tax of my predecessor. Rehoboam's arrogant answer to the deputation which waited on him to entreat an alleviation of "the yoke" laid on them by SOLOMON. The reply caused the revolt of all the tribes, except those of Judah and BENJAMIN.

Loki. The god of strife and spirit of evil in Norse mythology, son of the GIANT Farbauti and Laufey, and father of the MIDGARD snake, HEL, and FENRIR. It was he who artfully contrived the death of BALDER. He was finally chained to a rock and, according to one legend, there to remain until the Twilight of the Gods, when he will break his bonds; the heavens will disappear, the earth be swallowed up by the sea, fire shall consume the elements, and even ODIN, with all his kindred deities, shall perish. Another story has it that he was freed at RAGNAROK, and that he and HEIMDALL fought till both were slain.

Lollards. A name given to the followers of John Wyclif, and earlier to a sect in the Netherlands. It is probably from the Mid. Dut. *Lollaerd*, one who mumbles prayers or hymns. The word is recorded as having been used by William Courtenay, Archbishop of Canterbury, when he condemned their teachings in 1382.

The Lollards condemned TRANSUBSTANTIATION, INDULGENCES, clerical celibacy, the ecclesiastical hierarchy, and the temporal possessions of the church.

Lollipop man or lady. A schoolchildren's name for the traffic warden who conducts them across the road; from the striped pole, surmounted by a brightly coloured disc, which he or she carries.

Lombard. A banker or moneylender. In mediæval LONDON, Lombard Street became the home of Lombards and other Italian merchants who set up as goldsmiths, moneylenders, and bankers. From the 13th century they flourished as pawnbrokers and the three golden balls of the pawnshop are said to be taken from the armorial bearings of the MEDICI of Florence. *See* BALLS, THE THREE GOLDEN.

> This merchant, which that was ful war and wys.
> Creanced hath, and payd eek in Parys
> To certain Lumbardes redy in hir hond,
> The somme of gold, and hadde of hem his bond.
> CHAUCER: *Shipman's Tale*, i, 367.

All Lombard Street to a China orange. An old saying, implying very long odds, Lombard Street being the great centre of banking and mercantile transactions. To stake the wealth of LONDON against an orange is to stake great wealth against a trifle.

> "It is Lombard Street to a China orange," quoth Uncle Jack.
> BULWER LYTTON: *The Caxtons*, IV, iii.

London. The first surviving reference to London is to be found in Tacitus (*Annals*, Lib. XIV, ch. xxxiii) written A.D. 115–117, and referring to events in A.D. 61. It is the Roman name *Londinium*, which is from a CELTIC name of uncertain derivation.

London Bridge was built upon woolpacks. An old saying commemorating the fact that in the reign of Henry II the construction of a new stone bridge over the THAMES was begun, to be paid for by a tax on wool.

London Gazette. The official organ of the British government and the appointed medium for all official announcements. It dates from 1665 when Henry Muddiman started it as a daily newsletter or newspaper. It is now published on Tuesdays and Fridays. The *Iris Oifigiuil* (Dublin) and the *Belfast Gaz-*ette are similar official organs.

London Group. A society of artists founded in 1913 by some painters associated with Walter Sickert (1860–1942). Its aim was to break away from academic tradition and to draw inspiration from French Post-IMPRESSIONISM.

London Pride is the little red-and-white *Saxifraga umbrosa*, also called None-so-pretty and St. Patrick's Cabbage.

London Regiment. This regiment, now disbanded, comprised two regular battalions of the City of London Regiment (Royal Fusiliers) and a number of territorial battalions including the London Rifle Brigade, Kensingtons, Artists Rifles and London Scottish.

London Stone in Cannon Street is a most ancient relic of uncertain history. Camden thought it to be the point from which the Romans measured distances and another theory is that it is a Saxon ceremonial stone.

According to Holinshed, Jack CADE struck it with his sword when proclaiming himself master of the city and the incident is mentioned in Shakespeare's *Henry VI, Pt. II*, IV, vii. The stone was placed against the wall of St. SWITHIN's Church in 1798 as a safeguard against its destruction.

> Jack Straw at London-stone with all his rout
> Struck not the city with so loud a shout.
> DRYDEN: *The Cock and the Fox*, I, 742.

Londonderry. The Northern Ireland county and city of this name took their prefix "London" when in 1613 the confiscated lands of native chieftains were assigned to some of the London LIVERY COMPANIES and to the Corporation of LONDON.

Lone Star State. The State of Texas, U.S.A.

Long. Long chalk, dozen, odds, etc., *see these words.*

How long is a piece of string? *See under* STRING.

The long and the short of the matter. All that need be said; the essence or whole sum of the matter in brief.

So long. Good-bye, till we meet again.

To draw the longbow. *See under* BOW.

To make a long arm. To stretch for something, especially across the table.

Long Knives. *See under* NIGHT.

Long Meg of Westminster. A noted virago in the reign of Henry VIII, around whose exploits a comedy (since lost) was performed in LONDON in 1594.

> *Lord Proudly:* What d'ye this afternoon?
> *Lord Feesimple:* Faith, I have a great mind to see *Long Meg* and *The Ship* at the Fortune.
> NATHANIEL FIELD: *Amends for Ladie*
> II, i (1618)

Her name has been given to several articles of unusual size. Thus, the large blue-black marble in the south cloister of Westminster Abbey, over the grave of Gervasius de Blois, is called "Long Meg of Westminster". Fuller says the term is applied to things "of hop-pole height, wanting breadth proportionable thereunto", and refers to a great gun in the TOWER OF LONDON, so called, taken to Westminster in troublesome times; and in the *Edinburgh Antiquarian Magazine* (September 1769) we read of Peter Branan, aged 104, who was 6 ft. 6 in. high, and was commonly called *Long Meg of Westminster. See also* MAYPOLE; MEG.

Long Meg and her daughters. In the neighbourhood of Penrith, Cumbria is a prehistoric circle of 64 stones, some of them 10 ft. high. Some 17 paces off, on the south side, is a single stone, 15 ft. high, called *Long Meg*, the shorter ones being called *her daughters*.

Long Melford. A long stocking purse, such as was formerly carried by country folk. In boxing, according to Isopel Berners, it was a straight right-handed blow (Borrow: *Lavengro*, lxxxv). The village on Long Melford in Suffolk owes the epithet to the length of its main street.

Long Parliament. The most familiar of this name is the PARLIAMENT summoned by CHARLES I (3 November 1640), the remnant of which was not dissolved until 16 March 1660 (*see* RUMP). It was especially notable for its resistance to the king and its part in the GREAT REBELLION. The name is also applied to Henry IV's Parliament of 1406 (1 March–22 December), and to the CAVALIER PARLIAMENT (1661–1679) in Charles II's reign.

Long Range Desert Group. A British military force of volunteers in World War II who penetrated behind the enemy's lines in North Africa and carried out invaluable reconnaissance work through the uncharted desert. They helped to guide various forces to their objectives and facilitated the exploits of the *Special Air Service. Cp.* POPSKI'S PRIVATE ARMY.

Long stocking. To have a long stocking. To have a long purse; to have considerable monetary resources. *Cp.* LONG MELFORD.

Longchamps (long shong). The racecourse at the end of the Bois de Boulogne, Paris. An abbey formerly stood there, and it was long celebrated for the parade of smartly dressed Parisians which took place on the Wednesday, Thursday, and Friday of HOLY WEEK.

The custom dates from the time when all who could do so went to the abbey to hear the TENEBRÆ sung in HOLY WEEK; and it survives as an excellent opportunity to display the latest spring fashions.

Long-headed. Clever, sharp-witted. A long head was supposed to indicate shrewdness.

Longshanks. *See* HAMMER.

Longsword (*Longespée, Longepée, Longspée,* etc.). The surname of Wiliam, the first Duke of Normandy (d. 943). He was the great-great-grandfather of WILLIAM THE CONQUEROR. The name was also given to William, third Earl of Salisbury (d. 1226), a natural son of Henry II and (according to late tradition) Fair ROSAMOND.

Longtail, Cut and Longtail. One and another, all of every description. The phrase had its origin in the practice of cutting the tails of certain dogs and horses, and leaving others in their natural state, so that the cut and long-tail horses or dogs included all the species. Master Slender in Shakespeare's *Merry Wives of Windsor* (III, iv) says he will maintain Anne Page like a gentlewoman. "Ay!" says he. "That I will, come cut and long tail under the degree of a squire" [*i.e.* as well as anyone below the rank of squire].

How about the long-tailed beggar? A reproof to one who is drawing the longbow too freely (*see under* BOW). The tale is that a boy on returning from a short voyage pretended to have forgotten everything belonging to his home and asked his mother what she called that "long-tailed beggar", meaning the cat.

Long words. "Honorificabilitudinitatibus" has often been called the longest word in the English language; "quadradimensionality" is almost as long, and "antidisestablishmentarianism" beats it by one letter. While there is some limit to the coining of polysyllabic words by the conglomeration of prefixes, combining forms, and suffixes (*e.g.* deanthropomorphization, inanthropomorphizability), the chemists furnish us with such concatenations as "nitrophenylenediamine", and "tetramethyldiamidobenzhydrols". They are far surpassed, however, by the nonsense words found in Urquhart and Motteux's translation of Rabelais. The following comes from Ch. xv. of Bk. IV:

> He was grown quite esperruquanchurelebublouzerireliced down to his very heel ... (J.M. Cohen in Penguin Classics ... bruisedblueandcontused ...)

The film *Mary Poppins* (1963) provides us with "supercalifragilisticexpialidocious".
The longest place-name in Britain is that of a village in Anglesey, Llanfairpwllg-

wyngyllgogerychwyrndrobwllllantysiliogo-gogoch (58 letters). It is usually shortened to Llanfair P.G. The meaning is, "The church of St. Mary in a hollow of white hazel, near to the rapid whirlpool and St. Tysilio church, near to a red cave".

The longest English surname is said to be Featherstonehaugh, often pronounced "Fanshaw".

The German language lends itself to extensive agglomerations and the following would be hard to beat—"Lebens-mittelzuschusseinstellungskommissionsvor-sitzenderstellvertreter", *i.e.* Deputy-President of the Food-Rationing-Winding-up-Commission.

Longevity (lon jev' i ti). Among the traditional stock cases of longevity are Harry Jenkins, who is reputed to have lived 169 years; Thomas PARR, who died at the age of 152; Catherine, Countess of Desmond, who died at the age of 140; and Thomas Carn of Shoreditch, listed by Dr. Brewer as living 207 years and in the reign of ten sovereigns. Carn's actual dates were 1471 to 1578 (107 years), a figure "2" having been superimposed over a "1" on his tombstone.

It must be noted that all these cases belong to the days before the Registration Act of 1836 ensured a really efficient system of recording births, marriages, and deaths.

The longest authenticated life in the United Kingdom is that of Ada Roe (née Giddings, 1858–1970), who lived 111 years 339 days. The French Canadian, Pierre Joubert (1701–1814), has been proved to have lived 113 years 124 days.

Longinus, or **Longius.** The traditional name of the Roman soldier who smote Our Lord with his spear at the Crucifixion. The only authority for this is the apocryphal *Acts of Pilate*, dating from the 6th century. According to Arthurian Legend, this spear was brought by JOSEPH OF ARIMATHEA to Listenise, when he visited King Pellam, "who was nigh of Joseph's kin". Sir Balim the Savage seized this spear, with which he wounded King Pellam and destroyed three whole countries with that one stroke. William of Malmesbury says the spear was used by CHARLEMAGNE against the SARACENS.

Longwood. The residence on the island of St. Helena where the Emperor NAPOLEON passed the last years of his life in exile, dying there 5 May 1821.

Look. Black looks, To look blue, daggers, a gift-horse, etc., *see these words*.

Look alive! Make haste; be on the alert.

Look before you leap. Consider well before you act.

And look before you ere you leap.
For as you sow, you're like to reap.
BUTLER: *Hudibras*, Pt. II, canto ii, 502.

To look through blue glasses, or **coloured spectacles.** To regard actions in a wrong light; to view things distorted by prejudice.

To look through rose-coloured, or **rose-tinted spectacles.** To take an unduly favourable view of things which the circumstances do not warrant; to be over-optimistic.

To look up. To seek information in books; to visit an acquaintance; to pay a call. Things or persons are said to "look up" when they are improving.

It is unlucky to break a looking-glass. The nature of the ill-luck varies; thus, if a maiden, she will never marry; if a married woman, it betokens death, etc. This superstition arose from the use made of mirrors in former times by magicians, etc. If in their operations the mirror used was broken, the unlucky inquirer could receive no answer.

Looking-glass. As applied to words, a phrase implying that what is spoken or written is to be accepted in the reverse sense or turned upside down. Thus, as spoken by some, "We are prepared to negotiate" really means "We are willing to accept all our demands in full and concede nothing in return". Similarly "We believe in freedom of speech" really means "Only as long as you are on our side and say what we want to hear". The allusion is to Lewis Carroll's *Through the Looking-Glass. Cp.* MIRROR WRITING.

Loop. Looping the loop. The airman's term for the evolution which consists of describing a perpendicular circle in the air; at the top of the circle, or loop, the airman is upside down. The term is from a kind of switchback once popular at fairs in which a moving car or bicycle performed a similar evolution on a perpendicular circular track.

Loose. Figuratively, of lax morals; dissolute; dissipated.

A loose fish. *See under* FISH.

At a loose end. Without employment, or uncertain what to do next. **The loose ends** of any agreement or transaction are the final details requiring settlement, and **to tie up the loose ends** is to settle the outstanding points of detail.

Having a tile loose. *See under* TILE.

On the loose. Behaving in a dissolute fashion.

To cut loose. To break away from conventional restraints.

To play fast and loose. *See under* FAST.

Loose-strife. This name of several species of plants of the genera *Lysimachia* and *Lythrum* is due to mistranslation. The Greek name was *lusimachion*, from the personal name *Lusimachos*, and this was treated as though it were *lusi-*, from *luein*, to loose, and *mache*, strife. Pliny says that the plant has a soothing effect upon oxen that will not draw in the same yoke and that it keeps off flies and gnats, thus relieving horses and oxen from their irritation. Similarly in Fletcher's *Faithful Shepherdess* (II, ii) we read:

> Yellow Lysimachus, to give sweet rest
> To the faint shepherd, killing, where it comes,
> All busy gnats, and every fly that hums.

Lord. A nobleman, a peer of the realm; formerly (and in some connexions still), a ruler, a master, the holder of a manor. It is the O.E. *hlaford*, *hlaf*, loaf, and modern *ward*, *i.e.* the *bread-guardian* or *-keeper*, the head of the household (*cp.* LADY).

All members of the HOUSE OF LORDS are Lords; the archbishops and BISHOPS are Lords Spiritual, and the lay peers Lords Temporal. The word is used in COURTESY TITLES and as a title of honour to certain official personages, as the Lord Chief Justice and other Judges, the Lord Mayor, Lord Advocate, Lord Rector, etc. A BARON is called by his title of peerage (either a surname or territorial designation), prefixed by the title "Lord", as "Lord Dawson" or "Lord Islington". It may also be substituted in other than strictly ceremonial use for "MARQUESS", "EARL", or "VISCOUNT", the *of* being dropped, "Lord Salisbury" (for "The Marquess of Salisbury"), "Lord Derby" ("The Earl of Derby"), etc.; this cannot be done in the case of dukes.

Drunk as a lord. *See under* DRUNK.

In the year of our Lord. *See* ANNO DOMINI.

Lord Harry. *See* HARRY.

Lord Lieutenant. In the mid-16th century Lieutenants of the counties came into existence as Crown representatives for control of the military with the power of raising the MILITIA. Lords Lieutenant appointed by the Crown are now the chief executive authority in the counties with the right of recommending the appointment of magistrates. Their extensive control over the militia ended in 1871. Until 1922 the Viceroy was the Lord Lieutenant of Ireland.

Lord Look-on. A punning nickname given to Lord Lucan during the Crimean war for his cautiousness, particularly when he missed a splendid chance to charge a body of Russian cavalry on 5 October 1854.

Lord Lyon King of Arms. *See* HERALD.

Lord Mayor's Day. Originally the Lord Mayor of LONDON was elected on the Feast of St. SIMON and St. JUDE (28 October), and although the election day was altered, admittance to office continued to take place on that day until 1751. From 1752, owing to the adoption of the Gregorian CALENDAR, Lord Mayor's Day became 9 November. In recent years the Lord Mayor has been sworn in at Guildhall on the second Friday in November, being presented to the Lord Chief Justice on the following day (Saturday).

The Lord Mayor's Show. The annual procession which accompanies the Lord Mayor through the CITY to the Royal Courts of Justice on the second Saturday in November. It has developed in scale over the years, and from 1453 until 1856 a river pageant was part of the proceedings. A few days later the **Lord Mayor's Banquet** is held in the GUILDHALL where it is now customary for the Prime Minister to make a political speech. The bill for the Procession and Banquet is settled by the Lord Mayor and the Sheriffs.

Lord of the Ascendant. *See under* ASCENDANT.

Lord of Creation. Man.

> Replenish the earth, and subdue it: and have dominion over the fish of the sea, and over the fowl of the air, and over every living things that moveth upon the earth.... Behold, I have given you every herb bearing seed ... and every tree.
>
> *Gen.* i, 28, 29.

Lord of Hosts. In the Old Testament, a frequently used title for JEHOVAH, no doubt arising from the belief that He led their armies in battle.

Lord of the Isles. A title once borne by descendants of Somerled, Lord of Argyll, who ruled the Western Isles of Scotland as VASSALS of the King of Scotland in the 14th and 15th centuries.

The Lordship of the Isles was taken over by the Scottish crown in 1540 and it subsequently became one of the titles of the Prince of WALES. Scott has a poem called *The Lord of the Isles* (1814).

Lord of Misrule. *See* KING OF MISRULE.

The Lord of the Rings. Sauron the Great, the Dark Lord of Mordor in J.R.R. Tolkien's sequel (1954–55) the HOBBIT. Sauron's power depended on the possession of certain rings, especially the One Ring, the Ruling Ring, the Master Ring which he had lost many years ago and which he now sought to regain to give him strength to cover the land in a second darkness. This ring had eventually come into the hands of the Hobbit, Bilbo Baggins, who passed it on to Frodo Baggins, his adopted heir. If Sauron recovered it the Hobbits would be doomed and the only way to destroy the ring was to find the Cracks of Doom and cast it into the Fire-mountain. The saga essentially concerns Frodo's struggles, trials and adventures to achieve this.

The Lord's Day. SUNDAY.

The Lord's Prayer. The words in which Jesus taught his disciples to pray (*Matt*. vi, 9–13). *See* PATERNOSTER.

The Lord's Supper. A name given to the Holy Communion which commemorates the LAST SUPPER of Jesus with his disciples.

Lords and Ladies. The popular name of the wild arum. *Arum maculatum*. *See* CUCK-OO FLOWERS *under* CUCKOO.

Lords Spiritual. The bishops who have seats in the HOUSE OF LORDS.

Lords Temporal. The lay members of the HOUSE OF LORDS.

My Lord. The correct form to use in addressing Judges of the Supreme Court (usually slurred to "M'Lud"), also the respectful form of address to BISHOPS, noblemen under the rank of DUKE, Lord Mayors, Lord Provosts, and the Lord Advocate.

The Lord knows who, what, where, etc. Flippant expressions used to denote one's own entire ignorance of the matter.

> Great families of yesterday we show,
> And lords, whose parents were the Lord knows who.
> DEFOE: *The True-Born Englishman*, 374.

> Ask where's the north? At York, 'tis on the Tweed; In Scotland, at the Orcades; and there, At Greenland, Zembla, or the Lord knows where.
> POPE: *Essay on Man*, ii, 222.

To live like a lord. To fare luxuriously; to live like a fighting-cock (*see under* COCK).

To lord it, or **lord it over.** To play the lord; to ruly tyrannically, to domineer.

> You grey towers that still
> Rise up as if to lord it over air.
> WORDSWORTH: *Sonnets upon the Punishment of Death*, I.

When our Lord falls in our Lady's lap. When EASTER Sunday falls on the same date as LADY DAY (25 March). This is said to bode ill for England. In the 19th century this occured in 1883 and 1894; in the 20th, its sole occurrence has been in 1951.

Lord's. The Headquarters of the Marylebone Cricket Club (M.C.C.), and of CRICK-ET generally, is at St. John's Wood, London. The ground was opened by Thomas Lord (1757–1832) who was groundsman at the White Conduit Club, London, in 1780. In 1797 he started a cricket ground of his own on the site of what is now Dorset Square, moving the turf in 1811 to a new site near Regent's Canal, whence in 1814 he trans-ferred to the present ground.

> I doubt if there be any scene in the world more animating or delightful than a cricket-match—I do not mean a set match at Lord's ground for money, hard money, between a certain number of gentlemen and players, as they are called.
> MISS MITFORD: *Our Village* (*A Country Cricket-Match*) (1832).

Lorel. Also *losel*, a worthless person; a rake or profligate. The word is from *loren*, also *losen*, from the old *lesen*, to lose. It is chiefly remembered through "Cock Lorell". *See* COCK LORELL'S BOTE.

> Here I set before the good Reader the leud, lousey language of these lewtering Luskes and lasy Lorrels, wherewith they bye and sell the common people as they pas through the countrey. Whych language they term Peddelar's French.
> *Harman's Caveat* (1567).

Lorelie. The name of a steep rock, some 430 ft. high, on the right bank of the Rhine opposite St. Goar, noted for its remarkable echo. It is the traditional haunt of a SIREN who lures boatman to their death. Heine and others have poems on it, and Max Bruch made it the subject of an opera, *Die Lorelei*, produced in 1864. Mendelssohn has an incomplete opera of the same title.

Loreto. The house of Loreto. The Santa Casa or Holy House, the reputed house of the Virgin Mary at Nazareth. It was said to have been miraculously moved to Dalmatia in 1291, thence to Recanati in Italy in 1294, and finally to a site near Ancona in 1295. It was reputed to have been transported by AN-GELS to prevent its destruction by the Turks. The name is from the Lat. *lauretum*, a grove of laurels, in which it stood in Recanati. The Holy House itself is a small stone building, now surrounded by a marble screen.

Losel. *See* LOREL.

Loss. To be at a loss. To be unable to decide. To be puzzled or embarrassed.

Lost causes, The Home of. Oxford. Referred to as such by the poet Matthew Arnold (1822–1888) in his *Essays in Criticism* (*Preface* to the 1st Series).

> Whispering from her towers the last enchantments of the Middle Ages.... Home of lost causes, and forsaken beliefs, and unpopular names, and impossible loyalties!

Lost Generation. A name sometimes applied to the young men, especially of the cultivated upper and middle classes, who lost their lives in World War I. Rupert Brooke became their symbol; he was 27 when he died (not in battle, but of blood-poisoning).

Lost Tribes. The term applied to the ten tribes of Israel who were carried away from North Palestine (721 B.C.) into Assyria, about 140 years before the BABYLONIAN CAP-

TIVITY (586 B.C.) exiled the tribes of Judah. Their disappearance has caused much speculation, especially among those who look forward to a restoration of the Hebrews as foretold in the OLD TESTAMENT. In 1649, John Sadler suggested that the English were of Israelitish origin. This theory was expanded by Richard Brothers, the half-crazy enthusiast who declared himself Prince of the Hebrews and Ruler of the World (1792), and has since been developed by others. The British Israelite theory is still held by some without any serious supporting evidence.

Lost Sunday. Another name for SEPTUAGESIMA SUNDAY, from its having no special name.

Lothario. A gay Lothario. A gay LIBERTINE, a seducer of women, a debauchee. The character is from Rowe's tragedy *The Fair Penitent* (1703). He probably got the name from Davenant's *Cruel Brother* (1630) in which there is a similar character with this name. *Cp.* LOVELACE.

> Is this that haughty, gallant, gay Lothario?
> *Fair Penitent*, V, i.

Lothian, in SCOTLAND, traditionally takes its name from King Lot, or Lothus Llew, the brother-in-law of ARTHUR, and father of MODRED.

Lots. Casting Lots. To obtain a decision by casting (or drawing from) a set of objects selected for the purpose was a very old form of DIVINATION and an established practice in WITCHCRAFT. Lots were used in ancient Israel in deciding the division of property, appointing to office, the discovering of culprits, etc. (*See Lev*. xvi, 7–10) with the presupposition of divine influence affecting the result.

> The lot is cast into the lap; but the whole disposing thereof is of the Lord.
> *Prov*. xvi, 33.

Lotus. A name given to many plants, *e.g.* by the Egyptians to various species of water-lily, by the Hindus and Chinese to the Nelumbo (a water-bean), their "sacred lotus", and by the Greeks to *Zizyphus lotus*, a North African shrub of the order *Rhamnaceæ*, the fruit of which was used for food.

According to MOHAMMED, a lotus-tree stands in the seventh HEAVEN, on the right hand of the throne of God, and the Egyptians pictured the creator springing from the heart of a lotus flower. Iamblichus says the leaves and fruit of the lotus-tree, being round, represent "the motion of intellect", its towering up through mud symbolizes the eminency of divine intellect over matter; and the Deity sitting on it implies His intellectual sovereignty (*On the Egyptian Mysteries*, sec. vii, cap. ii).

The classic myth is that *Lotis*, a daughter of NEPTUNE fleeing from PRIAPUS was changed into a tree, called *Lotus* after her. Another story is that Dryope of Œchalia and her infant son Amphisus were each changed into a lotus.

Lotus-eaters, or **Lotophagi,** in Homeric legend, are a people who ate of the lotus-tree, the effect of which was to make them forget their friends and homes, and to lose all desire of returning to their native country, their only wish being to live in idleness in Lotus-land (*Odyssey*, XI). Hence a *lotus-eater* is one living in ease and luxury. One of Tennyson's greatest poems is *The Lotos-Eaters*.

Louis, St. Louis IX of France (1214, 1226–1270) is usually represented as holding the Saviour's crown of thorns and the cross; sometimes he is pictured with a pilgrim's staff and sometimes with the standard of the cross, the allusion in all cases being to the CRUSADES. He was canonized in 1297, his feast day being 25 August. He is considered a saint offering special protection to France.

Louisette. *See* GUILLOTINE.

Louisiana in the U.S.A. was named in compliment to Louis XIV of France and was originally applied to the French possessions in the Mississippi valley.

The Louisiana Purchase. The acquisition by the U.S. Government in 1803 of the French territory of Louisiana for the sum of about $15,000,000. Some 828,000 square miles, between the Mississippi and the Rocky Mountains, were thus obtained.

Lounge Lizard. *See* LIZARD.

Lourdes (loord). A famous centre of pilgrimage situated in the south-west of France. In 1858 Bernadette Soubirous, a simple peasant girl, claimed that the Virgin Mary had appeared to her on eighteen occasions. Investigations failed to shake her narrative, and a spring with miraculous healing properties that appeared at the same time began to draw invalids from all over the world. The pilgrimage received ecclesiastical recognition in 1862 and Bernadette was canonized in 1933.

Louvre (loo' vrè). The former royal palace of the French kings in Paris. Dagobert is said to have built there a hunting seat, but the present buildings were begun by Francis I in 1541. Since the French Revolution, the greater part of the Louvre has been used for the national museum and art gallery.

> He'll make your Paris Louvre shake for it.
> SHAKESPEARE: *Henry V*, II, iv.

Love. The word is from O.E. *lufu*, connected with Sans. *lubh*, to desire, and Lat. *lubet*, it pleases, etc.

The Abode of Love. *See* AGAPEMONE.

Cupboard love. *See* CUPBOARD.

The Family of Love. *See* FAMILISTS.

The God of Love. Generally implies either EROS or CUPID. Among the Scandinavians FREYJA was the goddess of sexual love, and among the Hindus Kama is the approximate equivalent of Eros.

Love's Girdle. The CESTUS.

A labour of love. Work undertaken for the love of the thing without regard to payment.

> Remembering without ceasing your work of faith, and labour of love, and patience of hope in our Lord Jesus Christ, in the sight of God and our Father.
> *I Thess.* i, 3.

Love and lordship never like fellowship. Neither lovers nor princes can brook a rival.

Love in a cottage. A marriage for love without sufficient means to maintain one's social status. "When povety comes in at the door, love flies out at the window."

> Love in a hut, with water and a crust,
> Is—Love, forgive us!—cinders, ashes, dust.
> Love in a palace is, perhaps, at last
> More grievous torment than a hermit's fast.
> KEATS: *Lamia*, Pt. II, i.

Love is blind. Lovers cannot see each other's weaknesses and shortcomings. *See* CUPID.

Love me, love my dog. If you love anyone, you will like all that belongs to him. St. BERNARD quotes this proverb in Latin, *Qui me amat, amat et canem meam*.

Not for love or money. Unobtainable, either for payment or for entreaties; not under any circumstances.

There is no love lost between so and so. The persons referred to dislike each other. Formerly the phrase was used in exactly the opposite sense—it was all love between them, and none of it went amissing. In the old ballad *The Children in the Wood* given in PERCY'S RELIQUES we have—

> No love between these two was lost,
> Each was to other kind.

To play for love. To play without stakes.

Love-apple. The tomato. The name was given by the Spaniards who introduced it to Europe from South America. It was alleged to have aphrodisiac properties.

Love Feast. *See* AGAPE.

Love-in-a-mist. The fennel flower, *Nigella damascena*, also called devil-in-a-bush and love-in-a-puzzle.

Love-in-idleness. The HEARTSEASE, *Viola tricolor*. Fable has it that it was originally white, but was changed to purple by Cupid.

> Yet marked I where the bolt of Cupid fell.
> It fell upon a little western flower.
> Before, milk-white, now purple with love's wound;
> And maidens call it Love-in-idleness.
> SHAKESPEARE: *A Midsummer Night's Dream*, II, i.

Love-lies-bleeding. The red AMARANTHS from their hanging inflorescences of small crimson flowers.

Love-lock. A small curl worn by women, fastened to the temples, also called a BOW-CATCHER. At the end of the 16th century the love-lock was a long lock of hair hanging in front of the shoulders, curled and decorated with bows and ribbons.

Loving, or **Grace Cup.** A large cup, tankard or goblet passed round from guest to guest at formal banquets. Agnes Strickland (1786–1874) says that Margaret Atheling, wife of Malcolm Canmore, in order to induce the Scots to remain for grace, devised the grace cup, which was filled with the choicest wine, and of which each guest was allowed to drink *ad libitum*, after grace had been said.

The monks took over the WASSAIL bowl of their heathen predecessors and called it *poculum caritatis*, or the loving-cup. At the Lord Mayor's or City Companies' banquets the loving-cup is a silver bowl with two handles, a napkin being tied to one of them. Two persons stand up, one to drink and the other to defend the drinker. Having taken his draught, the first wipes the cup with the napkin and passes it to his "defender", when the next person rises up to defend the new drinker, and so on.

At the universities of Oxford and Cambridge, the term Grace Cup is more general. The name is also applied to a strong brew of beer flavoured with lemon-peel, nutmeg and sugar, and very brown toast.

Lovel, the Dog. *See* RAT, CAT, AND DOG *under* RAT.

Lovelace. A LIBERTINE, a LOTHARIO. The name is taken from the principal male character in Richardson's *Clarissa, or the History of a Young Lady* (1748). He is a selfish voluptuary, a man of fashion, whose sole ambition is to seduce young women.

Low. To lay low is transitive, and means to overthrow or to kill; **to lie low** is intransitive, and means to be abased, or dead: and colloquially, to bide one's time, to do nothing for the moment.

In low water. Financially embarrassed; or in a bad state of health. The phrase comes from seafaring; *cp.* "stranded", "left HIGH AND DRY".

To give someone the lowdown. A colloquial expression meaning to impart inside information, to explain what the matter is really about. Possibly from the idea that it was mean, disreputable, or "low down" to give such information.

To lower your sail. To salute; to admit yourself submissive or conquered; to humble oneself. A nautical phrase which derives from the English sovereign's ancient claim to sovereignty of the British seas. Before the outbreak of the Third Dutch War (1672–1674) an ultimatum was sent to the Dutch on this issue and at the peace it was accepted that the Dutch lower their flags and strike their topsails in all seas between Cape Finisterre and Point Van Staten in Norway.

> His Majesty's ships shall not, on any account, lower their flags to any foreign ships whatsoever, unless the foreign ships shall first, or at the same time, lower their flags to them.
>
> *King's Regulations and Admiralty Instructions*, 1926.

Low-bell. A bell formerly used in night-fowling. The birds were first roused from their slumber by its tinkling, and then dazzled by a *low*, *i.e.*, a blaze or flame (Scottish and provincial English). The word *low-bell* was also applied to a small bell such as a sheep bell.

> There is also another method of fowling, which ... is performed with nets, and in the night time; and the darker the night the better.—"This sport we call in England, most commonly bird-batting, and some call it lowbelling; and the use of it is to go with a great light of cressets ... and carry it before you, on your breast, with a bell in your other hand, and of great bigness, made in the manner of a cow-bell."
>
> STRUTT: *Sports and Pastimes*, Bk. I, ch. ii (1801).

Low Church. The essentially PROTESTANT section of the CHURCH OF ENGLAND which gives a relatively low place to the claims of the priesthood, episcopate, etc., and has more in common with NONCONFORMIST than CATHOLIC teaching. It is used in contrast to HIGH CHURCH.

Low German. *See* HIGH GERMAN.

Low Latin. *See under* LATIN.

Low Mass. In the Western Church, MASS said by the celebrant without the assistance of other clergy. No part of the service is sung.

Low Sunday. The Sunday next after EASTER. So called probably because of the contrast to the "high" feast of EASTER Sunday. *Cp.* QUASIMODO SUNDAY.

Lower case. The printer's name for the small letters (minuscules) of a fount of type (*see* FONT), as opposed to the capitals; these were, in a type-setter's "case", on a *lower* level than the others.

Lower deck. In the Royal Navy, the rank and file of the ship's company as distinct from the officers. In the ships of former days the lower deck, above the orlop, was the lowest of the continuous gun decks where the crew had their messes and slung their hammocks.

Lower Empire. The later Roman, especially the Western Empire, from about the time of the foundation of the Eastern Empire in 330 to the fall of Constantinople in 1453.

The Lower House. The second of any two legislative chambers; in England, the HOUSE OF COMMONS.

Loyal. The Loyal North Lancashire Regiment was so called in 1793, the only British regiment given this designation

The Loyal Toast. This time-honoured toast to the King (or the Queen) is normally drunk while standing, but it is the Royal Navy's privilege to drink it sitting. The story is that this custom arose when George IV (or William IV), when acknowledging the toast in a ship, bumped his head on a beam as he stood up. However APOCRYPHAL such stories may be, it is probably due to the difficulty of standing upright between decks in the old wooden warships.

Loyola, St. Ignatius (1491–1556). Founder of the Society of Jesus, is depicted in art with the sacred monogram. I.H.S. on his breast, or as contemplating it, surrounded by glory in the skies, in allusion to his claim that he had a miraculous knowledge of the mystery of the TRINITY vouchsafed to him. He was the son of the Spanish ducal house of Loyola and, after being severely wounded at the siege of Pamplona (1521), left the army and dedicated himself to the service of the Virgin. *See* JESUIT.

Lubber's Hole. In sailing ships the open space in the top near the head of a lower mast through which seamen ascend to the top, to avoid the danger and difficulties of climbing over the rim by the futtock shrouds. It was once held only a fit method for timid GREENHORNS or lubbers. Hence, some way of evading or wriggling through one's difficulties.

Lubberkin, or **Lubrican.** *See* LEPRECHAUN.

Luce. Flower de Luce. A corruption of FLEUR-DE-LYS.

Lucian. The personification of the follies and vices of the age. Such was Lucian, the chief character in the GOLDEN ASS of Apuleius (2nd century A.D.).

Lucifer (Lat. lightbringer). VENUS, as the morning star. When she follows the SUN, and is an evening star, she is called HESPERUS.

Isaiah applied the epithet "Day-star" to the King of Babylon who proudly boasted he would ascend to the heavens and make himself equal to God, but who was fated to be cast down to the uttermost recesses of the pit. This epithet was translated into "Lucifer"—

> Take up this proverb against the king of Babylon and say, ... How art thou fallen from heaven, O Lucifer, son of the morning!
>
> *Is*. xiv, 4, 12.

By St. JEROME and other Fathers the name was applied to SATAN. Hence poets feign that Satan, before he was driven out of heaven for his pride, was called Lucifer. Milton, in *Paradise Lost* (X, 425), gives this name to the demon of "Sinful Pride", hence the phrase *Proud as Lucifer*.

Lucifer-match, or **Lucifer.** A match. The friction match was invented by John Walker in 1826 and first called a "friction light". The invention was copied by Samuel Jones of the STRAND and sold as the "Lucifer" (*c*. 1829). The term *match* was taken over from the name given to the spill used as secondary tinder in the days of the tinder-box. *Cp*. CONGREVES; LOCOFOCO; PROMETHEAN; SAFETY MATCHES.

Luciferians. A 4th-century sect, so called from their leader Lucifer, Bishop of Cagliari in Sardinia. They resisted all conciliation with repentant ARIANS.

Lucius. One of the mythical kings of Britain, the son of Coillus, and fabled as the first Christian British King according to Geoffrey of Monmouth.

Luck. Accidental good fortune (Dut. *luk*; Ger. *Glück*).

Down on one's luck. In adverse circumstances; short of funds, etc.

Give a man luck and throw him into the sea. Meaning that his luck will save him even in the greatest extremity. JONAH and ARION were cast into the sea, but were carried safely to land, the one by a whale and the other by a dolphin.

He has the luck of the Devil, or **the Devil's own luck.** He is extraordinarily lucky; everything he attempts is successful.

Luck money, or **luck penny.** A trifle returned to a purchaser for good luck after a deal; also a penny with a hole in it, supposed to ensure good luck. Picking up a pin or a piece of coal is also supposed to be lucky.

Not in luck's way. Not promoted unexpectedly, enriched, or otherwise benefited.

The luck of Eden Hall. See EDEN HALL.

There's luck in odd numbers. See ODD.

Luckie, or **Lucky.** In Scotland a term of familiar but respectful endearment for any elderly woman; often used of the landlady of an ale-house; a *luckie dad* is a grandfather.

A Lucky dip, or **bag.** A tub or other container, in which are placed various articles covered with bran, etc., much in use at bazaars and children's parties. The visitors "dip" and take what they get.

A lucky stone. A stone with a natural hole through it. John Aubrey (1697) tells us that flints with holes in them were hung on a horse or in its stall as a preservative against its being hag-ridden. *Cp*. LUCKY PENNY.

The lucky bone. The small bone of a sheep's head; once prized by beggars and tramps as it was supposed to bring good luck for the day of its acquisition.

To cut one's lucky (old slang). To decamp or make off quickly; to "cut one's stick". As luck means chance, the phrase may signify, "I must give up my chance and be off."

To strike lucky. *See* STRIKE.

Lucullus sups with Lucullus (lŭk ŭl′ ŭs). Said of a glutton who gourmandizes alone. Lucius Lucullus (*c*. 117–56 B.C.) was a successful Roman military leader and administrator whose latter years were given over to rich and elegant living. On one occasion a superb supper was prepared, and when asked who were to be his guests he replied, "Lucullus will sup tonight with Lucullus."

He was essentially a man of cultural tastes and more likely a *gourmet* than a GOURMAND.

Lucus a non lucendo (lū′ kŭs ā non loosen′ dō). An etymological contradiction; a phrase used by etymologists who accounted for words by deriving them from their opposites. It means literally "a grove (called *lucus*) from not being lucent" (*lux*, light; *luceo*, to shine). It was the Roman grammarian Honoratus Maurus (*fl*. end of 4th century A.D.) who provided this famous etymology. In the same way *ludus*, a school, may be said to come from *ludere*, to play, and our word *linen* from *lining*, because it is not used for linings.

> One *Tryphiodorus* ... composed an Epick Poem ... of four and twenty books, having entirely banished the letter A from his first book, which was called *Alpha* (as *Lucus a non lucendo*) because there was not an *Alpha* in it.
>
> ADDISON: *Spectator*, No. lix.

Lucy, St. Patron SAINT for those afflicted in the eyes. She is supposed to have lived in Syracuse and to have suffered martyrdom there about 304. One legend relates that a nobleman wanted to marry her for the beauty of her eyes; so she tore them out and gave them to him, saying, "Now let me live to God." Hence she is represented in art carrying a palm branch and a platter with two eyes on it.

Lucy Stoner. An American colloquialism for a married woman who insists on using her maiden name; after Lucy Stone (1818–1893), a famous U.S. SUFFRAGETTE. Her married name was Blackwell.

Lud. A mythical king of Britain. According to Geoffrey of Monmouth, the beautifier of LONDON who was buried by the gate which bears his name. It is also suggested that the name is that of a CELTIC river god.

General Lud. *See* LUDDITES.

Lud's Town. LONDON; so called from King LUD.

> And on the gates of Lud's town set your heads.
> SHAKESPEARE: *Cymbeline*, IV, ii.

Ludgate. One of the former western gates of the City of London, first mentioned in the 12th century. It stood halfway up Ludgate Hill, was rebuilt after extensive damage in 1586, and demolished 1760–1762. It was used as a prison for several centuries. The statues of LUD and his two sons which once adorned the gate are now in the entrance of St. Dunstan's School. The name probably derives from the O.E. *ludgeat*, a postern.

Luddites. The name given to the machine-breaking rioters in the manufacturing districts of Nottinghamshire, Lancashire, Cheshire, and Yorkshire, in the years 1811 to 1816. The textile workers blamed the new machinery for their unemployment and distress. They were called Luddites after their legendary leader, Ned Ludd, and the leadership of such rioters was often attributed to "General Ludd". *Cp.* CAPTAIN SWING *under* SWING.

Ludlam. *See* LAZY.

Luff (Dut. *loef*, weather-gauge). The *luff* of a fore-and-aft sail is its fore edge and the broadest part of a ship's bow is called the *luff* as well as the weather-gauge or part of the ship towards the wind. A tackle consisting of two hook blocks, one double and one single, is a *luff*.

Luff upon luff is to use a luff purchase with a second tackle on its hauling part, thus trebling or quadrupling the power.

To keep the luff is to continue close to the wind.

To luff is to bring the ship's head nearer the wind. A ship is said to **spring her luff** when she yields to the helm by sailing nearer the wind.

Lug. An old word for the ear, also for affected airs.

To blow in one's lug. To flatter, to wheedle.

To give him a lift on the lug. To give him a blow on the ear.

To put on the lugs. To give oneself airs, to be conceited.

Luke, St. Patron SAINT of artists and physi-

cians. Tradition says he painted a portrait of the Virgin Mary and *Col*. iv, 14, states that he was a physician. His day is 18 October. *See also* SYMBOLS OF SAINTS.

St. Luke's Club, or **The Virtuosi.** An artist's club, established in England by Vandyck about 1638 and held at the Rose Tavern, FLEET STREET. There was an academy of St. Luke founded by artists at Paris in 1391; one at ROME, founded in 1593, but based on the "Compagnia di San Luca" of Florence, founded in 1345; a similar one was established at Siena in 1355.

St. Luke's Summer. The latter end of autumn. *See* SUMMER.

As light as St. Luke's bird. Not light at all. In art St. LUKE is represented with an ox lying near him.

Luke's Iron Crown. A symbol of tyranny.

> The lifted axe, the agonising wheel,
> Luke's iron crown, and Damien's bed of steel,
> To men remote from power but rarely known,
> Leave reason, faith, and conscience all our own.
> GOLDSMITH: *The Traveller*, 435.

George and Luke Dosa headed an unsuccessful revolt in Hungary in the early part of the 16th century. George underwent the torture of the red-hot iron crown, as a punishment for allowing himself to be proclaimed king. Goldsmith errs in attributing the incident to Luke.

Lumber. Formerly a pawnbroker's shop (from LOMBARD). Thus Lady Murray (*Lives of the Baillies*, 1749) writes: "They put all the little plate they had in the lumber, which is pawning it, till the ships come home."

From its use as applied to old broken boards and bits of wood the word was extended to mean timber sawn and split, especially when the trees have been felled and sawn *in situ*.

Luminary of the English Church, The. Bishop Bartholomew of Exeter, a Breton (1161–1184), was so called by Pope Alexander III. He was one of the five bishops sent to Sens with Henry II's appeal to the Pope, after Archbishop Becket's flight to France in 1164. He conscientiously used his learning and abilities for the good of the Church.

Lump. If you don't like it, you may lump it. Whether you like to do it or not, no matter; you must take it as it is; you must put up with it, *i.e.* take it in a lump.

Lunar Month. From new moon to new moon, *i.e.* the time taken by the moon to revolve round the earth, about $29\frac{1}{2}$ days. Popularly, the lunar month is 28 days. In the JEWISH and MOHAMMEDAN CALENDARS (*see under* CALENDAR), the lunar month commences at sunset of the day when the new moon is first seen after sunset, and varies in length, being sometimes 29 and sometimes 30 days.

Lunar Year. Twelve lunar months, *i.e.* about 354⅓ days.

Lunatics. Literally, moon-struck persons. The Romans believed that the mind was affected by the moon, and that lunatics grew more and more frenzied as the moon increased to its full (Lat. *luna*, moon).

Lundi, St. *See* ST. MONDAY *under* MONDAY.

Lupercal, The. (lū′ pĕr kăl). In ancient ROME the spot where ROMULUS and Remus were suckled by the wolf (*lupus*). An annual festival, the *Lupercalia* was held there on 15 February, in honour of Lupercus the Lycæan PAN (so called because he protected the flocks from wolves). The name *Lupercal* is sometimes, inaccurately, used for the Lupercalia. It was on one of these occasions that Antony thrice offered JULIUS CÆSAR the crown, but he refused, saying, "JUPITER alone is king of Rome."

> You all did see that on the Lupercal,
> I thrice presented him a kingly crown,
> Which he did thrice refuse.
>
> SHAKESPEARE: *Julius Cæsar*, III, ii

Lurch. To leave in the lurch. To desert a person in a difficulty. In cribbage, one is left in the position called the *lurch* when one's adversary has run out his score of fifty-one holes before one has oneself turned the corner (or pegged out one's thirty-first hole).

Lush. Beer and other intoxicating drinks. A word of uncertain origin, said by some to be derived from the name of a London brewer called Lushington. Up to about 1895, there was a convivial society of actors called "The City of Lushington," which met in the Harp Tavern, Russell Street, and claimed to be 150 years old. It may also be the O.Fr. *vin louche*, thick or unsettled wine. *Lush* is also American slang for an alcoholic.

Lusiads, The. The Portuguese national epic, written by Camoëns, and published in 1572. It relates the stories of illustrious actions of the *Lusians* or Portuguese (*see* LUSUS), and primarily the exploits of Vasco da Gama and his comrades in their "discovery of India" (1497–1499). The intervention of VENUS and BACCHUS and other classical deities makes it far more than the narrative of a voyage. It has been said that Camoëns did for the Portuguese language what Dante did for Italian, and Chaucer for English. *See* LUSUS.

Lustral. Properly, pertaining to the LUSTRUM; hence purificatory, as *lustral water*, the water used in Christian as well as many pagan rites for aspersing worshippers. In ROME the priest used a small OLIVE or LAUREL branch for sprinkling infants and the people.

Lustrum. In ancient ROME the purificatory sacrifice made by the censors for the people once in five years, after the census had been taken (from *luere*, to wash, to purify); hence a period of five years.

Lusus. Pliny (III, i) tells us that Lusus was the companion of BACCHUS in his travels, and settled a colony in Portugal; whence the country was called *Lusitania*, and the inhabitants *Lusians*, or the sons of Lusus.

Lutestring. A glossy silk fabric; the French *lustrine* (from *lustre*).

Speaking in lutestring. Flash, or affected speech. Junius in Letter XLVIII says: "I was led to trouble you with these observations by a passage, which, to speak in lutestring, *I met with this morning in the course of my reading*." SHAKESPEARE has "taffeta phrases and silken terms precise". We call inflated speech "FUSTIAN or "BOMBAST"; say a man talks *stuff*; term a book or speech SHODDY; sailors call telling a story "spinning a yarn", etc.

Lutetia (Lat. *lutum*, mud). The ancient name of PARIS, which, in Roman times, was a collection of mud hovels. CÆSAR called it *Lutetia Parisiorum* (the mud town of the Parisii), which gives the present name *Paris*.

Lutin. A GOBLIN in the folklore of Normandy; similar to the house-spirits of Germany. The name was formerly *netun*, and is said to be derived from NEPTUNE. When the *lutin* assumes the form of a horse ready equipped, it is called *Le Cheval Bayard*. *See* BAYARD.

To lutin. To twist hair into ELF-LOCKS. These mischievous urchins are said to tangle the mane of a horse or the locks of a child so that the hair must be cut off.

Lutine Bell. H.M.S. *Lutine*, a captured French warship, re-commissioned by the British, left Yarmouth for Holland on 9 October 1799 with bullion and specie to the value of some £500,000. The same night, she was wrecked on a sandbank off the Zuyder Zee with the loss of every soul on board save one, who died as soon as rescued. It was a black day for LLOYD'S underwriters. In 1858 some £50,000 was salvaged, as well as the *Lutine*'s bell and rudder, among other things. The latter was made into the official chair for Lloyd's chairman and a secretary's desk. The bell was hung at Lloyd's and is rung once whenever a total wreck is reported, and twice for an overdue ship.

It was rung in 1963 to signal the death of President Kennedy and in 1965 for that of Sir Winston Churchill, who was an honorary member of Lloyd's.

Luz (lŭz). The indestructible bone of the human body according to Rabbinical legend; the nucleus of the resurrection body. A bone in the spine and the sacrum (sacred bone) may have been so called in allusion to it.

Lycanthropy (lī kăn' thrō pi). The insanity afflicting one who imagines himself to be some kind of animal and exhibits the tastes, voices, etc., of that animal. Formerly, the name given by the ancients to those who imagined themselves to be wolves (Gr. *lukos*, wolf; *anthropos*, man). The WEREWOLF has sometimes been called a *lycanthrope*; and *lycanthropy* was sometimes applied to the form of witchcraft by which WITCHES transformed themselves into wolves.

Lycaon (lī kā' on). In classical mythology, a king of ARCADIA, who, desirous of testing the divine knowledge of JOVE, served up human flesh on his table; for which the god changed him into a wolf. His daughter, CALISTO, was changed into the constellation the Bear, which is sometimes called *Lycaonis Arctos*.

Lycopodium (lī kō pō' di ùm). A genus of perennial plants comprising the club-mosses, so called from their fanciful resemblance to a wolf's foot (Gr. *lukos*, wolf; *pous, podos*, foot). The powder from the spore-cases of some of these is used in surgery as an absorbent and also (as it is highly inflammable) for stage-lighting. *Cp.* LIME-LIGHT.

Lyddite. A high explosive composed of picric acid and GUN-COTTON; so called from Lydd in Kent, where it was first tested on the artillery ranges in 1888.

Lydford Law. Punish first and try afterwards. Lydford was one of the four Saxon boroughs of Devon and its Norman castle became the prison of the STANNARIES. Offenders were confined in a dungeon so loathsome and dreary that they frequently died before they could be brought for trial. *Cp.* CUPAR JUSTICE; HULL; JEDDART; LYNCH LAW.

Lying for the whetstone. *See* WHETSTONE.

Lyke-wake. *See* LICH-WAKE.

Lyme-, or **Lyam-hound** (līm). The bloodhound, so called from *lyme*, or *lyam*, the leash (Lat. *ligare*, to tie). The *lymehound* was used by mediæval huntsmen for tracking down the wounded buck, and the *gazehound* for killing it.

Lynceus (lin' sūs). One of the ARGONAUTS. He was so sharp-sighted that he could see through the earth, and distinguish objects that were miles off.

> Non possis oculo quantum contendere Lynceus.
> HORACE : I *Epistles*, i, 28.

Also the name of the husband of HYPERMNESTRA. *See* DANAIDES.

Lynch Law. Mob-law, law administered by private individuals, and followed by summary execution. The origin of the term is unknown; none of the suggested derivations from James Lynch, a 15th-century Mayor of Galway in Ireland, or Charles Lynch (1736–1796) of Virginia, has been substantiated. From the 18th century the practice was particularly associated with the more lawless districts of the U.S.A. *Cp.* CUPAR JUSTICE; JEDDART; LYDFORD LAW.

Lynx (lingks). The animal proverbial for its piercing eyesight is a fabulous beast, half dog and half panther, but not like either in character. The cat-like animal now called a lynx is not remarkable for keen-sightedness. The word is probably related to Gr. *lussein*, to see *Cp.* LYNCEUS.

Lyon King of Arms, Lord. The chief heraldic officer for SCOTLAND; so called from the *lion rampant* in the Scottish royal arms. *See* HERALDRY; THE LION IN HERALDRY *under* LION.

Lyonesse. A rich tract of land fabled to stretch between Land's End and the Scilly Isles on which stood the *City of Lions* and some 140 churches. King ARTHUR came from this mythical country. "That sweet land of Lyonesse" was, according to Spenser (*the Faerie Queene*), the birthplace of TRISTRAM, and, according to Tennyson, the scene of King Arthur's death.

> Of Faery damsels met in forest wide
> By knights of Logres, or of Lyones,
> Lancelot, or Pelleas, or Pellenore.
> MILTON: *Paradise Regained*, II, 359.

Lyre. The most ancient of all stringed instruments. That of Terpander and Olympus had only three strings; the Scythian lyre had five; that of Simonides had eight, and that of Timotheus had twelve. It was played either with the fingers or with a plectrum. The lyre is called by poets a "shell", because the cords of the lyre used by ORPHEUS, AMPHION, and APOLLO were stretched on the shell of a tortoise. HERCULES used boxwood.

Amphion built Thebes with the music of his lyre.

Arion charmed the dolphins by the music of his lyre, and when the bard threw himself into the sea one of them carried him safely to Tænarus.

Hercules was taught music by Linus. One day, being reproved, the strong man broke the head of his master with his own lyre.

Orpheus charmed savage beasts, and even the infernal gods, with the music of his lyre. Mountains moved to hear his song and rivers ceased to flow.

Lysenkoism. *See* MICHURINISM.

M

M. The thirteenth letter of the English alphabet (the twelfth of the ancient Roman, and twentieth of the FUTHORC). M in the Phœnician character represented the wavy appearance of water, and is called in Hebrew *mem* (water). The Egyptian hieroglyphic represented the owl. In English M is always sounded, except in words from Greek in which it is followed by *n*, as *mnemonics*, *Mnason* (*Acts* xxi, 16).

In Roman numerals M stands for 1,000 (Lat. *mille*): MCMLXX = one thousand, nine hundred and seventy.

Persons convicted of manslaughter, and admitted to BENEFIT OF CLERGY, used to be branded with an M. It was burnt on the brawn of the left thumb.

What is your name? N or M. *See under* N.

M, to represent the human face. Add two dots for the eyes, thus, .M. These dots being equal to O's, we get OMO (*homo*), Latin for man.

> Who reads the name,
> For man upon his forehead, there the M
> Had traced most plainly.
> DANTE: *Purgatory*, xxiii.

M'. The first letter of certain CELTIC surnames (*M'Cabe, M'Ian, M'Mahon*, etc.) represents *Mac* (son) and should be so pronounced.

M.B. Waistcoat. A clerical cassock waistcoat was so called (*c.* 1830) when first introduced by the HIGH CHURCH party. M.B. means "MARK OF THE BEAST".

> He smiled at the folly which stigmatised an M.B. waistcoat.
> MRS. OLIPHANT: *Phœbe Junior*, II, iii.

M.C.C. The Marylebone Cricket Club, founded in 1787, which moved to LORD's in 1814.

MS. (pl. **MSS**). Manuscript; applied to literary works, etc., in handwriting, but erroneously to typescript (Lat. *manuscriptum*, that which is written by hand).

Mab (perhaps the Welsh *maban*, a baby). The "fairies' midwife"—*i.e.* employed by the fairies as midwife to deliver man's brain of dreams. Thus whem ROMEO says, "I dreamed a dream tonight," Mercutio replies, "Oh, then, I see Queen Mab hath been with you." When Mab is called "queen" it does not mean sovereign, for TITANIA as wife of King OBERON was Queen of Faery, but simply "female" (O.E. *quén* or *cwén*, modern *quean*).

Excellent descriptions of Mab are given by SHAKESPEARE (*Romeo and Juliet*, I, iv), by Ben Jonson, by Herrick, and by Drayton in *Nymphidea*.

Mabinogion. A collection of eleven mediæval CELTIC stories of which the Four Branches of the Mabinogi are the most outstanding. Originally they were probably essentially concerned with the life and death of Pryderi, but a considerable amount of additional material has complicated the structure. The tales are basically Welsh mythology and folklore together with ARTHURIAN ROMANCE. The title "Mabinogion" was given by Lady Charlotte Guest to her translations of these stories (1838–1849); but this only properly applies to the Four Branches (*Pwyll, Branwen, Manawydan*, and *Math*) and not the remainder. The last three stories, *The Lady of the Fountain, Peredur*, and *Gereint son of Erbin*, show marked Norman-French influence, often attributed to Chrétien de Troyes, but it is now thought that his material may have derived from Welsh sources.

Mabinogi is derived from *mab* (youth) and was applied to a "tale of youth", then to any "tale". Lady Guest's translation long held the field, but the best and most complete English translation is now that of Gwyn Jones and Thomas Jones (1948).

Macaber, or **Macabre, The Danse**. *See* DANCE OF DEATH.

Macadamize. A method of road-making introduced after 1810 by John L. Macadam (1756–1836), consisting of layers of broken stones of nearly uniform size, each being separately crushed into position by traffic, or (later) by a heavy roller.

Macaire. A French CHANSON DE GESTE of the 12th century. Macaire was the name of the murderer of Aubry de Montdidier and he was brought to justice by the sagacity of

AUBRY'S DOG (*see under* DOG). The story was transferred to the 14th century in another version and a 15th-century mural painting of the legend in the chateau of Montargis gave rise to Aubry's dog being called the "dog of Montargis".

Robert Macaire. A typical villain of French comedy; from the play of this name (a sequel to *L'Auberge des Adrets*, 1834) by Frédéric Lemaître and Benjamin Antier. Macaire is—

> le type de la perversité, de l'impudence, de la friponnerie audacieuse, le héros fanfaron du vol et de l'assassinat.

Macaroni. A COXCOMB (Ital. *un maccherone, see* next entry). The word is derived from the Macaroni Club, instituted in London about 1760 by a set of flashy men who had travelled in Italy, and introduced at AL-MACK's subscription table the new-fangled Italian food, *macaroni*. The Macaronies were exquisite fops; vicious, insolent, fond of gambling, drinking and duelling, and were (*c.* 1773) the curse of VAUXHALL GARDENS. *Cp.* MOHOCKS.

An American regiment raised in Maryland during the War of Independence was called *The Macaronies* from its showy uniform. *Cp.* YANKEE DOODLE.

Macaronic Latin. DOG-LATIN. From the Ital. *maccheroni* (macaroni), a mixture of coarse meal, eggs and cheese.

Macaroni verse. Verses in which foreign words are ludicrously distorted and jumbled together, as in Porson's lines on the threatened invasion of England by NAPOLEON or J. A. Morgan's "translation" of Canning's *The Elderly Gentleman*, the first two verses of which are—

> Prope ripan fluvii solus
> A senex silently sat
> Super capitum ecce his wig
> Et wig super, ecce his hat.
> Blew Zephyrus alte, acerbus,
> Dum elderly gentleman sat;
> Et a capite took up quite torve
> Et in rivum projecit his hat.

It seems to have been originated by Odaxius of Padua but was popularized by his pupil, Teofilo Folengo or Merlinus Coccaius (1491–1544), a Mantuan monk of noble family whose *Liber Macaronicorum* (1520), a poetical rhapsody, made up of words of different languages, treated of "pleasant matters" in a comical style.

Skelton's *Phyllyp Sparowe* (1512) contained somewhat similar verse. It begins—

> Pla ce bo,
> Who is there, who?
> Di le xi,
> Dame Margery

and Dunbar's *Testament of Andrew Kennedy* (1508)—

> I will na priestis for me sing,
> Dies illa, Dies iræ,
> Na yet na bellis for me ring,
> Sicut semper solet fieri—

though not true macaronic, is a near approach.

In 1801, A. Cunningham published *Delectus Macaronicorum Carminum*, a history of macaronic poetry.

Maccabæus. The surname given to Judas, the central figure in the Jewish struggle (*c.* 170–160 B.C.) against the SELEUCIDÆ, and hence to his family or clan. He was the third son of Mattathias the Hasmonæan. The most probable derivation of the name is from Heb. *makkabah*, hammer, just as Edward I was called '*Scotorum mallleus*'.

The Maccabees. The family of Jewish heroes descended from Mattathias the Hasmonæan and his five sons, John, Simon, Judas, Eleazar, and Jonathan, which delivered its race from the persecutions of the Syrian King, Antiochus Epiphanes (175–164 B.C.). It established a line of priest-kings which lasted till supplanted by Herod in 37 B.C. Their exploits are told in the four *Books of The Maccabees*, of which two are in the APOCRYPHA.

McCarthyism. Political WITCH-HUNTING; the hounding of Communist suspects to secure their removal from office and public affairs. So called after U.S. Senator Joseph McCarthy (1909–1957) who specialized in these activities somewhat unscrupulously.

McCoy, or **McKoy, The Real,** is used in the U.S.A., but formerly in Britain it was *the Real MacKay*. Various stories about an American boxer of the 1890s have been suggested as the origin of the phrase, but Eric Partridge in *From Sanskrit to Brazil* (1952), says with more probable truth that it dates from the 1880s and originated in SCOTLAND where it was applied to whisky, men, and things of the highest quality. The whisky was exported to both the U.S.A. and Canada where people of Scottish origin drank the whisky and kept the phrase alive. In the 1890s, however, there is no doubt that it was applied to an outstanding boxer whose name happened to be McCoy.

Macdonald. Lord Macdonald's breed. Parasites. It is said that Lord Macdonald (son of the LORD OF THE ISLES) once made a raid on the mainland. He and his followers replaced their own rags with the smarter clothes stripped off their enemies, with the result of being overrun with parasites.

Mace. Originally a club armed with iron, and

used in war; now a staff of office pertaining to certain dignitaries, as the SPEAKER of the HOUSE OF COMMONS, Lord Mayors, MAYORS, etc. Both sword and mace are symbols of dignity, suited to the times when men went about in armour, and sovereigns needed champions to vindicate their rights.

Macedonia's Madman. *See under* MAD.

Macedonians. A religious sect named after Macedonius (d. *c.* 362), Bishop of Constantinople, an upholder of semi-Arianism. He was deposed by the ARIAN Council of Constantinople in 360.

Macfarlane's Geese. The proverb is that, "MacFarlane's geese like their play better than their meat." The wild geese of Inch-Tavoe (Loch Lomond) used to be called *Macfarlane's Geese* because the MacFarlanes had a house on the island, and it is said that the geese never returned after the destruction of the house. One day James VI visited the chieftain and was highly amused by the gambols of the geese, but one served at table was so tough that the king exclaimed, "Macfarlane's geese like their play better than their meat."

MacGregor (mȧ greg' ŏr). The motto of the MacGregors is, "E'en do and spair nocht," said to have been given them in the 12th century by a king of SCOTLAND. While the king was hunting, he was attacked by a wild boar and Sir Malcolm asked permission to encounter the creature. "E'en do," said the king, "and spair nocht." Whereupon the baronet tore up an oak sapling and dispatched the enraged animal. For this the king gave Sir Malcolm permission to use the said motto, and, in place of a Scots fir, to adopt for crest *an oak tree eradicate, proper*.

Another motto of the MacGregors is *Srioghal mo dhream*, *i.e.* "Royal is my tribe."

The MacGregors furnish the only instance of a clan being deprived of its family name. In 1603, as a result of their ruthless ferocity at the battle of Glenfruin against the Colquhouns of Luss, it was proscribed by James VI and the clan assumed the names of neighbouring families such as the Campbells, Buchanans, Grahams, Murrays, etc. The laws against them were annulled by Charles II in 1661 but in 1693, under William and Mary, similar measures were enacted against them. These penalties were finally abolished by the British PARLIAMENT and John Murray of Lanrick resumed the name MacGregor as chief of the clan in 1822. *See* ROB ROY.

Robert (Rob Roy) MacGregor. *See* ROB ROY.

Machiavelli, Niccolò (ma kyȧ vel' i) (1469–1527). The celebrated Florentine statesman and author of *Il Principe* (The Prince), a treatise on the art of government addressed to Lorenzo de' MEDICI, putting forward the view that only a strong and ruthless prince could free Italy from devastation by foreigners. In view of the distracted state of the country, he held that terrorism and deceit were justifiable means of achieving a peaceful and prosperous Italy. Hence the use of his name as an epithet or synonym for an unscrupulous politician; and *Machiavellianism* and *Machiavellism* to denote political deceit and intrigue and the use of unscrupulous methods generally.

> Am I politic? am I subtle? am I a Machiavel?
> SHAKESPEARE: *The Merry Wives of Windsor,* III, i.

The Imperial Machiavelli. Tiberius, the Roman Emperor (42 B.C.–A.D. 37). His political axiom was: "He who knows not how to dissemble knows not how to reign." It was also the axiom of Louis XI of France.

Machismo (Sp. *Macho*, male). An American usage denoting assertive masculinity which emphasises such features as bravery, virility, and the domination of the opposite sex.

Mach Number. An expression of the ratio of flight speed to the speed of sound, devised by the Austrian physicist and psychologist, Ernst Mach (1838–1916). An aircraft flying at Mach 2 is travelling at twice the speed of sound.

Macintosh. Cloth waterproofed with rubber by a process patented in 1823 by Charles Macintosh (1766–1843); also a coat made of this or, loosely, any raincoat.

Mackerel. Mackerel Sky. A sky dappled with detached rounded masses of white cloud, something like the markings of a mackerel.

To throw a sprat to catch a mackerel. *See* SPRAT.

Mackworth's Inn. *See* BARNARD'S INN.

Macmillanites. A religious sect in Scotland which seceded from the CAMERONIANS in 1743 because they wished for stricter adherence to the principles of the REFORMATION in Scotland; so named from John Macmillan (1670–1753), their leader. They called themselves the "Reformed Presbytery".

MacPherson (mȧc'fēr' son). Fable has it that during the reign of David I of Scotland (1084, 1124–1153) a younger brother of the chief of the powerful clan Chattan became abbot of Kingussie. His elder brother died childless, and the chieftainship devolved on the abbot. He is supposed to have obtained a papal dispensation (a most improbable story) to marry the daughter of the thane of

Calder. A swarm of little "Kingussies" was the result. The people of Inverness-shire called them the Mac-phersons, *i.e.* the sons of the parson.

Macquarie Style. The late Georgian style of architecture favoured by General Lachlan Macquarie when Governor of New South Wales (1809–1821). His chief architect was Francis Howard Greenway, an ex-convict who designed St. James's Church, Sydney.

Macrocosm. (Gr., the great world). The ancients looked upon the universe as a living creature and the followers of PARACELSUS considered man a miniature representation of the universe. The one was termed the Macrocosm, the other the MICROCOSM.

Mad. Mad as a hatter. A phrase popularized by Lewis Carroll in *Alice in Wonderland*, (1865). It is found in Thackeray's *Pendennis* (1850) and is recorded in America in 1836. Mercurous nitrate was used in the making of felt hats and its effects can produce St. VITUS'S DANCE or lesser tremulous manifestations, hence the likely origin of the phrase. It has also been suggested that the original "mad hatter" was Robert Crab, a 17th-century eccentric living at Chesham, who gave all his goods to the poor and lived on dock leaves and grass.

Mad as a March Hare. *See under* HARE.

The Mad Cavalier. Prince Rupert (1619–1682), noted for his impetuous courage and impatience of control as the Royalist cavalry leader during the English CIVIL WAR. He was the son of James I's daughter, Elizabeth, and Frederick, the Elector of the PALATINATE.

The Mad Parliament. The PARLIAMENT which met at Oxford in 1258 and which produced the Provisions of Oxford to limit the power of Henry III. The epithet "Mad" seems to have arisen through error, probably a substitution of *insance* for *insigne* (famous) in a contemporary description.

The Mad Poet. Nathaniel Lee (*c.* 1653–1692), who towards the end of his life lost his reason through intemperance and was confined for five years in BEDLAM.

The Brilliant Madman, or **Madman of the North.** Charles XII of Sweden (1682, 1697–1718).

Heroes are much the same, the point's agreed
From Macedonia's madman to the Swede.
POPE : *Essay on Man, Epistle* iv.

Macedonia's Madman. ALEXANDER the Great.

Madame. The wife of Philippe, Duc d'Orléans (1640–1701), brother of Louis XIV, was so styled; the title was usually reserved for the eldest daughter of the king or the DAUPHIN. *Cp.* MONSIEUR.

Madame Tussaud's. The widely known LONDON exhibition of wax models of prominent as well as notorious people established by Marie Tussaud (née Grosholtz) in 1802. She was born at Berne in 1760 and was taught the art of wax-modelling at Paris and in due course gave lessons to Louis XVI's sister, Elizabeth. After a short imprisonment during the French Revolution she came to London where she died in 1850. The famous Chamber of Horrors is filled with figures of notorious murderers and instruments of torture.

Mademoiselle from Armenteers (Armentières). In the GREAT WAR Armentières in northern France was held by the British until the great German offensive of 1918. The army song "Mademoiselle from Armenteers, Parlez-vous", which became so widely known, originated in 1916. It was a modification of the much earlier song and tune "Three Prussian Officers Crossed the Rhine". As before it readily lent itself to improvisation, especially of a scurrilous nature.

'O Madam, have you any good wine?
Parlez-vous;
O Madam, have you any good wine?
Parlez-vous.
O Madam, have you any good wine?
Fit for a soldier of the line?
Inky-pinky, parlez-vous.'

Mademoiselle, La Grande. Anne, Duchesse de Montpensier (1627–1693), cousin to Louis XIV, and daughter of Gaston, Duc D'Orléans, noted for her wealth, position, and strength of character.

Madge. A MAGPIE; the abbreviated form of *Margaret. Cp.* MAG.

Madge-howlet, or **Madge-owl.** The barn owl.

I'll sit in a barn with madge-howlet, and catch mice first.
BEN JONSON : *Every Man in his Humour*, II, ii.

Madoc, or **Madog.** A Welsh prince, son of Owain Gwynedd, and legendary discoverer of America in 1170. He is supposed to have sailed from Aber-Cerrig-Gwynion near Rhos-on-Sea with two ships and reached Mobile Bay, Alabama. The Mandan Indians (extinct since the mid-19th century) have been held as the descendants of Madoc's voyagers, and there are fortifications north of Mobile Bay resembling Welsh pre-Norman castles. Madoc is also supposed to have made a second voyage to establish a colony, supposedly setting out from Lundy.

Southey has a poem called *Madoc* (1805) which also embodies the foundation of the Mexican Empire by the Aztecs from Aztlan.

The story is first found in a 15th-century Welsh poem.

Madonna (Ital., my lady). A title especially applied to the Virgin MARY.

Madras System. The MONITORIAL SYSTEM devised by Andrew Bell (1753–1832), when superintendent of the Madras Orphanage for sons of soldiers (1789–1797). The so-called LANCASTERIAN system was derived from it. Bell subsequently became Superintendent for the NATIONAL SOCIETY.

Mæander. *See* MEANDER.

Mæcenas (mē sē′ nǎs). A patron of letters; so called from the Roman statesman G. Mæcenas (d. 8 B.C.), who kept an open house for men of letters in the reign of Augustus. He was the special friend and patron of HORACE and VIRGIL. Nicholas Rowe so dubbed the Earl of Halifax on his installation to the Order of the GARTER (1714). *See* AUGUSTAN AGE.

The last English Mæcenas. Samuel Rogers (1763–1855), poet and banker.

Maelduin, or **Maeldune, The Voyage of.** In early Irish romance, Maeldune was the son of Ailill, who had been killed by a robber from Leix. As a young man, he set sail to seek the murderer and voyaged for three years and seven months visiting many islands and seeing marvels hitherto unknown. He eventually found the culprit, but took no vengeance, out of gratitude to God for his deliverance from such a variety of great dangers. The story has much in common with the voyage of St. BRANDAN.

Mænads (frenzied women). The Bacchæ or Bacchantes, female attendants of BACHUS. The name arises from their extravagant gestures and frenzied rites.

Mæonides (mēon′ i dēz), or **The Mæonian Poet.** HOMER either because he was the son of Mæon, or because he was born in Mæonia (Asia Minor).

Mæra, or **Mœra.** The dog of ICARIUS.

Maeve, or **Medb.** In Irish legend, a mythical queen of Connacht, wife of Ailill and mother of FINDABAIR who sought the downfall of CUCHULAIN and trained sorcerers to help bring this about. She instigated the Cattle Raid of Cuailnge, thus initiating the WAR OF THE BROWN BULL.

Mæviad. *See* BAVIAD.

Mae West. The name given by aircraft personnel in World War II to the inflatable lifejacket or vest worn when there was danger of being forced into the sea. It was an allusion to the somewhat buxom charms of the famous film star of this name.

Mafficking. Extravagant and boisterous celebration of an event, especially on an occasion of national rejoicing. From the uproarious scenes and unrestrained exultation that took place in the centre of London on the night of 18 May 1900, when the news of the relief of Mafeking (besieged by the Boers for 217 days) became known. The "heroic" character of Baden-Powell's defence has been questioned, but the impact made at the time is not in dispute.

Mafia. A network of Sicilian criminal organizations which became increasingly powerful during the 19th century. "Protection" by blackmail, boycotting, terrorization and the vendetta are characteristic, and Sicilian politics came to be dominated by the *mafiosi*. Its power was largely broken under Mussolini in the 1920s but it has not been exterminated. Sicilian immigrants introduced it into the United States, where it became a growing nuisance from the 1890s, and Mussolini's firm measures caused a fresh influx to join the BOOTLEGGERS and gangsters of the AL CAPONE era. These groups eventually adopted the name Cosa Nostra (Ital. our thing, our affair) controlling much of the drug racket, gambling and prostitution in the big cities, although its use is mainly confined to the eastern seaboard.

Mafia is apparently an Arabic word denoting "a place of refuge", and is a result of the Arab conquest of Sicily in the 9th century, many Sicilian families found a *mafia* in the hills where they duly became peasant bandits, with patriotic and family loyalties. Their resistance continued after the Norman conquest of the 11th century and later control by Spain. After the liberation and unification of Italy the Mafia made crime a fulltime pursuit.

Nowadays *mafia* is frequently misused, becoming a vogue word loosely applied to any clique, exclusive circle, or influential group. *Cp.* CAMORRA.

Mag. A contraction of MAGPIE. **What a mag you are!** You chatter like a magpie. A prating person is called "a mag".

Maga. A once familiar name for *Blackwood's Magazine*.

Magazine. A place for stores (Arab., *makhzan*, a storehouse) and this meaning is still retained in military usage. The word now commonly denotes a periodical publication containing contributions by various authors. How this came about is seen from the *Introduction* to *The Gentleman's Magazine* (1731)—the first to use the word in this way:

This Consideration has induced several Gentlemen to promote a Monthly Collection to treasure up, as in a Magazine, the most remarkable Pieces on the Subjects above mention'd.

Magdalene (măg' dà lēn). An asylum for reclaiming prostitutes; so called from Mary Magdalene, or Mary of Magdala, "out of whom He had cast seven devils" (*Mark* xvi, 9). It is probably a MISNOMER since the identification of Mary Magdalene with the sinner in *Luke* vii is very problematical. *See* MAUDLIN.

Magdalen College, Oxford (1458) and **Magdalene College, Cambridge** (1542), are pronounced mawd' lin.

Magdalenian (măg dė lē' nian). The name given to the late (upper) PALÆOLITHIC period from the district of La Madeleine, lower Vézère, France, where representative relics have been found. These people used wood and bone as well as flint, including bone needles and barbed harpoons. The cave paintings of Altamira in Spain belong to this period. In England, the Creswellian culture is akin to the Magdalenian.

Magdeburg Centuries. The first great PROTESTANT history of the Christian Church, compiled in Magdeburg under the direction of Matthias Flacius Ilyricus (1520–1575). It was written in Latin and first published at Basle (1559–1574) as the *Historia Ecclesiæ Christi*, and takes the story to 1400.

Magellan, Straits of (mà jel'àn). So called after Fernão de Magelhães (1480–1521), the Portuguese navigator, who undertook the first expedition to circumnavigate the globe, and who discovered them in 1520. He was killed in the Philippines.

Magenta (mà jen'tà). A brilliant red aniline dye derived from coal-tar, named in commemoration of the bloody battle of Magenta, when the Austrians were defeated by the French and Sardinians. This was just before the dye was discovered in 1859.

Maggot. There was an old idea that whimsical or crotchety persons had maggots in their brains:

> Are you not mad, my friend? What time o' th' moon is't?
> Have not you maggots in your brain?
> JOHN FLETCHER: *Women Pleased*, III, iv (1620).

Hence *maggoty*, whimsical, full of fancies. Fanciful dance tunes used to be called *maggots*, as in *The Dancing Master* (1716), where there are such titles as "Barker's maggots", "Cary's maggots", "Draper's maggots", etc., and in 1685 Samuel Wesley, father of John and Charles Wesley, published a volume called *Maggots; or Poems on Several Subjects*.

When the maggot bites. When the fancy takes us. Swift, making fun of the notion, says that if the bite is hexagonal it produces poetry; if circular, eloquence; if conical, politics.

Instead of maggots the Scots say, "His head is full of bees"; the French *Il a des rats dans la tête* (*cp*. our "rats in the garret" and "bats in the belfry"); and in Holland, "He has a mouse's nest in his head."

Magi (mā'jī) (Lat., pl. of *magus*). Literally "wise men"; specifically, the Three Wise Men of the East who brought gifts to the infant Saviour. Tradition calls them Melchior, Gaspar, and Balthazar, three kings of the East. The first offered GOLD, the emblem of royalty; the second, FRANKINCENSE in token of divinity; and the third, myrrh, in prophetic allusion to the persecution unto death which awaited the "Man of Sorrows".

> Melchior means "king of light"
> Gaspar or Caspar means "the white one".
> Balthazar means "the lord of treasures".

Mediæval legend calls them the *Three Kings of* COLOGNE, and the cathedral there claimed their relics. They are commemorated on 2, 3, and 4 January, and particularly at the Feast of the EPIPHANY.

Among the ancient Medes and Persians, the Magi were members of a priestly caste credited with great occult powers, and in Camoëns' LUSIAD (pub. 1572) the term denotes Indian BRAHMINS. Ammianus Marcellinus says the Persian magi derived their knowledge from the Brahmins of India (i, 23), and Arianus expressly calls the Brahmins "magi" (i, 7).

Magic Lantern. The old name for an optical instrument for the projection of slides and pictures. It is said to have been invented in 1636 by Athanasius Kircher.

The Great Magician, or **Wizard of the North.** Professor John Wilson ("Christopher North") gave Sir Walter Scott the name, because of the wonderful fascination of his writings.

Magician of the North. The title assumed by Johann Georg Hamann (1730–1788), a German philosopher and theologian.

Maginot Line (ma' zhi no). A zone of fortifications built along the eastern frontier of France between 1929 and 1934 and named after André Maginot (1877–1932), Minister of War, who sponsored its construction. The line, essentially to cover the returned territories of Alsace-Lorraine, extended from the Swiss border to that of Belgium and lulled the French into a belief that they were secure from any German threat of invasion. In the event, Hitler's troops entered France through Belgium in 1940. *Cp*. SIEGFRIED LINE.

Maginot mentality. Belief in a strategy of defence; also used contemptuously of one whose tactics are regarded as out of date.

Magna Carta (Lat.). The Great Charter of liberties extorted from King John in 1215. Its main effect was to secure the liberties of the English Church, the rights of the baronial classes, and to restrict abuses of royal power. It gained a new, but historically inaccurate, importance in the constitutional quarrels of the 17th century as a charter of "English liberty".

Magnanimous, The. Alfonso V of Aragon (c. 1394, 1416–1458).

Magnet. The loadstone or LODESTONE; so called from Magnesia in Lydia, where the magnetic iron ore was said to abound.

Magnetic Island. An island in Halifax Bay, Queensland, Australia, so named by Captain Cook because he thought his compass was affected by metallic ore in the rocks, although later navigators found no confirmation of this.

Magnetic Mountain. A mountain of mediæval legend which drew out the nails of any ship that approached within its influence. It is referred to in MANDEVILLE'S *Travels* and in other stories.

Magnificat. The hymn of the Virgin (*Luke i, 46–55*) *beginning* "My soul doth magnify the Lord" (*Magnificat anima mea Dominum*), used as part of the daily service of the Church since the beginning of the 6th century, and at Evening Prayer in England for over 800 years.

To correct Magnificat before one has learnt Te Deum. To try to do that for which one has no qualifications; to criticize presumptuously.

To sing the Magnificat at matins. To do things at the wrong time, or out of place. The Magnificat belongs to VESPERS, not to MATINS.

Magnificent, The. Lorenzo de' MEDICI (1449–1492), *Il Magnifico*, Duke of Florence.

Robert, Duke of Normandy (1028–1035), also called *Le Diable*.

Soliman or Suleiman I (c. 1494, 1520–1566), greatest of the Turkish sultans.

C'est magnifique, mais ce n'est pas la guerre. A magnificent gesture, but not really warfare. Admirable, but not according to rule. The comment on the field made by the French General Bosquet to A. H. Layard on the charge of the Light Brigade at Balaclava. It has frequently been attributed to Marshal Canrobert.

Magnolia. A genus of North American flowering trees, so called from Pierre Magnol (1638–1715), professor of Botany at Montpellier.

Magnum. A wine bottle, twice the size of an ordinary bottle, or two "reputed quarts". A Double Magnum holds the contents of four ordinary bottles. *Cp.* JEROBOAM.

Magnum bonum (Lat., "great and good"). A name given to certain choice potatoes and also plums.

Magnum opus (Lat. a great work). The chief or most important of one's learned or literary works.

> My magnum opus, the "Life of Dr. Johnson" ... is to be published on Monday, 16th May.
> BOSWELL: *Letter to Rev. W. Temple*, 1791.

Magog. *See* GOG.

Magpie. Formerly "maggot-pie", *maggot* representing *Margaret* (cp. *Robin* redbreast, *Tom*-tit, and the old *Phyllyp*-sparrow, and *pie* being *pied*, in allusion to its white and black plumage.

> Augurs and understood relations have
> (By maggot pies, and choughs, and rooks) brought forth
> The secret'st man of blood.
> SHAKESPEARE: *Macbeth*, III, iv.

The magpie has generally been regarded as an uncanny bird; in Sweden it is connected with WITCHCRAFT; in Devonshire it was a custom to spit three times to avert ill luck when the bird was sighted; in SCOTLAND magpies flying near the windows of a house foretold death. The old rhyme about magpies seen in the course of a walk says:

> One's sorrow, two's mirth,
> Three's a wedding, four's a birth,
> Five's a christening, six a dearth,
> Seven's heaven, eight is hell,
> And nine's the devil his ane sel'.

In target-shooting the score made by a shot striking the outermost division but one is called a *magpie* because it was customarily signalled by a black and white flag; and formerly BISHOPS were humorously or derisively called *magpies* because of their black and white vestments.

> Lawyers as Vultures, had soared up and down;
> Prelates, like Magpies, in the Air had flown.
> Howell's Letters: *Lines to the Knowing Reader* (1645).

Magus. *See* SIMON MAGUS; MAGI.

Mahabharata (ma ha ba ra' tà). One of the two great epic poems of ancient India, the other being the RAMAYANA. It is about eight times the combined length of the ILIAD and ODYSSEY. Its main story is the war between the Kauravas (descendants of Dhritarashtra) and the Pandavas (descendants of Pandu), but there are innumerable episodes. Dhritarashtra and Pandu were sons of

Kuru, a descendant of Bharata from whom the poem gets its name. It contains the BHA-GAVAD GITA.

Maha-pudma. *See* TORTOISE.

Mahâtma (mȧ hă t′ mȧ) (Sansk., "great soul").

Max Müller tells us that:

> Mahâtma is a well-known Sanskrit word applied to men who have retired from the world, who, by means of a long ascetic discipline, have subdued the passions of the flesh, and gained a reputation for sanctity and knowledge. That these men are able to perform most startling feats, and to suffer the most terrible tortures, is perfectly true.
>
> *Nineteenth Century*, May 1893.

By the Esoteric Buddhists the name is given to adepts of the highest order, a community of whom is supposed to exist in Tibet, and by Theosophists (*see* THEOSOPHY) to one who has reached perfection spiritually, intellectually, and physically. As his knowledge is perfect he can produce effects which, to the ordinary man, appear miraculous.

The title is particularly associated with Mohandas Karamchand Gandhi (1869–1948), the Hindu nationalist leader who identified himself with the poor, practised prayer and fasting, and sought to achieve his political ends by non-violence.

Mahayana ("Great Vehicle"). A development from the earlier form of BUDDHISM, which occurred about two thousand years ago. It enjoined, besides the pursuit of NIRVANA, that each individual should strive to become a Buddha, thereby becoming able to preach and serve the welfare of others.

Mahdi (Arab., "the divinely directed one"). The expected MESSIAH of the Mohammedans. There have been numerous bearers of this title since early on in the Mohammedan era and the Hidden IMAM (head of the true faith) of the Ismaelis was another such. The most popularly known to the British was Mohammed Ahmed, who led the revolt in the Sudan and who died in 1885. His tomb was destroyed after the battle of Omdurman in 1898. The most famous was Obaidallah al-Mahdi, first CALIPH of the Fatimite dynasty, who reigned from 909 to 933.

Mah-jongg. A Chinese game played with "tiles" like dominoes, made of ivory and bamboo, with usually four players. The tiles (136 or 144 in all) are made up of numbered *bamboos*, *circles*, and *characters*; *honours* (red, green and white dragons), *winds* (north, east, south and west), and additionally *flowers* and *seasons*.

It appears to be of 19th-century origin. The game was introduced to the U.S.A. by Joseph Babcock about 1919 under the trade name Mah-jongg, which he coined.

Mahogany. An old Cornish drink used by the fishermen on account of its warming quality; so called from its colour. The name has also been given to a strong concoction of brandy and water. Boswell at a dinner party at Sir Joshua Reynolds's says:

> "Mr Eliot mentioned a curious liquor peculiar to his country, which the Cornish fishermen drink. They call it Mahogany; and it is made of two parts gin, and one part treacle, well beaten together...I thought it very good liquor and said it was a counterpart of what is called Athol Porridge in the Highlands of Scotland, which is a mixture of whisky and honey. Johnson ... observed, "Mahogany must be a modern name; for it is not long since the wood called mahogany was known in this country".
>
> BOSWELL: *The Life of Dr. Johnson*, March 30, 1781.

Mahomet. *See* MOHAMMED.

Mahoun, Mahound. Name of contempt for MOHAMMED, a Moslem, a Moor, particularly in the romances of the CRUSADES. The name is sometimes used as a synonym for the DEVIL.

> Off-times by Termagant and Mahound swore.
>
> SPENSER: *The Faerie Queene*, VI, vii, 47.

Maia. The eldest and most lovely of the PLEIADES and mother, by JUPITER, of MERCURY. *See* MAY.

Maid. Maid Marian. A female character in the old May games and MORRIS DANCES, usually as Queen of the May. In the later ROBIN HOOD ballads she became attached to the cycle as the outlaw's sweetheart, probably through the performance of Robin Hood plays at MAY-DAY festivities. The part of Maid Marian, both in the games and the dance, was frequently played by a man in female costume.

> [The Courier] must, if the least spot of morphew come on his face, have his oil of tartar, his *lac virginis*, his camphor dissolved in verjuice, to make the foole as faire, for sooth, as if he were to play Maid Marian in a May-game or moris-dance.
>
> GREENE: *Quip for an Upstart Courtier* (1592).

Maid of all work. A female servant doing work of all kinds.

Maid of Athens. The girl immortalized in Byron's poem was Theresa Macri.

Maid of Buttermere. Mary Robinson, the beautiful and innocent daughter of an innkeeper in the valley of Buttermere, who married an unscrupulous impostor posing as the younger brother of the Earl of Hopetown in 1802. He proved to be a much-married confidence trickster and had served numerous prison sentences. Publicised and exposed by Coleridge, Hope was eventually hanged for forgery. The story was the subject of numerous songs, ballads and poems at the time. Wordsworth called Mary *The Maid of Buttermere* "unspoiled by commendation and the excess of public notice"

I mean, O distant friend a story drawn
From our own ground,—The Maid of
   Buttermere,—
And how, unfaithful to a virtuous wife
Deserted and deceived, the spoiler came
And wooed the artless daughter of the hills
And wedded her in cruel mockery....
WORDSWORTH: The Prelude, Bk. vii.

Maid of Honour. An unmarried lady in attendance upon a queen or princess. Also the name of a small almond-flavoured cheesecake.

Maid of Kent. *See* HOLY MAID OF KENT *under* HOLY.

Maid of Norway. Margaret (*c.* 1283–1290), daughter of Eric II and Margaret of Norway, acknowledged Queen of Scotland on the death of her maternal grandfather, Alexander III of Scotland (1285). She was betrothed to Prince Edward, son of Edward I of England, but died on the voyage to Scotland (1290).

Maid of Orleans. JOAN OF ARC.

Maid of Saragossa. Augustina Zaragoza, distinguished for her heroism when Saragossa was besieged in 1808 and 1809. (*See* BYRON, *Childe Harold*, I, liv, lvi.)

Old Maid. A spinster who remains unmarried, and also the name of a card game. The lapwing is so called, from the fancy that old maids are changed into lapwings after death.

Maiden. A form of GUILLOTINE used in SCOTLAND in the 16th and 17th centuries for beheading criminals; also called "the widow". It was introduced by Regent Morton for the purpose of beheading the laird of Pennycuik.

He who invented the maiden first hanselled it. Morton is erroneously said to have been the first to suffer by it; but Thomas Scott, one of Rizzio's murderers, was beheaded by it in 1566, and Morton not until 1581.

Maiden Assize. When there is nobody to be brought to trial. In a maiden assize, the sheriff of the county presented the judge with a pair of white gloves. We also have **maiden castle,** or **fortress,** one never taken; **maiden over,** an over in CRICKET from which no runs are made; **maiden speech,** One's first public speech; **maiden tree,** one never lopped; **maiden voyage,** the initial voyage of a ship; etc. *Maiden* conveys the sense of unspotted, unpolluted, innocent; thus Hubert says to the king:

This hand of mine
Is yet a maiden and an innocent hand,
Not painted with the crimson spots of blood.
SHAKESPEARE: King John, IV, ii.

Maiden Castle, Dorset, is the best surviving IRON AGE fortification in Britain occupying 120 acres and the site of earlier NEOLITHIC settlement.

Maiden King, The. Malcolm IV of Scotland (1141, 1153–1165).

Malcolm ... son of the brave and generous Prince Henry ... was so kind and generous in his disposition, that he was usually called Malcolm the Maiden.
SCOTT: Tales of a Grandfather, iv.

Maiden, or **Virgin Queen.** Elizabeth I, Queen of England, who never married (1533, 1558–1603).

Maiden Town. A town never taken by the enemy, but specifically Edinburgh, from the tradition that the maiden daughters of a Pictish king were sent there for protection during an intestine war.

Mail-cart. A small two-wheeled cart, drawn by one horse, in which mailbags were brought in from outlying districts in the 18th and early 19th centuries. The name was later applied to small vehicles and pushchairs in which children were taken for walks after they grew too large for a PERAMBULATOR.

Mailed Fist, The. Aggressive military might; from a phrase (*gepanzerte Faust*) used by William II of Germany when bidding adieu to Prince Henry of Prussia as he was starting on his tour of the Far East (16 December 1897):

Should anyone essay to detract from our just rights or to injure us, then up and at him with your mailed fist.

Cp. JACK-BOOT; PRUSSIANISM.

Maillotins (mī yō tan). Parisians who, in 1382, rose up against the taxes imposed by the regents early in the reign of Charles VI (1368–1422). They seized iron mallets (*maillets*) from the arsenal and killed the tax collectors but the insurrection was harshly suppressed.

Main. The main chance. Profit or money, probably from the game called hazard in which the first throw of the dice is called the *main*, which must be any number from 5 to 9 inclusive, the player then throwing his *chance*, which determines the main.

To have an eye to the main chance. *See under* EYE.

Main Plot. Lord Cobham's plot (1603) to replace James I by his English-born cousin Arabella Stuart. Sir Walter Ralegh was one of the conspirators and there were contacts with Spanish agents. They were tried with the contrivers of Watson's plot (*see* BYE PLOT). The names *Main* Plot and *Bye* Plot arose from their supposed connection.

Main Street. The principal thoroughfare in many of the smaller towns and cities of the

U.S.A. Sinclair Lewis's novel of this name (1920) epitomized the social and cultural life of these towns and gave the phrase a significance of its own.

Mainbrace. To splice the mainbrace. A naval expression denoting an extra tot of GROG all round, a very rare occurrence. Probably from the issue of an extra rum ration to those who performed the hard and difficult task of splicing the mainbrace, the brace attached to the main yard. It is also used more generally for celebrating and indulging in strong drink. The order *to splice the mainbrace* was given when Queen Elizabeth II reviewed the Fleet during the Silver Jubilee of 1977, and on 30 July, 1981 to toast the Prince and Princess of Wales, who were married on 29 July. *See* NELSON'S BLOOD *under* BLOOD.

Maintenance. (Fr. *main tenir*, to hold in the hand, maintain). Means of support or sustenance; in law, officious intermeddling in litigation with which one has rightfully nothing to do. It is not actionable except on proof of special damage.

Cap of Maintenance. *See under* CAP.

Maitland Club. A club of literary antiquaries, instituted at Glasgow in 1828. It published or reprinted works of Scottish historical and literary interest. *Cp.* BANNATYNE CLUB; ROXBURGHE CLUB.

Maize. American superstition had it that if a damsel found a blood-red ear of maize, she would have a suitor before the year was out.

> Even the blood-red ear to Evangeline brought not her lover.
> LONGFELLOW: *Evangeline*, II, iv.

Majesty. In mediæval England it was usual to refer to the king as "the Lord King". Henry VIII was the first English king styled "His Majesty", though it was not till the time of the Stuarts that this form of address became stereotyped, and in the Dedication to James I prefixed to the Authorized Version of the BIBLE (1611) the king is addressed also as "Your Highness".

> The Lord of Heaven and earth blesse your Majestie with many and happy dayes, that as his Heavenly hand has enriched your Highnesse, etc.

Henry IV was "His Grace"; Henry VI, "His Excellent Grace"; Edward IV, "High and Mighty Prince"; Henry VII, "His Grace" and "His Highness"; Henry VIII in the earlier years of his reign "His Highness". "His Sacred Majesty" was a title assumed by subsequent sovereigns, but was afterwards changed to "Most Excellent Majesty". The king of Spain was "His Catholic Majesty", and the king of France "His most Christian Majesty".

In HERALDRY, an eagle crowned and holding a sceptre is said to be "an eagle in his majesty".

Major. To Major Mitchell (Austr.) To ride a zigzag course across country, after Major Sir Thomas Mitchell (1792–1855), Surveyor-General to New South Wales, who made explorations into the Australian interior and proved the junction of the Murray and Darling, which he had set out to disprove. He also went adrift from his proper route.

Majority. He has joined the majority. He is dead. Blair says, in his *Grave*, "Tis long since Death had the majority."

Make (O.E. *macian*). In America this word is more frequently used with the meaning "put ready for use" than in England; as in *Have you made my room?* (*i.e.* put it tidy). We have, *to make the bed* and *cp.* Shakespeare's *make the door* (*see under* DOOR). *To make good, to make one's pile, to make a place* (*i.e.* to arrive there) are Americanisms, as is *to make a die of it* (to die).

> Why, tom, you don't mean to make a die of it?
> R.M. BIRD: *Nick of the Woods* (1837).

Make and break. A device which alternately closes (makes) and opens (breaks) an electric circuit.

Make and mend. In the Royal Navy, an afternoon free from work, originally, and still often, used for mending clothes.

Make dead men chew. An 18th-century naval expression, used of pursers who supposedly sold tobacco to dead men, thereby taking the profit. It was applied to the pay and victuals dishonestly drawn for men who were dead or had run.

Make or break. *This will either make or break you* means this will either bring you success or failure, ruin, etc.

On the make. Looking after one's own personal advantage or gain; intent on the MAIN CHANCE.

To make a board. In sailing, to make a distance, leg or tack when working to windward.

To make a book. To arrange or take bets on a particular event or occurrence.

To make a long arm. *See under* LONG.

To make away with. To take away, run off with; to squander; also, to murder; *to make away with oneself* is to commit suicide.

To make believe. To pretend; to play a game at. **Make-believe** is also a noun meaning "pretence".

To make bold. *See under* BOLD.

To make for. To conduce; as, "His actions make for peace"; also, to move towards; hence, in slang, to attack.

To make free with. To take liberties with, use as one's own.

To make good. To fulfil one's promises or to come up to expectations; to achieve success, often after an unpromising start.

> Whether or not the new woman Mayor would "make good" was of real interest to the country at large.
>
> *Evening Post* (New York), 14 September 1911.

Also to replace, repair, or compensate for; as, "My car was damaged through your carelessness and you will have to make it good".

To make heavy weather of. To make an undue labour of, from the labouring of a ship in rough seas.

To make it. To succeed in catching a train, keeping an appointment, etc., on time.

To make it up. To become reconciled.

To make off. To run away, to abscond.

To make out. To obtain an understanding of, as, "I can barely make out the meaning"; to assert, to establish by evidence or argument, as, "to make out one's case"; to draw up, prepare, as, "I am sick of making out income-tax returns." In the U.S.A., it is to achieve one's purposes, particularly amorous.

To make over. To transfer ownership; to refashion or renovate a garment.

To make tracks. To hurry away; to depart.

To make up to. To approach; to try to make friends with, usually for personal ends, to court.

> Young Bullock, ... who had been making up to Miss Maria the last two seasons.
>
> THACKERAY : *Vanity Fair*, xii.

What make you here? What do you want? What have you come here for?

> 'Twas in Margate last July, I walk'd upon the pier,
> I saw a little vulgar boy—I said, "What make you here?"
>
> BARHAM : *Ingoldsby Legends* (*Misadventures at Margate*).

Makeshift. A temporary improvisation during an emergency.

Make-up. As a verb and a noun denoting face cosmetics and their application, the term is of theatrical origin; an actor is said to be *made-up* for the stage after the requisite applications of greasepaint, etc. Hence, colloquially, the sum of one's characteristics, idiosyncrasies, etc. In printing the *make-up* is the arrangement of the printed matter in columns, pages, etc.

Make-weight. A small addition is compensation or an "extra", as a piece of meat, cheese, etc., put into the scale to make the weight correct.

Malachi Malagrowther. The signature of Sir Walter Scott to a series of letters contributed to the *Edinburgh Weekly Journal* in 1826 upon the lowest limitation of paper money to £5. They caused a great sensation at the time. He had previously called a querulous old courtier in *The Fortunes of Nigel* (1822) Sir Mungo Malagrowther. *Cp.* DRAPIER'S LETTERS.

Malakoff. This fortification, which was captured by the French (8 September 1855) during the Crimean War, was named from a Russian, Alexander Ivanovitch Malakoff, who kept a liquorshop outside Sebastopol. Other houses sprang up round it and "Malakoff", as the settlement came to be called, was ultimately fortified.

Malaprop, Mrs. The famous character in Sheridan's *The Rivals*. Noted for her blunders in the use of words (Fr. *mal à propos*). "As headstrong as an *allegory* [alligator] on the banks of the Nile", (III, iii), is one of her grotesque misapplications. Hence the words *malaprop* and *malapropism* to denote such mistakes.

Malbrouk, or **Marlborough.** The old French song, "*Marlbrouk s'en va-t-en guerre*" (Marlborough is off to the wars), is said to date from 1709 when the Duke of Marlborough was winning his battles in Flanders, but it did not become popular till it was applied to Charles Spencer, 3rd Duke of Marlborough, at the time of his failure against Cherbourg (1758). It was popularized by becoming a favourite of Marie Antoinette about 1780, and by its being introduced by Beaumarchais into *Le Mariage de Figaro* (1784). In Britain it is sung to the tune of "We won't go home till the morning" or "For he's a jolly good fellow". According to a tradition recorded by Chateaubriand, the air came from the Arabs, and the tale is a legend of Mambron, a crusader.

> Malbrouk s'en va-t-en guerre,
> Mironton, mironton, mirontaine;
> Malbrouk s'en va-t-en guerre,
> Ne sait quand reviendra.
> Il reviendra z'à Pâques—
> Mironton, mironton, mirontaine...
> Ou à la Trinité

Malebolge (ma là bol' jā). The eighth circle of Dante's *Inferno* (Canto xviii), containing ten *bolge* or pits. The name is used figuratively of any cesspool of filth or iniquity.

Malice. In addition to its common meaning *malice* is a term in English law to designate a wrongful act carried out against another intentionally, without just cause or excuse— this is commonly known as *malice prepens* or *malice aforethought*. *Malicious damage* is a legal term meaning damage done to property wilfully and purposely; *malicious prosecution* means the preferring a criminal prosecution or the presentation of a bankruptcy petition, maliciously and without reasonable cause.

Malignants. A term applied by the Parliamentarians to the Royalists who fought for CHARLES I and CHARLES II. They were also called DELINQUENTS.

Malkin. An old diminutive of Matilda; formerly used as a generic term for a kitchenwench or untidy slut; also for a cat (*see* GRIMALKIN), and for a scarecrow or grotesque puppet, from which latter meaning derives the mop called a *malkin*, used especially for cleaning a baker's oven.

> All tongues speak of him ...
> The kitchen malkin pins
> Her richest lochram 'bout her reechy neck,
> Clambering the walls to eye him.
> SHAKESPEARE: *Coriolanus*, II, i.

The name was also sometimes given to the Queen of the May (*see* MAID MARIAN).

> Put on the shape of order and humanity,
> Or you must marry Malkin, the May lady.
> BEAUMONT and FLETCHER: *Monsieur Thomas*, II, ii.

Mall, The. A broad thoroughfare in St. James's Park, London, so called because the game of PALL-MALL used to be played there by Charles II and his courtiers. The *mall* was the mallet with which the ball was struck.

> Noe persons shall after play carry their malls out of St. James's Parke without leave of the said keeper.
> *Order Book of General Monk* (1662).

Mallaby-Deeleys. A once popular term for "off the peg" clothes and suits; after Sir H. Mallaby-Deeley (1863–1937), M.P., who founded a firm for making cheap well-cut "ready-mades" for the middle classes after World War I. The venture ended in failure.

Malley's Cow (Austr.). Someone who disappears leaving no clue to his whereabouts. The story is that a certain Malley, who could not explain the disappearance of a cow he had been told to hold at a cattle muster, said, "She's a goner."

Malmesbury, The Philosopher of (mamz'-bĕri). Thomas Hobbes (1588–1679), author of LEVIATHAN, who was born in the vicinity of Malmesbury.

Malmsey (mam' zi or malm' zi). A strong, sweet wine from Greece, Spain, etc.; originally the wine of Malvasia (Gr. Monemvasia), in the Morea, which is the same name as *Malvoisie*.

George, Duke of Clarence, son of Richard, Duke of York, was, according to a London chronicle, put to death in the TOWER in 1478 by being drowned in a butt of malmsey by order of his brother, Edward IV. It is more likely that he was drowned in a bath. *See* Shakespeare's *Richard III*, I, iv.

> It is one of the more enjoyable freaks of history that the names of [Glarentza] ... and that of Monemva-

sia ... should both be familiar in their anglicized forms thanks to an incident in which the Duke of the former was drowned in a butt of the latter.
> OSBERT LANCASTER: *Classical Landscape with Figures* (1947).

Malt. A malt worm. A toper, especially a well-soaked beer drinker.

> I am joined with no foot-landrakers, no longstaff sixpenny strikers, none of these mad mustachio purple-hued malt worms: but with nobility and tranquility.
> SHAKESPEARE: *Henry IV, Pt. I*, II, i.

In meal or in malt. *See* MEAL.

When the malt gets aboon the meal. When persons, after dinner, get more or less fuddled.

Sermon on Malt. A famous sermon attributed to the PURITAN divine, John Dod (*c.* 1549–1645), rector of Fawsley, Northants, called *Decalogue Dod* from his exposition of the Ten Commandments (1604).

Malta. *See* GEORGE CROSS ISLAND.

Knights of Malta, or **Hospitallers of St. John of Jerusalem.** *See* HOSPITALLERS.

Maltese Cross. Made thus: ✠. Originally the badge of the Knights of Malta, formed of four barbed arrow-heads with their points meeting in the centre. In various forms it is the badge of many well-known Orders, etc., as the British VICTORIA CROSS and Order of MERIT, and the German Iron Cross. *See* CROSS.

Malthusian Doctrine. The idea that population tends to outrun the means of subsistence put forward by the Rev. T.R. Malthus (1766–1834) in his *Essay on Population* (1798). It was not novel, but his systematic exposition drew attention to the population problem.

Malum in Latin means *an apple* and *malus, mala, malum* means *evil*. Southey, in his *Commonplace Book*, quotes a witty etymon given by Nicolson and Burn, making the noun derive from the adjective, in allusion possibly to the apple eaten by EVE. There is also the schoolboy quatrain:

> *Malo*, I would rather be
> *Malo*, Up an apple tree
> *Malo*, Than a bad man
> *Malo*, In adversity.

Malum in se (Lat.). What of itself is wrong, and would be even if no law existed against its commission, as lying, murder, theft.

Malum prohibitum (Lat.). What is wrong merely because it is forbidden, as eating a particular fruit was wrong in ADAM and EVE, because they were commanded not to do so.

Mambrino. A pagan king of old romance, introduced by Ariosto into ORLANDO FURIOSO.

He had a helmet of pure gold which made the wearer invulnerable, and was taken possession of by RINALDO. This is frequently referred to in DON QUIXOTE, and we read that when the barber was caught in a shower, and clapped his brazen basin on his head, Don Quixote insisted that this was the enchanted helmet of the Moorish king.

Mamelukes (Arab. *mamluc*, a slave). The slaves brought from the Caucasus and Asia Minor to Egypt and formed into a bodyguard for the SULTAN, a descendant of SALADIN. In 1250 they set up one of their number as Sultan and the Mamelukes reigned until overthrown by the Turkish Sultan Selim I in 1517. The country was subsequently governed by twenty-four Mameluke beys under the PASHA but they retained virtual control. In 1811 they were exterminated by Mohammed Ali.

Mammet, or Maumet. An idol; hence a puppet, or doll (as in Shakespeare's *Romeo and Juliet*, III, v, and *Henry IV, Pt. I*, II, iii). The word is a corruption of *Mahomet*, hence to Christians it became a generic word to designate any false faith; even idolatry is called *mammetry*.

Mammon. The god of this world. The word in Syriac means riches, and it occurs in the BIBLE (*Matt.* vi, 24; *Luke* xvi, 13): "Ye cannot serve God and mammon." Spenser (*Faerie Queene*, II, vii), and Milton, who identifies him with VULCAN or MULCIBER (*Paradise Lost*, I, 738–51), both make Mammon the personification of the evils of wealth and miserliness.

> Mammon led them on—
> Mammon the least erected spirit that fell
> From Heaven; for even in Heaven his looks and
>   thoughts
> Were always downward bent; admiring more
> The riches of Heaven's pavement, trodden gold,
> Than aught divine or holy.
> MILTON: *Paradise Lost*, I, 678.

The Mammon of Unrighteousness. Money; see *Luke* xvi. 9.

Mammoth Cave. In Edmonson county, Kentucky; the largest known in the world, reputedly discovered in 1809, but known earlier. It comprises many chambers with connecting passages said to total 150 miles, and covers an area of nearly 10 miles in diameter. Rivers, streams, and lakes, add to the majesty and scenic variety of this vast limestone cave.

Man. Man in the Moon, Man of Blood, Brass, December, Sin, Straw. etc. *See these words*.

Man about town. A fashionable idler.

Man Friday. *See under* FRIDAY.

Man in the Iron Mask. *See* IRON MASK.

The Man in the Street. The ordinary citizen, the man or woman who in the aggregate makes public opinion.

The Man of Destiny. NAPOLEON I (1769–1821). He regarded himself as an instrument in the hands of destiny.

G.B. Shaw used the epithet as the title of a play about Napoleon.

Man of letters. An author, a literary scholar.

Man of Ross. *See* ROSS.

Man of Sorrows. Jesus Christ, from the prophecy in *Isaiah* liii, 3 that the MESSIAH would be "a man of sorrows, and acquainted with grief".

Man of the world. One versed in the ways of the world; no GREENHORN. Henry Mackenzie brought out a novel (1773) with this title and Charles Macklin a comedy (1871).

Man-of-war. A warship. Like other ships, a man-of-war is always referred to as "she". Formerly the term denoted a fighting man ("the Lord is a man of war", *Exod.* xv. 3).

The name of the "Man of War Rock", in the Scilly Isles, is a corruption of the Cornish *men* (*maen*) *an vawr*, meaning "big rock".

The popular name of the marine hydrozoan, *Physalia pelagica*, is the *Portuguese man-of-war*, or simply, *man-of-war*.

Man-of-war bird. The frigate-bird.

The man on the Clapham omnibus. In legal parlance, "the reasonable man". Possibly the phrase was first used by Sir Charles Bowen, Q.C. (later Lord Bowen), who was junior council against the claimant in the TICHBORNE CASE (1871–4).

Man to man. Frankly, as one man to another; in a manly fashion, as when two individuals fight "man to man".

The man who broke the bank at Monte Carlo. Joseph Hobson Jagger, who, in 1886, won over 2,000,000 francs in 8 days. An expert on spindles, he suspected one of the roulette wheels of a faulty spindle and had it watched for a week. Thereafter he staked on the numbers which were turning up with much more than mathematical probability and won a fortune. He died in 1892, probably mainly from boredom. His exploit became the subject of the famous Victorian MUSIC HALL ballad in the repertoire of the inimitable Charles Coborn, written and composed by Fred Gilbert.

> As I walk along the Bois Boolong, with an independent air,
> You can hear the girls declare—"He must be a millionaire";
> You can hear them sigh and wish to die,
> You can see them wink the other eye
> At the man who broke the bank at Monte Carlo.

The New Man. The regenerated man. In scripture phrase the unregenerated state is called *the old man*.

The Threefold Man. According to Diogenes Laertius, the body was composed of (1) a mortal part; (2) a divine and ethereal part called the *phren*; (3) an ethereal and vaporous part, called the *thumos*.

According to the Romans, man has a threefold soul, which at the dissolution of the body resolves itself into (1) the MANES; (2) the *Anima* or *Spirit*; (3) the *Umbra*. The Manes went either to ELYSIUM or TARTARUS; the Anima returned to the gods; but the umbra hovered about the body as unwilling to quit it.

According to the Jews, man consists of body, SOUL and spirit.

To a man. Without exception, all together, everyone, unanimously, as, "The audience applauded to a man."

To be one's own man again. To fully recover good health after illness, shock, etc.

Man proposes but God disposes. So we read in the *Imitatio Christi* (*Homo proponit, sed Deus disponit*, I, xix, 2). Herbert (*Jacula Prudentum*) has nearly the same words; as also has Montluc: *L'homme propose et Dieu dispose* (*Comédie de Proverbes*, iii, 7); and there are others.

Man, Isle of. One explanation of the name is that given by Richard of Cirencester— "Midway between the two countries [Britain and Ireland] is the island called Monœda, but now Monavia", *i.e.* that it is from *menagh* or *meanagh* meaning *middle*. Another is that it is from *Mannanan*, a wizard who kept the Land of *Mann* under mists when marauders threatened it.

Mañana (măn ya′ na) (Span., tomorrow). A word frequently used to imply some vague unspecified future date.

Mancha, La. *See* LA MANCHA.

Manchester. The name is formed from the old British *Mamucion* and *ceaster*, O.E. form of Lat. *castra*, denoting that it was once a Roman walled town. A native of Manchester is a *Mancunian*, from *Mancunium*, the mediæval Latin name of the city. *See* COTTONOPOLIS.

Manchester Martyrs. The name given to the three Irishmen who were hanged for attempting to rescue two FENIAN prisoners in Manchester (November 1867). In the course of the struggle a policeman was killed.

The Manchester Massacre. *See* PETERLOO.

The Manchester Poet. Charles Swain (1801–1874).

The Manchester School. A term applied to a group of RADICALS and free traders originating from business men of the Manchester Chamber of Commerce and sponsors of the Anti-Corn Law League. They were supporters of LAISSEZ-FAIRE and against the growth of the colonial empire. Led by Cobden and Bright, they were derisively so called by Disraeli in 1848, and the name came to be applied to Victorian advocates of FREE TRADE and a pacific foreign policy generally.

Mancus. An Anglo-Saxon coin in both gold and silver. In the reign of Ethelbert of Kent, money accounts were kept in pounds, mancuses, shillings, and pence. Five pence = one shilling; 30 pence = one mancus.

Mandæans. A GNOSTIC sect, also called *Nasoreans* and *Christians of St. John* which arose in the 1st or 2nd century and still found near Baghdad. Their teachings were akin to those of the MANICHÆANS, and St. JOHN THE BAPTIST featured prominently in their writings. They favoured frequent baptism.

Mandamus (Lat., we command). A writ of QUEEN'S BENCH, commanding the person or corporation, etc., named to do what the writ directs. So called from the opening word.

Mandarin. A name given by the Portuguese to the official called by the Chinese *Kuan*. It is from the Malay and Hindu *mantri*, a counsellor, or minister of state. The word is sometimes used derisively for overpompous officials, as, "The mandarins of our Foreign Office."

The nine ranks of mandarins were distinguished by the button in the cap: (1) ruby, (2) coral, (3) sapphire, (4) an opaque blue stone, (5) crystal, (6) an opaque white shell, (7) wrought gold, (8) plain gold, (9) silver.

Mandate (Lat. *mandatum*; *mandare*, to command). An authoritative charge or command. Also, the authority conferred upon certain "advanced nations" by the LEAGUE OF NATIONS after World War I, to administer the former German colonies and Turkish dependencies outside Europe. In practice "advanced nations" meant the victorious powers. After World War II, under the UNITED NATIONS, Mandates became *Trusteeships*.

Mandeville, Sir John (or **Jehan De**). The name assumed by the compiler of a famous and influential 14th-century book of travels, originally written in French. The author claimed to have been born at St. Albans and from 1322 to have travelled through Turkey, Armenia, Tartary, Persia, Syria, Arabia, Egypt, Libya, Ethiopia, Amazonia, India, to have visited Prestor John and served under the Emperor of China. The work contains many stories of fabulous monsters and legends, but was essentially derived from the writings of others, especially such noted mediæval travellers as Friar Odoric and John de Plano Carpini. The book was probably the work of a Liège physician, Jean de Bourgogne or Jehan à la Barbe. An English version had appeared by the beginning of the 15th century. *Cp.* MUNCHAUSEN.

Mandrake. The root of the mandrake, or mandragora, often divides in two, presenting a rough appearance of a man. In ancient times human figures were cut out of the root and wonderful virtues ascribed to them, such as the production of fecundity in women (*Gen.* xxx, 14–16). They could not be uprooted without supposedly producing fatal effects, so a cord used to be fixed to the root and round a dog's neck, and the dog when chased drew out the mandrake and died. A small dose was held to produce vanity in one's appearance, and a large dose, idiocy. The mandrake screamed when uprooted.

Of this latter property Thomas Newton, in his *Herball to the Bible*, says, "It is supposed to be a creature having life, engendered under the earth of the seed of some dead person put to death for murder."

> Shrieks like mandrakes, torn out of the earth.
> SHAKESPEARE: *Romeo and Juliet*, IV, iii.

He has eaten mandrake. Said of a very indolent and sleepy man, from the narcotic and stupefying properties of the plant, well-known to the ancients.

> Give me to drink mandragora...
> That I might sleep out this great gap of time
> My Antony is away.
> SHAKESPEARE: *Antony and Cleopatra*, I, v.

Mandrakes called love-apples. From the old notion that they were aphrodisiacs. Hence VENUS is called *Mandragoritis*, and the Emperor Julian, in his epistles, tells Calixenes that he drank its juice nightly as a love-potion.

Manes (mā′ nēz). **To appease his Manes.** To do when a person is dead what would have pleased him or was due to him when alive. The spirit or ghost of the dead was called by the Romans his *Manes*, which never slept quietly in the grave while survivors left its wishes unfulfilled. 19 February was the day when all the living sacrificed to the shades of dead relations and friends—a kind of pagan ALL SOULS' DAY.

Mangi. The name used by Marco Polo for southern China. *Cp.* CATHAY.

Manhattan. A COCKTAIL made from whisky and vermouth, with a dash of Angostura bit-

ters and Curaçao or Maraschino. Named from Manhattan Island, New York.

Mani (ma′ nē). The MOON. In Scandinavian mythology, the beautiful boy driver of the moon-car, the son of Mundilfœri. He is followed by a wolf, which, when time shall be no more, will devour both Mani and his sister SOL.

Mani, Manes, or **Manichæus.** The founder of MANICHÆISM, born in Persia (*c.* 215) and prominent in the reign of Shapur or Sapor I (*c.* 241–272). Mani began his teaching *c.* 240 and was put to death in 275.

Manichæans, or **Manichees.** Followers of Mani, who taught that the universe is controlled by two antagonistic powers, light or goodness (identified with God), and darkness, chaos, or evil. The system was based on the old Babylonian religion modified by Christian and Persian influences. St. AUGUSTINE was for nine years a Manichæan and Manichæism influenced many Christian heretical sects and was itself denounced as a heresy. One of Mani's claims was that, though Christ had been sent into the world to restore it to light and banish darkness, His APOSTLES had perverted his doctrine, and he, Mani, was sent as the PARACLETE to restore it. Manichæism survived in Turkestan until the 13th century.

Manitou (măn′ i too). The Great Spirit of certain American Indians, either the Great Good Spirit or the Great Evil Spirit. The word is Algonkian, meaning mystery, supernatural.

Manna. The miraculous food provided for the children of Israel on their journey from Egypt to the HOLY LAND.

> And when the children of Israel saw it, they said to one another, It is manna: for they wist not what it was. And Moses said unto them, This is the bread which the Lord hath given you to eat.
> *Exod.* xvi. 15.

The word is popularly said to be a corrupt form of *man-hu* (What is this?) but is probably Heb. *man*, a gift, and ultimately the Arab. *mann*, an exudation of the tamarisk.

> And the house of Israel called the name thereof Manna: and it was like coriander seed, white; and the taste of it was like wafers made with honey.
> *Exod.* xvi, 31.

Manna of St. Nicholas of Bari. AQUA TOFANA.

Manoa. The fabulous capital of EL DORADO, the houses of which city were said to be roofed with gold. There was numerous attempts by Sir Thomas Roe, Ralegh and others to locate it during the reigns of Elizabeth I and James I.

Manor (O.Fr. *manoir*, from Lat. *manere*, to

remain). A word introduced after the Norman Conquest and used of a dwelling of a man of substance, but not necessarily a large holding. It ultimately came to denote the self-contained estate in which the *demesne* (domain) land was worked for the lord's private benefit, the remainder being worked by free and unfree tenants (VILLEINS) who were subject to the COURT-BARON. *Cp.* MANSION; *See also* BOON WORK; COMMON; OPEN FIELD SYSTEM; WEEK-WORK.

Lord of the Manor. The person or corporation in whom the rights of a manor are vested.

Mansard Roof, also called *curb roof.* It was named after the French architect François Mansard (1598–1666), although used by Pierre Lescot at the Louvre *c.* 1550. Instead of forming an inverted V, the rafters are broken and the lower slope is almost perpendicular, the upper more nearly flat. It was in use in America in the old colonial days and there the term denotes a double-pitched roof, sloping up from the four sides of a building; where it ends in two gables it is called a GAMBREL roof.

Mansfield. The King and the Miller of Mansfield. This old ballad, given in PERCY'S RELIQUES, tells how Henry II, having lost his way, met a miller, who took him home to his cottage. Next morning the courtiers tracked the king, and the miller discovered the rank of his guest, who in merry mood knighted his host as "Sir John Cockle". On St. GEORGE's Day, Henry II invited the miller, his wife and son to a royal banquet, and after being amused with their rustic ways, made Sir John overseer of Sherwood Forest, with a salary of £300 a year.

Mansion (Lat. *mansio,* from *manere,* to remain, dwell). The Latin word means a stay or continuance, a halting-place or night-quarters; hence an inn or dwelling-place. *Cp.* MANOR.

The Mansion House. The official residence of the Lord Mayor of London, first used in 1753.

Manticore (Pers. *mardkhora,* man-eater). A fabulous beast usually given as having the head of a man, the body of a lion, a porcupine's quills and the tail of a scorpion. It is mentioned by Ctesias, a Greek living in the late 5th and early 4th centuries B.C., who wrote a history of Persia. It features in mediæval BESTIARIES and also in HERALDRY where it generally has horns and the tail and feet of a DRAGON. Martinus SCRIBLERUS says that it was "the most noxious animal that ever infested the earth".

Mantle. The Mantle of Elijah. A symbol of authority or leadership; when someone succeeds to the established authority of a predecessor, he is said to assume "the mantle of Elijah". Elijah the prophet cast his mantle upon Elisha to show he was his chosen successor (I *Kings* xix, 19).

Mantle of Fidelity. The old ballad *The Boy and the Mantle* in PERCY'S RELIQUES tells how a little boy showed King ARTHUR a curious mantle which should become no wife "that hath once done amisse". Queen GUINEVERE tried it, but it changed from green to red, and red to black, and seemed rent into shreds. Sir KAY's lady tried it, but fared no better; others followed, but only Sir Cradock's wife could wear it. The theme is a very common one in old story and was used by Spenser in the incident of Florimel's girdle. *Cp.* BRAWN.

Mantuan Swan, *or* **Bard.** VIRGIL.

Manu. In Hindu philosophy, one of a class of DEMIURGES of whom the first is identified with BRAHMA. Brahma divided himself into male and female, these produced *Viraj,* from whom sprang the first *Manu,* a kind of secondary creator. He gave rise to ten *Prajapatis* ("lords of all living"); from these came seven *Manus,* each of these presiding over a certain period, the seventh of these being *Manu Vaivasvata* ("the sun-born") who is now reigning and who is looked upon as the creator of the living races of beings. To him are ascribed the *Laws of Manu,* now called *Manavadharmashastra,* a section of the VEDAS containing a code of civil and religious law compiled by the Manavans. *See* DELUGE.

Manual seal. A signet. *See* SIGN.

Manumit (măn' ū mit). To set free; properly "to send from one's hand" (Lat. *e manu mittere*). One of the Roman ways of freeing a slave was to take him before the chief magistrate and say, "I wish this man to be free." The LICTOR or master then turned the slave round in a circle, struck him with a rod across the cheek and let him go. The ancient ceremony has a relic in the Roman Catholic rite of Confirmation when the BISHOP strikes the candidate lightly on the cheek, saying, "Peace be with you."

Manure (O.Fr. *manoverer*). Literally "handwork", hence tillage by manual labour, hence the dressing applied to land. Milton uses the word in its original sense in *Paradise Lost,* IV, 628:

> You flowery arbours...with branches overgrown
> That mock our scant manuring.

And in XI, 28, says that the repentant tears of ADAM brought forth better fruits than all the trees of PARADISE that his hands "manured" in the days of innocence.

Manx Cat. A tailless species of cat found in the Isle of MAN where it is popularly known as a *rumpee*. It was a practice to dock other cats in order to sell them to visitors as Manx cats. *See also* MODDEY DHOO.

Manxland (old Irish, *manu*). The Isle of Man.

Many a little makes a mickle. *See under* LITTLE.

Many men, many minds, *i.e.* there are as many opinions as there are men, as Terence says, *Quot homines tot sententiæ* (*Phormio*, II, iv, 14).

Too many for me, or **One too many for me**. More than a match. *Il est trop fort pour moi*.

Maple Leaf. The emblem of Canada.

Maquis (ma' kē). The thick scrubland in Corsica and Mediterranean coastal lands to which bandits retreat to avoid capture.

In World War II French patriots, who formed guerilla groups in the countryside during the German occupation (1940–1945), attacking their patrols, depots, etc., were known as *the Maquis*. *See* F.F.I.

Marabou. A large stork or heron of western Africa, from Arab. *murabit*, a hermit, because among the Arabs these birds were held sacred.

Marabouts. A priestly order of Morocco (Arab. *murabit*, a hermit) which in 1075 founded a dynasty and ruled over Morocco and part of Spain till it was put an end to by the Almohads in the 12th century.

Marais, Le. *See* PLAIN.

Maranatha (Syriac, the Lord will come—*i.e.* to execute judgement). A word which, with ANATHEMA, occurs in I *Cor.* xvi, 22, and has been erroneously taken as a form of anathematizing among the Jews; hence used for a terrible curse.

Marathon Race. A long-distance race, named after the battle of Marathon (490 B.C.), the result of which was announced at ATHENS by an unnamed courier who fell dead on his arrival, having run nearly 23 miles. This runner is sometimes cited as Pheidippides (or Philippides), who actually ran from ATHENS to Sparta to seek help against the Persians before the battle. In the modern OLYMPIC GAMES, the Marathon race was instituted in 1896, the distance being standardized at 26 miles 385 yards in 1924.

Maravedi (Span., ultimately from Arab. *Murabitin*, the name of a Moorish dynasty of Spain in the 11th and 12th centuries). Originally (11th century) a gold coin, later (16th–19th century) a very small Spanish copper coin worth less than a farthing.

Not worth a maravedi. Worthless.

Marble Arch. This famous LONDON landmark was originally erected in front of Buckingham Palace and moved to its present position at Cumberland Gate (formerly TYBURN Gate) in 1851. It is now on an "island" and contains a police station. It was designed by John Nash and it is said to be modelled on Constantine's Arch at ROME. The central entrance gates cost 3,000 guineas and the statue of George IV by Chantry (9,000 guineas), now in Trafalgar Square, was to have been placed upon it.

> The marble single arch in front of the Palace cost £100,000 and the gateway in Piccadilly cost £40,000. Can one be surprised at people becoming Radical with such specimens of royal prodigality before their eyes? to say nothing of the characters of such royalties themselves.
> CREEVEY: *Letter to Miss Ord*, 20 May 1835.

Marbles. *See* ARUNDELIAN; ELGIN.

March. The Month is so called from MARS.

The old Dutch name for it was *Lent-maand* (*see* LENT); the old Saxon name was *Hreth-monath* (rough-month, from its boisterous winds), subsequently changed to *Length-monath* (lengthening month); it was also called *Hlyd-monath* (boisterous month). In the French Republication CALENDAR it was called *Ventôse* (windy month, 20 February to 20 March).

A bushel of March dust is worth a king's ransom. Because we want plenty of dry windy weather in March for good tillage, it is worth much.

Mad as a March hare. *See under* HARE.

March borrowed three days from April. *See* BORROWED DAYS.

March comes in like a lion and goes out like a lamb. March begins with rough, boisterous weather and ends calmly.

March. He may be a rogue, but he's no fool on the march. Though his honesty may be in question he is a useful sort of person to have about.

To steal a march on one. *See* STEAL.

March table. A British military term for the instruction setting out the order in which parts of a convoy should proceed, the exact time each should pass a given starting point, and the average speed at which each should proceed.

Marching Watch. The guard of civilians enrolled in mediæval LONDON to keep order in the streets on the Vigils of St. PETER and St. JOHN THE BAPTIST during the festivities; used also of the festivities themselves.

Marches. The O.E. *mearc*, a mark, border; O.Fr. *marche*, a frontier. The boundaries between ENGLAND and WALES, and England and SCOTLAND, were called *marches*. Hence

Marcher lords, the powerful vassals with special rights who guarded the Welsh Marches at Hereford, Shrewsbury and Chester. The title *Earl of March* held by certain great feudal families is similarly derived. *Cp.* MARQUESS.

The word is still applied in the sense that a boundary is shared, *e.g.* Kent *marches* with Sussex, that is, the two counties are contiguous.

A territorial and historic division of Italy is called the *Marches*, which include Pesaro and Urbino, Ancona, Macerata, and Ascoli Piceno.

Riding the marches. In SCOTLAND, beating the BOUNDS of the parish.

Marchington (Staffordshire). Famous for a crumbling shortcake. Hence the saying that one of crusty temper is "as short as Marchington wake-cake".

Marchpane. The old name for the confection of almonds, sugar, etc., that we call *marzipan*, this being the German form of the original Ital. *marzapane*, which was adopted in the 19th century in preference to our well-established word because this confection was largely imported from Germany.

> *First Serv.* Away with the joint-stools, remove the court-cupboard, look to the plate. Good thou, save me a piece of marchpane.
> SHAKESPEARE: *Romeo and Juliet*, I, v.

Marcionites. An heretical sect founded by Marcion of Sinope in the 2nd century, and largely absorbed by the MANICHÆANS in the late 3rd century. They rejected the God of DEMI-URGE of the OLD TESTAMENT as a God of Law, and worshipped only Jesus Christ as the God of Love, whose mission was to overthrow the Demi-urge. Much of the NEW TESTAMENT was regarded by them as uncanonical and they had a certain kinship with Gnosticism (*see under* GNOSTICS).

Marcley Hill. Legend states that this hill in Herefordshire, at six o'clock in the evening on 7 February 1571, "roused itself with a roar, and by seven next morning had moved 40 paces". It kept on the move for three days, carrying all with it. It overthrew Kinnaston chapel and diverted two high roads at least 200 yards from their former route. Twenty-six acres of land are said to have been moved 400 yards (Speed: *Herefordshire*).

Marconigram. A message transmitted by wireless telegraphy, after Guglielmo Marconi (1874–1937), the inventor of this means of communication.

Mardi Gras (mar dē grái) (Fr., "fat Tuesday"). SHROVE TUESDAY, the last day of the LENT Carnival in France. At Paris, a fat ox, crowned with a fillet, used to be paraded through the streets. It was accompanied by mock priests and a band of tin instruments in imitation of a Roman sacrificial procession.

Marduk. The Babylonian god of HEAVEN and earth, light and life, and god of battle. He was identified with numerous other Babylonian deities. *See* BEL.

Mare. Away with the mare. Off with the blue devils, goodbye to care. This mare is the INCUBUS, called the *nightmare*.

The grey mare is the better horse. The woman is paramount, "she wears the trousers"; said of a wife who "bosses" her husband.

> As long as we have eyes, or hands, or breath,
> We'll look, or write, or talk you all to death,
> Yield, or she—Pegasus will gain her course.
> And the grey mare will prove the better horse.
> PRIOR: *Epilogue to Mrs. Manley's "Lucius"*.

The grey mare's tail. A cataract that is made by the stream which issues from Lochskene, in SCOTLAND so called from its appearance.

Money will make the mare go. You can do anything if only you have the money. As the old song says:

> "Will you lend me your mare to go a mile?"
> "No, she is lame leaping over a stile."
> "But if you will her to me spare,
> You shall have money for your mare."
> 'Oh ho! say you so?
> Money will make the mare to go."

Shanks's mare. One's legs or SHANKS.

The two-legged mare. The gallows.

To cry the mare (Herefordshire and Shropshire). The same as CRYING THE NECK. *See under* CRY.

To find a mare's nest is to make what you suppose to be a great discovery, but which proves to be no discovery or else all MOONSHINE. In some parts of SCOTLAND the expression is a *skate's nest*; in CORNWALL, *you have found a wee's nest and are laughing over the eggs*; in Devon, nonsense is called *a blind mare's nest*.

To win the mare or lose the halter. To play DOUBLE OR QUITS; all or nothing.

Whose mare's dead? What's the matter? Thus in Shakespeare's *Henry IV*, *Pt. II*, II, i, when Sir John Falstaff sees Mistress Quickly with the sheriff's officers, evidently in a state of great discomposure, he cries,

> How now? Whose mare's dead? What's the matter?

Mare (mar' i). The Latin word for *sea*. *Mare Clausum* is a closed sea or one that is closed by a certain power or powers to the unrestricted passage of foreign shipping. *Mare liberum* is the free and open sea. In 1635 John Selden (1584–1654) published a treatise called *Mare Clausum*.

FASCIST Italy called the Mediterranean *Mare Nostrum*, "our sea", in their expansionist heyday.

Marforio. *See* PASQUINADE.

Margaret. A country name for the MAGPIE; also for the daisy, marguerite (O.Fr. for a pearl), so called from its pearly whiteness.

St. Margaret. Virgin martyr of the 3rd century, known as St. Marina among the Greeks. It is said that Olybrius, governor of Antioch, captivated by her beauty, sought her in marriage but, being rejected, threw her into a dungeon, where the DEVIL came to her in the form of a DRAGON. She held up the cross and the dragon fled. Sometimes she is delineated as coming from the dragon's mouth, for one legend says that the monster swallowed her, but on her making the sign of the cross he suffered her to quit his maw.

She is the chosen type of female innocence and meekness, represented as a young woman of great beauty, bearing the martyr's palm and crown, or with the dragon as an attribute, sometimes standing upon it. She is the patron saint of the ancient borough of King's Lynn.

St. Margaret of Scotland (*c.* 1045–1093). The wife of Malcolm III of SCOTLAND and granddaughter of Edmund Ironside, King of England. She was noted for her services to the Church in Scotland and for her learning, piety and religious benefactions. She was canonized in 1250 and died on 16 November, which is her feast day.

Margin. In many old books a commentary was printed in the margin (as in the BIBLE); hence the word was often used for a commentary itself, as in Shakespeare's—

His face's own margent did quote such amazes.
Love's Labour's Lost, II, i.
I knew you must be edified by the margent.
Hamlet, V, ii.

Marguerite des Marguerites (the pearl of pearls). So Francis I called his sister, Marguerite d'Angoulême (1492–1549), authoress of the HEPTAMERON and a collection of poems entitled *Les Marguerites de la marguerite des princesses*, etc. She married twice; first the Duc d'Alençon, and then Henri d'Albret, King of Navarre, and was known for her PROTESTANT leanings.

Mari Lwyd (ma ri loo ed). *Singing with Mari Lwyd* (Holy Mary) is an old Welsh Christmastide custom still surviving at Llangynwyd, Glamorganshire, and may have derived from the old miracle plays (*see* MYSTERIES). The chief character wears a white cowl and a horse's skull bedecked with ribbons and is accompanied by two or three fantastically dressed followers. They sing outside houses, demanding an entrance. This is, at first, refused until the callers give evidence of their worth in song and repartee. They are then made welcome and suitably refreshed or recompensed.

Maria Marten. *See* RED BARN.

Mariage de convenance (Fr., marriage of expediency). A marriage for money and position. *Cp.* KNOBSTICK; SHOTGUN WEDDING.

Marian Year. The method of reckoning 25 March, the Feast of the ANNUNCIATION, as the first day of the year. This was used until the reform of the CALENDAR in 1752. The beginning of the financial year follows this reckoning; the eleven days added in 1752 make it 5 April.

Marie Celeste. Properly MARY CELESTE.

Marigold. The plant *Calendula officinalis* with its bright yellow or orange flowers is so called in honour of the Virgin Mary.

This riddle, Cuddy, if thou can'st, explain…
What flower is that which bears the Virgin's name,
The richest metal joined with the same?
JOHN GAY: *The Shepherd's Week* (Monday).

In 17th-century slang a marigold (or "marygold") meant a SOVEREIGN.

Marine. A "Sea-soldier". In the Royal Navy, the Marines have been an established force since 1755 although they had earlier origins in the Duke of York and Albany's Maritime Regiment of Foot (1664). A marine is familiarly known as a "JOLLY", "bootneck" "leatherneck", etc. The latter name arose from the leather lining of the stand-up collar of the old scarlet tunic (now only full-dress).

Empty bottles were at one time called "marines" (because the seamen regarded them as useless) but now, more usually, *dead marines*, or, in the U.S.A., *dead soldiers*.

According to the story, the Duke of York, when dining in the mess, said to the servant, "Here, take away these marines." A marine officer present asked for an explanation, and the duke replied, "They have done their duty, and are prepared to do it again."

A GREENHORN or land-lubber afloat is sometimes contemptuously called "a marine" by seamen.

The female Marine. Hannah Snell of Worcester (1723–1792) who, passing herself off as a Marine, took part in the attack on Pondicherry. It is said that she ultimately opened a public-house in Wapping, but retained her male attire. *See* HANNAH.

Marine Store. A place where old ship's materials and fittings such as canvas, cordage, and ironwork, were sold. Also applied generally to a junk shop or second-hand shop. *Cp.* DOLLY SHOP.

Tell that to the Marines. Said of a far-fetched yarn. The story is that Pepys, when re-telling stories gathered from the Navy to Charles II, mentioned flying fish. The courtiers were sceptical, but an officer of the Maritime Regiment of Foot said that he too had seen such. The king accepted this evidence and said, "From the very nature of their calling no class of our subjects can have so wide a knowledge of seas and lands as the officer and men of Our Loyal Maritime Regiment. Henceforward ere ever we cast doubts upon a tale that lacks likelihood we will first 'Tell it to the Marines'." *Cp.* HORSE MARINES *under* HORSE.

Mariner's Compass. China traditionally claims the invention of the compass in 2634 B.C. but the earliest authentic reference to the LODESTONE is in A.D. 121, and not until the 12th century is there mention of a compass in a ship. Claims for its discovery have also been made for the Arabs, Greeks, Italians, etc., but it may have arrived independently in both Europe and China. The belief that Marco Polo introduced it from China in 1260 is unfounded, as it was in use in Europe a century before this. *See* FLEUR-DE-LIS.

Marinism. Excessive literary ornateness and affectation. So named from Giambattista Marini (1569–1625), the Neapolitan poet, famous for his whimsical comparisons and pompous and over-wrought descriptions.

Maritimes. The Maritime Provinces of Canada: Nova Scotia, New Brunswick, and Prince Edward Island.

Marivaudage (ma rē vō dazh). An imitation of the style of Pierre Marivaux (1688–1763), author of several comedies and novels; an excessively refined style.

> Ce qui constitue le marivaudage, c'est une recherche affectée dans le style, une grande subtilité dans les sentiments, et une grande complication d'intrigues.
>
> BOUILLET:*Dict. Universel*, etc.

Marjoram. As a pig loves marjoram. Not at all. "How did you like it?" "Well, as a pig loves marjoram." Lucretius tells us (VI, 974), *Amaricinum fugitat sus*, swine shun marjoram.

Mark. Government equipment of various kinds issued to the armed services in the original form is labelled Mark I. Subsequent modifications of the same are labelled Mark II, Mark III, etc.

A man of mark. A notable or famous man; one who has "made his mark" in some walk of life.

Beside the mark. Not to the point; a phrase from archery, in which the mark was the target.

God bless, or **save the mark!** A kind of apology for introducing a disagreeable subject. Hotspur, apologizing to the king for not sending the prisoners according to command (SHAKESPEARE: *Henry IV, Pt. I*, I, iii), says the messenger was a "popinjay", who made him mad with his unmanly ways, and who talked

> So like a waiting-gentlewoman
> Of guns and drums and wounds,—God save the mark!

and in *Othello* (I,i) Iago says he was "God bless the mark! his Moorship's ancient", expressive of derision and contempt.

Sometimes the phrase is used to avert ill fortune or an evil omen, as in *Merchant of Venice* (II, ii):

> To be ruled by my conscience, I should stay with the Jew my master, who God bless the mark! is a kind of devil.

It is suggested that the "mark" is possibly the sign of the cross and the phrase a kind of supplication.

The mark of the beast. To set the "mark of the beast" on an object of pursuit (such as dancing, gambling, drinking, etc.) is to denounce it as an EVIL. The allusion is to Rev. xvi, 2; xix, 20.

The coloured flashes worn on the lapels of a midshipman's jacket are jocularly known as "marks of the beast".

See also M.B. WAISTCOAT *under* M.

Mark time. Raising the feet alternately as in marching, but without advancing or retreating. Also, to keep things going whilst awaiting for something to happen or for an opportunity.

Near the mark. Nearly correct, fairly close to the truth; a phrase derived from archery.

To make one's mark. To distinguish oneself, to achieve note.

It is an ancient practice for persons who cannot write to "make their mark". In old documents, the mark was the sign of the CROSS, which was followed by the name of the person concerned.

To toe the mark. To line up abreast of the others; so, to "fall in" and do one's duty.

Up to the mark. Generally used in the negative as "Not quite up to the mark", not good enough, not quite well; not up to the standard fixed by the ASSAY office for gold and silver articles.

Marks of gold and silver. *See* HALL MARK.

Marks in Printing. The various symbols used for styling a manuscript or typescript for the printer and for correcting printer's proofs.

Mark Banco. *see* BANCO.

Mark, *as a name.*

King Mark. In ARTHURIAN ROMANCE, a king of Cornwall, Sir TRISTRAM'S uncle. He lived at TINTAGEL, and is principally remembered for his treachery and cowardice, and as the husband of YSOLDE the Fair, who was passionately enamoured of Tristram.

Mark Twain. The pseudonym of the American novelist and humorist Samuel L. Clemens (1835–1910), who adopted it from the Mississippi river pilots' cry, "Mark twain!" when taking soundings.

St. Mark. The GOSPEL writer who died in prison *c.* 68 is represented in art as in the prime of life, sometimes habited as a BISHOP, and with a lion at his feet and scroll on which is written, "Peace be to thee, O Mark, My Evangelist." He is also represented with a pen in his right hand and in his left the Gospel. His day is 25 April.

St. Mark's Eve. An old custom in North-country villages was for people to sit in the church porch on this day (24 April) from 11 p.m. till 1 a.m. for three years running, in order to see on the third year the ghosts of those who were to die that year, pass into the church. In other parts this custom was observed on MIDSUMMER-eve.

Poor Robin's Almanack for 1770 refers to another superstition:

> On St. Mark's Eve, at twelve o'clock,
> The fair maid will watch her smock,
> To find her husband in the dark,
> By praying unto good St. Mark.

Keats has an unfinished poem on the subject, and he also refers to it in *Cap and Bells* (lvi).

Market-penny. A toll surreptitiously exacted by servants sent out to buy goods for their master; secret commission on goods obtained for an employer.

Maro. VIRGIL.

Marocco, or **Morocco.** The name of BANKS'S HORSE.

Maronites. A UNIAT body, mainly in the Lebanon, in communion with ROME and having their own liturgy. Although probably of 7th century origin, according to tradition, they arose in the early 5th century as followers of Maro, an anchorite living near Antioch. They became MONOTHELITES, but recognized Rome's authority in the 12th century.

Marplot. An officious person who defeats some design by gratuitous meddling. The name is given to a silly, cowardly, inquisitive Paul PRY, in *The Busybody* (1709), by Mrs. Centlivre. Similarly we have SHAKESPEARE'S "Sir Oliver Martext", the clergyman in *As You Like It*, and "Sir Martin Mar-All", the hero of Dryden and the Duke of Newcastle's comedy of that name, which was based on MOLIÈRE'S *L'Etourdi*.

Marprelate Controversy. The name given to the vituperative pamphlet war between the PURITAN writer "Martin Marprelate" and the supporters of the established Church. The Marprelate Tracts (1587–1589) were scurrilous attacks on the BISHOPS, secretly printed and distributed. They threatened to establish a "young Martin" in every parish "to mar a prelate". The Church commissioned John Lyly, Thomas Nashe and Robert Greene to launch a counter-attack. The tracts led to a Conventicle Act and another against seditious writings and the presumed chief author, John Penry, was caught and hanged in 1593.

Marque. *See under* LETTER.

Marquess, or Marquis (O.Fr. *marchis*, warden of the marches). A title of nobility in England below that of DUKE. It was first conferred on Richard II's favourite, Robert de Vere, Earl of Oxford, who was created Marquess of Dublin in 1385. A marquess is addressed as "The Most Honourable the Marquess of—". *See* COURTESY TITLE; COUSIN; MARCH.

Marriage. The Marriage knot. The bond of marriage effected by the legal marriage ceremony. The Latin phrase is *nodus Herculeus*, and part of the marriage service was for the bridegroom to loosen (*solvere*) the bride's girdle, not to tie it. In the Hindu marriage ceremony the bridegroom knots a ribbon round the bride's neck. Before the knot is tied the bride's father may refuse consent, but immediately it is tied the marriage is indissoluble. The PARSEES bind the hands of the bridegroom with a sevenfold cord, seven being a sacred number. The ancient Carthaginians tied the thumbs of the betrothed with a leather lace. *See* RICE.

Close seasons for marriage. These were of old, from ADVENT to St. Hilary's Day (13 January); SEPTUAGESIMA to LOW SUNDAY; ROGATION SUNDAY to TRINITY SUNDAY. They continued to be upheld in the English Church after the REFORMATION, but lapsed during the COMMONWEALTH.

> Advent marriage doth thee deny,
> But Hilary gives thee liberty.
> Septuagesima says thee nay,
> Eight days from Easter says you may.
> Rogation bids thee to contain,
> But Trinity sets thee free again.

The ROMAN CATHOLIC CHURCH does not allow nuptial MASS during what is left of the "close season", *i.e.* between the first Sunday of Advent and the Octave of the EPIPHANY, and from ASH WEDNESDAY to Low Sunday.

Marriages are made in Heaven. This implies that partners joined in marriage were foreordained to be so united. E. Hall (*c.* 1499–1547) says, "Consider the old proverbe to be true that saieth: Marriage is destinie." *Cp.* HANGING AND WIVING, etc. *under* HANG.

Marrow. A Scots and North-country word (obsolete except in dialect) for a mate or companion, hence a husband or wife, and (of things) an article that makes a pair with another.

> Busk ye, busk ye, my bonnie bonnie bride,
> Busk ye, busk ye, my winsome marrow.
> W. HAMILTON: *The Braes of Yarrow* (1724).

Down on your marrow-bones! Down on your knees! A good-humoured way of telling a person he had better beg pardon.

The Marrow-bone coach or stage. *To ride in the marrow-bone coach* is to walk. The leg-bone is the marrow-bone of beef and mutton, and the play is on MARYLEBONE (London) formerly pronounced "Marrybun". *Cp.* SHANK'S MARE.

Marrow Controversy. A controversy in the CHURCH OF SCOTLAND arising from the General Assembly's condemnation in 1720 of *The Marrow of Modern Divinity*, a book by "E.F." which first appeared in 1645 and which was considered to uphold ANTINO-MIAN doctrines and too free in its offer of salvation. Who "E.F." was is not known.

Marrow-men. The twelve ministers in the MARROW CONTROVERSY who protested against the General Assembly condemnation of the "Marrow". Thomas Boston, Ralph and Ebenezer Erskine were prominent among them.

Marry! An oath, meaning by Mary, the Virgin.

Marry come up! An exclamation of surprise, disapproval or incredulity, etc. May Mary come up to my assistance, or to your discomfort!

Mar's Year. The year 1715, that of the Earl of Mar's rebellion on behalf of the Old PRE-TENDER.

> Auld uncle John wha wedlock's joys
> Sin Mar's year did desire.
> BURNS: *Hallowe'en*, xxvii.

Mars. The Roman god of war; identified in certain aspects with the Greek ARES. He was also the patron of husbandmen.

The PLANET of this name was early so called because of its reddish tinge, and under it, says the *Compost of Ptholomeus*, "is borne theves and robbers...nyght walkers and quarell pykers, bosters, mockers, and skoffers; and these men of Mars causeth warre, and murther, and batayle. They wyll be gladly smythes or workers of yron...lyers, gret swerers."

Among the alchemists *Mars* designated iron, and in Camoëns' LUSIADS typified divine fortitude. *See also* MARTIANS.

The Mars of Portugal. Alfonso de Albuquerque (1453–1515), viceroy of India.

Marseillaise (Eng. mar se lāz'; Fr. mar sä yāz'). The hymn of the French Revolution and the national anthem of France. The words and music were written by Claude Rouget de Lisle (1760–1835), an artillery officer in the garrison at Strasbourg in 1792. It was first made known in Paris by troops from Marseilles, hence the name. *Cp.* CHANT DU DÉPART.

Marshal. (O.E. *mere*, mare; *scealc*, servant; O.Fr. *mareschal*). Originally a groom or farrier; now the title of high officials about the Court, in the armed forces, etc. In the Army, Field-Marshal is the highest rank, in the R.A.F., Marshal of the Royal Air Force; Air Chief Marshal, Air Marshal, and Air Vice-Marshal correspond to General, Lieutenant-General, and Major-General respectively. The military rank of Marshal of France was revived by NAPOLEON I who gave the baton to some of his most able generals. No Marshals were created after 1870 until 1916 when the title was given to General Joffre (1852–1931). Generals Foch (1851–1929), Lyautey (1854–1934), and Pétain (1856–1951) were also Marshals of France. *See also* EARL MARSHAL.

Marshal of the Army of God, and of Holy Church. The BARON Robert Fitzwalter, appointed by his brother barons to lead their forces in 1215, to obtain redress of grievances from King John. MAGNA CARTA was the result.

Marshal Vorwärts. *See* FORWARDS.

Marshall Plan. The popular name for the European Recovery Programme sponsored by U.S. Secretary of State G.C. Marshall, to bring economic aid to stricken Europe after World War II. It was inaugurated in June 1947. Most states other than Russia and her satellites participated. Britain ceased to receive Marshall Aid in 1950. *Cp.* LEND-LEASE.

Marshalsea Prison. An old prison in High Street, SOUTHWARK, the prison of the *Marshalsea Court*, which was originally a court of the HOUSEHOLD presided over by the *Earl Marshal*. The Court, with the *Knight-Marshal* for judge, existed until December 1849. From the 1430s, the prison also received admiralty prisoners and debtors. It moved to newer premises in 1799 and was closed in 1842. In 1381, its marshal was beheaded by the rebels under Wat Tyler; and Charles Dickens's father was imprisoned there in 1824.

> Necessarily, he was going out again directly, because the Marshalsea lock never turned upon a debtor who was not.
>
> DICKENS: *Little Dorrit*, ch. vi.

Marsyas (Mar' si ás). The Phrygian fluteplayer who challenged APOLLO to a contest of skill, and, being beaten by the god, was flayed alive for his presumption. From his blood arose the river so called. The flute on which Marsyas played had been discarded by MINERVA, and, being filled with the breath of the goddess, discoursed most beautiful music. The interpretation of this fable is as follows:

The DORIAN MODE, employed in the worship of Apollo, was performed on lutes; and the Phrygian mode, employed in the rites of CYBELE, was executed by flutes, the reeds of which grew on the river Marsyas. As the Dorian mode was preferred by the Greeks, they said that Apollo beat the flute-player.

Martel. The surname given to Charles (*c.* 688–741), son of Pippin II (MAYOR OF THE PALACE), probably because of his victory over the SARACENS, who had invaded France under Abd-el-Rahman in 732. It is said that Charles "knocked down the foe, and crushed them beneath his axe, as a martel or hammer crushes what it strikes."

Martello Towers. Round towers about 40 ft. high and of great strength. Many of them were built on the south-eastern coasts of England about 1803 against the threat of French invasion. They took their name from Mortella (Corsica), where a tower, from which these were designed, had proved extremely difficult to capture in 1794. *Cp.* PALMERSTON'S FOLLIES *under* FOLLY.

Mar-text. *See* MARPLOT.

Martha, St. Sister of St. LAZARUS and St. MARY MAGDALEN; patron saint of good housewives. She is represented in art in homely costume, bearing at her girdle a bunch of keys, and holding a ladle or pot of water in her hand. Like St. MARGARET she is accompanied by a DRAGON bound, for she is said to have destroyed one that ravaged the neighbourhood of Marseilles. She is commemorated on 29 July and is patron of Tarascon.

Martha's Vineyard. An island some 100 square miles in area off the S.E. coast of Massachusetts; so named in 1602 by the navigator Bartholomew Gosnold.

Martian Laws. Laws said to have been compiled by Martia, wife of King Guithelin of Brtain. According to Geoffrey of Monmouth (*Historia Britonum*) Martia was "a noble lady ... accomplished in all kinds of learning" and her work was translated into Saxon by King Alfred. *Cp.* MOLMUTINE LAWS.

Martians (mar' shánz). The hypothetical inhabitants of the planet MARS, which has a much less dense atmosphere than the Earth. In 1898 H. G. Wells wrote *The War of the Worlds*, in which he recounted the adventures and horrors of a war between the men of Mars and the dwellers on Earth.

Martin. One of the swallow family; probably so called from the Christian name Martin (*see* St. MARTIN'S BIRD below), but possibly because it appears in ENGLAND about March (the *Martian* month) and disappears about MARTINMAS.

Martin drunk. Very drunk indeed; Richard Baxter uses the name as a synonym of a drunkard. *See* St. MARTIN.

> The language of Martin is there [in heaven] a stranger.
>
> *Saint's Everlasting Rest* (1650).

St. Martin (of Tours). The patron SAINT of innkeepers and reformed drunkards, usually shown in art as a young mounted soldier dividing his cloak with a beggar; in allusion to the legend that in midwinter, when a military tribune at Amiens, he divided his cloak with a naked beggar who sought alms and that at night Christ appeared to him arrayed in this very garment. This effected his conversion.

He was born of heathen parents in Pannonia but was converted at ROME and became Bishop of Tours in 371, dying at Candes *c.* 400. His day is 11 November, the day of the Feast of Bacchus; hence his purely accidental patronage and also the phrase MARTIN DRUNK.

St. Martin's beads, jewellery, lace, rings, etc. Cheap counterfeit articles. When the old collegiate CHURCH of St. Martin's-le-Grand was demolished at the dissolution of the monasteries, hucksters established themselves on the site and carried on a considerable trade in artificial jewellery, and cheap ware generally. Hence the use of the saint's name in this connexion. *Cp.* TAWDRY.

> Certain lyght braynes ... wyll rather weare a Marten chayne, the pryce of viiid, then they woulde be unchayned.
>
> THOMAS BECON: *Jewel of Joy* (*c.* 1548).

St. Martin's bird. The hen-harrier, called *l'oiseau de Saint Martin* in France, because it makes its passage through the country about 11 November (St. Martin's day).

St. Martin's goose. St. Martin's day (11 November) was at one time the great goose feast in France. The legend is that St. MARTIN was annoyed by a goose which he ordered to be killed and served up for dinner. Hence, the goose was "sacrificed" to him on each anniversary. *Cp.* GOOSE FAIR; MICHAELMAS DAY.

St. Martin of Bullions. The St. SWITHIN of SCOTLAND. His day is 4 July, and the saying is that if it rains then, rain may be expected for forty days.

St. Martin's running footman. The DEVIL, traditionally assigned to St. Martin for such duties on a certain occasion.

> How do we know whether St. Martin's running footman is not brewing another storm?
> RABELAIS: *The Fourth Book: Pantagruel*, ch. xxiii.

St. Martin's summer. A late spell of fine weather. St. Martin's day is 11 November. *See* INDIAN SUMMER; SUMMER.

Martinmas. The feast of St. MARTIN, 11 November. **His Martinmas will come, as it does to every hog**—*i.e.* all must die. November was the great slaughtering time of the Anglo-Saxons when fodder was exhausted and oxen, sheep and hogs were killed and salted.

Martinet. A strict disciplinarian; so called from the Marquis de Martinet, colonel commanding Louis XIV's own regiment of infantry. The king required all young noblemen to command a platoon in this regiment before purchasing command of an infantry regiment. Martinet's system for training these wild young men in the principles of military discipline gained him lasting fame. He was slain at the siege of Duisburg in 1672.

Martini. A COCKTAIL essentially consisting of Martini Vermouth and gin, taking its name from the firm of *Martini and Rossi*, makers of vermouth. There are three forms of this cocktail, dry, medium, and sweet, each containing two parts gin to one of vermouth, the latter two cocktails having additional ingredients. In the U.S.A. the proportion of gin in a dry Martini is considerably higher.

Martyr (Gr.) simply means a witness, one who bears testimony; hence one who bears witness to his faith with his blood.

The Martyr King. CHARLES I of England, beheaded 30 January 1649.

Martyr to science. One who loses his health or life through his devotion to science.

Tolpuddle Martyrs. *See* TOLPUDDLE.

Marvedie. *See* MARAVEDI.

Marxism. The philosophical and political and economic theories or system propounded by Karl Marx (1818–1883) and Friedrich Engels (1820–1895) which form the basis of modern Communist dogma. It involves a materialist conception of history, a theory of class war, a belief in the ultimate destruction of capitalism and the formation of a classless society. *See* COMMUNISM; MATERIALISM.

Mary, the Mother of Christ, is represented in art as follows:

As *the Virgin*, with flowing hair, emblematical of her virginity.

As *Mater Dolorosa*. Somewhat elderly, clad in mourning, head draped, and weeping over the dead body of Christ.

As *Our Lady of Dolours*. Seated, her breast being pierced with seven swords, emblematic of her seven sorrows.

As *Our Lady of Mercy*. With arms extended, spreading out her mantle and gathering sinners beneath it.

As *The glorified Madonna*. Bearing a crown and sceptre, or an orb and CROSS, in rich robes and surrounded by angels.

Her seven joys. The ANNUNCIATION, VISITATION, NATIVITY, EPIPHANY, Finding in the Temple, Resurrection, Ascension.

Her seven sorrows. Simeon's Prophecy, the Flight into Egypt, the loss of the Holy Child, on meeting Our Lord on the way to CALVARY, the Crucifixion, the Taking Down from the CROSS, and the Entombment. Her festival is 8 September.

Bloody Mary. Queen Mary Tudor (1516, 1553–1558), for her persecution of PROTESTANTS. Some 300 suffered death, including Archbishop Cranmer. Also a COCKTAIL consisting of vodka and tomato juice.

Highland Mary. *See under* HIGHLANDS.

Little Mary. A euphemism for the stomach; from the play of that name by J. M. Barrie (1903).

The four Marys. The *Queen's Marys*, the companions of Mary Stewart, afterwards Queen of Scots. They were: Mary Beaton (or Bethune), Mary Livingstone (or Leuson), Mary Fleming (or Flemyng), and Mary Seaton (or Seyton). Mary Carmichael was not one of the four, although introduced in the well-known ballad.

> Yestre'en the queen had four Marys,
> This night she'll hae but three;
> There was Mary Beaton and Mary Seaton,
> Mary Carmichael, and me.

Mary Anne, or **Marianne.** A slang name for the guillotine, *see* MARY ANNE ASSOCIATIONS *below*.

Mary Anne Associations. Secret republican societies in France. The name was adopted by the Republican party because Ravaillac was moved to assassinate Henry

IV in 1610 by his reading *De Rege et Regio Institutione* by *Mariana* (*see* LIVY OF SPAIN).

Mary of Arnhem. The name used by Helen Sensburg in her NAZI propaganda broadcasts to British troops in N.W. Europe, 1944–1945. Her melting voice made her programmes very popular with the British, but without the results for which she hoped.

Mary Celeste. A brigantine found abandoned, with sails set, between the Azores and Portugal on 5th December, 1872. The ship's one boat, sextant, chronometer, register and crew were missing and no trace of them was ever found. It remains one of the unsolved mysteries of the sea.

Mary Magdalene, St. Patron SAINT of penitents, being herself the model penitent of GOSPEL story. Her feast is 22 July. *See* MAGDALENE; MAUDLIN.

In art she is represented either as young and beautiful, with a profusion of hair, and holding a box of ointment, or as a penitent, in a sequestered place, reading before a CROSS or skull.

Marybuds. The flower of the MARIGOLD. Like many other flowers, they open at daybreak and close at sunset.

> And winking marybuds begin
> To ope their golden eyes.
>
> SHAKESPEARE: *Cymbeline*, II, iii.

Marygold. *See* MARIGOLD.

Maryland (U.S.A.) was so named in compliment to Henrietta Maria, Queen of CHARLES I. In the Later charter it is called *Terra Mariæ*.

Marylebone. This London district was originally called TYBURN, being situated on that little river. The name derives from St. Mary-at-Bourne, a village near Tyburn river, also called Marybourne, Maryborne, Marybone, or Mary-le-bone.

Masada. The great rock on the edge of the Judæan desert, the site of Herod the Great's palace, where the ZEALOTS made their last heroic stand against the Romans. When defeat was certain their leader Eleazar ben Ya'ir persuaded them to draw lots to select 10 men to kill the remaining 960 defenders. One of these finally slew his nine fellows and then pushed his sword through his own body. The story is told by JOSEPHUS. Among the relics revealed by Professor Yigael Yadin's excavation exhibited at London in 1966 were eleven small potsherds inscribed with names, on one of which was the name "ben Ya'ir". They are probably the lots in question. *See* LOT.

Masaniello (măs an yel'ō). A corruption of *Tommaso Aniello*, a fisherman's son who led the Neapolitan revolt of July 1647 and ruled Naples for nine days. He was finally betrayed and shot. His body was flung into a ditch but was reclaimed and interred with great pomp and ceremony. The discontent was caused by excessive taxation and Masaniello's immediate grievance was the seizure of his property because his wife had smuggled flour. *See* LAZZARONE.

Auber's opera *La Muette de Portici* (1828) is based on these events.

Mascot. A person or thing that is supposed to bring good luck (*cp.* JETTATURA). The word is French slang (perhaps connected with Provençal *masco*, a sorcerer), and was popularized in England by Audran's opera, *La Mascotte* (1880).

> Ces envoyés du paradis
> Sont des Mascottes, mes amis,
> Heureux celui que le ciel dote d'une Mascotte.

Masculine ending. The stress or accent falling on the final syllable of a line of verse. *Cp.* FEMININE ENDING.

> I must go down to the seas again, to the lonely sea and the sky,
> And all I ask is a tall ship and a star to steer her by.
> MASEFIELD: *Sea Fever*, i.

Masher. An old-fashioned term for a "nut" or dude; an exquisite, a SWELL, a LADY-KILLER, or crusher. "Masher", the same as "crushing" or "killing", came into use in the 1880s.

Mask, The Man in the Iron. *See under* IRON.

Masochism. The name for the condition in which sexual gratification depends on the subject's self-humiliation and self-inflicted pain; after Leopold von Sacher-Masoch (1836–1895), the Austrian novelist who described this aberration. *Cp.* SADISM.

Mason and Dixon Line. The southern boundary line which separated Pennsylvania from MARYLAND, fixed at $39° 43' 26''$ N., marked out (1763–1767) by two English surveyors, Charles Mason and Jeremiah Dixon. From about 1820 it was popularly used to signify the boundary between North and South, "free" and "slave" states.

Mass (Lat. *missa*, a dismissal). The EUCHARIST. In the early Church the unbaptized were dismissed before the Eucharist proper began and the remaining congregation were solemnly dismissed at the end. By the 8th century the name *missa* had become transferred to the service as a whole, and the original meaning of the word faded out. The name *Mass* is used by the ROMAN CATHOLIC CHURCH and by High Churchmen of the CHURCH OF ENGLAND.

High Mass, or *Missa solemnis*, in which the celebrant is assisted by a deacon and subdeacon, requires the presence of choir and acolytes. Sung Mass, or *Missa Cantata*, is a simplification in which the celebrant and congregation sing the musical parts of the service, but without the deacon and subdeacon. The plain form of Mass is called Low Mass. A Pontifical High Mass is one celebrated by a BISHOP or higher prelate with very full ritual. A Nuptial Mass follows the marriage service and Requiem Mass is one offered for the dead. There are also other special forms of Mass.

Mass Observation is a British trade-mark name for a system of obtaining information as to popular opinion, similar to the GALLUP POLL. It grew out of a voluntary organization started by Charles Madge and Tom Harrison in 1937.

> In the two years of its existence M-O has been exploring new techniques for observing and analysing the ordinary. Through M-O you can already listen-in to the movements of popular habit and opinion.
> MADGE and HARRISON: *Britain by Mass-Observation*, i (1939).

Massacre of the Innocents. The slaughter of the male children of Bethlehem "from two years old and under" when Jesus was born (*Matt.* ii, 16). This was done at the command of Herod the Great in order to destroy "the babe" who was destined to become "King of the Jews".

In parliamentary parlance, the phrase denotes the withdrawal at the close of the session of the bills which there has been no time to consider or pass.

Mast. To serve before the mast. To serve as a common sailor, whose quarters are in the forepart of the ship, the FORECASTLE. An expression belonging to the days of sail.

Master (derived partly from O.E. *mægester* and partly from O.Fr. *maistre*; from the Lat. *magister*).

Little Masters. See under LITTLE.

Master-at-arms. In the Royal Navy, a chief petty officer of the Regulating Branch concerned with police and disciplinary duties. He takes precedence over other C.P.O.s.

Master of Arts, etc. One who holds a Master's degree of a university in arts. In the English universities it is the degree above that of Bachelor. At the modern universities it is awarded for further examination or research; at Oxford and Cambridge no further tests are required. In the Scottish universities it is a first degree. At most universities there are corresponding Master's degrees in other faculties.

Master of the Rolls. See ROLLS.

Master of the Sentences. See SENTENCES.

Master Mason. A FREEMASON who has been raised to the third degree.

Old Masters. The great painters (especially of Italy and the Low Countries) who worked from the 13th century to about the early 17th. Also their paintings.

Past Master. One who has held the office of dignity of *master*; hence an adept, one who is long-experienced in a craft, etc.

Matador. In bull-fights he is the final actor in the drama, his part being to play the bull alone and kill it.

In the game of OMBRE, *Spadille* (the ace of spades), *Manille* (the seven of trumps), and *Basto* (the ace of clubs) are called "Matadors".

> Now move to war her sable Matadores ...
> Spadillo first, unconquerable lord,
> Led off two captive trumps, and swept the board,
> As many more Manillo forced to yield,
> And marched a victor from the verdant field.
> Him Basto followed...
> POPE: *Rape of the Lock*, canto iii.

In the game of dominoes of this name, the double-blank and all the "stones" that of themselves make seven (6–1, 5–2, and 4–3) are "matadors", and can be played at any time.

Matamore. A POLTROON, a swagger, a BOBADIL. It is composed of two Spanish words *matar-Moros* (a slayer of Moors), See MOOR-SLAYER.

> Your followers catch your own humour, and must bandy and brawl in my court, and in my very presence, like so many Matamoros.
> SCOTT: *Kenilworth*, xvi.

Matapan Stew (Austr.). A meal concocted of left-overs, and so called from the fact that the cook of H.M.A.S. *Perth* served a scratch hot meal during the Battle of Matapan, 28 March 1941.

Mate. A man does not get his hands out of the tar by becoming second mate. In the days of sail a second mate was still expected to work with the tar-pot with the men. The first mate was exempt from this dirty work.

Maté (măt′ā). Paraguay tea made from the leaves of Brazilian holly (*Ilex paraguayenis*). Its full name is *Yerba de maté* (*yerba*, herb; *mate*, vessel) from the hollow gourd in which it was infused. It is also called *Brazil tea, Jesuit's tea* and *Yerba*.

The tea was drunk from the gourd through a *bombilla* or tube (S.Am. Span. *bomba*, a pump) and customarily the Paraguayan Indian host, after taking the first suck to signify that no treachery was possible, would pass the bombilla and gourd to his guests. *Cp.* CALUMET.

Mater Familias (mā′ tĕr fă mi li ăs) (Lat.). The mother of a family.

Materia medica (mă tēr′ i ă mĕd′ i kà) (Med. Lat., medical material). That branch of medicine which deals with the remedial substances employed for the cure and alleviation of disease, including their uses, properties and physiological effects. Dioscorides wrote his *Materia Medica* (1st century A.D.) giving the properties of some 600 medicinal plants and also animal products of medical and dietetic use which served to enlighten the herbalists of the 15th and 16th centuries.

Materialism. In philosophy, the doctrines of a *Materialist*, who maintains that there is nothing in the universe but matter, that mind is a phenomenon of matter, and that there is no ground for assuming a spiritual first cause. In general, Materialism is opposed to IDEALISM, free-will, and belief in God. In the ancient world, its chief exponents were EPICURUS and Lucretius, in modern times the 18th-century French philosophers La Mettrie and Holbach. In the 19th century Materialism was much influenced by the theory of evolution and became involved with problems of interpretation in science, while later Marx put forward DIALECTICAL MATERIALISM.

In everyday parlance "materialism" implies devotion to material things and interests.

Dialectical materialism. The Marxist adaptation of the Hegelian DIALECTIC to describe the way in which phenomena have, and therefore will, interact and develop; the general laws of motion which govern the evolution of nature and society. Every stage of history contains the germs of its own destruction, the thesis provokes its opposite or antithesis, and from the clash a new synthesis arises which preserves the best of both thesis and antithesis. The process then repeats itself. This conflict of opposites takes place gradually until a certain point, when quantitative change becomes qualitative change. By such processes is the classless society to be reached. It should be noted that ideas and institutions are the reflection of material conditions—the reverse of the Hegelian approach. *See* MARXISM.

Historical materialism. This is the application of DIALECTICAL MATERIALISM to the evolution of society. Broadly it comes down to a materialist or economic interpretation of history in which all historical developments are basically due to economic phenomena and all social, political and intellectual life, as well as religion, are basically determined by the material conditions of life. Furthermore, historical development is part of the dialectical process.

When we find that the most different modes of production, those of highly civilised nations as well as those of uncivilised warrior tribes, were, for a thousand years, compatible with the same ideology [Christianity], we are surely justified in concluding that the ideology of these nations was determined by some cause other than economics.

KARL FEDERN: *The Materialist Conception of History*, iii.

Materialize. In psychical research it denotes the assumption of bodily form of psychical phenomena. The principles governing materialization are as yet unknown.

Mathew, Father. Theobald Mathew (1796–1856), an Irish priest called *The Apostle of Temperance*. His work on behalf of total abstinence was truly remarkable. When the centenary of his death was celebrated in Cork (1956), 60,000 people gathered to honour his memory.

Matins. *See* MATTINS.

Matriculate (Lat. *matricula*, a roll or register). Students at universities matriculate when they enrol after fulfilling certain entrance requirements.

In common parlance, it used to mean to pass the entrance examination qualifying one to enter as a student at a university, although many sat for such examinations simply to obtain a qualification. This examination no longer exists.

In Scottish HERALDRY, when persons register their arms with the Lord LYON they are said *to matriculate*.

Matsya. *See* AVATAR.

Matter. A matter of course. Something one expects in the regular order of things; a natural consequence or accompaniment.

For that matter. As far as that is concerned.

No matter. It is of no consequence; regardless of, as in, "no matter what happens."

Matter-of-fact. Unvarnished truth; prosaic, unimaginative, as a "matter-of-fact swain".

Matterhorn. The German name of the mountain in the Pennine Alps known to the French as *Mont Cervin*, and to the Italians as *Monte Silvo*; so called from its peak (*Horn*) and the scanty patches of green meadow (*Matter*) which cluster round its base. Above a glacier-line, 11,000 ft. high, it rises in an almost inaccessible obelisk of rock to a total height of 14,703 ft. It was first scaled in 1865 by Edward Whymper (1840–1911), when four of his party lost their lives.

Figuratively used it applies to any danger, desperate situation threatening destruction, or LEAP IN THE DARK, as *the matrimonial Matterhorn*.

Matthew, St. Is represented in art as (1) an EVANGELIST, old and with a long beard, with an ANGEL generally standing near by dictating his GOSPEL; (2) an APOSTLE, bearing a purse in reference to his being a publican; sometimes carrying a spear, sometimes a carpenter's rule or square. His symbol is an angel or a man's face, and his day is 21 September.

One legend says that St. Matthew preached for 15 years in Judæa after the Ascension, and that he carried the Gospel to Ethiopia, where he was murdered.

In the last of Matthew. At the last gasp, on one's last legs. This is a German expression and arose thus: a Roman Catholic priest said in his sermon that Protestantism was in the last of Matthew, and, being asked what he meant, replied, "The last five words of the Gospel of St. Matthew are these: 'The end of this dispensation'." He quoted the Latin version; ours is less correctly translated "the end of the world".

Matthew Parker's Bible; Matthew's Bible. See BIBLE, THE ENGLISH.

Matthias, St. The APOSTLE chosen by lot to take the place left by the traitor Judas Iscariot (*Acts* i, 21–26). The name is a shortened form of *Mattathias*. His day is 14 May (formerly 24 February).

Mattins, or **Matins**. The BREVIARY office for the night called *Vigiliæ* until the 11th century, and originally held at midnight, but in the BENEDICTINE rule at 2 a.m. It is now anticipated and said the previous afternoon or evening. The name was retained in the BOOK OF COMMON PRAYER (1549) for the service of Morning Prayer which was derived from the ancient office. The name was discarded in the book of 1552.

Mattins of Bruges. The massacre of the French living in Bruges by the Flemings at daybreak, 18 May 1302.

Maudlin. Stupidly sentimental. *Maudlin drunk* is to be sentimentally drunk and inclined to tears. *Maudlin slip-slop* is sentimental chit-chat. The word is derived from the repentant tears of MARY MAGDALENE, who was often portrayed with eyes swollen after weeping. *Cp.* MAGDALENE.

Maul of Monks, The. Thomas Cromwell (1485–1540), VICAR-GENERAL (1535) who arranged for the visitation of the English monasteries and their subsequent dissolution.

Maumet, Maumetry. See MAMMET.

Maundy Thursday. The day before GOOD FRIDAY is so called from the first words of the antiphon for that day being *Mandatum novum do vobis*, a new commandment I give unto you (*St. John* xiii, 34), with which the ceremony of the washing of the feet begins. This is still carried out in Roman Catholic cathedrals and monasteries. It became the custom of popes, Catholic sovereigns, prelates, and priests to wash the feet of poor people. In England the sovereign did the same as late as the reign of James II. The word has been incorrectly derived from *maund* (a basket), because on the day before the great fast it was an ancient church custom to bring out food in maunds to distribute to the poor.

The Royal Maunds, or **Maundy Money.** Gifts in money given by the sovereign on MAUNDY THURSDAY to the number of aged poor men and women that corresponds with her (his) age. Broadcloth, fish, bread and wine were given in the reign of Elizabeth I, later clothing and provisions. The clothing was replaced by money in 1725 and the provisions in 1837. In due course the ceremony was transferred from the chapel at WHITEHALL to Westminster Abbey. Personal distribution of the doles ceased in 1688 until George V restarted it in 1932, as did Edward VIII in 1936. Queen Elizabeth II has made a personal distribution in most years since 1953 and the ceremony is no longer held at Westminster every year. Thus the 1979 service attended by the Queen and Prince Philip was held in Winchester Cathedral. The money is specially struck in silver pennies, twopennies, threepennies, and fourpences and is unaffected by decimalization.

Mauretania, or **Mauritania.** Parts of Morocco and Algiers, the land of the *Mauri* or Moors. The kingdom of Mauritania was annexed to the Roman Empire in A.D. 42 and finally disintegrated when overrun by the VANDALS in 429.

The modern Islamic Republic of Mauritania is situated in the S.W. Sahara.

Mausoleum. Originally the name of the tomb of *Mausolus*, King of Caria, to whom his wife Artemisia erected a splendid monument at Halicarnassus (353 B.C.). Parts of the sepulchre, one of the SEVEN WONDERS OF THE WORLD (*see* WONDER), are now in the BRITISH MUSEUM. The name is now applied to any magnificent tomb, usually with a sepulchral chamber.

Notable examples are: that of AUGUSTUS; of Hadrian, *i.e.* the castle of St. Angelo at Rome; that of St. Peter the Martyr in the church of St. Eustatius at Milan; that of Frederick William III and Queen Louisa at Charlottenburg near Berlin; that of the Prince Consort at Frogmore in Windsor Park.

Mauthe Dog. See MODDEY DHOO.

Mauther, mawther. An old East Anglian dialect word for a young girl; frequently altered to *Modder*, *Morther*, *Mor*, etc. Its etymology is obscure.

> Away! you talk like a foolish mauther.
> BEN JONSON: *The Alchemist*, IV, vii.
> When once a giggling morther you,
> And I a red-faced chubby boy...
> ROBERT BLOOMFIELD: *Richard and Kate*, xii.

Mauvais, mauvaise (mō va, mō vāz). Fr., bad.

Mauvais ton. Bad manners, ill-breeding, vulgar ways.

Mauvaise honte (awnt). Bad or silly shame; false modesty, bashfulness, sheepishness.

Mauvaise plaisanterie. A rude or illmannered jest; a jest in bad taste.

Maverick. An unbranded animal, a stray, a masterless person or rover. Samuel A. Maverick, a Texan cattle-raiser, did not bother to brand his cattle, hence the practice arose of calling unbranded calves *mavericks*, and the usage extended to other animals. In the U.S.A. it acquired a political connotation from the 1880s, applying to politicians who did not acknowledge any party leadership. Kipling called an imaginary regiment "The Mavericks". **To maverick** is to seize or brand *mavericks*, hence to appropriate anything without legal claim.

Mavournin. Irish (*mo mhurnin*) for "My darling"; *Erin go bragh* is "Ireland for ever".

> Land of my forefathers, Erin go bragh!...
> Erin mavournin, Erin go bragh!
> THOMAS CAMPBELL: *Exile of Erin*, v.

Mawworm. A hypocritical pretender to sanctity, a pious humbug. From the character of this name in Isaac Bickerstaffe's *The Hypocrite* (1769).

Maxim's. The most famous and elegant French restaurant, a symbol of gastronomic perfection and gaiety. Situated in the rue Royale, Paris, it was opened by Maxime Gaillard in 1893. His rich and famous clientèle grew steadily, aided by the patronage of fashionable courtesans. Its characteristically opulent ART NOUVEAU décor is still maintained but it is now more noted for food than frolics. It has featured in various productions including *The Merry Widow* and *Gigi*.

May. The Anglo-Saxons called this month *thrimilce*, because then cows can be milked three times a day; the present name is the Lat. *Maius*, probably from *Maia*, the goddess of growth and increase, connected with *major*. It was the fifth month in the Julian and Gregorian CALENDAR. The old Dutch name was *Blou-maand* (blossoming month). In the French Republican Calendar it was called *Floréal* (the time of flowers, 20 April to 20 May).

Cast not a clout till May is out. An old warning not to shed winter clothing too early in the year. *Clout* here is a rag or patch, hence a piece of clothing. *May* is also another name for hawthorn, which blossoms in May. Thus some hold that the proverb means "do not discard clothing until the hawthorn blossoms" but more likely it means "wait until the end of May". F.K. Robinson's *Whitby Glossary* (1855) has:

> The wind at North and East
> was never good for man nor beast,
> so never think to cast a clout
> until the month of May be out.

Here we go gathering nuts in May. See *under* NUT.

It's a case of January and May. See under JANUARY.

May unlucky for weddings. This is a Roman superstition, and is referred to by Ovid. In this month were held the festivals of *Bona Dea* (the goddess of chastity), and the feasts of the dead called *Lemuralia*.

> Nec viduæ tædis eadem, nec virginis apta
> Tempora; quæ nupsit, non diuturna fuit;
> Hæc quoque de causa, si te proverbia tangunt,
> Mente malum Maio nubere vulgus ait.
> OVID: *Fasti*, v, 487, etc.

Unlucky to wash blankets in May. This superstition still survives in parts of Britain, especially in the S.W. The old rhyme says:

> Wash a blanket in May
> Wash a dear one away.

May-day. Polydore Virgil says that the Roman youths used to go into the fields and spend the CALENDS of May in dancing and singing in honour of FLORA, goddess of fruits and flowers. The English celebrated Mayday with games and sports, particularly archery and MORRIS dancing and the setting up of the MAYPOLE. In due time ROBIN HOOD and MAID MARIAN came to preside as Lord and Lady of the May, and by the 16th century May-day was Robin Hood's day and Robin Hood plays became an integral part of the festivities.

May-day was also formerly the day of the London chimney-sweepers' festival. See *also* LABOR DAY.

Evil May Day. See DEVIL.

Mayfair. A fashionable district in the WEST END of London north of PICCADILLY, to Oxford Street and between Park Lane and Berkeley Square. It was originally Brookfield, but takes its present name from the May fair which occupied the site of the present Hertford Street, Curzon Street, and Shepherd Market. There was an annual fair in the area from the reign of Edward I, called

St. James's Fair, which began on the eve of St. JAMES and was suppressed in 1664. It was renewed by James II to commence on 1 May, hence the name. From the beginning of the 18th century it became a centre for drinking, gaming, etc., was temporarily suppressed in 1708, and finally abolished at the end of the 18th century.

May-Fair Marriages. "The Rev. Alexander Keith's Chapel" in Curzon Street, Mayfair, was notorious for its traffic in weddings until the Act of 1753 stopped the trade. Here the younger of the two beautiful Miss Gunnings was married to the sixth Duke of Hamilton in 1752. The ring was from a bed-curtain and the ceremony took place half an hour after midnight. *Cp.* FLEET MARRIAGES; GRETNA GREEN MARRIAGES.

Maypole, May Queen. etc. Dancing round the Maypole on MAY-DAY, "going-a-Maying", electing a May Queen, and lighting bonfires, are all ancient relics of nature-worship. In Cornhill, LONDON, before the Church of St. Andrew a great shaft or may-pole was set up, round which the people danced, whence the church came to be called St. Andrew Undershaft. In the first May morning people went "a-maying" to fetch fresh flowers and branches of hawthorn (hence its name *may*) to decorate their houses, and the fairest maid of the locality was crowned "Queen of the May".

A very tall ungainly woman is sometimes called a "Maypole", a term which was bestowed as a nickname on the Duchess of Kendal, one of George I's German mistresses.

The Maypole in the Strand. This once famous LONDON landmark was erected probably in the time of Elizabeth I, on a spot now occupied by the Church of St. Mary-le-Strand. Destroyed by the PURITANS in 1644, another (134 ft. high) was set up in 1661, it is said, by the farrier John Clarges to celebrate the marriage of his daughter to General Monck. By 1713 this was decayed, and another erected which was removed in 1718. It was bought by Sir Isaac Newton, who sent it to a friend in Wanstead, where it was erected in the park to support the then largest telescope in Europe.

May meetings. The annual gatherings, usually held in LONDON in May or June, of religious and charitable societies, to hear the annual reports and appeals for further support, etc. *See* EXETER HALL.

Maya. The mother of GAUTAMA who saw in a dream the future BUDDHA enter her womb in the shape of a little white elephant. Seven days after his birth she died from joy.

Mayflower. The 180-ton ship in which the PILGRIM FATHERS finally sailed from Plymouth, Devon, 6 September 1620. They arrived off Cape Cod, 11 November, and established their colony, although the original intention was to land on the shore of Delaware Bay. At Jordans, Buckinghamshire, the burial place of William Penn, there is a barn traditionally held to be built from the timber of this ship.

In 1957 a replica of the ship under the command of A. J. Villiers, and built of Devonshire oak and elm, sailed from Plymouth to Massachusetts following the route of its predecessor.

The Mayflower Compact. An agreement signed by 41 adults in the cabin of the *Mayflower* acknowledging their allegiance to the King of England and setting up a body politic "to frame just and equal laws" (21 November 1620).

Mayhem. An early form of *maim* and an archaic legal term for the crime of depriving a person of the use of an arm, leg, eye, etc. thus rendering him less able to defend himself in a violent struggle or to trouble his opponent. The word is now back in popular use for violent and injurious action.

Mayonnaise. A sauce made with pepper, salt, oil, vinegar, the yolk of egg, etc., beaten up together. When the Duc de Richelieu captured Port Mahon, Minorca, in 1756, he demanded food on landing; in the absence of a prepared meal, his chef took whatever he could find and beat it up together—hence the original form *mahonnaise*.

Mayor. The chief magistrate of a city, elected by the council, of which he becomes chairman. He holds office for twelve months.

The chief magistrate of LONDON is the Right Hon. the Lord Mayor, a Privy Councillor. York has had a Lord Mayor since 1389 and in more recent times the honour has been bestowed on Birmingham, Bradford, Bristol, Cardiff, Hull, Leeds, Leicester, Liverpool, Manchester, Newcastle upon Tyne, Norwich, Nottingham, Plymouth, Portsmouth, Sheffield and Stoke-on-Trent. The Norman *maire* (mayor) was introduced by Henry II and it supplanted the old name of PORTREEVE. *Cp.* LORD MAYOR'S DAY; LORD MAYOR'S SHOW.

Mayor of the Bull-ring. In the Dublin of former times, this official and his sheriffs were elected on MAY-DAY and St. PETER Eve "to be captaine and guardian of the batchelers, and the unwedded youth of the civitie". For the year the "Mayor" had authority to punish those who frequented houses of ill-fame. He was termed "Mayor of the Bull-ring" because he conducted any bachelor who married during his term of office to an iron ring in the market place to which bulls were tied for baiting, and made him kiss it.

Mayor of Garratt. *See* GARRATT.

Mayor of the Palace (*Maire du Palais*). Originally the *major domus* or steward of the Frankish Kings whose functions expanded into the affairs of state. By the 7th century, they were chief ministers until, in 751, Pippin III, son of Charles MARTEL, and mayor of the palace of Neustria and Burgundy, became King of the Franks and suppressed the office. He was the founder of the Carlovingian dynasty and father of CHARLEMAGNE.

Mazarin, Cardinal Jules (1602–1661), Italian-born successor to Cardinal Richelieu and minister to the Queen-Regent during the minority of Louis XIV.

Mazarin Bible. *See* BIBLE, SOME SPECIALLY NAMED EDITIONS.

Mazarin Library. The first public LIBRARY (1642) at Paris. The great Cardinal Mazarin left his collection of 40,000 books to the city on his death in 1661, and himself composed the rules for its conduct.

Mazarinades. Pamphlets in prose or verse published against Cardinal Mazarin (1602–1661) by supporters of the FRONDE.

Mazer. A large drinking vessel originally made of maple-wood, and so called from O.Fr. *masere*, O.H.Ger. *Masar*, a knot in wood, maple-wood.

> A mazer wrought of the maple ware.
> SPENSER: *Shepheard's Calendar (August)*.

Mazikeen, or **Shedeem.** A species of being in Jewish mythology resembling the Arabian JINN said to be agents of magic and enchantment. When ADAM fell, says the TALMUD, he was excommunicated for 130 years, during which time he begat demons and spectres.

Swells out like the Mazikeen ass. The allusion is to a Jewish tradition that a servant, whose task it was to rouse the neighbourhood to midnight prayer, one night mounted a stray ASS and neglected his duty. As he rode along the ass grew bigger and bigger, till at last it towered as high as the tallest edifice, where it left the man, and there next morning he was found.

Meal. In meal or in malt. Directly or indirectly; in one way or another. If much money passes through the hand, some profit will be sure to accrue either "in meal or in malt", and a certain percentage of one or the other is the miller's perquisite.

Meal Tub Plot. In 1679 during the POPISH PLOT scare, Thomas Dangerfield pretended to have discovered a WHIG plot to prevent the Duke of York's succession to the throne. The evidence was claimed to be concealed under the meal tub of his associate Mrs. Cellier. The falsity of this was discovered and he next accused prominent Roman Catholics of promoting the conspiracy as cover for a popish plot. Dangerfield was convicted of perjury and Mrs. Cellier finally pilloried for libel in connection with her trial.

Mealy-mouthed is the Greek *melimuthos* (honey-speech), and means velvet-tongued, afraid of giving offence, hypocritical, "smarmy".

Mean. Mean as hungry Tyson (Austr.). Very mean. In allusion too a very miserly Australian farmer, James Tyson (1819–1898).

Meander. To wind, to saunter about at random; so called from the Mæander, a winding river of Phrygia. It is said to have given DÆDALUS his idea for a LABYRINTH. The term is also applied to an ornamental pattern of winding lines, used as a border on pottery, wall decorations, etc.

Means Test. The principle of supplying evidence of need before qualifying for relief from public funds, *i.e.* a test of one's means. Such a test was introduced by the NATIONAL GOVERNMENT in 1931 when a person's unemployment benefit was exhausted, and the resulting inquisition was much resented by those concerned. It took note of any earnings by members of the household and all monetary assets, and penalized the provident. The regulations governing public assistance were modified after World War II.

Measure (O.Fr. *mesure*; Lat. *mensura*).

Beyond measure, or **out of all measure**. Beyond all reasonable degree; exceedingly, excessively.

> Thus out of measure sad.
> SHAKESPEARE: *Much Ado about Nothing*, I, iii.

To measure one's length on the ground. To fall flat on the ground; to be knocked down.

To measure other people's corn by one's own bushel. *See under* BUSHEL.

To measure strength. To wrestle together; to fight, to contest.

To measure swords. To try whether or not one is strong enough or sufficiently equally matched to contend against another. The phrase is from duelling, in which the seconds measure the swords to see that both are of the same length.

> So we measured swords and parted.
> SHAKESPEARE: *As You Like It*, V, iv.

To take the measure of one's foot. To ascertain how far a person will venture; to make a shrewd guess of another's character. The allusion is to *ex pede Herculem* (*see under* EX).

To tread a measure. A poetic and archaic expression meaning "to dance", especially a slow stately dance.

> "Now tread we a measure!" said young Lochinvar.
> SCOTT: *Marmion*, canto V, xii.

Meat, Bread. Both words can connote food in general. For Italians and Asiatics *bread* stands for food, an indication of their lower consumption of animal food. The English being greater consumers of *meat*, which simply means food, use the word almost exclusively for animal food. In the banquet given to his brethren, Joseph commanded the servants "to set on bread" (*Gen.* xliii, 31). In *Ps.* civ, 27, it is said of fishes, creeping things, and crocodiles that God gives them *meat* in due season.

In parts of Devonshire potatoes for the table are still called *meat* potatoes, as opposed to *seed* potatoes, and *feed* potatoes for livestock.

To carry off meat from the graves. To be as POOR as a church mouse; to be so poor as to descend to robbing the graves of offerings. The Greeks and Romans used to make feasts at certain seasons, when spirits were supposed to return to their graves, and the fragments were left on the tombs for them. Hence the Latin proverb *Eleemosynam sepulcri patris tui* (Alms on your father's grave).

Mebyon Kernow. (Sons of Cornwall). The society of Cornish nationalists, established in 1951. Their flag is the emblem of St. PIRAN—a white cross, which symbolises tin, on a black field which represents the ground rock from which it is extracted.

Mecca. The birthplace of MOHAMMED in Saudi Arabia. It is one of the two holy cities, the other being MEDINA and the most sacred pilgrimage for MOSLEMS. Hence, a place one ardently longs to visit, a place outstandingly frequented by the followers of a particular cult or pursuit. Thus Stratford-upon-Avon could be called a *Mecca* for the devotees of Shakespeare as could Wimbledon for tennis players.

Mecklenburg Declaration. The first declaration of independence in the U.S.A. made at Mecklenburg, N. Carolina, on 20 May 1775.

Medal of Honor. In the U.S.A., a medal instituted in 1862 for conspicuous acts of gallantry in the CIVIL WAR. It is the premier decoration of the United States, the equivalent of the VICTORIA CROSS.

Putty medal. Used in expressions such as

"that's worth a putty medal" and at first as a sarcastic comment implying that a putty medal was a suitable reward for an incompetent performance or attempt. Subsequently it became a jocular recognition of a praiseworthy effort and was intended to encourage.

Médard, St. (mā′ dar). The French St. SWITHIN; his day is 8 June.

> Quand il pleut à la Saint-Médard
> Il pleut quarante jours plus tard.

He was bishop of Noyon and Tournai in the 6th century and founded the Festival of the Rose at Salency, in which the most virtuous girl in the parish receives a crown of roses and a purse of money. Legend says that a sudden shower once fell which soaked everyone except St. Médard who remained dry as toast, for an EAGLE had spread its wings over him, and ever after he was termed *maître de la pluie*.

Medb. *See* MAEVE.

Medea (me dē′ à). In Greek legend, a sorceress, daughter of Æetes, king of Colchis. She married JASON, the leader of the ARGONAUTS, whom she aided to obtain the GOLDEN FLEECE, and was the mother of Medus, regarded by the Greeks as the ancestor of the Medes.

Medea's kettle, or **cauldron.** A means of restoring lost youth. MEDEA cut an old ram into pieces, threw the bits into her cauldron, and a young lamb came forth. The daughters of Pelias accordingly killed and cut up their father thinking to restore him to youth in the same way, but Medea refused to save the situation.

> Get thee Medea's kettle and be boiled anew.
> CONGREVE: *Love for Love*, IV, vii.

Medes and Persians. *See under* LAW.

Mediæval times. *See* MIDDLE AGES.

Medici (med′ i chi). A great and powerful family that ruled in Florence from the 15th to the 18th centuries, founded by Giovanni Medici, a banker, whose son Cosimo (1389–1464) was famous as a patron of art and learning. His grandson Lorenzo the Magnificent (1449–1492) was one of the outstanding figures of the RENAISSANCE.

From Lorenzo, brother of Cosimo the Elder, came the line of Grand Dukes of Tuscany, the first being his great-grandson Cosimo (1519–1574), who was regarded by many as the original of MACHIAVELLI's *Prince*. The Medici family gave three Popes to the Church, Leo X (1475–1521; POPE 1513–1521), in whose pontificate the REFORMATION began; Clement VII (1478–1534; Pope 1523–1534), who refused Henry VIII's divorce from Katharine of Aragon;

and Leo XI, who was Pope for only a few months in 1605.

Medicine. From Lat. *medicina*, which meant both the physician's art and his laboratory, and also a medicament. The alchemists applied the word to the PHILOSOPHER'S STONE and the ELIXIR OF LIFE; hence SHAKESPEARE'S.

> How much unlike art thou, Mark Antony!
> Yet, coming from him, the great medicine hath
> With his tinct gilded thee.
>
> *Antony and Cleopatra*, I, v.

The word was, and is, frequently used in a figurative sense, as

> The miserable have no other medicine
> But only hope.
>
> SHAKESPEARE: *Measure for Measure*, III, i.

Among the North American Indians *medicine* is a spell, charm, or FETISH, and sometimes even MANITOU himself, hence **Medicine-man,** a witch-doctor or magician.

The Father of Medicine. Aretæus of Cappadocia (2nd century A.D.) is sometimes so called, and especially HIPPOCRATES of Cos (*c.* 460–*c.* 377 B.C.).

Medicine Ball. A large, leather-covered, heavy ball tossed from one person to another as a form of exercise.

Medicine lodge. A tent or other form of structure used by North American Indians for ceremonial purposes.

Medicinal days. In ancient practice the 6th, 8th, 10th, 12th, 16th, 18th, etc., of a disease; so called because according to HIPPOCRATES no CRISIS occurs on these days and medicine may be safely administered.

Medicinal-finger. Also the leech-finger or leechman. The finger next to the little finger, the RING-finger; so called in mediæval times because of the notion that it contained a vein that led direct to the HEART.

Medina. The second holy city of the Mohammedans, called Yathrib before the Prophet fled thither from MECCA, but afterwards Medina-al-Nabi (the city of the prophet). *See* HEGIRA.

Mediterranean. The midland sea; the sea in the middle of the (Roman) earth (Lat. *medius*, middle; *terra*, land).

The Key of the Mediterranean. The Rock of GIBRALTAR.

Lighthouse of the Mediterranean. *See under* LIGHT.

Medmenham, Monks of. *See* HELL-FIRE CLUB.

Medusa. In classical mythology, the chief of the GORGONS. Her face was so terrible that all who looked on it were turned to stone. Her head was struck off by PERSEUS. Medusa

was the mother, by POSEIDON of Chrysaor and PEGASUS.

Meerschaum (mēr' shawm) (Ger., sea-froth). This mineral (used for making tobacco-pipes), from having been found on the seashore in rounded white lumps, was popularly supposed to be sea-froth petrified. It is a compound of silica, magnesia, lime, water and carbonic acid. When first dug it lathers like soap, and is used as soap by the Tartars.

Meg. Formerly slang for a GUINEA, and more recently for a halfpenny.

> No, no; Meggs are Guineas; Smelts are half-guineas.
>
> SHADWELL: *Squire of Alsatia*, I, i (1688).

Long Meg, etc. *See under* LONG.

Mons Meg. A great 15th-century piece of ordnance in Edinburgh Castle, made at Mons in Flanders and much esteemed by the Scots. It was taken to London about 1757 and restored to Edinburgh in 1829. (Gr. *megas*, great.)

Roaring Meg. Formerly any large gun that made a great noise when fired was so called, as MONS MEG herself. Burton says: "Music is a roaring Meg against melancholy" (Gr. *megas*, great).

> Drowning the noise of their consciences ... by ringing their greatest Bells, ... discharging their roaring-megs.
>
> TRAPP: *Comment on Job* (1656).

Megarians. The inhabitants of Megara and its territory, Megaris, Greece, were proverbial for their stupidity; hence the proverb "Wise as a Megarian", *i.e.* not wise at all; yet *see below*. *Cp.* ABDERA.

Megarian School. A philosophical school of the 4th-century B.C. founded by Euclid, a native of Megara, and disciple of SOCRATES. It combined the ethical doctrines of Socrates with the METAPHYSICS of the ELEATICS.

Megrims (mē' grimz). A corruption of the Gr. *hemi-crania* (half the skull), through the Fr. *migraine*. A neuralgic affection generally confined to one brow or to one side of the forehead; whims, fancies.

Meinie, or **Meiny** (mī' ni). A company of attendants; a household (from O.Fr. *meyné, mesnie*, from Lat. *mansio*, a house). Our word *menial* has much the same derivation and significance.

> They summon'd up their meiny, straight took horse.
>
> SHAKESPEARE: *King Lear*, II, iv.

Mein Kampf (mīn kămf) Ger., My Struggle). The name adopted by Adolf Hitler (1889–1945) for the book embodying his political and racial theories and misreadings of history, which in due course became the Nazi "Bible". The first part was written when he was in prison after the abortive "Beer Hall Putsch" of 1923. It was published in two parts (1925 and 1927). *Cp.* HITLERISM: MUNICH; NAZI.

Meiosis (mī ō sis). This word, coming from the Greek and meaning "lessening", denotes a figure of speech by which an impression is deliberately given that a thing is of less size or importance than it actually is. It is also used of LITOTES.

Meistersinger. (Mastersingers). Bürger poets of Germany, who, in the 14th to 16th centuries, attempted to revive the national minstrelsy of the MINNESINGER, which had fallen into decay. Hans Sachs, the cobbler (1494–1576), was the most celebrated. Wagner has an opera *Die Meistersinger von Nürnberg* (1868) in which he protested at his critics.

Melampode. Black Hellebore; so called from Melampus, a famous soothsayer and physician of Greek legend, who with it cured the daughters of Prœtus of their madness (VIRGIL: *Georgics*, iii, 550).

> My seely sheep, like well below,
> They need not melampode;
> For they been hale enough I trow,
> And liken their abode.
> SPENSER: *Shepheard's Calendar* (July).

Melancholy (Gr. *melas chole*). Lowness of spirits, supposed at one time to arise from a superfluity of black BILE.

> Hence, loathed Melancholy,
> Of Cerberus and blackest midnight born.
> MILTON: *L'Allegro*.

Melancholy Jacques. So Jean-Jacques Rousseau (1712–1778) was called for his morbid sensibilities and unhappy spirit. The expression is from SHAKESPEARE'S *As You Like It*.

Melanchthon is the Greek name by which Philipp Schwarzerd (black earth), the German reformer (1497–1560), was called. Similarly *Œcolampadius* is the Greek version of the German name *Hauschein*, and *Desiderius Erasmus* is one Latin and one Greek rendering of the name *Gheraerd Gheraerd*.

Melba. Melba toast, narrow slices of thin toast.

Peach, or **Pêche Melba,** a confection of peach on vanilla ice-cream, covered with raspberry purée.

These take their name from Dame Nellie Melba (1861–1931), the colourful Australian operatic soprano.

Meleager (mel ē ā' ger). A hero of Greek legend, son of Œneus of Calydon and Althæa, distinguished for throwing the javelin, for ·

slaying the Calydonian BOAR, and as one of the ARGONAUTS. *See* ALTHÆA'S BRAND.

Melibœan Dye. A rich purple. Melibœa, in Thessaly, was famous for the *ostrum*, a fish used in dyeing purple.

> A military vest of purple flowed,
> Livelier than Melibœan.
> MILTON: *Paradise Lost*, XI, 241.

Melicertes (mel i sĕr' tēz). Son of Ino, a sea deity of Greek legend. Athamas imagined his wife Ino to be a lioness, and her two sons to be lion's cubs. In his frenzy he slew one of the boys and drove Melicertes and his mother into the sea. *See* LEUCOTHEA.

Mélisande. *See* MELUSINA.

Mell Supper. In the northern counties, Harvest supper; usually called Kern or Churn Supper in Scotland. *See also* CRYING THE NECK; CORN DOLLY; HARVEST HOME; HARVEST THANKSGIVING; HOCKEY.

> Mell is plainly derived from the French word *mesler*, to mingle together, the master and servant promiscuously at the same table. At the mell-supper, Bourne tells us, "the servant and his master are alike, and everything is done with equal freedom; they sit at the same table, converse freely together, and spend the remaining part of the night in dancing and singing, without any difference or distinction".
> STRUTT: *Sports and Pastimes*, Bk. IV, ch. iii, xxvii.

Mellifluous Doctor. St. BERNARD of Clairvaux (1091–1153), the *Oracle of the Church*, whose writings were called a "river of Paradise". *See* DOCTORS OF LEARNING.

Melodrama (Gr. *melos*, a song). Properly (and in the early 19th century) a drama in which song and music were introduced, an OPERA. These pieces were usually of a sensational character and the musical parts were gradually dropped. The word now denotes a lurid, sensational and highly emotional play with a happy ending in which the villain gets all he richly deserves. *See* RED BARN.

Melon. The Mohammedans say that the eating of a melon produces a thousand good works. *See also* ELIJAH'S MELONS.

Melpomene (mel pom' e ni). The muse of TRAGEDY.

> Up then, Melpomene, thou mournfullest Muse of nine,
> Such cause of mourning never hadst afore.
> SPENSER: *Shepheard's Calendar* (November).

Melusina, or Mélisande. The most famous of all the fées of French romance, looked upon by the houses of Lusignan, Rohan, Luxembourg, and Sassenaye as their ancestor and founder. Having enclosed her father in a high mountain for offending her mother, she was condemned to become every Saturday a serpent from her waist downward. She married Raymond, count of Lusignan, and made her husband vow never to visit her on a Saturday; but the count hid himself on one of the forbidden days, and saw his wife's transformation. Melusina was now obliged to quit her husband, and was destined to wander about as a spectre till the day of doom, though some say that the count immured her in the dungeon of his castle.

A sudden scream is called *un cri de Mélusine*, in allusion to the scream of despair uttered by Melusina when she was discovered by her husband; and in Poitou certain gingerbread cakes bearing the impress of a beautiful woman "*bien coiffée*", with a serpent's tail, made by confectioners for the MAY fair in the neighbourhood of Lusignan, are still called *Mélusines*.

Memento mori (Lat., remember you must die). An emblem of mortality, such as a skull; something to put us in mind of the shortness and uncertainty of life.

> I make as good use of it [Bardolph's face] as many a man doth of a death's head or a memento mori.
> SHAKESPEARE: *Henry IV, Pt. I*, III, iii.

Memnon. The Oriental or Ethiopian prince who, in the TROJAN WAR, went to the assistance of his uncle PRIAM and was slain by ACHILLES. His mother Eos (the Dawn) was inconsolable for his death, and wept for him every morning. The Greeks called the statue of Amenophis III at Thebes that of Memnon. When first struck by the rays of the rising sun it is said to have produced a sound like the snapping asunder of a cord. Poetically, when Eos kissed her son at daybreak, the hero acknowledged the salutation with a musical murmur.

Memory. The Bard of Memory. Samuel Rogers (1763–1855), the banker-poet; author of *The Pleasures of Memory* (1792). *See* MÆCENAS.

Memory Woodfall. William Woodfall (1746–1803), brother of the Woodfall who controlled the *Public Advertiser* in which the *Letters of* JUNIUS appeared. He established *The Diary* (1789), the first journal to report parliamentary proceedings the morning after the occurrence. He would attend a debate, and, without notes, report it accurately. *See also* HANSARD.

The ever memorable. John Hales of Eton (1584–1656), scholar and Arminian divine.

Memorial Day, 30 May, also known as Decoration Day, observed in most states of the U.S.A. as a holiday to honour those killed in war; originally to commemorate those who fell in the CIVIL WAR. In VIRGINIA it is observed as Confederate Memorial Day. In Louisiana and Tennessee Confederate Memorial Day is 3 June, the birthday of Jefferson Davis; in Alabama, Florida, Georgia and Mississippi it is 26 April; and in the Carolinas, 10 May.

Menalcas. Any shepherd or rustic. The name figures in VIRGIL's *Eclogues* and the *Idylls* of Theocritus.

Mencius. *See* MENG-TSE.

Mendelism. The theory of heredity propounded by Gregor Johann Mendel (1822–1884), the Austrian scientist and Abbot of Brunn, showing that the characteristics of the parents of crossbred offspring reappear in certain proportions in successive generations according to definite laws.

Mendel's Law was promulgated in 1865 through experiments with peas. *Cp.* MICHURINISM.

Mendicant Orders, or **Begging Friars.** The orders of FRANCISCANS (Grey Friars), DOMINICANS (Black Friars), AUGUSTINIANS (Austin Friars), CARMELITES (White Friars), Servites, and other lesser orders.

Menechmians. Persons exactly like each other; so called from the Menæchmi of Plautus, the basis of SHAKESPEARE's *Comedy of Errors*, in which not only the two Dromios are exactly alike but Antipholus of Ephesus is the facsimile of his brother, Antipholus of Syracuse.

Menelaus (men a lā′ ŭs), son of Atreus, brother of AGEMEMNON, and husband of HELEN whose desertion of him brought about the TROJAN WAR. He was the king of Sparta or Lacadæmon.

Menevia. A form of the old name, *Mynyw*, of St. David's, Pembrokeshire (now part of Dyfed). Its present name is from Dewi, or DAVID.

> The sons of Liethali obtained the country of the Dimetæ, where is a city called Menavia.
> NENNIUS: *Historia Britonmum*.

Meng-tse (d. 290 B.C.). The Chinese philosopher who ranks next to Confucius. After his death, his teachings were gathered by his disciples to form the *Book of Meng-tse*, or the *Mencius*, the fourth of the sacred books of China. Confucius, or Kung-fu-tse, wrote the other three; *viz.*, *Ta-heo* (School of Adults), *Chong-yong* (The Golden Mean), and *Lun-yu* (The Book of Maxims).

Mother of Meng. A Chinese expression, meaning, "an admirable teacher". Meng's father died soon after the birth of the sage and he was brought up by his mother—the pattern of all mothers to the Chinese.

Menippus, the CYNIC, was born at Gadara, Syria, in the 3rd century B.C. He was called by Lucian the greatest snarler and snapper of all the dogs (*cynics*).

Varro wrote the *Satyræ Ménippeæ*, and, in imitation, a French political *Satyre Me-*

nippée was published in 1593. It was the work of Leroy, Gillot, Passerat, Rapin, Chrestien, Pithou, and Durant, and was directed against the CATHOLIC LEAGUE.

Mennonites. Followers of Simon Menno (1492–1561), a parish priest of Friesland, who joined the ANABAPTISTS in 1536. They still exist in Holland, Germany, and America and some other places. They reject church organization, infant baptism, and usually military service and the holding of public office.

Mensheviks. A Russian word for a minority party. The name was applied to the moderate Russian social democrats who opposed the BOLSHEVIKS in the Russian Revolution of 1917.

Menthu. *See* BAKHA.

Mention in Dispatches. A reference by name to an officer in British naval, army and air force dispatches commending his conduct in action. An officer so mentioned is entitled to wear a small bronze oak leaf on the left breast or upon the medal ribbon for that particular campaign.

Mentor. A guide, a wise and faithful counsellor; so called from Mentor, a friend of ULYSSES, whose form MINERVA assumed when she accompanied TELMACHUS in his search for his father.

Menu. *See* MANU.

Meo periculo (Lat., at my peril). On my responsibility; at my own risk.

Mephistopheles. A manufactured name (possibly from three Greek words meaning "not loving the light") of a DEVIL or familiar spirit which first appeared in the late mediæval FAUST legend; he is well known as the sneering, jeering, leering tempter in Goethe's *Faust*.

Mercantilism. A term embracing a wide range of policies at different times in various countries and first popularized by Adam Smith's attack on Britain's "Mercantile System" in his *The Wealth of Nations* (1776). Mercantilism held sway in Britain between the mid-16th and the mid-18th centuries and was bound up with ideas of state power and security. National self-sufficiency, a favourable balance of trade which would bring an influx of the precious metals, and protection, were all basic to it, and colonial trade was primarily regulated in the interest of the mother country. Adam Smith taught that labour, not trade, was the real source of wealth and aimed to replace mercantilism by FREE TRADE and LAISSEZ-FAIRE.

Mercator's Projection is a Mercator's chart or map for nautical purposes. The meridian lines are at right angles to the parallels of latitude. It is so called after its inventor Gerhard Kremer (= merchant, pedlar) (1512–1594), whose surname latinized is *Mercator*.

Merchant Adventurers. Local guilds of merchant adventurers were formed in the 14th century to develop English export of cloth to Europe and in 1407 a regulated company of Merchants Adventurers was formed at LONDON. It became a national organization with headquarters at Bruges, but political difficulties led to its removal at different times to other centres in the Low Countries and Germany. In the 16th century the company successfully rivalled the HANSE and it was not finally dissolved until 1808.

Mercia. One of the ancient Anglican Kingdoms of ENGLAND which first rose in importance under Penda in the first half of the 7th century; in the 8th century, under Ethelbald and Offa, it became the dominant kingdom of the HEPTARCHY, and Mercian kings were supreme south of the Humber; but in 829 it was temporarily incorporated with WESSEX under Egbert.

It was subjected to Danish attacks from 855. The Danes settled the eastern part and the remainder came under the control of Wessex by the early 10th century. The earldom of Wessex, created by Cnut (1016–1035), came to an end in 1070. The name is from O.E. *merce*, referring to the MARCH or frontier against the Britons (Welsh); Mercia occupied the land between the Humber and THAMES, WALES and East Anglia.

Mercury. The Roman counterpart of the Greek HERMES, son of MAIA and JUPITER, to whom he acted as messenger. He was the god of science and commerce, the patron of travellers and also of rogues, vagabonds and thieves. Hence, the name of the god is used to denote both a messenger and a thief.

> My father named me Autolycus; who being, as I am, littered under Mercury, was likewise a snapper-up of unconsidered trifles.
> SHAKESPEARE: *The Winter's Tale*, IV, iii.

Mercury is represented as a young man with winged hat and winged sandals (*talaria*), bearing the CADUCEUS, and sometimes a purse.

Posts with a marble head of Mercury used to be erected where two or more roads met, to point out the way (*Juvenal*, viii, 53).

In astrology, Mercury "signifieth subtill men, ingenious, inconstant: rymers, poets, advocates, orators, phylosophers, arithmeticians, and busie fellowes". The alchemists credited mercury (*cp.* QUICK-SILVER) with great powers and used it for many purposes, for which see Ben Jonson's masque, *Mercury Vindicated*.

Mercury fig (Lat. *Ficus ad Mercurium*). The Romans devoted the first fig gathered off a fig-tree to MERCURY. The proverbial saying was applied generally to all first fruits or first works.

You cannot make a Mercury of every log. PYTHAGORAS said: *Non ex quovis ligno Mercurius fit.* That is, "Not every mind will answer equally well to be trained into a scholar." The proper wood for a statue of Mercury was box—*Vel quod hominis pultorem præ se ferat, vel quod materies sit omnium maxime æterna* (Erasmus).

Mercurial. Light-hearted, gay, volatile; such were supposed by the astrologers to be born under the planet Mercury.

Mercurial finger. The little finger, which, if pointed, denotes eloquence; if square, sound judgment.

> The thumb in Chiromancy, we give Venus,
> The forefinger to Jove, the midst to Saturn,
> The ring to Sol, the least to Mercury.
>
> BEN JONSON: *Alchemist*, I, i.

Mercy. The seven corporal works of mercy are: (1) To tend the sick; (2) To feed the hungry; (3) To give drink to the thirsty; (4) To clothe the naked; (5) To harbour the stranger; (6) To minister to prisoners; (7) To bury the dead. *See Matt.* xxv, 35–45.

The seven spiritual works of mercy are: (1) To convert the sinner; (2) To instruct the ignorant; (3) To counsel those in doubt; (4) To comfort those in sorrow; (5) To bear wrongs patiently; (6) To forgive injuries; (7) To pray for the living and the dead.

The Merciless, or **Unmerciful Parliament** (3 Feburary to 3 June 1388). The PARLIAMENT in which the Lords Appellant secured the condemnation of Richard II's friends. Four knights of the King's chamber were executed and some of his supporters were exiled to Ireland.

Meredith. We're in, Meredith. A popular catch phrase derived from the very successful Fred KARNO sketch, *The Bailiff*, produced in 1907. It depicted the stratagems of a bailiff and his assistant Meredith attempting to enter a house for purposes of distraint. The phrase was used by the bailiff each time he thought he was on the verge of success.

Meridian. Sometimes applied, especially in SCOTLAND, to a noonday dram of spirits.

> "...get him over to John's coffee-house, man—gie him his meridian—keep him there, drunk or sober, till the hearing is ower."
>
> SCOTT: *Redgauntlet*, ch. i.

Merit, Order of. A British order for distinguished achievement in all callings founded by Edward VII in 1902, with two classes, civil and military. The Order is limited to 24 men and women and confers no precedence; it is designated by the letters O.M., following the first class of the Order of the BATH and precedes all letters designating membership of other Orders. The badge is a red and blue CROSS patté, with a blue medallion in the centre surrounded by a LAUREL wreath, and bears the words "For Merit". The ribbon is blue and crimson. Crossed swords are added to the badge for military members.

Merlin. The historical Merlin was a Welsh or British BARD, born towards the close of the 5th century, to whom a number of poems have been very doubtfully attributed. He is said to have become a bard of king ARTHUR and to have perished after a terrible battle about 570 between the Britons and their Romanized compatriots.

His story has been mingled with that of the enchanter Merlin of the ARTHURIAN ROMANCE. This Prince of Enchanters was the son of a damsel seduced by a friend, but was baptized by Blaise, and so rescued from the power of SATAN. He became an adept in NECROMANCY, but was beguiled by the enchantress Nimue who shut him up in a rock; and later Vivien, the LADY OF THE LAKE, entangled him in a thornbush by means of spells, and there he still sleeps, though his voice may be sometimes heard.

He first appears in Nennius as the boy Ambrosius and in Geoffrey of Monmouth's *Historia Britonum* and the *Vita Merlini*. There were developed by Robert Wace and Robert de Borron and later writers. See also Spenser's *The Faerie Queene* (III, iii) and Tennyson's *Idylls*.

> Now, though a Mechanist, whose skill
> Shames the degenerate grasp of modern science,
> Grave Merlin (and belike the more
> For practising occult and perilous lore)
> Was subject to a freakish will
> That sapped good thoughts, or scared them with defiance.
>
> WORDSWORTH: *The Egyptian Maid*, iv.

The English Merlin. William Lilly (1602–1681), the astrologer, who published two tracts under the name of "Merlinus Anglicus" and was the most famous CHARLATAN of his day.

Mermaid. The popular stories of this fabulous marine creature, half woman and half fish, allied to the SIREN of classical mythology, probably arose from sailors' accounts of the dugong, a cetacean whose head has a rude approach to the human outline. The mother while suckling her young holds it to her breast with one flipper, as a woman holds her infant in her arm. If disturbed, she suddenly dives under water, and tosses up her fish-like tail. *Cp.* MERROW.

In later 16th-century plays the term is often used for a courtesan. *See* Massinger's *Old Law*, IV, i, and SHAKESPEARE's *Comedy of Errors*, III, ii, etc.

The Mermaid Tavern. The famous meeting place (in Bread Street, Cheapside) of the wits, literary men, and men about town in the early 17th century. Among those who met there at a sort of early CLUB were Ben Jonson, Sir Walter Ralegh, Beaumont, Fletcher, John Selden, and in all probability SHAKESPEARE.

What things have we seen
Done at the Mermaid! Heard words that have been
So nimble, and so full of subtile flame,
As if that everyone from whence they came
Had meant to put his whole wit in a jest.
BEAUMONT: *Lines to Ben Jonson.*

Mermaid's glove. The largest of the British sponges (*Halichondria palmata*), so called because its branches resemble fingers.

Mermaid's purses. The horny egg cases of the ray, skate, or shark, frequently cast up by the waves on the sea-beach.

Merope (mer' ō pi). One of the PLEIADES; dimmer than the rest, because, according to Greek legend, she married SISYPHUS, a mortal. She was the mother of GLAUCUS.

Merops' Son. One who thinks he can set the world to rights, but can't. Agitators, demogogues, etc., are sons of Merops. The allusion is to PHÆTON, a reputed son of Merops (king of Ethiopia), who thought himself able to drive the car of PHŒBUS, but, in the attempt, nearly set the world on fire.

Merovingian Dynasty. The dynasty of Merovius, Merovech, or *Merwig* (great warrior), grandfather of Clovis, who ruled over the FRANKS in the 5th century. The dynasty rose to power under Clovis (d. 511) and gradually gave way before the MAYORS OF THE PALACE, until, in 751, the dynasty was brought to an end by Pippin the SHORT's usurpation.

Merrie England. *See* MERRY.

Merrow (Irish, *muirrúhgach*). A MERMAID, believed by Irish fishermen to forebode a coming storm.

It was rather annoying to Jack that, though living in a place where the merrows were as plenty as lobsters, he never could get a right view of one.
W.B. YEATS: *Irish Folk Stories and Fairy Tales.*

Merry. The original meaning is pleasing, delightful; hence, giving pleasure; hence, mirthful, joyous.

The old phrase MERRIE ENGLAND (*Merry London*, etc.) merely signified it was pleasant and delightful, not necessarily full of merriment; and so with the *merry month* of MAY.

The phrase *merry men*, meaning the companions at arms of a KNIGHT, or outlaw (especially of ROBIN HOOD), is really for merry MEINIE.

Merry Andrew. A buffoon, jester, or attendant on a QUACK doctor at fairs. Said by Thomas Hearne (1678–1735)—with no evidence—to derive from Andrew Boorde (*c.* 1490–1549), physician to Henry VIII, who to his vast learning added great eccentricity. Prior has a poem on "Merry Andrew". *Cp.* ANDREW.

Merry as a cricket, grig. *See* GRIG.

Merry begot. An old name for a BASTARD.

Merry Dancers. The NORTHERN LIGHTS, so called from their undulatory motion. The French call them *chèvres dansantes* (dancing goats).

Merry Greek. *See* GRIG.

Merry Maidens. An ancient circle of nineteen stones in St. Buryan parish, near Penzance, CORNWALL. Two pillar stones nearby, 120 ft. apart, are called *the Pipers*. The whole group was petrified for making sport on the SABBATH.

Merry Men. *See* MERRY.

Merry Men of May. An expanse of broken water which boils like a cauldron in the southern side of the Stroma Channel, Pentland Firth.

Merry Monarch. Charles II. *Cp.* OLD ROWLEY *under* ROWLEY.

Merry Monday. An old name for the day before SHROVE TUESDAY.

Merrythought. The furcula or wishing-bone in the breast of a fowl; sometimes pulled asunder by two persons, the one holding the larger portion being supposed to have his wish.

'Tis merry in hall, when beards wag all (Shakespeare: *Henry IV, Pt. II*, V, iii). It is a sure sign of mirth when the beards of the guests shake with laughter.

To make merry. To be jovial, festive; to make merry over, to treat with amusement, to be joyful; to ridicule, to make fun of.

Merton College. The oldest Oxford college, founded in 1264 by Walter de Merton, Bishop of Rochester and LORD HIGH CHANCELLOR (*see under* CHANCELLOR). He was, through this foundation, the originator of the collegiate system developed at Oxford and Cambridge. It was intended for training SECULAR CLERGY.

Meru. The "OLYMPUS" of the Hindus; a fabulous mountain in the centre of the world, 80,000 leagues high, the abode of VISHNU, and a perfect PARADISE.

Merveilleuse (mâr vä yĕrs) (Fr., marvellous). The sword of Doon of Mayence. It was so sharp that when placed edge downwards it would cut through a slab of wood without the use of force.

The term is also applied to the dress worn by the fops and ladies of the DIRECTORY period in France, who were noted for their extravagance and aping of classical Greek modes.

Mesmerism. So called from Franz Anton Mesmer (1734–1815), an Austrian physician who introduced his theory of "animal magnetism" at PARIS in 1778. It was the forerunner of HYPNOTISM which is increasingly studied for therapeutic purposes by the medical and psychiatric professions. Mesmerism is commonly used as a synonym for *hypnotism*.

Mesolithic Age (Gr. *mesos*, middle; *lithos*, stone). The Middle Stone Age in Europe, between the PALÆOLITHIC and NEOLITHIC periods.

Mesopotamia (Gr., the land between the rivers, *i.e.* the Euphrates and the Tigris), one of the cradles of civilization. It is now called Iraq.

The true "Mesopotamia" ring. Something high-sounding and pleasing, but wholly past comprehension. The allusion is to the story of the old woman who told her pastor that she "found great support in the blessed word *Mesopotamia*".

Mess. The usual meaning today is a dirty, untidy state of things, a muddle, a difficulty (*to get into a mess*); but the word originally signified a portion of food (Lat. *missum*, *mittere*, to send; *cp*. Fr. *mets*, viands, Ital. *messa*, a course of a meal); thence it came to mean mixed food, especially for an animal, and so a confusion, medley, jumble.

Another meaning was a small group of persons (usually four) who sat together at banquets and were served from the same dishes. This gave rise to army and navy *mess*, the place where meals are served and eaten, and to the Elizabethans using it in place of "four" or "a group of four". Thus, SHAKESPEARE says (*Love's Labour's Lost*, IV, iii), "You three fools lack'd me fool to make up the mess." In the INNS OF COURT, London, the members still dine in groups of four.

Mess of pottage. For such Esau sold his birthright to JACOB (*Gen.* xxv, 29–34); hence, figuratively, to obtain some material comfort or advantage at the expense of something of much greater value or lasting worth.

Mess traps. In the Royal Navy, the various utensils which make up the equipment of a mess, galley, or pantry.

Messalina. Wife of the Emperor Claudius of RÔME, executed by order of her husband in A.D. 48. Her name has become a byword for lasciviousness and incontinency. Catherine II of Russia (1729–1796) has been called *The Modern Messalina*.

Messiah (Heb. *mashiach*, one anointed). It is the title of the expected leader of the Jews who shall deliver the nation from its enemies and reign in permanent triumph and peace. Equivalent to the Greek word Christ, it is applied by Christians to Jesus. *Messiah* (incorrectly *The Messiah*) is the title of an oratorio by Handel, first produced in Dublin in 1742.

Mestizo (mĭs tī sō). A Spanish-American term of 16th-century origin for a half-breed, ultimately from Lat. *mixtus* (past participle of *miscere*, to mix). At first it denoted the offspring of a Spaniard and an American Indian; also later of a NEGRO.

Metals. Metals used to be divided into two classes, *Noble* and *Base*. The *Noble*, or *Perfect* metals were GOLD, SILVER and platinum, because they were not acted on by air (or oxygen) at any temperature. The *Base*, or *Imperfect* metals are subject to oxidation in air and change their character. The only metals used in HERALDRY are *or* (gold) and *argent* (silver).

The seven metals in alchemy:

Gold, APOLLO or the sun.
Silver, DIANA or the moon.
Quicksilver, MERCURY.
Copper, VENUS.
Iron, MARS.
Tin, JUPITER.
Lead, SATURN.

Metaphor (Gr., transference). A figure of speech in which a name or descriptive term is applied to an object, etc., to which it is not literally applicable as, "The ship spread its wings to the breeze."

A mixed metaphor is a figure of speech in which two or more inconsistent metaphors are combined, as "It is likely that the Government will bury its head in the sand and drive a bulldozer through the educational system."

Metaphysics (Gr., after-physics), so called because the name was posthumously given to ARISTOTLE'S "First Philosophy" which he wrote after his *Physics*. The science of metaphysics is that branch of speculation which deals with the first principles of existence, such as, being, substance, essence, the infinite, ultimate reality, etc.; the philosophy of being and knowing; the philosophy which establishes truth of existence by abstract reason. At various times the whole range of philosophical inquiry has been classed as metaphysics and the contrast between philosophy and science is comparatively modern.

Metaphysical Poets. A term used to describe certain poets of the 17th century, notably John Donne, George Herbert, Richard Crashaw, Henry Vaughan, and Andrew Marvell. They are characterized by subtlety of thought, expressed frequently in compressed though sometimes far-fetched images, and the use of complex versification. They mostly show strong religious feeling. The word *metaphysical* in relation to poetry was first used by William Drummond of Hawthornden about 1630, then applied to this particular group of poets by Dryden in 1693, and used derogatively of them by Dr. Johnson in 1781.

Metathesis (met à thē' sis). A Greek word meaning "transposition". A change in the relative order between sounds or letters in a word, as O.E. *bridd* becoming bird and *thrid* becoming third. *Cp.* SPOONERISM.

Methodists. A name given (1729) to the members of Charles Wesley's HOLY CLUB at Oxford, from the methodical way in which they observed their principles. They were originally members of the CHURCH OF ENGLAND and the separatist Methodist Church was not established until after John Wesley's death (1791). The movement was itself soon faced with secessions, the first being the Methodist New Connexion (1797), followed by the Independent Methodists (1805), Primitive Methodists (1810), the Bible Christians (1815), the Wesleyan Methodist Association (1835), and the Wesleyan Reformers (1849). Reunion began in 1857 with the formation of the United Methodist Free Church and was completed with the formation of the Methodist Church of Great Britain in 1932. Methodism was introduced into the U.S.A. in the 1760s and grew steadily in importance.

The name was at one time applied to the JESUITS, because they were the first to give systematic representations of the method of polemics.

Since 1965 the Church of England and the Methodist Church have been seeking reconciliation.

Methuselah (me' thū zė là). **Old as Methuselah**. Very old indeed, almost incredibly old. He is the oldest man mentioned in the BIBLE, where we are told (*Gen.*. v, 27) that he died at the age of 969.

Metonic Cycle, The. A cycle of nineteen years at the end of which period the new

moons fall on the same days of the year; so called because discovered by the Greek astronomer, Meton, 433 B.C. *See* CALLIPPIC PERIOD.

Metonymy (me ton' i mi). The use of one thing for another related to it, as "the Bench" for the magistrates or judges sitting in court, "a silk" for a QUEEN'S COUNSEL, "the bottle" for alcoholic liquor. The word is Greek, meaning "a change of name".

Metropolitan. A BISHOP who controls a province and its SUFFRAGANS. The two metropolitans of England are the archbishops of Canterbury and York, and in Ireland the archbishops of Armagh and Dublin. The Archbishop of Canterbury is *metropolitanus et primus totius Angliæ*, and the Archbishop of York *primus et metropolitanus Angliæ*. In the early Church the bishop of the civil metropolis (mother city) was usually given rights over the other bishops (suffragans) of the province. In the GREEK CHURCH a metropolitan ranks next below a PATRIARCH and next above an archbishop.

Meum and tuum (mē' ūm, tu' ūm) (Lat.). Mine and thine: that which belongs to me and that which is another's. If a man is said not to know the difference between *meum* and *tuum*, it is another way of saying he is a thief.

Meum est propositum in taberna mori. A famous drinking song usually accredited to Walter Map (*fl.* 1200), but by the anonymous German "Archpoet" (*fl.* 1160).

Meum est propositum in taberna mori;
Ubi vinum proximum morientis ori
Tunc cantabit lætius angelorum chori;
Deus sit propitius huic potatori (etc.).

"It is my intention to die in a tavern. May wine be placed to my dying lips, that when the choirs of angels shall come they may say, God be merciful to this drinker".

Mews. Stables, but properly a cage for hawks when moulting (O.Fr. *mue*; Lat. *mutare*, to change). The word acquired its new meaning because the royal stables built in the 17th century occupied the site of the King's Mews where formerly the king's hawks were kept. It is now the site of the National Gallery in Trafalgar Square. With the development of fashionable LONDON in the 19th century, rows of stabling, with accommodation above for the coachman, were built and called Mews. Since the 1920s these have been steadily converted into garages with flats or maisonettes.

Mexitl, or Mextli. The principal god of the ancient Mexicans (hence the name of their country), to whom hundreds of human beings were offered annually as sacrifices.

More usually called *Huitzilopochtli* (Humming-bird of the South, or He of the South), he was the god of war and storms and was born fully armed.

Mezzotint, or **Mezzo tinto** (Ital., medium tint). A process of engraving in which a copper plate is uniformly roughened so as to print a deep black, lights and half-lights being then produced by scraping away the burr; also a print from this, which is usually a good imitation of an indian-ink drawing.

Micah Rood's Apples. Apples with a spot of red in the heart. The story is that Micah Rood was a prosperous farmer at Franklin, Pennsylvania. In 1693 a pedlar with jewellery called at his house, and next day was found murdered under an apple-tree in Rood's orchard. The crime was never brought home to the farmer, but next autumn all the apples of the fatal tree bore inside a red blood-spot, called "Micah Rood's Curse", and the farmer died soon afterwards.

Micawber. An incurable optimist; from Dickens's Mr. Wilkins Micawber (*David Copperfield*), a great speechifier and letter-writer and projector of BUBBLE SCHEMES sure to lead to fortune, but always ending in grief. Notwithstanding his ill success, he never despaired, but felt certain that something would "turn up" to make his fortune. Having failed in every adventure in the old country, he emigrated to Australia, where he became a magistrate.

Michael, St. The ARCHANGEL. The great prince of all the ANGELS and leader of the celestial armies.

> Go, Michael, of celestial armies prince,
> And thou, in military prowess next,
> Gabriel; lead forth to battle these my sons
> Invincible; lead forth my armed saints
> By thousands and by millions ranged for fight.
> MILTON: *Paradise Lost*, VI, 44.

His day (St. Michael and All Angels) is 29 September (*see* MICHAELMAS DAY). He appears in the BIBLE in *Dan*. x, 13, and xii, 1; *Jude*, verse 9; and *Rev*. xii, 7–9, where he and his angels fight the DRAGON. His cult was popular in the MIDDLE AGES and he was also looked on as the presiding spirit of the planet MERCURY, and bringer to man of the gift of prudence.

In art St. Michael is depicted as a beautiful young man with severe countenance, winged, and clad in either white or armour, bearing a lance and shield, with which he combats a dragon. In the final judgment he is represented with scales, in which he weighs the souls of the risen dead.

St. Michael's Chair. An old beacon turret at the top of the chapel tower at St. Michael's

Mount, Cornwall. It is said that whichever of a newly-married couple first sits there will gain marital supremacy. There is also a rock on the island called St. Michael's Chair.

The Order of St. Michael and St. George. A British order of knighthood instituted in 1818 to honour natives of the Ionian Isles and Malta. In 1864 the Ionian Islands were restored to Greece and the order was remodelled and extended in 1868, 1879, and subsequently, to British subjects serving abroad or in British overseas possessions, but is now largely awarded to members of the Diplomatic and Foreign service and for administrative service in the COMMONWEALTH.

It is now limited to 100 Knights Commanders, 355 Knights, and 1,435 Companions.

Michael Angelo or **Michelangelo.** The pre-eminent Italian sculptor, celebrated painter, also architect and poet (1475–1564). His full name was Michelangelo Buonarroti.

Michel-Ange des Bamboches. Pieter van Laar, or Laer (c. 1592–c. 1642), Dutch painter, nicknamed *Il Bamboccio*, in allusion to his pictures of common life. *See* BAMBOCCIADES.

The Michelangelo of battle-scenes. Michelangelo Cerquozzi (1602–1660), a native of ROME, famous for his battle-scenes and shipwrecks.

Michelangelo of Music. Christoph Willibald von Gluck (1714–1787), the German composer.

Michelangelo of Sculptors. Pierre Puget (1620–1694), the French sculptor. Also René Slodtz (1705–1764).

Michaelmas Day. 29 September, the Festival of St. MICHAEL and all Angels, one of the QUARTER DAYS when rents are due and the day when magistrates are chosen.

The custom of eating goose at Michaelmas (*see also* St. MARTIN'S GOOSE) is very old and is probably due to geese being plentiful and in good condition at this season. We are told that tenants formerly presented their landlords with one to keep in their good graces. The popular story is that Queen Elizabeth I, on her way to Tilbury Fort on 29 September 1588, dined with Sir Neville Umfreyville, and partook of geese, afterwards calling for a bumper of Burgundy, and giving as a toast "Death to the Spanish Armada!" Scarcely had she spoken when a messenger announced the destruction of the fleet by a storm. The Queen demanded a second bumper, and said, "Henceforth shall a goose commemorate this great victory." The tale is marred by the fact that the Armada was dispersed by winds in July and the thanksgiving sermon for victory was preached at St. Paul's on 20 August.

George Gascoigne, the poet, who died in 1577, refers to the custom of goose-eating at Michaelmas:

At Christmas a capon, at Michaelmas, a goose.
And somewhat else at New Yere's tide for feare the lease flies loose.

Miching (M.E. *michynge*). Skulking, dodging, sneaking. It is derived from O.Fr. *muchier*, *mucier*, to hide. It is still a common term in the West Country and Wales for "truanting". Hence *to mich* is to truant, and a truant is a *micher*.

Ham: Marry, this is miching mallecho: it means mischief.
SHAKESPEARE: *Hamlet*, ii, ii.

Michurinism. A genetic theory, named after the Soviet horticulturalist I. V. Michurin (1855–1935), repudiating the laws of Mendel and essentially claiming that acquired characteristics can be inherited. It is alternatively called *Lysenkoism*, after T.D. Lysenko, the Soviet agriculturalist, whose pamphlet *Heredity and its Variability* attempted to discredit orthodox genetics. Its revolutionary character was more due to Marxist wishful thinking than scientific proof, and the acceptability of such teaching to the Soviet Government. Lysenkoism replaced orthodox genetics in the U.S.S.R. in 1948 but after 1952 lost ground. Lysenko was dismissed from his key position in 1956. *Cp.* MENDELISM.

Mickey Finn. A draught or powder slipped into liquor to render the drinker unconscious. The term comes from a notorious figure in 19th-century Chicago.

To take the mickey out of someone is to tease, and humiliate him; to undermine his self-esteem.

Mickleton Jury. A corruption of *mickletourn* (*magnus turnus*), *i.e.* the jury of court LEETS which were visited at EASTER and CHRISTMAS by the county sheriffs in their *tourns*. In Anglo-Saxon times the Great Council of the kings was known as the *micklemote* (great assembly).

Microcosm (Gr., little world). So man is called by PARACELSUS. The ancients considered the world (*see* MACROCOSM) as a living being; the SUN and MOON being its *two eyes*, the earth its *body*, the ether its *intellect*, and the sky its *wings*. When man was looked on as the world in miniature, it was thought that the movements of the world and of man corresponded, and if one could be ascertained, the other could be easily inferred; hence arose the system of ASTROLOGY, which

professed to interpret the events of a man's life by the corresponding movements, etc., of the stars.

Midas (mī' dăs). A legendary king of Phrygia who requested of the gods that everything that he touched might be turned to GOLD. His request was granted, but as his food became gold the moment he touched it, he prayed the gods to take their favour back. He was then ordered to bathe in the Pactolus, and the river ever after rolled over golden sands.

Another story told of him is, that when appointed to judge a musical contest between APOLLO and PAN, he gave judgment in favour of the SATYR; whereupon Apollo in contempt gave the king a pair of ass's ears. Midas hid them under his Phrygian cap; but his barber discovered them, and, not daring to mention the matter, dug a hole and relieved his mind by whispering in it "Midas has ass's ears", then covering it up again. Budæus gives a different version. He says that Midas kept spies to tell him everything that transpired throughout his kingdom, and the proverb "kings have long arms" was changed to "Midas has long ears".

A parallel of this tale is told of Portzmach, king of a part of Brittany. He had all the barbers of his kingdom put to death, lest they should announce to the public that he had the ears of a horse. An intimate friend was found willing to shave him, after swearing profound secrecy; but not able to contain himself he confided his secret to a river bank. The reeds of this river were used for pan-pipes and hautbois, which repeated the words, "Portzmach—King Portzmach has horse's ears".

Midden. A muck-heap, a kitchen refuse heap. *See* KITCHEN-MIDDENS.

Better marry over the midden than over the moor. Better seek a wife among your neighbours whom you know than among strangers of whom you know nothing.

Ilka cock craws loodest on its ain midden. The Scottish form of "Every COCK crows loudest on his own dunghill."

Middle. Middle Ages. A term used by historians to denote that period of European history between the downfall of the ancient classical civilization of Greece and Rome consequent upon the barbarian invasions and the Europe of the RENAISSANCE and REFORMATION, roughly a period of 1,000 years. It has no obvious beginning or end and is usually taken to begin about the 5th century and to extend to the late 15th. It is a term of convenience, but has resulted in popular misconceptions giving the mediæval period a spurious unity and distinctness which it did not really possess. *Cp.* DARK AGES.

Middle Kingdom. A term denoting that period of ancient Egyptian history covered by the XIIth-XIVth Dynasties from about 2130 to 1600 B.C. and essentially the period of the XIIIth Dynasty.

In the feudal period of Chinese history, the appellation *Chung Kwo*, "The Middle Kingdom", denoted the royal domain or the civilized states of China proper, and was not used in connexion with the idea that China was in the middle of the world.

Middle Passage. That part of the middle Atlantic between West Africa and the West Indies, the usual route for the slave traders of former days.

Middle Temple. *See* TEMPLE.

Middle West. In the U.S.A., properly, the states of Ohio, Indiana, Illinois, Michigan, and Wisconsin. It is the industrial centre of the United States and in many ways the political pivot of the country.

Middlesex. The original territory of the Middle Saxons, which seems to have included the area of the later counties of Middlesex and Hertford, between Essex and WESSEX. It became a SHIRE in the 10th century, was much reduced in area by the Local Government Act of 1888, and was finally absorbed by the Greater London Council, Surrey, and Hertfordshire in 1965.

Midgard. In Scandinavian mythology, the abode of the first pair, from whom sprang the human race. It was midway between NIFLHEIM and MUSPELHEIM, formed from the flesh and blood of YMIR and joined to ASGARD by the rainbow bridge BIFROST. *Cp.* UTGARD.

Mid-Lent Sunday. The fourth Sunday in LENT. It is called *dominica refectionis* (Refreshment Sunday) because the first lesson is the banquet given by Joseph to his brethren, and the GOSPEL of the day is the miraculous feeding of the five thousand. It is the day on which SIMNEL CAKES are eaten and it is also called MOTHERING SUNDAY.

Midnight Oil. Late hours.

Burning the midnight oil. Sitting up late, especially when engaged on literary work and study.

Smells of the midnight oil. *See* IT SMELLS OF THE LAMP *under* LAMP.

Midrash. Rabbinical commentary on, or exposition of, the OLD TESTAMENT writings, from the Heb. root meaning "to teach", "to investigate". *See* HAGGADAH. *Midrashim* of the 2nd century are the *Sifra* on *Leviticus*, the *Sifra* on *Numbers* and *Deuteronomy*, and the *Mekilta* on *Exodus*. *Cp.* MISHNAH.

Midsummer. The week or so round about the summer SOLSTICE (21 June). Midsummer Day is 24 June, St. JOHN THE BAPTIST'S DAY, and one of the QUARTERDAYS.

Midsummer ale. Festivities which used to take place in rural districts at this season. Here *ale* has the same extended meaning as in CHURCH-ALE.

Midsummer madness. The height of madness. Olivia says to Malvolio in SHAKESPEARE'S *Twelfth Night* (III,iv), "Why, this is very midsummer madness". The reference is to the heat of the sun or the wild celebrations on midsummer eve or possibly the midsummer moon when lunacy was held to be widespread. People who were inclined to be mad used to be said *to have but a mile to midsummer*.

Midsummer men. Orpine or Live-long, a plant of the *Sedum* tribe; so called because it used to be set in pots or shells on midsummer eve, and hung up in the house to tell damsels whether their sweethearts were true or not. If the leaves bent to the right, it was a sign of fidelity; if to the left, the "true-love's heart was cold and faithless".

Midsummer moon *"Tis midsummer moon with you"*; you are stark mad. Madness was supposed to be affected by the MOON, and to be aggravated by summer heat; so it naturally follows that the full moon at midsummer is the time when madness would be most pronounced.

> What's this, Midsummer moon?
> Is all the world gone a-madding?
>
> DRYDEN: *Amphitryon*, IV, i.

Midwife (O.E. *mid*, with; *wif*, woman). The nurse who is with the mother in her labour.

Midwife of men's thoughts. So SOCRATES termed himself, and, as Grote observed, "No man ever struck out of others so many sparks to set light to original thought." Out of his intellectual school sprang PLATO and the DIALECTIC school; Euclid and the MEGARIAN; Aristippus and the Cyrenaic; Antisthenes and the CYNIC.

Mihrab. *See* KIBLAH.

Mikado (mik á' dō) (Jap. *mi*, exalted; *kado*, gate or door). The title used by foreigners for the Emperor of Japan. The Japanese title is *Tenno*. *Cp.* SHOGUN. One of Gilbert and Sullivan's most popular comic operas is *The Mikado* (1885).

Mike. A short name for the microphone. *See also* BIDDY; DICKY.

To mike, or **to do a mike.** To idle away one's time, pretending to be waiting for a job or avoiding one. The word may be *miche*, to skulk. *See* MICHING.

Milan. The English form of Milano, the capital city of Lombardy, in Latin *Mediolanum*, "in the middle of the plain" (of Lombardy). In the MIDDLE AGES it was famous for its steel, used for making swords, chain armour, etc. *See* MILLINER.

The Edict of Milan. Proclaimed by Constantine after the conquest of Italy (313), to secure the Christians the restitution of their civil and religious rights.

The Milan Decrees. Decrees issued by NAPOLEON at Milan, 23 November and 17 December 1807. The second decree declared that all neutral shipping obeying the British Orders in Council (designed to prevent neutrals from trading with Napoleonic Europe) were lawful prizes if taken by France or her allies.

Milanion. *See* ATALANTA'S RACE.

Mile. A measure of length; in the British Commonwealth and the United States, 1,760 yd.; so called from Lat. *mille*, a thousand, the Roman lineal measure being 1,000 paces, or about 1680 yd. The old Irish and Scottish miles were a good deal longer than the standard English, that in Ireland (still in use in country parts) being 2,240 yd., the Scottish 1,980 yd.

The Nautical, or **Geographical Mile** is supposed to be one minute of a great CIRCLE of the earth; but as the earth is not a true sphere the minute is variable, so a mean length of 6,080 ft. (2,026 yd. 2ft.) was adopted by the British Admiralty. The Geographical Mile varies slightly with different nations, so there is a further *International Nautical Mile* of 1,852 metres.

The Square Mile. The City of LONDON, so called from its area (677 acres). A square mile consists of 640 acres.

Milesians. Properly, the inhabitants of *Miletus*; but the name has been given to the ancient Irish because of the legend that two sons of Milesius, a fabulous king of Spain, conquered the country, and repeopled it after exterminating the Firbolgs (the aborigines).

Milesian Fables. A Greek collection of witty but obscene short stories by Antonius Diogenes, no longer extant, and compiled by Aristides of *Miletus* (2nd cent. B.C.), whence the name. They were translated into Latin by Sidenna about the time of the civil wars of Marius and Sulla, and were greedily read by luxurious SYBARITES. Similar stories are still sometimes called *Milesian Tales*.

Milione, Il (Ital., the million) or **Marco Milione**. The name given by the Venetians to Marco Polo and his writings. It may have been a reference to his stories of CATHAY and its wonders, millions, etc.

Military Knights of Windsor. *See under* KNIGHT.

Militia. A development of the fyrd in the form of a national levy for defence, organized by the Lords-Lieutenant on a county basis, and so called in the 17th century. The obligation to provide men and arms was placed on property owners and those called upon to serve were allowed to call upon substitutes. It was never properly trained and became essentially a volunteer force after 1852. It came to an end with the passing of the Territorial and Reserve Forces Act of 1907, but the name was applied to the Special Reserve in 1921 and revived by the Military Training Act of 1939.

Milk. To. Slang for to extract money out of somebody in an underhand way; also to plunder one's creditors, and (in mining) to exhaust the veins of ore after selling the mine.

To milk the cow with a spanner. To open a tin of evaporated or condensed milk with a tin-opener.

A land of milk and honey. One abounding in all good things, or of extraordinary fertility. It is figuratively used to denote the blessings of HEAVEN.

> And I am come to deliver them out of the hand of the Egyptians, ... unto a land flowing with milk and honey.
>
> *Exod.* iii, 8.

Milk and water. Insipid, without energy or character, baby-pap, feeble stuff.

Milk teeth. The first, temporary teeth of a child.

The milk of human kindness. Sympathy, compassion.

> ... yet do I fear thy nature.
> It is too full o' th' milk of human kindness.
>
> SHAKESPEARE: *Macbeth*, I, v.

So that accounts for the milk in the coconut! Said when a sudden discovery of the reason for some action or state of things is made.

To cry over spilt milk. *See under* CRY.

Milk-run. An R.A.F. and R.A.A.F. expression of World War II for any sortie flown regularly day after day, or a sortie against an easy target on which inexperienced pilots could be used with impunity—as simple as delivering milk.

Milksop. An effeminate or babyish person; one without any backbone. The allusion is to young, helpless children, who are fed on pap.

Milky Way. *See* GALAXY.

Mill. To fight, or a fight. It is the same word as the mill that grinds flour (Lat. *molere*, to grind). Grinding was anciently performed by pulverizing with a stone or pounding with the hand. *To mill* is to beat with the fist, as persons used to beat corn with a stone.

To mill about is to move aimlessly in a circle, like a herd of cattle.

The mill cannot grind with water that is past. An old proverb, given in Herbert's *Collection* (1639). It implies that one must not miss one's opportunities and that it is no good *crying over spilt milk* (*see under* CRY).

The mills of God grind slowly. Retribution may be delayed, but it is sure to overtake the wicked. The *Adagia* of Erasmus puts it, *Sero molunt deorum molæ*, and the sentiment is to be found in many authors, ancient and modern.

> Though the mills of God grind slowly, yet they grind exceeding small;
> Though with patience He stands waiting, with exactness grinds He all.
>
> LONGFELLOW: *Retribution* (*Poetic Aphorisms*).

To go through the mill. To undergo hardship; to have been through difficulties and hardships or subjected to a severe course of probationary training.

Millenary Petition. An appeal to James I in 1603 from some, 1000 PURITAN clergy asking for certain changes in liturgy and worship, and for the prevention of pluralities and non-residence of clergy, etc. Their requests included the discontinuance of the sign of the CROSS in baptism, of the RING in marriage, and of Confirmation; also optional use of the cap and surplice, more scope for preaching, simplification of music, etc. As a result James summoned the HAMPTON COURT CONFERENCE.

Millennium. A thousand years (Lat. *mille, annus*). In *Rev.* xx, 2, it is said that an angel bound SATAN a thousand years, and in verse 4 we are told of certain martyrs who will come to life again who "lived and reigned with Christ a thousand years". "This", says St. JOHN, "is the first resurrection"; and this is what is meant by the millennium—the period of a thousand years during which Christ will return to earth and live with His saints, and finally take them to heaven.

Millenarians, or **Chiliasts** (Lat. *mille*, Gr. *chilioi*, a thousand) is the name applied to early Christian sects who believed in a future MILLENNIUM. Such views were held by some post-REFORMATION sects and by some of the 17th-century Independents in England, and more recently by MORMONS, IRVINGITES, and ADVENTISTS.

Millennial Church. *See* SHAKERS.

Miller. A Joe Miller. A stale jest. A certain John Mottley compiled a book of facetiæ in 1739, which (without permission) he en-titled *Joe Miller's Jest-Book*, from Joseph Miller (1684–1738), a popular comedian of the day who could neither read nor write. A "Joe Miller" is applied to a stale joke implying that it is stolen from Mottley's compilation. Byron, in *English Bards and Scotch Reviewers*, refers to critics who "take hackney'd jokes from Miller". *Cp.* CHESTNUT.

Every honest miller has a thumb of gold. *See under* THUMB.

More water glideth by the mill than wots the miller of (SHAKESPEARE: *Titus Andronicus*, II, i). Many things are done in a house which the master and mistress never dream of.

To drown the miller. To put too much water into spirits, or tea. The idea is that the supply of water is so great that even the miller, who uses a water wheel, is drowned with it.

To give someone to the miller. To engage him in conversation till enough people have gathered round him to set upon the victim with stones, dirt, garbage, and all the arms which haste supplies a mob with. *See* MILL.

To put the miller's eye out. To make a broth or pudding so thin that even a miller's eye would be puzzled to find the flour.

Lumps of unleavened flour in bread are sometimes called *miller's eyes*.

Miller's thumb. A small freshwater fish four or five inches long, *Cottus gobio*, also called the *Bullhead*, from its large head.

Millerites. Followers of William Miller of Massachusetts (1782–1849). *See* SEVENTH-DAY ADVENTISTS.

Milliner. A corruption of *Milaner*; so called from Milan in Italy, which at one time gave the law in Europe to all matters of taste, dress, and elegance.

Nowadays a milliner is expected to be a woman, but it was not always the case. Ben Jonson, in *Every Man in his Humour*, I, iii, speaks of a "milliner's wife".

Man-milliner. An effeminate fellow, or one who fusses over trifles.

> The *Morning Herald* sheds tears of joy over the fashionable virtues of the rising generation, and finds that we shall make better man-milliners, better lacqueys, and better courtiers than ever.
>
> HAZLITT: *Political Essays* (*On the Late War*) (1814).

Millstone. Hard as the nether millstone. Unfeeling, obdurate. The lower or "nether" of the two millstones is firmly fixed and very hard; the upper stone revolved round upon it on a shaft, and the corn, running down a tube inserted in the upper stone, was ground by the motion of the upper stone upon the lower one.

The millstones of Montisci. The stones

produce flour of themselves, whence the proverb, "Grace comes from God, but millstones from Montisci" (Boccaccio: *Decameron*, day viii, novel iii).

To carry a millstone round one's neck. To be burdened with some heavy obligation, tie, etc.; to be handicapped by a dependant or companion who cannot be shaken off.

To look, or **see through a millstone.** To be wonderfully sharpsighted.

> Then ... since your eies are so sharp that you can not only looke through a millstone, but cleane through the minds...
>
> LYLY: *Euphues*, ii.

To see through a millstone as well as most means that in a complicated problem one can see as good a solution as anyone, though that may not be very adequate.

To weep millstones. Not weep at all.

> Bid Glos'ter think on this, and he will weep—
> Aye, millstones as he lessoned us to weep.
>
> SHAKESPEARE: *Richard III*, I, iv.

Milner's Kindergarten. *See* KINDERGARTEN.

Milo (mī'lō). A celebrated Greek athlete of Crotona in the late 6th century B.C. It is said that he carried through the stadium at OLYMPIA a heifer four years old, and ate the whole of it afterwards. When old, he attempted to tear in two an oak-tree, but the parts closed upon his hands, and while held fast he was devoured by wolves.

Milton. "Milton", says Dryden, in the preface to his *Fables*, "was the poetical son of Spenser... Milton had acknowledged to me that Spenser was his original."

Milton of Germany. Friedrich G. Klopstock (1724–1803), author of *The Messiah* (1773). Coleridge says he is "a very German Milton indeed".

Mimosa (mi mō' zá). So called from the notion that it mimics the sensitivity of animals. The leaves fold upward at the slightest touch, hence the name *Sensitive Plant* for the most commonly cultivated variety, *M. pudica*.

> And one whose name I may not say,—
> For not Mimosa's tender tree
> Shrinks sooner from the touch than he.
>
> SCOTT: *Marmion, Intro. canto* IV.

Mince Pies at CHRISTMAS time are said to have been emblematical of the manger in which our Saviour was laid. The paste over the "offering" was made in the form of a cratch or hay-rack. Southey speaks of—

> Old bridges dangerously narrow and angles in them like the corners of an English mince-pie, for the foot-passengers to take shelter in.
>
> *Esprinella's Letters*, III, 384 (1807).

Mince pies is also RHYMING SLANG for "the eyes".

To mince matters. To avoid giving offence by speaking or censuring in mild terms. More commonly used in the negative to mean blunt speaking. From the mincing of meat to make it more digestible or pleasing.

A mincing manner. A prim manner, one of affected delicacy. Similarly we speak of *mincing ways*.

To make mincemeat of. Utterly to demolish; to completely defeat an opponent, literally or figuratively. Minced meat is meat cut up very fine.

Mincing Lane (London). Called in the 13th century *Menechinelane, Monechenlane*, etc., and in the time of Henry VIII *Mynchyn Lane*. The name is from O.E. *mynechenn*, a nun (fem. of *munuc*, monk), and the street is probably so called from the tenements held there by the nuns of St. Helen's, in Bishopsgate Street. Mincing Lane is the centre of the tea trade, for which it is often used as a generic term.

Mind. A month's mind. *See under* MONTH.

In my mind's eye; Mind your eye. *See under* EYE.

Mind your own business; keep to your own affairs and don't intermeddle with those of other people; don't interfere or "POKE YOUR NOSE IN" (*see under* NOSE).

Mind your P's and Q's. *See under* P.

To be in two minds over a matter is to be in doubt.

To give a person a piece of one's mind. To express disapproval plainly and forcibly; to castigate.

To have a good mind to do something. To feel strongly inclined to do it.

To have a mind for it. To desire to possess it; to wish for it. *Mind* meaning desire, intention, is a common usage: "I mind to tell him what I think"; "I shortly mind to leave you", occur in SHAKESPEARE's *Henry VI, Pt. III.* IV, i.

To set one's mind on. To be firmly resolved on; to greatly desire something.

To speak one's mind. To say clearly and emphatically what one thinks about the matter.

Minden Boys. *See* MINDEN REGIMENTS *under* REGIMENTAL AND DIVISIONAL NICKNAMES.

Minerva. The Roman goddess of wisdom and patroness of the arts and trades, fabled to have sprung, with a tremendous battle-cry, fully armed from the brain of JUPITER. She was subsequently identified by the Romans with the Greek ATHENE (Athena), the others being Jupiter and JUNO. She is represented as being grave and majestic, clad in a helmet and with drapery over a coat of mail, and bearing the ÆGIS on her breast. Phidias made a statue of her of ivory and gold 39 ft. high which was placed in the PARTHENON.

Invita Minerva (Lat., against the will of Minerva). Uninspired. Thus, Charles Kean acted comedy *invita Minerva*, his *forte* lying another way. Sir Philip Sidney attempted the Horatian metres in English verse *invita Minerva*. The phrase is from HORACE's *Ars Poetica*, i, 385, *Tu nihil invita dices faciesve Minerva*.

The Minerva Press. A printing establishment in Leadenhall Street, London, famous in the late 18th century for its trashy, ultra-sentimental novels, characterized by complicated plots, etc.

Miniature. Originally, a rubrication or a small painting in an illuminated MS., which was done with *minium* or red lead. Hence the word came to express any small portrait or picture on vellum or ivory. It is in no way connected with Lat. *minor* or *minimus*.

Minims (Lat. *Fratres Minimi*, least of the brethren). A term of self-abasement assumed by a mendicant order founded by St. Francis of Paula in 1453. They went bare-footed, and wore a coarse black woollen stuff, which they never took off, day or night. The FRANCISCANS had already adopted the title of *Fratres Minores* (inferior brothers). The superior of the minims is called *corrector*.

Minister. Literally, an inferior person, in opposition to *magister*, a superior. One is connected with the Lat. *minus*, and the other with *magis*. Our Lord says, "Whosoever will be great among you, let him be your minister", where the antithesis is well preserved. Gibbon has:

> a multitude of cooks, and inferior ministers, employed in the service of the kitchen.
> *Decline and Fall*, ch. xxi.

The minister of a church is one who serves the parish or congregation; and a minister of the crown is the sovereign's or state's servant.

Florimond de Remond, speaking of Albert Babinot, one of the disciples of Calvin, says, "He was student of the *Institutes*, read at the hall of the Equity school in Poitiers, and was called *la Ministerie*." Calvin, in allusion thereto, used to call him "Mr. Minister", whence not only Babinot but all the other clergy of the Calvinistic Church were called *ministers*.

Minnesinger. The poet-musicians of 12th—14th century Germany were so called, because the subject of their lyrics was *Minnesang* (love-ditty). The chief *Minnesinger* were Heinrich von Veldeke, Heinrich von Ofterdingen, Wolfram von Eshenbach, and Walter von der Vogelweide. All of them were men of noble birth and they were succeeded by the MEISTERSINGER.

Minoan. *See* MINOS.

Minories (London). So called from the abbey of the Minoresses of the Order of St. CLARE, which stood on the site until the dissolution of the monasteries.

Minoresses. *See* CLARE, ORDER OF ST.

Minorites, or **Minors.** *See* FRANCISCANS.

Minos (mī' nōs). A legendary king and law-giver of Crete, made at death supreme judge of the lower world, before whom all the dead appeared to give an account of their steward-ship, and to receive the reward of their deeds. He was the husband of PASIPHÆ and the owner of the LABYRINTH constructed by DÆDALUS. From his name we have the adjective *Minoan*, pertaining to Crete; the Minoan period is the Cretan bronze age, roughly about 2500–1200 B.C.

Minotaur (mīn' ō tôr). A mythical monster with the head of a bull and the body of a man, fabled to have been the offspring of PASIPHÆ and a bull that was sent to her by POSEIDON. MINOS kept it in his LABYRINTH and fed it on human flesh, seven youths and seven maidens being sent as tribute from Athens every year for the purpose. THESEUS slew this monster.

Minstrel. Originally, one who had some official duty to perform (Lat. *ministerialis*), but quite early in the MIDDLE AGES restricted to one whose duty it was to entertain his employer with music, storytelling, juggling, etc.; hence a travelling gleeman and entertainer.

Mint. The name of the herb is from Lat. *mentha* (Gr. *minthe*), so called from *Minthe*, a NYMPH of the COCYTUS, and beloved by PLUTO. This nymph was metamorphosed by PROSERPINE (Pluto's wife) out of jealousy, into the herb called after her.

The Mint, a place where money is coined, gets its name from O.E. *mynet*, representing Lat. *moneta*, money.

The chief seat of the Mint was at LONDON and was situated in the TOWER of London from its erection until 1810, when it moved to new premises upon Tower Hill and was one of the earliest public buildings lighted with gas. In Henry VIII's reign and in Saxon times, there was also a Mint at Southwark which later became a refuge or asylum for debtors and vagabonds, and a place for illicit marriages. (*Cp.* FLEET MARRIAGES; MAYFAIR MARRIAGES.) The Mint was removed to Llantrisant, west of Cardiff, in 1968. *See also* TRIAL OF THE PYX *under* PYX.

Minute (min' it). A minute of time (one-sixtieth part of an hour) is so called from Med. Lat. *pars minuta prima*, which, in the old system of sexagesimal fractions denoted one-sixtieth part of the unit. In the same way in geometry, etc., a *minute* is one-sixtieth part of a degree. *Cp.* SECOND.

A Minute gun. A signal of distress at sea, or a gun fired at the death of some distinguished person; so called because a minute elapses between the discharges.

Minute-men. American militiamen who, at the onset of the War of Independence, promised to take arms at a *minute*'s notice. Hence one who is similarly vigilant and ready to take prompt action. The name has been adopted by a small, secret, ultra-right-wing American organization armed to conduct guerrilla warfare in the event of a Communist invasion. *Minuteman* is also the name of a U.S. intercontinental ballistic missile.

Minute (mī nūt'), from the same Latin word, denotes something very small; hence a minute (min' it) of a speech, meeting, etc., is a brief draft taken down during the proceedings to be subsequently written up in the *minutes* as a summarised record of what was said and of any decisions taken.

Miocene (mī'ō sēn). The geological period immediately preceding the Pliocene, when the mastodon, *Dinotherium*, *Protohippus* and other creatures flourished.

Miracle plays. *See* MYSTERIES.

Miramolin (Commander of the Faithful). The title in the MIDDLE AGES of the Emperor of Morocco.

Mirror. Alasnam's mirror *See under* ALASNAM.

Cambuscan's mirror. Sent to CAMBUSCAN by the King of Araby and Ind; it warned of the approach of ill fortune, and told if love was returned (Chaucer: *Canterbury Tales*, "The Squires Tale").

Lao's mirror reflected the mind and its thoughts, as an ordinary mirror reflects the outward seeming (Goldsmith: *Citizen of the World*, xlv).

Merlin's magic mirror, given by MERLIN to King Ryence. It informed the king of treason, secret plots, and projected invasions (Spenser: *The Faerie Queene*, III, ii).

Reynard's wonderful mirror. This mirror existed only in the brain of Master Fox. He told the queen lion that whoever looked in it could see what was done a mile off. The wood of the frame was not subject to decay, being made of the same block as King Crampart's magic horse (REYNARD THE FOX, ch. xii).

Vulcan's mirror showed the past, the present, and the future. Sir John Davies tells us that CUPID gave it to ANTINOUS and Antinous gave it to PENELOPE, who saw therein "the court of Queen Elizabeth".

The Mirror for Magistrates. A large collection of poems (published 1555–1559) by William Baldwin, George Ferrers, and many others, with an "Induction" by Thomas Sackville. It contains in metrical form biographical accounts of British historical figures and the mirror reflects the falls of the great. It was much extended in four later editions up to 1587.

The Mirror of Diana. A lake in the Alban hills in the territory of ancient Aricia, in Italy, on the shores of which stood the earliest known temple of DIANA. The priest of this temple, called *Rex Nemorensis*, was either a gladiator or runaway slave who retained office until slain by a successor. The cult is described in the first chapter of Sir James Frazer's *Golden Bough*. The lake, *Nemorensis Lacus* (modern Nemi), is 110 ft. deep and some 3½ miles in diameter.

The Mirror of Human Salvation. See SPECULUM HUMANÆ SALVATIONIS.

The Hall of Mirrors. The famous state apartments of the Palace of VERSAILLES. It was here that King William I of Prussia was acclaimed German Emperor (18 January 1871) after the defeat of France under NAPOLEON III.

Mirror writing. Writing which is reversed and which can only be read when held before a mirror. It sometimes occurs in left-handed people and those with certain derangements. The MSS. of Leonardo da Vinci were written from right to left. *Cp.* LOOKING-GLASS.

Mirza (Pers., royal prince). When prefixed to a surname it is a title of honour, but when annexed to the surname it means a prince of the blood royal.

Miscreant (Fr. *mécréant*). A false believer; a term first applied to the Mohammedans who, in return, call Christian infidels, and associate with this word all that we imply by "miscreants".

Mise (mēz) (O.Fr., expenses). A word used to denote a payment or disbursement, and in particular the payment made by the COUNTY PALATINE of Chester to a new EARL, or by the Welsh to a new lord of the MARCHES and subsequently to a new Prince of WALES, who is also Earl of Chester.

The word is also applied to the settlement of a dispute by agreement or arbitration, as in the *Mise of Amiens* (1264), when Louis IX of France arbitrated between Henry III and the Montfortians, and the subsequent *Mise of Lewes* "for re-establishment of peace in the realm of England and the reconciliation of the discords which have arisen…".

Mise en scène (Fr., setting on stage). The stage setting of a play, including the scenery, properties, etc., and the general arrangement of the piece. Also used metaphorically.

Misère (mi zâr′) (Fr., misery, poverty). In solo WHIST and some other games, the declaration made when the caller undertakes to lose every trick.

Miserere (miz e rē′ re). The fifty-first psalm is so called because its opening words are *Miserere mei*, Deus (Have mercy upon me, O God. *See* NECK-VERSE). One of the evening services of LENT is called *miserere*, because this penitential psalm is sung, after which a sermon is given. The under side of a folding seat in choirstalls is called a *miserere*, or more properly, a **misericord**; when turned up it forms a ledge-seat sufficient to rest the aged in a standing position. A shorter dagger used by knights to end the agony of a wounded man was also known as a *misericord* (Lat. *misereri*, to have pity; *cor, cordis*, heart).

Misers. Among the most renowned are:

Baron Aguilar, or Ephraim Lopes Pereira d'Aguilar (1740–1802), born at Vienna and died at Islington, worth £200,000.

Daniel Dancer (1716–1794). His sister lived with him, and was a similar character, but died before him, and he left his wealth to the widow of Sir Henry Tempest, who nursed him in his last illness.

Sir Hervey Elwes, who died in 1763 worth £250,000, but never spent more than £110 a year. His sister-in-law inherited £100,000, but actually starved herself to death, and her son John (1714–1789), M.P., an eminent brewer in SOUTHWARK, never bought any clothes, never suffered his shoes to be cleaned, and grudged every penny spent on food.

Thomas Guy (*c.* 1645–1724), founder of Guy's Hospital.

William Jennings (1701–1797), a neighbour and friend of Elwes, died worth £200,000.

Mishna, or **Mishnah** ((Heb., learning, instruction, from *shana*, to learn). The collection of moral precepts, traditions, etc., forming the basis of the TALMUD; the second or oral law (*see* GEMARA). It is divided into six parts: (1) agriculture; (2) Sabbaths, fasts, and festivals; (3) marriage and divorce; (4) civil and penal laws; (5) sacrifices; (6) holy persons and things.

Misnomers. There are many such in English which have arisen through ignorance, confusion of ideas, or from the changes that time brings about. *Catgut* for instance, was in all probability once made from the intestines of a *cat* but now never is, although the name remains.

Many misnomers are to be found in this book. *See* CLEOPATRA'S NEEDLE, FORLORN HOPE, GERMAN SILVER, GUINEA-PIG, HUMBLE PIE, INDIAN (American), JERUSALEM ARTICHOKE, MEERSCHAUM, MOTHER-OF-PEARL, POMPEY'S PILLAR, SAND-BLIND, SLUG-HORN, VENTRILOQUISM, and WORMWOOD.

Some others are:

Blacklead is plumbago or graphite, a form of carbon, and has no LEAD in its composition.

Blindworms are neither blind nor worms. They are legless lizards.

China, as a name for porcelain, gives rise to the contradictory expressions Chelsea china, Nantgarw china, Sèvres china, Dresden china, etc.; like wooden or iron mile*stones*; brass shoe-*horns*; *silver* for our present cupro-nickel coins, etc.

Dutch clocks were of German (*Deutsch*), not Dutch, manufacture.

Elements. Fire, earth, air, and water, still often called "the four elements", are not elements at all.

Galvanized iron is not usually galvanized, but is simply iron dipped into molten zinc.

Guernsey lily (*Nerine sarniensis*) is not a native of Guernsey, but of South Africa. It is said that a ship bringing specimens to Europe was wrecked on the coast of Guernsey; some of the bulbs were washed ashore and took root, hence the misnomer.

Honeysuckle. So named from the old idea that bees extracted honey therefrom, but it is entirely useless to the bee.

India ink comes from China, not from India.

Isle of Portland, in Dorset, is a peninsula.

Japanese vellum is not vellum but a very costly handbeaten Japanese paper made from the inner bark of the mulberry tree.

Rice paper is not made from rice, but from the pith of a Formosan plant, *Fatsia papyrifera*.

Salts of lemon is in reality potassium acid oxalate, or potassium quadroxalate.

Slow-worm (or Blindworm). Is neither slow nor a worm.

Titmouse. Tit implies small and the second syllable represents O.E. *mase*, used of several small birds. It has no connexion with *mouse*.

Tonquin beans. A geographical blunder for they are the seeds of *Dipteryx odorata* from Tinka in Guyana, not Tonquin in Asia.

Turkeys do not come from Turkey, but from North America, and were brought to Spain from Mexico.

Turkish baths are not of Turkish origin though they were introduced from the Near East, which was associated with Turkish rule. The correct name of *Hammam* was commonly used in 17th-century England. HUMMUM's Hotel in COVENT GARDEN was on the site of a 17-century *Hammam*.

Whalebone is no bone at all but a horny substance (*baleen*) attached to the upper jaw of the whale which serves to strain the algæ, etc., which it consumes, from the water it takes into its mouth.

Misprision (Fr. *mépris*). Concealment, neglect of; in law, a serious offence.

Misprision of felony. Neglecting to reveal a felony when known.

Misprision of treason. Neglecting to disclose or purposely concealing a treasonable design.

Misrule, Feast of. *See* KING OF MISRULE *under* KING.

Miss, Mistress, Mrs. (lady-master). Miss used to be written Mis, and is the first syllable of Mistress; Mrs. is the contraction of *mistress* and is called Mis'ess. As late as the reign of George II, unmarried women used to be styled Mrs., as, Mrs. Lepel, Mrs. Bellenden, Mrs. Blount, all unmarried women (*see* Pope's *Letters*).

Mistress was originally an honourable term for sweetheart or lover ("Mistress mine, where are you roaming"), and in the 17th century "Miss" was often used for a paramour, *e.g.* Charles II's "misses". Mistress has since come to mean a concubine.

Mistress Roper. An old name for a MARINE; so called by sailors from their alleged handling of ropes in a womanly or unseamanlike fashion.

The Mistress of the Night. The tuberose is so called because it emits its strongest fragrance after sunset.

In the language of FLOWERS the tuberose signifies "the pleasures of love".

The Mistress of the World. Ancient ROME was so called because it controlled all the known world.

To kiss the mistress. To make a good hit, to shoot right into the eye of the target; in bowls, to graze another bowl with your own; the JACK used to be called the "mistress", and when one ball just touches another it is said "to kiss it".

Rub on, and kiss the mistress
SHAKESPEARE: *Troilus and Cressida*, III, ii.

Miss. To fail to hit or—in such phrases as I **miss you now you are gone**—to lack, to feel the want of.

A miss is as good as a mile. A failure is a failure be it ever so little, and is no more be it ever so great; a narrow escape is an escape. An old form of the phrase was *An inch in a miss is as good as an ell*.

To miss the bus, or **boat.** To miss an opportunity; to be too late to participate in something.

The missing link. A popular term for that stage in the evolution of man when he was developing characteristics that differentiated him from the other primates with whom he shared a common ancestry; the link between man and the ape. The expression is sometimes applied disparagingly or jocularly.

Missal (Lat. *liber missalis*, book of the mass). The book containing the liturgy of the MASS with ceremonial instructions as used in the ROMAN CATHOLIC CHURCH. *See* BREVIARY.

Mississippi Bubble. The French counterpart of our SOUTH SEA BUBBLE and equally disastrous. In 1716, John Law (1671—1729), a Scottish financier, obtained permission to establish a *Banque générale* in France and in 1717 set up the *Compagnie de la Louisiane ou d'Occident* and was granted control of the mint and the farming of the revenue. For these concessions he undertook the payment of the NATIONAL DEBT and at one time shares were selling at nearly 40 times their nominal value. The crash came in 1720 and many people were ruined.

Missouri. I'm from Missouri, you've got to show me. "I'm hard-headed and you have to show me", or "I won't believe anything without proof". First used in a speech in 1899 by Willard D. Vandiver, Congressman from Missouri.

Missouri Compromise. An arrangement whereby Missouri was in 1820 admitted to the UNION as a slave state, but with the proviso that there should be no slavery in the state north of 36°30′.

Mistletoe (mis′ él tō) (O.E. *mistiltan*; *mist* being both basil and mistletoe, and *tan*, a twig). The plant grows on various trees as a parasite, especially the apple-tree, and was held in great veneration by the DRUIDS when found on the OAK. Shakespeare calls it "the baleful mistletoe" (*Titus Andronicus*, II, iii), perhaps in allusion to the Scandinavian legend that it was with an arrow made of mistletoe that BALDUR was slain, or to the tradition that it was once a tree from which the wood of Christ's CROSS was formed; or possibly with reference to the popular belief that mistletoe berries are poisonous, or to the connexion of the plant with the human sacrifices of the Druids. It is probably for this latter reason it is excluded from church decorations. Culpeper says "some, for the virtues thereof, have called it *lignum sanctae crucis*, wood of the holy cross, as it cures falling sickness, apoplexy and palsy very speedily, not only to be inwardly taken, but to be hung at their neck". Mistletoe is said to have certain toxic qualities when taken in large doses.

Kissing under the mistletoe. An English CHRISTMAS-time custom, dating back at least to the early 17th century. The correct procedure, now seldom observed, is that a man should pluck a berry when he kisses a girl under the mistletoe, and when the last berry is gone there should be no more kissing.

Mistpoeffers. *See* BARISAL GUNS.

Mistress. *See* MISS.

Mithra, or **Mithras.** The god of light of the ancient Persians, one of their chief deities, and the ruler of the universe, sometimes used as a synonym for the SUN. The word means *friend*, and this deity is so called because he befriends man in this life, and protects him against evil spirits after death. He is represented as a young man with a Phrygian cap and plunging daggers into the neck of a bull that lies upon the ground.

Sir Thomas More called the Supreme Being of his *Utopia*, "Mithra" and the cult of Mithraism had certain affinities with Christianity.

Mithridate (mith' ri dāt). A concoction named from Mithridates VI, King of Pontus and Bithynia (d. *c.* 63 B.C.), who is said to have made himself immune from poisons by the constant use of antidotes. It was supposed to be an antidote against poisons and contained 46 or more ingredients.

> What brave spirit could be content to sit in his shop ... selling Mithridatum and dragon's water to infected houses?
>
> BEAUMONT and FLETCHER: *Knight of the Burning Pestle*, I (1608).

Mitre (mī' ter) (Gr. and Lat. *mitra*, a headband, turban). The episcopal mitre is supposed to symbolize the cloven tongues of fire which descended on the apostles on the day of PENTECOST (*Acts* ii, 1–12).

The Mitre Tavern. A famous tavern in FLEET STREET, London, first mentioned in 1603, but probably a good deal older. It was a frequent resort of Johnson and Boswell and ceased to be a tavern in 1788. Another Mitre, mentioned by Ben Jonson and Pepys, existed in Wood Street.

Mitten. To give one the mitten. To reject a sweetheart, to jilt. Possibly with a punning allusion to Lat. *mittere*, to send (about your business), whence *dismissal*.

Mittimus (Lat., we send). A command in writing to a jailer, to keep the person named in safe custody. Also a writ for removing a record from one court to another. So called from the first word of the writ.

Mizzentop, maintop, foretop. A "top" is a platform fixed over the head of a lower mast, resting on the trestle-trees, to spread the rigging of the topmast. The mizzenmast is the aftermast of a three-masted ship and the foremast is forward of the mainmast.

Mnemosyne (ne mos' i ni). Goddess of memory and mother by ZEUS of the nine MUSES of Greek Mythology. She was the daughter of heaven and earth. (URANUS and GÆA).

> To the Immortals every one
> A portion was assigned of all that is;
> But chief Mnemosyne did Maia's son
> Clothe in the light of his loud melodies.
> SHELLEY: *Homer's Hymn to Mercury*, lxxiii.

Moabite Stone, The. An ancient *stele*, bearing the oldest extant Semitic inscription, now in the LOUVRE, Paris. The inscription, of 34 lines in Hebrew-Phœnician characters, gives an account of the war of Mesha, King of Moab, who reigned about 850 B.C., against Omri, Ahab, and other kings of Israel (*see* II *Kings*, iii). Mesha sacrificed his eldest son on the city wall in view of the invading Israelites. The stone was found by F. Klein at Dibhan in 1868, and is 3 ft. 10 in. high, 2 ft. broad and 14½ in. thick. The Arabs resented its removal and splintered it into fragments, but it has been restored.

Moaning Minnie. A World War II term for a six-barrelled German mortar, from the rising shriek when it was fired. The name was also given to the air-raid warning siren from its repetitive wail and is colloquially applied to any constant moaner or habitual grumbler.

Mob. A contraction of the Lat. *mobile vulgus*, the fickle crowd. The term was first applied to the people by the members of the GREEN RIBBON Club.

In subsequent years the word was applied to an organized criminal gang.

Mob-cap. A bag-shaped cap formerly worn indoors by women and useful for concealing hair that was not yet "done". It was originally called *mab-cap*, from the old verb *mab*, to dress untidily.

Mock. Mock-beggar Hall, or **Manor.** A grand, ostentatious house, where no hospitality is afforded, neither is any charity given.

No times observed, nor charitable lawes,
The poor receive their answer from the dawes
Who, in their cawing language, call it plaine
Mock-beggar Manour, for they come in vaine.
TAYLOR: *The Water Cormorant* (1622).

Mock of the Church. When BANNS OF MAR-
RIAGE are called and none takes place. Formerly the churchwardens often fined the
offenders.

**Mockery. Trial by jury shall be a delu-
sion, a mockery, and a snare.** Thomas,
Lord Denman made this observation in his
judgment on the case of The Queen *v.*
O'Connell (1844).

Mock-up. A phrase originating in World
War II for a trial model or full-size working
model. In the American Air Force, a panel
mounted with models of aircraft parts and
used for instructional purposes was so
called.

Modality, in scholastic philosophy, means the
mode in which anything exists. Kant divides
our judgment into three modalities: (1) *Pro-
blematic*, touching possible events; (2) *As-
sertoric*, touching real events; (3) *Apodictic*,
touching necessary events.

Moddey Dhoo (pronounced Mawther Doo;
Manx' Black Dog). A ghostly black spaniel
that for many years haunted Peel Castle in
the Isle of MAN. It used to enter the guard
room as soon as candles were lighted, and
leave it at daybreak. While this spectre dog
was present, the soldiers forebore all oaths
and profane talk, but they always carried out
their nightly duties of locking up and conveying the keys to the captain accompanied
by one of their fellows. One night a drunken
trooper, from bravado, performed the
rounds alone but lost his speech and died in
three days. The dog never appeared again.

During excavations in 1871 the bones of
Simon, Bishop of Sodor and Man (died
1247) were uncovered, with the bones of a
dog at his feet.

Model Parliament. Summoned by Edward I
in 1295, it consisted of representatives of the
clergy, nobility and commonalty. It included twenty bishops, sixty-seven abbots,
seven earls and forty-one barons. In addition there were two knights from every SHIRE
and two burgesses from each city or BOR-
OUGH within a shire. It thus set the pattern
for subsequent parliaments.

Modernism. A movement in the ROMAN
CATHOLIC CHURCH which sought to interpret
the ancient teachings of the Church with due
regard to the current teachings of science,
modern philosophy, and history. It arose in
the late 19th century and was formally condemned by Pope Pius X in 1907 in the ency-
clical *Pascendi*, which stigmatized it as the
"synthesis of all heresies".

The term **Modernist** is also applied to
liberal and RADICAL critics of traditional
theology in other churches. The Modern
Churchmen's Union was founded in 1898
and was strongly critical of Anglo-Catholic
and Roman Catholic ideals. Dean Inge
(1860–1954) and Bishop Barnes (1874–
1953) were prominent among its members.

Modred. In ARTHURIAN ROMANCE, one of the
Knights of the ROUND TABLE, nephew and
betrayer of King ARTHUR. He is represented
as the treacherous knight. He revolted
against the king, whose wife he seduced, was
mortally wounded in the battle of CAMLAN
and was buried in AVALON. The story is told,
with a variation, in Tennyson's *Guinevere*
(*Idylls of the King*).

Mods. A contraction of *Moderations*, the first
public examination taken by candidates in
certain subjects for the BACHELOR OF ARTS
degree at Oxford. It is conducted by "Mod-
erators". Honour Moderations are now
taken in Greek and Latin Literature;
Mathematics; Theology; Biochemistry;
Physics, Mathematics, and Engineering Science. There are also Law Moderations. The
first public examination in other subjects is
the Preliminary Examination. *Cp.* LITTLE
GO; MATRICULATION; SMALLS.

Mods and Rockers. The *Mods* developed
as a teenage cult in London in the early
1960s initially putting their emphasis on
fastidiousness and extravagance in dress and
fashion. The rise of CARNABY STREET as their
dress centre was a consequence. Mainly devoid of social conscience, there was some association with homosexuality and PURPLE
HEARTS and their mode of life reflected the
less desirable results of the AFFLUENT SOCIE-
TY. With the rise of the rival gangs of
leather-jacketed *Rockers*, akin to the Teddy
Boys (*see* EDWARDIAN) of the 1950s, trouble
began. Bank holiday clashes between Mods
and Rockers, who arrived in their hordes on
scooters and motor-cycles, made certain seaside resorts hazardous places for the more
responsible elements in society. Loutishness
prevailed until the authorities took firm
measures against them. They were temporarily outmoded by the more recent cult of
the Flower-Children. *See* FLOWER POWER
under POWER.

Modus operandi (Lat.). The mode of operation; the way in which a thing is done, or
should be done.

Modus vivendi (Lat., way of living). A
working arrangement whereby persons, not
on friendly terms at the time, can be induced

737

to live peacefully. The term may be applied to individuals, societies, and peoples.

Mogul (Mongol). **The Great Mogul.** The name given to the ruler of the Mohammedan-Tartar Empire in India which began in 1526 with Baber, great-grandson of Timur, or TAMERLANE. It disintegrated after the death of Aurangzeb in 1707. Noteworthy among the Mogul emperors were Akbar, Jahangir and Shah Jahan. Wealthy business TYCOONS, etc., are sometimes called *moguls*.

Mogul cards. The best quality playing-cards were so called because the wrapper, or the "duty-card" (cards are subject to excise duty) was decorated with a representation of the Great Mogul. Inferior cards were called "Harrys", "Highlanders", and "Merry Andrews" for a similar reason.

Mohammed, Mahomet (Arab., "the praised one"). There are various spellings, the most correct being *Muhammmad*. It is the titular name of the founder of ISLAM or Mohammedanism, adopted by him at the time of the HEGIRA; his original name is given both as Kotham and as Halabi. He was born at MECCA *c*. 570 and died at MEDINA in 632.

Angel of. When Mohammed was transported to HEAVEN, he said: "I saw there an angel, the most gigantic of all created beings. It had 70,000 heads, each head had 70,000 faces, each face had 70,000 mouths, each mouth had 70,000 tongues, and each tongue spoke 70,000 languages; all were employed in singing God's praises."

Banner of. Sanjaksherif, kept in the Eyab mosque at Istanbul.

Bible of. The KORAN.

Camel (swiftest). Adha.

Cave. The cave in which GABRIEL appeared to Mohammed (610) was in the mountain of Hira, near Mecca.

Coffin. Legend held that Mohammed's coffin was suspended in mid-air at Medina without any support.

> Sp'ritual men are too transcendent...
> To hang, like Mahomet, in the air,
> Or St. Ignatius at his prayer,
> By pure geometry.
> BUTLER: *Hudibras*, III, ii, 602.

Daughter (favourite). Fatima.

Dove. Mohammed had a dove which he fed with wheat out of his ear.

Father of. Abdullah of the tribe of Koreish. He died just before or after the Prophet's birth.

Father-in-law of. Abu-Bekr (father of Ayesha) and the first CALIPH.

Flight from Mecca. The Hegira.

Horse of. Al Borak. *See* BORAK.

Miracles. Several are traditionally mentioned. The best known is that of the MOON. The story is that Habib the Wise asked Mohammed to prove his mission by cleaving the Moon in two. Mohammed raised his hands towards heaven and commanded the moon to do Habib's bidding. Accordingly it descended to the top of the KAABA, made seven circuits, and coming to the prophet, entered his right sleeve and came out of the left. It then entered the collar of his robe, descended to the skirt, and clove itself into two plaits, one of which appeared in the east of the skies and the other in the west. The two parts ultimately reunited.

Mother of. Amina, of the tribe of Koreish. She died when Mohammed was six years old.

Paradise of. The ten animals admitted to his paradise are:

(1) the dog Kratim, which accompanied the SEVEN SLEEPERS.

(2) BALAAM's ass, which spoke with the voice of a man to reprove the disobedient prophet.

(3) SOLOMON's ant, of which he said, "Go to the ant, thou sluggard ..."

(4) JONAH's whale.

(5) The ram caught in the thicket, and offered in sacrifice in lieu of Isaac.

(6) The calf of ABRAHAM.

(7) The camel of Saleb.

(8) The cuckoo of Bilkis.

(9) The ox of MOSES.

(10) Mohammed's steed, Al BORAK.

Stepping-stone. The stone upon which he placed his foot when he mounted Al Borak on his ascent to heaven. It rose as the beast rose, but Mohammed, putting his hand upon it, forbade it to follow him, whereupon it remained suspended in mid-air, where the True Believer, if he has faith enough, may still behold it.

Tribe. On both sides, the Koreish.

Uncle. Abu Tâlib, who took charge of Mohammed at the death of his grandfather.

Wives. Firstly, Kadija, a rich widow of the tribe of Koreish, who had been twice married already, and was forty years old. For twenty-five years she was his only wife, but he subsequently married a number of others, nine of whom survived him, the favourite being AYESHA. He also had concubines.

Year of Deputations. A.D. 630, the 8th of the Hegira.

If the mountain will not come to Mahomet, Mahomet must go to the mountain.
When Mohammed was asked by the Arab for miraculous proofs of his teaching he o

dered Mount Safa to come to him, and as it did not move, he said, "God is merciful. Had it obeyed my words, it would have fallen on us to our destruction. I will therefore go to the mountain and thank God that He has had mercy on a stiffnecked generation." The phrase is often used of one who, unable to get his own way, bows before the inevitable.

Mohocks. A class of ruffians who in the 18th century infested the streets of London. So called from the Mohawk Indians. One of their "new inventions" was to roll people down Snow Hill in a tub; another was to overturn coaches on rubbish-heaps. (*See* Gay: *Trivia*, III.)

A vivid picture of the misdoings of these and other brawlers is given in the *Spectator*, No. 324. *Cp.* MODS AND ROCKERS; TITYRE TUS.

Moira. Fate or Necessity, supreme even over the gods of OLYMPUS.

Moke. A donkey. *See* DICKY.

Mole. A small animal which burrows underground throwing up small heaps of soil called *molehills*. The name is currently applied to spies and traitors obtaining positions of trust in organizations, especially government departments, intelligence and secret service. The most notorious of these moles was Kim Philby (1912–1988), who worked for the U.S.S.R. as did his fellow Cantabrigians Anthony Blunt, Guy Burgess and Donald Maclean — quite a Labour of moles!

To make mountains out of molehills. *See under* MOUNTAIN.

Molech. *See* MOLOCH.

Molière. The name adopted by the great French comic dramatist and actor Jean Baptiste Poquelin (1622–1673). He was taken ill when acting in his latest comedy *Le Malade Imaginaire* and died the same night.

Molinism. The system of grace and election taught by the Spanish JESUIT, Louis Molina (1535–1600). His doctrine was that grace is a free gift to all, but consent of the will must be present before that grace can be effective. *Cp.* JANSENISTS.

Moll, Molly. Moll Cutpurse. *See* CUTPURSE.

Moll. An American term for a gunman's girl-friend; less commonly, for a prostitute.

Take away this bottle, it has Moll Thompson's mark on it. Moll Thompson is M.T. (*empty*).

Molly coddle. A pampered creature, a NAMBY PAMBY. To molly coddle is to fuss over or pamper.

Molly Maguires. An Irish secret society organized in 1843. Stout, active young Irishmen dressed up in women's clothes and otherwise disguised themselves to surprise rent-collectors. Their victims were ducked in bog-holes or more ruthlessly handled.

A similar Irish American secret society flourished in the mining districts of Pennsylvania between 1854 and 1877 which intimidated the German, Welsh, and English miners.

> The judge who tried the murderer was elected by the Molly Maguires; the jurors who assisted him were themselves Molly Maguires. A score of Molly Maguires came forward to swear the assassin was sixty miles from the spot on which he had been seen to fire at William Dunn … and the jurors returned a verdict of Not guilty.
>
> W. HEPWORTH DIXON: *New America*, II, xxviii.

Molly Mog. This celebrated beauty an innkeeper's daughter, at Oakingham, Berks. She was the toast of the gay sparks of the first half of the 18th century, and died unmarried in 1766, at the age of sixty-seven. Gay has a ballad on this *Fair Maid of the Inn*, in which the "swain" alluded to is Mr. Standen, of Arborfield, who died in 1730. It is said that Molly's sister Sally was the greater beauty. A portrait of Gay still stands in the inn.

Molloch, May, or **The Maid of the Hairy Arms.** An ELF of folklore who mingles in ordinary sports, and will even direct the master of the house how to play dominoes or draughts. Like the WHITE LADY of Avenel, May Molloch is a sort of BANSHEE.

> "Meg Mullack and Brownie mentioned in the end of it [this letter], are two Ghosts, which (as it is constantly reported) of old, haunted a Family in Strathspey of the Name of Grant. They appeared at first in the likeliness of a young Lass; the second of a young Lad."
>
> JOHN AUBREY: *Miscellanies*.

Molmutine Laws. According to Geoffrey of Monmouth, the laws of Dunwallo Molmutius, legendary king of Britain, son of Cloten, king of CORNWALL. *Cp.* MARTIAN LAWS.

> He enacted that the temples of the gods, as also cities, should have the privilege of giving sanctuary and protection to any fugitive or criminal, that should flee to them from his enemy.
>
> *Historia Britonum*, II, xvii.

Moloch (mō′ lok), or **Molech** (Heb., king). Any influence which demands from us the sacrifice of what we hold most dear. Thus, *war* is a Moloch, the *guillotine* was the Moloch of the French Revolution, *king Mob* is a Moloch, etc. The allusion is to the god of the AMMONITES, to whom children were made "to pass through the fire" (II *Kings* xxiii, 10). Milton says he was worshipped in Rabba, in Argob, and Basan, to the stream of utmost Arnon (*Paradise Lost*, I, 392–8). His victims were slain and burnt.

Molotov. The alias of the Russian diplomat

Vyacheslav Mikhailovich Skryabin was given in World War II to:

The **Molotov breadbasket.** A canister of incendiary bombs which, on being launched from a plane, opened and showered the bombs over a wide area. Also to the **Molotov cocktail,** a home-made anti-tank bomb, invented and first used by the Finns against the Russians in 1940 and developed in Britain as one of the weapons of the HOME GUARD. It consisted of a bottle filled with inflammable and glutinous liquid, with a slow match protruding from the top. When thrown at a tank the bottle burst, the liquid ignited and spread over the plating of the tank.

Moly. According to HOMER, the mythical herb given by HERMES to ULYSSES as an antidote against the sorceries of CIRCE.

> Black was the root, but milky white the flower,
> Moly the name, to mortals hard to find.
>
> POPE: *Odyssey*, X, 365.

The name is given to a number of plants, especially of the *Allium* (garlic) family, as the wild garlic, the Indian moly, the moly of Hungary, serpents moly, the yellow moly, Spanish purple moly, Spanish silver-capped moly, and Dioscorides' moly. They all flower in May except "the sweet moly of Montpelier", which blossoms in September.

Momus. (mō' mùs). One who carps at everything. Momus was the god of ridicule and the son of Nox (Night), who was driven out of HEAVEN for his criticisms of the gods. VENUS herself was censured for the noise made by her feet, although he could find no fault with her naked body.

Monday. The second day of the week until 1971, called by the Anglo-Saxons *Monandæg, i.e.* the day of the Moon. It is now the first. *See* SUNDAY.

St. Monday, or **St. Lundi.** A facetious name given to Monday (also called *Cobblers' Monday*) because it was observed by shoemakers and others as a holiday (*holy* day!).

There is a story in the *Journal of the Folklore Society* (Vol. I), that, while Cromwell lay encamped at Perth, one of his zealous partisans, named Monday, died and Cromwell offered a reward for the best lines on his death. A shoemaker of Perth brought the following:

> Blessed be the Sabbath Day,
> And cursed by worldly pelf,
> Tuesday will begin the week,
> Since Monday's hanged himself.

This so pleased Cromwell that he not only gave the promised reward but decreed that shoemakers should be allowed to make Monday a standing holiday.

Monday's child. The traditional rhyme says:

> Monday's child is fair of face,
> Tuesday's child is full of grace,
> Wednesday's child is full of woe,
> Thursday's child has far to go;
> Friday's child is loving and giving,
> Saturday's child works hard for a living;
> But the child that is born on the Sabbath-day
> Is bonny and blithe and good and gay.

Another rhyme says:

> If you sneeze on Monday, you sneeze for danger;
> Sneeze on Tuesday, kiss a stranger;
> Sneeze on Wednesday, sneeze for a letter;
> Sneeze on Thursday, something better;
> Sneeze on Friday, sneeze for sorrow;
> Sneeze on Saturday, see your sweetheart tomorrow.

That Monday morning feeling. Disinclination to start work after the week-end break (often employed in more strenuous exertion in the garden, etc.).

The swing-it-till-Monday basket. A nickname for the desk tray or basket for nonurgent matter or that which can safely be put aside until after the week-end.

Money. Shortly after the Gallic invasion of ROME, in 344 B.C., Lucius Furius (or according to other accounts, Camillus) built a temple to JUNO Moneta (the *Monitress*) on the spot where the house of Manlius Capitolinus stood; and to this temple was attached the first Roman mint, as the public treasury (*ærarium*) was attached to the temple of SATURN. Hence the "ases" there coined were called *moneta,* and hence our word *money*.

Juno is represented on medals with instruments of coinage, as the hammer, anvil, pincers, and die. *See Livy,* VII, xxviii, and Cicero, *De Divinitate,* i, 15.

The oldest coin of Greece bore the impress of an ox. Hence a bribe for silence was said to be an "ox on the tongue". Subsequently each state had its own impress:

Athens, an owl (the bird of wisdom); *Bœotia,* BACCHUS (the vineyard of Greece); *Delphos,* a dolphin; *Macedonia,* a buckler (from its love of war); *Rhodes,* the disc of the sun (the COLOSSUS was an image to the sun).

Rome had a different impress for each coin:

For the *As,* the head of JANUS on one side, and the prow of a ship on the reverse; the *Semi-as,* the head JUPITER and the letter S; the *Sextans,* the head of MERCURY and two points to denote two ounces; the *Triens* the head of a woman (? Rome or MINERVA) and three points to denote three ounces; the *Quadrans,* the head of HERCULES and four points to denote four ounces.

In every country there are popular nicknames for common coins and sums of money. Thus a *bawbee* in SCOTLAND means a halfpenny and also is applied to money generally. In ENGLAND money is called *brass*, current colloquialisms being *bread* and *lolly*, and we had (before decimalization) a copper (1*d*.); a joey (4*d*. and 3*d*.); a tanner, a tizzy (6*d*.); a bob (1*s*.); half a dollar, two and a kick (2*s*. 6*d*.); a dollar, a cartwheel (5*s*.); a QUID (20*s*.); a jimmy o'goblin (a SOVEREIGN); a fiver (£5); a tenner (£10); a pony (£25); a monkey (£500).

In N. America: a penny, a Red Indian (1*c*.); a nickel (5*c*.); a dime (10*c*.); a quarter, two bits (25*c*.); four bits (50*c*.); a buck (in silver, a cartwheel, a smacker) ($1.00); a SAWBUCK ($10.00); a century ($100.00); a monkey ($500.00); a grand, a G ($1000.00).

Money for old rope, or **money for jam.** An easy job, yielding a profitable reward for little effort.

Money is the root of all evil. Many people will do anything, however unscrupulous it may be, if there is money to be gained.

Money of account is a monetary denomination used in reckoning and often not employed as actual coin. For example, a GUINEA as British money of account, when no coin of this value was in circulation. The U.S.A. *mill*, being one-thousandth of a dollar or one-tenth of a cent, is money of account.

Money talks. The moneyed have considerable influence in many ways.

Money will make the mare go. *See* MARE.

Pin Money. *See under* PIN.

Ready money. Cash down; money available for immediate payment.

Mongrel Parliament. The PARLIAMENT that Charles II summoned at Oxford in 1681 to deprive the WHIGS of the support of the City of LONDON in their struggle to alter the succession, *i.e.*, to exclude the Duke of York, a Roman Catholic.

Monism. (mo′ nizm). The doctrine of the oneness of mind and matter which explains everything in terms of a single reality, ignoring all that is supernatural; any one of the philosophical theories that denies the dualism of mind and matter and seeks to deduce all the varied spiritual and physical phenomena from a single principle.

Monitor (Lat. from *monere*, one who reminds or admonishes, a preceptor, a tutor, etc.). So the Romans called the nursery teacher. The *Military Monitor* was an officer to tell young soldiers of the faults committed against the service. The *House Monitor* was a slave to rouse the family in the morning, etc. The term has long been applied to school pupils chosen to assist the staff in a variety of duties.

A shallow-draught ironclad with a flat deck, low freeboard and one or two revolving turrets of heavy guns, specially designed for coastal bombardment, was so called. The first such craft was designed by Captain John Ericsson in 1861 and used by the Federals in the American CIVIL WAR and was so called, as the designer said, because it was intended to "admonish the leaders of the Southern Rebellion" and to "prove a severe monitor" to them. The battle between the *Monitor* and the Confederate former frigate *Merrimac* (properly the *Virginia* as renamed after being rebuilt as an ironclad) in 1862 is notable as the first conflict between IRONCLADS.

The word is also used to designate a broadcasting official employed to listen in to foreign (especially enemy) radio transmissions in order to analyse the news announced and to study propaganda. In normal circumstances the duties of a monitor include checking the quality of transmissions.

Monitorial System. The name given to the system of instruction, originally called the *Madras System*, devised by Andrew Bell (1753–1832) when a superintendent of the Madras Orphanage (1789–1796). Owing to the dearth of suitably qualified masters, he used senior scholars or monitors to instruct their juniors. These monitors were taught to pass on factual information learned by rote, usually in the form of simple question and answer. The system was adopted in England by the early LANCASTERIAN and National Schools (*see* NATIONAL SOCIETY) for the same reasons that caused Bell to devise it in the first place.

Monk (O.E. *munuc*; Med. Lat. *monachus*, a solitary). In the Western Church, properly a member of those religious orders living a community life under vows of poverty, chastity, and obedience. *See* BENEDICTINES; CARTHUSIANS; CISTERCIANS. *Cp.* FRIARS; MENDICANT ORDERS.

In printing, a black smear or blotch made by leaving too much ink on the part is called a *monk*. Caxton set up his printing-press in the *scriptorium* of Westminster Abbey (*see* CHAPEL); and the association gave rise to the slang expressions *monk* and *friar* for black and white defects.

Monk Lewis. Matthew Gregory Lewis (1775–1818), so called from his highly coloured "Gothic novel called *Ambrosio, or the Monk* (1795).

Monkey. Slang for £500 or (in America) $500; also for a mortgage (sometimes extended to *a monkey with a long tail*), and among sailors the vessel which contained the full allowance of GROG for a MESS. A child, especially an active, meddlesome one, is often called "a little monkey"—for obvious reasons. In army parlance a *monkey* is a military policeman.

Blue Monkey. *See under* BLUE.

Monkey's allowance. MORE KICKS THAN HALFPENCE (*see under* KICKS).

Monkey board. In the old-fashioned knifeboard horse-omnibuses, the step on which the conductor stood, and on which he often skipped about "like a monkey".

Monkey jacket. A short jacket formerly worn by seamen. Possibly so called from its likeness to the jacket of the organ grinder's monkey of bygone days; or because it has no more tail than a monkey (or more strictly speaking, an ape).

Monkey puzzle. The Chilean pine, *Araucaria imbricata*, whose twisted and prickly branches puzzle even a monkey to climb.

Monkey spoons. Spoons having on the handle a heart surmounted by a monkey, at one time given in Holland at marriages to some immediate relative of the bride; at christenings and funerals to the officiating clergyman. *See* TO SUCK THE MONKEY, *below*.

Monkey suit. In the U.S.A. services, the term applied to full dress uniform, also to an aviator's overalls and sometimes to men's formal dress on important occasions.

Monkey tricks. Mischievous, ill-natured, or deceitful actions.

To get one's monkey up. To be riled or enraged; monkeys are often irritable and easily provoked. *Cp*. TO GET ONE'S GOAT *under* GOAT.

To monkey with, or **about.** To tamper with or play mischievous tricks. *To monkey with the cards* is to try to arrange them so that the deal will not be fair; *to monkey with the milk* is to add water to it and then sell it as pure and unadulterated.

To pay in monkey's money (Fr. *en monnaie de singe*). In goods, in personal work, in mumbling and grimace. In PARIS when a monkey passed the Petit Pont, if it was for sale four deniers' toll had to be paid; but if it belonged to a showman and was not for sale, it sufficed if the monkey went through his tricks.

> ... being an original by Master Charles Charmois, principal painter to King Megistus, paid for in court fashion with monkey's money.
>
> RABELAIS, IV, iii.

To suck the monkey. Among the Dutch, drinking is called "sucking the monkey", because the early morning appetizer of rum and salt was taken in a MONKEY SPOON. In sailor's slang "to suck the monkey" is to suck liquor from a cask through a straw; and when milk has been taken from a coconut, and rum has been substituted, "sucking the monkey" is drinking this rum.

> Besides, what the vulgar call "sucking the monkey"
> Has much less effect on a man when he's funky.
>
> BARHAM: *Ingoldsby Legends* (*The Black Mousquetaire*, II).

Monmouth. The town at the mouth of the Monnow; surname of Henry V of England, who was born there.

Monmouth cap. A soldier's cap.

> The Welchmen ... wearing leekes in their Monmouth caps.
>
> SHAKESPEARE: *Henry V*, IV, vii.
>
> The best caps were formerly made at Monmouth, where the capper's chapel doth still remain.
>
> FULLER: *Worthies of England*.

Monmouth Street, SOHO. This former London street was once noted for its second-hand clothes shops; hence the expression *Monmouth Street finery* for TAWDRY, pretentious clothes. *See* CARNABY STREET.

> [At the Venetian carnival] you may put on what-e'er
> You like by way of doublet, cape or cloak,
> Such as in Monmouth-street, or in Rag Fair
> Would rig you out in seriousness or joke.
>
> BYRON: *Beppo*, v.

Monmouth's Rebellion. The disastrous last throw of the Duke of Monmouth, the son of Charles II's mistress Lucy Walter, to overthrow James II as champion of the Protestant religion. He landed at Lyme in 1685 and was hailed as King at Taunton and Bridgwater, but was routed by James II's army at Sedgemoor (6 July). Monmouth was executed and his rustic followers were dealt with at the BLOODY ASSIZES.

Monophysites (Gr. *monos*, one; *phusis*, nature). A religious sect in the Levant which maintained that Jesus Christ had only one nature, and that divine and human were combined in much the same way as body and soul were combined in man. It arose upon the condemnation of the EUTYCHIAN heresy at the Council of Chalcedon, 451, and is still represented by the Coptic (*see* COPTS), Armenian, Abyssinian, Syrian, and Malabar JACOBITE Churches.

Monothelites (Gr. *monos*, one; *thelein*, to will). A 7th-century heretical sect holding that Christ had only one will, the divine. Monothelitism was akin to the teaching of the MONOPHYSITES, and was an attempt to reconcile the latter to their fellow-Christians of the eastern Empire against Persian and Mohammedan invaders. It was condemned finally by the Council of Constantinople (680).

Monroe Doctrine (mùn rō'). The doctrine first promulgated in 1823 by James Monroe (President of the U.S.A., 1817–1825), to the effect that the American States would not entangle themselves in the broils of the Old World, nor suffer European powers to interfere in the affairs of the New. There was to be no future colonization by any European powers.

The Monroe Doctrine was invoked by the UNITED STATES during the Anglo-Venezuelan boundary dispute over the limits of British Guiana (1894–1896).

The capture of Manila and the cession of the Philippines to the United States in 1898, and still more the part the Americans took in the World Wars have abrogated a large part of this famous Doctrine.

Mons Meg. *See under* MEG.

Mons Star. The British war medal ("The 1914 Star") given for service in France or Belgium in 1914, is popularly so called. The battle of Mons was fought on 23 August 1914.

Monseigneur. The title given to the DAUPHIN from the time of Louis XIV.

Monsieur. The eldest brother of the King of France was so called from the time of Louis XIV (1643–1715).

Monsieur de Paris. The public executioner or JACK KETCH of France.

Monsieur le Grand. The Great Equerry of France was so called.

The Peace of Monsieur. The peace that the HUGUENOTS, the POLITIQUES, and the Duke d'Alençon ("Monsieur") obliged Henry III of France to sign in 1576. By it the Huguenots and the Duke gained great concessions.

Monsignor (mon sē' nyôr) (pl. *Monsignori*). A title pertaining to all prelates in the ROMAN CATHOLIC CHURCH, which includes all prelates of the Roman court, active or honorary. Used with the surname, as "Monsignor Newman", it does away with the solecism of speaking of Bishop so-and-so, which is like calling the Duke of Marlborough "Duke Churchill".

Mont. (Fr., hill). The technical term in PALMISTRY for the eminences at the roots of the fingers.

> That at the root of the
> *thumb* is the Mont de Mars.
> *index finger* is the Mont de Jupiter.
> *long finger* is the Mont de Saturne.
> *ring finger* is the Mont du Soleil.
> *little finger* is the Mont de Vénus.
> The one between the thumb and the index finger is called the Mont de Mercure and the one opposite the Mont de la Lune.

Mont de Piété. A pawnshop in France; first instituted as *monti di pietà* (charity loans) at Rome under Leo X (1513–1521), by charitable persons who wished to rescue the poor from usurers. They advanced small sums of money on the security of pledges, at a rate of interest barely sufficient to cover the working expenses of the institution. Both the name and the system were introduced into France and Spain. Public granaries for the sale of corn were called in Italian *monti frumentarii*. "Monte" means a public or state loan; hence also a "bank".

Montagnards. *See* MOUNTAIN, THE.

Montanists. A short-lived 2nd-century heretical sect; so called from Montanus, a Phrygian, who asserted that he had received from the HOLY GHOST special knowledge that had not been vouchsafed to the APOSTLES. They were extreme ascetics and believed in the speedy coming of the Second ADVENT. *See* QUINTILIANS.

Monteer Cap. *See* MONTERO.

Monteith. A scalloped basin to cool and wash glasses in; a sort of punch-bowl, made of silver or pewter with a movable rim scalloped at the top; so called, according to Anthony Wood, in 1683 from "a fantastical Scot called 'monsieur Monteigh' who about that time wore the bottome of his coate so notched ∪∪∪∪."

> New things produce new names, and thus Monteith
> Has by one vessel saved his name from death.
> KING.

Montem. A custom observed triennially until 1847 by the boys of Eton College, who proceeded on Whit Tuesday *ad montem* (to a mound called Salt Hill), near Slough, and exacted a gratuity called *salt-money* from all who passed by. Sometimes as much as £1,000 was thus collected, and it was used to defray the expenses of the senior scholar at King's College, Cambridge.

Montero, or **Monteer Cap.** So called from the headgear worn by the *monteros de Espinosa* (mountaineers), who once formed the interior guard of the palace of the Spanish king. It had a spherical crown, and flaps that could be drawn over the ears, not unlike a Victorian shooting-cap.

Montessori Method. A system of training and educating young children evolved by the Italian educationist, Dr. Maria Montessori (1870–1952). Based on "free discipline", and the use of specially devised "educational apparatus" and "didactic material", it has exercised considerable influence on work with young children. *Cp.* FRŒBEL SYSTEM.

Montgomery's division, all on one side. This is a French proverb and refers to the

FREE COMPANIES, of which a Montgomery was a noted chief. The booty he took he kept himself. *Cp.* LION'S SHARE.

Month. One of the twelve divisions of a year. Anciently a new month started on the day of the new MOON, or the day after; hence the name (O.E. *monath*) which is connected with moon. For the individual months *see* their names; *see also* LUNAR MONTH.

The old mnemonic for remembering the number of days in each month runs:

> Thirty days hath September,
> April, June, and November,
> February eight-and-twenty all alone
> And all the rest have thirty-one,
> Unless that Leap Year doth combine
> And give to February twenty-nine.

This, with slight variations, is to be found in Grafton's *Chronicles* (1590), etc. In Harrison's *Description of England* (prefixed to Holinshed's *Chronicle*, 1577), is the Latin version:

> Junius, Aprilis, Septemque, Novemque, tricenos,
> Unum plus reliqui. Februus tenet octo vicenos,
> At si bissextus fuerit superadditur unus.

A month of Sundays. An indefinite but long time; NEVER.

A month's mind. Properly the Requiem MASS said for the deceased on the 30th day after death or burial. The term often occurs in old wills in connexion with charities to be disbursed on that day.

A *month's mind* was also used to denote an eager desire, as in:

> I have a month's mind, instead of this damnable iteration of guesses and forebodings, to give thee the history of a little adventure which befell me yesterday.
>
> SCOTT: *Redgauntlet, Letter* III.

Month in month out. Throughout all the months; constantly; all the time.

Montjoie St. Denis, or **Denys.** The war cry of mediæval France. *Montjoie* is a corruption of *Mons Jovis*, as the little mounds were called which served as direction-posts in ancient times; hence it was applied to whatever showed or indicated the way, as the banner of St. DENYS, called the ORIFLAMME. The Burgundians had for their war-cry, "Montjoie St. André"; the Dukes of Bourbon, "Montjoie Notre Dame"; and the Kings of England used to have "Montjoie St. George".

Montjoie was also the cry of the French heralds in the TOURNAMENTS, and the title of the French KING OF ARMS.

> Where is Mountjoy the herald? speed him hence:
> Let him greet England with our sharp defiance.
>
> SHAKESPEARE: *Henry V*, III, v.

Montpelier. The name is frequently found in English streets, squares, etc., due to the French town Montpellier being a fashionable resort in the 19th century.

Montserrat (Lat. *mons serratus*, the mountain jagged like a saw). The Catalonians aver that this mountain was riven and shattered at the Crucifixion. Every rift is filled with evergreens. The monastery of Montserrat is famous for its printing-press and for its Black Virgin.

Monument, The. The fluted Roman-Doric column of Portland stone (202 ft. high) designed by Sir Christopher Wren to commemorate the Great FIRE of London in 1666. It stands near the north end of London Bridge, near the spot where the fire started. It was erected between 1671 and 1677. In 1681 following inscription was made on the base (erased 1831):

> This Pillar was set up in perpetual remembrance of that most dreadful burning of this Protestant city, begun and carried out by ye treachery and malice of ye popish faction, in ye beginning of Septem in ye year of Our Lord 1666, in order to ye carrying on their horrid plott, for extirpating the Protestant religion and old English liberty, and the introducing Popery and slavery.

It was this that made Pope refer to it as:

> London's column pointing at the skies
> Like a tall bully, lifts the head, and lies.
>
> *Moral Essays*, III, 339.

Monuments and effigies in churches. The following points usually apply:

Founders of chapels, etc., lie with their monument built into the wall.

Figures with their hands on their breasts, and chalices, represent *priests*.

Figures with armour represent *knights*.

Figures with legs crossed represent either *crusaders* or *married men*, but those with a SCALLOP SHELL are certainly *crusaders*.

Female figures with a mantle and large ring represent *nuns*.

In the age of CHIVALRY the woman was placed on the man's right hand; but when chivalry declined she was placed on his left hand.

It may usually be taken that ancient inscriptions in Latin, cut in capitals, are of the first twelve centuries; those in Lombardic capitals and French, of the 13th; those in Old English text, of the 14th; while those in the English language and roman characters are subsequent to the 14th century.

Tablets against the wall came in with the REFORMATION; and brasses are mostly post-13th century.

Monumental City. Baltimore, Maryland, is so called because of its many monuments, churches, etc.

Moody and Sankey. Dwight Lyman Moody (1836–1899) was the son of a Massachusetts bricklayer who began his evangelical work in 1860. He was joined by Ira David Sankey (1840–1908) in 1870, who backed up Moody's preaching with singing and organ music. The famous "Sankey and Moody hymn book", first published in 1873, properly called *Sacred Songs and Solos*, was "compiled and sung" by Sankey. Their type of "Gospel Hymn" was partly popularized in Great Britain during their visits to this country and particularly by the SALVATION ARMY.

Moon. The word is probably connected with the Sanskrit root *me-*, to measure, because time was measured by it. It is common to all Teutonic languages (Goth. *mena*; O.Frisian *mona*; O.Norm. *mane*; O.E. *mona*, etc.) and is almost invariably masculine. In the EDDA the son of Mundilfœri is MANI (moon), and daughter SOL (sun); so it is still with the Lithuanians and Arabians, and so it was with the ancient Slavs, Mexicans, Hindus, etc., and the Germans still have *Frau Sonne* (Mrs. Sun) and *Herr Mond* (Mr. Moon).

The moon is represented in five different phases: (1) new; (2) full; (3) crescent or decrescent; (4) half; and (5) gibbous, or more than half. In pictures of the ASSUMPTION it is shown as a crescent under Our Lady's feet; in the Crucifixion it is eclipsed, and placed on one side of the CROSS, the SUN being on the other; in the Creation and Last JUDGMENT it is also depicted.

In classical mythology the moon was known as HECATE before she had risen and after she had set; as ASTARTE when crescent; as DIANA or CYNTHIA (she who "hunts the clouds") when in the open vault of heaven; as PHŒBE when looked upon as the sister of the sun (*i.e.* PHŒBUS); and was personified as SELENE or Luna, the lover of the sleeping ENDYMION, *i.e.* moonlight on the fields.

The moon is called *triform*, because it presents itself to us either round, or waxing with horns towards the east, or waning with horns towards the west.

One legend connected with the moon was that there was treasured everything wasted on earth, such as misspent time and wealth, broken vows, unanswered prayers, fruitless tears, unfulfilled desires and intentions, etc. In ARIOSTO'S ORLANDO FURIOSO, Astolpho found on his visit to the moon (Bk. XXXIV, lxx) that bribes were hung on gold and silver hooks; princes' favours were kept in bellows; wasted talent was kept in vases, each marked with the proper name, etc.; and in *The Rape of the Lock* (canto V) Pope tells us that when the Lock disappeared—

Some thought it mounted to the lunar sphere,
Since all things lost on earth are treasured there,
There heroes' wits are kept in pondr'ous vases,
And beaux' in snuff-boxes and tweezer-cases.
There broken vows and death-bed alms are found
And lovers' hearts with ends of riband bound,
The courtier's promises, and sick man's prayers,
The smiles of harlots, and the tears of heirs,
Cages for gnats, and chains to yoke a flea,
Dried butterflies, and tomes of casuistry.

Hence the phrase, the **limbus of the moon**. *Cp.* LIMBO.

The cycle of the moon. *See under* CYCLE.

The island of the moon. Madagascar is so named by the natives.

Mahomet and the moon. *See* MOHAMMED.

The man in the moon. Some say it is a man leaning on a fork, on which he is carrying a bundle of sticks picked up on a Sunday. The origin of this fable is from *Numb.* xv, 32–36. Some add a dog also; thus SHAKESPEARE'S *Midsummer Night's Dream* (V, i) says:

This man with lantern, dog, and bush of thorn,
Presenteth moonshine.

Another tradition says that the man is Cain, with his dog and thorn bush; the thorn bush being emblematical of the thorns and briars of the fall, and the dog being the "foul fiend". Some poets make out the "man" to be ENDYMION, taken to the moon by DIANA.

Minions of the moon. Thieves who rob by night (*See* SHAKESPEARE: *Henry IV, Pt. I*, I, ii).

Moon's men. Thieves and highwaymen who ply their trade by night.

The fortune of us that are Moon's-men doth ebb and flow like the sea.

SHAKESPEARE: *Henry IV, Pt. I*, I, ii.

The Mountains of the Moon means simply White Mountains. The Arabs call a white horse "moon-coloured".

I know no more about it than the man in the moon. I know nothing at all about the matter.

Once in a blue moon. *See* BLUE MOON *under* BLUE.

To aim, or **level at the moon.** To be very ambitious, as to aim, in shooting, at the moon.

To be over the moon. To be highly excited, extremely delighted, in raptures over something.

To cast beyond the moon. *See* CAST.

To cry for the moon. To crave for what is wholly beyond one's reach. The allusion is to foolish children who "cry for the moon to play with". The French say *Il veut prendre la lune avec les dents* (He wants to take the moon between his teeth), alluding to the old proverb about the "moon" and a "green cheese".

You have found an elephant in the

moon. You have found a MARE'S NEST. Sir Paul Neale, a conceited virtuoso of the 17th century, gave out that he had discovered "an elephant in the moon". It turned out that a mouse had crept into his telescope, and had been mistaken for an elephant in the moon. Samuel Butler has a satirical poem on the subject called *The Elephant in the Moon*.

You would have me believe that the moon is made of green cheese—*i.e.* the most absurd thing imaginable.

> You may as soon persuade some Country Peasants, that the Moon is made of Green Cheese (as we say) as that 'tis bigger than his Cart-wheel.
>
> WILKINS: *New World*, I (1638).

Moon-calf. An inanimate, shapeless abortion, formerly supposed to be produced prematurely owing to the malign influence of the moon; also a dolt or dunderhead.

> I hid me under the dead moon-calf's gaberdine for fear of the storm.
>
> SHAKESPEARE: *The Tempest*, II, ii.

Moon-drop. In Latin, *virus lunare*, a vaporous foam supposed anciently to be shed by the moon on certain herbs and objects, when influenced by incantations.

> Upon the corner of the moon
> There hangs a vaporous drop profound;
> I'll catch it ere it come to ground.
>
> SHAKESPEARE: *Macbeth*, III, v.

Cp. Lucan's *Pharsalia*, vi, 699, where Erichtho is introduced using it:

> Et virus large lunare ministrat.

Moonies. A religious sect, properly called the *Unification Church*, founded by Sun Myung Moon in South Korea in 1954. It spread to the U.S.A. in the 1960s and subsequently to Great Britain, Australia, etc. Moon claims to be the Second MESSIAH and his devotees will save mankind from SATAN. Funds built up by his followers by selling artificial flowers and other items were used by Moon to create a large property and business organization in America where he has dwelt since 1972. Tax avoidance led to his prosecution and imprisonment (1984–1985).

Moonlight. A moonlight flit. A clandestine removal of one's furniture during the night, to avoid paying one's rent or having the furniture seized in payment thereof.

Moonlighting. In the Ireland of former days, the name given to acts of agrarian violence at night. In Australia, riding after cattle by night and, in the U.S.A., holding a night job in addition to one's regular employment. In Great Britain the term is now somewhat loosely applied to the additional employment outside regular working hours predominantly undertaken by building workers, craftsmen, electricians, etc.; also

to undeclared employment by the registered unemployed. The employer usually pays in cash and tax evasion is thus possible.

Moonrakers. A nickname of Wiltshire folk; also of simpletons. From the story that Wiltshire yokels, with typical country guile, when raking a pond for kegs of smuggled brandy, feigned stupidity when surprised by the excise men, and said that they were trying to rake out the moon, which was reflected in the water.

Moonshine. In the U.S.A., especially Florida, a colloquial term for illicitly distilled liquor, the keeper of an illicit still being called a *moonshiner*. The liquor, called "corn", "shine", or "white lightning", is made from maize, sugar, and water. *See* BOOTLEGGER. In general colloquial usage the word means "nonsense", as in the phrase *It's all moonshine*; here the allusion is to the supposed effects of moonlight on mental stability. *Cp.* LUNATIC.

Moonstone. A variety of feldspar, so called on account of the play of light which it exhibits. It contains bluish-white spots, which, when held to the light, present a silvery play of colour not unlike that of the MOON.

Moor. The word is from Gr. and Lat. *Maurus*, an inhabitant of MAURITANIA. In the MIDDLE AGES, Europeans called all Mohammedans *Moors*, similarly the Eastern nations called all Europeans *Franks*. Camoëns, in the LUSIADS (Bk. VIII), gives the name to the Indians.

Moor-slayer, or **Mata-moros.** A name given to St. JAMES, the patron saint of Spain, because, as the legends say, in encounters with the Moors he came on his white horse to the aid of the Christians. *See also* MATAMORE.

Moot (O.E. *gemot*, a meeting). In Anglo-Saxon times, the assembly of freemen in a township, TITHING, etc. The main moots were those of the SHIRE and HUNDRED which served as units of local government. In a few towns, *e.g.* Aldeburgh, Suffolk, the town hall is still called the Moot Hall. *Cp.* WITENAGEMOT. In legal circles the name is given to the students' debates on supposed cases which formerly took place in the halls of the INNS OF COURT. The benchers and BARRISTERS took part, as well as the students.

Moot case, or **moot point.** A doubtful or unsettled question; one that is open to debate.

Mop, or **Mop Fair.** A statute or HIRING FAIR (*see under* FAIR). So called from the "mop" (a turf or tassel) worn as a badge by those seeking hire. Carters fastened a piece of whipcord to their hats; shepherds, a lock of wool; grooms, a piece of sponge, etc.

All mops and brooms. Intoxicated.

Mops and mows. Grimaces; here mop is connected with Dut. *moppen*, to pout.

Mopping-up operations. In military parlance means the final reduction of isolated pockets of enemy resistance.

Moral. The Moral Gower. John Gower (*c.* 1325–1408), the poet, is so called by Chaucer (*Troilus and Criseyde*, V).

Father of Moral Philosophy. St. THOMAS AQUINAS (*c.* 1225–1274).

Moral Re-armament (M.R.A.). A movement founded in 1938 by Frank Buchman, who had earlier founded the OXFORD GROUP. Its purpose is to counter the MATERIALISM of present-day society by persuading people to live according to the highest standards of morality and love, to obey God, and to unite in a worldwide association according to these principles.

Morality Play. An allegorical dramatic form in vogue from the 15th to the 16th centuries in which the vices (*see* SEVEN DEADLY SINS) and VIRTUES were personified and the victory of the latter clearly established. It was a development from the earlier MYSTERY Plays. EVERYMAN, a 15th-century play translated from the Dutch *Elkerlijk*, is the best-known. *Cp.* PASSION PLAY.

Moran's Collar. In Irish folk-tale, the collar of Moran, the wise councillor of King Feredach the Just, which strangled the wearer if he deviated from the strict rules of equity.

Moravians. A PROTESTANT Church which is a direct continuation of the BOHEMIAN BRETHREN. Theirs is a simple and unworldly form of religion and John Wesley was influenced by them. They are now to be found in Denmark, Holland, Germany, Switzerland, Great Britain, and America.

More. More or less. Approximately; in round numbers, etc.; as, "It is ten miles, more or less, from here to there," *i.e.*, "it is about ten miles."

The more one has, the more one desires, or **wants.** In French, *Plus il en a, plus il en veut.* In Latin, *Quo plus habent, eo plus cupiunt.*

> My more having would be a source
> To make me hunger more.
>
> SHAKESPEARE: *Macbeth*, IV, iii.

The more the merrier, the fewer the better cheer, or **fare.** The proverb is found in Heywood's *Collection* (1546) and Ray's (1670).

To be no more. To exist no longer; to be dead.

> Cassius is no more.
>
> SHAKESPEARE: *Julius Cæsar*, V, iii.

More of More Hall. *See* WANTLEY, DRAGON OF.

Morgan Le Fay. The fairy sister of King ARTHUR, a principal figure in CELTIC legend and ARTHURIAN ROMANCE, also known as *Morgane, Morganetta, Morgaine, Morgue la Faye* and (especially in ORLANDO FURIOSO) as *Morgana. See* FATA MORGANA.

It was Morgan le Fay who revealed to King Arthur the intrigues of LANCELOT and GUINEVERE. She gave him a cup containing a magic draught and he had no sooner drunk it than his eyes were opened to the perfidy of his wife and friend.

In *Orlando Furioso*, she is represented as living at the bottom of a lake, and dispensing her treasures to whom she liked. In ORLANDO INNAMORATO, she first appears as "Lady Fortune", but subsequently assumes her witch-like attributes. In TASSO, her three daughters, Morganetta, Nivetta, and Carvilia, are introduced.

In the romance of OGIER THE DANE she receives Ogier in the Isle of AVALON when he is over 100 years old, restores him to youth, and becomes his bride.

Morganatic Marriage. One between a man of high (usually royal) rank and a woman of lower station, as a result of which she does not acquire the husband's rank and neither she nor any children of the marriage are entitled to inherit the title or possessions; often called a "left-handed marriage" because the custom is for the man to pledge his troth with his left hand instead of his right. George William, Duke of Zell, married Eleanora d'Esmiers in this way, and she took the name and title of Lady Harburg; her daughter was Sophia Dorothea, the wife of George I. George, Duke of Cambridge (1819–1904), cousin of Queen Victoria, contracted a morganatic marriage in 1840. His children took the surname Fitz-George. The word comes from the Med. Lat. phrase *matrimonium ad morganaticam*, the last word representing O.H. Ger. *morgangeba*, the morning-gift, from husband to wife after the consummation of the marriage, and the wife's only claim to her husband's possessions.

Morgane, Morganetta. *See* MORGAN LE FAY.

Morgante Maggiore (môr gan' te mà̇jôr' è). A serio-comic romance in verse by Pulci of Florence (1482). The characters had appeared previously in many old romances; Morgante is a ferocious giant, converted by ORLANDO (the real hero) to Christianity. After performing the most wonderful feats, he dies at last from the bite of a crab.

Pulci was practically the inventor of this

burlesque form of poetry, called by the French BERNESQUE, from the Italian, Berni (1497–1535), who excelled in it.

Morgiana (môr ji ăn' à). In the ARABIAN NIGHTS (*Ali Baba and the Forty Thieves*), the clever, faithful slave of ALI BABA, who pries into the forty jars and discovers every jar but one contains a man. She takes the oil from the only jar containing it, and having made it boiling hot, pours enough into each jar to kill the thief therein. Finally she kills the captain of the gang and marries her master's son.

Morgue la Faye. The form of the name MORGAN LE FAY in OGIER THE DANE.

Morley, Mrs. The name under which Queen Anne corresponded with "Mrs. Freeman" (Sarah Churchill, Duchess of Marlborough).

Mormons. Properly the *Church of Jesus Christ of Latter-Day Saints* regarding itself as a restoration of the one and only Gospel of Christ.

Joseph Smith (1805–1844), a farmer's son of Western New York, claimed in 1820 that God the Father and his Son Jesus Christ had appeared to him and in 1823 that an account of the early inhabitants of America and of the everlasting Gospel inscribed on gold plates had been revealed to him and subsequently, in 1827, these plates were delivered to him. The result was the *Book of Mormon* produced at Palmyra, New York, in 1830, the book taking its name from the prophet Mormon, who had condensed earlier plates. In the same year Smith and his associates founded the Church. Smith was later murdered by a mob when imprisoned by his enemies in Carthage, Illinois, and his place was taken by Brigham Young (1801–1877), a carpenter. He led the persecuted "Saints" to the valley of the Salt Lake, 1,500 miles distant, generally called Utah, but by the Mormons, *Deseret* (Bee-country) the New Jerusalem where they have been settled since 1847, despite many disputes with the U.S. Government.

The Mormons accept the BIBLE as well as the *Book of Mormon* as authoritative, they hold doctrines of repentance and faith, that Zion will be built on the American continent, and believe in baptism, the EUCHARIST, the physical resurrection of the dead, and in the Second ADVENT when Christ will have the seat of His power in Utah. Marriage may be for "time and eternity". Popularly associated with polygamy the Mormons practised it until 1890 when the U.S. Supreme Court finally declared against it and this was accepted by the Church. Hence

the expression **a regular Mormon** for a promiscuous or flighty person who cannot keep to one wife or sweetheart.

After Smith's death those who refused to recognize Brigham Young's presidency subsequently established the *Reorganized Church of Jesus Christ of Latter-Day Saints* at Wisconsin in 1852. Notably it rejected polygamy, claiming that it was introduced by Brigham Young, and also that it is the true successor of the original Church. Its headquarters are now at Independence, Missouri.

Mormon missionaries first arrived in Britain in 1837 and there are now some 350 congregations in the United Kingdom following a strict code of behaviour and self-sufficiency.

Morning. The first glass of whisky drunk by Scottish fishermen in salutation to the dawn.

Morning Star. Byron's name for Mary Chaworth, his charming neighbour at Newstead, with whom he was in love early in his life.

Morning Star of the Reformation. John Wyclif (*c.* 1324–1384).

Morocco. Strong ale made from burnt malt, used in the annual feast at Levens Hall, Westmorland, on the opening of Milnthorpe Fair. It was put into a large glass of unique form, and the person whose turn it was to drink (called the "colt") had to "drink the constable", *i.e.* stand on one leg and say "Luck to Levens as long as Kent flows", then drain the glass or pay a forfeit. The custom ended in the late 1870s.

Morocco men. Men who, about the end of the 18th century, used to visit public-houses touting for illegal lottery insurances. Their rendezvous was a tavern in Oxford Market, at the Oxford Street end of Great Portland Street.

Moros. The name of the MOSLEM inhabitants of the island of Mindanao and the Sulu Archipelago in the Philippine Islands, and applied to them by the Spanish conquerors because of their supposed resemblance to MOORS.

Morpheus. Ovid's name for the son of Sleep, and god of dreams; so called from Gr. *morphe*, form, because he gives these airy nothings their form and fashion. Hence the name of the narcotic, *morphine*, or *morphia*.

Morrice, Gil, or **Childe.** The hero of an old Scottish ballad, a natural son of an earl and the wife of Lord Barnard, and brought up "in gude grene wode". Lord Barnard, thinking the Childe to be his wife's lover, slew him with a broadsword, and setting his head on a spear gave it to "the meanest man in a' his train" to carry to the lady. When she saw it she said to the baron, "Wi' that saim speir, O pierce my heart, and put me out o' pain"; but the baron replied, "Enouch of blood by me's bin spilt ... sair, sair I rew the deid," adding:

> I'll ay lament for Gill Morice,
> As gin he were mine ain;
> I'll neir forget the dreiry day
> On which the youth was slain.
>
> PERCY: *Reliques (Gil Morrice)*, xxvi.

Percy says this pathetic tale suggested to Home the plot of his tragedy, *Douglas*.

Morris Dance. A dance, popular in England in the 15th century and later, in which the dancers often represented characters from the ROBIN HOOD stories (*see* MAID MARIAN). Other stock characters were Bavian the fool, MALKIN the clown, the HOBBY-HORSE, or a DRAGON, and foreigners, probably MOORS or Moriscos. It was commonly part of the MAY-games and other pageants and festivals and the dancers were adorned with bells. It was brought from Spain in the reign of Edward III, and was originally a military dance of the Moors or Moriscos, hence its name.

Nine Men's Morris. An ancient game (similar to draughts) once popular with shepherds, still found in East Anglia, and either played on a board or on flat greensward. Two persons have each nine pieces or "men" which they place down alternately on

the spots (*see* diagram), and the aim of either player is to secure a row of three men on any line on the board, and to prevent his opponent achieving this by putting one of his own men on a line which looks like being completed, etc. Strutt says , "The rustics, when they have not materials at hand to make a table, cut the lines in the same form upon the ground, and make a small hole for every dot."

> The fold stands, empty in the drowned field,
> And crows are fatted with the murrain flock;
> The nine men's morris is fill'd up with mud.
>
> SHAKESPEARE: *A Midsummer Night's Dream*, II, ii.

It is also called *Merelles*.

Mortal. A mortal sin. A "deadly" sin, one which deserves everlasting punishment; opposed to VENIAL.

> Earth trembled from her entrails ... some sad drops
> Wept at completing of the mortal Sin
> Original; while Adam took no thought.
>
> MILTON: *Paradise Lost*, IX, 1003.

In slang and colloquial speech the word is used to express something very great or excessive, as, "He's in a mortal funk", "There was a mortal lot of people there", or as an emphatic expletive, "you can do any mortal thing you like."

Mortar-board. A college CAP surmounted by a square "board" usually covered with black cloth. The word is possibly connected with Fr. *mortier*, the cap worn by the ancient kings of France, and still used officially by the chief justice or president of the court of justice. It is perhaps more likely an allusion to the small square board or hawk on which a bricklayer or plasterer carries his mortar. *See* PHARISEES.

Morte d'Arthur, Le. *See* ARTHURIAN ROMANCES.

Morther. *See* MAUTHER.

Mortmain (O.Fr., Lat. *mortua manus*, dead hand). A term applied to land that was held inalienably by ecclesiastical or other corporations. In the 13th century, it was common for persons to make over their land to the Church and then receive it back as tenants, thus escaping their feudal obligations to the king or other lay lords.

In 1279 the Statute of Mortmain was passed prohibiting the practice without the king's licence.

Morton's Fork. John Morton (*c*. 1420–1500), CARDINAL and Archbishop of Canterbury and minister of Henry VII, when levying forced loans or BENEVOLENCES from rich men so arranged that none should escape. Those who were ostentatiously rich were forced to contribute on the ground that they could well afford it, those who lived without display on the ground that their economies must mean they had savings. The argument was dubbed "Morton's fork", which was two-pronged.

Mortstone. A rock off Morte Point, Devon.

He may remove Mortstone. A Devonshire proverb, said incredulously of husbands who pretend to be masters of their wives. It also means, "If you have done what you say, you can accomplish anything".

Mortuary. Formerly a gift of the second best beast of the deceased to the incumbent of the parish church, later of the first or second best possession. In due course mortuaries became fees and in 1529 PARLIAMENT limited them to moderate amounts. The custom lingered on in some parishes into the 18th century.

Mosaic Law. The laws given in the PENTATEUCH including the Ten Commandments.

Moses. The horns of Moses' face. Moses is conventionally represented with horns, owing to a blunder in translation. In *Exod.* xxxiv, 29, 30, where we are told that when Moses came down from Mount Sinai "the skin of his face shone", the Hebrew for this *shining* may be translated either as "*sent forth beams*" or "sent forth *horns*"; and the VULGATE took the latter as correct, rendering the passage: *quod cornuta esset facies sua*. *Cp. Hab.* iii, 4, "His brightness was as the light; he had horns [rays of light] coming out of his hand."

MICHAEL ANGELO followed the earlier painters in depicting Moses with horns.

Moses boat. A type of boat made at Salisbury, Massachusetts, by a famous boat-builder, Moses Lowell, in the 18th century. Farther south (in the West Indies), it is said to have been a boat of sufficient capacity to take a hogshead of sugar from shore to ship in one trip.

Moses' rod. The DIVINING ROD is sometimes so called, after the rod with which Moses worked wonders before Pharaoh (*Exod.* vii, 9), or the rod with which he smote the rock to bring forth water (*Exod.* xvii, 6).

Moslem, or **Muslim** (moz' lem, mŭz' lim). A Mohammedan, the president participle of Arab. *aslama*, to be safe, or at rest, whence ISLAM. The Arabic plural *Moslemin* is sometimes used, but *Moslems* is more common, and in English more correct.

Mosstrooper. A robber, a bandit; applied especially to the marauders who infested the borders of ENGLAND and SCOTLAND, who encamped on the *mosses* (O.E. *mos*, a bog).

Most. Most unkindest cut of all. Treachery from a friend; the proverbial "last straw". From SHAKESPEARE's *Julius Cæsar* (III, ii). When Mark Antony was showing the dagger cuts in Cæsar's mantle he thus referred to the thrust made by BRUTUS, whom he described as "Cæsar's angel".

> For when the noble Cæsar saw him stab,
> Ingratitude, more strong than traitor's arms,
> Quite vanquished him.

Mothball ships. Ships placed in reserve are so called from the post-World War II practice of spraying a plastic covering or cocoon over gun-mountings and other working parts, etc.

Mother. Properly a female parent (Sansk. *mātr*; Gr. *mētēr*; Lat. *mater*; O.E. *mōdor*; Ger. *Mutter*; Fr. *mère*; etc.) hence, figuratively, the origin of anything, the head or headquarters of a religious or other community, the source of, etc.

Mother is the name given to a stringy gummy substance, sometimes called *mother of vinegar*, which forms on the surface of a liquor undergoing acetous fermentation, consisting of the bacteria which are causing that fermentation.

Mother Ann, Bunch, Goose, Shipton, etc. *See* these names.

Mother Carey's Chickens. Sailor's name for stormy petrels, probably derived from *mater cara* or *madre cara* ("mother dear", with reference to the Virgin Mary). Sailors also call falling snow *Mother Carey's Chickens*. See Marryat's *Poor Jack* for an account of sailors' superstitions on such matters.

Mother Carey's Goose. The great black petrel or fulmar of the Pacific.

Mother Carey is plucking her goose. It is snowing. *Cp.* HULDA.

Mother Church. The church considered as the central fact, the head, the last court of appeal in all matters pertaining to conscience or religion. St. John LATERAN, at ROME, is known as the *Mother and Head of all churches,* Also, the principal or oldest church in a country or district; the cathedral of a diocese.

Mother country. One's native country; or the country whence one's ancestors came to settle. England is the *Mother country* of Australia, New Zealand, Canada, etc. The German term is *Fatherland*.

Mother Earth. When Junius BRUTUS (after the death of Lucretia) formed one of the deputation to DELPHI to ask the ORACLE which of the three would succeed TARQUIN, the response was, "He who should first kiss his mother." Junius instantly threw himself on the ground, exclaiming, "Thus, then, I kiss thee, Mother Earth", and he was elected consul.

Mothering Sunday. MID-LENT SUNDAY, LÆTARE SUNDAY, when the POPE blesses the GOLDEN ROSE, children feast on mothering cakes and SIMNEL CAKES. A bunch of violets is emblematic of this day, and it is customary for children to give small presents to their mothers. It is said that it is derived from the pre-Reformation custom of visiting the MOTHER CHURCH on that day. Children away from home, especially daughters in service, normally returned to their family.

The Mother of Believers. Among Mohammedans, AYESHA, the second and favourite wife of MOHAMMED, who was called the "Father of Believers". Mohammed's widows are also sometimes called "mothers of believers".

The Mother of Cities (Umm-al-Bulud). Balkh is so called.

Mother of Presidents. The state of Virginia. George Washington, first President of the U.S.A. (1789–1796), was a Virginian.

Mother's Day. In the U.S.A. the second Sunday in MAY is observed to remember one's mother by some act of grateful affection. In schools the preceding Friday is so observed. *Cp.* MOTHERING SUNDAY.

Mothers' meeting. A meeting of mothers held periodically in connexion with some church or denomination, at which the women can get advice or religious instruction, drink tea, gossip, and sometimes do needlework. Hence, facetiously, a gossiping group of people—men as well as women.

Mother's ruin. A nickname for GIN.

Mother's Union. A CHURCH OF ENGLAND women's society to safeguard and strengthen Christian family life, to uphold the lifelong vows of marriage, and generally to play a proper part in the life of the Church. It was incorporated by Royal Charter in 1926 and generally operates as a parish institution.

Does your mother know you're out? A jeering remark addressed to a presumptuous youth or to a simpleton. It is the title of a comic poem published in the *Mirror*, 28 April 1838. It became a catch phrase both in England and America and occurs in Barham's *Ingoldsby Legends* (*Misadventures at Margate*).

Oh mother, look at Dick! Said in derision when someone is showing off, or doing something easy with the intent of being applauded for his skill.

Tied to one's mother's apron-strings. *See under* APRON.

Mother-of-pearl. The inner iridescent layers of the shells of many bivalve molluscs, especially that of the pearl oyster.

Mother-sick. Hysterical. Hysteria in women used to be known as "the mother". It also means "pining for one's mother".

> She [Lady Bountiful] cures rheumatisms, ruptures and broken shins in men; green sickness, obstructions, and fits of the mother in women; the king's evil ... etc.
>
> FARQUHAR: *The Beaux' Stratagem*, I, i.

Mother-wit. Native wit, a ready reply; the wit which "our mother gave us".

Motion. The laws of motion, according to Galileo and Newton, are:

(1) If no force acts on a body in motion, it will continue to move uniformly in a straight line.

(2) If force acts on a body, it will produce a change of motion proportionate to the force, and in the same direction (as that in which the force acts).

(3) When one body exerts force on another, that other body reacts on it with equal and opposite force.

Motley. Men of Motley. Licensed fools; so called from their dress.

> Motley's the only wear.
>
> SHAKESPEARE: *As You Like It*, II, vii.

Motu proprio (Lat.). Of one's own motion; of one's own accord. Always applied to a rescript drawn up and issued by the POPE on his own initiative without the advice of others, and signed by him.

Mountain. The Mountain (Fr. *La Montagne*). The JACOBINS and extremists in the National Assembly at the time of the French Revolution, so called because they occupied the topmost benches on the left. Among its leaders were Robespierre, Danton, Marat, Collot-d'Herbois, Camille Desmoulins, Carnot, and St. Just. They gained ascendancy in the CONVENTION, supporting the execution of the king and the REIGN OF TERROR. The terms *Montagnard* and *Jacobin* were synonymous. Extreme RADICALS in France are still called *Montagnards Cp.* PLAIN.

> The Mountain, on the other hand, was resolved, less from ferocity than from calculation, that the king should die.
>
> LOUIS MADELIN: *The French Revolution*, ch. xxv.

Mountain Ash. *See* ROWAN.

Mountain-devil. The thorn lizard or thorn devil, *Moloch horridus*, a native of Australia, a grotesque and hideous reptile.

Tasmanians are nicknamed *mountain-devils*, and also called *Tassies* and *Apple-islanders*.

Mountain dew. Scotch whisky; formerly that from illicit stills hidden away in the mountains. *Cp.* MOONSHINE.

If the mountain will not come to Mohammed. *See under* MOHAMMED.

The mountain in labour. A mighty effort made for a small effect. The allusion is to the celebrated line "*Parturient montes, nascetur ridiculus mus*" (Mountains will be in labour and the birth will be a funny little mouse) by HORACE (*Ars Poetica*, 139). A similar quotation occurs in ÆSOP. Creech translates Horace, "The travailing mountain yields a silly mouse"; and Boileau, "*La montagne en travail enfante une souris*".

There is a story that the Egyptian king, Tachos, sustained a long war against Artaxerxes Ochus, and sent to the Lacedæmonians for aid. King Agesilaus went with a contingent, but when Tachos saw a little, ill-dressed, lame man, he said: "*Parturiebat mons; formidavat Jupiter; ille vero murem peperit.*" ("The Mountain laboured, JUPITER stood aghast, and a mouse ran out.") Agesilaus replied, "You call me a mouse, but I will soon show you I am a lion."

The Old Man of the Mountains (*Sheikh-al-Jebal*). Hasan ibn-al-Sabbah, or Hassan ben Sabbah, the founder of the ASSASSINS, who made his stronghold in the mountain fastnesses of Lebanon. He led an Ismaili revival against the SELJUKS and by the end of the 11th century his terrorists were well established throughout Persia and Iraq.

To make mountains out of molehills. To make a difficulty of trifles. Lat. *Arcem ex cloaca facere.* The corresponding French proverb is, *Faire d'une mouche un éléphant.*

Mountebank (Ital. *montambanco*). A vendor of quack medicines at FAIRS, etc., who attracts the crowd by his tricks and antics; hence any CHARLATAN or self-advertising pretender. The BANK, or bench, was the counter on which traders displayed their goods, and street-vendors used to *mount* on their *bank* to patter to the public.

Mourning. *Black.* To express the privation of light and joy, the midnight gloom of sorrow for the loss sustained. The colour of mourning in Europe; also in ancient Greece and the Roman Empire.

Black and white striped. To express sorrow and hope. The mourning of the South Sea Islanders.

Greyish-brown. The colour of the earth to which the dead return.

Pale brown. The colour of withered leaves. The mourning of Persia.

Sky blue. To express the assured hope that the deceased has gone to HEAVEN; used in Syria, Armenia, etc.

Deep blue. The colour of mourning in Bokhara, also that of the Romans of the Republic.

Purple and violet. To express royalty, "kings and priests to God". The colour of mourning for CARDINALS and the kings of France; in Turkey the colour is violet.

White. Emblem of "white-handed hope". Used by the ladies of ancient ROME and Sparta, also in Spain till the end of the 15th century. Henry VIII wore white for Anne Boleyn.

Yellow. The sere and yellow leaf. The colour of mourning in Egypt and in Burma, where it is also the colour of the monastic order. In Brittany, widows' caps among the *paysannes* are yellow. Anne Boleyn wore yellow mourning for Katharine of Aragon. Some say yellow is in token of exaltation. *See also* BLACK CAP.

Mournival. *See* GLEEK.

Mouse. The soul was of often anciently supposed to pass at death through the mouth of man in some animal form, sometimes a mouse or rat. A red mouse indicated a pure soul; a black mouse, a polluted soul; a pigeon or dove, a saintly soul.

Mouse is also slang for a black eye, and was formerly a common term of endearment, like *bird, birdie; duckie* and *lamb*.

> "God bless you, mouse," the bridegroom said,
> And smakt her on the lips.
>
> WARNER:*Albion's England*, II, x (1592).

It's a bold mouse that nestles in the cat's ear. Said of one who is taking an unnecessary risk. The proverb appears in Herbert's *Collection* (1640).

Poor as a church mouse. *See* POOR.

The mouse that hath but one hole is quickly taken. Have two strings to your BOW. The proverb occurs in Herbert's *Collection* (1640) and in many European languages. In Latin it was *Mus non uni fidit antro*, the mouse does not trust to one hole.

When the cat's away the mice will play. *See under* CAT.

The Mouse Tower. A mediæval watchtower on the Rhine, near Bingen, so called from the tradition that Archbishop HATTO was there devoured by mice. Actually it was built by Bishop Siegfried 200 years after Hatto's death, as a toll-house. The German *Maut* means "toll" (mouse is *Maus*), and the similarity of these words together with the unpopularity of the toll on corn gave rise to the legend.

Mousterian. A name given to the epoch of NEANDERTHAL MAN, from the cave of Le Moustier near Les Eyzies, on the right bank of the Vézère in France, where PALÆOLITHIC remains were found.

Mouth, Down in the mouth. *See* DOWN.

His heart was in his mouth. *See under* HEART.

His mouth was made. He was trained or reduced to obedience, like a horse trained to the bit.

> At first, of course, the fireworker showed fight ... but in the end "his mouth was made", his paces formed, and he became a very serviceable and willing animal.
>
> LEFANU:*House in the Churchyard*, ch. xcix.

Hold your mouth! or **Stop your mouth!** A rougher equivalent of "hold your tongue" be silent.

That makes my mouth water. The fragrance of appetizing food excites the salivary glands. The phrase means—that makes me long for it or desire it.

To be born with a silver spoon in one's mouth. *See under* BORN.

To laugh on the wrong side of one's face or **mouth.** *See under* LAUGH.

To live from hand to mouth. *See under* HAND.

To look a gift horse in the mouth. *See* GIFT-HORSE.

To make a mouth. To pull a wry face, to pout; to distort one's mouth in mockery.

To mouth one's words. To talk affectedly or pompously; to declaim.

> He mouths a sentence as curs mouth a bone.
> CHURCHILL: *The Rosciad*, 322.

To open one's mouth wide. To name too high a price; to strain after too big a prize.

To place oneself, or **one's head in the lion's mouth.** *See under* LION.

Moutons. Revenons à nos moutons (Fr., "Let us come back to our sheep"). A phrase used to express "Let us return to the subject". It is taken from the 14th century French comedy *La Farce de Maître Pathelin,* or *l'Avocat Pathelin* (line 1282), in which a woollen-draper charges a shepherd with ill-treating his sheep. In telling his story he continually ran away from the subject; and to throw discredit on the defendant's attorney (Pathelin), accused him of stealing a piece of cloth. The judge had to pull him up every moment, with "*Mais, mon ami, revenons à nos moutons*". The phrase is frequently quoted by Rabelais. *See* ENFANTS SANS SOUCI *under* SANS SOUCI.

Movable. The first movable. *See* PRIMUM MOBILE.

Movable Feasts. Annual church feasts which do not fall on a fixed date but are determined by certain established rules. EASTER Day is a notable example.

Move. Give me where to stand, and I will move the world. So said ARCHIMEDES of Syracuse; and the instrument he would have used is the lever.

To move the adjournment of the House (*i.e.* the HOUSE OF COMMONS). The House normally adjourns at the end of a day's sitting until the next day and motions of adjournment were formerly much used to hold up business. This form of obstruction is now prevented by STANDING ORDERS (*see under* STAND), etc. It is still open to a member "to move the adjournment on a definite matter of urgent public importance", although now a rare occurrence, and it can be disallowed by the SPEAKER. It is also customary to leave half an hour at the end of the day to allow M.P.s to raise matters "on the adjournment", thus giving scope for general debate and criticism. Occasionally the Government moves the adjournment after question-time as a concession to the Opposition and Private Members, thus leaving the day for discussion.

To move the previous question. *See under* QUESTION.

Mow (mō). The three *mows* in English are wholly distinct words. *Mow*, a heap of hay, etc. ("the barley-mow"), is O.E. *mūga*, connected with Icel. *müge*, a swath. *Mow*, to cut down grass, corn, etc., is O.E. *māwan* connected with Ger. *mähen*, Gr. *amân*, and Lat. *mětere*, to reap. *Mow*, to grimace (in "mops and mows"), is Fr. *moue*, a pout or grimace.

Much. The miller's son in the ROBIN HOOD stories. In the MORRIS-DANCE he played the part of the Fool, and his great feat was to bang the head of the gaping spectators with a bladder of peas.

Muckle. Many a mickle makes a muckle. *See under* LITTLE.

Muddied Oafs. Footballers. *See* FLANNELLED FOOLS.

Muff. One who is awkward at games and sports, or who is effeminate, dull or stupid; probably a sneering allusion to the use of muffs to keep one's hands warm. The term does not seem to be older than the early 19th century, but there is a Sir Harry Muff in Dudley's interlude, *The Rival Candidates* (1774), a stupid, blundering dolt.

Muffins and Crumpets. Muffins is probably Fr. *pain-moufflet*, soft bread. Du Cange describes the *panis mofletus* as bread of a more delicate nature than ordinary, and says it was made fresh every day. *Crumpet*, the unsweetened soft cake, is a word of uncertain origin; *crumpet* is also slang for the head, also a "bit of stuff". *See under* BIT.

Mufti. An Arabic word meaning an official, expounder of the KORAN and Mohammedan law: thus the Mufti of JERUSALEM is the chief religious official of the Moslems of Jerusalem; but used in English to denote civil, as distinct from military or official costume. Our meaning dates from the early 19th century, and probably arose from the resemblance that the flowered dressing-gown and tasselled smoking-cap, worn by off-duty officers in their quarters, bore to the stage get-up of an Eastern Mufti.

As soon as our morning talks were done I gobbled a hasty luncheon, changed into plain clothes (we were taught to abhor the word 'mufti', and such abominable expressions as 'civvies' were in those days unknown).

W. S. CHURCHILL: *My Early Life*, ch. iv.

Mug. The word is used as slang for "face" and also for one who is easily taken in, possibly coming from the GYPSY meaning, a simpleton or MUFF. **To mug up,** meaning to study hard for a specific purpose, *e.g.* to pass an examination, is an old university phrase. It has been suggested that it comes from the theatre where an actor, while making up his face or "mug", would hurriedly con over his lines.

Mugging. Now the common term for assault followed by robbery. From the old slang use of *mug* meaning to rob or swindle.

Mug-house. An ale-house was so called in the 18th century where many people gathered in the large tap-room to drink, sing and spout, one of their number being made chairman. Ale was served to the company in their own mugs, and the place where the mug was to stand was chalked on the table.

Muggins. Slang for a fool or simpleton—a juggins. Possibly an allusion to MUG.

Muggletonian. A follower of Lodovic Muggleton (1609–1698), a journeyman tailor, who, about 1651, set up for a prophet. He was sentenced for blasphemous writings to stand in the pillory, and was fined £500. The members of the sect, which maintained some existence until *c.* 1865, believed that their two founders, Muggleton and John Reeve, were the "two witnesses" spoken of in *Rev.* xi, 3.

Mugwump. An Algonkin word meaning a chief; in Eliot's Indian BIBLE the word "centurion" in the *Acts* is rendered *mugwump*. It is now applied in the U.S.A. to independent members of the Republican Party, those who refuse to follow the dictates of a CAUCUS, and all political PHARISEES whose party vote cannot be relied upon. It is also used in the sense of "big shot" or "BOSS".

Mulatto (mū lăt′ ō) (Span., from *mulo*, a mule). The offspring of a Negress by a white man; loosely applied to any half-breed. *Cp.* CREOLE.

Sally Brown, she's a bright mulatter,
Way-ay-y, Roll and go,
She drinks rum and chews terbaccer,
Spend my money on Sally Brown.

Sea Shanty.

Mulberry. Fable has it that the fruit was originally white and became blood-red from the blood of PYRAMUS and Thisbe. In the LANGUAGE OF FLOWERS, Black Mulberry (*Morus nigra*) means "I shall not survive you" and White Mulberry (*Morus alba*) signifies "widsom". Culpeper says that the tree is ruled by MERCURY and it is noted as a vermifuge. The old Gloucestershire proverb says, "After the mulberry-tree has shown green leaf, there will be no more frost". Silkworms are fed on the leaves of the mulberry, especially the white mulberry. The Paper Mulberry (*Broussonetia papyrifera*) is so called from its use in Japan and the Far East for making paper with the pulped shoots.

In the SEVEN CHAMPIONS (Pt. I, ch. iv), Eglantine, daughter of the King of Thessaly, was transformed into a mulberry-tree. *See* PYRAMUS.

In World War II **Mulberry** was the code name given to the prefabricated ports towed across to the Normandy coast to make possible the supply of the Allied armies in France in 1944 consequent upon the D-DAY landings. Submersible sections of concrete formed a breakwater and quay alongside which the transports were unloaded. The name was chosen at the time because it was the next in rotation on the British Admiralty's list of names available for warships. Two such Mulberries were set up, but the one serving the U.S. beaches was wrecked by a storm (19 June); that serving the British beaches was kept in service until Antwerp became available.

Here we go round the mulberry bush. An old game in which children take hand and dance round in a ring, singing the song of which this is the refrain.

Mulberry-faced. A person with a reddish-purple face.

Hired animalisms, vile as though that made
The mulberry-faced Dictator's orgie worse
Than aught they fable of the quiet Gods.

TENNYSON: *Lucretius*.

Mulciber. Among the Romans, a name of VULCAN; it means the softener, because he softened metals.

And round about him [Mammon] lay on every side
Great heaps of gold that never could be spent;
Of which some were rude ore, not purified
Of Mulciber's devouring element.

SPENSER: *The Faerie Queene*, II, vii, 5.

Mule. The offspring of a male ASS and a mare; hence a hybrid between other animals (or plants), as a *mule canary*, a cross between a canary and a goldfinch. The offspring of a stallion and a she-*ass* is not, properly speaking, a mule, but a *hinny*.

Very stubborn or obstinate people are sometimes called *mules*, in allusion to the reputed characteristic of the beast.

Crompton's mule, or **the Spinning-mule,** was invented by Samuel Crompton

(1753–1827) in 1779. His invention was pirated at the outset and he derived little financial benefit from his efforts. It was so called because it was:

> a kind of mixture of machinery between the warp-machine of Mr. Arkwright and the woof-machine or hand-jenny of Mr. Hargrave.
> *Encyclopædia Britannica*, 1797.

To shoe one's mule. To appropriate moneys committed to one's trust.

> He had the keeping and disposall of the moneys, and yet shod not his own mule.
> *History of Francion*, III (1655).

Mull. To make a mull of a job is to fail to do it properly. It is either a contraction of *muddle*, or from the old verb *to mull*, to reduce to powder.

Anglo-Indians in the service of the Madras Presidency were known as *Mulls*. Here the word stands for *mulligatawny*.

Mulled ale. Ale spiced and warmed; similarly *mulled wine*, etc. Possibly from M.E. *mold-ale*, a funeral feast (*mold*, the earth, the grave), but the derivation is uncertain.

Mulla. The Bard of Mulla's silver stream. So Spenser was called by Shenstone, because at one time his home in Ireland was on the banks of the Mulla, or Awbeg, a tributary of the Blackwater.

Mullah (Arab. *maula*). A title of respect given by Mohammedans to religious dignitaries versed in the sacred law.

The Mad Mullah. A nickname given to Mohammed bin Abdullah, a mullah who gave great trouble to the British in Somaliland at various times between 1899 and 1920. He claimed to be the MAHDI and made extensive raids on tribes friendly to the British. The DERVISH power was not finally broken until 1920 when the Mad Mullah escaped to Ethiopia, where he died in 1921.

Mulligan. The word has several colloquial uses in the U.S.A.: (1) a stew; (2) a nickname for an Irishman; (3) underworld term for a policeman; (4) a second drive, allowed by your opponent on the first tee of a round of golf if you miss the first one.

Mulmutine Laws. *See* MOLMUTINE.

Mulready Envelope. An envelope resembling a half-sheet of letter-paper when folded, having on the front an ornamental design by William Mulready (1786–1863), the artist. These were the stamped penny postage envelopes introduced in 1840 but the Mulreadies remained in circulation for one year only owing to ridicule of their ludicrous design. They are prized by stamp-collectors.

> A set of those odd-looking envelope-things,
> Where Britannia (who seems to be crucified) flings

> To her right and left, funny people with wings
> Amongst elephants, Quakers, and Catabaw Kings,—
> And a taper and wax, and small Queen's-heads in packs,
> Which, when notes are too big, you're to stick on their backs.
> BARHAM: *Ingoldsby Legends*, II, *A Row in an Omnibus (Box)*.

Multipliers. So alchemists, who pretended to multiply GOLD and SILVER, were called. An act was passed (2 Henry IV, C. IV) making the "art of multiplication" a felony. In the *Canterbury Tales* (*Canon's Yeoman's Tale*), the Canon's YEOMAN says he was reduced to poverty by ALCHEMY, adding: "Lo, such advantage is't to multiply".

Multitude, Nouns of. Dame Juliana Berners, in her *Booke of St. Albans* (1486), says, in designating companies we must not use the names of multitudes promiscuously, and examples her remark thus:

> We say a congregacyon of people, a hoost of men, a felyshyppynge of yeomen, and a bevy of ladyes; we must speak of a herde of deer, swannys, cranys, or wrenys, a sege of herons or bytourys, a muster of pe-cockes, a watche of nyghtyngales, a flyghte of doves, a claterynge of choughes, a pryde of lyons, a slewthe of beeres, a gagle of geys, a skulke of foxes, a sculle of frerys, a pontificalitye of prestys, and a super-fluyte of nonnes.

She adds that a strict regard to these niceties better distinguishes "gentylmen from un-gentylmen", than regard to the rules of grammar, or even to the moral law. *See* AS-SEMBLAGE, NOUNS OF.

Multum in parvo (Lat., much in little). Much "information" condensed into few words or into a small compass.

Mum. A strong beer made in Brunswick; said to be so called from Christian Mumme by whom it was first brewed in the late 15th century.

Mum's the word. Keep what is told you a profound secret. *See* MUMCHANCE.

> Seal up your lips, and give no words but—mum.
> SHAKESPEARE: *Henry, VI, Pt. II*, I, ii.

To keep mum. To keep silent; not to speak or to tell anyone.

Mumbudget. An old exclamation meaning "Silence, please"; perhaps from a children's game in which silence was occasionally necessary. *Cp.* BUDGET; DRY; MUMCHANCE; NAY-WORD.

> Have these bones rattled, and this head
> So often in thy quarrel bled?
> No did I ever wince or grudge it,
> For thy dear sake. Quoth she, Mumbudget.
> BUTLER: *Hudibras*, I, iii, 208.

Mumchance. Silence. Mumchance was a game of chance with dice, in which silence was indispensable. *Mum* is connected with *mumble* (Ger. *mummeln*; Dan. *mumle*, to mumble). *Cp.* MUMBUDGET.

Also one who has nothing to say—

> Methinks you look like Mumchance, that was hanged
> For saying nothing.
>
> SWIFT: *Polite Conversation*, i.

Mumbo Jumbo. The name given by Europeans (possibly from some lost native word) to a BOGY or grotesque idol venerated by certain African tribes; hence any object of blind unreasoning worship.

Mungo Park, in his *Travels in the Interior of Africa* (1795–1797), says (ch. iii) that Mumbo Jumbo "is a strange bugbear, common to all Mandingo towns, and much employed by the Pagan natives in keeping their wives in subjection". When the ladies of the household become too quarrelsome, Mumbo Jumbo is called in. He may be the husband or his agent suitably disguised, who comes at nightfall making hideous noises. When the women have been assembled and songs and dances performed. "Mumbo fixes on the offender", she is "stripped naked, tied to a post, and severely scourged with Mumbo's rod, amidst the shouts and derision of the whole assembly."

Mummer. A contemptuous name for an actor; from the parties that formerly went from house to house at CHRISTMAS-time *mumming, i.e.* giving a performance of St. GEORGE and the DRAGON, and the like, in dumb-show.

> Peel'd, patch'd and piebald, linsey-woolsey brothers,
> Grave mummers! sleeveless some, and shirtless others.
>
> POPE: *Dunciad, III*, 115.

Mummy is the Arabic *mum*, wax used for embalming; from the custom of anointing the body with wax and preparing it for burial.

Mummy wheat. Wheat (*Triticum compositum*) commonly grown on the southern shores of the Mediterranean, the seed of which is traditionally said to have been taken from ancient Egyptian tombs.

Mumpers. Beggars; from the old slang *to mump*, to cheat or to sponge on others; probably from Dut. *mompen*, to cheat. In Norwich, Christmas WAITS used to be called "Mumpers".

> A parcel of wretches hopping about by the assistance of their crutches, like so many Lincoln's Inn Fields mumpers, drawing into a body to attack the coach of some charitable lord.
>
> NED WARD: *The London Spy*, Pt. V.

Mumping Day. St. THOMAS's Day, 21 December, is so called in some parts of the country, because on this day the poor used to go about begging, or, as it was called, "a-gooding", that is, getting gifts to procure good things for CHRISTMAS, or begging corn. In Lincolnshire the name used to be applied to BOXING DAY; in Warwickshire the term used was "going a-corning".

Mumpsimus. Robert Graves, in *Impenetrability*, gives this word as an example of the practice of making new words by declaration. With the meaning, "an erroneous doctrinal view obstinately adhered to", *mumpsimus* was put into currency by Henry VIII in a speech from the throne in 1545. He remarked, "Some be too stiff in their old mumpsimus, others be too busy and curious in their sumpsimus." He referred to a familiar story in the jest-books of a priest who always read in the MASS *"quod in ore mumpsimus"* instead of *"sumpsimus"*, as his MISSAL was incorrectly copied. When his mistake was pointed out, he said that he had read it with an *m* for forty years, "and I will not change my old mumpsimus for your new sumpsimus." The word is now used to mean "an established manuscript-reading that, though obviously incorrect, is retained blindly by old-fashioned scholars".

Münchausen, Baron (min' chou zen). Karl Friedrich Hieronymus, Baron Münchausen (1720–1797) served in the Russian army against the Turks, and after his retirement told extraordinary stories of his war adventures. Rudolf Erich Raspe (1737–1794), a German scientist, antiquarian and writer, collected these tales, and when living in England as a mining engineer, published them in 1785 as *Baron Münchausen's Narrative of his Marvellous Travels and Campaigns in Russia*. The text of *Münchausen* as reprinted latterly contains *Sea Adventures*, an account of Baron de Tott (a character founded on a real French Hussar) partly written by Raspe, with much additional matter from various sources by other hands. *Cp.* MANDEVILLE.

Mundane Egg. *See* EGG.

Mundungus. Bad tobacco; originally offal or refuse, from Span. *mondongo*, black pudding.

In Sterne's *Sentimental Journey* (1768), the word is used as a name for Samuel Sharp, a surgeon, who published *Letters from Italy*; and Smollett, who published *Travels through France and Italy* (1766), "one continual snarl", was called "Smelfungus".

Mungo, St. An alternative name for St. KENTIGERN.

A superior kind of shoddy, made from second-hand woollens, is known as *mungo*.

Munich. Another Munich. A potentially disastrous, humiliating, or dishonourable act of appeasement or surrender. So called from the unfortunate act of appeasement, the Munich Pact or Agreement concluded between Great Britain, France, Germany, and Italy (30 September 1938) whereby the Sudetenland of Czechoslovakia was ceded to Germany.

Muratorian Fragment. A fragment of a late 2nd-century document found embodied in an 8th-century codex. Written in Latin, it reveals the NEW TESTAMENT canon of the period as consisting of the four Gospels, thirteen Epistles of Paul, two Epistles of John, the Epistle of Jude, the Apocalypse of John, and the Apocalypse of Peter. It was discovered by L. A. Muratori, librarian of the Ambrosian Library at Milan.

Murderer's Bible, The. *See* BIBLE, SOME SPECIALLY NAMED EDITIONS.

Murphy. A POTATO, from its long established prominence as a staple crop in Ireland.

Murphy's Law. Of uncertain origin but with an Irish implication, Murphy's Law can be summed up by the saying "that anything that can go wrong, will go wrong". Some typical examples of its use are: "interchangeable parts — won't; no good deed goes unpunished; you will always find something in the last place you look; the light at the end of the tunnel is the headlamp of an oncoming train; if you're feeling good, don't worry you'll get over it". It has a good deal in common with CATCH-22.

Murrumbidgee Whaler. An Australian term for a tramp, the origin of which is obscure. Some derive the term from the fact that tramps camped for long periods by such rivers as the Murrumbidgee and then told lies about the fish or "whales" they had caught.

Muscadins. Parisian exquisites who aped those of London about the time of the French Revolution. They used musk as a perfume, wore top-boots with long tails, and a high stiff collar, and carried a thick cudgel called a "constitution". It was thought "John Bullish" to assume a huskiness of voice, a discourtesy of manners, and a swaggering vulgarity of speech and behaviour.

Cockneys of London, Muscadins of Paris.
BYRON:*Don Juan*, viii, 124.

Muscular Christianity. Hearty or strong-minded Christianity, which braces a man to fight the battle of life bravely and manfully. The term was applied to the teachings of Charles Kingsley (1819–1875)—somewhat to his annoyance.

It is a school of which Mr. Kingsley is the ablest doctor; and its doctrine has been described fairly and cleverly as "muscular Christianity".
Edinburgh Review, Jan. 1858

Muses. In Greek mythology the nine daughters of ZEUS and MNEMOSYNE; originally goddesses of memory only, but later identified with individual arts and sciences. The paintings of Herculaneum show all nine in their respective attributes. Their names are: CALLIOPE, CLIO, EUTERPE, THALIA, MELPOMENE, TERPSICHORE, ERATO, POLYHYMNIA, URANIA. Three earlier Muses are sometimes given, *i.e.* Melete (Meditation), Mneme (Remembrance), and Aoide (Song).

Museum. Literally, a home or seat of the MUSES. The first building to have this name was the university erected at Alexandria by Ptolemy Soter about 300 B.C.

British Museum. *See under* BRITISH.

A museum piece. An object of historic or antiquarian interest and value, etc.; in a derogatory or facetious sense, any article which is antiquated or out of fashion, or an old-fashioned person.

Mushroom. Slang for an umbrella, on account of the similarity in shape; and as mushrooms are of very rapid growth, applied figuratively to anything that springs up "overnight", as a rapidly built housing estate, an upstart family, etc. In 1787, Bentham said, somewhat unjustly, "Sheffield is an oak, Birmingham is a mushroom."

To mushroom. To grow rapidly; to expand into a mushroom shape. Said especially of certain soft-nosed rifle bullets used in big-game shooting, or of a dense cloud of smoke that spreads out high in the sky, especially after an atomic explosion.

Music (Gr. *mousikē*, "art of the muses").

Father of Greek music. Terpander of Lesbos (*fl.* 676 B.C.).

Father of Modern Music. Mozart (1756–1791) has been so called.

Father of Musicians. Jubal, "the father of all such as handle the harp and organ" (*Gen.* iv, 21).

The Prince of Music. Giovanni Pierluigi da Palestrina (*c.* 1525–1594).

Music hath charms, etc. The opening line of Congreve's *Mourning Bride*.

Music hath charms to soothe the savage breast,
To soften rocks or bend a knotted oak.

The allusion is to ORPHEUS, who:
With his lute made trees,
And the mountain tops that freeze,
Bow themselves when he did sing.
SHAKESPEARE:*Henry VIII*, iii, i.

The music of the spheres. *See under* SPHERES.

To face the music. *See under* FACE.

Canned music. Recorded music on discs (records) or tapes for subsequent reproduction.

Live music. Music performed in one's presence, *i.e.* not reproduced.

Music Hall. This essentially popular form of variety entertainment had its origins in the "Free and Easy" of the public houses and in the song and supper rooms of early Victorian London. Food, drink, and the singsong were its first ingredients and its patrons came from the working classes. The first music hall proper, the *Canterbury*, was opened in 1852 by Charles Morton (1819–1905), "the Father of the Halls", and a native of Hackney. It was specially built for the purpose, consequent upon the success of his musical evenings at the "Canterbury Arms", Lambeth, of which he became the landlord in 1849. Music Halls eventually became more numerous in London and the provinces than the regular theatres and such names as Palladium, Palace, Alhambra, Coliseum, Empire, Hippodrome, etc., proclaim their former glories. Their best days were before 1914, after which revue, the cinema, wireless and, later, television, helped to bring about their eclipse. They have left a legacy of popular ballad and song, and memories of a host of great entertainers whose fame depended upon the intrinsic qualities of their individual acts. *Cp.* EVANS'S SUPPER ROOMS.

Musical Small-coal man. Thomas Britton (*c.* 1654–1714), a coal-dealer of CLERKENWELL, who established a musical club over his shop in which all the musical celebrities of the day took part.

The club met every Thursday night and was frequented by professional musicians such as Handel, talented amateurs such as Roger L'Estrange, and lovers of music.

Musits, or Musets (O.Fr. *muce*, a hiding-place). Gaps in a hedge, places through which a hare makes its way to escape the hounds, which is called *musing*.

> The many musits through the which he goes
> Are like a labyrinth to amaze his foes.
> SHAKESPEARE: *Venus and Adonis*, 683.

Muslim. *See* MOSLEM.

Muspelheim. In Scandinavian mythology, the "Home of Brightness" to the south of NIFLHEIM, where Surt (black smoke) ruled with his flaming sword and where dwelt the sons of Muspel the fire giant.

Mussulman. A Mohammedan, a MOSLEM. The plural is Mussulmans.

Mustard. So called because originally *must*, new wine (Lat. *mustus*, fresh, new), was used in mixing the paste.

After meat, mustard. Expressive of the sentiment that something that would have been welcome a little earlier has arrived too late and is no longer wanted. *C'est de la moutarde après dîner.*

> "Good folks," said Sancho, "my master does not want your hearkening; why do not you run in and help him? though I believe it is after-meat mustard; for sure the giant is dead by this time...."
> CERVANTES: *Don Quixote*, ch. xxix (*Translation by Motteux*).

Muster. To pass muster. To pass inspection: to "get by", to be allowed to pass.

Mutantur. *See* TEMPORA MUTANTUR.

Mutatis mutandis (Lat. *mutare*, to change). After making the necessary changes; more literally, those things have been changed which were to be changed.

Mute, To stand. An old legal term for a prisoner who, when arraigned for treason or felony, refused to plead or gave irrelevant answers.

Mutton (Fr. *mouton*, sheep). In old slang, a prostitute, frequently extended to *laced mutton*.

> *Speed:* Ay, sir: I, a lost mutton, gave your letter to her, a laced mutton; and she, a laced mutton, gave me, a lost mutton, nothing for my labour.
> SHAKESPEARE: *Two Gentlemen of Verona*, I, i.
> The old lecher hath gotten holy mutton to him, a nunne, my lord.
> GREENE: *Friar Bacon.*

It was with this meaning that John Wilmot, Earl of Rochester, wrote his mock epitaph on Charles II:

> Here lies our mutton-eating king,
> Whose word no man relies on;
> He never said a foolish thing,
> And never did a wise one.

Come and eat your mutton with me. Come and dine with me.

Dead as mutton. Absolutely dead.

Mutton Chops. Whiskers trimmed to the shape of mutton chops.

Mutton fist. A large, coarse red fist.

Mutton Lancers. *See* REGIMENTAL AND DIVISIONAL NICKNAMES.

To return to our muttons. *See* MOUTONS.

Mutual Friends. Can people have mutual friends? Strictly speaking not; but since Dickens adopted the solecism in the title of his novel *Our Mutual Friend* (1864), many people have objected to the correct term *common friends. Mutual* implies reciprocity from one to another (Lat. *mutare*, to change); the friendship between two friends should be mutual, but this mutuality cannot be extended to a third party.

> *Priest:* A contract of eternal bond of love,
> Confirmed by mutual joinder of your hands.
> SHAKESPEARE: *Twelfth Night*, V, i.

Mynheer (min âr′). The Dutch equivalent for "Mr."; hence sometimes used for a Dutchman.

'Tis thus I spend my moments here,
And wish myself a Dutch mynheer.
COWPER: *To Lady Austin.*

Myrmidons (lit. ant people, from Gk. *myrmix*) gained their name from the legend that when Ægina was depopulated by a plague, its king, Æacus, prayed to JUPITER that the ants running out of an OAK tree should be turned to men. According to one account they emigrated with Peleus to Thessaly, whence they followed ACHILLES to the siege of TROY. They were noted for their fierceness, diligence and devotion to their leader, hence their name is applied to a servant who carries out his orders remorselessly.

Myrmidons of the Law. Bailiffs, sheriffs' officers, policemen, and other servants of the law. Any rough fellow employed to annoy another is the employer's myrmidon.

Myron. A famous Greek sculptor noted for his realistic statues of gods, heroes, athletes, and animals. It is said that he made a cow so lifelike that even bulls were deceived and made their approaches. He was an older contemporary of Phidias.

Myrrha. The mother of ADONIS, in Greek legend. She is fabled to have had an unnatural love for her own father, and to have been changed into a MYRTLE. The resinous juice called *myrrh* is obtained from the Arabian myrtle (*Balsamodendron myrrha*).

Myrrophores (Gr., myrrh-bearers). The Marys who went to see the sepulchre, bearing spices, are represented in Christian art as carrying vases of myrrh (*see Mark* xvi, i).

Myrtle. A leaf of myrtle, viewed in a strong light, is seen to be pierced with innumerable little punctures. According to fable, PHÆDRA, wife of THESEUS, fell in love with HIPPOLYTUS, her stepson. When Hippolytus went to the arena to exercise his horses, Phædra repaired to a myrtle-tree in Trœzen to await his return, and beguiled the time by piercing the leaves with a hairpin.

In ORLANDO FURIOSO Astolpho is changed into a myrtle-tree by Acrisia. *Cp.* MYRRHA.

The ancient Jews believed that the eating of myrtle leaves conferred the power of detecting witches; and it was a superstition that if the leaves crackled in the hands the person beloved would prove faithful.

The myrtle which dropped blood. ÆNEAS (Virgil's *Æneid*, Bk. III) tells the story of how he tore up a myrtle to decorate a sacrificial altar, but was terrified to find it dripped blood, while a voice came from the ground saying, "Spare me, now that I am in my grave." It was that of Polydorus, the youngest son of PRIAM and HECUBA, who had been murdered with darts and arrows for the GOLD he possessed. The deed was perpetrated by Polymnestor, King of Thrace, to whose care Polydorus had been entrusted.

Mysteries of Udolpho. A romance by Mrs. Radcliffe (1764–1823), which was published in 1794 and founded the so-called "terror school" of English Romanticism, though Walpole's *Castle of Otranto* (1764) had broken the ground. *Cp.* FRANKENSTEIN.

Mysterium. The letters of this word, which, until the time of the REFORMATION, was engraved on the Pope's tiara, are said to make up the number 666. *See* NUMBER OF THE BEAST.

And upon her forehead was a name written, MYSTERY, BABYLON THE GREAT, THE MOTHER OF HARLOTS AND ABOMINATIONS OF THE EARTH.
Rev. xvii, 5.

Mystery. In English two distinct words are represented: *mystery*, the archaic term for a handicraft, as in *the art and mystery of printing*, is the same as the Fr. *métier* (trade, craft, profession), and is the M.E. *mistere*, from Med. Lat. *misterium*, *ministerium*, ministry. *Mystery*, meaning something hidden, inexplicable, or beyond human comprehension, is from Lat. *mysterium* (through French) and Gr. *mustēs*, from *muen*, to close the eyes or lips.

It is from this latter sense that the old miracle plays, mediæval dramas in which the characters and story were drawn from sacred history, came to be called **Mysteries**, though they were frequently presented by members of a guild or *mystery*. *Miracle plays* (as they were called at the time) developed from liturgical pageantry, especially in the CORPUS CHRISTI processions, and were taken over by the laity. They were performed in the streets on a wheeled stage or on stages erected along a processional route, and non-Biblical subjects were also introduced. They flourished in England from the 13th to the 15th century but MORALITY PLAYS continued into the 16th century. *Cp.* PASSION PLAY.

Mysteries of the Rosary. The fifteen subjects of meditation from the life of Christ and the Blessed Virgin Mary, connected with the decades of the ROSARY.

The three greater mysteries. The TRINITY, Original Sin, and the Incarnation.

Myton, The Chapter of Myton. So the battle of Myton (1319) in Yorkshire was called, when the clergy led out their flocks to repel the Scottish invaders. Many were slain and the Scots devastated the area.

N

N. The fourteenth letter of our alphabet; represented in Egyptian hieroglyphic by a water-line (〰). It was called *nun* (a fish) in Phœnician, whence the Greek *nu*.

N. A numeral; Gr. ν=50, but ͵ν=50,000. N (Med. Lat.)=90, or 900; but N̄=90,000, or 900,000.

n. The sign ~ (*tilde*) over an "n" indicates that the letter is to be pronounced as though followed by a "y", as *cañón=canyon*. It is used thus almost solely in words from Spanish. In Portuguese the accent (called *til*) is placed over vowels to indicate that they have a nasal value.

nth, or **nth plus one.** The expression is taken from the index of a mathematical formula, where *n* stands for any number, and *n*+1, one more than any number. Hence, *n-dimensional*, having an indefinite number of dimensions, *n-tuple* (on the analogy of *quadruple*, *quintuple* etc.), having an indefinite number of duplications.

n ephelkustic. The Greek *nu* (ν) added for euphony to the end of a word that terminates with a vowel when the next word in the sentence begins with a vowel.

N or M. The answer given to the first question in the CHURCH OF ENGLAND Catechism; and it means that here the person being catechized gives his or her *name* or *names*. Lat. *nomen vel nomina*. The abbreviation for the plural *nomina* was—as usual—the doubled initial (*cp*. "LL.D." for Doctor of Laws); and this when printed (as it was in old Prayer Books) in BLACK-LETTER and close together, N.N. came to be taken for M..

In the same way the M. and N. in the marriage-service ("I M. take thee N. to my wedded wife") merely indicate that the name is to be spoken in each case; but the M. and N. in the publication of banns ("I publish the BANNS OF MARRIAGE between M. of — and N. of —") stand for *maritus*, bridegroom, and *nupta*, bride.

N.B. (Lat. *nota bene*). Note well.

N.K.V.D. *See* OGPU.

Nab. Colloquial for to seize suddenly, without warning. (*Cp*. Norw. and Swed. *nappa*;

Dan. *nappe*.) Hence *nabman*, a sheriff's officer or police constable.

Ay, but so be if a man's nabbed, you know.
GOLDSMITH: *The Good-natured Man*, III.

Nabob (nā′ bob). Corruption of the Hind. *nawab*, deputy-governor; used of the governor or ruler of a province under the MOGUL Empire. Such men acquired great wealth and lived in splendour and eventually became independent princes. The name was sarcastically applied in the late 18th century to servants of the English East India Company who retired to England, having made their fortunes, bought estates and acquired seats in PARLIAMENT, etc.

Nabonassar, Era of. An era that was in use for centuries by the Chaldean astronomers, and was generally followed by Hipparchus and Ptolemy. It commenced at midday, Wednesday, 26 February, 747 B.C., the date of the accession of Nabonassar (d. 733 B.C.) as King of Babylonia. The year consisted of 12 months of 30 days each, with 5 complementary days added at the end. As no INTERCALARY day was allowed for, the first day of the year fell one day earlier every four years than the JULIAN year; consequently, to transpose a date from one era to another it is necessary to know the exact day and month of the Nabonassarian date, and to remember that 1,460 Julian years are equal to 1,461 Babylonian.

Naboth's Vineyard. The possession of another coveted by one who will use any means, however unscrupulous, to acquire it. (I *Kings* xxi.)

Nabu. *See* NEBO.

Nadir (nād′ ir). An Arabic word, signifying that point in the heavens which is directly opposite to the ZENITH, *i.e.* directly under our feet; hence, figuratively, the lowest point in one's fortunes, the lowest depths of degradation, etc.

Nævius. *See* ACCIUS NÆVIUS.

Nag's Head Consecration. An early 17th-century story designed to deride the validity of the APOSTOLIC SUCCESSION in the CHURCH OF ENGLAND and in particular the validity of

Archbishop Parker's consecration. The story is that on the passing of the Act of Uniformity of 1559 in Queen Elizabeth's reign, 14 bishops vacated their sees, and all the other sees were vacant except that of Llandaff, whose bishop refused to officiate at Parker's consecration. He was therefore irregularly consecrated at the "Nag's Head" tavern, in Cheapside, by John Scory who had been deprived of the SEE of Chichester under Mary. In fact the consecration took place at LAMBETH PALACE on 17 December 1559 by four bishops who had held sees under Edward VI (Barlow, Scory, Coverdale, and Hodgkin). Those who took part in the consecration apparently dined at the "Nag's Head" afterwards. The story was first put about in 1604 by C. Holywood, a JESUIT.

Naiad (nī' ăd). In classical mythology, a NYMPH of lake, fountain, river, or stream.

> You nymphs, call'd Naiads, of the wand'ring brooks,
> With your sedg'd crowns, and ever-harmless looks,
> Leave your crisp channels, and on this green land
> Answer your summons: Juno does command.
> SHAKESPEARE: *The Tempest*, IV, i.

Nail. A *nail* was formerly a measure of weight of 8lb. It was used for wool, hemp, beef, cheese, etc. It was also a measure of length of $2\frac{1}{4}$ inches.

> *Motto:* You shall have...a dozen beards, to stuffe two dozen cushions.
> *Licio:* Then they be big ones.
> *Dello:* They be halfe a yard broad, and a nayle, three quarters long, and a foote thick.
> LYLY: *Midas*, V, ii (1592).

In ancient ROME a nail was driven into the wall of the temple of JUPITER every 13 September. This was originally done to tally the year, but subsequently it became a religious ceremony for warding off calamities and plagues from the city. Originally the nail was driven by the *prætor maximus*, subsequently by one of the consuls, and lastly by the dictator (*see* LIVY, VII, iii).

In World War I patriotic Germans drove nails into a large wooden statue of Field-Marshal Hindenburg, buying each nail in support of a national fund.

The nails with which Our Lord was fastened to the Cross were, in the MIDDLE AGES, objects of great reverence. Sir John MANDEVILLE says, "He had two in his hondes, and two in his feet; and of on of theise the emperour of Constantynoble made a brydille to his hors, to bere him in bataylle; and throghe vertue thereof he overcam his enemyes" (*c.* viii). Fifteen are shown as relics. *See* IRON CROWN OF LOMBARDY *under* CROWN.

For want of a nail. "For want of a nail, the shoe is lost; for want of a shoe, the horse is lost; for want of a horse, the rider is lost." (Herbert: *Jacula Prudentum*).

Hard as nails. Stern, hard-hearted, unsympathetic; able to stand hard blows like nails. The phrase is used with both a physical and a figurative sense; a man in perfect training is "as hard as nails", and bigotry, straitlacedness, rigid puritanical pharisaism, make people "hard as nails".

Hung on the nail. Put in pawn. A reference to the old custom of hanging each pawn on a nail, with a number attached, and giving the customer a duplicate thereof.

I nailed him, or **it.** I pinned him, meaning I secured him, I fixed his attention or "got hold of him". *Is.* (xxii, 23) says, "I will fasten him as a nail in a sure place."

On the nail. Immediately, on the spot, as in, **to pay on the nail.** One meaning of nail (possibly from mediæval times) denoted a shallow vessel mounted on a stand and business was concluded by payment into the vessel. It may have been so named from the rough resemblance of the stand to a nail's shape.

Outside the Corn Exchange at Bristol such "nails" or pillars can still be seen and it is said that if a buyer was satisfied with the sample of grain shown on the nail he paid on the spot. (*Cp.* SUPERNACULUM.)

Nail drives out nail. A new interest or desire replaces what was previously felt for its predecessor; from the practice of using a new nail as a punch to drive out the old. An ancient proverb.

To drive a nail into one's coffin. *See under* COFFIN.

To hit the nail on the head. *See under* HEAD.

To nail to the counter. To convict and expose as false or spurious; as, "I nailed that lie to the counter at once." From the custom of shopkeepers nailing to the counter false money that was passed to them as a warning to others.

With colours nailed to the mast. *See under* COLOURS.

With tooth and nail. *See under* TOOTH.

Nail-paring. Superstitious people are particular as to the day on which they cut their nails. The old ryhme is:

> Cut them on Monday, you cut them for health;
> Cut them on Tuesday, you cut them for wealth;
> Cut them on Wednesday, you cut them for news;
> Cut them on Thursday, a new pair of shoes;
> Cut them on Friday, you cut them for sorrow;
> Cut them on Saturday, you see your true love tomorrow
> Cut them on Sunday, your safety seek,
> The devil will have you the rest of the week.

Another rhyme conveys an even stronger

warning on the danger of nail-cutting on a Sunday:

A man had better ne'er be born
As have his nails on a Sunday shorn.

Nain Rouge (nān roozh) (Fr., red dwarf). A LUTIN or house spirit of Normandy, kind to fishermen. There is another called *Le petit homme rouge* (the little red man).

Naked. O.E. *nacod*, connected with Lat. *nudus*, nude. Destitute of covering; hence, figuratively, defenceless, exposed; without extraneous assistance, as *with the naked eye*, *i.e.* without telescope or binoculars, etc.

Naked boy, or **lady.** The meadow saffron (*Colchicum autumnale*); so called because, like the almond, peach, etc., the flowers come out before the leaves. It is poetically called "the leafless orphan of the year", the flowers being orphaned or destitute of foliage.

The Naked Boy Courts, and **Alleys,** of which there are more than one in the City of London, are named from the PUBLIC-HOUSE SIGN OF CUPID.

The naked truth. The plain, unvarnished truth; truth without trimmings. The fable says that Truth and Falsehood went bathing; Falsehood came first out of the water, and dressed herself in Truth's garments. Truth, unwilling to take those of Falsehood, went naked.

Namby-pamby. Wishy-washy; insipid, weakly sentimental; said especially of authors. It was the nickname of Ambrose Philips (1674–1749), bestowed on him by Henry Carey, the dramatist, for his verses addressed to Lord Carteret's children, and was adopted by Pope. It is also applied to a MOLLY CODDLE.

Name.

What's in a name? That which we call a rose
By any other name would smell as sweet.
SHAKESPEARE: *Romeo and Juliet*, II, ii.

A name to conjure with. A very famous name, one of great influence. To conjure a name was to evoke a spirit. Thus Shakespeare says (*Julius Cæsar*, I, iii):

Write them together, yours is as fair a name;
Sound them, it doth become the mouth as well;
Weigh them, it is as heavy; conjure with 'em,
Brutus will start a spirit as soon as Cæsar.

Give a dog a bad name. See *under* DOG.

Give it a name. Tell me what it is you would like; said when offering a reward, a drink, etc.

In the name of. In reliance upon; or by the authority of.

Their name liveth for evermore. These consolatory words, frequently used on war memorials, are from the APOCRYPHA:

Their bodies are buried in peace; but their name liveth for evermore.
Ecclesiasticus xliv, 14.

To call a person names. To blackguard him by derogatory nicknames, or hurling opprobrious epithets at him.

Sticks and stones
May break my bones
But words can never hurt me.
Old Rhyme.

To lend one's name to. To authorize the use of one's name in support of a cause, venture, etc.

To name the day. To fix the day of the wedding—a privilege of the bride-to-be.

To take God's name in vain. To use it profanely, thoughtlessly, or irreverently.

Thou shalt not take the name of the Lord thy God in vain.
Exod. xx, 7.

Among primitive peoples, as well as the ancient Hebrews, the name of a deity is regarded as his manifestation, and is treated with the greatest respect and veneration. *See* ADONAI. Among savage tribes there is a reluctance in disclosing one's name because this might enable an enemy by magic to work one some deadly injury; the Greeks were particularly careful to disguise or reverse uncomplimentary names. *See* ERINYES; EUMENIDES; EUXINE.

Name-dropper. One who seeks to impress by casual reference to well-known or prominent people with the implication of friendly acquaintance.

Towards the end of his speech at the Museum of the Year award lunch, Norman St. John-Stevas, Arts Minister, is reliably reported as saying: "But I mustn't go on singling out names…One must not be a name-dropper, as Her Majesty remarked to me yesterday…"
Daily Telegraph, 21 June 1979.

Nana. In the story of PETER PAN, the gentle and faithful old dog who always looked after the children of the Darling family. When Mr. Darling played a trick on Nana by giving her unpleasant medicine, which he himself had promised to drink, the family did not appreciate his humour. This put him out of temper and Nana was chained up in the yard before he went out for the evening. As a consequence Peter Pan effected an entry into the children's bedroom. *See* IN THE DOGHOUSE *under* DOG.

Nancy, Miss. An effeminate, foppish youth. The celebrated actress "Mrs." Anne Oldfield (*see* NARCISSA) was nicknamed "Miss Nancy".

Nancy Boy. A homosexual.

Nankeen. So called from Nankin in China. It is the natural yellow colour of Nankin cotton. *Nankeens* are trousers made from this fabric.

Nantes (nănt). An old name for brandy, from its manufacture there.

Edict of Nantes. The decree of Henry IV of France, published from Nantes in 1598, giving guarantees to the HUGUENOTS and permitting them rights of worship in named towns, etc. The edict was revoked by Louis XIV in 1685. *See* CALAS; DRAGONNADES.

Nap. The doze or short sleep gets its name from O.E. *hnæppian*, to sleep lightly: the surface of cloth is so called from Mid. Dut. *noppe*; and *Nap*, the card game, is so called in honour of NAPOLEON III.

To be caught napping. *See under* CATCH.

To go nap. To set oneself to make five tricks (all one can) in the game of NAP; hence, to risk all you have on some venture, to back it through thick and thin.

Naphtha (năf' thà). The Greek name for an inflammable, bituminous substance coming from the ground in certain districts; in the MEDEA legend it is the name of the drug used by the witch for anointing the wedding robe of Glauce, daughter of King Creon, whereby she was burnt to death on the morning of her marriage with JASON.

Napier's Bones. The calculating square rods of bone, ivory, or boxwood with numerical tables on each of their sides, invented by the Scottish mathematician John Napier (1550–1617), laird of Merchiston, in 1615. This ingenious arrangement was used for shortening the labour of multiplications and divisions. The previous year he had invented logarithms. *Cp.* ABACUS.

Naples. See Naples and (then) die. An old Italian saying, implying that nothing more beautiful remains to be seen on earth. There is also a pun involved since Naples was once a centre of typhoid and cholera. *See* PARTHENOPE.

Napoleon Bonaparte (1769–1821). Emperor of the French (1804–1815). His reign is known in French history as the *First Empire* and his name is sometimes used to denote supremacy in a particular sphere as in, *a Napoleon of finance. Cp.* BONEY.

Code Napoléon. The code of laws prepared (1800–1804) under his direction, based on work begun by a committee of the CONVENTION and so called in 1807. It forms the basis of modern French law and is only second in importance to the code of Justinian. Equality in the eyes of the law, justice, and common sense are its keynotes.

Napoleon II, King of Rome (1811–1832). Francis Joseph Charles, the son of Napoleon and Marie Louise of Austria, never reigned but was known to the Bonapartists as Napoleon II. He was given the compensatory title of Duke of Reichstadt in 1818.

Napoleon III (1808–1873). His reign (1852–1870) is called the *Second Empire*. He was the third son of Louis Bonaparte, King of Holland (brother of NAPOLEON BONAPARTE) and Napoleon I's step-daughter Hortense de Beauharnais. Few men have had so many nicknames:

Man of December, so called because his COUP D'ETAT was 2 December 1851, and he was made emperor 2 December 1852.

Man of Sedan, and, by a pun, *M. Sedantaire*. It was at Sedan he surrendered his sword to William I, King of Prussia (1870).

Man of Silence, from his great taciturnity.

Comte d'Arenenberg, the name and title he assumed when he escaped from the fortress of Ham.

Badinguet, the name of the mason who changed clothes with him when he escaped from Ham. The emperor's partisans were called *Badingueux*, those of the empress were *Montijoyeaux*.

Boustrapa is a compound of Bou[logne], Stra[sbourg], and Pa[ris], the places of his noted escapades.

Rantipole, harum-scarum, half-fool and half-madman.

There are some curious numerical coincidences connected with Napoleon III and Eugénie. The last complete year of their reign was 1869. (In 1870 Napoleon was dethroned and exiled.)

Now, if to the year of coronation (1852) you add either the birth of Napoleon or the birth of Eugénie, or the date of marriage, or the capitulation of Paris, the sum will always be 1869. For example:

1852 {Coronation.}	1852	1852	1852
1 Birth	1 Birth	1 Date	1 Capit-
8 of	8 of	8 of	8 ulation
0 Napo-	2 Eugé-	5 Mar-	7 of
8 leon.	6 nie.	3 riage.	1 Paris.
1869	1869	1869	1869

And if to the year of *marriage* (1853) these dates are added, they will give 1870, the fatal year.

Napoleon of the Ring. James Belcher, the pugilist (1781–1811), who was remarkably like Napoleon in looks.

Napoo (na poo'). Soldier slang of World War I for something that is of no use or does not exist. It represents the French phrase *il n'y en a plus*, there is no more of it. It occurs in a popular song of 1917:

Bonsoir old thing, cheerio, chin-chin,
Nahpoo, toodle-oo, goodby-ee.

WESTON and LEE: *Good-Bye-Ee.*

Nappy ale. Strong ale has been so called for many centuries, probably because it contains a *nap* or frothy head.

Naraka (nar′ a kà). In Hindu mythology and BUDDHISM, the place of torture for departed evil-doers. It consists of many kinds of hells, hot and cold.

Narcissa. In Pope's *Moral Essays* "Narcissa" stands for the actress Anne Oldfield (1683–1730). When she died her remains lay in state attended by two noblemen. She was buried in Westminster Abbey in a very fine Brussels lace head-dress, a holland shift, with a tucker and double ruffles of the same lace, new kid gloves, etc. *See* NANCY.

> "Odious! In woollen! 'Twould a saint provoke"
> (Were the last words that poor Narcissa spoke).
> POPE: *Moral Essays*, i, 246.

"In woollen" is an allusion to the old law enacted for the benefit of the wool trade, that all shrouds were to be made of wool (*see under* WOOL).

Narcissus (nar sis′ us). In Greek mythology, the son of Cephisus; a beautiful youth who saw his reflection in a fountain, and thought it the presiding nymph of the place. He jumped in the fountain to reach it, where he died. The NYMPHS came to take up the body to pay it FUNERAL honours but found only flower, which they called by his name (Ovid: *Metamorphoses*, iii, 346, etc.).

Plutarch says the plant is called Narcissus from the Gr. *narkē*, numbness, and that it is properly *narcosis*, meaning the plant which produces numbness or palsy. ECHO fell in love with Narcissus.

> Sweet Echo, sweetest nymph that liv'st unseen...
> Canst thou not tell me of a gentle pair,
> That likest thy Narcissus are?
> MILTON: *Comus*, 230.

Narcissism is the psychoanalytical term for excessive love and admiration of oneself.

Nark, or **Copper's nark.** A police spy or informer; from a Romany word, *nak*, a nose, on the analogy of NOSEY Parker. The term is also applied to a policeman. In colloquial parlance, *to be narked* is to be angry or annoyed, and *nark it* means stop it, "give over".

Narrow. The Narrow Seas. The Irish Sea and the English Channel, especially the area around the Straits of Dover.

Narrowdale Noon. To do a thing *at Narrowdale noon* is to defer or delay it, to do it "late at noon". Narrowdale is in a deep limestone valley in Staffordshire near Dovedale, where for three months of the year there is virtually no sun at all and in the spring it does not appear until about one o'clock (2 p.m. B.S.T.). Hence *Narrowdale noon* as a proverbial expression when anything is delayed. *Cp*. GREEK CALENDS; NEVER.

Nasbys. A generic nickname in the U.S.A. for postal officials, particularly postmasters. The American humorist David Ross Locke (1833–1888) wrote a series of satirical articles in the form of letters which first appeared in 1861 in the *Jeffersonian*, published in Findlay, Ohio, and later in the *Blade*, published in Toledo, Ohio. These *Nasby Letters* purported to be those of a conservative, ignorant and whisky-drinking politician who hated Negroes and who was determined to be the postmaster of his little town. Comically spelled, and full of sly humour, the *Nasby Letters* were very popular, and soon gave rise to the generic title.

Naseby. Fable has it that this town in Northamptonshire is so called because it was considered the *navel* (O.E. *nafela*) or centre of ENGLAND, just as DELPHI was considered "the navel of the earth". In fact the town's name appears in DOMESDAY BOOK as *Navesberi*, showing that it was a burgh or dwelling of Hnæf, a Dane.

Naso (nā′ zō). Ovid (Publius Ovidius Naso, 43 B.C.–A.D. 18), the Roman poet, author of *Metamorphoses*. Naso means "nose", hence Holofernes' pun: "And why, indeed, Naso, but for smelling out the odoriferous flowers of fancy." (SHAKESPEARE: *Love's Labour's Lost*, IV, ii.)

Natheless, or **Nathless** (nāth′ les). An archaic form of nevertheless.

> Smote on him sore besides, vaulted with fire.
> Nathless he so endured.
> MILTON: *Paradise Lost*, I, 298.

National Anthem. The composition of "God Save the Queen", the British National Anthem, has been attributed to Dr. John Bull (d. 1628), organist at Antwerp Cathedral (1617–1628), and quite erroneously to Henry Carey, but the following, by Mme. de Brinon, was sung before Louis XIV in 1686:

> Grand Dieu sauvez le roi,
> Grand Dieu vengez le roi,
> Vive le roi!
> Qu'à jamais glorieux,
> Louis victorieux,
> Voie ses ennemis toujours soumis,
> Vive le roi!

The Authorized Version of the BIBLE has:

> And all the people shouted, and said, God save the king.
> I *Sam*. x, 24.

It became popular at the time of the FORTY-FIVE Rebellion as a demonstration of loyalty to George II and opposition to the JACOBITES, to whom the phrase "confound their politics" may well refer.

The following are examples of the National Anthems or principal patriotic songs of other nations:

Argentine: *Oíd, mortales, el grito sagrado Libertad*.

Australia: *God Save the Queen; Advance, Australia Fair*.

Austria: (After World War II) *Land der Berge, Land am Strome*.

Canada. *God Save the Queen; The Maple Leaf Forever; O Canada! terre de nos aïeux*.

Chile: *Dulce patria, recibe los votos*.

Denmark: *The Song of the Danebrog*; *Kong Christian stod ved højen Mast* (King Christian stood beside the lofty mast).

France: *The Marseillaise*.

Germany: (After World War I) *Deutschland über alles*.

German Democratic Republic: *Auferstanden aus Ruinen und der Zukunft zugewandt*.

German Federal Republic: *Einigkeit und Recht und Freiheit*.

Italy: *Inno di Mameli*.

Mexico: *Mexicanos, al grito de guerra*.

Netherlands: *Wilhelmus van Nassouwe*.

New Zealand: *God Defend New Zealand; God Save the Queen*.

Norway: *Ja, vi elsker dette Landet som det stiger frem* (Yes we love our country, just as it is).

Peru: *Somos libres, seámos lo siempre*.

Portugal: *Herois do mar*.

Russia (under the Tsars): *Bozhe Tsarya Khrani*.

Scotland: *Scots wha hae wi' Wallace bled*.

South Africa: *Die Stem van Suid-Afrika*.

Spain: *Marcha de Granaderos*.

Sweden: *Du gamla, du fria, du fjällhöga Nord, Du tysta, du glädjerika sköna Nord!* (Thou ancient, free, and mountainous North! Thou silent, joyous, and beautiful North!).

Switzerland: *Trittst im Morgenrot daher* (In the dawn you stride along).

U.S.A.: *The Star-spangled Banner. See* STARS AND STRIPES.

U.S.S.R.: *Soyuz nerushimy respublik svobodnykh*.

Wales: *Mae hen wlad fy nhadau* (Land of my Fathers); also *Men of Harlech*.

National Convention. For the French assembly of this name, *see* CONVENTION PARLIAMENTS.

In the U.S.A. the National Convention is the meeting of State delegates called by the national committees of the political parties which nominates candidates for President and Vice-President. The party platform is also drawn up.

National Debt. The public debt of the central government of a state and secured on the national revenue. The *Funded Debt* is the portion of the National Debt which is converted into bonds and annuities, etc. The remainder, essentially short-term debt, is called the *Floating Debt*.

The British National Debt assumed a permanent form in the reign of William III (1689–1702) and it has been managed by the Bank of England since 1750. The rapid increase of the National Debt has been mainly due to wars. *See* MISSISSIPPI BUBBLE; SINKING FUND; SOUTH SEA BUBBLE.

National Governments. As a result of the financial crises and the collapse of the labour Government in 1931, an all-party COALITION was formed under J. Ramsay MacDonald, the first of a series of governments called "National" which held office in succession until 1940, under MacDonald, then Baldwin, and lastly Chamberlain. Those LIBERAL and LABOUR M.P.s who supported these governments called themselves National Liberal candidates and National Labour candidates. The administrations became increasingly CONSERVATIVE in character.

National Guard. In France, the revolutionary leaders formed a National Guard at Paris in July 1789, and similar citizen armies were formed in the provinces. It supported Robespierre, but turned against the CONVENTION and was defeated by NAPOLEON with regular troops. Under Napoleon, a National Guard or militia was re-established which continued in existence until the Paris commune of 1871.

In the U.S.A., the National Guard is an organization of volunteer military units similar to the British Territorials. When called upon in a national emergency they become an integral part of the U.S. armed forces. The oldest unit is the 182nd infantry of Massachusetts which traces its origins back to 1636. *Cp.* MINUTE-MEN.

National Society. The shortened form of the name of the association formed in 1811 as the "National Society for the Education of the Poor in the Principles of the Established Church". It played a great part in the development of English education, especially before direct state participation and control. Principally known for the establishment of Church schools, or "National Schools", and teacher training colleges, it still continues its work. *See* MONITORIAL SYSTEM; VOLUNTARY SCHOOLS.

Nations, Battle of the. A name given to the battle of Leipzig (16–19 October 1813) which led to the first overthrow of NAPO-

LEON. Prussians, Russians, Austrians and Swedes took part against the French.

Native. To go native. To abandon civilized ways and to share the life and habits of a more primitive society.

Nativity, The. CHRISTMAS Day, the day set apart in honour of the Nativity or Birth of Christ.

The Cave of the Nativity. The "Cave of the Nativity" at Bethlehem, discovered, according to Eusebius, by the empress HELENA, is under the chancel of the BASILICA of the "Church of the Nativity". It is a hollow scraped out of rock, and there is a stone slab above the ground with a star cut in it to mark the supposed spot where Jesus was laid. There are no grounds for connecting the Nativity with a cave.

To cast a man's nativity. The astrologers' term for constructing a plan or map of the position of the twelve "houses" which belong to him and explaining its significance. *See* HOUSES, ASTROLOGICAL.

Nature. In a state of nature. Nude or naked.

A natural. A born idiot, *i.e.* someone who is born half-witted. The word is now commonly used to denote one who is naturally adept at some particular skill, especially at games.

> For this drivelling love is like a great natural that runs lolling up and down to hide his bauble in a hole.
> SHAKESPEARE: *Romeo and Juliet*, II, iv.

In music, a *natural* is a white key on the pianoforte, etc., as distinguished from a black key. In musical notation the sign ♮ is employed to counteract the following note from a sharp or flat in the signature, and from a preceding accidental sharp or flat in the same bar.

A natural child. A BASTARD. The Romans called the children of concubines *naturales*, children according to nature and not according to law.

Natural increase. In population statistics, etc., the excess of births over deaths in a given period, usually a year. *Cp.* MALTHUSIAN DOCTRINE.

Natural Philosophy. *See* EXPERIMENTAL PHILOSOPHY.

Naught, Nought. These are merely variants of the same word, naught representing O.E. *na whil* and nought, *no whit*. In most senses they are interchangeable; but nowadays *naught* is the more common form, except for the name of the cipher, which is usually *nought*.

Naught was formerly applied to things that were bad or worthless, as in II *Kings* ii, 19, "The water is naught and the ground

barren", and it is with this sense that Jeremiah (xxiv, 2) speaks of "naughty figs":

> One basket had very good figs, even like the figs that are first ripe...The other basket had very naughty figs, which could not be eaten.

The REVISED VERSION did away with the old "naughty" and substituted "bad"; and in the next verse, where the Authorized calls the figs "EVIL", the Douai Version has:

> The good figges, exceeding good and the naughtie figges, exceeding naught: which cannot be eaten because they are naught.

Naughty Nineties, The. The 1890s in England, when the puritanical Victorian code of behaviour and conduct gave way in certain wealthy and fashionable circles to growing laxity in sexual morals, a growing cult of hedonism, and a more light-hearted approach to life. MUSIC HALLS were at the height of their popularity and the EMPIRE PROMENADE was in its heyday.

> Those again concerned with the fashionable surface of life and letters in London are struck by the revulsion from puritanism to raffishness, and speak of the "naughty nineties"—the epoch of the *Yellow Book* and the Oscar Wilde case and of a more flaunting West End vice.
> SIR ROBERT ENSOR: *England 1870–1914*, ch. X.

Nausicaa (naw sik ā′ a). The Greek heroine whose story is told in the ODYSSEY. She was the daughter of Alcinous, king of the Phæacians, and the shipwrecked Odysseus found her playing ball with her maidens on the shore. Pitying his plight he conducted him to her father, by whom he was entertained.

Nautical mile. *See under* MILE.

Navvy. A labourer employed on heavy work such as excavating, trenching, etc.; a contraction of *navigator*. The name derives from the days of canal construction, as the canals were called *navigations*.

> This navigation really consists of two sections—the Forth and Clyde Navigation, and the Monkland Navigation. The former, authorized in 1768, and opened in 1790...
> E. A. PRATT: *British Canals*, ch. iv.

Nay-word. A byword, a password.

> If I do not gull him into a nayword, and make him a common recreation, do not think I have wit enough to lie straight in my bed.
> SHAKESPEARE: *Twelfth Night*, II, iii.
> We have a nay-word how to know one another; I come to her in white and cry mum; she cries budget; and by that we know one another.
> SHAKESPEARE: *Merry Wives of Windsor*, V, ii.

Nazarene. A native of Nazareth; Our Lord is so called (*John* xviii, 5, 7). He was brought up in Nazareth, but was born in Bethlehem (*see Matt.* ii, 23). Hence the early Christians were called *Nazarenes* (*Acts* xxiv, 5); also an early sect of Jewish Christians, who believed Christ to be the MESSIAH, but who nevertheless conformed to much of the Jewish law.

Can any good thing come out of Nazareth? (*John* i, 46). A general insinuation against any family or place of ill repute. Can any great man come from such an insignificant village as Nazareth?

Nazarites (Heb. *'nazar*, to separate). A body of Israelites set apart to the Lord under vows. They refrained from strong drink, and allowed their hair to grow. (*See Numb.* vi, 1–21.)

Nazi (nat' zi, naz' i). The shortened form of *National-Sozialist*, the name given to Adolf Hitler's party. *See* FÜHRER; HITLERISM; MEIN KAMPF; NIGHT OF THE LONG KNIVES; SWASTIKA.

Ne plus ultra (nē plŭs ŭl' trà) (Lat., nothing further, *i.e.* perfection). The most perfect state to which a thing can be brought. *See* PLUS ULTRA.

Neæra (ne ē' rà). Any sweetheart or lady love. She is mentioned by HORACE, VIRGIL, and Tibullus.

> To sport with Amaryllis in the shade,
> Or with the tangles of Neæra's hair?
> MILTON: *Lycidas*.

Neanderthal Man (ni ăn' děr tal). A species of PALÆOLITHIC man inhabiting Europe during the MOUSTERIAN period. It was named from the bones discovered in a grotto of the Neanderthal ravine near Düsseldorf, in 1856. Similar remains have been found in many parts of Europe.

Neap Tides. Those tides which attain the least rise and fall at or near the first and last quarters of the moon. The high water rises little more than half as high above the mean level as it does at SPRING TIDES, and the low water sinks about half as little below it.

Near, meaning *mean*, is rather a curious play on the word *close* (close-fisted). What is "close by" is near.

Near side, and **Off side.** In Britain, left side and right side when facing forward. "Near wheel" means that to the driver's left hand; and "near horse" (in a pair) means that to the left hand of the driver. In a four-in-hand the two horses on the left side of the coachman are the near wheeler and the near leader. Those on the right-hand side are "off" horses. This, which seems an anomaly, arose when the driver walked beside his team. The teamster always walks with his right arm nearest the horse, and therefore, in a pair of horses, the horse on the left side is nearer than the one on his right. *See* OFF.

Nebo (nē' bō). A god of the Babylonians (properly, *Nabu*) mentioned in *Is.* xlvi, 1.

He was the patron of Borsippa, near Babylon, and was regarded as the inventor of writing, as well as the god of wisdom. The name occurs in many Babylonian royal names, as, Nebuchadrezzar, Nebushasban (*Jer.* xxxix, 13), Nebuzaradan (II *Kings* xxv, 8), etc.

Nebuchadnezzar (neb ū kăd nez' àr). An incorrect form of *Nebuchadrezzar* (as it appears in *Jer.* xxi, 2, etc.). The name means NEBO *protects the crown*.

Nebuchadnezzar was the greatest king of Babylon and reigned from 604 to 561 B.C. He restored his country to its former prosperity and importance, practically rebuilt Babylon, restored the temple of BEL, erected a new palace, embanked the Euphrates, and probably built the HANGING GARDENS. His name became the centre of many legends.

> The king spake, and said, Is not this great Babylon, that I have built for the house of the kingdom by the might of my power, and for the honour of my majesty?
> While the word was in the king's mouth, there fell a voice from heaven, saying, O king Nebuchadnezzar, to thee it is spoken; the kingdom is departed from Thee.
> *Daniel* iv, 30, 31.

Necessary. The 17th- and 18th-century term for a privy. In large houses the emptying and cleaning of this was carried out by a servant known as the *Necessary Woman*.

Necessitarians. Those who deny free will, holding that all action is determined by antecedent causes. Those who believe in free will are called *libertarians*.

Necessity. Necessity knows no law. These were the words used by the German Chancellor Bethmann-Hollweg in the Reichstag on 4 August 1914, as a justification for the infringement of Belgian neutrality.

> Gentlemen, we are now in a state of necessity, and necessity knows no law. Our troops have occupied Luxembourg and perhaps have already entered Belgian territory.

To quote Milton:

> So spake the Fiend, and with necessitie,
> The Tyrant's plea, excus'd his devilish deeds.
> MILTON: *Paradise Lost*, IV, 393.

The phrase is common to most languages. Publilius Syrus has *Necessitas dat legem, non ipsa accipit* (Necessity gives the law, but does not herself accept it), and the Latin proverb *Necessitas non habet legem* appears in Piers Plowman (14th century) as, "Neede hath no law."

To make a virtue of necessity. To grin and bear it; "what can't be cured must be endured".

> Thanne is it wisdom, as it thinketh me
> To maken virtu of necessitee.
> CHAUCER: *Knight's Tale*, 3041.

Quintilian has *laudem virtutis necessitati damus*; St. Jerome (epistle liv, section vi), *Fac de necessitate virtutem*. In the *Roman de la Rose* (line 14058) we find *S'il ne fait de nécessité virtu*, and Boccaccio has *Si come savia fatta della necessità*.

Neck. Slang for cheek, impudence.

Neck and crop. Entirely. The crop is the gorge of a bird; a variant of the phrase is *neck and heels*, as, "I bundled him out neck and heels." There was once a punishment which consisted in bringing the chin and knees of the culprit forcibly together, and then thrusting him into a cage.

Neck and neck. Very close competitors, very near in merit. A phrase from the TURF, when two or more horses run each other very closely.

Neck of the woods (U.S.A.). A settlement in the forest, or slang for any area.

Neck or nothing. Desperate. An all-out attempt; to win by a neck or to be nowhere; a racing phrase.

Oh that the Roman people had but one neck! The words of CALIGULA, the Roman Emperor. He wished that he could slay them all with one stroke.

Stiff-necked. Obstinate and self-willed. In the *Psalms* we read: "Speak not with a stiff neck" (lxxv, 5); and *Jer.* xvii, 23, "They obeyed not...but made their neck stiff'; and *Isaiah* xlviii, 4, says: "Thy neck is an iron sinew." The allusion is to a wilful horse, ox, or ass, which will not answer to the reins.

To get it in the neck. To be thoroughly castigated; to be severely reprimanded. The phrase is an Americanism—I got it where the chicken got the axe—"in the neck".

To stick one's neck out. To ask for trouble; to expose oneself to being hurt, as a chicken might stick out its neck for the axe.

To talk through the back of one's neck. To be utterly wrong or inaccurate, to talk rubbish, to be hopelessly wide of the mark.

Necking. A common expression for amorous "petting". In the Western States of the U.S.A., *necking* is to tie a restless animal by the neck to a tame one in order to render it more tractable. *Necking* is also part of a column between the shaft and capital, as the annulets of a DORIC capital.

Neck-tie party (U.S.A.). A hanging, particularly by LYNCH LAW.

Neck verse. The first verse of *Ps.* li. *See* MISERERE. "Have mercy upon me, O God, according to thy loving kindness: according unto the multitude of thy tender mercies blot out my transgressions."

He [a treacherous Italian interpreter] by a fine cunny-catching corrupt translation, made us plainly to confess, and cry *Miserere*, ere we had need of our necke-verse.
NASH: *The Unfortunate Traveller* (1594).

This verse was so called because it was the trial-verse of those who claimed BENEFIT OF CLERGY, and if they could read it, the ORDINARY of the prison said, "*Legit ut clericus*" (he reads like a clerk) and the prisoner saved his neck, but by an Act of Henry VII convicted clerks were branded on the hand before release.

Necklace. A necklace of coral or white bryony beads used to be worn by children to aid their teething. Necklaces of hyoscyamus or henbane-root have been recommended for the same purpose.

Diamond Necklace. *See under* DIAMOND.

The Fatal Necklace. The necklace which CADMUS gave to HARMONIA; some say that VULCAN, and others that Europa, gave it to him. It possessed the property of stirring up strife and bloodshed. It is said to have eventually become the property of Phaÿllus, who gave it to his mistress. Her youngest son set fire to the house and mother, son, and the necklace were destroyed.

Necromancy (nek' rō man si) (Gr. *nekros*, the dead; *manteia*, prophecy). Prophesying by calling up the dead, as the WITCH OF ENDOR called up Samuel (I *Sam.* xxviii, 7 ff.). Also the art of magic generally, the BLACK ART. *See* DIVINATION.

Nectar. (Gr.). In classical mythology, the drink of the gods. Like their food AMBROSIA, it conferred immortality, hence the name of the *nectarine*, so called because it is as "sweet as nectar".

Neddy. Little Edward, an old familiar name for a DONKEY. *Cp.* CUDDY; DICKY; DOBBIN.

"Neddy" is also the popular name for the National Economic Development Council set up by the Government in 1962; and the numerous Economic Development Committees for particular industries which subsequently appeared were called "Little Neddies" (21 by 1968).

Need. Needfire. Fire obtained by friction; a beacon. It was formerly supposed to defeat sorcery, and cure diseases ascribed to WITCHCRAFT, especially cattle diseases. We are told in Henderson's *Agricultural Survey of Caithness* (1812), that as late as 1785 it was so used as a charm when stock were seized with the murrain.

The ready page, with hurried hand,
Awaked the need-fire's slumbering brand.
SCOTT: *The Lay of the Last Minstrel*,
Canto Third, xxix.

Needs must. Necessity compels. A shortening of the old saying, "Needs must when the devil drives." *See under* DEVIL.

Needful, The. Ready money, cash.

Needham. You are on the high-road to Needham—to ruin or poverty. The pun is on *need* and there is no reference to Needham in Suffolk. *Cp.* LAND OF NOD.

Needle. Looking for a needle, etc. *See under* BOTTLE.

The eye of a needle. *See under* CAMEL.

To get the needle. To become thoroughly vexed, or even enraged, and to show it. A variant of the phrase is *to get the spike*.

To hit the needle. To hit the nail right on the head, to make a perfect hit. A term in archery, equivalent to hitting the bull's-eye.

To needle. In the U.S.A., to provoke, goad or tease.

Needle time. The time allocated to the broadcasting of recorded music and entertainment.

Negative. The answer is in the negative. The Parliamentary circumlocution for *No*.

Negro. Negro offspring. White father and Negro mother: MULATTO.

White father and mulatto mother: quadroon.

White father and quadroon mother: quintero.

White father and quintero mother: white.

White parent and quadroon parent: octoroon.

Negus (nē' gus). The drink—port or SHERRY, with hot water, sugar and spices—is so called from a Colonel Francis Negus (d.1732), who first concocted it.

The ruler of Ethiopia was entitled *the Negus*, from the native *n'gus*, meaning crowned.

Neiges d'Antan, Les (nāzh don tan) (Fr.). A thing of the past. Literally "last year's snows", from the refrain of François Villon's well-known *Ballade des Dames du Temps Jadis*:

Prince, n'enquerez de sepmaine
Ou elles sont, ne de cest an,
Que ce reffrain ne vous remaine:
Mais ou sont les neiges d'antan?
(Where are the snows of yester-year?)

Neighbourhood Watch. *See under* WATCH.

Neither. Neither here nor there. Irrelevant to the subject under discussion; a matter of no moment.

Nelly. A popular name in Australia for MOTHER CAREY'S GOOSE.

Not on your Nellie or **Nelly.** Not likely, not on any account, not on your life or "puff". Probably from RHYMING SLANG, "Not on your Nellie Duff", Duff rhyming with "puff" which is old slang for "breath" and life itself.

Nelson's blood. *See under* BLOOD.

Nelson's Pillar. *See under* PILLAR.

Nemean (nem' ē àn). **Nemean Games.** One of the four great festivals of ancient Greece, held in the valley of Nemea in Argolis every alternate year, the first and third of each OLYMPIAD. Legend states that they were instituted in memory of Archemorus who died from the bite of a serpent as the expedition of the SEVEN AGAINST THEBES was passing through the valley. It was customary for the games to open with a funeral oration in his honour. After HERCULES had slain the NEMEAN LION the games were held in honour of ZEUS. Athletic contests were added after the model of the OLYMPIC GAMES. The victor's reward was at first a crown of OLIVES, later of green parsley. PINDAR has eleven odes in honour of victors.

The Nemean Lion. A terrible lion which kept the people of the valley of Nemea in constant alarm. The first of the Twelve Labours of HERCULES was to slay it; he could make no impression on the beast with his club, so he caught it in his arms and squeezed it to death. Hercules ever after wore the skin as a mantle.

> My fate cries out,
> And makes each petty artery in this body
> As hardy as the Nemean lion's nerve.
> SHAKESPEARE: *Hamlet*, I, iv.

Nemesis. The Greek goddess, daughter of Nox; a divinity of vengeance who rewarded virtue and punished the wicked and all kinds of impiety; the personification of divine retribution. Hence, retributive justice generally, as *the Nemesis of Nations*, the fate which, sooner or later, overtakes every great nation.

> And though circuitous and obscure
> The feet of Nemesis how sure!
> SIR WILLIAM WATSON: *Europe at the Play*.

Nemine contradicente (usually contracted to **nem. con.**) (Lat.). No one opposing, unanimously.

Nemine dissentiente (**nem. diss.**) (Lat.). Without a dissentient voice.

Nemo me impune lacessit (Lat.). No one provokes me with impunity. The motto of the Order of the THISTLE and of the kings of SCOTLAND.

Nenni Telegram. The telegram of support sent by John Platts-Mills, Konni Zilliacus, and twenty other members of the LABOUR Party to the pro-Communist socialist Signor Nenni at the time of the Italian general election of April 1948. The Labour Party officially supported the right-wing Italian socialists; as a result Platts-Mills was expelled from the party and subsequently Zilliacus also.

Neolithic Age (Gr. *neos*, new; *lithos*, stone). The later STONE AGE of Europe. Neolithic stone implements are polished, more highly finished and more various than those of the PALÆOLITHIC Age; man knew something of agriculture, kept domestic animals, used boats, slings, and bows and arrows. It was superseded by the Bronze Age.

Nepenthe, or **Nepenthes** (Gr. *ne*, not; *penthos*, grief). An Egyptian drug mentioned in the ODYSSEY (IV, 228) that was fabled to drive away care and make people forget their woes. Polydamna, wife of Thonis, King of Egypt, gave it to HELEN.

> That nepenthes which the wife of Thone
> In Egypt gave to Jove-born Helena.
> MILTON: *Comus*, 675–6.

Nephew (Fr. *neveu*; Lat. *nepos*). Both in Latin and archaic English the word means grandchild or descendant; hence *nepotism*, the undue favouring and promotion of one's relations. In the Authorized Version of the BIBLE, I *Tim.* v, 4, reads—"if any widow have children or nephews", but in the RE-VISED VERSION "grandchildren".

Niece (Lat. *neptis*) similarly means granddaughter or female descendant.

Nepman. A term applied in the U.S.S.R. to the man allowed to engage in private-enterprise business under the New Economic Policy (N.E.P.) begun in 1921.

Nepomuk. *See* St. JOHN OF NEPOMUK *under* JOHN.

Nepotism (Ital. *nepote*, nephew). The practice of favouring relatives in matters of employment, promotion, etc. The usage derives from the days when Popes and high ecclesiastics gave preferment and advancement to their nephews as their illegitimate sons were euphemistically labelled.

Neptune. The Roman god of the sea corresponding to the Greek POSEIDON, hence, allusively, the sea itself. Neptune is represented as an elderly man of stately mien, bearded, carrying a trident, and sometimes astride a dolphin or horse. *See* HIPPOCAMPUS; PLANETS.

Neptunian, or **Neptunist.** The name given to certain 18th-century geologists, who held the opinion of Abraham Gottlob Werner (1750–1817), that all the great rocks of the earth were once held in solution in water and were deposited as sediment. *Cp.* VULCANIST.

Nereus. "THE OLD MAN OF THE SEA", a sea-god of Greek mythology represented as a very old man. He was the father of the NEREIDS and his special dominion was the Ægean Sea.

Nereids. The sea-nymphs of Greek mythology, the fifty daughters of NEREUS and "grey-eyed" Doris. The best known are AMPHITRITE, THETIS, and GALATEA. Milton refers to another, Panope, in his *Lycidas* (line 99):

> The air was calm and on the level brine
> Sleek Panope with all her sisters played.

And the names of all will be found in Spenser's *The Faerie Queene*, Bk. IV, c. xi, verses 48–51.

Neri. *See* BIANCHI.

Nero, A. Any bloody-minded man, relentless tyrant, or evil-doer of extraordinary cruelty; from the depraved and infamous Roman Emperor, C. Claudius Nero (A.D. 37, 54–68), whom contemporaries believed to be the instigator of the great fire that destroyed most of ROME in A.D. 64, and to have recited his own poetry and played his lyre while enjoying the spectacle. Nero blamed the Christians.

Nero of the North. Christian II of Denmark (1481–1559), also called "The Cruel". He conquered Sweden in 1520 and massacred over 80 nobles and others in "the blood-bath" at Stockholm. Several hundred prominent people were put to death subsequently. The Danish oppressors were driven out by Gustavus Vasa in 1523.

Neroli. The essential oil of orange blossoms, used in EAU DE COLOGNE and other perfumes, is said to have been named after an Italian princess of the Neroli family.

Nerthus, or **Hertha.** The name given by Tacitus to a German or Scandinavian goddess of fertility, or "Mother Earth", who was worshipped on the island of Rügen. She roughly corresponds with the classical CYBELE; and is probably confused with the Scandinavian god *Njorthr* or NIORDHR, the protector of sailors and fishermen. *Nerthus* and *Njorthr* alike mean "benefactor".

Nessus. Shirt of Nessus. A source of misfortune from which there is no escape. The shirt of Nessus killed HERCULES. *See* DEIANIRA; *cp.* HARMONIA.

Nest-egg. Money laid by. The allusion is to the custom of placing an egg in a hen's nest to induce her to lay her eggs there. If a person has saved a little money, it serves as an inducement to him to increase his store.

Nestor. King of Pylos, in Greece; the oldest and most experienced of the chieftains who went to the siege of TROY. Hence the name is frequently applied as an epithet to the oldest and wisest man of a class or company. Samuel Rogers, for instance, who lived to be 92, was called "the Nestor of English poets".

Nestorians. Followers of Nestorius, Patriarch

of Constantinople, 428–431 (d. *c.* 451). He is traditionally supposed to have asserted that Christ had two distinct natures and that Mary was the mother of his human nature. His teaching was condemned by Pope Celestine I in 430. A separate Nestorian Church was established which spread to Asia where most of their churches were destroyed by Timur (TAMBURLAINE) about 1400. A small group called Assyrian Christians survived in parts of Asia Minor and Persia.

Nettle. To grasp the nettle. To face up firmly to a difficulty, to tackle a situation boldly. A nettle is less likely to sting when grasped firmly as the lines written by Aaron Hill (1685–1750) tell us:

> Tender-handed stroke a nettle,
> And it stings you for your pains;
> Grasp it like a man of mettle,
> And it soft as silk remains.

Neustria. The western portion of the ancient Frankish Kingdom, originally corresponding to north-western France between the Loire and the mouth of the Scheldt. In the 8th century the name was applied to Western Lombardy.

Never. There are numerous locutions to express this idea, as:

> At the coming of the COCQCIGRUES.
> At the Latter LAMMAS.
> NARROWDALE NOON.
> In the reign of QUEEN DICK.
> On ST. TIB'S EVE.
> In a MONTH OF SUNDAYS.
> When two Fridays or three Sundays come together.
> When Dover and Calais meet.
> When pigs fly.
> When the world grows honest.
> When the Yellow river runs clear.

On the never never. To get or buy something on the never never is to obtain it on hire purchase, a system of deferred payment.

Never had it so good. Earlier current in the U.S.A., the phrase became popular in Britain after its use by Harold Macmillan, Conservative Prime Minister (1957–1964), in a speech at Bedford (20 July 1957). Referring to the overall prosperity and general improvement of living standards, he said, "Most of our people have never had it so good."

Never Never Land. The land where the Lost Boys and Red Indians lived, and where Pirates sailed up the lake in J. M. Barrie's PETER PAN (1904). The phrase was applied to the whole of the Australian outback, but since the publication of *We of the Never Never* (1908) by Mrs. Aeneas Gunn it was restricted to the Northern Territory.

New. New Atlantis. *See under* ATLANTIS.

New Deal. The name given to President Roosevelt's policy of economic reconstruction announced in his first presidential campaign (1932). "I pledge you, I pledge myself, to a new deal for the American people." A relief and recovery programme known as the "First New Deal" was inaugurated in March 1933, and a "Second New Deal" concerned with social reform in January 1935. The "Third New Deal" of 1938 sought to preserve such gains made by its predecessors.

New England. The collective name of the north-eastern states of the U.S.A.—Connecticut, Massachusetts, Rhode Island, Vermont, New Hampshire, and Maine. In colonial days, Plymouth and New Haven formed part of the group before they lost their separate identities as part of Massachusetts and Connecticut respectively. The name was given to the area by Captain John Smith in 1614 and colonization was begun by the PILGRIM FATHERS after the Plymouth Company of Virginia had been revived as the Council for New England. During the English CIVIL WAR a New England Confederation was set up consisting of Massachusetts, Plymouth, Connecticut, and New Haven to maintain a common front. James II formed a short-lived Dominion of New England (1687–1689), consisting of Massachusetts, Rhode Island, Connecticut, Plymouth, Maine, and New Hampshire, to which NEW YORK and New Jersey were added.

New Jersey tea. The popular name for *Ceanothus americanus*, a white-flowered plant found in the north-eastern areas of the U.S.A. The name derives from the fact that Indians and colonists made a kind of tea from the plant, the former regarding the drink as possessing medicinal properties. According to tradition, some colonists used this tea to avoid the British tax on imported tea.

New Jerusalem. The city of HEAVEN foretold in *Rev.* xxi, 2, "coming down from God out of heaven, prepared as a bride adorned for her husband". Hence, figuratively, the perfect society.

The New Jerusalem Church. The name chosen (*c.* 1784) by Richard Hindmarsh for the sect founded by him on the doctrines of Emanuel Swedenborg. *See* SWEDENBORGIANS.

New Learning. The name given to the revival of Greek and Latin classical learning during the period of the 15th- and 16th-century RENAISSANCE.

New lease of life. Renewed health and vigour, especially applied to someone who appears to gain his "second wind" after a serious illness or change of circumstances.

New Look. The name given to the long-skirted women's dress of 1948. The style was reminiscent of Edwardian days and was short-lived.

New Model, The. In the CIVIL WAR, the Parliamentary army organized in 1645 under Sir Thomas Fairfax in place of a variety of local forces. Most of the officers were IN-DEPENDENTS and the troopers of the EAST-ERN ASSOCIATION became its backbone. Initially more than half of the infantry were pressed men. Regular pay (not available to the CAVALIERS) resulted in better discipline. Cromwell took command in 1650.

New Morality. A popular term of the 1960s implying that the hitherto publicly accepted canons of morality are no longer relevant to present-day society, owing to the rapid spread of social and technical change, the advent of the PILL, and more "enlightened" attitudes generally. Such thinking was induced by the growth of the AFFLUENT SOCIE-TY, the diminishing of individual responsibility occasioned by the WELFARE STATE, the declining influence of Christian standards and "middle-class morality", and the championship of hedonism and self-indulgence by AVANT-GARDE writers and scientific theorists, who seem to lack the balance of historical perspective. In the sphere of sexual behaviour it has been neatly defined by Lord Shawcross as "the old immorality"; and, in general, its effect has been to deprive many of the young of a sense of direction, duty, and that self-discipline which helps to distinguish man from the animal. The growth of the PERMISSIVE SOCIETY has not as yet produced much of a credit balance. *Cp.* SCAR-LET LETTER.

New Style. *See* GREGORIAN YEAR; STILO NOVO.

New Testament, The. The name given to the second group of sacred writings in the BIBLE comprising 27 books in all (the four Gospels, The Acts of the Apostles, 21 Epistles and the Revelation of St. John the Divine), but which more correctly could be called "The New Covenant" or "The New Dispensation".

The religion of Israel was regarded as a covenant between Jehovah and his chosen people and in due time a new covenant was promised by the prophets:

> Behold, the days come, saith the Lord, that I will make a new covenant with the house of Israel, and the house of Judah.—*Jeremiah* xxi, 31.

This new covenant, for the Christians, was established by the life and death of Christ, and towards the end of the 2nd century a generally accepted collection of new scriptures, worthy of complementing the OLD TESTAMENT, was evolving. The present canon is that established by the Council of Carthage in 397. The name *Testament* is from the Lat. *testamentum* which is an inaccurate rendering of the Gr. *diathēkē*, "disposition" or "covenant". Thus we have in the *Authorized Version* (*Luke* xxii, 20): "This cup is the new testament in my blood, which is shed for you." This in the *Revised Version* reads "This cup is the new covenant in my blood, even that which is poured out for you." *See* APOCRYPHA.

New Thought. A general term for a system of therapeutics based on the theory that the mental and physical problems of life should be met, regulated and controlled by the suggestion of right thoughts. This system has nothing in common with CHRISTIAN SCI-ENCE, auto-suggestion or psychotherapy.

New World. The Americas; the Eastern Hemisphere is called the Old World.

I have called the New World into existence to redress the balance of the Old. The famous words used by George Canning (1777–1827), British Foreign Secretary, in 1826 to justify his allowing a French occupation of Spain, but not of the former Spanish colonies in South America, whose independence he had recognized in 1823. "Contemplating Spain, such as our ancestors had known her, I resolved that if France had Spain, it should not be Spain with the Indies. I called the New World into existence to redress the balance of the Old." *Cp.* MON-ROE DOCTRINE.

New Year's Day. 1 January. The Romans began their year in March; hence *September, October, November, December* for the 7th, 8th, 9th, 10th months. Since the introduction of the Christian era, CHRISTMAS Day, LADY DAY, EASTER Day, 1 March and 25 March have in turns been considered as New Year's Day. With the introduction of the GREGORIAN YEAR, 1 January was accepted as New Year's Day by most Christian countries, but not until 1600 in Scotland, and 1752 in England.

New Year's gifts. The giving of presents at this time was a custom among both the Greeks and the Romans, the latter calling them *strenæ*, whence the French term *étrenne* (a New Year's gift). Nonius Marcellus says that Tatius, King of the SABINES, was presented with some branches of trees cut from the forest sacred to the goddess STRENIA (strength) on New Year's Day, and from this incident the custom arose.

Our forefathers used to bribe the magistrates with gifts on New Year's Day—a custom abolished by law in 1290, but even down to the reign of James II the monarchs received their "tokens".

New York. Formerly New Amsterdam, so named in honour of James, Duke of York, brother of Charles II, to whom it was granted after its capture by the British in 1664.

New Zealand. The name of this former British colony is derived from the Dutch province of *Zeeland* as a result of its discovery in 1642 by Abel Tasman, the great Dutch navigator. *See* WAITANGI DAY.

Newcastle. To carry coals to Newcastle. *See under* COAL.

Newgate. According to Stow, this was first built in the city wall of LONDON in the time of Henry I, but excavations have shown that there was a Roman gate here about 31 ft. in width. It may have fallen into disuse, and have been repaired by Henry I, the present name being given at the time.

Newgate Gaol. The first prison (over the gate) existed in the reign of King John. The last prison on the site (designed in 1770) was closed in 1880 and demolished in 1902, and it was for long the prison for the City of LONDON and County of Middlesex. Many notorious criminals and state prisoners were confined there, as well as debtors. Condemned criminals were executed in the street outside, "condemned sermons" being preached the preceding Sunday, to which the public were formerly admitted.

From its prominence, Newgate came to be applied as a general name for gaols, and Nash, in his *Pierce Pennilesse* (1592), says it is "a common name for all prisons, as *homo* is a common name for a man or woman".

The Newgate Calendar. A biographical record of the more notorious criminals confined at Newgate; begun in 1773 and continued at intervals for many years. In 1824–1828 A. Knapp and Wm. Baldwin published, in 4 vols., *The Newgate Calendar, comprising Memoirs of Notorious Characters*, partly compiled by George Borrow; and in 1886, C. Pelham published his *Chronicles of Crime or the New Newgate Calendar* (2 vols.). Another such calendar was published in 1969. The term is often used as a comprehensive expression embracing crime of every sort.

> I also felt that I had committed every crime in the Newgate Calendar.
> DICKENS: *Our Mutual Friend*, ch. xiv.

Newgate fashion. Two by two. Prisoners used to be conveyed to Newgate linked together in twos.

> Must we all march?
> Yea, two and two, Newgate fashion.
> SHAKESPEARE: *Henry IV, Pt. I*, III, iii.

Newgate fringe. The hair worn under the chin, or between the chin and the neck. So called because it occupies the position of the rope when men are about to be hanged.

Newgate knocker. A lock of hair twisted into a curl, once worn by COSTERMONGERS and persons of similar status. So called because it resembles a knocker, and the wearers were too often inmates of Newgate.

News. The letters E $\frac{N}{S}$ W used to be prefixed to newspapers to show that they obtained information from the four quarters of the world, and the supposition that our word *news* is thence derived is an ingenious conceit but destroyed by the old spelling *newes*; it is from the Fr. *nouvelles*.

> News is conveyed by letter, word or mouth
> And comes to us from North, East, West and South.
> *Witt's Recreations.*

The word is now nearly always construed as singular ("the news is very good"), but it was formerly treated as a plural, and in the *Letters of Queen Victoria* the Queen and most of her correspondents so treated it:

> The news from Austria are very sad, and make one very anxious.
> *To the King of the Belgians*, 20 August 1861.

Newspeak. Language in which the words change their meaning to accord with the official party-political views of the state. Coined by George Orwell (1903–1950) in his *1984*. *Cp.* LOOKING-GLASS.

Newt. *See* NICKNAMES.

Newtonian Philosophy. The astronomical system that in the late 17th century displaced COPERNICANISM, and also the theory of universal gravitation. So called after Sir Isaac Newton (1642–1727), who established the former and discovered the latter.

> Nature and Nature's laws lay hid in night;
> God said "Let Newton be", and all was light.
> POPE: *Intended for Sir Isaac Newton.*

Next of Kin. The legal term for a person's nearest relative, more especially where estate is left by an intestate. In English law the next of kin in priority is: Husband or wife; children; father or mother (equally if both alive); brothers and sisters; grandparents; uncles and aunts; half uncles and aunts; the Crown.

Next friend, in law, is an adult (usually a relation) who brings an action in a court of law on behalf of a minor or a person of unsound mind.

Nibelungenlied, The (nē be lung' en lēd). A

great mediæval German epic poem founded on old Scandinavian legends contained in the *Volsunga Saga* and the EDDA.

Nibelung was a mythical king of a race of Scandinavian dwarfs dwelling in *Nibelheim* (*i.e.* "the home of darkness, or mist"). These *Nibelungs* or *Nibelungers* were the possessors of the wonderful "Hoard" of gold and precious stones guarded by the dwarf ALBERICH, and their name passed to later holders of the Hoard, SIEGFRIED's following and the Burgundians being in turn called "the Nibelungs".

Siegfried, the hero of the first part of the poem, became possessed of the Hoard and married KRIEMHILD, sister of GUNTHER, King of Worms, whom he helped to secure the hand of BRUNHILD of Iceland. After Siegfried's murder by Hagen at Brunhild's instigation, Kriemhild carried the treasure to Worms where it was seized by Gunther and his retainer Hagen. They buried it in the Rhine, intending later to enjoy it; but they were both slain for refusing to reveal its whereabouts, and the Hoard remains for ever in the keeping of the Rhine Maidens. The second part of the Nibelungenlied tells of the marriage of the widow Kriemhild with King Atli or ETZEL (Attila), her invitation of the Burgundians to the court of the Hunnish King, and the slaughter of all the principal characters, including Gunther, Hagen and Kriemhild.

Nic Frog. *See under* FROG.

Nicæa. The Council of Nicæa. The first ŒCUMENICAL COUNCIL of the Christian Church held under Constantine the Great in 325 at Nicæa in Bithynia, Asia Minor, primarily to deal with the ARIAN heresy, which it condemned. The second Council of Nicæa (787), the seventh General Council of the Church, was summoned by The Empress Irene to end the Iconoclastic Controversy (*see* ICONOCLASTS).

Nicene Creed. The creed properly so called was a comparatively short statement of beliefs issued in 325 by the COUNCIL OF NICÆA to combat the ARIAN heresy. The "Nicene Creed" commonly referred to is that properly called the *Niceno-Constantinopolitan Creed*, referred to in Article VIII of the THIRTY-NINE ARTICLES given in the BOOK OF COMMON PRAYER, which ultimately derives from the Baptismal Creed of JERUSALEM. It is used in the EUCHARIST of the ROMAN CATHOLIC CHURCH, the CHURCH OF ENGLAND, and the EASTERN CHURCH, where it still forms part of the service of Baptism. It was first used at Antioch in the late 5th century and gradually gained acceptance in both East and West. *See also* FILIOQUE CONTROVERSY. *Cp.* APOSTLES' CREED; ATHANASIAN CREED.

Nicholas, St. One of the most popular saints in Christendom, especially in the East. He is the patron SAINT of Russia, of Aberdeen, of parish clerks, of scholars (who used to be called clerks), of pawnbrokers (because of the three bags of gold—transformed to the three gold BALLS—that he gave to the daughters of a poor man to save them from earning their dowers in a disreputable way), of little boys (because he once restored to life three little boys who had been cut up and pickled in a salting-tub to serve for bacon), and is invoked by sailors (because he allayed a storm during a voyage to the HOLY LAND) and against fire. Finally he is the original of SANTA CLAUS.

Little is known of his life but he is said to have been Bishop of Myra (Lycia) in the early 4th century, and one story relates that he was present at the COUNCIL OF NICÆA (325) and buffeted Arius on the jaw. His day is 6 December, and he is represented in episcopal robes with either three purses of gold, three gold balls, or three small boys, in allusion to one or other of the above legends. *Cp.* LOMBARD.

St. Nicholas's Bishop. *See* BOY BISHOP.

St. Nicholas's Clerks. Old slang for thieves and highwaymen. It has been suggested that it may be an allusion to the liberties taken by choristers on St. Nicholas's day when they chose their BOY BISHOP.

> Sirrah, if they meet not with Saint Nicholas' clerks,
> I'll give thee this neck.
> SHAKESPEARE: *Henry IV, Pt. I*, II, i.

Nick. Slang for to pilfer; in the 18th century those who delighted to break windows by throwing halfpence at them were called *nickers*.

> His scattered pence the flying Nicker flings,
> And with the copper shower the casement rings.
> GAY: *Trivia*, III, 323.

Old Nick. The DEVIL. The term was in use in the 17th century, and is perhaps connected with the German *Nickel*, a GOBLIN, or in some forgotten way with St. NICHOLAS. Butler's derivation from Niccolò Machiavelli is, of course, poetical licence:

> Nick Machiavel had ne'er a trick
> (Though he gave name to our old Nick).
> *Hudibras*, III, i.

He nicked it. Won, hit, accomplished it. A *nick* is a winning throw of dice in the old game of hazard. Also, he stole it (*see* NICK *above*).

In the nick. In prison, in custody.

In the nick of time. Just in time, at the

right moment. The allusion is to tallies marked with nicks or notches. (*See* TALLY.)

To nick the nick. To hit the exact moment. Tallies used to be called "nick-sticks". Hence, to make a record of anything is "to nick it down", as the publicans used to nick a score on a TALLY.

Nicka-Nan Night. The night preceding SHROVE TUESDAY was so called in CORNWALL because boys played tricks and practical jokes on that night. The following night they went from house to house singing—

Nicka, nicka nan,
Give me some pancake and then I'll be gone;
But if you give me none
I'll throw a great stone
And down your doors shall come.

Nickel. The metal is so called from the Ger. *Kupfernickel*, the name given to the ore from which it was first obtained (1751) by Axel F. von Cronstedt. *Kupfer* means copper, and *Nickel* is the name of a mischievous GOBLIN fabled to inhabit mines in Germany; the name was given to it because, although it was copper-coloured, no copper could be got from it, and so the *Nickel* was blamed.

In the U.S.A. a *nickel* is a coin of 5 cents, so called from being made of an alloy of nickel and copper.

Nickelodeon. The first cinema theatre called a "Nickelodeon" (because the admission price was only five cents), was that opened by John P. Harris and Harry Davis at McKeesport, near Pittsburgh, Pennsylvania, in 1905. The picture shown was *The Great Train Robbery*. It was the first real motion-picture theatre and thousands more nickelodeons soon sprang up throughout the U.S.A. Hence, a cheap entertainment, and also its application to a juke-box.

Nicker, or **Nix.** In Scandinavian folklore, a water-wraith, or KELPIE, inhabiting sea, lake, river, and waterfall. They are sometimes represented as half-child, half-horse, the hoofs being reversed, and sometimes as old men sitting on rocks wringing the water from their hair. The female nicker is a *nixy*.

Nickname. Originally *an eke-name*, *eke* being an adverb meaning "also", O.E. *eac*, connected with *iecan*, to supply deficiencies in or to make up for. *A newt* was formed in the same way (*an ewt*). The "eke" of a bee-hive is a piece added to the bottom to enlarge the hive. *Cp.* APRON; NONCE. Surnames as such were not common in England before the 13th century; hence identification was helped by nicknames such as "Long", "Brown", "Bull", "Russell" (red-haired), "Sour milk", "Barefoot", etc.

National Nicknames. Among the best known are:

For an American of the U.S.A., "BROTHER JONATHAN", a "YANKEE"; for the U.S.A. personified, "UNCLE SAM" (*see under* SAM).

For an Australian, "AUSSIE", "DIGGER".

For a Dutchman, "NIC FROG" (*see under* FROG) and "Mynheer Closh".

For an Englishman, "JOHN BULL", "LIMEY", "POMMIE".

For a Frenchman, "Crapaud" (*see* FLEUR-DE-LYS), "Froggie" or "FROG", "Johnny" or "Jean", "Robert MACAIRE", "Mossoo".

For a French Canadian, "Jean Baptiste", "CANUCK".

For French peasantry, "Jacques Bonhomme".

For French reformers, "BRISSOTINS".

For a German, "COUSIN MICHAEL" or "Michel", "Boche", "HUN", "Fritz", "Heinie", "Kraut", "JERRY."

For an Irishman, "PADDY".

For an Italian, "Antonio", or "Tony". *Cp.* WOP.

For a Scot, "Sandy", "Mac", or "Jock".

For a Spaniard or Portuguese, "Dago" (Diego).

For a Welshman, "TAFFY".

Traditional Nicknames of those with a particular surname are numerous. Among them are:

Dinger or Daisy Bell; Nobby Clark; Cocky Ducros (Austr.); Pincher Martin; Dusty Miller; Spud Murphy; Spud Thomson; Knocker White.

In Australia fair-headed people are called "Snowy" and red-headed "Blue".

Nickneven. A gigantic malignant hag of Scottish superstition. Dunbar has well described this spirit in his *Flyting of Dunbar and Kennedy*.

Nicodemus, Gospel of. *See under* GOSPEL.

Nicodemused into nothing. To have one's prospects in life ruined by a silly name; according to the proverb, "Give a DOG a bad name and hang him." It is from Sterne's *Tristram Shandy* (vol. I, 19):

How many Cæsars and Pompeys...by mere inspiration of the names have been rendered worthy of them; and how many...might have done...well in the world...had they not been Nicodemused into nothing.

Nicotine. So named from *Nicotiana*, the Latin name of the tobacco plant, given to it in honour of Jean Nicot (*c.* 1530–1600), French ambassador to Portugal, who introduced tobacco into France about 1560.

Niece. *See* NEPHEW.

Niflheim (nif' êl hīm) (*i.e.* mist-home). In

Scandinavian mythology, the region of endless cold and everlasting night, ruled over by the goddess HEL. It consisted of nine worlds, to which were consigned those who die of disease or old age; it existed in the north and out of its spring Hvergelmir flowed twelve ice-cold streams. *Cp.* MUSPELHEIM.

Nigger (Lat. *niger*, black). A Negro or anyone of very dark skin. It is now an offensive term.

Nigger Minstrels. The common name for the once-popular "coon" shows of the MUSIC HALL and seaside concert party who drew their inspiration from the CHRISTY MINSTREL shows. The Kentucky Minstrels and Black and White Minstrels are more recent revivals of this type of performance. Their songs were characterized by humour and pathos, plantation life was romanticized but it was essentially good-humoured and without any offensive intent. *See also* UNCLE TOM'S CABIN.

A nigger in the woodpile. Originally a way of accounting for the disappearance of fuel; it now denotes something deceitful or underhanded; a concealed troublemaker or suspicious circumstance.

Night of the Long Knives, The. A descriptive phrase applied to the night of 30 June 1934 when Hitler, assisted by Göring and Himmler's GESTAPO, secured the murder of the leaders of the BROWNSHIRTS (S.A.) and some Catholic leaders. The shootings (mainly at Munich and Berlin) actually began on the Friday night of the 29th and continued through the Sunday. The estimates of those killed vary between 60 and 400 and Röhm and Schleicher were among them. Hitler had decided to rely on the *Reichswehr* rather than risk dependence on Röhm and the S.A. Himmler presented the assassins with "daggers of honour" inscribed with his name.

George Borrow, referring to a treacherous murder of South British chieftains by Hengist in 472, says:

> This infernal carnage the Welsh have appropriately denominated the treachery of the long knives. It will be as well to observe that the Saxons derived their name from the saxes, or long knives, which they wore at their sides, and at the use of which they were terribly proficient.
>
> *Wild Wales* (1862), ch. lii.

The phrase is now applied allusively to ruthless or relentless deeds and actions.

Nightingale. The Greek legend is that Tereus, King of Thrace, fetched Philomela to visit his wife, Procne, who was her sister; but when he reached the "solitudes of Heleas" he dishonoured her, and cut out her tongue that she might not reveal his con-duct. Tereus told his wife that Philomela was dead, but Philomela made her story known by weaving it into a robe, which she sent to Procne. Procne, in revenge, cut up her own son and served him to Tereus, and as soon as the king discovered it he pursued his wife, who fled to Philomela; whereupon the gods changed all three into birds; Tereus became the hawk, his wife the swallow, and Philomela, the nightingale, which is still called Philomel (lit., lover of song) by the poets.

> Youths and maidens most poetical...
> Full of meek sympathy must heave their sighs
> O'er Philomela's pity-pleading strains.
> COLERIDGE: *The Nightingale.*

The Swedish Nightingale. The operatic singer, Jenny Lind (1820–1887), afterwards Mme Goldschmidt. She was a native of Stockholm.

Nightmare. A sensation in sleep as if something heavy were sitting on one's breast, formerly supposed to be caused by a monster who actually did this. It was not infrequently called the *night-hag*, or the *riding of the witch*. The second syllable is the O.E. *mare* (old Norse *mara*), an INCUBUS, and it appears in the Fr. *cauchemar*, "the fiend that tramples". The word now usually denotes a frightening dream, a night terror.

The Nightmare of Europe. NAPOLEON BONAPARTE was so called.

Nihil. Nihil obstat. The words by which a Roman Catholic censor of books (*Censor Librorum*) declares that he has found nothing contrary to faith or good morals in the book in question. The full Latin phrase is *nihil obstat quominus imprimatur*, nothing hinders it from being printed.

The IMPRIMATUR is granted by the BISHOP or his delegate.

Nihilism (nī' hil izm) (Lat. *nihil*, nothing). The name given to an essentially philosophical and literary movement in Russia which questioned and protested against conventional and established values, etc. The term was popularized by Turgenev's novel *Fathers and Sons* (1862) and was subsequently confused with a kind of revolutionary anarchism. Although nihilism proper was basically non-political, it strengthened revolutionary trends. The term was not new having long been applied to negative systems of philosophy.

Nike (nī' kē). The Greek winged goddess of victory, according to Hesiod, the daughter of PALLAS and STYX. A U.S.A. army ground-to-air missile for use against high-flying attacking planes is so named from this goddess.

Nine

Nil admirari (Lat.). To be stolidly indifferent. Neither to wonder at anything, nor yet to admire anything. The tag is from HORACE (*Ep.* I, vi, 1):

> Nil admirari prope res est una, Numici,
> Solaque, quæ possit facere et servare beatum.

> (Not to admire, Numicius, is the best—
> The only way to make and keep men blest.)
> *Conington.*

Nil desperandum (Lat.). Never say die; never give up in despair; a tag from HORACE (*Carmen*, I, vii, 27):

> Nil desperandum Teucro duce et auspice Teucro.

> (There is naught to be despaired of when we are under Teucer's leadership and auspices.)

Nile. The Egyptians used to say that the rising of the Nile was caused by the tears of ISIS. The feast of Isis was celebrated at the anniversary of the death of OSIRIS, when Isis was supposed to mourn for her husband.

The Hero of the Nile. Horatio, Lord Nelson (1758–1805), from his great victory at Aboukir Bay (1798), for which he was made Baron Nelson of the Nile.

Nimbus (Lat., a cloud). In Christian art a HALO of light placed round the head of an eminent personage. There are three forms: (1) *Vesica piscis*, or fish form (*cp.* ICHTHYS), used in representations of Christ and occasionally of the Virgin Mary, extending round the whole figure; (2) a circular halo; (3) radiated like a star or sun. The enrichments are: (1) for our Lord, a CROSS; (2) for the Virgin, a circlet of stars; (3) for ANGELS, a circlet of small rays, and an outer circle of quatrefoils; (4) the same for SAINTS and martyrs, but with the name often inscribed round the circumference; (5) for the Deity the rays diverge in a triangular direction. Nimbi of a square form signify that the persons so represented were living when they were painted.

The nimbus was used by heathen nations long before painters introduced it into sacred pictures of saints, the TRINITY, and the Virgin Mary. PROSERPINE was represented with a nimbus; the Roman EMPERORS were also decorated in the same manner because they were *divi*. Cp. AUREOLE.

Nimini-pimini. Affected simplicity. Lady Emily, in General Burgoyne's *The Heiress*, III, ii (1786), tells Miss Alscrip to stand before a glass and keep pronouncing *nimini-pimini*—"The lips cannot fail to take the right plie."

A similar conceit is used by Dickens in *Little Dorrit* (Bk. II, ii), where Mrs. General tells Amy Dorrit:

> Papa gives a pretty form to the lips. Papa, potatoes,

poultry, prunes, and *prism* are all very good words for the lips; especially *prunes* and *prism*.

W.S. Gilbert has the form (*Patience*, II):

> A miminy-piminy, *Je-ne-sais-quoi* young man.

Nimrod. Any daring or outstanding hunter; from the "mighty hunter before the Lord" (*Gen.* x, 9), which the TARGUM says means a "sinful hunting of the sons of men". Pope says of him, he was "a mighty hunter, and his prey was man" (*Windsor Forest*, 62); so also Milton interprets the phrase (*Paradise Lost*, XII, 24, etc.).

The legend is that the tomb of Nimrod still exists in Damascus, and that no dew ever falls upon it, even though all its surroundings are saturated.

Nimrod was the pseudonym of Major Charles Apperley (1779–1843), a devotee of hunting and contributor to the *Sporting Magazine*. His best-known works are *The Life of John Mytton Esq.*, *The Chase, the Turf, and the Road*, and the *Life of a Sportsman*.

Nine. Nine, FIVE, THREE are mystical numbers—the DIAPASON, *diapente*, and *diatrion* of the Greeks. Nine consists of a trinity of trinities. According to the Pythagoreans man is a full chord, or eight notes, and deity comes next. Three, being the TRINITY, represents a perfect *unity*; twice three is the perfect *dual*; and thrice three is the perfect *plural*. This explains why nine is a mystical number.

From ancient times the number nine has been held of particular significance. DEUCALION'S ark was tossed about for *nine* days when it stranded on the top of Mount PARNASSUS. There were *nine* MUSES, *nine* Gallicenæ or virgin priestesses of the ancient Gallic ORACLE; and Lars Porsena swore by *nine* gods.

NIOBE'S children lay *nine* days in their blood before they were buried; the HYDRA had *nine* heads; at the *Lemuria*, held by the Romans on 9, 11, and 13 May, persons haunted threw black beans over their heads, pronouncing *nine* times the words: "Avaunt, ye spectres, from this house!" and the EXORCISM was complete (*see* Ovid's *Fasti*).

There were *nine* rivers of HELL, or, according to some accounts, the STYX encompassed the infernal regions in *nine* circles; and Milton makes the gates of HELL "thrice three-fold", "three folds were brass, three iron, three of adamantine rock". They had *nine* folds, *nine* plates, and *nine* linings (*Paradise Lost*, II, 645).

VULCAN, when kicked from OLYMPUS, was *nine* days falling to the island of LEMNOS; and when the fallen ANGELS were cast out of

HEAVEN Milton says "*Nine* days they fell" (*Paradise Lost*, VI, 871).

In the early Ptolemaic system of astronomy, before the PRIMUM MOBILE was added, there were *nine* SPHERES; hence Milton, in his *Arcades*, speaks of

The celestial siren's harmony,
That sat upon the nine enfolded spheres.

In Scandinavian mythology there were *nine* earths, HEL being the goddess of the ninth; there were *nine* worlds in NIFLHEIM, and ODIN'S ring dropped eight other rings every *ninth* night.

In folk-lore *nine* appears frequently. The ABRACADABRA was worn *nine* days, and then flung into a river; in order to see the FAIRIES one is directed to put "*nine* grains of wheat on a four-leaved clover"; *nine* knots are made on black wool as a charm for a sprained ankle; if a servant finds *nine* green peas in a peascod, she lays it on the lintel of the kitchen door, and the first man that enters is to be her cavalier; to see *nine* magpies is most unlucky; a cat has *nine* lives (*see also* CAT-O'-NINE-TAILS); and the *nine* of Diamonds is known as the CURSE OF SCOTLAND.

The weird sisters in Shakespeare's *Macbeth* (I, iii) sang, as they danced round the cauldron, "Thrice to thine, and thrice to mine, and thrice again to make up nine"; and then declared "the charm wound up"; and we drink a *Three-times-three* to those most highly honoured.

Leases are sometimes granted for 999 years, that is *three* times *three-three-three*. Many run for 99 years, the dual of a trinity of trinities.

See also the NINE POINTS OF THE LAW *below*, and the NINE WORTHIES *under* WORTHIES. There are *nine* orders of angels; in HERALDRY there are *nine* marks of cadency and *nine* different crowns recognized.

Dressed up to the nines. *See* DRESSED.

Nine days' Queen. Lady Jane Grey. She was proclaimed queen in London on 10 July 1553; Queen Mary was proclaimed in London on 19 July.

Nine days' wonder. Something that causes a great sensation for a few days, and then passes into the LIMBO of things forgotten. An old proverb is: "A wonder lasts nine days, and then the puppy's eyes are open," alluding to dogs, which like cats, are born blind. As much as to say, the eyes of the public are blind in astonishment for nine days, but then their eyes are open, and they see too much to wonder any longer.

King: You'd think it strange if I should marry her.
Gloster: That would be ten days' wonder, at the least.

Clar.: That's a day longer than a wonder lasts.
SHAKESPEARE: *Henry VI, Pt. III*, III, ii.

The Nine First Fridays. In the ROMAN CATHOLIC CHURCH the special observance of the first FRIDAY in each of nine consecutive months, marked by receiving the EUCHARIST. The practice derives from St. Mary Alacoque (*see* SACRED HEART *under* HEART), who held that Christ told her that special grace would be granted to those fulfilling this observance.

Nine Men's Morris. *See under* MORRIS.

The Nine Worthies. *See* WORTHIES.

Nine-tail bruiser. Prison slang for the CAT-O'-NINE-TAILS.

Nine tailors make a man. *See* TAILOR.

Nine times out of ten. Far more often than not.

Possession is nine points of the law. It is every advantage a person can have short of actual right. The "nine points of the law" have been given as: (1) a good deal of money; (2) a good deal of patience; (3) a good cause; (4) a good lawyer; (5) a good counsel; (6) good witnesses; (7) a good jury; (8) a good judge; and (9) good luck.

To look nine ways. To squint.

Ninepence. Commendation Ninepence. *See* COMMENDATION.

Nice as ninepence. A corruption of "Nice as nine-pins". In the game of nine-pins, the "men" are set in three rows with the utmost exactitude or nicety.

Nimble as ninepence. Silver ninepences were common till the year 1696, when all unmilled coin was called in. These ninepences were very *pliable* or "nimble", and, being bent, were given as love tokens, the usual formula of presentation being *To my love, from my love*. There is an old proverb, *A nimble ninepence is better than a slow shilling*.

Ninepence to a shilling. An old rustic phrase in the West of England meaning that the person referred to is deficient in common sense or intelligence.

Right as ninepence. Perfectly well; in perfect condition.

Ninus. Son of Belus, husband of SEMIRAMIS, and the reputed builder of Nineveh. It is at his tomb that the lovers meet in the PYRAMUS and Thisbe travesty:

Pyr.: Wilt thou at Ninny's tomb meet me straightway?
This.: 'Tide life, 'tide death, I come without delay.
SHAKESPEARE: *Midsummer Night's Dream*, V, i.

Niobe (nī' o bē). The personification of maternal sorrow. According to Greek legend, Niobe, the daughter of TANTALUS and wife of AMPHION, King of THEBES, was the mother of fourteen children, and taunted LATONA because she had but two—APOLLO and DIANA. Latona commanded her children to avenge the insult and they consequently destroyed Niobe's sons and daughters. Niobe, inconsolable, wept herself to death, and was changed into a stone, from which ran water, "Like Niobe, all tears" (SHAKESPEARE: *Hamlet*, I, ii).

The Niobe of Nations. So BYRON styles ROME, the "lone mother of dead empires", with "broken thrones and temples"; a "chaos of ruins"; a "desert where we steer stumbling o'er recollections" (*Childe Harold*, iv, 79).

Niord, Niordhr, or **Njorthr.** A Scandinavian god, protector of wealth and ships, who dwelt at Noatun by the sea-shore. His wife Skadi lived in the mountains, for the gulls disturbed her sleep! *See* CUP OF VOWS; NERTHUS.

Nip. A nip of whisky, etc. Short for **Nipperkin.** A small wine and beer measure containing about half a pint, or a little under; now frequently called "a nip".

> His hawk-economy won't thank him for't
> Which stops his petty nipperkin of port.
> PETER PINDAR: *Hair Powder*.

The traditional Devon and Cornish song *The Barley Mow* starts with drinking the health out of the "jolly brown bowl", and at each chorus increases the size of the receptacle until in the sixteenth and last we have:

> We'll drink it out of the ocean, my boys,
> Here's a health to the barley mow!
> The ocean, the river, the well, the pipe, the hogshead, the half-hogshead, the anker, the halfanker, the gallon, the half-gallon, the pottle, the quart, the pint, the half pint, the quarter pint, the nipperkin, and the jolly brown bowl!

Nip and tuck. A NECK-AND-NECK race: a close fight.

Number Nip. Another name for RÜBEZAHL.

To nip in the bud. To destroy before it has had time to develop; to stop something in its early stages, as a bud is nipped by frost or pests, etc., thus preventing further growth.

Nip-cheese, or **Nip-farthing.** A miser, who nips or pinches closely his cheese and farthings. Among sailors the purser is nicknamed "Nip-cheese". (Dutch *nypen*.)

Nipper. Slang for a small boy.

Nippon. The Japanese name for Japan, "the great land of the rising sun".

Nirvana (Sansk., a blowing out, or extinction). In BUDDHISM, the cessation of individual existence; the attainment of a calm, sinless state of mind achieved by the extinction of passion, a state which can be attained during life.

Nisei (nē' sā). A person born in the U.S.A. of Japanese descent but a loyal American.

Nisi (nī' sī) (Lat., unless). In Law a "rule nisi" is a rule unless cause be shown to the contrary.

Decree nisi. A decree of divorce granted on the condition that it does not take effect until made *absolute*, which is done in due course, unless reasons why it should not have meantime come to light. Every decree of divorce is, in the first instance, a *decree nisi*.

Nisi prius (Lat., unless previously). Originally a writ commanding a SHERIFF to empanel a jury which should be at the Court of WESTMINSTER on a certain day unless the justices of assize have previously come to his county.

The second Statute of Westminster (1285) instituted Judges of *nisi prius*, who were appointed to travel through the shires three times a year to hear civil causes. A trial at *nisi prius* is now a trial by jury in a civil cause before a single judge.

Nisroch. The Assyrian god in whose temple Sennacherib was worshipping when he was slain (II *Kings* xix, 37). Nothing is known of this god but the name is probably a corruption of *Asur* or a by-form of *Asuraku*. *Cp.* ASSHER.

Nisus and Euryalus. An example of proverbial friendship comparable to that of PYLADES and Orestes. Nisus with a Trojan friend raided the camp of the Rutulians and slaughtered many of the enemy in their drunken sleep, but the youthful Euryalus was killed by Volscens. Nisus rushed to avenge his death and in slaying Volscens was himself killed (*Æneid*, IX).

Nitouch (ni toosh'). **Faire la Sainte Nitouche,** to pretend to great sanctity, to look as though BUTTER would not melt in one's mouth. Sainte Nitouche, a contraction of *n'y touche*, is a name given in France to a hypocrite.

Nivetta. *See* MORGAN LE FAY.

Nivôse (nē vōz) (Lat. *nivosus*, very snowy). The fourth month of the FRENCH REVOLUTIONARY CALENDAR (*see under* CALENDAR), lasting from 21 December to 19 January.

Nix. *See* NICKER. The word is also slang for "nothing" (Ger. *nichts*, nothing). "He won't work for nix" means he won't work without payment.

Nizam (ni zăm'). The title of sovereignty of the ruler of the former state of Hyderabad, India; contracted from *Nizam-ul-mulk* (regulator of the state), in 1713 the title of Asaf Jah, who later became independent of MOGUL control.

Njorthr. *See* NIORD.

No. No can do. I cannot do it.

No dice (U.S.A.). Nothing doing.

No Man's Land. The name given to the area between hostile lines of entrenchments or to any space contested by both sides and belonging to neither. In the OPEN FIELD system, odd scraps of land, also called "Jack's land" or "anyone's land".

Noah. Noah's Ark. A name given by sailors to a white band of cloud spanning the sky like a rainbow and in shape something like the hull of a ship. If east and west, expect dry weather, if north and south, expect wet. Noah's Ark is also used as a PUBLIC-HOUSE SIGN.

Noah's wife. According to legend she was unwilling to go into the ark, and the quarrel between the patriarch and his wife forms a prominent feature of *Noah's Flood*, in the Chester and Townley MYSTERIES.

> Hastow not herd, quod Nicholas, also
> The sorwe of Noe with his felawshipe
> Er that he mighte gete his wyf to shipe?
> CHAUCER: *Miller's Tale*, 352.

Nobbler. An Australian colloquial term for a short drink, one-fifth of a gill or a fluid ounce.

Nobby. Smart, elegant, neat; from NOB, a slang term for one of the upper classes, a contraction of *noble* or *nobility*.

Noble. A former English gold coin, from the superior quality of its GOLD. First minted by Edward III (1344), possibly in commemoration of the Battle of Sluys (1340). It was originally valued at 6s. 8d. and replaced by the *royal* or *rose noble* in 1465.

The Noble. Charles III of Navarre (1361–1425).

The Noble Duke of York of nursery rhyme fame was George III's second son.

> The noble Duke of York,
> He had ten thousand men;
> He marched 'em up to the top of the hill,
> And he marched 'em down again.

The rhyme was a derisive commentary on his abortive operations in Flanders (1794) against the French. He was young at the time, although some versions refer to "the rare old Duke" or "the grand old Duke". The land was flat, otherwise the rhyme is fair comment. He was made Commander-in-Chief in 1798. *See* DUKE OF YORK'S COLUMN *under* COLUMN.

The Noble Science. The old epithet for fencing or boxing, sometimes called "The Noble Art of Self-Defence".

> ...a bold defiance
> Shall meet him, were he of the noble science.
> BEAUMONT and FLETCHER:
> *Knight of the Burning Pestle*, II, i.

The Noble Yachtsman. A nickname given to the 7th Earl of CARDIGAN, during the Crimean War, who for some weeks lived aboard his yacht in Balaclava harbour, thus escaping the hardships ashore.

Noblesse oblige (nō bles' ō blēzh') (Fr.). Noble birth imposes the obligation of high-minded principles and noble actions.

Noctes Ambrosianæ. *See* AMBROSIAN NIGHTS.

Nod. A nod is as good as a wink to a blind horse. *See under* HORSE.

On the nod. On credit. To get a thing on the nod is to get it without paying for it at the time. The phrase is from the auction room where one signifies a bid by a mere nod of the head, the formalities of paying being attended to later. *Cp.* ON THE NEVER NEVER *under* NEVER.

The land of Nod. *See under* LAND.

A nodding acquaintance. A slight acquaintance, a person with whom one exchanges a nod for recognition when passing without seeking to become more closely acquainted. When used of one's acquaintance with literary works, etc., it means a superficial or slight knowledge.

Noddy. A Tom Noddy is a very foolish or half-witted person, "a noodle". The marine birds called noddies are so silly that anyone can go up to them and knock them down with a stick. It seems more than likely that the word is connected with *to nod*, but it has been suggested that it was originally a pet form of *Nicodemus*.

Noddy is a well-known, somewhat simple, "nodding-man" in Enid Blyton's children's books and it is also an old name for cribbage.

Noel (nō' el). In English (also written *Nowell*), a Christmas CAROL, or the shout of joy in a carol; in French, Christmas Day. The word is Provençal *nadal*, from Lat. *natalem*, natal.

> Nowells, nowells, nowells!
> Sing all we may,
> Because that Christ, the King,
> Was born this blessed day.
> *Old Carol.*

Nokes. *See* JOHN-A-NOKES.

Nolens volens (no' lenz vo' lenz). Whether willing or not. Two Latin participles meaning "being unwilling (or) willing". *Cp.* WILLY-NILLY.

Noli me tangere (nol' i mē tǎn' jer i) (Lat., touch me not). The words Christ used to MARY MAGDALENE after his resurrection (*John* xx, 17) and given as a name to a plant of the genus *Impatiens*. The seed vessels consist of one cell in five divisions, and when the seed is ripe each of these, on being touched, suddenly folds itself into a spiral form, and leaps from the stalk. *See* Darwin's *Loves of the Plants*, II, iii.

Noll. Old Noll. Oliver Cromwell was so called, Noll being a familiar form of *Oliver*.

Nolle prosequi (nol′ i prō sek′ wi) (Lat., to be unwilling to prosecute). A petition from a plaintiff to stay a suit. *Cp.* NON PROS.

Nolo contendere (nō′ lō kon ten′ dĕ rē) (Lat., I am unwilling to contend). A plea in law by which the defendant, while not admitting guilt, declares he will not offer any defence. A plea tantamount to that of "guilty".

Nolo episcopari (nō′ lō p isk ō pâ′ ri) (Lat., I am unwilling to be made a BISHOP). The formal reply supposed to be returned to the royal offer of bishopric. Chamberlayne says (*Present State of England*, 1669) that in former times the person about to be elected modestly refused the office twice, and if he did so a third time his refusal was accepted.

Nom. Nom de guerre (Fr. "war name"). An assumed name. It was once customary for every entrant into the French army to assume a name, especially in the times of CHI-VALRY, when knights were known by the device on their shields.

Nom de plume. English-French for "penname" or pseudonym, the name assumed by a writer, cartoonist, etc., who does not choose to use his own name; as Currer Bell (Charlotte Brontë); Stendhal (Marie Henri Beyle). *See* CARAN D'ACHE; GEORGE ELIOT; GEORGE SAND; PHIZ; VOLTAIRE.

Nominalism. The SCHOOLMEN'S name for the theory of knowledge which denies the objective existence of abstract ideas. A form of Nominalism was put forward by Roscelin in the 11th century, but in its more pronounced form by WILLIAM OF OCCAM in the 14th century. Those who held the opposite view were called Realists (*see* REALISM).

Non. The Latin negative, *not*; adopted in English and very widely employed as a prefix of negation, *e.g. non*-abstainer, *non*-conformist, *non*-existent, *non*-residence, *non*sense, etc.

Non amo te, Zabidi. *See* FELL.

Non Angli sed angeli. *See* ANGLES.

Non assumpsit (Lat., he has not undertaken). The legal term for a plea denying a promise or undertaking.

Non-com. A non-commissioned officer in the army (more usual in the U.S.A.).

Non compos mentis (Lat., not of sound mind). Said of a lunatic, idiot, drunkard, or one who has lost memory and understanding by accident or disease.

Non-ego. *See* EGO.

Non est. A contraction of Lat. *non est in-ventus* (not to be found). They are the words which the sheriff writes on a writ when the defendant is not to be found in his bailiwick.

Non mi ricordo (I do not remember). A shuffling way of saying, "I don't choose to answer that question." It was the usual answer of the Italian witnesses when under examination at the trial of Queen Caroline, wife of George IV, in 1820.

Non placet (Lat., it is unpleasing). The formula used, especially by the governing body of a University, for expressing a negative vote.

Non pros. for Lat. *non prosequitur*, he does not follow up. Judgment *non pros.* for a defendant was pronounced in an action when the plaintiff failed to take the necessary steps in time.

Non sequitur (Lat., it does not follow). A conclusion which does not follow from the premises stated; an inconsequent statement, such as Artemus Ward's:

> I met a man in Oregon who hadn't any teeth—not a tooth in his head—yet that man could play on the bass drum better than any man I ever met.

Nonce. M.E. for *than anes*, for the once. *Cp.* NICKNAME.

Nonce-word. A word coined for a particular occasion, such as BIRRELLISM, LIMEHOUSE, PUSEYITE.

Non-conformists. In England, members of PROTESTANT bodies who do not conform to the doctrines of the CHURCH OF ENGLAND. They had their origins in the BROWNISTS and BAPTISTS of Elizabeth I's reign and among the 17th-century PURITANS and sectaries. After the RESTORATION and the subsequent Act of Uniformity of 1662, which enforced strict observance of the BOOK OF COMMON PRAYER, some 2,000 clergy were ejected and a lasting division resulted. The DISSENTERS or Nonconformists were subjected to the CLARENDON CODE until relief came with the Toleration Act of 1689 and later measures. Nonconformity received further recruits particularly with the advent of the METHODISTS.

Nonconformist Conscience. *See under* CONSCIENCE.

Nones (nōnz). In the ancient Roman CALENDAR, the *ninth* (Lat. *nonus*) day before IDES; in the ROMAN CATHOLIC CHURCH, the office for the *ninth* hour after sunrise, *i.e.* between noon and 3 p.m.

Non-jurors. Those HIGH CHURCH clergy who refused to take the oath of allegiance to William and Mary after the Revolution of 1688 and who were deprived of their livings in 1690. Their numbers included Archbishop

Sancroft and five other bishops. They maintained their own episcopal succession until the death of their last bishop in 1805. *Cp.* SEVEN BISHOPS.

Non-resistance. In the CHURCH OF ENGLAND passive obedience to royal commands was a natural corollary of the DIVINE RIGHT OF KINGS but it acquired a particular importance after the RESTORATION, when TORY-minded clergy advocated non-resistance to combat NONCONFORMIST doctrines and WHIG policies. When James II tried to promote Roman Catholicism, many advocates of non-resistance abandoned their support of the monarchy and others became NON-JURORS after the accession of William of Orange.

Norman French. The old French dialect spoken in Normandy at the time of the CONQUEST and spoken by the dominant class in ENGLAND for some two centuries subsequently. Vestiges remain, particularly in legal terminology, and in other connections, such as "Fitz" (*fils*, son) that precedes certain family surnames. The royal assent to bills passed by PARLIAMENT is still given in Norman French, *La Reine remercie ses bons sujets, accepte leur benevolence, et ainsi le veult*, etc.

Norns, The. The fates, dispensers of destiny in Norse mythology. They lived at the foot of the ash-tree YGGDRASIL which they watered daily from the fountain called Urd. These sisters eventually became three in number in imitation of the three FATES of classical legend.

Norroy (*i.e.* north *roy*, or king). The third King of Arms (*see* HERALD) is so called, because his jurisdiction is on the north side of the river Trent; that to the south is exercised by CLARENCEUX. In 1943, the office of UL-STER KING OF ARMS was united with that of Norroy.

North. There was an old belief that only evil-doers should be buried on the north side of a churchyard, which probably arose from the lack of sun on this side. The east was *God*'s side, where his throne is set; the west, *man*'s side, the GALILEE of the Gentiles; the south, the side of the "*spirits made just*", where the sun shines in his strength; and the north, the *devil*'s side. *Cp.* THE DEVIL'S DOOR *under* DEVIL.

> As men die, so shall they arise; if in faith in the Lord, towards the south…and shall arise in glory; if in unbelief…towards the north, then they are past all hope.
>
> COVERDALE: *Praying for the Dead*.

North, Christopher. *See* AMBROSIAN NIGHTS.

He's too far north for me. Too canny, too cunning to be taken in; a very hard bargainer. The inhabitants of Yorkshire are supposed to be very canny, especially in driving a bargain; and when you get to Aberdeen—!

North Briton. A periodical founded by John Wilkes in 1762 to air his animosity against Lord Bute and the Scottish nation. *See* NUMBER 45 *under* FORTY; GENERAL WARRANTS.

The North-East Passage. A hoped-for route to the East round the north extremity of Asia. It was first attempted by Willoughby and Chancellor (1553–1554) and its only practical result was the establishment of the Muscovy Company (1555). The passage was traversed by the Swedish ship *Vega* in 1897.

> That everlasting cassock, that has worn
> As many servants out as the North-east Passage
> Has consumed sailors.
> BEAUMONT and FLETCHER: *The Woman's Prize*, II, ii.

The North Pole was first reached on 6 April 1909, by the American explorer Robert Edwin Peary (1856–1920). In May 1933, the North Pole was claimed by the Russians and four years later they established a Polar station there under Prof. Otto Schmidt.

The North-West Frontier. Particularly, the north-west frontier of British India and the province of that name, now part of PAKISTAN. Owing to the warlike nature of the local tribesmen and the Russian advance in central Asia, it gained an especial importance from the later 19th century, and was a constant drain in men and money.

The North-West Passage. The name given to the long-sought-for route to the East round the north of the American continent, the search for which began with Sebastian Cabot's voyage of 1509. Search continued through the centuries by men such as Frobisher, Davis, Hudson, Baffin and Bylot, Cook, and Vancouver. It was first traversed by the Norwegian Roald Amundsen (1903–1905).

The Northern Bear. Tsarist Russia was so called.

The Northern Gate of the Sun. The sign of CANCER, or summer SOLSTICE; so called because it marks the northern tropic.

The Northern Lights. The AURORA BOREALIS.

The Northern Wagoner. The genius presiding over the GREAT BEAR (*see under* BEAR) or CHARLES'S WAIN, which contains seven large stars.

> By this the northern wagoner had set

His sevenfold team behind the stedfast star [the pole-star].

SPENSER: *The Faerie Queene*, Bk. I, ii, 1.

Dryden calls the Great Bear the *Northern Car*, and similarly the crown in Ariadne has been called the *Northern Crown. Cp.* CYNOSURE.

Northamptonshire Poet. *See* PEASANT POET.

Northumbria. The Anglo-Saxon kingdom formed in the early 7th century, which included all ENGLAND north of the Humber, and S.W. and E. SCOTLAND to the Firth of Forth. For most of the 7th century it was the most powerful English kingdom and its kings Edwin, Oswald, and Oswy held the office of BRETWALDA. Its dominance was replaced by that of MERCIA. It was long noted as a centre of learning.

Norway, Maid of. *See* MAID.

Norwich. Do you know the Bishop of Norwich? *See under* KNOW.

Nose. A nose of wax. *See under* WAX.

As plain as the nose on your face. Extremely obvious, patent to all.

Bleeding of the nose. According to some, a sign that one is in love. Grose says if it bleeds one drop only it forebodes sickness, if three drops the omen is still worse; but Melton, in his *Astrologaster*, says, "If a man's nose bleeds one drop at the left nostril it is a sign of good luck, and vice versa."

Cleopatra's nose. *See under* CLEOPATRA.

Golden nose. Tycho Brahe (d. 1601), the Danish astronomer. He lost his nose in a duel, so adopted a golden one, which he attached to his face by a cement which he carried about with him.

The bloodthirsty Emperor Justinian II, nicknamed Rhinotmetus, had a golden nose in place of the nose that had been cut off by his general Leontius before he ascended the imperial throne. It used to be said that when Justinian cleansed this golden nose, those who were present knew that the death of someone had been decided upon.

Led by the nose. Said of one who has no will of his own but follows tamely the guidance of a stronger character, as horses, asses, etc., are led by the nose by bit and bridle. Hence SHAKESPEARE's Iago says of Othello, he was "led by the nose as asses are" (I, iii). Bulls, buffaloes, camels, and bears are led by a ring through their nostrils. *Isaiah* xxxvii, 29, says: "Because thy rage against me...is come up into mine ears, therefore will I put my hook in thy nose...and...I will turn thee back."

Nose tax. It is said that in the 9th century the Danes imposed a poll tax in IRELAND, and that this was called the "Nose Tax", because those who neglected to pay were punished by having their noses slit.

On the nose. An American expression meaning exactly on time. It originated in the broadcasting studio, where the producer, when signalling to the performers, puts his finger on his nose when the programme is running to schedule time.

The Pope's nose. The rump of a fowl, which is also called the *parson's nose*. The phrase is said to have originated during the years following James II's reign (1685–1688), when anti-Catholic feeling was high.

To bite, or **snap one's nose off.** To speak snappishly. To *pull* (or *wring*) *the nose* is to affront by an act of indignity; to *snap one's nose* is to affront by speech. Snarling dogs snap at each other's noses.

To count noses. A horse-dealer counts horses by the *nose*, as cattle are counted by the *head*; hence, the expression is sometimes ironically used of numbering votes, as in the Division lobbies.

To cut off your nose to spite your face, or **to be revenged on your face.** To act out of pique in such a way as to bring harm to yourself.

To follow one's nose. To go straight ahead; to proceed without deviating from the path.

To keep one's nose clean. To ensure that one does not get involved in dealings or practices of a dubious or shady character; to avoid any suspicion of malpractice.

To keep one's nose to the grindstone. To keep hard at work. Tools, such as scythes, chisels, etc., are constantly sharpened on a stone or with a grindstone.

Be to the poor like onie whunstane,
And haud their noses to the gruntstane.
BURNS: *Dedication to Gavin Hamilton*.

To look down one's nose. To treat disdainfully, to regard with disapproval; from the customary attitude of disapproval of lowering one's eyelids and looking down one's nose.

To pay through the nose. To pay too much. Of many conjectured origins, the most likely is that this phrase derives from the NOSE TAX (*see above*).

To poke, or **thrust one's nose in.** Officiously to intermeddle with other people's affairs; to intrude where one is not wanted.

To put one's nose out of joint. To supplant a person in another's good grace; to upset one's plans; to humiliate or bring disgruntlement to someone.

To take pepper i' the nose. *See under* PEPPER.

To turn up one's nose. To express contempt. When a person sneers he turns up the nose by curling the upper lip.

To wipe one's nose. *See under* WIPE.

Unable to see beyond the end of one's nose. Totally lacking in foresight, perception and discernment; obtuse.

Under one's very nose. Right before one. In full view.

Nosey. Very inquisitive; overfond of poking one's nose into the business of others. One who does this is a **Nosey Parker,** possibly an allusion to Matthew Parker, Archbishop of Canterbury (1504, 1559–1575). He was noted for the detailed articles of inquiry concerning ecclesiastical affairs generally and the conduct of the clergy, which he issued for the Visitations of his province and diocese. The Duke of Wellington was called "Old Nosey" by his troops from his strongly accentuated aquiline nose. The nickname was also given to Oliver Cromwell. *See* COPPER NOSE.

Nostradamus. The name assumed by Michel de Nostradame, French physician and astrologer (1503–1566) who published an annual "Almanack" as well as the famous *Les Centuries* (1555) which suffered papal condemnation in 1781. His controversial prophecies were couched in very ambiguous language. Hence the saying "*as good a prophet as Nostradamus*", *i.e.*, so obscure that your meaning cannot be understood.

Notables, The Assembly of. In French history, an assembly of persons of distinction and political weight summoned by the VALOIS kings at their pleasure instead of convening the STATES GENERAL. It was the only concession made to consulting the will of the nation. They were called together by Richelieu in 1626–1627 and not again until 1787, when Louis XVI was harassed by impending financial collapse. The last time they met was 6 November 1788. *Cp.* PARLIAMENT.

Notarikon (Gr. *notarikon*; Lat. *notarius*, a shorthand writer). A cabalistic word denoting the old Jewish art of using each letter in a word to form another word, or using the initials of the words in a sentence to form another word, etc., as the word CABAL itself was fabled to have been from Clifford, Ashley, Buckingham, Arlington, and Lauderdale; and as the term ICHTHYS was applied to the Saviour. Other instances are: A.E.I.O.U.; CLIO; HEMPE; LIMP; SMECTYMNUUS. *Cp.* HIP! HIP! HURRAH!

Notch. Out of all Scotch and Notch. *See under* SCOTCH.

Note. To compare notes. To exchange opinions, observations, etc., on a particular matter or subject, with someone else. Here the reference is to the written note.

To strike the right note. To say, write, or to do the particularly appropriate thing to suit the occasion; the allusion is to the note in music.

Notes of the Church. The four characteristic marks of the Church, *i.e. one*, *holy*, *catholic*, and *apostolic*, as set forth in the NICENE CREED. These "notes" were used by Roman Catholic theologians and others, and by the TRACTARIANS to demonstrate their claims.

Note-shaver (U.S.A.). A discounter of bills, an usurer.

Nothing. Mere nothings. Trifles; unimportant things or events.

Next to nothing. A very little, as, "It will cost next to nothing"; "He eats next to nothing."

Nothing doing! Used to imply that your request is refused; your wishes cannot be met, etc.

Nothing venture, nothing have, or **win.** An old proverb, if you won't take a chance, you cannot expect to gain anything; if you daren't throw a SPRAT you mustn't expect to catch a mackerel.

Out of nothing one can get nothing; the Latin *Ex nihilo nihil fit*—*i.e.* every effect must have a cause. It was the dictum by which Xenophanes, founder of the ELEATIC School, postulated his theory of the eternity of matter. Persius (*Satires*, iii, 84) has *De nihilo nihilum, in nihilum nil posse reverti*, From nothing nothing, and into nothing can nothing return.

We now use the phrase as equivalent to "You cannot get blood from a stone", or expect good work from one who has no brains.

That's nothing to you, or **to do with you.** It's none of your business; it is not your concern.

There's nothing for it but to... There's no alternative, there is only one thing to do.

To come to nothing. To turn out a failure; to result in naught.

To make nothing of. To fail to understand; not to do anything with; not to make a fuss about.

To think nothing of. To regard as unimportant, or easy.

Nought. *See* NAUGHT.

Nous (nous) (Gr., mind, intellect). Adopted in English and used to denote "intelligence", "horse-sense", "understanding".

Thine is the genuine head of many a house,
And much divinity without a NOUS.
POPE: *Dunciad*, IV, 244.

Nous was the Platonic term for mind, or the first cause, and the system of divinity referred to above is that which springs from blind nature.

Nous avons changé tout cela (noo zăv on shon′ zhã too sela) (Fr., We have changed all that). A facetious reproof to one who lays down the law upon everything, and talks contemptuously of old customs, old authors, old artists, etc. The phrase is taken from MOLIÈRE's *Médecin Malgré Lui*, II, vi.

Nouveaux riches (noo′ vō rēsh′) (Fr., the new rich). A phrase with derogatory implications applied to those who have newly acquired considerable affluence and who often seek to use their money for social climbing, etc. Cobbett wrote of the "damned aristocracy of money" in this connexion and in his *Rural Rides* (30 October 1821) he describes "a park" belonging to a Mr. Montague with Dutch gardens and pseudo-Gothic dwelling and says: "I do not know who this gentleman is. I suppose he is some honest person from the 'Change or its neighbourhood; and that these *gothic arches* are to denote the *antiquity of his origin*!"

Nova Scotia. *See* ACADIA.

Novatians (nō vā′ shánz). Followers of Novatian, a presbyter of ROME in the 3rd century. They were doctrinally orthodox, but objected to the readmission into the Church of those who had dallied with paganism. They were excommunicated, but Novatianist churches persisted until after the 5th century.

Novel disseisin ("Seisin" is possession, hence "new dispossession"). A petty assize introduced by Henry II (*c.* 1166) to provide quick remedy for the man *disseised, i.e.* ejected from his FREEHOLD. If juries decided a man was wrongly disseised, he was restored to possession. It was particularly welcome after the anarchy of Stephen's reign and as time progressed the period covered by "novel" was increasingly extended until it lost meaning.

Novella. A diminutive from Lat. *novus*, new. A short story of the kind contained in Boccaccio's *Decameron*, and immensely popular in the 16th and 17th centuries. Such stories were the forerunners of the long novel and also of the short story of more recent times.

November (Lat. *novem*, nine). The ninth month in the ancient Roman CALENDAR, when the year began in MARCH; now the eleventh. The old Dutch name was *Slaghtmaand* (slaughter-month, the time when the beasts were slain and salted down for winter use); the old Saxon *Wind-monath* (wind-month, when the fishermen drew their boats ashore, and gave over fishing till

the next spring); it was also called *Blotmonath*—the same as *Slaghtmaand*. In the French Republican Calendar it was called *Brumaire* (fog-month, 23 October to 21 November).

> No sun—no moon!
> No morn—no noon—
> No dawn—no dusk—no proper time of day.
> No warmth, no cheerfulness, no healthful ease,
> No comfortable feel in any member—
> No shade, no shine, no butterflies, no bees,
> No fruits, no flowers, no leaves, no birds!—
> November!
> T. HOOD: *No!* (1844).

Novena (nō vē′ nà) (Lat. *novenus*, nine each). In Roman Catholic devotions, a prayer for some special object or occasion extended over a period of nine days.

Nowell. *See* NOEL.

Noyades (nwa′ yad) (Fr., drownings). During the REIGN OF TERROR in France (1793–1794), Carrier at Nantes drowned many of his victims in the Loire by stowing them in boats and removing the plugs. NERO, at the suggestion of Anicetus, attempted to drown his mother in the same manner.

Null and void. No longer of binding force; having no further validity.

Nulla linea. *See* NO DAY WITHOUT ITS LINE *under* LINE.

Nullarbor Plain, The Great (Lat. *nulla arbor*, no tree). The vast bare plain north of the Australian Bight, so named from its treeless character.

Nulli secundus (Lat., second to none). The motto of the COLDSTREAM GUARDS, which regiment is hence sometimes spoken of as the *Nulli Secundus Club*.

Numbers, Numerals. PYTHAGORAS looked on numbers as influential principles; in his system:

> 1 was Unity, and represented Deity, which has no parts.
> 2 was Diversity, and therefore disorder; the principle of strife and all EVIL.
> 3 was Perfect Harmony; or the union of unity and diversity.
> 4 was Perfection; it is the first square (2 × 2=4).
> 5 was the prevailing number in Nature and Art.
> 6 was Justice.
> 7 was the CLIMACTERIC number in all diseases.

With the ancient Romans 2 was the most fatal of all the numbers; they dedicated the second month to PLUTO, and the second day of the month to the MANES.

In old ecclesiastical symbolism the numbers from 1 to 13 were held to denote the following:

> 1 The Unity of God.
> 2 The hypostatic union of Christ, both God and man.
> 3 The TRINITY.
> 4 The number of the EVANGELISTS.
> 5 The wounds of the Redeemer;

two in the hands, two in the feet, one in the side.
6 The creative week.
7 The gifts of the HOLY GHOST and the seven times
  Christ spoke on the CROSS.
8 The number of BEATITUDES (*Matt.* v, 3–11).
9 The nine orders of ANGELS.
10 The number of the Commandments.
11 The number of the APOSTLES who remained faithful.
12 The original college.
13 The final number after the conversion of Paul.

All our numerals and ordinals up to a million (with one exception) are Anglo-Saxon. The one exception is *Second*, which is French. The Anglo-Saxon word was *other*, as First, Other, Third, etc., but as this was ambiguous, the Fr. *seconde* was early adopted. Million is from Lat. *mille*, a thousand.

The primitive method of counting was by the fingers (*cp.* DIGITS); thus, in the Roman system of numeration, the first four were simply i, ii, iii, iiii; five was the outline of the hand simplified into a v; the next four figures were the four combined, thus, vi, vii, viii, viiii; and ten was a double v, thus x. At a later period iiii and viiii were expressed by one less than five (i−v) and one less than ten (i−x); nineteen was ten-plus-nine (x+ix) etc. *See also* ARABIC FIGURES.

Abundant Number. *See* ABUNDANT.

Apocalyptic number, 666. *See* NUMBER OF THE BEAST, *below.*

Back number. Any number of a paper or periodical previous to the current issue; hence an out-of-date or old-fashioned person or thing; one no longer IN THE SWIM (*see under* SWIM).

Book of Numbers. In the OLD TESTAMENT, the Fourth Book of Moses, from the "numbering" of the Israelites in chapters iii and xxvi.

Cyclic number. A number the final digit of whose square is the same; 5 (25) and 6 (36) are examples.

Deficient Number. *See* DEFICIENT.

Golden numbers. *See under* GOLDEN.

Mach Number. *See* MACH.

Medical number. In the Pythagorean system (*see* NUMBER *above*), 7.

Number One. *See under* ONE.

Perfect Number. *See under* PERFECT.

The Number of the Beast. 666; a mystical number of unknown meaning but referring to some man mentioned by St. JOHN.

Let him that hath understanding count the number of the beast: for it is the number of a man: and his number is Six hundred threescore and six.
Rev. xiii, 18.

One of the most plausible suggestions is that it refers to Neron Cæsar, which in Hebrew characters with numerical value gives 666, whereas NERO, without the final "n", as in Latin, gives 616 (n=50), the number given in many early MSS., according to Irenæus.

Among the CABBALISTS, every letter represented a number, and one's number was the sum of these equivalents to the letters in one's name. If, as is probable, the *Revelation* was written in Hebrew, the number would suit either Nero, Hadrian, or Trajan—all persecutors; if in Greek, it would fit Caligula or *Lateinos*, *i.e.* the Roman Empire; but almost any name in any language can be twisted into this number, and it has been applied to many persons assumed to have been ANTICHRIST or Apostates, Diocletian, Evanthas, JULIAN THE APOSTATE, Luther, Mohammed, Paul V, Silvester II, NAPOLEON Bonaparte, Charles Bradlaugh, William II of Germany, and several others; as well as to certain phrases supposed to be descriptive of "the Man of Sin", as Vicar-General of God, Kakos Odegos (bad guide), Abinu Kadescha Papa (our holy father the pope), *e.g.*—

M	a	o	m	e	t	i	s		
40	1	70	40	5	300	10	200	=	666

L	a	t	e	i	n	o	s		
30	1	300	5	10	50	70	200	=	666

One suggestion is that St. John chose the number 666 because it just fell short of the holy number 7 in every particular; it was straining at every point to get there, but never could. *See also* MYSTERIUM.

His days are numbered. They are drawing to a close; he is near death.

God hath numbered thy kingdom, and finished it.
Dan. v, 26.

Not to have one's number on it. An expression used by members of the armed forces when one has a narrow escape from a bullet or other missile, since it was not supposedly earmarked by fate for one's extinction. *Cp.* YOUR NUMBER'S UP.

There's luck in odd numbers. This is an ancient fancy. According to the Pythagorean system nine represents Deity. A major chord consists of a fundamental or tonic, its major third, and its just fifth. As the odd numbers are the fundamental notes of nature, the last being the Deity, it is understandable how they came to be considered the great or lucky numbers. *Cp.* DIAPASON; NUMBERS.

Good luck lies in odd numbers...They say, there is divinity in odd numbers, either in nativity, chance or death.
SHAKESPEARE: *The Merry Wives of Windsor*, V, i.

The odd numbers 1, 3, 5, 7, 9 (which

see), seem to play a far more important part than the even numbers. VIRGIL (*Eclogues*, viii, 75) says *Numero Deus impare gaudet* (the god delights in odd numbers). THREE indicates the "beginning, middle, and the end". The Godhead has three persons; so in classical mythology HECATE had threefold power; JOVE's symbol was a triple thunderbolt, NEPTUNE's a sea-trident, PLUTO's a three-headed dog; the Horæ three. There are SEVEN notes, NINE planets, nine orders of ANGELS, seven days a week, thirteen lunar months, or 365 days a year, etc.; FIVE senses, five fingers, five toes, five continents, etc.

To consult the Book of Numbers. A facetious way of saying "to put it to the vote".

Your number's up. You are caught, or about to die. A soldier's phrase; in the American army a soldier who has just been killed or has died is said to have "lost his mess number". An older phrase in the Royal Navy was "to lose the number of his mess". *Cp.* NOT TO HAVE ONE'S NUMBER ON IT, *above*. *See also* TO HAVE HAD IT *under* HAD.

Nunawading Messiah. James Cowley Morgan Fisher (*c.* 1832–1915) of Nunawading, Victoria, Australia was so called. The son of Gloucestershire immigrants, he ran away to sea at the age of 14 and settled at Nunawading in the mid-1850s. In the 1860s he succeeded his mother-in-law as head of the New Church of the Firstborn. In a law suit of 1871 he was accused of claiming to be the Messiah or the Christ and of practising polygamy, with three sisters as his wives. His following was small, estimated at about 100 in 1871, but was probably less. *Cp.* SOUTHCOTTIANS.

Nunc dimittis. The Song of Simeon (*Luke* ii, 29), "Lord, now lettest thou thy servant depart in peace", so called from the opening words of the Latin version, *Nunc dimittis servum tuum, Domine*.

Hence, *to receive one's Nunc dimittis*, to be given permission to go; *to sing one's Nunc dimittis*, to show satisfaction at departing.

The Canticle is sung at Evening Prayer in the CHURCH OF ENGLAND, and has been anciently used at COMPLINE or VESPERS throughout the Church.

> But, above all, believe it, the sweetest canticle is, 'Nunc dimittis' when a man hath obtained worthy ends and expectations.
>
> BACON: *Essays (Of Death)*.

Nuncheon. Properly, "the noon-tide draught"; M.E. *noneschench* (*none*, noon; *schench*, a cup or draught); hence, light refreshments between meals, lunch. The word *luncheon* has been affected by the older *nuncheon*. Cp. BEVER; TIFFIN.

> Laying by their swords and truncheons,
> They took their breakfasts, or their nuncheons.
>
> BUTLER: *Hudibras*, I, i, 345.

Nunky. Slang for Uncle, especially as meaning a pawnbroker; or for UNCLE SAM (*see under* SAM).

Nunky pays for all. The American government (*see* UNCLE SAM *under* SAM) has to "stand the RACKET".

Nuremberg. Nuremberg Eggs. Watches, which were invented at Nuremberg about 1500, and were egg-shaped.

Nuremberg Laws. The infamous NAZI laws promulgated in September 1935. Jews, and all those of Jewish extraction, were deprived of all rights of German citizenship, and regulations were made against those of partial Jewish ancestry. Marriage between JEW and "German" was forbidden. Nuremberg was the centre of the annual Nazi Party convention.

Nuremberg Trials. The trial of 23 NAZI leaders conducted by an Inter-Allied tribunal at Nuremberg after World War II (September 1945—May 1946). Three were acquitted. Göring, Ribbentrop and nine others were condemned to death, and the remainder sentenced to various terms of imprisonment. Hitler, Himmler, and Goebbels avoided retribution by committing suicide, as did Göring.

Nurr and Spell. *See* KNURR.

Nursery. A room set apart for the use of young children (Lat. *nutrire*, to nourish); hence, a garden for rearing plants (tended by a *nurseryman*).

In horse-racing, *Nurseries* are races for two-year-olds; and figuratively the word is used of any place or school of training for the professions, etc.

Nursery cannons. In billiards, a series of cannons played so that the balls move as little as possible.

Nursery rhymes. The traditional metrical jingles learned by children "in the nursery" and frequently used in their games. They contain survivals of folklore, ancient superstitions, festival games, and local customs, history, etc. Most of them are very old, but some are more recent, such as OLD MOTHER HUBBARD and the NOBLE DUKE OF YORK.

Nursery slopes. Easy hillsides on which beginners learn to ski.

Nut. Slang for the head; perhaps from its shape. Also slang for a DUDE, a swell young man about town; in this sense it is sometimes spelled *Knut*, from an early 20th-century song featured by Basil Hallam, "I'm Gilbert the Filbert, the colonel of the K-nuts".

A hard nut to crack. A difficult question to answer; a hard problem to solve.

A nut case. Crazy, daft.

A tough nut. A difficult one to handle or convince.

He who would eat the nut must first crack the shell. The gods give nothing to man without great labour.

Here we go gathering nuts in May. This burden of the old children's game is a corruption of "Here we go gathering *knots* of may", referring to the old custom of gathering knots of flowers on MAY-DAY *i.e.* "to go a-maying". There are no nuts to be gathered in May.

It is time to lay our nuts aside (Lat. *relinquere nuces*). To leave off our follies, to relinquish boyish pursuits. The allusion is to an old Roman marriage ceremony, in which the bridegroom, as he led his bride home, scattered nuts to the crowd, as if to symbolize that he gave up boyish playthings.

That's nuts to him. A great pleasure, a fine treat, "meat and drink".

> To edge his way along the crowded paths of life,
> warning all human sympathy to keep its distance,
> was what the knowing ones call nuts to Scrooge.
> DICKENS: *A Christmas Carol*, i.

To be dead nuts on, or **nuts on.** To be highly gratified with; to be very keen on.

> My aunt is awful nuts on Marcus Aurelius; I beg
> your pardon, you don't know the phrase; my aunt
> makes Marcus Aurelius her Bible.
> WILLIAM BLACK: *Princess of Thule*, xi.

To be off one's nut, to be nuts. Crazy, demented. Hence, **Nut house,** a lunatic asylum.

To use a sledgehammer to crack a nut. To take quite disproportionate steps to settle what is really a very small matter; virtually the same as "to break a butterfly on a wheel" (*see under* BREAK).

The Nut-brown Maid. An English ballad probably dating from the late 15th century, first printed (*c.* 1520) in Arnold's *Chronicle* at Antwerp. It tells how the "Not-browne Mayd" was wooed and won by a knight who gave out that he was a banished man. After describing the hardships she would have to undergo if she married him, and finding her love true to the test, he revealed himself to be an earl's son, with large estates in Westmorland.

The ballad is given in PERCY'S RELIQUES, and forms the basis of Matthew Prior's *Henry and Emma*.

Nutcrack Night. ALL HALLOWS' EVE from the customary cracking of nuts.

Nutcrackers. *See* REGIMENTAL AND DIVISIONAL NICKNAMES.

The "Iliad" in a nutshell. Pliny (vii, 21) tells us that the ILIAD was copied in so small a hand that the whole work could lie in a walnut shell; his authority is Cicero (*Apud Gellium*, ix, 421).

> Whilst they (as Homer's *Iliad* in a nut)
> A world of wonders in one closet shut.
> *On the Tradescant Monument, Lambeth Churchyard.*

Huet, Bishop of Avranches (d.1721), proved by experiment that a parchment 27 by 21 centimetres could contain the entire *Iliad*, and that such a parchment would go into a common-sized nut; he wrote 80 verses of the *Iliad* (which contains in all 501,930 letters) on a single line of a page similar to this Dictionary. This would be 19,000 verses to the page, or 2,000 more than the *Iliad* contains.

In the Harleian MSS. (530) is an account of Peter Bales, a clerk of the Court of CHANCERY about 1590, who wrote a BIBLE so small that he enclosed it in a walnut shell of English growth. Lalanne described, in his *Curiosités Bibliographiques*, an edition of la Rochefoucauld's *Maximes*, published by Didot in 1829, on pages one inch square, each page containing 26 lines, and each line 44 letters. Charles Toppan, of New York, engraved on a plate one-eighth of an inch square 12,000 letters; the *Iliad* would occupy 42 such plates engraved on both sides. George P. Marsh says, in his Lectures, he has seen the entire KORAN in a parchment roll four inches wide and half an inch in diameter.

To lie in a nutshell. To be explained in a few words; to be capable of easy solution.

Nutmeg State. The nickname of CONNECTICUT, where wooden nutmegs were allegedly manufactured for export.

Nutter's Dance. A dance still performed at Bacup, Lancashire, on EASTER Saturday. The "nutters" are eight men clad in black, with white skirts and stockings, with wooden "nuts" fastened to their hands, waist and knees. The dance is performed to music and time is kept by clapping the nuts.

Nymphs (nimfs) (Gr., young maidens). In classical mythology, minor female divinities of nature, of woods, groves, springs, streams, rivers, etc. They were young and beautiful maidens and well disposed towards mortals. They were not immortal, but their life span was several thousand years. Particular kinds of nymphs were associated with the various provinces of nature. *See* DRYADS; HAMADRYADS; NAIADS; NEREIDS; OCEANIDS; OREADS.

O

O. The fifteenth letter of our alphabet, the fourteenth of the ancient Roman, and the sixteenth of the Phœnician and Semitic (in which it was called "the eye"). Its name in O.E. was *oedel*, home. As a mediæval Latin numeral o represents 11.

> A headless man had a letter [O] to write,
> He who read it [naught] had lost his sight,
> The dumb repeated it [naught] word for word,
> And deaf was the man who listened and heard [naught].
>
> DR. WHEWELL.

Round as Giotto's O. Said of work that is perfect and complete, but done with little effort. *See* GIOTTO.

The fifteen O's, or **The O's of St. Bridget.** Fifteen meditations on the PASSION composed by St. Bridget. Each begins with *O Jesu*, or a similar invocation.

The Seven O's, or **The Great O's of Advent.** The seven antiphons to the MAGNIFICAT sung during the week preceding CHRISTMAS. They commence respectively with *O Sapientia, O Adonai, O Radix Jesse, O Clavis David, O Oriens Splendor, O Rex gentium*, and *O Emmanuel*. They are sometimes called *The Christmas O's.*

O'. An Irish patronymic. (Gael. *ogha*; Ir. *oa*, a descendant.)

O' in *tam-o'-shanter, what's o'clock? cat-o'-nine-tails*, etc., stands for *of*; but in such phrases as *He comes home late o' night, I go to church o' Sundays*, it represents M.E. *on.*

O.K. All correct, all right; a reassuring affirmative that, coming from the U.S.A. to England, has spread colloquially throughout several European languages. Its first recorded use occurs in 1839. Commonly regarded as standing for "*Orl Korrect*" (all correct), it was said to derive from the political society called "Democratic O.K.", the "O.K." signifying "Old Kinderhook", a nickname of the Democratic leader, Martin Van Buren (1782–1862). Most probably it is from black American English *i.e.* of Afro-American origin. In Mandingo *O ke* signifies "all right", "that's it"; in Wolof *waw kay* means "yes indeed". Its use in New England in the late 1830s was probably due to the steady influx of refugees from the Southern slave states.

O.P. Riots. When COVENT GARDEN Theatre was reopened in 1809 after the disastrous fire of the preceding year, the charges of admission were increased; but night after night for three months, a throng crowded the pit, shouting "O.P." (old prices); much damage was done, and the manager was obliged at last to give way.

O tempora! O mores! (ō tem′ pôr ȧ-ȯ môr′ ēz) (Lat.). Alas! how the times have changed for the worse! Alas! how the morals of the people have degenerated! The tag is from Cicero's *In Catilinam*, i, 1.

O Yes! O Yes! O Yes! *See* OYEZ.

Oaf. A corruption of *ouph* (elf). A foolish lout or dolt is so called from the notion that idiots are CHANGELINGS, left by the FAIRIES in place of the stolen ones.

Oak. The oak was in ancient times sacred to the god of thunder because these trees are said to be more likely to be struck by lightning than any other. The DRUIDS held the oak in greatest veneration and the WOODEN WALLS of England depended upon it. About 3,500 full-grown oaks or 900 acres of oak forest were used in selecting the timber for a large three-decker line-of-battle ship. (*See* HEART OF OAK.) The strength, hardness, and durability of the timber, as well as the longevity of the tree, have given the oak a special significance to Englishmen, hence its name the *Monarch of the Forest.*

> I sit beneath your leaves, old oak,
> You mighty one of all the trees;
> Within whose hollow trunk a man
> Could stable his big horse with ease.
>
> W. H. DAVIES: *The Old Oak Tree.*

Among the famous oaks of Britain are:

The *Abbot's Oak*, near Woburn Abbey, was so called because the abbot of Woburn was hanged on one of its branches, in 1537, by order of Henry VIII.

The *Boscobel Oak. See* OAK-APPLE DAY.

The *Bull Oak*, Wedgenock Park, was growing at the time of the CONQUEST.

Cowthorpe Oak, near Wetherby, Yorkshire, will hold 70 persons in its hollow. It is said to be over 1,600 years old.

The *Ellerslie Oak*, near Paisley, is reported to have sheltered Sir William WALLACE and 300 of his men.

FAIRLOP OAK. *See* FAIRLOP.

Herne's Oak. An oak in Windsor Great Park, reputed to be haunted by the ghost of Herne the Hunter (*see* WILD HUNTSMAN). It was supposed to be 650 years old when blown down in 1863. Queen Victoria planted a young oak on the site.

Honour Oak. This boundary oak still standing at Whitchurch, Tavistock, marked the Tavistock limit for French prisoners on parole from Princetown prison during the years 1803–1814, when England was at war with France. It was also the place where money was left in exchange for food during the cholera epidemic of 1832.

King Oak. See William the Conqueror's Oak, below.

The *Major Oak*, Sherwood Forest, Edwinstowe, is supposed to have been a full-grown tree in the reign of King John. The hollow of the trunk will hold 15 persons, but new bark has considerably diminished the opening. Its girth is 37 or 38 ft., and the head covers a circumference of 240 ft. ROBIN HOOD is supposed to have hidden in it. Originally called the *Queen Oak*, its present name may be a tribute to Major Rooke, an 18th century antiquarian, who was particularly fond of this tree in the DUKERIES.

Meavy Oak. A venerable oak in front of the lych-gate of Meavy Church, near Yelverton, Devon, some 25 ft. in circumference, in the hollow of which nine persons are once reputed to have dined. According to tradition it dates back to Saxon times.

Owen Glendower's Oak, at Shelton, near Shrewsbury, was in full growth in 1403, for in this tree Owen Glendower witnessed the great battle between Henry IV and Henry Percy. Six or eight persons can stand in the hollow of its trunk. Its girth is 40¼ ft.

The *Parliament Oak*, Clipston, in Sherwood Forest, was the tree under which Edward I held a PARLIAMENT in 1282. He was hunting when a messenger announced the Welsh were in revolt under Llewelyn ap Gruffydd. He hastily convened his nobles under the oak and it was resolved to march against the Welsh at once. The tree no longer exists.

Queen's Oak, Huntingfield, Suffolk, is so named because near this tree Queen Elizabeth I shot a buck.

The *Reformation Oak*, on Mousehold Heath, near Norwich, is where the rebel Ket

held his court in 1549, and when the rebellion was stamped out nine of the ringleaders were hanged on this tree.

Robin Hood's Larder was an oak in Sherwood Forest. The tradition is that ROBIN HOOD used its hollow trunk as a hiding-place for the deer he had slain. Late in the last century some schoolgirls boiled their kettle in it, and burnt down a large part of the tree, which was reputed to be 1,000 years old. It was blown down in 1966, and the Duke of Portland gave a suitably inscribed remnant to the Mayor of Toronto.

The *Royal Oak. See* OAK-APPLE DAY.

Sir Philip Sidney's Oak, near Penshurst, Kent, was planted at his birth in 1554, and was commemorated by Ben Jonson and Waller.

The *Swilcar Oak*, in Needwood Forest, Staffordshire, is between 600 and 700 years old.

The *Watch Oak*, in Windsor Great Park, said to be 800 years old. So called because the Duke of Cumberland (3rd son of George II, who defeated the Jacobites at Culloden in 1745) was said to have stationed a look-out in its branches during target practices to signal the accuracy of the cannon shots.

William the Conqueror's Oak, or the King Oak, in Windsor Great Park, which is supposed to have afforded him shelter, is 38 ft. in girth.

Heart of Oak. *See under* HEART.

Oak before the Ash. The old proverbial forecast, referring to whichever is in leaf first, says:

> If the oak's before the ash
> Then you'll only get a splash;
> If the ash precedes the oak,
> Then you may expect a soak.

i.e. a wet summer is to be expected.

To sport one's oak. An old university custom signifying that one is "not at home" to visitors by closing the *oak* or outer door of one's rooms.

> Mr. Verdant Green had for the first time "sported his oak". Under any circumstances it would have been a mere form, since his bashful politeness would have induced him to open it to any comer;...
> "CUTHBERT BEDE": *The Adventures of Mr. Verdant Green*, ch. viii.

Oak-apple Day (also called **Royal Oak Day**). 29 May, the birthday of Charles II and the day when he entered London at the RESTORATION; commanded by Act of PARLIAMENT in 1664 to be observed as a day of thanksgiving. A special service (expunged in 1859) was inserted in the BOOK OF COMMON PRAYER and people wore sprigs of oak with gilded oak-apples on that day.

It commemorates Charles II's conceal

ment with Major Careless in the "Royal Oak" at Boscobel, near Shifnal, Salop, after his defeat at Worcester (3 September 1651).

Oak boys. Bands of PROTESTANT agrarian rioters in ULSTER in the 1760s, so called from the oak sprays worn in their hats. The main grievance was against the TITHE system. *Cp.* STEELBOYS.

Oakes's Oath (Austr.). Unreliable testimony delivered on oath. The phrase is said to derive from one, Oakes, who was asked in a Court of Law if he could identify a pair of horns as belonging to one of his own cattle. After hesitating a moment he is reported to have said, "I'll chance it; Yes!"

Oakley, Annie. An expert American markswoman (1860–1926), who in BUFFALO BILL'S Wild West Show, using a playing card as a target, centred a shot in each of the pips. From this performance of hers, and the resemblance of the card to a punched ticket, springs the American use of the name "Annie Oakley" to mean a complimentary ticket to a show, a meal ticket, or a pass on a railway.

Oaks, The. The "Ladies' Race", one of the CLASSIC RACES of the turf; it is for three-year-old fillies, and is run at Epsom two days after the DERBY. It was instituted in 1779 and so called from an estate of the Earl of Derby near Epsom named "The Oaks".

Oakum. Picking Oakum. An old employment given to prisoners, the picking and unravelling of old rope, which was used for caulking the seams of wooden ships. It is the O.E. *acumbe*, off-combings.

Oannes (ō ǎn' ēz). A Babylonian god having a fish's body and a human head and feet. In the daytime he lived with men to instruct them in the arts and sciences, but at night returned to the depths of the Persian Gulf.

Oar. To put your oar into my boat. To interfere in my affairs.

To rest on one's oars. To take a rest or breathing space after hard work or strenuous effort. A boating phrase.

To toss the oars. To raise them vertically, resing on the handles. It is a form of salute.

Oasis (ō ā' sis) (Coptic *ouahe*; from *ouih*, to dwell). A fertile spot in the midst of desert country where water and vegetation are to be found. A delightful spot, or a charming and sheltered retreat from a drab or noisy environment, is sometimes called "a perfect oasis".

Oaten pipe. A rustic musical pipe made of an oat straw so cut as to be stopped at one end with a knot, the other end being left open. A slit made in the straw near the knot was so cut as to form a reed.

Meanwhile the rural ditties were not mute,
Temper'd to the oaten flute.

MILTON: Lycidas.

Oatmeals. A 17th-century nickname given to profligate bands in the streets of London. *Cp.* MOHOCKS; TITYRE TUS.

Do mad pranks
With roaring boys and Oatmeals.

DEKKER and FORD: Sun's Darling, I, i.

Oatmeal Monday. The mid-term Monday at the Scottish Universities when the father of a poor student would bring him a sack of oatmeal to provide his staple diet for the rest of the term.

Oats. To sow one's wild oats. To indulge in youthful excesses and dissipations. The reference is to sowing bad grain (wild) instead of good (cultivated).

Obadiah. An old slang name for a QUAKER.

Obeah, Obi. The belief in and practice of *obeah*, *i.e.* a kind of sorcery or witchcraft prevalent in West Africa and formerly in the West Indies. *Obeah* is a native word and signifies something put into the ground, to bring about sickness, death, or other disaster. *Cp.* VOODOO.

Obelisk. A tapering pillar of stone, originally erected by the Egyptians, who placed them in pairs before temple portals. The base was usually one-tenth of the height and the apex was copper-sheathed. Each of the four faces bore incised HIEROGLYPHS. The best known in England is CLEOPATRA'S NEEDLE.

The tallest obelisk (nearly 110 ft.) is at ROME, taken there from Heliopolis by the Emperor CALIGULA (37–41 A.D.) and later (1586) re-erected in the piazza of St. Peter's by order of Pope Sixtus V. Weighing some 320 tons, it was moved bodily on rollers. Spectators were forbidden to utter a sound on pain of death during the operation but when the ropes were straining to breaking point, one of the workmen, a sailor from San Remo, is said to have shouted *"Acqua alle funi"* (Water on the ropes), so saving the situation at risk of the death penalty.

The Obelisk of Luxor, in the Place de la Concorde, PARIS, came from Thebes, and was presented to Louis Philippe in 1831, by the then KHEDIVE of Egypt. Its hieroglyphs record the deeds of Rameses II (12th century B.C.). *Cp.* COLUMN.

Oberammergau. *See* PASSION PLAY.

Obermann. The impersonation of high moral worth without talent, and the tortures endured by the consciousness of this defect. From Senancour's psychological romance of this name (1804), in which Obermann, the hero, is a dreamer perpetually trying to escape the actual.

Oberon. King of the FAIRIES, husband of TITANIA. Shakespeare introduced them in his *Midsummer Night's Dream*. The name is probably connected with ALBERICH, the king of the elves.

He first appeared in the mediæval French romance, *Huon de Bordeaux*, where he is the son of Julius CÆSAR and MORGAN LE FAY. He was only three feet high, but of angelic face, and was the lord and king of Mommur. At his birth, the fairies bestowed their gifts—one was insight into men's thoughts, and another was the power of transporting himself to any place instantaneously; and in the fullness of time legions of ANGELS conveyed his soul to PARADISE.

Obi. *See* OBEAH.

Obiter dictum (ob' i tèr dik' tùm) (Lat.). An incidental remark, something said in passing; a judge's expression of opinion backed by his knowledge and experience, but not forming part of a judgement and therefore not legally binding. *Obiter* means "in passing", the more common plural form of the phrase being *obiter dicta*.

Object; Objective. *See* SUBJECT.

Oblong (U.S.A.). A late 19th-century slang term for a bank note.

Obolus. An ancient Greek bronze or silver coin of small value; also a mediæval silver coin of small value. *See* BELISARIUS.

Observantins. *See* FRANCISCANS.

Obverse. That side of a coin or medal which contains the principal device. Thus, the obverse of our coins is the side which contains the sovereign's head; the other side is the *reverse*.

Occam's Razor. *Entia non sunt multiplicanda praeter necessitatem* (entities ought not to be multiplied except from necessity), which means that all unnecessary facts or constituents in the subject being analysed are to be eliminated. These exact words do not appear in Occam's works but the principle expressed occurs in several other forms. Occam's razor cuts away superfluities.

William of Occam, the *Doctor Singularis et Invincibilis* (d. 1349), the great FRANCISCAN scholastic philosopher, was probably born at Ockham, Surrey, *Occam* being the latinized form of the name. *See also* SCHOLASTICISM.

Occasion. To improve the occasion. To draw a moral lesson from some event or occurrence.

To rise to the occasion. To show oneself equal to a demanding situation or task; to speak or act as the emergency requires.

Occult Sciences (Lat. *occultus*; related to *celare*, to hide). Magic, ALCHEMY, ASTROLOGY, palmistry, DIVINATION, etc.; so called because they were hidden mysteries.

Oceanids, or **Oceanides.** In Greek mythology, sea-NYMPHS, daughters of OCEANUS and Tethys, among whom were DORIS, Electra, and AMPHITRITE. Offerings were made to them by mariners.

Oceanus (ō sē' à nus). A Greek sea-god; also the river of the world which circles the earth and as such is represented as a snake with its tail in its mouth. As a sea-god, he is an old man with a long beard and with bull's horns on his head.

Ockham. *See* OCCAM.

October. The eighth month of the ancient Roman CALENDAR (Lat. *octo*, eight) when the year began in MARCH; the tenth of ours. The old Dutch name was *Wynmaand*; the O.E. *Winmonath* (Wine-month, or the time of vintage); also *Teomonath* (tenth month) and *Winter-fylleth* (winter full-moon). In the French Revolutionary Calendar it was *Vendémiaire* (time of vintage, 22 September to 21 October).

A tankard of October. A tankard of the best and strongest ale, brewed in October.

October Club. In the reign of Queen Anne, a group of High TORY M.P.s who met at a tavern near PARLIAMENT to drink October ALE and to abuse the WHIGS. It became politically prominent about 1710 although it had probably existed from the end of William III's reign.

Also a left-wing political club at Oxford in the 1930s of Communist sympathies, taking its name from the OCTOBER REVOLUTION.

Octobrists. A "constitutionalist" centre party in Russia supported by the landlords and wealthy mercantile interests, prominent in the dumas between 1907 and 1914, after the Tsar's famous liberal manifesto published in October 1905.

October Revolution. In Russian history, the BOLSHEVIK revolution of October 1917 (November in the western Calendar) which led to the overthrow of Kerensky and the MENSHEVIKS and the triumph of Lenin.

Od. *See* ODYLE.

Odal. *See* UDAL TENURE.

Odd. Odd Fellows. A FRIENDLY SOCIETY of 18th-century origins, first formed at London. During the period of the French Revolutionary Wars many lodges were prosecuted for alleged "seditious" activities, as were many harmless organizations. In 1813, the Independent Order at Odd Fellows was formed at Manchester and it became the most influential in England. The movement spread to the United States and Canada and allied bodies now exist in various European countries.

Sette of Odd Volumes. A literary dining Society at London, founded in 1884.

At odds. At variance.

By long odds. By a great difference; as, "He is the best man by long odds." In horse-racing, odds are the ratio by which the amount staked by one party to a bet exceeds that of the other; hence long odds indicates a big variance in this ratio.

Odd man out. The one of a group who fails to get selected or included when numbers are made up; one who does not fit into a group or gathering owing to difference of interests, temperament, position, etc.

Odds and ends. *see* END.

That makes no odds. No difference; never mind, that is no excuse. An application of the betting phrase.

There's luck in odd numbers. *See under* NUMBERS.

To shout the odds. To make a noisy protest or fuss; as a bookmaker noisily proclaims the odds.

Odin (ō′ din). The Scandinavian name of the GOD called by the Anglo-Saxons WODEN. He was god of wisdom, poetry, war, and agriculture. As god of the dead, he presided over banquets of those slain in battle. (*See* VALHALLA.) He became the All-wise by drinking of Mimir's fountain, but purchased the distinction at the pledge of one eye, and is often represented as a one-eyed man wearing a hat and carrying a staff. His remaining eye is the SUN, his horse Sleipnir. He was master of magic and discovered the RUNES.

The promise of Odin. The most binding of all oaths to a Norseman. In making it the hand was passed through a massive silver ring kept for the purpose; or through a sacrificial stone, like that called the "Circle of Stennis". *Cp.* THE STANDING STONES OF STENNESS *under* STONE.

The vow of Odin. A matrimonial or other vow made before the "Stone of Odin" in the Orkneys. This was an oval stone, with a hole in it large enough to admit a man's hand. Anyone who violated a vow made before this stone was held infamous.

Odium theologicum (ō′ di ùm thē ō - loj′ ikùm) (Lat.). The bitter hatred of rival theologians. No wars so sanguinary as holy wars; no persecutions so relentless as religious persecutions; no hatred so bitter as theological hatred.

Odor lucri (ō′ dôr lū′ krî) (Lat.). The sweets of gain; the delights of money-making.

Odour. In good odour; in bad odour. In favour, out of favour; in good repute, in bad repute.

The odour of sanctity. In the MIDDLE AGES it was held that a sweet and delightful odour was given off by the bodies of saintly persons at their death, and also when their bodies, if "translated", were distinterred. Hence the phrase, *he died in the odour of sanctity, i.e.* he died a saint. The SWEDENBORGIANS say that when the celestial ANGELS are present at a deathbed, what is then cadaverous excites a sensation of what is aromatic.

There is an "odour of iniquity" as well and SHAKESPEARE has a strong passage on the odour of impiety. Antiochus and his wicked daughter were killed by lightning and Shakespeare says (*Pericles, Prince of Tyre*, II, iv):

> A fire from heaven came and shrivelled up
> Their bodies, e'en to loathing; for they so stunk
> That all those eyes adored them ere their fall
> Scorn now their hand should give them burial.

See also COMPARISONS ARE ODOROUS.

Od's, used in oaths, as:

Od's bodikins! or *Odsbody!* means "God's body".

Od's pittikins! God's pity.

Od's plessed will! (*Merry Wives of Windsor*, I, i). God's blessed will.

Od rot'em! See DRAT.

Od-zounds! God's wounds.

Odyle (od′ îl). The name formerly given to the hypothetical force which emanates from a medium to produce the phenomena connected with MESMERISM, spirit-rapping, table-turning, and so on. Baron von Reichenbach (1788–1869) called it *Od force*, and taught that it pervaded all nature, especially heat, light, crystals, magnets, etc., and was developed in chemical action; and also that it streamed from the fingers of specially sensitive persons.

> That od-force of German Reichenbach
> Which still from female finger-tips burns blue.
> MRS. BROWNING: *Aurora Leigh*, vii, 566.

Odyssey (od′ i si). The epic poem of HOMER which records the adventures of Odysseus (ULYSSES) on his homeward voyage from TROY. The word implies the things or adventures of ULYSSES.

Œcumenical Councils (ē kū men′ ik àl) (Gr. *oikoumenikos*, the whole inhabited world— *ge*, earth, being understood). Ecclesiastical councils whose findings are—or were— recognized as binding on all Christians.

Those commonly recognized in the East and West, which dealt with the heresies indicated, are:

Nicæa, 325 (Arianism); Constantinople, 381 (Apollinarianism); Ephesus, 431 (Nestorianism); Chalcedon, 451 (Eutychianism); Constantinople,

533 and 680–1 (Monothelitism); Nicæa, 787 (Iconoclasm).

The ROMAN CATHOLIC CHURCH also recognizes:

Constantinople, 869–870; Lateran, 1123, 1139, 1179, 1215; Lyons, 1245, 1274; Vienne, 1311–1312; Constance 1414–1418; Ferrara-Florence, 1438–1439; Trent, 1545–1563 (Protestantism and Reform); Vatican, 1869–1870 (Papal Infallibility); Vatican, 1962–1965.

The Second VATICAN COUNCIL was attended by observers from the CHURCH OF ENGLAND and 26 other denominations.

Œcumenical Movement. The movement towards re-unity among the various Christian Churches, which has gathered strength in recent years, especially since the Second Vatican Council and the establishment of the World Council of Churches inaugurated at Amsterdam in 1948 which comprises most of the prominent Christian bodies.

Œdipus (ē di pús) was the son of Laius, King of Thebes, and of Jocasta the Queen. To avert the fulfilment of the prophecy that he would murder his father and marry his mother, Œdipus was exposed on the mountains as an infant and taken in and reared by the shepherds. When grown to manhood he unwittingly slew his father; then, having solved the riddle of the SPHINX, he became King of THEBES, thereby gaining the hand in marriage of Jocasta, his mother, of whose relationship to himself they were both ignorant. When the facts came to light Jocasta hanged herself and Œdipus tore out his own eyes.

An Œdipus complex is the psychoanalytical term for the sexual desire (usually unrecognized by himself) of a son for his mother and conversely an equally unrecognized jealous hatred of his father.

Œil-de-Bœuf (ĕē de bĕrf) (Fr., "bull's-eye"). A large reception room (*salle*) in the Palace of VERSAILLES was so named from its round "bull's-eye" window. The ceiling, decorated by Van der Meulen, contains likenesses of Louis XIV's children. It was the ante-room where courtiers waited and gossiped, hence the name became associated with BACKSTAIRS intrigue.

Les Fastes de l'Œil-de-Bœuf. The annals of the courtiers of the *Grand Monarque*; hence the anecdotes of courtiers generally.

Œnone (ēnō' nē). A NYMPH of Mount IDA, the wife of PARIS before he abducted HELEN. She prophesied the disastrous consequences of his voyage to Greece and, on the death of Paris, killed herself.

Off (Lat. *ab*, from, away). The house is a *mile off*—*i.e.* is "away" or "from" us a mile. The word preceding *off* defines its scope. To be "*well off*" is to be away or on the way towards prosperity or well-being; to be "*badly off*" is the reverse.

The off-side of a motor-car is that to the right hand of the driver (*cp.* NEAR); in Association Football the referee signals *Off-side* and awards a free kick when the ball is played and a player of the attacking side is nearer to his opponent's goal-line and there are not two of his opponents between himself and the goal.

An act of behaviour, a thing, a person, etc., is said to be *a bit off* when it is not quite up to proper standards. (*See* OFF COLOUR *under* COLOUR.)

Offa's Dyke. An earthwork running from the Wye, near Monmouth, to near Prestatyn (now in Clwyd), probably built by Offa of MERCIA (*c*. 784–796) as a boundary between him and the Welsh. *Cp.* GRAHAME'S DYKE; GRIM'S DITCH; WANSDYKE.

Office, The Divine. The obligatory prayers, etc., of the Church said by priests and the religious. The Divine Office (*horae canonicae*) of the ROMAN CATHOLIC CHURCH is contained in the BREVIARY.

Office, The Holy. *See* INQUISITION.

Offing. In the offing. Said of a ship visible at sea off the land. Such a ship is often approaching port, hence the phrase is used figuratively to mean "about to happen", "likely to occur" or "likely to take place", etc.

Og, King of Bashan, according to Rabbinical legend, was an antediluvian GIANT, saved from the Flood (*see* DELUGE) by climbing on the roof of the ark. After the passage of the Red Sea, MOSES first conquered Sihon, and then advanced against the giant Og whose bedstead, made of iron, was 9 cubits long and 4 cubits broad (*Deut.* iii, 11). The legend says that Og plucked up a mountain to hurl at the Israelites, but he got so entangled with his burden that Moses was able to kill him without much difficulty.

In Dryden's *Absalom and Achitophel*, Og is used for Thomas Shadwell, who was very large and fat.

Ogam, or **Ogham.** The alphabet in use among the ancient Irish and British peoples. There were 20 characters, each of which was composed of a number (from one to five) of

794

thin strokes arranged and grouped above, below, or across a horizontal line.

The word is connected with *Ogmius*, the name of a Gaulish god, likened to HERCULES by Lucian, who performed his feats through eloquence and the gift of languages. *Cp*. RUNE.

Ogier the Dane (ō' ji ėr). One of the great heroes of mediaeval romance whose exploits are chronicled in the CHANSONS DE GESTE; son of Geoffrey, King of Denmark, of which country (as Holger Danske) he is still the national hero. In one account his son was slain by CHARLEMAGNE'S son Charlot and in revenge Ogier killed the king's nephew and was only prevented from slaying Charlemagne himself. He eventually returned from exile to defend France against the Saracen chief Brehus. In another romance, it is said, FAIRIES attended his birth, among them MORGAN LE FAY, who eventually took him to AVALON where he dwelt for 200 years. She then sent him to defend France against invasion, after which she took him back to Avalon. William Morris gives a rendering of this romance in his *Earthly Paradise (August)*.

Ogpu, or **G.P.U.** The secret police of the U.S.S.R. which succeeded the Cheka in 1922. The initials stand for *Obedinennoe Gosudarstvennoe Politicheskoe Upravlenie* (United State Political Administration). It was renamed the N.K.V.D., *Narodnyi Komissariat Vnutrennykh Dyel* (People's Commissariat for Internal Affairs), in 1934. In 1944 it became the M.V.D., changing to the K.G.B. in 1954.

Ogres of nursery story are GIANTS of very malignant disposition, who live on human flesh. The word was first used (and probably invented) by Perrault in his *Histoires ou Contes du temps passé* (1697), and is thought to be made up from *Orcus*, a name of PLUTO.

Ogygia (ō jij' i a). *See* CALYPSO.

Ogygian Deluge. In Greek legend, a flood said to have occurred when Ogyges was King of Bœotia, some 200 years before DEUCALION'S flood. Varro says that the planet VENUS underwent a great change in the reign of Ogyges. It changed its diameter, its colour, its figure, and its course.

Oi Polloi, properly HOI POLLOI.

Oil. Fixed oils. *See under* FIX.

Oil of Angels. Money used as a bribe or douceur; in allusion to the old coin called an ANGEL.

Oil of Palms. *See* PALM-OIL.

Burning the midnight oil. *See* MIDNIGHT OIL.

To be well oiled. Pretty well drunk.

To oil the knocker. To fee the porter. The expression is from Racine's *Les Plaideurs:* *"On n'entre point chez lui sans graisser le marteau"* (no one enters his house without oiling the knocker).

To pour oil on troubled waters. To soothe by gentle words; to use tact and diplomacy to restore calm after excited anger and quarrelsome argument.

The allusion is to the well-known fact that the violence of waves is much decreased when oil is poured upon them. In Bede's *Ecclesiastical History* (731) it is said that St. Aidan gave a young priest, who was to escort a maiden destined for the bride of King Oswy, a cruse of oil to pour on the sea if the waves became stormy. The priest did this when a storm arose and thereby calmed the waters.

To strike oil. To make a lucky or valuable discovery; to come upon good fortune in some form or other. The phrase refers to the finding of mineral oil deposits, always a source of wealth.

Old. Used colloquially as a term of endearment or friendship, as in *My dear old chap*, *my old man* (*i.e.* my husband); as a general disparagement, as in *old cat*, *old fogy*, *old geezer, old stick-in-the-mud*; and as a common intensive, as in SHAKESPEARE'S "Here will be an old abusing of God's patience and the King's English" (*The Merry Wives of Windsor*, I, iv), and in the modern "any old thing will do".

For names such as Old Grog, Harry, Noll, Nosey, Rowley, Scratch, Tom, etc., *see under these words*.

Old Bags. John Scott Eldon (1751–1838), Lord CHANCELLOR; so called from his carrying home with him in different bags the cases still pending his judgement.

Old Bailey. The Central Criminal Court of the City of LONDON and of (approximately) the Greater London area, situated in the thoroughfare of this name. It is probably from Med. Lat. *ballium*, enclosure; the enclosure of the City wall between LUDGATE and NEWGATE. The area has historic associations with crime owing to the proximity of NEWGATE GAOL and its being the site of public executions, the last victim being a FENIAN executed by William Calcraft in 1868. It was also the site of a pillory.

Old Believers. Those members of the Russian ORTHODOX CHURCH who rejected the liturgical reforms of the patriarch Nikon and were excommunicated in 1667. They were subjected to violent persecution and eventually resolved into two groups, the *Popovtsy*, and the *Bespopovtsy*, the latter rejecting the priesthood altogether. The former attained state recognition in 1881.

Old Bill. *See* 'OLE, A BETTER.

Old Blood and guts. General G. S. Patton. *See* BLOOD AND GUTS.

Old Bold Fifth. *See* REGIMENTAL AND DIVISIONAL NICKNAMES.

Old Bona Fide. Louis XIV (1638, 1643–1715).

Old Boots. *See under* BOOTS.

Old Boy. A friendly colloquial form of address between men of any age; the term also denotes a former pupil of a particular school, hence "old boys' clubs", "old boys' dinners", etc. *Old girl* is similarly used to denote old scholars, and by men as an affectionate term of address to members of the opposite sex. It is also applied to certain female animals, especially horses. Both terms are applied in the obvious sense to elderly men and women. *See* OLD SCHOOL TIE.

Old Boy net or **network.** To arrange something on the "Old Boy network" is to fix it through a social contact (properly someone from one's old school) instead of through the usual channels.

Old Braggs. *See* REGIMENTAL AND DIVISIONAL NICKNAMES.

Old Bullion. Thomas Hart Benton (1782–1858), Jacksonian Democrat and statesman. He opposed the establishment of a national bank and was nicknamed "Old Bullion" for his championship of the virtues of "hard money" (*see* HARD CURRENCY).

Old Catholics. *See under* CATHOLIC.

Old Chapel, The. *See under* CHAPEL.

Old Contemptibles. *See* CONTEMPTIBLES.

Old Country, The. In the days of the British Empire, Great Britain, the mother country.

Old Cracow Bible. *See* BIBLE, SOME SPECIALLY NAMED EDITIONS.

Old Dominion. *See under* DOMINION.

Old Dozen. *See* REGIMENTAL AND DIVISIONAL NICKNAMES.

Old Fogs. *See* REGIMENTAL AND DIVISIONAL NICKNAMES.

Old Fox. A nickname of George Washington and Marshal Soult.

Old Glory. The United States Flag. *See* STARS AND STRIPES.

Old Guard. The veteran regiments of NAPOLEON's Imperial Guard, the flower of the French army. Devoted to their Emperor, the Old Guard could be relied upon in any desperate strait, and it was they who made the last charge of the French at Waterloo. Figuratively, the phrase *Old Guard* is used for the stalwarts of any party or movement.

The Imperial Guard was composed of four regi ments of the Young Guard, four of the Middl Guard, four of the Old Guard, four cavalry regi ments, and 96 pieces of artillery.
NAPOLEON: *The Waterloo Campaign*, II, iv

Old hat. *See under* HAT.

Old Hickory. The nickname of Genera Andrew Jackson (1767–1845), 7th Presiden of the U.S.A. (1828–1837); it arose from hi staunchness and strength of character. *Se* KITCHEN CABINET.

Old Hundredth. *See under* HUNDRED.

Old Ironsides. *See* IRONSIDES.

Old King Cole. *See* COLE.

Old Lady of the Bund. The nickname gi ven by British residents in China to *Th North China Daily News*, published a Shanghai (1855–1950).

Old Lady of Threadneedle Street. *Se under* THREADNEEDLE STREET.

Old Man Eloquent. MILTON so called Iso crates. When he heard of the result of th battle of Chæronea, which was fatal to Gre cian liberty, he died of grief.

That dishonest victory
At Chæronea, fatal to liberty,
Killed with report that Old Man Eloquent.
MILTON: *Sonnet*, x

The name was also applied to Joh Quincy Adams (1767–1848), 6th Presiden of the U.S.A. (1825–1829).

Old Man of the Mountain. *See unde* MOUNTAIN.

Old Man of the Sea. In the story of *Sinba the Sailor* (ARABIAN NIGHTS), the Old Ma of the Sea hoisted himself on Sinbad's shoul ders and clung there for many days an nights, much to the discomfort of Sinbac who finally got rid of the Old Man by makin him drunk. Hence, any burden, figurativ or actual, of which it is impossible to fre oneself without the greatest exertions called an Old Man of the Sea. *Cp.* NEREUS

Old Masters. *See under* MASTER.

Old Mo, The. The Middlesex MUSIC HALL Drury Lane, was so called after the Mogu Tavern which was incorporated in the pre mises. After rebuilding in 1911 it becam the New Middlesex and in 1919 the Wint Garden Theatre.

Old Mother Hubbard. This lastingly pop ular NURSERY RHYME is one of definite known origin and was first published i 1805. It was written by Sarah Catherin Martin (1768–1821) while staying with he brother-in-law, J. P. Bastard of Kitle Yealmpton, South Devon. It is traditional said that Mother Hubbard was the hous keeper at Kitley and there is a cottage Yealmpton purporting to be her one-tim residence.

> Old Mother Hubbard
> Went to the cupboard
> To fetch her poor dog a bone;
> But when she came there
> The cupboard was bare
> And so the poor dog had none.

Old Nick. *See under* NICK.

Old Pretender. *See* PRETENDER.

Old Reekie. *See* AULD REEKIE.

Old Rough and Ready. General Zachary Taylor (1784–1850), 12th President of the U.S.A., 1849–1850.

Old School Tie. Literally a distinguishing necktie worn by OLD BOYS of a particular school. Such ties being essentially associated with the public schools and the older grammar schools led to *old school tie* being given a pejorative use as a symbol of class distinction, *e.g.* "the old school tie brigade", meaning the members of a privileged class. *Cp.* OLD BOY NET.

Old stager. One of long experience, an old hand at the game; originally an experienced stage player.

> All the girls declare
> That I'm a gay old stager,
> Hey! Hey! clear the way
> Here comes the galloping major!
>
> F. W. LEIGH and G. BASTOW:
> *The Galloping Major.*

Old Style, New Style. Terms used in chronology. *Old Style* refers to dating by the JULIAN CALENDAR and *New Style* by the GREGORIAN CALENDAR. *See* STILO NOVO.

Old Testament, The. The collective name (*see* NEW TESTAMENT) of the first 39 books in the BIBLE inherited as sacred scripture from the Jewish church, and referred to by Christ and his disciples as "the Scriptures". *Matt.* xxi, 42 has:

> Jesus saith unto them, Did ye never read in the scriptures ...

The Hebrew canon, which is that of the Reformed churches and comprises the 39 books printed in most bibles, is substantially that adopted by a Jewish council at Jamnia (*c.* 90 A.D.). The Roman Catholic canon includes the APOCRYPHA.

Old Vic. The theatre in Waterloo Road, LONDON, which became famous for its Shakespearean productions under the management of Lilian Baylis, who took over from her aunt, Emma Cons, in 1912, and who died in 1937. It was opened in 1818 as the Coburg and was renamed the Royal Victoria Hall in 1833. In 1963 it became the temporary home of the National Theatre. *See* SADLER'S WELLS.

Old wives' tales. Superstitious stories and beliefs such as are kept alive and spread by credulous old women.

Old woman. Colloquially, a fusspot, an old ditherer, as, "he is a proper old woman."

Old World. So Europe, Asia, and Africa are called when contrasted with the NEW WORLD.

Oldenburg Horn. A horn long in the possession of the reigning princes of the House of Oldenburg, but now in the collection of the King of Denmark. According to tradition, Count Otto of Oldenburg, in 967, was offered drink in this silver-gilt horn by a "wild woman", at the Osenborg. As he did not like the look of the liquor, he threw it away, and rode off with the horn.

'Ole, A Better. Old Bill, a walrus-moustached, disillusioned old soldier, in the 1914–1918 war, portrayed by Captain Bruce Bairnsfather (1887–1959), artist and journalist, in his publications *Old Bill* and *The Better 'Ole.* Cowering in a muddy shell-hole in the midst of a withering bombardment, he says to his grousing pal Bert, "If you know of a better 'ole, go to it." The joke and Old Bill struck the public fancy and Old Bill became the embodiment of a familiar type of simple, cynical, long-suffering, honest old grouser.

Olet lucernam (ō' let loo sĕr' năm). A Latin proverb, *see* IT SMELLS OF THE LAMP *under* LAMP.

Olio (ō' li ō) (Span. *olla*, a stew, or the pot in which it is cooked; from Lat. *olla*, a pot). In Spain a mixture of meat, vegetables, spices, etc., boiled together and highly seasoned; hence any HOTCHPOTCH of various ingredients, as a miscellaneous collection of verses, drawings, pieces of music, etc.

Olive. In ancient Greece the olive was sacred to PALLAS, in allusion to the story that at the naming of ATHENS she presented it with an olive branch. It was the symbol of peace and fecundity, brides wearing or carrying an olive garland as ours do a wreath of ORANGE BLOSSOM. A crown of olive was the highest distinction of a citizen who deserved well of his country, and was the highest prize in the OLYMPIC GAMES.

In the OLD TESTAMENT, the subsiding of the FLOOD was demonstrated to Noah by the return of a DOVE bearing an olive leaf in her beak (*Gen.* viii, 11).

Olive Branch Petition. A peace move adopted by Congress (5 July 1775) after Bunker Hill to secure reconciliation with Great Britain and drawn up by John Dickinson. Lord North's conciliation proposals were rejected by the Americans and George III refused to receive the Olive Branch Petition.

Olive branches. A facetious term for children in relation to their parents; the allusion is to "Thy wife shall be as a fruitful vine ...

thy children like olive plants round about thy table" (*Ps*. cxxviii, 3).

> The wife and olive branches of one Mr. Kenwigs.
> DICKENS: *Nicholas Nickleby, xiv*.

To hold out the olive branch. To make overtures for peace; in allusion to the olive being an ancient symbol of peace. In some of Numa's medals the king is represented holding an olive twig, indicative of a peaceful reign.

Oliver. CHARLEMAGNE's favourite PALADIN, who, with ROLAND, rode by his side. He was the son of Regnier, Duke of Genoa (another of the paladins), and brother of the beautiful Aude. His sword was called *Hauteclaire*, and his horse *Ferrant d'Espagne*.

A Roland for an Oliver. *See under* RO-LAND.

Olivet or **the Mount of Olives.** The range of hills to the east of Jerusalem, closely connected with ancient Jewish ceremonies and intimately associated with the events of the NEW TESTAMENT. Here Jesus retired for prayer and meditation and to talk to his disciples and here he came on the night of his betrayal.

> And in the daytime he was teaching in the temple, and at night he went out, and abode in the mount that is called the Mount of Olives.
> *Luke* xxi, 37.

Olivetan. Pierre Robert (*c*. 1506–1538), a cousin of Calvin, PROTESTANT reformer and translator of the OLD TESTAMENT; called "Olivetanus" in allusion to his "burning the midnight oil".

Olivetans. Brethren of Our Lady of Mount Olivet, an offshoot of the BENEDICTINES. The order was founded in 1319 by St. Bernard Ptolemei. For a time they were total abstainers.

Olla Podrida (ol′ yå pod rē′ då) (Span., putrid pot). Odds and ends, a mixture of scraps or *pot-au-feu*, into which every sort of eatable is thrown and stewed. *Cp*. OLIO. Figuratively, the term means an incongruous mixture, a miscellaneous collection of any kind, a medley.

> However, I shall not take it amiss, if Master Sewer will now and then get me one of these olla podridas (and the stronger they are the better), where all sorts of good things are stewed, and, as it were, lost in one another.
> CERVANTES: *Don Quixote*, ch. lxxxi
> (*Translation by Motteu*)

Olympia. The ancient name of a valley in Elis, Peloponnesus, so called from the famous games held there in honour of the OLYMPIAN ZEUS. The ALTIS, an enclosure of about 500 ft. by 600 ft., was built in the valley, containing the temple of Zeus, the Heræum, the Metroum, etc., the STADIUM, with gymnasia, baths, etc. Hence the name is applied to large buildings for sporting events, exhibitions, etc., such as the Olympia at Kensington, London.

Olympiad. Among the ancient Greeks, a period of four years, being the interval between the celebrations of the OLYMPIC GAMES. The first Olympiad began in 776 B.C., and the last (the 293rd) in A.D. 392.

Olympian Zeus, or **Jove.** A statue by Phidias, one of the "Seven Wonders of the World" (*see under* WONDER). Pausanias (vii, 2) says when the sculptor placed it in the temple at OLYMPIA (433 B.C.), he prayed to the god to indicate whether he was satisfied with it, and immediately a thunderbolt fell on the floor of the temple without doing the slightest harm.

It was a chryselephantine statue, *i.e.* made of ivory and GOLD; and, though seated on a throne, was 60 ft. in height. The left hand rested on a sceptre, and the right palm held a statue of Victory in solid gold. The robes were of gold and so were the four lions which supported the footstool. The throne was of cedar, embellished with ebony, ivory, gold, and precious stones.

It was removed to Constantinople in the 5th century A.D., and perished in the great fire of 475.

Olympic Games. The greatest of the four sacred festivals of the ancient Greeks, held every fourth year at OLYMPIA in July. After suitable sacrifices, racing, wrestling, and other contests followed, ending on the fifth day with processions, sacrifices, and banquets and OLIVE garlands for the victors.

The games were revived in 1896 as international sporting contests, the first being held at Athens, and subsequently at Paris (1900), St. Louis (1904), London (1908), Stockholm (1912), Antwerp (1920), Paris (1924), Amsterdam (1928), Los Angeles (1932), Berlin (1936), London (1948), Helsinki (1952), Melbourne (1956), Rome (1960), Tokyo (1964), Mexico City (1968), Munich (1972), Montreal (1976), Moscow (1980), Los Angeles (1984), Seoul (1988).

Winter Olympic Games were inaugurated in 1924.

Olympus. The home of the gods of ancient Greece, where ZEUS held his court, a mountain about 9,800 ft. high on the confines of Macedonia and Thessaly. The name is used for any PANTHEON, as, "ODIN, HORT, BALDER, and the rest of the Northern Olympus."

Om. Among the BRAHMINS, the mystic equivalent for the name of the Deity; it has been adopted by modern occultists to denote absolute goodness and truth or the spiritual essence.

Om mani padme hum ("Omm, the jewel, is in the lotus: Amen"). The mystic formula of the Tibetans and northern Buddhists used as a charm and for many religious purposes. They are the first words taught to a child and the last uttered on the death-bed of the pious. The LOTUS symbolizes universal being, and the jewel the individuality of the utterer.

Omar Khayyam (ō′ mar kî yăm′), Persian poet, astronomer, and mathematician, lived at Nishapur, where he died at about the age of 50 in A.D. 1123. He was known chiefly for his work on algebra until Edward Fitzgerald published a poetical translation of his poems in 1859. Little notice of this was taken, however, until the early '90s when the RUBAIYAT took Britain and America by storm. It is frankly hedonistic in tone, but touched with a melancholy that attunes with eastern and western pessimism alike. Fitzgerald never pretended that his work was other than a free version of the original; he made several revisions, but did not improve on his first text.

Ombre (om′ bẽr) (Span. *hombre*, man). A card-game, introduced into England from Spain in the 17th century, and very popular till it was supplanted by QUADRILLE, about 1730. It was usually played by three persons, and the eights, nines, and tens of each suit were left out. Prior has an epigram on the game; he was playing with two ladies, and Fortune gave him "success in every suit but hearts". Pope immortalized the game in his *Rape of the Lock*.

Ombudsman (om′ boods man) (Swed. *ombudsman*, a commissioner). In Scandinavian countries, an official appointed by the legislature whose duty it is to protect the rights of the citizen against infringement by the government. Sweden has had once since 1809, Denmark since 1955, and Norway since 1962. New Zealand was the first COMMONWEALTH country to appoint such a commissioner (1962) and Great Britain appointed a Parliamentary Commissioner for Administration in 1967, commonly known as the "Ombudsman".

Omega (ō′ meg à). *See* ALPHA.

Omelet (om′lĕt). **You can't make omelets without breaking eggs.** Said by way of warning to one who is trying to "get something for nothing"—to accomplish some desired object without being willing to take the necessary trouble or make the necessary sacrifice. The phrase is a translation of the French *On ne saurait faire une omelette sans casser des œufs*.

Omens. Phenomena or unusual events taken as a prognostication of either good or EVIL; prophetic signs or auguries. *Omen* is a Latin word adopted in the 16th century. Some traditional examples of accepting what appeared to be evil omens, as of good AUGURY, are:

> Leotychides II, of Sparta, was told by his augurs that his projected expedition would fail because a viper had got entangled in the handle of the city key "Not so," he replied, "the key caught the viper."

> When Julius Cæsar landed at Adrumetum he tripped and fell on his face. This would have been considered a fatal omen by his army, but, with admirable presence of mind, he explained, "Thus I take possession of thee, O Africa!" A similar story is told of Scipio.

> When William the Conqueror leaped upon the English shore he fell on his face and a great cry went forth that it was an ill-omen; but the duke exclaimed, "I have taken seisin of this land with both my hands".

Omnibus (Lat., for all, dative pl. of *omnis*, all). The name was first applied to the public vehicle in France in 1828. In the following year it was adopted by Shillibeer for the vehicles which he started on the Paddington (now MARYLEBONE) Road, London. The plural is *omnibuses*, and the word is generally abbreviated to *bus*, without an initial apostrophe—just as *cabriolet* became *cab*, not *cab'*.

Omnibus Bill. The Parliamentary term for a BILL embracing clauses that deal with a number of different subjects, as a Revenue Bill dealing with Customs, Taxes, Stamps, Excise, etc.

Omnibus box. A box at a theatre for which the subscription is paid by several different parties, each of which has the right of using it.

Omnibus train. An old name for a train that stops at all stations—a train for all, as apart from the specials and the expresses that ran between only a few stations. *Cp.* JERKWATER.

Omnibus volume. A collection in one volume of an author's works, of short stories, essays, etc.

Omnium (Lat., of all). The particulars *of all* the items, or the assignment *of all* the securities, of a government loan.

Omnium gatherum. DOG-LATIN for a *gathering* or collection of *all* sorts of persons and things; a miscellaneous gathering together without regard to suitability or order.

Omphale (om′ fà lē). In Greek legend, the Queen of Lydia of masculine inclinations to whom HERCULES was bound a slave for three years. He fell in love with her and led a submissive life spinning wool. Omphale wore the lion's skin while Hercules wore a female garment.

On. A little bit on. Slightly drunk.

It's not on. It cannot be done. A phrase from snooker, used when the object ball is obscured.

It's not on today. It's not on the menu, "it's off", *i.e.*, not available.

On the beach. Retired from naval service; in the Merchant Service it is to be without a ship, *i.e.* unemployed.

On the binge. ON THE SPREE.

On the loose. *See under* LOOSE.

On the shelf. *See* SHELF.

On the spree. Out for a frolic, *on the binge*, out carousing.

To have something on a person. To possess damaging evidence or information about him as, defiantly, "you've got nothing on me", meaning, "you know nothing that can incriminate me".

On dit (ong dē) (Fr., they say). A rumour, a report, a bit of gossip. "There is an *on dit* that the prince is to marry soon."

Once. Once and for all. Finally, emphatically, and decisively, as, "Let us settle this affair once and for all."

Once bitten twice shy. I am not to be caught again; I have learned by previous experience and am not going to be made a fool of twice.

Once in a while. Only occasionally.

Once upon a time. The traditional opening phrase in fairy stories, at some indefinite time long ago.

To give someone, or **something the once-over.** To make a quick examination or assessment of.

One. One is Deity. *The Evil One* is the DEVIL.

By one and one. Singly, one at a time; entirely by oneself.

He was one too many for me. He was a little too clever for me, he outwitted me.

Number one. Oneself; hence **to look after number one;** to be selfish; to seek one's own interest.

In the Royal Navy, the first lieutenant of a ship or establishment is colloquially known as "Number One" or "Jimmy the One".

One and all. Everybody, individually and jointly. The phrase is the motto of Cornishmen.

One for the road. *See under* ROAD.

One in the eye, on the nose, in the bread-basket, etc. A blow on the spot named—the last being slang for the stomach. *One in the eye* is also used figuratively, for a telling blow.

One of these days. Some day, at some unspecified time in the future.

There is One above. A reference to the Deity.

To go one better than he did. To improve upon another's lead, performance, action, story, etc. The phrase is from card-playing; at poker if one wishes to continue betting one has to "go" at least "one better", *i.e.* raise the stake.

One-armed bandit. A gambling or "fruit" machine operated by the insertion of coins and the pulling of an arm or lever. So called because it frequently "robs" one of loose change.

One-horse town. A very small town with few amenities. An expression of American origin when a small community might only boast of one horse. Now used figuratively of any small, amateurish affair as "a one-horse show", "a one-horse outfit".*Cp*.JERKWATER.

One-night stand. A single evening performance by a touring theatrical company, circus, etc., at a town only likely to provide an audience for one night.

One-track mind. A mind with one dominant preoccupation which constantly reverts to the one subject, as a single-track railway only allows traffic in one direction at a time.

Oneida Community, The. *See* PERFECTIONISTS.

Oneiromancy (Gr. *oneiros*, a dream; *manteia*, prophecy). DIVINATION from dreams.

Onomatopeia (on ō măt ōpē' à) (Gr. *onomatopoiia*, word-making). The forming of a word by imitating the sound associated with the object designated, or a word that appears to suggest its nature or qualities. "Cuckoo", "murmur", "tingle" are examples.

Onus (ō' nus) (Lat.). The burden, the responsibility; as, "The whole onus must rest on your shoulders."

Onus probandi (Lat., the burden of proving). The obligation of proving some proposition, accusation, etc.; as, "The *onus probandi* rests with the accuser."

Onyx (on' iks) is Greek for a finger-nail; so called because the colour of the onyx resembles that of the finger-nail.

Oom Paul. "Uncle" Paul, the name familiarly applied to Paul Kruger (1825–1904), President of the Transvaal Republic and leader of Boer resistance to British rule in South Africa.

Op. cit. (Lat. *opere citato*). In the work quoted.

Opal (Gr. *opallios*; probably from Sansk. *upala*, a gem). This semi-PRECIOUS STONE, well known for its play of iridescent colours a vitreous form of hydrous silica, has long been deemed to bring ill-luck. Alphonso XII of Spain (1857, 1874–1885) presented an opal ring to his wife on his wedding-day, and her death occurred soon afterwards. Before the funeral he gave the ring to his sister, who died a few days later. The king then presented it to his sister-in-law, and she died within three months. Alphonso, astounded at these fatalities, resolved to wear the ring himself, and within a very short time he, too, was dead. The Queen Regent then suspended it from the neck of the Virgin of Almudena of Madrid.

Open. Open City. A city which is completely demilitarized and left open to occupation, either because of its historic treasures and importance or because it is a centre for hospitals and wounded.

Open diplomacy, as opposed to secret diplomacy, is defined in the first of Woodrow Wilson's FOURTEEN POINTS, "open covenants of peace openly arrived at, after which there shall be no private international understandings of any kind". It is perhaps significant that the Treaty of VERSAILLES was an "open treaty" negotiated in secret, ultimately by President Wilson, Clemenceau and Lloyd George.

Open door. In political parlance, the principle of admitting all nations to a share in a country's trade, etc. Also any loophole left for the possibility of negotiation between contending parties, nations, etc.

Open field system. The old manorial common-field system of agriculture in which the villages cultivated their individual "strips" in the unfenced (open) arable fields. It was essentially a three-field system based on a triennial crop rotation. From the 15th century, and expecially in the 18th and 19th centuries, the system gave way to enclosures. It still survives at Laxton in Nottinghamshire. *Cp.* COMMON; MANOR.

Open letter. A letter to a particular person but published in a newspaper or periodical so that its contents may be publicly known, usually of a critical nature or as a protest.

Open question. *See under* QUESTION.

Open secret. *See* SECRET.

Open Sesame. *See* SESAME.

Open shop. *See under* SHOP.

To keep open house. *See under* HOUSE.

Opera. Drama set to music, the latter being an integral part of the composition. Dialogue is mostly verse and sung to orchestral accompaniment; lyrics are an important element and in older operas a ballet was often included. The rise of opera dates from the end of the 16th century and it became popular after the first opera house was opened at Venice, in 1637. Alessandro Scarlatti (1659–1725) established the aria as a legiti-

mate form of soliloquy, and introduced the recitativo. Henry Purcell (*c.* 1658–1695) was the father of English opera, writing some 42 musical works for the stage, including some semi-operas and one full opera, *Dido and Aeneas* (1689).

Grand opera. Opera in which the entire libretto is set to music.

Opéra bouffe (Fr. *bouffe*, buffoon) is a form of French comic opera or operetta light in construction and of slight musical value.

Opera buffa, a form of light Italian comedy with musical numbers and dialogue in recitative; comic opera.

Opéra comique is a French type of opera which contains spoken dialogue. It does not necessarily imply "comic opera".

Operetta. Short opera, light opera, usually with spoken dialogue. The works of Gilbert and Sullivan may be included in this category.

Ophir. An unidentified territory, famed in the OLD TESTAMENT for its fine GOLD, possibly in S.E. Arabia. (*See* I *Kings* ix, 26–28.)

Opinicus. A fabulous monster in HERALDRY, compounded from DRAGON, CAMEL and LION. It forms the crest of the Barber-Surgeons of London. The name seems to be corruption of *Ophinicus*, the classical name of the constellation, the serpent (Gr. *ophis*).

Opium-eater. Thomas de Quincey (1785–1859), author of *The Confessions of an English Opium-Eater* (1821).

Opium War. The name given to the war between Great Britain and China, the First Chinese War, 1839–1842. The British government did not contest the Chinese right to prohibit trade in opium, but the demand that foreign merchants should agree that if opium were found on a British ship the culprits would be handed over for execution and the ship or cargo confiscated. Hostilities began when the British refused to surrender an innocent British subject for execution after the death of a Chinaman in a brawl. *Cp.* HONG MERCHANTS.

The Opium of the People. A CATCHPHRASE applied to religion. It is derived from Karl Marx (*On Hegel's Philosophy of Law*).

> Religion is the sigh of the hard-pressed creature, the heart of a heartless world, as it is the soul of soulless circumstances. It is the opium of the people.

Oppidan (Lat. *oppidum*, town). At Eton College, all those who are not collegers (King's Scholars). Originally those not on the foundation boarded in the town.

Opponency. *See* ACT OF OPPONENCY.

Opposition. The constitutional term for whichever of the major political parties is out of power. The leader of the Opposition receives a salary as such. In the HOUSE OF COMMONS, the Opposition sits on the benches to the SPEAKER's left, its leader occupying the FRONT BENCH (*see under* BENCH).

Ops. The old SABINE fertility goddess and wife of SATURN. She was later identified with RHEA.

Optime (op' ti mē). In Cambridge phraseology, a graduate in the second or third division of the Mathematical TRIPOS, the former being *Senior Optime* and the latter *Junior Optime*. The term comes from the Latin phrase formerly used—*Optime disputasi* (You have disputed very well). The class above the Optimes is composed of WRANGLERS.

Optimism. The doctrine that "whatever is, is right", that everything which happens is for the best. It was originally set forth by Leibnitz (1646–1716) from the postulate of the omnipotence of God, and is cleverly travestied by VOLTAIRE in his CANDIDE. *See* PANGLOSS.

Opus (ō' pus) (Lat., a work). *See* MAGNUM OPUS.

Opus Anglicanum. Rich mediæval embroidery dominated by work in silver and gold thread; so called because the reputation of England was unrivalled in this art which revealed the skill of the English gold and silver wiresmiths. It was mostly employed on ecclesiastical vestments and frontals, but also on banners, palls, robes, and hangings.

Opus operantis, opus operatum; ex opere operato (Lat.). Theological terms long used in relation to the effectiveness of acts relating to the sacraments. *Opus operantis* means the "act of doer"; *opus operatum*, the "act done" irrespective of the qualities or disposition of the recipient. Thus baptism is held to convey regeneration to an infant. To hold that a SACRAMENT gives grace *ex opere operato* (from the act of being done) means that the sacrament, properly performed, itself conveys grace, irrespective of the merits of the performer or recipient.

Or. The heraldic term for the metal GOLD. *See* HERALDRY.

Oracle (Lat. *oraculum*; from *orare*, to speak, to pray). The answer of a god or inspired priest to an inquiry respecting the future; the deity giving responses; the place where the deity could be consulted, etc.; hence, a person whose utterances are regarded as profoundly wise and authoritative.

> I am Sir Oracle,
> And when I open my lips let no dog bark.
> SHAKESPEARE: *The Merchant of Venice*, I, i.

The most famous of the very numerous oracles of ancient Greece were those of:

APOLLO, at DELPHI, the priestess of which was called the Pythoness; at DELOS, and at Claros.
DIANA, at Colchis.
ÆSCULAPIUS, at Epidaurus, and at ROME.
HERCULES, at ATHENS and Gades.
JUPITER, at DODONA (the most noted), AMMON in Libya, and in CRETE.
MARS, in Thrace.
MINERVA, at Mycenæ.
PAN, in ARCADIA.
TROPHONIUS, in BŒOTIA, where only men made the responses.
VENUS, at Paphos, another at Aphæa, etc.

In most of the temples, women, sitting on a tripod, made the responses, many of which were ambiguous and so obscure as to be misleading; to this day, our word *oracular* is still used of obscure as well as of authoritative pronouncements. Examples are:

When CRŒSUS consulted the Delphic oracle respecting a projected war, he received for answer, "*Crœsus Halyn penetrans magnum pervertet opum vim*" (When Crœsus crosses over the river Halys, he will overthrow the strength of an empire). Crœsus supposed the oracle meant he would overthrow the enemy's empire, but it was his own that he destroyed when defeated by Cyrus.

Pyrrhus, being about to make war against Rome, was told by the oracle: "*Credo te, Æacide, Romanos vincere posse*" (I believe, Pyrrhus, that you the Romans can conquer), which may mean either "You, Pyrrhus, can overthrow the Romans", or "Pyrrhus, the Romans can overthrow you".

Another prince, consulting the oracle on a similar occasion, received for answer. "*Ibis redibis nunquam per bella peribis*" (You shall go you shall return never you shall perish by the war), the interpretation of which depends on the position of the comma; it may be "You shall return, you shall never perish in the war", or "You shall return never, you shall perish in the war", which latter was the fact.

Philip of Macedon sent to ask the oracle of Delphi if his Persian expedition would prove successful, and received for answer—

> The ready victim crowned for death
> Before the altar stands

Philip took it for granted that the "ready victim" was the King of Persia, but it was Philip himself.

When the Greeks sent to Delphi to know if they would succeed against the Persians they were told

> Seed-time and harvest, weeping sires shall tell
> How thousands fought at Salamis and fell.

But whether the Greeks or the Persians were to be the "weeping sires", no indication was given, nor whether the thousands "about to fall" were to be Greeks or Persians. *See also* WOODEN WALLS *under* WOOD.

When Maxentius was about to encounter Constantine, he consulted the guardians of the SIBYLLINE BOOKS as to the fate of the battle, and the prophetess told him, *"Illo die hostem Romanorum esse periturum"*, but whether Maxentius or Constantine was the "enemy of the Roman people" the oracle left undecided.

In the BIBLE (I *Kings* xxii, 15, 35) we are told that when Ahab, King of Israel, was about to wage war on the King of Syria, and asked Micaiah if Ramoth-Gilead would fall into his hands, the prophet replied, "Go, for the Lord will deliver the city into the hand of the king." In the event, the city fell into the hands of the King of Syria.

The Oracle of the Church. St. BERNARD of Clairvaux (1091–1153). *Cp.* MELLIFLUOUS DOCTOR.

The Oracle of the Holy Bottle. The oracle to which Rabelais (Bks. IV and V) sent PANURGE and a large party to obtain an answer to a question which had been put to SIBYL and poet, monk and fool, philosopher and witch, judge and fortune-teller: "whether Panurge should marry or not?" The oracle was situated at BACBUC "near Catay in Upper India", and the story has been interpreted as a satire on the Church. The celibacy of the clergy was for long a moot point, and the "Holy Bottle" or cup to the laity was one of the moving causes of the schisms from the Church. The crew setting sail for the Bottle refers to Anthony, Duke of Vendôme, afterwards King of Navarre, setting out in search of religious truth.

The oracle of the sieve and shears. *See* SIEVE.

To work the oracle. To succeed in persuading another to favour some plan or to join in a project, etc., when the chances seemed slender. Also, in slang, to raise money.

> They fetched a rattling price through Starlight's working the oracle with those swells.
> BOLDREWOOD: *Robbery Under Arms*, ch. xii.

Orange. William III's territorial name originally came from Orange (anciently Arausio), a town on the Rhône north of Avignon; his ancestors acquired it through marriage. The House of Orange still reigns in the Netherlands.

Orange blossom. The conventional decoration for the bride at a wedding, introduced as a custom into ENGLAND from France about 1820. The *orange* is said to indicate the hope of fruitfulness, few trees being more prolific; while the *white blossoms* are symbolic of innocence. Hence the phrase, **to go gathering orange blossoms,** to look for a wife.

Orange Lilies. *See* REGIMENTAL AND DIVISIONAL NICKNAMES.

Orange Lodges. *See* ORANGEMEN.

Orangemen, Orange Order. A society founded in 1795 in ULSTER to maintain "the PROTESTANT Constitution, and to defend the King and his heirs as long as they maintain the Protestant ascendancy". It was formed after an armed clash between Roman Catholics and Protestants in Armagh, known as the Battle of the Diamond. The name commemorated William of Orange (William III), who defeated James II and his Catholic supporters at the Battle of the Boyne in 1690. Orange Lodges or clubs of militant Protestants spread throughout the province, their members being known as *Orangemen*, an earlier association of this name having been formed in the reign of William III. Gladstone's championship of HOME RULE after 1886 led to a revival of the movement. The Orange Order still flourishes, imposing ethical obligations on its members.

Orange Peel. A nickname given to Sir Robert Peel when Chief Secretary for Ireland (1812–1818), on account of his PROTESTANT bias and opposition to Roman Catholic emancipation.

Orange-tawny. The ancient colour appropriated to clerks and persons of inferior condition, also the colour worn by Jews. Hence Bacon says: "Usurers should have orange-tawny bonnets, because they do judaise" (*Essay* xli).

Orator. Orator Henley. John Henley (1692–1756), who for about 30 years delivered lectures on theological, political, and literary subjects.

Orator Hunt. Henry Hunt (1773–1835), RADICAL politician. He presided at the famous PETERLOO meeting, and as M.P. for Preston (1830–1833) presented the first petition to PARLIAMENT in favour of women's rights. *See* A WHITE HAT *under* HAT.

The Orator of the Human Race. *See* ANACHARSIS CLOOTS.

Oratorians. (Med. Lat. *oratorium*, a place of prayer). A congregation founded at ROME by St. Philip Neri (1515–1595), but with origins in the late 1550s. Now called the Institute of the Oratory of St. Philip Neri, membership consists of secular priests and lay brothers, who take no vows but live communally, and are free to leave if, and when, they wish. Each oratory is autonomous and its members work under the ORDINARY of their diocese. Dr. J. H. Newman was so impressed with the Oratory at Rome that he obtained papal permission to found the Birmingham Oratory in 1847 and in 1849 sent F. W. Faber to found the London Oratory, which moved to Brompton in 1854. *See* ORATORIO.

Oratorio is sacred story or drama set to music, in which solo voices, chorus, and instrumental music are employed. St. Philip Neri introduced the acting and singing of sacred dramas in his Oratory at ROME in the late 16th century, and it is from this that the term comes.

Orc. A sea-monster fabled by ARIOSTO, Drayton, Sylvester, etc., to devour men and women. The name was sometimes used for a whale.

> An island salt and bare,
> The haunt of seals and orcs, and sea-mews clang.
> MILTON: *Paradise Lost*, XI, 829.

Orcades. The Roman name for the Orkneys, probably connected with the old ORC, a whale.

Orcus. A Latin name for HADES. Spenser speaks of a DRAGON whose mouth was:

> All set with iron teeth in ranges twain,
> That terrified his foes, and armed him,
> Appearing like the mouth of Orcus grisely grim.
> *The Faerie Queene*, VI, xii, 26.

Ordeal (O.E. *ordel*, judgment). The ancient Anglo-Saxon and Teutonic practice of referring disputed questions of criminality to supernatural decision, by subjecting the accused to physical trials in the belief that God would defend the right, even by miracle if needful. Hence, figuratively, an experience testing endurance, patience, courage, etc. All ordeals, except that by battle and cold water for witches, were abolished in ENGLAND in the early 13th century when trial by jury took their place. Similar methods of trial are found among other races. *See* ACT OF TRUTH.

Ordeal, or **wager of battle.** The accused was obliged to fight his accuser. Lords often chose vassals to represent them and priests and women were allowed champions. It was legally abolished in 1818 when the right was claimed by a person charged with murder.

Ordeal of boiling water was usual for the common people and involved plunging the hand into hot water either up to the wrist or elbow and guilt was presumed if the skin was injured.

Ordeal by cold water. The accused was bound and tossed into water. If he floated he was guilty. If he sank he was hauled out. This became a common test for WITCHCRAFT.

Ordeal of fire was for persons of high rank. Carrying a red-hot iron or walking barefoot and blindfolded over red-hot plough-shares were the usual forms. If the accused showed no wound after three days he was adjudged innocent.

Ordeal of the bier. A suspected murderer was required to touch the corpse and was deemed guilty if blood flowed from the body.

Ordeal of the Corsned. *See* CORSNED.

Ordeal of the cross. The accuser and accused stood upright before a CROSS and he who moved first was adjudged guilty. *See also* JUDICIUM CRUCIS.

Ordeal of the Eucharist was for priests. It was believed that if the guilty partook of the SACRAMENT divine punishment would follow for the sacrilege commited.

Order! When members of the HOUSE OF COMMONS and other debators call out *Order!* they mean that the person speaking is in some way breaking the rule of *order* of the assembly, and has to be *called to order*.

The Order of the Day. The prevailing state of things.

The Orders of the Day. In the HOUSE OF COMMONS, the items of business set down for a particular day on the Order Papers, the main business of the day.

To move for the Orders of the Day, as a substantive motion in the HOUSE OF COMMONS, is now obsolete. "That this House do pass to the orders of the day" is used as an amendment on a motion introduced before the ordinary business of the day (*e.g.* a PRIVILEGE motion), to prevent debate.

Architectural Orders. *See* ARCHITECTURE.

Holy Orders. A clergyman is said to be in *holy orders* because he belongs to one of the *orders* or ranks of the Church. In the CHURCH OF ENGLAND these are three, *viz.*, Deacon, Priest, and BISHOP; in the ROMAN CATHOLIC CHURCH there is a fourth, that of Sub-deacon.

In ecclesiastical use the term also denotes a fraternity of monks or friars (as the *Franciscan Order*), and also the Rule by which the fraternity is governed.

To take orders. To enter HOLY ORDERS by ordination.

Order of battle. *See* LINE OF BATTLE.

Orders in Council. Orders issued by the PRIVY COUNCIL with the sanction of the SOVEREIGN under the royal prerogative. In practice they are drawn up on the advice of Ministers who are answerable to PARLIAMENT, usually to deal with matters demanding immediate attention. Orders in Council are also issued on matters of administrative detail under certain Acts of Parliament.

Orders of Knighthood. *See* KNIGHT.

Ordinal Numbers. *See* CARDINAL NUMBERS.

Ordinary. In the CHURCH OF ENGLAND, an ecclesiastic who has *ordinary* or regular jurisdiction in his own right and not by depute, usually the BISHOP of a diocese and the archbishops. The Chaplain of NEWGATE GAOL was called the Ordinary thereof. In the ROMAN CATHOLIC CHURCH, the POPE, diocesan bishops, abbots, apostolic vicars, etc., are classed as ordinaries. In SCOTLAND certain judges of the Court of Sessions are called *Lords Ordinary* and those legal experts appointed to aid the HOUSE OF LORDS in the determination of appeals are called *Lords of Appeal in Ordinary*.

A meal prepared at an eating-house at a fixed rate for all comers was called "an ordinary"; hence, the place providing such meals.

> 'Tis almost dinner; I know they stay for you at the ordinary.
> BEAUMONT and FLETCHER: *The Scornful Lady*, IV, i.

In HERALDRY the "ordinary" is a simple charge, such as the chief, pale, fesse, bend, bar, chevron, cross or saltire.

The Ordinary of the Mass. That part of the MASS which varies in accordance with the Church Calendar as opposed to the CANON OF THE MASS which does not change.

Oreads (ôr' ē adz) or **Oreades.** NYMPHS of the mountains (Gr. *oros*, mountain).

> The Ocean-nymphs and Hamadryades,
> Oreads and Naiads, with long weedy locks,
> Offered to do her bidding through the seas,
> Under the earth, and in the hollow rocks.
> SHELLEY: *Witch of Atlas*, xxii.

Oregon Trail. A famous pioneer route some 2,000 miles long from Independence, Missouri, across the plains, thence up the North Platte, through South Pass, Wyoming, along the Snake River, across southern Idaho and the Blue Mountains to the Columbia river and finally by raft to the mouth of the Willamette. It was first followed by Nathaniel Wyeth of Massachusetts in 1833 and in the 1840s it became a regular emigrant route and was also used as the overland route to the Californian goldfields.

The modern highway called the "Oregon Trail" follows a slightly different route.

Orellana (or el ā' nà). A former name of the river Amazon, after Francisco do Orellana, lieutenant of Pizarro, who first explored it in 1541.

Oremus. *See* LEGEM PONE.

Orestes. *See* PYLADES.

Orgies (ôr' jēz). Drunken revels, riotous feasts, wild or licentious extravagance. So called from the Gr. *orgia*, the secret nocturnal festivals in honour of BACCHUS.

Orgoglio (ôr gō' lyō) (Ital., Arrogant Pride, or Man of Sin). In Spenser's *Faerie Queene* (I, vii and viii), a hideous giant as tall as three men, son of Earth and Wind, who typifies the tyrannical power of the Church of ROME.

Oriana. The beloved of AMADIS OF GAUL, who called himself Beltenebros when he retired to the Poor Rock (*Amadis de Gaula*, ii, 6).

Queen Elizabeth I is sometimes called the "peerless Oriana", especially in the madrigals entitled the *Triumphs of Oriana* (1601).

Orientation (Lat. *oriens*, the east). The placing of the east window of a church due east so that the rising sun may shine on the altar. Anciently, churches were built with their axes pointing to the rising sun on the saint's day; so that a church dedicated to St. JOHN was not parallel to one dedicated to St. PETER, but in the building of modern churches the saint's day is not, as a rule, regarded.

Figuratively, *orientation* is the correct placing of one's ideas, mental processes, etc., in relation with each other and with current thought—the ascertainment of one's "bearings".

Oriflamme (Fr., "flame of gold"). The ancient banner of the Kings of France, first used in battle in 1124, which replaced the blue hood of St. MARTIN. It was the standard of the abbey of St. DENYS and was a crimson flag on a gilded staff, and said by some writers to have had three points or tongues with tassels of green silk. It was last used in the field at Agincourt (1415) and was replaced by a blue standard powdered with FLEUR-DE-LIS.

It is reputed that infidels were blinded by merely looking at it. In the *Roman de Garin* the Saracens cry, "If we only set eyes on it we are all dead men"; and Froissart records that it was no sooner unfurled at Rosbecq than the fog cleared away from the French, leaving their enemies in misty darkness.

Original Sin. *See under* SIN.

Orinda, The Matchless. Katherine Philips *née* Fowler (1631–1664), poetess and letter-writer. She first adopted the signature "Orinda" in her correspondence with Sir Charles Cotterell, and afterwards used it for general purposes. Her praises were sung by Cowley, Dryden, and others.

Orion (o rī' on). A giant hunter of Greek mythology, noted for his beauty. He was blinded by Œnopion, but VULCAN sent Cedalion to be his guide, and his sight was restored by exposing his eyeballs to the sun. Being slain by DIANA, he was made one of the constellations and is supposed to be attended with stormy weather. His wife was named Side and his dogs Arctophonus and Ptoophagus.

The constellation Orion is pictured as a giant hunter with belt and sword surrounded by his dogs and animals. Betelgeuse and Bellatrix are the "shoulder" stars and three bright stars in a line form the belt, below which is the sword-handle containing a remarkable nebula.

Orkneys. *See* ORCADES.

Orlando. The Italian form of ROLAND, one of the great heroes of mediaeval romance, and the most celebrated of CHARLEMAGNE'S PALADINS.

Orlando Furioso (Orlando mad). An epic poem in 45 cantos, by ARIOSTO (published 1516–1533). Orlando's madness is caused by the faithlessness of ANGELICA, but the main subject of the work is the seige of PARIS by Agramant the MOOR, when the Saracens were overthrown.

The epic is full of anachronisms. We have CHARLEMAGNE (d. 814) and his paladins joined by King Edward IV of England, Richard Earl of Warwick, etc. (Bk. VI). Cannon are employed by Cymosco, King of Friza (Bk. IV). In Bk. XVII the late mediæval PRESTER JOHN appears (*see under* JOHN), and in the last three books Constantine the Great, who died in 337.

Among English translations are those of Sir John Harington, by command of Queen Elizabeth I (1591), John Hoole (1783), and W. S. Rose (1823–1831).

About 1589 a play (printed 1594) by Robert Greene entitled The Historie of Orlando Furioso was produced. In this version Orlando marries Angelica.

Orlando Innamorato (Orlando in love). An unfinished romance by Boiardo (1434–1494) featuring the love of ROLAND and ANGELICA. ARIOSTO wrote his *Orlando Furioso* as a sequel and in 1541 Berni turned Boiardo's work into a burlesque.

Ormulum. A long poem in Transition, or Early Middle, English, of which only a "fragment" of some 20,000 lines is extant. It is so called from its author *Orm* or *Ormin*, an Austin canon who wrote about 1200. It consists of a simple narrative of the gospels appointed to be read in church each with a homily upon it and expositions out of Aelfric, BEDE, and St. AUGUSTINE. It is preserved in the BODLEIAN LIBRARY and its orthography makes it particularly valuable evidence of the vowel-length at the time.

> This boc iss nemmed Ormulum
> Forrthi that Orm itt wrohhte.

Ormuzd, or **Ahura Mazda.** In ZOROASTRIANISM, the principle or ANGEL of light and good, and creator of all things and judge of the world. He is in perpetual conflict with AHRIMAN but in the end will triumph.

> And Oromaze, Joshua, and Mahomet,
> Moses and Buddha, Zerdusht, and Brahm, and Foh,
> A tumult of strange names, which never met
> Before, as watchwords of a single woe,
> Arose.
> SHELLEY: *Revolt of Islam*, X, xxxi.

Orosius. An early 5th-century Spanish presbyter and historian whose *Historia Adversus Paganos*, from the Creation to A.D. 417, was translated into Anglo-Saxon from the Latin by King ALFRED. It was a popular textbook of general history in the MIDDLE AGES. He presented some of his works to St. AUGUSTINE when he visited him in 415.

Orpheus (ôr' fūs). In Greek legend, a Thracian poet, son of Œagrus and CALLIOPE (held by some to be a son of APOLLO), who could move even inanimate things by his music—a power that was also claimed for the Scandinavian ODIN. When his wife EURYDICE died he went into the infernal regions and so charmed PLUTO that she was released on the condition that he would not look back till they reached the earth. When about to place his foot on the earth he turned round and Eurydice vanished instantly.

> That Orpheus' self may ... hear
> Such strains as would have won the ear
> Of Pluto, to have quite set free
> His half regain'd Eurydice.
> MILTON: *L'Allegro*, 145–50

The prolonged grief of Orpheus at his second loss so enraged the Thracian women that in one of their Bacchanalian ORGIES they tore him to pieces. The fragments of his body were collected by the MUSES and buried at the foot of Mount OLYMPUS, but his head, thrown into the river Hebrus, was carried into the sea, and so to Lesbos, where it was buried.

> What could the Muse herself that Orpheus bore,
> The Muse herself, for her enchanting son,
> Whom universal nature did lament,
> When by the rout that made the hideous roar
> His gory visage down the stream was sent,
> Down the swift Hebrus to the Lesbian shore?
> MILTON: *Lycidas*, 58.

Orpheus of Highwaymen. So John Gay (1685–1732) has been called on account of his *Beggar's Opera* (1728).

The Orphic Egg. *See* MUNDANE EGG *under* EGG.

Orphism. A movement in painting started by Robert Delaunay (1885–1941), characterized by patches and swirls of intense and contrasting colours. *Cp.* CUBISM; DADAISM;

FAUVISM; FUTURISM; IMPRESSIONISM; SUR-REALISM; SYNCHRONISM; VORTICISM.

Orrery (or' ĕr i). A complicated piece of mechanism showing by means of clockwork the movements of the planets, etc., round the SUN. It was invented about 1700 by George Graham, who sent his model to Rowley, an instrument maker, to make one for Prince Eugene. Rowley made a copy of it for Charles Boyle (1676–1731), third Earl of Orrery, in whose honour it was named. One of the best is Fulton's, in Kelvin Grove Museum, Glasgow.

Orson (Fr. *ourson*, a little bear). Twin brother of Valentine in the old romance of VALEN-TINE AND ORSON.

Orthodox. The Orthodox Church. The Eastern Church, properly, The Holy Orthodox Catholic Apostolic Eastern Church. Its separation from the Western Church was partly due to the historic division of the Empire by Constantine; but also to the differences arising between "Greek" and "Latin" Christianity which culminated in complete separation in 1054 over the FILIOQUE CONTROVERSY. The Eastern Church now consists of seven patriarchates and is oligarchical in structure. *See* CATHOLIC CHURCH; GREEK CHURCH.

Orthodox Sunday, or **Feast of Orthodoxy,** in the Eastern Church, is the First Sunday in LENT, to commemorate the restoration of the icons in 842. *See* ICONOCLASTS.

Orthos, or **Orthrus.** The dog of GERYON, destroyed by HERCULES. *See* ECHIDNA.

Orts. Crumbs; refuse. (Low Ger. *Ort*, what is left after eating.)

I shall not eat your orts—*i.e.* your leavings.

> Let him have time a beggar's orts to crave.
> SHAKESPEARE: *Rape of Lucrece*, 895.

Orvietan, or **Venice Treacle,** once held to be a sovereign remedy against poison, an electuary of unknown composition. It took its name from a charlatan of Orvieto, Italy, who used to pretend to poison himself and effect a cure with his potion.

Orwell, George. The pseudonym adopted by Eric Arthur Blair (1903–1950), Old Etonian and socialist; author of *The Road to Wigan Pier*, ANIMAL FARM, *Nineteen Eighty-Four*, etc. *See* DOUBLE-THINK.

Os sacrum (Lat.). The sacred bone. A triangular bone at the lower part of the vertebral column. *See* LUZ.

Oscar. A gold-plated figurine awarded annually by the American Academy of Motion Picture Arts and Sciences for the best filmacting, writing, or production of the year.

There are two claims for the origin of this name. One is that in 1931 the future executive secretary of the Academy, Mrs. Margaret Herrick, joined as librarian; on seeing the then nameless gold statue for the first time she exclaimed "it reminds me of my Uncle Oscar"—the name stuck.

The other claim is that it derives indirectly from Oscar Wilde. When on a lecture tour of the U.S.A. he was asked if he had won the Newdigate Prize for Poetry, and he replied, "Yes, but while many people have won the Newdigate, it is seldom that the Newdigate gets an Oscar." When Helen Hayes was presented with the award, her husband Charles MacArthur, a noted wit and playwright, said, "Ah, I see you've got an Oscar", and the name stuck.

Osiris (ō sī' ris). One of the chief gods of ancient Egypt; son of Nut, brother of SET, his jealous and constant foe, and husband of ISIS. Set encompassed his death, but Osiris underwent resurrection with the aid of THOTH. His son HORUS became his avenger. He was the god of the dead and of the afterlife and resurrection.

The name means *Many-eyed* and Osiris is usually depicted as a man wearing the White Crown and holding a sceptre and flail, as a mummy.

Osmand. A necromancer in *The Seven Champions of Christendom*, I, xix, who by enchantment raised an army to resist the Christians. Six of the Champions fell, whereupon St. GEORGE restored them; Osmand tore out his own hair, in which lay his magic power, bit his tongue in two, disembowelled himself, cut off his arms and then died. *See* SEVEN CHAMPIONS.

Ossa. *See* PELION.

Ossian, or **Oisin.** The legendary Gaelic bard and celebrated warrior hero of the 3rd century, the son of Fionn Mac Cumhail (FINGAL). He is best known from the publications (1760–1763) of James Macpherson born at Ruthven, Inverness (1736–1796), purporting to be translations of poems by Ossian, the son of Fingal, from original MSS. Macpherson became famous and his works were widely translated, but their authenticity was challenged by Dr. Johnson in his *Journey to the Western Islands of Scotland*, and others. They seem to have been essentially made up by Macpherson himself with some use of ancient sources.

> "I [Johnson] look upon M'Pherson's Fingal to be as gross an imposition as ever the world was troubled with."
> BOSWELL: *The Journal of a Tour to the Hebrides* (Wed., 22 Sept.).

Ostracism (Gr. *ostrakon,* a potsherd). Black-balling, boycotting; exclusion from society, etc. The word arose from the ancient Greek custom of banishing, by a popular vote, one whose power was a danger to the state, the citizens writing the name of one whose banishment was deemed desirable on a sherd. *Cp.* BLACK-BALLED; BOYCOTT.

Ostrich. At one time the ostrich was fabled, when hunted, to run a certain distance and then thrust his head into the sand, thinking because it cannot see that it cannot be seen (*cp.* CROCODILE); hence the application of *ostrich-like, ostrich-head, ostrich belief,* etc., to various forms of self-delusion.

The ostrich also has the habit of eating indigestible things such as stones and hard objects to assist the functions of its gizzard. This has given rise to such phrases as **to have a digestion like an ostrich** or **to have an ostrich-stomach,** *i.e.* to be able to digest anything.

> But I'll make thee eat iron like an ostrich, and swallow my sword like a great pin, ere thou and I part.
> SHAKESPEARE: *Henry VI, Pt. II,* IV, x.

Ostrich eggs are often suspended in Eastern churches as symbols of God's watchful care. It used to be thought that the ostrich hatches her eggs by gazing on them, and if she suspends her gaze even for a minute or so the eggs are addled. Furthermore, we are told that if an egg is bad the ostrich will break it; so will GOD deal with EVIL men.

> Oh! even with such a look as fables say
> The mother ostrich fixes on her egg,
> Till that intense affection
> Kindle its light of life.
> SOUTHEY: *Thalaba,* III, 24.

Ostrog Bible, The. *See* BIBLE, SOME SPECIALLY NAMED EDITIONS.

Othello's occupation's gone. A phrase from SHAKESPEARE's *Othello* (III, iii), sometimes used when one is "laid on the shelf;", no longer "the observed of all observers".

Other Club, The. A dining CLUB founded in 1911 by Sir Winston Churchill and F.E. Smith (Lord Birkenhead), and said to be so called because they were not wanted at an existing fraternity known as *The Club.* It still meets at the Savoy and membership is not confined to Tories or politicians.

Other Day, The. Originally this meant "the second day" either forward or backward, *other* being the Old English equivalent for *second,* as in Latin *unus, alter, tertius*; or *proximus, alter, tertius.* Starting from to-day, and going backwards, yesterday was the *proximus ab illo*; the day before yesterday was the *alterus ab illo,* or the other day; and the day preceding that was *tertius ab*

illo, or three days ago. Now the phrase is used to express "a few days ago", "not so long since".

Otium cum dignitate (ō' ti ùm kūm dig ni-tā' ti) (Lat., leisure with dignity). Retirement after a person has worked and saved enough to live upon in comfort.

> *Otium cum dignitate* is to be had with £500 a year as well as with £5,000.
> BOLINGBROKE to Swift, 19 November 1729.

Ottava Rima (o ta' và rē' mà). A stanza of eight ten-syllable lines, rhyming *a b a b a b c c,* as used by Keats in his *Isabella,* BYRON in *Don Juan,* etc. It originated in Italy and was used by TASSO and ARIOSTO and many others, the lines being eleven-syllable.

Ottoman Empire. The Turkish empire founded by Othman or Osman I (1288–1320), which lasted until 1919.

Otus. *See* EPHIALTES.

Ouida (wē' dà). The pseudonym of Maria Louise de la Ramée (1839–1908), originally Maria Louise Ramée, a prolific writer of romantic novels of high society, the best known being *Under Two Flags* (1867). She was an unconventional, and later eccentric character, herself unlucky in pursuit of romance. She was born at Bury St. Edmunds, the daughter of a French father and an English mother, the name *Ouida* being her early childhood attempt to produce "Louise".

Ouija (wē' jà). A device employed by spiritualists for receiving spirit messages. It consists of a small piece of wood on wheels, placed on a board marked with the letters of the alphabet and certain commonly-used words. When the fingers of the communicators are placed on the Ouija board it moves from letter to letter and thus spells out sentences. The word is a combination of Fr. *oui* and Ger. *ja,* both meaning "yes". Ouija is a registered trade mark in the United States of America.

Out. Murder will out. The secret is bound to be revealed; "be sure your sins will find you out".

> O blisful god, that art so just and trewe!
> Lo, how that thou biwreyest mordre alway,
> Mordre wol out, that see we day by day.
> CHAUCER: *Nun's Priests's Tale.* 284.

Out and away. By far, incomparably, as, "He is out and away the best batsman."

Out and out. Thoroughly, absolutely, without qualification, thus an "out and out liar" is a complete and utter liar.

Out of it. Left on one side, not included.

Out on a limb. Isolated, stranded, cut off; as an animal on the end of a branch of a tree.

Outed. Expelled, ejected.

To be out for. To have one's mind set on

achieving some particular end.

To go all out. To make every effort, to do one's utmost.

To have it out. To contest either physically or verbally with another to the utmost of one's ability; as, "I mean to have it out with him one of these days"; "I had it out with him"—*i.e.* "I spoke my mind freely and without reserve." The idea is that of letting loose pent-up disapprobation.

To out-Herod Herod. *See* HEROD.

To outrun the Constable. *See under* CONSTABLE.

Outback. The more remote and sparsely populated areas in the Australian interior, the bush.

Outsider, An. One who is not a member of a particular circle or group, one not considered a socially desirable companion; also a horse or person not thought to be in the running. The usage comes from coaching days when the humbler passengers travelled outside (other than on the box next to the coachman).

Ouzelum Bird. This fanciful bird is reputed to fly backwards and thus does not know where it is going but likes to know where it has been.

Oval, The. The famous cricket ground at Kennington, LONDON, the headquarters of the Surrey Cricket Club, a former market garden, was opened in 1846. It was after Australia's victory at the Oval in 1882 that the ASHES came into being.

Ovation. An enthusiastic display of popular favour, so called from the ancient Roman *ovatio*, a minor form of TRIUMPH in which the conqueror entered the city on horseback or on foot wearing a crown of MYRTLE instead of GOLD.

Oven-wood. Brushwood; wood only fit for burning or heating the oven for bread-making, etc. Long an obsolete term except in certain country districts where it lingered.

> A narrow brook, by rushy banks concealed,
> Runs in a bottom and divides the field;
> Oaks intersperse it, that had once a head,
> But now wear crests of oven-wood instead.
>
> COWPER: *The Needless Alarm.*

Over. Half seas over. *See under* HALF.

It's all over with him. He's finished, he can't go any farther, he's "shot his bolt". Said also of one who has been given up by the doctors.

Over and above. In addition to; besides.

Over and over again. Very frequently, repeatedly. In Lat., *Iterum iterumque.*

Over the left. *See under* LEFT.

Overlander. An Australian term for those stockmen employed in driving cattle or sheep from one station to another. Tramps and settlers who arrived "overland" were called "overland men". As the 19th-century ballad says:

> We're not fenced in with walls or gates,
> No monarch's realms are grander.
> Our sheep and cattle eat their fill,
> And wander blithely at their will
> O'er forest, valley, plain or hill,
> Free as an Overlander.
>
> *The Overlander.*

Overlord. The famous code name given to the Allied operation for the invasion of N.W. Europe, which began on D-DAY 1944.

Overture (Fr. *ouvert*, O.F. *overt*, past part. of *ouvrir*, to open). An opening, a preliminary proposal; a piece of music for the opening of an OPERA. Independent pieces of instrumental music in overture style are called *concert overtures.*

To make overtures is to be the first to make an advance, as with a view to acquaintanceship, some business deal, or a reconciliation.

Overy, or Overie. The priory church of St. Mary Overy, renamed St. Saviour's in 1540, and which became SOUTHWARK Cathedral in 1905, was legendarily founded by a ferryman's daughter called Mary (or Mary Overs). Her miserly father Awdrey feigned death in the hope that sorrow would restrain his household's consumption of victuals. Instead they rejoiced and made merry, whereupon Awdrey rose up in anger, only to be slain as a ghost. Mary, now possessed of his fortune, sent for her lover, but he was thrown from his horse and was killed. In sorrow she founded the nunnery which she entered. *Overy* is probably a corruption of "over the river".

Owain. The hero of a 12th-century legend, *The Descent of Owain*, written by Henry of Saltrey, an English CISTERCIAN. Owain was an Irish KNIGHT of Stephen's court who, by way of penance for a wicked life, entered and passed through ST. PATRICK'S PURGATORY.

Owl. The emblem of ATHENS, where owls abounded. Hence MINERVA (ATHENE) was given the owl for her symbol. The Greeks had a proverb, **To send owls to Athens,** which meant the same as our *To carry coals to Newcastle* (*see under* COAL). *See also* MADGE.

I live too near a wood to be scared by an owl. I am too old to be frightened by a BOGY. **Like an owl in an ivy-bush.** Having a sapient, vacant look, as some persons have when in their cups; having a stupid vacant stare. Owls are proverbial for their judge-like solemnity; IVY is the favourite plant of BACCHUS, and was supposed to be the favourite haunt of owls.

> Good ivy, say to us, what birds hast thou?
> None but the owlet that cries "How How!"
> *Carol* (15th century).

Gray, in his *Elegy*, and numerous other poets bracket the two:

> From yonder ivy-mantled tower
> The moping owl doth to the moon complain.

The owl was a baker's daughter. According to a Gloucestershire legend, our Saviour went into a baker's shop for something to eat. The mistress put a cake into the oven for Him, but her daughter said it was too large, and reduced it by half. The dough, however, swelled to an enormous size, and the daughter cried out, "Heugh! heugh! heugh!" and was transformed into an OWL. Ophelia alludes to the tradition:

> Well, God 'ield you! They say the owl was a baker's daughter.
> SHAKESPEARE: *Hamlet*, IV, v.

Owlglass. *See* EULENSPIEGEL.

Owl Jug. A large pot-bellied earthenware container with two ear-handles, once common in Dorset, used for carrying water, cider, etc.

Owl light. Dusk; the gloaming, "BLIND MAN'S HOLIDAY". Fr. *Entre chien et loup*.

Ox. One of the four figures which made up the cherubim in *Ezekiel* i, 10. It is the emblem of the priesthood, and was assigned to St. LUKE as his symbol because he begins his GOSPEL with the Jewish priest sacrificing in the TEMPLE.

It is also an emblem of St. Frideswide, St. LEONARD, St. Sylvester, St. MEDARD, St. Julietta, and St. Blandina.

The dumb ox. *See under* DUMB.

Off-ox. A stupid or clumsy person. In an ox-team the off-ox is the one farthest away from the driver. *See* NEAR.

He has an ox on his tongue. *See* MONEY.

The black ox hath trod on your foot, or **hath trampled on you.** Misfortune has come to you or your house; sometimes, you are henpecked. A black ox was sacrificed to PLUTO, the infernal god, as a white one was to JUPITER.

> Venus waxeth old; and then she was a pretie wench, when Juno was a young wife; now crowes foote is on her eye, and the blacke oxe hath trod on her foot.
> LYLY: *Sapho and Phao*, IV, ii.

Thou shalt not muzzle the ox when he treadeth out the corn (*Deut.* xxv, 4). In other words, do not grudge him the mouthful he may snatch when working for you; do not deprive a man of his little perquisites.

To play the giddy ox. To act the fool generally; to behave in an irresponsible or over-hilarious manner. There was an old phrase,

to make an ox of one, meaning *to make a fool of one*; and in SHAKESPEARE's *Merry Wives of Windsor* (V, v) we have:

> Fal.: I do begin to perceive that I am made an ass.
> Ford: Ay, and an ox too; both the proofs are extant.

Ox-bow. A horseshoe bend in a river.

Ox-eye. A sailor's name for a cloudy speck which indicates the approach of a storm.

Oxgang. An Anglo-Saxon measure of no very definite quantity; as much as an ox could *gang* over or cultivate. Also called a *bovate*. Eight oxgangs made a *carucate*. An oxgang became a conventional unit varying from about 10 to 25 acres in different places. The Lat. *jugum* was a similar term, according to Varro, "Quod juncti boves uno die exarare possunt."

Oxbridge. A word widely used as an abbreviation for Oxford and Cambridge collectively, and for the type of historic English university. For some it is a convenient term, for others it has tendentious and snobbish implications. *Cp.* CAMFORD; REDBRICK.

> Repeated differences with the university authorities caused Mr. Foker to quit Oxbridge in an untimely manner.
> THACKERY: *Pendennis*, ch. xviii.

> Sixth Forms and Oxbridge Entry.
> *The Times* (Heading of 5 February 1968).

Oxford. Oxford bags. Very wide-bottomed flannel trousers first fashionable among Oxford undergraduates in the 1920s.

Oxford Blues. *See* REGIMENTAL AND DIVISIONAL NICKNAMES.

Oxford frame. A picture frame the sides of which cross each other at the corners forming a cross-like projection; once much used for photographs of college groups, etc.

Oxford Group. The name first adopted in South Africa by the followers of Frank Buchman (1878–1961), also called *Buchmanism* which developed into the MORAL RE-ARMAMENT movement. He had a considerable following at Cambridge in the 1920s, but later wider support at Oxford. The movement was EVANGELICAL in character and also became concerned with social, industrial, and international questions.

Oxford Movement. A High Church revival movement in the CHURCH OF ENGLAND "started and guided" by Oxford clerics, especially John Keble, J. H. Newman, R. H. Froude, and E. B. Pusey (hence *Puseyism* as another name for the movement). They were dissatisfied with the decline of Church standards, and with the increase of liberal theology, and feared that the Catholic Emancipation Act of 1829 endangered the English Church. The movement began in 1833 with Keble's sermon against the suppression of ten Irish bishoprics. It was published under the title of *National Apostasy*. Three tracts setting forth their views were published in 1833 and many *Tracts for the Times* followed, hence the name *Tractarianism*. They stressed the historical continuity of the Church of England and the importance of the priesthood and the sacraments. "PROTESTANT" and EVANGELICAL hostility was aroused, especially after Newman's reception into the ROMAN CATHOLIC CHURCH in 1845, but in spite of much official opposition the movement had a lasting influence on the standards and ceremonial of the Church.

> Whether we call it by the ill name of the Oxford counter-reformation or the friendlier name of catholic revival, it remains a striking landmark in the varied notions of English religious thought and feeling for the three-quarters of a century since the still unfinished journey first began.
>
> MORLEY: *Life of Gladstone*, Bk. II, iv, iii (1903).

Provisions of Oxford. *See* MAD PARLIAMENT.

Oxymoron. A rhetorical figure in which effect is produced by the juxtaposition of contradictory terms, such as "Make haste slowly", "Faith unfaithful kept him falsely true". The word is the Gr. for "pointedly foolish".

Oyer and terminer (oi′ ĕr, t′ min ĕr). An Anglo-French legal phase meaning "to hear and determine". *Commissions* or *Writs of oyer and terminer* were issued to judges on circuit twice a year in every county directing them to hold courts for the trial of offences.

Oyez! Oyez! Oyez! (ō yes) (O. Fr., Hear ye!). The call made by the public crier, court officer, etc., to attract attention when a proclamation is about to be read out. Sometimes written *O yes!*

Oyster. And did you ever see an oyster walk upstairs? A satirical query sometimes addressed to one who has been telling unbelievable yarns about his own experiences.

Close as a Kentish oyster. Absolutely secret; hermetically sealed. Kentish oysters are proverbially good, and all good oysters are fast closed.

Never eat an oyster unless there's an R in the month. Good advice which limits the eating of native oysters to the months from September to April, the normal marketing time. The legal close time for oysters in ENGLAND and SCOTLAND, however, extends only from 15 June to 4 August. The advice does not necessarily apply to imported oysters.

> "I think oysters are more beautiful than any religion."
>
> SAKI: *The Chronicles of Clovis*.

The world's mine oyster. The world is the place from which to extract profit, etc., as a pearl can be extracted from an oyster. SHAKESPEARE uses the phrase (*The Merry Wives of Windsor*, II, ii).

Who eats oysters on St. James's Day will never want. ST. JAMES's Day, 25 July, falls during what is now the close season (*see* NEVER EAT AN OYSTER, *above*). It may be supposed that oysters obtainable so unseasonably early would be a luxury only eaten by the rich.

Oz, Wizard of. *See under* WIZARD.

P

P. The sixteenth letter in the English alphabet called *pe*, "mouth", by the Phœnicians and ancient Hebrews, and represented in Egyptian hieroglyphs by a shutter.

In the 16th century, Placentius, a DOMINICAN friar, wrote a poem of 253 HEXAMETER verses, called *Pugna Porcorum*, every word of which begins with the letter *p*. It opens thus:

> Plaudite, Porcelli, porcorum pigra propago—

which may be translated:

> Piglets, praise pigs' prolonged progeny.

P as a mediæval numeral stands for 400, $\overline{P}$ stands for 400,000. P is also the abbreviation for "new penny" in the British decimal currency.

The Four PP or P's. A "merry interlude" by John Heywood, written *c.* 1540. The four principal characters are "a Palmer, a Pardoner, a Potticary (apothecary), and a Pedlar".

The Five P's. William Oxberry (1784–1824) was so called, because he was Printer, Poet, Publisher, Publican, and Player.

p, pp, ppp (in music). *p=piano* (Ital., soft); *pp* and *ppp=pianissimo* (Ital., very soft).

P.C. The Roman *patres conscripti. See* CONSCRIPT FATHERS.

P.P.C. *See* CONGÉ

P.S. (Lat. *post-scriptum*). Written afterwards—*i.e.* after the letter or book was finished.

P's and Q's. Mind your P's and Q's. Be very circumspect in your behaviour. Most probably it derives from an admonition to children learning the alphabet to be careful to distinguish between the forms of *p* and *q* or to printers' apprentices in handling and sorting type. More fancifully it is suggested that in public houses accounts were scored up for beer "P" for pints and "Q" for quarts and a customer needed "to mind his P's and Q's" when the reckoning came. Another is that in the France of Louis XIV, when huge WIGS were fashionable, dancing masters would warn their pupils to "Mind your P's (*i.e. pieds*, feet) and Q's (*i.e. queues*, wigs)"

lest the latter fall off when bending low to make a formal bow.

Pace (pā' si). From Lat. *pax*, meaning peace or pardon, is used in the sense, of "with the permission of" when preceding the mention of some person who disagrees with what is being done.

Pace-eggs. *See under* PASCH.

Pace. To be put through one's paces. To test one's capabilities, as a horse might be tried out by an intending purchaser.

To set the pace. To set the standard of achievement for others to emulate or keep up with, as in a race.

Pacific, The. Amadeus VIII, duke of Savoy (1383, 1391–1439; d. 1451). As Felix V (1440–1449) he was an ANTI-POPE.

Frederick III, Emperor of Germany (1415, 1440–1493).

Olaf III of Norway (1030–1093).

Pacific Ocean. So named by MAGELLAN in 1520, because there he enjoyed calm weather, and a placid sea after the stormy and tempestuous passage of the Straits of Magellan. It was first sighted by Balboa in 1513.

Pacifico, Don. David Pacifico, a Portuguese Jew born at GIBRALTAR claimed exorbitant damages of £26,618 from the Greek government when his house at ATHENS was burned down by rioters. They refused payment, whereupon he asserted his British citizenship and, in January 1850, Palmerston sent the Mediterranean fleet to the Piræus which seized Greek shipping. Eventually compensation was agreed at some £5,000, it being found that Pacifico claimed as much as £150 for a bedstead and £10 for a pillowcase. The handling of the affair aroused a vigorous criticism in PARLIAMENT. *See* CIVIS ROMANUS SUM.

Pack (U.S.A.). To carry, as, *to pack a gun.*

Pack and Penny Day. The last day of a FAIR when traders were packing up their stalls and prepared to dispose of their remaining goods cheaply. A day for bargains.

Pack-Rag-Day. Old MAY DAY; so called in Lincolnshire, because servants hired for the

Asia Minor, where it was used for writing material when Ptolemy prohibited the exportation of PAPYRUS from Egypt.

Pardon Bell. The ANGELUS bell. So called because of the INDULGENCE once given for reciting certain prayers forming the Angelus.

Pardoner. A mediæval cleric licensed to preach and collect money for a definite object such as a CRUSADE or the building of a church, for contributing to which letters of INDULGENCE were exchanged. By many they were regarded as licences to sin and were denounced by Chaucer, Langland, and Wycliff.

The pardoner's mitten. Whoever put this mitten on would be sure to thrive in all things.

> He that his hondë put in this metayn,
> He shal have multiplying of his grayn,
> Whan he hath sowen, be it whete or otes,
> So that he offre pans [pence] or ellës grootes.
> CHAUCER: *Prologue to the Pardoner's Tale.*

Pari mutuel (pa′ ri mū tū el′) (Fr., mutual stake). The name first given to the totalizator, which ensures that the winners of a race share the money staked on the horses, etc., after the cost of management, taxes, etc., have been deducted.

Pari passu (Lat., at the same pace). At the same time; in equal degrees. Two or more schemes carried on at once and driven forward with equal energy are said to be carried on *pari passu.*

Pariah. A low-caste Hindu of southern India, from a native word meaning "a drummer", because such Hindus beat the drums at certain festivals. Europeans extended the term to those of no caste at all; hence its application to outcasts generally. Cp. UNTOUCHABLES.

Parian. Pertaining to the island of *Paros*, one of the Cyclades, renowned for its white marble; hence a fine white porcelain used for making statuettes, vases, etc.

Parian Chronicle. One of the ARUNDELIAN MARBLES, found on the island of *Paros*, and bearing an inscription which contains a chronological register of the chief events of the mythology and history of ancient Greece from the reign of Cecrops (c. 1580 B.C.) to the archonship of Diognetus (264 B.C.), of which approximately the last 100 years is missing.

Paris. In Greek legend, the son of PRIAM, King of TROY, and HECUBA; and through his abduction of HELEN the cause of the siege of Troy. Hecuba dreamed that she was to bring forth a firebrand, and as this was interpreted to mean that the unborn child would bring destruction to his house, the infant Paris was exposed on Mount IDA. He was, however, brought up by a shepherd and grew to perfection of beautiful manhood. At the judgment on the APPLE OF DISCORD, HERA, APHRODITE, and ATHENE had each offered him a bribe—the first power, the second the most beautiful of women, and the third martial glory. In return for her victory, Aphrodite assisted him in the abduction of Helen, for whom he deserted his wife ŒNONE, daughter of the river-god, Cebren. At Troy, Paris, having killed ACHILLES, was fatally wounded with a poisoned arrow by PHILOCTETES at the taking of the city.

Paris, the capital of France (*see* LUTETIA). Rabelais gives a whimsical derivation of the name. He tells (I, xvii) how GARGANTUA played a disgusting practical joke on the Parisians who came to stare at him, and the men said that it was a sport "*par ris*" (to be laughed at); wherefore the city was called Par'is.

The heraldic device of the city of Paris is a ship. As Sauval says, "*L'île de la cité est faite comme un grand navire enfoncé dans la vase, échoué au fil de l'eau vers le milieu de la Seine.*" This form of a ship struck the authorities, who, in the later MIDDLE AGES, emblazoned it on the shield of the city.

Monsieur de Paris. *See under* MONSIEUR.

Paris green, or **French green.** A vivid light green pigment composed of aceto-arsenite of copper, also used as an insecticide. Named from the French capital, where it was manufactured.

Plaster of Paris. Gypsum, especially calcined gypsum used for making statuary casts, keeping broken limbs rigid for setting, etc. The name derives from the gypsum quarries of Montmartre, Paris.

Paris-Garden. A bear-garden; a noisy disorderly place. In allusion to the famous Tudor bull-baiting and bear-baiting gardens of that name at BANKSIDE, on the site of a house owned by Robert de Paris, who held the manor in the reign of Richard II. About 1595 the *Swan Theatre* was erected here and, in 1613, this gave way to *The Hope.*

> Do you take the court for Paris-garden?
> SHAKESPEARE: *Henry VIII*, V, iv.

The Parisian Wedding. The massacre of St. BARTHOLOMEW which took place (24 August 1572) during the festivities at the marriage of Henry of Navarre and Margaret of France.

> Charles IX, too, although it was not possible for him to recall to life the countless victims of the Parisian wedding, was yet ready to explain those murders to the satisfaction of every unprejudiced mind.
> MOTLEY: *The Rise of the Dutch Republic*, III, ix.

Parkinson's Law. As satirically promulgated by C. Northcote Parkinson in his book with that title (1957), it states that the amount of work done is in inverse proportion to the number of people employed; in other words, something similar to the Law of Diminishing Returns takes effect. The "law" is directed mainly at public administration, but it is aimed also at inefficient business administration.

Parlement. Under the old régime in France, the sovereign court of justice at Paris, where councillors were allowed to plead, and where justice was administered in the king's name. It was a development of the *curia regis*. In due course, twelve provincial *parlements* were created. They had not the function of a court of peers as had the Parlement of Paris, but they had certain administrative powers. The Paris Parlement received appeals from all inferior tribunals, but its own judgments were final. It took cognizance of all offences against the crown, the peers, the BISHOPS, the corporations, and all high officers of state. It had no legislative power, but had to register the royal edicts before they could become law. The Parlements were abolished by the CONSTITUENT ASSEMBLY in 1790.

Parliament (Fr. *parlement*, Med. Lat. *parliamentum*, a talk, meeting, discussion). Its application to assemblies of the king and his magnates, etc., becomes common in 13th-century England and a representative element was introduced at these meetings. It became an established institution during the 14th century.

A number of Parliaments have been given characteristic names for various reasons. *See under* ADDLED; BAREBONES; CAVALIER; CONVENTION; DEVIL'S; DRUNKEN; DUNCES; GOOD; GRATTAN'S; LONG; MAD; MERCILESS; MODEL; MONGREL; PENSIONARY; RUMP; SHORT; UNLEARNED; USELESS; WONDERMAKING, etc.

A hung Parliament. One in which no party has an overall majority and that which forms the government is dependent on the support of one or more of the smaller parties. Such a government is likely to prove unstable and is usually due to the existence of minority parties, especially where there is proportional representation.

Parliamentary language, *i.e.* restrained and seemly language, such as is properly required of any member speaking in Parliament.

Parliamentary Train. By the Regulation of Railways Act of 1855 every railway in Great Britain was obliged to run at least one train a day over its system, at a minimum speed of 12 m.p.h., calling at every station, at a fare not greater than 1*d*. a mile. This was repealed in 1915. *Cp.* JERKWATER.

Parlour. Originally the reception room in a monastery, etc., where the inmates could see and speak (Fr. *parler*) to their friends.

Parlour boarder. Said of one in a privileged position; from the pupil at a boarding school who resided with the principal and received extra care and attention.

Parlour tricks. Accomplishments that are useful in company, at parties, etc. "Don't try any of your parlour tricks here" is used in the sense of, "Don't try any of your games or nonsense with me".

Parnassus. A mountain near DELPHI, Greece, with two summits, one of which was consecrated to APOLLO and the MUSES, the other to BACCHUS. It is supposedly named from Parnassus, a son of NEPTUNE, and DEUCALION's ark came to rest there after the flood. Owing to its connexion with the Muses it came to be regarded as the seat of poetry and music, hence **To climb Parnassus** is "to write poetry".

The Legislator, or **Solon of Parnassus.** Nicolas Boileau (1636–1711) was so called by VOLTAIRE, because of his *Art of Poetry*, a production unequalled in the whole art of didactic poetry.

Gradus ad Parnassum (Lat., steps to Parnassus). The fanciful title of a once popular dictionary of Latin prosody used in schools for the teaching of Latin verse. It was also the title of a well-known treatise on musical composition written in Latin by Johan Joseph Fux, published at Vienna in 1725, and for Clementi's collection of piano studies.

Parnassian School. The name given to a group of French poets flourishing from about 1850 to 1890, from a collection of their poems entitled *Le Parnasse contemporain* (1866). They included Théophile Gautier, Leconte de Lisle, Baudelaire, François Coppée, Sully Prudhomme and Verlaine.

They were nicknamed *les impassibles* for their supposed devotion to "art for art's sake" and represented a reaction against the romanticism of Hugo and Lamartine.

In England, the group of poets following Rossetti and William Morris have sometimes been referred to as "the Parnassians". *Cp.* PRE-RAPHAELITE BROTHERHOOD.

Parody. Father of Parody. Hipponax of Ephesus (6th century B.C.). *Parody* means an ode which perverts the meaning of another ode (Gr. *para ode*).

Parolles (pà rol' ēz). **He was a mere Par-**

olles. A pretender, a man of words, and a pedant. The allusion is to the faithless, bragging, slandering villain who dubs himself "captain", pretends to knowledge which he has not, and to sentiments he never feels, in SHAKESPEARE's *All's Well That Ends Well*.

Parquet (par' kā). The word is a diminutive of O.Fr. *parc*, an enclosure (in Mod. Fr. it has the meanings of both BAR and BENCH). In England it is commonly used of a form of wooden flooring made up of blocks laid in a pattern; in the U.S.A. it denotes the ground floor of a theatre (more commonly called the "orchestra" nowadays) corresponding to the English "pit", the latter deriving from the bear-baiting pit of the 16th century.

Parr. Thomas Parr, the "old, old, very old man", was said to have lived in the reigns of ten sovereigns, to have done penance for incontinence at the age of 105, to have married a second wife when he was 122 years old, and to have had a child by her. He was a husbandman, reputedly born at Alberbury, near Shrewsbury, in 1483, and died in 1635. He was taken to the court of CHARLES I by the Earl of Arundel in 1635, and the change of his mode of life killed him. He was buried in the south transept of Westminster Abbey. There is no real evidence supporting his alleged age of 152, but he was doubtless a very old man. *See* LONGEVITY.

Parsees. GUEBRES or fire-worshippers; descendants of Persians who fled to India during the Mohammedan persecution of the 7th and 8th centuries, and still adherents of Zoroastrianism. The word means *People of Pars, i.e.* Persia. *See* TOWERS OF SILENCE *under* SILENCE.

Parsifal, Parsival. *See* PERCIVAL, SIR.

Parsley. He has need now of nothing but a little parsley, *i.e.* he is dead. A Greek saying; the Greeks decked tombs with parsley, because it keeps green a long time.

Parson. *See* CLERICAL TITLES.

Grey-coat parson. An impropriator; a layman who owned the TITHES.

Parson Adams. A leading character in Fielding's *Joseph Andrews* (1742), often taken as the type of the good-natured, hardworking, and learned country CURATE who is totally ignorant of "the ways of the world".

He was drawn from Fielding's friend, the Rev. William Young, who edited Ainsworth's *Latin Dictionary* (1752).

Parson and Clerk. An old children's game played with burnt paper, the sparks representing persons.

So when a child (as playful children use)
Has burnt to tinder a stale last-year's news,
The flame extinct, he views the roving fire—

There goes my lady, and there goes the squire,
There goes the parson, oh illustrious spark!
And there, scarce less illustrious, goes the clerk!
COWPER: *On observing Some Names of Little Note*.

Two red sandstone rocks at Dawlish are known as the *Parson and Clerk*. The story is that an inland parson used to visit a certain BISHOP of Exeter who was in ill health in the hope that he might gain the see on the bishop's death. One winter's night, when on his now customary errand guided by the parish clerk, they lost their way, but with the aid of a rustic eventually found shelter at Dawlish. Among rough company they passed the night in carousal, and in the morning heard that the bishop was dead. In haste the parson pushed his clerk into the saddle, but the horses refused to budge. "I believe the DEVIL is in the horses," said the parson; "I believe he is," answered the clerk, only to be greeted with laughter from the company who had now turned into jeering demons. The house disappeared and they found themselves on the seashore, the horses still ignored the whip and they both lost consciousness. Neither parson nor clerk returned to their parish, but two strange rocks now stood on the shore.

Parson's nose. The rump of a fowl. Also called the "POPE'S nose".

Parson's Pleasure. The well-known bathing enclosure on the bank of the Cherwell at Oxford, known as *Paten's Pleasure* in the 17th century, it was acquired by the university in 1865, eventually coming to be called *Parson's Pleasure* from its use by local clergy. As a men only enclosure, bathing in the nude became the common practice.

Part. A portion, a piece, a fragment.

For my part. As far as concerns me.

For the most part. Generally, as a rule.

In good part. Favourably, graciously, not to be offended though one might well be. **To take in ill** or **bad part** has the opposite meaning.

Part and parcel. An essential part, portion, or element.

Parts of speech. A grammatical class of words of a particular character. The old rhyme by which children used to be taught the parts of speech is:

Three little words you often see
Are ARTICLES, *a, an*, and *the*.
A NOUN's the name of anything;
As *school* or *garden, hoop* or *swing*.
ADJECTIVES tell the kind of noun;
As *great, small, pretty, white*, or *brown*.
Instead of nouns the PRONOUNS stand;
Her head, *his* face, *our* arms, *your* hand.
VERBS tell of something being done;
To *read, count, sing, laugh, jump*, or *run*.
How things are done the ADVERBS tell;

As *slowly, quickly, ill,* or *well.*
CONJUNCTIONS join the words together;
As, men *and* women, wind *or* weather.
The PREPOSITION stands before
A noun, as *in* or *through* a door.
The INTERJECTION shows surprise;
As, *oh*! how pretty! *ah*! how wise!
The whole are called nine parts of speech,
Which reading, writing, speaking teach.

Lines 7 and 8 are now completely misleading as the so-called "pronouns" here function as possessive adjectives; but it must be
remembered that *her, his, our, your,* etc.,
were formerly regarded as personal pronouns of the possessive or genitive case.

Part up! Slang for "hand over", as in, "If
you don't part up with the money, there will
be trouble". An extension of the use is the
old saying (George Buchanan, tutor to
James VI), *A fool and his money are soon
parted.*

Till death us do part. *See* DEPART.

To play a part. To perform some duty or
pursue some course of action; also, to act deceitfully. The phrase is from the stage,
where an actor's *part* is the words or the
character assigned to him.

To take part. To assist; to participate.

To take the part of. To side with, to support the cause of.

A man of parts. An accomplished man;
one who is clever, talented, or of high intellectual ability.

The parting of the ways. Said of a critical
moment when one has to choose between
two different courses of action. The allusion, of course, is to a place at which a road
branches off in different directions.

Partant pour la Syrie (Fr., Departing for
Syria). The official march of the French
troops in the Second Empire. The words
were by Count Alexander de Laborde
(1774–1842), and the music—attributed to
Queen Hortense, mother of NAPOLEON—
was probably by the flautist Philip Drouet
(1792–1873). The ballad tells how young
Dunois followed his lord to Syria, and
prayed the Virgin "that he might prove
the bravest warrior, and love the fairest
maiden". Afterwards the count said to Dunois, "To thee we owe the victory, and my
daughter I give to thee". The refrain was:
*Amour à la plus belle; honneur au plus vail-
lant.*

Parthenon (par' thé non) (Gr., "The maiden's chamber"). The great temple of
ATHENE at ATHENS, many of the sculptured
friezes and fragments of pediments of which
are now in the BRITISH MUSEUM among the
ELGIN MARBLES. The temple was begun by
the architect Ictinus about 445 B.C. and was

mainly embellished by Phidias, whose colossal chryselephantine statue of Athene was its
chief treasure. The Parthenon was destroyed during the siege of Athens in 1687
by the Venetians, when the powder stored in
it by the Turks exploded.

Parthenope (par then' ō pi). Naples; so
called from Parthenope, the SIREN, who
threw herself into the sea out of love for
ULYSSES, and was cast up in the Bay of
Naples. Parthenope was an early Greek settlement, later called *Palæopolis* (the old
city), after subsequent settlers had established *Neapolis* (the new city), from which
Naples derives its name.

Parthenopean Republic. The transitory
Republic of Naples, established with the aid
of the French in 1799, and overthrown by
the Allies in the following June, when the
BOURBONS were restored.

Parthian shot, or **shaft.** A parting shot; a telling or wounding remark made on departure,
giving one's adversary no time to reply. An
allusion to the ancient practice of Parthian
horsemen turning in flight, to discharge arrows and missiles at their pursuers.

Parti pris (par' ti prē) (Fr., choice or side
having been taken). A preconceived opinion, bias.

Particularists. Those who hold the doctrine
of particular election and redemption, *i.e.*
the election and redemption of some, not all,
of the human race.

**Partington. Dame Partington and her
mop.** A taunt against those who try to withstand progress or the inevitable. Sidney
SMITH speaking at Taunton in October
1831, on the rejection of the Reform Bill by
the Lords, compared them to Dame Partington, who, during a great storm at Sid-
mouth in 1824, tried to push back the Atlantic with her mop. "She was excellent at a
slop, or a puddle," he said, "but she should
not have meddled with a tempest. Gentlemen, be at your ease—be quiet and steady.
You will beat Mrs. Partington."

   B.P. Shillaber, the American humorist,
published *The Life and Sayings of Mrs. Partington* (1854), the old lady, like Mrs. MAL-
APROP, constantly misusing words.

Partlet (O.Fr. *Pertelote,* a feminine proper
name). A neckerchief or ruff worn in the
16th century by women. Also used as the
name of a hen with reference to the frill-like
feathers round the neck of some hens. The
hen in Chaucer's *Nun's Priest's Tale* is
called Partlet.

Partridge, always partridge! *See* PERDRIX.

St. Partridge's Day. 1 September, when
partridge shooting begins. *See* GLORIOUS

TWELFTH; SPORTING SEASONS.

> 'Well, this *is* friendship! What on earth brings you here, old fellow? Why aren't you in the stubbles celebrating St. Partridge?"
>
> MRS HUMPHRY WARD: *Robert Elsmere*, ch. xlviii.

Parturient montes, etc. *See* THE MOUNTAIN IN LABOUR *under* MOUNTAIN.

Party. Person or persons under consideration. "This is the next party, your worship"—*i.e.* the next case to be examined.

As a Victorian colloquialism *party* was synonymous with person—"That dull old party in the corner"—and is still often used in this sense. When a sailor goes ashore to meet his "party" he means his "lady friend".

Party line. The official "line" or policy of a political party; also a telephone line shared by two or more subscribers. **To toe the party line** is to follow or be coerced into following party policy.

Parvenu (par' ve nū) (Fr., arrived). An upstart; one who has risen from the ranks. The word was made popular in France by Marivaux's *Paysan Parvenu* (1735).

> The insolence of the successful *parvenu* is only the necessary continuance of the career of the needy struggler.
>
> THACKERAY: *Pendennis*, II, xxi.

Parvis (par' vis) (*Parvisus*, a Low Latin corruption of *paradisus*, a church close, especially the court in front of St. Peter's at ROME in the MIDDLE AGES). The "place" or court before the main entrance of a cathedral. In the parvis of St. Paul's lawyers used to meet for consultation as brokers do in exchange. The word is now applied to the room above the church porch.

> A sergeant of lawe, war and wys,
> That often hadde ben atte parvys.
>
> CHAUCER: *Canterbury Tales*, line 309.

Pasch. EASTER, from the Greek form of the Hebrew *Pesach*, PASSOVER.

Pasch eggs, or **Pace eggs.** EASTER eggs, given as an emblem of the Resurrection.

Paschal Lamb. The lamb sacrificed and eaten at the Jewish PASSOVER. For Christians, Jesus Christ is called the *Paschal Lamb* because He was called the "Lamb of God" by *John* (i, 29) and in allusion to I *Cor.* v, 7—"For even Christ our passover is sacrificed for us."

In HERALDRY, a white lamb *passant* carrying a banner of St. GEORGE.

Pasha (păsh' a). A Turkish title borne by governors of provinces and certain military and civil officers of high rank. There were three grades of pashas, which were distinguished by the number of horsetails carried before them and planted in front of their tents. The highest rank were those of *three tails*; the grand VIZIER was always such a pasha, as also were commanding generals and admirals; generals of divisions, etc., were pashas of *two tails*; and generals of brigades, rear-admirals, and petty provincial governors were pashas of *one tail. Cp.* BASHAW.

Pasiphæ (păs' i fē). In Greek legend, a daughter of the SUN and wife of MINOS, King of Crete. She was the mother of ARIADNE, and also through intercourse with a white bull (given by POSEIDON to Minos) of the MINOTAUR.

Pasque eggs. *See* PASCH EGGS.

Pasquinade (păs kwin ād'). A LAMPOON or political squib, having ridicule for its object; so called from Pasquino, an Italian tailor or barber of the 15th century, noted for his caustic wit. After his death, a mutilated statue was dug up and placed near the Piazza Navona. As it was not clear whom the statue represented, and as it stood opposite Pasquin's house, it came to be called "Pasquin". The people of ROME affixed their political, religious, and personal satires to it, hence the name. At the other end of the city was an ancient statue of MARS, called *Marforio*, to which were affixed replies to the Pasquinades.

Pass. A pass, or **A common pass.** At the universities, an ordinary degree, one without honours, a pass degree, the recipient being called a *passman*.

A pretty pass. A difficult or deplorable state of affairs.

To pass current. To be generally accepted as genuine or credible.

To pass the buck. To evade responsibility, to pass responsibility on to someone else. An American phrase, coming from the game of poker. The "buck", perhaps a piece of buckshot or a "bucktail", was passed from one player to another as a reminder that the recipient was to be the next dealer. The earliest recorded use of the phrase is by Mark Twain in 1872.

To pass the time of day. To exchange a greeting by some remark appropriate to the time of day or the weather, as "Good morning", "It's a lovely day", etc.

Passing Bell. *See under* BELL.

Passepartout (pas' par too) (Fr., pass everywhere). A master-key; also a simple kind of picture-framing in which the picture is placed between a sheet of cardboard and a piece of glass, the whole being held together by strips of fabric pasted round the edges. Also the name of Phileas Fogg's French valet in Jules Verne's novel *Round the World in Eighty Days*.

Passes, St. Bernard. Two Alpine passes into Italy, the Great St. Bernard from Switzerland, the little St. Bernard from France. On the former is the famous hospice founded by St. Bernard of Menthon (923–1008, canonized 1681), served by the AUGUSTINIAN CANONS. From early days they have succoured pilgrims and others crossing the pass, for this purpose breeding the large and handsome **St. Bernard dog,** trained to track and aid travellers lost in the snow. In May 1800, NAPOLEON made his famous passage of the Alps across the Great St. Bernard pass with 30,000 men, the only track then being a bridle path.

Passim (pǎs′ im) (Lat., here and there, in many places). A direction often found in annotated books which tells the reader that reference to the matter in hand will be found in many passages in the book mentioned.

Passion, The. The sufferings of Jesus Christ which had their culmination in His death on the CROSS.

Passion Flower. A plant of the genus *Passiflora*, whose flowers bear a fancied resemblance to the instruments of the PASSION. *Cp.* PIKE. It seems to have been given the name by 16th-century Spanish missionaries to South Africa.

> The *leaf* symbolizes the spear.
> The five *petals* and five *sepals*, the ten apostles (Peter who denied, and Judas who betrayed, being omitted).
> The five *anthers*, the five wounds.
> The *tendrils*, the scourges.
> The column of the *ovary*, the pillar of the cross.
> The *stamens*, the hammers.
> The three *stigmas*, the three nails.
> The *filaments* within the flower, the crown of thorns.
> The *calyx*, the glory or nimbus.
> The *white* tint, purity.
> The *blue* tint, HEAVEN.

It keeps open three days, symbolizing the three years' ministry.

Passion Play. A development of the mediæval MYSTERY play with especial reference to the story of our Lord's passion and death. The best-known survival of such plays, which were common in 14th-century France, is the Oberammergau Passion Play, which takes place every ten years. In 1633 the BLACK DEATH swept over the village of Oberammergau; when it abated the inhabitants vowed to enact the PASSION every ten years and this has been done with one or two exceptions. It is now a highly commercial undertaking although the cast is still taken from the villagers.

Passion Sunday. *See* JUDICA.

Passionists. Members of the Congregation of Discalced Clerks of the Most Holy Cross and Passion of Our Lord Jesus Christ, founded by St. Paul of the Cross in 1720. The first house, at Monte Argentario, an island off the coast of Tuscany, was opened in 1737. Their chief work is in the holding of retreats and missions. The fathers wear on the breast of their black habit a white heart with the inscription *Jesu Xpi Passio*, surmounted by a CROSS.

Passover. A Jewish festival to commemorate the deliverance of the Israelites, when the ANGEL of death (that slew the firstborn of the Egyptians) passed over their houses, and spared all who did as MOSES commanded them. The festival began on 14th of Nisan (*i.e.* about 12 April) when the PASCHAL LAMB was eaten, and the Festival of Unleavened Bread lasted seven days.

Patch. A fool; so called from the nickname of Cardinal Wolsey's jester, Sexton, who got his name either from Ital. *pazzo*, a fool, or from the motley or patched dress worn by licensed fools.

> What a pied ninny's this! thou scurvy patch!
> SHAKESPEARE: *The Tempest*, III, ii.

Cross-patch. An ill-tempered person.

Face patches. One of the more absurd fashions of the 17th and early 18th centuries was the wearing of face patches by women and sometimes by men. Round black patches were the most popular but diamond and other shapes were also used, sometimes to hide blemishes but usually intended as an adornment.

Not a patch upon. Not to be compared with; as, "His horse is not a patch upon mine."

To patch up a quarrel. To arrange the matter in a not very satisfactory way; a coat that has been torn and then "patched up" is pretty sure to break out again; so is a quarrel. *Cp.* PAPER OVER THE CRACKS.

Patent (through Fr. from Lat. *patentem*, lying open). Open to the perusal of anybody. A thing that is *patented* is protected by LETTERS PATENT.

Letters patent. Documents from the SOVEREIGN or a crown office conferring a title, right, privilege, etc., such as a title of nobility, or the exclusive right to make or sell for a given number of years some new invention. So called because they are written upon open sheets of parchment, with the seal of the sovereign or party by whom they were issued pendent at the bottom.

Patent Rolls. CHANCERY enrolment of LETTERS PATENT under the GREAT SEAL collected on parchment rolls and first dating from 1201. Each roll contains a year, though in some cases the roll is subdivided into two or more parts. Each sheet of parchment is numbered and called a membrane; for example the 8th sheet, say, of the 10th year of Henry III is cited thus: "Pat. 10 Hen. III, m.8". If the document is on the back of the roll it is called *dorso*, and "d" is added to the citation. Patents of invention were last enrolled in 1853 and they are now registered at the Patent Office. *Cp.* CLOSE ROLLS.

Paternoster (Lat., Our Father). The Lord's Prayer; from the first two words in the Latin version. Every eleventh bead of a ROSARY is so called, because at that bead the Lord's Prayer is repeated; the name is also given to a certain kind of fishing tackle, in which hooks and weights to suit them are fixed alternately on the line somewhat in rosary fashion.

A Paternoster-while. Quite a short time; the time it takes to say a paternoster.

Paternoster Row (LONDON) was probably so named from the ROSARY or paternoster makers. There is mention as early as 1374 of a Richard Russell, a "paternosterer", who dwelt there, and we read of "one Robert Nikke, a paternoster maker and citizen", in the reign of Henry IV. Another suggestion is that it was so called because funeral processions on their way to St. Paul's began their *Pater noster* at the beginning of the Row. For three centuries Paternoster Row was the home of publishers and booksellers. It was totally destroyed in an air raid in December 1940.

To say the Devil's paternoster. *See under* DEVIL.

Pathetic Fallacy. A term coined by John Ruskin (1819–1900) to describe the figure of speech that attributes human feelings to nature.

Pathfinder. One of the names of Natty Bumppo in Fenimore Cooper's LEATHER-STOCKING Novels. It was given to the American Major-General John Charles Fremont (1813–1890) who conducted four expeditions across the Rocky Mountains. In World War II, R.A.F. pilots who identified targets and dropped flares to guide the attacking force were called "Pathfinders".

Patient Grisel. *See* GRISELDA.

Patmos. The island of the Sporades in the Ægean Sea (now called *Patmo* or *Patino*), to which St. JOHN retired—or was exiled (*Rev.* i, 9). Hence the name is used allusively for a place of banishment or solitude.

Patres Conscripti. *See* CONSCRIPT FATHERS.

Patriarch (Gr. *patria*, family; *archein*, to rule). The head of a tribe or family who rules by paternal right; applied specially (after *Acts* vii, 8) to the twelve sons of Jacob, and to ABRAHAM, Isaac, and Jacob and their forefathers. In one passage (*Acts* ii, 29) David is spoken of as a patriarch.

In the early Church, "Patriarch", first mentioned in the Council of Chalcedon, but virtually existing from about the time of the Council of Nicæa, was the title of the highest Church officers. A Patriarch ordained METROPOLITANS, convened councils, received appeals, and was the chief BISHOP over several countries or provinces, as an archbishop is over several dioceses. It was also the title given by the POPES to the archbishops of Lisbon and Venice, in order to make the patriarchal dignity appear lower and distinct from the papal. It is also the title of the chief bishop of various Eastern churches, as the JACOBITES, Armenians and MARONITES.

In the ORTHODOX Eastern Church the bishops of Constantinople, Alexandria, Antioch, and JERUSALEM are patriarchs, the Patriarch of Constantinople bearing the style of Œcumenical Patriarch. Within a religious order the title is given to the founder, as St. Benedict, St. FRANCIS, and St. DOMINIC.

Patrician. Properly, one of the *patres* (fathers) or senators of ROME (*see* CONSCRIPT FATHERS), and their descendants. As for long they held all the honours of the state, the word came to signify the magnates or nobility of a nation, the aristocrats or "patrician class". *Cp.* PLEBEIAN; PROLETARIAT.

Patrick, St. The apostle and patron SAINT of IRELAND (commemorated on 17 March) was not an Irishman but was born at Bannavem (*c.* 389). Its location is unknown but it may have been in Glamorgan and his father, Calpurnius, was a Roman official and deacon. As a boy he was captured in a Pictish raid and sold as a slave in Ireland. He escaped to GAUL where he probably studied in the monastery of Lérins before returning to Britain. After receiving a supernatural call to preach to the heathen of Ireland, he returned to Gaul and was ordained deacon. He landed in Wicklow (432) and going north converted the people of ULSTER and later those of other parts of Ireland. He established many communities and churches including the cathedral church of Armagh. He is said to have died in 461 and to have been buried at Down in Ulster.

St. Patrick left his name to many places and numerous legends are told of his miraculous powers. Perhaps the best known tradition is that he cleared Ireland of its vermin. The story goes that one old SERPENT resisted him, so he made a box and invited the serpent to enter it. The serpent objected, saying it was too small; but St. Patrick insisted it was quite large enough to be comfortable. Eventually the serpent got in to prove it was too small, whereupon St. Patrick slammed down the lid and cast the box into the sea.

In commemoration of this he is usually represented banishing the serpents, and with a SHAMROCK leaf.

St. Patrick's Cross. The same shape as St. Andrew's CROSS (**X**), only different in colour, viz. red on a white ground.

St. Patrick's Purgatory. A cave on Station Island in Lough Derg, Co. Donegal, a resort of pilgrims from the 13th century. The legend is that Christ revealed it to St. Patrick and told him that all who visited it in penitence and faith would gain a full INDULGENCE of their sins and they would gain sight of the torments of HELL and the joys of HEAVEN. Henry of Saltrey tells how Sir OWAIN visited it, and Fortunatus, of CHAP-BOOK fame, was one of the adventurers. It was blocked up by order of the POPE on St. Patrick's Day, 1497. Calderón (1600–1681) has a play on the subject, *El Purgatorio de San Patricio*.

> Why then should all your chimney-sweepers be Irishmen?...
> Faith, that's soon answered, for St. Patrick, you know, keeps purgatory; he makes the fire, and his countrymen could do nothing if they cannot sweep chimneys.
> DEKKER: *The Honest Whore*, Pt. II, I, i.

The Order of St. Patrick. A British order of knighthood instituted by George III in 1783, originally consisting of the Sovereign, the Lord Lieutenant, and 15 knights (enlarged to 22 in 1833). Its motto is *Quis Separabit*? In 1968 the Order consisted of the Sovereign and 2 knights. There have been no elections since 1924. The Order ceased with the death of the Duke of Gloucester in 1974.

Patriots' Day. In the U.S.A. the anniversary of the battle of Lexington, 19 April 1775, the first battle in the War of Independence. It is a public holiday in Massachusetts and Maine.

Patroclus. The gentle and amiable friend of ACHILLES. When the latter refused to fight in order to annoy AGAMEMNON, Patroclus appeared in the armour of Achilles at the head of the MYRMIDONS and was slain by HECTOR.

Patroon (Dut., a patron). A landowner in New Jersey and New York when they were Dutch colonies. The patroon had certain manorial rights and privileges which were abolished about 1850.

Patter. To chatter, to clack, also the running talk of CHEAP-JACKS, conjurers, entertainers and comedians, etc., is from PATERNOSTER. When saying MASS the priest often recited in a low rapid mechanical way until he came to the words "and lead us not into temptation", which he spoke clearly and deliberately.

The patter of feet, of rain, etc., is not connected with the above. It is a frequentative of *pat*, to strike gently.

Pattern. From the same root as *patron* (Lat. *pater*, father). As the *patron* ought to be an example, so pattern has come to signify a model.

Paul, St. Patron saint of preachers and tent-makers (see *Acts* xviii, 3). Originally called Saul, his name, according to tradition, was changed in honour of Sergius Paulus, whom he converted (*Acts* xiii, 6–12).

His symbols are a sword and open book, the former the instrument of his martyrdom and the latter indicative of the new law propagated by him as the apostle of the Gentiles. He is represented as of short stature, with bald head and grey, bushy beard; and legend relates that when he was beheaded at ROME (*c.* A.D. 66) after having converted one of NERO's favourite concubines, milk instead of blood flowed from his veins. He is commemorated on 25 January. *Cp.* WINIFRED.

St. Paul the Hermit. The first of the Egyptian hermits. When 113 years old, he was visited by St. ANTONY, himself over 90, and when he died in 341, St. Antony wrapped his body in the cloak given to him by St. Athanasius, and his grave was dug by two lions. He lived in a cave, and he is represented as an old man, clothed with palm-leaves, and seated under a palm-tree, near which are a river and loaf of bread.

A Paul's man. A braggart; a captain out of service, with a long rapier; so called because the Walk down the centre of Old St. Paul's LONDON, was at one time the haunt of stale knights and other characters. These loungers were also known as *Paul's Walkers*; Jonson called BOBADIL a Paul's man.

Paul's Cross. A pulpit in the open air situated on the north side of Old St. Paul's Cathedral, in which, from 1259 to 1643, eminent divines preached in the presence of the Lord Mayor and Aldermen every Sunday. The cross was demolished in 1643 by order of PARLIAMENT. A new pulpit and CROSS were erected on the site in 1910.

Paul Jones. A dance which became popular in Britain in the 1920s in which the ladies formed an outward facing circle moving in the opposite direction to the men, who faced inwards. The couples facing each other when the music stopped became partners for the next part of the dance, this pattern being repeated several times. It was earlier one of the "sets" in American barn-dancing, perhaps named after the naval adventurer John Paul Jones (1747–1792).

Paul Pry. *See* PRY.

To rob Peter to pay Paul. *See* ROB.

Pavan, or **Pavin** (pa′ van). A stately Spanish dance of the 16th and 17th centuries, said to be so called because in it the dancers stalked like peacocks (Lat. *pavones*), the gentlemen with their long robes of office, and the ladies with trains like peacock's tails. The pavan, like the minuet, ended with a quick movement called the *galliard*, a sort of gavotte. The etymology is uncertain and it is also suggested that the name is from *Padova* (Padua).

Every pavan has its galliard. Every sage has his moments of folly. Every white must have its black, and every sweet its sour.

Pawnbroker's Sign, The. *See* BALLS, THE THREE GOLDEN.

Pawnee (paw′ nē). Anglo-Indian for water (Hind. *pani*, water). It is also the name of a North American Indian tribe.

Brandy pawnee. Brandy and water.

Pax (păks) (Lat., peace). The "kiss of peace", which is given at MASS. It is omitted on MAUNDY THURSDAY.

Also a sacred utensil used when mass is celebrated by a high dignitary. It is sometimes a crucifix, sometimes a tablet, and sometimes a reliquary, and is handed round to be kissed as a symbolic substitute for the "kiss of peace".

The old custom of "kissing the bride", which took place immediately before the Communion of the newly married couple and still obtains in some churches, is derived from the Salisbury rubric concerning the Pax in the Missa Sponsalium:

Tunc amoto pallio, surgant ambo sponsus et sponsa; et accipiat sponsus pacem a sacerdote, et ferat sponsæ osculans eam et neminem alium, nec ipse, nec ipsa; sed statim diaconus vel clericus a presbytero pacem accipiens, ferat aliis sicut solitum est.

Pax! The schoolboy's cry of truce.

Pax Britannica. The peace formerly imposed by British rule in her colonial empire. The phrase is modelled on the Latin **Pax Romana**, the peace existing between the different parts of the Roman empire.

The *pax Britannica* was an umbrella that sheltered all colonists, one which they neither wished nor could afford to dispense with.

A.P. THORNTON: *The Imperial Idea and Its Enemies*, iii.

Since the U.S.A. increasingly took over Britain's former role, the term **Pax Americana** came into vogue.

Pax vobis(cum) (Peace be unto you). The formula used by a BISHOP instead of "The Lord be with you", wherever this versicle occurs in Divine service. They are the words used by Christ to His APOSTLES on the first EASTER morning.

Pay, to discharge a debt, is through O.Fr. *paier*, from Lat. *pax*, peace, by way of *pacare*, to appease. The nautical *pay*, to cover with hot tar when caulking, represents O.Fr. *peier*, from Lat. *picare*, to cover with pitch (Lat. *pix*).

He who pays the piper calls the tune. The one who foots the bill has the control. The allusion is obvious.

Here's the devil to pay, and no pitch hot. *See under* DEVIL.

I'll pay him out. I'll be a match for him, I'll punish him.

To pay in his own coin. To treat him as he has treated you; to settle with him by the methods he himself employs; a TIT FOR TAT.

To pay off old scores. *See under* SCORE.

To pay on the nail. *See under* NAIL.

To pay out a rope is to let it out gradually.

To pay with the roll of the drum. Not to pay at all. No soldier can be arrested for debt when on the march.

How happy the soldier who lives on his pay,
And spends half-a-crown out of sixpence a day;
He cares not for justices, beadles, or bum,
But pays all his debts with the roll of the drum.
O'KEEFE.

Who's to pay the piper? Who is to pay the score? When a piper amused guests at inns or on the green he expected payment for his efforts.

You can put paid to that. You can treat it as finished, it's all over and done with. A phrase from the counting-house; when "Paid" is put to an account it is settled. Similarly **that's put paid to him** means "that's settled him".

Pay dirt. A mining term for ground which pays for working.

Payload. The goods or passengers carried in a ship, aeroplane, etc., which pay for their carriage, as opposed to crew and equipment, etc.

Paynim (pā′ nim), from the O.Fr. *paienime*, Lat. *paganismus*, a heathen, was the recognized chivalric term for a MOSLEM.

Peace. A Bill of Peace. A bill intended to secure relief from perpetual litigation. It is brought by one who wishes to establish and perpetuate a right which he claims, but which, from its nature, is controversial.

Justices of the Peace. *See under* JUSTICE.

Peace at any price. Lord Palmerston sneered at the QUAKER statesman John Bright, as a "peace-at-any-price man". *Cp.* CONCHY.

> Though not a "peace-at-any-price" man, I am not ashamed to say I am a peace-at-almost-any-price man.
>
> LORD AVEBURY: *The Use of Life*, xi (1894).

Peace Ballot. A national ballot (27 June 1935) organized by the "National Declaration Committee" under the chairmanship of Lord Cecil (closely linked with the League of Nations Union), on certain questions of peace and disarmament. Over $11\frac{1}{2}$ million votes were in favour of adherence to the League of Nations and over 10 million voted for a reduction in armaments. The ballot was misinterpreted by the AXIS powers as a sign of British weakness.

Peace in our time. The unfortunate phrase used by Prime Minister Neville Chamberlain, on his return from MUNICH, 30 September 1938. It comes from the versicle in Morning Prayer, "Give peace in our time, O Lord."

Peace Pledge Union. A body pledged to renounce war, organized by Canon Dick Sheppard of St. Martin-in-the-Fields in 1936.

Peace with honour. A phrase popularized by Lord Beaconsfield on his return from the Congress of Berlin (1878), when he said:

> Lord Salisbury and myself have brought you back peace—but a peace I hope with honour, which may satisfy our Sovereign and tend to the welfare of the country.

SHAKESPEARE has:

> We have made peace
> With no less honour to the Antiates
> Than shame to the Romans.
>
> *Coriolanus*, V, v.

The Kiss of Peace. *See* PAX.

The Perpetual Peace. The peace concluded 24 June 1502 between ENGLAND and SCOTLAND, whereby Margaret, daughter of Henry VII, was betrothed to James IV of Scotland; but the Scots invaded England in 1513! The name has been given to other treaties, as that between Austria and Switzerland in 1474, and between France and Switzerland in 1516.

The Queen's, or **King's Peace.** The peace of law-abiding subjects; originally the protection secured by the king to those employed on his business.

> To kill an alien, a Jew, or an outlaw, who are all under the king's peace or protection, is as much murder as to kill the most regular born Englishman.
>
> *Blackstone's Commentaries*, IV, xiv.

If you want peace, prepare for war. A translation of the Latin proverb, *Si vis pacem, para bellum*. It goes a step further than the advice given by POLONIUS to his son (*Hamlet*, I, iii), for you are told, whether you are "in a quarrel' or not, always bear yourself so that all possible opposers "may beware of thee".

To hold one's peace. To keep silent, to refrain from speaking.

To keep the peace. To refrain from disturbing the public peace, to prevent strife or commotion. Wrongdoers are sometimes bound over to keep the peace for a certain time by a magistrate, subject to entering into a recognizance.

Peacock. A peacock in his pride. A peacock with his tail fully displayed.

By the peacock! An obsolete oath which at one time was thought to be blasphemous. The fabled incorruptibility of the peacock's flesh caused the bird to be adopted as a type of the resurrection.

There is a story that when George III had partly recovered from one of his bouts of "insanity" his Ministers got him to read the King's speech, and he ended every sentence with the word *peacock*. The Minister who drilled him said that *peacock* was an excellent word for ending a sentence, only kings should not let subjects hear it, but should whisper it softly. The resulting pause at the close of each sentence had an excellent effect.

The Peacock's feather. An emblem of vain-glory, and in some Eastern countries a mark of rank.

As a literary term the expression is used of a borrowed ornament of style spatchcocked into the composition; the allusion being to the fable of the jay who decked herself out in a peacock's feathers, making herself an object of ridicule.

The peacock's tail is an emblem of an EVIL EYE, or an ever-vigilant traitor; hence the feathers are considered unlucky. *Cp.* ARGUS-EYED.

Peal. To ring a peal. Correctly speaking a set of bells is called a *ring* of bells and the sound made is a *peal*. Specifically, *to ring a peal* is to ring a series of CHANGES on a set of bells, although the expression is commonly used more loosely.

Pearls. Dioscorides and Pliny mention the belief that pearls are formed by drops of rain falling into oyster-shells while open; the raindrops thus received being hardened into pearls by some secretions of the animal. They are actually a secretion forming a coating and repeated so often that they attain considerable thickness, caused by the attempts of marine and fresh-water molluscs to get rid of a foreign object (*e.g.* a grain of sand or tiny parasitic worm).

According to HORACE (II *Satires*, iii, 239), Clodius, son of Æsop the tragedian, drew a pearl of great value from his ear, melted it in vinegar, and drank to the health of Cecilia Metella. This story is referred to by Valerius Maximus, Macrobius, and Pliny. *Cp.* CLEOPATRA AND HER PEARL.

A pearl of great price. Something highly treasured or of especial value. One of the doctrinal works of the MORMONS is called *The Pearl of Great Price.*

To cast pearls before swine. To offer something of a quality which the uncultured PHILISTINE is unable to appreciate; to offer one's "pearls of wisdom" to an unappreciative audience.

> Give not that which is holy unto the dogs, neither cast ye your pearls before swine.
> *Matt.* vii, 6.

The Pearl Coast. So the early Spanish explorers named the Venezuelan coast from Cumana to Trinidad; the islands off this coast were called the *Pearl Islands*. This area was the site of large pearl-fisheries.

Pearl Mosque. At Agra, India; built of white marble at the orders of Shah Jehan, who also ordered the more famous Taj Mahal in the same city. There is another Pearl Mosque at Delhi, which was Aurangzeb's private place of prayer.

Pearlies. The coster "kings" and "queens", "princes" and "princesses" of the LONDON boroughs, so named from their glittering attire studded with innumerable pearl buttons. Since the Festival of Britain (1951), there has been a Pearly King of London. Originally elected by the street-traders of London to safeguard their rights from interlopers and bullies, they now devote their efforts to collecting and working for charities.

Their tradition is an old one and they are a reminder of the more colourful London when barrow-boys were more prevalent than supermarkets. *See* COSTERMONGER.

Peasant Poet. John Clare (1793–1864), the son of a labourer, who began work as a herd boy at the age of seven, was so called. His first publication, *Poems Descriptive of Rural Life and Scenery*, 1820, attracted attention and *The Village Minstrel* followed in 1821. His unsuccessful *Shepherd's Calendar* appeared in 1827 and *The Rural Muse* in 1835. He drifted through various occupations and was dogged by poverty. Mental disturbances began in 1836 and he eventually died in Northampton Asylum. He was born at Helpston, Huntingdonshire and was there

buried. "Peasant Poet" is inscribed on his tombstone.

Peasants' Revolt. The name given to the English peasant risings of 1381 which were immediately occasioned by an unpopular poll-tax at a time when there was a growing spirit of social revolt. Its chief centre was south-eastern England, especially Kent and Essex. Wat Tyler's men beheaded the Archbishop of Canterbury (Sudbury) and temporarily held LONDON, and John Ball joined the Kentish rebels. King Richard II promised free pardon and redress of grievances (abolition of villeinage, etc.). Wat Tyler was slain by Walworth, the MAYOR of London, severe retribution followed, and the boy King's promises were not kept.

In Germany the *Peasants' Revolt* or *Peasant War* of 1524–1525 was caused by tyranny and oppression by the nobility and further stimulated by the seeming encouragement of religious reformers. Luther disowned the peasants and threw in his lot with the princes, and the risings were put down with great severity.

Peascod. Winter for shoeing, peascod for wooing. The allusion in the latter clause is to the custom of placing a peascod with nine peas in it on the door-lintel, under the notion that the first man who entered through the door would be the husband of the person who placed the peascodd. Another custom is alluded to by William Browne of Tavistock (1592–1643):

> The peascod greene oft with no little toyle
> Hee'd seeke for in the fattest, fertil'st soile,
> And rend it from the stalke to bring it to her
> And in her bosome for acceptance woo her.
> *Britannia's Pastorals*, II, s.

Pec. Old Eton slang for money. A contraction of Lat. *pecunia. See* PECUNIARY.

Peccavi. To cry peccavi. To acknowledge oneself in the wrong. Sir Charles Napier, in 1843, sent a preliminary despatch with the single word "Peccavi" (I have sinned, *i.e.* I have Sind) announcing his conquest by the victory of Miani.

Pecker. Keep you pecker up. As the mouth is in the head, *pecker* (the mouth) means the head; and to "keep your pecker up" means to keep your head up, or more familiarly, "keep your chin up", "never say die".

Peckham. All holiday at Peckham, *i.e.* no appetite, not peckish; a pun on the word *peck*, as "going to Bedfordshire" is a pun on the word *bed*.

Going to Peckham. Going to dinner.

Peckish. Hungry, or desirous of something to eat. "Peck" refers to fowls, etc., which peck their food.

Pecksniff. A canting hypocrite, who speaks homilies of morality, does the most heartless things "as a duty to society", and forgives wrongdoing in nobody but himself (Dickens, *Martin Chuzzlewit*). *Cp.* PODSNAP.

Pecos Bill (pe' kos). A cowboy of American legend who performed superhuman prodigies on the frontier in early days. One of his feats was to dig the Rio Grande river.

Pectoral Cross. *See* CRUX PECTORALIS.

Peculiar. A parish or group of parishes exempt from the jurisdiction of the ORDINARY of the diocese. There were many such in mediæval England, e.g. monastic peculiars, royal peculiars, archiepiscopal, and diocesan, peculiars, peculiars belonging to Orders, and cathedral peculiars. In 1832 there were still over 300 peculiars which were abolished between 1838 and 1850, the exceptions being cathedral peculiars, Westminster Abbey and those of the royal residences including the Chapel Royal of the Savoy. *See also* DEAN OF THE ARCHES; DEANS OF PECULIARS.

Court of Peculiars. In particular, a branch of the Court of ARCHES which had jurisdiction over the PECULIARS of the Archbishop of Canterbury.

The Peculiar People. Properly, the Jews, the "Chosen people". The title was also assumed by a London sect, the "Plumstead Peculiars", founded in 1838. They refuse medical, but not surgical aid and rely on the efficacy of prayer and on anointing with oil by the elders. The name is based on *Titus* ii, 14—"Purify unto himself a peculiar people".

Pecuniary (Lat. *pecuniarius* from *pecunia*, money). The word is ultimately from Lat. *pecus*, cattle, sheep, etc. Varro says that sheep were the ancient medium of barter and standard of value. Ancient coin was commonly marked with the image of an ox or sheep.

Pedagogue (Gr. *pais*, boy; *agein*, to lead). A "boy-leader", hence a schoolmaster—now usually one who is pompous and pedantic. In ancient Greece the *pedagogos* was a slave whose duty it was to attend his master's son whenever he left home.

Pedestal. To set on a pedestal. To idolize or to idealize. From the custom of showing reverence to figures of SAINTS and others set on pedestals.

Pedlar. This word for an itinerant vendor of small wares is not from Lat. *pedes*, feet, but is probably from *ped*, basket, in which his goods were carried. In Norwich, Ped-market was where women used to display eggs, butter, cheese, etc., in open hampers.

Pedlar's Acre. A portion of Lambeth Marsh bequeathed to the parish church of St. Mary, and possibly originally a "squatting-place" of pedlars. In the church is a window containing a representation of a pedlar and his dog and the story is that a pedlar bequeathed "his acre" to the church on the condition that he and his dog were commemorated in a window. It has been suggested that it is a REBUS on Chapman, the name of a benefactor. There is a similar representation in Swaffham Church, Norfolk, of one John Chapman, and a similar tradition persists there.

Pedlars' French. The jargon or CANT of thieves, rogues, and vagabonds. "French" was formerly widely used to denote anything or anyone that was foreign, and even Bracton uses the word "Frenchman" as a synonym of foreigner.

> Instead of Pedlars' French, gives him plain language.
>
> *Faithful Friends* (17th century), I, ii.

Peel. A fortified keep or tower, particularly one built in the 16th century along the border areas of ENGLAND and SCOTLAND as a defence against raids. It derives from Lat. *palus*, a stake. Perhaps the best known is the Peel on St. Patrick's Isle, off the Isle of Man, connected to the main island by a causeway. *See* MODDEY DHOO.

A Peel Parish. In the CHURCH OF ENGLAND, a district taken out of an existing parish which may with due formalities be constituted a new parish. So called from the fact that Sir Robert Peel was Prime Minister when the ACT OF PARLIAMENT (1843) authorizing such changes was passed.

Peeler. Slang for a policeman; first applied to the Irish constabulary founded by Sir Robert Peel when Chief Secretary for IRELAND (1812–1818), and later to the Metropolitan Police which he established in 1829 when Home Secretary. *Cp.* BOBBY; *see* ORANGE PEEL.

In the 16th century the word was applied to robbers, from *peel* (later *pill*), to plunder, strip of possessions, rob. Holinshed, in his *Scottish Chronicle* (1570) refers to Patrick Dunbar, who "delivered the countrie of these peelers". *Cp. also* Milton's *Paradise Regained*, IV, 136:

> That people ... who, once just,
> Frugal, and mild, and temperate, conquered well
> But govern ill the nations under yoke,
> Peeling their provinces, exhausted all
> By lust and rapine.

Peelites. Those CONSERVATIVES who supported and remained loyal to Sir Robert Peel at the time of the Repeal of the Corn Laws.

Among them were Aberdeen, Gladstone, Goulburn, Graham, and Sidney Herbert and they did not return to the Conservative party after the rift in 1846.

Peep-o'-Day Boys. The Irish PROTESTANT faction in ULSTER of the 1780s and 1790s; so called because they used to visit the houses of the DEFENDERS at "peep of day" searching for arms or plunder, etc. *Cp.* ORANGEMEN.

Peeping Tom of Coventry. *See* GODIVA, LADY.

Peers of the Realm. The five orders of DUKE, MARQUESS, EARL, VISCOUNT and BARON. The word peer is the Lat. *pares* (equals), and in feudal times all great vassals were held as equals.

The Twelve Peers of Charlemagne. *See* PALADINS.

Peewits' Pinch. The same as "BLACKTHORN WINTER", the short cold spell that usually occurs in MARCH, when peewits are about to begin nesting, and feel their "pinch" when frost and cold winds come upon them at this time. Peewits nest on the ground.

Peg. A square peg in a round hole. One who is doing (or trying to do) a job for which he is not suited; *e.g.* a BISHOP refereeing a prize-fight.

I am a peg too low. I am low-spirited, moody; I want another draught to cheer me up. Our Saxon ancestors used tankards with pegs inserted at equal intervals, so that when two or more drank from the same bowl no one might exceed his fair allowance (*cp.* IN MERRY PIN *under* PIN). We are told that St. DUNSTAN introduced the fashion to prevent brawling.

> Come, old fellow, drink down to your peg!
> But do not drink any farther, I beg.
> LONGFELLOW: *Golden Legend*, iv.

To peg a price. To fix or maintain a market price, as by buying, selling or subsidy.

To peg away at it. To stick at it persistently, often in spite of difficulties and discouragement. Probably derived from the use of the peg tankard.

To peg out. To die. From the game of cribbage where the game is ended by a player pegging out the last holes.

To take one down a peg. To take the conceit out of a braggart or pretentious person; to lower their self-esteem. The allusion is to a ship's colours, which used to be raised and lowered by pegs; the higher the colours are raised the greater the honour, and to take them down a peg would be to diminish the honour. An earlier explanation refers to the ancient practice of sharing drink from a pegged container down to one's allotted peg. *See above* I AM A PEG TOO LOW.

> Trepanned your party with intrigue,
> And took your grandees down a peg.
> BUTLER: *Hudibras*, II, ii.

Peg-leg. A wooden legged person; from the days when wooden legs were rods strapped at the knee.

Pegasus. The winged horse on which BELLEROPHON rode against the CHIMÆRA. When the MUSES contended with the daughters of Pieros, HELICON rose heavenward with delight; but Pegasus gave it a kick, stopped its ascent, and brought out of the mountain the soul-inspiring waters of HIPPO-CRENE; hence, the name is used for the inspiration of poetry.

> Then who so will with vertuous deeds assay
> To mount to heaven, on Pegasus must ride,
> And with sweete Poets verse be glorified.
> SPENSER: *Ruines of Time*, 425.

In World War II, the horse, with Bellerophon on his back, in pale blue on a maroon ground, was adopted as the insignia of all British Airborne troops.

Peine forte et dure (pān fort ā dūr). A species of torture applied to contumacious felons who refused to plead; it usually took the form of pressing the accused between boards until he accepted a trial by jury or died. Juliana Quick (1442), Anthony Arrowsmith (1598), Walter Calverly (1605), and Major Strangeways (1657) suffered death in this way. Even in 1741 this torture was invoked at the Cambridge assizes. It was abolished in 1772. (Lat. *pœna*, punishment; *fortis et dura*, intense and severe.)

Peking Man (*Sinanthropus pekinensis*). The name given to remains of a skull found near Peking in 1929 which in many respects showed resemblances to that of PITHECAN-THROPUS *erectus* and held as being intermediate between Java and NEANDERTHAL MAN.

Pelagians. Heretical followers of the British monk Pelagius (a Latinized form of his Welsh name *Morgan*, the sea). They denied the doctrine of ORIGINAL SIN (*see under* SIN) or the taint of ADAM, and maintained that we have power of ourselves to receive or reject the GOSPEL. They were opposed by St. AU-GUSTINE and condemned by Pope Innocent I in 417 and again by Pope Zosimus in 418.

Pelf. Filthy Pelf. Money; usually with a contemptuous implication—as we speak of "filthy lucre", or "Who steals my purse steals trash".

The word is from O.Fr. *pelfre*, connected with our *pilfer*, and was originally used of stolen or pilfered goods, ill-gotten gains.

Pelican. In Christian art, a symbol of charity; also an emblem of Jesus Christ, by "whose blood we are healed". St. JEROME gives the story of the pelican restoring its young ones destroyed by serpents, and his own salvation by the blood of Christ. The popular fallacy that pelicans feed their young with their blood arose from the fact that the parent bird transfers macerated food from the large bag under its bill to its young. The correct term for the heraldic representation of the bird in this act is **a pelican in her piety,** *piety* having the classical meaning of filial devotion.

The mediæval BESTIARY tells us that the pelican is very fond of its brood, but, when they grow, they often rebel against the male bird and provoke his anger, so that he kills them; the mother returns to the nest in three days, sits on the dead birds, pours her blood over them, revives them, and they feed on her blood.

> Then sayd the Pellycane,
> When my byrdis be slayne
> With my bloude I them reuyue [revive].
> Scripture doth record
> The same dyd our Lord,
> And rose from death to lyue.
>
> SKELTON: *Armoury of Birdis.*

The Pelican State. Louisiana, U.S.A., which has a pelican in its device. Pelicans are plentiful on its coasts.

Pelion (pē' li on). **Heaping Pelion upon Ossa.** Adding difficulty to difficulty, embarrassment to embarrassment, etc. When the giants tried to scale HEAVEN, they placed Mount Pelion upon Mount Ossa, two peaks in Thessaly, for a scaling ladder (*Odyssey,* XI, 315).

Pell-mell. Headlong; in reckless confusion. From the players of PALL-MALL, who rushed heedlessly to strike the ball.

Pelleas, Sir. One of the Knights of the ROUND TABLE, famed for his great strength. He is introduced in Spenser's *The Faerie Queene* (VI, xii) as going after the BLATANT BEAST. *See also* Tennyson's *Pelleas and Ettare.*

Pells, Clerk of the Pells. An officer of the EXCHEQUER, whose duty it was to make entries of receipts and disbursements on the *pells* or parchment rolls. The office was abolished in 1834 (O.Fr. *pel, peau,* skin or hide).

Pelmanism. A system of mind and memory training originated by W.J. Ennever in the closing years of the 19th century, and so called because it is an easy name to remember. Owing to its very extensive advertising, the verb *to pelmanize,* meaning to obtain good results by training the memory, was coined. It has also given its name to a card game, popular with children, which largely depends on mental concentration and memory.

Pelops. Son of TANTALUS, and father of Atreus and Thyestes. He was king of Pisa in Elis, and was cut to pieces and served as food to the gods. The Morea was called *Peloponnesus,* "the island of Pelops", from this mythical king.

The ivory shoulder of Pelops. The distinguishing or distinctive mark of anyone. The tale is that DEMETER ate the shoulder of Pelops when it was served by TANTALUS; when the gods put the body back into the cauldron to restore it to life, this portion was lacking, whereupon Demeter supplied one of ivory.

Pen is the Lat. *penna,* a feather, both words being derived from the Sanskrit root *pet-* to fly. *Pet-* gave Sansk. *Patra* (feather); this became Lat. *penna* (Eng. *pen*), and in O. Teut. *fethro* (Ger. *Feder;* Dut. *veder;* Eng. *feather*). In O.Fr. *penne* meant both *feather* and *pen,* but in Mod. Fr. it is restricted to the long wing- and tail-feathers and to heraldic plumes on crests, while *pen* is *plume.* Thus the French and English usage has been vice versa, English using *plume* in HERALDRY, French using *penne,* the English writing implement being a *pen* and the French, *plume.*

Pen-name. A pseudonym. *See* NOM DE PLUME.

Penalty envelopes. In the U.S.A., envelopes franked for official use by government departments like those stamped O.H.M.S. (On Her Majesty's Service) in Britain. "Penalty" refers to the penalty for their misuse.

Penates. *See* DII PENATES; LARES AND PENATES.

Pencil. Originally a painter's brush, and still used of very fine paint-brushes, from Lat. *penicillum,* a paint-brush, diminutive of *peniculus,* a brush, which itself is a diminutive of *penis,* a tail. When the modern pencil came into use in the early 17th century it was known as a *dry pencil* or a *pencil with black lead.*

Knight of the Pencil. A bookmaker; a reporter; also anyone who makes his living by scribbling.

Pencil of rays. All the rays of light that issue from one point or can be found at one point; so called because a representation of them has the appearance of a pointed pencil.

Pendant, Pennant, Pennon. *Pennon* (Lat. *penna,* feather), denoting the small pointed or swallow-tailed flag borne on the lance of a knight, and later adopted by Lancer regiments, led to the custom of noblemen flying their banners or pennons from the masthead when afloat. In the Royal Navy it came to be called a *pendant* (Lat. *pendere,* to hang) and it is applied to the broad pendant of a commodore and to the long narrow flag flown at the masthead of a warship. There are also special pendants used in naval signalling. It is pronounced *pennant* and this latter and more general spelling arose from a fusion of *pennon* and *pendant*. A pennant, sometimes called a *streamer* and also a *coach-whip*, is taken as the "whip" with which the English Admiral Blake nullified Van Tromp's boast to sweep the English from the seas, when he hoisted a BROOM at the masthead during the Dutch War of 1652–1653. The story is almost certainly legendary.

Pendente lite (pen den′ ti lī te) (Lat.). Pending the trial; while the suit is going on.

Pendragon. A title conferred on several British chiefs in times of great danger when they were invested with supreme power, especially (in ARTHURIAN ROMANCES) to UTHER Pendragon, father of King ARTHUR. The word is Welsh *pen*, head, and *dragon* (referring to the war-chief's dragon standard). It corresponded to the Roman *dux bellorum*.

Geoffrey of Monmouth relates that when Aurelius, the British king, was poisoned by Ambron, during the invasion of Pascentius, son of Vortigern, "there appeared a star of wonderful magnitude and brightness, darting forth a ray, at the end of which was a globe of fire in the form of a dragon, out of whose mouth issued forth two rays; one of which seemed to stretch itself beyond the extent of Gaul, the other towards the Irish Sea, and ended in seven lesser rays" (Bk. VIII, ch. xiv). Uther, brother of Aurelius and his predestined successor, ordered two golden dragons to be made, one of which he presented to Winchester Cathedral, and the other "to be carried along with him to his wars", whence he was called Uther Pendragon.

Penelope (pė nel′ ō pi). The wife of ULYSSES and mother of TELEMACHUS in Homeric legend. She was a model of all the domestic virtues.

The Web of Penelope. A work "never ending, still beginning"; never done, but ever in hand. Penelope, according to HOMER, was pestered with suitors at Ithaca while ULYSSES was absent at the siege of TROY. To relieve herself of their importunities, she promised to make a choice of one as soon as she had finished a shroud for her father-in-law. Every night she unravelled what she had done in the day, and so deferred making any choice until Ulysses returned and slew the suitors.

Penetralia (pen e trā′li à) (Lat., the innermost parts). The private rooms of a house; the secrets of a family. Properly, the part of a Roman TEMPLE to which the priest alone had access, where the sacred images were housed, the responses of the ORACLES made, and the sacred mysteries performed. The HOLY OF HOLIES was the *penetralia* of the Jewish Temple.

Penguin. The name of this flightless bird is applied to a training aircraft used on the ground; also, jocularly, to a member of the Women's Royal Air Force, a "FLAPPER" who does not fly. *Cp.* KIWI.

Penitential Psalms. The seven psalms expressive of contrition (vi, xxxii, xxxviii, li, cii, cxxx, cxliii). From TIME IMMEMORIAL they have all been used at the ASH WEDNESDAY services; the first three at MATINS, the 51st at the Commination, and the last three at Evensong.

Pennant, Pennon. See PENDANT.

Pennsylvania Dutch (Ger. *Deutsche(r)*, German). The name given to the German settlers in Pennsylvania who first began to arrive in 1683 and whose immigration was actively promoted by William Penn. A steady influx continued through much of the 18th century—in some parts a German patois is still spoken—and the influence of their culture and industry has been notable. *See* MENNONITES; TUNKERS.

Penny (O.E. *pening*). The English coin, before decimalization (*see* DECIMAL CURRENCY) worth one-twelfth of a SHILLING, was originally made of SILVER and was used by the Anglo-Saxons. A few silver pennies are still coined as MAUNDY MONEY, but they were last struck for general circulation in the reign of Charles II. A few GOLD pennies (worth 20 silver pennies) were struck in the reign of Henry III. The first English COPPER penny was made in 1797 by Boulton at the Soho Mint, Birmingham, hence *a copper* as a common synonym for a penny. In 1860 bronze coins were substituted for copper.

The plural *pennies* is used of the number of coins and *pence* of the value. A penny is sometimes used to denote low-value coins of other nations, such as in *Luke* xx, 24, where it stands for the Roman *denarius* from which the symbol *d* for a penny is derived. (*See also* P.)

A penny for your thoughts! Tell me what you are thinking about. Addressed humorously to one in a BROWN STUDY. The phrase occurs in Heywood's *Proverbs* (1546).

A penny saved is a penny gained, or **earned,** etc. An old adage intended to encourage thrift in the young.

A pretty penny. A considerable sum of money, an unpleasantly large sum.

He has got his pennyworth. He has got good value for his money; sometimes said of one who has received a good drubbing.

In for a penny, in for a pound. Once involved the matter must be carried through whatever obstacles or difficulties may arise—there can be no drawing back.

In penny numbers. In small amounts, or little by little. From the stories eked out in serial form in the penny periodicals of former days.

No penny, no paternoster. No pay, no work; you'll get nothing for nothing. The allusion is to pre-REFORMATION days, when priests would not perform services without payment.

Not a penny to bless himself with. *See* BLESS.

Penny plain, twopence coloured. A phrase originating in the shop of a maker of toy theatres in East London. The scenery and characters for the plays to be "acted" were printed on sheets of thick paper ready to be cut out, these being sold at 1*d*. if plain, 2*d*. if coloured.

Penny wise and pound foolish. Said of one who is in danger of "spoiling the ship for a ha'porth of tar". One who is thrifty in small matters and careless over large ones is said to be *penny wise*.

Take care of the pence and the pounds will take care of themselves. An excellent piece of advice, which Chesterfield records in his Letter to his son (5 February 1750) as having been given by "old Mr. Lowndes, the famous Secretary of the Treasury, in the reigns of King William, Queen Anne, and George I". Chesterfield adds:

> To this maxim, which he not only preached, but practised, his two grandsons, at this time, owe the very considerable fortunes that he left them.

The saying was parodied in the *Advice to a Poet*, which goes, "Take care of the *sense* and the *sounds* will take care of themselves".

To turn an honest penny. To earn an honest penny by working for it.

Penny-a-liner. The old name for a contributor to the newspapers who was not on the staff and was paid a penny a line. As it was in his interest to "pad" as much as possible, the word is still used in a contemptuous way for a second-rate writer or newspaper HACK.

Penny-dreadful, or **-horrible.** A cheap boy's paper full of crude situations and highly coloured excitement. Still used of such trashy periodicals although they are no longer available for a penny. A "shilling shocker" was a similar but more expensive publication.

Penny-father. A miser, a penurious person who "husbands" his pence.

> To nothing fitter can I thee compare
> Than to the son of some rich penny-father,
> Who having now brought on his end with care,
> Leaves to his son all he had heap'd together.
> DRAYTON: *Idea*, X, i.

Penny farthing. The nickname of what was also called the "ordinary" bicycle that came into vogue in 1872; the front wheel being sometimes as much as 5 ft. in diameter, while the rear was only 12 in., hence the name. The drive was on the front wheel, the seat being directly above it and slightly back from the perpendicular of the axle. The "Safety" bicycle, much on the lines of the usual cycle of today, was introduced in 1885.

Penny fish. A name given to the JOHN DORY because of the round spots on each side left by St. PETER'S FINGERS.

Penny gaff. A concert or crude music-hall entertainment for which the entrance charge was one penny. *See* GAFF.

> My grandfather ran his own penny-gaff — a very famous actor, who might have took the stage with the best if he'd only been known about.
> EDEN PHILPOTTS: *The Broom Squires*, ch.iii.

Penny-leaf. A country name for the navelwort or wall pennywort (*Cotyledon umbilicus*), from its round leaves.

Penny-pies. A name given to the moneywort (*Sibthorpia europœa*), and to the PENNY-LEAF.

Penny readings. Parochial entertainments consisting of readings, music, etc., for which one penny admission was charged.

Penny weddings. Weddings formerly in vogue among the poor in SCOTLAND and WALES at which each guest paid a small sum of money not exceeding a shilling. After defraying expenses, the residue went to the newly-weds to aid in furnishing their home.

> Vera true, vera true. We'll have a' to pay ... a sort of penny-wedding it will prove, where all men contribute to the young folk's maintenance.
> SCOTT: *The Fortunes of Nigel*, xxvii.

Pennyroyal. A species of mint (*Mentha pulegium*). It is a corruption of *pulyole ryale*, from Lat. *pulegium*, flea-bane (so called from *pulex*, a flea, because it was supposed to be harmful to fleas), and Anglo-French *real*, royal. The French call the herb *pouliot*, also from Lat. *pulegium*.

Pennyweight. 24 grains, *i.e.* one-hundred-and-fortieth of a pound TROY; so called because it was formerly the same proportion of the old TOWER POUND (*i.e.* 22½ grains), which was the exact weight of a new SILVER penny. The abbreviation is dwt., *denarius* weight. *Cp.* PENNY.

Pension. Etymologically, that which is weighed out (Lat. *pensionem*, payment; from *pendere*, to weigh; also *to pay*, because payment was originally weighed out. *Cp.* our *pound*, both a weight and a piece of money).

Pension, a boarding house (to live *en pension, i.e.* as a boarder), though now pronounced and treated as French (pon si on), was, in the 17th century, ordinary English; this use arose because *pension* was the term for any regular payment made for services rendered such as for board and lodging.

Pensioner. The counterpart at Cambridge of the Oxford COMMONER, *i.e.* one who pays for his own commons.

At the INNS OF COURT, the *pensioner* is the officer who collects the periodical payments made by the members for the upkeep of the Inn.

Chelsea Pensioner. The popular name for the In-Pensioners of the Royal Hospital, Chelsea, founded by Charles II at the instigation of Sir Stephen Fox, the Paymaster General of the Forces. It is maintained for selected veterans of the regular army and was opened in 1692. The legend that Nell GWYN suggested the foundation is apparently imaginary.

Gentlemen Pensioners. The old name for the members of the Honourable Corps of GENTLEMEN AT ARMS.

The Pensioner, or **Pensionary Parliament.** The LONG PARLIAMENT or CAVALIER PARLIAMENT of Charles II (1661–1679), so called from the bribes or pensions accepted by many of its members and noted for the growth of party faction.

Pentacle. A five-pointed star, or five-sided figure, used in sorcery as a TALISMAN against WITCHES, etc., and sometimes worn as a folded headdress of fine linen, as a defence against demons in the act of conjuration. It is also called the *Wizard's Foot*, and is supposed to typify the five senses, though as it resolves itself into three triangles, its efficacy may spring from its being a triple symbol of the TRINITY.

It is also a candlestick with five branches. *Cp.* SOLOMON'S SEAL.

> And on her head, lest spirits should invade,
> A pentacle, for more assurance, laid.
> ROSE: *Orlando Furioso*, III, xxi.

The Holy Pentacles numbered forty-four, of which seven were consecrated to each of the planets SATURN, JUPITER, MARS, and the SUN; five to both VENUS and MERCURY; and six to the MOON. The divers figures were enclosed in a double circle, containing the name of God in Hebrew, and other mystical words.

Pentagon. A vast five-sided building erected in Washington, D.C., to house government officials. It now houses the U.S. Department of Defense, and the word Pentagon is a synonym for the official American attitude in military matters.

Pentameron. A collection of fifty folk tales modelled on the DECAMERON and written in the Neapolitan dialect by Giambattista Basile (*c.* 1575–1632) and first published at Naples in 1637. The stories were supposed to have been told by ten old women during five days, to a Moorish slave who had taken the place of the true princess.

The Pentameron (1837) of Walter Savage Landor (1775–1864) was a collection of five long imaginary conversations.

Pentameter (pen tăm' i tẽr). In prosody, a line of five feet, DACTYLS or spondees divided by a cæsura into two parts of two-and-a-half feet each—the line used in alternation with the HEXAMETER in Latin elegiac verse. The name is sometimes wrongly applied to the English five-foot IAMBIC line.

> In the hexameter rises the fountain's silvery
> column,
> In the pentameter aye falling in melody back.
> COLERIDGE: *Example of Elegiac Metre*.

Pentateuch (pen' ta tūk). The first five books of the OLD TESTAMENT, anciently attributed to MOSES (Gr. *penta*, five; *teuchos*, a tool, book).

The Samaritan Pentateuch. The Hebrew text of the Pentateuch as preserved by the Samaritans; said to date from the 4th century B.C.

Pentathlon. An athletic contest of five events, usually the jump, javelin throw, 200-metre race, discus throw, and 1,500-metre flat race. In the ancient OLYMPIC GAMES the contest consisted of running, jumping, throwing the discus and javelin, and wrestling.

Pentecost (Gr. *pentecoste* fiftieth). The festival held by the Jews on the fiftieth day after the second day of the PASSOVER; our WHIT-SUNDAY.

Pentecostal Churches. PROTESTANT sects associated with manifestations of the gift of tongues such as had occurred at PENTECOST (*see Acts* ii, 1–4), and evangelical and healing campaigns.

Pentecostals. In mediæval England, offerings made to the parish priest at WHITSUN-TIDE were called *Pentecostals*, or *Whitsun-farthings*. The term is also used of offerings paid by the parish church to the cathedral of the diocese. *Cp.* DOWELLING MONEY; PETER'S PENCE; SMOKE-FARTHINGS.

Penthesilea. Queen of the AMAZONS who, in the post-Homeric legends, fought for TROY; she was slain by ACHILLES. Hence any strong, commanding woman. Sir Toby Belch in SHAKESPEARE's *Twelfth Night* (II, iii) calls Maria by this name.

Peony. According to fable, so called from Pæon, the physician who cured the wounds received by the gods in the Trojan war. The seeds were, at one time, worn round the neck as a charm against the powers of darkness.

> About an Infant's neck hang Peonie,
> It cures Alcydes cruell maladie.
> SYLVESTER: *Du Bartas*, I, iii, 712.

People. Chosen People. The Israelites, the Jews.

The good, or **little people.** FAIRIES, ELVES, etc.

People's Charter. *See* CHARTISM.

Pepin the Short. *See* SHORT.

Pepper. To pepper one well. To give one a good basting or thrashing; also to sprinkle with pellets or shot.

To take pepper i' the nose. To take offence. The French say, *La moutarde lui monte au nez.*

> Take your pepper in the nose, you mar our sport.
> MIDDLETON: *The Spanish Gipsy*, IV, iii.

When your daughter is stolen, close Pepper Gate. The equivalent of "locking the stable door when the horse has bolted". Pepper Gate used to be on the east side of the city of Chester. It is said that the mayor's daughter eloped and the mayor ordered the gate to be shut.

Pepper-and-salt. A cloth mixture of light and dark wools making a pattern of light and dark dots.

Peppercorn rent. A nominal rent. A peppercorn is of very slight value and is a token rental; virtually free possession without the ownership of the freehold.

Cowper makes a figurative use of the custom.

> True. While they live, the courtly laureate pays
> His quit-rent ode, his pepper-corn of praise.
> *Table-talk*, 110.

Pepperpot. A stew of tripe, dumplings, and vegetables originating in Philadelphia; also a celebrated West Indian dish of cassareep, fish, vegetables (chiefly the unripe pods of the okra) and chillies.

Per contra (Lat.). A commercial term for "on the opposite side of the account". Used also of arguments, etc.

Per saltum (Lat., by a leap). A promotion or degree given without going through the usual stages; as the ordination of a man to the priesthood who is not yet a deacon. Such ordinations, now prohibited, were common in earlier times.

> For the same reason, those that are advanced by degrees are less envied than those that are advanced suddenly, and "per saltum".
> BACON: *Essays (Of Envy).*

Perambulator. A wooden wheel which, when pushed along by a man on foot, records exactly the distance traversed. Such apparatuses were used by the employees of John Cary in the production of the first accurate *Itinerary of the Great Roads of England and Wales* (1798). The name, usually abbreviated "pram", has been attached to the vehicle in which babies are taken for walks.

Perceforest (pĕrs' for est). An early 14th-century French prose romance (said to be the longest in existence), belonging to the Arthurian cycle, but mingling with it the ALEXANDER romance. After Alexander's war in India, he comes to England, of which he makes Perceforest, one of his knights, king. The romance tells how Perceforest establishes the Knights of the Franc Palais, how his grandson brings the GRAIL to England, and includes many popular tales, such as that of the SLEEPING BEAUTY.

Percival, Sir. The Knight of the ROUND TABLE who, according to Malory's *Morte d'Arthur* (and Tennyson's *Idylls of the King*) finally won a sight of the Holy GRAIL. He was the son of Sir Pellinore and brother of Sir Lamerocke. In the earlier French romances (based probably on the MABINOGION and other CELTIC originals) he has no connexion with the Grail, but here (as in the English also) he sees the lance dripping with blood, and the severed head surrounded with blood in a dish. The French version of the romance is by Chrétien de Troyes (12th century), which formed the basis of Sebastian Evans's *The High History of the Holy Graal* (1893). The German version, *Parsifal* or *Parzival*, was written some 50 years later by Wolfram von Eschenbach and it is principally on this version that Wagner drew for his opera, *Parsifal* (1882).

Percy. When Malcolm III of SCOTLAND invaded ENGLAND and reduced the castle of Alnwick, Robert de Mowbray brought to him the keys of the castle suspended on his lance; and handing them from the wall, thrust his lance into the king's eye; from which circumstance, the tradition says, he received the name of "Pierce-eye", which has ever since been borne by the Dukes of Northumberland.

> This is all a fable. The Percies are descended from a great Norman baron, who came over with William, and who took his name from his castle and estate in Normandy.
> SCOTT: *Tales of a Grandfather*, iv.

Percy's Reliques. The famous collection of old ballads and poems published as *Reliques of Ancient English Poetry* by Thomas Percy in 1765. He became Bishop of Dromore in 1782 and died in 1811. He was encouraged in his project by Shenstone, Johnson, Garrick and others, and Scott acknowledged his debt to Percy's work: "To read and to remember was in this instance the same thing, and henceforth I overwhelmed my schoolfellows, and all who would hearken to me, with tragical recitations from the ballads of Percy."

Perdita. In SHAKESPEARE's *A Winter's Tale*, the daughter of Leontes and Hermione of Sicily. She was abandoned by order of her father, and put in a vessel which drifted to "the sea-coast of Bohemia" where the infant was discovered by a shepherd, who brought her up as his own daughter. In time, FLORIZEL, the son and heir of the Bohemian King Polixenes, fell in love with the supposed shepherdess. The match was forbidden by Polixenes and the young lovers fled to Sicily. Here the story is cleared up, and all ends happily in the restoration of Perdita to her parents, and her marriage with Florizel.

Mrs. Robinson, the actress and mistress of George IV when Prince of Wales, was specially successful in the part of Perdita, by which name she came to be known, the Prince being known as Florizel.

Perdrix, toujours perdrix (pâr′ drē-too zhoor pâr′ drē). Too much of the same thing. According to Horace Walpole, the confessor of one of the French kings reproved him for conjugal infidelity, and was asked by the king what he liked best. "Partridge", replied the priest, and the king ordered him to be served with partridge every day, till he quite loathed the sight of his favourite dish. When the king eventually visited him, and hoped he had been well served, the confessor replied, "*Mais oui, perdrix, toujours perdrix.*" "Ah! ah!", replied the amorous monarch, "and one mistress is all very well, but not '*perdrix, toujours perdrix*'."

Soup for dinner, soup for supper, and soup for breakfast again.

FARQUHAR: *The Inconstant*, V, ii.

Père Lachaise (pâr la shāz). This great Parisian cemetery is on the site of a religious settlement founded by the JESUITS in 1626, and later enlarged by Louis XIV's confessor, Père Lachaise. After the Revolution, the grounds were laid out as a cemetery and were first used in 1804. It was here that the Communards made their last stand in 1871.

Peregrine Falcon. A falcon of wide distribution, formerly held in great esteem for hawking, and so called (13th century) because taken when on passage or *peregrination*, from the breeding place, instead of straight off the nest, as was the case with most others (Lat. *peregrinus*, a foreigner, one coming from foreign parts). The hen is the *falcon* of falconers; the cock the *tercel. See* HAWK.

The word *peregrine* was formerly used as synonymous with *pilgrim*, and (adjectivally) for one travelling about.

Perestroika (Russ. restructuring). A policy, linked with GLASNOST, much publicized since 1986 when it became Mikhail Gorbachev's intent to introduce economic and political reform and allow greater freedom of expression, which included the publication of formerly banned books. Gorbachev became President and Communist Party Leader in the autumn of 1988.

Referring to the differences within his own politburo, he said, "Every member of our leadership is deeply committed to the cause of perestroika."

Daily Telegraph, 23 May 1988.

Perfect. Perfect number. One of which the sum of all its divisors exactly measures itself, as 6, the divisors of which are 1, 2, 3=6. These are very scarce; indeed, from 1 to 40 million there are only five, viz., 6; 28; 496; 8,128 and 33,550,336.

Perfect rhyme is a rhyme of two words spelled or pronounced alike but with different meanings, as "rain" and "reign", "thyme" and "time".

Perfectibilist. See ILLUMINATI.

Perfectionists. Members of a communistic sect formed by J.H. Noyes (1811–1886) in Vermont about 1834, and removed by him and settled at Oneida, New York, 1847–1848. Its chief features were that the community was held to be one family, mutual criticism and public opinion took the place of government, and wives were—theoretically, at least—held in common, till 1879, when, owing to opposition, this was abandoned. In 1881 the sect, which had prospered exceedingly through its thrift and industry, voluntarily dissolved and was organized as a joint-stock company.

Perfide Albion. See under ALBION.

Perfume means simply "from smoke" (Lat. *per fumum*), the first perfumes having been obtained by the combustion of aromatic woods and gums. Their original use was in sacrifices to counteract the offensive odours of burning flesh.

Peri (pē′ ri). Originally, a beautiful but malevolent sprite of Persian myth, one of a class which was responsible for comets, eclipses, failure of crops, etc.; in later times applied to delicate, gentle, fairy-like beings, begotten by fallen spirits who direct with a wand the pure in mind the way to HEAVEN. These lovely creatures, according to the KORAN, are under the sovereignty of EBLIS; and MOHAMMED was sent for their conversion, as well as for that of man.

The name used sometimes to be applied to any beautiful girl.

Paradise and the Peri. The second tale in Moore's *Lalla Rookh*. The Peri laments her expulsion from HEAVEN, and is told she will be readmitted if she will bring to the gate of heaven the "gift most dear to the Almighty". After a number of unavailing offerings she brought a guilty old man, who wept with repentance, and knelt to pray. The Peri offered the Repentant Tear, and the gates flew open.

Perillus and the Brazen Bull. *See under* INVENTORS.

Perilous Castle. The castle of "the good" Lord Douglas was so called in the reign of Edward I, because DOUGLAS destroyed several English garrisons stationed there, and vowed to be revenged on anyone who should dare to take possession of it. Scott calls it "Castle Dangerous" (*see* Introduction of *Castle Dangerous*).

Peripatetic School (per i pà tet' ik). The school or system of philosophy founded by ARISTOTLE, who used to walk about (Gr. *peri*, about; *patein*, to walk) as he taught his disciples in the covered walk of the Lyceum. This colonnade was called the *peripatos*.

Periphrasis (pe rif' rà sis). A roundabout or long-winded form of expression (Gr. *peri*, around, about; *phrasis*, speech). A fair example is: "Persons prejudicial to the public peace may be assigned by administrative process to definite places of residence', *i.e.* breakers of the law may be sent to gaol.

Perish the thought! Do not entertain such an idea for a moment! A quotation from Colley Cibber's version of SHAKESPEARE'S *Richard III*, V, v.

Periwinkle. The plant name is from Lat. *vincire*, to bind around. It is a trailing plant. In Italy it used to be wreathed round dead infants and was thus called *fiore di morto*.

The sea-snail of this name was called in O.E. *pinewinkle*, the first syllable probably being cognate with Lat. *pina*, a mussel, and *winkle* from O.E. *wincel*, a corner, with reference to its much convoluted shell.

Perk. Possibly allied to *perch*; also, in the plural, a contraction of "perquisites".

To perk up. To get more lively, to feel better.

Permissive Society. A term widely used in Britain in the 1960s to denote the increasingly tolerant and liberal attitudes in society which tend to blur the distinctions between right and wrong. Gambling clubs, strip clubs, the legalizing of homosexual practices between "consenting adults", and the growing use of "bad language" and obscenities in publications, in the theatre and on television, are all evidences. The borderline between permissiveness and decadence is not always apparent. *See* AVANT GARDE; NEW MORALITY.

> There is nothing either good or bad, but thinking makes it so.
>
> SHAKESPEARE: *Hamlet*, II, ii.

Perpetual Motion. The term applied to some theoretical force that will move a machine for ever of itself—a mirage which holds attractions for some minds much as did the search for the PHILOSOPHER'S STONE, the ELIXIR OF LIFE, and the FOUNTAIN OF (perpetual) YOUTH. According to the laws of thermodynamics it is impossible.

Persecutions, The Ten Great. According to Orosius: (1) under Nero, A.D. 64; (2) Domitian, 95; (3) Trajan, 98–117; (4) Marcus Aurelius, 177; (5) Septimius Severus, 193–211; (6) Maximinus Thrax, 235; (7) Decius, 250; (8) Valerian, 258; (9) Aurelian, 272; (10) Diocletian, 303–305. In fact neither Trajan nor Severus were active persecutors.

These were all persecutions of Christians, but Christians persecuted each other before they slowly learned toleration. *See* ALBIGENSES; BARTHOLOMEW, MASSACRE OF ST.; DRAGONNADES; HUGUENOT; INQUISITION; WALDENSIANS; etc.

Jews, particularly, have suffered persecution for religious and other reasons, the worst of all being perpetrated by the NAZI régime, when possibly some 10 million were exterminated. Political persecutions have been common through the ages and in modern times totalitarian and Communist countries have relied on this weapon.

Persephone. *See* PROSERPINA.

Persepolis. The capital of the ancient Persian empire. It was situated some 35 miles N.E. of Shiraz. The palaces and other public buildings were some miles from the city and were approached by magnificent flights of steps.

Perseus. In Greek legend, the son of ZEUS and DANAË. He and his mother were set adrift in a chest but rescued by the intervention of Zeus. He was brought up by King Polydectes, who, wishing to secure DANAË, got rid of him by encouraging him in the almost hopeless task of obtaining the head of the MEDUSA. With the help of the gods, he was successful, and with the head (which turned all that looked on it into stone) he rescued

ANDROMEDA, and later metamorphosed Polydectes and his guests to stone.

Before his birth, an ORACLE had foretold that Acrisius, father of Danaë, would be slain by Danaë's son (hence Perseus being originally cast adrift to perish). This came to pass, for while taking part in the games at Larissa, Perseus accidentally slew his grandfather with a discus.

Person. From Lat. *persona*, which meant originally a mask worn by actors (perhaps from *per sonare*, to sound through), and later transferred to the character or personage represented by the actor (*cp.* our *dramatis personæ*), and so to any definite character, at which stage the word was adopted in English through O.Fr. *persone*.

Confounding the Persons. The heresy of Sabellius (*see* SABELLIANISM), who declared that Father, Son, and Holy Ghost were but three names, aspects, or manifestations of one God, the orthodox doctrine being that of the ATHANASIAN CREED:

> We worship one God in Trinity, and Trinity in Unity; Neither confounding the Persons, nor dividing the Substance (*Neque confundentes personas, neque substantiam separantes*).

Persona grata (Lat.). An acceptable person; one liked. When a diplomatic representative becomes no longer acceptable to the government to which he is accredited he is no longer *persona grata*, which virtually requests his recall. *Persona non grata* is the reverse of *persona grata*.

Perth. The Five Articles of Perth (1618) were imposed on the CHURCH OF SCOTLAND by James VI and I, enjoining kneeling at communion; the observance of CHRISTMAS, GOOD FRIDAY, EASTER, and PENTECOST; confirmation; communion for the dying; and early baptism of infants. They were ratified by the Scottish Parliament, 4 August 1621, called BLACK SATURDAY, and condemned by the General Assembly at Glasgow in 1638.

Peru. From China to Peru. From one end of the world to the other; world-wide. Equivalent to the biblical "from Dan to Beersheba". The phrase comes from the opening of Johnson's *Vanity of Human Wishes:*

> Let observation with extensive view
> Survey mankind from China to Peru.

Boileau (*Sat.* viii, 3) had previously written:

> De Paris au Pérou, du Japon jusqu'à Rome.

Peruvian Bark, CHINCHONA bark, called also *Jesuit's Bark*, because it was introduced into Spain by the JESUITS. "Quinine", from the same tree, is called by the Indians *quinquina*.

Petard. Hoist with his own petard. Beaten with his own weapons, caught in his own trap; involved in the danger intended for others, as were some designers of instruments of torture. *See under* INVENTORS. The petard was a thick iron engine of war, filled with gunpowder, and fastened to gates, barricades, etc., to blow them up. The danger was lest the engineer who fired the petard should be blown up by the explosion.

> Let it work;
> For 'tis sport, to have the engineer
> Hoist with his own petard; and it shall go hard
> But I will delve one yard below their mines,
> And blow them at the moon.
> SHAKESPEARE: *Hamlet*, III, iv.

Pétaud (pā' tō). **'Tis the court of King Pétaud, where everyone is master.** There is no order or discipline at all. In France in earlier times King Pétaud (Lat. *peto*, to beg) was the name jokingly given by beggars to their chief, but who was without any authority.

Peter. St. Peter. The patron saint of fishermen, being himself a fisherman; the "Prince of the APOSTLES". His feast is kept universally on 29 June, and he is usually represented as an old man, bald, but with a flowing beard, dressed in a white mantle and blue tunic, and holding in his hand a book or scroll. His peculiar symbols are the keys, and a sword (*Matt.* xvi, 19, and *John* xviii, 10).

Tradition tells that he confuted SIMON MAGUS, who was at NERO's court as a magician, and that in A.D. 65 he was crucified with his head downwards at his own request, as he said he was not worthy to suffer the same death as Our Lord. The location of his bones under the high altar of St. Peter's, ROME, was announced in 1950 and the POPE confirmed their authenticity in 1968.

St. Peter's Fingers. The fingers of a thief. The allusion is to the fish caught by St. Peter with a piece of money in its mouth. It is said that a thief has a fish-hook on every finger.

St. Peter's Fish. The JOHN DORY; also the HADDOCK.

Peter's Pence. An annual tribute of one PENNY, paid at the feast of St. Peter to the see of ROME, collected at first from every family, but afterwards restricted to those "who had the value of thirty pence in quick or livestock". This tax was collected in England from the late 8th century until its abolition by Henry VIII in 1534. It was also called *Rome-Scot, Rome fardynges*, or *Peter's farthings*. Much of it never got as far as Rome. *Cp.* PENTECOSTALS.

Peter's Pence now consists of voluntary offerings made to the HOLY SEE by Roman Catholics.

Great Peter. A bell in York Minster, weighing 10¾ tons, and hung in 1845.

Peter-boat; Peterman. A fishing boat made to go either way, with stem and stern alike. So called from *Peterman*, an old term for a fisherman.

> I hope to live to see dog's meat made of the old usurer's flesh ... his skin is too thick to make parchment, 'twould make good boots for a peterman to catch salmon in.
>
> CHAPMAN: *Eastward Ho*, II, ii.

Peterhouse, or **St. Peter's College,** the oldest of the Cambridge colleges, having been founded in 1284 by Hugo de Basham, Bishop of Ely.

Peter the Hermit (*c.* 1050–1115). Preacher of the first CRUSADE. He took part in the siege of Antioch (1098) and entered JERUSALEM with the victorious crusaders. He afterwards became Prior of Huy.

Peter Pan. The little boy who never grew up, the central character of Sir J.M. Barrie's famous play of this name (1904). One night Peter entered the nursery window of the house of the Darling family to recover his shadow. He flew back to NEVER NEVER LAND accompanied by the Darling children, to rejoin the Lost Boys. Eventually all were captured by the pirates, except Peter, who secured their release and the defeat of the pirates. The children, by now homesick, flew back to the nursery with their new friends but Peter refused to stay as he did not wish to grow up. In their absence Mr. Darling lived in the dog kennel as penance for having taken NANA away, thus making possible the children's disappearance in the first . instance.

Frampton's statue of Peter Pan in Kensington Gardens was placed there by Barrie in 1912.

Peter Pindar. *See under* PINDAR.

Peter-see-me. A favourite Spanish wine so called in the 17th century. The name is a corruption of *Pedro Ximenes*, the name of a grower who introduced a special grape.

> Peter-see-me shall wash thy noul
> And malaga glasses fox thee;
> If, poet, thou toss not bowl for bowl
> Thou shalt not kiss a doxy.
>
> MIDDLETON: *Spanish Gipsy*, III.

Peter the Wild Boy. In 1724 a boy was found walking on his hands and feet and climbing trees like a squirrel in a wood near Hameln, Hanover. He was taken to George I, who brought him to England and put him under the care of Dr. Arbuthnot, who had him christened "Peter". He never became articulate and eventually lived with a farmer who equipped him with a brass collar inscribed "Peter the Wild Boy, Broadway Farm, Berkhamsted". On the farmer's death (1785) Peter refused food and soon died. *Cp.* GAZELLE BOY.

To peter out. To come gradually to an end, to give out. A phrase from the American mining camps of the 1840s of unknown origin.

To rob Peter to pay Paul. *See* ROB.

Peterloo, or **the Manchester Massacre.** On 16 August 1819 a large crowd (about 50,000 to 60,000) gathered at St. Peter's Field, Manchester, to hear ORATOR HUNT address them on Parliamentary reform, and fearing a riot the magistrates ordered the YEOMANRY to disperse the assembly. Eleven people were killed including two women, and some 600 injured. Hunt was arrested and given three years' imprisonment. The "massacre" caused great indignation throughout England.

The name was founded on *Waterloo*, then fresh in the public mind.

Petit Sergeanty. *See under* SERGEANTY.

Petitio principii (Lat.). A BEGGING OF THE QUESTION, or assuming in the premises the question you undertake to prove. In mediæval logic, a *principium* was an essential, self-evident principle from which particular truths were deducible; the assumption of this principle was the *petitio, i.e.* begging of it. It is the same as "arguing in a circle".

> Petitio Principii, as defined by Archbishop Whately, is the fallacy in which the premise either appears manifestly to be the same as the conclusion, or is actually proved from the conclusion, or is such as would naturally and properly so be proved.
>
> J.S. MILL: *System of Logic*, II, p. 389.

Petitioners and Abhorrers. Names given to political groupings in the reign of Charles II, eventually superseded by WHIGS and TORIES. When Charles II prorogued a newly elected Parliament in October 1679, Shaftesbury and the Country party *petitioned* the King to summon Parliament. The Court party *abhorred* this attempt to encroach on the royal prerogative. Hence the names as party labels.

Petrel. The stormy petrel. A small seabird. (*Procellaria pelagica*), traditionally so named from Ital. *Petrello*, little Peter, because during storms these birds seem to be able to fly patting the water with each foot alternately as though walking on it, reminiscent of St. PETER, who walked on the lake of Gennesareth. Sailors call them MOTHER CAREY'S CHICKENS. The term is used figuratively of one whose coming always portends trouble.

Petticoat Government is control by women, *i.e.* when women "wear the trousers".

Petticoat Lane. The Sunday street-market, since the 1840s officially called Middlesex Street, and originally known as Hogham Lane, situated between Aldgate and Bishopsgate. It was settled by HUGUE-NOT silk-weavers, later by Jews, and became a noted centre for second-hand clothes and general goods. It continues as a market for clothes, fruit, toys, cheap jewellery, etc., and is still a popular East End feature. The name derives from the trade in women's petticoats.

Petto. In petto. In secrecy, in reserve (Ital., in the breast). The Pope creates cardinals *in petto, i.e.* in his own mind, and keeps the appointment to himself till he thinks proper to announce it. On the declaration of their names their seniority dates from their appointment *in petto.* It is claimed that the English historian Lingard was made cardinal *in petto* by Leo XII, who died before announcing the fact.

Peutingerian Table. A map on parchment of the military roads of the Western Roman Empire supposed to be a copy of one made in the 3rd century A.D. This copy was found by Konrad Celtes in 1494, who bequeathed it to his friend Konrad Peutinger (1465–1547) of Augsburg.

Pewter. To scour the pewter. To do one's work.

> But if she neatly scour her pewter,
> Give her the money that is due t'her.
> KING: *Orpheus and Eurydice.*

Pfister's Bible. See BIBLE, SOME SPECIALLY NAMED EDITIONS.

Phædra (fē' drà). Daughter of MINOS and PASIPHÆ, who became enamoured of her stepson HIPPOLYTUS. On her rejection by him she brought about his death by slandering him to her husband THESEUS. She subsequently killed herself in remorse. *See* MYRTLE.

Phædrus (fē' drùs). A freedman of AUGUSTUS, who, in the reign of Tiberius, translated ÆSOP'S FABLES into Latin verse, interspersing them with anecdotes of his own. A prose version of his work, written about the 10th century, served as a model for the mediæval fabulists.

Phaeton (fā' tòn). In classical myth, the son of PHŒBUS (the Sun); he undertook to drive his father's chariot, and was upset. He thereby caused Libya to be parched into barren sands, and all Africa to be more or less injured, the inhabitants blackened, and vegetation nearly destroyed; he would have set the world on fire had not ZEUS transfixed him with a thunderbolt.

> Gallop apace, you fiery-footed steeds,
> Towards Phœbus' lodging; such a waggoner
> As Phaeton would whip you to the west,
> And bring in cloudy night immediately.
> SHAKESPEARE: *Romeo and Juliet*, III, ii.

The name was given to a light, four-wheeled open carriage usually drawn by two horses.

Phaeton's Bird. The swan. Cygnus, son of NEPTUNE, was the friend of PHAETON and lamented his fate so grievously that APOLLO changed him into a swan, and placed him among the constellations.

Phalanx (făl' ăngks). The BATTLE order of the heavy infantry (hoplites) of ancient Greece, first used by the Spartans and made famous by Philip of Macedon and Alexander the Great. The hoplites with lances of 16 ft. length or longer and with shields joined, were drawn up in from 12 to 16 close parallel lines. Alexander used a 16-rank formation, the first five ranks carrying their spears horizontally and the remainder carrying theirs across the shoulder. Much resistant to hostile onset, the phalanx lacked mobility. Hence any number of people presenting an unyielding front or distinguished for firmness and solidity of union.

Phalaris (făl' a ris). **The brazen bull of Phalaris.** *See under* INVENTORS.

The Epistles of Phalaris. A series of 148 letters said to have been written by Phalaris, Tyrant of Agrigentum, Sicily, in the 6th century B.C. and edited by Charles Boyle in 1695. Boyle maintained them to be genuine, but Richard Bentley, applying methods of historical criticism, proved that they were forgeries, probably of the 2nd century A.D. *See* BOYLE CONTROVERSY; FORGERY.

Phantom. A spirit or apparition, an illusory appearance; from M.E. and O.Fr. *fantosme,* Gr. *phantasma* (*phainein,* to show).

Phantom corn. The mere ghost of corn; corn that has as little body as a spectre.

Phantom fellow. One who is under the ban of some HOBGOBLIN; a half-witted person.

Phantom flesh. Flesh that hangs loose and flabby; formerly supposed to be bewitched.

The Phantom Ship. The FLYING DUTCHMAN.

Pharamond (făr' à mond). In the ARTHURIAN ROMANCES, a KNIGHT of the ROUND TABLE, said to have been the first king of France and to have reigned in the early 5th century. He was the son of Marcomir and father of Clodion.

La Calprenède's novel *Pharamond, ou l'Histoire de France* was published in 1661.

Pharaoh (făr' ō). An expression meaning the "great house", applied to the kings of ancient Egypt in much the same way as "the HOLY

SEE" came to be used for the Pope, or "the Sublime PORTE" for the government of the Sultan of Turkey. Its popular use stems from the BIBLE but its use as a term for the King of Egypt begins during the 18th dynasty with Akhnaton. In hieroglyphics the old usage of four or five titles persisted.

The Pharaohs of the Bible are mostly not identifiable owing to vagueness of reference and absence of reliable chronological data, but the Pharaoh of the Oppression is usually taken to be Ramses II of the 19th dynasty, and his son Merenptah, the Pharaoh of the Exodus.

According to the TALMUD, the name of Pharaoh's daughter who brought up MOSES was Bathia.

In Dryden and Tate's *Absalom and Achitophel*, "Pharaoh" stands for Louis XIV of France.

Pharaoh's chicken, or **hen.** The Egyptian vulture, so called from its frequent representation in Egyptian HIEROGLYPHS.

Pharaoh's corn. The grains of wheat sometimes found in mummy cases. *Cp.* MUMMY WHEAT.

Pharaoh's rat. *See* ICHNEUMON.

Pharaoh's serpent. A chemical toy consisting of sulpho-cyanide of mercury, which fuses into a serpentine shape when lighted; so called in allusion to the magic serpents of *Exod.* vii, 9–12.

Pharisees (făr' i sēz) (Heb. *perusim*; from *perash*, to separate) means "those who have been set apart". The Jewish party of this name first appeared in Judea in the reign of John Hyrcanus I (135–104 B.C.) and strove to ensure that the state was governed in strict accordance with the TORAH. Their influence in the development of orthodox Judaism was profound. The condemnations of Jesus were essentially against the more extremist followers of the Pharisee Shammai, who were open to charges of narrow literalism and hypocrisy. The TALMUD mentions the following groups:

(1) The "Dashers" or "Bandy-legged" (*Nikfi*), who scarcely lifted their feet from the ground in walking, but "dashed them against the stones", that people might think them absorbed in holy thought (*Matt.* xxi, 44).

(2) The "Mortars", who wore a "mortier" or cap, which would not allow them to see the passersby, that their meditations might not be disturbed. "Having eyes they saw not" (*Mark* viii, 18).

(3) The "Bleeders", who inserted thorns in the borders of their gaberdines to prick their legs in walking.

(4) The "Cryers", or "Inquirers", who went about crying out, "Let me know my duty, and I will do it" (*Matt.* xix, 16–22).

(5) The "Almsgivers", who had a trumpet sounded before them to summon the poor together (*Matt.* vi, 2).

(6) The "Stumblers", or "Bloody-browed" (*Kizai*), who shut their eyes when they went abroad that they might see no women, being "blind leaders of the blind" (*Matt.* xv, 14). Our Lord calls them "blind Pharisees", "fools and blind".

(7) The "Immovables", who stood like statues for hours together, "Praying in the market places" (*Matt.* vi, 5).

(8) The "Pestle Pharisees" (*Medinkia*), who kept themselves bent double like the handle of a pestle.

(9) The "Strong-shouldered" (*Shikmi*), who walked with their back bent as if carrying on their shoulders the whole burden of the law.

(10) The "Dyed Pharisees", called by Our Lord "Whited Sepulchres", whose externals of devotion cloaked hypocrisy and moral uncleanliness. (*Talmud of Jerusalem, Berakoth*, ix; *Sota*, v, 7; *Talmud of Babylon, Sota*, 22b.)

Pharos (fâr' os). A lighthouse; so called from the lighthouse (*see* SEVEN WONDERS OF THE WORLD *under* WONDER) built by Ptolemy Philadelphus on the island of Pharos, off Alexandria, Egypt. It was 450 ft. high, and according to JOSEPHUS could be seen at a distance of 42 miles. Part was blown down in 793 and it was totally destroyed by an earthquake in 1375.

Pharsalia (far sā' lia). An epic in Latin hexameters by Lucan. It tells of the civil war between Pompey and CÆSAR, and of the battle of Pharsalus (48 B.C.) in which Pompey, with 45,000 legionaries, 7,000 cavalry, and a large number of auxiliaries, was decisively defeated by Cæsar, who had only 22,000 legionaries and 1,000 cavalry. Pompey's battle-cry was *Hercules invictus*: that of Cæsar, *Venus victrix*.

Phasian Bird. The pheasant (*Phasianus colchicus*); so called from Phasis, a river of Colchis, whence the bird is said to have been introduced elsewhere in Europe by the ARGONAUTS.

Pheidippides. *See* MARATHON.

Phigalian Marbles (fi gā' li ăn). A series of 23 sculptures in ALTO-RELIEVO, forming part of the ELGIN MARBLES. They were removed from the temple of APOLLO at Bassæ, near Phigalia, in 1812, and represent the combat of the CENTAURS and the LAPITHÆ, and that of the Greeks and AMAZONS.

Philadelphia (fil à del' fi à). The first city of the State of Pennsylvania, founded in 1682 by William Penn (1644–1718) and others of the SOCIETY OF FRIENDS and so named from the Greek *philadelphia*, brotherly love. It was also the Greek name of two ancient cities: (1) Rabbath-Ammon (now Amman) in south-eastern Palestine; (2) in Asia Minor, named after Attalus II, King of Pergamum (159–138 B.C.), called *Philadelphus* for his devotion to his brother and predecessor, Eumenes II. This city was the seat of one of the SEVEN CHURCHES (*Rev.* iii, 7).

Philadelphia lawyer. A lawyer of outstanding ability, with a keen scent for the weaknesses in an adversary's case, and a thorough knowledge of the intricacies of the law. "You will have to get a Philadelphia lawyer to solve that" is a familiar American phrase. It is said that in 1735, in a case of criminal libel, the only counsel who would undertake the defence was Andrew Hamilton, the famous Philadelphia barrister, who obtained his client's acquittal in face of apparently irrefutable evidence, and charged no fee. In NEW ENGLAND there was a saying that three Philadelphia lawyers were a match for the DEVIL.

Philadelphists. *See* BEHMENISTS.

Philandering (fi lăn' dèr ing). Coquetting with a woman; paying court, and leading her to think you love her, but never declaring your preference. *Philander* literally means "a lover of men" (Gr. *philos*, loving; *andros*, man), but as the word was made into a proper noun and used for a lover by Ariosto in ORLANDO FURIOSO (followed by Beaumont and Fletcher in *The Laws of Candy*), it obtained its present significance. In Norton and Sackville's GORBODUC (1561), Philander is the name of a staid old counsellor.

Philemon and Baucis. Poor cottagers of Phrygia (husband and wife), who, in Ovid's story (*Metamorphoses*, viii, 631), entertained JUPITER and MERCURY, in the guise of travellers, so hospitably that Jupiter transformed their cottage into a TEMPLE, making them its priest and priestess. They asked that they might die together, and it was so. Philemon became an OAK, Baucis a linden tree, and their branches intertwined at the top.

Philip, St., is usually represented bearing a large CROSS, or a basket containing loaves in allusion to *John* vi, 5–7. He is commemorated with ST. JAMES THE LESS on 1 May (since 1985, 11 May by Roman Catholics).

The name Philip is also applied to a sparrow.

Philip, remember thou art mortal. A sentence repeated to the Macedonian king every time he gave an audience.

Philip sober. When a woman, who asked Philip of Macedon to do her justice, was snubbed by the petulant monarch, she exclaimed, "Philip, I shall appeal against this judgment." "Appeal!" thundered the enraged king, "and to whom will you appeal?" "To Philip sober", was her reply.

Philippe Égalité. *See* ÉGALITÉ.

Philippic. A severe scolding; a speech full of acrimonious invective. So called from the orations of Demosthenes against Philip of Macedon, to rouse the Athenians to resist his encroachments. The orations of CICERO against Antony are called "Philippics".

Philistines. Properly, a warlike immigrant people of ancient Palestine or *Philistia* who contested its possession with the Israelites, hence a heathen foe. Its application to the ill-behaved and ignorant, those lacking culture and sensibility or of base and materialistic outlook stems from the term *Philister* as used by German university students to denote the townspeople, the "outsiders". This is said to have arisen at Jena, because of a TOWN AND GOWN row in 1693, which resulted in a number of deaths, when the university preacher took for his text, "The Philistines be upon thee" (*Judges* xvi, 12). Its use was much popularized in England by Matthew Arnold's frequent employment of the term in his *Culture and Anarchy* (1869).

> The people who believe most that our greatness and welfare are proved by our being very rich, and who most give their lives and thoughts to becoming rich, are just the very people whom we call Philistines.
> *Culture and Anarchy*, ch. i.

Philoctetes. The most famous archer in the TROJAN WAR, to whom HERCULES, at death, gave his arrows. In the tenth year of the siege Odysseus (ULYSSES) commanded that he should be sent for, as an ORACLE had declared that TROY could not be taken without the arrows of Hercules. Philoctetes accordingly went to Troy, slew PARIS and Troy fell.

The *Philoctetes* of Sophocles is one of the most famous Greek tragedies.

Philomel. *See* NIGHTINGALE.

Philopena. From the German *Vielliebchen*, darling, sweetheart. A philopena is a double almond.

> One evening we invited him to dine at our table, and we ate a philopena together.
> MRS. MACKIN: *Two Continents* (1898).

The word is also applied to a game in which each of two persons tries to inveigle the other into paying a forfeit.

Philosopher. The sages of Greece used to be called *sophoi* (wise men), but PYTHAGORAS thought the word too arrogant, and adopted the compound *philosophos* (lover of wisdom), whence "philosopher", one who courts or loves wisdom.

Marcus Aurelius (121–180) was surnamed *The Philosopher* by Justin Martyr, and the name was also conferred on Leo VI, Emperor of the East (d. 911), and Porphyry, the Neoplatonic opponent of Christianity (d. *c.* 305).

The leading philosophers and Schools of Philosophy in Ancient Greece were:

Philosophers of the Academic sect. PLATO, Speusippos, Xenocrates (*see* XENOCRATIC), Polemo, Crates of Athens, Crantor, Arcesilaos, Carneades, Clitomachos, Philo, and Antiochos.

Philosophers of the Cynic sect. ANTISTHENES, DIOGENES of Sinope, Monimos, Onesicritos, Crates of Thebes, Metrocles, Hipparchia, MENIPPUS, and Menedemos of Lampsacos.

Philosophers of the Cyrenaic sect. Aristippos, Hegesias, Anniceris, Theodoros, and Bion.

Philosophers of the Eleac and Eretriac sects. Phædo, Plisthenes, and Menedemos of Eretria.

Philosophers of the Eleatic sect. Xenophanes, Parmenides, Melissos, ZENO of Tarsus, Leucippos, DEMOCRITUS, Protagoras, and Anaxarchos.

Philosophers of the Epicurean sect. EPICURUS, and a host of disciples.

Philosophers of the Heraclitan sect. Heraclitos; the names of his disciples are unknown.

Philosophers of the Ionic sect. Anaximander, Anaximenes, Anaxagoras, and Archelaos.

Philosophers of the Italic sect. PYTHAGORAS, EMPEDOCLES, Epicharmos, Archytas, Alcmæon, Hippasos, Philolaos, and Eudoxos.

Philosophers of the Megaric sect. Euclid, Eubulides, Alexinos, Euphantos, Apollonius Chronosis, Diodorus, Ichthyas, Clinomachos, and Stilpo.

Philosophers of the Peripatetic sect. ARISTOTLE, Theophrastos, Strato, Lyco, Aristoxenus, Critolaos and Diodoros.

Philosophers of the Sceptic sect. Pyrrho (*see* PYRRHONISM) and Timon.

Philosophers of the Socratic sect. SOCRATES, Xenophon, Æschines, Crito, Simon, Glauco, Simmias, and Cebes.

Philosophers of the Stoic sect. ZENO, Cleanthes, CHRYSIPPUS, Zeno the Less, Diogenes of Babylon, Antipater, Panætios, Epictetus, Marcus Aurelius, Posidonios and Seneca.

Philosopher's Egg. A mediæval preservative against poison and a cure for the plague. The shell of a new egg was pricked, the white blown out, and the space filled with saffron or a yolk of an egg mixed with saffron.

Philosophers' Stone. The hypothetical substance which, according to the alchemists, would convert all baser metals into GOLD; by many it was thought to be compounded of the purest sulphur and mercury. Mediæval experimenters toiled endlessly in the search, thus laying the foundations of the science of chemistry, among other inventions. It was in this quest that Bötticher stumbled on the manufacture of DRESDEN porcelain, Roger Bacon on the composition of gunpowder, Geber on the properties of acids, Van Helmont on the nature of gas, and Dr. GLAUBER on the "salts" which bear his name.

In Ripley's treatise, *The Compound of Alchemie* (*c.* 1471), we are told the 12 stages or "gates" in the transmutation of metals are: (1) Calcination; (2) Dissolution; (3) Separation; (4) Conjunction; (5) Putrefaction; (6) Congelation; (7) Cibation; (8) Sublimation; (9) Fermentation; (10) Exaltation; (11) Multiplication; and (12) Projection. Of these the last two were much the most important; the former consisting of the ELIXIR, the latter in the penetration and transfiguration of metals in fusion by casting the powder of the philosophers' stone upon them, which is then called the "powder of projection". According to one legend, Noah was commanded to hang up the true philosophers' stone in the ark, to give light to every living creature therein; while another related that DEUCALION had it in a bag over his shoulder, but threw it away and lost it. *Cp.* ALKAHEST: PARACELSUS.

Philosopher's Tree, or **Diana's Tree.** An amalgam of crystallized SILVER, obtained from mercury in a solution of silver; so called by the alchemists, with whom DIANA stood for silver.

Philter (Gr. *philtron*; from *philein*, to love). A draught or charm to incite in another the passion of love. The Thessalian philters were the most renowned, but both Greeks and Romans used these dangerous potions, which sometimes produced insanity. Lucretius is said to have been driven mad by one, and CALIGULA's death is attributed to some philters administered by his wife, Cæsonia. Brabantio says to Othello:

> Thou has practised on her [Desdemona] with foul charms,
> Abused her delicate youth with drugs or minerals
> That weaken motion.
>
> SHAKESPEARE: *Othello*, I, ii.

Phiz, the face, is a contraction of physiognomy.

> Th' emphatic speaker dearly loves t' oppose
> In contact inconvenient, nose to nose,
> As if the gnomon on his neighbour's phiz,
> Touch'd with a magnet, had attracted his.
>
> COWPER: *Conversation*, 269.

Phiz was the pseudonym assumed by the artist Hablot Knight Browne (1815–1882), who became well-known for his amusing and clever book illustrations. He adopted the name when he began illustrating the works of Charles Dickens (to match up with BOZ).

Phlegethon (Gr. *phlego*, to burn). A river of liquid fire in HADES, flowing into the ACHERON.

> Fierce Phlegethon,
> Whose waves of torrent fire inflame with rage.
> MILTON: *Paradise Lost*, II, 580.

Phlogiston (flō jis' ton) (Gr., "combustible"). The inflammable substance that was supposed to be a constituent of all combustible material. A theory originated by German chemist J.J.Becher (1635–1682) and developed by G.E. Stahl in 1702. It held sway until overthrown in the 1770s by Lavoisier with the theory of oxygenation.

Phœbe (fē' bi). A female TITAN of classical myth, daughter of URANUS and GÆA; also a name of DIANA, as goddess of the MOON.

Phœbus (Gr., the Shining One). An epithet of APOLLO, god of the SUN. In poetry the name is sometimes used of the sun itself, sometimes of Apollo as leader of the MUSES.

> The Rosy Morne long since left Tithones bed,
> All ready to her silver coche to clyme;
> And Phœbus gins to shew his glorious hed.
> SPENSER: *Epithalamion*.

Phœnix (fē' niks). A fabulous Egyptian (Arabian, or Indian, etc.) bird, the only one of its kind, according to Greek legend said to live a certain number of years, at the close of which it makes in Egypt (or ARABIA, etc.) a nest of spices, sings a melodious dirge, flaps its wings to set fire to the pile, burns itself to ashes, and comes forth with new life. It is to this bird that SHAKESPEARE refers in *Cymbeline* (I, vi):

> If she be furnished with a mind so rare,
> She is alone the Arabian bird.

The Phœnix and Turtle (attributed to Shakespeare) is based on the legendary love and death of this bird and the turtledove.

The phœnix was adopted as a sign over chemists' shops through the association of this fabulous bird with ALCHEMY. PARACELSUS wrote about it, and several of the alchemists employed it to symbolize their vocation.

The phœnix is also a symbol of the Resurrection.

Phœnix, the son of Amyntor king of Argos, was tutor to ACHILLES.

Phœnix dactylifera. The date-palm; so called from the ancient idea that this tree, if burnt down or if it falls through old age, will rejuvenate itself and spring up fairer than ever.

Phœnix period, or **cycle,** generally supposed to be 500 years; Tacitus tells us it was 500 years; R. Stuart Poole that it was 1,460 Julian years, like the SOTHIC PERIOD; and Lipsius that it was 1,500 years. Opinions vary between 250 and 7,000 years. Tacitus (*Annales*, vi, 28) mentions four appearances of the bird in Egypt.

Phœnix Park (Dublin). A corruption of the Gaelic *Fionn-uisge*, the clear water, so called from a spring at one time resorted to as a chalybeate spa.

The Phœnix Park Murders. The assassination (6 May 1882) of Lord Frederick Cavendish, Chief Secretary for Ireland, and Mr. Burke, Under-Secretary, by Irish INVINCIBLES, when walking in Phœnix Park near the Vice-regal lodge. They were hacked to death by surgical knives on the day of Lord Spencer's arrival in Dublin as viceroy. James Carey, a Dublin councillor, one of the Invincibles, turned QUEEN'S EVIDENCE and five of the gang were hanged, others being given life sentences. Carey was shot later by an avenger. The affair aroused great horror and proved a great embarrassment to the Irish leader, Parnell.

Phoney, or **phony.** Fraudulent, bogus, insincere; an American colloquialism and slang term that became anglicized about 1920. It derives from *fawney*, an obsolete underworld CANT word meaning the imitation gold ring used by confidence tricksters. During World War II, the period of comparative inactivity, from the outbreak to the invasion of Norway and Denmark, was characterized by American journalists as the "Phoney War".

Phonograph. In Britain, the name of the old sound-reproducing machine with cylindrical records which gave place to the gramophone, which in turn was supplanted by the electrical record-player. In America the flat-disc gramophone is called a phonograph.

Phony. *See* PHONEY.

Photo-finish. The end of a race so closely contested that the winner can be discovered with certainty only by means of a photograph taken at the finish. Most race-courses are equipped to take such photographs.

Phrygians (frij' yànz). An early Christian sect of the late 2nd century, so called from Phrygia, where they abounded; also called MONTANISTS.

Phrygian cap. The CAP OF LIBERTY.

Phrygian mode. In music, the second of the "authentic" ecclesiastical modes. It had its "final" on E and its "dominant" on C, and was derived from the ancient Greek mode of this name, which was war-like.

Phryne (frī′ ne). A famous Athenian courtesan of the 4th century B.C., who acquired so much wealth by her beauty that she offered to rebuild the walls of Thebes if she might put on them the inscription: "ALEXANDER destroyed them, but Phryne the hetæra rebuilt them." It is recorded of her that, when she was being tried on a capital charge, her defender, who failed to move the judges by his eloquence, asked her to uncover her bosom. She did so, and the judges, struck by her beauty, acquitted her on the spot.

She is said to have been the model for Praxiteles' Cnidian VENUS, and also for APELLES' picture of Venus Rising from the Sea.

Phylactery (Gr. *phylacterion*; from *phylasso*, I watch). A charm or amulet worn by conforming Jews on the forehead and arm during morning prayer. It consisted of four slips of parchment, each bearing a text of Scripture, enclosed in two black leather cases. One case contained *Exod.* xiii, 1–10, 11–16; and the other case *Deut.* vi, 4–9, xi, 13–21. The practice arose from the command of Moses, "Therefore shall ye lay up these my words in your heart ... and bind them for a sign upon your hand ... as frontlets between your eyes" (*Deut.* xi, 18).

Phynnodderee. A Manx HOBGOBLIN combining the properties of the Scandinavian TROLL, the Scottish BROWNIE and the Irish LEPRECHAUN. He drives home straying sheep and helps in the harvesting if a storm is brewing, and is possessed of great strength for his size.

Physician (Gr. *phusis*, nature). **The Beloved Physician.** St. LUKE, so called by St. PAUL in *Col.* iv, 14.

The Physician finger. The third. *See* MEDICINAL FINGER.

The Prince of Physicians. AVICENNA.

Physiocrats. A school of French political economists in the second half of the 18th century founded by François Quesnay (1694–1774), a court physician. They attacked the economic regulations of MERCANTILISM, and held that wealth consisted in the products of the soil, not in coin or bullion. They advocated a predominantly agricultural society, FREE TRADE, and LAISSEZ-FAIRE. All revenue was to be raised by a land tax. The word is from the Greek, meaning "government according to nature".

Piazza (pi ăt′ ză). An Italian word meaning square, or market-place, such as the *piazza* of COVENT GARDEN. In America it is applied to the verandah of a dwelling-house.

Great Piazza Coffee House. A flourishing COFFEE house at the N.E. angle of the COVENT GARDEN piazza opened in 1756, previously (1754–1756) known as Macklin's. It was here that, in 1809, Sheridan watched the fire at the DRURY LANE Theatre saying: "A man may surely be allowed to take a glass of wine at his own fireside." It became a hotel in 1840 and was pulled down to make way for the Floral Hall in 1865.

Pica. *See* PIE.

Picards. An extremist early 15th-century sect prevalent in Bohemia and the VAUDOIS, said to be so called from Picard of Flanders, their founder, who called himself the New ADAM and tried to introduce the custom of living in the nude, like Adam in PARADISE. They were suppressed by Ziska in 1421. *Cp.* ADAMITES.

Picaresque (pik à resk′). The term applied to the class of literature that deals sympathetically with the adventures of clever and amusing rogues (Span. *picaresco*, roguish, knavish). The Spanish novel *Lazarillo de Tormes* (1553) is the earliest example of its kind and Le Sage's *Gil Blas* (1715) is perhaps the best known. Nash's *Jack Wilton* (1594) is the earliest English example, and others are Defoe's *Moll Flanders* and *Colonel Jack.*

Picayune. Formerly, in FLORIDA and Louisiana, the Spanish half-real, from the Fr. *picaillon*, an old small coin of Piedmont. Hence the use of the word for anything of trifling value or contemptible character.

Piccadilly. The famous London street takes its name after a *Piccadilly Hall* that existed in the vicinity in the early 17th century, the home of Robert Baker, a tailor. The name is derived from *pickadils* or *peccadilloes*, which, according to Blount's *Glossographia* (1656), were the round hems about the edge of a skirt or garment, also a kind of stiff collar or band for the neck and shoulders. The name may be in allusion to the tailor's source of wealth or that it was the "skirt house" or outermost house in the district.

Piccadilly Weepers. *See* WEEP.

Piccinists. *See* GLUCKISTS.

Pick-a-back. On the back or shoulders, as a pack is carried. The term dates at least from the early 16th century, but its precise origin, and the force of the *pick-*, are unknown. Other forms of it are *a-pigga-back, piggy-back, pick-back,* etc.

Pickle. A rod in pickle. One ready to chastise with at any moment; one "preserved" for use.

I'm in a pretty pickle. In a sorry plight, or state of disorder.

How cam'st thou in this pickle?
SHAKESPEARE: *The Tempest*, V, i.

To be pickled. A colloquial term for being drunk.

Pickle-herring. The German term for a CLOWN or buffoon, from a humorous character of that name in an early 17th-century play. It was adopted in ENGLAND through Addison's mention in *The Spectator* (No. 47, 1711), where he wrongly attributes it to the Dutch.

Pickwickian. In a Pickwickian sense. Said of words or epithets, usually of a derogatory or insulting kind, that, in the circumstances in which they are employed, are not to be taken as having quite the same force or implication as they naturally would have. The allusion is to the scene in ch. i. of *Pickwick Papers* when Mr. Pickwick accused Mr. Blotton of acting in "a vile and calumnious manner", whereupon Mr. Blotton retorted by calling Mr. Pickwick "a humbug". It finally was made to appear that both had used the offensive words only in a Pickwickian sense, and that each had, in fact, the highest regard and esteem for each other.

Picts. Ancient inhabitants of SCOTLAND before the coming of the Scots (Goidelic-speaking Celts) from Northern Ireland, in the 5th century. The Scots settled in Dalriada (Argyll) and the Pictish kingdom survived until the mid-9th century when it was conquered by Kenneth Mac Alpine, King of Dalriada. The name is the Lat. *picti*, painted, *i.e.* "tattooed men".

Picts' houses. Underground prehistoric dwellings found in the Orkneys and on the east coast of SCOTLAND, and attributed to the Picts.

Picture (Lat. *pictura*; from *pictus*, past participle of *pingere*, to paint). A model, or BEAU IDEAL, as, *He is the picture of health; The bride looked a picture.*

Picture Bible. A name given to the BIBLIA PAUPERUM.

The pictures. A colloquial term for the cinema or "picture-house".

To put someone in the picture. To inform someone of the proceedings or developments to date.

To see the picture whole. To be able to appreciate fully a situation, case, etc., in its entirety, based on a proper appreciation of its constituent elements.

Pidgin English. Originally a form of Anglo-Chinese jargon which developed on the China coast from the 17th century as a consequence of contact with English traders and businessmen. It is essentially a form of basic English with some Chinese, and additions from other tongues, but with certain Chinese constructions and a characteristic Chinese pronunciation, *i.e. ploper* for "proper", *solly* for "sorry", *makee* for "make", *tinkee* for "think", etc. Pidgin is a corruption of "business", hence, **this is not my pidgin,** this is not my business, not my responsibility, not my affair.

Similar forms, of largely independent growth, using the same basic words, have become widespread in the Pacific, Australia, Africa and elsewhere.

Pie or Pi. A printer's term to describe the mix-up of types (as when dropped), or a jumble of letters when a word or sentence is badly printed. It may be an allusion to the mixed ingredients in a pie, or it may come from the assortment of types used in the old *pie* or pre-REFORMATION books of rules for finding the prayers, etc. proper for the day. The ordinal was called the *pica* or *pie* from the colour and confused appearance of the rules which were printed in old black-letter type on white paper, thus giving a pied appearance (Lat. *pica*, a magpie).

Pie, or **pi** is also an epithet applied to a smugly or irritatingly pious person.

Pie in the sky. The good time or good things promised which never come; that which will never be realized.

> You will eat, bye and bye,
> In the glorious land above the sky!
> Work and pray,
> Live on hay,
> You'll get pie in the sky when you die!
> JOE HILL: *The Preacher and the Slave.*

To eat humble pie. See under EAT.

Piece. Piece goods. Fabrics woven in recognized lengths for certain purposes for sale by the *piece.*

Piece of goods. Often a somewhat disparaging term for a woman, but not necessarily so; thus for example "she's a flighty piece of goods", a "slovenly piece of goods", "a handsome piece of goods". See SKIRT; STUFF.

Pièce de résistance (pi ās dè rā zēs tôns) (Fr., piece of resistance). The "substantial piece" *i.e.* the main dish of a meal; the joint or meat dish. Figuratively, the most important feature, the main event, the best part of the show, the outstanding item.

Pieces of Eight. The old Spanish silver *peso* (piastre) or DOLLAR of 8 reals of the 17th and 18th centuries. It was marked with an 8.

To give a person a piece of one's mind. See under MIND.

Piece work. A term used when an industrial worker is paid by the *piece* or job, instead of by the hour, etc.

Pied. Au pied de la lettre (Fr., to the foot of the letter). Quite literally, close to the letter.

A wild enthusiastic young fellow, whose opinions one must not take *au pied de la lettre*.

THACKERAY: *Pendennis*, I, xi.

Pied-à-terre (pē ā då târ′) (Fr. foot on the ground). A temporary lodging or a country residence, a footing.

Mr. Harding, however, did not allow himself to be talked over into giving up his own and only little *pied-à-terre* in the High Street.

TROLLOPE: *Barchester Towers*, ch. xliv.

Pied Piper of Hamelin. The legend is that the town of Hamelin (Westphalia) was infested with rats in 1284, that a mysterious piper in a parti-coloured suit appeared in the town and offered to rid it of vermin for a certain sum, which offer was accepted by the townspeople. The Pied Piper fulfilled his contract but payment was not forthcoming. On the following St. John's Day he reappeared, and again played his pipe. This time all the children followed him and he led them to a mountain cave where all disappeared save two—one blind, the other dumb, or lame. Another version is that they were led to Transylvania where they formed a German colony. The story, familiar in ENGLAND from Robert Browning's poem, appeared earlier in James Howell's *Familiar Letters* (1645–1655). The legend has its roots in the story of the CHILDREN'S CRUSADE (*see under* CRUSADES).

Piepowder Court. A court of justice formerly held at FAIRS, which dealt with disputes between buyers and sellers. Literally a "wayfarer's court", piepowder being from F. *pied-poudreux*, dusty-footed (also a vagabond).

Is this well, goody Joan, to interrupt my market in the midst, and call away my customers? Can you answer this at the pie-poudres?

BEN JONSON: *Bartholomew Fair*, III, i.

Pierrot (pē′ rō) (*i.e.* "Little Peter"). A traditional character in French PANTOMIME, a kind of idealized clown. He is generally tall and thin, has his face covered with white powder or flour, and wears a white costume with very long sleeves and a row of big buttons down the front. *Cp.* HARLEQUIN.

Piers Plowman. *See* VISION OF PIERS PLOWMAN.

Pietà (pē ā ta′). A representation of the Virgin embracing the dead body of her Son. Filial or parental love was called *pietas* by the Romans.

Pietists. A 17th-century Lutheran movement seeking to revive the life of the Lutheran Church in Germany. It was started by P.J. Spener (1635–1705) and the name was applied derisively by the orthodox in the same way as the term METHODIST was used in England.

Pig. The pig was held sacred by the ancient Cretans because JUPITER was suckled by a sow; it was immolated in the ELEUSINIAN MYSTERIES; was sacrificed to HERCULES, to VENUS, and to the LARES by all who sought relief from bodily ailments. The sow was sacrificed to CERES "because it taught men to turn up the earth". The pig is unclean to Jews and Moslems.

The five dark marks on the inner side of each of a pig's forelegs are supposed to be the marks of the DEVIL's claws when they entered the swine (*Mark* v, 11–15). *See also* HOG; SOW.

A pig in a poke. A blind bargain. The reference is to a common trick of yore of trying to palm off on a GREENHORN a cat for a sucking-pig. If he opened the poke or sack he "let the cat out of the bag", and the trick was disclosed. The use is referred to in Thomas Tusser's *Five Hundreth Good Pointes of Husbandrie* (1580). The French *chat en poche* refers to the fact, while our proverb refers to the trick. *Pocket* is a diminutive of *poke*.

A pig's whisper. A very short space of time; properly a grunt—which doesn't take long.

You'll find yourself in bed in something less than a pig's whisper.

DICKENS: *Pickwick Papers*, ch. xxxii.

Bartholomew pig. *See under* BARTHOLOMEW.

He has brought his pigs to a pretty market. He has made a very bad bargain; he has managed his affairs badly. Pigs were for long a principal article of sale among country folk.

Pig-a-back. *See* PICK-A-BACK.

Pig and Whistle. *See* PUBLIC-HOUSE SIGNS.

Pigs and whistles. Trifles. *To go to pigs and whistles* is to be ruined, to go to the DEUCE.

I would be nane suprised to hear the morn that Nebuchadnezzar was a' gane to pigs and whistles, and driven out with the divors bill to the barren pastures of bankruptcy.

GALT: *The Entail*, I, ix.

Pig's ear. In RHYMING SLANG, beer.

Pig-headed. Obstinate, contrary.

Pig Iron. Iron cast in oblong ingots now called *pigs* but formerly *sows*. *Sow* is now applied to the main channel in which the molten liquid runs, the smaller branches which diverge from it being called *pigs*, and it is the iron from these which is called *pig iron*.

Pigs in clover. People who have money but don't know how to behave decently. Also, a game consisting of a box divided into recesses into which one has to roll marbles by tilting the box.

Please the pigs. If circumstances permit, *Deo volente*. An alliterative form which has been given several laboured explanations, such as "please the PYX", or "please the PIX-IES".

St. Anthony's pig. *See under* ANTHONY.

The Pig and the Tinderbox. An old colloquial name for the ELEPHANT AND CASTLE public-house; in allusion to its sign of a pig-like elephant surmounted by the representation of a castle which might pass as a tinderbox.

To drive one's pigs to market. To snore very loudly.

To drive pigs. To snore.

To pig it. To eat in a greedy fashion, to bolt one's food; to live in a slovenly piggish fashion, in ill-kept and ill-provided circumstances.

To pig together. To huddle together like pigs in a sty. To share and share alike, especially in lodgings in a small way; formerly it meant to sleep two (or more) in the same bed.

To stare like a stuck pig. With open mouth and staring eyes, as a pig that is being killed; in the utmost astonishment, mingled sometimes with fear.

When pigs fly. NEVER.

Pigskin. A saddle, the best being made of pigskin. "To throw a leg across a pigskin" is to mount a horse.

Pigtail. In England the word first appeared (17th century) as the name of a tobacco that was twisted into a thin rope; and it was used of the plait of twisted hair worn by sailors till the early 19th century, as it is still used of that worn by schoolgirls (*see* FLAPPER).

When the Manchu invaded and conquered China in the 17th century the Chinese were required to wear queues or pigtails as a sign of servitude until the advent of the republic in 1912.

Pig-wife. A woman who sold crockery. A *piggin* was a small pail, especially a milkpail; and a *pig* a small bowl, cup or mug.

Piggy-bank. The traditional pig-shaped money-box, still manufactured, nowadays often in plastic but formerly of earthenware or glass. Such money-boxes, with a coin or coins inside, were given to apprentices in Tudor times as CHRISTMAS BOXES.

Pigeon. Slang for a dupe, an easily gullible person, a GULL. To *pigeon* is to cheat or gull one out of his money by fairly transparent hoaxes. Pigeons are very easily caught by snares, and in the sporting world rogues and their dupes are called "rooks and pigeons".

Thackeray has a story entitled "Captain Rook and Mr. Pigeon".

The Black Pigeons of Dodona. *See under* DODONA.

Flying the pigeons. Stealing the coals from a cart or sack between the coal-dealer's yard and the house of the customer.

That's not my pigeon. That is not my responsibility; that's not my job; also used in the form, "That's someone else's pigeon". *Pigeon* here is an incorrect variant spelling of "pidgin". *See* PIDGIN ENGLISH.

To pluck a pigeon. To cheat a gullible person of his money; to fleece a GREENHORN.

To put the cat among the pigeons. *See under* CAT.

Pigeon, or **Pigeon's Blood.** Soy sauce; also the colour of a fine dark RUBY.

Pigeon English. An incorrect form of PIDGIN ENGLISH.

Pigeon Pair. Boy and girl twins. It was once supposed that pigeons always sit on two eggs which produce a male and a female, and these twin birds live together in love the rest of their lives.

Pigeon's milk. Partly digested food, regurgitated by pigeons for their young; also a non-existent liquid which gullible children and APRIL FOOLS are sometimes sent to fetch. *Cp.* ELBOW-GREASE.

Pigeon-hole. A small compartment for filing papers; hence, a matter that has been put on one side is often said to have been *pigeon-holed*. In dovecots a small hole is left for the pigeons to walk in and out.

Pigeon-livered. Timid, easily frightened, like a pigeon. *See* LIVER.

> It cannot be
> But I am pigeon-livered, and lack gall
> To make oppression bitter; or, ere this,
> I should have fatted all the region kites
> With this slave's offal.
>
> SHAKESPEARE: *Hamlet*, II, ii.

Piggin. *See* PIG-WIFE.

Pigmies. *See* PYGMIES.

Pigott Forgeries. *See under* FORGERY.

Pigwidgin, or **Pigwiggen.** A FAIRY or DWARF; anything very small.

> Pigwiggen, was this Fairy Knight,
> One wond'rous gracious in the sight
> Of fair Queen Mab, which day and night
> He amorously observed.
>
> DRAYTON: *Nymphidia*, I, 89.

Pike. The Germans have a tradition that when Christ was crucified all fishes dived under the water in terror, except the pike, which, out of curiosity, lifted up its head and beheld the whole scene; hence the fancy that in a pike's head all the parts of the Crucifixion are represented, the CROSS, three nails, and a sword being clearly delineated. *Cp.* PASSION FLOWER.

Pikestaff. Plain as a Pikestaff. Quite clear, obvious, and unmistakable. The earlier form of the phrase (mid-16th century) was *plain as a packstaff, i.e.* the staff on which a pedlar carried his pack, which was worn plain and smooth.

> O Lord! what absurdities! as plain as any packstaff.
> DRYDEN: *Amphitryon*, III, i.

Pilate. One tradition has it that Pontius Pilate's later life was so full of misfortune that in CALIGULA'S time he committed suicide at ROME. His body was thrown into the Tiber, but evil spirits so disturbed the water that it was retrieved and taken to Vienne, where it was cast into the Rhône, eventually coming to rest in the recesses of a lake on Mount PILATUS. Another legend is that he committed suicide to avoid the sentence of death passed on him by Tiberius because of his having ordered the crucifixion of Christ. His wife is given as Claudia Procula, or Procla, and by some she has been identified with Claudia of II *Tim.* iv, 21: there is a story that they both became penitent and died peaceably in the faith.

In the Coptic Church he is regarded as a martyr, and his feast day is 25 June. Procla has been canonized in the GREEK CHURCH.

The Acts of Pilate. An apocryphal work, probably of the 4th century, recounting the trial, death, and resurrection of Christ. In combination with another treatise on the *Descent of Christ into Hades*, the two are known as the *Gospel of Nicodemus*.

Pilate voice. A loud ranting voice. In the old mysteries all TYRANTS were made to speak in a rough ranting manner. Similarly SHAKESPEARE has "out-herods HEROD" (*Hamlet*, III, ii), and "This is Ercles' vein, a tyrant's vein" (*Midsummer Night's Dream*, I, ii).

> The Miller, that for-drunken was al pale...
> in Pilates vois he gan to crye,
> And swoor by armes and by blood and bones,
> "I can a noble tale for the nones
> With which I wol now quyte the Knightes tale."
> CHAUCER: *Miller's Prologue*, 12–19.

Pilatus, Mount. In Switzerland, between the canton of Lucerne and Unterwalden. So called because during westerly winds it is covered with a white "cap" of cloud (Lat. *pileatus*, covered with the *pileus*, or felt cap). The similarity of the name gave rise to a fabled connexion with PILATE. One tradition is that Pilate was banished to GAUL by Tiberius and threw himself into the lake near the summit of this mountain, where he appears annually. Whoever sees the ghost will die before the year is out. In the 16th century a law was passed forbidding anyone to throw stones into the lake for fear of bringing a tempest on the country.

Pilgarlic, or **Pill'd Garlic.** In the 16th and 17th centuries, a term for a bald-headed man, especially one who had lost his hair through disease, and left a head that was suggestive of peeled garlic. Stow says of one getting bald: "He will soon be peeled garlic like myself." The term was later used of any poor wretch forsaken by his fellows, and in a humorous and self-pitying way, of oneself.

> After this [feast] we jogged off to bed for the night; but never a bit could poor pilgarlic sleep one wink, for the everlasting jingle of bells.
> RABELAIS: *Pantagruel*, V, viii.

Pilgrim Fathers. The term (first used in 1799) applied to the emigrants who founded the colony of Plymouth, NEW ENGLAND, in 1620. In 1608 a PURITAN congregation from Scrooby (Notts.) settled at Leiden and eventually decided to migrate to America. They finally left Plymouth in the MAYFLOWER. Of the 102 settlers, 24 were women, and only 35 of the party were Puritans. Their tradition is part of American folklore.

The Pilgrims is a club founded in honour of the Pilgrim Fathers in 1902 with one branch in London and the other in New York.

The Pilgrim's Progress. The allegorical masterpiece of John Bunyan, the first part of which appeared in 1678 and the second in 1684. It tells of Christian's pilgrimage, beset with trials and temptations, but with incidental encouragement, until he reached the Celestial City where he was later joined by his wife and children. The rustic simplicity and directness of its story gave it lasting appeal and many expressions have become part of the language. "The Slough of Despond", "Vanity Fair", "Mr. Worldly Wiseman" and "Mr. Facing-both-ways" are notable examples.

Pilgrim's Way. The road from Winchester in Hampshire to Canterbury in Kent, used by pilgrims from Europe and the south and west of England when visiting the shrine of Archbishop Becket. The route followed by mediæval pilgrims follows a much more ancient trackway.

Pilgrimage. A journey to a sacred place undertaken as an act of religious devotion, either as an act of veneration or penance, or to ask for the fulfilment of some prayer. In the MIDDLE AGES the chief venues in the West were Walsingham and Canterbury (England), Fourvière, Le Puy, and St. Denis (France); ROME, Loreto, and Assisi (Italy); COMPOSTELA, Guadalupe, and Montserrat (Spain); Mariazell (Austria); Cologne, Trier (Germany); Einsiedeln

(Switzerland). The pre-eminent pilgrimage was of course to the HOLY LAND. LOURDES became a noted place of pilgrimage for Roman Catholics after 1858.

Miraculous cures were sometimes effected upon those who worshipped at these shrines and spiritual and bodily welfare was the main concern of most pilgrims; for others a pilgrimage was an occasion for a holiday and an opportunity to visit distant parts or foreign lands. *Cp.* CANTERBURY TALES; COCKLE HAT; CRUSADES; PALMER.

> Whan that Aprille with his shoures soote
> The droghte of Marche hath perced to the roote...
> Than longen folk to goon on pilgrimages,
> (And palmers for to seken straunge strondes)...
> CHAUCER: *Canterbury Tales (Prologue)*.

The Pilgrimage of Grace. A rising in Yorkshire (1536–1537) due to political unrest among the gentry occasioned by inclosures, etc., and the religious changes culminating in the dissolution of the monasteries. Under Robert Aske, the "pilgrims" took the five wounds of Christ as their banner and captured York and Hull. Among the insurgents were the Archbishop of York, Lords Darcy, Latimer, Lumley, Scrope, and Sir Thomas Percy. The Duke of Norfolk effected a truce based on promises of redress which were not kept. A full pardon was offered but further outbreaks in 1537 gave Henry VIII the excuse to execute some 220 rebels.

Pill, The. Since the introduction of the oral contraceptive in the early 1960s its impact has caused it to be known as *the pill*, to the exclusion of all others. In Victorian England pills were popular "universal remedies" for many maladies, but especially associated with liver complaints and constipation. Thomas Holloway and Thomas Beecham were the two richest pill magnates of the day, the former entering the market in 1837 and the latter in 1857. Aloes, ginger, and soap formed the basis of their products, and both became millionaires.

To gild the pill. To soften the blow; to make a disagreeable task less offensive, as pills used to be gilded (and are now sugar-coated) to make them more palatable.

Pillar. From pillar to post. Hither and thither; from one thing to another without definite purpose; harassed and badgered. The phrase was originally *from post to pillar*, and comes from the old tennis-courts in allusion to the banging about of the balls.

Nelson's Pillar. Formerly Dublin's most controversial monument, erected in honour of the great sailor by a committee of bankers and merchants in 1808–9, who raised the funds by public subscription. It was sited in Sackville Street (now O'Connell Street) and the statue of Nelson on the top was the work of Thomas Kirk. The column contained a spiral staircase leading to the top of the doric abacus and somewhat fresher air. The whole monument was 134 ft. high. It was blown up by young Republican extremists on 8 March 1966, and the 50 ft. of masonry left standing was demolished by army engineers. Nelson's head was removed to a Corporation depot whence it was taken by a group of art students and flown to London for subsequent sale to an antique dealer. *Cp.* NELSON'S COLUMN *under* COLUMN.

Pillar Saints. *See* STYLITES.

The Pillars of Hercules. The opposite rocks at the entrance to the Mediterranean, one in Spain and the other in Africa, anciently called Calpe and Abyla, now Gibraltar and Mount Hacho (on which stands the fortress of Ceuta). The tale is that they were bound together till HERCULES tore them asunder in order to get to Gades (Cadiz). Macrobius ascribes the feat of making the division to Sesostris (the Egyptian Hercules), Lucan follows the same tradition; and the Phœnicians are said to have set on the opposing rocks two large pyramidal columns to serve as seamarks, one dedicated to Hercules and the other to ASTARTE.

I will follow you even to the Pillars of Hercules. To the end of the world. The ancients supposed that these rocks marked the utmost limits of the habitable globe.

Pompey's Pillar. *See under* POMPEY.

Pillory. Punishment by the pillory was not finally abolished in England till 1837, but since 1815 it had been used only for cases of perjury. In Delaware, U.S.A., it was a legal punishment down to 1905. It was abolished in France in 1832. It was a popular punishment for libel, and among those pilloried for this offence were Prynne, Bastwick, Defoe and, in 1797, Thomas Evans, the preacher, for singing a seditious Welsh song.

Pilot. Through Fr. from Ital. *pilota*, formerly *pedota*, which is probably connected with Gr. *pedon*, a rudder.

Pilot balloon. A small balloon sent up to find the direction of the wind; hence, figuratively, a feeler; a hint thrown out to ascertain public opinion on some point.

Pilot engine. The leading engine when two are needed to draw a railway train; also an engine sent ahead of a train carrying important personages, etc., to ensure that the line is clear.

Pilot fish. The small sea-fish *Naucrates ductor*, so called because it is supposed to pilot the shark to its prey.

Pilot scheme, project. An experimental try-out.

The pilot that weathered the storm. William Pitt the younger, who as Prime Minister steered the country through much of the European storm stirred up by the French Revolution. It derives from Canning's *Song for the Inauguration of the Pitt Club.*

Pilpay, or **Bidpay.** The name given as that of the author of *Kalilah and Dimnah* (otherwise known as *The Fables of Pilpay*), which is the 8th-century Arabic version of the Sanskrit *Panchatantra*. The word is not a true name, but means "wise man" (Arab. *bidbah*), and was applied to the chief scholar at the court of an Indian prince.

Piltdown Man, or **Piltdown Skull.** *See under* FORGERY.

Pimlico (London). Formerly the pleasure gardens of Hoxton, but the better-known Pimlico is the district of WESTMINSTER between Knightsbridge and the Thames and St. James's Park and Chelsea. It was once noted for its pleasure gardens, such as the Mulberry Garden (now the site of Buckingham Palace), RANELAGH, and Jenny's Whim. The name in Hoxton derives from Ben Pimlico, a local brewer and tavern keeper, famous for his ales. A tract of 1598, *Newes from Hogsden*, has: "Have at thee, then, my merrie boys, and hey for old Ben Pimlico's nut-browne." He apparently eventually settled just south of the site occupied by the present Victoria Station which may account for the name of this district of Westminster.

Pin. At a pin's fee. At an extremely low estimate; valueless.

> I do not set my life at a pin's fee.
> SHAKESPEARE: *Hamlet*, I, iv.

I don't care a pin, or **a pin's point.** I don't care in the least.

I do not pin my faith upon your sleeve. I am not going to take your IPSE DIXIT for gospel. In feudal times badges were worn on the sleeve by a leader's partisans and sometimes badges were changed for some reason, hence people were chary of judging by appearances and would say, "You wear the badge, but I do not intend to pin my faith on your sleeve."

In merry pin. In merry mood, in good spirits.

> The calender, right glad to find
> His friend in merry pin,
> Return'd him not a single word,
> But to the house went in.
> COWPER: *John Gilpin*, st. xlv.

Pin here may refer to the pin or key of a stringed instrument by which it is kept at the right pitch, or it may be an allusion to the pins or pegs of peg-tankards (*cp.* I AM A PEG TOO LOW *under* PEG). By the rules of good fellowship a drinker was supposed to stop *only at a pin*, and if he went beyond it, he was to drink to the next one. As it was hard to stop exactly at the pin, the effort gave rise to much mirth, and the drinker had usually to drain the tankard.

> No song, no laugh, no jovial din
> Of drinking wassail to the pin.
> LONGFELLOW: *The Golden Legend*, I.

Not worth a pin. Wholly worthless.

There's not a pin to choose between them. They're as like as two peas, practically no difference between them.

To tirl at the pin. *See under* TIRL.

To pin a person down. To "nail him down", to compel him to reveal his intentions or to state clearly his views, etc.

To pin something on a person. To fasten the blame, guilt, or responsibility on him.

Weak on his pins. Weak in his legs, the legs being a man's "pins" or pegs.

You could have heard a pin drop. Said of a state—especially a sudden state in the midst of din—of complete silence. Leigh Hunt speaks of "a pin-drop silence" (*Rimini*, I, 144).

Pin money. A woman's allowance of money for her own personal expenditure. Pins were once very expensive, and in 14th- and 15th-century wills there were often special bequests for the express purpose of buying pins; when they became cheap, women spent their allowances on other fancies but the term *pin money* remained in vogue.

> *Miss Hoyden:* Now, nurse, if he gives me two hundred a year to buy pins, what do you think he'll give me to buy fine petticoats?
> *Nurse:* Ah, my dearest, he deceives thee foully, and he's no better than a rogue for his pains! These Londoners have got a gibberage with 'em would confound a gipsy. That which they call pin-money is to buy their wives everything in the versal world, down to their very shoe-ties.
> VANBRUGH: *The Relapse*, V, v (1697).

Pins and needles. The tingling that comes over a limb when it has been numbed or is "asleep".

On pins and needles. On TENTERHOOKS; in a state of fearful expectation or great uneasiness.

Policy of pin pricks. A policy of petty annoyance to wear someone down. The term came into prominence during the period of strained relations between Britain and France in 1898 at the time of the Fashoda incident. It is an anglicization of a much older French phrase, *un coup d'épingle*.

Pin-up Girl. In World War II servicemen used to pin up in their quarters pictures of film stars and actresses (often scantily clad) or their own particular girl-friends. These were called "pin-up girls".

Pinch. A pinch for stale news. A punishment for telling as news what is well known.

At a pinch. In an urgent case; if hard pressed. There are things that one cannot do in the ordinary way, but that one may manage "at a pinch".

Peewits' pinch. *See* PEEWIT.

Pinch, punch, first of the month, and no returns. An old established children's trick, usually carried out fairly gently, on their fellows on the first of a month. The final phrase is a safeguard against retaliation. *Cp* APRIL FOOL.

To be pinched for money. To be in financial straits, hard up. Hence *to pinch and scrape* or *to pinch it*, to economize, to cheesepare.

To pinch. Slang for to steal.

Where the shoe pinches. *See under* SHOE.

Pinch-hitter. A person who substitutes for another in a crisis. The term is from baseball where the pinch-hitter—a man who always hits the ball hard—is put in to bat when the team is in desperate straits.

Pinchbeck. An alloy of copper (5 parts) and zinc (1 part), closely resembling GOLD, so called from Christopher Pinchbeck (1670–1732), a manufacturer of trinkets, watches, and jewellery in FLEET STREET, London. The term is used figuratively of anything spurious, of deceptive appearance, or low quality.

Pindar (*c.* 522–443 B.C.). A renowned lyric poet of THEBES who achieved great respect and public honour for his verse from his contemporaries.

Pindaric Verse (pin dar′ ik). Irregular verse; a poem of various metres, and of lofty style; after the fashion started by Abraham Cowley in the mid-17th century, who inaccurately imitated in English the Greek versification of Pindar. He published fifteen *Pindarique Odes* in 1656 and the style was copied by many, including Dryden and Pope.

Pindar, Pinder, or **Pinner of Wakefield.** *See* AS GOOD AS GEORGE-A-GREEN *under* GEORGE.

Peter Pindar. The pseudonym of Dr. John Wolcot (1738–1819), one-time physician-general in Jamaica and incumbent of Vere, Jamaica. He obtained an M.D. at Aberdeen in 1767 and was ordained in London in 1769. He returned to practise medicine at Truro but removed to London in 1780 to devote his time to the writing of satirical verse and caricatures on the WHIG side. He had few

scruples or convictions and George III was a victim of his pen. His verses include *The Lousiad, Whitbread's Brewery visited by their Majesties*, and *Bozzy and Piozzi*.

Pine-tree shilling. A coin struck (1652-1684), contrary to English law, by the mint established by Massachusetts. Other shillings bore the devices of the oak-tree and willow. Charles II became aware of the practice, but as the royal OAK was used as a device took no action. The export of coins from Great Britain was forbidden and the early colonists relied on barter in wampum, beaver skins, corn, tobacco, etc., or on foreign coinage.

Pine-tree State. Maine, which has forests of these trees, and bears a pine-tree on its COAT OF ARMS.

Pink. The flower is so called because the edges of the petals are *pinked* or notched. The verb *to pink* means to pierce or perforate, also to ornament dress material by punching holes in it so that the lining can be seen, scalloping the edges, etc. In the 17th century it was commonly used of stabbing an adversary, especially in a duel.

> "There went another eyelet-hole to his broidered jerkin!"—"Fairly pinked, by G—d!" In fact, the last exclamation was uttered amid a general roar of applause, accompanying a successful and conclusive lunge, by which Peveril ran his gigantic antagonist through the body.
>
> SCOTT: *Peveril of the Peak*, ch. xxxii.

In pink. In the scarlet coat of a fox-hunter. The colour is not pink, but no hunting man would call it anything else. *Cp.* REDCOATS.

> Pen rode well to hounds, appeared in pink, as became a young buck...
>
> W.M. THACKERAY: *Pendennis* (1850), ch. xviii.

In the pink. In excellent health. An abbreviation of the modern phrase "in the pink of condition", deriving from SHAKESPEARE's "the very pink of courtesy" (*Romeo and Juliet*, II, iv), Steele's "the pink of courtesy" (*Tatler*, no. 204), Goldsmith's "the very pink of perfection" (*She Stoops to Conquer*, I), and Burns's "the pink o' womankind" (*The Posie*).

Pinkerton. Pinkerton's National Detective Agency was founded at Chicago (1852) by Allan Pinkerton (1819–1884), Glasgow-born deputy sheriff of Kane County, Illinois, who had proved himself a detective of some resource. It came to the forefront during the CIVIL WAR, when, in 1861, Pinkerton's men uncovered a plot to assassinate Lincoln, the President-elect. Pinkerton also found the means of obtaining military and political information from the Southern States during the war and eventually organized the Federal Secret Service. His most sensational coups were the discovery of the thieves of $700,000 stolen from the Adams Express in 1866, and the breaking-up of the MOLLY MAGUIRES (1877), an Irish-American secret society with many subversive and lawless deeds to their discredit.

Pinocchio (pē nō' kiō). The mischievous hero of the famous puppet story *Le Avventure di Pinocchio* (1883) by G. Lorenzini, who wrote under the name of "Collodi", which was taken from his birthplace.

The story tells how a carpenter found a piece of wood that laughed and cried like a child and gave it to his friend Geppetto who fashioned from it the puppet Pinocchio. His creation proved unusually mischievous and had many bizarre adventures including having his feet burned off, his nose elongated, and being transformed into a donkey. Eventually he learned to show sympathy and goodness and "the fairy" changed him to a real boy back at home with Geppetto.

Pious. The Romans called a man who revered his father *pius*; hence Antoninus was called *pius*, because he requested that his adoptive father (Hadrian) might be ranked among the gods. ÆNEAS was called *Pius* because he rescued his father from the burning city of TROY. The Italian word PIETÀ has a similar meaning.

The Pious. Ernest I, founder of the House of Gotha (1601–1674).

Robert II, son of Hugh Capet (*c.* 970, 966–1031).

Louis I of France. *See* DEBONAIR.

Eric IX of Sweden (reigned 1150–1160).

Frederick III, Elector of Palatine (1515, 1559–1576).

Pip. The pips on cards and dice were named from the seeds of fruit (earlier *peep*, origin obscure). This is merely an abbreviated form of *pippin*, which denoted the seed long before it denoted apples raised from seed.

To be pipped is to be BLACKBALLED or defeated, the black ball being the pip. **To be pipped at the post** is to be defeated when victory seemed in sight.

Till the pips squeak. To put extreme pressure on someone, literally or metaphorically. An allusion to the squeezing of such fruits as oranges and lemons.

To get one's second pip. In the army, to be promoted from second to first lieutenant, these ranks and that of captain being marked by "pips", a nickname for the stars on the shoulder straps.

To have, or **to get the pip.** To be thoroughly "fed up", downhearted and miserable. Probably connected with *pip*, the poultry disease which causes fowls to pine away.

Pip emma. Military usage in World War I for P.M. Originally telephonese; "ten pip emma" avoids any possibility of misunderstanding. In the same way *ack emma* stands for A.M. *Cp.* TOC H.

Pipe. As you pipe, I must dance. I must accommodate myself to your wishes. "He who pays the piper calls the tune."

Pipe down! Stop being aggressive or noisy, stop talking. A naval colloquialism derived from the boatswain's call of this name meaning "hands turn in", *i.e.* "lights out".

Pipe dream. Originating with opium smoking, an impossible, imaginary and fanciful hope or plan indulged in at one's ease when smoking a pipe.

Piping hot. Hot as water which pipes or sings; hence, new, only just out.

Piping times of peace (SHAKESPEARE, *Richard III*, I, i). Times when there was no thought of war, and the pastoral pipe instead of the martial trumpet was heard on the village greens.

Put that in your pipe and smoke it. Digest that if you can. "Swallow that one!" An expression used by one who has given an adversary a severe rebuke or given him "something to think about".

The pipe of peace. *See* CALUMET.

To pipe one's eye. To snivel, weep.

To put one's pipe out. To spoil his piping; to make him change his key or sing a different tune; "to take his shine out".

Pipeclay. Routine; excessive attention to "parade-ground" correctness in dress, drill, SPIT AND POLISH, etc. (*cp.* RED TAPE). Pipeclay was formerly much in evidence on soldiers' belts, gloves, and other accoutrements. *See* BLANCO WHITE *under* WHITE.

Pipe-laying (U.S.A.). Swaying the issue in an election by slipping in voters who are not on the electoral roll.

Pipeline. In the pipeline. Already under way; in process of manufacture or delivery, etc. From the transport of oil by pipeline.

Pipe Rolls, or **Great Rolls of the Pipe.** The name given to a class of EXCHEQUER records on account of their being kept in rolls in the form of a pipe. They begin in 1131 and continue till 1831, and contain the annual accounts of SHERIFFS with the Exchequer, county by county. They are now in the Public Record Office, Chancery Lane, London.

Piper. Piper's news. Stale news; FIDDLER'S NEWS.

The Pied Piper. *See* PIED.

Tom Piper. So the piper is called in the MORRIS DANCE.

Who's to pay the piper? *See under* PAY.

Pippin. *See* PIP.

Pippin the Short. *See under* SHORT.

Piran, St. (5th or 6th century). The patron saint of Cornish miners, said to have been sent to CORNWALL by St. PATRICK. According to another legend he was cast into the sea by his fellow Irishmen bound to a millstone and landed at Perranzabuloe (St. Piran in the Sands) near Perranporth. He set up a hermitage and discovered tin when he saw it streaming from the stone of his fireplace. Two churches of St. Piran were buried in the sand dunes and the remains of one have been uncovered, hence legends of bells ringing in the sand. His day is 5th March. *See* MEBYON KERNOW.

Pis-aller (pēz ăl′ ā) (Fr., worst course). A makeshift; something for want of a better; a last expedient.

Pisces (pis′kēz, pī′sēz) (Lat. the fishes). A constellation and the twelfth sign of the ZODIAC.

Piso's Justice (pī′ zō). Verbally right, but morally wrong. Seneca says that Piso condemned a man on circumstantial evidence for murder; but when the execution was about to take place, the man supposed to have been murdered appeared. The centurion sent the prisoner to Piso, and explained the situation to him; whereupon Piso condemned all three to death, saying, *Fiat justitia* (Lat., let justice be done). The condemned man was executed because he had been sentenced, the centurion because he had disobeyed orders, and the man supposed to have been murdered because he had been the cause of death to two innocent men.

Pistol. Formerly *pistolet*; so called from the old *pistolese*, a dagger or hanger (a short cut-and-thrust sword), for the manufacture of which Pistoia, in Tuscany, was famous.

Pocket pistol. *See under* POCKET.

To fire one's pistol in the air. Purposely to refrain from injuring an adversary. The phrase is often used of argument, and refers to the old practice of duellists doing this when they wished to discharge a "debt of honour" without incurring risks or wounding their opponent.

> A steady voice said "Fire"; and the Duke raised his pistol. But Winchilsea's was still pointing at the ground. The Duke paused for an instant, fired, and hit his coat. Then Winchilsea fired in the air.
> P. GUEDALLA: *The Duke*, viii, iii.

Pit-a-pat. My heart goes pit-a-pat. Throbs, palpitates. An echoic or a RICOCHET word, as "fiddle-faddle", "harum-scarum", "ding-dong", etc.

> Anything like the sound of a rat
> Makes my heart go pit-a-pat.
> BROWNING: *Pied Piper of Hamelin*.

Pitch. The black resinous substance gets its name from Lat. *pix*; the verb (to fling, settle, etc.) is the M.E. *pichen*, *pykken*.

The devil to pay and no pitch hot. *See under* DEVIL.

He that touches pitch will be defiled. A rotten apple injures its companions. "Evil communications corrupt good manners." The saying occurs in *Ecclesiasticus* (xii, 1), "he that toucheth pitch shall be defiled therewith".

Pitch and pay. Pay up at once. There is a suppressed pun in the phrase: "to pay a ship" was to cover the oakum in the seams with pitch.

> Look to my chattels and my movables.
> Let senses rule; the word is "Pitch and pay".
> Trust none.
> SHAKESPEARE: *Henry V*, II, iii.

Pitch and toss. A game in which coins are pitched at a mark, the player getting nearest having the right to toss all the other's coins into the air and take those that come down with heads up. Hence, *to play pitch and toss* with one's money, prospects, etc., is to gamble recklessly, to play DUCKS AND DRAKES.

> The bounding pinnace played a game
> Of dreary pitch and toss;
> A game that, on the good dry land,
> Is apt to bring a loss.
> THOS. HOOD: *The Sea Spell*.

To pitch into one. To assail him vigorously; to give it him hot.

To queer one's pitch. *See under* QUEER.

A pitched battle. *See* BATTLE.

Pitcher. From Med. Lat. *picarium* or *bicarium*; the word is a doublet of beaker.

Little pitchers have long ears. Little folk or children hear what is said when you little think it. The *ear* of a pitcher is the handle, made somewhat in the shape of a man's ear.

The pitcher went once too often to the well. The dodge was tried once too often, and utterly failed. The sentiment is proverbial in most European languages.

Pithecanthropus (pith e kăn′throp ŭs) or **Java Man.** The name given by Haeckel in 1868 to the hypothetical MISSING LINK; from Gr. *pithekos*, ape, and *anthropos*, man. Later *pithecanthropus* was the generic name given to the remains of the extinct man-like ape discovered near Trinil, Java, in 1891. *Cp.* PEKING MAN.

Pitt Diamond. A DIAMOND of just under 137 CARATS found at the Parteal mines, India, and bought by Thomas Pitt (*see* DIAMOND PITT) in 1702 from a thief for a sum (said to have been £20,400) far below its real value. Hence Pope's reference:

Asleep and naked as an Indian lay,
An honest factor stole a gem away.
Moral Essays, Ep. iii, 361.

Pitt sold the diamond in 1717 to the Regent Orleans (hence its alternative name the "Regent Diamond") for £135,000; it later adorned the sword-hilt of NAPOLEON, and is still in the possession of France. Its original weight before cutting was 410 carats.

Pitt's Pictures. "Blind" windows were so called because many window spaces were blocked up when Pitt the younger greatly increased the window tax in 1782 and 1797, although houses with fewer than seven windows were exempted in 1792.

Pixie, or **Pixy.** A sprite or FAIRY of folklore, especially in CORNWALL and Devon, where some held pixies to be the spirits of infants who died before baptism. In Cornwall and West Devon figures of "piskeys" or pixies are still very much in evidence at "beauty spots" as souvenirs and lucky charms for tourists.

Place. Place-makers' Bible. *See* BIBLE, SOME SPECIALLY NAMED EDITIONS.

Place aux dames (Fr.). Make way for the ladies; ladies first.

Placebo (plăs ē′ bō) (Lat., I shall please, or be acceptable). VESPERS for the dead; because the first antiphon at Vespers of the office of the Dead began with the words *Placebo Domino in regione vivorum*, "I will walk before the Lord in the land of the living" (*Ps.* cxvi, 9).

As sycophants and those who hoped to get something out of the relatives of the departed used to make a point of attending this service and singing the *Placebo*, the phrase *to sing placebo* came to mean to play the flatterer or sycophant. Chaucer gives the name to such a parasite in the *Merchant's Tale* and in the *Parson's Tale* says, "Flattereres been the develes chapelleyns that singen evere *Placebo*" (§xl).

A king when he presides in council, let him beware how he opens his own inclination too much in that which he propoundeth; for else counsellors ... instead of giving free counsel, will sing him a song of "placebo".
BACON: *Essays (Of Counsel).*

An innocuous medicine designed to humour a patient, and which may have a beneficial psychological and physical effect is called a *placebo*.

Placemen. A name given to those members of the HOUSE OF COMMONS who held "places" or offices of profit under the Crown. Their numbers grew steadily after the RESTORATION with the corrupt use of Crown patronage by the Treasury to gain support for the government of the day. (*See* WHIG BIBLE *under* BIBLE). Placemen included ministers, civil servants, court officials, contractors, army and navy officers, etc. Attempts to limit their influence by Place Bills excluding them from the Commons were frequent, particularly from the 1690s until the 1740s, but few were passed. The objective was mainly secured by administrative reforms (1782–1870) which abolished places. The problem of patronage, however, still exists.

But what is said far too seldom is that the whole development of government intervention into so many aspects of economic and social affairs has meant a huge proliferation of jobs, salaries or honorifics, available for distribution to party loyalists.
MAX BELOFF: article in *The Times*, 16 April 1968.

Plagiarist (plā′ jà rist), one who appropriates another's ideas, etc., in literature, music, and so on, means strictly a kidnapper or manstealer. Martial applies it to a literary thief.

Plaid Cymru (plīd kŭm rē) (W. Party of Wales). The Welsh nationalist party set up in 1925 with the object of achieving Welsh home rule. Support grew in the 1960s and the party gained three seats in the HOUSE OF COMMONS in 1974, but only two in 1979 and 1983 and three in 1987.

Plain, The. The GIRONDISTS were so called in the French Revolutionary National Convention, because they sat on the level floor or *plain* of the hall. After their overthrow this part of the House was called the *marais* or swamp, and included such members as were under the control of the MOUNTAIN.

The Cities of the Plain. *See under* CITY.

It's all plain sailing. It's perfectly straightforward; there need be no hesitation about the course of action. A nautical phrase which should be written *plane*, not *plain*. **Plane sailing** is the art of determining a ship's position on the assumption that the earth is flat and she is sailing, therefore, on a plane, instead of a spherical surface, which is a simple and easy method of determining the course and distance over short passages.

Plains Indians is the name given to the Indian tribes of the central prairie areas of North America from Alberta to Texas— once the land of the American bison or buffalo. They are the redskins of popular fame, with their feather head-dresses, teepees, and peace pipes. Among the numerous tribes are the Dakota, BLACKFEET, Cheyenne, Comanche, PAWNEE and APACHE.

Planets. The heavenly bodies that revolve round the SUN in approximately circular orbits; so called from Gr. *planes*, wanderer, because to the ancients, they appeared to wander about among the stars instead of having fixed places.

The *primary planets* are MERCURY, VENUS, the Earth, MARS, JUPITER, SATURN, URANUS, NEPTUNE and PLUTO (discovered in 1930); these are known as the *major planets*, the asteroids between the orbits of Mars and Jupiter being the *minor planets*.

The *secondary planets* are the satellites, or moons revolving round a primary.

Mercury and Venus are called *inferior planets* since their orbits are nearer to the sun than the Earth's; the remaining planets are *superior planets*. Only five of the planets were known to the ancients (the Earth not being reckoned), *viz*. Mercury, Venus, Mars, Jupiter, and Saturn; but to these were added the Sun and MOON, making seven in all.

For the relation of metals and precious stones to the planets *see* PRECIOUS STONES.

Planet-struck. A blighted tree is said to be planet-struck. Epilepsy, paralysis, lunacy, etc., are attributed to the malignant aspects of the planets. Horses are said to be *planet-struck* when they seem stupefied, whether from want of food, colic, or stoppage.

> They with speed
> Their course through thickest constellations held,
> Spreading their bane; the blasted stars looked wan,
> And planets, planet-strook, real eclipse
> Then suffered.
> MILTON: *Paradise Lost*, X, 410.

To be born under a lucky, or **unlucky planet.** According to ASTROLOGY, some planet, at the birth of every individual, presides over his destiny. Some of the planets, like JUPITER, are lucky; and others like SATURN, are unlucky. *See* HOUSES, ASTROLOGICAL.

Plank. Any one portion or principle of a political PLATFORM.

To walk the plank. To be put to the supreme test; also, to be about to die. Walking the plank was a mode of disposing of prisoners at sea, much in vogue among pirates in the 17th century.

Plantagenet (plăn tăj′ ĕ net). A name commonly given since the mid-17th century to the royal line now more properly called ANGEVIN and to the LANCASTRIAN and YORKIST kings from Henry IV to Richard III; the descendants of Geoffrey, Count of Anjou, and Matilda, daughter of Henry I. It may have arisen from Geoffrey of Anjou's habit of wearing a sprig of broom (*plante genêt*) in his cap, or that he planted BROOM to improve his hunting covers. Henry II was Geoffrey's son. The *House of Plantagenet* therefore includes the following kings: Henry II, Richard I, John, Henry III, Edward I, II, and III, Richard II, Henry IV, V, VI, Edward IV and V, and Richard III. It was historically only a nickname, first used as a surname by Richard Duke of York, father of Edward IV.

Plate. In horse-racing, the GOLD or SILVER cup forming the prize; hence the race for such a prize.

A lot on one's plate. Slang for having much to do or worry about.

Plates of meat. RHYMING SLANG for "feet"; often abbreviated to *plates*.

Selling plate. A race in which owners of starters have to agree beforehand that the winners shall be sold at a previously fixed price.

Platform. The policy or declaration of a political party, that on which the party stands (*cp*. PLANK). In this sense it is an Americanism dating from before the mid-19th century. It was, however, used in the late 16th century of a plan or scheme of church government, and Milton says, "some ... do not think it for the ease of their inconsequent opinions to grant that the Church-discipline is platformed in the Bible, but that it is left to the discretion of men" (*Church Government*).

Plato (*c*. 428–348 B.C.). The great Athenian philosopher, pupil of SOCRATES, and founder of the ACADEMY. Of his numerous writings the REPUBLIC has perhaps been the most influential. He was originally called Aristocles but the name Plato is said to have been bestowed by his gymnastic teacher, from his broad shoulders. Some say it arose from the breadth of his forehead.

Platonic bodies. An old name for the five regular geometric solids described by PLATO, *viz*. the tetrahedron, hexahedron, octahedron, dodecahedron, and icosahedron, all of which are bounded by like, equal, and regular planes.

Platonic love. Spiritual love between persons of opposite sexes; the friendship of man and woman, without any sexual implications. The phrase is founded on a passage towards the end of the *Symposium* in which PLATO was extolling not the non-sexual love of a man for a woman but the loving interest that SOCRATES took in young men—which was pure, and therefore noteworthy in the Greece of the period.

> I am convinced, and always was, that Platonic Love is Platonic nonsense.
> RICHARDSON: *Pamela*, III, lxxviii.

The Platonic Year. *See* PLATONIC CYCLE *under* CYCLE.

Platonism is characterized by the doctrine of pre-existing eternal ideas, and teaches the immortality and pre-existence of the soul, the dependence of virtue upon discipline, and the trustworthiness of cognition.

Plattdeutsch (plăt doich). Low German, which, until 1500, was the business language of northern Europe. *See* HIGH GERMAN.

Play. "This may be play to you, 'tis death to us." The allusion is to ÆSOP'S FABLE of the boys throwing stones at some frogs.

As good as a play. Intensely amusing. Said to have been the remark of Charles II at the HOUSE OF LORDS debate on Lord Ross's Divorce Bill (1670).

He played his cards well. *See under* CARD.

Played out. Exhausted; out of date; no longer in VOGUE.

Playing possum. *See* POSSUM.

To play for time. To prolong or delay negotiations, coming to a decision, in the hope of staving off defeat, failure, etc.; as in CRICKET, when victory for the batting team is no longer possible in the remaining time, but cautious play may lead to a drawn game instead of defeat.

To play into someone's hands. *See under* HAND.

To play someone up. To be a nuisance to them, to harass and annoy, to behave in a troublesome fashion, as schoolchildren are wont to "play up" certain of their teachers.

To play to the gallery, or **to the gods.** *See* GALLERY, *and* AMONG THE GODS *under* GOD.

To play up to someone. To seek to ingratiate oneself with a person by flattery, etc. Probably of theatrical origin.

Pleader, Pleading. *See* SPECIAL PLEADING.

Plebeian (ple bē' an). One of, or appertaining to, the common people; properly a free citizen of ROME, neither PATRICIAN nor client. From Lat. *plebs*, the common people.

Plebiscite (pleb'i sit). In Roman history, a law enacted by the "comitia" or assembly of tribes; nowadays it means the direct vote of the whole body of citizens of a state on some definite question; thus Louis Napoleon's COUP D'ÉTAT (2 December 1851) was confirmed by a carefully "rigged" plebiscite and in November 1852 another plebiscite approved the re-establishment of the Empire.

Pledge. To guarantee; to assign as security; hence in drinking a toast, to give assurance of friendship by the act of drinking.

> Drink to me only with thine eyes,
> And I will pledge with mine.
>
> BEN JONSON: *To Celia*.

To sign, or **take the pledge.** To bind oneself by one's pledged word to abstain from intoxicating liquors. Such a pledge was taken by members of the BAND OF HOPE.

Pleiades (plī' a dēz). In classical myth, the seven daughters of ATLAS and Pleione, sisters of the HYADES. They were transformed into stars, one of which, MEROPE, is invisible, out of shame, because she married a mortal man; while others say it is ELECTRA who hides herself from grief for the destruction of TROY and its royal race. Electra is known as "the lost Pleiad".

> One of these forms which flit by us, when we
> Are young, and fix our eyes on every face ...
> Whose course and home we know not, nor shall know,
> Like the lost Pleiad seen no more below.
>
> BYRON: *Beppo*, xiv.

The great cluster of stars in the constellation TAURUS, especially the seven larger ones, were called **the Pleiades** by the Greeks from the word *plein*, to sail, because they considered navigation safe at the rising of the constellation, and their setting marked the close of the sailing season.

The Pleiad. A name frequently given to groups of seven particularly illustrious persons.

The Philosophical Pleiad. The Seven WISE MEN OF GREECE are sometimes so called.

The Pleiad of Alexandria. A group of seven contemporary poets in the 3rd century B.C., *viz*. Callimachus, Apollonius of Rhodes, Aratus, Philiscus (called HOMER the Younger), Lycophron, Nicander, and THEOCRITUS.

Charlemagne's Pleiad, the group of scholars with which the Emperor surrounded himself, *viz*. CHARLEMAGNE (who, in this circle, was known as "David"), Alcuin ("Albinus"), Adelard ("Augustine"), Angilbert ("Homer"), Riculfe ("Damætas"), Varnefrid, and Eginhard.

The French Pleiad of the 16th century, who wrote poetry in the metres, style, etc., of the ancient Greeks and Romans. Ronsard was their leader, the others being Daurat, Du Bellay, Belleau, Baïf, Jodelle, and Pontus de Tyard. Scévole de Sainte-Marthe and Muretus are sometimes given instead of Jodelle and Pontus de Tyard.

The second French Pleiad. Some contemporary poets in the reign of Louis XIII (1610–1643), very inferior to the "First Pleiad". They are Rapin, Commire, Larue, Santeuil, Ménage, Dupérier, and Petit.

Plimsoll Line, or **Mark.** The mark fixing the maximum load line of a merchant vessel in salt water. It takes its name from Samuel Plimsoll (1824–1898), M.P. for Derby, who from 1870 led a campaign of protest against the over-loading and over-insuring of unsafe shipping. His sensational outburst when

Disraeli's government decided to drop the Shipping Bill in 1875 led to the Merchant Shipping (Plimsoll) Act of 1876.

Plon-plon. The sobriquet of Prince Napoleon Joseph Charles Paul Bonaparte (1822–1891), son of Jerome Bonaparte, an adaptation of *Craint-plon* (Fear-bullet), the nickname he earned in the Crimean War.

Plonk. Also "RED BIDDY" or "Pinkie". An Australian term for cheap red wine fortified by methylated spirit. It is popularly applied to any cheap red wine.

Plough. Another name for the GREAT BEAR (*see under* BEAR).

Fond, Fool, or **White Plough.** The plough dragged about a village on PLOUGH MONDAY. Called *white*, because the MUMMERS were dressed in white, gaudily trimmed with flowers and ribbons. Called *fond*, or *fool*, because the procession is fond or foolish—*i.e.* not serious or of a business character.

Plough alms. In mediæval England, a payment of one penny for each plough team in the parish, paid to the priest a fortnight after EASTER.

Plough Monday. The first MONDAY after Twelfth Day is so called because it was the end of the CHRISTMAS holidays when men returned to their plough or daily work. It was customary for farm labourers to draw a plough (*see* FOND *above*) from door to door and solicit "plough-money" to spend in a frolic. The queen of the banquet was called Bessy. *Cp.* ST. DISTAFF'S DAY *under* DISTAFF.

Speed the plough, or **God speed the plough.** A wish for success and prosperity in some undertaking. It is a very old phrase, and occurs in the song sung by ploughmen on PLOUGH MONDAY.

To be ploughed. To fail to pass an examination (*see* PLUCK).

To plough the sands. To engage in some altogether fruitless labour.

To plough with another's heifer. To use information obtained by unfair means, *e.g.* through a treacherous friend. A Biblical phrase. When the men of Timnath gave Samson the answer to his riddle, he replied:

> If ye had not ploughed with my heifer, ye had not found out my riddle.
>
> *Judges* xiv, 18.

To put one's hand to the plough. To undertake a task; to commence operations in earnest. Only by keeping one's eyes on an object ahead is it possible to plough straight.

> And Jesus said unto him, No man, having put his hand to the plough, and looking back, is fit for the kingdom of God.
>
> *Luke* ix, 62.

To put the plough before the oxen. Another way of saying "to put the cart before the horse" (*see* CART).

Ploughbote. A bote or estover dating back to Saxon times, the tenant-right of taking wood from the estate for repairing the tools of husbandry; originally for the maintenance of the woodwork of the plough.

Plover. An old synonym for a dupe or GULL; also for a courtesan.

To live like a plover. To live on nothing, to live on air. Plovers, however, live on small insects and worms, which they hunt for in newly ploughed fields.

Plowden. "The case is altered," quoth **Plowden.** There is more than one story accounting for the origin of this old phrase—used by Jonson as the title of one of his comedies (1598). One is that Edmund Plowden (1518–1585), the great lawyer, was defending a gentleman who was accused of hearing MASS, and elicited the fact that the service was performed by a layman masquerading in priestly vestments for the purpose of informing against the worshippers. Thereupon the brilliant lawyer observed, "The case is altered, no priest, no mass", thus securing the acquittal of his client. Another version is that Plowden was asked what legal remedy there was against some hogs that trespassed on a complainant's ground. "There is a very good remedy," began the lawyer, but when informed that they were the complainant's own hogs, said, "Nay, then, the case is altered." *See* PUBLIC-HOUSE SIGNS.

Pluck, meaning courage, determination, was originally pugilistic slang of the late 18th century, and meant much the same as heart. A "pug" who was lacking in pluck was a coward; the *pluck* of an animal is the HEART, liver, and lungs, that can be removed by one pull or *pluck*. *Cp.* the expressions bold *heart*, lily-livered (*see* LIVER), a man of another KIDNEY, BOWELS OF MERCY, a *vein* of fun, it raised his BILE, etc.

A rejected candidate at an examination is said to be *plucked*, because formerly at the ancient universities, when degrees were conferred and the names were read out before presentation to the Vice-Chancellor, the PROCTOR walked once up and down the room, and anyone who objected might signify his dissent by plucking the proctor's gown. This was occasionally done by tradesmen to whom the candidate was in debt.

> "No, it isn't that, sir. I'm not afraid of being shot; I wish to God anybody would shoot me. I have not got my degree. I—I'm plucked, sir".
>
> THACKERAY: *Pendennis*, ch. xx.

A plucked pigeon. One fleeced out of his

money; one plucked by a ROOK or sharper.

> There were no smart fellows whom fortune had tumbled…no plucked pigeons, or winged rooks— no disappointed speculators—no ruined miners.
> SCOTT: *Peveril of the Peak*, ch. xi.

He's a plucked'un. He's a plucky chap; there's no frightening him.

I'll pluck his goose for him. I'll cut his crest, lower his pride, make him EAT HUMBLE PIE. Comparing the person to a GOOSE, the threat is to pluck off his feathers in which he prides himself.

Plug. Plug song. A song given publicity, as on the radio. To *plug* in this connexion is to publicize somewhat excessively.

Plugged in. *Au fait* with the latest trends in fashion or popular trends generally. "Switched on" is similarly used; both are derived from electrical appliances.

Plug ugly. A rowdy, unpleasant character, a term said to have originated at Baltimore.

Plum. Old slang for a very large sum of money (properly £100,000), or for its possession. Nowadays the figurative use of the word means the very best part of anything, the prize, the "pick of the basket", a WINDFALL.

Plumes. In borrowed plumes. Assumed merit; airs and graces not merited. The allusion is to the fable of the jay who dressed up in peacock's feathers.

To plume oneself on something. To be proud of it, conceited about it; to boast of it. A plume is a feather, and *to plume oneself* is to feather one's own conceit.

Plump. To give all one's votes to a single candidate, or to vote for one only when one has the right to vote for more. The earlier phrase was **to give a plumper**, or **to vote plump**.

Plunger. One who *plunges*, *i.e.* gambles recklessly, and goes on when he can't afford it in the hope that his luck will turn. The 4th and last Marquess of Hastings was the first person so called by the TURF. He was the original of CHAMPAGNE CHARLIE and the most notorious spendthrift and wastrel of the mid-19th century. One night he lost three games of draughts for £1,000 a game. He then cut a pack of cards for £500 a cut, and lost £5,000 in an hour and a half. He paid both debts before he left the room.

Plus fours. Loose KNICKERBOCKERS overlapping the knee-band and thereby giving added freedom for active outdoor sports. They were particularly popular with golfers in the 1920s. The name derives from the four extra inches of cloth required below the knee in tailoring.

Plus ultra. The motto in the Spanish royal arms. It was once *Ne plus ultra* ("thus far and no farther") in allusion to the PILLARS OF HERCULES, the *ne plus ultra* of the world; but after the discovery of America, and when Charles V inherited the crown of Aragon and Castile, with all the vast American possessions, he struck out *ne*, and assumed the words *plus ultra* for the national motto, the suggestion being that Spain *could* go farther.

Pluto. In Roman mythology, the ruler of the infernal regions, son of SATURN, brother of JUPITER and NEPTUNE, and husband of PROSERPINE; hence, the grave, the place where the dead go before they are admitted into ELYSIUM or sent to TARTARUS.

In World War II, *Pluto* was the codename (from the initials of Pipe Line Under The Ocean) given to the pipelines to carry oil fuel laid across the bed of the English Channel—from Sandown to Cherbourg and from Dungeness to Boulogne.

Plutonian or **Plutonist.** *See* VULCANIST.

Plutonic Rocks. Granites, certain porphyries and other igneous unstratified crystalline rocks, supposed to have been formed at a great depth and pressure, as distinguished from the volcanic rocks which were formed near the surface. So called from PLUTO, as the lord of elemental fire. Richard Kirwan used the term in his *Elements of Mineralogy*, 1796.

Plutus. In Greek mythology, the god of riches. Hence, *rich as Plutus*, and *plutocrat*, one who exercises influence or possesses power through his wealth. The legend is that he was blinded by ZEUS so that his gifts should be equally distributed and not go only to those who merited them.

Plymouth Brethren. A sect of Evangelical Christians founded in IRELAND about 1828 by J.N. Darby, one-time Anglican priest (hence they are sometimes called Darbyites), and deriving their name from Plymouth, the first centre set up in England (1830). In 1849 they split up into "Open Brethren" and "Exclusive Brethren". They have no organized ministry and lay emphasis on the Breaking of Bread each SUNDAY.

Pocahontas (pok à hon′ tăs). Daughter of Powhatan, an Indian chief of Virginia. She is said to have rescued Captain John Smith when her father was on the point of killing him. She subsequently married John Rolfe, the first Englishman to plant and cure tobacco. In 1616 she came to ENGLAND with her husband and infant son and was presented to James I and the Queen. She died off Gravesend (21 March 1617) when about to return to Virginia, and was buried in St George's Church. Curiously enough sh passed her stay at the Bell-Savage (*see* L

864

BELLE SAUVAGE).

The blessed
Pocahontas, as the historian calls her,
And great King's daughter of Virginia.
BEN JONSON: *Staple of News*, II, v (1625).

Pocket (M.E. *poket*, a pouch, small bag, etc.). From its attributive use for small articles designed to be carried in the *pockets* of a garment, as *pocket handkerchief*, *pocket watch*, it is figuratively used of numerous things and people of less than normal or average size. Thus, Germany, forbidden to build warships of over 10,000 tons by the Treaty of VERSAILLES (1919), constructed several formidable battleships purporting to be within this limit which were known as **pocket battleships**.

Pocket borough. Before the Reform Act of 1832, a borough where the electorate was so small that the local magnate had the borough "in his pocket", *i.e.* he was able to return his own nominee.

Pocket judgment. A bond under the hand of the debtor, countersigned by the sovereign. It could be enforced without legal process, but has for long fallen into disuse.

Pocket pistol. Colloquial for a flask carried in "self-defence", because one may not be able to get a dram on the road.

Queen Elizabeth's Pocket Pistol. An ancient bronze cannon given to Elizabeth I by the Netherlands in recognition of her help against Philip II of Spain. It used to overlook the Channel from the Dover Cliffs and is now in Dover Castle.

Pocket veto. When the President of the U.S.A. refuses to sign a Bill which has passed both Houses, he is said to *pocket* it.

Put your pride in your pocket. Lay it aside for the nonce.

To be in, or **out of pocket.** To be a gainer or loser by some transaction.

To have someone in one's pocket. To have complete influence over a person; to be sure of his ready complaisance in any matter.

To line one's pockets. To make a good deal of money, TO FEATHER ONE'S NEST (*see under* FEATHER); often with the implication of profiting at the expense of others. *See* LINING.

To pocket an insult. To submit to an insult without showing annoyance.

To put one's hand in one's pocket. To give money (often to a charity).

Pococurante (pō kō kū răn' ti). (Ital. *poco curante*, caring little). Insouciant, DEVIL-MAY-CARE (*see under* DEVIL PHRASES), easy-go-lucky. Hence, *pococurantism*, indifference to matters of importance but concern about trifles. Also used for one who in arguments leaves the main gist and rides off on some minor and indifferent point.

Podsnap. A pompous, self-satisfied man in Dickens's *Our Mutual Friend*, the type of one who is overburdened with stiff-starched etiquette and self-importance. Hence, *Podsnappery*. *Cp.* PECKSNIFF.

He always knew exactly what providence meant. Inferior and less respectable men might fall short of that mark, but Mr. Podsnap was always up to it. And it was very remarkable (and must have been very comfortable) that what Providence meant was invariably what Mr. Podsnap meant.
Our Mutual Friend, Bk. I, ch. xi.

Podunk. A term for a little American ONE-HORSE TOWN; from the place near Hartford, Connecticut, of this name, which is of American Indian origin.

Poet. Poet Laureate. A court official, now appointed by the PRIME MINISTER, who composes odes in celebration of royal birthdays and State occasions. The appointment essentially dates from the time of James I, but in earlier times there had been an occasional *Versificator Regis* and the universities gave the LAUREL wreath to graduates in rhetoric and Latin versification and to meritorious poets, among whom Skelton was styled *Laureatus*. The laurel crown was anciently a mark of distinction and honour. The following is the list of Poets Laureate:

Ben Jonson, 1619–1637
Sir William Davenant, 1638–1668
John Dryden, 1670–1688
Thomas Shadwell, 1688–1692
Nahum Tate, 1692–1715
Nicholas Rowe, 1715–1718
Laurence Eusden, 1718–1730
Colley Cibber, 1730–1757
William Whitehead, 1757–1785
Thomas Warton, 1785–1790
Henry James Pye, 1790–1813
Robert Southey, 1813–1843
William Wordsworth, 1843–1850
Alfred Tennyson, 1850–1892
Alfred Austin, 1896–1913
Robert Bridges, 1913–1930
John Masefield, 1930–1967
Cecil Day Lewis, 1968–1972
John Betjeman, 1972–1984
Ted Hughes, 1984–

Peasant Poet. *See* PEASANT.

Postman Poet. *See* DEVONSHIRE POET.

Poeta nascitur, non fit. Poets are born, not made. *See under* BORN.

Poet's Corner. The southern end of the south transept of Westminster Abbey, first so called by Oliver Goldsmith because it contained the tomb of Chaucer. Addison had previously (*The Spectator*, No.26, 1711) alluded to it as the "poetical quarter", in which he says—

I found there were Poets who had no Monuments, and Monuments which had no poets.

Among writers buried here are Spenser, Dryden, Dr. Johnson, Sheridan, Dickens, Browning, Tennyson, Macaulay, Hardy, and Kipling. There are many monuments to writers not buried here. Ben Jonson was buried in the north aisle of the Abbey, and Addison in Henry VII's Chapel.

The term *Poet's Corner* is also facetiously applied to the part of a newspaper in which poetical contributions are printed.

Point. Defined by EUCLID as "that which hath no parts". Playfair defined it as "that which has position but not magnitude", and Legendre says it "is a limit terminating a line", which suggests that a point could not exist without a line, and presupposes that we know what a line is.

A point of honour. *See under* HONOUR.

A point of order. In a formal deliberative assembly, a question raised as to whether a particular proceeding is in accordance with the rules of the body itself.

A point-to-point race. A race, especially a STEEPLECHASE, direct from one point to another; a cross-country race.

On points. A World War II expression relating to the system of rationing food, clothing, etc. Apart from direct rationing of meat, bacon, sugar, fats and tea, miscellaneous groceries, etc., were given "points" values and each ration-book holder was given a certain number of points to spend in an allotted period. Hence "it's on points" was a common reference to many commodities.

Point of no return. The point in an aircraft's flight at which it has not enough fuel to return to its point of departure and must continue. Hence its figurative application, a point or situation from which there is no going back.

Armed at all points. Armed to the teeth; having no parts undefended.

> A figure like your Father,
> Arm'd at all points exactly, *cap-a-pe*,
> Appears before them.
> SHAKESPEARE: *Hamlet*, I, ii.

In point of fact. A stronger way of saying "As a fact", or "As a matter of fact".

Not to put too fine a point upon it. Not to be over delicate in stating it; the prelude to a blunt though truthful remark. The allusion here is to the sharp end of a tool or weapon, etc.

To carry one's point. To attain the desired end; to get one's way.

To come to the point. To speak out plainly, to avoid circumlocution; to get to the gist of the matter; not TO BEAT ABOUT THE BUSH. (*See under* BEAT.)

To dine on potatoes and point. To have potatoes without any relish or extras, a very meagre dinner indeed. When viands were scarce parents used to tell their children to point their potato to the salt, cheese, bacon, etc. (as imaginary extras) and then eat the potato. *Bread and point* was a similar expression, akin to the more recent "bread and pull-it".

To give one points. To be able to accord him an advantage and yet beat him; to be considerably better than he.

To make a point of doing something. To treat it as a matter of duty, or to make it a special object. The phrase is a translation of the older French *faire un point de*.

To stand on points. On punctilios; delicacy of behaviour. SHAKESPEARE puns on the phrase in the following quotation, the side allusion being that Quince, in the delivery of his Prologue, had taken no notice of the stops, or *points*:

> This fellow doth not stand upon points.
> *A Midsummer Night's Dream*, V, i.

To stretch a point. To exceed what is strictly right or proper. It may allude to the tagged laces called *points*, formerly used in costume; to "truss a point" was to tie the laces which fastened the garment; to "stretch a point", to stretch these laces, so as to adjust for growth or the temporary fulness after good feeding.

To truss his points. To tie the points of garments, especially hose. The *points* were cords tagged like shoe-laces, attached to doublets and hose, etc.; being very numerous, some second person was required to "truss" them or fasten them properly.

Point-blank. Direct. A term from gunnery; when a cannon is so placed that the line of sight is parallel to the axis and horizontal, the discharge is point-blank, and was supposed to go direct, without curve, to an object within a certain distance. In French *point blanc* is the white mark or BULL'S-EYE of a target, to hit which the ball or arrow must not deviate in the least.

> Now art thou within point-blank of our jurisdiction regal.
> SHAKESPEARE: *Henry VI, Pt. II*, IV, ii.

Point d'appui (pwăn dă pwē'). A standpoint, a fulcrum, a base for action; a pretext to conceal the real intention. Literally, the point of support.

Point-device. An archaic expression meaning punctilious, minutely exact.

> Men's behaviour should be like their apparel, no too strait or point device, but free for exercise o motion.
> BACON: *Essays (Of Ceremonies and Respects)*

Pointillism (pwăn' til izm) (Fr. *pointiller*, to dot, to stipple). A Neo-Impressionist technique of painting with dots of pure colour, popularized by the French painter Georges Seurat (1859–1891). It is also known as the Divisionist technique. *Cp.* IMPRESSIONISM.

Poison. *See* MITHRIDATE.

Box-office poison. An American expression for an unsuccessful play, etc.

One man's meat is another man's poison. What is palatable or beneficial to one man is distasteful or harmful to another.

Poisson d'Avril (pwa' son dȧ vril) (Fr., April fish). The French equivalent of our APRIL FOOL.

Poke. A bag, pouch, or sack—from which comes our *pocket*, a little poke. The word is virtually obsolete except in the phrase *to buy* A PIG IN A POKE (*see under* PIG).

Poke bonnet. A long, straight, projecting bonnet, commonly worn by women in the early 19th century and later by SALVATION ARMY lassies and old-fashioned QUAKER women. Perhaps so called because it projects or pokes out in front.

To poke fun at one. To ridicule.

Poker face. An expressionless face characteristic of the good poker-player, who assumes it to conceal from his adversaries any idea of what cards he may be holding.

Poky. Cramped, narrow, confined, as *a poky little room*. Also poor and shabby.

> The ladies were in their pokiest old headgear.
> THACKERAY: *The Newcomes*, ch. lvii.

As a noun it is U.S. slang for a prison.

Polack (pō' lăk). An inhabitant of Poland, a term now superseded by *Pole*, although humorously used in the U.S.A.

> So frowned he once, when, in an angry parle,
> He smote the sledded Polacks on the ice.
> SHAKESPEARE: *Hamlet*, I, i.

Poland. There are many legends of early Poland. One is that Prince Popiel invited all his family to a banquet and when they were drunk killed them off with poisoned wine. He was duly punished when millions of mice entered his castle and devoured him. The chiefs then elected one Piast, a wheelmaker, to be their ruler, it having been reported that when he had been sitting in the garden with his wife two young men with white wings on their shoulders were with them, and this was deemed a favourable omen. The two ANGELS were Cyril and Methodius, the APOSTLES of central Europe. The Piast dynasty ruled from 880 until 1370. *See also* LAND OF THE WHITE EAGLE.

The Polish Corridor. The territory given to Poland by the Treaty of VERSAILLES (1919) to give her access to the Baltic Sea west of Danzig. The Corridor cut off East Prussia from the rest of Germany and proved to be a bone of contention from the outset. It followed roughly the line of the Vistula.

Pole. The stake, mast, measure (16½ ft.), etc., gets its name from Lat. *palus*, a pale or stake; *pole*—the *North Pole*, *magnetic pole*, etc., is from Gr. *polos*, axis, pivot.

Barber's pole. *See under* BARBER.

The Poles are the vintagers in Normandy. The Norman vintage consists of apples beaten down by poles. The French say *En Normandie l'on vendange avec la gaule*, a play on the words *Gaule* (Gaul) and *gaule*, meaning a pole. During the German occupation of Paris (1941–1944) students once marched through the streets carrying two posts (*deux gaules*) and it took the Germans some time to realise that this was a play on the name De Gaulle—then a symbol of French nationality and liberty.

Under bare poles. *See* BARE POLES.

Polichinelle, Un Secret de. *See under* SECRET.

Polish. Polish off. To finish out of hand. In allusion to articles polished.

I'll polish him off in no time. I'll soon deal with him, give him a good drubbing.

To polish off a meal. To eat it quickly; to finish it off.

Spit and polish. *See* SPIT.

Politbureau, -buro. Formerly, the chief policy-making body of the Communist Party in the U.S.S.R., first formed in 1917. It examined matters before they were submitted to the government and consisted of five members. It was superseded by the PRESIDIUM of the Central Committee of the Communist Party in 1952.

Politeness of Kings. *See* PUNCTUAL.

Politiques (pol i tēk'). In French history, a party of "moderates", formed after the Massacre of St. BARTHOLOMEW around the Duke of Montmorency and the Marshal de Cossé-Brissac, who reacted against the fanaticism of CATHOLIC LEAGUE and HUGUENOT alike, and sought to bring the wars of religion to an end. The *Satyre Ménippée* (*see* MENIPPUS) was their work and it championed the cause of Henry of Navarre as the future king of France.

Polka. A round dance said to have been invented about 1830 by a Bohemian servant girl, which soon took Europe by storm. It is danced by couples in 2/4 time, the characteristic feature being the rest on the second beat.

Poll (pōl) (of Teutonic origin) means the head; hence, the number of persons in a crowd ascertained by counting heads, hence the counting of voters at an election, and such phrases as **to go to the polls**, to stand for election, and POLL TAX, a tax levied on everybody.

The Cambridge term, **the Poll**, meaning students who obtain a pass degree, *i.e.* a degree without honours, is probably from Gr. *hoi polloi*, the common herd. These students—*poll men*, were said to *go out in the poll*, and to take a *poll degree*.

Poll tax. A graduated tax levied per head in England in 1377 led to the PEASANTS' REVOLT in 1381. Another was imposed in 1513 and on subsequent occasions but it was abolished in 1689. In most of the Southern States of the U.S.A. it was used as a condition of suffrage from 1889 and was still imposed by a few well into the 20th century. A poll tax replaces domestic rates in Scotland in 1989 and in the remainder of Great Britain in 1990.

Clod poll. A blockhead, a stupid fellow.

> Therefore this letter, being so excellently ignorant, will breed no terror in this youth: he will find it comes from a clodpole.
>
> SHAKESPEARE: *Twelfth Night*, III, iv.

Pollux. In classical mythology the twin brother of CASTOR.

Polly, Mary. The change of M for P in pet names is by no means rare, *e.g.*—

> *Margaret*. Maggie or Meggy, becomes Peggie, and Pegg or Peg.
>
> *Martha*. Matty becomes Patty.

In the case of *Mary—Polly* we see another change by no means unusual—that of *r* into *l* or *ll*. Similarly, *Sarah* becomes Sally; *Dorothea*, Dora, becomes Dolly; *Henry*, Hal.

Polonius. A garrulous old courtier in SHAKESPEARE'S HAMLET, typical of the pompous, sententious old man. He was the father of Ophelia and lord chamberlain to the king of Denmark.

Poltergeist (pol tĕr gīst). A household spirit well known to spiritualists, remarkable for throwing things about, plucking the bedclothes, making noises, etc. It is a German term—*Polter*, noise; *Geist*, spirit. *See* SAMPFORD GHOST.

Polt-foot. A club-foot. Ben Jonson calls VULCAN, who was lame, the "polt-footed philosopher". Variant spellings are *poult* and *powlt*, and its literal meaning is chicken-foot.

> Venus was content to take the blake Smith [Vulcan] with his powlt foote.
>
> LYLY: *Euphues*.

Poltroon. A coward; from Ital. *poltro*, a bed, because cowards are sluggards and feign themselves sick a-bed in times of war.

In falconry the name was given to a bird of prey, with the talons of the hind toes cut off to prevent it flying at game, probably from the old idea that the word was the Lat. *pollice truncus*, maimed in the thumb.

Polycarp, St. One of the most noted martyrs of the 2nd century whose life was linked with the Apostolic age. Born *c*.69, he was probably converted to Christianity by ST. JOHN THE EVANGELIST and was Bishop of Smyrna for over 40 years where he became a staunch and vigorous leader. Persecution of Christians arose in Smyrna in 155 and the mob soon demanded Polycarp, "the father of the Christians" as their next victim. The proconsul, Statius Quadratus, had him arrested and he was burnt alive after refusing to deny his faith. His faithfulness to the Apostolic tradition is recorded by Irenæus, his disciple. Polycarp's only surviving writing is his *Epistle to the Philippians*. His day is 26 January.

Polycrates (pol i krā′ tēz). *See* AMASIS.

Polyhymnia, or **Polymnia.** The Muse of lyric poetry and the inventor of the lyre. She invented harmony and presided over singing. *See* MUSES.

Polyphemus (pol i fē′ mŭs). One of the CYCLOPS, who ruled over Sicily. When ULYSSES landed on the island the monster made him and twelve of his crew captives; six of them he ate, and then Ulysses contrived to blind him and escape with the rest of the crew (*cp.* LESTRIGONS). *See also* ACIS; GALATEA.

Pomander (pom ăn dèr). From the Fr. *pomme d'ambre*, apple of AMBER or ambergris. A ball made of perfume, such as ambergris, which was worn or carried in a perforated case in order to ward off infection or counteract bad smells. The cases, usually of gold or silver, were also called "pomanders".

Pomatum (po mā′ tŭm). Another name for pomade, so called because originally made by macerating over-ripe apples (Fr. *pommes*) in grease.

> There is likewise made an ointment with the pulpe of Apples and Swines grease and Rose water, which is used to beautifie the face ... called in shops, *pomatum*, of the Apples whereof it is made.
>
> GERARD: *Herbal*, III, xcv (1597).

Pomfret Cakes. *See* PONTEFRACT.

Pommard. A red Burgundy wine, so called from a village of that name in the Côte d'Or, France. The word is sometimes colloquially used for cider, the pun being on *pomme*, apple.

Pommel. The pommel of a sword is the rounded knob terminating the hilt, so called from its apple-like shape (Fr. *pomme*, apple); and to *pommel* or *pummel* one, to pound him with your fists, was originally to beat him with the pommel of your sword.

Pommie, Pommy. An Australian and New Zealand term for an Englishman, used both affectionately and disparagingly. Of uncertain origin, it may derive ultimately from *pomme* (apple) or *pomegranate*, possibly in allusion to the pink and white complexions of the English in contrast to their own tanned countenances. Another possible suggestion is that it arose in the days when English convicts were transported to Australia and it was formed from the initials P.O.M.E. — Prisoner of Mother England.

Pomona (po mō′ nȧ). The Roman goddess of fruits and fruit-trees (Lat. *pomum*), hence fruit generally.

Pompadour (pom′ pa dôr), as a colour, is claret purple, so called from Louis XV's mistress, the Marquise de Pompadour (1721–1764).

There is an old song supposed to be an elegy on John Broadwood, a QUAKER, which introduces the word:

> Sometimes he wore an old brown coat,
> Sometimes a pompadore,
> Sometimes 'twas buttoned up behind,
> And sometimes down before.

The word is also applied to a fashion of hairdressing in which the hair is raised (often on a pad) in a wave above the forehead.

Pompey (pom′ pi). In British naval slang, Portsmouth.

It is also a generic name formerly used of a black footman, as ABIGAIL used to be a lady's maid. (One of Hood's jocular book-titles was *Pompeii, or Memoirs of a Black Footman*, by *Sir W. Gill* (Sir W. Gell wrote a book on Pompeii).)

Pompey's Pillar. A Corinthian column of red granite, nearly 100 ft. high, erected at Alexandria by Publius, Prefect of Egypt, in honour of Diocletian and to record the conquest of Alexandria in 296. It was probably miscalled by travellers through ignorance. *Cp.* CLEOPATRA'S NEEDLE.

Pongo. In the old romance of THE SEVEN CHAMPIONS of Christendom he was an amphibious monster of Sicily who preyed on the inhabitants of the island for many years. He was slain by the three sons of St. GEORGE.

Pongo was also a nickname for a monkey, an Australian aborigine name for flying squirrel, and one-time sailors' slang for a marine (now a *bootneck*), and then for a soldier.

> Then an old 'possum would sing out, or a black-furred flying squirrel — pongoes, the blacks call 'em

— would come sailing down from the top of an iron-bark tree ...
> BOLDREWOOD: *Robbery Under Arms*, ch xx.

Pons Asinorum (ponz ăs i nôr′ ŭm). (Lat., the asses' bridge). The fifth proposition, Bk. I, of EUCLID—the first difficult theorem, which dunces rarely got over for the first time without stumbling. It is anything but a "bridge"; it is really *pedica asinorum*, the "dolts' stumbling-block".

Pontefract, or **Pomfret Cakes.** Liquorice lozenges impressed with a castle and made at Pontefract since the 16th century. The name of the town is still frequently pronounced *pumfret*, representing the Anglo-Norman and M.E. *Pontfret*. The place was called *Fractus Pons* by Orderic (1097) and *Pontefractus* by John of Hexham (*c.* 1165), in allusion to the old Roman bridge over the Aire, broken down by William I in 1069, remains of which were still visible in the 16th century.

Pontiff. The term formerly applied to any BISHOP but now only to the POPE—the Supreme Pontiff. It means literally one who has charge of the bridges (Lat. *pons, pontis*, a bridge), and these were under the care of the principal college of priests in ancient Rome, the head of which was the *Pontifex Maximus*.

Pontius Pilate's Bodyguard. *See* REGIMENTAL AND DIVISIONAL NICKNAMES.

Pony. Slang for £25; also (especially in the U.S.A.) for a translation CRIB; also for a small beer-glass holding slightly less than a gill.

In card games the person on the right hand of the dealer is called the *pony*, from Lat. *pone*, "behind", being behind the dealer.

Pony Express. This was the U.S. government mail system across the continent just before the days of railways and telegraphs. It ran from St. Joseph, Missouri, to the Pacific Coast and was inaugurated in 1860; less than two years later it was superseded by the electric telegraph. The schedule time for the whole distance was ten days, but Lincoln's inaugural address was taken across the continent in 7 days 17 hours. Fleet horses were used, not ponies, ridden for stages of 10 to 15 miles, the rider doing three stages before handing over the wallet. The service was operated by the firm of Russell, Majors and Waddell.

Pooh Bah, A. One who holds numerous offices simultaneously, usually from motives of self-interest. Pooh Bah, The Lord High Everything Else, is a character in Gilbert and Sullivan's *Mikado*, who was First Lord of the Treasury, Lord Chief Justice,

Commander-in-Chief, Lord High Admiral, Master of the Buckhounds, Groom of the Back Stairs, Archbishop of Titipu, and Lord Mayor.

Poor. Poor as a church mouse? In a church there is no cupboard or pantry where a mouse may take his pickings and he thus has a lean time.

Poor as Job. The allusion is to JOB being deprived by SATAN of everything he possessed.

Poor as Lazarus. This is the beggar LAZARUS, full of sores, who was laid at the rich man's gate and desired to be fed with crumbs that fell from DIVES' table. (*Luke* xvi, 19–31).

Poor Clares. *See* CLARE.

Poor Jack, or **John.** Dried hake. We have "JOHN DORY", a "jack" (pike), a "jack shark", etc., and *Jack* may be here a play on the word "Hake", and *John* a substitute for *Jack*.

> 'Tis well thou art not fish; if thou hadst, thou hadst been poor-john.
>
> SHAKESPEARE: *Romeo and Juliet*, I. i.

Cp. the jocular proof that an eel pie is a fish pie, a fish pie may be a jack pie, a jack pie is a john pie, and john pie is a pie john (pigeon).

Poor man. Scottish term for the bladebone of a shoulder of mutton. In some parts of England it is termed a "poor knight of Windsor", because it holds the same relation to "Sir Loin" (*see* SIRLOIN) as a Windsor Knight does to a BARONET. Scott (*Bride of Lammermoor, Note* to ch. xix) tells of a laird terrifying an English landlord by saying that he "could relish a morsel of poor man" for his dinner. (*See* KNIGHTS OF WINDSOR).

Poor Richard. The assumed name of Benjamin Franklin in a series of ALMANACS from 1732 to 1757. They contained maxims and precepts on temperance, economy, cleanliness, chastity, and other virtues; and several ended with the words "as poor Richard says".

Poor Robin's Almanack. A humorous ALMANAC, parodying those who seriously indulged in prophecy, published at intervals from 1662 to as late as 1828. The early issues were almost certainly the work of William Winstanley (*c.* 1628–1698). As a specimen of the "predictions", the following, for January 1664, may be cited:

> Strong Beer and good Fires are fit for this Season as a Halter for a Thiefe; and, when every Man is pleas'd, then 'twill be a Merry World indeed...This month we may expect to hear of the Death of some Man, Woman, or Child, either in Kent or Christendom.

There are none poor but those whom God hates. This does not mean that poverty is a punishment, but that those whom

God loves are rich in his love. In this sense DIVES may be the poor man, and LAZARUS abounding in that "blessing of the Lord which maketh rich".

Pop goes the weasel. *See under* WEASEL.

Pope. The word represents the O.E. *papa*, from ecclesiastical Latin, and Gr. *pappas*, the infants' word for father.

In the early Church the title was given to many bishops; Leo I, the Great (440–461) was the first to use it officially, and in the time of Gregory VII (1073–1085) it was, by decree, specially reserved to the Bishop of Rome. *Cp.* PONTIFF.

According to Platina, Sergius II (844–847) was the first pope who changed his name on assuming office. Some accounts have it that his name was Hogsmouth, others that it was "Peter de Porca" and he changed it out of deference to St. PETER, thinking it arrogant to style himself Peter II. However, the first clear case of changed name was when Peter, Bishop of Pavia, on election (983) changed his name for that of John XIV.

Gregory the Great (590–604) was the first pope to adopt the title *Servus Servorum Dei* (the Servant of the Servants of God). It is founded on *Mark* x, 44.

The title *Vicar of Christ*, or *Vicar of God*, was adopted by Innocent III, 1198.

Including John Paul II, there are commonly 263 popes enumerated, and the nationality of two of them is unknown. Of the remainder, 209 were Italians, 15 Frenchmen, 12 Greeks, 6 Germans, 6 Syrians, 3 Africans, 3 Spaniards, 2 Dalmatians, and 1 each Dutch, English, Polish, Portuguese, and Jew (St. Peter).

For the drink called a *Pope*, *see* BISHOP.

The Black Pope. The General of the JESUITS.

The Pope of Geneva. A name given to Calvin (1509–1564).

The Red Pope. The Prefect of the PROPAGANDA.

The Pope's eye. The tender piece of meat (the lymphatic gland) surrounded by fat in the middle of a leg of an ox or a sheep. The French call it *Judas's eye*, and the Germans *the priest's tit-bit*.

The Pope's nose. Another name for the PARSON'S NOSE.

The Pope's slave. So Cardinal Cajetan (d. 1534) called the Church.

Pope Joan. A mythical female POPE first recorded in the 13th century by the Dominican Stephen de Bourbon (d. *c.* 1261) who is said to have derived the story from Jean de Mailly. It was widely and long accepted. She was said to have been born in Germany of English parents and eventually went to ROME after living with a monk at Athens. Passing under the name of Johannes Anglicus, her wide learning gained her election to the papacy in 855 as John VIII. She was supposed to have died in childbirth during a solemn procession. The Calvinist scholar David Blondel exploded the myth in 1647 and it was finally demolished by Döllinger in 1863. Emmanuel Royidis published his novel *Papissa Joanna* on the subject in 1886.

Pope Joan is the name of a once popular card game played with an ordinary pack minus the eight of diamonds (the nine of diamonds is called the "Pope"); also with a circular revolving tray with eight compartments.

Popish Plot (1678). A fictitious JESUIT plot to murder Charles II and others, enthrone the Duke of York, fire the CITY of LONDON, after which, with the aid of French and Irish troops, a PROTESTANT massacre was to ensue. The plot was invented by the scoundrelly Titus Oates (1649–1705) and before the anti-Catholic panic abated in 1681 some 35 Catholics were judicially murdered, including the Roman Catholic Primate of Ireland. Oates was eventually pilloried, whipped, and imprisoned when James II became king.

Popinjay. An old name for a parrot (ultimately of Arabic origin; Gr. *papagos*), hence, a conceited or empty-headed fop.

> I then, all smarting with my wounds being cold,
> To be so pester'd with a popinjay,
> Out of my grief and my impatience,
> Answered neglectingly I know not what,
> He should, or he should not.
>
> SHAKESPEARE: *Henry IV, Pt. I*, I, iii.

The Festival of the Popinjay. The first SUNDAY in MAY, when a figure of a popinjay, decked with parti-coloured feathers and suspended from a pole, served as a target for shooting practice. He whose ball or arrow brought down the bird, by cutting the string by which it was hung, received the proud title of "Captain Popinjay" for the rest of the day, and was escorted home in triumph.

Poplar. The poplar was consecrated to HERCULES, because he destroyed Kakos in a cavern of Mount Aventine, which was covered with poplars. In the moment of triumph, the hero plucked a branch from one of the trees and bound it round his head. When he descended to the infernal regions, the heat caused a profuse perspiration which blanched the under surface of the leaves, while the smoke of the eternal flames blackened the upper surface. Hence the leaves of the poplar are dark on one side and white on the other.

The white poplar is fabled to have originally been the NYMPH Leuce, beloved by PLUTO. He changed her into this at death.

Poppy Day. *See* REMEMBRANCE DAY.

Popski's Private Army. A British raiding and reconnaissance force of *c.* 120 men formed in October 1942 under Lt. Col. Vladimir Peniakoff, who had previously worked with the Libyan Arab Force. Familiarly known as "Popski", his men wore the initials P.P.A. on their shoulders. He was born in Belgium of Russian parents, educated at Cambridge and resident in Egypt since 1924. Popski and a small element of his force, together with the LONG RANGE DESERT GROUP, reconnoitred the route by which Montgomery conducted his surprise attack around the Mareth Line, and subsequently operated in Italy and Austria.

Popular Front. A political alliance of left-wing parties (communists, socialists, liberals, radicals, etc.) against reactionary government, especially dictatorship. The idea of an anti-FASCIST Popular Front was proposed by the Communist International in 1935. Such a government was set up in Spain in 1936, but CIVIL WAR soon followed. The French Popular Front government, set up by Blum in 1936, ended in 1938.

Populist. A term applied in the U.S.A. to a member of the People's Party, an agrarian protest movement formed at St. Louis in 1891. They demanded free and unlimited silver currency, the prohibition of alien land ownership, state control of transport, etc.

Porcelain. Ital. *porcellana*, from *porcella*, a little pig, the name given by the early Portuguese traders to cowrie-shells, the shape of which is not unlike a pig's back, and later to Chinese earthenware, which is white and glossy, like the inside of these shells.

Porch, The. A philosophic sect, generally called STOICS (Gr. *stoa*, a porch), because ZENO, the founder, gave his lectures in the public ambulatory, *Stoa poikile* (the painted colonnade), in the agora or market-place of ATHENS.

> The successors of Socrates formed societies which lasted several centuries; the Academy, the Porch, the Garden.
>
> SEELEY: *Ecce Homo*.

Pork, Pig. The former is Norman, the latter Saxon. As in the case of most edible domestic animals, the Norman word is used for the meat and the Saxon for the live animal. *See* PIG.

Pork Barrel. An American term applied to legislation, normally achieved by LOG-ROLLING which makes available Federal funds for local improvements or developments in the district of the congressman who promotes the measure to maintain popularity with the electorate. It is an allusion to old plantation days when slaves assembled at the pork barrel for the allowance of pork reserved for them and "pork barrel" for the congressman is a reward for party service.

Porphyrogenitus (pôr fi ro jen′ i tŭs). A surname of the Byzantine Emperor, Constantine VII (905–959). It signifies "born in the purple" (Gr. *porphuros* purple; *genetos*, born), and a son born to a sovereign after his accession is so designated. It was specifically an epithet of the Byzantine emperors born while their father was reigning and the term refers to the purple room used by the empress for her accouchement.

Porridge. Everything tastes of porridge. However we may deceive ourselves, whatever CASTLES IN THE AIR we may construct, the facts of home life will always intrude.

He has supped all his porridge. Eaten his last meal; he is dead.

Keep, or **save your breath to cool your porridge.** A blunt remark to one who is giving unwanted or unsought advice.

> Well, Friar, spare your breath to cool your porridge; come, let us now talk with deliberation, fairly and softly.
>
> RABELAIS: *Pantagruel*, etc., V, xxviii.

Not to earn salt for one's porridge. To earn practically nothing; to be a "waster" or "layabout".

To do porridge. A slang expression for serving time in prison.

Port, meaning the left-hand side of a vessel when facing forward, is probably *port*, harbour, and it replaced the earlier *larboard* which was so easily confused with STARBOARD, so called from the days when the *steerboard* or rudder was carried over the right-hand side, and it was therefore necessary to come alongside on the larboard side. It is presumed the term *port* derives from the fact that the larboard was thus towards the side of the port.

A vessel's **port-holes** are so called from Lat. *porta*, a door; the harbour is called a *port* from Lat. *portus*, a haven; the dark red wine gets its name from *Oporto*, Portugal (which is again the Lat. *portus*), and *port*, the way of bearing oneself, is from Lat. *portare*, to carry.

Any port in a storm. Said when one is in a difficulty and has to take whatever refuge, literal or metaphorical, offers itself.

Port-Royal. A convent of CISTERCIAN nuns about 8 miles S.W. of VERSAILLES, which in the 17th century became a centre of the JAN-

SENIST influence. In 1626 the community had moved to PARIS and Port-Royal des Champs was occupied mostly by laymen living a semi-monastic existence, among them many distinguished scholars. In 1648 some of the nuns returned and the hermits moved elsewhere in the neighbourhood.

From 1653 it came under papal condemnation for its adherence to Jansenism, and Louis XIV began active persecution from 1661. By 1669 the conformist nuns were all at the Paris house and the supporters of Jansen remained at Port-Royal des Champs until forcibly removed in 1709. The buildings were duly destroyed but Port-Royal-de-Paris remained in being till the French Revolution.

Porte, or **Sublime Porte.** Originally the official name of the OTTOMAN Court at Constantinople, and later used as a synonym for the Turkish government. The word is the French translation of an Arabic word for "gate", the gate in question being the Imperial Gate or "High" (sublime) gate of the SERAGLIO at Constantinople.

Porteous Riots. At Edinburgh, in September 1736, a smuggler awaiting death for robbing an excise-collector escaped with the aid of Andrew Wilson, a fellow culprit. At the latter's execution, Lieutenant Porteous ordered the town guard to fire on the mob, which had become tumultuous; about six people were killed and eleven injured. Porteous was condemned to death but temporarily reprieved; whereupon some citizens burst into the gaol and, dragging him to the Grassmarket, hanged him by torchlight on a barber's pole. The Lord Provost was dismissed as a consequence and the city fined £2,000. The episode is featured in Scott's *Heart of Midlothian*.

Porter. *See* ENTIRE; STOUT.

Portia (pôr′ shà). A rich heiress and "lady barrister" in Shakespeare's *Merchant of Venice*, in love with Bassanio. Her name is often used for a female advocate.

Portland Vase. A cinerary urn of transparent blue glass, coated with opaque white glass cut in cameo fashion, found in a tomb (supposed to be that of Alexander Severus) near ROME in the 17th century. In 1770 it was purchased from the Barberini Palace by Sir William Hamilton for 1,000 guineas, and came afterwards into the possession of the Duke of Portland, one of the trustees of the BRITISH MUSEUM, who placed it in that institution for exhibition. In 1845 a lunatic named Lloyd dashed it to pieces, but it was so skilfully repaired that the damage is barely visible. It is ten inches high, and six in diameter at the broadest part.

Portmanteau Word. An artificial word made up of parts of others, and expressive of a combination denoted by those parts—such as SQUARSON, a cross between a *squire* and *parson*. Lewis Carroll invented the term in *Through the Looking-glass*, ch. vi; *slithy*, he says means *lithe* and *slimy*, *mimsy* is *flimsy* and *miserable*, etc. So called because there are two meanings "packed up" in the one word.

Portreeve. In Saxon times and later, the chief magistrate of a town or BOROUGH, *port* here meaning town. *See also* REEVE.

Portsmouth. The Portsmouth Defence. This is a ploy whereby a man accused of assault pleads guilty but in defence says that he was outraged by a homosexual advance being made to him. It stems, of course, from Portsmouth being the chief port of the British Navy, where many men of all sorts and conditions are thrown together.

Portsoken Ward. The most easterly ward of the City of LONDON. (*Port*, town; *soke*, franchise.) It was the soke of the old KNIGHTENGUILD outside the wall in the parish of St. Botolph, Aldgate.

Portumnus. *See* PALÆMON.

Poseidon (pò sī′ don). In Greek mythology, the god of the sea, the counterpart of the Roman NEPTUNE. He was the son of CRONOS and RHEA, brother of ZEUS and HADES, and husband of AMPHITRITE. It was he who, with APOLLO, built the walls of TROY, and as the Trojans refused to give him his reward he hated them and took part against them in the TROJAN WAR. Earthquakes were attributed to him, and he was said to have created the first HORSE.

Poser. Formerly used of an examiner, one who poses (*i.e.* "opposes") questions, especially a BISHOP's examining chaplain, and of each of the two representatives of the FELLOWS of King's College, Cambridge, among the examiners for scholarships to the Foundation of Eton and King's in the days when scholarships at King's were closed to all except scholars of Eton.

> The examination [for an Eton scholarship] was conducted by the Provosts of Eton and King's, the Fellows of Eton and two representatives of the Fellows of King's called Posers, so called either because they posed you with questions you could not answer, or because they placed you on the list.
>
> OSCAR BROWNING, *Memoirs of Sixty Years* (1910).

Nowadays the word usually denotes a puzzling question or proposition.

Posh. This colloquialism for "grand", "SWELL", or "first rate" was supposed to have originated in the old days of constant steamship travel between England and In-

dia. Passengers travelling by the P. & O. (Peninsular and Oriental) would, at some cost, book their return passage with the arrangement "PORT Outward STARBOARD Homeward", thus ensuring cabins on the cooler side of the ship, as it was usually quite unbearably hot when crossing the Indian Ocean. Passages were booked "P.O.S.H." accordingly, and *Posh* soon came to be applied to a first-class passenger who could afford this luxury. This traditional explanation is apparently fictitious.

Positivism. A term originally applied to the system of Auguste Comte (1798–1857), which only recognized observable ("positive") facts scientifically established and disregarded metaphysical and theological considerations. Its chief English exponent was Frederic Harrison (1831–1923) who actively promoted it as a religious system centred on the worship of humanity.

In the wider sense, Positivism applies to any philosophical approach which rejects metaphysics and confines itself to the facts of experience.

Posse (pos′ i) (Lat., to be able). A body of men—especially CONSTABLES—who are armed with legal authority.

Posse Comitatus. The whole power of a county—that is, all male members of the county over 15 years of age with the exception of clergymen and peers, summoned by a SHERIFF to assist in preventing a riot, or enforcing process. In modern times assistance is provided by constables and special constables.

Possum. To play possum is to lie low, to feign quiescence, to dissemble. The phrase comes from the opossum's habitual attempt to avoid capture by feigning death. *See* GUM.

Post. Post-and-rail. Wooden fencing made of posts and rails. In Australia, strong tea as made in the BUSH or OUTBACK in which the stalks are floating is called *post-and-rail* tea.

Post Captain. A term used in the Royal Navy from about 1730 to 1815 to distinguish an officer who held a captain's commission (post) from one of inferior rank who had been given the title by courtesy because he was in command of a small ship or was acting as captain. Ships below the size of a frigate were not entitled to a post captain.

Post paper. Before metrication, a standard size of paper measuring 15 × 19¼ in. in writing papers, and 15½ × 19¼ in. in printings; so called from an ancient watermark which has been supposed to represent a post-horn. This horn or bugle mark was, however, in use as early as 1314, long before anything in the nature of a postman or his horn existed.

It is probably the famous horn of ROLAND.

Beaten on the post. Only just beaten: a racing term, the "post" being the winning-post.

By return of post. By the next mail in the opposite direction; originally the phrase referred to the messenger, or "post", who brought the dispatch and would return with the answer.

From pillar to post. *See* PILLAR.

Knight of the post. *See under* KNIGHT.

Post haste. With great speed or expedition. The allusion is to postal messengers galloping in to the inn yards with the cry "Post haste!", which gave them priority in the selection of horses available. The term was current by the early 16th century, signifying the quickest journey possible.

To be posted in a club is to have one's name put upon the notice board as no longer a member, for non-payment of dues or other irregularity. In the Army and R.A.F. it means to be assigned to a specific post or appointment; the naval term is to be *drafted*.

To be well posted. To be thoroughly acquainted with it, well informed. Originally an American colloquialism, probably from the counting-house, where ledgers are *posted*. In the U.S.A. it means that hunting and fishing are prohibited—*land posted with signs*.

To run your head against a post. To go ahead heedlessly and stupidly, or as if you had no eyes. *Cp.* TO RUN ONE'S HEAD AGAINST A BRICK WALL *under* HEAD.

Post (Lat., after). **Post factum** (Lat.). After the act has been committed.

Post hoc, ergo propter hoc (Lat.). After this, therefore because of this; expressive of the fallacy that because one thing follows another, the former is the cause of the latter. Because a man drinks a glass of beer and then falls over it does not follow that the beer was the cause of his fall. He *may* have actually slipped on a banana skin.

Post meridiem (Lat.). After noon; usually contracted to "P.M." *See* PIP EMMA.

Post mortem (Lat.). After death; as, a *post-mortem examination*, for the purpose of ascertaining the cause of death.

A post-mortem degree. In old university slang, a degree given to a candidate after having failed at the POLL.

Post nati (Lat., those born after). Historically, a term referring to a judicial decision of 1607 which decided that all those born in SCOTLAND after James VI's accession as James I of ENGLAND (1603) were natural born subjects of the king of England. James unsuccessfully tried to bring about the

union of England and Scotland and to get the English Parliament to agree to the naturalization of his Scottish subjects.

Post obit (Lat. *post obitus*, after decease, *i.e.* of the person named in the bond). An agreement to pay for a loan by a larger sum to be paid on the death of the person specified from whom the borrower has expectations.

Post term (Lat. *post terminum*, after the term). The legal expression for the return of a writ after the term, and for the fee that then is payable for its being filed.

Post-Impressionism. The name applied to the phase of painting that followed IMPRESSIONISM. The chief exponents were Cézanne, Gauguin, Van Gogh, and Seurat. It aimed at synthesis and the expression of the material and spiritual significance of the subject free from restraint. *Cp.* POINTILLISM.

Poste restante (pōst res tant') (Fr., remaining post). A department at a post office to which letters may be addressed for callers, and where they will remain (within certain limits) until called for.

Posteriori. *See* A POSTERIORI.

Postman Poet. *See* DEVONSHIRE POET.

Postman's knock. An old parlour kissing game. The girls are each given a number. The "postman" knocks on the door a certain number of times and the girl whose number corresponds with the number of knocks has to kiss the postman.

Posy properly means a verse or sentence inscribed on a ring or other object and is a contraction of *poesy*. The meaning of a bunch of flowers, a nosegay, probably comes from the custom of sending verses with gifts of flowers. *Cp.* GARLAND.

> About a hoop of gold, a paltry ring
> That she did give me; whose posy was,
> For all the world, like cutler's poetry
> Upon a knife, *Love me, and leave me not.*
> SHAKESPEARE: *The Merchant of Venice*, V, i.

Pot. Apart from designating a variety of vessels and containers, the word *pot* is one of the many slang terms for the drug marijuana.

A big pot. An important person; also descriptive of a big belly.

A little pot is soon hot. A little person is quickly "riled". Grumio makes humorous use of the phrase in SHAKESPEARE's *The Taming of the Shrew* (IV. i).

A pot of money. A large amount of money; especially a large stake on a horse.

A watched pot never boils. Said as a mild reproof to one who is showing impatience; watching and anxiety won't hasten matters.

Gone to pot. Ruined, gone to the bad. The

allusion is to the pot in which left-overs of cooked meat are put ready for their last appearance as a hash.

In the melting pot. Affairs are in a state of flux or transition; the outcome is still not apparent. The allusion is obvious.

The pot calling the kettle black. Said of one accusing another of faults similar to those committed by himself.

The pot of hospitality. The pot or cauldron hanging over the fire, which in IRE-LAND used to be dipped into by anyone who dropped in at meal-times, or required refreshment.

To keep the pot a-boiling. To keep things going briskly, to see that the interest does not flag; also to go on paying one's way and making enough to live on.

To take pot luck. To share a meal of whatever food is available, one that has not been specially prepared for visitors; to take a chance. It comes from the days when the family cooking pot, containing a variety of edibles, was kept boiling over the fire. When it was ladled out at meal-times what anyone received was "pot luck".

Pot-boiler. Anything done merely for the sake of the money it will bring in—because it will "keep the pot a-boiling", *i.e.* help to provide the means of livelihood; applied especially to work of small merit by artists and writers.

Pot-hook. The hook over an open fire on which hung the pot. The term was applied to a "hooked" stroke used in writing, especially to the stroke terminating in a curve formerly practised by children in learning to write, as in the second element of *n*.

Pot-hunter. One whose main aim is the collecting of prizes rather than enjoying a sport or activity for its own sake, the *pot* being the silver cup commonly awarded for sporting events, etc.

Pot-valour. Courage provided by liquor, DUTCH COURAGE; one so fortified is said to be *pot valiant*.

Pot-wallopers. Before the Reform Act of 1832, those who possessed a vote as householders because they had boiled their own *pot* at their own fireplace in the constituency for at least six months. The earlier form was *pot-waller*, from O.E. *weallan*, to boil.

Potato. This very useful and common vegetable (*Solanum tuberosum*) was introduced from S. America into Europe by the Spaniards in the latter part of the 16th century. Sir Walter Ralegh is supposed to have introduced it on his Irish lands from Virginia about 1585 but it did not arrive in Virginia until more than a century later. Potatoes

were introduced to N. America from IRE-LAND in 1719. Sir John Hawkins brought back the sweet potato from the Caribbean in 1565. This latter plant, *Ipomœa batatas*, from which the word *potato* is derived, is supposed to have aphrodisiac qualities and Falstaff refers to this when he says, "Let the sky rain potatoes" (SHAKESPEARE: *Merry Wives of Windsor*, V, v).

Both *spud* and *murphy* are slang terms for a potato and anyone with the name Murphy is always nicknamed "Spud".

> Only two things in this world are too serious to be jested on—potatoes and matrimony.
>
> *Irish Aphorism.*

A set of circumstances or an issue which is difficult, risky, or disagreeable to handle is colloquially called a *hot potato*. In the U.S.A. *cold potato* means "cold fish".

Potato Jones. Captain D.J. Jones, who died in 1962 aged 92. In 1937, with his steamer *Marie Llewellyn* loaded with potatoes, he tried to run General Franco's blockade off Spain, but was prevented by a British warship. Two other blockade-running captains were called Ham-and-Egg Jones and Corncob Jones.

Potato War. The Prussian name for the War of the Bavarian Succession (1778–1779), because the operations largely revolved around the acquisition or denial to the enemy of supplies.

Potatoes and Point. *See under* POINT.

To think small potatoes of it. To think very little of it, to account it of very slight worth or importance.

Potato-bogle. So the Scots call a scarecrow, the head of these bird-bogies being a big potato or turnip.

Poteen, Potheen (po tēn′) (Irish *poitín*, little pot). Illicitly distilled Irish whiskey, usually in small amounts. The practice arose in the late 18th century when the government refused to license small stills.

> An' that I tould yer Honour whativer I hard an' seen,
> Yer Honour 'ill give me a thrifle to drink yer health in potheen.
>
> TENNYSON: *Tomorrow*, xvi.

Potent. Cross potent. A heraldic CROSS each limb of which has an additional cross-piece like the head of an old-fashioned crutch; so called from Fr. *potence*, a crutch. It is also known as a *Jerusalem cross*.

Potichomania (po tēsh′ō mā′ni à). The name is a combination of Fr. *potiche*, glass vase, and *manie*, craze or fad. It denotes the art of decorating plain glass vases, etc., on the inside with patterned paper designs to imitate decorated porcelain of various kinds.

Glass panels, cheval-screens, chiffoniers, and other furniture was similarly dealt with. The art spread from France to ENGLAND in the early 19th century and is fully described in Cassell's *Household Guide* of 1875. A debased form of potichomania consisted in sticking figures on the outside of pottery jars and varnishing over the whole. Such jars were called "Dolly Varden" jars.

Potiphar's Wife (pot' i fàr) is unnamed both in the BIBLE (*Gen.* xxxix, 7) and the KORAN. Some Arabian commentators have called her Rahil, others ZULEIKA, and it is this latter name that the 15th-century Persian poet gives her in his *Yusuf and Zulaikha*.

In C. J. Wells's poetic drama *Joseph and His Brethren* (1824), of which she is the heroine, she is named Phraxanor.

Potlatch. Among certain North American Indians of the north-west coast, a feast at which gifts are distributed lavishly to the guests while the hosts sometimes destroy some of their own valuable possessions. It is a social barbarity to refuse an invitation to a potlatch, or not to give one in return.

Potpourri (pō poo' rē) (Fr.). A mixture of dried sweet-smelling flower-petals and herbs preserved in a vase. *Pourri* means rotten and *potpourri* is literally the vase containing the "rotten" flowers. It is also a HOTCH-POTCH or OLLA PODRIDA; and in music, a medley of favourite tunes strung together.

Pott. Before metrication, a size of printing and writing paper ($15\frac{1}{2} \times 12\frac{1}{2}$ in.); so called from its originally watermark, a *pot*, which really represented the Holy GRAIL.

Potter's Field. A name applied to a burial ground formerly reserved for strangers and the friendless poor. It is an allusion to the field bought by the chief priests with the thirty pieces of silver returned to them by the repentant JUDAS (*Matt.* xxvii, 7).

> And they took counsel, and bought with them the potter's field, to bury strangers in.

Poulaines (poo' lānz). The long pointed toes of the 14th century. They were put on the feet of suits of armour for purposes of defence. They appeared also on the fashionable *souliers à la poulaine*. The fashion is thought to have come from Poland—*poulaine* being O.Fr. for Polish.

Poult (pōlt). A chicken, or the young of the turkey, guinea-fowl, etc. The word is a contraction of *pullet*, from the Late Lat. *pulla*, a hen, whence *poultry*, *poulterer*, etc.

Poulter's Measure. In prosody, a metre consisting of alternate ALEXANDRINES and fourteeners, *i.e.* twelve-syllable and fourteen-syllable lines. The name was given to it by Gascoigne (1576) because, it is said, poulterers—then called *poulters*—used sometimes to give twelve to the dozen and sometimes fourteen. The following specimen is from Surrey's *Complaint of the absence of her lover, being upon the sea:*

> Good ladies, ye that have your pleasure in exile.
> Step in your foot, come take a place, and mourn with me awhile,
> And such as by their lords do set but little price
> Let them sit still, it skills them not what chance come on the dice.

Pound. The unit of weight (Lat. *pondus*, weight); also, before the decimalization of the British currency, cash to the value of twenty SHILLINGS sterling, because in the CARLOVINGIAN period the Roman pound (twelve ounces) of pure SILVER was coined into 240 silver pennies. The symbols £ and *lb.* are for *libra*, the Latin for a pound. *See also* DECIMAL CURRENCY.

In for a penny, in for a pound. *See under* PENNY.

Pound of flesh. The whole of the bargain, to the last letter of the agreement, the bond *literatim et verbatim*. The allusion is to Shakespeare's *The Merchant of Venice* (IV, i), where Shylock bargained with Antonio for a "pound of flesh" but was foiled in his suit by PORTIA, who said the bond was expressly a pound of flesh, and therefore (1) the Jew must cut the exact quantity, neither more nor less than a just pound; and (2) in so doing he must not shed a drop of blood.

Pour. To pour down the drain. Figuratively, to waste one's resources, especially money, on useless, totally unproductive or unprofitable projects.

Poverty. When poverty comes in at the door, love flies out at the window. An old proverb, given in Ray's *Collection* (1742), and appearing in many languages. Keats says much the same in *Lamia* (Pt. II):

> Love in a hut, with water and a crust
> Is—Love forgive us—cinders, ashes, dust.

Powder. I'll powder your jacket for you. A corruption of Fr. *poudrer*, to dust. *Cp.* I'LL DUST YOUR JACKET FOR YOU *under* DUST.

Not worth powder and shot. Not worth the trouble; the thing aimed at is not worth the cost of the ammunition.

Power. Black Power. An emotive concept originating among certain sections of Negro opinion in the U.S.A. since 1966, whose advocates aim at redressing racial injustice by militant black nationalism that allows for violence and race war.

Flower Power. The power of the "Flower Children", based on the slogan "Make Love not War"; the Flower Children or Beautiful People being a new form of HIPPY movement whose adherents were characterized by the wearing of bells and flowers. The Flower Children appeared in Britain in 1967, taking their pattern from San Francisco.

The powers that be. A common expression applied to those in authority, especially those who exercise control of society as a whole. The phrase is taken from *Rom.* xiii, 1—"The powers that be are ordained of God."

Pow-wow. A consultation. Derived from the North American Indians.

Præmonstratensian. *See* PREMONSTRATENSIAN.

Præmunire (prē mū nī' rè). The title of numerous statutes passed from 1353, and especially that of 1393 designed to assert the rights of the Crown against encroachments from the Papacy, particularly rights of patronage, the removal of cases from the King's courts, and EXCOMMUNICATION. The name also denotes the offence, the writs, and the punishment under these statutes. The writ begins with the words *præmunire facias*, "that you cause to be forewarned". The most famous case of præmunire was when Henry VIII invoked the statute against Cardinal Wolsey in 1529 on account of his activities as Papal legate. A peer so charged cannot be tried by his peers, but must accept a jury. The last statute involving præmunire was the Royal Marriage Act of 1772.

Prætorian Guard, or **Prætorians.** Prætor was the title given to a provincial consul who had military powers and the general's bodyguard was the *cohors prætoria*. From the time of AUGUSTUS to that of Constantine, the Prætorians were the household guard of the Roman emperors. In due course they acquired a dangerous power of making and unmaking emperors in times of crisis and they were eventually (312) dispersed among the legions. *Cp.* JANISSARIES.

Pragmatic Sanction (Gr. *pragmatikos*, business-like, official). A term originating in the BYZANTINE EMPIRE to denote a public decree and later used by European sovereigns for important declarations defining their powers, settling the succession, etc. Prominent among such was the *Pragmatic Sanction* of St. Louis, 1269, and that of Charles VII in 1438, asserting the rights of the Gallican Church against the Papacy; that which settled the Empire of Germany in the House of Austria in 1439; the instrument by which Charles VI of Austria settled the succession of his daughter, Maria Theresa, in 1713; and that of Naples, 1759, whereby Charles III of Spain ceded the succession to the Kingdom of Naples to his third son and his

heirs in perpetuity. The *Pragmatic Sanction* of 1713 is the most usually referred to unless some qualification is added.

Pragmatism (Gr. *pragma*, deed). The philosophical doctrine that the only test of the truth of human cognitions or philosophical principles is their practical results, *i.e.* their workableness. It does not admit absolute truth, as all truths change their trueness as their practical utility increases or decreases. The word was introduced in this connexion about 1875 by the American logician C.S. Peirce (1839–1914) and was popularized by William James, whose *Pragmatism* was published in 1907.

Prairie Schooner. A large covered wagon, drawn by oxen or mules, used to transport settlers across the North American continent during the mid-19th century, and usually built water-tight for crossing rivers.

Praise the Lord and Pass the Ammunition. A World War II phrase said to have been used by an American Naval chaplain during the Japanese attack on Pearl Harbor, though the actual identity of the chaplain has since been in dispute. Made the subject of a popular song in 1942.

Prajapatis. *See* MANU.

Prang. R.A.F. slang in World War II, meaning to bomb a target with evident success; to shoot down another or to crash one's own aircraft; and generally to collide with, or bump into, any vehicle. Hence, also, *wizard prang*, for a wonderful or extremely accurate hit, etc.

Pratique (prăt ēk'). The licence given to an incoming vessel when she can show a clean BILL OF HEALTH or has fulfilled the necessary QUARANTINE regulations. *See* YELLOW JACK.

Prayer wheel. A device used by the Tibetan Buddhists as an aid or substitute for prayer, supposedly founded on a misconception of the BUDDHA'S instructions to his followers that they should "turn the wheel of the law"—*i.e.* preach BUDDHISM incessantly. It varies from a small pasteboard cylinder inscribed with prayers to a larger water-wheel. Among the many prayers is the mystic formula OM MANI PADME HUM, and each revolution represents one repetition of the prayers. *Cp.* ROSARY.

It is also another name for the mediæval WHEEL OF FORTUNE.

Pre-Adamites. The name given by Isaac de la Peyrère (1655) to a race of men whom he supposed to have existed before the days of ADAM. He held that only the Jews are descended from Adam, and that the Gentiles derive from these "Pre-Adamites".

Prebend (Late Lat. *præbenda*, a grant, pen

sion). A cathedral BENEFICE, its holder being a *prebendary*. In the 19th century nearly all prebends became honorary offices only, and members of CHAPTERS came to be designated CANONS.

Precariæ. *See* BOON WORK.

Precarious (Lat. *precarius*, obtained by prayer) is applied to what depends on our prayers or requests. A *precarious tenure* is one that depends solely on the will of the owner to concede to our prayer; hence, uncertain, not to be depended on.

Preceptor. Among the Knights TEMPLAR a *preceptory* was a subordinate house or community (the larger being a *commandery*) under a *Preceptor* or *Knight Preceptor*. The *Grand Preceptor* was the head of all the preceptories in a province, those of Jerusalem, Tripolis, and Antioch being the highest ranking.

Précieuses, Les (prā sē ĕrz) (Fr.). The ladies of the intellectual circle that centred about the Hôtel de RAMBOUILLET in 17th-century Paris. It may be interpreted as "persons of distinguished merit". Their affected airs were the subject of MOLIÈRE'S comedy *Les Précieuses Ridicules* (1659), and they were further satirized in *Les Femmes Savantes* (1672).

Precious Stones. The ancients divided precious stones into male and female, the darker being the males and the light ones the females. Male sapphires approach indigo in colour, but the females are sky-blue. Theophrastus mentions the distinction.

> And the tent shook, for mighty Saul shuddered—
> and sparkles 'gan dart
> From the jewels that woke in his turban, at once
> with a start—
> All its lordly male-sapphires, and rubies courageous
> at heart.
>
> BROWNING: *Saul*, viii.

According to the Poles, each month is under the influence of a precious stone:

January	Garnet	*Constancy*
February	Amethyst	*Sincerity*
March	Bloodstone	*Courage*
April	DIAMOND	*Innocence*
May	Emerald	*Success in love*
June	Agate	*Health and long life*
July	Cornelian	*Content*
August	Sardonyx	*Conjugal felicity*
September	Chrysolite	*Antidote to madness*
October	Opal	*Hope*
November	Topaz	*Fidelity*
December	Turquoise	*Prosperity*

In relation to the signs of the ZODIAC:

Aries	Ruby	Libra	Jacinth
Taurus	Topaz	Scorpio	Agate
Gemini	Carbuncle	Sagittarius	Amethyst
Cancer	Emerald	Capricornus	Beryl
Leo	Sapphire	Aquarius	Onyx
Virgo	Diamond	Pisces	Jasper

In relation to the planets:

Saturn	Turquoise	*Lead*
Jupiter	Cornelian	*Tin*
Mars	Emerald	*Iron*
Sun	Diamond	GOLD
Venus	Amethyst	*Copper*
Moon	Crystal	SILVER
Mercury	Loadstone	*Quicksilver*

In HERALDRY:

The topaz represents "or" (*gold*), or Sol, the Sun.
The pearl or crystal represents "argent" (*silver*), or Luna, the Moon.
The ruby represents "gules" (*red*), or the planet Mars.
The sapphire represents "azure" (*blue*), or the planet Jupiter.
The diamond represents "sable" (*black*), or the planet Saturn.
The emerald represents "vert" (*green*), or the planet Venus.
The amethyst represents "purpure" (*purple*), or the planet Mercury.

Many precious stones were held to have curative and magical properties, e.g. *loadstone* prevented quarrels between brothers; *jasper* worn by the ploughman ensured the fertility of a field; *turquoise* protected the wearer from injury if he fell; *jade* for the Chinese was the most pure and divine of natural materials and had many properties, including stimulating the flow of milk in nursing mothers when powdered and mixed with milk and honey.

Precocious means early ripened (Lat. *præ*, before; *coquere*, to cook); hence, premature; development of mind or body before one's age.

> Many precocious trees, and such as have their spring in the winter, may be found in most parts of Europe.
>
> SIR THOS. BROWNE: *Vulgar Errors*, ii, 6.

Premier (pre' mi ėr). First, chief (Fr. *premier* from Lat. *primus*, first). Hence the Prime Minister (Fr. *premier ministre*), the first minister of the Crown.

Première (pre mi âr'). The feminine form of the Fr. *premier*, commonly denotes the first performance of a play or film.

Première danseuse. The leading female dancer in a ballet.

Ce n'est que le premier pas qui coûte (Fr.). It is only the first step that costs anything. An observation made by Mme. du Deffand (1697–1780) on hearing the Cardinal de Polignac's description of the miraculous walk of St. DENYS after decapitation. PYTHAGORAS used to say, The beginning is half the whole.

> Incipe dimidium facti est cœpisse.
>
> AUSONIUS.
>
> Dimidium facti, qui cœpit, habet.
>
> HORACE: *Ep.*, I, ii, 41.

"Well begun is half done".

Premillenarians. *See* SECOND ADVENTISTS.

Premonstratensian (prē mon strȧ ten′ sian) or *Norbertine Order*. An order founded by St. Norbert in 1120 in the diocese of Laon, France, which adopted the rule of St. AUGUSTINE. A spot was pointed out to him in a vision, hence the name *Pré montré* or *Pratum Monstratum* (the meadow pointed out). In England the order possessed 35 houses before the dissolution and its members were called "White Canons".

Prepense (prē pens′). **Malice prepense.** MALICE aforethought; malice designed or deliberate (Lat. *præ*, before; *pensare*, to think).

Pre-Raphaelite Brotherhood, The. A group of artists formed in London in 1848 consisting of Holman Hunt, Millais, D. G. Rossetti, and the sculptor Thomas Woolner. It was later joined by J. Collinson, W. H. Deverell, F. G. Stephen and W. M. Rossetti; Ford Madox Brown and Ruskin supported their movement, which espoused a closer study of nature than was practised by those tied to academical rules, and the study of the method and spirit of the artists before Raphael (1483–1520). Nevertheless, their works contained much artificiality of literary origins. The group was attacked by many artists and critics, especially by Charles Dickens in *Household Words* in 1850. From this date D. G. Rossetti ceased to exhibit publicly. Their works are characterized by exaggerated attention to detail and a high degree of finish, and their earlier lives, at least, by BOHEMIAN activities.

> ... a society which unfortunately, or rather unwisely, has given itself the name of "Pre-Raphaelite"; unfortunately, because the principles on which its members are working are neither pre-nor post-Raphaelite, but everlasting. They are endeavouring to paint with the highest possible degree of completion, what they see in nature, without reference to conventional or established rules; but by no means to imitate the style of any past epoch.
> RUSKIN: *Modern Painters*, pt. II, sect. vi, ch. iii, § xvi.

Presbyterians. Members of a church governed by elders or presbyters (Gr. *presbuteros*, elder), and ministers in a hierarchy of representative courts. Their doctrine is fundamentally Calvinistic. The CHURCH OF SCOTLAND (*see under* CHURCH) became presbyterian after the REFORMATION but the growth of Presbyterianism in 17th-century England was checked by the rise of the INDEPENDENTS and the Act of Uniformity of 1662. The Presbyterian Church of Wales is of 18th-century origin.

New Presbyter is but Old Priest writ large. There is no difference other than in the name; the name may be different but both things are essentially the same. The word *priest* actually derives from the same root as *presbyter*. The phrase is from Milton's *New Forcers of Conscience*.

Presence. *See* REAL PRESENCE.

Presents (prez′ ents). **Know all men by these presents**—*i.e.* by the writings or documents now present (Lat. *per presentes*, by the [writings] present).

Presidium. In the U.S.S.R. the Presidium of the Supreme Soviet, since 1936 a body elected by the Supreme Soviet which fulfils the role of constitutional head of the State. Its chairman is its representative in ceremonial affairs and it issues ordinances when the Supreme Soviet is not in session. *See* POLITBURO.

Press-gang. The name given particularly to those naval parties who carried out the task of *impressment*, an ancient and arbitrary method of obtaining men for military service dating back to the early 13th century. Individual captains of ships provided their own parties until the demands of the 18th-century Navy led to the establishment of an Impress Service with depots where seafarers abounded. Apart from seizing men from taverns, they seized merchant sailors from ships at sea, etc., and *Pressed men* formed about half of a ship's crew. The Royal Navy relied on this method until the 1830s, when improvements in pay and conditions encouraged adequate voluntary enlistment, although impressment has never been abolished. The word has nothing to do with "pressing" in the sense of "forcing" but derives from the *prest* or *imprest* money (Fr. *prêter*, to lend) advanced on enlistment, rather like the army's "KING'S SHILLING".

> But woe is me! the press-gang came,
> And forc'd my love away
> Just when we named next morning fair
> To be our wedding day.
> *The Banks of the Shannon* (an Irish ballad of 1785).

To be press-ganged into it. To be forced to do something or to take part against one's will or inclination.

Prester John. *See under* JOHN.

Prestige (pres tēzh). A word with a curiously metamorphosed meaning. The Lat. *præstigiæ*, from which it is derived, means juggling tricks, hence the extension to illusion, fascination, charm and so to the present meaning of standing, influence, reputation, based upon past achievements and associations, etc.

Presto. The name frequently applied to himself by Swift in his *Journal to Stella*. According to his own account (*Journal*, 1 August 1711) it was given him by the notorious

Duchess of Shrewsbury, an Italian:

> The Duchess of Shrewsbury asked him, was not that Dr. —, Dr. —, and she could not say my name in English, but said Dr. Presto, which is Italian for Swift.

Preston and his Mastiffs. To oppose Preston and his mastiffs is to be foolhardy, to resist what is irresistible. Christopher Preston established the Bear Garden at HOCKLEY-IN-THE-HOLE in the time of Charles II, and was killed in 1700 by one of his own bears.

> ...I'd as good oppose
> Myself to Preston and his mastiffs loose.
>> JOHN OLDHAM: *Satyr in Imitation of the Third of Juvenal* (1683).

Pretender. The Old Pretender. James Francis Edward Stewart or Stuart (1688–1766), son of James II, the WARMING-PAN BABY, and known as the Old Chevalier. He was called James III by the JACOBITES on the death of his father in 1701. The word "Pretender" here denotes one who makes a claim or pretension to a title.

The Young Pretender. Charles Edward Stuart (1720–1788), son of the OLD PRETENDER, and popularly known as Bonnie Prince Charlie or the Young Chevalier. *See* THE FORTY-FIVE *under* FORTY.

Pretext. A pretence or excuse. From the Lat. *prætexta*, a dress embroidered in the front, worn by Roman magistrates, priests, and children of the aristocracy between the age of 13 and 17. The *prætextatæ* were dramas in which actors personated those who wore the *prætexta*; hence persons who pretended to be what they were not.

Prevarication. The Lat. word *varico* means I straddle, and *prævaricor*, I go zigzag or crooked. The verb, says Pliny, was first applied to men who ploughed crooked ridges, and afterwards to men who gave crooked answers in the law courts, or deviated from the straight line of truth. *Cp.* DELIRIUM.

Previous Question. *See under* QUESTION.

Priam (prī′ am). King of TROY when that city was sacked by the Greeks, husband of HECUBA, and father of 50 children, the eldest of whom was HECTOR. When the gates of Troy were thrown open by the Greeks who had been concealed in the wooden horse, Pyrrhus, the son of ACHILLES, slew the aged Priam.

Priapus (prī ā′pŭs). In Greek mythology, the son of DIONYSUS and APHRODITE, the god of reproductive power and fertility (hence of gardens), the protector of shepherds, fishermen and farmers. He was later regarded as the chief deity of lasciviousness and obscenity and the phallus was his attribute.

Prick. The prick of conscience. Remorse; tormenting reflection on one's misdeeds. In the 14th century Richard of Hampole wrote a devotional treatise with this title.

Prick the Garter. *See under* GARTER.

To kick against the pricks. To strive against odds, especially against authority. *Prick* here is an ox-goad, and the allusion is to *Acts* ix, 5—"It is hard for thee to kick against the pricks."

To prick up one's ears. To pay particular attention; to do one's best to listen to what is going on. In allusion to the twitching of a horse's ears when its attention is suddenly attracted.

Pricking for sheriffs. The annual choosing of SHERIFFS used to be done by the king, who marked the names on a list by pricking them with a bodkin at random. Sheriffs are still "pricked" by the sovereign, but the names are chosen beforehand.

Prick-eared. Said of a dog with upstanding ears. The PURITANS or ROUNDHEADS were so called because they had their hair cut short and covered their heads with a black skullcap drawn down tight, leaving the ears exposed.

Pricklouse. An old contemptuous name for a tailor.

Prick-song. Written music for singing as distinguished from music learnt by ear. So called because the notes were originally pricked in on parchment. The term has long been obsolete.

> He fights as you sing prick-song, keeps time, distance, and proportion.
>> SHAKESPEARE: *Romeo and Juliet*, II, iv.

Pride (M.E. *pryde*). Overweening self-esteem, arrogance of bearing; also a proper sense of what is proper or becoming to oneself. It has further the meaning ostentation, finery, magnificence, etc., or that which persons are proud of; thus Spenser (*The Faerie Queene*, I, i, 7) talks of "loftie trees yclad with sommer's pride" (verdure); Pope (*Odyssey*, viii, 439), of a "sword whose ivory sheath [was] inwrought with curious pride" (ornamentation).

A pride of lions. A company or group of lions.

Fly pride, says the peacock (SHAKESPEARE, *Comedy of Errors*, IV, iii). A bird proverbial for pride, the POT CALLING THE KETTLE BLACK. *See under* POT.

The heraldic peacock is said to be *in his pride* when depicted with the tail displayed and the wings drooping.

Pride goes before a fall. An adaptation of *Proverbs* xvi, 18—"Pride goeth before destruction, and an haughty spirit before a fall."

The pride of the morning. The early mist or shower which promises a fine day. The morning is too proud to come out in her glory all at once—or the proud beauty being thwarted weeps and pouts awhile.

Pride's Purge (6 December 1648). When CHARLES I was a captive, after his defeat in the field, the LONG PARLIAMENT declared for a reconciliation (5 December), whereupon a body of soldiers under Colonel Pride arrested 45 M.P.s and debarred 78 others from entry. Another 20 refused to sit and the RUMP was prepared to serve the Army's purposes.

Prig. An old CANT word (probably a variant of PRICK) for to filch or steal, also for a thief. In SHAKESPEARE's *The Winter's Tale* (IV, ii) the clown calls AUTOLYCUS a "prig" who "haunts wakes, fairs, and bear-baitings".

Shadwell (*The Squire of Alsatia*, I, i) uses the term of a pert COXCOMB, "and thou shalt shine, and be as gay as any spruce prig that ever walked the street".

Nowadays *prig* denotes a conceited, formal or didactic person—one who tries to teach others how to behave, etc., one of narrow-mindedly precise morals.

Prima Donna (prē' ma don' a) (Ital., first lady). The principal female singer in an opera.

Prima facie (Lat.). At first sight. A *prima facie* case is a case or statement which, without minute examination into its merits, seems plausible and correct.

Primary colours. See under COLOURS.

Primate. The title of the BISHOP of the "first" or chief see of a state (Lat. *prima sedes*); originally the METROPOLITAN of a province. The Archbishop of York is called *Primate of England* and the Archbishop of Canterbury *Primate of All England*.

Prime (Lat. *primus*, first). In the Western Church, the office appointed for the first hour (6 a.m.), the first of the CANONICAL HOURS. Milton terms sunrise "that sweet hour of prime" (*Paradise Lost*, V, 170); and the word is used in a general way of the first beginnings of anything, especially of the world itself. *Cp.* Tennyson's "dragons of the prime" (*In Memoriam*, lvi).

In my prime. In my youth; at the best period of my life.

Prime Minister. The first minister of the Crown; the PREMIER.

Prime Numbers. The GOLDEN NUMBER, also called simply the "Prime". In mathematics a prime number is any positive number which cannot be expressed as the product of two others, *e.g.* 1, 3, 5, 7, 11, etc.

Primed. Fully prepared and ready to deliver a speech or to cope in an argument, etc. A man whose head is full of his subject is said to be "primed to the muzzle". The allusion is to firearms. Primed is also a euphemism for "drunk".

Primer. Originally the name of a book of devotions used by the laity in pre-REFORMATION England; this was used as a first reading book. The name was then applied to a small book by which children were taught to read and pray and hence to an elementary school book on any subject.

This litel child his litel book lerninge
As he sat in the scole at his prymer.
CHAUCER: *Canterbury Tales*
(*The Prioress's Tale*, I, 72).

Great primer (prim' ėr). A large-sized type, rather smaller than 18 point, 4¼ lines to the inch (2.54 cm.).

Long primer. A smaller-sized type, 9½ point, 7½ lines to the inch (2.54 cm.).

Primero (prim ēr' ō). A very popular card game for about a hundred years after 1530, in which the cards had three times their usual value, four were dealt to each player, the principal groups being flush, prime, and point. *Flush* was the same as in poker, *prime* was one card of each suit, and *point* was reckoned as in piquet.

I ... left him at primero with the Duke of Suffolk.
SHAKESPEARE: *Henry VIII*, V, i.

Primrose. A curious corruption of Norman *primerole*, which is the name of the flower in M.E. This is from the Late Lat. *primula*, and the *rose* (as though from *prima rosa*, the first, or earliest rose) is due to a popular error.

Primrose Day. 19 April, the anniversary of the death of Benjamin Disraeli, Earl of Beaconsfield, the season when primroses are at their best. *See* PRIMROSE LEAGUE.

The Primrose League. A Conservative party organization founded by members of the FOURTH PARTY in 1883, having as its objects "the maintenance of religion, of the estates of the realm, and of the imperial ascendancy". The name was taken in the mistaken belief that the primrose was Lord Beaconsfield's favourite flower, from the wreath of primroses sent to his funeral with the words, "His favourite flowers from Osborne, a tribute of affection from Queen Victoria". The league had its greatest influence and popularity in the days before World War I when imperial sentiment was at its height.

Primrose path. The easy way, the path of pleasure and self-indulgence. SHAKESPEARE refers to the "primrose path of dalliance" (*Hamlet*, I, iii), and to "the primrose way to the everlasting bonfire" (*Macbeth*, II, i).

Primum mobile (prī' mum mō' bile) (Lat., the first moving thing), in the PTOLEMAIC SYSTEM of astronomy, the ninth (later the tenth) sphere. It was supposed to revolve round the earth from east to west in 24 hours, carrying with it all the other spheres. Milton refers to it as "that first mov'd" (*Paradise Lost*, III, 483) and Sir Thomas Browne (*Religio Medici*) used the phrase, "Beyond the first movable", meaning outside the material creation. According to Ptolemy, the *primum mobile* was the boundary of creation, above which came the EMPYREAN, or seat of God.

The term is figuratively applied to any machine which communicates motion to others; and also to any great sources of motion or in the development of ideas, etc. Thus, SOCRATES may be called the *primum mobile* of the Dialectic, MEGARIAN, Cyrenaic, and CYNIC systems of philosophy.

Primus (prī' mus) (Lat., first). The presiding BISHOP of the Episcopal Church of Scotland. He is elected by the other six bishops, and presides in Convocation, and at meetings relative to Church matters.

Primus inter pares (Lat.). The first among equals.

Prince (Lat. *princeps*, chief, leader). A royal title which, in England, is now limited to the sons of the sovereign and their sons. *Princess* is limited to the sovereign's daughters and his sons' (but not daughters') daughters.

Black Prince. See under BLACK.

Crown Prince. The title of the heir-apparent to the throne in some countries, as Sweden, Denmark, and Japan (formerly also in Germany).

Prince Consort. A prince who is the husband of the reigning queen.

Prince Imperial. The title of the heir-apparent in the French Empire of NAPOLEON III (1852–1870).

Prince Regent. A prince ruling on behalf of the legal sovereign; in British history George, PRINCE OF WALES (*see under* WALES), who acted as regent for his father, George III. See REGENCY.

Prince of the Asturias. Traditional title of the heir-apparent to the Spanish throne.

Prince of the Church. A CARDINAL.

Prince of Darkness. The DEVIL; SATAN.

Prince of Peace. The MESSIAH; Jesus Christ.

> For unto us a child is born, unto us a son is given ... and his name shall be called Wonderful, Counsel-lor, The mighty God, The everlasting Father, The Prince of Peace.
> *Isaiah* ix, 6.

The Spanish statesman Manuel de Godoy (1767–1851) was called *Prince of the Peace* for his negotiations with France in the Treaty of Basle, 1795.

Prince of Physicians. A title given to AVICENNA.

Prince of Piedmont. The heir-apparent to the House of Savoy, former kings of Italy.

Prince of Wales. *See under* WALES.

Prince Rupert's drops. See RUPERT.

Prince's Metal. See RUPERT.

Princess Royal. The title of an eldest daughter of a British sovereign. On the death of a Princess Royal the eldest daughter of the then reigning monarch customarily receives the title and retains it for life, no matter how many sovereigns with daughters may occupy the throne during her lifetime. George III's daughter Charlotte, Queen of Württemberg, was Princess Royal until her death in 1828; neither George IV nor William IV having daughters, the title was in abeyance until 1840 when Queen Victoria's daughter, Princess Victoria (later the Empress Frederick of Germany), succeeded to it. She remained Princess Royal until her death in 1901, when King Edward's daughter, Princess Louise, Duchess of Fife, succeeded. On her death in 1931 the title passed to Princess Mary, Countess of Harewood, daughter of George V. She died in 1965, and the title was given to Princess Anne on 13 June 1987.

Principalities. Members of one of the nine orders of angels in mediæval angelology. *See* ANGEL.

> In the assembly next upstood
> Nisroch, of Principalities the prime.
> MILTON: *Paradise Lost*, VI, 447.

Printer. The Printer's Bible. See BIBLE, SOME SPECIALLY NAMED EDITIONS.

Printers' marks.

? is $\frac{q}{o}$—that is, the first and last letters of *quæstio* (question).

! is $\frac{I}{o}$. *Io* in Latin is the interjection or joy.

¶ is the initial letter of *paragraph* (reversed).

§ the S-mark or section mark.

* is used by the Greek grammarians to arrest attention to something striking (*asterisk* or star).

† is used by the Greek grammarians to indicate something objectionable (*obelisk* or dagger). Both marks are now used to indicate footnotes.

Printing House Square. Often used as synonymous with *The Times* newspaper, which was produced there from its inception until 1974. It began in 1785 as *The Daily Universal Register*, which became *The Times* in 1788. Printing House Square is at Blackfriars in the City of London and was earlier the site of the King's Printing-House.

Priori. *See* A PRIORI.

Prisca, St. A Roman Christian maiden tortured and beheaded (*c*. 270) under the Emperor Claudius II. There is a church of St. Prisca at ROME. She is represented between two lions who, it is said, refused to attack her.

    St. Priscilla, a Christian convert of the 1st century, and mentioned several times in the NEW TESTAMENT (*Acts* xviii, *Rom*. xvi, I *Cor*. xvi, 2 *Tim*. iv), is also known as St. Prisca.

Priscian's Head (prish' ȧn). **To break Priscan's head** (Lat. *diminuere Priscianis caput*). To violate the rules of grammar. Priscian was a great grammarian of the early 6th century, whose name is almost synonymous with grammar.

    And hold no sin so deeply red
    As that of breaking Prisician's head.
               BUTLER: *Hudibras*, Pt. II, ii.
  Sir Nathaniel: Laus Deo, bone intelligo.
  Holofernes: Bone!—*bone* for *bene*: Priscian a
                little scratch'd; 'twill serve.
        SHAKESPEARE: *Love's Labour's Lost*, V, i.

Prisoner. Prisoner of Chillon. *See* CHILLON. **Prisoner of the Vatican.** *See under* VATICAN; LATERAN TREATY.

Privateer. A privately owned vessel commissioned under LETTERS OF MARQUE by a belligerent state to wage war on the enemy's commerce. The practice of issuing such commissions ceased as a result of the Declaration of Paris, 1856, but it did not finally become obsolete until the Hague Convention of 1907.

Privilege. In the Parliamentary sense applies to PARLIAMENT'S right to regulate its own proceedings and in the case of the Commons the right to regulate membership; also the right to punish for *breach of privilege* or contempt, the right to freedom of speech, and freedom from civil arrest. In addition there is still the freedom of access as a body to the sovereign to present an address and the request for a favourable construction on its proceedings.

Privy Council. The council chosen by the SOVEREIGN originally to administer public affairs, but now never summoned to assemble as a whole except to proclaim the successor to the Crown on the death of the Sovereign, or to listen to the Sovereign's announcement of intention to marry. It usually includes Princes of the Blood, the two PRIMATES, the Bishop of London, the great officers of State and of the Royal Household, the Lord CHANCELLOR and Judges of the Courts of Equity, the Chief Justices of the Courts of COMMON LAW, the Judge Advocate, some of the PUISNE JUDGES, the SPEAKER of the HOUSE OF COMMONS, the Lord Mayor of London, Ambassadors, Governors of Colonies, and many politicians. The business of the Privy Council is nowadays to give formal effect to Proclamations and ORDERS-IN-COUNCIL; for this a quorum of three suffices. The CABINET and the Judicial Committee are, in theory, merely committees of the Privy Council. Privy Councillors are entitled to the prefix "the Right Honourable", and to the use of the initials "P.C." after their names; they rank next after Knights of the GARTER who may be commoners. The Lord President of the Council is the fourth great officer of State.

Privy Seal. The seal which the sovereign uses in proof of assent to a document, kept in the charge of a high officer of State known as the Lord Privy Seal. In matters of minor importance it is sufficient to pass the Privy Seal, but instruments of greater moment must have the GREAT SEAL also.

Prize Court. A court of law set up in time of war to examine the validity of capture of ships and goods made at sea by the navy.

Prize money. The name given to the net proceeds of the sale of enemy shipping and property captured at sea. Prior to 1914 the distribution was confined to the ships of the Royal Navy actually making the capture; since that date all prize money has been pooled and shared out among the navy as a whole. Prize money was paid at the end of World War II for the last time.

The prize ring is the boxing ring in which a *prize fight* takes place, a prize fight being a boxing match for a money prize or trophy.

Pro (Lat., for, on behalf of). *Pro* is also a common shortening of "professional" as, "He is a golf pro."

Pro and con (Lat.). For and against. "Con" is a contraction of *contra*. The *pros and cons* of a matter are all that can be said for or against it.

Pro bono publico (prō bō' nō pub' lik ō) (Lat.). For the public good or benefit.

Pro rata (prō rā' ta) (Lat.). Proportional or proportionally.

Pro tanto (Lat.). As an instalment, good enough as far as it goes, but not final; for what it is worth.

  I heard Mr. Parnell accept the Bill of 1886 as a measure that would close the differences between the two countries; but since then he stated that he had accepted it as a *pro tanto* measure ... It was a parliamentary bet, and he hoped to make future amendments on it.

JOSEPH CHAMBERLAIN, *April 1893*.

Pro tempore (Lat.). Temporarily; for the time being, till something is permanently settled. Contracted into *pro tem*.

Procès-verbal (prō sā vâr' bal) (Fr.). A detailed and official statement of some fact; especially a written and authenticated statement of facts in support of a criminal charge.

Procne. *See* NIGHTINGALE.

Proconsul. A magistrate of ancient ROME who was invested with the power of a consul and charged with the command of an army or the administration of a province. The name has often been applied to some of the great colonial administrators of the former British Empire.

Procris (prok' ris). **Unerring as the dart of Procris.** When Procris fled from CEPHALUS out of shame, DIANA gave her a dog (Lælaps) that never failed to secure its prey, and a dart which not only never missed aim, but which always returned of its own accord to the shooter.

Procrustes' Bed (prō krus' tēz). Procrustes, in Greek legend, was a robber of Attica, who placed all who fell into his hands upon an iron bed. If they were longer than the bed he cut off the overhanging parts, if shorter he stretched them till they fitted it. He was slain by THESEUS. Hence, any attempt to reduce men to one standard, one way of thinking, or one way of acting, is called *placing them on Procrustes' bed*. *Cp*. DAMIENS' BED OF STEEL.

> Tyrants more cruel than Procrustes old,
> Who to his iron-bed by torture fits
> Their nobler parts, the souls of suffering wits.
> MALLET: *Verbal Criticism* (1733).

Proctor. Literally this is one who manages the affairs of another, the word being a contraction of "procurator". At the universities of Oxford and Cambridge the proctors are two officials whose duties include the maintaining of discipline. Representatives of ecclesiastical bodies in Convocation are called Proctors.

The King's or **Queen's Proctor.** *See under* KING.

Procyon (prō' si on). The Lesser DOG-STAR (*see under* DOG(5)), *alpha* in *Canis Minor*, so called because it rises before the Dog-Star (Gr. *pro*, before; *kyon*, dog). It is the eighth brightest star in the heavens. *See* ICARIUS.

Prodigal. Festus the Latin lexicographer (2nd century A.D.) says the Romans called victims wholly consumed by fire *prodigæ hostiæ* (victims prodigalized), and adds that those who waste their substance are therefore called prodigals. This derivation is incorrect. Prodigal is Lat. *pro-ago* or *prod-igo*, I drive forth, and persons who had spent all their patrimony were "driven forth" to be sold as slaves to their creditors.

Prodigy (Lat. *prodigium*, a portent, prophetic sign). One endowed with surprising qualities.

The Prodigy of France. Guillaume Budé (1467–1540), the French humanist, was so called by Erasmus.

The Prodigy of Learning. Samuel Hahnemann (1755–1843), the German physician and scholar, was so named by J. Paul Richter.

Producer's Goods. An economist's term for goods such as tools and raw material, which satisfy needs only indirectly, through making other goods.

Profane means literally before or outside the temple (Lat. *pro fano*); hence *profanus* was applied to those persons who came to the temple and, remaining outside and unattached, were not initiated. Hence the idea of irreverence, disregard of sacred things, blasphemous, secular, etc.

Profile (prō' fīl) means shown by a thread (Ital. *profilo*; Lat. *filum*, a thread). A profile is an outline, but especially a view, or drawing or some other representation of the human face outlined by the median line. The term "profile", for an essay setting forth the outstanding characteristics of an individual—a verbal outline, so to speak—came into use in the 1940s.

Profound. The Profound Doctor. Thomas Bradwardine, Richard Middleton, and other 14th-century scholastic philosophers were given the title.

Most Profound Doctor. Ægidius de Colemna (d. 1316), a Sicilian SCHOOLMAN.

Prog. The verb was used in the 16th century for "to poke about" for anything, especially to forage for food; hence the noun is slang for food, but its origin is unknown. Burke says, "You are the lion, and I have been endeavouring to prog for you."

> So saying, with a smile she left the rogue,
> To weave more lines of death, and plan for prog.
> DR. WOLCOT: *Spider and Fly*.

Prog is also university slang for PROCTOR.

Programme Music is instrumental music based on a literary, historical, or pictorial subject and intended to describe or illustrate this theme musically.

Projection. Powder of projection. A form of the PHILOSOPHERS' STONE, which was supposed to have the virtue of changing baser metals into GOLD. A little of this powder, being cast into the molten metal, was to *project* from it pure gold.

Proletariat (prō le târ′ i ăt). The labouring classes; the unpropertied wage-earning classes. In ancient ROME the *proletarii* could hold no office, and were ineligible for the army and only served the State with their offspring (*proles*).

> The proletariat, the lowest stratum of our present society, cannot stir, cannot raise itself up, without the whole superincumbent strata of official society being sprung into the air.
>
> MARX and ENGELS: *Communist Manifesto*, I.

Prom, or **Promenade Concert.** A concert in which some of the audience stand in an open area of the concert-room floor. Promenade Concerts, familiarly called "Proms", date back to the days of the London pleasure gardens such as VAUXHALL and RANELAGH. Mansard had conducted similar concerts at Paris in the 1830s and from 1838 his example was followed at London. In 1895 Sir Henry Wood (1869–1944) began the concerts at the Queen's Hall which he conducted for over half a century and which became a regular feature of London life. In 1927 the B.B.C. took over their management from Chappell's. The destruction of the hall by enemy action in 1941 caused a break in the concerts but they were renewed at the Royal Albert Hall.

In the U.S.A. *going to a prom* means attending a dance given by members of a class at school or college.

Prometheus (prō mē′ thūs) (Gr., Forethought). One of the TITANS of Greek myth, son of IAPETOS and the ocean-nymph Clymene, and famous as a benefactor to man. It is said that ZEUS, having been tricked by Prometheus over his share of a sacrificial ox, denied mankind the use of fire. Prometheus then stole fire from HEPHÆSTUS to save the human race. For this he was chained by Zeus to Mount Caucasus, where an EAGLE preyed on his liver all day, the liver being renewed at night. He was eventually released by HERCULES, who slew the eagle. It was to counterbalance the gift of fire to mankind that Zeus sent PANDORA to earth with her box of evils.

Promethean. Capable of producing fire; pertaining to PROMETHEUS.

A somewhat dangerous match invented in 1828 was known as a "Promethean". It consisted of a small glass bulb containing sulphuric acid, the outside being coated with potassium chlorate, sugar, and gum surrounded by a paper wrapping in the form of a spill. When the glass was bitten with the teeth the chlorate fired the paper. *Cp.* LUCIFER-MATCH.

> I carried with me some promethean matches, which I ignited by biting; it was thought so wonderful that a man should strike fire with his teeth, that it was usual to collect the whole family to see it.
>
> DARWIN: *The Voyage of the "Beagle"* (1839), ch. iii.

Promethean fire. The vital principle; the fire with which PROMETHEUS quickened into life his clay images.

> I know not where is that Promethean heat
> That can thy light relume.
>
> SHAKESPEARE: *Othello*, V, ii.

Promethean unguent. Made from a herb on which some of the blood of PROMETHEUS had fallen. MEDEA gave JASON some of it, and thus rendered his body proof against fire and warlike instruments.

Promised Land, or **Land of Promise.** Canaan; so called because God promised ABRAHAM, Isaac, and Jacob that their offspring should possess it. Figuratively, HEAVEN or any place of expected happiness or fulfilment.

Proof. A printed sheet to be examined and approved before it is finally printed. The first, or *foul*, proof is that which contains all the compositor's errors; when these are corrected the impression next taken is called a *clean* proof and is submitted to the author; the final impression, which is corrected by the reader, is termed the *press* proof.

The Proof Bible. *See* BIBLE, SOME SPECIALLY NAMED EDITIONS.

Proof prints. The first impressions of an engraving. *India proofs* are those taken off on *India paper*.

Proofs before lettering are those taken off before any inscription is engraved on the plate. After the proofs the connoisseur's order of value is—(1) prints which have the letters only in outline; (2) those in which the letters are shaded with a black line; (3) those in which some slight ornament is introduced into the letters; (4) those in which the letters are filled up quite black.

Proof spirit. A term applied to a standard mixture of alcohol and water used as a basis for customs and excise purposes. It is legally defined as having a specific gravity of $^{12}/_{13}$ at 51°F. When the mixture has more alcohol it is said to be *over proof*, and when less *under proof*. In earlier days proof spirit was held to be that which if poured over gunpowder and ignited would eventually ignite the powder. If the spirit was under proof the water remaining would prevent the firing of the powder.

Prooshan Blue. A term of great endearment, when after the battle of Waterloo the Prussians were immensely popular in England. Sam Weller in *Pickwick Papers* (ch. xxxiii) addresses his father as "Vell, my Prooshan

Blue." *See* PRUSSIAN BLUE.

Prop, To. An Australian term used to describe when horses come to a sudden stop. Hence, generally, to JIB, to refuse to co-operate.

Propaganda. The Congregation or College of the Propaganda (*Congregatio de propaganda fide*) is a committee of cardinals established at Rome by Gregory XV in 1622 for propagating the Faith throughout the world. Hence the term is applied to any scheme, association, publication, etc., for making PROSELYTES or influencing public opinion in political, social, and religious matters, etc.

Property Plot, in theatrical language, means a list of all the "properties" or articles which are needed for the production of a particular play. Everything used on the stage is termed a "prop." "Actor's props" are articles of personal use, the remainder are termed "manager's props".

Prophet, The. The special title of MOHAMMED. According to the KORAN there have been 200,000 prophets, but only six of them brought new laws or dispensations, *viz.* ADAM, Noah, ABRAHAM, MOSES, Jesus, and Mohammed.

The Great, or **Major Prophets.** Isaiah, JEREMIAH, Ezekiel, and DANIEL; so called because their writings are more extensive than the prophecies of the other twelve.

The Minor, or **Lesser Prophets.** Hosea, Joel, Amos, Obadiah, Micah, JONAH, Nahum, Habakkuk, Zephaniah, Haggai, Zechariah, and Malachi, whose writings are less extensive than those of the four GREAT PROPHETS.

Props. *See* PROPERTY PLOT.

Proscription. Outlawry, the denunciation of citizens as public enemies, etc.; so called from the Roman practice of writing the names of the *proscribed* on tablets which were posted up in the forum, sometimes with the offer of a reward for those who should aid in bringing them to court. If the proscribed did not answer the summons, their goods were confiscated and their persons outlawed. In this case the name was engraved on brass or marble, the offence stated, and the tablet placed conspicuously in the market-place.

Prose means straightforward speaking or writing (Lat. *oratio prosa*), in opposition to foot-bound speaking or writing, *oratio vincta* (fettered speech, *i.e.* poetry).

It was Monsieur Jourdain, in MOLIÈRE'S comedy *Le Bourgeois Gentilhomme*, who suddenly discovered that he had been talking prose for forty years without knowing it.

Proselytes (pros' e līts). From Gr. *proselu-*

tos, one who has come to a place; hence, a convert, especially (in its original application) to Judaism. Among the Jews proselytes were of two kinds—*viz.* "The proselyte of righteousness" and the "stranger that is within thy gates" (Hellenes). The former submitted to circumcision and conformed to the laws of MOSES; the latter went no farther than to refrain from offering sacrifice to heathen gods, and from working on the SABBATH.

Proserpina, or **Proserpine** (pro sĕr' pi nȧ, pros' er pīn). The Roman counterpart of the Greek goddess Persephone, queen of the infernal regions and wife of PLUTO (*see* DAFFODIL), and sometimes identified with HECATE.

Prosit (prō' sit) (Lat., "May it benefit you"). Good luck to you! A salutation used in drinking a person's health, and particularly associated with German university students.

Prosperity Robinson. F. J. Robinson (1782–1859), Viscount Goderich, afterwards first Earl of Ripon, Chancellor of the Exchequer 1823–1827, so called by Cobbett who also dubbed him later "Goody Goderich". In 1825 he boasted in the House of the prosperity of the nation, but unfortunately the autumn and winter were marked by bank failures, bankruptcies and STOCK EXCHANGE collapse. However, his economic policies were generally progressive.

Protean. *See* PROTEUS.

Protectionist. One who advocates the imposition of import duties, to "protect" home produce and manufactures. *Cp.* MERCANTILISM.

Protector, The. A title sometimes given in England to the regent during the sovereign's minority.

John of Lancaster, Duke of Bedford, was made Regent of France and Protector of England during the minority (1422–1442) of his nephew, Henry VI; and Humphrey, Duke of Gloucester, was Protector during Bedford's absence in France, which was, in fact, for most of the time.

Richard, Duke of Gloucester, was Protector from 1483 until his assumption of the crown as Richard III. He took Edward V into his custody on the death of Edward IV.

Edward Seymour, Duke of Somerset, was Protector (1547–1550) and Lord Treasurer in the reign of his nephew, Edward VI.

The Lord Protector of the Commonwealth. Oliver Cromwell (1599–1658) was declared such in 1653. His son Richard succeeded to the title in 1658, but resigned in May 1659.

The Protectorate. *See* COMMONWEALTH.

Protestant. A member of a Christian Church upholding the principles of the REFORMA-TION or (loosely) of any Church not in communion with ROME. In the time of Luther his followers called themselves "evangelicals". The name arose from the Lutheran *protest* against the recess of the Diet of Spires (1529) which declared that the religious STATUS QUO must be maintained.

The Protestant Pope. Clement XIV (1769–1775), who ordered the suppression of the JESUITS in 1773. He was a patron of art and a liberal-minded statesman but was under pressure from the BOURBON kings.

Proteus (prō′ tūs). In Greek legend, NEP-TUNE'S herdsman, an old man and a prophet, famous for his power of assuming different shapes at will. Hence the phrase, *As many shapes as Proteus, i.e.* full of shifts, aliases, disguises, etc., and the adjective **protean,** readily taking on different aspects, ever-changing, versatile.

Proteus lived in a vast cave, and his custom was to tell over his herds of sea-calves at noon, and then to sleep. There was no way of catching him but by stealing upon him at this time and binding him; otherwise he would elude anyone by a rapid change of shape.

Protevangelium (prō te văn jē′ li um). The first (Gr. *protos*) GOSPEL; a term applied to an apocryphal gospel which has been attributed to St. JAMES THE LESS. It was supposed by some critics that all the gospels were based upon this, but it appears to be the compilation of a Jewish Christian from a variety of sources and dates from the 2nd century. The name is also given to the curse upon the SERPENT in *Gen.* iii, 15, which has been regarded as the earliest utterance of the gospel:

> And I will put enmity between thee and the woman, and between thy seed and her seed; it shall bruise thy head, and thou shalt bruise his heel.

See APOCRYPHA.

Prothalamion (prō thả lā′ mi ùn). The term coined by Spenser (from Gr. *thalamos*, a bridal chamber) as a title for his "Spousall Verse" (1596) in honour of the double marriage of Lady Elizabeth and Lady Katharine Somerset, daughters of the Earl of Worcester, to Henry Gilford and William Peter, Esquires. Hence a song sung in honour of the bride and bridegroom before the wedding. *Cp.* EPITHALAMIUM.

Protocol (prō′ tō kol). In diplomacy, the original draft of a diplomatic document such as a dispatch or treaty; from Gr. *protos*, first, *kolla*, glue, a sheet glued to the front of a manuscript, or the case containing it, giving certain descriptive particulars. The word also denotes the code of correct procedure, etiquette, and ceremonial to be observed in official international intercourse.

The Protocols of the Elders of Zion. Forged material published by Serge Nilus in Russia in 1905, based on an earlier FORGERY of 1903, purporting to outline secret Jewish plans for achieving world power by undermining Gentile morality, family life and health, and by securing a monopoly in international finance, etc. Their falsity was first exposed by Philip Graves, *The Times* correspondent in Constantinople, in 1921 and later judicially, at Berne (1934–1935). Their influence in inciting anti-semitism notably among the Russians, and later providing Hitler and his associates with an excuse they knew to be a myth, provide tragic evidence of the power of the "big lie".

Proto-martyr. The first martyr (Gr. *protos*, first). STEPHEN the deacon is so called (*Acts* vi, vii), and St. ALBAN is known as the proto-martyr of Britain.

Proud, The. Otto IV, Emperor of Germany (*c.* 1182, 1208–1218).

Tarquin II of Rome. *Superbus.* (Reigned 535–510 B.C., d. 496).

The Proud Duke. Charles Seymour, 6th Duke of Somerset (1662–1748). He would never suffer his children to sit in his presence, and would never communicate with his servants except by signs.

To do someone proud. To treat them lavishly; to give them first-class hospitality, etc.

To stand proud. In engineering and the practical skills, said of something which sticks out further than it should or above a particular plane.

Provincial. One who lives in the provinces, at a distance from the metropolis, hence the meaning of narrow, unpolished.

The Provincial of an Order. In a religious order, one who has authority over all the houses of that order in a province or given area. He is usually elected by the provincial CHAPTER.

Proxime accessit (Lat. *proxime*, next; *accessit*, he approached). An expression used in prize lists, etc., for the runner-up, the one who came very near the winner.

Prud'homme (proo′ dom) in O.Fr. meant a man endowed with all the knightly virtues (*preux homme*), but later implied a man of proven honesty, experience and knowledge in his craft or trade, whence its specialized meaning in Mod. Fr. for a member of an Industrial Arbitration Board.

Prudhommerie is the loud and pompous

enunciation of the obvious, derived from the character Joseph Prud'homme, created by the French writer Henri Monnier (1830).

Prunella (proo nel′ a). A dark, smooth, woollen stuff of which clergymen's and barristers' gowns used to be made, also gaiters and the uppers of boots; probably so named from its plum colour (Fr. *prunelle*, sloe).

All leather and prunella. See LEATHER.

Prunes and prisms. See NIMINI-PIMINI.

Prussian Blue. So called because it was discovered by a Prussian, Diesbach, a colourman of Berlin, in 1704. It was sometimes called *Berlin blue*. It is made by adding ferrous sulphate solution to one of potassium ferrocyanide to which ferric chloride is subsequently introduced. *Prussic acid* (hydrocyanic acid) can be made by distilling Prussian blue. *Cp.* PROOSHAN BLUE.

Prussianism. A term denoting the arrogance and overbearing methods associated with the Prussian military machine and governmental attitudes from the days of Frederick the Great (1712–1786) until World War I. Unfortunately there was a return to Prussianism in Germany under the NAZIS. *Cp.* JACK-BOOT; MAILED FIST.

> In its simplest form, Prussianism is blind submission. It is a philosophy of a military Order that sought primarily to maintain its position against the possible revolt of the conquered. It is the spirit of an army carried over into a bureaucracy and into society itself ... It is discipline—and servility. Standardized.
>
> EDGAR MOWRER: *Germany Puts the Clock Back*, ch. v.

Pry, Paul. An idle meddlesome fellow, who has no occupation of his own, and is always interfering with other folk's business. The term comes from the hero of John Poole's comedy, *Paul Pry* (1825).

Psalmanazar, George. A classical example of the impostor. A Frenchman whose real name is unknown to this day, he appeared in London in 1703 claiming to be a native of Formosa, at that time an almost unknown island. In 1704 he published an account of Formosa with a grammar of the language, which from beginning to end was a fabrication of his own. The literary and critical world of London was taken in, but his imposture was soon exposed by Roman Catholic missionaries who had laboured in Formosa, and after a time Psalmanazar publicly confessed his fraud. He turned over a new leaf and applied himself to the study of Hebrew and other genuine labours, ending his days in 1763 as a man of some repute and the friend of Dr. Johnson. See FORGERY; OSSIAN; PROTOCOLS OF THE ELDERS OF ZION.

Psalms. Of the 150 songs in the *Book of Psalms*, 73 are inscribed with David's name,

12 with that of Asaph the singer, 11 are attributed to the sons of Korah, a family of singers, and one (*Psalm* xc) to Moses. The whole compilation is divided into five books: Bk. 1, from i to xli; Bk. 2, from xlii to lxxii; Bk. 3, from lxxiii to lxxxix; Bk. 4, from xc to cvi; Bk. 5, from cvii to cl.

Much of the *Book of Psalms* was for centuries attributed to David (hence called the sweet psalmist of Israel) but it is doubtful whether he wrote any of them. The tradition comes from the author of *Chronicles*, and II *Sam.* xxii is a psalm attributed to David that is identical with *Ps.* xviii. Also, the last verse of *Ps.* lxxii ("The prayers of David the son of Jesse are ended") seems to suggest that he was the author up to that point.

In explanation of the confusion between the Roman Catholic and PROTESTANT psalters, it should be noted that *Psalms* ix and x in the BOOK OF COMMON PRAYER version (also in the BIBLE, AUTHORIZED VERSION and REVISED VERSION) are combined in the Roman Catholic Psalter to form *Psalm* ix, and *Psalms* cxiv and cxv in the *Book of Common Prayer* are combined in the Roman Catholic Psalter to form *Psalm* cxiii. Again, *Psalm* cxvi in the *Book of Common Prayer* is split to form *Psalms* cxiv and cxv in the Roman Catholic Psalter, and *Psalm* cxlvii in the *Book of Common Prayer* is split to form *Psalms* cxlvi and cxlvii in the Roman Catholic Psalter. Thus only the first eight and the last three *Psalms* coincide numerically in both psalters. *See also* GRADUAL PSALMS; PENITENTIAL PSALMS.

Pschent. See EGYPT.

Pseudepigrapha (sū de pig′ rà fà). (Gr., falsely inscribed or ascribed). In Biblical scholarship, a term applied to certain pseudonymous Jewish writings such as the "Book of Enoch", the "Assumption of MOSES", the "Psalms of SOLOMON", the "Fourth Book of the MACCABEES" (*see under* MACCABÆUS), etc., which were excluded from the CANON of the OLD TESTAMENT and the APOCRYPHA.

Pseudonym. See NOM DE PLUME.

Psyche (sī′ kē) (Gr., breath; hence, life, or soul itself). In "the latest-born of the myths", *Cupid and Psyche*, an episode in the GOLDEN ASS, Psyche is a beautiful maiden beloved by CUPID, who visited her every night but departed at sunrise. Cupid bade her never seek to know who he was, but one night curiosity got the better of her; she lit the lamp to look at him, a drop of hot oil fell on his shoulder and he awoke and fled. The abandoned Psyche then wandered far and wide in search of her lover; she became the slave of VENUS, who imposed on her heartless tasks and treated her most cruelly. Ultimately she was united to Cupid and became immortal. The tale appears in Walter Pater's *Marius the Epicurean*.

Psychedelic experiences. In the jargon of the BEATNIK fringe and world of HIPPIES and pop groups, "mind-expanding" experiences produced by drugs, flashing lights, music, dancing, etc., usually in combination. The expression was imported into Britain in 1966.

Psychological Moment, The. The moment when the mind is readiest to receive suggestions from another. It is an inaccurate translation of the German *das Momentum*, which means *momentum*, not *moment*. It is incorrectly applied when the idea of mental receptivity is absent, but it is popularly used to mean "the opportune moment", "just at the right time", etc.

Ptolemaic System (to le mā' ik). The system to account for the apparent motion of the heavenly bodies expounded in the 2nd century by Ptolemy, the famous astronomer of Alexandria. He taught that the earth is fixed in the centre of the universe, and the heavens revolve round it from east to west, carrying with them the SUN, PLANETS, and fixed stars, in their respective spheres, which he imagined as solid coverings (like so many skins of an onion) each revolving at different velocities. The tenth or outer sphere was the PRIMUM MOBILE. This theory was an attempt to systematize theories long held by PLATO, ARISTOTLE, Hipparchus, and others, and it substantially held sway until replaced by the COPERNICAN SYSTEM.

Public (Lat. *publicus*, from *populus*, the people). The people, generally and collectively, of a state, nation or community. Also a colloquial contraction of "public house", more usually contracted to "pub".

> The simple life I can't afford,
> Besides, I do not like the grub—
> I want a mash and sausage, "scored"—
> Will someone take me to a pub?
> G. K. CHESTERTON: *Ballad of an Anti-Puritan*.

Pub-crawl. Colloquially, *to go on a pub-crawl* is to partake in a drinking session in which one progresses, after suitable refreshment, from one public house to another, the number of such visited obviously depending on the length of stay at each and the capacity of the "crawler" to stay the course. *Cp.* BUSH-SHANTY.

Public-house signs are in themselves a fascinating study and much of Britain's history may be gleaned from them, as well as folklore, HERALDRY, social customs, etc. Many are a compliment to the lord of the manor or a nobleman or his cognizance, as the *Warwick Arms*, the BEAR AND RAGGED STAFF. Others pay tribute to distinguished warriors or their battles, as *The Marquis of Granby*, the *Duke of Wellington*, the *Waterloo*, the *Keppel's Head*, the *Trafalgar*. Royalty is conspicuously represented by the *Crown*, the *King's Arms*, the *Prince Regent*, the *Prince of Wales*, the *Victoria*, the *Albert*, the *George*, etc. Literary names are less conspicuous, but there is a *Shakespeare*, *Milton Arms*, *Macaulay Arms*, *Sir Richard Steele*, and *Sir Walter Scott*, as well as *The Miller of Mansfield*, *Pindar of Wakefield*, *Sir John Falstaff*, *Robinson Crusoe*, and *Valentine and Orson*. *Simon the Tanner*, *The Good Samaritan*, *Noah's Ark*, the *Gospel Oak*, the *Angel* have a Biblical flavour, and myth and legend are represented by *The Apollo*, *Hercules*, *Phœnix*, *King Lud*, *Merlin's Cave*, *The Man in the Moon*, *Punch*, *Robin Hood*, the *Moonrakers*, *Cat and the Fiddle*, etc.

Some signs indicate sporting associations, such as the *Cricketers*, the *Bat and Ball*, the *Bowling Green*, the *Angler's Rest*, the *Huntsman*; or trades associations as *Coopers'*, *Bricklayers'*, *Plumbers'*, *Carpenters'*, *Masons'* Arms, etc. Others show a whimsical turn as *The Who'd a Thought It*, *The Five Alls*, *The World Turned Upside Down*, *The Good Woman*.

The following list will serve to exemplify the subject:

The Bag o'Nails. From a tradesman's sign — that of an ironmonger. Said by some 19th-century writers to be a corruption of "Bacchanals".

The Bear. From the popular sport of bear-baiting.

The Bell. Mostly derived from the national addiction to bell-ringing.

The Bell Savage. See LA BELLE SAUVAGE.

The Blue Boar. See under BLUE.

The Blue Lion. Denmark (possibly a compliment to James I's queen, Anne of Denmark), also the badge of the Earl of Mortimer.

Bolt in Tun. The punning heraldic badge of Prior Bolton, last of the clerical rulers of St.Bartholomew's before the REFORMATION.

The Bull and Dog. From the sport of bull-baiting.

The Bull and Gate. See under BULL.

The Case is Altered. Apart from the explanation that the circumstances of a particular inn have altered substantially, there are various supposed origins of the sign. One is (as at Ravensden, Bedfordshire) that it is from PLOWDEN's use of the expression. Another (as in Middlesex) is that it is a corruption of

Casa Alta (Sp. High House), which was said to be used as a public house name when soldiers of the 57th Foot returned to Middlesex after the Peninsular War.

The Cat and Fiddle. See under CAT.

The Cat and Kittens. See under CAT.

The Cat and Wheel. A corruption of St. "CATHERINE'S Wheel".

The Chequers. See CHEQUERS.

The Coach and Horses. A favourite sign of a posting-house or stage-coach inn.

The Cock and Bottle. See under COCK.

The Cross Keys. See under KEY.

The Devil. See GO TO THE DEVIL *under* DEVIL.

Dirty Dick's. See under DIRT.

The Dog and Duck, or *The Duck in the Pond,* indicating that the sport so called could be seen there. A duck was put into the water, and a dog set to hunt it; the fun was to see the duck diving and the dog following it under water.

The Five Alls consists of a king (I rule all), a priest (I pray for all), a soldier (I fight for all), a JOHN BULL or a farmer (I pay for all), and a lawyer (I plead for all).

The Four Alls. The first four of the FIVE ALLS, above.

The Fox and Goose. Sometimes signifying that there were arrangements within for playing the game of Fox and Goose.

The Golden Fleece. An allusion to the fable of the GOLDEN FLEECE and to the woollen trade.

The Golden Lion. The badge of Henry I and the PERCYS of Northumberland.

The Goat and the Compass. See under GOAT.

The Golden Cross. A reference to the emblems carried by the crusaders.

The Goose and Gridiron. See under GOOSE.

The Green Man, The Green Man and Still. See under GREEN.

Hearts of Oak. A compliment to the British naval tradition. *See under* HEART.

The Hole in the Wall. Perhaps an allusion to the hole in the wall of a prison through which the inmates received donations, or a reference to the narrow alley or passage by which the tavern was approached.

The Horse and Jockey. An obvious allusion to the TURF.

The Man with a Load of Mischief. A sign in Oxford Street, London, nearly opposite Hanway Yard, said to have been painted by Hogarth, showing a man carrying a woman with a glass of gin in her hand, a magpie, and a monkey, etc.

The Marquis of Granby. In compliment to John Manners (*see* GRANBY), eldest son of John, third Duke of Rutland—a bluff, brave soldier, generous and greatly beloved by his men.

> What conquest now will Britain boast
> Or where display her banners?
> Alas! in Granby she has lost
> True courage and good Manners.

The Pig and Tinderbox. See under PIG.

The Pig and Whistle. Said by some to be a corruption of *pig and wassail, pig* being an abbreviation of *piggin,* an earthen vessel; or a facetious form of the BEAR AND RAGGED STAFF, etc.; but possibly a sign-painter's whimsy.

The Plum and Feathers. A corruption of *The Plume and Feathers,* the *Prince of Wales's Feathers* (*see under* WALES).

The Queen of Bohemia. In honour of James I's daughter Elizabeth who married Frederick, Elector of the Palatinate, who was chosen King of Bohemia in 1619.

The Red Cow. Possibly because at one time red cows were more esteemed in England than the more common "black".

The Red Lion. Rampant, Scotland; also the badge of John of Gaunt, Duke of Lancaster.

The Rising Sun. A badge of Edward III.

The Rose. A symbol of England.

The Rose and Crown. One of the "loyal" public-house signs.

The Running Footman. From the liveried servant who used to run before the nobleman's carriage.

St. George and the Dragon. In compliment to the patron saint of ENGLAND.

The Salutation. Refers to the angel saluting the Virgin MARY.

The Saracen's Head. Reminiscent of the CRUSADES.

The Seven Stars. An astrological sign.

The Ship and Shovel. Said to be a corruption of Sir Cloudesley Shovel, the admiral of Queen Anne's reign, but probably refers to the shovels used for unloading coal, etc.

The Star and Garter. The insignia of the Order of the Garter.

The Swan and Antelope. Supporters of the arms of Henry IV.

The Swan and Harp. See GOOSE AND GRIDIRON *under* GOOSE.

The Swan with Two Necks. See under SWAN.

The Tabard. A sleeveless coat, worn by noblemen and heralds, upon which a coat of arms was embroidered. The tavern with this sign at Southwark was where Chaucer's pilgrims "assembled".

The Talbot (a hound). The arms of the

Talbot family.

The Three Kings. An allusion to the three kings of COLOGNE, the MAGI.

The Turk's Head. Like the Saracen's Head, an allusion to the CRUSADES.

The Two Chairmen. Found in the neighbourhood of fashionable quarters when sedan chairs were in vogue.

The Unicorn. The Scottish supporter in the royal arms of Great Britain.

The White Hart. The cognizance of Richard II.

The White Lion. The cognizance of Edward IV as Earl of March. Also the device of the Dukes of Norfolk, the Earls of Surrey, etc.

See also THE OLD CHAPEL *under* CHAPEL; A COCK AND BULL STORY *under* COCK; MERMAID TAVERN.

Publicans (Lat. *publicani*). In the Roman Empire, wealthy businessmen who contracted to manage State monopolies or to farm the taxes, which often led to abuses. Hence their unpopularity in the provinces and their being associated with sinners in the NEW TESTAMENT.

Pucelle, La (pū sel') (Fr., "The Maid"), *i.e.* of Orleans, JOAN OF ARC. Chapelain and VOLTAIRE wrote a poem with this title.

Puck. A mischievous sprite of popular folklore, also called ROBIN GOODFELLOW. In Spenser's *Epithalamion* he is an evil goblin:

Ne let the Pouke, nor other evill sprights,

but SHAKESPEARE'S *Midsummer Night's Dream* (II,i) shows him as:

that shrewd and knavish sprite
Call'd Robin Goodfellow; are not you he
That frights the maidens of the villagery;
Skim milk, and sometimes labour in the quern
And bootless make the breathless housewife churn;
And sometime make the drink to bear no barm;
Mislead night wanderers, laughing at their harm?
Those that Hobgoblin call you, and sweet Puck,
You do their work, and they should have good luck.

Pudding. Pudding-time. Dinner-time, the time at which pudding, anciently the first dish, was set on the table; hence the critical time, the nick of time, the opportune moment. *Cp.* PSYCHOLOGICAL MOMENT.

When George in pudding-time came o'er,
And moderate men looked big, sir.
The Vicar of Bray.

The proof of the pudding is in the eating. An old proverb meaning that performance is the true test, not appearances, promises, etc.; just as the best test of a pudding is to eat it, not just to look at it.

Pudens (pū' denz). A soldier in the Roman army, mentioned in II *Tim.* iv, 21, in connexion with Linus and Claudia. According to tradition, Claudia, the wife of Pudens, was a British lady; Linus, otherwise Cyllen, was her brother; and Lucius "the British king", the grandson of Linus. Tradition further adds that Lucius wrote to Eleutherus, Bishop of ROME, to send missionaries to Britain to convert the people.

Pueblo (pweb' lō). The Spanish word meaning "people" (Lat. *populus*), hence a town or village. It has been applied particularly to the peace-loving Indians of New Mexico and Arizona, and to their communal villages.

Puff. An onomatopœic word, suggestive of the sound made by puffing wind from the mouth; since at least the early 17th century, applied to extravagantly worded advertisements, reviews, etc., with the implication that they have as much lasting value as a "puff of wind".

In Sheridan's *The Critic* (1779), Puff, who, he himself says, is "a practitioner in panegyric, or, to speak more plainly, a professor of the art of puffing", gives a catalogue of puffs:

Yes, sir—puffing is of various sorts, the principal are, the puff direct, the puff preliminary, the puff collateral, the puff collusive and the puff oblique, or puff by implication. These all assume, as circumstances require, the various forms of letter to the editor, occasional anecdote, impartial critique, observation from correspondent, or advertisement from the party.
The Critic, I, ii.

Puffed up. Conceited; elated with conceit or praise; filled with wind. A *puff* is a tartlet with a very light or puffy crust.

That no one of you be puffed up for one against another.
I *Cor.* iv, 6.

Puff-ball. A fungus of the genus *Lycoperdon*, so called because it is ball-shaped and when it is ripe it bursts and the spores come out in a "puff" of fine powder.

Puisne Judges (pū' ni). Formerly justices and barons of the COMMON LAW courts at Westminster other than the Chief Justices; by the Judicature Act of 1877, Judges of the High Court other than the Lord CHANCELLOR, the Lord Chief Justice, the MASTER OF THE ROLLS, the Lord Chief Justice of the Common Pleas and the Lord Chief Baron (the last two offices becoming defunct). Since the Judicature Act of 1925 the term applies to Judges of the High Court other than the Lord Chancellor, the Lord Chief Justice, and the President of the Probate Division, but is not usually attached to the Master of the Rolls. *Puisne* is etymologically the same as *puny*; it is the O.Fr. *puisne*, subsequently born (Lat. *post natus*) and signifies "junior" or "inferior in rank".

Pulitzer Prizes, for literary work, journalism,

drama, and music, are awarded annually from funds left for the purpose by Joseph Pulitzer (1847–1911), a prominent and wealthy American editor and newspaper proprietor.

Pull. The act of drawing or tugging to oneself; hence, figuratively, "influence", especially with those in control. *See* TO PULL THE STRINGS *below*.

A long pull, a strong pull, and a pull all together—*i.e.* a steady, energetic, and systematic co-operation. The reference may be to the oarsmen in a boat, or to a TUG-OF-WAR, or the act of hauling with a rope, for all of which a simultaneous strong pull is required.

The long pull. The extra quantity of beer supplied by a publican to his customer over and above the exact quantity ordered and paid for. In the U.S.A. the term is applied to long and diligent effort.

Pull devil, pull baker. Said in encouragement of a contest, usually over the possession of something. *See under* DEVIL.

To have the pull of, or **over one.** To have the advantage over him; to be able to dictate terms or make him do what you wish.

To pull a fast one. To obtain an advantage by a trick or by somewhat questionable means.

To pull bacon. TO COCK A SNOOK (*see under* COCK).

To pull one's punches. Not to be as blunt as one could be; to soften the blow and to avoid offence by holding back a little. In boxing, blows delivered intentionally ineffectively are said to be "pulled".

To pull one's socks up. TO PULL ONESELF TOGETHER and endeavour to do better.

To pull one's weight. To do the very best one can, to play one's proper part. A phrase from rowing; an oarsman who does not put all his weight into the stroke is a drag on the rest of the crew and something of a passenger.

To pull oneself together. To rouse oneself to renewed activity; to shake off depression or inertia.

To pull out all the stops. To make a supreme effort to achieve one's objective. An expression derived from the organ player who has to be extremely dexterous to manipulate the many stops of his organ.

To pull someone's leg. To delude him in a humorous way, lead him astray by chaff, exaggeration, etc.

To pull the chestnuts out of the fire. To retrieve a difficult situation for someone; to get someone out of an embarrassment. The allusion is to the fable of the monkey and the cat. *See* TO BE MADE A CATSPAW OF *under* CAT.

To pull the strings. To use private influence "behind the scenes". From the puppet-master who controls the movements of the puppets by the strings attached to them. *Cp.* TO PULL THE WIRES *under* WIRE.

To pull the wool over someone's eyes. To deceive or hoodwink; to blind him temporarily to what is going on.

To pull through. To get oneself well out of difficulty or serious illness.

To pull together. To co-operate harmoniously.

To pull up one's hooks. To cut adrift from one's local ties and to move from the district. Possibly from the idea of weighing anchor in a ship and sailing on, "hook" being nautical slang for an anchor. **To pull up stakes** is a similar American phrase conveying the idea of striking camp and moving on.

Pullman. Properly a well-fitted railway saloon or sleeping-car built at the Pullman Carriage Works, Illinois; so called from the designer, George M. Pullman (1831–1897) of Chicago.

The word is now applied to other luxurious railway saloons and motor transport.

Pummel. *See* POMMEL.

Pump. To prime the pump. To give financial aid to an enterprise in the hope that it will become self-supporting. From starting a pump working by pouring in water to establish suction.

To pump someone is to extract information out of him by artful questions; to draw from him all he knows, as one draws water from a well by gradual pumping. Ben Jonson in *A Tale of a Tub* (IV, iii) has, "I'll stand aside whilst thou pump'st out of him his business."

Pumpernickel. The coarse rye-bread ("brown George") eaten in Germany, especially in Westphalia. Thackeray applied the term as a satirical nickname to petty German princelings ("His Transparency, the Duke of Pumpernickel") who made a great show with the court officials and etiquette, but whose revenue was almost nil.

Pun. He who would make a pun would pick a pocket. Dr. Johnson is usually credited with this silly dictum, but the correct version is: "Any man who would make such an execrable pun would not scruple to pick my pocket", the remark addressed by the critic John Dennis (1657–1734) to Purcell. See the *Public Advertiser*, 12 January 1779, and the *Gentleman's Magazine*, vol. II, p. 324; also the note to Pope's *Dunciad*, bk. I, l.63.

The "execrable pun" was this: Purcell rang the bell for the drawer or waiter, but no one answered it. Purcell, tapping the table, asked Dennis "why the table was like the tavern!" Ans. "Because there is no drawer in it."

Punch. The name of this beverage, which was introduced into England in the early 17th century, is usually held to derive from Hind. *panch*, five, because it has five principal ingredients (spirit, water, spice, sugar, and some acid fruit juice). It may equally derive from *puncheon*, the large wine cask.

Punch and Judy. The name of Mr. Punch, the hero of the puppet play, probably comes from Ital. *pulcinello*, a diminutive of *pulcino*, a young chicken. His identification with Pontius Pilate and of Judy with JUDAS is imaginary. The story roughly in its present form is attributed to an Italian comedian, Silvio Fiorillo (about 1600), and it appeared in ENGLAND about the time of the RESTORATION. Punch, in a fit of jealousy, strangles his infant child, whereupon his wife Judy belabours him with a bludgeon until he retaliates and beats her to death. He flings both bodies into the street, but is arrested and shut in prison whence he escapes by means of a golden key. The rest is an allegory showing how the light-hearted Punch triumphs over (1) Ennui, in the shape of a dog; (2) Disease, in the disguise of a doctor; (3) Death, who is beaten to death; and (4) the DEVIL himself, who is outwitted. In subsequent English versions JACK KETCH, instead of hanging Punch, gets hanged himself.

The satirical humorous weekly paper, *Punch*, or *The London Charivari*, is, of course, named after Mr. Punch, who naturally featured prominently on the cover design for very many issues. It first appeared in July 1841 under the editorship of Mark Lemon and Henry Mayhew.

Pleased as Punch. Greatly delighted. Punch is always singing with self-satisfaction at the success of his EVIL actions.

Suffolk Punch. A short-legged, sturdy, thick-set cart horse. The term was formerly applied to any short fat man, and is probably a dialect variant of *bunch*.

[I] did them call their fat child Punch, which pleased me mightily, that word being become a word of common use for everything that is thick and short.

PEPYS: *Diary*, 30 April 1669.

Punch line. A vivid, often startling climax to an anecdote, joke, story, etc., which gives point to the foregoing. The figurative "punch" suggests that the listener is struck by this line.

To be punch drunk. To experience a form of concussion to which boxers are liable, causing unsteadiness of gait resembling drunkenness, used figuratively of one "reeling from heavy punishment".

Punctual. No bigger than a point, exact to a point or moment (Lat. *ad punctum*). Hence the ANGEL, describing this earth to ADAM calls it, "This spacious earth, this punctual spot"—*i.e.* a spot not bigger than a point (Milton: *Paradise Lost*, VIII, 23).

Punctuality is the politeness of kings (Fr. *L'exactitude est la politesse des rois*). A favourite maxim of Louis XVIII, but erroneously attributed by Samuel Smiles to Louis XIV.

Pundit (Hind. *pandit*). In India, a learned man, one versed in Sanskrit, law, religion, etc. We use the word for a learned man, an expert, an authority.

Punic Apple. A pomegranate or apple belonging to the genus *Punica*.

Punic Faith (Lat. *punica fides*). Treachery, violation of faith, the faith of the Carthaginians. The Phœnicians (Lat. *Punicus*, a Phœnician) founded Carthage and the long-drawn-out **Punic Wars** between Rome and Carthage ended in the latter's destruction. The Roman accusations of breach of faith were classic instances of the POT CALLING THE KETTLE BLACK. *Cp.* ATTIC FAITH.

Our Punic Faith
Is infamous, and branded to a proverb.
ADDISON: *Cato*, II.

Punk. An old word for a harlot, a worthless person or thing. Currently applied to certain young people wearing grotesque and bizarre clothes and hair style. *Cp.* HELL'S ANGELS; MODS AND ROCKERS; SKINHEADS.

Punk rock. A form of pop music of a violent and aggressive character.

Pup. Slang for a *pupil*, especially an undergraduate studying with a tutor.

As applied to the young of dogs, the word is an abbreviation of *puppy*, which represents Fr. *poupée*, a dressed doll, a plaything.

An empty-headed, impertinent young fellow is frequently called a *young puppy*, hence Douglas Jerrold's epigram in his *Man Made of Money*—

Dogmatism is puppyism come to its full growth.

To be sold a pup. To be swindled.

Pure, Simon. *See* SIMON PURE.

Purgatory. The doctrine of Purgatory, according to which the souls of the departed suffer for a time till they are purged of their sin, is of ancient standing, and in certain phases of Jewish belief GEHENNA seems to have been regarded partly as a place of purgatory.

The early Church Fathers developed the

concept of purgatory and support for the doctrine was adduced from *2 Macc.* xii, 39–45; *Matt.* xii, 32; 1 *Cor.* iii, 11–13; etc. The first decree on the subject was promulgated by the Council of Florence in 1439. It was rejected by the CHURCH OF ENGLAND in 1562 by the XXIInd of the *Articles of Religion*.

St. Patrick's Purgatory. *See under* PATRICK.

Purification, Feast of. *See* CANDLEMAS DAY.

Puritans. The more extreme PROTESTANTS inside and outside the CHURCH OF ENGLAND who found the Elizabethan religious settlement unacceptable and wished a further "purification" of religion. They looked more and more to the BIBLE as the sole authority, rejecting all tradition in matters of public worship, and were mainly Calvinist in outlook and theology. They feature in the 16th and 17th century as BROWNISTS, BARROWISTS, PRESBYTERIANS, BAPTISTS, SEPARATISTS, and Independents, and were sometimes called *Precisionists* from their punctiliousness over religious rules and observances. After the RESTORATION and the Act of Uniformity (1662), they became collectively known as DISSENTERS or NONCONFORMISTS.

Purlieu (pĕr' lū). The outlying parts of a place, the environs; originally the borders or outskirts of a forest, especially that which was formerly part of the forest. It is a corruption of the O.Fr. *pourallée*, a going through; the *lieu*, as though for *place*, being an erroneous addition due to English pronunciation and spelling of the French. Thus Henry III allowed certain portions around the forests, acquired by his predecessors by unlawful encroachment, to be freed from the forest-laws and restored to former owners. The boundaries were then settled by a perambulation or *pourallée*. *See* FOREST COURTS.

> In the purlieus of this forest stands
> A sheepcote fenced about with olive-trees.
> SHAKESPEARE: *As You Like It*, IV, iii.

Purple. A synonym for the rank of Roman emperor, derived from the colour of the emperor's dyed woollen robe, hence phrases such as "raised to the purple". Purple robes were a mark of dignity among the ancient Greeks and Romans and were worn by kings, magistrates, and military commanders, hence purple became a symbol of luxury and power. It was obtained from shellfish (*Buccinum*, *Murex*) and the deep colour was termed *purpura* (from the name of one of these molluscs). The famous *Tyrian purple* was made from a mixture of these shellfish

and was very costly to produce. Differing shades were obtained by various combinations and methods. Since Roman times, purple was used in the insignia of emperors, kings and prelates, and a priest is said to be **raised to the purple** when he is created CARDINAL, though his insignia are actually red. *Purpure* is one of the tinctures used in HERALDRY, and in engravings it is shown by lines running diagonally from sinister to dexter (*i.e.* from right to left as one looks at it). *See* COLOURS.

Born in, or **to the purple.** *See* PORPHYROGENITUS.

Purple Emperor. One of the largest and most richly coloured British butterflies, *Apatura iris*. Only the male has the purple sheen.

Purple Heart. A U.S. army medal awarded for wounds received by enemy action while on active service. It consists of a silver heart bearing the effigy of George Washington, suspended from a purple ribbon with white edges. The heartwood of *Copaifera pubiflora* and *C. bracteata* is called *Purple Heart* or *Purple Wood*. It is a native of Guyana and a rich plum colour, and was used in making ramrods for guns. *Purple Heart* is also the popular name of a stimulant pill (Drinamyl) favoured by youthful drug-takers, so called from its shape and colour.

Purple patches. Highly coloured or florid patches in a literary work which is generally undistinguished. The allusion is to Horace's *De Arte Poetica*, 14:

> Inceptis gravibus plerumque et magna professis
> Purpureus, late qui splendeat, unus et alter
> Adsuitur pannus.
> (Often to weighty enterprises and such as profess great objects, one or two purple patches are sewn on to make a fine display in the distance.)

Pursuivant (pĕr' swi vȧnt). The lowest grade of the officers of arms comprising the Heralds' College, the others, under the EARL MARSHAL, being (1) the Kings of Arms, and (2) the HERALDS.

ENGLAND has four Pursuivants, *viz. Rouge Croix*, *Bluemantle*, *Rouge Dragon*, and *Portcullis*; SCOTLAND has three, *viz. Carrick*, *Kintyre*, and *Unicorn*.

Purveyance. A doublet of *providence*, from Lat. *providentia*, foresight. Historically, the Crown prerogative of purchasing provisions etc. for the HOUSEHOLD at an appraised price and of impressing horses and vehicles. With an itinerant court such compulsory purchases caused much local hardship, especially as ready payment was rare, and from the late 13th century protests led to statutes against its abuse. It was largely abolished in 1660 but the purveyance of horses by the army was practised in World War I and this and the right of impressment of vehicles still exist for the Services. The current use of *compulsory purchase orders* on properties has much in common with practices denounced under the early Stuart kings.

Puseyite (pū'zi īt). A HIGH CHURCH follower of E. B. Pusey (1800–1882), Professor of Hebrew at Oxford, one of the leaders of the OXFORD MOVEMENT, and a contributor to *Tracts for the Times*. Hence **Puseyism** as an unfriendly name for Tractarianism.

Push. To give one the push. To give him his CONGÉ, to give him the sack (*see under* SACK).

To push off. To depart, to commence the operations. A phrase from boating—one starts by pushing the boat off from the bank. Used imperatively, *Push off* means "Go away", "Get out of here".

To push the boat out. A popular expression meaning to celebrate by treating one's acquaintances to a drinking session. Of nautical origin, probably from the idea of a final celebration before sailing, to give impetus to one's departure.

Push-button civilization. A phrase descriptive of the highly industrialized nations of the world where household chores are performed and entertainment provided, etc., by electrical appliances operated by "push-button" controls.

Push-button, or **press-button war.** A war carried on with guided missiles controlled by pushing or pressing a button.

Puss. A conventional call-name for a cat, possibly imitative of a cat-like sound; also applied in the 17th century and since to hares. The derivation from Lat. *lepus*, a hare, Frenchified into *le pus*, is, of course, only humorous.

Puss in Boots. This nursery tale, *Le Chat Botté*, is from Straparola's *Nights* (1530), No. xi, where Constantine's cat procures his master a fine castle and the king's heiress. It was translated from the Italian into French, in 1585, and appeared in Perrault's *Les contes de ma Mère l'Oye* (1697), through which medium it reached England. In the story the clever cat secures a fortune and a royal partner for his master, who passes off as the Marquis of Carabas, but is in reality a young miller without a penny in the world.

Puss in the Corner. An old game recorded in Strutt's *Sports and Pastimes of the People of England*. A boy or girl stands in each corner of a room and a fifth player in the middle. Those in the corners change positions in a succession and the centre player tries to oc-

cupy a corner before another can reach it. If achieved the loser occupies the centre.

Pussyfoot. A person with a soft, cat-like sneaking tread, and from PUSSYFOOT JOHNSON (*below*), now applied as a noun to advocates of, and as an adjective to opinions, legislation, etc., promoting total abstinence.

Pussyfoot Johnson. W. E. Johnson (1862–1945), the temperance advocate, gained his nickname from his "cat-like" policies in pursuing law-breakers in gambling saloons, etc., in Indian territory when serving as Chief Special Officer of the U.S. Indian Service (1908–1911). After this he devoted his energies to the cause of prohibition and gave over 4,000 lectures on temperance.

Put. A clown, a silly shallow-pate, a butt; one easily "put upon".

> As he gave the good-night to two or three young fellows before landing, one of them, instead of returning the civility, asked us what queer old put we had in the boat.
> ADDISON: *Sir Roger at Spring Gardens*.

Put and Take. A game of chance played with a modification of the old "tee-to-tum", one side of which is marked *Put*—signifying that the player pays—and another *Take*. It was popular in the early 1920s.

To put one's shoulder to the wheel. To make a determined effort; as a carter would put his shoulder to the wheel to assist his horses hauling his waggon out of a rut.

To put two and two together. To draw conclusions from facts, events, etc.; two and two make four, hence the suggestion of a simple and obvious deduction.

To stay put. To remain firmly in a position, literally or figuratively.

Putsch (pooch). A German word, the same as our *push*, applied to a COUP DE MAIN or political uprising.

Pygmalion (pig mā' li ón). In Greek legend, a sculptor and king of Cyprus. According to Ovid's *Metamorphoses*, he fell in love with his own ivory statue of his own ideal woman. At his earnest prayer the goddess APHRODITE gave life to the statue and he married it. The story is found in Marston's *Metamorphosis of Pygmalion's Image* (1598). Morris retold it in *The Earthly Paradise* (*August*), and W. S. Gilbert adapted it in his comedy of *Pygmalion and Galatea* (1871), in which the sculptor is a married man. His wife, Cynisca, was jealous of the animated statue (Galatea), which, after considerable trouble, voluntarily returned to its original state. The name was used figuratively by G. B. Shaw for a play produced in 1912 from which the popular musical *My Fair Lady* was derived.

Pygmy (pig' mi). The name used by HOMER

and other classical writers for a supposed race of DWARFS said to dwell in Ethiopia, Africa, or India; from Gr. *pugme*, the length of the arm from elbow to the knuckles. They cut down corn with hatchets and made war against cranes which came annually to plunder them. When HERCULES visited their country they climbed up his goblet by ladders to drink from it, and while he was asleep two whole armies of pygmies fell upon his right hand and two on his left and were rolled up by Hercules in the skin of the NEMEAN LION. Swift's debt to this legend is apparent in his *Gulliver's Travels*.

The term is now applied to certain dwarfish races of central Africa (whose existence was established late in the 19th century), Malaysia, etc.; also to small members of a species, as the *pygmy hippopotamus*.

Pylades and Orestes (pī′ lă dēz, ō res′ tēz). Two friends in Homeric legend, whose names have become proverbial for friendship, like those of DAMON AND PYTHIAS, DAVID AND JONATHAN. Orestes was the son, and Pylades the nephew, of AGAMEMNON, after whose murder Orestes was put in the care of Pylades' father (Strophius), and the two became fast friends. Pylades assisted Orestes in obtaining vengeance on Ægisthus and CLYTEMNESTRA, and afterwards married ELECTRA, his friend's sister.

Pylon. Properly a monumental gateway (Gr. *pulon*, a gateway), especially of an Egyptian temple, consisting of two massive towers joined by a bridge over the doorway; now usually applied to the obelisks that mark out the course on an airfield or to the standards for electric cables, etc.

Pyramid (pir′ à mid) (Gr. *pyramis*, a wheaten cake). The Greek name of these massive royal tombs of ancient Egypt was probably of humorous application. Zoser's step-pyramid at Saqqara (IIIrd Dynasty) was the forerunner of the true pyramid. The next stage was when the step-pyramid at Meidum was covered with a uniform slope from base to top by filling in the steps (*c.* 2670 B.C.). The famous Great Pyramid at Giza, covering some 13 acres and originally rising to a height of 481 ft., was built by Cheops or Khufu (*c.* 2650 B.C.). That of Chephren or Khafra (*c.* 2620 B.C.), his son, is slightly smaller, and the third, the tomb of Mycerinius or Menkaura (*c.* 2600 B.C.), is 204 ft. high. Each contains entrances with passages leading to an antechamber and the burial chamber. Other pyramids are to be found at Abusir, Saqqara, Dahshur, Lisht, and in the Faiyum.

The kings of the XIth Dynasty built small brick pyramids at Thebes.

Pyramus (pir′ à mùs). A Babylonian youth in classic story (*see* Ovid's *Metamorphoses*, iv), the lover of Thisbe. Thisbe was to meet him at the white MULBERRY-tree near the tomb of Ninus, but she, scared by a lion, fled and left her veil, which the lion besmeared with blood. Pyramus, thinking his lady-love had been devoured, slew himself, and Thisbe, coming up soon afterwards, stabbed herself also. The blood of the lovers stained the white fruit of the mulberry-tree into its present colour. The "tedious brief scene" and "very tragical mirth" presented by the rustics in SHAKESPEARE's *Midsummer Night's Dream* is a travesty of this legend.

Pyrography. The art of decorating woodwork, furniture, panelling, etc., by designs and pictures burnt in with hot steel points. Some of the best work was as fine in detail as a good etching. Pyrography dates from the 17th century and reached its highest standard in the 19th century. In its crude form it is pokerwork.

Pyromancy (Gr. *pur*, fire; *manteia*, divination). DIVINATION by fire or the shapes observed in fire.

Pyrrha (pi′ rà). The wife of DEUCALION.

Pyrrhic Dance (pi′ rik). The famous war-dance of the Greeks; so called from its inventor, Pyrrichos, a Dorian. It was a quick dance, performed in full armour to the flute, and its name is still used for a metrical foot of two short "dancing" syllables. The *Romaika*, still danced in Greece, is a relic of the ancient Pyrrhic dance.

> Ye have the Pyrrhic dance as yet;
> Where is the Pyrrhic phalanx gone?
> BYRON: *Don Juan*, canto III (*The Isles of Greece*, l.56).

Pyrrhic victory. A victory won at too heavy a price, like the costly victory won by Pyrrhus, King of Epirus, at Asculum in 279 B.C. ("One more such victory and we are lost."). Pyrrhus lost all his best officers and many men.

Pyrrhonism. Scepticism, or philosophic doubt; so named from Pyrrho (4th century B.C.), the founder of the first Greek school of sceptical philosophy. Pyrrho maintained that nothing was capable of proof and admitted the reality of nothing but sensations.

Pythagoras (pī thăg′ or às). The Greek philosopher and mathematician of the 6th century B.C. (born at Samos), to whom was attributed the enunciation of the doctrines of the TRANSMIGRATION OF SOULS and of the harmony of the spheres, and also the proof of the 47th proposition in the 1st book of EUCLID, which is hence called the *Pythagorean* *proposition.* He taught that the SUN, MOON, and PLANETS have a motion independent of their daily rotation but seems to have held that the universe was earth-centred (*see* PYTHAGOREAN SYSTEM).

Pythagoras was noted for his manly beauty and long hair. Many stories are related of him, such as that he distinctly recollected previous existences of his own, having been (1) Æthelides, son of MERCURY; (2) Euphorbus the Phrygian, son of Panthous, in which form he ran PATROCLUS through with a lance, leaving HECTOR to kill him; (3) Hermotimus, the prophet of Clazomenæ; and (4) a fisherman. To prove his Phrygian existence he was taken to the temple of HERA, in Argos, and asked to point out the shield of the son of Panthous, which he did without hesitation. Rosalind alludes to this story in Shakespeare's *As You Like It* (III, ii) when she says:

> I was never so be-rhymed since Pythagoras' time, that I was an Irish rat, which I can hardly remember.

It is also elaborated in *Twelfth Night* (IV, ii):

> *Clown:* What is the opinion of Pythagoras concerning wild fowl?
> *Mal.:* That the soul of our grandam might haply inhabit a bird.
> *Clown:* What thinkest thou of his opinion?
> *Mal.:* I think nobly of the soul, and no way approve his opinion.

Other legends assert that one of his thighs was of GOLD, and that he showed it to ABARIS, and exhibited it in the OLYMPIC GAMES.

It was also said that Pythagoras used to write on a looking-glass in blood and place it opposite the MOON, when the inscription would appear reflected on the moon's disc; and that he tamed a savage Daunian bear by "stroking it gently with his hand", subdued an EAGLE by the same means, and held absolute dominion over beasts and birds by "the power of his voice" or "influence of his touch".

At Croton he became the centre of the *Pythagorean brotherhood* which sought the moral reformation of society, practising temperance and abstinence from fleshly food.

The letter of Pythagoras. The Greek letter upsilon, y, so called because it was used by him as a symbol of the divergent paths of virtue and vice.

The Pythagorean System. The astronomical system so called which held the universe to be spherical in shape with fire at its centre, around which revolved the counter-earth, the earth, then the MOON, the SUN, the five PLANETS, and lastly the sphere of fixed stars. It is a forerunner of the COPERNICAN SYSTEM and seems to be a later hypothesis of the Pythagoreans and not to have been originated by Pythagoras himself.

The Pythagorean Tables. *See* TABLE OF PYTHAGORAS.

The Theorem of Pythagoras. That the square on the hypotenuse of a right-angled triangle is equal to the sum of the squares on the other two sides.

Pythia (pith' i à). The priestess of APOLLO at DELPHI who delivered ORACLES. Inspiration was obtained by inhaling sulphureous vapours which issued from the ground from a hole over which she sat on a three-legged stool or tripod. Oracles were only available in the spring and were originally spoken in HEXAMETER verses.

Pythian Games. The Greek games held in honour of APOLLO at Pytho in Phocis, subsequently called DELPHI. They took place every fourth year, in the third year of each OLYMPIAD, and were next in importance to the OLYMPIC GAMES.

Pythias. *See* DAMON.

The Knights of Pythias. A benevolent fraternity in the U.S.A. and Canada, founded at Washington, D.C., in 1864. The *Pythian Sisters*, founded in 1888, are recruited from female relatives of the Knights.

Python (pī' thon). The monster serpent hatched from the mud of DEUCALION's deluge, and slain by APOLLO at DELPHI (Pytho).

Pyx (piks) (Gr. *pyxis*, a boxwood vessel). A small metal receptacle or box in which the reserved HOST is taken to sick people. It is also the vessel in which the Host is reserved in the Tabernacle in Roman Catholic (and some Anglican) churches.

Trial of the Pyx. In ENGLAND, out of every 15 lb. TROY WEIGHT of GOLD and every 60 lb. of "silver" minted a coin was put into the *pyx* or box for annual testing at Goldsmiths' Hall in the City of London. The *trial of the pyx* is conducted in the presence of the QUEEN's REMEMBRANCER and a jury of goldsmiths. Their verdict is delivered in the presence of the CHANCELLOR OF THE EXCHEQUER. The trial was initiated in the reign of Edward I and formerly took place in the Chapel of the Pyx in Westminster Abbey. Samples are now taken and coins are not assayed separately. Silver was replaced by cupronickel in 1947.

Q

Q. The seventeenth letter of the English alphabet, and nineteenth of the Phœnician and Hebrew. In English *q* is invariably followed by *u* except in transliteration of some Arabic words, as in *Qatar*. *Qu* in English normally represents the sound *kw* as in *quinquennial* but occasionally *k* as in *perique*, *grotesque*, and *quay* (pronounced kē). Without the *u* it is pronounced *k* as in *Iraq*. Formerly, in Scotland, *qu* replaced *hw* as in *quhat*, or *hwat* (what). Q as a mediæval Latin numeral represents 500.

"Q". In Biblical criticism, the symbol used for the theoretical document used by MATTHEW or LUKE or both. In the SYNOPTIC GOSPELS there is much material common to both Matthew and Luke, which is designated "Q" (usually held to be the German *Quelle*, source). These passages mainly consist of the sayings of Jesus.

Q. The *nom de plume* of Sir Arthur Quiller-Couch (1863–1944), Cornish author and novelist, King Edward VII Professor of English Literature at Cambridge (1912–1944) and one-time editor of the *Oxford Book of English Verse*.

Old Q. William Douglas, third Earl of March, and fourth Duke of Queensberry (1724–1810), notorious for his dissolute life and escapades, especially on the TURF.

Q in a corner. An old children's game, perhaps the same as our PUSS IN THE CORNER; also something not seen at first but subsequently brought to notice.

In a merry Q (cue). Humour, temper; thus Shakespeare says, "My cue is villainous melancholy" (*King Lear*, I, ii).

To mind one's P's and Q's. *See under* P.

Q.C. QUEEN'S COUNCIL.

Q.E.D. (Lat. *quod erat demonstrandum*, which was to be demonstrated). Appended to the theorems of EUCLID: Thus have we proved the proposition stated above, as we were required to do. In schoolboy parlance, "Quite easily done."

Q.E.F. (Lat. *quod erat faciendum*, which was to be done). Appended to the problems of EUCLID: Thus have we done the operation required.

Q.P. (Lat. *quantum placet*). Used in prescriptions to signify that the quantity may be as little or as much as you like. Thus, in a cup of tea we might say. "Milk and sugar *q.p.*"

Q.S. (Lat. *quantum sufficit*, as much as suffices). Thus, after giving the drugs in minute proportions, the apothecary may be told to "mix in liquorice, *q.s.*"

Q ships. In World War I, the name given to war vessels camouflaged as tramps. These "mystery ships" were used to lure U-BOATS to their destruction.

Q.T. On the strict Q.T. With complete secrecy. "Q.T." stands for "quiet".

Q.V. (Lat. *quantum vis*). As much as you like, or *quantum valeat*, as much as is proper.

q.v. (Lat. *quod vide*). Which see.

Quack, or **Quack doctor;** once called *quacksalver*. A puffer of salves; an itinerant drug vendor at FAIRS who "quacked" forth the praises of his wares to the credulous rustics. Hence, a CHARLATAN.

Quad. The university contraction for quadrangle, the college ground; hence, *to be in quad* is to be confined to your college grounds. The word *quad* is also applied to one of a family of quadruplets. *Cp.* QUOD.

Quadragesima (kwod ra jes' i ma). The forty days of LENT.

Quadragesima Sunday. The first Sunday in LENT; so called because it is, in round numbers, the fortieth day before EASTER.

Quadragesimals. The farthings or payments formerly made in commutation of a personal visit to the Mother-church on Mid-Lent Sunday. *Cp.* PENTECOSTALS. *See also* MOTHERING SUNDAY.

Quadrant, The. The name given to the curved southern end of Regent Street, London. It was designed by John Nash (1752–1835) in 1813, and when built had two DORIC colonades, the cast-iron columns being made at the Carron iron-works; these were removed in 1848. The original buildings were, regrettably, demolished in 1928.

Quadriga (kwod' ri ga). A contraction of *quadrijugae* (Lat. *quattuor*, *quadri-*, four;

jugum, yoke). In classical antiquity, a two-wheeled chariot drawn by four horses harnessed abreast. A spirited representation of Peace riding in a quadriga, executed in bronze by Adrian Jones in 1912, surmounts the arch at the west end of Constitution Hill, London.

Quadrilateral. The four fortresses of Peschiera and Mantua on the Mincio, with Verona and Legnago on the Adige. Now demolished.

Lambeth Quadrilateral. The four points suggested by the LAMBETH Conference of 1888 as a basis for Christian reunion; the BIBLE, the Apostolic and NICENE CREEDS, two Sacraments (BAPTISM and the EUCHARIST), and the historic Episcopate.

Quadrille (kwod ril'). An old card game played by four persons with an ordinary pack of cards from which the eights, nines, and tens have been withdrawn. It displaced OMBRE in popular favour about 1730, and was followed by WHIST.

The square dance of the same name was of French origin, and was introduced into England in 1813 by the Duke of Devonshire.

Quadrivium (kwod riv' i um). The collective name given by the SCHOOLMEN of the MIDDLE AGES to the four "liberal arts" (Lat. *quadri-*, four; *via*, way), viz., arithmetic, music, geometry, and astronomy. The quadrivium was the "fourfold way" to knowledge; the TRIVIUM, the "threefold way" to eloquence; both together comprehended the *Seven Liberal Arts* enumerated in the following hexameter:

> Lingua, Tropus, Ratio, Numerus, Tonus,
> Angulus, Astra.

And in the two following:

> Gram. loquitur, Dia. vera docet, Rhet. verba
> colorat;
> Mus. cadit, Ar. numerat, Geo. ponderat, Ast. colit
> astra.

Quadroon *See* NEGRO.

Quai d'Orsay (kā dôr sā). The quay in Paris running along the left bank of the Seine where are situated the departments of Foreign Affairs and other government offices. The name is applied to the French Foreign Office and sometimes to the French government as a whole.

Quail. This bird was formerly supposed to be of an inordinately amorous disposition, hence its name was given to a courtesan.

> Here's Agamemnon, an honest fellow enough, and
> one that loves quails.
> SHAKESPEARE: *Troilus and Cressida*, V, i.

Quaker. A familiar name for a member of the Society of Friends, a religious body having no definite creed and no regular ministry, founded by George Fox, who began his preaching in 1647. His followers created an organized society during the 1650s and 1660s. It appears from the founder's *Journal* that they first obtained the appellation (1650) from the following circumstances: "Justice Bennet, of Derby," says Fox, "was the first to call us Quakers, because I bid them Tremble at the Word of the Lord."

> Quakers (that, like to lanterns, bear
> Their light within them) will not swear.
> BUTLER: *Hudibras*, II, ii.

The name was previously applied to a sect whose adherents shook and trembled with religious emotion and was generally applied in the COMMONWEALTH period as an abusive term to religious and political radicals. *Cp.* SHAKERS.

Quaker City. PHILADELPHIA, which was founded by a group of Quakers led by William Penn and intended as a haven of religious freedom.

Quaker guns. Dummy guns made of wood, for drill purposes or camouflage; an allusion to the Quaker reprobation of the use of force.

The Quaker Poet. Bernard Barton (1784–1849); also John Greenleaf Whittier (1807–1892).

Quarantine (Ital. *quaranta*, forty). The period, originally forty days, that a ship suspected of being infected with some contagious disorder is obliged to lie off port. Now applied to any period of segregation to prevent infection.

In law, the term is applied to the forty days during which a widow who is entitled to a dower may remain in the chief mansion-house of her deceased husband. *See also* YELLOW ADMIRAL *under* ADMIRAL; YELLOW JACK.

To perform quarantine is to ride off port during the time of quarantine.

Quare impedit (Lat., wherefore he hinders). A form of legal action by which the right of presentation to a Church of England BENEFICE is tried (from the opening words of the writ). When a BISHOP has failed to institute a clergyman presented by the patron of the benefice, the latter may apply for a writ of *Quare impedit* against the bishop. It is now only used where the bishop's objections relate to matters of doctrine and ritual.

Quarrel (O.Fr. *quarel*; from Late Lat. *quadrellus*, diminutive of *quadrus*, a square). A square or lozenge; a small square or diamond-shaped tile, or a similarly shaped pane of glass as used in lattice-windows; also a short stout square-headed bolt or arrow used in the crossbow.

Quarrel. To engage in contention, to fall out (from O.Fr. *querele*; Lat. *querela*, complaint).

To quarrel over the bishop's cope— over something which cannot possibly do you any good; over goat's wool. A newly appointed Bishop of Bruges entered the town in his cope, which he gave to the people; and the people, to part it among themselves, tore it to shreds, each taking a piece.

To quarrel with your bread and butter. To act against your best interest; to follow a course which may prejudice your livelihood.

Quarry. An object of chase, especially the bird flown at in hawking or the animal pursued by hounds or hunters. Originally the word (O.Fr. *cuirée*, skinned) denoted the entrails, etc., of the deer which were placed on the animal's skin after it had been flayed, and given to the hounds as a reward.

> Your castle is surprized; your wife and babes
> Savagely slaughtered; to relate the manner,
> Were, on the quarry of these murder'd deer,
> To add the death of you.
>
> SHAKESPEARE: *Macbeth*, IV, iii.

The place where slate, stone, etc., is dug out is called a *quarry* from O.Fr. *quarrière*, Lat. *quadrare*, to square, because the stones were squared on the spot. *Cp.* QUARREL.

Quart d'heure (kar děr). **Un mauvais quart d'heure** (Fr., a bad quarter of an hour). Used of a short, disagreeable experience.

Quarter. The fourth part of anything, as of a year or an hour or any material thing. In weights a *quarter* is 28 lb., *i.e.* a fourth of a hundredweight; as a measure of capacity for grain it is 8 bushels, which used to be one-fourth, but is now one-fifth of a load. In the meat trade a *quarter* of a beast is a fourth part, which includes one of the legs. A *quarter* in the U.S. coinage is the fourth part of a DOLLAR; in a heraldic shield or on a flag the *quarters* are the divisions made by central lines drawn at right angles across them. When looking at a shield the 1st and 4th quarters are in the *dexter chief* and *sinister base* (left-hand top and right-hand bottom), and the 2nd and 3rd in the *sinister chief* and *dexter base*.

Quarter, as exemption from death upon surrender.

To cry quarter. To beg for mercy.

To grant quarter. To spare the life of an enemy in your power. The old suggestion that it derives from an agreement anciently made between the Dutch and Spaniards, that the ransom of a soldier should be the *quarter* of his pay, is not borne out. It is possibly due to the fact that the victor would have to provide his captive with temporary QUARTERS.

Quarter, Quarters. Residence or place of abode.

A district of a town or city is often known as a quarter, as the *poor quarter*, the *native quarter*. The **Quartier Latin** (Latin quarter) of Paris is the university area. Although popularly renowned as the cosmopolitan and BOHEMIAN quarter, it derives its name from its ancient fame as a centre of learning when Latin was the common language for the students, who came from all over Europe.

Winter quarters is the place where an army lodges during the winter months; *married quarters*, barrack accommodation, etc., for married service men and their families. **Come to my quarters** was a common phrase among bachelors as an invitation to their rooms. In the Southern U.S.A. the word was used of that part of a plantation allotted to the Negroes.

> There shall no leavened bread to be seen with thee, neither shall there be leaven seen...in all thy quarters.
>
> *Exod.* xiii, 7.

Quarter Days. (1) New Style LADY DAY (25 March), MIDSUMMER Day (24 June), MICHAELMAS DAY (29 September), and CHRISTMAS Day (25 December).

(2) Old Style—Lady Day (6 April), Old Midsummer Day (6 July), Old Michaelmas Day (11 October), and Old Christmas Day (6 January).

Quarter Days in Scotland. CANDLEMAS DAY (2 February), WHITSUNDAY (15 May), LAMMAS DAY (1 August), and MARTINMAS Day (11 November).

Quarter Sessions. From the mid-14th century JUSTICES OF THE PEACE sat four times a year in Quarter Sessions to deal with appeals from Petty Sessions, criminal charges, and some civil cases as well as administrative work. Generally trial was by jury before two or more justices, but in 1882 a qualified barrister known as a Recorder replaced them in the boroughs, and from 1962 the chairman in other courts of Quarter Sessions had to be a qualified lawyer. In 1842 the more serious criminal cases were transferred to the Assizes and most of their administrative work was lost to the County Councils by the Local Government Act of 1888. Quarter Sessions were abolished by the Courts Act of 1971.

Quartered. *See* DRAWN AND QUARTERED.

Quarterdeck. The upper deck of a ship from the mainmast to the stern. In the Royal Navy it is the promenade reserved for officers. Hence, *to behave as though he were on his own quarterdeck*, to behave as though he owned the place. The naval custom of saluting the quarterdeck is of uncertain origin, one suggestion being that anciently a shrine was kept in this part of the ship. *Cp.* FORECASTLE.

Quarterly, The. A common name for the *Quarterly Review*, a literary and political review first published by John Murray at Edinburgh in 1809. It was a TORY rival of the EDINBURGH REVIEW. Its first editor was William Gifford (1756—1826) and Scott and Southey were principal contributors. J. G. Lockhart took over the editorship from S. T. Coleridge in 1825 and continued in office until 1853. It ceased publication in 1967.

Quartermaster. In the army, the officer whose duty it is to attend to the QUARTERS of the soldiers. He superintends the issue of all stores and equipment.

In the navy, the rating or petty officer who supervises the steering of the ship at sea and in harbour keeps watch under the Officer of the WATCH.

Quarto. A size of paper made by folding the sheet twice, giving *four* leaves, or eight pages; hence, a book composed of sheets folded thus. *Cp.* FOLIO; OCTAVO. The word is often written "4to".

Quashee (kwosh′ē). A generic name of a Negro; from West African *Kwasi*, a name often given to a child born on a Sunday. *Cp.* QUASSIA.

Quasi (kwā′ zī) (Lat., as if). Prefixed to indicate "seeming", "as it were", that what it qualifies is not the real thing but has some of its qualities. Thus a *quasi-historical account* is seemingly historical but not accurately so, or only partially so.

Quasi contract. In law, an obligation similar to that created by a formal contract.

Quasi tenant. The tenant of a house sublet.

Quasimodo Sunday (kwā zī mō dō′). The first Sunday after EASTER or LOW SUNDAY; so called from the Introit at MASS on this day which begins *Quasi modo geniti infantes*, as newborn babes (I *Pet.* ii, 2). *Cp.* CANTATE SUNDAY.

Quasimodo was also the name of the hunchback in Victor Hugo's *Notre-Dame de Paris* (1831).

Quassia (kwash′ yà *or* kwosh′ yà). An American plant, or rather genus of plants, named after Quassi, a Negro, who, in 1730, was the first to make its medicinal properties as a tonic known. *See* QUASHEE.

Linnæus applied this name to a tree of Surinam in honour of a negro, Quassi...who employed its bark as a remedy for fever; and enjoyed such a reputation among the natives as to be almost worshipped by some.
LINDLEY and MOORE:
Treatise of Botany, Pt. II, p. 947.

Quattrocento (Ital. from Lat. *quattuor*, four; *centum*, hundred). An abbreviation of *mille quattrocento*, 1400. The name given to the Fifteenth Century as a period of art and literature, especially with reference to Italy. *Cp.* CINQUENCENTO.

Que sçais-je? (kĕ sāzh) (Fr., What do I know?). The motto adopted by Michel-Eyquem de Montaigne (1533–1592), the great French essayist, as expressing the sceptical and inquiring nature of his writings.

Queen. A female sovereign or a king's wife (also nowadays, slightingly, of a male homosexual); from O.E. *cwen*, a woman (which also gives *quean*, a word still sometimes used slightingly or contemptuously of a woman), from an ancient Aryan root that gave the Old Teutonic stem *kwen-*, Zend *gena*, Gr. *gyne*, Slavonic *zena*, etc., all meaning "woman". *Cp.* KING; *see* MAB.

Queen Anne. Daughter of James II and his first wife Anne Hyde. Her reign extended from 1702 to 1714 and her name is still used in certain phrases.

Queen Anne is dead. A slighting retort made to a teller of stale news.

Queen Anne style. The style in buildings, decoration, furniture, silverware, etc., characteristic of her period.

Queen Anne's Bounty. A fund established by Queen Anne in 1704 for the relief of the poorer clergy of the CHURCH OF ENGLAND. It was created out of the firstfruits (*see* ANNATES) and tenths, formerly given to the papacy, which were annexed to the Crown by Henry VIII. In 1809 there were 860 incumbents still getting less than £50 per annum and the fund was increased by Parliamentary grants (1809–1820). Queen Anne's Bounty was merged with the Ecclesiastical Commission in 1948 to form the Church Commissioners.

Queen Anne's fan. TO COCK A SNOOK. *See under* COCK.

Queen Anne's footstool. A name given to St. John's Church, Smith Square, Westminster; a fine specimen of baroque architecture by Thomas Archer, completed in 1728. There is an apocryphal story that Queen Anne, when interviewing the architect, kicked over her footstool and said "Make it like that", the four up-turned legs representing the towers. In reality, the building began to settle during construction and to stabilize it a tower and lantern-turret were added at each corner. Lord Chesterfield likened the church to an elephant thrown on its back with its four feet erect. It was burnt out in 1742, and again in 1941 after which it was re-opened in 1969 as a concert and lecture hall.

Queen City. Cincinnati.

Queen Consort. The wife of a reigning king.

Queen Dick. Richard Cromwell (1626–1712), son of Protector Oliver Cromwell, was sometimes so called; also known as "King Dick".

In the reign of Queen Dick. See QUEEN DICK; also DICK.

Queen Dowager. The widow of a deceased king.

Queen Mab. See MAB.

Queen Mother. The consort of a king is so called after her husband's death and when her son or daughter has succeeded to the throne.

Queen of the Blues. A nickname given by Dr. Johnson to Mrs. Elizabeth Montagu (1720–1800), a noted BLUE-STOCKING.

Queen of Glory. An epithet of the Virgin MARY.

Queen of Hearts. Elizabeth (1596–1662), daughter of James I, wife of the Elector of the PALATINATE, and ill-starred Queen of BOHEMIA; so called in the Low Countries from her amiable character and engaging manners, even in her misfortune.

Queen of Heaven. The Virgin MARY. In ancient times, among the Phœnicians, ASTARTE; Greeks, HERA; Romans, JUNO; HECATE; the Egyptian ISIS, etc., were also so called; but as a general title it applied to DIANA, or the MOON also called *Queen of the Night*, and *Queen of the Tides*. In *Jer*. vii, 18, we read: "The children gather wood...and the women knead dough, to make cakes to the queen of heaven", *i.e.* the Moon.

Queen of Love. APHRODITE or VENUS.

> Poor queen of love in thine own law forlorn
> To love a cheek that smiles at thee in scorn!
> SHAKESPEARE: *Venus and Adonis*, 251.

Queen of the May. See under MAY.

Queen Regnant. A queen who holds the crown in her own right, in contradistinction to a QUEEN CONSORT.

Queen of Scots' Pillar. A column in the Peak Cavern, Derbyshire, as clear as alabaster. So called because on one occasion when going to throw herself on the mercy of Elizabeth I, the Queen of Scots proceeded thus far and then turned back.

Queen of the Suburbs. Ealing, on the western outskirts of Edwardian London,

was so called from the social status or genteel quality of its residents. *Cp*. GARDEN SUBURB.

Queen's or **King's Bench.** The Supreme Court of COMMON LAW; so called because at one time the SOVEREIGN presided in this court, and the court followed the sovereign when he moved from one place to another. Originally called the *Aulia Regia*, it is now a division of the High Court of Justice.

Queen's College (Oxford), **Queens' College** (Cambridge). Note the position of the apostrophe in each case. The Oxford College was founded (1340) by Robert de Eglesfield in honour of Queen Philippa, consort of Edward III, to whom he was confessor. The Cambridge College numbers two Queens as its founders, *viz.*, Margaret of Anjou, consort of Henry VI (1448), and Elizabeth Woodville, Edward IV's consort, who refounded the college in 1465.

Queen's, or **King's Colour.** The UNION JACK, except in the case of foot guards, the first of the two colours borne by regiments. In the GUARDS it is a crimson flag bearing the royal cipher. The first colour was called "King's" in 1751, "Royal" in 1837, with the accession of Queen Victoria, and "Queen's" in 1892. *See also* REGIMENTAL COLOURS *under* COLOUR.

Queen's, or **King's Counsel.** In ENGLAND a member of the BAR appointed by the Crown or the nomination of the Lord CHANCELLOR; in SCOTLAND on the recommendation of the Lord Justice General. A Q.C. wears a silk gown and is thus often called a *silk*. He takes precedence over the junior Bar, and in a case must have a junior barrister with him.

Queen's County. See KING'S COUNTY.

Queen's Day. 17 November, the day of the accession of Queen Elizabeth I, first publicly celebrated in 1570, and for over three centuries kept as a holiday in Government offices and at Westminster School.

17 November at Merchant Taylors' School is a holiday also, now called Sir Thomas White's Founder's Day.

Queen's English. See under ENGLISH.

Queen's Evidence. See EVIDENCE.

Queen's, or **King's Messenger** is an official of the British Foreign Office whose duty it is to carry personally confidential messages from London to any embassy or legation abroad. He carries as his badge of office a silver greyhound, and though he receives courtesies and help in the countries across which he travels, he enjoys no diplomatic immunities or privileges except that of passing through the customs the "diplomatic bag" he is carrying.

The Queen's, or **King's Picture.** *See under* KING.

Queen's, or **King's Remembrancer.** Originally an EXCHEQUER clerk sharing the work of establishing and collecting fixed revenues and debts with the Lord Treasurer's Remembrancer. In 1323 the King's Remembrancer was assigned to casual crown revenues, proceedings against defaulters, etc., and other duties were added later. In 1877 the office was transferred to the Supreme Court and is now held by the Senior Master of the QUEEN'S BENCH division. His duties are concerned with the selection of SHERIFFS, the swearing-in of the Lord MAYOR of London and with revenue cases.

Queen's or **King's Shilling.** *See under* SHILLING.

The Queen's or **King's Speech.** The speech from the throne in the HOUSE OF LORDS made at the opening of a parliamentary session outlining the government's programme for the session. It is always addressed to both Houses but the special clause relating to finance is addressed to the Commons alone.

Queen's or **King's Tobacco-pipe.** A jocular name given to a kiln which used to be situated at the corner of the tobacco Warehouse at the London Docks. It was used for the periodic and wasteful destruction of contraband, and damaged tobacco, tea, smuggled books, etc. It went out of use in the late 19th century.

Queen's ware. Glazed Wedgewood earthenware of a creamy colour.

Queen's weather. When a fête, etc., takes place on a fine day; so called because Queen Victoria was, for the most part, fortunate in having fine weather when she appeared in public.

The White Queen. Mary Queen of Scots; so called because she dressed in *white* mourning for her French husband, Francis II (1544–1560).

The Winter Queen. *See under* WINTER.

Queen Square Hermit. Jeremy Bentham (1748–1832), the philosopher and father of UTILITARIANISM, who lived at No. 1 Queen Square, London. His embalmed figure, seated and fully clad, is preserved at University College, London.

Queenhithe. The hithe, or landing-place, or wharf off Upper Thames Street, on the north bank of the Thames upstream of SOUTHWARK Bridge. It is mentioned in a charter of ALFRED THE GREAT as *Aetheredes hyd* and eventually became the property of Queen Adeliza, second wife of Henry I, and subsequently it came to be called queen's hithe or Queenhithe. In early times it was a flourishing port, mainly handling corn and fish.

Queensberry Rules. The regulations governing boxing matches in which gloves were worn, formulated by John Sholto Douglas, eighth Marquess of Queensberry, and John G. Chambers (1843–1883) in 1867. They were first fully used at a London tournament in 1872. The present rules governing glove contests are those issued by the British Boxing Board of Control in 1929. *See* BELT.

Queer. Colloquial for "out of sorts", "not up to the mark", also thieves' CANT for anything base and worthless, and a modern term for a homosexual.

A queer cove. An eccentric person, a rum customer; also *queer card*.

As queer as Dick's hatband. *See* DICK'S HATBAND.

In Queer Street. In financial difficulties. The punning suggestion has been made that the origin of the phrase is to be found in a query (?) with which a tradesman might mark the name of such a one on his ledger.

To come over all queer. To feel suddenly giddy, faint, etc.

To queer one's pitch. To forestall him; to render his efforts nugatory by underhand means; as a street or market vendor might find his trade spoilt by the interloper.

Querno (kwĕr' nō). Camillo Querno, of Apulia, hearing that Pope Leo X (1475, 1513–1522) was a great patron of poets, went to ROME with a harp in his hand and sang a poem called *Alexias* containing 20,000 verses. He was introduced to the POPE as a buffoon, but was promoted to the LAUREL and became a constant frequenter of the Pope's table.

> Rome in her Capitol saw Querno sit,
> Thron'd on seven hills the Antichrist of wit.
> POPE: *Dunciad*, II, i, 15.

Querpo (kĕr' pō). **In querpo.** In one's shirt-sleeves; in undress (Sp. *en cuerpo*, without a cloak).

> Boy, my cloak and rapier; it fits not a gentleman of my rank to walk the streets in querpo.
> BEAUMONT and FLETCHER: *Love's Cure*, II, i.

Question. When members of the HOUSE OF COMMONS or other debaters call out *Question*, they mean that the speaker is wandering away from the subject under consideration.

A leading question. *See under* LEADER.

An open question. A statement, proposal, doctrine, or supposed fact where differences of opinion are permissible. In the HOUSE OF COMMONS every member may vote as he likes, regardless of party considerations, on an open question.

Out of the question. Not worth discussing, not to be thought of, or considered.

The previous question. The question whether the matter under debate shall be put to the vote or not. In the HOUSE OF COMMONS to "move the previous question" is to move "that the question be not now put". If the motion is carried the question that was previously before the house is abandoned, but if not carried the question concerned must be put forthwith. The motion is now rarely used. The previous question may not be moved on an amendment or business motion, nor in committee.

To beg the question. *See* BEG.

To pop the question. To propose or make an offer of marriage. As this request is supposedly unexpected, the question is said to be "popped".

Questionists. In the examinations for degrees at Cambridge it was customary, at the beginning of the January term, to hold "Acts", and the candidates for the Bachelor's degree were called "Questionists". They were examined by a moderator, and afterwards the fathers of other colleges "questioned" them for three hours in Latin, and the dismissal uttered by the REGIUS PROFESSOR indicated what class each would be placed in, or if a respondent was plucked (*see* PLUCK), in which case the words were simply *Descendus domine*.

Quetzalcoatl. An Aztec deity whose name means "feathered serpent", a god of the air or a sun-god and a benefactor of their race who instructed them in the use of agriculture, metals, etc. According to one account, he was driven from the country by a superior god and on reaching the shores of the Mexican Gulf promised his followers that he would return. He then embarked on his magic skiff for the land of Tlapallan. Prescott (*Conquest of Mexico*, ch. III) tells us that "He was said to have been tall in stature, with a white skin, long, dark hair, and a flowing beard. The Mexicans looked confidently to the return of the benevolent deity; and this remarkable tradition, deeply cherished in their hearts, prepared...for the future success of the Spaniards."

Quey (kwā). A female calf, a young heifer (O.Scand. *kviga*).

Quey calves are dear veal. An old proverb, somewhat analogous to "killing the GOOSE which lays the golden eggs". Female calves should be kept and reared for milking.

Qui s'excuse, s'accuse (Fr.). He who excuses himself, accuses himself.

Qui vive (kē vēv) (Fr., who lives?). The French sentry's equivalent of Who goes there? which in French would be *Qui va là?*.

To be on the qui vive. On the alert; to be quick and sharp; to be expectantly on the lookout like a sentinel.

Quia Emptores (kwī' à emp tôr ēz) (Lat., because purchasers). A statute passed in the reign of Edward I (1290), taking its name from its opening words, to insure the lord his feudal incidents when tenants sold lands held of them. It allowed free sale on condition that the purchaser should hold from the superior lord thus preventing subinfeudation. It resulted in a great increase of landowners holding direct from the Crown.

Quick. Living; hence, animated, lively; also, fast, active, brisk (O.E. *cwic*, living, alive). "Look alive" means "Be brisk."

Cut to the quick. Figuratively, deeply hurt. The reference here is to the sensitive flesh below the nails or skin, hence the seat of feeling.

The quick and the dead. The living and the dead.

Quicksand is sand which shifts its place as if it were alive. *See* QUICK.

Quickset is living hawthorn set in a hedge, instead of dead wood, hurdles, and palings. *See* QUICK.

Quicksilver is *argentum vivum* (living silver), silver that moves about like a living thing (O.E. *cwic seolfor*), i.e. mercury.

> That, swift as quicksilver, it courses through
> The natural gates and alleys of the body.
> SHAKESPEARE: *Hamlet*, I, v.

Quickie. In film parlance, a cheaply produced film to catch the less discriminating and make a quick return on the money invested. In everyday speech a "quickie" usually means a quick drink as in, "Come and have a quickie (or quick one)."

Quid. Slang for a SOVEREIGN (or a pound note). It occurs in Shadwell's *Squire of Alsatia* (1688), but its origin is unknown.

In *a quid of tobacco*, meaning a piece for chewing, *quid* is another form of *cud*.

Quids. *See* QUIDDISTS.

Quids in. Extremely lucky, very profitable, to have everything turn out favourably.

Quidlibet. *See* QUODLIBET.

Quid pro quo (Lat., something for something). A return made for something, an equivalent, a TIT FOR TAT; in legal parlance, a consideration.

Quid rides? (Lat., Why are you laughing?). It is said that Lundy Foot, a Dublin tobacconist, set up his carriage, and that Curran, when asked to furnish him with a motto, suggested this. The witticism is also attributed to H. Callender, who, it is asserted, supplied it to one Brandon, a London tobacconist. The application of *quid* to a tobacconist is obvious. In the Latin both syllables of "rides" are pronounced.

Quiddists, or **Quids.** In the U.S.A., sectionalists of the Democratic-Republican party under John Randolph who sought to maintain the ascendancy of Virginia and its planter aristocracy against the more democratic elements. Active between 1805 and 1811, they opposed Madison's succession to Jefferson as party leader. The name was from *tertium quid*, "a third something or other" opposed to the Federalists and administration Republicans.

Quiddity. The essence of a thing, or that which differentiates it from other things— "the Correggiosity of Corregio", "the Freeness of the Free". Hence used of subtle, trifling distinctions, quibbles, or captious argumentation. SCHOOLMEN say *Quid est?* (what is it?) and the reply is, the *Quid* is so and so, the *What* or the nature of the thing is as follows. The latter *quid* being formed into a barbarous Latin noun becomes *Quidditas*. Hence *Quid est?* (What is it?). Answer: *Talis est quidditas* (Its essence is as follows).

> He knew...
> Where entity and quiddity
> (The ghosts of defunct bodies) fly.
> BUTLER: *Hudibras*, I, i.

Quidnunc (Lat., What now?). One who is curious to know everything that's going on, or pretends to know it; a self-important newsmonger and gossip. It is the name of the leading character in Murphy's farce *The Upholsterer*, or *What News?*

Quién sabe? (kien sa' be) (Sp.). Who knows? Sometimes used as a response in the sense of "How should I know?"

Quieta non movere (Lat.). Literally, do not disturb the peace; *i.e.* let sleeping dogs lie (*see under* DOG). It was the favourite maxim of Sir Robert Walpole (1676–1745), traditionally regarded as the first prime minister (1721–1742). Lord Melbourne (1779–1848), the early Victorian prime minister, had a similar watchword, "Why not let it alone?".

Quietism. A form of religious mysticism based on the doctrine that the essence of religion consists in the withdrawal of the SOUL from external objects, and in fixing it upon the contemplation of God; especially that taught by Miguel Molinos (1640–1696), who taught the direct relationship between the soul and God. His followers were called Molinists or *Quietists*. Outward acts of mortification were held superfluous and when a person has attained the mystic state

by mental prayer, even if he transgresses in the accepted sense, he does not sin, since his will has been extinguished. *See* MOLINISM.

Quietus (Late Lat. *quietus est*, he is quit). The writ of discharge formerly granted to those BARONS and KNIGHTS who personally attended the king on a foreign expedition, exempting them also from the claim of SCUTAGE or knight's fee. Subsequently the term was applied to the acquittance which a SHERIFF receives on settling his account at the EXCHEQUER; and, later still, to any discharge, as of an account, or even of life itself.

> You had the trick in audit-time to be sick till I had signed your quietus
> WEBSTER: *Duchess of Malfi*, III, ii (1623).
> When he himself might his quietus make
> With a bare bodkin?
> SHAKESPEARE: *Hamlet*, III, i.

Quill-drivers. Writing clerks.

Quinapalus (kwin ăp' á lus). A highsounding, pedantic name invented by Feste, the Clown in SHAKESPEARE's *Twelfth Night*, when he wished to give some saying the weight of authority. Hence someone "dragged in" when one wishes to clench an argument by some supposed quotation.

> What says Quinapalus: "Better a witty fool, than a foolish wit."
> *Twelfth Night*, I, v.

Quinine. *See* CINCHONA.

Quinquagesima Sunday (kwin kwà jes' i mà) (Lat., fiftieth). Shrove Sunday, or the first day of the week which contains ASH WEDNESDAY. It is so called because in round numbers it is the fiftieth day before EASTER.

Quins, or **Quints** (U.S.A.), **The.** The popular name for the famous Dionne quintuplets, Marie, Emilie, Yvonne, Cécile, and Annette. Daughters born (1934) to a farmer's wife in Callander, Ontario, they became wards of King George VI, who, with his Queen, received them during his visit to Canada in 1939. There were seven other children in the family.

Quinsy. This is from the Med. Lat. *quinancia* derived from Gr. *kynagkhē*, dog-throttling, because those suffering from quinsy throw open the mouth like dogs, especially mad dogs. It appeared in English (14th century) as *qwinaci*, and later forms were *quynnancy* and *squinancy*. *Squinancy-wort* is still a name given to the small woodruff (*Asperula cynanchica*), which was used as a cure for quinsy by the herbalists.

Quintain (kwin' tin). **Tilting at the quintain.** An ancient military exercise and pastime, particularly practised by mediæval KNIGHTS. A dummy figure or just a head, often representing a Turk or SARACEN, was fastened to pivot or swing horizontally from an upright stake fixed in the ground. The knight tilted at the figure and if he did not strike it in the right place with his lance it moved round at speed and struck him in the back before he could pass on. There were various forms of quintain and in the 14th century Londoners used to tilt from boats, the quintain being fixed to a mast erected in the Thames. Tilting at the quintain remained a rustic sport, associated particularly with wedding festivities, until the outbreak of the English CIVIL WARS. The word is probably from Lat. *quintana*, fifth, a street in a Roman camp between the fifth and sixth maniples where the camp market was situated, supposedly a place for martial exercise.

Quintessence. The fifth essence. The ancient Greeks said that there are four elements or forms in which matter can exist—fire, air, water, and earth (*see* ELEMENTS); the Pythagoreans (*see* PYTHAGOREAN SYSTEM) added a fifth, the fifth essence—quintessence—ether, more subtle and pure than fire, and possessed of an orbicular motion, which flew upwards at creation and formed the basis of the stars. Hence the word stands for the essential principle or the most subtle extract of a body that can be procured. HORACE speaks of "kisses that Venus has imbued with the quintessence of her own nectar".

> Swift to their several quarters haste then
> The cumbrous elements, earth, flood, aire, fire;
> And this ethereal quintessence of heaven
> Flew upward...and turned to stars
> Numberless as thou seest.
> MILTON: *Paradise Lost*, III, 714.

Quintilians (kwin'til'yans). Members of a 2nd-century heretical sect of MONTANISTS, said to have been founded by one Quintilia, a prophetess. They made the EUCHARIST of bread and cheese, and allowed women to become priests and BISHOPS. *See* HERETIC.

Quip Modest, The. "Sir, it was done to please myself," in SHAKESPEARE's *As You Like It* (V, iv). Touchstone's reasoning is as follows: If I sent a person word that his beard was not well cut and he replied he cut it to please himself, he would answer with a Quip Modest, which is six removes from the lie direct. Shakespeare is satirizing the formalities and code of honour of the Italianate style of duelling, then in vogue, in which the "lie direct" involved a settlement by fighting. The other degrees of lie provided an opportunity for disputants to wax valiant but to retreat from the risk of bloodshed. *See* COUNTERCHECK QUARRELSOME; REPLY CHURLISH; RETORT COURTEOUS.

Quipu (ke' poor or kwi' poo). An ancient Peruvian device used for keeping accounts, recording information, etc. The word means a knot, and the quipu was a length of cord, about two feet long, made of different coloured threads and tied with knots. The various threads and knots represented simple objects and numerical combinations.

> The Quipus, thus used, might be regarded as the Peruvian system of mnemonics
> PRESCOTT: *Conquest of Peru*, I, iv.

Quirinal (kwi' ri nal). One of the seven hills of ancient ROME, named after Quirinus, the SABINE name of MARS, and given to ROMULUS after deification. It is now called Monte Cavallo. Also the name of the palace originally built on its slopes as a Papal summer residence and subsequently used by the Kings of Italy and now by the President. The term was applied emblematically to the Italian kingdom and government as opposed to the VATICAN, the seat of Papal authority and ecclesiastical government.

Quis (Lat). Who? Formerly commonly used, especially among schoolboys, when offering to give away something. When only one thing was being offered, the first to call *Ego*—I [do]—after the cry *Quis?*—Who [wants]—gained the reward.

Quis custodiet ipsos custodes? (Lat., Who will watch over the watchers themselves?) The shepherds keep watch over the sheep but who is there to keep watch over the shepherds? Said when one is uncertain of the person whom one has placed in a position of trust. The phrase is from Juvenal (*Satires*, VI, 347) and is used to question the wisdom of setting guards over wives to prevent infidelities.

Quis separabit? (Lat., Who shall separate us?) The motto adopted by the Most Illustrious ORDER OF ST. PATRICK (*see under* PATRICK) when it was founded.

Quisling (kwiz' ling). A traitor or fifth columnist, from Vidkun Quisling, the Norwegian admirer of Mussolini and Hitler, who acted as advance agent for the German invasion of Norway in 1940. He duly became puppet Minister-President. He surrendered (9 May 1945) after the German defeat and was tried and shot (24 October).

Quit. (Fr. *quitter*, to leave, to depart). In general this word is more commonly used in the sense of to leave a job or place.

Cry quits. When two boys quarrel, and one has had enough, he says, "Cry Quits", meaning "Let us leave off, and call it a drawn game". So in an unequal distribution, he who has the largest share restores a portion and "cries quits", meaning that he has made the distribution equal. Here *quit* means "acquittal" or discharge.

Double or quits. *See under* DOUBLE.

To be quit of. To be free from, to be rid of.

Quit rent. A rent formerly paid to the lord of a MANOR by freeholders and copy-holders which was an *acquittal* of all other services. Nowadays a token or nominal rent. The ancient ceremony of rendering the quit-rent service due to the Crown by the Corporation of the City of London is still held before the QUEEN'S REMEMBRANCER.

Quixote, Don (kwik' zot). The hero of the famous romance of this name by Miguel de Cervantes Saavedra (1547–1616). It was published at Madrid in 1605 with the continuation or second part in 1615. It ridicules the more tedious chivalric romances. Don Quixote is a gaunt country gentleman of La Mancha, gentle and dignified, affectionate and simple-minded, but so crazed by reading books of knight-errantry that he believes himself called upon to redress the wrong of the whole world. Hence a **quixotic** man is a romantic idealist, one with impractical ideas of honour or schemes for the general good. *See also* SANCHO PANZA.

The Quixote of the North. Charles XII of Sweden (1682, 1697–1718) also called *The Madman.*

Quiz. One who banters or chaffs another. The origin of the word, which appeared about 1780, is unknown; but fable accounts for it by saying that a Mr. Daly, manager of a Dublin theatre, laid a wager that he would introduce into the language within twenty-four hours a new word of no meaning. Accordingly on every wall, or all places accessible, were chalked up the four mystic letters, and all Dublin was inquiring what they meant. The wager was won and the word became part of the language. A monocular eye-glass with, or without, a handle was called a *quizzing-glass*, and any odd or ridiculous person or thing a *quiz.*

Quiz is also applied to a test, usually competitive, of knowledge, general or otherwise. Hence the American expression, **Quiz Kid,** from such children appearing on radio or television in *quiz programmes.*

Quo vadis? *See* DOMINE, QUO VADIS?

Quo warranto (kwō war ăn' tō) (Lat.). A writ against a defendant (whether an individual or a corporation) who lays claim to something he has no right to; so named because the offender is called upon to show *quo warranto (rem) usurpavit* (by what right

or authority he lays claim to the matter of dispute).

The writ has long been displaced by "the information in the nature of a writ of quo warranto" which can be brought by a private person.

Quoad hoc (kwō' ăd hok) (Lat.). To this extent, with respect to this.

Quod. Slang for prison. Probably the same word as QUAD, which is a contraction of *quadrangle*, the enclosure in which prisoners are allowed to walk, and where whippings used to be inflicted. The word was in use in the 17th century.

Quodlibet, or **Quidlibet** (Lat., what you please). Originally a philosophical or theological question proposed for purposes of scholastic debate; hence a nice and knotty point, a subtlety.

Quondam (Lat., former). We say, He is a quondam schoolfellow (a former schoolfellow); my quondam friend, the quondam chancellor, etc.

Quorum (kwôr' um) (Lat., of whom). The lowest number of members of a committee or board, etc., the presence of whom is necessary before business may be transacted; formerly, also certain JUSTICES OF THE PEACE (*See under* PEACE), hence known as Justices of the Quorum, chosen for their special ability, one or more of whom had to be on the Bench at trials before the others could act. SHAKESPEARE's Slender calls Justice Shallow "justice of the peace, and coram" (*Merry Wives of Windsor*, I, i).

> I must not omit that Sir Roger is a justice of the quorum.
>
> ADDISON: *Spectator*, No. 2.

Quos ego (kwōs eg' ō). A threat of punishment for disobedience. The words, from VIRGIL's *Æneid* (I, 135), were uttered by NEPTUNE to the disobedient and rebellious winds, and are sometimes given as an example of aposiopesis, *i.e.* a stopping short for rhetorical effort. "Whom I—," said Neptune, the "will punish" being left to the imagination.

Quot. Quot homines, tot sententiæ (Lat.). As many minds as men; there are as many opinions as there are men to hold them. The phrase is from Terence's *Phormio* (II, iv, 14).

Quot linguas calles, tot homines vales (Lat.). As many languages as you know, so many separate individuals you are worth. Attributed to Charles V.

R

R. The eighteenth letter of the English alphabet (seventeenth of the Roman) representing the twentieth of the Phœnician and Hebrew. As a mediæval Roman numeral, R stood for 80 and R̄ for 80,000. In England it was formerly used as a branding mark for rogues.

It has been called the "snarling letter" or "dog letter", because a dog in snarling utters a sound resembling *r-r-r*, etc., or *gr-r-r-r*.

> Irritata canis quod R R quam plurima dicat.
>
> LUCILIUS.

In his *English Grammar made for the benefit of all Strangers* Ben Jonson says:

> R is the dog's letter and hurreth in the sound; the tongue striking the inner palate, with a trembling about the teeth.

And see the Nurse's remark about R in SHAKESPEARE's *Romeo and Juliet*, II, iv.

R in prescriptions. The ornamental part of this letter is the symbol of JUPITER (♃), under whose special protection all medicines were placed. The letter itself (*Recipe*, take) and its flourish may thus be paraphrased: "Under the good auspices of JOVE, the patron of medicines, take the following drugs in the proportions set down."

The R months. *See under* OYSTER.

The three R's. Reading, writing, and arithmetic. The phrase is said to have been originated by Sir William Curtis (1752–1829), an illiterate alderman and Lord MAYOR of London, who gave this as a toast, *i.e.* "Riting, Reading and Rithmetic".

> Within the limits set by the code [The REVISED CODE, 1862], and by the ideal which most people then had of education for the poor, viz. an elementary knowledge of the three R's, Mr. Lowe had more than redeemed his promises.
>
> H. HOLMAN: *English National Education*, ch. viii (1898).

R.A.P. Rupees, annas, and pies, in India; corresponding to the former £.s.d. in Britain.

R.I.P. *Requiescat in pace.* Latin for "May he (or she) rest in peace"; a symbol used on mourning cards, tombstones, etc.

Ra, or **Re**. The sun-god of ancient Egypt, and from the time of Chephren (IVth Dynasty) the supposed ancestor of all the PHARAOHS.

His chief centre was at HELIOPOLIS where he was also known as Atum. His great enemy was the serpent Apep with whom he fought continually, but always eventually defeated. According to one legend, Ra was born as a child every morning and died at night as an old man. His name and cult was assimilated with that of Amen (AMEN-RA) and many others and he was commonly represented with the head of a falcon surmounted by a solar disc surrounded with the Uræus, the sacred flame-spitting asp which destroyed his enemies.

Rabbit. To produce the rabbit out of the hat. To produce unexpectedly an answer or solution, etc., when success appears impossible or the situation seems hopeless. An allusion to the conjuror's art.

Rabelaisian. Coarsely and boisterously satirical; grotesque, extravagant and licentious in language; reminiscent in literary style of the great French satirist François Rabelais (1495–1553). When *Rabelaisian* is used it implies coarseness and complete frankness and ignores Rabelais's humanism. *See* PANTAGRUEL.

The English Rabelais. A title somewhat unsuitably given to Dean Swift (1667–1745), Thomas Amory (*c.* 1691–1788, author of John Buncle), and Laurence Sterne (1713–1768).

Raboin. *See* TAILED MEN.

Races. The principal horse-races in England are chiefly run at Newmarket, Doncaster, Epsom, Goodwood, and Ascot (*see* CLASSIC RACES). The GRAND NATIONAL is the greatest event in STEEPLE CHASING. The following is a selection of the main races, with distance and venue:

> Alexandra Stakes (Ascot), 2 m. 6 fur. 75 yd.
> Ascot Gold Cup, 2½ m.
> Ascot Stakes, 2½ m.
> The Cambridgeshire (Newmarket), 9 fur.
> The Cesarewitch (Newmarket), 2¼ m.
> Champagne Stakes (Doncaster), 6 fur.
> Champion Stakes (Newmarket), 1¼ m.
> Cheltenham Gold Cup, 3 m. 2 fur. 76 yd.
> Chester Cup, 2¼ m. 77yd.
> Chesterfield Cup (Goodwood), 1 m. 2 fur.
> Cheveley Park Stakes (Newmarket), 6 fur.

City and Suburban Handicap (Epsom), 1¼ m.
Coventry Stakes (Ascot), 5 fur.
Craven Stakes (Newmarket), 1 m.
Criterion Stakes (Newmarket), 6 fur.
The Derby (Epsom), 1½ m.
Dewhurst Stakes (Newmarket), 7 fur.
Doncaster Cup, 2 m. 2 fur.
Ebor Handicap (York), 1¾ m.
Eclipse Stakes (Sandown), 1¼ m.
Goodwood Cup, 2 m. 5 fur.
Goodwood Stakes, 2 m. 3 fur.
Grand Military Gold Cup (Sandown), 3 m. 125 yd.
Grand National (Aintree), 4 m. 856 yd.
Great Metropolitan Handicap (Epsom), 2¼ m.
Jockey Club Stakes (Newmarket), 1½ m.
Jubilee Handicap (Kempton), 1¼ m.
July Stakes (Newmarket), 5 fur. 140 yd.
Lincolnshire Handicap (Doncaster), 1 m.
Liverpool Summer Cup, 1 m. 2 fur.
Middle Park Stakes (Newmarket), 6 fur.
New Stakes (Ascot), 5 fur.
Northumberland Plate (Newcastle), 2 m.
The Oaks (Epsom), 1½ m.
The One Thousand Guineas (Newmarket), 1 m.
Ovaltine Manchester Handicap, 1½ m.
Portland Handicap (Doncaster), 5 fur. 152 yd.
Prince of Wales' Stakes (Newmarket), 1½ m.
Royal Hunt Cup (Ascot), 7 fur. 166 yd.
The St. Leger (Doncaster), 1 m. 6 fur. 132 yd.
Stewards' Cup (Goodwood), 6 fur.
The Two Thousand Guineas (Newmarket), 1 m.

Rache (răch). In mediæval England, a hound that hunts by scent (O.E. *raecc*, a hound); they were later called "running hounds" (*canes currentes*). *Cp.* ALANS.

> At first I will begin with raches and their nature, and then greyhounds and their nature, and then alaunts and their nature ... and then I shall devise and tell the sickness of hounds and their diseases.
> EDWARD, 2ND DUKE OF YORK: *The Master of Game,*
> *Prologue* (c. 1410).

Rachel (ra shel'). A famous French actress whose real name was Elizabeth Felix (1821–1858). She was the daughter of poor Jewish pedlars, but going on the stage as a girl, she won a great triumph in 1843 in the name part of Racine's *Phèdre*. As Adrienne Lecouvreur, in Scribe's play of that name (1849), she confirmed her position as one of the greatest tragic actresses in Europe. The cosmetics bearing the name "Rachel" immortalize a Parisian beauty specialist of the SECOND EMPIRE.

Rachmanism. RACK-RENTING, extortion, and general exploitation of tenants and purchasers of house-property. After Peter Rachman (1920–1962), a Polish immigrant whose undesirable activities of this kind in the Paddington area of London were brought to light in 1962–1963.

Rack. The instrument of torture so called (connected with Ger. *recken*, to strain) was a frame in which a man was fastened and his arms and legs stretched by windlass arrangements. Not infrequently the limbs were forced thereby out of their sockets. Its use in England was abolished in 1640. *See* THE

DUKE OF EXETER'S DAUGHTER *under* DUKE.

Rack and ruin. Utter decay or destitution. Here "rack" is a variant of *wrack* and *wreck*.

Rack-rent. Legally regarded as the annual rent which can be reasonably charged for a property, being that which it can command in the open market; an excessive rent, one which is "racked" or stretched. *See* RACHMANISM.

To lie at rack and manger. To live without thought of the morrow, like cattle or horses whose food is placed before them without themselves taking thought; hence, to live at reckless expense.

To rack one's brains. To strain them to find out or recollect something; to puzzle about something.

Racket. Noise or confusion. The word is probably imitative, like crack, bang, splash, etc. Also, colloquially, game, line of business, BLACKMAIL and extortion.

Racketeer. From the practice (of American origin) of creating a noise, commotion or *racket* to enable a theft or crime to be carried out without attracting attention, the organizers of such came to be known as *racketeers*. The term was next applied to blackmailers and extortioners and their activities became *rackets*.

To stand the racket. To bear the expense; to put up with the consequences.

Radar. A name formed from Radio Detection and Ranging; a means of detecting the direction and range of aircraft, ships, etc., by the reflection of radio waves. It is particularly valuable at night or in fog when the eye is of no avail. It was first developed effectively for the purposes by Sir Robert Watson-Watt in 1934–1935 (and independently in the U.S.A., France and Germany) and was of great importance during World War II, especially during the BATTLE OF BRITAIN.

Radcliffe Library. A library at Oxford, founded with a bequest of £40,000 left for the purpose by Dr. John Radcliffe (1650–1714), and originally intended for a medical library. Dr. Radcliffe was a prominent London physician, famous for his candour. When summoned to QUEEN ANNE he told her that there was nothing the matter with her but "vapours", and he refused to attend her on her deathbed.

Radegonde, or **Radegund, St.** (răd' e gond). Wife of Clotaire, King of the FRANKS (558–561). Disgusted with the crimes of the royal family, she founded the monastery of St. Croix at Poitiers. Her feast day is 13 August.

St. Radegonde's lifted stone. A stone 60 ft. in circumference, placed on five supporting stones, said by the historians of Poitou to have been so arranged in 1478, to commemorate a great FAIR held on the spot in October of that year. The country people insist that Queen Radegonde brought the impost stone on her head, and the five uprights in her apron, and arranged them all as they appear to this day.

Radevore (răd' e vôr). A kind of cloth, probably tapestry, known in the 14th century. It has been suggested (Skeat) that it was named from Vaur, in LANGUEDOC; *ras* (Eng. *rash*, a smooth—*rased*—textile fabric) *de Vor*.

> This woful lady ylern'd had in youthe
> So that she worken and embrowden kouthe,
> And weven in hire stole the radevore
> As hyt of wommen had be y-woved yore.
> CHAUCER: *Legend of Good Women*, 2351.

Radical. A political label denoting an ultra-liberal which came into use about 1816 and is applicable to ORATOR HUNT, Major Cartwright, William Cobbett and many others of that period. The early radicals drew their inspiration mainly from the French Revolution but John Wilkes may be considered representative of a somewhat earlier tradition.

> If the Whigs most inclined to popular courses adhere steadily to their determination of having no communication with the Radicals of any description, I trust the session may pass over without any schism among Opposition ...
> *Letter from Mr. Allen to Mr. Creevey* (20 November 1816).

Radical Jack. John George Lambton (1792–1840), 1st Earl of Durham. Prominent in the Whig party, he acquired the nickname for his persistent advocacy of radical reforms, and took a major part in the struggle for the Reform Act of 1832.

Radiocarbon dating. A scientific method of estimating the age of organic materials. Carbon dioxide from the atmosphere, which contains the radioactive isotope Carbon-14, is taken up by all living matter. After the organism has died the amount of Carbon-14 diminishes at a known rate, thus the age of the material can be approximately dated.

Rag. A tatter, hence a remnant (as "not a rag of decency", "not a rag of evidence"), hence a vagabond or RAGAMUFFIN.

> Lash hence these overweening rags of France.
> SHAKESPEARE: *Richard III*, V, iii.

The word was old CANT for a FARTHING, and was also used generally to express scarcity—or absence—of money:

> Money by me? Heart and goodwill you might,
> But surely, master, not a rag of money
> SHAKESPEARE: *Comedy of Errors*, IV, iv.

In university slang (now general) *a rag* is a boisterous escapade, jollification, etc.,

usually involving horseplay and practical jokes. **To rag** a person is to tease and torment him, TO BADGER him (*see under* BADGER).

The Rag. The nickname of the Army and Navy Club, PALL MALL. It is said to have originated in the remark of a dissatisfied member who described the entertainment there as "rag and famish". Another suggestion is that the "rag" is the flag.

> We ... drove back to the town together,
> De Vigne to dine at the Rag ...
> OUIDA: *Held in Bondage*, ch. xiii.

The local rag. A colloquial term for the local newspaper.

The Rag Trade. The clothing and fashion industries.

Rag water. In thieves' jargon, whisky.

Glad rags. *See under* GLAD.

To chew the rag. A slang expression for "grousing", complaining, or talking at length on one particular subject. In the U.S.A., it means simply "to chat".

Rag-tag and bob-tail. The RIFF-RAFF, the rabble, "the great UNWASHED". The common expression in the 16th and 17th centuries was *the rag and tag*.

Ragtime. Medium tempo syncopated music of American Negro origin, properly solo piano music although also played by bands. Scott Joplin's *Maple Leaf Rag* (1899) was the first of its kind. *Cp.* BLUES; BOOGIE-WOOGIE; JAZZ; SWING.

Ragamuffin. A *muffin* is a poor thing of a creature, a "regular muff"; so that a *ragamuffin* is a sorry creature in rags.

> I have led my ragamuffins where they are peppered.
> SHAKESPEARE: *Henry IV, Pt. I*, V, iii.

Ragged Robin. A wild flower (*Lychnis flos-cuculi*), from the ragged appearance of its fringed petals. The word is used by Tennyson for a pretty damsel in ragged clothes.

> The prince
> Hath picked a ragged robin from the hedge.
> TENNYSON: *Idylls of the King* (*The Marriage of Geraint*).

Ragged schools. VOLUNTARY SCHOOLS for the education of destitute children, originated by John Pounds, a Portsmouth shoemaker, about 1818. Ragged Sunday Schools, Day Schools, and Evening Schools made an important contribution to the welfare of the STREET ARABS (*see under* ARABIA) of 19th-century LONDON and elsewhere. The seventh Earl of Shaftesbury was a notable benefactor.

Raglan. An overcoat which has no shoulder seams, the sleeves extending up to the neck. First worn by Lord Raglan, the British commander in the Crimean War.

Ragman Rolls. The returns of each HUNDRED to Edward I's inquest of 1274–1275, also called Hundred Rolls; their colloquial name is from the ragged appearance due to their numerous pendant seals. The roll of Homage and Fealty made by the Scottish clergy and barons to Edward I at Berwick in 1297 is likewise so called. *See* RIGMAROLE.

Ragnarok (răg′ na rok). The *Götterdämmerung* or Twilight of the Gods in Scandinavian mythology. The day of doom, when the old world and all its inhabitants were annihilated. Out of the destruction a new world was born, a world at peace. Of the old gods BALDER returned, and ODIN'S two sons VIDAR and Vail, Vili and Ve (Odin's brother's sons), Magni and Modi, sons of THOR, and Hœnir (Odin's companion).

Rahu (ra′ hū). The demon that, according to Hindu legend, causes eclipses. One day he quaffed some of the NECTAR of immortality, but was discovered by the SUN and MOON, who informed against him, and VISHNU cut off his head. As he had already taken some of the nectar into his mouth, the head was immortal, and he ever afterwards hunted the sun and moon, which he sometimes caught, thus causing eclipses.

Railroad, Railway. Both terms were originally used in England; but *railway* has long been the normal English usage while *railroad* is the accepted American form.

> Alas! even the giddiness attendant on a journey on this Manchester rail-road is not so perilous to the nerves, as that too frequent exercise in the merry-go-round of the ideal world.
> SCOTT: *Count Robert of Paris: Introductory Address* (1832).

To railroad (U.S.A.). To hustle someone through (as of school) or out (as of an assembly) with unseemly haste and without reference to the proper formalities.

Underground Railroad. In the U.S.A. the name given (*c.* 1830) to the secret and changing system of hiding places and routes organized for helping runaway slaves to escape to the Northern States and Canada. An **Underground Road** was its forerunner.

The Railway King. George Hudson (1800–1871), chairman of the York and North Midland Railway Company, Midland Railway Company, etc., whose ventures in railway amalgamations and speculations at first proved so profitable that he dominated the market. Thrice Mayor of York and M.P. for Sunderland, the railway mania of 1847–1848 brought his ruin. Accused of "cooking the books", legal proceedings stripped him of his fortune. He remained an M.P. until 1859.

What a way to run a railway! What an inefficient, chaotic or disorderly way of doing things.

Rain. It never rains but it pours. One occurrence is frequently the harbinger of many such; strokes of good or ill fortune are often accompanied by additional benefits or misfortunes. An 18th-century proverb.

To put something by for a rainy day. To save something against bad times.

To rain cats and dogs. In northern mythology the CAT is supposed to have great influence on the weather and "The cat has a gale of wind in her tail" is a seafarer's expression for when a cat is unusually frisky. Witches that rode on storms were said to assume the form of cats. The DOG is a signal of wind, like the WOLF, both of which were attendants of ODIN, the storm god.

Thus cat may be taken as a symbol of the down-pouring rain, and dog of the strong gusts of wind accompanying a rainstorm.

Rain Check (U.S.A.). A receipt or the counterfoil of a ticket entitling one to see another baseball game if the original match for which the ticket was purchased is rained off. The phrase is now in general use of a promise to accept an invitation at a later date, *e.g.* when invited and one cannot accept, one says, "I'll take a rain-check."

Raining-tree, or **Rain-tree.** Old travellers to the Canaries told of a linden tree from which sufficient water to supply all the men and beasts of the island of Hierro was said to fall. In certain weather conditions moisture condenses and collects on the broad leaves of many trees. The genisaro or guango, *Pithecolobium saman*, or ornamental tropical tree, one of the Leguminosæ, is known as the rain-tree. In this case ejections of juice by the cicadas are responsible for the "rain" under its branches. Another is the *Andira inermis*, found in tropical Africa and America.

Rainbow. The old legend is that if one reaches the spot where a rainbow touches the earth and digs there one will be sure to find a pot of GOLD. Hence visionaries, wool-gatherers, day-dreamers, etc., are sometimes called *rainbow chasers*, because of their habit of hoping for impossible things.

Rainbow Corner. In World War II Messrs. Lyons' Corner House in Shaftesbury Avenue, London, was taken over and turned into a large café and lounge for American servicemen under this name, and it became a general meeting place for Americans in London. The name was in reference to the RAINBOW DIVISION (*see* UNITED STATES ARMY *under* REGIMENTAL AND DIVISIONAL NICKNAMES), and the rainbow in the insignia of SHAEF (Supreme Headquarters Allied Expeditionary Forces).

Raison d'état (rā' zon dā' tă) (Fr., reason of state). The doctrine that the interests of the State take precedence even at the expense of moral considerations.

Raison d'être (rā' zon de tr) (Fr.). The reason for a thing's existence, its rational ground for being; as, "If crime were abolished there would be no *raison d'être* for the police."

Rajah (ra' ja). Sanskrit for king, cognate with Lat. *rex*. The title of an Indian king or prince, given later to tribal chiefs and comparatively minor rulers; also to Malayan and Javanese chiefs. *Maharajah* means the "great rajah".

Ralph Robinson. *See* FARMER GEORGE.

Ralph Roister Doister. The name of the earliest English comedy on classical lines; so called from the chief character. It probably appeared in 1552 or 1553 and was written by Nicholas Udall, headmaster of Eton, 1534–1541, and headmaster of Westminster, 1555–1556.

Ram. Formerly, the usual prize at wrestling matches. Thus Chaucer says of his miller, "At wrastlynge he wolde bere awey the ram" (*Canterbury Tales: Prologue*, 548).

The Ram Feast. Formerly held on MAY morning at Holne, Dartmoor, when a ram was run down in the "Ploy Field" and roasted, complete with fleece, close by a granite pillar. At midday, a scramble took place for a slice, which was supposed to bring luck to those who got it. At Kingsteignton, Devon, a decorated carcase is still escorted through the town on Whit Monday and afterwards roasted in the open.

The Ram and Teazle. A PUBLIC-HOUSE SIGN, in compliment to the Clothworkers' Company. The *ram* is emblematical of wool and the *teazle* is used for raising the nap of woollen cloth.

The Ram of the Zodiac. This is the famous Chrysomallus, whose GOLDEN FLEECE was stolen by JASON. *See* ARIES.

Rama. The seventh incarnation of VISHNU (*see* AVATAR). His beautiful wife, Sita, was abducted by Ravana, the demon-king of Ceylon. With the aid of a nation of monkeys who collected trees and rocks, a bridge, Adam's bridge, was built across the straits. Rama and his invading army gradually overcame the enemy and Rama's arrow slew the demon-monster. The story is told in the RAMAYANA.

Ramachandra. *See* AVATAR.

Ramadan (răm ȧ dăn). The ninth month of the Mohammedan year, and the Moslem LENT or Holy Month. It is the month in which the KORAN was revealed. The MOSLEM year being lunar sometimes means the Ramadan falls in midsummer when the fast causes much discomfort, since it involves abstinence from drinking.

Ramayana (ra' ma ya' na) (*i.e.* the deeds of Rama). The history of RAMA, the great epic poem of ancient India, ranking with the MAHABHARATA, and almost with the ILIAD. It is ascribed to the poet Valmiki and contains 24,000 verses in seven books.

Rambouillet, Hôtel de (răm bwē yā). The house in Paris where, about 1615, the Marquise de Rambouillet, disgusted with the immoral and puerile tone of the time, founded the salon out of which grew the Académie Française. Mme de Sévigné, Malherbe, Corneille, the Duchesse de Longueville, and La Rochefoucauld were among the members. They had a refinement of language of their own, but preciosity, pedantry, and affectation eventually led to disintegration of the coterie. The women were known as *Les* PRÉCIEUSES and the men as *Esprits doux*.

Ramilie, Ramillies (răm' i li). A name given to certain articles of dress in commemoration of the Duke of Marlborough's victory over the French at Ramillies in 1706. The *Ramillies hat* was the cocked hat worn between 1714 and 1740 with the brim turned up in three equal-sized cocks. The *Ramillies wig*, that lasted on until after 1760, had a long gradually diminishing plait, called the *Ramillies plait*, with a large bow at the top and a smaller one at the bottom.

Rampage. On the rampage. Acting in a violently excited or angry manner. The word was originally Scottish, and is probably connected with *ramp*, to storm and rage.

Rampallion (răm păl' yon). A term of contempt; probably a PORTMANTEAU WORD of *ramp* and *rapscallion*; in Davenport's *A New Trick to Cheat the Devil* (1639) we have: "and bold rampallion-like, swear and drink drunk."

> Away, you scullion! you rampallion! you fustilarian! I'll tickle your catastrophe.
> SHAKESPEARE: *Henry IV, Pt. II*, II, i.

Rampant. The heraldic term for an animal especially a LION, shown rearing up with the forepaws in the air; strictly, a LION RAMPANT should stand on the SINISTER hind-leg, with both forelegs elevated, and the head in profile.

Ran. *See* ÆGIR.

Ranch. A dude ranch. One run as a resort, where city-dwellers can spend their holidays playing at being COWBOYS.

Randan. On the randan or **ran-tan.** On the spree; having a high old time in town. *Randan* is a variant of *random*.

Formerly, at Cold Aston, Derbyshire, when a man was **ran-tanned**, a straw likeness was made and carried round the village on three successive nights, accompanied by people banging tin cans and making a general din. The image was burnt after the last parade. Matrimonial upsets usually provided the occasion for such performances. *Cp.* RIDING; SHALLAL; SKIMMINGTON; STANG.

Randem-tandem. Three horses driven TANDEM fashion.

Ranee, or **Rani.** A Hindu queen; the feminine of RAJAH.

Ranelagh (răn' ė là). An old LONDON place of amusement on the site that now forms part of the grounds of Chelsea Hospital. It was named after Richard Jones, 1st Earl of Ranelagh, who built a house and laid out gardens there in 1690. From 1742 to 1803, Ranelagh rivalled VAUXHALL GARDENS for concerts, masquerades, etc. A notable feature was the Rotunda, built in 1742. It was not unlike the Albert Hall in design, and was 185 ft. across with numerous boxes in which refreshments were served, while the brightly lit floor formed a thronged promenade. There was also a Venetian pavilion in the centre of a lake.

The Ranelagh Club was established in 1894 in Barn Elms Park, S.W., to provide facilities for polo, tennis, golf, etc.

Rangers. Picked men in the U.S. Army who worked with British COMMANDOS. They were named after ROGERS' RANGERS, an intrepid body of frontiersmen organized by Major Robert Rogers (1731–1795). Rangers first appeared at the Dieppe Raid in 1942 on which a small party went as armed observers. *See* GIRL GUIDES.

Rank. A row, a line (especially of soldiers); also high station, dignity, eminence, as:

The rank is but the guinea's stamp,
The man's the gowd for a' that!
BURNS: *Is there for Honest Poverty?* 431.

Rank and fashion. People of high social standing; the "UPPER TEN" (*see under* TEN).

Rank and file. *See under* FILE.

Risen from the ranks. Said of a commissioned officer of the army who has worked his way up from a private soldier, often called a *ranker*. Hence applied to a SELF-MADE MAN in any walk of life.

Ransom. In origin the same word as *redemption*, from Lat. *redemptionem*, through O.Fr. *rançon*, earlier *redempçon*.

A king's ransom. A very large sum of money.

Ran-tan. *See* RANDAN.

Rantipole (răn' ti pōl). A HARUM-SCARUM fellow, a madcap. Probably from *ranty* or *randy*, riotous, disorderly, etc., and *poll*, a head or person. NAPOLEON III was called *Rantipole* for his escapades at Strasbourg and Boulogne.

Ranz des vaches (rans dā vash). Literally the air or tune for the cows. Simple melodies sung by the Swiss cowherds or played on the Alpenhorn when they drive their cows to pasture or bring them home.

Rap. Not worth a rap. Worth nothing at all. The rap was a base halfpenny, intrinsically worth about half a FARTHING circulated in Ireland in 1721, because small coin was so very scarce.

Many counterfeits passed about under the name of raps.
SWIFT: *Drapier's Letters*, i.

Why the coin was so called is not known.

To rap the knuckles. Figuratively, to administer a sharp rebuff. From the once common practice in schools, when children were punished for a misdemeanour in class by a sharp rap on the knuckles from the teacher's ruler.

Rape. One of the six divisions into which Sussex is divided, intermediate between HUNDRED and SHIRE; it is said that each had its own river, forest, and castle. *Herepp* is Norwegian for a parish district and *rape* in DOMESDAY BOOK is used for a district under military jurisdiction, but connexion between the two words is doubtful. *Cp.* LATHE.

Rape of the Lock. Lord Petre, in a thoughtless moment of frolic and gallantry, cut off a lock of Arabella Fermor's hair, and this liberty gave rise to the bitter feud between the two families which Alexander Pope worked up into the best heroic-comic poem of the language. The first sketch was published in 1712 in two cantos, and the complete work, including the most happily conceived machinery of SYLPHS and GNOMES, in five cantos in 1714. Pope, under the name of Esdras Barnevelt, apothecary, later pretended that the poem was a covert satire on QUEEN ANNE and the Barrier Treaty.

Say what strange motive, goddess! could compel
A well-bred lord t'assault a gentle belle?
O say what stranger cause, yet unexplored,
Could make a gentle belle reject a lord?
The Rape of the Lock, Canto I, l.7.

Raphael (răf' ā el). One of the principal ANGELS of Jewish angelology. In the book of TOBIT we are told how he travelled with Tobias into Media and back again, instructing him on the way how to marry Sara and to drive away the wicked spirit. Milton calls him the "sociable spirit" and the "affable archangel" (*Paradise Lost*, VII, 40), and it was he who was sent by God to warn ADAM of his danger.

> Raphael, the sociable spirit that deigned
> To travel with Tobias, and secured
> His marriage with the seven-times-wedded maid.
> *Paradise Lost*, V, 221.

Raphael is usually distinguished in art by a pilgrim's staff or carrying a fish, in allusion to his aiding Tobias to capture the fish which performed the miraculous cure of his father's eyesight.

Raphaelesque. In the style of the great Italian painter Raphael (1483–1520), who was specially notable for his supreme excellence in the equable development of all the essential qualities of art—composition, expression, design, and colouring.

Rapparee (răp′ á rē′). A wild Irish plunderer; so called from his being armed with a *rapaire*, or half-pike.

Rappee. A coarse kind of snuff manufactured from dried tobacco by an instrument called in French a *râpe*, or rasp; so called because it is *râpé*, rasped.

Rara avis (râr′ á ā′ vis) (Lat., a rare bird). A phenomenon; a prodigy; something quite out of the ordinary. First applied by Juvenal to the black swan, which until its discovery in Australia was unknown.

> Rara avis in terris nigroque simillima cygne (a bird rarely seen on the earth, and very like a black swan).
> JUVENAL, vi, 165.

Rare. Underdone, as of a steak; or lightly cooked, as of an egg. It is the M.E. *rere*, underdone.

Rare Ben. The inscription on the tomb of Ben Jonson (1573–1637), the dramatist, in the north nave aisle of Westminster Abbey. "O rare Ben Jonson", was, says Aubrey, "done at the charge of Jack Young (afterwards knighted), who, walking there when the grave was covering, gave the fellow eighteenpence to cut it." *Rare* here is Lat. *rarus*, uncommon, remarkable.

Raree Show. A peep-show; a show carried about in a box. In the 17th century, most of the travelling showmen were Savoyards, and perhaps this represents their attempt at pronunciation of *rare* or *rarity*.

Rascal. Originally a collective term for the rabble of an army, the commonalty, the mob, this word was early (14th century) adopted as a term of the chase, and for long almost exclusively denoted the lean, worthless deer of a herd. In the late 16th century it

was retransferred to people, and so to its present meaning, a mean rogue, a scamp, a base fellow. SHAKESPEARE says, "Horns? the noblest deer has them as huge as the rascal" (*As You Like It*, III, iii); and "Come, you thin thing; come, you rascal" (*Henry IV, Pt. II*, V, iv).

Rascal counters. Pitiful £ s. d., "filthy lucre". Brutus calls money paltry compared with friendship, etc.

> When Marcus Brutus grows so covetous
> To lock such rascal counters from his friends,
> Be ready, gods, with all your thunderbolts,
> Dash him to pieces!
> SHAKESPEARE: *Julius Cæsar*, IV, iii.

Raspberry, To give the. A 20th-century slang expression for showing contempt of someone. In action, *to give a raspberry* is to put one's tongue between the closed lips and expel air forcibly with a resulting rude noise. It is otherwise known as a BRONX CHEER. *Cp.* TO COCK A SNOOK *under* COCK; *see also* RHYMING SLANG.

Rasputin. Gregory Efimovitch (1871–1916), the Siberian monk notorious for his baneful influence over the Russian monarchy in its last years, was apparently so called by his fellow villagers. Rasputin means "the dissolute" and he lived up to his nickname until the end. His easy conquests over women were helped by his assertion that physical contact with him was itself a purification. His incredible indecencies and disgusting coarseness did not prevent his excessive familiarity with the Empress Alexandra and Tsar Nicholas II which arose from his undoubted success in healing and sustaining the Tsarevich Alexis, a tragic victim of hæmophilia. Rasputin was first called to the palace in 1905 and his power increased stead- ily until his murder by Prince Yusupov and associates in 1916—itself a story reminiscent of Hollywood rather than real life.

Rastafarians. Members of the *Ras Tafari*, a black political and religious group originating in the 1920s in Jamaica. They recognized Haile Selassie, Emperor of Ethiopia (1930–1974) as a god. They consider blacks are superior to whites, that Ethiopia is heaven, and that Haile Selassie will arrange that all of African origin will find a homeland in Ethiopia. *Ras* means duke and *Tafari* was a family name of Haile Selassie (Might of the Trinity). There are now Rastafarians in the West Indies, the U.S.A., Canada and Europe, conspicuous by their long matted curls (dreadlocks).

Rat. The Egyptians and Phrygians deified rats. In Egypt the rat symbolized utter destruction, and also wise judgement, the latter because rats always choose the best bread.

Pliny tells us (VIII, lvii) that the Romans drew presages from rats and to see a white rat foreboded good fortune. Clothing or equipment gnawed by rats presaged ill fortune.

It was an old superstition among sailors that rats deserted a ship before she set out on a voyage that was to end in her loss. Similarly rats were said to leave a falling house.

> In few, they hurried us aboard a bark,
> Bore us some leagues to sea; where they prepared
> A rotten carcass of a butt, not rigg'd,
> Nor tackle, sail, nor mast; the very rats
> Instinctively have quit it.
> SHAKESPEARE: *The Tempest*, I, ii.

As wet as, or **like a drowned rat.** Soaking wet; looking exceedingly dejected.

I smell a rat. I perceive some underhand work or treachery afoot. The allusion is to a cat *smelling* a rat, while unable to *see* it.

Irish rats rhymed to death. It was once a common belief that rats in pasturages could be destroyed by anathematizing them in rhyming verse or by metrical charms. Thus Ben Jonson (*Poetaster, Apologetical Dialogue*) says: "Rhime them to death, as they do Irish rats." Sir Philip Sidney says (*Defence of Poesie*): "I will not wish unto you … to be rimed to death, as is said to be done in Ireland"; and SHAKESPEARE makes Rosalind say (*As You Like It*, III, ii): "I was never so be-rhymed since Pythagoras' time, that I was an Irish rat."

Pharaoh's rat. *See* ICHNEUMON.

Rat, Cat, and Dog.

> The cat, the rat, and Lovel our dog,
> Rule all England under an hog.

The famous lines affixed to the door of St. Paul's and other places in the City of London in 1484 at the instigation of William Colyngburne, for which, according to the *Great Chronicle of London*, "he was drawn unto the Tower Hill and there full cruelly put to death, at first hanged and straight cut down and ripped, and his bowels cast into the fire". The rhyme implied that the kingdom was ruled by Francis, Viscount Lovel, the king's "spaniel" or dog; Sir Richard Ratcliffe, the Rat; and William Catesby, SPEAKER of the HOUSE OF COMMONS, the Cat. The Hog was the white boar or cognizance of Richard III. *See* BLUE BOAR.

Rats! Nonsense! etc.; or an exclamation of annoyance.

To rat. To forsake a losing side for the stronger party, as rats are said to forsake unseaworthy ships; to become a renegade; to "squeal" or to inform.

To take a rat by the tail (*prendre un rat par la queue*). An ancient French colloquialism for "to cut a purse". *See* CUT-PURSE.

Rat-catcher. A colloquial term for unorthodox hunting dress.

Rat-killer. APOLLO received this derogatory title from the following incident: Apollo sent a swarm of rats against Crinis, one of his priests, for neglect of his office; but the priest seeing the invaders coming, repented and obtained pardon and the god annihilated the rats with his far-darting arrows.

Rat-race. The relentless struggle to get ahead of one's rivals, particularly in professional and commercial occupations. *Rat* is used generally as a derogatory epithet.

Rattening. Destroying or taking away another workman's tools, or otherwise incapacitating him from doing his work, with the object of forcing him to join a TRADE UNION or to obey its rules. The term was once common in Yorkshire and is of unknown origin.

Rattler. A train, usually a local one, made up of old rolling stock. A term long used in Australia and the U.S.A., and in the latter, it also denotes a rattlesnake.

Raven. A bird of ill omen; fabled to forbode death, and to bring infection and bad luck.

> The raven himself is hoarse
> That croaks the fatal entrance of Duncan
> Under my battlements.
> SHAKESPEARE: *Macbeth*, I, v.
>
> The boding raven on her cottage sat,
> And with hoarse croakings warned us of our fate.
> GAY: *Pastorals; The Dirge*.

CICERO was forewarned of his death by the fluttering of ravens, and Macaulay relates the legend that a raven entered the chamber of the great orator the very day of his murder and pulled the clothes off his bed. Like many other birds, ravens indicate the approach of foul weather. When ravens forsake their normal abode we may look for famine and mortality, because ravens bear the characters of SATURN, the author of these calamities, and have a very early knowledge of the bad disposition of that planet.

According to Roman legend, ravens were once as white as swans and not inferior in size; but one day a raven told APOLLO that CORONIS, a Thessalian NYMPH whom he passionately loved, was faithless. The god shot the nymph with his dart; but hating the tell-tale bird:

> He blacked the raven o'er,
> And bid him prate in his white plumes no more.
> ADDISON: *Translation of Ovid*, Bk. II.

In Christian art, the raven is an emblem of God's Providence, in allusion to the ravens which fed ELIJAH. St. Oswald holds in his hand a raven with a ring in its mouth; St.

Benedict has a raven at his feet; ST. PAUL THE HERMIT is drawn with a raven bringing him a loaf of bread.

The fatal raven, consecrated to ODIN, the Danish war-god, was the emblem of the Danish Standard, *Landeyda* (the desolation of the country), and was said to have been woven and embroidered in one noontide by the daughters of Ragnar Lodbrok, son of SIGURD. If the Danish arms were destined to defeat, the raven hung his wings; if victory was to attend them, he stood erect and soaring, as if inviting the warriors to follow.

> The Danish raven, lured by annual prey,
> Hung o'er the land incessant.
> JAMES THOMSON: *Liberty*, Pt. IV.

The two ravens that sit on the shoulders of Odin are called Huginn and Muninn (Mind and Memory).

Ravenstone (Ger. *Rabenstein*). The old stone gibbet of Germany; so called from the ravens which were wont to perch on it.

> Do not think
> I'll honour you so much as save your throat
> From the Ravenstone, by choking you myself.
> BYRON: *Werner*, II, ii.

Raw. Johnny Raw. A raw recruit; a "new chum", a GREENHORN.

A raw deal. A transaction which is harsh or unfair to a person, perhaps from the idea that it leaves him feeling "raw" or hurt.

To touch one on the raw. To mention something that makes a person wince, like touching a horse on a raw place in currying him.

Rawhead and Bloody-bones. A BOGY at one time the terror of children.

> The indiscretion of servants, whose usual method is to awe children and keep them in subjection, by telling them of *raw-head* and *bloody-bones*.
> LOCKE: *Thoughts on Education*.

Razee. An old naval term for a ship of war cut down (or *razed*) to a smaller size, as a seventy-four reduced to a frigate.

Razor. On the razor's edge. To be in a hazardous position or a critical situation.

To cut blocks with a razor. *See under* CUT.

Razzia (ră' zi à). An incursion made by the military into enemy territory for the purpose of carrying off cattle or slaves, or for enforcing tribute. It is the French form of an Arabic word usually employed in connexion with Algerian and North African affairs.

Razzle-dazzle. A boisterous spree, a jollification.

On the razzle, or **razzle-dazzle.** On the spree, on a hilarious drunken frolic.

Re (rē) (Lat.). Respecting; in reference to; as "re Brown", in reference to the case of Brown.

Reach of a river. The part which lies between two points or bends; so called because it *reaches* from point to point.

> We are now well along Halfway Reach, the portion of the water street to London which is the midway point between the City and Gravesend.
> A. G. LINNEY: *The Lure and Lore of London's River*, ch. vii.

Read. To read between the lines. *See under* LINE.

To read oneself in. Said of an Anglican clergyman on entering upon a new incumbency, because one of his first duties is to give a public reading of the THIRTY-NINE ARTICLES in the church to which he has been appointed, and to make the Declaration of Assent.

Reader. The designation of certain senior lecturers at many of the universities; at the INNS OF COURT, one who reads lectures in law. In printing, one who reads and corrects proof sheets before publication. In a publisher's office, one who reads and reports on manuscripts submitted for publication.

Lay Reader. In the CHURCH OF ENGLAND, a layman licensed by the BISHOP to conduct church services; namely, Morning and Evening Prayer (except the absolution and the blessing) and the Litany. A Lay Reader may also publish BANNS OF MARRIAGE, preach, catechize children, etc. The modern office dates from 1866.

Ready. An elliptical expression for ready money.

> Lord Strutt was not flush in ready, either to go to law, or clear old debts.
> ARBUTHNOT: *History of John Bull*.

Real Presence. The doctrine that Christ Himself is present in the bread and wine of the EUCHARIST after consecration, as contrasted with doctrines that maintain the Body and Blood are only symbolically present.

Realism. In mediæval scholastic philosophy the opposite of NOMINALISM; the belief that abstract concepts or universals are real things existing independently of our conceptions and their expression. It was a development from PLATO'S metaphysic and was held in varying forms by ERIGENA, REMIGIUS, St. Anselm, ABELARD, Albertus Magnus, THOMAS AQUINAS, Duns Scotus, and others. *See* DUNCE; SCHOLASTICISM.

In literature and art it denotes the attempt to present life as it is, however unpleasant, ugly or distasteful. Zola and Maupassant were leaders of this school in France at the end of the 19th century. The brutality and outspokenness of their writings led to an outcry, thus Anatole France described

Zola's novel *La Terre* as "a heap of ordure". Realism often tends to emphasize the crude, the perverted, and the immoral somewhat disproportionately, at the expense of the more balanced, admirable or beautiful.

Realpolitik (rē al po′ li tēk′) (Ger.). Practical politics, political realism; politics based on national "interests" or material considerations as distinct from moral objectives.

Reaper. The grim reaper. Death; often depicted, like Time, with a scythe.

Rearmouse, or **Reremouse.** The bat (O.E. *hreremus*, probably the fluttering-mouse; from *hrerean*, to move or flutter). The bat is not, of course, a flying mouse.

Reason. Age of Reason. *See under* AGE.

It stands to reason. It is logically manifest; this is the Lat. *constat* (*constare*, to stand together).

The Goddess of Reason. The central figure in an attempt to supersede Christianity during the French Revolution. The first Feast of Reason was held on 20th BRUMAIRE, 1793, when the "goddess" Mlle Candeille of the Opera was enthroned in the cathedral of Notre-Dame which became the Temple of Reason. She was dressed in white, with a red Phrygian cap and the pike of Jupiter-Peuple in her hand. Mme Momoro, wife of a member of the CONVENTION, was later installed at St. Sulpice. Goddesses of Liberty and Reason were soon set up throughout France, one allegedly wearing a fillet bearing the words "Turn me not into Licence!" SATURNALIA of a disgusting kind accompanied these installations.

The woman's reason. I think so just because I *do* think so. (*See* SHAKESPEARE's *Two Gentlemen of Verona*, I, ii.)

> First then a woman will, or won't, depend on't;
> If she will do't, she will, and there's an end on't.
>   AARON HILL: *Epilogue to "Zara".*

Rebeccaites (re bek′ a īts). Bands of Welsh tenant-farmers dressed as women were responsible for the **Rebecca Riots** of 1839 and 1842–1843, which were suppressed with military aid. They demolished turnpike gates and were largely a reaction against tolls, rates, TITHES, rents and an unfair system of landholding. These riots occurred in Carmarthenshire, Pembroke, and Brecon, and the rioters took their name from *Gen.* xxiv, 60; when Rebecca left her father's house, Laban and his family "blessed her", and said, "Let thy seed possess the gate of those which hate them."

Rebellion, The Great. In English history, the period of the Civil Wars which ended in the execution of CHARLES I in 1649 (30 January). *See* RESTORATION; FIFTEEN; THE

FORTY-FIVE *under* FORTY.

Rebus (rē′ bús) (Lat., with things). A hieroglyphic riddle, *non verbis sed rebus*. The origin of the word has, somewhat doubtfully, been traced to the lawyers of Paris, who, during the carnival, used to satirize the follies of the day in SQUIBS called *De rebus quæ geruntur* (on the current events), and, to avoid libel actions, employed hieroglyphics either wholly or in part.

In HERALDRY the name is given to punning devices on a coat of arms suggesting the name of the family to whom it belongs; as the broken spear on the shield of Nicholas Breakspear (Pope Adrian IV).

Recessional. The music or words, or both, accompanying the procession of clergy and choir when they retire after a service. Rudyard Kipling's *Recessional* (1897) written for Queen Victoria's Diamond JUBILEE begins:

> God of our fathers, known of old—
> Lord of our far-flung battle-line—
> Beneath whose awful Hand we hold
> Dominion over palm and pine—
> Lord God of Hosts, be with us yet,
> Lest we forget, lest we forget!

Rechabites (rek′ a bīts). Members of a teetotal benefit society (the Independent Order of Rechabites), founded in 1835, and so named from Rechab, who enjoined his family to abstain from wine and to dwell in tents (*Jer.* xxxv, 6, 7).

Recipe, Receipt. *Recipe* is Latin for "take", and contracted into ℞ is used in doctors' prescriptions. *See* ℞.

Reckon. I reckon, in the sense of "I guess" (suppose), was in use in England by the early 17th century and later became widely used in the U.S.A.

Day of reckoning. Settlement day; when one has to pay up one's account or fulfil one's obligation; also used of the Day of JUDGMENT.

Dead reckoning. *See under* DEAD.

Out of one's reckoning. Having made a mistake in the date, in one's expectation, etc., or an error of judgment.

To reckon without your host. *See under* HOST.

Recollects. The name given (1) to a reformed branch of the FRANCISCAN Observants first formed in France; and (2) a reformed group of AUGUSTINIAN Hermits founded in Spain. Both orders were first formed in the late 16th century.

Record. That which is recorded, originally "got by heart" (Lat. *cor, cordis*, heart); hence the best performance or most striking event of its kind known, especially in such phrases as **to beat,** or **break the record, to**

do it in record time, etc.; also the disc on which music or words are recorded for re-transmission by gramophone or record-player.

Court of Record. A court where proceedings are officially recorded and can be produced as evidence. The Supreme Court is a superior court of record.

For the record. To make a statement of one's views, etc., for public consumption or publication.

Off the record. Originally a legal term whereby a judge directs that improper or irrelevant evidence shall be struck off the record. This later became commonly synonymous with "in confidence", an un-official expression of views.

Recreant is one who yields (from O.Fr. *re-croire*, to yield in trial by combat); alluding to the judicial combats, when the person who wished to give in cried for mercy, and was held a coward and infamous.

Rector. *See* CLERICAL TITLES.

Recusants (rek' ū zánts). The name given from the reign of Elizabeth I to those who refused to attend the services of the CHURCH OF ENGLAND (Lat. *recusare*, to refuse). The term commonly denoted "popish recusants" although properly it included PROTESTANT dissenters. Fines were first exacted under statute in 1552 and 1559 at the rate of 1s. per Sunday but raised to the exorbitant sum of £20 per month in 1587. Fortunately they were intermittently imposed, and the last fines for recusancy were those in 1782 on two Yorkshire labourers and their wives.

Red. One of the primary colours (*see under* COLOURS); in HERALDRY said to signify magnanimity and fortitude; in liturgical use worn at certain seasons; and in popular folk-lore the colour of magic.

> Red is the colour of magic in every country, and has been so from the very earliest times. The caps of fairies and musicians are well-nigh always red.
> YEATS: *Fairy and Folk Tales of the Irish Peasantry (The Trooping Fairies—The Merrow).*

Nowadays it is more often symbolical of anarchy and revolution—"Red ruin, and the breaking up of laws" (Tennyson: *Guinevere*, 421). In the French Revolution the *Red Republicans* were those extremists who never hesitated to dye their hands in blood. In Russia red is supposed to be the beautiful colour, but in general red is regarded as the colour of radicalism, socialism (*see* RED FLAG *under* FLAG), and revolution.

Red is the colour of the royal livery; and it is said that this colour was adopted by huntsmen because fox-hunting was declared a royal sport by Henry II. (*See* IN PINK *under* PINK.)

In the old ballads *red* was frequently applied to gold ("the gude red gowd"), and in thieves' CANT a gold watch is a *red kettle*, and the chain a *red tackle*. One of the names given by the alchemists to the PHILOSOPHER'S STONE was the *red tincture*, because with its help they hoped to transmute the base metals into gold.

In the red. Overdrawn at the bank; in debt; or said of a business running at a loss. From the banking practice of showing overdrawn accounts in red.

To paint the town red. *See under* PAINT.

To see red. To give way to excessive passion or anger; to be violently moved, TO RUN AMOK (*see under* RUN).

To see the red light. To be aware of approaching disaster; to realize it is time to desist; to take warning. From the railway signal, where the red light signifies danger.

Admiral of the Red. *See under* ADMIRAL.

Red Barn, The murder in the. A sensational murder at Polstead, near Ipswich, that achieved lasting notoriety in melodrama and story. *The Red Barn* or *The Gypsy's Curse* was first performed at Weymouth in 1828 and gained immediate and widespread popularity. The theme, essentially that of the innocent village maiden, seduced, and later murdered, by a local man of property, next appeared in book form as *The Awful Adventure of Maria Monk*, and in other titles. They are all founded on the murder of Maria Marten, a mole-catcher's daughter of loose morals who first bore a child to Thomas Corder, the son of a prosperous farmer. Later William Corder, younger brother of Thomas, became enamoured of her with the inevitable consequences, but avoided marriage. In May 1827 it seems that arrangements were made for Maria to meet him at the Red Barn on his farm with the intention of going to Ipswich to be married. Maria was not seen alive again, but Corder decamped to London and married one Mary Moore, who kept a school. Eventually Maria's body was discovered in the Red Barn and William Corder was hanged for her murder at Bury St. Edmunds in August 1828.

Red Biddy. *See under* BIDDY.

Red Book. A directory relating to the court, the nobility, and the "UPPER TEN" (*see under* TEN) generally. *The Royal Kalendar*, published from 1767 to 1893, was known by this name, as also Webster's *Royal Red Book*, a similar work first issued in 1847.

The name is also given to certain special works covered in red, such as the official parliamentary records of the old Austro-

Hungarian Empire, similar to our BLUE BOOKS, etc.

The Red Book of the Exchequer. *Liber ruber Scaccarii* in the Public Record Office. A collection of EXCHEQUER documents compiled by Alexander of Swerford in the earlier part of the 13th century with subsequent additions. It contains material from the 12th to the 16th centuries and includes such important documents as the Laws of Henry I, the *Dialogue of the Exchequer*, and the *Carte Baronum* (the returns of TENANTS-IN-CHIEF in 1166 certifying how many knights' fees they held and the services due to the king, etc.).

The Red Book of Hergest (*Llyfr Coch Hergest*). A Welsh manuscript of the late 14th or early 15th century containing the MABINOGION, poems by TALIESIN and Llywarch Hen, a history of the world from ADAM to 1318, etc. It is now in the library of Jesus College, Oxford.

Red Button. In the former Chinese Empire, a MANDARIN of the first class wore a button or knob of red coral or ruby as a badge of honour in his cap. *Cp.* THE NINE RANKS OF MANDARIN *under* MANDARIN; PANJANDRUM.

Red cent. Not a red cent. No money at all; "stony broke". An Americanism; the cent used to be copper, but is now an alloy of copper, tin and zinc. Hence, *not worth a red cent*, worth nothing at all.

Red Comyn. Sir John Comyn the younger of Badenoch, nephew of John Balliol, king of SCOTLAND, so called from his ruddy complexion and red hair, and son of Black Comyn, John Comyn the elder, who was swarthy and black-haired. He was stabbed by Robert Bruce in 1306 in the church of the Minorites at Dumfries, and afterwards dispatched by Lindsay and Kirkpatrick.

The Red Crescent, Lion and Sun. The equivalent in non-Christian countries of the RED CROSS, *i.e.* the military hospital service.

Red Cross. *See under* CROSS.

The Red Cross Knight in Spenser's *Faerie Queene* (Bk. I) is a personification of St. GEORGE, the patron saint of ENGLAND. He typifies Christian holiness and his adventures are an allegory of the CHURCH OF ENGLAND. The knight is sent by the Queen to destroy a DRAGON which was ravaging the kingdom of Una's father. After many adventures and trials Una and the knight are united in marriage.

Red Dragon. Anciently the badge of the Parthians, it was introduced in Britain by the Romans. In the 7th century it became the standard of King Cadwaladr and later was one of the supporters of the Tudor arms. The present Welsh flag consists of a red dragon *passant* on a ground of two horizontal strips (white over green). *See* DRAGON; RED DRAGONS *under* REGIMENTAL AND DIVISIONAL NICKNAMES; ROUGE DRAGON; UNICORN.

Red Duster. The Red Ensign, the flag of British merchant ships since 1674, but also the senior ensign of the Royal Navy until 1864 where it was used as squadronal colour. Its use was solely reserved for the Merchant Navy in 1864. It is a red flag with a union device in the upper canton, but before 1707 it bore a St. GEORGE'S CROSS.

Red Eye (U.S.A.). Cheap whiskey.

Red Feathers. *See* REGIMENTAL AND DIVISIONAL NICKNAMES.

Red Flag. *See under* FLAG.

Red Friday. Friday 31 July 1925, when a stoppage in the coal industry, planned to meet the threat of wage cuts, was averted by promise of government subsidies to support wages, etc. It was so called by the Labour press to distinguish it from BLACK FRIDAY of 15 April 1921, when union leaders called off an impending strike of railwaymen and transport workers designed to help the miners who were locked out.

Red Hand of Ulster. *See under* ULSTER.

The Red Hat. The flat broad-brimmed hat formerly bestowed upon cardinals, hence the office of CARDINAL.

Red Herring. *See* DRAWING A RED HERRING *under* HERRING.

Red Indians. The North American Indians; so called because of their copper-coloured skin; also called *Redskins* and *Red men*.

Red Lamp, or **Red Light district.** The brothel-quarter of a large town; from the red light frequently displayed outside a bawdy-house.

The Red Laws. The civil code of ancient ROME. Juvenal says, *Per lege rubras majoram leges* (*Satires*, xiv, 193). The civil laws, being written in vermilion, were called *rubrica*, and *rubrica vetavit* means: It is forbidden by the civil laws.

The prætor's laws were inscribed in white letters and imperial rescripts were written in purple.

The Red Letter. *See* THE ZINOVIEV LETTER *under* FORGERY.

Red-letter day. A lucky day; a day to be recalled with delight. In ALMANACS, and more commonly in ecclesiastical calendars, important FEAST days and saints' days were printed in red, other days in black.

Red Man. A term in ALCHEMY, used in conjunction with "white woman" to express the affinity and interaction of chemicals. In the long list of terms that Surly scoffingly gives (Ben Jonson's *The Alchemist*, II, iii) "your red man and your white woman" are mentioned.

The French say that a red man commands the elements, and wrecks off the coasts of Brittany those whom he dooms to death. The legend affirms that he appeared to NAPOLEON and foretold his downfall. *See also* RED INDIANS, *above*.

Red rag. Old slang for the tongue.

> Discovering in his mouth a tongue,
> He must not his palaver balk;
> So keeps it running all day long,
> And fancies his red rag can talk.
> > PETER PINDAR: *Lord B. and his Motions*.

Also in the phrase **Like a red rag to a bull,** anything that is calculated to excite rage. Toreadors' capes are lined with red.

Red Sea. So called by the Romans (*Mare rubrum*) and by the Greeks, as a translation of the Semitic name, the reason for which is uncertain. One explanation is that it was the "sea of reeds", another that it is from the corals on its bed; or again, from the reflection of the eastern sky in its waters, etc.

Red Shirt. *See* GARIBALDI.

Red snow. Snow reddened by the presence of a minute alga, *Protococcus nivalis*, not uncommon in arctic and alpine regions where its sanguine colour formerly caused it to be regarded as a portent of evil.

Red tape. Official formality, or rigid adherence to rules and regulations, carried to excess; so called because lawyers and government officials tie their papers together with red tape. Charles Dickens is said to have introduced the expression; but the scorn poured on this EVIL of officialdom by Carlyle brought the term into popular use. Hence **to have a red tape mind** is to be rigidly bound by the rules even if they do not sensibly apply; to be hidebound; to lack imaginative insight.

Redbreasts. The old BOW STREET RUNNERS. Dickens says:

> The Bow Street Runners ceased out of the land soon after the introduction of the new police. I remember them very well as standing about the door of the office in Bow Street. They had no other uniform than a blue dress-coat, brass buttons ... and a bright red cloth waistcoat ... The slang name for them was "Redbreasts" in consequence.
> > *Letters*.

Redbrick. A term much favoured by journalists and often used in scholastic circles; it is loosely applied to all English universities other than those of Oxford and Cambridge. The name was introduced by Bruce Truscot

(Professor E. Allison Peers: d. 1952) in his book *Redbrick University*, 1943). He was primarily dealing with the universities of Birmingham, Bristol, Leeds, Liverpool, Manchester, Reading, and Sheffield, and expressly excluded London. In his *Introduction* he says: "So unique has the University of London become and so essentially its own are the problems which it has to solve, that in this book very little specific mention will be made of it." Of the term itself: "Though red brick, rather than dingy stone, has been chosen as the symbol of the new foundations, it must be categorically stated that no one university alone has been in the author's mind." *Cp.* CAMFORD; OXBRIDGE.

> There is nothing that makes me more angry than to hear the University of London associated with that hideous, snobbish term "Red Brick". The term itself ought not to be used but looking at this Senate House, or indeed at the classical portico of University College, I think it must be some flight of imagination that describes these, even architecturally, as "Red Brick".
> > SIR IFOR EVANS: *Address to Convocation* (*University of London*), 9 January 1960.

Redcap. A colloquial term for British military police, who wear red covers to their caps; in the U.S.A., a porter at a railway- or bus-station.

Redcoats. British soldiers, from the colour of their uniforms in line regiments before the introduction of KHAKI. Cromwell's New Model Army was the first to wear red coats as a uniform. Regiments were distinguished by the colour of their facings—Blue, Green, Buff, etc. *See* REGIMENTAL AND DIVISIONAL NICKNAMES.

Red-haired persons. For centuries the red-haired have been popularly held to be unreliable, deceitful, and quick-tempered (*see* HAIR). The fat of a dead red-haired person used to be in demand as an ingredient for poisons (*see* Middleton's *The Witch*, V, ii) and Chapman says that flattery, like the plague—

> Strikes into the brain of man,
> And rageth in his entrails when he can,
> Worse than the poison of a red-hair'd man.
> > *Bussy d'Ambois*, III, i.

Red-handed. To be caught red-handed is to be caught in the act, IN FLAGRANTE DELICTO, as if with blood on the hands.

Red-laced. A red-laced jacket. Old military slang for a flogging.

Red-lattice phrases. Pot-house talk. A red lattice at the doors and windows was formerly the sign that an ale-house was duly licensed; see the page's quip on Bardolph in *Henry IV, Pt. II*, ii—"'a called me e'en now, my lord, through a red lattice, and I could discern no part of his face from the window."

> I, I, I myself sometimes leaving the fear of heaven on the left hand ... am fain to shuffle, to hedge and to lurch; and yet you, rogue, will ensconce your rags ... your red-lattice phrases ... under the shelter of your honour.
>
> SHAKESPEARE: *The Merry Wives of Windsor*, II, ii.

Redneck. In the U.S.A., a disparaging term for one of the "uneducated" masses. *Cp.* ROOINEK.

Redskins. *See* RED INDIANS.

Redder. One who tries to separate parties fighting, the adviser, the person who *redes* or settles a quarrel (M.E. *reden*, put in order).

> "But father," said Jenny, "if they come to lounder ilk ither [thump each other] as they did last time, sildna I cry on you?" "At no hand, Jenny; the redder gets aye the warst lick in the fray."
>
> SCOTT: *Old Mortality*, ch. iv.

Rede (O.E. *raed*). Archaic word meaning counsel, advice; also a verb.

To reck one's own rede. To be governed by one's own better judgment.

> Do not, as some ungracious pastors do,
> Show me the steep and thorny way to heaven,
> Whilst, like a puffed and reckless libertine,
> Himself the primrose path of dalliance treads,
> And recks not his own rede.
>
> SHAKESPEARE: *Hamlet*, I, iii.

Ethelred II, King of England (968, 978–1016) was nicknamed the "Redeless" or "Unready", *i.e.* destitute of counsel.

Redemptioner. An immigrant who was obliged to pay back his passage money out of his earnings after landing in the new country, or who paid the master of the ship by his services.

Redemptionists. Members of a religious order whose object was to redeem Christian captives and slaves from the Mohammedans. They are also known as TRINITARIANS.

Redemptorists. Members of the Congregation of the Most Holy Redeemer, a religious order founded at Scala, Italy, in 1732 by St. Alphonsus Maria di Liguori. They are largely concerned with mission work among the poor and foreign missions.

Reductio ad absurdum (Lat.). Proof of the falsity of a principle by demonstrating that its logical consequence involves an absurdity. It is used loosely of taking an argument or principle to impractical lengths. "The more sleep one has the longer one lives. To sleep all the time ensures the longest possible life."

Reduplicated, or **Ricochet Words.** There are probably some hundreds of these words in English, which usually have an intensifying force, such as: chit-chat, click-clack, clitter-clatter, dilly-dally, ding-dong, drip-drop, fal-lal, fiddle-faddle, flim-flam, flip-flap, flip-flop, hanky-panky, harum-scarum, helter-skelter, higgledy-piggledy, hob-nob, hodge-podge, hoity-toity, hubble-bubble, hugger-mugger, hurly-burly, mingle-mangle, mish-mash, namby-pamby, niminy-piminy, nosy-posy, pell-mell, ping-pong, pit-pat, pitter-patter, pribbles and prabbles, random-tandem, randy-dandy, razzle-dazzle, riff-raff, roly-poly, shilly-shally, slip-slop, slish-slosh, tick-tack, tip-top, tittle-tattle, wibble-wobble, wig-wag, wiggle-waggle, wish-wash, wishy-washy.

Ree. An interjection formerly used by teamsters when they wanted the horses to go to the right. "Heck" or "Hey!" was used for the contrary direction. In the U.S.A., the interjections are "Gee! Gee!" and "Haw! Haw!" for right and left respectively.

> Who with a hey and ree the beasts command.
>
> MIDDLETON: *Micro Cynicon*, VIII, 121.

Reed. A broken, or **bruised reed.** Something not to be trusted for support; a weak adherent. Egypt is called a broken reed, in which Hezekiah could not trust if the Assyrians made war on Jerusalem: "which broken reed if a man leans on, it will go into his hand and pierce it." *See* II *Kings* xviii, 21; *Is.* xxxvi, 6.

A reed shaken by the wind. A person blown about by every wind of doctrine. John the Baptist (said Christ) was not a "reed shaken by the wind", but from the very first had a firm belief in the Messiahship of the Son of MARY, and this conviction was not shaken by fear or favour. *See Matt.* xi, 7.

Reef. He must take in a reef or so. He must retrench; he must reduce his expenses. The reef of a sail is that part which is rolled and tied up by the reef points to reduce the area caught by the wind.

Reefer. An old name for a midshipman because they attended to reefing in the tops; and a closely fitting double-breasted jacket or short coat as worn by seamen. The name also denotes an oyster that grows on reefs; in Australia, one searching for GOLD; and it is slang for a marijuana cigarette, possibly from Mexican *grifa* or *grif*, a person intoxicated from this or similar drugs.

Reekie, Auld. *See* AULD REEKIE.

Reel. Right off the reel. Without intermission, continuously. From the use of a reel (O.E. *hreol*) for winding rope, etc.

> We've been travelling best part of twenty-four hours right off the reel.
>
> BOLDREWOOD: *Robbery under Arms*, ch. xxxi.

The Scottish dance called a *reel* is from Gaelic *righil* or *ruidhil*, which may be from

O.E. *hreol*.

Reeve (O.E. *gerefa*). The local officer and representative of his lord. The manorial reeve was generally a VILLEIN elected by his fellows. He was responsible for organizing the daily work of the MANOR and it was his duty to see that people were at their tasks. The *shire-reeve* or SHERIFF was an official of the SHIRE and the PORT-REEVE, of a town. There was a port-reeve in Tavistock as late as 1886.

> His lordes sheep, his cattle, his dayerie,
> His swyn, his hors, his store, and his poultrie,
> Was wholly in this reeves governynge.
>
> CHAUCER: *Canterbury Tales* (*Prologue*).

Reformation, The. Specifically, the religious revolution of the 16th century which destroyed the religious unity of Western Europe and resulted in the establishment of "Reformed" or PROTESTANT churches. It aimed at reforming the abuses in the Roman Church and ended in schism, its chief leaders being Luther, Zwingli, and Calvin (*see* CALVINISM, ROMAN CATHOLIC CHURCH).

The Counter-Reformation. A name given by historians to the movement for reform within the Roman Church (much stimulated by the REFORMATION) and the measures taken to combat the spread of Protestantism and to regain lost ground. It is usually reckoned to extend from the mid-16th century, when the Council of Trent (1545–1563) strengthened and reawakened the life and discipline of the Church, until the time of the THIRTY YEARS WAR (1618–48). The JESUITS played a major role, whilst the INQUISITION and the INDEX strengthened Papal influence.

Refresher. An extra fee paid to a BARRISTER during long cases in addition to his retaining fee, originally to remind him of the case entrusted to his charge.

Refreshment Sunday. *See* MID-LENT SUNDAY.

Regan. The second of King LEAR's unfilial daughters. In SHAKESPEARE's *King Lear* (IV, ii) called "most barbarous, most degenerate". She was married to the Duke of Cornwall, and in Geoffrey of Monmouth, from whose *Historia Britonum* the story originally comes, she is called *Regau*. *See* CORDELIA; GONERIL.

Regard, or **Reguard.** A forest visitation held triennially to review (regard) the forest boundaries, matters affecting the king's rights, and to inquire of dogs kept in the forest, which had to be lawed (*i.e.* to have the three talons cut from each front foot). Reguard was carried out by 12 selected KNIGHTS. *See* FOREST COURTS.

Regatta. A boat-race, or organized series of boat races; the name originally given to the races held between Venetian gondoliers, the Italian *regata* meaning "strife" or "contention".

Regency. In British history, architecture, and decoration the term is usually applied to the period 1811–1820 when George, PRINCE OF WALES (afterwards George IV), acted as regent during his father's (George III) illness. In French history it refers to the years from 1715 to 1723 when the Duke of Orleans was regent for the minor Louis XV.

Regent's Park (London). This park, formerly called Marylebone Park Fields, covering 410 acres of crown property, was laid out by John Nash from 1812 for the PRINCE REGENT, who had the ultimate intention of building a palace there. Regent Street was the connecting link with Carlton House.

Regicides. The name given to those 67 men who sat in judgment on CHARLES I in 1649 and especially the 58 who signed his death warrant. After the RESTORATION 10 were executed and 25 others imprisoned, the majority for life. The remainder escaped or were dead. The bodies of Cromwell, Ireton, and Bradshaw were disinterred, and after a solemn trial for treason were dismembered and exhibited at TYBURN and elsewhere.

Regimental and Divisional Nicknames. British Army

Assaye Regiment. The 74th Foot, later 2nd Battalion Highland Light Infantry, now part of the Royal Highland Fusiliers (Princess Margaret's Own Glasgow and Ayrshire Regiment). The regiment distinguished itself at the Battle of Assaye (1803) when 2,000 British and 2,500 Sepoy troops under Wellesley defeated 50,000 Mahrattas.

Barrell's Blues. The 4th Foot or King's Own Royal Regiment; so called from their blue facings and blue breeches and William Barrell, colonel of the regiment (1734–1739).

Belfast Regiment. The old 35th Foot, later 1st Battalion Royal Sussex Regiment, now 3rd Battalion The Queen's Regiment, was raised in Belfast in 1701.

Bengal Tigers. The 17th Foot, later The Royal Leicestershire Regiment, now 4th Battalion Royal Anglian Regiment, was granted a badge of a royal tiger to honour their services in India (1804–1823).

Bingham's Dandies. The 17th Lancers, now 17th/21st Lancers. When the regiment was commanded by Lord Bingham (later the Earl of Lucan) from 1826 to 1837, it was noted for its smart appearance.

Bird Catchers. This name is used for three regiments, each of which captured a French

EAGLE Standard: (1) 1st Dragoons, later Royal Dragoons (1st Dragoons), captured an Eagle at Waterloo. The regiment merged with the Royal Horse Guards (The Blues) in 1969 to form "The Blues and Royals"; (2) 2nd Dragoons, the GREYS (*see below*), captured an Eagle at Waterloo; (3) 87th Foot, later Royal Irish Fusiliers, captured an Eagle at Barossa (1811). Disbanded 1968.

Black Horse. The 7th Dragoon Guards, now the 4th/7th Royal Dragoon Guards, from their black facings.

Black Watch. In 1725, six companies of clansmen loyal to the King were raised, and were stationed in small detachments to keep watch on the HIGHLANDS and the clans. Their tartan was dark, and their name was coined from a combination of this and their function, and was used to distinguish them from the English troops performing the same duty. These companies later became the 42nd Foot, now The Black Watch (Royal Highland Regiment). *Black Watch* has been a part of the official regimental title for over one hundred years.

Blayney's Bloodhounds. The 87th Foot, the Royal Irish Fusiliers (Princess Victoria's). The regiment received this name for their success in capturing Irish rebels in 1798 when commanded by Lord Blayney. Disbanded 1968.

Blind Half-Hundred. Many of the men of the 50th Foot suffered from ophthalmia (a common cause of blindness) during the Egyptian campaign of 1801. The regiment later became 1st Battalion Queen's Own Royal West Kent Regiment, and is now part of the 2nd Battalion The Queen's Regiment.

Bloody Eleventh. The 11th Foot, later Devonshire Regiment, now part of the Devonshire and Dorset Regiment. After their stubborn fight in the Battle of Salamanca (1812), the regiment had 71 out of over 400 men left fit for duty, and many of these survivors were wounded.

Blues, The. *See* OXFORD BLUES, *below*.

Bob's Own. The Irish Guards. Field-Marshal Earl Roberts (known to the Army as "Bobs") was the first Colonel of the regiment.

Brickdusts. The name is derived from the brick-red facings of the 53rd Foot King's Shropshire Light Infantry. The regiment became the 3rd Battalion The Light Infantry in 1958, and is also known as the "Five and Threepennies", a play on their old number and the old rate of an Ensign's pay.

Buckmaster's Light Infantry. The 3rd West India Regiment (disbanded 1870) was so called after Buckmaster, a tailor who sold unauthorized Light Infantry uniforms to the officers of the regiment.

Buffs, The. The 3rd Foot was descended from a regiment raised for Dutch service in 1572 and the London TRAIN-BANDS, all of which had buff uniforms or facings. The name became part of the official regimental title some 300 years ago, but in recent times the regiment has been titled The Buffs (Royal East Kent Regiment) and is now part of the 2nd Battalion The Queen's Regiment.

Cheesemongers. The 1st Life Guards; from 1788 when the regiment was re-modelled, some commissions were refused because certain officers were the sons of merchants and were not "gentlemen". The 1st and 2nd Life Guards were amalgamated in 1922 to form the present regiment.

Cherry-Pickers. This name was given to the 11th Hussars when a detachment was surprised by French cavalry while picking cherries in a Spanish orchard in 1811 and had to fight a dismounted action. This regiment amalgamated with the 10th Royal Hussars to form the Royal Hussars (Prince of Wales's Own) in 1969.

Cherubims. The 11th Hussars, also called **Cherry-breeches** and **Cherrybums** from the very tight pink trousers enforced upon their officers in 1840 by their regimental commander, the 7th Earl of Cardigan. *See* CHERRY-PICKERS *above*.

Crossbelts. 8th Hussars, now part of the Queen's Royal Irish Hussars. During the Battle of Almenara (1710), the regiment almost destroyed a Spanish cavalry regiment. The 8th Hussars removed the Spaniards' crossbelts and wore them over the right shoulder.

Death or Glory Boys. The 17th Lancers, now 17th/21st Lancers. The regimental badge, chosen by the first Colonel in memory of General Wolfe, is a Death's Head with the motto "Or Glory".

Delhi Spearmen. The 9th (Queen's) Royal Lancers, amalgamated in 1960 with the 12th Lancers to form the 9th/12th Royal Lancers. The name was acquired at the time of the Indian Mutiny when the regiment was surprised in bivouac by the mutineers who were dispersed so effectively that they fled shouting "Delhi Bhala Wallah" (Delhi Spear Man).

Desert Rats. The name associated with the 7th Armoured Division, whose divisional sign was the desert rat (jerboa), which was adopted during its "scurrying and biting" tactics in Libya. The final design of the badge was a red rat outlined on a black background. The division served throughout the North Africa campaign, and in North-West

Europe from Normandy to Berlin.

Devil's Own. Has been given to two regiments. Tradition has it that it was given to the INNS OF COURT and Bloomsbury Volunteers, later renamed the Inns of Court Rifles (now a Territorial unit) by George III when he found that the regiment consisted mainly of lawyers. It was also applied to the 88th Foot, later 1st Battalion Connaught Rangers (disbanded in 1922), by General Picton in honour of their bravery in the Peninsular War.

Die-Hards. At the Battle of Albuera (1811), the 57th Foot, later 1st Battalion Middlesex Regiment, now 4th Battalion The Queen's Regiment, had three-quarters of the officers and men either killed or wounded. Colonel Inglis was badly wounded, but refused to be moved, instead he lay where he had fallen crying, "Die hard, my men, die hard."

Dirty Half-Hundred. The 50th Foot, later 1st Battalion Royal West Kent Regiment, now part of the 2nd Battalion The Queen's Regiment. At Vimiera in 1808, the men wiped their sweating faces on their cuffs, transferring the black dye from their facings.

Dirty Shirts. The 101st Foot, later 1st Battalion Royal Munster Fusiliers (disbanded 1922), fought in their shirt-sleeves at Delhi during the Indian Mutiny (1857).

Duke of Wellington's Bodyguard. The 5th Foot, Royal Northumberland Fusiliers. The name dates from the Peninsular War, when the regiment was attached to Army Headquarters for a long period. The regiment became the 1st Battalion Royal Regiment of Fusiliers in 1968.

Earl of Mar's Grey-Breeks. The 21st Foot, later Royal Scots Fusiliers, now part of the Royal Highland Fusiliers (Princess Margaret's Own Glasgow and Ayrshire Regiment), from the colour of their breeches when the regiment was raised by the Earl of Mar in 1678.

Elegant Extracts. The 105th Foot, the King's Shropshire Light Infantry, was re-modelled in 1813 when the officers were removed after a number of courts–martial. New officers were selected from other regiments to take their places. This regiment became the 3rd Battalion The Light Infantry in 1958.

Eliott's Tailors. The 15th (King's) Hussars, now part of the 15th/19th King's Royal Hussars. In 1759, Lt.-Col. Eliott (later Lord Heathfield) enlisted a large number of London tailors into a new cavalry regiment modelled on the Prussian Hussars. In 1768,

the regiment was granted the title of the "King's Light Dragoons"; the later title was adopted in 1806.

Emperor's Chambermaids. The 14th King's Hussars, now the 14th/20th King's Hussars, who captured Joseph Bonaparte's carriage and retained a silver chamber-pot as a trophy after the Battle of Vittoria (1813).

Eversworded 29th. The 29th Foot, the Worcestershire Regiment. When the regiment was serving in North America in 1746, the officers were attacked in their Mess by Indians who had been thought to be loyal. The Indians were beaten off, but to guard against any similar attack in the future, the unique custom of officers wearing swords at dinner in the Mess was instituted. The custom is now observed by the Captain of the Week and the Orderly Officer at dinner and on certain other occasions. This regiment amalgamated with the Sherwood Foresters to form the Worcestershire and Sherwood Foresters' Regiment in 1970.

Fighting Fifth. The 5th Foot, the Royal Northumberland Fusiliers. The name came from a saying attributed to the Duke of Wellington, "The Ever-Fighting, Never-Failing Fifth". The Regiment became the 1st Battalion Royal Regiment of Fusiliers in 1968. Also called the "Old Bold Fifth".

Flamers, The. The 54th Foot, later 2nd Battalion Dorset Regiment, now part of the Devonshire and Dorset Regiment. In September 1781, the 54th Foot was part of a force which captured the privateer base of New London, Connecticut, after a fierce fight. The force burnt the town and a number of ships in the harbour.

Green Dragoons. The name given to the 13th Dragoons in the period 1715–1784 when they wore green facings; later the 13th Hussars. Now part of the 13th/18th Royal Hussars (Queen Mary's Own); the facings later changed to buff and are now white. (*See also* LILYWHITES, *below*.)

Green Howards. The 19th Foot, from their facings and Sir Charles Howard, Colonel of the Regiment 1738–1748. The name became part of the official title of the regiment in 1920, the present title is The Green Howards (Alexandra, Princess of Wales's Own Yorkshire Regiment).

Green Linnets. The 39th Foot, later 1st Battalion Dorset Regiment, now part of the Devonshire and Dorset Regiment. The name refers to the green facings of the regiment and dates from *c.* 1741.

Greys, The. The Royal Scots Greys (2nd Dragoons) were raised in 1678. It is now uncertain whether the name comes from the grey horses or uniform, but within 30 years of formation the regiment was known as the "Grey Dragoons". "Scots Greys" has been part of the official title since 1866, with "Royal" being added 11 years later. By 1971 they were amalgamated with the 3rd Carabiniers (Princess of Wales's Dragoon Guards) to form the Royal Scots Dragoon Guards (Carabiniers and Greys).

Heavies, The. The heavy cavalry, especially the Dragoon Guards, which consisted of men of greater build and height than Lancers and Hussars. This term has been applied to the larger guns manned by the Royal Artillery and one of its predecessors, the Royal Garrison Artillery.

Hindustan Regiment. The 76th Foot, now the Duke of Wellington's Regiment (West Riding), was so called because the Regiment distinguished itself in the Hindustan campaign of 1803–1805.

Holy Boys. The 9th Foot, later Royal Norfolk Regiment, now part of the 1st Battalion Royal Anglian Regiment. During the Peninsular War, the Spaniards thought that the regimental badge of Britannia represented the Virgin MARY.

Horse Marines. The 17th Lancers, now 17th/21st Lancers. In 1795, two troops of the regiment served on board the frigate H.M.S. *Hermione* on the West Indies Station. *See also under* HORSE.

Immortals, The. The 76th Foot, now Duke of Wellington's Regiment (West Riding). During the Mahratta War (1803–1805), almost every man had one or more wounds.

Kiddies, The. A name given to the Scots Guards, when in 1686 James II formed a large camp on Hounslow Heath as a precaution against unrest in London. The (then) three existing Guards regiments were present, and the Scots, being the junior of the three, were given this name.

Kirke's Lambs. The 2nd Foot, later Queen's Royal Regiment (West Surrey), now 1st Battalion The Queen's Regiment. Raised in 1661 for service in Tangier, which had become a British possession as part of the dowry of Charles II's Queen, Catherine of Braganza, and ranged against Moslem forces, the badge adopted was the Christian emblem of the PASCHAL LAMB. After MONMOUTH'S REBELLION (1685), the regiment under Colonel Percy Kirke (hence Kirke's Lambs) was noted for its ruthlessness against the defeated rebels in Somerset and adjacent areas. *Kirke's Lambs* were also nicknamed the **Tangerines** in allusion to their origin, and **Mutton Lancers** from their badge.

Lacedæmonians, The. A nickname of the 46th Foot, later 2nd Battalion Duke of Cornwall's Light Infantry, then part of the Somerset and Cornwall Light Infantry. In 1777, during the American War of Independence, their Colonel is supposed to have made a long speech under heavy fire on Spartan discipline and the military system of the Lacedæmonians. In 1968 this regiment became the 1st Battalion The Light Infantry.

Lilywhites, The. The 13th Hussars, now 13th/18th Hussars. When the regiment was converted from Light Dragoons to Hussars in 1861, buff facings were adopted, but for some reason they were pipeclayed white. When the 13th Hussars and the 18th Hussars were amalgamated in 1922, the nickname was adopted by the new regiment.

Minden Regiments. (1) 12th Foot, later Suffolk Regiment, now 1st Battalion Royal Anglian Regiment. (2) 20th Foot—the Lancashire Fusiliers, known as "the Minden boys", later the (disbanded) 4th Battalion Royal Regiment of Fusiliers. (3) 23rd Foot—the Royal Welch Fusiliers. (4) 25th Foot—King's Own Scottish Borderers. (5) 37th Foot—later Royal Hampshire Regiment. (6) 51st Foot—King's Own Yorkshire Light Infantry, who became the 2nd Battalion The Light Infantry in 1968.

On 1 August 1759, these six regiments won the most spectacular victory of the SEVEN YEARS WAR by attacking and defeating a superior force of French Cavalry. As the regiments advanced to the attack across Minden Heath, the men picked wild roses and stuck them in their caps. To commemorate this victory, the regiments (with the exception of the Royal Welch Fusiliers) wear roses in their caps on Minden Day.

Moonrakers. *See* SPRINGERS, *below*.

Mutton Lancers. *See* KIRKE'S LAMBS *above*.

Nanny-Goats, or **Royal Goats.** The 23rd Foot, now the Royal Welch Fusiliers, which has a regimental mascot, a goat, supplied from the Royal herd. *See* RED DRAGONS *below*.

Nutcrackers. The 3rd Foot, later The Buffs (Royal East Kent Regiment), now 2nd Battalion The Queen's Regiment, from their exploits against the French during the Peninsular War.

Old Bold Fifth. *See* FIGHTING FIFTH *above*.

Old Braggs. *See* SLASHERS, *below*.

Old Dozen. The 12th Foot, later the Suffolk Regiment, now part of the 1st Battalion Royal Anglian Regiment.

Old Fogs. The 87th Foot, the Royal Irish Fusiliers (Princess Victoria's); the name comes from their war-cry at Barossa (1811)—"Faugh-a-Ballagh" (Clear the Way). Disbanded 1968.

Orange Lilies. 35th Foot, later 1st Battalion Royal Sussex Regiment, now 3rd Battalion The Queen's Regiment. The regiment was raised in Belfast in 1701 by the Earl of Donegal, who chose orange facings in honour of William III. The lilies come from the white plumes which the regiment took from the French Regiment of Royal Roussillon, whom they defeated at Quebec (1759).

Oxford Blues, The. The Royal Horse Guards were so called in 1690, from the Earl of Oxford, their commander, and the blue uniform which dates from 1661. The nickname was later shortened to "The Blues" and was incorporated in the regiment's title as The Royal Horse Guards (The Blues). In March 1969, the regiment amalgamated with the Royal Dragoons (1st Dragoons) to form The Blues and Royals (Royal Horse Guards and 1st Dragoons).

Paget's Irregular Horse. The 4th Hussars, now part of the Queen's Royal Irish Hussars. When the regiment returned to England in 1842 under Colonel Paget, it had lost almost 900 officers and men in its 20 years in India. As the replacements were not as highly trained as the original men, the general standard of drill fell, and the name was coined.

Pompadours, The. The 56th Foot, later 2nd Battalion Essex Regiment, now part of the 3rd Battalion Royal Anglian Regiment. When the regiment was raised in 1755, the facings chosen were purple, the favourite colour of Madame de POMPADOUR, the mistress of Louis XV.

Pontius Pilate's Bodyguard. The 1st Foot, now the Royal Scots (The Royal Regiment). Tradition states that when in French service as *Le Régiment de Douglas*, a dispute arose with the *Régiment de Picardie* as to seniority, and an officer of the latter claimed that his regiment was on duty on the night of the Crucifixion, to which an officer of Douglas's replied, "Had we been on duty, we would not have slept at our post."

Queen's Bays. The 2nd Dragoon Guards. From 1767 the regiment was mounted on bay-coloured horses, while other cavalry regiments had black horses. In 1870 the name became official, the regiment being titled 2nd Dragoon Guards (Queen's Bays); it is now part of the 1st (Queen's) Dragoon Guards.

Red Dragons. The Royal Welch Fusiliers, the 23rd Foot, so named from the Welsh national emblem, the Red Dragon, which forms part of their badge. Since 1958 included in the Welsh Brigade. *See* NANNY-GOATS *above*.

Red Feathers. The 46th Foot, later 2nd Battalion Duke of Cornwall's Light Infantry, then part of the Somerset and Cornwall Light Infantry. During the American War of Independence, the 46th Foot defeated an American force at Brandywine (1777). The Americans promised to have their revenge, so the regiment dyed their cap feathers red to aid identification by the enemy. The regiment became the 1st Battalion The Light Infantry in 1968.

Ross-Shire Buffs. The 78th Foot, later 2nd Battalion Seaforth Highlanders (Ross-shire Buffs, the Duke of Albany's), now part of the Queen's Own Highlanders (Seaforth and Camerons). This name became part of the official title soon after the formation of the regiment, and commemorates the colour of their facings and the recruiting area.

Sankey's Horse. The 39th Foot, later 1st Battalion Dorset Regiment, now part of the Devonshire and Dorset Regiment. Sankey was Colonel of the regiment when in Spain (1708–1711), and tradition has it that he mounted the men on mules to enable them to reach the scene of a battle in time to take part.

Saucy Seventh. The 7th Queen's Own Hussars, now part of the Queen's Own Hussars. A regimental recruiting poster of *c.* 1809 uses this name, an allusion to the regiment's smart appearance.

Saucy Sixth. The 6th Foot, the Royal Warwickshire Regiment. In 1795 the Regiment returned from the West Indies and recruited in Warwickshire, but the required standard was so high that few recruits were found, and the name was coined. In 1968 this regiment became the 2nd Battalion Royal Regiment of Fusiliers.

Scarlet Lancers. The 16th Lancers, whose tunic was red. Now the 16th/5th The Queen's Royal Lancers. They were the only Lancer regiment to retain the DRAGOON's scarlet tunic in the latter half of the 19th century.

Slashers, The. The 28th Foot, later Gloucestershire Regiment. When the regiment was stationed in Canada in 1764, a magistrate harassed the soldiers and their families. A party of heavily disguised soldiers broke into the magistrate's house one night, and during a scuffle the man's ear was cut off. Officially, the identity of the culprits was never discovered, but the 28th acquired the nickname of "The Slashers". Two other names attached to the regiment are "The Braggs" and the "Old Braggs", from Lieut.-General Philip Bragg, Colonel of the regiment 1734–1759.

Snappers, The. The 15th Foot, later East Yorkshire Regiment, now part of the Prince of Wales's Own Regiment of Yorkshire. During the Battle of Brandywine (1777), with ammunition exhausted, the men "snapped" their muskets to give the impression that they were firing; this misled the Americans, and they retired.

Springers, The. The 62nd Foot, later 1st Battalion Wiltshire Regiment, now part of the Duke of Edinburgh's Royal Regiment (Berkshire and Wiltshire). In 1775–1776, during the American War of Independence, the 62nd were used as Light Infantry and the nickname commemorates their alertness and speed in their temporary role. Perhaps, however, better known as the MOONRAKERS.

Tangerines, The. *See* KIRKE'S LAMBS *above*.

Vein-Openers, The. The 29th Foot, later Worcestershire Regiment, now part of the Worcestershire and Sherwood Foresters' Regiment. In 1770, when American colonial discontent with England was increasing, the 29th were in Boston, and while a detachment was guarding the Customs House it was pelted by a mob. During a scuffle a soldier mistook a shout from the crowd for an order and he fired. Other shots followed and four rioters were killed and several wounded. The name was given to the regiment by the Americans for their part in what was called the "Boston Massacre".

Virgin Mary's Bodyguard. The 7th Dragoon Guards, now part of the 4th/7th Royal Dragoon Guards. During the reign of George II the regiment was sent to assist the Archduchess Maria Theresa of Austria.

Wolfe's Own. The 47th Foot, later the Loyal Regiment (North Lancashire), so called for their distinguished service under General Wolfe at Quebec (1759), now, with the Lancashire Regiment (Prince of Wales's Volunteers), the Queen's Lancashire Regiment.

United States Army

In the following representative selection all are Infantry Divisions unless otherwise stated. Unofficial nicknames are marked thus *.

1st: The Big Red One. Name given it by the Germans, who saw the red "1" on their shoulder patch. According to legend, the original red "1" was improvised from the cap of an enemy soldier killed by a 1st Division DOUGHBOY in World War I when the division earned the right to proclaim itself the first American division (1918) in France, first to fire on the enemy, first to suffer casualties, first to take prisoners, first to stage a major offensive, and first to enter Germany.

2nd: Indianhead. A long-forgotten truck driver of the division in World War I adorned the side of his vehicle with a handsome shield framing an Indian head which was adopted by the division as its shoulder insignia. Hence the name "Indian Division".

3rd: Marne Division. In World War I, because of its impregnable stand against the Germans' last counter-offensive. The three diagonal stripes in its insignia symbolize its participation in three major battles in 1918.

4th: Ivy Division. From its insignia. The selection of that design is one of the few known instances of authorized military frivolity. "I-vy" is simply spelling out in a letter form the Roman numeral for "four".

5th: Red Diamond. From its insignia. The Red Diamond was selected at the suggestion of Major Charles. A. Meals that their insignia be the "Ace of Diamonds, less the Ace". Originally there was a white "5" in the centre. This was removed when they reached France.

8th: Pathfinder. From their insignia, which is a golden arrow through a figure "8" pointing the way. Also called the "Golden Arrow Division".

9th: Hitler's Nemesis*. A newspaper at home dubbed them this. Also called "Old Reliable"* and "Varsity"*.

10th: Mountaineers (formerly 10th Mountain division). This division was given the task of dislodging crack German mountain troops from the heights of Mt. Belvedere. It was composed of famous American skiers, climbers, forest rangers, and Wild Life Service men.

13th: (Airborne). Blackcats*. Gets its name from its flaunting of superstition. Its number is "13", and it was reactivated on Friday the 13th.

17th: (Airborne). Golden Talon* from its shoulder patch, stretching golden talons on a black field, representing ability to seize; black suggests darkness, under which many operations are effected. Also called "Thunderbolt"*.

23rd: The America Division. Although without a nickname, it was the only Division in U.S. Army history with a name and not a number, until the war in Vietnam. It was formed from Task Force 6814 in New Caledonia and joined in the invasion of Guadalcanal in 1942 subsequently fighting in Leyte and other Philippine Islands. It won an arrowhead for the invasion of Cebu.

24th: Victory. The Filipinos on Leyte greeted them with the "V" sign.

25th: Tropic Lightning. Activated from elements of the Hawaiian Division, Regular Army troops.

26th: Yankee. Originally composed of National Guard troops from the New England (YANKEE) States.

28th: Keystone. Troops from Pennsylvania, which is known as the "Keystone State".

29th: Blue and Gray. Organized in World War I from National Guardsmen of New Jersey, Delaware, Virginia, Maryland, and the District of Columbia. Its shoulder patch of blue and grey, the colours of the rival armies in the CIVIL WAR, symbolizes unity of former embattled states. They are combined in a monad, the Korean symbol for eternal life.

30th: Old Hickory. Composed after World War I from National Guardsmen of the Carolinas, Georgia, and Tennessee, Andrew Jackson's old stamping grounds. He was known as "OLD HICKORY".

31st: Dixie. Originally composed of men of the "Deep South" or "Dixie".

32nd: Red Arrow. On tactical maps the enemies' lines are indicated in red. Their patch is a reminder to those who wear it that the enemy has never stopped them. Another name "Les Terribles", was given them by an admiring French general during World War I, when they earned four battle streamers and were first to crack the Hindenburg line.

34th: Red Bull. Its patch is a red bull's skull on an olla, a Mexican water bottle. Inspired by the desert country of the South-west where it trained in World War I.

35th: Santa Fe. So called because the ancestors of its personnel blazed the old Santa Fe trail. Insignia is the original marker used on the trail.

36th: Texas. Personnel was from Oklahoma and Texas. The arrowhead of its insignia represented Oklahoma and the "T" was for Texas.

37th: Buckeye. Composed of Ohio troops. Ohio is known as the "Buckeye State". Insignia is that of the state flag.

38th: Cyclone. Got its name in 1917 at Shelby, Mississippi, when the tent city in which it was bivouacked was levelled by winds. The division struck like a cyclone when it landed in Luzon.

42nd: Rainbow. Nickname originated from the fact that the division was composed of military groups from the District of Columbia, and 25 states, representing several sections, nationalities, religions, and viewpoints. They blended themselves into one harmonious unit. A major in World War I, noting its various origins, said, "This division will stretch over the land like a rainbow."

43rd: Winged Victory. Received its name on Luzon. It is formed from the name of its commanding general, Maj.-Gen. Leonard F. Wing, and the ultimate goal of the division.

63rd: Blood and Fire. When the division was activated in June 1943 following the Casablanca Conference they adopted the Conference's resolution, to make their enemies "bleed and burn in expiation of their crimes against humanity", as their symbol.

65th: Battle-Axe*. Its patch is a white halbert on a white shield. The halbert, a sharp-pointed battle-axe, was a potent weapon of the 15th-century foot soldier, being suitable either for a powerful cutting smash or for a quick thrust. It is an emblem that signifies both the shock action and the speed of the modern infantry division.

66th: Black Panther*. The black panther on its shoulder patch symbolizes the attributes of a good infantryman: ability to kill, to be aggressive, alert, stealthy, cunning, agile, and strong.

70th: Trailblazer. Their insignia combines an axe, a snowy mountain, and a green fir-tree, symbols of the pioneers who blazed the trail to Oregon and the Willamette Valley, where most of their training was accomplished.

76th: Onaway. The alert call of the Chippewa Indians in whose hunting grounds they trained. Also unofficially called "Liberty Bell"* from the shoulder patch of a Liberty Bell worn in World War I. The 76th was the first draft division from civilian ranks and in 1919 their device became a shield with a white label, indicating the eldest son.

77th: Statue of Liberty. Their insignia bears the picture of the Statue of Liberty, because most of the personnel in World War I were from New York City.

78th: Lightning. The shoulder patch originated in World War I because the battles of that division were likened by the French to bolt of lightning, leaving the field blood red

79th: Cross of Lorraine. Having distinguished itself at Montfaucon in Lorraine the division selected the CROSS of Lorraine, symbol of triumph, as its insignia.

80th: Blue Ridge. Its insignia symbolizes the three Blue Ridge states, Pennsylvania, Virginia, and West Virginia, from which most of its World War I personnel were drawn.

81st: Wildcat. Gets its name from Wildcat Creek that flows through Fort Jackson, S.C. It is generally credited as the first to wear the shoulder patch.

82nd: (Airborne). All American. In World War I the division was composed of men from every state in the union. Originally an infantry division, when it was reactivated as an airborne division it retained its insignia, adding the word "Airborne" above.

84th: Railsplitters. Primarily made up of National Guard units from Illinois, Kentucky and Indiana, the Lincoln states. They called themselves the Lincoln Division. Their insignia is a red disc with a white axe which splits a rail. In World War II they called themselves the "Railsplitters". The Germans called them the "Hatchet-men".

85th: Custer. The initials on its insignia "CD" stand for Custer Division, because they were activated at Camp Custer, Michigan, in World War I.

86th: Blackhawk*. Its insignia is a black hawk with wings outspread superimposed on a red shield. On the breast of the hawk is a small red shield with black letters "BH" for its nickname. Its personnel in World War I were drawn from Illinois, Wisconsin, and Minnesota, the territory inhabited by Chief Blackhawk and his tribe. The bird symbolizes keenness, cunning and tenacity.

87th: Golden Acorn. Their patch is a green field with a golden acorn which symbolizes strength.

88th: Blue Devil. Their patch is a blue four-leaf clover formed from two crossed arabic numerals, "88".

89th: Rolling W*. The "W" on its insignia within a circle forms an "M" when it is inverted, the two letters standing for Middle West, the section of the country from which its personnel were drawn. The circle indicates speed and stability. Also called "Middle West"*.

90th: Tough 'Ombres. The letter "T" of its insignia, standing for Texas, bisects the letter "O" for Oklahoma. The men of the division say it stands for "Tough 'Ombres".

92nd: Buffalo*. Insignia is a black buffalo on an olive drab background with black border. In the days of Indian warfare the Indians called Negro soldiers "Black Buffaloes" from their kinky hair similar to that on a buffalo's neck. The men of this Negro division in WORLD WAR I were trained at Fort Huachuca in the same locality.

96th: Deadeye*. Their name came from their perfect marksmanship while in training.

97th: Trident*. Their insignia is a trident, white on a blue field. NEPTUNE's trident represents the coastal states of Maine, Vermont, and New Hampshire, from which they came. There is a prong for each state. The blue represents their freshwater lakes, and the white their snowy mountains.

98th: Iroquois. Its patch consists of a shield in the shape of the great seal of the State of New York. The head of the Iroquois Indian chief is in orange. These are the colours of the Dutch House of Nassau, which was responsible for the settlement of New Amsterdam, later New York. The five feathers worn by the Indian represent the FIVE NATIONS who formed the Iroquois Confederacy. The personnel were from New York.

99th: Checkerboard*. The blue and white squares resembling a checkerboard formed part of the coat of arms of William Pitt (sable, a fess chequé or and AZURE between 3 BEZANTS). The home station of the division was Pittsburgh.

101st: (Airborne). Screaming Eagle. Its white eagle's head with gold beak on a black shield is based on CIVIL WAR tradition. The black shield recalls the "Iron Brigade", one regiment of which possessed the famous eagle "Old Abe" which went into battle with them as their screaming mascot.

102nd: Ozark. A large golden "O" on a field of blue. Within the "O" is the letter "Z", from which is suspended an arc. This represents the word "Ozark". The personnel came from the Ozark Mountain region.

103rd: Cactus. A green Saguaro cactus in a blue base superimposed on a yellow disc was adopted by this Reserve division which had its headquarters in Denver, Colorado. Yellow disc represents the golden sky, while the green cactus growing in the blue sage-covered earth is characteristic of the Southwest.

106th: Golden Lion*. Their patch represents a golden lion's face on a blue background encircled by white and red borders. The blue represents the infantry, red the supporting artillery, and the lion's face strength and power.

Regium donum (Lat., royal gift). An annual grant paid by the Crown from 1670 until 1871 to help PRESBYTERIAN ministers in ULSTER. It was, however, withdrawn by James II and again in 1714. An English *regium donum* was introduced by Walpole in 1723 for the benefit of the widows of Dissenting ministers. NON-CONFORMIST unease led to its discontinuance in 1851.

> The English "Regium Donum" had all the demoralizing effects of a bribe. For more than a century and a quarter it continued to be a source of weakness, strife, discontent, and reproach.
>
> SKEATS and MIALL: *History of the Free Churches of England*, ch. V.

Regius Professor (Lat. *regius*, royal). At Oxford and Cambridge, one who holds a professorship founded by Henry VIII and certain others of subsequent foundation. At the Scottish universities, any professorship instituted by the Crown.

Regnal Year. *See under* YEAR.

Regular (U.S.A.). In the early 19th century this meant thorough, well founded; in the 20th century, more often applied to people as, *a regular guy*, a straightforward, dependable person.

Regulars. All men of the British (and U.S.) armed forces who adopt their respective service as a career, as opposed to members of reserve forces, and conscripts.

Rehoboam (II *Chron*. xiii, 7). As a wine measure, the equivalent of six bottles. *See* BOTTLE; JEROBOAM; TAPPIT-HEN.

Charlotte Brontë—why is not known—applied the name to a clerical SHOVEL HAT.

> He [Mr. Helstone] was short of stature [and wore] a rehoboam, or shovel hat, which he did not ... remove.
>
> *Shirley*, ch. i.

Reign of Terror. The period in the French Revolution from April 1793 until July 1794, when supreme power was in the hands of the Committee of Public Safety, and the JACOBINS, dominated by Robespierre, St. Just, and Couthon. During this period, Taine estimated that 17,000 people were put to death, although this is perhaps an exaggeration, but some 2,600 were sentenced at Paris alone. The excuse was the external threat from the European coalition, "royalist plots", etc. Robespierre formulated the doctrine that "in times of peace the springs of popular government are in virtue, but in times of revolution, they are both in virtue and terror".

Reilly, To lead a life of. To live luxuriously. From a comic song, "Is That Mr. Reilly", by Pat Rooney, popular in the U.S.A. in the 1880s. The song described what the hero would do if he "struck it rich".

Rein (connected with *retain*, from Lat. *retinere*, to hold back). The strap attached to the bit, used in guiding a HORSE.

To draw rein. To tighten the reins; hence to slacken pace, to stop.

To give the reins, or **to give free rein to.** To let go unrestrained; to give licence.

To take the reins. To assume the guidance of direction; to assume control.

Reins (Lat. *renes*). The kidneys, supposed by the Hebrews and others to be the seat of knowledge, pleasure, and pain. The Psalmist says (xvi, 7), "My reins instruct me in the night seasons." SOLOMON (*Prov*. xxiii, 16), "My reins shall rejoice, when thy lips speak right things," and Jeremiah says (*Lam*. iii, 13), God "caused his arrows to enter into my reins," *i.e.* sent pain into my kidneys.

Relic, Christian. The corpse of a saint, or any part thereof; any part of his clothing; or anything ultimately connected with him. The veneration of Christian relics goes back to the 2nd century and led to many spurious relics being brought back from the HOLY LAND. Miracle-working relics brought wealth to many monasteries and churches and the remains of saints were often dismembered and trickery and violence were used to obtain them. Relics such as the tip of LUCIFER'S tail, the blood of Christ, the candle which the ANGEL of the Lord lit in Christ's tomb, were among the many accepted by the credulous.

Relief Church. A secession from the CHURCH OF SCOTLAND led in 1752 by Thomas Gillespie (1708–1774). He offered passive obedience respecting the settlement of ministers. The "Presbytery of Relief" was constituted in 1761; in 1847 the sect was embodied in the United Presbyterian Church of Scotland.

Religious. His Most Religious Majesty. The title by which the kings of England were formerly addressed by the POPE. It still survives in the BOOK OF COMMON PRAYER in the Prayer "for the High Court of Parliament under our most religious and gracious Queen at this time assembled" (which was written, probably by hand, in 1625), and in James I's *Act for Thanksgiving on the Fifth of November* occurs the expression "most great, learned, and religious King".

Similarly the Pope addressed the King of France as "Most Christian", the Emperor of Austria as "Most Apostolic", the king of Portugal as "Most Faithful", etc. *See* MAJESTY.

Reliquary. A receptacle of various kinds for RELICS. The smaller relics were preserved in monstrances, pyxes, pectoral reliquaries (usually in the form of a CROSS), shapes of arms and legs, etc. (*see* ARM-SHRINES). The entire remains of a saint were kept in shrines.

Reliques of Ancient English Poetry. *See* PERCY'S RELIQUES.

Remember! The mysterious injunction of CHARLES I, on the scaffold, to Bishop Juxon. Not his "last words". *See* DYING SAYINGS.

Remembrance Day, Remembrance Sunday. After World War I ARMISTICE DAY, or Remembrance Day, commemorating the fallen was observed on 11 November; also called "Poppy Day" from the artificial poppies (recalling the poppies of Flanders fields) sold by the British LEGION in aid of ex-servicemen. From 1945 to 1956 Remembrance Sunday was observed instead on the first or second Sunday of November, commemorating the fallen of World Wars I and II. In 1956 it was fixed on the second Sunday of November.

Remigius, or Remy, St. (re mij' i ūs, re'mi) (438–533), BISHOP and confessor, and apostle of the FRANKS. He is represented as carrying a vessel of holy oil, or in the act of anointing therewith Clovis, who kneels before him. He is said to have given Clovis the power of touching for the KING'S EVIL. His day is 1 October.

Remittance men. In 19th-century Australia and other colonial territories, a name given to middle-class immigrants, well-connected Englishmen, and ne'er-do-wells who were often impractical, unsuccessful, and not at home in the BUSH; so called from their dependence on money sent from home. They were also called "colonial experiencers".

Remonstrants. Another name for the ARMINIANS. In Scottish history, the name is also given to those who presented a remonstrance to the Committee of Estates in 1650 refusing to acknowledge Charles II as king until he had established his good faith and devotion to the Covenant (*see* COVENANTERS).

Remus. *See* ROMULUS.

Renaissance, The (Fr., rebirth). The term applied to the intellectual movement characteristic of that period of European history marking the transition between the mediæval and modern. Chronologically it is usually taken to fall in the 15th and 16th centuries, occurring earliest in Italy and later in England. In a more limited sense it implies what was formerly called the REVIVAL OF LEARNING.

The period is particularly marked by a rediscovery of the classics, questioning of religious dogmas, the growth of a more scientific outlook, major developments in art and literature, new inventions and overseas discoveries, and a general assertion and emancipation of the human intellect.

The name is now also given to certain earlier periods, such as "the Twelfth-century Renaissance".

Renard (ren' ard). **Une queue de renard** (Fr., a fox's tail). A mockery. At one time it was a common practical joke to fasten a fox's tail behind a person against whom a laugh was designed. PANURGE never lost a chance of attaching a fox's tail, or the ears of a leveret, behind a Master of Arts or Doctor of Divinity (*Gargantua*, II, xvi). *See also* REYNARD.

C'est une petite vipère
Qui n'épargneroit pas son père
Et qui par nature ou par art
Sçait couper la queue au renard.
BEAUCAIRE: *L'Embarras de la Foire*.

Repenter Curls. The long ringlets of a lady's hair. *Repentir* is the French for penitence, and *les repenties* are the girls doing penance for their misdemeanours. MARY MAGDALENE had such long hair that she wiped off her tears from the feet of Jesus therewith. Hence the association of long curls and reformed (*repenties*) prostitutes.

Reply Churlish. "Sir, you are no judge; your opinion has no weight with me." Or, to paraphrase Touchstone's illustration (SHAKESPEARE: *As You Like It*, V, iv): "If I tell a courtier his beard is not well cut, and he disables my judgment, he gives me the reply churlish, which is the fifth remove from the lie direct, or rather, the lie direct in the fifth degree." *Cp.* COUNTERCHECK QUARRELSOME; QUIP MODEST; REPROOF VALIANT; RETORT COURTEOUS.

Reproof Valiant. "Sir, allow me to tell you that is not the truth." This is Touchstone's fourth remove from the lie direct, or, rather, the lie direct in the fourth degree. *See* COUNTERCHECK QUARRELSOME; QUIP MODEST; REPLY CHURLISH; RETORT COURTEOUS.

Republic, The. The English name for PLATO'S best-known work, the *Politeia* (Commonwealth), written in the 4th century B.C. It is his ideal Commonwealth and *The Republic* is especially regarded for its philosophical and ethical teachings. It gave Sir Thomas More the inspiration for his UTOPIA. *See* IDEAL COMMONWEALTHS *under* COMMONWEALTH.

The Republic of Letters. The world of literature; authors generally and their influence. Goldsmith, in *The Citizen of the World*, No. 20 (1760), says "it is a very common expression among Europeans"; it is found in MOLIÈRE'S *Le Mariage Forcé*, Sc. vi (1664).

The Republican Queen. Sophia Charlotte (1668–1705), wife of Frederick I of Prussia, was so nicknamed on account of her advanced political views. She was the sister of George I of Britain, the friend of Leibniz, and a woman of remarkable culture. Charlottenburg was named after her.

Requests, Court of. A minor court of equity hearing poor men's causes, which fell into disuse at the time of the CIVIL WARS. Also certain local COURTS OF CONSCIENCE (*see under* CONSCIENCE).

Requiem (re' kwi em). The first word of the prayer *Requiem aeternam dona eis, domine, et lux perpetua luceat eis* (Eternal rest give them, O Lord, and let everlasting light shine upon them) used as the introit of a MASS for the Dead; hence a Requiem Mass.

Reremouse. *See* REARMOUSE.

Resolute. The Resolute Doctor. John Baconthorpe (d. 1346), grand-nephew of Roger Bacon, head of the CARMELITES in England (1329–1333) and commentator on ARISTOTLE, the BIBLE, etc.

The Most Resolute Doctor. Guillaume Durandus de St. Pourçain (d. 1332), a French DOMINICAN philosopher, bishop of Meaux (1326), and author of *Commentaires sur Pierre Lombard*.

Respects. To pay one's respects. To show polite regard for someone, usually by making a call.

To pay one's last respects. To show respect for one who is dead, particularly by being present at the funeral.

Responsions. *See* SMALLS.

Rest. Laid to rest. Buried.

Restoration, The. In British history, the recall of the Stuarts to the throne in 1660 in the person of Charles II, thus bringing the Puritan COMMONWEALTH to an end. The Restoration period was marked by a relaxation in standards of conduct but scholarship, science, literature and the arts blossomed and flourished with the cessation of PURITAN restraints.

In France, the royal house of Bourbon was restored after the fall of NAPOLEON in 1815 in the person of Louis XVIII, brother of the late King Louis XVI, whose son, dynastically known as Louis XVII, did not survive to rule.

Resurrectionists, or **Resurrection Men.** Body-snatchers, those who broke open the coffins of the newly buried to supply the demands of the surgical and medical schools. The first recorded instance of the practice was in 1742 and it flourished particularly until the passing of the Anatomy Act of 1832. The Resurrectionist took the corpse naked, this being in law a misdemeanour, as opposed to a felony if garments were taken as well. Murders were sometimes committed for the same market. *See* BURKE.

Retiarius (rē ti âr' i us) (Lat.). A gladiator who made use of a net (*rete*), which he threw over his adversary. *See also* TRIDENT.

As in the thronged amphitheatre of old
The wary Retiarius trapped his foe.
THOMSON: *Castle of Indolence*, canto ii.

Retort Courteous, The. "Sir, I am not of your opinion; I beg to differ from you" or, to use Touchstone's illustration (SHAKESPEARE: *As You Like It*, V, iv), "If I said his beard was not cut well, he was in the mind it was." The lie seven times removed, or rather, the lie direct in the seventh degree. *See* COUNTERCHECK QUARRELSOME; QUIP MODEST; REPLY CHURLISH; REPROOF VALIANT.

Returned Letter Office. *See* BLIND DEPARTMENT.

Reuters. The premier international news agency, reputed for its integrity and impartiality, founded by Paul Julius Reuter (1816–1899), a native of Cassel, Germany. The agency was established at London in 1851, taking full advantage of the developing telegraph service, although links had to be completed by railway and pigeon-post. He developed a world-wide service in the ensuing years and in 1871 was made Baron de Reuter by the Duke of Saxe-Coburg and Gotha. It became a private trust in 1916 and was later (1926–1941) taken over by the British Press Association, the Newspaper Publishers Association, the Australian Associated Press and the New Zealand Press Association, becoming a public company in 1984.

Reveille (re văl' i) (Fr. *réveiller*, to awaken). The bugle call used in the armed forces announcing that it is time to rise.

Revenant (rev' e non) (Fr., present participle of *revenir*, to come back). One who returns after long exile; an apparition, a ghost, one who returns from the dead.

Revenons à nos moutons. *See* MOUTONS.

Reverend. An archbishop is *the Most Reverend* (Father in God); a BISHOP, *the Right Reverend*; a DEAN, *the Very Reverend*; an archdeacon, *the Venerable*; all the other CLERGY, *the Reverend*. A person in orders should always be referred to as "the Reverend Mr. Jones", or "the Reverend John Jones"; never "Reverend", or "the Reverend Jones".

Revised code. The regulations governing English elementary education issued in 1862 when the many existing directives were gathered together and systematically arranged. It introduced the notorious system of "payment by results" whereby the grant to schools was dependent upon tests in THE THREE R'S (*see under* R) given to the pupils by H.M. Inspectors. Its effects on the teaching of grammar, geography, and history were disastrous as their teaching did not affect a school's revenues.

The Revised Version. *See* BIBLE, THE ENG-LISH.

Revival of Learning, or **Letters.** A term applied to that aspect of the RENAISSANCE which involved the revival of classical learning, especially of Greek literature, freed from the cramping influences of mediæval SCHOLASTICISM and ecclesiastical restraint. Humanism, which demanded that human reason should be free to pursue its intellectual and aesthetic purposes, was its keynote. Marked by the enthusiastic pursuit of scholarship, the investigation of manuscript sources, and the establishment of libraries and museums, it received added impetus from the invention of printing (*c.* 1440). Italy was the centre of this European revival, where it was in evidence by the late 14th century, reaching its full development in the early 16th century.

Rexists. A Belgian political party formed by Léon Degrelle in 1936 advocating FASCIST methods. Markedly collaborationist during the German occupation of Belgium, it was accordingly suppressed when the Germans were expelled in 1944. The name is an adaptation of "Christus Rex", Christ the King, the watchword of a Catholic Young People's Action Society founded in 1925. *Cp.* QUISLING.

Reynard (rā' nard). A fox. Caxton's form of the name in his translation (from the Dutch) of the *Roman de Renart* (*see* REYNARD THE FOX, *below*). *Renart* was the Old French form, from Ger. *Reginhart*, a personal name; the M. Dutch was *Reynaerd* or *Reynaert*.

Reynard the Fox. A mediæval beast-epic satirizing contemporary life and events, found in French, Dutch, and German literature. Chaucer's *Nun's Priest's Tale* is part of the Reynard tradition. Most of the names in the Reynard cycle are German but it found its greatest vogue in France as the *Roman de Renart*. Caxton's *Hystorie of Reynart the Foxe* (1481) was based on a Dutch version published at Gouda in 1479. The oldest version (12th century) is in Latin.

Reynard's Globe of Glass. Reynard, in REYNARD THE FOX, said he had sent this invaluable treasure to her majesty the QUEEN as a present; but it never came to hand as it had no existence except in the imagination of the fox. It was supposed to reveal what was being done—no matter how far off—and also to afford information on any subject that the person consulting it wished to know. **Your gift was like the globe of glass of Master Reynard.** A great promise but no performance.

Reynard's Wonderful ring. *See* RINGS NOTED IN FABLE *under* RING.

Rhabdomancy. A form of DIVINATION by means of a rod or wand, dowsing (Gr. *rhabdomanteia*; *rhabdos*, rod; *manteia*, prophecy). *See* DOWSE.

Rhadamanthus. In Greek mythology, one of the three judges of HELL; MINOS and Æacus being the other two.

Rhapsody meant originally "songs strung together" (Gr. *rapto*, to sew or string together; *ode*, a song). The term was applied to portions of the ILIAD and ODYSSEY, which bards recited.

Rhea. In Greek mythology, Mother of the gods, daughter of URANUS and GÆA, and sister of KRONOS by whom she bore ZEUS, HADES, POSEIDON, HERA, Hestia, and DEMETER. She is identified with CYBELE and also known as AGDISTIS.

Rhea Sylvia. The mother of ROMULUS and Remus.

Rheims-Douai Version, The. *See* THE DOUAI BIBLE, *under* BIBLE, THE ENGLISH.

Rhetorical Question. A question asked for the sake of effect rather than demanding an answer as, "Who worries about that?" *i.e.* nobody worries.

Rhino (rī' nō). Slang for money; the term was in use in the 17th century. Its origin is uncertain but one plausible suggestion is that it derives from an Eastern belief that the powdered horn of the rhinoceros increased sexual potency and therefore commanded a high price.

> Some, as I know,
> Have parted with their ready rhino.
> *The Seaman's Adieu* (1670).

Rhodesia. Named after Cecil Rhodes (1853–1902), the former territories of Matabeleland and Mashonaland, which became part of the British Empire by 1894 through the enterprise of Rhodes and his British South Africa Company. In 1964 Northern Rhodesia was renamed Zambia and Southern Rhodesia became Zimbabwe in 1980. Both are independent republics within the COMMONWEALTH. *See* JAMESON RAID.

Rhodes Scholars. Students holding a scholarship at Oxford under the will of Cecil Rhodes, whose wealth largely accumulated from his mining activities in South Africa. These scholars are selected from candidates in the British COMMONWEALTH, the U.S.A. and Germany.

Rhodian Bully. The COLOSSUS of Rhodes.

> Yet fain wouldst thou the crouching world bestride,

Just like the Rhodian bully o'er the tide.
JOHN WOLCOT: *The Lousiad*, canto ii.

The Rhodian Law. The earliest system of maritime law known to history; compiled by the Rhodians about 900 B.C.

Rhopalic Verse (Gr. *rhopalon*, a club which is much thicker at one end than the other). Verse consisting of lines in which each successive word has more syllables than the one preceding it.

Rem tibi confeci doctissime dulcisonorum
Spes deus aeternæ-est stationis conciliator
AUSONIUS.
Hope ever solaces miserable individuals.

Rhyme. Neither rhyme nor reason. Fit neither for amusement nor instruction. An author took his book to Sir Thomas More, CHANCELLOR of Henry VIII, and asked his opinion. Sir Thomas told the author to turn it into rhyme. He did so, and submitted it again to the Lord Chancellor. "Ay! ay!" said the witty satirist, "that will do, that will do. 'Tis rhyme now, but before it was neither rhyme nor reason."

See also WHAT! ALL THIS FOR A SONG? *under* SONG.

Rhyming slang. Slang, much used by the COCKNEY, in which the word intended is replaced by one that rhymes with it, as "plates of meat" for *feet*, "Rory O'More" for *door*, "dicky dirt" for *shirt*, "dicky-bird" for *word*. When the rhyme is a compound word the rhyming part is often dropped, leaving the uninitiated somewhat puzzled. Thus Chivy (Chevy) Chase rhymes with "face", by dropping "chase" *Chivy* remains. Similarly *daisies* are *boots*, from "daisy roots", the "roots" being dropped. Raspberry is *heart* (or vulgarly, *fart*), contracted from "raspberry tart". Numerous colloquial expressions derive from it, as "that's a fiddle", from "Yiddisher fiddle" (the musical instrument) which rhymed with *diddle*.

Rhyming to death. *See* IRISH RATS *under* RAT.

Thomas the Rhymer. Thomas Ercildoune, 13th-century border poet and seer, also called Thomas Learmont. He is the reputed author of a number of poems, including one on TRISTRAM (which Scott believed to be genuine), and is fabled to have predicted the death of Alexander III of SCOTLAND, the Battle of Bannockburn, the accession of James VI to the English throne, etc. He is not to be confused with Thomas Rymer (d. 1713), Historiographer Royal to William III.

Ribbon development. Single-depth building, chiefly houses, along main roads extending out of built-up areas. Such development was stopped by the Town and Country Planning Act of 1947.

Ribbonism. The activities, aims, etc., of the Ribbon or Riband societies, secret Irish CATHOLIC associations flourishing from *c.* 1820 to 1870, and at their peak *c.* 1835–1855. Ribbonism began in ULSTER to defend Catholics against ORANGEMEN, but spread south and by the 1830s was essentially agrarian; but its character and methods varied somewhat from district to district. It was basically a movement of the lower classes concerned with sporadic acts of outrage and took the place of the Whitefeet, MOLLY MAGUIRES, TERRY ALTS, etc. The name arose from the green ribbon worn as a badge.

Ribston Pippin. So called from Ribston, in Yorkshire, where the first pippins, introduced from Normandy about 1707, were planted. It is said that Sir Henry Goodriche planted three pips; two died, and from the third came all the Ribston apple-trees in England.

Rice. The custom of throwing rice after a bride comes from India, rice being, with the Hindus, an emblem of fecundity. The bridegroom throws three handfuls over the bride, and the bride does the same over the bridegroom. *Cp.* MARRIAGE KNOT.

Rice Christians. Converts to Christianity for worldly benefits, such as a supply of rice to Indians. Profession of Christianity born of gain, not faith.

Rice-paper. *See* MISNOMERS.

Richard Roe. *See* DOE.

Richmond. Another Richmond in the field. Said when another unexpected adversary turns up. The reference is to SHAKESPEARE'S *Richard III*, V, iv, where the king, speaking of Henry of Richmond (afterwards Henry VII), says:

I think there be six Richmonds in the field;
Five have I slain to-day, instead of him.

Rick Mould. Fetching the rick mould. An old catch played during the hay harvest. The GREENHORN was sent to borrow a rick-mould with strict injunctions not to drop it. Something very heavy was put in a sack and hoisted on to his back; when he had carried it carefully in the hot sun to the hayfield he was laughed at for his pains. *Cp.* ELBOW GREASE; PIGEON'S MILK.

Ricochet (rik′ ō shā). The bound of a bullet or other projectile after striking, the skipping of a flung stone over water ("DUCKS AND DRAKES"); hence applied to anything repeated again and again. Marshal Vauban introduced ricochet firing at Philipsburg in 1688.

Ricochet words. *See* REDUPLICATED.

Riddle. Josephus relates how Hiram, King of Tyre, and SOLOMON once had a contest in riddles, when Solomon won a large sum of money, but subsequently lost it to Abdemon, one of Hiram's subjects.

Plutarch says that HOMER died of chagrin because he could not solve a certain riddle. *See* SPHINX.

A riddle of claret. Thirteen bottles, a MAGNUM and twelve quarts; said to be so called because in certain old golf clubs, magistrates invited to the celebration dinner presented the club with this amount, sending it in a *riddle* or sieve.

Riddle me, riddle me ree. Expound my riddle rightly.

Ride (O.E. *ridan*). To go on horseback, to be carried in a vehicle, etc. In the U.S.A. *to ride* is also used to mean to oppress, to pick on and irritate a person.

Riding. In Cornwall a "riding" was a practice similar to the SKIMMINGTON, designed to shame and publicize those guilty of marital infidelity. Two people, representing the offenders, were driven through the streets in a cart pulled by a donkey with a suitable accompanying din. *Cp.* RANDAN; SHALLAL; STANG.

The three historic divisions of Yorkshire called **ridings**, because each formed a third part of the country, derive from the Danish occupation. Originally *thriding*; the initial *th-* of the word being lost through the amalgamation with *east*, *west*, or *north*. The divisions of Tipperary are (and those of Lincolnshire formerly were) also called ridings. *Cp.* LATHE; RAPE.

Riding the marches. *See* BOUNDS, BEATING THE.

To ride abroad with St. George, but at home with St. Michael. Said of a henpecked braggart. St. GEORGE is represented as riding on a war charger; St. MICHAEL on a DRAGON. Away a man rides, like St. George, on a horse which he can control and govern; but at home he has "a dragon" to manage, like St. Michael.

To ride and tie. Said of a couple of travellers with only one horse between them. One rides on ahead and then ties the horse up and walks on, the other takes his turn on the horse when he has reached it.

To ride backwards up Holborn Hill. *See under* HOLBORN.

To ride bodkin. *See under* BODKIN.

To ride for a fall. To proceed with one's business recklessly, usually regardless of the consequences; almost to invite trouble by thoughtless or reckless actions.

To ride in the marrow-bone coach. *See under* MARROW.

To ride roughshod. *See under* ROUGH.

To take for a ride. "To take for a trot", to pull someone's leg; to make the butt of a joke; but it has also become a gangster EUPHEMISM for murder. The victim is induced or forced into a vehicle and murdered in the course of the ride. Such methods were used by the NAZI régime in Germany.

Rider of the Shires, The. William Cobbett (1762–1835), the warm-hearted countryman and radical journalist, has been so designated. His journeys on horseback through many of the counties of England are described in his *Rural Rides*, which were written after days in the saddle.

> I saw great Cobbett riding,
> The horseman of the shires;
> And his face was red with judgment
> And a light of Luddite fires.
> ....
> A trailing meteor on the Downs he rides above the rotting towns,
> The Horseman of Apocalypse, the Rider of the Shires.
> G. K. CHESTERTON: *The Old Song.*

Ridgeback. A native-born Rhodesian of white stock; probably from the native ridge-backed hunting dog, as a Britisher is sometimes similarly termed a "British BULLDOG". *See* RHODESIA.

Ridiculous. There is but one step from the sublime to the ridiculous. In his *Age of Reason* (1794), Pt. II, *note*, Tom Paine said, "The sublime and the ridiculous are often so nearly related that it is difficult to class them separately. One step above the sublime makes the ridiculous, and one step above the ridiculous makes the sublime again."

NAPOLEON, who was a great admirer of Tom Paine, used to say, "*Du sublime au ridicule il n'y a qu'un pas.*"

Ridotto (Ital.). A social assembly; a gathering for music and dancing (*cp.* Fr. *redoute*). In music, "reduced" from the full score, *i.e.* arranged for a smaller group of performers. It is ultimately from Lat. *reducere*, to bring back, reduce.

Riff-Raff. Sweepings, refuse; the offscourings of society, the rabble. The old French term was *rif et raf*, whence the phrase *Il n'a laissé ni rif ni raf* (he has left nothing behind him). "Raff" may be Swed. *rafs*, sweepings, rubbish, etc.

Rift in the lute. A rift is a split or crack, hence a defect betokening the beginning of disharmony or incipient dissension.

> Unfaith in aught is want of faith in all,
> It is the little rift within the lute
> That by-and-by will make the music mute,
> And ever widening slowly silence all.
> TENNYSON: *Merlin and Vivien*, l.387.

Rig. There is more than one word *rig* but their etymology and division are not clear-cut. In the sense of dressing, it was originally applied to a ship which is said to be *well-rigged*, *fully-rigged*, etc. The ropes, stays, shrouds, braces, halyards, etc., used to stay its masts and work the sails are its *rigging*; also the cordage, masts and sails as a whole. Hence, **a good rig-out,** first-rate outfit in clothes, equipment, etc.

In the U.S.A. before the days of the motor-car a *rig* was a carriage or private conveyance.

The word was also formerly used of a strumpet, and a lewd woman was said to be *riggish*.

Also, a hoax or dodge; hence a swindle, and the phrase **to rig the market,** to arrange prices by underhand methods in order to make a profit.

To run the rig. To have a bit of fun, or indulge in practical jokes.

> He little thought when he set out
> Of running such a rig.
> COWPER: *John Gilpin.*

Rigadoon. A lively dance for two people, said to have been invented towards the close of the 17th century by a dancing-master of Marseilles called Rigaud.

> Dance she would, not in such court-like measures as she had learned abroad, but some highplaced jig, or hopskip rigadoon, befitting the brisk lasses at a rustic merrymaking.
> HAWTHORNE: *Seven Gables*, xiii.

Right. In politics the right is the CONSERVATIVE side. *See* LEFT.

Petition of Right (1628). A document presented by PARLIAMENT to CHARLES I which eventually gained his assent. It forbade the raising of gifts, loans, BENEVOLENCES and taxes without parliamentary consent and forbade arbitrary imprisonment, compulsory billeting of soldiers and sailors and the issue of commissions of martial law.

In one's right mind. Sane; in a normal state after mental excitement. The phrase comes from *Mark* v, 15:

> And they ... see him that was possessed with the devil, and had the legion, sitting and clothed, and in his right mind.

It'll all come right in the end. The cry of the optimist when things go wrong.

Miner's right. The Australian term for a licence to dig for GOLD.

Right as a trivet. Quite right; in an excellent state. The trivet was originally a three-legged stand—a tripod—and the allusion is to it standing firmly on its three legs.

Right foot foremost. It is considered un-lucky to enter a house, or even a room, on the left foot, and in ancient ROME a boy was stationed at the door of a wealthy man's home to caution visitors not to cross the threshold with the left foot.

Right-hand man. An invaluable or chief assistant, as indispensable as one's right hand. A very old expression.

Right Honourable. *See under* HONOURABLE.

Right now. At this very moment. Immediately.

Righto! or Right ho! All right, a colloquial form of cheerful assent; *right you are* is a similar exclamation.

Right of way. The right of passing through the land of another. A highway is a public right. A private right is either customary or an easement (a legal right for the benefit of an adjoining owner). Rights of way may be for special purposes as an agricultural way, a way to church, a footway, a carriage way, etc.

To do one right. To be perfectly fair to him, to do him justice.

> King Charles, and who'll do him right now?
> BROWNING: *Cavalier Tunes*, II (*Give a Rouse*).

In Elizabethan literature the phrase is very common, and meant to answer when one's health had been drunk.

> *Falstaff* [To *Silence*, who drinks a bumper]: Why, now you have done me right.
> SHAKESPEARE: *Henry IV, Pt. II*, V, iii.

To send one to the right about. To clear him off, send him packing.

Rights. Declaration of Rights. An instrument submitted to William and Mary, after the GLORIOUS REVOLUTION, and accepted by them (13 February 1689). It sought to remove the specific grievances which arose from the arbitrary acts of James II such as the use of the dispensing and suspending power, the maintenance of a standing army in time of peace, taxation without parliamentary consent, freedom of elections, etc. The Declaration, together with a settlement of the succession, etc., was passed into law (October) as the **Bill of Rights.** It emphasized the importance of PARLIAMENT in the constitution which no king subsequently dared to question. *See also* RIGHTS OF MAN.

The Rights of Man. According to political philosophers of the 17th and 18th centuries, certain inalienable human rights—as stated by Locke—the right to life, liberty, and property. The social contract theorists also included the right to resistance from tyranny. Such rights were formally embodied in the French DECLARATION OF THE RIGHTS OF MAN and a *Declaration of Rights* was drawn up by the First American Continental Congress in 1774. The American Declaration of Independence, 1776, says:

We hold these truths to be self-evident, that all men are created equal, that they are endowed by their Creator with certain inalienable Rights, that among these are Life, Liberty, and the pursuit of happiness.

Mazzini, the Italian republican idealist, preached a less popular doctrine:

But I know, and you who are good and unspoiled by false doctrine and riches will understand before long, that every *right* you have can only spring from a *duty* fulfilled.
The Duties of Man (*To the Italian Working Class*).

Declaration of the Rights of Man. A manifesto of the French National Assembly (August 1789) embodying the "principles" of the revolution. Thus, all citizens are born equal and are equal in the eyes of the law, with rights of liberty, property, and security, and the right to resist tyranny; the nation is sovereign and laws are the expression of the general will; every citizen has the right to freedom of opinion, speech, writing, etc. These rights were not, of course, honoured in practice, as the REIGN OF TERROR was to make manifest.

Universal Declaration of Human Rights. A document adopted by the General Assembly of the UNITED NATIONS in 1948 setting forth basic rights and fundamental freedoms to which all are entitled. They include the right to life, liberty, freedom from servitude, fair trial, marriage, ownership of property, freedom of thought and conscience, freedom of expression; the right to vote, work, education, etc.

To put things to rights. To tidy up, to put everything in its proper place.

Rigmarie (rig ma′ rē). An old Scottish coin of low value. The word originated from one of the "billon" coins struck in the reign of Queen Mary, which bore the words *Reg. Maria* as part of the legend.

Billon is mixed metal for coinage, especially silver largely alloyed with copper.

Rigmarole (rig′ mȧ rōl). A rambling disconnected account, an unending yarn; said to be a popular corruption of RAGMAN ROLL. It is recorded from the early 18th century.

You never heard such a rigmarole ... He said he thought he was certain he had seen somebody by the rick and it was Tom Bakewell who was the only man he knew who had a grudge against Farmer Blaize and if the object had been a little bigger he would not mind swearing to Tom and would swear to him for he was dead certain it was Tom only what he saw looked smaller and it was pitch dark at the time ... etc.

MEREDITH: *Richard Feverel*, ch. ix.

Rig-veda. *See* VEDAS.

Rile. A dialect word, common in Norfolk and other parts, for stirring up water to make it muddy; hence, to excite or disturb, and hence the colloquial meaning, to vex, annoy, make angry. It comes from O.Fr. *roillier*, to roll or flow (of a stream).

Rimmon. The Babylonian god who presided over storms. Milton identifies him with one of the fallen angels:

Him followed Rimmon, whose delightful seat
Was fair Damascus, on the fertile bank
Of Abbana and Pharphar, lucid streams.
Paradise Lost, Bk. I, 467.

To bow down in the house of Rimmon. To palter with one's conscience; to do that which one knows to be wrong so as to save one's face. The allusion is to Naaman obtaining Elisha's permission to worship the god when with his master (II *Kings* v, 18).

Rinaldo. One of the great heroes of mediæval romance (also called Renault of Montauban, Regnault, etc.), a PALADIN of CHARLEMAGNE, cousin of ORLANDO, and one of the four sons of AYMON. He was the owner of the famous horse BAYARDO, and is always painted with the characteristics of a borderer—valiant, ingenious, rapacious, and unscrupulous.

Tasso's romantic epic *Rinaldo* appeared in 1562 and his masterpiece JERUSALEM DELIVERED, in which Rinaldo was the ACHILLES of the Christian army, despising GOLD and power but craving renown, was published (without permission) in 1581.

In Ariosto's ORLANDO FURIOSO (1516), Rinaldo appears as the son of the fourth Marquis d'Este, Lord of Mount Auban or Albano, eldest son of Amon or Aymon, nephew of Charlemagne. He was the rival of his cousin Orlando.

Ring. The noun (meaning a circlet) is the O.E. *hring*; the verb (to sound a bell, or as a bell) is from O.E. *hringan*, to clash, ring, connected with Lat. *clangere*, to clang.

A ring worn on the forefinger is supposed to indicate a haughty, bold, and overbearing spirit; on the long finger, prudence, dignity and discretion; on the marriage finger, love and affection; on the little finger, a masterful spirit. *Cp.* WEDDING FINGER.

The wearing of a wedding-ring by married women is now universal in Christian countries, but the custom varies greatly in detail. It appears to have originated in the betrothal rings given as secular pledges by the Romans. Until the end of the 16th century it was the custom in England to wear the wedding-ring on the third finger of the right hand.

As the forefinger was held to be symbolical of the HOLY GHOST, priests used to wear their ring on this in token of their spiritual office. Episcopal rings, worn by CARDINALS, BISHOPS and abbots, are of GOLD with a stone—cardinals a sapphire, bishops and abbots an AMETHYST— and are worn upon the third finger of the right hand. The POPE wears a similar ring, usually with a cameo, EMERALD, or RUBY. A plain gold ring is put upon the third finger of the right hand of a nun on her profession.

In ancient ROME, the free Roman had the right to wear an iron ring, only senators, chief magistrates and in later times KNIGHTS (*equites*), enjoyed the *jus annuli aurei*, the right to wear a ring of gold. The emperors conferred this upon whom they pleased and Justinian extended the privilege to all Roman citizens. *See also* CRAMP-RINGS.

Rings noted in Fable and Legend

Agramant's Ring. This enchanted ring was given by Agramant to the dwarf Brunello from whom it was stolen by BRADAMANT and given to Melissa. It passed successively into the hands of ROGERO and ANGELICA, who carried it in her mouth (ORLANDO FURIOSO).

The Ring of Amasis. See AMASIS.

Cambalo's Ring. See CAMBALO.

The Doge's Ring. See BRIDE OF THE SEA.

The Ring of Edward the Confessor. It is said that Edward the Confessor was once asked for alms by an old man, and gave him his ring. In time some English pilgrims went to the HOLY LAND and happened to meet the same old man, who told them he was JOHN THE EVANGELIST, and gave them the identical ring to take to "Saint" Edward. It was preserved in Westminster Abbey.

The Ring of Gyges. See GYGES.

The Ring of Innocent. On 29 May 1205, Innocent III sent John, King of England, four gold rings set with precious stones, and explained that the *rotundity* signifies *eternity*—"remember we are passing through time into eternity"; the *number* signifies the *four* virtues which make up constancy of mind—*viz.* justice, fortitude, prudence, and temperance; the *material* signifies "the wisdom from on high", which is as gold purified in the fire; the *green* emerald is emblem of "faith", the *blue* sapphire of "hope", the *red* garnet of "charity", and the *bright* topaz of "good works" (Rymer: *Fædera*, vol. I, 139).

Luned's Ring rendered the wearer invisible. Luned gave it to Owain, one of King ARTHUR'S knights.

Take this ring and put it on thy finger, and put this stone in thy hand, and close thy fist over the stone; and so long as thou conceal it, it will conceal thee too.

MABINOGION (*Lady of the Fountain*).

The Ring of Ogier was given him by MORGAN LE FAY. It removed all infirmities, and restored the aged to youth again.

Otnit's Ring of Invisibility belonged to Otnit, King of Lombardy, and was given to him by the queen-mother when he went to gain the soldan's daughter in marriage. The stone had the virtue of directing the wearer the right road to take in travelling (the HELDENBUCH).

Polycrates' Ring. See AMASIS.

Reynard's Wonderful Ring. This ring, which existed only in the brain of REYNARD, had a stone of three colours—red, white, and green. The red made the night as clear as day; the white cured all manner of diseases; and the green rendered the wearer invisible (*Reynard the Fox*, ch. xii).

Solomon's Ring enabled the monarch to overcome all opponents, to transport himself to the celestial spheres where he learned the secrets of the universe. It also sealed up the refractory JINN in jars and cast them into the Red Sea, and conferred upon the wearer the ability to understand and converse with the animal world.

The talking ring in Basque legend was given by Tartaro, the Basque CYCLOPS, to a girl whom he wished to marry. Immediately she put it on, it kept incessantly saying, "You there, and I here." In order to get rid of the nuisance, the girl cut off her finger and threw it and the ring into a pond. The story is given in Campbell's *Popular Tales of the West Highlands*, and in Grimm's *Tales* (*The Robber and His Sons*).

Ring a ring o'roses. *See* BLACK DEATH.

Ring of the Fisherman. *See* FISHERMAN'S RING *under* FISH.

Ring of the Nibelung, or **Ring Cycle.** The Festival cycle by Wagner first performed at Bayreuth in 1876. Its constituent parts are *Das Rheingold*, 1869; *Die Walküre*, 1870; *Siegfried*, 1876; *Götterdämmerung* (The Dusk of the Gods), 1876. *Cp.* NIBELUNGENLIED.

Ring posies, or **mottoes.** These were commonly inscribed on the inside of rings in the 16th, 17th and 18th centuries.

(1) AEI (Greek for "Always").
(2) For ever and for aye.
(3) In thee my choice, I do rejoice.
(4) Let love increase.
(5) May God above Increase our love.
(6) Not two but one Till life is gone.
(7) My heart and I, Until I die.
(8) When this you see, Then think of me.
(9) Love is heaven, and heaven is love.

(10) Wedlock, 'tis said In heaven is made.

The Ring. Bookmakers or pugilists collectively, and the sports they represent, because the spectators at a prize-fight or race form a ring around the competitors. Specifically, *The Ring* was the hall for prize-fights in the Blackfriars Road.

In Australia in the early 19th century *The Ring* denoted a group of the most hard-bitten convicts at the Norfolk Island penitentiary, who exercised an EVIL influence over their fellows. This use antedates by some 30 years that of the U.S.A.

Also applied to unscrupulous dealers, as a group, who FORM, or MAKE A RING. Wagner's RING OF THE NIBELUNG is often called *The Ring*.

A ring of bells. A set of bells from 5 to 12 in number for CHANGE ringing.

It has the true ring. It has intrinsic merit; it bears the mark of real talent. A metaphor taken from the custom of judging genuine coin by its "ring" or sound.

Ring off! The expression commonly used to end a telephone conversation or connexion by hanging up or replacing the receiver, as "I must ring off now", "Ring off please", etc.

Ring up. To ring up is to make a telephone call.

To ring up the curtain. In the theatre, to order the curtain to be raised or opened; the signal originally being the ringing of a bell. Metaphorically, to initiate or inaugurate an enterprise, etc. Similarly **to ring down the curtain** is to terminate or bring to an end.

The Ringing island. Britain was once so called from the excellence of its church bell-ringers at CHANGE ringing.

Ringing the changes. *See* CHANGE.

Figuratively the phrase usually means to try many different ways of doing a thing for the sake of variety, but it also means to swindle someone over a transaction by confusing him in the changing of money. For example: a man bought a glass of beer for 1s. 4d. and gave the barmaid a ten-shilling note, receiving 8s. 8d. in change. "Oh!" said the man, "give me the note back, I have such a lot of change". He offered ten shillings in silver when handed the note, but before pocketing it put note and silver together and said: "There, let's have a QUID instead of the note and silver." If the barmaid was not quick enough to spot the trick she lost ten shillings by the deal.

That rings a bell. That recalls something to mind, that stirs a recollection.

To form, or **make a ring.** To act together in order to control the price of a given arti-cle, usually to enhance the price and ensure greater profit. Dealers at auctions sometimes form such a ring and do not outbid each other, thus ensuring articles being knocked down cheaply. After the auction, the dealers' ring then organizes a sale or distribution among its members.

To make rings, or **run rings round one.** To defeat him completely in some sport or competition, etc.; to outclass him easily. In Australia the fastest shearer in the shed is called a *ringer* as he is "the man who runs rings round the rest".

Ringer. A one-ringer, etc. In the Royal Navy and Royal Air Force the rank of an officer is designated by the braided rings worn round the lower part of the sleeve. One ring denotes a Sub-Lieutenant and a Flying Officer; two rings, a Lieutenant and a Flight Lieutenant, etc.; called colloquially a *one-ringer*, *two-ringer*, etc. Warrant officers and pilot officers wear a thin ring, hence the term *half-ringer*. Lieutenant-Commanders and Squadron Leaders wear two rings with a narrow one between them and are thus called *two-and-a-half-ringers*. In the Navy a *four-ringed* Captain denotes one of Captain's rank as opposed to the "Captain" of a ship, who may be of much lower rank.

The term *ringer* is also applied on the racecourse, running-track, etc., to a runner who is entered for a race by means of a false return with regard to the detailed conditions of entry; to a person or thing which closely resembles another: hence, *dead ringer* (U.S.A.), for an exact resemblance.

Ringleader. The moving spirit, the chief in some enterprise, especially of a mutinous character; from the old phrase to *lead the ring*, the *ring* being a group of associated persons.

Riot. To read the Riot Act. Legally, when 12 or more persons are committing a riot it is the duty of the magistrates to command them to disperse in the Queen's name and anyone who obstructs or continues to riot for one hour afterwards is guilty of a felony. Such a proclamation is read in accordance with the Riot Act of 1715. Figuratively to *read the riot act* is to check noise, commotion and misbehaviour of children and others by vigorous and forceful protests, to threaten them with the consequences of disobedience, etc.

To run riot. To act without restraint or control; to act in a very disorderly way. The phrase was originally used of hounds which had lost the scent.

Rip. A regular rip. A thorough roisterer, rake, or debauchee; rip seems to be a perversion of *rep*, rep-robate. *Cp.* DEMI-REP.

> Some forlorn, worn-out old rips, broken-kneed and broken-winded.
>
> GEORGE DU MAURIER: *Peter Ibbetson*, Pt. VI.

Let her rip. Let it (an engine, etc.) go as fast as it can.

Rip Van Winkle. The famous character whose fabled adventures are recounted in Washington Irving's *Sketch Book* (1819). The tale is represented as being found among the papers of one Diedrich Knickerbocker, a Dutch antiquary of New York. Rip Van Winkle was a happy-go-lucky, hen-pecked husband of a "well-oiled" disposition. During a ramble on the Kaatskill Mountains he met some quaint personages dressed in the old Flemish style playing at ninepins. Unobserved he took a draught of their Hollands and soon fell asleep. He awoke to find himself alone, even his dog had disappeared and his firearm was heavy with rust. He made his way homewards in trepidation only to find his house deserted and none of his former companions about. He had apparently slept for 20 years and after establishing his identity became a village patriarch. He had set out as a subject of George III and returned as a free citizen of the United States!

Ripon. True as Ripon steel. Ripon, Yorkshire, used to be famous for its steel spurs, which were the best in the world. The spikes of a Ripon spur would strike through a SHILLING piece without turning the point.

Rise. On the rise. Going up in price; becoming more valuable, especially of stocks and shares.

To get a rise. To have an increase in salary or wages.

To take the rise out of one. To raise a laugh at his expense, to make him a butt. Hotten says this is a metaphor from fly-fishing; the fish *rise* to the fly, and are caught. In the U.S.A. a pay increase is called a *raise*, and to *get a raise* out of someone is to call forth the desired reaction or response.

Rising in the air. *See* LEVITATION.

Risorgimento (ri sôr ji men′ tō) (Ital., resurrection). The name given to the 19th-century movement for Italian liberation. It can be said to have had its roots in the enlightened despotism of the 18th century and the influence of the French Revolution and French occupation. The CARBONARI in Naples and Sicily, the *Federati* in Sardinia, and Mazzini's YOUNG ITALY all played a part, and the *Risorgimento* was strengthened by the revolutionary events of 1848–1849. Its political aims were largely achieved by

Cavour in the events of 1859–1860 and Garibaldi's radicalism made a further contribution, but the idealism of the *Risorgimento* was submerged by Cavour's realistic policies.

Ritzy. In colloquial usage, fashionable and luxurious. After the standards of the Ritz-Carlton Hotel, New York, the Ritz Hotel, Paris, and the Ritz Hotel, Piccadilly, London, which became identified with wealth. The latter hotel was established by the Swiss hotelier, César Ritz, in 1906. Hence "to dine at the Ritz" is the ultimate luxury in dining out.

Rivals. Originally "persons dwelling on opposite sides of a river" (Lat. *rivalis*, a riverman). Cælius says there was no more fruitful source of contention than river-right, both with beasts and men, not only for the benefit of its waters, but also because rivers are natural boundaries.

River. To be sent up the river. In American colloquial usage, to be sent to prison; from the fact that Sing Sing, one of the most widely known prisons, is up the Hudson River from New York.

To sell down the river. To let down, to betray. From the days when American owners sold domestic slaves to plantation owners lower down the Mississippi, where harsh conditions often prevailed.

Roach. Sound as a roach. An old saying; a translation of the French *Sain comme un gardon*.

To roach is to trim a horse's mane to within an inch or so of the hide. The word is also applied in this sense to a style of cutting a man's hair, the same as TO HOG (*see under* HOG).

Road, The. The name by which CHARING CROSS Road, in its heyday as the centre of the second-hand book trade in London, was known to booksellers and bibliophiles.

All roads lead to Rome. All efforts of thought converge in a common centre. As from the centre of the Roman world roads radiated to every part of the Empire, so any road, if followed to its source, must lead to the great capital city, ROME.

Gentlemen of the road, or **knights of the road.** Highwaymen. In parts of North America a highwayman was called a *road agent* and the term is still sometimes applied to bandits who hold up trains, motorcars, etc.

One for the road. One last drink before departing, a popular call at the end of a night ON THE SPREE.

On the road. Progressing towards; as, "on the road to recovery"; said also of actors on tour and of commercial travellers.

Road hog. *See* HOG.

Roman roads. *See under* ROMAN.

The rule of the road.

> The rule of the road is a paradox quite,
> In riding or driving along;
> If you go to the left you are sure to go right,
> If you go to the right you go wrong.

This is still the rule in Great Britain, and IRELAND. In all other European countries and in the U.S.A. traffic keeps to the right.

To take to the road. To become a highwayman or a tramp.

Roadhouse. An inn, hotel, etc., by the roadside, usually at some distance outside a town, where parties can go out by car for meals, dancing, etc.

Roads or **Roadstead,** as "Yarmouth Roads", a place where ships can safely ride at anchor. *Road*, O.E. *rad*, comes from *ridan*, to ride.

Roan Barbary. *See* BARBARY ROAN.

Roar. Roarer. A broken-winded horse is so called from the noise it makes in breathing.

Bull-roarer. *See under* BULL.

He drives a roaring trade. He does a great business.

Roaring boys. The riotous blades of Ben Jonson's time, whose delight it was to annoy quiet folk. At one time their pranks in London were carried on to an alarming extent.

> A very unthrift, master Thorney; one of the Country roaring lads, we have such as well as the city, and as arrant rakehells as they are, though not so nimble at their prizes of wit.
> FORD and DEKKER: *Witch of Edmonton*, I, ii.

Dekker and Middleton wrote a play (1611) on Moll Cutpurse (*see under* CUTPURSE), which they called *The Roaring Girl*. *Cp.* MOHAWK; MODS AND ROCKERS.

The Roaring Forties. *See under* FORTY.

The roaring game. Curling, so called because the Scots when playing or watching support their side with noisy cheering, and because the stones (made of granite or whinstone and shaped like a Dutch cheese) roar as they traverse the ice.

Roaring Meg. *See under* MEG.

Roast. To roast a person is to banter him unmercifully; also to give him a dressing-down.

To rule the roast. To have the chief direction, to be paramount. The phrase was common in the 16th century apparently deriving from the master of the household, as head of the table, carving the joint. It has been suggested that the expression is really *to rule the roost* (the common form nowadays) from the cock deciding which hen is to roost near him; but "roost" is more likely a corruption of "roast", the old spelling for which was "rost", or "roste". In Thomas Heywood's *History of Women* (*c*.1630) we read of "her that ruled the roast in the kitchen". *Cp.* TROUSERS.

> Suffolk, the new-made duke that rules the roast.
> SHAKESPEARE: *Henry VI, Pt. II*, I, i.
> Ah, I do domineer, and rule the roast.
> CHAPMAN: *Gentleman Usher*, V, i (1606).

Rob. To rob Peter to pay Paul. To take away from one person in order to give to another; or merely to shift a debt—to pay it off by incurring another one. Fable has it that the phrase alludes to the fact that on 17 December 1540 the abbey church of St. Peter, Westminster, was advanced to the dignity of a cathedral by LETTERS PATENT (*see under* PATENT); but ten years later was joined to the diocese of London, and many of its estates appropriated to the repairs of St. Paul's Cathedral. But it was a common saying long before and was used by Wyclif about 1380:

> How should God approve that you rob Peter, and give this robbery to Paul in the name of Christ.
> *Select Works*, III, 174.

The hint of the President Viglius to the Duke of Alva when he was seeking to impose ruinous taxation in the Netherlands (1569) was that:

> It was not desirable to rob Saint Peter's altar in order to build one to St. Paul.
> MOTLEY: *The Rise of the Dutch Republic*, Pt. III, ch. V.

Rob Roy (Robert the Red). Nickname of Robert M'Gregor (1671–1734), Scottish outlaw and FREEBOOTER, on account of his red hair. He assumed the name of Campbell about 1716, and was protected by the Duke of Argyll. He may be termed the ROBIN HOOD of Scotland.

> Rather beneath the middle size than above it, his limbs were formed upon the very strongest model that is consistent with agility ... Two points in his person interfered with the rules of symmetry:—his shoulders were so broad ... as ... gave him something the air of being too square in respect to his stature; and his arms, tough, round, sinewy, and strong, were so very long as to be rather a deformity.
> SCOTT: *Rob Roy*, ch. xxiii.

Robert. A name sometimes applied to a policeman, "the man in blue", in allusion to Sir Robert Peel. *Cp.* BOBBY; PEELER.

Highwaymen and bandits are called *Robert's men* from ROBIN HOOD.

King Robert of Sicily. A metrical romance taken from the *Story of the Emperor Jovinian* in the GESTA ROMANORUM, and borrowed from the TALMUD. It is also found in the ARABIAN NIGHTS, the Turkish *Tutinameh*, the Sanskrit *Panchatantra*, and was utilized by Longfellow in his *Tales of a Way-*

side Inn.

Robert the Devil, or **Le Diable.** Robert, sixth Duke of Normandy (1028–1035), father of WILLIAM THE CONQUEROR. He supported the English athelings against Canute, and made the PILGRIMAGE TO JERUSALEM. He got his name for his daring and cruelty. He is also called *Robert the Magnificent*. A Norman tradition is that his wandering ghost will not be allowed to rest till the Day of Judgment (*see* JUDGMENT, THE LAST) and he became a subject of legend and romance. Meyerbeer's opera *Roberto il Diavolo* (1831) portrays the struggle between the virtue inherited from his mother and the vice imparted by his father.

Robert François DAMIENS (1715–1757), who attempted to assassinate Louis XV, was also called "Robert le Diable".

Robin. A diminutive of Robert.

Ragged Robin. *See under* RAG.

Robin Goodfellow. Another name for PUCK. His character and activities are given fully in the ballad of this name in PERCY'S RELIQUES, as exemplified in the following verse:

When house or harth doth sluttish lye,
I pinch the maidens black and blue;
The bed-clothes from the bedd pull I,
And lay them naked all to view.
'Twixt sleepe and wake,
I do them take,
And on the key-cold floor them throw.
If out they cry
Then forth I fly,
And loudly laugh out, ho, ho, ho!

Robin Gray, Auld. Words by Lady Anne Lindsay, daughter of the Earl of Balcarres, and afterwards Lady Barnard, written (1771) to an old Scotch tune called "The bridegroom grat when the sun gaed down". Auld Robin Gray was the herdsman of her father. When Lady Anne had written a part, she called her younger sister for advice. She said, "I am writing a ballad of virtuous distress in humble life. I have oppressed my heroine with sundry troubles: for example, I have sent her Jamie to sea, broken her father's arm, made her mother sick, given her Auld Robin Gray for a lover, and want a fifth sorrow; can you help me to one?" "Steal the cow, sister Anne," said the little Elizabeth; so the cow was stolen awa', and the song completed. Lady Anne later wrote a sequel in which Auld Robin Gray died, Jeannie married Jamie and all turned to a happy ending.

Robin Hood. This traditional outlaw and hero of English ballads is mentioned by Langland in the *Vision of Piers Plowman*, Bk. V, 402 (1377), and there are several mid-15th-century poems about him. The first published collection of ballads about him, *A Lytell Geste of Robyn Hode* was printed by Wynkyn de Worde (*c.* 1489). The earliest tales were set in Barnsdale, Yorkshire, or in Sherwood Forest, Nottinghamshire, and his adventures have been variously assigned from the reign of Richard I (1189–1199) to that of Edward II (1307–1327). One popular legend was that he was the outlawed Earl of Huntingdon, Robert Fitzooth, in disguise. The name may have been that of an actual outlaw around whose name the legends accumulated. He suffered no woman to be molested and he is credited with robbing the rich and helping the poor.

Robin's earlier companions included LITTLE JOHN, Will Scarlet, MUCH, the miller's son, Allen-a-dale, George-a-Green (*see* AS GOOD AS GEORGE-A-GREEN *under* GEORGE), and later FRIAR TUCK and MAID MARIAN.

The stories formed the basis of early dramatic representations and were later amalgamated with the MORRIS dancers' MAY-DAY revels. *Cp.* TWM SHON CATTI.

Robyn was a proude outlawe,
Whyles he walked on grounde,
So curteyse an outlawe as he was one
Was never none yfounde.
A Lytell Geste of Robyn Hode, I.

Bow and arrow of Robin Hood. The traditional bow and arrow of Robin Hood are religiously preserved at Kirklees Hall, Yorkshire, the seat of the Armytage family; and the site of his grave is pointed out in the park.

Death of Robin Hood. He was reputedly bled to death treacherously by a nun, instigated to the foul deed by his kinswoman, the prioress of Kirklees, near Halifax (1247).

Many talk of Robin Hood who never shot with his bow. Many brag of deeds in which they took no part.

Robin Hood and Guy of Gisborne. A ballad given in PERCY'S RELIQUES. ROBIN HOOD and LITTLE JOHN, having had a tiff, part company, when Little John falls into the hands of the SHERIFF of Nottingham, who binds him to a tree. Meanwhile Robin Hood meets with Guy of Gisborne, sworn to slay the "bold forrester". The two bowmen struggle together, but Guy is slain and Robin Hood rides till he comes to the tree where Little John is bound. The sheriff mistakes him for Guy of Gisborne, and gives him charge of the prisoner. Robin cuts the cord, hands Guy's bow to Little John, and the two soon put to flight the sheriff and his men.

A Robin Hood wind. A thaw-wind which is particularly raw and piercing being saturated with moisture scarcely above freezing-point. Tradition runs that ROBIN HOOD used to say he could bear any cold except that which a thaw-wind brought with it.

Robin Hood's Bay, between Whitby and Scarborough, Yorkshire, is mentioned by Leland. Robin Hood is supposed to have kept fishing boats there to put to sea when pursued by the soldiery. He also went fishing in them in the summer.

Robin Hood's Larder. *See under* OAK.

To go round Robin Hood's barn. To arrive at the right conclusion by circuitous methods.

To sell Robin Hood's pennyworth is to sell things at half their value. As Robin Hood stole his wares he sold them under their intrinsic value, for what he could get.

Robin Redbreast. The tradition is that when Our Lord was on His way to CALVARY, a robin picked a thorn out of His crown, and the blood which issued from the wound falling on the bird dyed its breast red.

Another fable is that the robin covers the dead with leaves; this is referred to in Webster's *White Devil*, V, i (1612):

Call for the robin-red-breast and the wren,
Since o'er shady groves they hover,
And with leaves and flowers do cover
The friendless bodies of unburied men.

When so covering Christ's body, their white breasts touched his blood and they have ever since been red.

And in the ballad of the *Children in the Wood* (PERCY'S RELIQUES):

No burial this pretty pair
Of any man receives,
Till Robin-red-breast piously
Did cover them with leaves.

Cp. RUDDOCK.

Robin Redbreasts. *See* REDBREASTS.

Robin and Makyne. An ancient Scottish pastoral given in PERCY'S RELIQUES. Robin is a shepherd for whom Makyne sighs. She goes to him and tells her love, but Robin turns a deaf ear, and the damsel goes home to weep. After a time the tables are turned, and Robin goes to Makyne to plead for her heart and hand; but the damsel replies:

The man that will not when he may,
Sall have nocht when he wald.

A round robin. *See under* ROUND.

Poor Robin's Almanack. *See under* POOR.

Robinson Crusoe. The ever-popular castaway of Defoe's novel of this name (1719) was suggested by the adventures of Alexander SELKIRK. Crusoe's Island was not Juan Fernandez in the South Pacific where Sel-kirk was put ashore, but an imaginary island near Trinidad; Defoe's description most nearly fits Tobago.

Robinson, Before you can say Jack. *See under* JACK.

Robot (rō′ bot) (Czech *robota*, forced labour). An automaton with semi-human powers and intelligence. From this the term is often extended to mean a person who works automatically without employing initiative. The name comes from the mechanical creatures in Karel Capek's play *R.U.R.* (Rossum's Universal Robots), which was successfully produced in London in 1923. The word was also applied to various forms of "flying bombs", "Buzz-bombs" or "Doodle-bugs" sent against England by the Germans in World War II.

Roc. In Arabian legend, a fabulous white bird of enormous size and such strength that it can "truss elephants in its talons", and carry them to its mountain nest, where it devours them. It is described in the ARABIAN NIGHTS (SINBAD THE SAILOR).

Roch, or **Roque, St.** (rōsh, rōk). Patron of those afflicted with the plague, because "he worked miracles on the plague-stricken, while he was himself smitten with the same judgment". He is depicted in a pilgrim's habit, lifting his dress, to display a plague-spot on his thigh, which an ANGEL is touching that he may cure it. Sometimes he is accompanied by a DOG bringing bread in his mouth, in allusion to the legend that a hound brought him bread daily while he was perishing of pestilence in a forest.

His feast day, 16 August, was formerly celebrated in England as a general HARVEST-HOME, and styled "the great August festival".

St. Roch et son chien (Fr., St. Roch and his dog). Inseparables; DARBY AND JOAN.

Rochdale Pioneers, The. The name given to the sponsors of the first financially successful co-operative store. In December 1844, a group of 28 weavers calling themselves the Equitable Pioneers opened their store in Toad Lane, Rochdale, Lancashire, with a capital of £28. They sold their wares at market prices and gave a dividend to purchasers in proportion to their expenditure. It was on this device that the co-operative movement grew.

Roche (rōsh). **Sir Boyle Roche's bird.** Sir Boyle Roche (1743–1807) was an Irish M.P., noted for his "BULLS". On one occasion in the House, quoting from Jevon's play, *The Devil of a Wife*, he said, "Mr. Speaker, it is impossible I could have been in two places at once, unless I were a bird."

The phrase is probably of earlier origin.

Rochelle Salt. Seidlitz powder, a tartrate of sodium or potassium, so called because it was discovered by an apothecary of La Rochelle, named Seignette, in 1672. In France it is called *sel de Seignette* or *sel des tombeaux*.

Rock. A symbol of solidity and strength.

> Thou art Peter, and upon this rock I will build my church; and the gates of hell shall not prevail against it.
>
> *Matt*. xvi. 18.

It is the Lat. *petra*, rock, from which the name Peter is derived. *Cp.* ROCK OF AGES, below.

Gibraltar is commonly known as "The Rock"(*see* ROCK ENGLISH *below*).

Alcatraz Island in San Francisco Bay, the site of the former American prison for the most dangerous criminals, consists of 12 acres of solid rock and became known as "The Rock". It is now part of a recreation area.

In U.S.A. thieves' slang a *rock* is a diamond or other precious stone. *See also* ROCK DAY; ROCK 'N' ROLL.

A house builded upon rock. Typical of a person or a thing whose foundations are sure. The allusion is to *Matt*. vii, 24.

The Ladies' Rock. A crag under the castle rock of Stirling, where ladies used to witness tournaments.

On the rocks. "Stony broke", having no money; a phrase from seafaring: a ship that is on the rocks will very quickly go to pieces unless she can be floated off.

People of the Rock. The inhabitants of Hejaz of ARABIA Petræa.

Rock Day. "St. Distaff's Day" (*see under* DISTAFF); *Cp.* PLOUGH MONDAY.

Rock Dove. The London Pigeon is a semi-domesticated Rock Dove. The wild *rock* is confined to cliffs, hence the name. It can be distinguished from the STOCK DOVE in that it has no black wing tips.

Rock English. The mixed patois of Spanish and English spoken by the native inhabitants of Gibraltar—colloquially referred to as *Rock Lizards* or ROCK SCORPIONS. Similarly, Malta or Mediterranean fever, which is common in Gibraltar, is also called *Rock fever*.

Rock of Ages. Christ, as the unshakeable and eternal foundation. In a marginal note to *Is*. xxvi, 4, the words "everlasting strength" are stated to be in Hebrew "rock of ages". In one of his hymns Wesley wrote (1788)—

> Hell in vain against us rages;
> Can it shock

> Christ the Rock
> Of eternal Ages?
>
> *Praise by all to Christ is given.*

Southey also has:

> These waters are the well of life and lo!
> The Rock of Ages, there, from whence they flow.
>
> *Pilgrimage to Waterloo*, Pt. II, iii.

The well-known hymn *Rock of ages, cleft for me*, was written by Augustus Montague TOPLADY (1740–1778) and first published in *The Gospel Magazine* (1775). One account says that he wrote it while seated by a great cleft of rock near Cheddar, Somerset; a more unlikely story is that the first verse was written on the ten of diamonds in the interval between two rubbers of WHIST at Bath.

Rock Scorpion. A colloquial name for a Gibraltarian. Gibraltar is commonly known as "the Rock". *See* GARLIC WALL.

It's like the Rock of Gibraltar. Said of something that is firmly fixed, solid and immovable; also sometimes applied to food that is hard and tough.

That is the rock you'll split on. That is the danger, or the more or less hidden or eventual difficulty. A phrase of nautical origin.

To rock the boat. To unsettle the stability of a situation; to create difficulties for one's associates, companions or partners.

Rock 'n' roll (Rock and Roll), or just *Rock*, was the "pop" music of the latter half of the 1950s, characterized by its swing or rhythm and the style of dancing that went with it. Its fans were called "rockers" and they belonged to the days of the *teddy boy* (*see* EDWARDIAN), before the advent of the Mods. *Cp.* MODS AND ROCKERS.

Rocking Stones. *See* LOGAN STONES.

Rocket. To give someone a rocket. To reprimand severely, "to blow him sky high".

Rococo (rō kō' kō). A style in the fine and decorative arts, particularly characterized by motifs taken from shells, which developed in 18th-century France and spread to Germany, Austria and Spain. The name is from Fr. *rocaille*, rockwork, grotto work, as exemplified in the extravagances at VERSAILLES. At its best it was a lighter and more graceful development from Baroque as is seen in the furniture and architecture of France during the reign of Louis XV (1715–1774). At its worst, it was florid and ornate, hence the use of the word *rococo* to denote anything in art and literature that is pretentious and tasteless.

Rod. A rod in pickle. A scolding or punishment in store. Birch-rods used to be laid in brine to keep the twigs pliable.

... and therefore let everyone carry an even hand, and mind their hits, or else I would have them to know there are rods in pickle for them.

CERVANTES: *Don Quixote*, ch. lxxi (Translation by Motteux).

Spare the rod and spoil the child. An old saying drawing attention to the folly of allowing childish faults to go unreproved; founded on *Prov.* xiii, 24, "He that spareth his rod hateth his son; but he that loveth him chasteneth him betimes."

To kiss the rod. To submit to punishment or misfortune meekly and without murmuring.

To make a rod for one's own back. Doing something which will lead to trouble, difficulties or hardship for oneself in the future.

Rodeo (rō' di ō, *or* rō dā' ō) (Span. *rodear*, to go around). A contest or exhibition of skill among COWBOYS, a feature of the ROUND-UP. As a travelling show it was first introduced by BUFFALO BILL and depends for its popularity upon professional skill with the lasso, the riding of broncos and steers, etc.

Roderick, or **Rodrigo.** A Spanish hero round whom many legends have collected. He was the last of the Visigothic kings. He came to the throne in 710, and was routed, and probably slain, by the Moors under Tarik in 711. Southey took him as the hero of his *Roderick, the last of the Goths* (1814), where he appears as the son of Theodofred.

According to legend he violated Florinda, daughter of Count Julian of Ceuta, who called in the SARACENS by way of revenge. It is related that he survived to spend the rest of his life in penance and was eventually devoured by snakes until his sin was atoned for. It was also held that he would return in triumph to save his country.

Rodomontade. Bluster, brag, or a blustering and bragging speech; from Rodomont, the brave but braggart leader of the SARACENS in Boiardo's ORLANDO INNAMORATO and Ariosto's ORLANDO FURIOSO.

Rodrigo. *See* RODERICK.

Roe, Richard. *See* DOE.

Rogation Days. Rogation Sunday is the SUNDAY before ASCENSION DAY, the Rogation days are the Monday, Tuesday, and Wednesday following Rogation Sunday. Rogation is the Latin equivalent of the Greek *litaneia*, supplication or litany (Lat. *rogatio*), and in the ROMAN CATHOLIC CHURCH on the three Rogation days "the Litany of the Saints" is appointed to be sung by the clergy and people in public procession.

The Rogation Days used to be called *Gang Days*, from the custom of *ganging* round the country parishes to beat the BOUNDS at this time. Similarly the weed milkwort is called *Rogation* or *Gangflower* from the custom of decorating the pole carried on such occasions with these flowers.

Roger. The Jolly Roger. The black flag with skull and cross-bones, the pirate flag.

Sir Roger de Coverley. The simple, good, and lovable country squire created by Steele as the chief character in the club that was supposed to write for the *Spectator*, but essentially portrayed by Addison. Sir Roger de Coverley has left his name to a popular country dance which, he tells us, was invented by his great-grandfather. Coverley is intended for Cowley, near Oxford.

As Sir Roger is landlord to the whole congregation, he keeps them in very good order, and will suffer no body to sleep in it besides himself.

ADDISON: *A Sunday in the Country*.

Rogero, Ruggiero, or **Rizieri** (ro jâr' ō, ruj-âr' o, ritz i âr' i) of Risa (in Ariosto's ORLANDO FURIOSO), was brother of Marphisa, and son of Rogero and Galacella. His mother was slain by Agolant and his sons, and he was nursed by a lioness. He deserted from the Moorish army to CHARLEMAGNE, and was baptized. His marriage with BRADAMANTE, Charlemagne's niece, and election to the crown of Bulgaria conclude the poem.

Rogers' Rangers. A body of daring American frontiersmen raised by Major Robert Rogers to fight with the British troops during the French and Indian war of 1756–1763. They took possession of Detroit and other posts. During the War of Independence, the uncertainty of Rogers's allegiance led to his rejection by both sides and his undoubted abilities were wasted. He died at London in drunken obscurity (1795).

Rogue. One of the "canting" words first used in the 16th century to describe sturdy beggars and vagrants (perhaps from some outstanding member of the class named Roger). There is a good description of them in Harman's *Caveat for Warening for Commen Corsetors, Vulgarely called Vagabones*, ch. iv. The expression *rogues and vagabonds* has since 1572 been applied in the Vagrancy Acts to all sorts of wandering, disorderly, or dissolute persons.

Rogue elephant. A vicious dangerous elephant that lives apart from the herd.

Rogue in grain. A Knave in the GRAIN.

Rogue's badge. A race-horse or a hunter that becomes obstinate and refuses to do its work is known as a *rogue*, and the blinkers that it is made to wear are the *rogue's badge*.

Rogue's Latin. The same as thieves' Latin. *See under* LATIN.

Rogue's March. The tune played when an

undesirable soldier was drummed out of his regiment; hence, an ignominious dismissal.

Rogue's yarn. The name given to the coloured strand forming part of a government rope inserted to deter thieves. In the former main dockyard roperies *yellow* denoted Chatham cordage, *blue* Portsmouth, and *red* Devonport. *Cp.* BROAD ARROW.

Roi Panade (Fr., King of Slops). Louis XVIII (1755, 1814–1824) was so nicknamed. Literally, panade is bread soup.

Roland, or (in Ital.) **Orlando.** The most famous of Charlemagne's PALADINS, called "the Christian THESEUS" and "the ACHILLES of the West". He was Count of Mans and knight of Blaives, and son of Duke Milo of Aiglant, his mother being Bertha, the sister of CHARLEMAGNE. Fable has it that he was eight feet high, and had an open countenance which invited confidence, but inspired respect. When Charlemagne was returning from his expedition against Pamplona and Saragossa the army fell into a natural trap at Roncesvalles, in the Pyrenees, and Roland, who commanded the rearguard, was slain with all the flower of the Frankish CHIVALRY (778).

His achievements are recorded in the Chronicle attributed to Turpin (d. 794), Archbishop of Rheims, which was not written till the 11th or 12th century. He is the hero of the SONG OF ROLAND (*see below*), Boiardo's ORLANDO INNAMORATO, and Ariosto's ORLANDO FURIOSO. He is also a principal character in Pulci's MORGANTE MAGGIORE and converts the giant Morgante to Christianity.

A Roland for an Oliver. A blow for a blow, TIT FOR TAT. The exploits of these two PALADINS are so similar that it is difficult to keep them distinct. What Roland did Oliver did, and what Oliver did Roland did. At length the two met in single combat, and fought for five consecutive days, but neither gained the least advantage. SHAKESPEARE alludes to the phrase: "England all Olivers and Rolands bred" (*Henry VI, Pt. I*, I, ii) and Edward Hall, the historian, almost a century before Shakespeare, writes:

> But to have a Roland to resist an Oliver, he sent solempne ambassadors to the King of Englande, offerying hym hys doughter in mariage.
>
> *Henry VI.*

Childe Roland. Youngest brother of the "fair burd Helen" in the old Scottish ballad. Guided by MERLIN, he successfully undertook to bring his sister from Elfland, whither the fairies had carried her.

> Childe Roland to the dark tower came;
> His word was still "Fie, foh, fum,

I smell the blood of a British man."
> SHAKESPEARE: *King Lear*, III, iv.

Browning's poem, *Child Roland to the Dark Tower Came*, is not connected, other than by the first line, with the old ballad.

Like the blast of Roland's horn. Roland had a wonderful ivory horn, named "Olivant", that he won from the giant Jutmundus. When he was attacked by the Saracens at Roncesvalles (Roncesvaux) he sounded it to give CHARLEMAGNE notice of his danger. At the third blast it cracked in two, but it was so loud that birds fell dead and the whole SARACEN army was panic-struck. Charlemagne heard the sound at St.-Jean-Pied-de-Port, and rushed to the rescue, but arrived too late.

> Oh, for a blast of that dread horn
> On Fontarabian echoes borne,
> That to King Charles did come.
>
> SCOTT: *Marmion*, vi, xxxiii.

Roland's sword. Duranda, Durindana or Durandal, etc., which was fabled to have once belonged to HECTOR, and which, like the horn, ROLAND won from the giant Jutmundus. It had in its hilt a thread from the Virgin Mary's cloak, a tooth of ST. PETER, one of ST. DENYS'S hairs, and a drop of St. Basil's blood. Legend relates that Roland, after he had received his death wound, strove to break Durandal on a rock to prevent it falling to the SARACENS; but it was unbreakable so he hurled it into a poisoned stream, where it remains for ever.

The Song (Chanson) of Roland. The 11th-century CHANSON DE GESTE ascribed to the Norman TROUVÈRE Théroulde or Turoldus, which tells the story of the death of ROLAND and all the PALADINS at Roncesvalles, and of CHARLEMAGNE's vengeance. When Charlemagne had been six years in Spain he sent GANELON on an embassy to Marsillus, the pagan king of Saragossa Ganelon, out of jealousy, betrayed to Marsillus the route which the Christian army designed to take on its way home, and the pagan king arrived at Roncesvalles just as Roland was conducting through the pass a rearguard of 20,000 men. He fought till 100,000 SARACENS lay slain, and only 50 of his own men survived, when another army of 50,000 men poured from the mountains. Roland now blew his enchanted horn. Charlemagne heard the blast but Ganelon persuaded him that Roland was but hunting deer. Thus Roland was left to his fate.

The *Chanson* runs to 4,000 lines, the oldest manuscript being preserved in the BODLEIAN LIBRARY, and Wace (*Roman de Rou*) tells us that the Norman minstrel sang parts of this to encourage William's soldiers at the Battle of Hastings.

> Taillefer, the minstrel-knight, bestrode
> A gallant steed, and swiftly rode
> Before the Duke, and sang the song
> Of Charlemagne, of Roland strong,
> Of Oliver, and those beside
> Brave knights at Roncesvaux that died.
> *A. S. Way's rendering.*

To die like Roland. To die of starvation or thirst. One legend has it that ROLAND escaped the general slaughter in the defile of Roncesvalles, and died of hunger and thirst in seeking to cross the Pyrenees. He was buried at Blayes, in the church of St. Raymond; but his body was removed afterwards to Roncesvalles.

Rolandseck Tower, opposite the Drachenfels on the Rhine, 22 miles above Cologne. The legend is that when ROLAND went to the wars, a false report of his death was brought to his betrothed, who retired to a convent in the isle of Nonnenwerth. When he returned flushed with glory and found she had taken the veil, he built the castle to overlook the nunnery, that he might gain a glimpse of his lost love.

Roll. The flying roll of Zechariah (v, 1-5). Predictions of evils to come on a nation are likened to the "flying roll of Zechariah" which was 20 cubits long and ten wide and full of maledictions, threats, and calamities about to befall the Jews. The parchment being unrolled fluttered in the air.

A rolling stone. *See under* STONE.

Rolling stock. All the wheeled equipment of a railway that is fitted to run on rails: the locomotives, passenger coaches, vans, goods trucks, etc.

Rollright Stones. An ancient stone circle between the villages of Great and Little Rollright on the Oxfordshire-Warwickshire border. The structure consists of the King Stone, a circle of about 70 stones called the King's Men, and a few others called the Whispering Knights. "The King" at this point could look over Oxfordshire and said:

> When Long Compton I shall see,
> King of England I shall be.

But he and his men were petrified by a witch.

Rolls. Chapel of the Rolls (Chancery Lane). Formerly the Chapel of the House of the Converts, founded by Henry III in 1232 for the reception of Jewish converts to Christianity. Edward I expelled the Jews and by 1377 the House of the Converts was allocated to the Keeper of the Rolls of CHANCERY, who was an ecclesiastic. The chapel remained a place of worship, but was also increasingly used for storing records. Most of the documents were transferred to the adjoining and newly-built Public Record Office in 1856 and it was replaced by the Museum of the Public Record Office. The name derives from the practice of keeping parchment documents in rolls for convenience of storing.

Master of the Rolls. A title of 15th-century origin for the keeper of CHANCERY records or rolls and legal assistant to the CHANCELLOR. In the 19th century he became the chief judge of the Chancery division and (since 1838) the custodian of all public records. In 1958 his jurisdiction again reverted to Chancery records only.

It runs like a Rolls. It runs perfectly and with the utmost smoothness. Usually said of a motor-car or of other power-driven vehicles; a tribute to the traditional superiority and quality of Rolls-Royce motors.

To be struck off the rolls. To be removed from the official list of qualified solicitors, and so prohibited from practising. This is done in cases of professional misconduct.

Roly-poly. A suet crust with jam rolled up into a pudding; a little fat child. *Roly* is a thing rolled with the diminutive added. In some parts of SCOTLAND the game of ninepins is called *rouly-pouly*.

Romaic. Modern or romanized Greek.

Roman. Pertaining to ROME, especially ancient Rome, or to the ROMAN CATHOLIC CHURCH. As a surname or distinctive title the adjective has been applied to:

Giulio Pippi, *Giulio Romano* (1492–1546), the Italian artist.

Adrian von Roomen (1581–1615), the famous mathematician, *Adrianus Romanus*.

Stephen Picart (1631–1721), the French engraver, *le Romain*.

Jean Dumont (1700–1781), the French painter, *le Romain*.

Marcus Terentius Varro (116–27 B.C.) was called the *Most Learned of the Romans*, and Rienzi or Rienzo (1313–1354), the Italian patriot and "last of the Tribunes", was known as *Ultimus Romanorum*, the LAST OF THE ROMANS (*see under* LAST).

Roman architecture. A style of architecture distinguished by its massive character and abundance of ornament, largely derived from the Greek and Etruscan. The Greek orders were adapted and the IONIC and CORINTHIAN were combined to form what came to be called the *Roman* or *Composite* order. Their greatest works were baths, amphitheatres, basilicas, aqueducts, bridges, triumphal arches and gateways.

Roman birds. Eagles; so called because the ensign of the Roman legion was an EAGLE.

Roman Catholic Church. A name introduced by "non-Catholics" for members of the CATHOLIC or western Church under the jurisdiction of the papacy. The term is a consequence of the REFORMATION and came into use at about the end of the 16th century. *See also* POPE.

Roman Empire. Properly, the Empire established by AUGUSTUS in 27 B.C., on the ruins of the Republic. It was finally divided into the Western or Latin Empire and the Eastern or Greek in A.D. 395. The Western Empire was eventually extinguished in 475, the last nominal emperor being Romulus Augustulus. The term "Roman empire" is also applied to the territories and dominions of the ROMAN REPUBLIC. *See* BYZANTINE EMPIRE.

Roman Empire, The Holy. *See under* HOLY.

Roman figures. *See* NUMBERS.

Roman holiday. An allusion to Byron's *Childe Harold's Pilgrimage*, IV, cxli, where he describes the death of a gladiator in the arena, "Butchered to make a Roman holiday".

The Roman Republic was established in 509 B.C. after the overthrow of the last of the seven kings, Tarquinius Superbus. It was superseded by the Empire (27 B.C.).

For a few months in 1849, after the flight of Pius IX, the people of Rome declared themselves a republic under the triumvirate of Mazzini, Saffi, and Armellini. *See also* YOUNG ITALY.

Roman roads. *See* ERMINE; FOSSE; ICKNIELD; WATLING.

Roman type. The first printing types were based upon the national or local handwriting. Roman type, the character in which this book is printed, developed from the *littera antiqua*, the conscious revival of the old Roman capital and the CAROLINGIAN minuscule which the Humanist scholars of the Italian RENAISSANCE considered more appropriate for the transcription of recently discovered Classical manuscripts than the everyday forms of Gothic handwriting. First used in print about 1465, Roman type had virtually superseded Gothic letter in less than 100 years in all parts of Europe except Germany, the British Isles, and Scandinavia. Roman type steadily took over in Britain from the late 16th century.

Romans. King of the Romans. The title usually assumed by the sovereign of the HOLY ROMAN EMPIRE previous to his actual coronation at ROME. NAPOLEON's son, afterwards the Duke of Reichstadt, was styled the *King of Rome* at his birth in 1811.

Last of the Romans. *See under* LAST.

Roman de la Rose. *See* ROSE, ROMANCE OF THE.

Romance. Applied in linguistics (*see* ROMANCE LANGUAGES, *below*) to the languages, especially Old French, sprung from the Latin spoken in the European provinces of the ROMAN EMPIRE; hence, as a noun, the word came to mean a mediæval tale in Old French or Provençal describing usually in mixed prose and verse the marvellous adventures of a hero of CHIVALRY. The modern application to a work of fiction containing incidents more or less removed from ordinary life, or to a love story or love affair, followed from this.

The mediæval romances fall into three main groups or cycles, *viz.* the Arthurian (*see under* ARTHUR), the CHARLEMAGNE cycle, and the cycle of ALEXANDER THE GREAT.

Romance languages. Those languages which are the immediate offspring of Latin, as Italian, Spanish, Portuguese, French, and Rumanian. Early French is emphatically so called; hence Bouillet says, "*Le roman était universellement parlé en Gaule au dixième siècle.*"

You are romancing. You are making it up, stretching it, telling falsehoods or stories, etc. From *romance* as an imaginative story.

Romanes Lecture, at Oxford University, an annual lecture by an eminent authority on a literary or scientific subject. Founded in 1891 by C. J. Romanes (1848–1894).

Romanesque Architecture (rō măn esk'). This term embraces the style of architecture in Western Europe from the virtual collapse of Roman rule in the 6th century until the emergence of the GOTHIC style in the late 12th century. A style with considerable regional variations, *e.g.* SAXON and Norman in England, CAROLINGIAN and Rhenish in Germany, it is characterized by the round arch, great thickness of walls, shallow (if any) buttressing, and in later phases by profuse decoration or arcades and other features.

Romantic Movement, The. The literary movement that began in Germany in the last quarter of the 18th century, having for its object a return from the AUGUSTAN or classical formalism of the time, to the freer fancies and methods of ROMANCE. It was led by Schiller, Goethe, Novalis, and Tieck, and spread to England where it influenced the work of Collins and Gray and received an impetus from the publication of PERCY'S RELIQUES and Macpherson's OSSIAN. It was immensely stimulated by the French Revolution and effected a transformation of English literature through the writings of Keats, Byron, Wordsworth, Shelley, Coleridge, Scott, etc. In France its chief exponents were Rousseau, Chateaubriand, Mme de Staël, Lamartine, Musset, Vigny, and Victor Hugo.

Romany. A GYPSY; or the gypsy language, the speech of the Roma or Zincali. The word is from Gypsy *rom*, a man, or husband.

> "Aukko to pios adrey Rommanis. Here is your health in Rommany, brother," said Mr. Petulengro; who having refilled the cup, now emptied it at a draught.
>
> BORROW: *Lavengro*, ch. liv.

Romany rye. One who enters into the GYPSY spirit, learns their language, lives with them as one of themselves, etc. *Rye* is gypsy for gentleman. George Borrow's book with this title (a sequel to *Lavengro*) was published in 1857.

Rome. The greatest city of the ancient world, according to legend founded in 753 B.C. by ROMULUS and named after him; but in all probability so called from Greek *rhoma* (strength), a suggestion supported by its other name Valentia (Lat. *valens*, strong). It acquired a new significance as the seat of the papacy.

All roads lead to Rome. *See under* ROAD.

Oh, that all Rome had but one head, that I might strike it off at a blow. Caligula, the Roman Emperor (A.D. 12, 37–41), is said to have uttered this sentiment.

Rome-Berlin Axis. *See* AXIS.

Rome penny, or **Rome scot.** The same as PETER'S PENCE.

Rome's best wealth is its patriotism. So said Mettius Curtius (*c.* 360 B.C.) who jumped into the wide gap which appeared in the Forum when the ORACLE gave out that it would never close till ROME threw therein its most precious possession.

Rome was not built in a day. Achievements of great moment, worthwhile tasks, etc., are not accomplished without patient perseverance and a considerable interval of time. It is an old saying, and occurs in Heywood's *Collection* (1562).

'Tis ill sitting at Rome and striving with the Pope. Don't TREAD ON SOMEONE'S CORNS when you are living with him or are in close touch with him—especially if he is powerful.

To fiddle while Rome burns. To trifle during an emergency or crisis. An allusion to NERO's reputed behaviour during the burning of ROME in A.D. 64 when he sang to his lyre and enjoyed the spectacle from the top of a high tower.

When at Rome, do as Rome does. Conform to the manners and customs of those amongst whom you live; "Don't wear a brown hat in Friesland." St. Monica and her son St. Augustine said to St. AMBROSE: "At Rome they fast on Saturday, but not at Milan; which practice ought to be observed?" To which St. Ambrose replied: "When I am at Milan, I do as they do at Milan; but when I go to Rome, I do as Rome does!" (*Epistle* xxxvi). *Cp.* II *Kings* v, 18.

The saying is to be found in that great storehouse of proverbs, Porter's *Two Angry Women of Abingdon* (1599).

Romeo and Juliet. A typification of romantic love as exemplified in SHAKESPEARE's famous play of this title. Romeo, of the house of Montague, falls in love with Juliet, one of the Capulet family, long-standing enemies of the Montagues. Romeo and Juliet are secretly married, but Romeo is banished from Verona before their wedding day is over as punishment for the unfortunate slaughter of a Capulet in an affray. Old Capulet now orders Juliet to prepare for marriage with Count Paris forthwith, and to avoid this, she drugs herself into a death-like trance. Romeo, hearing of her "death", returns, enters the tomb where Juliet lies, and kills himself. Juliet awakens, sees her lover dead, and dispatches herself with Romeo's dagger. Shakespeare closely based his play upon Arthur Brooke's long narrative poem, *The Tragicall History of Romeo and Juliet* (1562), which was derived ultimately from an earlier Italian story (1535) by Luigi da Porto, through a French version (1559) by Pierre Boisteau.

A regular Romeo. Said banteringly of one who fancies himself as a LADYKILLER.

Romulus (rom'ū lŭs). With his twin brother Remus, the legendary and eponymous founder of ROME. They were sons of MARS and Rhea Sylvia (Ilia), who, because she was a VESTAL virgin, was condemned to death, while the sons were exposed. They were, however, suckled by a she-wolf, and eventually set about founding a city, but quarrelled over the plans and Remus was slain by his brother in anger. Romulus was later taken to the heavens by his father, MARS, in a fiery chariot, and was worshipped by the Romans under the name of Quirinus.

The Second Romulus. Camillus was so called because he saved ROME from the Gauls, 365 B.C.

The Third Romulus. Caius Marius, who saved ROME from the Teutons and Cimbri in 101 B.C.

We need no Romulus to account for Rome. We require no hypothetical person to account for a plain fact.

Roncesvalles. *See* THE SONG OF ROLAND, *under* ROLAND.

Ronyon, or **Runnion** (ron´ yŏn, rŭn´ yŏn). A term of contempt for a woman. It is probably the Fr. *rogneux* (scabby, mangy). Shakespeare has:

> You hag, you baggage, you polecat, you ronyon! out, out!
> *The Merry Wives of Windsor*, IV, ii.

> "Aroint thee, witch!" the rump-fed ronyon cries.
> *Macbeth*, I, iii.

Rood (connected with *rod*). The Cross of the Crucifixion; or a crucifix, especially the large one that was formerly set on the stone or timber *rood-screen* that divides the nave from the choir in many churches. This is usually richly decorated with statues, and carvings of saints, emblems, etc., and frequently surmounted by a gallery called the *rood-loft*.

> And then to see the rood-loft,
> Zo bravely zet with saints.
> PERCY: *Reliques* (*Plain Truth, and Blind Ignorance*).

By the rood: by the holy rood. Old expletives used by way of asseveration. In SHAKESPEARE's *Hamlet*, when the Queen asks Hamlet if he has forgotten her he answers "No, by the rood, not so" (III, iv).

Rood Day. HOLY ROOD DAY; 14 September, the EXALTATION OF THE CROSS; or 3 May, the INVENTION OF THE CROSS (*see under* CROSS).

Roof of the World. A name given to the Pamirs, the great region of mountains covering 30,000 square miles, devoid of trees and shrubs, and most of it in the Soviet Socialist Republic of Tadzhikistan. The name is a translation of *Bam-i-Dunya*, bestowed by the natives of this region. The name also applies to Tibet.

To raise the roof. To be very noisy; to make a real hullabaloo.

Rooinek (Afrikaans, "red-neck"). A name given by the Boers to the British in the South African War, and used later to mean any British or European immigrant to South Africa.

Rook, a cheat. "To rook", to cheat; "to rook a pigeon", to fleece a GREENHORN. Sometimes it simply means to win from another at a game of chance or skill.

Rook, the castle in CHESS, is through Fr. and Span., from Persian *rukh*, which is said to have meant a warrior.

Rookery. Any low, densely populated neighbourhood, especially one frequented by thieves and vagabonds. The allusion is to the way in which rooks build their nests closely together. Colonies of seals, and places where seals or seabirds collect in their breeding season are also known as *Rookeries*. *See* ALSATIA.

Rookie. In army slang, a recruit, a novice or GREENHORN. In the U.S.A., the name given to a raw beginner in professional sport. It is probably from *rook*, a rookie being a guileless greenhorn who is easily *rooked*, swindled, or "taken in".

Room. Your room is better than your company. Your absence is more to be wished than your presence. An old phrase; it occurs in Stanyhurst's *Description of Ireland* (1577), Greene's *Quip for an Upstart Courtier* (1592), etc.

Roost. To rule the roost. *See under* ROAST.

Root. Root and Branch. The whole of it without any exceptions or omissions; "LOCK, STOCK, AND BARREL". The Puritans who supported the Root and Branch Bill of 1641 to abolish EPISCOPACY were known as "Root-and-branch men", or "Rooters", and the term has since been applied to other political factions who are anxious TO GO THE WHOLE HOG (*see under* HOG).

The root of the matter. Its true inwardness, its actual base and foundation. The phrase comes from *Job* xix, 28:

> But ye should say, Why persecute we him, seeing the root of the matter is found in me?

To root for (U.S.A.). To support a sporting team. Also used of giving active support to a campaigning politician.

To take, or **strike root.** To become permanently or firmly established.

Rope. Fought back to the ropes. Fought to the bitter end. A phrase from the prize-ring, the "ropes" forming the boundary of the "ring". Hence the expression **on the ropes,** meaning on the verge of ruin or collapse.

> It is a battle that must be fought game, and right back to the ropes.
> BOLDREWOOD: *Robbery Under Arms*, ch. xxxiii.

Money for old rope. Easy money, money for nothing or very little; something which can be effected easily. The derivation is obvious.

Ropes of sand. *See* SAND.

She is on her high ropes. In a distant and haughty temper; "HIGH AND MIGHTY". The allusion is to a rope-dancer, who looks down on the spectators.

A taste of the rope's end. A flogging. A nautical expression, where it was formerly a routine punishment to administer a flogging with the end of a rope.

To come to the end of one's rope, or **tether.** *See* TETHER.

To fight with a rope round one's neck. To fight with a certainty of death if one loses.

You must send in a large force; ... for, as he fights with a rope round his neck, he will struggle to the last.

KINGSTON: *The Three Admirals*, ch. viii.

To give one rope enough. To allow a person to continue on a certain course of action (usually EVIL) till he reaps the consequences of his folly or wrongdoing. "Give him enough rope and he will hang himself" is the common saying.

To know the ropes. To be thoroughly familiar with what is to be done; to be up to all the tricks and dodges. It derives from the days of sail when a sailor or apprentice had to become thoroughly familiar with the details of the rigging and how to handle the ropes.

To rope one in. To get him to take part in some scheme, enterprise, etc. An expression from the cattle lands of America, where animals are roped in with a lasso.

You carry a rope in your pocket. Said of a person very lucky at cards, from the superstition that a bit of rope with which a man has been hanged, carried in the pocket, secures luck at cards.

The Rope-walk. Former barristers' slang for an OLD BAILEY practice. Thus "Gone into the Rope-walk" means, he has taken up practice in the OLD BAILEY. The allusion is to the murder trials there, and to the convicted murderer "getting the rope".

Ropeable. In Australia, a term now applied to one who is in a bad temper. Originally it meant cattle so wild that they could be controllable only by roping.

Ropey. A slang expression meaning inferior, worn-out, tatty, dubious, etc., as a "ropey outfit", a "ropey character".

Roper. Mistress Roper. A CANT name given to the MARINES by British sailors, from the allegedly awkward way Marines handled the ship's ropes—a fiction rather than fact.

To marry Mistress Roper is to enlist in the Royal Marines.

Roque, St. *See* ROCH.

Roquelaure (rōk´ lōr). A cloak for men, reaching to the knees. It was worn in the 18th century, and so named from Antoine-Gaston, Duc de Roquelaure (1656–1738), a Marshal of France.

> "Your honour's roquelaure", replied the corporal, "has not once been had on since the night before your honour received your wound."
>
> STERNE: *Tristram Shandy; Story of Le Fever*.

Rory O'More. *See* RHYMING SLANG.

Rosabelle. The favourite palfrey of Mary Queen of Scots.

Rosalia, or **Rosalie, St.** (rō zā´ li a, roz´ a lē). The patron saint of Palermo, in art depicted in a cave with a CROSS and skull, or else in

the act of receiving a ROSARY or chaplet of roses from the Virgin. She lived in the 13th century, and is said to have been carried by ANGELS to an inaccessible mountain, where she dwelt for many years in the cleft of a rock, a part of which she wore away with her knees in her devotions. A CHAPEL has been built there, with a marble statue, to commemorate the event.

Rosamond, The Fair (roz´ a mund). Higden, monk of Chester, writing about 1350, says: "she was the fayre daughter of Walter, Lord Clifford, concubine of Henry II, and poisoned by Queen Eleanor, A.D. 1177. Henry made for her a house of wonderful working, so that no man or woman might come to her. This house was named Labyrinthus, and was wrought like unto a knot in a garden called a maze. But the queen came to her by a clue of thredde, and so dealt with her that she lived not long after. She was buried at Godstow, in an house of nunnes, with these verses upon her tombe:

> Hic jacet in tumba Rosa mundi, non Rosa munda;
> Non redolet, sed olet, quæ redolere solet."

> Here Rose the graced, not Rose the chaste, reposes;
> The smell that rises is no smell of roses.
>
> E.C.B.

The legend of her murder by Queen Eleanor first appears in the 14th century and the story of the LABYRINTH even later. There is no evidence to support the stories that Fair Rosamond was the mother of William Longsword and Geoffrey, Archbishop of York. A subterranean labyrinth in Blenheim Park, near Woodstock, is still pointed out as "Rosamond's Bower".

> Jane Clifford was her name, as books aver:
> Fair Rosamond was but her *nom de guerre*.
>
> DRYDEN: *Epilogue to Henry II*.

Rosary (rō´ zàr i) (Lat. *rosarium*, rose garden, garland). The bead-roll used by Roman Catholics for keeping count of the recitation of certain prayers; also the prayers themselves. The usual modern rosary consists of five decades of ten recitations, or one-third of the complete rosary known as a *corona* or *chaplet*. The full rosary comprises 15 decades of *Aves* (Hail Marys—small beads), each preceded by a *Pater* (Our Father—large bead), and followed by a *Gloria* (Glory be to the Father—large bead). While the first chaplet is being recited the five joyful MYSTERIES are contemplated; during the second chaplet, the five sorrowful mysteries; and during the third, the five glorious mysteries. Only one group of five mysteries is usually contemplated. Traditionally the devotion of the rosary is said to have begun with St. DOMINIC early in the 13th century but this is not established. Sometimes the Venerable BEDE is credited with its introduction but quite erroneously; the idea is based upon the fanciful derivation of bead from *Beda*. *Cp.* GAUDY; PATERNOSTER.

Rosciad, The (ros'i åd). A satire by Charles Churchill, published in 1761, on well-known metropolitan actors. Churchill was a member of the HELL-FIRE CLUB.

Roscius (ros'i us). A first-rate actor; after Quintus Roscius (d. *c.* 62 B.C.), the Roman actor unrivalled for his grace of action, melody of voice, conception of character, and delivery.

> What scene of death has Roscius now to act?
> SHAKESPEARE: *Henry VI, Pt. III*, V, vi.

Another Roscius. So Camden terms Richard Burbage (d. 1619).

The British Roscius. Thomas Betterton (1635–1710), of whom Cibber says, "He alone was born to speak what only Shakespeare knew to write." Garrick was also given the title.

The Roscius of France. Michel Boyron (1635–1729), generally called Baron.

The Young Roscius. William Henry West Betty (1791–1874). He first appeared publicly in 1803 as Oswyn in *Zara*, and after achieving astonishing success, left the stage in 1824.

Rose. Mediæval legend asserts that the first roses appeared miraculously at Bethlehem as the result of the prayers of a "fayre Mayden" who had been falsely accused and sentenced to death by burning. As Sir John MANDEVILLE tells the tale (*Travels*, ch. vi), after her prayer:

> sche entered into the Fuyer; and anon was the Fuyr quenched and oute; and the Brondes that weren brennynge, becomen red Roseres; and the Brondes that weren not kyndled, becomen white Roseres, fulle of Roses. And these weren the first Roseres and Roses, both white and rede, that evere any Man saughe. And was this Mayden saved be the Grace of God.

In Christian symbolism the *Rose*, as being emblematic of a paragon or one without peer, is peculiarly appropriated to the Virgin MARY, one of whose titles is "The Mystical Rose". It is also the attribute of St. DOROTHEA, who carries roses in a basket; of St. Casilda, St. Elizabeth of Portugal, and St. Rose of Viterbo, who carry roses in either their hands or caps; of St. Thérèse of Lisieux, who scatters red roses; and of ST. ROSALIE, St. Angelus, St. Rose of Lima, and St. Victoria, who wear crowns of roses.

The Rose is an emblem of ENGLAND and in HERALDRY is used as the mark of cadency for a seventh son. *See* RED ROSE; TUDOR ROSE; WHITE ROSE, *below.*

In the language of FLOWERS, different roses have a different signification as:

The Burgundy Rose signifies simplicity and beauty.

The China Rose, grace or beauty ever fresh.

The Daily Rose, a smile.

The Dog Rose, pleasure mixed with pain.

A Faded Rose, beauty is fleeting.

The Japan Rose, beauty your sole attraction.

The Moss Rose, voluptuous love.

The Musk Rose, capricious beauty.

The Provence Rose, my heart is in flames.

The White Rose Bud, too young to love.

The White Rose full of buds, secrecy.

A Wreath of Roses, beauty and virtue rewarded.

The Yellow Rose, infidelity. *See* ST. ANTHONY'S FIRE *under* ANTHONY.

Golden Rose. *See under* GOLDEN.

The Red Rose was one of several badges of the House of Lancaster, but not especially the most prominent. It was used by Edmund, Earl of Lancaster (1245–1296), called Crouchback, second son of Henry III, and it was one of the badges of Henry IV and Henry V, but it does not appear to have been used by Henry VI. The rose-plucking scene in SHAKESPEARE's *Henry VI, Pt. I*, II, iv, is essentially a fiction.

The Tudor Rose. Henry of Richmond (1457–1509), son of Edmund Tudor, Earl of Richmond, and head of the House of Lancaster after the death of Henry VI, adopted the red rose to emphasize his LANCASTRIAN claims. After his victory at Bosworth (1485), he became king as Henry VII and in 1486 married Princess Elizabeth of York. The union of the two Houses gave rise to the Tudor Rose, a superimposition of the white rose on the red. *See* WARS OF THE ROSES, *below.*

The White Rose was used as a badge by Richard, Duke of York (1411–1460), and was derived from his Mortimer ancestors. It was one of the numerous badges used by his son Edward IV and was used by his descendants, but Richard III's badge was the white BOAR. It was also adopted by the JACOBITES as an emblem of the PRETENDER, because his adherents were obliged to abet him SUB ROSA (*see below*). Cecily Neville, wife of Richard, Duke of York, and grand-daughter of John of Gaunt, was known as *The White Rose of Raby. Cp.* RED ROSE, *above*; WARS OF THE ROSES, *below.*

The Rose Alley Ambuscade. The attack on Dryden by masked ruffians, probably in the employ of Rochester and the Duchess of Portsmouth, on 18 December 1679, in revenge for an anonymous *Essay on Satire* attacking King Charles II, Rochester, and the Duchesses of Cleveland and Portsmouth, which was erroneously attributed to Dryden but actually written by Lord Mulgrave.

The Rose Coffee House. The tavern standing at the corner of Russell Street and Bridge Street, COVENT GARDEN, from about 1651. *See* WILL'S COFFEE HOUSE.

Rose Noble. A gold coin, also called a *ryal*, or *royal*, so named because it bore a rose in a sun on the reverse. It was first minted in 1465 and was valued at 10*s*., but the issue ceased by 1470. It was revived by Henry VII and again by Mary and Elizabeth I. A *rose-ryal* was issued by James I.

The Rose of Jericho. The popular name of *Anastatica hierochuntina*, a small branching plant, native to the sandy deserts of ARABIA, Egypt, and Syria. When it is dry, if it is exposed to moisture, the branches uncurl. Also called the *rose of the Virgin*, or *Rosa Mariæ*.

Rose of Sharon. St. John's Wort, *Hypericum calycinum*, a small shrub-like plant with a yellow flower. The rose of Sharon in *The Song of Solomon* (II,i) was probably a bulbous plant.

Rose, The Romance of the. An early French poem of over 20,000 lines; an elaborate allegory on the Art of Love beneath which can be seen a faithful picture of contemporary life. It was begun by Guillaume de Lorris in the latter half of the 13th century, and continued by Jean de Meung in the early part of the 14th. The poet is accosted by Dame Idleness, who conducts him to the Palace of Pleasure, where he meets Love, accompanied by Sweet-looks, Riches, Jollity, Courtesy, Liberality, and Youth, who spend their time in dancing, singing and other amusements. By this retinue the poet is conducted to a bed of roses, where he singles out one and attempts to pluck it, when an arrow from CUPID'S bow stretches him fainting on the ground, and he is carried far from the flower of his choice. As soon as he recovers, he finds himself alone, and resolves to return to his rose. Welcome goes with him; but Danger, Shame-face, Fear and Slander obstruct him at every turn. Reason advises him to abandon the pursuit, but this he will not do; whereupon Pity and Liberality aid him in reaching the rose of his choice, and VENUS permits him to touch it with his lips. Meanwhile Slander rouses up Jealousy, who seizes Welcome, and casts him into a strong castle, giving the key of the castle door to an old hag. Here the poet is left to mourn over his fate, and the original poem ends.

In the second part—which is much the longer—the same characters appear, but the spirit of the poem is altogether different, the author being interested in life as a whole instead of solely love; and directing his satire especially against women.

An English version, *The Romaunt of the Rose*, was translated by Chaucer, but in the extant version (first printed in 1532) it is generally held that only the first 1,700 lines or so are his.

Rose Sunday. The fourth Sunday in LENT, when the POPE blesses the GOLDEN ROSE.

A rose by any other name would smell as sweet. The name is of little consequence, it does not affect the inherent qualities of the person or thing under consideration. Thus SHAKESPEARE's Juliet says:

> What's in a name? that which we call a rose,
> By any other name would smell as sweet;
> So Romeo would, were he not Romeo call'd.
> *Romeo and Juliet*, II, ii.

The expression is now commonly used sarcastically.

No rose without a thorn. There is always something to detract from pleasure—"every sweet has its sour", "there is a crook in every lot" (*see under* CROOK).

Sing Old Rose and burn the bellows. "Old Rose" was the title of a song now unknown; Isaak Walton refers to it:

> And now let's go to an honest alehouse, where we may have a cup of good barley wine, and sing "Old Rose", and all of us rejoice together.
> *The Compleat Angler*, Pt. I, ch. ii (1653).

Burn the bellows may be a schoolboys' perversion of *burn libellos*. At breaking-up time the boys might say, "Let's sing *Old Rose* and burn our *libellos*" (school-books). This does not accord ill with the meaning of the well-known catch:

> Now we're met like jovial fellows,
> Let us do as wise men tell us,
> Sing *Old Rose* and burn the bellows.

Sub rosa (Lat.), or **Under the rose.** In strict confidence. The origin of the phrase is obscure but the story is that CUPID gave HARPOCRATES (the god of silence) a ROSE, to bribe him not to betray the amours of VENUS. Hence the flower became the emblem of silence and was sculptured on the ceilings of banquet-rooms, to remind the guests that what was spoken *sub vino* was not to be repeated SUB DIVO. In the 16th century it was placed over confessionals.

A bed of roses. *See under* BED.

The Wars of the Roses. The usual name

given to the CIVIL WARS in England (1455–1485) between LANCASTRIANS and YORKISTS which ended in the triumph of Henry Tudor at Bosworth. The wars were partly dynastic and partly private wars of the nobility, occasioned by the weakness of government and the collapse of law and order. The name is not really historical and appears to derive from Scott.

> He now turned his eyes to the regaining of those rich and valuable foreign possessions which had been lost during the administration of the feeble Henry VI, and the civil discords so dreadfully prosecuted in the wars of the White and Red Roses.
>
> *Anne of Geierstein*, ch. vii.

There is no contemporary record of the use of the term for these struggles for political control. *See* THE RED ROSE; THE TUDOR ROSE; THE WHITE ROSE, *above*.

Rose-red City. Petra, ancient capital of the Nabatæan Kings from which Arabia Petræa took its name. It was occupied by the Romans in 105 A.D. and is noted for its ancient tomb and temple ruins as well as Roman remains. The epithet derives from the famous line of J. W. Burgon's Newdigate Prize poem of 1845:

> "A rose-red city half as old as time".

The local rocks are essentially red and much enhanced by red sunsets.

Rosemary (rōz' mà ri) (Lat. *Ros marinus*, sea-dew). The shrub (*Rosmarinus officinalis*) is said to be useful in love-making. As VENUS, the love goddess, was sprung from the foam of the sea, rosemary or sea-dew would have amatory qualities.

> The sea his mother Venus came on;
> And hence some rev'rend men approve
> Of rosemary in making love.
>
> BUTLER: *Hudibras*, Pt. II, Canto i, l. 843.

Rosemary, an emblem of remembrance. In SHAKESPEARE's *Hamlet* (IV, v) Ophelia says, "There's rosemary, that's for remembrance." According to Culpeper, "It quickens a weak memory, and the senses." As HUNGARY WATER, it was once extensively taken to quieten the nerves. It was much used in weddings, and to wear rosemary in ancient times was as significant of a wedding as to wear a white favour. When the Nurse in Shakespeare's *Romeo and Juliet* (II, iv) asks, "Doth not rosemary and Romeo begin both with a [*i.e.* the same] letter?" She refers to the emblematical characteristics of the herb. In the language of FLOWERS it means "Fidelity in love".

Rosemodres Circle. The MERRY MAIDENS.

Rosetta Stone, The (rō zet' à). A stone found in 1799 by M. Boussard, a French officer of engineers, in an excavation made at Fort St.

Julien, near Rosetta, in the Nile delta. It has an inscription in three different languages—the hieroglyphic, the demotic, and the Greek. It was erected (195 B.C.) in honour of Ptolemy Epiphanes, because he remitted the dues of the sacerdotal body. The great value of the stone is that it furnished the key whereby the Egyptian HIEROGLYPHS were deciphered.

Rosherville Gardens. In Victorian times "the place to spend a happy day". These gardens were established by Mr. Rosher in disused chalk quarries at Gravesend. A theatre, zoological collections, and music formed part of their attraction, and the gardens were particularly favoured by river excursionists. The site has long been given over to industry. *Cp.* CREMORNE GARDENS; VAUXHALL GARDENS.

Rosicrusians (roz i kroo' shànz). A secret society of CABBALISTS, occultists and alchemists that is first heard of in 1614 when the anonymous *Fama fraternitatis des löblichen Ordens des Rosenkreuzes* was published at Cassel, duly followed by the *Confessio* and *The Chemical Wedding of Christian Rosenkreutz*. The Rosicrucian Order was reputedly founded by the mythical Rosenkreutz (the cross of roses) in 1459. In FREEMASONRY there is still a degree known as the *Rose Croix*. Rosicrucian philosophy played a part in the early struggle for intellectual progress by clothing its progressive ideas in mystical guise. It seems to have influenced the Elizabethan, Dr. John Dee, and Sir Francis Bacon among others, and to have some links with the work of PARACELSUS.

> As for the Rosicross philosophers,
> Whom you will have to be but sorcerers,
> What they pretend to is no more
> Than Trismegistus did before,
> Pythagoras, old Zoroaster,
> And Apollonius their master.
>
> BUTLER: *Hudibras*, Pt. II, iii, l. 651.

Rosicrucian societies still exist.

Rosin Bible. *See* BIBLE, SOME SPECIALLY NAMED EDITIONS.

Rosinante. *See* ROZINANTE.

Ross, Betsy (1752–1836). She is said to have made the first STARS AND STRIPES in 1776. The story is that George Washington, with Robert Morris and General George Ross, visited Betsy's upholstery shop in Philadelphia and asked her to make a flag from their design. The stars had six points but Betsy said they would look better with five. This was agreed and in due course she produced the flag.

Ross. The Fair Maid of Ross. Amy, the daughter of Captain Browne, the warden of

Ross Castle, Killarney, was known as "The Fair Maid of Ross" and attracted the attention of most of the young officers, especially Raymond Villiers whom her father wanted her to marry, but she was already in love with Donough McCarthy whose estates had been seized by the enemy. When the castle was beseiged by the Cromwellians in 1652, Villiers, having been refused by Amy, resolved to betray Ross Castle to Ludlow, Cromwell's general, but when engaged on this mission Amy followed him and learned of his treason. When Villiers finally left the castle Amy again followed him but was wounded by his pistol shot. In a subsequent skirmish McCarthy killed Villiers and Captain Browne surrendered the castle on honourable terms. In due course McCarthy recovered his land and married Amy.

The Man of Ross. John Kyrle (1637–1724) who spent most of his life at Ross, Herefordshire. He was famous for his benevolence and for supplying needy parishes with churches. The KYRLE SOCIETY was named in his honour.

> Who taught the heaven-directed spire to rise?
> "The Man of Ross", each lisping babe replies.
> Behold the market-place with poor o'erspread!
> He feeds yon alms-house, neat, but void of state,
> Where Age and Want sit smiling at the gate;
> Him portioned maids, apprenticed orphans blest,
> The young who labour, and the old who rest.
>
> POPE: *Moral Essays*, Epistle III, l. 261.

Rosse. A famous sword which the dwarf AL-BERICH gave to Otwit, King of Lombardy. It struck so fine a cut that it left no "gap", shone like glass, and was adorned with gold.

> This sword to thee I give: it is all bright of hue;
> Whatever it may cleave, no gap will there ensue,
> From Almari I brought it, and Rosse is its name;
> Wherever swords are drawn, 'twill put them all to
> shame.
>
> *The Heldenbuch.*

Rostrum. A pulpit, or stand for public speakers. The Lat. *rostrum* is the bill or beak of a bird, also the beak or curved prow of a ship. In the Forum at ROME, the platform from which orators addressed the public was ornamented with *rostra*, or ship-prows taken from the Antiates in 338 B.C., hence this use of the word.

Rota (rō' tà). A short-lived political club founded in London in 1659 by James Harrington. Its republican principles are outlined in his *Oceana* and it advocated rotation of government offices and voting by ballot. It met at the Turk's Head in New Palace Yard and did not survive the RESTORATION.

Rota Sacra Romana. A Roman Catholic ecclesiastical court of mediæval origin composed of auditors under the presidency of a DEAN. It was reconstituted by Pius X in 1908 and appears to take its name from the circular table originally used by the judges at Avignon. It tries cases and hears appeals from ecclesiastical tribunals.

Rotary Club. A movement among business men which takes for its motto "Service above Self". The idea originated with Paul Harris, a Chicago lawyer, in 1905. In 1911 it took root in Britain and there are now clubs in most towns, membership being limited to one member each of any trade, calling, or profession. Lectures are delivered at weekly meetings by guest speakers. The name derives from the early practice of holding meetings in rotation at the offices or business premises of its members. The Rotary Clubs are now members of one association called Rotary International.

Rote. To learn by rote is to learn by means of repetition, *i.e.* by going over the same beaten track or *route* again and again. *Rote* is really the same word as *route*.

Rothschild. I am not a Rothschild. I am not a millionaire. I am not "rolling in money". This and similar phrases are in allusion to the great wealth of the famous international banking family of Rothschild, whose name derives from the red shield by which their parent house at Frankfurt was known. The family banking business really stems from the activities of Meyer Amschel Rothschild (1743–1812) who made a fortune during the Napoleonic wars. His five sons separated, extending the business throughout Europe. Nathan Meyer Rothschild (1777–1836) established a branch at London in 1798 and made a financial scoop by his advance knowledge of the defeat of NAPOLEON at Waterloo. His son Lionel (1808–1879) was best known for his work for Jewish emancipation in Great Britain. Lionel's son Nathaniel Meyer (1840–1915) was made a baron in 1885.

Rotten Row. The famous equestrian track in Hyde Park, London, is said to be so called from O.Fr. *route le roi* or *route du roi*, because it formed part of the old royal route from the palace of the PLANTAGENET Kings at WESTMINSTER to the royal forests. Camden derives the word from *rotteran*, to muster, as the place where soldiers mustered. The reason for the name is obscure.

Roué (roo' ā). The profligate Duke of Orleans, Regent of France, first used this word in its modern sense about 1720. It was his ambition to collect round him companions as worthless as himself, and he used facetiously to boast that there was not one of them who did not deserve to be broken on the *wheel*; hence these profligates went by the name of Orleans' *roués*. The most notorious *roués* were the Dukes of Richelieu, Broglie, Biron, and Brancas, together with Canillac and Nocé.

Rouen (roo' on). **Aller à Rouen.** To go to ruin. A French pun comparable to our *You are on the road to* NEEDHAM (a market town in Suffolk), *i.e.* your courses will lead you to poverty.

The Bloody Feast of Rouen (1356). Charles the DAUPHIN (later Charles V) gave a banquet to his friends at Rouen, to which his brother-in-law Charles the BAD of Navarre was invited. While the guests were at table King John the Good entered the room with an escort, exclaiming, "Traitor, thou art not worthy to sit at table with my son!" Then, turning to his guards, he added, "Take him hence! By holy Paul, I will neither eat nor drink till his head be brought to me!" Then, seizing an iron mace from one of the men-at-arms, he struck another of the guests between the shoulders, saying, "Out, proud traitor! by the soul of my father, thou shalt not live!" Four of the guests were beheaded on the spot and Charles of Navarre was taken a prisoner to Paris.

Rouge (roozh) (Fr., red). **Rouge Croix.** One of the PURSUIVANTS of the Heralds' College. So called from the red cross of St. GEORGE, the patron saint of ENGLAND. Rouge Croix was instituted by Henry V.

Rouge Dragon. The PURSUIVANT established by Henry VII. The RED DRAGON was the ensign of the Welsh princes from whom Henry VII traced his ancestry.

Rouge et Noir (Fr., red and black). A game of chance; so called because of the red and black diamond-shaped compartments on the board. After the stakes have been placed on the table the cards are dealt in the prescribed manner and the player whose "pips" amount nearest to 31 is the winner. The game is also called *Trente-et-un* (31) or *Trente-et-Quarante* (30 and 40).

Rough. A rough diamond. *See under* DIAMOND.

A rough house. A disorderly scrimmage or brawl.

Rough music. A din or noisy uproar made by clanging together pots and pans and other noise-producing instruments usually as a protest outside the house of a person who has outraged propriety. In Somersetshire it was called skimmity-riding, by the Basques *toberac*, and in France CHARIVARI. *Cp.* SKIMMINGTON.

Rough Riders. The First Regiment of U.S. Cavalry Volunteers under Colonel Leonard Wood and Lieut.-Colonel Theodore Roosevelt were so designated in the Spanish-

American War (1898), noted for their successful charge up San Juan Hill. The force was made up from COWBOYS, Indians, rangers, and college students.

In the British cavalry rough-riders were non-commissioned officers and highly skilled horsemen who acted as assistants to the regimental riding master. They owed their position to their abilities in riding unbroken (rough) horses.

Rough and Ready. Rough in manner but prompt in action; not elaborate, roughly adequate. General Zachary Taylor (1784–1860), twelfth president of the United States, was called **Old Rough and Ready**, a name he won in the Seminole Wars.

To cut up rough. *See under* CUT.

To ride rough-shod over one. To treat one without the least consideration; to completely disregard another's interests or feelings, etc. The shoes of a horse that is *rough-shod* for slippery weather are equipped with points or calks.

Rough-hewn. Shaped in the rough, not finished, unpolished, ill-mannered, raw; as a "rough-hewn seaman".

> There's a divinity that shapes our ends,
> Rough-hew them how we will.
> SHAKESPEARE: *Hamlet*, V, ii.

Rouncival, or **Rounceval** (rown' si val). Very large or strong; of gigantic size. Certain large bones said to have been dug up at Roncesvalles (*see* THE SONG OF ROLAND *under* ROLAND) were believed to have belonged to the heroes who fell with Roland, hence the usage. "Rouncival peas" are the large marrowfat peas and a very big woman is called a *rouncival*.

Round. There is an archaic verb *to round* (O.E. *runian*) meaning to whisper, or to communicate confidentially. Browning used it more than once:

> First make a laughing-stock of me and mine,
> Then round us in the ears from morn to night
> (Because we show wry faces at your mirth)
> That you are robbed, starved, beaten and what
> not!
> *The Ring and the Book*, iv, 599.

SHAKESPEARE has:

> And France...rounded in the ear
> With that same purpose-changer, that sly devil;
> That broker, that still breaks the pate of faith...
> *King John*, II, i.

Cp. also:

> And ner the feend he drough as nought ne were,
> Full privëly, and rounëd in his eere,
> "Herkë, my brother, herkë, by thi faith..."
> CHAUCER: *Friar's Tale*, 249.

The Round Table. The Table fabled to have been made by MERLIN at Carduel for

UTHER Pendragon. Uther gave it to King Leodegraunce of Cameliard, who gave it to King ARTHUR when the latter married GUINEVERE, his daughter. It was circular to prevent any jealousy on the score of precedency; it seated 150 knights, and a place was left in it for the SANGRAIL. The first reference to it is in Wace's *Roman de Brut* (1155); these legendary details are from Malory's *Morte d'Arthur*, III, i and ii.

The table shown at Winchester was recognized as ancient in the time of Henry III, but its anterior history is unknown. It is of wedge-shaped oak planks, and is 17 ft. in diameter and $2\frac{3}{4}$ in. thick. At the back are 12 mortice holes in which 12 legs probably used to fit. It was for the accommodation of 12 favourite knights. Henry VIII showed it to Francis I, telling him that it was the one used by the British king. The Round Table was not peculiar to the reign of Arthur. Thus the king of Ireland, father of the fair Cristabelle, says in the ballad given in PERCY'S RELIQUES:

> Is there never a Knighte of my round table
> This matter will undergo?
> *Sir Cauline* (Part the Second).

In the eighth year of Edward I, Roger de Mortimer established a Round Table at Kenilworth for "the encouragement of military pastimes". At this foundation, 100 knights and as many ladies were entertained at the founder's expense. About 70 years later, Edward III erected a splendid table at Windsor. It was 200 ft. in diameter, and the expense of entertaining the knights thereof amounted to £100 a week. *Cp.* JOHN O'GROATS.

Knights of the Round Table. According to Malory (*Morte d'Arthur*, III, i and ii) there were 150 knights who had "sieges" at the table. King Leodegraunce brought 100 when he gave the table to King ARTHUR; MERLIN filled up 28 of the vacant seats, and the king elected GAWAIN and Tor; the remaining 20 were left for those who might prove worthy.

A list of the knights (151) and a description of their armour is given in the *Theatre of Honour* (1622) by Andrew Fairne. These knights went forth in quest of adventures, but their chief exploits were concerned with the quest of the Holy GRAIL.

Sir LANCELOT is meant for a model of fidelity, bravery, frailty in love, and repentance; Sir GALAHAD of chastity; Sir GAWAIN of courtesy; Sir KAY of a rude, boastful knight, and Sir MODRED of treachery.

There is still a "Knights of the Round Table" Club which claims to be the oldest social club in the world, having been founded in 1721. Garrick, Dickens, Toole, Sir Henry Irving, and Tenniel are among those who have been members.

A round table conference. A conference in which no participant has precedence and at which it is agreed that the question in dispute shall be settled amicably with the maximum amount of "give and take" on each side.

The expression came into prominence in connexion with a private conference in the house of Sir William Harcourt, 14 January 1887, with the view of trying to reunite the Liberal party after the split occasioned by Gladstone's advocacy of Irish Home Rule. Other politically notable Round Table Conferences were those on Indian government held in London (1931–1932).

A good round sum. A large sum of money.

> Three thousand ducats; 'tis a good round sum.
> SHAKESPEARE: *Merchant of Venice*, I, iii.

A round peg in a square hole. The same as a square peg in a round hole. *See* PEG.

A round robin. A petition or protest signed in a circular form, so that no name heads the list. The device is French, and the term seems to be a corruption of *rond* (round), *ruban* (a ribbon), and originally used by sailors.

At a round pace, or **rate.** Briskly, rapidly, smartly.

> He cried again,
> "To the wilds!" and Enid leading down the
> tracks...
> Round was their pace at first, but slacken'd soon.
> TENNYSON: *Geraint and Enid*.

In round figures, or **numbers.** Disregarding fractions, units, etc., in tens, hundreds, etc., thus with the quantity ending in an o or round number. Thus we say, "His income in round figures was £5,000", although strictly accurately it may be £4,975, or, "The population of Haiti in 1962 was four millions in round numbers."

In the round. In the theatre, the production of plays on a central stage surrounded by the audience as in an arena, without proscenium arch or curtains.

Round dealing. Honest, straightforward dealing, without branching off into underhand tricks. The same as square dealing.

Round-up (Western U.S.A.). The gathering up of cattle by riding round them and driving them in. Hence, a gathering-in of scattered objects, or persons such as criminals. *See* RODEO.

Sellinger's round. *See* SELLINGER'S.

To get round one. To take advantage of

him by cajoling or flattery; to have one's own way through deception.

To round on one. To turn on him; to inform against him.

To walk the Round. Lawyers used frequently to give interviews to their clients in the Round Church in the TEMPLE; and "walking the Round" meant loitering about the church, in the hope of being hired for a witness.

Roundabout. A large revolving machine at FAIRS, circuses, etc., with wooden horses or the like which go round and round and are ridden by passengers to the strains of music, known in the U.S.A. as a *carousel*. From this arises the device at crossroads, whereby traffic circulates in one direction only.

What you lose on the swings you gain on the roundabouts. *See under* SWING.

Roundel, or **Roundle,** in HERALDRY, is a charge of a circular form. There are a number of varieties, distinguished by their colours or tinctures, as—a *Bezant*, tincture "or"; *Plate*, "argent"; *Torteau*, "gules"; *Hurt*, "azure"; *Ogress* or *Pellet*, "sable"; *Pomey* (because supposed to resemble an apple, Fr. *pomme*), "vert"; *Golpe*, "purpure"; *Guze*, "sanguine"; *Orange*, "tenney".

Roundheads. PURITANS of the time of the CIVIL WARS; especially Cromwell's soldiers. So called from their close-cropped hair as contrasted with the long hair fashionable among the Royalists or CAVALIERS. The name appears in 1641 in the affrays at WESTMINSTER when the mobs of apprentices were demonstrating against the EPISCOPACY.

Roundsmen. In the 18th century, the name given to those able-bodied paupers who were sent from house to house to find temporary employment. House occupiers and farmers paid the wages fixed by the parish but were reimbursed from the poor rate for all monies paid beyond a certain amount. Usually about half the wages came from the employer and half from the parish. The system was also known as the *billet* or *ticket* system from the chit for employment issued to the pauper by the parish overseer. This practice ended in 1834.

Roup, a name given to an auction in SCOTLAND. It is of Scandinavian origin and is connected with M. Swed. *ropa*, to shout.

Rout. A common term in the 18th century for a large evening party or fashionable assemblage. *Cp.* DRUM; HURRICANE, etc.

Routiers, or **Rutters** (roo' ti erz, rut' erz). Mediæval adventurers who made war a trade and let themselves out to anyone who would pay them. So called because they were always on the *route* or moving from place to place. (*Cp.* CONDOTTIERI.) Also the name given to early manuals of pilotage.

Rove. The original meaning was to shoot with arrows at marks that were selected at haphazard, the distance being unknown, with the object of practising judging distance.

Running at rovers. Running wild, at random, being without restraint.

To shoot at rovers. To shoot at random, without any distinct aim.

Rowan, or **Mountain Ash** (rou' an, rō' an). Called in Westmorland the "Wiggentree". It was greatly venerated by the DRUIDS and was formerly known as the "Witchen" because it was supposed to ward off WITCHES.

> Rowan-tree or reed
> Put the witches to speed.

Many mountain-ash berries are said to denote a deficient harvest. In Aberdeenshire it was customary to make crosses of rowan twigs on the eve of the INVENTION OF THE CROSS (*see under* CROSS) and to put them over doors and windows to ward off witches and evil spirits.

Rowley. Old Rowley. Charles II was so called after his favourite stallion. A portion of the Newmarket race-course is still called Rowley Mile and the Rowley Stakes are also held there.

> "Old Rowley himself, madam," said the King, entering the apartment with his usual air of easy composure.
>> SCOTT: *Peveril of the Peak*, ch. xxxi.

The Rowley Poems. *See under* FORGERY.

Roxburghe Club, The (roks' brŏ). An association of bibliophiles founded in 1812 for the purpose of printing rare works or MSS. It was named after John, Duke of Roxburghe, a celebrated collector of ancient literature (1740–1804), and remains the most distinguished gathering of bibliophiles in the world. It was the forerunner of a number of similar printing societies, as the Camden, Chetham, Percy, Shakespeare, Surtees, and Wharton, in ENGLAND; the Abbotsford, BANNATYNE, MAITLAND, and Spalding, in SCOTLAND; and the Celtic Society of IRELAND.

Roy, Le, or **La Reine s'avisera** (The king (or queen) will consider it). This is the royal veto on a parliamentary bill, last put into force 11 March 1707, when Queen Anne refused her assent to a Scottish Militia Bill. *See* ROYAL ASSENT.

Royal. Before metrication, a standard size of writing paper measuring 19 × 24 in. In printing it was 20 × 25 in. or 20 × 25½ in.; hence a royal octavo book measures 10 × 6½ in. (untrimmed).

Super Royal in printing papers measured (with slight variations) 20 × 27 in., and in writing papers 19 × 27 in.

Royal Academy. Founded in 1768, with Sir Joshua Reynolds as the first president, "for the purpose of cultivating and improving the arts of painting, sculpture and architecture".

Royal American Regiment. The original name of the King's Royal Rifle Corps, which was first raised under that title in Maryland and Pennsylvania, 1755. Now the 2nd Battalion The Royal Green Jackets.

Royal and Ancient. The name by which the game of golf has been known since early days when the Scottish kings practised it. James IV of SCOTLAND is the first recorded royal patron and Mary, Queen of Scots, was playing golf when news was brought to her of Lord Darnley's death.

Royal Assent to parliamentary bills is still given in Norman French. The form of assent to public and private bills is *Le Roy*, or *La Reine le veult*; to personal bills *Soit fait comme il est désiré*; and to taxation and supply, *Le Roy* or *La Reine remercie ses bons sujets, accepte leur benevolence, et ainsi le veult*. *Cp.* LE ROY S'AVISERA.

Royal Bounty. A part of the CIVIL LIST out of which the British sovereign makes gifts to charities and pays for official subscriptions.

Royal Exchange, Cornhill, London. The original exchange, founded by Sir Thomas Gresham, whose crest was a GRASSHOPPER, was opened by Queen Elizabeth I in 1568 and was modelled on the Bourse at Antwerp as a place for London Merchants to transact their business. It was burnt down during the GREAT FIRE and a new exchange was opened in 1670 but this was again destroyed by fire in 1838. It is said that before the bells fell they had chimed *There's nae luck aboot the hoose*. The third building was opened by Queen Victoria in 1844. In 1928 the building was taken over by the Royal Exchange Assurance Corporation which had occupied offices there since 1720.

Royal Flush. In poker, a hand consisting of the ace, king, queen, jack, and ten of one suit.

Royal game of goose. *See under* GOOSE.

Royal Merchants. The wealthy, mediæval families such as the MEDICI of Florence and the Grimaldi of Genoa.

> Glancing an eye of pity on his losses,
> That have of late so huddled on his back,
> Enow to press a royal merchant down.
> SHAKESPEARE: *Merchant of Venice*, IV, i.

Sir Thomas Gresham, founder of the ROYAL EXCHANGE, was called a "royal merchant"

from his wealth and influence; and in 1767, Fletcher's comedy, *The Beggar's Bush* (1622), was produced as an opera with the title *The Royal Merchant*.

Royal Oak. *See* OAK-APPLE DAY.

Royal road to learning, etc. A direct and easy way. Royal roads were generally straighter and better than most roads.

Royal Society. The premier scientific society in Great Britain. It was established in 1660 and incorporated as the Royal Society in 1662, but its origins can be traced to the meetings of philosophers and scientists held at Gresham College in 1645. It met at the college until 1710 and then moved to Crane Court, FLEET STREET. In 1780 it transferred to SOMERSET HOUSE and thence to Burlington House in 1857. Fellowship of the Royal Society is the most coveted honour among scientists.

Royal Titles. *See* TITLES OF.

Royalists. *See* CAVALIERS.

Royston. A Royston horse and Cambridge Master of Arts will give way to no one. A Cambridgeshire proverb. Royston was famous for malt which was sent to LONDON on horseback. These heavy-laden beasts never moved out of the way. The Masters of Arts, or Cambridge dons, had the wall conceded to them by the townsfolk out of courtesy.

Rozinante, Rocinante (roz i năn' ti). The wretched JADE of a riding-horse belonging to Don QUIXOTE. Although it was nothing but skin and bone—and worn out at that—he regarded it as a priceless charger surpassing "the BUCEPHALUS of ALEXANDER and the Babieca of the CID". The name, which is applied to similar hacks, is from Span. *rocin*, a jade, the *ante* (before) implying that once upon a time, perhaps, it had been a horse.

Rub. An impediment. The expression is taken from bowls where "rub" means that something hinders the free movement of your wood.

> We sometimes had those little rubs which Providence sends to enhance the value of its favours.
> GOLDSMITH: *The Vicar of Wakefield*, ch. i.

Don't rub it in! Yes, I know I've made a mistake, but you needn't go on emphasizing the fact.

Rub of the green. *See under* GREEN.

To rub shoulders with. To mix closely in company.

To rub up. To refresh the memory, to revive one's knowledge of a subject.

To rub up the wrong way. To annoy, to irritate by lack of tact, etc.; as a cat is irritated when its fur is rubbed the wrong way.

Rubaiyát (plural of *Ruba'i*), means quatrains, much used by Arabic poets, and familiar to

English readers through Fitzgerald's *Rubaiyát* of OMAR KHAYYAM (1859).

Rubber. In WHIST, bridge, and some other games, a set of three games, the best two of three, or the third game of the set. The origin of the term is uncertain, but it may be a transference from bowls, in which the collision of two woods is a *rubber*, because they RUB against each other.

Those who play at bowls must look out for rubbers. There is always some risk in anything you undertake, and you've got to be prepared to meet it; you must take the rough with the smooth.

To rubber-stamp. To authorize as a matter of routine, to approve automatically, without any personal examination or check. From the use of rubber stamps on routine documents, etc., in place of a written authorization.

Rubberneck-wagon. An excursion or sightseeing-bus in which the passengers stretch their necks to look at views or monuments.

Rübezahl. A mountain spirit of German folk-lore, ruler of the weather, also called Herr Johannes, whose home is in the Riesengebirge (Giant Mountains), the mountain range which separates Prussian Silesia (now in Poland) and Bohemia (Czecho-|slovakia).

Rubicon. To cross the Rubicon. To take an irrevocable step; as when the Germans crossed the Belgian frontier in August 1914, which led to war with Great Britain. The Rubicon was a small river which separated ancient Italy from Cisalpine GAUL (the province allotted to Julius CÆSAR). When Cæsar crossed this stream in 49 B.C. he passed beyond the limits of his province and became an invader in Italy, thus precipitating war with Pompey and the Senate.

Rubric (roo'brik) (Lat. *rubrica*, red ochre or vermilion). The Romans called an ordinance or law a rubric, because it was written with vermilion.

The liturgical directions, titles, etc., in a Prayer Book are known as the *Rubrics* because these were (and sometimes still are) printed in red (*cp.* RED-LETTER DAY).

> No date prefix'd
> Directs me in the starry rubric set.
> MILTON: *Paradise Regained*, IV, 392.

The directions given on formal examination papers concerning the selection of questions to be answered, etc., are called the *rubrics*.

Ruby. The ancients considered the ruby to be an antidote to poison, to preserve persons from plague, to banish grief, to repress the ill effects of luxuries, and to divert the mind from EVIL thoughts.

It has always been a valuable stone, and even today a fine Burma ruby will cost more than a diamond of the same size.

> Who can find a virtuous woman? for her price is far above rubies.
> *Prov.* xxxi, 10; *cp.* also *Job* xxviii, 18, and *Prov.* viii, 11.

Marco Polo said that the king of Ceylon had the finest ruby he had ever seen. "It is a span long, as thick as a man's arm, and without a flaw." Kublai Khan offered the value of a city for it, but the king would not part with it, though all the treasures of the world were to be laid at his feet.

The perfect ruby. An alchemist's term for the ELIXIR, or PHILOSOPHER'S STONE.

> He that has once the flower of the sun,
> The perfect ruby which we call elixir,...
> Can confer honour, love, respect, long life,
> Give safety, valour, yea, and victory,
> To whom he will.
> BEN JONSON: *The Alchemist*, II, i.

Rudder. Who won't be ruled by the rudder must be ruled by the rock. He who won't listen to reason must bear the consequences, like a ship that runs upon a rock if it will not answer the helm.

Ruddock. The redbreast "sacred to the household gods"; *see* ROBIN REDBREAST. The word is ultimately from O.E. *rudu*, redness, whence *ruddy*. SHAKESPEARE makes Arviragus say over Imogen:

> Thou shalt not lack
> The flower that's like thy face, pale prim rose;
> nor
> The azur'd hare-bell...the ruddock would,
> With charitable bill...bring thee all this.
> *Cymbeline*, IV, ii.

Rudolphine Tables, The (roo dol' fin). Astronomical calculations begun by Tycho Brahe, continued by Kepler, and published in 1627. They were named after Kepler's patron, Kaiser Rudolph II.

Rue (roo), called HERB OF GRACE, because it was employed for sprinkling holy water.

See also DIFFERENCE. Ophelia says:

> There's rue for you, and here's some for me! we may call it "herb of grace" o' Sundays.
> SHAKESPEARE: *Hamlet*, IV, v.

Ruff. An early forerunner of WHIST, very popular in the late 16th and early 17th centuries, later called *slamm*. The act of trumping at whist, etc., is still called "the ruff".

Ruffian's Hall. A CANT term for West SMITHFIELD.

> The field commonly called West-Smith field, was for many yeares called Ruffians Hall, by reason it was the usuall place of Frayes and common fighting, during the Time that Sword-and-Bucklers were in use.
> *Howe's continuation of Stow's "Annals"* (1631), p. 1024.

Rufus (The Red). William II of England (1056, 1087–1100).

Otto II of Germany (955, 967–983), son of the emperor Otto the Great.

Gilbert de Clare, Earl of Gloucester (1243–1295).

Ruggiero. *See* ROGERO.

Rule, or **Regulus, St.** A priest of Patræ in Achaia, who is said to have come to SCOT-LAND in the 4th century, bringing with him relics of ST. ANDREW, and to have founded the town and bishopric of St. Andrews. The name Killrule (*Cella Reguli*) perpetuates his memory.

Rule. Rule, Britannia. Words by James Thomson (1700–1748), author of *The Seasons*; music by Dr. Arne (1710–1778). It first appeared in a masque entitled *Alfred* produced in August 1740 at Maidenhead at Cliveden House. It was written at the command of the PRINCE OF WALES and performed before him. The original opening was:

When Britain first, at Heaven's command,
Arose from out the azure main,
This was the charter of the land,
And guardian angels sung this strain:
"Rule, Britannia, rule the waves;
Britons never will be slaves."

In the rising of 1745 "Rule, Britannia" was sung by the JACOBITES with modifications appropriate to their cause.

Rule nisi (nī' sī). A "rule" is an order from one of the superior courts, and a "rule nisi" (*cp.* NISI) is such an order "to show cause". That is, the rule is to be held absolute *unless* the party to whom it applies can "show cause" why it should not be so.

Rule of the Road. *See under* ROAD.

Rule of thumb. *See under* THUMB.

Rule the roost. *See under* ROAST.

Twelve Good Rules. (1) Urge no healths; (2) Profane no divine ordinances; (3) Touch no state matters; (4) Reveal no secrets; (5) Pick no quarrels; (6) Make no comparisons; (7) Maintain no ill opinions; (8) Keep no bad company; (9) Encourage no vice; (10) Make no long meals; (11) Repeat no grievances; (12) Lay no wagers.

The rules were framed and displayed in many taverns in the 18th century and derived from a broadside showing a rough-cut of the execution of CHARLES I and were said to have been "found in the study of King Charles the First, of Blessed Memory". Goldsmith refers to them in *The Deserted Village* (line 232).

Rulers, Titles of. The following titles are (1) designations that approximately correspond to our *King* or *Emperor* (*e.g. Bey, Mikado, Sultan*), and (2) appellatives that were originally the proper name of some individual ruler (*e.g. Cæsar*). Some are now, of course, obsolete.

Abgarus. A title of the kings of Edessa (99 B.C.-A.D. 217).

Abimelech (father of counsel). A title of the king of the ancient Philistines.

Akhoond. King and high priest of the Swat (N.W. provinces of India).

Ameer, Amir. Ruler of Afghanistan, Sind, and certain other Mohammedan princes.

Archon. Chief of the nine magistrates of ancient ATHENS. The next in rank was called *Basileus*.

Augustus. The title of the Roman Emperor when the heir-presumptive was styled *Cæsar*.

Beglerbeg. See BEY *below.*

Begum. A queen, princess, or lady of high rank in India.

Bey—of Tunis. In the Turkish Empire, a bey was usually a superior military officer, or the governor of a minor province or *sanjak*.

Brenn, or *Brenhin.* A war-chief of the ancient Gauls. A dictator appointed by the DRUIDS in times of danger.

Bretwalda. See BRETWALDA.

Cacique. See CAZIQUE, *below.*

Cæsar. Originally a surname of the Julian family, then assumed by successive Roman emperors and later by their heir-presumptive. *Cp.* AUGUSTUS, *above.*

Caliph, or *Calif* (successor). Successors of MOHAMMED in temporal and spiritual affairs. After the first four successors the caliphate passed to the Omayyad dynasty (660), thence to the ABBASSIDES (670–1538). The supposed transfer to the OTTOMANS is not authenticated and, in 1924, the caliphate was suppressed by the Turkish assembly.

Candace. A title of the queens of Meroe in Upper Nubia.

Caudillo. See CAUDILLO.

Cazique, or *Cacique.* A native prince of the ancient Peruvians, Cubans, Mexicans, etc., also applied to chiefs of Indian tribes in South America and the West Indies.

Chagan. The chief of the Avars.

Cham. See KHAN, *below.*

Czar. See TSAR, *below.*

Dey. Governor of Algiers before it was annexed to France in 1830; also the 16th-century rulers of Tunis and Tripoli.

Divan. The native chief of Palanpur, India.

Doge (Duke). The ruler of the old Venetian Republic (*c.* 700–1797); also that of Genoa (1339–1797).

Duce. See DUCE.

Duke. The ruler of a duchy (Lat. *dux, a*

leader); formerly in many European countries of sovereign rank.

Elector. A prince of the HOLY ROMAN EMPIRE of sovereign rank entitled to take part in the election of the Emperor.

Emir. The independent chieftain of certain Arabian provinces as Bokhara, Nejd, etc.; also given to Arab chiefs who claim descent from MOHAMMED.

Emperor. The ruler of an empire, especially of the HOLY ROMAN EMPIRE from Lat. *Imperator*, one who commands.

Exarch. The title of a viceroy of the BYZANTINE EMPIRE, especially the *Exarch* of Ravenna, who was *de facto* governor of Italy.

Führer. See FÜHRER.

Gaekwar. Formerly the title of the ruler of the Mahrattas; then that of the ruler of Baroda (his son being *Gaekwad*). The word is Marathi for a cowherd.

Gauleiter (Ger., "region leader"). The ruler of a province under the NAZI régime (1933–45).

Holkar. The title of the Maharajah of Indore.

Hospodar. The title borne by the princes of Moldavia and Wallachia before their union with Rumania (Slavic, "lord, master").

Imperator. See EMPEROR, *above*.

Inca. The title of the sovereigns of Peru up to the conquest by Pizarro (1532).

Kabaka. The native ruler in the Buganda province of Uganda.

Kaiser. The German form of CÆSAR (*see above*); the old title of the HOLY ROMAN EMPEROR and of the later Austrian and German Emperors.

Khan. The chief rulers of Tartar, Mongol, and Turkish tribes, as successors of Genghis Khan (d. 1227). The word means "lord" or "prince".

Khedive. The title meaning "prince" or "sovereign" conferred in 1867 by the SULTAN of Turkey on the viceroy or governor of Egypt. It was abandoned in favour of *Sultan* in 1914. *Cp.* VALI, *below*.

King. See KING.

Lama. See LAMA.

Maharajah (Hind., "the great king"). The title of many of the native rulers of Indian states.

Maharao. The title of the rulers of Cutch, Kotah, and Sirohi, India.

Maharao Rajah. The ruler of Bundi, India.

Maharawal. The rulers of Banswana, Dungarpur, Jaisalmer, and Partabgarh, India.

Mikado. See MIKADO. *Cp.* SHOGUN; TYCOON.

Mir. The ruler of Khairpur, India.

Mogul. See MOGUL.

Mpret. The old title of the Albanian rulers (from Lat. *imperator*), revived in 1913 in favour of Prince William of Wied, whose Mpretship lasted only a few months.

Nawab. The native rulers of Bhopal, Tonk, Jaora, etc.; and formerly of Bengal.

Negus (properly *Negus Negust*, "King of Kings"). The native name of the Emperor of Ethiopia.

Nizam. The title of the ruler of Hyderabad.

Padishah (Pers., "protecting lord"). A title of the former SULTAN of Turkey, the Shah of Persia, and of the former Great MOGULS.

Pendragon. See PENDRAGON.

Pharaoh. See PHARAOH.

Prince. Formerly in common use as the title of a reigning sovereign, and still used in a few cases, *e.g.* the Prince of Monaco, the Prince of Liechtenstein.

Rajah. Hindustani for "King" (*cp.* MAHARAJAH, *above*); the title of the rulers of Cochin, Ratlam, Tippera, Chamba, Faridkot, Mandi, Pudukota, Rajgarh, Rajpipla, Sailana, and Tehri (Garhwal). *Cp.* REX, *below*.

Rex. The Latin equivalent of "King", connected with *regere*, to rule, and with Sans. *rajan* (whence RAJAH), a king.

Sachem, Sagamore. Chieftains of certain tribes of Northern American Indians.

Satrap. The governor of a province in ancient Persia.

Shah (Pers., king). The supreme ruler of Persia and some other Eastern countries. *Cp.* PADISHAH, *above*.

Shaikh or *Sheikh*. An Arab chief, or head man of a tribe.

Shogun. See SHOGUN.

Sindhia. The special title of the Maharajah of Gwalior.

Sirdar. The commander-in-chief of the Egyptian army and military governor of Egypt (a British officer during the occupation, 1882–1922). Also applied to certain nobles in India (Pers. *sardar*, leader, officer).

Stadtholder. Originally a provincial viceroy in the Netherlands, later the chief executive officer of the United Provinces.

Sultan (also *Soldan*). The title of the rulers of certain Mohammedan states.

Tetrarch. The governor of the fourth part of a province in the ancient Roman Empire

Thakur Sahib. The title of the native rule

of Gondal, India.

Tsar, or *Czar*. The common title of the former Emperors of Russia, first assumed by Ivan the Terrible in 1547 (Lat. *Cæsar*). His wife was the *Tsarina*, his son the *Tsare-vitch*, and his daughter the *Tsarevna*. The latter titles were eventually reserved for the eldest son and his wife respectively.

Tycoon. See TYCOON.

Vali. The title of the governors of Egypt prior to their holding of the style KHEDIVE (*see above*).

Voivode, or *Vaivode* (Russ., "the leader of an army"). A title once used by the princes of Moldavia and Wallachia, later called HOS-PODARS (*see above*).

Wali. A title of the ruler or Khan of Kalat, India.

It should be noted that many of these titles now refer to former rulers (*e.g.* those of Indian States and Persia).

Rum-Runners. During the prohibition era in the U.S.A., those engaged in smuggling illicit liquor by speedboats across the lakes from Canada or from ships outside the THREE-MILE LIMIT. The limit was subsequently increased to twelve miles by agreement with other powers and enforced by U.S.N. destroyers. These, when over-age, were passed to Great Britain in 1940 under the LEND-LEASE arrangements. *See* BOOT-LEGGER; MOONSHINER.

Ruminate. To think, to meditate upon some subject; literally, "to chew the cud" (Lat. *rumino*; from *rumen*, the throat).

> He chew'd
> The thrice-turn'd cud of wrath, and cook'd his
> spleen.
> TENNYSON: *The Princess*, Pt. I, i.64.

Rump, The. The end of the backbone, with the buttocks. The term was applied contemptuously to the remnant of the LONG PARLIAMENT that was left after PRIDE'S PURGE. It first numbered less than 60 M.P.s and, when augmented, not more than 125. It abolished the HOUSE OF LORDS and the monarchy and declared England a COMMON-WEALTH. It was dismissed by Cromwell in 1653, but resumed its sitting in 1659 and in 1660 Monck secured the recall of its purged members. It was finally dissolved in March 1660.

Rump and dozen. A rump of beef and a dozen of CLARET; or a rump steak and a dozen oysters. A not uncommon wager among sportsmen of the late 18th and early 19th centuries.

Rumpelstiltskin, or **Rumpelstilzchen** (rum pèl stilts' kin). A passionate little deformed DWARF of German folk-tale. A mill-

er's daughter was enjoined by a king to spin straw into GOLD, and the dwarf did it for her, on condition that she would give him her first child. The maiden married the king, and grieved so bitterly when the child was born that the dwarf promised to relent if within three days she could find out his name. Two days were spent in vain guesses, but the third day one of the queen's servants heard a strange voice singing:

> Little dreams my dainty dame
> Rumpelstilzchen is my name.

The child was saved, and the dwarf killed himself with rage.

Run. A long run, a short run. Said of a theatrical or film show. "It had a long run" means it was performed repeatedly over a long period, owing to its popularity. The allusion is to a long-distance run or race. A *short run* means that the show did not take on with the public and was soon withdrawn.

He that runs may read. The BIBLE quotation in *Hab.* ii, 2, is, "Write the vision, and make it plain upon tables, that he may run that readeth it."

Cowper says:

> But truths, on which depends our main concern...
> Shine by the side of every path we tread
> With such a lustre, he that runs may read.
> *Tirocinium*, 1.77.

In the long run. Eventually, in the final result. The allusion is to the runner who may be outpaced at the start but who draws ahead before the finish. The hare got the start, but in the long run the patient perseverance of the tortoise won the race.

On the run. Moving from place to place and hiding from the authorities; said especially of criminals, etc.

Run of the mill. The expected or usual type, or sequence of events. Provided that a steady flow of water issued from the mill-pond, the mill would run smoothly and normally.

To be run in. To be arrested and taken to the lock-up.

To give someone a run for his money. To make him expend considerable effort, to lead him a pretty dance.

To go with a run. To go swimmingly; "without a HITCH". As a rope goes with a run when let go free, instead of being paid out gradually.

To have a run for one's money. To obtain satisfaction or pleasure from one's expenditure or efforts, even if the outcome is not entirely successful; as a bet on a horse may give the backer some excitement whether it wins or not.

To have the run of the house. To have

free access and liberty to make full use of what it offers.

To run amok, or amuck. To indulge in physical violence while in a state of frenzy. *Amuck* or *amok* is the Malay *amog*, a state of frenzy.

To run down. To cease to go or act from lack of motive force, as a clock when the spring is fully unwound. *See also* TO RUN A MAN DOWN *under* DOWN.

To run into the ground. To pursue too far; to exhaust a topic.

To run rings round. To outclass completely. To be so much better than one's rival that one can run round him and still reach the winning post first.

To run riot. *See under* RIOT.

To run the rig. *See under* RIG.

To run the show. To take charge of it, to make oneself responsible for its success.

To run through. "To run through one's inheritance" is to squander it at a rapid rate; "to run through one's part in a play" is to read or rehearse it; "to run through the accounts" is to make a quick general survey of them. "To run a person through" is to pass one's sword or rapier through his body.

To run to earth. To discover in a hiding-place; to get to the bottom of a matter. A METAPHOR from fox-hunting when the quarry is run to its "earth" or lair.

Runners. *See* REDBREASTS.

Runners of Classic Renown. *See* HUNTERS AND RUNNERS *under* HUNT.

Runner-up. The competitor or team that finishes in second place; after the winner.

Runcible Hat, Spoon. In Edward Lear's *How Pleasant to know Mr. Lear* there is mention of a runcible hat and in the *Owl and the Pussycat* a runcible spoon. What *runcible* denotes is not apparent. Some who profess to know describe the spoon as a kind of fork having three broad prongs, one of which has a sharp cutting edge.

> They dined on mince and slices of quince
> Which they ate with a runcible spoon.
> *The Owl and the Pussycat.*

Rune (roon). A letter or character of the earliest alphabet in use among the Gothic tribes of northern Europe. Runic inscriptions most commonly occur in Scandinavia and parts of the British Isles. Runes were employed for purposes of secrecy, charms, or DIVINATION; and the word is also applied to ancient lore or poetry expressed in runes. *Rune* is related to O.E. *rūn*, secret. The deeds of warriors were recorded on runic staves and knowledge of rune writing was supposed to have been introduced by ODIN. *See* FUTHORC; OGAM.

Runic Staff, or Wand. *See* CLOG ALMANAC.

Running. Running footmen. Men servants in the early part of the 18th century whose duty was to run beside the slow-moving coach horses and advise the innkeeper of his approaching guests, bear torches, pay turnpikes, etc. The pole which they carried was to help the cumbrous coach out of the numerous sloughs. OLD Q (*see under* Q) was said to be the last to employ them. The "Running Footman" used as a PUBLIC-HOUSE SIGN derives from the old Tudor foot postmen.

Running the Hood, or the Hood Game. It is said that (in the 13th century) Lady Mowbray was passing over Haxey Hill (Lincolnshire) when the wind blew away her hood. It was recovered by 12 rustics who tossed it from one to the other. The event is celebrated annually on 6 January, when the participants called *boggans* play a curious kind of rugby with rolled canvas hoods.

Running Thursday. 13 December 1688, two days after the flight of James II. A rumour ran that the French and Irish papists had landed; panic ensued and many people ran for their lives into the country.

Running water. No enchantment can subsist in a living stream; if, therefore, a person can interpose a brook betwixt himself and the witches, sprites, or GOBLINS chasing him, he is in perfect safety. Burns's tale of *Tam o'Shanter* turns upon this superstition.

His shoes are made of running leather. *See under* SHOE.

Quite out of the running. Quite out of the competition; not worthy of consideration; like a horse that has been SCRATCHED for a race and is thus not "in the running".

To make the running. To set the pace or standard.

Rupert. Prince Rupert's drops. Bubbles made by dropping molten glass into water. Their form is that of a tadpole, and if the smallest portion of the "tail" is nipped off, the whole flies into fine dust with explosive violence. They were introduced into ENGLAND by Prince Rupert (1619–1682), grandson of James I and Royalist cavalry leader during the CIVIL WARS. *Prince's metal*, seemingly an alloy of brass or copper, was also his invention.

Rupert of Debate. Edward Stanley, fourteenth Earl of Derby (1799–1869). It was when he was Mr. Stanley, and the opponent of Daniel O'Connell, that Lord Lytton so described him, in allusion to the brilliant Royalist cavalry leader, Prince Rupert.

> The brilliant chief, irregularly great,
> Frank, haughty, bold—the Rupert of Debate.
> LYTTON: *New Timon*, Pt. VI.

Ruptured Duck. The nickname in World War II for the American ex-service lapel button issued to all demobilized from the forces. The expression is also applied, not unkindly, to persons with some disablement.

Ruritania (roo ri tā′ nya). An imaginary kingdom in pre-World War I Europe where Anthony Hope placed the adventures of his hero in the novels *The Prisoner of Zenda* (1894) and *Rupert of Hentzau* (1898). The name is frequently applied to any small state where politics and intrigues of a melodramatic and romantic interest are the natural order of the day.

Rush. Friar Rush. *See under* FRIAR.

It's a regular rush. A barefaced swindle, an exorbitant charge. Said when one is "rushed" into paying a good deal more for something than it is worth.

Not worth a rush. Worthless; not worth a STRAW. When floors used to be strewn with rushes, distinguished guests were given clean rushes, but those of inferior standing were left with used rushes or none at all, being considered "not worth a rush".

> Keep your wisdom and your righteousness and piety for yourself. I do not value them a rush; but your love I will have.
> S. BARING-GOULD: *In the Roar of the Sea*, ch.xxxi.

Rush-bearing Sunday. A SUNDAY, generally near the festival of the SAINT to whom the church is dedicated, when anciently it was customary to renew the rushes with which the church floor was strewn. The custom is still observed at St. Mary Redcliffe, Bristol, on WHIT SUNDAY and at Ambleside, Grasmere, and elsewhere in Westmorland.

At Ambleside, a rush-bearing procession is held on the Saturday nearest St. Anne's Day (26 July), the church being dedicated to St. Anne.

Russel. A common name given to a fox, from its russet colour.

> And daun Russell the fox stirte up at ones
> And by the gargat hente Chauntecleer,
> And on his bak toward the wode hym beer.
> CHAUCER: *The Nonnes Preestes Tale*, 1. 514.

Rustam, and **Rustem.** The Persian HERCULES, the son of Zal, prince of Sedjistan, famous for his victory over the white DRAGON Asdeev. His combat for two days with Prince Isfendiar is a favourite subject with the Persian poets. Matthew Arnold's poem *Sohrab and Rustam* gives an account of Rustam fighting with and killing his son Sohrab.

> Let Zal and Rustrum bluster as they will,
> Or Hatim call to Supper—heed not you.
> FITZGERALD: *Omar Khayyám*, x.

Rusty. To turn rusty. Like a rusty bolt, which sticks and will not move; to become obstinate, or surly and ill-tempered. **To cut up rusty** is a similar expression.

Rye-house Plot. A conspiracy in 1683 to murder Charles II and his brother James on their return from Newmarket near the Rye House, Hoddesdon, Hertfordshire, the home of Rumbold, a Cromwellian, where the plot was hatched. It was the work of WHIG extremists and former Cromwellians but miscarried because the royal party left sooner than planned. Lord William Russell and Algernon Sidney, although not active participants, were executed for complicity.

Rymenhild. *See* KING HORN.

S

S. The nineteenth letter of the English alphabet (eighteenth of the ancient Roman), representing the Greek *sigma* from the Phoenician and Hebrew *shin*. As a mediæval Roman numeral S stood for 7, also 70; and S for 70,000.

Collar of S.S., S's or **Esses.** *See under* COL-LAR.

'S. A euphemistic abbreviation of *God's*, formerly common in oaths and expletives; as *'Sdeath* (God's death), *'Sblood* (God's blood), *'Sdeins* (God's *dignes*, *i.e.* dignity), *'Sfoot*, etc.

> 'Sdeins, I know not what I should say to him, in the whole world! He values me at a crack'd three farthings, for aught I see.
> BEN JONSON *Every Man in His Humour*, II, i.

$ The typographical sign for the DOLLAR, is thought to be a variation of the 8 with which pieces of eight were stamped, and was in use in the United States before the adoption of the Federal currency in 1785. Another, perhaps fanciful, derivation is from the letters U.S.

S.A. *See* S.S.; NIGHT OF THE LONG KNIVES.

S.J. (*Societas Jesu*). The Society of Jesus; denoting that the priest after whose name those letters are placed is a JESUIT.

S O S. The Morse code signal (3 dots, 3 dashes, 3 dots, ...———...) used by shipping, etc., in distress to summon immediate aid; hence any urgent appeal for help.

The letters, in morse a convenient combination, have been popularly held to stand for *save our souls* or *save our ship*.

S.P.Q.R. *Senatus Populusque Romanus* (The Roman Senate and People). Letters inscribed on the standards, etc., of ancient ROME. Facetiously, "small profits and quick returns".

S.S. (Ger.). *Schutz Staffeln*, an armed force that originated as part of Hitler's bodyguard in 1923 with the predominant S.A. (*Sturm Abteilung*). In 1929, Heinrich Himmler took on the S.S. and defining its duties as "to find out, to fight and to destroy all open and secret enemies of the FÜHRER, the National Socialist Movement, and our racial resurrec-

tion", raised it to a position of dominating power and great numerical strength. During World War II, S.S. Divisions fought with fanatical zeal. *See also* NIGHT OF THE LONG KNIVES.

S.T.P. (*Sacræ Theologiæ Professor*). "Professor of Sacred Theology". "D.D."—*i.e.* Doctor of Divinity—is the English equivalent of "S.T.P."

Sabæans, Sabeans (så bē' ånz). The ancient people of Yemen in south-western Arabia; from Arabic Saba', or SHEBA (*see Job* vi, 19).

Sabaism (såb' å izm). The worship of the stars, or the "host of heaven" (from Heb. *caba*, host). The term is also sometimes applied to the religion of the SABIANS.

Sabaoth (så bā' oth). The Bible phrase *Lord God of Sabaoth* means *Lord God of Hosts* not *of the Sabbath*, *Sabaoth* being Hebrew for "armies" or "hosts". The epithet has been frequently misunderstood, as in the last stanza of Spenser's *Faerie Queene* (VII, viii, 21):

> All that moveth doth in change delight:
> But thenceforth all shall rest eternally
> With him that is God of Sabaoth hight:
> O! that great Sabaoth God, grant me that
> Sabbath's sight.

Sabbatæans. The disciples of Sabbatai Sebi (1626–1676) or Zebi of Smyrna who proclaimed himself MESSIAH in 1648. He was arrested at Constantinople in 1666 and accepted the MOSLEM faith. His learning and personal appeal were extraordinary and in his heyday he had thousands of followers. He was a Jew of Spanish descent.

Sabbath (såb' åth) (Heb. *shabath*, to rest). Properly, the seventh day of the week, enjoined on the ancient Hebrews by the fourth Commandment (*Exod*. xx, 8–11) as a day of rest and worship; the Christian SUNDAY, "the Lord's Day", the first day of the week, is often inaccurately referred to as "the Sabbath". For Mohammedans, FRIDAY is the weekly day of rest.

A Sabbath Day's Journey (*Acts* i, 12) with the Jews was not to exceed the distance between the ark and the extreme end of the camp. This was 2,000 cubits, about 1,000 yards. It arose from the injunction (*Exod.* xvi, 29) against journeying on the Sabbath with that (*Jos.* iii, 4) providing for a distance of 2,000 cubits between the ark and the people when they travelled in the wilderness. As their tents were this distance from the ark, it was held that they might properly travel this distance, since the injunction could not have been intended to prevent their attendance at worship.

Sabbatarians. Those who observe the day of rest with excessive strictness, a peculiar feature of English and Scottish Puritanism enforced during the period of the COMMONWEALTH when sport and recreation was forbidden. Some relaxation occurred after the RESTORATION, but the Lord's Day Observance Act of 1782 closed all places of entertainment on a SUNDAY where an admission fee was charged. A Sunday Entertainments Act, 1932, empowered local authorities to license the Sunday opening of cinemas and musical entertainments; the opening of museums, etc., was permitted. The Bill was opposed by the Lord's Day Observance Society.

Sabbatians. Members of a 4th-century NOVATIAN sect, followers of Sabbatius. They followed the Quartodeciman rule.

Sabbatical Year (sȧ băt' i kȧl). One year in seven, when all the land, according to Mosaic law, was to lie fallow (*Exod.* xxiii, 10, etc.; *Lev.* xxv, 2–7; *Deut.* xv, 1–11). The term is used in universities, etc., for a specified period of freedom from academic duties, during which time a professor or lecturer is released to study or travel.

Sabean. *See* SABÆANS.

Sabellianism (sȧ bel' i ȧn izm). The tenets of the **Sabellians,** an obscure sect founded in the 3rd century by Sabellius, a Libyan priest. Little is known of their beliefs, but they were UNITARIANS and held that the TRINITY merely expressed three relations or states of one and the same God. *See* CONFOUNDING THE PERSONS *under* PERSON.

Sabians. A semi-Christian sect of Babylonia, akin to the MANDÆANS or Christians of St. John, a GNOSTIC sect which arose in the 2nd and 3rd centuries and still survives south of Baghdad.

Sabines, The (săb' īnz). An ancient people of central Italy, living in the Apennines, N. and NE. of ROME, and subjugated by the Romans about 290 B.C.

The Rape of the Sabine Women. The legend, connected with the foundation of ROME, is that, as ROMULUS had difficulty in providing his followers with wives, he invited the men of the neighbouring tribes to a festival. In the absence of the menfolk, the Roman youths raided the Sabine territory and carried off all the women they could find. The incident has frequently been depicted in art; Rubens's canvas in the National Gallery, London, is one of the best known examples.

Sable. The heraldic term for *black*, shown in engraving by horizontal lines crossing perpendicular ones. The fur of the animal of this name is brown, but it is probable that in the 15th century, when the heraldic term was first used, the fur was dyed black, as seal fur is today. Sable fur was always much sought after, and very expensive.

A suit of sables. A rich courtly dress. By the Statute of Apparel (24 Henry VIII c. 13) it is ordained that none under the degree of EARL shall use sables. Ben Jonson says (*Discoveries*), "Would you not laugh to meet a great councillor of state in a flat cap, with trunk hose...and yond haberdasher in a velvet gown trimmed with sables?"

> So long? Nay, then, let the devil wear black, for I'll have a suit of sables.
> SHAKESPEARE: *Hamlet*, III, ii.

Sabotage (săb' ō tazh). Wilfull and malicious destruction of machinery, plant, disruption of plans and projects, etc., by strikers, rebels, fifth columnists, etc. The term came into use after the great French railway strike in 1912, when the strikers cut the shoes (*sabots*) holding the railway lines.

Sabres. *See* BAYONETS.

Sabreur (sa brer'). **Le beau sabreur** (Fr.), the handsome swordsman. This was the name given to Joachim Murat (1767–1815), King of Naples and brother-in-law of NAPOLEON BONAPARTE. He was cavalry commander in many of Napoleon's greatest battles.

Sabrina (sa brī' nȧ). The Roman name of the river Severn, but according to Geoffrey of Monmouth (*Historia Britonum*) it is from Sabre, daughter of Locrin and his concubine Estrildis, whom he married after divorcing Guendolœna. The ex-Queen gathered an army and Locrin was slain. Estrildis and Sabre were consigned to the waters of the Severn. NEREUS took pity on Sabre, or Sabrina, and made here the river goddess.

> There is a gentle nymph not far from hence,
> That with moist curb sways the smooth Severn stream,
> Sabrina is her name, a virgin pure.
> MILTON: *Comus*, 824.

Sac and Soc. *Sac* is O.E. *sacu*, strife, contention, litigation; *soc* is O.E. *soc*, the inquiry or investigation, a jurisdiction. The expression was common both before and after the

Norman CONQUEST and used in grants of land to denote the conveyance of rights in private jurisdiction to the grantee.

Saccharissa (săk à ris' á). A name bestowed by Edmund Waller on Lady Dorothy Sidney (b. 1617), eldest daughter of the Earl of Leicester, who, in 1639, married Lord Spencer of Wormleighton, afterwards Earl of Sunderland. Aubrey says that Waller was passionately in love with the lady, but the poems themselves give the impression that the affair was merely a poetical pose.

Sacco Benedetto, or **Saco Bendito** (săk' ō ben é det' ō, ben dē' tō) (Ital., Sp., blessed sack, or cloak). The yellow linen robe with two crosses on it, and painted over with flames and devils, worn by those going to the stake after condemnation by the Spanish INQUISITION. *See* AUTO DA FÉ. Penitents who had been taken before the Inquisition had to wear this habit for a stated period. Those worn by Jews, sorcerers, and renegades bore a St. Andrew's CROSS in red on back and front.

Sachem (sā' chem). A chief among some of the North American Indian tribes. *Sagamore* is a similar title. Sachem was also applied to certain high officials of the TAMMANY Society of New York.

Sacheverell. The Sacheverell Affair. On 5 November 1709, the anniversary of William III's landing at Torbay, Dr. Henry Sacheverell (*c. 1674–1724*) preached a sermon in St. Paul's before the Lord Mayor of London reasserting the doctrine of non-resistance and by implication attacking the principles of the GLORIOUS REVOLUTION and the DISSENTERS. The sermon, *The Perils of False Brethren*, was subsequently printed and the WHIG ministry ill-advisedly impeached him (1710). The affair aroused tremendous excitement; Queen Anne attended Westminster Hall daily, and the London mob burnt Dissenters' chapels. Sacheverell was declared guilty by 69 votes to 52 and sentenced to abstain from preaching for three years and to have his sermon burnt by the common hangman. It was substantially a moral victory for Sacheverell and his TORY adherents.

Sack (Lat. *saccus*). A bag. According to tradition, it was the last word uttered before the tongues were confounded at BABEL. Also applied to certain loose garments and ladies' gowns hanging from the shoulders.

Friars of the Sack (Lat. *fratres saccati*). Also known as *De Penitencia*, or friars of the Penance of Jesus Christ, and so called from their sackcloth garment. They were abolished in 1274 but some remained in England until 1317.

A sack race. A contest in which each runner is put up to the armpits in a sack to jump or run as well as the size of the sack permits.

To get the sack, or **To be sacked.** To be dismissed from employment. The phrase was current in 17th-century France (*On luy a donné son sac*); and the probable explanation of the term is that workmen carried their implements in a bag or sack, and when discharged took up their bag of tools and departed to seek a job elsewhere. The SULTAN used to put in a sack, and throw into the BOSPORUS any one of his harem he wished to be rid of; but this has no connexion with the phrase.

To wear sackcloth and ashes. Metaphorically, an expression of contrition and penitence. An allusion to the Hebrew custom of wearing sackcloth and ashes as suitably humble attire for religious ceremonies, mourning, penitence, etc. The sackcloth in question was a coarse dark haircloth from which sacks were made.

> And I set my face unto the Lord God, to seek by prayer and supplications, with fasting, and sackcloth, and ashes.
>
> *Dan.* ix, 3.

Sack. The old name for dry wines of the sherry type such as Madeira sack, Canary sack, Palm sack. It appears to be derived from span. *saca*, export, not from Fr. *sec*, dry.

Sackerson. The famous bear kept at PARISGARDEN in SHAKESPEARE's time.

Saco Bendito. *See* SACCO BENEDETTO.

Sacrament (Lat. *sacramentum*). Originally "a military oath" taken by the Roman soldiers not to desert their standard, turn their back on the enemy, or abandon their general. Traces of this meaning survive in early Christian usage but its present meaning comes from its employment in the Latin NEW TESTAMENT to mean "sacred mystery". Hence its application to baptism, confirmation, the EUCHARIST, etc.

The five sacraments are Confirmation, Penance, Orders, Matrimony, and EXTREME UNCTION. These are not counted "Sacraments of the GOSPEL". (*See Book of Common Prayer, Articles of Religion*, XXV.)

The seven sacraments are BAPTISM, Confirmation, the EUCHARIST, Penance, Orders, Matrimony, and EXTREME UNCTION.

The two sacraments of the PROTESTANT Churches are BAPTISM and the Lord's Supper.

Sacramentarians. The name given by Luther to those who maintained that no change took place in the eucharistic elements after consecration but that the bread and wine are only the body and blood of

Christ in a metaphorical sense. The name was thus applied in the 16th century to those who did not accept the REAL PRESENCE.

Sacred (Lat. *sacrare*, to consecrate). That which is consecrated or dedicated to religious use.

The Sacred Band. A body of 300 Theban "Ironsides" who fought against Sparta in the 4th century B.C. They specially distinguished themselves at Leuctra (371), and the Band was annihilated at Chæronea (338).

The Sacred City. See HOLY CITY.

The Sacred College. The College of Cardinals (*see under* CARDINAL).

A sacred cow. Any institution, long-cherished practice, custom, etc., treated as immune from criticism, modification, or abolition. An allusion to the fact that the cow is held sacred by the Hindus.

The Sacred Heart. See under HEART.

The Sacred Isle, or **Holy Island.** IRELAND was so called from its many SAINTS and Guernsey from its many monks. The island referred to by Moore in his *Irish Melodies* is Scattery, to which St. Senanus retired and vowed no woman should set foot thereon.

> Oh, haste and leave this sacred isle,
> Unholy bark, ere morning smile.
> > *St. Senanus and the Lady.*

Enhallow (Norse *Eyinhalga*, holy isle) is a small island in the Orkney group where cells fo the Irish anchorite fathers are still said to exist. *See also* HOLY ISLAND.

Sacred Majesty. See MAJESTY.

The Sacred War. In Greek history, one of the wars waged by the AMPHICTYONIC League in defence of the temple and ORACLE of DELPHI.

(1) Against the Cirrhæans (594–587 B.C.).

(2) For the restoration of Delphi to the Phocians, from whom it had been taken (448–447 B.C.).

(3) Against Philip of Macedon (346 B.C.).

The Sacred Way. *See* SACRA VIA *under* VIA.

The Sacred Weed. VERVAIN (*see also* HERBA SACRA), or—humorously—tobacco, also called "divine".

Sacring Bell (săk' ring). From the obsolete verb to *sacre*, to consecrate, used especially of sovereigns and BISHOPS. The bell rung in churches to draw attention to the most solemn parts of the MASS. In mediæval times it served to announce to those outside that the Mass was in progress, and for this purpose often a handbell was rung out of a side window. It is more usually called the **Sanctus bell** because it was rung at the saying of the *Sanctus* at the beginning of the CANON OF THE MASS (*see under* CANON), and also at the Consecration and Elevation and other moments. It is still used in the ROMAN CATHOLIC CHURCH and certain other Churches.

> He heard a little sacring bell ring to the elevation of a to-morrow mass.
> > REGINALD SCOTT:
> > *Discoverie of Witchcraft* (1584).

Sacy's Bible. See BIBLE, SOME SPECIALLY NAMED EDITIONS.

Sad. He's a sad dog. A playful way of saying a man is a debauchee.

Sad bread (Lat. *panis gravis*). Heavy bread, bread that has not risen properly. SHAKESPEARE calls it "distressful bread"—not the bread of distress, but the *panis gravis* or ill-made bread eaten by those who cannot get better. In America unleavened cakes are known as *sad cakes*.

Saddle. A saddle of mutton. The two loins with the connecting vertebræ.

Boot and saddle. *See under* BOOT.

I will lose the horse or win the saddle. *See under* HORSE.

Saddle-bag furniture. Chairs, etc., upholstered in a cheap kind of carpeting, the design of which is based on that of saddle-bags carried by camels in the East.

Set the saddle on the right horse. Lay the blame on those who deserve it.

To be in the saddle. To be in office, to be in a position of authority; also to be ready for work and eager to get on with it.

To saddle with responsibility. To put the responsibility on, to make responsible for.

Sadducees (săd' ū sēz). A Jewish party opposed to the PHARISEES. They did not accept oral tradition, but only the written Law, denied the existence of ANGELS and spirits and rejected the idea of future punishments in an after-life, as well as the resurrection of the body. They were major opponents of Christ and His disciples and were involved in the events leading to His death. Substantially, they represented the interests and attitudes of the privileged and wealthy and nothing more is heard of them after the destruction of Jerusalem (A.D. 70).

The name is said to be from Zadok (*see* II *Sam.* viii, 17), who was high priest at the time of SOLOMON.

Sadism. The term for the obtaining of sexual satisfaction through the infliction of pain or humiliation on another person, or even an animal; also the morbid pleasure those in certain psychological states experience in being cruel or in watching certain acts of cruelty. The name derives from the Marquis de Sade (1740–1814), a vicious pervert and writer of plays and obscene novels, notably *Justine* (1791), *Philosophie dans le boudoir*

(1793), and *Les Crimes de l'amour* (1800). *Cp.* MASOCHISM.

Sadler's Wells. There was once a Holy Well at this place belonging to St. John's Priory, CLERKENWELL; it was blocked up at the RE-FORMATION but rediscovered by Mr. Sadler in 1683 when workmen were digging for gravel. The waters were pronounced to be chalybeate and the discovery was turned to immediate profit; when however attendance at the well declined, MUSIC HALL entertainment was provided, and from the 1690s this became the chief attraction under James Miles. In 1765, a builder named Rosoman erected a proper theatre which became famous for burlettas, musical interludes, and PANTOMIMES. Edmund Kean, Dibdin, and Grimaldi all appeared there. In 1844 Samual Phelps took over and produced SHAKE-SPEARE, but after his retirement the boom in WEST END theatres cast the Wells into the shade and it eventually became a cinema, which closed in 1916. A new theatre was built with the help of the Carnegie United Kingdom Trust which opened in 1931 under Lilian Baylis of the OLD VIC and it became one of the leading houses in London for the production of ballet and opera. In 1946 the ballet company transferred to the Royal Opera House, COVENT GARDEN, and in 1968 the opera company moved to the London Coliseum (*see* COLOSSEUM).

Sadler's Wells features in Smollett's *Humphry Clinker*.

Safari. On safari (Swahili from Arab. *safar*, journey). On a hunting expedition in Africa; often used in the sense of "on trek" in the wilds with a company of followers.

Safety. Safety bicycle. *See* PENNY FARTHING.

Safety Matches. Matches which only light when struck on the specially prepared surface on the side of the box, *i.e.* the match head only contains part of the ingredients of combustion. They derive from the discovery of amorphous phosphorus by Anton von Schrotte in 1845. J.E. Lundstrom of Sweden is credited with their introduction. *Cp.* LUCIFER-MATCH; PROMETHEAN.

Saffron. He hath slept in a bed of saffron (Lat. *dormivit in sacco croci*). He has a very light heart, in reference to the exhilarating effects of saffron.

Saga (pl. *sagas*) (sa' gà). In Icelandic the word is applied to any kind of narrative, but in English it particularly denotes heroic biographies written in Iceland and Norway mainly during the 12th, 13th, and 14th centuries. From this comes its English application to a story of heroic adventure.

The sagas are a compound of history and myth in varying proportions, the *King's Sagas* being the oldest, the *First Saga of King Olaf* dating from 1180. Other notable examples are the *Saga of Hallfred*, the *Saga of Björn*, the *Grettis Saga*, the *Saga of Burnt Njáll*, the *Egils Saga* the *Islendinga Saga*, the *Ynglinga Saga*, the *Volsunga Saga*, *Tristram's Saga*, and the *Karlomagnus Saga*. Snorri Sturluson's *Heimskringla* (Orb of the World) is a collection of biographies of Norwegian kings from the 9th to the 12th century. *See* EDDA.

Sagamore. *See* SACHEM.

Sage. The Sage of Chelsea. Thomas Carlyle (1795–1881), essayist and historian, was so called. He and his wife Jane moved from Dumfriesshire to No. 5 (now 24) Cheyne Row, Chelsea in 1834, where they lived for the remainder of their lives.

The Seven Sages. *See* WISE MEN OF GREECE.

Sagittarius (săj i târ' i ûs) (Lat. the archer). One of the old constellations, the ninth sign of the ZODIAC, which the sun enters about 22 November. *See* CHIRON.

Sagittary (săj' i tà ri). The name given in mediæval romances to the CENTAUR, whose eyes sparkled like fire and struck dead like lightning, fabled to have been introduced into the TROJAN armies.

> The dreadful Sagittary
> Appals our numbers.
>
> SHAKESPEARE: *Troilus and Cressida*, V, v.

The "sagittary" referred to in *Othello* I, i:

> Lead to the Sagittary the raised search,
> and there will I be with him,

was probably an inn, but may have been the arsenal.

Sahib (sab, sa' ib) (Urdu, friend). A form of address used by Hindus to Europeans in India corresponding to our "Sir" in "Thank you, sir." Also an Englishman or European, a woman being *Mem-sahib*. The word is also used colloquially to describe a cultured, refined man. *Pukka sahib* denotes a gentleman.

Sail. Sailing under false colours. Pretending to be what you are not with the object of personal advantage. The allusion is to pirate vessels sailing under false colours to escape detection.

To sail against the wind. To swim against the tide, to oppose popular or current trends, opinions, etc.

To sail before the wind. To prosper, to go on swimmingly, to meet with great success, as a ship sails smoothly and rapidly with a following wind.

To sail close to the wind. To keep the vessel's head as near the quarter from which the wind is blowing as possible yet keeping the sails filled; figuratively to go to the verge of what decency or propriety allow; to act so as just to escape the letter or infringement of the law; to take a risk.

To sail into. "To sail into someone" is to attack or reprimand him forcefully, "to sail into a task", etc., is to set about it vigorously, as the attackers "sailing into" the enemy to commence a naval engagement.

To set sail. To start a voyage.

To strike sail. To acknowledge oneself beaten; to eat humble pie (*see under* EAT). When a ship in a fight, or on meeting another ship, lowered her topsails at least half-mast high, she was said to *strike*, meaning that she submitted or paid respect to another.

> Now Margaret
> Must strike her sail, and learn awhile to serve
> Where kings command.
> SHAKESPEARE: *Henry VI, Pt. III*, III, iii.

To trim one's sails. To modify or reshape one's policy or opinion to meet the circumstances, as the sails of a ship are "trimmed" or adjusted according to the wind.

You may hoist sail. Be off. Maria saucily says to Viola, dressed in man's apparel:

> Will you hoist sail, sir? Here lies your way.
> SHAKESPEARE: *Twelfth Night*, I, v.

Sailor King, The. William IV of England (1765, 1830–1837), also called *Silly Billy*, who entered the navy as a midshipman in 1779, and was made Lord High Admiral in 1827.

Saint. Individual saints are entered under their respective names.

The title of saint was from early Christian times applied to APOSTLES, EVANGELISTS, MARTYRS and Confessors of remarkable virtue, especially martyrs. In due course the need arose for BISHOPS to intervene against local recognition of the undeserving and eventually Pope Alexander III (1159–1181) asserted the exclusive right of the Papacy to add to the roll of saints. Nowadays canonization is dependent upon a lengthy legal process where the case for the canonization of a particular person is thoroughly explored and contested. JOAN OF ARC was canonized in 1920; Sir Thomas More (1478–1535) and John Fisher (1459–1535), Bishop of Rochester, in 1935.

In Christian art, saints are often depicted with a NIMBUS, AUREOLE, or glory and individual symbols by which they can be recognized. *See* SYMBOLS OF SAINTS, *below*.

Popes numbered among the saints.

From the time of St. PETER to the end of the 4th century all the Popes (with a few minor and doubtful exceptions) are popularly entitled "Saint"; since then the follow-

ing are the chief of those given the honour:

Innocent I (402–417).
Leo the Great (440–461).
John I (523–526).
GREGORY THE GREAT (590–604).
Deusdedit I (615–619).
Martin I (649–654).
Leo II (682–683).
Sergius I (687–701).
Zacharias (741–752).
Paul I (757–767).
Leo III (795–816).
Paschal I (817–824).
Nicholas the Great (858–867).
Leo IX (1049–1054).
Gregory VII, HILDEBRAND (1073–1085).
Celestine V (1294).
Pius V (1566–1572).
Pius X (1903–1914).

Kings and Queens honoured as Saints.
Among them are:

Edward the Martyr (961, 975–978).
Edward the Confessor (1004, 1042–1066).
Eric VIII of Sweden (1150–1160).
Ethelred I, King of Wessex (866–871).
Ferdinand III of Castile and Leon (1200, 1217–1252).
Louis IX of France (1215, 1226–1270).
Margaret, Queen of Scotland (d. 1093), wife of Malcolm III.
Olaf II of Norway (1015–1030).
Stephen I of Hungary (979, 997–1038).

Patron Saints. (1) a selected list of trades and professions with their patron saints:

Accountants, bankers, book-keepers	St. MATTHEW
Actors	St. Genesius
Advertising	St. Bernadine of Siena
Airmen	Our Lady of Loreto, SS. Thérèse of Liesiux, Joseph Cupertino
Architects	SS. THOMAS Ap., Barbara
Artists	St. LUKE
Athletes (and Archers)	St. SEBASTIAN
Authors and Journalists	St. Francis de Sales
Bakers	SS. ELIZABETH OF HUNGARY, NICHOLAS
Barbers	SS. Cosmas and Damian, Louis
Blacksmiths	St. DUNSTAN
Booksellers	St. JOHN OF GOD
Brewers	SS. AUGUSTINE of Hippo, Luke, NICHOLAS of Myra
Bricklayers	St. STEPHEN
Builders	St. Vincent Ferrer
Cab-drivers	St. Fiacre
Carpenters	St. JOSEPH
Children	St. Nicholas
Comedians	St. VITUS
Cooks	SS. LAWRENCE, Martha
Dentists	St. Apollonia
Dieticians (Medical)	St. MARTHA
Domestic Servants	St. Zita

Editors	St. John Bosco
Engineers	St. Ferdinand III
Farmers	SS. GEORGE, Isidore
Firemen	St. Florian
Florists	SS DOROTHEA, Thérèse
Funeral Directors	SS. JOSEPH OF ARIMATHEA, DYSMAS
Gardeners	SS. Dorothea, Adelard, Tryphon, Fiacre, Phocas
Goldsmiths and Metalworkers	SS. Dunstan, Anastasius
Gravediggers	St. ANTHONY (Ab.)
Grocers	St. MICHAEL
Gunners	St. Barbara
Housewives	St. Anne
Hunters	St. HUBERT
Infantrymen	St. Maurice
Innkeepers and Wine merchants	St Amand
Jewellers	St. ELOI
Lawyers	SS. Ivo, Genesius, Thomas More
Librarians	St. JEROME
Lighthousekeepers	St. Venerius
Miners	St. Barbara
Motorcyclists	Our Lady of Grace
Motorists	SS. Frances of Rome, CHRISTOPHER
Musicians and Singers	SS. Gregory the Great, CECILIA, Dunstan
Nurses	SS. Camillus of Lellis, JOHN OF GOD, AGATHA, Alexius, RAPHAEL
Paratroopers	St. Michael
Pawnbrokers	St. Nicholas
Physicians	SS. Pantaleon, Cosmas and Damian, LUKE, Raphael
Poets	SS. DAVID, Cecilia
Policemen	St. Michael
Postal, Radio, Tele-communications and Telephone, Telegraph and Television Workers	St. Gabriel
Printers	SS JOHN OF GOD, AUGUSTINE of Hippo
Sailors	SS. CUTHBERT, Brendan, Eulalia, Christopher, Peter Gonzales, Erasmus
Scholars	St. Bridget
Scientists	St. Albert
Scouts	St. GEORGE
Sculptors	St. Claude
Secretaries	SS. Genesius, Cassian
Shoemakers	SS. CRISPIN and Crispinianus
Soldiers	SS. Adrian, GEORGE, Ignatius, SEBASTIAN, MARTIN, JOAN OF ARC
Speleologists	St. BENEDICT
Students	SS. THOMAS AQUINAS, Catherine
Surgeons	SS. Cosmas and Damian
Tailors	St. Homobonus
Tax-collectors	St. MATTHEW
Teachers	SS. Gregory the Great, CATHERINE, John Baptist de la Salle
Television	St. CLARE
Travellers	SS. ANTHONY OF PADUA, NICHOLAS, CHRISTOPHER, RAPHAEL
Wine-growers	St. VINCENT
Workers	St. JOSEPH
Yachtsmen	St. Adjutor

(2) Some European and COMMONWEALTH Countries with their patron saints:

Australia	Our Lady Help of Christians
Belgium	St. JOSEPH
Canada	SS. Joseph, Anne
Czechoslovakia	SS. Wenceslas, JOHN OF NEPOMUK, Procopius
Denmark	SS. Asgar, Canute
England	St. GEORGE
France	Our Lady of the ASSUMPTION, SS. JOAN OF ARC, DENYS, LOUIS, Thérèse (see TERESA). There is no official patron saint of France, those listed are recognised as patron saints by the Church.
Germany	SS. BONIFACE, Michael
Greece	SS. NICHOLAS, ANDREW
Holland	St. Willibrord
Hungary	Our Lady, St. STEPHEN
India	Out Lady of the Assumption
Ireland	St. PATRICK
Italy	SS. FRANCIS of Assisi, Catherine of Siena
New Zealand	Out Lady Help of Christians
Norway	St. Olaf
Poland	Our Lady of Czestochowa, SS. Casimir, Stanislaus
Portugal	Immaculate Conception, SS. Francis Borgia, ANTHONY OF PADUA, George, VINCENT
Russia	SS. Andrew, NICHOLAS, Thérèse of Lisieux
Scotland	SS. Andrew, Columba
South Africa	Our Lady of the Assumption
Spain	SS. JAMES, Teresa
Sweden	SS. Bridget, Eric
Wales	St. DAVID
West Indies	St. Gertrude

Symbols of Saints. The symbol common to all saints is the NIMBUS which encircles the head. MARTYRS alone have the common symbols of the CROWN of eternal life won by their heroism and the PALM of triumph. With these is generally associated with some symbol peculiar to the individual saint, often the instrument of his martyrdom, such as the GRIDIRON of St. LAWRENCE or the windlass on which the bowels were drawn from St. Erasmus' body.

Saints not martyrs will be depicted with an object symbolizing their particular virtue (St. AMBROSE has the behive emblematic of eloquence) or relating to some incident in their lives (as St. DUNSTAN pinching the DEVIL's nose). All saints are depicted in their proper dress, as soldiers in armour, bishops or priests in appropriate vestments, kings robed and crowned, religious in the habits of their order.

Below is a selection of some of the many symbols of saints with some of the saints to which they are applied. (*See also* APOSTLES, MARY *and entries for individual saints.*)

Alms-box: *hung round his neck:* St. JOHN OF GOD

Anchor: SS. Clement, Felix, NICHOLAS

Angel(s): Singly or in their host, angels have constantly appeared to aid and protect the saints and are their companions in sacred iconography. For example: *Angel holding plough:* St. Isidore of Madrid;—*fish on a plate:* St. Bertold;—*crosier:* St. BERNARD;—*basket of flowers:* St. DOROTHEA;—*bottle:* St. Leontius; *Angel playing violin:* St. FRANCIS of Assisi;—*organ:* St. CECILIA; *Angel bringing monastic rule:* SS.Pachomius, Paphnutius;—*fish:* SS. Bertold, Boniface, Congal; *Angel defending from lightning:* St. HUGH OF LINCOLN

Anvil: SS. Adrian, ELOI

Apple: Malachy; *three golden:* St. Nicholas

Arrow(s): *as instruments of martyrdom:* SS. Anastasius, Canute, Christina, Edmund, Faustus, SEBASTIAN, URSULA MM.; *two, piercing heart:* St. Augustine; *bunch held:* St. Otto;—and bent bow: St. Mackesoge

Ass: SS. Gerlach, Germanus, Philibert;—*kneeling to Blessed Sacrament:* St. ANTHONY OF PADUA

Axe: *as instrument of martyrdom:* SS. Anastasius, Josophat, Malchus, Martian, MATTHEW, MATTHIAS, Proculus, Rufus

Barge: St. Bertulphus

Barn: SS. Ansovinus, Bridget of Kildare

Barrell: SS. Antonia, Bercher; *cross in*—: St. Willibrord

Basket: SS. Frances, Joanna, JOHN DAMASCENE;—*of bread:* SS. *Philip, Romanus;—of flowers:* St. DOROTHEA;—*of fruit:* SS. Ann, Dorothea, Sitha;—*of roses:* St. ELIZABETH OF HUNGARY

Bear: SS. Columba, Edmund, Gallus, Humbert, Maximinus;—*keeping sheep:* St. Florentius;—*laden with baggage:* SS. Corbinian, Maximinus;—*ploughing:* St. James

Beard: *obtained by prayers of* SS. Galla, Paula Barbata, Wilgefortis (*see* UNCUMBER)

Bed of Iron: St. Faith

Behive: SS. AMBROSE, BERNARD, JOHN CHRYSOSTOM

Bell: SS. ANTHONY THE GREAT, Gildas, Kenan;—*and fishes:* St. Winwaloc;—*in fish's mouth:* St. Paul de Leon

Bellows: *held by devil:* St. Genevieve

Boar: St. Emilion

Boat: SS. Bertin, JUDE, MARY MAGDALENE

Boathook: St. JUDE

Bodkin: SS. Leger, Simon of Trent

Book: Common attribute of Apostles, Abbots, Abbeses, Bishops etc.; specifically:—*with child Jesus standing on it:* St. ANTHONY OF PADUA;—*with hunting horn or stag with crucifix between horns:* St. HUBERT;—*with wine vessel on it:* St. Urban;—*in bag:* SS. Antoninus, Sitha

Broom: SS. Gisella, Martin of Siguenza, Petronilla

Bull: SS. Adolphus, Regnier, Sylvester; *tossed or gored by*—; SS. Blandina, Marciana, Saturninus

Calves: *two at feet:* St. WALSTAN

Camel: SS. Aphrodicius, Hormisdas; *bound to:* St. Julian of Cilicia

Candle: St. Beatrix

Cauldron: *as an instrument of martyrdom by boiling in lead, oil, pitch, water, etc.:* SS. Boniface, CECILIA, Emilian, Erasmus, Felicity, LUCY, VITUS MM.; JOHN THE EVANGELIST

Chafing dish: St. AGATHA

Church: A common symbol of Abbots, Abbesses, Bishops, etc., as builders of churches and monasteries

City: The attribute of a saint as protector of a particular city

Club(s) *as instrument of martyrdom:* Boniface, Ewald the White, Eusebius, Fabian, Lambert, Magnus, Nicomedes, Panteleon, VALENTINE, Vitalis MM.

Colt: St. MEDARD

Cow: SS. Berlinda, Bridget, Modwena, Perpetua

Crocodile: SS. Helenus, Theodore

Crow: St. VINCENT

Cup and Serpent: *symbolizing poison detected by:* SS. BENEDICT, James of Marchia, John the Evangelist, John a Facundo

Dagger: *as instrument of martyrdom:* SS. Agnes, Canute, Edward, Irene, Kilian, Olave, Solange MM.

Deer: St. Henry

Devil(s): In Christian art the Devil is shown both tormenting the saints (throwing St. Euphrasia down a well, disturbing the prayers of SS. CUTHBERT or Madalberte, for example), and worsted by their virtue (holding a candle for St. DOMINIC or seized by the nose in St. DUNSTAN's pincers). The incidents are too various for separate mention.

Distaff: SS. Genevieve, Rosalie

Doe: SS. Fructuosus, Mammas, Maximus of Turin

Dog: SS. Benignus, BERNARD;—*with loaf:* St. ROCH;—*with torch:* St. Dominic

Dolphin: St. Martianus;—*bearing corpse:* St. Adrian;—*supporting:* St. Calistratus

Dove: *on or over:* SS. AMBROSE, BASILE, Bridget of Sweden, CATHERINE, Catherine of Siena, Cunibert, DAVID, DUNSTAN, GREGORY THE GREAT, Hilary of Arles, John Columbini, Lo, Louis, MEDARD, Oswald, Peter of Alcantara, Peter Celestin, Sampson, THOMAS AQUINAS

Eagle: SS. Augustine, GREGORY THE GREAT, John the Evangelist, Prisca

Ear(s) of Corn: SS. Bridget, Fara, Walburge

Falcon or Hawk: SS. Bavo, Edward, JULIAN Hospitator:—*on cottage:* St. Otto

Feather: St. Barbara

Firebrand: St. ANTHONY THE GREAT

Fish(es): SS. ANDREW, Eanswide, Gregory of Tours, John of Burlington, RAPHAEL, SIMON. *See also* Angel, Bell, Key

Fish hooks: St. Zeno

Flail: St. Varus

Flower(s): SS. Dorothea, Hugh of Lincoln, Louis of Toulouse;—*in apron:* St. Zita

Fountain: *obtained by prayer:* SS. Alton, Antoninus of Toulouse, Apollinaris, Augustine of Canterbury, Clement, Egwin, Guntilda, Humbert, Isidore of Madrid, Julian of Mans, LEONARD, Nicholas of Tolentino, Omer, Philip Beniti, Riquier, Servatius, Trond, Venantius, Wolfgang;—*springing from their blood:* SS. Boniface, Eric MM.

Frog(s): SS. Huvas, Rieul, Sinorina, Ulphia

Goose: St. MARTIN

Gosling: St Pharaildis

Gridiron: *as instrument of martyrdom:* SS. Cyprian, Donatilla, Erasmus, Faith, LAWRENCE, Vincent MM.

Hammer: SS. Adrian, Reinoldus;—*and chalice:* SS. Bernward, ELOI

Hare: St. Albert of Siena

Harp: SS. Cecilia, Dunstan

Hatchet: SS. Adjutus, Matthew, Matthias

Heart: SS. Augustine, Catherine of Siena, Francis de Sales, Jane Frances;—*with sacred monogram:* SS. IGNATIUS, Teresa

Hen: St. Pharaildis

Hind: SS. Catherine of Sweden, Genevieve of Brabant, Lupus of Sens;—*with two fawns:* St. Bassian

Hoe: St. Isidore of Madrid

Hook: *as instrument of martyrdom:* SS. AGATHA, EULALIA, Felician, Vincent MM.

Hops: St. Arnold of Soissons

Horse: SS. Barochus, Irene, Severus of Avranches

Hourglass: SS. Hilarion, Theodosius

Ink-bottle: St. JEROME

Jug or Pitcher: SS. Agatha, Bede, BENEDICT, Elizabeth

of Portugal, Vincent

Key: SS. Ferdinand, Germanus of Paris, HUBERT, PETER, Raymond of Pannafort;—and book: St. Petronilla;—and rosary: St. Sitha;—in fish's mouth: St. Egwin

Keys: two: SS. Hippolytus, Maurilius, Riquier; bunch of: B.V.M., SS. Genevieve, JAMES THE GREAT, MARTHA, Nothburge

Knife: SS. Agatha, BARTHOLOMEW, Christina, Ebba, Peter Martyr

Ladder: SS. Emmeran, John Climacus

Ladle: St. MARTHA

Lamp: SS. FRANCIS, LUCY;—and book: St. Hiltrudis

Lance or Spear: as instrument of martyrdom: SS. BARBARA, Canute, Emmeran, Gerhard, Germanus, Hippolytus, John of Goto, Lambert, Longinus, Matthias, Oswin, THOMAS MM.

Lantern: SS. Gudule, Hugh, Mary of Cabeza

Leopard: and ox, or lions: St. Marciana

Lily: SS. Anthony of Padua, Cajetan, Casimir, Catherine of Sweden, CLARE, DOMINIC, JOSEPH, KENELM, SEBASTIAN, Vincent Ferrer

Lion(s): SS. Adrian, DOROTHEA, Euphemia, Germanus, Ignatius, JEROME, MARK, Prisca

Loom: SS. ANASTASIA, GUDULE

Mason's tools: St. Marinus

Nail(s): as instrument of martyrdom, held or piercing the body: Alexander, DENYS, Fausta, Gemellus, Julian of Emesa, Pantaleon, Quintin, Severus of Rome, WILLIAM OF NORWICH, MM.

Oar: St. JUDE

Organ: St. Cecilia

Ox(en): SS. Blandina, Otto, Frideswide, Fursey, Julitta, LEONARD, Lucy, LUKE, MEDARD

Padlock: on lips: St. JOHN OF NEPOMUK

Pickaxe: St. Leger

Pig: St. Anthony the Great

Pilgrim's Staff: SS. DOMINIC, Louis

Pincers: SS. Agatha, Apollonia, LUCY

Plough: SS. Exuperius, Richard

Purse: St. Cyril of Jerusalem; three: SS. Brieruc, NICHOLAS

Rats: St. GERTRUDE OF NIVELLES

Raven: St. BENEDICT;—bringing food: SS. Erasmus, PAUL THE HERMIT;—with ring in beak: SS. Ida, Oswald

Razor: St. Pamphilius

Ring: SS. BARBARA, Damascus, Edward

Saw: SS. JAMES THE LESS, SIMON

Scales: St. Manous; weighing souls in—: St. MICHAEL

Scourge: SS. AMBROSE, BONIFACE, Dorotheus, Gervase, GUTHLAC, Peter Damian

Scythe: SS. Guntilda, Nothburge, Walstan;—and well: St. Sidwell

Shears: SS. Agatha, Fortunatus, Marca;—and bottle: SS. Cosmas and Damian

Shovel: bakers': SS. Aubert, Honorius

Sieve: SS. BENEDICT, Hippolytus

Spade: St. Fiacre

Sparrow: St. Dominic

Spit: SS. Gengulph, Quentin

Stag(s): SS. Aidan, Eustace, HUBERT, JULIAN Hospitator, Osyth, Rieul; ploughing with—: SS. Kenan, KENTIGERN

Star: on or over: SS. Anastasia, Bernadin, Bruno, Dominic, Humbert, Nicholas of Tolentino, Thomas Aquinas

Swan(2): SS. Cuthbert, Hugh of Grenoble, Kentigern

Sword: as instrument of martyrdom; piercing head or body: SS. Boniface, Euphemia, Lucy, Thomas of Canterbury;—held: SS. AGNES, Aquila, Prisca, CATHERINE, Irene, JAMES THE GREAT, PAUL;—and chalice: St. Ewald the Black;—and club: St. Arcadius;—and crosier or dagger: St. Kilian;—

and hammer: St. Adrian;—and stone(s): SS. Beztert, Pancras;—and vase: St. Pantaleon;—and wheel or book: St. Catherine MM.

Taper: St. GUDULE

Thistle: SS. Caroline, Narcissus

Tongs: SS. Christina, Felician, Martina

Torch: SS. Aidan, Barbara, Dorothea, Eutropia, Irenæus, MEDARD

Tower: St. Barbara, Praxedes

Trowel: SS. Winibald, WILLIAM OF MONTEVERGINE

Trumpet: St. Vincent Ferrer

Vine: SS. Elpidius, Urban, Urban of Langres

Weavers' Loom: St. Severus of Ravenna

Wheel: SS. Catherine, Euphemia;—broken: St. Quentin

Wolf: St. William of Montevergine;—bringing child: St. Simpertus;—bringing goose: St. Vedast;—stealing pig: St. Blaise

Wolfdog: St. Donatus

Woolcomb: St. Blaise

The Battle of the Saints (12 April 1782). Rodney's victory over the French fleet during the American War of Independence which restored British supremacy in the West Indies. It was fought off Les Saintes near Gualdeloupe.

The City of Saints. See under CITY.

The Island of Saints. So IRELAND was called in the MIDDLE AGES.

The Latter-day Saints. See MORMONS.

Saint-Simonism. The social and political theories derived from the teachings of Claude Henri, Comte de Saint-Simon (1760–1825), the French utopian socialist. He advocated a social order based on large-scale industrial production controlled by benevolent industrial leaders. The aim of his society was to improve the lot of the poorest. His disciples advocated that the State should become the sole proprietor, and a form of socialism in which social groups were to manage the state properties. Each man was to be placed and rewarded in their social heirarchy according to his capacities.

Sake. A form of the obsolete word sac. See SAC AND SOC.

In the common phrases For God's sake, for goodness' sake, for conscience's sake, etc., it means "out of consideration for" God, goodness, etc.

For old sake's sake. For the sake of old acquaintance, past times.

For one's name's sake. Out of regard for one's reputation or good name.

Sakes! or **Sakes alive!** Expression of surprise, admiration, etc. Commoner in the United States than England.

Saker (sā' ker). A piece of light artillery, used especially on board ship, in the 16th and 17th centuries. The word is borrowed from the saker hawk (falcon).

> The cannon, blunderbuss, and saker,
> He was the inventor of and maker.
> BUTLER: Hudibras, I, ii, 355.

Saki. The pseudonym of H. H. Munro (1870–1916), the author of *The Westminster Alice* (1902), *Reginald* (1904), *The Chronicles of Clovis* (1911), *The Unbearable Bassington* (1912), etc., and numerous other short stories. His style was often bitingly satirical.

Sakuntala (sà kun' ta la). The heroine of Kalidasa's great Sanskrit drama *Abhijnanasakuntala*. She was the daughter of a sage, Viswamita, and Menaka, a water-nymph, and was brought up by a hermit. One day King Dushyanta came to the hermitage during a hunt, and persuaded her to marry him; and later, giving her a ring, returned to his throne. A son was born and Sakuntala set out with him to find his father. On the way, while bathing, she lost the ring, and the king did not recognize her owing to enchantment. Subsequently it was found by a fisherman in a fish he had caught (*cp.* KENTIGERN), the king recognized his wife, she was publicly proclaimed his queen, and Bharata, his son and heir, became the founder of the glorious race of the Bharatus. Sir William Jones (1746–1794) translated it into English.

Sakya-Muni. One of the names of Gautama Siddartha, the BUDDAH.

Salad. A pen'orth of salad oil. A strapping; a castigation. It was a joke on All Fools' Day (*see* APRIL FOOL) to send one to the saddler's for "a pen'orth of salad oil" (*cp.* ELBOW GREASE; PIGEON'S MILK). The pun is between "salad oil", and the French *avoir de la salade*, "to be flogged". The French *saler* and *salade* are derived from the O.Fr. word for the saddle on which schoolboys were at one time birched. *See also* RICK MOULD.

Salad days. Days of inexperience, when persons are very green.

> My salad days,
> When I was green in judgment.
> SHAKESPEARE: *Antony and Cleopatra*, I, v.

Saladin (Arab. *Salah ud-Din*, "Honour of the Faith") (1138–1193). SULTAN of Egypt and Syria and founder of the Ayubite dynasty, whose capture of JERUSALEM in 1187 led to the Third CRUSADE. He appears in Scott's *Talisman* as a chivalrous warrior.

Saladin tithe. The tax levied by Henry II in 1188 for the recovery of JERUSALEM after its capture by SALADIN.

Salamander (săl' à măn der) (Gr. *salamandra*, a kind of lizard). The name is now given to a genus of amphibious Urodela (newts, etc.), but anciently to a mythical lizard-like monster that was supposed to be able to live in fire, which, however, it quenched by the chill of its body. Pliny refers to this belief (*Nat. Hist.* x, 86; xxix, 23). It was adopted by PARACELSUS as the name of the elemental being inhabiting fire (GNOMES being those of the earth, SYLPHS of the air, and UNDINES of the water), and was hence taken over by the ROSICRUCIAN system, from which source Pope introduced salamanders into his *Rape of the Lock* (i, 60).

Francis I of France adopted as his badge a lizard in the midst of flames, with the legend *Nutrisco et extinguo* (I nourish and extinguish). The Italian motto from which it derived was *Nutrisco il buono e spengo il reo* (I nourish the good and extinguish the bad). Fire purifies good metal, but consumes rubbish.

SHAKESPEARES's Falstaff calls Bardolph's nose "a burning lamp", "a salamander", and the drink that made such "a fiery meteor" he calls "fire".

> I have maintained that salamander of yours with fire any time this two-and-thirty years.
> *Henry IV, Pt. I*, III, iii.

Salamanders wool. Asbestos, a fibrous mineral, affirmed by the TARTARS to be made "of the root of a tree". It is sometimes called "mountain flax", and is not combustible.

Salary. Originally "salt rations" (Lat. *salarium* from *sal*, salt). The ancient Romans served out rations of salt and other necessaries to their soldiers and civil servants. These were collectively known as *salt*, and when money was substituted for the rations, the stipend went by the same name.

The salariat. Salaried employees collectively, such as civil servants, etc.

Sales promotion. A commercial term for all the methods used to increase the sale of commodities and to break down **sales resistance,** the negative attitude of a possible buyer which hinders or prevents the sale of a commodity.

Salic (săl' ik). Pertaining to the Salian FRANKS, a tribe of Franks who in the 4th century established themselves on the banks of the Sala (now known as the Yssel), and from whom the MEROVINGIAN Kings of France descended.

> Which Salique, as I said, 'twixt Elbe and Sala,
> Is at this day in Germany called Meisen.
> SHAKESPEARE: *Henry V*, I, ii.

The Salic Law. The compilation of laws of the Salian Franks supposedly begun in the 5th century, with later additions. Several Latin texts of what was essentially a penal code still exist. *Lex Salica* LIX stated that a wife could not inherit the land of her husband. This proviso regarding Salic lands in no way applied to the succession to the

French crown. The so-called "Salic Law" invoked in 1316 to exclude the daughters of Louis X and later Philip V from the throne of France never existed. Subsequent exclusions of females from European thrones rested on precedent rather than Salic Law. The so called "Spanish Salic Law", an Act of Philip V published in 1713 giving preference to male succession, was to satisfy European pressure and aimed at preventing the future union of the French and Spanish thrones. This law was abrogated by Charles IV in 1789, although the fact was not made public until 1830.

Salii, or **Saliens.** In ancient ROME, a college of twelve priests of MARS traditionally instituted as guardians of the ANCILE. Every year these young patricians paraded the city with song and dance, finishing the day with a banquet, insomuch that *saliares cœna* became proverbial for a sumptuous feast. The word *saliens* means dancing.

> Nunc est bibendum...
> ...nunc Saliaribus
> Ornare pulvinar Deorum
> Tempus est dapibus sodales.
>
> HORACE: I *Odes*, xxxvii, 1–4

Salisbury Crags. The range of cliffs on the flank of ARTHUR'S SEAT, Edinburgh, are so called from the Earl of Salisbury who accompanied Edward III in an expedition against the Scots.

Sallee-man, or **Sallee rover.** A pirate-ship; so called from Sallee, a seaport near Rabat on the west coast of Morocco, formerly a notorious nest of pirates.

Sally Army. A nickname of the SALVATION ARMY. *See* POKE BONNET.

Sally Lunn. A tea cake; so called from a woman pastrycook of that name who used to cry them in the streets of Bath at the close of the 18th century. Dalmer, a baker and musician, bought her business and made a song about the buns. Sally Lunn's house still exists in Lilliput Alley.

Salmacis. *See* HERMAPHRODITE.

Salmagundi (săl′ mà gŭn′ di). A mixture of minced veal, chicken, or turkey, anchovies or pickled herrings, and onions, all chopped together and served with lemon-juice and oil. The word appeared in the 17th century; its origin is unknown, but fable has it that it was the name of one of the ladies attached to the suite of Marie de′ MEDICI, wife of Henry IV of France, who either invented or popularized the dish.

In 1807 Washington Irving published a humorous periodical with this as the title.

Salon des Refusés. The exhibition of paintings opened at PARIS in 1863 at the instigation of NAPOLEON III, of works from artists (especially Claude Monet) rejected by the French Salon. Monet's picture *Impressions* gave rise to the term IMPRESSIONISM which was coined in derision by a journalist.

Salop. *See* SHROPSHIRE.

Salt. Flavour, smack. The "salt of youth" is that vigour and strong passion which then predominates.

> Though we are justices and doctors, and churchmen, Master Page, we have some salt of our youth in us.
>
> SHAKESPEARE:
> *The Merry Wives of Windsor, II, iii.*

Shakespeare uses the term on several occasions for strong amorous passion. Thus Iago refers to it as "hot as monkeys, salt as wolves in pride" (*Othello*, III, iii). The Duke calls Angelo's base passion his "salt imagination", because he supposed his victim to be Isabella, and not his betrothed wife whom the Duke forced him to marry (*Measure for Measure*, V, i).

Salt Hill. The mound where boys at Eton used to collect money for the Captain at the MONTEM. All the money collected was called salt (*see* SALARY).

Salt lick. A place where salt is found naturally and in a position where animals which resort thither may lick it from the rocks. etc.

To salt an account, invoice, etc. To put the extreme value upon each article, and even something more, to give it piquancy and raise its market value.

To salt a mine. To introduce pieces of ore, etc., into the workings so as to delude prospective purchasers or shareholders into the idea that a worthless mine is in reality a profitable investment.

To salt away, or **down.** To store or preserve for future use, especially money.

A covenant of salt (*Numb.* xviii, 19). A covenant which could not be broken. As salt was a symbol of incorruption it symbolized perpetuity.

> The Lord God of Israel gave the kingdom...to David...by a covenant of salt
>
> II *Chron.* xiii, 5.

An old salt. A long-experienced sailor. One who has been well salted by the sea.

Attic salt. *See under* ATTIC.

The Pillar of Salt. Lot's wife, when escaping from Sodom with her husband and daughters, looked back on the cities of SODOM AND GOMORRAH against God's command and "She became a pillar of salt" (*Gen.* xix, 26). Our Lord, when teaching indifference to worldly affairs and material possessions, refers to the episode saying, "Remember Lot's wife" (*Luke* xvii, 32).

The salt of the earth. The perfect, the elect; the best of mankind. Our Lord told his disciples they were "the salt of the earth" (Matt. v, 13).

To eat a man's salt. To partake of his hospitality. Among the Arabs, to eat a man's salt created a sacred bond between host and guest. No one who has eaten of another's salt should speak ill of him or do him an ill turn.

> Why dost thou shun the salt? that sacred pledge,
> Which, once partaken, blunts the sabre's edge,
> Makes even contending tribes in peace unite,
> And hated hosts seem brethren to the sight!
> BYRON: *The Corsair*, II, iv.

He won't earn salt for his porridge. He will never earn a penny.

If the salt have lost its savour, wherewith shall it be salted? (*Matt.* v, 13). If men fall from grace, how shall they be restored? The reference is to rock salt which loses its saltness if exposed to the hot sun.

Not worth your salt. Not worth your wages. The reference is to the SALARY issued to Roman soldiers, etc.

Put some salt on his tail. Catch or apprehend him. The phrase is from the advice given to young children to lay salt on a bird's tail if they want to catch it.

Spilling salt was held to be an unlucky omen by the Romans, and the superstition remains, but EVIL may be averted if he who spills the salt throws a pinch of it over the left shoulder with the right hand. In Leonardo da Vinci's picture of the LAST SUPPER, JUDAS Iscariot is known by the salt-cellar knocked over accidently by his arm. Salt was used in sacrifice by the Jews, as well as by the Greeks and Romans. It was an emblem of purity and the sanctifying influence of a holy life on others owing to its preservative quality; also a sign of incorruptibility. It is used for the preparation of HOLY WATER and it was not uncommon to put salt into a coffin; for it is said that SATAN hates salt. It was long customary to throw a handful of salt on the top of the mash when brewing to keep the witches from it.

To row a man up Salt River (U.S.A.). To discomfit or defeat him, especially a political opponent at an election. There is a story that when Henry Clay was Presidential candidate in 1832, the boatman hired to row him up the Ohio to Louisville, to address a meeting, took him up the Salt River, a tributary, instead. This caused him to lose Kentucky and the election. The phrase, however, is older than this.

To sit above the salt. To sit in a place of distinction. Formerly the family *saler* (salt cellar) was of massive silver, and placed in the middle of the table. Persons of distinction sat above the "saler"—*i.e.* between it and the head of the table; dependants and inferior guests sat below.

True to his salt. Faithful to his employers. Here *salt* means salary.

With a grain, or **pinch of salt.** (Lat. *cum grano salis*). With great reservations or limitation; allowing it a mere grain of truth. A pinch of salt with something may help one to swallow it.

Salutation, Salute (Lat. *salutare*, to keep safe, to greet). Military salutes take various forms according to the occasion, and include touching the CAP, presenting arms, the lowering of sword-points, lowering the FLAG, the firing of guns, etc. The number of guns fired for a Royal Salute in the Royal Navy is 21, in the Army 101. The lowering of swords indicates a willingness to put yourself in the power of the person saluted, as does the presenting of arms.

Other common forms of salutation are the kiss, rubbing noses, bowing, curtseying, shaking hands, the removal or touching of the hat, etc.

Salvation Army. A religious organization founded by William Booth (1829–1912), originally a METHODIST minister. Its origins are to be found in 1865 in his Christian Mission, WHITECHAPEL, and the movement took its present name in 1878. Booth himself became the "General" and the "Army" was planned on semi-military lines. The motto adopted was "Through Blood and Fire" and the activities were directed at the poor, outcast, and destitute. The movement became world-wide, and its brass bands and open-air meetings became a familiar feature of the street scene, as did the bonnets of the Salvation Army "lasses". Immense good has been done by the selfless devotion of its rank and file.

Salve. Latin, "hail", "welcome". The word is sometimes woven on door-mats.

Salve, Regina. An ancient antiphonal hymn recited at the end of some of the canonical hours and still widely used in Roman Catholic Churches. So called from the opening words, *Salve, regina mater misericordiæ* (Hail, O Queen, Mother of Mercy).

Sam. To stand Sam. To pay the reckoning. The phrase is said to have arisen from the letters U.S. on the knapsacks of American soldiers. The government of "Uncle Sam" has to pay, or "stand Sam" for all; hence also the phrase *Nunky pays for all.*

Uncle Sam. Nickname for the collective citizens of the U.S.A. It arose in the neighbourhood of Troy, N.Y., about 1812 partly from the frequent appearance of the initials U.S. on government supplies to the army, etc. The other contributory factor to the derivaton is puzzling, but some have maintained that there was someone in the district who had a connexion with army supplies and who was actually known as Uncle Sam.

Upon my Sam, or **Sammy!** A humourous form of asseveration; also, *'pon my sacred Sam!*

Sam Browne belt. The leather belt with a strap over the shoulder and originally with a sword-frog, compulsory for officers and warrant officers in the British Army up to 1939, when it was declared optional. This belt was invented by General Sir Sam Browne, V.C. (1824–1901), a veteran of the INDIAN MUTINY. Its pattern has been adopted by almost every military power in the world.

Samanids. A Persian dynasty founded by Ismail at Samani. They ruled from 892 to 1005 and were notable patrons of Persian literature.

Samaritan. A good Samaritan. A philanthropist, one who helps the poor and needy (*see Luke* x, 30–7).

The Samaritans. An organization founded by the Rev. Chad Varah of St. Stephen, Walbrook, London, in 1953, to help the despairing and suicidal. It now has nearly 200 centres in the British Isles as well as some overseas. Trained volunteers give their help at any hour to those who make their needs known by telephone, letter, or by a personal visit.

Sambo. A pet name given to one of NEGRO race; properly applied to the male offspring of a Negro and Mulatto (Span. *zambo*, bow-legged).

Samian (sā'mi ån). **The Samian Letter.** The letter Y, the Letter of Pythagoras (*see under* PYTHAGORAS).

When reason doubtful like the Samian letter,
Points him two ways, the narrower the better.
POPE: *Dunciad*, IV.

The Samian Poet. Simonides of Amorgos, Greek iambic poet and native of Samos, who flourished in the mid-7th century B.C.

The Samian Sage, or **The Samian.** PYTHAGORAS, who was born at Samos.

Not so the Samian sage; to him belongs
The brightest witness of recording Fame.
THOMSON: *Liberty*, Pt. III.

Samite (săm' īt). A rich silk fabric with a warp of six threads, generally interwoven with GOLD, held in high esteem in the MIDDLE AGES. So called after the Gr. *hexamiton*: *Hex*, six; *Mitos*, a thread. *Cp.* DIMITY.

But ere he dipt the surface, rose an arm
Clothed in white samite, mystic, wonderful,
And caught him by the hilt,...
TENNYSON: *Morte d'Arthur*.

Sampford Ghost. An uncommonly persistent POLTERGEIST which haunted a thatched house (destroyed by fire *c*. 1942) at Sampford Peverell, Devon, for about three years until 1810. Besides the usual knockings the inmates were beaten, curtains agitated and damaged, levitations occurred, and in one instance an "unattached arm" flung a folio Greek Testament from a bed into the middle of the room. The Rev. Charles Caleb Colton, rector of the Prior's Portion, Tiverton (credited as author of these freaks), offered £100 to anyone who could explain the matter except on supernatural grounds. No one claimed the reward.

Sampo. *See* KALEVALA.

Sampson. A Dominie Sampson. A humble, pedantic scholar, awkward, irascible, and very old-fashioned. A character in Scott's *Guy Mannering*.

Samson. Any man of unusual strength; so called from the ancient Hebrew hero (*Judges xiii—xvi*). The name has been specially applied to Thomas Topham, the "British Samson", son of a London carpenter. He lifted three hogsheads of water (1,836 lb.) in the presence of thousands of spectators at COLDBATH FIELDS, 28 May 1741. He stabbed his wife and committed suicide in 1749; also to Richard Joy, the "Kentish Samson", who died in 1742 at the age of 67. His tombstone is in St. Peter's churchyard, Isle of Thanet.

Samurai (săm' ū rī). The military class of old Japan. In early feudal times the term (which means "guard") was applied to all who bore arms, but eventually the Samurai became warrior knights and administrators as retainers of the *daimyo* or nobles. From 1869 the rigid feudal stratification of society came to an end, and in 1876 they were forbidden to wear two swords, the symbol of a warrior. With the creation of a new nobility in 1884 they became *shizoku* ("gentry") and many took posts in administration and industry. The formal reorganization of society into *kazoku* (nobility), *shizoku* (gentry) and *heimin* (common people) set up in 1869, and subsequently modified, was abolished in 1947. *See also* HARA-KIRI.

San Benito. *See* SACCO BENEDETTO.

Sance Bell. The Sanctus bell. *See* SACRING BELL.

Sancho Panza (săn' chō păn' zà). The squire of Don QUIXOTE in Cervantes' romance. A short pot-bellied rustic, full of common sense, but without a grain of "spirituality", he became governor of BARATARIA. He rode upon an ass, DAPPLE, and was famous for his proverbs. *Panza*, in Spanish, means *paunch*. Hence a *Sancho Panza* as a rough-and-ready, sharp and humorous justice of the peace, an allusion to Sancho, as judge in the isle of Barataria.

Sanchoniathon (sang ko ni' à thon). The *Fragments of Sanchoniathon* are the literary remains of a supposed ancient Phœnician philosopher (alleged to have lived before the TROJAN WAR), which are incorporated in the *Phœnician History* by Philo of Byblos (1st and 2nd centuries A.D.), and which was drawn upon by Eusebius (*c*. 260–*c*. 340), the "Father of Church History". The name is Greek and may mean "the whole law of Chon" or alternatively may be a proper name. It is likely that the name was invented by Philo to give ancient authority to his writings.

Sanctuary, Right of. In Anglo-Saxon ENG-LAND all churches and churchyards generally provided refuge for fugitives for 40 days; while permanent refuge was available at the great LIBERTIES of Beverley, Durham, and Ripon. Sanctuary for treason was disallowed in 1486 and most of the remaining rights were severely restricted by Henry VIII. Eight cities of refuge were finally provided on the biblical model—Chester, Derby, Launceston, Northampton, Norwich, Wells, Westminster, and York. Sanctuary for criminals was abolished in 1623 and for civil offenders by acts of 1697 and 1723. These latter measures were aimed at such rookeries as ALSATIA, the SAVOY, the CLINK, the MINT, etc.

In SCOTLAND the most famous sanctuaries were those of the church of Wedale (Stow), near Galashiels, and that of Lesmahagow, Lanark. These were abolished at the REFORMATION. The abbey of Holyrood House remained a sanctuary for debtors until the late 19th century.

Sanctum Sanctorum. Latin for HOLY OF HOLIES. *Cp*. ADYTUM.

Sanctus Bell. *See* SACRING BELL.

Sancy Diamond, The. A famous DIAMOND (55 carats), said to have once belonged to Charles the Bold of Burgundy, and named after the French ambassador in Constantinople, Nicholas de Harlay, Sieur de Sancy, who, about 1575, bought it for 70,000 francs. Later it was owned by Henri III and Henri IV of France, then by Queen Elizabeth I; James II took it with him in his flight to France in 1688 and sold it to Louis XIV for £25,000. Louis XV wore it at his corona-

tion, but during the French Revolution it was stolen and, in 1828, sold to Prince Paul Demidoff for £80,000. In 1865, it was bought by Sir Jamsetjee Jeejeebhoy, but was on the market again in 1889 and rumoured to have been subsequently acquired by the Tsar of Russia. Its present fate is unknown.

Sand. A rope of sand. A proverbially weak link or tie, a union which is easily broken; that which is virtually worthless and untrustworthy.

Happy as a sand-boy. *See under* HAPPY.

The sands are running out. Time is getting short; there will be little opportunity for doing what you have to do unless you take the chance now. Often used in reference to one who has evidently not much longer to live. The allusion is to the hour-glass.

To plough, or **to number the sands.** To undertake an endless or impossible task.

> Alas! poor duke, the task he undertakes
> Is numbering sands and drinking oceans dry.
>
> SHAKESPEARE: *Richard II*, II, ii.

Sand-blind. Dim-sighted; not exactly blind, but with eyes of very little use. *Sand* here is a corruption of the obsolete prefix *sam-* meaning "half", as in the old *sam-dead*, *sam-ripe*, etc., and *sam-sodden*, which still survives in some dialects. In SHAKESPEARES *Merchant of Venice* (II, ii) Launcelot Gobbo connects it with *sand*, the gritty earth—

> This is my true-begotten father, who, being more than sand-blind, high gravel blind, knows me not.

The sand-man is about. A playful remark addressed to children who are tired and "sleepy-eyed". *Cp*. THE DUSTMAN HAS ARRIVED *under* DUST.

Sandgropers Nickname for the inhabitants of Western Australia, originally applied to the gold rush pioneers.

Sand, George Sand. *See under* GEORGE.

Sandabar, or **Sindibad.** Names given to a mediæval collection of tales much the same as those in the Greek *Syntipas the Philosopher* and the Arabic *Romance of the Seven Viziers* known in Western Europe as *The Seven Sages* (SEVEN WISE MASTERS), and derived from the *Fables of Bidpay*. These names probably result from Hebrew mistransliterations of the Arabic equivalent of Bidpay or PILPAY.

Sandal. A man without sandals. A prodigal; so called by the ancient Jews, because the seller gave his sandals to the buyer as a ratification of his bargain (*Ruth* iv, 7).

He wears the sandals of Theramenes. Said of a TRIMMER, an opportunist. Theramenes (put to death *c*. 404 B.C.) was one of the Athenian oligarchy, and was nicknamed

Cothurnus (*i.e.* a sandal or boot which might be worn on either foot), because no dependence could be put on him. He "blew hot and cold with the same breath" (*see under* BLOW).

Sandemanians, or **Glasites** (sănd e măn' i ănz). A religious party expelled from the CHURCH OF SCOTLAND under John Glas (1695–1773) for maintaining that national churches, being "kingdoms of this world" are unscriptural. He was suspended in 1728 and expelled in 1730. Eventually the leadership passed to his son-in-law Robert Sandeman, whence the more common name *Sandemanians*. They believe in salvation through grace and abstain from all animal food which has not been drained of blood. Love feasts (AGAPE) are held and the kiss of charity is enjoined.

Sandford and Merton. The schoolboy heroes of Thomas Day's old-fashioned children's tale of this name (published in three parts, 1783–1789). "Master" Tommy Merton is rich, selfish, untruthful, and generally objectionable; Harry Sandford, the farmer's son, is depicted as being the reverse in every aspect. Tommy was duly reformed under the guidance of Mr. Barlow the local clergyman, and by association with Harry. In the last paragraph of the book Tommy says to Harry:

> "to your example I owe most of the little good that I can boast; you have taught me how much better it is to be useful than rich or fine; how much more amiable to be good than great".

Sandwich. Meat or other filling between two slices of bread, so called from the fourth Earl of Sandwich (1718–1792), the notorious "Jemmy TWITCHER". He passed whole days in gambling, bidding the waiter to bring him for refreshment a piece of ham between two slices of bread, which he ate without stopping play.

Sandwich man. A perambulating advertisement displayer, "sandwiched" between advertisement boards carried before and behind.

Sang-de-bœuf (săng de berf) (Fr., bullock's blood). The deep red with which ancient Chinese porcelain is often coloured.

Sang-froid (Fr., cold blood). Freedom from excitement or agitation. One does a thing "with perfect *sangfroid*" when one does it coolly and collectedly.

> ...cross-legg'd with great sang-froid
> Among the scorching ruins he sat smoking
> Tobacco on the little carpet.
> BYRON: *Don Juan*, VIII, cxxi.

Sanger's Circus. One of the most spectacular entertainments of Victorian England. In 1845 the brothers John (1816–1889) and George (1827–1911) Sanger began a conjuring exhibition at Birmingham and from this they ventured into a travelling circus business. Their success was such that they were eventually able to lease the Agricultural Hall, Islington, and in 1871 purchased ASTLEY'S. Their mammoth shows were a distinctive feature of the entertainment world but they subsequently dissolved partnership and after John's death only "Lord" George's circus continued on the road.

Sangrado, Dr. (săn gra' dō). A name applied to an ignorant or "fossilized" medical practitioner, from the humbug in Le Sage's *Gil Blas* (1715), a tall, meagre, pale man, of very solemn appearance, who weighed every word he uttered and gave an emphasis to his sage "dicta". "His reasoning was geometrical, and his opinions angular." He prescribed warm water and bleeding for every ailment, for his great theory was that, "It is a gross error to suppose that blood is necessary for life."

Sangrail, or **Sangreal** (săn grāl). The Holy GRAIL. Popular etymology used to explain the word as meaning the real blood of Christ, *sang-real*, or the wine used in the LAST SUPPER; and a tradition arose that part of this wine-blood was preserved by JOSEPH OF ARIMATHÆA in the Saint, or Holy Grail.

Sanguine (săng' gwin) (Lat. *sanguis, sanguinis*, blood). The term used in HERALDRY for the deep red or purplish colour usually known as *murrey* (from the mulberry). In engravings it is indicated by lines of vert and purpure crossed, that is, diagonals from left to right. This is a word with a curious history. Its actual meaning is bloody, or of the colour of blood, hence it came to be applied to one who was ruddy, whose cheeks were red with good health and well-being. From this it was easy to extend the meaning to one who was full of vitality, vivacious, confident and hopeful. An artist's drawing in red chalk or crayon is called a *sanguine*, also the chalk itself.

Sanhedrin (săn i drin), or **Sanhedrim** (Gr. *syn*, together; *hedra*, a seat; *i.e.* a sitting together). The supreme council and highest court of justice of the ancient Jews held at JERUSALEM. It consisted of 70 priests and elders and a president, dealt with religious questions, and acted as a civil court for Jerusalem. It was the Sanhedrin that condemned Christ to death. The Sanhedrin proper came to an end with the fall of the Jewish state (A.D. 70). Some authorities, taking their evidence from the MISHNA, hold that there was a *Great Sanhedrin* of 71 members possessing civil authority and a little Sanhedrin of 23 with religious authority under the High priest.

In Dryden's *Absalom and Achitophel*, the *Sanhedrin* stands for the English PARLIA-MENT.

Sans (Fr., without). SHAKESPEARE (*As You Like It*, II, vii) describes second childhood as "sans teeth, sans eyes, sans taste, sans everything".

Sans Culottes (Fr., without knee-breeches). A name given during the French Revolution to the extremists of the working classes. Hence *Sansculottism*, the principles, etc., of "red republicans".

Sans culottides. The five complementary days added to the 12 months of the Revolutionary Calendar (*see under* CALENDAR), each month being made to consist of 30 days. The days were named in honour of the *sans culottes*, and made idle days or holidays.

Sans-Gêne, Madame. The nickname of the wife of Lefebvre, Duke and Dantzic (1755–1820), one of NAPOLEON's marshals. She was originally a washer-woman, and followed her husband—then in the ranks—as a VIVANDIÈRE. She was kind and pleasant, but her rough-and-ready ways and ignorance and etiquette soon made her the butt of the court, and earned her the nickname, which means "without constraint" or "free and easy".

Sans peur et sans reproche (Fr., without fear and without reproach). The Chevalier Bayard (*see under* BAYARD) was known as *Le chevalier sans peur et sans reproche*.

Sans Souci (Fr.). Free and easy, void of care. It is the name given by Frederick the Great to the palace he built near Potsdam (1747).

The Philosopher of Sans-Souci. Frederick the Great (1712, 1740–1786).

Enfants Sans Souci. A mediæval French society of actors, mainly young men of good family, largely devoted to the production of the *Sotie*, a kind of political comedy in which public characters and the manners of the day were turned to ridicule. The head of the "Care-for-Nothings" (*sans souci*) was called "The Prince of Fools" (*Prince des Sots*), an office held for years by Pierre Gringoire (*c.* 1475–1539). *Cp.* BASOCHIANS.

Sansei (săn' sā). An American citizen whose grandparents were immigrants to the U.S.A.; from a Japanese word meaning "third generation". *Cp.* NISEI.

Santa Casa. *See* LORETO.

Santa Claus. A contraction of Santa Nikolaus (St. NICHOLAS), the patron saint of German children. His feast-day is 6 December, and the vigil is still held in some places, but for the most part his name is now associated with Christmastide. The custom used to be for someone, on 5 December, to assume the costume of a BISHOP, and distribute small gifts to "good children". The present custom, introduced into England from Germany about 1840, is to put toys and other small presents into a stocking late on CHRISTMAS Eve, when the children are asleep, and when they wake on Christmas morn they find at the bedside the gifts brought by Santa Claus, who supposedly travels around in a sleigh pulled by reindeer.

Santa Fe Trail, The. The wagon trail between Independence, Missouri, and Santa Fe, New Mexico, used by Missouri traders. The first wagon train traversed the trail in 1821–1822 and a steady trade in mules, furs, silver, etc., developed. For several years detachments of troops were used to protect the caravans against Indian attacks. The railway reached Santa Fe in 1880.

Sapho (săf' ō). Mlle de Scudéry (1607–1701), the French novelist and poet, went by this name among her own circle.

Sappho (săf' ō). The Greek poetess of Lesbos, known as "the Tenth MUSE". She lived about 600 B.C., and is fabled to have thrown herself into the sea from the Leucadian promontory in consequence of her advances having been rejected by the beautiful youth Phaon.

Pope used the name in his *Moral Essays* (II) for Lady Mary Whortley Montagu (*cp.* ATOSSA). *See also* SAPHO, *above*.

The Sappho of Toulouse. Clémence Isaure, a lady of Toulouse who composed an *Ode to Spring* and who is legendarily supposed to have founded and endowed the *Jeux Floraux*, the Toulouse Academy which gives an annual prize of poetry. In fact the Academy was founded by the TROUBADOURS in 1323 and originally known as the *Consistoire du Gai Savoir*.

Sapphics. A four-lined stanza-form of classical lyric poetry, named after SAPPHO of Lesbos, who employed it, the fourth line being an Adonic. There must be a cæsura after the fifth syllable of each of the first three lines which run thus:

—∪|— —|—||∪∪|—∪|—∪

The Adonic is:

—∪∪|—∪ or — —

The first and third stanzas of the famous *Ode* of HORACE, *Integer vitæ* (i, 22), may be translated thus, preserving the metre:

He of sound life, who ne'er with singers wendeth,
Needs no Moorish bow, such as malice bendeth,

Nor with poisoned darts life from harm defendeth.
Fuscus, believe me.
Once I, unarmed, was in a forest roaming,
Singing love lays, when i' the secret gloaming
Rushed a huge wolf, which though in fury foaming
Did not aggrieve me.

E.C.B.

Probably the best example of Sapphics in English is Canning's *Needy Knife-grinder*.

Sapphism. Another name for Lesbianism. *See* LESBIAN.

Saracen (săr′ à sen) (Late Gr. *Sarakenos*, possibly from Arab. *sharqi*, an "oriental"). Applied to Arabs generally by mediæval writers, especially those of Syria and Palestine; also applied to all infidel nations who opposed the CRUSADERS. The name was given by the Greeks and Romans to the nomadic tribes of the Syro-Arabian desert.

Saragossa, The Maid of. *See under* MAID.

Sarah. The Divine Sarah. Sarah Bernhardt (1845–1923), French actress of international repute. Her original name was Rosine Bernard.

Saratoga Trunk (săr à tō′ gà). A huge trunk, such as used to be taken by fashionable ladies to the watering place of that name in New York State.

Sarcenet. *See* SARSENET.

Sarcophagus (sar kof′ à gus) (Gr. *sarx*, flesh; *phagein*, to eat). A stone coffin; so called because it was made of stone which, according to Pliny, consumed the flesh in a few weeks. The stone was sometimes called *lapis Assius*, because it was found at Assos in Lycia.

Sardanapalus. A name applied to any luxurious, extravagant, self-willed tyrant. It is the Greek name of Asurbanipal (mentioned in *Ezra* iv, 10, as *Asnappar*), king of Assyria in the 7th century B.C. Byron, in his poetic drama of the name, makes him a voluptuous tyrant whose effeminacy led Arbaces, the Mede, to conspire against him. Myrra, his favourite concubine, roused him to appear at the head of his armies. He won three successive battles, but was then defeated, and was induced by Myrra to place himself on a funeral pyre. She set fire to it, and jumping into the flames, perished with him. The famous painting *Sardanapalus* (1827) by Delacroix was inspired by Byron's drama (1821).

Sardonic smile, or **laughter.** A smile of contempt; bitter, mocking laughter; so used by HOMER.

The *Herba Sardonia* (so called from Sardis, in Asia Minor) is so acrid that it produces a convulsive movement of the nerves of the face, resembling a painful grin; but the word is probably Gr. *sardanios*, a bitter laugh.

Tis envy's safest, surest rule
To hide her rage in ridicule;
The vulgar eye the best beguiles
When all her snakes are decked with smiles,
Sardonic smiles by rancour raised.

SWIFT: *Pheasant and Lark*.

Sardonyx (sar′ don iks). A precious stone composed of white chalcedony alternating with layers of sard, which is an orange-brown variety of cornelian. Pliny says it is called *sard* from Sardis, in Asia Minor, where it is found, the *onyx*, the nail, because its colour resembles that of the skin under the nail (*Nat. Hist. xxxvii*, 31).

Sarsen Stones (sar′ sen). The sandstone boulders of Wiltshire and Berkshire are so called. The early Christian Saxons used the word *Saresyn* (*i.e.* SARACEN) as a synonym of pagan or heathen, and as these stones were popularly associated with DRUID worship, they were called *Saresyn* (or heathen) stones. Robert Ricart says of Duke Rollo, "He was a Saresyn come out of Denmark into France." In the tin mining areas of Cornwall old attle or rock waste was called *Sarsen* or *Jews' leavings* on the assumption that Saracens, Jews and Phœnicians had once worked there.

Sarsenet (sar′ sen et). A very fine, soft, silk material, so called from its Saracenic or Oriental origin. The word is sometimes used adjectivally of soft and gentle speech.

Sassanides (săs ăn′ i dēz). A powerful Persian dynasty, ruling from about A.D. 225 to 641; so named because Ardeshir, the founder, was son of Sassan, a lineal descendant of XERXES.

Sassenach (săs′ năk). The common form of *Sassunnach*, Gaelic for "English" or "an Englishman".

Satan (sā′ tàn), in Hebrew, means adversary or enemy, and is traditionally applied to the DEVIL, the personification of EVIL.

To whom the Arch-enemy
(And thence in heaven called Satan).

MILTON: *Paradise Lost, Bk. I, 81*.

He appears as the SERPENT, tempter of mankind in *Gen.* iii, 1, and the existence of Satan as the centre of evil is part of the teaching of bot the Old and NEW TESTAMENT,

But when they have heard, Satan cometh immediately, and taketh away the word that was sown in their hearts.

Mark iv, 15.

The name is often used of a tempter or of a person of whom one is expressing abhorrence. Thus the Clown says to Malvolio:

Fie, thou dishonest Satan! I call thee by the most modest terms; for I am one of those gentle ones that will use the devil himself with courtesy.

SHAKESPEARE: *Twelfth Night*, IV, ii

Satan rebuking sin. THE POT CALLING THE KETTLE BLACK (*under* POT).

The Satanic School. So Southey called BYRON, Shelley, and those of their followers who set at defiance the generally received notions of religion. See the Preface to his *Vision of Judgment*.

Satire (săt′ īr). Scaliger's derivation from SATYR is quite untenable. It is Lat. *satura* (full of variety); originally *lanx satura*, a dish of varied fruits, a medley. The term was applied to a medley or hotchpotch in verse; later to compositions in verse or prose in which folly, vice, or individuals are held up to ridicule. See Dryden's Dedication prefixed to his *Satires*.

Father of Satire. Archilochus of Paros, 7th century B.C.

Father of French Satire. Mathurin Régnier (1573–1613).

Father of Roman Satire. Lucilius (*c.* 175–103 B.C.)

> Lucilius was the man who, bravely bold,
> To Roman vices did this mirror hold;
> Protected humble goodness from reproach,
> Showed worth on foot, and rascals in a coach.
> DRYDEN:*Art of Poetry*, c. ii.

Saturday. The seventh day of the week until 1971 when it became the sixth (see Sunday); called by the Anglo-Saxons *Sæterdæg*, after the Latin *Saturni dies*, the day of SATURN. *See* BLACK SATURDAY.

Saturn (săt′ ŭrn). A Roman deity, identified with the Greek KRONOS (time). He devoured all his children except JUPITER (air), NEPTUNE (water), and PLUTO (the grave). These Time cannot consume. The reign of Saturn was celebrated by the poets as a "GOLDEN AGE". According to the old alchemists and astrologers Saturn typified LEAD, and was a very EVIL planet to be born under. He was the god of seedtime and harvest and his symbol was a scythe, and he was finally banished from his throne by his son Jupiter.

Saturn red. Red lead.

Saturn's tree. An alchemist's name for the Tree of DIANA, or PHILOSOPHER'S TREE.

Saturnalia. The ancient Roman festival of SATURN, celebrated on 19 December and eventually prolonged for seven days, was a time of freedom from restraint, merrymaking, and often riot and debauchery. During its continuance public business was suspended, the law courts and schools were closed and no criminals were punished.

Saturnian. Pertaining to Saturn; with reference to the "GOLDEN AGE", to the god's sluggishness, or to the baleful influence attributed to him by the astrologers.

> Then rose the seed of Chaos and of Night
> To blot out order and extinguish light.
> Of dull and venal a new world to mould,
> And bring Saturnian days of lead and gold.
> POPE:*Dunciad*, IV, 13.

Saturnian verses. A rude metre in use among the Romans before the introduction of Greek metres. Also a peculiar metre consisting of three iambics and a syllable over, joined to three trochees, as:

> The queen was in the par-lour...
> The maids were in the garden...

> The Fescennine and Saturnian were the same, for as they were called Saturnian from their ancientness, when Saturn reigned in Italy, they were called Fescennine, from Fescennia [*sic*] where they were first practised.
> DRYDEN:Essay on Satire.

Saturnine. Grave, phlegmatic, gloomy, dull and glowering. Astrologers affirm that such is the disposition of those who are born under the influence of the leaden planet SATURN.

Satyr (săt′ īr). One of a body of forest gods or demons who, in classical mythology, were the attendants of BACCHUS. Like the FAUNS, they are represented as having the legs and hind-quarters of a GOAT, budding horns, and goat-like ears, and they were very lascivious.

Hence, the term is applied to a brutish or lustful man; and the psychological condition among males characterized by excessive venereal desire is known as *satyriasis*.

Sauce (Lat. *salsus*) means "salted food", for giving a relish to meat, as pickled roots, herbs, etc.

In familiar usage it means "cheek", impertinence, of the sort one expects from an impudent youngster or *saucebox*.

The sauce was better than the fish. The accessories were better than the main part.

To serve the same sauce. To retaliate; to give as good as you get; to serve in the same manner.

What is sauce for the goose is sauce for the gander. The same principle applies in both cases; what is fitting for the husband, should be fitting for the wife.

Saucer. Originally a dish for holding sauce, the Roman *salsarium*.

Saucer eyes. Big, round, glaring eyes.

> Yet when a child (good Lord!) I thought
> That thou a pair of horns had'st got
> With eyes like saucers staring.
> PETER PINDAR:*Ode to the Devil*.

Saucer oath. When a Chinese is put in the witness-box, he says: "If I do not speak the truth may my soul be cracked and broken like this saucer." So saying, he dashes the saucer on the ground. The Jewish marriage custom of breaking a wineglass is of a similar character.

Flying saucers. Alleged mysterious objects resembling revolving, partially luminous discs that shoot across the sky at a high velocity and at a great height. "Flying saucers" have been reported on a number of occasions in recent years but their actuality remains as elusive as that of the LOCH NESS MONSTER. *Cp.* U.F.O.

Saul. Is Saul also among the prophets? (I *Sam*. x, 11). Said of one who unexpectedly bears tribute to a party or doctrine that he has hitherto vigorously assailed. At the conversion of Saul, afterwards called PAUL, the Jews said in substance, "Is it possible that Saul can be a convert?". (*Acts* ix, 21).

Sauve qui peut (sōv kē pėr) (Fr., save himself who can). One of the first uses of the phrase is by Boileau (1636–1711). The phrase thus came to mean a rout. Thackeray (*The Four Georges*, ch. 41) writes of "that general *sauve qui peut* among the Tory party".

Save. To save appearances. To do something to obviate or prevent embarrassment or exposure.

Save the mark! *See* GOD BLESS *under* MARK.

To save one's bacon, face, skin. *See under these words.*

Savoir-faire (săv′ wa fâr) (Fr.). Readiness in doing the right thing; address, tact, skill.

Savoir-vivre (săv′ wa vēvr). Good breeding; being at ease in society and knowing what to do.

Savonarola. *See* WEEPERS.

Savoy, The. A precinct off the STRAND, London, between the present ADELPHI and the TEMPLE; so called after Peter of Savoy, the uncle of Henry III's queen, Eleanor of Provence. Henry granted it to Peter in 1245 and, after his departure in 1263, it became the residence of Eleanor of Castile, wife of Prince Edward (afterwards Edward I) and it was later given to Queen Eleanor's second son, Edmund of Lancaster. On the accession of Henry IV in 1399, it was annexed to the crown as part of the estates of the Duchy of Lancaster. Most of the original buildings were destroyed by Wat Tyler's followers in 1381, but Henry VII bequeathed funds for reconstruction of the palace as a hospital for the poor under the name of St. John's Hospital. It became a military hospital, then a barracks under Charles II, but this was demolished with the construction of Rennie's Waterloo Bridge (1811–1817).

In the late 17th century, the Savoy precinct became a notorious ROOKERY for evildoers claiming rights of SANCTUARY (*cp.* ALSATIA). The Savoy Hotel and Savoy Theatre now occupy part of the area.

The Savoy Chapel was first built in 1505 and, after the destruction of St. Mary le Strand by Protector Somerset, became known as St. Mary le Savoy. It was repaired and restored several times in the 18th century and again by Queen Victoria in 1843 and 1864.

Savoy Conference. After the RESTORATION, the conference at the Savoy (1661) between the BISHOPS and PRESBYTERIAN clergy to review the BOOK OF COMMON PRAYER. It only resulted in minor changes which were included in the revised book of 1662. Most of the Presbyterian demands were rejected and attempts at comprehension came to naught.

Savoy Hill. The site of the first studios of the British Broadcasting Company (1922) and until 1932 the headquarters of the British Broadcasting Corporation, the original B.B.C. callsign being 2LO.

Savoy Operas. The comic operas with words by W.S. Gilbert (1836–1911) and music by Arthur Sullivan (1842–1900), produced by R. D'Oyly Carte; most of them first appeared at the Savoy Theatre which D'Oyly Carte built specially for his productions. The players performing in these operas were known as the "Savoyards".

Saw In Christian art an attribute of St. SIMON and St. JAMES THE LESS, in allusion to the tradition of their being sawn to death.

Sawbuck. In American usage, a ten-dollar bill. A sawbuck is a sawing horse used for cutting up firewood, the legs at each end of which are crossed and bolted in an X-shape. Before note issue became a monopoly of the Federal Reserve Bank, many had an X instead of a 10 to show the denomination. A *double sawbuck* is a twenty-dollar bill.

Saxifrage (săks′ i frāj). A member of a genus of small plants (*Saxifraga*) probably so called because they grow in the clefts of rocks (Lat. *saxum*, a rock; *frangere*, to break). Pliny, and later writers following him, held that the name was due to the supposed fact that the plant had a medicinal value in the breaking up and dispersal of stone in the bladder.

Saxons. A Germanic people who invaded Britain in the late 5th and early 6th centuries; also the general name given by the Romans to the Teutonic raiders who from the 2nd century ravaged the coasts of Roman Britain. Essex, Sussex, Middlesex, and Wessex are names that commemorate their settlements.

Saxon Shore. The coast of Norfolk, Suffolk, Essex, Kent, Sussex and Hampshire fortified by the Romans against the attacks of Saxon and Frisian pirates, under the charge of the Count of the Saxon shore (*Comes Littoris Saxonici per Britanniam*). His garrisons were at Brancaster (*Branodunum*) in Norfolk, Burgh Castle (*Gariannonum*) and Walton Castle in Suffolk; Bradwell (*Othona*) in Essex; Reculver (*Regulbium*), Richborough (*Rutupiæ*), Dover (*Dubria*), and Lympne (*Portus Lemanis*) on the Kent coast, Pevensey (*Anderida*) on the Sussex coast, and [?] Porchester (*Portus Adurni*) near Portsmouth.

Saxo Grammaticus (Saxo the Scholar or Grammarian). A famous Danish chronicler living in the latter part of the 12th century (died c. 1208). His *Gesta Danorum*, a chronicle of the early Danish kings to 1185 is a valuable source of the times nearer his own, the earlier parts, derived from old songs, traditions and Runic inscriptions (*see* RUNE), are less reliable.

Say. To take the say. To taste meat or wine before it is presented, in order to prove that it is not poisoned. *Say* is short for *assay*, a test; the phrase was common in the reign of Queen Elizabeth I.

Scævola (skē′ vō là) (Lat., left-handed). So Gaius Mucius and his house were called because he had burnt off his right hand. Purposing to kill Lars Porsena, who was besieging ROME, he entered that king's camp but slew Porsena's secretary by mistake. He was captured and taken before the king and sentenced to the flames. He deliberately held his hand over the sacrificial fire till it was destroyed to show the Etruscan he would not shrink from torture. This fortitude was so remarkable that Porsena at once ordered his release and made peace with the Romans.

Scales. From time immemorial the scales have been one of the principal attributes of Justice, it being impossible to outweigh even a little Right with any quantity of Wrong.

> ...first the right he put into the scale,
> And then the Giant strove with puissance strong
> To fill the other scale with so much wrong
> But all the wrongs that he therein could lay,
> Might not it peise.
>
> SPENSER: *The Faerie Queene*, V, ii, 46.

According to the KORAN, at the Judgement Day everyone will be weighed in the scales of the archangel GABRIEL. The good deeds will be put in the scale called "Light", and the EVIL ones in the scale called "Darkness", after which they have to cross the bridge AL-SIRAT, not wider than the edge of a scimitar. The faithful will pass over in safety, but the rest will fall into the dreary realms of GEHENNA.

The scales fell from his eyes. The cause of his inability to recognise the truth having been removed, he now saw the facts clearly. *Scale* here is the shell or thin covering, a scab; it is cognate with the scale or dish of a balance.

After Ananias put his hands on Saul (St. PAUL) we are told:

> And immediately there fell from his eyes as it had been scales; and he received sight forthwith.
>
> *Acts* ix, 18.

To hold the scales even, or **true.** To judge impartially.

> King Providence attends with generous aid...
> And weighs the nations in an even scale.
>
> COWPER: *Table Talk*, 251.

To turn the scale. Just to outweigh the other side.

> Thy presence turns the scale of doubtful fight,
> Tremendous God of battles, Lord of Hosts!
>
> WORDSWORTH: *Ode* (1815), 112.

Scallop shell. The emblem of St. JAMES of Compostela, adopted, says Erasmus, because the shore of the adjacent sea abounds in them; also the emblem of the pilgrims to his shrine and of mediæval pilgrims generally. *See* COCKLE HAT.

> Give me my scallop-shell of quiet,
> My staff of faith to walk upon,
> My scrip of joy, immortal diet,
> My bottle of salvation,
> My gown of glory, hope's true gage,
> And thus I'll take my pilgrimage.
>
> SIR WALTER RALEGH: *The Pilgrimage*.

Scalp Lock. A long lock of hair allowed to grow on the scalp by men of certain North American Indian tribes as a challenge to their scalp-hunting enemies.

Scambling Days. *See* SKIMBLE-SKAMBLE.

Scammozzi's Rule (skà mot′ ziz). The jointed two-foot rule used by builders, and said to have been invented by Vincenzo Scammozzi (1552–1616), the famous Italian architect.

Scandal (Gr. *skandalon*) means properly a pitfall or snare laid out for an enemy; hence a stumbling-block, and morally an aspersion.

In *Matt*. xiii, 41–2, we are told that the angels "shall gather all things that offend...and shall cast them into a furnace"; here the Greek word is *skandalon*, and *scandals* is given as an alternative in the margin; the REVISED VERSION renders the word "all things that cause stumbling". *Cp. also* I *Cor*. i, 23.

The Hill of Scandal. So Milton (*Paradise Lost*, I, 415) calls the Mount of Olives, because King SOLOMON built thereon "an high place for Chemosh, the abomination of the children of Ammon" (I *Kings* xi, 7).

Scandal broth. Tea. The reference is to the gossip held by some of the womenfolk over their tea. Also called "chatterbroth".

Scandalum Magnatum (skăn' dȧ lum măg nā' tùm) (Lat., scandal of magnates). Words in derogation of the Crown, PEERS, judges, and other great officers of the realm, made a legal offence in the time of Richard II. What St. PAUL calls "speaking evil of dignities"; popularly contracted to *scanmag*.

Scanderbeg. A name given by the Turks to George Castriota (1403–1468), the patriot chief of Epirus. The name is a corruption of *Iskander* (Alexander) *beg* or *bey*.

Scanderbeg's sword must have Scanderbeg's arm. None but ULYSSES can draw Ulysses' bow. MOHAMMED I wanted to see Scanderbeg's scimitar, but when presented no one could draw it; whereupon the Turkish emperor, deeming himself imposed upon, sent it back; Scanderbeg replied he had sent his majesty his sword, not the arm that drew it.

Scapegoat. Part of the ancient ritual among the Hebrews for the DAY OF ATONEMENT laid down by Mosaic Law (*see Lev.* xvi) was as follows: two goats were brought to the altar of the TABERNACLE and the high priest cast lots, one for the Lord, and the other for AZA-ZEL. The Lord's goat was sacrificed, the other was the scapegoat; and the high priest having, by confession, transferred his own sins and the sins of the people to it, it was taken to the wilderness and suffered to escape.

Scaphism (skā' fizm) (Gr. *skaphe*, anything scooped out). A mode of torture formerly practised in Persia. The victim was enclosed in the hollow trunk of a tree, the head, hands, and legs projecting. These were anointed with honey to invite the wasps. In this situation the sufferer must linger in the burning sun for several days.

Scarab (scă' rȧb). A trinket in the form of a dung-beetle, especially *Scarabæus sacer*. It originated in ancient Egypt as an AMULET, being made of polished or glazed stone, metal, or glazed faience, and was perforated lengthwise for suspension. By the XIIIth Dynasty, scarabs became used as seals, worn as pendants, or mounted on signet rings. The insect was supposed to conceal in itself the secret of eternal life, since the scarab was believed to be only of the male sex, hence their use as amulets. They are still the most popular of Egyptian souvenirs.

Scaramouch (skăr' ȧ mouch). The English form of Ital. *Scaramuccia* (through Fr. *Scaramouche*), a stock character in old Italian farce, introduced into England soon after 1670. He was a braggart and fool, very valiant in words, but a POLTROON, and was usually dressed in a black Spanish costume caricaturing the dons. The Neapolitan actor Tiberior Fiurelli (1608–1694) was surnamed *Scaramouch Fiurelli*. He came to England in 1673, and astonished JOHN BULL with feats of agility. *Cp.* COLUMBINE; HARLEQUIN.

> Stout Scaramoucha with rush lance rode in,
> And ran a tilt at centaur Arlequin.
> DRYDEN: *Epilogue to the University of Oxford.*

Scarborough Warning. No warning at all; blow first, warning after. In Scarborough robbers were said to be dealt with in a very summery manner by a sort of HALIFAX GIBBET-LAW, LYNCH LAW, or an *à la lanterne*. (*See under* LANTERN.)

Fuller says that the expression arose from Thomas Stafford's unexpected seizure of Scarborough Castle in 1557, but the phrase occurs earlier than this. *Cp.* JEDDART; LYDFORD LAW.

Scarlet. The colour of certain official costumes as those of judges, CARDINALS, holders of certain academic qualifications, etc.; hence sometimes applied to these dignitaries. *Cp.* PINK; PURPLE.

Dyeing scarlet. Heavy drinking, which in time will dye the face scarlet.

> They call drinking deep, dyeing scarlet.
> SHAKESPEARE: *Henry IV, Pt. I*, II, iv.

Scarlet Hat. A CARDINAL; from his once traditional red hat.

The Scarlet Lancers. *See* REGIMENTAL AND DIVISIONAL NICKNAMES.

Scarlet Letter. In the early days in Puritan New England a scarlet "A" for "adulteress" used to be branded or sewn on a guilty woman's dress.

> She turned her eyes downwards at the scarlet letter, and even touched it with her finger, to assure herself that the infant and the shame was real.
> HAWTHORNE: *The Scarlet Letter*, ch. II.

Scarlet Pimpernel. A plant of the primrose family, *Anagallis arvensis*. The hero of Baroness Orczy's novel, *The Scarlet Pimpernel* (1905), and of several others in the series, took his nickname from the use of the pimpernel as his emblem.

The Scarlet Woman, or Scarlet Whore. The woman seen by St. JOHN in his vision "arrayed in purple and scarlet colour", sitting "upon a scarlet coloured beast, full of names of blasphemy, having seven heads and ten horns", "drunken with the blood of the saints, and with the blood of the martyrs", upon whose forehead was written "Mystery, Babylon the Great, The Mother of Harlots and Abominations of The Earth' (*Rev.* xvii, 1–6).

St. John was probably referring to ROMI which, at the time he was writing, wa:

"drunken with the blood of the saints; some controversial PROTESTANTS have applied the words to the Church of Rome, and some RO-MAN CATHOLICS to the Protestant churches generally.

Will Scarlet. One of the companions of ROBIN HOOD.

Scat singing. In JAZZ a form of singing without words, using the voice as a musical instrument. Said to have been started by Louis Armstrong in the 1920s when he forgot the words or dropped the paper on which they were written while singing a number; Jelly Roll Morton, on the other hand, claimed to have sung scat as early as 1906.

Scavenger's Daughter. An instrument of torture invented by Sir Leonard Skevington, Lieutenant of the TOWER in the reign of Henry VIII. The machine compressed the body by bringing the head to the knees, and so forced blood out of the nose and ears.

Scent. We are not yet on the right scent. We have not yet got the right clue. The allusion is to dogs following game by scent.

Sceptic (skep′tik) literally means one who thinks for himself, and does not receive on another's testimony (from Gr. *skeptesthai*, to examine). Pyrrho founded the philosophic sect called "Sceptics", and Epictetus combated their dogmas. In theology we apply the word to those who do not accept revelation. *See* PYRRHONISM.

Sceptre (sep′ter) (Gr., a staff). The GOLD and jewelled wand carried by a SOVEREIGN as an emblem of royalty; hence, royal authority and dignity.

> This hand was made to handle nought but gold:
> I cannot give due action to my words,
> Except a sword, or sceptre, balance it.
> A sceptre shall it have, have I a soul,
> On which I'll toss the flower-de-luce of France.
> SHAKESPEARE: *Henry VI, Pt. II*, V, i.

The sceptre of the kings and emperors of ROME was of ivory, bound with gold and surmounted by a golden EAGLE; the British sceptre is of richly jewelled gold, and bears immediately beneath the CROSS and ball the the great CULLINAN DIAMOND.

HOMER says that AGAMEMNON's sceptre was made by VULCAN, who gave it to the son of SATURN. It passed successively to JUPITER, MERCURY, PELOPS, Atreus and THYESTES till it came to Agamemnon. It was looked on with great reverence, and several miracles were attributed to it.

Schadenfreude (sha′den froi de) (Ger.). A malicious delight in the bad luck of others (*Schaden*, damage; *Freude*, joy).

Scheherazade (she hēr′ a zad a). The mouthpiece of the tales related in the ARABIAN NIGHTS, daughter of the grand VIZIER of the Indies. The SULTAN Schahriah, having discovered the infidelity of his sultana, resolved to have a fresh wife every night and have her strangled at daybreak. Scheherazade entreated to become his wife, and so amused him with tales for a thousand and one nights that he revoked his cruel decree, bestowed his affection on her, and called her "the liberator of the sex".

> I had noticed that the young girl—the story writer, our Scheherazade, as I call her—looked as if she had been crying or lying awake half the night.
> O.W. HOLMES: *The Poet at the Breakfast-table*, ch. iii.

Schelhorn's Bible. *See* BIBLE, SOME SPECIALLY NAMED EDITIONS.

Schiedam (skī dăm′). Hollands gin, so called from Schiedam, a town where it is principally manufactured.

Schism, The Great. The split in the CATHOLIC CHURCH when there were rival popes at Avignon and ROME. It began in 1378 and ended in 1417. After the death of Gregory XI, the last of the AVIGNON POPES proper, Urban VI (1378–1389) alienated the French cardinals and their adherents, and they established an antipope, Clement VII, at Anagni. Clement soon retired to Avignon with his supporters, where the ANTI-POPE remained until the schism ended.

Schlemihl, Peter (shlem′il). The man who sold his shadow to the DEVIL, in Chamisso's tale so called (1814). The name is a synonym for any person who makes a desperate and silly bargain. *Schlemihl* is Yiddish for a clumsy person.

Scholasticism. The term usually denotes the philosophy and doctrines of the mediæval SCHOOLMEN from the 9th to the early 15th century. It was very much concerned with applying Aristotelian logic to Christian theology. On the whole, reason took second place to faith and the apparent reconciliation and harmony between the two established by St. THOMAS AQUINAS in his *Summa Theologica* was undermined by Duns Scotus and WILLIAM OF OCCAM. It taught men to discipline their thought and classify their knowledge. Scholasticism owed much of its decline to its own internal quibblings, verbal subtleties, and intellectual exhaustion, but it never completely lost its vitality and still attracts theologians, especially in the ROMAN CATHOLIC CHURCH. *Cp.* NOMINALISM: REALISM; DIALECTIC.

Schoolboards. The name given to the special local committees elected under Forster's Education Act of 1870 to administer the undenominational elementary schools set up under the Act, hence the term BOARD SCHOOLS. Schoolboards were abolished by the Balfour Act of 1902 and their work was taken over by education committees of the various local government authorities. These schools then became known as "council schools".

Schoolgirl. That schoolgirl complexion. A popular phrase used in compliment or in jest which owes its familiarity to its long use in advertisements for a well-known soap.

Schoolmaster. The schoolmaster is abroad. Education is spreading and it will bear fruit. Lord Brougham, a champion of popular education, said in a speech to the HOUSE OF COMMONS (1828) on the general diffusion of education, and of the intelligence arising therefrom, "Let the soldier be abroad, if he will; he can do nothing in this age. There is another personage abroad...the schoolmaster is abroad, and I trust to him, armed with his primer, against the soldier in full military array." It must be noted that the phrase lends itself to ironical usage to explain a state of ignorance.

Schoolmen. The name given to the teachers of philosophy and theology who lectured in the ecclesiastical schools attached to certain abbeys and cathedrals as instituted by CHARLEMAGNE, and in the mediæval universities (*see* SCHOLASTICISM). Among the most famous are:

Flaccus Alcuin or Albinus (735–804).

Johannes Scotus ERIGENA or John the Scot (*c.* 815–*c.* 877).

Gerbert of Aurillac (*c.* 950–1003), Pope Sylvester II (999–1003).

Berengar of Tours (*c.* 998–1088).

Lanfranc (*c.* 1005–1089), Archbishop of Canterbury (1070–1089).

Anselm (*c.* 1033–1109), Archbishop of Canterbury (1093–1109).

Roscellinus of Compiègne (*c.* 1050–*c.* 1122).

Peter ABELARD (1079–1142).

Peter Lombard (*c.* 1100–*c.* 1160).

John of Salisbury (*c.* 1115–1180).

Alain de Lille (*c.* 1128–1202).

Alexander of Hales (*c.* 1175–1245).

Albertus Magnus (*c.* 1206–1280).

St. Bonaventura or John of Fidanza (1221–1274).

THOMAS AQUINAS (*c.* 1225–1274).

Raymond Lully (*c.* 1235–1315).

Duns Scotus (*c.* 1265–1308).

William of Occam (*c.* 1280–1349).

Thomas Bradwardine (*c.* 1290–1349).

Robert Holcot (*d.* 1349).

Jean Buridan (*c.* 1300–*c.* 1368).

See also DOCTORS OF LEARNING; DUNCE; OCCAM'S RAZOR; SENTENCES.

School-pence. The small weekly sum paid for tuition in elementary schools. The Education Act of 1870 limited them to ninepence per week and a permissive Act of 1891, giving parents the right to claim free education for their children, practically resulted in their abolition, but such fees were not legally abolished until 1918.

> If a child came to school one Monday morning without the school-pence, what was the teacher to do?
> ODGERS and NALDRETT: *Local Government*, ch. vii.

Schooner (skoo′ner). In the U.S.A. a tall glass for beer, etc.; it is also applied to a standard pint-size beer glass in Australia.

Prairie schooner. *See* PRAIRIE.

Science. Literally "knowledge", it is Lat. *scientia* from *scire*, to know. SHAKESPEARE uses it in this old, wide meaning:

> Plutus himself,
> That knows the tinct and multiplying medicine,
> Hath not in nature's mystery more science
> Than I have on this ring.
> *All's Well That Ends Well*, V, iii.

The Science. Pugilism.

The Dismal Science. Economics, so named by Carlyle:

> The social science—not a "gay science", but a rueful—which finds the secret of this Universe in "supply and demand"...what we might call, by way of eminence, the dismal science.
> CARLYLE: *On the nigger question* (1849).

The Gay Science. *See under* GAY.

Hard and **Soft Science.** NATURAL SCIENCE, physics, etc. are sometimes called "hard science" as opposed to "soft science", a term applied to sociology, economics, psychology, political science and other social and behavioural sciences.

Natural Science. Empirical science as distinct from mathematics, logic, mental and moral science, etc. Its general principles are commonly called "the laws of nature".

The Noble Science. Boxing, or fencing; the "noble art of self-defence".

The Seven Sciences, or **Seven Liberal Sciences.** The same as the *Seven Liberal Arts. See* QUADRIVIUM.

Science persecuted. Anaxagoras of Clazomenæ (d. *c.* 430 B.C.) held opinions in NATURAL SCIENCE (*see above*) so far in advance of his age that he was accused of impiety and condemned to death. Pericles, with great difficulty, got his sentence commuted to fine and banishment.

Galileo (1564–1642) was imprisoned by the INQUISITION for maintaining that the earth moved, but recanted to gain his liberty. *See* EPPUR SI MUOVE.

Roger Bacon (*c.* 1214–1294) was excommunicated and imprisoned for diabolic knowledge, chiefly on account of his chem cal researches. Dr. DEE was imprisoned under Queen Mary for using enchantments to compass the Queen's death. Averroes, the Arabian philosopher, who flourished in the 12th century, was denounced as a lunatic and degraded solely on account of his great eminence in natural philosophy and medicine.

Scio's Blind Old Bard (sī' o). HOMER. Scio is the Italianized name of Chios, in the Ægean Sea, one of the "seven cities" that claimed the honour of being his birthplace. Anciently, one of the most flourishing Ionian states.

> Smyrna, Chios, Colophon, Salamis, Rhodos, Argos, Anthenæ
> Your just right to call Homer your son you must settle between ye

Scire facias (sī' re fā' si ȧs) (Lat., make [him] to know). A writ founded upon record (*i.e.* judgment, letters PATENT, etc.) directing the SHERIFF to make known (*scire facias*) to the person against whom it is brought to show why the person bringing the writ should not have the benefit of the record. It is now largely obsolete.

Sciron (sī' ron). A robber of Greek legend, slain by THESEUS. He infested the parts about Megara, and forced travellers over the rocks into the sea, where they were devoured by a sea monster.

Scissors. *See* KNIFE.

Scissors and paste. Compilation as distinct from original literary work. The allusion is obvious.

Scissors to grind. Work to do; purpose to serve. *I have my own scissors to grind* is a way of saying, "I've got my own work to do, or my own troubles, and can't be bothered with yours".

Scogan's Jests (skō' gȧn). A popular jestbook in the 16th century, said by Andrew Boorde (who published it) to be the work of one John Scogan, reputed to have been court fool to Edward IV. He is referred to (anachronously) by Justice Shallow in *Henry IV*, *Pt. II*, III, ii, and must not be confused with Henry Scogan (d. 1407), the poet-disciple of Chaucer to whom Ben Jonson alludes:

> Scogan? What was he?
> Oh, a fine gentleman, and a master of arts
> Of Henry the Fourth's times, that made disguises
> For the king's sons, and writ in ballad royal
> Daintily well.
> *The Fortunate Isles* (1642).

Scold's bridle. *See under* BRIDLE.

Sconce (skons). A word with several meanings: a lantern, a candlestick, a wall candle-bracket for one or more candles (from O. Fr. *esconse*, lantern); a small fortified earthwork or fort (from Dut. *schans*, a fort); also

a noun meaning a fire, and a verb meaning to mulct (derivation uncertain).

To be sconced. At Oxford, to pay a forfeit of ale to the company for a breach of table etiquette. Formerly, university officials imposed sconces or fines for breaches of discipline.

To build up a sconce. To incur or run-up a bill and dodge payment; to defraud.

Scone (skoon). **The Stone of Scone.** The great coronation stone, the Stone of Destiny, on which the Scottish kings were formerly crowned at Scone, near Perth. It was removed by Edward I in 1296 and brought to Westminster Abbey, and has ever since been housed under the Chair of St. Edward. It was stolen on the night of 24–25 December 1950, but restored to its place in February 1952.

It is also, traditionally, called JACOB'S STONE. It is of reddish-grey sandstone and is fabled to have been once kept at Dunstaffnage in Argyll and removed to Scone by Kenneth MacAlpin in 843. *Cp.* TANIST STONE.

Scorched Earth Policy. A policy of burning and destroying crops and anything that may be of use to an invading force.

Score (O.E. *scoru*, a notch). Especially applied to a notch on a TALLY, hence a reckoning or account. As the number 20, probably from the special score or mark on a tally which indicated that figure. Drovers passing their animals through a toll-gate always based their counting on twenties or *scores*.

To pay off old scores. To settle accounts; used sometimes of money debts, but usually in the sense of revenging an injury, "getting even" with one.

Scorpio, Scorpion (skôr' pi ō). Scorpio is the eighth sign of the ZODIAC, which the sun enters about 24 October. ORION had boasted that he could kill any animal the earth produced. A scorpion was sent to punish his vanity and it stung Orion to death. JUPITER later raised the scorpion to HEAVEN.

Fable has it that scorpions carry with them an oil which is a remedy against their stings. *Cp.* THE TOAD, UGLY AND VENOMOUS *under* TOADS.

> 'Tis true, a scorpion's oil is said
> To cure the wounds the venom made,
> And weapons dress'd with salves restore
> And heal the hurts they gave before.
> BUTLER: *Hudibras*, III, ii, 1029.

The oil was extracted from the flesh and given to the sufferer as a medicine; it was also supposed to be very useful to bring away the descending stone of the kidneys. Another belief was that if a scorpion was surrounded by a circle of fire it would sting itself to death with its own tail. Byron, in the *Giaour* (1.422), extracts a simile from the legend:

> The mind that broods o'er guilty woes
> Is like the Scorpion girt by fire;
> One sad and sole relief she knows,
> The sting she nourished for her foes,
> Whose venom never yet was vain,
> Gives but one pang, and cures all pain.

A lash, or scourge of scorpions. A specially severe punishment, in allusion to the Biblical passage:

> My father hath chastised you with whips, but I will chastise you with scorpions.
>
> I *Kings* xii, 11.

In the MIDDLE AGES a scourge of four or five thongs set with steel spikes and leaden weights was called a *scorpion*.

Scot. Payment, reckoning. The same word as SHOT; we still speak of *paying one's shot*.

Scot and lot. The rough equivalent of the modern rates, *i.e.* payments by householders for local and national purposes. They became in due course a qualification for the franchise. *Scot* is the tax and *lot* the allotment or portion alloted. Scot came from the Old Norse *skot*, a contribution, corresponding to O.E. *sceot. Cp.* CHURCH SCOT.

To go scot-free. To be let off payment; to escape payment or punishment, etc.

Scotch, Scots, Scottish. These three adjectives all mean belonging to, native of, or characteristic of SCOTLAND, but their application varies and the Scots usually prefer Scottish rather than Scotch, which is applied to whisky and **A Scotch breakfast,** a substantial meal of sundry good things to eat and drink. *Scotch*, however, is a proper English word for the Scottish.

Broad Scotch (Braid Scots). The vernacular of the lowlands of SCOTLAND; very different from the enunciation of Edinburgh and from the peculiarity of the Glasgow dialect.

Scotch mist. Fine, misty, rain. The phrase *What do you think this is—Scotch mist?* is addressed sarcastically to one who cannot see or grasp what stares him in the face.

Scotch Plot. An alleged conspiracy, called the Queensberry Plot in SCOTLAND, for a JACOBITE rising and invasion of Scotland in 1703. Simon Fraser, Lord Lovat, after intriguing at St. GERMAIN and VERSAILLES, returned to Scotland with a letter from Mary of Modena (James II's widow) to be delivered to an unnamed nobleman. He addressed it to John Murray, Duke of Atholl, his pesonal enemy, and then took it to the Duke of Queensberry, Atholl's rival in the Scottish Ministry. This broke up the ministry and drove Atholl over to the Jacobites. It led to disputes between the English and Scottish parliaments but no punitive action was taken.

Scotch-Irish. The American name for the PRESBYTERIAN immigrants from ULSTER who mainly settled in Pennsylvania and the Carolinas during the 18th century. The name derives from the Scottish ancestry of the Ulstermen.

A pound Scots. English and Scottish coins were of equal value until 1355 after which the Scottish coinage steadily depreciated, and when James VI of SCOTLAND became James I of ENGLAND (1603) the pound Scots was worth 1s. 8d., one-twelfth the value of an English pound. A pound Scots was divided into 20 *Scots shillings* each worth an English penny. The Scottish Mint closed in 1709.

The Scots Greys. *See* GREYS *under* REGIMENTAL AND DIVISIONAL NICKNAMES.

A Scots pint was about equivalent to three English imperial pints.

Scotch. To make a scotch is to cut with shallow incisions, to slash. SHAKESPEARE's *Macbeth* (III, ii) has, "We have scotch'd the snake, not killed it", but in the 1st Folio the word appears *scorch'd*. Isaac Walton's *Compleat Angler* tells us that to dress a chub, "Give him three or four scotches or cuts on the back with your knife, and broil him on charcoal." The derivation of the word is uncertain.

Out of all scotch and notch. Beyond all bounds; *scotch* was the line marked upon the ground in certain games, as **hopscotch.**

The word *scotch* is also applied to a wedge or block placed under a wheel, etc., to prevent it moving.

Scotists (skō′ tists). followers of Duns Scotus (*see* DUNCE), who maintained the doctrine of the IMMACULATE CONCEPTION in opposition to THOMAS AQUINAS.

Scotland. St. ANDREW is the patron saint of Scotland and tradition says that his remains were brought by Regulus (St. RULE) to the coast of Fife in 368.

The old royal arms of Scotland were: Or, a lion rampant gules, armed and langued azure, within a double tressure flory counter-flory of fleur-de-lis of the second. *Crest.* An imperial crown proper, surmounted by a lion sejant affronté gules crowned or, holding in his dexter paw a naked sword and in the sinister a sceptre both proper. *Supporters.* Two UNICORNS argent, armed, crined, and unguled or, imperially crowned, gorged with open crown with chains reflexed over the back of the last the dexter supporting a banner charged with the arms of Scotland, the sinister supporting a similar banner azure, thereupon a saltire argent. *Mottoes.* NEMO ME IMPUNE LACESSIT and over the crest *In Defens*.

In Scotland now, the royal arms of Great Britain are used with certain alterations; the collar of the THISTLE encircles that of the GARTER, the Scottish crest takes the place of the English, and the unicorn supporter crowned and gorged takes precedence of the lion (*see* HERALDRY).

The last Scottish coronation was that of Charles II at SCONE, 1 January 1651.

Scotland Yard. As commonly used it denotes the Criminal Investigation Department of the Metropolitan Police; from the fact that Great Scotland Yard, WHITEHALL, was the headquarters of the Metropolitan Police from *c.* 1842 to 1891 and thereafter New Scotland Yard, Parliament Street, until 1967 when "Scotland Yard" was transferred to Broadway, WESTMINSTER. The name of the original Scotland Yard comes from the fact that it was the residence of the kings of Scotland when they came to London.

To call in Scotland Yard, or the Yard. To summon the aid of the C.I.D. at Metropolitan Police Headquarters, the centre of crime detection.

> Norris was already at the factory when the Yard men arrived and reported that Holman was in the building and had been at work for about half an hour.
> JOSEPHINE BELL: *The Port of London Murders*, ch. XI.

Scotus, Duns. *See* DUNCE; SCOTISTS.

Scourge. A whip or lash; commonly applied to diseases that carry off great numbers, as "the scourge of influenza", etc., and to persons who seem to be the instruments of divine punishment, etc. Spenser, in his *Sonnet upon Scanderbeg*, calls him "The Scourge of the Turkes and plague of infidels".

The Scourge of God (Lat. *flagellum Dei*). ATTILA (d. 453), king of the HUNS, so called by mediæval writers because of the widespread havoc and destruction caused by his armies.

The Scourge of Homer. The carping critic ZOILUS.

The Scourge of Princes. Pietro Aretino (1492–1556), the Italian satirist.

Scouse (skous). A name applied to a native of the port of Liverpool; also to Liverpudlian speech and mannerisms. The word is the shortened form of *lobscouse*, a sailor's name for a stew, particularly of meat, vegetables, and ship's biscuit. Hence *lobscouser* as a name for a sailor.

Scout. This word comes from the old French *escoute*, a spy or eavesdropper, akin to the modern French *écouter*, to listen. It is applied to an individual, an aeroplane, warship, etc., sent to observe enemy movements or to obtain information. In the early days of CRICKET, the fielders were called scouts; college servants at Oxford are still called scouts; and it was also used for a member of the BOY SCOUTS whose association is now officially called the *Scout Association*.

Scowerers. A set of rakes (*c.* 1670–1720), who with the Nickers (*see* NICK) and MOHOCKS, committed great annoyances in London and other large towns.

> Who has not heard the Scowerers' midnight fame?
> Who has not trembled at Mohocks' name?
> Was there a watchman took his hourly rounds,
> Safe from their blows and new-invented wounds?
> GAY: *Trivia*, III, 325.

Scrap. The Scrap of Paper. The Treaty of 1839 maintaining the independence of Belgium; signed by Lord Palmerston for Great Britain; Count Sebastiani for France, Baron Bülow for Prussia; Count Pozzi di Borgo for Russia; Count Senfft for Austria; and M. Van de Weyer for Belgium. It was this treaty that the Germans violated when they invaded Belgium in August 1914. This brought Great Britain into the struggle and the German Chancellor Bethmann-Hollweg declared that Great Britain had entered the war "just for a scrap of paper".

Scrape. Bread and scrape. Bread and butter with the butter spread very thinly. *See* TO DINE ON POTATOES AND POINT *under* POINT.

I've got into a bad scrape. An awkward predicament, an embarrassing difficulty.

To scrape along. To get along in the world with difficulty, finding it hard to "make both ends meet".

To scrape an acquaintance with. To get on terms of familiarity with by currying favour and by methods of insinuation. The *Gentleman's Magazine* (N.S. xxxix, 230), says that Hadrian went one day to the public baths and saw an old soldier, well known to him, scraping himself with a potsherd for want of a flesh-brush. The emperor sent him a sum of money. Next day Hadrian found the bath crowded with soldiers scraping themselves with potsherds, and said, "Scrape on, gentlemen, but you'll not scrape acquaintance with me."

To scrape through. To pass an examination, etc., "by the skin of one's teeth" just to escape failure.

Scratch. There are two colloquial sporting uses of this word: (1) a horse or other entrant in a race or sporting event when withdrawn is said to be *scratched;* (2) a person starting from *scratch* in a sporting event is one starting from the usual starting point (*i.e.* the line marked—originally scratched out), whereas his fellow competitors would be starting ahead of him with handicaps awarded to their respective merits. In golf the term *par* is used instead of scratch. *To start from scratch* in general usage means to start from nothing or without particular advantages.

Scratch cradle. Another form of CAT'S CRADLE. *See under* CAT.

A scratch crew, side, etc. One scraped together *ad hoc*; not a regular team.

Old Scratch. OLD NICK (*see under* NICK), the DEVIL. From *skratta*, an old Scandinavian word for a GOBLIN or monster (modern Icelandic *skratti*, a devil).

A scratch race. A race of horses, men, boys, etc., without restrictions as to age, weight, previous winnings, etc., who all start from scratch.

To come up to (the) scratch. To be ready or good enough in any test; to make the grade. Under the London Prize Ring Rules, introduced in 1839, a round in a prize fight ended when one of the fighters was knocked down. After a 30-second interval this fighter was allowed eight seconds in which to make his way unaided to a mark scratched in the centre of the ring; if he failed to do so, he "had not come up to scratch" and was declared beaten.

Screw. Slang for wages, salary; possibly because in some employments it was handed out "screwed up in paper" or because it was "screwed out" of one's employer; it is also slang for a prison warder, from the days when the locks were operated with a screw-like movement.

An old screw. A skinflint; a miser who has amassed his wealth by "putting on the screw" (*see below*), and who keeps his money tight.

He has a screw loose. He is "not quite all there", he's "a little touched" or mad. His mind, like a piece of machinery, is in need of adjustment.

His head is screwed on the right way. He is clear-headed and right-thinking; he knows what he's about.

There's a screw loose somewhere. All is not quite right, there's something amiss. A figurative phrase from machinery, where one screw not tightened up may be the cause of a disaster.

To put on the screw. A phrase surviving from the days when the thumb-screw was used as a form of torture to extract confessions or money. To press for payment, as a screw presses by gradually increasing pressure. Hence *to apply the screw, to give the screw another turn*, to take steps (or additional steps) to enforce one's demands.

To screw oneself up to it. To force oneself to face it, etc.; to get oneself into the right frame of mind for doing some unpleasant or difficult job.

The Screw Plot. The story is that before Queen Anne went to St. Paul's in 1708 to offer thanksgiving for the victory of Oudenarde, conspirators removed certain screwbolts from the roof beams of the cathedral that the fabric might fall on the queen and her suite and kill them. In fact it appears that certain iron fastenings were omitted by one of the workmen as he thought the timbers were already sufficiently secured.

Screw-ball. A colloquial term for an erratic, eccentric, or unconventional person. It is also a baseball term for a ball pitched to break with a particular kind of slant away from the apparent curve of flight.

Screwed. Intoxicated. A playful synonym of *tight*.

Scribe. In the NEW TESTAMENT, it means a Jewish doctor of the law, and Scribes were generally coupled with the PHARISEES as upholders of the ancient ceremonial tradition. In *Matt.* xxii, 35, we read, "then one of them, which was a *lawyer*, asked Him...which is the great commandment in the law?" *Mark* (xii, 28) says, "And one of the *scribes* came, and...asked him, Which is the first commandment of all?"

In the OLD TESTAMENT the word has a wider application. In II *Sam.* viii, 17, it is used in the sense of "secretary", and again in *Jer.* xxxvi, 10, 12, 20, 21, etc. In II *Kings* xxv, 19, it applies to the military muster-master and *Is*. xxxiii, 18, a tax-official, etc. More commonly it denotes those occupied in literary study, copying and editing of the SCRIPTURES, and especially of the Law, this being akin to the New Testament usage.

Scriblerus, Martinus (mar ti nùs skrib lēr' ùs). A merciless satire on the false taste in literature current in the time of Pope, for the most part written by Arbuthnot, and published in 1741. Cornelius Scriblerus, the father of Martin, was a pedant, who entertained all sorts of absurdities about the education of his son. Martin grew up a man of capacity; but though he had read everything, his judgment was vile and taste atrocious. Pope, Swift, and Arbuthnot founded a *Scriblerus club* with the object of pillorying all literary incompetence.

Scrimshaw. A word from sailing ship days (derivation unknown) applied to carved scratched engraving on shells, bone, ivory, etc., to while away the time at sea. To *scrimshaw* is to make any ingenious useful article on shipboard.

Scriptores Decem (skrip tôr′ ēz′ dē sem). A collection of ten ancient chronicles on English history edited by Sir Roger Twysden (1597–1672) and published in 1652 as *Historiæ Anglicanæ Scriptores Decem* with the "Glossary" of William Somner, the first Anglo-Saxon word-list. The chroniclers are Simeon of Durham, John of Hexham, Richard of Hexham, Ailred of Rieval, Ralph de Diceto (Archdeacon of London), John Brompton of Jorval, Gervase of Canterbury, Thomas Stubbs, William Thorn of Canterbury, and Henry Knighton of Leicester.

Thomas Gale (*c.* 1635–1702) published a similar collection of five chronicles, *Historiæ Anglicanæ Scriptores Quinque* in 1687, and in 1691 *Historiæ Britannicæ Saxonicæ Danicæ Scriptores Quindecim*.

Scriptorium (skrip tôr′ i ūm) (Lat. from *scriptus*, past part. of *scribere*, to write). A writing-room, especially the chamber set apart in the mediæval monasteries for the copying of MSS., etc. Sir James Murray (1837–1915) gave the name to the corrugated-iron outhouse in his garden at Mill Hill, in which he started the great *New English Dictionary*.

Scriptures, The, or **Holy Scripture** (Lat. *scriptura*, a writing). The BIBLE; hence appleid allusively to the sacred writings of other creeds, as the KORAN, *the Scripture of the Mohammedans*, the VEDAS and ZEND-AVESTA, of the Hindus and Persians, etc.

Scripturists. A name given to the Karaites ("Readers of the Scripture"), those Jewish literalists who kept Biblical injunctions, etc., to the letter. For them "an eye for an eye" meant just this, and "Ye shall kindle no fire throughout your habitations upon the sabbath day" (*Exod.* xxxv, 3) left them to shiver in the winter. The movement began in the 8th century under Anan ben David, and spread from Babylonia to Persia and Egypt. Its decline set in from the 10th century, although it has lingered on in isolated pockets.

Scrooge, A regular Scrooge. A miserable skinflint, a proper miser. The allusion is to Ebenezer Scrooge in Dickens's *Christmas Carol* (1843).

> Oh! But he was a tight-fisted hand at the grindstone, Scrooge! a squeezing, wrenching, grasping, scraping, clutching, covetous old sinner!
> *Christmas Carol*, Stave One.

Scruple. The name of the weight (20 grains,

or ¹/₂₄ oz.), and the term for doubt or hesitation (as in *a scruple of conscience*), both come from Lat. *scrupulus*, meaning a sharp little pebble, such as will cause great uneasiness if it gets into one's shoe. The second is the figurative use; with the name of the little weight compare that of the big one—*stone*.

Scullabogue. The Barn of Scullabogue, (skŭl à bōg′). In the Irish rebellion of 1798 which largely degenerated into a war between CATHOLICS and PROTESTANTS, revenge was taken after the repulse of the rebels at New Ross. The barn at Scullabogue, containing over 180 Protestant loyalists, was set on fire and all its inmates perished.

Scunner. A Scottish term for a feeling of distaste amounting almost to loathing. *To take a scunner at something* is to conceive a violent dislike to it.

Scurry. In horse-racing, a SCRATCH RACE for inferior mounts, etc.; a short, quick race.

Hurry-scurry. A confused bustle through lack of time; in a confused bustle. A RICOCHET word.

Scutage (skū′ tij), or **Escuage.** In feudal times, a payment in commutation of KNIGHT-SERVICE (*i.e.* military service). It developed after the Norman CONQUEST but the term, from Lat. *scutum*, a shield, did not come into use until the beginning of the 12th century. The method of assessment was regularized in the reign of Henry II and TENANTS-IN-CHIEF passed on the levy to their tenants. Scutage came to an end in 1327.

Scuttle. The scuttle for coals is O.E. *scutel*, a dish, from Lat. *scutella*, a dish or platter. The scuttle or opening in the side or deck of a ship is Sp. *escotilla*, a hatchway.

To scuttle a ship is to hole it in order to make it sink. This is from SCUTTLE in the sense of a hatch-opening or hole.

To scuttle off. To make off hurriedly. This was originally *to scuddle off*, scuddle being a frequentative of *scud*, to run or skim along.

Scylla. In Greek legend the name of a daughter of King Nisus of Megara; also a sea monster.

The daughter of Nisus promised to deliver Megara into the hands of her lover, MINOS, and, to effect this, cut off a golden hair on her father's head while he was asleep. Minos despised her for this treachery, and Scylla threw herself from a rock into the sea. Other accounts say she was changed into a lark by the gods and her father into a hawk.

Scylla, the sea monster, was a beautiful NYMPH beloved by GLAUCUS, who applied to CIRCE for a love-potion, but Circe became enamoured of him and metamorphosed her rival into a hideous creature with twelve feet and six heads, each with three rows of teeth. Below the waist her body was made up of hideous monsters, like dogs, which barked unceasingly. She dwelt on the rock of Scylla, opposite CHARYBDIS, on the Italian side of the Straits of Messina and was a terror to ships and sailors. Whenever a ship passed, each of her heads would seize one of the crew.

Avoiding Scylla, he fell into Charybdis. *See* CHARYBDIS

Between Scylla and Charybdis. *See* CHARYBDIS.

To fall from Scylla into Charybdis—out of the FRYING-PAN into the fire. *See* CHARYBDIS.

Scythian (sith' i àn). Pertaining to the peoples or region of Scythia, the ancient name of a great part of European and Asiatic Russia.

Scythian defiance. When DARIUS approached Scythia, an ambassador was sent to his tent with a bird, a frog, a mouse, and five arrows, then left without uttering a word. Darius, wondering what was meant, was told by Gobrias it meant this: Either fly away like a bird, hide your head in a hole like a mouse, or swim across the river like a frog, or in five days you will be laid prostrate by the Scythian arrows.

The Scythian or **Tartarian Lamb.** *See under* LAMB.

'Sdeath, 'Sdeins. *See* 's.

Sea. Any large expanse of water, more or less enclosed; hence the expression "molten sea" meaning the great brazen vessel which stood in SOLOMON'S TEMPLE (II *Chron*. iv, 2, and I *Kings*, vii, 23); even the NILE, the Euphrates, and the Tigris are sometimes called *sea* by the prophets. The world of water is the *Ocean*.

At sea, or **all at sea.** Wide of the mark, in a state of uncertainty or error; like one at sea who has lost his bearings.

The four seas. The seas surrounding Great Britain, on the north, south, east, and west.

Half-seas over. *See under* HALF.

The high seas. The open sea, the "main"; especially that part of the sea beyond "the THREE-MILE LIMIT, which forms a free highway to all nations.

The Old Man of the Sea. *See under* OLD.

The Seven Seas. *See under* SEVEN.

Sea Deities. In classical myth, besides the fifty NEREIDS, the OCEANIDS, the SIRENS, etc., there were numerous deities connected with the sea. Chief among them are: AMPHITRITE; GLAUCUS; Ino (*see* LEUCOTHEA); NEPTUNE; NEREUS and his wife TETHYS; Por-

tumnus (*see* PALÆMON); POSEIDON (the Greek Neptune); PROTEUS; THETIS; TRITON.

Sea Lawyer. A seaman who is constantly arguing about his rights, a captious person, a troublemaker. It is also nautical slang for a shark.

Sea legs. To get one's sea legs. To acquire the ability to walk steadily in a ship at sea despite the rolling and pitching of the vessel.

Sea serpent. A serpentine monster supposed to inhabit the depths of the ocean. Many reports of such a creature have been made by mariners over the centuries but its existence has never been established; thus J. G. Lockhart (*Mysteries of the Sea: The Great Sea-Serpent*) writes: "We thus conclude with at least three sea-serpents, one in 1857, one in 1875, and one in 1905, for which we have reasonably satisfactory evidence ... Most of the witnesses agree on certain outstanding features; it is a long serpentine creature; it has a series of humps; its head is rather like a horse's; its colour is dark on the top and light below; it appears during the summer months; and unlike the sea monster it is harmless, for it never actually attacked anybody even under provocation". *Cp.* LOCH NESS MONSTER.

The Sea-born City. Venice.

The Sea-born goddess. APHRODITE.

The Sea-girt isle. ENGLAND. So called because, as SHAKESPEARE has it, it is "hedged in with the main, that water-walled bulwark" (*King John*, II, i).

> This precious stone set in the silver sea,
> Which serves it in the office of a wall,
> Or as a moat defensive to a house,
> Against the envy of less happier lands.
> *Richard II*, II, i.

Sea-green Incorruptible, The. So Carlyle called Robespierre in his *French Revolution*. He was of a sallow, unhealthy complexion.

Sea-island cotton. A fine long-stapled cotton, so called from its being grown on the islands off the coast of South Carolina and Georgia.

Seal. The sire is called a *bull*, his females are *cows*, the offspring are called *pups*; the breeding-place is called a *rookery*, a group of young seals a *pod*, and a colony of seals a *herd*. The immature male is called a *bachelor*. A *sealer* is a seal-hunter, and seal hunting is called *sealing*.

Seal (O.Fr. *seel* from Lat. *sigillum*). An impressed device, in wax, lead, etc.

Great Seal. *See under* GREAT.

Solomon's Seal. *See under* SOLOMON.

To set one's seal to. To give one's authority, to authenticate. From the affixing seals to documents as an official sign of their authenticity.

Under my hand and seal. A legal phrase indicating that the document in question is both signed and sealed by the person on whose behalf it has been drawn up.

Sealed Orders. Orders delivered in a sealed package to naval and military commanders which they must not open before a certain time, or reaching a certain locality, etc.

Seamy side. The "wrong" or worst side; as the "seamy side of London", the "seamy side of life". In velvet, Brussels carpets, tapestry, etc., the "wrong" side shows the seams or threads of the pattern exhibited on the right side.

Seasons, The Four. Spring, Summer, Autumn, and Winter. *Spring* starts (officially) on 21 March, the Spring Equinox, when the sun enters ARIES; *Summer* on 22 June, the Summer SOLSTICE, when the sun enters CANCER; *Autumn* on 23 September, the Autumn Equinox, the sun entering LIBRA; the *Winter* on 22 December, when the sun enters CAPRICORN. *See* ZODIAC.

The ancient Greeks characterized Spring by MERCURY, Summer by APOLLO, Autumn by BACCHUS, and Winter by HERCULES.

James Thomson's poetic series *The Seasons* was not published as a collection until 1730. *Winter* first appeared in 1726 and fetched three guineas from the publisher, but gave Thomson a reputation. *Summer*, dedicated to Bob Dodington, was published in 1727, *Spring* in 1728, and *Autumn* in 1730.

In and out of season. Always or all the time, constantly.

The London Season. The part of the year when the Court and fashionable society generally is in town—May, June, July.

The silly season. *See under* SILLY.

Season-ticket. A ticket giving the holder certain specified rights (in connection with travelling, entrance to an exhibition, etc.) for a certain specified period.

Seat. To take a back seat. *See under* BACK.

Sebastian, St. Patron SAINT of archers, martyrd in 288. He was bound to a tree and shot at with arrows and finally beaten to death. As the arrows stuck in his body as pins in a pin-cushion, he was also made the patron saint of pin-makers. As he was a captain of the guard, he is the patron saint of soldiers. His feast, coupled with that of St. Fabian, is kept on 20 January.

The English St. Sebastian. St. Edmund, the martyr-king of East Anglia (855—870) who is said to have been tied to a tree by the Danes and shot dead with arrows at Hoxne,

Suffolk, because he refused to rule as a Danish vassal. His body was taken to the royal manor of Bedricsworth which came to be called St. Edmund's Burgh and his remains, miraculously incorrupt, became the chief relic of the abbey of Bury St. Edmunds.

Second. The next after the first (Lat. *secundus*).

In duelling the *second* is the representative of the principal; he carries the challenge, selects the ground, sees that the weapons are in order, and is responsible for all the arrangements.

A second of time is so called because the division of the minute into sixtieths is the second of the sexagesimal operations, the first being the division of the hour into minutes.

One's second self. One's ALTER EGO; one whose tastes, opinions, habits, etc., correspond so entirely with one's own that there is practically no distinction.

The Second Adam. Jesus Christ.

Second Adventists. Those who believe that the Second Coming of Christ (*cp.* 1 *Thess.* iv, 15) will precede the MILLENNIUM; hence sometimes also called Premillenarians.

Second Chamber. In a legislature of two houses the non-elected or indirectly elected house is so called. In Great Britain the HOUSE OF LORDS is the Second Chamber and in the U.S.A. it is the Senate.

Second Empire. *See* NAPOLEON III.

Second Floor. Two flights above the ground floor. In the U.S.A. the second floor is the English first floor.

Second-hand. Not new or original; what has already been the property of another, as "second-hand" books, clothes, opinions, etc.

Second nature. Said of a habit, way of doing things, etc., that has become so ingrained that it is instinctive.

Second pair back. The back room on the floor two flights of stairs above the ground floor; similarly the front room is called the *second pair front*.

Second sight. The power of seeing things invisible to others; the power of foreseeing future events.

Second Wind. *See under* WIND.

To second an officer (accent on last syllable) is, in military parlance, to remove him temporarily from his present duties to take up another extra-regimental or staff appointment.

Secondary colours. *See under* COLOURS.

Secret. An open secret. A piece of information generally known, but not formally announced.

Un secret de polichinelle. No secret at all; an open secret. *Polichinelle* is the PUNCH of the old French puppet-shows, and his secrets are STAGE WHISPERS told to all the audience.

Secret Service. The popular name for governmental intelligence, espionage and counter-espionage organizations. The U.S. Secret Service, under the Treasury Department, is mainly concerned with Federal crime.

Secular. From Lat. *sæcularis*, pertaining to a *sæculum* or age, a generation; also a period of 100 years (the longest duration of man's life), any long period of indefinite length. This gives us our meanings of "occurring once in an age", "lasting indefinitely", "occurring once in a hundred years" and "lasting for a hundred years". The meaning "lay", "temporal", "of this world", is from Late Latin when *sæcularis* had acquired the meaning of "belonging to the world", "worldly".

Secular clergy. Clergy living "in the world" as opposed to the regular clergy of the cloister, who live under a rule. In the ROMAN CATHOLIC CHURCH secular clergy take precedence over the regular clergy.

Secular games (Lat. *Ludi sæculares*). In ancient ROME, the public games lasting three days and three nights, that took place once in an age (*sæculum*) or every 100 years (sometimes every 110 years).

They were instituted in obedience to the SIBYLLINE verses with the promise that "the empire should remain in safety so long as this admonition was observed". They derived from the Tarentine Games instituted in 249 B.C. to propitiate PLUTO and PROSERPINE.

> Date, quæ precamur
> Tempore sacro
> Quo Sibyllini monuere versus.
>
> HORACE: *Carmen Sæculare*, A.U.C. 737.

Secularism. The name given in 1846 by George Jacob Holyoake (1817–1906) to an ethical system founded on "natural morality" and opposed to the tenets of revealed religion and ecclesiasticism.

Security Risk. Governmental security is concerned with the prevention of leakages of confidential information, and *a security risk* denotes one of doubtful loyalty, whose background and associations make employment in state service inadvisable, especially in posts which involve access to confidential information likely to be of use to a potentially hostile government.

> The abrupt departure of two young Foreign Office officials, Burgess and Maclean, to their spiritual home in Moscow on 25 May 1951 could also not be blamed on Morrison, but it did reflect on the security arrangements for which his predecessor had been responsible.
>
> W. N. MEDLICOTT: *Contemporary England*, ch. 12.

Sedan chair (se dăn'). The covered seat, so called, carried by two bearers back and front, originated in Italy in the late 16th century, and was introduced into England by Sir S. Duncombe in 1634.

The name is probably derived from Lat. *sedere*, to sit; but Johnson's suggestion that it is connected with the French town, *Sedan*, is a possibility.

The Man of Sedan. NAPOLEON III was so called because he surrendered his sword to William I, King of Prussia, after the battle of Sedan (2 September 1870).

Sedulous. To play the sedulous ape to. To study the style of another, and model one's own on his as faithfully and meticulously as possible; said, usually with more or less contempt, of literary men. The phrase is taken from R. L. Stevenson, who, in his essay, "A College Magazine" (*Memories and Portraits*), said that he had:

> Played the sedulous ape to Hazlitt, to Lamb, to Wordsworth, to sir Thomas Browne, to Defoe, to Hawthorne; to Montaigne, to Baudelaire, and to Obermann...That, like it or not, is the way to learn to write.

See (Lat. *sedes*). The seat or throne of a BISHOP, hence the town or place where the bishop's cathedral is located and from which he takes his title; and so has to be distinguished from diocese, the territory over which he has jurisdiction.

The Holy See. *See under* HOLY.

See (O.E. *seon*). To perceive by the eye.

To see a person through. To help him through a difficulty.

To see into the matter. To investigate.

To see off. To accompany someone to the point of departure on a journey; also, colloquially, to outwit or get the better of someone by sharp practice, etc.; or to get the better of someone physically, as a dog "sees off" unwanted prowlers.

To see through a person. To perceive his true character and motives, "not to be taken in".

To see to. To attend to.

Seeded players. Those players regarded by the organizers of a tournament (*e.g.* lawn tennis at the All England Club, Wimbledon) as likely to reach the final stages, and who are so placed in the order of play that they do not meet each other until the closing rounds. These players are numbered in the order of likelihood. Of course it sometimes happens that seeded players are defeated early in a tournament.

Seekers. A 17th-century PURITAN sect akin to the QUAKERS in their outlook who rejected the existing church and claimed to seek the true church which God would reveal in his own time. Roger Williams (*c.* 1603–1683) founded Providence, NEW ENGLAND, as a refuge for the sect.

Seel. To close the eyelids of a HAWK by running a thread through them; to hoodwink (Fr. *ciller*; *cil*, the eyelash).

> She that so young could give out such a seeming,
> To seel her fathers eyes up, close as oak.
>
> SHAKESPEARE: *Othello*, III, iii.

Seian Horse, The (sī àn). A possession which invariably brought ill luck with it. Hence the Latin proverb *Ille homo habet equum Seianum*. Cneius Seius had an Argive horse, of the breed of Diomed, of a bay colour and surpassing beauty, but it was fatal to its possessor. Seius was put to death by Mark Antony. Its next owner, Cornelius Dolabella, who bought it for 100,000 sesterces, was killed in Syria during the civil wars. Caius Cassius, who next took possession of it, perished after the battle of Philippi by the very sword which stabbed CÆSAR. Antony had the horse next, and after the battle of Actium slew himself.

Likewise the gold of Tolosa (*see under* GOLD) *and* HARMONIA'S NECKLACE were fatal possessions. *Cp.* NESSUS; OPAL.

Selah (sē la). A Hebrew word occurring often in thd *Psalms* (and three times in *Habakkuk* iii), indicating some musical or liturgical direction, such as a pause, a repetition, or the end of a section.

Select men. Town officers in NEW ENGLAND deputed to be responsible for certain local concerns. They are elected annually at town meetings and their office derives from the select vestrymen of former days.

Selene (se lē' nē). The moon goddess of Greek mythology, daughter of HYPERION and Theia, corresponding approximately to the Roman DIANA. Selene had 50 daughters by ENDYMION and three by ZEUS, including Erse, the Jew. Selene is represented with a diadem and wings on her shoulders, driving in a chariot drawn by two white horses; Diana is represented with a bow and arrow running after a stag.

Seleucidæ (se lū' si dē). The dynasty of Seleucus Nicator (*c.* 358–281 B.C.), one of ALEXANDER's generals who in 312 conquered Babylon and succeeded to part of Alexander's vast empire. The monarchy consisted of Syria, a large part of Asia Minor, and all the eastern provinces (Persia, Bacteria, etc.). The last of the line was dispossessed by the Romans in 64 B.C.

Self. The Self-denying Ordinance. The measure passed by the LONG PARLIAMENT (April 1645) providing that Members of either House should give up their military commands and civil offices within 40 days. Nothing was said to prevent their reappointment. The indecisive second battle of Newbury in 1644 led to this measure which was directed against incompetent commanders, particularly in the HOUSE OF LORDS.

Self-determination. In politics, the concept that every nation, no matter how small or weak, has the right to decide upon its own form of government and to manage its own affairs. The phrase acquired this significance during the attempts to resettle Europe after World War I.

A self-made man. One who has risen from poverty and obscurity to comparative opulence or a position of importance by his own efforts.

Seljuks (sel' jŭks). The name of several Turkish dynasties descended from Seljuk, a Ghuzz chieftain, and which ruled in Persia, Syria and Asia Minor between the 11th and 13th centuries. In 1055 Togrul Beg, grandson of Seljuk, was made "Commander of the Faithful" (*see* CALIPH) for coming to the assistance of the ABBASSIDE Caliph of Baghdad. His successor Alp Arslan took Syria and Palestine, and a large part of Anatolia from the BYZANTINE Emperor. The territories were eventually partitioned among branches of the family, but were subject to Mongol onslaughts from 1243. Their power steadily declined and their place was eventually taken by the OTTOMANS.

Sell. Slang for a swindle, a hoax, a first-of-April trick; and the person hoaxed is said to be *sold*.

To sell down the river. See RIVER.

Selling out. In stockbroking, to sell in open exchange shares which a purchaser failed to take up at the specified time, the original purchaser having to make good the difference between the original contract price and the price at which they are actually sold. Also applied to officer's retirement from the Army in the days when commissions were bought and sold.

To sell a person up. To dispose of his goods by order of the court because he cannot pay his debts, the proceeds going to his creditors.

To sell short. See *under* SHORT.

A selling race. See SELLING PLATE *under* PLATE.

Selling the pass. Betraying one's own side. The phrase was originally Irish and applied to those who turned King's EVIDENCE, or who impeached their comrades for money. The tradition is that a regiment was sent by Crotha, "lord of Atha", to hold a pass against the invading army of Trathal, "King of Cael". The pass was betrayed for money; the Firbolgs (*see* MILESIANS) were subdued, and Trathal assumed the title of "King of Ireland".

Sellinger's Round. An old country dance, very popular in Elizabethan times, in which:

> the dancers take hands, go round twice and back again; then all set, turn, and repeat; then lead all forward, and back, and repeat; two singles and back, set and turn single and repeat; arms all and repeat.
>
> JOHN PLAYFORD: *The English Dancing Master* (1651).

It is said to be so called either from Sir Thomas Sellynger, buried in St. George's Chapel, Windsor, about 1470, or from Sir Anthony St. Leger, Lord Deputy of Ireland (d.1559).

Semele (sem′ e lē). In Greek mythology, the daughter of CADMUS and HARMONIA. By ZEUS she was the mother of DIONYSUS and was slain by lightning when he granted her request to visit her in his majesty.

Semiramis (se mir′ à mis). In ancient legend, daughter of the goddess Derceto and a young Assyrian. She married Menones, but he hanged himself when NINUS, king of Assyria and founder of Nineveh, demanded Semiramis from him. She forthwith married NINUS who was so enamoured that he resigned the CROWN to her. After this she put him to death, but was herself ultimately slain by her son Ninyas. She is sometimes identified with ISHTAR and her doves. These and other legends accumulated round an Assyrian princess of this name who lived *c.* 800 B.C.

The Semiramis of the North. Margaret of Denmark, Sweden, and Norway (1353–1412), and Catherine II of Russia (1729–1796) have both been so called.

Semitic (se mit′ ic). Pertaining to the descendants of SHEM (*see Gen*. x), *viz*., the Hebrews, Arabs, Assyrians, Aramæans, etc.; nowadays applied to the Jews.

The Semitic languages are the ancient Assyrian and Chaldee, Aramaic, Syriac, Arabic, Hebrew, Samaritan, Ethiopic, and old Phœnician. The great characteristic of this family of languages is that the roots of words consist of three consonants.

Senatus consultum (sen a′ tus kon sŭl′tum). A decree of the Senate of Ancient ROME. The term was sometimes applied to a decree of any senate, especially that of the First Empire in France.

Send. That sends me. Amateurs of JAZZ use this phrase, meaning: The music sends me out of myself, or into ecstasies.

Se'nnight. A week; seven nights. *Fort'night*, fourteen nights. These words are relics of the ancient CELTIC custom of beginning the day at sunset, a custom observed by the ancient Greeks, Babylonians, Persians, Syrians, and Jews, and by the modern heirs of these peoples. In *Gen*. i, 5, we find the evening precedes the morning: as, "The evening and the morning were the first day", etc.

> He shall live a man forbid:
> Weary se'n-nights nine times nine
> Shall he dwindle, peak and pine.
>
> SHAKESPEARE: *Macbeth*, I, iii.

Sense. Common sense. *See under* COMMON.

Scared out of my seven senses. Utterly scared, scared out of my wits. *See* SEVEN SENSES.

Sensitive Plant. *See* MIMOSA.

Sentences, Master of the. The SCHOOLMAN, Peter Lombard (*c*. 1100–1160), and Italian theologian and BISHOP of Paris, author of *The Four Books of Sentences* (*Sententiarum libri IV*), a compilation from the Fathers of the leading arguments PRO AND CON, bearing on the hair-splitting theological questions of the MIDDLE AGES.

The mediæval graduates in theology, of the second order, whose duty it was to lecture on the *Sentences*, were called *Sententiatory Bachelors*.

Separatists. A name given to the BROWNISTS and Independents of the 17th century who separated from the Established Church.

Sephardim. The Jews of Spain and Portugal, as distinct from those of Poland and Germany called *Ashkenazim* (from the location given in *Gen*. x, 3). The name is from *Sepharad* (*Obad*. 20) where Jews were in captivity. The TARGUM of Jonathan wrongly identified it with Spain, possibly from some similarity with Hesperis, hence the application of the name to Spanish Jews.

Sept, from O.Fr. *septe*, possibly a variant of *secte* or sect; a term especially applied to an Irish CLAN which was a division of the tribe. The freemen of the sept bore the clan name with the prefix "Ua", grandson, written in English as "O".

September. The seventh month from MARCH, where the year used to commence.

The old Dutch name was *Herst-maand* (autumn-month), the old Saxon, *Gerst-monath* (barley-month), or *Hæfest-monath*; and after the introduction of Christianity *Halig-monath* (holy-month, the nativity of the Virgin MARY being on the 8th, the EXALTATION OF THE CROSS or Holy Cross Day on the 14th and St. MICHAEL's Day on the

29th). In the French Republican CALENDER it was called *fructidor* (fruit-month, 18 August to 16 September).

September Bible. *See* BIBLE, SOME SPECIALLY NAMED EDITIONS.

September Massacres. An indiscriminate slaughter during the French Revolution, directed at the royalists confined in the Abbaye and other prisons, lasting from 2 to 7 September 1792. Over 1,500 were massacred with revolting brutalities. It was occasioned by the dismay at the fall of Verdun to the Prussians. Those taking part in the atrocities were called Septembrists.

Septentrional Signs (sep ten' tri ō nàl). The first six signs of the ZODIAC, because they belong to the *northern* celestial hemisphere. The north was called the *septentrion* from the seven stars of the Great Bear (Lat. *septem*, seven; *triones*, plough oxen). *Cp.* URSA MAJOR.

Septuagesima Sunday (sep tū à jes' i mà). The third Sunday before LENT; in round numbers, 70 (in fact 64) days (Lat. *septuagesima dies*) before EASTER.

Septuagint (sep' tū à jint) (Lat. *septuaginta*, seventy). The most important Greek version of the OLD TESTAMENT and APOCRYPHA, so called because it was traditionally said to have been translated from the Hebrew SCRIPTURES by 72 learned Jews in the 3rd century B.C., at the command of Ptolemy Philadelphus for the Alexandrian LIBRARY. They worked on the island of PHAROS and completed the task in 72 days.

The name Septuagint is commonly abbreviated as LXX. It is probably the work of Jewish scholars at Alexandria working over a long period of time.

Sepulchre, The Holy. The cave outside the walls of old JERUSALEM in which the body of Christ is believed to have lain between His burial and Resurrection. The tomb is said to have been discovered by St. HELENA and from at least the 4th century (*see* INVENTION OF THE CROSS *under* CROSS) the spot has been covered by a Christian Church, where today Greek, Catholic, Armenian, Syrian, and Coptic Christians have their rights of occupation.

Knights of the Holy Sepulchre. An order of military knights founded by Godfrey of Bouillon in 1099 to guard the Holy Sepulchre.

Seraglio (sè ra' lyō). The word is Italian and means "enclosure" and especially denotes the former palace of the SULTANS at Constantinople, situated on the GOLDEN HORN and enclosed by walls containing many buildings. The chief entrance was the Sublime Gate (*see* PORTE); and the chief edifice the Harem or "forbidden spot" which contained numerous dwellings, for the sultan's wives, and for his concubines. The Seraglio might be visited by strangers, not so the Harem.

Seraphic (se rǎf' ik). **Seraphic Blessing.** The blessing written by St. FRANCIS OF ASSISI at the request of Brother Leo on Mt. Alverna in 1224. It is based on *Numbers* vi, 24: "May the Lord bless thee and keep thee. May he show His face to thee and have mercy on thee. May he turn his countanance on thee and give thee peace. May the Lord bless thee, Brother Leo."

The Seraphic Doctor. The Scholastic philosopher, St. Bonaventura (1221–1274).

The Seraphic Father, or **Saint.** St. FRANCIS OF ASSISI (1182–1226); whence the FRANCISCANS are sometimes called the *Seraphic Order*.

The Seraphic Hymn. The Sanctus, 'Holy, holy, holy" (*Is.* vi, 3), which was sung by the SERAPHIM.

Seraphim. The highest of the nine choirs of ANGELS, so named from the seraphim of *Is.* vi, 2. The word is probably the same as *saraph*, a serpent, from *saraph*, to burn (in allusion to its bite); and this connexion with burning suggested to early Christian interpreters that the seraphim were specially distinguished by the ardency of their zeal and love.

Seraphim is a plural form; the singular, *seraph*, was first used in English by Milton. ABDIEL was,

The flaming Seraph, fearless, though alone,
Encompassed round with foes.
Paradise Lost, V, 875.

Serapis (se rā' pis). The Ptolemaic form of APIS, an Egyptian deity who, when dead, was honoured under the attributes of OSIRIS and thus became "osirified Apis" or [O] Sorapis. He was lord of the underworld, and was identified by the Greeks with HADES.

Serat, Al. *See* AL-SIRAT.

Serbonian Bog, The (sèr bō' ni àn). A great morass, now covered with shifting sand, between the isthmus of Suez, the MEDITERRANEAN, and the delta of the Nile. In Strabo's time it was a lake stated by him to be 200 stadia long and 50 broad, and by Pliny to be 150 miles in length. TYPHON was said to dwell at the bottom of it, hence its other name, *Typhon's Breathing Hole*.

A gulf profound as that Serbonian bog,
Betwixt Damiata and Mount Cassius old,
Where armies whole have sunk.
MILTON: *Paradise Lost*, II, 592.

The term is used figuratively of a mess

from which there is no way of extricating oneself.

Serendipity (se ren dip′ i ti). A happy coinage by Horace Walpole to denote the faculty of making lucky and unexpected "finds" by accident. In a letter to Mann (28 January 1754) he says that he formed it on the title of a fairy story, *The Three Princes of Serendip*, because the princes:

> were always making discoveries, by accidents and sagacity, of things they were not in quest of.

Serendip is an ancient name of Ceylon.

Serene (Lat. *serenus*, clear, calm). A title mainly given formerly to certain German princes. Those who used to hold it under the empire were entitled *Serene* or *Most Serene Highnesses*.

It's all serene, or **all sereno.** All right, all is well (Span. *sereno*, all right—the sentinel's countersign).

The drop serene. *See under* DROP.

Sergeanty, or **Serjeanty.** Various forms of land tenure akin to KNIGHT service involving military service or some form of household service for the king or lord, sometimes nominal. *Serjeanty* comes from Norman French *serjantie* (Lat. *serviens*, a servant). They eventually came to be classed as **Grand serjeanties** and **Petty Serjeanties,** the latter involving some obligation such as the rendering of a bow or a sword. (Woodstock was granted to the Duke of Marlborough in grand serjeanty, in return for the rendering of a French standard to the crown on the anniversary of Blenheim.) These services were retained when military tenures were abolished in 1661. The incidents were preserved by the Law of Property Acts, 1922 and 1925.

Serjeants-at-Arms. Officials of the Royal HOUSEHOLD with certain ceremonial functions, eight in number. In addition there is the SPEAKER's Serjeant-at-Arms in the HOUSE OF COMMONS, who carries the MACE and acts as the disciplinary officer, and another who carries the mace of the Lord CHANCELLOR in the HOUSE OF LORDS.

Serjeants-at-law. A superior order of barristers superseded by QUEEN'S COUNSEL in 1877. From the Low Latin *servientes ad legem*, one who serves the king in matters of law. They formed an Inn called Serjeants Inn which was in FLEET STREET and later Chancery Lane. *See* COIF.

Serpent. The serpent is symbolical of:

(1) Deity, because, says Plutarch, "it feeds upon its own body; even so all things spring from God, and will be resolved into deity again" (*De Iside et Osiride*, i, 2, p. 5; and *Philo Byblius*).

(2) Eternity, as a corollary of the former. It is represented as forming a circle, holding its tail in its mouth.

(3) Renovation and the healing art. It is said that when old it has the power of growing young again "like the eagle", by casting its slough, which is done by squeezing itself between two rocks. It was sacred to ÆSCULAPIUS, and was supposed to have the power of discovering healing herbs. *See* CADUCEUS.

(4) Guardian spirit. It was thus employed by the ancient Greeks and Romans, and not infrequently the figure of a serpent was depicted on their altars.

In the temple of Athena at ATHENS, a serpent, supposed to be animated by the soul of Erichthonius, was kept in a cage, and called "the Guardian Spirit of the Temple".

(5) Wisdom. "Be ye therefore wise as serpents, and harmless as doves" (*Matt.* x, 16).

(6) Subtlety. "Now the serpent was more subtil than any beast of the field" (*Gen.* iii, i).

(7) The DEVIL. As the Tempter (*Gen.* iii, 1–6). In early pictures the serpent is sometimes placed under the feet of the Virgin, in allusion to the promise made to EVE after the fall (*Gen.* iii, 15).

In Christian art it is an attribute of St. CECILIA, St. Euphemia, St. PATRICK, and many other SAINTS, either because they trampled on SATAN, or because they miraculously cleared some country of snakes.

Fable has it that the cerastes (horned viper) hides in sand that it may bite the horse's foot and get the rider thrown. In allusion to this belief, Jacob says, "Dan shall be…an adder in the path, that biteth the horse heels, so that his rider shall fall backward" (*Gen.* xlix, 17). The Bible also tells us that the serpent stops up its ears that it may not be charmed by the charmers, "charming never so wisely" (*Ps.* lxiii, 4).

Another old idea about snakes was that when attacked they would swallow their young and not eject them until reaching a place of safety.

It was in the form of a serpent, says the legend, that Jupiter AMMON appeared to OLYMPIA and became by her the father of ALEXANDER THE GREAT. *See also* SNAKE.

The old Serpent. SATAN.

> And he laid hold on the dragon, that old serpent, which is the Devil, and Satan, and bound him a thousand years.
>
> *Rev.* xx, 2.

Pharaoh's serpent. *See under* PHARAOH.
Sea serpent. *See under* SEA.
The serpent of old Nile. CLEOPATRA, so called by Antony.

> He's speaking now,
> Or murmuring "Where's my serpent of old Nile?"
> for so he calls me.
>
> SHAKESPEARE: *Antony and Cleopatra*, I, v.

Their ears have been serpent-licked.
They have the gift of foreseeing events, the
power of seeing into futurity. This is a
Greek superstition. It is said that CASSAN-
DRA and Helenus were gifted with the power
of prophecy, because serpents licked their
ears while sleeping in the temple of APOLLO.

To cherish a serpent in your bosom. To
show kindness to one who proves ungrateful. The Greeks say that a husbandman
found a frozen serpent, which he put into his
bosom. The snake was revived by the
warmth, and stung its benefactor. SHAKE-
SPEARE applies the tale to a serpent's egg:

> Therefore think him as a serpent's egg
> Which, hatched, would (as his kind) grow danger-
> ous.
>
> *Julius Cæsar*, II, i.

Serpentine Verses. Such as end with the
same word as they begin with. The following are examples:

> Crescit amor nummi, quantum ipsa pecunia crescit.
> (Greater grows the love of pelf, as pelf itself grows
> greater).
> Ambo florentes ætatibus, Arcades ambo.
> (Both in the spring of life, arcadians both).

The allusion is to the old representations
of snakes with their tails in their mouths—
no beginning and no end.

Serve. I'll serve him out—give him a good
QUID PRO QUO. This is the French *desservir*,
to do an ill turn to one.

Serves you right! You've got just what you
deserved.

To serve a mare. To place a stallion to her.

To serve a rope is to wind it round with
spunyarn or other suitable cord or twine, to
protect it from wet or chafe. Serving is always put on against the lay of the rope.

To serve a sentence. To undergo the punishment awarded.

To serve a writ on. To deliver into the
hands of the person concerned a legal writ.

To serve its turn. Said of something which
is used to satisfy a purpose or fulfil a need,
and then discarded.

To serve one out. To punish, to get revenge on, to get one's own back.

To serve one's time. To hold an office or
appointment for the full period allowed; to
go through one's apprenticeship; to go
through one's length of service in the armed
forces; to serve one's sentence in a prison.

Servus servorum (sĕr' vŭs sĕr vôr' ŭm)
(Lat.). The slave of slaves, the drudge of a
servant. *Servus servorum Dei* (the servant

of the servants of God) is one of the honorific
epithets of the POPE; it was first adopted by
GREGORY THE GREAT (540, 590–604).

Sesame (ses' à mi). **Open, Sesame!** The
password at which the door of the robbers'
cave flew open in the tale of *The Forty
Thieves* (ARABIAN NIGHTS); hence, a key to a
mystery, or anything that acts like magic in
obtaining favour, admission, recognition,
etc.

Sesame is an East Indian annual herb,
with an oily seed which is used as food, a
laxative, etc. In Egypt they eat sesame
cakes, and the Jews frequently add the seed
to their bread.

Sesquipedalian (ses kwi pĕ dā' li àn) is
sometimes applied in heavy irony to cumbersome and pedantic words. It comes from
HORACE's *sesquipedalia verba*, words a foot
and a half long.

Session, Court of. *See under* COURT.

Sestina (ses tē' nà). A set form of poem, usually rhymed, with six stanzas of six lines each
and a final triplet. The terminal words of
stanzas 2–6 are the same as those of stanza 1
but arranged differently. Sestinas were invented by the Provençal TROUBADOUR Ar-
naut Daniel (13th century); DANTE, Petrarch, and others employed them in Italy,
Cervantes and Camoëns in the Peninsula,
and an early use in English was by Drummond of Hawthornden. Swinburne's sestinas are probably the best in English.

Set, or Seth. The Egyptian original of the
Greek TYPHON. He was the jealous brother
of OSIRIS whom he murdered by tricking him
into a coffer, nailing the lid, and having it
sealed with molten lead. He was later castrated by HORUS and came to be regarded as
the incarnation of evil. He is represented as
having the body of a man with a thin curved
snout and square shaped ears, and sometimes with a tail and the body of an animal
which has not been identified with any certainty.

Set. All set. All ready to begin.

He'll never set the Thames on fire. *See
under* THAMES.

A set scene. In theatrical parlance, a scene
built up by the stage carpenters, or a furnished interior, as a drawing-room, as distinguished from an ordinary or shifting
scene. **To set the scene** is to indicate to an
audience where the action of the play is taking place, and what has prompted it.

A set to. A fight; a real tussle, literally or
verbally. In pugilism the combatants were
by their seconds "set to the scratch" or line
marked on the ground (*see* TO COME UP TO
(THE) SCRATCH *under* SCRATCH).

To set off to advantage. To display a thing in its best light.

To set on foot. *See under* FOOT.

To set one's face against something. *See under* FACE.

To set one's hand to. To sign; to begin a task.

To set one's heart upon. *See under* HEART.

Setting a hen. Giving her a certain number of eggs to hatch. The clutch of eggs is called a *sitting*.

Setting a saw. Bending the teeth alternately to the right and left in order to make it clear a path through the wood or metal to prevent jamming.

Setting her cap at him. *See under* CAP.

The setting of a jewel. The frame or mount of GOLD or SILVER surrounding a jewel in a ring, brooch, etc.

> This precious stone set in the silver sea.
> SHAKESPEARE: *Richard II*, II, i.

The setting of the sun, moon, or **stars.** Their sinking below the horizon.

The Empire on which the sun never sets. This, and similar phrases applied to the British Empire in the imperialist heyday, was not original. Thus in the *Pastor Fido* (1590) Guarini speaks of Philip II of Spain as "that proud monarch to whom when it grows dark [elsewhere], the sun never sets." Captain John Smith in his *Advertisements for the Unexperienced* notes that:

> the brave Spanish soldiers brag, The sunne never sets in the Spanish dominions, but ever shineth on one part or other we have conquered for our king:

and Thomas Gage in his Epistle Dedicatory to his *New Survey; of the West Indies* (1648) writes:

> It may be said of them [the Dutch], as of the Spaniards, that the Sun never sets upon their Dominions.

Setebos (set' e bos). A god or DEVIL worshipped by the Patagonians, and introduced by SHAKESPEARE into his *Tempest* as the god of Sycorax, CALIBAN's mother.

> His art is of such power,
> It would control my dam's god, Setebos,
> And make a vassal of him.
> *The Tempest*, I, ii.

The cult of Setebos was first known in Europe through MAGELLAN's voyage round the world, 1519–1521.

Settler. Settler's clock. The Laughing Jackass or Kookaburra, the Australian Great Kingfisher; so called because it tends to utter its cry more especially at sunrise and sunset than at other times.

Settler's matches. The long strips of stringy bark which hang from the eucalyptus are so called in Australia, since they make easily ignited kindling.

The remnant of an old Bush Ballad says:

> Stringy-bark will light your fire
> Green-hide will never fail yer,
> Stringy-bark and green-hide
> Are the mainstay of Australia.

Greenhide or untanned hide had a wide variety of uses among the early settlers.

Seven. A mystic or sacred number; it is composed of four and three, which among the Pythagoreans were, and from time immemorial have been, accounted lucky numbers. Among the Babylonians, Egyptians, and other ancient peoples there were seven sacred planets; and the Hebrew verb to swear means literally "to come under the influence of seven things"; thus seven ewe lambs figure in the oath between Abraham and Abimelech at Beersheba (*Gen*. xxi, 28), and Herodotus (III, viii) describes an Arabian oath in which seven stones are smeared with blood.

There are seven days in creation, seven days in the week, seven VIRTUES, seven divisions in the Lord's Prayer, seven sages in the life of man, CLIMATERIC years are seven and nine with their multiples by odd numbers, and the seventh son of a seventh son was always held notable.

Among the Hebrews every seventh year was SABBATICAL, and seven times seven years was the JUBILEE. The three great Jewish feasts lasted seven days, and between the first and second were seven weeks. Levitical purifications lasted seven days. The number is associated with a variety of occurrences in the OLD TESTAMENT.

In the *Apocalypse* we have SEVEN CHURCHES OF ASIA, seven candlesticks, seven stars, seven trumpets, seven spirits before the throne of God, seven horns, seven vials, seven plagues, a seven-headed monster, and the Lamb with seven eyes.

The old astrologers and alchemists recognized seven PLANETS, each having its own "heaven":

> The bodies seven, eek, lo hem heer anoon;
> Sol gold is, and Luna silver we threpe,
> Mars yren, Mercurie quyksilver we clepe;
> Saturnus leed, and Jubitur is tyn;
> And Venus coper, by my fader kyn.
> CHAUCER: *The Canon's Yeoman's Tale*, 472.

The Seven. Used of groups of seven people, especially (1) the "men of honest report" chosen by the APOSTLES to be the first Deacons (*Acts* vi, 5), *viz*. Stephen, Philip, Prochorus, Nicanor, Timon, Parmenas, and Nicholas; (2) the SEVEN BISHOPS (*see below*); or (3) the Seven Sages of Greece (*see* WISE MEN).

The original members of the European

free Trade Association (EFTA) formed in 1959, namely, Denmark, Norway, Sweden, Austria, Portugal, Switzerland, and the UNITED KINGDOM, were known as "The Seven" as distinct from THE SIX.

The Seven against Thebes. The seven Argive heroes (ADRASTUS, Polynices, Tydeus, Amphiaraus, Capaneus, Hippomedon and Parthenopæus), who, according to Greek legend, made war on Thebes with the object of restoring Polynices (son of ŒDIPUS), who had been expelled by his brother Eteocles. All perished except Adrastus, and the brothers slew each other in single combat. The legend is the subject of one of the tragedies of ÆSCHYLUS. *See* NEMEAN GAMES.

The Seven Bishops. Archbishop Sancroft of Canterbury, and Bishops Lloyd of St. Asaph, Turner of Ely, Ken of Bath and Wells, White of Peterborough, Lake of Chichester, and Trelawney of Bristol, who petitioned James II against the order to have his second Declaration of Indulgence read in every church on two successive Sundays (May 1688). James foolishly sent them to the TOWER and had them duly tried on a charge of seditious libel; they were acquitted amidst universal rejoicing. Cf. NONJURORS.

> And have they fix'd the where and when? and shall
>   Trelawny die?
> Here's twenty thousand Cornish men will know the
>   reason why.
> *Song of the Western Men.*

The Seven Champions. The mediæval designation of the national patron SAINTS of ENGLAND, SCOTLAND, WALES, IRELAND, France, Spain, and Italy. In 1596 Richard Johnson published a chap-book *The Famous History of the Seven Champions of Christendom*. In this he relates that St. GEORGE of England was seven years imprisoned by the Almidor, the black king of Morocco; St. DENYS of France lived seven years in the form of a hart; St. JAMES of Spain was seven years dumb out of love for a fair Jewess; St. Anthony of Italy, with the other champions, was enchanted into a deep sleep in the Black Castle, and was released by St. George's three sons, who quenched the seven lamps by water from the enchanted fountain; St. ANDREW of Scotland delivered six ladies who had lived seven years under the form of white swans; St. PATRICK of Ireland was immured in a cell where he scratched his grave with his own nails; and St. DAVID of Wales slept seven years in the enchanted garden of Ormandine, and was redeemed by St. George.

The Seven Churches of Asia. Those mentioned in *Rev.* i, 11, viz.:

(1) Ephesus, founded by St. PAUL, 57, in a ruinous state in the time of Justinian.

(2) Smyrna. Polycarp was its first bishop.

(3) Pergamos, renowned for its library.

(4) Thyatira, now called Ak-hissar (the White Castle).

(5) Sardis, now Sart, a small village.

(6) Philadelphia, now called Allah Shehr (City of God).

(7) Laodicea, now a deserted place called Eski-hissar (the Old Castle).

Seven cities warred for Homer being dead. *See* HOMER.

The Island of the Seven Cities. A land of Spanish fable, where seven BISHOPS, who quitted Spain during the dominion of the MOORS, founded seven cities. The legend says that many have visited the island, but no one has ever quitted it.

The Seven Deacons. In *Acts* vi, 1–6, the "seven men of honest report, full of the Holy Ghost and wisdom" (*see* THE SEVEN). These are held to be the first deacons of the Church.

The Seven Deadly, or **Capital Sins.** Pride, Wrath, Envy, Lust, Gluttony, Avarice, Sloth.

Seven Dials, St. Giles in the Fields, HOLBORN. When first developed in the reign of Charles II a DORIC pillar with (actually) six sun-dials stood facing the seven streets radiating therefrom, two of the streets opening on one face of the dialstone. The column and dials were removed in 1773 and later set up on Weybridge Green.

The district came to be notorious for squalor, vice, crime, and degradation generally and was long the headquarters of the ballad printers and balladmongers.

> Where famed St. Giles's ancient limits spread,
> An in-rail'd column rears its lofty head;
> Here to seven streets seven dials count their day,
> And from each other catch the circling ray.
> GAY: *Trivia*, ii.

The Seven Gifts of the Spirit, or **Holy Ghost.** Wisdom, Understanding, Counsel, Fortitude, Knowledge, Righteousness, Fear of the Lord.

The Seven Gods of Luck. In Japanese folklore, Benten, goddess of love; Bishamon, god of war; Daikoku, of wealth; Ebisu, of self-effacement; Fukurokuji and Jojorin, gods of longevity; and Hotei, of joviality.

The Seven Heavens. *See under* HEAVEN.

To be in the Seventh Heaven. *See under* HEAVEN.

The Seven Hills of Rome. The Palatine, Capitoline, Aventine, Cælian, Esquiline, Viminal, and QUIRINAL or Colline. The walls of ancient ROME were built about them.

The Seven Joys of Mary, or the Virgin. *See* MARY.

The Seven Liberal Arts. *See* QUADRIVIUM.

The Seven Planets. *See* PLANETS.

The Seven Sacraments. *See under* SACRAMENT.

The Seven Sages of Greece. *See* WISE MEN OF GREECE.

The Seven Sciences. The same as the *Seven Liberal Arts*. *See* QUADRIVIUM.

The Seven Seas. The Arctic and Antarctic, North and South PACIFIC, North and South ATLANTIC, and the Indian Oceans.

The Seven Senses. According to ancient teaching the SOUL of man, or his "inward holy body" is compounded of seven properties which are under the influence of the seven PLANETS. Fire animates, earth gives the sense of feeling, water gives speech, air gives taste, mist gives sight, flowers give hearing, the south wind gives smelling. Hence the seven senses are animation, feeling, speech, taste, sight, hearing, and smelling (*see Ecclus*. xvii, 5).

The Seven Sisters. An old name of the PLEIADES; also given to a set of seven cannon, cast by one Robert Borthwick and used at Flodden (1513); and to the chalk cliffs between Cuckmere Haven and Beachy Head on the Sussex coast.

The Seven Sleepers. Seven Christian youths of Ephesus, according to the legend, who fled during the Diocletian persecution (250) to a cave in Mt. Celion. The cave was walled up by their pursuers and they fell asleep. In the reign of Theodosius II, some 200 years later, they awoke and one of them went into the city for provisions. They fell to sleep again, this time until the resurrection. Their names are given as Constantius, Dionysius, Joannes, Maximianus, Malchus, Martinianus, and Serapion. The legend was current in the 6th century and is referred to by Gregory of Tours.

The Seven Sorrows. *See* MARY.

The Seven Stars. Used formerly of the PLANETS; also of the PLEIADES and the GREAT BEAR (*see under* BEAR).

> *Fool:* The reason why the seven stars are no more than seven is a pretty reason.
> *Lear:* Because they are not eight?
> *Fool:* Yes, indeed; thou wouldst make a good fool
> SHAKESPEARE: *King Lear*, I, v.

The Seven Virtues. *See under* VIRTUE.

The Seven Weeks' War. The war between Austria and Prussia, 14 June–26 July 1866. Austria and her allies were decisively defeated at Sadowa or Königgrätz (3 July) and the war ended with the Treaty of Prague (23 August). Austria withdrew from the German Confederation and Prussia was left to assume the leadership of Germany.

The Seven Wise Masters. A collection of oriental tales (*see* SANDABAR) supposed to be told to the king by his advisers. The king's son returned to court after being educated in the SEVEN LIBERAL ARTS by the Seven Wise Masters. By consulting the STARS, he learned that his life was in danger if he spoke before the elapse of seven days. One of the royal consorts then endeavoured to seduce him without success, whereupon she denounced him to the sovereign and the prince was condemned to death. The Wise Masters, by their tales against women, secured a suspension of the sentence for one day. The woman then told a contrary tale to secure the confirmation of Prince Lucien's punishment. The Wise Masters counteracted this with further tales and so on, until the seventh day, when the prince revealed the truth and his accuser was sentenced to death instead. There are numerous variant versions of these stories, which date from 10th century. *Cp.* SCHEHERAZADE.

The Seven Wonders of the World. *See under* WONDER.

The Seven Works of Mercy. *See* MERCY.

The Seven Years War (1756–1763). A war fought over European and colonial and commercial rivalries by France, Austria, the Empire, Russia, Poland and Sweden against Prussia, Great Britain, and Hanover. Spain joined in 1761 and attacked Portugal. It began with Frederick the Great's invasion of Saxony and was ended by the Treaty of Paris between Great Britain, France, Portugal, and Spain, which gave Canada and other colonial territories to Great Britain, New Orleans to Spain, etc. By the Peace of Hubertusburg between Austria and Prussia, the latter retained Silesia.

Seveners. The Isma'ilis, a SHI'ITE following of Isma'il, whom they hold to be the seventh IMAM; they include the ASSASSINS, Carmathians, DRUSES, and FATIMITES. *Cp.* TWELVERS.

Seventh-day Adventists. A sect of Adventists which grew out of a movement begun by William Miller in the United States in 1831. He preached that the present world would end about 1843. The Seventh-day Adventists adopted their name in 1860, and were formally organized from 1863. They observe Saturday as their SABBATH and insist on temperance and abstinence from alcohol, tobacco, etc., and a strict adherence to the SCRIPTURES.

Seventh-day Baptists. In the U.S.A., a group of German Baptist brethren who keep

Saturday, the seventh day of the week, as their SABBATH.

Severn. *See* SABRINA.

Severus. The Wall of Severus. The Emperor Severus (146–211), who spent the last three years of his life in Britain, thoroughly strengthened the fortified line between the Tyne and Solway originally constructed by Hadrian. His work was so extensive that some ancient authorities speak of him as its original builder. *See* HADRIAN'S WALL.

Sèvres Ware (sevr). Fine-quality porcelain made at the French state factory at Sèvres near Paris. It was first opened at Vincennes in 1745, and moved to Sèvres in 1756, and the King (Louis XV) became the proprietor in 1760. The king took a personal interest in the manufactory, and expositions were held at VERSAILLES for the sale of the products to the nobility at court. There is a story that Louis XV one day noticed a nobleman quietly pocket a pretty cup; the next day a servant attended upon him and presented him with a saucer together with an invoice.

Sexagesima Sunday (seks à jes' i mà). The second Sunday before LENT so called because in round numbers it is 60 days (Lat. *sexagesima dies*) before EASTER.

Sextile (seks' tīl). The aspect of two PLANETS when distant from each other 60 degrees or two signs. This position is marked by astrologers thus ★.

> In sextile, square, and trine, and opposite
> Of noxious efficacy.
> MILTON: *Paradise Lost*, X, 659.

Sez (says) you. A contemptuous exclamation expressing disbelief in what someone has said, holding it up to ridicule. An expression of American origin popular in England in the 1930s.

Shades. The abode of the departed or HADES; also the spirits or ghosts of the departed.

> Peter Bell excited his spleen to such a degree that he evoked the shades of Pope and Dryden.
> MACAULAY: *Moore's Life of Lord Byron*.

Wine vaults with a bar attached are often known as *shades*. The term originated at Brighton, when the Old Bank in 1819 was turned into a smoking room and bar. There was an entrance by the Pavilion Shades, or Arcade, and the name was soon transferred to the bar.

To put someone in the shade. To outdo him; eclipse him; to attract to yourself all the applause and encomiums he had been enjoying.

Shadow. A word with numerous figurative and applied meanings, such as, a ghost; Macbeth says to the ghost of Banquo:

> Hence, horrible shadow! unreal mockery, hence!
> SHAKESPEARE: *Macbeth*, III, iv.

An imperfect or faint representation, as, "I haven't the shadow of a doubt"; a constant attendant, as in Milton's "Sin and her shadow Death" (*Paradise Lost*, IX, 12); moral darkness or gloom, as, "He has outsoar'd the shadow of our night" (Shelley: *Adonais*, xl, 1); protecting influence:

> Hither, like yon ancient Tower,
> Watching o'er the River's bed,
> Fling the shadow of thy power,
> Else we sleep among the dead.
> WORDSWORTH: *Hymn (Jesu! bless)*.

Gone to the bad for the shadow of an ass. "If you must quarrel let it be for something better than the shadow of an ass." *See* WRANGLE FOR AN ASS'S SHADOW *under* ASS.

May your shadow never grow less! May your prosperity always continue and increase. A phrase of Eastern origin. Fable has it that when those studying the black arts had made certain progress, they were chased through a subterranean hall by the DEVIL. If he caught only their shadow, or part of it, they lost all or part of it, but became first-rate magicians. This would make the expression mean, "May you escape wholly and entirely from the clutches of the devil", but a more simple explanation is, "May you never waste away, but always remain healthy and robust." *See* SCHLEMIHL.

To be reduced to a shadow. Of people, to become thoroughly emaciated; of things, to become an empty form from which the substance has departed.

To shadow. To follow about like a shadow, especially as a detective, with the object of spying out all one's doings.

Shady. A shady character. A person of very doubtful reputation; one whose character would scarcely bear investigation in the light of day.

On the shady side of forty. The wrong side, meaning more than forty.

Shaggy. A shaggy dog story. A would-be funny story told laboriously at great length with an unexpected twist at the end. So called from the shaggy dog featured in many stories of this genre popular in the 1940s.

Shagroon. In New Zealand, an original settler, other than those from England, who were called *Pilgrims*. The word is probably from the Irish *seachran*, wandering.

Shah. *See* RULERS, TITLES OF.

Shake (O.E. *scacan*). To agitate, move violently or quickly.

Give me a shake. Wake me up (at the requested time).

A good shake up. Something sudden that startles one out of one's lethargy and rouses one to action.

I'll do it in a brace of shakes. Instantly, as soon as you can shake the dice-box twice.

In two shakes of a lamb's tail. Instantly. An expression originating in the U.S.A. in the early 19th century.

No great shakes. Nothing extraordinary or particularly clever; not very good. Commonly said to derive from gambling with dice; but Admiral Smyth's *Sailor's Word-Book* (1867) says it comes from "shaking a cask", which is to dismantle it and pick up the staves or shakes, a condition in which it has little value.

A shake of the head. An indication of refusal, disapproval, annoyance, etc.

To shake hands. A very old method of SAL-UTATION and farewell; when one was shaking hands one could not get at one's sword to strike a treacherous blow. When Jehu asked Jehonadab if his "heart was right" with him, he said, "If it be, give me thine hand", and Jehonadab gave him his hand (II *Kings* x, 15). NESTOR shook hands with ULYSSES on his return to the Grecian camp with the stolen horses of Rhesus; ÆNEAS, in the temple of DIDO, sees his lost companions enter, who *avidi conjugere dextras ardebant* (*Æneid*, I, 514); and HORACE, strolling along the VIA SA-CRA, shook hands with an acquaintance: *Arreptaque manu*, "*Quid agis dulcissime rerum?*"

To shake in one's shoes. *See under* SHOE.

To shake one's sides. To be convulsed with laughter; *cp.* Milton's "Laughter holding both his sides" (*L'Allegro*).

To shake the dust from one's feet. *See under* DUST.

Come and have a shakedown at my place. A bed for the night, especially a makeshift one on the floor, sofa, etc. The allusion is to the time when men slept upon litter or clean straw.

Shake-out. On the Stock Exchange, a crisis which drives the weaker speculators out of the market; also currently applied to the reduction of the labour force in an industry, trade, etc.

Shakers. A sect of Adventists started by James and Jane Wardley at Manchester in 1747 who seceded from the QUAKERS, and from their excited behaviour were derisively dubbed "Shakers". Ann Lee, known as Mother Ann, the "bride of the Lamb" and the "Female Christ", soon became their acknowledged leader and the sect left for America in 1774. They practised celibacy, temperance, communal living, etc., and a few small communities still survive.

Another sect of English Shakers was founded at Battersea by Mary Anne Girling (1827–1886), a farmer's daughter. The "Children of God" settled in the New Forest but the sect petered out after Mrs. Girling's death.

Shakespeare, William (1564–1616). The greatest poetic dramatist. The Shakespearian canon comprises the 36 plays of the First Folio (1623), which include collaborative contributions that cannot be determined with certainty; the *Sonnets*, *The Rape of Lucrece*, *Venus and Adonis*, a few lyrics and the 16 lines contributed to the play of *Sir Thomas More*.

The theory that Shakespeare was not the writer of the works attributed to him, based on the assumption that he did not possess the knowledge and culture revealed in those works, was first put forward by Herbert Lawrence in 1769. In 1857 Willian Henry Smith suggested that the only writer of that age competent to produce such writings was Francis Bacon, thus the **Baconian theory** began its lengthy career. In 1887 Ignatius Donnelly published *The Great Cryptogram* which professed to show that cryptograms in the plays revealed Bacon as the undoubted author, and the cryptographic method was further advanced by Sir Edwin Durning-Lawrence and others. The Baconians still persist and others have put forward many additional candidates, including a distributist school of thought which assigns Shakespear's work to a group of seven writers. *See also* DARK LADY OF THE SONNETS *under* LADY.

The German Shakespeare. Kotzebue (1761–1819) has been so styled.

The Spanish Shakespeare. Calderón (1600–1681).

The Shakespeare of Divines. Jeremy Taylor (1613–1667).

The Shakespeare of Eloquence. So Barnave happily characterized the Comte de Mirabeau (1749–1791).

Shakuntala. *See* SAKUNTALA.

Shallal. In former days in Cornwall, a band of ROUGH MUSIC which visited newly-married couples and those suspected of immorality. *Cp.* RIDING; SKIMMINGTON; STANG.

Shalott, The Lady of (shà lot'). A maiden in the ARTHURIAN ROMANCES (*see under* ARTHUR), who fell in love with Sir LANCELOT OF THE LAKE, and died because her love was not returned. Tennyson has a poem on the subject; and the story of ELAINE is substantially the same.

Shamanism (sha' mà nizm). A primitiv form of religion, in which is is believed tha the world is governed by good and EVIL spir its who can be propitiated through the intervention of a *Shaman*, a priest or sorcerer. The word is Slavonic, the cult being practised by the Samoyeds and other Siberian peoples.

Shamrock. The symbol of IRELAND, because it was selected by St. PATRICK to illustrate to the Irish the doctrine of the TRINITY. According to the elder Pliny no serpent will touch this plant.

Shamus. U.S. slang for a policeman or private detective. It may derive from *Shammash*, the sexton of a SYNAGOGUE, or be an anglicization of the Iris *Séamus* (James), or a mixture of both.

Shan Van Voght. This excellent song (composed in 1798) has been called the Irish MARSEILLAISE. The title is a corruption of *An tsean bhean bhoct* (the poor old woman—*i.e.* IRELAND). The last verse is:

> Will Ireland then be free?
> Said the San Van Voght. [repeat]
> Yes, Ireland shall be free
> From the centre to the sea,
> Hurrah for liberty!
> Said the Shan Van Voght.

Shandean (shăn′ dē ăn). Characteristic of Tristram Shandy or the Shandy family in Sterne's novel, *Tristram Shandy* (9 vols., 1759–1767). Tristram's father, Walter Shandy, is a metaphysical Don QUIXOTE in his way, full of superstitious and idle conceits. He believes in long noses and propitious names, but his son's nose is crushed, and his name becomes Tristram instead of Trismegistus. Tristram's Uncle Toby was wounded at the siege of Namur, and is benevolent and generous, simple as a child, brave as a lion, and gallant as a courtier. His modesty with Widow Wadman and his military tastes are admirable. He is said to be drawn from Sterne's father. The mother was the *beau idéal* of nonentity; and of Tristram himself we hear almost more before he was born than after he had burst upon an astonished world.

Shandon, The Bells of. Those of St. Anne's Church, Shandon, Cork, made famous in the lines of "Father Prout" (1804–1866).

> ...the bells of Shandon
> That sound so grand
> On the quiet waters
> Of the river Lee.

The old church was destroyed in the siege of 1690 and rebuilt (1722–1726).

There is an old saying in *Lean's Collectanea*:

> Party-coloured like the people,
> Red and white stands Shandon's steeple.

Shanghai, To (shang hī′). An old nautical phrase, meaning to make a man drunk or to drug him insensible and to get him on board an outward-bound vessel in need of crew. It originated on the west coast of the U.S.A. where Shanghai was a likely destination for a crimped sailor.

Shangri La (shăng gri la′). The hidden Buddhist lama PARADISE described in James Hilton's *Lost Horizon* (1933). The name was applied to F. D. Roosevelt's mountain refuge in Maryland, and to the secret "base" used for the great American air raid on Tokyo in 1942.

Shank's Mare. To ride Shank's mare or **pony** is to walk or go on foot, the shanks being the legs; the same as "Going by the MARROW-BONE STAGE" or by "Walker's bus".

Shannon. Dipped in the Shannon. One who has been dipped in the Shannon is said to lose all bashfulness. *Cp.* TO KISS THE BLARNEY STONE *under* BLARNEY.

Shanties, Chanties. Songs of the days of sail sung by a "shanty man" to help rhythmical action among sailors hauling on ropes, working the capstan, etc. The workers joined in the choruses. The word is probably from Fr. *chanter*, to sing. The chorus of one of the most popular runs thus:

> Then away, love, away,
> Away down Rio.
> O fare ye well my pretty young gel,
> For we're bound for the Rio Grande.

A *shanty* is also a small wooden house or hut, from Canadian-French *chantier*, loghut, workshop (Fr., timber-yard).

Sharecropper (U.S.A.). After the CIVIL WAR, Southern plantations were divided into one-man holdings worked by a freedman and his family, or by a white, usually planting cotton or tobacco. They were called *sharecroppers* because the planter or storekeeper, from whom they obtained their supplies, usually took from one-quarter to one-half of the crop, according to the service rendered. From the 1940s, with the growth of mechanization in agriculture and the spread of industry in the South, many Negroes moved to the cities of the North. Sharecropping, however, is still a common form of rent payment in many parts of the U.S.A.

Shark. A swindler, a pilferer, an extortionate dealer, landlord, etc.; one who snaps up things like a shark, which swallows its food alive or dead, regardlessly.

To shark up. To get a number of people, etc., together promiscuously, without consideration of their fitness.

> Now sir, young Fortinbras...
> Hath in the skirts of Norway here and there
> Shark'd up a list of lawless resolutes,
> For food and diet, to some enterprise

That hath a stomach in't.
SHAKESPEARE: *Hamlet*, I. i.

Sharp. A regular Becky Sharp. An unprincipled, scheming young woman, who by cunning, hypocrisy, and low smartness raises herself from obscurity and poverty to some position in SOCIETY, and falls therefrom in due course after having maintained a more or less precarious foothold. Of course she is good-looking, and superficial amiability is a SINE QUA NON. Becky Sharp, the original of this, is the principal character in Thackeray's *Vanity Fair* (1848).

Sharp practice. Over-smart, underhand or dishonourable dealing; low-down trickery intended to advantage oneself.

Sharp's the word! Look alive, there! No hanging about.

Sharp-set. Hungry; formerly used of HAWKS when hungry for their food.

Shave. Just a grazing touch; *a near* or *close shave*, a narrow escape; *to shave through an examination*, only just to get through, narrowly to escape being *plucked* (*see* PLUCK). At Oxford a pass degree was sometimes called *a shave*.

A good lather is half the shave. Your work is half done if you've laid your plans and made your preparations properly.

To shave a customer. It was once a draper's expression for overcharging; it is said that when the manager saw a chance of doing this he stroked his chin as the sign to the assistant that he might fleece the customer.

To shave an egg. To attempt to extort the uttermost FARTHING; to "SKIN a flint".

Shaveling. Used in contempt of a young man and—especially after the REFORMATION—of a priest. At a time when the laity wore beards and moustaches the clergy were not only usually clean shaven but they also wore large shaven TONSURES.

It maketh no matter how thou live here, so thou have the favour of the pope and his shavelings.
JOHN BRADFORD (1510–1555):
Works, II (*Parker Soc.*, 1853).

Shavian (shā'vi ản). After the manner of George Bernard Shaw (1856–1950), or descriptive of his philosophy and style of humour.

She. The She Bible. *See* BIBLE, SOME SPECIALLY NAMED EDITIONS.

The She-Wolf of France. *See under* WOLF.

Shear. God tempers the wind to the shorn lamb. *See under* GOD.

Ordeal by sieve and shears. *See* SIEVE.

Sheathe. To sheathe the sword. To cease hostilities, make peace.

Sheba, The Queen of (shē' bả). The queen who visited SOLOMON (I *Kings* x) is known to the Arabs as BALKIS, Queen of Sheba (KORAN, ch. xxvii). Sheba was thought by the Romans to have been the capital of what is now YEMEN; and the people over whom the queen reigned were the SABÆANS.

She thinks she's the Queen of Sheba. She thinks she is somebody; she gives herself airs. We are told (I *Kings* x, 2): "she came to Jerusalem with a very great train".

Shebang (she băng'). **Fed up with the whole shebang.** Tired of the whole concern and everything connected with it. *Shebang* is American slang for a hut or one's quarters; also for a cart; and in a humorous depreciatory way, for almost anything.

Shebeen (she bēn'). A place (originally only in IRELAND) where liquor is sold without a licence; hence applied to any low-class public house. Possibly from Irish *sibin*, a little drinking mug.

You've been takin' a dhrop of the crathur' an' Danny says "Troth, an' I been
Dhrinking yer health wid Shamus O'Shea at Katty's shebeen."
TENNYSON: *To-morrow*, ii.

Shedeem. *See* MAZIKEEN.

Sheep. *Ram* or *tup*, the sire; *ewe*, the dam; *lamb*, the young till weaned, when it is called a *tup-hogget* or *ewe-hogget*, as the case may be, or, if the tup is castrated, a *wether-hogget*.

After the removal of the *first* fleece, the tup-hogget becomes a *shearling*, the ewe-hogget a *gimmer*, and the wether-hogget a *dinmont*.

After the removal of the *second* fleece, the shearling becomes a *two-shear tup*, the gimmer a *ewe*, and the dinmont a *wether*.

After the removal of the *third* fleece, the ewe is called a *twinter-ewe*; and when it ceases to breed, a *draft-ewe*.

The Black Sheep (*Kara-Koyunlu*) and the **White Sheep** (*Ak-Koyunlu*). Two rival confederacies among the Turkomans of Azerbaijan and Armenia in the late 14th and the 15th centuries. They were so called from the devices on their standards.

The black sheep of the family. The ne'er-do-well; the one who brings disgrace on the family.

There's a black sheep in every flock. In every group or community of people there is sure to be at least one shady character.

Vegetable sheep. *See* THE VEGETABLE LAMB *under* LAMB.

As well be hanged for a sheep as a lamb. Don't stop at half measures; in for a PENNY in for a POUND; if we are destined for trouble let's have our fling first.

Like a sheep's head, all jaw. Said of a

tediously garrulous person.

Sheep dressed up as lamb. Said of a woman of some maturity who "dolls herself up" to give the appearance of being much younger.

To cast, or **make sheep's eyes.** To look askance, in a SHEEPISH way, at a person to whom you feel lovingly inclined.

> A fig for their nonsense and chatter!—suffice it, her
> Charms will excuse one for casting sheep's eyes at
> her!
> BARHAM: *Ingoldsby Legends*, II (*The Knight and the Lady*).

Sheepish. Awkward and shy; bashful through not knowing how to deport oneself in the circumstances.

Sheep's head. A fool, a simpleton.

> What, no more compliment? Kiss her, you sheep's
> head!
> CHAPMAN: *All Fools*, II, i.

Sheepskin (U.S.A.). A college diploma.

Sheer, or **Shere Thursday.** MAUNDY THURSDAY. It is generally supposed to be from M.E. *schere*, clean, *i.e.* free from guilt, from the custom of receiving absolution, or of cleansing the altars on this day. The *Liber Festivalis*, however, says:

> Hit is also in English tong "Schere Thursday", for
> in owr elde fadur days men wold on yᵗ day makon
> scheron hem honest, and dode here hedes ond cly-
> pon here berdes and poll here hedes, ond so makon
> hem honest agen Estur day.

Sheet. Three sheets in the wind. Very drunk. The *sheet* is the rope attached to the clew of a sail used for trimming sail. If the sheet is quite free, leaving the sail free to flap without restraint, the sheet is said to be "in the wind", and "a sheet in the wind" is a colloquial nautical expression for being tipsy; thus to have "three sheets in the wind" is to be very drunk.

> Captain Cuttle looking, candle in hand, at Bunsby
> more attentively, perceived that he was three sheets
> in the wind, or, in plain words, drunk.
> DICKENS: *Dombey and Son*, ch. xxxix.

That was my sheet anchor. My best hope, chief stay, last refuge. The *sheet anchor*, once the heaviest anchor carried, but long since the same weight as the bower anchors, is a spare bower anchor available for use in emergency when the ship is moored. It is carried abaft the starboard bower anchor and in the days of sail abaft the fore rigging. Sheet is probably a corruption of *shoot* or *shot*, from the fact that it was shot, or let go, from the ship when needed.

Sheffield. Sheffield Plate. A process of fusing silver on copper discovered by Thomas Boulsover, a Sheffield cutler, about 1742. Domestic articles such as candlesticks, coffee-pots, trays and dishes of quality were produced by Sheffield craftsmen until the industry gave way to electro-plated products and came to an end about 1865.

A Sheffield whittle. So the general-purpose knife was often called in Chaucer's day.

Sheikh (shāk). A title of respect among the Arabs (Like the Ital. *signore*, Fr. *sieur*, Span. *señor*, etc.), but properly the head of a BEDOUIN clan, family, or tribe, or the headman of an Arab village.

Sheikh-ul-Islam. The Grand MUFTI, or supreme head of the Mohammedan hierarchy in Turkey.

Shekels (shek' ĕlz). Colloquial for money. It was anciently part of the Babylonian weight and monetary systems, and in general use among the peoples of Mesopotamia and Syria. The Hebrew heavy gold shekel weighed *c*. 252 grains TROY and the light gold shekel *c*. 126 grains; the heavy silver shekel weighed *c*. 224 grains troy and the light silver shekel *c*. 112 grains. The standard English gold SOVEREIGN was *c*. 123 grains troy. Phœnician shekels of *c*. 224 and *c*. 112 grains were also commonly found throughout the Near East.

Shekinah (she kī' nȧ) (Heb., that which dwells or resides). A word used frequently in the TARGUMS as an equivalent for the Divine Being or God. It does not occur in the BIBLE. The Shekinah is God's omnipresence and is everywhere. God is not identical with the world, He is of the world and yet afar off. Thus when Jacob says (*Gen*. xxviii, 16), "The Lord is in this place", the Targum says, "The glory of the Shekinah of J is in this place."

Sheldonian Theatre. The Senate House of Oxford University; so called from Gilbert Sheldon (1598–1677), Archbishop of Canterbury, who provided the money for the building designed by Sir Christopher Wren and opened in 1699. Formerly their meetings were held in St. Mary's Church. *See* ENCÆNIA.

Shelf. Laid, or **put on the shelf.** Put aside as of no further use; superannuated. Said of officials and others no longer actively employed; a project, etc., begun and set aside; also, a pawn at the brokers. A SPINSTER beyond the average age of marriage is said to be *on the shelf*.

Shell (O.E. *scell*). The hard outside covering of nuts, eggs, molluscs, etc.; hence applied to other hollow coverings, as the hollow projectile filled with explosives. It is also applied to a form or class in some public and endowed schools, usually an intermediate form of some kind between those distinguished by numbers. This latter usage derives from Westminster School, where the intermediate form between the V and VI occupied a schoolroom, one end of which was shell-shaped or apsidal.

Cockle shell. See under COCKLE.

Eggshells. Many persons, after eating a boiled egg, break or crush the shell. This, according to Sir Thomas Browne:

> is but a superstitious relict...and the intent thereof was to prevent witchcraft; for lest witches should draw or prick their names therein, and veneficiously mischief their persons, they broke the shell.
>
> *Pseudodoxia Epidemica*, V, xxiii.

Scallop shells. See SCALLOP.

Shellback. Nautical slang for a hardened and seasoned sailor, an "old salt". In the U.S. Navy the term is reserved for one who has crossed the line and been duly initiated. See TO CROSS THE LINE under CROSS.

Shell jacket. A short tight-fitting undress military jacket reaching only to the waist at the back; also an officer's mess jacket.

Shell shock. An acute neurasthenic condition due to the explosion of a shell or bomb at close quarters. A term originating in World War I.

To lie in a nutshell. See under NUT.

To retire into one's shell. To become reticent and uncommunicative, to withdraw from the society of one's fellows. The allusion is to the tortoise, which, once it has "got into its shell", is quite unget-at-able. **To come out of one's shell** is the reverse process, *i.e.* to become friendly and communicative.

To shell out. To pay or "stump up", to "fork out"; as peas are shelled out of a pod.

Shem. The traditional ancestor of the Hebrews and other kindred peoples. *Semite* and SEMITIC derive from Shem, the eldest of the three sons of Noah (*Gen.* ix, 18).

Shemozzle (shi moz'l). **There was a bit of a shemozzle.** There was something of a fuss, a bit of a rumpus or a rough and tumble. *Shemozzle* (bad luck) is a YIDDISH term.

Sheol. See HADES.

Shepherd. The Good shepherd. Jesus Christ.

> I am the good shepherd: the good shepherd giveth his life for the sheep.
>
> *John* x, 11.

The Ettrick Shepherd. See ETTRICK.

The Shepherd Lord. Henry, fourteenth Baron Clifford (*c.* 1455–1523), sent by his mother to be brought up as a shepherd, in order to save him from the fury of the YORKISTS. At the accession of Henry VII he was restored to all his rights and seigniories. He is celebrated in Wordsworth's *The Song for the Feast of Brougham Castle*, and *The White Doe of Rylstone*.

The Shepherd of Banbury. The ostensible author of a Weather Guide (published 1744), written by John Claridge, which attained considerable popularity at the time.

The Shepherd of Hermas. An allegorical work of the mid-2nd century, essentially a collection of instructions and revelations from an angelic guide for the benefit of good Christians. It has been called "the Pilgrim's Progress of the Early Church". The identity of Hermas is largely a matter of conjecture.

The Shepherd of the Ocean. So Sir Walter Ralegh was called by Spencer.

> Whom when I asked from what place he came,
> And how he hight, himselfe he did ycleepe
> The shepheard of the Ocean by name,
> And said he came far from the main-sea deepe.
>
> *Colin Clout's Come Home Againe*, 64.

The Shepherd of Salisbury Plain. A famous religious tract by Mrs. Hannah More, first published in *The Cheap Repository* (1795), a series of moral "tales for the people". It had enormous popularity; the story is said to be founded on the life of one David Saunders, who was noted for his homely wisdom and practical piety, whom she turns into a sort of Christian ARCADIAN.

The Shepherd's Sundial. The SCARLET PIMPERNEL, which opens at a little past seven in the morning and closes at a little past two. When rain is at hand, or the weather is unfavourable, it does not open at all. It is also called the Shepherd's Calendar, Clock, and Watch, and the Shepherd's Weatherglass.

The Shepherd's Warning.

> Red sky at night is the shepherd's delight,
> Red sky in the morning is the shepherd's warning.

The Italian saying is *Sera rossa e bianco mattino, allegro il pellegrino* (a red evening and a white morning rejoice the pilgrim).

Sheppard, Jack (1702–1724). A notorious thief, son of a carpenter in SMITHFIELD and brought up in Bishopsgate workhouse. He was famous for his prison escapes, especially when he broke out of "the Castle" of NEWGATE via the chimney. He was soon afterwards taken and hanged at TYBURN.

> "I say, master, did you ever hear tell of Mr Wood's famous 'prentice?"
> "What apprentice?" asked the stranger, in surprise
> "Why, Jack Sheppard, the notorious housebreaker–him as has robbed half Lunnon to be sure.
>
> W.H. AINSWORTH: *Jack Sheppard*, III, i.

Shere Thursday. See SHEER.

Sherif (she rēf'). A descendant of the Prophet MOHAMMED through his daughter FATIMA. also formerly applied to the chief magistrate of MECCA. The title was also adopted by the rulers of Morocco, who claimed descent from the Prophet through his grandson Hasan.

Sheriff (sher' if) (O.E. *scirgerefa*). In mediæval and later times the sheriff (shire REEVE) was an official who looked after the royal demesne in the SHIRE and, by the 11th century, the chief official for local adminstration. After the 13th century, the sheriffs declined in importance with the rise of new courts and officials, and today they are largely of ceremonial and minor judicial importance. The sheriff is still the chief officer of the Crown in the County. The City of London has two sheriffs and certain ancient cities (Norwich, Bristol, York, Oxford, etc.) still have one. In the U.S.A. the sheriff, usually elected, has administrative and limited judicial functions. *See* PRICKING FOR SHERIFFS *under* PRICK.

Sheriffmuir. There was mair lost at the Shirramuir. Don't grieve for your losses, for worse have befallen others before now. The battle of Sheriffmuir, in 1715, between the JACOBITES and Hanoverians was very bloody; both sides sustained heavy losses, and both sides claimed the victory.

Sherlock Holmes. The most famous figure in detective fiction, the creation of Arthur Conan Doyle (1859–1930). His solutions of crime and mysteries were related in a series of 60 stories that appeared in the *Strand Magazine* between 1891 and 1927. The character was based on Dr. Joseph Bell of the Edinburgh Infirmary, whose methods of deduction suggested a system that Holmes developed into a science—the observation of the minutest details and apparently insignificant circumstances scientifically interpreted. Dr. Watson, Holmes's friend and assistant, was a skit on Doyle himself and Baker Street acquired lasting fame through his writings.

> Let me have a report by wire at Baker Street before evening.
> And now, Watson, it only remains for us to find out by wire the identity of the cabman.
> SIR A. CONAN DOYLE: *The Hound of the Baskervilles*, ch. iv.

A Sherlock or **a regular Sherlock.** One who shows an unusual ability in observation and deduction and in solving apparent mysteries; sometimes used derisively. *Sherlock* is also used of a private detective.

Sherrick. Yorkshire for something very small. Used in Australia for a small amount of anything, particularly money.

Sherry. *See* JEREZ; SACK.

Shewbread. The name adopted by Tyndale, modelled on Luther's *Schaubrot*; more correctly *presence-bread*. Tyndale explains it as "alway in the presence and sight of the Lorde". Shrewbread denotes the 12 loaves for the 12 tribes, arranged in two piles on the table of shittim wood set beside the altar each week and when they were removed only the priest was allowed to partake of them. This ancient oblation is referred to in *Exod.* xxv, 30; *Lev.* xxiv, 5–9, etc.

Shibboleth (shib' o leth). A test word; a catchword or principle to which members of a group adhere long after its original significance has ceased; hence a worn-out or discredited doctrine. *Shibboleth* (meaning "ear of wheat", "stream", or "flood") was the word the Ephraimites could not pronounce when they were challenged at the ford on the Jordan by their pursuers, Jephthah and the Gileadites. The Ephraimites could only say *Sibboleth*, thus revealing themselves to the enemy (*see Judges* xii, 1–6).

Shick-shack Day. Royal Oak Day, 29 May, also called *shig-shag*. The origin of the name is obscure. *See* OAK-APPLE DAY.

Shield. The most famous shields in story are the Shield of ACHILLES described by HOMER, of HERCULES described by Hesiod, of ÆNEAS described by Virgil, and the ÆGIS.

Others are that of:

> AGAMEMNON, a GORGON.
> Amycos (son of POSEIDON), a crayfish, symbol of prudence.
> CADMUS and his descendants, a DRAGON, to indicate their descent from the dragon's teeth.
> *Eteocles*, a man scaling a wall.
> HECTOR, a LION.
> IDOMENEUS, a COCK.
> *Menelaus*, a SERPENT at his heart; alluding to the elopement of his wife with PARIS.
> *Parthenopœus*, one of the SEVEN AGAINST THEBES, a SPHINX holding a man in its claws.
> ULYSSES, a DOLPHIN. Whence he is sometimes called Delphinosemos.

Servius says that in the siege of TROY the Greeks had, as a rule, NEPTUNE on their bucklers, and the Trojans MINERVA.

It was a common custom, after a great victory, for the victorious general to hang his shield on the wall of some temple.

The clang of shields. When a CELTIC chief doomed a man to death, he struck his shield with the blunt end of his spear by way of notice to the royal BARD to begin his death-song.

> Cairbar rises in his arms,
> The clang of shields is heard.
> OSSIAN: *Temora*, I.

The Gold and Silver Shield. A mediæval allegory tells how two knights coming from opposite directions stopped in sight of a shield suspended from a tree branch, one side of which was GOLD and the other SILVER, and disputed about its metal, proceeding from words to blows. Luckily a third knight came up: the point was referred to him, and the disputants were informed that the shield was silver on one side and gold on the other. Hence the sayings, *The other side of the shield, It depends on which side of the shield you are looking at*, etc.

The Shield of David. *See* STAR OF DAVID.

The Shield of Expectation. The perfectly plain shield given to a young warrior on his maiden campaign. As he achieved glory, his deeds were recorded or symbolized on it.

Shi'ites (Arab. *shi'ah*, a sect). Those Mohammedans who regard ALI, MOHAMMED's son-in-law, as the first rightful IMAM and CALIPH. They reject the first three Sunni caliphs and all SUNNITE tradition.

Shillelagh (shi lā' la). The conventional cudgel of the Irishman made from OAK or blackthorn; so called from the village of this name in County Wicklow which is supposed to have supplied the roof timbers for WESTMINSTER Hall from its once extensive oak forest.

Shilling (O.E. *scilling*; which is connected with O.Teut *skel-*, to resound or ring, or *skil-*, to divide). The shilling, as such, dates from 1504, and was originally made with a deeply indented cross, and could be easily divided into halves and quarters.

Cut off with a shilling. *See under* CUT.

To take the Queen's or **King's shilling.** to enlist; in allusion to the former practice of giving each recruit a shilling when he was sworn in.

Shilling shocker. *See* PENNY-DREADFUL.

Shilly shally. To hesitate, act in an undecided, irresolute way; a corruption of "Will I, shall I," or "Shall I, shall I?"

> There's no delay, they ne'er stand shall I, shall I,
> Hermogenes with Dallila doth dally.
> JOHN TAYLOR: *Workes*, iii, 3 (1630).

Shin Plaster. An old American and also Australian phrase still occasionally used for paper tokens issued by rural stores as small change. It is said that some storekeepers baked them to make them brittle so that they would powder to nothing in the recipients' pockets.

Shindig (shin' dig). A slang term for a dance, a noisy celebration party, etc.

Shindy. To kick up a shindy. To make a row or to create a disturbance. The word is probably connected with *shinty* or *shinny*, a primitive kind of hockey played in SCOTLAND and the north of ENGLAND.

Shine. To take the shine out of one. To humiliate him, "take him down a PEG or two"; to outshine him.

Shingle. To hang out one's shingle. An American colloquialism meaning "to begin one's professional career". *Shingle*, properly a kind of wooden tile, refers to the small signboard displayed outside premises by professional men and others.

Shintoism ("The way of the Gods"). The ancient national religion of Japan, now partly supplanted by BUDDHISM. The chief of innumerable deities in Amaterasuōmikami, the sun goddess, from whom the imperial dynasty supposedly descended. In 1946 the Emperor divested himself of any divine attributes.

Ship. In the printing-house, the body of compositors engaged for the time being on one definite piece of work is known as a *ship*; this is said to be short for *companionship*, but it is worth noting that many printing-house terms (*cp.* CHAPEL; FRIAR; MONK) have an ecclesiastical origin, and *ship* was an old name for the nave of a church.

Private ship. In the Royal Navy, a ship other than a FLAG SHIP. A term in use by the early 17th century.

The Ship of the Desert. The camel.

The Ship of Fools. Alexander Barclay's adaptation of Sebastian Brant's *Narrenschiff* (1494), published as *The Shyp of Folys of the Worlde* (1509). The ship was manned by fools of various types and the device was used for a satire on the vices and follies of the times. It had a considerable vogue and was imitated by W. H. Ireland in his *Modern Ship of Fools* (1807). *See* COCK LORELL'S BOTE.

Ship of the line. A man-of-war with sufficient gun-power to take a place in "line of battle". Fighting ships were not grouped specifically for this purpose before the mid-18th century when line battleships were divided into First Rates (three-deckers with at least 100 guns), Second Rates (three-deckers with 90 guns), Third Rates (two-deckers with 64 or 74 guns).

Losing, or **spoiling a ship for a ha'porth o' tar.** By saving a little to lose much. to mar a job, etc., in order to skimp. 'Ship' here is a dialect version of *sheep* and refers to the smearing of tar on sheep against various infections—a practice common in SHAKESPEARE's day, *e.g.*:

> And they [the hands] are often tarred over with the surgery of our sheep.
> *As You Like it*, III, ii.

Ships that pass in the night. Chance acquaintances only encountered once. The phrase is from Longfellow.

> Ships that pass in the night, and speak each other in passing,
> Only a signal shown and a distant voice in the dark-

ness;
So on the ocean of life we pass and speak one an-
other,
Only a look and a voice; then darkness again and a
silence.
Tales of a Wayside Inn, III. *Theologian's Tale*.

To take ship or **shipping.** To embark, to
take passage in a ship.

When my ship comes home. When my
fortune is made. The allusion is to the ARGO-
SY returning from foreign parts laden with
rich freight, and so enriching the merchant
who sent it forth.

And I have better news in store for you
Than you expect: unseal this letter soon;
There you shall find three of your argosies
Are richly come to harbour suddenly.
SHAKESPEARE: *The Merchant of Venice*, V, i.

Ship keeper. The watchman who takes care
of a ship in port.

Ship money. An old-established levy exacted from maritime towns and countries to
strengthen the navy in time of need.
CHARLES I extended the demand to inland
areas in 1635, which resulted in John Hampden's famous refusal (1637) to pay his due of
20s. The judges decided against Hampden,
contrary to the Petition of Right. Ship-
money was made illegal by the LONG PARLIA-
MENT in 1641.

Shipshape. In proper order, as methodic-
ally as things in a ship. When a sailing vessel
was properly rigged and equipped it was said
to be "shipshape". *Cp*. ALL SHIPSHAPE AND
BRISTOL FASHION *under* ALL.

Ship's husband. The agent on land who represents the owners and arranges the berthing, repairs, provisioning, etc., of the
ship. Now usually carried out by a Marine
Superintendent.

Shippen, Shippon. From O.E. *scypen*, a
shed or stall and connected with shop, a stall
or booth. Sometimes the word is said to be
obsolete and also mistakenly derived from
sheep-pen. It is normal west country usage
for a cowhouse or cowshed.

Kester got up from his three-legged stool, on seeing
what the others did not — that the dip-candle in the
lantern was coming to an end — and that in two or
three minutes the shippen would be in darkness,
and so his pails of milk endangered.
MRS GASKELL: *Sylvia's Lovers*, ch. XV.

Shipton, Mother. A prophetess and WITCH of
legendary fame first recorded in a pamphlet
of 1641, who is said to have foretold the
death of Wolsey, Lord Percy, and others,
and to have predicted the steam-engine and
telegraph, etc. In 1677 Richard Head
brought out a *Life and Death of Mother
Shipton*. She was born in a cave at Knaresborough, Yorkshire, in 1488, baptized as
Ursula Southiel and married Tony Shipton

when she was 24. There is a fake "Mother
Shipton's tomb" at Williton, Somerset.

Shire (O.E. *scir*). The main unit of local government in Anglo-Saxon England, presided
over by an ealdorman but from the 10th century by a SHERIFF. Shires were divided into
HUNDREDS or WAPENTAKES and after the
Norman CONQUEST the name *county* was applied to shire.

The Shires. The English counties whose
names terminate in -*shire*; but, in a narrower
sense, the Midland counties noted for fox-
hunting, especially Leicestershire, Northamptonshire, Rutland. The inhabitants of
East Anglia, Kent, Sussex, Essex and Surrey apply this term to the rest of ENGLAND.

To come out of the shires. To come from a
considerable distance; a phrase from Kent,
which was surrounded by Surrey, Sussex,
Middlesex, and Essex, none of which is
suffixed with *shire*.

Knight of the Shire. *See under* KNIGHT.

The Rider of the Shires. *See* RIDER.

Shire horse. The old breed of large, heavily
built cart-horse, originally bred in the Midlands.

Shire Moot. *See* MOOT.

Shirt. A boiled shirt. A white shirt, or more
usually a dress shirt.

Hair shirt. A shirt made of haircloth worn
by penitents. *See* TO WEAR SACKCLOTH AND
ASHES *under* SACK.

The shirt of Nessus. *See* NESSUS.

A stuffed shirt. Said of a pompous nonentity; a bore.

Close sits my shirt, but closer my skin.
An old proverb meaning that self-interest
comes first.

Not a shirt to one's name. "Not a RAG to
one's back." Penniless.

To give the shirt off one's back. All one
has.

To keep one's shirt on. To keep one's temper.

To put one's shirt on a horse. To back it
with all the money one possesses.

To take the shirt off someone's back. To
strip him of all he has.

Shirts as party emblems. *See* BLACK-
SHIRTS; BLUE SHIRTS; BROWN SHIRTS; GARI-
BALDI'S RED SHIRT; GREENSHIRT.

Shirty. Bad-tempered; very cross and offended; in the state you are in when somebody has "got your shirt out".

Shiva. *See* SIVA.

Shivaree (shiv' ĕrē). the word is a corruption
of CHARIVARI, and in the U.S.A. means the
mocking serenade accorded to newly married people.

Shiver. Shiver my timbers. An imprecation

used by "stage-sailors" and popular with children's story writers. Presumably of nautical origin, *shiver* here is used in the sense of "to shatter" or "splinter into pieces", the timbers being those of the ship.

Shivering Mountain. Mam Tor, a hill about 1700 ft. above sea-level, one of the "Seven Wonders of the Peak District"; so called from the waste of its mass by "shivering"—that is, breaking away in "shivers" or small pieces. This has been going on for ages, as the hill consists of alternate layers of shale and gritstone. The former, being soft, is easily reduced to powder, and as it crumbles small "shivers" of the gritstone break away for want of support.

Shoe. It was once thought unlucky to put on the left shoe before the right, or to put either shoe on the wrong foot.

It has long been a custom to throw an old shoe at the bride and bridegroom when the depart from the wedding breakfast or when they go to church to get married. Now it is more usual to tie an old shoe to their carriage or motor-car. To throw a shoe after someone is an ancient way of bringing good luck. The custom has been variously interpreted.

In Anglo-Saxon marriages, the father delivered the bride's shoe to the bridegroom who touched her on the head with it to show his authority.

Loosing the shoe (*cp. Josh.* v, 15) is a mark of respect in the East. The MOSLEM leaves his slippers outside the mosque. In *Deut.* xxv, 5–10, we read that the widow refused by her husband's surviving brother, asserted her independence by "loosing his shoe"; and in the story of *Ruth* (iv, 7) we are told that it was the custom in exchange to deliver a shoe in token of confirmation. "A man without sandals" was a proverbial expression among the Jews for a prodigal, from the custom of giving one's sandals in confirmation of a bargain.

Scot (*Discoverie of Witchcraft*, 1584) tells us that "many will go to bed again if they sneeze before their shoes be on their feet".

A shoe too large trips one up. A Latin proverb, *Calceus major subvertit.* An empire too large falls to pieces; a business too large comes to grief; an ambition too large fails altogether.

Another man's shoes. "To stand in another man's shoes" is to occupy the place of another. Among the ancient Northmen, when a man adopted a son, the person adopted put on the shoes of the adopter.

In REYNARD THE FOX, Reynard, having turned the tables on Sir Bruin the Bear, asked the queen to let him have the shoes of the disgraced minister; so Bruin's shoes were torn off and put upon the new favourite.

Another pair of shoes. A different thing altogether; quite another matter.

His shoes are made of running leather. He is given to roving.

Over Edom will I cast out my shoe (*Ps.* lx, 8; cviii, 9), *i.e.* will I march and triumph.

Over shoes, over boots. "In for a penny, in for a pound." *See under* PENNY.

> Where true courage roots
> The proverb says, "once over shoes, o'er boots."
> JOHN TAYLOR: *Workes*, ii, 145 (1630).

To die in one's shoes. To die a violent death, especially one on th escaffold. *Cp.* TO DIE IN HARNESS *under* HARNESS.

> And there is M'Fuze, and Lieutenant Tregooze,
> And there is Sir Carnaby Jenks of the Blues,
> All come to see a man die in his shoes.
> BARHAM: *Ingoldsby Legends* (*The Execution*).

To shake in one's shoes. To be in a state of fear or nervous terror.

To shoe the anchor. To cover the flukes of an anchor with a broad triangular piece of a plank, in order that the anchor may have a stronger hold in soft ground.

To shoe the cobbler. To give a quick peculiar movement with the front foot in sliding.

To shoe a goose. To engage in a silly and fruitless task.

To shoe the wild colt. To exact a fine called "footing" from a newcomer, who is called the "colt". Colt is a common synonym for a GREENHORN, or a youth not broken in.

Waiting for dead men's shoes. Looking out for a legacy; waiting to take the place of another when he has passed on to retirement or death.

Where the shoe pinches. "No one knows where the shoe pinches like the wearer" is the reputed saying of a Roman sage who was blamed for divorcing his wife, with whom he seemed to live happily.

> For, God it wot, he sat ful still and song
> When that his scho ful bitterly him wrong.
> CHAUCER: *Wife of Bath's Tale, Prologue*, 492.

The cause of the trouble, or where the difficulty lies, is called "the place where the shoe pinches".

Whose shoes I am not worthy to bear (*Matt.* iii, 11). This means, "I am not worthy to be his humblest slave." It was the business of a slave recently purchased to loose and carry his master's sandals.

Shoemakers. Shoemaking is called the GENTLE CRAFT and its patron saint is CRISPIN.

Shoestring. To live on a shoestring. To manage on very little money.

Shofar (shō' far). A Hebrew trumpet still used in the modern SYNAGOGUE. It is made of the horn of a ram or any ceremonially clean animal, and produces only the natural series of harmonics from its fundamental note.

Shogun (shō' gŭn) ("Army leader"). The Shoguns were hereditary commanders-in-chief who seized political power in Japan at the end of the 12th century. The MIKADO did not fully regain power until 1868. *Cp.* TYCOON.

Shoot (M.E. *shoten*, dart forth, rush). *See also* SHOT.

Shoot! Go ahead; say what you have to say. Let's have it! In film studios it is the word used for the cameras to begin turning.

To go the whole shoot. To do all there is to do, go the whole HOG, run through the gamut.

To shoot down in flames. To refute the arguments of an opponent devastatingly and completely. A METAPHOR from aerial warfare.

To shoot a line. To boast extravagantly.

To shoot one's linen. To display an unnecessary amount of shirt-cuff; to show off.

To shoot the moon. To remove one's household goods by night to avoid distraint; to "do a MOONLIGHT flit".

To shoot Niagara. To embark on a desperate enterprise.

To shoot the sun. A nautical colloquialism meaning to take the sun's altitude with a sextant.

Shooting-iron. Slang (originally American) for a firearm, especially a revolver.

Shooting stars. Incandescent meteors shooting across the sky, formerly, like comets, fabled to presage disaster:

> A little ere the mightiest Julius fell,
> The graves stood tenantless, and the sheeted dead
> Did squeak and gibber in the Roman streets;
> As stars with trains of fire and dews of blood,
> Disasters with the sun.
>
> SHAKESPEARE: *Hamlet*, I, i.

They were called in ancient legends the "fiery tears of St. LAWRENCE", because one of the periodic swarms of these meteors is between 9 and 14 AUGUST, about the time of St. Lawrence's festival, which is on the 10th. Other periods are from 12 to 14 November, and from 6 to 12 December.

Shooting stars are said by the Arabs to be firebrands hurled by the ANGELS against the inquisitive genii, who are forever clambering up on the constellations to peep into HEAVEN.

Shooting war. A real war as distinct from a COLD WAR.

Shop. The Shop. In military slang, the former Royal Military Academy at Woolwich which removed to Sandhurst in 1946; on the Stock Exchange it is the South African gold market.

All over the shop. Scattered in every direction, all over the place; or pursuing an erratic course.

Closed shop. A term, first used in the U.S.A., to characterize shops or factories from which non-union labour is excluded.

On the shop floor. Among the industrial workers of a workshop, factory, etc.

Open shop. The reverse of a CLOSED SHOP.

To shop a person. To put him in prison, or inform against him so that he is arrested, similarly, a billiard player will speak of "shopping the white", *i.e.* putting his opponent's ball down in the pocket.

To shop around. To look for the "best buy", to visit a variety of shops comparing prices and quality before making one's choice.

To shut up shop. To retire or withdraw from participation in an undertaking.

To talk shop. To talk about one's trade, occupation, business, etc.

You've come to the wrong shop. I can't help you, I can't give you the information, and so on, you require.

Shop steward. The elected trade union representative of a factory or workshop who acts as the link with the local union branch, keeps watch on union membership, etc., and has certain negotiating functions with the management.

Shopkeepers. A nation of shopkeepers. This phrase, applied to Englishmen by NAPOLEON in contempt, comes from Adam Smith's *The Wealth Nations* (iv, 7). This book, well known to the Emperor, says:

> To found a great empire for the sole purpose of raising up a people of customers, may at first sight appear a project fit only for a nation of shopkeepers.

Shoreditch. The legend that this LONDON district takes its name from Edward IV's mistress, Jane Shore, derives from a ballad in the Pepys' collection, a version of which is given in PERCY'S RELIQUES:

> Thus, weary of my life, at lengthe
> I yielded up my vital strength
> Within a ditch of oathsome scent,
> Where carrion dogs did much frequent:
> The which now since my dying daye,
> Is Shoreditch called, as writers saye.

It is also suggested that the name comes from *Soerdich*, or *Shorditch*, the family who once held the manor, and Bishop Percy says it is "from its being a common sewer (vulgarly 'shore') or drain"; but it is most probably "the ditch leading to the shore" (of the Thames). According to the old ballad it was in Shoreditch that George BARNWELL was led astray:

> Good Barnwell, then quoth she,
> Do thou to Shoreditch come,
> And ask for Mrs. Millwood's house,
> Next door unto the Gun.

The Duke of Shoreditch. An archer of this parish is said to have been so called by Henry VIII for his success in an archery contest at Windsor. The title was long playfully applied to the Captain of the Company of Archers of London.

Shorne, or **Schorne, John.** Rector of North Marston, Buckinghamshire (*c.* 1290–1314), in the church of which was once a shrine in his honour. He was renowned for his piety and miraculous powers. He blessed a local well giving it legendary healing properties and also "conjured the DEVIL into a boot". His shrine became so frequented by pilgrims that, in 1481, the DEAN and CHAPTER of Windsor, owners of the ADVOWSON, with papal permission, removed his shrine and relics to Windsor.

Short. Pepin, or **Pippin the Short.** Pippin III, MAYOR OF THE PALACE, father of CHARLEMAGNE and founder of the CAROLINGIAN dynasty of French kings. He deposed the last of the MEROVINGIANS, Childeric III, in 751 and reigned as King of the FRANKS until 768. He was the son of Charles Martel.

Short commons. *See* COMMONS.

Short Parliament (13 April–5 May 1640). The abortive PARLIAMENT summoned by CHARLES I after his ELEVEN YEARS TYRANNY to procure supplies to fight the Scots. The Commons insisted on redress of grievances and Charles dissolved Parliament.

Short thigh. *See* CURTHOSE.

A drop of something short. A tot of whisky, gin, etc., as opposed to a "long drink" such as a glass of beer.

Cut it short! Don't be so prolix, come to the point; "cut the cackle and come to the 'osses". Said to a speaker who goes round and round his subject.

My name is Short. I'm in a hurry and cannot wait.

> Well, but let us hear the wishes (said the old man); my name is short, and I cannot stay much longer.
> W.B. YEATS: *Fairy Tales of the Irish Peasant* (*The Devil, The Three Wishes*).

The short cut is often the longest way round. It does not always pay to avoid taking a little trouble; short cuts don't always pay. Francis Bacon says:

> It is in life, as it is in ways, the shortest way is commonly the foulest, and surely the faire way is not much about.
> *Advancement of Learning.*

To break off short. Abruptly, without warning, but completely.

To make short work of it. To dispose of it quickly, to deal summarily with it.

To sell short. A STOCK EXCHANGE phrase meaning to sell stock that one does not at the moment possess, on the chance that it may be acquired at a lower rate before the date of delivery; the same as "selling for a fall", or "selling a BEAR".

To win by a short head. Only just to outdistance one's competitors, to win with practically nothing to spare. The phrase is from horse-racing.

To short-circuit. Metaphorically to take a short cut, especially when dealing with officialdom; a figure from electrics in which a short-circuit is a deviation of current along a path of lower resistance.

Shorter Catechism. One of the two Catechisms (the *Larger* and *Shorter*) drawn up by the WESTMINSTER ASSEMBLY in 1647 and adopted by the English PARLIAMENT and the Scottish General Assembly. The *Shorter Catechism* proved its instructional worth and came into regular use among PRESBYTERIANS, Baptists, and later, WESLEYANS.

Shot (O.E. *sceot*, arrow, dart, etc.). A missile weapon.

A big shot. An important person. A development of the 19th-century "great gun" or "big bug".

The fool's bolt is soon shot. *See under* BOLT.

He shot wide of the mark. He was altogether wrong. The allusion to target shooting is obvious.

I haven't a shot in the locker. My last resources are spent; I've run right out of food, drink, money, etc. The reference is to the ammunition locker of a warship.

Like a shot. With great rapidity; or, without hesitation; most willingly.

A long shot. A remote chance, such as hazarding a highly improbable guess.

Parthian shot. *See* PARTHIAN.

A shot in the arm. A drink of whisky, etc., something which puts new life into one; an allusion to hypodermic injections or morphine, cocaine, etc.

A shot in the dark. A wild guess, a random conjecture.

To have a shot at. To have a try, to make an attempt at something in which you make no particular claim to expertise.

To have shot one's bolt. *See under* BOLT.

Shot. Akin to *Scot* (*see* SCOT AND LOT). A reckoning, share of an ale-house bill, etc.

To stand shot. To pay the bill.

Shotgun Wedding. One forced upon the couple, usually by the bride's parents, when the bride is pregnant.

Shotten Herring. A lean, spiritless creature, a JACK-O-LENT, like a herring that has *shot*, or ejected, its spawn. Herrings gutted and dried are likewise so called.

> Though they like shotten-herrings are to see,
> Yet such tall souldiers of their teeth they be,
> That two of them, like greedy cormorants,
> Devour more than sixe honest Protestants.
>> TAYLOR: *Workes*, iii, 5 (1630).

Shoulder. The government shall be upon his shoulder (*Is.* ix, 6). An allusion to the key slung on the shoulder of Jewish stewards on public occasions. *See* THE KEY SHALL BE UPON HIS SHOULDER *under* KEY.

Straight from the shoulder. With full force, physically, or verbally. A term from boxing.

To set, or put one's shoulder to the wheel. *See under* PUT.

Shout, To (Austr.). To stand a round of drinks.

All over but the shouting. Success is so certain that only the applause is lacking. The phrase, perhaps, derives from elections.

Shovel Board. The "two Edward shovel-boards" mentioned in SHAKESPEARE's *Merry Wives of Windsor* (I, i), were the broad shillings of Edward VI used in playing the game "shove groat", "shovel board" or "slyp groat". Strutt (*Sports and Pastimes*, Bk. IV, ch. i) distinguishes between shovel board and shove groat. The former, he says, was played on a very long table, the players shoving flat weights.

> I have seen a shovel-board table...thirty-nine feet two inches in length.

Shove groat, played on a much smaller table, was "only practised by such as frequent the tap-rooms". These games were the forerunners of *shove-halfpenny*.

Shovel Hat. A broad-brimmed black hat curved up at the sides producing a shovel-like projection at back and front; formerly favoured by CLERGY. Hence *shovel-hat* as a colloquialism for an ecclesiastic.

Show (Austr.). A gold mine. "Give him a show", give him a chance, *i.e.* originally, let him stake out his own claim.

To have a show-down. To reveal the strength of one's position; to have a final confrontation in a dispute to settle the matter or to clear the air. As in poker, cards are put face upwards on the table.

To show one's hand. To reveal one's motives or intentions, as in displaying one's hand at cards.

Shrew-mouse. This small insectivorous animal was fabled to have the power of harming

cattle, etc., by running over their backs and to lame the foot over which it ran. Gilbert White tells of a shrew-ash, the twigs of which, if applied to the limbs of beasts harmed by the shrew-mouse, give relief. This tree was one in which a deep hole had been bored and a shrew-mouse thrust in alive; the hole was then plugged (*Natural History of Selbourne*, Letter xxviii). It was also ill luck to encounter a shrew-mouse when beginning a journey.

Shrift, Shrive. To shrive a person was to prescribe penance after confession and to absolve. *Cp.* SHROVETIDE.

To give short shrift to. To make short work of. *Short shrift* was the few minutes in which a criminal about to be executed was allowed to make his confession.

Shropshire. The O.E. name for the county was *Scrobbesbyrigscir*, "the shire with Shrewsbury as its head". The Norman name was *Salopescira*, hence *Salop* as a synonym for the county and *Salopian* for a native.

Shrovetide. The three days just before the opening of LENT, when people went to confession and afterwards indulged in all sorts of sports and merry-making.

Shrove Tuesday. The day before ASH WEDNESDAY; "PANCAKE DAY". It used to the great "DERBY DAY" of COCK-FIGHTING in England.

> Or martyr beat, like Shrovetide cocks, with bats.
>> PETER PINDAR: *Subjects for Painters*: *Scene, The Royal Academy*, III.

Shut up. Slang for "HOLD your tongue"; shut up your mouth.

Shy. To have a shy at anything. To fling at it. To have a go, to take a chance and see how it turns out.

Shylock, A (shī' lok). A grasping, stony-hearted moneylender; in allusion to the Jew in SHAKESPEARE's *Merchant of Venice*.

> A stony adversary, an inhuman wretch
> Uncapable of pity, void and empty
> From any dreams of mercy
>> IV, i.

Si (sē). *See* ARETINIAN SYLLABLES.

Si Quis (sī kwis) (Lat., if anyone). A notice to all whom it may concern, given in the parish church before ordination that a resident means to offer himself as a candidate for HOLY ORDERS (*see under* ORDERS); and if anyone knows any just cause or impediment thereto, he is to declare the same to the BISHOP.

Siamese twins. Identical twins physically joined together when born and often inseparable. The name originated with two children, Eng and Chang, born (1811) in Siam of Chinese parents. Joined in the area of the waist, they were duly sold by their mother and exhibited in America (where they eventually settled), England and Europe. They married two sisters and fathered offspring and died in 1874 within two and a half hours of each other.

Sibyl (sib'il). A prophetess of classical legend, who was supposed to prophesy under the inspiration of a deity; the name is now applied to any prophetess or woman fortune-teller. There were a number of sibyls, and they had their seats in widely separate parts of the world—Greece, Italy, Babylonia, Egypt, etc.

PLATO mentions only one, *viz.* the *Erythræan*—identified with AMALTHEA, the *Cumæan* sibyl, who was consulted by ÆNEAS and accompanied him into HADES and who sold the SIBYLLINE BOOKS to TARQUIN; Martin Capella speaks of two, the *Erythræan* and the *Phrygian*; Ælian of four, the *Erythræan*, *Samian*, *Egyptian*, and *Sardian*; Varro tells us that there were ten, *viz.* the *Cumæan*, the *Delphic*, *Egyptian*, *Erythræan*, *Hellespontine*, *Libyan*, *Persian*, *Phrygian*, *Samian*, and *Tiburtine*.

> How know we but that she may be an eleventh Sibyl or a second Cassandra?
> RABELAIS: *Gargantua and Pantagruel*, III, xvi.

The mediæval monks "adopted" the sibyls—as they did so much of pagan myth; they made them 12, and gave to each a separate prophecy and distinct emblem:

(1) The *Libyan*: "The day shall come when men shall see the King of all living things." *Emblem*, a lighted taper.

(2) The *Samian*: "The Rich One shall be born of a pure virgin." *Emblem*, a ROSE.

(3) The *Cuman*: "Jesus Christ shall come from heaven, and live and reign in poverty on earth." *Emblem*, a CROWN.

(4) The *Cumæan*: "God shall be born of a pure virgin, and hold converse with sinners." *Emblem*, a cradle.

(5) The *Erythræan*: "Jesus Christ, Son of God, the Saviour." *Emblem*, a horn.

(6) The *Persian*: "Satan shall be overcome by a true prophet." *Emblem*, a DRAGON under the sibyl's feet, and a lantern.

(7) The *Tiburtine*: "The Highest shall descend from HEAVEN and a virgin be shown in the valleys of the deserts." *Emblem*, a dove.

(8) The *Delphic*: "The Prophet born of the virgin shall be crowned with thorns." *Emblem*, a crown of thorns.

(9) The *Phrygian*: "Our Lord shall rise again." *Emblem*, a banner and a CROSS.

(10) The *European*: "A virgin and her Son shall flee into Egypt." *Emblem*, a sword.

(11) The *Agrippine*: "Jesus Christ shall be

outraged and scourged." *Emblem*, a whip.

(12) The *Hellespontic*: "Jesus Christ shall suffer shame upon the cross." *Emblem*, a T cross.

Sibylline Books, The. A collection of oracular utterances preserved in ancient ROME and consulted by the Senate in times of emergency or disaster. According to Livy, there were orginally NINE books offered to TARQUIN by the SIBYL of Cumæ but the offer was rejected, and she burnt three of them. She offered the remaining six at the same price. Again, being refused, she burnt three more. The remaining three were then bought by the King for the original sum.

The three books were preserved in a vault of the temple of JUPITER Capitolinus, and committed to the charge of custodians, ultimately 15 in number. These books were destroyed by fire in 83 B.C. A new collection of verses was made from those preserved in the cities of Greece, Italy, and Asia Minor, and deposited in the rebuilt temple. These were transferred to the temple of APOLLO by AUGUSTUS in 12 B.C. and were said to have been destroyed by Stilicho (*c.* 405).

Sibylline Oracles. A collection of 15 books, 12 of which are extant, of 2nd- and 3rd-century authorship, and written by Jews and Christians in imitation of the SIBYLLINE BOOKS. Their aim was to gain converts to their respective faiths.

Sic (sik) (Lat., thus, so). A word used by reviewers, quoters, etc., after a doubtful word or phrase, or a misspelling, to indicate that it is here printed exactly as in the original and to call attention to the fact that it is wrong in some way.

Sic transit gloria mundi. *See under* GLORIA.

Sicilies, The Two. The old name for the Spanish Bourbon Kingdom of Naples and Sicily formerly united under their Angevin rulers in the 13th century. The Two Sicilies were annexed to the Kingdom of Italy in 1860.

Sicilian Vespers. The massacre of the French in Sicily on EASTER Monday (30 March) 1282, which began on the stroke of the vesper-bell. It was occasioned by the brutality and tyranny of Charles of Anjou's rule.

Sick. Sick joke. A sadistic, gruesome joke — not really funny but the product of a warped sense of humour.

Sick Man, The. So Nicholas I of Russia (in 1844 and subsequently) called the Turkish Empire, which had long been in decline. His hints to Great Britain in 1853 of a partition were ignored.

I repeat to you that the sick man is dying; and we must never allow such an event to take us by surprise.

Annual Register, 1853.

Don John, Governor-General of the Netherlands, so spoke of his charge when writing to his master Philip II in 1579.

"Money is the gruel," said he, "with which we must cure this sick man."
MOTLEY: *Rise of the Dutch Republic*, Pt. V, ch. ii.

Side. On the side of the angels. The famous phrase with which Disraeli thought he had settled the problems raised by Darwin's theory of the origin of species. It occurred in his speech at the Oxford Diocesan Conference in 1864:

The quest is this: Is man an ape or an angel? Now I am on the side of the angels.

It was the same statesman who said in the HOUSE OF COMMONS (14 May 1866), "Ignorance never settles a question."

Putting on side. Giving oneself airs; being bumptious. *To put on side* in billiards is to give your ball a twist or spin with the cue as you strike it.

To side-track. Originally an American RAIL-ROAD term; hence to divert, to put on one side, to shelve.

Sideburns. Short side-whiskers, originally called *burnsides* after the American Federal General Ambrose Everett Burnside (1824–1881) who wore side-whiskers.

Siege Perilous. In the cycle of ARTHURIAN ROMANCES a seat at the ROUND TABLE which was kept vacant for him who should accomplish the quest of the Holy GRAIL. For any less a person to sit in it was fatal. At the crown of his achievement Sir GALAHAD took his seat in the Siege Perilous.

Siegfried (zēg' frēd), or **Sigurd.** Hero of the first part of the NIBELUNGENLIED. He was the youngest son of Siegmund and Sieglind, King and Queen of the Netherlands.

Siegfried's cloak of invisibility, called "*Tarnkappe*" (*tarnen*, to conceal; *Kappe*, a cloak). It not only made the wearer invisible, but also gave him the strength of 12 men.

Siegfried Line. The defences built by the Germans on their western frontier before and after 1939 as a reply to France's MAGINOT LINE. The British song, popular in 1939, "We're gonna hang out the washing on the Siegfried Line" was somewhat premature. When Canadian troops penetrated the Line in 1945 they hung up a number of sheets with a large notice on which was written "The Washing".

Sieve and Shears. An ancient form of DIVINATION mentioned by THEOCRITUS. The points of the shears were stuck in the wooden rim of the sieve and two persons supported it upright with the tips of their two fingers. Then a verse of the BIBLE was read aloud, and St. PETER and St. PAUL were asked if the guilty person was A, B, or C (naming those suspected). When the guilty person was named the sieve would suddenly turn round. This method was also used to tell if a couple would marry, etc.

Searching for things lost with a sieve and shears.
BEN JONSON: *Alchemist*, I, i.

Sight. In archaic usage, it often denotes a "multitude" or large number of persons or objects.

Second sight. *See under* SECOND.

A sight for sore eyes. Something that it is very pleasurable to see or witness, especially something unexpected.

Though lost to sight, to memory dear. This occurs in a song by George Linley (*c*. 1835), but is found as an "axiom" in the *Monthly Magazine*, January 1827, and is probably earlier than this.

To do a thing on sight. At once, without any hesitation.

Sign. Royal Sign Manual. The signature of the monarch used on orders, commissions, and warrants. The earliest known royal signature is that of Edward III, prior to which marks or seals were used. Under certain restrictions a stamp is used for minor documents.

To sign off. In the 19th century this denoted finally leaving one religious organization for another. It is generally used to mean terminating attendances, registering when leaving work, finishing broadcasting, etc.

To sign on the dotted line. To fully accept the terms offered; from the space indicated by dots reserved for a person's signature on printed forms.

Signature tune. A musical theme played regularly as a means of identification to introduce a dance band, artist, or regularly broadcast programme, etc.

Significavit (sig ni fi cā' vit). An obsolete CHANCERY writ given by the ORDINARY to keep an excommunicate (*see* EXCOMMUNICATION) in prison till he submitted to the authority of the Church. From its opening words *Significavit nobis venerabilis pater*. Chaucer says of his Sompnour:

And also ware him of a significavit.
Canterbury Tales (Prologue), 664.

Sigurd. The SIEGFRIED of the Volsunga SAGA, the Scandinavian version of the NIBELUNGENLIED. He falls in love with BRUNHILD but under the influence of a love-potion marries GUDRUN, a union with fateful consequences.

Sikes, Bill. The type of a ruffianly housebreaker, from the character of that name in Dickens's *Oliver Twist*.

Silence. Amyclæan Silence. *See* AMY-CLÆAN.

The Argument of Silence (Lat. *argumentum e silentio*). The conclusion that, if the works of an author omit all reference to a particular subject, the writer was unaware of it.

Silence gives consent. A saying, common to many languages, founded on the old Latin legal maxim—*Qui tacet consentire videtur* (who is silent is held to consent).

> But that you shall not say I yield, being silent,
> I would not speak.
>
> SHAKESPEARE: *Cymbeline*, II, iii.

Silence is golden. *See* SPEECH.

The rest is silence. The last words of the dying Hamlet (SHAKESPEARE: *Hamlet*, V, ii).

Towers of Silence. The small towers on which the PARSEES and ZOROASTRIANS place their dead to be consumed by birds of prey. The bones are picked clean in the course of a day, and are then thrown into a receptacle covered with charcoal.

Parsees do not burn or bury their dead, because they consider a corpse impure, and they will not defile any of the elements. They carry it on a bier to the tower. At the entrance they look their last on the body, and the corpse-bearers carry it within the precincts and lay it down to be devoured by vultures which are constantly on the watch.

Two-minute silence. The cessation of traffic and all other activities for two minutes at 11 a.m. on 11 November to commemorate those who died in World War I. First observed in 1919, it remained a central feature of REMEMBRANCE DAY.

William the Silent. Prince William of Orange (1533–1584), so called because when (1559) Henry II of France, thinking that he would be a ready accomplice, revealed to him the plans for a general massacre of PROTESTANTS:

> the Prince, although horror-struck and indignant at the Royal revelations, held his peace, and kept his countenance ... William of Orange earned the name of "the Silent", from the manner in which he received the communications of Henry without revealing to the monarch by word or look, the enormous blunder which he had committed.
>
> MOTLEY: *The Rise of the Dutch Republic*, Pt. II, i.

Silenus (sī lē' nůs). The drunken attendant and nurse of BACCHUS, represented as a fat, jovial old man, always full of liquor, riding an ass.

> Within his car, aloft, young Bacchus stood,
> Trifling his ivy-dart, in dancing mood,
> With sidelong laughing;...
> And near him rode Silenus on his ass,
> Pelted with flowers as he on did pass
> Tipsily quaffing.
>
> KEATS: *Endymion*, IV, 209.

Silhouette. A profile drawing of a person giving the outline only, and all within the outline in black; hence a shadow and, figuratively, a slight literary sketch of a person or other subject. Derived from the French minister of Finance, Etienne de Silhouette (1709–1767), noted for his parsimony in public expenditure. His name was applied to things made cheaply.

Silk. The Silk Road. The ancient caravan route along which silk was carried from China, through central Asia, thence to Antioch and the eastern Mediterranean and eventually to other parts of Europe It was in use for about 1500 years, particularly in the days of the Roman Empire. Parts of it were traversed by Marco Polo on his visits to China in the late 13th century.

To take silk. Said of a BARRISTER who has been appointed a QUEEN'S COUNSEL (Q.C.) because he then exchanges his stuff gown for a silk one.

You cannot make a silk purse out of a sow's ear. You cannot make something good of what is by nature bad or inferior in quality. "You cannot make a horn of a pig's tail."

Silly is the German *selig* (blessed) and used to mean in English "happy through being innocent"; whence the infant Jesus was termed "the harmless silly babe", and sheep were called "silly". As the innocent are easily taken in by worldly cunning, the word came to signify "gullible", "foolish".

Silly Billy. A nickname applied to William IV (1765, 1830–1837); also to William Frederick, Duke of Gloucester (1776–1834).

Silly-how. An old name—still used in SCOTLAND—for a child's caul. It is a rough translation of the German term *Glückshaube*, lucky cap. The caul has always been supposed to bring luck to its original possessor.

The silly season. An obsolescent journalistic expression for the part of the year when PARLIAMENT and the Law Courts are not sitting (about August and September), when, through lack of news, the papers had to fill their columns with trivial items—such as news of giant gooseberries and sea serpents— and long correspondence on subjects of evanescent (if any) interest.

Silly Suffolk. Possibly so called from its many churches and religious houses. *See*

SILLY *above*.

Silurian. Of or pertaining to the ancient British tribe, the Silures, or the district they inhabited, *viz.* Monmouth, Glamorgan, Brecon, Radnor and Hereford. The "sparkling wines of the Silurian vats" are cider and perry.

> From Silurian vats, high-sparkling wines
> Foam in transparent floods.
> THOMSON: *The Seasons (Autumn,* 656).

Silurian rocks. A name given by Sir Roderick Murchison (1835) to what miners call *gray-wacke* and Werner termed *transition rocks*, because it was in the SILURIAN district (English-Welsh border) that he first investigated their structure.

The Silurist. A surname adopted by the mystical poet Henry Vaughan (1621–1695), who was born and died in Brecknockshire.

Silver. In England *standard silver (i.e.* that used for coinage) formerly consisted of thirty-seven-fortieths of fine silver and three-fortieths of alloy (fineness, 925); in 1925 the proportions were changed to one-half silver, one-half alloy (fineness, 500). In 1946 cupro-nickel coins were introduced to replace silver. *See* HALL MARK; LEGAL TENDER.

Among the ancient alchemists silver represented the MOON or DIANA; in HERALDRY it is known by its French name ARGENT (which also gives its chemical symbol, Ag), and is indicated on engravings by the silver (argent) portion being left blank.

The Silver Age. According to Hesiod and the Greek and Roman poets, the second of the AGES of the World; fabled as a period that was voluptuous and godless, and much inferior in simplicity and true happinesss to the GOLDEN AGE.

The silver cooper. A kidnapper. "To play the silver cooper", to kidnap. A cooper is one who "coops up" another.

Silver of Guthrum. *See* GUTHRUM.

Silver Star. A United States military decoration for gallantry in action. It consists of a bronze star bearing a small silver star in its centre.

The Silver Streak. The English Channel.

Silver Wedding. The twenty-fifth anniversary, when presents of silver plate (in Germany a silver wreath) are given to the happy pair.

Thirty pieces of silver. The sum of money that JUDAS Iscariot received from the chief priests for the betrayal of his Master (*Matt.* xxvi, 5); hence used proverbially of a bribe or "BLOOD-MONEY" (*see under* BLOOD).

Born with a silver spoon in one's mouth.

See under BORN.

A silver lining. The prospect of better things and happier times. The saying **Every cloud has a silver lining** is an old one; thus in Milton's *Comus* (I, 221–222) the lady lost in the wood resolves to hope on, and sees:

> Was I deceiv'd, or did a sable cloud
> Turn forth her silver lining on the night?

Speech is silver. *See under* SPEECH.

With silver weapons you may conquer the world. The Delphic ORACLE to Philip of Macedon, when he went to consult it. Philip, acting on this advice, sat down before a fortress which his staff pronounced to be impregnable. "You shall see," said the king, "how an ass laden with silver will find an entrance."

The Silver-Fork School. A name given in amused contempt (*c.* 1830) to the novelists who were sticklers for the etiquette and graces of the UPPER TEN (*see under* TEN) and showed great respect for the affectations of gentility. Theodore Hook, Lady Blessington, and Bulwer Lytton might be taken as representatives of it.

Silver-tongued. An epithet bestowed on many persons famed for eloquence; especially William Bates, the PURITAN divine (1625–1699); Anthony Hammond, the poet (1688–1738); Henry Smith, preacher (*c.* 1550–1591); and Joshua Sylvester (1563–1618), translator of Du Bartas.

Simeon, St. (sim′ ē ón), the son of Cleophas, is usually depicted as bearing in his arms the infant Jesus or receiving Him in the TEMPLE. His feast day is 18 February.

St. Simeon Stylites. *See* STYLITES.

Similia similibus curantur (sim il′ ia simil′i bús kū răn′ ter) (Lat.). Like cures like; or as we say. "Take a hair of the dog that bit you." (*See under* HAIR.)

Sim(p)kin. Anglo-Indian for champagne—of which word it is an Urdu mispronunciation.

Simnel Cakes. Rich cakes formerly eaten (especially in Lancashire) on MID-LENT SUNDAY (MOTHERING SUNDAY), EASTER, and CHRISTMAS DAY. They were ornamented with scallops, and were eaten at Mid-Lent in commemoration of the banquet given by Joseph to his brethren, which forms the first lesson of Mid-Lent Sunday, and the feeding of the five thousand, which forms the GOSPEL of the day.

The word *simnel* is through O.Fr. from Late Lat. *siminellus,* fine bread, Lat. *simila,* the finest wheat flour.

Simon, St. (Zelotes) is represented with a saw in his hand, in allusion to the instrument of his martyrdom. He sometimes bears fish in his other hand, in allusion to his occupation as a fisherman. His feast day is 28 October.

Simon Magus. Isidore tells us that Simon Magus died in the reign of NERO, and adds that he had proposed a dispute with PETER and PAUL, and had promised to fly up to HEAVEN. He succeeded in rising high into the air, but at the prayers of the two APOSTLES he was cast down to earth by the evil spirits who had enabled him to rise.

Milman, in his *History of Christianity* (ii) tells another story. He says that Simon offered to be buried alive, and declared that he would reappear on the third day. He was actually buried in a deep trench, "but to this day," says Hippolytus, "his disciples have failed to witness his resurrection".

His followers were known as *Simonians*, and the sin of which he was guilty, *viz.* the trafficking in sacred things, the buying and selling of ecclesiastical offices (*see Acts* viii, 18) is still called *simony*.

Simon Pure. The real man, the authentic article, etc. In Mrs. Centlivre's *Bold Stroke for a Wife*, a Colonel Feignwell passes himself off for Simon Pure, a QUAKER, and wins the heart of Miss Lovely. No sooner does he get the assent of her guardian than the Quaker turns up, and proves beyond a doubt he is the "real Simon Pure". In modern usage, a hypocrite, making a great parade of virtue.

Simple Simon. A simpleton, a gullible booby; from the character in the well-known anonymous nursery tale, who "met a pieman".

Simonism. *See* SAINT-SIMONISM.

Simple, The. Charles III of France (879, 893–929). He was dethroned in 923.

The simple life. A mode of living in which the object is to eliminate as far as possible all luxuries and extraneous aids to happiness, etc., returning to the simplicity of life as imagined by the pastoral poets.

Sin, according to Milton, is twin keeper with Death of the gates of HELL. She sprang fullgrown from the head of SATAN.

> ... Woman to the waist, and fair
> But ending foul in many a scaly fold
> Voluminous and vast, a serpent armed
> With mortal sting.
> *Paradise Lost*, II, 650–3.

Original Sin. That corruption which is born with us, and is the inheritance of all the offspring of ADAM. Theology teaches that as Adam was founder of his race, when Adam fell the taint and penalty of his disobedience passed to all posterity.

The Man of Sin (II *Thess*. ii, 3). Generally held to signify ANTICHRIST, and applied by the PURITANS to the POPE, by the FIFTH MON-

ARCHY MEN to Cromwell, etc.

Mortal Sins. The same as deadly sins.

The seven deadly sins. *See under* SEVEN.

Sin-eaters. Poor persons hired at funerals in olden days, to eat beside the corpse and so take upon themselves the sins of the deceased, that the soul might be delivered from PURGATORY. In Carmarthenshire the sin-eater used to rest a plate of salt on the breast of the deceased and place a piece of bread on the salt. After saying an incantation over the bread the sin-eater consumed it and with it the sins of the dead.

"Sin on" Bible. *See* BIBLE, SOME SPECIALLY NAMED EDITIONS.

Sin rent. In mediæval England, a fine imposed upon the laity by the Church for living in sin, *i.e.*, for concubinage. *Cp.* CRADLE CROWN.

To earn the wages of sin. To be hanged or condemned to death.

> The wages of sin is death.
> *Rom*. vi, 23.

To sin one's mercies. To be ungrateful for the gifts of Providence.

Sinbad the Sailor. The hero of the story of this name in THE ARABIAN NIGHTS ENTERTAINMENTS. He was a wealthy citizen of Baghdad, called "The Sailor" because of his seven voyages in which, among many adventures, he discovered the ROC's egg and the Valley of Diamonds, and killed the OLD MAN OF THE SEA.

Sine (Lat.). Without.

Sine die (Lat.). No time being fixed; indefinitely in regard to time. When a proposal is deferred *sine die*, it is deferred without fixing a day for its reconsideration, which is virtually "for ever".

Sine qua non (Lat.). An indispensable condition. Lat. *Sine qua non potest esse* or *fieri* (that without which [the thing] cannot be, or be done).

Sinecure (Lat. *sine cura*, without cure, or care). An enjoyment of the emoluments attached to a benefice without having the trouble of the "cure"; applied to any office to which a salary is attached without any duties to perform. Government sinecures were a particular feature of 18th-century political life. *Cp.* PLACEMEN.

Sinews of War. Essential funds for the prosecution of a war. Troops have to be paid and fed and the materials of war are costly.

The English phrase comes from Cicero's *Nervos belli pecuniam* (*Phil.* V, ii, 5), money makes the sinews of war. Rabelais (I, xlvi) uses the same idiom—*les nerfs des batailles sont les pécunes*.

Victuals and ammunition,
And money too, the sinews of the war,
Are stored up in the magazine.
BEAUMONT and FLETCHER:
Fair Maid of the Inn, I, i.

Sing. Singing bread (Fr. *pain à chanter*). An old term for the larger altar bread used in celebration of the MASS, because singing or chanting was in progress during its manufacture; also called *singing cake* and *singing loaf*.

Swans sing before they die. *See* SWAN.

To make someone sing another tune. To make him change his behaviour altogether; to make him submit or humble himself.

To sing in agony, or **tribulation**. Old slang for to confess when put to the torture.

One of the guards said to him, "Signor Cavalier, to sing in agony means, in the cant of these rogues, to confess upon the rack."
CERVANTES: *Don Quixote*, xviii
(*Translation by Motteux*).

To sing out. To cry or squeal from chastisement; to shout or call out.

To sing Placebo. *See* PLACEBO.

To sing small. To cease boasting and assume a quieter tone.

Singe. Singeing the King of Spain's beard. Sir Francis Drake's daring attack on the Spanish ships and stores at Cadiz (1587), which delayed the sailing of the Armada until 1588. He referred to it as his "singeing of the Spanish King's beard".

Single. Single-speech Hamilton. William Gerard Hamilton (1729–1796), who was Chancellor of the Exchequer in IRELAND, 1763–1784. So called from his maiden speech in Parliament (1755), a masterly torrent of eloquence which astounded everyone.

Single Tax. The doctrine that land rent alone should be subject to taxation, propounded by Henry George in *Progress and Poverty* (1879).

Sinis (sī' nis). A Corinthian robber of Greek legend, known as the *Pinebender*, because he used to fasten his victims to two pine-trees bent towards the earth, and then leave them to be rent asunder when the trees were released. He was captured by THESEUS and put to death in the same way.

Sinister (sin' is ter) (Lat., on the left hand). Foreboding of ill; ill-omened. According to AUGURY, birds, etc., appearing on the left-hand side forbode ill luck; but on the right-hand side, good luck. Plutarch, following PLATO and ARISTOTLE, gives as the reason that the west (or left side of the augur) was towards the setting or departing sun.

In HERALDRY it denotes the left side of the shield viewed from the position of its bearer,

i.e. in illustrations it is the right-hand side.

Bar Sinister. *See under* BAR.

Cornix sinistra (Lat., a crow on the left hand) is a sign of ill luck which belongs to English superstitions as much as to the ancient Roman or Etruscan (VIRGIL, *Eclogues*, ix, 15).

That raven on yon left-hand oak
(Curse on his ill-betiding croak)
Bodes me no good.
GAY: *Fable* xxxvii, 27.

Sinking Fund. The name given to the government fund established in 1717, the interest from which was to "sink" or pay off the NATIONAL DEBT. The fund was re-established by Pitt the Younger in 1786, which, as a result of the French Revolutionary Wars, created a loss and was abandoned in 1828. A new fund was set up in 1875 which was remodelled in 1923 and 1928.

Sinn Fein (shin fān) (Irish, "Ourselves alone"). The Irish nationalist movement formed in 1905 which set up the Irish Republic (1919) under De Valera and carried on guerrilla warfare with the English until the treaty of 1922. Disagreements over this settlement disrupted the party, which still aims to bring ULSTER into the Republic.

Sinon (sī' non). The Greek who induced the Trojans to receive the WOODEN HORSE (VIRGIL, *Æneid*, II, 102, etc.). Anyone deceiving to betray is called "a Sinon".

Sir. Lat. *senex*; Span. *señor*; Ital. *signore*; Fr. *sieur*, sire.

As a title of honour prefixed to the Christian name of BARONETS and KNIGHTS, *Sir* is of great antiquity; and the CLERGY had at one time *Sir* prefixed to their name. This is merely a translation of the university word *dominus* given to graduates, as "Dominus Hugh Evans", etc. Spenser uses the title as a substantive, meaning a parson:

But this good Sir did follow the plaine word.
Mother Hubberds Tale, 390.

Sirat, Al. *See* AL-SIRAT.

Siren (sī' rėn). One of the mythical monsters, half woman and half bird, said by Greek poets (*see Odyssey*, XII) to entice seamen by the sweetness of their song to such a degree that the listeners forgot everything and died of hunger (Gr. *sirenes*, entanglers); hence applied to any dangerous, alluring woman.

In Homeric mythology there were but two sirens; later writers name three, viz. PARTHENOPE, Ligea, and Leucosia; and the number was still further augmented by others.

ULYSSES escaped their blandishments by filling his companions' ears with wax and lashing himself to the mast of his ship.

> What Song the Syrens sang, or what name Achilles assumed when he hid himself among women, though puzzling questions, are not beyond all conjecture.
>
> SIR THOS. BROWNE: *Urn Burial*, v.

PLATO says there were three kinds of sirens—the *celestial*, the *generative*, and the *cathartic*. The first were under the government of JUPITER, the second under that of NEPTUNE, and the third of PLUTO. When the SOUL is in HEAVEN the sirens seek, by harmonic motion, to unite it to the divine life of the celestial host; and when in HADES, to conform it to the infernal regimen; but on earth they produce generation, of which the sea is emblematic (Proclus: *On the Theology of Plato*, Bk. VI).

In more recent times the word has been applied to the loud mechanical whistle sounded at a factory, etc., to indicate that work is to be started or finished for the day. Sirens with two or more recognizable notes were employed in World War II to give warning of the approach or departure of hostile aircraft.

Siren suit. A one-piece lined and warm garment on the lines of a boiler suit, sometimes worn in London during the air raids of World War II. It was much favoured by Sir Winston Churchill and so named from its being slipped on over night clothes at the first wail of the SIREN.

Sirius (sir′ i ùs). The DOG-STAR; so called by the Greeks from the adjective *seirios*, hot and scorching. The Romans called it *canicula*, whence our CANICULAR DAYS, and the Egyptians *sept*, which gave the Greek alternative *sothis*. *See* SOTHIC YEAR.

Sirloin. Properly *surloin*, from Fr. *surlonge*, above the loin. The mistaken spelling *sir*- has given rise to a number of stories of the joint having been 'knighted' because of its estimable qualities. Thomas Fuller (1608–1661) tells us that Henry VIII did so:

> Dining with the Abbot of Reading, he [Henry VIII] ate so heartily of a loin of beef that the abbot said he would give 1,000 marks for such a stomach. "Done!" said the king, and kept the abbot a prisoner in the Tower, won his 1,000 marks, and knighted the beef.
>
> *Church History*, VI, ii (1655).

Another tradition fathers the joke on James I:

> "I vow, 'tis a noble sirloin!"
> "Ay, here's cut and come again."
> "But pray, why is it called a sirloin?"
> "Why you must know that our King James I, who loved good eating, being invited to dinner by one of his nobles, and seeing a large loin of beef at his table, he drew out his sword, and in a frolic knighted it. Few people know the secret of this."
>
> JONATHAN SWIFT: *Polite Conversation*, ii.

He is said to have performed this act in 1617 when passing the night at Hoghton Tower, near Blackburn, as the guest of Sir Richard Hoghton.

And yet another on Charles II.

In any case the joke is an old one; in Taylor the WATER POET's *Great Eater of Kent* (1680), we read of one who:

> should presently enter combate with a worthy knight, called Sir Loyne of Beefe, and overthrow him.

Sirocco. *See* AUSTER.

Sise Lane. *See* TOOLEY STREET.

Sistine (sis′ tin, sis′ tēn). **The Sistine Chapel.** The principal chapel in the VATICAN, reserved for ceremonies at which the POPE is present, so called because it was built by Pope Sixtus IV (1471–1484). It is decorated with frescoes by MICHELANGELO and others.

Sistine Madonna, The (*Madonna di San Sisto*). The Madonna painted by Raphael (*c*. 1518) for the church of St. Sixtus (San Sisto) at Piacenza; St. Sixtus is shown kneeling at the right of the Virgin. The picture is now in the Royal Gallery, Dresden.

Sisyphus (sis′ i fùs) ("The Crafty"). In Greek legend, the son of ÆOLUS and husband of MEROPE; in post-Homeric legend, the father of Odysseus (ULYSSES). His punishment in the world of the SHADES was to roll a huge stone up a hill to the top. As it constantly rolled down again just as it reached the summit, his task was everlasting; hence "a labour of Sisyphus" or "Sisyphean toil" is an endless, heart-breaking job. The reasons given for this punishment vary. *See* AUTOLYCUS.

Sit. To make one sit up. To astonish or disconcert one considerably; to subject to punishment or hard work.

To sit down under. To submit tamely to; to put up with.

To sit like patience on a monument. To be exceptionally patient and long suffering. From the apparent patience of a statue.

> She sat like patience on a monument,
> Smiling at grief.
>
> SHAKESPEARE: *Twelfth Night*, II, iv.

To sit on, or **upon.** To snub, squash, smother, put in his place. *Sit on* has other meanings also; thus *to sit on a corpse* is to hold a coroner's inquest on it; *to sit on the bench* is to occupy a seat as a judge or magistrate.

To sit on the fence. *See under* FENCE.

To sit tight. Not to give up your seat; to keep your counsel; to remain in or as in hiding. The phrase is from poker, where, if a player does not want to continue betting and at the same time does not wish to throw in his cards, he "sits tight".

To sit under. To be one of the congregation of the clergyman named; to listen to.

There would also appear in pulpits other visages, other gestures, and stuff otherwise wrought than what we now sit under, oft-times to as great a trial of our patience as any other that they preach to us.

MILTON: *Of Education* (1644).

Sit down strike. A strike in which the workers remain at their factory, etc., but refuse to work themselves or allow others to do so. A tactic begun in the 1930s.

A Sit-in. Similar to a sit-down strike, currently applied to students occupying college premises, but boycotting lectures, etc., with the object of redressing grievances or dictating policy. *See* BOYCOTT.

Sitting Bull (*c.* 1834–1890). A famous Sioux chief who resisted the governmental policy of reservations for his tribe. He defeated Custer in 1876 (*See* CUSTER'S LAST STAND) and later appeared in BUFFALO BILL'S show. He was killed while resisting arrest during the Sioux rebellion of 1890.

Sitzkrieg (sits' krēg). The "sitting war", the descriptive term applied (in contrast to *Blitzkrieg*) to the period of comparative quiet and seeming military inactivity at the outset of World War II (September 1939–April 1940); the period of the PHONEY war.

Siva, or **Shiva** (sē' va, shē' va). The third member of the Hindu TRIMURTI, representing the destructive principle in life and also the reproductive or renovating power. He has other contrasting qualities, being a god of ascetics as well as of music, dancing, and learning; in all a god of many attributes and functions. Siva, which means "The Benevolent", is only one of his many names. He is generally represented with three eyes and four arms and his symbol is the *lingam*.

Six. The Six. The six countries—Belgium, France, Germany, Italy, the Netherlands, and Luxemburg, who were the original participants in three economic communities. These are: the European Coal and Steel Community, 1951 (ECSC); the European Economic Community or Common Market (EEC), set up by the Treaty of Rome, 1957; and the European Atomic Energy Community or Euratom, 1957. *Cp.* THE SEVEN.

Les Six. A group of French composers formed at Paris in 1918 under the ÆGIS of Jean Cocteau and Erik Satie, in order to further their interests and those of modern music generally. The group lost its cohesion in the 1920s. Its members were Honegger, Milhaud, Poulenc, Durey, Auric, and Tailleferre.

The Six Acts. The name given to the six measures sponsored by the Liverpool Ministry in 1819 to curb RADICAL agitation and popular disorder after PETERLOO. They were not all unreasonable. These measures restricted public meetings; shortened procedures in bringing cases to trial (to deal with political agitators more speedily); forbade the drilling of private persons; empowered magistrates to seize blasphemous and seditious literature; authorized the seizure of arms; and extended the stamp duties on newspapers and periodicals.

The Six Articles. The so-called "Whip with six strings", otherwise known as the "Bloody Bill", the Statute of Six Articles passed in 1539 to secure uniformity in matters of religion. It was repealed in 1547 under Edward VI. The articles maintained (1) TRANSUBSTANTIATION; (2) the sufficiency of Communion in one kind; (3) clerical celibacy; (4) the obligation of monastic vows; (5) the propriety of private masses; (6) the necessity of auricular confession. Penalties were imposed for non-observance including death at the stake for those who spoke against transubstantiation.

Six Clerks Office. An old name for the Court of CHANCERY, from the six clerks who received and filed all Chancery proceedings, each of whom had ten subordinates. The Six Clerks, who also had charge of causes in court, were abolished in 1842.

The Six Counties. Another name for ULSTER or Northern Ireland, *i.e.* Armagh, Antrim, Down, Derry, Fermanagh and Tyrone.

The Six Nations. The FIVE NATIONS together with the Tuscaroras.

The Six Points of Ritualism. Altar lights, eucharistic vestments, the mixed chalice, incense, unleavened bread, and the eastward position. So called when English Ritualists and upholders of the OXFORD MOVEMENT sought to reintroduce them in the 1870s.

The six-foot way. The strip of ground between two sets of railway lines.

A six-hooped pot. A two-quart pot. Quart pots were bound with three hoops, and when three men joined in drinking, each man drank his hoop. Mine host of the Black Bear (Scott: *Kenilworth*, ch. iii), calls Tressilian "a six-hooped pot of a traveller", meaning a first-class guest, because he paid freely, and made no complaints.

Six-Principle Baptists. A sect of Arminian Baptists, founded about 1639, who based their creed on the six principles enunciated in *Heb.* vi, 1–2: repentance, faith, BAPTISM, laying on of hands, the resurrection of the dead, and eternal judgment.

The Six-stringed Whip. The SIX ARTICLES (*see above*).

At sixes and sevens. Higgledy-piggledy, in a state of confusion; or of persons, unable to come to an agreement, at LOGGERHEADS. The phrase comes from dicing. Udall (*Erasmus' Apothegmes*, 1542) says "There is a proverb *Omnem jacere aleam*, to cast all dice by which is signified to set all on six and seven … assaying the wild chance of fortune, be it good, be it bad".

It is also traditionally held that the expression arose out of a dispute between two of the great LIVERY COMPANIES, the Merchant Taylors and the Skinners as to which was sixth and which seventh in the order of the companies going in processions in THE CITY, both companies having been chartered in 1327 within a few days of each other. In 1484 they submitted the matter to the judgment of the Mayor, Sir Robert Billesden, and the Aldermen. The award was that the Master and Wardens of both companies were to dine each other annually and that the Skinners were to precede the Taylors in that year's procession. The next year the Taylors were to take the sixth place and this alternation was to continue "ever more".

> Lat not this wreched wo thyne herte gnawe,
> But manly, set the world on six and sevene,
> And if thou deye a martyr, to go hevene.
> CHAUCER: *Troilus*, iv, 622 (*c.* 1386).

The six-o'clock swill. In parts of Australia bars formerly closed at 6 p.m. Drinkers leaving their jobs at 5.30 therefore tended to guzzle rapidly to beat the clock. This was termed the six-o'clock swill.

Six of one and half a dozen of the other. There is nothing to choose between them, they|are|both in the wrong—ARCADES AMBO.

Six of the best. In the earlier decades of the present century, when corporal chastisement was still the normal and usually effective way of punishing schoolboys for wrongdoing and bad behaviour, it meant six strokes of the cane across the delinquent's posterior given by the headmaster or one of his assistants.

Sixpence. *See* TANNER.

Sixteen-string Jack. John Rann, a highwayman (hanged 1774), noted for his foppery. He wore 16 tags, eight at each knee.

Sixty-four (or **Sixty-four thousand**) **dollar question** (U.S.A.). The last and most difficult question, the crux of the problem; from the stake money awarded in a QUIZ for answering the final question.

Did that mean the whole area had extractable tin underneath it? "That's the 64,000 dollar question".
> *Sunday Telegraph* (5 August 1979).

Sizar (sī′ zàr). An undergraduate of Cambridge, or of Trinity College, Dublin, who receives a grant from his college to assist in paying his expenses. Formerly sizars were expected to undertake certain menial duties now performed by college servants; and the name is taken to show that one so assisted received his sizes or SIZINGS free.

Sizings. The allowance of food provided by the college for undergraduates at a meal; a pound loaf, two inches of butter, and a pot of milk used to be the "sizings" for breakfast; meat was provided for dinner, but any extras had to be *sized* for. The word is a contraction of *assize*, a statute to regulate the size or weight of articles sold.

Skains-mate. The meaning of the word is uncertain but *skene* or *skean* is the long dagger formerly carried by the Irish and Scots, so it may mean a dagger-comrade or fellow cutthroat. Swift, describing an Irish feast (1720), says, "A cubit at least the length of their skains", and Greene, in his *Quip for an Upstart Courtier* (1592), speaks of "an ill-favoured knave, who wore by his side a skane, like a brewer's bung knife".

> Scurvy knave! I am none of his flirt-gills; I am none of his skains-mates.
> SHAKESPEARE: *Romeo and Juliet*, II, iv.

Skanda. *See* KARTTIKEYA.

Skeleton. The family skeleton, or **the skeleton in the cupboard.** Some domestic source of worry or shame which the family conspires to keep to itself; every family is said to have at least one!

The story is that someone without a single care or trouble in the world had to be found. After long and unsuccessful search a lady was discovered who all thought would "fill the bill"; but to the great surprise of the inquirers, after she had satisfied them on all points and the quest seemed to be achieved, she took them upstairs and there opened a closet which contained a human skeleton. "I try", said she, "to keep my trouble to myself, but every night my husband compels me to kiss that skeleton." She then explained that the skeleton was once her husband's rival, killed in a duel. The expression was given literary use by Thackeray—

> And it is from these that we shall arrive at some particulars regarding the Newcome family, which will show us that they have a skeleton or two in their closets as well as their neighbours.
> *The Newcomes* (1855) ch. lv.

The skeleton at the feast. The thing or person that acts as a reminder that there are troubles as well as pleasures in life. Plutarch says in his *Moralia* that the Egyptians always had a skeleton placed in a prominent position at their banquets.

Skevington's daughter. *See* SCAVENGER'S.

Skid Row. An American expression applied to a district abounding in vicious characters and down-and-outs. In the lumber industry a *skid row* was a row of logs down which other felled timber was slid or skidded. Early on, Tacoma, near Seattle, flourished on its lumber production and in due course liquor and loose women became available for loggers descending the skid row. The usage may well derive from this situation.

Skidbladnir. In Scandinavian mythology, the magic ship made by the DWARFS for FREYR. It was big enough to take all the ÆSIR with their weapons and equipment, yet when not in use could be folded up and carried by Freyr in his pouch. It sailed through both air and water, and went straight to its destination as soon as the sails were hoisted. *Cp.* CARPET.

Skiddaw (skid′ aw). **Whenever Skiddaw hath a cap, Scruffell wots full well of that** (Fuller, *Worthies*). When my neighbour's house is on fire mine is threatened; when you are in misfortune I am also a sufferer; when you mourn I have cause also to lament. When Skiddaw is capped with clouds, it will be sure to rain ere long at Scawfell.

Skiffle. A name given to a style of JAZZ of the 1920s, and more recently to a type of jazz folk-music current in Britain in the late 1950s played by a skiffle group, consisting of guitar, drums, kazoo, washboard, and other improvised instruments.

Skills. It skills not (archaic). It makes no difference; it doesn't matter one way or the other.

> Whether he [Callimachus] be now lying I know not but whether he be or no, it skilleth not.
>> LYLY: *Euphues and His England* (1580).

Similarly, **What skills talking?** What is the use of talking?

Skimble-skamble. Rambling, worthless. "Skamble" is merely a variant of *scramble*, hence "scambling days", those days in LENT when no regular meals are provided, but each person "scrambles" or shifts for himself. "Skimble" is added to give force.

> And such a deal of skimble-skamble stuff
> As put me from my faith.
>> SHAKESPEARE: *Henry IV, Pt.* I, III, i.

Skimmington. It was an old custom in rural ENGLAND and SCOTLAND to make an example of nagging wives by forming a ludicrous procession through the village accompanied by ROUGH MUSIC to ridicule the offender. A man, mounted on a horse with a distaff in his hand, rode behind the woman with his face to the horse's tail, while the woman beat him about the jowls with a ladle. As the procession passed a house where the woman was paramount the participants gave the threshold a sweep. The event was called *riding the Skimmington* (*cp.* To ride the STANG). The origin of the name is uncertain, but in an illustration of 1639 the woman is shown belabouring her husband with a skimming-ladle. Unfaithful husbands were similarly put to scorn. The procession is fully described in Butler's *Hudibras*, II, ii:

> Near whom the Amazon triumphant
> Bestrid her beast, and, on the rump on't,
> Sat face to tail and bum to bum,
> The warrior whilom overcome,
> Arm'd with a spindle and a distaff,
> Which, as he rode, she made him twist off:
> And when he loiter'd, o'er her shoulder
> Chastis'd the reformado soldier.

Scott alludes to it in the *Fortunes of Nigel*, ch. xxi:

> "Remember I am none of your husband—and, if I were, you would do well not to forget whose threshold was swept when they last rode the Skimmington upon such another scolding jade as yourself."

For another example see Hardy's *Mayor of Casterbridge*, ch. xxxix, where the *skimmity ride* causes the death of Lucetta Farfrae. *Cp.* RIDING; SHALLAL.

Skin. By the skin of one's teeth. Only just, by a mere hair's breadth. The phrase comes from the book of *Job* (xix, 20):

> My bone cleaveth to my skin, and to my flesh, and I am escaped with the skin of my teeth.

Coverdale's rendering of the passage is:

> My bone hangeth to my skynne, and the flesh is awaye only there is left me the skynne aboute my teth.

To get under one's skin. To irritate, to annoy. Probably an allusion to the activities of such larvæ as harvest-bugs, etc., which cause intense irritation "under the skin".

To have a thick skin. To be insensitive or indifferent to jibes, criticism or even insults; "to have a hide like a rhinoceros". Similarly **to have a thin skin** is to be hypersensitive about such things.

To save one's skin. To get off with one's life.

To sell the skin before you have caught the bear. To count your chickens before they are hatched. SHAKESPEARE alludes to a similar practice:

> The man that once did sell the lion's skin
> While the beast lived, was killed with hunting him.
>> *Henry V*, IV, iii.

To skin a flint. To be very exacting in making a bargain. The French say, *Tondre sur un œuf*. The Latin *lana caprina* (goat's wool) means something as worthless as the skin of a flint or fleece of an eggshell. Hence a **skinflint**, a pinch-farthing, a niggard.

Skin game. A swindling trick. Presumably from the sense of *skin* meaning to fleece or strip someone of their money by sharp practice or fraud. John Galsworthy has a play of this title (1920).

Skinhead. A young person, usually member of a gang, with hair very closely cropped or shaved off, making their appearance from the late 1960s. *Cp.* MODS AND ROCKERS; PUNK.

Skinners. A predatory band in the American Revolutionary War which roamed over Westchester County, New York, robbing and fleecing those who refused to take the oath of fidelity to the Republic. *See also* LIV-ERY COMPANIES.

Skirt. A skirt, or **a piece of skirt** is English slang for a girl or young woman.

To sit upon one's skirt. To insult, or seek occasion of quarrel. Tarlton, the clown, told his audience the reason why he wore a jacket was that "no one might sit upon his skirt". Sitting on one's skirt is, like "stamping on one's coat" in IRELAND a friutful source of quarrels, often provoked. *Cp.* To trail one's COAT.

> Crosse me not, Liza, neither be so perte,
> For if thou dost, I'll sit upon thy skirte.
> *The Abortive of an Idle Houre* (1620).

Skull. Skull and Crossbones. An emblem of mortality; specifically, the pirate's flag. The "crossbones" are two human thigh-bones laid across one another.

Sky. RHYMING SLANG for pocket, the missing word being *rocket*.

If tke sky falls we shall catch larks. A bantering reply to those who suggest some very improbable or wild scheme.

Lauded to the skies. Extravagantly praised; praised to the heights.

Out of a clear sky. Unexpectedly, without warning, "out of the blue".

Skyhook. Where an overhead hook could be useful or necessary in certain work operations, a GREENHORN is despatched by his more experienced workmates to fetch a "sky-hook". *Cp.* GOLDEN RIVET.

Skyjacker. A criminal who secures passage on an airliner with the intent to terrorise the crew into furthering his particular ends. Skyjackers are mostly anarchists or terrorists but robbers and lunatics are also among them. *Cp.* HIJACKER.

Sky-pilot. A clergyman or padre. Originally a sailor's expression in use from late-Victorian days. The allusion is obvious.

Skysail. In a square-rigged ship, a sail next above the fore-royal, the main-royal, or the mizzen royal.

Skyscraper. A very tall building, especially one in New York or some other American city. Some of them run to a hundred floors, and more. Also applied by sailors to a SKY-SAIL.

To skylark about. To amuse oneself in a frolicsome way, jump around and be merry, indulge in mild horseplay. The phrase was originally nautical and referred to the sports of the boys among the rigging after work was done.

Slam. A term in card-playing denoting winning all the tricks in a deal. In bridge this is called *Grand slam*, and winning all but one, *Little or Small slam*. *Cp.* RUFF.

Slam. To slam the door (in someone's face). To refuse discussion; to dismiss abruptly; to put an end to the possibility of further negotiations.

Slang. As denoting language or jargon of a low or colloquial type the word first appeared in the 18th century; it is perhaps connected with *sling* (*cp.* *mud-slinging*, for hurling abuse). Slang is of various kinds, professional, sporting, schoolboy, nautical, thieves', etc., and usually has some element of humour about it. *See* BACK-SLANG; CANT; RHYMING SLANG.

A slanging match. A lengthy exchange of abuse and insulting language.

To slang a person. To abuse him, give him a piece of your mind.

Slap. Slap-bang. At once, without hesitation—done with a *slap* and a *bang*. The term was formerly applied to cheap eating-houses, where one *slapped* one's money down as the food was *banged* on the table.

> They lived in the same street, walked to town every morning at the same hour, dined at the same slap-bang every day.
> DICKENS: *Sketches by Boz*, iii, 36.

Slap-dash. In an off-hand manner, done hurriedly as with a *slap* and a *dash*. Rooms used to be decorated by *slapping* and *dashing* the walls so as to imitate paper, and at one time *slap-dash* walls were very common.

Slap-happy. Foolish and irresponsible, as one who is dazed, akin to PUNCH-DRUNK.

Slapstick. Literally the two or more laths bound together at one end with which HAR-LEQUINS, CLOWNS, etc., strike other performers with a resounding *slap* or crack; but more often applied to any broad comedy with knock-about action and horseplay.

Slap-up. First-rate, grand, stylish.

The more slap-up still have the two shields painted on the panels with the coronet over.

THACKERAY: *The Newcomes*, xxxi.

Slate. On the slate. On the account, to be paid for later. From the custom of chalking up debts on a *slate* in shops and public houses.

Slate Club. A sick benefit club for working-men. Originally the names of the members and the money paid in were entered on a folding *slate*.

To have a slate, or **tile loose.** *See under* TILE.

To slate one. To reprove, abuse, or criticize one savagely. It is not known how the term arose, but perhaps it is because at school the names of bad boys were chalked up on the *slate* as an exposure.

The journalists there lead each other a dance,
If one man "slates" another for what he has done,
It is pistols for two, and then coffin for one.
Punch (The Pugnacious Penmen), 1885.

To start with a clean slate. To be given another chance, one's past misdeeds having been forgiven and expunged, as writing is sponged from a *slate*. **To wipe the slate clean** is a similar expression, meaning to cancel past debts or offences.

Slave. An example of the way words acquire changed meanings. The *Slavi* or *Slavs* were a tribe which once dwelt on the banks of the Dnieper; but as, in later days of the Roman Empire, many of them were spread over Europe as captives, the word acquired its present meaning.

The Slave Coast. The west coast of Africa around the Bight of Benin, between the River Volta and Mount Cameroon; for 350 years the chief source of African slaves.

The Slave States. A phrase current in the period before the American CIVIL WAR (1861–1865) and applied to the states where domestic slavery was practised, *i.e.* Delaware, Maryland, Virginia, North Carolina, South Carolina, Georgia, Florida, Alabama, Mississippi, Louisiana, Texas, Arkansas, Missouri, Kentucky, and Tennessee.

Chinese Slavery. *See* CHINESE.

Sledge-hammer. A sledge-hammer argument. A clincher; an argument which annihilates opposition at a blow. The sledge-hammer (O.E. *slecge*) is the largest hammer used by smiths, etc., and is wielded in both hands.

To use a sledge-hammer to crack a nut. *See under* NUT.

Sleep. To let sleeping dogs lie. *See under* DOG.

To put to sleep. Commonly used as a EUPHEMISM for painlessly putting to death pet animals.

To sleep away. To pass away in sleep, to consume in sleeping; as "To sleep one's life away."

To sleep like a log, or **top.** To sleep very soundly, excellently, go the night through without waking or discomfort. When peg-tops are at the ACME of their gyration, they become so steady and quiet that they do not seem to move; in this state they are said to "sleep". Congreve plays on the two meanings:

Hang him, no, he a dragon! If he be, 'tis a very peaceful one. I can ensure his anger dormant, or should he seem to rouse, 'tis but well lashing him and he will sleep like a top.
Old Bachelor, I, v.

To sleep off. To get rid of by sleep, especially the after-effects of alcohol.

To sleep on a matter. To let a decision on it stand over until tomorrow.

The Sleeper. EPIMENIDES, the Greek poet, is said to have fallen asleep in a cave when a boy, and not to have waked for 57 years, when he found himself possessed of all wisdom.

In mediæval legend, stories of those who have gone to sleep and have been—or are to be—awakened after many years are very numerous. Such legends are associated with King ARTHUR, CHARLEMAGNE, and BARBAROSSA. *Cp.* also the stories of the SEVEN SLEEPERS of Ephesus, TANNHÄUSER, OGIER THE DANE, and RIP VAN WINKLE.

The Seven Sleepers. *See under* SEVEN.

The Sleeper Awakened. *See* SLY, CHRISTOPHER.

Sleepers. In Britain the supports for the chairs (usually of timber) which carry railway lines (from the Norwegian *sleip*, a roller or timber laid along a road). In the U.S.A. these supports are called *ties*. A *sleeper* also denotes a railway sleeping-car.

The Sleeping Beauty. This charming nursery tale comes from the French *La Belle au Bois Dormant*, by Charles Perrault (1628–1703) (*Contes de ma mère l'Oye*, 1697). The Princess is shut up by enchantment in a castle, where she sleeps a hundred years, during which time an impenetrable wood springs up around. Ultimately she is released by the kiss of a young prince, who marries her.

Sleeping partner. A partner in a business who takes no active share in running it beyond supplying capital; also called a *silent partner* in the U.S.A.

Sleeping sickness. A West African disease caused by a parasite, *Trypanosoma gambiense*, characterized by fever and great sleepiness, and often terminating fatally. The disease known in England, which shows similar symptoms, is usually called *Sleeping illness* or *Sleepy sickness* as a means of distinction; its scientific name is *Encephalitis lethargica*.

Sleepy. Said of pears and other fruits when they are beginning to rot.

Sleepy Hollow. Any village far removed from the active concerns of the outside world. From Washington Irving's story "The Legend of Sleepy Hollow" (*Sketch Book*), which deals with a quiet old-world village on the Hudson.

Sleepy sickness. *See* SLEEPING SICKNESS above.

Sleeve. To hang on one's sleeve. To listen devoutly to what one says; to surrender freedom of thought and action to the judgment of another.

To have up one's sleeve. To hold in reserve; to have ready to bring out in a case of emergency. The allusion is to conjurers, who frequently conceal in the sleeve the means by which they do the trick.

To laugh in, or **up one's sleeve.** To laugh inwardly; to hold in derision secretly. At one time it was quite possible to conceal amusement by hiding the face in the large loose sleeves then worn. The French say, *rire sous cape*.

To pin to one's sleeve, as "I shan't pin my faith to your sleeve", meaning, "I shall not slavishly believe or follow you". The allusion is to the practice of KNIGHTS, in the days of CHIVALRY, pinning to their sleeve some token given them by their lady-love. This token was a pledge that they would do or die.

To wear one's heart on one's sleeve. To expose all one's feelings to the eyes of the world; to be lacking in normal reserve.

> But I will wear my heart upon my sleeve
> For daws to peck at: I am not what I am.
> SHAKESPEARE: *Othello*, I, i.

Sleeveless. In the 16th and 17th centuries *sleeveless* was commonly used to signify fruitless, bootless, unprofitable, as *a sleeveless message*, *a sleeveless errand*, etc. The reason for this usage is uncertain.

Sleuth-hound. A blood-hound which follows the *sleuth* (Old Norse *sloth*, our more modern *slot*) or track of an animal. Hence used, especially in America, of a detective.

Sliding scale. A scale of duties, prices, payments, etc., which "slides" upwards and downwards in relation to the fluctuations in the cost of the article, etc., to which it relates. Thus in the famous Sliding-scale CORN LAW (*see under* CORN) of 1828, the duty varied inversely to the home price of corn, *i.e.* as the price of corn went up the duty went down.

Slip. Many a slip 'twixt the cup and the lip. Everything is uncertain till you possess it. *Cp.* ANCÆUS.

To give one the slip. To steal off unperceived; to elude pursuit. Probably from the idea of a hound slipping its collar or from the slipping of an anchor when it is necessary to get away quickly from an uncomfortable berth. The normal practice in such circumstances is to buoy the cable before letting it slip through the hawse-pipe, so that anchor and cable are recoverable subsequently.

To let it slip through one's fingers. To fail to seize a chance at the favourable moment, as an unprepared fielder drops a catch in CRICKET.

To let slip. To tell unintentionally when off one's guard, as a hound might be let slip unintentionally in coursing.

To slip one over on. To deceive or hoodwink; to "put one over" on someone; to "pull a fast one" (*see under* FAST).

To slip the cable, To slip one's cable. *See under* CABLE.

To slip up. Metaphorically, to make a mistake, usually through an oversight.

Sloane Ranger. A young upper class or upper-middle class person who is disciplined, good mannered, well educated, speaking B.B.C. English of the days of Sir John Reith's management (1922–1938). Sloanes are conservative in dress, the women having no freakish hair styles and the men being clean shaven. The women wear informal country clothes and the men the clothes of a City gentleman or country squire, those in town living around Sloane Street, Holland Park and Kensington. The name was originated by Peter York, author of *Style Wear* (1982). *The Sloane Ranger Handbook* by Ann Barr and Peter York elaborated the theme.

Slogan (slō′găn). The war-cry of the old Highland CLANS (Gael. *sluagh*, host; *ghairm*, outcry). Hence, any war-cry; and in later use, a political party cry, an advertising catchphrase, etc. *Cp.* SLUG-HORN.

Slop, Dr. So William Hone called Sir John Stoddart (1773–1856), a choleric lawyer and journalist who assailed NAPOLEON most virulently in *The Times* (1812–1816). The allusion was to Dr. Slop, the ignorant man-midwife in Sterne's *Tristram Shandy*.

Slope. The slippery slope. The broad and easy way "that leadeth to destruction". *See* AVERNUS.

Slops. Police; originally "ecilop". *See* BACK-

> I dragged you in here and saved you,
> And sent out a gal for the slops;
> Ha! they're acomin', sir! Listen!
> The noise and the shoutin' stops.
>
> SIMS: *Ballads of Babylon* (*The Matron's Story*).

Slops is also an old name for a loose garment (O.E. *slyp*, *slype*) and in the Royal Navy the term *slops* has long been applied to the clothing, towels, blankets, etc., sold from the ship's store which is known as the *slop-shop*.

Slough of Despond. A period of, or fit of, great depression. In Bunyan's *Pilgrim's Progress*, Pt. I, it is a deep bog which Christian has to cross in order to get to the Wicket Gate. Help comes to his aid, but Neighbour Pliable turns back.

Slow. Slow-coach. A dawdler; also one who is mentally slow. A usage from the old coaching days.

Slow-worm. *See* MISNOMERS.

Slubberdegullion (slŭb er de gŭl′ yon). A base fellow, a nasty oaf. To *slubber* is to do things carelessly, in a slovenly way; *degullion* is a fanciful addition, *gullion* being a variant of *cullion*, a base fellow.

> Quoth she, Although thou hast deserved,
> Base-slubber degullion, to be served
> As thou didst vow to deal with me.
>
> BUTLER: *Hudibras*, I, iii.

Slugabed. A late riser. To *slug* used to be quite good English for "to be thoroughly lazy". Sylvester has:

> The Soldier, slugging long at home in Peace
> His wonted courage quickly doth decrease.
>
> DU BARTAS: *Collected Works*, I, vii, 340 (1592).

Slug-horn. A battle-trumpet; the word being the result of an erroneous reading by Chatterton of the GAELIC *slogan*. He thought the word sounded rather well; and as he did not know what it meant, gave it a meaning that suited him:

> Some caught a slughorne and an onsett wounde.
>
> *The Battle of Hastings*, ii, 99.

Browning adopted it in the last line but one of his *Childe Rolande to the Dark Tower Came*, and thus this "GHOSTWORD" got a footing in the language.

Sly, Christopher. A keeper of bears and a tinker, son of a pedlar, and a sad drunken sot in the *Induction* of *The Taming of the Shrew*. SHAKESPEARE mentions him as a well-known character of Wincot, a hamlet near Stratford-on-Avon, and it is more than probable that in him we have an actual portrait of a contemporary.

Sly is found dead drunk by a lord, who commands his servants to put him to bed, and on his waking to attend upon him like a lord and bamboozle him into the belief that he is a great man; the play is performed for his delectation. The same trick was played by the Caliph HAROUN AL-RASCHID on ABOU HASSAN, the rich merchant, in *The Sleeper Awakened* (ARABIAN NIGHTS).

Sly. On the sly. In a sly, secretive manner.

You're a sly dog. You're a knowing one; you pretend to be discontented, but I can "read between the lines". (*See under* LINE).

Sly-boots. A cunning one, a WAG. A similar compound to *lazy-boots*, *clumsy-boots*, etc.

Smack. A slang term for heroin. *Cp.* GRASS.

Small. Small arms (Lat. *arma*, arms, fittings). Weapons fired from the hand or shoulder such as revolvers and rifles, also light portable machine-guns, etc.

Small-back. Death. So called because he is usually drawn as a skeleton.

Small beer. Properly, beer of only slight alcoholic strength; hence, trivialities, persons or things of small consequence.

Small clothes. Once a term for breeches, now for underclothes or "smalls".

Small coal. Coal in very small pieces, slack.

Small-endians. *See* BIG-ENDIANS.

Small fry. A humorous way of referring to a number of small children, from the numerous *fry* or young of fish and other creatures.

Small holding. A small plot of agricultural land bigger than an allotment, but not big enough to be called a farm. The term received legal significance under the Small Holdings Act of 1892, which permitted County Councils to provide them for letting. The Small Holdings and Allotments Act of 1926 defined them as of not less than an acre and not more than 50, and of not more than £100 in annual value.

The small hours. The hours from 1 a.m. to 4 or 5 a.m., when you are still in the *small*, or low numbers.

The small of the back. The slenderer, narrower part, just above the buttocks.

Small talk. Trifling conversation, social chit-chat.

A small and early. An evening party on a modest scale, with not many guests, and not late hours.

To feel small. To feel humiliated, "taken down a PEG or two".

To sing small. To adopt a humble tone; to withdraw some sturdy assertion and apologize for having made it.

Smalls. The undergraduate name at Oxford for *Responsions*, at one time the first of the three examinations for the B.A. degree, similar to the Cambridge LITTLE-GO; the final examination being called *Greats* (*see* GREAT-GO). It later became the official university entrance examination until the growing use of the School Certificate, and later General Certificate of Education, examinations led to its discontinuance. Smalls were last held in September 1960. *See* SMALL CLOTHES *above*.

Smart Alec(k). An American term for a bumptious, conceited know-all. The name goes back to the 1860s, but no record now remains of Alec's identity.

Smart Money. Money paid by a person to obtain exemption from some disagreeable office or duty. It was applied to money paid by an army recruit to obtain release before being sworn in, and also to money paid to soldiers and sailors for wounds. In law it denotes heavy damages. It is something which makes the person "smart" (*i.e.* suffer), or which is received in payment for "smarting".

Smear. A smear campaign. A planned or organized attempt to tarnish someone's character or reputation.

Smectymnuus (smek tim′ nū ŭs). The name under which was published (1641) an anti-episcopal tract in answer to Bishop Hall's *Humble Remonstrance*. The name was composed of the initials of its authors, *viz.* Stephen Marshall, Edward Calamy, Thomas Young, Matthew Newcomen, and William Spurstow.

Thomas Young was Milton's former tutor, and Milton seems to have had a part in it and wrote pamphlets in defence of the Smectymnuans.

> The handkerchief about the neck,
> Canonical cravat of Smec.
> BUTLER: *Hudibras*, I, iii, 1165.

Smell, To. Often used figuratively for to suspect, to discern intuitively, as in *I smell a rat, I smell treason*, etc.

SHAKESPEARE has, "Do you smell a fault?" (*King Lear*, I, i); and Iago says to Othello, "One may smell in such a will most rank" (III, iii). St. JEROME says that St. Hilarion had the gift of knowing what sins and vices anyone was inclined to by smelling either the person or his garments, and by the same faculty could discern good feelings and virtuous propensities.

It smells of the lamp. *See under* LAMP.

Smiler. Another name for shandy-gaff—a mixture of ale and lemonade or ginger-beer.

Smith. The Smith of Smiths. The Rev. Sydney Smith (1771—1845) was so called by Macaulay. Famous Whig clergyman and canon of St. Paul's, he was renowned as a conversationalist for his drollery and brilliance of wit as well as for the incisive quality of his writings. *See* PARTINGTON.

Smith of Nottingham. Applied to conceited persons who imagine that no one is able to compete with themselves. Ray, in his *Collection of Proverbs*, has the following couplet:

> The little Smith of Nottingham
> Who doth the work that no man can.

Smithfield. The smooth field (O.E. *smethe*, smooth), called in Latin *Campus Planus* and described by Fitz-Stephen in the 12th century as a "plain field where every Friday there is a celebrated rendezvous of fine horses brought thither to be sold". It was originally outside the CITY wall and used for races, QUINTAIN-matches, TOURNAMENTS, etc., as well as a market. BARTHOLOMEW FAIR was held here until 1855, at which time the cattle market was transferred to the CALEDONIAN MARKET. Its less pleasant associations were the gibbet and the stake, and most of the Marian MARTYRS suffered death at Smithfield. It is now the central meat market of London.

The fires of Smithfield. An allusion to the burning of HERETICS at Smithfield during the Marian persecution of PROTESTANTS. Death at the stake was used at Smithfield as late as 1611.

Smoke, or Big Smoke, The. London. An old slang name of obvious origins. *Cp.* AULD REEKIE.

> Till that last awful winter!...when the farmers had been mostly ruined, and half the able-bodied men of Mellor had tramped "up into the smoke", as the village put it, in search of London work...
> MRS HUMPHRY WARD: *Marcella*, Bk. I, ch. ix.

Cape smoke. A cheap and villainous kind of whisky sold in South Africa.

Smoke-farthings, smoke silver. An old church rate, the contribution of each house or hearth; also another name for PENTECOSTALS, the WHITSUNTIDE offering to the parish priest. Also called *smoke-money*, and *smoke-penny*, it appears in records as a contribution to the parochial purse as well as to the priest.

Much smoke, little fire. Said of one who makes a great fuss, commotion or protest but whose actions do not correspond.

No smoke without fire. Every slander or rumour has some foundation. The reverse proverb, **No fire without smoke,** means no good without some drawback.

Put that in your pipe and smoke it. *See under* PIPE.

To end in, or **up in smoke.** To come to no practical result; to come to nothing.

To smoke out. To drive someone out of hiding, literally or metaphorically.

To smoke the pipe of peace. *See* CALU-

MET.

To put up a smokescreen. To take steps to conceal one's basic motives from one's opponents or rivals, or from the public at large. The allusion is obvious.

Snack (a variant of *snatch*).

To go snacks. To share and share alike.

To take a snack. To have a little to eat; "snatch a bite of something".

Snag. To come against a snag. To encounter some obstacle in your progress.

Snake. RHYMING SLANG for a looking-glass, the missing portion being "in the grass".

It was an old idea that snakes in casting their sloughs annually gained new vigour and fresh strength; hence SHAKESPEARE's allusion:

> When the mind is quicken'd out of doubt,
> The organs, though defunct and dead before,
> Break up their drowsy grave, and newly move
> With casted slough and fresh legerity.
> *Henry V*, IV, i.

Another notion was that one could regain one's youth by feeding on snakes:

> You have eat a snake
> And are grown young, gamesome and rampant.
> BEAUMONT and FLETCHER:
> *Elder Brother*, IV, iv.

Snake stones. AMMONITES, from the old belief that these were coiled snakes petrified.

A snake in the grass. A hidden or hypocritical enemy, a disguised danger. The phrase is from VIRGIL (*Ecl*. iii, 93), *Latet anguis in herba*, a snake is lurking in the grass.

Great snakes! An exclamation of surprise.

To see snakes, to have snakes in one's boots, etc. To suffer from delirium tremens. This is one of the delusions common to those so afflicted.

Snake-eyes (U.S.A.). In throwing dice, a double one.

Snap. A snap vote. A vote taken unexpectedly, especially in PARLIAMENT. The result of a "snap vote" has, before now, been the overthrow of a ministry.

Not worth a snap of the fingers. Utterly worthless and negligible.

To snap a person's head off. Virtually the same as *To snap one's nose off. See* TO BITE ONE'S NOSE OFF *under* NOSE.

To snap one's fingers at. To brush aside contemptuously, to disregard authority.

To snap out of it. To shake off a fit of depression, to regain one's good humour, to pull oneself together, etc.

Snapdragon. The same as FLAPDRAGON; also a plant of the genus *Antirrhinum* with a flower opening like a dragon's mouth.

Snapshot. Formerly applied to a shot fired without taking aim, but now almost exclus-

ively to an instantaneous photograph. Hence *to snapshot a person*, to take an instantaneous photograph of him.

Snark. The imaginary animal invented by Lewis Carroll as the subject of his mock-heroic poem *The Hunting of the Snark* (1876). It was most elusive and gave endless trouble, and when eventually the hunters thought they had tracked it down, their quarry proved to be but a Boojum. The name (a "PORTMANTEAU WORD" of snake and shark) has sometimes been given to the quests of dreamers and visionaries.

It was one of Rossetti's delusions that in *The Hunting of the Snark* Lewis Carroll was caricaturing him.

Snarling Letter (Lat. *litera canina*). The letter *r*, *see* R.

Sneck posset. To give one a sneck posset is to give one a cold reception, to slam the door in one's face (Cumbria). The "sneck" is the latch of the door, and to "sneck the door in one's face" is to shut a person out.

Snell, Hannah. *See* THE FEMALE MARINE *under* MARINE.

Sneeze. St. GREGORY has been credited with originating the custom of saying "God bless you" after sneezing, the story being that he enjoined its use during a pestilence in which sneezing was a mortal symptom. ARISTOTLE, however, mentions a similar custom among the Greeks; and Thucydides tells us that sneezing was a crisis symptom of the great Athenian plague.

The Romans followed the same custom, their usual exclamation being *Absit omen!* The PARSEES hold that sneezing indicates that EVIL spirits are abroad, and we find similar beliefs in India, Africa, ancient and modern Persia, among the North American Indian tribes, etc.

We are told that when the Spaniards arrived in FLORIDA the Cacique sneezed, and all the court lifted up their hands and implored the sun to avert the evil omen. The nursery rhyme says:

> If you sneeze on Monday you sneeze for danger;
> Sneeze on Tuesday, kiss a stranger,
> Sneeze on Wednesday, sneeze for a letter,
> Sneeze on Thursday, something better,
> Sneeze on Friday, sneeze for sorrow,
> Sneeze on Saturday, see your sweetheart tomorrow.

It is not to be sneezed at. Not to be despised.

Snood. The lassie lost her silken snood. The snood was a ribbon with which a Scots lass braided her hair, and was the emblem of her maiden character. When she married, she changed the snood for the curch or coif; but if she lost the name of virgin before she obtained that of wife, she "lost her silken snood" and was not privileged to assume the curch.

In more recent times the word has been applied to the net in which women confine their hair.

Snooks. An exclamation of incredulity or derision.

To cock a snook. *See under* COCK.

Snottie. Naval slang for a midshipman; allegedly from their habit of wiping their noses on their sleeves; and it is said that the three buttons on the cuffs of their jackets were to prevent them doing this. New entries were called *warts* and the Lieutenant who overlooked the gunroom was known as the *snottie nurse*.

Snow. A slang term for cocaine, heroin or morphine.

Snow King. So the Austrians called Gustavus Adolphus of Sweden (1594, 1611–1632), because, said they, he "was kept together by the cold, but would melt and disappear as he approached a warmer soil".

Snow-line. The line above which a mountain is continually under snow.

Snuff. To be snuffed out. Put down, eclipsed, killed.

To snuff it is to die, the allusion being to the snuffing out of a candle.

> 'Tis strange the mind, that very fiery particle,
> Should let itself be snuffed out by an article.
> BYRON : *Don Juan*, xi, 60.

Took it in snuff: In anger, in huff, expressed by sneezing. Snuff here being the powder made from tobacco, which may make the unwary sneeze.

> Who, therewith angry, when it next came there,
> Took it in snuff.
> SHAKESPEARE : *Henry IV, Pt. I*, I, iii.

Up to snuff. Wide awake, knowing, sharp; not easily taken in or imposed upon. An allusion to the tobacco preparation.

So. So what? What of it? A colloquialism of American origin.

Soap, or **Soft soap.** Flattery, especially of an oily, unctuous kind.

How are you off for soap? A common street-saying of the mid-19th century, of indeterminate meaning. It may mean "What are you good for?" in the way of cash, or anything else; and it was often just a general piece of cheek. *Cp.* "What! No soap?" in Foote's nonsense passage (*see* PANJANDRUM).

In soaped-pig fashion. Vague; a method of speaking or writing which always leaves a way of escape. The allusion is to the custom at FAIRS, etc., of soaping the tail of a pig before turning it out to be caught by the tail.

He is vague as may be; writing in what is called the "soaped-pig" fashion.
> CARLYLE :
> *The Diamond Necklace*, ch. iv (*Footnote*).

Soap-box oratory. Tub-thumping, demagogic utterance. From the use of a "soap-box" as a stand or platform. Soap was formerly packed in strong wooden boxes.

Soap-lock (U.S.A.). A lock of HAIR worn on the temple and kept in position with soap, a 19th-century fashion; any such lock of hair.

Soap opera. A somewhat disparaging term for a sentimental type of play, usually in episodic serial form, as used by commercial radio and television in advertising soap and other commodities.

Soapy Sam. Samuel Wilberforce (1805–1873), Bishop of Oxford, and afterwards of Winchester; so called because of his persuasive and unctuous way of speaking. It is somewhat remarkable that the floral decorations above the stall of the bishop and of the principal of Cuddesdon were S.O.A.P., the initials of Sam Oxon and Alfred Port.

Someone asking the bishop why he was so called received the answer, "Because I am often in hot water and always come out with clean hands."

Sob stuff. A phrase describing newspaper, film, or other stories of a highly sentimental kind; cheap or tear-jerking pathos.

Sob sister. A journalist who conducts an "answers to correspondents" column in a woman's magazine; one who writes tear-provoking sentimentalities.

Sobersides. A grave, steady-going, serious-minded person, called by some "a stick-in-the-mud"; usually **Old Sobersides**.

Socage (sok′ aj). A free feudal non-military tenure, held in FEE SIMPLE (*see under* FEE), service being in the form of rent or some form of agricultural duty. It is from O.E. *soc*, jurisdiction, franchise.

Sociable. A horse-drawn carriage so named because its side seats faced each other; also a tricycle for two to ride side by side.

> The Queen has had a most providential escape. The carriage, a sociable, very low and safe, was overturned last night after dark, on her way back from an expedition of seven or eight hours.
> GLADSTONE : *Diary*, 8 October 1863.

Social and Liberal Democrats. *See* GANG OF FOUR (2), LIBERAL.

Social Democratic Party. *See* GANG OF FOUR (2), LIBERAL.

Society. In the restricted sense, the world of fashion, high society; the UPPER TEN (*see under* TEN).

Society of Friends. *See* QUAKERS.

Society verse. *See* VERS DE SOCIÉTÉ

Socinianism (so sin′ yàn izm). A form of Unitarianism (*see* UNITARIANS) which, on the one hand, does not altogether deny the supernatural character of Christ, but, on the other, goes farther than Arianism (*see* ARIANS) which, while upholding His divinity denies that He is coequal with the Father. So called from the Italian theologians Laelius Socinus (1525–1562) and his nephew Faustus Socinus (1539–1604) who developed these tenets. Socinus is the latinized form of *Sozzini*.

Sock. The light shoe worn by the comic actors of Greece and ROME (Lat. *soccus*); hence applied to comedy itself.

> Then to the well-trod stage anon,
> If Jonson's learned sock be on.
>
> MILTON: *L'Allegro*.

The difference between the sock of comedy and the BUSKIN of tragedy was that the sock reached only to the ankle, but the buskin extended to the knee.

Put a sock in it. Be quiet, shut up, make less noise — a slang expression. In the late 19th century and earlier years of the 20th, when gramophones or phonographs amplified the sound through large horns, woollen socks were often stuffed in them to cut down the noise.

To pull one's socks up. *See under* PULL.

Socrates (sok′ rà tēz). The great Greek philosopher of ATHENS (*c.* 470–399 B.C.). He used to call himself "the midwife of men's thoughts"; and out of his intellectual school sprang those of PLATO and the Dialectic system, Euclid and the MEGARIAN, Aristippus and the Cyrenaic, ANTISTHENES and the CYNIC, and the Elean and Eretrian schools. Phædo and Xenophon were also among his disciples. Cicero said of him, "he brought down philosophy from the heavens to earth"; and he was the first to teach that "the proper study of mankind is man". He was condemned to death for the corruption of youth by introducing new gods (thus being guilty of impiety) and drank hemlock in prison in the presence of his followers.

Socratic irony. Leading on your opponent in an argument by simulating ignorance, so that he "ties himself in knots" and eventually falls an easy prey—a form of procedure used with great effect by Socrates.

The Socratic method. The method of conducting an argument, imparting information, etc., by means of question and answer.

Soda-jerker. An attendant at an ice-cream soda fountain in the U.S.A.

From Soda to hock. A western U.S.A. phrase. In Faro the first card shown face-up before the bets are placed is known as *Soda*, while the last card left in the box is said to be "in hock", *i.e.* in pawn. The phrase is thus equivalent to "from A to Z".

Sodom and Gomorrah. Figuratively, any town or towns regarded as exceptional centres of vice and immorality. An allusion to the cities which God destroyed (*see Gen.* xviii, xix).

Soft, or **softy.** A mentally retarded or underdeveloped person; one whose brain shows signs of "softening".

A soft fire makes a sweet malt. Too much hurry or precipitation spoils work, just as too fierce a fire would burn the malt and destroy its sweetness. "Soft and fair goes far", "the more haste the less speed", are sayings of similar meaning.

Soft sawder. Flattery, adulation. *Sawder* being solder, and soft solder a combination of tin and LEAD used for soldering zinc, lead, and tin. Its origin is obscure.

A soft touch. One who is soft-hearted and easily imposed upon, especially one easy to "touch" for money.

Soft or **fair words butter no parsnips.** *See under* BUTTER.

Software. Computer programmes; also video cassettes and discs. *See* HARDWARE.

Soho! An exclamation used by huntsmen, especially in hare-coursing when a hare has been started. It is a very old call dating from at least the 13th century, and corresponds to the "TALLY-HO!" of foxhunters when the fox breaks cover. It was the pass-word used by Monmouth's forces in their ill-starred night attack at Sedgemoor in 1685. (*See* MONMOUTH'S REBELLION).

Soho. This famous cosmopolitan area of LONDON apparently derives its name from the old hunting cry when Soho fields were used for hunting. Its first use as a place-name is found in 1636. Its first foreign influx was that of the HUGUENOTS after the revocation of the EDICT OF NANTES in 1685 and in the 1860s and 1870s Germans and Italians came to settle, followed by Swiss, Russians, Poles, and Greeks, etc. It has long been a noted centre for foreign restaurants and delicatessen shops and a haunt of gastronomes, but in recent years they have given ground to STRIP-TEASE shows, near-beer clubs and CLIP-JOINTS.

Soi-disant (swa dē′ zon) (Fr.). Self-styled, would-be.

Soil. A son of the soil. One native to a district whose family has well-established local roots; one who works on the land.

To take soil. A hunting term, signifying that the quarry, usually a deer, has taken to the water. *Soil* here is Fr. *souille*, the mire in which a wild boar wallows.

> Fida went downe the dale to seeke the hinde,
> And founde her taking soyle within a flood.
> WM. BROWNE: *Britannia's Pastorals*, I, iv, 40.

Sol (Lat. *sol*, sun). The Roman SUN god; the sun itself. In Scandanivian mythology Sol was the maiden who drove the chariot of the sun.

The name was given by the alchemists to GOLD and in HERALDRY it represents *or* (gold). It is also the monetary unit of Peru. In music *sol* is the fifth note of the diatonic scale.

Solano (so la′ nō). **Ask no favour during the solano.** A popular Spanish proverb meaning—Ask no favour during a time of trouble or adversity. The *solano* is an extremely hot south-east wind loaded with fine dust which produces giddiness and irritation. *Cp.* AUSTER.

Sold down the river. *See* TO SELL DOWN THE RIVER *under* RIVER.

Soldier. Originally a hireling; one paid a wage, especially for military service (Med. Lat. *solidus*, a gold coin, hence pay).
An old soldier. An empty bottle. *Cp.* DEAD MARINES.
Soldiers' battles. Engagements which are essentially hand-to-hand encounters between the opposing soldiers themselves, the commander usually being prevented by circumstances from making effective dispositions. Inkerman (1854), which was fought in a fog, is known as **the Soldiers' Battle**.
Soldiers of fortune. Men who live by their wits; *chevaliers d'industrie*. Referring to those men in mediæval times who let themselves for hire to any army.
Soldier's wind. *See under* WIND.
To come the old(er) soldier over one. To dictate peremptorily and profess superiority of knowledge and experience; also to impose on one.

> But you needn't try to come the old soldier over me,
> I'm not quite such a fool as that.
> HUGHES: *Tom Brown at Oxford*, II, xvii.

To soldier on. To keep going in spite of discouragements and difficulties; to plod on steadily like a good soldier.

Solecism (sŏ′ lĕ sizm). A deviation from correct idiom or grammar; from the Greek *soloikos*, speaking incorrectly, so named from Soloi, a town in Cilicia, the ATTIC colonists of which spoke a debased form of Greek.

The word is also applied to any impropriety or breach of good manners.

Solemn. The Solemn League and Covenant. An agreement between the English PARLIAMENT and the Scots in 1643 to strengthen their position in the struggle against CHARLES I. Presbyterianism was to be established in England and Ireland and the Scots undertook to provide an army in return for payment. Charles II swore to abide by the Covenant when he was crowned at SCONE in 1651, but after the RESTORATION it became a dead letter. *See* COVENANTERS.

Sol-fa. *See* TONIC SOL-FA.

Solicitor. *See* ATTORNEY.

Solicitor-General. The second law officer of the Crown and deputy of the ATTORNEY-GENERAL. He is a member of the HOUSE OF COMMONS and his period of office terminates with the fall of the ministry. It is customary to confer a knighthood on the holder of this office.

Solid (Lat. *solidus*, firm, dense, compact). As applied to individuals it commonly denoted soundness, as in a "man of solid worth", or grave and profound; also a man of substance. In more recent colloquial usage it implies mental slowness, obtuseness, as in such expressions as, "he is solid from the neck up".
The Solid Doctor. Richard Middleton (*fl.* 1280), a Franciscan SCHOOLMAN, author of works on theology and canon law. *Solid* here means profound. *See* DOCTORS OF LEARNING.

Solipsism (sō lip′ sizm) (Lat. *solus*, alone; *ipse*, self). Absolute egoism; the metaphysical theory that the only knowledge possible is that of oneself.

Solomon. King of Israel (d. *c.* 930 B.C.). He was specially noted for his wisdom, hence his name has been used for wise men generally.
The English Solomon. James I (1566, 1603–1625), who was a Scot, also called by Sully "the wisest fool in Christendom".
The Solomon of France. Charles V (1338, 1364–1380), *le Sage*.
Solomon's Carpet. *See* CARPET.
Solomon's Ring. *See under* RING.
Solomon's Seal. *Polygonatum multiflorum*, a plant with drooping white flowers. As the stems decay, the rootstock becomes marked with scars that have some resemblance to seals; this is one explanation of the name; another is that the root has medicinal value in *sealing* up and closing green wounds. It is also another name for the STAR OF DAVID.

Solon. Athenian statesman and sage (*c.* 638– *c.* 558 B.C.), a great law giver and one of the Seven Sages of Greece (*see* WISE MEN).

The Solon of Parnassus. So VOLTAIRE called Nicolas Boileau (1636–1711), in allusion to his *Art of Poetry*.

Solstice (sol' stis). The summer solstice is 21 JUNE; the winter solstice is 22 DECEMBER; so called because on or about these dates the sun reaches its extreme northern and southern points in the ECLIPTIC and appears to stand still (Lat. *sol*, sun; *sistit*, stands) before it turns back on its apparent course.

Soma (sō' ma). An intoxicating drink anciently made, with mystic rites and incantations, from the juice of some Indian plant by the priests, and drunk by the BRAHMINS as well as offered as libations to their gods. It was fabled to have been brought from HEAVEN by a falcon, or by the daughters of the SUN; and it was itself personified as a god, and represented the MOON. The plant was probably a species of *Asclepias*.

To drink the Soma. To become immortal, or as a god.

Some. Some pumpkins (U.S.A.). Substantial, important; the opposite of "small potatoes".

Somerset House. The present building off the STRAND, housing the Board of Inland Revenue, the Registrar-General (until 1974), and the Principal Probate Registry, was built (1776–1786) by Sir William Chambers. It occupies the site of the former princely mansion of Protector Somerset, brother of Jane Seymour and uncle of Edward VI. It became crown property after Somerset's execution (1552) and was later renamed Denmark House by James I, in honour of his queen, Anne of Denmark. It was occupied in turn by three Queens, Anne of Denmark, Henrietta Maria, and Catherine of Braganza.

Somoreen. *See* ZAMORIN.

Son. Son of God. Christ; one of the regenerate.

> As many as are led by the Spirit of God, they are the sons of God.
>
> *Rom*. viii, 14.

Son of a gun. *See under* GUN.

Sons of Liberty. American secret radical associations formed after the passing of the Stamp Act (1765) to resist British attempts at taxation. They had considerable influence in arousing revolutionary feeling.

Son of Man. In the GOSPELS, a title of Christ.

Every mother's son. All, without exception; every one of you.

Son et lumière (sô ā loo mē âr') (Fr.). Sound and lights. Pageantry and dramatic spectacles presented after dark and, most advantageously, in an appropriate natural or historic setting. They are accompanied by, and dependent upon lighting effects, suitable music and narrative.

Song. A song or **an old song.** A mere trifle, something hardly worth reckoning, as "it went for a song", it was sold for practically nothing. It probably derives from the trifling cost of the old ballad sheets or the small change given to itinerant songsters outside inns and public houses.

The Songs of Degrees. Another name for the GRADUAL PSALMS.

The Song of Roland. *See under* ROLAND.

The Song of Songs. The *Song of Solomon* in the OLD TESTAMENT, also known as *Canticles*.

The Song of the Three Holy Children. An APOCRYPHAL book in the SEPTUAGINT and the VULGATE included as part of the *Book of Daniel*. It contains the prayer of Azarias and a narrative of the three Hebrews in the fiery furnace ending with the thanksgiving for their deliverance. The canticle known as the *Benedicite* is taken from this.

Don't make such a song about it! Be more reasonable in your complaints; don't make such a fuss about it.

What! all this for a song? The reputed comment of Lord Burghley, the Lord High Treasurer when he heard of Queen Elizabeth I's proposed bounty of £500 to Edmund Spenser, author of the *Faerie Queene*. The story is told by Edward Phillips in his *Theatrum Poetarum Anglicanorum* (1675), and he says that Burghley owed Spenser a grudge and had the grant cut to £100. An earlier account in Fuller's *Worthies of England* (1662) says that Elizabeth initially commanded the treasurer to give Spenser £100 but Burghley objected to the amount. So the Queen told him to give "what is reason". Payment was neglected so Spenser presented this petition to the Queen:

> I was promis'd on a time,
> To have reason for my rhyme;
> From that time unto this season,
> I receiv'd nor rhyme nor reason.

"Hereupon the queen gave strict order ... for the present payment of the hundred pounds the first intended unto him."

Sonnet. Prince of the Sonnet. Joachim du Bellay, "Apollo of the PLEIAD" (1522–1560), French sonneteer, was so called.

Dark Lady of the Sonnets. *See under* LADY.

Sooner. Slang for a sponger, one who lives on his wits and will do anything *sooner* than work for his living.

In the U.S.A., whose who acquired the

best land in Oklahoma before the rush in 1889, by evading the regulations, were called **Sooners** and Oklahoma came to be known as the *Sooner State*.

Sooterkin. A kind of false birth fabled to be produced by Dutch women through sitting over their stoves; hence an abortive proposal or scheme, and, as applied to literature, an imperfect or a supplementary work.

> For knaves and fools being near of kin
> As Dutch boors are t'a sooterkin,
> Both parties join'd to do their best
> To damn the public interest.
>
> BUTLER: *Hudibras*, III, ii, 145.

Sop. A sop in the pan. A tit-bit, dainty morsel; a piece of bread soaked in the dripping of meat caught in the dripping pan; a bribe.

To give a sop to Cerberus. To give a bribe; to quiet a troublesome customer. CERBERUS is PLUTO's three-headed dog, stationed at the gates of the infernal regions. When persons died the Greeks and Romans used to put a cake in their hands as a sop to Cerberus to allow them to pass without molestation.

Soph. A contraction of *sophister*. At Cambridge, a second-year student was formerly called a Junior Soph and in his third year a Senior Soph. These students had to maintain a given question in the schools by opposing the orthodox view of it (*see* ACT OF OPPONENCY). The word is from Greek and Latin *sophister*, a sophist.

In American universities *Soph* is an abbreviation of *Sophomore*, a term applied to second-year students.

Sophia, Santa (sō fi' à). The great metropolitan cathedral of the ORTHODOX CHURCH at Istanbul. It was built by Justinian (532–537), but since the capture of the city by the Turks (1453) has been used as a mosque and is now a museum. It was not dedicated to a saint named Sophia, but to the "Logos", or Second Person of the TRINITY, called *Hagia Sophia* (Sacred Wisdom).

Sophist, Sophistry, Sophism, Sophisticator, etc. These words have quite departed from their original meaning. The *seven sages* (*see* WISE MEN OF GREECE) were called *sophists* (wise men) and in the 5th and 4th centuries B.C. the term denoted those who made a profession of teaching the various branches of learning. PYTHAGORAS (*fl. c.* 540–*c.* 510 B.C.) out of modesty called himself a PHILOSOPHER (a wisdom-lover). A century later Protagoras of Abdera resumed the title and the sophists became hostile to the philosophers. Their hypercritical attitudes eventually led to sophistry falling into contempt, as the less able increasingly appeared

as a set of quibblers. Hence *sophos* and its derivatives came to be applied to "wisdom falsely so called", and *philo-sophos* to the "modest search after truth". Current uses of *sophisticated* implying "worldly-wise", "disillusioned", "with the most technically up-to-date systems or devices", reveal a further drift in meaning of what is now a vogue word.

Sophy, The. An old title of the rulers of Persia, first given as an epithet to Sheik Junaid, whose grandson, Ismail I, founded the Safawid dynasty (1502–1736). It is derived from Arab. *Çafi-ud-din*, purity of religion. *See also* RULERS, TITLES OF.

Sorbonne. The usual name for the University of Paris, which derives from the ancient college of this name, the *Collegium Pauperum Magistrorum* founded by Robert de Sorbon *c.* 1257. He was confessor of St. LOUIS and the college was for the advanced study of theology. It was suppressed in 1792, but re-established by NAPOLEON in 1808 as a theological faculty which lasted until 1882.

Sorites (sò rī' tēz). A "heaped-up" (Gr. *soros*, a heap) or cumulative SYLLOGISM, the predicate of one forming the subject of that which follows, the subject of the first being ultimately united with the predicate of the last. The following will serve as an example:

All men who believe shall be saved.

All who are saved must be free from sin.

All who are free from sin are innocent in the sight of God.

All who are innocent in the sight of God are meet for HEAVEN.

All who are meet for heaven will be admitted into heaven.

Therefore all who believe will be admitted into heaven.

The famous Sorites of Themistocles was:

That his infant son commanded the whole world, proved thus;

My infant son rules his mother.

His mother rules me.

I rule the Athenians.

The Athenians rule the Greeks.

The Greeks rule Europe.

And Europe rules the world.

Sorrow. The Seven Sorrows of the Virgin. *See* MARY.

Sort. Out of sorts. Not in good health and spirits. The French *être dérangé* explains the METAPHOR. If cards are out of sorts they are deranged, and if a person is out of sorts the health or spirits are out of order.

In printer's language *sorts* is applied to particular pieces of type considered as part of the fount, and a printer is *out of sorts* when he has run short of some particular letters, figures, stops, etc.

To run upon sorts. In printing, said of work which requires an unusual number of certain letters, etc.; as an index, which may require a disproportionate number of capitals.

Sortes (sôr′ tēz) (Lat. *sors, sortis*, chance, lot). A species of DIVINATION performed by selecting passages from a book haphazard. VIRGIL's *Æneid* was anciently the favourite work for the purpose. (*Sortes Virgilianæ*), but the BIBLE (*Sortes Biblicæ*) has also been in common use.

The method is to open the book at random, and the passage you touch by chance with your finger is the oracular response. Severus consulted Virgil and read these words: "Forget not thou, O Roman, to rule the people with royal sway." Gordianus, who reigned only a few days, hit upon this verse: "Fate only showed him on this earth, and suffered him not to tarry"; and Dr. Wellwood gives an instance respecting CHARLES I and Lord Falkland. Falkland, to amuse the king, suggested this kind of AUGURY, and the king hit upon IV, 615–20, the gist of which is that "evil wars would break out, and the king lose his life". Falkland, to laugh the matter off, said he would show his Majesty how ridiculously the "lot" would foretell the next fate, and he lighted on XI, 152–81, the lament of Evander for the untimely death of his son Pallas. King Charles soon after mourned over his noble friend who was slain at Newbury (1643).

In Rabelais (III, x), PANURGE consults the *Sortes Virgilianæ et Homericæ* on the burning question, whether or not he should marry. In Cornelius Agrippa's *De Vanitate Scientiarum*, c. iv, there is a passage violently reprobating the *Sortes*.

Soter (sō′ tĕr). Ptolemy I of Egypt (d. 283 B.C.) was given this surname, meaning *the Preserver*, by the Rhodians because he compelled Demetrius to raise the siege of Rhodes (304 B.C.).

Sothic Period, Year. The Sothic year was the fixed year of the ancient Egyptians, the CANICULAR year, determined from one heliacal rising of the DOG-STAR Sirius (*Sothis*) to the next. Since Sothis rose one day later every four years their CALENDAR did not accord with the solar year until after 1,460 (365 × 4) solar years when their first day of the year had worked through the seasons and come back into line. This was the Sothic or CANICULAR PERIOD.

Soul. The idea of the soul as the immaterial and immortal part of man surviving after death as a ghost or spirit was an ancient and widespread belief. The ancient Egyptians represented it as a bird with a human head. With ARISTOTLE the soul is essentially the vital principle and the Neoplatonists held that it was located in the whole body and in every part. It has also been located in the blood, heart, brain, bowels, liver, kidneys, etc.

The MOSLEMS say that the souls of the faithful assume the forms of snow-white birds, and nestle under the throne of ALLAH until the resurrection.

All Souls' Day. 2 November, the day following ALL SAINTS' Day, set apart by the ROMAN CATHOLIC CHURCH for a solemn service for the repose of the departed. In England it was formerly observed by ringing the soul bell (*see* PASSING-BELL *under* BELL), by making and distributing SOUL CAKES, blessing beans, etc.

Soul Cakes. Sweet cakes formerly distributed at the church door on ALL SOULS' DAY to the poor who went *a-souling, i.e.* begging for soul cakes. The words used were:

> Soul, soul, for soul-cake,
> Pray you, good mistress, a soul cake.

Soul-papers. Papers requesting prayers for the souls of the departed named thereon which were given away with SOUL CAKES.

Soup. In the soup. In a mess, in trouble.

Sour grapes. *See* GRAPES.

South Bank religion. A journalistic label for the religoius activities in the diocese of SOUTHWARK associated with Dr. Arthur Mervyn Stockwood, Bishop of Southwark (1959–1980), Dr. John Robinson, Suffragan Bishop of Woolwich (1959–1969), author of *Honest to God* (1963), and some of their diocesan clergy. Characterized by outspokenness on moral and political issues often from a socialist angle, and energetic attempts to bring the Church into closer relation to contemporary society and its problems, South Bank religion is not without its critics and the label is often applied disparagingly by opponents. Dr. Stockwood was appointed under Mr. Macmillan's TORY government in 1958 and the appellation *South Bank* derives from the fact that the Southwark diocese borders on the south bank of the Thames.

> That is rather the new idea inside the Church. I should definitely say you were a South Banker.
> AUBERON WAUGH: *Consider the Lilies*, ch. 9.

South Sea Bubble. The speculative mania associated with South Sea Company and other stock in 1720 which ended disastrously in the ruin of many. The South Sea Company, founded in 1711, was given the monopoly of trade with Spanish America in return for an undertaking to convert part of the NATIONAL DEBT to a lower rate of interest. In 1720 the company's monopoly was extended to the South Seas and at the same time it offered to take over the whole National Debt. This led to gross over-speculation and many other preposterous companies were floated. £100 shares of the company ran up to £890 and ultimately £1,000 with the inevitable consequences, and Ministers were involved. The South Sea Company continued its existence until 1856. *Cp.* MISSISSIPPI BUBBLE.

Southcottians. The followers of Joanna Southcott (1750–1814), one-time domestic servant at Exeter. Starting as a METHODIST, she became a prophetess and declared herself to be the "woman clothed with the sun, and the moon under her feet, and upon her head a crown of twelve stars" (*Rev.* xii, 1). At the age of 64 she announced that she was to be delivered of a son, the Shiloh of *Gen.* xlix, 10:

> The sceptre shall not depart from Judah, nor a law-giver from between his feet, until Shiloh come; and unto him shall the gathering of the people be.

19 October 1814 was the date fixed for the birth, which did not take place, but the prophetess died in a trance soon afterwards and was buried in the churchyard of St. John's Wood Chapel. She left a locked wooden box usually known as **Joanna Southcott's Box** which was not to be opened until a time of national crisis, and then only in the presence of all the bishops in England. Attempts were made to persuade the episcopate to open it during the Crimean War and again in World War I. It was opened in 1927 in the presence of one reluctant prelate, and found to contain a few oddments and unimportant papers, and among them a lottery ticket. It is claimed by some that the box opened was not the authentic one. *Cp.* NUNAWADING MESSIAH.

Southpaw. In American usage, a left-handed baseball player, especially a pitcher; also meaning sometimes any left-handed person. In both American and British usage it describes a boxer who leads with his right hand.

Southwark. The ancient suburb on the south bank of the Thames annexed to the City of London in 1327 and once known as "The BOROUGH". It has a wealth of historical associations including the site of the TABARD INN of Chaucer's *Canterbury Tales*, the Globe Theatre on BANKSIDE, the CLINK, the MARSHALSEA, and PARIS GARDEN, as well as the church of St. Mary OVERIE, the George Inn, etc. Southwark possessed two MINTS and an annual fair (1550–1763), and it became an independent borough in 1899. As a DIOCESE, it was formed out of Rochester in 1905. The name means "Southern fort" and is of Saxon origin. *See* SOUTH BANK RELIGION.

Sovereign. A strangely evolved word from Lat. *superanus*, supreme; the last syllable being assimilated to *reign*. The Fr. *souverain* is nearer the Latin; Ital. *sovrano*; Span. *soberano*.

The gold coin of this name valued at 20 shillings, first issued by Henry VII, was so called from its representation of the monarch enthroned and was replaced by the UNITE in the reign of James I. A smaller sovereign was issued from 1817 until 1917.

Sow (sou). **A pig of my own sow.** Said of that which is the result of one's own action.

A still sow. A cunning and selfish man; one wise in his own interest; one who avoids talking at meals that he may enjoy his food the better. So called from the old proverb, "The still sows eats the wash" or "draff".

> We do not act that often jest and laugh;
> 'Tis old, but true, "Still swine eats all the draff."
> SHAKESPEARE: *Merry Wives of Windsor*, IV, ii.

As drunk as David's, or **Davy's sow.** *See* DAVY'S SOW.

To get the wrong sow by the ear. To capture the wrong individual, to take "the wrong end of the STICK", hit upon the wrong thing.

To send a sow to Minerva. To "teach your grandmother to suck eggs" (*see under* EGG), to instruct one more learned in the subject than oneself. From the old Latin proverb, *Sus Minervam docet* (a pig teaching MINERVA); Minerva being the goddess of wisdom.

You cannot make a silk purse out of a sow's ear. *See under* SILK.

Sow (sō). **Sow the wind and reap the whirlwind.** To provoke serious consequences through one's heedless actions.

Spade. The spade of playing-cards is so called from Span. *espada*, a sword, the suit in Spanish packs being marked with short swords; in French and British cards the mark—largely through similarity in name—has been altered to the shape of a pointed spade.

Spade guinea. An English gold coin, value 21*s.*, minted 1787–1799, so called because it bears a shield shaped like the spade on playing-cards on the reverse. The legend is M.B.F. ET. H. REX. F.D. B. ET. L.D. S.R.I.A.T. ET. E.—Magnæ Britanniæ, Franciæ, et Hiberniæ Rex; Fidei Defensor; Brunsvicensis et Lunenburgensis Dux; Sacri Romani Imperii Archi Thesaurarius et Elector.

To call a spade a spade. To be outspoken, blunt, even to the point of rudeness; to call things by their proper names without any "beating about the bush" (*see under* BEAT).

Spagyric (spà jir' ik). Pertaining to ALCHEMY; the term seems to have been invented by PARACELSUS. Alchemy is "the spagyric art", and an alchemist a "spagyrist".

Spagyric food. CAGLIOSTRO's name for the ELIXIR of immortal youth.

Spain. Castles in Spain. *See* CASTLE.

Patron Saint of Spain. St. JAMES the Great, who is said to have preached the GOSPEL in Spain and to have his relics preserved at COMPOSTELA.

Spanish fly. The cantharis, a coleopterous insect used in medicine. Cantharides are dried and used externally as a blister and internally as a stimulant to the genito-urinary organs; they were formerly considered to act as an aphrodisiac.

Spanish Inquisition. *See* INQUISITION.

The Spanish Main. Properly, the northeast coast of South America from the mouth of the Orinoco to the Isthmus of Panama; the mainland bordering the Caribbean Sea, called by the Spanish conquerors *Tierra Firme*. The term is often more loosely applied to the area of the Caribbean Sea and its islands.

> Then up and spake an old Sailor,
> Had sailed the Spanish Main.
> LONGFELLOW: *The Wreck of the Hesperus*.

Spanish moss. A plant of the family *Bromeliaceæ* which hangs in long grey festoons from the branches of trees, especially the live oak, in tropical and subtropical American forests.

Spanish worm. An old name for a nail concealed in a piece of wood, against which a carpenter blunts his saw or chisel.

To ride the Spanish mare. An old nautical punishment. The victim was put astride a boom with the stay slackened off when the ship was at sea. A hazardous position and of great discomfort.

To walk Spanish. To walk on tiptoe, being lifted and pushed by a more powerful person; to walk under compulsion; to walk GINGERLY. From the behaviour of pirates of the SPANISH MAIN towards captives. *Cp*. FROG MARCH.

Span New. *See* SPICK.

Spaniel. The "Spanish dog", from *español*, through the French.

Spanker. Used of a fast horse, also colloquially—of something or someone that is an exceptionally fine specimen, a "stunner".

In nautical language the spanker is the fore-and-aft sail set upon the mizen-mast of a three-masted vessel, and the jiggermast of a four-masted vessel. There is no spanker in a one- or two-masted vessel of any rig.

Spare the rod and spoil the child. *See under* ROD.

Sparker, or **Sparks.** A colloquial term for a ship's wireless operator; in the Royal Navy formerly called a Telegraphist, now called a Radio Operator. *Cp*. BUNTING-TOSSER.

Spartacists. An extreme Socialist group in Germany that flourished between 1916 and 1919. It was founded by Karl Liebknecht who, with Rosa Luxemburg, led an attempted revolution in January of the latter year, in the suppression of which they were both killed. The movement was finally crushed by Ebert's government in the April. It took its name from the Thracian GLADIATOR, Spartacus, who in 73 B.C. led a slave rebellion against ROME, which was not suppressed until 71 B.C. During the uprising, he defeated five Roman armies and devastated whole tracts of Italy.

Spartan. The inhabitants of ancient Sparta, one of the leading city-states of Greece, were noted for their frugality, courage, and stern discipline; hence one who can bear pain unflinchingly is termed "a Spartan", a very frugal diet is "Spartan fare", etc. It was a Spartan mother, who, on handing her son the shield he was to carry into battle, said that he was to come back either with it or on it.

Spartan dog. A blood-hound; a blood-thirsty man.

> O Spartan dog
> More fell than anguish, hunger or the sea.
> SHAKESPEARE: *Othello*, V, ii.

Spasmodic School, The. A name applied by W. E. Aytoun in 1854 to certain writers of the 19th century whose style was marked by sentimentality, forced conceits, and a certain lack of taste. Among them were P.J. Bailey, Sydney Dobell, Ernest Jones, Ebenezer Jones, and Alexander Smith.

Speak. It speaks for itself. There is no need for further explanation, evidence or discussion. It is sufficiently clear in itself.

Speak for yourself. Limit yourself to speaking about your own part in the matter or to expressing your own views. Don't involve or compromise other people.

To speak the same language. To understand each other perfectly, to hold the same views.

English as she is spoke. Used of ungrammatical or unidiomatic English. Andrew White Tuer (1838–1900) chose this as a title of a reprint of the English part of a book purporting to be a guide to conversation in English and Portuguese by Cavolino (first published at Paris, 1855). The gross distortions of English are said to have suggested the title.

Speak-easy. A place where alcoholic liquors are sold illegally. An American term widely current in the years of prohibition (1920–1934). *See* BOOTLEGGER; CAPONE.

> The place of the saloon was taken by speak-easies which ranged all the way from dingy back rooms to palatial establishments, but all tolerated by the police.
>
> L.D. BALDWIN:
> *The Stream of American History*, Vol. II, ch. xlv

Speaker. The title of the presiding officer and official spokesman of the British HOUSE OF COMMONS, the United States House of Representatives, and of some other legislative assemblies.

The Speaker of the House of Commons has autocratic power in the control of debates and internal arrangements of the House, etc.; he is elected by the members irrespective party, and ceases to be a "party man", having no vote—except in cases of a tie, when he can give a CASTING VOTE. He holds the office for the duration of that PARLIAMENT, but by custom (not law) is reappointed unless he wishes to resign (in which case he goes to the HOUSE OF LORDS).

The LORD CHANCELLOR (*see under* CHANCELLOR) is *ex officio* Speaker of the HOUSE OF LORDS.

To catch the Speaker's eye. The rule in the HOUSE OF COMMONS is that the member whose rising to address the House is first observed by the SPEAKER is allowed precedence.

Speaking. A speaking likeness. A very good and lifelike portrait; one that makes you imagine that the subject is just going to speak to you.

Properly speaking. Speaking in the strict and accurate meaning of the words: speaking without qualification.

Speaking Heads. Fables and romance tell of a variety of artificial heads that could speak: among the best known are:

The statue of MEMNON, in Egypt, which uttered musical sounds when the morning sun darted on it (*see* THEBES).

That of ORPHEUS, at Lesbos, which is said to have predicted the bloody death that terminated the expedition of Cyrus the Great into Scythia.

The head of MINOS, fabled to have been brought by ODIN to Scandinavia, and to have uttered responses.

The BRAZEN HEAD of Roger Bacon, and that of Gerbert, afterwards Pope Sylvester

II (10th century).

An earthen head made by Albertus Magnus in the 13th century, which both spoke and moved. THOMAS AQUINAS broke it, whereupon the mechanist exclaimed: "There goes the labour of thirty years!"

Alexander's statue of ÆSCULAPIUS; it was supposed to speak, but Lucian says the sounds were uttered by a concealed man, and conveyed by tubes to the statue.

They are not on speaking terms. Said of those who have fallen out.

Spear. If a KNIGHT kept the point of a spear forward when he entered a strange land, it was a declaration of war; if he carried it on his shoulder with the point behind him, it was a token of friendship. In OSSIAN (*Temora*, I), Cairbar asks if FINGAL comes in peace, to which Morannal replies: "In peace he comes not, king of ERIN, I have seen his forward spear."

The spear of Achilles. *See* ACHILLES' SPEAR.

The spear side. The male line of descent, called by Anglo-Saxons *sperehealfe*. *Cp.* DISTAFF SIDE; SPINDLE SIDE.

To break a spear. To fight a TOURNAMENT.

To pass under the spear. To be sold by auction, sold "under the hammer". Writing to Pepys (12 August 1689), Evelyn speaks of "the noblest library that ever passed under the speare". The phrase is from the Lat. *sub hasta vendere*.

Special Pleading. Specious argument; making your own argument good by forcing certain words and phrases from their obvious and ordinary meaning. A pleading in law means a written statement of a cause PRO AND CON, and "special pleaders" are persons who have been called to the BAR, but do not speak as advocates. They advise on evidence, draw up affidavits, state the merits and demerits of a cause, and so on. After a time most special pleaders go to the bar and many get advanced to the BENCH.

Specie, Species, means literally "what is visible" (Lat. *species*, appearance). As things are distinguished by their visible forms, it has come to mean *kind* or *class*. As drugs and condiments at one time formed the most important articles of merchandise, they were called *species*—still retained in the French *épices*, and English *spices*. Again, as banknotes represent money, money itself is called *specie*, the thing represented.

Spectacles. In CRICKET, when a batsman makes no score in either innings of a match, he is said **to make a pair of spectacles.** *Cp.* DUCK'S EGG *under* DUCK.

Spectre of the Brocken. An optical illusion,

first observed on the Brocken (the highest peak of the Hartz range in Saxony), in which shadows of the spectators, greatly magnified, are projected on the mists about the summit of the mountain opposite. In one of De Quincey's opium-dreams, there is a powerful description of the Brocken spectre.

Speculum Humanæ Salvationis (The Mirror of Human Salvation). A similar book to the BIBLIA PAUPERUM on a somewhat more extensive scale, telling pictorially the BIBLE story from the fall of LUCIFER to the Redemption of Man, with explanations of each picture in Latin rhymes. Its illustrations were copied in church sculptures, wall paintings, altar-pieces and stained-glass windows. Copies of the 13th century and earlier are extant and it was one of the earliest of printed books (c. 1467). See also BLOCK BOOKS.

Speech. Parts of Speech. See under PART.

Speech Day. The annual prize-giving day at a school when it is customary to invite a guest to make a speech and to distribute the prizes. The Headmaster or Headmistress also makes a report on the school's record for the preceding year, and sundry other worthies manage to contribute (often lengthy) votes of thanks, etc.

The speech from the throne. See QUEEN'S OR KING'S SPEECH.

Speech is silver, or **silvern, silence is golden.** An old proverb, said to be of oriental origin, pointing to the advantage of keeping one's own counsel. The Hebrew equivalent is: "If a word be worth one shekel, silence is worth two."

Speech was given to man to disguise his thoughts. This epigram was attributed to Talleyrand by Barrère in his Memoirs; but though Talleyrand no doubt used it, he was not its originator. VOLTAIRE, in his XIVth Dialogue (Le Chapon et la Poularde), had said:

Men use thought only as authority for their injustice, and employ speech only to conceal their thoughts.

and Goldsmith in The Bee, III (1759), has:

The true use of speech is not so much to express our wants as to conceal them.

Speenhamland System. The system of outdoor relief initiated by the magistrates of Speenhamland, Berkshire, in 1795 to counter distress among the agricultural labourers. Wages were to be supplemented by rate-aid according to a minimum-wage scale related to the price of bread and the size of the family. Outdoor relief was not new, but the Speenhamland System spread rapidly, particularly in the south. It tended to depress wages and demoralize its beneficiaries and sharply increased the poor rate. The Poor Law Amendment Act (1834) sought to terminate outdoor relief, but never wholly succeeded.

Speewah, The. A mythical cattle station somewhere in Australia where everything is bigger and better than anywhere else in the world. A series of legends comparable only with the adventures of Baron MÜNCHAUSEN are associated with it.

Spell. Spell ho! An exclamation to signify that the allotted time has expired for a spell of work, and the men are to be relieved by others. Spell here is from O.E. spelian. To spell meaning to relieve another at work is now rare. To spell, meaning to write or name the letters that make a word, is from O. Fr. espeler.

Spell (O.E. spel, a saying, fable, etc.). Spells as charms and incantations are found the world over in folk-lore and superstition. They form part of the stock-in-trade of WITCHES, WIZARDS, magicians, sorcerers, GYPSY crones, etc., and many FAIRY stories revolve round their use.

The component words of the spells used by mediæval sorcerers were usually taken from Hebrew, Greek, and Latin, but mere gibberish was often employed. Cp. ABRACADABRA; ABRAXAS.

Spellbinders. Orators who hold their audience spellbound, that is fascinated, charmed. The word came into use in America in the presidential election of 1888.

Spencean Philanthropists. Followers of Thomas Spence (1750–1814) who, in 1775, devised a system of land nationalization on socialist lines. They formed the Society of Spencean Philanthropists in 1812 and thought that their plan heralded the MILLENNIUM. Spence denounced the landed aristocracy and was constantly in trouble for his views and pamphlets. It was the Spenceans who advocated seizing power by force; they addressed the Spa Fields meeting of 2 December 1816 which ended in the plundering of gunsmiths' shops, and they were prominent in the CATO STREET CONSPIRACY of 1820.

Spencer. Now applied to a close-fitting bodice worn by women, but formerly the name of an outer coat without skirts worn by men; so named from the second Earl Spencer (1758–1834).

Spencerian Handwriting is the name given to a style of calligraphy introduced by Platt Rogers Spencer (1800–1861), an American calligrapher. Written with a fine pen, with the down-strokes tapering from top to bottom and large loops, the writing has a forward slope and marked terminal flourishes. Spencer taught this style in many parts of U.S.A. and it is said to have had a marked influence on American calligraphy.

Spenserian Stanza. The stanza devised by Edmund Spenser for the *Faerie Queene* (1590). It may have been founded on the Italian *ottava rima*, or on Chaucer's stanza in the *Monk's Tale*. The Old French ballad has been suggested as another source. It is a stanza of nine IAMBIC lines, all of ten syllables except the last, which is an ALEXANDRINE. Only three different rhymes are admitted into a stanza and these are disposed: a b a b b c b c c.

Among those who used this stanza are Akenside (*Virtuoso*), Thomson (*Castle of Indolence*), Byron (*Childe Harold*), Shelley (*Adonais*, *The Revolt of Islam*), and Keats (*The Eve of St. Agnes*).

Spheres. In the PTOLEMAIC SYSTEM of astronomy the nine spheres were those carrying (1) DIANA or the MOON, (2) MERCURY, (3) VENUS, (4) APOLLO or the SUN, (5) MARS, (6) JUPITER, (7) SATURN, (8) the fixed stars—the Starry Sphere, and (9) the CRYSTALLINE SPHERE—introduced by Hipparchus, to account for the precession of the equinoxes. The PRIMUM MOBILE was added in the MIDDLE AGES.

The Music, or Harmony of the Spheres. PYTHAGORAS, having ascertained that the pitch of notes depends on the rapidity of vibrations, and also that the planets move at different rates of motion, concluded that the planets must make sounds in their motion according to their different rates; and that, as all things in nature are harmoniously made, the different sounds must harmonize; whence the old theory of the "harmony of the spheres". Kepler has a treatise on the subject.

> There's not the smallest orb which thou behold'st
> But in his motion like an angel sings,
> Still quiring to the young-eyed cherubims.
> SHAKESPEARE: *Merchant of Venice*, V, i.

Sphinx (sfingks). The sphinx of Greek mythology, quite distinct from the Egyptian sphinx, was a monster with the head and breasts of a woman, the body of a dog or LION, the wings of a bird, a SERPENT's tail, and lion's paws. It had a human voice and was said to be the daughter of Orthos and TYPHON (or the CHIMÆRA). She inhabited the vicinity of THEBES, setting the inhabitants riddles and devouring those unable to find solutions. The Thebans were told by the oracles that she would kill herself if the following riddle was solved:

> What goes on four feet, on two feet, and three,
> But the more feet it goes on the weaker it be?

It was at length solved by ŒDIPUS with the answer that it was a man, who as an infant crawls upon all fours, in manhood goes erect on two feet, and in old age supports his tottering legs with a staff. Thus were the Thebans delivered and this is the riddle of the sphinx.

The Egyptian sphinx was a lion, usually with a PHARAOH's head, symbolizing royal power and came to be associated with "HORUS in the Horizon" or Harmakhis. The famous Sphinx at Gizeh was hewn out of limestone rock by order of Khephren or Khafre (c. 2620 B.C.) and is some 60 ft. high and 180 ft. long.

Spice Islands. The Moluccas and most of the islands of the Malay Archipelago, whose chief products are spices of all kinds, much sought-after by 15th- and 16th-century navigators and traders when spices were highly prized commodities in Europe.

Spick and Span New. Quite and entirely new. A *spic* is a spike or nail, and a *span* is a chip. So that a spick and span new ship is one in which every nail and chip is new. The more common expression today is spick and span, meaning all neat, clean, bright, and tidy.

Spider. There are many old wives' tales about spiders, the most widespread being that they are venomous.

> Let thy spiders, that suck up thy venom,
> And heavy-gaited toads lie in their way.
> SHAKESPEARE: *Richard II*, III, ii.
> There may be in the cup
> A spider steep'd, and one may drink, depart,
> And yet partake no venom.
> SHAKESPEARE *The Winter's Tale*, II, i.

During the examination into the murder (1613) of Sir Thomas Overbury, one of the witnesses deposed "that the countess wished him to get the strongest poison that he could …". Accordingly he brought seven great spiders. There are few spiders poisonous to man, but the American Black Widow spider is a notable exception.

Other tales were that fever could be cured by wearing a spider in a nutshell round the neck, and a common cure for jaundice was to swallow a large live house-spider rolled up in butter. In IRELAND this was a remedy for ague. A spider on one's clothes was a sign of good luck or that money was coming and the very small spider is called a *money-spider*.

Yet another story was that spiders spin only on dark days.

> The subtle spider never spins,
> But on dark days, his slimy gins.
> S. BUTLER: *On a Nonconformist*, iv, 445.

Bruce and the spider. In 1306 Robert Bruce began a resistance to Edward I's domination of SCOTLAND and was crowned King at SCONE. The story is that, when in hiding in the island of Rathlin, he noticed a spider try six times to fix its web on a beam in the ceiling. "Now shall this spider (said Bruce) teach me what I am to do, for I also have failed six times." The spider made a seventh effort and succeeded. Bruce thereupon left the island (1307), with 300 followers, landed at Carrick, and at midnight surprised the English garrison in Turnberry Castle. His successes steadily grew until, in 1314, he routed the English at the great victory of Bannockburn.

Frederick the Great and the spider. While Frederick II was at SANS-SOUCI, he went into his ante-room to drink a cup of chocolate, but set his cup down to fetch a handkerchief. On his return he found a great spider had fallen from the ceiling into his cup. He called for fresh chocolate and the next moment heard the report of a pistol. The cook had been suborned to poison the chocolate and, supposing he had been found out, shot himself. On the ceiling of the room in Sans-Souci a spider has been painted (according to tradition) in remembrance of this event.

Mohammed and the spider. When MOHAMMED fled from MECCA he hid in a certain cave, with the Koreishites close upon him. Suddenly an acacia in full leaf sprang up at the mouth of the cave, a wood-pigeon had its nest in the branches, and a spider had WOVEN its net between the tree and the cave. When the Koreishites saw this, they felt persuaded that no one could have entered recently, and went on.

Spigot. Spare at the spigot and spill at the bung. To be parsimonious in trifles and wasteful in great matters, like a man who stops his beer-tub at the vent-hole and leaves it running at the bung hole.

Spike. Slang for the workhouse; **to go on the spike,** to become a workhouse inmate. A *spike* is also a colloquialism for a high churchman, and the *Church Times* is colloquially known as *Spiky Bits*.

To spike a drink. To add strong spirits to increase the alcoholic content.

To spike one's guns for him. To render his plans abortive, frustrate the scheme he has been laying, "draw his teeth". The allusion is to the old way of making a gun useless by driving a spike into the touch-hole.

Spill. To spill the beans. To reveal a secret prematurely.

It's no good crying over spilt milk. *See under* CRY.

Spin a yarn, To. To tell a story. A nautical expression, from the days when sailors whiled away the time telling stories while sitting on the deck making spun yarn and other rope work.

Spindle side. The female line of descent. The spindle was the pin on which the thread was wound from the spinning-wheel. *Cp.* DISTAFF SIDE; SPEAR SIDE; SPINSTER.

Spinner. Come in, Spinner. From the Australian national game of "Two up"—spinning two coins, on which enormous sums are bet. When all bets are laid against the man who wishes to spin, he is told to come in (or spin) by the "boxer" (referee in charge of the game). The phrase is used derisively by one who has been taken in by a joke or trick.

Spinster. An unmarried woman. In Saxon times, spinning was a routine winter occupation of the female section of the household. ALFRED THE GREAT, in his will, calls the female part of his family the SPINDLE SIDE; and it was reckoned by our forefathers that no young woman was fit to be a wife till she had spun herself a set of body, table, and bed linen. Hence the maiden was termed a *spinner* or *spinster*.

It is said that the heraldic lozenge, in which the armorial bearings of a woman are depicted originally represented a spindle. Among the Romans the bride carried a DISTAFF, and HOMER tell us that Kryseis was to spin and share the king's bed.

Spirit. Properly, the breath of life, from Lat. *spiritus* (*spirare*, to breathe, blow):

> And the Lord God formed man of the dust of the ground, and breathed into his nostrils the breath of life; and man became a living soul.
>
> *Gen.* ii, 7.

Hence, life or the life principle, the SOUL; a disembodied soul (a ghost or apparition), or an immaterial being that never was supposed to have had a body (sprite), as a GNOME, ELF, or FAIRY; also, the temper or disposition of mind as animated by the breath of life, as in *good spirits*, *high-spirited*, *a man of spirit*.

The mediæval physiological notion (adopted from Galen) was that spirit existed in the body in three kinds, *viz.* (1) the *Natural spirit*, the principle of the "natural functions"—growth, nutrition, and generation, said to be a vapour rising from the blood and having its seat in the liver; (2) the *Vital spirit*, which arose in the heart by a mixture of the air breathed in with the natural spirit and supplied the body with heat and life; and (3) the *Animal spirit*, which was responsible for the power of motion and sensation, and for the rational principle generally; this was a modification of the vital spirit, effected in the brain.

The **Elemental spirits** of PARACELSUS and the ROSICRUCIANS, *i.e.* those which presided over the four elements, were—the SALAMANDERS (or fire), GNOMES (earth), SYLPHS (air), and UNDINES (water).

Spirit also came to mean any volatile agent or essence; and hence, from the alchemists, is still used of solutions in alcohol and of any strong alcoholic liquor. The alchemists named four substances only as "spirits"—MERCURY, arsenic, sal ammoniac, and sulphur.

> The first spirit quyksilver called is:
> The second orpiment; the third y-wis
> Sal armoniac; and the ferth bremstoon.
> CHAUCER: *Canon's Yeoman's Tale*, 102.

Out of spirits. Depressed and despondent.

To spirit away. To kidnap, abduct; to make away with speedily and secretly. The phrase first came into use in the 17th century, in connexion with kidnapping youths and transporting them to the West Indian plantations.

Spiritualism. The belief that communication between the living and the spirits of the departed can and does take place, usually through the agency of a specially qualified person (a medium) and often by means of rapping, table-turning, or automatic writing; the system, doctrines, practice, etc., arising from this belief. *Cp.* OUIJA.

In philosophy, spiritualism—the antithesis of materialism—is the doctrine that the spirit exists as distinct from matter, or as the only reality.

Spit. The dead spit of his father, etc. The exact counterpart; the equivalent of SPIT AND IMAGE.

Spit and image, or **spitting image.** An exact likeness or resemblance—just as if one person were to spit out of another's mouth.

Spit and polish. To give something "a bit of spit and polish" is to clean it up, to make it shine, etc. To spit on leather, etc., and rub it to give it a shine was once common practice; an expression of army origin, the army being properly concerned with the maintenance of smartness of equipment. *See* BULL.

Spitting for luck. Spitting was a charm against enchantment among the ancient Greeks and Romans. Pliny says it averted WITCHCRAFT, and availed in giving an enemy a shrewder blow. People sometimes spit for luck on a piece of money given to them or found; boxers spit on their hands, and traders were wont to spit on the first money

taken in the day. There are numerous other instances of spitting for luck and it was also common to spit for defiance or as a challenge, etc.

Spitting image. *See* SPIT AND IMAGE.

Spital, or **Spittle.** Contractions for hospital. The London district of **Spitalfields** which included parts of Bethnal Green, SHOREDITCH, WHITECHAPEL, and Mile End, was named from its being the property of the Priory and hospital of St. Mary Spittle founded by Walter Brune and his wife Rosia in 1197. HUGUENOT refugees settled there after the revocation (1685) of the EDICT OF NANTES (*see under* NANTES) and it became a centre for silk and velvet manufacture.

Spital Sermons. Sermons originally preached on GOOD FRIDAY and on the following Monday, Tuesday and Wednesday from the Pulpit Cross, Spitalfields, which were attended by the Lord Mayor and Aldermen and the boys of Christ's Hospital. The pulpit was destroyed in the CIVIL WARS and at the RESTORATION the Spital Sermons were revived at St. Bride's, Fleet Street. From 1797 they were delivered at Christ Church, Newgate Street and reduced to two. This church was destroyed by incendiary bombs in 1941. The one Spital Sermon is now given in the Corporation Church of St. Lawrence Jewry. The boys of Christ's Hospital, Horsham, and the girls from Hertford now attend the St. MATTHEW's Day service at the Church of the Holy Sepulchre without Newgate, which incorporates the former parish of Christ Church.

Spiv. A shady character who lives by his wits without working. A word used by racecourse gangs since the 1890s. Probably an abbreviation of *spiffing*, an old slang word meaning "fine", "excellent"; an allusion to the flash, dandified appearance of the characteristic spiv.

Spleen. The soft vascular organ placed to the left of the stomach and acting on the blood, once believed to be the seat of melancholy and ill humour. The fern *spleenwort* was supposed to remove splenic disorders.

Splice. To marry, to join together. A phrase of nautical origin. *Splice* is probably derived from Ger. *spleissen*, to split, as ropes are split or unlayed prior to their being united or interwoven or "spliced".

To splice the main brace. *See* MAINBRACE.

Split. Colloquially, to give away one's accomplices, to betray secrets, to tell tales, to PEACH.

To split hairs. *See under* HAIR.

To split the infinitive. To interpose words between *to* and the verb, as, "to thoroughl understand the subject". This construction is branded as a SOLECISM by pedants and purists, but it is long established and has been used by many accomplished writers.

> Without permitting himself to actually mention the name.
>
> MATTHEW ARNOLD: *On Translating Homer*, iii.
>
> It becomes a truth again, after all, as he happens to newly consider it.
>
> BROWNING: *A Soul's Tragedy*, Pt. II.

To split with laughter. To laugh uproariously or unrestrainedly; to "split one's sides".

Spoils System. The practice in the United States by which the victorious party in an election rewards its supporters by appointments to public office. It takes its name from the phrase "to the victor belong the spoils" which was popularized by Senator Marcy in 1831. Andrew Jackson was not the originator of the practice, nor did he noticeably extend it. It was first used by Jefferson (1801–1809) and used on a big scale from 1841. The Pendleton Act of 1883 and subsequent legislation proved ineffective checks.

To spoil the Egyptians. To plunder one's enemies by force or trickery, as the Jewish women were instructed to do (*Exod.* iii, 22) before their departure from Egypt.

> And the Lord gave the people favour in the sight of the Egyptians, so that they lent unto them such things as they required. And they spoiled the Egyptians.
>
> *Exod.* xii, 36.

To spoil the ship for a ha'porth o' tar. *See under* SHIP.

Spoke. To put a spoke in one's wheel. To interfere with one's projects and frustrate them; to thwart one. When solid wheels were used, the driver was provided with a pin or spoke, which was thrust into one of the three holes made to receive it, to skid the cart when it went down-hill. "To put a sprag in one's wheel" is the same thing and has the same meaning.

Sponge. To sponge on a man. To live on him like a parasite, sucking up all he has as a dry sponge will suck up water.

To throw up the sponge. Give up; confess oneself beaten. The METAPHOR is from boxing matches, for when a second tossed a sponge (used to refresh a contestant) into the air it was a sign that his man was beaten.

A sponger is a mean parasite who is always accepting the hospitality of those who will give it and never makes any adequate return.

A Sponging House. A house where persons arrested for debt were kept for 24 hours, before being sent to prison. They were generally kept by a bailiff, and the person lodged was "sponged" of all his money before leaving.

Spoon. A simpleton, a shallow prating duffer used to be called a *spoon*, and hence the name came to be applied to one who indulged in foolish, sentimental love-making, and such a one is said to be *spoony*, and to be *spoons on* the girl.

In nautical phrase *to spoon* is to scud before the wind; and in sculling, to dip the sculls so lightly in the water as to do little more than skim the surface.

Apostle spoons. *See under* APOSTLE.

Love spoons. The giving of elaborately carved love spoons by a lover to his lady as a token during courtship was common in 18th-century Wales and later.

Born with a silver spoon in his mouth. *See under* BORN.

The Wooden Spoon. *See under* WOOD.

He needs a long spoon who sups with the Devil. You will want all your wits about you if you ally or associate yourself with EVIL. SHAKESPEARE alludes to this proverb in the *Comedy of Errors*, IV, iii, and again in *The Tempest*, II, ii, where Stephano says: "Mercy! mercy! this is a devil ... I will leave him, I have no long spoon."

> Therefor behoveth hire a ful long spoon
> The schal ete with a feend
>
> CHAUCER: *Squire's Tale*, 594.

Spoonerism. A form of METATHESIS that consists of transposing the initial sounds of words so as to form some ludicrous combination, often the accidental result of mental tiredness or absent-mindedness; so called from the Rev. W. A. Spooner (1844–1930), Warden of New College, Oxford. Some of the best attributed to him are: "We all know what it is to have a half-warmed fish within us" (for "half-formed wish"); "Yes, indeed; the Lord is a shoving leopard"; and "Kinkering Kongs their titles take." Sometimes the term is applied to the accidental transposition of whole words, as when the tea-shop waitress was asked for "a glass bun and a bath of milk". *Cp.* MALAPROP.

Sport. To sport one's oak. *See under* OAK.

Sporting Seasons in England. The lawful season for venery, which began at Midsummer and lasted till HOLY ROOD DAY, used to be called the *Time of Grace*. The fox and wolf might be hunted from the NATIVITY to the ANNUNCIATION; the roebuck from EASTER to MICHAELMAS; the roe from Michaelmas to CANDLEMAS; the hare from Michaelmas to Midsummer; and the boar from the Nativity to the PURIFICATION.

The times for hunting and shooting are now fixed as follows: those marked thus (*) are fixed by Act of Parliament.

BLACK GAME*, from 20 August to 10 December; but in Somerset, Devon, and the New Forest, from 1 September to 10 December.

Deer, about 12 August to 12 October for stags and from 10 November to 31 March for hinds.

Fox-hunting, early November until April.

Grouse shooting*, 12 August to 10 December.

Otter hunting, mid-April to mid-September.

Patridge shooting*, 1 September to 1 February.

Pheasant shooting*, 1 October to 1 February.

There is no close season for the shooting of rabbits, hares, woodcock, snipe, quail, etc., but it is illegal for shops to sell hares between 1 March and 31 July.

There are special game laws for IRELAND and SCOTLAND and permitted seasons for the taking of trout, salmon, oysters, chub, carp, etc.

Spot. In a spot. In a jam or difficulty, up against it.

On the spot. Immediately, then and there, ready and alert; without having time to move away or do anything else. "He answered on the spot", immediately, without hesitation. **To put on the spot** (U.S.A.), to mark down for assassination; to give one a grilling; to put one in a very difficult position, or virtually inextricable situation.

To knock spots off someone. To excel someone completely in something; originally an Americanism.

Spot cash. Ready money, money down.

Spot check. A surprise check on the spot without notice being given; a random check to serve as a basis for conclusions on a wider basis.

Spot dance. A dance in which the couple focused in the spotlight when the music stops, gain a prize; or, when there is no spotlight, the couple are on a particular spot on the floor not previously revealed to the dancers.

Spot on. Exactly right, right on the mark.

Spouse, one who has promised (Lat. *sponsus*, past part. of *spondere*, to promise). In ancient ROME, the friends of the parties about to be married met at the house of the woman's father to settle the marriage contract. This contract was called *sponsalia* (espousal); the man, *sponsus*, and the woman, *sponsa*.

The spouse of Jesus. St. TERESA of Avila (1515–1582) was given this title by some of her contemporaries.

All thy good works ... shall
Weave a constellation
Of Crowns with which the King thy spouse
Shall build up thy triumphant brows.
CRASHAW: *Hymn to St. Theresa* (1652).

Spout. To spout. To utter in a bombastic, declamatory manner; to declaim.

Up the spout. At the pawnbroker's or more usually nowadays "down the drain", gone, lost, ruined, etc. An allusion to the "spout" up which brokers sent the articles ticketed. When redeemed they returned down the spout—*i.e.* from the storeroom to the shop. It is also a vulgarism meaning "pregnant".

Sprag. To put a sprag in one's wheel. *See* SPOKE.

Sprat. To throw a sprat to catch a mackerel. To give a trifle, to make a concession, etc., in the hope of a bigger return.

Spread-eagle, spread-eaglism, spread-eagled. *See under* EAGLE.

Spring. The season of young growth between WINTER and SUMMER. In the Northern hemisphere, March, April and May; astronomically from 21/22 March to 21/22 June.

Sweet spring, full of sweet days and roses,
A box where sweets compacted lie.
GEORGE HERBERT: *Virtue*.

Spring Tides. The tides that *spring* or rise up higher than other tides. They occur just after new and full MOON, when the gravitational attraction of both SUN and moon acts in a direct line. *Cp.* NEAP TIDES.

Spring, Tom (1795–1851). One of the great pugilists of the English prize ring who claimed the title of English champion on the retirement of Tom Cribb. His real name was Winter, and on retiring (1828) he became landlord of the Castle Tavern, HOLBORN.

Hail to thee, Tom of Bedford, or to by whatever name it may please thee to be called, Spring or Winter ... Hail to thee, last of England's bruisers ... 'Tis a treat to see thee, Tom of Bedford, in thy "public" in Holborn way, whither thou hast retired with thy well-earned bays.
BORROW: *Lavengro*, ch. xxvi.

Springers, The. *See* REGIMENTAL AND DIVISIONAL NICKNAMES.

Sprite. *See* SPIRIT.

Spruce. Smart, dandified. The word is from the old Fr. *Pruce* (Ger. *Preussen*), Prussia, and was originally (16th century) applied to Prussian leather of which particularly neat and smart-looking jerkins were made.

And after them came, syr Edward Haward, then admyral, and with him sir Thomas Parre, in doblettes of Crimosin velvet, voyded lowe on the backe, and before to the cannell bone, laced on the breastes with chaynes of silver, and over that shorte clokes of Crimosyn satyne, and on their heades hattes after dauncers fashion, with fesauntes fethers in theim; They were appareyled after the fashion of Prussia or Spruce.
Hall's Chronicle: Henry VII, year 1 (1542).

Spruce beer is made from the leaves of the spruce fir, this being a rendering of the German name of the tree, *Sprossenfichte*, literally "sprouts-fir".

Spunging House. *See* SPONGING HOUSE.

Spur. The Battle of the Spurs. A name given (1) to the Battle of Courtrai (1302) when the

French were defeated by the Flemings, so called from the thousands of spurs collected as trophies after the battle; (2) to the Battle of Guinegate (1513) when the French spurred away from their vanquishers, the forces of Henry VIII of England and the Emperor Maximilian.

On the spur of the moment. Instantly; without stopping to take thought.

Spur money. A small fine formerly imposed on those who entered a church wearing spurs, because of the interruption caused to divine service by their ringing. It was collected by the choirboys or the BEADLES.

To dish up the spurs. In SCOTLAND, during the times of the BORDER feuds, when any of the great families had come to the end of their provisions, the lady of the house sent up a pair of spurs for the last course, to intimate that it was time to put spurs to the horses and make a raid upon ENGLAND for more cattle.

To ride whip, or **switch and spur.** To ride with all possible speed; to trample down obstacles ruthlessly.

To win his spurs. To gain the rank of knighthood; hence to win entitlement to recognition by one's efforts. When a man was knighted, the person who dubbed him presented him with a pair of gilt spurs.

Sputnik (Russ. travelling-companion). A Russian man-made earth satellite. Sputnik 1, launched 4 October 1957, was the first satellite to be projected successfully into orbit round the earth.

Spy Wednesday. A name given in IRELAND to the Wednesday before GOOD FRIDAY, when JUDAS bargained to become the spy of the Jewish SANHEDRIN (*Matt.* xxvi, 3–5, 14–16).

Squab. Short and fat, plump; a person, cushion, etc., like this (a fat woman is *squabba* in Swedish). A young pigeon—especially an unfledged one—is called a *squab*.

Poet Squab. So Rochester called Dryden, who was very corpulent.

Squab-pie. Pigeon pie, or a pie of mutton, apples and onions.

> Cornwall squab-pie and Devon white-pot brings,
> And Leicester beans and bacon, fit for kings.
> WILLIAM KING: *Art of Cookery*.

Squad, Squadron. *See* AWKWARD SQUAD.

Squalls. Look out for squalls. Expect to meet with difficulties. A nautical term, a squall being a succession of sudden violent gusts of wind (Icel. *skvata*).

Square, A. In modern slang, one who likes orthodox music and not JAZZ and its derivatives; one of "bourgeois" tastes; one who is

not in with current trends, fashions, and hence old-fashioned. There are several suggestions for the origin of these usages none of which is particularly convincing, the most likely being associated with the patrons of the traditional square dance as opposed to the devotees of rocking and rolling, jiving and twisting, etc.

A square deal. A fair deal, one that is straight and above board. Similarly **a square meal** is one that is adequate and satisfying. In both these expressions "square" conveys the idea of "straight", "right", and hence "satisfying".

To square an account. To settle it; to pay the amount owing.

To square accounts with a person. To get even with; to be revenged upon.

To square the circle. To attempt an impossibility. The allusion is to the impossibility of exactly determining the precise ratio (π) between the diameter and the circumference of a circle, and thus constructing a circle of the same area as a given square. Approximately p is 3.14159, but the next decimals would be 26537, and the numbers would go on *ad infinitum*.

To square a person. To bribe him, or to pay him for some extra trouble he has taken.

To square up to a person. To put oneself in a fighting attitude.

> Are you such fools
> To square for this?
> SHAKESPEARE: *Titus Andronicus*, II, i.

Square-bashing. A slang expression used by the armed services for parade-ground drill.

Square rig. *See* FORE AND AFT.

Squarson. A 19th-century usage for a clergyman who was both squire and parson of the parish. The Revd. Sabine Baring-Gould (1834–1924), Vicar of Lew Trenchard, Devon, was a classic example of this combination. He was also a novelist, investigator of prehistoric sites, collector of West-country songs and author of the hymn *Onward Christian Soldiers*. *Cp.* JACK RUSSELL.

Squeeze-box. A colloquial name for a concertina which is operated by opening and closing (squeezing) its bellows. It was invented in 1829 by Sir Charles Wheatstone, F.R.S. (1802–1875), a pioneer of the electric telegraph, and son of a musical instrument maker.

Squib. A small firework thrown by hand; a LAMPOON, a short SATIRE.

A damp squib. Said of an enterprise or joke, etc., that fails to come off or satisfy the expectations aroused, just as a damp squib disappointingly fails to explode.

Squinancy. *See* QUINSY.

Squintum, Doctor. George Whitefield (1714–1770), so called by Foote in his farce *The Minor.*

Theodore Hook applied the sobriquet to Edward Irving the preacher (1792–1834), who had an obliquity of the eyes.

Squire. In mediæval times a youth of gentle birth attendant on a KNIGHT (*see* ESQUIRE). From the later 16th century the term is applied to country landowners who exercised sway, mostly paternal, over a district. The squirearchy as such has largely been extinguished by the rise of a more democratic urbanized society on the one hand and rapacious taxation on the other. Addison's benevolent Sir ROGER DE COVERLEY, Fielding's Squire Western in *Tom Jones* and Squire Jawleyford, the creation of Surtees, himself a Northumbrian squire, provide lively portraits of varying traditions.

Squire of dames. Any CAVALIER who is devoted to ladies. Spenser introduces "the Squyre of Dames" in the *Faerie Queene* (Bk. III, Canto vii, stanza 51). *Cp.* CAVALIERE SERVENTE.

Stabat Mater (sta′ băt ma′ ter) (Lat., The Mother was standing). The Latin hymn reciting the SEVEN SORROWS of the Virgin at the CROSS, so called from its opening words, forming part of the service during Passion week in the ROMAN CATHOLIC CHURCH. It is of unknown authorship and in addition to its traditional plainsong there are settings by Palestrina, Pergolesi, Haydn, Rossini, and others.

Stable. To lock the stable door, etc. *See under* HORSE.

Stadium. This word is from Gr. *stadion*, a length of 600 Greek feet (about 606 English feet), which was the length of the foot-race course at OLYMPIA; hence applied to the race, then the place where it was run. The Olympic stadium had terraced seats along its length and the length of the course was traditionally said to have been fixed by HERCULES.

Staff. I keep the staff in my own hand. I keep possession; I retain the right. The staff was the ancient SCEPTRE, and therefore, figuratively, it means power, authority, dignity, etc.

> Give up your staff, sir, and the king his realm.
>
> SHAKESPEARE: *Henry VI, Pt. II*, ii, iii.

The staff of life. Bread, which is the support of life.

> "Bread," says he, "dear brothers, is the staff of life."
>
> SWIFT: *Tale of a Tub*, iv.

To put down one's staff in a place. To abide for a while, to set down one's staff, as a traveller at an inn. The phrase introduced by Thomas Adams (*fl.* 1612–1653), a divine, called by Southey "the prose SHAKESPEARE of PURITAN theologians".

To strike staff. To lodge for the time being.

Stafford. He has had a treat in Stafford Court. He has been thoroughly cudgelled, a pun on the word *staff*, a stick. The French have a similar phrase: *Il a été au festin de Martin Baston* (he has been to JACK DRUM'S ENTERTAINMENT).

Similarly, **Stafford law** is club law—a good beating.

Stag. A male deer or hart.

Baldfaced Stag. *See under* BALD.

The Stag in Christian art. The attribute of St. JULIAN Hospitaller, St. Felix of Valois, and St. Aidan. When it has a crucifix between its horns it alludes to the legend of St. HUBERT. When luminous it belongs to St. Eustachius.

Stag line. An American term for the line of men at the edge of the dance floor, without partners, and waiting to claim one from among those dancing.

Stag party. A gathering of men only—usually out on the spree, and especially on the eve of a wedding.

Stags, in Stock Exchange phraseology, are persons who apply for an allotment of new shares, not because they wish to hold the shares, but because they hope to sell the allotment at a premium.

Stage whispers. A "whisper" intended to be heard by other than those to whom it is addressed, as one on the stage is heard by the audience.

Stagirite, or **Stagyrite, The** (stăj′ i rīt). ARISTOTLE, who was born at Stagira, in Macedon (4th century B.C.).

> And rules as strict his laboured work confine
> As if the Stagirite o'erlooked each line.
>
> POPE: *Essay on Criticism*, i. 137.

Stairs. Below stairs. In the basement among the servants. In most of the town houses built from the end of the 18th century for the well-to-do, the kitchens and servants' daytime quarters were in the basement, hence the phrase. **Above stairs** has the opposite implications and associations. *Cp.* UPSTAIRS.

Stakhanovism (stăk ăn′ ō vizm). In the U.S.S.R., a movement for specially raising the output of labour on a basis of specialized efficiency, after Alexei Stakhanov, a Donetz coal-miner who substantially increased his daily output by rationalization. In 1935 Stalin held a conference of Stakhanovites in which he extolled the working-man.

Stalemate. To stalemate a person. To bring him to a standstill, render his projects worthless or abortive. The phrase is from CHESS, *stalemate* being the position in which the king is the only moveable piece and he, though not in CHECK, cannot move without becoming so. *Stale* in this word is probably from O.Fr. *estal* (our *stall*), a fixed position.

Stalingrad. Formerly Tsaritsyn, on the Volga, renamed to commemorate its defence by Stalin, in 1917, against the WHITE RUSSIANS. Stalin died in 1953 and in 1962 the name was changed to Volgograd. In 1943 it was the scene of the decisive defeat of the German VI Army.

Stalking-horse. A mask to conceal some design; a person put forward to mislead; a sham. Sportsmen often used to conceal themselves behind horses, and go on stalking step by step till they got within shot of the game.

> He uses his folly like a stalking-horse, and under the presentation of that he shoots his wit.
> SHAKESPEARE: *As You Like It*, V, iv.

Stammerer, The. Louis II of France, *le Bègue* (846, 877–879).

Michael II, Emperor of the East (820–829).

Balbus Notker, monk of St. Gall (surnamed Balbulus) (*c*. 840–912).

Stamp. 'Tis of the right stamp. Has the stamp of genuine merit. A METAPHOR taken from current coin, which is stamped with a recognized stamp and superscription.

> I weigh the man, not his title, 'tis not the king's stamp can make the metal heavier or better.
> WYCHERLEY: *The Plain Dealer*, I, i (1677).
> The rank is but the guinea's stamp;
> The man's the gowd for a'that!
> BURNS: *Is There For Honest Poverty?*

Stand. To be at a stand. To be in doubt as to further progress, perplexed at what to do next.

To let a thing stand over. To defer consideration of it to a more favourable opportunity.

To stand by. To be ready to give assistance in case of need. A *stand-by* is a person or thing on which one can confidently rely.

To stand for a child. To be sponsor for it; to stand in its place and answer for it.

To stand in with. To go shares, to become a party to.

To stand it out. Persist in what one says. A translation of "persist" (Lat. *per-sisto* or *per-sto*).

To stand off and on. To sail away from the shore and then towards it, repeatedly, usually to keep a particular mark in sight.

To stand Sam, stand to reason, stand treat, etc. *See these words*.

To stand to one's guns. To persist in a statement; not to give way. A military phrase.

To stand up for. To support, to uphold.

To stand up for one's privilege, or on **punctilios.** Quietly to insist on one's position, etc., being recognized; this is the Latin *insisto*.

A stand-in. A substitute.

Stand-offish. Unsociable, rather snobbishly reserved.

Standing orders. Rules or instructions constantly in force, as those of a commanding officer or those rules of the Houses of PARLIAMENT for the conduct of proceedings which stand in force till they are rescinded or superseded. The suspension of the latter is generally caused by a desire to hurry through a BILL with unusual expedition.

The Standing Fishes Bible. *See* BIBLE, SOME SPECIALLY NAMED EDITIONS.

Standard. Properly a large flag tapering towards the fly, slit at the end and flown by personages of rank. It bore the owner's badges and its length depended upon the owner's rank.

The personal *Royal Standard* of the British Sovereign is a banner in shape and quarterings. The word is from Lat. *extendere*, to stretch out, through O.Fr. *estandard*. *See* THE BATTLE OF THE STANDARD, *below*.

Standard is also applied to a measure of extent, weight, value, etc., which is established by law or custom as an example or criterion for others; and, in figurative use from this, to any criterion or principle, as, "the standard of political rectitude". The weights and measures were formerly known as "the king's standard", as being official and recognized by royal authority.

In uses such as an *electric-light standard* (the lamp-post), *standard rose* (*i.e.* one that stands on its own stem and is not trained to a wall or espalier), etc., the word is the result of confusion with *stand*.

The Battle of the Standard. Between the English and Scots at Cowton Moor, near Northallerton (22 August 1138). Here David I, fighting on behalf of Matilda, was defeated by King Stephen's army under Thurstan, Archbishop of York, and Raoul, Bishop of Durham. It received its name from the mast (erected on a wagon) carrying the banners of St. PETER of York, St. JOHN OF BEVERLEY, and St. WILFRED of Ripon, surmounted by a PYX containing the HOST. It was this occasion which introduced the word *standard* into the English language.

Gold Standard. *See under* GOLD.

The standard of living. A conventional term to express the supposed degree of comfort or luxury usually enjoyed by a man, a family, or a nation: this may be high or low according to circumstances.

Standard Time, or **Zone Time.** A system of time-keeping in most parts of the world based on 24 meridians, each 15° apart, starting from Greenwich, thus giving an exact difference of an hour between any two adjacent zones (certain countries have adopted zones involving half-hour differences). Such a system was first adopted by the chief railway companies of Canada and the U.S.A. in 1883 to overcome the obvious inconveniences causd by the differing local times on their routes. *Cp.* DAYLIGHT SAVING; GREENWICH TIME.

Stang. To ride the stang. At one time in SCOTLAND and the north of ENGLAND a man who ill-treated his wife (or sometimes a HEN-PECKED husband) was made to sit on a *stang* (O.E. *staeng*, a pole) hoisted on men's shoulders. On this uneasy conveyance the "stanger" was carried in procession amidst the hootings and jeerings of his neighbours. *Cp.* RANDAN; RIDING; ROUGH MUSIC; SHALLAL; SKIMMINGTON.

Stanhope (stăn' ŏp). The **Stanhope lens,** a cylindrical lens with spherical ends of different radii, and the **Stanhope press,** the first iron printing press to be used (1798), are so called from the inventor, Charles, third Earl of Stanhope (1753–1816).

Stannaries, The. The tin-mining areas of Devon and Cornwall (Lat. *stannum*, tin), an appanage of the Crown, and after 1337 of the Duchy of Cornwall. There were four in Cornwall and four in Devon (covering Dartmoor and surrounding areas). A warden was appointed in 1198 and in 1201 King John issued their first charter confirming the tinners' privileges and making the Warden the only magistrate to have jurisdiction over them. The tinners had their own representative meetings or "parliaments" as late as 1752 and were subject to special *Stannary Courts* which were not finally abolished until 1897. The courts, under the Lord Warden, vice-warden, and stewards were also concerned with regulation of the trade. The miners were anciently called *stannators*; their privileges arose from the king's aim to increase tin production.

Star. In ecclesiastical art a number of SAINTS are depicted with a star; thus, St. Bruno bears one on his breast, St. DOMINIC, St. Humbert, St. Peter of Alcantara, one over the head, or on the forehead, etc. *See also* BLAZE.

A star of some form constitutes part of the insignia of every order of Knighthood; the *Star and Garter*, a common PUBLIC-HOUSE SIGN, being in reference to the Most Noble Order of the GARTER.

Star is also figuratively applied to a noted performer, especially a film actor; hence the **star part,** the part taken by the leading actor; who is the **star turn.**

The stars were said by the old astrologers to have almost omnipotent influence on the lives and destinies of man (*cp. Judges* v, 20: "The stars in their courses fought against Sisera"), and to this belief is due a number of phrases as: **Bless my stars! You may thank your lucky stars; star-crossed** (not favoured by the stars, unfortunate); **to be born under an unlucky star,** etc.

Star Chamber. A court of mediæval origin, composed of the King's Council, reinforced by judges, which developed criminal jurisdiction. So named from its meeting place, the Star Chamber in the Palace of WESTMINSTER, the ceiling or roof of which was decorated with stars. The reputation it acquired for harshness was largely unjustified and it was frequently attacked by the Common Lawyers who resented its jurisdiction. It was abolished by the LONG PARLIAMENT in 1641.

Star of Bethlehem. A bulbous plant of the lily family (*Ornithogallum umbellatum*), with star-shaped white flowers. The French peasants call it *La dame d'onze heures*, because it opens at eleven o'clock.

Star of David, or **Shield of David.** A symbol of obscure origin (also called SOLOMON'S SEAL) made up of two superimposed equilateral triangles thus: ✡. It was adopted by the first Zionist Conference in 1897 and is the symbol on the flag of Israel. It is found as early as the 3rd century but is not mentioned in the BIBLE or the TALMUD. Jews were made to wear such a cloth star under the NAZI régime and, to show his disapproval of this racial indignity, King Christian X of Denmark wore a Star of David during the German occupation of his country.

Star of India. A British order of knighthood, The Most Exalted Order of the Star of India, instituted by Queen Victoria in 1861. Its motto is "Heaven's Light our Guide" and it was a means of recognizing services to India and the loyalty of its princely rulers. No appointments have been made since 1947 and it is now obsolescent.

Star of South Africa. A pear-shaped DIAMOND discovered near the Orange River in 1869, also called the *Dudley diamond* after the Earl of Dudley, its first purchaser. It weighs 47.7 carats but was 85.75 carats when uncut.

Stars and Bars. The flag of the 11 CON-FEDERATE STATES of America which broke away from the UNION in 1861. It consisted of two horizontal red bars with a narrow white bar between them; in the top left corner a blue union bearing eleven white stars arranged in a circle.

Stars and Stripes, or the Star-spangled Banner. The flag of the United States of America. The *stripes* are emblematic of the original 13 states, and the *stars*—of which there are 50—of the States that now constitute the UNION. It is also popularly called *Old Glory*, a name said to have been given by William Driver, a Salem skipper, in 1831.

At the outset of the American Revolution each state adopted its own flag, that of Massachusetts bearing a pine tree and that of South Carolina a rattlesnake with the words "Don't tread on me". In 1776 a national flag of 13 red and white stripes with crosses of St. GEORGE and St. ANDREW in a canton was adopted.

By act of Congress, 14 June 1777, a flag of 13 alternate red and white stripes, with a union of 13 white stars on a blue field was adopted, the stars arranged in a circle representing "a new constellation". It was apparently designed by Francis Hopkinson and the story that it was first embroidered by Betsy Ross is now discredited.

In 1794 (after the admission of Vermont and Kentucky), the stripes and stars were increased to 15, but in 1818 it was decided that the original 13 stripes should be restored, and stars added to signify the number of States in the Union. The stars were also squared up for the first time.

The *Stars and Stripes forever* is the name of Sousa's most popular military band tune, and the *Star-Spangled Banner* was adopted as the official anthem of the United States in 1931. The words were written by Francis Scott Key in 1814, the tune being that of 'ANACREON in Heaven", a popular drinking song composed by J. S. Smith for the Anacreontic Society of London.

His star is in the ascendant. He is in luck's way; said of a person to whom some good fortune has fallen and who is very prosperous. According to ASTROLOGY, those leading stars which are above the horizon at a person's birth influence his life and fortune; when those stars are in the ASCENDANT, he is strong, healthy, and lucky; but when they are in the descendant below the horizon, his stars do not shine on him, he is in the shade and subject to ill fortune. *Cp.* HOUSES,

ASTROLOGICAL.

I'll make you see stars! "I'll put you through it"; literally, will give you such a blow in the eye with my fist that, when you are struck, you'll experience the optical illusion of seeing brilliant streaks, radiating and darting in all directions.

Star-gazy, of Starry-gazy pie. An old Cornish dish of pilchards baked in a pie with their heads poking through the crust.

Starboard and Larboard. *Star-* is the O.E. *steor*, paddle, rudder, and *bord*, side. Larboard is perhaps from *ladebord*, the lading side. *See* PORT.

Stare. To stare like a stuck pig. *See under* PIG.

Starvation Dundas. Henry Dundas, first Viscount Melville (1742–1811), was so called. He first used the word *starvation* or brought it to popular notice in a Parliamentary speech (1775) concerned with the placing of restrictions on American colonial trade.

Starved with cold. Half dead with cold (O.E. *steofan*, to die).

States, The. A common term for the UNITED STATES OF AMERICA.

States General. In France, the national consultative assembly (*États Généraux*), of 14th-century origin, but not summoned between 1614 and 1789. It consisted of three estates, Clergy, Nobility and Third Estate (*le tiers état*) or commoners (the vast majority of deputies being from the bourgeoisie when the Revolution began in 1789).

The name is still applied to the PARLIAMENT of the Netherlands consisting of two chambers, the upper elected by members of the Provincial States and the second chamber elected by the people.

Station (Lat. *statio*, a place of standing, station, etc.). This word with the meaning of a place where people assemble for a specific duty or purpose has many applications; *e.g.* a railway station (U.S.A. depot; a police station, a lifeboat station, etc. In Australia, it was used as early as 1830 in the sense of a cattle farm or ranch. Thus, **station black,** an aboriginal; **station jack,** a sort of meat pudding; **station mark,** a brand; **station super,** a manager.

The Stations of the Cross; known as the *via Calvaria* or *via Crucis*. Each station represents, by fresco, picture, or otherwise, some incident in the passage of Christ from the judgment hall to CALVARY, and at each one prayers are offered up in memory of the event represented. They are as follows:

(1) The condemnation to death.
(2) Christ is made to bear His CROSS.

(3) His first fall under the cross.
(4) The meeting with the Virgin.
(5) Simon the Cyrenean helps to carry the cross.
(6) Veronica wipes the sacred face.
(7) The second fall.
(8) Christ speaks to the daughters of Jerusalem.
(9) The third fall.
(10) Christ is stripped of His garments.
(11) The nailing to the cross.
(12) The giving up of the Spirit.
(13) Christ is taken down from the cross.
(14) The deposition in the sepulchre.

Stator (stā′tôr) (Lat., the stopper or arrester). When the Romans fled from the SABINES, they stopped at a certain place and made terms with the victors. On this spot they afterwards built a temple to JUPITER, and called it the temple of Jupiter Stator, or Jupiter who caused them to stop in their flight.

Status quo (stā′tùs kwō) (Lat.). The state in which, the existing state or condition.

Status quo ante (Lat.). The previous position.

In statu quo (Lat.). In the same state (as before).

Status symbol. A possession, privilege, etc., which is a mark of one's social standing; generally used caustically of a fashionable, expensive, material object, the possession of which is designed to impress others and to flatter one's own self-esteem. *Cp.* KEEPING UP WITH THE JONESES *under* KEEP.

Statute (Lat. *statutum*; from *statuere*, to cause to stand; the same word, etymologically, as *statue*). A law enacted by a legislative body, an ACT OF PARLIAMENT; also laws enacted by the king and council before there were any regular parliaments. Hence, a *statute mile* is the measure as by law established and not according to local custom.

On the statute book. Included among the laws of the nation; the *statute book* is the whole body of the laws.

Statute fair. A mop fair. *See* HIRING FAIR *under* FAIR.

Steaks, Sublime Society of the. *See* BEEFSTEAK CLUB.

Steal. One man may steal a horse, while another may not look over the hedge. *See under* HORSE.

To steal a march on one. To obtain an advantage by stealth, as when an army appears unexpectedly before an enemy.

To steal the show. To win the greatest applause or acclamation; to surpass or outshine all other performers or players. An expression at first limited to performers in stage shows.

Stolen sweets are always sweeter. Things procured by stealth, and game illicitly taken, have the charm of illegality to make them the more palatable. SOLOMON says, "Stolen waters are sweet, and bread eaten in secret is pleasant" (*Prov.* ix, 17). In one of the songs in Act III, sc. iv, of Randolph's *Amyntos* (1638) are the lines:

Furto cuncta magis bella,
Furto dulcior Puella,
Furto omnia decora,
Furto poma dulciora,

which were translated by Leigh Hunt as:

Stolen sweets are always sweeter,
Stolen kisses much completer,
Stolen looks are nice in chapels,
Stolen, stolen, be your apples.

Steam. To let off steam. To give vent to anger; to work off one's feelings; to work off energy; as steam pressure is released from an engine or boiler.

Steelboys. Bands of ULSTER insurgents who committed agrarian outrages in protest against the TITHE system in the early 1770s. Probably named from their "hearts of steel". *Cp.* OAK BOYS; WHITEBOYS.

Steelyard. The London depot of the HANSE from 1320 to 1597, occupying premises between Upper Thames Street and the river. The buildings were ultimately sold in 1853 and demolished ten years later to make way for Cannon Street Station. The name is a mistranslation of Ger. *Stalhof*, a sample yard or hall.

Steelyard, the weighing machine with unequal arms, in which the article to be weighed is hung from the shorter arm and a weight moved along the other till they balance, is named from the metal and the measure (O.E. *gyrd, gerd*, a stick).

Steenie. A nickname given by James I to his handsome favourite, George Villiers, Duke of Buckingham, with whom he was infatuated. "Steenie" is a Scotticism for STEPHEN, the allusion being to *Acts* vi, 15, where those who looked on Stephen the martyr "saw his face as it had been the face of an angel".

Steeplechase. Originally a horse race across fields, hedges, ditches and other obstacles, now run over a prepared course. The term is said to have originated from the frolic of a party of foxhunters in IRELAND (1803) who decided to race in a straight line to a distant steeple. The term is also applied to a cross-country race of this kind on foot. *See* RACES.

Steeple house. An old PURITAN epithet for a church.

Steering committee. A committee which decides the programme and order of business. A term of American origin.

Stentor (sten′tôr). **The Voice of a Stentor.** A very loud voice. Stentor was a Greek herald in the Trojan war. According to HOMER (*Iliad*, V, 783), his voice was as loud as that of 50 men combined; hence *stentorian*, loud-voiced.

Step-. A prefix used before *father, mother, brother, sister, son, daughter*, etc., to indicate that the person spoken of is a relative only by the marriage of a parent, and not by blood (O.E. *steop*, connected with *astieped*, bereaved). Thus, a man who marries a widow with children becomes *stepfather* to those children and, if he has children by her, these and those of the widow's earlier marriage are *stepbrothers* or *stepsisters*. The latter are also called *half-brothers* and *half-sisters*; but some make a distinction between the terms, *half-brother* being kept for what we have already defined as a *stepbrother*, this latter term being applied only between the children of former marriages when both parents have been previously married.

I feel like a stepchild. Said by one who is being left out of the fun or getting none of the titbits. Stepchildren are proverbially treated by the step-parent with somewhat less consideration than the others.

Stephen, St. (d. *c.* 35). The first Christian martyr—the "protomartyr". He was accused of blasphemy and stoned to death (*see Acts* vi–viii). He is commemorated on 26 December; the name means "wreath" or "crown" (Gr. *stephanos*).

The Crown of St. Stephen. The crown of Hungary, this St. Stephen being the first King of Hungary (975, 998–1038). He became a Christian in 985 and set out to convert his country. He was canonized in 1083 and his day is 16 August. The existing crown is probably of 13th-century origin. It was removed to the U.S.A. in 1944.

St. Stephen's. PARLIAMENT is still sometimes so called, because for nearly 300 years prior to its destruction by fire in 1834, the Commons used to sit in the Chapel of St. Stephen in the Palace of WESTMINSTER. *See* BIG BEN.

St. Stephen's loaves. Stones.

Fed with St. Stephen's bread. Stoned.

Sterling. A term applied to British money and also to GOLD and SILVER plate denoting that they are of standard value or purity; hence applied figuratively to anything of sound intrinsic worth, as *A man of sterling qualities*. The word, first met with in the 12th century, has been held to be a corruption of *Easterling*, a name given to the HANSE merchants trading with England; but it is probably from O.E. *steorling*, a coin with a star, from the fact that some of the early Norman pennies had a small star on them.

Stern reality. *See* BISHOP.

Stern. To sit at the stern; At the stern of public affairs. Having the management of public affairs. The stern (O.E. *steorne*) is the steering place, hence the helm.

> Sit at chiefest stern of public weal.
> SHAKESPEARE: *Henry VI, Pt. I*, I, i.

Sternold and Hopkins. The old metrical version of the Psalms that used to be bound up with the BOOK OF COMMON PRAYER and sung in churches. They were mainly the work of Thomas Sternhold (d. 1549) and John Hopkins (d. 1570). The completed version appeared in 1562.

> Mistaken choirs refuse the solemn strain
> Of ancient Sternhold.
> CRABBE: *The Borough*, III, 1. 130.

Stet (Lat., let it stand). A direction to cancel a correction or deletion previously made in a MS., proof, etc.

Stetson. A large-brimmed hat habitually worn by cattle-men in the U.S.A., so called from the best-known manufacturer, John B. Stetson.

Stevenographs. Coloured silk pictures woven on a special Jacquard loom, first made in 1879 by Thomas Stevens, a Coventry silk weaver. Some 180 designs were produced on popular subjects including Dick TURPIN on Black Bess, and the London-York stage-coach. The factory was destroyed by bombing in 1940.

Stew. In a stew. In a fix, a flurry; in a state of mental agitation.

Irish stew. A stew of mutton, onions, and potatoes; called "Irish" from the predominance of potatoes, regarded as the Irishman's staple diet.

To stew in one's own juice. To suffer the natural consequences of one's own actions; to reap as one has sown. Chaucer has:

> In his own gress I mad him frie
> For anger and for very jalousie.
> *Wife of Bath's Tale (Prologue)*, 1. 487.

Stick. An old stick-in-the-mud. A dull, unprogressive person, sometimes but not always "old". *Cp.* SQUARE.

It sticks out a mile! It is absolutely obvious, one cannot miss it, there is no mistake about it, as, "Anyone can see he's a rogue—it sticks out a mile!"

It sticks out like a sore thumb. It hits you in the eye, it looks very much out of place.

Over the sticks. Over the hurdles; hence a hurdle-race or a STEEPLECHASE.

The policy of the big stick. One backed by threat of force. *See* BIG STICK DIPLOMACY *under* BIG.

The wrong end of the stick. Not the true facts; a distorted version. To *have got hold of* *the wrong end of the stick* is to have mis-understood the story.

To have, or **get the dirty end of the stick.** To come off badly; to be left to bear the brunt of things; not to be treated fairly.

To stick at it. To persevere.

To stick at nothing. To be heedless of all obstacles in accomplishing one's desire; to be utterly unscrupulous.

To stick in one's gullet. Something difficult to swallow or digest, literally or metaphorically; something repugnant or unacceptable. **To stick in one's gizzard** and **to stick in one's craw** (a bird's crop) are similar expressions.

To stick it up. Old slang for leaving one's "SCORE" at the tavern to be paid later; a note of it was stuck, or chalked up, on the back of the door.

To stick to, or **in his fingers.** To appropriate improperly or unlawfully (usually money); to embezzle.

To stick up. To waylay and rob a coach, etc.; originally Australian BUSH-RANGER'S slang; in common use nowadays for armed robbery when the victims are covered with revolvers and told to "stick 'em up", *i.e.* to hold their hands above their heads.

The sticking-place. The point at which a screw becomes tight; hence, the point aimed at. SHAKESPEARE'S use of the word is probably an allusion to the peg of a musical instrument, which is not much use unless it is actually in the "sticking-place".

> We fail!
> But screw your courage to the sticking-place,
> And we'll not fail.
>
> *Macbeth*, I, vii.

The sticks. An American colloquialism meaning "countryside"; "rural area"; "wilds", etc. *Cp.* OUTBACK.

Stuck up. Said of pretentious people who give themselves airs, nobodies who assume to be somebodies. The allusion is to the peacock, which sticks up its train allegedly to add to its "importance" and overawe antagonists.

Stickit. A Scotticism for "stuck (*stick-ed*) half-way", as a *stickit job*, one that is unfinished or unsatisfactory; hence, applied to persons who have given up their work through lack of means or capacity or some other reason, as a *stickit minister*, one who has failed to get a pastoral charge, or to obtain preferment. S. R. Crockett wrote a novel called *The Stickit Minister* (1893).

Stickler. A stickler over trifles. One particular about things of no moment. *Sticklers* were the umpires in tournaments, or seconds in single combats, very punctilious about the minutest points of etiquette. The word is connected with O.E. *stihtan*, to arrange, regulate.

Stiff. Slang for a corpse; also for a horse that is sure to lose in a race; also (with reference to the stiff interest exacted by moneylenders) an I O U, a bill of acceptance.

> His "stiff" was floating about in too many directions, at too many high figures.
>
> OUIDA: *Under Two Flags*, ch. vii.

Stigmata (stig′ mà tà). Marks developed on the body of certain persons, which correspond to some or all of the wounds received by our Saviour in His trial and crucifixion. It is a well-known psychological phenomenon and has been demonstrated in many modern instances. From Gr. *stigma*, the brand with which slaves and criminals in ancient Greece and ROME were marked; hence our verb *stigmatize*, to mark as with a brand of disgrace.

Among those who are said to have been marked with the stigmata are: (1) *Men*. St. PAUL, who said "I bear in my body the marks of the Lord Jesus" (*Gal.* vi, 17); Angelo del Paz (all the marks); Benedict of Reggio (the CROWN OF THORNS), 1602; Carlo di Saeta (the lance-wound); FRANCIS of Assisi (all the marks), 15 September 1224; and Nicholas of Ravenna. Francesco Forgione (1887–1968), who became a Capuchin friar in 1902 taking the name of brother Pio, is said to have received stigmata on his hands in 1902. (2) *Women*. Bianca de Gazeran; Catherine of Siena; Catharine di Raconisco (the CROWN OF THORNS), 1538; Cecilia di Nobili of Nocera, 1655; Clara di Pugny (mark of the spear), 1514; "Estatica" of Caldaro (all the marks), 1842; Gabriella da Piezolo of Aquila (the spear-mark), 1472; Hieronyma Carvaglio (the spear-mark, which bled every Friday); Joanna Maria of the Cross; Maria Razzi of Chio (marks of the thorny crown); Maria Villani (ditto); Mary Magdalen di Pazzi; Mechtildis von Stanz; Ursula of Valencia; Veronica Giuliani (all the marks), 1694; Vincenza Ferreri of Valencia; Anna Emmerich of Dülmen, Westphalia (d. 1824); Maria von Mörl (in 1839); Louise Lateau (1868), and Anne Girling, the foundress of the English SHAKERS. Theresa Neumann, of Kounersreuth, Germany (1898–1962), received her first stigmata on the tops of her hands and feet, on GOOD FRIDAY, 1926. In subsequent years more marks appeared, on her side, shoulders, and brow. Stigmata as studied in her case, never heal and never suppurate.

Stilo Novo (stī′ lō nō′ vō) (Lat., in the new style). Newfangled notions. When the CALENDAR was reformed by Gregory XIII

(1582), letters used to be dated *stilo novo*, which grew in time to be a CANT phrase for any innovation. *See* OLD STYLE.

> And so I leave you to your *stilo novo*.
>
> BEAUMONT and FLETCHER:
> *Woman's Prize*, IV, iv.

Stir Up Sunday. The last SUNDAY after TRINITY. So called from the first two words of the collect: "Stir up, we beseech thee, O Lord, the wills of thy faithful people ...". It was an old custom to stir the CHRISTMAS plum pudding on this day, hence the old schoolboy rhyme, beginning, "Stir up, we beseech thee, the pudding in the pot."

Stirrup. Literally, a rope to climb by (O.E. *stirap*; from *stigan*, to climb, and *rap*, a rope).

Stirrup cup. A "parting cup" given to guests on leaving, when their feet were in the stirrups. *Cp.* DOCH-AN-DORIS.

> Lord Marmion's bugles blew to horse;
> Then came the stirrup-cup in course;
> Between the baron and his host,
> No point of courtesy was lost.
>
> SCOTT: *Marmion*, I, 31.

Among the ancient Romans a "parting cup" was drunk to ensure sound sleep (*see* Ovid, *Fasti*, ii, 35).

Stirrup oil. A beating; a variety of STRAP OIL.

Stiver (stī′ vẽr). **Not a stiver.** Not a penny, not a cent. The stiver (*stuiver*) was a Dutch coin, equal to about a penny.

> Set him free,
> And you shall have your money to a stiver
> And present payment.
>
> FLETCHER: *Beggars' Bush*, I, iii.

Stock. Originally a tree-trunk, or stem (connected with *stick*); hence, in figurative use, something fixed, also regarded as the origin of families, groups, etc.; as **He comes of a good stock,** from a good stem, of good line of descent, **Languages of Indo-Germanic stock,** etc.

To worship stocks and stones is to worship idols, *stock* here being taken as a type of a motionless fixed thing like a tree-stump. The village **stocks,** in which petty offenders were confined by the wrists and ankles, are so called from the stakes or posts at the side. *Stock* in the sense of a fund or capital derives from that part of the old wooden TALLY which the creditor took with him as evidence of the king's debt, the other portion, known as the *counterstock*, remaining in the EXCHEQUER. The word was then applied to the money which this tally represented, *i.e.* money lent to the government.

His stocks are good. His reputation is sound, he is held in good estimation. An allusion to stocks as investments.

It is on the stocks. It is in hand, but not yet finished. The stocks is the frame in which a ship is placed during building and so long as it is in hand it is said to be, or to lie, *on the stocks*.

Live stock. In colloquial usage, lice or other parasitic vermin.

Lock, stock, and barrel. *See* LOCK.

Stock in trade. The goods kept for sale by a shopkeeper; the equipment, tools, etc., for a trade or profession.

To take stock. To ascertain how one's business stands by taking an inventory of all goods and so on in hand, balancing one's books, etc.; hence, to survey one's position and prospects.

Stock-broker, Stock-jobber. The *broker* was engaged in the purchase of stocks and shares for clients on commission; the *jobber* speculated in stocks and shares so as to profit by market fluctuations, acting as an intermediary between buying and selling brokers. The jobber had to be a member of the Stock Exchange but a broker not necessarily; if the latter was not, he was known as an "outside broker" or "kerbstone operator". These differentiations were markedly changed by the BIG BANG. *See also* BUCKETSHOP.

Stock Dove. Also called a blue rock, very similar to a ROCK DOVE; so called from its nesting in old tree stumps or from the erroneous idea that it was the ancestor of varieties of the domestic pigeon.

> The murmuring stockdove's melancholy coo,
> When they their loved mates lament or woo.
>
> THOMSON: *On a Country Life*.

Stock Exchange. A market in which stocks and shares are bought and sold. Such markets had long existed in LONDON (and elsewhere) and in the 18th century speculators and dealers met at JONATHAN's and various other premises. In 1773 they formed an association or Stock Exchange meeting in Sweeting's Alley in what came to be known as the Stock Exchange Coffee-house or tavern. In 1801 it was decided that a more suitable building was needed and the Stock Exchange in CAPEL COURT was opened in 1802, considerably enlarged in 1853–4, and subsequently. The London Stock Exchange, known in the City as the HOUSE is the oldest in the world and was not rivalled by that of New York (originating in 1792) until the 20th century. *See* BACKWARDATION; BEAR; BIG BANG; CONTANGO; STOCKBROKER; STOCKJOBBER; WALL STREET.

Stockfish. Dried cod, cured without salt, supposed to derive the name from its being beaten with a stock or club to make it more tender. Till beaten it was very tough and was called *buckhorn*. Hence the expression **I will beat thee like a stockfish.**

> Peace, thou'lt be beaten like a stockfish else.
> JONSON: *Every Man in His Humour*, III, i.

In SHAKESPEARE's day the word was often used as abuse; thus Falstaff shouts at Prince Henry:

> 'Sblood, you starveling, you elf-skin, you dried neat's tongue, you bull's pizzle, you stock-fish!
> *Henry IV, I*, II, iv.

Stock-rider. The Australian term for one in charge of cattle, *i.e.* stock. He uses a *stock-whip*, and herds his beasts in a *stockyard*.

Stocking. Used of one's savings or "NEST-EGG", because formerly money used to be hoarded up in an old stocking, which was frequently hung up the chimney for safety. *See* LONG STOCKING *under* LONG.

Blue stocking. *See under* BLUE.

Stockwell Ghost. A supposed ghost that created a great sensation in Stockwell (London) in 1772, then a village. The author of the strange noises was Anne Robinson, a servant. *Cp.* COCK LANE GHOST; SAMPFORD GHOST.

Stoic. (stō′ ik). A school of Greek philosophers founded by ZENO (*c.* 308 B.C.) who held that virtue was the highest good, and that the passions and appetites should be rigidly subdued. *See* PORCH. The later Stoic school of the Romans is represented by Seneca, Epictetus, and Marcus Aurelius.

> The ancient Stoics in their porch
> With fierce dispute maintained their church,
> Beat out their brains in fight and study
> To prove that virtue is a body,
> That *bonum* is an animal,
> Made good with stout polemic bawl.
> BUTLER: *Hudibras*, II, ii, 15.

Stole (Lat. *stola*). An ecclesiastical vestment, also called the Orarium. Deacons wear the stole over the left shoulder like a sash. Priests normally wear it round the neck, both ends hanging loose in front. With Eucharistic vestments the ends are crossed over the chest.

Stole, Groom of the. Formerly, the first lord of the bedchamber, a high officer of the Royal HOUSEHOLD ranking next after the vice-chamberlain. In the reign of Queen Anne it was held by a woman, and on the accession of Queen Victoria the office was replaced by that of the *Mistress of the Robes*.

Stole here is not connected with Lat. *stola*, a robe, but refers to the King's *stool* or privy. As late as the 16th century, when the king made a royal progress his close-stool formed part of the baggage and was in charge of a special officer or groom.

Stolen sweets. *See under* STEAL.

Stomach. Used figuratively of inclination. Thus SHAKESPEARE has:

> He which hath no stomach for this fight.
> *Henry V*, IV, iii.
> He [Wolsey] was a man of an unbounded stomach.
> *Henry VIII*, IV, ii.
> Let me praise you while I have the stomach.
> *Merchant of Venice*, III, v.

An army marches on its stomach. The troops need to be well provisioned if they are to be fighting fit.

To stomach an insult. To swallow or put up with an insult.

Stone. Used figuratively when some characteristic of a stone is implied as, *stone blind*, *stone cold*, *stone dead*, *stone deaf*, *stone still*, etc., as blind, cold, dead, deaf, or still as a stone.

> I will not struggle; I will stand stone still.
> SHAKESPEARE: *King John*, IV, i.

In all parts of the world primitive peoples have set up stones, especially those of meteoric origin (fabled to have fallen from HEAVEN), in connexion with religious rites. Anaxagoras mentions a stone that fell from JUPITER in Thrace, a description of which is given by Pliny. The Ephesians asserted that their image of DIANA came from Jupiter. The stone at Emessa, in Syria, worshipped as a symbol of the SUN, was a similar meteorite, and there were similar stones at Abydos and Potidæa. At Corinth one was venerated as ZEUS, and Tacitus describes one in Cyprus dedicated to VENUS. The famous BLACK STONE set in the KAABA is also a meteorite.

The great stone circles of Avebury, STONEHENGE, and the STANDING STONES OF STENNESS, are particularly noteworthy examples of the industry and ingenuity of early man, each having their mythological and religious associations. *See also* ÆTITES; PHILOSOPHER'S STONE; PRECIOUS STONES; TOUCH-STONE; etc.

Hag-stones. Flints naturally perforated used in country places as charms against witches, the EVIL EYE, etc. They are hung on the key of an outer door, round the neck for luck, on the bed-post to prevent nightmare, on a horse's collar to ward off disease, etc.

London Stone. *See under* LONDON.

The Standing Stones of Stenness, in Orkney, some 4 miles from Stromness, comprise a NEOLITHIC stone-circle 340 ft. in diameter of which only 13 stones of a probable 60 are still standing, the tallest being 14 ft high. Scott in a note (*The Pirate*, ch xxxviii) says "One of the pillars ... is perforated with a circular hole, through which loving couples are wont to join hands when they take the *Promise of* ODIN." The *Eyrbig* *gia Saga* gives an account of the setting apart of the Helga Fels, or Holy Rock, by the pontiff Thorolf for solemn meetings.

The Stone Age. The period when stone implements were used by primitive man, before the discovery of metals. Its dating varies considerably over the continents, the use of bows and arrows, stone axes, bone tools, etc., persisting in Papua, New Guinea, etc., in the present century. *See* PALÆOLITHIC; NEOLITHIC.

The Stone of Destiny. *See* SCONE.

Stone frigate. A sailor's name for barracks, or a shore establishment. *Cp.* BARRACK STANCHION.

The stone jacket, or jug. *See* JUG.

Stone lilies. *See* St. CUTHBERT'S BEADS.

Stone soup, or St. Bernard's soup. The story goes that a beggar asked alms at a lordly mansion, but was told by the servants that they had nothing to give him. "Sorry for it," said the man, "but will you let me boil a little water to make some soup of this stone?" This was so novel a proceeding, that the curiosity of the servants was aroused, and the man was readily furnished with a saucepan, water, and a spoon. In he popped the stone, and begged for a little salt and pepper for flavouring. Stirring the water and tasting it, he said it would be the better for any fragments of meat and vegetables they might happen to have. These were supplied, and ultimately he asked for a little ketchup or other sauce. When ready the servants tasted it, and declared that "stone soup" was excellent.

This story, which was a great favourite in the 16th and 17th centuries, was told with many variations, horseshoes, nails, ram's-horns, etc., taking the place of the stone as narrated above.

A rolling stone gathers no moss. One who is always on the move and does not settle down will never become prosperous or wealthy. A common proverb. Tusser in his *Five Hundred Points of Good Husbandrie* (1573) has:

> The stone that is rolling can gather no moss.
> For master and servant oft changing is loss.

Stone of stumbling. An obstacle, stumbling-block, or an occasion for being hindered. The phrase is from *Is.* viii, 14:

> He shall be...for a stone of stumbling and for a rock of offence to both the houses of Israel.

To cast the first stone. To take the lead in criticizing, fault-finding, quarrelling, etc. The phrase is from *John* viii, 7:

> He that is without sin among you, let him first cast a stone at her.

To kill two birds with one stone. *See under* BIRD.

To leave no stone unturned. To spare no trouble, time, expense, etc., in endeavouring to accomplish your aim. After the defeat of Mardonius at Platæa (477 B.C.), a report was current that the Persian general had left great treasures in his tent. Polycrates the Theban sought long, but found them not. The ORACLE of Delphi, being consulted, told him "to leave no stone unturned", and the treasures were discovered.

You have stones in your mouth. Applied to one who stutters or speaks very indistinctly. Demosthenes cured himself of stuttering by putting pebbles in his mouth and declaiming on the seashore.

> The orator who once
> Did fill his mouth with pebble stones
> When he harangued.
> BUTLER: *Hudibras*, I, i, 115.

Stony Arabia. A mistranslation of *Arabia Petræa*, where Petræa is supposed to be an adjective formed from Gr. *petros*, a stone. The name really derives from the city of Petra, the capital of the Nabathæans. *Cp.* YEMEN.

Stonehenge. The most famous prehistoric monument in Britain, although covering a smaller area than Avebury. It is situated on Salisbury Plain, 2 miles west of Amesbury. The name is from O.E. *hengen*, in reference to something hung up, in this case the horizontal lintel stones. At various times regarded as having been built by the DRUIDS, the Romans and the Danes, it is originally of late NEOLITHIC construction and was later reconstructed by the Beaker folk and subsequently. It seems to have last been used *c.* 1400 B.C. It finally consisted of an outer circle of local SARSEN STONES and two inner circles of Blue Stones, apparently from the Prescelly Mountains in Pembrokeshire. The first and third circles are capped with stone lintels. The whole is surrounded by a ditch, inside the bank of which are 56 pits known as *Aubrey holes*. The Hele Stone, over which the sun rises on MIDSUMMER Day, stands in isolation outside the circles. It is certain that Stonehenge was a centre of worship, probably connected with the sun, and it has recently been suggested that it was a massive kind of astronomical clock. Scientific examination of the site did not begin until 1901.

> Three years after this, he himself [Constantine, King of Britain] ... was killed by Conan, and buried close by Uther Pendragon within the structure of stones, which was set up with wonderful art not far from Salisbury, and called in the English tongue, Stonehenge.
> GEOFFREY OF MONMOUTH: *Historia Britonum*, XI, iv.

Stonewall, To. A cricketer's term for adopting purely defensive measures when at the wicket, blocking every ball and not attempting to score. It was originally Australian political slang and was used of obstructing business. In general usage, *stonewalling* is to employ obstructive or delaying tactics.

Stonewall Jackson. Thomas J. Jackson (1824–1863), one of the Confederate generals in the American CIVIL WAR; so called from his firmness at the Battle of Bull Run (1861), when a fellow officer observed him with his brigade standing "like a stone wall".

Stool. Stool Pigeon. A police spy or informer; a decoy.

Stool of Repentance. The cutty stool, a low stool placed in front of the pulpit in Scottish churches, on which persons who had incurred ecclesiastical censure were placed during divine service. When the service was over the penitent had to stand on the stool and receive the minister's rebuke.

Store. Store cattle. Beasts kept on a farm for breeding purposes, or lean cattle bought for fattening.

Store is no sore. Things stored up for future use are no EVIL. *Sore* means grief as well as wound, our *Sorrow*.

To set store by. To value highly.

Stork. According to Swedish legend, the stork received its name from flying round the cross of the crucified Redeemer, crying *Styrka! styrka!* (Strengthen, strengthen!).

Lyly in his *Euphues* (1580) says of this bird:

Ladies use their lovers as the stork doth her young ones who pecketh them till they bleed with her bill, and then healeth them with her tongue.

Also:

Constancy is like unto the stork, who wheresoever she fly cometh into no nest but her own.

And:

It fareth with me ... as with the stork, who, when she is least able, carrieth the greatest burden.

It is an old tale to children that babies are brought by storks and they still feature prominently on cards of congratulation to a baby's parents. It was also a belief that a stork will kill a snake "on sight".

King Stork. A tyrant that devours his subjects, and makes them submissive with fear and trembling. The allusion is to the fable of *The Frogs desiring a King. See* A KING LOG *under* LOG.

Storm (Austr.). Young grass which has grown after a rainfall in dry areas. Travelling from storm to storm is to **storm along.**

A Brain-storm. A sudden and violent upheaval in the brain, causing temporary loss of control, or even madness. *Nervestorm* is used in much the same way of the nerves.

The Cape of Storms. So Bartholomew Diaz named the south cape of Africa in 1486, but John II of Portugal (d. 1495) changed it to the *Cape of Good Hope*.

Storm and Stress. *See* STURM UND DRANG.

A storm in a teacup. A mighty to-do about a trifle; making a great fuss about nothing.

To take by storm. To seize by a sudden and irresistible attack; a military term used figuratively, as of one who becomes suddenly famous or popular; an actor, suddenly springing to fame, "takes the town by storm".

Stormy Petrel. *See* PETREL.

Storting or **Stirthing,** (stôr′ ting). The Norwegian PARLIAMENT, elected every fourth year (*stor*, great; *thing*, assembly).

Stout. A dark beer made with roasted malt. Porter, a light stout, is still sold on draught in Ireland and stout derives its name from being a *strong* or *stout* porter. *See* ALE; ENTIRE.

Stove plants. An old name for hothouse plants which need artificial heat.

Stovepipe Hat. An old-fashioned tall silk hat, a chimney-pot hat. A name of American origin.

Strad. A colloquial name for a violin made by Antonio Stradivarius (1644–1737) of CREMONA, now much prized. His best violins were made between 1700 and 1723. *Cp.* AMATI.

Strafe (straf) (Ger. *strafen*, to punish). A word borrowed in good-humoured contempt from the Germans during World War I. One of their favourite slogans was *Gott strafe England!* The word was applied to any sharp and sudden bombardment, and also used by Americans in World War II for the machine-gunning of troops or civilians by low-flying aircraft.

Strain. The quality of mercy is not strained (SHAKESPEARE: *Merchant of Venice*, IV, i)—not constrained or forced, but comes down freely as the rain, which is God's gift.

To strain a point. To go beyond one's usual, or the proper limits; to give way a bit more than one ought.

To strain at a gnat and swallow a camel. To make much fuss about little peccadilloes, but commit offences of real magnitude. The proverb comes from *Matt.* xxiii, 24, which in Tyndale's, Coverdale's, and other early versions of the BIBLE reads *strain out*, *i.e.* to filter out a gnat before drinking the wine. The REVISED VERSION also adopts this form but the AUTHORIZED VERSION's rendering is *which strain at a gnat*, which was not a mistake but established usage at the time.

Greene in his *Mamillia* (1583) speaks of "straining at a gnat and letting pass an elephant".

To strain courtesy. To stand upon ceremony. Here *strain* is to *stretch*, as parchment is strained on a drum-head.

Strand, The. One of the most famous of London's thoroughfares joining THE CITY of LONDON to WESTMINSTER along the riverside, whence its name. Its many great inns or houses had riverside approaches (the Victoria Embankment was not begun until 1864). Its many historic buildings have almost entirely ceased to exist although names still survive as in Essex Street, the SAVOY Hotel, etc. There is still a Roman bath in Strand Lane. Its boundary with FLEET STREET was formerly marked by the gateway at TEMPLE BAR.

> Through the long Strand together let us stray;
> With thee conversing, I forget the way.
> Behold that narrow street which steep descends,
> Whose building to the slimy shore extends.
> . . . .
> There Essex's stately pile adorned the shore,
> There Cecil's, Bedford's, Villiers',—now no more.
> — GAY: *Trivia.*

Stranger. Originally, a foreigner; from O.Fr. *estrangier* (Mod. Fr. *étranger*), which is the Lat. *extraneus*, one without.

It is said that BUSIRIS, King of Egypt sacrificed to his gods all strangers who set foot on his territories. DIOMEDES gave strangers to his horses for food.

Floating tea-leaves in one's cup, charred pieces of wick that make the candle gutter, little bits of soot hanging from the grate, etc., are called "strangers", because they are supposed to foretell the coming of visitors.

I spy strangers! The recognized form of words by which a Member of PARLIAMENT conveys to the SPEAKER the information that there is an unauthorized person in the House.

The little stranger. A new-born infant.

The stranger that is within thy gates. *See* PROSELYTES.

Strap. A taste of the strap. A strapping or flogging, properly with a leather strap.

A strapping young fellow. A big sturdy chap; just as we speak of a "thumping" or "whacking great chap"; a vigorous young woman is similarly called a *strapper*.

Straphanger. One who stands in a bus, train, etc., when the seats are fully occupied, holding on to the strap hanging from the roof.

Strap oil. Slang for a thrashing with a strap.

Strappado (strǎ pä' dō) (Ital. *strappare*, to pull). A mode of torture formerly practised for extracting confessions, retractions, etc.

The hands were tied behind the back, and the victim was pulled up to a beam by a rope tied to them and then let down suddenly; by this means a limb was not infrequently dislocated.

> An I were at the strappado, or all the racks in the world, I would not tell you on compulsion.
> SHAKESPEARE: *Henry IV, Pt. I*, II, iv.

Strasbourg Goose. A goose fattened, crammed, and confined in order to enlarge its liver, from which is made true pâté de foie gras.

Straw. Straw was proverbially regarded as worthless, something blown about by the wind; hence used in phrases as, **Not worth a straw,** quite valueless, not worth a RAP, a FIG, etc.; **to care not a straw,** not to care at all.

Straw Polls. An early form of public opinion poll sponsored by the American press as early as 1824 when reporters of the *Harrisburg Pennsylvanian* were sent to inquire from the townsfolk of Wilmington which candidate they favoured for the presidency. Such polls were subsequently used on a much larger scale and postal voting came to be employed. The name derives from the idea of a straw "showing which way the wind blows". *Cp.* GALLUP POLL.

Straw vote. A vote of no official value taken casually at a meeting, etc., as an indication of opinion.

I have a straw to break with you. I have something to quarrel with you about; I am displeased with you; I have a reproof to give you. An obsolete expression.

In the straw. Applied to women in childbirth. The allusion is to the straw with which beds were once stuffed before the introduction of feather beds.

The last straw. "This is the last straw that breaks the camel's back." There is an ultimate point of endurance beyond which calamity breaks a man down.

A man of straw. A man without means, with no more substance than a straw doll; also, an imaginary or fictitious person put forward for some reason.

A straw shows which way the wind blows. Mere trifles often indicate the coming of momentous events. They are shadows cast before coming events.

To catch at a straw. A FORLORN HOPE. A drowning man will catch at a straw.

To make bricks without straw. To attempt to do something without the proper or necessary materials. The allusion is to the exaction of the Egyptian taskmasters mentioned in *Exod.* v, 6–14.

To pick straws. To show fatigue or weariness, as birds pick up straws to make their nests (or bed).

> Their eyelids did not once pick straws,
> And wink, and sink away;
> No, no; they were as brisk as bees,
> And loving things did say.
> PETER PINDAR: *Orson and Ellen*, canto v.

To stumble at a straw. To be pulled up short by a trifle.

To throw straws against the wind. To contend uselessly and feebly against what is irresistible; to "sweep back the Atlantic with a besom". *Cp.* PARTINGTON.

Strawberry. Of this fruit Izaak Walton (*Compleat Angler*, ch. v) says:

> We may say of angling as Dr. Boteler said of strawberries, "doubtless God could have made a better berry, but doubtless God never did."

Crushed strawberry. A crimson red colour of dullish hue.

The strawberry leaves. A dukedom; the honour, rank, etc., of a DUKE. The ducal CORONET is ornamented with eight strawberry leaves.

Strawberry mark. A birthmark something like a strawberry. In J. M. Morton's BOX AND COX the two heroes eventually recognize each other as long-lost brothers through one of them having a strawberry mark on his left arm.

Strawberry preachers. So Latimer called the non-resident country clergy, because they "come but once a year and tarie not long" (*Sermon on the Plough*, 1549).

Stream of Consciousness. A technique of novel writing, first deliberately employed by Dorothy Richardson in *Pointed Roofs* (1915) and developed by James Joyce and Virginia Woolf. By this technique the writer presents life as seen through impressions on the mind of one person.

To swim with the stream. *See under* SWIM.

Street. Right up my street. "Just my handwriting", in my particular province or field; "just my line of country". As familiar to a person as his own street.

Streets ahead. Well ahead; much in advance. The phrase conveys the idea of long distance.

Street Arab. *See under* ARABIA. *Cp.* BEDOUINS.

To be in easy street. In a very comfortable situation and of considerable affluence.

Strenia (strē' ni à). A SABINE goddess identified with the Roman Salus, to whom gifts (*strenæ*) were taken at the New Year, consisting of figs, dates, and honey. The custom is said to have been instituted by the Sabine King Tatius, who entered ROME on NEW YEAR'S DAY and received from some augurs palms cut from the sacred grove dedicated to her. The French *étrenne*, a New Year's gift, is from this goddess.

Strephon (stref' òn). A stock name for a rustic lover; from the languishing lover of that name in Sidney's *Arcadia*.

Strike (O.E. *strican*, to go, advance swiftly, to strike). This verb is now mainly used in the sense of to hit, to deliver a blow, or to act swiftly.

The noun *strike* has numerous specialized meanings, *e.g.* an old grain measure varying locally from half a bushel to four bushels; also the wooden straight-edged implement for levelling off a measure of grain by "striking it off" but it is most commonly used nowadays to denote a cessation of work by a body of employees for coercive purposes; strikes over delayed payment were not unknown among the workmen employed on the royal tombs in ancient Egypt.

It strikes me that ... It occurs to me that ..., it comes into my mind that ...

Strike-a-light. The flint formerly used with tinder-boxes for striking fire; also, the shaped piece of metal used to strike the flint. The latter's similarity with the links of the collar of the Order of the GOLDEN FLEECE gave rise to the nickname "the collar of strike-a-lights". *Strike a light* is also commonly used as an exclamation.

Strike, but hear me! (Lat. *verbera, sed audi*). Carry out your threats—if you must—but at least hear what I have to say. The phrase comes from Plutarch's life of Themistocles. He strongly opposed the proposal of Eurybiades to quit the Bay of Salamis. The hot-headed SPARTAN insultingly remarked that "those who in the public games rise up before the proper signal are scourged". "True," said Themistocles, "but those who lag behind win no laurels." On this, Eurybiades lifted up his staff to strike him, when Themistocles earnestly exclaimed, "Strike, but hear me!"

Bacon (*Advancement of Learning*, ii) calls this "that ancient and patient request".

Strike me dead! blind! etc. Vulgar expletives, or exclamations of surprise, dismay, wonder, and so on. *Strike me dead* is also sailor's slang for thin, wishy-washy beer.

Strike while the iron is hot. Act while the time or the opportunity presents; a METAPHOR from the blacksmith's shop. Similar proverbs are: "Make hay while the sun shines", "Take time by the forelock".

To be struck all of a heap. *See* HEAP.

To be struck on a person. To like or be much interested in, or inclined to be enamoured of a person.

To strike an attitude. To pose, to assume an exaggerated or theatrical attitude.

To strike a balance. *See under* BALANCE.

To strike a bargain (*Cp*. Lat. *fœdus ferire*). To make or conclude a transaction; "I have just struck a bargain" is also used in the sense, "I have just come across an advantageous purchase".

To strike at the foundations. To attempt to undermine the whole thing, to overthrow it utterly.

To strike camp. To take down the tents and move off.

To strike the flag. *See under* FLAG.

To strike hands upon a bargain is to confirm it by shaking or "striking hands".

To strike lucky. To have unexpected good fortune; a phrase from the miners' camps. *Cp.* TO STRIKE OIL *under* OIL.

To strike out in another direction. To open up a new way for oneself, to start a new approach, to open out into a new line of business.

To strike sail. *See under* SAIL.

To strike up. To begin, start operations; as to *strike up an acquaintance*, to set acquaintanceship going. Originally of an orchestra or company of singers, who "struck up" the music.

Willing to wound, and yet afraid to strike. Said of one who dare not do the injury or take the revenge that he wishes. The "tag" is from Pope's *Epistle to Dr. Arbuthnot*, 1.204 (1735).

Strike-breaker. A "BLACKLEG", a "scab"; a worker induced by the employer to carry on working when the other employees are on strike.

String. Always harping on one string. Always talking on the same subject; always repeating or referring to the same thing. The allusion is obvious.

He has two strings to his bow. *See under* BOW.

How long is a piece of string? Who knows? How can one tell? Said to someone who asks a question to which there is no accurate or worthwhile answer.

To pull the strings. *See under* PULL.

To string along with. To accompany; to join up with, *i.e.* to join the line or "string".

Stringy-bark. *See* SETTLER'S MATCHES.

Strip. Comic strip; strip cartoon. A series or strip of drawings in a newspaper, telling a story, usually one episode per issue.

Strip Jack Naked. Another name for "Beat Your Neighbour Out of Doors", a simple card game popular with children.

To strip a cow. To milk it to the last drop.

To tear someone off a strip. To give one a severe castigation; to reprimand angrily.

Strip-tease. A theatrical or cabaret performance in which an actress slowly and provocatively undresses herself. One who does this is called a *stripper*.

Stroke. The oarsman nearest the stern facing the COXSWAIN, who sets the time of the stroke for the rest.

To stroke one (up) the wrong way. To vex him, ruffle his temper.

Strong. A strong verb is one that forms inflexions by internal vowel-change (*bind*, *bound*; *speak*, *spoke*); weak verbs add a syllable, or letter (as *love*, *loved*; *refund*, *refunded*).

Going strong. Prospering, getting on famously; in an excellent state of health.

To come it strong. *See under* COME.

Struldbrugs (strŭld'brŭgz). Wretched inhabitants of Luggnagg (in Swift's *Gulliver's Travels*), who had the privilege of immortality without having eternal vigour, strength, and intellect.

Stubble Geese. The geese turned into the stubble-fields to pick up the corn left after harvest.

Stuck up. *See under* STICK.

Stuff. A bit, or **piece of stuff.** The same as a SKIRT.

Stuff Gown. A BARRISTER who has not yet taken SILK.

Stuffed shirt. *See under* SHIRT.

Stumer (stū'mer). A swindle, or a swindler, a forged banknote or "dud" cheque; a fictitious bet recorded by the bookmakers, and published in the papers, to deceive the public by running up the odds on a horse which is not expected to win. From 1914, in military parlance, a dud shell was called a *stumer*. The word is of unknown origin.

Stump. The Black Stump. *This side of the Black Stump* or *The other side of the Black Stump* are Australian expressions implying "a long way off", "a considerable, but unspecified distance". The *Black Stump* refers to the undefined stump left after a bush fire. There is an actual place bearing the name, south of Hillston in New South Wales.

A stump speaker, or **orator.** A speaker who harangues all who will listen to him from some improvised vantage point; often with the implications of rant and bombast of the tub-thumping variety. The phrase is of American origin, where it has not necessarily derogatory implications. It originates from the days when a tree stump was often the most readily available platform for political speeches. Hence such phrases as to *stump the country*, *to take to the stump*, to go from place to place making inflammatory or provocative speeches, etc. So-called **stump speeches** were once favoured by entertainers, minstrel shows, etc., and usually somewhat laboured in their humour.

To be stumped. Outwitted; at a loss, defeated. A term borrowed from CRICKET.

To stir one's stumps. To get on faster; to set about something expeditiously. *Stumps* here are one's legs; also the wooden stump or peg-leg once fastened to multilated limbs, or the mutilated limbs themselves.

> For Witherington needs must I wayle, as one in
> doleful dumpes;
> For when his leggs were smitten off, He fought
> upon his stumpes.
>
> PERCY: *Reliques*
> (*The More Modern Ballad of Chevy Chase*).

To stump up. To pay one's reckoning, to pay what is due. Ready money is called *stumpy* or *stumps*. An Americanism, meaning money paid down on the spot—*i.e.* on the stump of a tree. *Cp. On the* NAIL.

Stupor Mundi (Lat., "The amazement of the world"). So the Emperor Frederick II (1194, 1215–1250) was called as being the greatest sovereign, soldier, and patron of artists and scholars in the 13th century.

Sturm und Drang (shtoorm unt drŭng) (Ger., storm and stress). The name given to the German literary movement of the late 18th century with which Goethe, Schiller, and Herder were closely associated, from a tragedy of this title (1776) by Frederick Maximilian von Klinger (1752–1831). The dramas of the period are typified by the extravagant passion of the characters, and the movement had considerable effect upon the subsequent ROMANTIC MOVEMENT.

Stygian (sti' ji ăn). Infernal, gloomy; pertaining to the river STYX.

> At that so sudden blaze the Stygian throng
> Bent their aspect.
>
> MILTON: *Paradise Lost*, X, 453.

Style is from the Latin *stylus* (a metal pencil for writing on waxen tablets, etc.). The characteristic of a person's writing is called his *style*. Metaphorically it is applied to composition and speech. Good writing is *stylish*, and, by extension, smartness of dress and deportment is so called.

> Style is the dress of thoughts, and well-dressed
> thought, like a well-dressed man, appears to great
> advantage.
>
> LORD CHESTERFIELD: *Letters*, clvi (1751).

New Style, Old Style. *See* OLD STYLE *under* OLD; STILO NOVO.

The style is the man. A mistranslation of "Le style est l'homme même" from the discourse of Buffon (1707–1788) on his reception into the French Academy.

To do a thing in style. To do it splendidly, regardless of expense.

Styles. Tom Styles, or **John a Styles,** connected with JOHN-A-NOKES, an imaginary plaintiff or defendant in a lawsuit in the same way as John DOE and Richard ROE.

> And, like blind Fortune, with a sleight
> Convey men's interest and right
> From Stiles's pocket into Nokes's.
>
> BUTLER: *Hudibras*, III, iii, i. 713.

Stylites, or **Pillar Saints** (stī lī' tēz). A class of ascetics found especially in Syria, Mesopotamia, Egypt and Greece between the 5th and 10th centuries. They took up their abode on the tops of pillars, which were sometimes equipped with a small hut, from which they never descended. They take their name from St. Simeon Stylites of Syria (390–459) who spent some 30 years on a pillar which was gradually increased to the height of 40 cubits. St. Daniel, his most famous disciple, spent 33 years on a pillar near Constantinople. Tennyson wrote a poem on St. Simeon Stylites.

Stymie. A golfing term, obsolete since 1952. A player was *laid a stymie* if, on the putting-green, the opponent's ball fell in the line of his path to the hole (providing the balls were not within 6 in. of each other). To hole out could only be achieved by a very difficult lofting stroke. Hence several still current expressions. **A stymie** is a frustrating situation, a discouragingly difficult position and **to be stymied** is to be in such a position; and **to stymie** is to hinder or thwart; also to put one in the position of having to negotiate.

Styx (stiks). The river of Hate (Gr. *stugein*, to hate)—called by Milton "abhorred Styx, the flood of deadly hate" (*Paradise Lost*, II, 577)—that, according to classical mythology, flowed nine times round the infernal regions. Some say it was a river in ARCADIA whose waters were poisonous and dissolved any vessel put upon them. When a god swore falsely by the Styx, he was made to drink a draught of its water which made him lie speechless for a year. The river was said to take its name from Styx, the eldest daughter of OCEANUS and TETHYS, and wife of Pallas, by whome she had three daughters, Victory, Strength, and Valour. *See* ACHERON; CHARON.

> By the black infernal Styx I swear
> (That dreadful oath which binds the Thunderer)
> 'Tis fixed!
>
> POPE: *Thebais of Statius*, I, 411.

Suaviter (swā vi ter) **in modo, fortiter in re** (Lat.). Gentle in manner, resolute in action. Said of one who does what is to be done with unflinching firmness, but in the most inoffensive manner possible. Lord Chesterfield takes it as his theme in one of his letters (ch. xi).

> He is firm, but gentle; and practises that most excellent maxim, *suaviter in modo, fortiter in re.*
>
> LORD CHESTERFIELD: *Letters*, cxciv (1752).

Sub divo (Lat. *divum*, sky). Under the open sky; in the open air.

Sub hasta (sŭb hăs tà) (Lat.). By auction. When an auction took place among the Romans, it was customary to stick a spear in the ground to give notice of it to the public; literally, under the spear. *See* SPEAR.

Sub Jove (Lat.). Under Jove; in the open air. JUPITER is the god of the upper regions of the air, as JUNO is of the lower regions, NEPTUNE of the waters of the sea, VESTA of the earth, CERES of the surface soil, and HADES of the invisible or underworld.

Sub judice (sŭb joo' di sē) (Lat.). Under consideration; not yet decided in a court of law.

Sub rosa. *See under* ROSE.

Subject and Object. In METAPHYSICS the *Subject* is the ego, the mind, the conscious self, the substance or substratum to which attributes must be referred; the *Object* is an external as distinct from the ego, a thing or idea brought before the consciousness. Hence **subjective criticism, art,** etc., is that which proceeds from the individual mind and is consequently individualistic, fanciful, imaginative; while **objective criticism** is that which is based on knowledge of the externals.

Subject-object. The immediate object of thought, the thought itself as distinct from the *object-object,* the real object as it is in fact.

Sublapsarian, or **Infralapsarian** (sŭb-lăp sâr' i àn). A Calvinist who maintains that God devised His scheme of redemption after he had permitted the "lapse" or fall of ADAM, when He elected some to salvation and left others to run their course. The *supra*lapsarian maintains that all this was ordained by God from the foundation of the world, and therefore before the "lapse" or fall of Adam.

Sublime. From Lat. *sub*, up to, *limen*, the lintel; hence, lofty, elevated in thought or tone.

The Sublime Porte. *See* PORTE.

The Sublime Society of Steaks. *See* BEEFSTEAK CLUB.

There is but one step from the sublime to the ridiculous. *See under* RIDICULOUS.

Submarine. *See* BUSHNELL'S TURTLE.

Submerged. The Submerged Tenth. The very poor; sunk or submerged in poverty.

Subpœna (sŭb pē' nà) (Lat., under penalty) is a writ commanding a man to appear in court, usually unwillingly, to bear witness or give evidence on a certain trial named. It is so called because the party summoned is bound to appear *sub pœna centum librorum* (under a penalty of £100). We have also the verb *to subpœna.*

Subsidy. (Lat. *sub-sedere*, to sit down). The *subsidii* of the Roman army were the troops held in reserve, the auxiliaries, supports; hence the word came to be applied to a support granted by PARLIAMENT to the King. It now usually applies to state aid in support of industries, etc., of public importance. *Subsidiary*, auxiliary, supplemental, is of the same origin.

Subtle Doctor. *See* DOCTORS OF LEARNING; DUNCE.

Subtopia. A word coined (from *suburb*) and *Utopia*) by Ian Nairn in 1954 to denote the sprawling suburban housing estates built to satisfy the town workers' yearning for country surroundings while clinging to the amenities of the town. The term includes all the paraphernalia of concrete posts, lamp standards, chain link fencing, and other uglinesses associated with a disfigured landscape.

Succotash (U.S.A.). A dish of Indian corn and beans boiled together. Originally an American-Indian dish.

Succoth, or **Sukkoth** (Heb. *sukkoth*, booths). The Jewish name for the feast of the Tabernacles (*see under* TABERNACLE).

Succubus (suk' ū bus) (Med. Lat. masculine form of Late Lat. *succuba*, from *succumbere*, to lie under). A female demon fabled to have sexual relations with sleeping men. *Cp.* INCUBUS.

Suck, or **Suck-in.** A swindle, hoax, deception, fiasco. **To be sucked in** is to be taken in, deceived, tricked, and one who is thus gulled is said to be a *sucker*. A **suck-up** or **sucker-up** is a TOADY or creep.

Sucking was formerly used (after *sucking-pig*) of the young and inexperienced, those in training, etc., as a *sucking lawyer* (an articled clerk), etc.

> The very curates ... she, in her pure, sincere enthusiasm, looked upon as sucking saints.
>
> CHARLOTTE BRONTË: *Shirley*, xiv.

Teach your grandmother to suck eggs. *See under* EGG.

To suck the monkey. *See under* MONKEY.

Suède (swād). Undressed kid-skin; so called because the gloves made of this originally came from Sweden (Fr. *gants de Suède*).

Suffering. The Meeting for Sufferings. The standing representative committee of the Yearly Meeting of the Society of Friends, so called because originally its chief function was to relieve the sufferings imposed upon QUAKERS by distraint of TITHES and other petty persecutions.

Suffragan (sŭf' rà gàn). An auxiliary BISHOP; one who has not a see of his own but is appointed to assist a bishop in a portion of his SEE. In relation to a METROPOLITAN or archbishop all bishops are suffragans; and they were so called because they could be summoned to a synod to give their SUFFRAGE.

Suffrage. One's vote, approval, consent; or one's right to vote, especially at parliamentary and municipal elections. The word is from Lat. *suffragium*, voting tablet, probably from *suffrago*, the hock or ankle-bone of a horse, which may have been used by the Romans for balloting. *Cp.* BEANS; CALCULATE.

Hence **Suffragettes** as the name for the militant women who agitated for the parliamentary vote, in the period 1906–1914. *See* CAT AND MOUSE ACT.

Sugar. Sugar Daddy. An elderly, wealthy man who lavishes expensive gifts on a much younger woman. From U.S. slang.

Sui generis (sū' i jen' er is) (Lat., of its own kind). Having a distinct character of its own; unlike aything else.

Sui juris (Lat.). Of one's own right; the state of being able to exercise one's legal rights—*i.e.* freedom from legal disability.

Suicide (Lat. *sui*, of oneself; *-cidium*, from *cædere*, to kill). Until 1823, a suicide was buried at the CROSS-ROADS with a stake thrust through the body.

Suit. A suit of dittoes. *See under* DITTO.

To follow suit. To follow the leader; to do as those do who are taken as your exemplars. The term is from games of cards.

Sukkoth. *See* SUCCOTH.

Sultan (Arab., King). Until 1923 the title of the ruler of the former Turkish Empire and, until 1957, of the King of Morocco. It is still in use in certain lesser Mohammedan states, as Muscat and Oman, Kishen and Socotra, etc. In mediæval writings *sultan* is often corrupted to **Soldan** or **Sowdan**. The wife (also mother, sister or concubine) of the sultan is called **Sultana**, a name which is also sometimes applied to a mistress.

> While Charles flirted with his three sultanas, Hortensia's French page, a handsome boy, whose vocal performances were the delight of Whitehall, … warbled some amorous verses.
>
> MACAULAY: *History of England*, ch. iv.

Sultana is also the name of a seedless raisin; a form of necklace worn by women in the latter half of the 18th century; an old

musical instrument like a zither; both sultan and sultana denote the *hyacinthine gallinule*, a brilliantly coloured bird of the Rallidæ family, and a kind of white domestic hen.

Summer. The warmest season of the year. In Britain, June, July, and August; astronomically, from the summer SOLSTICE to the autumn equinox (*c.* 22 September).

> From bright'ning fields of ether fair disclosed,
> Child of the Sun, refulgent Summer comes.
>
> THOMSON: *The Seasons* (*Summer*).

St. LUKE's little summer is a period of mild weather around mid-October, St. Luke's Day being 18 October. *See also* ALL-HALLOWS SUMMER; INDIAN SUMMER; St. MARTIN'S SUMMER.

Summer Time. *See* DAYLIGHT SAVING.

Summit. A summit conference. One between the chief representatives of the participating powers.

Summum bonum (sŭm' ŭm bō' nŭm). (Lat., the highest good). The chief excellence; the highest attainable good. The STOIC School held that virtue and its attainment was the highest end.

SOCRATES said knowledge is virtue, and ignorance is vice.

ARISTOTLE said that happiness is the greatest good.

Bernard de Mandeville and *Helvetius* contended that self-interest is the perfection of the ethical end.

Bentham and *Mill* were for the greatest happiness of the greatest number.

Herbert Spencer placed it in those actions which best tend to the survival of the individual and the race; and

Robert Browning (see his poem of this name) "in the kiss of one girl".

Sumptuary Laws. Laws to limit the expenses of food and dress, or any luxury. The Romans had their *leges sumptuarii*, and they have been enacted in many states at various times. Those of England were all repealed by 1 James I, c. 25; but during the two World Wars, with the rationing of food, coals, etc., and the compulsory lowering of the strength of beer and whisky, we had a temporary return to sumptuary legislation.

Sun. The source of light and heat, and consequently of life to the whole world; hence regarded as a deity and worshipped as such by all primitive peoples and having a leading place in their mythologies. *Shamash* was the principal sun-god of the Assyrians and Babylonians, MITHRAS of the Persians, RA of the Egyptians, *Tezcatlipoca* (Smoking Mirror) of the Aztecs, HELIOS of the Greeks, known to the Romans as SOL and usually identified with PHŒBUS and APOLLO.

The City of the Sun. *See under* CITY.

The Southern Gate of the Sun. The sign Capricornus or winter SOLSTICE. So called because it is the most southern limit of the sun's course in the ECLIPTIC.

The Sun of Righteousness. Jesus Christ (*Mal*. iv. 2).

The empire on which the sun never sets. *See under* SET.

Heaven cannot support two suns, nor earth two masters. So said ALEXANDER the Great when DARIUS (before the battle of Arbela) sent to offer terms of peace. *Cp.* SHAKESPEARE:

> Two stars keep not their motion in one sphere;
> Nor can one England brook a double reign,
> Of Harry Percy and the Prince of Wales.
> *Henry IV, Pt. I*, V, iv.

More worship the rising than the setting sun. More persons pay honour to ascendant than to fallen greatness. The saying is attributed to Pompey.

> I should fear those that dance before me now
> Would one day stamp upon me; it has been done;
> Men shut their doors against a setting sun.
> SHAKESPEARE: *Timon of Athens*, I, ii.

A place in the sun. A favourable position that allows for development; a share in what one has a natural right to. The phrase achieved a particular significance when William II of Germany spoke of his nation taking steps to ensure that "no one can dispute with us the place in the sun that is our due."

Out of God's blessing into the warm sun. One of Ray's proverbs, meaning from good to less good. In Shakespeare's *Hamlet* (I, ii), when the king says to Hamlet, "How is it that the clouds still hang on you?" the prince answers, "Not so, my lord; I am too much i' the sun", meaning, "I have lost God's blessing, for too much of the sun"— *i.e.* this far inferior state.

> Thou out of heaven's benediction comest
> To the warm sun.
> SHAKESPEARE: *King Lear*, II, i.

The sun is over the foreyard or **yardarm.** An expression among naval officers indicating that the time has come to have a drink. In home waters and northern latitudes the sun would be over the yardarm towards noon.

To have been out in the sun, or **to have the sun in one's eyes.** To be slightly inebriated.

To make hay while the sun shines. *See under* HAY.

Sundowner. In Australia, a tramp. In the early days one who went from one settlement to another arriving at *sundown*, so it is said, to be too late for work, but in time for food. In Africa and India, a *sundowner* denotes a drink of spirits, etc., taken just after sundown; in the U.S.A., an official who works late at the office.

Sunday (O.E. *sunnen dæg*). For centuries the first day of the week, anciently dedicated to the sun. In 1971 it became the seventh when Britain adopted the decision of the International Standardisation Organisation to call MONDAY the first day. *See* WEEK, DAYS OF THE; SABBATH.

Sunday Letters. *See* DOMINICAL LETTERS.

Sunday School. Nowadays, classes for children organized by church and chapel for a fairly short time on Sundays for religious instruction. They were first established in the 18th century to teach working class children their letters in order that they might learn to read the BIBLE, to improve their behaviour through moral instruction and to keep them off the streets all day. The movement gained considerable impetus when Robert Raikes founded his school in Gloucester in 1780 and William Fox set up the Sunday School Society in 1785. Sunday Schools became particularly strong in Wales.

Not in a month of Sundays. Not in a very long time.

One's Sunday best, Sunday suit, Sunday-go-to-meeting togs. One's best clothes, as worn on Sundays.

Sunday saint. One who observes the ordinances of religion, and goes to church on a Sunday, but is worldly, grasping, "indifferent honest", the following six days.

When three Sundays come together. NEVER.

Sunflower State. Kansas.

Sunna (Arab., custom, divine law). The traditional sayings and example of MOHAMMED and his immediate followers as set forth in the HADITH.

Sunnis, Sunnites. Orthodox MOSLEMS who consider the SUNNA as authentic as the KORAN itself and acknowledge the first four CALIPHS to be the rightful successors of MOHAMMED. They form by far the largest section of Mohammedans. *Cp.* SHI'ITES.

Sup. To sup with Sir Thomas Gresham. *See* HUMPHREY.

Supererogation, Works of. A theological expression for good works which are not enjoined or of obligation and therefore "better" (Lat. *super*, over, above; *erogare*, to pay out). The phrase is commonly applied to acts performed beyond the bounds of duty.

Superman. A hypothetical superior human being of high intellectual and moral attainment, fancied as evolved from the normally existing type. The term (*Übermensch*) was invented by the German philosopher Nietzsche (d. 1900), and was popularized in England by George Bernard Shaw's play, *Man and Superman* (1903).

The wide popularity of the term gave rise to many compounds, such as *super-woman, super-critic, super-tramp, super-Dreadnought*, and *super-tax*.

Supernaculum. The very best wine. Sham Latin for "upon the nail" (Ger. *auf den Nagel*), meaning that the wine is so good the drinker leaves only enough in his glass to make a bead on his nail. The French say of first-class wine, *Faire rubis sur l'ongle*, "It is only fit to make a ruby on the nail." Nashe (*Pierce Penilesse*, 1592) says that after a man had drunk his glass, it was usual, in the North, to turn the cup upside down, and let a drop fall upon the thumb-nail. If the drop rolled off, the drinker was obliged to fill and drink again.

Hence **to drink supernaculum** is to leave no HEEL-TAPS: to leave just enough not to roll off one's thumb-nail if poured upon it.

Supplies. In Parliamentary parlance, the various grants and moneys authorized annually by PARLIAMENT other than those paid out of the CONSOLIDATED FUND or permitted by an Act during the session.

Supply. The law of supply and demand. The economic statement that the competition of buyers and sellers tends to make such changes in price that the demand for any article in a given market will become equal to the supply. In other words, if the demand exceeds the supply the price rises, operating so as to reduce the demand and so enable the supply to meet it, and VICE VERSA.

Supralapsarian. *See* SUBLAPSARIAN.

Surfeit Water. An old name for a "water" used to cure "surfeits", *i.e.* the effects of gluttony. Hannah Glasse's 18th-century recipe requires 4 gallons of brandy and 27 other ingredients, mostly herbs. This surfeit water was drunk from special tapering fluted glasses, and two spoonfuls was the dose of this highly alcoholic pick-me-up.

Surloin. *See* SIRLOIN.

Surname. The name added to, or given over and above, the Christian name (O. Fr. *sur-*; from Lat. *super-*, over, above). Surnames, as names passed from father to son, were not widespread until the 13th century, and grew from the custom of adding the place of domicile or provenance, trade or some descriptive characteristic, to the Christian name to assist identification, *e.g.* York, Butcher, Large, Russell (red-haired), etc. Yet another category derives from family relationship, *e.g.* Williamson, Macgregor, O'Brien.

Surplice. Over the *pelisse* or fur robe (Lat. *superpellicium*, from *pellis*, skin). The white linen vestment worn by CLERGY, acolytes, choristers, etc., so fashioned for its ease of wearing over fur dress worn in northern Europe in mediæval times. The shorter *cotta* is a development from this.

Surplice fees. The fees for marriage and burials which are the right of the incumbent of a BENEFICE.

> With tithes his barns replete he sees,
> And chuckles o'er his surplice fees
>
> T. WARTON:
> *The Progress of Discontent*, 89 (1750).

Surrealism. A movement in art and the literary world which began in 1924 and flourished between the two World Wars under the leadership of the poet André Breton. In painting it falls into two groups: hand-painted dream scenes as exemplified by Chirico, Dali, and Magritte: and the creation of abstract forms by the practice of complete spontaniety of technique as well as subject-matter by the use of contrast as with Arp, Roy, Miró and Dali. They sought to express thought uncontrolled by reason and aesthetic and moral concepts. *Cp.* CUBISM; DADAISM; FAUVISM; FUTURISM; IMPRESSIONISM; ORPHISM; SYNCHRONISM; VORTICISM.

Susanna and the Elders. *See* DANIEL.

Sussex weeds. A name for oak-trees, still plentiful in Sussex.

Sutras (sū' trăz) (Sansk, *sutra*, a thread). In Sanskrit literature, certain aphoristic writings giving the rules of systems of philosophy, grammar, etc.; and in Brahmanic use, directions concerning religious ritual and ceremonial customs which are part of the VEDA.

Suttee (Sansk. *sati*, a virtuous wife). The Hindu custom of burning the widow on the funeral pyre of her deceased husband; also, the widow so put to death. Women with child and mothers of children not yet of age could not perform suttee. This ancient practice was prohibited in British India by Lord William Bentinck in 1829, but was practised as late as 1877 in Nepal.

Sutton Hoo Treasure. An Anglo-Saxon ship-burial of the early 7th century, discovered at Sutton Hoo near Woodbridge, Suffolk, in 1939. It is one of the richest ever found and the treasure, consisting of a sword and sheath, helmet, bowls and other objects in precious metals, is now in the BRITISH MUSEUM. The find is of considerable archæological and historical importance.

Swaddlers. An early nickname for Wesleyans, and applied later by Roman Catholics to DISSENTERS and PROTESTANTS generally. Southey (*Life of Wesley*, ii) explains its origin as follows:

> It happened that Cennick, preaching on Christmas Day, took for his text these words from St. Luke's Gospel: "And this shall be a sign unto you; ye shall find the babe wrapped in swaddling clothes lying in a manger." A Catholic who was present, and to whom the language of scripture was a novelty, thought this so ridiculous that he called the preacher a swaddler in derision, and this unmeaning word became a nickname for "Protestant", and had all the effect of the most opprobrious appellation.

Swag (connected with Norwegian *svagga*, to sway from side to side). One's goods carried in a pack or bundle; hence the booty obtained from a burglary, often carried away in a sack. **To get away with the swag** is used figuratively to imply profiting by one's cleverness or sharp practice.

Swagman. The Australian term for the numerous itinerant labourers who tramped from sheep station to sheep station in former times carrying their "swag" (*i.e.* bundle of clothes, blankets, etc.), seeking employment from the squatters. *Cp.* SUNDOWNER.

> And you think of the days out on the track when you and Tom sat on your swags under a mulga at midday, and ate mutton and johnny-cake with clasp-knives, and drank by turns out of the old, battered, leaky billy.
>
> HENRY LAWSON:
> *On the Track* (*Meeting Old Mates*).

Swag-shop. A place kept by a "FENCE"; where thieves can dispose of their "SWAG"; also, a low-class shop where cheap and trashy articles are sold.

Swagger (frequentative of SWAG). To strut about with a superior or defiant air; to bluster, make oneself out a very important person; hence, ostentatiously smart or "SWELL"; as *a swagger dinner, a swagger car*, etc.

Swagger-stick. The small cane a soldier was formerly obliged to carry when walking out.

Swainmote. *See* SWANIMOTE.

Swallow. According to Scandinavian tradition, this bird hovered over the cross of our Lord, crying "*Svala! svala!*" (Console! console!), whence it was called *svalow* (the bird of consolation).

Ælian says that the swallow was sacred to the PENATES or household gods, and therefore to injure one would be to bring wrath upon your own house. It is still considered a sign of good luck if a swallow or martin builds under the eaves of one's house.

> Perhaps you failed in your foreseeing skill,
> For swallows are unlucky birds to kill.
> DRYDEN: *Hind and Panther*, Pt. III.

Longfellow refers to another old fable regarding this bird:

> Seeking with eager eyes that wondrous stone which the swallow
> Brings from the shore of the sea to restore the sight of its fledglings.
> *Evangeline*, Pt. I, 119.

One swallow does not make a summer. You are not to suppose summer has come to stay just because you have seen a swallow; nor that the troubles of life are over because you have surmounted one difficulty. The Greek proverb, "One swallow does not make a spring", is to be found in ARISTOTLE's *Nicomachœan Ethics* (I, vii, 16).

Swan. The fable that the swan sings beautifully just before it dies is very ancient, but baseless. The only one for which a song of any kind can be claimed is the Whistling Swan (Cygnus musicus). The superstition was credited by PLATO, ARISTOTLE, Euripides, Cicero, Seneca, Martial, etc., and doubted by Pliny and Ælian. SHAKESPEARE refers to it more than once; Emilia, just before she dies, says:

> I will play the swan,
> And die in music.
> *Othello*, V, ii.

Spenser speaks of the swan as a bird that sings:

> He, were he not with love so ill bedight,
> Woulde mount as high, and sing as soote [sweetly] as Swanne.
> *Shephearde's Calendar* (*October*, 89).

Coleridge (*On a Volunteer Singer*), referring to poetasters of the time, gives the old superstition an epigrammatic turn:

> Swans sing before they die; 'twere no bad thing
> Did certain persons die before they sing.

One Greek legend has it that the soul of APOLLO, the god of music, passed into a swan, hence the Pythagorean fable that the souls of all good poets passed into swans (*See* SWAN OF AVON, MANTUA etc., *below*).

The male swan is called a *cob*, the female, a *pen*; a young swan, a *cygnet*. *See also* FIONNUALA; LEDA; LOHENGRIN.

The Knight of the Swan. LOHENGRIN.

The Order of the Swan. An order of knighthood founded by Frederick II of Brandenburg in 1440 (and shortly after in Cleves) in honour of the LOHENGRIN legend. It died out in the 16th century but was revived by Frederick William IV of Prussia in 1843. After the arrival of Anne of Cleves in ENGLAND the *White Swan* was adopted as a PUBLIC-HOUSE SIGN. The badge of the Order was a silver swan surmounted by an image of the Virgin.

The Swan of Avon. SHAKESPEARE; so called (Ben Jonson) in allusion to his birthplace at Stratford-upon-Avon and the legend that APOLLO was changed into a swan.

The Swan of Lichfield. The name given to Anna Seward (1747–1809) the poetess.

The Swan of Mantua. VIRGIL, who was born at Mantua.

The Swan of Meander. HOMER, who is supposed to have lived on the banks of the MEANDER.

The Swan of Usk. So Henry Vaughan, the SILURIST (1622–1695), was called, having given one of his volumes of verse this name: *Olor Iscanus*.

The Swan with Two Necks. An old tavern sign, said to be a corruption of "two nicks" with which the Vintners' Company mark the beaks of their swans. In coaching days, the *Swan with Two Necks* in Lad Lane (now Gresham Street) was the chief London departure point for the North.

All your swans are geese. All your fine promises or expectations have proved fallacious. "Hope told a flattering tale." The converse, **All your geese are swans**, means all your children are paragons, and whatever you do is in your own eyes superlative work.

To swan about, or **around.** To move around aimlessly. A phrase popular among troops in World War II to describe a tank moving apparently aimlessly across the battlefield or to denote taking a vehicle off for a meandering drive when off duty.

Swan-maidens. Fairies of northern folklore, who can become maidens or swans at will by means of the *swan shift*, a magic garment of swan's feathers. Many stories are told of how the swan shift was stolen, and the FAIRY was obliged to remain thrall to the thief until rescued by a KNIGHT.

Swan song. The song fabled to be sung by a dying swan; hence, the last work or appearance of a poet, composer, actor, etc.

Swan-upping. A taking up of swans and placing the marks of ownership on their beaks. The term is specially applied to annual expeditions for this purpose up the THAMES, when the marks of the owners (*viz.* the Crown and the Dyers' and Vintners' Companies) are made. The royal swans are marked with five nicks—two lengthwise, and three across the bill—and the Companies' swans with two nicks. Also called *swan-hopping*.

Swanimote (swǎn' i mōt). A court held thrice a year before forest verderers by the steward of the court. So called from O.E. *swangemot*, a meeting of swine-herds, because, under the *Charta de Foresta* (1217), it was a meeting of the keepers of the royal forests to arrange for the depasturing of pigs in autumn, the clearance of cattle during the deer's fawning season, etc. *See* FOREIGN COURTS.

Swap. To swap, or **change horses in midstream.** To change leaders at the height of a crisis. Abraham Lincoln, in an address, 9 June 1864, referring to the fact that his fellow Republicans, though many were dissatisfied with his conduct of the CIVIL WAR, had renominated him for President, said that the Convention had concluded "that it is best not to swap horses while crossing the river".

Swashbuckler. A ruffian; a swaggerer. "From swashing," says Fuller (*Worthies*, III, 1662), "and making a noise on the buckler." The sword-players used to "swash" or tap their shield as fencers tap their foot upon the ground when they attack. *Cp.* SWINGE-BUCKLER.

Swastika. The GAMMADION or FYLFOT, an elaborate cross-shaped design (*see* CROSSES) used as a charm to ward off evil and bring good luck. It was adopted by Hitler as the NAZI emblem about 1920, probably from the German Baltic Corps, who wore it on their helmets after service in Finland, where it was used as a distinguishing mark on Finnish aeroplanes. It is from Sanskrit *svasti*, good fortune.

Swear to. Originally used only for solemn affirmations by the invocation of God or some sacred personage, etc.; hence to take an oath. Later extended to profanities and bad language by the use of sacred expressions as intensives and expletives.

Swearing on the horns. *See under* HORN.

To swear black and blue. To assert vigorously and emphatically.

To swear black is white. To swear to any falsehood.

To swear like a trooper. To indulge in very strong blasphemy or profanity, as a soldier sometimes does.

Sweat. An old sweat. An experienced soldier of long service, an old soldier.

To sweat a coin was to shake up GOLD or SILVER coins to remove particles of metal from them without the diminution of weight being noticeable.

To sweat a person is to exact the maximum amount of labour out of a person for a minimum wage. Also to bleed or fleece a person. Hence **sweating system** to denote the overworking of operatives in the clothing trades, etc., of earlier days. In the U.S. **to sweat it out of a person** is to extort a confession by threats and violence.

Sweater girl. A young woman with a well-developed bust, which is made apparent by the wearing of a clinging *sweater* or jumper.

Sweating sickness, or **English sweat.** A fatal disease characterized by its symptoms—the onset of shivers followed by intense sweating, etc., which brought death in a few hours. It first appeared in England in 1485, and the last outbreak was in 1551. Although infrequent in its occurrence (five visitations in all), the mortality was considerable. It first reached the Continent in 1528. *Cp.* BLACK DEATH.

Swedenborgians. Followers of Emanuel Swedenborg (1688–1772), distinguished Swedish scientist and mystic, who in middle life came to hold himself appointed to reveal the Lord's teachings to mankind. He taught that Christ is the one God and that the Divine Trinity was present in him. The New Jerusalem Church or New Church was set up in ENGLAND in 1787 to propagate his teachings, which differ considerably from those of accepted Christianity. There are branches of the New Church in the U.S.A., Australia, New Zealand, and in Europe. Swedenborg wrote all his works in Latin and he claimed to have witnessed the Last Judgment.

Sweep. To sweep the board. In gaming, to win everything, to pocket all the stakes. Hence applied to one who carries all before him, wins all the prizes, etc.

To sweep the threshold. To announce to the world that the woman of the house is paramount. *See* SKIMMINGTON.

To sweep under the carpet. See *under* CARPET.

Sweepstakes. A race in which stakes are made by the owners of horses engaged, to be awarded to the winner or other horse in the race. Entrance money has to be paid to the race fund. If the horse runs, the full stake must be paid; but if it is withdrawn, a forfeit only is imposed.

Also a gambling arrangement in which a number of persons stake money on some event (usually a horse-race), each of whom draws a lot for every share bought, the total sum deposited being divided among the drawers of winners (or sometimes of starters).

St. Leger Sweepstakes. A horse-race for three-year-olds run at Doncaster early in September. It was instituted in 1776 by Colonel Anthony St. Leger, of Park Hill, near Doncaster, but was not called the "St. Leger" till two years later. *See* CLASSIC RACES; RACES.

Sweet. The sweet singer of Israel. King David, traditional author of the PSALMS.

To be sweet on. To be enamoured of, in love with.

To have a sweet tooth. To be very fond of dainties and sweet things generally.

Sweetness and light. A phrase much favoured by Matthew Arnold, particularly in his *Culture and Anarchy*:

> What we want is a fuller harmonious development of our humanity, a free play of thought upon our routine notions, spontaneity of consciousness, sweetness and light, and these are just what culture generates (ch. V).

The phrase was used by Swift (BATTLE OF THE BOOKS, 1697) in an imaginary fable by ÆSOP as to the merits of the bee (the ancients) and the spider (the moderns). It concludes:

> The difference is that instead of dirt and poison, we have rather chosen to fill our hives with honey and wax, thus furnishing mankind with the two noblest of things, which are sweetness and light (*Preface*).

Swell. A person showily dressed; one who puffs himself out beyond his proper dimensions, like the frog in the fable; hence, a fashionable person, one of high standing or importance. In American usage as an adjective, fine, stylish, first rate, just right.

Swell mob. An old term for the better-dressed thieves and pickpockets.

Swelled head. An exaggerated sense of one's own dignity, usefulness, importance, etc.

Swim. In the swim. In a favourable position in SOCIETY of any kind; in with those who matter or from whom advantages may be gained; a phrase from angling. A lot of fish gathered together is called a *swim*, and when an angler can pitch his hook in such a place he is said to be "in a good swim".

Sink or swim. No matter what happens; convicted WITCHES were thrown into the water to "sink or swim"; if they sank they were drowned; if they swam it was clear proof they were in league with the Evil One; so it did not much matter, one way or the other.

To swim with the stream. To allow one's actions and principles to be guided solely by the force of prevailing public opinion.

Swindle. To cheat, defraud, gain a mean advantage by trickery. The verb is formed from the noun *swindler*, which was introduced into England by German Jews about 1760, from Ger. *Schwindler*, a cheating company promoter (from *schwindeln*, to lie, to deceive).

Swing, with reference to JAZZ music is to play, either solo or ensemble, in such a manner over a regular pulse beat as to give the impression of a forward-moving rhythmic momentum. *To swing* is to play jazz music in this particular way and the term swing, although not new, gained a wide currency in the early 1930s from a popular number beginning "It don't mean a thing if it ain't got that swing". *Cp.* BOOGIE-WOOGIE; RAGTIME.

Captain Swing. The name assumed (1830–1833) by those who promoted the **Swing Riots** in the southern counties, resulting from the distressed condition of the agricultural labourers, and touched off by the introduction of new threshing machines which threatened to aggravate their situation. Menacing letters were sent to farmers, the machines were smashed, and ricks fired, and Captain Swing became the bogey of the propertied countryfolk. Although lives of Captain Swing appeared in 1830 and 1831, he seems to have been an imaginary character. *Cp.* LUDDITES.

> The neighbours thought all was not right,
> Scarcely one with him ventured to parley,
> And Captain Swing came in the night,
> And burnt all his beans and his barley.
> BARHAM: *Ingoldsby Legends (Babes in the Wood)*.

I don't care if I swing for him! A bitterly vengeful remark implying that the speaker will go to any length to get even—even if hanging be the consequence!

In full swing. Going splendidly; everything prosperous and in perfect order.

It went with a swing. Said of a ceremony, function, entertainment, etc., that passed off without a hitch and was a great success.

The swing-it-till-Monday basket. *See under* MONDAY.

To swing a ship. To check the compass deviation of a ship by swinging the vessel in as small a circle as possible through the points of the compass and taking bearings on suitable distant objects, and comparing the apparent with the true bearings. This is best done when the vessel is riding at a single anchor or at a buoy. There are other methods.

What you lose on the swings you gain on the roundabouts. What you lose on one venture you recoup on another. A way of stating the law of averages.

Swinge-buckler. A roisterer, a rake, a SWASH-BUCKLER.

> There was I, and Little John Doit of Staffordshire, and black George Barnes, and Francis Pickbone, and Will Squele, a Cotswold man; you had not four such swinge-bucklers in all the Inns-of-Court; and, I may say to you, we knew where the bona-robas were.
> SHAKESPEARE: *Henry IV, Pt. II, III, ii.*

Swiss. Swiss Guard. The Bourbon kings of France maintained a Guard of Swiss mercenaries until the Revolution. Pope Julius II (1503–13) instituted a Swiss Guard supplied by the cantons of Lucerne and Zürich. Some 100 men are still maintained as a papal escort drawn from the various Swiss cantons. Their formal uniform is still of MICHELANGELO's design.

No money—no Swiss—*i.e.* no assistance. The Swiss were for centuries the mercenaries of Europe—willing to serve anyone for pay—and were usually called in England *Switzers*, as in SHAKESPEARE's "Where are my Switzers? Let them guard the door" (*Hamlet*, IV, v). In France an hotel-porter—also the BEADLE of a church—is called *un suisse*. *Cp.* GNOMES OF ZÜRICH.

Swipes. An old name for a thin, washy, cheap beer; now used in slang for beer in general.

Switched on. AU FAIT with contemporary fashionable and popular cults, thoroughly up to date and responsive to current trends and tendencies. The expression is also applied to someone under the influence of drugs.

Swithin, St. If it rains on St. Swithin's Day (15 July), there will be rain for forty days.

> St. Swithin's day, gif ye do rain, for forty days it will remain;
> St. Swithin's day an ye be fair, for forty days 'twill rain nae mair.

The legend is that St. Swithin (or Swithun), Bishop of Winchester and adviser of Egbert of Wessex, who died in 862, desired to be buried in the churchyard of the minster, that the "sweet rain of heaven might fall upon his grave". At CANONIZATION, the monks thought to honour the SAINT by removing his body into the cathedral choir and fixed 15 July 971 for the ceremony, but it rained day after day for 40 days, thereby, according to some, delaying the proceedings. His shrine was destroyed during the REFORMATION and a new one was dedicated in 1962. Those who hold to this superstition ignore the fact that it is based upon the dating of the JULIAN Calendar and therefore could not hold for 40 days from the current 15 July which is based on the GREGORIAN YEAR.

The St. Swithin of France is St. Gervais (*see also* St. MÉDARD). The rainy saint in Flanders is St. Godelève; in Germany, the SEVEN SLEEPERS have this attribute.

Switzers. *See* SWISS.

Sword. In the days of CHIVALRY and romance a KNIGHT's horse and sword were his two most carefully prized possessions and it was customary to give each a name. Among the most noted of such swords are:

> Balisarda, ROGERO's sword, made by a sorceress.

Balmung, one of the swords of SIEGFRIED, made by Wieland.

Chrysaor (sword as good as gold), ARTEGAL's sword in Spenser's *Faerie Queene*.

Corrouge. Otuel's sword.

Courtain (the short sword), one of the swords of OGIER THE DANE; *Sauvagine* was the other, and they both took Munifican three years to make.

Durandal. See ROLAND'S SWORD *under* ROLAND.

Flamberge or Floberge (the flame-cutter), the name of one of CHARLEMAGNE's swords, and also of RINALDO and Maugis.

Frusberta, RINALDO's sword.

Glorious, OLIVER's sword, which hacked to pieces the nine swords made by Ansias, Galas, and Munifican.

Gram (grief), one of the swords of SIEGFRIED.

Greysteel, the sword of Koll the Thrall.

Haute-claire (very bright), both OLIVER's and Closamont's swords were so called.

Mimung, the sword that Wittich lent SIEGFRIED.

Morglay (big glaive), Sir BEVIS's sword.

Nagelring (nail-ring), DIETRICH's sword.

Philippan, the sword of Antony, one of the triumvirs.

Quern-biter (a foot-breadth), both Haco I and Thoralf Skolinson had a sword of this name.

Sanglamore (the big bloody glaive), BRAGGADOCHIO's sword (Spenser's *Faerie Queene*).

Sauvagine (the relentless), *see* COURTAIN *above*.

Tizona, the CID's sword.

See also ANGURVADEL; ARONDIGHT; AZOTH; CALIBURN; CURTANA; EXCALIBUR; JOYEUSE; MERVEILLEUSE; ROSSE.

Sword dance. A Scottish dance performed over two swords laid crosswise on the floor, or sometimes danced among swords placed point downwards in the ground; also a dance in which the men brandish swords and clash them together, the women passing under them when crossed.

Sword dollar. A Scottish silver coin of James VI marked with a sword on the reverse. It was worth 30s Scots (2s. 6d. English) in contemporary coin.

The Sword of Damocles. See DAMOCLES.

The Sword of God. Khaled-ibn-al-Walid (d. 642), Mohammedan leader, was so called for his prowess at the battle of Muta (629), when he defeated the Emperor Heraclius, after a fierce two days' engagement.

The Sword of Rome. Marcellus, who opposed Hannibal (216–214 B.C.).

The Sword of the Spirit. The Word of God (*Eph.* vi, 17). Also the name of a Roman Catholic social movement founded in 1940.

At sword's point. In deadly hostility, ready to fight each other with swords.

Fire and sword. Rapine and destruction perpetrated by an invading army.

Flaming swords. See FLAMING.

Poke not fire with a sword. This was a

precept of PYTHAGORAS, meaning add not fuel to fire, or do not irritate an angry man by sharp words which will only increase his rage. (*See* Iamblichus: *Protrepticus*, symbol ix.).

Sword and buckler. An old epithet for brag and bluster; as *a sword and buckler voice, sword and buckler men*, etc. Hotspur says of the future Henry V:

> And that same sword and buckler Prince of Wales,
> . . . .
> I'd have him poisoned with a pot of ale.
> SHAKESPEARE: *Henry IV, Pt. I*, I, iii.

To put to the sword. To slay.

To sheathe the sword. Figuratively, to put aside enmity, to make peace.

Your tongue is a double-edged sword. Whatever you say wounds; your argument cuts both ways. The allusion is to the double-edged sword out of the mouth of the Son of Man—one edge to condemn, and the other to save (*Rev.* i, 16).

Yours is a Delphic sword—it cuts both ways. Erasmus says a Delphic sword is that which accommodates itself to the PRO OR CON of a subject. The reference is to the double meanings of the Delphic ORACLES.

Sybarite (sĭ' bår ĭt). A self-indulgent person; a sensualist. The inhabitants of Sybaris, in south Italy, were proverbial for their luxurious living and self-indulgence. A tale is told by Seneca, of a Sybarite who complained that he could not rest comfortably at night, and being asked why, replied that, "He found a rose-leaf doubled under him, and it hurt him."

Sybil. A perverted spelling of SIBYL, in classical mythology a prophetess, especially the prophetesses of APOLLO (*see* SIBYLLINE BOOKS). GEORGE ELIOT was known to her friends as *The Sybil*.

Sycophant (sĭk' ō fănt). A SPONGER, parasite or servile flatterer; the Greek *sukophantes* (*sukon*, fig; *phainein*, to show), which is said to have meant one who informed against those who exported figs contrary to law or robbed the sacred fig-trees. Hence, by extension, a tale-bearer, flatterer, etc. This explanation is difficult to substantiate.

At ATHENS, *sycophantes* were a class of professional prosecutors who often blackmailed the wealthy with threats of prosecution or litigation and thus their name may include the added allusion of "shaking a fig-tree" to expose the fruit, as a blackmailer might shake his wealthy victim to produce the cash. This has no direct connexion with our use of the word.

Sydney or the Bush. An Australian expression meaning you either go for the very best or its the worst, there is no half-way house.

Syllogism (sil′ ō jizm). A form of argument consisting of three propositions, a *major premise* or general statement, a *minor premise* or instance, and the *conclusion*, which is deducted from these.

Sylph (silf). An elemental spirit of air; so named in the MIDDLE AGES by the ROSICRUCIANS and CABBALISTS, from the Greek *silphe*, beetle or larva. *Cp.* SALAMANDER.

Any mortal who has preserved inviolate chastity might enjoy intimate familiarity with these gentle spirits, and deceased coquettes were said to become sylphs, "and sport and flutter in the fields of air".

> Whoever, fair and chaste,
> Rejects mankind, is by some sylph embraced.
> POPE: *The Rape of the Lock*, i, 67.

Symbolists. A group of French writers who, towards the end of the 19th century, revolted against Naturalism and Parnassianism (*see* PARNASSIAN SCHOOL *under* PARNASSUS). Their aim was to suggest rather than to depict or transcribe, and their watchword was Verlaine's, "Pas de couleur, rien que la nuance." Their precursors were Baudelaire, Banville, G. de Nerval and Villiers de l'Isle-Adam. Chief Symbolists: in verse, Verlaine, Rimbaud, Mallarmé; in prose, Huysmans.

Symbols of Saints. *See under* SAINTS.

Symplegades. Another name for the CYANEAN ROCKS.

Symposium (sim pō′ zi ům). Properly, a drinking together (Gr. *syn*, together; *posis*, drink); hence, a convivial meeting for social and intellectual entertainment; hence, a discussion upon a subject, and the collected opinions of different authorities printed and published in a review, etc.

The Symposium is the title given to a dialogue by PLATO, and another by Xenophon, in which the conversation of SOCRATES and others is recorded.

Synagogue (Gr. *synagoge*, assembly or place of assembly). In Jewish communities, the institution for worship, the study of Judaism, and social life and service which had its origins at the time of the BABYLONIAN CAPTIVITY. The most notable of its special symbols are the Ark, in which scrolls of the Law are kept, the ever-burning lamp, and the Reading Desk, usually in the middle of the building. It is managed by a board of elders. *See* TABERNACLE; TEMPLE.

The Great Synagogue. According to Jewish tradition a body of 120 men in the time of Ezra and Nehemiah (5th century B.C.) who were engaged in remodelling the religious life of the Jews after the return from exile and in establishing the text and canon of the Hebrew SCRIPTURES.

Synchronism. A form of abstract art resembling ORPHISM begun by two Americans, Morgan Russell and S. MacDonald Wright, in 1913, characterized by movements of pure colour moving by gradations or rhythms from the primaries to the intermediary colours. Their painting depended on colour and its immediate effects. *Cp.* CUBISM; DADAISM; FAUVISM; FUTURISM; IMPRESSIONISM; SURREALISM; VORTICISM.

Syndicalism (Fr. *syndicalisme*, trade unionism). A trade-union movement originating in France about 1890 where it was known as *Syndicalisme révolutionnaire*. It was opposed to State socialism, the means of production being taken over by the TRADE UNIONS and not by the State, and government was to be by a federation of trade-union bodies. The syndicalists aimed at achieving their objectives by widespread STRIKES, GO-SLOWS, etc. Syndicalism played an important part in fomenting the trade-union unrest in Great Britain immediately preceding World War I, and syndicalists were a prominent element in Spain in the 1930s.

Synecdoche (si nek′ dō ki). The figure of speech which consists of putting a part for the whole, the whole for the part, a more comprehensive for a less comprehensive term, or *vice versa*. Thus, *a hundred bayonets* (for *a hundred soldiers*), *the town was starving* (for *the people in the town*).

> Now will I remember you farther of that manner of speech which the Greeks call *Synecdoche*, and we the figure of quick conceite ... as when one would tell me how the French king was overthrown at Saint Quintans. I am enforced to think that it was not the king himselfe in person, but the Constable of Fraunce with the French kings power.
>
> |PUTTENHAM: *Arte of English Poesie*, Bk. III, ch. xviii (1589).

Synoptic Gospels. Those of MATTHEW, MARK, and LUKE; so called because, taken together and apart from that of JOHN, they form a *synopsis* (Gr., a seeing together), *i.e.* a general and harmonized account of the life of Christ.

The Synoptic Problem. The problems of the origin and relationship of the three SYNOPTIC GOSPELS arising from large sections of material, and often phrasing, being common to them. There is general agreement that MARK is the earliest of the GOSPELS, and that it provides much of the material for MATTHEW and LUKE. The latter two contain material not found in Mark (*see* "Q"). There are varying theories among Biblical scholars to account for this parallelism, etc.

Syntax, Dr. (sin′ tăks). The pious, henpecked clergyman, very simple-minded, but of excellent taste and scholarship, created by William Combe (1741–1823) to accompany a series of coloured comic illustrations by Rowlandson. His adventures are told in eight-syllabled verse in the *Three Tours of Dr. Syntax* (1812, 1820, and 1821).

Syrinx (sī′ ringks). An Arcadian NYMPH of Greek legend. On being pursued by PAN she took refuge in the river Ladon, and prayed to be changed into a reed; the prayer was granted, and of the reed Pan made his pipes. Hence the name is given to the PAN-PIPE, or reed mouth-organ, and also to the vocal organ of birds.

T

T. The twentieth letter of the alphabet, representing Semitic and Greek *tau*, which meant "a sign or a mark". Our T is a modification of the earlier form, X. *See also* TAU.

As a mediæval numeral T represents 160, and T 160,000.

It fits to a T. Exactly. The allusion is to the use of a *T-square* for the accurate drawing of right-angles, parallel lines, etc.

Marked with a T. Notified as a felon. Persons convicted of felony, and admitted to the BENEFIT OF CLERGY, were branded on the thumb with the letter T (thief). The law authorizing this was abolished in 1827.

Taal (tahl). Cape Dutch later known as Afrikaans, derived from 17th-century Dutch of the province of South Holland.

Tab. A flap, tag; a tally.

To keep tabs on someone is to keep check on him.

Tabard. An outer coat of rough, heavy material once worn by poor people; also a loose outer garment, with or without short sleeves, worn like a cloak by KNIGHTS over their armour—what Chaucer called *cote-armour* often emblazoned with heraldic devices. It survives in the tabard worn by Heralds and PURSUIVANTS.

The Tabard Inn. The inn where pilgrims from LONDON used to set out on their journey to Canterbury; it was on the London estate of the abbots of Hyde (near Winchester), and lay in the SOUTHWARK (now BOROUGH) High Street, a little to the south of LONDON BRIDGE. The site is marked by a commemorative plaque. The inn and its host Harry Baily are immortalized in Chaucer's *Canterbury Tales*.

Tabardar, or **Taberder.** A scholar on the foundation of Queen's College, Oxford: so called because they wore gowns with tabard sleeves—that is, loose, terminating a little below the elbow in a point.

Tabby. Originally the name (from Arabic) of a silk material with a "watered" surface, giving an effect of wavy lines; applied to the brownish cat with dark stripes, because its markings resemble this material.

Demurest of the tabby kind,
The pensive Selima reclined.
GRAY: *On the Death of a Favourite Cat.*

Tabernacle. (Lat. *tabernaculum*, a tent). The portable shrine instituted by MOSES during the wanderings of the Jews in the wilderness. It was divided by a veil or hanging, behind which, in the "HOLY OF HOLIES", was the Ark. The outer division was called the Holy Place. When set up in camp the whole was surrounded by an enclosure. *See Exod.* xxv–xxxi; xxxiii, 7–10; xxxv–xl.

In Roman Catholic churches, the tabernacle is the ornamental receptacle on the High Altar, in which the vessels containing the Blessed Sacrament are reserved. The name derives from the application of the word *tabernaculum* in church ornamentation to a variety of canopied forms.

The Feast of the Tabernacles. One of the three main feasts of the Jewish year lasting seven days followed by an eighth day of "holy convocation" (see *Lev.* xxiii. 34–43; *Numb.* xxix, 12–34). It commemorates the way the Jews dwelt in booths or tents in the wilderness and also celebrates the final ingathering of the harvest and the vintage. It begins on the 15th Tishri (September—October).

Tin Tabernacles. The name given to the corrugated iron Nonconformist chapels and other churches which were erected in the 19th and early 20th centuries to meet the needs of developing or scattered Christian communities.

Table. Apelles' Table. A pictured board (Lat. *tabula*) or table, representing the excellency of sobriety on the one side and the deformity of intemperance on the other.

Archbishop Parker's Table. The table of prohibited degrees within which marriage was forbidden, published in 1563, and to be found as the *Table of Kindred and Affinity* in the BOOK OF COMMON PRAYER. Matthew Parker was Archbishop of Canterbury from 1559 to 1575 (*See* NAG'S HEAD CONSECRATION; VESTIARIAN CONTROVERSY.)

The Lord's Table. The communion table

or ALTAR.

The Round Table, or **Table Round.** *See under* ROUND.

Table d'hôte (Fr., the host's table). The "ORDINARY" at an hotel or restaurant; the meal for which one pays a fixed price whether one partakes of all the courses or not. In the MIDDLE AGES, and even down to the reign of Louis XIV, the landlord's or host's table was the only public dining place known in Germany and France.

Table of Pythagoras. The common multiplication table, carried up to ten. The table is divided into a hundred little squares. The name is taken from a corrupt text of Boethius, who was really referring to the ABACUS.

Alphonsine Tables. *See* ALPHONSINE; TABULÆ TOLETANÆ.

Table of Cebes. Cebes was a Theban philosopher and disciple of SOCRATES. His *Tabula* presents a picture of human life depicted with great accuracy of judgment and splendour of sentiment.

The Table of Toledo. *See* TABULÆ TOLETANÆ.

The Twelve Tables. The tables of the Roman laws engraved on brass, brought from ATHENS to ROME by the decemvirs.

Table money, or **charge.** A charge additional to that of the meal made at restaurants, etc., towards the cost of attendance; or a small fee charged to players at Bridge clubs; also, in the Army and navy, an allowance made to senior officers to assist in meeting the expenses of official entertaining.

Table Mountain. A flat topped mountain, especially that overlooking Cape Town.

Table-rapping. The occurrence of knocking sounds on a table without apparent source but coming from the departed, according to spiritualists, who use them as a supposed means of contacting the dead.

Table-talk. Small talk, chit-chat, familiar conversation.

Table-turning. The turning of tables without the application of mechanical force, which in the early days of SPIRITUALISM was commonly practised at seances, and sank to the level of a parlour trick. It was said by some to be the work of departed spirits, and by others to be due to a force akin to MESMERISM.

To fence the tables. In Scottish usage, to debar those unworthy from communion.

To lay on the table. The parliamentary phrase for postponing consideration of a motion, proposal, BILL, etc., indefinitely. Hence *to table a matter* is to defer it *sine die*. It is also used to mean submitting something for discussion.

To turn the tables. To reverse the conditions or relations; as, for instance, to rebut a charge by bringing forth a counter-charge. The phrase comes from the old custom of reversing the *table* or board, in games such as CHESS and draughts, so that the opponent's relative position is altogether changed.

Tableaux vivants (Fr., living pictures). Representations of statuary groups by living persons; said to have been invented by Madame de Genlis (1746–1830) while she had charge of the children of the Duc d'Orléans.

Taboo, tabu. A Polynesian word signifying that which is banned; the prohibition of the use of certain persons, animals, things, etc., or the utterance of certain names and words. Thus a temple is *taboo*, and so is he who violates a temple and everyone and everything connected with what is taboo becomes taboo also. Captain Cook was made *taboo* when he tried to set up an observatory in the Sandwich Islands. The idea of taboo is not, of course, peculiar to the Polynesians and is found among the ancient Egyptians, Jews, etc. Hence a person who is ostracized or an action, custom, etc., that is altogether forbidden by society, is said to be *taboo* or *tabooed*.

> For several days after entering the valley I had been saluted at least fifty times in twenty-four hours with the talismanic word "Taboo" shrieked in my ears, at some gross violation of its provions, of which I had unconsciously been guilty.
>
> HERMAN MELVILLE: *Typee*, ch. xxx.

Tabouret, Right of (tăb′ oo rā′). In the old French court certain ladies of the highest rank had the *droit de tabouret* (the right of sitting on a tabouret or low stool) in the presence of the queen. Gentlemen similarly privileged had the *droit de fauteuil* (the right of sitting in an armchair).

Tabula rasa (tăb′ ū lȧ rā′ zȧ) (Lat., a scraped tablet). A clean slate—literally and figuratively—on which anything can be written. Thus, we say that the mind of a person who has been badly taught must become a *tabula rasa* before he can learn anything properly.

Tabulæ Toletanæ. The ALPHONSINE TABLES, so called because they were compiled at Toledo.

> His Tables Tolletanes forth he brought,
> Ful wel corrected ne ther lakked nought.
> CHAUCER: *Franklin's Tale*, 545.

Tace is Latin for candle. Silence is most discreet. "MUM'S THE WORD". *Tace* is Latin for "be silent", and *candle* is symbolical of light. The phrase means "keep it dark", do not throw light upon it. Fielding, in *Amelia* (ch. x), has—"*Tace*, madam," answered Murphy, "is Latin for a candle".

It was customary at one time to express disapprobation of a play or an actor by throwing a candle on to the stage thus sometimes causing the curtain to be drawn.

Tack. The use of the word, particularly by sailors, soldiers, etc., to denote food is of unknown origin. It is used in such phrases as **poor tack, hard tack** (especially ship's biscuit) as opposed to **soft tack** (bread or other more palatable fare).

On the right tack, or **on the wrong tack.** Taking the right (or wrong) line or course of action. A nautical phrase, *tack* here being the course of a ship when "tacking", *i.e.* steering a zigzag course when sailing to windward.

Taffeta, or **taffety** (tăf′ e tà, tăf′ e ti). A material made of silk; at one time it was watered; hence Taylor says, "No taffaty more changeable than they." The word is from the Persian *taftan*, to twist or cure.

The fabric has often changed its character. At one time it was silk and linen, at another silk and wool. In the 18th century it was lustrous silk, sometimes striped with gold.

Taffeta phrases. Smooth, sleek phrases, EUPHEMISMS. We also use the words FUSTIAN, *stuff, silken, shoddy,* BUCKRAM, *velvet,* etc., to qualify phrases and literary compositions spoken or written.

> Taffeta phrases, silken terms precise,
> Three-piled hyperboles.
> SHAKESPEARE: *Love's Labour's Lost,* V, ii.

Taffy. A Welshman, from *Davy* (*Dafydd,* David), a common name in Wales; perhaps it is best known among the English from the old rhyme in allusion to the days of border cattle raids.

> Taffy was a Welshman,
> Taffy was a thief,
> Taffy came to my house
> And stole a leg of beef.

Tag. A children's game of catch in which from the outset each person touched or "caught" joins the line to catch those remaining.

Tag Days. The American equivalent of British FLAG DAYS.

Tag, rag and bobtail. *See* RAG-TAG AND BOBTAIL.

Tages (tā′ jēz). In Etruscan mythology, a mysterious boy with the wisdom of an old man who was ploughed up, or who sprang from the ground, at Tarquinii. He is said to have been the grandson of JUPITER and to have instructed the Etruscans in the art of AUGURY. The latter wrote down his teaching in 12 books, which were known as "the books of Tages", or "the Acherontian books".

Tail. According to an old fable lions wipe out their footsteps with their tail, that they may not be tracked.

Out of the tail of one's eye. With a sidelong glance; just to see a thing "out of the corner of your eye."

Tail male, tail female. *See* ENTAIL.

To put salt on the tail. *see* PUT SOME SALT ON HIS TAIL *under* SALT.

To tail a person is to follow someone and not to lose sight of them.

To turn tail. To turn one's back and make off.

To twist the lion's tail. *See under* LION.

With his tail between his legs. Very dejected, quite downcast. The allusion is to dogs.

With a sting in its tail. In speech or writing, that which contains a sting or rebuke at the end: an unexpected catch, snag or hurt at the end of the matter. The bee has a sting in its tail, so have the sting-ray and the scorpion. *See* TELEGONUS.

Tailed men. It was an old belief in mediæval times that such creatures existed and among continentals Englishmen were once reputed to have tails. It was long a saying that the men of Kent were born with tails, as a punishment for the murder of Thomas á Becket.

> A *Warwickshire* Man will be known by his Grinn, as Roman-Catholics imagine a *Kentish* man by his Tail.

Peter Pindar (*Epistle to the Pope,* 41) fastens the legend on the town of Strood:

> As Becket that good saint, sublimely rode,
> Thoughtless of insult, through the town of Strode,
> What did the mob? Attacked his horse's rump
> And cut the tail, so flowing, to the stump.
> What does the saint? Quoth he, "For this vile trick
> The town of Strode shall heartily be sick".
> And lo! by power divine, a curse prevails—
> The babes of Strode are born with horse's tails.

Jews and Cornishmen were also held to have tails, the appendage also being borne by the DEVIL. In the former case from a confusion of *rabbi* with *raboin* or *rabuino,* the devil, from Span. *rabo,* a tail.

Tail-end Charlie. An R.A.F. phrase in World War II for the rear-gunner in the tail of an aircraft; also for the aircraft at the rear of a group, or the last ship in a flotilla.

Taillefer (tī a fâr). The Norman TROUVÈRE who accompanied William of Normandy's army to England in 1066. He begged leave to strike the first blow and rode far ahead of the other horsemen singing of CHARLEMAGNE and ROLAND and playing like a juggler with his sword. After overcoming his first two opponents he charged into the Saxon host and was cut to pieces.

Tailor. Nine tailors make a man. An old expression of contempt at the expense of tailors, implying such physical feebleness that it would take nine of them to make a man of good physique, the occupation not being conducive to sound physical developement. It has been suggested that *tailor* is a facetious adaptation of *teller*, a *teller* being a stroke on the funeral bell, three being given for a child, six for a woman, and nine for a man.

The number mentioned is sometimes only three:

> Some foolish knave, I thinke, at first began
> The slander that three taylors are one man.
> TAYLOR: *Workes*, iii, 73 (1630).

The Three Tailors of Tooley Street. Canning says that three tailors of Tooley Street, SOUTHWARK, addressed a petition of grievances to the HOUSE OF COMMONS, beginning: "We, the people of England". Hence the phrase is used of any pettifogging côterie that fancies it represents the nation.

Tai-ping. The word means "Great peace", and the Tai-pings were the Chinese followers of Hung Hsiu-ch'uan (Heavenly Prince) in the rebellion of 1851–1864 against the Manchu dynasty. Hung, a Christian of a kind, who claimed to be the Younger Brother of Christ, set out to establish the "Great Peace" and captured Nanking in 1853. The rebellion was finally crushed, after millions had been killed by the Emperor's forces aided by CHINESE GORDON and his EVER-VICTORIOUS ARMY.

Take. To be taken aback. *See* ABACK.

To have taking ways. To be of an ingratiating disposition; readily able to make oneself liked. *Fetching ways, winning ways* amount to the same thing.

To take after. To have a strong resemblance to, physically, mentally, etc. "Doesn't little Johnny take after his father?" "Most of Lawrence's paintings seem to take after Romney."

To take back one's words. To withdraw them; to recant.

To take in. To deceive, gull. Hence, *a regular take-in*, a hoax, swindle.

To take in one's stride. Effortlessly or unflurriedly, without disrupting one's normal activities or routine.

To take it. To withstand suffering, hardship, punishment, insult, etc. "Britain can take it" was a popular slogan during the air attacks of World War II.

To take it lying down. To submit to insult or oppression without protest or resistance, like a dog when it is cowed.

To take it out of someone. To exact the utmost from, to give someone a real drubbing; to exact satisfaction from, to get one's own back. Also to become thoroughly exhausted, as, "Working after midnight does take it out of me."

To take it out on someone. Colloquially, to work off one's irritation, frustration, etc., by being unpleasant to someone else.

To take it upon oneself. To make oneself responsible (perhaps unwarrantably), to assume control.

To take off. To mimic or ridicule; also to start, especially of an aeroplane or of one in an athletic contest, as jumping or racing.

To take on. To undertake to perform, to assume, or, colloquially, to be upset or considerably affected as in, "Don't take on so" (*i.e.* don't distress yourself so); to make a fuss.

To take one down a peg. *See under* PEG.

To take over. To assume the management, control, or ownership.

To take someone at his word. To regard what he has said as trustworthy.

To take to. To develop an immediate liking for someone; to begin to develop a habit, as, "He has taken to drink since his wife absconded."

To take to task. To blame or censure, to call to account.

To take up. To pick up, to raise; to arrest; to begin to cultivate a hobby, study, etc.; also used of beginning to patronize or "adopt" people, usually for their advancement in society or business, etc.

> "Yes, Lady Rockminster has took us up," said Lady Clavering.
> "Taken us up, Mamma," cried Blanche, in a shrill voice.
> "Well, taken us up, then," said my lady, "it's very kind of her, and I dare say we shall like it when we get used to it, only at first one don't fancy being took—well, taken up, at all."
> THACKERAY: *Pendennis*, ch. xxxvii.

To take up with. To commence to associate with.

You can't take it with you, *i.e.* to the grave; in other words make use of your resources, material and financial, while you have the chance.

You must take us as you find us. Said to an unexpected visitor before whose arrival there has been no time to make special preparations.

Take-home pay. That which is left to the wage earner after the depredations of the CHANCELLOR OF THE EXCHEQUER and the exaction of the various levies for social insurance.

A take-over bid. A favourable offer to the shareholders of a company by another company which wishes to secure control of it.

Tale (O.E. *talu*). A number, a reckoning; a story. In *Exod.* v, 8, we have *tale of bricks*, a measure by number, as of a shepherd counting sheep:

> And every shepherd tells his tale
> Under the hawthorn in the dale.
> MILTON: *L'Allegro*, 67.

An old wives' tale. Legendary lore, or a story usually involving the marvellous, and only accepted by the credulous. George Peele has a play *The Old Wives' Tale* (1595) and Arnold Bennett a novel (1908) of the same title.

A tale of a tub. *See under* TUB.

To tell tales out of school. To utter abroad affairs not meant for the public ear; to reveal confidential matters.

Out of tale, without tale. More than can be numbered.

Talent. Ability, aptitude, a "gift" for something or other. The word is borrowed from the parable in *Matt.* xxv, 14–30, and was originally the name of a weight and piece of money in Assyria, Greece, ROME, etc. (Gr. *talanton*, a balance). The value varied, the later Attic talent weighing about 57 lb. troy, and being worth about £250.

The Ministry of all the Talents. *See* ALL THE TALENTS.

Tales (tā′ lēz). Persons in the court from whom selection is made to supply the place of jurors who have been empanelled, but are not in attendance. It is the first word of the Latin sentence providing for this contingency—*Tales de circumstantibus, i.e.* "from such (persons) as are standing about". Those who supplement the jury are called *talesmen* and their names are set down in the *talesbook*.

> To serve for jurymen or tales.
> BUTLER: *Hudibras*, III, viii.

To pray a tales. To pray that the number of jurymen may be completed.

In the celebrated action Bardell *v.* Pickwick:

> It was discovered that only ten special jurymen were present. Upon this, Mr. Serjeant Buzfuz prayed a *tales*; the gentlemen in black then proceeded to press into the special jury, two of the common jurymen; and a greengrocer and a chemist were caught directly.
> DICKENS: *Pickwick Papers*, ch. xxxiv.

Taliesin (tăl i ēs′ in). A Welsh BARD of the late 16th century about whom very little is known. The so-called *Book of Taliesin* is of the 13th century and its contents are the work of various authors. The village of Taliesin in Cardiganshire is named after him. The story is that Prince Elphin, son of the King of Gwynedd, was given the right to net a certain weir near the mouth of the Dovey once a year, and on this occasion his net was brought ashore without a single salmon in it. While bewailing his constant misfortune, he noticed a leather wallet suspended from the timber of the weir and upon opening it found therein a youth of such lustrous brow that Elphin named him Taliesin (radiant brow). Taliesin brought wonderful prosperity to Elphin and became the greatest of the British bards at the court of King ARTHUR at CAERLEON.

Talisman. A charm or magical figure or word, such as the ABRAXAS which is cut on metal or stone under the influence of certain planets; it is supposed to be sympathetic and to communicate to the wearer influence from the planets.

> "Know, then, that the medicine to which thou, Sir King, and many one beside, owe their recovery, is a talisman, composed under certain aspects of the heavens, when the Divine Intelligences are most propitious. I am but the poor administrator of its virtues."
> SCOTT: *The Talisman*, xviii.

In order to free a place of vermin, a talisman consisting of the obnoxious creature was made in wax or consecrated metal, in a planetary hour.

> Swore you had broke, and robb'd his house,
> And stole his talismanic louse.
> BUTLER: *Hudibras*, III, i.

The word is the Arabic *tilsam* from late Greek *telesma*, mystery.

Tall. A tall story. An incredible tale.

To walk tall. *See under* WALK.

Tally, To. To correspond. In England the tally, a notched piece of wood (Fr. *taille* a notch or incision) used for reckoning, had a particular importance as an EXCHEQUER record and receipt down to 1826 (usually of money loaned to the Government). The notch on one side was an acknowledgement of the sum paid, two other sides were marked with the date, the name of the payer, etc., and the whole was cleft longitudinally so that each half contained one written side and the half of every notch. One part was retained at the Exchequer (the *counterstock*) and the other (the *stock*) was issued. When payment was required the two parts were compared if they "tallied" all was in order.

In 1834, the mass of these valuable records were burnt in the stoves which heated the HOUSE OF LORDS; an unintelligent action causing the disastrous fire which destroyed the old PARLIAMENT buildings.

Tallyman. A travelling hawker who calls at private houses to sell wares on the *tally system*—that is, part payment on account, and other parts when the man calls again, so called because he keeps a *tally* or SCORE of his transactions.

To live tally, or **make a tally bargain.** Said of a couple who live together as man and wife without being married—presumably because they do so as their tastes *tally*, and not from any reason of compulsion. *Cp.* COMMON LAW WIFE.

Tally-ho! The cry of fox-hunters on catching sight of the fox. It is an English form of Fr. *taiaut*, which was similarly used in deer-hunting.

Talmud, The (tăl′ mŭd) (Heb., instruction). The collection of Jewish civil and religious law, religious and moral doctrine, and ritual founded on SCRIPTURE. It consists of the MISHNAH and the GEMARA and there are two recensions, the Babylonian and the Palestinian, or Jerusalem. The Babylonian Talmud, about three times the volume of the Palestinian, is held to be the more important and it was completed towards the end of the 5th century A.D.. The Palestine Talmud was produced in the mid-4th century A.D. After the BIBLE, the Talmud is the most important influence in Jewish life.

Talus (tā′ lŭs). *See* MAN OF BRASS *under* BRASS.

Tamberlane, Tamerlane. Names under which the renowned Tartar conqueror Timur, or Timur i Leng, *i.e.* Timur the Lame (1336–1405), is commonly known. He had his capital at Samarkand, and conquered most of Persia and India, Georgia and other Caucasian lands, and was preparing to conquer China when he died. The story of his confinement of the Sultan Bayezid, or Bajazet, in an iron cage is probably legendary. He is the hero of Marlowe's blank verse tragedy *Tamburlaine the Great* (acted 1587). In Rowe's play *Tamerlane* (1702), the warrior appears as a calm philosophic prince—out of compliment to William III.

Tammany Hall. The headquarters (in 14th Street, New York) of the Democratic Party organization in New York City and State. In the 19th century, it became a powerful influence in the party as a whole and in the 1870s, under W.M. Tweed, was associated with widespread corruption, and this and other incidents led to *Tammany Hall* being used figuratively for wholeseale and widespread political or municipal malpractice.

Tammany Hall was the survivor of numerous Tammany societies which sprang up at the time of the American Revolution as patriotic anti-British organizations and "St. Tammany" became the patron of the SONS OF LIBERTY clubs.

Tammuz. *See* THAMMUZ.

Tam-o'-Shanter. The hero of Burns's poem of that name; the soft cloth headdress is so called from him.

Remember Tam-o'-Shanter's mare. You may pay too dear for your WHISTLE, as Meg lost her tail, pulled off by Nannie of the "CUTTY SARK", in Burns's poem.

> Think, ye may buy the joys owre dear—
> Remember Tam-o'-Shanter's mare.
> BURNS: *Tam-o'-Shanter.*

Tancred (d. 1112). One of the chief heroes of the First CRUSADE, and a leading character in TASSO'S JERUSALEM DELIVERED. He was the son of Otho the Good and Emma (sister of Robert Guiscard). In the epic he was the greatest of all Christian warriors except RINALDO.

Disraeli's strange romance, *Tancred* (1847), tells of an early-19th-century heir to a dukedom who went on a "New Crusade" to the HOLY LAND.

Tangie. A water-spirit of the Orkneys appearing as a man covered with seaweed (Dan. *tang*, seaweed) or as a little seahorse.

Tanist (Ir. and Gael., *tanaiste*). The lord or chief of a territory, or his elected heir. It was an ancient custom in IRELAND and among CELTIC peoples for the family or CLAN to elect a successor to the lands from among their number, usually the nearest male relative of the existing chieftain unless he were a minor or otherwise unsuitable. This mode of tenure is called **tanistry.**

Tanist Stone. The monolith erected by the ancient GAELIC kings at their coronation, especially that called LIA-FAIL, which, according to tradition, is identical with the famous Stone of SCONE. It is said to have been set up at Icolmkil for the coronation of Fergus I of SCOTLAND, a contemporary of ALEXANDER THE GREAT and son of Ferchard, King of Ireland.

Tank. The heavily armoured motorized combat vehicle running on caterpillar tracks was first introduced on the battlefield by the British in the Battle of the Somme (1916). It owes its name to *tank* being used as a code word for these vehicles in order not to arouse enemy suspicions and to achieve a complete surprise.

Tanner. Slang for a sixpenny piece. Originally a silver coin, first minted in 1551. It survived after the introduction of DECIMAL CURRENCY with a value of 2½p. until its withdrawal in 1980. It was so called after John Sigismund Tanner (d. 1775), an engraver at the MINT. *Cp.* TESTER.

Tannhäuser (tăn′ hoi zer). A lyrical poet, or MINNESINGER of Germany, who flourished in the second half of the 13th century. He led a wandering life, and is said even to have visited the Far East; this fact, together with his *Busslied* (song of repentance), and the general character of his poems, probably gave rise to the legend about him—which first appeared in a 16th-century German ballad. This related how he spends a voluptuous year with VENUS, in the VENUSBERG, a magic land reached through a subterranean cave; at last he obtains leave to visit the upper world, and goes to POPE Urban IV for absolution. "No", says His Holiness, "you can no more hope for mercy than this dry staff can be expected to bud again." Tannhäuser departs in despair; but on the third day the papal staff bursts into blossom; the Pope sends in every direction for Tannhäuser, but the KNIGHT is nowhere to be found, for, mercy having been refused, he has returned to end his days in the arms of Venus. *See* ECKHARDT THE FAITHFUL.

Wagner's opera of this name was first produced in 1845.

Tantalus (tăn′ tă lus). In Greek mythology, the son of ZEUS and a NYMPH. He was a Lydian king, highly honoured and prosperous; but, because he divulged to mortals the secrets of the gods, he was plunged up to the chin in a river of HADES, a tree hung with clusters of fruit being just above his head. As every time he tried to drink the waters receded from him, and as the fruit was just out of reach, he suffered agony from thirst, hunger, and unfulfilled anticipation.

Hence, our verb, *to tantalize*, to excite a hope and disappoint it; and hence the name *tantalus* applied to a lock-up spirit chest in which the bottles are visible but un-get-atable without the key.

Tantivy, or **Tantivy Man** (tăn tiv′ i). A name given TORY High churchmen in the time of James II. They were caricatured as being mounted on the CHURCH OF ENGLAND riding "tantivy" to ROME. *To ride tantivy* is a hunting term meaning to ride at full gallop.

Tantony pig. The smallest pig of a litter, which, according to the old proverb, will follow its owner anywhere. So called in honour of St. ANTHONY, who was the patron SAINT of swineherds, and is frequently represented with a little pig at his side.

Tantony is also applied to a small church bell—or to any hand bell—for there is usually a bell round the neck of St. Anthony's pig or attached to the TAU CROSS he carries.

Tantras, The. Sanskrit religious books (6th and 7th century A.D.) of the Shaktas, a Hindu cult whose adherents worship the female principle, usually centring round Siva's wife, Parvati. They are mostly in the form of a dialogue between SIVA and his wife.

Tantra is Sanskrit for thread, or warp, and hence is used of groundwork, order or doctrine of religion.

Taoism (tā′ ō izm) (*tao*, the way). One of the three religious systems of China along with Confucianism and BUDDHISM. It derives from the philosphical system of Lao-tsze (6th century B.C.).

Tap. On tap. Available, ready for use; as liquor is from a cask when it has been tapped.

To tap the admiral. To broach a cask of liquor surreptitiously. From the story of the sailors who are supposed to have tapped the cask of spirits in which an admiral's body was being brought back to England.

Tap-up Sunday. An old local name for the Sunday preceding 2 October, when a fair was held on St. Catherine's Hill, near Guildford. So called because any person, with or without a licence, might open a "tap", or sell beer on the hill for that one day.

Taped. To have a person taped. Fully appraised or summed up, completely "weighed up" or assessed; as if measured with a tape. When one has a situation "taped" it also implies having things under control.

Tapis (tăp′ ē). **On the tapis.** Literally, on the table-cloth, hence under consideration. An English-French phrase.

My business comes now upon the tapis.
FARQUHAR: *The Beaux' Stratagem*, III, iii.

Tapley, Mark. Martin's servant and companion in Dickens's *Martin Chuzzlewit*, sometimes taken to typify anyone cheerful under all circumstances.

Tappit-hen. A Scots term, properly for a hen with a crest or tuft on its head, but generally used for a large beer or wine measure. Readers of Scott's *Waverley* will remember (in ch. xi) the Baron Bradwardine's tappit-hen of claret "containing at least three English quarts".

Weel she lo'ed a Harwick gill
And leugh to see a tappit-hen.

Cp. JEROBOAM.

To have a tappit-hen under the belt is to have swallowed three quarts.

Tar. Jack Tar. *See under* TARPAULIN.

A touch of the tar brush. A strain of Negro blood in one's ancestry indicated by dark skin. It is used less frequently of Indian or other coloured ancestry.

All tarred with the same brush. All alike to blame, all having the same faults; all sheep of the same flock. The allusion is to the former treatment of sores, etc., on sheep, with a brush dipped in tar.

Losing or **spoiling a ship for a ha'porth o' tar.** *See under* SHIP.

Tarred and feathered. Stripped to the skin, daubed with tar, and then rolled in feathers so that the feathers adhere; a common popular punishment in primitive communities, and still occasionally resorted to.

The first record of this punishment is in 1189 (1 Rich. I). A statute was made that any robber voyaging with the crusaders "shall be first shaved, then boiling pitch shall be poured on his head, and a cushion of feathers shook over it". The wretch was then to be put on shore at the very first place the ship came to (Rymer: *Fœdera*, I, 65).

Tar-heel. The colloquial name for a native of North Carolina, the Tar-heel State; so called from the early production of rosin, turpentine, and tar from its pine-woods.

Tarpaulin (O.E. *teoru*, tar; *paulin* from Lat. *pallium*, cloak or mantle). Properly, canvas sheeting made waterproof with tar; also, in former days, a sailor's hat made of tarred cloth (as were their water-proof jackets and trousers); hence a colloquial term for a sailor, often abbreviated to *tar*, and so JACK TAR.

Tara. The Hill of Tara, County Meath, some 20 miles north of Dublin, was the ancient seat of the High Kings of IRELAND until the 6th century A.D. Only a series of earthworks now remain to mark the site of "Tara's halls". Here were held a national assembly, the Feis of Tara, and gatherings for music, games and literary contests. Here too was the LIA-FAIL which is supposed to have been Jacob's pillow taken from Tara to SCOTLAND. *See* TANIST STONE.

> The harp that once through Tara's halls
>   The soul of music shed
> Now hangs as mute on Tara's walls
>   As if that soul were fled.
>
> T. MOORE.

Tarantella (tăr ĕn tel′ à). A very quick Neapolitan dance (or its music) for one couple, said to have been based on the gyrations practised by those whom the TARANTULA had poisoned.

Tarantula (tà răn′ tū là). A large and hairy venomous spider (so called from *Taranto*, Lat. *Tarentum*, a town in Apulia, Italy, where they abound), whose bite was formerly supposed to be the cause of the dancing mania hence known as *tarantism*. This was an hysterical disease, common, epidemically, in Southern Europe from the 15th to the 17th centuries.

Targums (Aramaic, interpretations). The name given to the various Aramaic (Chaldean) interpretations and translations of the OLD TESTAMENT, made in Babylon and Palestine when Hebrew was ceasing to be the everyday speech of the Jews. They were transmitted orally and the oldest, that of Oneklos on the PENTATEUCH, is probably of the 2nd century A.D..

Tariff Reform. a political movement in Great Britain inaugurated in 1903 by Joseph Chamberlain (1836–1914) for the reintroduction of a tariff or scale of duties on imported goods, originally with the idea of strengthening the bonds of empire on a basis of Imperial Preference. Return to protection did not take place on any scale until 1932 consequent upon the financial crisis of 1931.

Tarot, or Tarok Cards. Italian playing cards, first used in the 14th century and still occasionally employed in fortune-telling. The pack originally contained 78 cards: four suits of numeral cards with four COAT CARDS, *i.e.* king, queen, chevalier, and valet, and in addition to the four suits 22 *atutti* cards, or trumps, known as *tarots*.

The modern pack contains 54 cards: 32 suit cards, 21 tarots, and 1 joker.

Tarpeian Rock (tar pē′ àn). An ancient rock or peak (no longer in existence) of the Capitoline Hill, ROME; so called from Tarpeia, the faithless daughter of the governor of the citadel (*see* CRUSHED BY HIS HONOURS *under* HONOUR), who was flung from this rock by the SABINES. It became the traditional place from which traitors were hurled.

> Bear him to the rock Tarpeian, and from thence
> Into destruction cast him.
>
> SHAKESPEARE: *Coriolanus*, III, i.

Tarquin (tar′ kwin). The family name of a legendary line of early Roman kings. Tarquinius Priscus, the fifth king of ROME is dated 617–578 B.C. His son, Tarquinius Superbus, was the seventh (and last) king of Rome, and it was his son, Tarquinius Sextus, who committed the rape on Lucretia, in revenge for which the Tarquins were expelled from Rome and a Republic established.

Tarquin is also the name of a "recreant knight" figuring in the ARTHURIAN ROMANCES.

Tarroo-Ushtey. In MANXLAND, an amphibious bull which frequented the curraghs (fens) and sometimes mingled with the cattle in the fields to lure the finest heifer to death.

Tart. As applied to a harlot or girl of loose sexual morals this word, a contraction of "sweetheart", came into use in the later Victorian period.

Tartar, or Tatar. The Asiatic tribes of this name are properly called *Tatars*, the form *Tartar* probably deriving from association with TARTARUS, HELL, the Tatars being part of the Asiatic host under Jenghiz Khan which threatened 13th-century Europe. Hence a savage, irritable or excessively severe person is called a *tartar*; when applied to a woman it denotes a VIXEN or shrew.

To catch a tartar. *See under* CATCH.

Tartarian Lamb. *See under* LAMB.

Tartarus. The infernal regions of classical mythology; used as equivalent to HADES by later writers, but by HOMER placed as far beneath Hades as Hades is beneath the earth. It was here that ZEUS confined the TITANS. *Cp.* HELL.

Tassel-gentle. The male goshawk trained for falconry; *tassel* being a corruption of *tiercel*, a male hawk, which is a third (*tierce*) less in size than the female, and called *gentle* because of its tractable disposition.

SHAKESPEARE uses the term figuratively for a sweetheart:

> O for a falconer's voice
> To lure this tassel-gentle back again!
> *Romeo and Juliet*, II, ii.

Tassies. Tasmanians. *See* APPLE-ISLANDERS.

Tasso, Torquato (1544–1595). The celebrated Italian poet, author of *Rinaldo* (1562) and JERUSALEM DELIVERED (1575). He became the idol of the brilliant court of Ferrara but his exhausting literary labours and the excitement and stresses of court life caused mental breakdown, and he spent most of the rest of his life in confinement, exile, and poverty. His *Jerusalem Delivered* was pirated in 1580 and he received no payment for his masterpiece. He died as a pensioner of Pope Clement VIII.

Tattoo. The beat of the drum at night to recall soldiers to barracks is from Dutch *taptoe*, and "to beat the taptoe" was the signal to put the tap to, *i.e.* shut, public houses. When the word came into use in the mid-17th century it was written *taptoo, tapp-too*, etc.

Tattoo, as the indelible marking of the skin, is one of our few words from Polynesian. It is the Tahitian *tatau*, mark, and was introduced by Captain Cook in 1769.

Beating the devil's tattoo. *See under* DEVIL (phrases).

Torchlight tattoo. A military entertainment, carried out at night in the open air with illuminations, evolutions, and martial music.

Tau. The letter T in Greek and the SEMITIC languages. Anciently it was the last letter of the Greek alphabet (as it still is of the Hebrew); and in Middle English literature the phrase *Alpha to Omega* was not infrequently rendered *Alpha to Tau*.

Tau cross. A T-shaped CROSS, especially St. ANTHONY's cross.

Tauchnitz (tou*ch'* nits). The famous library of British and American books in English, bound in paper for circulation on the Continent of Europe, was founded by the Freiherr Christian Bernhard Tauchnitz (1816–1895) in 1841, at Leipzig. He came of a family which had been in the publishing business for several generations.

Taurus (taw' rŭs) (Lat., the bull). The second zodiacal constellation, and the second sign of the ZODIAC, which the sun enters about 21 April.

> As bees
> In spring-time, when the sun with Taurus rides,
> Pour forth their populous youth about the hive
> In clusters.
> MILTON: *Paradise Lost*, I, 768.

Taverner's Bible. *See* BIBLE, THE ENGLISH.

Tawdry. A corruption of St. Audrey (*Audrey* itself being a corruption of *Etheldrida*). At the annual fair of St. Audrey, in the Isle of Ely, cheap jewellery and showy lace called *St. Audrey's lace* were sold; hence *tawdry*, which is applied to anything gaudy, in bad taste, and of little value. *Cp.* TANTONY.

> Come, you promised me a tawdry lace and a pair of sweet gloves.
> SHAKESPEARE: *The Winter's Tale*, IV, iv.

Taxi, Short for *taximeter*, is the accepted term for a motor-cab, which takes its name from the meter which was installed on French horse-drawn cabs or *fiacres* long before motor-cabs appeared on the road. In Britain it only became common with the introduction of motor-cabs and was thus associated with them.

An aeroplane is said **to taxi** when it moves along the ground under its own power.

Te Deum, The (tē dē' um). So called from the opening words *Te Deum laudamus* (Thee, God, we praise). This Latin hymn was traditionally assigned to SS. AMBROSE and AUGUSTINE, and was supposed to have been improvised by St. Ambrose while baptizing St. Augustine (386). Hence it is sometimes called "the Ambrosian Hymn" and in some early psalters it is entitled "*Canticum Ambrosii et Augustini*". It is now generally thought to have been written by Niceta, Bishop of Remesiana (d. *c.* 414). It is used in various offices and at MATTINS.

Te Igitur (Lat.) "Thee therefore". In the ROMAN CATHOLIC CHURCH, the first words of the old form of the CANON OF THE MASS, and consequently the name for the first section of the canon.

Oaths upon the Te Igitur. Oaths sworn on this part of the MISSAL, which were regarded as especially sacred.

Tea. A nice old cup of tea. Sometimes applied ironically to awkward occurences, unpleasant situations, or muddles, but when we say "she's a nice old cup of tea" we mean "she is a dear" or "pleasant old soul".

Not for all the tea in China. Under no circumstances, not for any consideration.

Not my cup of tea. Not at all in my line, not what I want or am suited for.

A storm in a teacup. *See under* STORM.

A tea fight. A tea-party; especially a church or chapel gathering at which tea and buns, etc., are provided.

That's another cup of tea. That is a very different matter.

Tea-kettle broth. "Poor man's soup", consisting of hot water, bread, and a small lump of butter, with pepper and salt; the French *soupe maigre*.

Tea-room party. During the passage of Disraeli's Parliamentary Reform Act of 1867 Gladstone objected to certain items and proposed a limit of £5 rating in the BOROUGHS as a voting qualification. This was opposed by some fifty WHIGS and RADICALS known as *the tea-room party* because they met in the tea-room of the HOUSE OF COMMONS.

Teapoy (tē′ poi). A small, three- or four-legged occasional table. Though largely used for standing a tea-tray upon, the teapoy has really nothing to do with tea, the name coming from Hindustani *teen*, three, and the Persian *pae*, a foot.

Teach-in. An American name for a series of lectures and discussions on a particular theme led by experts. The expression became current in England in the 1960s.

Teague. A contemptuous name for an Irishman (from the Irish personal name), rarely used nowadays but common in the 17th and 18th centuries.

> Was't Carwell, brother James, or Teague,
> That made thee break the Triple League?
> ROCHESTER: *History of Insipids*.

Tear (târ). **To tear Christ's body.** To use imprecations. The common oaths of mediæval times were by different parts of the Lord's body; hence the preachers used to talk of "tearing God's body by imprecations".

> Hir others been so grete and so dampnable
> That it is grisly for her to heere hem swere;
> Our blissed Lordes body thay to-tere.
> CHAUCER: *Pardoner's Tale*, 144.

To tear someone off a strip. *See under* STRIP.

Tear (tēr). St. LAWRENCE's tears. *See* SHOOTING STARS.

Tears of Eos. The dewdrops of the morning were so called by the Greeks. Eos was the mother of MEMNON, and wept for him every morning.

The Vale of Tears. This world. *Cp.* BACA.

Tear-jerker. A novel, play, or film with a very sad or sentimental theme.

Ted, or **Teddy.** A pet-form of Edward.

A ted, teddy boy, teddy girl. *See* EDWARDIAN.

Teddy-bear. A child's toy bear, said to have been named after Theodore (Teddy) Roosevelt, who was fond of bear-hunting.

Teeny-bopper. An American colloquialism, applied usually to girls in their early teens, who adopt current eccentricities in dress and are devotees of "pop" music and extravagances generally.

Teeth. *See* TOOTH.

Teetotal. A word expressive of total abstinence from alcoholic liquors. The origin of the word has two explanations. Dick Turner, a Lancashire artisan of Preston, coined it about 1833 (some accounts say that he stuttered!) and his tombstone bears the inscription:

> Beneath this stone are deposited the remains of Richard Turner, author of the word *Teetotal* as applied to abstinence from all intoxicating liquors, who departed this life on the 27th day of October, 1846, aged 56 years.

The word also seems to have arisen independently in America, perhaps a little earlier, from the practice introduced by a New York Temperance Society of getting members to sign the pledge. "O.P." against a name stood for "Old Pledge" (abstinence from distilled spirits only) and "T" for total abstinence. Frequent reference to "T-total" gave rise to the word.

Teian Muse, The (tī′ ăn). ANACREON, who was born at Teos, Asia Minor.

> The Scian and the Teian muse,
> The hero's heart, the lover's lute,
> Have found the fame your shores refuse.
> BYRON: *The Isles of Greece*, ii.

Telamones (tel a mō′ nēz). Large, sculptured male figures (*cp.* ATLANTES; CARYATIDES) serving as architectural columns or pilasters. So called from the Greek legendary hero Telamon (father of AJAX) who took part in the Calydonian hunt (*see* CALYDONIAN BOAR *under* BOAR), and the expedition of the ARGONAUTS.

Telegonus (tē leg′ on ŭs). The son of ULYSSES and CIRCE, who was sent to find his father. On coming to Ithaca, he began to plunder the fields when Ulysses and TELEMACHUS appeared in arms to prevent him. Telegonus killed his father, who was unknown to him, with a lance pointed with the spine of a trygon, or sting-ray which Circe had given him. He subsequently married PENELOPE.

Tel el Amarna Tablets. Cuneiform tablets found in 1887 at Tel el Armarna, the modern name for the abandoned site of Akheta-ton, the short-lived capital built (*c.* 1360 B.C.) by Ikhnaton (Amenophis IV) in place of THEBES. These important sources of historical evidence concern a period before the exodus of the Israelities from Egypt and consist of letters from Egyptian governors in Syria and Palestine, from the kings of Assyria and Babylon, and others. About two-thirds of the 230 or so tablets went to the Berlin Museum, the remainder to the BRITISH MUSEUM.

Telemachus (tel lem´ăkus). The only son of ULYSSES and PENELOPE. After the fall of TROY he went, attended by ATHENE in the guise of MENTOR, in quest of his father. He ultimately found him, and the two returned to Ithaca and slew Penelope's suitors.

Telepathy (tĕ lep´ ă thi). The word invented in 1882 by F.W.H. Myers to describe "the communication of impressions of any kind from one mind to another independently of the recognized channels of sense". The term "thought-transference" is often used for this phenomenon and more nearly expresses its implications, for it indicates the communication of thought from one person to another without the medium of speech.

Telephus. *See* ACHILLEA.

Tell, William. The legendary national hero of Switzerland whose deeds appear to be an invention of the 15th century and are paralleled in numerous European myths and legends.

The story is that Tell was the champion of the Swiss in the struggle against Albert I (slain 1308), Duke of Austria. Tell refused to salute the cap of Gessler, Albert's tyrannical steward, and for this act of independence was sentenced to shoot with his bow and arrow an apple from the head of his own son. He achieved this feat and Gessler demanded what his second arrow was for, whereupon Tell boldly replied, "To shoot you with, had I killed my son." Gessler had him conveyed to Küssnacht castle, but he escaped on the way and later killed Gessler in ambush. A rising followed which established the independence of Switzerland.

The story has been systematically exposed as having no foundation in fact, and similar feats are recorded in the Norse legend of Toki. The popularity of tales of the "master shot" is evidence by the stories of Adam Bell, CLYM OF THE CLOUGH, WILLIAM CLOUDESLEY and EGIL.

Teller. Anciently, one who kept the tallies (Anglo-Fr. *talier*) and counted the money; now, a bank-clerk who receives and pays out money at the counter.

Up to 1834 there were four officers of the EXCHEQUER known as *Tellers of the Exchequer*, whose duty was to receive and pay out moneys. *See* TALLY.

> When shall our prayers end?
> I tell thee (priest) …
> When proud surveyors take no parting pence,
> When Silver sticks not on the Teller's fingers
> And when receivers pay as they receive.
>
> GASCOIGNE: *The Steele Glas* (1576).

Telstar. The name given to the satellite launched in 1962 for relaying transatlantic telephone messages and television pictures.

Temperance, The Apostle of. *See* MATHEW.

Templars, or **Knights Templar.** In 1119, nine French KNIGHTS bound themselves to protect pilgrims on their way to the HOLY PLACES and took monastic vows. They received the name TEMPLARS because they had their headquarters in a building on the site of the old TEMPLE OF SOLOMON at JERUSALEM.

Their habit was a long white mantle ornamented with a red cross on the left shoulder. Their seal showed two knights riding on one horse, the story being that the first Master was so poor that he had to share a horse with one of his followers. Their banner, called *Le Beauseant* or *Bauceant* (an old French name for a piebald horse), was half black, half white, and charged with a red CROSS.

Their bravery in the field was unquestionable, as was in due course the wealth and power of the Order which had houses throughout Europe, but the fall of Acre (1291) marked the ultimate failure of their efforts. Jealousy of their power and wealth rather than the internal corruption of their Order resulted in their suppression and extinction in 1312, in France accompanied by particular cruelties.

In England the Order had its first house (*c.* 1121) near Holborn Bars, London, but it later settled on the site still called the TEMPLE.

At Paris, the stronghold of the Knights Templar was taken over by the Knights of St. John. The old tower later became a prison where, in 1792, the royal family of France was incarcerated prior to execution and the DAUPHIN (Louis XVII) probably died within its walls. *See* THE SOCIETY OF THE TEMPLE, *below*.

Temple. This is the Lat. *templum*, from Gr. *temenos*, a sacred enclosure, *i.e.* a space cut off from its surroundings (Gr. *temnein*, to cut). The Lat. *templum* originally denoted the space marked out by the augurs within which the sign was to occur.

Temple, The. The site between FLEET STREET and the THAMES formerly occupied by the building of the TEMPLARS (*c.*

1160–1312) of which the Temple Church, one of the four circular churches built in England by them, is the only portion remaining. On the suppression of the Order, the site was granted to the Knights HOSPI-TALLERS and, from 1346, it has been occupied by practitioners and students of law who, since 1609, have formed two separate INNS OF COURT known as the Inner and Middle Temples. The badge of the former is the Winged Horse (*Pegasus*), that of the latter the Lamb (*Agnus Dei*).

Temple Bar. The old FLEET STREET gateway into the CITY, formerly situated close to the entrance into the TEMPLE on the spot since 1880 occupied by the monument known as the "Griffin". The old "bar" was destroyed in the GREAT FIRE and a new one erected (1670–1672) by Sir Christopher Wren. This was removed and re-erected in Theobald's Park, Herts, in 1878. Until 1746, heads of rebels and conspirators were displayed on iron spikes above the pediment; the last shrivelled head seems to have fallen off about 1772.

The Temple, or The Society of the Temple. At Paris in the early 18th century, a gay and dissipated côterie at the Temple (*see* TEMPLARS presided over by the Duke of Vendôme and his brother Phillippe, Grand Prior of the Knights of Malta in France. The Abbé Chaulieu was a prominent member and VOLTAIRE was introduced to it in his youth.

Anacreon of the Temple. *See under* ANA-CREON.

The Temple of Reason During the REIGN OF TERROR (1793–1794) the Paris Commune enthroned a dancer on the high altar of Notre Dame Cathedral as the Goddess of Reason. She was draped in a tricolour flag and the cathedral became the *Temple of Reason*. There was much desecration and plundering of Notre Dame by the Paris mob.

The Temple of Solomon. The national shrine of the Jews at JERUSALEM, erected by SOLOMON and his Tyrian workmen on Mount Moriah in the 10th century B.C.. It was destroyed in the siege of Jerusalem by NEBUCHADNEZZAR (558 B.C.), and some 70 years later the new **Temple of Zerubbabel** was completed on its site. The third building, the **Temple of Herod** begun in 20 B.C., was the grandest and was that of NEW TESTA-MENT times. It is said to have covered 19 acres. In the holy place were kept the golden candlestick, the altar of incense, and the table of the SHEWBREAD; within the HOLY OF HOLIES, the ark of the covenant and the mercy-seat. It was destroyed by fire by the

Romans under Titus, A.D. 70. The site has long been covered by a MOSLEM shrine. *See* JACHIN AND BOAZ.

Tempora mutantur (Lat., the times are changed). The tag is founded on *Omnia mutantur, nos et mutamur in illis* (all things are changed, and we with them), a saying of Nicholas Borbonius, a Latin poet of the 16th century. Lothair, EMPEROR of the HOLY ROMAN EMPIRE, had, it is stated, already said, *Tempora mutantur, nos et mutamur in illis*.

Tempus fugit (tem' pus fū' jit) (Lat.). Time flies.

Ten. The Council of Ten. A secret tribunal exercising unlimited powers in the old Venetial republic. Instituted in 1310 with ten members, it was enlarged to 17, and continued in active existence till the fall of the republic in 1797.

The Ten Commandments. *See* COMMANDMENT; DECALOGUE.

Ten to one. The chances are very much in favour of; there is a very strong probability that, as, "It's ten to one that it will rain tonight," *i.e.* there is a ten to one chance of rain.

The Upper Ten. The aristocracy, the cream of society. Short for *the upper ten thousand*. The term was first used by N.P. Willis (1806–1867), a spirited American journalist, in speaking of the fashionables of New York.

Ten-cent Jimmy. James Buchanan (1791–1868), fifteenth President of the U.S.A. (1857–1861), was so nicknamed on account of his advocacy of low tariffs and low wages.

Ten-gallon hat. The original tall-crowned, wide-brimmed hat worn by cowboys. Doubtless a jocular allusion to its capacity.

Tenner. A ten-pound note; as *fiver* is a five-pound note. In the U.S.A. a *tenner* is a ten-dollar note or bill.

Tenpenny nails. Large-sized nails, originally so called because they were sold at 10*d*. a hundred. Smaller nails used to be known as *eightpenny, sixpenny, fourpenny nails*.

Tenant (Fr. *tenant*, holding, from *tenir*, to hold). One who holds property or premise.

Tenant at will. One who at any moment can be dispossessed of his tenancy at the will of the landlord or lessor.

Tenant in chief. One who held land direct from the king.

Tenant-right. The right of an outgoing tenant to claim compensation from an incoming tenant for improvements, manuring, crops left in the ground, etc. In earlier times, the term denoted the right of passing on a tenancy, at decease, to the eldest surviving issue. It is also applied to the right of a well-behaved tenant to compensation if deprived of his tenancy.

Tender. *See* LEGAL TENDER.

Tendon of Achilles. *See* ACHILLES TENDON.

Tenebræ (ten' ē brē) (Lat., darkness, gloom). In the Western Church the MATTINS and LAUDS of the following day sung on the Wednesday, Thursday, and Friday of HOLY WEEK. The lights of 15 candles are extinguished one by one at the end of each psalm, the last after the *Benedictus*. The MISERERE is then sung in darkness. This ritual goes back to the 8th century and symbolizes dramatically Christ's PASSION and Death.

Tennis-Court Oath, The (20 June 1789). The famous oath taken by the Third ESTATE in the Tennis Court at VERSAILLES—never to separate, and to meet wherever circumstances might make it necessary for it to meet, until the Constitution had been established and set on a firm foundation. The occasion was when Louis XVI excluded the deputies from their assembly hall and they met in the neighbouring building, the royal tennis court. It was another step towards revolution.

Tenson. A contention in verse between rival TROUBADOURS before a court of love; a metrical dialogue consisting of smart repartees, usually on women and love; also a subdivision of the troubadours' love lyrics (Lat. *tensio*, a struggle).

Tenterden. Tenterden steeple was the cause of Goodwin Sands. A satirical remark when some ridiculous reason is given for a thing. The story, according to one of Latimer's sermons, is that Sir Thomas More, being sent into Kent to ascertain the cause of the GOODWIN SANDS, called together the oldest inhabitants to ask their opinion. A very old man said, "I believe Tenterden steeple is the cause," and went on to explain that in his early days there was no Tenterden steeple, and there were no complaints about the sands. This reason seems ridiculous enough, but the fact seems to be that the Bishops of Rochester applied to the building of Tenterden steeple moneys raised in the county for the purpose of keeping Sandwich haven clear, so that when they found the harbour was getting blocked up there was no money for taking the necessary countermeasures.

Tenterhooks. To be on tenterhooks. In suspense, most curious or anxious to hear the outcome. An allusion to newly-woven cloth being stretched or "tentered" on hooks passed through the selvedges (Lat. *tentus*,

stretched, hence "tent", canvas stretched).

Tenth. The Submerged, or **Tenth legion.** *See* SUBMERGED.

The Tenth Muse. A name given originally to SAPPHO, there being *nine* true MUSES and afterwards applied to literary women, as Mme de la Garde Deshoulières (1638–1694), Mlle de Scudéry (1607–1701), Queen Christina of Sweden (1626–1689), and the English novelist and essay writer, Hannah More (1745–1833).

The tenth wave. *See* WAVE.

Tenths. In English ecclesiastical usage, the tenth part of the annual profit of every living originally paid to the POPE and transferred to the Crown after the breach with ROME, later to QUEEN ANNE'S BOUNTY. *Cp.* ANNATES. Also, in former days, a tax levied by the Crown of one-tenth of every man's personal property.

Teocalli (Mexican, house of a god). A temple of earth and stone or brick used by the aborigines of Mexico, built like a four-sided truncated pyramid on a platform at the top of terraces. The best known is the pyramid of Cholula which is 177ft. high.

Teraphim (ter' à fim). The idols or images of the ancient Hebrews and other Semitic peoples, worshipped by them as household gods or individual protecting deities (*see Judges* xviii, 5; *Hosea* iii, 4). It was her father Laban's teraphim that Rachel stole and hid in the camel's saddle in *Gen.* xxxi, 17–35. *Cp.* LARES AND PENATES. That they were also used for DIVINATION and soothsaying seems apparent. *See Ezek.* xxi, 21; *Zec.* x.2.

Teresa, St. The name of two Carmelite nuns of remarkable qualities: (1) St. Teresa of Avila (1515–1582) or St. Teresa of Jesus, whose life combined great practical achievement with continual prayer and religious sanctity in which she reached a state of "spiritual marriage". She was responsible for the reform of the Carmelite Order and founded 32 convents as well as writing outstanding works on prayer and meditation. She was canonized in 1622 and in 1970 the first woman to be made a DOCTOR OF THE CHURCH. Her day is 15 October. (*See* ST. JOHN OF THE CROSS *under* JOHN.) (2) St. Teresa of Lisieux (1873–1897), a Carmelite nun, professed in 1890, who died of tuberculosis, and who is associated with miracles of healing and prophecy. Her autobiography, *L'Histoire d'une âme*, made her famous and she was canonized in 1925. She was associated with JOAN OF ARC as patroness of France in 1947 and in England she is known as "The Little Flower".

Term. To be on good (or **bad**) **terms** with a person is to be on a good (or bad) footing with them.

To bring to terms. To force a person to accept one's conditions.

To come to terms. To make an agreement with; decide the terms of a bargain.

To keep a term. To attend a term of study at a college or university.

Termagant. The name given by the Crusaders, and in mediæval romances, to an idol or deity that the SARACENS were popularly supposed to worship. He was introduced into the MORALITY PLAYS as a most violent and turbulent person in long, flowing Eastern robes, a dress that led to his acceptance as a woman, whence the name came to be applied to a shrewish, violently abusive VIRAGO. The origin of the word is uncertain.

> 'Twas time to counterfeit, or that hot termagant
> Scot [Douglas] had paid me scot and lot too.
>
> SHAKESPEARE: *Henry IV, Pt. I*, V, iv.

O'erdoing Termagant (*Hamlet*, III, ii). In old drama, the degree of rant was the measure of villainy. TERMAGANT and HEROD, being considered the BEAU IDEAL of all that is bad, were represented as settling everything by CLUB-LAW, and bawling so as to split the ears of the groundlings.

That beats Termagant. Your ranting, raging pomposity, or exaggeration, surpasses that of TERMAGANT of the old MORALITY PLAYS.

Terpsichore (tĕrp sik′ ôr i). One of the nine MUSES of ancient Greece, the Muse of dancing and the dramatic chorus, and later of lyric poetry. Hence *Terpsichorean*, pertaining to dancing. She is usually represented seated, and holding a lyre.

Terra firma (Lat.). Dry land—in opposition to water; the continents as distinguished from islands. The Venetians so called the mainland of Italy under their sway, and the continental parts of America belonging to Spain were called by the same term.

Terrapin War (ter′ a pin). An American name for the war with Britain of 1812–1814, so called because, through the blockade, the U.S.A. was shut up in its shell like a terrapin (a tide-water turtle).

Terrible, The. *See* IVAN THE TERRIBLE.

Terrier. A dog that "takes the earth", or unearths his prey (Lat. *terra*, earth); also formerly applied to the burrows of foxes, badgers, rabbits, etc.

A land-roll or list of lands belonging to an individual or corporation, especially the latter, is called a *terrier* (O. Fr. *papier terrier*, a register of the lord's tenants). Also, by extension, any inventory of property or goods.

Terrier is also the popular name for a member of the Territorial Army, which under the Territorial and Reserve Forces Act (1907) superseded the old Militia, Yeomanry, and Volunteers on a territorial basis until it was absorbed into the newly created Territorial and Army Volunteer Reserve in 1967. The old "Territorial" element was much diminished in the ensuing years.

Terror, The, or **The Reign of Terror.** *See* REIGN.

Terry Alts. One of the numerous secret societies of Irish insurrectionists similar to the Blackfeet, Lady Clares, and MOLLY MAGUIRES, etc. It was active in County Clare in the early 19th century. *See* WHITEBOYS.

Ter-Sanctus. *See* TRISAGION.

Tertiaries. Members of "a third order", an institution which began with the FRANCISCANS in the 13th century for lay folk who wished to strive for Christian perfection in their day-to-day life in accordance with the spirit and teaching of St. FRANCIS. The system spread to other Orders such as the DOMINICANS, AUGUSTINIANS, and CARMELITES. Tertiaries are obedient to a rule and take a solemn promise. There are also Regular Tertiaries who live in communities under vows and are fully "religious" in the technical sense. The name *Third Order* arises from the Friars and Nuns being classed as the First and Second Orders.

Tertium quid. A third party which shall be nameless; a third thing resulting from the combination of two things, but different from both. Fable has it that the expression originated with PYTHAGORAS, who, defining bipeds, said:

> Sunt bipes homo, et avis, et tertium quid.
> A man is a biped, so is a bird, and a third thing
> (which shall be nameless).

Iamblichus said this third thing was Pythagoras himself.

In chemistry, when two substances chemically unite, the new substance is called a *tertium quid*, as a neutral salt produced by the mixture of an acid and an alkali.

Terza Rima. An Italian verse-form in triplets, the second line rhyming with the first and third of the succeeding triplet. In the first triplet lines 1 and 3 rhyme, and in the last there is an extra line, rhyming with its second.

Dante's *Divine Comedy* is in this metre: it was introduced into ENGLAND by Sir Thomas Wyatt in the 16th century, and was largely employed by Shelley, as also by Byron in *The Prophecy of Dante*.

Test Acts. A name given to the various Acts of PARLIAMENT designed to exclude Roman

Catholics, Protestant NONCONFORMISTS, and "disaffected persons" from public offices, etc. They include Acts of Abjuration, Allegiance, and Supremacy, the Corporation Act, 1661, the Act of Uniformity, 1662, as well as those specifically named *Test Acts*. Those named "Test Acts" were: (1) that of 1673 which insisted that all holders of civil and military office must be communicants of the CHURCH OF ENGLAND as well as taking the oaths of Allegiance and Supremacy; (2) that of 1678 which excluded all Roman Catholics, other than the Duke of York, from Parliament; (3) that for Scotland (1681) which made all state and municipal officials affirm their belief in the PROTESTANT faith. These Acts were repealed in 1828. *See also* UNIVERSITY TESTS ACT.

Test Match. In CRICKET one of the matches between selected national teams arranged by the International Conference, which replaced the Imperial Cricket Conference (1909–1965) after South Africa left the COMMONWEALTH (1961). *See* THE ASHES *under* ASHES.

England *v*. Australia. First played 1876.

England *v*. South Africa. First played 1888.

England *v*. West Indies. First played 1928.

England *v*. New Zealand. First played 1929.

England *v*. India. First played, 1932.

England *v*. Pakistan. First played 1952.

Tester. A sixpenny piece; so-called from the *teston* or *testoon* (a shilling) first introduced by Henry VII. As the coinage depreciated, it later came to be applied to a sixpence. The teston took its name from the sovereign's head (Ital. *testa*) stamped on one side. Similarly the head canopy of a bed is called its *tester. Cp.* TANNER.

Hold, there's a tester for thee.
SHAKESPEARE: *Henry IV, Pt. II*, III, ii.

Testers are gone to Oxford, to study at Brasenose. When Henry VIII debased the silver testers, the alloy broke out in red pimples through the silver, giving the royal likeness in the coin a blotchy appearance; hence the punning proverb.

Testudo. *See* TORTOISE.

Tête-à-tête (Fr., head to head). A confidential conversation, a heart-to-heart talk.

Tête-de-mouton (Fr., sheep's head). A 17th-century head-dress, the hair being arranged in short, thick curls.

Tête du pont. The barbican or watch-tower placed on the head of a drawbridge.

Tether He has come to the end of his tether. He has come to the end of his resources; he has exhausted his fortune etc. The reference is to a tethered animal which can only graze as far as the rope allows.

HORACE calls the end of life *ultima linea rerum*, the final goal, referring to the white chalk mark at the end of a racecourse. *Cp.* BITTER END.

Tethys. A sea goddess, wife of OCEANUS hence, the sea itself. She was the daughter of URANUS and GÆA, and mother of the OCEANIDES.

Tetragrammaton. A word of four letters, especially the Jewish name of the Deity JHVH, which the Jews never pronounced but substituted the word ADONAI instead (usually rendered in the BIBLE as *Lord*). Its probable pronunciation was *Yahweh* and from the 16th century was corrupted into JEHOVAH by combining the vowels of Adonai with JHVH.

PYTHAGORAS called Deity a Tetrad or Tetracys, meaning the "four sacred letters". The Greek *Zeus* and θεος, in Latin *Jove* and *Deus*; Fr. *Dieu*, Ger. *Gott*, Sansk. *Deva*, Span. *Dios*, Scand. *Odin*, and our *Lord* are tetragrams.

Such was the sacred Tetragrammaton.
Things worthy silence must not be revealed.
DRYDEN: *Britannia Rediviva*, 197.

Tetrarch (tet' rark). Originally meaning the rule of one of four parts of a region (Gr. *tettares*, four; *archein*, to rule), under the Roman Empire the term came to be applied to minor rulers, especially to the princes of Syria subject to the Roman Emperor.

Teucer. In the ILIAD, the son of Telamon, and stepbrother of AJAX; he went with the allied Greeks to the siege of TROY, and on his return was banished by his father for not avenging on Odysseus (ULYSSES) the death of his brother.

Teutons. The name of an ancient tribe of northern Europe called by the Romans *Teutones* or *Teutoni*. The adjective *Teutonic* is also applied to the Germanic peoples generally and in the widest sense includes both Scandinavians and Anglo-Saxons.

Teutonic Cross. A CROSS potent, the badge of the order of TEUTONIC KNIGHTS. *See* POTENT.

Teutonic Knights. The third great military crusading Order which has its origin in the time of the Third CRUSADE. It developed from the provision of a hospital service by Germans at the siege of Acre (1190) which became the German Hospital of St. Mary at JERUSALEM. It was made a Knightly Order in 1198, thenceforward confined to those of noble birth. In 1229 they began the conquest of heathen Prussia and after 1291 their contact with the East ceased. They survived as a powerful and wealthy body until their disastrous defeat by the Poles and Lithuanians at Tannenberg in 1410. The Order lingered on until its suppression in 1809, but was revived in Austria in 1840 but with HABSBURG associations.

Texas Rangers. A constabulary force first organized in Texas in 1835 and much developed by General Sam Houston a few years later. They wore no uniform and especially proved their worth in 1870 against rustlers and raiders. Their resourcefulness in the saddle, their toughness, and colourful exploits have given them legendary fame.

Th (θ, *theta*). The sign given in the verdict of the AREOPAGUS of condemnation to death (THANATOS).

Thais (thā' is). The Athenian courtesan who, it is said, induced ALEXANDER THE GREAT when excited with wine, to set fire to the palace of the Persian kings at Persepolis. After Alexander's death, she married Ptolemy Lagus, king of Egypt, by whom she had seven children.

> The king seized a flambeau with zeal to destroy;
> Thais led the way to light him to his prey,
> And, like another Helen, fired another Troy.
> DRYDEN: *Alexander's Feast*, iv.

This is also the title of an historico-political novel (1890) by Anatole France, and of an opera by Massenet (1894) based upon it.

Thales. *See* WISE MEN OF GREECE.

Thalestris (thȧ les' tris). A queen of the AMAZONS who went with 300 women to meet ALEXANDER THE GREAT, in the hope of raising a race of Alexanders.

Thalia (thȧ lī' ȧ). One of the MUSES who presided over comedy and pastoral poetry. She also favoured rural pursuits and is represented holding a comic mask and a shepherd's crook. Thalia is also the name of one of THE THREE GRACES (*see under* GRACE) or *Charites*.

Thames (temz). The second longest river in Britain, called *Tamesis* by the Romans, who based the name on the existing British name. At Oxford and upstream it is often called *Isis*, an artificial development from Tamesis.

He'll never set the Thames on fire. He'll never make any figure in the world; never do anything wonderful and print his footsteps on the sands of time. The popular explanation is that the word Thames is a pun on the word *temse*, a corn-sieve; and that the parallel French locution *He will never set the Seine on fire* is a pun on *seine*, a drag-net; but these solutions are not tenable. There is

a Latin saw, *Tiberum accendere nequaquam potest*, which is probably the *fons et origo* of other parallel sayings; and the Germans had *Den Rhein anzünden* (to set the Rhine on fire) as early as 1630.

Thammuz (thăm' ŭz). A Sumerian, Babylonian and Assyrian god who died every year and rose again in the spring. He is identified with the Babylonian MARDUK and the Greek ADONIS. In *Ezek*. viii, 14, reference is made to the heathen "women weeping for Tammuz".

> Thammuz came next behind,
> Whose annual wound in Lebanon allured
> The Syrian damsels to lament his fate
> In amorous ditties all a summer's day,
> While smooth Adonis from his native rock
> Ran purple to the sea, supposed with blood
> Of Thammuz yearly wounded.
> MILTON: *Paradise Lost*, I, 446.

Thamyris (thăm' i ris). A Thracian bard mentioned by HOMER (*Iliad*, II, 595). He challenged the MUSES to a trial of skill, and, being overcome in the contest, was deprived by them of his sight and powers of song. He is represented with a broken lyre in his hand.

> Blind Thamyris and blind Mæonides [Homer]
> And Tiresias and Phineus, prophets old.
> MILTON: *Paradise Lost*, III, 35.

Thanatos. The Greek personification of death, twin brother of Sleep (*Hypnos*). Hesiod says he was born of Night with no father.

Thane. The name given in Anglo-Saxon England to a class of soldiers and land-holders ranking between the earl and the churl. The rank of thane could be obtained by a man of lower degree. After the Norman Conquest the word disappeared in ENGLAND, giving place to KNIGHT. In SCOTLAND, a thane ranked with an earl's son, holding his land direct from the king; the title was given also to the chief of a CLAN who became one of the king's barons.

Thanksgiving Day. An annual holiday in the U.S.A. usually held on the last Thursday in NOVEMBER and observed as an acknowledgement of the divine favours received during the year. It was first celebrated by the Plymouth Colony in 1621. After the Revolution, its observance became general and from 1863 it was annually recommended by the President. In 1941 it was fixed as a public holiday for the fourth Thursday in November. Pumpkin pies and turkey are part of the traditional fare.

That. Seven "thats" may follow each other, and make sense.

> For be it known that we may safely write
> Or say that "that *that*" that that man wrote was
> right;

Nay, e'en that that *that*, that "that THAT" has followed,
Through six repeats, the grammar's rule has hallowed;
And that *that* that *that* "that THAT" began
Repeated seven times is right, deny't who can.
My Lords (says he) with humble Submission, *That*
that I say is this; that *That* that, that gentleman has
advanced is not *That*, that he should have proved to
your Lordships.

Spectator, No. 80.

And that's that! A colloquial way of emphatically and triumphantly making one's
point, closing the argument, etc.

Thaumaturgus (thaw ma tĕr′ gus) (Gr., a
wonder-worker). A miracle-worker; applied
to SAINTS and others who are reputed to have
performed miracles, and especially Gregory, Bishop of Neo-Cæsarea, called Thaumaturgus (*c.* 213–*c.* 270) whose miracles included the moving of a mountain. St BER-
NARD of Clairvaux (1090–1153) was called
"The Thaumaturgus of the West".

Thé dansant. An afternoon tea party with
dancing.

Thebes, called *The Hundred-Gated*, was not
Thebes of Bœotia, but the chief town of the
Thebaid, on the Nile in Upper Egypt, said
to have extended over 23 miles of land.
HOMER says out of each gate the Thebans
could send forth 200 war-chariots.

The world's great empress on the Egyptian plain,
That spreads her conquests o'er a thousand states,
And pours her heroes through a hundred gates,
Two hundred horsemen and two hundred cars
From each wide portal issuing to the wars,

POPE: *Iliad*, I.

It is here that the vocal statue of MEMNON
stood. The sound was caused by internal vibrations resulting from a split in the statue
after an earthquake. Here too is the VALLEY
OF THE KINGS, including the tomb of TU-
TANKHAMUN, the Temple of Luxor and
those of Karnak. It is now a favourite tourist
centre.

The Seven Against Thebes. An expedition in Greek legend fabled to have taken
place against Thebes of Bœotia before the
TROJAN WAR. The Seven were the Argive
chiefs ADRASTUS, Polynices, Tydeus, Amphiaraus, Hippomedon, Capaneus and
Parthenopæus.

When ŒDIPUS abdicated, his two sons
agreed to reign alternate years; but at the expiration of the first year, the elder, Eteocles,
refused to give up the throne, whereupon
Polynices, the younger brother, induced the
six chiefs to espouse his cause. The allied
army laid siege to Thebes, but without success, and all the heroes perished except
Adrastus. Subsequently, seven sons of the
chiefs, resolved to avenge their fathers'
deaths, marched against the city, took it,

and placed Terpander, one of their number
on the throne. These are known as the *Epigoni* (Gr., descendants). The Greek tragic
poets ÆSCHYLUS and Euripides dramatized
the legend.

Theban Bard, or **Eagle, The.** PINDAR,
born at Thebes (*c.* 522–443 B.C.).

Theban Legion, The. Another name for
the THUNDERING LEGION, which was raised
in the Thebaid of Egypt, led by St. Maurice.

Theban Sphinx. *See* SPHINX.

Thecla, St. (thek′ là). One of the most famous
saints of the 1st century, the first woman
martyr. All that is known of her is from the
Acts of Paul and Thecla, pronounced APO-
CRYPHAL by Pope Gelasius. According to the
legend, she was born of a noble family at
Iconium and was converted by St. PAUL.

Theist, Deist, Atheist, Agnostic. A *theist*
believes there is a God who made and governs all creation; Christians, Jews, and Mohammedans are included among *theists*.

A *deist* believes there is a God who
created all things, but does not believe in His
superintendence and government. He
thinks the Creator implanted in all things
certain immutable laws, called the *Laws of
Nature*, which act *per se*, as a watch acts
without the supervision of its maker. He
does not believe in the doctrine of the TRIN-
ITY, nor in a divine revelation.

The *atheist* disbelieves even the existence
of a God. He thinks matter is eternal, and
what we call "creation" is the result of natural laws.

The *agnostic* believes only what is know-
able. He rejects revelation and the doctrine
of the Trinity as "past human understanding". He is neither theist, deist, nor atheist,
as all these subscribe to doctrines that are incapable of scientific proof.

Thellusson Act (thel′ u son). The 39th and
40th George III, cap. 98. An Act (1800) to
prevent testators from leaving their property
to accumulate for more than 21 years. It was
passed in reference to the will of Peter Thellusson, a London banker who died in 1797
and left £600,000 and £4,500 a year to accumulate for the benefit of his eldest great-
grandson after the death of all his sons and
grandsons. The last grandson died in 1856,
and the expense of the legal actions that followed swallowed up all the accumulated interest, so that Thellusson's eldest son's eldest grandson received barely the amount of
the original legacy.

Theme song. A song which recurs during the
course of a musical play or film which generally reflects the mood or *theme* of the production.

Themis. A daughter of URANUS and GÆA and a wife of JUPITER, mother of the HORÆ and PARCÆ. With Jupiter she presides over law and order. She also is protector of hospitality and the oppressed and has oracular powers.

Theocritus. A Greek poet of Syracuse (3rd century B.C.), the creator of pastoral poetry, whose verse was imitated by VIRGIL.

Theodoric (thē od' ō rik). King of the Ostrogoths (c. 454–526), who became celebrated in German legend as DIETRICH OF BERN, and also has a place in the Norse romances and the *Nibelungen Saga*. He invaded Italy, slew Odoacer (493), and became sole ruler.

Theon (thē' on). A satirical poet of ancient ROME, noted for his mordant writings. Hence **Theon's tooth**, the bite of an ill-natured or carping critic. Thus:

> *Dente Theonino circumroditur* (HORACE: I *Epist.* xviii, 82), meaning "is slandered, calumniated".

Theophany. See TIFFANY.

Theosophy (Gr., the wisdom of God). The name adopted by the Theosophical Society (founded in 1875 by Mme Blavatsky, Col. H.S. Olcott, William Q. Judge, and others) to define their religious or philosophical system, which aims at the knowledge of God by means of intuition and contemplative illumination, or by direct communion. *Esoteric Buddhism* is another name for it; and its adherents claim that the doctrines of the great world religions are merely the *exoteric* expressions of their own *esoteric* traditions.

> The Theosophist is a man who, whatever be his race, creed, or condition, aspires to reach this height of wisdom and beatitude by self-development.
> H.S. OLCOTT: *Theosophy*, p. 144 (1885).

The name was formerly applied to the philosophical system of Jakob Boehme (1575–1624).

Théot, Catherine. See under CATHERINE.

Theramenes. See HE WEARS THE SANDALS OF THERAMENES *under* SANDAL.

Therapeutæ (thēr a pū' tē) (Gr., servants, ministers). A sect of Jewish ascetics in Egypt described in Philo's *De Vita Contemplativa*. They lived in a community near Alexandria run on monastic lines which was developed long before the rise of Christianity. *Cp.* ESSENES.

Thermidor (thēr' mi dôr). The eleventh month of the French Republican CALENDAR 20 July—18 August. So named from Gr. *therme*, heat; *doron*, a gift.

Thermidorians. The French Revolutionaries who took part in the COUP D'ETAT which effected the fall of Robespierre, on 9th Thermidor of the second Republican year (27 July 1794), thus ending the REIGN OF TERROR.

Thermopylæ (thĕr mop' i li). The famous pass from Thessaly to Locris, only 25 ft. wide at its narrowest part, celebrated for its heroic defence (480 B.C.) by LEONIDAS, with some 300 Spartans and 700 Thespians against XERXES and the Persian Host. Eventually, treachery allowed the Persians to get to the rear of the Greeks and the Spartan king and his band were all slain. The pass took its name from the hot baths nearby.

Thermopylae of America. See ALAMO.

Thersites (thĕ sī' tēz). A deformed, scurrilous officer in the Greek army at the siege of TROY. He was always railing at the chiefs; hence the name is applied to any dastardly, malevolent, impudent railer against the powers that be. ACHILLES felled him to the earth with his fist and killed him.

In SHAKESPEARE's *Troilus and Cressida* (I, iii) he is "A slave whose gall coins slanders like a mint."

Theseus (thē' sūs). The chief hero of Attica in ancient Greek legend; son of ÆGEUS, and the centre of countless exploits. Among them are the capture of the Marathonian bull, the slaying of the MINOTAUR, his war against the AMAZONS, and the hunting of the CALYDONIAN BOAR (*see under* BOAR). He was eventually murdered by Lycomedes in Scyros. See SINIS.

Theseus is also the name of the Duke of Athens in Chaucer's *Knight's Tale*. He married Hippolita, and as he returned home with his bride, and Emily her sister, was accosted by a crowd of female suppliants who complained of Creon, King of Thebes. The Duke forthwith set out for Thebes, slew Creon, and took the city by assault. Many captives fell into his hands, amongst whom were the two knights, Palamon and ARCITE.

SHAKESPEARE gives the same name to the Duke of Athens in *A Midsummer Night's Dream*.

Thespians (thes' pi ànz). Actors; so called from Thespis, an Attic poet of the 6th century B.C., reputed to be the father of Greek TRAGEDY.

> Thespis, the first professor of our art,
> At country wakes sang ballads from a cart.
> DRYDEN: *Prologue to Sophonisba*.

Thestylis (thes' ti lis). A stock poetic name for a rustic maiden; from a young female slave of that name in the *Idylls* of THEOCRITUS.

> And then in haste her bower she leaves,
> With Thestylis to bind the sheaves.
> MILTON: *L'Allegro*, 87.

Thetis (thē′ tis). The chief of the NEREIDS of Greek legend. By Peleus she was the mother of ACHILLES.

Thetis's hair-stone. A fancy name given to pieces of rock-crystal enclosing hair-like filaments.

Thick. As thick as a doorpost. Dull-witted, unintelligent.

As thick as two short planks. Very obtuse.

It's a bit thick. More than one can be expected to tolerate.

Thick 'un. Slang for a SOVEREIGN.

Those two are very thick. They are very good friends, on excellent terms with one another. **As thick as thieves** is a similar saying.

Through thick and thin. Despite all difficulties; under any conditions; unwaveringly.

> A griesly foster forth did rush
> Through thick and thin, both over bank and bush,
> In hope her to attain by hook or crook.
> SPENSER: *The Faerie Queene*, III, i, 17.

To be thick. Not to be very bright or intelligent; to be slow on the uptake.

To lay it on thick. To flatter extravagantly; also to blame or punish excessively.

Thick-skinned. Not sensitive; not irritated by rebukes or slanders. *Thin-skinned*, on the contrary means impatient of reproof or censure, having skin so thin that it is an annoyance to be touched.

Thief, The Penitent. *See* DYSMAS.

Thieves' Latin. Slang; gibberish.

Thimble. From O.E. *thymel*, a thumbstall; so called because it was originally worn on the thumb, as is the "thimble" of a sailmaker's palm.

Just a thimble or **thimbleful.** A very little drop, just a taste—usually with reference to spirits.

> 'Tis true to her cottage still they came ...
> And never swallow'd a thimble the less
> Of something the Reader is left to guess.
> HOOD: *A Tale of a Trumpet*, 130.

Thimble-rigging. A form of cheating, carried on with three thimbles and a pea, formerly mainly practised on or about race-courses. A pea is put on a table, and the manipulator places three thimbles over it in succession, and then, setting them on the table, asks you to say under which thimble the pea is. You are sure to guess wrong.

The term *thimble-rigging* is used allusively of any kind of mean cheating or JIGGERY-POKERY.

Thin. It's a lot too thin! Said of an excuse, explanation, story, etc., that sounds plausible but is quite unacceptable. The idea is that it is so thin as to be transparent—it is easily seen through.

The thin end of the wedge. An action, innovation, etc., of apparently small consequence which may lead to major undesirable developments. The reference is to wedges used for splitting blocks of stone or wood.

The thin red line. *See under* LINE.

Thin-skinned. *See* THICK-SKINNED.

Thing. The Old Norse word for the assembly of the people, PARLIAMENT, etc. It is etymologically the same word as our *thing* (an object), the original meaning of which was a discussion (from *thingian*, to discuss), hence a cause, an object.

The Parliament of Norway is still called the *Storting* which divides itself into the *Lagting* and the *Odelsting*.

Just the thing, or **the very thing.** Just what I was wanting; exactly what will meet the case.

Old thing. A familiar mode of address between friends.

One's things. One's minor belongings, especially clothes, or personal luggage.

A poor thing. A person (or sometimes an inanimate object) that is regarded with pity or disparagement. Touchstone's remark about Audrey—"An ill-favoured thing, sir, but mine own" (SHAKESPEARE: *As You Like It*, V, iv)—is frequently misquoted, "A poor thing, but mine own", when employed in half-ironical disparagement of one's own work.

The thing. The proper thing to do; as, "it's not the thing to play leapfrog down Bond Street in a top-hat and spats."

To do the handsome thing. To treat generously.

To know a thing or two. To be sharp, shrewd, not easily taken in; knowing, experienced.

To make a good thing of. To make a success of; to develop into something worthwhile; to make a profit out of.

You can have too much of a good thing. "Enough is as good as a feast."

> People may have too much of a good thing—
> Full as an egg of wisdom thus I sing.
> PETER PINDAR: *The Gentleman and His Wife*, i.

Think-tank. A popular term for a group of people with specialized knowledge and ability, set up to carry out research into particular problems (usually social, political and technological) and to provide ideas and possible solutions.

Third. *See also* THREE.

Third Degree. The highest degree, that of Master Mason, in British FREE-MASONRY. In the U.S.A. the term is applied to the use of exhaustive questioning and cross-questioning by the police in an endeavour to extort a confession of compromising information from a criminal, accomplice, or witness.

Third Estate. *See under* ESTATE.

Third Order. *See* TERTIARIES.

Third Republic. The French Republic established in 1870 after the capitulation of NAPOLEON III at Sedan (4 September). It came to an end with another French capitulation to Germany in 1940, when a collaborationist government was set up under Marshal Pétain at VICHY.

Third World. *See under* WORLD.

Thirteeen. It is said that the origin of sitting down 13 at a table being deemed unlucky is because, at a banquet in VALHALLA, LOKI once intruded, making 13 guests, and BALDER was slain.

In Christian countries, the superstition was confirmed by the LAST SUPPER of Christ and His twelve APOSTLES.

Addison, *On Popular Superstitions* (*Spectator*), says:

> I remember I was once in a mixed assembly that was full of noise and mirth, when on a sudden an old woman unluckily observed there were thirteen of us in company. This remark struck a panic terror into several who were present, insomuch that one or two of the ladies were going to leave the room; but a friend of mine, taking notice that one of our female companions was big with child, affirmed there were fourteen in the room, and that, instead of portending one of the company should die, it plainly forebode one of them should be born. Had not my friend found this expedient to break the omen, I question not but half the women in the company would have fallen sick that night.

It is traditionally regarded as unlucky for a ship to begin a voyage on the 13th, especially if it happens to be FRIDAY.

Thirteenpence-halfpenny. A hangan. So called because thirteenpence-halfpenny was at one time his wages for hanging a man.

Thirty. The Thirty Tyrants. *See under* TYRANT.

The Thirty Years War. The wars in Germany which began in Bohemia in 1618 and were terminated by the peace of Westphalia in 1648. Traditionally regarded as a struggle initially between German PROTESTANTS and Catholics, which was exploited by foreign powers, it was more essentially part of a contest between BOURBON and HABSBURG dynastic interests combined with constitutional struggles inside the Habsburg Empire waged under the cloak of religion. The idea that "Germany" was universally devastated is largely a myth.

The Thirty-nine Articles. The *Articles* of Religion in the BOOK OF COMMON PRAYER largely defining the CHURCH OF ENGLAND's position in certain matters of dogma which were in dispute at the time. They were first issued in 1563, based on the Forty-two Articles of 1553, and revised in 1571. Clergy had to subscribe to them, but since 1865 a more general affirmation has been substituted.

Thirty-six-Line Bible. *See* BIBLE, SOME SPECIALLY NAMED EDITIONS.

A man at thirty must be either a fool or a physician. A saying attributed to Tacitus (*Annals*, VI, xlvi) to the Emperor Tiberius, who died at the age of 78 in A.D. 37 (Plutarch gives the story, but changes the age to 60). The idea seems to be that if a man has not learned to look after his health by the time he is 30 he must be a fool.

Thisbe. *See* PYRAMUS.

Thistle. The heraldic emblem of SCOTLAND which seems to have been adopted by James III (1451, 1460–1488), possibly as a symbol of defence. The motto *Nemo me impune lacessit*, "Nobody touches (or provokes) me with impunity", first appeared on the coinage of James VI (1566, 1567–1603).

Thistles, especially "Our Lady's Thistle", are said to be a cure for stitch in the side. According to the doctrine of signatures, Nature has labelled every plant, and the prickles of the thistle tell us that the plant is efficacious for *prickles* or the stitch. The species called *Silybum marianum*, we are told, owes the white markings on its leaves to milk from Our Lady's breast, some of which fell thereon and left a white mark behind.

The "Most Ancient" Order of the Thistle. This Scottish Order of knighthood (ranking second to the Order of the GARTER) is not very ancient, being instituted by James VII and II in 1687. It is inaccurately said to have been "refounded" then; legend has it that it was founded by Achaius, King of the Scots in 787. It fell into abeyance after 1688 but was revived by QUEEN ANNE in 1703 and now consists of 16 KNIGHTS (besides royalty). Its officers are the DEAN, the secretary, the LYON KING OF ARMS, and the Gentleman Usher of the Green Rod. Its insignia comprise the Badge (an elongated eight-pointed star with a figure of St. ANDREW and his CROSS), Star, Collar of golden thistles and sprigs of RUE, Mantle, and dark green ribbon.

It is sometimes called the Order of St. Andrew.

Thomas. St. Thomas. The Apostle who doubted (*John* xx, 25); hence the phrase, **a doubting Thomas,** applied to a sceptic.

The story told of him in the APOCRYPHAL *Acts of St. Thomas* is that he was deputed to go as a missionary to India, and, on refusing, Christ appeared and sold him as a slave to an Indian prince who was visiting JERUSALEM. He was taken to India, where he baptized the prince and many others, and was finally martyred at Mylapore.

Another legend has it that Gundaphorus, an Indian king, gave him a large sum of money to build a palace. St. Thomas spent it on the poor, "thus creating a superb palace in heaven". On account of this he is the patron SAINT of masons and architects, and his symbol is a builder's square.

Another story is that he once saw a huge beam of timber floating on the sea near the coast, and the king unsuccessfully endeavouring, with men and elephants, to haul it ashore. St. Thomas desired leave to use it in building a church, and, his request being granted, he dragged it easily ashore with a piece of packthread.

His feast day is 3 July (formerly 21 December). His relics are now said to be at Ortona in the Abruzzi.

Christians of St. Thomas. According to tradition, St. THOMAS founded the Christian churches of Malabar and then moved on to Mylapore (Madras), thus Christian communities were there to welcome the Portuguese when Vasco da Gama arrived in 1498. They called themselves "Christians of St. Thomas" and may be descendants of Christians converted by NESTORIAN missions, although the claim that they were evangelized by St. Thomas is not entirely improbable.

Thomasing. Collecting small sums of money or obtaining drink from employers on St. Thomas's Day. In THE CITY OF LONDON, every one of the Common Council has to be elected or re-elected on St. Thomas's Day, which used to be observed on 21 December.

Thomas Aquinas, St. (*c.* 1225–1274). DOMINICAN scholastic philosopher and theologian, of outstanding authority and intellectual distinction among his contemporaries, and whose teachings have been a major influence on the doctrines of the ROMAN CATHOLIC CHURCH. He was the youngest son of Count Landulf of Aquino (midway between ROME and Naples) and became a Dominican in the face of strong family opposition. He was a pupil of Albertus Magnus and subsequently taught at PARIS, ROME, Bologna and Pisa. First nicknamed the DUMB OX he became *Doctor Angelicus* and "the Fifth Doctor of the Church". Among his many writings his *Summa Theologica* is his classic work. He drew a clear distinction between Faith and Reason and was considerably influenced by the philosophy of ARISTOTLE. He was canonized in 1323 and his feast day is 28 January.

Thomists. Followers of St. THOMAS AQUINAS (*c.* 1225–1274). They were opponents of the SCOTISTS, or followers of Duns Scotus (*see* DUNCE).

> Scotists and Thomists now in peace remain.
> POPE: *Essay on Criticism*, 444.

Thomas the Rhymer. *See under* RHYME.

Thone, or **Thonis.** In Greek mythology, the governor of a province of Egypt to which, it is said by post-Homeric poets, PARIS took HELEN, who was given by Polydamnia, wife to Thone, the drug NEPENTHES, to make her forget her sorrows.

> Not that nepenthes which the wife of Thone,
> In Egypt gave to Jove-born Helena
> Is of such power to stir up joy as this.
> MILTON: *Comus*, 675–7.

Thopas, Rime of Sir (thō′ păs). A burlesque on contemporary metrical romances, told as Chaucer's own tale in the *Canterbury Tales*.

Thor (thôr). Son of WODEN, god of war, and the second god in the PANTHEON of the ancient Scandinavians—their VULCAN, and god of thunder. He had three principal possessions, a Hammer (*Mjolnir*), typifying thunder and lightning, and having the virtue of returning to him after it was thrown; a Belt (*Meginjardir*) which doubled his strength; and Iron Gloves to aid him in throwing his hammer.

He was a god of the household, and of peasants, and was married to Sif, a typical peasant woman. His name is still perpetuated in our THURSDAY, and in a number of place-names such as *Thorsby* (Cumberland), *Torthorwald* (Dumfries), and *Thurso* (Caithness).

Thorn. The Crown of Thorns. That with which Our Saviour was crowned in mockery (*Matt.* xxvii, 29); hence sometimes used of a very special affliction with which one is unjustly burdened.

Calvin (*Admonitio de Reliquiis*) gives a long list of places claiming to possess one or more of the thorns which composed the Saviour's crown. *See* GLASTONBURY.

Glastonbury Thorn. *See* GLASTONBURY.

A thorn in the flesh. A source of constant irritation, annoyance, or affliction; said of objectionable and parasitical acquaintances, obnoxious conditions, etc. There was a sect of the PHARISEES which used to insert thorns in the borders of their gaberdines to prick their legs in walking and make them bleed. The phrase is taken from St. PAUL'S reference to some physical complaint or misfortune (II *Cor.* xii, 7).

On thorns. In a state of painful anxiety and suspense; "on pins"; fearful that something is going wrong. *Cp.* TENTERHOOKS.

Thorough. The name given to the methods of government associated with Strafford and Laud, especially the former's policy in IRELAND (1632–1639). It was characterized by firm, efficient and orderly government, but was also associated with corruption and tyrannical methods. *Through* and *thorough* were then interchangeable terms.

Thoroughbred. Of pure or unmixed breed, especially said of horses and cattle. A *thoroughbred* is a racehorse of English breed remotely derived by crossing with Arab and other strains.

Thoth. The Egyptian lunar god, usually with the head of an IBIS but sometimes that of a baboon. His chief centre was Hermapolis (modern Ashmunein) and he was identified with HERMES by the Greeks. He was the master over writing, languages, laws, annals, calculations, etc., and patron of scribes and magicians. He made the CALENDAR and his control over HIEROGLYPHS and divine words enhanced his magical powers. He acted as secretary of the gods. At the judgement after death he weighed the heart.

Thousand. Thousand and One Nights. *See* ARABIAN NIGHTS.

He's one in a thousand. Said of a man who is specially distinguished by his excellent qualities; similarly, *a wife in a thousand,* a perfect wife, or one that exactly suits the speaker's ideas of what a wife should be.

Thrash. To thrash out. To decide and settle by discussion and argument the points at issue. A METAPHOR from the threshing of corn to separate the grain from the chaff.

Thread. The thread of destiny. That on which destiny depends; the imaginary thread or span of life provided by the FATES.

The Triple Thread. Brahminism. The ancient Brahmins wore a symbol of three threads, reaching from the right shoulder to the left. João de Faria says that their religion sprang from fishermen, who left the charge of the temples to their successors on the condition of their wearing some threads of their nets in remembrance of their vocation.

To lose the thread. To lose the train of thought or issue of argument, etc., owing to a digression, interruption, mental aberration, etc.

To pick up the threads. To resume one's line of argument, etc., also to get back into the way of things after absence, illness, etc.

Threadneedle Street. The street in THE CITY of LONDON leading from Bishopsgate to the BANK of England. The name first appears as *Three needle Street* in 1598, and previously it seems to have been called *Broad Street,* forming part of the present *Old Broad Street.* The name is usually said to derive from a signboard with three needles on it, or from the arms of the Needlemakers' Company; but it may derive from the children's game of thread-the-needle having been played there.

The Old Lady of Threadneedle Street. A synonym for the BANK of England, which stands in this street. The term dates from the late 18th century, and there is a caricature by Gilray, dated 22 May 1797, entitled *The Old Lady in Threadneedle Street in Danger,* which refers to the temporary stopping of cash payments, 26 February 1797, and to the issue of one-pound banknotes on 4 March of the same year.

William Cobbett (*Rural Rides*: From Petersfield to Kensington, 20 Nov., 1825) says:

> Great apologies are due to the OLD LADY from me on account of my apparent inattention towards her during her ... present fit of that tormenting disorder which ... comes upon her by *spells.*

Three. PYTHAGORAS calls three the perfect number, expressive of "beginning, middle, and end", wherefore he makes it a symbol of Deity.

A TRINITY is by no means confined to the CHRISTIAN creed. The BRAHMINS represent their god with three heads; the world was supposed by the ancients to be under the rule of three gods, *viz.* JUPITER (HEAVEN), NEPTUNE (sea), and PLUTO (HADES). Jove is represented with three-forked lightning, Neptune with a trident, and Pluto with a three-headed dog. The FATES are three, the FURIES three, the Graces three (*see under* GRACE), the Harpies three (*see* HARPY), the SIBYLLINE BOOKS three times three (of which only three survived); the fountain from which HYLAS drew water was presided over by three NYMPHS; the MUSES were three times three; in Scandinavian mythology we hear of "the Mysterious Three", *viz* "Har" (High), "Jafenhar" (Equally High), and "Thridi" (the third), who sat on three thrones in ASGARD.

Man is threefold (body, mind, and spirit); the world is threefold (earth, sea, and air); the enemies of man are threefold (the world, the flesh, and the DEVIL); the Christian graces are threefold (Faith, Hope, and Charity); the Kingdoms of Nature are threefold (animal, vegetable and mineral); the CARDINAL colours are three in number (RED, YELLOW, and BLUE), etc. *Cp.* NINE which is three times three.

Rule of Three. The method of finding the fourth term of a proportion where three are given, the numbers being such that the first is to the second as the third is to the fourth. By multiplying the second and third terms together and dividing the result by the first, the fourth term is arrived at.

Three acres and a cow. A phrase particularly associated with Jesse Collings (1831–1920), and his advocacy of radical agrarian policies in the 1880s and the small holdings movement in general.

The Three Bashaws of Somerset House. *See under* BASHAW.

Three Choirs Festival. A festival for the performance of sacred music given since 1724 by the choirs of the cathedrals of Gloucester, Worcester, and Hereford, held in each of the three cities in rotation.

Three Emperors. The Battle of the Three Emperors. The Battle of Austerlitz (2 December 1805), when the French Emperor NAPOLEON routed the Emperors of Austria and Russia, all three being personally present on the field.

The League of the Three Emperors. The *Dreikaiserbund* of 1872 whereby the Emperors of Germany, Austria, and Russia agreed to co-operate in maintaining the STATUS QUO in Europe, and a formal treaty was signed at Berlin in 1881 on policy with regard to possible war between one of them and a fourth Great Power, and also on matters in the Near East. The treaty was renewed in 1884, but terminated in 1888.

The Three Estates of the Realm. *See* ESTATES OF THE REALM.

The Three F's. Fair rent, free sale, and fixity of tenure, which were demanded by the Irish LAND LEAGUE and conceded by Gladstone's Land Act of 1881.

Three Kings' Day. EPIPHANY or Twelfth Day, designed to commemorate the visit of the "three kings" or Wise Men of the East to the infant Jesus. *See* MAGI.

Three-Mile Limit. The usual limit of territorial waters around their coasts claimed by maritime states including Great Britain and the U.S.A. Some states claim much wider jurisdiction and disputes over territorial waters are not infrequent.

The three Musketeers. Athos, Porthos, and Aramis, the three heroes of Dumas's novels *The Three Musketeers*, 1844; *Twenty Years After*, 1845; and *Vicomte de Bragelonne*, 1848–1850. The Musketeers were a mounted guard of gentlemen in the service of the kings of France from 1661 until the Revolution caused their abolition in 1791. They formed two companies, called the

Grey and the Black from the colour of their horses. The uniform was scarlet, hence their quarters were known as *La Maison Rouge*. In peacetime the Musketeers formed the king's bodyguard, but in war they fought on foot or on horseback with the army. Their ranks included many Scots, either JACOBITE exiles or mere soldiers of fortune.

The Three R's. *See under* R.

The Three Tailors of Tooley Street. *See under* TAILOR.

The Three Tongues. Those in which the inscription on the CROSS was written, *viz*. Hebrew, Greek, and Latin. In the MIDDLE AGES it was considered that a thorough knowledge of these was necessary before one could begin to understand theology.

A three-cornered fight. A parliamentary (or other) contest in which there are three participants.

A three-decker. Properly, in the days of sail, a warship having three gun decks. Also applied to other triplicates arranged in tiers such as the old-fashioned pulpit, reading-desk, and clerk's desk arranged one above the other; and to the three-volume novel—the usual way of publishing the 19th-century novel.

> In the early 'eighties there had never been fewer than 190 three-deckers published annually in London; in 1888 for the first time the figure dropped to 165, in 1895 it was 52, in 1897 four.
> S. NOWELL-SMITH: *The House of Cassell*, ch. viii.

The name is also given to a sandwich with three slices of bread.

Three-field system. The system of crop rotation under the old OPEN-FIELD SYSTEM of agriculture which persisted from manorial times until well into the reign of George III. The three open arable fields were successively used for wheat or rye, then peas, beans, barley, oats, etc., and left fallow for the third season.

The three-legged mare. In obsolete slang, the gallows, which at TYBURN was a triple erection in triangular plan.

Three score years and ten. A ripe old age—not necessarily (in allusive use) exactly 70 years. The reference is to *Ps*. xc, 10:

> The days of our years are three score years and ten; and if by reason of strength they be fourscore years, yet is their strength labour and sorrow; for it is soon cut off, and we fly away.

Three sheets in the wind. *See* SHEET.

Three-tailed Bashaw. *See under* BASHAW.

To give one three times three. To give him a rousing ovation, cheer after cheer.

We three. "Did you never see the picture of We Three?" asks Sir Andrew Aguecheek (SHAKESPEARE: *Twelfth Night*, II, iii)—not meaning himself, Sir Toby Belch, and the clown, but referring to a PUBLIC-HOUSE SIGN of *Two* LOGGERHEADS with the inscription, "We three loggerheads be," the third being the spectator. "When shall we three meet again?"—the title of a picture of two asses—is a similar "joke".

Throat. Clergyman's throat. Chronic inflammation of the pharynx, to which clergymen and others who are habitually liable to overstrain the vocal organs are specially prone.

To cut one's own throat. Figuratively, to adopt a policy, or take action that ruins one's own chances, plans, etc. Similarly, **to cut one another's throat** is to ruin one another by excessive competition.

To have a bone in one's throat. A pretended excuse for being unwilling to talk.

To jump down a person's throat. To interrupt and affront him, suddenly, sharply, and decisively.

To lie in one's throat. To lie most outrageously, well knowing that you are lying, and meaning to do so.

To ram, or **thrust down a person's throat.** To force an opinion or point of view upon another which he may be reluctant to accept or "swallow"; to assert insistently without allowing an opportunity for reply or being prepared to listen.

The words stuck in his throat. *See under* WORD.

Throgmorton Street. The financial world at large, or the STOCK EXCHANGE, which is situated in this narrow LONDON street. So named from Sir Nicholas Throckmorton (1515–1571), head of the ancient Warwickshire family, and ambassador to France in the reign of Elizabeth I.

Throne, The. A comprehensive name for the office of Queen or KING, *e.g. The throne is above party politics.*

The Speech from the Throne. *See* QUEEN'S SPEECH.

Thrones, Principalities, and Powers. According to Dionysius the Areopagite, three of the nine orders of ANGELS. These names or their liguistic counterparts occur frequently in Jewish-Christian writings around NEW TESTAMENT times.

> The host of the heavens and all the holy ones above, and the host of God...all the angels of power, and all the angels of principalities
> *Enoch* vi, 10.

Through. *See* THOROUGH.

Throw. To throw a spanner in the works. To deliberately sabotage a plan or enterprise or spoil a scheme by creating difficulties, obstructions, etc., designed to promote failure, as some machinery can be wrecked by literally throwing a spanner or a piece of metal into moving parts.

To throw away one's money. to spend it carelessly, recklessly, extravagantly.

To throw back. To revert to ancestral traits; *a throw-back* is one who does this. "To throw back at someone" is to retort.

To throw good money after bad. Having already lost money on a scheme, investment or project, to continue to spend more on what is bound to result in loss.

To throw in one's hand. To abandon a project; to give up. A METAPHOR from card-playing.

To throw oneself on someone. to commit oneself to his protection, favour, mercy, etc.

To throw the helve after the hatchet. *See* HELVE.

To throw to the wolves. *See under* WOLF.

To throw up the sponge. *See* SPONGE.

Thrums. The fringe of warp threads left when the web has been cut off; weaver's ends and FAG-ENDS of carpet, used for common rugs.

Thread and thrum. Everything, good and bad together.

> O Fates, come, come, cut thread and thrum;
> Quail, crush, conclude and quell!
> SHAKESPEARE: *A Midsummer Night's Dream*, V, i.

The town featured by Sir James Barrie in *A Window in Thrums* (1889) is Kirriemuir, Forfarshire, his birthplace.

Thug. A worshipper of KALI, who practised *thuggee*, the strangling of human victims in the name of religion. Robbery of the victim provided the means of livelihood. They were also called *Phansigars* (Noose operators) from the method employed. Vigorous suppression was begun by Lord William Bentinck in 1828, but the fraternity did not become completely extinct for another 50 years or so.

In common parlance the word is used for any violent "tough".

Thule. The name given by the ancients to an island, or point of land, six days' sail north of Britain, and considered by them to be the extreme northern limit of the world. The name is first found in the account by Polybius (*c.* 150 B.C.) of the voyage made by Pytheas in the late 4th century B.C. Pliny says, "It is an island in the Northern Ocean discovered by Pytheas, after sailing six days from the Orcades." Others, like Camden, consider it to be Shetland, in which opinion they agree with Marinus, and the descriptions of Ptolemy and Tacitus; and still others that it was some part of the coast of Norway. The etymology of the word is unknown.

Ultima Thule. The end of the world; the last extremity.

> Tibi serviat Ultima Thule.
>
> VIRGIL: *Georgics*, I, 30.

Thumb. In the ancient Roman combats, when a GLADIATOR was vanquished it rested with the spectators to decide whether he should be slain or not. If they wished him to live, they shut up their thumbs in their fists (*pollice compresso favor judicabatur*); if to be slain they turned out their thumbs. *See* Juvenal, iii, 36; Horace, I *Epist*, xviii, 66.

> Influenced by the rabble's bloody will,
> With thumbs bent back they popularly kill.
>
> DRYDEN: *Third Satire of Juvenal*.

Our popular saying **Thumbs up!** expressive of pleasure or approval is probably a development from this custom.

Rule of thumb. A rough, guesswork measure; practice or experience, as distinguished from theory; in allusion to the use of the thumb for rough measurements.

Thumb index. Grooves cut in the pages of a book showing initial letters or other particulars to enable the reader to find a reference easily.

Thumb-nail. Used attributively of various things, especially sketches, portraits, and so on, that are on a very small scale.

Tom Thumb. *see under* TOM.

Every honest miller has a thumb of gold. Even an honest miller grows rich with what he filches; for he simply cannot help some of the flour that ought to go into the loaf sticking to his thumb! Chaucer says of his miller:

> Wel koude he stelen corn and tollen thries,
> And yet he hadde a thombe of gold pardee.
>
> *Canterbury Tales: Prologue*, 562.

The pricking of one's thumb. In popular superstition, a portent of evil. The Second Witch in SHAKESPEARE's *Macbeth* (IV, i) says:

> By the pricking of my thumbs
> Something wicked this way comes.

And Macbeth enters.

Another proverb says, **My little finger told me that.** When your *ears tingle* it is to indicate that someone is speaking about you; when a sudden fit of *shivering* occurs, it is because someone is treading over the place which is to form your grave; when the *eye twitches*, it indicates the visit of a friend; when the *palm itches* it shows that a present will shortly be received; and when the *bones ache* a storm is prognosticated. Sudden pains and prickings are the warnings of evil on the road; sudden glows and pleasurable sensations are the couriers to tell us of joy close at hand.

In ancient ROME, the augurs (*see* AUGURY) took special notice of the palpitation of the heart, the flickering of the eye, and the pricking of the thumb. In regard to the last, if the pricking was on the left hand it was considered a very bad sign, indicating mischief at hand.

To bite one's thumb at one. To insult him. Formerly a way of expressing defiance and contempt by snapping the finger or putting the thumb in the mouth. Both these acts are terms a FICO. *Cp.* HE BIT HIS GLOVE *under* GLOVE.

> I will bite my thumb at them; which is a disgrace to them, if they bear it.
>
> SHAKESPEARE: *Romeo and Juliet*, I, i.

To thumb a lift. to ask for or to "scrounge" a ride from a passing vehicle by holding out the hand with the thumb pointing upwards and moving in the direction of intended travel.

To thumb the nose. To COCK A SNOOK.

To twiddle one's thumbs. To sit in a state of bored inactivity, often against one's inclination; to be wasting time or to have to waste one's time. An allusion to the habit at such times, of sitting with the hands interlaced in one's lap idly rotating the thumbs round each other.

Under one's thumb. Under the influence or power of the person named.

Thumbikins, Thumbscrew. An instrument of torture used largely by the INQUISITION, whereby the thumbs are compressed between two bars of iron, by means of a screw. William Carstares (1649–1715) was the last person put to the torture in Britain; as the Law of ENGLAND would not permit torture, he was sent by the PRIVY COUNCIL for examination in Edinburgh, to elicit the names of the accomplices in the RYE HOUSE PLOT.

Thunder. Used figuratively of any loud noise, also of vehement denunciations or threats, as, "the thunders of the VATICAN", meaning the anathemas and denunciations of the POPE.

THOR was the Scandinavian god of thunder, and JUPITER in Roman mythology; hence Dryden's allusion to the inactivity of Louis XIV:

> And threatening France, placed like a painted Jove,
> Kept idle thunder in his lifted hand.
>
> *Annus Mirabilis*, XXXIX.

Sons of Thunder. See BOANERGES.

To steal one's thunder. To forestall him; or to adopt his own special methods as one's own. The phrase comes from the anecdote of John Dennis (1657–1734), the critic and playwright who invented an effective device for producing stage thunder for his play *Appius and Virginia*. The play was a failure and was withdrawn, but shortly afterwards Dennis heard his thunder used in a performance of *Macbeth*. "My God," he exclaimed, "The villains will play my thunder but not my plays!"

Thunderbolt. A missile or mass of heated matter that was formerly supposed to be discharged from thunder-clouds during a storm; used figuratively of an irresistible blow, a sudden and overwhelming shock. *cp.* A BOLT FROM THE BLUE *under* BOLT.

JUPITER was depicted by the ancients as a man seated on a throne, holding a sceptre in his left hand and thunderbolts in his right.

> Be ready, gods, with all your thunderbolts;
> Dash him to pieces!
> SHAKESPEARE: *Julius Cæsar*, IV, iii.

The Thunderbolt of Italy. Gaston de Foix, duc de Nemours (1489–1512), nephew of Louis XII, was so called because of his brilliant campaign in Italy (1512).

Thunderday. *See* THURSDAY.

Thunderer, The. A name facetiously applied to *The Times* newspaper in the mid-19th century, in allusion to an article by the assistant editor, Edward Sterling (1773–1847), which began, "We thundered forth the other day an article on the subject of social and political reform." *See* PRINTING HOUSE SQUARE.

> He [Edward Sterling], more than any other man or circumstances, *was* the *Times* Newspaper, and thundered through it to the shaking of the spheres.
> CARLYLE: *John Sterling*, III, v (1851).

Thundering Legion, The. The XIIth Legion of the Roman army; probably so called because its ensign was a representation of JUPITER TONANS.

The name *Fulminata* dates from the time of Augustus (31 B.C.—A.D. 14) but fable relates it to the time of Marcus Aurelius. The story is that in this emperor's expedition against the Marcomanni, Quadi, etc. (172), the XIIth Legion, consisting of Christians, saved the whole army from a disastrous drought by praying for rain. A terrible thunderstorm burst and not only provided abundance of water but dispersed the enemy with lightning and THUNDERBOLTS. Hence the legion's name.

> What wonders, yea, what apparent miracles did the prayers of former Christians procure! hence the Christian soldiers in their Army were called the Thundering Legion; they could do more by their prayers than the rest by their arms.
> BAXTER: *Saints' Everlasting Rest*, II, vi, 6.

Thursday. The fifth day of the weeek until 1971, now the fourth (*see* SUNDAY). The day of the god THOR, called by the French *jeudi*, that is, Jove's day. Both JOVE and THOR were gods of thunder, and formerly Thursday was sometimes called *Thunderday*. *See also* BLACK, HOLY, MAUNDY THURSDAY.

When three Thursdays come together. One of the many circumlocutions for NEVER.

Thyestes (thī' es tēz). Brother of Atreus, and son of PELOPS and HIPPODAMIA. He seduced his brother's wife and also contrived a situation which led to Atreus slaying his own son. By way of revenge, Atreus invited Thyestes to a banquet in which the limbs of two of his sons, slain by Atreus, were served as a dish. Hence a *Thyestean feast*: one at which human flesh is served.

Thyrsus (ther' sus). The staff carried by DIONYSUS and his attendants, topped with a pine cone and decorated with vine and ivy leaves. *See* TORSO.

Ti. *See* ARETINIAN SYLLABLES.

Tiara (tē ar' à). Anciently the turban-like head-dress worn erect by the Persian kings and turned down by lords and priests; now applied to a coronet-like head ornament, especially to the triple CROWN of the POPE. The latter resembles the old-style beehive in shape and is worn on other than liturgical occasions. It typifies the temporal or sovereign power of the Papacy and is composed of GOLD cloth encircled by three crowns and surmounted by a golden globe and CROSS. It is first mentioned in the early 8th century and was a kind of cap called *camelaucum*. By the 11th century, a coronet had been added to the rim with two pendants or lappets hanging down at the back. The second circlet was added by Boniface VIII (1294–1303), perhaps to symbolize both temporal and spiritual powers, and the third coronet seems to have been added either by Benedict XI (1303–1304) or Clement V (1305–1314). An early representation of the triple crown is in an effigy of Benedict XII (d. 1342) and its symbolism is variously interpreted. The tiara is very richly ornamented and contains 146 jewels of all COLOURS, 11 brilliants, and 540 pearls.

Tib. The ace of trumps in the game of GLEEK. Tom is the KNAVE.

> That gamester needs must overcome,
> That can play both Tib and Tom.
> RANDOLPH: *Hermaphrodite*.

St. Tib's Eve. NEVER. There is no such SAINT in the CALENDAR, her eve is nonexistent like the GREEK CALENDS.

Tich. A diminutive person; from celebrated dwarfish music-hall comedian Harry Ralph (1868–1928), known as Little Tich. As a podgy infant at the time of the TICHBORNE CASE, he was nicknamed "Tichborne" or

"Tich" in allusion to the Tichborne claimant, who was very corpulent. As he remained a "TOM THUMB" he came to be called "Little Tich", a name he used professionally. He first appeared at ROSHERVILLE GARDENS playing a tin-whistle and then as a NIGGER-MINSTREL. He became renowned for his stage pranks and satirical humour and in due course appeared at the DRURY LANE with Dan Leno and Marie Lloyd. His popularity in Paris gained him the LEGION OF HONOUR.

Tichborne Case. The most celebrated impersonation case in English law. In March 1853, Roger Charles Tichborne, heir to an ancient Hampshire baronetcy, sailed for Valparaiso, and after travelling a while in S. America embarked on 20 April 1854 in a sailing ship named the *Bella*, bound for Jamaica. The ship went down and nothing more was heard or seen of Roger Tichborne. In October 1865, "R.C. Richborne" turned up at Wagga Wagga, in Australia, in the person of a man locally known as Tom Castro. On Christmas Day 1866, he landed in England as a claimant to the Tichborne baronetcy, asserting that he was the lost Roger. Lady Tichborne, the real Roger's mother, professed to recognize him, but the family could not be deceived. The case came into the courts where the fellow's claims were proved to be false and he himself identified as Arthur Orton, the son of a Wapping butcher. A further trial for perjury, lasting 188 days, ended in his being sentenced to 14 years' penal servitude. *See* B. OF B.K..

Tichborne Dole. An ancient charity maintained by the Tichborne family said to have been instituted by Lady Mabel Tichborne in 1150. The legend is that, when dying, she begged her husband to provide for the poor from the produce of the estate and he promised to give the value of the land she could encircle while holding a burning torch. She rose from her deathbed and encompassed 23 acres and prophesied that if the charity were allowed to lapse, seven sons would be born to the family followed by seven daughters and the title would lapse. The dole was stopped after 644 years and the then baronet had seven sons and his heir seven daughters. The third son changed his name to Doughty and revived the dole and escaped the full consequences of the curse. The title became extinct in 1968 with the death of Sir Anthony Doughty-Tichborne, the fourteenth baronet.

Tick. To get, or **go on tick.** To get on credit, to owe for what one buys. In the 17th century *ticket* was the ordinary term for the written acknowledgement of a debt, and one living on credit was said to be living *on ticket* or *tick*.

> A poor wretch that goes on tick for the paper he writes his Lampoons on, and the very Ale and Coffee that inspires him, as they say.
> WYCHERLEY: *Love in a Wood*, iii, 1.

To tick someone off. To rebuke or "tell off" sharply; both "tick off" and "'tell off'" involve the idea of enumerating or checking off a list of complaints or offences.

What makes it tick? The child's question, asked about a watch or clock, has given rise to a figurative use: "What makes him (her or it) tick?" meaning, "What keeps him on the go?" Sometimes the question is asked with wider implications, such as, what are a person's beliefs and interests?

Ticket (U.S.A.). The party list of candidates in an election. "I intend to vote for the straight Republican ticket."

Ticket of leave. A warrant given to convicts to have their liberty on condition of good behaviour; hence, *Ticket-of-leave man*, a convict freed from prison but obliged to report himself to the police from to time until his sentence was completed. The system is now discontinued.

That's the ticket, or **that's the ticket for soup.** That's the right thing, that's just what is wanted, from the custom among 19th-century charities of issuing to the needy tickets exchangeable for soup, clothing, coal, etc.

To get one's ticket. In the Merchant Service the expression denotes becoming a qualified mate or master, etc., of a ship, *i.e.* to get one's certificate as such. Thus **to lose one's ticket** is to have one's certificate withdrawn as a result of incompetence causing the hazarding of a ship etc.

To work one's ticket. An army expression meaning to secure one's discharge before the contract of service has expired.

All tickety-boo. Everything is in order, everything is fine and as it should be. An expression of uncertain origin, possibly from *ticket* as in THAT'S THE TICKET (*above*).

Tiddy-oggie. The prevalent local name for the Cornish pasty of meat and potato. *Tiddy* is the dialect word for potato (*cp. tater*) and oggie is a pasty (a dinner-cake or baked pastry is called *hogen*). The Cornish miner's lunch usually consisted of a pasty and its crust was formerly supposed to be sufficiently hard to be dropped down the mine shaft to the man below.

Tide (O.E. *tid*, time, season, tide of the sea). The word is cognate with TIME. *See also* TIDY. It is used figuratively of a tendency, a current or flow of events, etc., as in a tide of feeling, and in SHAKESPEARE'S:

There is a tide in the affairs of men,
Which, taken at the flood, leads on to fortune.
Julius Cæsar, IV, iii.

Lose not a tide. Waste no time; set off at once on the business.

Time and tide wait for no man. *See under* TIME.

To tide over a difficulty, hard times, etc. To surmount the difficulty, to get by.

Tide-waiter. Also called a *tidesman*, a Customs officer who boards ships entering port to ensure that the customs regulations are observed. The term is figuratively applied to one who waits to see the trend of events before taking action, or which way the "tide of opinion is flowing".

Tidy means in TIDE, in season, in time, as in eventide, springtide, etc. Tusser has the phrase, "If the weather be fair and tidy", meaning seasonable. Things done in their proper season are sure to be done orderly and properly; hence, by association, *tidy* came to imply methodical, neat, well arranged.

The word is also used in the sense of a thing being worth consideration: **a tidy penny,** quite a good sum; **a tidy fortune,** an inheritance worth having.

Tied House. A retail business, especially a public house *tied* by agreement to obtain its supplies from a particular firm.

Tiercel. *see* TASSELL-GENTLE.

Tiffany. A kind of thin silk-like gauze. The word is supposed to be a corruption of *Theophany* (Gr. *theos*, god; *phainein*, to show), the manifestation of God to man, the EPIPHANY; and the material was so called because it used to be worn at the TWELFTH NIGHT (Epiphany) revels.

Tiffin. An old north of ENGLAND provincialism for a small draught of liquor; also a lunch or slight repast between breakfast and dinner. In Anglo-Indian usage it denotes a light meal or lunch, especially of curried dishes, chutney and fruit.

"I bought a pineapple at the same time, which I gave to Sambo. Let's have it for tiffin; very cool and nice this hot weather."
THACKERAY: *Vanity Fair*, iv.

Tiger. The NICKNAME of the French statesman Georges Clemenceau (1841–1929). The warlike and ruthless Tipu Sahib, Sultan of Mysore (1750, 1782–1799), was also nicknamed *The Tiger*.

A liveried servant who rides out with his master used to be called a *tiger*, also a boy in buttons, a page. In America it is applied to a final yell in a round of cheering.

In poker, *tiger* is the lowest hand that can be drawn—six high, ace low, without pair, straight or flush. Great nerve is required to hold and bluff on such a hand, and the expression is responsible for the title of the famous JAZZ classic *Tiger Rag. Cf.* YARBOROUGH.

Paper Tiger. *See under* PAPER.

Tight. In colloquial usage, "intoxicated".

Blow me tight! An old expression of surprised wonder, incredulity, etc.

'If there's a soul will give me food, or find me in employ,
By day or night, then blow me tight!' (he was a vulgar Boy).
BARHAM: *Ingoldsby Legends (Misadventures at Margate*, 21).

Tike, or **Tyke.** A provincial word (from Old Norse) for a dog or cur; hence used of a low or rough-mannered fellow, as in the contemptuous insults, "you dirty tike", "you measly tyke".

A Yorkshire tike. An established name for a Yorkshireman, nowadays without any derogatory implications; it formerly specially denoted a clownish rustic of that county.

Tilbury. A once fashionable well-sprung, two-wheeled horse carriage or gig, without top or cover. Designed by John Tilbury of London in the early 19th century. He was a horse-dealer and later a job-master and both NIMROD and John Mytton used his mounts.

Tile. Old slang for a hat, this being to the head what tiles are to a house. The once very popular MUSIC HALL song by J. Rolmaz begins, "Where did you get that hat? Where did you get that tile?"

Out on the tiles. On a late night spree, on the loose, on a nocturnal drinking bout.

To have a tile loose. To be not quite *compos mentis*, not "all there".

To tile a lodge, in FREEMASONRY is to close and guard the doors to prevent anyone uninitiated from entering, the officer who does this being called the *Tiler*, sometimes spelled *tyler*.

Tilt. At full tilt. At full speed. From the encounter at full gallop of KNIGHTS in a tilt. *See* QUINTAIN.

To tilt at windmills. *See under* WINDMILL.

Tim Bobbin. A native of Lancashire.

Timber. To take the tall timber. To depart or escape suddenly and unceremoniously (U.S.A.).

Belly timber. *See under* BELLY.

Timber-toes. A name for a person with a wooden leg.

Timbuctoo, or **Timbuktu.** An ancient African city on the southern edge of the Sahara, "the part of the Sudan in the Sahara", which first began as a settlement in the 11th century and subsequently developed as a mart for GOLD, etc., and achieved legendary repute. It was the last great goal of 19th century European travellers searching for fabulous wealth and splendour. Major Gordon Laing having reached it from Tripoli in 1826 was put to death, but René Caillé of Bordeaux, to whom its then ruinous condition became apparent, made a safe return in 1828. It was occupied by the French in 1894 and is now in the Republic of Mali.

Go to Timbuctoo. Virtually the same as "GO TO HALIFAX".

Time. Greenwich Time. *See under* GREENWICH. **Summer Time.** *See* DAYLIGHT SAVING.

Time lag. The term given to the pause that elapses between a cause and its effect.

Time of Grace. *See* SPORTING SEASONS.

Time of Troubles. In Russian history, the years 1584–1613, a period of monarchical instability, foreign intervention, social disorder and economic crises. It began with the accession of Ivan IV's son Feodor, who was incapable of exercising his office, with resultant intrigues among the boyars, and did not end until the accession of Michael Romanov in 1613. Boris Godunov was proclaimed Tsar in 1598 and ruled until his death in 1605, but from 1604 various Pretenders intrigued for the throne. In 1609 King Sigismund of Poland intervened until Patriarch Hermogen stimulated national resistance, which led to the election of Michael by the Zemsky Sobor, and the expulsion of the Poles.

Time zone. *See* STANDARD TIME.

Take time by the forelock. Seize the present moment; CARPE DIEM. Time, called by SHAKESPEARE "that bald sexton" (*King John*, *III*, i), is represented with a lock of hair on his forehead but none on the rest of his head, to signify that time past cannot be used, but time present may be seized by the forelock. The saying is attributed to Pittacus of Mitylene, one of the SEVEN SAGES OF GREECE. It is also suggested that the statue of Opportunity by Lysippus inspired the phrase.

Time and tide wait for no man. One of many sayings pointing the folly of procrastination. It appears in Ray's *Scottish Proverbs* as, "Time bides na man."

Time, gentlemen, please! The traditional announcement for closing time in bars and public houses.

Time Immemorial. Since ancient times, beyond memory. In English law, beyond "legal memory", *i.e.* before the reign of Richard I (1189–1199), because the Statute of Westminister of 1275 fixed this reign as the time limit for bringing certain types of action.

Time is, Time was, Time's past. *See* BRAZEN HEAD.

Time out of mind. TIME IMMEMORIAL; time longer than anyone can remember.

To have had one's time. In World War II, a British soldier's expression for being ripe for death, to expect imminent disaster. In the Royal Navy, part of the traditional "Wakey, Wakey" chant when calling the hands is, "You've had your time", *i.e.* your allotted period of rest.

To know the time o'day. to be smart, wide awake.

Time-expired. Applied to soldiers whose term of service is completed. Also used of convicts who have served their sentences.

Time-honoured Lancaster. Old John of Gaunt, Duke of Lancaster (*c.* 1340–1399), so called by SHAKESPEARE (*Richard II*, I, i) because his memory had been honoured by Time. His father was Edward III, his son Henry IV, his nephew Richard II, and through his great granddaughter, Margaret Beaufort, he is the ancestor of all our sovereigns from Henry VII, Margaret's son. Shakespeare calls him "old"; he was only 59 at his death.

Timeo Danaos. *See* GREEK GIFT.

Timoleon (tī mō′ lē ȯn). The Greek general and statesman (d. *c.* 336 B.C.) who so hated tyranny that he voted for the death of his own brother Timophanes when he attempted to make himself absolute in Corinth.

> The fair Corinthian boast,
> Timoleon, happy temper, mild and firm,
> Who wept the brother while the tyrant bled.
>
> THOMSON: *The Seasons* (*Winter*), 476.

Timon of Athens (tī′ mon). An Athenian misanthrope of the late 5th century B.C., and the principal figure in SHAKESPEARE's play so called.

Macaulay uses the expression to "out-Timon Timon"—*i.e.* to be more misanthropical than even Timon.

Timur. *See* TAMBERLANE.

Tin. Money. A depreciating synonym for SILVER, called by alchemists "JUPITER".

Tin fish. Naval slang for a torpedo.

Tin hat. A soldier's name for his protective metal helmet. **To put the tin hat on it,** to bring something to an abrupt and conclusive end.

Tin topee. *See* BATTLE BOWLER.

Tin-pan Alley. The district of New York City, originally in the area of 14th Street, where popular music is published. In England, Denmark Street, off CHARING CROSS Road, was so called as the centre of the popular music industry. The name has been said to derive from the rattling of tins by rivals when a performance was too loud and too protracted. The "Alley" is now largely deserted by song writers and music publishers who have moved to bigger premises. *See* OLD GREY WHISTLE TEST under GREY.

Tin Tabernacle. *See under* TABERNACLE.

Tintype. A positive photograph taken on a sensitized sheet of enamelled tin. Tintypes were cheap and very popular at FAIRS, amusement parks, etc.

Tincture. In HERALDRY, the hues or colours of the shield and its charges. It include metals, colours, and furs.

Tine-man, The. Archibald Douglas, 4th Earl of Douglas, who died in 1424.

In old Scottish a *tiner* was a loser, and Douglas was said to have lost almost every battle or skirmish in which he took part.

Tinker. Not worth a tinker's damn, or **curse.** Absolutely worthless. It has been suggested that the term derives from the old-time tinker's custom of blocking up the hole in the article he was mending with a pellet of bread, thus making a dam which would prevent the solder from escaping. This pellet was discarded as useless when the job was finished.

Tintagel (tin tăj′ ĕl). The castle on the north coast of Cornwall fabled as King ARTHUR'S Castle and according to Geoffrey of Monmouth (*Historia Britonum*, XIX) the birthplace of King Arthur. The present ruin upon the cliff is of mid-12th century origin.

Tip. A small present of money, such as that given to a waiter, porter, or schoolboy; from the CANT verb (common in the 16th and 17th centuries) *to tip*, meaning to hand over, which also gives rise to the other signification of the verb, *viz.* private warning, such secret information as may guide the person *tipped* to make successful bets or gain some other advantage. *A straight tip* comes straight or direct from the owner or trainer of a horse, or from one in a position to know.

Tip and Run raid. A phrase used in World War II to denote a hurried and often indiscriminate air raid when the enemy sped homeward after jettisoning their bombs. So called from the light-hearted form of CRICKET in which the batsman is forced to run every time he hits the ball.

Tip-off. To warn or give a hint, especially timely warning of a police raid.

To have a thing on the tip of one's tongue. *See under* TONGUE.

To tip one the wink. To give a signal to another by a wink; to tip one off, *i.e.* to give him a hint or warning.

Tip-top. First rate, capital, splendid.

Tiphany. The name given in the old romances to the mother of the MAGI. It is a corruption of EPIPHANY. *Cp.* TIFFANY.

Tiphys. The pilot of the ARGONAUTS, hence a generic name for pilots.

"Tipperary". This song, inseparably associated with World War I, was composed by Jack Judge (d. 1938), of Oldbury, Birmingham. The words were by Harry J. Williams of Temple Balsall, Warwickshire, and the first line of the refrain was engraved on his tombstone. It was composed in 1912 and was already popular in the MUSIC HALL by 1914; it was sung by troops embarking for France and on the front.

> It's a long way to Tipperary,
> It's a long way to go,
> It's a long way to Tipperary,
> To the sweetest girl I know;
> Goodbye, Piccadilly; farewell, Leicester Square;
> It's a long, long way to Tipperary,
> But my heart's right there.

Tipperary Rifle. A SHILLELAGH or stick made of blackthorn.

Tippling House. A contemptuous name for a tavern or public house. A *tippler* was formerly a tavern-keeper or tapster, and the tavern was called a *tippling house*. At Boston, Lincolnshire, in 1577, five persons were appointed "tipplers of Lincoln beer", and no "other tippler [might] draw or sell beer..." under penalties.

Tipstaff. A constable, BAILIFF, or SHERIFF'S officer; so called because he carried a staff tipped with a bull's horn or with metal. In the documents of Edward III allusion is often made to his staff.

Tirant lo Blanch. A romance of CHIVALRY by Johannot Martorell and Johan de Galba, written in Catalan and produced at Valencia in 1490. A favourite book of Cervantes, and one which figures in Don QUIXOTE'S library.

Tiresias (tī rē′ si ás). A Theban of Greek legend, who by accident saw ATHENE bathing, and was therefore struck with blindness by her splashing water in his face. She afterwards repented, and, as she could not restore his sight, conferred on him the power of soothsaying and of understanding the language of birds, giving him a staff with which he could walk as safely as if he had his sight. He found death at last by drinking from the well of Tilphosa.

Another story is that he had been temporarily changed into a woman (for seven years) and was therefore called upon by JUPITER and JUNO to settle an argument as to which of the sexes derived the greatest pleasure from the married state. Tiresias, speaking from experience, declared in favour of the female, whereupon Juno struck him blind.

Tirl. A Scottish variant of *twirl*.

To tirl at the pin. To twiddle or rattle the latch before opening the door. The pin was part of the door-latch and it was a signal that one wished to enter.

Tironian (ti rō′ ni àn). Pertaining to a system of shorthand said to have been invented by Tiro, the freedman and amanuensis of CI-CERO. Our "&" (*see* AMPERSAND) is still sometimes called the *Tironian sign*, for it represents the contraction of Latin *et* introduced by Tiro.

Tirynthian (ti rin′ thi àn). HERCULES is called by Spenser the *Tirynthian Swain* (*Fairie Queene*, VI, xii, 35), and the *Tirynthian Groom* (*Epithalamium*, 329), because he generally resided at Tiryns, an ancient city of Argolis in Greece.

Tisiphone. *See* FURIES.

Tit for Tat. Retaliation; probably representing *tip for tap, i.e.* blow for blow. J. Bellenden Ker says this is the Dutch *dit vor dat* (this for that), Lat. QUID PRO QUO. Heywood uses the phrase *tit for tat*, perhaps the French *tant pour tant*.

Titania (tī tan′ yà). Wife of OBERON, and Queen of the Fairies. SHAKESPEARE uses the name in his *A Midsummer Night's Dream*.

Titans (tī′tànz). In Greek mythology, children of URANUS and GÆA, of enormous size and strength, and typical of lawlessness and the power of force. There were 12, six male (OCEANUS, Cœus, Crius, CRONUS, HYPERION, and Japetus or IAPETOS) and six female (Theia, RHEA, THEMIS, MNEMOSYNE, PHŒBE, and TETHYS). This is according to Hesiod, but the number is variously given by other writers.

Incited by their mother, they overthrew Uranus and emasculated him, and set up Cronus as king. Cronus was in turn overthrown by his son ZEUS. After the long struggle which some of the Titans carried on against Zeus, they were finally hurled down into TARTARUS. *See* GIANTS' WAR WITH ZEUS.

By VIRGIL and Ovid the SUN was sometimes surnamed *Titan*; hence SHAKE-SPEARE'S:

> And flecked Darkness like a drunkard reels
> From forth Day's path and Titan's fiery wheels.
> *Romeo and Juliet*, II, iii.

Tithes. One-tenth of the produce of the land given to the Church, at first voluntarily but made compulsory by the end of the 8th century. The *great* tithes were those of the major crops, the *small* consisting of lesser produce. With the growth of the parochial system, they became an important item in the income of the parson and source of friction between clergy and their parishioners. With the rise of the PURITANS and later Nonconformity a new grievance arose. Commutation of tithes began before 1600, and an attempt to commute tithes to a single rent charge was begun by an Act of 1836. Acts of 1937 and 1951 commuted them to a lump sum redeemable by instalments up to A.D. 2000. *Cp.* TENTHS; *see* VICAR.

Tithing. King Cnut (1017–1035) provided that all free men over the age of 12 should be put in a tithing, a group of ten upon which rested the responsibility of securing the good behaviour of the group, etc.

Tithonus (ti thō′ nùs). A beautiful Trojan of Greek legend, brother to Laomedon, and beloved by Eos (AURORA). At his prayer, the goddess granted him immortality, but as he had forgotten to ask for youth and vigour he grew old, and life became insupportable. He now prayed Eos to remove him from the world; this, however, she could not do, but she changed him into a GRASSHOPPER.

Titi, Prince (tē′ tē). The nickname of Frederick, PRINCE OF WALES (1707–1751), eldest son of George II. In constant opposition to his father, he wrote an *Histoire du Prince Titi* (1735) which contained gross and unmanly caricatures of his father and mother. Two English translations of this offensive work appeared in 1736.

Titles of Kings. *See* RULERS; RELIGIOUS.

Title-Role, in a play, opera or film, is the part or role from which the title is taken, *e.g.* HAMLET, *Carmen,* KING KONG.

Titmouse. *See* MISNOMERS.

Titular Bishops. The Roman Catholic dignitaries formerly known as bishops IN PARTIBUS.

Titus (tī′ tùs). An alternative name for DYS-MAS. Also the name of one of St. PAUL'S disciples to whom he wrote one of his *Epistles*. The latter is traditionally regarded as the first bishop of Crete, where he died. His head was eventually carried off by the Venetians and the skull was returned to the ORTHODOX CHURCH in Crete in 1964.

The Arch of Titus. The arch built in ROME in commemoration of the capture of JERUSALEM (A.D. 70) by Titus and his father Vespasian. Titus became Emperor in A.D. 79. The arch is richly sculptured, and the trophies taken at the destruction of the TEMPLE are shown in relief.

Tityre Tus (tit′ i rē tūz). Dissolute young scapegraces of the late 17th century (*cp.* MO-HOCKS) whose delight was to annoy the watchmen, upset SEDANS, wrench knockers off doors, and insult pretty women. The name comes from the first line of VIRGIL'S first *Eclogue, Tityre, tu patulæ recubans sub tegmine fagi*, because the Tityre Tus loved to lurk in the dark night looking for mischief.

Tityrus (tit′ i rus). A poetical surname for a shepherd; from its use in Greek idylls and VIRGIL'S first *Eclogue*. In *The Shephearde's Calendar* (Feb., June, and Dec.) Spenser calls Chaucer by this name.

> Heroes and their feats
> Fatigue me, never weary of the pipe
> Of Tityrus, assembling as he sang
> The rustic throng beneath his favourite beech.
> COWPER: *The Task (the Winter Evening)*, 705.

Tityus (tit′ i ŭs). In Greek mythology, a gigantic son of ZEUS and GÆA whose body covered nine acres of land. He tried to defile LATONA, but APOLLO cast him into TARTARUS, where a vulture fed on his liver which grew as fast as it was devoured (*cp*. PROMETHEUS).

Tiu, Tiw, or **Tyr.** In Scandinavian mythology, son of ODIN and a younger brother of THOR. He had his hand bitten off when chaining up the wolf FENRIR. He was identified with MARS, the Roman god of war, and his name is found in our *Tuesday* (Fr. *mardi*). Philologists have generallly equated the name with Gr. ZEUS, Lat. *Deus*, Sansk. *devas*.

Tizzy. A sixpenny-piece; a variant of TESTER. *See* TANNER.

Tmesis (tmē′ sis). The grammatical term for the separation of the parts of a compound word by inserting between them other words, or the rearrangement in this manner of the words of a phrase; *e.g. A large meal and rich*, instead of, "A large, rich meal"; *The greatness of his power to us-ward (Eph.* i, 19), instead of, "The greatness of his power toward us".

To-do. Here's a pretty to-do. Here's a ′fine rumpus or disturbance.

To-remain Bible. *See* BIBLE, SOME SPECIALLY NAMED EDITIONS.

Toads. The device of Clovis was three toads (or *botes*, as they were called in O. Fr.); legend relates that after his conversion and BAPTISM the ARIANS assembled a large army under King Candat against him. While on his way to meet the heretics, Clovis saw in the heavens his device miraculously changed into three lilies *or* on a banner *azure*. He instantly had such a banner made, and called it his ORIFLAMME, and even before his army came in sight of King Candat, the host of the HERETIC lay dead, slain, like the army of Sennacherib, by a blast from the God of Battles (Raoul de Presles, *Grans Croniques de France*).

The toad, ugly and venomous, wears yet a precious jewel in its head. Nashe (*Anatomie of Absurditie*, 1589) says, "It fareth with finer wits as it doth with the pearl, which is affirmed to be in the head of the toad", and SHAKESPEARE says:

> Sweet are the uses of adversity,
> Which, like the toad, ugly and venomous,
> Wears yet a precious jewel in its head.
> *As You Like It*, II, i.

Thomas Lupton, in his *One Thousand Notable Things* (1579), speaks of the virtues of the *toadstone* which the toad carried inside its head. "A toad-stone (*crapaudina*) touching any part envenomed, hurt, or stung with rat, spider, wasp, or any other venomous beast, ceaseth the pain or swelling thereof." Such stones, toad-like in shape or colour, believed to have come from the toad, were used as amulets and set in rings.

Toads were also generally held to be poisonous.

Toads unknown in Ireland. It is said that St. PATRICK cleared the island of all vermin by his malediction.

Toad-eater or **Toady.** A cringing parasite, an obsequious lickspittle. The old MOUNTEBANKS used to take around with them a boy who ate—or pretended to eat—toads, then believed to be poisonous. This gave the master the chance to exhibit his skill in expelling poison.

> Be the most scorn'd Jack-Pudding of the pack,
> And turn toad-eater to some foreign quack.
> TOM BROWN: *Satire on an Ignorant Quack (Works* I, 71).

Toad-in-the-hole. A piece of beef, sausage, chop, etc., baked in batter.

Toast. The person, cause, object, etc., to which guests are invited to drink in compliment, as well as the drink itself. The word is taken from the piece of toast which used at one time to be put into the tankard, and which still floats in the LOVING-CUPS at the ancient universities.

The story goes that, in the reign of Charles II, a certain beau pledged a noted beauty in a glass of water taken from her bath; whereupon another roysterer cried out he would have nothing to do with the liquor, but would have the toast—*i.e.* the lady herself (*Tatler*, No. 24).

> Let the toast pass, drink to the lass.
> SHERIDAN: *School for Scandal*, III, iii.

> Say, why are beauties praised and honoured most,
> The wise man's passion and the vain man's toast.
> POPE: *The Rape of the Lock*, canto V, 9.

Toast-master. The official who announces the after-dinner speakers at a formal banquet. He must be a man of stentorian voice and enjoy a nice knowledge of precedence.

Toaster. Toasting-iron. *See* CHEESE-TOASTER.

Tobacco Baron. In prison slang a *baron* is a prisoner who traffics in various items such as sweets, cigarettes, tobacco, etc. Tobacco is the most sought-after commodity, and rations, etc., are often mortgaged for a smoke. The term *Tobacco baron*, for one who wields power by trading in tobacco, or *snout*, is a term more commonly used by journalists than the prisoners themselves.

Tobit. The central character of the popular story in the *Book of Tobit*, in the Old Testament APOCRYPHA. Tobit is a scrupulous and pious Jew who practised good works, but, while sleeping in his courtyard, being unclean from burying a Jew found strangled in the street, was blinded by sparrows which "muted warm dung in his eyes". His son Tobias was attacked on the Tigris by a fish, which leapt out of the water and which he caught at the bidding of the angel RAPHAEL, his mentor. Tobit's blindness was cured by applying to his eyes the gall of the fish. Father and son prepared to reward Azarias (Raphael), whereupon the ANGEL revealed his identity and returned to HEAVEN.

Tobit's dog. *See* CAMEL.

Toby. The dog in the puppet-show of PUNCH AND JUDY. He wears a frill garnished with bells to frighten away the DEVIL from his master.

The high toby, the high road; **the low toby,** the by-road. A highwayman is a "high tobyman"; a mere footpad is a "low tobyman". This is probably from the Shelta (*i.e.* tinkers' jargon) word for road, *tobar*.

Toby jug. A small jug in the form of a squat old man in 18th-century dress, wearing a three-cornered hat, one corner of which forms the lip. The name comes from a poem (1761) about one "Toby Philpot", adapted from the Latin by Francis Fawkes; and the design of the jug from a print sold by Carrington Bowles, a London print-seller, to Ralph Wood, the potter, who turned out a great number of Toby Jugs.

Toc H. The morse pronunciation of the letters T.H., the initials of Talbot House. The term was used in World War I, when the first Talbot House was founded, in December 1915, at Poperinghe, in memory of Gilbert Talbot, son of the Bishop of Winchester, who had been killed at Hooge in the preceding July. The Rev. P.B. Clayton, M.C., made it a famous rest and recreation centre. In 1920, he founded a similar centre in London, also known as Toc H, which developed into an interdenominational association for Christian social service. *See* PIP EMMA.

Tod. To be on one's tod. To be alone; a contraction of Tod Sloan in cockney rhyming slang. (Tod Sloan was a famous jockey).

Toddy. Properly the juice obtained by tapping certain palms, fermented so as to become intoxicating (Hindu *tadi*; from *tar*, a palm). It is also applied to a beverage compounded of spirits, hot water, and sugar, a kind of PUNCH.

Toe. From top to toe. From head to foot.

To toe the line. To submit to discipline or regulations, to come into line with the rest. In foot races the runners are made to assemble with toes up to the start line.

To tread on someone'e toes. To upset, to offend; to vex or annoy.

To turn up one's toes. To die.

Tofana. *See* AQUA TOFANA.

Toga. The distinctive public garb of the Roman citizen consisting of a single semicircular piece of white woollen cloth worn in a flowing fashion round the shoulders and body. The Romans were hence the *Gens togata*, the "togaed people". It was also worn by freedwomen and prostitutes. Respectable women wore the *stola*. *Cp.* GALLIA BRACATA; GENS BRACATA; PALLIUM.

Toga candida. A new toga whitened with chalk, worn by candidates for public office when they appeared before the people.

Toga picta. The toga embroidered with golden stars that was worn by the emperor on special occasions, by a victorious general at his "TRIUMPH", etc.

Toga prætexta. The toga bordered (*prætexta*) with purple that was worn by children, by those engaged in sacred rites, magistrates on duty, etc.

Toga virilis. The toga worn by men (*virilis*, manly), assumed at the age of 15.

Togs. Slang for clothes; hence *togged out in his best*, dressed in his best clothes; *toggery*, finery. The word may be connected with TOGA.

Token payment. A small payment made as a formal and binding acknowledgment of indebtedness. The word "token" is often used to describe some action or phrase used in lieu of—but acknowledging—a greater obligation.

Tokyo Rose. The name given by U.S. servicemen to a woman broadcaster of propaganda from Japan during World War II. Several U.S.A.-born Japanese (NISEI) girls were suspected of taking part in these broadcasts but only one was found guilty. *Cp.* LORD HAW-HAW.

Tolbooth, or **Tollbooth** (tōl′ booth). Originally a booth or stall where taxes were collected.

> And whanne Jesus passide fro thennis, he saw a
> man, Matheu bi name, sittingge in a tolbothe.
> WYCLIF, *Matt*, ix, 9.

In SCOTLAND, the term was applied to the town gaol, from the custom of confining offenders against the laws of a fair or market in the booth where market dues were collected.

Toledo (tô lē′ dō). A sword made at Toledo in Spain, which place, long before and after the MIDDLE AGES, was specially famous for them. *Cp.* ANDREA FERRARA; BILBO.

> I give him three years and a day to match my
> Toledo,
> And then we'll fight like dragons.
> MASSINGER: *The Maid of Honour*, II, ii.

Tolosa (to lō′ sà). **He has got gold of Tolosa**. *See under* GOLD.

Tolpuddle Martyrs. Six agricultural labourers of Tolpuddle, Dorset, who formed a TRADE UNION to resist wage cuts. They were sentenced to seven years' transportation to Australia in 1834 on a concocted charge of administering illegal oaths. After continuous protests they were pardoned in 1836.

Tom. Tommy. Short for *Thomas*; used for the male of certain animals (especially the cat), and generically, like JACK, for a man. It sometimes has a somewhat contemptuous implication, as in TOM O'BEDLAM, TOM-FOOL.

> The man that hails you Tom or Jack,
> And proves by thumps upon your back
> How he esteems your merit,
> Is such a friend, that one had need
> Be very much his friend indeed
> To pardon or to bear it.
> COWPER: *Friendship, 169*.

Great Tom of Lincoln. A bell at Lincoln Cathedral weighing 5 tons 12 cwt.

Great Tom of Oxford. A bell in TOM GATE Tower, Oxford, tolled every night. It weighs 7 tons 12 cwt.

Long Tom. A familiar term for any gun of great length; especially the naval 4.7s used on land in the South African War (1899–1902). A brush for painting, on a long handle of the broomstick variety, is also called a long tom.

Old Tom. A specially potent gin. The story goes that a Thomas Norris, employed in Messrs. Hodges' distillery, opened a GIN-PALACE in Great Russell Street, COVENT GARDEN, in the late 18th century, and called the gin concocted by Thomas Chamberlain, one of the firm of Hodges, "Old Tom", in compliment to his former master.

Tom and Jerry. Types of roystering young men about town; from Pierce Egan's *Life in London; or, The Day and Night Scenes of Jerry Hawthorn, Esq., and his Elegant Friend Corinthian Tom* (1821). *Cp.* JERRY-SHOP.

Also a hot, spiced drink made from eggs, sugar, rum, cinnamon, etc.

Tom Collins. *See* JOHN COLLINS.

Tom, Dick and Harry. A Victorian term for the "MAN IN THE STREET", more particularly persons of no note; persons unworthy of notice. BROWN, JONES AND ROBINSON are for other men; they are the vulgar rich, who give themselves airs, especially abroad, and look with scorn on all foreign manners and customs which differ from their own.

Tom Fool. A clumsy, witless fool, fond of stupid practical jokes; hence *tom-foolery*.

Tom Gate. The great gate of Christ Church, Oxford, begun by Wolsey and completed (1682) by Wren. In its tower is GREAT TOM (*see above*).

Tom Long. Any lazy, dilatory man. *To be kept waiting for Tom Long* is to be kept hanging about for a wearisome time.

Tom Noddy. A puffing, fuming, stupid creature.

Tom o'Bedlam. A mendicant who levies charity on the plea of insanity. In the 16th and 17th centuries many harmless inmates of BEDLAM were let out to beg and such a beggar was called an ABRAM-MAN.

One of the greatest of Elizabethan anonymous poems is called *Tom of Bedlam's Song*.

Tom Quad. The great quadrangle of Christ Church, Oxford.

Tom Thumb. Any dwarfish or insignificant person is so called from the tiny hero of the old nursery tale, popular in the 16th century. *The History of Tom Thumb* was published by Richard Johnson in 1621, and there was a similar tale by Perrault, *Le Petit Poucet*, 1697.

Fielding wrote a burlesque (acted 1730) entitled *Tom Thumb the Great*. The American dwarf Charles Sherwood Stratton (1838–1883) was called "General Tom Thumb" when first exhibited by Phineas T. Barnum. The "General" was then under 5 years of age and less than 24 inches in height but eventually grew to 40 inches. When at London he was summoned to Buckingham Palace by Queen Victoria and subsequently visited King Louis Philippe in France. He married another American dwarf, Lavinia Warren, in 1863. *See also* BOAST OF ENGLAND.

Tom Tiddler's Ground. A place where it is easy to pick up a fortune or make a place in the world for oneself; from the old children's game in which a base-keeper, who is called *Tom Tiddler*, tries to keep the other children who sing:

> Here we are on Tom Tiddler's ground
> Picking up gold and silver,

from crossing the boundary into his base.

Tom Tiler, or **Tyler.** A hen-pecked husband.

Tom's. A noted COFFEE-house of the late 18th century, that was in existence in Russell Street, COVENT GARDEN, as late as 1865. It was owned and named after Thomas West; and here in 1764 was founded *Tom's Club*, which included most of the literary and social Notabilities of the time.

Uncle Tom. *See* UNCLE TOM'S CABIN under UNCLE.

Tomboy. A romping girl. The word was also used of a loose or immodest woman, whence the slang, *Tom*, applied to a prostitute.

> A lady
> So fair...to be partner'd
> With tomboys.
> SHAKESPEARE: *Cymbeline*, I, vi.

Tommy, or **Tommy Atkins.** A British army private soldier as a JACK TAR is a British sailor. From 1815 and throughout the 19th century *Thomas Atkins* was the name used in the specimen form, accompanying the official manual issued to all army recruits, supplied to show them how their own form requiring details of name, age, date of enlistment, etc., should be filled in.

> O' it's Tommy this an' Tommy that, an' Tommy, go away";
> But it's "Thank you, Mister Atkins", when the band begins to play.
> KIPLING: *Tommy* (*Barrack Room Ballads*, 1892).

In the early 19th century *tommy* was also a soldier's term for under-baked sticky bread.

Tommy bar. This is a small bar of rounded metal used for inserting into and turning box-spanners and similar tools.

Tommy-cooker. A small individual stove using solid fuel invented in the time of World War I and issued to Allied troops in World War II. It was also the name given by the Germans to the Sherman tank, which caught fire very easily when hit.

Tommy Dodd. The "odd" man who, in tossing up, either wins or loses according to agreement with this confederate.

To go to Tommy Dodd for drinks, etc., is to toss "odd man out", the odd man dropping out until there are only two left, who toss for who pays.

Tommy gun. A Thompson short-barrelled sub-machine-gun.

Tommy rot. Utter nonsense, rubbish; a COCK AND BULL STORY.

Tommy shop. A shop where vouchers, given by an employer in lieu of money, can be exchanged for goods; commonly run by large employers of labour before the TRUCK SYSTEM was made illegal. *Tommy* here is a slang term for bread, provisions, etc.

Tomahawk (tom' à hawk). The war axe of the North American Indians, prehistorically made of stone or deer-horn, but after the coming of the white man, of iron or steel with a wooden handle. Sometimes the blunt end of the head was hollowed into a pipe-bowl, the handle being bored to form a stem. *See* BURY THE HATCHET.

Tongue. Confusion of tongues. According to the BIBLE (*Gen*. xi, 1–9), the people of the earth originally spoke one language and lived together. They built a city and a tower as a rallying point, but God, seeing this as the beginning of ambition, "did confound the language of all the earth" and scattered them abroad and hence the town was called BABEL. This was taken as an explanation of the diversity of languages and the dispersal of mankind and the origin of the name BABYLON.

The gift of tongues. Command of foreign languages; also the power claimed by the early church and by some later mystics (as the IRVINGITES) of conversing in and understanding unknown tongues (from the miracle at PENTECOST—*Acts* ii, 4, the implications of which are obscure).

One's mother tongue. One's native language.

The Three Tongues. *See under* THREE.

The tongue of the trump. The spokesman or leader of a party. The trump here is the Jew's HARP and the tongue is its most important part.

> The tongue o' the trump to them a'.
> BURNS: *Mr. Heron's Election Ballads*, ii, 10.

A lick with the rough side of the tongue. A severe reprimand, a good slating.

To bite one's tongue. To repress one's speech, to remain silent under provocation.

To find one's tongue. To speak after recovery from initial shyness.

To give someone the length of one's tongue. To tell him in unmeasured language what you really think of him.

To give tongue. Properly used of a dog barking when on the scent; hence sometimes applied to people. Thus POLONIUS says to his son:

> Give thy thoughts no tongue,
> Nor any unproportioned thought his act.
> SHAKESPEARE: *Hamlet*, I, iii.

To have a long tongue. To be talkative or indiscreet in one's utterance.

To have something on the tip of one's

tongue. To be just about to utter it or to have it on the verge of one's memory but escaping utterance.

To hold one's tongue. To keep silent when one might speak; to keep a secret.

To lose one's tongue. To become tongue-tied or speechless through shyness, fear, etc.

To speak with one's tongue in one's cheek. Insincerely; saying one thing and meaning another.

To wag one's tongue. To talk continuously or indiscreetly.

You've got a tongue in your head (or **mouth**). Why did you not speak or say something at the time and miss the opportunity? It is no good complaining now.

Tonic Sol-fa. A system of musical notation and sight singing in which diatonic scales are written always in one way (the keynote being indicated), the tones being represented by syllables or initials, and time and accents by dashes and colons. *Tonic* is a musical term denoting pertaining to or founded on the keynote; *sol* and *fa* are two of the ARETINIAN SYLLABLES. *See also* DOH; GAMUT.

The system was developed about 1850 by the Rev. John Curwen (1816–1860), a CONGREGATIONALIST minister who made use of the earlier work of Miss Sarah Ann Glover (1785–1867).

Tonnage or **Tunnage.** From the 12th century English imports of Bordeaux wine increased steadily and the ships carried it in huge casks or *tuns* containing 252 gallons, occupying some 60 cubic feet in the holds. In due course this became the unit of measurement of the stowage or tonnage of a ship.

Nowadays tonnage is either *Displacement Tonnage*—the weight of water displaced by the ship; *Gross Tonnage*—the internal capacity of the vessel in tons of 100 cubic feet, *Net* or *Register Tonnage* which is essentially its carrying capacity as recorded in Lloyd's Register (now independent of LLOYD'S).

Tonnage and Poundage. Customs duties levied from the early years of the 14th century and granted to the sovereign by PARLIAMENT from 1373 until their abolition in 1787 (except during the reign of Charles I when they were levied without Parliamentary consent). *Tonnage* came to be fixed at 3 shillings on a cask or *tun* of wine and *Poundage* a 5% duty on all imports and exports.

Tonquin Bean. *See* MISNOMERS.

Tonsure (Lat. *tonsura*, a shearing). The shaving of part of the head among CATHOLIC clergy became customary in the 6th and 7th centuries as a mark of the clerical state. It is not retained in such countries as Britain and the U.S.A. where it is not in accordance with custom. The western form of tonsure leaving a circle of hair around the head is supposed to symbolize the CROWN OF THORNS. The CELTIC tonsure consisted of shaving off all the hair in front of a line extending over the head from ear to ear. In the East the whole head was shorn. The modern Roman Catholic tonsure varies among the different Orders and that of the secular clergy is a small circle on the crown of the head.

Tontine (ton' tēn). A form of annuity shared by several subscribers, in which the shares of those who die are added to the holdings of the survivors till the last survivor inherits all. So named from Lorenzo Tonti, a Neopolitan banker who introduced the system into France in 1653. In 1765 the HOUSE OF COMMONS raised £300,000 by way of tontine annuities at 3 per cent; and as late as 1871 the *Daily News* announced a proposed tontine to raise £650,000 to purchase the Alexandra Palace and 100 acres of land (*see* ALLY PALLY).

Tool. To tool a coach. To drive; generally applied to a gentleman who undertook stage-coach driving for his own amusement. *Tool* here is a fanciful application implying the use of skill.

Tooley Street. A corruption of St. Olaf—*i.e.* 'T-olaf, Tolay, Tooley. Similarly, Sise Lane is St. Osyth's Lane.

The three tailors of Tooley Street. *See under* TAILOR.

Toom Tabard. (Scot. empty jacket). A NICKNAME given to John Baliol (1249—1315), because of his poor spirit, and sleeveless appointment to the throne of Scotland. The honour was an "empty jacket", which he enjoyed only from 1292 to 1296. He died in Normandy.

Tooth, Teeth. Milk teeth. A child's first set of teeth.

By the skin of one's teeth. *See* SKIN.

From the teeth outwards. Merely talk; insincerity, not from the heart. An archaic expression.

He has cut his eye-teeth. He is "wide awake"; he has acquired wordly wisdom, is quite sophisticated. The eye-teeth are cut late, the first set about 16 months, the second set at 12 years. *Cp.* WISDOM TEETH under WISDOM.

His teeth are drawn. His power of doing mischief is taken from him. The phrase comes from the fable of the LION in love, who consented to have his teeth drawn and his claws cut, in order that a fair damsel might marry him. When this was done the girl's father fell on the lion and slew him.

In spite of his teeth. In opposition to his

settled purpose or resolution; even though he snarl and show his teeth like an angry dog. *Cp.* WORTH A JEW'S EYE *under* JEW.

> In despite of the teeth of all the rhyme and reason.
> SHAKESPEARE: *Merry Wives of Windsor*, V, iv.

In the teeth of the wind. With the wind dead against one, blowing in or against one's teeth.

> To strive with all the tempest in my teeth.
> POPE: *Epistles of Horace*, II, ii.

To cast into one's teeth. To utter reproaches; to throw it back at him.

> All his faults observed,
> Set in a note-book, learned, and conned by rote,
> To cast into my teeth.
> SHAKESPEARE: *Julius Cæsar*, IV, iii.

To draw one's eye-teeth. To take the conceit out of a person; to fleece without mercy.

To get one's teeth into something. To get to grips with it, to set to work with energy and determination.

To have a sweet tooth. To be addicted to sweet things.

To lie in one's teeth. To lie flagrantly.

To put teeth into. Said of a law regulation, etc., when steps are taken to make it effective.

To set one's teeth on edge. *See under* EDGE.

To show one's teeth. To adopt a menacing tone or attitude; as a dog shows its teeth when it snarls.

To take the bit between one's teeth. *See* BIT.

With tooth and nail. In right good earnest, with one's utmost power; as though biting and scratching.

Tooth and egg. An obsolete corruption of *tutenag* (from Arab. *tutiya*), an alloy rich in zinc, coming from the East Indies, much used for the lining of tea chests.

Top. *See also* MIZZENTOP.

The Big Top. The great circus tent in which the main performance takes place.

Can you top that? (U.S.A.) Can you beat or surpass that, especially in the telling of outlandish stories.

Out of the top drawer. *See under* DRAWER.

The top o'the morning to ye! A cheery greeting on a fine day, especially in IRELAND. It is about the same as, "The best of everything to you!"

To be on top of the world. Said of the feeling of elation experienced when one is in the best of care-free good health and when all one's affairs are flourishing.

To blow one's top. To lose one's temper excessively; to lose all self-control.

To go over the top. To take the final plunge. A phrase from the trench warfare of World War I, when, at ZERO HOUR, troops climbed over the parapet of the front-line trenches to advance across NO-MAN'S LAND to attack the enemy front line.

To sleep like a top. *See under* SLEEP.

Top dog. The one who by skill, personality or violence obtains the mastery, as the dog who is on top of his adversary in a fight.

Top-heavy. Liable to tip over because the centre of gravity is too high; intoxicated.

Top sawyer. A first-rate fellow, a distinguished man. Literally, the sawyer who works the upper handle in a sawpit; hence one who holds a superior position.

Top secret. Service or governmental information about which the greatest secrecy is to be observed. *Cp.* HUSH-HUSH.

Topping out. Traditional drinking ceremony when the framework of a building is completed.

Topham. Take him, Topham. Catch him if you can; lay hold of him, TIPSTAFF. Topham was the BLACK ROD of the HOUSE OF COMMONS in the reign of Charles II, very active in apprehending suspects during the supposed conspiracy revealed by Titus Oates. "Take him, Topham", became a proverbial saying of the time.

Tophet (tō' fet). The valley of the children of Hinnom through which children were made "to pass through the fire of MOLECH" (II *Kings* xxiii, 10). Isaiah (xxx, 31), in prophesying the destruction of the Assyrians, foretold that their king would be destroyed by fire in Tophet. It is a loathsome place associated with horror and defilement, a place of human sacrifice, but its location is a matter of surmise. The name is taken as symbolical of HELL and it may mean "a place to be spat upon" or "the place of burning".

> The pleasant valley of Hinnom, Tophet thence
> And black Gehenna call'd the Type of Hell.
> MILTON: *Paradise Lost*, I, 404.

Toplady Ring. A ring set with stones in the form of the pips on the ten of diamonds; named after Augustus Montague Toplady in allusion to the story of his beginning to write the ROCK OF AGES on this playing card.

Topsy. The little slave girl in Harriet Beecher Stowe's UNCLE TOM'S CABIN (1852); chiefly remembered because when asked by "Aunt Ophelia" about her parents she maintained that she had neither father nor mother, her solution of her existence being, "I 'spect I grow'd."

Topsy-turvy. Upside down; probably *top* with *so* and obsolete *terve*, connected with O.E. *tearflian*, to turn or roll over. SHAKESPEARE says (*Henry IV, Pt. I*, iv, i), "Turn it topsy-turvy down."

Torah (tôr' à) (Heb., the law). The Jewish term for the PENTATEUCH which contains the Mosaic Law; the revealed will of God as contained in the Jewish SCRIPTURES.

Torch. The code-name for the Allied plan for the North African landings which began on 8 November 1942.

To carry the torch (U.S.A.). To suffer unrequited love, the torch being the torch of love. *A torch singer* is a female who sings sentimental ditties of such love.

To hand on the torch. To maintain and transmit knowledge, learning, etc., to the succeeding generation. The allusion is to the runners at ancient Greek festivals passing on the torch in relays.

Torpids. The name given to the LENT boat races at Oxford, between the second crews of colleges. A second-class racing eight is called a *torpid*, at Cambridge a *slogger*.

> The torpid being filled with the refuse of the rowing men—generallly awkward or very young oarsmen.
> T. HUGHES: *Tom Brown at Oxford*, II, iv (1861).

Torricelli. An Italian physicist and mathematician (1608–1647), noted for his explanation of the rise of mercury in a common barometer. Galileo explained the phenomenon by the IPSE DIXIT of "Nature abhors a vacuum."

Torso. A statue or human body devoid of head and limbs. The word is Ital. for a trunk or stalk, from Lat. *thyrsus*, the attribute of BACCHUS.

The Torso Belvedere, the famous torso of HERCULES in the VATICAN, was discovered in the 15th century. It is said that MICHAELANGELO greatly admired it.

Tortoise. This animal is frequently taken as the type of plodding persistence—"slow but sure".

In Hindu myth, the tortoise Chukwa supports the ELEPHANT Maha-pudma, which in its turn supports the world.

The name *tortoise* (Lat. *testudo*) is also given to the ancient Roman protective shelter formed by soldiers with shields overlapping above their heads when attacking a fort.

Achilles and the tortoise. *See under* ACHILLES.

The hare and the tortoise. *See under* HARE.

Tory (tôr'i) (Irish *toiridhe, toruidhe*, a pursuer, plunderer). The name applied in the 17th century to Irish ROMAN CATHOLIC outlaws and bandits who harassed the English in IRELAND. In the reign of Charles II, the name came to be applied as an abusive term to the supporters of the Crown and its prerogatives at the time of the struggle over the Exclusion Bills. As supporters of the CHURCH OF ENGLAND they opposed NONCONFORMIST and Roman Catholic alike, but most of them acquiesced in the Revolution of 1688. Tory extremists remained JACOBITES at the time of the Hanoverian succession which led to a WHIG monopoly of political power during the reign of George I and George II, after which they regained office under Pitt the Younger and remained dominant throughout the period of the French Revolutionary and Napoleonic Wars. From about 1830, the Tory party under the leadership of Peel came to be called CONSERVATIVE, the older name being associated with reaction. Nowadays *Tory* and *Conservative* are essentially interchangeable terms. *Cp.* DIEHARD; LIBERAL; UNIONIST.

Toss. A toss up. An even chance; a matter of heads or tails as in the spinning of a coin.

Totem (tō' tem). A North American Indian (Algonkian) word for some natural object, usually an animal, taken as the EMBLEM of a person or CLAN on account of a supposed relationship. Persons bearing the same totem were not allowed to marry, thus totemism prevented intermarriage between near relations. The animal borne as one's totem must neither be killed nor eaten. Totemism is common among primitive peoples.

Totem pole. The post standing before a dwelling on which grotesque and frequently brilliantly coloured representations of the TOTEM were carved or hung. It is often of great size, and sometimes so broad at the base that an archway is cut through it.

Touch. A soft touch. *See under* SOFT.

Not to touch it with a barge pole. Not to have anything to do with it under any circumstances, to avoid it at all costs, the pole used for propelling a barge being a very lengthy one.

To be in, or **keep in touch.** To maintain contact with someone either in person, or by correspondence, etc.

To touch wood. *See under* WOOD.

Touch and go. A very narrow escape; a METAPHOR derived, perhaps, from driving when the wheel of one vehicle touches that of another passing vehicle without doing mischief. It was a touch, but neither vehicle was stopped, each could go on.

Touch down. In Rugby and American football, to score by touching the ball on the ground within a certain defined area behind the opponent's goal posts.

When an aircraft lands it is said to *touch down*.

Touch pieces. *See* KING'S EVIL.

Touché (too' shā) (Fr., touched). An acknowledgment of a telling remark or rejoinder by one's opponent in an argument. It is the fencing term denoting a hit or touch.

Touchstone. A dark, flinty schist, jasper, or basanite (the *Lapis Lydius* of the ancients); so called because GOLD was assayed by comparing the streak made on it by the sample of gold with those made by *touch-needles* of known gold content, after all the streaks had been treated with nitric acid. The needles were made of varying proportions of gold and SILVER, gold and copper, or of all three metals. Hence the use of *touchstone* as any criterion or standard.

Ovid (*Metamorphoses*, Bk. II, xi) tells us that Battus saw MERCURY steal APOLLO'S oxen, and Mercury gave him a cow to secure his silence, but, being distrustful of the man, changed himself into a peasant, and offered him a cow and an ox if he would tell him where he got the cow. Battus, caught in the trap, told the secret, and Mercury changed him into a touchstone.

> Men have a touchstone whereby to try gold; but gold is the touchstone whereby to try men.
> FULLER: *The Holy State and the Profane State* (*The Good Judge*).

Touchstone is the name given to the clown in SHAKESPEARE'S *As You Like It*.

Tour. The Grand Tour. In the 17th, 18th, and early 19th centuries it was the custom of families of rank and substance to finish their sons' education by sending them under the guardianship of a tutor or BEAR-LEADER on a tour through France, Switzerland, Italy, and home through western Germany. This was known as the Grand Tour and sometimes a couple of years or more were devoted to it. The young men were supposed to study the history, language, etc., of each country they visited and such travel was a distinguishing mark between the great landowners and the ordinary squire.

Tour de force (Fr.). A feat of strength or skill.

Tournament (O.Fr. *torneiement*; from Lat. *tornare*, to turn). In the days of CHIVALRY, a martial sport or contest among knights of jousting or tilting; the chief art being to manœuvre or turn your horse away to avoid the adversary's blow. Usually blunted weapons were used and the contests came to be associated with elaborate pageantry. *See* QUINTAIN.

The Eglinton Tournament. A revival or replica of a mediæval tournament at Eglinton Castle, Ayrshire, in August 1839. Lady Seymour was made Queen of Love and Beauty and the ladies wore fashions of the 14th and 15th centuries. The Marquess of Londonderry was King of the Tournament and society men practised the role of KNIGHT, among them Prince Louis Napoleon (afterward NAPOLEON III). The affair is substantially depicted in Disraeli's *Endymion*.

> Then on a barded Arab, herself dressed in cloth of gold parti-coloured with violet and crimson, came, amid tremendous cheering, the Queen of Beauty herself. Twelve attendants bore aloft a silken canopy, which did not conceal from the enraptured multitude the lustre of her matchless loveliness.
> *Endymion*, ch. lix.

The tournament of Tottenham. A comic romance, given in PERCY'S RELIQUES. A number of clowns are introduced, practising warlike games, and making vows like KNIGHTS of high degree. They tilt on cart-horses, fight with plough-shares and flails, and wear for armour wooden bowls and saucepan-lids.

Tours (toor). Geoffrey of Monmouth (*Historia Britonum*, xvi) says that BRUTUS had a nephew called Turonus who slew 600 men before being overwhelmed by the Gauls. "From him the city of Tours derived its name, because he was buried there." The name, in fact, derives from the Turones, a people of Gallia Lugdunensis.

Tout ensemble (too ton sombl) (Fr.). The whole massed together; the general effect.

Tower, The. Specifically, the Tower of LONDON the oldest part of which is the great keep known as the WHITE TOWER (*see below*) built by WILLIAM THE CONQUEROR, traditionally on the site of a fort erected by Julius CÆSAR.

> Ye Towers of Julius, London's lasting shame,
> With many a foul and midnight murther fed.
> GRAY: *The Bard*.

As well as a fortress, it has a special place in English history, both as a royal residence down to the reign of James I, and as a state prison. It has also housed the Royal MINT (until 1810), a menagerie and the Public Records, and is still the home of the Crown Jewels. Among those buried in its chapel are Protector Somerset, the Duke of Northumberland, Anne Boleyn, Katharine Howard, Lord Guildford Dudley, Lady Jane Grey, the Duke of Monmouth, and Lords Kilmarnock, Balmerino, and Lovat (supporters of the FORTY-FIVE REBELLION). State prisoners confined there range from Ralf Flambard to Sir Walter Ralegh, Sir Roger Casement, and Rudolf Hess. W. Harrison Ainsworth's novel *The Tower of London* was first published in 1840. *See also* BEEFEATERS; CEREMONY OF THE KEYS *under* KEY; TRAITORS' GATE.

The Bloody Tower. Built as the *Garden Tower*, this addition to the TOWER of London dates from the reign of Richard I (1377–1399). It had won its present name b

1597 from the supposition that it witnessed the murder of the PRINCES IN THE TOWER. It subsequently housed such famous prisoners as Sir Walter Ralegh, Archbishop Laud and Judge Jeffreys.

Leaning Tower. *See under* LEANING.

The Princes in the Tower. The boy King Edward V and his younger brother Richard, Duke of York, who were lodged in the TOWER (May—June 1483), after which their uncle Richard, Duke of Gloucester, assumed the CROWN as Richard III. The princes disappeared at this time and are generally presumed to have been murdered by their uncle, but there is no conclusive evidence. Bones found during excavations near the WHITE TOWER in 1674 were transferred to Westminster Abbey. In 1933, experts proclaimed them to be bones of children of ages corresponding to those of the princes.

Tower Liberty. The Tower of London with the fortifications and Tower Hill. This formed part of the ancient demesne of the Crown, with jurisdiction and privileges distinct from and independent of the CITY. Its bounds are still beaten triennially by choirboys and children after a service in the Royal Chapel of St. Peter ad Vincula. Governor, Chaplain, Warders and residents accompany them and at each of the 31 boundary stones the Chaplain exclaims, "Cursed is he who removeth his neighbours' landmark." The Chief Warder then says: "Whack it, boys, whack it."

The White Tower. The approximately square keep of the Tower of London, the oldest part of the fortress begun by WILLIAM THE CONQUEROR. There is a turret at each corner and the sides are over 100 ft. wide, the walls being 15 ft. thick in the lower parts and 11 ft. thick in the upper storey. It has housed many notable prisoners. *See also* THE PRINCES IN THE TOWER *above*.

Tower of Babel. *See* BABEL; CONFUSION OF TONGUES *under* TONGUE.

Towers of Silence. *See under* SILENCE.

Tower pound. The legal pound of 5,400 grains ($11\frac{1}{4}$ oz. TROY WEIGHT), used in England until the adoption of the Troy pound in 1526. So called from the standard pound kept in the TOWER of London. *See* PENNYWEIGHT.

Town (O.E. *tun*, Ger. *Zaun*, a hedge or enclosure). Originally a group of dwellings surrounded by a hedge or wall.

Town and Gown. The two sections of a university town, composed of those not connected with the university and those who are members of it; hence *a town and gown row*, a collision or brawl between the students and non-gownsmen. *See* PHILISTINES.

> Here another Town and Gown party had fought their way from the Corn-market; and the Gown getting considerably the worse of the conflict, had taken refuge within Exeter College by the express order of the Senior Proctor, The Rev. Thomas Tozer, more familiarly known as "old Towser".
> "CUTHBERT BEDE": *The Adventures of Mr. Verdant Green*, II, iv.

Town bull. The parish bull, kept for breeding purposes.

> And so, brother Toby, this poor Bull of mine…might have been driven into Doctors' Commons and lost his character—which to a Town Bull, brother Toby, is the very same thing as his life.
> STERNE: *Tristram Shandy*, IX, xxxiii.

Town crier, also called a bellman, a town official, usually in a robe, ringing a bell and crying OYEZ! OYEZ! to attract attention to his public announcements and proclamations. The earlier bellman was a night watchman whose duty was to parade the streets at night and call out the hours, etc.

Going to town. Letting oneself go in a lighthearted fashion. To go to town on something is to GO THE WHOLE HOG (*see under* HOG), to exploit the situation to the full. The expression is of American origin, probably originating among those in the backwoods who went to town for a spree.

A man about town. *See under* MAN.

Town is empty. The season is over; SOCIETY has left town for the country. *See* LONDON SEASON *under* SEASON.

A woman of the town. A prostitute.

Toyshop of Europe, The. So Burke called Birmingham. Here the word "toy" does not refer to playthings for children, but to trinkets, knick-knacks, and similar articles.

Trachtenberg System. A system of speedy mathematical calculations based upon simple counting according to prescribed keys or formulæ which need to be memorized. There is no division or multiplication as such, and complicated calculations can be more easily and rapidly handled than by normal processes. The system was devised by Jakow Trachtenberg (b. 1888) during his seven long years in a NAZI concentration camp. He was born at Odessa and trained as an engineer and became a refugee in German after the Russian Revolution. *See* CALCULATOR.

Tractarians. *See* OXFORD MOVEMENT.

Tracy. All the Tracys have the wind in their faces. Those who do wrong will always meet with punishment. William de Tracy was the most active of the four KNIGHTS who slew Thomas à Becket, and for this misdeed all who bore the name were saddled by the Church with this ban:

> Wherever by the sea or land they go

For ever the wind in their face shall blow.

Trade. The Trade. Usually the liquor trade, especially those engaged in brewing and distilling; also applied to those engaged in the particular trade under consideration.

The Balance of Trade. *See under* BALANCE.

Board of Trade. A government department concerned with the various aspects of trade, first set up in 1786. It developed from the various PRIVY COUNCIL Committees of Trade appointed from 1622 onwards which were then much concerned with colonial matters. In 1974 most of its functions were absorbed by the Department of Trade and Industry.

Free Trade. *See under* FREE.

Trade board. A committee representing workers and management set up under Act of PARLIAMENT to regulate conditions of labour in a particular industry.

Trade dollar. A United States silver DOLLAR formerly coined specially for Oriental trade. It weighed 420 gr., instead of the 412.5 gr. of the ordinary dollar, and has not been coined since 1887.

Trade mark. The name or distinctive device for an article made for sale indicating that it was made by the holder of that device. Trade marks are usually registered and protected by law.

Trade Union. An association of employees formed for the promotion and protection of their working conditions, wages, etc., by collective bargaining, and sometimes also acting as Friendly Societies to their members. Nowadays they constitute powerful pressure groups. They are essentially a byproduct of the INDUSTRIAL REVOLUTION. *Cp.* TOLPUDDLE MARTYRS.

Trade winds. Winds that *blow trade, i.e.* regularly in one track or direction (Low Ger. *Trade*, track). In the Northern Hemisphere they blow from the *northeast*, and in the Southern Hemisphere from the *southeast*, about 30 degrees each side of the Equator. In some places they blow six months in one direction, and six months in the opposite.

To blow trade. *See* TRADE WINDS *above*.

To trade something in. To hand over a part-worn article (*e.g.* a cooking stove or motor-car) in part payment for a new one.

To trade something off. To barter or exchange it; to sell it as a "JOB LOT".

To trade upon. To make use of so as to gain some advantage, as in making unscrupulous use of private knowledge, or using a personal affliction to arouse sympathy, other people's kindness and generosity, etc.

Trade follows the flag. Wherever the flag flies trade with the mother country develops and prospers; where the flag is established trade will grow up.

> Colonists did not follow the flag; they pushed forward into new fields from the centres that had first been annexed, and the flag had to follow them despite the reluctance of the Home Government to extend its territorial responsibilities.
> A. P. NEWTON: *A Hundred Years of the British Empire*, I.

Tragedy. Literally, a goat-song (Gr. *tragos*, goat; *ode*, song), though why so called is not clear. HORACE (*Ars Poetica*, 220) says, because the winner at choral competitions received a goat as a prize, but the explanation has no authority. *Cp.* COMEDY.

It was ARISTOTLE (in his *Poetics*) who said that tragedy should move one "by pity and terror":

> The plot ought to be so constructed that, even without the aid of the eye, he who hears the tale told will thrill with horror and melt to pity at what takes place.
> ARISTOTLE: *Poetics*, xix (*Butcher*).

The Father of Tragedy. A title given to ÆSCHYLUS (d. 456 B.C.), author of the Orestean trilogy and many other tragedies, and to Thespis. *See* THESPIANS.

Trahison des clercs (tra ēz ôn dā klâr) (Fr. the treason or treachery of the intellectuals.) The incursion of the intelligentsia, who should be concerned with the pursuit of truth and guided by abstract principle, into the field of partisan politics and propaganda.

Trail. To trail one's coat. *See under* COAT.

Train-bands. Locally-raised bodies of citizen soldiers or MILITIA of little military value, with the exception of those of London. They derived from an order of Elizabeth I (1573) that a "convenient number" in every county were to be organized in bands and trained. They were not willing to leave their districts and were seldom suitably trained.

> John Gilpin was a citizen
> Of credit and renown,
> A train-band captain eke was he
> Of famous London town.
> COWPER: *John Gilpin*.

Traitors' Gate. The old water gate under St. Thomas's Tower to the THAMES under which many state prisoners were brought to imprisonment or death in the TOWER of London. An old proverb says:

> A loyal heart may be landed at the Traitors' Gate.

Trajan (trā' jàn). Marcus Ulpius Trajanus, Roman Emperor (*c.* 53, 88–117), notable for his campaigns against the Dacians and Parthians, and for his buildings and public works.

Trajan's Arch. There are two arches

known by this name, commemorating the triumphs of Trajan. One, the finest ancient arch in existence, was erected in A.D. 114 over the APPIAN WAY at Benevento, and the other in 112 at Ancona. Both are of white marble.

Trajan's Column. *See under* COLUMN.

Trajan's Wall. A line of fortifications stretching across the Dobrudja from Czernavoda to the BLACK SEA.

Tram. The old "popular" derivation of this word from the name of Benjamin Outram, who ran vehicles on stone rails at Little Eaton, Derbyshire, in 1800, is discredited. The word is connected with Low Ger. *Traam*, a baulk or beam, and was applied as early as the 16th century to trucks used in coal mines, and run on long wooden beams as rails.

> Trams are a kind of sledge on which coals are brought from the place where they are hewn to the shaft. A tram has four wheels but a sledge is without wheels.
>
> BRAND: *History of Newcastle-upon-Tyne*, vol. II, p. 681 (1789).

Tramontana (tra mon ta' na). The north wind; so called by the Italians, because to them it comes from over the mountains (Lat. *trans*, across; *montem*, mountain).

Tramontane (tra mon' tān). Beyond the mountain, *i.e.* on the other side of the Alps from ROME; hence, barbarous, foreign; as a noun, a barbarian or foreigner. *See* ULTRA-MONTANE.

Transept. An architectural term (from the Lat. *trans*, across; *septum*, enclosure) for the transverse portion of any building lying across the main body of that building. The transept became common in ecclesiastical architecture in the MIDDLE AGES and almost universal in the GOTHIC period. The CROSS is often surmounted by a tower, spire, or dome. In a BASILICA church the transept is the transverse portion in front of the choir.

Transfiguration. The word applied to the miraculous transformation of Christ's appearance which occurred on a mountain where He was praying. It was witnessed by PETER, JAMES and JOHN and is celebrated on the 6th of August.

Translator-General. So Fuller, in his *Worthies* (1662), calls Philemon Holland (1552–1637), who translated works by Pliny, Livy, Plutarch, and a large number of other Greek and Latin classics.

Transmigration of Souls. An ancient belief concerning the transition of the soul after death to another body or substance, usually human or animal; also known as metempsychosis. BRAHMINS and Buddhists accept human descent into plants as well as animals, and the BUDDHA underwent 550 births in different forms. The ancient Egyptians held to a form of transmigration in which the soul could inhabit another form to allow temporary revisiting the earth. *See* PYTHAGORAS.

Transubstantiation (trăn sub stan shi ā'-shon). A change from one substance into another. Theologically, the change of the whole substance of the bread and wine in the EUCHARIST to the body and blood of Christ, only their outward form or ACCIDENTS remaining.

Trap. Slang for the mouth; also old slang for a policeman; **shut your trap,** be quiet.

Trappists. Properly, the CISTERCIANS of the French abbey at Soligny La Trappe (founded 1140) after their reform and reorganization in 1664. They were absorbed by the CISTERCIANS of the Strict Observance in 1892, to whom the name is now applied. They are noted for extreme austerity, their rule including absolute silence, a common dormitory, and no recreation.

Traps. Luggage; one's personal belongings, etc., as in *Leave your traps at the station*. *Traps* being short for *trappings*, bits of additional finery for decoration, especially the ornamental harness or caparison of a horse (Fr. *drap*, cloth).

Traskites. A sect of Puritan SABBATARIANS founded by John Trask, a Somerset man, about 1620. They believed that the law as laid down for the ancient Hebrews was to be taken literally and applied to themselves and all men. Trask was brought before the STAR CHAMBER and pilloried. He is said to have recanted later and to have become an ANTINOMIAN, and his followers became absorbed by the SEVENTH-DAY BAPTISTS.

Traveller's Joy (*Clematis vitalba*). A plant with rope-like stems found in hedgerows in southern England, the Midlands and Wales. It has greenish flowers with feathery fruit.

Travellers' Tales. Tall yarns; exaggerated stories of wonderful adventures and sights. Telling such tales used to be called *tipping one the traveller*.

Travelogue (trăv' ė log). A lecture or running commentary delivered to accompany a travel film.

Tre, Pol, Pen. *See* CORNISH NAMES.

Treacle properly means an antidote against the bite of wild beasts (Gr. *theriake*; from *ther*, a wild beast). The ancients gave the name to several sorts of antidotes, but ultimately it was applied chiefly to Venice treacle (*theriaca androchi*), a compound of some 64 drugs in honey.

Sir Thomas More speaks of "a most

strong treacle [*i.e.* antidote] against these venomous heresies". *See also* TREACLE BIBLE, *under* BIBLE, SOME SPECIALLY NAMED EDITIONS.

Tread. To tread on his corns. *See under* CORN.

To tread on someone's neck. To oppress or tyrannise over a person.

To tread the boards. To perform on the stage; to be an actor; the *boards* being the planks of the stage.

To tread the light fantastic. To dance.

> Come and trip it as ye go
> On the light fantastic toe.
>
> MILTON: *L'Allegro*.

Treason. Betrayal of a trust or of a person.

High treason is an act of treachery against the SOVEREIGN of the State, a violation of one's allegiance. **Petty treason** is the same against a subject, as the murder of a master by his servant. *See also* MISPRISION OF TREASON.

Treasure. These are my treasures; meaning the sick and the poor. So said St. LAWRENCE when the Roman prætor commanded him to deliver up his treasures. *See also* CORNELIA.

Treasure trove (O. Fr. *trove*, found). The term applied to coins and other valuables of GOLD or SILVER found in the ground or other place of concealment. Gold ornaments, etc., found in tombs where there is no purpose of concealment are not treasure trove. Treasure trove belongs to the Crown, but in practice the finder is usually given the market value of his find. A recent find is thus reported (*The Times*, 25 Sept. 1968):

> Mainly nobles, they are part of the "Fishpool Hoard" of 1,237 coins, which were found on a building site near Newstead Abbey in Nottinghamshire in March, 1966.
> The hoard, which is described by the British Museum as "the largest find of mediæval gold coins so far recorded in England and of quite exceptional importance," was declared to be treasure trove by a coroner's jury.

Treasury, Treasury Bills are a form of British government security issued in multiples of £1,000 and repayable in 3, 6, 9, or 12 months.

Treasury Bonds are for money borrowed for a number of years.

Treasury Notes were issued by the Treasury from 1924 to 1928 for £1 and 10*s*. Their place was taken by notes issued by the Bank of England. *See* BRADBURY.

Treasury of the Church, Treasury of Merits, or **Satisfactions.** The theological term for the superabundant store of merits and satisfactions of Christ which were beyond the needs of the salvation of the human race. To these are added the excess of merits and satisfactions of the B.V.M. and the SAINTS. It is by drawing on this treasury that the Church grants INDULGENCES.

Treat. To stand treat. To pay the expenses of some entertainment; especially to pay for drinks consumed by others.

Tree. For particulars of some famous and patriarchal trees *see under* OAK *and* YEW.

In the Natural History Museum, South Kensington, is the section of a *Sequoia gigantea* with 1,335 rings, representing that number of years, and the Jardin des Plantes at Paris has a similar section. There are yet older trees still in full life in the forests of America.

The CROSS on which Our Lord was crucified is frequently spoken of in hymns and poetry as *the tree*. *See Acts* v, 30, "... Jesus, whom ye slew and hanged on a tree'; and I *Pet*. ii, 24, "Who his own self bare our sins in his own body on the tree".

The gallows is also called *the tree*, or *the fatal tree*. *See* TYBURN TREE.

One proverb says, "If on the trees the leaves still hold, the coming winter will be cold," and another, "When caught by the tempest, wherever it be, if it lightens and thunders beware of a tree." *See also under* WOOD.

The Tree of Buddha, or **of Wisdom.** The BO-TREE.

The Tree of Diana. *See* PHILOSOPHER'S TREE.

The Tree of Knowledge. The tree which God planted, together with the *Tree of Life*, in the Garden of EDEN.

"But of the tree of the knowledge of good and evil, thou shalt not eat of it; for in the day that thou eatest thereof thou shalt surely die" (*Gen*. ii, 17). EVE partook of the forbidden fruit and gave some to ADAM; "And the Lord God said, Behold, the man is become as one of us, to know good and evil: and now, lest he put forth his hand, and take also of the tree of life, and eat, and live for ever" (*Gen*. iii, 22); and so the first man and the first woman were driven from the garden and the woes of mankind began.

The Tree of Liberty. A post or tree set up by the people, hung with flags and devices and crowned with a CAP OF LIBERTY. In the United States, poplars and other trees were planted during the War of Independence "as growing symbols of growing freedom". The JACOBINS in Paris planted their first trees of liberty in 1790, and used to decorate them with tri-coloured ribbons, circles to indicate unity, triangles to signify equality, and Caps of Liberty. Trees of liberty were also planted by the Italians in the revolution of 1848.

The Tree of Life. *See* TREE OF KNOWLEDGE.

The Tree of the Universe. YGGDRASIL.

At the top of the tree. At the highest position attainable in one's profession, calling, etc.

The tree is known by its fruit. One is judged by what one does, not by what one says. The saying is from *Matt.* xii, 33.

A tree must be bent while it is young. "You can't teach an old dog new tricks." (*See under* DOG). The Scots say, "Thraw the wand while it is green."

The treeness of the tree. The essential qualities that compose a tree; in the absence of which the tree would cease to be a tree. Hence, the absolute essentials of anything. The phrase is evidently modelled on Sterne's "Correggiosity of Correggio" (*Tristram Shandy*, III, xii).

Up a tree. In a difficulty, in a mess, nonplussed. An American phrase, from 'coon hunting. As soon as the 'coon is driven up a tree he is helpless.

It is said that Spurgeon used to exercise his students in extempore preaching, and that one of his young men, on reaching the desk and opening the note containing his text, read the single word "Zacchæus". He thought for a minute or two, and then delivered himself thus:

> Zacchæus was a little man, so am I; Zacchæus was up a tree, so am I; Zacchæus made haste and came down, and so do I.

You cannot judge of a tree by its bark. Don't go by appearances; an old proverb.

Tregeagle (Trē gā' gul). A kind of Cornish BLUEBEARD who sold his soul to the DEVIL and married and murdered numerous rich heiresses, and whose ghost haunts various parts of Cornwall. His allotted task is to bale out Dozmary Pool on Bodmin Moor with a leaky limpet shell. Hence *to bale out Dozmary Pool with a limpet shell* as a local expression for an impossibility. When the wintry blast howls over the moor, the people say it is Tregeagle roaring, and a child crying lustily is said to be "roaring worse than Tregeagle".

Trench fever. A remittent or relapsing fever affecting men living in trenches, dug-outs, etc., and transmitted by the excrement of lice. It first appeared in World War I, in the static warfare on the Western Front.

Trencher. Trencher cap. The MORTARBOARD worn at college; so called from the trenchered or split boards which form the top.

Trencher friends. Persons who cultivate the friendship of others for the sake of sitting at their board, and the good things they can get.

Trencher knight. A table KNIGHT, a suitor from CUPBOARD LOVE.

A good trencher-man. Usually said of a good eater, his opposite being a *poor trencher-man*. The trencher was the platter on which food was cut (Fr. *trancher*, to cut) or served, and the term *trencher-man* is sometimes applied to a cook or table companion.

He that waits for another's trencher eats many a late dinner. He who is dependent on others must wait, and wait, and wait, happy if after waiting he gets anything at all.

Trenchmore. A popular dance in the 16th and 17th centuries.

> Like one dancing the trenchmore he stamped up and downe the yard holding his hips in his hands.
> T. DELONEY: *The Gentle Craft*, Pt. II, ii (1597).

Trente et quarante. *See* ROUGE ET NOIR.

Tressure. A border within an heraldic shield and surrounding the bearings. The origin of the "double-tressure flory-counterflory gules" in the royal arms of SCOTLAND is traced by old heralds to the 9th century. They assert that CHARLEMAGNE granted it to King Achaius of Scotland in token of alliance, and as an assurance that "the lilies of France should be a defence to the lion of Scotland".

Trèves. The Holy Coat of Trèves. *See under* HOLY.

Tria Juncta in Uno (Lat., three combined in one). The motto of the Order of the BATH. It refers to the three classes of which the order consists, *viz.* Knights Grand Cross, Knights Commander, and Companions.

Triads. Three subjects more or less connected, treated as a group; as the Creation, Redemption, and Resurrection; BRAHMA, VISHNU, and SIVA; ALEXANDER THE GREAT, JULIUS CÆSAR, and NAPOLEON; Law, Physic, and Divinity.

The Welsh *Triads* are collections of historic facts, mythological traditions, moral maxims, or rules of poetry disposed in groups of three for mnemonic purposes.

The anciently established Chinese secret society known as "The Hung" or "The Society of Heaven and Earth", is also called "The Triad" from the trinity of HEAVEN, earth and man, and the use of the triangle in its ritual.

Trial at Bar. *See under* BAR.

Trial of the Pyx. *See under* PYX.

Tribune (trib' ūn). A chief magistrate and very powerful official among the ancient Romans. During the revolt of the plebs in 494 B.C. they appointed two tribunes as protectors against the PATRICIANS' oppression; later the number was increased to ten and their office put on a proper footing. They were personally inviolable, and could separately VETO measures and proceedings.

As a military title *tribune* denoted the commander of a cohort.

A tribune of the people. A democratic leader.

The Last of the Tribunes. *See under* LAST.

Trice. In a trice. In an instant; in a twinkling.

> To tell you what conceyte
> I had then in a tryce
> The matter were too nyse.
> SKELTON: *Phyllyp Sparowe*, 1130 (c. 1508).

It is probably *trice*, to haul, to tie up; the idea being "at a single tug". The older expression was *at a trice*.

> The howndis...pluckid downe deere all at a tryse.
> *Ipomydon*, 392 (c. 1440).

Tricolour. A FLAG of three broad stripes of different COLOURS, especially the national standard of France, blue, white, and red. The first flag of the Republicans was *green*. The tricolour was adopted 11 July 1789, when the people were disgusted with the king for dismissing Necker; the popular tale is that the insurgents had adopted for their flag the two colours, *red* and *blue* (the colour of the city of Paris), but that Lafayette persuaded them to add the BOURBON *white*, to show that they bore no hostility to the king.

Other tricolours are the flags of:

*Afghanistan, black, red, green; divided horizontally.
*Andorra, blue, yellow, red; vertically.
Belgium, black, yellow, red; vertically.
*Bolivia, red, yellow, green; horizontally.
*Bulgaria, white, green, red; horizontally.
*Cameroun, green, red, yellow; vertically.
*Cape Verde, vertical red in hoist, then horizontal yellow and green.
Chad, blue, yellow, red; vertically.
Colombia, yellow, blue, red; horizontally.
*Ecuador, yellow, blue, red; horizontally.
*Egypt, red, white, black; horizontally.
Ethiopia, green, yellow, red; horizontally.
Gabon, green, gold, blue; horizontally.
*German Democratic Republic, black, red, gold; horizontally.
German Federal Republic, black, red, gold; horizontally.
*Ghana, red, gold, green; horizontally.
Guinea, red, yellow, green; vertically.
*Guinea-Bissau, vertical red in hoist, then horizontal yellow and green.

Hungary, red, white, green; horizontally.
*India, saffron, white, green; horizontally.
*Iran, green, white, red; horizontally.
*Iraq, red, white, black; horizontally.
Ireland, green, white, orange; vertically.
Italy, green, white, red, vertically.
Ivory Coast, orange, white, green; vertically.
*Lesotho, white, blue, green, diagonally.
Luxembourg, red, white, blue; horizontally.
Malagasy Republic, vertical white in hoist, then horizontal red and green.
*Malawi, black, red, green; horizontally.
Mali, green, gold, red; vertically.
*Mexico, green, white, red; vertically.
Netherlands, red, white, blue; horizontally.
*Niger, orange, white, green; horizontally.
*Paraguay, red, white, blue; horizontally.
*Rumania, blue, yellow, red; vertically.
*Rwanda, red, yellow, green; vertically.
*Senegal, green, gold, red; vertically.
Sierra Leone, green, white, blue; horizontally.
*South Africa, orange, white, blue; horizontally.
*St Vincent, blue, yellow, green; vertically.
*Syria, red, white, black; horizontally.
*Venezuela, yellow, blue, red; horizontally.
*Yemen, red, white, black; horizontally.
*Yugoslavia, blue, white, red; horizontally.

Those bearing devices and emblems are marked thus*

Flags divided vertically have the colour given from the hoist outwards; for those divided horizontally the first colour given is at the top.

Tricoteuses (trē kot ĕrz'). Parisian women who, during the French Revolution, used to attend the meetings of the CONVENTION and, while they went on with their *tricotage* (knitting), encouraged the leaders in their bloodthirsty excesses. They gained for themselves the additional title, *Furies of the Guillotine*.

Trident. In Greek mythology, the three-pronged spear which POSEIDON (Roman NEPTUNE), god of the sea, bore as the symbol of his sovereignty. It has come to be regarded as the emblem of sea power and as such is borne by BRITANNIA. In gladiatorial combats in ROME, the trident was used by the RETIARIUS, whose skill lay in entangling his opponent in a net, and then despatching him with his trident.

Trigon (trī' gon). In ASTROLOGY, the junction of three signs. The ZODIAC is partitioned into four trigons, named respectively after the four elements: the *watery* trigon includes CANCER, SCORPIO, and Pisces; the *fiery*, ARIES, Leo, and SAGITTARIUS; the *earthly*, TAURUS, Virgo (*see* VIRGIN), and CAPRICORN; and the *airy*, GEMINI, LIBRA, and AQUARIUS.

Trilogy (tril′ ō ji). A group of three tragedies. Everyone in Greece who took part in the poetic contest had to produce a trilogy and a satiric drama. The only complete specimen extant contains the *Agamemnon*, the *Choephorœ*, and the *Eumenides*, by ÆSCHYLUS.

Hence, any literary, dramatic, or operatic work consisting of three self-contained parts but related to a central theme, such as SHAKESPEARE's *Henry VI* or Schiller's *Wallenstein*.

Trimalchio (tri măl′ ki ō). The vulgar, ostentatious, and fabulously rich parvenu of Petronius Arbiter's satirical romance, *Petronii Arbitri Satiricon* (1st century A.D.); the subject of allusion on account of the colossal and extravagant banquet (Dinner of Trimalchio) that he gave.

Trimmer. One who "runs with the hare and hunts with the hounds." (*See under* HARE.) George Savile, Marquis of Halifax (1633–1695), circulated a pamphlet in 1688 called *On the Character of a Trimmer* in which he defended his policy of "trimming" or avoiding party extremes and excesses. Owing to his frequent changes of side he was called **Halifax the Trimmer** although fundamentally he strove for a policy of moderation.

Trimurti (Sansk. *tri*, three; *mirti*, form). The Hindu TRIAD of BRAHMA, VISHNU, and SIVA as a unity, represented as one body with three heads. It bears only a forced resemblance to the idea of a TRINITY.

Trine (Lat. *trinus*, threefold). In ASTROLOGY, a PLANET distant from another one-third of the circle is said to be in trine; one-fourth, it is in square; one-sixth or two signs, it is in sextile; but when one-half distant, it is said to be "opposite".

> In sextile, square, and trine, and opposite
> Of noxious efficacy.
> MILTON: *Paradise Lost*, X, 659.

Planets distant from each other six signs or half a circle have opposite influences, and are therefore opposed to each other.

Trinitarians. Believers in the doctrine of the Holy TRINITY as distinct from UNITARIANS. Also, members of the Order of the Most Holy Trinity, or Mathurins, founded by St. John of Matha and St. Felix of Valois in 1198, concerned with the ransoming of captives and slaves and sometimes known as REDEMPTIONISTS. Their rule is an austere form of the AUGUSTINIAN.

Trinity, The. The three Persons in one God—God the Father, God the Son, and God the HOLY GHOST. *See also* CONFOUNDING THE PERSONS *under* PERSON; THREE.

> And in this Trinity none is afore, or after other; none is greater, or less than another; but the whole three Persons are co-eternal together: and co-equal.
> *The Athanasian Creed.*

The term TRIAD was first used by Theophilus of Antioch (*c.* 180) for this concept; the term *Trinity* was introduced by Tertullian about 217 in his treatise *Adversus Praxean.*

Trinity, or Trinity Sunday. The SUNDAY next after WHIT SUNDAY; widely observed as a feast in honour of the Trinity since the MIDDLE AGES, its general observance was enjoined by Pope John XXII in 1334. The EPISTLE and GOSPEL used in the CHURCH OF ENGLAND on this day are the same as those in the Lectionary of St. JEROME, and the Collect comes from the Sacramentary of St. GREGORY. The Church of England followed the Sarum Use in reckoning Sundays after Trinity, the ROMAN CATHOLIC CHURCH reckons them after PENTECOST (now adopted in the ALTERNATIVE SERVICES BOOK).

Trinity House, Corporation of. The chief pilotage authority of the UNITED KINGDOM controlling the lighting and marking of British coastal waters and certain maritime charities. Its headquarters are at Tower Hill, London, and its work is controlled by Elder Brethren consisting of nine master mariners and one senior officer of the Royal Navy. It developed from the gild of mariners and lodesmen of Deptford Strond, Kent, who obtained a charter from Henry VIII in 1512, and it acquired the Lord High Admiral's rights of buoyage and beaconage in 1594. Private lighthouses were acquired under an Act of 1836.

Trinity Term. The period of law sittings in England from the first TUESDAY after TRINITY SUNDAY to the end of JULY.

Trinobantes (trin ō băn′ tēz). A tribe, referred to in Cæsar's Gallic Wars, inhabiting the area of Essex and the southern part of Suffolk. The name was corrupted into *Trinovantes*. *See* TROYNOVANT.

Tripehound. In Australian slang, a DOG on a sheep station; in England the word has been adopted as a term of opprobrium.

Tripitaka (trip it′ a ka) (Pali, "the threefold basket"). The three classes into which the sacred writings of the Buddhists are divided—viz. the *Vinayapitaka* (Basket of Disciplinary Directions for the monks), the *Sutrapitaka* (Basket of Aphorisms or Discourses), and the *Abhidhammapitaka* (Basket of Metaphysics).

Tripos (trī' pos) (Lat. *tripus*, a three-footed stool). A Cambridge term, meaning the three honour classes in which candidates are grouped at the final examination, whether of Mathematics, Law, Theology, or Natural Science, etc. So called because the B.A. who disputed with the "Father" in the Philosophy School on ASH WEDNESDAY sat on a three-legged stool and was called "Mr. Tripos".

Triptolemus (trip tol' ē mŭs). A Greek hero and demi-god who was born at Eleusis and was taught the arts of agriculture by CERES. He established the ELEUSINIAN MYSTERIES and festivals.

Trisagion (tris ăg' i on) (Gr., thrice holy). A hymn in the liturgies of the Greek and Eastern Churches in which (after *Is*. v, 3) a threefold invocation to the Deity is the burden—"Holy God, Holy and Mighty, Holy and Immortal, have mercy on us."

The name is sometimes applied to Bishop Heber's hymn for Trinity Sunday—

Holy, Holy, Holy! Lord God Almighty,
Early in the morning our song shall rise to Thee;

which is more properly called the *Ter-Sanctus*.

Triskelion (tri skel' i on) (Gr., three-legged). The emblem of the Isle of MAN, and of Sicily; three human legs, bent at the knee, and joined at the thigh.

Trismegistus. *See* HERMETIC ART.

Tristram Sir (Tristam, Tristan, or **Tristem).** A hero of mediæval romance whose exploits, though originally unconnected with it, became attached to the ARTHURIAN cycle, he himself being named as one of the KNIGHTS of the ROUND TABLE. There are many versions of his story, which is, roughly, that he was cured of a wound by Iseult, or YSOLDE, daughter of the king of IRELAND, and on his return to CORNWALL told his uncle, King MARK, of the beautiful princess. Mark sent him to solicit her hand in marriage, and was accepted. Tristram escorted her to ENGLAND, but on the way they both unknowingly partook of a magic potion and became irretrievably enamoured of each other. Iseult married the king, and on Mark's discovering their liaison Tristram fled to Brittany and married Iseult, daughter of the Duke of Brittany. Wounded by a poisoned weapon, he sent for Iseult of Ireland to come and heal him. The vessel in which she was to come had orders to hoist a white sail if she was on board, otherwise a black sail. Tristram's wife, seeing the vessel approach, told her husband, from jealousy,

that it bore a black sail. In despair Tristram died; Iseult of Ireland, arriving too late, killed herself.

The name was originally *Drystan*, from the Pictish name *Drostan*, and the initial was changed to *T* apparently to connect it with Lat. *tristis*, sad. Wagner's opera *Tristan and Isolde* was first produced in 1865.

Triton. Son of POSEIDON and AMPHITRITE, represented as a fish with a human head. It is this sea-god that makes the roaring of the ocean by blowing through his shell.

A Triton among the minnows. A great man among a host of inferiors.

Triumph. A word formed from Gr. *thriambos*, the Dionysiac hymn, *Triumphe* being an exclamation used in the solemn processions of the ARVAL BROTHERS.

> Some...have assigned the origin of...triumphal processions to the mythic pomps of Dionysus, after his conquests in the East, the very word triumph being...the Dionysiac hymn.
> PATER: *Marius the Epicurean*, ch. xii.

The old Roman *triumphus* was the solemn and magnificent entrance of a general into ROME after having obtained a great or decisive victory. *Cp*. OVATION.

Triumvir (trī'ŭm 'vĕr). In ancient ROME, one of a group of three men (Lat. *trium*, gen. of *tres*, three; *vir*, man) acting as joint magistrates for some special purpose or function. In Roman history the most famous triumvirate was that of Octavian, Antony, and Lepidus (43 B.C.), which was known as the *Second Triumvirate* to distinguish it from the combination of CÆSAR, Pompey and Crassus in 60 B.C., which is known as the *First Triumvirate*.

Trivet. Right as a trivet. *See under* RIGHT.

Trivia. Gay's name for his invented goddess of streets and ways (Lat. *trivius*, of three roads). His burlesque in three books so entitled (1716) is a mine of information on the outdoor life of QUEEN ANNE'S time.

> I sing: Thou, Trivia, Goddess, aid my song.
> Through spacious streets conduct thy bard along...
> To pave thy realm, and smooth the broken ways,
> Earth from her womb a flinty tribute pays.
> *Trivia*, Bk. I, 5.

Trivium (Lat. *tres*, three; *via*, a road). In the MIDDLE AGES, the three roads to learning, *i.e.* Grammar, Rhetoric, and Logic; forming the lower division of the seven liberal arts. *See* QUADRIVIUM.

Trochilus. A small Egyptian bird said by the ancients to enter with impunity the mouth of the CROCODILE and to pick its teeth, especially of a leech which greatly tormented the creature.

It is now known as the Crocodile-bird,

Pluvianus ægyptus, a species of plover which not only picks the crocodile's teeth but by its cry gives warning of an approaching foe.

Troglodytes (Gr. *trogle*, cave; *duein*, to go into). A name given by the ancient Greeks to races of uncivilized men who dwelt in caves or holes in the ground. Strabo mentions troglodytes in Syria and Arabia, and Pliny (v, 8) asserts that they fed on serpents. The best-known were those of southern Egypt and Ethiopia. The term is applied to other cave-dwellers, and, figuratively, to those who dwell in seclusion.

In ornithology, wrens, which mostly build their nests in holes, are named *troglodytes*.

Troilus. The prince of CHIVALRY, one of the sons of PRIAM, killed by ACHILLES in the TROJAN WAR.

The loves of Troilus and CRESSIDA, celebrated by Chaucer and SHAKESPEARE, form no part of the old classic tale. This story appears for the first time in the *Roman de Troie* by the 12th century TROUVÉRE Benoit de Ste. More. Guido delle Colonne included it in his *Historia Trojana* (1287), it thence passed to Boccaccio, whose *Il Filostrato* (1338)—where Pandarus first appears—was the basis of Chaucer's *Troilus and Criseyde*. **As true as Troilus.** Troilus is meant by SHAKESPEARE to be the type of constancy, and Cressida the type of female inconstancy.

> After all comparisons of truth...
> "As true as Troilus" shall crown up the verse.
> And sanctify the numbers.
> *Troilus and Cressida*, III, ii.

Trojan. Trojan Horse. *See* WOODEN HORSE OF TROY.

Trojan War. The legendary war sung by HOMER in the ILIAD as having been waged for ten years by the confederated Greeks against the men of TROY and their allies, in consequence of PARIS, son of PRIAM, the Trojan king, having carried off HELEN, wife of MENELAUS. The last year of the siege is the subject of the *Iliad*; the burning of Troy and the flight of ÆNEAS is told by VIRGIL in his ÆNEID.

There is no doubt that the story of the siege of Troy, much doubted in the 19th century, has an historical basis and probably took place during the 13th and 12th centuries B.C.

He is a regular Trojan. A fine fellow, with courage and spirit, who works very hard, usually at some uncongenial task, indeed, doing more than could be expected of him. The Trojans in Homer's ILIAD and Virgil's ÆNEID are described as truthful, brave, patriotic, and confiding.

> There they say right, and like true Trojans.
> BUTLER: *Hudibras*, I, i.

Troll-madam, or **Troll-my-dames.** A popular indoor game in the 16th and 17th centuries (also known as *trunks*, *pigeon-holes*, or *nine-holes*), borrowed from the French and called by them *trou* (hole) *madame*. It resembled bagatelle, and was played on a board having at one end a number of arches, like pigeon-holes, into which the balls were rolled. SHAKESPEARE has a reference to it in *The Winter's Tale* (IV, ii).

Trolls. In Icelandic myth, malignant one-eyed giants; in Scandinavian folklore, mischievous DWARFS, some cunning and treacherous, some fair and good to men, akin to the Scottish BROWNIE. They were wonderfully skilled in working metals and lived in the hills, and had a propensity for stealing, even carrying off women and children. They were especially averse to noise, from a recollection of the time when THOR used to be forever flinging his hammer after them.

Trompe l'oeil (trômp lĕĕ′) (Fr.). A trick of the eye, a visual deception. It is applied to art which gives a distinct impression of reality, as, for example, perspective art which can give a sense of distance, solidity and space. The apparent dimensions of an interior can be imagnified by such decorative effects.

Trooping. The trooping season. The season when annual reliefs of the British forces in India were made, from September to late February or March, the purpose being to avoid travel in the hottest months.

Trooping the Colour. The annual ceremony on Horse Guards Parade, WHITEHALL, in which the colour or regimental FLAG is carried between files of troops and received by the sovereign. It takes place on the sovereign's official birthday.

The ceremony dates from the 18th century (probably from Marlborough's time), and was originally a guard-mounting ceremony, the battalion providing the guards for the day "trooping" the colour to be carried on King's guard.

Trophonius (trō fō′ ni us). An architect, celebrated in Greek legend as the builder of the TEMPLE of APOLLO at DELPHI. After his death he was deified, and had an ORACLE in a cave near Lebadeia, Bœotia, which was so awe-inspiring that those who entered and consulted the oracle never smiled again. Hence a melancholy or habitually terrified man was said to have visited the cave of *Trophonius*.

Trophy. Originally the arms of a vanquished foe, collected and set up by the victors on the field of battle. The captured standards were hung from the branches of an OAK-tree, a portion of the booty being laid at the foot of the tree and dedicated to the tutelary deity. The Romans frequently bore their trophies to ROME; under the Empire the triumphs of the victorious generals were also celebrated with arches and columns.

Troubadours. Poets of the south of France in the 11th to 14th centuries whose works were often performed and sung by wandering minstrels or JONGLEURS; so called from the Provencal verb *trobar*, to find or invent (*cp.* "poet", which means "a maker"). They wrote in the LANGUE D'OC or Provencal, principally on love and CHIVALRY. *Cp.* TROUVÈRES.

Trouble-shooter. An American coinage for one expert in locating and mending "trouble", mechanical or otherwise; hence its application to those brought into industry to mend relations between employer and employee.

Trousers. She's the one who wears the trousers. Said of a married woman who lords it over her husband, from the days when only men normally wore trousers and were usually the dominant partners. In recent decades, having largely become a GENS BRACATA, the phrase is perhaps somewhat less expressive.

Trouvères (troo′ vâr). Court poets in central and northern France in the 12th to 14th centuries, writing chiefly of love. So called from F. *trouver*, to find or invent (*cp.* TROUBADOURS). They wrote in the LANGUE D'OÏL or *langue d'oui*.

Trows, or **Drows.** DWARFS of Orkney and Shetland mythology, similar to the Scandinavian TROLLS. There are land-trows and sea-trows. "Trow tak' thee" is a phrase still used by the island women when angry with their children.

> When I hung around the neck that gifted chain, which all in our isles know was wrought by no earthly artist, but by the Drows, in the secret recesses of their caverns, thou wert then but fifteen years old.
>
> SCOTT: *The Pirate*, ch. x.

Troy. The fortress city of Homer's ILIAD in the extreme north-west corner of Asia Minor overlooking the strait of the Dardanelles; also the land of Troy or the *Troad*, with Ilium as its chief city.

The siege of Troy. *See* ACHILLES; ILIAD; HELEN; TROJAN WAR; ULYSSES; WOODEN HORSE OF TROY (*under* HORSE), etc.

Troy town. A Cornish expression for a labyrinth of streets, a regular maze. Sir Arthur Quiller-Couch in his writings uses the name for a disguise for Fowey (pronounced Foy). *Troy* was formerly used figuratively of any scene of disorder or confusion; thus a room in disarray would be called a *Troy fair*.

Troy weight. The system of weights used in weighing precious metals and gems, the pound of 12 ounces weighing 5,760 grains as compared with the pound *avoirdupois* which weighs 7,000 grains and is divided into 16 ounces. Why it is so called is not certainly known, but probably it was the system used at the great FAIRS at Troyes, in France. 1 lb. troy = 0.822861 lb.av., rather over four-fifths. *See* TOWER POUND.

Troynovant. The name given by the early chroniclers to LONDON, anciently the city of the TRINOBANTES; a corruption of *Trinovant*, *Troynovant* was assumed to mean *The New Troy*, which Geoffrey of Monmouth (*Historia Britonum*, Bk. I, ch. xvii) tells us was built by BRUTUS, a Trojan refugee (from whom is derived the name *Britain*). Afterwards LUD surrounded it with walls and called it *Caer-Lud*, or the City of Lud (London).

> For noble Britons sprong from Trojans bold,
> And Troynovant was built of old Troyes ashes cold.
> SPENSER: *The Fairie Queene*, III, ix, 38.

Truce of God. In the MIDDLE AGES, a suspension of private warfare decreed by the CHURCH on certain days or for certain seasons such as ADVENT and LENT. In 1027 hostilities between Saturday night and Monday morning were forbidden and the *Truce of God* was reaffirmed and extended by various Councils including the LATERAN COUNCIL of 1179. It was only partly effective and was eventually superseded by the King's peace.

Truck System, The. The system of paying employees wholly or in part in goods and tokens valid only at a TOMMY SHOP connected with their employers. The system was controlled and essentially abolished by insisting on payment in coin by Acts of 1831, 1881, and 1896. An Act of 1960 authorized payment other than in current coin, *i.e.*, by cheque, or bank transfer.

True. A true bill. *see under* BILL.

True blue, *i.e.* lasting blue; hence a type of constancy. A true blue is one who is constant, steadfast, loyal, faithful, etc. There are other allusions as in *True as Coventry Blue.* (*see* COVENTRY), *'Twas Presbyterian true blue.* (*See under* BLUE.)

True-lovers' knot. A complicated double KNOT with two interlacing bows on each side and two ends, used as a symbol of love.

> Three times a true-love's knot I tie secure;

Firm be the knot, firm may his love endure.
GAY: *Pastorals, The Spell*, 506.

Truepenny. An honest fellow, true as a genuine penny.

Ha, ha, boy! say'st thou so? art thou there, truepenny?
SHAKESPEARE: *Hamlet*, I, v.

True Thomas. THOMAS THE RHYMER (*see under* RHYME).

Trump. This word in such phrases as *a trumped-up affair* (falsely concocted, etc.), *trumpery* (showy finery, worthless stuff), etc., is the same word as *trumpet*; from Fr. *trompe*, a trumpet, whence *tromper*, which, originally meaning "to play on a trumpet", came to mean to beguile, deceive, impose upon.

Trump in cards, is from Fr. *triomphe* (triumph), the name of an old variant of écarté.

Jew's trump. A JEW'S HARP.

The last trump. The final end of all things earthly; the Day of JUDGMENT.

We shall not all sleep, but we shall all be changed, in a moment, in the twinkling of an eye, at the last trump.
I Cor. xv, 51, 52.

To play one's last trump. To be reduced to one's last expedient; a phrase from card-playing.

To turn up trumps. Unexpectedly to prove very friendly and helpful; to be much better than anticipated. An allusion to card-playing.

Trumpet. *See* TRUMP.

The Feast of Trumpets. A Jewish festival held on the first two days of Tishri (about mid-SEPTEMBER to mid-OCTOBER), the beginning of the Jewish ecclesiastical year, at which the blowing of trumpets formed a prominent part of the ritual. *See Num.* xxix, I.

A flourish of trumpets. An ostentatious introduction, preliminary, or arrival. From the fanfare announcing the arrival of one of high rank or distinction.

To blow one's own trumpet. To indulge in self-advertisement, to publish one's own praises, etc. The allusion is to HERALDS, who used to announce with a flourish of trumpets the KNIGHTS who entered a list. Similarly, **Your trumpeter is dead** means that you are obliged to sound your own praises because no one will do it for you.

Trunk. In its sense of denominating the main body as opposed to the roots and branches, the word is used to describe the main lines of railway, postal, and telephone systems, from which branch lines radiate. **A trunk call** is a telephone call on a trunk line from one town to another.

Trunk road is a main highway between two principal towns.

Trunk hose were a style of breeches worn in the 16th and 17th centuries, reaching from the waist to the middle of the thigh.

Trunk drawers, or **trunks,** are pants reaching only to the knee or, more recently, men's bathing-drawers.

Trust. A combination of a number of companies or businesses doing similar trade, for the purpose of defeating competition or creating a monopoly, under one general control. So called because each member is *on trust* not to undersell the others, but to remain faithful to the terms agreed on.

Truth. PILATE said, "What is truth?" (*John* xviii, 38). This was the great question of the Platonists. PLATO said we could know truth if we could sublimate our minds to their original purity. Arcesilaus said that man's understanding is not capable of knowing what truth is. Carneades maintained that not only our understanding could not comprehend it, but even our senses are wholly inadequate to help us in the investigation. Gorgias the SOPHIST said "What is right but what we prove to be right? and what is truth but what we believe to be truth?"

"What is truth?" said jesting Pilate, and would not stay for an answer.
BACON: *Essays, Of Truth.*

Act of Truth. *See under* ACT.

Truth drug. Alkaloid scopolamine. An American doctor, R. E. House (1875–1930), used this drug to induce a state of lethargic intoxication in which the patient lost many of his defences and spoke the truth concerning matters about which he would normally have lied or prevaricated. The value of this and other truth drugs in penology has by no means been established.

Truth lies at the bottom of the well. This expression has been attributed to Heraclitus, Cleanthes, DEMOCRITUS the Derider, and others.

Naturam accusa, quæ in profundo veritatem (ut ait Democritus) penitus abstruserit.
CICERO: *Academics*, i, 10.

Trygon. *See* TELEGONUS.

Tu autem (tū aw′ tem) (Lat., But thou). A hint to leave off; "hurry up and come to the last clause". In the long Latin grace at St. John's College, Cambridge, the last clause used to be *Tu autem miserere mei, Domine, Amen*, and it was not unusual, when a scholar read slowly, for the senior Fellow to whisper *Tu autem, i.e.* Skip all the rest and give us only the last sentence.

Tu quoque (tū kwo′ kwē) (Lat., You too). A retort implying that the one addressed is in the same case as the speaker—no better and no worse.

The tu quoque style of argument. Personal invective; the argument of personal application; *argumentum ad hominem*.

Tuatha De Danann (twa' thà de dăn' àn). A legendary race of superhuman heroes which invaded IRELAND, overthrew the Firbolgs and Fomors, and were themselves overthrown by the MILESIANS, who later worshipped them as gods.

Tub. Tubs, in college rowing slang, are gig pairs of college boat clubs, who practise for the term's races, and **tubbing** is taking out pairs under the supervision of a coach for training.

A tale of a tub. A COCK-AND-BULL STORY, a RIGMAROLE; a nonsensical romance.

There is a comedy of this name by Ben Jonson (produced 1633), and a prose satire by Swift (1704) which portrays allegorically the failings of the English, Roman, and PRESBYTERIAN Churches.

To throw a tub to the whale. To create a diversion in order to avoid a real danger; to bamboozle or mislead an enemy. In whaling, according to Swift, when a ship was threatened by a school of whales, it was usual to throw a tub into the sea to divert their attention.

A tub of naked children. Emblematical in religious paintings of St. NICHOLAS.

Tub-thumper. A ranter, a SOAP-BOX ORATOR or STUMP ORATOR; in allusion to the upturned tub once used as a platform at open-air meetings.

Tuck. In the sense of eatables *tuck* is a mid-18th-century slang word, especially used by boys in boarding schools whose *tuck-box*, supplied from home, supplemented the school fare. **To tuck in** is to eat heartily and with relish. In Australia the word became **tucker** for any kind of food, especially that carried on journeys in one's *tucker bag*.

To tuck one up. To finish him, do for him. Possibly from the duellist's rapier formerly called a *tuck* (O. Fr. *estoc*, stock), or from *tuck up* in the sense of to draw up, this being old slang meaning to hang a person.

Tuck, Friar. See FRIAR TUCK.

Tuckahoe (tŭk' à hō) (U.S.A.). An inhabitant of that part of the State of Virginia that lies east of the Blue Ridge Mountains.

Tucker. The ornamental frill of lace or muslin worn by women in the 17th and 18th centuries round the top of their dresses to cover the neck and shoulders. Hence, **with clean,** or **best bib and tucker,** dressed in one's best, looking fresh and spruce. *See also* TUCK.

Tuesday. The third day of the week until 1971

when it became the second. *See* SUNDAY; TIU.

Tuffet. A dialect variant of *tuft*, which was formerly used of a small grassy mound or hillock.

> Little Miss Muffet
> Sat on a tuffet
> Eating her curds and whey.
> *Nursery Rhyme.*

Tuft. The name formerly given at Oxford University to a peer's son or a fellow COMMONER, because he wore a GOLD tassel or *tuft* on his college CAP. The practice was discontinued in 1870.

Tuft-hunter. One who tries to curry favour with the wealthy or great for the sake of feeding on the crumbs which fall from the rich man's table. *See* TUFT.

Tug. A name by which Collegers are known at Eton; from the *tog* (*i.e. toga*) worn by them to distinguish them from the rest of the school.

Tug of war. A sporting activity in which a number of men, divided into two teams, lay hold of a strong rope and pull against each other till one side has tugged the other over the dividing line.

When Greek meets Greek then is the tug of war. *See under* GREEK.

Tuileries (twē' lè rē). A former palace in Paris, so named from the tile-yards (*tuileries*) once on the site. It stood between the LOUVRE and the Place de la Concorde. The palace was designed by Philibert de l'Orme for Catherine de' MEDICI, 1564, and long served as a residence for the sovereigns of France. In 1871 it was burned down by the Communards, but the gardens remain as a pleasant public open space.

Tulchan Bishops. Certain titular Scottish BISHOPS introduced by the PRESBYTERIANS in 1572 and whose office had ceased by 1580. A *tulchan* is a stuffed calf-skin placed under a cow that holds her milk to deceive her into yielding into the pail. The bishops were contemptuously so called because their title was but an empty one, their revenues being mainly absorbed by nobles as lay patrons.

Tulip Mania. A reckless mania for the purchase of tulip-bulbs that arose in Holland in the 17th century and was at its greatest height about 1633–1637. A bulb of the species called *Viceroy* sold for £250; *Semper Augustus* more than double that sum. The mania spread all over Europe, and became a mere stock-jobbing speculation. *La Tulipe Noire* (1850) by Alexandre Dumas the elder, centres around the black tulip and a tulip-fancier, Cornelius van Baerle, of the period of the "tulipo-mania". He succeeded in growing a black tulip thereby winning a prize of one hundred thousand florins.

To number the streaks of the tulip. To devote too much attention to minute details—characteristic, in the view of 18th-century critics, of a bad poet. The phrase comes from Imlac's dissertation on poetry in Johnson's *Rasselas* (ch. x) where the principle is laid down that a poet must examine not the individual but the species, and concern himself with the general rather than the particular.

Tumbledown Dick. *See under* DICK.

Tumbler. The flat-bottomed stemless glass derives its name from the fact that it was originally made with a rounded bottom which made it tumble over if set down on a table; hence requiring that it should be held till emptied.

Tune. The man who pays the piper calls the tune. He who foots the bill decides what is to be done. An old proverb.

To change one's tune, or **to make one sing another tune.** *See under* SING.

The tune the old cow died of. Advice instead of relief; remonstrance instead of help.

> The reference is to the song:
>
> There was an old man, and he had an old cow,
> But he had no fodder to give her,
> So he took up his fiddle and played her the tune;
> "Consider, good cow, consider,
> This isn't the time for the grass to grow,
> Consider, good cow, consider."

To the tune of. To the amount of; as, "I had to pay up to the tune of £500."

Tuneful Nine, The. The nine MUSES.

> When thy young Muse invok'd the tuneful Nine,
> To say how Louis did not pass the RHINE,
> What Work had we with WAGENINGHEN, ARN-
> HEIM,
> Places that could not be reduced to Rhime?
> PRIOR: *Letter to Boileau Despréaux*, l.18 (1704).

Tunkers, Dunkers, or **Dunkards** (Ger., dippers). A religious sect also known as the German Baptists, founded in Germany in 1708 by Alexander Mack. In 1719 they emigrated to Pennsylvania and spread westwards and into Canada. They reject infant baptism, the taking of oaths or bearing of ARMS, and practise triple immersion, the AGAPE, etc. They are now called the Church of the Brethren. The SEVENTH-DAY BAPTISTS (1728) are an offshoot.

Tunnage. *See* TONNAGE.

Turf, The. The race-course, horse-racing; the horse-racing world; in allusion to the *turf* or grass of the course. A *turfite* is a devotee of horse-racing or one who gets his living from it; a supporter of the turf.

Turk. Formerly applied to the barbarous, savage, and cruel, from the European association of the Old Ottoman Empire with bar-

baric practices, from mediæval times until the early years of the 20th century; now usually applied to mischievous and unruly children; as, *You little Turk!* or, *You young Turk!*

> Fierce revolt against intolerable misrule slowly blazed upon Bosnia and Herzegovina, and a rising in Bulgaria, not dangerous in itself, was put down by Turkish troops despatched for the purpose from Constantinople, with deeds described by the British agent who investigated them on the spot, as the most heinous crimes that had stained the history of the century.
> MORLEY: *Life of Gladstone*, VII, iv.

The Young Turks. A Turkish reforming party seeking to transform the decadent Turkish Empire into a modern European state and to give it a parliamentary constitution. It had its origins in a committee formed at Geneva in 1891 and the party, considerably supported by students, raised the standard of revolt at Salonika in 1908, deposed Sultan Abdul Hamid, and replaced him by his brother as Mohammed V (1909). Their "liberalism" was not dominant but they remained the major force in Turkish politics until the end of World War I, when the party was dissolved. Turkey was proclaimed a republic in 1923.

Turk Gregory. Falstaff's *ne plus ultra* of military valour—a humorous combination of the SULTAN with Gregory VII (HILDE-BRAND), probably the strongest of all the POPES.

> Turk Gregory never did such deeds in arms as I have done this day.
> SHAKESPEARE: *Henry IV, Pt. I*, V, iii.

To turn Turk. To become a MOSLEM, to turn renegade, to change very much for the worse.

Turkey. *See* MISNOMERS.

To talk turkey (U.S.A.). To talk plainly or seriously. Also, **that's cold turkey,** the frank details, the straight truth.

Turkey-work. Knotted carpeting work used for covering chairs and stools, especially in the first half of the 17th century, introduced as a result of the importation of Turkish carpets.

Turn. Done to a turn. Cooked exactly right; another turn on the spit would be too much.

He felt that the hour for the upturning of his glass was at hand. He knew that the sand of life was nearly run out, and that death was about to turn his hourglass upside down.

One good turn deserves another. A benefit received ought to be repaid.

To serve its turn. To answer the purpose; to be sufficient for the occasion; sometimes with the implication of being a makeshift or barely meeting requirements.

To turn down. To reject, as, "She turned down his marriage proposal", or, "His application for the post was turned down."

In Eastern countries a glass is turned down at convivial gatherings as a memento of a recently departed companion.

> And when thyself with shining feet shalt pass
> Among the guests star-scattered on the grass
> And in the joyous errand reach the spot
> Where I made one—turn down an empty glass!
> FITZGERALD: *Omar Khayyám* (1859).

To turn in. Colloquially, to go to bed.

To turn the tables. *See under* TABLE.

To turn to. To carry on with one's work; to get to work.

To turn turtle. To turn completely over, upside down, TOPSY-TURVY. Usually said of boats, from the fact that a turtle, when turned on its back, is quite helpless.

To turn up. To arrive, often unexpectedly; to appear.

A turn-up for the book. A bit of good luck, unexpected good fortune.

Waiting for something to turn up. Expectant that luck will change, that good fortune will arrive without much effort on one's own part. Mr. MICAWBER's philosophy of life:

> "And then", said Mr. Micawber, who was present, "I have no doubt I shall, please Heaven, begin to be beforehand with the world, and to live in a perfectly new manner, if—in short, if anything turns up."
> DICKENS: *David Copperfield*, ch. xi.

Turncoat. A renegade; one who deserts his principles or party.

Fable has it that a certain Duke of Saxony, whose dominions were bounded in part by France, hit upon the device of a coat *blue* one side, and *white* the other. When he wished to be thought in the French interest he wore the white outside; otherwise the blue. Hence a SAXON was nicknamed *Emmanuel Turncoat*.

Turnspit. One who has all the work but none of the profit; he *turns* the *spit* but eats not of the roast. The allusion is to the turnspit, a small dog which was used to turn the roasting-spit by means of a kind of treadwheel. Topsell says, "They go into a wheel, which they turn round about with the weight of their bodies, so diligently...that no drudge...can do the feat more cunningly" (1607).

Turnip. Common slang for a large, old-fashioned silver watch.

Turpin. Archbishop of Rheims, who appears in several CHANSONS DE GESTE as a friend and companion of CHARLEMAGNE. He was formerly supposed to be the writer of the *Historia de vita Caroli et Rolandi*. In the *Chanson de Roland* Turpin dies with the hero and is buried with him. He is most likely the same as Tilpin, archbishop of Rheims in the 8th century (*c*. 753–*c*. 800).

Dick Turpin (1705–1739). The "King of the Road" was born at the Bell Inn, Hempstead, Essex, and apprenticed to a butcher at WHITECHAPEL at the age of 16. He soon became a footpad to supplement his earnings and, after his marriage in 1728, set up as a butcher in Essex. He took to stocking his shop with stolen cattle and sheep and, on discovery, joined a gang of smugglers near Canvey Island and there turned to housebreaking with Gregory's Gang in Epping Forest. In 1735 he became a highwayman working around the south of LONDON, and in 1736 began his partnership with Tom King; his effrontery became a public legend as did his activities in Epping Forest and Hounslow Heath. After the death of King in 1737, he shifted to Lincolnshire and thence to Yorkshire where he was finally apprehended and hanged at the Mount, outside the walls of York. The legend of Black BESS and the ride to York derives from Harrison Ainsworth's *Rookwood* (1834) although that of the ride has historical precedents.

> And the fame of Dick Turpin had been something less
> If he'd ne'er rode to York on his bonnie Black Bess.
> ELIZA COOK: *Black Bess*.

Tuscan Order. In architecture, essentially a simplified form of Roman DORIC, plain and lacking in ornament. The columns are never fluted. *See* CORINTHIAN; IONIC.

Tusitala. Teller of tales; the name given by the Samoans to R. L. Stevenson.

Tut. A word used in Lincolnshire for a phantom, as the *Spittal Hill Tut*. *Tom Tut will get you* is a threat to frighten children. *Tutgotten* is panic-struck.

Tutankhamun. *See* VALLEY OF THE KINGS.

Tutankhamun's Curse. *See under* CURSE.

Tutivillus, or **Titivil** (tū ti vil' ŭs). The demon of mediæval legend who collects all the words skipped over or mutilated by priests in the celebration of the MASS. These scraps or shreds he deposits in that pit which is said to be paved with "good intentions" never brought to effect.

Tuxedo. The American name for a dinner-jacket; so called because it was first taken to the U.S.A. from ENGLAND by Griswold Lorillard, in 1886, and introduced by him at the Tuxedo Club, Tuxedo, N.Y.

Twain, Mark. The pen-name of Samuel Langhorne Clemens (1835–1910), the famous humorist, creator of Tom Sawyer and

Huckleberry Finn. The name "Mark Twain" is from the calls used by Mississippi pilots when taking sounds—in this case the two-fathom mark on the lead-line.

Tweed. The origin of this name of a woollen cloth used for garments is to be found in a blunder. It should have been *tweel*, the Scots form of *twill*; but when the Scottish manufacturer sent a consignment to James Locke of London, in 1826, the name was badly written and misread; and as the cloth was made on the banks of the Tweed, *tweed* was accordingly adopted. *Twill* like DIMITY, means "two-threaded".

The Tweed Ring. In American history, the political ring under W. M. ("Boss") Tweed which by wholesale graft and corruption controlled the New York Democratic party and municipal finances (1869–1871). Boss Tweed died in prison (1878). *See* TAMMANY HALL.

Tweedledum and Tweedledee. Names invented by John Byrom (1692–1763) to satirize two quarrelling schools of musicians between whom the real difference was negligible. Hence used of people whose persons or opinions are "as like as two peas".

> Some say compared to Bononcini
> That mynheer Handel's but a ninny;
> Others aver that he to Handel
> Is scarcely fit to hold a candle.
> Strange all this difference should be
> 'Twixt Tweedledum and Tweedledee.
> J. BYROM: *Feud between Handel and Bononcini*.

The Duke of Marlborough and most of the nobility took the side of G. B. Bononcini (d. *c.* 1752), but the Prince of Wales, with Pope and Arbuthnot, was for Handel. *Cp.* GLUCKISTS.

Lewis Carroll uses the names for two fat little men in his *Through the Looking-Glass*.

Twelve, Twelfth. The Glorious Twelfth. *See* GLORIOUS.

Twelfth man. The reserve chosen for a team of 11, especially in CRICKET, hence, anyone who just misses distinction.

Twelfth Night. 5 January, the eve of the Twelfth Day after CHRISTMAS or Feast of the EPIPHANY. Formerly this was a time of great merrymaking when the BEAN-KING was appointed, and the celebrations and festivities seemingly derive from the SATURNALIA of old Roman times which were held at the same season. By the JULIAN CALENDAR Twelfth Day is Old CHRISTMAS Day.

SHAKESPEARE's play of this name (produced 1600–1601) was so called because it was written for acting at the Twelfth Night revels.

The Twelve Tables. The earliest code of Roman law, compiled by the Decemviri

(451–450 B.C.), and engraved on 12 tablets. Originally ten, to which two were added, they were supposed to comprise the basis of all Roman law. In CICERO's boyhood it was still customary for them to be learnt by heart (Livy: III, lvii; Diodorus, xii, 56).

Each English archer carries twelve Scotsmen under his girdle. This was a common saying at one time, because the English were unerring archers, and each carried 12 arrows in his belt.

The Twelvers. A sect of SHI'ITES who accept *twelve* of the descendants of ALI as Imams. The 12th IMAM, MOHAMMED, it is held, disappeared (*c.* 874) but is still alive and will return at the end to set up the Shi'ite faith through the world.

Twickenham. The Bard of Twickenham. Alexander Pope (1688–1744), who lived there for 25 years. Contemporaries sometimes called him the *Wasp of Twickenham* because of his acerbity.

Twickers. *See* BILLY WILLIAMS'S CABBAGE PATCH.

Twig. I twig you. I catch your meaning; I understand (Irish *tuigim*, I understand). The Irish word is pronounced *tigim*.

Twilight Twilight of the Gods. *See* RAGNAROK.

Twilight Sleep. A state of semiconsciousness produced by injection of scopolamine and morphia in which a woman can undergo childbirth with comparatively little pain. *See also* TRUTH DRUG.

Twins, The. *See* GEMINI.

Twirl. In prison parlance, the same as a SCREW, and for a similar reason.

Twist. The twist. A dance popular about 1962, so called from the contortions performed.

Like Oliver Twist, asking for more. Oliver Twist, the workhouse-boy hero of Dickens's famous novel of that name (1838), astonished the workhouse-master and caused general consternation by once actually asking for more gruel (*see* chap. ii).

To twist a person. Slang for to swindle him or to bamboozle him to one's own advantage. Also (with allusion to giving the screw another twist), to extract from a person all one can and a bit over.

To twist a person's arm. To coerce or persuade a person to do something against their inclination.

To twist a person round one's (little) finger. To be able to influence him at will; to have him in complete subjection.

To twist the lion's tail. *See under* LION.

Twitcher, Jemmy. A cunning, treacherous highwayman in Gay's *Beggar's Opera*. The name was given about 1765, in a poem by Gray, to John, Lord SANDWICH (1718–1792), noted for his liaison with Miss Ray, who was shot by the Rev. "Captain" Hackman out of jealousy.

Twm Shon Catti (tum shòn kati). A kind of Welsh ROBIN HOOD who was born about 1530. He is mentioned in George Borrow's *Wild Wales*. There are many tales of his exploits and he is said to have eventually married an heiress and ended up as a squire and magistrate.

Two. The evil principle of PYTHAGORAS. Accordingly the second day of the second month of the year was sacred to PLUTO, and was esteemed unlucky.

Two bits. American term for 25 cents, otherwise known as a *quarter*. The origin of the term is in British slang "bit" (*e.g.* three-penny bit), which was adopted in the south and west of the U.S.A. for the old Mexican *real* worth 12½ cents.

The Two cultures. *See* CULTURES.

The two eyes of Greece. ATHENS and Sparta.

He has two strings to his bow. *See under* BOW.

To put two and two together. To come to an inference or conclusion (usually fairly obvious) from the facts of the matter.

Two heads are better than one. Another's advice is often very useful. To the saying is sometimes added—*or why do folks marry?*

Two is company, three is none. An old saying, much used by lovers; it is given in Heywood's collection of proverbs (1546).

Two of a trade did never agree. A very old proverb (it occurs in Hesiod's *Works and Days*).

> In every age and clime we see
> Two of a trade can ne'er agree.
>   GAY: *Fables*, I, xxi, 43.

Two may keep counsel–if one of them's dead. A caustic saying expressive of the great difficulty of being certain that the secret is not told once it is imparted to someone else. SHAKESPEARE has:

> Two may keep counsel when the third's away.
>   *Titus Andronicus*, IV, ii.

In Thomas Usk's *Testament of Love* (formerly attributed to Chaucer) is:

> For thre may kepe a counsel, if twain be awaie.

When two Fridays come together. One of a number of circumlocutions for NEVER!

Twopenny. Often used slightingly of things of very little value.

Twopenny Damn. *See* DAMN.

The Twopenny Tube. The Central London Railway was so called, because for some years after its opening (1900) the fare be-

tween any two stations was 2*d*.

Tuck in your twopenny! Mind your head! A schoolboy's warning to the boy over whose back the leap is to be made in leap-frog.

Tybalt (tib' ălt). An old name given to a cat (*see* GIB CAT). Hence the allusions to cats in connexion with Tybalt, one of the CAPULET family in SHAKESPEARE's *Romeo and Juliet* (III, i). Mercutio says, "Tybalt, you rat-catcher, will you walk?"; and again, when Tybalt asks, "What wouldst thou have with me?" Mercutio answers, "Good King of Cats! nothing but one of your nine lives."

Tyburn (tī' běrn). A famous tributary of the THAMES rising at Hampstead, which gave its name to the village that was later called MARYLEBONE and to a place of execution. Hence **Tyburn tree,** the gallows (at Tyburn); **to take a ride to Tyburn,** to go to one's hanging; **Lord of the Manor of Tyburn,** the common hangman, etc.

The site of the gallows is marked by three brass triangles let into the pavement at the corner of Edgware Road and Bayswater Road. The last criminal to be hanged there was John Austin in 1783; after that executions were carried out at NEWGATE until its demolition.

Tyburn ticket. A certificate which, under a statute of William III (10 W. III, c.12), 1698, was granted to prosecutors who had secured a capital conviction against a criminal, exempting them from all parish and ward offices within the parish in which the felony had been committed. This, with the privilege it conferred, might be sold once, and once only, and the *Stamford Mercury* for 27 March 1818 announced the sale of one for £280. The Act was repealed in 1818, but as late as 1856 Mr Pratt of Bond Street claimed exemption from serving on an OLD BAILEY jury on the strength of the possession of a Tyburn Ticket and was successful.

Tyburnia. A district of LONDON near the old TYBURN gallows was so called. It comprised approximately the area between what is now Paddington Station and MARBLE ARCH.

Tycoon (tī'koon'). A title of the SHOGUN; also applied to an industrial or business magnate.

Tyke. *See* TIKE.

Tyler grippe. An obsolescent American term for influenza. When John Tyler was President (1841–1845) of the U.S.A. a man called at the WHITE HOUSE and a few hours later contracted influenza, which is also, but less familiarly, known by the Fr. word *grippe*. This man jokingly told his friends that he had caught cold from shaking hands with the President, who was noted for the formality of his manners. The play on the words *grip* and *grippe* led to influenza being called the *Tyler grippe*.

Tyler's Insurrection. The main rebellion of the English PEASANTS' REVOLT.

Tylwyth Teg (tŭl with tāg) (Welsh *tylwyth*, family; *teg*, fair). The fairies of Welsh folklore, friendly but mischievous, who live in caves and on the mountains, who communicate by signs and never speak. They are versed in country lore, but if they touch iron, vanish away.

Tyndale's Bible. *See* BIBLE, THE ENGLISH.

Tynwald. The Court of Tynwald constitutes the governing body of the Isle of MAN. It consists of the Lieutenant-Governor, a Crown appointment; the Legislative Council, consisting of the Bishop of Sodor and Man, two DEEMSTERS, the Attorney-General, two of the Governor's nominees, and five members of the House of Keys; and the House of Keys, which is composed of 24 members elected by adult suffrage. No British Act of PARLIAMENT applies to the island unless specifically stated. The House of Keys was self-elected until 1866. *Tyn* is from THING and *Wald*, the *wold* or down on which it assembled. The origin of *Keys* is a matter of conjecture; in the 15th century the 24 keys are referred to as *Keys of Man and Keys of the Law*.

Typhœus (tī fē' ŭs), or **Typhon** (tī' fon). A monster of Greek mythology, son of GÆA and TARTARUS, with a hundred heads, each with a terrible voice. He made war on ZEUS, who killed him with a THUNDERBOLT. According to one legend, he lies buried under Mount ETNA. By ECHIDNA he fathered ORTHOS, CERBERUS, the Lernæan HYDRA, the CHIMÆRA, the Theban SPHINX, and the NEMEAN LION. *See* SET.

Tyr. *See* TIU.

Tyrant. In ancient Greece the *tyrant* was merely the absolute ruler, the *despot*, of a state, and at first the word had no implication of cruelty or what we call tyranny. Many of the Greek tyrants were pattern rulers, as Pisistratus and Pericles of ATHENS; Periander of Corinth; Dionysius the Younger, Gelon, and his brother Hiero of Syracuse; Phidon of Argos; Polycrates of Samos (*see* AMASIS), etc. The word (*turannos*) soon, however, obtained much the same meaning as it has with us.

The Thirty Tyrants. The 30 magistrates appointed by Sparta over ATHENS, at the termination of the Peloponnesian War. This "reign of terror", after one year's continuance, was overthrown by Thasybulus (403 B.C.).

In Roman history, those military leaders who endeavoured in the reigns of Valerian and Gallienus (A.D. 253–268) to make themselves independent princes are also known as *the Thirty Tyrants*, although the number is loosely applied.

A tyrant's vein. A ranting, bullying manner. In the old MORALITY PLAYS the tyrants were made to rant, and the loudness of their rant was proportionate to the villainy of their dispositions.

Tyrian Purple. *See* PURPLE.

Tyrtæus (tĕr tē' ŭs). A lame schoolmaster and elegiac poet of ATHENS who is said to have so inspired the Spartans by his songs that they defeated the Messenians (7th century B.C.). The name has hence been given to many martial poets who have urged on their countrymen to deeds of ARMS and victory.

U

U. The twenty-first letter of the English alphabet; in form a modification of V with which for many centuries it was interchangeable. Words beginning with U and V were (like those in I and J) not separated in English dictionaries till about 1800 and later. *A Dictionary of the English Language* published by Henry Washbourne, London, 1847, still adhered to the old practice. In 16th- and early 17th-century books spellings such as *vpon* and *haue* are the rule rather than the exception. The following from the title-page of *Polymanteia* (anon., 1595) is a good example of the confusion:

> Polymanteia, or, The meanes … to ivdge of the fall of a Commonwealth, against the friuoulous and foolish coniectures of this age. Whereunto is added, a Letter … perswading them to a constant vnitie … for the defence of our … natiue country … *Printed by John Legate, Printer to the Vniversitie of Cambridge*, 1595.

U.F.O. Unidentified flying object; the name given to objects claimed to have been sighted in the sky such as FLYING SAUCERS (*see under* SAUCER) etc., or picked up on radar screens, the exact nature of which is uncertain. Study and observation of U.F.O.s is termed *ufology* by enthusiasts.

U and Non-U. A semi-humorous mark of distinction between social classess in England based on the usage of certain words. "U" is Upper Class, "Non-U" being non-Upper Class. It is "U" to say "luncheon" for what "Non-U" folk call "lunch"; "napkin" and "serviette", "cycle" and "bike" are samples of this snobbism. The terms owe their popularity to Nancy Mitford, who quoted them in an article in the magazine *Encounter* in September 1955; but they were invented by Professor A.S.C. Ross in 1954 and appear in his article "Linguistic class indicators in present-day English".

> No wonder show-jumping had recently attracted so many enthusiasts: it is the gipsy life of modern times, nomadic, transitory and glamorous, in which the gentry can take part as legitimately as the professional, where it is just as 'U' to sleep on straw in a horse-box as it is in the smartest hotel.
> MOYRA WILLIAMS: *Adventures Unbridled* (1960), ch. xi.

U-boat. A German submarine; the term is adapted from the German *Unterseeboot* (under-water vessel). *Cp.* E-BOAT.

Uberrimæ fidei (Lat., of the fullest confidence, complete faith). A legal expression used of contracts in which the fullest and frankest information must be disclosed by the applicant or promisee. All insurance contracts are governed by this principle in order that the insurers may judge whether or not to accept the proposal.

Udal Tenure (Icel. *othal*). More correctly *odal* tenure, the same as "allodial tenure", a sort of FREEHOLD tenure depending on attested long-term undisturbed possession, as in the ORKNEYS and Shetlands. It was quite distinct from feudal forms of tenure. A *Udaller* is one holding such a tenure.

> The Udallers are the allodial possessors of Zetland, who hold their possessions under the old Norwegian law, instead of the feudal tenures introduced among them from Scotland.
> SCOTT: *The Pirate*, ch. I (footnote).

Ugly Duckling. An unpromising child who develops into a beautiful or handsome adult; also anything of an unprepossessing character that may change with time into something attractive. The expression is taken from Hans Andersen's story of the *Ugly Duckling* that endured many embarrassments but grew into a beautiful swan.

Uisnech. *See* USNECH.

Uitlander (oit lan' dĕr). The Boer term for a foreigner (Outlander), and especially those Europeans resident in the Transvaal and Orange Free State (mostly British subjects) after the discoveries of GOLD, who were not given political rights.

Their situation led to the JAMESON RAID of 1895 and the subsequent Boer War of 1899–1902.

Ulema (ū lē' mà). The learned classes in Mohammedan countries, interpreters of the KORAN and the law, from whose numbers came the MULLAHS, MUFTIS, IMAMS, cadis, etc. (teachers of religion, of law, and administrators of justice). *Ulema* is the plural of Arab. *alim*, a wise man.

Ullage (ŭl′ àj). The difference between the amount of liquid a vessel can contain and what it actually does contain (O.Fr. *œiller*, to fill up). The term is applied to a bottle of wine of which part of the contents have evaporated. Colloquially it is applied to *dregs*, or *rubbish* generally.

Ulster. The northernmost province of IRELAND which was forfeited to the Crown in James I's reign in consequence of the rebellions of Tyrconnell and Tyrone and planted by English and Scottish settlers (1609–1612). Under Acts of 1920 and 1922, as Northern Ireland, it was made a separate political division of the United Kingdom while still sending 12 M.P.s to WESTMINSTER.

The Red, or **Bloody Hand of Ulster.** The badge of ULSTER, a sinister hand, erect, open, and couped at the wrist, gules; the Red Hand of the O'Neills. *See* BARONET.

Ulster King of Arms. Formerly the chief heraldic officer for IRELAND and Registrar to the ORDER OF ST. PATRICK (*see under* PATRICK), created by Edward VI in 1553. The office was united with that of the NORROY King of Arms in 1943. His present jurisdiction is restricted to the SIX COUNTIES. Eire appointed its own Chief Herald of Ireland in 1943 who occupies the former office of the Ulster King in Dublin Castle.

Ultima Thule. *See under* THULE.

Ultimus Romanorum (ŭl′ ti mùs rō mà nôr′ ùm) (Lat.). The LAST OF THE ROMANS.

Ultor (ŭl′ tôr) (Lat., the Avenger). A title given to MARS when, after defeating the murderers of Julius CÆSAR at Philippi, Augustus built a temple to him in the Forum at ROME.

Ultra vires (ŭl′ tra vī′ rēz) (Lat. *ultra*, beyond; *vires*, the powers). In excess of the authority given by law, hence invalid in the legal sense. Thus if the BANK of England were to set up a MINT on its premises it would be acting *ultra vires*.

Ultramontane Party. The extreme party in the Church of ROME. *Ultramontane* opinions or tendencies are those which favour the high "Catholic" party. *Ultramontane* (beyond the mountains, *i.e.* the Alps) means Italy or the old Papal States. The term was first used by the French, to distinguish those who look upon the POPE as the fountain of all power in the Church, in contradistinction to the Gallican school, which maintained the right of self-government by national churches. *Cp.* TRAMONTANE.

Ulysses, or **Odysseus** (ū′ lis ēz, o dis′ūs) ("the hater"). A mythical king of Ithaca, a small rocky island of Greece, one of the leading chieftains of the Greeks in HOMER's ILIAD, and the hero of his ODYSSEY, represented by Homer as wise, eloquent, and full of artifices.

According to VIRGIL, it was he who suggested the device of the WOODEN HORSE (*see under* HORSE) through which TROY was ultimately taken. *See* TELEGONUS.

Ulysses' Bow. Only ULYSSES could draw his own bow, and he could shoot an arrow through 12 rings. By this sign PENELOPE recognized her husband after an absence of 20 years. He was also recognized by his dog, Argus.

The bow was prophetic. It belonged at one time to Eurytus of Œchalia.

Umble pie. *See* TO EAT HUMBLE PIE *under* EAT.

Umbrage. To take umbrage (Lat. *umbra*, shade). Originally to feel overshadowed, slighted, and hence to take offence.

Umbrella (Lat. *umbra*, shade). Used in ancient China, Babylon, Egypt, etc., but not commonly in use in England until after Jonas Hanway (1712–1786), the philanthropist, publicized it from about 1750 by carrying one regularly in the streets of London to keep off the rain. He incurred a good deal of ridicule in the process.

Umbrellas were not, however, unknown. Drayton says in his *Muses' Elizium* (1630):

> And like umbrellas, with their feathers,
> Shield you in all sorts of weathers.

Quarles in his *Emblems* (1635) used the word to signify the Deity hidden in the manhood of Christ—"Nature is made th'umbrella of the Deity" (iv, 14). Further mention is in Swift's *City Shower* (1710), in Gay's *Trivia* (1716), and *The Female Tatler* (12 Dec. 1709) contains this notice:

> The young gentleman belonging to the Custom House, that for fear of rain, borrowed the Umbrella at Will's Coffee House in Cornhill of the Mistress, is hereby advertised that to be dry from head to foot on the like occasion he shall be welcome to the Maid's pattens.

Under the umbrella of So-and-so. Under his dominion, regimen, influence, protection. The allusion is to the umbrella carried over certain African potentates as an EMBLEM of sovereignty. In 1876, the sacred umbrella of King Koffee of the Ashantis was captured and placed in the South Kensington Museum.

In World War II the term *umbrella* was used to denote air-cover to ground or sea operations.

Umlaut (um′ lout). The change or modification of sound characteristic of cetain Germanic languages occasioned when a vowel is influenced by a following vowel. The second or modifying vowel can appear, or it can be replaced by a diæresis, itself called an *um-*

laut, as Goethe, Göthe; Duerer, Dürer. The word was invented by Grimm, the philologist.

Umpire. *See* APRON.

Unam sanctam (Lat., One holy). The opening words of Boniface VIII's BULL of 1302 declaring that there was "One holy Catholic and Apostolic Church", membership of which was necessary for salvation. It is notable for its assertion of papal claims and of the authority of the spiritual power over the temporal.

Unaneled. Unanointed; without having had extreme unction (O.E. *ele*, oil; from Lat. *oleum*). *See* HOUSEL.

> Unhouseled, disappointed, unaneled.
> SHAKESPEARE: *Hamlet*, I, v.

Uncials (ŭn' si àlz). A form of majuscule (large) script used in MSS. dating from about the 4th century A.D. to the 8th century; so called from Lat. *uncia*, twelfth part, inch, because the letters were about an inch high. There were also half-uncials.

Uncle. Slang for a pawnbroker, in use as early as 1756. Its origin is unknown. An article that has *gone to uncle's* is in pawn.

Old Uncle Tom Cobleigh. The last named of the seven village worthies who borrowed Tom Pearce's grey mare on which to ride to WIDECOMBE FAIR and whose names form the refrain of the famous ballad of that name which has become as much the county song of Devon as "D'ye ken John Peel" is of Cumberland.

> When the wind whistles cold on the moor of a night,
> All along, down along, out along lee,
> Tom Pearce's old mare doth appear gashly white,
> Wi' Bill Brewer, Jan Stewer, Peter Gurney,
> Peter Davy, Dan'l Whidden, Harry Hawk,
> Old Uncle Tom Cobleigh and all,
> Old Uncle Tom Cobleigh and all.

Uncle George. King George III (1738, 1760–1820).

Uncle Joe. A British (World War II) nickname for Joseph Stalin, head of the Government of the U.S.S.R. (1941–1953).

Uncle Remus (rē' mùs). The old plantation negro whose quaint and proverbial wisdom, and stories of Br'er Rabbit and BR'ER FOX, were related by Joel Chandler Harris (1848–1908) in *Uncle Remus, his Songs and Sayings* (1880), and *Nights with Uncle Remus* (1883).

Uncle Sam. *See under* SAM.

Uncle Tom's Cabin. A story by Mrs. Harriet Beecher Stowe (1811–1896) that appeared in 1852. It tells of the sale of a pious and faithful old Negro slave to a bad owner. By its emphasis on the worst sides of Negro slavery, the book helped in no small degree to arouse the American nation to an understanding of the iniquities of the system. The original of Uncle Tom was a slave subsequently ordained as the Rev. J. Henson. He came to London in 1876 and was presented to Queen Victoria. **Uncle Tom** is now used by Black Nationalists to denote Negroes who are over-subservient to the white ESTABLISHMENT.

Welsh uncle. The husband of a parent's cousin; sometimes a parent's first cousin.

Don't come the uncle over me. In Latin, *Ne sis patruus mihi* (HORACE, II *Sat.*, iii, 88), *i.e.* do not overdo your privilege of reproving or castigating me. The Roman notion of a *patruus* or uncle acting as guardian was that of a severe castigator. Similarly their idea of a STEP-mother was a woman of stern and unsympathetic nature, often unjust to her step-children.

To talk like a Dutch uncle. *See under* DUTCH.

Unclubable, or **unclubbable.** "A very unclubable man." One who is very unsocial, lacking in urbanity. A word coined by Dr. Johnson and applied by him to Sir John Hawkins, one of the original members of the Literary CLUB founded in 1763, which met at the Turk's Head, Gerrard Street, SOHO.

Unco. A Scottish variant of *uncouth* (unknown; hence, strange, extraordinary). It has two meanings: as an adjective it means unknown, strange, unusual, but as an adverb it means very—as *unco good, unco glad*, etc. The "unco guid" are the PINCHBECK saints, too good by half.

Unconscious, The. In psychology, the mental processes which the individual cannot bring into consciousness—they are, indeed, often unknown to him.

Uncumber, St. The Portuguese St. Wilgefortis, about whom little is known with any accuracy and so called according to Sir Thomas More "because they [women] reken that for a pecke of oats she will not faile to uncumber them of their husbondys". Traditionally, she was one of seven beautiful princesses, and wishing to lead a single life prayed that she might have a beard. The prayer was granted and she was no more cumbered with suitors, but one of them, a prince of Sicily, was so enraged that he had her crucified.

Undecimilla *See* URSULA, St.

Under. Under the counter. Said of actions that are surreptitious and savouring of dishonest practice; in World War II, rationing led to considerable "under the counter" transactions by some shopkeepers who kept back goods for privileged customers or BLACK MARKET transactions "under the counter".

Under cover. Working out of sight, in secret. An under-cover agent is one who pursues his inquiries or work unknown to any but his employer.

Underground. A political or military movement carried on in secret against an oppressor government of an occupying enemy administration, especially in World War II.

Underground Railroad. *See under* RAILROAD.

Undertaker. Originally any contractor. The application of this word to one who carries out funerals—in the U.S.A. termed a mortician—dates from the 17th century. The principal English and Scottish grantees of land during the plantation of ULSTER (1609–1612) were called *Undertakers*, as were those who undertook to secure the return to PARLIAMENT of members favourable to the policies of James I in 1614. The term was also applied to the 18th-century magnates who monopolized political power in Ireland and who controlled the Irish Parliament.

> "There's a Providence in it all," said Sam. "O' course there is," replied his father with a nod of grave approval. "Wot 'ud become of the undertakers without it, Sammy?"
>
> DICKENS: *Pickwick Papers*, ch. lii.

Underwriter. One who engages to buy at a certain prearranged price all the stock in a new company, of a new issue, etc., that is not taken up by the public. An underwriter at LLOYD'S is one who insures a ship or its merchandise and undertakes other insurance to a stated amount. So called because he writes his name under the policy.

Undine (ŭn' dēn). One of the elemental spirits of PARACELSUS, the spirit of the waters. She was created without a soul; but had this privilege, that by marrying a mortal and bearing him a child she obtained a soul, and with it all the pains and penalties of the human race. She is the subject of a tale (*Undine*, 1811) by Friedrich de la Motte Fouqué (1777–1843). *Cp.* SYLPH.

Unearned increment. The increase in the value of land, houses, etc., not attributable to the owner's efforts or outlay, as from the building of roads, growth of population, etc.

Unfinished Symphony. Schubert's Symphony No. 8 in B Minor (1822), of which only two movements were completed. The phrase is applied figuratively and humorously to various unfinished compositions.

Unfrock. In ecclesiastical parlance, to deprive a priest of his clerical robes and reduce him to lay estate.

Unguem (ŭn' gwem). **Ad unguem.** To a nicety, exactly. To finish a statue *ad unguem* is to finish it so smoothly and perfectly that when the nail is run over the surface it can detect no imperfection. *See* TO HAVE IT AT ONE'S FINGERS' ENDS *under* FINGER.

Unhinged. To be quite unhinged. To have one's nerves badly shaken, one's balance of mind disturbed; like a door which has lost one of its hinges.

Unhouseled. *See under* HOUSEL.

Uniat, or **Uniate Churches** (Lat. *unus*, one). Churches of Eastern Christendom which are in communion with ROME but retain their own rights, languages, and canon law.

Unicorn (ū' ni kôrn) (Lat. *unum cornu*, one horn). A mythical and heraldic animal, represented by mediæval writers as having the legs of a buck, the tail of a LION, the head and body of a HORSE, and a single horn, white at the base, black in the middle, and red at the tip, in the middle of its forehead. The body is white, the head red, and eyes blue. The earliest author that describes it is Ctesias (400 B.C.); the mediæval notions concerning it are well summarized in the following extract:

> The unicorn has but one horn in the middle of its forehead. It is the only animal that ventures to attack the elephant; and so sharp is the nail of its foot, that with one blow it can rip the belly of the beast. Hunters can catch the unicorn only by placing a young virgin in his haunts. No sooner does he see the damsel, than he runs towards her, and lies down at her feet, and so suffers himself to be captured by the hunters. The unicorn represents Jesus Christ, who took on Him our nature in the virgin's womb, was betrayed by the Jews and delivered into the hands of Pontius Pilate. Its one horn signifies the Gospel of Truth.
>
> *Le Bestiaire Divin de Guillaume,*
> *Clerc de Normandie* (13th century).

Another popular belief was that the unicorn by dipping its horn into a liquid could detect whether or not it contained poison. In the designs for GOLD and SILVER plate made for the Emperor Rudolph II by Ottavio Strada is a cup on which a unicorn stands as if to assay the liquid.

The supporters of the old royal ARMS of SCOTLAND are two Unicorns; when James VI of Scotland came to reign over ENGLAND (1603) he brought one of the Unicorns with him, and with it supplanted the RED DRAGON which, as representing WALES, was one of the supporters of the English shield, the other being the Lion.

The animosity which existed between the lion and the unicorn referred to by Spenser in his *Faerie Queene* (II, v, 10):

> Like as a lyon, whose imperiall powre
> A prowd rebellious unicorn defyes—

is allegorical of that which once existed between England and Scotland.

Driving unicorn. Two wheelers and one leader. The leader is the one horn.

Unigenitus (ū ni jen′ i tus) (Lat., the Only-Begotten). A Papal BULL, so called from its opening sentence *Unigenitus, Dei Filius*, issued in 1713 by Clement XI in condemnation of Quesnel's *Réflexions Morales*, which favoured Jansenism. It was a *damnatio in globo*—i.e. a condemnation of the whole book without exception. It was confirmed in 1725, but in 1730 the bull was condemned by the civil authorities of PARIS and this clerical controversy died out.

Union, The. A short term for the United States of America; in ENGLAND, a once familiar colloquialism for the workhouse, from its being maintained by a group of parishes formed into a *Union* in accordance with the Poor Law Amendment Act of 1834.

The Act of Union. Specifically the Act of Union of 1707 declaring that on and after 1 May 1707 ENGLAND and SCOTLAND "for ever after be united into One Kingdom by the Name of Great Britain". It provided for one PARLIAMENT for both countries. There had been a common sovereign since 1603.

The term also applies to the Act of 1536, incorporating WALES with England, and the Act of 1800, which united the Kingdoms of Great Britain and IRELAND on and after 1 January 1801, a union which came to an end in 1922.

Union Jack. The national banner of the UNITED KINGDOM. It consists of three united crosses—that of St. GEORGE for ENGLAND, the saltire of St. ANDREW for Scotland (added by James I), and the CROSS of St. PATRICK for Ireland (added at the Union in 1801).

The white edging of St. George's cross shows the white field. In the saltire the cross is reversed on each side, showing that the other half of the cross is covered over. The broad white band is the St. Andrew's cross and should be uppermost at the top left-hand corner of the flag (*i.e.* the hoist). The narrow white edge is the white field of St. Patrick's cross.

The Union Jack is technically described thus:

The Union Flag shall be azure, the Crosses saltire of St. Andrew and St. Patrick quarterly per saltire, counter-changed, argent and gules, the latter fimbriated of the second, surmounted by the Cross of St. George of the third fimbriated as the saltire.—*By order of the Council.*

See JACK (4).

Union of South Africa. The union of the former self-governing colonies of the Cape of Good Hope, Natal, the Transvaal, and the Orange River Colony, with its PARLIA-

MENT at Cape Town. The title was changed to the Republic of South Africa on 31 May 1961, when South Africa left the British COMMONWEALTH.

The Union Rose. The Tudor Rose. *See under* ROSE.

Union is strength (Lat. *unitate fortior*). The wise saw of Periander, tyrant of Corinth between *c.* 627 and 586 B.C.

Unionists. In 1886, when Gladstone introduced his first Home Rule Bill for Ireland, 78 LIBERALS under Joseph Chamberlain and Lord Hartington allied with the CONSERVATIVES as Liberal Unionists to uphold the union with IRELAND (*see* ACT OF UNION, *above*). From 1886, the Conservative Party was also called the Unionist Party; it adopted the official name of *Conservative and Unionist Party* in 1909.

Unitarians. Originally Christians who denied the existence of the TRINITY, maintaining that God existed in one person only. Many of the early heretical sects were unitarian in belief if not in name, and at the time of the REFORMATION unitarianism had numerous exponents who may be regarded as the founders of the modern movement.

In ENGLAND, John Biddle (1615–1662) is generally regarded as the founding father and among the famous men who have been Unitarians are Dr. Samuel Clarke, Joseph Priestley, Dr. Lardner, James Martineau, Sir Edgar Bowring, and Joseph Chamberlain. Modern Unitarianism is not based on Scriptural authority, but on reason and conscience and includes AGNOSTICS and humanists among its members. There is no formal dogma or creed.

Unite. A GOLD coin worth 20*s.*, also called a *broad*, from its size. It was first minted by James I in 1604 in place of the SOVEREIGN, named from the union of the crowns of ENGLAND and SCOTLAND (1603), and bore the motto *"Faciam eos in gentem unam"* (I will make them one people. *Ezek.* xxxvii, 22). It was replaced by the GUINEA in 1663. *See* JACOBUS.

United. United Empire Loyalists. Many of those American colonists who remained loyal to the mother country during the American War of Independence subsequently migrated to Ontario and the Maritime Provinces. They formed the nucleus of British Canada and were given the honourable title of *United Empire Loyalists*.

United Irishmen. A society formed by Theobald Wolfe Tone in 1791 with its first headquarters at Belfast and with the objects of securing a representative national PARLIAMENT, to unite all Irishmen against British influence, etc. Membership included both PROTESTANTS and Roman Catholics, but it soon became revolutionary and was largely responsible for the rebellion of 1798.

United Kingdom. The name adopted on 1 January 1801, when Great Britain and IRELAND were united. *See* ACT OF UNION *under* UNION.

United Nations. The successor to the LEAGUE OF NATIONS as a world organization primarily concerned with the maintenance of peace but with numerous other functions and agencies. It sprang from the Dumbarton Oaks conversations (1944) between the UNITED STATES, Great Britain, and Soviet Russia, and was formally inaugurated in 1945. Its headquarters is in New York City.

United Provinces. Guelderland, Utrecht, Friesland, Overyssel, Groningen, Zeeland, and Holland; the seven provinces whose independence was recognized by Spain in 1648 and who first came together in the *Union of Utrecht* (1579), thus laying the foundation of the United Kingdom of the Netherlands. They became the Batavian Republic in 1795 and the Kingdom of Holland under Louis Bonaparte in 1806. At the end of the Napoleonic Wars (1814), the Kingdom of the Netherlands was reconstituted with the addition of the Southern Netherlands. Belgium secured its independence after the revolt in 1830 and was formally recognized in 1839.

The United Provinces of Agra and Oudh (1902) were entitled the United Provinces in 1935, changed to Uttar Pradesh in 1950.

United Reformed Church. The church formed in 1972 from the union of the Congregational Church of England and Wales (*see* CONGREGATIONALISTS) with the English PRESBYTERIAN Church.

United States of America. The Federal republic of 50 States and one Federal District which has developed from the original 13 States (marked with an asterisk in the list below) which secured their independence from Great Britain in 1783. Its government is based upon the Constitution of 1787. *See also* UNCLE SAM *under* SAM; YANK.

All States except three have official abbreviations and NICKNAMES which are shown below, together with the dates of admission to the UNION.

Alabama (Ala.), Cotton. (1819).
Alaska. (1959).
Arizona (Ariz.), Apache. (1912).
Arkansas (Ark.), Wonder. (1836).
California (Calif.), Golden. (1850).
Colorado (Colo.), Centennial. (1876).
*Connecticut (Conn.), Nutmeg. (1788).

*Delaware (Del.), Diamond. (1787).
Florida (Fla.), Peninsula. (1845).
*Georgia (Ga.), Empire State of the South. (1788).
Hawaii. (1959).
Idaho (Id., Ida.), Gem. (1890).
Illinois (Ill.), Prairie. (1818).
Indiana (Ind.), Hoosier. (1816).
Iowa (Ia., Io.), Hawkeye. (1846).
Kansas (Kans.), Sunflower. (1861).
Kentucky (Ky.), Blue Grass. (1792).
Louisiana (La.), Pelican. (1812).
Maine (Me.), Pine Tree. (1820).
*Maryland (Md.), Old Line. (1788).
*Massachusetts (Mass.), Bay. (1788).
Michigan (Mich.), Wolverine. (1837).
Minnesota (Minn.), Gopher. (1858).
Mississippi (Miss.), Magnolia (1817).
Missouri (Mo.), Show-me. (1821).
Montana (Mont.), Treasure. (1889).
Nebraska (Nebr.), Cornhusker. (1867).
Nevada (Nev.), Sagebrush. (1864).
*New Hampshire (N.H.), Granite. (1788).
*New Jersey (N.J.), Garden. (1787).
New Mexico (N. Mex.), Sunshine. (1912).
*New York (N.Y.), Empire. (1788).
*North Carolina (N.C.), Tar Heel. (1789).
North Dakota (N.D.), Flickertail. (1889).
Ohio (O.), Buckeye. (1803).
Oklahoma (Okla.), Sooner. (1907).
Oregon (Ore., Oreg.), Beaver. (1859).
*Pennsylvania (Pa.), Keystone. (1787).
*Rhode Island (R.I.), Little Rhody. (1790).
*South Carolina (S.C.), Palmetto. (1788).
South Dakota (S.D.), Coyote. (1889).
Tennessee (Tenn.), Volunteer. (1796).
Texas (Tex.), Lone Star. (1845).
Utah, Mormon. (1896).
Vermont (Vt.), Green Mountain. (1791).
*Virginia (Va.), Old Dominion. (1788).
Washington (Wash.), Evergreen. (1889).
West Virginia (W. Va.,), Panhandle. (1863).
Wisconsin (Wis.), Badger. (1848).
Wyoming (Wyo.), Equality. (1890).
District of Columbia (D.C.). (1791).

There are other outlying territories and other nicknames.

Unities, The Dramatic. *See under* DRAMA.

Universal Doctor. Alain de Lille (*c.* 1128–1202), French theologian, so called for his varied learning.

Albertus Magnus (*c.* 1206–1280), the scholastic philosopher, was also called *doc-*

tor universalis.

University. Generally applied to collegiate societies of learning from the 14th century, from Med. Lat. *universitas*, a community or corporation, in this case a corporation of teachers and scholars. Oxford University has its origins in the 12th century and that of Cambridge early in the 13th century. The more common and earlier term was *studium* or *studium generale*, places of instruction of general resort, *i.e.* for students from all parts. They were essentially ecclesiastical institutions.

The University Tests Act. An Act passed in 1871 abolishing in the Universities of Oxford, Cambridge, and Durham subscriptions to the Thirty-nine *Articles of Religion*, all declarations and oaths concerning religious belief, and all compulsory attendance at public worship except for those taking divinity degrees. The Act also applied to all holders of lay posts.

Unknown. The Great Unknown. *See under* GREAT.

The Unknown Prime Minister. A name given to A. Bonar Law (1858–1923), who held office as CONSERVATIVE leader in 1922–1923.

The Unknown Warrior. The body of an unknown British soldier of World War I brought home from one of the battlefields of the Western Front and "buried among the kings" in Westminster Abbey (11 November 1920). Part of the inscription on the gravestone reads: "Thus are commemorated the many multitudes who during the Great War of 1914–1918 gave the most that man can give, Life itself...." Similar tombs were set up in the National Cemetery at Arlington, Virginia; beneath the Arc de Triomphe at Paris; and in the Unter den Linden, Berlin. In 1958 the bodies of two more unknown American servicemen were placed in the **Tomb of the Unknowns** at Arlington—one who died in World War II, and one in the Korean war.

Unlearned Parliament, The. Henry IV's second PARLIAMENT of 1404, also called the *Lawless Parliament*, and *Parliament of Dunces*, because the king hoped for a more tractable assembly by directing the sheriffs not to return any lawyers.

Unmentionables. One of the 19th-century humorous colloquialisms for trousers, pantaloons, breeches; also known as *inexpressibles*. *See* GENS BRACATA

Unmerciful Parliament, The. The MERCILESS PARLIAMENT (*see under* MERCY); also called the WONDERFUL PARLIAMENT.

Unready, The. Ethelred II, King of England (978–1016), called the *redeless*, or deficient in counsel. *Unready* is a modern corruption. Ethelred means "noble-counsel". His nickname is first found in the 13th century.

Unrighteous Bible, The. *See* BIBLE, SOME SPECIALLY NAMED EDITIONS.

Untouchables. The lowest CASTE in India, excluded from social and religious contact with Hinduism and subjected to many indignities. Their touch was supposed to sully the higher castes. Largely through the teaching of Mahatma Gandhi, untouchability was legally ended in 1949. *Cp.* PARIAH.

Unwashed, The Great. Usually a derogatory reference to the lower classes of former days or to the less hygienic habits of our ancestors.

> There are individuals still alive who sneer at the people and speak of them with epithets of scorn. Gentlemen, there can be but little doubt that your ancestors were the Great Unwashed.
>
> THACKERAY: *Pendennis*, ch. xxix.

Unwritten Law. Uncodified custom which rests for its authority on the supposed right of the individual to take into his hands the avenging of personal wrongs; also applied to understood and long-standing custom or convention. COMMON LAW is sometimes so called, which rests upon judicial decision as opposed to written statute.

Up. A.B. is up. A.B. is actually making a speech in PARLIAMENT.

The House is up. The business of the day is ended, and members of PARLIAMENT may go home.

It is up to him. It is for him to take the initiative or decide what is to be done.

Up country. In the interior, away from the coast, inland. The term is sometimes used in America and Australia with slighting implications, meaning unsophisticated, rustic.

"Up, Guards, and at them!" The somewhat APOCRYPHAL order attributed to Wellington as his order to the Guards at the battle of Waterloo (18 June 1815). Creasy gives this rendering in his *Fifteen Decisive Battles*.

Up stage. As a technical theatrical direction this means at the back of the stage which in many theatres slopes down slightly to the footlights. Colloquially the phrase *up-stage* means aloof, putting on airs of consequence or superiority; an actor up stage of another has the advantage, the latter having to act with his back to the audience.

Up State. In the U.S.A., the part of a State farthest north or distant from the coast; the term is used more particularly of the northern parts of New York State.

Upper storey or **story. Not quite right in**

his upper storey. Somewhat mentally unsound, not quite *all there*; something wrong *up top*, *i.e.* in the head or brain.

> But Doctor Plot does not think it necessary to explain, — and the steward, who, before this, has begun to suspect that the old gentleman is not quite right in his upper story, is now confirmed in the impression.
>
> W. HARRISON AINSWORTH: *The Flitch of Bacon* (1854), ch. vii.

The Upper House. *See under* HOUSE.

The Upper Ten. *See under* TEN.

Down on or **on one's uppers.** Impoverished; as typified by the worn-out condition of one's footwear. *Cp.* DOWN AT HEEL.

Upanishads (ū păn′ i shădz). Part of the oldest speculative literature of the Hindus, a collection of treatises on the nature of the universe, the deity, and man. They form the VEDANTA, or last part of the VEDA, and date from about 500 B.C. The name is Sanskrit, and means "a sitting down" (at another's feet), hence "a confidential talk", "esoteric doctrine".

Upas Tree (ū′ păs). The Javanese tree, *Antiaris toxicaria*, the milky juice of which contains a virulent poison and is used for tipping arrows.

Fable has it that a putrid steam rises from it, and that whatever the vapour touches dies. Foersch, a Dutch physician, wrote in 1783, "Not a tree, nor blade of grass is to be found in the valley or surrounding mountains. Not a beast or bird, reptile or living thing, lives in the vicinity." He adds that on "one occasion 1,600 refugees encamped within 14 miles of it, and all but 300 died within two months". This "traveller's tale" has given rise to the figurative use of *upas* for a corrupting or pernicious influence.

Upsee. Used in combination with *Dutch*, *Freeze*, *English*, as jesting terms for drinking or tippling. *Upsee Dutch* is "in the manner of the Dutch", *upsee Freeze*, "in the manner of a Frisian", etc.

> I do not like the dulness of your eye,
> It hath a heavy cast; 'tis upsee-Dutch,
> And says you are a lumpish whoremaster.
>
> BEN JONSON: *The Alchemist*, IV, iv.

Upset price. The price at which goods sold by auction are first offered for competition. If no advance is made they fall to the person who made the upset price. *Reserved bid* is virtually the same thing.

Upstairs. To kick upstairs. To get rid of an embarrassing colleague in the CABINET or HOUSE OF COMMONS by giving him a peerage, thereby removing him to the HOUSE OF LORDS. Thus any promotion given to get rid of someone.

Urania (ū rā′ ni à). One of the MUSES in Greek mythology who presides over ASTROLOGY; usually represented pointing at a celestial globe with a staff. Also an epithet of APHRODITE or VENUS. The name means "heavenly" or "celestial". Milton (*Paradise Lost*, VII, 1–39) makes her the spirit of the loftiest poetry, and calls her "heavenly born" and the sister of Wisdom.

Uranus (ū′ rà nus). In Greek mythology, the personification of HEAVEN, son and husband of GÆA (Earth), and father of the TITANS, the CYCLOPS, etc. He hated his children and confined them in the body of Earth who begged them to avenge her, and his son KRONOS unmanned him with a sickle and dethroned him.

The planet Uranus was discovered in 1781 by Herschel, and named by him *Georgium Sidus* in honour of George III. Its five satellites are named *Ariel*, *Umbriel*, *Titania*, *Oberon*, and *Miranda*.

Urbanists. *See* FRANCISCANS.

Urbi et Orbi (ĕr′ bī et ôr′ bī). (Lat., to the city [Rome] and the world). A phrase applied to the solemn blessing publicly given by the POPE from the balcony of St. Peter's on special occasions, such as his election. The custom fell into abeyance after 1870 but was revived by Pope Pius XI after his election in 1922.

Urdu. The form of Hindustani spoken by Mohammedans and Hindus in contact with them; from *urdu zaban*, "the language of the camp", which grew up as the means of communication between the MOSLEM conquerors and their subject population.

Uriah (ū rī′ à). **Letter of Uriah.** A treacherous letter, importing friendship but in reality a death warrant. (*See* II *Sam.* xi, 15.)

Uriel (ū′ ri ĕl). One of the seven ARCHANGELS of rabbinical angelology, sent by God to answer the questions of Esdras (II *Esdras* iv). In Milton's *Paradise Lost* (III, 690) he is the "Regent of the Sun", and "sharpest-sighted spirit of all in HEAVEN".

Urim and Thummim (ū′ rim, thŭm′ im). Sacred LOTS of unknown nature used for DIVINATION by the ancient Hebrews as a means of ascertaining the will of God. They are mentioned in *Exod.* xxviii, 30; *Deut.* xxxiii, 8; I *Sam.* xxviii, 6; *Ezra* ii, 63, etc., but fell out of use as more spiritual conceptions of the Deity developed and there is no mention of them after the time of David.

Ursa Major. The GREAT BEAR (*see under* BEAR), or CHARLES'S WAIN, the most conspicuous of the northern constellations.

Boswell's father used to call Dr. Johnson *Ursa Major*.

Ursa Minor. The Little Bear; the northern

constellation known also as Cynosura or Dog's tail, from its circular sweep. The Pole star is α in the tail. *See* CYNOSURE; GREAT BEAR *under* BEAR.

Ursula, St. A 5th-century British princess, according to legend, who went with 11,000 virgins on a pilgrimage to ROME and was massacred with all her companions by the Huns at Cologne. One explanation of the story is that *Undecimilla* (mistaken for *undecim millia,* 11,000) was one of Ursula's companions.

Ursulines. An order of nuns founded by St. Angela Merici of Brescia in 1535, from their patron SAINT, St. URSULA. They were primarily concerned with the education of girls.

Use. To have no use for a person. Used idiomatically, implies active dislike mingled with contempt—one is not prepared to make use of him for any purpose. "To have no time for a person" is a similar expression.

Useless Parliament, The. The PARLIAMENT convened by CHARLES I, on 8 June 1625; adjourned to Oxford, 1 August; and dissolved 12 August; having done nothing but quarrel with the KING.

Usher. From Fr. *huissier*, a door-keeper.
   Gentleman Usher of the Black Rod. *See* BLACK ROD.
   Usher of the Green Rod. An officer in attendance on the Knights of the Thistle at their chapters. (*See* THE "MOST ANCIENT" ORDER OF THE THISTLE *under* THISTLE).

Usnech, or **Uisnech, The Sons of.** Naoise (or Noisi), Ainle, and Ardan. DEIRDRE was told by her foster-father that she would fall in love with a man who had hair as black as a raven, cheeks as red as blood, and a body white as snow. Naoise was such a man and Deirdre eloped with him.

Usquebaugh (us' kwē baw). Whisky (Ir. *uisgebeatha*, water of life). Similar to the Lat. *aqua vitæ* and Fr. *eau de vie*.

Utgard. In Scandinavian mythology, the abode of the giants, where Utgard-LOKI had his castle.

Uther. According to Geoffrey of Monmouth (*Historia Britonum*), King of Britain and father of King ARTHUR by an adulterous amour with Igerna, wife of Gorlois, Duke of Cornwall, at TINTAGEL. *See* PENDRAGON.

Uti possidetis (ū' tī pos i dē' tis) (Lat., as you possess). The principle that the property remains with its present possessor; in international law that the belligerents retain possession of their acquisitions in war.

Uticensis (ū ti sen' sis). Cato the Younger (95–46 B.C.) was so called from Utica, the place of his death.

Utility. The official name given during and after World War II to clothing, furniture, etc., made according to government specification and sold at controlled prices. The name was a sign of the austerity of the times, practical qualities being more important than ornamentation, etc.

Utilitarianism. The ethical doctrine that actions are right in proportion to their usefulness or as they tend to promote happiness; the doctrine that the end and criterion of public action is "the greatest happiness of the greatest number".

The term originated with Jeremy Bentham (1748–1832), whose ideas were expounded by his disciple James Mill (1773–1836) and by the latter's son John Stuart Mill (1806–1873), in his *Utilitarianism* (1869), who also introduced quantitative and qualitative distinctions in pleasures. *See* PANOPTICON.

Utnapishtim. The Babylonian counterpart of Noah, whose story is told in the GILGAMESH EPIC, and which has many notable resemblances to the BIBLE story. The Hebrews almost certainly derived their account from Babylonia.

Utopia. Nowhere (Gr. *ou*, not; *topos*, a place). The name given by Sir Thomas More to the imaginary island in his political romance of the same name (1516), where everything is perfect—the laws, the morals, the politics, etc., and in which the evils of existing laws, etc., are shown by contrast. *See* IDEAL COMMONWEALTHS *under* COMMONWEALTH.

Hence *Utopian*, applied to any idealistic but impractical scheme.

Rabelais (Bk. II, ch. xxiv) sends PANTAGRUEL and his companions to Utopia, where they find the citizens of its capital, Amaurot, most hospitable.

Utraquists (Lat. *utraque specie*, in both kinds). HUSSITES or CALIXTENES, so called because they insisted that both elements should be administered to communicants in the EUCHARIST.

Utter and Inner Barristers. An *utter* or *outer* BARRISTER is one who has not taken SILK. An *inner* barrister means a student.

Uzziel. One of the principal ANGELS of rabbinical angelology, the name meaning "Strength of God". He was next in command to GABRIEL, and in Milton's *Paradise Lost* (IV, 782) is commanded by Gabriel to "coast the south with strictest watch".

V

V. The twenty-second letter of the alphabet formerly sharing its form with U.

In the Roman notation it stands for 5 and represents ideographically the four fingers and thumb with the latter extended. V̄ represents 5,000.

V for Victory. On 14 January 1941, M. Victor de Lavaleye, a member of the exiled Belgian government in London, proposed in a broadcast to Belgium that the letter V, standing for Victory in all European languages, be substituted for the letters R.A.F. which were being chalked up on walls, etc., in Belgium. The plan was immediately adopted and the Morse Code V (...—) was featured in every B.B.C. broadcast to Europe followed by the opening bar of Beethoven's 5th Symphony which has the same rhythm. "Colonel Britton" (D. E. Ritchie), director of the B.B.C. European news service, was responsible for the diffusion of the V-sign propaganda which gave hope to those under the NAZI yoke. Sir Winston Churchill greatly popularized the sign of two upraised fingers in the form of a V.

V-1. Jet-propelled ROBOT plane bomb sent against Britain by the Germans, June–August 1944; subsequently sent by them against Antwerp. V = *Vergeltungswaffe* (reprisal weapon).

V-2. Long-range rocket with an explosive warhead, projected against England by the Germans in autumn, 1944.

V.C. *See* VICTORIA CROSS.

V.D.M.I.Æ. Lat. *Verbum Dei manet in æternum, i.e.* the word of God endureth for ever. The inscription on the liveries of the servants of the Duke of Saxony and Landgrave of Hesse, the Lutheran princes, at the Diet of Spires (Speier) in 1526.

V.E. Day. The end of hostilities in Europe after World War II, 8 May 1945.

V.I.P. Very Important Person. This well-established usage was coined by a Station Commander of Transport Command in 1944 who was responsible for the movement of a plane-load of important individuals, including Lord Mountbatten, to the Middle East and so described them in his movement orders to avoid disclosing their identity.

V.J. Day. The end of hostilities in the Far East, 15 August 1945.

V.P. Vice-President. In U.S.A. often called *Veep*.

VXL. A punning monogram on lockets, etc., standing for UXL (you excel). U and V were formerly interchangeable.

Vacuum (Lat. *vacare*, to be empty). The word is commonly used for a vacuum-cleaner and to *vacuum* is to clean up with this instrument. *Cp.* HOOVER.

Nature abhors a vacuum. This maxim is used by Spinoza in his *Ethics* (1677) and by Rabelais in its Latin form, *natura abhorret vacuum*, in his GARGANTUA (ch. V). *See* TORRICELLI.

Vade mecum (vā' dē mē' kŭm) (Lat., go-with-me). A pocket-book, memorandum-book, pocket cyclopædia, lady's pocket companion, or anything else which contains many things of daily use in a small compass.

Væ Victis! (vē vik' tis) (Lat.). Woe to the vanquished! So much the worse for the conquered! This was the exclamation of Brennus, the Gaulish chief, on throwing his sword into the balance as a make-weight, when determining the price of peace with ROME (390 B.C.).

Vagitanus. *See* BABES, PROTECTING DEITIES OF.

Vail. To lower; to cast down. From Fr. *avaler*, to descend.

> The time is come
> That France must vail her lofty plumed crest.
> SHAKESPEARE: *Henry VI, Pt. I*, V, iii.

Vails, or **Vales,** an obsolete term for a tip given to servants, from Fr. *valoir*, Lat. *valere*, to be worth. The older form was *avails*.

> 2. *Fish:* Ay, but hark you, my friend; 'twas we that made up this garment through the rough seams of the waters: there are certain condolements, certain vails. I hope, sir, if you thrive, you'll remember from whence you had it.
> SHAKESPEARE: *Pericles*, II, i.

Vale! Farewell! 2nd pers, sing. imp. of Lat. *valere*, to be worth, or to fare well.

I thought once againe heare to have made an ende,
with a heartie *Vale* of the best fashion.
SPENSER: *Letter to Gabriel Harvey* (1580).

Ave atque vale! Hail and farewell! The
words of Catullus at his brother's tomb.

Vale of the White Horse. *See under* HORSE.

Valentine, St. A priest of ROME who was imprisoned for succouring persecuted Christians. He became a convert and, although he
is supposed to have restored the sight of the
gaoler's blind daughter, he was clubbed to
death (*c.* 270). His day is 14 February, as is
that of St. Valentine, bishop of Terni, who
was martyred a few years later. There are
several other saints of this name.

The ancient custom of choosing *Valen-
tines* has only accidental relation to either
SAINT, being essentially a relic of the old Roman *Lupercalia* (*see* LUPERCAL), or from association with the mating season of birds. It
was marked by the giving of presents and
nowadays by the sending of a card on which
CUPIDS, transfixed hearts, etc., are depicted.

Chaucer refers to this in his *Assembly of
Fowls* (310):

For this was on Saint Valentine's Day,
When ev'ry fowl cometh to choose her make,

and SHAKESPEARE (*Midsummer Night's
Dream*, IV, i) has:

Good morrow, friends! St. Valentine is past;
Begin these wood-birds but to couple now?

Valentine and Orson. An old French RO-
MANCE connected with the Carolingian
cycle.

The heroes, from whom it is named, were
the twin sons of Bellisant, sister of King
Pepin, and Alexander, and were born in a
forest near Orléans. Orson (Fr. *ourson*, a little bear) was carried off by a bear and became a wild man and the terror of France.
While the mother was searching for him,
Valentine was carried off by his uncle,
the KING. The brothers had many adventures and Orson was reclaimed by Valentine. Orson married Fezon, daughter of
Duke Savary of Aquitaine, and Valentine,
Clerimond, sister of the Green Knight.

Valhalla. In Scandinavian mythology, the
hall in the celestial regions whither the souls
of heroes slain in battle were borne by the
VALKYRIES, to spend eternity in joy and
feasting (*valr*, the slain, and *hall*).

Hence the name is applied to buildings,
such as Westminster Abbey, used as the last
resting-place of a nation's great men.

Valkyries (Old Norse, the choosers of the
slain). The nine (or seven, or twelve) hand-
maidens of ODIN, who, mounted on swift
horses and holding drawn swords, rushed
into the *mêlée* of battle and selected those

destined to death. These heroes they conducted to VALHALLA, where they waited
upon them and served them with mead and
ALE in the skulls of the vanquished.

Vallary Crown (Lat. *vallum*, a mound, rampart). The same as a *mural* CROWN.

Valley of Ten Thousand Smokes. A volcanic valley in the region of Mount Katmai,
Alaska. Shortly before Mount Katmai blew
up on 6 June 1912 there were many bursts of
molten matter in the valley, and these
fissures have since discharged hot gases,
hence the name of the valley. It has been a
National Monument since 1918.

The Valley of the Kings. A site in the Theban Hills, north-west of THEBES, Egypt,
containing the tombs of PHARAOHS of the
New Kingdom. Thutmosis I (1530–1520
B.C.) was the first to build his tomb there.
The wadi was guarded by small forts and the
tombs were walled up with rubble, but pillaging began as the New Kingdom declined.
The many tombs uncovered include that of
Tutankhamun, revealed with its remarkable
treasures in 1922–3 by Howard Carter who,
with Lord Carnarvon, had been engaged in
excavations there since 1906. *See* CURSE OF
TUTANKHAMUN.

The Valley of the Queens. The less spectacular cemetery of the wives and daughters
of Pharaohs of the XXth Dynasty. It lies to
the south of the VALLEY OF THE KINGS.

Valois (văl' wa). The reigning dynasty in
France from 1328 to 1589, taking its name
from Philip, Duke of Valois, the first of the
line. They were a branch of the CAPET family
and were succeeded by the BOURBON line
when Henry of Navarre, husband of Marguerite of Valois, became King as Henry IV
in 1589.

Valois head-dress. A mid-19th-century
women's hair style, the hair being pulled
back from the forehead to form a roll on the
crown of the head.

Vamana. *See* AVATAR.

Vamp. To vamp is properly to put new
uppers to old boots; and *vamps* were short
hose covering the feet and ankles (Fr.
avant-pied, the forepart of the foot).

To vamp up an old story, to refurbish it; *to
vamp* an accompaniment to a song is to improvise as one goes along. Another verb *to
vamp*, derived from VAMPIRE, means to flirt
outrageously or allure with the intent of
gaining some personal end.

Vampire. A fabulous being, supposed to be
the ghost of a heretic, criminal, etc., who returned from the grave in the guise of a monstrous bat to suck the blood of sleeping persons who usually became vampires them-

selves. The only way to destroy them was to drive a stake through their body. The superstition is essentially Slavonic.

> But first on earth, as vampire sent,
> Thy corse shall from its tomb be rent,
> Then ghastly haunt thy native place
> And suck the blood of all thy race.
>
> BYRON: *The Giaour*, 755.

The word is applied to one who preys upon his fellows—a "blood-sucker".

One of the classic horror stories, Bram Stoker's *Dracula* (1897), centres on vampirism. The Dracula of Transylvanian legend appears to originate from Vlad V of Wallachia (1456–1476), known as Vlad the Impaler, although he was not a vampire. It is suggested that Stoker's Count Dracula was a composite figure derived from Vlad the Impaler and the Countess Báthori, who was arrested in 1610 for murdering girls. It was her habit to wash in the blood of her several hundred girl victims in order to maintain her skin in a youthful condition. The name comes from Vlad's membership of the Order of the Dragon, although *dracul* in Rumanian also means *devil*.

Van Diemen's Land. The former name for Tasmania, given by its Dutch discoverer Abel Jans Tasman in 1642 in honour of his patron, the Dutch Governor-General of Batavia. It became a British settlement in 1803, and its name was changed to Tasmania in 1853, to obliterate memories of its associations with BUSHRANGERS and convicts, transportation having ceased at that time.

Vandals. A Teutonic race first recorded in north-east Germany which in the 5th century ravaged GAUL, Spain, and North Africa, and in 455 ROME itself, when they despoiled it of its treasures of art and literature.

The name is hence applied to those who wilfully or ignorantly indulge in destruction of works of art, etc. *Vandalism* is now applied to most forms of wanton damage.

Vandyke (văn dīk'). To scallop an edge after the fashion of the collars painted by Van Dyck in the reign of CHARLES I. The scalloped edges are said to be *vandyked*.

Vandyke beard. A pointed beard such as those frequently shown in Van Dyck's portraits, especially of CHARLES I.

Vanessa (vă nes' à). Dean Swift's name for his friend and correspondent, Esther Vanhomrigh, made by compounding Van, the first syllable of her surname, with Essa, the pet form of Esther. Swift called himself Cadenus, an anagram on Decanus (Lat. for DEAN).

Vanguard. See AVANT-GARDE.

Vanir. A Scandinavian race of gods of peaceful and benevolent functions in contrast to the ÆSIR, who were essentially warriors. Among them were NJÖRD, FREYR, and FREYJA.

Vanity Fair. In Bunyan's *Pilgrim's Progress*, a fair established by BEELZEBUB, Apollyon, and Legion, in the town of Vanity, and lasting all the year round. Here were sold houses, lands, trades, places, honours, preferments, titles, countries, kingdoms, lusts, pleasures, and delights of all sorts.

Thackeray adopted the name for the title of his novel (1847) satirizing the weaknesses and follies of human nature.

Vantage loaf. The thirteenth loaf of a baker's dozen.

Varaha. See AVATAR.

Variety is the spice of life. It is variety in all its aspects that makes life interesting—an established aphorism which tends to be forgotten nowadays by planners, egalitarians, and disciples of the COMMON MARKET.

> Variety's the very spice of life,
> That gives it all its flavour.
>
> COWPER: *The Task* II, 606.

Variorum Edition (Lat. *variorum*, of various persons). An edition of a literary text giving the variant readings, notes, and comments of different scholars.

'Varsity. A shortened form of *university*; but, in England, properly used only of Oxford or Cambridge.

Varuna. In Hindu mythology, the brother of Mitra, one of the ADITYAS. Varuna shines at night and is linked with the MOON. He is represented as a white man riding on a sea monster, is the witness of everything, orders the seasons and controls the rains. Mitra is linked with the sun and shines or sees by day.

Vassal. A feudal TENANT with military obligations to his superior; hence, a dependant, retainer, servant, etc.

Vathek. The hero of the outstanding oriental novel of this name by William Beckford (1760–1844) of Fonthill (*see* FOLLY). It was written in French and first appeared in English in 1786. Vathek, the ninth caliph of the ABBASSIDE dynasty, is a haughty, effeminate monarch, induced by a malignant genius to commit all sorts of crimes. He abjured faith, and offered allegiance to EBLIS, under the hope of obtaining the throne of the pre-Adamite sultans. This he gained, only to find that it was a place of torture and that he was doomed to remain in it for ever.

Vatican (văt' i kàn). The palace of the POPE; so called because it stands on the *Vaticanus Mons* (Vatican Hill) of ancient ROME, which got its name through being the headquarters of the *vaticinatores*, or soothsayers.

The Vatican City State. The area of ROME occupied by the city of the VATICAN, recognized by the LATERAN TREATY (1929) as constituting the territorial extent of the temporal power of the HOLY SEE. It consists of the Papal palace, the LIBRARY, archives, and museums, the Piazza of St. PETER, and contiguous buildings including a railway station, in all an area of just under a square mile. It has about 900 inhabitants and its own coinage. Certain other buildings outside the Vatican enjoy extraterritorial rights.

The Vatican Council. The twentieth ŒCUMENICAL COUNCIL of the ROMAN CATHOLIC CHURCH (1869–1870), summoned by Pius IX and suspended when the Italians occupied ROME after the withdrawal of the French garrison. It was notable for its definition of Papal INFALLIBILITY which was limited to when the Pope speaks *ex cathedra* regarding faith or morals.

A second Vatican Council was opened by Pope John XXIII in October 1962 and concluded by Paul VI in December 1965. Among numerous controversial proposals for change, it was notably concerned with the need for Christian unity, liturgical reforms, and matters of church government. One special feature was the presence of observers from non-Roman Catholic Churches. *See* ŒCUMENICAL COUNCILS.

The Prisoner of the Vatican. The POPE was so called after 1870, when Pius IX retired into the VATICAN after the occupation of ROME. He proclaimed himself a prisoner for conscience' sake and his successors remained in the precincts of the Vatican until the LATERAN TREATY of 1929.

The Thunders of the Vatican. *See* THUNDER.

Vaudeville (vō' divil). A corruption of *Val de vire* or in O.Fr. *Vau de vire*, valley of the Vire, the native valley of Olivier Basselin, a Norman poet (d. 1418) and author of convivial songs which were so named from the place where he composed them. It is now applied to variety entertainment made of songs, dances, sketches, etc.

Vaudois. *See* WALDENSIANS. *Cp.* VOODOO.

Vauxhall (vawks' or vox' awl). A part of LAMBETH, London, so called from Falkes de Bréauté who was lord of the manor in the early 13th century.

Vauxhall Gardens. A very popular pleasure resort for Londoners, first laid out in 1661 as Spring Gardens and finally closed in 1859. Pepys refers to it as Fox Hall. It finds mention in the *Spectator*, Dickens's *Sketches by Boz*, Thackeray's *Vanity Fair*,

etc. It provided ample refreshment, musical entertainment, fireworks, displays of pictures and statuary, etc., and at night was lit by over 1,000 lamps. *Cp.* CREMORNE GARDENS; ROSHERVILLE GARDENS.

Vedanta (Sansk., "The end of the Veda"). The UPANISHADS, the philosophy of the Upanishads; the system of Hindu philosophy based on the VEDAS.

Vedas. The four sacred books of the BRAHMINS, comprising (1) the *Rigveda*; (2) the *Samaveda*; (3) the *Yajurveda*; and (4) the *Atharvaveda*. The first consists of hymns, the second of chants, the third mainly of sacrificial prayers in prose and verse, and the fourth largely of hymns and spells concerned with superstitious practices.

The word *Veda* means knowledge.

Veep. *See* V.P.

Vehmgerichte (fām' gĕ rich tĕ). Also *Fehmgerichte*. Courts or tribunals conducted by groups of free men under the presidency of a *Freigraf* (free count) which flourished in Germany (especially in Westphalia) between the 12th and 16th centuries. They were restricted to Westphalia in the 16th century and their last vestiges abolished in 1811. They dealt with serious crimes (punishable by death), heresy and witchcraft. Generally portrayed as sinister institutions, for the most part they did not abuse their power. In secret session the only punishment awarded was the death sentence which was carried out on the guilty forthwith.

"And was that opinion", said the presiding Judge, "favourable or otherwise to the Holy and Secret Vehme–gericht? Let truth rule your tongue—remember, life is short, Judgment is eternal."
SCOTT: *Anne of Geierstein*, ch. xx.

Veil. Beyond the veil. The unknown state of those who have departed this life.

To take the veil. To become a nun; from the traditional head-dress of women in religious orders.

Velvet. The iron hand in the velvet glove. Absolute firmness concealed by mildness of approach.

The little gentleman in velvet. The MOLE. *See under* LITTLE.

Velveteens. An old nickname for a gamekeeper, from his once common velveteen jacket—velveteen being a sort of FUSTIAN of twilled cotton with a pile.

"I'm the new under-keeper, and master's told me to keep a sharp look-out on all o' you young chaps. And I tells 'ee I means business, and you'd better keep on your own side, or we shall fall out."
"Well, that's right, Velveteens—speak out, and let's know your mind at once."
HUGHES: *Tom Brown's Schooldays*, I, ix.

Vendémiaire (von dä mē âr). The first month in the FRENCH REVOLUTIONARY CALENDAR (*see under* CALENDAR); from 22 SEPTEMBER to 21 OCTOBER. The word means "Vintage month".

Vendue (ven dū') (U.S.A.). A word of obvious French origin for a public auction sale, used from about the mid-18th century to the mid-19th century.

> We'd better take maysures for shettin' up shop,
> An' put off our stock by a vendoo or swop.
> LOWELL: *Biglow Papers, Series 2*, V, 133–134.

Venerable (Lat. *venerabilis*, worthy of honour). The title applied to archdeacons in formally addressing them ("The Venerable the Archdeacon of Barset", or "The Venerable E. L. Brown"); and in the ROMAN CATHOLIC CHURCH, the title of one who has attained the first of the three degrees of CANONIZATION.

It belongs especially to BEDE, the monk of Jarrow, an English ecclesiastical historian (d. 735), and to William of Champeaux (d. 1121), the French scholastic philosopher and opponent of ABELARD.

Veni, Creator Spiritus (vä nē' krä a'tôr spē' ri tùs). A hymn to the HOLY GHOST in the Roman BREVIARY, probably of the 9th century and often attributed to Rabanus Maurus (d. 856), Archbishop of Mainz. It is sung at VESPERS and Terce during PENTECOST and on other occasions such as the consecration of a church or of a BISHOP. The popular English version beginning "Come, Holy Ghost, our souls inspire" is by John Cosin (1594–1672), Bishop of Durham.

Veni, Sancte Spiritus (Lat., Come, Holy Spirit). A mediæval Latin hymn, used as a sequence at PENTECOST in the ROMAN CATHOLIC CHURCH.

Veni, vidi, vici (Lat., I came, I saw, I conquered). According to Plutarch, it was thus that Julius CÆSAR announced to his friend Amintius his victory at Zela (47 B.C.), in Asia Minor, over Pharnaces, son of Mithridates, who had rendered aid to Pompey.

Venial Sin. One that does not forfeit grace. In the ROMAN CATHOLIC CHURCH sins are of two sorts, MORTAL and venial (Lat. *venia*, grace, pardon). See *Matt*. xii, 31.

Venice Glass. The drinking-glasses of the MIDDLE AGES, made at Venice, were said to break into shivers if poison were put into them.

> *Doge:* 'Tis said that our Venetian crystal has
> Such pure antipathy to poison, as
> To burst, if aught of venom touches it.
> BYRON: *The Two Foscari*, V, i.

Venire facias (Lat., cause to come). An ancient writ directing a SHERIFF to assemble a jury.

Venison. Anything taken in hunting or by the chase. Hence Isaac bids Esau to go and get venison such as he loved (*Gen.* xxvii, 3), meaning the wild kid. The word is the Lat. *venatio*, hunting, but is now restricted to the flesh of deer.

Venite (vē nī' tē). Psalm 95, from its opening words *Venite, exultemus Domino*, "O come, let us sing unto the Lord". It is said or sung at MATTINS.

Venner's Rising. The last futile attempt of some 80 men under Thomas Venner to set up the FIFTH MONARCHY in January 1661. They fought desperately and Venner and 16 of his accomplices were executed.

Venom. The Venom is in the tail. The real difficulty is the conclusion; *with a sting in its tail* is a similar expression. (*See* TAIL).

Ventôse (von' tōz) (Fr., windy). The sixth month of the FRENCH REVOLUTIONARY CALENDAR (*see under* CALENDAR).

Ventre-saint-Gris (vontr sǎng grē). The usual oath of Henri IV of France, *Gris* being a euphemism for Christ, and *ventre*, stomach. Oaths not infrequently took this form of blasphemy—*God's nails*, *God's teeth*, etc., were common in England.

A similar oath is *Par le ventre de Dieu*. Rabelais has *Par sainct Gris*; and the suggestion has been made that the allusion was to FRANCIS of Assisi, who was *ceint* (girdled) and clad in *gris* (grey).

Ventriloquism. The trick of producing vocal sounds so that they appear to come, not from the person producing them, but from some other quarter. So called from Lat. *venter*, belly, *loqui*, to speak (speaking from the belly), with the erroneous notion that the voice of the ventriloquist proceeded from his stomach.

Venus. The Roman goddess of beauty and sensual love, identified with APHRODITE, in some accounts said to have sprung from the foam of the sea, in others to have been the daughter of JUPITER and DIONE, a NYMPH. VULCAN was her husband, but she had amours with MARS and many other gods and demigods. By MERCURY she was the mother of CUPID, and by the hero Anchises, the mother of ÆNEAS, through whom she was regarded by the Romans as the foundress of their race. Her chief festival is 1 April. *See* VENUS VERTICORDIA, *below*.

Her name is given to the second planet from the SUN (*see* HESPERUS), and in ASTROLOGY "signifiethe white men or browne ... joyfull, laughter, liberall, pleasers, dauncers, entertayners of women, players, perfumers, musitions, messengers of love".

Venus loveth ryot and dispence.
CHAUCER: *Wife of Bath's Prol.*, 700.

By the alchemists *copper* was designated *Venus*, probably because mirrors were anciently made of copper. A mirror is still the astronomical symbol of the planet Venus.

The best cast at dice (three sixes) used to be called *Venus*, and the worst (three aces), *Canis* (dog); hence the phrase, "His Venus has turned out a whelp" equivalent to, "ALL HIS SWANS ARE GEESE" (*see under* GOOSE).

Venus Anadyomene. VENUS rising from the sea, accompanied by dolphins. The name is given to the famous lost painting by APELLES, and to that by Botticelli in the Accademia delle Belle Arti at Florence.

Venus Callipyge (Gr., with the beautiful buttocks). The name given to a late Greek statue in the Museo Nazionale at Naples. There is no real ground for connecting the statue with VENUS.

Venus de' Medici. A famous statue, since 1860 in the Uffizi Gallery, Florence, ranking as a canon of female beauty. It is supposed to date from the time of AUGUSTUS, and was dug up in the 17th century in the villa of Hadrian, near Tivoli, in 11 pieces. It was kept in the MEDICI Palace at ROME till its removal to Florence by Cosimo III.

Venus Genetrix (Lat., she that has borne). VENUS worshipped as a symbol of marriage and motherhood. CÆSAR erected a temple to Venus Genetrix in the Forum at ROME and there are several statues of this name. She is represented as raising her light drapery and holding an apple, the emblem of fecundity.

Venus of Cnidus. The nude statue of Praxiteles, purchased by the ancient Cnidians, who refused to part with it, although Nicomedes, king of Bithynia, offered to pay off their national debt as its price. It was subsequently removed to Constantinople, and perished in the great fire during the reign of Justinian (A.D. 532); but an ancient reproduction is in the VATICAN.

Venus of Milo, or Melos. This statue, with three of HERMES, was discovered by the French admiral Dumond d'Urville in Milo or Melos, one of the Greek islands. It dates from the 2nd century B.C. and is probably the finest single work of ancient art extant. It is now in the LOUVRE.

Venus Verticordia. One of the surnames of VENUS because she was invoked to "turn the hearts" of women to virtue and chastity (Lat. *vertere*, to turn; *cor, cordis*, heart).

Venus Victrix. VENUS, as goddess of victory, represented on numerous Roman coins.

Venus's Fly-trap. A plant (*Dionœa musci-*

pula) which feeds on insects, and is found in Carolina.

Venus's girdle. The CESTUS.

Venus's hair. The maidenhair fern, *Adiantum capillus-Veneris*.

Venus's hair-stone, or **pencil.** Rock-crystal or quartz penetrated by acicular crystals of rutile which show through as hair-like filaments.

Venus's Looking-glass (*Specularia hybrida*). A rare small plant growing in the south and east of England on chalky soil. It has blue or purple flowers.

Venusberg. The Hörselberg, or mountain of delight and love, situated between Eisenach and Gotha, in the caverns of which, according to mediæval German legend, the Lady Venus held her court. Human visitors were sometimes allowed in, such as Thomas of Ercildoune and TANNHÄUSER, but they ran the risk of eternal perdition. ECKHARDT the Faithful sat outside to warn them against entering.

Vera causa (vē′ rà kaw′ zà) (Lat., a true cause). A cause in harmony with other causes already known. A fairy godmother may be assigned in story as the cause of certain marvellous effects, but is not a *vera causa*. The revolution of the earth round the sun may be assigned as the cause of the four seasons, and is a *vera causa*.

Verb. sap., or **Verb. sat.** The abbreviations of the Lat. *verbum sapienti sat est*, a word to the wise is enough. A hint is sufficient to any intelligent person.

Verbatim et litteratim (Lat.). "Word for word and letter for letter." Accurately rendered.

Verbena. *See* VERVAIN.

Verdant Green. An excessively "green" or unsophisticated young man. The character was epitomized in *The Adventures of Mr. Verdant Green* (1853) by "Cuthbert Bede, B.A." (Rev. Edward Bradley). Verdant's adventures at Oxford, whither he goes as a very green freshman, the victim of endless practical jokes and impostures, make an entertaining and enlightening commentary on life at the University in the mid-19th century.

> "Looks ferociously mild in his gig-lamps!" remarked a third, alluding to Mr Verdant Green's spectacles. "And jolly green all over!" wound up a fourth. (ch. iii).

Verderer. In English forest law (*see under* FOREST COURTS), an official having jurisdiction in the royal forests with especial charge of trees and undergrowth.

Vere adeptus (Lat., one who has truly attained). A title assumed by one admitted to the fraternity of the ROSICRUCIANS.

> In Rosicrucian lore as learned
> As he the vere-adeptus earned.
> BUTLER: *Hudibras*, I, i, 539.

Verger. The BEADLE in a church who carries the rod or staff, which was formerly called the *verge* (Lat. *virga*, a rod).

Vergil. *See* VIRGIL.

Vermeer Forgery. *See under* FORGERY.

Veronica, St. According to late mediæval legend, a woman of JERUSALEM who handed her head-cloth to Our Lord on His way to CALVARY. He wiped His brow and returned it to the giver when it was found to bear a perfect likeness of the Saviour impressed upon it and was called *Vera-Icon* (true likeness); the woman became St. *Veronica*. It is one of the relics at St. Peter's, ROME. In Spanish bull-fighting the most classic movement with the cape is called the *Veronica*, the cape being swung so slowly before the face of the charging bull that it resembles St. Veronica's wiping of the Holy Face.

Vers de société (Fr., Society verse). Light poetry of a witty or fanciful kind, generally with a slight vein of social satire running through it.

Vers libre. *See* FREE VERSE.

Versailles (vâr sī'). The great palace built by Louis XIV, in the town of that name to the S.W. of Paris. It was begun by Louis XIII, but in 1661 the great enlargement was started that made it the greatest palace in Europe. The gardens were planned by Le Nôtre and the original park contained the Grand Trianon and the Petit Trianon. Its fountains, water-courses, statuary, and shrubberies were all on a grand scale.

It was the scene of many historic occasions including the signing of the armistice between Great Britain and the United States with their French allies in 1783, and the taking of the TENNIS COURT OATH by the States General in 1789. Here, too, in the famous Galerie des Glaces, William I of Prussia was crowned first German Emperor, and the Treaty of Versailles between the Allied Powers and Germany was signed after World War I. *See also* ŒIL-DE-BŒUF.

Versi Berneschi. *See* BERNESQUE.

Vert (vĕrt). The heraldic term (from French) for *green*, said to signify love, joy, and abundance; in engravings it is indicated by lines running diagonally across the shield from right to left.

Vertumnus (vĕr tŭm' nus). The ancient Roman god of the seasons, and the deity presiding over gardens and orchards. He was the husband of POMONA. 12 August was his festival.

Vervain (vĕr' vān). Called "holy herb", from its use in ancient rites. Also called "pigeons' grass", "Juno's tears", and "simpler's joy". *Verbena* is its botanical name. *See* HERBA SACRA.

Vesica Piscis (ves' i ka pis'is). (Lat., fishbladder). The ovoidal frame or glory which, in the 12th century, was much used, especially in painted windows, to surround pictures of the Virgin Mary and of Our Lord. It is meant to represent a fish, from the acronym ICHTHUS. *See* ICHTHYS.

Vespers. The sixth of the canonical hours in the Greek and Roman Churches; sometimes also used of the Evening Service in the English Church. From Lat. *vesperus*, the evening, cognate with HESPERUS, Gr. *Hesperos*, the evening star.

The Fatal Vespers. 26 October 1623. A congregation of some 300 had assembled in an upper room in the residence of the French ambassador, at Blackfriars, to hear Father Drury, a JESUIT, preach. The flooring gave way, and Drury with another priest and about 100 of the congregation were killed. This accident was attributed to God's judgment against the Jesuits.

The Sicilian Vespers. *See* SICILIAN.

Vesta. The virgin goddess of the hearth in Roman mythology, corresponding to the Greek Hestia, one of the 12 great Olympians. She was custodian of the sacred fire brought by ÆNEAS from TROY, which was never permitted to go out lest a national calamity should follow.

Wax matches are named from her.

Vestals. The six spotless virgins who tended the sacred fire brought by ÆNEAS from TROY, and preserved by the state in a sanctuary in the Forum at ROME. They were chosen by lot from maidens between the ages of six and ten and served under strict discipline for 30 years, after which they were free to marry, although few took this step. In the event of their losing their virginity they were buried alive.

The word *vestal* has been figuratively applied by poets to any woman of spotless chastity. SHAKESPEARE bestowed the epithet on Elizabeth I.

> A fair vestal enthroned by the west.
> *A Midsummer Night's Dream*, II, i.

Vestiarian Controversy. The name given to the dispute about the wearing of clerical vestments raised by puritan-minded clergy in the reign of Edward VI and again in the reign of Elizabeth I. The simplest vestments such as the surplice and gown were described as the livery of ANTICHRIST. Archbishop Parker sought to enforce conformity by his *Advertisements* of 1566 ordering the wearing of the four-cornered cap, scholar's gown, and surplice, but many refused and deprivations followed. Diversity of practice remained and the controversy became merged with the puritan agitation against EPISCOPACY.

Vestry (Lat. *vestiarium*, robing-room). A room in a church in which the vestments, registers, altar vessels, etc., are kept and used as a robing-room by the clergy. Some larger churches contain a priests' vestry, wardens' vestry, and choir vestry. From the habit of parishioners meeting to conduct parish business in the vestry, both the body of parishioners and the meeting were called the *Vestry*.

Up to 1894 the Vestry was the final authority in all parish matters, civil and ecclesiastical. The parish priest presided over the meeting which elected churchwardens and other parish officers and the property of the parish was usually vested in the churchwardens. The *Common Vestry* consisted of the general assembly of ratepayers and the *Select Vestry* of a body of *vestrymen* elected to represent the parish, the usual procedure in many of the larger parishes. With the passing of the Local Government Act of 1894, secular Parish Councils were elected to take over the civil administrative functions of the rural parishes and in the towns such work was subsequently transferred to Urban Councils. In 1921 ecclesiastical administration passed to the newly created Parochial Church Councils, although the meeting which elects the churchwardens is still called a *Vestry Meeting*.

Veteran. In Britain this word is applied only to soldiers with long experience under arms, but in the U.S.A. it is bestowed upon one who has had any service, however brief, in some field of warfare.

In the U.S.A. the abbreviation **vet**. stands for *veteran* and *veterinarian*, but in Britain it is an abbreviation for *veterinary surgeon*.

Veteran's Day. See ARMISTICE DAY.

Veto (vē' tō) (Lat., I forbid). Louis XVI and Marie Antoinette were called *Monsieur* and *Madame Veto* by the Republicans, because the CONSTITUENT ASSEMBLY (1791) allowed the king to have the power, which he abused, of putting his veto upon any decree submitted to him.

Vexillum (veks il' ŭm) (Lat., a standard). The standard borne by troops of the Roman army. In particular it was the red flag flown on the general's tent as a signal for marching or for battle.

Via (Lat., a way). Our use of the word, in *I'll go via Chester, i.e.* "by way of Chester", is the ablative of *via*.

Sacra Via (Lat., The Holy Street). The street in ancient ROME where ROMULUS and Tatius (the SABINE) swore mutual alliance.

Via Appia. The APPIAN WAY.

Via Dolorosa (Lat., Dolorous way). The route Our Lord went from the place of judgment to CALVARY, now marked by the fourteen STATIONS OF THE CROSS.

Via Flaminia. The FLAMINIAN WAY.

Via Lactea (Lat.). The Milky Way. See GALAXY.

Via Media (Lat., The Middle Way). The mean between two extremes. The Elizabethan Church Settlement of the 16th century is often so called, the CHURCH OF ENGLAND being regarded as the mean between extreme Protestantism and Roman Catholicism.

Vial. Vials of wrath. Vengeance, the execution of wrath on the wicked. The allusion is to the seven ANGELS who pour out upon the earth their vials full of wrath (*Rev.* xvi).

Viaticum (Lat.). The EUCHARIST administered to the dying. The word means "provision for a journey", and its application is obvious.

Vicar (Lat. *vicarius*, a substitute). The priest of a parish where the TITHES were appropriated in pre-REFORMATION times, usually to monasteries. The monastery retained the *Rectorial* or great tithes and reserved the small tithes (*Vicarial* tithes) for the incumbent. After the Dissolution such Rectorial tithes were granted to CHAPTERS, COLLEGES, laymen, etc., known as impropriators (*see* IMPROPRIATION), who were under obligation to appoint vicars to carry out the ecclesiastical duties. The title is also given to Perpetual Curates. *Cp.* CLERICAL TITLES.

In the U.S. Episcopal Church a vicar is head of a chapel dependent on a parish church. In the ROMAN CATHOLIC CHURCH he is an ecclesiastic representing a BISHOP.

Lay Vicar. A cathedral officer who sings those portions of the liturgy not reserved for the clergy. Formerly called a *clerk vicar*.

Vicar Apostolic. In the ROMAN CATHOLIC CHURCH, a titular BISHOP appointed to a place where no episcopate has been established, or where the succession has been interrupted. In 1585 the English hierarchy came to an end and until 1594 Catholics came under the jurisdiction of Cardinal Allen, then that of archpriests from 1599 until 1621; but from 1623 until 1850 the Roman Catholic Church in ENGLAND was governed by vicars apostolic. The term formerly de noted a bishop to whom the POPE delegated some part of his jurisdiction.

Vicar Choral. One of the minor clergy, or a layman, attached to a cathedral for singing certain portions of the service.

Vicar Forane. A priest appointed by a Roman Catholic BISHOP to exercise limited (usually disciplinary) jurisdiction in a particular part of his diocese. The office is similar to that of RURAL DEAN (*see under* DEAN). *Forane* is a form of "foreign", hence outlying, rural.

Vicar-General. An ecclesiastical functionary assisting a BISHOP or archbishop in the exercise of his jurisdiction. In 1535 Thomas Cromwell was appointed Vicar-General to carry out Henry VIII's ecclesiastical policies.

The Vicar of Bray. This popular (probably early 18th-century) song depicting a time-serving VICAR of the 17th–18th century is based upon a 16th-century Vicar of Bray, Berkshire, who managed to retain his living during the religious changes of the reigns of Henry VIII, Edward VI, Mary, and Elizabeth.

> And this is the law I will maintain,
> Until my dying day, Sir,
> That whatsoever king shall reign,
> I'll still be the Vicar of Bray, Sir.

The Vicar of Christ. A title given to the POPE, an allusion to his claim to be the representative of Christ on earth.

The Vicar of Hell. A name playfully given by Henry VIII to John Skelton, his "poet laureate", perhaps because Skelton was rector of Diss, in Norfolk, the pun being on *Dis* (PLUTO). Milton refers to the story in his *Areopagitica*:

> I name not him for posterity's sake, whom Henry the Eighth named in merriment his vicar of hell.

Vice. The buffoon in the old English MORALITY PLAYS. He wore a cap with ass's ears, and was generally named after some particular vice, Gluttony, Pride, etc.

Vice versa (vī' si vĕr' sà) (Lat. *vicis*, change; *versa*, turned). The reverse; the terms of the case being reversed.

Vichy (vē shē). A town in the Department of Allier, in central France, formerly fashionable on account of its thermal and medicinal springs, *Vichy water* being a considerable export and taken for various forms of indigestion, catarrh, etc.

Vichy acquired a new significance during World War II as the seat of Marshal Pétain's collaborationist government (1940–1944), after the German occupation.

Vicious circle. A chain of circumstances, in which the solving of a problem creates a new problem, which makes the original problem more difficult of solution.

In logic, the fallacy of proving one statement by another which itself rests on the first for proof.

Vicisti, Galilæe. *See* GALILEAN.

Victoria Cross. The premier British award for conspicous bravery in the presence of the enemy, instituted by Queen Victoria in 1856. The ribbon is now claret coloured, but was formerly blue for the Royal Navy and red for the Army. It is a bronze Maltese CROSS with the royal crown surmounted by a LION in its centre under which is a scroll bearing the words "For Valour". It is worn on the left breast and takes precedence over all other decorations. The crosses were made from the metal of guns captured in the Crimean War at Sebastopol (1855).

Victory Medal (World War I). A bronze medal with a winged figure of Victory on the obverse; awarded in 1919 to all allied service personnel who had served in a theatre of war, also to certain women's formations.

Vidar. In Scandinavian mythology, a son of ODIN, noted for his taciturnity and fearless destruction of FENRIR.

Videlicet (vi del' i set) (Lat. *videre licet*, it is permitted to see). To wit, that is to say, namely. Abbreviated to VIZ.

Vigilance Committee. A privately formed citizen group taking upon themselves to assist in the maintenance of law and order, etc.; sometimes found in the Southern States of the U.S.A. as a body intimidating Negroes. During the CIVIL WAR (1861–1865) they also strove to suppress the activities of loyalists to the Northern cause. Members of such committees are called *Vigilantes*.

Vigiliæ. *See* MATTINS.

Villain, or **Villein** (Late Lat. *villanus*, a farm-servant, from *villa*, a farm). Originally the unfree peasant of feudal times was called a *villein*. He was bound to the MANOR and owed service to its lord. As the latter's personal chattel, he could be sold or transferred, but he had shares in the village fields. From the time of the BLACK DEATH shortage of labour led to the villein improving his status into that of a copyholder. *Cp.* BORDAR; COTTAR. *See* BOON WORK; WEEK-WORK.

The notion of rascality, wickedness, and worthlessness now associated with *villain* is a result of aristocratic condescension and sense of superiority.

> I am no villain; I am the youngest son of Sir Rowland de Boys; he was my father, and he is thrice a villain that says such a father begot villains.
> SHAKESPEARE: *As You Like It*, I, i.

Vim. Slang for energy, force, "go"; usually in

the phrase *vim and vigour*. It is the accusative of Lat. *vis*, strength.

Vin (Fr., wine). **Vin ordinaire**. The French name for inexpensive table wine of no particular regional origin. It is often a blend of different regional wines and not usually of any particular VINTAGE. It is generally a red wine, but not necessarily so.

Vin rosé. Pink wine, usually made by leaving the black skins of the grape in the juice long enough to produce the required colour, but sometimes from a mixture of red and white wine or by the addition of artificial colouring. In certain parts of France this is called *vin gris*.

Vinalia. Roman wine festivals in honour of JUPITER and also associated with VENUS as a goddess of vineyards. The first such festival was held on 23 APRIL when the wine of the previous season was broached and the second on 19 AUGUST when the VINTAGE began (Lat. *vinalis*, pertaining to wine).

Vinayapitaka. *See* TRIPITAKA.

Vincent, St. A deacon of Saragossa, martyred in *c.* 304 during the persecution under Diocletian. His day is 22 January. He is a patron SAINT of drunkards for no apparent reason; an old rhyme says:

> If on St. Vincent's Day the sky is clear
> More wine than water will crown the year.

Vincentian. A Lazarist or Lazarite, a member of the Congregation of Priests of the Mission founded (1625) by St. Vincent de Paul (*c.* 1580–1660).

Vine. The Rabbis say that the fiend buried a LION, a LAMB, and a hog at the foot of the first vine planted by NOAH; and that hence men receive from wine ferocity, mildness, or wallowing in the mire.

Vinegar. Livy tells us that when Hannibal led his army over the Alps from Spain into Italy in 218 B.C. he splintered the rocks with fire and vinegar to create a zigzag road for the descent. The vinegar or sour wine may have been used for lack of water.

The Vinegar Bible. *See* BIBLE, SOME SPECIALLY NAMED EDITIONS.

Vinegar Joe. The World War II nickname of General Joseph W. Stilwell (1883–1946), U.S. Commander of troops in China.

Vinegar Hill. A hill some 389 ft. high near Enniscorthy, Wexford. An insurrection organized by the UNITED IRISHMEN in the spring of 1798 was soon suppressed after General Lake's victory over the rebels at the battle of Vinegar Hill on 21 June.

Vingt-et-un (vant' ā ŭn') (Fr., twenty-one). A card game in which the object is to get as near as possible to 21 without exceeding it. The court cards count as ten and the ace as one or 11.

Vinland. The name (Wineland) given to that portion of North America known to the Norsemen and first discovered by Leif Ericsson about A.D. 1000. Its location is uncertain and is generally held to have been in the region of Newfoundland, but its estimated position ranges between Labrador and VIRGINIA. Some account for much of the discrepancy in Scandinavian writings by positing a Vinland I and Vinland II. *Vinland* may well refer to pasture-land, thus obviating the difficulties presented by the association of the name with the vine.

Vinland Map. *See under* FORGERY.

Vino. In vino veritas (Lat.). In wine is truth, meaning when persons are intoxicated they utter many things they would at other times seek to conceal or disguise.

Vintage (Fr. *vendange*). The gathering of the grapes; the year in which a certain wine was made. The wine of a good vintage year is known as *vintage wine* and hence "a vintage year" is a memorable and notable year in any context.

Vintry Ward. One of the 25 electoral WARDS of the City of LONDON. So called, according to Stowe, from the site occupied by the wine-merchants from Bordeaux, who anciently settled on this part of the THAMES bank around QUEENHITHE. The Vintners built large houses with vaults and the great house built by Sir John Stodie (Mayor in 1357) was called *The Vintry*.

Vinum Theologicum (vī' num thē ōloj' i kum) (Lat.). An old term for the best wine obtainable. Holinshed says it was so called because religious men would be sure "neither to drinke nor be served of the worst, or such as was anie wais vined by the vintner; naie, the merchant would have thought that his soule would have gone streightwaie to the devil if he would have served them with other than the best."

Violet. A flower usually taken as the type of modesty, but fabled by the ancients to have sprung from the blood of the boaster AJAX.

The colour indicates the love of truth and the truth of love. For ecclesiastical and symbolical uses, *see* COLOURS.

In the language of FLOWERS the white violet is emblematical of innocence, and the blue violet of faithful love.

The City of the Violet Crown. *See under* CITY.

Corporal Violet. NAPOLEON Bonaparte; because when banished to Elba he told his friends he would return with the violets. "Corporal Violet" became a favourite toast of his partisans, and when he reached Fréjus a gang of women assembled with violets, which were freely sold. The SHIBBOLETH was, "Do you like violets?" If the answer given was "*Oui*," the person was known not to be a confederate; but if the answer was "*Eh bien*", the respondent was recognized as an adherent.

The violet on the tyrant's grave (Tennyson, "Aylmer's Field", line 845). The reference is to NERO. It is said that some unknown hand went by night and strewed violets over his grave. We are told that at his death his statues were "crowned with garlands of flowers".

Violin. See AMATI; CREMONA; STRAD; FIDDLE.

Viper (U.S.A.). A slang term for a smoker of marijuana.

Viper and File. The biter bit. ÆSOP says a viper found a file, and tried to bite it, under the supposition that it was good food; but the file said that its province was to bite others, and not to be bitten.

Virago (vi ra' gō). Literally, a man-like woman, but a term usually employed to designate a turbulent or scolding shrew.

Viraj. See MANU.

Virgate (Lat. *virga*, a rod). An old English measure of land, usually about 30 acres—*i.e.* one-quarter of a HIDE; but differing considerably in different districts. Also called *yardland*.

Virgil (věr' jil). The greatest poet of ancient ROME, Publius Virgilius Maro (70–19 B.C.), born near Mantua (hence called *The Mantuan Swan*), a master of epic, didactic, and idyllic poetry. His chief works are the ÆNEID, the *Eclogues* or *Bucolics*, and the *Georgics*. From the *Æneid*, grammarians illustrated their rules and rhetoricians selected the subjects of their declamations; and even Christians looked on the poet as half inspired; hence the use of his poems in DIVINATION. See SORTES.

In the MIDDLE AGES Virgil came to be represented as a magician and enchanter, hence Dante's conception in his *Divina Commedia* of making Virgil, as the personification of human wisdom, his guide through the infernal regions.

Virgil was wise, and as craft was considered a part of wisdom, especially overreaching the spirit of EVIL, so he is represented by mediæval writers as outwitting the demon. Much of this legend grew out of Neapolitan folklore and one story says that he beguiled the DEVIL into a glass bottle and kept him there until he had learned the devil's magic arts. The tale has much in common with that of the *Fisherman and the Genie* in the ARABIAN NIGHTS. Virgil's magi-

cal exploits are recounted in numerous mediæval romances and poems and there is an account of Virgil's NECROMANCY in the *Gesta Romanorum*.

The Christian Virgil. Marco Girolamo Vida (d. 1566), an Italian Latin poet, author of *Christiads* in six books (1535), an imitation of the ÆNEID.

The Virgil and Horace of the Christians. So Bentley calls Aurelius Clemens Prudentius (*fl. c.* 400). He was a native of Spain and the author of several Latin hymns and religious poems reminiscent of VIRGIL and HORACE.

Virgin. The Virgin Birth. The belief that Christ had no human father and that His miraculous birth did not impair the virginity of his mother, the Blessed Virgin Mary (*see Matt.* i, 18; *Luke* i, 27–35).

The Virgin Mary's Bodyguard. See REGIMENTAL AND DIVISIONAL NICKNAMES.

The Virgin Queen. Elizabeth I (1558–1603); also called by SHAKESPEARE "the fair Vestal" (*see* VESTALS).

Virginal. A quilled keyboard instrument of the harpsichord family in use in the 16th and early 17th century; often referred to as *a pair of virginals*. It has been suggested that it was so called because it was used in convents to lead the *virginals* or hymns to the Virgin, but its name probably arises from the fact that it was mostly played by girls.

Virginia. The first securely established English colony in North America, founded at Jamestown in 1607. It took its name from the earlier attempt (1584–1587) of Sir Walter Raleigh to found a colony on Roanoke Island (now in North Carolina) which was named after the VIRGIN QUEEN. In the early days of settlement, the name *Virginia* was applied to the whole coast between FLORIDA and NOVA SCOTIA.

Virginia fence. An irregular fence made of roughly laid logs. Benjamin Franklin describes a drunkard's uncertain progression as resembling a Virginia fence.

Virgo (Lat., Virgin). One of the ancient constellations and the sixth sign of the ZODIAC (23 August–22 September). The constellation is the metamorphosis of ASTRÆA. *See also* ICARIUS.

Virtue. Moral virtue. An ethical virtue as opposed to the *theological* virtues. *See below*.

The Seven Virtues. Faith, Hope, Charity, Justice, Fortitude, Prudence, and Temperance. The first three are called the *supernatural, theological* or *Christian* virtues; the remaining four are PLATO's *cardinal* or *natural* virtues. *Cp.* SEVEN DEADLY SINS.

Virtuosi. See ST. LUKE'S CLUB *under* LUKE.

Virtuoso (věr tū ō′ zō). An Italian word meaning one who excels; it is applied to those with expert knowledge or appreciation for works of art or *virtu*. It is especially applied to instrumental performers of the highest ability; hence *virtuoso music*, that which demands exceptional skill from the performer.

Vis à vis (vēz′ a vē′) (Fr., face to face). Properly applied to persons facing one another, as in a railway carriage; also an old name for a carriage or coach which enables the occupants to face one another. The phrase is now often used in the sense of "in relation to", "as regards".

Vis inertiæ (vis in ĕr′ shē) (Lat., the power of inactivity). It is a common mistake to imagine that *inertia* means absence of motion; *inertia* is that property of matter which makes it resist any change. Thus it is hard to set in motion what is still, or to stop what is in motion. Figuratively, it applies to that unwillingness to change which makes men rather bear those ills they have than fly to others that they know not of.

Viscount (vī′ kount) (O. Fr. *viconte* from Lat. *vice*, *comes*, the deputy of a count). In Britain, a peer ranking next below an EARL and above a BARON. The title was first granted to John Lord Beaumont in 1440. The CORONET of a Viscount bears 16 pearls set around the rim. He is styled "Right Honourable" and addressed by the Sovereign as "Our right trusty and well-beloved Cousin". *See also* COURTESY TITLES.

Vishnu. The Preserver; the second in the Hindu TRIMURTI, though worshipped by many Hindus as the supreme deity. He originally appears as sun-god. He is beneficent to man and has made numerous incarnations or "descents", ten being the number most generally reckoned. (*See* AVATAR). He is usually represented as four-armed and carrying a mace, a conch-shell, a disc, and a LOTUS, and often riding the EAGLE Garuda. His wife is LAKSHMI, born from the sea.

Vision of Piers Plowman, The. A long allegorical poem in Middle English alliterative verse, written by William Langland (*c.* 1332–*c.* 1400), who was born probably in the West Midlands. The poet's dream or vision gives a vivid insight into 14th-century conditions and the current social and religious evils. Properly, *The Vision of William concerning Piers the Plowman*; in the earlier part Piers typifies the simple, pious English labourer, and in the latter, Christ Himself. Piers is the subject, not the author of the poem. There are several texts.

Visitation, The, or **The Visitation of Our Lady.** The Blessed Virgin's visit to her cousin St. Elisabeth before the birth of St. JOHN THE BAPTIST (*Luke* I, 39–56). It is celebrated on 2 July.

The Order of the Visitation, or **Visitandines.** A contemplative Order for women founded by St. Francis de Sales and St. Jane Frances de Chantal in 1610. They adopted a modification of the AUGUSTINIAN Rule and their chief work is now concerned with education.

Vital Statistics. Properly, population statistics concerned with births, marriages, deaths, divorces, etc. (Lat. *vita*, life). It is now applied humorously to a woman's bust, waist, and hip measurements.

Vitex (Lat. *vitis*, a vine, from *viere*, to twist). A genus of plants of the family Verbenaceæ; the *Agnus castus* (Lat., chaste lamb) or *chaste-tree*, also called *Abraham's balm*, *monk's pepper-tree*, and *hemp-tree*. In the language of FLOWERS it means "insensibility to love". Dioscorides, Pliny, and Galen mention the plant as a mild anaphrodisiac and say that Grecian ladies used to strew their couches with its leaves as a guard against impure thoughts. A syrup concocted from its fruits was also used in convents for similar reasons.

> And wreaths of Agnus castus others bore;
> These last, who with those virgin crowns were dressed,
> Appeared in higher honour than the rest.
> DRYDEN: *The Flower and the Leaf*, 172.

Vitus, St. (vī′ tùs). A Sicilian youth who was martyred with Modestus, his tutor, and Crescentia, his nurse, during the Diocletian persecution, *c.* 303.

St. Vitus's Dance. In Germany in the 17th century it was believed that good health for the year could be secured by anyone who danced before a statue of St. VITUS on his feast-day; such dancing to excess is said to have come to be confused with chorea, hence its name, *St. Vitus's Dance*, the SAINT being invoked against it.

Viva! (vī′ và, vē′ và). An exclamation of applause or joy; Italian, meaning (long) live. A VIVA VOCE examination is usually called a "*viva*".

Viva voce (Lat., with the living voice). Orally; by word of mouth. A *viva voce* examination is one in which the respondent gives spoken answers.

Vivat regina, or **rex!** (Lat.). Long live the Queen, or King! At the coronation of British sovereigns the boys of Westminster School have the privilege of acclaiming the King or Queen with shouts of "*Vivat Rex*, or *Regina!*".

Vivandière (vē von dē âr'). A woman formerly officially attached to a French (and other continental) regiment for the purpose of selling liquor and food to the soldiers. OUIDA portrays the vivandière, Cigarette, in *Under Two Flags* (1866).

Vivien. An enchantress of ARTHURIAN ROMANCE, the LADY OF THE LAKE.

Vixen (O.E. *fyxen*). A female fox. Metaphorically, a shrewish woman, one of villainous and ungovernable temper.

Vixere fortes ante Agamemnona. *See under* AGAMEMNON.

Viz. A contraction of VIDELICET. The *z* represents 3, a common mark of contraction in writing in the MIDDLE AGES; as oṁib 3—*omnibus*.

Vizier (vi zēr', viz' i ẽr) (Arab. *wazir*, bearer of the burden). A name given to the chief minister of the ABBASSIDE caliphs and to officials serving other MOSLEM rulers. The title was also formerly given to Turkish ministers and governors; the chief minister (until 1878) was called the *Grand Vizier*.

Vogue (vōg). A loan-word from the French. In *vogue* means in fashion, in popular favour, current, etc. The verb *voguer* means to be carried forward on the water by oar or by sail, hence the idea of sailing with the tide.

Vogue la galère (Fr., lit., row the galley). Let the world go how it will; let us keep on, whatever happens; *advienne que pourra*.

Vol-au-vent (vol' ō von) (Fr., flight on the wind). A small case of very light puff-pastry with a savoury filling.

Volapük (vol' à pūk). An artificial language invented in 1879 by a German pastor, J. M. Schleyer. It was based on European languages, about one-third from English, and the remainder from Latin, German, and the ROMANCE LANGUAGES. The words were cut down so that no original is recognizable: *Volapük* is supposed to be *Vol*, from "English" *world*; *pük*, from "English" *speech*. After about ten years its place was taken by ESPERANTO. *See also* INTERLINGUA.

Vole (Fr. *voler*, to fly). **He has gone the vole.** He has been everything by turns. *Vole* is a deal at cards that draws all the tricks. *To go the vole* is to take any risk for the sake of gain.

Voltaire. The assumed name of François Marie Arouet (1694–1778), the great French philosopher, poet, dramatist, and author. He began to use the name on his release from imprisonment in the Bastille in 1718. It is probably an anagram of Arouet l(*e*) j(*eune*). *See* CANDIDE.

Volte-face (volt' fas) (Fr., a turning of the head, a turn-about). Used of a complete about-face or change of front in argument, opinions, views, etc.

Volume. The word shows its ancestry for it comes from Lat. *volvere*, to roll. The ancient form of books was of written sheets fastened together and rolled up on a stick or roller.

Volund. *See* WAYLAND.

Voluntary Schools. The name for schools established by the Voluntary Societies such as the NATIONAL SOCIETY and the British and Foreign Schools Society, religious bodies, etc., as opposed to those established by local public authorities which were formerly called *council schools*, and until 1902, BOARD SCHOOLS. All primary and secondary schools maintained by a local education authority are still classified as county or voluntary schools according to their origins, although the voluntary principle in education has largely been submerged.

Voodoo, or **Voodooism.** A mixture of superstition, magic, WITCHCRAFT, serpent-worship, etc., derived from African rites and some Christian beliefs. It still survives among some Negro groups in Haiti, and other parts of the West Indies and the Americas.

The name is said to have been first given to it by missionaries, from Fr. *Vaudois*, a WALDENSIAN, as these were accused of sorcery; but Sir Richard Burton derived it from *vodun*, a dialect form of Ashanti *obosum*, a fetish or tutelary spirit. *Cp.* OBEAH.

Vorticism. An artistic movement which began in England in 1914, somewhat akin to CUBISM and FUTURISM and embracing art and literature. It was iconoclastic and regarded the question of representation as irrelevant; its designs are in straight lines and angular patterns. Concern with machinery was also a feature. Among its representatives, P. Wyndham Lewis and Edward Wadsworth were the most notable. The name was bestowed by Ezra Pound. *Cp.* DADAISM; FAUVISM; IMPRESSIONISM; ORPHISM; SURREALISM; SYNCHRONISM.

Votive offerings. *See* ANATHEMA.

Vox. Vox et præterea nihil (Lat., a voice, and nothing more). Empty words—"full of sound and fury, signifying nothing"; a threat not followed out. When the Lacedæmonian plucked the nightingale, on seeing so little substance he exclaimed, *Vox tu es, et nihil præterea* (Plutarch, *Apophthegmata Laconica*).

Vox populi vox Dei (Lat., the voice of the people is the voice of God). This does not mean that the voice of the many is wise and good, but only that it is irresistible. After Edward II had been dethroned by the people in favour of his son (Edward III), Walter Reynolds (d. 1327), Archbishop of Canterbury, preached at the coronation of Edward III with these words as his text.

Voyageur (vwa ya zhĕr´). A French Canadian or half-breed, accustomed to portage his canoe when necessary; formerly employed by the Hudson's Bay Company and Northwest Company to maintain supplies and communications between their trading stations.

> The voyageurs were a hardy class of men, trained from boyhood to use the paddle. Many of them were Iroquois Indians—pure or with an admixture of white blood. But the French Canadians, too, became noted for their expert management of the canoe...
>
> GEORGE BRYCE: *The Remarkable History of the Hudson's Bay Company*, ch. xxxi.

Vulcan. A son of JUPITER and JUNO, and GOD of fire, and the working of METALS, and patron of handicraftsmen in metals, identified with the Gr. Hephæstus, and called also MULCIBER, *i.e.* the softener.

His workshops were under Mount ETNA and other volcanoes where the CYCLOPS assisted him in forging thunderbolts for JOVE. It is said that he took the part of Juno against Jupiter who hurled him out of HEAVEN. He was nine days in falling and was saved by the people of Lemnos from crashing to earth, but one leg was broken, hence his lameness. VENUS was his wife and, in consequence of her amour with MARS, he came to be regarded as the special patron of CUCKOLDS. He was the father of CUPID and the Cecrops, and created PANDORA from clay.

Vulcanist. One who supports the Vulcanian or Plutonian theory, which ascribes the changes on the Earth's surface to the agency of fire. These theorists say the earth was once in a state of igneous fusion, and that the crust has gradually cooled down to its present temperature. *Cp.* NEPTUNIAN.

Vulgate, The. The Latin translation of the Bible, made about 384–404 by St. JEROME, originally to establish a standard text. The first printed edition was the MAZARIN BIBLE (1456) (*see* BIBLE, SOME SPECIALLY NAMED EDITIONS). A revised edition was issued by Clement VIII in 1592 and a new edition was commissioned by Pius X in 1908. *Genesis* was published in 1926 and the work is still in progress. The name is the Lat. *editio vulgata*, the common edition sanctioned by the ROMAN CATHOLIC CHURCH.

W

W. The twenty-third letter of the English alphabet. The form is simply a ligature of two Vs (VV); hence the name; for V was formerly the symbol of U (*q.v.*) as well as of V.

Waac (wăk). The familiar name of a member of the Women's Army Auxiliary Corps, a body of women raised for non-combatant army service in World War I. In World War II they were termed A.T.S., Auxiliary Territorial Service. This became the W.R.A.C. (Women's Royal Army Corps) in 1949.

Waaf (wăf). The familiar name of a member of the Women's Auxiliary Air Force, or the force itself, which was established in 1939. It became the W.R.A.F. (Women's Royal Air Force) in 1949. There was an earlier W.R.A.F. in World War I.

W.A.C. (U.S.A.). In World War II the Women's Army Corps, equivalent to the British A.T.S. *Cp.* WAVES.

W.V.S. The Women's Voluntary Service set up in 1938, primarily to help with air raid precautions. It became the W.R.V.S. (Women's Royal Voluntary Service) in 1949. It continues to do valuable social and welfare work with the aged and infirm and gives help in emergencies. It is particularly noted for its "Meals on Wheels" service.

Wad. A roll of paper money, and hence the money itself.

Wade. General Wade. The old rhyme:

> Had you seen but these roads before they were made,
> You would hold up your hands and bless General Wade,

refers to Field-Marshal George Wade (1673–1748), famous for his construction of military roads in the HIGHLANDS (*c.* 1724–1730) as a precaution against JACOBITE insurrection.

> Soon afterwards we came to the *General's Hut*, so called because it was the temporary abode of Wade, while he superintended the works upon the road.
> JOHNSON: *A Journey to the Western Highlands*, etc.
> (*Lough Ness*).

Wade's boat.

> They can so mochë craft of Wadës boot,
> So mochë broken harm whan that hem list,
> That with hem schuld I never lyv in rest.
> CHAUCER: *Merchant's Tale*, 180.

Wade was a hero of mediæval romance, whose adventures were a favourite theme in the 16th century. His famous boat was named *Guingelot*.

Wafer. Ecclesiastically a thin disc of unleavened bread used in the EUCHARIST.

Before the device of gummed envelope flaps was introduced, thin round discs of dried paste or gelatine were inserted between the flap and the envelope—or earlier still, between the outer sides of the folded letter—and having been moistened and pressed with a seal served the same purpose of keeping the paper closed.

Wag. Meaning a humorous person, one given to jest, is the O.E. *wagge*, probably from the facetious use of *waghalter*, a droll, a rascal—one who wags or shakes a halter.

To hop, or **play the wag.** To play truant—probably some allusion to *waghalter* (*see* WAG *above*).

Wager (wā' jĕr). Anything staked or hazarded on the event of a contest, etc. Connected with *gage* and *wage* (Low Lat. *wadiare*, to pledge).

Wager of battle. *see* ORDEAL OF BATTLE.

Wagga blanket. A sort of sleeping-bag made of two corn sacks cut open and stitched together. The name is taken from the town of Wagga Wagga, N.S.W., Australia.

Waggoner. An old name for a volume of sea-charts, Dalrymple's Charts being known as the *English Waggoner*. A corruption of *Wagenaar*, from a collection of such charts published at Leyden by Lukas Wagenaar (1584).

Wagoner. See BOÖTES.

Wahabis, or **Wahabites.** Adherents of a MOSLEM movement seeking to purify ISLAM and restore it to its primitive simplicity; so called from the founder Ibn-abd-ul-Wahab who began his activities about 1760. The sect centres upon Saudi Arabia.

Wailing Wall. The length of high stone wall at Jerusalem, said to be a relic of the TEMPLE OF HEROD which was destroyed in A.D. 70. After the Jews returned, it eventually became a tradition to gather there every FRI-

DAY for prayer and lamentations for the Dispersion and lost glories of Israel.

Wait. Wait and See. A phrase often humorously used with reference to H. H. Asquith (Earl of Oxford and Asquith), thus "What did Asquith say?" is another way of saying "Wait and see." Asquith used the phrase in answer to a question in the HOUSE OF COMMONS, 4 April 1910, and took to repeating it—subsequently when faced with an awkward question. Eventually the OPPOSITION took it up and chanted it back at him when questions were put to him.

Lords in Waiting, Gentlemen in Waiting, Grooms in Waiting, etc., are functionaries in the Royal HOUSEHOLD for personal attendance upon the sovereign.

Ladies in Waiting (in the Queen's Household) are officially styled *Ladies of the Bedchamber, Bedchamber Women,* and MAIDS OF HONOUR.

Waits. A name now given to parties of singers and musicians who perform outside people's houses at CHRISTMAS-time. They derive their name from those watchmen of former times called *waits* who sounded a horn or played a tune to mark the passing hours. Waits were employed at the royal court "to pipe the watch" and also by town corporations. The household expenses of Edward IV provide for "A *wayte,* that nightelye from Mychelmas to Shreve Thorsdaye pipe the watche withen this courte fower tymes in the somere nightes three tymes" (Rymer, *Fœdera*).

Waits duly came to provide a uniformed band for their town for civic occasions, and played to the public at Christmas-time, hence the current usage. The hautboy was also called a *wayte* or *wait,* from its being their chief instrument.

> I had scarcely got into bed when a strain of music seemed to break forth in the air just below the window. I listened, and found it proceeded from a band which I concluded to be the waits from some neighboring village.
> IRVING: *Sketch Book (Christmas Eve).*

Waitangi Day. 6th February; since 1960 celebrated as NEW ZEALAND's national day. It is a public holiday and commemorates the day on which the Treaty of Waitangi was made in 1840 by the British governor, William Hobson, with the Maori chiefs. They recognised British sovereignty in return for the tribes being guaranteed possession of their lands.

Wake. A watch or vigil. The name was early applied to the all-night watch kept in church before certain holy days and to the festival kept at the annual commemoration of the dedication of a church. In due course the festive element predominated and the name came to be associated with annual FAIRS and revelries held at such times. Some towns in the North country still observe local holidays called *wakes.*

In IRELAND, the term denotes the watching of the body of the deceased before the funeral, and the feasting which follows, a custom formerly also common in WALES and SCOTLAND.

Wake-robin. In ENGLAND an arum, usually the cuckoo-pint. In the U.S.A. a trillium, or jack-in-the-pulpit.

Waking a witch. If a witch were obdurate, the most effectual way of obtaining a confession was by what was termed *waking* her. An iron bridle or hoop was bound across her face with prongs thrust into her mouth; this was fastened to the wall by a chain in such a manner that the victim was unable to lie down; and men were constantly by to keep her awake, sometimes for several days. *See* WITCHCRAFT.

Waldensians, or **Waldenses** (wol den′siȧnz, wol den′ sēz). Also known by their French name as the *Vaudois.* Followers of Peter Waldo of Lyons who sought to govern their life by the teaching of the GOSPELS and who came to be known as the "Poor Men of Lyons". The movement began about 1170 and papal prohibition of their preaching culminated in Waldo's EXCOMMUNICATION. Various heretical teachings followed and papal authority was completely rejected. Active persecution scattered them to other parts of France, Italy, and Spain, etc., and it continued till the late 17th century. Their doctrinal descendants still exist, principally in the Alpine Valleys of Piedmont.

> Avenge O Lord thy slaughter's Saints, whose bones
> Lie scatter'd on the Alpine mountains cold.
> MILTON: *On the Late Massacre in Piedmont* (1655).

Waler. A strong, heavy horse bred in Australia specially for the Indian army of former days. So called from the fact that about 1840 when the breed was developed most Australian life centred in New South Wales, which then also included Victoria and Queensland. Walers owed their best qualities to the English thoroughbred which was derived from the pure-bred Arab horse.

Wales. From O.E. *Wealas,* plural of *wealh,* foreigner, applied to the Britons by the Anglo-Saxons. The O.E. name for CORNWALL was *Cornwealas* (the Welsh in Cornwall). The WELSH name for their own land is CYMRU (kŭm′ rē).

The Prince of Wales. When Edward I extinguished WELSH independence (1282–

1283) he is popularly said to have presented WALES with a new prince in the form of his son Edward who was born at Caernarvon (1284). In fact Edward was created Prince of Wales in 1301. The last native prince, Llywelyn ap Gruffydd, was killed at Builth in 1282.

Since 1337 the king's or queen's eldest son has been born Duke of Cornwall and the title Prince of Wales has been conferred upon him subsequently.

The Prince of Wales's feathers. *See* ICH DIEN.

Walhalla. *See* VALHALLA.

Walk. This word comes from O.E. *wealcan*, to roll; whence we get *wealcare*, a fuller of cloth, and thus the surname *Walker* has the same origin as *Fuller*.

> She curst the weaver and the walker
> The clothe that they had wrought.
> PERCY: *Reliques* (*The Boy and the Mantle*).

Cock of the Walk. *See under* COCK.

To make a man walk Spanish. *See under* SPANISH.

To walk into. To attack vigorously, to thrash; also to eat heartily of, as, "He walked into the apple tart." *To wade into* has similar meanings. *To walk into a trap*, either verbal or physical, is to be caught unsuspectingly.

To walk off with. To filch and decamp with.

To walk out with. To court, as a preliminary to marriage.

To walk tall. To hold one's head high, to maintain one's proper sense of pride and self-respect.

To walk the chalk. An old-established method of testing sobriety by making the suspected inebriate walk between two parallel lines chalked on the floor without stepping on either line. Hence, figuratively, to keep on the straight and narrow path of rectitude.

To walk the hospitals. To attend the hospitals as a medical student; from the practice of accompanying the hospital doctors when visiting patients in the wards.

To walk the plank. *See under* PLANK.

To walk through one's part. To repeat one's part at rehearsal verbally, but without dressing for it or acting it; to do anything appointed you in a listless, indifferent manner.

Walk not in the public ways. The fifth symbol of the *Protreptics* of Iamblichus, meaning, follow not the multitude in their EVIL ways; or, wide is the path of sin and narrow the path of virtue, few being those who find it.

> Broad is the way that leadeth to destruction.
> *Matt.* vii, 13.

A walk-out. To down tools and go on strike.

A walk-over. Properly, an uncontested race, won by the only competitor perambulating the course; hence applied to a very easy victory with little serious competition.

Hookey Walker! An early Victorian derisive exclamation meaning *Nonsense! Incredible!* used when hearing a "tall story" or some statement that cannot be trusted. Many ingenious and patently inaccurate stories have been advanced to explain this phrase; its origin is unknown.

To go by Walker's bus. To walk. Similar expressions are, "To go by the MARROWBONE stage", "To ride SHANKS'S MARE or pony".

Walkie-Talkie. A small portable short-range wireless containing receiver and transmitter as used by the fighting services, the police, etc.

Walking Stewart. The nickname of John Stewart (1749–1822). The son of a LONDON linen-draper, he secured a post in the East India Company and went to Madras. After serious quarrels with his superiors, he resigned and started out on his travels. During the following years he went on foot through Hindustan, Persia, Nubia, Abyssinia, across the Arabian Desert, through Europe from Constantinople to ENGLAND, passing through most of the continental countries. In 1791 he crossed to America and walked through what was then known of Canada and the United States. De Quincey says of him:

> A most interesting man ... contemplative and crazy ... yet sublime and divinely benignant in his visionariness. This man as a pedestrian traveller had seen more of the earth's surface than any man before or since.

A walking-on part. A part in a play in which the actor has only to walk about on the stage, sometimes with a word or two to say.

Walking-out dress. Uniform, smarter than that used on duty, worn by British soldiers when out of barracks, etc.

Wall. The Roman Wall. *See* ANTONINE'S WALL; GRAHAME'S DYKE; HADRIAN'S WALL; SEVERUS.

Wall Street. The street in New York City which contains the STOCK EXCHANGE and offices of major banking and insurance concerns etc. It is the financial centre of the U.S.A., hence the name is a synonym for the American Stock market and "big business" generally. The street is on the site of a *wall* or palisade built in 1652 by the Dutch against a possible English attack.

To drive someone up the wall. *See under* DRIVE.

To drive to the wall. See under DRIVE.

To give the wall. To allow another, as a matter of courtesy, to pass by on the pavement at the side furthest from the gutter; hence, to be courteous. At one time pedestrians *gave the wall* to persons of a higher rank than themselves. Nathaniel Bailey says (1721) it is:

> a compliment paid to the female sex, or those to whom one would show respect, by letting them go nearest the wall or houses, upon a supposition of its being the cleanest. This custom is chiefly peculiar to England, for in most parts abroad they will give them the right hand, though at the same time they thrust them into the kennel.

Cp. TO TAKE THE WALL, *below*.

To go to the wall. To be put on one side; to be shelved. This is in allusion to another phrase, **laid by the wall**, *i.e.* dead but not buried; put out of the way.

To hang by the wall. To hang up neglected; not to be made use of.

To run one's head against a brick or **stone wall.** See under HEAD.

To take the wall. To take the place of honour.

> I will take the wall of any man or maid of Montague's
>
> SHAKESPEARE: *Romeo and Juliet* , I, i.

Cp. TO GIVE THE WALL, *above*.

The weakest go to the wall. The saying is explained by Halliwell as deriving from the placing of beds along the side of the room and putting the youngest or feeblest in the safest place—*i.e.* against the wall. Another explanation is that, in the days when few churches had pews, except maybe for the gentry, there were benches along the walls for the aged. Pews were not installed generally until the late 17th century and subsequently.

The Writing on the wall. See under WRITE.

Walls have ears. Things uttered in secret get rumoured abroad; there are listeners everywhere, and you'd better be careful. Certain rooms in the LOUVRE were said to be so constructed in the time of Catherine de' MEDICI, that what was said in one room could be heard distinctly in another. It was by this contrivance that the suspicious queen became acquainted with state secrets and plots. The tubes of communication were called the *auriculaires*. *Cp*. DIONYSIUS'S EAR *under* EAR.

Wooden Walls. See under WOOD.

Wall-eyed. The M.E. *wald-eyed*, a corruption of Icel. *vald eygthr*, having a beam in the eye (*vagl*, beam). Persons are wall-eyed when the white is unusually large, and the sight defective, due to opacity of the cornea, or when they have a divergent squint. SHAKESPEARE has *wall-eyed wrath or staring rage* (*King John*, IV, iii). The term is particularly used of horses.

> To this proposal I objected that walking would be twenty times more genteel than such a paltry conveyance, as Blackberry was wall-eyed, and the colt wanted a tail.
>
> GOLDSMITH: *The Vicar of Wakefield*, ch. X.

Wallflower. So called because it grows on old walls, etc. Similarly *wall-cress*, *wall creeper*, etc., are plants which grow on dry, stony places, or on walls. *Wall fruit* is fruit trained against a wall. *Cp*. WALNUT.

Girls who sit along the wall without partners during a dance are called wallflowers.

Wallaby. A small Australian kangaroo.

On the wallaby, or, **on the wallaby track.** On the tramp—usually because out of work.

Wallace, Sir William (*c*. 1274–1305). The Scottish hero who won a great victory over the English at Stirling Bridge in 1297 but was eventually hanged, disembowelled, beheaded and quartered at West SMITHFIELD.

Wallace's Larder. See under LARDER.

Wallace's Line. A line of demarcation running between Bali and Lombok, through the Straits of Macassar, between Borneo and the Celebes, then northeastward between Mindanao and Gilolo, separating the fauna of the Indo-Malayan region from the widely divergent species of the Australian region which includes New Guinea and the islands to the eastward. It is named after Alfred Russel Wallace (1823–1913), the famous naturalist who defined it.

Wallah (wol' à). Anglo-Indian for a man of specified attributes or duties, as *dhobi-wallah*, the Indian washerman; *bathroom-wallah*, the man who looks after the bathrooms in an hotel; *punka-wallah*, the man who waves a fan, etc. A *Competition wallah* was the old nickname for a successful competitor in the Indian Civil Service examinations introduced in 1856, in contrast to those who obtained their appointments under the old system of influence. *Wallah* is a Hindu suffix denoting an agent, as *-er* in English.

Wallop (wol' òp). To thrash; properly, to boil with a noisy bubbling sound. *Gallop* is a variant of *wallop*. It is also a slang term for ALE.

To pack a (powerful) wallop (U.S.A.). To have great power.

Walnut. The foreign nut; called in M.E. *wal-note*, from O.E. *wealh*, foreign, since it came from Persia.

> Some difficulty there is in cracking the name thereof. Why walnuts, having no affinity to a wall, should

be so called. The truth is, *gual* or *wall*, in the old Dutch signifieth "strange" or "exotic" (whence *Welsh* foreigners); these nuts being no natives of England or Europe.

FULLER: *Worthies of England*.

It is said that the walnut tree thrives best if the nuts are beaten off with sticks, and not picked. There is an old saying that:

A woman, a dog, and a walnut tree,
The more you beat them the better they be.

Walpurgis Night (wol pēr' gis). The eve of MAY DAY, when the witch-world was supposed to hold high revelry under its chief, the DEVIL, on certain high places, particularly the Brocken, the highest point of the Harz Mountains. Walpurgis was an English nun who went as a missionary to Germany and became abbess of Heidenheim (d. *c.* 788). Her day is 1 May, hence her coincidental association with the rites of an earlier pagan festival.

Walpurgis oil. A bituminous kind of oil exuding from the rock at Eichstatt in which the relics of St. Walpurgis were deposited. It was supposed to have miraculous healing and curative properties.

Walstan, St. In ENGLAND, the patron SAINT of husbandmen. He worked as a farm labourer in Norfolk and was noted for the austerity and piety of his life and for his charity. He died in 1016 and is usually depicted with a scythe in his hand and cattle in the background.

Waltham Blacks. *See* BLACK ACT.

Waltzing Matilda. An Australian phrase made famous by the Australian poet A. B. (Banjo) Paterson (1864–1941). It means carrying or humping one's bag or pack as a tramp does. Henry Lawson (*The Romance of Song*) says, "Travelling with SWAG in Australia is variously and picturesquely described as 'humping bluey', 'walking Matilda', 'humping Matilda', 'humping your drum', 'being on the wallaby' ..."

The reason for the tramp's roll being called a "Matilda" is obscure; to *waltz* conveys the impression of tramping along with one's pack jogging up and down with one's steps. *See* BILLABONG.

Once a jolly swagman camped by a billabong
Under the shade of a coolibah tree,
And he sang as he watched and waited till his billy boiled,
"You'll come a-waltzing Matilda with me."

Wampum (wom' pùm). Shell beads made and strung for ornament, currency, ceremonial gift belts, etc., by North American Indian tribes. They were used as money as late as the 19th century, but machine-made mass-produced "wampum" with resultant inflation first caused its obsolescence in the eastern states. The name comes from the Algonkian *wompi*, white.

When he came in triumph homeward
With the sacred Belt of Wampum.

LONGFELLOW: *The Song of Hiawatha*, II.

Wandering Jew, The. The central figure of the widespread later-mediæval legend which tells of a JEW who insulted or spurned Christ when He was bearing the cross to CALVARY, and was condemned to wander over the face of the earth till JUDGMENT Day.

The usual form of the legend says that he was AHASUERUS, a cobbler, who refused to allow Christ to rest at his door, saying, "Get off! Away with you, away!" Our Lord replied, "Truly I go away, and that quickly, but tarry thou till I come."

An earlier tradition has it that the Wandering Jew was Cartaphilus, the doorkeeper of the judgment hall in the service of Pontius Pilate. He struck our Lord as he led Him forth, saying, "Go on faster, Jesus"; whereupon the MAN OF SORROWS replied, "I am going, but thou shalt tarry till I come again." (*Chronicle of St. Alban's Abbey*, 1228). The same Chronicle, continued by Matthew Paris, tells us that Cartaphilus was baptized by Ananias, and received the name of Joseph. At the end of every hundred years he falls into a trance, and wakes up a young man about 30.

In German legend he is associated with John Buttadæus, seen at Antwerp in the 13th century, again in the 15th, and the third time in the 16th. His last appearance was in 1774 at Brussels. In the French version he is named Isaac Laquedom or Lakedion; another story has it that he was Salathiel ben-Sadi, who appeared and disappeared towards the close of the 16th century at Venice, in so sudden a manner as to attract the notice of all Europe; and another connects him with the WILD HUNTSMAN.

"I'll rest, sayd hee, but thou shalt walke;"
So doth this wandring Jew
From place to place, but cannot rest
For seeing countries newe.

PERCY: *Reliques* (*The Wandering Jew*).

There are several plants called *The Wandering Jew*.

Wanion. With a wanion. An old imprecation; the word is the present participle of *wanion*, to wane, and meant misfortune, ill-luck.

Look how thou stirrest now! come away, or I'll fetch thee with a wannion.

SHAKESPEARE: *Pericles*, II, i.

Wansdyke. Woden's dyke. A system of dykes, perhaps built by the Romano-Britons, stretching some 60 miles from Inkpen in

Berkshire to Maesbury in Somerset. It was probably a defence against the English invaders. *See* GRAHAME'S DYKE; GRIM'S DITCH; OFFA'S DYKE.

Wantley, The Dragon of. An old story, preserved in PERCY'S RELIQUES, tells of this monster who was slain by More of More Hall. He procured a suit of armour studded with spikes, and kicked the DRAGON in the backside, where alone it was vulnerable. Percy says the Dragon stands for a greedy renter of the TITHES of the Wortley family who attempted to take the tithes in kind from the parishioners and More was the man who conducted the suit against him. There are other theories. Wantley is Wharncliffe in Yorkshire.

Wapenshaw, Wappenshaw, or **Wapinshaw,** etc. A weapon show, the early spelling being *Wappinschaw.* Formerly the Scottish term for the review of men under ARMS to check that they were properly equipped according to rank. It is now used of a rifle-shooting competition.

Wapentake (wop′ en tāk). A subdivision of a county similar to a HUNDRED, found in Yorkshire and other areas of once strong Danish influence—Derbyshire, Leicestershire, Lincolnshire, Nottinghamshire and the former county of Rutland. The word is of Scandinavian origin meaning "a taking" or "grasping of weapons" signifying the clash of ARMS made by an assembly to signify assent.

War. Civil War. *See under* CIVIL.

Cold War. *See under* COLD.

A Holy war. Properly a war undertaken from religious motives, such as the CRUSADES. As such wars were fiercely and often bitterly contested the expression is often colloquially applied to relentless crusades of various kinds.

Hundred Years War. *See* HUNDRED.

Thirty Years War. *See under* THIRTY.

The War of the Brown Bull. Also known as the "Cattle raid of Cooley" or "Cuailnge". In Irish legend, the struggle provoked by Queen MAEVE (Medb) of Connaught who led the forces of four provinces to capture the great bull, the Brown One of Cuailnge belonging to an ULSTER chief. Her husband Ailill had a great white bull called Finnbennach and she wished to equal his possessions. The Brown Bull was taken by stratagem but Maeve's forces were driven into retreat by CUCHULAIN and the men of Ulster. The Brown One fought the White Bull all over IRELAND until the latter was slain, and the Brown Bull then rushed northwards until its heart burst.

The Wars of the Roses. *See under* ROSE.

War baby. A baby born in wartime; especially the illegitimate offspring of a serviceman.

War game. Originally known by its German name *Kriegsspiel*, it was introduced by a Prussian officer, Lieutenant von Reiswitz, in 1824, who completed and improved upon his father's design. It depends upon the use of maps as battlefields in miniature and blocks or counters representing troops, etc., for the purpose of instructing officers in military tactics. In modern times the computer is used to this end.

War-hawk (U.S.A.). One who is eager for war. *See* HAWKS AND DOVES.

War-head. The explosive head of a torpedo or bomb.

War-horse. A veteran or old warrier; a "FIRE-EATER". An allusion to the charger formerly used in battle.

War-paint. The paint applied to their faces by RED INDIANS and other peoples to make their appearance terrifying before going out ON THE WARPATH. Putting on one's war paint is a phrase applied figuratively to getting ready to enter energetically into a dispute or, of a woman, to putting on lipstick, powder, etc., in order to overcome her rivals.

On the warpath. Thoroughly roused and incensed; looking for one's adversary or victim with every intention of exacting retribution.

War of nerves. Planned measures to undermine morale by threats, rumours, SABOTAGE, etc.

Ward (O.E. *weard*, keeping watch, guard, etc.). A district under the charge of a warden. The word is applied to subdivisions of Cumberland, Westmorland, and Durham, also in some counties of SCOTLAND. In mediæval times, the Wardens were appointed by the English and Scottish governments to watch over the border districts.

The word is also applied to administrative divisions of a town or city, a large room or division of a hospital; a part of a lock or of a key which prevents the door being opened by the wrong key; a minor placed under the care of a guardian, etc. *See* WATCH AND WARD.

Ward room. In British warships, a mess shared by the Commander unless he is the captain of the ship, and other officers.

The name is not found before the 18th century and derives from the compartment known as the *Ward Robe* which was used as a store for valuables captured from prizes. It came to be used for officers of the rank of Lieutenant upwards. *Cp.* GUN ROOM.

Ward, Artemus. The pseudonym used by Charles Farrar Browne (1834–1867), the American journalist, humorist and comic writer. He often wrote with grotesque spelling and clever satire.

Warden Pie. Pie made of the Warden pear; a pear said to be so called from Warden in Bedfordshire, but quite probably from O.Fr. *wardant*, keeping, because they are good keeping pears.

> My self by denial I mortify,
> With a good dainty bit of Warden pie.
> JOHN O'KEEFE: *The Friar of Orders Grey*.

Wardour Street English. The affected use of archaic words and phrases. A term first applied by William Morris in 1888 to a translation of the ODYSSEY, couched in language which reminded him of the pseudo-antique furniture that in those days was sold in Wardour Street, LONDON. This thoroughfare in the present century came to be associated with the film industry.

Warlock. An evil spirit; a WIZARD. O.E. *wærloga*, a traitor, one who breaks his word.

Warm. Used colloquially with much the same force as HOT, as a *warm member*, said of a man who "goes the pace", of a sharper, or of one who is particularly notable in connexion with whatever happens to be the subject of discussion.

Warm thanks are hearty thanks; *he's in a warm corner* means he's in an awkward position.

A British warm. A thick overcoat worn by army officers.

A house-warming. An entertainment given by new occupiers of a house; a first welcoming of friends to a fresh residence.

Warming the bell. *See under* BELL.

Warming-pan. One who holds a place temporarily for another; sometimes applied to a clergyman who officiates while the actual holder of the living is qualifying. In public schools it used to be the custom to make a FAG warm his "superior's" bed by lying in it till the proper occupant was ready to turn him out.

The Warming-pan baby. The Old PRETENDER, because of the widely circulated story that he was introduced into the lying-in chamber of Mary of Modena, queen of James II, in a warming-pan, and that her own child was stillborn. Hence **warming-pans** as a nickname for JACOBITES.

Warrior Queen, The. BOADICEA.

Wart. An army name for a 2nd Lieutenant, from the single 'pip' or badge of rank on his shoulders. *See* SNOTTIE.

Warts and all. Said of a description, biography, etc., which seeks to give the rounded portrait, including the blemishes and defects. Oliver Cromwell, whose face was not without blemishes, when having his portrait painted by Lely, apparently told him to "Remark all these roughnesses, pimples, warts, and everything as you see me".

Warwick the King-maker. *See* KINGMAKER *under* KING.

Wash. It will all come out in the wash. Everything will turn out all right in the end, as dirt and stains, etc., are removed by washing.

It's got lost in the wash. It has just disappeared in the welter of things, in the proceedings, etc., as items get lost in the laundry. The expression is also sometimes punningly used with reference to King John's loss of royal treasure and baggage when his convoy of horses and waggons was caught and swallowed up by the incoming tide on the sands of the Wash in 1216.

That (story) won't wash. That story or excuse won't do at all; you'll have to think of a better tale than that! Said of an explanation or excuse that is palpably false, far-fetched, or exaggerated.

To take in one another's washing. To do each other reciprocal favours; to help each other out.

To wash a brick. To engage in an utterly unprofitable enterprise; to do useless work. An old Latin proverbial expression (*laterem lavere*, Terence's *Phormio*, I, iv, 9).

To wash one's dirty linen in public. To expose the family SKELETON to the public gaze; openly to discuss private affairs that are more or less discreditable.

To wash one's hands of a thing. *See under* HAND.

To give one's head for the washing. To yield, to submit to insult.

Washed out. Exhausted, done up, with no strength or spirit left. **Washed up** has similar implications.

Head-washing. An old provincialism for drinking a new infant's health. *To wet the baby's head* is a colloquialism for the same thing.

A wash-out. A fiasco, a failure. As an imperative verb, it means cancel, disregard, from the times when naval signal messages were taken down on a slate which was washed clean when the message had been transmitted to the proper quarters.

Wassail (O.E. *wæs hael*, be whole, be well). A salutation, especially over the spiced ale cup at the New Year, hence called the "wassail bowl". *See also* HEALTH.

Strutt (*Sports and Pastimes of the People of England*, III, iv) says: "Wassail, or rather the wassail bowl, which was a bowl of spiced ale, formerly carried about by young women on New-year's eve, who went from door to door in their several parishes singing a few couplets of homely verses composed for the purpose, and presented the liquor to the inhabitants of the house where they called, expecting a small gratuity in return ..."

> The King doth wake tonight and takes his rouse,
> keeps wassail.
>
> SHAKESPEARE: *Hamlet*, I, iv.

Hence *Wassailers*, those who join a wassail; revellers, drunkards.

Wat. An old name for a hare, short for *Walter*. *Cp.* TOM for cat, NEDDY for a donkey, *Jenny* wren etc.

> By this poor Wat, far off upon a hill,
> Stands on his hinder legs, with listening ear.
>
> SHAKESPEARE: *Venus and Adonis*, 697.

Watch. In nautical usage, the time during which part of a ship's complement is on duty; usually four hours except during the DOG WATCHES of two hours each, by which the variation in the watches kept by any individual is effected. Ship's companies are arranged in two watches, port and starboard, each of which is usually subdivided thus providing four groups for normal watch-keeping duties. The day is regulated according to the following watches:

1200–1600 (12 noon to 4 p.m.)	Afternoon Watch
1600–1800 (4 to 6 p.m.)	First Dog Watch
1800–2000 (6 to 8 p.m.)	Second Dog Watch
2000–2400 (8 to 12 midnight)	First Watch
2400–0400 (12 to 4 a.m.)	Middle Watch
0400–0800 (4 to 8 a.m.)	Morning Watch
0800–1200 (8 to 12 noon)	Forenoon Watch

Formerly the First Watch was usually called the "First Night Watch". Sometimes duties are arranged in three watches but this does not, of course, affect the time-keeping system shown above. *See also* AT THREE BELLS; ONE BELL IN THE LAST DOG WATCH, *under* BELL.

Historically, *the Watch* refers to the body of men in towns who patrolled the streets at night before the introduction of police forces, which, in the boroughs, were under the control of the Watch Committee until their amalgamation with the County Police in 1967. *See also* COCK-CROW; WAKE; WATCH AND WARD.

The Black Watch. *See under* BLACK.

Neighbourhood Watch. As a result of increasing crime, especially burglary, residents in particular areas began organising *Neighbourhood Watch* groups from the early 1980s with police co-operation. Suspicious activities and circumstances are reported to the police and some worthwhile impact on burglary has resulted. The idea was copied from similar schemes in the U.S.A.

Watch Night. 31 December, to see the Old Year out and the New Year in by a religious service. John Wesley introduced it among the METHODISTS and it has been adopted by other Christian denominations.

The Watch on the Rhine (*Die Wacht am Rhein*). A German national song which achieved a place of honour with *Deutschland über Alles* (Germany over all) in the former German Empire. It was written by Max Schneckenburger in 1840 at a time when French policies were suspect.

Watch and Ward. Continuous vigilance; *watch* and *ward* being the terms formerly used to denote guard by *night* and by *day* respectively. Townships were made responsible for appointing watchmen in the 13th century. *See* WATCH.

Watchful waiting. The phrase used by Woodrow Wilson in 1913 to describe his policy of non-recognition of the Mexican Government of General Huerta. It did not last long as, in 1914, the Americans occupied Vera Cruz. The phrase was previously used by President Jackson (OLD HICKORY) in 1836.

Watchword. A word given to sentries as a signal that one has the right of admission, a password; hence, a motto, word, or phrase symbolizing or epitomizing the principles of a party, etc. *Cp.* SHIBBOLETH.

Water. The Water of Jealousy. If a woman was known to have committed adultery she was to be put to death, according to the Mosaic law (*Deut.* xxii, 22). If, however, the husband had no proof, but only suspected his wife of infidelity, he might take her before the SANHEDRIN to be examined, and "bitter water" was prepared from holy water and the dust of the floor of the tabernacle. The priest then said to the woman, "If thou hast not gone aside to uncleanness with another instead of thy husband, be thou free from this bitter water that causeth the curse." If she had "gone aside" the priest wrote the curses on a roll, sprinkled it with water, and gave the woman the "water of jealousy" to drink (*Numb.* v, 11–29).

The Water Poet. John Taylor (1580–1654), the witty and sometimes scurrilous Thames WATERMAN who early left Gloucester Grammar School for London, having failed at Latin accidence. He wrote fourscore books and verse pamphlets and in his closing days kept an ale-house in Long Acre.

> Taylor, their better Charon, lends an oar,
> (Once swan of Thames, tho' now he sings no more).
> POPE: *Dunciad*, III, 19.

The Father of the Waters. The Mississippi, the chief river of North America. The Missouri is its child. The Irrawaddy (in Burma) is also thus named.

Territorial Waters. *See* THREE-MILE LIMIT.

Blood is thicker than water. *See under* BLOOD.

Court holy water. *See under* COURT.

I am for all waters (SHAKESPEARE, *Twelfth Night*, IV, ii). I am a JACK OF ALL TRADES, can turn my hand to anything. Like a fish which can live in salt or fresh water.

In deep water. In difficulties; in great perplexity; similarly, *in smooth water* means all is PLAIN SAILING, one's troubles and anxieties are things of the past.

In low water. *See under* LOW.

It makes my mouth water. It is very alluring; it makes me long for it. Saliva is excited in the mouth by appetizing food.

More water glideth by the mill than wots the miller. The Scots say, "Mickle water goes by the miller when he sleeps". *See under* MILLER.

Of the first water. Of the highest type, superlative. *See* DIAMOND OF THE FIRST WATER *under* DIAMOND.

Smooth, or **still waters run deep.** Deep thinkers are persons of few words; he (or she) thinks a good deal more than is suspected; silent conspirators are the most dangerous; BARKING DOGS SELDOM BITE. A calm exterior is far more to be feared than a tongue-doughty BOBADIL.

> Smooth runs the water where the brook is deep;
> And in his simple show he harbours treason.
> The fox barks not when he would steal the lamb;
> No, no my sovereign, Gloucester is a man
> Unsounded yet, and full of deep deceit.
> SHAKESPEARE: *Henry VI, Pt. II*, III, i.

That won't hold water. That is not correct; it is not tenable. It is a vessel which leaks. *Cp.* THAT WON'T WASH *under* WASH.

To back water. To row backwards in order to reverse or stay a boat's motion; hence, to go easy, to retrace one's steps, to retreat.

To carry water to the river. To carry coals to Newcastle. *See under* COAL.

To fish in troubled waters. *See under* FISH.

To get into hot water. *See under* HOT.

To keep one's head above water. *See under* HEAD.

To pour oil on troubled waters. *See under* OIL.

To take the waters. To visit a spa for health reasons, a common routine among fashionable folk in the 18th and 19th centuries.

To throw cold water on a scheme. To discourage the proposal; to dwell upon its weaknesses and disadvantages; to speak slightingly of it.

To tread water. In swimming, to keep the body erect moving the hands and feet up and down, thus keeping one's head above water.

To turn on the waterworks. To cry, to blubber.

To water stock. To add extra shares. Suppose a trust consists of 1,000 shares of £50 each, and the profit available for dividend is 40 per cent; the managers "water the stock", that is, add another 1,000 fully paid-up shares to the original 1,000. There are now 2,000 shares, and the dividend, instead of £40 per cent, is reduced to £20; but the shares are more easily sold, and the shareholders are increased in number.

Water-gall. The dark rim round the eyes after much weeping; a peculiar appearance in a rainbow which indicates more rain at hand.

> And round about her tear-distained eye
> Blue circles streamed, like rainbows in the sky;
> These watergalls ... foretell new storms.
> SHAKESPEARE: *The Rape of Lucrece*, 1. 1586.

Watergate. In the U.S.A. an area of flats and offices, etc. beside the river Potomac, Washington, which gave its name to a major political scandal. An illegal bugging attempt was made by Republicans at the Watergate headquarters of the Democratic Party during the 1972 elections followed by attempts to cover-up the affair. The subsequent resignation and prosecution of senior WHITE HOUSE officials and further evidence of corruption eventually led to the resignation of the Republican President Richard Nixon when threatened with impeachment.

Water-sky. The term used by Arctic navigators to denote a dark or brown sky, indicating an open sea. An ice-sky is a white one, or a sky tinted with orange or rose-colour, indicative of a frozen sea (*cp.* ICE-BLINK).

Water-witch. Another name for a dowser (*see* DOWSE).

Waterman. A boatman, especially one who rows a boat for hire. The Thames watermen were a feature of old LONDON. *See* DOGGET.

Hackney-coach stands and cab ranks were each supplied with a licensed waterman whose duty it was to water the cab-horses, etc.

Watermark. A design impressed into paper by fine wire during manufacture and while the paper is still wet. Watermarks were used as early as 1282 and served to identify the products of each paper mill.

The watermark has in many instances been the origin of paper-trade nomenclature; thus the mark of the *cap and bells* gave us *Foolscap*, the *Post-horn*, *Post*, the *Pot*, *Pott*, and the *Crown* and *Elephant* similarly came to denote sizes of paper.

Waterloo. He met his Waterloo. He came up against it; he suffered a crushing defeat; an allusion to the final defeat of NAPOLEON by WELLINGTON and Blücher (*see* FORWARDS, MARSHAL) at Waterloo (1815).

The Waterloo Cup. The "Derby" (*see* DERBY STAKES) of the coursing fraternity; the great dog-race held annually at Altcar during three days in February. It was founded in 1836 by a man named Lynn, the sporting owner of the *Waterloo Hotel* in Liverpool (whence its name). Lynn was also the founder of the GRAND NATIONAL, run at Aintree.

Watling Street. The great Roman road beginning at Dover and running through Canterbury to LONDON, thence through St.Albans and Dunstable, along the boundary of Leicester and Warwick to Wroxeter on the Severn. In the late 9th century it became the boundary between English and Danish territory. There are several other sections of road so called.

The name is from O.E. *Wæclingastraet*, the road leading to *Wæclingaceaster* (now St. Albans).

Watson, Dr. *See* SHERLOCK HOLMES.

Watson's Plot. *See* BYE PLOT.

Wattle. Australian settlers built wattle-and-daub huts after the English manner from twigs of the abundant acacia trees which hence became known as *wattles*. *Wattle Day* is a national festival in Australia, held on 1 August or 1 September, according to the peak of the flowering of the wattle in each State.

Wave. The tenth wave. A notion prevails that the waves keep increasing in regular series till the maximum arrives, and then the series begins again. No doubt when two waves coalesce they form a large one, but this does not occur at fixed intervals.

The most common theory is that the tenth wave is the largest, but Tennyson says the ninth:

> And then the two
> Dropt to the cove, and watch'd the great sea fall,
> Wave after wave, each mightier than the last,
> Till last, a ninth one, gathering half the deep
> And full of voices, slowly rose and plunged
> Roaring, and all the wave was in a flame.
> *Idylls of the King, The Coming of Arthur.*

Waves. In the U.S.A., the women's section of the Naval Reserve. The name is formed by the initial letters of *Women Appointed for Voluntary Emergency Service*.

Wavy Navy. The popular name for the former Royal Naval Volunteer Reserve (R.N.V.R.), whose officers wore gold distinction lace made in wavy lines instead of straight, as worn on the sleeves of regular officers belonging to the "Straight Navy". The R.N.V.R. lost its separate existence, after a brilliant wartime record, in December 1957, when it was combined with the Royal Naval Reserve (R.N.R.). *Cp.* WRENS; WAVES.

Waverley Novels. The novels of Sir Walter Scott (1771–1832), which took their name from the first of the series, the title of which was derived from the ruined Waverley Abbey, near Farnham, Surrey. *See* GREAT UNKNOWN.

Wax. Slang for temper, anger; *he's in an awful wax*, he's in a regular rage. Hence **waxy**, irritated, vexed, angry.

A man of wax. A model man; like one fashioned in wax. HORACE speaks of the "waxen arms of Telephus", meaning model arms, or of perfect shape and colour; and in SHAKESPEARE'S *Romeo and Juliet* (I, iii), the nurse says of Paris, "Why, he's a man of wax," which she explains by saying, "Nay, he's a flower, i' faith a very flower."

A nose of wax. Of a pliable and yielding character; mutable and accommodating. A waxen nose may be twisted in any way.

Way. In the family way. With child, pregnant.

The way of all flesh. To die, Samuel Butler (1835–1902) has a novel of this title published posthumously in 1903.

The Way of the Cross. *See* STATIONS OF THE CROSS.

To mend one's ways. To improve one's hitherto unsatisfactory habits and behaviour; TO TURN OVER A NEW LEAF (*see under* LEAF).

Under way. Said of a ship in motion, one which is making headway. *To lose way* is to lose speed when sailing and *to gather way* is to pick up speed.

Way enough! The call to oarsmen to complete their stroke and cease rowing, *i.e.* the boat has enough "way on" (motion through the water) for the given circumstances.

Ways and means. Methods and means of accomplishing one's purposes; resources; facilities.

The Committee of Ways and Means. The name given in the HOUSE OF COMMONS to a Committee of the whole House which authorizes the Government to raise money for the upkeep of public services and approves new, altered, or revised forms of taxation. It also authorizes payments from the CONSOLIDATED FUND for these purposes. The uses to which the money is are controlled by the *Committee of Supply*.

The Chairman of Ways and Means is the Chairman of Committees, the Deputy SPEAKER.

Wayland Smith. The English form of the Scandinavian Volund (Ger. *Wieland*), a wonderful and supernatural smith and lord of the elves (*see* ELF), a kind of VULCAN. The legend is found in the EDDA and is alluded to in BEOWULF. He was bound apprentice to Mimir, the smith. King Nidung cut the sinews in his feet in order to retain his services but he eventually flew away in a feather robe which had been first tested out by his brother EGIL. The legend has much in common with that of DÆDALUS.

Tradition has placed his forge in a megalithic monument known as *Wayland Smith's Cave* near the WHITE HORSE in Berkshire, where it was said that if a traveller tied up his horse there, left sixpence for fee, and retired from sight, he would find the horse shod on his return.

> Neither the tradition of Alfred's Victory, or of the celebrated Pusey Horn, are better preserved in Berkshire than the wild legend of Wayland Smith.
> SCOTT: *Kenilworth*, ch. xiii.

Wayzgoose. An annual dinner, picnic, or BEANFEAST especially one given to, or held by, those employed in a printing-house. *Wayz (wase)* is an obsolete word for a bundle of hay, straw, stubble; hence a "STUBBLE GOOSE", a harvest goose or fat goose, which is the crowning dish of the entertainment.

We. Used of himself by a Sovereign, the "royal we", said to have been used first by Richard I. His Charter to Winchester (1190) reads, "Sciatis *nos* concessisse civibus *nostris* Wintoniæ..." while an earlier charter of his father, Henry II, reads "Sciatis *me* concessisse civibus *meis* Wyntoniæ...".

We is also used by the editor of a newspaper or the writer of unsigned articles, as representing the journal for which he is writing and to avoid the appearance of egotism.

"We are not amused!" A reproof attributed to Queen Victoria and frequently used as an ironical rebuke. There appears to be no evidence that Queen Victoria ever used the expression.

Weapon Salve. A salve said to cure wounds by sympathy; applied not to the wound, but to the instrument which gave the wound. The direction "Bind the wound and grease the nail" is still common. Sir Kenelm Digby says the salve is sympathetic, and quotes several instances to prove that "as the sword is treated the wound inflicted by it feels. Thus, if the instrument is kept wet, the wound will feel cool; if held to the fire, it will feel hot", etc.

> But she has ta'en the broken lance,
> And wash'd it from the clotted gore,
> And salved the splinter o'er and o'er.
> SCOTT: *The Lay of the Last Minstrel*, III, xxiii.

Weapon-schaw. *See* WAPENSHAW.

Wearing of the Green, The. *See under* GREEN.

Weasel. Weasels suck eggs; hence SHAKESPEARE'S:

> I can suck melancholy out of a song, as a weasel sucks eggs.
> *As You Like It*, II, v.

Pop goes the Weasel. Now regarded as a children's song, was obviously originally intended for their parents:

> Up and down the City Road,
> In and out the Eagle.
> That's the way the money goes,
> Pop goes the weasel.

The Eagle was a tavern and old-time MUSIC HALL in the City Road, LONDON, and a popular rendezvous for singing and Saturday night drinking, which explains the need to "pop" or pawn the "weasel". Whatever the "weasel" was is not clear, but it may have been slang for a tailor's iron.

To catch a weasel asleep. To deceive a very vigilant person or to catch him off his guard.

Weasel words. Words of convenient ambiguity, or a statement from which the original meaning has been sucked or retracted. Theodore Roosevelt popularized the term by using it in a speech in 1916 when criticizing President Wilson. A quotation from the speech provides a good example: "You can have universal training, or you can have voluntary training, but when you use the word *voluntary* to qualify the word *universal*, you are using a weasel word; it has sucked all the meaning out of *universal*. The two words flatly contradict one another."

Roosevelt was indebted to a story by Stewart Chaplin, "Stained-Glass political Platform", which appeared in the *Century Magazine* in June 1900, and in which occurs the sentence: "Why, weasel words are words that suck the life out of the words next to them, just as a weasel sucks the egg and leaves the shell." In the U.S.A. a politician who sits on the fence is sometimes called a *weasler*.

Weather. A-weather. To windward.

Clerk of the Weather. *See under* CLERK.

Fair weather friends. Those that stick to you when you are flourishing but desert as soon as your fortunes change.

I have my weather-eye open. I have my wits about me, I am keeping a good look out, I am on my guard. The weather-eye is towards the wind, supposedly to observe the weather and to be on the look out for squalls.

The peasant's, or **shepherd's weatherglass.** Another name for the SHEPHERD'S SUNDIAL.

Queen's weather. *See under* QUEEN.

To get the weather-gage of a person. To get the advantage over him. In the days of sail a fighting-ship that had the weather-gage of an enemy was to windward of him, thus having the tactical advantage.

> Then, were the line
> Of Rokeby once combined with mine,
> I gain the weather-gage of fate.
> SCOTT: *Rokeby*, xxiv.

To keep the weather of. To get round, or get the better of. A phrase from the seaman's vocabulary.

> Mine honour keeps the weather of my fate:
> Life every man holds dear; but the dear man
> Holds honour far more precious dear than life.
> SHAKESPEARE: *Troilus and Cressida*, V, iii.

To make fair weather. To flatter, conciliate; to make the best of things.

> But I must make fair weather yet awhile,
> Till Henry be more weak, and I more strong.
> SHAKESPEARE: *Henry VI, Pt. II,* V, i.

To make heavy weather of something. To find it a trial, to make a burden of it; to make heavy going of it.

Under the weather. To feel unwell or out of sorts; a condition affected by the weather. Also a colloquialism for being tipsy.

A weather breeder. A day of unusual fineness coming suddenly after a series of damp, dull days, especially at the time of year when such a genial day is not looked for. Such a day is generally followed by foul weather.

Weathercock. By a Papal enactment made in the middle of the 9th century, the figure of a cock was set up on every church steeple as the EMBLEM of St. PETER. The emblem is in allusion to his denial of our Lord thrice before the cock crew twice. On the second crowing of the cock the warning of his Master flashed across his memory, and the repentant apostle "went out and wept bitterly".

A person who is always changing his mind is, figuratively, a *weathercock*.

> Ther is no feith that may your herte embrace;
> But, as a wedercock, that turneth his face
> With every wind, ye fare.
> CHAUCER(?): *Balade Against Women Unconstant*.

Web. The Web of Life. The destiny of an individual from the cradle to the grave. An allusion to the three FATES who, according to Roman mythology, spin the thread of life, the pattern being the events which are to occur.

Web and pin. An old name for cataract, or a disease of the eye resulting in opacity of the lens.

> This is the foul fiend Flibbertigibbet ... he gives the web and pin, squints the eye, and makes the harelip.
> SHAKESPEARE: *King Lear*, III, iv.

Wed, Wedding. *Wed* is Old English, and means a pledge. The ring is the pledge given by the man to avouch that he will perform his part of the contract. *See* MARRIAGE.

The Blood-red wedding. The marriage of Henry of Navarre and Margaret of Valois (18 August 1572), which was followed a week later by the Massacre of St. BARTHOLOMEW.

Penny Weddings. *See under* PENNY.

Wedding anniversaries. Fanciful names have been given to many wedding anniversaries, the popular idea being that they designate the nature of the gifts suitable for the occasion. The following is not without variants for the lesser anniversaries. Most of them are observed by few other than the twenty-fifth and fiftieth.

First	...	Cotton Wedding.
Second	...	Paper Wedding.
Third	...	Leather Wedding.
Fourth	...	Flower or Fruit Wedding.
Fifth	...	Wooden Wedding.
Sixth	...	Iron or Sugar-candy Wedding.
Seventh	...	Woollen Wedding.
Eighth	...	Bronze or Electrical Appliances Wedding.
Ninth	...	Copper or Pottery Wedding.
Tenth	...	Tin Wedding.
Eleventh	...	Steel Wedding.
Twelfth	...	Silk and Fine Linen Wedding.
Thirteenth	...	Lace Wedding.
Fourteenth	...	Ivory Wedding.
Fifteenth	...	Crystal Wedding.
Twentieth	...	China Wedding.
Twenty-fifth	...	Silver Wedding.
Thirtieth	...	Pearl Wedding.
Thirty-fifth	...	Coral Wedding.
Fortieth	...	Ruby Wedding.
Forty-fifth	...	Sapphire Wedding.
Fiftieth	...	Golden Wedding.
Fifty-fifth	...	Emerald Wedding.
Sixtieth	...	Diamond Wedding.
Seventy-fifth	...	Diamond Wedding.

The sixtieth anniversary is often reckoned the "Diamond Wedding" in place of the seventy-fifth, as the sixtieth anniversary of Queen Victoria's accession was her "Diamond Jubilee".

Wedding Finger. The fourth finger of the left hand. Macrobius says the thumb is too busy to be set apart, the forefinger and little finger are only half protected, the middle finger is called *medicus*, and is too opprobrious for the purpose of honour, so the only finger left is the *pronubus*.

Aulus Gellius tells us that Appianus asserts in his Egyptian books that a very delicate nerve runs from the fourth finger on the left hand to the heart, on which account this finger is used for the marriage ring.

> The finger on which the ring [the wedding-ring] is to be worn is the fourth finger on the left hand, next unto the little finger; because by the received opinion of the learned ... in ripping up and anatomising men's bodies, there is a vein of blood, called *vena amoris*, which passeth from that finger to the heart.
> HENRY SWINBURNE: *Treaties of Spousals* (1680).

In the ROMAN CATHOLIC CHURCH, the thumb and next two fingers represent the TRINITY; thus the bridegroom says, "In the name of the Father," and touches the thumb; "in the name of the Son," and touches the index finger; and "in the name of the Holy Ghost," and he touches the long or third finger; with the word "Amen" he then puts it on the fourth finger and leaves it there. In some countries the wedding ring is worn on the right hand; this was the custom generally in ENGLAND until the end of the 16th century, and among Roman Catholics until much later.

In the Hereford, York, and Salisbury missals, the ring is directed to be put first on the thumb, then on the index finger, then on the long finger, and lastly on the ring-finger, *quia in illo digito est quædam vena procedens usque ad cor.*

No herring, no wedding. A bad fishing season discourages marriage among fisherfolk.

Wedge, The Wooden. *See under* WOOD. *Cp.* WOODEN SPOON.

The thin end of the wedge. *See under* THIN.

Wedlock. This word comes from O.E. *wed*, a pledge, and *lac*, action, the whole meaning the marriage vow and hence the married state. It does not imply the unopenable lock of marriage, as has sometimes been supposed.

Wednesday. The fourth day of the week until 1971 when it became the third (*see* SUNDAY); Woden's Day or ODIN's Day, called by the French *mercredi*, Mercury's Day. The Persians regard it as a "RED-LETTER DAY" because the MOON was created on the fourth day (*Gen.* i, 14–19).

Wee Frees. *See under* FREE.

Weeds. Widow's weeds. The mourning worn by a widow; from O.E. *wæde*, a garment. Spenser (*Fairie Queene*, II, iii, 21)

speaks of "A goodly lady clad in hunter's weed".

SHAKESPEARE (*Midsummer Night's Dream*, II, i) has:

> And there the snake throws her enamell'd skin,
> Weed wide enough to wrap a fairy in.

And in *Titus Andronicus* (I, i) we get the modern meaning:

> Hail, Rome, victorious in thy mourning weeds!

Week, Days of the. The names of these days are of Anglo-Saxon origin while those of the months are derived from the Romans. See the individual entries SUNDAY, MONDAY, etc., also JANUARY, FEBRUARY, etc.

A week of Sundays. A long time, an indefinite period. *See* SUNDAY.

Week-work. Under FEUDALISM, compulsory work by the unfree TENANT on his lord's land for so many days a week, usually three days. It was the chief mark of serfdom or villeinage. *Cp.* BOON WORK. *See* VILLEIN.

Weep. Weeper. In the more elaborate and formal funeral ceremonial of the 19th century, undertakers attending (called *mutes*) and the principal male mourners wore long black streamers hanging from the hatband; these were commonly known as weepers, as was also the widow's long black veil. In humorous allusion to the former, the long side whiskers in fashion in the 1860s were called *Piccadilly weepers*.

Weepers. The derisive title (Ital. *Piagnoni*, weepers or snivellers) given to the supporters of Savonarola (1452–1498) and the popular government in Florence in the 1490s, from their penitential practices and professions.

Weeping. A notion long prevailed in this country that it augured ill for future married happiness if the bride did not weep profusely at the wedding.

As no WITCH could shed more than three tears, and those from her left eye only, a copious flow of tears gave assurance to the husband that the lady had not "plighted her troth" to SATAN, and was no witch.

Weeping Cross. A cross set up by the roadside for penitential devotions.

To come home, or to return by Weeping Cross. To suffer grievous disappointment, defeat, or failure; hence, to repent of one's actions.

> The tyme will come when comming home by weeping crosse, thou shalt confesse, that it is better to be at home in the cave of an Hermit than abroad in the court of an Emperor.
> LYLY: *Euphues and his England* (1580).

The Weeping Philosopher. Heraclitus (d. *c.* 475 B.C.), so called because he grieved at the folly of man.

The Weeping Saint. St. SWITHIN, because of the tradition of forty days' rain if it rains on his day (15 July).

Weigh (O.E. *wegan*, to carry). **To weigh anchor.** To haul up the anchor preparatory to sailing.

Weighed in the balance and found wanting. Tested and proved to be at fault, or a failure. The phrase is from Daniel's interpretation of the vision of Belshazzar (*Dan.* v, 27).

Dead weight. *See under* DEAD.

A weight-for-age race. A sort of handicap in which the weights carried are apportioned according to certain conditions. Horses of the same age carry similar weights, *ceteris paribus*.

Weimar Republic, The. The German federal republic established under the Constitution of 1919, which lasted until it was overthrown by Hitler in 1933. So called from the Thuringian town, particularly associated with Goethe, where the constitution was adopted by the National Assembly.

Welch. An old spelling of *Welsh*; surviving in such names as the *Welch Fusiliers*, the *Welch Regiment*, etc.

Welcome Nugget. One of the largest nuggets of GOLD ever discovered. It was found at Baker's Hill, Ballarat, 11 June 1858, and weighed 2,217 oz.

Welcome Stranger. The largest gold nugget found to date. It weighed 2,520 oz. and was found in Victoria, Australia, in 1869.

To wear out one's welcome. To visit too frequently or to stay too long so that one's presence is no longer appreciated or desired.

Welfare State, The. A term applied to Britain after the implementation of the *Beveridge Report* (1942) providing for nation-wide social security services for sickness, unemployment, retirement, want, etc., and essentially based upon the National Insurance Act of 1946. The system depends upon compulsory contributions and taxation and was built up on the less sweeping Liberal legislation of 1908–14.

Well. Well-beloved. Charles VI of France, *le Bien-aimé* (1368, 1380–1422); also applied to Louis XV (1710, 1715–1764). *See also* COUSIN.

Well heeled. Materially prosperous as indicated by one's being well shod; the reverse of DOWN-AT-HEEL.

Wellington. The Duke of Wellington (1769–1852) is commemorated in the name of types of riding-boots and topboots, a tree of the sequóia family (the *Wellingtonia*), and as a term in cards. Thus in "Nap" a call of *Wellington* doubles *Napoleon*—*i.e.* the call-

er has to take all five tricks and wins (or loses) double stakes. Wellington College (opened 1853, as a public school for the sons of officers) was also named after him, as were also many thoroughfares, public-houses, etc.

Wells-Fargo. The famous American company founded by William George Fargo (1818–1881) and Henry Wells (1805–1878) in 1852. It carried on the stage express business between New York and San Francisco via the isthmus of Panama. It absorbed the PONY EXPRESS and took over the Overland Mail Company in 1866, and was also an agency for the transport of bullion. It amalgamated with the Adams Express in 1918 as the American Railway Express Company. *Cp.* COBB AND CO.

Welsh. *See* WALES; TAFFY.

Welsh, welsher. *To welsh* is to decamp from a racecourse without settling one's debts; to avoid settling a debt. A *welsher* is one who does this. The origin of the term is uncertain.

Welsh cake. A small, flat cake or GIRDLE CAKE cooked on a bakestone, or an iron pan. It is made from flour, fat, currants, egg, milk, salt, and sugar.

Welsh harp. The musical instrument of the ancient Welsh bards; a large harp with three rows of strings, two tuned diatonically in unison, the third supplying the chromatic sharps and flats.

Also applied loosely to the Brent Reservoir, in Middlesex, from the public-house of that name in the vicinity.

Welsh Main. In COCKFIGHTING, a form of BATTLE ROYAL in which eight pairs were matched, next the eight winners, then four, and finally the last two, until only one was left alive.

Welsh mortgage. A pledge of land in which no day is fixed for redemption.

Welsh rabbit. Cheese melted with butter, milk, Worcester sauce, etc., spread on buttered toast. *Rabbit* is not a corruption of *rare-bit*; the term is on a par with "mock-turtle", "BOMBAY DUCK", etc.

Welter-weight. A boxer between light and middle weight, about 147 lb. In racing the term is applied to any extra heavy weight.

Weltpolitik (velt' pol i tēk). The German phrase (world politics) for the policy a nation pursues in its relations with the world at large.

Wen, The, or **The Great Wen.** London. A name used by William Cobbett (1762–1835) in his *Rural Rides*, meaning that it was an abnormal growth or blotch on the land. To him the sprawl and growth of any town was "a wen". Thus he says "Chatham has had some monstrous wens stuck on to it by the lavish expenditure of the war" (4 December 1821); and, "Croydon is a good market-town; but is, by the funds, swelled out into a wen" (8 January 1822).

Wenceslas, St. (*c.* 907–929). The Bohemian martyr-prince made famous in ENGLAND by the 19th-century carol *Good King Wenceslas*. He was noted for his piety and was murdered by Boleslav, his brother. He became recognized as the patron of Bohemia and his day is 28 September.

Werewolf. *See* WERWOLF.

Wergild. The BLOOD-MONEY (*wer*, man; *gild*, payment) paid in Anglo-Saxon times by the kindred of the slayer to the kindred of the slain to avoid a blood-feud in cases of murder or manslaughter. There was a fixed scale, as 1,200 shillings for a thegn, 200 shillings for a ceorl, etc.

Werwolf. A "man-wolf" (O.E. *wer*, man), *i.e.* a man who, according to ancient superstition, was turned—or could at will turn himself—into a WOLF (the *loupgarou* of France). It had the appetite of a wolf, and roamed about at night devouring infants and sometimes exhuming corpses. Its skin was proof against shot or steel, unless the weapon had been blessed in a chapel dedicated to St. HUBERT.

Ovid tells the story of LYCAON, King of ARCADIA, turned into a wolf because he tested the divinity of JUPITER by serving up to him a "hash of human flesh"; Herodotus describes the Neuri as having the power of assuming once a year the shape of wolves; Pliny relates that one of the family of ANTÆUS was chosen annually, by lot, to be transformed into a wolf, in which shape he continued for nine years; and St. PATRICK, we are told, converted Vereticus, King of WALES, into a wolf.

Hence the term *lycanthropy* (Gr. *lukos*, wolf; *anthropos*, man) for this supposed transformation and for the form of insanity in which the subject exhibits depraved animal traits.

Tigers, hyenas, and leopards had the same associations in other parts of the world, and after the disappearance of the wolf in England WITCHES were commonly "transformed" into cats.

Wesleyan. A member of the NONCONFORMIST church which grew out of the evangelical movement started by John Wesley (1703–1791) and his associates, although there was no real break with the CHURCH OF ENGLAND until 1795. *See* METHODISTS.

Wessex. The ancient kingdom of the West Saxons, founded by Cerdic in the 6th century. Its nucleus was the modern Berkshire and Hampshire, and it later spread to CORNWALL in the west and to Kent and Essex in the east. The Danish invasions of the 9th century destroyed the other English kingdoms and ALFRED THE GREAT came to be recognized as King of all the English outside the Danish areas. The subsequent reconquest of the DANELAW resulted in the king of Wessex becoming king of ENGLAND.

The Novelist of Wessex. Thomas Hardy (1840–1928), the scenes of whose novels are set in this area.

West. The West End. The western district of inner LONDON, noted for its fashionable shopping, theatres, clubs, hotels, restaurants, the expensive residential district of MAYFAIR, SOHO, etc. It includes largely the area between Hyde Park and CHARING CROSS Road. *Cp.* EAST END *under* END.

To go west. Of persons, to die; of things, to be lost, rendered useless or unattainable, as, "My chance of promotion has gone west." The reference is to the setting sun, which "goes west", and then sinks or expires, or possibly TYBURN.

West, Mae. *See* MAE WEST.

The Western Church. The CATHOLIC CHURCH.

The Western Empire. The western division of the ROMAN EMPIRE with ROME as its capital, after the division into the Eastern and Western Empire by Theodosius in 395.

Westerns. *see* WILD WEST.

Westminster. The seat of government in ENGLAND since the time of Canute (1016–35). From the time of WILLIAM THE CONQUEROR the sovereign has been crowned in Westminster Abbey and it later became the home of the Mother of Parliaments. Hence, like WHITEHALL and DOWNING STREET, it is sometimes used as a synonym for government or PARLIAMENT.

The Palace of Westminster. Until 1512, a royal residence and the place to which PARLIAMENT was summoned; now the seat of Parliament. In 1547 St. Stephen's Chapel within the Palace became the home of the HOUSE OF COMMONS until the fire of 1834, when new buildings were erected. The House of Commons Chamber was again destroyed by enemy bombing in 1940. The LORDS occupied other parts of the Palace which ceased to be a royal residence after a serious fire in 1512. STAR CHAMBER stood in these precincts, but the only ancient building now remaining is Westminster Hall, parts of which date from 1097.

The Westminster Assembly. The assembly appointed by the LONG PARLIAMENT to reform the English Church. It consisted of 30 laymen and 120 clergy and met in Westminster Abbey precincts (1643–53). Its most important achievement was the WESTMINSTER CONFESSION. *See also* ERASTIANISM.

The Westminster Confession. The PRESBYTERIAN Confession of faith adopted by the WESTMINSTER ASSEMBLY in 1646 and approved by PARLIAMENT in 1648. It became a standard definition of Presbyterian doctrine.

Wet. Slang for a drink; hence **to have a wet** is to have a drink, and **to wet one's whistle** means the same thing; Chaucer has, "So was her joly whistle wel y-wet" (*Reeve's Tale*, 235).

In the U.S.A. *wet* States were those which did not support the prohibition of the sale of alcoholic drinks.

In colloquial speech *wet* also denotes stupidity, foolishness, thus **he is pretty wet** means he is fairly stupid and **don't talk wet** means don't talk such nonsense, don't be silly. The more liberal element in the TORY party, which does not favour all the IRON LADY's policies, are called "wets".

A wet blanket. *See under* BLANKET.

Wetback. An illegal immigrant to the U.S.A. from Mexico. The term originates in the fact that such interlopers usually had to swim the Rio Grande.

Wet bob. At Eton, a wet bob is a boy who goes in for boating; a dry bob one who chooses CRICKET.

Wet nurse. A woman employed to suckle children not her own.

To wet the baby's head. To celebrate a baptism with a social gathering to drink to the health of the newly born baby.

W. H., Mr. When SHAKESPEARE's *Sonnets* appeared in 1609 they were dedicated to a Mr. W. H., called their "onlie begetter". The identity of Shakespeare's friend is uncertain. Various names have been put forward and for long the most favoured were William Herbert, third Earl of Pembroke, to whom (with his brother) the First Folio Shakespeare was dedicated, and Henry Wriothesley, third Earl of Southampton, to whom *Venus and Adonis* and *Lucrece* were dedicated. In 1964 Dr. Leslie Hotson put forward a case for William Hatcliffe of Lincolnshire, "Prince of Purpoole" in the GRAY'S INN revels of 1588. According to Dr. A. L. Rowse, Master W. H. is Sir William Harvey, the Earl of Southampton's stepfather.

Whale. To throw a tub to a whale. *See under* TUB.

Very like a whale. Very much like a COCK-AND-BULL STORY. In SHAKESPEARE's *Hamlet* (III, ii), the Prince chaffs POLONIUS by comparing a cloud to a camel, and then to a weasel, and when the courtier assents Hamlet adds, "Or like a whale"; to which Polonius answers, "Very like a whale."

A whale of a lot. A great amount. Colloquially *whale* is used of something very fine or big as *we had a whale of a time*, a fine time, or *a whale of a job*, a very considerable task.

Whalebone. *See* MISNOMERS.

White as whalebone. An old simile; whalebone is far from white. Our forefathers seemed to confuse walrus with whale; and "white as whalebone" is really a blunder for "white as walrus-ivory".

What. He knows what's what. He is a shrewd fellow, not to be imposed upon. One of the senseless questions of logic was *Quid est quid*?

> He knew what's what, and that's as high
> As metaphysic wit can fly.
> BUTLER: *Hudibras*, I, i.

What makes it tick. *See under* TICK.

What we gave we have. The epitaph on "the Good Earl of Courtenay" (see Gibbon's *Decline and Fall*, vol. VI, ch. lxi):

> What wee gave, wee have;
> What wee spent, wee had;
> What wee left, wee lost.

is a free rendering of Martial's:

> Extra fortunam est quidquid donatur amicis
> Quas dederis, solas semper habebis opes.

There are similar epitaphs in many churches; one in St. George's, Doncaster, runs thus:

> How now, who is here?
> I, Robin of Doncastere
> And Margaret, my feere.
> That I spent, that I had;
> That I gave, that I have;
> That I left, that I lost.

Whatever are you at? So Dr. W. G. Grace is reported to have called out when, in 1896, Ernest Jones, the Australian fast bowler, bowled through W.G.'s beard.

What-not. A small stand with shelves for photographs, knick-knacks, china ornaments, and "what-not" (*i.e.* etc.), popular in Victorian and Edwardian times.

Wheatear. A bird with a white rump and base of tail, one of the thrush family. The name has no connection with either *wheat* or *ear*, but it is the O.E. *hwit*, white; *ears*—still in vulgar use as *arse*—the buttocks or rump. The French name of the bird, *culblanc*, signifies exactly the same thing.

Wheel. Emblematical of St. CATHERINE, who was broken on a spiked wheel.

St. Donatus bears a wheel set round with lights.

St. Euphemia and St. Willigis both carry wheels.

St. Quintin is sometimes represented with a broken wheel at his feet.

Broken on the wheel. *See under* BREAK.

To break a butterfly on a wheel. *See under* BREAK.

To put a spoke in one's wheel. *See* SPOKE.

To put one's shoulder to the wheel. *See under* PUT.

The wheel is come full circle. Just retribution has followed. The line is from SHAKE-SPEARE's *King Lear*, V, iii.

The wheel of Fortune. Fortuna, the goddess, is represented on ancient monuments with a wheel in her hand, emblematical of her inconstancy.

> Though fortune's malice overthrow my state,
> My mind exceeds the compass of her wheel.
> SHAKESPEARE: Henry VI, Pt. III, iv, iii.

See also PRAYING-WHEEL, *below*.

Wheels within wheels. A complex of motives and influences and circumstances at work which are not always apparent. The allusion is to *Ezekiel* i, 16.

Praying-wheel. A revolving wheel or cylinder, used for purposes of prayer among Buddhists, upon which written prayers are set, each turn of the wheel being reckoned as a prayer. In Europe, a wheel with bells (sometimes called a WHEEL OF FORTUNE), used as a means of DIVINATION, a favourable or unfavourable response being indicated by the position at which it came to rest.

Wheel-horse, or **Wheeler.** Figuratively, one who does the hard work or bears the brunt. The wheel-horse is the one nearest the front wheels of a vehicle and is harnessed to the pole or shafts, as distinct from the leader who is the front horse.

Wheeler-dealer. One who "wheels and deals". Wheel in American slang signifies a leader, one who takes charge, a "big shot". Hence one of great influence in a particular field (usually business or politics); a shrewd and influential operator and manipulator.

Wherewithal. In older writings this is a form of *wherewith* as in:

> Wherewithal shall a young man cleanse his way?
> Ps. cxix, 9.

It is now used as a noun in the sense of *means, money*.

Whetstone. *See* ACCIUS NAEVIUS.

Lying for the whetstone. Said of a person who is grossly exaggerating or falsifying a statement. One of the WHITSUN amusements of our forefathers was the lie-wage or lie-match; he who could tell the greatest lie was rewarded with a whetstone to sharpen his wit. The nature of these contests may be illustrated by the following: one of the combatants declared he could see a fly on the top of a church steeple; the other replied, "Oh, yes, I saw him wink his eye."

The Whetstone of Witte. A famous treatise on algebra (1557) by Robert Recorde. The old name for algebra was the "Cossic Art", and *Cos ingenii* rendered into English is "the Whetstone of Wit". In Scott's *Fortunes of Nigel* (ch. xxiv), the servant told Nigel that she knew of no other books in the house "than her mistress's Bible ...; and her Master's Whetstone of Witte, being the second part of Arithmetic, by Robert Record, with the Cossike Practice and Rule of Equation.".

Whig. A name applied to Scottish cattle rustlers and horse thieves, then to the Presbyterian COVENANTERS and later, in the reign of Charles II (1660–1685), to those seeking to exclude the Duke of York from succession to the throne. The name was used abusively by their TORY opponents. From the time of the GLORIOUS REVOLUTION the Whigs were upholders of parliamentary supremacy and toleration for NONCONFORMISTS. They supported the Hanoverian succession and enjoyed a monopoly of political power until the reign of George III, when they were superseded by the Tories after 1783 and did not recover the ascendancy until 1830, the time of the Reform Bill. By 1868 the name LIBERAL had largely replaced that of Whig.

The origin of the word is obscure but it is probably a shortened form of *whiggamore*, a horse drover.

In American usage, *Whig* denotes a supporter of the American Revolution; also a member of the American Whig party formed in 1834 from the old National Republican Party against President Andrew Jackson and "executive tyranny". The part disintegrated by 1854 over the question of "free soil" and slavery.

The Whig Bible. *See* BIBLE, SOME SPECIALLY NAMED EDITIONS.

Whip. In British parliamentary usage, M.P.s appointed by a party, whose duty it is to see that the members of their party vote at important divisions and to discipline them if they do not attend, or vote against the party.

Whip also denotes the notice sent by party whips to members requesting their attendance in the HOUSE, and the degree of urgency is indicated by one, two, or three lines shown under the summons. The name derives from the *whipper-in* at a fox-hunt.

The ship with six strings. *See* THE SIX ARTICLES under SIX.

Whip-dog Day. 18 October, St. LUKE'S day. Brand (*Popular Antiquities*, II) says that it is so called because a priest about to celebrated MASS on St. Luke's Day happened to drop the PYX, which was snatched up by a dog.

A whip-round. An impromptu collection for some benevolent object.

To whip-saw. To have or take the advantage over an opponent; especially in faro, to win two different bets at one turn.

Whip-sawing is also an American term for accepting bribes from two opposing interests at the same time. The whip-saw is a long narrow frame-saw with a handle at either end so that it cuts both ways.

Whipper-snapper. An inexperienced, insignificant and often intrusive young person. The word probably derives from *whip snapper*, one who has nothing to do but crack a whip.

Whipping Boy. A boy kept to be whipped when a prince deserved chastisement. Fuller (*Church History*, II) says Barnaby Fitzpatrick so stood for Edward VI, and Mungo Murray for CHARLES I. When Henry IV of France abjured Protestantism and was received into the ROMAN CATHOLIC CHURCH in 1593, Bishop Duperron and Cardinal d'Ossat were sent to ROME to obtain the King's absolution. They knelt in the portico of St. Peter's singing the MISERERE. At each verse a blow with a switch was given on their shoulders.

Whisky. SCOTCH. In Ireland and the U.S.A. spelt *whiskey*. *See* USQUEBAUGH. The light one-horse gig called a whisky is from *whisk*, to move briskly.

Whisky Insurrection. An outbreak in Western Pennsylvania in 1794 when the Federal Government tried to enforce the excise tax of 1791 which was opposed by farmers in the area who distilled whisky to make use of surplus grain. It culminated in riot and destruction of private property and some federal excise officers were tarred and feathered until suppressed by the militia.

Whisky Money. The name given to the money diverted to county and county borough councils in 1890, for the development of technical education in accordance with the Technical Instruction Act, 1889. It was derived from the extra duty (6*d*. per gallon) levied on spirits in 1890 as part of an abortive scheme to compensate licensees of redundant public-houses, but was used instead for technical and secondary education. As a consequence, temperance did not help education.

Whisper. Pig's whisper. *See under* PIG.

To give the whisper. To give the tip, the warning; to pass some bit of secret information.

Whist. The card game originated in England (16th century) and was first called *Triumph* (whence *trump*), then *Ruff* or *Honours*, and then, early in the 17th century, *Whisk*, in allusion to the sweeping up of the cards. Whist, the later name, appears in Butler's *Hudibras* (1663), and was adopted through confusion with *Whist!* meaning Hush! Silence!

> Let nice Piquette the boast of France remain,
> And studious Ombre be the pride of Spain!
> Invention's praise shall England yield to none,
> While she can call delightful Whist her own.
> ALEXANDER THOMAS: *Whist* (2nd edn., 1792).

See WHITECHAPEL.

Whistle. To wet one's whistle. *See* WET.

To whistle down the wind. To abandon; to talk or argue purposelessly. From the releasing of a HAWK down wind.

To whistle for it. It was an old superstition among sailors that when a ship was becalmed a wind could be raised by whistling, but to many seamen whistling was "the Devil's music" which could raise a gale. It was, therefore, not tolerated. More rationally the phrase "you can whistle for it" now means "You won't get it".

Worth the whistle. Worth calling; worth inviting; worth notice. The dog is worth the pains of whistling for. Thus Heywood, in one of his dialogues consisting entirely of proverbs, says, "It is a poor dog that is not worth the whistling." Goneril says to Albany:

> I have been worth the whistle.
> SHAKESPEARE: *King Lear*, IV, ii.

You paid too dearly for your whistle. You paid dearly for something you fancied, but found that it did not answer your expectation. The allusion is to a story told by Benjamin Franklin of his nephew, who set his mind on a common whistle, which he bought of a boy for four times its value.

Whistle-stop tour. In the U.S.A., to conduct a brief campaign, usually political, by travelling the country visiting the smaller communities, often talking from the rear platform of a train. A *whistle-stop* being a small town on a rail-road where the train only stopped on a given signal. *Cp.* JERKWATER.

Whitsunday. *White* Sunday. The seventh SUNDAY after EASTER, to commemorate the descent of the HOLY GHOST on the day of PENTECOST. It was one of the great seasons for baptism and the candidates wore white garments, hence the name.

Whitsuntide. The whole week following WHITSUNDAY.

Whitsun farthings. *See* PENTECOSTALS.

Whitsun-ale. The most important CHURCH-ALE, celebrated with much revelry.

White denotes purity, simplicity, and candour; innocence, truth, and hope. For its ecclesiastical use, symbolism, etc., *see* COLOURS.

Generally, the priests of antiquity wore white vestments, and Bardic costume, supposedly derived from the DRUIDS, is always white. OSIRIS, the ancient Egyptian god, wore a white crown; the priests of JUPITER were clad in white, and at the death of a CÆSAR the national mourning was white. The Persians affirm that the divinities are clothed in white.

Blanco White. In the British army, the popular designation of personnel named White. It derives from the trade name "Blanco" for the preparation which replaced pipeclay as the universal substance for whitening the webbing in a soldier's equipment. It was made by a Sheffield firm called Pickering from about 1881 until the 1960s. "Khaki Blanco" was also much used.

The white bird. Conscience, or the SOUL of man. The Mohammedans have preserved the old idea that the souls of the just lie under the throne of GOD, like white birds, till the resurrection morn. *Cp.* DOVE.

White Canons. *See* PREMONSTRATENSIAN.

The White Cockade. The badge worn by the followers of Charles Edward, the Young PRETENDER.

The White Company. In 13th-century France, a band of cut-throats organized by Folquet, bishop of Toulouse, to extirpate heretics in his diocese. The name is better known for its association with the FREE COMPANIES of the late 14th century: that which Bertrand du Guesclin led against Pedro the Cruel of Castile in 1367, whose members wore a white CROSS on the shoulder; and that under Sir John Hawkwood in Italy. Sir Arthur Conan Doyle's notable story, *The White Company*, was first published in 1891. *See also* CONDOTTIERI.

White elephant. *See under* ELEPHANT.

White Ensign. A St. George's CROSS on a white ground with the UNION JACK in a canton, since 1864 the ensign of the Royal Navy but also used by members of the Royal Yacht Squadron who have the requisite warrant.

White Fathers. Members of the French Society of Missionaries of Africa established at Algiers in 1868. So called from their white tunic.

White flag. An all-white flag is universally used as the signal of surrender or desiring to parley and its bearer is by international custom immune from harm.

White Friars. The CARMELITES, so called from their white MANTLE worn over a brown habit. One of their houses founded in LONDON on the south side of FLEET STREET in 1241 gave its name to the district called *Whitefriars* or ALSATIA which was long a SANCTUARY.

White harvest. A late harvest, when the ground is white of a morning with hoar frost.

The White Horse. *See under* HORSE.

White horses. *See under* HORSE.

The White House. The Presidential mansion at Washington, D.C. It is a building of freestone, painted white. The cornerstone was laid by George Washington. Figuratively it means the Presidency of the U.S.A.

White Lady. A kind of spectre, the appearance of which generally forebodes death in the house. It is a relic of Teutonic mythology, representing HULDA or BERCHTA, the goddess who received the SOULS of maidens and young children. She is dressed in white and carries a bunch of keys at her side.

The first recorded instance of this apparition was in the 15th century, and the name given to the lady is Bertha von Rosenberg. She last appeared, it is said, in 1879. German legend says that when the castle of Neuhaus, Bohemia, was being built a white lady appeared and promised the workmen a sweep soup and a carp on the completion of the castle. In remembrance thereof, these dainties were for long given to the poor on MAUNDY THURSDAY.

In Normandy the White Ladies lurk in ravines, fords, bridges, etc., and ask the wayfarer to dance, and if refused fling him into a ditch. The most famous of these ladies are *La Dame d'Aprigny*, who used to occupy the site of the Rue St. Quentin, at Bayeux, and *La Dame Abonde*.

The *White Lady of Avenel*, in Scott's *The Monastery*, is based upon these legends.

White Ladies. A popular name for the CISTERCIAN nuns in mediæval ENGLAND, from the colour of their habit, and for the Magdalenes. Also applied to the French Order of the Sisters of the Presentation of Mary (1796).

White League. A name for the KU KLUX KLAN.

A white lie. *See under* LIE.

White magic. Sorcery in which the DEVIL is not invoked and plays no part, as distinct from *black* magic.

A white man. A thoroughly straightforward and honourable man.

The White Man's Burden. In the days of imperialism, the duty supposed to be imposed upon the white races, especially the British, to govern and to educate the less-civilized or backward coloured peoples.

> Take up the White Man's Burden—
> Send forth the best you breed,
> Go bind your sons to exile
> To serve the captives' need.
> KIPLING: *The White Man's Burden.*

The White Man's Grave. The unhealthy areas of equatorial West Africa, especially Sierra Leone.

White Monks. The CISTERCIAN monks, whose habit was made from white wool.

A white night. A sleepless night; the French have the phrase *Passer une nuit blanche.*

White Paper. A government publication printed for the information of PARLIAMENT. Such a report, statement of policy, etc., is not bulky enough to warrant the protective covers of a BLUE BOOK. White Papers are available to the public through H.M. Stationery Office.

White rent. Rent paid in silver money. Also the duty of eightpence per head formerly paid by the tin-miners of Devon and CORNWALL to the Duke of Cornwall. These dues were abolished in 1838. *See* STANNARIES.

The White Rose. *See under* ROSE.

White Russian. An inhabitant of White Russia or Byelorussia (Russ. *byely*, white), one of the republics of the U.S.S.R. A *"White"* Russian also denotes a counter-revolutionary or *émigré* at the time of the BOLSHEVIK revolution, and their army was known as the **White Army.**

White Satin. An old nickname for GIN.

White sheep. *See* BLACK SHEEP *under* SHEEP.

The White Ship. The ship carrying Henry I's son William from Normandy to ENGLAND, which struck a rock off Barfleur (25 November 1120) and sank. William was drowned with the resultant conflict for the crown between Stephen and Matilda. The disaster was due to the drunken laxity of the crew.

White Sisters. The Congregation of the Daughters of the HOLY GHOST, founded in Brittany in 1706, so called from the colour of their habit. Also the Congregation of the Missionary Sisters of Our Lady of Africa (1869), the counterpart of the WHITE FATHERS.

White Slave. A woman who is sold or forced into prostitution, especially when taken abroad.

A white squall. One which produces no diminution of light, in contradistinction to a *black* squall, in which the clouds are black and heavy. Also a small whirlwind, usually occurring in the tropics.

White tincture. The alchemist's name for a preparation that should convert any base metal into SILVER. It is also called the Stone of the Second Order, the Little Elixir, and the Little Magisterium. *See* RED.

The White Tower. *See under* TOWER.

White wedding. A wedding in which the bride wears the traditional white wedding dress and veil, white symbolizing purity and virginity. For the same reason, grey horses were formerly used for the wedding carriage and the postboys wore white hats. Wedding cake is coated with white icing and invitations, etc., are usually printed in silver. It is also said to be unlucky to be married in anything but white.

White wine. Any wine of a light colour as distinct from *red* wine, *e.g.*: Champagne, hock, Sauternes, Moselle, Graves, Chablis, etc.

White witch. One who practises WHITE MAGIC only.

White's. A chocolate-house and later a fashionable club, first opened by Francis White (d. 1711) on the east side of St. James's Street in 1693, moving across the street to larger premises in 1697. The fashionable fraternity soon congregated upstairs to avoid the general company of the Chocolate-house which after 1711 was in the hands of the Arthur family. Early on it earned notoriety as a gaming-house, and for the exclusiveness of its upstairs clientele, from which in due course White's Club developed. The transition was virtually complete by the mid-18th century and it can with some justification be regarded as the first of the London Clubs, moving to larger premises in 1755. Gambling and gaming excesses continued until the accession of George III (1760) when they were reduced to more modest proportions in keeping with the changed tone of the court. At this juncture a group of the more extravagant younger men from White's became the patrons of ALMACK'S.

Days marked with a white stone. Days to be remembered with gratification. The Romans used a white stone or piece of chalk to mark their lucky days on the calendar. Unlucky days were marked with charcoal. *Cp.* RED-LETTER DAY.

To hit the white. To be quite right, make a good shot. The phrase is from the old days of archery, the white being the inner circle of the target—the BULL'S EYE.

To show the white feather. To show cowardice; a phrase from COCKFIGHTING, a white feather in a gamecock's tail being taken as a sign of degenerate stock, not a true game-bird.

To stand in a white sheet. Part of the ancient penance for incontinence was to stand before the congregation at MASS robed in a white sheet. The term now designates the utmost penitence.

Washing the Blackamoor white. *See* BLACKAMOOR.

White-collar worker. The professional or clerical worker, whose calling demands a certain nicety of attire typified by the wearing of a white shirt and collar. *Cp* BLACK-COATED WORKER.

A white tie affair. A social function at which the men wear formal evening dress with a white bow-tie and swallow-tailed coat.

A whited sepulchre. A hypocrite, especially one who conceals wickedness under a cloak of virtue.

In Biblical times, Jewish sepulchres were whitened to make them conspicuous so that passers-by might avoid ritual defilement by near approach. Thus Jesus (*Matt.* xxiii, 27) says: "Ye are like unto whited sepulchres, which indeed appear beautiful outward, but are within full of dead men's bones, and of all uncleanness."

White-face. A nickname for a man from Hereford; from the white faces of Herefordshire cattle.

White-livered. Cowardly, from the old notion that the livers of cowards were bloodless.

> How many cowards, whose hearts are all as false
> As stairs of sand, wear yet upon their chins
> The beards of Hercules and frowning Mars,
> Who, inward search'd, have livers white as milk!
> SHAKESPEARE: *Merchant of Venice*, III, ii.

Whitebait Dinner. A dinner of CABINET Ministers and prominent politicians which, until the early 1890s, was held at Blackwall or Greenwich towards the close of the parliamentary session. The time of meeting was TRINITY Monday, or as near Trinity Monday as was convenient. Blackwall and Greenwich were formerly much resorted to by Londoners to enjoy whitebait.

Whiteboys. Irish Catholic peasant organizations first appearing in Munster in the 1760s, whose outrages were a protest against RACK-RENTING, TITHES, enclosures, etc. They again terrorized southern IRELAND from the late 1780s until the end of the century. So called because they wore white frocks over their clothing. In the Isle of MAN,

Christmas mummers were known as *White Boys*.

Whitechapel. A district of Stepney in the East END of London, east of Aldgate, and a noted Jewish quarter. It contains part of PETTICOAT LANE and was the scene of the notorious **Whitechapel Murders** by JACK THE RIPPER. It is also notable for its bell-foundry. It takes its name from the colour of the original chapel-of-ease to Stepney built there.

In WHIST, *Whitechapel* denotes unskilful play such as leading out with winning cards, or leading from a one-card suit in order to trump.

Whitechapel cart. A light, two-wheeled spring cart, once used by tradesmen for delivering goods.

Whitehall. This famous thoroughfare takes its name from the royal palace sited there, which was in use from the time of Henry VIII to William III. It was mostly destroyed by fire in 1698 and only the banqueting hall, built by Inigo Jones, still stands. The palace was formerly Wolsey's mansion called York Place, but was named *White Hall* after its confiscation by Henry VIII.

> You must no more call it York Place, that's past:
> For, since the cardinal fell, that title's lost;
> 'Tis now the King's, and call'd Whitehall.
> SHAKESPEARE: *King Henry VIII*, IV, i.

From its being the site of the major Government offices the name is often used as a synonym for the British government.

Whitewash. Figuratively, excuses made in palliation of bad conduct; a false colouring given to a person's character or memory, a stained reputation, etc.

The term is also applied to the clearance by a bankrupt of his debts, not by paying them but by judicial process.

Whitsun. *See under* WHIT.

Whittington, Dick. According to the popular legend and PANTOMIME story, a poor boy who made his way to LONDON when he heard that the streets were paved with GOLD and SILVER. He found shelter as a scullion in the house of a rich merchant who permitted each of his servants to partake in sending a cargo of merchandise to Barbary. Dick sent his CAT, but subsequently ran away owing to ill-treatment below STAIRS. He was recalled by BOW BELLS seeming to say:

> Turn again Whittington
> Thrice Lord Mayor of London.

He returned to find his cat had been purchased for a vast sum by the King of Barbary, who was much plagued by rats and mice. He married his master's daughter Alice, prospered exceedingly, and became thrice Lord Mayor.

In fact, he was the youngest son of Sir William Whittington of Pauntley in Gloucestershire and duly became a mercer of London, having married Alice, the daughter of Sir Ivo Fitzwaryn. He became very wealthy, the richest merchant of his day, and was made Lord MAYOR of London in 1397–1398, 1406–1407, and 1419–1420. He died in 1423 leaving his vast wealth for charitable and public purposes.

The part of the cat in the story has been carefully explained: that he traded in coals brought to London in *cats* (a type of sailing-vessel), and that it is a confusion with Fr. *achat*, "purchase" (a term then used for trading at a profit). Whatever be the truth, Dick Whittington and his cat are now inseparables.

Whizz or **Whiz Kid.** A highly intelligent young person, one who achieves rapid success, the onomatopoeic word *whizz* being the sound of something moving through the air with great rapidity.

Who dun it. A colloquialism originating in the U.S.A. for a detective story (in American usage, a mystery).

Whoopee (woo pē'). **To make whoopee.** To enjoy oneself uproariously, to go on the RAZZLE or spree.

Wicked. Probably connected with O.E. *wicca*, a WIZARD.

The Wicked Bible. *See* BIBLE, SOME SPECIALLY NAMED EDITIONS.

The Wicked Prayer Book. Printed 1686, octavo. In the Epistle for the Fourteenth Sunday after TRINITY the following passage occurs:

> Now the works of the flesh are manifest, which are these, adultery, fornication, uncleanness, idolatry...they who do such things shall inherit the kingdom of God.

("shall inherit" should be "shall not inherit".)

Wicket. To bat on a sticky wicket. To be confronted with a difficult situation which demands coolness and judgment. An allusion to the game of CRICKET when a soft pitch causes greater difficulties for the batsman when the ball is delivered.

Widdershins. *See* WITHERSHINS.

Wide. Slang for cunning, artful, or for one who is very wide-awake. Hence **wide boy,** a plebeian type of SMART-ALEC who needs watching, one who tries "to see you off." *Cp.* SPIV.

Wideawake. Types of felt hat, with a low crown and wide brim, common in Victorian times. Punningly so called because they never had a *nap*.

Widecombe Fair. The famous fair held annually on the second Tuesday of September at Widecombe-in-the-Moor. The long established sheep and pony fair in this DARTMOOR parish became widely known from the old folk song telling the story of UNCLE TOM COBLEIGH. He still appears in the modern carnival dressed in an old linen smock astride the old grey mare giving rides to young children.

Widow, The. Old slang for the gallows. Also Victorian slang for champagne, in allusion to the well-known brand Veuve Clicquot, so called from "Widow" Clicquot who, at the age of 27, took over the firm in 1806 on the death of her husband François, and with her associates made it an outstanding success. The House of Clicquot was founded by Philippe Clicquot in 1772 and eventually renamed Veuve Cliquot-Ponsardin in 1810.

The Widow at Windsor. A name applied to Queen Victoria whose husband Albert, the PRINCE CONSORT, died at the end of 1861. Her remaining 39 years were largely spent in seclusion and she never ceased to mourn her loss. The name *The Widow at Windsor* was applied by Rudyard Kipling in his *Barrack-Room Ballad* of that name (1892).

> Then 'ere's to the Widow at Windsor,
> An' 'ere's to the stores an' the guns,
> The men an' the 'orses what makes up the forces
> O' Missis Victorier's sons.

Widow bench. An obsolete law term for the share of her husband's estate allowed to a widow over and above her jointure.

The widow's cruse. A small supply of anything which, by good management, is made to go a long way and to be apparently inexhaustible. In allusion to the miracle of the cruse of oil in II *Kings* iv.

Widow's man. Old naval slang for a nonexistent seaman whose name was borne on the ship's book, his pay, PRIZEMONEY, etc., going to Greenwich Hospital or to a fund for widows.

Widow's mite. An offering, small in itself but representing self-sacrifice on the part of the giver; a small contribution from one who is unable to give much. An allusion to *Mark* xii, 42. Lord John Russell, 1st Earl Russell (1792–1878), of Reform Bill fame was nicknamed the *Widow's mite* from his small stature and his marriage in 1835 to the widow of the 2nd Lord Ribblesdale.

Widow's peak. A V-shaped point of hair over the forehead reminiscent of the front cusp of the cap formerly worn by widows.

Widow's weeds. *See* WEEDS.

Wieland *See* WAYLAND SMITH.

Wife. O.E. *wif*, a woman. The ultimate root of the word is obscure; but it is "certainly not allied to *weave* (O.E. *weafn*), as the fable runs" (Skeat).

The old meaning, a *woman*, still appears in such combinations as *fish-wife, house-wife,* etc., and **old-wives' tales** for unconvincing stories or proverbial legend.

> But refuse profane and old wives' fables, and exercise thyself rather unto godliness.
>
> I *Tim*. iv, 7.

The Wife-hater Bible. *See* BIBLE, SOME SPECIALLY NAMED EDITIONS.

Wig. A shortened form of *periwig* (earlier, *perwig*), from Fr. *perrugue*. The long flowing wig of Louis XIV's time was called the *allonge* (lengthening) and in the 18th century there were thirty or forty different styles and names: as the artichoke, bag, barrister's, bishop's, Blenheim, brush, buckle, busby, bush (buzz), campaigning, cauliflower, chain, chancellor's corded, Count Saxe's mode, crutch, cut bob, Dalmahoy (a bob wig worn by tradesmen), detached buckle, drop, Dutch, full, half natural, Jansenist bob, judge's, ladder, long bob, Louis, pigeon's wing, rhinoceros, rose, she-dragon, small back, spinach seed, staircase, wild boar's back, wolf's paw.

A bigwig. A magnate, someone of importance; in allusion to the large wigs that in the 17th and 18th centuries encumbered the head and shoulders of the aristocracy of England and France, etc. They are still worn by the Lord CHANCELLOR, judges, and the SPEAKER of the HOUSE OF COMMONS; BISHOPS continued to wear them in the HOUSE OF LORDS until 1880.

Scratch wig. A small one just large enough to cover the bald patch, as opposed to the full-bottomed wig.

Tie-wig. The small wig as worn by barristers.

Welsh wig. A worsted cap.

Dash my wig! A mild imprecation, formerly very common.

Wigs on the green. A serious disagreement likely to lead to a scrimmage; a rumpus.

Wigging. A scolding, a reprimand. Possibly from the idea of dislodging or ruffling someone's wig, or from a reproof by a BIGWIG or a *wigged* superior.

Wiggen tree. *See* ROWAN.

Wight (wīt). An Old English word meaning a person, a human being. It chiefly survives in the phrase "luckless wight", one for whom everything goes wrong.

Wild. Wild Bill. James Butler Hickok (1837–1876) American soldier and scout was so called. A renowned pistol shot in his early days he served as a stage driver and later in the Union army during the Civil War as a scout and sharpshooter. He became a deputy marshal in 1866 and served as a scout for General CUSTER and others. From 1869–1871 he was marshal in Kansas. Of great strength and courage he shot many thieves and outlaws and in 1872–1873 toured in the east with BUFFALO BILL. He was killed from behind, at Deadwood, Dakota in 1876.

Wild Boy. *See* GAZELLE BOY; PETER THE WILD BOY.

Wildcat. A female of fierce and uncontrolled temper is often called a wildcat for obvious reasons and the expression is variously applied to reckless, uncontrolled, and unsound activities, ventures, etc. Thus, *wildcat strike*, an impromptu or unofficial strike; *wildcat scheme*, a rash and hazardous scheme, especially financial; *wildcat banking*, financially unsound; etc. The usage is of colloquial American origin and in the U.S.A. a prospect well for oil or natural gas is also called a *wildcat*.

The Wild Huntsman. A spectral hunter of mediæval legend, who with a pack of spectral dogs frequents certain forests and occasionally appears to mortals. It takes numerous forms in Germany, France, and England, and the wild huntsman is often identified with various heroes of national legend. In England, there is notably Herne the Hunter, onetime keeper in Windsor Forest. SHAKESPEARE says he "walks" in winter-time, about midnight, blasts trees and takes cattle. He wears horns and rattles a chain (*Merry Wives of Windsor*, IV, iv). Herne is also featured in Harrison Ainsworth's *Windsor Castle*. *See* HERNE OAK *under* OAK.

There is a Midnight Hunter of Dartmoor accompanied by the WISH HOUNDS. *Cp.* GABRIEL'S HOUNDS; MAUTHE DOG.

A wild-goose chase. An impracticable or useless pursuit of something; an absurd enterprise. A wild-goose is very difficult to catch. *Cp.* WILDCAT.

To sow one's wild oats. *See* OATS.

Wildfire. A very old English description of a composition of inflammable materials that catch fire quickly. It is now used figuratively in the phrase **To catch like wildfire,** to take on with the public instantaneously.

Wild men. A term often applied in politics to party intransigents or extremists. Women who took part in the campaign for women's rights, especially the militant SUFFRAGETTES, were sometimes called **wild women.**

Wild West. In 19th-century America, the moving western frontier, before orderly settlement was established under governmental control. It was an area of action and adventure, of desperadoes and cattle rustlers, noted for hard drinking, gambling, and violence and crime generally. Since romanticized in stories and films (called *Westerns*), it has its own folk heroes varying from the Lone Ranger to Deadwood Dick.

Wilderness. To go into the Wilderness. A figurative description of being deprived of political office through a change of government.

Wilfrid, St. (*c*. 634–709). A Northumbrian, educated at Lindisfarne, he subsequently visited Canterbury and ROME, learning the Roman liturgy. He became Abbot of Ripon and was largely responsible for the adoption of Roman usages in preference to CELTIC at the Synod of Whitby, 664. Soon afterwards he became BISHOP of York and finally of Hexham. His day is 12 October.

St. Wilfrid's Needle. A narrow passage in the crypt of Ripon cathedral, built by Odo, Archbishop of Canterbury, and said to have been used to test a woman's chastity, as none but a virgin was able to squeeze through.

Wilgefortis. *See* UNCUMBER.

Wilhelmstrasse (vil' helm shtra sė). A street in Berlin where the principal government offices, including the Foreign Office, were situated. Hence used figuratively for the German Foreign Office and its policies. Most of the street was destroyed by Allied bombing in World War II.

Will-o'-the-wisp. *See* IGNIS FATUUS.

William. One of the most popular of Christian names; Fr. *Guillaume*, Ger. *Wilhelm*, it means a protector; literally, a resolute helmet (Ger. *Wille Helm*).

St. William of Maleval. A Frenchman of the 12th century who died in Tuscany in 1157. He went as a pilgrim to the HOLY LAND and on his return adopted the religious life. He was noted for his piety and asceticism and for his gifts of prayer and prophecy. His day is 10 February.

St. William of Montevergine. A 12th-century hermit of Piedmont who built himself a cell on Montevergine and subsequently founded several monasteries. He died in 1142 and his day is 25 June.

St. William of Norwich (1132–1144). A tanner's apprentice of Norwich, alleged to have been crucified and murdered by Jews during the PASSOVER. It was said at the time that it was part of Jewish ritual to sacrifice a Christian every year. (*See* Drayton's *Polyolbion*, song xxiv.)

St. William of York (d. 1154). William Fitzherbert, chaplain to King Stephen and Archbishop of York (1142). He was cano-

nized by Honorius III in 1227, largely on account of the miracles reported to have been performed at his tomb.

William of Cloudeslie. A noted outlaw and archer of the "north country". *See* CLYM OF THE CLOUGH.

William of Malmesbury (*c*. 1080–1143). A monk and librarian of Malmesbury Abbey and noted chronicler and historian. Among his numerous works his two most important are his *De Gestis Regum Anglorum* (Chronicle of the Kings of England, to 1125) and *De Gestis Pontificum Anglorum* (The History of the Prelates of England, to 1122).

William of Occam (*c*. 1300–*c*. 1349). The famous NOMINALIST philosopher, a native of Ockham, Surrey; also called *Doctor Invincibilis*. *See* OCCAM'S RAZOR

William of Wykeham. *See* WYKEHAMIST.

William Rufus (the Red). King William II of England (*c*. 1056, 1087–1100); so called from his ruddy complexion.

William the Conqueror. King William I of England (*c*. 1027, 1066–1087), who as Duke of Normandy invaded and conquered the English in 1066. Also called William the Bastard, from his parentage.

William the Lyon. King of SCOTLAND (1143, 1165–1214). The reason for this appellation is not known, but it is popularly supposed that he was the first Scottish king to adopt the LION as his achievement.

William the Silent. *See under* SILENCE.

William Tell. *See* TELL.

Sweet William. An old English garden flower, *Dianthus barbatus*, a member of the pink family.

> Some with sweet-williams red, some with bear's-foot and the like low flowers, being withal sweet and sightly.
>
> BACON: *Essays* (*Of Gardens*).

The William pear. Properly the *Williams's pear*, or *Bon Chrétien*, so called after the name of its introducer into England from France. For a like reason it is known in the U.S.A. as the *Bartlett pear*.

Willie-Wastle. This child's game is said to be named from William Wastle, governor of Hume Castle, Haddington. When Cromwell summoned him to surrender, he is said to have replied:

> Here I, Willie Wastle,
> Stand firm in my castle,
> And all the dogs in the town
> Shan't pull willie Wastle down.

Willis's Rooms. *See* ALMACK'S.

Willow. Willow Pattern. This celebrated design for porcelain in blue and white was introduced by Thomas Turner of Caughley in 1780. It imitated the Chinese style of decoration but was not an exact copy of any Chinese original. It takes its name from the willow tree being a main feature of the design.

To handle, or **wield the willow.** To play CRICKET, cricket-bats being made of willow; hence the game is sometimes called *King Willow* (see the Harrow School song of that name).

To wear the willow. To go into mourning, especially for a sweetheart or bride, to bewail a lost lover.

The willow, especially the weeping willow, has anciently been associated with sorrow and ever since the BABYLONIAN CAPTIVITY the latter is said to have drooped its branches. *Psalm* cxxxvii says:

> By the rivers of Babylon, there we sat down, yea, we wept, when we remembered Zion.
> We hanged our harps upon the willows in the midst thereof.

The refrain of the well-known song *There is a Tavern in a Town* has the phrase, "I'll hang my harp on the weeping willow tree."

In SHAKESPEARE's *Othello* (IV, iii), Desdemona says:

> My mother had a maid call'd Barbara;
> She was in love, and he she lov'd prov'd mad
> And did forsake her; she had a song of "willow";
> An old thing 'twas, but it expressed her fortune,
> And she died singing it.

And then comes the song:

> The poor soul sat sighing by a sycamore tree,
> Sing all a green willow;
> Her hand on her bosom, her head on her knee,
> Sing willow, willow, willow;
> The fresh streams ran by her, and murmur'd her moans;
> Sing willow, willow, willow;
> Her salt tears fell from her, and soften'd the stones;
> Sing willow, willow, willow.

This reminds us of W. S. Gilbert's song *The Suicide's Grave* in *The Mikado* (Willow, tit-willow, tit-willow).

Will's Coffee House. A famous resort in the time of Dryden, who added much to its popularity. It stood on the corner of Bow Street and Russell Street, COVENT GARDEN. Formerly called the *Red Cow*, then the *Rose*, it took its name from Will Urwin who was its proprietor at the time of the RESTORATION. Known as the "Wits Coffee House", it was the headquarters of TORY men of letters but from 1714 was rivalled by BUTTON'S COFFEE HOUSE, the home of the WHIG literati. Pepys in his *Diary* (3 February 1664) notes meeting "Dryden, the poet I knew at Cambridge, and all the wits of the town". Confusion sometimes arises from the coexistence of five or more coffee houses of this name but this is undoubtedly the Will's associated with the *Spectator*. It closed some time before the middle years of the 18th century.

Willy-nilly. *Nolens volens*; willing or not. Will-he, nill-he, *nill* being *n'* (negative) *will*, just as Lat. *nolens* is *n'-volens*.

Willy-willy. The Australian aboriginal term for the sudden whirlwinds which are common on the north-west coast. They can be seen approaching in a high circular column of leaves and dust from a great distance.

Wimbledon. A name synonymous with lawn tennis and tennis championships; a London suburb, and home of the All England Croquet Club. In the middle of the 1870s the Club, being in low water, added "Lawn Tennis" to its title, this being then a new game increasing in popularity. On the Club's courts, the first lawn tennis Championship in the world was held in 1877. The annual tournament run by the All England Club at Wimbledon ranks as the premier championship.

Win, To. Colloquially, to acquire, often by dubious means, to filch surreptitiously; a somewhat more questionable form of "scrounging", which does not always bear inspection.

Winchester. Identified by Malory and other old writers with the CAMELOT of ARTHURIAN ROMANCE. It was King Alfred's capital. *See also* SWITHIN; WYKEHAMIST.

Wind. According to classical mythology, the north, south, east, and west winds (BOREAS, *Notus*, EURUS, and ZEPHYRUS) were under the rule of ÆOLUS, who kept them confined in a cave on Mount Hæmus, Thrace. Other strong winds of a more destructive nature were the brood of TYPHŒUS.

The story says that Æolus gave ULYSSES a bag tied with a silver string, in which were all the hurtful and unfavourable winds, so that he might arrive home without being delayed by tempests. His crew, however, opened the bag in the belief that it contained treasure, the winds escaped, and a terrible storm at once arose, driving the vessel out of its course and back to the island of Æolus.

Aquilo is another Latin name for the north wind, as AUSTER is of the south and FAVONIUS of the west. *Thrascias* is a north-north-west wind and *Libs* a west-south-west wind, CAURUS or *Corus* a north-west wind (also personified as *Argestes*), *Volturnus* a south-east wind and *Africus* and *Afer ventus* a south-west wind.

> Boreas and Cæcias, and Argestes loud,
> And Thrascias rend the woods, and seas upturn...
> Notus and Afer, black with thunderous clouds,
> From Serraliona; thwart of these, as fierce,
> Forth rush...Eurus and Zephyr...
> Sirocco and Libecchio.
> MILTON: *Paradise Lost*, X, 699–706.

See also ETESIAN WIND; SOLANO; TRADE WINDS; WILLY-WILLY.

A rasher of wind. A phrase widely current in late-Victorian times and subsequently, used to describe a very slight or thin person or something of very little account.

Soldier's wind. A nautical term for a fair wind for going and returning, *i.e.* a side wind.

A wind egg. An egg without a shell, or with a soft shell, or an unfertilized one; from the old superstition that the hen that lays it was impregnated, like the "Thracian mares", by the wind.

Wind of change. A new current of opinion, a markedly reformist or novel trend, etc. A phrase popularized by Harold Macmillan in his speech to the South African Parliament (3 February 1960), with reference to the social and political ferment in the African continent.

> The wind of change is blowing through this continent, and, whether we like it or not, this growth of national consciousness is a political fact.

In the wind's eye. *See under* EYE.

There's something in the wind. There are signs that something is about to happen; something is being prepared or concocted without one's knowledge.

Three sheets in the wind. *See* SHEET.

'Tis an ill wind that blows nobody any good. Someone profits by every loss; someone usually benefits by every misfortune.

To get one's second wind. To recover and go about one's pursuits with renewed vigour; as a runner, after initial breathlessness, warms up and regains more regular respiration known as his second wind.

To get the wind up. To become thoroughly alarmed, nervous, over-anxious, and frightened.

To get wind of something. To get advance knowledge of something which has not yet happened. From an animal's ability to detect the approach of others by their scent on the wind.

To have the wind. *See* TO TAKE, etc., *below*.

To know which way the wind blows. To be aware of the true state of affairs.

To raise the wind. To obtain necessary money or funds.

To sail against, or **before the wind, To sail close to the wind,** etc. *See under* SAIL.

To take, or **have the wind.** To get or keep the upper hand. *To have the wind* also means to have flatulence.

To take the wind out of one's sails. To forestall him, "to steal his thunder" (*see under*

der THUNDER), frustrate him by utilizing his own material or methods. Literally, it is to sail to windward of a ship and so rob its sails of the wind.

To temper the wind to the shorn lamb. To exercise forbearance and moderation towards someone who is vulnerable and likely to be hurt. Shorn lambs are obviously more susceptible to rough weather than well-coated sheep. It is ultimately from the French proverb "*A brebis tondue Dieu mesure le vent*."

To whistle down the wind. *See under* WHISTLE.

Windbag. A long-winded, bombastic speaker, who uses inflated phrases and promises far more than he can perform.

Windfall. An unexpected piece of good luck, especially an unexpected legacy; something worth having that comes to one without any personal exertion—like fruit which has fallen from the tree and so does not have to be picked.

Windjammer. A sailing ship, or one of its crew. The term is a modern one, born since steam superseded sail.

Windy City. Chicago.

Windmill. To have windmills in your head. To be full of fancies; TO HAVE A BEE IN YOUR BONNET (*see under* BEE). SANCHO PANZA says:

> Did I not tell you they were windmills, and that nobody could think otherwise, unless he had also windmills in his head?
> CERVANTES: *Don Quixote*, Pt. I, ch. viii.

To tilt at windmills. To face imaginary adversaries, combat CHIMÆRAS. The allusion is to *Don* QUIXOTE (Pt. I, ch. viii) when the crazy knight imagines them to be GIANTS and gives battle.

Window. Window Dressing. Properly the display of goods in a shop window for the purpose of attracting customers. Figuratively, a specious display to present oneself or one's case, etc., in a favourable light.

Window Tax. A tax first imposed in 1691 and abolished in 1851, which accounts for the blocked-up window spaces in many old houses. It took the place of the Hearth Tax and was greatly increased in 1782 and 1797, and reduced in 1823. Houses with less than seven windows were exempt in 1782 and with less than eight in 1825.

All his goods in the window is much the same as WINDOW DRESSING, implying that a man is displaying all his superficial merits, etc., to view with nothing substantial to back them up.

Windsor. The House of Windsor. The style of the British Royal House adopted in 1917 in deference to anti-German sentiment to replace the then existing style of Saxe-Coburg-Gotha derived from Albert the PRINCE CONSORT. It was changed in 1960 to Mountbatten-Windsor for the descendants of Queen Elizabeth II, other than those entitled to the style of Royal Highness or of Prince and Princess.

After his abdication, 11 December 1936, King Edward VIII was created Duke of Windsor.

The Knights of Windsor. *See under* KNIGHT.

Windsor Herald. One of six heralds of the College of Arms, and others being Chester, Lancaster, Richmond, Somerset and York. *See* HERALDRY.

The Widow at Windsor. *See under* WIDOW.

Wine. A wine. At the old universities a once-common name for a wine-party.

Wine of Ape. In Chaucer's Prologue to the *Manciple's Tale*, the Manciple says, "I trow that ye have drunken wine of ape"—*i.e.* wine to make you foolishly drunk; in French *vin de singe*. According to Rabbinical tradition SATAN came to Noah when he was planting vines, and slew a *lamb*, a *lion*, a *pig*, and an *ape*, to teach Noah that man, in turn, reveals the characteristics of all four according to the amount of liquor consumed.

To put new wine in old bottles. To impose new practices, principles, etc., on people or things too old or unfit to stand the strain. A reference to the unwisdom of putting new fermentations in old wine-skins which are bound to crack under the pressure.

> Neither do men put new wine into old bottles; else the bottles break, and the wine runneth out, and the bottles perish: but they put new wine into new bottles, and both are preserved.
> *Matt.* ix, 17.

Wing. In the R.A.F., a group of three squadrons.

The wings of Azrael. *See under* AZRAEL.

Don't try to fly without wings. Attempt nothing you are not fit for or until you are properly equipped to do so. A Latin saying; Plautus has (*Pœnulus*, IV, ii, 47): *Sine pennis volare haud facile est*, It is by no means easy to fly without wings.

On the wing. Flying, in motion, or about to depart or take flight.

To clip one's wings. To take down one's conceit; to hamper one's freedom of action.

To lend wings. To spur one's speed.

To take one under your wing. To assume patronage of, to protect. The allusion is to a hen gathering her chicks under her wing.

To take wing. To fly away; to depart without warning.

> Oh, God! it is a fearful thing
> To see the human soul take wing.
> BYRON: *The Prisoner of Chillon*, 176.

Winifred, or Winefride, St. Patron SAINT of North Wales and virgin martyr. According to the story she was the daughter of a Welsh chieftain and was instructed by St. Beuno. Prince Caradoc made violent advances to her and she fled to the church for safety. Caradoc pursued her and struck off her head, but it was replaced on her body by St. Beuno who breathed life into her again. She died a second time about 660. The miraculous healing spring of Holywell (Flintshire) gushed forth where her head had come to rest, and it became a regular resort of pilgrims. *Cp*. PAUL, St.

Wink. Forty winks. A short nap, a doze.

Like winking. Very quickly, in a flash.

A nod is as good as a wink to a blind horse. *See* NOD.

To tip one the wink. To give him a hint privately; to give a signal or secret hint.

To wink at. To connive at, or to affect not to notice.

> He knows not how to wink at human frailty
> Or pardon weakness that he never felt.
> ADDISON: *Cato*, 102.

Winkle, Rip Van. *See* RIP VAN WINKLE.

Winkle-pickers. Shoes with very elongated and pointed toes, affected by some in the early 1960s. The allusion is to the use of a pin for picking winkles out of their shells.

Winter. The coldest part of the year. In the Northern Hemisphere DECEMBER, JANUARY, FEBRUARY; astronomically from 21/22 December to 21/22 March.

> From winter, plague and pestilence, good lord, deliver us!
> THOMAS NASHE: *Summer's Last Will and Testament*.

Winter's King and Queen. Frederick V, Elector Palatine, and his wife Elizabeth, who reigned in Bohemia from November 1619 to November 1620. Elizabeth was the daughter of James I of England and her beauty inspired Sir Henry Wotton's lyric, *Elizabeth of Bohemia*.

Wipe. Old slang for a pocket-handkerchief.

To wipe one's nose. To affront him; to give him a blow on the nose. Similarly, **to wipe a person's eye,** to steal a march on him; **to fetch one a wipe over the knuckles,** to give him a good rap.

To wipe the floor with someone. To defeat him completely and ignominiously, literally or figuratively; to demolish utterly all his arguments, to floor him absolutely.

Wiped out. Destroyed, annihilated; quite obliterated.

Wire. Used as a verb, meaning to telegraph. "Wire me without delay", telegraph to me at once.

A live wire. A wire charged with electricity; hence, a very lively person abounding with energy.

To pull the wires, wire-pulling. The same as TO PULL THE STRINGS (*see under* PULL).

Wireless. Applied to radio transmission or broadcasting, since the signals are not transmitted along wires.

Wisdom. The Wisdom of Solomon. A book of the Old Testament APOCRYPHA, probably written by an Alexandrian Jew between 100 B.C. and A.D. 50. It seems to be a reply to the Stoicism and Epicureanism reflected in the Book of *Ecclesiastes*, and is designed to reawaken loyalty and zeal for the old Jewish faith among apostates and waverers.

The wisdom of many and the wit of one. Lord John Russell (1792–1878) thus defined a proverb.

Wisdom tooth. The popular name for the third molar in each jaw. Wisdom teeth usually appear between the ages of 17 and 25, hence the name from association with years of discretion.

To cut your wisdom teeth. To reach the years of discretion.

Wise, The. The following have been thus surnamed:

Albert II, Duke of Austria, called *The Lame and Wise* (1293, 1330–1358).

Alfonso X of Leon, and IV of Castile, called *The Wise* and *The Astronomer* (1202, 1252–1284).

Charles V of France, called *Le Sage* (1337, 1364–1380).

Frederick II, Elector of Palatine (1482, 1544–1556).

Frederick III, Elector of Saxony (1463, 1486–1525).

Wise Men of the East. *See* MAGI.

Wise Men of Gotham. *See* GOTHAM.

The Wise Men of Greece. Also known as *The Seven Sages*, all of whom flourished in the 6th century B.C..

Bias of Priene, one of whose sayings was: "Most men are bad."

Chilo of Sparta. "Consider the end." *See* DE MORTUIS.

Cleobulus of Lindos. "The golden mean" or "Avoid extremes."

Periander of Corinth. "Nothing is impossible to industry."

Pittacus of Mitylene. "Seize time by the forelock."

Solon of Athens (*c.* 640–*c.* 558 B.C.). "Know thyself."

Thales of Miletus. "Who hateth suretyship is sure."

The Wisest Man of Greece. So the Delphic ORACLE pronounced SOCRATES to be, and Socrates modestly made answer: "'Tis because I alone of all the Greeks know that I know nothing."

The Wisest fool in Christendom. James I of ENGLAND (1566, 1603–1625); so called by Henry IV of France.

Wiseacre (Ger. *Weissager*, a soothsayer or prophet). This word, like SOPHIST, has quite lost its original meaning and is applied to dunces, wise only in their own conceit.

There is a story told that Ben Jonson, at the *Devil*, in FLEET STREET, said to a country gentleman who boasted of his estates, "What care we for your dirt and clods? Where you have an acre of land, I have ten acres of wit." The landed gentleman retorted by calling Ben "Good Mr. Wiseacre." The story may pass for what it is worth.

Wisecrack. A colloquialism for a facetious or witty remark.

Wish. Wish Hounds, or **Yell Hounds.** Spectral hounds that hunt the wildest parts of Dartmoor on moonless nights, urged on by the "Midnight Hunter of the Moor" on his huge horse which breathes fire and flame. The baying of these hounds, held by some to be headless, if heard, spells death to the hearer within the year. The Abbot's Way, an ancient track across the southern part of the moor, is said to be their favourite path. *See* WILD HUNTSMAN.

The wish is father to the thought. We are always ready to believe what we most want to believe. When the Prince says to his dying father, "I never thought to hear you speak again," Henry IV replies:

Thy wish was father, Harry, to that thought.
I stay too long for thee, I weary thee.
SHAKESPEARE: *Henry IV, Pt. II*, IV, iv.

To wish one farther. To prefer his room to his company; to wish him gone.

Wishful thinking. A popular psychoanalytical term describing the unconscious expression of one's desire in accordance with one's wishes; the thinking of a thing to be true because one wants it to be so.

Wishing bone. *See* MERRYTHOUGHT.

Wishing Cap. *See* FORTUNATUS.

Wit. Understanding, from O.E. *witan*, to know.

The five wits. *See under* FIVE.

At one's wits' end. Quite at a loss as to what to say or what to do next; "flummoxed".

To live on one's wits. To live by temporary shifts and expedients rather than by honest work.

To have one's wits about one. To be wide awake; observant of all that is going on and prepared to take advantage of any opportunity that offers.

To wit. Namely; that is to say.

Witch. Waking a witch. See WAKING.

Witchcraft. (O.E. *wiccian*, to practise sorcery). Belief in witchcraft, prevalent into the 18th century and later, was a legacy from pagan times and is found in the BIBLE (*see* WITCH OF ENDOR). DIVINATION of all kinds was a fundamental aspect of witchcraft. Even St. AUGUSTINE believed in it; in 1258, Pope Alexander IV instructed the INQUISITION to deal with witchcraft when allied to heresy and Innocent VIII's celebrated bull (*Summis Desiderantes*, 1484) encouraged the Inquisition to severe measures against witches. Countless people suffered death from this superstition, especially old women. Witchcraft was made a felony in ENGLAND in 1542, causing death by witchcraft became a capital offence in 1563, and in the same year witchcraft became subject to the death penalty in SCOTLAND.

Witch-hunting was a particular pastime of 17th-century PRESBYTERIANS until after the RESTORATION. The notorious "witch-finder" Matthew Hopkins travelled through the eastern counties in the 1640s to hunt out witches and is said to have hanged 60 in one year in Essex alone. In 1647 he was tested by his own methods; when cast into the river, he floated, and so was hanged as a WIZARD. *Cp.* MCCARTHYISM.

The last trial for witchcraft in ENGLAND occurred in 1712, and in SCOTLAND in 1722. English and Scottish laws against witchcraft were repealed in 1736.

Witch balls. The popular name for the lustred glass globes in use since the 16th century as domestic ornaments. They mirror in miniature the contents of a room, and the name is probably a fanciful corruption of *watch* ball. The inside of the ball was usually coated with a preparation largely made up of mercury.

The Witch of Endor. The woman who had "a familiar spirit" through whom Saul sought communication with the dead Samuel. She brought Samuel up "out of the earth" (a classic case of NECROMANCY) having first secured a promise from Saul that he would take no action against her as a witch (*see* I *Sam.* xxviii).

The Witch of Wookey. See WOOKEY HOLE.

Witches' Sabbath. A midnight meeting of witches, demons, etc., supposed to have been held annually. Mediæval devotees of the witchcraft cult held sabbaths at CANDLEMAS, Roodmas, LAMMAS, and ALL HALLOWS' EVE, and their celebrations lasted until dawn. The rites were lead by the "Coven", a group of 12 members and one DEVIL.

Witch-hunting. In political usage it denotes the searching out and exposure of opponents alleged to be disloyal to the State, often amounting to persecution. *See* MCCARTHYISM.

Witchen. See ROWAN.

Witenagemot (wit' ė na gė mōt). The Anglo-Saxon national assembly of higher clerics and laymen (ealdormen, thegns, etc.) which gave advice and consent on legislation, taxation, important judicial matters, etc., and which formally elected a new king. *Witan* is O.E. for *wise men* (connected with *wit*, knowledge); *gemote* is *ge-*, together; *moot*, meet hence "an assembly of wise men".

Withershins or **Widdershins** (O.E. *wither*, against; *sith*, journey). An old English word, still in use in SCOTLAND and in north-country dialects, denoting a movement in a contrary direction to that of the SUN—as of a clock whose hands are going backwards. Witches and warlocks were supposed to approach the DEVIL *withershins*.

The opposite of withershins is *deasil* meaning righthandwise or sunwise (Gael. *deiseil*).

Wivern (wī' vern). A fabulous creature of HERALDRY consisting of a winged DRAGON ending in a barbed, serpent's tail.

Wizard. A magician, one adept in the black arts; the male counterpart of a WITCH. It is derived from *wise*.

Wizard is popularly used to express admiration, etc., as, *a wizard performance*, a wonderful performance; *absolutely wizard*, absolutely splendid.

The Wizard of the North. A nickname given to Sir Walter Scott. *See* WAVERLEY.

The Wizard of Oz. The central figure in the very popular children's book, *The Wonderful Wizard of Oz* (1900), by Lyman Frank Baum (1856–1919), a well-known American journalist. The musical comedy of the same name (1901) was a great success, which was carried on to the film of some years later.

Wobblies, The. The Industrial Workers of the World or I.W.W. were so nicknamed. This American revolutionary labour organization was formed in 1905 and reached its peak before World War I, but largely petered out after the war. They drew their main support from migratory farmers, textile workers, and dockers. Noted for their songs, the best-known are "Pie in the Sky" and "Hallelujah, I'm a Bum." They were also known as "The Bummery".

Wobbly is apparently derived from *Wow* (*workers of the world*).

Woden. *See* ODIN; WEDNESDAY.

Woden's dyke. *See* WANSDYKE.

Woe. Woe worth the day! Cursed be the day! EVIL betide it. *Worth* here is O.E. *weorthan*, to become.

> Thus saith the Lord God: Howl ye, Woe worth the day!
>
> *Ezek.* xxx, 2.

Woebegone. Overwhelmed by woe, especially applied to the appearance—*a woebegone countenance.* It does not mean "woe, go away, be gone"; *begone* here is from the O.E. verb *began*, to beset, surround. It thus means "beset with woe."

Wog. A colloquial name applied to blacks, Arabs, Egyptians, etc. Possibly a contraction of *golliwog.* In naval parlance held to stand for *wily oriental gentleman.* Another assertion is that is was formerly applied by the British army to its Egyptian labourers and is an abbreviation of "workers on government service".

Wolf. WILLIAM OF MALMESBURY (*Chronicles of the Kings of England*, Bk. ii, ch. viii) says that the tribute of 300 wolves payable yearly by the king of WALES to Edgar the Peaceful (959—975) ceased after the third year because "he could find no more"; but they are recorded in ENGLAND as late as the 15th century and in IRELAND and SCOTLAND they seem to have lingered on until the 18th century.

Dryden gave the name to the Presbytery in *The Hind and the Panther* (I. 152).

> Unkennelled range in the Polonian plains
> A fiercer foe the insatiate Wolf remains.

In music, a discordant sound (due to the system of tuning or temperament), in certain keyboard instruments, was called a *wolf*; also the jarring note sometimes heard from bowed instruments. Said by Ferne (*Blazon of Gentrie*, 1586), in the case of a harp, to be caused by the use of a string made from the entrails of a wolf. The squeak made in reed instruments by unskilled players is termed a "goose".

The She-wolf of France. Isabella of France (1292–1358), daughter of Philip the Fair and adulterous wife of Edward II. She executed the Despensers and procured her husband's death (1327) at Berkeley Castle. His murderers are said to have thrust a hot iron into his bowels.

> She-wolf of France, with unrelenting fangs
> That tear'st the bowels of thy mangled Mate.
>
> GRAY: *The Bard*, II, i.

Wolf Cub. The long-established and original name for a member of the Junior branch of the SCOUT Movement, now called Cub Scouts (age range 8–11 years). The conception owes much to Kipling's *Jungle Books*.

Wolf month, or **Wolf-monath.** *See* JANUARY.

A wolf pack. A term applied in World War II to German submarines in a group.

Wolf whistle. An oafish call made by a male at the sight of a female. It implies admiration.

Between dog and wolf. Neither daylight nor dark, the BLIND MAN'S HOLIDAY. Generally applied to the evening dusk. In Latin, *Inter canem et lupum*; in French, *Entre chien et loup*.

Dark as a wolf's mouth. Pitch dark.

He has seen a wolf. Something or other has frightened him, formerly said of a person who had lost his voice. Our forefathers believed that if a man saw a wolf before the wolf saw him, he became dumb, at least for a time.

To see a wolf was also a good sign, inasmuch as the wolf was dedicated to ODIN, the giver of victory. *Cp.* FENRIR.

He put his head into the wolf's mouth. He exposed himself to needless danger. The allusion is to ÆSOP's fable of the crane that put its head into a wolf's (or fox's) mouth in order to extract a bone.

Holding a wolf by the ears. An old Greek saying; AUGUSTUS used it of his situation at ROME, meaning it was equally dangerous to keep hold or to let go.

> He that goes to law (as the proverb is) holds a wolf by the ears.
>
> BURTON: *Anatomy of Melancholy* (*Democritus to the Reader*).

To cry "Wolf!" To give a false alarm. The allusion is to the fable of the shepherd lad who so often called "Wolf!" merely to make fun of the neighbours, that when at last the wolf came no one would believe him. This fable appears in almost every nation the world over.

To keep the wolf from the door. To ward off starvation. We say of a ravenous person, "He has a wolf in his stomach", and one who eats voraciously is said *to wolf* his food. French *manger comme un loup* is to eat voraciously.

To throw to the wolves. To sacrifice someone (a companion, colleague, sub-ordinate), usually to divert criticism or opposition from the "thrower"; to make someone the SCAPEGOAT. As a traveller in a sleigh, pursued by a pack of wolves, might throw food or other objects in the hope of gaining his escape.

Wake not a sleeping wolf! (SHAKESPEARE: *Henry IV, Pt. II*, I, ii). A variant of "Let sleeping dogs lie!"—Let well alone.

A wolf in sheep's clothing. An enemy posing a a friend. The phrase is taken from the well-known fable of ÆSOP.

Wolfe's Own. *See* REGIMENTAL AND DIVISIONAL NICKNAMES.

Women. Hell hath no fury like a woman scorned. A popular saying derived from Congreve's *The Mourning Bride* (1697), III, viii.

> Heav'n has no rage, like love to hatred turn'd,
> Nor Hell a fury, like a woman scorn'd.

Colley Cibber's *Love's Last Shaft* (1696) has, "we shall find no fiend in hell can match the fury of a disappointed women,—scorned, slighted, dismissed without a parting pang."

Womble cropped. An expression current in America about 1800, denoting a feeling of uneasiness about anything. It is found as *wamblecropt* in Richard Huluoet's *Abecedarium* (1552).

Wonder. The Seven Wonders of the World. In the ancient world:
The PYRAMIDS of Egypt.
The HANGING GARDENS OF BABYLON.
The Tomb of Mausolus (MAUSOLEUM).
The Temple of DIANA at Ephesus.
The COLOSSUS of Rhodes.
The Statue of JUPITER by Phidias.
The PHAROS of Alexandria.
A later list gives:
The Coliseum of Rome (*see* COLOSSEUM).
The Catacombs of Alexandria.
The Great Wall of China.
STONEHENGE.
The LEANING TOWER of Pisa.
The Porcelain Tower of Nanking.
The Mosque of San Sophia at Constantinople (Istanbul).

The Wonder of the World. The title given to Otto III, Holy Roman EMPEROR (980, 983–1002), on account of his brilliant intellectual endowment. The title was also applied to Frederick II (*see* STUPOR MUNDI).

The Wonderful Doctor. Roger Bacon, also called the ADMIRABLE DOCTOR.

The Wonderful, or **Wondermaking Parliament.** Also called the MERCILESS PARLIAMENT (1388), when Richard II's favourites were condemned for treason.

Wonder-worker. *See* THAUMATURGUS.

Wonky. This slang word, meaning unsteady, unsound, unstable, comes from O.E. *wancol* of the same meaning.

Wood. Don't cry, or **halloo till you are out of the wood.** Do not rejoice for having escaped danger till the danger has passed away. "Don't count your CHICKENS before they are hatched"; "there's many a slip 'twixt the CUP and the lip."

Drawn from the wood. Said of beer and wines served directly from the cask. Beer barrels have now largely been supplanted by metal containers and their contents dispensed through pressurized beer-engines, a matter of regret to connoisoeurs of good ALE.

One can't see the wood for the trees. It is difficult to pick out the essentials from the surrounding mass of detail; the main issues are not readily apparent.

To touch wood. An old superstition to avert bad luck or misfortune or to make sure of something good; also when feeling pleased with one's achievement or when bragging. Traditionally, certain trees such as the OAK, ash, hazel, HAWTHORN and willow had a sacred significance, and thus protective powers. Properly these should be the ones touched but this detail has largely passed into oblivion and any wood is put to use. Often, jocularly, the forehead is touched.

Wooden. Used of one who is awkward or ungainly; or of a spiritless, emotionless person.

The Wooden Horse. *See under* HORSE.

The Wooden Horse of Troy. *See under* HORSE.

The Wooden Mare. An instrument used for military punishments, also called the WOODEN HORSE (*see under* HORSE).

Wooden Nickels. Like WOODEN NUTMEGS, these were said to have been made in the U.S.A. by those unwilling to earn an honest living. As the nickel piece of 1857 was only worth a cent it was an unrewarding enterprise, but it gave rise to the phrase **Don't take any wooden nickels** as a friendly warning to the unsuspecting or easily duped.

Wooden nutmegs. In the early 19th century Connecticut, the Nutmeg State, was referred to derisively as the land of wooden nutmegs because certain dishonest merchants were said to have exported nutmegs made of wood.

The wooden spoon. A booby prize gained by the student last in the mathematical TRIPOS list at Cambridge. *Cp.* WOODEN WEDGE *below*.

Wooden Walls. The wooden warships of the Royal Navy were so called before the days of ironclads, and it is said that some 3,500 oak-trees were used in the construction of the big THREE-DECKERS. The *Victory* now at Portsmouth is perhaps the most famous of these vessels. The screw wood ship H.M.S. *Duncan* was launched in 1869 and the well-known training ship *Mercury*, associated with C. B. Fry, was built as late as 1878.

When the Greeks consulted the Delphic ORACLE to ask how they were to defend themselves against XERXES, who had invaded their country, the evasive answer was to this effect:

> Pallas hath urged, and Zeus, the sire of all,
> Hath safety promised in a wooden wall;
> Seed-time and harvest, weeping sires shall tell
> How thousands fought at Salamis and fell.

Themistocles interpreted "wooden wall" to mean the Greek ships in the Bay of Salamis and so won a decisive victory over the Persians.

The wooden wedge. Last in the classical TRIPOS. When, in 1824, the classical Tripos was instituted at Cambridge, it was debated by what name to call the last on the list. It so happened that the last on the list was *Wedgwood*, and the name was adopted in this slightly modified form. *Cp.* THE WOODEN SPOON, *above*.

Woodbine. A common name for the wild honeysuckle, *Lonicera periclymenum*; also applied to other plants that bind or wind themselves around trees.

The Packet of Woodbines. The nickname given to the Russian cruiser *Askold* from its five long thin funnels — Woodbine cigarettes being thin and sold in packets of five. She was taken from the Bolsheviks after the October Revolution of 1917 and used by the R.N. against the revolutionaries in the White Sea.

Woodbine Willie. The Rev. G. A. Studdert-Kennedy (1883–1929) was so called from the well-liked brand of small cigarettes named Woodbines, which he gave to the men in the trenches in the Great War of 1914–18 when serving as Chaplain to the Forces (1916–19). He was perhaps the most well-liked and well-known PADRE of the war.

Woodcock. Old slang for a simpleton; from the ease with which he is ensnared. POLONIUS tells his daughter that protestations of love are "springes to catch woodcocks" (SHAKESPEARE: *Hamlet*, I, iii).

Wood's Halfpence. The copper coinage which William Wood began to introduce into IRELAND (1723) under a patent purchased from the Duchess of Kendal, George I's mistress, to whom it had been granted. The outcry against Wood's Half-

pence, supported by Swift in his DRAPIER'S LETTERS, led to the withdrawal of the patent in 1725. The Irish PARLIAMENT and government were not informed of the scheme in advance and it was feared that the flood of COPPER coins would drive out the existing small stocks of GOLD and SILVER.

Woodser. *See* JIMMY WOODSER.

Wookey Hole. A famous cavern near Wells in Somerset, which has given rise to numerous legends. *Wicked as the Witch of Wookey* is an old local simile. Her repulsiveness led to her directing her spells against "the youth of either sex" as well as blasting every plant and blistering every flock. She was turned into a stone by a "lerned wight" from "Glaston" but left her curse behind, since the girls of Wookey found "that men are wondrous scant".

> Here's beauty, wit and sense combin'd,
> With all that's good and virtuous join'd
> Yet hardly one gallant.
> PERCY: *Reliques* (*The Witch of Wookey*).

Wool. All wool and a yard wide. Genuine, of real quality; no sham or substitute.

Dyed in the wool. Cloth which is wool-dyed, not piece-dyed, and true throughout. Hence the phrase is used to mean through and through, genuine, out and out, as "dyed-in-the-wool teetotaller", a completely convinced and genuine teetotaller. *Cp.* A KNAVE IN THE GRAIN *under* GRAIN.

Great cry and little wool. *See under* CRY.

No wool is so white that a dyer cannot blacken it. No one is so free from faults that slander can find nothing to say against him; no book is so perfect as to be free from adverse criticism.

To be wool-gathering. To let one's mind wander from the matter in hand; to be absent-minded. As children sent to gather wool from hedges wander hither and thither, apparently aimlessly.

To go for wool and come home shorn. To have the tables turned on one.

To pull the wool over one's eyes. To delude or deceive; from the idea of obscuring one's vision.

Burial in Woollen. Under Acts of 1666 and 1678 corpses were not to be buried "in any shirt, shift, sheet, or shroud" other than of wool nor was the coffin to be lined with any other material. It was intended for the encouragement of English woollen manufacturers and was eventually repealed in 1814, after it had largely fallen into abeyance; it had long been ignored by those able and willing to pay the fines for its non-observance:

"Odious! in woollen! 'twould a saint provoke!"
(Were the last words that poor Narcissa spoke).
"No! let a charming chintz and Brussels lace
Wrap my cold limbs, and shade my lifeless face.
One would not, sure, be frightful when one's dead;
And—Betty—give this cheek a little red."

POPE: *Moral Essays*, Ep. I, iii (1733).

The Woolsack. The official seat of the Lord CHANCELLOR as SPEAKER of the HOUSE OF LORDS. It is a large red square bag of wool, rather like an enlarged hassock. There were originally four, probably introduced in the reign of Edward III as symbols of England's staple trade, on which sat the Judges, the Barons of the EXCHEQUER, the SERJEANTS-AT-LAW, and the Masters in CHANCERY. The woolsacks were technically outside the precincts of the House, as these officials had no voice in the proceedings; thus when the Lord Chancellor wishes to speak as a peer he goes to his place in the House.

The term *woolsack* is often applied to the office of Lord Chancellor.

Woomera. The name of the rocket testing range in South Australia, appropriately an aborigine word for a spear-throwing stick.

Woopies. An acronym current in the late 1980s signifying "well off old people" but applicable to less than 20 percent of old age or retirement pensioners.

Wop. In the original American slang usage it meant an uncouth or aggressive person and was later used as a derogatory term for Italians and those of similar complexion.

Word. The Word. The SCRIPTURES; Christ as the Logos.

In the beginning was the Word, and the Word was with God, and the Word was God.

John i, 1.

By word of mouth. Orally. As, "the message was passed by word of mouth", *i.e.* spoken, not written.

I take you at your word. I accept what you say and rely on what you tell me.

Make no words about it. Don't mention it; make no fuss about it.

A man of his word. One whose word may be depended on; trustworthy; "he is as good as his word" and "his word is as good as his bond".

Many words will not fill a bushel. Mere promises will not help the needy. If we say to a beggar, "Be thou filled," is he filled?

The object of words is to conceal thoughts. See SPEECH WAS GIVEN TO MAN TO DISGUISE HIS THOUGHTS.

Put in a good word for me, please! Do your best to get me some privilege or favour; put my claims, my deeds, etc., in the best light possible.

Soft words butter no parsnips. See BUTTER.

To eat one's words. See *under* EAT.

To give, or **pass one's word.** To give a definite undertaking, make a binding promise.

To have words with one. To quarrel; to have an angry discussion. **To have a word with one** is to have a brief conversation with him.

To take the words out of one's mouth. When someone else says what one is about to say oneself.

Upon my word. Assuredly; by my troth. As an exclamation it implies outraged surprise or irritation.

Upon my word and, or **of honour.** A strong affirmation of the speaker as to the truth of what he asserts.

Weasel words. See *under* WEASEL.

A word to the wise! Said when giving advice as a hint that it would be well for the recipient to follow it. See VERB. SAP.

The words stuck in his throat. He was unable to utter them owing to nervousness or great reluctance.

Work. Seven Works of Mercy. See MERCY.

To give someone the works. To subject a person to rigorous or extreme treatment, either verbally or physically, even to the point of murder. A slang phrase of American origin.

To have one's work cut out. To have difficulty in completing or carrying out a task owing to circumstances.

To shoot the works. To stake one's all in a game of chance; to make an all-out effort. A slang phrase from the U.S.A.

To work double tides. See *under* DOUBLE.

Working to rule. In trade-union parlance, to fulfil all the regulations relating to one's work literally and pedantically, in order to bring about delays in working, and frustration generally; another form of GO-SLOW tactics.

World. All the world and his wife. Everyone without exception.

A man, or **woman of the world.** One who is acquainted with the "ways of the world", a socially experienced, practical person. **A worldly man,** or **woman,** denotes one who only cares for the material things of this world.

In SHAKESPEARE's time *a woman of the world* signified a married woman.

Touchstone: To-morrow will we be married.
Audrey: I do desire it with all my heart; and I hope it is no dishonest desire to be a woman of the world.

As You Like It, V, iii.

Out of this world. Something quite exceptional, quite out of the ordinary, indescribably luxurious, beautiful, etc. A 20th-century vogue phrase.

To be on top of the world. *See under* TOP.

To go to the world. To be married. *See* A MAN OF THE WORLD, *above*.

The world, the flesh, and the devil. "The world" is the material things of this world as opposed to the things of the spirit; "the flesh", sensual pleasures; the DEVIL", EVIL of every kind.

> From all the deceits of the world, the flesh, and the devil, Good Lord, deliver us.
> *The Litany (Book of Common Prayer).*

The Third World. An expression coined in France (*le Tiers-Monde*) and applied to those less developed countries of Africa, Asia and Latin America which are not substantially aligned with the capitalist or communist "worlds" or political groupings.

> ...the new countries which he [Mr Lee Kuan Yew, Prime Minister of Singapore] described as "the poor, strife-ridden, chaotic third world in Africa, south and south-east Asia and Latin America".
> *The Times*, 21 July 1969.

The Workshop of the World. England in its 19th century heyday as the leading industrial nation. In the days of CHARTISM F.D.Maurice and Charles Kingsley produced a poster in 1848 addressing the workers "...Englishmen! Saxons! Workers of the great cool-headed, strongheaded nation of England, the workshop of the world..."

The World Turned Upside Down. An inn sign illustrating an unnatural state of affairs, and also an allusion to the antipodes. It often took the form of a man walking at the South Pole.

It was also the name of the tune played by the military band when Cornwallis surrendered to the Americans at Yorktown in 1781.

World Wars. The name given to the wars of 1914–1918 (The Great War or World War I) and of 1939–1945 (World War II) in which participation was world-wide.

Worm. The word was formerly used of DRAGONS and great SERPENTS especially those of Teutonic and old Norse legend; it is now figuratively applied to miserable, grovelling creatures; also to the ligament under a dog's tongue.

Even a worm will turn. The most abject of creatures will turn upon its tormentors if driven to extremity.

Idle worms. It was once supposed that little worms were bred in the fingers of idle servants. To this SHAKESPEARE alludes:

> A round little worm

> Pricked from the lazy finger of a maid.
> *Romeo and Juliet*, I, iv.

To be food for worms. To be dead.

> Your worm is your only emperor for diet: we fat all creatures else, to fat us; and we fat ourselves for maggots.
> SHAKESPEARE: *Hamlet*, IV, iii.

To have a worm in one's tongue. To be cantankerous; to snarl and bite like a mad dog.

> There is one easy artifice
> That seldom has been known to miss—
> To snarl at all things right or wrong,
> Like a mad dog that has a worm in's tongue.
> BUTLER: *Upon Modern Critics*, IV.

To satisfy the worm. To appease one's hunger.

To worm oneself into another's favour. To insinuate oneself into the good graces of another.

To worm out information. To extract it piecemeal or indirectly.

Wormwood. The common name for the aromatic herbs of the genus *Artemisia*, especially *A. absinthium*, from which absinthe and vermouth are concocted. Culpeper recommends it as a specific against worms. It is said to have been so called because this plant, according to legend, sprang up in the track of the SERPENT as it writhed along the ground when driven out of PARADISE. The word is also used figuratively to denote bitterness or its cause.

Worship. Literally "worth-ship", honour, dignity, reverence; in its highest and now usual sense, the respect and reverence man pays to God.

At one time the word carried a sense of personal respect, as in, "Thou shalt have worship in the presence of them that sit at meat with thee" (*Luke* xiv, 10), and in the marriage service (*Book of Common Prayer*), the man says to the woman: "With my body I thee worship, and with all my worldly goods I thee endow."

Magistrates and MAYORS are addressed as *Your Worship* and referred to as *the Worshipful Mayor of...*

Worst. If the worst comes to the worst. Even if the very worst occurs.

To get the worst of it. To be beaten, defeated; to come off second best.

Worsted (wus'ted). This varity of woollen thread formed of regular parallel strands takes its name from Worsted (now Worstead) near Norwich, once an important woollen centre. The name occurs as early as the 13th century.

Worthies, The Nine. Nine heroes—three from the BIBLE, three from the classics, and three from romance; or three pagans, three Jews, and three Christians, who were bracketed together by writers like the SEVEN WONDERS OF THE WORLD (*see under* WORLD). They are usually given as HECTOR, ALEXANDER, and Julius CAESAR; Joshua, DAVID, and Judas MACCABÆUS; ARTHUR, CHARLEMAGNE, and Godfrey of Bouillon. SHAKESPEARE's Pageant of the Nine Worthies in *Love's Labour's Lost* (V, ii) has an incomplete list of five which includes Pompey and Hercules, who are not on the traditional list.

> Nine worthies were they called, of different rites,
> Three Jews, three pagans, and three Christian Knights.
>
> DRYDEN: *The Flower and the Leaf*, 535.

The Nine Worthies of London. A kind of chronicle-history in mixed verse and prose of nine prominent citizens of LONDON, published in 1592 by Richard Johnson, author of *The* SEVEN CHAMPIONS *of Christendom.* His worthies are:

Sir William Walworth, who stabbed Wat Tyler the rebel, and was twice Lord Mayor of London (1374, 1381).

Sir Henry Pritchard, who (in 1357) feasted Edward III (with 5,000 followers), Edward the BLACK PRINCE, John, King of France, the King of Cyprus, and David, King of SCOTLAND.

Sir William Sevenoke, who fought with the DAUPHIN of France and was Lord Mayor in 1418 and who endowed a grammar school.

Sir Thomas White, a merchant tailor, who was Lord Mayor in 1553 and founder of St. John's College, Oxford; also a founder of Merchant Taylors' School.

Sir John Bonham, entrusted with a valuable cargo for the Danish market, and made commander of an army raised to stop the progress of the great Solyman.

Christopher Croker, famous at the siege of Bordeaux, and companion of the Black Prince when he helped Don Pedro to the throne of Castile.

Sir John Hawkwood, famous soldier and commander of the WHITE COMPANY in Italy. He died in 1394 and is known in Italian history as *Giovanni Acuto Cavaliero*.

Sir Hugh Calveley (d. 1393), soldier and commander of FREE COMPANIES. He fought under the Black Prince against the French and became governor of the Channel Islands and famous for ridding Poland of a monstrous bear.

Sir Henry Maleverer, generally called Henry of Cornhill, who lived in the reign of Henry IV. He was a crusader, and became the guardian of "Jacob's well".

The above are essentially noted for military rather than civic achievement.

Wound. Bind the wound, and grease the weapon. A Rosicrucian maxim. *See* WEAPON SALVE.

Wove. Applied to papers made on an ordinary dandy roll or mould in which the wires are woven. Used in contradistinction to LAID.

Wraith (rāth). The phantom or spectral appearance of one still living, usually taken as a warning that this person's death is imminent. It appears to persons at a distance and forewarns them of the event. In general, a spectre, a ghost.

Wrangler. The Cambridge term for one who has obtained a place in the highest class of the mathematical TRIPOS. The first man was (until 1909) called the *Senior Wrangler*. A *wrangler* is a disputant and the name arises from the former public disputations in which candidates were required to take part. *See* ACT OF OPPONENCY; OPTIME.

> "Senior Wrangler, indeed; that's at the other shop."
> "What is the other shop, my dear child?" said the lady.
> "Senior Wrangler's at Cambridge, not Oxford," said the scholar, with a knowing air.
>
> THACKERAY: *Vanity Fair*, XXXIV.

In the western U.S.A. a *wrangler* is the herder of the saddle horses.

Wrath money. *See* WROTH.

Wren. A member of the Women's Royal Naval Service. *Cp.* WAAC; W.A.C., WAAF, etc.

Wrenning Day. St. Stephen's Day (26 December) used to be so called, because it was a local custom among villagers to stone a wren to death on that day in commemoration of the stoning of St. STEPHEN.

Wright. Do you know Dr. Wright of Norwich? A reproof given to a person who stops the decanter at dinner. Dr. Wright of Norwich was said to have been a great diner-out and an excellent talker. When a person stops the bottle and is asked this question, it implies that Dr. Wright had this privilege because of his entertaining conversation, but you are no Dr. Wright, except in stopping the circulation of the wine.

Write. O.E. *writan*, connected with Icel. *rita*, to tear, cut, scratch out, etc.

To write down, to commit to writing, also to criticize unfavourably, to depreciate. Contrariwise **to write up** is to puff, to bring into public notice or estimation by favourable criticism or accounts.

To write off a debt. To cancel it.

To write oneself out. To exhaust one's powers of literary production.

Writer. In SCOTLAND, a legal practitioner in a small town. In the Royal Navy a writer is a rating engaged for clerical duties.

Writer to the Signet. A member of an anciently-established society of solicitors in SCOTLAND who still have the sole right of preparing crown writs.

The writing on the wall. Said of something foreshadowing trouble or disaster. The reference is to *Dan*. v, 5–31, when a mysterious hand appeared writing on the wall while Belshazzar was feasting. Daniel interpreted the words to him as portending his downfall and that of his kingdom. Belshazzar was slain that night.

Wrong. The king can do no wrong. The legal and constitutional principle that the Crown acts on the advice and consent of ministers and therefore the Sovereign cannot be held responsible. It is another way of expressing the principle of ministerial responsibiity. Nor, according to Dicey (*Law of the Constitution*), "can the king be made personally responsible at law for any act done by him."

Wrong'un. A swindler, a cheat, a palpably dishonest person; also applied to false coin and other fakes; also a horse which has run in any flat-race meeting not recognized by the JOCKEY CLUB, and so is boycotted by the Club.

In CRICKET, a *wrong'un* is a ball which breaks the opposite way from what the batsman is led to expect from his observation of the bowler's grip of the ball and manner of delivery.

Wroth Money, or Wroth Silver. Money paid to the lord in lieu of castleward, *i.e.* a feudal obligation in return for protection, *castle ward* or *guard* being KNIGHT SERVICE for defending the lord's castle. It was a local name for what is also called *warth money* or *ward silver*. Such a feudal rent was collected by the Duke of Buccleuch as lord of the HUNDRED of Knightlow in Warwickshire.

Wulfstan, or Wulstan. There are two English saints of this name. (1) Wulfstan, Archbishop of York (d. 1023), and formerly Bishop of Worcester, best known for his homily in Old English prose *Lupi Sermo ad Anglos*, etc., portraying the miseries of the year 1014 during the Danish onslaught. (2) Wulfstan, Bishop of Worcester (d. 1095), noted, in association with Lanfranc, for suppression of the slave trade between ENGLAND and IRELAND.

Wuyck's Bible. See BIBLE, SOME SPECIALLY NAMED EDITIONS.

Wycliffite (wik′ lif īt). A LOLLARD, a follower of Wyclif (*c.* 1320–1384), who was called "The Morning Star of the REFORMATION". He condemned TRANSUBSTANTIATION, and monasticism, and held that only the righteous have the right to dominion and property. He attacked the Papacy and the BISHOPS, and advocated the use of the BIBLE in English.

Wykehamist (wik′ ȧm ist). A member of Winchester College, past or present, which was founded in 1378 by William of Wykeham (1324–1404), Bishop of Winchester and CHANCELLOR of England. He also founded New College, Oxford, and was born at Wickham in Hampshire.

Wysiwyg. Computer slang for "What you see is what you get" *i.e.* what you see on the screen is exactly what will appear in computer-printed form.

Wyvern. See WIVERN.

X

X. The twenty-fourth letter of the alphabet, representing the twenty-second letter of the Greek alphabet (*chi*), and denoting in Roman numeration 10, or, on its side (✕) 1,000 and with a dash over it ($\overline{X}$) 10,000.

In algebra and mathematics generally *x* denotes an unknown quantity. The reason for this is that algebra came into use in Europe from Arabia and that the Arab. *shei*, a thing, a something, used to designate the mathematically "unknown" was transcribed as *xei*. (*Cp.* COSS)

X as an abbreviation stands for Christ as in Xmas.

X on beer casks formerly indicated beer which had paid the old 10*s*. duty, and hence it came to mean beer of a given quality. Two or three crosses are mere trade-marks intended to convey an impression of its extra strength.

X.Y.Z. Affair. In 1797 the American President, John Adams, sent his commissioners, Pinckney, Marshall, and Gerry to France to negotiate on certain maritime frictions. From Paris they reported that three French agents had intercepted them and demanded a large sum of money and an American loan before the DIRECTORY would receive them. The Americans refused and the whole correspondence with the three French agents, designated X, Y, and Z, was published at Washington. This led to undeclared maritime hostility with France (1798–1800).

Xanthian Marbles, The (zăn′ thi ăn). A collection of ancient sculptures and friezes discovered by Sir Charles Fellows in 1838 at Xanthus, a Greek city of Lycia, Asia Minor, and now in the BRITISH MUSEUM.

Xanthippe, or **Xantippe** (zăn tip′ i). Wife of the philosoper SOCRATES. Her bad temper shown towards her husband has rendered her name proverbial for a conjugal scold.

> Be she as foul as was Florentius' love,
> As old as Sibyl, and as curst and shrewd
> As Socrates' Xanthippe, or a worse,
> She moves me not.
> SHAKESPEARE: *Taming of the Shrew*, I, ii.

Xanthus, or **Xanthos** (zăn′ thŭs) (Gr.,

reddish-yellow). ACHILLES' wonderful HORSE brother of Balios, Achilles' other horse, and offspring of ZEPHYRUS and the harpy, Podarge. Being chid by his master for leaving PATROCLUS on the field of battle, Xanthus turned his head reproachfully, and told Achilles that he also would soon be numbered with the dead, not from any fault of his horse, but by the decree of inexorable destiny (ILIAD, XIX).

Xanthus is also the ancient name of the Scamander, and of a city on its banks. Ælian and Pliny say that HOMER called the Scamander "Xanthos", or the "Gold-red river", because it coloured with such a tinge the fleeces of sheep washed in its waters. Others maintain that it was so called because a Greek hero of this name defeated a body of TROJANS on its banks, and pushed half of them into the stream.

Xaverian Brothers, The (zăv ēr′ i ăn). A Roman Catholic congregation founded at Bruges in 1839, concerned chiefly with the education of youth. It was founded by Theodore James Ryken who took the name Brother Francis Xavier after St. Francis Xavier (1506–1552), one of the earliest of the JESUITS, celebrated as the "Apostle of the Indies" and "the Apostle of Japan".

Xenocratic (zen ō krăt′ ik). Pertaining to the doctrine of Xenocrates (396–314 B.C.), a disciple of PLATO, noted for his continence and contempt of wealth. He combined Pythagoreanism with Platonism. Even the courtesan LAIS failed to tempt him from the path of virtue.

> Warmed by such youthful beauty, the severe
> Xenocrates would not have more been chaste.
> ARIOSTO: *Orlando Furioso*, xi, 3.

Xerxes (zĕrks′ ēz). A Greek way of writing the Persian *Ksathra* or *Kshatra*. Xerxes I, the great Xerxes, King of Persia (485–465 B.C.), is identical with the Ahasuerus of the BIBLE.

When Xerxes invaded Greece he constructed a pontoon bridge across the Dardanelles, which was swept away by the force of the waves; this so enraged the Persian despot that he "inflicted 300 lashes on the rebellious sea, and cast chains of iron across it". This story is a Greek myth, founded on the peculiar construction of Xerxes' second bridge, which consisted of 300 boats, lashed by iron chains to two ships serving as supporters.

Another story tells us that when he reviewed his enormous army before starting for Greece, he wept at the thought of the slaughter about to take place. "Of all this multitude, who shall say how many will return?"

Ximena (zim ē′ nà). The CID's bride.

Xiphias (zif′ i às) (Gr. *xiphos*, a sword). The name used in mediæval times for a sword-shaped comet; also for the southern constellation now called Dorado; and a poetical name given to the swordfish (genus *Xiphias*).

> Strong is the horse upon his speed;
> Strong in pursuit the rapid glede,
> Which makes at once his game;
> Strong the tall ostrich on the ground;
> Strong through the turbulent profound
> Shoots Xiphias to his aim.
> CHRIS. SMART: *Song to David*, LXXV.

Xylomancy (zī′ lō măn si). A form of DIVINATION using twigs, rods, etc. (Gr. *xylon*, wood; *manteia*, prophecy).

Y

Y. The twenty-fifth letter of the alphabet, derived from the Greek *Y* (*upsilon*), added by the Greeks to the Phœnician alphabet. *See* SAMIAN LETTER. It is used to represent both consonantal and vowel sounds.

As a mediæval numeral Y represents 150 and Ȳ, 150,000.

In algebra it denotes the second unknown quantity (*cp*. X). *See also* YE.

Y-Gun. A Y-shaped gun mounted in ships for firing a pair of depth-charges.

Yachtsman, The Noble. *See under* NOBLE.

Yahoo (ya hoo′). Swift's name, in *Gulliver's Travels*, for brutes with human forms and vicious propensities. They are subject to the HOUYHNHNMS, the horses with human reason. Hence applied to coarse, brutish or degraded persons.

Yahweh. *See* JEHOVAH.

Yama. In Hindu mythology, the first of the dead, born from the SUN, judge of men and king of the dead. His kingdom is the PARADISE for the worthy where friends and relations are reunited. His twin sister is called Yami and he is usually represented as four-armed and riding a buffalo.

Yank, Yankee (yăng′ ki). A citizen of the U.S.A., properly a New Englander. The derivation is uncertain but probably from Dut. *Janke*, a diminutive of John, perhaps used originally of the Dutch of New Amsterdam. The word was popularized by the song YANKEE DOODLE. America is often referred to as *Yankee-land*.

Yankee Doodle. A popular mid-18th-century song perhaps first introduced by British troops during the Anglo-French war (1755–63). It is now a quasi-national air of the United States.

There are several suggested origins of the tune which was first printed in England in 1778 and in America in 1794, but none is conclusive.

> Yankee Doodle went to town
> Riding on a pony;
> He stuck a feather in his cap
> And called it MACARONI.

Yarborough. A hand at bridge in which there is no card higher than a nine. So called because the second Lord Yarborough (1809–1862) used to lay 1,000 to 1 against such an occurence in any named hand. The actual mathematical odds are 1,827 to 1 against. *Cp*. TIGER.

Yard, Yard of tin. The coach horn, sounded by the guard, which was a yard long. It was used to summon passengers, to warn other traffic, and to signal the turnpikemen to open their gates.

Yardland. *See* VIRGATE.

Yarra-yabbies. Nickname for the inhabitants of Victoria, Australia, who are also known as the *Cabbage-patchers*. The Yarra-Yarra flows through Melbourne into Port Phillip Bay.

Yclept (i klept′). An old English word meaning called, named, styled. It is now only used in a sort of arch facetiousness that Fowler calls "Worn-out Humour".

Ye. An archaic way of writing *the*, the *y* representing O.E.Ʒ. Early printers used *y* as a substitute for the letter *Þ*, the character representing our *th*, hence the use of *ye* for *the* and *yt* as an abbreviation for *that*. It was always pronounced *the*.

Ye is also, of course, the archaic nominative plural of the second person.

Year (connected with Gr. *horos*, a season, and Lat. *hora*, an hour). The period of time occupied by the revolution of the Earth round the SUN.

The Astronomical, Equinoctial, Natural, Solar, or Tropical year is the time taken by the Sun in returning to the same equinox, in mean length, 365 days 5 hours 48 min. and 46 sec.

The Astral or Sidereal year is the time in which the Sun returns from a given star to the same star again: 365 days 6 hours 9 min. and 9.6 sec.

The Platonic, Great, or Perfect year (*Annus magnus*), a great cycle of years (estimated by early Greek astronomers at about 26,000 years) at the end of which all the heavenly bodies were imagined to return to the same places as they occupied at the Crea-

tion. *See also* CALENDAR; CANICULAR PER-
IOD; EMBOLISMIC; LEAP YEAR; SOTHIC PER-
IOD; SABBATICAL YEAR.

Academic Year. The university year, usually beginning in October.

Financial Year. In the United Kingdom,
the year ending 31 March. The taxation
year, however, ends on 5 April as a consequence of the transition to the Gregorian CA-
LENDAR. Until 1752, the year began on 25
March and the transition from the JULIAN
Calendar was effected by omitting Eleven
Days from the September of that year. Tax-
payers objected to paying on a year thus
shortened and so the taxation was correspondingly adjusted to end on 5 April.

Gregorian Year. *See* GREGORIAN.

Julian Year. *See* JULIAN.

Regnal Year. The year beginning with a
monarch's accession. In Great Britain Acts
of PARLIAMENT are still referred to by the regnal year in which they were passed; thus
the Local Government Act 1929, is also
dated 19 Geo. 5, the 19th year of the reign of
George V.

Year Books. The name given to annual
publications summarizing the events,
changes, etc., of the preceding year in the
world at large, or some particular subject,
profession, trade, industry, etc., *e.g. The
Statesman's Year Book, Whitaker's Almanack, The Brewers' Almanack, The Mining
Year Book.*

Historically, the term denotes the unique
series of reports of cases decided in the
courts of COMMON LAW, written in Norman
French, and covering the period 1292–1534.

Year of Confusion. 46 B.C., when the JU-
LIAN CALENDAR was introduced, a year of
445 days.

Year of Grace. *See under* GRACE.

Year of Our Lord. A year of the Christian
era.

For a year and a day. In law the period of
time which in certain matters determines a
right or liability. Thus the Crown formerly
had the right to hold the land of felons for a
year and a day, and if a person wounded does
not die within a year and a day, the assailant
is not guilty of murder.

Year in year out. Continuously, all the
time.

Yell Hounds. *See* WISH HOUNDS.

Yellow (O.E. *geolo*, connected with Gr.
chloros, green, and with *gall*, the yellowish
fluid secreted by the liver). In symbolism it
indicates jealousy, inconstancy, adultery,
perfidy, and cowardice. In France, the
doors of traitors used to be daubed with yellow and in some countries the laws ordained

that Jews must be clothed in yellow, because
they betrayed Jesus, and in mediæval pictures JUDAS is arrayed in yellow. In Spain at
an AUTO DA FE, the victims wore yellow, to
denote heresy and treason. *See* COLOURS.

In HERALDRY and ecclesiastical symbolism yellow is frequently used in place of
GOLD.

Yellow Admiral. *See under* ADMIRAL.

The Yellow Book. A yellow-covered quarterly magazine published (1894–1897) by
John Lane, the title being chosen to suggest
certain qualities of the "yellow-back"
French novel. Edited by Henry Harland, its
contributors included Arnold Bennett, A.C.
Benson, Edmund Gosse, Henry James,
George Moore, Arthur Symons and Oscar
Wilde. Aubrey Beardsley and Max Beer-
bohm contributed drawings, Beardsley's
work having erotic implications. The Yellow Book became the AVANT-GARDE reading
of the NAUGHTY NINETIES.

Yellow Books. Official documents, Government reports, etc., in France, corresponding to British BLUE BOOKS; so called
from the colour of their covers.

Yellow bounder. A hired post-chaise for
two passengers, nearly always painted yellow. Coachmen called the travelling carriages of the rich, "bounders" and those who
did not have their own barouches and were
above using a public vehicle, hired "yellow
bounders".

Yellow boy. Old slang for a golden SOVER-
EIGN, once fairly common in Great Britain.

> John did not starve the cause: there wanted not
> yellow-boys to fee counsel.
>
> ARBUTHNOT: *John Bull* (1712).

Yellow dog contracts. An American name
for agreements made by the employers with
employees to prevent the latter from joining
labour unions. Such contracts became invalid under an Act of 1932.

Yellow fever. A tropical fever accompanied by jaundice and black vomit; also called
YELLOW JACK. In Australia the name was given to the gold-prospecting mania of colonial days.

Yellow Jack. The YELLOW FEVER; also the
yellow flag displayed from lazarettos and
commonly, but somewhat inaccurately,
called the QUARANTINE flag, probably because it was the flag usually flown by vessels
liable to the performance of quarantine. By
an act of 1825, the yellow flag was adopted as
one of three quarantine flags and when flown
signified a clean bill of health. A yellow flag
with a black ball in the centre signified the
converse, and the yellow and black quartered flat meant dangerous plague or disease

on board. In the current International Code of Signals (1931), the yellow (Q) flag, when flown by a ship entering territorial waters from abroad, still has the same meaning— "My ship is healthy and I request free PRATI-QUE". Flag Q flown over the first substitute (QQ) means, in short, "My ship is suspect", and Flag Q flown over L (QL) means "My ship is infected".

The Yellow Peril. A scare, originally raised in Germany in the late 1890s, that the yellow races of China and Japan would rapidly increase in population and overrun the territories occupied by the white races with fearful consequences.

The Yellow Press. The sensationalist newspapers. The name arose in the United States when W. R. Hearst's *Journal*, during the circulation battle with Pulitzer's *World*, introduced a comic picture feature called "The Yellow Kid". This rivalry was dubbed "yellow journalism" and came to be characterized by scare headlines, sensational articles, lavish illustrations, comic features, Sunday supplements, etc.

The Yellow River. The Hwang-Ho in China, so called from the yellow earth or loess that it carries in suspension. It is also an epithet of the Tiber.

Yellow-back. A cheap novel, especially of the sensational kind. So called from the yellow board binding familiar on the railway bookstalls of Victorian days.

Yellow-bellies. A name given to people of the fenlands of the counties of Lincoln, Huntingdon, Cambridge, Suffolk, and Norfolk. The Mexicans are also so called.

Yellow-hammer. A bunting with yellowish head, neck, and breast (O.E. *amore*; Ger. *Ammer*, a bunting). The tradition is that the bird fluttered about the CROSS, and got its plumage stained with the Blood; by way of punishment its eggs were doomed ever after to bear marks of blood. Because the bird was "cursed", boys were taught that it was right and proper to destroy its eggs.

Yen. To have a yen for. An expression of American origin, to have an intense desire or longing for. From the Chinese *yen*, opium smoke.

Yeoman. Historically, a middle class of small freeholders, variously defined at different periods and later applied to the class of "forty-shilling freeholders".

Yeoman service. Effectual service, characterized by hard and steady work. The reference is to the service of yeomen in the English armies of former days.

> It did me yeoman's service.
> SHAKESPEARE: *Hamlet*, V, ii.

Yeoman of the Guard. *See* BEEFEATERS.

Yeomanry. British volunteer cavalry units were so called from 1761, although not effectively formed until 1794. In the 19th century they were largely used for suppressing riots and were essentially maintained by private benevolence and voluntary efforts. Most of them were former members of the regular cavalry. The Yeomanry were absorbed in the Territorial Army in 1907. *See* TERRIER.

Yes-man. An expressive colloquialism for one who always expresses agreement with his superior, irrespective of his private opinions.

Yeti. Tibetan name for the ABOMINABLE SNOW-MAN.

Yew. The yew is a native British tree (*Taxus baccata*), and is commonly planted in churchyards because, as an evergreen, it is a symbol of immortality. The practice was also encouraged to provide a supply of bowstaves from the hard, elastic wood resulting from the slow growth of this tree, which lives to a great age. To decorate the house with yew was held to lead to a death in the family. Yew leaves and berries are poisonous.

Some famous Yews.

That of *Brabourne*, in Kent; in Evelyn's time reputed to be nearly 59 ft. in girth.

That of *Darley churchyard*, Derbyshire; claimed to be well over 2,000 years old and 33 ft. in girth.

The *Scotch Yew at Fortingal*, in Perthshire; it was claimed to be between 2,000 and 3,000 years old.

The three at *Fountains Abbey*, Yorkshire, are said to have existed before the abbey was built in the 12th century.

J. Lowe's *The Yew Trees of Great Britain and Ireland* (1897) lists the oldest and biggest Yew trees and of the 211 given of over 10 ft. in girth, 36 were in Wales. The largest tree in the famous grove at *Mamhilad*, Monmouthshire, is over 31 ft. in girth.

Yggdrasil (ig drà sil). The world tree of Scandinavian mythology that, with its roots and branches, binds together HEAVEN, earth, and HELL. It is an ash, and is evergreen, and at the root is a fountain of wonderful virtues. In the tree, which drops honey, sit an EAGLE, a squirrel, and four stags. It is the tree of life and knowledge, and of time and space.

Yiddish (Ger. *jüdisch*, Jewish). A Middle German dialect developed in Poland under Hebrew and Slavonic influence, written in Hebrew characters, and used as a language by Eastern European Jews. As a result of the latter's widespread dispersal Yiddish became the *lingua franca* of world Jewry. Hence *Yid* as a term for a JEW.

Ymir (im ir). The primæval being of Scandinavian mythology, father of all the GIANTS. He was nourished by the four milky streams which flowed from the cow Audhumla. From his body the world was created and his skull became the vault of the heavens.

Yob. *See* BACK-SLANG.

Yodel (yō′ dĕl). To sing with frequent alternations between the ordinary voice and falsetto. It is properly peculiar to Switzerland and is a development of Switzerland and the Tyrolese.

Yoga (yō′ gà). A practice of Hindu philosophy, the withdrawal of the physical senses from external objects. Adepts in yoga are able to hold their breath for protracted periods and do other things in apparent contravention of natural requirements. Hypnotism and self-mortification are part of the cult. Union with the Deity became its object (Sans. *yoga*, union, devotion). A *yogi* is one who practises yoga.

Yoke. To pass under the yoke. To make a humiliating submission; to suffer the disgrace of a vanquished army. The Romans made a yoke of three spears—two upright and one resting on them. When an army was vanquished, the soldiers had to lay down their arms and pass under this archway of spears.

Yom Kippur (yom ki pĕr′). *See* DAY OF ATONEMENT *under* ATONEMENT.

Yorkist. A partisan of the House of York in the WARS OF THE ROSES (*see under* ROSE).

Yorkshire. I'se Yorkshire, too. *See* TO COME YORKSHIRE OVER ONE *under* COME.

Yorkshire slavery. *See* FACTORY KING.

The Yorkshireman's toast. "Here's tiv us, all on us; may we never want nowt, noan on us; nor me nawther."

Yorker. In CRICKET, a deceptive ball delivered so that it pitches directly beneath the bat and is thus likely to be missed by the batsman. Perhaps from its first being developed by a Yorkshire bowler.

Young. Often used as an epithet in the names of political parties who aim to effect sweeping political changes or to reawaken the national spirit.

Young England. A group of young TORY politicians of the early 1840s who sought to revive a somewhat romantic concept of paternal feudalism and to idealize the functions of the territorial aristocracy. They saw their movement as a safeguard against revolution and the triumph of the LAISSEZ FAIRE doctrines of the MANCHESTER SCHOOL. Their leaders were Lord John Manners and George Smythe; Disraeli also joined their ranks. The EGLINTON TOURNAMENT (*see under* TOURNAMENT) was one of their more extravagant ventures.

Young Germany. A German school of the 1830s whose aim was to liberate politics, religion and manners from the old conventional trammels. Heinrich Heine was its most prominent representative.

Young Ireland. An Irish nationalist movement of the 1840s taking its name in imitation of Mazzini's YOUNG ITALY. There aims included the revival of Irish language and literature and national independence. Including both Protestants and Catholics, they were responsible for the futile rising of 1848. Their leaders included Smith O'Brien, Gavan Duffy, John Mitchel, Thomas Francis Meagher, and Fintan Lalor.

Young Italy. (*Giovine Italia*). A republican nationalist movement inspired by the exiled Mazzini and seeking to promote an Italian revolution. Founded in 1831 and imbued by its leader with fervent idealism, it never gained the support of the masses, but it did much to develop the spirit of nationalism in the 1830s and 1840s. *See* CARBONARI.

Young Pretender. *See under* PRETENDER.

The Young Turks. *See under* TURK.

Yours truly. This conventional ending to letters is sometimes used to indicate the speaker—"There were X, Y, and Yours truly."

Ysolde (**Yseult, Isolde,** etc.). The name of two heroines of ARTHURIAN ROMANCE, *Ysolde the Fair*, daughter of the king of IRELAND, wife of King MARK and lover of TRISTRAM, the other *Ysolde of the White Hands* or *Ysolde of Brittany*.

Yuga. One of the four ages of the world into which, according to Hindu cosmogony, mundane time is divided.

Yule, Yuletide. CHRISTMAS-TIME. O.E. *gēol*, from Icel. *jōl*, the name of a heathen festival at the winter SOLSTICE.

Yule log, or **Yule clog.** A great log of wood formerly laid across the hearth with great ceremony on Christmas Eve and lit with a brand from the previous year's log. There followed drinking and merriment.

Yummie. An acronym from the 1980s for a young upwardly mobile Marxist.

Yuppie. A young urban (or upwardly mobile) professional person. A popular acronym from the 1980s. *Cp.* CLIMBING THE LADDER.

Yves, or **Yvo, St.** (ēv, ē′ vō) (1253–1303). Patron SAINT of lawyers, being himself a lawyer. He became an ecclesiastical judge at Rennes and in 1285 entered the priesthood. His work for orphans and widows earned him the title of "Advocate of the Poor". He was canonized in 1347 and his day is 19 May.

Yvetot (ēv′ tō). **The King of Yvetot.** A man of mighty pretensions but little merit. Yvetot is a town in Normandy; the "King" was the lord of the town, and the title was in use from the 14th to the 16th century. The ballad of this title by Béranger, with satirical allusions to NAPOLEON, appeared in 1813 and became a type of the "*roi bon enfant*".

Z

Z. The last letter of the alphabet, called *zed* in England, but in America *zee*. Its older English name was *izzard*. It was the seventh letter of the Greek alphabet, *zeta*.

> Thou whoreson zed! thou unnecessary letter!
> SHAKESPEARE: *King Lear*, II, ii.

In mathematics it denotes the third unknown quantity; and as a mediæval numeral it represents 2,000. It is also used as a contraction mark as in *viz.*, *oz.*

Zadkiel (zăd' ki el). In Rabbinical angelology, the ANGEL of the planet JUPITER. The name was adopted as a pseudonym by the astrologer Richard James Morrison (1795–1874), a naval lieutenant, author of the *Herald of Astrology* (1831), continued as **Zadkiel's Almanack.**

Zamorin (zăm' or in). The title of the one-time ruler of Calicut.

Zany (zā' ni). The buffoon who mimicked the clown in the Commedia dell'Arte; hence, a simpleton, one who "acts the goat". The name is the Ital. *zanni*, a buffoon, a familiar form of *Giovanni* (*i.e.* John).

> For indeed,
> He's like the zani to a tumbler
> That tries tricks after him to make men laugh.
> JONSON: *Every Man out of his Humour*, IV, i.

Zarathustra. See ZORASTRIANS.

Zealots, or **Cananæans.** A Jewish sect founded by Judas of Gamala in the early years of the 1st century A.D., who fiercely opposed Roman domination. They fought fanatically during the great rebellion which ended in the destruction of Jerusalem in A.D. 70. See MASADA.

Zebi. See SABBATÆANS.

Zedland. An old designation of the West-country shires of Devon, Dorset and Somerset, where *s* is still often pronounced as *z*.

Zeitgeist (zīt' gīst) (Ger. *Zeit*, time; *Geist*, spirit). The spirit of the time; the moral or intellectual tendency characteristic of the period.

Zem Zem. The sacred well near the KAABA at MECCA. According to Arab tradition, this is the very well that was shown to Hagar when ISHMAEL was perishing of thirst.

Zemindar. Under the MOGUL emperors of India, one of a class of tax farmers, responsible for the revenues of land held in common. They were treated as landlords by the British and made proprietors paying a fixed annual tax. This change, introduced by Lord Cornwallis in Bengal in 1793, did not prevent RACK-RENTING of the peasantry by the zemindars.

Zemstvo (Russ. *zemlya*, land). The name given to the elected District Assemblies and provincial councils (elected by the District Assemblies) in Russia, introduced by Alexander II in 1864. They dealt with local taxation, primary education, famine precautions, roads and bridges, etc.

Zen. A Japanese Buddhist sect which believes that the ultimate truth is greater than words and is therefore not to be wholly found in the sacred writings, but must be sought through the "inner light" and self-mastery. It originated in the 6th century in China.

Zend-Avesta. The sacred writings of Zoroaster that formed the basis of the religion that prevailed in Persia from the 6th century B.C. to the 7th century A.D. *Avesta* means the lore, or sacred writings, and *Zend*, the commentary. Hence the application of *Zend* to the ancient Iranian language in which the *Zend-Avesta* is written. See ZOROASTRIANS.

Zenith, Nadir (Arab.). *Zenith* is the point of the heavens immediately over the head of the spectator. NADIR is the opposite point immediately beneath the spectator's feet. Hence, *to go from the zenith of one's fortunes to the nadir* is to fall from the height of fortune to the depth of poverty.

Zeno. The name of several PHILOSOPHERS. Zeno of Elia, who flourished about 500 B.C., was a disciple of Parmenides and one of the ELEATIC school. He is said to have been the inventor of DIALECTIC. When tortured for conspiring against the tyrant Nearchus he bit off his tongue and spat it in the tyrant's face.

Zeno of Citium (342–270 B.C.) was founder of the STOIC school at ATHENS. One of his maxims was that we are given two ears, and only one mouth, to tell us that we should listen more than we should speak.

Zeno of Tarsus, the STOIC, and Zeno of Sidon, an Epicurean, are of lesser note.

Zephyr (zef′ir). **Zephyrus.** In classical mythology, the west wind, son of Astræus and AURORA, and lover of Flora, identified with the Roman FAVONIUS; hence, any soft, gentle wind.

> Fair laughs the Morn and soft the Zephyr blows,
> While proudly riding o'er the azure realm
> In gallant trim the gilded vessel goes;
> Youth on the prow, and Pleasure at the helm.
> GRAY: *The Bard*, 71.

Zero (zē′ rō) (Arabic, a cipher). The figure o; nothing; especially the point on a scale (such as that of a thermometer) from which positive and negative quantites are measured; on the Centigrade and Réaumur thermometers fixed at the freezing-point of water; on the Fahrenheit 32° below freezing-point.

Absolute zero is the point at which it would be impossible to get any colder; *i.e.* that at which it is totally devoid of heat (estimated at about —273° C).

Zero hour. A military term (first used in World War I) for the exact time at which an attack, etc., is to be begun. From this are timed the subsequent operations, *e.g.* zero +3 means 3 minutes after zero hour. Succeeded in World War II by H-hour.

Zeugma (zūg′ mà) (Gr. *zeugnumi*, yoke). In grammar and logic, a term for a phrase in which one word modifies or governs two or more not connected in meaning. A well-known example is, "Miss Bolo went straight home in a flood of tears and a sedan chair." (Dickens, *Pickwick Papers*, xxxv.)

Zeus (zūs). The Greek equivalent of JUPITER. The root meaning of the word is "bright".

Zimri. The name given by Dryden in *Absalom and Achitophel* to George Villiers, 2nd Duke of Buckingham (1628–1687), in allusion to the King of Israel who "slew his master" and was himself overthrown (I *Kings* xvi).

Zingari. Gypsies; so called in Italy. The name is thought to derive from *Sinte* or *sind* (India) and *calo* (black).

> Zingaro is Sanscrit, and signifies a man of mixed race, a mongrel.
> BORROW: *Lavengro* (*Preface of 1872*).

I Zingari (I.Z.). An exclusive nomadic CRICKET club, founded in 1845 by William Bolland. The club has no ground of its own, no subscription is payable, and Bolland is its perpetual president.

Zinoviev Letter. *See under* FORGERY.

Zion (Heb. *Tsiyon*, a hill). Figuratively, the chosen people, the Israelites; the church of God, the kingdom of HEAVEN. The city of David stood on Mount Zion.

In *Pilgrim's Progress* Bunyan calls the Celestial City (*i.e.* heaven) *Mount Zion*.

Daughter of Zion. JERUSALEM or its people.

Zionism. The Jewish movement for the establishment of the "national home" in Palestine. The Zionist movement was founded by Dr. Theodore Herzl of Vienna in 1895 and the Balfour Declaration of 1917 recognized Zionist aspirations. From 1920 to 1948 Palestine was a British mandate, administered under great difficulties arising from the friction between Jews and Arabs. The independent state of Israel was established in 1948.

Zip code. In the U.S.A., the system used to differentiate the mail delivery zones based on five-digit numbers. The name 'Zip' is derived from the initial letters of the name of the system, Zone Improvement Plan. The British Post Code composed of letters and numbers is a similar system.

Zodiac (Gr. *zodiakos*, pertaining to animals; from *zoon*, an animal). The imaginary belt or zone of the heavens, extending about eight degrees each side of the ECLIPTIC, which the SUN traverses annually.

Signs of the Zodiac. The zodiac was divided by the ancients into 12 equal parts, proceeding from west to east, each part of 30 degrees, and distinguished by a sign; these originally corresponded to the zodiacal constellations bearing the same names, but now, through the precession of the equinoxes, they coincide with the constellations bearing the names next in order.

Beginning with ARIES, we have first six on the north side and six on the south side of the Equator; beginning with CAPRICORNUS, we have six ascending and then six descending signs—*i.e.* six which ascend higher and higher towards the north, and six which descend lower and lower towards the south. The six northern signs are: *Aries* (the ram), TAURUS (the bull), GEMINI (the twins), spring signs; CANCER (the crab), *Leo* (the lion), VIRGO (the virgin), summer signs. The six southern are: LIBRA (the balance), SCORPIO (the scorpion), SAGGITARIUS (the archer), autumn signs; *Capricornus* (the goat), AQUARIUS (the water-bearer), and *Pisces* (the fishes), winter signs.

> Our vernal signs the RAM begins,
> Then comes the BULL, in May the TWINS;
> The CRAB in June, next LEO shines,
> And VIRGO ends the northern signs.
> The BALANCE brings autumnal fruits,
> The SCORPION stings, the ARCHER shoots;
> December's GOAT brings wintry blast,
> AQUARIUS rain, the FISH come last.
> E.C.B.

Zoilus. A Greek rhetorician of the 4th century B.C., a literary THERSITES, shrewd, witty, and spiteful, nicknamed *Homeromastix* (Homer's scourge), because he mercilessly assailed the epics of HOMER, and called the companions of ULYSSES in the island of CIRCE "weeping porkers". He also attacked PLATO and ISOCRATES. His name is applied to a spiteful and carping critic. *See* THRACIAN DOG *under* DOG.

Zollverein (Ger. *Zoll*, duty; *Verein*, union). A customs union. In German history, the Prussian Zollverein, which developed from 1819, is of particular importance. By 1852 it included practically the whole of Germany with the notable exclusion of Austria. Attempts to form rival unions were stillborn and the Zollverein was used by Prussia as an economic prelude to the struggle with Austria.

Zombie. The python god of certain West African tribes. Its worship was carried to the West Indies with the slave trade, and still somewhat covertly survives in VOODOO ceremonies in Haiti and some of the Southern States of the U.S.A.

The word *zombie* is also applied to an alleged dead body brought to life in a more or less cataleptic or automaton state by Voodoo magic; also, colloquially, to a half-wit or thick-head.

Zone time. *See* STANDARD TIME.

Zoot-suit (U.S.A.). An exaggerated style of clothing adopted in the late 1930s by HEPCATS and followers of fashionable SWING music. It usually consisted of baggy trousers caught in at the bottom, a long coat resembling a frock coat, a broad-brimmed hat, and a flowing tie, all in vivid colours. An essential article of equipment was a vast key-chain.

Zoroastrians. Followers of Zoroaster or Zarathustra, founder of the ancient Persian religion called Zoroastrianism. Zoroaster's teachings are contained in the AVESTA and he taught that ORMUZD, the creator and ANGEL of GOOD, will triumph over AHRIMAN, the spirit of EVIL. Man's state after death will depend on the good and evil in his life. Sacred fire-altars were used in their ritual, hence their inaccurate appellation of "fire-worshippers". *See* GUEBRES; PARSEES.

Zounds! A minced oath, euphemistic for *God's wounds*.

Zucchetto (zu ket′ ō). The small skullcap worn by Roman Catholic clergy; white for the POPE, red for a CARDINAL, purple for a BISHOP, and black for others.

Zuleika. The name traditionally ascribed to POTIPHAR'S WIFE, and a very common name in Persian poetry.

Zürich. The Zürich Bible. *See* BIBLE, SOME SPECIALLY NAMED EDITIONS.

Gnomes of Zurich. *See under* GNOME.

Zwickau Prophets, The. An early sect of ANABAPTISTS at Zwickau in Saxony, who sought to establish a Christian commonwealth. *See also* ABECEDARIAN.

Zwinglian. Pertaining to the teachings of Ulrich (Huldreich) Zwingli (1484–1531), the Swiss religious reformer and minister at Zurich. The term **Zwinglianism** refers especially to his teachings on the EUCHARIST. He maintained a completely symbolic interpretation and rejected all forms of local or corporeal presence, including Luther's doctrine of Consubstantiation. *see* IMPANATION; TRANSUBSTANTIATION.

A.M.D.G.

GUIDE TO INDEX

This index is necessarily selective; otherwise it would have grown to be as long as the book itself. The main aim has been to make more accessible the vast store of information and anecdote tucked away under unlikely headings. In addition a limited number of topic headings have been chosen, listing where to find information on subjects that have particularly interested Dr Brewer and his editors.

J.M. Cresswell

HOW TO USE THIS INDEX

Where the words 'see also' follow a headword, this indicates that there is an entry under this word in the text of the Dictionary, but that additional information on the subject can be found under the entries listed. Cross-references that are listed in the Dictionary entry have not been included in the index.

Where brackets are used in a reference, these indicate that the phrase is to be found listed under the word outside the brackets. Thus the entry 'Alchemy see also (Seven) bodies' tells you that there is already an entry in the Dictionary under Alchemy, but that further information can be found under the heading 'Bodies', where the phrase 'Seven bodies' will be found.

Occasionally it has been necessary to phrase an entry in the style 'Adonics see Sapphics s.v. Sappho'. This means that information on Adonics appears under the sub-heading 'Sapphics' which is found under the main entry 'Sappho'.

Index

Index

Index

Index

Index